Department of Economic and
Social Affairs
Statistics Division

Département des affaires économiques
et sociales
Division de statistique

Statistical Yearbook
Forty-fifth issue

1998
Data available as of
30 November 2000

Annuaire statistique
Quarante-cinquième édition

Données disponibles
au 30 novembre 2000

United Nations/Nations Unies   New York, 2001

Note

The designations employed and the presentation of material in this publication do not imply the expression of any opinion whatsoever on the part of the Secretariat of the United Nations concerning the legal status of any country, territory, city or area or of its authorities, or concerning the delimitation of its frontiers or boundaries.

In general, statistics contained in the present publication are those available to the United Nations Secretariat up to November 2000 and refer to 1998/1999 or earlier. They therefore reflect country nomenclature in use in 2000.

The term "country" as used in this publication also refers, as appropriate, to territories or areas.

The designations "developed" and "developing" are intended for statistical convenience and do not necessarily express a judgment about the stage reached by a particular country or area in the development process.

Symbols of United Nations documents are composed of capital letters combined with figures.

Note

Les appellations employées dans la présente publication et la présentation des données qui y figurent n'impliquent, de la part du Secrétariat de l'Organisation des Nations Unies, aucune prise de position quant au statut juridique des pays, territoires, villes ou zones, ou de leurs autorités, ni quant au tracé de leurs frontières ou limites.

En règle générale, les statistiques contenues dans la présente publication sont celles dont disposait le Secrétariat de l'Organisation des Nations Unies jusqu'à novembre 2000 et portent sur la période finissant à 1999. Elles reflètent donc la nomenclature des pays en vigueur à l'époque.

Le terme "pays", tel qu'il est utilisé ci-après, peut également désigner des territoires ou des zones.

Les appellations "développées" et "en développement" sont employées à des fins exclusivement statistiques et n'expriment pas nécessairement un jugement quant au niveau de développement atteint par tel pays ou telle région.

Les cotes des documents de l'Organisation des Nations Unies se composent de lettres majuscules et de chiffres.

ST/ESA/STAT/SER.S/21

UNITED NATIONS PUBLICATION
Sales No. E/F.00.XVII.1

PUBLICATION DES NATIONS UNIES
Numéro de vente : E/F.00.XVII.1

ISBN 92-1-061189-6
ISSN 0082-8459

Inquiries should be directed to:

SALES SECTION
PUBLISHING DIVISION
UNITED NATIONS
NEW YORK 10017
USA

Adresser toutes demandes de renseignements à la :

SECTION DE VENTES
DIVISION DES PUBLICATIONS
NATIONS UNIES
NEW YORK 10017
ÉTATS-UNIS D'AMÉRIQUE

E-mail: publications@un.org
Internet: http://www.un.org/Pubs

Preface

This is the forty-fifth issue of the United Nations *Statistical Yearbook,* prepared by the Statistics Division, Department of Economic and Social Affairs of the United Nations Secretariat, since 1948. The present issue contains series covering, in general, 1989–1998 or 1990–1999, using statistics available to the Statistics Division up to 30 November 2000.

The *Yearbook* is based on data compiled by the Statistics Division from over 40 different international and national sources. These include the United Nations Statistics Division in the fields of national accounts, industry, energy, transport and international trade; the United Nations Statistics Division and Population Division in the field of demographic statistics; and data provided by over 20 offices of the United Nations system and international organizations in other specialized fields.

United Nations agencies and other international organizations which furnished data are listed under "Statistical sources and references" at the end of the *Yearbook.* Acknowledgement is gratefully made for their generous cooperation in providing data.

The Statistics Division also publishes the *Monthly Bulletin of Statistics* [25]*, which provides a valuable complement to the *Yearbook* covering current international economic statistics for most countries and areas of the world and quarterly world and regional aggregates. Subscribers to the *Monthly Bulletin of Statistics* may also access the *Bulletin* on-line via the World Wide Web on Internet. *MBS On-line* allows time-sensitive statistics to reach users much faster than the traditional print publication. For further information see <http://www.un.org/Depts/unsd/>.

The present issue of the *Yearbook* reflects a phased programme of major changes in its organization and presentation undertaken in 1990 which until then was relatively unchanged since the first issue was released in 1948. One result of this process has been to reduce the total number of tables from 140 in the 37th issue to 80 in the present issue and to include an index.

Recognizing the tremendous worldwide growth in recent years in the use of microcomputers and the corresponding interest in obtaining statistics in machine-readable form for further study and analysis by users, the *Yearbook* has also been published on CD-ROM for IBM-compatible microcomputers, since the thirty-eighth issue. The latest issue on CD-ROM is the forty-fourth[1]. The present issue will also be published on CD-ROM in 2001. Ad hoc or standing orders

---

* Numbers in brackets refer to numbered entries in the section Statistical sources and references at the end of this book.

Préface

La présente édition est la quarante-cinquième de l'*Annuaire statistique* des Nations Unies, établi depuis 1948 par la Division de statistique du Département des affaires économiques et sociales du Secrétariat de l'Organisation des Nations Unies. Elle contient des séries qui portent d'une manière générale sur la période 1989 à 1998 ou 1990 à 1999 et pour lesquelles ont été utilisées les informations dont disposait la Division de statistique au 30 novembre 2000.

L'*Annuaire* est établi à partir des données que la Division de statistique a recueillies auprès de plus de 40 sources différentes, internationales et nationales. Ces sources sont: la Division de statistique du Secrétariat de l'Organisation des Nations Unies pour ce qui concerne les comptabilités nationales, l'industrie, l'énergie, les transports et le commerce international; la Division de statistique et la Division de la population du Secrétariat de l'Organisation des Nations Unies pour les statistiques démographiques; et plus de 20 bureaux du système des Nations Unies et d'organisations internationales pour les autres domaines spécialisés.

Les institutions spécialisées des Nations Unies et les autres organisations internationales qui ont fourni des données sont énumérées dans la section "Sources et références statistiques" figurant à la fin de l'ouvrage. Les auteurs de l'*Annuaire statistique* les remercient de leur généreuse coopération.

La Division de Statistique publie également le *Bulletin Mensuel de Statistiques* [25]*, qui est un complément intéressant à l'*Annuaire Statistique* qui couvre les statistiques économiques courantes sur la plupart des pays et zones du monde et des aggrégats trimestriels, au niveau du monde et des grandes régions. Les abonnés au *Bulletin Mensuel de Statistiques* ont aussi à leur disposition le *Bulletin* en ligne, accessible sur Internet par le "World Wide Web". Grâce à "BMS en ligne" les utilisateurs disposent plus rapidement des données conjoncturelles que par la voie traditionnelle de la publication imprimée. Pour des informations supplémentaires, voir <http://www.un.org/Depts/unsd/>.

La présente édition de l'*Annuaire* tient compte des importantes transformations qui, depuis 1990, ont été apportées par étapes successives à son organisation et à sa présentation, lesquelles étaient restées pratiquement inchangées depuis la première édition parue en 1948. Ce processus a ainsi permis de ramener le nombre de tableau de 140 dans la trente-septième édition à 80 dans l'édition actuelle et à inclure un index (en anglais seulement).

---

* Les chiffres entre crochets se réfèrent aux entrées numérotées dans la liste des sources et références statistiques à la fin de l'ouvrage.

for the *Yearbook* in hard copy and on CD-ROM may be placed with United Nations Publications sales offices in New York and Geneva. A full list of machine-readable products in statistics available from the United Nations Statistics Division may be obtained, upon request, from the Statistics Division of the United Nations Secretariat, New York or from the Division's Internet home page <http://www.un.org/Depts/unsd/>. The Division has also prepared an inventory of over 100 international statistical databases with some form of public access, *StatBase Locator on Disk—UNSTAT's Guide to International Computerized Statistical Databases.*[2]

The organization of the *Yearbook*, described in the Introduction below in more detail, consists of four parts. Part One: World and Region Summary, consists of key world and regional aggregates and totals and is essentially unchanged from previous issues. In the remaining parts, the main subject matter is generally presented according to countries or areas, with world and regions aggregates also shown in some cases. Parts two, three and four cover, respectively, population and social topics, national economic activity and international economic relations. The organization of the population and social topics generally follows the arrangement of subject matter in the United Nations *Handbook on Social Indicators* [45]; economic activity is taken up according to the classes of the United Nations International Standard Industrial Classification of All Economic Activities (ISIC) [47]; and tables on international economic relations cover merchandise trade, international tourism (a major factor in international trade in services and balance of payments) and financial transactions including development assistance. Each chapter ends with brief technical notes on statistical sources and methods for the tables it includes. References to sources and related methodological publications are provided at the end of the *Yearbook* in the section "Statistical sources and references".

Annex I provides complete information on country and area nomenclature, and regional and other groupings used in the *Yearbook*, and annex II lists conversion coefficients and factors used in various tables. Symbols and conventions used in the *Yearbook* are shown in the section "Explanatory notes", preceding the Introduction.

The complete list of tables added to or omitted from the last issue of the *Yearbook* is given in annex III. Tables for which a sufficient amount of new data is not available are not being published in this *Yearbook*. Their titles nevertheless are still listed in the table of contents since it is planned that they will be published in a later issue as new data are compiled by the collecting agency. However, the complete set of tables is retained in the CD-ROM version of the *Yearbook*.

As described more fully in the Introduction below, every attempt has been made to ensure that the series contained in the *Yearbook* are sufficiently comparable to provide a reliable general description of eco-

En raison de l'expansion extraordinaire que la micro-informatique a connue ces dernières années et de l'intérêt croissant que suscite la présentation de statistiques sur des supports lisibles en machine et exploitables directement par l'utilisateur, l'*Annuaire* a été publiée sur disque compact (CD/ROM) pour micro-ordinateurs IBM et compatibles depuis la publication de la trente-huitième édition. La plus récente édition sur disque compact (CD/ROM) est la quarante-quatrième[1]. La présente édition sera également publiée sur CD/ROM en 2001. Les commandes individuelles et les abonnements à l'*Annuaire statistique* (édition imprimée ou sur CD/ROM) peuvent être adressées aux bureaux de vente des publications des Nations Unies à New York et à Genève ou sur Internet page d'accueil de la Division <http://www.un.org/Depts/unsd/>. La Division de statistique du Secrétariat de l'Organisation des Nations Unies à New York fournit sur demande la liste complète de produits statistiques disponibles sur supports lisibles en machine. La Division publie également *StatBase Locator on Disk — UNSTAT's Guide to International Computerized Databases,*[2] inventaire de plus de 100 bases de données statistiques internationales accessibles au public.

Le plan de l'*Annuaire*, qui est décrit ci-après de manière plus détaillée dans l'introduction, comprend quatre parties. La première partie, "Aperçu mondial et régional", qui se compose des principaux agrégats et totaux aux niveaux mondial et régional, est reprise presque sans changement des éditions précédentes; les trois autres sont consacrées à la population et aux questions sociales (deuxième partie), à l'activité économique nationale (troisième partie) et aux relations économiques internationales (quatrième partie). L'organisation de la deuxième partie, "Population et questions sociales", suit généralement le plan adopté par l'ONU "*Manuel des indicateurs sociaux*" [45]; dans la troisième partie, l'activité économique est présentée conformément aux catégories adoptées par l'ONU dans la *Classification internationale type, par industrie, de toutes les branches d'activité économique* [47]; les tableaux de la quatrième partie, consacrée aux relations économiques internationales, portent sur le commerce des marchandises, le tourisme international (élément essentiel du secteur international des services et balance des paiements) et les opérations financières, y compris l'aide au développement. Chaque chapitre termine avec une brève note technique sur les sources et méthodes statistiques utilisées pour les tableaux du chapitre. On trouvera à la fin de l'*Annuaire*, dans la section "Sources et références statistiques", des références aux sources et publications méthodologiques connexes.

L'annexe I donne des renseignements complets sur la nomenclature des pays et des zones et sur la façon dont ceux-ci ont été regroupés pour former les régions et autres entités géographiques utilisées dans l'*Annuaire*; l'annexe II fournit des renseignements sur les coefficients et facteurs de conversion employés dans les différents tableaux. Les divers symboles et conventions utili-

nomic and social topics throughout the world. Nevertheless, the reader should carefully consult the footnotes and technical notes for any given table for explanations of general limitations of series presented and specific limitations affecting particular data items; the section "comparability of statistics" should also be consulted. Readers interested in more detailed figures than those shown in the present publication, and in further information on the full range of internationally assembled statistics in specialized fields, should also consult the specialized publications listed in the "Statistical sources and references" at the end of the *Yearbook*.

Needless to say, much more can be done to improve the *Yearbook*'s scope, coverage, timeliness, design, and technical notes. The process is inevitably an evolutionary one. Comments on the present *Yearbook* and its future evolution are welcome and should be addressed to the Director, United Nations Statistics Division, New York 10017 USA, or via e-mail to statistics@un.org .

sés dans l'*Annuaire* sont présentés dans la section "Notes explicatives" qui précède l'introduction.

La liste complète des tableaux ajoutés et supprimés depuis la dernière édition de l'*Annuaire* figure à l'annexe III. Les tableaux pour lesquels on ne dispose pas d'une quantité suffisante des données nouvelles, n'ont pas été publiés dans cet *Annuaire*. Comme ils seront repris dans une prochaine édition à mesure que des données nouvelles seront dépouillées par l'office statistique d'origine, ses titres figurent toujours dans la table des matières. Tous les tableaux sont cependant repris dans l'édition publiée sur CD/ROM.

Comme il est précisé ci-après dans l'introduction, aucun effort n'a été épargné afin que les séries figurant dans l'*Annuaire* soient suffisamment comparables pour fournir une description générale fiable de la situation économique et sociale dans le monde entier. Néanmoins, le lecteur devra consulter avec soins les renvois individuels et les notes techniques de chaque tableau pour y trouver l'explication des limites générales imposées aux séries présentées et des limites particulières propres à certains types de données; aussi le lecteur devra consulter la section "comparabilité des statistiques". Les lecteurs qui souhaitent avoir des chiffres plus détaillés que ceux figurant dans le présent volume ou qui désirent se procurer des renseignements sur la gamme complète des statistiques qui ont été compilées à l'échelon international dans tel ou tel domaine particulier devraient consulter les publications énumérées dans la section "Sources et références statistiques".

Inutile de dire qu'il reste beaucoup à faire pour mettre l'*Annuaire* pleinement à jour en ce qui concerne son champ, sa couverture, sa mise à jour, sa conception générale, et ses notes techniques. Il s'agit là inévitablement d'un processus évolutif. Les observations sur la présente édition de l'*Annuaire* et les modifications suggérées pour l'avenir seront reçues avec intérêt et doivent être adressées au Directeur de la Division de statistique de l'ONU, New York, N.Y. 10017 (États-Unis d'Amérique), ou e-mail à statistics@un.org .

---

1   *Statistical Yearbook, forty-fourth issue, CD-ROM*, (United Nations publication, Sales No. E.00.XVII.2).
2   United Nations publication, Sales No. E.94.XVII.8 (issued on one 3 1/2" diskette for IBM-compatible microcomputers).

---

1   *L'Annuaire statistique, quarante-quatrième édition sur CD-ROM* (Publication des Nations Unies, numéro de vente E.00.XVII.2).
2   Publication des Nations Unies, numéro de vente E.94.XVII.8 (sur une disquette de 3,5 inches pour micro-ordinateurs IBM et compatibles).

Contents

Table des matières

Part Four
International Economic Relations

Quatrième partie
Relations économiques internationales

List of tables

Part One
World and Region Summary

Part Two
Population and Social Statistics

Liste des tableaux

Première partie
Aperçu mondial et régional

Deuxième partie
Population et statistiques sociales

Part Three
Economic Activity

Troisième partie
Activité économique

---

*   This symbol identifies tables presented in previous issues
of the *Statistical Yearbook* but not contained in the present
issue because of insufficient new data. These tables will
be updated in future issues of the *Yearbook* when new data
become available.

*   Ce symbole indique les tableaux publiés dans les éditions
précédentes de l'*Annuaire statistique* mais qui n'ont pas été
repris dans la présente édition fautes de données nouvelles
suffisantes. Ces tableaux seront actualisés dans les futures
livraisons de l'*Annuaire* à mesure que des données nouvelles deviendront disponibles.

Explanatory notes

The metric system of weights and measures has been employed throughout the *Statistical Yearbook*. For conversion coefficients and factors, see annex II.

In some cases, the comparability of the statistics is affected by geographical changes. As a general rule, the data relate to a given country or area within its present de facto boundaries. Where statistically important, attention is called to changes in territory by means of a footnote. The reader is referred to annex I, concerning country and area nomenclature, where changes in designation are listed.

Numbers in brackets refer to numbered entries in the section "Statistical sources and references" at the end of this book.

In general, the statistics presented in the present publication are based on information available to the Statistics Division of the United Nations Secretariat up to 30 November 2000.

Symbols and conventions used in the tables:
A point (.) is used to indicate decimals.
A hyphen (-) between years, e.g., 1994-1995, indicates the full period involved, including the beginning and end years; a slash (/) indicates a financial year, school year or crop year, e.g., 1994/95.

Not applicable or not separately reported	..
Data not available	...
Magnitude zero	-
Less than half of unit employed	0 or 0.0
Provisional or estimated figure	*
United Nations estimate	x
Marked break in series	#

Details and percentages in the tables do not necessarily add to totals because of rounding.

Notes explicatives

Le système métrique de poids et mesures a été utilisé dans tout l'*Annuaire statistique*. On trouvera à l'annexe II les coefficients et facteurs de conversion.

Dans certains cas, les changements géographiques intervenus influent sur la comparabilité des statistiques. En règle générale, les données renvoient au pays ou zone en question dans ses frontières actuelles effectives. Une note appelle l'attention sur les changements territoriaux, si cela importe du point de vue statistique. Le lecteur est renvoyé à l'annexe I (nomenclature des pays et zones et groupements régionaux) où il trouvera une liste des changements de désignation.

Les chiffres figurant entre crochets se réfèrent aux entrées numérotées dans la liste des sources et références statistiques à la fin de l'ouvrage.

En général, les statistiques qui figurent dans la présente publication sont fondées sur les informations dont disposait la Division de statistique du Secrétariat de l'ONU au 30 novembre 2000.

Signes et conventions employés dans les tableaux:
Les décimales sont précédées d'un point (.).
Un tiret (-) entre des années, par exemple "1994-1995", indique que la période est embrassée dans sa totalité, y compris la première et la dernière année; une barre oblique (/) renvoie à un exercice financier, à une année scolaire ou à une campagne agricole, par exemple "1994/95".

Non applicable ou non communiqué séparément	..
Données non disponibles	...
Néant	-
Valeur inférieure à la moitié de la dernière unité retenue	0 ou 0.0
Chiffre provisoire ou estimatif	*
Estimation des Nations Unies	x
Discontinuité notable dans la série	#

Les chiffres étant arrondis, les totaux ne correspondent pas toujours à la somme exacte des éléments ou pourcentages figurant dans les tableaux.

Introduction

This is the forty-fifth issue of the United Nations *Statistical Yearbook*, prepared by the Statistics Division, Department of Economic and Social Affairs of the United Nations Secretariat. It contains series covering, in general, 1989-1998 or 1990-1999, based on statistics available to the Statistics Division up to 30 November 2000.

The major purpose of the *Statistical Yearbook* is to provide in a single volume a comprehensive compilation of internationally available statistics on social and economic conditions and activities, at world, regional and national levels, covering roughly a ten-year period.

Most of the statistics presented in the *Yearbook* are extracted from more detailed, specialized publications prepared by the Statistics Division and by many other international statistical services. Thus, while the specialized publications concentrate on monitoring topics and trends in particular social and economic fields, the *Statistical Yearbook* tables provide data for a more comprehensive, overall description of social and economic structures, conditions, changes and activities. The objective has been to collect, systematize and coordinate the most essential components of comparable statistical information which can give a broad and, to the extent feasible, a consistent picture of social and economic processes at world, regional and national levels.

More specifically, the *Statistical Yearbook* provides systematic information on a wide range of social and economic issues which are of concern in the United Nations system and among the governments and peoples of the world. A particular value of the *Yearbook*, but also its greatest challenge, is that these issues are extensively interrelated. Meaningful analysis of these issues requires systematization and coordination of the data across many fields. These issues include:

— General economic growth and related economic conditions;

— Economic situation in developing countries and progress towards the objectives adopted for the United Nations development decades;

— Population and urbanization, and their growth and impact;

— Employment, inflation and wages;

— Energy production and consumption and the development of new energy sources;

— Expansion of trade;

— Supply of food and alleviation of hunger;

— Financial situation and external payments and receipts;

— Education, training and eradication of illiteracy;

— Improvement in general living conditions;

— Pollution and protection of the environment;

— Assistance provided to developing countries for social and economic development purposes.

Introduction

La présente édition est la quarante-cinquième de l'*Annuaire statistique* des Nations Unies, établi par la Division de statistique du Département des affaires économiques et sociales du Secrétariat de l'Organisation des Nations Unies. Elle contient des séries de données qui portent d'une manière générale sur les années 1989 à 1998 ou 1990 à 1999, et pour lesquelles ont été utilisées les informations dont disposait la Division de statistique au 30 novembre 2000.

L'*Annuaire statistique* a principalement pour objet de présenter en un seul volume un inventaire complet de statistiques disponibles sur le plan international et concernant la situation et les activités sociales et économiques aux échelons mondial, régional et national, pour une période d'environ 10 ans.

Une bonne partie des données qui figurent dans l'*Annuaire* existent sous une forme plus détaillée dans les publications spécialisées établies par la Division de statistique et par bien d'autres services statistiques internationaux. Alors que les publications spécialisées suivent essentiellement l'évolution dans certains domaines socio-économiques précis, l'*Annuaire statistique* présente les données de manière à fournir une description plus globale et exhaustive des structures, conditions, transformations et activités socio-économiques. On a cherché à recueillir, systématiser et coordonner les principaux éléments de renseignements statistiques comparables, de manière à dresser un tableau général et autant que possible cohérent des processus socio-économiques en cours aux échelons mondial, régional et national.

Plus précisément, l'*Annuaire statistique* a pour objet de présenter des renseignements systématiques sur toutes sortes de questions socio-économiques qui sont liées aux préoccupations actuelles du système des Nations Unies ainsi que des gouvernements et des peuples du monde. Le principal avantage de l'*Annuaire* — et aussi la principale difficulté à surmonter — tient à ce que ces questions sont étroitement interdépendantes. Pour en faire une analyse utile, il est essentiel de systématiser et de coordonner les données se rapportant à de nombreux domaines différents. Ces questions sont notamment les suivantes:

— La croissance économique générale et les aspects connexes de l'économie;

— La situation économique dans les pays en développement et les progrès accomplis vers la réalisation des objectifs des décennies des Nations Unies pour le développement;

— La population et l'urbanisation, leur croissance et leur impact;

— L'emploi, l'inflation et les salaires;

— La production et la consommation d'énergie et la mise en valeur des énergies nouvelles;

— L'expansion des échanges;

— La pollution et la protection de l'environnement;

Organization of the *Yearbook*

The contents of the *Statistical Yearbook* are planned to serve a general readership. The *Yearbook* endeavours to provide information for various bodies of the United Nations system as well as for other international organizations, for governments and non-governmental organizations, for national statistical, economic and social policy bodies, for scientific and educational institutions, for libraries and for the public. Data published in the *Statistical Yearbook* are also of interest to companies and enterprises and to agencies engaged in marketing research.

The 80 tables of the *Yearbook* are grouped into four broad parts:

— World and Region Summary (chapter I: tables 1-7);

— Population and Social Statistics (chapters II-V: tables 8-17);

— Economic Activity (chapters VI-XV: tables 18-68);

— International Economic Relations (chapters XVI-XX: tables 69-80).

These four parts present data at two levels of aggregation. The more aggregated information shown in Part One provides an overall picture of development at the world and region levels. More specific and detailed information for analysis concerning individual countries or areas is presented in the three following parts. Each of these is divided into more specific chapters, by topic, and each chapter includes a section, "Technical notes". These notes provide brief descriptions of major statistical concepts, definitions and classifications required for interpretation and analysis of the data. Systematic information on the methodology used for the computation of the figures can be found in the publications on methodology of the United Nations and its agencies, listed in the section "Statistical sources and references" at the end of the *Yearbook*. Additional general information on statistical methodology is provided in the section below on "Comparability of statistics" and in the explanatory notes following the Introduction.

Part One, World and Region Summary, comprises seven tables highlighting the principal trends in the world as a whole as well as in regions and in the major economic and social sectors. It contains global totals of important aggregate statistics needed for the analysis of economic growth, the structure of the world economy, major changes in world population and expansion of external merchandise trade. The global totals are, as a rule, subdivided into major geographical areas.

Part Two, Population and Social Statistics, comprises 10 tables which contain more detailed statistical series on social conditions and levels of living, for example, data on education and cultural activities.

Part Three, Economic Activity, provides data in 24 tables of statistics on national accounts, index numbers

— Les approvisionnements alimentaires et la lutte contre la faim;

— La situation financière, les paiements extérieurs et les recettes extérieures;

— L'éducation, la formation et l'élimination de l'analphabétisme;

— L'assistance fournie aux pays en développement à des fins socio-économiques.

Présentation de l'*Annuaire*

Le contenu de l'*Annuaire statistique* a été préparé à l'intention de tous les lecteurs intéressés. Les renseignements fournis devraient pouvoir être utilisés par les divers organismes du système des Nations Unies ainsi que par d'autres organisations internationales, par les gouvernements et les organisations non gouvernementales, par les organismes nationaux de statistique et de politique économique et sociale, par les institutions scientifiques et les établissements d'enseignement, les bibliothèques et les particuliers. Les données publiées dans l'*Annuaire statistique* peuvent également intéresser les sociétés et entreprises, et les organismes spécialisés dans les études de marché.

Les 80 tableaux de l'*Annuaire* sont groupés en quatre parties:

— Aperçu mondial et régional (chapitre I: tableaux 1 à 7);

— Statistiques démographiques et sociales (chapitres II à V: tableaux 8 à 17);

— Activité économique (chapitres VI à XV: tableaux 18 à 68);

— Relations économiques internationales (chapitres XVI à XX: tableaux 69 à 80).

Ces quatre parties présentent les données à deux niveaux d'agrégation: les valeurs les plus agrégées qui figurent dans la première partie donnent un tableau global du développement à l'échelon mondial et régional, tandis que les trois autres parties contiennent des renseignements plus précis et détaillés qui se prêtent mieux à une analyse par pays ou par zones. Chacune de ces trois parties est divisée en chapitres portant sur des sujets donnés, et chaque chapitre comprend une section intitulée "Notes techniques" où l'on trouve une brève description des principales notions, définitions et classifications statistiques nécessaires pour interpréter et analyser les données. Les méthodes de calcul utilisées sont décrites de façon systématique dans les publications se référant à la méthodologie des Nations Unies et de leurs organismes, énumérées à la fin de l'*Annuaire* dans la section "Sources et références statistiques". Le lecteur trouvera un complément d'informations générales ci-après dans la section intitulée "Comparabilité des statistiques", ainsi que dans les notes explicatives qui suivent l'introduction.

La première partie, intitulée "Aperçu mondial et régional", comprend sept tableaux présentant les principales tendances dans le monde et dans les régions ainsi

of industrial production, interest rates, labour force, wages and prices, transport, energy, environment and intellectual property; and in 27 tables on production in the major branches of the economy (using, in general, the International Standard Industrial Classification, ISIC), namely agriculture, hunting, forestry and fishing; mining and quarrying; manufacturing; and transport and communications. In an innovation in the general approach of the *Yearbook*, consumption data are now being combined with the production data in tables on specific commodities, where feasible.

Part Four, International Economic Relations, comprises 12 tables on international merchandise trade, balance of payments, tourism, finance and development assistance. It focuses on the growth and structure of exports and imports by countries or areas, international tourism, balance of payments and development assistance provided by multilateral and bilateral agencies to individual recipients.

An index (in English only) is provided at the end of the *Yearbook*.

Annexes and regional groupings of countries or areas

The annexes to the *Statistical Yearbook* and the section "Explanatory notes" preceding the Introduction, provide additional essential information on the *Yearbook*'s contents and presentation of data.

Annex I provides information on countries or areas covered in the *Yearbook* tables and on their grouping into geographical regions. The geographical groupings shown in the *Yearbook* are generally based on continental regions unless otherwise indicated. However, strict consistency in this regard is impossible. A wide range of classifications is used for different purposes in the various international agencies and other sources of statistics for the *Yearbook*. These classifications vary in response to administrative and analytical requirements.

Neither is there a common agreement in the United Nations system concerning the terms "developed" and "developing", when referring to the stage of development reached by any given country or area and its corresponding classification in one or the other grouping. Thus, the *Yearbook* refers more generally to "developed" or "developing" regions on the basis of conventional practice. Following this practice, "developed regions" comprises Northern America, Europe and the former USSR, Australia, Japan and New Zealand, while all of Africa and the remainder of the Americas, Asia and Oceania comprise the "developing regions". These designations are intended for statistical convenience and do not necessarily express a judgement about the stage reached by a particular country or area in the development process.

Annex II provides detailed information on conversion coefficients and factors used in various tables, and annex III provides listings of tables added and omitted in the present edition of the *Yearbook*.

que dans les principaux secteurs économiques et sociaux. Elle fournit des chiffres mondiaux pour les principaux agrégats statistiques nécessaires pour analyser la croissance économique, la structure de l'économie mondiale, les principaux changements dans la population mondiale et l'expansion du commerce extérieur de marchandises. En règle générale, les chiffres mondiaux sont ventilés par grandes régions géographiques.

La deuxième partie, intitulée "Statistiques démographiques et sociales", comporte 10 tableaux où figurent des séries plus détaillées concernant les conditions sociales et les niveaux de vie, notamment des données sur l'éducation et les activités culturelles.

La troisième partie, intitulée "Activité économique", présente en 24 tableaux des statistiques concernant les comptes nationaux, les nombres indices relatifs à la production industrielle, les taux d'intérêt, la population active, les prix et les salaires, le transport, l'énergie, l'environnement, et la propriété intellectuelle; et en 27 tableaux des données sur la production des principales branches d'activité économique (en utilisant en général la *Classification internationale type, par industrie, de toutes les branches d'activité économique*): agriculture, chasse, sylviculture et pêche; mines et carrières; industries manufacturières; transports et communications. Une innovation a été introduite dans la présentation générale de l'*Annuaire* en ce sens que les tableaux traitant de certains produits de base associent autant que possible les données relatives à la consommation aux valeurs concernant la production.

La quatrième partie, intitulée "Relations économiques internationales", comprend 12 tableaux relatifs au commerce international de marchandises, aux balances des paiements, au tourisme, aux finances et à l'aide au développement. Elle est consacrée essentiellement à la croissance et à la structure des exportations et des importations par pays et par zone, au tourisme international, aux balances des paiements et à l'aide au développement fournie aux pays par les organismes multilatéraux et bilatéraux.

Un index (en anglais seulement) figure à la fin de l'*Annuaire*.

Annexes et groupements régionaux des pays et zones

Les annexes à l'*Annuaire statistique* et la section intitulée "Notes explicatives" qui précède l'introduction, offrent d'importantes informations complémentaires quant à la teneur et à la présentation des données figurant dans le présent ouvrage.

L'annexe I donne des renseignements sur les pays ou zones couverts par les tableaux de l'*Annuaire* et sur leur regroupement en régions géographiques. Sauf indication contraire, les groupements géographiques figurant dans l'*Annuaire* sont généralement fondés sur les régions continentales, mais une présentation absolument systématique est impossible à cet égard car les diverses institutions internationales et autres sources de statisti-

Comparability of statistics

One major aim of the *Statistical Yearbook* is to present series which are as nearly comparable across countries as the available statistics permit. Considerable efforts are also made among the international suppliers of data and by the staff of the *Yearbook* to ensure the compatibility of various series by coordinating time periods, base years, prices chosen for valuation and so on. This is indispensable in relating various bodies of data to each other and to facilitate analysis across different sectors. Thus, for example, relating data on economic output to those on employment makes it possible to derive some trends in the field of productivity; relating data on exports and imports to those on national product allows an evaluation of the relative importance of external trade in different countries and reveals changes in the role of trade over time.

In general, the data presented reflect the methodological recommendations of the United Nations Statistical Commission, issued in various United Nations publications, and of other international bodies concerned with statistics. Publications containing these recommendations and guidelines are listed in the section "Statistical sources and references" at the end of the *Yearbook*. Use of international recommendations not only promotes international comparability of the data but also ensures a degree of compatibility regarding the underlying concepts, definitions and classifications relating to different series. However, much work remains to be done in this area and, for this reason, some tables can serve only as a first source of data, which require further adjustment before being used for more in-depth analytical studies. While on the whole, a significant degree of comparability has been achieved in international statistics, there are many limitations, for a variety of reasons.

One common cause of non-comparability of economic data is different valuations of statistical aggregates such as national income, wages and salaries, output of industries and so forth. Conversion of these and similar series originally expressed in national prices into a common currency, for example into United States dollars, through the use of exchange rates, is not always satisfactory owing to frequent wide fluctuations in market rates and differences between official rates and rates which would be indicated by unofficial markets or purchasing power parities. For this reason, data on national income in United States dollars which are published in the *Yearbook* are subject to certain distortions and can be used as only a rough approximation of the relative magnitudes involved.

The use of different kinds of sources for obtaining data is another cause of incomparability. This is true, for example, in the case of employment and unemployment, where data are collected from such non-comparable sources as sample surveys, social insurance statistics and establishment surveys.

ques employées pour la confection de l'*Annuaire* emploient, selon l'objet de l'exercice, des classifications fort différentes en réponse à diverses exigences d'ordre administratif ou analytique.

Il n'existe pas non plus dans le système des Nations Unies de définition commune des termes "développé" et "en développement" pour décrire le niveau atteint en la matière par un pays ou une zone donnés ni pour les classifier dans l'un ou l'autre de ces groupes. Ainsi, dans l'*Annuaire*, on s'en remet à l'usage pour qualifier les régions de "développées" ou "en développement". Selon cet usage, les régions développées sont l'Amérique septentrionale, l'Europe et l'ancienne URSS, l'Australie, le Japon et la Nouvelle-Zélande, alors que toute l'Afrique et le reste des Amériques, l'Asie et l'Océanie constituent les régions en développement. Ces appellations sont utilisées pour plus de commodité dans la présentation des statistiques et n'impliquent pas nécessairement un jugement quant au stade de développement auquel est parvenu tel pays ou telle zone.

L'annexe II fournit des renseignements sur les coefficients et facteurs de conversion employés dans les différents tableaux, et l'annexe III contient les listes de tableaux qui ont été ajoutés ou omis dans la présente édition de l'*Annuaire*.

Comparabilité des statistiques

L'*Annuaire statistique* a principalement pour objet de présenter des statistiques aussi comparables d'un pays à l'autre que les données le permettent. Les sources internationales de données et les auteurs de l'*Annuaire* ont réalisés des efforts considérables pour faire en sorte que les diverses séries soient compatibles en harmonisant les périodes de référence, les années de base, les prix utilisés pour les évaluations, etc. Cette démarche est indispensable si l'on veut rapprocher divers ensembles de données pour faciliter l'analyse intersectorielle de l'économie. Ainsi, en liant les données concernant la production à celles de l'emploi, on parvient à dégager certaines tendances dans le domaine de la productivité; de même, en associant les données concernant les exportations et importations aux valeurs du produit national, on obtient une évaluation de l'importance relative des échanges extérieurs dans différents pays et de l'évolution du rôle joué par le commerce.

De façon générale, les données sont présentées selon les recommandations méthodologiques formulées par la Commission de statistique de l'ONU et par les autres organisations internationales qui s'intéressent aux statistiques. Les titres des publications contenant ces recommandations et lignes directrices figurent à la fin de l'ouvrage dans la section intitulée "Sources et références statistiques". Le respect des recommandations internationales tend non seulement à promouvoir la comparabilité des données à l'échelon international, mais elle assure également une certaine comparabilité entre les concepts, les définitions et classifications utilisés. Mais comme il

Non-comparability of data may also result from differences in the institutional patterns of countries. Certain variations in social and economic organization and institutions may have an impact on the comparability of the data even if the underlying concepts and definitions are identical.

These and other causes of non-comparability of the data are briefly explained in the technical notes to each chapter.

Statistical sources and reliability and timeliness of data

Statistics and indicators have been compiled mainly from official national and international sources, as these are more authoritative and comprehensive, more generally available as time series and more comparable among countries than other sources. In a few cases, official sources are supplemented by other sources and estimates, where these have been subjected to professional scrutiny and debate and are consistent with other independent sources. The comprehensive international data sources used for most of the tables are presented in the list of "Statistical sources and references" at the end of the *Yearbook*.

Users of international statistics are often concerned about the apparent lack of timeliness in the available data. Unfortunately, most international data are only available with a delay of at least one to three years after the latest year to which they refer. The reasons for the delay are that the data must first be processed by the national statistical services at the country level, then forwarded to the international statistical services and processed again to ensure as much consistency across countries and over time as possible.

reste encore beaucoup à faire dans ce domaine, les données présentées dans certains tableaux n'ont qu'une valeur indicative et nécessiteront des ajustements plus poussés avant de pouvoir servir à des analyses approfondies. Bien que l'on soit parvenu, dans l'ensemble, à un degré de comparabilité appréciable en matière de statistiques internationales, diverses raisons expliquent que subsistent encore de nombreuses limitations.

Une cause commune de non-comparabilité des données réside dans la diversité des méthodes d'évaluation employées pour comptabiliser des agrégats tels que le revenu national, les salaires et traitements, la production des différentes branches d'activité industrielle, etc. Il n'est pas toujours satisfaisant de ramener la valeur des séries de ce type — exprimée à l'origine en prix nationaux — à une monnaie commune (par exemple le dollar des États-Unis) car les taux de change du marché connaissent fréquemment de fortes fluctuations tandis que les taux officiels ne coïncident pas avec ceux des marchés officieux ni avec les parités réelles de pouvoir d'achat. C'est pourquoi les données relatives au revenu national, qui sont publiées dans l'*Annuaire* en dollars des États-Unis, souffrent de certaines distorsions et ne peuvent servir qu'à donner une idée approximative des ordres de grandeur relatifs.

Le recours à des sources diverses pour la collecte des données est une autre facteur qui limite la comparabilité, en particulier dans les secteurs de l'emploi et du chômage où les statistiques sont obtenues par des moyens aussi peu comparables que les sondages, le dépouillement des registres d'assurances sociales et les enquêtes auprès des entreprises.

Dans certains cas, les données ne sont pas comparables en raison de différences entre les structures institutionnelles des pays. Certaines variations dans l'organisation et les institutions économiques et sociales peuvent affecter la comparabilité des données même si les concepts et définitions sont fondamentalement identiques.

Ces causes de non-comparabilité des données sont parmi celles qui sont brièvement expliquées dans les notes techniques de chaque chapitre.

Origine, fiabilité et actualité des données

Les statistiques et les indicateurs sont fondés essentiellement sur des données provenant de sources officielles nationales et internationales; c'est en effet la meilleure source si l'on veut des données fiables, complètes et comparables et si l'on a besoin de séries chronologiques. Dans quelques cas, les données officielles sont complétées par des informations et des estimations provenant d'autres sources qui ont été examinées par des spécialistes et confirmées par des sources indépendantes. On trouvera à la fin de l'*Annuaire* la liste des "Sources statistiques et références", qui récapitule les sources des données internationales utilisées pour la plupart des tableaux.

Les utilisateurs des statistiques internationales se plaignent souvent du fait que les données disponibles ne sont pas actualisées. Malheureusement, la plupart des données internationales ne sont disponibles qu'avec un délai de deux ou trois ans après la dernière année à laquelle elles se rapportent. S'l en est ainsi, c'est parce que les données sont d'abord traitées par les services statistiques nationaux avant d'être transmises aux services statistiques internationaux, qui les traitent à nouveau pour assurer la plus grande comparabilité possible entre les pays et entre les périodes.

Part One
World and Region Summary

I
World and region summary (tables 1-7)

This part of the *Statistical Yearbook* presents selected aggregate series on principal economic and social topics for the world as a whole and for the major regions. The topics include population and surface area, agricultural and industrial production, motor vehicles in use, external trade, government financial reserves, and energy production and consumption. More detailed data on individual countries and areas are provided in the subsequent parts of the present *Yearbook*. These comprise Part Two: Population and Social Statistics; Part Three: Economic Activity; and Part Four: International Economic Relations.

Regional totals may contain incomparabilities between series owing to differences in definitions of regions and lack of data for particular regional components. General information on regional groupings is provided in annex I of the *Yearbook*. Supplementary information on regional groupings used in specific series is provided, as necessary, in table footnotes and in the technical notes at the end of chapter I.

Première partie
Aperçu mondial et régional

I
Aperçu mondial et régional (tableaux 1 à 7)

Cette partie de l'*Annuaire statistique* présente, pour le monde entier et ses principales subdivisions, un choix d'agrégats ayant trait à des questions économiques et sociales essentielles: population et superficie, production agricole et industrielle, véhicules automobiles en circulation, commerce extérieur, réserves financières publiques, et la production et la consommation d'énergie. Des statistiques plus détaillées pour divers pays ou zones figurent dans les parties ultérieures de l'*Annuaire*, c'est-à-dire dans les deuxième, troisième et quatrième parties intitulées respectivement: population et statistiques sociales, activités économiques et relations économiques internationales.

Les totaux régionaux peuvent présenter des incomparabilités entre les séries en raison de différences dans la définition des régions et de l'absence de données sur tel ou tel élément régional. A l'annexe I de l'*Annuaire*, on trouvera des renseignements généraux sur les groupements régionaux. Des informations complémentaires sur les groupements régionaux pour certaines séries bien précises sont fournies, lorsqu'il y a lieu, dans les notes figurant au bas des tableaux et dans les notes techniques à la fin du chapitre I.

1
Selected series of world statistics
Séries principales de statistiques mondiales
Population, production, transport, external trade and finance
Population, production, transports, commerce extérieur et finances

Series / Séries	Unit or base / Unité ou base	1990	1991	1992	1993	1994	1995	1996	1997	1998	1999
World population [1] **Population mondiale** [1]	million	5282	5385	5480	5572	5630	5687	5768	5849	5901	5978

Agriculture, forestry and fishing production • Production agricole, forestière et de la pêche

Index numbers · Indices

Series / Séries	Unit or base / Unité ou base	1990	1991	1992	1993	1994	1995	1996	1997	1998	1999
All commodities Tous produits	1989−91=100	101	101	103	104	107	109	114	116	118	119
Food Produits alimentaires	1989−91=100	101	101	104	105	108	110	115	117	119	120
Crops Cultures	1989−91=100	101	101	104	104	107	108	115	117	117	120
Cereals Céréales	1989−91=100	103	99	103	100	103	100	109	111	110	111
Livestock products Produits de l'élevage	1989−91=100	101	102	102	103	106	109	110	113	116	119

Quantities · Quantités

Series / Séries	Unit or base / Unité ou base	1990	1991	1992	1993	1994	1995	1996	1997	1998	1999
Oil crops Cultures d'huile	million t.	74	76	77	80	88	91	93	97	101	104
Meat Viande	million t.	135	137	138	141	144	146	147	152	158	159
Roundwood Bois rond	million m³	3326	3208	3146	3141	3162	3214	3219	3298	3550	3591
Fish catches Quantités pêchées	million t.	98.6	98.2	100.8	104.4	112.3	116.1	120.3	122.4	117.2	...

Industrial production • Production industrielle

Index numbers [2] · Indices [2]

Series / Séries	Unit or base / Unité ou base	1990	1991	1992	1993	1994	1995	1996	1997	1998	1999
All commodities Tous produits	1990=100	100	100	101	102	107	111	115	121	124	129
Mining Mines	1990=100	100	101	103	104	107	109	112	115	115	115
Manufacturing Manufactures	1990=100	100	100	101	101	106	111	115	122	125	130

Quantities · Quantités

Series / Séries	Unit or base / Unité ou base	1990	1991	1992	1993	1994	1995	1996	1997	1998	1999
Coal Houille	million t.	3513	3460	3526	3462	3592	3741	3804	3836	...	...
Lignite and brown coal Lignite et charbon brun	million t.	1194	1056	1040	995	1002	942	950	933	...	...
Crude petroleum Pétrole brut	million t.	3005	2987	3019	3003	3055	3077	3120	3193	...	...
Natural gas Gaz naturel	petajoules pétajoules	74428	76750	76117	78521	80785	86513	90129	90231	...	...
Pig−iron and ferro−alloys Fonte et ferro−alliages	million t.	522	491	491	494	505	523	515	538	532	...
Fabrics · Tissus Cellulosic and non−cellulosic fibres Cellulosiques et non cellulosiques	million m²	17997	15836	16293	14864	14799	15350	15135	15475	15389	...
Cotton and wool Coton et laines	million m²	70588	68435	67087	67475	67639	74348	74007	76665	78208	...
Leather footwear Chaussures de cuir	million pairs	4544	4271	4200	3869	3602	3547	3364	3374	3404	...
Sulphuric acid Acide sulfurique	million t.	132	98	90	81	81	87	88	91	92	...
Soap Savons	million t.	24	25	24	25	25	26	26	27	27	...
Refrigerators Réfrigérateurs	million	53	53	53	56	61	63	63	67	66	...
Washing machines Machines à laver	million	46	46	44	48	49	46	49	53	53	...

1
Selected series of world statistics
Population, production, transport, external trade and finance [*cont.*]
Séries principales de statistiques mondiales
Population, production, transports, commerce extérieur et finances [*suite*]

Series Séries	Unit or base Unité ou base	1990	1991	1992	1993	1994	1995	1996	1997	1998	1999
Machine tools · Machines outils											
Drilling and boring machines	thousands										
Perceuses	milliers	98	118	95	88	72	75	66	66	49	...
Lathes	thousands										
Tours	milliers	91	89	63	50	52	66	65	62	58	...
Lorries · Camions											
Assembled	thousands										
Assemblés	milliers	689	701	665	742	740	765	816	858	802	...
Produced	thousands										
Fabriqués	milliers	11748	11070	11645	10504	10516	10119	10080	10375	10064	...
Aluminium	thousands t.										
Aluminium	milliers t.	23404	23877	24652	24974	25160	25661	25694	28044	28859	...
Cement											
Ciment	million t3	1141	1160	1214	1278	1350	1420	1459	1508	1502	
Electricity [3]	billion kWh										
Electricité [3]	milliard kWh	11810	12041	12141	12403	12697	13133	13673	13947	...	...
Fertilizers [4]											
Engrais [4]	million t.	147.6	144.5	137.8	132.3	135.8	142.2	147.3	146.4	147.3	...
Sugar, raw											
Sucre, brut	million t.	111.2	113.1	115.7	109.6	108.0	118.5	125.8	126.4	129.5	134.3
Woodpulp											
Pâte de bois	million t.	155.1	155.2	152.0	151.3	161.9	161.7	156.4	162.5	160.1	163.2
Sawnwood											
Sciages	million m³	505	457	437	431	433	426	431	431	421	434
Motor vehicles · Véhicules automobiles											
Passenger											
Tourisme	million	34.99	33.63	33.81	31.98	33.60	33.14	33.94	34.20	32.93	...
Commercial											
Utilitaires	million	12.19	11.51	12.13	11.04	11.07	10.72	10.74	10.07	10.74	...

Transport · Transports

	Motor vehicles in use · Véhicules automobiles en service										
Passenger cars	thousands										
Voitures de tourisme	milliers	441958	451928	445742	449990	469303	457763	470587	481755	...	...
Commercial vehicles	thousands										
Véhicules utilitaires	milliers	137869	141930	139575	141023	149548	165368	186867	196056	...	...

External trade · Commerce extérieur

	Value, billion US$ · Valeur, milliard $E.–U.										
Imports, c.i.f.											
Importations c.a.f.		3557.0	3563.9	3798.6	3755.6	4279.1	5052.7	5310.9	5533.4	5449.9	5664.9
Exports, f.o.b.											
Exportations f.o.b.		3437.6	3444.4	3685.6	3707.9	4228.5	5007.8	5205.6	5447.6	5371.1	5546.3
	Quantum: index of exports · Quantum : indice des exportations										
All commodities											
Tous produits	1990=100	100	105	110	113	123	136	143	160	169	179
Manufactures											
Produits manufacturés	1990=100	100	105	111	115	130	141	152	172	171	...
	Unit value: index of exports [5] · Valeur unitaire : indice des exportations [5]										
All commodities											
Tous produits	1990=100	100	98	100	97	101	109	108	101	94	93
Manufactures											
Produits manufacturés	1990=100	100	100	103	99	101	110	106	98	96	...
	Primary commodities: price indexes [5 6] · Produits de base : indices des prix [5 6]										
All commodities											
Tous produits	1980=100	79	69	71	65	66	72	76	71	56	63
Food											
Produits alimentaires	1980=100	88	85	87	82	87	92	92	89	82	76
Non–food: of agricultural origin											
Non alimentaire: d'origine agricole	1980=100	100	93	91	84	95	106	98	90	81	73
Minerals											
Minéraux	1980=100	72	59	62	55	53	58	67	62	43	57

1

Selected series of world statistics
Population, production, transport, external trade and finance [*cont.*]
Séries principales de statistiques mondiales
Population, production, transports, commerce extérieur et finances [*suite*]

Series Séries	Unit or base Unité ou base	1990	1991	1992	1993	1994	1995	1996	1997	1998	1999
Finance • Finances											
International reserves minus gold, billion SDR [7] · Réserves internationales moins l'or, milliard de DTS [7]											
All countries	billion SDR										
Tous les pays	milliard DTS	637.7	692.3	720.1	797.8	859.0	988.4	1142.2	1261.2	1242.9	1366.6
Position in IMF	billion SDR										
Disponibilité au FMI	milliard DTS	23.8	25.9	33.9	32.8	31.7	36.7	38.0	47.1	60.6	54.8
Foreign exchange	billion SDR										
Devises	milliard DTS	593.6	646.2	673.5	750.4	811.5	932.0	1085.7	1193.6	1162.0	1293.4
SDR (special drawing rights)	billion SDR										
DTS (droits de tirage spéciaux)	milliard DTS	20.4	20.6	12.9	14.6	15.8	19.8	18.5	20.5	20.4	18.5

Sources:
Databases of the Food and Agriculture Organization of the United Nations
(FAO), Rome; the International Monetary Fund (IMF), Washington, D.C.;
and the Statistics Division of the United Nations Secretariat, New York.

Sources:
Les bases de données de l'Organisation des Nations Unies pour
l'alimentation et l'agriculture (FAO), Rome; du Fonds Monétaire
International (FMI), Washington, D.C.; et de la Division de statistique
du Secrétariat de l'Organisation des Nations Unies, New York.

1 Annual data: mid−year estimates.
2 Excluding China and the countries of the former USSR (except
   Russian Federation and Ukraine).
3 Electricity generated by establishments for public or private use.
4 Year beginning 1 July.
5 Indexes computed in US dollars.
6 Export price indexes.
7 End of period.

1 Données annuelles : estimations au milieu de l'année.
2 Non compris la Chine et les pays de l'ancienne URSS (sauf
   la Fédération de Russie et Ukraine).
3 L'électricité produite par des entreprises d'utilisation publique
   ou privée.
4 L'année commençant le 1er juillet.
5 Indice calculé en dollars des Etats−Unis.
6 Indice des prix à l'exportation.
7 Fin de la période.

2
Population, rate of increase, birth and death rates, surface area and density
Population, taux d'accroissement, taux de natalité et taux de mortalité, superficie et densité

Major areas and regions Grandes régions et régions	Mid-year population estimates (millions) Estimations de population au milieu de l'année (millions)								Annual rate of increase Taux d'accrois-sement annuel % 1995	Birth rate Taux de natalité (0/000) –2000	Death rate Taux de mortalité (0/000)	Surface area (km²) Superficie (km²) (000's) 1998	Density[1] Densité[1] 2000
	1950	1960	1970	1980	1990	1995	1998	2000					
World													
Monde	**2521**	**3022**	**3696**	**4440**	**5266**	**5666**	**5901**	**6055**	**1.3**	**22**	**9**	**135641**	**45**
Africa													
Afrique	**221**	**277**	**357**	**467**	**615**	**700**	**749**	**784**	**2.4**	**38**	**14**	**30306**	**26**
Eastern Africa Afrique orientale	65	82	108	144	192	217	235	247	2.6	42	18	6356	39
Middle Africa Afrique centrale	26	32	40	52	70	84	91	96	2.7	45	15	6613	14
Northern Africa Afrique septentrionale	53	67	85	110	142	157	167	173	2.0	28	7	8525	20
Southern Africa Afrique méridionale	16	20	25	31	39	43	46	47	1.6	28	12	2675	18
Western Africa Afrique occidentale	61	76	98	128	172	196	211	222	2.5	40	15	6138	36
Northern America[2]													
Amérique septentrionale	**172**	**204**	**232**	**255**	**282**	**297**	**305**	**310**	**0.9**	**14**	**8**	**21517**	**14**
Latin America													
Amérique latine	**167**	**218**	**285**	**361**	**440**	**480**	**504**	**519**	**1.6**	**23**	**6**	**20533**	**25**
Caribbean Caraïbes	17	20	25	29	34	36	37	38	1.1	21	8	235	162
Central America Amérique centrale	37	49	67	90	111	123	130	135	1.9	27	5	2480	55
South America Amérique du Sud	113	145	192	242	295	321	336	346	1.5	22	7	17819	19
Asia[3]													
Asie[3]	**1402**	**1702**	**2147**	**2641**	**3181**	**3436**	**3585**	**3683**	**1.4**	**22**	**8**	**31764**	**116**
Eastern Asia Asie orientale	671	791	987	1178	1350	1422	1461	1485	0.9	16	7	11762	126
South Central Asia Asie central méridionale	499	621	788	990	1239	1365	1441	1491	1.8	27	9	10776	138
South Eastern Asia Asie mériodionale orientale	182	225	287	360	441	480	504	519	1.5	23	7	4495	115
Western Asia[3] Asie occidentale[3]	50	66	86	113	150	168	180	188	2.2	30	7	4731	40
Europe[3]													
Europe[3]	**547**	**605**	**656**	**693**	**722**	**728**	**729**	**729**	**0.0**	**10**	**11**	**22986**	**32**
Eastern Europe Europe orientale	219	253	276	295	311	310	308	307	−0.2	10	13	18813	16
Northern Europe Europe septentrionale	78	82	87	90	92	94	94	94	0.1	12	11	1749	54
Southern Europe Europe mériodionale	109	118	128	138	143	143	144	144	0.1	10	10	1316	110
Western Europe Europe occidentale	141	152	165	170	176	181	183	183	0.3	11	10	1107	166
Oceania[2]													
Océanie[2]	**12.6**	**15.7**	**19.3**	**22.7**	**26.4**	**28.5**	**29.6**	**30.4**	**1.3**	**18**	**8**	**8537**	**4**
Australia and New Zealand Australie et Nouvelle–Zélande	10.1	12.6	15.4	17.7	20.2	21.6	22.3	22.7	1.0	14	8	7984	3
Melanesia Mélanésie	2.1	2.6	3.3	4.2	5.2	5.8	6.2	6.5	2.2	31	9	541	12
Micronesia Micronésie	0.2	0.2	0.3	0.3	0.4	0.5	0.5	0.5	2.6	36	5	3	181
Polynesia Polynésie	0.2	0.3	0.4	0.5	0.5	0.6	0.6	0.6	1.6	25	5	9	70

2
Population, rate of increase, birth and death rates, surface area and density [*cont.*]
Population, taux d'accroissement, taux de natalité et taux de
mortalité, superficie et densité [*suite*]

Source:
United Nations Secretariat, "Demographic Yearbook 1998"
and the demographic statistics database of the Statistics
Division.

1   Population per square kilometre of surface area. Figures
    are merely the quotients of population divided by surface
    area and are not to be considered as either reflecting
    density in the urban sense or as indicating the supporting
    power of a territory's land and resources.
2   Hawaii, a state of the United States of America, is included
    in Northern America rather than Oceania.
3   The European portion of Turkey is included in Western
    Asia rather than Europe.

Source:
Secrétariat de l'Organisation des Nations Unies, "Annuaire démographique
1998" et la base de données pour les statistiques démographiques de
la Division de statistique.

1   Habitants per kilomètre carré. Il s'agit simplement du quotient calculé
    en divisant la population par la superficie et n'est pas considéré
    comme indiquant la densité au sens urbain du mot ni l'effectif de
    population que les terres et les ressources du territoire sont capables
    de nourrir.
2   Hawaii, un Etat des Etats–Unis d'Amérique, est compris en Amérique
    septentrionale plutôt qu'en Océanie.
3   La partie européenne de la Turquie est comprise en Asie Occidentale
    plutôt qu'en Europe.

3
Index numbers of total agricultural and food production
Indices de la production agricole totale et de la production alimentaire

1989–1991 = 100

Country or area Pays ou zone	1990	1991	1992	1993	1994	1995	1996	1997	1998	1999
A. Total agricultural production · Production agricole totale										
World *Monde*	101	101	103	104	107	109	114	116	118	119
Africa Afrique	98	105	103	106	109	110	122	119	123	125
America, North Amérique du Nord	102	101	108	101	114	110	114	118	119	120
America, South Amérique du Sud	99	103	105	106	112	118	122	126	128	131
Asia Asie	101	103	112	117	122	127	132	137	139	141
Europe Europe	100	100	94	91	86	86	88	88	86	86
Oceania Océanie	101	101	105	107	102	109	116	119	121	120
former USSR † l'ex–URSS †	105	91	...	...	...	...	...	...	...	...
B. Food Production · Production alimentaire										
World *Monde*	101	101	104	105	108	110	115	117	119	120
Africa Afrique	98	105	103	107	110	111	122	119	124	126
America, North Amérique du Nord	101	101	108	101	114	110	114	118	120	121
America, South Amérique du Sud	99	102	106	107	114	121	125	130	132	135
Asia Asie	101	103	112	117	122	128	133	137	141	143
Europe Europe	100	100	94	91	86	86	88	88	86	86
Oceania Océanie	101	101	108	112	107	117	126	128	132	130
former USSR † l'ex–URSS †	105	91	...	...	...	...	...	...	...	...

Source:
Food and Agriculture Organization of the United Nations (FAO), Rome, "FAO Production Yearbook 1999" and the FAOSTAT database.

Source:
Organisation des Nations Unies pour l'alimentation et l'agriculture (FAO), Rome, "Annuaire FAO de la production 1999 "et la base de données FAOSTAT.

† For information on recent changes in country or area nomenclature pertaining to former Czechoslovakia, Germany, Hong Kong Special Administrative Region (SAR) of China, Macao Special Administrative Region (SAR) of China, SFR of Yugoslavia and the former USSR, see Annex I – Country or area nomenclature, regional and other groupings.

† Pour les modifications récentes de nomenclature de pays ou de zone concernant l'Allemagne, Hong Kong région administrative spéciale (RAS) de Chine, Macao région administrative spéciale (RAS) de Chine, l'ex–Tchécoslovaquie. l'ex–URSS et l'ex–Rfs de Yougoslavie, voir annexe I – Nomenclature des pays ou des zones, groupements régionaux et autres groupements.

4
Index numbers of per capita total agricultural and food production
Indices de la production agricole totale et de la production alimentaire par habitant

1989–1991 = 100

Country or area Pays ou zone	1990	1991	1992	1993	1994	1995	1996	1997	1998	1999
A. Per capita total agricultural production · Production agricole totale par habitant										
World *Monde*	101	100	100	99	101	102	104	105	105	105
Africa Afrique	98	102	98	99	98	97	105	100	101	100
America, North Amérique du Nord	102	100	105	97	108	103	106	108	107	107
America, South Amérique du Sud	99	101	102	100	105	109	111	112	113	114
Asia Asie	101	101	106	109	112	115	118	120	121	121
Europe Europe	100	100	64	63	59	59	60	61	59	59
Oceania Océanie	101	100	102	102	96	101	106	107	108	106
former USSR † l'ex–URSS †	104	91	...	...	...	...	...	...	...	...
B. Per capita food production · Production alimentaire par habitant										
World *Monde*	101	99	101	100	102	102	105	106	106	106
Africa Afrique	98	102	98	99	99	98	105	100	102	101
America, North Amérique du Nord	101	100	105	97	108	103	106	108	109	108
America, South Amérique du Sud	99	101	102	102	107	111	114	116	116	117
Asia Asie	101	101	106	110	113	116	119	121	123	122
Europe Europe	100	100	64	63	59	59	60	61	59	59
Oceania Océanie	101	99	105	107	100	109	116	116	118	114
former USSR † l'ex–URSS †	105	90	...	...	...	...	...	...	...	...

Source:
Food and Agriculture Organization of the United Nations (FAO), Rome, "FAO Production Yearbook 1999" and the FAOSTAT database.

Source:
Organisation des Nations Unies pour l'alimentation et l'agriculture (FAO), Rome, "Annuaire FAO de la production 1999 "et la base de données FAOSTAT.

† For information on recent changes in country or area nomenclature pertaining to former Czechoslovakia, Germany, Hong Kong Special Administrative Region (SAR) of China, Macao Special Administrative Region (SAR) of China, SFR of Yugoslavia and the former USSR, see Annex I – Country or area nomenclature, regional and other groupings.

† Pour les modifications récentes de nomenclature de pays ou de zone concernant l'Allemagne, Hong Kong région administrative spéciale (RAS) de Chine, Macao région administrative spéciale (RAS) de Chine, l'ex–Tchécoslovaquie, l'ex–URSS et l'ex–Rfs de Yougoslavie, voir annexe I – Nomenclature des pays ou des zones, groupements régionaux et autres groupements.

5

Index numbers of industrial production: world and regions
Indices de la production industrielle: monde et régions
1990=100

Region and industry [ISIC Rev.3] Région et industrie [CITI Rév.3]	Weight(%) Pond.(%)	1991	1992	1993	1994	1995	1996	1997	1998	1999
World · Monde										
Total industry [CDE]										
Total, industrie [CDE]	**100.0**	**100.3**	**101.3**	**102.1**	**106.7**	**111.2**	**114.9**	**121.0**	**123.6**	**128.6**
Total mining [C]										
Total, industries extractives[C]	**9.8**	**101.3**	**102.7**	**103.8**	**107.1**	**109.3**	**112.3**	**114.5**	**115.0**	**114.8**
Coal										
Houille	1.2	98.7	96.2	91.6	92.7	94.7	95.1	96.2	95.6	95.8
Crude petroleum and natural gas										
Pétrole brut et gaz naturel	6.6	102.2	104.7	107.2	110.7	112.6	115.7	118.0	118.0	117.4
Metal ores										
Minerais métalliques	1.0	98.7	97.4	91.6	91.5	95.7	101.3	104.0	108.1	107.2
Total manufacturing [D]										
Total, industries manufacturières[D]	**81.6**	**99.9**	**100.7**	**101.3**	**106.3**	**111.1**	**114.9**	**121.8**	**124.6**	**130.4**
Food, beverages, tobacco										
Industries alimentaires, boissons, tabac	10.0	102.1	103.7	104.5	108.3	111.1	113.2	116.4	118.5	125.1
Textiles										
Textiles	3.9	100.8	102.2	101.0	104.6	105.4	106.1	109.5	106.1	106.1
Wearing apparel, leather and footwear										
Articles d'habillement, cuir et chaussures	2.9	98.2	96.3	94.8	95.5	94.7	92.5	91.1	86.9	82.5
Wood and wood products										
Bois et articles en bois	1.8	95.7	97.5	97.9	102.4	103.5	103.5	106.6	107.1	108.5
Paper, printing, publishing and recorded media										
Papier, imprimerie, édition et supports enregistrés	6.3	99.5	101.1	103.1	105.8	107.3	107.4	111.2	111.8	113.0
Chemicals and related products										
Produits chimiques et alliés	12.7	100.5	103.9	105.6	110.9	114.8	118.4	124.6	126.1	130.8
Non–metallic mineral products										
Produits minéraux non métalliques	3.5	98.4	99.2	99.3	103.9	108.1	111.0	114.7	112.8	115.3
Basic metals										
Métallurgie de base	4.9	98.1	96.4	98.0	104.2	108.2	110.2	116.5	113.3	113.3
Fabricated metal products										
Fabrications d'ouvrages en métaux	12.2	97.4	96.2	97.0	104.3	112.2	116.1	121.7	122.3	120.7
Office and related electrical products										
Machines de bureau et autres appareils élect.	12.3	102.7	102.0	103.1	111.3	125.1	138.7	156.3	175.5	205.1
Transport equipment										
Equipement de transports	7.8	99.5	100.9	98.2	102.0	104.9	107.2	117.8	121.4	125.2
Electricity, gas, water [E]										
Electricité, gaz et eau [E]	**8.6**	**103.9**	**104.8**	**107.6**	**110.4**	**114.2**	**118.6**	**120.6**	**123.1**	**126.5**
Developed regions [1] · Régions developpées [1]										
Total industry [CDE]										
Total, industrie [CDE]	**100.0**	**99.2**	**99.4**	**99.3**	**103.7**	**107.8**	**110.7**	**116.1**	**119.4**	**123.3**
Total mining [C]										
Total, industries extractives [C]	**5.6**	**100.4**	**99.5**	**100.5**	**104.4**	**105.6**	**108.4**	**109.5**	**107.9**	**104.7**
Coal										
Houille	0.9	98.1	94.5	88.8	89.3	89.6	89.3	89.7	88.0	87.3
Crude petroleum and natural gas										
Pétrole brut et gaz naturel	3.3	101.5	101.0	104.4	109.6	111.2	115.5	116.5	113.3	108.8
Metal ores										
Minerais métalliques	0.6	101.2	102.8	101.7	100.1	99.0	100.9	102.5	102.3	94.5
Total manufacturing [D]										
Total, industries manufacturières [D]	**85.9**	**98.7**	**98.9**	**98.5**	**103.2**	**107.6**	**110.4**	**116.6**	**120.3**	**124.9**
Food, beverages, tobacco										
Industries alimentaires, boissons, tabac	9.9	101.3	102.2	102.4	105.4	107.0	107.4	109.3	109.7	110.3
Textiles										
Textiles	2.3	97.4	98.3	95.4	98.3	97.1	94.2	97.5	95.1	92.6
Wearing apparel, leather and footwear										
Articles d'habillement, cuir et chaussures	2.6	97.8	95.8	93.6	94.7	93.7	90.6	88.6	83.9	78.3
Wood and wood products										
Bois et articles en bois	2.0	95.1	97.2	97.0	101.9	103.0	102.8	106.3	108.2	110.7

5

Index numbers of industrial production: world and regions [*cont.*]
Indices de la production industrielle: monde et régions [*suite*]
1990=100

Region and industry [ISIC Rev.3] Région et industrie [CITI Rév.3]	Weight(%) Pond.(%)	1991	1992	1993	1994	1995	1996	1997	1998	1999
Paper, printing, publishing and recorded media Papier, imprimerie, édition et supports enregistrés	8.8	98.9	100.1	101.7	104.0	105.1	105.0	108.7	109.4	110.3
Chemicals and related products Produits chimiques et alliés	13.5	100.1	102.8	103.5	108.6	112.4	114.7	119.9	121.7	125.3
Non-metallic mineral products Produits minéraux non métalliques	3.2	95.8	94.6	93.1	97.7	100.0	100.9	103.3	103.8	106.3
Basic metals Métallurgie de base	4.7	97.6	95.2	94.8	100.1	103.0	103.1	108.8	105.8	105.1
Fabricated metal products Fabrications d'ouvrages en métaux	13.6	96.1	94.6	94.9	102.2	110.7	114.1	119.2	120.9	118.1
Office and related electrical products Machines de bureau et autres appareils élect.	12.7	102.0	101.1	101.6	109.5	122.9	136.5	153.9	174.7	203.7
Transport equipment Equipement de transports	9.4	96.4	96.9	92.8	96.8	97.9	99.4	107.5	111.7	114.1
Electricity, gas, water [E] **Electricité, gaz et eau[E]**	**8.6**	**103.7**	**104.1**	**106.1**	**107.9**	**111.1**	**114.8**	**115.8**	**117.6**	**119.9**

Developing countries [2] · Pays en développement [2]

	Weight(%) Pond.(%)	1991	1992	1993	1994	1995	1996	1997	1998	1999
Total industry [CDE] **Total, industrie [CDE]**	**100.0**	**105.0**	**108.8**	**113.0**	**118.6**	**124.9**	**131.9**	**140.4**	**140.4**	**149.4**
Total mining [C] **Total, industries extractives [C]**	**24.7**	**102.1**	**105.5**	**106.9**	**109.5**	**112.6**	**115.7**	**119.0**	**121.4**	**123.8**
Coal Houille	1.1	100.9	101.6	100.8	103.8	111.3	113.7	117.4	119.9	123.4
Crude petroleum and natural gas Pétrole brut et gaz naturel	20.0	102.7	107.1	109.0	111.4	113.5	115.8	119.1	121.1	123.1
Metal ores Minerais métalliques	2.2	96.0	91.8	80.9	82.4	92.1	101.7	105.6	114.2	120.8
Total manufacturing [D] **Total, industries manufacturières [D]**	**69.4**	**105.9**	**110.0**	**115.0**	**121.3**	**128.6**	**137.0**	**147.3**	**146.0**	**157.3**
Food, beverages, tobacco Industries alimentaires, boissons, tabac	13.0	104.3	108.2	110.6	117.3	123.5	130.5	137.8	144.9	169.9
Textiles Textiles	7.0	105.1	107.3	108.3	112.7	116.1	121.3	124.9	120.3	123.4
Wearing apparel, leather and footwear Articles d'habillement, cuir et chaussures	3.6	99.4	97.6	98.2	98.0	97.5	97.8	98.5	95.5	94.8
Wood and wood products Bois et articles bois	1.2	99.7	99.0	103.8	106.2	107.3	108.6	108.7	100.1	93.9
Paper, printing, publishing and recorded media Papier, imprimerie, édition et supports enregistrés	3.0	105.8	113.1	119.4	127.0	131.9	134.6	139.8	139.6	143.0
Chemicals and related products Produits chimiques et alliés	13.7	102.1	107.9	113.7	119.8	124.6	132.8	143.0	143.5	152.2
Non-metallic mineral products Produits minéraux non métalliques	4.0	106.8	114.0	119.0	124.0	133.8	143.2	151.5	141.4	144.2
Basic metals Métallurgie de base	4.7	100.2	101.2	110.8	120.4	128.8	138.0	146.5	142.5	145.3
Fabricated metal products Fabrications d'ouvrages en métaux	6.7	107.5	109.1	113.7	121.4	124.1	132.3	142.5	134.4	141.1
Office and related electrical products Machines de bureau et autres appareils élect.	6.2	108.1	109.6	115.2	126.1	142.7	156.7	175.5	182.2	216.8
Transport equipment Equipement de transports	4.0	128.1	138.5	149.2	150.1	171.4	180.5	214.2	212.3	228.8
Electricity, gas, water [E] **Electricité, gaz et eau [E]**	**5.9**	**105.6**	**108.7**	**116.2**	**124.6**	**132.0**	**140.1**	**148.7**	**155.0**	**164.2**

Northern America [3] · Amérique septentrionale [3]

	Weight(%) Pond.(%)	1991	1992	1993	1994	1995	1996	1997	1998	1999
Total industry [CDE] **Total, industrie [CDE]**	**100.0**	**97.7**	**100.5**	**103.9**	**109.4**	**114.4**	**119.1**	**126.8**	**133.2**	**139.9**
Total mining [C] **Total, industries extractives [C]**	**8.0**	**98.5**	**96.4**	**96.8**	**99.3**	**99.4**	**100.8**	**103.1**	**101.1**	**95.8**
Coal Houille	1.0	96.6	95.7	90.7	99.1	99.0	101.3	104.5	105.7	104.0

5
Index numbers of industrial production: world and regions [*cont.*]
Indices de la production industrielle: monde et régions [*suite*]
1990=100

Region and industry [ISIC Rev.3] Région et industrie [CITI Rév.3]	Weight(%) Pond.(%)	1991	1992	1993	1994	1995	1996	1997	1998	1999
Crude petroleum and natural gas										
Pétrole brut et gaz naturel	5.6	99.0	95.5	97.2	98.5	97.8	99.1	100.7	97.3	90.9
Metal ores										
Minerais métalliques	0.7	102.0	104.9	101.5	99.8	100.8	103.6	106.4	105.3	94.4
Total manufacturing [D]										
Total, industries manufacturières [D]	**83.8**	**97.2**	**100.7**	**104.4**	**110.6**	**116.1**	**121.4**	**130.3**	**138.0**	**146.3**
Food, beverages, tobacco										
Industries alimentaires, boissons, tabac	10.9	100.5	102.1	102.0	105.9	108.6	108.3	110.2	111.0	110.4
Textiles										
Textiles	1.6	98.9	107.1	112.7	118.8	118.9	117.2	121.1	120.2	120.4
Wearing apparel, leather and footwear										
Articles d'habillement, cuir et chaussures	2.4	98.5	100.4	102.6	105.1	105.2	102.7	101.0	95.6	89.6
Wood and wood products										
Bois et articles bois	2.3	92.6	97.9	99.0	103.8	105.5	107.7	112.8	116.1	119.8
Paper, printing, publishing and recorded media										
Papier, imprimerie, édition et supports enregistrés	11.4	97.1	98.7	100.4	102.0	102.8	102.6	106.8	106.8	107.0
Chemicals and related products										
Produits chimiques et alliés	14.6	98.6	103.2	106.4	111.0	113.7	116.6	121.5	123.5	126.4
Non−metallic mineral products										
Produits minéraux non métalliques	2.4	91.9	94.2	96.1	101.4	104.2	110.9	115.1	120.0	123.7
Basic metals										
Métallurgie de base	3.6	93.5	97.1	102.1	109.8	112.2	115.4	122.2	121.3	122.4
Fabricated metal products										
Fabrications d'ouvrages en métaux	12.2	94.4	97.3	104.4	115.7	125.9	132.5	141.1	145.5	140.5
Office and related electrical products										
Machines de bureau et autres appareils élect.	10.0	101.5	108.3	114.8	127.4	150.9	178.8	214.1	263.3	331.5
Transport equipment										
Equipement de transports	9.8	94.1	97.1	100.9	105.6	105.6	106.4	115.9	120.3	122.8
Electricity, gas, water [E]										
Electricité, gaz et eau [E]	**8.2**	**102.5**	**101.7**	**105.5**	**107.1**	**110.9**	**114.4**	**114.4**	**115.6**	**117.1**

Latin America and the Caribbean
Amérique latine et Caraïbes

Total industry [CDE]										
Total, industrie [CDE]	**100.0**	**102.3**	**103.7**	**108.3**	**115.7**	**117.1**	**123.2**	**130.5**	**132.0**	**130.9**
Total mining [C]										
Total, industries extractives [C]	**11.7**	**104.9**	**104.7**	**109.5**	**114.1**	**124.4**	**134.4**	**141.0**	**146.7**	**154.7**
Coal										
Houille	0.5	96.2	95.1	95.2	103.7	110.3	116.6	125.7	129.4	139.2
Crude petroleum and natural gas										
Pétrole brut et gaz naturel	7.2	108.8	109.3	111.7	116.6	125.7	134.6	142.1	148.8	155.9
Metal ores										
Minerais métalliques	2.7	104.6	105.1	104.7	107.8	117.1	128.2	133.5	138.1	149.9
Total manufacturing [D]										
Total, industries manufacturières [D]	**80.8**	**101.8**	**103.9**	**108.4**	**116.0**	**115.8**	**121.3**	**128.8**	**129.2**	**125.9**
Food, beverages, tobacco										
Industries alimentaires, boissons, tabac	18.2	105.3	108.5	109.2	113.9	117.5	121.1	124.9	127.4	130.1
Textiles										
Textiles	4.1	104.0	101.7	97.2	101.0	96.9	99.6	99.0	94.5	93.0
Wearing apparel, leather and footwear										
Articles d'habillement, cuir et chaussures	4.1	97.0	95.5	97.8	100.0	94.7	97.4	97.3	95.9	90.1
Wood and wood products										
Bois et articles bois	1.2	106.6	104.0	110.5	120.2	116.9	129.0	138.3	142.3	137.4
Paper, printing, publishing and recorded media										
Papier, imprimerie, édition et supports enregistrés	4.9	107.2	112.6	119.0	126.0	126.9	129.2	134.3	136.0	135.1
Chemicals and related products										
Produits chimiques et alliés	16.5	99.9	102.2	106.0	112.3	111.2	118.2	125.9	129.7	129.0
Non−metallic mineral products										
Produits minéraux non métalliques	3.9	103.4	105.8	111.9	117.6	114.8	121.2	130.4	132.3	128.8
Basic metals										
Métallurgie de base	5.0	94.4	94.9	99.7	108.8	111.2	120.0	130.3	131.2	126.9

5

Index numbers of industrial production: world and regions [*cont.*]
Indices de la production industrielle: monde et régions [*suite*]
1990=100

Region and industry [ISIC Rev.3] Région et industrie [CITI Rév.3]	Weight(%) Pond.(%)	1991	1992	1993	1994	1995	1996	1997	1998	1999
Fabricated metal products										
Fabrications d'ouvrages en métaux	7.1	97.5	98.3	105.8	117.3	111.6	112.4	121.9	122.4	116.9
Office and related electrical products										
Machines de bureau et autres appareils élect.	7.4	97.2	90.6	98.6	112.6	122.5	132.3	135.4	128.1	117.8
Transport equipment										
Equipement de transports	5.0	105.1	114.7	129.3	144.5	135.6	143.9	168.6	164.5	151.4
Electricity, gas, water [E]										
Electricité, gaz et eau [E]	**7.4**	**103.9**	**100.5**	**105.9**	**114.1**	**119.5**	**126.5**	**133.2**	**139.4**	**147.5**

Asia · Asie

Total industry [CDE]										
Total, industrie [CDE]	**100.0**	**103.8**	**103.4**	**103.2**	**105.8**	**111.0**	**115.5**	**121.2**	**117.1**	**123.2**
Total mining [C]										
Total, industries extractives [C]	**12.7**	**102.4**	**107.7**	**109.9**	**113.1**	**114.6**	**116.2**	**118.8**	**121.0**	**122.2**
Coal										
Houille	0.7	102.0	102.4	100.7	101.3	107.5	108.7	107.1	108.1	109.7
Crude petroleum and natural gas										
Pétrole brut et gaz naturel	10.5	102.0	107.9	110.4	113.2	114.2	115.1	117.8	119.5	120.5
Metal ores										
Minerais métalliques	0.5	118.2	123.3	123.9	138.2	165.8	188.0	194.8	232.8	240.8
Total manufacturing [D]										
Total, industries manufacturières [D]	**80.3**	**103.9**	**102.1**	**101.2**	**103.2**	**109.0**	**113.8**	**120.0**	**114.3**	**121.1**
Food, beverages, tobacco										
Industries alimentaires, boissons, tabac	8.9	101.8	104.3	105.8	111.1	115.0	120.2	124.9	128.5	152.1
Textiles										
Textiles	4.9	103.1	104.9	103.3	105.8	108.8	113.4	117.0	110.8	113.3
Wearing apparel, leather and footwear										
Articles d'habillement, cuir et chaussures	2.7	100.3	97.4	92.6	89.4	87.3	85.1	81.5	74.1	72.1
Wood and wood products										
Bois et articles bois	1.1	98.6	96.6	95.7	94.0	93.1	91.1	88.1	75.2	70.4
Paper, printing, publishing and recorded media										
Papier, imprimerie, édition et supports enregistrés	5.0	103.5	105.6	109.0	111.5	115.4	117.6	119.6	116.6	116.6
Chemicals and related products										
Produits chimiques et alliés	11.9	102.8	106.3	108.6	113.4	120.2	124.8	131.8	128.4	136.4
Non-metallic mineral products										
Produits minéraux non métalliques	3.8	104.1	104.5	104.6	107.2	114.4	119.1	122.7	108.6	111.2
Basic metals										
Métallurgie de base	6.2	102.3	95.6	96.5	97.8	103.0	103.8	108.5	97.3	98.8
Fabricated metal products										
Fabrications d'ouvrages en métaux	9.7	104.0	96.5	92.3	94.7	99.7	104.6	107.5	96.6	97.1
Office and related electrical products										
Machines de bureau et autres appareils élect.	15.1	107.9	100.2	97.7	102.4	113.3	122.6	133.4	132.2	146.9
Transport equipment										
Equipement de transports	6.9	109.5	111.3	107.3	102.5	110.6	114.7	129.0	122.4	131.3
Electricity, gas, water [E]										
Electricité, gaz et eau [E]	**7.0**	**105.7**	**110.3**	**114.7**	**122.6**	**127.8**	**133.9**	**139.9**	**143.4**	**148.6**

Asia excluding Israel and Japan
Asie à l'exception de l'Israël et du Japon

Total industry [CDE]										
Total, industrie [CDE]	**100.0**	**107.8**	**114.1**	**119.4**	**124.8**	**135.4**	**144.1**	**154.5**	**153.0**	**170.3**
Total mining [C]										
Total, industries extractives [C]	**26.7**	**102.3**	**107.9**	**110.3**	**113.7**	**115.3**	**116.9**	**119.7**	**122.0**	**123.3**
Coal										
Houille	1.5	102.6	103.8	102.6	103.7	111.8	112.9	114.8	117.0	118.4
Crude petroleum and natural gas										
Pétrole brut et gaz naturel	23.0	102.0	107.9	110.4	113.2	114.2	115.1	117.8	119.5	120.6
Metal ores										
Minerais métalliques	1.0	118.8	124.1	125.0	140.7	170.6	195.1	202.8	243.8	252.8
Total manufacturing [D]										
Total, industries manufacturières [D]	**68.3**	**110.0**	**116.3**	**122.3**	**128.3**	**142.4**	**153.7**	**167.1**	**163.5**	**187.5**

5
Index numbers of industrial production: world and regions [*cont.*]
Indices de la production industrielle: monde et régions [*suite*]
1990=100

Region and industry [ISIC Rev.3] Région et industrie [CITI Rév.3]	Weight(%) Pond.(%)	1991	1992	1993	1994	1995	1996	1997	1998	1999
Food, beverages, tobacco Industries alimentaires, boissons, tabac	10.5	104.2	109.9	115.1	126.6	137.9	150.6	164.0	177.8	239.2
Textiles Textiles	8.7	105.7	110.2	113.5	119.0	125.7	133.4	138.5	133.2	138.5
Wearing apparel, leather and footwear Articles d'habillement, cuir et chaussures	3.3	102.0	101.0	99.9	96.8	100.0	99.1	97.0	89.3	91.0
Wood and wood products Bois et articles bois	1.1	101.2	102.9	106.7	107.0	111.2	108.0	108.4	92.9	85.4
Paper, printing, publishing and recorded media Papier, imprimerie, édition et supports enregistrés	2.4	104.0	115.7	123.3	132.4	145.1	148.8	154.5	150.8	162.0
Chemicals and related products Produits chimiques et alliés	13.4	103.4	112.1	119.9	126.0	135.3	144.5	156.7	154.8	170.0
Non-metallic mineral products Produits minéraux non métalliques	4.3	109.7	119.9	124.9	129.9	147.0	158.3	167.5	147.9	154.4
Basic metals Métallurgie de base	5.1	106.5	109.2	126.6	136.7	153.4	163.2	170.3	158.5	170.6
Fabricated metal products Fabrications d'ouvrages en métaux	7.1	115.5	118.0	120.9	126.0	134.9	148.6	159.2	143.0	157.7
Office and related electrical products Machines de bureau et autres appareils élect.	6.4	116.4	124.0	128.4	137.1	159.0	176.4	207.0	223.9	292.4
Transport equipment Equipement de transports	3.9	147.6	159.6	167.9	157.7	203.8	213.8	256.2	256.0	296.9
Electricity, gas, water [E] **Electricité, gaz et eau [E]**	**5.1**	**108.0**	**117.1**	**127.6**	**137.1**	**146.9**	**156.8**	**168.1**	**174.8**	**185.8**

Europe · Europe

	Weight(%) Pond.(%)	1991	1992	1993	1994	1995	1996	1997	1998	1999
Total industry [CDE] **Total, industrie [CDE]**	**100.0**	**97.8**	**95.6**	**92.1**	**93.2**	**95.8**	**95.9**	**98.9**	**101.9**	**103.7**
Total mining [C] **Total, industries extractives [C]**	**6.0**	**99.9**	**99.9**	**99.9**	**104.5**	**106.8**	**110.8**	**108.7**	**105.1**	**104.8**
Coal Houille	1.9	93.3	86.9	78.8	69.4	66.9	63.1	58.6	50.9	47.3
Crude petroleum and natural gas Pétrole brut et gaz naturel	2.8	106.7	113.4	121.0	135.9	142.2	154.2	153.3	149.7	150.7
Metal ores Minerais métalliques	0.5	87.6	81.4	69.4	62.7	61.2	55.0	50.6	46.3	41.3
Total manufacturing [D] **Total, industries manufacturières [D]**	**85.8**	**97.1**	**94.6**	**90.6**	**91.7**	**94.3**	**93.9**	**97.6**	**101.1**	**103.1**
Food, beverages, tobacco Industries alimentaires, boissons, tabac	10.2	99.7	98.1	97.7	97.6	97.3	97.2	98.7	99.7	100.4
Textiles Textiles	4.2	91.5	83.7	75.2	68.7	65.4	61.5	63.1	60.8	57.5
Wearing apparel, leather and footwear Articles d'habillement, cuir et chaussures	3.3	94.6	88.8	82.6	76.7	73.4	70.1	68.7	64.6	59.6
Wood and wood products Bois et articles bois	2.1	95.6	93.0	88.8	88.5	90.3	86.6	88.2	91.1	92.3
Paper, printing, publishing and recorded media Papier, imprimerie, édition et supports enregistrés	5.6	99.4	99.9	100.3	103.0	104.3	103.2	107.3	110.7	114.0
Chemicals and related products Produits chimiques et alliés	12.8	98.5	98.0	94.8	98.2	102.1	103.3	108.5	111.7	115.0
Non-metallic mineral products Produits minéraux non métalliques	4.2	95.9	93.9	90.6	93.9	95.9	93.5	95.1	97.0	99.0
Basic metals Métallurgie de base	4.8	94.8	89.3	83.1	85.7	88.8	86.5	90.6	90.8	87.6
Fabricated metal products Fabrications d'ouvrages en métaux	15.7	94.5	90.6	86.3	84.9	90.3	88.2	90.0	92.3	91.5
Office and related electrical products Machines de bureau et autres appareils élect.	11.7	99.5	97.4	95.5	98.9	104.6	108.5	116.3	127.9	139.2
Transport equipment Equipement de transports	8.2	96.9	95.0	84.2	89.1	91.6	93.2	99.9	109.4	112.2
Electricity, gas, water [E] **Electricité, gaz et eau [E]**	**8.3**	**102.7**	**102.7**	**102.5**	**101.1**	**103.3**	**105.9**	**106.3**	**107.8**	**110.1**

5

Index numbers of industrial production: world and regions [cont.]

Indices de la production industrielle: monde et régions [suite]

1990 = 100

Region and industry [ISIC Rev.3] Région et industrie [CITI Rév.3]	Weight(%) Pond.(%)	1991	1992	1993	1994	1995	1996	1997	1998	1999
European Union ' · Union européenne '										
Total industry [CDE] **Total, industrie [CDE]**	**100.0**	**99.5**	**98.8**	**96.0**	**100.8**	**104.6**	**105.5**	**109.7**	**114.0**	**116.6**
Total mining [C] **Total, industries extractives [C]**	**3.7**	**101.7**	**100.2**	**101.7**	**108.5**	**110.7**	**113.5**	**111.3**	**110.3**	**111.6**
Coal Houille	1.0	97.9	89.0	80.5	71.6	70.8	66.6	64.3	57.7	55.6
Crude petroleum and natural gas Pétrole brut et gaz naturel	1.8	105.9	110.7	119.6	135.7	139.8	148.9	145.5	144.9	146.4
Metal ores Minerais métalliques	0.1	99.2	95.4	79.2	82.3	84.1	77.6	76.4	73.0	68.5
Total manufacturing [D] **Total, industries manufacturières [D]**	**87.7**	**98.8**	**98.1**	**94.7**	**99.9**	**103.9**	**104.3**	**109.1**	**113.8**	**116.4**
Food, beverages, tobacco Industries alimentaires, boissons, tabac	9.8	102.7	103.0	104.0	106.3	107.2	108.1	111.2	112.2	114.0
Textiles Textiles	3.3	96.7	95.2	90.1	93.1	92.0	88.4	92.4	90.8	87.3
Wearing apparel, leather and footwear Articles d'habillement, cuir et chaussures	3.1	96.7	92.4	88.0	89.1	88.7	85.3	83.6	80.5	74.4
Wood and wood products Bois et articles bois	1.8	98.3	98.7	98.0	104.9	107.0	103.7	107.5	111.7	115.1
Paper, printing, publishing and recorded media Papier, imprimerie, édition et supports enregistrés	6.9	100.0	101.1	101.8	105.3	106.0	104.9	109.3	112.8	116.4
Chemicals and related products Produits chimiques et alliés	14.0	101.0	102.9	101.2	107.2	111.4	113.3	119.5	123.4	127.7
Non-metallic mineral products Produits minéraux non métalliques	4.1	96.8	95.6	92.4	97.9	100.8	98.2	100.6	103.2	105.7
Basic metals Métallurgie de base	4.4	98.4	95.4	91.3	99.2	102.4	100.1	106.2	107.2	104.0
Fabricated metal products Fabrications d'ouvrages en métaux	16.8	95.6	93.6	89.7	95.4	104.6	104.7	108.1	112.3	112.3
Office and related electrical products Machines de bureau et autres appareils élect.	11.0	99.2	97.9	95.8	102.3	109.6	114.1	121.9	134.2	144.0
Transport equipment Equipement de transports	9.4	96.9	95.3	82.7	89.8	93.0	94.7	102.1	112.3	115.6
Electricity, gas, water [E] **Electricité, gaz et eau [E]**	**8.6**	**104.8**	**105.7**	**106.5**	**107.0**	**109.8**	**114.1**	**114.9**	**117.4**	**120.7**
Oceania · Océanie										
Total industry [CDE] **Total, industrie [CDE]**	**100.0**	**99.7**	**99.3**	**100.9**	**104.8**	**108.1**	**110.8**	**112.8**	**116.5**	**118.2**
Total mining [C] **Total, industries extractives [C]**	**18.5**	**105.4**	**109.9**	**110.7**	**111.0**	**116.7**	**120.7**	**122.6**	**129.9**	**127.9**
Coal Houille	5.0	105.1	112.5	112.4	113.8	120.9	124.6	124.8	131.0	140.7
Crude petroleum and natural gas Pétrole brut et gaz naturel	5.3	101.1	101.6	102.0	100.4	109.7	108.6	109.8	118.3	104.6
Metal ores Minerais métalliques	7.5	110.7	116.1	118.1	120.6	119.5	131.0	138.7	144.5	145.2
Total manufacturing [D] **Total, industries manufacturières [D]**	**66.8**	**97.7**	**95.0**	**97.4**	**102.3**	**105.0**	**107.4**	**109.3**	**112.6**	**115.8**
Food, beverages, tobacco Industries alimentaires, boissons, tabac	12.8	102.6	102.8	104.3	108.1	109.9	113.4	114.6	120.6	124.3
Textiles Textiles	1.9	96.3	91.5	88.5	90.1	89.0	84.3	83.8	83.9	84.9
Wearing apparel, leather and footwear Articles d'habillement, cuir et chaussures	2.1	95.6	91.3	88.5	90.3	89.4	84.7	84.0	83.6	84.4
Wood and wood products Bois et articles bois	2.3	96.0	95.1	101.9	106.0	111.2	111.9	114.5	116.2	117.9
Paper, printing, publishing and recorded media Papier, imprimerie, édition et supports enregistrés	6.8	97.2	92.9	97.3	100.3	104.8	106.1	107.0	108.5	111.5

5
Index numbers of industrial production: world and regions [*cont.*]
Indices de la production industrielle: monde et régions [*suite*]
1990=100

Region and industry [ISIC Rev.3] Région et industrie [CITI Rév.3]	Weight(%) Pond.(%)	1991	1992	1993	1994	1995	1996	1997	1998	1999
Chemicals and related products										
Produits chimiques et alliés	9.4	101.5	98.4	100.4	106.1	110.5	116.1	117.3	118.6	123.4
Non—metallic mineral products										
Produits minéraux non métalliques	3.4	91.0	88.2	95.6	98.3	99.7	93.9	94.7	96.8	104.1
Basic metals										
Métallurgie de base	7.2	97.5	96.3	99.0	104.0	102.5	105.1	108.5	112.7	117.1
Fabricated metal products										
Fabrications d'ouvrages en métaux	8.8	96.2	93.4	96.6	103.2	105.2	108.3	111.8	115.4	118.0
Office and related electrical products										
Machines de bureau et autres appareils élect.	3.2	94.7	89.5	90.8	98.3	105.0	109.0	112.3	115.7	117.2
Transport equipment										
Equipement de transports	6.8	95.2	90.1	91.1	98.7	105.2	109.5	112.7	116.0	118.2
Electricity, gas, water [E]										
Electricité, gaz et eau [E]	**14.6**	**102.1**	**105.9**	**105.0**	**108.6**	**111.0**	**114.3**	**115.9**	**117.8**	**116.6**

Source:
United Nations Secretariat, industrial statistics database
of the Statistics Division.

1 Northern America (Canada and the United States), Europe, Australia,
  Israel, Japan, New Zealand and South Africa.
2 Latin America and the Caribbean, Africa (excluding South
  Africa), Asia (excluding Israel and Japan), Oceania (excluding
  Australia and New Zealand).
3 Canada and the United States only.
4 Austria, Belgium, Denmark, Finland, France, Germany,
  Greece, Ireland, Italy, Luxembourg, Netherlands, Portugal,
  Spain, Sweden and the United Kingdom.

Source :
Secrétariat de l'Organisation des Nations Unies, la base de données
de statistiques industrielles de la Division de statistique.

1 Amérique septentrionale (le Canada et les Etats—Unis), Europe,
  l'Australie, l'Israël, la Nouvelle—Zélande et l'Afrique du Sud.
2 Amérique latine et Caraïbes, Afrique (non compris
  l'Afrique du Sud), Asie (non compris l'Israël et le Japon), Océanie
  (non compris l'Australie et la Nouvelle—Zélande).
3 Le Canada et les Etats—Unis seulement.
4 L'Autriche, la Belgique, le Danemark, la Finlande, la France,
  l' Allemagne, la Grèce, l'Irlande, l'Italie, le Luxembourg,
  les Pays—Bas, le Portugal, l'Espagne, la Suède et le Royaume—Uni.

Table 6 follows overleaf

Le tableau 6 est présenté au verso

6
Production, trade and consumption of commercial energy
Production, commerce et consommation d'énergie commerciale
Thousand metric tons of oil equivalent and kilograms per capita
Milliers de tonnes d'équivalent pétrole et kilogrammes par habitant

Regions	Year	Primary energy production – Production d'énergie primaire					Changes in stocks	Imports	Exports
		Total Totale	Solids Solides	Liquids Liquides	Gas Gaz	Electricity Electricité	Variations des stocks	Imports Importations	Exports Exportations
World	1991	8 015 298	2 218 499	3 199 755	1 833 894	763 150	29 058	2 516 389	2 453 440
	1992	8 028 872	2 196 304	3 226 440	1 828 852	777 276	46 260	2 923 525	2 809 947
	1993	8 068 815	2 145 470	3 235 810	1 886 814	800 721	−2 762	2 978 205	2 865 906
	1994	8 262 109	2 224 045	3 295 097	1 929 519	813 448	44 374	2 999 937	2 908 648
	1995	8 517 778	2 291 139	3 326 687	2 052 164	847 788	14 802	3 075 475	3 025 045
	1996	8 743 802	2 330 496	3 371 941	2 152 705	888 659	3 876	3 251 140	3 170 360
	1997	8 840 353	2 349 117	3 449 857	2 155 122	886 257	51 314	3 364 732	3 272 922
Africa	1991	517 278	99 940	339 269	70 612	7 458	738	49 581	344 921
	1992	519 617	97 933	344 353	69 826	7 505	−4 508	48 312	343 675
	1993	522 054	101 897	340 519	72 692	6 946	−4 574	49 550	342 902
	1994	526 339	109 312	338 828	70 483	7 715	−2 371	53 832	342 861
	1995	554 667	115 036	347 587	83 921	8 122	−1 177	56 044	370 686
	1996	567 066	114 880	353 302	90 353	8 532	−3 732	55 385	382 611
	1997	589 166	120 896	359 660	99 862	8 748	−2 044	56 248	395 151
America, North	1991	2 111 226	563 491	690 381	602 250	255 104	−2 845	538 626	333 482
	1992	2 110 054	558 989	680 793	615 444	254 828	−9 427	566 893	334 912
	1993	2 100 759	525 851	680 053	634 813	260 042	−20 952	632 903	329 019
	1994	2 189 660	575 967	676 551	668 594	268 548	21 589	665 461	332 107
	1995	2 206 264	573 332	672 864	680 679	279 389	−10 902	655 502	354 493
	1996	2 254 645	590 424	665 213	701 207	297 800	−7 514	690 841	368 321
	1997	2 272 937	606 037	677 442	707 404	282 054	8 337	737 602	383 740
America, South	1991	343 377	18 872	232 891	57 066	34 547	−438	59 149	155 418
	1992	355 057	19 844	239 798	60 324	35 091	2 911	60 955	155 115
	1993	380 001	19 693	253 698	68 836	37 775	1 289	67 283	170 140
	1994	407 044	21 433	269 966	75 965	39 679	−2 304	71 315	184 313
	1995	427 641	23 395	283 637	78 715	41 894	−6 902	74 257	203 549
	1996	446 445	24 836	295 619	82 398	43 593	−4 899	79 771	213 495
	1997	480 139	28 489	314 746	91 424	45 480	−3 046	84 865	231 350
Asia	1991	2 291 101	785 508	1 160 346	219 372	125 875	24 690	775 709	926 884
	1992	2 607 057	866 438	1 279 338	329 183	132 098	20 257	916 065	1 085 411
	1993	2 700 857	889 600	1 313 415	352 974	144 867	26 602	941 783	1 125 755
	1994	2 813 836	938 566	1 356 720	364 765	153 784	19 979	954 636	1 103 956
	1995	2 930 182	1 003 485	1 367 320	392 601	166 777	24 272	1 006 693	1 126 858
	1996	3 028 425	1 036 360	1 390 604	427 644	173 818	23 865	1 082 887	1 163 206
	1997	3 073 395	1 032 859	1 427 901	432 270	180 365	30 014	1 140 871	1 210 461
Europe	1991	1 032 083	341 418	223 891	207 351	259 423	6 260	1 069 862	407 380
	1992	2 258 212	541 410	646 720	727 523	342 559	37 414	1 308 967	798 469
	1993	2 183 447	495 748	612 596	729 448	345 655	−3 189	1 259 484	800 252
	1994	2 134 684	457 429	618 990	720 193	338 071	9 805	1 226 449	840 499
	1995	2 193 858	442 371	621 292	784 173	346 022	7 293	1 254 299	855 789
	1996	2 238 412	428 198	633 125	817 693	359 395	−3 062	1 310 391	927 003
	1997	2 206 313	415 733	635 807	790 549	364 225	16 042	1 312 357	929 708
Oceania	1991	167 866	105 489	34 482	22 516	5 380	653	20 252	85 506
	1992	178 876	111 691	35 438	26 551	5 195	−387	22 262	92 366
	1993	181 696	112 680	35 528	28 052	5 436	−1 938	27 132	97 836
	1994	190 548	121 338	34 042	29 518	5 650	−2 324	28 173	104 913
	1995	205 166	133 519	33 987	32 075	5 584	2 219	28 607	113 670
	1996	208 809	135 798	34 078	33 411	5 522	−783	31 790	115 724
	1997	218 403	145 102	34 301	33 615	5 385	2 011	32 717	122 510

Source:
United Nations Secretariat, "Energy Statistics Yearbook 1997" and the energy statistics database of the Statistics Division.

Source:
Secrétariat de l'Organisation des Nations Unies, "Annuaire des statistiques de l'énergie 1997" et la base de données pour les statistiques énergétiques de la Division de statistique.

Bunkers – Soutes			Consumption – Consommation							
Air Avion	Sea Maritime	Unallocated Nondistribué	Per capita Par habitant	Total Totale	Solids Solides	Liquids Liquides	Gas Gaz	Electricity Electricité	Année	Régions
41 288	**117 507**	**220 557**	**1 389**	**7 669 835**	**2 230 774**	**2 837 666**	**1 837 746**	**763 650**	**1991**	***Monde***
46 091	**122 291**	**283 249**	**1 402**	**7 644 558**	**2 201 828**	**2 822 923**	**1 842 631**	**777 176**	**1992**	
48 942	**123 281**	**293 033**	**1 396**	**7 718 620**	**2 205 531**	**2 832 156**	**1 880 486**	**800 446**	**1993**	
51 296	**125 385**	**311 972**	**1 395**	**7 820 371**	**2 244 729**	**2 842 044**	**1 920 180**	**813 417**	**1994**	
53 441	**132 236**	**305 396**	**1 418**	**8 062 332**	**2 299 602**	**2 858 149**	**2 056 720**	**847 861**	**1995**	
56 017	**136 507**	**315 365**	**1 442**	**8 312 817**	**2 366 930**	**2 920 459**	**2 137 740**	**887 689**	**1996**	
58 176	**139 811**	**344 937**	**1 427**	**8 337 926**	**2 346 286**	**2 953 472**	**2 151 710**	**886 458**	**1997**	
2 243	3 660	13 275	319	202 023	72 742	83 709	38 158	7 414	1991	Afrique
2 222	3 964	23 535	306	199 041	70 858	84 921	35 929	7 334	1992	
2 319	6 069	24 558	300	200 331	67 629	86 330	39 544	6 827	1993	
2 441	6 342	23 361	305	207 537	73 814	85 049	41 028	7 646	1994	
2 386	6 341	20 812	303	211 663	69 290	85 253	49 055	8 065	1995	
2 620	6 913	15 973	305	218 067	69 354	87 809	52 595	8 309	1996	
2 551	7 095	14 629	312	228 032	75 410	90 167	53 924	8 531	1997	
1 299	34 515	24 398	5 215	2 259 002	490 634	906 941	606 110	255 317	1991	Amerique du Nord
1 348	35 714	16 225	5 236	2 298 175	494 034	926 070	623 038	255 032	1992	
1 258	31 709	48 374	5 271	2 344 254	506 648	942 428	635 107	260 071	1993	
1 323	31 380	59 075	5 348	2 409 647	508 171	965 934	666 995	268 547	1994	
1 379	33 063	49 983	5 335	2 433 750	510 637	950 547	693 105	279 461	1995	
1 563	31 367	53 382	5 410	2 498 367	534 621	964 398	701 542	297 806	1996	
1 406	27 691	65 598	5 402	2 523 767	551 399	982 680	707 209	282 479	1997	
968	2 773	13 737	766	230 068	17 807	120 891	56 894	34 476	1991	Amerique du Sud
939	2 019	17 490	778	237 538	17 519	124 756	60 291	34 972	1992	
1 016	2 105	18 516	819	254 218	17 841	130 215	68 501	37 661	1993	
1 177	2 183	21 710	860	271 279	18 752	136 935	76 012	39 581	1994	
1 278	2 424	17 388	886	284 160	19 868	143 708	78 702	41 882	1995	
1 412	2 712	19 716	902	293 780	20 048	147 905	82 264	43 564	1996	
1 428	3 043	17 530	952	314 698	21 864	156 018	91 344	45 472	1997	
12 038	39 567	116 714	611	1 946 917	892 113	704 086	224 858	125 861	1991	Asie
14 437	42 371	152 044	669	2 208 601	958 039	798 517	319 237	132 809	1992	
14 228	44 416	149 613	680	2 282 025	987 316	821 392	328 297	145 021	1993	
14 931	47 506	159 153	712	2 422 947	1 051 734	851 546	364 871	154 796	1994	
16 099	50 995	164 378	739	2 554 273	1 113 985	882 548	390 305	167 435	1995	
17 099	53 278	171 794	765	2 682 071	1 157 887	926 109	423 728	174 346	1996	
17 585	55 642	190 777	762	2 709 786	1 146 075	942 704	440 069	180 938	1997	
22 313	35 771	9 046	2 491	1 621 176	429 162	606 722	323 790	261 502	1991	Europe
24 629	36 978	76 813	3 573	2 592 875	619 215	848 619	783 207	341 833	1992	
27 470	37 666	54 285	3 477	2 526 447	585 052	808 372	787 592	345 430	1993	
28 725	36 452	49 811	3 294	2 395 840	548 874	760 352	749 417	337 198	1994	
29 390	37 865	54 955	3 383	2 462 865	541 124	753 659	822 650	345 434	1995	
30 239	40 693	54 678	3 431	2 499 252	536 673	750 403	854 033	358 142	1996	
32 024	44 845	54 692	3 350	2 441 359	501 307	741 245	835 154	363 653	1997	
2 427	1 156	−5 161	3 861	103 537	39 943	39 675	18 540	5 380	1991	Oceanie
2 516	1 179	−2 859	3 973	108 322	42 163	40 035	20 929	5 195	1992	
2 651	1 251	−2 313	4 022	111 340	41 044	43 414	21 445	5 436	1993	
2 698	1 457	−1 138	4 025	113 115	43 384	42 224	21 858	5 650	1994	
2 909	1 481	−2 120	4 055	115 614	44 699	42 429	22 902	5 584	1995	
3 084	1 477	− 177	4 195	121 274	48 347	43 828	23 578	5 522	1996	
3 183	1 426	1 710	4 107	120 279	50 231	40 653	24 011	5 385	1997	

7
Total exports and imports: index numbers
Exportations et importations totales: indices
Quantum, unit value and terms of trade (1990 = 100)
Quantum, valeur unitaire et termes de l'échange (1990 = 100)

Regions [1] Régions [1]	1989	1991	1992	1993	1994	1995	1996	1997	1998	1999
A. Exports · Exportations										
Quantum indices [2] · Indices du quantum [2]										
Total	95	105	110	113	123	136	143	160	169	179
Developed economies [3]										
Economies développées [3]	95	103	106	107	117	127	133	149	155	163
North America										
Amérique du Nord	95	105	112	117	127	137	145	161	165	176
Europe										
Europe	95	102	104	104	115	127	133	151	160	168
EU+										
UE+	95	103	105	105	116	128	134	153	163	171
EFTA+										
AELE+	93	101	102	108	117	136	127	143	144	154
Africa [4]										
Afrique [4]	100	99	97	106	112	165	187	...	...	...
Asia										
Asie	94	102	104	102	104	108	109	119	117	120
Oceania										
Océanie	94	114	120	127	136	139	155	167	166	173
Developing economies [3]										
Economies en développement [3]	96	110	121	131	143	163	172	192	210	227
America										
Amérique	105	107	117	117	124	166	160	164	176	177
Europe [5]										
Europe [5]	104	...	...	...	...	...	...	...	...	...
Africa										
Afrique	88	102	101	102	99	108	121	121	143	132
Asia										
Asie	95	113	125	138	154	170	184	210	229	255
Middle East										
Moyen−Orient	104	107	114	138	135	137	143	164	200	206
Other Asia										
Autres pays d'Asie	92	114	127	137	157	177	192	219	234	264
Unit value indices in US dollars [6] · Indices de la valeur unitaire en dollars E.−U. [6]										
Total	92	98	100	97	101	109	108	101	94	93
Developed economies [3]										
Economies développées [3]	91	99	101	98	101	109	107	99	95	94
North America										
Amérique du Nord	99	100	100	99	101	107	108	106	102	100
Europe										
Europe	87	97	100	93	96	105	103	92	90	88
EU+										
UE+	87	97	100	94	97	106	104	93	91	89
EFTA+										
AELE+	87	97	97	85	88	90	100	86	82	80
Africa [4]										
Afrique [4]	94	99	101	97	96	71	66	...	...	...

7

Total exports and imports: index numbers
Quantum, unit value and terms of trade (1990 = 100) [*cont.*]
Exportations et importations totales: indices
Quantum, valeur unitaire et termes de l'échange (1990 = 100) [*suite*]

Regions [1] Régions [1]	1989	1991	1992	1993	1994	1995	1996	1997	1998	1999
Asia Asie	101	107	113	123	132	143	132	123	115	121
Oceania Océanie	100	92	89	85	89	97	98	93	82	79
Developing economies [3] **Economies en développement [3]**	**92**	**95**	**96**	**95**	**101**	**109**	**110**	**106**	**92**	**91**
America Amérique	89	90	86	89	97	103	119	129	119	126
Europe [5] Europe [5]	90	...	...	...	...	...	...	...	...	...
Africa Afrique	83	91	89	81	87	95	93	93	71	79
Asia Asie	94	97	99	98	104	112	110	103	88	86
Middle East Moyen−Orient	81	86	89	83	84	93	101	95	68	80
Other Asia Autres pays d'Asie	97	100	102	102	108	116	112	105	93	88

B. Imports · Importations
Quantum indices [2] · Indices du quantum [2]

	1989	1991	1992	1993	1994	1995	1996	1997	1998	1999
Total	95	104	111	114	126	138	145	158	167	174
Developed economies [3] **Economies développées [3]**	**96**	**103**	**106**	**107**	**118**	**128**	**134**	**149**	**160**	**168**
North America Amérique du Nord	100	98	106	116	129	137	144	162	179	196
Europe Europe	94	104	106	103	112	122	127	144	157	160
EU+ UE+	94	105	108	104	114	123	129	146	159	162
EFTA+ AELE+	96	98	90	93	102	124	104	124	135	140
Africa [4] Afrique [4]	109	98	100	107	124	150	165	...	...	...
Asia Asie	95	105	105	108	123	138	143	146	138	151
Oceania Océanie	107	96	103	107	121	130	140	148	157	169
Developing economies [3] **Economies en développement [3]**	**92**	**111**	**128**	**139**	**152**	**168**	**179**	**190**	**188**	**193**
Europe [5] Europe [5]	87	...	...	...	...	...	...	...	...	...

Unit value indices in US dollars [6] · Indices de la valeur unitaire en dollars E.−U. [6]

	1989	1991	1992	1993	1994	1995	1996	1997	1998	1999
Total	92	98	99	94	97	105	105	99	93	93
Developed economies [3] **Economies développées [3]**	**91**	**98**	**99**	**92**	**95**	**102**	**101**	**94**	**90**	**90**
North America Amérique du Nord	97	100	101	100	101	106	106	104	99	100

7
Total exports and imports: index numbers
Quantum, unit value and terms of trade (1990 = 100) [*cont.*]
Exportations et importations totales: indices
Quantum, valeur unitaire et termes de l'échange (1990 = 100) [*suite*]

Regions [1] Régions [1]	1989	1991	1992	1993	1994	1995	1996	1997	1998	1999
Europe Europe	88	97	99	89	92	100	99	89	86	85
EU+ UE+	88	97	99	89	92	100	99	89	86	85
EFTA+ AELE+	88	97	100	90	92	91	109	89	85	81
Africa [4] Afrique [4]	92	103	106	101	103	112	100	...	...	...
Asia Asie	94	97	96	96	97	105	105	99	87	88
Oceania Océanie	98	100	99	99	104	110	110	104	95	95
Developing economies [3][7] **Economies en développement [3][7]**	**96**	**99**	99	97	100	113	113	112	102	104
Europe [5] Europe [5]	90	...	...	...	...	...	...	...	...	...

C. Terms of trade [8] · Termes de l'échange [8]

	1989	1991	1992	1993	1994	1995	1996	1997	1998	1999
Developed economies [3] **Economies développées [3]**	**100**	**101**	**102**	**106**	**106**	**107**	**105**	**105**	**106**	**105**
North America Amérique du Nord	102	100	99	100	100	101	101	102	103	100
Europe Europe	99	100	101	105	105	105	104	104	105	104
EU+ UE+	99	100	101	106	105	105	105	104	106	105
EFTA+ AELE+	99	99	97	95	95	99	92	97	96	99
Africa [4] Afrique [4]	102	96	96	96	93	100	104	...	...	...
Asia Asie	107	110	118	128	137	136	126	124	132	138
Oceania Océanie	102	91	90	86	85	88	88	89	87	83
Developing economies [3] **Economies en développement [3]**	**96**	**97**	**97**	**98**	**101**	**97**	**98**	**95**	**90**	**88**
Europe [5] Europe [5]	99	...	...	...	...	...	...	...	...	...

Source:
United Nations Secretariat, trade statistics database of the Statistics Division.

Source:
Secrétariat de l'Organisation des Nations Unies, la base de données pour les statistiques de commerce extérieur de la Division de statistique.

+   For Member States of this grouping, see Annex I − Other groupings.

+   Pour les Etats membres de ce groupement, voir annexe I − Autres groupements.

1   The regional analysis in this table is in accordance with the groupings of countries or areas specified in table 69.
2   Quantum indices are derived from value data and unit value indices. They are base period weighted.

1 L'analyse régionale dans ce tableau est conforme aux groupes des pays ou zones paraissant dans le tableau 69.
2 Les indices du quantum sont calculés à partir des chiffres de la valeur et des indices de valeur unitaire. Ils sont à coéfficients de pondération correspondant à la périod en base.

7

Total exports and imports: index numbers
Quantum, unit value and terms of trade (1990 = 100) [*cont.*]
Exportations et importations totales: indices
Quantum, valeur unitaire et termes de l'échange (1990 = 100) [*suite*]

3   This classification is intended for statistical convenience and does not necessarily express a judgement about the stage reached by a particular country in the development process.
4   South African Customs Union.
5   Data refer to the Socialist Federal Republic of Yugoslavia.

6   Regional aggregates are current period weighted.

7   Indices, except those for Europe, are based on estimates prepared by the International Monetary Fund.

8   Unit value index of exports divided by unit value index of imports.

3 Cette classification est utilisée pour plus de commodité dans la présentation des statistiques et n'implique pas nécessairement un jugement quant au stage de développement auquel est parvenu un pays donné.
4 L'Union douanière d'Afrique australe.
5 Les données se rapportent à la République fédérative socialiste de Yougoslavie.

6 Les totaux régionaux sont à coéfficients de pondération correspondant à la période en cours.
7 Le calcul des indices, sauf ceux pour l'Europe, sont basés sur les estimations preparées par le Fonds monétaire international.
8 Indices de la valeur unitaire des exportations divisé par l'indice de la valeur unitaire des importations.

Technical notes, tables 1-7

Table 1: The series of world aggregates on population, production, transport, external trade and finance have been compiled from statistical publications and databases of the United Nations and the specialized agencies and other institutions [1, 6, 8, 9, 13, 21, 22, 23, 24]. Reference should be made to these sources for details on compilation and coverage.

Table 2 presents estimates of population size, rates of population increase, crude birth and death rates, surface area and population density for the world and regions. Unless otherwise specified, all figures are estimates of the order of magnitude and are subject to a substantial margin of error.

All population estimates and rates presented in this table were prepared by the Population Division of the United Nations Secretariat and published in *World Population Prospects: 1998 Revision* [28].

The average annual percentage rates of population growth were calculated by the Population Division of the United Nations Secretariat, using an exponential rate of increase formula.

Crude birth and crude death rates are expressed in terms of the average annual number of births and deaths respectively, per 1,000 mid-year population. These rates are estimated.

Surface area totals were obtained by summing the figures for the individual countries or areas.

Density is the number of persons in the 2000 total population per square kilometre of total surface area.

The scheme of regionalization used for the purpose of making these estimates is presented in annex I. Although some continental totals are given, and all can be derived, the basic scheme presents eight macro regions that are so drawn as to obtain greater homogeneity in sizes of population, types of demographic circumstances and accuracy of demographic statistics.

Tables 3-4: The index numbers in table 3 refer to agricultural production, which is defined to include both crop and livestock products. Seeds and feed are excluded. The index numbers of food refer to commodities which are considered edible and contain nutrients. Coffee, tea and other inedible commodities are excluded.

The index numbers of total agricultural and food production in table 3 are calculated by the Laspeyres formula with the base year period 1989-1991. The latter is provided in order to diminish the impact of annual fluctuations in agricultural output during base years on the indices for the period. Production quantities of each commodity are weighted by 1989-1991 average national producer prices and summed for each year. The index numbers are based on production data for a calendar year.

Notes techniques, tableaux 1 à 7

Tableau 1: Les séries d'agrégats mondiaux sur la population, la production, les transports, le commerce extérieur et les finances ont été établies à partir de publications statistiques et bases de données des Nations Unies et les institutions spécialisées et autres organismes [1, 6, 8, 9, 13, 21, 22, 23, 24]. On doit se référer à ces sources pour tous renseignements détaillés sur les méthodes de calcul et la portée des statistiques.

Le *Tableau 2* présente les estimations mondiales et régionales de la population, des taux d'accroissement de la population, des taux bruts de natalité et de mortalité, de la superficie et de la densité de population. Sauf indication contraire, tous les chiffres sont des estimations de l'ordre de grandeur et comportent une assez grande marge d'erreur.

Toutes les estimations de la population et tous les taux présentés dans ce tableau ont été établis par la Division de la population du Secrétariat des Nations Unies et publiés dans "*World Population Prospects: 1998 Revision*" [28].

Les pourcentages annuels moyens de l'accroissement de la population ont été calculés par la Division de la population du Secrétariat des Nations Unies, sur la base d'une formule de taux d'accroissement exponentiel.

Les taux bruts de natalité et de mortalité sont exprimés, respectivement, sur la base du nombre annuel moyen de naissances et de décès par tranche de 1.000 habitants au milieu de l'année. Ces taux sont estimatifs.

On a déterminé les superficies totales en additionnant les chiffres correspondant aux différents pays ou régions.

La densité est le nombre de personnes de la population totale de 2000 par kilomètre carré de la superficie totale.

Le schéma de régionalisation utilisé aux fins de l'établissement de ces estimations est présenté dans l'annexe I. Bien que les totaux de certains continents soient donnés et que tous puissent être déterminés, le schéma de base présente huit grandes régions qui sont établies de manière à obtenir une plus grande homogénéité en ce qui concerne l'ampleur des populations, les types de conditions démographiques et la précision des statistiques démographiques.

Tableaux 3-4: Les indices du tableau 3 se rapportent à la production agricole, qui est définie comme comprenant à la fois les produits de l'agriculture et de l'élevage. Les semences et les aliments pour les animaux sont exclus de cette définition. Les indices de la production alimentaire se rapportent aux produits considérés comme

As in the past, the series include a large number of estimates made by FAO in cases where figures are not available from official country sources.

Index numbers for the world and regions are computed in a similar way to the country index numbers except that instead of using different commodity prices for each country group, "international commodity prices" derived from the Gheary-Khamis formula are used for all country groupings. This method assigns a single "price" to each commodity.

The indexes in table 4 are calculated as a ratio between the index numbers of total agricultural and food production in table 3 described above and the corresponding index numbers of population.

For further information on the series presented in these tables, see the FAO *Production Yearbook* [6].

Table 5: The index numbers of industrial production are classified according to tabulation categories, divisions and combinations of divisions of the International Standard Industrial Classification of All Economic Activities, Revision 3, (ISIC Rev. 3) [47] for mining (category C), manufacturing (category D), and electricity, gas and water (category E).

The indices indicate trends in value added in constant US dollars. The measure of value added used is the national accounts concept, which is defined as gross output less the cost of materials, supplies, fuel and electricity consumed and services received.

Each series is compiled using the Laspeyres formula, that is, the indices are base-weighted arithmetic means. The weight base year is 1990 and value added, generally at factor values, is used in weighting.

For most countries the estimates of value added used as weights are derived from the results of national industrial censuses or similar inquiries relating to 1990. These data, in national currency, are adjusted to the ISIC where necessary and are subsequently converted into US dollars.

Within each of the ISIC categories (tabulation categories, divisions and combinations of divisions) shown in the tables, the indices for the country aggregations (regions or economic groupings) are calculated directly from the country data. The indices for the World, however, are calculated from the aggregated indices for the groupings of developed and developing countries.

China and the countries of the former USSR (except Russian Federation and Ukraine) are excluded from their respective regions.

Table 6: For a description of the series in table 6, see the technical notes to chapter XIII.

comestibles et contenant des éléments nutritifs. Le café, le thé et les produits non comestibles sont exclus.

Les indices de la production agricole et de la production alimentaire présentés au tableau 3 sont calculés selon la formule de Laspeyres avec les années 1989-1991 comme période de référence, cela afin de limiter l'incidence, sur les indices correspondant à la période considérée, des fluctuations annuelles de la production agricole enregistrée pendant les années de référence. Les chiffres de production de chaque produit sont pondérés par les prix nationaux moyens à la production pour la période 1989-1991 et additionnés pour chaque année. Les indices sont fondés sur les données de production de l'année civile. Comme dans le passé, les séries comprennent un grand nombre d'estimations établies par la FAO lorsqu'elle n'avait pu obtenir de chiffres de sources officielles dans les pays eux-mêmes.

Les indices pour le monde et les régions sont calculés de la même façon que les indices par pays, mais au lieu d'appliquer des prix différents aux produits de base pour chaque groupe de pays, on a utilisé des "prix internationaux" établis d'après la formule de Gheary-Khamis pour tous les groupes de pays. Cette méthode attribue un seul "prix" à chaque produit de base.

Les indices du tableau 4 sont calculés comme ratio entre les indices de la production alimentaire et de la production agricole totale du tableau 3 décrits ci-dessus et les indices de population correspondants.

Pour tout renseignement complémentaire sur les séries présentées dans ces tableaux, voir l'*Annuaire FAO de la production* [6].

Tableau 5: Les indices de la production industrielle sont classés selon les catégories de classement, les divisions ou des combinaisons des divisions de la Classification Internationale type, par industrie, de toutes les branches d'activité économique, Révision 3 (CITI Rev. 3) [47] qui concernent les industries extractives (la catégorie C) et les industries manufacturières (la catégorie D), ainsi que l'électricité, le gaz et l'eau (la catégorie E).

Ces indices représentent les tendances de la valeur ajoutée en dollars constants des Etats-Unis. La mesure utilisée pour la valeur ajoutée correspond à celle qui est appliquée aux fins de la comptabilité nationale, c'est-à-dire égale à la valeur de la production brute diminuée des coûts des matériaux, des fournitures, de la consommation de carburant et d'électricité ainsi que des services reçus.

Chaque série a été établie au moyen de la formule de Laspeyres, ce qui signifie que les indices sont des moyennes arithmétiques affectées de coefficients de pondération. L'année de base de pondération est l'année 1990 et on utilise généralement pour la pondération la valeur ajoutée aux coûts des facteurs.

Table 7: For a description of the series in table 7, see the technical notes to chapter XVI. The composition of the regions is presented in table 69.

Pour la plupart des pays, les estimations de la valeur ajoutée qui sont utilisées comme coefficients de pondération sont tirées des résultats des recensements industriels nationaux ou enquêtes analogues concernant l'année 1990. Ces données, en monnaie nationale, sont ajustées s'il y a lieu aux normes de la CITI et ultérieurement converties en dollars des Etats-Unis.

A l'intérieur de chacune des subdivisions de la CITI (catégories de classement, divisions et combinaisons des divisions) indiquées dans les tableaux, les indices relatifs aux assemblages de pays (régions géographiques ou groupements économiques) sont calculés directement à partir des données des pays. Toutefois, les indices concernant le *Monde* sont calculés à partir des indices agrégés applicables aux groupements de pays développés et de pays en développement.

La Chine et les pays de l'ancienne URSS (sauf la Fédération de Russie et Ukraine) sont exclus de leurs régions respectives.

Tableau 6: On trouvera une description de la série de statistiques du tableau 6 dans les notes techniques du chapitre XIII.

Tableau 7: On trouvera une description de la série de statistiques du tableau 7 dans les notes techniques du chapitre XVI. La composition des régions est présentée au tableau 69.

Part Two
Population and Social Statistics

II
Population (table 8)
III
Education and literacy (tables 9-11)
IV
Health and nutrition
(tables 12 and 13)
V
Culture and communication
(tables 14-17)

Part Two of the *Yearbook* presents statistical series on a wide range of population and social topics for all countries or areas of the world for which data are available. These include population and population growth, surface area and density; primary, secondary and tertiary education, public expenditure on education, and the illiterate population; AIDS cases and food supply; cinemas, fax machines, telephones, and Internet users.

Deuxième partie
Population et statistiques sociales

II
Population (tableau 8)
III
Instruction et alphabétisation
(tableaux 9 à 11)
IV
Santé et nutrition (tableaux 12 et 13)
V
Culture et communication
(tableaux 14 à 17)

La deuxième partie de l'*Annuaire* présente, pour tous les pays ou zones du monde pour lesquels des données sont disponibles, des séries statistiques intéressant une large gamme de questions démographiques et sociales: population et croissance démographique, superficie et densité; enseignement primaire, secondaire et supérieur, dépenses publiques d'éducation, et la population analphabète; cas de SIDA et disponibilités alimentaires; cinémas, télécopieurs, téléphones, et usagers d'Internet.

8
Population by sex, rate of population increase, surface area and density
Population selon le sexe, taux d'accroissement de la population, superficie et densité

Country or area Pays ou zone	Latest census Dernier recensement Date	Both sexes Les deux sexes	Male Masculin	Female Féminin	Mid-year estimates (thousands) Estimations au milieu de l'année (milliers) 1993	1998	Annual rate of increase Taux d'accrois-sement annuel % 1993–98	Surface area (km²) Superficie (km²) 1998	Density Densité 1998[1]
Africa · Afrique									
Algeria[2] Algérie[2]	25 VI 1998	*29 276 767	*14 766 371	*14 510 396	26 894	*29 800	2.1	2 381 741	13
Angola[3] Angola[3]	15 XII 1970	5 646 166	2 943 974	2 702 192	x10 237	x12 092	3.3	1 246 700	10
Benin Bénin	15 II 1992	4 915 555	2 390 336	2 525 219	5 075	*6 044	3.5	112 622	54
Botswana Botswana	21 VIII 1991	1 326 796	634 400	692 396	1 391	*1 572	2.4	581 730	3
Burkina Faso [4] Burkina Faso [4]	10 XII 1996	10 312 609	4 970 882	5 341 727	9 682	*10 683	...	274 000	39
Burundi Burundi	16 VIII 1990	5 139 073	2 473 599	2 665 474	5 769	*6 300	1.8	27 834	226
Cameroon Cameroun	11 IV 1987	10 493 655	...	...	x12 473	x14 305	2.7	475 442	30
Cape Verde Cap–Vert	23 VI 1990	341 491	161 494	179 997	x364	*417	2.7	4 033	103
Central African Republic République centrafricaine	8 XII 1988	2 463 616	1 210 734	1 252 882	x3 151	x3 485	2.0	622 984	6
Chad [5] Tchad [5]	8 IV 1993	6 279 931	...	...	6 098	x7 270	3.5	1 284 000	6
Comoros [6] Comores [6]	15 IX 1991	446 817	221 152	225 665	x573	x658	2.8	2 235	294
Congo Congo	22 XII 1984	1 843 421	...	...	x2 419	x2 785	2.8	342 000	8
Côte d'Ivoire [4] Côte d'Ivoire [4]	1 III 1988	10 815 694	5 527 343	5 288 351	13 175	x14 292	...	322 463	44
Dem. Rep. of the Congo Rép. dém du Congo	1 VII 1984	29 916 800	14 543 800	15 373 000	x42 245	x49 139	3.0	2 344 858	21
Djibouti Djibouti	1960	81 200	...	...	x574	x623	1.6	23 200	27
Egypt [4] Egypte [4]	19 XI 1996	59 312 914	30 351 390	28 961 524	55 201	x65 978	...	1 001 449	66
Equatorial Guinea [7] Guinée équatoriale [7]	4 VII 1983	300 000	144 760	155 240	x379	x431	2.6	28 051	15
Eritrea Erythrée	9 V 1984	2 748 304	1 374 452	1 373 852	x3 028	x3 577	3.3	117 600	30
Ethiopia Ethiopie	11 X 1994	53 477 265	26 910 698	26 566 567	53 236	*59 882	2.4	1 104 300	54
Gabon Gabon	31 VII 1993	1 014 976	501 784	513 192	x1 019	*1 188	3.1	267 668	4
Gambia Gambie	13 IV 1993	1 025 867	514 530	511 337	x1 034	x1 229	3.5	11 295	109
Ghana Ghana	11 III 1984	12 296 081	6 063 848	6 232 233	x16 624	x19 162	2.8	238 533	80
Guinea [8] Guinée [8]	4 II 1983	4 533 240	...	...	x6 660	x7 337	1.9	245 857	30
Guinea–Bissau Guinée–Bissau	1 XII 1991	983 367	476 210	507 157	x1 039	x1 161	2.2	36 125	32
Kenya [4] Kenya [4]	24 VIII 1989	21 443 636	10 628 368	10 815 268	28 113	x29 008	...	580 367	50
Lesotho Lesotho	12 IV 1986	1 447 000	...	...	x1 843	x2 062	2.2	30 355	68
Liberia Libéria	1 II 1984	2 101 628	1 063 127	1 038 501	2 640	x2 666	0.2	111 369	24
Libyan Arab Jamahiriya Jamahiriya arabe libyenne	11 VIII 1995	4 404 986	2 236 943	2 168 043	4 700	x5 339	2.6	1 759 540	3

8
Population by sex, rate of population increase, surface area and density [*cont.*]
Population selon le sexe, taux d'accroissement de la population,
superficie et densité [*suite*]

Country or area Pays ou zone	Latest census Dernier recensement Date	Both sexes Les deux sexes	Male Masculin	Female Féminin	Mid–year estimates (thousands) Estimations au milieu de l'année (milliers) 1993	1998	Annual rate of increase Taux d'accrois- sement annuel % 1993–98	Surface area (km²) Superficie (km²) 1998	Density Densité 1998[1]
Madagascar Madagascar	1 VIII 1993	12 092 157	5 991 171	6 100 986	x12 860	x15 057	3.2	587 041	26
Malawi [4] Malawi [4]	1 IX 1987	7 988 507	3 867 136	4 121 371	9 135	x10 346	...	118 484	87
Mali [9] Mali [9]	17 IV 1998	9 790 492	4 847 436	4 943 056	x9 479	x10 694	2.4	1 240 192	9
Mauritania [10] Mauritanie [10]	5 IV 1988	1 864 236	923 175	941 061	2 148	x2 529	3.3	1 025 520	2
Mauritius Maurice	1 VII 1990	1 056 660	527 760	528 900	1 097	*1 160	1.1	2 040	569
Morocco Maroc	2 IX 1994	25 926 000	12 895 000	13 031 000	26 069	*27 775	1.3	446 550	62
Mozambique[4][8] Mozambique[4][8]	1 VIII 1997	16 099 246	7 714 306	8 384 940	15 583	*16 917	...	801 590	21
Namibia Namibie	21 X 1991	1 409 920	686 327	723 593	x1 465	x1 660	2.5	824 292	2
Niger Niger	20 V 1988	*7 248 100	*3 590 070	*3 658 030	x8 555	x10 078	3.3	1 267 000	8
Nigeria Nigéria	26 XI 1991	88 992 220	44 529 608	44 462 612	x94 107	x106 409	2.5	923 768	115
Reunion[2] Réunion[2]	15 III 1990	597 828	294 256	303 572	632	x682	1.5	2 510	272
Rwanda Rwanda	15 VIII 1991	7 142 755	...	...	x5 740	x6 604	2.8	26 338	251
St. Helena ex. dep. Sainte–Hélène sans dép.	8 III 1998	5 157	2 612	2 545	6	...	...	122	...
Ascension Ascension	31 XII 1978	849	608	241	...	...	...	88	...
Tristan da Cunha Tristan da Cunha	22 II 1987	296	139	157	–	...	...	...	...
Sao Tome and Principe Sao Tomé–et–Principe	4 VIII 1991	116 998	57 837	59 161	122	x141	2.9	964	146
Senegal Sénégal	27 V 1988	6 896 808	3 353 599	3 543 209	7 913	*9 038	2.7	196 722	46
Seychelles Seychelles	26 VIII 1994	74 331	37 128	37 203	72	*79	1.7	455	173
Sierra Leone[8] Sierra Leone[8]	15 XII 1985	3 515 812	1 746 055	1 769 757	x4 083	x4 568	2.2	71 740	64
Somalia Somalie	15 II 1987	7 114 431	3 741 664	3 372 767	x7 962	x9 237	3.0	637 657	14
South Africa[8] Afrique du Sud[8]	10 X 1996	40 583 573	19 520 887	21 062 686	37 802	*42 130	2.2	1 221 037	35
Sudan [4] Soudan [4]	15 IV 1993	24 940 683	12 518 638	12 422 045	28 129	x28 292	...	2 505 813	11
Swaziland Swaziland	11 V 1997	*965 859	...	...	851	x952	2.3	17 364	55
Togo Togo	22 XI 1981	2 703 250	...	...	x3 837	x4 397	2.7	56 785	77
Tunisia Tunisie	20 IV 1994	*8 785 711	*4 439 289	*4 346 422	8 657	*9 333	1.5	163 610	57
Uganda Ouganda	12 I 1991	16 671 705	8 185 747	8 485 958	x17 882	*21 029	3.2	241 038	87
United Rep. of Tanzania Rép.–Unie de Tanzanie	28 VIII 1988	23 126 310	11 217 723	11 908 587	26 732	x32 102	3.7	883 749	36
Western Sahara [11] Sahara occidental [11]	31 XII 1970	76 425	43 981	32 444	x230	x275	3.5	266 000	1
Zambia Zambie	20 VIII 1990	7 383 097	3 617 577	3 765 520	x7 804	x8 781	2.4	752 618	12
Zimbabwe Zimbabwe	18 VIII 1992	10 412 548	5 083 537	5 329 011	10 779	*12 685	3.3	390 757	32

8
Population by sex, rate of population increase, surface area and density [*cont.*]
Population selon le sexe, taux d'accroissement de la population,
superficie et densité [*suite*]

Country or area Pays ou zone	Latest census Dernier recensement Date	Both sexes Les deux sexes	Male Masculin	Female Féminin	Mid-year estimates (thousands) Estimations au milieu de l'année (milliers) 1993	1998	Annual rate of increase Taux d'accrois-sement annuel % 1993–98	Surface area (km²) Superficie (km²) 1998	Density Densité 1998[1]
America, North · Amérique du Nord									
Anguilla Anguilla	10 IV 1984	6 987	3 428	3 559	9	x8	−2.5	96	84
Antigua and Barbuda Antigua−et−Barbuda	28 V 1991	62 922	...	...	66	x67	0.4	442	151
Aruba [2] Aruba [2]	6 X 1991	66 687	32 821	33 866	75	*92	4.1	193	477
Bahamas Bahamas	1 V 1990	255 095	124 992	130 103	269	*298	2.0	13 878	21
Barbados Barbade	2 V 1990	257 082	...	...	264	x268	0.3	430	624
Belize Belize	12 V 1991	189 774	96 289	93 485	205	*238	3.0	22 696	11
Bermuda [12] Bermudes [12]	20 V 1991	74 837	...	...	59	x64	1.4	53	1 199
British Virgin Islands Iles Vierges britanniques	12 V 1991	17 809	...	...	x18	x20	2.8	151	134
Canada [2 8] Canada [2 8]	14 V 1996	28 846 760	14 170 030	14 676 735	28 703	*30 247	1.0	9 970 610	3
Cayman Islands [2] Iles Caïmanes [2]	15 X 1989	25 355	12 372	12 983	31	x36	3.1	264	135
Costa Rica [2] Costa Rica [2]	10 VI 1984	2 416 809	1 208 216	1 208 593	3 005	*3 341	2.1	51 100	65
Cuba Cuba	11 IX 1981	9 723 605	4 914 873	4 808 732	10 904	x11 116	0.4	110 861	100
Dominica Dominique	12 V 1991	71 794	35 927	35 867	73	*76	0.9	751	101
Dominican Republic Rép. dominicaine	24 IX 1993	7 293 390	3 550 797	3 742 593	7 620	*8 105	4.0	48 511	167
El Salvador El Salvador	27 IX 1992	5 118 599	2 485 613	2 632 986	x5 429	x6 032	2.1	21 041	287
Greenland [2] Groenland [2]	26 X 1976	49 630	26 856	22 774	55	56	0.3	2 175 600	–
Grenada [13] Grenade [13]	12 V 1991	85 123	41 893	43 230	x92	x93	0.3	344	271
Guadeloupe [2 14] Guadeloupe [2 14]	15 III 1990	387 034	189 187	197 847	x411	x443	1.5	1 705	260
Guatemala [4] Guatemala [4]	17 IV 1994	8 322 051	...	...	10 030	*10 799	...	108 889	99
Haiti [2] Haïti [2]	30 VIII 1982	5 053 792	2 448 370	2 605 422	6 903	*7 647	2.0	27 750	276
Honduras Honduras	29 V 1988	4 248 561	2 110 106	2 138 455	5 248	*6 180	2.0	112 088	55
Jamaica Jamaïque	7 IV 1991	2 314 479	1 134 386	1 180 093	2 446	x2 538	0.7	10 990	231
Martinique [2] Martinique [2]	15 III 1990	359 579	173 878	185 701	377	x389	0.6	1 102	353
Mexico [2] Mexique [2]	12 III 1990	81 249 645	39 893 969	41 355 676	x87 976	x95 831	1.7	1 958 201	49
Montserrat Montserrat	12 V 1991	10 639	5 290	5 349	x11	x11	−0.3	102	105
Netherlands Antilles [2 15] Antilles néerlandaises [2 15]	27 I 1992	189 474	90 707	98 767	195	x213	1.7	800	266
Nicaragua [2] Nicaragua [2]	25 IV 1995	4 357 099	2 147 105	2 209 994	4 265	x4 807	2.4	130 000	37
Panama Panama	13 V 1990	2 329 329	1 178 790	1 150 539	2 535	2 764	1.7	75 517	37
Puerto Rico [2 16] Porto Rico [2 16]	1 IV 1990	3 522 037	1 705 642	1 816 395	3 622	*3 860	1.3	8 875	435

8
Population by sex, rate of population increase, surface area and density [*cont.*]
Population selon le sexe, taux d'accroissement de la population,
superficie et densité [*suite*]

Country or area Pays ou zone	Latest census Dernier recensement				Mid-year estimates (thousands) Estimations au milieu de l'année (milliers)		Annual rate of increase Taux d'accrois- sement annuel %	Surface area (km²) Superficie (km²)	Density Densité
	Date	Both sexes Les deux sexes	Male Masculin	Female Féminin	1993	1998	1993–98	1998	1998[1]
Saint Kitts and Nevis Saint–Kitts–et–Nevis	12 V 1991	40 618	19 933	20 685	44	x39	−2.2	261	150
Saint Lucia Sainte–Lucie	12 V 1991	133 308	64 645	68 663	x140	*152	1.6	622	244
St. Pierre and Miquelon Saint–Pierre et Miquelon	5 III 1990	6 392	...	...	7	x7	−	242	27
St. Vincent and Grenadines [17] St.–Vincent–et–Grenadines [17]	12 V 1991	106 499	53 165	53 334	110	*111	0.2	388	286
Trinidad and Tobago Trinité–et–Tobago	2 V 1990	1 169 572	584 445	585 127	1 247	x1 283	0.6	5 130	250
Turks and Caicos Islands Iles Turques et Caïques	31 V 1990	12 350	6 289	6 061	x13	x16	3.7	430	36
United States [18] Etats–Unis [18]	1 IV 1990	248 709 873	121 239 418	127 470 455	258 083	*270 561	0.9	9 363 520	29
United States Virgin Islands [2][16] Iles Vierges américaines [2][16]	1 IV 1990	101 809	49 210	52 599	x99	x94	−1.0	347	272
America, South · Amérique du Sud									
Argentina Argentine	15 V 1991	32 615 528	15 937 980	16 677 548	33 869	*36 125	1.3	2 780 400	13
Bolivia[8] Bolivie[8]	3 VI 1992	6 420 792	3 171 265	3 249 527	7 065	*7 950	2.4	1 098 581	7
Brazil [9][19] Brésil [9][19]	1 IX 1991	146 825 475	72 485 122	74 340 353	151 572	*161 790	1.3	8 547 403	19
Chile Chili	22 IV 1992	13 348 401	6 553 254	6 795 147	13 771	*14 822	1.5	756 626	20
Colombia Colombie	24 X 1993	33 109 840	16 296 539	16 813 301	33 951	*36 705	1.6	1 138 914	32
Ecuador[20] Equateur[20]	25 XI 1990	9 648 189	4 796 412	4 851 777	10 981	*12 175	2.1	283 561	43
Falkland Is. (Malvinas)[21][22] Iles Falkland (Malvinas) [21][22]	24 IV 1996	2 564	1 447	1 117	x2	x2	0.6	12 173	−
French Guyana[2] Guyane française[2]	15 III 1990	114 808	59 798	55 010	x134	x167	4.3	90 000	2
Guyana Guyana	12 V 1991	701 704	344 928	356 776	x814	x850	0.9	214 969	4
Paraguay[8] Paraguay[8]	26 VIII 1992	4 152 588	2 085 905	2 066 683	4 575	*5 219	2.6	406 752	13
Peru[8][19] Pérou[8][19]	11 VII 1993	22 048 356	10 956 375	11 091 981	x22 739	*24 801	1.7	1 285 216	19
Suriname Suriname	1 VII 1980	355 240	...	...	404	x414	0.5	163 265	3
Uruguay Uruguay	22 V 1996	3 163 763	1 532 288	1 631 475	3 172	*3 289	0.7	175 016	19
Venezuela[19] Venezuela[19]	20 X 1990	18 105 265	9 019 757	9 085 508	20 910	*23 242	2.1	912 050	25
Asia · Asie									
Afghanistan [23] Afghanistan [23]	23 VI 1979	13 051 358	6 712 377	6 338 981	x17 633	x21 354	3.8	652 090	33
Armenia [9] Arménie [9]	12 I 1989	3 304 776	1 619 308	1 685 468	3 731	x3 536	−1.1	29 800	119
Azerbaijan [9] Azerbaïdjan [9]	27 I 1999	*7 953 000	*4 119 000	*3 834 000	7 399	*7 665	0.7	86 600	89
Bahrain Bahreïn	16 XI 1991	508 037	294 346	213 691	537	*643	3.6	694	927
Bangladesh Bangladesh	11 III 1991	111 455 185	57 313 929	54 141 256	x114 900	x124 774	1.6	143 998	866
Bhutan Bhoutan	11 XI 1969	1 034 774	...	...	x1 781	x2 004	2.4	47 000	43
Brunei Darussalam[8] Brunéi Darussalam[8]	7 VIII 1991	260 482	137 616	122 866	276	x315	2.6	5 765	55

8
Population by sex, rate of population increase, surface area and density [*cont.*]
Population selon le sexe, taux d'accroissement de la population,
superficie et densité [*suite*]

Country or area Pays ou zone	Latest census Dernier recensement Date	Both sexes Les deux sexes	Male Masculin	Female Féminin	Mid-year estimates (thousands) Estimations au milieu de l'année (milliers) 1993	1998	Annual rate of increase Taux d'accrois- sement annuel % 1993–98	Surface area (km^2) Superficie (km^2) 1998	Density Densité 1998[1]
Cambodia [24] Cambodge[24]	3 III 1998	*11 437 656	*5 511 408	*5 926 248	9 308	x10 716	2.8	181 035	59
China [25] [26] Chine [25] [26]	1 VII 1990	1 160 044 618	...	...	x1 196 305	x1 255 698	1.0	9 596 961	131
China, Hong Kong SAR † Chine, Hong Kong RAS †	15 III 1996	6 217 556	3 108 107	3 109 449	5 901	*6 687	2.5	1 075	6 221
China, Macao SAR Chine, Macao RAS	30 VIII 1991	385 089	...	...	384	*424	2.0	18	23 556
Cyprus [27] Chypre[27]	1 X 1992	602 025	299 614	302 411	718	*749	0.8	9 251	81
East Timor Timor oriental	31 X 1990	747 750	386 939	360 811	x785	x857	1.8	14 874	58
Georgia [4] [9] Géorgie [4] [9]	12 I 1989	5 400 841	2 562 040	2 838 801	5 440	x5 059	...	69 700	73
India[28] Inde[28]	1 III 1991	846 302 688	439 230 458	407 072 230	883 910	*970 933	1.9	3 287 263	295
Indonesia[29] Indonésie[29]	31 X 1990	179 378 946	89 463 545	89 915 401	187 589	*202 907	1.6	1 904 569	107
Iran (Islamic Republic of) Iran (Rép. islamique d')	1 X 1996	60 055 488	30 515 159	29 540 329	58 481	*61 626	1.0	1 648 195	37
Iraq Iraq	17 X 1987	16 335 199	8 395 889	7 939 310	x19 260	x21 800	2.5	438 317	50
Israel[2] [30] Israël[2] [30]	4 XI 1995	5 548 523	2 738 175	2 810 348	5 261	*5 963	2.5	21 056	283
Japan[31] Japon[31]	1 X 1995	125 570 246	61 574 398	63 995 848	124 829	*126 410	0.3	377 829	335
Jordan[32] [33] Jordanie[32] [33]	10 XII 1994	4 095 579	2 135 883	1 959 696	x5 261	x6 304	3.6	97 740	64
Kazakhstan [4] Kazakhstan [4]	12 I 1989	16 536 511	8 012 985	8 523 526	16 479	*15 073	...	2 724 900	6
Korea, Dem. People's Rep. Corée, Rép. pop. dém. de	31 XII 1993	21 213 378	10 329 699	10 883 679	x21 506	x23 348	1.6	120 538	194
Korea, Republic of [8] [34] Corée, Rép. de [8] [34]	1 XI 1995	44 608 726	22 389 324	22 219 402	44 195	*46 430	1.0	99 268	468
Kuwait Koweït	20 IV 1995	1 575 983	914 324	661 659	1 461	*2 027	6.6	17 818	114
Kyrgyzstan [9] Kirghizistan [9]	12 I 1989	4 257 755	2 077 623	2 180 132	4 482	*4 797	1.4	199 900	24
Lao People's Dem. Rep. Rép. dém. populaire lao	1 III 1985	3 584 803	1 757 115	1 827 688	x4 520	x5 163	2.7	236 800	22
Lebanon[35] [36] Liban[35] [36]	15 XI 1970	2 126 325	1 080 015	1 046 310	x2 807	x3 191	2.6	10 400	307
Malaysia Malaisie	14 VIII 1991	17 563 420	8 876 829	8 686 591	19 564	*22 180	2.5	329 758	67
Maldives Maldives	25 III 1995	244 814	124 622	120 192	238	x271	2.6	298	909
Mongolia Mongolie	5 I 1989	2 043 400	...	...	2 232	*2 404	1.5	1 566 500	2
Myanmar [4] [9] Myanmar [4] [9]	31 III 1983	35 307 913	17 518 255	17 789 658	43 116	x44 497	...	676 578	66
Nepal Népal	22 VI 1991	18 491 097	9 220 974	9 270 123	19 275	*21 813	2.5	147 181	148
Occupied Palestinian Territory[37] [38] Territoire palestinien occupé[37] [38]	9 XII 1997	2 601 669	1 322 264	1 279 405	...	...	...	...	...
Oman Oman	1 XII 1993	2 018 074	...	...	2 020	*2 135	1.1	309 500	7
Pakistan[4] [39] Pakistan[4] [39]	2 III 1998	130 579 571	67 840 137	62 739 434	122 795	*131 510	...	796 095	165
Philippines[2] Philippines[2]	1 IX 1995	68 616 536	34 584 170	34 032 366	66 982	*75 155	2.3	300 000	251

8

Population by sex, rate of population increase, surface area and density [*cont.*]
Population selon le sexe, taux d'accroissement de la population,
superficie et densité [*suite*]

Country or area Pays ou zone	Latest census Dernier recensement				Mid-year estimates (thousands) Estimations au milieu de l'année (milliers)		Annual rate of increase Taux d'accrois- sement annuel %	Surface area (km²) Superficie (km²)	Density Densité
	Date	Both sexes Les deux sexes	Male Masculin	Female Féminin	1993	1998	1993–98	1998	1998[1]
Qatar [4] Qatar [4]	1 III 1997	522 023	342 459	179 564	559	x579	...	11 000	53
Saudi Arabia Arabie saoudite	27 IX 1992	16 948 388	9 479 973	7 468 415	x17 350	x20 181	3.0	2 149 690	9
Singapore [40] Singapour [40]	30 VI 1990	2 705 115	1 370 059	1 335 056	3 259	*3 866	3.4	618	6 255
Sri Lanka Sri Lanka	17 III 1981	14 846 750	7 568 253	7 278 497	17 619	*18 774	1.3	65 610	286
Syrian Arab Republic[41] Rép. arabe syrienne[41]	3 IX 1994	13 782 315	7 048 906	6 733 409	13 393	*15 597	3.0	185 180	84
Tajikistan Tadjikistan	12 I 1989	5 092 603	2 530 245	2 562 358	5 638	x6 015	1.3	143 100	42
Thailand Thaïlande	1 IV 1990	*54 532 300	*27 031 200	*27 501 100	58 010	*61 201	1.1	513 115	119
Turkey Turquie	21 X 1990	56 473 035	28 607 047	27 865 988	58 812	*63 451	1.5	774 815	82
Turkmenistan Turkménistan	10 I 1995	4 483 251	2 225 331	2 257 920	4 308	*4 859	2.4	488 100	10
United Arab Emirates [4] [42] Emirats arabes unis [4] [42]	11 XII 1995	2 377 453	1 579 743	797 710	x2 102	*2 724	...	83 600	33
Uzbekistan [9] Ouzbékistan [9]	12 I 1989	19 810 077	9 784 156	10 025 921	21 852	*24 051	1.9	447 400	54
Viet Nam Viet Nam	1 IV 1989	64 411 713	31 336 568	33 075 145	71 026	x77 562	1.8	331 689	234
Yemen [4] Yémen [4]	16 XII 1994	14 587 807	7 473 540	7 114 267	12 302	*17 071	...	527 968	32
Europe · Europe									
Albania Albanie	12 IV 1989	3 182 400	1 638 900	1 543 500	3 485	*3 791	1.7	28 748	132
Andorra Andorre	11 XI 1954	5 664	...	...	63	x72	2.6	468	154
Austria[2] Autriche[2]	15 V 1991	7 795 786	3 753 989	4 041 797	7 991	*8 077	0.2	83 859	96
Belarus Bélarus	12 I 1989	10 199 709	4 775 835	5 423 874	10 356	*10 191	−0.3	207 600	49
Belgium[2] Belgique[2]	1 III 1991	9 978 681	4 875 982	5 102 699	10 084	*10 214	0.3	30 528	335
Bosnia and Herzegovina [2] Bosnie–Herzégovine [2]	31 III 1991	4 377 033	2 183 795	2 193 238	4 434	*4 211	−1.0	51 197	82
Bulgaria Bulgarie	4 XII 1992	8 472 724	...	...	8 472	*8 257	−0.5	110 912	74
Channel Islands Iles Anglo–Normandes	10 III 1996	143 831	69 638	74 193	142	x151	1.2	195	774
Croatia [2] Croatie [2]	31 III 1991	4 784 265	2 318 623	2 465 642	4 641	*4 572	−0.3	56 538	81
Czech Republic [2] Rép. tchéque [2]	3 III 1991	10 302 215	4 999 935	5 302 280	10 331	*10 295	−0.1	78 866	131
Denmark [2] [43] Danemark [2] [43]	1 I 1998	5 294 860	2 615 669	2 679 191	5 189	*5 301	0.4	43 094	123
Estonia [9] Estonie [9]	12 I 1989	1 565 662	731 392	834 270	1 517	*1 450	−0.9	45 100	32
Faeroe Islands [2] Iles Féroé [2]	22 IX 1977	41 969	21 997	19 972	x46	x43	−1.0	1 399	31
Finland [2] Finlande [2]	31 XII 1990	4 998 478	2 426 204	2 572 274	5 066	*5 153	0.3	338 145	15
France [44] [45] [46] France [44] [45] [46]	5 III 1990	56 634 299	27 553 788	29 080 511	57 654	*58 847	0.4	551 500	107

8
Population by sex, rate of population increase, surface area and density [*cont.*]
Population selon le sexe, taux d'accroissement de la population,
superficie et densité [*suite*]

Country or area Pays ou zone	Latest census Dernier recensement Date	Both sexes Les deux sexes	Male Masculin	Female Féminin	Mid-year estimates (thousands) Estimations au milieu de l'année (milliers) 1993	1998	Annual rate of increase Taux d'accrois- sement annuel % 1993–98	Surface area (km²) Superficie (km²) 1998	Density Densité 1998[1]
Germany † [2] [47] Allemagne † [2] [47]		...	...	...	81 187	*82 024	0.2	357 022	230
Federal Rep. of Germany [2] Rép. féd. d'Allemagne [2]	25 V 1987	61 077 042	29 322 923	31 754 119	...	...	...	248 647	...
former German Dem Rep. [2] l'ex–R. d. allemande [2]	31 XII 1981	16 705 635	7 849 112	8 856 523	...	...	...	108 333	...
Gibraltar [48] Gibraltar [48]	14 X 1991	26 703	13 628	13 075	28	x25	−2.0	6	4 239
Greece [49] [50] Grèce [49] [50]	17 III 1991	10 259 900	5 055 408	5 204 492	10 379	*10 515	0.3	131 957	80
Holy See [51] Saint–Siège [51]	30 IV 1948	890	548	342	x1	*1	5.1	–	...
Hungary Hongrie	1 I 1990	10 374 823	4 984 904	5 389 919	10 294	*10 114	−0.4	93 032	109
Iceland [9] Islande [9]	1 XII 1970	204 930	103 621	101 309	264	*274	0.7	103 000	3
Ireland Irlande	28 IV 1996	3 626 087	1 800 232	1 825 855	3 574	*3 705	0.7	70 273	53
Isle of Man Ile de Man	14 IV 1996	71 714	34 797	36 917	71	*74	0.9	572	129
Italy Italie	20 X 1991	59 103 833	...	...	57 049	*57 369	0.1	301 318	190
Latvia [9] Lettonie [9]	12 I 1989	2 666 567	1 238 806	1 427 761	2 586	*2 449	−1.1	64 600	38
Liechtenstein Liechtenstein	2 XII 1980	25 215	...	...	x30	x32	1.4	160	200
Lithuania [9] Lithuanie [9]	12 I 1989	3 674 802	1 738 953	1 935 849	3 730	*3 702	−0.2	65 200	57
Luxembourg[2] Luxembourg[2]	31 III 1991	384 634	188 570	196 064	398	*426	1.4	2 586	165
Malta [52] Malte [52]	16 XI 1985	345 418	169 832	175 586	365	*377	0.7	316	1 194
Monaco [2] Monaco [2]	23 VII 1990	29 972	14 237	15 735	x31	x33	1.1	1	32 894
Netherlands [2] [53] Pays–Bas [2] [53]	1 I 1991	15 010 445	7 419 501	7 590 944	15 290	*15 694	0.5	41 526	378
Norway [2] Norvège [2]	3 XI 1990	4 247 546	2 099 881	2 147 665	4 312	*4 431	0.5	323 877	14
Poland [54] Pologne [54]	6 XII 1988	37 878 641	18 464 373	19 414 268	38 459	*38 666	0.1	323 250	120
Portugal [55] Portugal [55]	15 IV 1991	9 862 540	4 754 632	5 107 908	9 881	*9 957	0.2	91 982	108
Republic of Moldova [4] République de Moldova[4]	12 I 1989	4 337 592	2 058 160	2 279 432	4 348	*3 652	...	33 851	108
Romania Roumanie	7 I 1992	22 810 035	11 213 763	11 596 272	22 755	*22 503	−0.2	238 391	94
Russian Federation [9] Fédération de Russie [9]	12 I 1989	147 021 869	68 713 869	78 308 000	148 146	*146 539	−0.2	17 075 400	9
San Marino Saint–Marin	30 XI 1976	19 149	9 654	9 495	24	x26	1.2	61	424
Slovakia [2] Slovaquie [2]	3 III 1991	5 274 335	2 574 061	2 700 274	5 325	*5 391	0.2	49 012	110
Slovenia [2] Slovénie [2]	31 III 1991	1 965 986	952 611	1 013 375	1 991	*1 982	−0.1	20 256	98
Spain [56] Espagne [56]	1 III 1991	39 433 942	19 338 083	20 095 859	39 086	*39 371	0.1	505 992	78
Svalbard and Jan Mayen Isl. [57] Svalbard et Ile Jan–Mayen [57]	1 XI 1960	3 431	2 545	886	...	...	...	62 422	...

8
Population by sex, rate of population increase, surface area and density [cont.]
Population selon le sexe, taux d'accroissement de la population,
superficie et densité [suite]

Country or area Pays ou zone	Latest census Dernier recensement Date	Both sexes Les deux sexes	Male Masculin	Female Féminin	Mid-year estimates (thousands) Estimations au milieu de l'année (milliers) 1993	1998	Annual rate of increase Taux d'accrois- sement annuel % 1993–98	Surface area (km²) Superficie (km²) 1998	Density Densité 1998[1]
Sweden [2] Suède [2]	1 IX 1990	8 587 353	4 242 351	4 345 002	8 719	*8 851	0.3	449 964	20
Switzerland [2] Suisse [2]	4 XII 1990	6 873 687	3 390 212	3 483 475	6 938	*7 110	0.5	41 284	172
TFYR of Macedonia [2] L'ex–R.y. Macédoine [2]	20 VI 1994	1 945 932	974 255	971 677	x1 943	x1 999	0.6	25 713	78
Ukraine [9] Ukraine [9]	12 I 1989	51 452 034	23 745 108	27 706 926	52 179	*50 500	−0.7	603 700	84
United Kingdom [4][58] Royaume–Uni [4][58]	21 IV 1991	56 352 200	...	...	58 191	x58 649	...	242 900	241
Yugoslavia [2] Yougoslavie [2]	31 III 1991	10 394 026	5 157 120	5 236 906	10 482	*10 616	0.3	102 173	104
Oceania · Océanie									
American Samoa [2][16] Samoa américaines [2][16]	1 IV 1990	46 773	24 023	22 750	53	x63	3.6	199	319
Australia Australie	30 VI 1996	17 892 423	8 849 224	9 043 199	17 667	*18 751	1.2	7 741 220	2
Cook Islands [59] Iles Cook [59]	1 XII 1996	19 103	9 842	9 261	20	*17	−2.9	236	72
Fiji Fidji	25 VIII 1996	775 077	393 931	381 146	771	x796	0.6	18 274	44
French Polynesia [60] Polynésie française [60]	3 IX 1996	219 521	113 830	105 691	210	x227	1.6	4 000	57
Guam [2][4][16] Guam [2][4][16]	1 IV 1990	133 152	70 945	62 207	143	*149	...	549	271
Kiribati [61] Kiribati [61]	7 XI 1995	77 658	38 478	39 180	x76	x81	1.4	726	112
Marshall Islands Iles Marshall	13 XI 1988	43 380	22 181	21 199	52	*63	3.9	181	350
Micronesia (Federated States of) Micronésie (Etats fédérés de)	18 IX 1994	105 506	53 923	51 583	x102	x114	2.2	702	162
Nauru Nauru	17 IV 1992	9 919	...	...	10	x11	1.7	21	529
New Caledonia [62] Nouvelle–Calédonie [62]	4 IV 1989	164 173	83 862	80 311	181	*196	1.6	18 575	11
New Zealand [63] Nouvelle–Zélande [63]	5 III 1996	3 618 303	1 777 464	1 840 839	3 554	*3 791	1.3	270 534	14
Niue Nioué	17 VIII 1997	2 088	1 053	1 035	x2	x2	−2.1	...	...
Norfolk Island Ile Norfolk	30 VI 1986	2 367	1 170	1 197	...	...	...	36	...
Northern Mariana Islands Iles Mariannes du Nord	1 IV 1990	43 345	...	...	x53	x70	5.5	464	151
Palau Palaos	9 IX 1995	17 225	...	...	x16	x19	2.5	459	40
Papua New Guinea [64] Papouasie–Nouv.–Guinée[64]	11 VII 1990	3 761 954	...	...	3 922	x4 600	3.2	462 840	10
Pitcairn Pitcairn	31 XII 1991	66	...	...	–	–	−2.8	5	9
Samoa Samoa	5 XI 1991	161 298	...	...	x164	*168	0.5	2 831	59
Solomon Islands [65] Iles Salomon [65]	23 XI 1986	285 176	147 972	137 204	x355	x417	3.2	28 896	14
Tokelau Tokélaou	1991	1 577	...	...	x2	x1	−0.6	12	124
Tonga Tonga	30 XI 1996	97 784	49 615	48 169	97	x98	0.3	650	151
Tuvalu Tuvalu	17 IX 1991	9 043	4 376	4 667	x10	x11	2.8	26	428

8
Population by sex, rate of population increase, surface area and density [*cont.*]
Population selon le sexe, taux d'accroissement de la population,
superficie et densité [*suite*]

| Country or area Pays ou zone | Latest census Dernier recensement | | | | Mid-year estimates (thousands) Estimations au milieu de l'année (milliers) | | Annual rate of increase Taux d'accrois- sement annuel % | Surface area (km²) Superficie (km²) | Density Densité |
	Date	Both sexes Les deux sexes	Male Masculin	Female Féminin	1993	1998	1993–98	1998	1998[1]
Vanuatu Vanuatu	16 V 1989	142 944	73 674	69 270	156	x182	3.0	12 189	15
Wallis and Futuna Islands Iles Wallis et Futuna	1990	13 705	...	...	x14	x14	0.5	200	72

Source:
United Nations Secretariat, "Demographic Yearbook 1998" and the demographic statistics database of the Statistics Division.

† For information on recent changes in country or area nomenclature pertaining to former Czechoslovakia, Germany, Hong Kong Special Administrative Region (SAR) of China, Macao Special Administrative Region (SAR) of China, SFR of Yugolasvia and the former USSR, see Annex I – Country or area nomenclature, regional and other groupings.

* Provisional.
x Estimate for 1995–2000 prepared by the Population Division of the United Nations.
1 Population per square kilometre of surface area in 1998. Figures are merely the quotients of population divided by surface area and are not to be considered either as reflecting density in the urban sense or as indicating the supporting power of a territory's land and resources.
2 De jure population.
3 Including the enclave of Cabinda.
4 Rate not computed because of apparent lack of comparability between estimates shown for 1993 and 1998.
5 Census results have been adjusted for under–enumeration estimated at 1.4 per cent.
6 Census results, excluding Mayotte.
7 Comprising Bioko (which includes Pagalu) and Rio Muni (which includes Corisco and Elobeys).
8 Mid–year estimates have been adjusted for under–enumeration. Census data have not been adjusted for under–enumeration, estimated as follows: Bolivia (6.92), Brunei Darussalam (1.06), Canada (...), Guinea (...), Korea, Republic of (1.9), Mozambique (5.1), Paraguay (7.40), Peru (2.35), South Africa (6.8), Sierra Leone (9.0).

9 Census results for de jure population.
10 Census results, including an estimate of 224 095 for nomad population.

11 Comprising the Northern Region (former Saguia el Hamra) and Southern Region (former Rio de Oro).
12 Mid–year estimates for de jure population, but excluding persons residing in institutions.
13 Including Carriacou and other dependencies in the Grenadines.

14 Including dependencies: Marie–Galante, la Désirade, les Saintes, Petite–Terre, St. Barthélemy and French part of St. Martin.

Source:
Secrétariat de l'Organisation des Nations Unies, "Annuaire démographique 1998" et la base de données pour les statistiques démographiques de la Division de statistique.

† Pour les modifications récentes de nomenclature de pays ou de zone concernant l'Allemagne, Hong–Kong (Région administrative spéciale de Chine), Macao (Région administrative spéciale de Chine), l'ex–Tchécoslovaquie, l'ex–URSS, Rfs de Yougoslavie, voir annexe I – Nomenclature des pays ou des zones, groupements régionaux et autres groupements.

* Données provisoires.
x Estimations pour 1995–2000 établie par la Division de la population de l'Organisation des Nations Unies.
1 Nombre d'habitants au kilomètre carré en 1998. Il s'agit simplement du quotient du chiffre de la population divisé par celui de la superficie: il ne faut pas y voir d'indication de la densité au sens urbain du terme ni de l'effectif de population que les terres et les ressources du territoire sont capables de nourrir.
2 Population de droit.
3 Y compris l'enclave de Cabinda.
4 On n'a pas calculé le taux parce que les estimations pour 1993 et 1998 ne paraissent pas comparables.
5 Les résultats du recensement ont été ajustés pour compenser les lacunes du dénombrement estimées à 1,4 p. 100.
6 Les résultats du recensement, non compris Mayotte.
7 Comprend Bioko (qui comprend Pagalu) et Rio Muni (qui comprend Corisco et Elobeys).
8 Les estimations au milieu de l'année tiennent compte d'un ajustement destiné à compenser les lacunes du dénombrement. Les données de recensement ne tiennent pas compte de cet ajustement. En voici le détail: Bolive (6,92), Brunéi Darussalam (1,06), Canada (...), Guinée (...), Corée Rép. de (1,9), Mozambique (5,1), Paraguay (7,40), Pérou (2,35), Afrique de Sud (6,8), Sierra Leone (9,0).

9 Les résultats du recensement. Population de droit.
10 Les résultats du recensement, y compris une estimation de 224 095 personnes pour la population nomade.

11 Comprend la région septentrionale (ancien Saguia–el–Hamra) et la région méridionale (ancien Rio de Oro).
12 Estimations au milieu de l'année pour la Population de droit, mais non compris les personnes dans les institutions.
13 Y compris Carriacou et les autres dépendances du groupe des îles Grenadines.

14 Y compris les dépendances: Marie–Galante, la Désirade, les Saintes, Petite–Terre, Saint–Barthélemy et la partie française de Saint–Martin.

8
Population by sex, rate of population increase, surface area and density [*cont.*]
Population selon le sexe, taux d'accroissement de la population,
superficie et densité [*suite*]

15　Comprising Bonaire, Curaçao, Saba, St. Eustatius and Dutch part of St. Martin.	15　Comprend Bonaire, Curaçao, Saba, Saint—Eustache et la partie néederlandaise de Saint—Martin.
16　Including armed forces stationed in the area.	16　Y compris les militaires en garnison sur le territoire.
17　Including Bequia and other islands in the Grenadines.	17　Y compris Bequia et des autres îles dans les Grenadines.
18　De jure population, but excluding civilian citizens absent from country for extended period of time. Census figures also exclude armed forces overseas.	18　Population de droit, mais non compris les civils hors du pays pendant une période prolongée. Les chiffres de recensement ne comprennent pas également les militaires à l'étranger.
19　Excluding Indian jungle population.	19　Non compris les Indiens de la jungle.
20　Excluding nomadic Indian tribes.	20　Non compris les tribus d'Indiens nomades.
21　Excluding dependencies, of which South Georgia (area 3 755 km²) had an estimated population of 499 in 1964 (494 males, 5 females). The other dependencies namely, the South Sandwich group (surface area 337 km²) and a number of smaller islands, are presumed to be uninhabited.	21　Non compris les dépendances, parmi lesquelles figure la Georgie du Sud (3 755 km²) avec une population estimée à 499 personnes en 1964 (494 du sexe masculin et 5 du sexe féminin). Les autres dépendances, c'est—à—dire le groupe des Sandwich de Sud (superficie: 337 km²) et certaines petites—îles, sont présumées inhabitées.
22　A dispute exists between the governments of Argentina and the United Kingdom of Great Britain and Northern Ireland concerning sovereignty over the Falkland Islands (Malvinas).	22　La souveraineté sur les îles Falkland (Malvinas) fait l'objet d'un différend entre le Gouvernement argentin et le Gouvernement du Royaume—Uni de Grande—Bretagne et d'Irlande du Nord.
23　Census results, excluding nomad population.	23　Les résultats du recensement, non compris la population nomade.
24　Excluding foreign diplomatic personnel and their dependants.	24　Non compris le personnel diplomatique étranger et les membres de leur famille les accompagnant.
25　For statistical purposes, the data for China do not include those for the Hong Kong Special Administrative Region (Hong Kong SAR) and Macao special Administrative Region (Macao SAR).	25　Pour la présentation des statistiques, les données pour Chine ne comprend pas la Région Administrative Spéciale de Hong Kong (Hong Kong RAS) et la Région Administrative Spéciale de Macao (Macao RAS).
26　Census figures for China, as given in the communiqué of the State Statistical Bureau releasing the major figures of the census, includes a population of 6 130 000 for Hong Kong and Macao.	26　Les chiffres du recensement de la Chine, qui figurent dans le communiqué du Bureau du statistique de l'Etat publiant les principaux chiffres du recensement, comprennent la population de Hong Kong et Macao qui s'élève à 6 130 000 personnes.
27　Census results, for government controlled areas.	27　Les résultats du recensement, pour les zones contrôlées par le Gouvernement.
28　Including data for the Indian—held part of Jammu and Kashmir, the final status of which has not yet been determined.	28　Y compris les données pour la partie du Jammu et du Cachemire occupée par l'Inde dont le statut définitif n'a pas encore été déterminé.
29　Figures provided by Indonesia including East Timor, shown separately.	29　Les chiffres fournis par l'Indonesie comprennent le Timor oriental, qui fait l'objet d'une rubrique distincte.
30　Including data for East Jerusalem and Israeli residents in certain other territories under occupation by Israeli military forces since June 1967.	30　Y compris les données pour Jérusalem—Est et les résidents israéliens dans certains autres territoires occupés depuis juin 1967 pour les forces armées israéliennes.
31　Comprising Hokkaido, Honshu, Shikoku, Kyushu. Excluding diplomatic personnel outside the country and foreign military and civilian personnel and their dependants stationed in the area.	31　Comprend Hokkaido, Honshu, Shikoku, Kyushu. Non compris le personnel diplomatique hors du pays, les militaires et agents civils étrangers en poste sur le territoire et les membres de leur famille les accompagnant.
32　Including military and diplomatic personnel and their families abroad, numbering 933 at 1961 census, but excluding foreign military and diplomatic personnel and their families in the country, numbering 389 at 1961 census. Also including registered Palestinian refugees numbering 654 092 and 722 687 at 30 June 1963 and 31 May 1967, respectively.	32　Y compris les militaires et le personnel diplomatique à l'ètranger et les membres de leur famille les accompagnant, au nombre de 933 personnes au recensement de 1961, mais non compris les militaires et le personnel diplomatique étrangers sur le territoire et les membres de leur famille les accompagnant, au nombre de 389 personnes au recensement de 1961. Y compris également les réfugiés de Palestine immatriculés: 654 092 au 30 juin 1963 et 722 687 au 31 mai 1967.
33　Census results, excluding data for Jordanian territory under occupation since June 1967 by Israeli military forces.	33　Les résultats du recensement, non compris les données pour le territoire jordanien occupé depuis juin 1967 par les forces armées israéliennes.
34　Excluding alien armed forces, civilian aliens employed by armed forces, foreign diplomatic personnel and their dependants and Korean diplomatic personnel and their dependants outside the country.	34　Non compris les militaires étrangers, les civils étrangers employés par les forces armées, le personnel diplomatique étranger et les membres de leur famille les accompagnant et le personnel diplomatique coréen hors du pays et les membres de leur familles les accompagnant.
35　Excluding Palestinian refugees in camps.	35　Non compris les réfugiés de Palestine dans les camps.

8

Population by sex, rate of population increase, surface area and density [*cont.*]

Population selon le sexe, taux d'accroissement de la population,
superficie et densité [*suite*]

36 Based on results of sample survey.	36 D'après les résultats d'une enquête par sondage.
37 The figures were received from the Palestinian Authority and refer to the Palestinian population.	37 Les chiffres sont fournis par l'autorité palestinienne et comprennent la population palestinienne.
38 Census results exclude an estimate for under–enumeration estimated at 2.4 per cent.	38 Les résultats du recensement n'ont pas été ajustées pour compenser les lacunes de denombrement, estimées à 2,4 p. 100.
39 Excluding data for Jammu and Kashmir, the final status of which has not yet been determined, Junagardh, Manavadar, Gilgit and Baltistan.	39 Non compris les données pour le Jammu et le Cachemire, dont le statut définitif n'a pas encore été déterminé, le Junagardja, la Manavadar, le Gilgit et le Batistan.
40 Census results, excluding transients afloat and non–locally domiciled military and civilian services personnel and their dependants and visitors.	40 Les résultats du recensement, non compris les personnes de passage à bord de navires, les militaires et agents civils non résidents et les membres de leur famille les accompagnant, et les visiteurs.
41 Including Palestinian refugees.	41 Y compris les réfugiés de Palestine.
42 Comprising 7 sheikdoms of Abu Dhabi, Dubai, Sharjah, Ajaman, Umm al Qaiwain, Ras al Khaimah and Fujairah, and the area lying within the modified Riyadh line as announced in October 1955.	42 Comprend les sept cheikhats de Abou Dhabi, Dabai, Ghârdja, Adjmân, Oumm–al–Quiwaïn, Ras al Khaïma et Foudjaïra, ainsi que la zone délimitée par la ligne de Riad modifiée comme il a été annoncé en octobre 1955.
43 Excluding Faeroe Islands and Greenland.	43 Non compris les îles Féroé et le Groenland.
44 Excluding Overseas Departments, namely French Guiana, Guadeloupe, Martinique and Réunion, shown separately.	44 Non compris les départements d'outre–mer, c'est–à–dire la Guyane française, la Guadeloupe, la Martinique et la Réunion, qui font l'objet de rubriques distinctes.
45 De jure population, but excluding diplomatic personnel outside the country and including foreign diplomatic personnel not living in embassies or consulates.	45 Population de droit, non compris le personnel diplomatique hors du pays et y compris le personnel diplomatique étranger qui ne vivent pas dans les ambassades ou les consulats.
46 Excluding military personnel stationed outside the country who do not have a personal residence in France.	46 Non compris les militaires en garnison hors du pays et sans résidence personnelle en France.
47 All data shown pertaining to Germany prior to 3 October 1990 are indicated separately for the Federal Republic of Germany and the former German Democratic Republic based on their respective territories at the time indicated.	47 Toutes les données se rapportant à l'Allemagne avant le 3 octobre 1990 figurent dans deux rubriques séparées basées sur les territoires respectifs de la République fédérale d'Allemagne et l'ancienne République démocratique allemande selon la période indiquée.
48 Excluding armed forces.	48 Non compris les militaires.
49 Census results, include armed forces stationed outside the country, but excluding alien armed forces stationed in the area.	49 Les résultats du recensement, y compris les militaires en garnison hors du pays, mais non compris les militaires étrangers en garnison sur le territoire.
50 Estimates include armed forces stationed outside the country, but including alien armed forces stationed in the area.	50 Les estimations de la population, y compris les militaires en garnison hors du pays, mais y compris les militaires étrangers en garnison sur le territoire.
51 Data refer to the Vatican City State.	51 Les données se rapportent à l'Etat de la Cité du Vatican.
52 Including Gozo and Comino Islands and civilian nationals temporarily outside the country.	52 Y compris les îles de Gozo et de Comino et les civils nationaux temporairement hors du pays.
53 Census results, based on compilation of continuous accounting and sample surveys.	53 Les résultats du recensement, d'après les résultats des dénombrements et enquêtes par sondage continue.
54 Excluding civilian aliens within the country, but including civilian nationals temporarily outside the country.	54 Non compris les civils étrangers dans le pays, mais y compris les civils nationaux temporairement hors du pays.
55 Including the Azores and Madeira Islands.	55 Y compris les Açores et Madère.
56 Including the Balearic and Canary Islands, and Alhucemas, Ceuta, Chafarinas, Melilla and Penon de Vélez de la Gomera.	56 Y compris les Baléares et les Canaries, Al Hoceima, Ceuta, les îles Zaffarines, Melilla et Penon de Vélez de la Gomera.
57 Inhabited only during the winter season. Census data are for total population while estimates refer to Norwegian population only. Included also in the de jure population of Norway.	57 N'est habitée que pendant la saison d'hiver. Les données de recensement se rapportent à la population totale, mais les estimations ne concernent que la population norvégienne, comprise également dans la population de droit de la Norvège.
58 Excluding Channel Islands and Isle of Man, shown separately.	58 Non compris les îles Anglo–Normandes et l'île de Man, qui font l'objet de rubriques distinctes.
59 Excluding Niue, shown separately, which is part of Cook Islands, but because of remoteness is administered separately.	59 Non compris Nioué, qui fait l'objet d'une rubrique distincte et qui fait partie des îles Cook, mais qui, en raison de son éloignement, est administrée séparément.
60 Comprising Austral, Gambier, Marquesas, Rapa, Society and Tuamotu Islands.	60 Comprend les îles Australes, Gambier, Marquises, Rapa, de la Societé et Tuamotou.
61 Including Christmas, Fanning, Ocean and Washington Islands.	61 Y compris les îles Christmas, Fanning, Océan et Washington.

8
Population by sex, rate of population increase, surface area and density [*cont.*]
Population selon le sexe, taux d'accroissement de la population,
superficie et densité [*suite*]

62 Including the islands of Huon, Chesterfield, Loyalty, Walpole
    and Belep Archipelago.
63 Including Campbell and Kermadec Islands (population 20 in 1961,
    surface area 148 km²) as well as Antipodes, Auckland, Bounty,
    Snares, Solander and Three Kings island, all of which are uninhabited.
    Excluding diplomatic personnel and armed forces outside the country,
    the latter numbering 1 936 at 1966 census; also excluding alien
    armed forces within the country.

64 Comprising eastern part of New Guinea, the Bismarck
    Archipelago, Bougainville and Buka of Solomon Islands
    group and about 600 smaller islands.
65 Comprising the Solomon Islands group (except Bougainville
    and Buka which are included with Papua New Guinea shown
    separately), Ontong, Java, Rennel and Santa Cruz Islands.

62 Y compris les îles Huon, Chesterfield, Loyauté et Walpole, et
    l'archipel Belep.
63 Y compris les îles Campbell et Kermadec (20 habitants en 1961,
    superficie: 148 km²) ainsi que les îles Antipodes, Auckland,
    Bounty, Snares, Solander et Three Kings, qui sont toutes
    inhabitées. Non compris les personnel diplomatique et les
    militaires hors du pays, ces derniers au nombre de 1 936 au
    recensement de 1966; non compris également les militaires
    étrangers dans le pays.
64 Comprend l'est de la Nouvelle–Guinée, l'archipel Bismarck,
    Bougainville et Buka (ces deux dernières du group des Salomon)
    et environ 600 îlots.
65 Comprend les îles Salomon (à l'exception de Bougainville et
    de Buka dont la population est comprise dans celle de
    Papouasie–Nouvelle Guinée qui font l'objet d'une rubrique
    distincte), ainsi que les îles Ontong, Java, Rennel
    et Santa Cruz.

Technical notes, table 8

Table 8 is based on detailed data on population and its growth and distribution published in the United Nations *Demographic Yearbook* [21], which also provides a comprehensive description of methods of evaluation and limitations of the data.

Unless otherwise indicated, figures refer to de facto (present-in-area) population for the present territory; surface area estimates include inland waters.

Notes techniques, tableau 8

Le *tableau 8* est fondé sur des données détaillées sur la population, sa croissance et sa distribution, publiées dans l'*Annuaire démographique* des Nations Unies [21], qui offre également une description complète des méthodes d'évaluation et une indication des limites des données.

Sauf indication contraire, les chiffres se rapportent à la population effectivement présente sur le territoire tel qu'il est actuellement défini; les estimations de superficie comprennent les étendues d'eau intérieures.

9
Education at the primary, secondary and tertiary levels
Enseignement primaire, secondaire et supérieur
Number of students and percentage female
Nombre d'étudiants et étudiantes en pourcentage

Country or area / Pays ou zone	Years / Années	Primary education Enseignement primaire Total	%F	Years / Années	Secondary education Enseignement secondaire Total	%F	Years / Années	Tertiary education Enseignement supérieur Total	%F
Africa · Afrique									
Algeria	1990/91	4189152	45	1990/91	2175580	43	1990/91	285930	...
Algérie	1995/96	4617728	46	1995/96	2544864	46	1994/95	298767	...
	1996/97	4674947	46	1996/97	2618242	48	1995/96	347410	...
Angola	1990/91	990155	*48	1985/86	178910	...	1985/86	5034	...
Angola	1991/92	989444	46	1990/91	187436	...	1991/92	6331	...
	1997/98	910734	*47	1991/92	218987	...	1997/98	7916	39
Benin	1990/91	490129	33	1990/91[1 2]	72256	27	1990	10873	13
Bénin	1996/97	784887	37	1995/96[2]	128256	30	1995	11227	18
	1997/98	843340	38	1996/97[2]	146135	30	1996	14055	19
Botswana	1990	283516	52	1990	61767	53	1991/92	5364	42
Botswana	1996	*318629	*50	1996[4]	111006	53	1995/96	7920	48
	1997	322268	50	1997[8]	124906	52	1996/97	8850	47
Burkina Faso	1990/91	504414	38	1990/91	*98929	*34	1990/91	5425	23
Burkina Faso	1995/96	700995	39	1992/93	*115753	*35	1995/96	9388	24
	1997/98	777691	40	1993/94[5]	124841	35	1996/97	8911	23
Burundi	1990/91	633203	46	1990/91	44207	37	1990/91	3592	27
Burundi	1997/98	554981	45	1992/93	55713	39	1992/93	4256	26
	1998/99	670882	44	1994/95[2]	47636	...	1997/98	4415	29
Cameroon	1990/91	1964146	46	1990/91	500272	41	1980/81[16]	11686	...
Cameroun	1997/98	2023809	45	1996/97[5]	549569	44	1985/86[3]	17071	...
	1998/99	2133707	...	1997/98[8]	587611	42	1990/91	33177	...
Cape Verde	1990/91	69832	...	1985/86[5]	5302	45	...	...	...
Cap–Vert	1997/98	91777	49	1991/92[5 13]	11458	...	...	...	...
	1998/99	92523	49	1993/94	14097	49	...	...	...
Central African Rep.	1985/86	309656	39	1985/86	59273	27	1985/86	2651	11
Rép. centrafricaine	1990/91	308409	39	1990/91	50930	29	1990/91	3840	13
	1991/92	277961	40	1991/92[1]	43740	29	1991/92	3684	15
Chad	1990/91	525165	31	1990/91[5]	62658	16	1995/96	3446	13
Tchad	1996/97	680909	34	1996/97	99789	20	1996/97	3798	15
	1997/98	786537	35	1997/98[8]	112964	21	1997/98	4799	14
Comoros	1990/91	72824	42	1991/92	15878	...	1991/92	223	28
Comores	1993/94	77837	45	1993/94	17637	...	1992/93	229	...
	1995/96	78527	...	1995/96[2]	21192	...	1995/96	348	...
Congo	1990/91	493918	47	1990/91	182967	...	1990/91	10671	18
Congo	1994/95	*518400	*46	1993/94	212850	...	1991/92	12045	19
	1995/96	497305	48	1995/96	214650	43	1992/93	13806	...
Côte d'Ivoire	1990/91	1414865	41	1990/91[4]	361032	32	1991/92[6]	30064	...
Côte d'Ivoire	1996/97	1735814	42	1995/96[4]	489740	33	1993/94[6]	51215	23
	1997/98	1807503	43	1996/97[4]	534214	32	1994/95[6]	52228	24
Dem. Rep. of the Congo	1990/91	4562430	43	1991/92	1097095	32	1985/86	40878	...
Rép. dém du Congo	1993/94	4939297	43	1993/94	1341446	31	1990/91	80233	...
	1994/95	5417506	41	1994/95	1514323	38	1994/95	93266	...
Djibouti	1990/91	31706	41	1990/91	9513	...	1991/92	53	30
Djibouti	1995/96	36223	42	1995/96	11860	42	1995/96	130	47
	1996/97	36896	42	1996/97	13311	41	1996/97	161	44
Egypt	1990/91	6964306	44	1990/91	5507257	43	1990/91[17]	628233	36
Egypte	1996/97	8243137	45	1995/96	6142651	46	1994/95[1 3 7]	696988	39
	1997/98	7499303	46	1996/97	6726738	45	1995/96[1 3 7]	850051	42
Equatorial Guinea	1992/93[1]	72725	48	1992/93[4 3]	17535	30	1981/82	1140	10
Guinée équatoriale	1993/94	75751	49	1993/94	16616	35	1990/91	578	13
Eritrea	1990/91	109087	49	1990/91[5]	60029	48		...	...
Erythrée	1995/96[13]	241725	45	1995/96	80182	42	1994/95	3137	14
	1996/97	240737	45	1996/97	89087	42	1995/96	3020	12
Ethiopia	1990/91	2466464	40	1990/91	866016	43	1990/91	34076	18
Ethiopie	1996/97	4007694	36	1996/97[5]	892574	42	1995/96	35027	19
	1997/98[24]	*5092770	*37	1997/98[8]	*477940	*41	1996/97	42226	20
Gabon	1991/92	210000	50	1991/92[5]	51348	...	1991/92[3]	3000	28
Gabon	1995/96	250693	50	1994/95	65718	45	1993/94[3]	3977	...
	1996/97	256171	50	1995/96	80552	47	1994/95[3]	4655	...
Gambia	1990/91	86307	*41	1990/91	20400	33	...	...	...
Gambie	1995/96	124513	44	1995/96	32097	38	...	...	...
	1998/99	141569	45	1998/99[2 8]	39573	38	1994/95	1591	36

9

Education at the primary, secondary and tertiary levels
Number of students and percentage female [*cont.*]
Enseignement primaire, secondaire et supérieur
Nombre d'étudiants et étudiantes en pourcentage [*suite*]

Country or area Pays ou zone	Years Années	Primary education Enseignement primaire Total	%F	Years Années	Secondary education Enseignement secondaire Total	%F	Years Années	Tertiary education Enseignement supérieur Total	%F
Ghana	1990/91	1945422	45	1990/91[1][2]	768603	39	1990/91	13700	23
Ghana	1995/96	2197172	...	1993/94[2]	922078	40	1992/93	19531	19
	1996/97	2333347	...	1994/95	940948	41	1993/94	20338	23
Guinea	1990/91	346807	32	1990/91	85942	24	1990/91	5366	7
Guinée	1997/98	674732	37	1996/97[2]	143243	26	1996/97	8151	11
	1998/99	726561	38	1997/98[8]	160049	26	1997/98	8272	12
Guinea-Bissau	1991/92	79882	36	1984/85	9384	21	...	...	...
Guinée-Bissau	1993/94	91103	36	1987/88	5468	26	...	...	...
	1994/95	100369	37	1988/89	6330	32	1988/89	404	6
Kenya	1990	5392319	49	1990[4]	635534	43	1980/81	12986	...
Kenya	1997	5764855	49	1994[2]	619839	46	1985/86	21756	26
	1998	5919721	49	1995[2]	*632388	*46	1990/91[3]	35421	28
Lesotho	1990	351632	55	1990	48209	60	1990/91	2029	58
Lesotho	1996	374628	52	1996	68132	59	1995/96	4384	55
	1997	368895	52	1997[8]	72170	59	1996/97	4614	54
Liberia	1984	132889	35	1980	54623	28			
Libéria	1986[1]	80048	...	1984[2]	43273	...	...	...	...
Libyan Arab Jamahiriya	1990/91	1175229	48	1990/91	257120	...	1980/81	20166	25
Jamah. arabe libyenne	1992/93	1254242	48	1992/93	310556	...	1985/86	*30000	...
	1993/94	1357040	49	1993/94[46]	147689	81	1991/92	72899	46
Madagascar	1990/91	1570721	49	1990/91[5]	339805	49	1990/91	35824	45
Madagascar	1995/96	1638187	49	1995/96[5][44]	310173	50	1996/97	26715	45
	1997/98	1889885	49	1997/98[8]	356555	49	1997/98	30781	45
Malawi	1990/91	1400682	45	1990/91	60701	...	1990/91	4829	26
Malawi	1994/95[10]	2860819	47	1994/95	108682	18	1994/95	5358	30
	1995/96[10]	2887107	47	1995/96	141911	...	1995/96	5561	30
Mali	1990/91	395334	37	1990/91	84220	33	1990/91	4780	14
Mali	1996/97	778450	39	1995/96	151554	34	1996/97	13679	19
	1997/98	862875	41	1996/97	168898	33	1997/98	13847	20
Mauritania	1990/91	167229	42	1990/91[11]	37653	32	1990/91	5339	14
Mauritanie	1997/98	330199	48	1995/96[11]	51765	34	1995/96	8496	17
	1998/99	346222	48	1997/98[8][20]	1911	38	1997/98	9240	16
Mauritius	1990	137491	49	1990	79229	50	1990/91	3485	37
Maurice	1997	127109	49	1997[8]	97405	...	1997/98	7099	47
	1998	130505	49	1998	99005	50	1998/99	7149	46
Morocco	1990/91	2483691	40	1990/91	1194377	41	1990/91	255667	36
Maroc	1996/97	3160907	42	1996/97	1442049	42	1996/97	311743	41
	1997/98	3254354	43	1997/98[8]	1504774	43	1997/98	256016	42
Mozambique	1990	1260218	43	1990	160177	36	1992/93	4600	26
Mozambique	1994	1301833	42	1994	169520	38	1995/96	6639	25
	1995	1415428	42	1995	185181	39	1996/97	7143	24
Namibia	1990	314105	52	1990	62399	56	1991	4157	64
Namibie	1997	380537	50	1996	104613	54	1994	9714	61
	1998	400325	50	1997[8]	110140	53	1995	11344	61
Niger	1990/91	368732	36	1990/91	76758	29	1980/81	1435	20
Niger	1996/97	464267	38	1996/97	97675	35	1986/87	3317	18
	1997/98	482065	39	1997/98[8]	98978	37	1991/92	4513	...
Nigeria	1990	13607249	43	1990	2908466	43	1980/81	150072	...
Nigéria	1995	15741078	45	1993	4032083	46	1985/86	266679	27
	1996	14078473	45	1994	4451329	46	1993/94[3]	207982	...
Réunion	1990/91	71966	...	1985/86	69863	54	...	...	...
Réunion	1994/95[12]	73250	...	1994/95	90033	50	...	...	...
	1995/96	73702	...	1995/96	91548	50	...	...	...
Rwanda	1985/86	836877	49	1985/86	46998	42	1980/81	1243	10
Rwanda	1990/91	1100437	50	1990/91	70400	43	1985/86	1987	14
	1991/92[13]	1104902	50	1991/92	94586	44	1989/90	3389	19
Saint Helena	1980/81	717	51	1980/81	638	48	1980/81	36	24
Sainte-Hélène	1985/86	582	55	1985/86	513	49	1981/82	37	13
Sao Tome and Principe	1986/87	17010	48	1986/87	5255	...	...	...	...
Sao Tomé-et-Principe	1989/90	19822	47	1989/90[5]	7547	46	...	...	...
Senegal	1990/91	708448	42	1990/91[5]	179818	34	1990/91[3]	18689	...
Sénégal	1997/98	1026570	45	1997/98[8]	216066	38	1996/97[3]	22797	...
	1998/99	1034065	45	1998/99	236133	39	1997/98[3]	25865	27

9
Education at the primary, secondary and tertiary levels
Number of students and percentage female [*cont.*]
Enseignement primaire, secondaire et supérieur
Nombre d'étudiants et étudiantes en pourcentage [*suite*]

Country or area Pays ou zone	Years Années	Primary education Enseignement primaire Total	%F	Years Années	Secondary education Enseignement secondaire Total	%F	Years Années	Tertiary education Enseignement supérieur Total	%F
Seychelles	1990[1]	14362	...	1990	4396	...	...	...	...
Seychelles	1995[13]	9885	49	1995[29]	8931	49	...	...	...
	1996	9886	49	1996	9099	49	1980	144	88
Sierra Leone	1985/86	421689	...	1985/86	94717	...	1980/81	2166	...
Sierra Leone	1989/90[14]	391152	41	1989/90	101726	35	1985/86	5690	...
	1990/91[14]	367426	41	1990/91	102474	37	1990/91	4742	...
Somalia	1980/81	271704	36	1980/81	43841	27	...	...	...
Somalie	1985/86	196496	34	1985/86	45686	35	1986/87	15672	20
South Africa	1990	6951777	50	1990	2742105	54	1990[15]	439007	44
Afrique du Sud	1995	8159430	49	1994	3571395	54	1994	617897	48
	1997[1]	8091295	49	1995[4]	3749449	54	1997[15]	667775	53
Sudan	1990/91	2042743	43	1990/91	731624	43	1980/81	28788	27
Soudan	1995/96[35]	2930328	45	1995/96[34]	378139	46	1990/91[3]	59824	48
	1996/97	3000048	45	1996/97	405583	47	1995/96	125713	47
Swaziland	1990	166454	50	1990[4]	41128	50	1990/91	3198	43
Swaziland	1997	205829	49	1997[8]	58197	50	1996/97	5658	52
	1998	208779	49	1998	62471	50	1998/99	3428	49
Togo	1990/91	646962	40	1990/91	125545	25	1990/91	8969	14
Togo	1996/97	859574	41	1995/96	169481	26	1995/96	11639	15
	1997/98	888012	42	1996/97	178254	27	1997/98	14322	17
Tunisia	1990/91	1405665	46	1990/91	564540	43	1990/91	68535	39
Tunisie	1996/97	1450916	47	1996/97	882730	48	1996/97	121787	45
	1997/98	1478241	*47	1997/98[8]	989919	...	1997/98	137024	46
Uganda	1990	*2401590	*44	1990[43]	267520	36	1990/91	17578	28
Ouganda	1996	3068625	46	1995[43]	292321	...	1995/96	30266	33
	1997[10]	5303564	47	1996[4]	333000	39	1996/97[18]	34773	33
United Rep. Tanzania	1990[47]	3379000	50	1990	167150	42	1991/92	7468	16
Rép.–Unie de Tanzanie	1996[47]	3942888	49	1996	211664	46	1996/97	14882	18
	1997[47]	4057965	50	1997[8]	271260	...	1997/98	15928	20
Zambia	1990	1461206	...	1990	189796	...	1985[3]	4680	17
Zambie	1994	1507660	48	1994[43]	208640	...	1990	15343	...
	1995	1506349	48	1995[9]	5208	...	1994[3 9]	10489	30
Zimbabwe	1990	2116414	50	1990	661066	47	1990/91	49361	...
Zimbabwe	1997	2510605	...	1995	711094	46	1995/96[1]	45593	35
	1998	2507098	...	1996	751349	46	1996/97[1]	46673	36
America, North · Amerique du Nord									
Anguilla	1992/93	1407	50	1992/93	836	53	...	...	...
Anguilla	1996/97	1557	49	1996/97	1062	55	...	...	...
Antigua and Barbuda	1991/92	9298	49						
Antigua–et–Barbuda	1994/95	10727	...	1991/92	5845	50	...	...	...
Bahamas	1990/91	32873	...	1991/92	29559	50	1985/86	4531	...
Bahamas	1994/95	32684	49	1994/95	28435	49	1987/88	5305	68
	1996/97	34199	...	1996/97	27970	...	1994/95	3960	72
Barbados	1984/85	30161	48	1984/85	28695	50	1990/91	6651	...
Barbade	1988/89	29584	49	1989/90	24004	47	1995/96[3]	3064	62
	1991/92	26662	49	1990/91[46]	161	25	1996/97[3]	*3275	...
Belize	1990/91[17]	46023	*48	1990/91	7904	53	...	...	...
Belize	1995/96[17]	52994	48	1995/96[2]	10648	53	...	...	...
	1996/97[17]	53110	49	1996/97[2]	10912	52	...	...	...
Bermuda	1983/84	5530	50	1980/81[4]	4374	50	...	...	...
Bermudes	1994/95	5962	49	1994/95[4]	3553	50	...	...	...
	1996/97	5883	49	1996/97[4]	3726	51	1980/81	608	51
British Virgin Islands	1990/91	2340	47	1990/91	1124	53	...	...	...
Iles Vierges britanniques	1993/94	2502	48	1991/92	1134	55	...	...	...
	1994/95	2625	48	1993/94	1309	51	...	...	...
Canada	1990/91	2375704	48	1990/91	2292497	49	1990/91	1916801	54
Canada	1995/96	2448144	48	1995/96[49]	2505389	49	1995/96[49]	1763105	53
	1997/98	2401590	49	1997/98[8]	2949298	48	1997/98	1179395	56
Costa Rica	1990	435205	49	1990	130553	50	1990[21 22]	74681	...
Costa Rica	1997	525273	49	1996	183162	51	1992[21]	88324	...
	1998	529637	49	1997[8]	192678	51	1994[3 21 23]	78819	...
Cuba	1990/91	887737	48	1990/91	1002338	52	1990/91	242434	57
Cuba	1996/97[12]	1094868	48	1996/97	712897	52	1996/97	111587	60
	1997/98[12]	1081085	48	1997/98[8]	779911	52	1997/98	104595	61

9
Education at the primary, secondary and tertiary levels
Number of students and percentage female [cont.]
Enseignement primaire, secondaire et supérieur
Nombre d'étudiants et étudiantes en pourcentage [suite]

Country or area Pays ou zone	Years Années	Primary education Enseignement primaire		Years Années	Secondary education Enseignement secondaire		Years Années	Tertiary education Enseignement supérieur	
		Total	%F		Total	%F		Total	%F
Dominica	1990/91	12836	49	1990/91[4]	4749	52	1990/91[5]	430	41
Dominique	1993/94	12822	50	1993/94[4]	6431	49	1991/92[5]	658	55
	1994/95	12627	50	1994/95[4]	6493	51	1992/93[5]	484	47
Dominican Republic	1990/91[1]	948186	...	1992/93[2]	205943	...	...	...	...
Rép. dominicaine	1996/97	1360044	49	1996/97[29]	*333760	6	1985/86	123748	...
	1997/98	1492596	49	1997/98[8]	359888	56	1996/97	176995	57
El Salvador	1991	1000671	50	1991	94268	55	1990	78211	...
El Salvador	1996	1130900	49	1995	144078	52	1996	112266	50
	1997	1191052	49	1996	143588	53	1998	117991	55
Grenada	1990/91	19811	*45	1990/91	9776	53	...	...	...
Grenade	1991/92	21365	*44	1991/92	9896	54	...	...	...
	1992/93	22345	*49	1992/93	10213	54	...	...	...
Guadeloupe	1990/91	38531	49	1990/91	49846	53	...	...	...
Guadeloupe	1993/94	37330	49	1993/94	50174	52	...	...	...
	1994/95[12]	38332	...	1994/95	50899	52	...	...	...
Guatemala	1990	1164937	...	1991	294907	...	1992/93	70431	...
Guatemala	1996	1510811	46	1995	372006	...	1994/95	77051	...
	1997	1544709	46	1996	375528	47	1995/96	80228	...
Haiti	1990/91	865415	48	1990/91[2]	184968	49	1980/81	4671	30
Haïti	1996/97	1429280	48	1995/96[2]	307417	...	1983/84	6289	34
	1997/98	1485722	49	1996/97[2]	327978	48	1985/86	6288	26
Honduras	1991	908446	50	1986	179444	...	1990	43117	43
Honduras	1993	990352	50	1991	194083	55	1993	47562	45
	1994	1008181	50	1993	203192	...	1994	54106	44
Jamaica	1990/91[1]	323378	50	1985/86[4]	229023	52	1990/91	16018	...
Jamaïque	1995/96[1]	300931	49	1990/91	238345	...	1995/96[3]	8191	38
	1996/97[1]	293863	49	1992/93	235071	51	1996/97[3]	*8434	...
Martinique	1990/91	32744	...	1991/92	46373	52	...	...	...
Martinique	1994/95[12]	33917	...	1994/95	46178	50	...	...	...
	1995/96[12]	34559	49	1995/96	47706	51	...	...	...
Mexico	1990/91	14401588	49	1990/91	6704297	50	1990/91	1310835	...
Mexique	1996/97	14650521	48	1996/97	7914165	49	1996/97[35]	1612318	48
	1997/98	14647797	49	1997/98[8]	8406782	50	1997/98	1727484	48
Montserrat	1990/91	1593	...	1990/91[46]	43	33	...	...	...
Montserrat	1992/93	1566	...	1992/93	888	...	...	...	...
	1993/94	1525	46	1993/94[4]	905	49	...	...	...
Netherlands Antilles	1980/81	32856	49	1980/81[5]	21959	52	...	...	...
Antilles néerlandaises	1991/92	22410	...	1991/92	14987	...	...	...	...
Nicaragua	1990	632882	51	1990	184101	49	1990	30733	52
Nicaragua	1997	777917	50	1996[2]	233410	54	1992	35730	50
	1998	783002	50	1997[8]	287156	54	1995	50769	51
Panama	1990	351021	48	1990	195903	51	1990	53235	...
Panama	1995[12]	361877	...	1995	216210	...	1995	76798	...
	1996[12]	371250	...	1996	221022	...	1996	80980	...
Saint Kitts and Nevis	1985/86	7810	42[1]	1985/86	4197	49	1985/86	212	42
Saint-Kitts-et-Nevis	1991/92	7236	48	1991/92	4396	51	1991/92	225	54
	1992/93	7068	49	1992/93	4402	51	1992/93	394	55
Saint Lucia	1990/91	33006	*49	1990/91	*8230	59	1986/87	67	55
Sainte-Lucie	1995/96	*31800	*49	1992/93	10356	63	1992/93	870	61
	1996/97	31615	49	1996/97	11753	56	1995/96	2760	72
Saint Pierre and Miquelon	1990/91	556	...	1980/81	748	52	...	...	...
Saint-Pierre-et-Miquelon	1992/93	529	...	1985/86	821	53	...	...	...
	1994/95	492	...	1986/87	800	53	...	...	...
St. Vincent and the Grenadines	1985/86[25]	24561	49	1986/87	8785	56	1985/86	736	69
Saint-Vincent-Grenadines	1990/91	22030	49	1990/91	10719	55	1986/87	795	63
	1993/94	21386	49	1993/94[2]	9870	56	1989/90	677	68
Trinidad and Tobago	1990/91[17 26]	193992	49	1990/91	97493	50	1990/91	7249	44
Trinité-et-Tobago	1995/96[17 26]	186000	49	1995/96[2]	103016	51	1995/96[3]	5348	54
	1996/97[17 26]	181030	49	1996/97[2]	104349	51	1996/97[3]	6007	55
Turks and Caicos Islands	1984/85[1]	1429	49	1980/81	691	...	...	...	...
Iles Turques et Caïques	1993/94[1]	1211	50	1993/94	1032	50	...	...	...
	1996/97	1573	49	1996/97[4]	1028	50	...	...	...
United States	1990/91	22429000	48	1990/91	19270000	49	1990/91	13710150	54
Etats-Unis	1995/96	24045967	49	1995/96	21473692	49	1995/96	14261778	56
	1998/99	24691431	49	1997/98[8]	23840692	50	1997/98	13284002	56

9
Education at the primary, secondary and tertiary levels
Number of students and percentage female [*cont.*]
Enseignement primaire, secondaire et supérieur
Nombre d'étudiants et étudiantes en pourcentage [*suite*]

Country or area Pays ou zone	Years Années	Primary education Enseignement primaire		Years Années	Secondary education Enseignement secondaire		Years Années	Tertiary education Enseignement supérieur	
		Total	%F		Total	%F		Total	%F
US Virgin Islands	1985/86	14948	...	1985/86	13548	...	1985/86	2602	72
Iles Vierges américaines	1990/91	14319	40[1]	1990/91[1]	10050	55	1990/91	2466	75
	1992/93	14544	47	1992/93	12502	50	1992/93	2924	74
America, South · Amerique du Sud									
Argentina	1990	4965395	...	1990	2160410	...	1985	846145	53
Argentine	1996[12]	5250329	49	1994	2307821	...	1991	1008231	...
	1997[12]	5153256	49	1996	2594329	52	1994	1069617	...
Bolivia	1986	1204534	47				1991[3]	109503	...
Bolivie	1990	1278775	47	1990	219232	46	1996	188645	...
Brazil	1990	28943619	...	1990	3498777	...	1990[22]	1540080	52
Brésil	1997	34229388	...	1994	4510199	...	1994	1716263	53[22]
	1998	35838372	...	1996	5739077	...	1996[22]	1868529	...
Chile	1990	1991178	49	1990	719819	51	1991	261800	...
Chili	1995[12]	2149501	49	1995	679165	51	1995	342788	46
	1996[12]	2241536	48	1996	739316	51	1996	367094	46
Colombia	1990	4246658	53	1991	2377947	54	1990	487448	...
Colombie	1995	4692614	49	1995	3025350	53	1996	644188	52
	1996	*4916934	*49	1996	3525128	50	1997	772291	53
Ecuador	1990/91	1846338	...	1990/91[2]	785844	...	1990/91	206541	...
Equateur	1996/97[27]	1888172	49	1995/96	806096	50	1994/95	202682	...
	1997/98[27]	1882945	49	1997/98[8]	866606	50	1996/97	213496	...
Falkland Islands (Malvinas)	1980	223	58	1980	90	56	...	...	...
Iles Falkland (Malvinas)	1995	199	47	1995	147	49	...	...	...
French Guiana	1990/91	14256	...	1990/91	10722	...	...	...	...
Guyane française	1994/95[12]	16449	...	1994/95	15034	50	...	...	...
	1995/96[12]	17006	49	1995/96	15989	50	...	...	...
Guyana	1990/91	104241	49	1990/91	69696	52	1993/94	7503	46
Guyana	1995/96	100252	49	1995/96	63365	51	1995/96	7680	47
	1996/97	102000	49	1996/97	62043	51	1996/97	8965	51
Paraguay	1990	687331	48	1990	163734	50	1990	32884	...
Paraguay	1996	895777	48	1995	267485	51	1995[28]	40913	...
	1997	905813	48	1996	293651	51	1996[28]	42302	55
Peru	1990	3855282	...	1990	1697943	...	1990	678236	...
Pérou	1997[12]	4163180	...	1997[8]	1969501	...	1997	657586	...
	1998[12]	4236594	49	1998	2062543	48	1998	734392	48
Suriname	1990/91	60085	49	1990/91	33561	53	1980/81	2378	...
Suriname	1992/93	79162	48	1992/93	30016	53	1985/86	2751	54
	1993/94	87882	49	1993/94[4]	18165	60	1989/90	4319	53
Uruguay	1990	346416	49	1990	265947	...	1990	71612	...
Uruguay	1995	341197	49	1995	263616	54	1992	68227	...
	1996	345573	49	1996	269826	...	1996	79691	...
Venezuela	1990/91	4052947	50	1990/91	281419	57	1985	443064	41
Venezuela	1995/96	4120418	50	1995/96	329287	58	1990	550030	...
	1996/97	4262221	50	1996/97	377984	58	1991	550783	...
Asia · Asie									
Afghanistan	1990	622513	34	1990	182340	...	1982	19652	...
Afghanistan	1994	1161444	32	1994	497762	20	1986	22306	14
	1995	1312197	32	1995	512851	25	1990	24333	31
Armenia	1993/94	266076	51	1993/94	343096	...	1987/88	55700	...
Arménie	1995/96	249872	...	1995/96	326585	...	1995/96	39592	51
	1996/97	256475	...	1996/97	372187	...	1996/97	35517	56
Azerbaijan	1990/91	527370	49	1990/91	867386	49	1990/91	163901	39
Azerbaïdjan	1996/97[29]	719013	48	1996/97	819625	51	1996/97	115116	50
	1997/98	711127	48	1997/98[8]	886999	49	1997/98	135505	47
Bahrain	1990/91	66597	49	1990/91	47005	50	1990/91	6868	56
Bahreïn	1996/97	72876	49	1996/97	57184	51	1994/95	7701	59
	1997/98	74058	49	1997/98[8]	58547	51	1995/96	8096	60
Bangladesh	1980	8240169	37	1980	2659208	24	1980	240181	14
Bangladesh	1985	8920292	40	1985	3125219	28	1985	461073	19
	1990	11939949	45	1990	*3592995	33	1990	434309	16
Bhutan	1992	51411	...	1985	6094	...	1980	322	22
Bhoutan	1993	56773	43	1993[4]	5440	36	1983	288	17
	1994	60089	43	1994[4]	7459	38	1984[3]	220	20

9
Education at the primary, secondary and tertiary levels
Number of students and percentage female [*cont.*]
Enseignement primaire, secondaire et supérieur
Nombre d'étudiants et étudiantes en pourcentage [*suite*]

Country or area Pays ou zone	Years Années	Primary education Enseignement primaire		Years Années	Secondary education Enseignement secondaire		Years Années	Tertiary education Enseignement supérieur	
		Total	%F		Total	%F		Total	%F
Brunei Darussalam	1991	38933	47	1991	25699	50	1992/93	1388	57
Brunéi Darussalam	1996	43291	47	1995	30889	51	1994/95	1539	58
	1997	43540	47	1996	30470	52	1995/96	*1642	*58
Cambodia	1990/91	1329573	...	1990/91	264419	...	1990/91	6659	...
Cambodge	1997/98[30]	2011772	45	1996/97[5]	331951	36	1996/97	10019	16
	1998/99	2094000	46	1997/98[8]	312779	35	1997/98	9208	19
China ††	1990/91	122413800	46	1990/91	52385600	41	1990/91	3822371	...
Chine ††	1997/98	140272002	48	1996/97	68275438	45	1996/97	5826636	...
	1998/99[40]	139538000	48	1997/98[8]	72617219	50	1997/98	6074953	...
China, Hong Kong SAR †	1990/91	524919	*48	1990/91[4][3]	431381	...	1991/92	85214	40
Chine, Hong Kong RAS †	1994/95	476847	*49	1994/95[4][3]	458199	...	1992/93	88950	42
	1995/96	467718	48	1995/96	473817	49	1993/94	97392	43
China, Macao SAR †	1990/91	34972	48	...	...	...	1990/91	7425	41
Chine, Macao RAS †	1991/92	37872	48	1991/92[5]	18978	52	1993/94	6517	45
	1992/93	40665	48	1992/93[5]	20383	53	1996/97	7485	49
Cyprus[32]	1990/91	62962	48	1990/91	44614	49	1990/91	6554	52
Chypre[32]	1995/96	64660	48	1995/96	59845	49	1995/96	8874	59
	1996/97	64761	48	1996/97	61266	49	1996/97	9982	56
Georgia	1990/91	352393	49	1990/91	567998	48	1990/91	148391	46[22]
Géorgie	1995/96	288509	49	1995/96	441557	49	1995/96	155033	53
	1996/97	293325	48	1996/97	444058	49	1996/97	163345	51[22]
India	1990/91	99118320	41	1990/91[4]	54180391	36	1990/91	4950974	33
Inde	1996/97	110390406	43	1996/97	68872393	38	1995/96	5695780	36
	1997/98	108781792	44	1997/98[8]	67619483	39	1996/97	6060418	36
Indonesia	1990/91	29753576	49	1990/91	10965430	45	1991/92	1773459	...
Indonésie	1995/96	29447990	48	1995/96	13095913	46	1994/95	2229796	38
	1996/97	29236283	48	1996/97	14209974	...	1995/96	2303469	35
Iran (Islamic Rep. of)	1990/91	9369646	46	1990/91	5084832	41	1990/91[28]	312076	27
Iran (Rép. islamique d')	1996/97	9238393	47	1996/97	8776792	46	1996/97[28]	579070	36
	1998/99	8667147	47	1998/99[8]	9593269	45	1997/98[28]	625380	38
Iraq	1990/91	3328212	44	1990/91[2]	1023710	39	1985/86	169665	36
Iraq	1992/93	2857467	45	1992/93	1144938	38	1987/88	183608	40
	1995/96	2903923	45	1995/96	1160421	38	1988/89	209818	38
Israel	1990/91	724502	49	1990/91	309098	51	1990/91	134885	49
Israël	1995/96[33]	631916	...	1995/96[34]	541737	...	1995/96	198766	...
	1997/98	702637	49	1997/98[8]	562285	49	1997/98	233991	56
Japan	1990/91	9373295	49	1990/91	11025720	49	1991/92	2899143	40
Japon	1996/97	8105629	49	1994/95	9878568	49	1994/95[35]	3917709	44
	1997/98	7883565	49	1997/98[8]	9187545	49	1997/98	3963658	45
Jordan[36]	1990/91	926445	48	1990/91	100953	47	1990/91	80442	48
Jordanie[36]	1996/97	1086641	49	1995/96	143014	50	1995/96	99020	46
	1997/98	1121866	49	1996/97	149063	50	1996/97	112959	47
Kazakhstan	1990/91	1197300	...	1990/91	2144400	...	1990/91	537491	...
Kazakhstan	1996/97	1342035	49	1996/97	1921302	52	1994/95	482690	55
	1997/98	1290810	50	1997/98[8]	2040127	51	1995/96[39]	419460	55
Korea, Republic of	1990/91	4868520	49	1990/91	4559557	48	1990/91	1691429	32
Corée, République de	1997/98	3794447	47	1997/98[8]	4567366	48	1996/97[35]	2541659	37
	1998/99	3844949	47	1998/99	4367683	48	1997/98	2792410	38
Kuwait	1990/91	124996	48	1990/91[4]	140324	49	1991/92	21171	65
Koweït	1996/97[12]	143286	49	1996/97[12]	216223	49	1995/96	28705	62
	1997/98[12]	142308	49	1997/98[8]	223035	50	1996/97	29509	62
Kyrgyzstan	1990/91	354700	50	1990/91	651200	50	1990/91	57563	...
Kirghizistan	1994/95	386829	50	1994/95	606381	...	1993/94	55229	52
	1995/96[29]	473077	49	1995/96	530854	...	1995/96	49744	52
Lao People's Dem. Rep.	1990/91	576472	43	1990/91[2]	127231	38	1992/93	6071	29
Rép. dém. pop. lao	1996/97	786335	44	1996/97	187867	39	1996/97	12732	30
	1997/98	821546	45	1997/98[8]	216906	40	1997/98	10293	30
Lebanon	1991/92	345662	48	1991/92[5]	285500	51	1985/86	*79500	...
Liban	1996/97	*382309	*48	1996/97	347850	52	1991/92	85495	48
	1997/98	397905	48	1997/98[8]	388667	52	1995/96	81588	49
Malaysia	1990	2455525	49	1990	1456497	51	1990/91	121412	...
Malaisie	1997[17]	*2840667	*49	1995[1]	1651684	51	1994/95	191290	...
	1998[17]	*2870667	*49	1996[1]	*1736414	51	1995/96	210724	...

9

Education at the primary, secondary and tertiary levels
Number of students and percentage female [cont.]
Enseignement primaire, secondaire et supérieur
Nombre d'étudiants et étudiantes en pourcentage [suite]

Country or area Pays ou zone	Years Années	Primary education Enseignement primaire		Years Années	Secondary education Enseignement secondaire		Years Années	Tertiary education Enseignement supérieur	
		Total	%F		Total	%F		Total	%F
Maldives	1992	45333	49	1992[5]	16087	49	...	...	...
Maldives	1997	50230	48	1995	23889	50	...	...	...
	1998	48895	48	1996	26701	50	...	...	...
Mongolia	1990/91	166349	50	1990/91	301131	53	1990/91	31434	65
Mongolie	1996/97[30]	234193	51	1996/97[30]	195408	57	1996/97	44088	69
	1997/98	244815	50	1997/98[8]	206992	57	1997/98	46535	68
Myanmar	1990/91	5384539	49	1990/91	1281165	49	1991/92	196052	55
Myanmar	1994/95	5530502	48	1994/95	1752510	50	1993/94	235256	...
	1995/96	5413752	...	1995/96[2]	1923323	...	1994/95[37]	245317	61
Nepal	1990	2788644	36	1990	708663	29	1990/91	93753	23
Népal	1995	3263050	40	1995	1016443	36	1995/96	93176	...
	1996	3447607	41	1996	1121335	37	1996/97	105694	...
Occupied Palestinian Terr.	1994/95	572529	49	1994/95	45339	46	1995/96	40916	44
Territoire palestinien occupé	1995/96	611857	49	1995/96	50770	46	1996/97	49599	44
	1996/97	656353	49	1996/97	56467	48	1997/98	56726	44
Oman	1990/91	262989	47	1990/91	101567	44	1990/91	6208	45
Oman	1997/98	313516	48	1997/98[8]	217246	49	1996/97	12251	46
	1998/99	315557	48	1998/99	230701	49	1997/98	16032	45
Pakistan	1990/91[38]	11451000	32	1990/91	4345464	31	1985/86	267742	26
Pakistan	1996/97[38]	13724000	39	1993/94[20]	*92000	*33	1989/90	336689	33
	1997/98[38]	15050000	39	1995/96	5554973	35	1991/92[19]	221313	20
Philippines	1990/91	10427077	49	1990/91	4033597	...	1990/91	1709486	...
Philippines	1996/97	11902501	...	1995/96	4809863	...	1994/95[3]	1832553	57
	1997/98	12159495	...	1996/97	4888246	...	1995/96	2022106	57
Qatar	1990/91	48650	48	1990/91	30031	50	1990/91	6485	69
Qatar	1995/96	53631	49	1995/96	38594	49	1996/97	8475	73
	1997/98	59912	47	1997/98[8]	42438	49	1997/98	8590	72
Saudi Arabia	1990/91	1876916	46	1990/91	892585	44	1990/91	153967	43
Arabie saoudite	1996/97	2256185	48	1996/97	1542989	46	1996/97	273992	47
	1997/98	2243613	48	1997/98[8]	1736442	...	1997/98	296927	52
Singapore	1990	257932	47	1990	220561	47	1990	55672	41
Singapour	1995	261648	...	1995	213138	...	1995	83914	44
	1996	269668	48	1996	215952	...	1996	92140	...
Sri Lanka	1990	2112023	48	1990	2081842	51	1991[39]	55190	32
Sri Lanka	1995	1962498	48	1994	2315541	51	1994	80704	...
	1996	1843848	48	1995	2314054	51	1995[39]	63660	44
Syrian Arab Republic	1990/91	2452086	46	1990/91	914250	41	1990/91	221628	39
Rép. arabe syrienne	1996/97	2690205	47	1996/97	957664	46	1993/94	216211	41
	1997/98	2695452	47	1997/98[8]	1014412	48	1994/95	215734	41
Tajikistan	1990/91	507354	49	1990/91	829479	...	1990/91	109653	*38
Tadjikistan	1994/95	593526	49	1994/95	724056	...	1993/94	107402	*32
	1996/97	638674	49	1996/97[4][40]	688150	47	1994/95	108203	*33
Thailand	1990/91	6956717	49	1990/91	2230403	48	1992/93	1156174	53
Thaïlande	1996/97	5909618	...	1995/96	3794290	...	1995/96	1220481	...
	1997/98	5927902	...	1996/97	3925923	...	1996/97	1332767	...
Turkey	1990/91	6861711	47	1990/91	3808142	37	1990/91	749921	34
Turquie	1996/97	6389060	47	1996/97	4760892	40	1996/97	1434033	35
	1997/98[24]	7170832	47	1997/98[8]	4043772	40	1997/98	1409627	40
Turkmenistan	...	...	...	...	...	...	1985/86[22]	75800	...
Turkménistan	...	...	...	...	...	...	1990/91[22]	76000	...
United Arab Emirates	1990/91	228980	48	1990/91	107881	50	1990/91	10196	70
Emirats arabes unis	1996/97	259509	48	1996/97	180764	50	1992/93	10641	70
	1997/98	262653	48	1997/98[8]	190576	50	1996/97[3]	16213	72
Uzbekistan	1990/91	1777900	49	1990/91	3194600	...	1985/86	567200	...
Ouzbékistan	1993/94	1852841	49	1993/94	3218800	...	1990/91	602700	...
	1994/95	1905693	49	1994/95	3318900	...	1991/92	638200	...
Viet Nam	1990/91	8862292	...	1990/91[5]	3371392	...	1990/91	129600	...
Viet Nam	1996/97	10431300	...	1996/97[5]	6167700	...	1996/97	509300	...
	1997/98	10435508	48	1997/98[8]	7014722	47	1997/98	599275	39
Yemen	1993/94	2678863	28	1993/94	212129	18	1991/92	53082	17
Yémen	1996/97	2699788	28	1996/97	354288	20	1996/97	65675	13
Europe · Europe									
Albania	1990/91	551294	48	1990/91	205774	45	1990/91	22059	52
Albanie	1994/95	550737	48	1994/95	93830	49	1993/94	30185	53
	1995/96	558101	48	1995/96	89895	49	1996/97	34257	57

9
Education at the primary, secondary and tertiary levels
Number of students and percentage female [*cont.*]
Enseignement primaire, secondaire et supérieur
Nombre d'étudiants et étudiantes en pourcentage [*suite*]

| Country or area | Years | Primary education Enseignement primaire | | Years | Secondary education Enseignement secondaire | | Years | Tertiary education Enseignement supérieur | |
Pays ou zone	Années	Total	%F	Années	Total	%F	Années	Total	%F
Austria	1990/91	370210	49	1990/91	746272	47	1990/91	205767	46
Autriche	1996/97	381927	49	1996/97	793485	48	1996/97[35]	240632	49
	1997/98	385309	49	1997/98[8]	793249	48	1997/98	247498	49
Belarus	1990/91	614800	...	1990/91	968200	...	1990/91	335284	...
Bélarus	1996/97	625000	48	1996/97	1064700	...	1996/97	328746	55
	1997/98	614700	48	1997/98[8]	1091500	...	1997/98	361075	55
Belgium	1990/91	719372	49	1990/91	769438	49	1990/91	276248	48
Belgique	1994/95	738768	48	1994/95[49]	1061790	51	1994/95[49]	352630	49
	1995/96	742796	49	1995/96	1058998	51	1995/96	358214	50
Bulgaria	1990/91	960681	48	1990/91	391550	50	1990/91	188479	51
Bulgarie	1996/97[29]	431790	48	1996/97[29]	733362	49	1996/97	262757	61
	1997/98	425511	48	1997/98[8]	717894	48	1997/98	260487	61
Croatia	1990/91	431586	49	1990/91	186090	51	1990/91[22]	72342	...
Croatie	1996/97[29]	203933	49	1996/97[29]	416829	49	1996/97[22]	85752	51
	1997/98	206121	49	1997/98[8]	416907	49	1997/98[48]	90021	50
Czech Republic	1990/91	545814	49	1990/91	1267699	48	1990/91[42]	118194	44
République tchèque	1996/97[30]	659263	49	1996/97	1067160	50	1996/97[35]	207221	48
	1997/98	662647	49	1997/98[8]	1036241	50	1997/98	215041	48
Denmark	1990/91	340267	49	1990/91	464555	49	1990/91	142968	52
Danemark	1995/96	336690	49	1995/96	438809	49	1995/96[49]	174975	54
	1997/98	360683	49	1997/98[8]	428737	50	1997/98	183274	55
Estonia	1990/91	127389	48	1990/91	134463	...	1990/91	25900	50
Estonie	1996/97	126800	48	1996/97[2]	95877	53	1996/97[33]	43468	53
	1997/98	127823	48	1997/98[8]	119057	51	1997/98	43064	57
Finland	1990/91	390587	49	1990/91	426864	53	1990/91	165714	52
Finlande	1996/97	380932	49	1996/97	469933	52	1996/97[49]	226458	53
	1997/98	381078	49	1997/98[8]	469495	51	1997/98	250047	54
France	1990/91	4149143	48	1990/91	5521862	50	1990/91	1698938	53
France	1996/97	4004704	49	1996/97	5979690	49	1996/97[49]	2062495	55
	1997/98	3979453	49	1997/98[8]	6001745	49	1997/98	2027422	55
Germany	1990/91	3431385	...	1990/91	7398011	...	1990/91[22]	2048627	...
Allemagne	1996/97	3859490	49	1996/97	8382335	48	1996/97[22]	2131907	46
	1997/98	3865724	49	1997/98[8]	8534099	48	1997/98[48]	2097694	46
Gibraltar	1984/85	2830	48	1996/97[4]	1781	48	...	...	...
Gibraltar	1996/97	2729	47	1997/98[8]	2074	47	...	...	...
Greece	1990/91	813353	48	1990/91	851353	48	1990/91	283415	...
Grèce	1996/97	652040	48	1996/97	817566	49	1996/97	363150	48
	1997/98	648608	49	1997/98[8]	881597	49	1997/98	374122	50
Holy See [45]	...	...	...	...	...	...	1990/91	10938	32
Saint–Siège [45]	...	...	...	...	...	...	1995/96	14403	25
	...	...	...	...	...	...	1997/98	12769	30
Hungary	1990/91	1130656	49	1990/91	514076	49	1990/91	102387	50
Hongrie	1996/97[35]	502555	48	1996/97[35]	1103907	50	1996/97[35]	215115	53
	1997/98	504046	49	1997/98[8]	1096333	50	1997/98	254693	54
Iceland	1990/91	29816	...	1990/91	29465	48	1990/91	5225	57
Islande	1996/97	29342	49	1996/97[2]	25477	52	1996/97	7908	58
	1997/98	29705	49	1997/98[8]	33497	49	1997/98	8100	60
Ireland	1990/91	416747	49	1990/91	345941	51	1990/91	90296	46
Irlande	1996/97	358830	49	1996/97	389353	51	1996/97[49]	134566	52
	1997/98[38]	468328	49	1997/98[8]	392074	51	1997/98	142774	53
Italy	1990/91	3055883	49	1990/91	5117897	49	1990/91	1452286	48[22]
Italie	1996/97	2810158	48	1996/97	4602243	49	1996/97[35]	1892542	54
	1997/98	2818053	48	1997/98[8]	4515195	49	1997/98	1869101	56
Latvia	1990/91	143338	49	1990/91	264475	49	1990/91	45953	55
Lettonie	1996/97	146653	48	1996/97	239318	51	1996/97	56187	60
	1997/98	146650	48	1997/98[8]	253751	50	1997/98	70233	59
Lithuania	1990/91	202222	47[40]	1990/91[12]	396036	...	1990/91[22]	88668	...
Lituanie	1996/97	225701	48	1996/97[12]	378754	50	1996/97	83645	59
	1997/98	222278	49	1997/98[8]	394092	50	1997/98	96371	60
Luxembourg	1990/91	23465	51	1990/91[2]	7594	...	...	...	...
Luxembourg	1996/97	28437	...	1996/97	28796	50	...	...	...
	1997/98	29094	...	1997/98[8]	30868	...	...	...	...

9
Education at the primary, secondary and tertiary levels
Number of students and percentage female [*cont.*]
Enseignement primaire, secondaire et supérieur
Nombre d'étudiants et étudiantes en pourcentage [*suite*]

Country or area Pays ou zone	Years Années	Primary education Enseignement primaire		Years Années	Secondary education Enseignement secondaire		Years Années	Tertiary education Enseignement supérieur	
		Total	%F		Total	%F		Total	%F
Malta	1990/91	36899	48	1990/91	32544	47	1990/91	3123	44
Malte	1996/97	35374	48	1996/97	36103	48	1996/97	6368	51
	1997/98	35261	49	1997/98[8]	36522	...	1997/98	7441	49
Monaco	1990/91	1773	51	1990/91	2785	49	...	...	...
Monaco	1996/97	1919	47	1996/97	2886	51	...	...	...
	1997/98	1956	47	1997/98[8]	2912	...	...	...	...
Netherlands	1990/91	1082022	50	1990/91	1401739	47	1990/91	478869	44
Pays–Bas	1995/96	1207896	48	1995/96	1479682	47	1995/96[35]	491748	47
	1996/97	1230987	48	1996/97	1415712	48	1996/97	468970	48
Norway	1990/91	309432	49	1990/91	370779	50	1990/91	142521	53
Norvège	1996/97	330619	49	1996/97	368074	48	1996/97[35]	185320	56
	1997/98[24]	401577	49	1997/98[8]	373163	48	1997/98	183026	57
Poland	1990/91	5189118	49	1990/91	1887667	50	1990/91	544893	56
Pologne	1996/97	5021378	48	1996/97	2547383	49	1996/97	1182360	58
	1997/98	4905367	48	1997/98[8]	2778828	50	1997/98	1191099	57
Portugal	1990/91	1019794	48	1990/91	670035	53	1990/91	185762	56
Portugal	1995/96	867253	48	1995/96	947478	51	1995/96[49]	319525	56
	1997/98	832696	48	1997/98[8]	891773	51	1997/98	351784	56
Republic of Moldova	1990/91	301653	49	1990/91	459701	52	1990/91	104800	...
Moldova, Rép. de	1995/96[12]	*320055	*49	1995/96	*440622	*50	1995/96	87700	56
	1996/97[12]	*320725	*49	1996/97	*445501	*50	1996/97	93759	55
Romania	1990/91	1253480	49	1990/91	2837948	49	1990/91	192810	47
Roumanie	1996/97	1405308	49	1996/97	2212090	49	1994/95	369662	33[1]
	1997/98	1373079	49	1997/98[8]	2286129	50	1996/97	411687	53
Russian Federation	1990/91	7596000	49	1990/91	13956000	...	1990/91	5100000	55
Fédération de Russie	1993/94	7738000	49	1992/93	13724000	...	1993/94	4587045	55
	1994/95	7849000	49	1993/94	13732000	...	1994/95	4458363	56
San Marino	1990/91	1212	47	1990/91	1182	52	...	...	...
Saint–Marin	1995/96	1134	48	1995/96	1199	48	...	...	...
	1996/97	1170	48	1996/97	1192	48	...	...	...
Slovakia	1992/93	350604	49	1992/93	657010	50	1992/93	66002	48
Slovaquie	1996/97	329880	48[40]	1996/97	677377	49[40]	1996/97	101764	50
	1997/98	324311	49	1997/98[8]	668429	50	1997/98	112837	51
Slovenia	1990/91	112134	...	1990/91	208905	...	1990/91	33565	56
Slovénie	1996/97	98866	49	1996/97	212458	49	1996/97[48]	53483	56
	1997/98	95812	49	1997/98[8]	210078	50	1997/98[48]	68126	55
Spain	1990/91	2820497	48	1990/91	4755322	50	1990/91	1222089	51
Espagne	1996/97[29]	2702553	...	1996/97[29]	3852102	50	1996/97[49]	1684445	53
	1997/98	2633678	48	1997/98[8]	3786935	50	1997/98	1745170	53
Sweden	1990/91	578359	49	1990/91	588474	50	1990/91	192611	54
Suède	1996/97	690630	49	1996/97	829295	53	1996/97	275217	56
	1997/98	746164	50	1997/98[8]	930748	54	1997/98	280712	56
Switzerland	1990/91	404154	49	1990/91	567396	47	1990/91	137486	35
Suisse	1995/96	477643	49	1995/96	559924	47	1995/96[49]	148024	38
	1997/98	522741	49	1997/98[8]	557366	47	1997/98	152653	41
TFYR Macedonia	1990/91	266813	48	1990/91	70696	...	1990/91[22]	26515	52
L'ex–R.y. Macédoine	1996/97	260917	48	1996/97	83746	48	1995/96[22]	29583	54
	1997/98[24]	131501	48	1997/98[8]	215374	48	1996/97[22]	30754	54
Ukraine	1990/91	3990500	49	1990/91	3407500	...	1990/91	1651700	...
Ukraine	1993/94[49]	2658800	49	1993/94[49]	4731200	...	1995/96	1541000	...
	1997/98	2339118	49	1997/98[8]	5734262	50	1997/98[41]	1130627	50
United Kingdom	1990/91	4532500	49	1990/91	4335600	50	1990/91	1258188	48
Royaume–Uni	1996/97[33]	5328219	49	1996/97	6548786	52	1996/97[49]	1891450	52
	1997/98	4664429	49	1997/98[8]	6634735	52	1997/98	1938423	53
Yugoslavia	1990/91[27]	466692	49	1990/91	788170	49	1991/92[22]	133331	52
Yougoslavie	1995/96	449192	49	1995/96	831758	49	1996/97[22]	172313	54
	1996/97	437780	49	1996/97	815029	50	1997/98[48]	189554	54
Oceania · Océanie									
American Samoa	1985/86	7704	47	1986/87	3295	49	1985/86	758	52
Samoa américaines	1991/92	7884	48	1991/92	3643	46	1988/89	909	54
Australia	1990	1583024	49	1990	1278163	50	1990[50]	485075	53
Australie	1997[29]	1855789	49	1996	2280274	49	1996[35]	1002476	51
	1998	1869852	49	1997[8]	2618506	49	1998[35]	869172	54

9
Education at the primary, secondary and tertiary levels
Number of students and percentage female [cont.]
Enseignement primaire, secondaire et supérieur
Nombre d'étudiants et étudiantes en pourcentage [suite]

Country or area Pays ou zone	Years Années	Primary education Enseignement primaire		Years Années	Secondary education Enseignement secondaire		Years Années	Tertiary education Enseignement supérieur	
		Total	%F		Total	%F		Total	%F
Cook Islands	1985	2713	...	1985[1]	2559	...			
Iles Cook	1998	2711	48	1998[8]	1779	50	1980	360	45
Fiji	1990	143552	...	1985	45093	50	1980	1666	...
Fidji	1991	144924	49	1991	61614	48	1985	2313	38
	1992	145630	49	1992	66890	49	1991	7908	...
French Polynesia	1990/91	28270	48	1986/87	17878	55	1980/81	27	25
Polynésie française	1994/95	30037	48	1990/91	20311	53	1983/84	180	...
	1995/96	29415	48	1992/93	22366	55	1991/92	301	50
Guam	1985/86	16783	...	...	...	...	1986/87	7052	53
Guam	1988/89	15516	...	...	...	...	1988/89[3]	4257	59
Kiribati	1990	14709	50	1990	3003	49	...	...	...
Kiribati	1997	17594	49	1996	4341	54	...	...	...
	1998	17557	49	1998[8]	*5159	*54	...	...	...
Nauru									
Nauru	1985	1451	47	1985	482	50	...	...	...
New Caledonia	1990	22958	48	1985	18351	52	1980	438	39
Nouvelle – Calédonie	1992	21865	...	1990	20673	52	1984	660	38
	1994	22308	...	1991	21908	52	1985	761	44
New Zealand	1990	318568	48	1990	340915	49	1990	111504	52
Nouvelle – Zélande	1997	357569	49	1996	430526	50	1996	162350	56
	1998	362413	49	1998[8]	449001	50	1998	161288	58
Niue	1980	666	...	1980	397	...	...	...	...
Nioué	1985	503	...	1985	321	...	...	...	...
	1991[13]	371	...	1991[13]	302	53	...	...	...
Papua New Guinea	1990	415195	44	1990	65643	38	1980	5040	22
Papouasie – Nvl – Guinée	1994	505153	45	1994	83252	39	1995	14158	31
	1995	516797	45	1995	78759	39	1996	16118	39
Samoa	1990	35763	49	1990	10450	51	...	...	...
Samoa	1996[29]	35378	47	1995[29]	13241	50	1981	644	7
	1997	35649	48	1996	12672	50	1983	562	47
Solomon Islands	1990	47598	44	1990	5636	37	...	...	...
Iles Salomon	1993	57264	44	1993	7351	36	...	...	...
	1994	60493	45	1994[1]	7811	38	...	...	...
Tokelau	1981	434	49	1983	488	50			
Tokélaou	1991	361	50	1991[4]	113	47			
Tonga	1990	16522	48	1990	14749	48	1981	693	43
Tonga	1992	16658	48	1992[4]	13544	48	1984	680	56
	1993	16792	48	1993	16570	48	1985	705	56
Tuvalu	1990[1 51]	1485	48	1984[4]	243	56	...	...	...
Tuvalu	1993	1752	48	1987[4]	293	57	...	...	...
	1994	1906	49	1990	345	52	...	...	...
Vanuatu	1990	24471	47	1990[46]	293	38	...	...	...
Vanuatu	1991	24952	47	1991	4184	43	...	...	...
	1992	26267	47	1992[5]	4713	43	...	...	...

Source:
United Nations Educational, Scientific and Cultural Organization (UNESCO) Institute for Statistics, Paris, the UNESCO statistics database.

Source:
L'Institut de statistique de l'Organisation des Nations Unies pour l'éducation, la science et la culture (UNESCO), Paris, la base de données de l'UNESCO.

† For information on the recent changes in country or area nomenclature pertaining to former Czechoslovakia, Germany, Hong Kong Special Administrative Region (SAR) of China, Macao Special Administrative Region (SAR) of China, SFR of Yugoslavia and the former USSR, see Annex I – Country or area nomenclature, regional and other groupings.

† Pour les modifications récentes de nomenclature de pays ou de zone concernant l'Allemagne, Hong Kong, région administrative spéciale (RAS) de Chine, Macao région administrative spéciale (RAS) de Chine, l'ex – Tchécoslovaquie, l'ex – URSS et l'ex – Rfs de Yougoslavie, voir annex I – Nomenclature des pays ou des zones, groupements régionaux et autres groupements.

†† For statistical purposes the data for China do not include those for Hong Kong Special Administrative Region (Hong Kong SAR), Macao Special Administrative Region (Macao SAR) and Taiwan province of China.

†† Les données statistiques relatives à la Chine ne comprennent pas celles qui concernent la région administrative spéciale de Hong Kong (la RAS de Hong Kong), la région administrative spéciale de Macao (la RAS de Macao), et la province chinoise de Taiwan.

9
Education at the primary, secondary and tertiary levels
Number of students and percentage female [*cont.*]
Enseignement primaire, secondaire et supérieur
Nombre d'étudiants et étudiantes en pourcentage [*suite*]

1 Public education only.	1 Enseignement public seulement.
2 General education only.	2 L'enseignement général seulement.
3 Universities only.	3 Universitaires seulement.
4 Not including vocational education.	4 Non compris l'enseignement technique et professionnel.
5 Not including teacher training.	5 Non compris la formation d'enseignants.
6 Data refer only to institutions under the authority of the Ministry of Higher Education and Scientific Research.	6 Les données se réfèrent seulement aux institutions sous la tutelle du Ministère de l'Enseignement Supérieur de la Recherche Scientifique.
7 Not including Al Azhar university.	7 Non compris l'université Al Azhar.
8 Beginning 1997, secondary education includes post−secondary non−tertiary education.	8 A partir de 1997, l'enseignement postsecondaire qui n'est pas du supérieur est inclus dans l'enseignement secondaire.
9 Teacher training only.	9 La formation d'enseignants seulement.
10 Primary education exempt of school fees.	10 Les frais de scolarité sont supprimés pour l'enseignement primaire.
11 Not including health−related programmes.	11 Non compris les programmes relatifs à la santé.
12 Including special education.	12 Y compris l'enseignement spécial.
13 As from 1991, change in structure.	13 A partir de 1991, changement de structure.
14 Data refer to approximately 95% of the total number of schools.	14 Les données se réfèrent à environ 95% du nombre total des écoles.
15 Not including the former independent states (Transkei, Bophuthatswana, Venda and Ciskei).	15 Non compris les anciens états indépendants (Transkei, Bophuthatswana, Venda et Ciskei).
16 Not including the 'Ecole Nationale d'Administration et de Magistrature'.	16 Non compris l'Ecole Nationale d'Administration et de Magistrature.
17 Public and aided education only.	17 Enseignement public et subventionné seulement.
18 Not including private non−university institutions.	18 Non compris les institutions privées non universitaires.
19 Not including arts and science colleges.	19 Non compris le premier cycle universitaire d'enseignement classique.
20 Vocational education only.	20 L'enseignement technique et professionnel seulement.
21 Data refer only to institutions recognised by the national council for higher education.	21 Les données se réfèrent seulement aux institutions reconnues par le Conseil National pour l'Education Supérieure.
22 Not including students enrolled in the second stage of tertiary education.	22 Non compris les étudiants inscrits dans le deuxième niveau de l'enseignement supérieur.
23 Including distance−learning university institutions.	23 Y compris les institutions universitaires d'enseignement à distance.
24 As from 1997, change in structure.	24 A partir de 1997, changement de structure.
25 Including secondary classes attached to primary schools.	25 Y compris les classes secondaires rattachées aux écoles primaires.
26 Including post−primary classes.	26 Y compris les classes post−primaires.
27 Data refer to the end of school year.	27 Les données se réfèrent à la fin de l'année scolaire.
28 Not including private universities.	28 Non compris les universités privées.
29 As from 1995, change in structure.	29 A partir de 1995, changement de structure.
30 As from 1996, change in structure.	30 A partir de 1996, changement de structure.
31 Day schools only.	31 Ecoles de jour seulement.
32 Not including Turkish schools.	32 Non compris les écoles turques.
33 As from 1994/95 (Israel), 1995/96 (Estonia) and 1992/93 (United Kingdom), change in classification of one or more national programmes of education.	33 A partir de 1994/95 (Israël), 1995/96 (Estonie) et 1992/93 (Royaume−Uni), la classification d'un ou de plusieurs programmes nationaux d'enseignement a changé.
34 As from 1994, change in structure.	34 A partir de 1994, changement de structure.
35 As from 1993, change in structure.	35 A partir de 1993, changement de structure.
36 East Bank only.	36 Rive orientale seulement.
37 Not including medical science.	37 Non compris les science médicales.
38 Including pre−primary education.	38 Y compris l'enseignement préprimaire.
39 Not including some non−university institutions.	39 Non compris quelques institutions supérieures non universitaires.
40 Not including special education.	40 Non compris l'enseignement spécial.
41 Not including foreign students.	41 Non compris les étudiants étrangers.
42 Full−time only.	42 Plein temps seulement.
43 Not including private general education.	43 Non compris l'enseignement général privé.
44 Not including private vocational education.	44 Non compris l'enseignement technique privé.
45 Data refer to institutions under the authority of the Holy See.	45 Les données se réfèrent aux institutions sous l'autorité du Saint −Siège.
46 Not including general education.	46 Non compris l'enseignement général.
47 Tanzanian mainland only.	47 Tanzanie continentale seulement.
48 Not including students enrolled in doctoral studies.	48 Non compris les étudiants inscrits en doctorat.
49 As from 1992, change in structure.	49 A partir de 1992, changement de structure.
50 Data do not include Vocational Education and Training Institutes (VETS).	50 Les données n'incluent pas l'Education Technique et les Instituts de Formation Professionnelle (VETS).
51 Including 3 years of education provided in community training centres.	51 Y compris 3 années d'enseignement dispensé dans les centres de formation locaux.

10
Public expenditure on education: total and current, percentage of GNP and government expenditure
Dépenses publiques afférentes à l'éducation: totales et ordinaires, pourcentage par rapport au PNB et aux dépenses du gouvernement

Country or area Pays ou zone	Year Année	Total expenditure on education Dépenses totales d'éducation			Current expenditure on education Dépenses ordinaires d'éducation		
		In national currency (millions) En monnaie nationale (millions)	As % of GNP En % du PNB	As % of total government expenditure En % des dépenses totales du gouvernement	In national currency (millions) En monnaie nationale (millions)	As % of GNP En % du PNB	As % of current government expenditure En % des dépenses ordinaires du gouvernement
Africa · Afrique							
Algeria [1]	1994	85390	6.0	18.8	75190	5.3	23.3
Algérie [1]	1995	108100	5.8	14.7	95920	5.2	21.9
	1996	122500	5.1	16.4	106900	4.5	35.4
Angola	1986	12880	7.3	12.6	12460	7.1	15.6
Angola	1987	12850	6.2	13.8	11570	5.6	15.5
	1990[2]	12080	4.9	10.7	10860	4.4	...
Benin	1980	...	...	...	12430	4.2	36.8
Bénin	1995	31070	3.2	15.2	26610	2.7	21.1
Botswana	1995	1071	8.6	20.5	819	6.6	23.1
Botswana	1996	1471	10.3	21.8	1101	7.7	24.8
	1997	1502	8.6	20.6	1200	6.9	24.6
Burkina Faso	1992	23580	3.0	...	22000	2.8	...
Burkina Faso	1994	36320	3.6	11.1	30020	2.9	17.4
	1997	...	...	...	33190	2.4	...
Burundi	1994	10670	4.6	...	10440	4.5	...
Burundi	1995	12530	5.1	...	11490	4.7	...
	1996	10740	4.0	18.3	10440	3.9	20.3
Cameroon	1990	108000	3.4	19.6	97950	3.1	26.9
Cameroun	1991	91890	2.9	16.9	81720	2.6	21.6
	1996	...	...	...	98420	2.3	12.8
Cape Verde	1985	341	3.6	...	325	3.5	15.2
Cap–Vert	1987	493	2.9	14.8	472	2.8	15.3
	1991	903	4.0	19.9	890	3.9	20.0
Central African Rep. [2]	1993	...	...	...	7808	2.2	...
Rép. centrafricaine [2]	1994	...	...	...	7850	1.7	...
	1995	...	...	...	8820	1.6	...
Chad	1994	10800	1.7	...	10690	1.7	15.1
Tchad	1996	...	...	...	11790	1.4	15.8
	1997	20496	2.2	...	12043	1.3	...
Comoros [2]	1993	...	...	...	2938	3.9	20.5
Comores [2]	1994	...	...	...	3285	4.2	21.6
	1995	...	...	...	3381	4.2	21.1
Congo	1993	59640	9.1	...	58390	8.9	...
Congo	1994	63050	7.5	15.5	58500	7.0	18.2
	1995	52270	6.1	14.7	51000	5.9	15.0
Côte d'Ivoire	1995	236200	5.3	28.8	212600	4.7	...
Côte d'Ivoire	1996	251900	5.0	24.0	231400	4.6	...
	1997	275800	5.0	24.9	250300	4.5	...
Dem. Rep. of the Congo	1986	3874	0.9	6.9	3833	0.9	6.9
Rép. dém. du Congo	1987	8239	1.0	8.2	7926	1.0	8.2
	1988	15010	1.0	6.4	14360	0.9	6.4
Djibouti	1989	...	...	...	2596	...	10.7
Djibouti	1990	...	...	...	2614	...	10.5
	1991	...	...	...	2872	3.6	11.1
Egypt	1994	8057	4.7	13.8	7204	4.2	15.0
Egypte	1995	9530	4.8	14.9	8767	4.4	16.7
	1996	...	...	...	10150	4.4	...
Equatorial Guinea	1988	620	1.7	3.9	527	1.5	3.5
Guinée équatoriale	1993	734	1.7	5.6	721	1.7	5.8
Eritrea [1]	1994	...	...	...	59	1.3	...
Erythrée [1]	1995	...	...	...	90	1.9	...
	1996	91	1.8	...	70	1.4	...
Ethiopia	1994	1297	4.6	13.0	885	3.2	16.5
Ethiopie	1995	1339	4.0	13.9	945	2.8	16.6
	1996	1497	4.0	13.7	1016	2.7	...

10
Public expenditure on education: total and current, [*cont.*]
percentage of GNP and government expenditure
Dépenses publiques afférentes à l'éducation: totales et ordinaires, [*suite*]
pourcentage par rapport au PNB et aux dépenses du gouvernement

Country or area Pays ou zone	Year Année	Total expenditure on education Dépenses totales d'éducation			Current expenditure on education Dépenses ordinaires d'éducation		
		In national currency (millions) En monnaie nationale (millions)	As % of GNP En % du PNB	As % of total government expenditure En % des dépenses totales du gouvernement	In national currency (millions) En monnaie nationale (millions)	As % of GNP En % du PNB	As % of current government expenditure En % des dépenses ordinaires du gouvernement
Gabon	1992	41530	3.2	...	34410	2.7	...
Gabon [1]	1994	56790	2.8	...	45830	2.2	...
	1995	61250	2.9	...	46090	2.2	
Gambia	1994	183	5.3	16.0	113	3.3	12.9
Gambie	1995	202	5.6		121	3.4	
	1996	186	4.9	21.2	133	3.5	...
Ghana	1994	218900	4.3	19.2	213900	4.2	25.3
Ghana	1995	362800	4.8	21.4	330400	4.3	25.4
	1996	462700	4.2	19.9	449700	4.0	24.1
Guinea	1995	69440	2.0	27.7	...	...	...
Guinée	1996	71850	1.9	25.6	...	...	...
	1997	76700	1.9	26.8	...	...	...
Guinea–Bissau	1983	...	...	...	276	1.9	12.4
Guinée–Bissau	1984	...	...	...	539	2.1	11.2
	1987	2533	1.8	...	2473	1.7	...
Kenya	1994	26890	7.1	16.4	25390	6.7	...
Kenya	1995	30120	6.7	16.9	28450	6.4	...
	1996	33550	6.5	16.7	31350	6.1	...
Lesotho	1994	272	6.7	...	241	6.0	...
Lesotho	1995	...	...	...	336	7.3	...
	1996	462	8.4	...	349	6.4	...
Liberia Libéria	1980	62	5.7	24.3	53	4.9	27.0
Libyan Arab Jamahiriya	1984	484	6.6	13.6	350	4.7	24.3
Jamah. arabe libyenne	1985	575	7.1	19.8	457	5.7	38.1
	1986	636	9.6	20.8	506	7.7	37.1
Madagascar	1992	122600	2.3	...	...	...	...
Madagascar	1993	138100	2.2	16.1	...	...	...
	1997	333900	1.9	...	...	...	...
Malawi	1993	396	4.4	20.0	313	3.5	20.7
Malawi	1994	426	4.3	18.3	337	3.4	20.8
	1995	1163	5.4	...	958	4.4	...
Mali	1994	...	...	...	22820	2.3	20.1
Mali	1995	26190	2.2	...	25600	2.1	21.2
	1996	29450	2.2	...	...	...	...
Mauritania [2]	1994	6291	5.2	16.2	4660	3.9	...
Mauritanie [2]	1995	6674	5.1	16.2	4917	3.7	22.1
	1996	...	...	...	5266	3.7	24.9
Mauritius	1995	2884	4.2	16.8	2432	3.5	16.9
Maurice	1996	3510	4.6	17.4	2755	3.6	16.3
	1997 [1]	...	...	...	2767	3.3	...
Morocco [2]	1994	14950	5.6	22.6	13370	5.0	28.4
Maroc [2]	1995	15780	5.8	24.7	14380	5.3	...
	1996	16370	5.3	24.9	15120	4.9	29.9
Mozambique	1988	25200	3.0	8.1	17000	2.1	11.3
Mozambique	1989	44570	3.5	9.3	30370	2.4	12.3
	1990	72260	4.1	12.0	46060	2.6	17.5
Namibia	1995	1068	8.5	24.6	996	7.9	...
Namibie	1996	1299	9.3	25.6	1208	8.6	...
	1997	1396	9.1	...	1301	8.5	...
Niger [1]	1995	26780	2.9	16.4	...	...	...
Niger [1]	1996	26390	2.6	15.2	...	...	...
	1997	24850	2.3	12.8	...	...	...
Nigeria [3]	1993	7999	0.9	...	6437	0.7	...
Nigéria [3]	1994	10280	0.9	14.8	7878	0.7	...
	1995	12820	0.7	11.5	9798	0.5	...
Rwanda	1987	6010	3.5	22.9	5642	3.3	25.0
Rwanda	1988	6138	3.4	22.2	5653	3.1	25.0
	1989	7222	3.8	25.4	6793	3.5	29.1

10
Public expenditure on education: total and current, [*cont.*]
percentage of GNP and government expenditure
Dépenses publiques afférentes à l'éducation: totales et ordinaires, [*suite*]
pourcentage par rapport au PNB et aux dépenses du gouvernement

Country or area Pays ou zone	Year Année	Total expenditure on education Dépenses totales d'éducation			Current expenditure on education Dépenses ordinaires d'éducation		
		In national currency (millions) En monnaie nationale (millions)	As % of GNP En % du PNB	As % of total government expenditure En % des dépenses totales du gouvernement	In national currency (millions) En monnaie nationale (millions)	As % of GNP En % du PNB	As % of current government expenditure En % des dépenses ordinaires du gouvernement
Sao Tome and Principe	1981	91	8.0	...	...	...	...
Sao Tomé–et–Principe	1982	91	6.3	...	...	...	...
	1986	100	3.8	18.8	...	...	...
Senegal	1995	85700	4.0	33.1	84440	3.9	38.6
Sénégal	1996	89600	3.7	...	88520	3.7	...
	1997	...	...	...	88870	3.4	...
Seychelles	1994	222	9.3	16.8	181	7.6	16.0
Seychelles	1995	187	8.0	16.3	152	6.5	15.7
	1996	195	7.9	...	156	6.3	...
Sierra Leone	1987	432	1.7	...	417	1.6	...
Sierra Leone	1988	529	1.3	...	499	1.2	...
	1989	604	0.9	...	577	0.9	...
Somalia [1]	1984	344	0.6	5.3	285	0.5	...
Somalie [1]	1985	371	0.5	4.1	274	0.3	...
	1986	434	0.4	2.8	290	0.3	...
South Africa	1995	32290	6.8	20.5	30360	6.4	...
Afrique du Sud	1996	42050	8.0	23.9	39910	7.5	...
	1997	43943	7.6	22.0	41626	7.2	...
Sudan	1980	187	4.3	9.1	172	3.9	12.6
Soudan	1995	50770	1.4	...	50470	1.4	...
Swaziland	1994	285	7.7	18.3	241	6.5	...
Swaziland	1995	309	6.3	19.9	268	5.5	23.5
	1996	326	5.7	18.1	290	5.1	...
Togo	1992	27000	6.1	21.6	26310	6.0	29.0
Togo	1995	...	...	...	26890	4.3	...
	1996	33080	4.5	24.6	30730	4.2	24.1
Tunisia	1995	1103	6.8	17.4	958	5.9	...
Tunisie	1996	1207	6.7	17.4	1035	5.7	25.9
	1997	1532	7.7	19.9	1323	6.6	30.4
Uganda	1990 [2]	20190	1.5	11.5	18530	1.4	15.1
Ouganda	1991 [2]	35030	1.9	15.0	33010	1.8	16.5
	1995	136100	2.6	...	129900	2.4	...
United Rep. of Tanzania	1992	...	...	...	35000	3.0	14.6
Rep.–Unie de Tanzanie	1993	...	...	...	45920	3.1	17.9
	1994	...	...	...	72000	3.7	23.0
Zambia	1993	28920	2.1	9.2	27380	2.0	...
Zambie	1994	44330	2.1	6.5	38130	1.8	...
	1995	61040	2.2	7.1	56510	2.0	...
Zimbabwe	1994	...	...	...	4029	7.5	...
Zimbabwe	1995 [1]	...	...	...	3896	6.6	...
	1996 [1]	...	...	...	5619	6.9	...
America, North · Amérique du Nord							
Antigua and Barbuda	1984	12	2.7	...	11	2.6	...
Antigua–et–Barbuda	1987	...	...	...	19	2.8	...
	1988	...	...	...	31	3.7	...
Aruba	1995	104	...	16.2	84	...	15.8
Aruba	1996	103	...	11.8	90	...	12.2
	1997	103	...	12.8	90	...	14.0
Bahamas	1990	125	4.3	17.8	112	3.8	...
Bahamas	1991	114	4.0	16.3	103	3.6	...
	1996	119	...	13.2	110	...	14.4
Barbados	1992	215	6.9	16.9	192	6.2	17.5
Barbade	1993	238	7.5	18.7	230	7.3	20.0
	1994	242	7.2	19.0	...	...	...
Belize	1994	63	5.9	19.9	60	5.7	...
Belize	1995	60	5.3	19.6	59	5.1	...
	1996	61	5.0	19.5	59	4.8	...
Bermuda	1989	51	3.4	16.7	44	2.9	15.9
Bermudes	1990	53	3.3	14.5	49	3.1	15.7
	1991	60	3.7	...	54	3.3	...

10
Public expenditure on education: total and current, [*cont.*]
percentage of GNP and government expenditure
Dépenses publiques afférentes à l'éducation: totales et ordinaires, [*suite*]
pourcentage par rapport au PNB et aux dépenses du gouvernement

Country or area Pays ou zone	Year Année	Total expenditure on education Dépenses totales d'éducation			Current expenditure on education Dépenses ordinaires d'éducation		
		In national currency (millions) En monnaie nationale (millions)	As % of GNP En % du PNB	As % of total government expenditure En % des dépenses totales du gouvernement	In national currency (millions) En monnaie nationale (millions)	As % of GNP En % du PNB	As % of current government expenditure En % des dépenses ordinaires du gouvernement
British Virgin Islands	1989	7	...	11.9	6	...	...
Iles Vierges brit.	1990	8	...	12.2	7	...	...
	1991	11	...	15.4	9	...	...
Canada [7]	1992	49960	7.5	14.3	46520	7.0	...
Canada [7]	# 1993	49740	7.2	13.2			
	1994	49930	6.9	12.9	46120	6.4	...
Costa Rica	1994	58700	4.6	19.2	...	...	...
Costa Rica	1995	73520	4.6	19.8	...	...	...
	1996	99630	5.4	22.8	...	...	...
Cuba	1994	1444	7.5	10.2	1434	7.5	12.5
Cuba	1995	1475	6.8	10.9	1463	6.7	12.5
	1996	1535	6.7	12.6	1521	6.7	15.0
Dominica	1987	19	5.6	14.1	18	5.2	17.5
Dominique	1988	...	...	...	18	4.7	17.5
	1989	22	5.5	10.6	20	5.0	19.9
Dominican Republic	1995	3019	1.9	13.2	...	...	...
Rép. dominicaine	1996	3537	2.0	13.4	3107	1.7	21.8
	1997	4778	2.3	13.8	4383	2.1	19.3
El Salvador	1995	1806	2.2	15.3	1793	2.2	...
El Salvador	1996	2086	2.3	14.1	...	...	...
	1997	2447	2.5	16.0	...	...	...
Grenada	1994	32	4.6	12.5	...	...	...
Grenade	1995	33	4.6	11.2	...	...	...
	1996	36	4.7	10.6	...	...	...
Guatemala [2]	1994	1139	1.5	14.7	1064	1.4	...
Guatemala [2]	1995	1429	1.7	16.0	1354	1.6	...
	1996	1560	1.7	15.8	1478	1.6	...
Haiti	1988	199	1.8	20.4	198	1.8	20.6
Haïti	1989	213	1.7	19.7	213	1.7	20.0
	1990	216	1.5	20.0	216	1.5	20.1
Honduras	1991	621	4.1	...	606	4.0	...
Honduras	1994	988	3.5	16.0	971	3.4	...
	1995	1353	3.6	16.5	1327	3.5	...
Jamaica	1994	7078	5.7	10.4	6239	5.0	16.1
Jamaïque	1995	10110	6.4	7.7	9184	5.8	17.9
	1996	14640	7.5	12.9	13380	6.8	20.6
Mexico [78]	1993	62410000	5.1	...	...	...	...
Mexique [78]	# 1994	64970	4.7	26.0	61670	4.5	...
	1995	85350	4.9	23.0	80340	4.6	...
Montserrat	1991	...	...	...	8	...	19.5
Montserrat	1992	...	...	...	8	...	19.3
	1993	...	...	...	7	...	18.8
Nicaragua [1]	1995	433	3.7	9.9	349	3.0	...
Nicaragua [1]	1996	515	3.7	10.2	373	2.6	...
	1997	681	3.9	8.8	...	...	...
Panama	1995	395	5.2	22.1	360	4.8	23.9
Panama	1996	423	5.3	20.9	395	5.0	22.3
	1997	429	5.1	16.3	399	4.8	17.2
Saint Kitts and Nevis	1992	15	3.2	...	14	3.1	...
Saint-Kitts-et-Nevis	1995	22	3.7	9.8	21	3.6	14.9
	1996	24	3.8	8.8	22	3.5	13.8
Saint Lucia	1992	...	...	...	63	5.2	23.2
Sainte Lucie	1993	...	...	...	70	5.7	23.7
	1994	128	9.8	22.2	85	6.5	24.9
Saint Vincent and the Grenadines	1986	19	6.0	11.6	18	5.6	16.8
Saint-Vincent-et-Grenadines	1989	26	5.7	10.5	23	5.0	17.1
	1991	34	6.3	13.8	26	4.7	17.2
Trinidad and Tobago	1992	811	3.8	10.3	772	3.6	10.7
Trinité-et-Tobago	1993	836	3.7	...	805	3.5	...
	1994	1170	4.4	...	1061	4.0	...

10
Public expenditure on education: total and current, [*cont.*]
percentage of GNP and government expenditure
Dépenses publiques afférentes à l'éducation: totales et ordinaires, [*suite*]
pourcentage par rapport au PNB et aux dépenses du gouvernement

Country or area Pays ou zone	Year Année	Total expenditure on education Dépenses totales d'éducation			Current expenditure on education Dépenses ordinaires d'éducation		
		In national currency (millions) En monnaie nationale (millions)	As % of GNP En % du PNB	As % of total government expenditure En % des dépenses totales du gouvernement	In national currency (millions) En monnaie nationale (millions)	As % of GNP En % du PNB	As % of current government expenditure En % des dépenses ordinaires du gouvernement
Turks and Caicos Islands							
Iles Turques et Caïques	1983	1	...	10.3	1	...	12.4
United States [7]	# 1992	328400	5.4	14.1	...	...	...
Etats–Unis [7]	1993	335300	5.3	14.0	...	...	...
	1994	361200	5.4	14.4	...	...	...
US Virgin Islands	1982	72	8.6	...	...	...	...
Iles Vierges américaines	1983	70	7.7	...	...	...	...
	1984	74	7.5	...	...	...	...
America, South · Amérique du Sud							
Argentina	1993	8310	3.3	12.4	...	...	...
Argentine	1994	10470	3.8	14.0	...	...	...
	1996	10160	3.5	12.6	9320	3.2	...
Bolivia	1994	1322	4.9	11.2	1293	4.8	15.1
Bolivie	1995	1848	5.9	...	1601	5.1	...
	1996	1812	4.9	11.1	1794	4.8	14.2
Brazil [4]	1988	3550000	4.3	...	...	...	...
Brésil [4]	1989	56100000	4.5	...	...	...	...
	1995	32250	5.1	...	30020	4.7	...
Chile	1995	767600	3.1	14.0	726900	2.9	15.6
Chili	1996	927200	3.4	14.8	870800	3.2	16.5
	1997	1109000	3.6	15.5	1061000	3.4	17.8
Colombia [2]	1994	1923000	3.4	16.0	1632000	2.9	...
Colombie [2]	1995	2607000	3.7	19.0	2076000	2.9	...
	1996	3531000	4.1	16.6	2653000	3.1	...
Ecuador	1994	1150000	3.4	19.2	1128000	3.4	...
Equateur	1995	1473000	3.4	15.2	1321000	3.1	...
	1996	1957000	3.5	13.0	1787000	3.2	...
Falkland Islands (Malvimas)							
Iles Falkland (Malvinas)	1996	3	...	5.4	2	...	9.6
Guyana	1994	2857	4.5	7.1	2080	3.3	7.1
Guyana	1995	3267	4.3	8.1	2546	3.3	8.9
	1996	4590	5.0	10.0	3026	3.3	9.9
Paraguay [2]	1995	588300	3.4	18.0	...	...	...
Paraguay [2]	1996	777700	3.9	18.6	683800	3.5	25.0
	1997	863200	4.0	19.8	...	...	...
Peru	1993	2081	2.6	...	...	...	...
Pérou	1994	4098	3.9	...	3818	3.6	...
	1996	4279	2.9	19.2	3784	2.6	26.9
Suriname	1991	266	7.5	...	265	7.4	...
Suriname	1992	362	7.2	...	360	7.1	...
	1993	384	3.5	...	380	3.4	...
Uruguay	1994	2049000	2.5	13.3	1981000	2.5	13.3
Uruguay	1995	3122000	2.8	...	2750000	2.5	...
	1996	4778000	3.3	15.5	4352000	3.0	15.8
Venezuela	1993	242800	4.6	22.0	...	...	...
Venezuela	1994	434300	5.2	22.4	419500	5.0	31.2
	1995	...	...	...	661000	5.0	23.5
Asia · Asie							
Afghanistan	1982	2363	...	6.4	2191	...	6.9
Afghanistan	1987	3810	...	4.0	3150	...	3.7
	1990	5667	...	...	5282	...	...
Armenia	1990	4	7.3	20.5	...	...	...
Arménie	1993	...	...	...	136	3.5	...
	1996	13250	2.0	10.3	12410	1.8	11.5
Azerbaijan	1995	375800	2.9	17.5	342300	2.7	16.9
Azerbaïdjan	1996	512000	3.3	21.3	466900	3.0	21.0
	1997	547200	3.0	18.8	...	...	...
Bahrain	1995	80	4.3	12.8	73	4.0	14.1
Bahreïn	1996	80	4.2	12.8	76	4.0	...
	1997	85	4.4	12.0	82	4.2	14.8

10
Public expenditure on education: total and current, [cont.]
percentage of GNP and government expenditure
Dépenses publiques afférentes à l'éducation: totales et ordinaires, [suite]
pourcentage par rapport au PNB et aux dépenses du gouvernement

Country or area Pays ou zone	Year Année	Total expenditure on education Dépenses totales d'éducation			Current expenditure on education Dépenses ordinaires d'éducation		
		In national currency (millions) En monnaie nationale (millions)	As % of GNP En % du PNB	As % of total government expenditure En % des dépenses totales du gouvernement	In national currency (millions) En monnaie nationale (millions)	As % of GNP En % du PNB	As % of current government expenditure En % des dépenses ordinaires du gouvernement
Bangladesh [2]	1992	21000	1.7	8.7	16740	1.4	10.4
Bangladesh [2]	1996	38120	2.2	...	22290	1.3	...
	1997	39933	2.2	13.8	23428	1.3	14.6
Bhutan	1995	...	...	...	255	2.9	...
Bhoutan	1996	...	...	...	289	2.8	...
	1997	492	4.1	7.0	283	2.4	8.8
Brunei Darussalam	1987	280	...	...	253	...	...
Brunéi Darussalam	1988	296	...	...	272	...	...
	1990	253	2.5	...	229	2.3	...
Cambodia Cambodge	1996	236600	2.9	...	150300	1.8	...
China ††	1994	111800	2.4	...	100100	2.1	...
Chine ††	1995	130700	2.3	...	115200	2.0	...
	1996	155600	2.3	...	136100	2.0	...
China, Hong Kong SAR †	1992	22190	2.8	17.4	20350	2.6	...
Chine, Hong Kong RAS †	1993	25010	2.8	17.0	...	...	...
	1995	31400	2.9	...	29850	2.8	...
China, Macao SAR †	1990	444	...	10.7	...	...	...
Chine, Macao RAS †	1991	602	...	10.4	...	...	...
	1992	601	...	8.9	...	...	...
Cyprus [5]	1993	139	4.2	13.5	127	3.9	13.8
Chypre [5]	1994	156	4.4	13.8	143	4.0	14.1
	1995	173	4.5	13.2	158	4.1	13.7
Georgia Géorgie	1994	69	5.2	6.9	57	4.3	7.5
India	1994	336700	3.5	11.8	333400	3.5	...
Inde	1995	365600	3.3	11.6	361800	3.3	12.7
	1996	401400	3.2	...	...	...	...
Indonesia [3]	1994	5241000	1.4	7.5	2263000	0.6	5.3
Indonésie [3]	1995	6052000	1.4	7.8	2786000	0.6	5.9
	1996	7139000	1.4	7.9	3280000	0.6	5.8
Iran (Islamic Rep. of)	1993	4979000	5.4	22.8	4069000	4.4	26.4
Iran (Rép. islamique d')	1994	5839000	4.7	18.1	4793000	3.8	22.7
	1995	7292000	4.0	17.8	6044000	3.3	21.6
Iraq	1988	690	5.1	...	625	4.6	...
Iraq	1991	804	...	...	711	...	...
	1992	902	...	...	896	...	...
Israel [7]	1992	10850	6.8	11.8	9932	6.3	12.6
Israël [7]	# 1993	12810	7.0	12.3	11690	6.4	13.0
	1994	16740	7.6	...	15300	6.9	...
Japan [7]	# 1992	16980000	3.6	10.4	...	...	...
Japon [7]	1993	18010000	3.8	10.8	...	...	...
	1994	17380000	3.6	9.9	...	...	...
Jordan	1994	311	7.7	19.6	240	5.9	...
Jordanie	1995	393	8.7	21.4	275	6.1	...
	1996	369	7.9	19.8	298	6.4	...
Kazakhstan	1995	45830	4.6	17.6	45790	4.6	18.2
Kazakhstan	1996	65770	4.7	...	64480	4.6	...
	1997	73130	4.4	...	...	...	...
Korea, Republic of [7]	1993	11760000	4.4	16.0	9345000	3.5	17.7
Corée, République de [7]	# 1994	11240000	3.7	17.4	...	...	...
	1995	12830000	3.7	17.5	...	...	...
Kuwait	1995	484	5.2	11.7	...	...	...
Koweït	1996	526	4.8	13.5	...	...	...
	1997	556	5.0	14.0	...	...	...
Kyrgyzstan	1994	731	6.2	25.6	697	5.9	25.2
Kirghizistan	1995	1065	6.7	23.1	1030	6.5	24.2
	1996	1223	5.3	23.5	1173	5.1	24.1
Lao People's Dem. Rep.	1995	32580	2.3	...	27750	2.0	...
Rep. dém. pop. lao	1996	41930	2.5	10.3	35510	2.1	17.8
	1997	46890	2.1	8.7	40220	1.8	16.0

10
Public expenditure on education: total and current, [cont.]
percentage of GNP and government expenditure
Dépenses publiques afférentes à l'éducation: totales et ordinaires, [suite]
pourcentage par rapport au PNB et aux dépenses du gouvernement

Country or area Pays ou zone	Year Année	Total expenditure on education Dépenses totales d'éducation			Current expenditure on education Dépenses ordinaires d'éducation		
		In national currency (millions) En monnaie nationale (millions)	As % of GNP En % du PNB	As % of total government expenditure En % des dépenses totales du gouvernement	In national currency (millions) En monnaie nationale (millions)	As % of GNP En % du PNB	As % of current government expenditure En % des dépenses ordinaires du gouvernement
Lebanon [2] Liban [2]	1994	316700	2.0	7.5	240100	1.5	...
	1995	491500	2.6	8.7	...	...	...
	1996	526700	2.5	8.2	...	...	...
Malaysia Malaysie	1995	9735	4.7	...	7901	3.8	...
	1996	12470	5.2	15.4	10130	4.3	...
	1997	13020	4.9	...	10780	4.1	...
Maldives Maldives	1992	220	11.9	16.0	...	...	...
	1993	183	8.4	13.6	132	6.1	18.0
	1995	190	6.4	10.5	145	4.9	16.5
Mongolia Mongolie	1995	25330	6.0	17.0	...	...	...
	1996	33670	6.4	15.9	...	...	...
	1997	44080	5.7	15.1	...	...	...
Myanmar [2] Myanmar [2]	1988	1318	1.7	...	1139	1.5	...
	1989	2948	2.4	...	2699	2.2	...
	1994	5685	1.2	14.4	4436	0.9	19.0
Nepal Népal	1995	7230	3.3	14.0	4729	2.2	...
	1996	7759	3.1	13.5	5079	2.0	...
	1997	8945	3.2	...	...	...	...
Oman Oman	1995	183	4.5	16.7	164	4.1	19.8
	1996	189	...	18.9	178	...	20.8
	1997	204	...	16.4	191	...	22.1
Pakistan Pakistan	1995	52640	2.8	7.1	45130	2.4	7.1
	1996	64430	3.0	8.1	51800	2.4	7.6
	1997	65620	2.7	7.1	56510	2.3	7.1
Philippines Philippines	1995	57980	3.0	15.6	49320	2.5	...
	1996	73040	3.2	17.6	63110	2.8	...
	1997	86470	3.4	15.7	73470	2.9	17.4
Qatar Qatar	1992	957	3.3	...	896	3.1	...
	1993	976	3.6	...	891	3.3	...
	1994	889	3.4	...	816	3.1	...
Saudi Arabia Arabie saoudite	1995	26540	5.4	17.7	25340	5.2	...
	1996	27210	5.1	17.0	25400	4.8	...
	1997	41260	7.5	22.8	39330	7.2	...
Singapore Singapour	1993	2903	3.1	23.1	2210	2.4	24.2
	1994	3319	3.0	23.5	2486	2.3	25.6
	1995	3633	3.0	23.3	2760	2.3	25.4
Sri Lanka Sri Lanka	1994	18260	3.2	9.4	15310	2.7	13.2
	1995	20080	3.0	8.1	16130	2.4	11.5
	1996	26060	3.4	8.9	21610	2.9	11.6
Syrian Arab Republic Rép. arabe syrienne	1995[1]	18180	3.3	11.2	...	...	...
	1996	25560	4.2	13.6	...	...	...
	1997[1]	21160	3.1	...	...	...	...
Tajikistan Tadjikistan	1993	600	8.6	17.8	542	7.8	18.8
	1995	1524	2.4	16.1	1452	2.3	18.5
	1996	6639	2.2	11.5	6294	2.0	12.1
Thailand Thaïlande	1994	135400	3.8	18.9	108500	3.0	21.1
	1995	169600	4.1	20.1	133300	3.3	25.8
	1996	215600	4.8	...	162100	3.6	...
Turkey [7] Turquie [7]	# 1993	66700000	3.3	...	62940000	3.2	...
	1994	132500000	3.4	14.7	123600000	3.2	...
	1995	174700000	2.2	...	...	...	...
Turkmenistan Turkménistan	1989	1	4.2	27.1	...	...	...
	1990	1	4.3	21.0	...	...	...
	1991	1	3.9	19.7	...	...	...
United Arab Emirates Emirats arabes unis	1995	2927	1.8	16.3	2702	1.7	15.9
	1996	3045	1.6	16.7	2806	1.5	16.1
	1997	3206	1.7	20.3	2990	1.6	19.6
Uzbekistan Ouzbékistan	1994	5390	8.3	24.9	5162	8.0	...
	1995	22460	7.4	22.8	20790	6.9	...
	1996	42870	7.7	21.1	41350	7.4	...

10
Public expenditure on education: total and current, [*cont.*]
percentage of GNP and government expenditure
Dépenses publiques afférentes à l'éducation: totales et ordinaires, [*suite*]
pourcentage par rapport au PNB et aux dépenses du gouvernement

Country or area Pays ou zone	Year Année	Total expenditure on education Dépenses totales d'éducation			Current expenditure on education Dépenses ordinaires d'éducation		
		In national currency (millions) En monnaie nationale (millions)	As % of GNP En % du PNB	As % of total government expenditure En % des dépenses totales du gouvernement	In national currency (millions) En monnaie nationale (millions)	As % of GNP En % du PNB	As % of current government expenditure En % des dépenses ordinaires du gouvernement
Viet Nam	1995	6535000	3.0	...	6180000	2.8	...
Viet Nam	1996	7422000	2.9	...	6935000	2.7	...
	1997	8719000	3.0	...	8100000	2.8	...
Yemen	1995	23030	5.4	...	21800	5.1	...
Yémen	1996	37260	6.3	...	33510	5.7	...
	1997	46110	7.0	...	36940	5.6	...
Europe · Europe							
Albania	1989	937	...	...	...	...	...
Albanie	1990	984	5.8	...	...	...	...
	1994	5893	3.1	...	5353	2.8	...
Austria [7]	# 1993	115800	5.5	...	102200	4.8	...
Autriche [7]	1995	131300	5.6	10.6	120000	5.2	...
	1996	131500	5.4	10.4	120000	5.0	...
Belarus	1994	1228000	7.0	17.3	1020000	5.8	...
Bélarus	1995	6631000	5.6	17.1	6333000	5.3	...
	1996	10870000	5.9	17.8	9905000	5.4	18.5
Belgium [7]	# 1994	439600	5.6	10.4	435600	5.6	...
Belgique [7]	1995[6]	251600	3.1	5.8	246000	3.0	...
	1996[6]	261400	3.1	6.0	256000	3.0	...
Bulgaria	1994	24000	4.7	...	22620	4.4	...
Bulgarie	1995	33520	3.9	...	31480	3.7	...
	1996	53420	3.2	7.0	51010	3.0	6.9
Croatia	1992	105	4.1	...	...	...	...
Croatie	1994	4246	5.0	...	...	...	...
	1995	4972	5.3	...	...	...	...
Czech Republic [7]	# 1994	64050	5.6	13.8	57370	5.0	...
Rép. tchèque [7]	1995	72110	5.4	13.6	63540	4.7	...
	1996	77650	5.1	...	67070	4.4	...
Denmark [7]	# 1994	74210	7.8	12.5	69790	7.4	...
Danemark [7]	1995	77440	7.7	13.1	72990	7.3	...
	1996	85790	8.1	...	80710	7.7	...
Estonia	1995	2871	7.0	25.5	2545	6.2	26.7
Estonie	1996	3811	7.3	22.4	3327	6.3	22.5
	1997	4536	7.2	25.5	4008	6.4	26.2
Finland [7]	# 1994	37040	7.6	11.9	34980	7.1	...
Finlande [7]	1995	39950	7.5	12.2	37760	7.1	...
	1996	41680	7.5	12.2	38920	7.0	...
France [7]	# 1994	435500	5.9	10.8	397900	5.4	...
France [7]	1995	462800	6.1	11.1	421100	5.5	...
	1996	472900	6.0	10.9	436500	5.6	...
Germany [7]	# 1994	155300	4.7	9.4	140600	4.2	...
Allemagne [7]	1995	164300	4.8	8.4	149200	4.3	...
	1996	169000	4.8	9.6	153500	4.4	...
Gibraltar	1982	6	7.9	...	4	5.8	...
Gibraltar	1983	5	6.0	...	5	5.6	...
	1984	5	6.0	...	...	...	...
Greece [7]	# 1994	585200	2.4	7.0	...	...	...
Grèce [7]	1995	780600	2.9	8.2	...	...	...
	1996	918800	3.1	...	...	...	...
Hungary [7]	1994	278300	6.6	6.9	262900	6.2	7.9
Hongrie [7]	# 1995	282900	5.2	...	263100	4.9	...
	1996	308700	4.6	...	284000	4.3	...
Iceland [7]	# 1994	21250	5.0	12.0	18680	4.4	...
Islande [7]	1995	22030	5.0	12.3	19650	4.5	...
	1996	25770	5.4	13.6	22580	4.8	...
Ireland [7]	# 1994	1981	6.3	13.3	1880	6.0	...
Irlande [7]	1995	2101	6.0	13.5	1998	5.7	...
	1996	2252	6.0	...	2140	5.7	...

10
Public expenditure on education: total and current, [*cont.*]
percentage of GNP and government expenditure
Dépenses publiques afférentes à l'éducation: totales et ordinaires, [*suite*]
pourcentage par rapport au PNB et aux dépenses du gouvernement

Country or area Pays ou zone	Year Année	Total expenditure on education Dépenses totales d'éducation			Current expenditure on education Dépenses ordinaires d'éducation		
		In national currency (millions) En monnaie nationale (millions)	As % of GNP En % du PNB	As % of total government expenditure En % des dépenses totales du gouvernement	In national currency (millions) En monnaie nationale (millions)	As % of GNP En % du PNB	As % of current government expenditure En % des dépenses ordinaires du gouvernement
Italy [7]	# 1994	78650000	4.9	8.7	75370000	4.7	...
Italie [7]	1995	82710000	4.7	8.9	79090000	4.5	...
	1996	90150000	4.9	9.1	85900000	4.6	...
Latvia	1995	158	6.7	16.8	157	6.7	17.0
Lettonie	1996	179	6.3	14.1	173	6.1	14.3
	1997	209	6.5	16.5	...	...	...
Lithuania	1995	1350	5.6	21.8	1263	5.3	24.0
Lituanie	1996	1713	5.5	22.8	1628	5.2	24.3
	1997	2206	5.9	...	2107	5.6	...
Luxembourg [7]	1994 [2]	16590	3.1	11.5	...	...	...
Luxembourg [7]	# 1995	22500	4.1	...	20270	3.7	...
	1996	22500	4.0	...	21010	3.7	...
Malta	1994	54	5.2	11.4	50	4.9	12.3
Malte	1995	60	5.2	11.4	56	4.8	12.3
	1996	62	5.1	10.8	57	4.7	11.3
Monaco	1995	213	...	6.7	197	...	8.4
Monaco	1996	221	...	6.3	205	...	7.9
	1997	201	...	5.3	183	...	7.0
Netherlands [7]	# 1994	32180	5.2	9.4	31130	5.1	...
Pays-Bas [7]	1995	33250	5.2	8.7	32160	5.0	...
	1996	34130	5.1	9.8	32780	4.9	...
Norway [7]	# 1995	74120	8.1	16.2	67270	7.3	...
Norvège [7]	1996	75280	7.4	15.8	69340	6.9	...
	1997	83360	7.7	16.8	72770	6.8	...
Poland [7]	# 1994	11090	5.3	13.2	10430	5.0	13.5
Pologne [7]	1995	14940	5.2	16.4	...	...	...
	1996	27030	7.5	24.8	...	...	...
Portugal [7]	# 1994	773200	5.3	12.1	724100	5.0	...
Portugal [7]	1995	823600	5.3	11.7	752800	4.8	...
	1996	958300	5.8	...	889000	5.3	...
Republic of Moldova	1994	426	9.0	28.9	403	8.6	25.1
République de Moldova	1995	583	9.2	22.9	555	8.7	24.3
	1996	795	10.6	28.1	769	10.3	29.7
Romania	1993	637000	3.2	9.1	606700	3.0	9.8
Roumanie	1994 [3]	1491000	3.0	13.6	...	...	...
	1996	3882000	3.6	10.5	3592000	3.3	11.5
Russian Federation [7]	1992	679400	3.7	...	...	...	...
Fédération de Russie [7]	1993	6918000	4.1	9.6	6609000	4.0	10.0
	# 1995	55150	3.5	...	...	...	...
San Marino	1994	35990	...	...	35480	...	...
Saint-Marin	1995	38910	...	...	38260	...	...
	1996	42210	...	...	41030	...	...
Slovakia	1995	26370	5.1	...	20700	4.0	...
Slovaquie	1996	28590	5.0	...	26560	4.6	...
	1997	30372	4.7	14.6	28292	4.4	...
Slovenia	1993	83180	5.8	12.4	76590	5.4	...
Slovénie	1994	102500	5.5	12.0	92720	4.9	...
	1995	128700	5.7	12.6	120200	5.4	...
Spain [7]	# 1994	3193000	5.0	10.5	2942000	4.6	...
Espagne [7]	1995	3404000	4.9	10.6	3133000	4.5	...
	1996	3634000	5.0	11.0	3341000	4.6	...
Sweden [7]	# 1994	117200	8.0	11.0	...	...	...
Suède [7]	1995	127900	8.1	11.6	...	...	...
	1996	133800	8.3	12.2	...	...	...
Switzerland [7]	# 1994	20230	5.5	15.2	18120	4.9	...
Suisse [7]	1995	20500	5.4	15.4	18410	4.9	...
	1996	20690	5.4	15.4	18730	4.9	...
TFYR of Macedonia	1994	6970	5.2	18.3	6807	5.1	18.5
L'ex-R.y. Macédoine	1995	7618	5.0	18.7	7285	4.8	18.5
	1996	7989	5.1	20.0	7653	4.9	20.2

10
Public expenditure on education: total and current, [*cont.*]
percentage of GNP and government expenditure
Dépenses publiques afférentes à l'éducation: totales et ordinaires, [*suite*]
pourcentage par rapport au PNB et aux dépenses du gouvernement

Country or area Pays ou zone	Year Année	Total expenditure on education Dépenses totales d'éducation			Current expenditure on education Dépenses ordinaires d'éducation		
		In national currency (millions) En monnaie nationale (millions)	As % of GNP En % du PNB	As % of total government expenditure En % des dépenses totales du gouvernement	In national currency (millions) En monnaie nationale (millions)	As % of GNP En % du PNB	As % of current government expenditure En % des dépenses ordinaires du gouvernement
Ukraine	1994	84710000	7.1	...	70300000	5.9	...
Ukraine	1995	389800000	7.3	...	341200000	6.4	...
	1997	509400000	5.6	14.8	492300000	5.4	14.7
United Kingdom [7]	# 1993	34330	5.5	11.4	...	...	...
Royaume–Uni [7]	1994	36060	5.4	11.4	...	...	...
	1995	37300	5.3	11.6	...	...	...
Oceania · Océanie							
American Samoa	1981	11	8.2	16.0	11	8.1	17.9
Samoa américaines	1987	22	...	21.2	...	...	...
	1988	26	...	23.7	...	...	...
Australia [7]	# 1993	23300	5.6	13.2	22320	5.3	...
Australie [7]	1994	23900	5.4	12.9	22820	5.1	...
	1995	25920	5.5	13.5	24780	5.2	...
Cook Islands	1986	5	...	9.5	4	...	9.5
Iles Cook	1991	8	...	12.4	8	...	12.7
	1997	6	...	14.0	6	...	...
Fiji [2]	1990	94	4.7	...	93	4.7	...
Fidji [2]	1991	105	4.8	...	98	4.5	...
	1992	128	5.4	18.6	124	5.2	...
French Polynesia	1983	905	10.0	...	821	9.1	...
Polynésie française	1984	1030	9.8	...	935	8.9	...
Guam	1981	49	8.0	...	48	7.9	...
Guam	1985	60	8.5	...	59	8.3	...
Kiribati	1994	...	...	...	6	6.3	17.6
Kiribati	1995	...	...	...	9	9.9	...
	1996	...	...	...	11	11.4	...
New Caledonia	1985	1007	13.5	...	919	12.3	...
Nouvelle–Calédonie	1986	1036	13.3	...	975	12.5	...
	1987	1140	13.3	...	1073	12.5	...
New Zealand [7]	# 1994	5526	6.8	...	5270	6.5	...
Nouvelle–Zélande [7]	1995	6454	7.5	...	6045	7.1	...
	1996	6454	7.3	...	6045	6.9	...
Niue	1987	1	...	11.2	1	...	...
Nioué	1988	1	...	10.8	1	...	10.1
	1991	1	...	10.2	1	...	10.8
Norfolk Island	1980	0	...	15.1	...	...	...
Ile Norfolk	1981	1	...	19.8	1	...	21.5
	1982	0	...	14.0	...	...	...
Samoa							
Samoa	1990	15	4.2	10.7	14	4.0	15.8
Solomon Islands	1983	7	5.0	11.6	4	2.6	8.4
Iles Salomon	1984	10	4.7	12.4	4	1.9	8.0
	1991	24	3.8	7.9	...	...	...
Tonga	1985	4	4.1	16.1	...	...	...
Tonga	1986	4	4.0	...	...	...	...
	1992	9	4.7	17.3	...	...	...
Tuvalu	1989	1	...	18.5	...	...	...
Tuvalu	1990	1	...	16.2	...	...	...
Vanuatu	1991	929	4.8	18.8	...	...	...
Vanuatu	1994	1120	5.0	...	...	...	...
	1995	1179	4.8	...	...	...	...

Source:
United Nations Educational, Scientific and Cultural Organization
(UNESCO) Institute for Statistics, Paris, and the UNESCO
statistics database.

Source:
L'Institut de statistique de l'Organisation des Nations Unies pour
l'éducation, la science et la culture (UNESCO), Paris, la base de données
de l'UNESCO.

10
Public expenditure on education: total and current, [*cont.*]
percentage of GNP and government expenditure
Dépenses publiques afférentes à l'éducation: totales et ordinaires, [*suite*]
pourcentage par rapport au PNB et aux dépenses du gouvernement

† For information on recent changes in country or area
nomenclature pertaining to former Czechoslovakia, Germany,
Hong Kong Special Administrative Region (SAR) of China,
Macao Special Administrative Region (SAR) of China, SFR of
Yugoslavia, and the former USSR, see Annex I – Country or
area nomenclature, regional and other groupings.

†† For statistical purposes, the data for China do not
include those for the Hong Kong Special Administrative Region,
(Hong Kong SAR), Macao Special Administrative Region
(Macao SAR) and Taiwan province of China.

1 Not including expenditure on tertiary education.
2 Ministry of Education only.
3 Central government only.
4 For the years 1988 and 1989, data are expressed in Cruzeiros. In
  1995 data are expressed in Reais (1 Reais = 2750 Cruzeiros).
5 Expenditure of the Office of Greek Education only.
6 Flemish Community only.
7 For countries participating in the UNESCO/OECD/Eurostat
  survey there may be a break in the series due to methodological
  changes. This is indicated by a marked break in series (#).
8 In 1993, data are expressed in Pesos. For the years 1994 and
  and 1995, data are expressed in New Pesos (1 New Peso =
  1000 Pesos).

† Pour les modifications récentes de nomenclature de pays ou de zone
concernant l'Allemagne, Hong Kong région administrative spéciale (RAS)
de Chine, Macao région administrative spéciale (RAS) de Chine, l'ex–
Tchécoslovaquie, l'ex–URSS et l'ex–Rfs de Yougoslavie, voir annexe I –
Nomenclature des pays ou des zones, groupements régionaux et autres
groupements.

†† Les données statistiques relatives à la Chine ne comprennent pas celles qui
concernent la région administrative spéciale de Hong Kong (la RAS de
Hong Kong) la région spéciale de Macao (la RAS de Macao) et la province
chinoise de Taiwan.

1 Non compris les dépenses de l'enseignement supérieur.
2 Ministère de l'Education seulement.
3 Gouvernement central seulement.
4 Pour les années 1988 et 1989, les données sont exprimées en cruzeiros. Pour
  1995, les données sont exprimées en reais (1 reais = 2750 cruzeiros).
5 Les dépenses du bureau grec de l'éducation seulement.
6 Communauté flamande seulement.
7 Pour les pays qui participent à l'enquête de l'UNESCO/OCDE/Eurostat,
  peut y avoir rapture dans les séries temporelles due à des changements
  méthodologiques. Ceci est indiqué par discontinuité notable dans la série (#).
8 Pour 1993, les données sont exprimées en pesos. Pour les années 1994 et
  1995, les données sont exprimées en nouveaux pesos (1 nouveau peso =
  1000 anciens pesos).

11
Illiterate population by sex, aged 15 years and over, estimates and projections
Population analphabète selon le sexe, âgée de 15 ans et plus, estimations et projections

Country or area Pays ou zone	Year [1] Année [1]	Illiterate population (000) Population analphabète (000)			Percentage of illiterates Pourcentage d'analphabètes		
		Total	M	F	Total	M	F
Africa · Afrique							
Algeria	1985	6532	2396	4136	53.3	39.0	67.6
Algérie	1995	6567	2282	4286	38.5	26.6	50.6
	2000	6427	2187	4240	32.2	21.8	42.9
Benin	1985	1650	691	959	77.0	66.3	87.0
Bénin	1995	1843	691	1152	66.2	51.3	80.2
	2000	1972	691	1281	59.7	43.1	75.3
Botswana	1985	207	101	106	36.6	38.4	35.0
Botswana	1995	227	119	108	27.3	29.9	25.0
	2000	213	116	98	22.8	25.6	20.1
Burkina Faso	1985	3582	1602	1980	86.6	78.8	94.1
Burkina Faso	1995	4379	1906	2474	80.2	70.8	89.4
	2000	4786	2056	2730	76.1	66.1	85.9
Burundi	1985	1745	658	1087	66.4	53.2	78.2
Burundi	1995	1890	743	1147	57.0	46.8	66.4
	2000	1856	748	1108	51.7	43.4	59.3
Cameroon	1985	2481	918	1563	45.1	34.2	55.6
Cameroun	1995	2230	817	1414	30.3	22.6	37.7
	2000	2050	752	1298	24.1	17.9	30.0
Cape Verde	1985	74	21	53	42.9	29.0	52.9
Cap–Vert	1995	67	18	49	30.2	19.0	38.7
	2000	66	17	49	25.8	15.2	33.8
Central African Republic	1985	1082	414	668	72.1	58.3	84.6
Rép. centrafricaine	1995	1127	411	716	60.2	46.3	72.7
	2000	1107	398	709	53.3	40.2	65.1
Chad	1985	2266	982	1284	78.2	69.5	86.5
Tchad	1995	2362	989	1373	65.4	56.0	74.3
	2000	2391	987	1405	57.4	48.4	66.0
Comoros	1985	116	47	69	49.2	40.9	57.2
Comores	1995	145	59	86	43.3	35.7	50.6
	2000	162	67	95	40.4	33.5	47.2
Congo	1985	433	149	284	41.1	29.4	51.9
Congo	1995	354	115	238	25.6	17.3	33.2
	2000	304	95	209	19.3	12.5	25.6
Côte d'Ivoire	1985	3715	1657	2058	71.6	61.6	82.3
Côte d'Ivoire	1995	4437	1953	2484	59.6	50.7	69.3
	2000	4428	1936	2491	52.9	45.1	61.2
Democratic Republic of the Congo	1985	10022	3658	6364	59.4	44.9	72.9
Rép. dém. du Congo	1995	10898	3794	7103	45.4	32.4	57.7
	2000	10301	3506	6795	38.6	26.9	49.8
Djibouti	1985	117	41	76	53.3	38.2	67.6
Djibouti	1995	146	50	96	41.1	28.8	52.8
	2000	131	43	88	35.4	24.4	45.6
Egypt	1985	17082	6504	10579	56.8	43.0	70.8
Egypte	1995	18771	7070	11701	48.8	36.5	61.4
	2000	19747	7436	12311	44.6	33.3	56.1
Equatorial Guinea	1985	61	16	45	33.3	18.2	47.6
Guinée équatoriale	1995	51	12	39	22.2	10.5	32.9
	2000	43	9	33	16.8	7.5	25.6
Eritrea	1985	880	344	536	58.1	46.2	69.7
Erythrée	1995	867	322	545	48.9	37.0	60.5
	2000	952	345	607	44.3	32.7	55.5
Ethiopia	1985	17259	7679	9580	76.3	68.0	84.6
Ethiopie	1995	20108	9107	11002	67.0	60.3	73.8
	2000	20741	9541	11199	61.6	56.4	66.8
Gambia	1985	335	152	182	79.5	73.8	84.8
Gambie	1995	451	199	252	69.0	62.0	75.7
	2000	494	213	280	63.4	56.0	70.6
Ghana	1985	3451	1248	2203	48.9	36.0	61.4
Ghana	1995	3395	1176	2219	34.9	24.5	45.0
	2000	3271	1114	2157	28.5	19.7	37.1

11
Illiterate population by sex, aged 15 and over,
estimates and projections [*cont.*]
Population analphabète selon le sexe, âgée de 15 ans et plus,
estimations et projections [*suite*]

Country or area Pays ou zone	Year [1] Année [1]	Illiterate population (000) Population analphabète (000)			Percentage of illiterates Pourcentage d'analphabètes		
		Total	M	F	Total	M	F
Guinea–Bissau	1985	398	154	244	76.3	60.6	91.2
Guinée–Bissau	1995	415	142	273	66.7	47.0	85.3
	2000	426	137	289	61.2	40.3	81.0
Kenya	1985	3587	1185	2401	36.1	24.1	48.0
Kenya	1995	3366	1072	2295	22.9	14.7	31.1
	2000	3011	947	2064	17.6	11.1	24.0
Lesotho	1985	225	163	62	25.2	38.5	13.2
Lesotho	1995	221	172	49	19.2	31.0	8.2
	2000	216	173	43	16.7	27.6	6.4
Liberia	1985	795	309	486	66.5	51.3	81.9
Libéria	1995	509	181	328	54.4	38.2	71.1
	2000	838	274	564	46.0	29.9	62.3
Libyan Arab Jamahiriya	1985	793	247	546	39.1	22.4	58.9
Jamahiriya arabe libyenne	1995	738	194	544	25.4	12.7	39.6
	2000	697	167	530	19.9	9.2	31.7
Madagascar	1985	2718	1070	1648	47.2	38.1	55.8
Madagascar	1995	2904	1126	1778	37.7	29.9	45.2
	2000	2966	1151	1815	33.5	26.4	40.3
Malawi	1985	1986	615	1371	51.8	33.7	68.2
Malawi	1995	2249	700	1549	44.1	28.4	58.8
	2000	2301	720	1582	39.9	25.5	53.5
Mali	1985	3413	1508	1905	80.8	74.2	87.0
Mali	1995	3514	1510	2005	66.8	59.2	74.0
	2000	3534	1501	2033	58.6	51.1	65.6
Mauritania	1985	643	263	379	66.4	55.9	76.3
Mauritanie	1995	784	316	468	60.6	50.0	70.8
	2000	872	350	522	57.7	47.2	67.9
Mauritius	1985	159	58	100	22.8	16.9	28.5
Maurice	1995	142	54	88	17.6	13.5	21.6
	2000	134	52	81	15.4	12.1	18.6
Morocco	1985	8422	3286	5136	66.5	52.6	80.1
Maroc	1995	9456	3542	5914	56.0	42.3	69.5
	2000	9770	3615	6155	51.1	38.1	63.9
Mozambique	1985	5425	2080	3346	71.1	56.0	85.5
Mozambique	1995	5902	2119	3783	61.5	45.3	76.9
	2000	6067	2112	3955	56.0	39.9	71.3
Namibia	1985	195	83	112	29.2	25.5	32.7
Namibie	1995	192	87	105	21.5	19.8	23.1
	2000	181	86	96	18.0	17.2	18.8
Niger	1985	3152	1431	1721	90.4	84.4	96.2
Niger	1995	4086	1828	2258	86.5	79.3	93.4
	2000	4674	2074	2600	84.1	76.2	91.6
Nigeria	1985	24325	9559	14766	59.2	47.6	70.4
Nigéria	1995	23902	9080	14823	43.6	33.8	53.1
	2000	22886	8602	14283	36.1	27.6	44.2
Réunion	1985	78	41	37	21.1	23.2	19.2
Réunion	1995	67	37	30	14.4	16.5	12.5
	2000	61	34	27	12.1	14.0	10.3
Rwanda	1985	1662	648	1014	53.4	42.5	63.9
Rwanda	1995	1108	425	682	39.8	31.4	47.9
	2000	1403	545	858	33.2	26.4	39.8
Senegal	1985	2618	1134	1484	75.5	65.8	85.1
Sénégal	1995	3062	1289	1774	67.2	57.2	77.0
	2000	3284	1364	1920	62.6	52.7	72.3
South Africa	1985	3991	1855	2136	21.1	19.9	22.3
Afrique du Sud	1995	3982	1843	2139	16.7	15.8	17.5
	2000	3865	1787	2079	14.7	14.0	15.4

11
Illiterate population by sex, aged 15 and over,
estimates and projections [cont.]
Population analphabète selon le sexe, âgée de 15 ans et plus,
estimations et projections [suite]

Country or area Pays ou zone	Year [1] Année [1]	Illiterate population (000) Population analphabète (000)			Percentage of illiterates Pourcentage d'analphabètes		
		Total	M	F	Total	M	F
Sudan Soudan	1985	7163	2661	4502	59.6	44.3	75.1
	1995	7407	2664	4743	48.0	34.7	61.2
	2000	7504	2686	4818	42.0	30.2	53.7
Swaziland Swaziland	1985	115	48	67	33.9	31.5	35.8
	1995	117	51	66	24.0	22.5	25.3
	2000	117	52	66	20.4	19.3	21.4
Togo Togo	1985	990	340	650	59.3	41.7	76.1
	1995	1060	329	731	48.4	30.7	65.4
	2000	1068	313	755	42.7	25.5	59.2
Tunisia Tunisie	1985	2101	758	1343	47.4	34.0	61.0
	1995	2085	712	1373	35.3	24.0	46.7
	2000	1936	623	1312	29.0	18.6	39.4
Uganda Ouganda	1985	3778	1318	2460	49.2	35.0	62.9
	1995	3660	1240	2420	38.2	26.3	49.8
	2000	3575	1203	2372	32.9	22.4	43.1
United Rep.Tanzania Rép.– Unie de Tanzanie	1985	4934	1569	3365	42.9	27.9	57.0
	1995	4838	1498	3340	30.0	19.0	40.5
	2000	4434	1368	3065	24.2	15.3	32.9
Zambia Zambie	1985	1188	385	803	36.7	25.0	47.5
	1995	1135	366	769	26.8	18.0	34.9
	2000	1060	348	711	21.9	14.8	28.6
Zimbabwe Zimbabwe	1985	1096	386	710	24.3	17.3	31.0
	1995	937	308	629	15.2	10.2	20.1
	2000	775	243	531	11.3	7.2	15.3
America, North · Amérique du Nord							
Bahamas Bahamas	1985	9	5	4	5.9	6.5	5.4
	1995	9	5	4	4.7	5.4	4.1
	2000	9	5	4	4.3	5.0	3.6
Belize Belize	1985	12	5	7	13.6	12.3	15.0
	1995	11	5	6	8.4	7.7	9.1
	2000	10	5	5	6.8	6.7	6.8
Costa Rica Costa Rica	1985	118	58	59	7.1	6.9	7.2
	1995	120	61	60	5.2	5.2	5.2
	2000	119	61	58	4.4	4.4	4.3
Cuba Cuba	1985	446	222	224	6.0	6.0	6.0
	1995	344	168	176	4.0	4.0	4.1
	2000	290	139	151	3.3	3.2	3.4
Dominican Republic Rép. dominicaine	1985	898	444	455	23.1	22.5	23.8
	1995	935	471	464	18.4	18.2	18.6
	2000	933	475	458	16.4	16.4	16.4
El Salvador El Salvador	1985	830	343	487	30.9	26.6	34.8
	1995	851	352	499	24.0	20.7	27.0
	2000	856	356	500	21.2	18.3	23.8
Guatemala Guatemala	1985	1780	727	1053	42.8	34.8	51.0
	1995	1911	745	1165	34.9	27.2	42.6
	2000	2006	762	1244	31.2	23.8	38.7
Haiti Haïti	1985	2262	1030	1231	64.9	61.6	67.9
	1995	2373	1086	1287	55.2	52.7	57.6
	2000	2444	1123	1321	50.2	48.0	52.1
Honduras Honduras	1985	783	377	406	34.8	33.6	36.0
	1995	901	447	454	28.3	28.1	28.6
	2000	962	485	477	25.4	25.6	25.2
Jamaica Jamaïque	1985	300	175	124	20.6	24.7	16.7
	1995	253	157	96	15.3	19.5	11.3
	2000	235	150	85	13.2	17.1	9.3
Martinique Martinique	1985	14	8	7	5.7	6.4	5.1
	1995	10	6	4	3.5	4.0	2.9
	2000	8	4	3	2.6	3.0	2.2
Mexico Mexique	1985	6424	2453	3971	14.8	11.5	17.9
	1995	6016	2267	3749	10.2	7.9	12.5
	2000	5728	2145	3584	8.7	6.7	10.6

11
Illiterate population by sex, aged 15 and over,
estimates and projections [cont.]
Population analphabète selon le sexe, âgée de 15 ans et plus,
estimations et projections [suite]

Country or area Pays ou zone	Year [1] Année [1]	Illiterate population (000) Population analphabète (000)			Percentage of illiterates Pourcentage d'analphabètes		
		Total	M	F	Total	M	F
Netherlands Antilles	1985	6	3	3	5.0	4.9	5.0
Antilles néerlandaises	1995	6	3	3	3.9	3.9	3.9
	2000	6	3	3	3.5	3.5	3.5
Nicaragua	1985	660	329	331	36.9	37.4	36.5
Nicaragua	1995	808	410	398	33.2	34.5	32.0
	2000	913	470	443	31.4	33.1	29.8
Panama	1985	174	83	91	12.9	12.1	13.6
Panama	1995	165	77	88	9.4	8.7	10.1
	2000	158	73	85	8.1	7.5	8.7
Puerto Rico	1985	232	109	124	9.8	9.5	10.0
Porto Rico	1995	202	98	105	7.3	7.4	7.2
	2000	184	90	94	6.3	6.5	6.1
Trinidad and Tobago	1985	77	25	51	9.8	6.5	13.1
Trinité−et−Tobago	1995	64	22	42	7.3	5.1	9.5
	2000	61	21	39	6.2	4.5	7.9
America, South · Amérique du Sud							
Argentina	1985	1027	471	556	4.9	4.6	5.2
Argentine	1995	904	427	477	3.7	3.6	3.7
	2000	846	407	439	3.2	3.1	3.2
Bolivia	1985	892	270	623	26.2	16.3	35.6
Bolivie	1995	780	218	562	17.7	10.1	24.9
	2000	723	195	528	14.4	7.9	20.6
Brazil	1985	18502	8583	9918	21.6	20.3	22.9
Brésil	1995	18211	8773	9438	16.8	16.5	17.0
	2000	17859	8781	9078	14.8	14.9	14.6
Chile	1985	582	262	320	7.0	6.5	7.5
Chili	1995	508	234	273	5.1	4.8	5.3
	2000	465	217	247	4.3	4.1	4.5
Colombia	1985	2618	1227	1391	13.3	12.7	13.9
Colombie	1995	2445	1174	1272	9.7	9.5	9.8
	2000	2336	1140	1195	8.2	8.2	8.2
Ecuador	1985	815	327	488	15.2	12.2	18.2
Equateur	1995	765	305	460	10.5	8.4	12.6
	2000	730	290	440	8.7	6.9	10.5
Guyana	1985	20	6	13	3.9	2.6	5.1
Guyana	1995	12	4	8	2.1	1.4	2.8
	2000	9	3	6	1.5	1.1	1.9
Paraguay	1985	243	93	150	11.6	8.9	14.3
Paraguay	1995	228	93	135	8.1	6.6	9.6
	2000	223	94	130	6.7	5.6	7.8
Peru	1985	2006	561	1445	17.2	9.7	24.7
Pérou	1995	1822	483	1339	12.1	6.5	17.4
	2000	1719	447	1272	10.1	5.3	14.6
Uruguay	1985	92	49	43	4.2	4.7	3.7
Uruguay	1995	66	36	29	2.7	3.2	2.3
	2000	56	32	24	2.2	2.6	1.8
Venezuela	1985	1376	608	768	13.2	11.6	14.8
Venezuela	1995	1255	573	682	9.0	8.2	9.8
	2000	1174	550	625	7.4	6.9	7.8
Asia · Asie							
Afghanistan	1985	6570	2811	3759	77.8	64.6	91.7
Afghanistan	1995	7885	3172	4712	67.8	53.1	83.2
	2000	8012	3152	4860	62.7	48.1	78.1
Armenia	1985	75	15	60	3.2	1.3	5.0
Arménie	1995	51	11	40	2.0	0.9	3.0
	2000	42	9	33	1.6	0.7	2.4
Bahrain	1985	65	29	36	23.2	16.7	33.6
Bahreïn	1995	57	25	31	14.7	10.8	20.6
	2000	54	23	31	12.4	9.0	17.4
Bangladesh	1985	36377	15556	20821	68.0	56.5	80.1
Bangladesh	1995	44046	18453	25593	61.9	50.7	73.5
	2000	49142	20464	28678	58.6	47.7	70.1

11
Illiterate population by sex, aged 15 and over,
estimates and projections [*cont.*]
Population analphabète selon le sexe, âgée de 15 ans et plus,
estimations et projections [*suite*]

Country or area Pays ou zone	Year [1] Année [1]	Illiterate population (000) Population analphabète (000)			Percentage of illiterates Pourcentage d'analphabètes		
		Total	M	F	Total	M	F
Brunei Darussalam	1985	27	9	18	19.1	11.9	27.1
Brunéi Darussalam	1995	21	7	14	10.9	6.9	15.4
	2000	19	6	12	8.5	5.4	11.9
China ††	1985	209520	66109	143411	28.1	17.2	39.6
Chine ††	1995	172484	49178	123306	19.2	10.7	28.1
	2000	152111	40818	111292	15.8	8.3	23.7
China, Hong Kong SAR †	1985	508	114	394	12.2	5.3	19.5
Chine, Hong Kong RAS †	1995	409	105	303	8.2	4.1	12.6
	2000	370	105	265	6.5	3.5	9.8
Cyprus	1985	36	7	29	7.5	3.0	11.8
Chypre	1995	23	5	18	4.1	1.7	6.5
	2000	18	4	14	2.9	1.3	4.5
India	1985	262937	103368	159570	54.8	41.7	68.8
Inde	1995	281887	108449	173439	46.7	34.8	59.4
	2000	289106	110334	178772	42.8	31.6	54.6
Indonesia	1985	25885	8412	17473	25.2	16.7	33.5
Indonésie	1995	21599	6760	14839	16.3	10.3	22.2
	2000	19241	5912	13330	13.1	8.1	17.9
Iran (Islamic Rep. of)	1985	11208	4392	6816	43.2	33.6	53.0
Iran (Rép. islamique d')	1995	10525	3888	6638	29.2	21.4	37.1
	2000	10028	3592	6436	23.2	16.5	30.1
Iraq	1985	5048	2030	3018	60.2	47.8	72.9
Iraq	1995	5676	2247	3429	49.4	38.6	60.5
	2000	5982	2365	3617	44.1	34.4	54.1
Israel	1985	218	59	159	7.6	4.2	10.9
Israël	1995	197	51	146	5.0	2.7	7.2
	2000	180	46	134	4.0	2.1	5.8
Jordan	1985	545	162	382	24.9	14.2	36.7
Jordanie	1995	442	120	323	13.6	7.1	20.7
	2000	396	104	293	10.2	5.2	15.7
Korea, Republic of	1985	1565	317	1248	5.5	2.2	8.7
Corée, République de	1995	1049	201	848	3.0	1.2	4.9
	2000	822	157	664	2.2	0.9	3.6
Kuwait	1985	290	149	141	26.7	22.8	32.7
Koweït	1995	209	93	117	20.3	17.2	23.6
	2000	228	108	120	17.4	15.4	19.7
Lao People's Dem. Rep.	1985	1427	548	879	69.3	53.2	85.4
Rép. dém. pop. lao	1995	1535	550	985	57.8	41.5	74.0
	2000	1563	547	1016	51.3	35.9	66.8
Lebanon	1985	395	114	281	23.7	14.5	31.8
Liban	1995	330	91	239	16.7	9.6	23.1
	2000	309	83	226	14.0	7.9	19.6
Malaysia	1985	2259	765	1494	23.5	16.0	31.0
Malaisie	1995	2003	685	1318	15.6	10.6	20.6
	2000	1835	633	1202	12.5	8.6	16.5
Maldives	1985	7	4	4	7.5	7.1	7.9
Maldives	1995	6	3	3	4.8	4.7	4.9
	2000	6	3	3	3.6	3.7	3.6
Myanmar	1985	4957	1518	3438	21.7	13.6	29.6
Myanmar	1995	5008	1704	3303	17.1	11.8	22.3
	2000	5027	1797	3230	15.3	11.0	19.4
Nepal	1985	6851	2728	4123	73.2	57.1	89.9
Népal	1995	7823	2813	5011	64.1	46.6	81.4
	2000	8257	2882	5376	58.5	40.8	76.1
Oman	1985	426	178	248	54.5	40.1	73.5
Oman	1995	424	167	256	36.3	25.8	49.5
	2000	401	154	247	28.2	19.8	38.4
Pakistan	1985	39391	16614	22777	68.2	54.9	82.8
Pakistan	1995	45916	18283	27633	58.8	44.8	74.1
	2000	49109	18983	30126	53.9	40.1	68.9

11
Illiterate population by sex, aged 15 and over,
estimates and projections [cont.]
Population analphabète selon le sexe, âgée de 15 ans et plus,
estimations et projections [suite]

Country or area Pays ou zone	Year [1] Année [1]	Illiterate population (000) Population analphabète (000)			Percentage of illiterates Pourcentage d'analphabètes		
		Total	M	F	Total	M	F
Philippines	1985	2918	1335	1583	9.0	8.3	9.8
Philippines	1995	2508	1185	1323	6.0	5.6	6.3
	2000	2249	1083	1166	4.7	4.5	4.8
Qatar	1985	66	46	20	25.6	24.5	28.6
Qatar	1995	83	60	22	20.8	21.0	20.1
	2000	83	61	22	18.8	19.6	16.9
Saudi Arabia	1985	2853	1167	1685	39.5	27.0	58.3
Arabie saoudite	1995	2971	1216	1755	27.8	19.2	40.3
	2000	2951	1187	1764	23.0	15.9	32.8
Singapore	1985	293	73	220	14.3	7.0	21.7
Singapour	1995	237	58	180	9.2	4.5	13.9
	2000	212	51	161	7.6	3.7	11.6
Sri Lanka	1985	1356	424	932	12.9	8.0	17.8
Sri Lanka	1995	1229	391	837	9.7	6.3	13.0
	2000	1161	379	782	8.3	5.6	11.0
Syrian Arab Republic	1985	2182	610	1572	40.5	22.4	59.2
Rép. arabe syrienne	1995	2358	576	1782	30.1	14.6	45.8
	2000	2439	563	1876	25.5	11.7	39.5
Tajikistan	1985	74	16	58	2.8	1.3	4.3
Tadjikistan	1995	40	9	31	1.2	0.6	1.8
	2000	30	8	22	0.8	0.4	1.2
Thailand	1985	3194	958	2236	9.7	5.9	13.5
Thaïlande	1995	2469	760	1708	5.8	3.6	8.0
	2000	2057	646	1411	4.5	2.8	6.1
Turkey	1985	8309	2241	6067	25.9	13.6	39.1
Turquie	1995	7602	1763	5839	18.0	8.3	27.9
	2000	7095	1557	5538	14.9	6.5	23.4
United Arab Emirates	1985	355	245	109	31.8	30.7	34.6
Emirats arabes unis	1995	418	298	120	27.1	27.7	25.7
	2000	428	309	118	24.4	25.9	21.1
Uzbekistan	1985	2231	699	1533	20.6	13.3	27.5
Ouzbékistan	1995	1846	551	1295	13.6	8.3	18.7
	2000	1681	491	1189	11.1	6.6	15.3
Viet Nam	1985	3961	1018	2942	11.1	6.1	15.7
Viet Nam	1995	3708	1113	2595	7.9	5.0	10.7
	2000	3532	1154	2378	6.6	4.5	8.6
Yemen	1985	3645	1196	2449	74.1	53.4	91.5
Yémen	1995	4724	1483	3241	59.9	37.9	81.6
	2000	5027	1519	3508	53.7	32.5	74.8
Europe · Europe							
Albania	1985	548	170	378	28.3	17.1	40.1
Albanie	1995	411	114	297	18.8	10.3	27.7
	2000	336	88	248	15.3	7.9	23.0
Belarus	1985	74	13	60	1.0	0.4	1.4
Bélarus	1995	45	11	34	0.5	0.3	0.8
	2000	35	10	25	0.4	0.3	0.6
Bulgaria	1985	261	75	186	3.7	2.2	5.2
Bulgarie	1995	147	45	102	2.1	1.3	2.9
	2000	109	34	75	1.6	1.0	2.1
Croatia	1985	150	21	128	4.2	1.3	6.9
Croatie	1995	85	14	71	2.3	0.8	3.7
	2000	64	12	52	1.7	0.7	2.7
Greece	1985	524	110	414	6.7	2.9	10.3
Grèce	1995	320	77	243	3.7	1.8	5.4
	2000	248	65	184	2.7	1.5	4.0
Hungary	1985	97	36	62	1.2	0.9	1.4
Hongrie	1995	65	24	41	0.8	0.6	0.9
	2000	56	21	36	0.7	0.5	0.8
Italy	1985	1326	459	866	2.9	2.1	3.6
Italie	1995	892	311	581	1.8	1.3	2.3
	2000	764	264	500	1.6	1.1	2.0
Latvia	1985	4	2	2	0.2	0.2	0.2
Lettonie	1995	4	2	2	0.2	0.2	0.2
	2000	4	2	2	0.2	0.2	0.2

11
Illiterate population by sex, aged 15 and over,
estimates and projections [cont.]
Population analphabète selon le sexe, âgée de 15 ans et plus,
estimations et projections [suite]

Country or area Pays ou zone	Year [1] Année [1]	Illiterate population (000) Population analphabète (000)			Percentage of illiterates Pourcentage d'analphabètes		
		Total	M	F	Total	M	F
Lithuania	1985	24	7	16	0.9	0.6	1.1
Lituanie	1995	16	6	10	0.5	0.4	0.7
	2000	13	5	8	0.4	0.3	0.5
Malta	1985	36	17	19	13.8	13.9	13.7
Malte	1995	28	14	13	9.5	10.1	8.9
	2000	25	13	12	7.9	8.6	7.2
Poland	1985	171	62	109	0.6	0.5	0.8
Pologne	1995	96	42	54	0.3	0.3	0.4
	2000	84	38	46	0.3	0.3	0.3
Portugal	1985	1178	397	781	15.5	11.0	19.5
Portugal	1995	806	264	542	9.9	6.8	12.7
	2000	636	203	433	7.7	5.2	10.0
Republic of Moldova	1985	113	19	94	3.7	1.3	5.7
République de Moldova	1995	55	10	46	1.7	0.6	2.7
	2000	38	7	31	1.1	0.5	1.7
Romania	1985	645	142	503	3.8	1.7	5.7
Roumanie	1995	437	103	334	2.4	1.2	3.6
	2000	347	87	261	1.9	1.0	2.8
Russian Federation	1985	1059	228	831	1.0	0.5	1.4
Fédération de Russie	1995	699	178	521	0.6	0.3	0.8
	2000	539	159	379	0.4	0.3	0.6
Slovenia	1985	7	3	4	0.5	0.4	0.6
Slovénie	1995	6	3	4	0.4	0.4	0.4
	2000	6	3	3	0.4	0.3	0.4
Spain	1985	1372	383	989	4.6	2.7	6.5
Espagne	1995	969	282	687	2.9	1.8	4.0
	2000	790	235	556	2.3	1.4	3.2
Ukraine	1985	286	59	228	0.7	0.3	1.0
Ukraine	1995	196	51	145	0.5	0.3	0.6
	2000	163	47	115	0.4	0.3	0.5
Oceania · Océanie							
Fiji	1985	60	23	37	13.9	10.4	17.4
Fidji	1995	45	16	28	9.0	6.5	11.5
	2000	40	14	25	7.1	5.1	9.2
Papua New Guinea	1985	946	409	538	47.3	39.0	56.4
Papouasie – Nvl – Guinée	1995	1031	437	594	39.7	32.4	47.5
	2000	1065	448	618	36.1	29.4	43.2
Samoa	1985	23	11	12	26.5	24.5	28.6
Samoa	1995	22	11	11	22.1	20.9	23.5
	2000	22	11	11	19.8	18.8	21.0

Source:
United Nations Educational, Scientific and Cultural Organization
(UNESCO) Institute for Statistics, Paris, the UNESCO statistics
database.

† For information on the recent changes in country or area
nomenclature pertaining to former Czechoslovakia,
Germany, Hong Kong Special Administrative Region (SAR)
of China, Macao Special Administrative Region (SAR) of
China, SFR of Yugoslavia and the former USSR, see
Annex I – Country or area nomenclature, regional and
other groupings.

†† For statistical purposes the data for China do not include
those for Hong Kong Special Administrative Region
(Hong Kong SAR), Macao Special Administrative
Region (Macao SAR) and Taiwan province of China.

1 Estimates and projections of UNESCO, as assessed in 1999 based
on statistics collected during national population censuses.

Source:
L'Institut de statistique de l'Organisation des Nations Unies pour
l'education, la science et la culture (UNESCO), Paris, la base de
données de l'UNESCO.

† Pour les modifications récentes de nomenclature de pays ou de
zone concernant l'Allemagne, Hong Kong, région administrative
spéciale (RAS) de Chine, Macao, région administrative spéciale
(RAS) de Chine, l'ex–Tchécoslovaquie, l'ex–URSS et l'ex–Rfs de
Yougoslavie, voir annexe I – Nomenclature des pays ou des zones,
groupements régionaux et autres groupements.

†† Les données statistiques relatives à la Chine ne comprennent pas
celles qui concernent la région administrative spéciale de Hong
Kong (la RAS de Hong Kong), la région administrative spéciale de
Macao (la RAS de Macao) et la province chinoise de Taiwan.

1 Estimations et projections de l'UNESCO, révisées en 1999 et
basées sur les données collectées au cours des recensements
nationaux de la population.

Technical notes, tables 9-11

Detailed data on education and literacy accompanied by explanatory notes can be found in the *UNESCO Statistical Yearbook* [29]. Brief notes which pertain to the statistical information shown in the tables in this chapter are given below.

Table 9: The definitions and classifications applied by UNESCO are those set out in the *Revised Recommendation concerning the International Standardization of Education Statistics* (1978) and the1976 and 1997 versions of the *International Standard Classification of Education* (ISCED). The data reported for the years prior to 1997 follow the criteria of the 1976 version of the ISCED; beginning 1997, the data are based on the criteria of the revised version of the ISCED (ISCED-97). Data are presented in Table 9 according to the revised terminology of the ISCED-97, in which the terms "primary", "secondary", and "tertiary" education replace the old terms "first", "second", and "third" level.

According to the ISCED, these three levels are defined as follows:

Primary education (ISCED level 1), of which the main function is to provide the basic elements of education at such establishments as elementary schools or primary schools.

Secondary education (ISCED levels 2 and 3), providing general and/or specialized instruction at middle schools, secondary schools, high schools, teaching training schools and schools of a vocational or technical nature.

Tertiary education (ISCED levels 5, 6 and 7) provided at universities, teachers' colleges, and higher professional schools, which requires, as a minimum condition of admission, the successful completion of secondary education or evidence of the attainment of an equivalent level of knowledge.

The ISCED-97 also introduces a new category or level between upper secondary and tertiary education called post-secondary non-tertiary education (ISCED level 4). Beginning 1997, this level is included in secondary education in Table 9 for those countries footnoted accordingly. It is assumed that the programmes which countries now report separately to UNESCO as post-secondary non-tertiary have also been reported in the past, in either secondary or tertiary education depending on the country. These programmes typically fall into two categories: (a) second cycle programmes at upper secondary and (b) access or foundation programmmes for entry to tertiary programmes. Countries with type (a) programmes will typically have reported them in the past as secondary programmes whilst countries with type (b) programmes will more often have reported them

Notes techniques, tableaux 9 à 11

On trouvera des données détaillées sur l'instruction, assorties de notes explicatives, dans l'*Annuaire statistique de l'UNESCO* [29]. Ci-après figurent des notes sommaires, relatives aux principaux éléments d'information statistique figurant dans les tableaux.

Tableau 9: Les définitions et classifications appliquées par l'UNESCO sont tirées de la *Recommandation révisée concernant la normalisation internationale des statistiques de l'éducation* (1978) et des versions de 1976 et de 1997 de la *Classification internationale type de l'éducation* (CITE). Les chiffres des années antérieures à 1997 sont calculés selon les critères de la version de 1976; à compter de 1997, ils suivent les critères de la version révisée (CITE-1997). La terminologie utilisée dans le tableau 9 est celle de la CITE-1997, où les termes "enseignement primaire", "secondaire" et "supérieur" remplacent les anciennes appellations "premier degré", "second degré" et "troisième degré".

Dans la CITE, ces trois niveaux sont définis comme suit:

Enseignement primaire (niveau 1 de la CITE), dispensé par exemple dans les écoles élémentaires ou les écoles primaires, et dont la fonction principale est de fournir un enseignement de base.

Enseignement secondaire (niveaux 2 et 3 de la CITE), dispensé par exemple dans les écoles moyennes, les écoles secondaires, les lycées, les collèges, les écoles de formation des maîtres et les écoles professionnelles ou techniques.

Enseignement supérieur (niveaux 5, 6 et 7 de la CITE), dispensé par exemple dans les universités, les établissements d'enseignement pédagogique et d'enseignement spécialisé, exigeant comme condition minimale d'admission d'avoir achevé avec succès des études secondaires ou de faire preuve de connaissances équivalentes.

La CITE de 1997 introduit également une catégorie nouvelle, à savoir un niveau intermédiaire entre le deuxième cycle de l'enseignement secondaire et l'enseignement supérieur, appelé "enseignement post secondaire qui n'est pas du supérieur" (niveau 4 de la CITE). À compter de 1997, dans le tableau 9, pour les pays marqués d'une note à cet effet, ce niveau est inclus dans l'enseignement secondaire. On suppose que les programmes que les pays signalent désormais à l'UNESCO comme programmes d'enseignement post secondaire qui n'est pas du supérieur l'étaient par le passé comme programmes d'enseignement soit secondaire soit supérieur selon le pays. Ils relèvent généralement de l'une ou l'autre des deux catégories suivan-

as tertiary in the past. Some countries will have both types of programmes.

In general, the statistics shown in Table 9 refer to both public and private education. Since 1994, special needs education is, in principle, included in the statistics reported.

Table 10: Data on total expenditure on education refer to public expenditure on public education plus subsidies for private education. Total expenditures cover both current and capital expenditure.

Current expenditures include expenditures on administration, emoluments of teachers and supporting teaching staff, school books and other teaching materials, scholarships, welfare services and maintenance of school buildings.

Capital expenditures include outlays on purchases of land, building construction expenditures and so forth; loan transactions are also included.

Data include, unless otherwise indicated, educational expenditure at every level of administration. In general, the data do not include development assistance expenditures on education. Data on gross national product (GNP) used to derive the ratio of total public expenditure on education to GNP are World Bank estimates.

Table 11: Data on the illiterate population by sex refer to the population 15 years of age and over. The ability to both read and write a simple sentence on everyday life is used as the criterion of literacy; hence semi-literates (persons who can read but not write) are included with illiterates. Persons for whom literacy is not known are excluded from calculations; consequently the percentage of illiteracy for a given country is based on the number of reported illiterates, divided by the total number of reported literates and illiterates.

The data are the latest illiteracy estimates and projections of UNESCO, as assessed in 1999 based on statistics collected during national population censuses.

tes: (a) programmes de deuxième cycle du secondaire, et (b) cours de base ou de transition préparant à l'enseignement supérieur. Les pays où ces programmes relèvent du type (a) les auront normalement inclus dans l'enseignement secondaire avant 1997, les pays où ils relèvent du type (b) les auront souvent inclus dans l'enseignement supérieur. Dans certains pays, il y a des programmes de niveau 4 relevant de l'un et de l'autre type.

En règle générale, les statistiques du tableau 9 portent sur l'enseignement public et privé. Depuis 1994, l'éducation répondant à des besoins spéciaux est en principe incluse dans les statistiques communiquées par les pays.

Tableau 10: Les données relatives aux dépenses totales d'éducation se rapportent aux dépenses publiques consacrées à l'enseignement public et aux subventions à l'enseignement privé. Les totaux englobent à la fois les dépenses ordinaires et les dépenses d'équipement.

Les dépenses ordinaires comprennent les dépenses d'administration, les émoluments du personnel enseignant et auxiliaire, les manuels scolaires et autres matériels didactiques, les bourses d'études, les services sociaux et l'entretien des bâtiments scolaires.

Les dépenses d'équipement comprennent les dépenses consacrées à l'achat de terrains, à la construction de bâtiments, etc.; les transactions de prêt sont également incluses.

Sauf indication contraire, les données comprennent les dépenses effectuées à tous les niveaux administratifs. En règle générale, elles ne comprennent pas les dépenses d'enseignement financées au titre de l'aide au développement. Les données relatives au produit national brut (PNB), utilisées pour déterminer le ratio du volume total de dépenses publiques consacrées à l'éducation au PNB, sont des estimations de la Banque mondiale.

Tableau 11: Les données sur la population analphabète selon le sexe se réfèrent à la population âgée de 15 ans et plus. On utilise l'aptitude à lire et à écrire une phrase simple sur la vie quotidienne comme critère d'alphabétisme; par conséquent, les semi-alphabètes (c'est-à-dire les personnes qui savent lire, mais non écrire) sont assimilés aux analphabètes. Les personnes dont on ne sait pas si elles savent lire ou écrire sont exclues de ces calculs; par conséquent, le pourcentage d'analphabétisme d'un pays donné est fondé sur le nombre d'analphabètes connus divisé par le total des alphabètes et analphabètes connus.

Les données sont les dernières estimations et projections de l'UNESCO sur l'analphabétisme, révisées en 1999 et basées sur les données collectées au cours des recensements nationaux de la population.

12
Estimates of cumulative HIV/AIDS infections and AIDS deaths, and reported AIDS cases
Chiffres estimatifs du nombre cumulé de personnes infectées par le VIH ou le SIDA et de décès dus au SIDA, et cas déclarés de SIDA

A. Estimated cumulative HIV/AIDS infections, AIDS deaths and people newly infected with HIV in 2000
Chiffres estimatifs cumulés du nombre de personnes infectées par le VIH ou le SIDA, et de décès dus au SIDA et nouveaux cas d'infection à VIH en 2000

	Number of cases (millions) Nombre de cas (millions)		
	Total	M	F
Cumulative HIV/AIDS infections **Cumulé de personnes infectées par le VIH**	36.1	...	...
Adults Adultes	34.7	18.3	16.4
Children Enfants	1.4	...	...
Cumulative AIDS deaths **Cumulé de décès dus au SIDA**	21.8	...	...
Adults Adultes	17.5	8.5	9.0
Children Enfants	4.3	...	...
Aids deaths in 2000 **Décès dus au SIDA en 2000**	3.0	...	...
Adults Adultes	2.5	1.2	1.3
Children Enfants	0.5	...	...
People newly infected with HIV in 2000 **Nouveaux cas d'infection à VIH en 2000**	5.3	...	...
Adults Adultes	4.7	2.5	2.2
Children Enfants	0.6	...	...

B. Reported AIDS cases to the World Health Organization
Cas de SIDA déclarés à l'Organisation mondiale de la santé

Regions Régions	Total reported cases to 1990 Nombre total de cas déclarés jusqu' au 1990	New cases reported in: / Nombre de cas nouveaux déclarés en:								Cumulative total Nombre total cumulé
		1991	1992	1993	1994	1995	1996	1997	1998	
World **Monde**	464371	183469	212720	224012	227244	246914	232972	219341	197870	2214182[1]
Africa Afrique	155531	80782	81396	84210	79914	94624	84854	85865	95702	843061[1]
North America Amérique du Nord	227603	68374	88679	88989	82336	79254	69631	59824	44786	809952[1]
South America Amérique du Sud	30621	14617	18606	20652	23716	24275	25621	22176	10858	192139[1]
Asia Asie	1946	848	2056	6777	14501	21843	27304	31693	31685	141355[1]
Europe Europe	45670	17924	21119	22435	25724	26008	24739	19230	14269	218029[1]
Oceania Océanie	3000	924	864	949	1053	910	823	553	570	9646[1]

12 C. Reported AIDS cases • Cas de SIDA déclarés

Country or area Pays ou zone	Total reported cases to 1990 Nombre total de cas déclarés jusqu' au 1990	1991	1992	1993	1994	1995	1996	1997	1998	1999
		New cases reported in:/ Nombre de cas nouveaux déclarés en:								
Africa • Afrique										
Algeria Algérie	65	35	34	31	53	32	48	39	49	24
Angola Angola	291	130	147	135	157	321	329	416	507	...
Benin Bénin	134	113	218	277	324	214	503	1030	...	...
Botswana Botswana	167	270	534	876	575	1172	1368	2224	2992	...
Burkina Faso Burkina Faso	978	835	1073	836	1892	1684	1838	2216	2166	...
Burundi Burundi	3615	1565	1583	799	443	1358	2239	3510	4092	4395
Cameroon Cameroun	317	604	1308	1385	1761	2766	1485	3950	5410	...
Cape Verde Cap–Vert	63	15	15	18	16	24	36	39	43	12
Central African Rep. Rép. centrafricaine	2474	840	636	290	50	649	2077	...	...	...
Chad Tchad	59	165	363	1010	1268	1132	1242	2748	2030	1282
Comoros Comores	2	1	3	4	3	2	0	3	2	...
Congo Congo	7425	3482	5267	6473	7773	10223	...	...	...	...
Côte d'Ivoire Côte d'Ivoire	6896	3894	3863	4015	6566	6727	5935	5949	5685	6427
Dem. Rep. of the Congo Rép. dém. du Congo	16519	4482	2070	4215	1707	4689	5159	4948	3746	22
Djibouti Djibouti	58	107	144	144	196	231	358	434	111	...
Egypt Egypte	27	12	23	29	22	16	14	25	33	34
Equatorial Guinea Guinée équatoriale	...	...	...	24	16	98	74	...	189	...
Eritrea Erythrée	74	76	219	300	625	727	896	1260	1610	1086
Ethiopia Ethiopie	742	897	3256	5132	6927	3793	832	7981	8314	...
Gabon Gabon	117	98	178	128	204	334	601	0	...	...
Gambia Gambie	124	56	56	38	53	32	78	84	126	...
Ghana Ghana	5144	2442	2699	2391	2330	2578	3295	3833	4854	7752
Guinea Guinée	221	220	236	328	543	610	922	1005	1222	...
Guinea–Bissau Guinée–Bissau	142	30	118	165	254	77	37	217	...	120
Kenya Kenya	16150	9554	11569	12204	8588	9133	6844	4885	2565	...
Lesotho Lesotho	23	29	139	166	238	341	936	2203	3242	...
Liberia Libéria	5	14	8	4	12	67	18	104	40	...
Libyan Arab Jamah. Jamah. arabe libyenne	5	2	3	2	3	2	3	7	5	...
Madagascar Madagascar	0	0	0	0	9	6	1	6	2	...
Malawi Malawi	14861	7439	4655	4916	4732	5209	5406	3705	...	...
Mali Mali	476	377	460	672	609	454	594	711	620	290
Mauritania Mauritanie	30	15	18	94	56	103	98	...	...	...

12 C. Reported AIDS cases [*cont.*] · Cas de SIDA déclarés [*suite*]

Country or area Pays ou zone	Total reported cases to 1990 Nombre total de cas déclarés jusqu' au 1990	New cases reported in:/ Nombre de cas nouveaux déclarés en:								
		1991	1992	1993	1994	1995	1996	1997	1998	1999
Mauritius Maurice	5	5	5	3	7	7	5	6	1	7
Morocco Maroc	70	28	30	44	77	57	66	92	93	...
Mozambique Mozambique	162	178	322	164	534	1380	2086	1661	4376	3952
Namibia Namibie	...	...	430	355	452	1836	2687	3797	5158	4726
Niger Niger	293	212	304	453	467	621	652	217	425	940
Nigeria Nigéria	222	129	412	719	908	2829	838	745	18490	984
Réunion Réunion	59	13	16	25	23	30	0	0	...	...
Rwanda Rwanda	4489	2089	2908	1220	0	0	3847	1350	...	...
Sao Tome and Principe Sao Tomé−et−Principe	4	5	2	2	1	4	6	11	25	10
Senegal Sénégal	425	127	96	263	534	396	141	411	151	144
Seychelles Seychelles	...	0	1	3	3	6	6	5	5	8
Sierra Leone Sierra Leone	34	17	37	23	22	29	62	67	26	...
Somalia Somalie	13	...	...	...	...	...	...	...	...	...
South Africa Afrique du Sud	734	549	887	1882	3816	4219	738	...	...	...
Sudan Soudan	320	188	184	191	201	257	221	270	511	392
Swaziland Swaziland	30	31	216	165	120	154	613	1466	733	...
Togo Togo	650	628	824	1330	1284	1710	1527	1211	1623	998
Tunisia Tunisie	98	36	38	52	50	65	54	62	44	42
Uganda Ouganda	19955	10235	6362	4641	4927	2192	3032	1962	1406	...
United Rep. Tanzania Rép. Unie de Tanzanie	25503	18692	15871	13506	5873	4722	8426	10592	8867	...
Zambia Zambie	19267	5264	3376	2894	1963	5950	4552	1676	...	...
Zimbabwe Zimbabwe	5994	4557	8180	9174	10647	13356	12029	6732	4113	...
America, North · Amérique du Nord										
Anguilla Anguilla	5	0	0	0	0	0	0	0	...	...
Antigua and Barbuda Antigua−et−Barbuda	13	6	14	18	16	7	13	7	2	7
Aruba Aruba	10	1	3	1	0	6	1	2	...	...
Bahamas Bahamas	608	230	254	297	322	390	374	389	234	...
Barbados Barbade	172	80	78	88	119	95	130	113	168	...
Belize Belize	45	15	13	24	18	28	38	0	...	...
Bermuda Bermudes	156	23	17	15	44	48	17	13	5	6
British Virgin Islands Iles Vierges britanniques	3	1	1	2	1	3	1	3	1	0
Canada Canada	6195	1548	1717	1749	1706	1572	1050	661	552	325
Cayman Islands Iles Caïmanes	7	4	4	0	3	0	3	1	2	...

12 C. Reported AIDS cases [*cont.*] · Cas de SIDA déclarés [*suite*]

Country or area Pays ou zone	Total reported cases to 1990 Nombre total de cas déclarés jusqu' au 1990	1991	1992	1993	1994	1995	1996	1997	1998	1999
Costa Rica Costa Rica	238	93	127	128	164	212	204	233	162	19
Cuba Cuba	71	37	71	82	102	116	99	128	140	...
Dominica Dominique	12	0	0	14	6	5	14	19	12	5
Dominican Republic Rép. dominicaine	1516	315	388	403	423	492	427	392	320	...
El Salvador El Salvador	183	132	132	155	387	380	417	409	146	...
Grenada Grenade	24	7	4	21	7	18	18	4	...	...
Guadeloupe Guadeloupe	183	128	81	77	104	106	73	38	...	...
Guatemala Guatemala	181	96	94	178	110	141	835	649	397	730
Haiti Haïti	3669	492	806	0	0	0	0	3932	...	...
Honduras Honduras	1209	515	851	1183	1058	1138	978	929		
Jamaica Jamaïque	199	134	100	236	359	505	527	370	320	225
Martinique Martinique	157	36	44	44	49	41	42	23		...
Mexico Mexique	11012	3625	3988	3950	4129	4106	3810	3550	3498	1094
Montserrat Montserrat	4	2	0	1	0	0	0	0	1	...
Netherlands Antilles Antilles néerlandaises	77	23	10	47	0	76	0	0	...	...
Nicaragua Nicaragua	16	13	10	24	38	21	25	18	10	2
Panama Panama	272	89	117	220	192	215	252	341	195	49
Saint Kitts and Nevis Saint–Kitts–et–Nevis	30	1	4	3	5	5	6	4	...	...
Saint Lucia Sainte–Lucie	27	6	8	12	13	10	14	15	6	...
St. Vincent and the Grenadines St. Vincent–et–Grenadines	27	14	5	8	8	6	19	24	28	...
Trinidad and Tobago Trinité–et–Tobago	736	234	257	243	269	340	412	118		...
Turks and Caicos Islands Iles Turques et Caïques	19	2	4	14	0	0	0	0	...	...
United States Etats–Unis	200525	60472	79477	79752	72684	69172	59832	47439	38587	25434
America, South · Amérique du Sud										
Argentina Argentine	1146	738	1128	1469	2172	2162	2520	2058	1492	259
Bolivia Bolivie	30	17	19	21	19	15	28	21	9	...
Brazil Brésil	23652	11374	14345	16096	17504	18383	19222	17187	7564	...
Chile Chili	360	177	200	247	315	350	421	522	395	163
Colombia Colombie	1941	863	934	740	1361	910	1095	589	...	...
Ecuador Equateur	143	55	69	90	117	69	67	128	134	...
French Guiana Guyane française	212	59	73	52	70	78	62	35	...	...
Guyana Guyana	145	85	160	107	105	96	144	115	96	...
Paraguay Paraguay	52	19	28	45	24	23	54	96	34	...

12 C. Reported AIDS cases [*cont.*] • Cas de SIDA déclarés [*suite*]

Country or area Pays ou zone	Total reported cases to 1990 Nombre total de cas déclarés jusqu' au 1990	New cases reported in:/ Nombre de cas nouveaux déclarés en:								
		1991	1992	1993	1994	1995	1996	1997	1998	1999
Peru Pérou	942	398	646	669	789	1070	1183	1058	954	310
Suriname Suriname	90	16	28	35	20	20	2	0	...	...
Uruguay Uruguay	159	86	90	103	119	127	156	173	180	...
Venezuela Venezuela	1749	730	886	978	1101	972	667	194	...	...
Asia · Asie										
Armenia Arménie	3	0	0	0	0	0	7	2	2	8
Azerbaijan Azerbaïdjan	...	0	0	0	1	1	2	5	3	8
Bahrain Bahreïn	4	0	6	3	6	10	11	14	11	9
Bangladesh Bangladesh	1	0	0	0	0	6	0	3	0	...
Bhutan Bhoutan	0	0	0	0	0	0	...	...	...	...
Brunei Darussalam Brunéi Darussalam	2	0	0	1	2	4	2	2	0	1
Cambodia Cambodge	906	...	...	1	14	91	300	572	1494	2256
China †† Chine ††	5	3	5	23	29	52	38	126	136	230
China, Hong Kong SAR † Chine, Hong Kong RAS †	46	14	14	19	37	45	70	64	63	53
China, Macao SAR † Chine, Macao RAS †	1	1	2	2	2	0	1	2	4	2
Cyprus Chypre	25	7	2	7	11	5	18	10	6	6
Georgia Géorgie	4	1	4	0	2	3	2	6	2	7
India Inde	57	45	140	252	523	1091	888	2108	1148	...
Indonesia Indonésie	12	12	10	17	16	20	32	34	74	38
Iran (Islamic Rep. of) Iran (Rép. islamique d')	19	25	16	32	19	16	27	40	21	...
Iraq Iraq	0	7	6	21	37	16	15	2	4	...
Israel Israël	135	28	46	47	32	45	67	45	36	137
Japan Japon	91	38	51	86	136	169	234	250	231	300
Jordan Jordanie	12	8	7	8	6	2	4	12	11	3
Kazakhstan Kazakhstan	...	0	0	1	0	3	3	8	9	1
Korea, Dem.People's Rep. Corée, Rép. pop. dém. de	0	0	0	0	0	0	0	0	...	...
Korea, Republic of Corée, République de	7	1	2	6	11	14	22	33	35	34
Kuwait Koweït	3	3	2	2	5	4	5	2	19	1
Kyrgyzstan Kirghizistan	14	1	0	0	0	2	2	2	6	...
Lao People's Dem. Rep. Rép. dém. populaire lao	0	1	0	5	4	4	16	48	27	...
Lebanon Liban	27	13	7	22	12	18	5	8	35	...
Malaysia Malaisie	22	60	73	71	105	233	347	568	875	1200
Maldives Maldives	0	0	0	0	1	1	2	1	0	...

12 C. Reported AIDS cases [*cont.*] • Cas de SIDA déclarés [*suite*]

Country or area Pays ou zone	Total reported cases to 1990 Nombre total de cas déclarés jusqu' au 1990	New cases reported in:/ Nombre de cas nouveaux déclarés en:							
		1991	1992	1993	1994	1995	1996	1997	1998	1999
Mongolia Mongolie	...	...	...	...	...	...	...	...	...	1
Myanmar Myanmar	0	6	41	142	286	618	690	554	231	...
Nepal Népal	4	5	5	10	11	15	32	101	42	...
Occupied Palestinian Terr. Terr. palestinien occupé	5	1	6	1	3	3	1	9	3	1
Oman Oman	91	25	32	37	51	28	24	36	33	10
Pakistan Pakistan	30	16	18	16	9	20	19	19	23	3
Philippines Philippines	72	13	19	36	56	52	52	23	42	77
Qatar Qatar	52	10	3	7	6	4	2	4	1	4
Saudi Arabia Arabie saoudite	34	10	6	12	38	37	100	112	39	26
Singapore Singapour	23	12	18	22	48	56	92	88	125	140
Sri Lanka Sri Lanka	9	3	10	11	14	11	11	9	15	...
Syrian Arab Republic Rép. arabe syrienne	13	7	3	3	4	6	9	8	8	7
Thailand Thaïlande	165	453	1466	5713	12807	18890	23664	26000	25847	13601
Turkey Turquie	43	18	28	29	34	35	34	33	34	38
Turkmenistan Turkménistan	...	0	1	0	0	0	0	0	...	...
United Arab Emirates Emirats arabes unis	8	1	3	1	2	1	2	1	1	2
Uzbekistan Ouzbékistan	...	0	1	1	0	0	2	1	2	0
Viet Nam Viet Nam	...	...	...	106	118	201	390	688	953	639
Yemen Yémen	1	0	3	4	3	11	60	40	34	...
Europe • Europe										
Albania Albanie	0	0	0	0	2	5	1	2	1	0
Austria Autriche	515	175	199	210	188	214	142	130	110	86
Belarus Bélarus	0	2	6	2	2	3	0	2	4	5
Belgium Belgique	822	227	250	224	237	236	217	136	166	84
Bosnia & Herzegovina Bosnie–Herzégovine	1	0	0	2	3	4	3	5	4	3
Bulgaria Bulgarie	10	2	6	6	10	1	10	8	3	11
Croatia Croatie	28	11	8	13	16	16	16	12	17	15
Czech Republic République tchèque	21	2	9	15	12	13	18	21	8	16
Denmark Danemark	716	209	194	236	249	229	161	108	71	73
Estonia Estonie	...	0	1	1	1	4	7	3	4	2
Finland Finlande	72	24	23	24	46	37	25	17	20	10
France France	13146	4565	5141	5583	5798	5486	4840	2836	2026	...
Germany Allemagne	5129	1708	1638	1849	1868	1784	1638	1413	922	575

12 C. Reported AIDS cases [*cont.*] • Cas de SIDA déclarés [*suite*]

Country or area Pays ou zone	Total reported cases to 1990 Nombre total de cas déclarés jusqu' au 1990	New cases reported in:/ Nombre de cas nouveaux déclarés en:								
		1991	1992	1993	1994	1995	1996	1997	1998	1999
Greece Grèce	404	139	148	160	123	309	215	237	143	137
Hungary Hongrie	48	30	33	35	23	31	45	32	35	38
Iceland Islande	16	5	4	6	4	3	3	2	2	5
Ireland Irlande	178	61	69	75	62	54	79	31	41	41
Italy Italie	7300	3371	4147	4533	5440	6062	5378	3782	2484	2200
Latvia Lettonie	2	1	1	3	2	0	8	3	11	17
Lithuania Lituanie	2	1	1	1	2	0	4	3	8	6
Luxembourg Luxembourg	33	12	12	20	13	15	12	10	10	5
Malta Malte	15	7	4	3	5	3	4	2	4	0
Monaco Monaco	5	2	10	7	9	4	2	1	0	0
Netherlands Pays–Bas	1521	422	533	435	461	468	448	342	291	234
Norway Norvège	194	57	54	62	74	70	50	38	39	25
Poland Pologne	50	35	40	42	94	120	96	117	132	113
Portugal Portugal	572	232	386	452	580	698	861	919	888	970
Republic of Moldova République de Moldova	2	0	0	2	0	2	1	10	4	5
Romania Roumanie	1166	539	535	410	507	684	644	650	648	306
Russian Federation Fédération de Russie	32	16	54	21	27	39	57	13	98	43
San Marino Saint–Marin	0	0	0	0	0	0	4	4	4	2
Slovakia Slovaquie	3	0	1	3	4	2	0	5	3	2
Slovenia Slovénie	12	7	4	7	6	14	10	1	14	9
Spain Espagne	7351	3904	5273	5477	7071	6757	6935	6064	4197	3462
Sweden Suède	508	137	126	175	181	198	156	77	63	73
Switzerland Suisse	1608	612	643	672	711	736	543	565	426	264
TFYR Macedonia L'ex–R.y. Macédonie	2	0	4	5	8	2	1	1	3	5
Ukraine Ukraine	4	4	4	10	10	35	159	193	287	571
United Kingdom Royaume–Uni	4063	1350	1471	1600	1773	1571	1854	1379	964	788
Yugoslavia Yougoslavie	119	55	87	54	102	99	92	56	114	57
Oceania · Océanie										
American Samoa Samoa américaines	0	0	0	0	0	0	0	0	0	0
Australia Australie	2625	804	788	844	954	805	658	371	301	154
Fiji Fidji	3	1	1	1	2	0	0	0	0	0
French Polynesia Polynésie française	50	4	3	5	1	4	2	2	2	0
Guam Guam	8	4	2	5	11	2	10	5	7	8

12 C. Reported AIDS cases [*cont.*] · Cas de SIDA déclarés [*suite*]

Country or area Pays ou zone	Total reported cases to 1990 Nombre total de cas déclarés jusqu' au 1990	New cases reported in:/ Nombre de cas nouveaux déclarés en:								
		1991	1992	1993	1994	1995	1996	1997	1998	1999
Kiribati Kiribati	0	2	0	0	0	0	1	2	4	5
Marshall Islands Iles Marshall	2	...	...	...	...	...	...	...	...	...
Micronesia (Federated States of) Micronésie (Etats fédérés de)	2	...	...	...	...	...	...	...	...	1
Nauru Nauru	0	...	...	...	...	...	...	...	...	...
New Caledonia Nouvelle–Calédonie	23	9	1	10	9	5	2	9	3	4
New Zealand Nouvelle–Zélande	247	78	50	70	44	49	76	43	29	33
Niue Nioué	0	...	...	...	...	...	...	...	...	...
Northern Mariana Islands Iles Mariannes du Nord	3	1	0	0	2	0	1	1	3	2
Palau Palaos	0	...	...				...			
Papua New Guinea Papouasie–Nvl–Guinée	34	21	19	12	26	44	69	120	220	207
Samoa Samoa	1	...	...	...	2	1	2	...	...	...
Solomon Islands Iles Salomon	0	...	...	...	...	...	...	...	...	...
Tokelau Tokélaou	0	...	...	...	...	...	...	...	...	...
Tonga Tonga	2	...	...	1	2	...	2	...	1	...
Tuvalu Tuvalu	0	...	...	...	...	...	...	...	...	...
Vanuatu Vanuatu	0	...	...	...	...	...	...	...	...	...
Wallis and Futuna Islands Iles Wallis–et–Futuna	0	...	...	1	...	...	...	...	...	...

Source:
Joint United Nations Programme on HIV/AIDS (UNAIDS) and
World Health Organization (WHO), Geneva, "Aids epidemic
update: December 2000" and the UNAIDS/WHO HIV/AIDS
database.

† For information on recent changes in country or area
nomenclature pertaining to former Czechoslovakia, Germany,
Hong Kong Special Administrative Region (SAR) of China,
Macao Special Administrative Region (SAR) of China,
SFR of Yugoslavia and the former USSR, see Annex I – Country
or area nomenclature, regional and other groupings.

†† For statistical purposes, the data for China do not
include those for the Hong Kong Special Administrative
Region (Hong Kong SAR), Macao Special Administrative
Region (Hong Kong SAR) and Taiwan province of China.

1 Total includes AIDS cases with unreported year of diagnosis.

Source:
Programme commun des Nations Unies sur le VIH/SIDA (ONUSIDA)
et l'Organisation mondiale de la santé (OMS), Genève,
"Le point sur l'épidémie de SIDA: décembre 2000" et la base
de données sur le VIH et le SIDA de l'ONUSIDA/OMS.

† Pour les modifications récentes de nomenclature de pays
ou de zone concernant l'Allemagne, Hong Kong région
administrative spéciale (RAS) de Chine, Macao région administrative
spéciale (RAS) de Chine, l'ex–Tchécoslovaquie, l'ex–URSS et l'ex–
Rfs de Yougoslavie, voir annex I – Nomenclature des pays ou des
zones, groupements régionaux et autres groupments.

††Les données statistiques relatives à la Chine ne comprennent
pas celles qui concernent la région administrative spéciale de
Hong Kong (la RAS de Hong Kong), la région administrative
spéciale de Macao (la RAS de Macao) et la province chinoise
de Taiwan.

1 Y compris les cas de SIDA pour lesquels l'année de diagnostic n'a pas
été précisée.

13
Food Supply
Disponibilités alimentaires
Calories, protein and fat: per capita per day
Calories, protéine et lipides : par habitant, par jour

Country or area Pays ou zone	Calories (number) Calories (nombre)			Protein (grams) Protéine (grammes)			Fat (grams) Lipides (grammes)		
	1980−82	1986−88	1996−98	1980−82	1986−88	1996−98	1980−82	1986−88	1996−98
World **Monde**	**2561**	**2670**	**2783**	**67.4**	**70.6**	**74.6**	**60.2**	**65.8**	**72.7**
Africa · Afrique									
Algeria Algérie	2681	2776	2980	68.4	75.2	81.1	66.4	60.5	69.3
Angola Angola	2064	1845	1912	51.2	46.0	40.9	48.3	44.8	39.3
Benin Bénin	1998	2046	2538	47.8	51.1	60.5	49.9	41.0	43.6
Botswana Botswana	2116	2349	2212	66.4	70.9	70.6	47.7	52.8	59.1
Burkino Faso Burkina Faso	1688	2149	2161	50.0	64.6	63.5	33.0	46.3	48.3
Burundi Burundi	2010	2029	1635	66.8	63.4	49.6	15.8	15.2	11.0
Cameroon Cameroun	2321	2200	2186	57.7	52.4	50.6	48.7	45.5	43.7
Cape Verde Cap−Vert	2604	2969	3051	70.0	75.0	68.5	54.1	70.1	90.4
Central African Rep. Rép. centrafricaine	2290	1922	1999	35.6	37.9	43.5	64.5	62.1	63.4
Chad Tchad	1619	1648	2053	48.5	46.3	59.4	37.2	37.7	60.8
Comoros Comores	1788	1813	1849	39.3	39.3	42.2	34.1	36.3	41.9
Congo Congo	2257	2328	2168	41.9	47.2	43.3	48.4	55.0	51.3
Côte d'Ivoire Côte d'Ivoire	2836	2707	2611	59.5	56.8	50.7	53.1	52.9	54.3
Dem. Rep. of the Congo Rép. dém. du Congo	2077	2120	1752	33.9	34.3	27.8	33.4	32.6	25.4
Djibouti Djibouti	1877	1840	2064	49.0	46.9	43.4	43.9	42.3	59.9
Egypt Egypte	2991	3103	3282	74.9	81.1	89.7	67.0	63.5	55.9
Eritrea Erythrée	...	...	1645	...	...	52.9	...	...	19.8
Ethiopia Ethiopie	...	...	1845	...	...	54.1	...	...	23.0
Ethiopia including Eritrea Ethiopie y compris Erythrée	1837	1719	...	57.7	49.7	...	24.7	24.7	...
Gabon Gabon	2447	2500	2535	72.6	75.1	73.5	46.0	44.7	52.1
Gambia Gambie	1853	2506	2520	44.4	54.6	53.0	42.7	51.8	64.3
Ghana Ghana	1721	1975	2670	39.8	44.0	51.6	36.6	38.9	32.9
Guinea Guinée	2271	2092	2309	50.9	48.0	49.4	51.1	42.8	56.5
Guinea−Bissau Guinée−Bissau	2098	2365	2424	44.5	47.9	47.5	52.8	63.3	59.6
Kenya Kenya	2130	2037	1969	55.6	55.2	51.8	41.3	41.7	46.5
Lesotho Lesotho	2240	2245	2226	65.1	63.6	62.3	32.8	36.2	31.9
Liberia Libéria	2523	2381	2001	49.1	44.1	36.6	47.8	53.6	59.5
Libyan Arab Jamahirya Jamah. arabe libyenne	3457	3313	3250	91.4	81.4	80.9	111.7	104.8	101.3
Madagascar Madagascar	2428	2286	2008	58.0	54.6	47.0	34.9	31.9	30.3
Malawi Malawi	2269	2020	2171	65.8	57.8	54.7	39.4	30.8	30.4

13

Food Supply
Calories, protein and fat: per capita per day [cont.]
    Disponibilités alimentaires
    Calories, protéine et lipides : par habitant, par jour [suite]

Country or area	Calories (number) Calories (nombre)			Protein (grams) Protéine (grammes)			Fat (grams) Lipides (grammes)		
Pays ou zone	1980−82	1986−88	1996−98	1980−82	1986−88	1996−98	1980−82	1986−88	1996−98
Mali Mali	1753	1953	2153	53.0	57.1	63.7	43.3	40.3	44.6
Mauritania Mauritanie	2157	2505	2633	74.6	77.9	75.2	60.0	64.3	63.5
Mauritius Maurice	2661	2749	2939	60.0	64.0	74.2	68.4	68.9	86.2
Morocco Maroc	2779	3077	3127	73.1	83.7	83.1	52.8	60.4	62.8
Mozambique Mozambique	1883	1789	1860	32.0	32.6	35.9	32.4	36.4	32.7
Namibia Namibie	2196	2180	2126	65.4	62.4	57.7	39.5	36.5	35.1
Niger Niger	2155	2039	1937	63.6	56.3	52.6	34.9	30.1	34.0
Nigeria Nigéria	2003	2091	2758	46.1	47.9	62.3	58.4	56.8	72.1
Rwanda Rwanda	2286	2026	2030	54.0	49.3	47.0	15.1	16.0	23.0
Sao Tome and Principe Sao Tomé−et−Principe	2043	2069	2174	45.7	43.0	43.2	65.5	88.9	66.1
Senegal Sénégal	2372	2222	2293	67.6	69.5	64.6	65.0	53.4	69.1
Seychelles Seychelles	2304	2296	2462	66.5	66.0	77.8	45.6	47.3	71.5
Sierra Leone Sierra Leone	2114	1990	2047	45.1	42.0	43.6	61.6	60.4	56.4
Somalia Somalie	1973	1937	1550	62.5	62.6	50.4	72.8	67.9	56.9
South Africa Afrique du Sud	2905	2935	2942	77.0	76.0	74.5	68.7	76.1	75.1
Sudan Soudan	2229	2287	2434	65.6	66.5	77.3	75.5	67.6	75.9
Swaziland Swaziland	2492	2601	2493	64.2	65.3	60.9	45.1	47.8	50.1
Togo Togo	2165	2054	2456	48.8	49.2	59.6	31.6	36.4	48.6
Tunisia Tunisie	2843	3103	3263	77.2	85.0	88.0	74.4	82.6	89.8
Uganda Ouganda	2160	2128	2143	47.3	47.7	47.1	21.4	24.2	28.3
United Rep. Tanzania Rép. Unie de Tanzanie	2271	2261	2001	55.1	55.8	49.0	31.4	32.1	31.9
Zambia Zambie	2144	2013	1960	56.0	52.6	50.3	35.2	30.6	29.5
Zimbabwe Zimbabwe	2252	2149	2142	59.2	53.7	52.7	53.9	50.2	53.4
America, North · Amérique du Nord									
Antigua and Barbuda Antigua et Barbuda	2252	2303	2422	70.6	81.7	79.0	81.8	91.3	91.5
Bahamas Bahamas	2637	2786	2537	76.5	83.4	79.3	85.2	95.6	81.4
Barbados Barbade	3089	3168	3110	87.5	95.8	87.1	99.6	103.8	101.7
Belize Belize	2738	2528	2895	68.9	67.4	63.9	74.2	73.6	73.8
Bermuda Bermudes	3050	3103	2917	107.0	108.7	91.0	134.7	128.9	123.6
Canada Canada	2896	3048	3118	92.7	95.6	98.1	120.7	129.6	126.0
Costa Rica Costa Rica	2558	2711	2745	62.2	64.4	74.7	60.6	66.9	77.6
Cuba Cuba	3003	3088	2415	72.8	72.5	49.6	80.5	82.1	46.2
Dominica Dominique	2334	2884	3033	59.0	72.3	83.7	60.3	78.5	79.2

13

Food Supply
Calories, protein and fat: per capita per day [*cont.*]
Disponibilités alimentaires
Calories, protéine et lipides : par habitant, par jour [*suite*]

Country or area	Calories (number) Calories (nombre)			Protein (grams) Protéine (grammes)			Fat (grams) Lipides (grammes)		
Pays ou zone	1980−82	1986−88	1996−98	1980−82	1986−88	1996−98	1980−82	1986−88	1996−98
Dominican Republic Rép. dominicaine	2281	2335	2270	49.4	50.4	50.0	58.4	57.6	74.8
El Salvador El Salvador	2315	2335	2536	55.7	55.2	62.8	50.2	52.6	55.6
Grenada Grenade	2285	2530	2687	62.2	70.9	67.4	71.3	87.9	95.9
Guatemala Guatemala	2333	2390	2180	58.6	61.7	56.5	43.8	41.9	43.4
Haiti Haïti	2040	1856	1842	47.8	48.2	42.0	34.6	32.6	34.2
Honduras Honduras	2111	2216	2342	52.2	52.0	57.0	44.0	56.5	61.0
Jamaica Jamaïque	2622	2604	2663	63.5	64.3	65.1	63.4	67.4	74.6
Mexico Mexique	3207	3098	3131	86.5	81.1	84.3	83.7	84.5	88.1
Netherlands Antilles Antilles néerlandaises	3105	2652	2629	98.2	83.4	82.8	101.1	94.4	98.6
Nicaragua Nicaragua	2282	2345	2190	60.0	57.9	50.7	42.7	43.7	45.9
Panama Panama	2324	2399	2453	58.9	61.4	64.6	67.4	68.7	72.8
Saint Kitts and Nevis Saint−Kitts−et−Nevis	2256	2546	2748	63.2	67.5	76.1	68.6	86.9	94.2
Saint Lucia Sainte−Lucie	2209	2498	2828	57.5	73.3	85.7	61.8	59.3	73.0
St. Vincent and Grenadines St. Vincent−et−Grenadines	2490	2465	2544	56.4	60.3	66.6	60.7	65.4	76.1
Trinidad and Tobago Trinité−et−Tobago	3012	2927	2687	81.0	73.5	62.3	77.5	79.3	72.8
United States Etats−Unis	3173	3414	3708	98.3	106.1	113.6	129.3	139.7	143.3
America, South · Amérique du Sud									
Argentina Argentine	3175	3079	3145	104.3	99.5	99.0	114.0	108.9	113.5
Bolivia Bolivie	2115	2126	2204	55.3	55.2	56.6	53.0	48.0	57.0
Brazil Brésil	2647	2739	2960	62.2	65.6	76.7	64.8	73.8	85.7
Chile Chili	2646	2498	2818	71.1	66.4	78.7	60.5	55.9	84.4
Colombia Colombie	2320	2310	2578	49.9	50.3	61.2	48.0	52.1	65.9
Ecuador Equateur	2371	2457	2710	49.2	50.2	57.4	63.4	74.9	96.8
Guyana Guyana	2506	2439	2448	60.3	56.0	70.0	49.7	31.1	49.7
Paraguay Paraguay	2545	2550	2566	72.7	68.7	75.1	71.3	66.2	83.7
Peru Pérou	2143	2292	2392	54.7	57.3	61.1	41.9	50.5	51.0
Suriname Suriname	2400	2436	2643	62.5	60.0	64.1	51.1	47.6	62.8
Uruguay Uruguay	2815	2593	2813	85.0	80.5	86.0	102.6	90.5	103.0
Venezuela Venezuela	2732	2612	2358	70.6	64.5	59.8	78.2	78.8	65.6
Asia · Asie									
Afghanistan Afghanistan	2171	2138	1619	61.0	58.8	45.0	38.6	35.5	24.1
Armenia Arménie	...	...	2349	...	...	64.7	...	...	52.7
Azerbaijan Azerbaïdjan	...	...	2193	...	...	66.4	...	...	34.3
Bangladesh Bangladesh	1899	2025	2065	41.6	43.3	45.0	14.4	18.5	20.6

13

Food Supply
Calories, protein and fat: per capita per day [cont.]
Disponibilités alimentaires
Calories, protéine et lipides : par habitant, par jour [suite]

Country or area Pays ou zone	Calories (number) Calories (nombre)			Protein (grams) Protéine (grammes)			Fat (grams) Lipides (grammes)		
	1980–82	1986–88	1996–98	1980–82	1986–88	1996–98	1980–82	1986–88	1996–98
Brunei Darussalam Brunéi Darussalam	2674	2856	2851	75.3	86.7	84.0	57.2	74.4	83.3
Cambodia Cambodge	1765	1837	2059	40.5	44.4	47.4	14.4	20.7	33.5
China †† Chine ††	2396	2622	2935	55.9	63.1	79.9	34.4	45.9	74.5
China, Hong Kong SAR † Chine, Hong Kong RAS †	2964	3209	3201	89.3	94.4	100.7	106.5	123.0	135.9
China, Macao SAR † Chine, Macao RAS †	2811	2571	2536	82.3	72.1	67.3	98.1	97.2	113.8
Cyprus Chypre	2908	3099	3422	82.3	95.8	109.3	112.4	133.1	143.6
Georgia Géorgie	...	...	2315	...	...	66.4	...	...	37.1
India Inde	2065	2238	2474	50.5	55.1	59.4	33.9	37.9	46.3
Indonesia Indonésie	2218	2472	2883	46.9	54.2	65.9	36.4	45.9	57.3
Iran (Islamic Rep. of) Iran (Rép. islamique d')	2679	2631	2827	69.9	68.1	74.6	63.7	61.0	65.3
Iraq Iraq	2954	3414	2340	78.2	87.0	50.2	62.4	78.4	72.2
Israel Israël	3016	3116	3434	101.0	102.4	111.3	107.1	118.0	125.6
Japan Japon	2756	2874	2901	87.0	93.0	94.8	70.3	77.7	82.4
Jordan Jordanie	2691	2782	2789	70.3	76.6	72.8	65.3	73.4	81.1
Kazakhstan Kazakhstan	...	...	2861	...	...	90.2	...	...	64.8
Korea, Dem. People's Rep. Corée, Rép. pop. dém. de	2426	2505	1864	74.9	79.9	54.9	37.2	43.5	32.2
Korea, Republic of Corée, République de	2969	3092	3115	82.0	83.8	84.5	42.8	54.9	78.2
Kuwait Koweït	3010	3026	3053	92.1	90.8	95.8	91.7	97.9	92.5
Kyrgyzstan Kirghizistan	...	...	2487	...	...	83.0	...	...	49.8
Lao People's Dem. Rep. Rép. dém. populaire lao	2093	2055	2117	51.2	49.7	52.5	23.0	21.8	25.9
Lebanon Liban	2788	3056	3269	78.0	78.1	84.6	87.2	95.9	104.8
Malaysia Malaisie	2719	2634	2885	57.9	59.1	74.2	80.5	88.0	81.8
Maldives Maldives	2221	2256	2474	69.6	85.4	92.9	32.1	40.7	49.6
Mongolia Mongolie	2374	2281	1961	78.0	74.8	72.0	83.2	75.8	70.4
Myanmar Myanmar	2388	2705	2832	61.3	69.2	72.2	37.4	46.4	45.2
Nepal Népal	1922	2139	2189	51.5	55.6	56.9	26.8	28.3	30.2
Pakistan Pakistan	2147	2175	2427	51.8	51.6	61.4	44.6	57.4	62.1
Philippines Philippines	2250	2223	2392	52.3	51.7	57.1	35.4	34.8	46.1
Saudi Arabia Arabie saoudite	2885	2560	2855	75.4	72.6	77.4	79.3	78.6	74.4
Sri Lanka Sri Lanka	2292	2268	2299	46.2	47.7	51.3	45.8	42.9	46.2
Syrian Arab Republic Rép. arabe syrienne	3111	3159	3354	84.6	85.1	86.7	88.6	85.3	94.1
Tajikistan Tadjikistan	...	...	2159	...	...	55.8	...	...	44.8
Thailand Thaïlande	2224	2196	2439	48.9	49.2	56.8	33.2	39.3	50.5
Turkey Turquie	3328	3496	3499	97.4	101.7	97.7	83.0	90.7	98.5

13
Food Supply
Calories, protein and fat: per capita per day [*cont.*]
Disponibilités alimentaires
Calories, protéine et lipides : par habitant, par jour [*suite*]

Country or area Pays ou zone	Calories (number) Calories (nombre)			Protein (grams) Protéine (grammes)			Fat (grams) Lipides (grammes)		
	1980–82	1986–88	1996–98	1980–82	1986–88	1996–98	1980–82	1986–88	1996–98
Turkmenistan Turkménistan	...	...	2615	...	...	72.6	...	...	82.8
United Arab Emirates Emirats arabes unis	3430	3089	3371	107.2	98.6	105.3	120.7	96.4	107.4
Uzbekistan Ouzbékistan	...	...	2545	...	...	71.5	...	...	76.3
Viet Nam Viet Nam	2159	2214	2408	48.0	49.9	56.4	20.6	25.9	35.9
Yemen Yémen	1965	2143	2047	58.4	59.4	55.5	38.4	37.1	36.3
Europe · Europe									
Albania Albanie	2706	2651	3031	79.9	78.7	101.1	60.7	60.3	84.4
Austria Autriche	3361	3418	3538	95.8	97.9	104.8	149.2	153.3	160.2
Belarus Bélarus	...	...	3160	...	...	90.8	...	...	92.9
Belgium–Luxembourg Belgique–Luxembourg	3338	3477	3618	102.0	102.6	103.0	141.8	154.6	159.3
Bosnia and Herzegovina Bosnie–Herzégovine	...	...	2655	...	...	76.1	...	...	45.5
Bulgaria Bulgarie	3636	3701	2703	105.2	110.4	82.6	109.0	121.9	92.6
Croatia Croatie	...	...	2611	...	...	64.0	...	...	69.7
former Czechoslovakia † l'ex–Tchécoslovaquie †	3391	3522	...	99.1	104.2	...	124.4	134.1	...
Czech Republic République tchèque	...	...	3277	...	...	94.7	...	...	111.9
Denmark Danemark	3117	3198	3374	88.1	101.5	104.3	133.7	130.2	132.4
Estonia Estonie	...	...	2947	...	...	95.9	...	...	95.5
Finland Finlande	3075	2999	3100	94.5	95.5	101.3	131.4	124.9	127.6
France France	3405	3527	3528	112.5	115.8	114.0	149.1	159.3	163.8
Germany Allemagne	3345	3487	3400	96.0	101.5	96.6	137.1	141.2	146.4
Greece Grèce	3328	3459	3588	105.6	107.8	115.2	124.8	136.7	149.1
Hungary Hongrie	3485	3681	3350	96.8	105.5	86.8	132.8	150.0	135.5
Iceland Islande	3293	3210	3135	132.7	124.1	109.2	143.5	130.7	124.3
Ireland Irlande	3649	3630	3585	113.4	117.6	110.5	146.8	142.3	132.3
Italy Italie	3493	3512	3561	105.1	107.3	109.9	128.7	145.8	149.2
Latvia Lettonie	...	...	2932	...	...	80.7	...	...	92.7
Lithuania Lituanie	...	...	3107	...	...	94.3	...	...	78.0
Malta Malte	3238	3171	3361	99.7	96.4	109.0	110.6	111.5	109.2
Netherlands Pays–Bas	3050	3123	3283	94.0	94.8	106.5	131.3	133.0	142.0
Norway Norvège	3276	3223	3378	101.9	100.4	104.3	143.1	135.4	139.1
Poland Pologne	3429	3464	3329	106.6	105.3	98.6	111.2	116.9	111.3
Portugal Portugal	2854	3332	3665	77.9	97.2	114.8	90.5	106.2	130.6
Republic of Moldova République de Moldova	...	...	2693	...	...	65.4	...	...	55.1
Romania Roumanie	3129	2951	3280	95.4	91.7	100.4	91.1	88.6	87.1

13

Food Supply
Calories, protein and fat: per capita per day [*cont.*]
Disponibilités alimentaires
Calories, protéine et lipides : par habitant, par jour [*suite*]

Country or area	Calories (number) Calories (nombre)			Protein (grams) Protéine (grammes)			Fat (grams) Lipides (grammes)		
Pays ou zone	1980−82	1986−88	1996−98	1980−82	1986−88	1996−98	1980−82	1986−88	1996−98
Russian Federation Fédération de Russie	...	...	2840	...	...	87.9	...	...	76.7
Slovakia Slovaquie	...	...	2955	...	...	79.6	...	...	108.9
Slovenia Slovénie	...	...	2968	...	...	99.3	...	...	101.8
Spain Espagne	3048	3142	3340	96.4	100.5	109.5	116.2	129.5	145.3
Sweden Suède	2977	2938	3100	97.1	95.0	99.2	123.3	123.1	126.6
Switzerland Suisse	3480	3357	3257	97.5	95.0	89.5	158.8	153.4	146.0
TFYR Macedonia L'ex−R.y. Macédoine	...	...	2784	...	...	71.5	...	...	80.0
Ukraine Ukraine	...	...	2829	...	...	80.3	...	...	71.8
United Kingdom Royaume−Uni	3111	3215	3253	87.3	92.4	95.1	134.3	137.4	141.4
Yugoslavia, SFR † Yougoslavie, Rfs †	3661	3667	...	105.1	103.0	...	105.2	117.2	...
Yugoslavia Yougoslavie	...	...	3035	...	...	90.3	...	...	125.4
former USSR † l'ex−URSS †	3360	3382	...	102.4	106.3	...	93.5	102.8	...
Oceania · Océanie									
Australia Australie	3075	3158	3206	104.8	108.9	107.3	114.8	125.9	130.5
Fiji Fidji	2531	2630	2849	64.0	66.1	69.8	88.0	88.9	105.9
French Polynesia Polynésie française	2733	2810	2927	74.4	81.9	96.2	90.6	101.9	104.5
Kiribati Kiribati	2579	2499	2919	61.8	62.1	70.9	94.6	90.2	101.5
New Caledonia Nouvelle−Calédonie	2913	2888	2808	79.5	78.6	83.8	100.4	106.3	111.4
New Zealand Nouvelle−Zélande	3098	3145	3334	98.7	96.0	105.8	125.6	125.2	137.7
Papua New Guinea Papouasie−Nvl−Guinée	2110	2139	2141	44.7	46.6	46.1	35.0	40.9	42.3
Solomon Islands Iles Salomon	2226	2220	2166	57.9	56.5	51.2	51.3	44.6	41.4
Vanuatu Vanuatu	2561	2734	2729	62.4	62.7	59.8	98.6	100.4	96.7

Source:
Food and Agriculture Organization of the United Nations (FAO), Rome,
FAOSTAT Nutrition database.

† For information on the recent changes in country or area
  nomenclature pertaining to former Czechoslovakia,
  Germany, Hong Kong Special Administrative Region (SAR)
  of China, Macao Special Administrative Region (SAR) of
  China, SFR of Yugoslavia and the former USSR, see
  Annex I − Country or area nomenclature, regional and
  other groupings.

†† For statistical purposes, the data for China do not include
   those for Hong Kong Special Administrative Region
   (Hong Kong SAR) and Macao Special Administrative
   Region (Macao SAR).

Source:
Organisation des Nations Unies pour l'alimentation et l'agriculture
(FAO), Rome, les données alimentaires de FAOSTAT.

† Pour les modifications récentes de nomenclature de pays ou de
  zone concernant l'Allemagne, Hong Kong, région administrative
  spéciale (RAS) de Chine, Macao, région administrative spéciale
  (RAS) de Chine, l'ex−Tchécoslovaquie, l'ex−URSS et l'ex−Rfs d
  Yougoslavie, voir annex I − Nomenclature des pays ou des zones,
  groupements régionaux et autres groupements.

†† Les données statistiques relatives à la Chine ne comprennent
   pas celles qui concernent la région administrative spéciale de
   Hong Kong (la RAS de Hong Kong) et la région administrative
   spéciale de Macao (la RAS de Macao).

Technical notes, tables 12 and 13

Table 12: Data on acquired immunodeficiency syndrome (AIDS) have been compiled and estimated by the Joint United Nations Programme on HIV/AIDS (UNAIDS) and the World Health Organization (WHO). UNAIDS is composed of the United Nations Children's Fund, the United Nations Development Programme, the United Nations Population Fund, the United Nations International Drug Control Programme, the United Nations Educational, Scientific and Cultural Organization, the World Health Organization and the World Bank. Data are published in the *AIDS epidemic update* [30].

Table 13: Estimates on food supply are published by the Food and Agriculture Organization of the United Nations in *Food Balance Sheets* [5], in which the data give estimates of total and per caput food supplies per day available for human consumption during the reference period in terms of quantity and, by applying appropriate food composition factors for all primary and processed products, also in terms of caloric value and protein and fat content. Calorie supplies are reported in kilocalories. The traditional unit of calories is being retained for the time being until the proposed kilojoule gains wider acceptance and understanding (1 calorie = 4.19 kilojoules). Per caput supplies in terms of product weight are derived from the total supplies available for human consumption (i.e. Food) by dividing the quantities of Food by the total population actually partaking of the food supplies during the reference period, i.e. the present in-area (de facto) population within the present geographical boundaries of the country. In other words, nationals living abroad during the reference period are excluded, but foreigners living in the country are included. Adjustments are made wherever possible for part-time presence or absence, such as temporary migrants, tourists and refugees supported by special schemes (if it has not been possible to allow for the amounts provided by such schemes under imports). In almost all cases, the population figures used are the mid-year estimates published by the United Nations Population Division.

Per caput supply figures shown in the commodity balances therefore represent only the average supply available for the population as a whole and do not necessarily indicate what is actually consumed by individuals. Even if they are taken as an approximation of per caput consumption, it is important to bear in mind that there could be considerable variation in consumption between individuals.

Notes techniques, tableaux 12 et 13

Tableau 12: Les données sur le syndrome d'immunodéficience acquise (SIDA) ont été compilées et estimées par le Programme commun des Nations Unies sur le VIH/SIDA (ONUSIDA) et l'Organisation mondiale de la santé (OMS). L'ONUSIDA se compose du Fonds des Nations Unies pour l'enfance, du Programme des Nations Unies pour le développement, du Fonds des Nations Unies pour la population, du Programme des Nations Unies pour le contrôle international des drogues, de l'Organisation des Nations pour l'éducation, la science et la culture, de l'Organisation mondiale de la santé et de la Banque mondiale. Les données sont publiées dans "*AIDS epidemic update*" [30].

Tableau 13: Les estimations sur les disponibilités alimentaires sont publiées par l'Organisation des Nations Unies pour l'alimentation et l'agriculture dans les *Bilans alimentaires* [5] où les données donnent des estimations des disponibilités alimentaires totales et par habitant par jour pour la consommation humaine durant la période de référence, en quantité, en calories, en protéines et en lipides. Les calories sont exprimées en kilocalories. L'unité traditionnelle pour les calories n'est pas utilisée pour l'instant jusqu'à ce que le kilojoule soit plus largement accepté (1 calorie = 4,19 kilojoules). Les disponibilités par habitant exprimées en poids du produit sont calculées à partir des disponibilités totales pour la consommation humaine (c'est-à-dire "Alimentation humaine") en divisant ce chiffre par la population totale qui a effectivement eu accès aux approvisionnements alimentaires durant la période de référence, c'est-à-dire par la population présente (de facto) dans les limites géographiques actuelles du pays. En d'autres termes, les ressortissants du pays vivant à l'étranger durant la période de référence sont exclus, mais les étrangers vivant dans le pays sont inclus. Des ajustements ont été opérés chaque fois que possible pour tenir compte des présences ou des absences de durée limitée, comme dans le cas des imigrants/émigrants temporaires, des touristes et des réfugiés bénéficiant de programmes alimentaires spéciaux (s'il n'a pas été possible de tenir compte des vivres fournis à ce titre à travers les importations). Dans la plupart des cas, les données démographiques utilisés sont les estimations au milieu de l'année publiées par la Division de la population des Nations Unies.

Les disponibilités alimentaires par habitant figurant dans les bilans ne représentent donc que les disponibilités moyennes pour l'ensemble de la population et n'indiquent pas nécessairement la consommation effective des individus. Même si elles sont considérées comme une estimation approximative de la consommation par habitant, il importe de ne pas oublier que la consommation peut varier beaucoup selon les individus.

14
Cinemas: number, seating capacity, annual attendance and box office receipts
Cinémas: nombre d'établissements, nombre de sièges, fréquentation annuelle et recettes guichet

Country or area Pays ou zone	Year Année	Cinemas - Cinémas Number Nombre	Seating capacity Sièges No. (000)	P. 1000	Annual attendance Fréquentation annuelle No. (000000)	P. capita P. habitant	Gross receipts Recettes brutes Total (000000)	Currency Monnaie
Africa · Afrique								
Algeria	1985	216	110.0	5.0	20.5	0.9	109.0	Dinar
Algérie	1996	136	...	...	0.6	0.0	...	
	1997	136	...	...	0.6	0.0		
Benin	1993	23[1]	9.4	1.9	0.7	0.1	116.0	Franc C.F.A
Bénin	1996	3	2.5	0.5	0.3	0.1	56.0	
	1997	3	2.5	0.4	0.3	0.0	58.0	
Burkina Faso	1986	23	24.0	3.0	6.2	0.8	890.0	Franc C.F.A
Burkina Faso	1996	35	55.0	5.1	4.7	0.4	838.0	
	1997	35	55.0	5.0	4.9	0.4	870.0	
Cameroon	1985	197[1]	39.8	4.0	...	...	...	Franc C.F.A
Cameroun	1990	230[1]	38.9	3.4	...	...	...	
	1991	232[1]	39.9	3.4	...	...	...	
Congo	1994	28[1]	11.2	4.5	...	...	...	Franc C.F.A
Congo	1995	30[1]	4.4	1.7	...	...	...	
Côte d'Ivoire	1992	60	70.0	5.6	7.9	0.6	...	Franc C.F.A
Côte d'Ivoire	1993	60	70.0	5.5	7.3	0.6		
Egypt	1991	149	126.0	2.2	16.5	0.3	23.0	Pound
Egypte	1994	138	106.0	1.7	12.9	0.2	37.0	
	1996	122	96.1	1.5	10.6	0.2	46.0	
Guinea	1985	29	61.2	12.3	2.6	0.5	...	Syli
Guinée	1990	88	46.4	8.1	4.4	0.8	897.0	
	1991	80	41.0	6.8	3.9	0.6	793.0	
Kenya	1992	42[1]	7.0	0.3	8.0	0.3	...	Shilling
Kenya	1993	42[1]	7.0	0.3	5.8	0.2		
Madagascar	1990	20	...	...	0.7	0.1	356.0	Franc
Madagascar	1991	11	...	...	0.4	0.0	209.0	
Mauritius	1991	15	13.0	12.2	0.6	0.6	*15.0	Rupee
Maurice	1992	15	14.0	13.0	0.7	0.7	*22.0	
	1993	16	14.0	12.8	0.7	0.7	*22.0	
Morocco	1995	185	131.0	5.0	17.3	0.7	103.0	Dirham
Maroc	1996	183	130.0	4.9	16.3	0.6	114.0	
	1997	175	124.0	4.6	14.3	0.5	111.0	
Rwanda	1980	10	3.1	0.6	0.3	0.1	52.0	Franc
Rwanda	1985	34	9.3	1.5	...	...	...	
	1990	4	1.9	0.3	...		...	
United Rep. Tanzania	1986	31	16.4	0.7	4.2	0.2	167.0	Shilling
Rép.–Unie de Tanzanie	1990	28	12.4	0.5	1.9	*0.1	183.0	
	1991	28	12.4	0.5	1.9	*0.1	148.0	
Zimbabwe	1990	24	12.3	1.2	1.7	0.2	6.7	Dollar
Zimbabwe	1991	24	12.2	1.2	1.8	0.2	7.6	
America, North · Amérique du Nord								
Barbados	1990	3	...	...	0.0	0.0	...	Dollar
Barbade	1991	4	...	...	0.0	0.0	...	
Canada	1980	1 298	1 163.1	47.3	101.2	4.1	306.0[2]	Dollar
Canada	1986	898	906.0	34.5	76.1	2.9	305.0[2]	
	1990	742	722.0	26.0	79.0	2.8	439.0[2]	
Costa Rica	1985	105	...	...	0.2	*0.1	...	Colon
Costa Rica	1994	38	...	...	1.5	0.4	760.0	
	1995	39	...	...	1.7	0.5	1 058.0	
Cuba	1993	903[1]	187.9	17.3	23.8	2.2	6.4	Peso
Cuba	1996	944	193.3	17.5	10.8	1.0	5.8	
	1997	782	172.5	15.6	9.2	0.8	6.4	
Mexico	1995	1 495	774.0	8.5	63.0	0.7	888.0	New Peso
Mexique	1996	1 639	...	...	80.0	0.9	...	
	1997	1 842	...	...	95.0	1.0	...	
United States	1992	25 105	...	...	971.2	3.7	4 650.0	Dollar
Etats–Unis	1993	25 737	...	...	1 180.0	4.5	4 980.0	
	1994	26 586	...	...	1 210.0	4.6	5 250.0	

14

Cinemas: number, seating capacity, annual attendance and box office receipts [*cont.*]
Cinémas: nombre d'établissements, nombre de sièges, fréquentation annuelle et recettes guichet [*suite*]

Country or area Pays ou zone	Year Année	Cinemas – Cinémas Number Nombre	Seating capacity Sièges No. (000)	P. 1000	Annual attendance Fréquentation annuelle No. (000000)	P. capita P. habitant	Total (000000)	Gross receipts Recettes brutes Currency Monnaie
America, South · Amérique du Sud								
Argentina	1992	280	...	...	7.8	0.2	...	Peso
Argentine	1996	523	...	...	21.5	0.6	...	
	1997	635	...	...	26.6	0.7	...	
Bolivia	1993	130¹	...	...	2.2	*0.3	...	Boliviano
Bolivie	1996	76	...	...	1.2	0.2	11.0	
	1997	72	...	...	1.2	0.2	11.0	
Chile	1991	*154	*89.0	*6.7	10.0	*0.7	...	Peso
Chili	1992	*137	*83.5	*6.2	8.4	*0.6	...	
	1993	*133	*75.9	*5.5	8.0	*0.6	...	
Colombia	1980	418	...	...	60.7	2.1	1 721.0	Peso
Colombie	1985	586	277.3	8.8	56.1	1.8	4 642.0	
Ecuador	1986	118	110.0	11.8	11.1	1.2	884.0	Sucre
Equateur	1990	161	77.6	7.6	7.8	0.8	3 162.0	
	1991	134	75.3	7.2	6.8	0.6	4 949.0	
Peru	1996	124	...	...	3.0	0.1	19.0	Inti
Pérou	1997	116	...	...	4.1	0.2	25.0	
Suriname	1996	1	0.8	1.9	0.2	0.4	...	Guilder
Suriname	1997	1	0.8	1.9	0.1	0.3	...	
Venezuela	1993	218	132.0	6.3	18.3	0.9	1 896.0	Bolivar
Venezuela	1996	220	1 387.0	62.2	6.2	0.3	6 142.0	
	1997	241	1 394.7	61.2	6.4	0.3	10 353.0	
Asia · Asie								
Armenia	1993	577¹	118.5	33.1	...	...	44.0	Dram
Arménie	1994	599¹	124.9	34.9	...	...	...	
	1995	599¹	124.9	34.9	...	...	...	
Azerbaijan	1993	100	348.0	46.9	1.9	0.3	...	Manat
Azerbaïdjan	1996	236	378.0	49.7	2.1	0.3	2 208.0	
	1997	234	376.0	49.2	1.9	0.3	1 785.0	
Bahrain	1980	6	4.0	11.5	...	...	...	Dinar
Bahreïn	1985	6	4.0	9.7	1.1	2.6	...	
	1989	6	3.2	6.7	0.6	1.3	...	
China ††	1985	182 948¹	...	...	21 756.4	20.3	...	Yuan
Chine ††	1990	146 184¹	...	...	16 107.3	13.9	2 225.0	
	1991	139 639¹	...	...	14 428.4	12.3	2 365.0	
China, Hong Kong SAR †	1991	166	...	...	...	...	1 557.0	Dollar
Chine, Hong Kong RAS †	1994	186	99.9	16.4	35.0	5.7	1 449.0	
	1995	184	94.8	15.2	28.0	4.5	1 368.0	
Cyprus	1995	35	8.4	11.3	0.8	1.0	1.8	Pound
Chypre	1996	30	9.0	11.9	0.9	1.2	...	
	1997	29	8.0	10.5	0.9	1.2	...	
Georgia	1993	290¹	106.8	19.9	30.4	5.7	91 093.0	Coupon of Georgia
Géorgie	1996	97	22.8	4.4	20.5	4.0	...	
	1997	97	22.8	4.5	18.7	3.7	...	
India	1985	12 696¹	6 034.3	7.9	4 921.0	6.4	4 500.0	Rupee
Inde	1990	*13 550¹	*6611.4	*7.8	4 300.0	5.1	...	
	1991	*13 448¹	*6751.4	*7.8	4 300.0	5.0	...	
Indonesia	1985	1 902	962.1	5.7	...	...	...	Rupiah
Indonésie	1996	1 009	674.4	3.4	...	...	...	
	1997	1 009	674.4	3.3	...	...	...	
Iran (Islamic Rep. of)	1993	277	171.4	2.9	29.0	0.5	12 616.0	Rial
Iran (Rép. islamique de)	1994	294	197.0	3.2	56.0	0.9	...	
	1995	287	173.0	2.8	26.0	0.4	...	
Israel	1992	241	71.1	14.2	...	...	...	Shekel
Israël	1993	256	63.9	12.3	...	...	...	
	1994	266	62.5	11.6	10.0	1.9	...	
Japan	1993	1 734	...	...	130.7	1.0	163 700.0	Yen
Japon	1994	1 747	...	...	123.0	1.0	153 590.0	
	1995	1 776	...	...	127.0	1.0	...	

14
Cinemas: number, seating capacity, annual attendance and box office receipts [*cont.*]
Cinémas: nombre d'établissements, nombre de sièges, fréquentation annuelle et recettes guichet [*suite*]

Country or area Pays ou zone	Year Année	Cinemas – Cinémas Number Nombre	Seating capacity Sièges No. (000)	P. 1000	Annual attendance Fréquentation annuelle No. (000000)	P. capita P. habitant	Total (000000)	Gross receipts Recettes brutes Currency Monnaie
Jordan	1989	61	94.0	20.9	1.0	0.2	...	Dinar
Jordanie	1992	35	...	...	0.2	0.0	...	
	1993	35	...	...	0.2	0.0	...	
Kazakhstan	1993	5 947[1]	...	...	39.4	2.4	2.3	Tenge
Kazakhstan	1994	1 896	389.8	23.5	13.2	0.8	24.0	
	1995	1 580	346.7	21.0	6.2	0.4	39.0	
Korea, Republic of	1993	640	212.0	4.8	...	...	...	Won
Corée, République de	1996	272	...	...	42.3	0.9	204 180.0	
	1997	241	...	...	47.5	1.0	238 446.0	
Kuwait	1992	14	...	...	0.4	0.2	...	Dinar
Kowëit	1993	7	...	...	0.7	0.4	...	
	1994	6	...	...	0.8	0.5	...	
Kyrgyzstan	1995	385[1]	87.8	19.2	0.6	0.1	2.0	Som
Kirghizistan	1996	582[1]	80.3	17.5	0.4	0.1	1.9	
	1997	571[1]	80.8	17.5	0.4	0.1	2.1	
Lao People's Dem. Rep.	1990	31[1]	6.6	1.6	1.4	0.3	340.0	Kip
Rép. dém. pop. lao	1991	31[1]	6.6	1.5	1.0	0.2	245.0	
Lebanon	1993	79[1]	26.8	9.5	99.2	35.3	691 733.0	Pound
Liban	1996	36	35.6	11.5	35.6	11.5	249 163.0	
	1997	36	35.6	11.3	35.6	11.3	249 163.0	
Malaysia	1993	261	157.0	8.2	39.4	2.1	...	Ringgit
Malaisie	1996	170	37.6	1.8	16.1	0.8	...	
	1997	106	37.6	1.8	16.1	0.8	...	
Mongolia	1980	520	...	...	15.3	9.2	...	Tughrik
Mongolie	1985	562	...	...	19.1	10.0	...	
	1989	581	...	...	20.1	9.3	...	
Myanmar	1991	163	127.2	3.1	...	...	...	Kyat
Myanmar	1992	162	125.3	3.0	...	...	...	
	1993	163	126.0	3.0	...	...	...	
Pakistan	1985	702	458.2	4.5	...	...	...	Rupee
Pakistan	1996	652	...	...	9.7	0.1	213.0	
	1997	652	...	...	9.7	0.1	243.0	
Qatar	1980	4	4	17.4	1.2	5.2	7.7	Riyal
Qatar	1989	4	4	8.6	0.3	0.6	...	
Singapore	1993	80	...	...	20.0	6.2	...	Dollar
Singapour	1994	80	...	...	17.9	5.5	...	
	1995	80	...	...	18.1	5.5	...	
Sri Lanka	1985	318	201.0	12.5	36.5	2.3	39.0	Rupee
Sri Lanka	1992	255	142.0	8.2	29.2	1.7	222.0	
	1993	259	143.0	8.1	27.2	1.5	223.0	
Syrian Arab Republic	1989	77	40.0	3.3	7.0	0.6	...	Pound
Rép. arabe syrienne	1992	56	24.8	1.9	4.0	0.3	9.5	
	1993	55	23.8	1.8	3.9	0.3	12.0	
Tajikistan	1993	916[1]	200.2	35.8	12.7	2.3	235.0	Rouble
Tadjikistan	1994	514[1]	108.0	19.1	2.5	0.4	3.3	
	1995	172[1]	39.0	6.8	0.4	0.1	6.0	
Turkey	1993	320	...	...	15.0	0.3	392 135.0	Lira
Turquie	1996	300	115.0	1.8	9.5	0.2	...	
	1997	344	118.0	1.9	11.3	0.2	...	
Uzbekistan	1992	3 357	669.2	31.4	64.2	3.0	...	Rouble
Ouzbékistan	1993	2 777	609.3	28.0	29.0	1.3	...	
Viet Nam	1980	1 107[1]	...	...	288.9	5.4	...	Dong
Viet Nam	1985	1 394[1]	...	...	345.8	5.8	...	
	1988	1 451[1]	...	...	240.0	3.8	...	
Europe · Europe								
Austria	1995	412[1]	72.7	9.1	11.9	1.5	847.0	Schilling
Autriche	1996	423[1]	64.2	8.0	12.3	1.5	904.0	
	1997	441[1]	73.3	9.0	13.7	1.7	1 025.0	
Belarus	1993	4 168	744.3	71.8	29.5	2.8	2 581.0	B. Rouble
Bélarus	1994	3 900	712.9	68.6	18.7	1.8	3 515.0	
	1995	3 780	700.1	67.4	12.5	1.2	19 290.0	
Belgium	1995	423	...	...	19.2	1.9	3 526.0	Franc
Belgique	1996	440	...	...	21.2	2.1	3 988.0	
	1997	438	...	...	22.1	2.2	4 157.0	

14
Cinemas: number, seating capacity, annual attendance and box office receipts [cont.]
Cinémas: nombre d'établissements, nombre de sièges, fréquentation annuelle et recettes guichet [suite]

Country or area Pays ou zone	Year Année	Cinemas – Cinémas			Annual attendance Fréquentation annuelle			Gross receipts Recettes brutes
		Number Nombre	Seating capacity Sièges				Total (000000)	Currency Monnaie
			No. (000)	P. 1000	No. (000000)	P. capita P. habitant		
Bulgaria	1995	232	108.0	12.7	4.7	0.6	219.0	Lev
Bulgarie	1996	219	99.0	11.7	3.7	0.4	369.0	
	1997	216	98.0	11.7	3.2	0.4	4 389.0	
Croatia	1995	151[1]	55.0	12.2	3.7	0.8	75.0	Kuna
Croatie	1996	145[1]	53.0	11.8	3.3	0.7	52.0	
	1997	146[1]	53.0	11.8	3.2	0.7	53.0	
Czech Republic	1995	940	330.0	32.0	9.3	0.9	255.0	C. Krouny
République tchèque	1996	870	300.0	29.1	9.0	0.9	309.0	
	1997	851	300.0	29.1	9.8	1.0	437.0	
Denmark	1995	315[1]	50.0	9.6	8.8	1.7	289.0	Krone
Danemark	1996	323[1]	50.0	9.5	9.9	1.9	352.0	
	1997	321[1]	51.0	9.7	10.8	2.1	390.0	
Estonia	1995	220	...	...	1.0	0.7	16.0	Krooni
Estonie	1996	200			1.0	0.7	26.0	
	1997	200	...	...	1.0	0.7	29.0	
Finland	1995	330	58.4	11.4	5.3	1.0	194.0	Markka
Finlande	1996	325	57.2	11.2	5.5	1.1	197.0	
	1997	321	55.5	10.8	5.9	1.1	217.0	
France	1995	4 365	919.2	15.8	130.1	2.2	4 523.0	Franc
France	1996	3 214	954.0	16.4	137.0	2.3	4 762.0	
	1997	4 655	942.0	16.1	148.0	2.5	5 143.0	
Germany	1995	3 861[1]	730.0	8.9	124.5	1.5	1 183.0	Deutsche Mark
Allemagne	1996	4 089[1]	760.0	9.3	133.0	1.6	1 314.0	
	1997	4 182[1]	772.0	9.4	143.0	1.7	1 469.0	
Gibraltar Gibraltar	1980	4	2.3	80.7	0.2	6.7	...	Pound Stg.
Greece	1990	584	392.0	38.4	...	...	...	Drachma
Grèce	1991	584	392.0	38.1	...	...	...	
	1994	320	...	...	6.5	0.6	8 800.0	
Hungary	1995	597[1]	116.0	11.3	14.0	1.4	2 311.0	Forint
Hongrie	1996	558	117.0	11.5	13.3	1.3	2 884.0	
	1997	652	121.0	11.9	16.6	1.6	4 727.0	
Iceland	1995	23	6.0	22.4	1.2	4.5	665.0	Krona
Islande	1996	33	11.0	40.6	1.4	5.3	736.0	
	1997	32	10.0	36.6	1.5	5.4	800.0	
Ireland	1992	189	43.0	12.2	8.3	2.3	21.0	Pound
Irlande	1993	184	...	...	9.3	2.6	24.0	
	1994	191	...	...	10.4	2.9	27.0	
Italy	1994	3 617	...	...	98.2	1.7	823 727.0	Lira
Italie	1995	3 816	...	...	90.7	1.6	797 396.0	
	1996	4 004	472.0	8.2	96.5	1.7	875 154.0	
Latvia	1995	245	54.0	21.3	1.0	0.4	0.7	Lat
Lettonie	1996	137	28.0	11.2	1.0	0.4	0.8	
	1997	118	23.0	9.3	1.3	0.5	1.2	
Lithuania	1995	174[1]	38.2	10.3	0.7	0.2	1.4	Lita
Lituanie	1996	117	26.1	7.0	0.4	0.1	1.1	
	1997	124	28.2	7.6	0.5	0.1	2.2	
Luxembourg	1992	17	3.1	7.9	0.6	1.5	114.0	Franc
Luxembourg	1993	17	3.1	7.8	0.7	1.8	134.0	
	1994	17	3.1	7.7	0.7	1.8	133.0	
Malta	1990	10	7.0	19.8	0.3	0.7	...	Lira
Malte	1991	10	7.0	19.6	0.3	0.7	...	
	1992	10	7.0	19.3	0.3	0.8	...	
Monaco	1980	3	1.4	52.7	0.1	3.8	...	F. Franc
Monaco	1990	4	1.6	53.4	0.1	3.7	3.9	
Netherlands	1994	423	90.6	5.9	16.0	1.0	188.0	Guilder
Pays – Bas	1996	440	90.8	5.8	16.8	1.1	202.0	
	1997	444	88.8	5.7	18.9	1.2	233.0	
Norway	1994	394	92.6	21.4	11.6	2.7	446.0	Krone
Norvège	1996	630	92.2	21.1	11.5	2.6	485.0	
	1997	631	90.1	20.5	10.9	2.5	487.0	

14

Cinemas: number, seating capacity, annual attendance and box office receipts [*cont.*]

Cinémas: nombre d'établissements, nombre de sièges, fréquentation annuelle et recettes guichet [*suite*]

Country or area Pays ou zone	Year Année	Cinemas – Cinémas			Annual attendance Fréquentation annuelle			Gross receipts Recettes brutes
		Number Nombre	Seating capacity Sièges				Total (000000)	Currency Monnaie
			No. (000)	P. 1000	No. (000000)	P. capita P. habitant		
Poland	1994	773[1]	233.0	6.0	17.0	0.4	578 000.0	Zloty
Pologne	1996	706	206.0	5.3	21.5	0.6	123.0	
	1997	686	200.0	5.2	24.3	0.6	168.0	
Portugal	1994	263	84.7	8.6	6.4	0.6	3 066.0	Escudo
Portugal	1996	558	90.1	9.1	...	...	...	
	1997	595	97.1	9.8	...	...	...	
Republic of Moldova	1995	68	22.3	5.1	1.4	0.3	1.8	Lei
République de Moldova	1996	49	22.9	5.2	0.5	0.1	0.8	
	1997	50	23.0	5.3	0.2	0.0	0.3	
Romania	1995	626[1]	162.0	7.1	17.0	0.7	...	Leu
Roumanie	1996	494	150.0	6.6	12.6	0.6	21 907.0	
	1997	469	149.0	6.6	9.5	0.4	36 333.0	
Russian Federation	1995	2 016	875.8	5.9	140.1	0.9	...	Rouble
Fédération de Russie	1996	1 866	850.8	5.8	20.0	0.1	48.0	
	1997	1 746	778.9	5.3	16.2	0.1	49.0	
San Marino	1995	2	1.8	72.3	0.1	2.0	253.0	Lira
Saint–Marin	1996	3	1.8	70.6	0.1	2.7	354.0	
	1997	3	1.9	74.4	0.1	3.0	468.0	
Slovakia	1995	326	85.0	15.9	5.6	1.1	152.0	S. Koruny
Slovaquie	1996	334	90.0	16.8	4.9	0.9	154.0	
	1997	296	83.6	15.6	4.0	0.8	159.0	
Slovenia	1995	98	29.0	14.6	2.9	1.5	890.0	Tolar
Slovénie	1996	97	28.0	14.0	2.7	1.4	957.0	
	1997	91	27.0	13.5	2.5	1.3	1 376.0	
Spain	1995	2 090	...	...	94.6	2.4	48 229.0	Peseta
Espagne	1996	2 354	...	...	104.0	2.6	55 286.0	
	1997	2 530	...	...	101.0	2.6	56 841.0	
Sweden	1995	1 176	...	...	15.2	1.7	905.0	Krona
Suède	1996	1 165	445.0	50.4	15.4	1.7	...	
	1997	1 164	435.0	49.1	15.2	1.7	...	
Switzerland	1995	439	100.7	14.1	...	...	...	Franc
Suisse	1996	485	107.5	14.9	15.1	2.1	199.0	
	1997	502	110.9	15.3	15.6	2.1	205.0	
TFYR Macedonia	1995	38	14.0	7.1	0.2	0.1	22.0	Dinar
L'ex–R.Y. Macédoine	1996	39	14.0	7.1	0.3	0.1	26.0	
	1997	37	10.0	5.0	0.5	0.2	45.0	
Ukraine	1995	14 997[1]	3 298.0	64.1	30.8	0.6	567 688.0	Hryvnias
Ukraine	1996	13 358[1]	2 979.0	58.1	13.8	0.3	4.9	
	1997	10 768[1]	2 477.0	48.5	7.3	0.1	3.3	
United Kingdom	1993	1 890	...	...	113.4	2.0	343.0	Pound Stg.
Royaume–Uni	1994	1 969	553.0	9.5	124.4	2.1	364.0	
	1995	2 019	...	...	114.6	2.0	384.0	
Yugoslavia	1995	146[1]	73.0	6.9	2.2	0.2	...	Dinar
Yougoslavie	1996	156[1]	70.0	6.6	4.1	0.4	26.0	
	1997	195[1]	80.0	7.5	5.3	0.5	55.0	
Oceania • Océanie								
Australia	1995	1 137	332.0	18.5	69.0	3.8	502.0	Dollar
Australie	1996	1 251	356.0	19.6	74.0	4.1	537.0	
	1997	1 422	387.0	21.1	76.0	4.1	584.0	
New Zealand	1995	255	...	...	14.1	3.8	82.0	Dollar
Nouvelle–Zélande	1996	270	...	...	14.3	3.8	93.0	
	1997	285	...	...	16.5	4.4	112.0	

Source:
United Nations Educational, Scientific and Cultural Organization (UNESCO) Institute for Statistics, Paris, the UNESCO statistics database.

Source:
L'Institut de statistiques de l'Organisation des Nations Unies pour l'éducation, la science et la culture (UNESCO), Paris, la base de données de l'UNESCO.

14
Cinemas: number, seating capacity, annual attendance and box office receipts [*cont.*]
Cinémas: nombre d'établissements, nombre de sièges, fréquentation annuelle et recettes guichet [*suite*]

† For information on recent changes in country or area
nomenclature pertaining to former Czechoslovakia,
Germany, Hong Kong Special Administrative Region (SAR) of
China, Macao Special Administrative Region (SAR) of China, SFR
of Yugoslavia and former USSR, see Annex I − Country or area
nomenclature, regional and other groupings.

†† For statistical purposes, the data for China do not include those
for the Hong Kong Special Administrative Region (Hong Kong SAR),
Macao Special Administrative Region (Macao SAR) and Taiwan
province of China.

1 Data on number of cinemas include mobile units used for
non−commercial exhibitions.
2 Receipts do not include taxes.

† Pour les modifications récentes de nomenclature de pays
ou de zone concernant l'Allemagne, Hong Kong, région
administrative spéciale (RAS) de Chine, Macao région
administrative spéciale (RAS) de Chine, l'ex−Tchécoslovaquie
l'ex−URSS, et l'ex−Rfs de Yougoslavie voir annex I − ou
des pays ou des zones, groupements régionaux et autres
groupements.

†† Les données statistiques relatives à la Chine ne comprennent
pas celles qui concernent la région administrative spéciale de
Hong Kong (la RAS de Hong Kong), la région administrative
spécial de Macao (la RAS de Macao) et la province chinoise de
Taiwan.

1 Les données sur le nombre de cinémas comprennent les cinémas
itinérants non commerciaux.
2 Les recettes ne tiennent pas compte des taxes.

15
Facsimile machines and mobile cellular telephone subscribers
Télécopieurs et abonnés au téléphone mobile

Country or area Pays ou zone	Facsimile machines (number) Télécopieurs (nombre)					Mobile cellular telephone subscribers (number) Abonnés au téléphone mobile (nombre)				
	1994	1995	1996	1997	1998	1994	1995	1996	1997	1998
Africa · Afrique										
Algeria Algérie	4138[1]	5200	6200	7000	...	1348	4691	11700	17400	18000
Angola Angola	...	...	...	...	...	1824	1994	3298	7052	9820
Benin Bénin	600	800	1064	...	...	...	1050	2707	4295	6286
Botswana [2] Botswana [2]	2100[3]	3149[3]	3413[3]	3529	...	...	...	...	...	22980
Burkina Faso Burkina Faso	...	...	...	...	...	...	...	525	1503	2730
Burundi Burundi	2000	3000	4000	...	...	378	564	561	619	620
Cameroon Cameroun	...	...	...	...	...	1600	2800	3500	4200	...
Cape Verde Cap–Vert	400	500	1000	...	...	...	...	...	20	1020
Central African Rep. Rép. centrafricaine	103[4]	136[4]	222[4]	281[4]	316[4]	...	44	471	570	710
Chad Tchad	140	174	175	185	...	...	...	...	...	...
Comoros Comores	...	...	...	166	173	...	...	...	...	...
Congo Congo	...	...	...	...	...	...	...	1000	...	3390
Côte d'Ivoire Côte d'Ivoire	...	...	...	...	...	...	...	13549	36000	91212
Dem. Rep. of the Congo Rép. dém. du Congo	...	5000[1]	...	...	...	...	8500[1]	7200[3]	8900[3]	10000[3]
Djibouti Djibouti	93	94	70[5]	345	...	...	...	110	203	220
Egypt [7] Egypte [7]	21591	27332	31394	30720	33068	7371	7368	7369	65378	90786
Equatorial Guinea Guinée équatoriale	100	100	...	...	65	...	...	61	300	297
Eritrea Erythrée	505	777	1101	1388	1615	...	...	...	...	...
Ethiopia [7] Ethiopie [7]	1057	1445	1624	2038	2502	...	...	...	...	...
Gabon Gabon	...	360	503	501	...	2581	4000	6800	9500	9694
Gambia [2] Gambie [2]	700	1030	1096	1149	...	812	1442	3096	4734	5048
Ghana Ghana	4500[3]	5000[3]	...	...	...	3336	6200	12766	21866	41753
Guinea Guinée	...	...	1000	2018	2812	812	950	950	2868	21567
Guinea–Bissau Guinée–Bissau	480	500	500	480	500	...	...	...	...	...
Kenya [7] Kenya [7]	3500[3]	3800[3]	...	...	...	1990	2279	2826	5345	6819
Lesotho [2] Lesotho [2]	480	569	...	...	...	...	...	1262	3500	9831
Libyan Arab Jamahirya Jamah. arabe libyenne	...	...	...	...	...	...	...	...	10000[3]	20000
Madagascar Madagascar	...	...	...	...	...	300	1300	2300	4100	12784
Malawi Malawi	924	1086	1192	1250	1271	...	382	3700	7000	10500
Mali Mali	...	...	...	...	...	...	...	1187	2842	4473
Mauritania Mauritanie	...	302	2700	3200	4300	...	...	...	...	...

15
Facsimile machines and mobile cellular telephone subscribers [*cont.*]
Télécopieurs et abonnés au téléphone mobile [*suite*]

Country or area Pays ou zone	Facsimile machines (number) Télécopieurs (nombre)					Mobile cellular telephone subscribers (number) Abonnés au téléphone mobile (nombre)				
	1994	1995	1996	1997	1998	1994	1995	1996	1997	1998
Mauritius Maurice	18000	20000	25000	28000	30000	5706	11735	20843	37000	60482
Morocco Maroc	10000¹	13000¹	15000¹	18000¹	...	13794	29511	42942	74472	116645
Mozambique Mozambique	7182	...	...	...	...	...	...	...	2500	6725
Namibia ¹⁴ Namibie ¹⁴	...	...	...	...	...	...	3500	6644	12500	19500
Niger Niger	333	327	...	...	...	...	...	...	98	1349
Nigeria Nigéria	...	...	...	...	...	12800	13000	14000	15000	20000
Réunion Réunion	...	...	9164	...	...	...	5500	14000	26700	50300
Rwanda Rwanda	...	800	800	850	900	...	...	...	...	5000
Sao Tome and Principe Sao Tomé−et−Principe	145	170	...	212	320	...	...	...	...	...
Senegal Sénégal	...	...	...	...	...	98	122	1412	6942	22110
Seychelles ² Seychelles ²	552	609	645	...	...	...	326	1149	2615	3810
Sierra Leone Sierra Leone	800	1000	1700	1900	2500	...	...	...	...	...
South Africa ² Afrique du Sud ²	75000	100000	125000	150000	...	340000	535000	953000	1574000	2600000
Sudan Soudan	5000	5800	7000	12000	18000	...	...	2200	3800	8600
Swaziland ² Swaziland ²	922	...	1201	...	...	...	...	...	...	4700
Togo Togo	4000	10000	16000	17000	18000	...	...	...	2995	7500
Tunisia Tunisie	20000	25000	28000	31000	...	2709	3185	5439	7656	38998
Uganda ⁷ Ouganda ⁷	2000¹	2500¹	3000¹	...	...	...	1747	4000	5000	30000
United Rep. of Tanzania Rép.− Unie de Tanzanie	...	...	...	...	...	371	3500	9038	20200	37940
Zambia ² Zambie ²	570¹	600¹	650¹	855¹	1005¹	...	1547	2721	3752	5161
Zimbabwe ⁷ Zimbabwe ⁷	3500	4100	...	...	...	...	...	...	5734	19000
America, North · Amérique du Nord										
Antigua and Barbuda ² Antigua−et−Barbuda ²	...	...	850	...	...	...	...	1300	...	1500¹
Aruba Aruba	...	...	...	...	...	...	1718	3000	3402	5380
Bahamas Bahamas	...	...	...	...	...	...	4100	4948	6152	8072
Barbados ² Barbade ²	1610	1781	...	...	...	2967	4614	6283	8013	12000
Belize ² Belize ²	...	...	...	...	...	832	1547	2184	3023	3438
Bermuda ² Bermudes ²	...	...	...	...	...	5127	6324	7980	...	12572
British Virgin Islands ² Iles vierges britanniques ²	...	...	1200	...	...	...	...	...	...	...
Canada Canada	600000³	700000³	800000³	1000000³	1075000³	1865779	2589780	3420318	4266000	5320000
Cayman Islands ² Iles Caïmanes ²	...	...	...	...	...	1813	2534	...	4109	5170
Costa Rica Costa Rica	5000	6000	7500	8500	...	6985	18750	46531	64387	108770
Cuba Cuba	...	...	...	...	...	1152	1939	2427	2994	4056
Dominica ² Dominique ²	...	298	396	...	...	...	...	461	...	650

15
Facsimile machines and mobile cellular telephone subscribers [*cont.*]
Télécopieurs et abonnés au téléphone mobile [*suite*]

Country or area	Facsimile machines (number) Télécopieurs (nombre)					Mobile cellular telephone subscribers (number) Abonnés au téléphone mobile (nombre)				
Pays ou zone	1994	1995	1996	1997	1998	1994	1995	1996	1997	1998
Dominican Republic Rép. dominicaine	...	...	2300	...	...	20990	55979	73402	133463	255912
El Salvador El Salvador	...	...	...	...	...	4868	13475	23270	40163	106114
Greenland Groenland	...	...	...	...	...	964	2052	4122	6481	8899
Grenada Grenade	...	225	270	...	...	350	400	570	976	1410
Guadeloupe Guadeloupe	3441	...	...	...	...	...	...	...	...	14227
Guatemala Guatemala	10000					10462	29999	43421	64194	111445
Haiti Haïti	...	...	...	...	...	...	...	...	...	10000
Honduras Honduras	...	...	...	...	...	...	...	2311	14427	34896
Jamaica [2] Jamaïque [2]	...	...	...	...	...	26106	45178	54640	65995	78624
Martinique Martinique	3373	3859	4315	5200	...	...	...	...	15000	55000
Mexico Mexique	200000	220000	250000	285000	...	569251	688513	1021900	1740814	3349475
Netherlands Antilles Antilles néerlandaises	...	...	...	...	...	8486	11698	13977	...	16000
Nicaragua Nicaragua	...	...	...	...	...	2183	4400	5100	7911	31000
Panama Panama	...	...	...	...	...	...	...	7000	17000	80000
Puerto Rico [6] Porto Rico [6]	...	...	...	...	...	175000	287000	329000	367000	580000
Saint Kitts and Nevis [2] Saint−Kitts−et−Nevis [2]	...	...	450	...	...	...	...	300	205	440
Saint Lucia [2] Sainte−Lucie [2]	...	...	...	...	...	524	1000	1400	1600	1900
St. Vincent & the Grenadines [2] St. Vincent−et−Grenadines [2]	670	737	1500	...	...	...	...	...	346	750
Trinidad and Tobago [2] Trinité−et−Tobago [2]	1959[8]	2023[8]	2100[8]	2400[8]	5024[8]	2599	6353	14000	17547	26287
United States Etats−Unis	14052000[3]	17000000[3]	19000000[3]	21000000[3]	...	24134421	33785661	44042992	55312293	69209321
United States Virgin Islands Iles Vierges américaines	...	...	...	...	...	...	...	...	16000	25000
America, South · Amérique du Sud										
Argentina [14] Argentine [14]	40000[3]	50000[3]	60000[3]	75000[3]	87000[3]	241163	340743	568000	1588000	2530000
Bolivia Bolivie	...	...	...	...	...	4056	10000	20300	118433	239272
Brazil Brésil	230000[3]	270000[3]	350000[3]	500000[3]	...	574009	1285533	2498154	4550000	7760563
Chile Chili	19000[3]	25000[3]	32000[3]	40000[3]	...	100000	197314	319470	409740	964248
Colombia Colombie	79700[3]	100000[3]	140600[3]	172960[3]	...	86805	274590	522857	1264763	1800229
Ecuador Equateur	...	...	...	...	...	18920	54380	59779	126505	242812
French Guiana Guyane française	...	...	...	...	...	...	...	...	...	4000
Guyana Guyana	...	...	...	...	...	1251	1243	1200	1400	1454
Paraguay Paraguay	...	...	...	...	...	7660	15807	32860	84240	231520
Peru Pérou	7000[3]	15000[3]	...	...	...	52200	73543	200972	421814	742642
Suriname Suriname	550	700	800	...	...	1382	1687	2416	2258	6007
Uruguay Uruguay	9500	11000	...	...	...	6825	39904	79701	99318	154505

15
Facsimile machines and mobile cellular telephone subscribers [*cont.*]
Télécopieurs et abonnés au téléphone mobile [*suite*]

Country or area	Facsimile machines (number) Télécopieurs (nombre)					Mobile cellular telephone subscribers (number) Abonnés au téléphone mobile (nombre)				
Pays ou zone	1994	1995	1996	1997	1998	1994	1995	1996	1997	1998
Venezuela Venezuela	25000	35000	50000	70000	...	319000[1]	403800[1]	581700[1]	1071900[1]	2015000[1]
Asia · Asie										
Armenia Arménie	300	...	350	...	...	...	...	300	5000	7000
Azerbaijan Azerbaïdjan	2500	...	...	...	...	500	6000	17000	40000	65000
Bahrain Bahreïn	5388[9]	6299[9]	6341[9]	6620[9]	6687[9]	17616	27600	40080	58543	92063
Bangladesh [7] Bangladesh [7]	3000[1]	4000[1]	...	...	...	1104	2500	4000[3]	26000[3]	75000
Bhutan Bhoutan	300	...	1000	1000	1500	...	...	...	...	...
Brunei Darussalam Brunéi Darussalam	1500[1]	2000[1]	...	...	...	15623	35881	43524	45000	49129
Cambodia Cambodge	526	884	1470	2995	...	10239	14100	23098	33556	61345
China †† Chine ††	204000	270000	1500000	2000000	...	1568000	3629000	6853000	13233000	23863000
China, Hong Kong SAR † [2] Chine, Hong Kong RAS † [2]	256957	284926	314258	346016	362850	484823	798373	1361861	2229862	3174369
China, Macao SAR † Chine, Macao RAS †	7170	7301	7380	7313	6751	21445	35881	44788	50624	65320
Cyprus Chypre	...	...	...	...	...	22938	44453	70781	91968	116429
Georgia Géorgie	457	...	...	...	...	...	150	2300	30000	60000
India [2] Inde [2]	50000	70000	100000	150000	...	...	76680	327967	881839	1195400
Indonesia Indonésie	55000[3]	85000[3]	125000[3]	185000[3]	...	78024	210643	562517	916173	1065820
Iran (Islamic Rep. of) [11] Iran (Rép. islamique d') [11]	30000[3]	...	...	...	...	9200	15902	59967	238942	389974
Israel Israël	110000	140000	...	...	...	133425	445456	1047582	1672442	2147000
Japan [2] Japon [2]	10900000	12800000	14300000	16000000	...	4331369	11712137	26906511	38253893	47307592
Jordan Jordanie	31000[1]	32000[1]	35000[1]	42067[1]	51604[1]	1446	12400	16100	42100[3]	70498
Kazakhstan Kazakhstan	1504	2917	2646	1620	...	400	4600	9798	11202	29700
Korea, Dem. People's Rep. Corée, Rép. pop. dém. de	3000[1]	...	...	...	...	...	...	...	...	...
Korea, Republic of Corée, République de	375000[1]	400000[1]	...	...	...	960258	1641293	3180989	6878786	14018612
Kuwait Koweït	30000	35000	40000	42000	50000	85195	117609	151063	210000	250000
Kyrgyzstan Kirghizistan	...	...	...	...	...	...	...	...	...	1350
Lao People's Dem. Rep. Rép. dém. populaire lao	500[1]	...	...	...	...	625	1539	3790	4915	6453
Lebanon Liban	...	...	...	...	...	...	120000[1]	200000[1]	425000[1]	500000
Malaysia Malaisie	58090[1]	100000[3]	125000[3]	150000[3]	175000[3]	571720	1005066	1520320	2000000	2200000
Maldives Maldives	480	3500	...	...	...	...	...	20	1290	1600
Mongolia Mongolie	350	2150	5300	6436	...	...	...	900	2000	5300
Myanmar Myanmar	879	1339	1599	2029	2278	1920	2766	7260	8492	8516
Nepal [13] Népal [13]	900[1]	1100[1]	2000[1]	3500[1]	5000[1]	...	...	...	...	...
Occupied Palestinian Terr. Terr. palestinien occupé	...	...	15000	18000	...	...	20000[17]	25000[17]	40000[17]	...
Oman Oman	2683	2889	5778	6356	...	6751	8052	12934	59822	103032

15
Facsimile machines and mobile cellular telephone subscribers [*cont.*]
Télécopieurs et abonnés au téléphone mobile [*suite*]

Country or area	Facsimile machines (number) Télécopieurs (nombre)					Mobile cellular telephone subscribers (number) Abonnés au téléphone mobile (nombre)				
Pays ou zone	1994	1995	1996	1997	1998	1994	1995	1996	1997	1998
Pakistan [7] Pakistan [7]	130000	159000	175000	206000	268000	26000	43000	65000	110000	202000
Philippines Philippines	35000[3]	50000[3]	...	...	...	171903	493862	959024	1343620	1733652
Qatar Qatar	8000	9400	10400	...	...	9790	18469	28772	43476	65786
Saudi Arabia Arabie saoudite	100000[1]	150000[1]	...	...	...	15959	16008	190736	332068	627321
Singapore [2] Singapour [2]	60000[3]	70000[3]	80000[3]	90000[3]	100000[3]	235630	306000	431010	848600	1094700
Sri Lanka Sri Lanka	11000[1]	...	...	...	...	29182	53124	71029	114888	174202
Syrian Arab Republic Rép. arabe syrienne	4200	5000	21000	21000	22000	...	...	...	...	...
Tajikistan Tadjikistan	1200	1300	1500	1800	2000	...	...	102	320	420
Thailand [14] Thaïlande [14]	75000	100000	125000	150000	...	737283	1297826	1844627	2203905	1957249
Turkey Turquie	87978	99146	102111	108014	...	174779	437130	806339	1609809	3506127
Turkmenistan Turkménistan	...	...	...	...	...	...	...	...	2500	3000
United Arab Emirates Emirats arabes unis	35000[3]	40000[3]	45000[3]	50000[3]	...	91488	128968	193834	309373	493278
Uzbekistan Ouzbékistan	437	1037	1342	1658	1799	902	3731	9510	17232	26826
Viet Nam Viet Nam	13200[1]	14900[1]	19800[1]	...	...	12500	23500	68910	133946	187000
Yemen Yémen	1926[4]	2784[3]	...	...	...	8191	8250	8810	8810	18000
Europe · Europe										
Albania Albanie	...	...	6000	9000	13500	...	...	2300	3300	5600
Andorra Andorre	...	2800	3000	...	5000	784	2825	5488	8618	14117
Austria Autriche	240000	284738	...	...	...	278199	383535	598708	1159700	2292900
Belarus Bélarus	5770	8901	12259	15270	19472	1724	5897	6548	8167	12155
Belgium Belgique	170000	180000	190000	...	...	128071	235258	478172	974494	1756287
Bosnia and Herzegovina Bosnie – Herzégovine	...	...	...	...	...	...	...	1500	9000	25181
Bulgaria Bulgarie	12000[3]	15000[3]	...	...	...	6500	20920	26588	70000	127000
Croatia Croatie	28988	39072	45259	50237	...	21664	33688	64943	120420	182500
Czech Republic République tchèque	58463	73552	79499	103084	106604	30429	48900	200315	526339	965476
Denmark Danemark	210000[1]	250000[1]	...	...	...	503500	822264	1316592	1444016	1931101
Estonia Estonie	10000	13000	...	...	...	13774	30452	69500	144200	247000
Faeroe Islands Iles Féroé	...	...	...	...	...	1960	2558	3265	4701	6516
Finland Finlande	132000	161000	179000	198000	...	675565	1039126	1502003	2162574	2946948
France France	1600000[3]	1900000[3]	2400000[3]	2800000[3]	...	883000	1302496	2462700	5817300	11210100
Germany Allemagne	3300000[1]	4000000[1]	4900000[1]	5600000[1]	6000000[1]	2490500	3725000	5512000	8276000	13913000
Greece Grèce	20000[3]	30000[3]	40000[3]	...	...	167000	273000	550000	937700	2057000
Hungary Hongrie	40000[3]	50000[3]	80000[3]	120000[3]	180000[3]	143000	265000	473100	705786	1070154
Iceland Islande	...	...	...	...	...	21845	30883	46805	65368	91468

15
Facsimile machines and mobile cellular telephone subscribers [*cont.*]
Télécopieurs et abonnés au téléphone mobile [*suite*]

Country or area	Facsimile machines (number) Télécopieurs (nombre)					Mobile cellular telephone subscribers (number) Abonnés au téléphone mobile (nombre)				
Pays ou zone	1994	1995	1996	1997	1998	1994	1995	1996	1997	1998
Ireland [2] Irlande [2]	85000[1]	90000[1]	95000[1]	100000[1]	...	88000	158000	288600	533000	946000
Italy Italie	1350000[3]	1500000[3]	1650000[3]	1800000[3]	...	2240000	3923000	6422000	11737904	20489000
Latvia Lettonie	804	874	...	...	...	8364	15003	28500	77100	167460
Liechtenstein Liechtenstein	...	...	...	...	...	...	...	...	...	...
Lithuania Lituanie	2986	3830	5610	6200	...	4512[12]	14795[12]	50973[12]	165337[12]	267615[12]
Luxembourg [3] Luxembourg [3]	6500	7000	15000	17155	20000	12895	26838	45000	67208	130500
Malta Malte	4000[3]	5000[3]	6000[3]	...	...	7500	10791	12500	17691	22531
Netherlands Pays–Bas	450000	500000	550000	600000	...	321000	539000	1016000	1717000	3351000
Norway Norvège	150000[1]	170000[1]	190000[1]	220000[1]	...	588478	981305	1261445	1676763	2106414
Poland Pologne	40000[3]	55000[3]	...	...	...	38942	75000	216900	812200	1928042
Portugal Portugal	40000	50000	60000	70000	...	173508	340845	663651	1506958	3075633
Republic of Moldova République de Moldova	415	549	446	645	722	...	14	920	2200	7000
Romania Roumanie	18311	20746	...	...	...	2775	9068	17000	201000	643000
Russian Federation Fédération de Russie	18618	30610	65246	57600	52900	27744	88526	223002	484883	747160
Slovakia Slovaquie	37903	44682	55395	56359	54037	5946	12315	28658	200140	465364
Slovenia Slovénie	13241[4]	15541[4]	17727[4]	19464[4]	20754[4]	16332	27301	41205	93611	161606
Spain Espagne	600000[3]	650000[3]	700000[3]	...	...	411930	944955	2997645	4337696	7051264
Sweden Suède	350000[3]	400000[3]	450000[3]	...	...	1381000	2008000	2492000	3169000	4108000
Switzerland Suisse	175000[8]	197000[8]	207000[8]	...	...	332165	447167	662713	1044379	1672300
TFYR Macedonia L'ex–R.y. Macédoine	1777[10]	1777	2600	3000	...	...	...	1058	12362	30087
Ukraine Ukraine	11774	100	130	175	...	5000	14000	30000	57200	115500
United Kingdom Royaume–Uni	1425000[3]	1747000[3]	1992000[3]	...	...	3940000[2]	5735785[2]	7248355[2]	8841000[2]	14878000[2]
Yugoslavia Yougoslavie	13718	15000	14498	14798	20000	...	...	14800[1]	87000[1]	240000[1]
Oceania · Océanie										
Australia [7] Australie [7]	600000	700000	800000	900000	...	1220000	2242000	3990000	4578000	5342000
Cook Islands [2] Iles Cook [2]	...	...	...	...	...	...	...	182[18]	196	285
Fiji Fidji	2500[1]	3000[1]	3500[1]	3800[1]	3381[1]	1100	2200	3700	5200	8000
French Polynesia Polynésie française	1221[16]	1993[16]	2280[16]	2974[16]	3000[16]	...	1150	2719	5427	11060
Guam Guam	...	...	...	...	...	4098	4965	5803	5673	...
Kiribati Kiribati	125	185	...	...	...	...	...	...	...	22
Marshall Islands Iles Marshall	...	145	160	...	...	280	264	365	466	345
Micronesia (Fed. States of) Micronésie (Etats féd. de)	...	...	470	507	540	...	...	...	...	...
New Caledonia Nouvelle–Calédonie	2200	...	...	...	...	...	825	2060	5198	13040
New Zealand [2] Nouvelle–Zélande [2]	50000	65000	...	...	...	239200	365000	492800	566200	790000

15
Facsimile machines and mobile cellular telephone subscribers [*cont.*]
Télécopieurs et abonnés au téléphone mobile [*suite*]

Country or area Pays ou zone	Facsimile machines (number) Télécopieurs (nombre)					Mobile cellular telephone subscribers (number) Abonnés au téléphone mobile (nombre)				
	1994	1995	1996	1997	1998	1994	1995	1996	1997	1998
Northern Mariana Islands Iles Mariannes du Nord	1200	1200	...	...	...	765	1200	...	...	...
Papua New Guinea Papouasie−Nvl−Guinée	795	...	...	...	...			3053	...	...
Samoa Samoa	410[1]	430	450	490	500	...	...	...	1545[15]	3000
Solomon Islands [2] Iles Salomon [2]	728[4]	789[4]	840[4]	950[4]	698[4]	144	230	337	658	702
Tonga Tonga	180[1]	250[1]	250[1]	...	...	...	300	302	...	...
Vanuatu Vanuatu	...	...	...	...	...	64	121	154	207	220

Source:
International Telecommunication Union (ITU), Geneva, "Yearbook of Statistics, Telecommunication Services, Chronological Time Series 1989 − 1998" and the ITU database.

Source:
Union internationale des télécommunications (UIT), Genève. "Yearbook of Statistics, Telecommunication Services, Chronological Time Series 1989 − 1998" et la base de données de l'UIT.

† For information on the recent changes in country or area nomenclature pertaining to former Czechoslovakia, Germany, Hong Kong Special Administrative Region (SAR) of China, Macao Special Administrative Region (SAR) of China, SFR of Yugoslavia and the former USSR, see Annex I − Country or area nomenclature, regional and other groupings.

†† For statistical purposes the data for China do not include those for Hong Kong Special Administrative Region (Hong Kong SAR), Macao Special Administrative Region (Macao SAR) and Taiwan province of China.

1   Estimate.
2   Data refer to fiscal years beginning 1 April of the year indicated.

3   ITU estimate.
4   Fax subscribers.
5   Public facsimile machines.
6   Data refer to Puerto Rico Telephone Authority.
7   Data refer to fiscal years ending 30 June of the year indicated.

8   According to telefax directory.
9   Number of fax lines.
10   Registered facsimile machines.
11   Data refer to fiscal years beginning 22 March of the year indicated.

12   Not including radiotelephone connections of "Altaj" System.
13   Data refer to fiscal years ending 15 July of the year indicated.

14   Data refer to fiscal years ending 30 September of the year indicated.

15   As of 10 February 1998.
16   Facsimile machines provided by operator.
17   Users use Israel's cellular network.
18   As of May 1997.

† Pour les modifications récentes de nomenclature de pays ou de zone concernant l'Allemagne, Hong Kong, région administrative spéciale (RAS) de Chine, Macao, région administrative spéciale (RAS) de Chine, l'ex−Tchécoslovaquie, l'ex−URSS et l'ex−Rfs de Yougoslavie, voir annexe I − Nomenclature des pays ou des zones, groupements régionaux et autres groupements.

†† Les données statistiques relatives à la Chine ne comprennent pas celles qui concernent la région administrative spéciale de Hong Kong (la RAS de Hong Kong), la région administrative spéciale de Macao (la RAS de Macao), et la province chinoise de Taiwan.

1   Estimation.
2   Les données se réfèrent aux années fiscales commençant le 1er avril de l'année indiquée.
3   Estimations de l'UIT.
4   Abonnés à télécopie.
5   Télécopieurs publics.
6   Les données se réfèrent à "Puerto Rico Telephone Authority."
7   Les données se réfèrent aux années fiscales finissant le 30e juin de l'année indiquée.
8   Selon les annuaires de télécopie.
9   Nombre de lignes de télécopie.
10   Télécopieurs immatriculés.
11   Les données se réfèrent aux années fiscales commençant le 22e mars de l'année indiquée.
12   Non compris les connections radio−téléphonique du systéme d'Altaj.
13   Les données se réfèrent aux années fiscales finissant le 15e juillet de l'année indiquée.
14   Les données se réfèrent aux années fiscales finissant le 30e septembre de l'année indiquée.
15   Dès le 10 février 1998.
16   Télécopieurs fournis par l'agent.
17   Les abonnés utilisent le réseau israélien de téléphonie mobile.
18   Dès mai 1997.

16
Telephones
Téléphones

Main telephone lines in operation and per 100 inhabitants
Nombre de lignes téléphoniques en service et pour 100 habitants

Country or area Pays ou zone	Number (000) Nombre (000)					Per 100 inhabitants Pour 100 habitants				
	1994	1995	1996	1997	1998	1994	1995	1996	1997	1998
Africa · Afrique										
Algeria Algérie	1 122	1 176	1 278	1 400	1 477	4.1	4.1	4.4	4.8	4.9
Angola Angola	53	53[1]	53[1]	62[1]	72[1]	0.5	0.5	0.5	0.5	0.6
Benin Bénin	24	28	33	36	38	0.5	0.5	0.6	0.7	0.7
Botswana[2] Botswana[2]	50	60	72	86	102	3.5	4.1	4.8	5.6	6.5
Burkina Faso Burkina Faso	26	30	34	36	41	0.3	0.3	0.3	0.3	0.4
Burundi Burundi	16	17	15	16	18	0.3	0.3	0.3	0.3	0.3
Cameroon Cameroun	58	66	71	75	94	0.5	0.5	0.5	0.5	0.7
Cape Verde Cap-Vert	18	22	25	33	40	4.8	5.5	6.4	8.2	9.8
Central African Rep. Rép. centrafricaine	7	8	10	10	10	0.2	0.3	0.3	0.3	0.3
Chad Tchad	5	5	6	7	9	0.1	0.1	0.1	0.1	0.1
Comoros Comores	4	4	5	6	6	0.7	0.7	0.8	0.8	1.0
Congo Congo	21	21	* 22	* 22	22	0.8	0.8	0.8	0.8	0.8
Côte d'Ivoire Côte d'Ivoire	103	116	130	142	170	0.8	0.9	1.0	1.0	1.2
Dem. Rep. of the Congo Rép. dém. du Congo	* 36	* 36	* 36	* 21	* 20	0.1	0.1	0.1	0.0	0.0
Djibouti Djibouti	8	8	8	8	8	1.3	1.3	1.3	1.3	1.3
Egypt[3] Egypte[3]	2 456	2 716	3 025	3 453	3 972	4.3	4.6	5.0	5.5	6.0
Equatorial Guinea Guinée équatoriale	* 3	* 3[4]	* 4	* 4	* 6	0.7	0.6[4]	0.9	0.9	1.3
Eritrea Erythrée	15	18	19	22	24	0.4	0.5	0.5	0.6	0.7
Ethiopia[3] Ethiopie[3]	138	142	149	157	164	0.3	0.3	0.3	0.3	0.3
Gabon Gabon	31	32	35	37	39	3.0	3.0	3.2	3.3	3.3
Gambia[2 5] Gambie[2 5]	18	19	21	25	26	1.7	1.8	1.9	2.1	2.1
Ghana Ghana	50	63	78	106	144	0.3	0.4	0.4	0.6	0.8
Guinea Guinée	9	11	16	20	37	0.1	0.2	0.2	0.3	0.5
Guinea-Bissau Guinée-Bissau	7	7	8	8	8	0.7	0.7	0.7	0.7	0.7

16
Telephones
Main telephone lines in operation and per 100 inhabitants [cont.]
Téléphones
Nombre de lignes téléphoniques en service et pour 100 habitants [suite]

Country or area	Number (000) Nombre (000)					Per 100 inhabitants Pour 100 habitants				
Pays ou zone	1994	1995	1996	1997	1998	1994	1995	1996	1997	1998
Kenya[3] Kenya[3]	229	256	267	272	288	0.8	0.8	0.9	0.9	1.0
Lesotho[2] Lesotho[2]	* 16	18	16	20	20	0.8	0.9	0.8	1.0	1.0
Liberia Libéria	* 5	* 5	5	6	* 7	0.2	0.2	0.2	0.2	0.2
Libyan Arab Jamah. Jamah. arabe libyenne	264	318	380	...	500	5.1	5.9	6.8	...	9.1
Madagascar Madagascar	34	37	39	43	47	0.2	0.3	0.3	0.3	0.3
Malawi Malawi	33	34	35	37	37	0.4	0.4	0.4	0.4	0.4
Mali Mali	15	17	21	23	27	0.2	0.2	0.2	0.2	0.3
Mauritania Mauritanie	8	9	10	13	15	0.4	0.4	0.4	0.6	0.6
Mauritius Maurice	129	148	184	223	245	11.6	13.2	16.2	19.5	21.4
Mayotte Mayotte	5	5	7	9	12	4.2	4.7	5.6	7.6	9.5
Morocco Maroc	1 007	1 158	1 251	1 301	1 393	3.9	4.4	4.6	4.7	5.0
Mozambique Mozambique	57	61	61	66	75	0.4	0.4	0.3	0.4	0.4
Namibia[6] Namibie[6]	70	79	86	100	106	4.7	5.1	5.4	6.2	6.4
Niger Niger	12	14	15	16	18	0.1	0.2	0.2	0.2	0.2
Nigeria Nigéria	369	405	413	400	407	0.4	0.4	0.4	0.4	0.4
Réunion Réunion	210	219	226	236	243	32.1	33.1	33.9	35.1	35.6
Rwanda Rwanda	* 10	* 7	10	12	11	0.2	0.1	0.2	0.2	0.2
Saint Helena[2] Sainte-Hélène[2]	2	2	2	2	2	26.4	28.8	29.8	31.1	31.9
Sao Tome and Principe Sao Tomé-et-Principe	2	3	3	3	3	2.0	2.0	1.9	2.1	2.2
Senegal Sénégal	72	82	95	116	140	0.9	1.0	1.1	1.3	1.6
Seychelles[2] Seychelles[2]	12	14	15	16	19	16.8	18.0	19.5	20.6	24.8
Sierra Leone Sierra Leone	16	17	17	17	17	0.4	0.4	0.4	0.4	0.4
Somalia Somalie	* 15	* 15	* 15	* 15	* 15	0.2	0.2	0.2	0.2	0.2
South Africa[2] Afrique du Sud[2]	3 775	4 002	4 259	4 645	5 075	9.3	9.7	10.1	11.2	12.5

16
Telephones
Main telephone lines in operation and per 100 inhabitants [cont.]
Téléphones
Nombre de lignes téléphoniques en service et pour 100 habitants [suite]

Country or area Pays ou zone	Number (000) Nombre (000)					Per 100 inhabitants Pour 100 habitants				
	1994	1995	1996	1997	1998	1994	1995	1996	1997	1998
Sudan Soudan	64	75	99	113	162	0.3	0.3	0.4	0.4	0.6
Swaziland[2] Swaziland[2]	18	21	23	25	29	2.1	2.3	2.4	2.7	3.1
Togo Togo	21	22	24	25	31	0.5	0.5	0.6	0.6	0.7
Tunisia Tunisie	474	522	585	654	752	5.4	5.8	6.4	7.1	8.1
Uganda[3] Ouganda[3]	30	39	48	54	57	0.2	0.2	0.2	0.3	0.3
United Rep.Tanzania Rép.-Unie de Tanzanie	88	90	93	105	122	0.3	0.3	0.3	0.3	0.4
Zambia[2] Zambie[2]	80	77	78	77	78	1.0	1.0	0.9	0.9	0.9
Zimbabwe[3] Zimbabwe[3]	135	152	175	212	237	1.3	1.4	1.6	1.9	2.1
America, North · Amérique du Nord										
Anguilla[2] Anguilla[2]	4	4	4	5	6	48.5	51.3	55.2	67.8	68.9
Antigua and Barbuda[2] Antigua-et-Barbuda[2]	24	26	28	31	34	37.0	38.8	40.8	43.9	46.8
Aruba Aruba	22	* 27	34	33	35	27.2	33.5	39.1	36.7	37.3
Bahamas Bahamas	* 79	84	89	98	106	29.0	30.0	31.5	34.0	35.8
Barbados[2] Barbade[2]	85	90	97	108	113	32.7	34.5	36.5	40.8	42.2
Belize[2] Belize[2]	28	29	30	31	32	13.4	13.4	13.3	13.7	13.8
Bermuda[2] Bermudes[2]	44	46	49	52	54	70.7	73.7	75.8	81.0	84.0
British Virgin Islands[2] Iles Vierges britanniques[2]	9	9	10	...	...	46.7	50.1	50.6	...	...
Canada Canada	17 250	17 763	17 974	18 353	19 206	59.4	60.5	60.6	61.2	63.5
Cayman Islands[2] Iles Caïmanes[2]	18	19	...	19	25	58.8	62.7	...	52.0	65.4
Costa Rica Costa Rica	430	479	526	584	660	13.2	14.4	15.5	16.2	17.2
Cuba Cuba	349	353	356	371	388	3.2	3.2	3.2	3.4	3.5
Dominica[2] Dominique[2]	17	18	19	...	20	22.8	24.1	25.2	...	26.5
Dominican Republic Rép. dominicaine	555	583	618	706	764	7.2	7.4	7.7	8.7	9.3
El Salvador El Salvador	236	285	325	360	483	4.3	5.0	5.6	6.1	8.0
Greenland Groenland	18	20	21	23	25	33.2	35.1	37.7	41.7	44.5

16
Telephones
Main telephone lines in operation and per 100 inhabitants [cont.]
Téléphones
Nombre de lignes téléphoniques en service et pour 100 habitants [suite]

Country or area Pays ou zone	Number (000) Nombre (000)					Per 100 inhabitants Pour 100 habitants				
	1994	1995	1996	1997	1998	1994	1995	1996	1997	1998
Grenada Grenade	21	23	24	27	27	23.8	26.0	26.7	29.0	29.8
Guadeloupe Guadeloupe	159	165	171	...	197	38.1	39.0	39.6	...	44.5
Guatemala Guatemala	245	286	338	430	* 517	2.5	2.9	3.3	4.1	4.8
Haiti Haïti	* 50	* 60	* 60	* 60	* 65	0.7	0.8	0.8	0.8	0.8
Honduras Honduras	131	161	190	234	250	2.3	2.7	3.1	3.8	4.0
Jamaica[2] Jamaïque[2]	251	292	353	419	470	10.1	11.7	14.0	16.6	18.5
Martinique Martinique	155	161	163	170	172	40.4	41.7	42.2	43.8	44.3
Mexico[7] Mexique[7]	8 493	8 801	8 826	9 254	9 927	9.2	9.4	9.3	9.7	10.4
Montserrat Montserrat	5	5	5	4	...	43.6	43.0	42.1	34.5	...
Netherlands Antilles Antilles néerlandaises	* 71	* 76	76	* 77	* 78	36.0	36.6	36.3	36.5	36.7
Nicaragua Nicaragua	85	97	111	128	140	2.0	2.2	2.6	2.9	3.0
Panama Panama	287	304	325	366	419	11.1	11.6	12.2	13.4	15.1
Puerto Rico[89] Porto Rico[89]	1 130	1 196	1 254	1 323	1 262	30.7	32.1	33.2	34.6	32.7
Saint Kitts and Nevis[2] Saint-Kitts-et-Nevis[2]	14	14	16	17	18	34.1	36.3	39.7	43.8	47.1
Saint Lucia[2] Sainte-Lucie[2]	25	31	34	37	40	17.5	21.0	23.0	24.7	26.6
Saint Pierre and Miquelon[2] Saint-Pierre-et-Miquelon[2]	4	...	4	4	4	56.6	...	61.0	66.0	65.8
St. Vincent-Grenadines[2] St. Vincent-Grenadines[2]	17	18	19	21	21	15.6	16.5	17.4	18.4	18.8
Trinidad and Tobago[2] Trinité-et-Tobago[2]	204	209	220	243	264	16.6	16.8	17.4	19.1	20.6
United States[10] Etats-Unis[10]	153 448	159 735	165 047	172 453	179 822	58.9	60.7	62.2	64.4	66.1
United States Virgin Is. Iles Vierges américaines	59	58	59	62	65	52.6	51.2	51.5	53.2	54.8
America, South · Amérique du Sud										
Argentina[6] Argentine[6]	4 694	5 532	6 120	6 699	7 132	13.7	15.9	17.4	18.8	19.7
Bolivia Bolivie	* 243	247	* 349	384	452	3.4	3.3	4.6	4.9	5.7
Brazil[11] Brésil[11]	12 269	13 263	15 106	17 039	19 987	8.0	8.5	9.6	10.7	12.1
Chile Chili	1 587	1 818	2 151	2 693	3 046	11.3	12.7	14.9	18.4	20.6

16
Telephones
Main telephone lines in operation and per 100 inhabitants [*cont.*]
Téléphones
Nombre de lignes téléphoniques en service et pour 100 habitants [*suite*]

Country or area Pays ou zone	Number (000) Nombre (000)					Per 100 inhabitants Pour 100 habitants				
	1994	1995	1996	1997	1998	1994	1995	1996	1997	1998
Colombia Colombie	3 513	3 873	4 645	5 395	6 367	10.2	11.0	13.0	14.4	16.1
Ecuador Equateur	658	698	750	819	991	5.9	6.1	6.4	6.9	8.1
Falkland Is. (Malvinas)[2] Iles Falkland (Malvinas)[2]	1	2	2	2	2	74.1	72.9	74.7	84.0	94.8
French Guiana Guyane française	40	42	44	47	46	27.7	27.9	28.9	29.2	27.7
Guyana Guyana	44	45	50	55	60	5.3	5.4	6.0	6.5	7.1
Paraguay Paraguay	151	167	176	218	289	3.2	3.5	3.6	4.3	5.5
Peru Pérou	772	1 109	1 435	1 646	1 555	3.3	4.7	6.0	6.8	6.3
Suriname Suriname	51	54	57	64	67	12.1	13.2	13.8	15.5	16.3
Uruguay Uruguay	582	622	669	761	824	18.4	19.5	20.9	23.5	25.0
Venezuela Venezuela	2 334	2 463	2 667	2 804	2 712	10.9	11.4	11.7	12.2	11.7
Asia · Asie										
Afghanistan Afghanistan	* 29	* 29	* 29	* 29	* 29	0.2	0.2	0.1	0.1	0.1
Armenia Arménie	587	583	580	568	556	15.6	15.5	15.3	15.0	15.7
Azerbaijan Azerbaïdjan	635	640	645	658	680	8.5	8.5	8.5	8.6	8.9
Bahrain Bahreïn	136	141	144	152	158	24.3	24.2	24.1	24.6	24.6
Bangladesh[3] Bangladesh[3]	262	287	316	375	378	0.2	0.2	0.3	0.3	0.3
Bhutan Bhoutan	5	5	6	6	10	0.8	0.9	1.0	1.0	1.6
Brunei Darussalam Brunéi Darussalam	62	68	79	77	78	22.1	24.0	25.8	25.0	24.7
Cambodia[12] Cambodge[12]	7	9	15	11	20	0.1	0.1	0.2	0.1	0.2
China †† Chine ††	27 295	40 706	54 947	70 310	87 421	2.3	3.3	4.4	5.6	7.0
China, Hong Kong SAR†[2] Chine, Hong Kong RAS†[2]	3 149	3 278	3 451	3 647	3 729	52.2	53.3	54.7	56.1	55.8
China, Macao SAR † Chine, Macao RAS †	145	153	161	170	174	36.6	37.5	38.8	40.2	40.4
Cyprus Chypre	330[13]	347[13]	366[13]	386	405	52.4	53.8	54.2	54.5	54.5
Georgia Géorgie	526	554	567	617	629	9.7	10.2	10.5	11.3	11.6
India[2] Inde[2]	9 795	11 978	14 543	17 802	21 594	1.1	1.3	1.6	1.9	2.2

16
Telephones
Main telephone lines in operation and per 100 inhabitants [*cont.*]
Téléphones
Nombre de lignes téléphoniques en service et pour 100 habitants [*suite*]

Country or area Pays ou zone	Number (000) Nombre (000)					Per 100 inhabitants Pour 100 habitants				
	1994	1995	1996	1997	1998	1994	1995	1996	1997	1998
Indonesia Indonésie	2 463	3 291	4 186	4 982	5 572	1.3	1.7	2.1	2.5	2.7
Iran (Islamic Rep. of)[14] Iran (Rép. islamique d')[14]	4 320	5 090	5 825	6 503	7 355	7.2	8.3	9.3	10.1	11.2
Iraq[3] Iraq[3]	* 675	* 675	675	675	675	3.4	3.4	3.3	3.2	3.1
Israel Israël	2 138	2 343	2 539	2 656	2 819	38.3	41.7	44.1	45.0	47.1
Japan[2] Japon[2]	59 936	61 106	63 126[15]	62 781[15]	62 550[15]	47.9	48.7	50.2	49.8	49.5
Jordan Jordanie	305	317	345	416	511	5.9	5.8	6.2	7.2	8.3
Kazakhstan Kazakhstan	1 987	1 963	1 917	1 805	1 775	11.9	11.9	11.6	11.0	10.9
Korea, Dem. P. R. Corée, R. p. dém. de	* 1 100	* 1 100	* 1 100	* 1 100	* 1 100	5.1	5.0	4.9	4.8	4.7
Korea, Republic of[16] Corée, République de[16]	17 647	18 600	19 601	20 422	20 089	39.3	41.2	43.0	44.4	43.3
Kuwait Koweït	373	382	392	412	427	23.0	22.6	22.4	23.1	23.6
Kyrgyzstan Kirghizistan	339	357	342	351	355	7.6	7.9	7.5	7.6	7.6
Lao People's Dem. Rep. Rép. dém. pop. lao	18	17	19	25	28	0.4	0.4	0.4	0.5	0.6
Lebanon Liban	* 330	* 330	461	562	620	11.3	11.0	14.9	17.9	19.4
Malaysia Malaisie	2 864	3 332	3 771	4 223	4 384	14.6	16.6	17.8	19.5	20.2
Maldives Maldives	12	14	15	18	20	5.0	5.7	5.8	6.6	7.3
Mongolia Mongolie	69	78	84	87	96	3.0	3.4	3.6	3.7	3.8
Myanmar Myanmar	137	158	179	214	229	0.3	0.4	0.4	0.5	0.5
Nepal[17] Népal[17]	76	84	113	140	208	0.4	0.4	0.5	0.6	0.9
Occupied Palestinian Terr. Terr. palestinien occupé	78	80	83	112	167	3.7	3.5	3.3	4.1	5.8
Oman Oman	158	170	198	201	220	7.6	7.9	8.6	8.6	9.2
Pakistan[3] Pakistan[3]	1 830	2 127	2 377	2 558	2 756	1.5	1.7	1.9	2.0	2.1
Philippines Philippines	1 110	1 410	1 787[18]	2 078[18]	2 512[18]	1.7	2.1	2.6	2.9	3.4
Qatar Qatar	116	123	134	142	151	21.6	22.3	23.9	24.9	26.0
Saudi Arabia Arabie saoudite	1 676	1 719	2 004	2 285	2 878	9.4	9.4	10.6	11.7	14.3

16
Telephones
Main telephone lines in operation and per 100 inhabitants [cont.]
Téléphones
Nombre de lignes téléphoniques en service et pour 100 habitants [suite]

Country or area Pays ou zone	Number (000) Nombre (000)					Per 100 inhabitants Pour 100 habitants				
	1994	1995	1996	1997	1998	1994	1995	1996	1997	1998
Singapore[2] Singapour[2]	1 332	1 429	1 563	1 685	1 778	45.5	47.8	51.3	54.3	56.2
Sri Lanka Sri Lanka	181	206	255	342	524	1.0	1.1	1.4	1.9	2.8
Syrian Arab Republic Rép. arabe syrienne	686	958	1 199	1 313	1 463	5.0	6.8	8.2	8.8	9.5
Tajikistan Tadjikistan	268	263	247	226	221	4.7	4.5	4.2	3.8	3.7
Thailand[6] Thaïlande[6]	2 751	3 482	4 200	4 827	5 038	4.7	5.9	7.0	8.0	8.4
Turkey Turquie	12 195	13 216	14 286	15 744	16 960	19.9	21.1	22.4	25.0	25.4
Turkmenistan Turkménistan	305	320	338	354	354	6.9	7.1	7.4	8.0	8.2
United Arab Emirates Emirats arabes unis	615	672	738	835	915[19]	28.5	29.1	32.7	35.1	38.9
Uzbekistan Ouzbékistan	1 557	1 544	1 531	1 541	1 537	7.0	6.8	6.6	6.5	6.5
Viet Nam Viet Nam	442	775	1 186	1 587	2 000	0.6	1.1	1.6	2.1	2.6
Yemen Yémen	173	187	205	220	250	1.2	1.2	1.3	1.3	1.5
Europe · Europe										
Albania Albanie	42	42	64	87	116	1.2	1.2	1.7	2.3	3.1
Andorra Andorre	28	30	31	32	33	44.0	43.8	43.6	43.1	44.1
Austria[20] Autriche[20]	3 692	3 797	3 902	3 969	3 997	46.0	47.2	48.4	49.2	49.1
Belarus Bélarus	1 890	1 968	2 128	2 313	2 490	18.3	19.2	20.8	22.6	24.3
Belgium[20] Belgique[20]	4 543	4 682	4 814	4 964	5 073	45.0	46.2	47.4	48.7	50.0
Bosnia and Herzegovina Bosnie-Herzégovine	250[21]	238	272	303	333	6.1	6.0	7.0	8.0	9.1
Bulgaria Bulgarie	2 488	2 563	2 647	2 681	2 742	29.5	30.5	31.7	32.3	32.9
Croatia Croatie	1 205	1 287	1 389	1 488	1 558	26.2	28.3	30.9	33.2	34.8
Czech Republic République tchèque	2 178	2 444	2 817	3 280	3 741	21.1	23.7	27.3	31.8	36.4
Denmark Danemark	3 123	3 193	3 251	3 341	3 496	60.1	61.2	61.9	63.3	66.0
Estonia Estonie	378	412	439	469	499	25.2	27.7	29.9	32.1	34.4
Faeroe Islands Iles Féroé	23	22	23	24	24	50.7	50.5	52.7	53.8	54.4
Finland[16] Finlande[16]	2 791	2 799	2 802	2 850	2 842	54.7	54.1	54.6	55.4	55.1

16
Telephones
Main telephone lines in operation and per 100 inhabitants [cont.]
Téléphones
Nombre de lignes téléphoniques en service et pour 100 habitants [suite]

Country or area Pays ou zone	Number (000) Nombre (000)					Per 100 inhabitants Pour 100 habitants				
	1994	1995	1996	1997	1998	1994	1995	1996	1997	1998
France[20] France[20]	31 700	32 400	32 900	33 700	34 099	54.8	55.7	56.4	57.1	57.1
Germany[22] Allemagne[22]	38 800	42 000	44 100	45 200	46 660	47.6	51.3	53.8	55.1	56.9
Gibraltar Gibraltar	15	17	18	19	20	56.3	61.2	64.6	68.5	74.8
Greece Grèce	4 976	5 163	5 329	5 431	5 536	47.7	49.4	50.9	51.6	52.2
Hungary Hongrie	1 774	2 157	2 651	3 095	3 423	17.3	21.1	26.0	30.4	33.6
Iceland[23] Islande[23]	148	149	155	168	178	55.6	55.5	57.6	61.4	64.7
Ireland[2] Irlande[2]	1 240	1 310	1 390	1 500	1 600	34.6	36.3	38.3	41.1	43.5
Italy Italie	24 542	24 845	25 259	25 698	25 986	42.9	43.3	44.0	44.8	45.3
Latvia Lettonie	667	705	739	748	741	26.0	27.9	29.6	30.2	30.2
Lithuania[5] Lituanie[5]	898	941	993	1 048	1 110	24.1	25.4	26.8	28.3	30.0
Luxembourg[24] Luxembourg[24]	223	234	258	280	293	55.2	57.3	62.6	66.9	69.2
Malta Malte	163	171	181	187	192	44.1	45.9	48.3	49.3	49.9
Monaco Monaco	30	31	32	32	33	96.3	97.0	99.0	96.4	99.1
Netherlands[20] Pays-Bas[20]	7 859	8 124	8 431	8 860	9 337	51.1	52.4	54.0	56.6	59.3
Norway[20] Norvège[20]	2 401	2 476	2 589	2 735	2 935	55.4	56.8	59.1	62.1	66.0
Poland Pologne	5 006	5 729	6 532	7 510	8 812	13.0	14.8	16.9	19.4	22.8
Portugal[20] Portugal[20]	3 474	3 643	3 822	4 002	4 117	35.1	36.7	38.5	40.3	41.4
Republic of Moldova République de Moldova	546	566	593	627	657	12.6	13.0	13.7	14.4	15.0
Romania Roumanie	2 806	2 968	3 176	3 398	3 599	12.3	13.1	14.1	15.1	16.0
Russian Federation Fédération de Russie	24 097	25 019	25 915	28 250	29 031	16.3	16.9	17.6	19.2	19.7
San Marino Saint-Marin	14	16	17	18	19	58.7	64.3	68.3	70.2	77.3
Slovakia Slovaquie	1 004	1 118	1 246	1 392	1 539	18.7	20.8	23.2	25.9	28.6
Slovenia Slovénie	577	615	664	722	757	29.0	30.9	33.4	36.4	38.0
Spain Espagne	14 685	15 095	15 413	15 854	16 289	37.5	38.5	39.3	40.3	41.4

16

Telephones
Main telephone lines in operation and per 100 inhabitants [*cont.*]
Téléphones
Nombre de lignes téléphoniques en service et pour 100 habitants [*suite*]

Country or area Pays ou zone	Number (000) Nombre (000)					Per 100 inhabitants Pour 100 habitants				
	1994	1995	1996	1997	1998	1994	1995	1996	1997	1998
Sweden Suède	5 967	6 013	6 032	6 010	5 965	68.3	68.1	68.2	67.9	67.4
Switzerland[20] Suisse[20]	4 258	4 480	4 571	4 688	4 803	57.8	63.4	64.6	66.1	67.4
TFYR Macedonia L'ex-R.y. Macédoine	337	351	367	408	439	17.3	17.9	18.5	19.9	22.0
Ukraine Ukraine	8 066	8 311	9 241	9 410	9 698	15.5	16.1	18.1	18.5	19.1
United Kingdom[2] Royaume-Uni[2]	28 358	29 411	30 678	31 879	32 829	48.6	50.3	52.2	54.2	55.7
Yugoslavia Yougoslavie	1 970	2 017	2 082	2 182	2 319	18.8	19.2	19.7	20.6	21.8
Oceania · Océanie										
American Samoa Samoa américaines	10	10	13	13	14	17.4	18.5	21.6	22.1	21.4
Australia[3] Australie[3]	8 850	8 900	9 170	9 498	9 844	49.6	49.3	50.1	51.3	52.6
Cook Islands[2] Iles Cook[2]	5	5	5	5	5	25.5	27.1	26.9	26.9	27.5
Fiji Fidji	59	65	70	72	77	7.8	8.4	9.0	9.2	9.8
French Polynesia Polynésie française	47	49	51	52	53	21.9	22.1	23.0	23.0	23.2
Guam Guam	64	69	70	71	75	43.4	46.1	45.8	45.3	46.6
Kiribati Kiribati	2	2	2	2	3	2.5	2.6	2.6	3.1	3.4
Marshall Islands Iles Marshall	3	3	3	3	4	5.5	5.7	5.9	5.8	6.2
Micronesia (Fed. States of) Micron (Etats fédérés de)	7	8	8	8	9	6.8	7.4	7.6	7.6	8.0
Nauru Nauru	2	...	2	2	2	15.7	...	14.3	14.5	15.0
New Caledonia Nouvelle-Calédonie	42	44	46	47	49	23.3	23.6	24.1	24.1	23.9
New Zealand[2] Nouvelle-Zélande[2]	1 658	1 719	1 782	1 840	1 868	46.3	47.3	48.4	48.6	49.1
Northern Mariana Islands Iles Marianas du Nord	14	15	21	20	21	30.5	32.2	42.8	40.0	40.4
Papua New Guinea Papouasie-Nvl-Guinée	40	44	47	...	...	1.0	1.1	1.1	...	...
Samoa Samoa	7	8	8	8	8	4.5	4.7	5.0	5.0	4.9
Solomon Islands[2 25] Iles Salomon[2 25]	6	7	7	8	8	1.6	1.7	1.8	1.9	1.9
Tonga Tonga	6	7	8	...	...	6.6	6.7	7.9	...	...

16
Telephones
Main telephone lines in operation and per 100 inhabitants [cont.]
Téléphones
Nombre de lignes téléphoniques en service et pour 100 habitants [suite]

Country or area	Number (000) Nombre (000)					Per 100 inhabitants Pour 100 habitants				
Pays ou zone	1994	1995	1996	1997	1998	1994	1995	1996	1997	1998
Vanuatu Vanuatu	4	4	4	5	5	2.7	2.5	2.6	2.7	2.8
Wallis and Futuna Islands Iles Wallis et Futuna	1	1	1	1	1	7.4	9.6	10.3	9.9	9.8

Source:
International Telecommunication Union (ITU), Geneva,
"Yearbook of Statistics, Telecommunication Services,
Chronological Time Series 1989-1998" and the ITU database.

† For information on recent changes in country or
area nomenclature pertaining to former Czechoslovakia,
Germany, Hong Kong Special Administrative Region (SAR) of
China, Macao Special Administrative Region (SAR) of China,
SFR of Yugoslavia and the former USSR, see Annex I - Country
or area nomenclature, regional and other groupings.

†† For statistical purposes, the data for
China do not include those for Hong Kong Special
Administrative Region (Hong Kong SAR), Macao Special
Administrative Region (Macao SAR) and Taiwan province of
China.

1 Data refer to Angola Telecom.
2 Data refer to fiscal years beginning 1 April of the year
   indicated.
3 Data refer to fiscal years ending 30 June of the year
   indicated.
4 Malabo and Bata.
5 Excluding public call offices.
6 Data refer to fiscal years ending 30 September of the year
   indicated.
7 Lines in service.
8 Data refer to Puerto Rico Telephone Authority.
9 Switched access lines.
10 Data for 1980 refer to main stations reported by FCC. From
   1981, data refer to "Local Loops".
11 Conventional telephony terminals in service.
12 From 1994 WLL lines included.
13 Does not include 8,960 main lines in the occupied areas.

14 Data refer to fiscal years beginning 22 March of the year
   indicated.
15 Main lines with ISDN channels.
16 Telephone subscriber lines. (Finland: from 1996 the basis
   for the compilation of the statistics changed).
17 Data refer to fiscal years ending 15 July of the year
   indicated.
18 ITU estimate.
19 OFTEL estimate.
20 Including ISDN channels.
21 Temporary data; refers only to the part of the country under
   legal control of the government.
22 Only Deutsche Telekom.
23 Including PABX.
24 Including digital lines.
25 Billable lines.

Source:
Union internationale des télécommunications (UIT), Genève,
"Yearbook of Statistics, Telecommunication Services,
Chronological Time Series 1989-1998" et la base de données
de l'UIT.

† Pour les modifications récentes de nomenclature
de pays ou de zone concernant l'Allemagne, Hong Kong, région
administrative spéciale (RAS) de Chine, Macao, région
administrative spéciale (RAS) de Chine,
l'ex-Tchécoslovaquie, l'ex-URSS et l'ex-Rfs de Yougoslavie,
voir annexe I - Nomenclature des pays ou des zones,
groupements régionaux et autres groupements.

†† Les données statistiques relatives à
la Chine ne comprennent pas celles qui concernent la région
administrative spéciale de Hong Kong (la RAS de Hong Kong),
la région administrative spéciale de Macao (la RAS de Macao)
et la province chinoise de Taiwan.

1 Les données se réfèrent à "Angola Telecom".
2 Les données se réfèrent aux années fiscales commençant le
   1er avril de l'année indiquée.
3 Les données se réfèrent aux années fiscales finissant le 30e
   juin de l'année indiquée.
4 Malabo et Bata.
5 Cabines publiques exclues.
6 Les données se réfèrent aux années fiscales finissant le 30e
   septembre de l'année indiquée.
7 Lignes en service.
8 Les données se réfèrent à "Puerto Rico Telephone Authority".
9 Lignes d'accès par communication.
10 Les données pour 1980 se réfèrent aux stations principales.
   Dès 1981, les données se réfèrent aux "Local Loops".
11 Terminaux classiques en service.
12 Dès 1994, y compris les lignes "WLL".
13 Non compris 8 960 lignes principales dans les territoires
   occupés.
14 Les données se réfèrent aux années fiscales commençant le
   22e mars de l'année indiquée.
15 Lignes principales inclu RNIS.
16 Lignes d'abonnés au téléphone. (Finland : a compter de 1996,
   la base de calcul des statistiques à changé).
17 Les données se réfèrent aux années fiscales finissant le 15e
   juillet de l'année indiquée.
18 Estimation de l'UIT.
19 Estimation de l'OFTEL.
20 RNIS inclu.
21 Données provisoires; se rapportent à la partie du territoire
   du pays sur laquelle le Gouvernement exerce son contrôle.
22 Deutsche Telekom seulement.
23 PABX inclu.
24 Y compris lignes digitales.
25 Lignes payables.

17
Internet users
Usagers d'Internet
Estimated number
Nombre estimatif

Country or area Pays ou zone	1990	1991	1992	1993	1994	1995	1996	1997	1998	1999
Africa · Afrique										
Algeria Algérie	...	...	...	...	100	500	500	1 000	2 000	20 000
Angola Angola	...	...	...	...	...	...	100	750	2 500	10 000
Benin Bénin	...	...	...	...	...	...	100	500	2 000	10 000
Botswana[1] Botswana[1]	0	0	0	0	...	1 000	2 500	5 000	10 000	12 000
Burkina Faso Burkina Faso	...	...	...	...	...	...	100	800	1 000	4 000
Burundi Burundi	...	...	...	...	0	0	50	75	150	2 000
Cameroon Cameroun	...	...	...	...	...	...	...	1 000	2 000	20 000
Cape Verde Cap-Vert	...	...	...	...	...	...	...	1 000	2 000	5 000
Central African Rep. Rép. centrafricaine	...	...	...	...	...	...	59	200	200	1 000
Chad Tchad	...	...	...	...	...	...	...	50	335	1 000
Comoros Comores	...	...	...	...	...	...	...	0	200	800
Congo Congo	...	...	...	...	...	...	100	100	100	500
Côte d'Ivoire Côte d'Ivoire	...	...	...	...	...	30	1 300	3 000	10 000	20 000
Dem. Rep. of the Congo Rép. dém. du Congo	...	...	...	...	...	...	50	100	200	500
Djibouti Djibouti	...	...	...	...	...	100	200	400	500	1 000
Egypt[2] Egypte[2]	...	...	...	600	4 000	20 000	40 000	60 000	100 000	200 000
Equatorial Guinea Guinée équatoriale	...	...	...	...	...	...	...	200	470	500
Eritrea Erythrée	...	...	...	0	0	0	0	300	300	500
Ethiopia[2] Ethiopie[2]	...	...	...	...	...	10	1 000	3 000	6 000	8 000
Gabon[3] Gabon[3]	...	...	...	...	...	...	0	550	2 000	5 000
Gambia[1] Gambie[1]	...	...	...	...	...	100	400	600	2 500	4 000
Ghana Ghana	...	...	...	...	...	60	1 000	5 000	6 000	20 000
Guinea Guinée	...	...	...	...	10	50	150	300	500	5 000
Guinea-Bissau Guinée-Bissau	...	...	...	...	...	...	...	200	300	1 500

17
Internet users
Estimated number [*cont.*]
Usagers d'Internet
Nombre estimatif [*suite*]

Country or area Pays ou zone	1990	1991	1992	1993	1994	1995	1996	1997	1998	1999
Kenya[2] Kenya[2]	...	...	...	...	...	200	2 500	10 000	15 000	35 000
Lesotho[1] Lesotho[1]	...	...	...	...	...	...	50	100	200	1 000
Liberia Libéria	...	...	...	...	...	...	...	100	100	300
Libyan Arab Jamah. Jamah. arabe libyenne	...	...	...	...	...	...	...	0	0	7 000
Madagascar Madagascar	...	...	...	...	...	...	500	2 000	3 000	8 000
Malawi Malawi	...	...	...	...	...	...	...	500	2 000	10 000
Mali Mali	...	...	...	...	...	...	200	1 000	1 000	10 000
Mauritania Mauritanie	...	...	...	...	...	...	...	100	1 000	12 500
Mauritius Maurice	...	...	...	...	...	...	2 100	5 500	30 000	55 000
Morocco Maroc	...	...	...	...	...	1 000	1 552	6 000	40 000	50 000
Mozambique Mozambique	...	...	...	...	...	...	500	2 000	3 500	15 000
Namibia[4] Namibie[4]	...	...	...	...	...	110	116	1 000	5 000	6 000
Niger Niger	...	...	...	...	...	...	100	200	300	3 000
Nigeria Nigéria	...	...	...	...	...	...	10 000	20 000	30 000	100 000
Réunion Réunion	...	...	...	...	...	...	...	0	9 000	10 000
Rwanda Rwanda	...	...	...	...	...	...	50	100	800	5 000
Sao Tome and Principe Sao Tomé-et-Principe	...	...	...	...	...	...	...	0	400	500
Senegal Sénégal	...	...	...	...	...	60	1 000	2 500	7 500	30 000
Seychelles[1] Seychelles[1]	...	...	...	...	...	...	500	1 000	2 000	5 000
Sierra Leone Sierra Leone	...	...	...	0	0	0	100	200	600	2 000
Somalia Somalie	...	...	...	...	...	0	0	0	100	200
South Africa[1] Afrique du Sud[1]	...	10 000	60 000	140 000	330 000	460 000	618 000	800 000	1 266 000	1 820 000
Sudan Soudan	...	...	...	...	0	0	0	300	500	5 000
Swaziland[1] Swaziland[1]	...	...	...	...	...	10	500	900	1 000	5 000
Togo Togo	0	0	0	0	0	0	100	1 500	75 000	100 000

17
Internet users
Estimated number [*cont.*]
Usagers d'Internet
Nombre estimatif [*suite*]

Country or area Pays ou zone	1990	1991	1992	1993	1994	1995	1996	1997	1998	1999
Tunisia Tunisie	...	...	...	...	650	1 000	2 500	4 000	10 000	30 000
Uganda[2] Ouganda[2]	...	...	...	...	...	600	1 000	2 300	15 000	25 000
United Rep.Tanzania Rép.-Unie de Tanzanie	...	...	...	...	...	...	500	2 500	3 000	25 000
Zambia[1] Zambie[1]	...	...	...	...	600	800	850	900	3 000	15 000
Zimbabwe[2] Zimbabwe[2]	...	...	...	...	200	900	2 000	4 000	10 000	20 000
America, North · Amérique du Nord										
Antigua and Barbuda[1] Antigua-et-Barbuda[1]	...	...	...	...	...	1 500	2 000	2 500	3 000	4 000
Aruba Aruba	...	...	...	...	...	...	2 300	...	...	4 000
Bahamas Bahamas	...	...	...	...	...	2 700	5 000	3 967	6 908	11 307
Barbados[1] Barbade[1]	...	...	...	...	...	20	1 000	2 000	5 000	6 000
Belize[1] Belize[1]	...	...	...	...	...	10	1 582	5 000	10 000	12 000
Bermuda[1] Bermudes[1]	...	...	...	...	...	4 200	10 000	15 000	20 000	25 000
Canada Canada	...	160 000	260 000	340 000	690 000	1 220 000	2 000 000	4 500 000	7 500 000	11 000 000
Costa Rica Costa Rica	...	...	36	2 700	9 500	14 500	30 000	60 000	100 000	150 000
Cuba Cuba	...	...	...	...	...	10	3 500	7 500	25 000	34 800
Dominica[1] Dominique[1]	...	...	...	...	...	377	800	...	2 000	2 000
Dominican Republic Rép. dominicaine	...	...	...	...	...	1 400	6 200	10 000	20 000	25 000
El Salvador El Salvador	...	...	...	...	...	...	2 628	10 000	30 000	40 000
Greenland Groenland	...	...	...	...	36	30	1 000	...	...	...
Grenada Grenade	...	...	0	0	0	0	300	1 000	1 500	2 500
Guadeloupe Guadeloupe	...	...	...	...	...	...	100	1 000	2 000	4 000
Guatemala Guatemala	...	...	...	...	...	300	2 000	10 000	50 000	65 000
Haiti Haïti	...	...	...	...	...	...	600	...	2 000	6 000
Honduras Honduras	...	...	...	...	...	2 055	2 500	10 000	18 000	20 000
Jamaica[1] Jamaïque[1]	...	...	...	...	900	2 700	14 700	20 000	50 000	60 000

17
Internet users
Estimated number [*cont.*]
Usagers d'Internet
Nombre estimatif [*suite*]

Country or area Pays ou zone	1990	1991	1992	1993	1994	1995	1996	1997	1998	1999
Martinique Martinique	...	...	...	...	...	...	...	...	2 000	5 000
Mexico Mexique	...	5 000	15 000	45 000	80 000	140 000	270 000	595 700	1 306 700	2 452 000
Netherlands Antilles Antilles néerlandaises	...	...	...	...	...	...	500	...	...	2 000
Nicaragua Nicaragua	...	...	...	...	600	1 400	4 000	10 000	15 000	20 000
Panama Panama	...	...	...	...	200	1 500	6 000	15 000	30 000	45 000
Puerto Rico Porto Rico	...	...	...	...	1 000	5 000	10 000	50 000	100 000	200 000
Saint Kitts and Nevis[1] Saint-Kitts-et-Nevis[1]	...	...	...	...	...	...	850	1 000	1 500	2 000
Saint Lucia[1] Sainte-Lucie[1]	...	...	...	...	...	450	1 000	1 500	2 000	3 000
St. Vincent-Grenadines[1] St. Vincent-Grenadines[1]	...	...	...	...	...	139	522	1 000	2 000	3 000
Trinidad and Tobago[1] Trinité-et-Tobago[1]	...	...	...	...	...	1 960	5 000	10 000	20 000	30 000
United States Etats-Unis	...	3 000 000	4 500 000	5 500 000	8 500 000	20 000 000	30 000 000	40 000 000	60 000 000	110 000 000
United States Virgin Is. Iles Vierges américaines	...	...	...	...	1 000	3 000	5 000	7 500	10 000	12 000

America, South · Amérique du Sud

Country or area Pays ou zone	1990	1991	1992	1993	1994	1995	1996	1997	1998	1999
Argentina[4] Argentine[4]	...	...	1 000	10 000	15 000	30 000	50 000	100 000	200 000	900 000
Bolivia Bolivie	...	...	...	...	...	650	5 000	10 000	17 000	35 000
Brazil Brésil	...	5 000	20 000	40 000	60 000	170 000	740 000	1 310 000	2 500 000	3 500 000
Chile Chili	...	...	5 000	10 000	20 000	50 000	100 000	150 000	250 000	625 000
Colombia Colombie	...	...	...	...	13 000	28 000	130 000	200 000	350 000	600 000
Ecuador Equateur	...	...	550	1 800	3 900	5 000	10 000	13 000	15 000	35 000
French Guiana Guyane française	...	...	...	...	...	...	500	1 000	1 500	2 000
Guyana Guyana	...	...	...	...	...	...	500	1 000	2 000	3 000
Paraguay Paraguay	...	...	...	...	...	...	1 000	5 000	10 000	20 000
Peru Pérou	...	...	...	...	2 000	8 000	60 000	100 000	200 000	400 000
Suriname Suriname	...	...	...	...	...	500	1 000	4 494	7 236	10 000
Uruguay Uruguay	...	...	...	...	2 000	8 000	75 000	100 000	230 000	300 000

17
Internet users
Estimated number [cont.]
Usagers d'Internet
Nombre estimatif [suite]

Country or area Pays ou zone	1990	1991	1992	1993	1994	1995	1996	1997	1998	1999
Venezuela Venezuela	...	...	1 000	5 000	6 000	10 000	20 000	35 000	350 000	400 000
Asia · Asie										
Armenia Arménie	...	...	...	...	300	1 700	3 000	3 500	4 000	30 000
Azerbaijan Azerbaïdjan	...	...	...	...	110	160	500	2 000	3 000	8 000
Bahrain Bahreïn	...	...	...	...	...	2 000	5 000	10 000	20 000	30 000
Bangladesh[2] Bangladesh[2]	...	...	...	...	...	...	...	1 000	5 000	50 000
Bhutan Bhoutan	...	...	...	...	...	...	...	...	...	500
Brunei Darussalam Brunéi Darussalam	...	...	...	...	...	3 000	10 000	15 000	20 000	25 000
Cambodia Cambodge	...	...	...	...	...	...	...	700	2 000	4 000
China †† Chine ††	...	...	2 000	14 000	60 000	160 000	400 000	2 100 000	8 900 000	
China, Hong Kong SAR†[1] Chine, Hong Kong RAS†[1]	...	7 000	50 000	80 000	170 000	200 000	300 000	675 000	947 000	2 430 000
China, Macao SAR † Chine, Macao RAS †	...	...	...	...	150	1 153	3 037	10 000	30 000	40 000
Cyprus Chypre	...	...	350	400	800	3 000	5 000	33 000	68 000	88 000
Georgia Géorgie	...	...	...	...	...	600	2 000	3 000	5 000	20 000
India[1] Inde[1]	...	...	1 000	2 000	10 000	250 000	450 000	700 000	1 400 000	2 800 000
Indonesia Indonésie	...	...	...	...	2 000	50 000	100 000	250 000	500 000	900 000
Iran (Islamic Rep. of)[5] Iran (Rép. islamique d')[5]	...	...	...	...	250	2 600	10 000	30 000	65 000	100 000
Israel Israël	5 000	10 000	15 000	20 000	40 000	80 000	150 000	300 000	450 000	1 000 000
Japan[1] Japon[1]	...	50 000	120 000	500 000	1 000 000	2 000 000	5 500 000	11 550 000	16 940 000	27 060 000
Jordan Jordanie	...	...	...	...	...	1 000	2 000	27 354	60 816	120 000
Kazakhstan Kazakhstan	...	...	...	...	84	1 800	5 000	10 000	20 000	70 000
Korea, Republic of Corée, République de	...	20 000	43 000	110 000	138 000	366 000	731 000	1 634 000	3 103 000	10 860 000
Kuwait Koweït	...	...	...	1 700	2 600	3 500	15 000	40 000	60 000	100 000
Kyrgyzstan Kirghizistan	...	...	...	...	...	...	...	...	3 500	10 000
Lao People's Dem. Rep. Rép. dém. pop. lao	...	...	...	...	...	...	...	...	500	2 000

17
Internet users
Estimated number [*cont.*]
Usagers d'Internet
Nombre estimatif [*suite*]

Country or area Pays ou zone	1990	1991	1992	1993	1994	1995	1996	1997	1998	1999
Lebanon Liban	...	...	...	...	...	2 500	5 000	45 000	100 000	200 000
Malaysia Malaisie	...	...	200	5 000	20 000	40 000	200 000	600 000	800 000	1 500 000
Maldives Maldives	0	0	0	0	0	0	575	800	1 500	3 000
Mongolia Mongolie	...	...	...	...	...	200	415	2 600	3 400	6 000
Myanmar Myanmar	...	...	...	...	...	...	...	...	...	500
Nepal[6] Népal[6]	0	0	0	0	0	200	1 000	5 000	15 000	35 000
Oman Oman	...	...	...	...	...	...	...	10 000	20 000	50 000
Pakistan[2] Pakistan[2]	...	...	...	...	...	160	4 000	37 800	61 900	80 000
Philippines Philippines	...	...	...	...	4 000	20 000	40 000	100 000	150 000	500 000
Qatar Qatar	...	...	...	...	...	1 000	5 000	17 000	20 000	24 000
Saudi Arabia Arabie saoudite	...	...	...	...	...	2 000	5 000	10 000	20 000	300 000
Singapore[1] Singapour[1]	...	5 000	15 000	25 000	40 000	100 000	300 000	500 000	750 000	950 000
Sri Lanka Sri Lanka	...	...	...	...	500	1 000	10 000	30 000	55 000	65 000
Syrian Arab Republic Rép. arabe syrienne	0	0	0	0	0	0	0	5 000	10 000	20 000
Tajikistan Tadjikistan	...	...	...	...	...	...	...	...	...	2 000
Thailand[4] Thaïlande[4]	...	...	60	5 000	20 000	40 000	80 000	150 000	200 000	800 000
Turkey Turquie	...	...	...	5 000	30 000	50 000	120 000	300 000	450 000	1 500 000
Turkmenistan Turkménistan	...	...	...	...	...	...	...	...	...	2 000
United Arab Emirates Emirats arabes unis	...	...	...	...	...	2 503	9 669	90 000	200 000	400 000
Uzbekistan Ouzbékistan	...	...	...	...	...	350	1 000	2 500	5 000	7 500
Viet Nam Viet Nam	...	...	...	...	...	...	100	3 000	10 000	100 000
Yemen Yémen	...	...	...	...	...	...	100	2 500	4 000	10 000
Europe · Europe										
Albania Albanie	...	...	...	...	...	350	1 000	1 500	2 000	2 500
Andorra Andorre	...	...	...	...	...	...	1 000	2 000	4 500	5 000

17
Internet users
Estimated number [*cont.*]
Usagers d'Internet
Nombre estimatif [*suite*]

Country or area Pays ou zone	1990	1991	1992	1993	1994	1995	1996	1997	1998	1999
Austria Autriche	...	20 000	50 000	60 000	110 000	150 000	200 000	760 000	1 230 000	1 840 000
Belarus Bélarus	...	...	...	...	50	300	3 000	5 000	7 500	50 000
Belgium Belgique	...	2 000	10 000	20 000	70 000	100 000	300 000	500 000	800 000	1 400 000
Bosnia and Herzegovina Bosnie-Herzégovine	...	...	...	...	...	...	500	800	1 200	3 500
Bulgaria Bulgarie	...	...	...	200	1 650	10 000	60 000	100 000	150 000	200 000
Croatia Croatie	...	...	...	4 500	12 500	24 000	40 000	80 000	150 000	200 000
Czech Republic République tchèque	...	...	...	60 000	130 000	150 000	200 000	300 000	400 000	700 000
Denmark Danemark	...	10 000	20 000	30 000	70 000	200 000	300 000	600 000	1 000 000	1 500 000
Estonia Estonie	...	...	1 000	4 500	17 000	40 000	50 000	80 000	150 000	200 000
Faeroe Islands Iles Féroé	...	...	...	...	...	...	500	1 000	2 000	3 000
Finland Finlande	...	70 000	95 000	130 000	250 000	710 000	860 000	1 000 000	1 737 000	2 143 000
France France	...	80 000	130 000	130 000	350 000	500 000	800 000	1 000 000	3 500 000	5 660 000
Germany Allemagne	...	200 000	350 000	375 000	750 000	1 500 000	2 500 000	5 500 000	8 100 000	14 400 000
Greece Grèce	...	5 000	5 000	20 000	40 000	80 000	150 000	200 000	350 000	750 000
Hungary Hongrie	...	...	5 000	20 000	50 000	70 000	100 000	200 000	400 000	600 000
Iceland Islande	...	1 000	4 000	7 000	18 000	30 000	40 000	75 000	100 000	150 000
Ireland[1] Irlande[1]	...	2 000	6 000	10 000	20 000	40 000	80 000	150 000	300 000	444 000
Italy Italie	...	20 000	40 000	70 000	110 000	300 000	585 000	1 300 000	2 600 000	7 000 000
Latvia Lettonie	...	...	...	...	...	...	20 000	50 000	80 000	105 000
Lithuania Lituanie	...	...	...	...	...	...	10 000	35 000	70 000	103 000
Luxembourg Luxembourg	...	...	600	1 200	2 000	6 500	23 000	30 000	50 000	75 000
Malta Malte	...	...	...	...	...	850	4 000	7 000	9 000	15 000
Netherlands Pays-Bas	...	80 000	130 000	160 000	330 000	600 000	900 000	1 000 000	1 600 000	3 000 000
Norway Norvège	...	60 000	95 000	120 000	180 000	280 000	800 000	1 300 000	1 600 000	2 000 000
Poland Pologne	...	2 000	20 000	50 000	150 000	250 000	500 000	800 000	1 581 000	2 100 000

17
Internet users
Estimated number [*cont.*]
Usagers d'Internet
Nombre estimatif [*suite*]

Country or area Pays ou zone	1990	1991	1992	1993	1994	1995	1996	1997	1998	1999
Portugal Portugal	...	10 000	25 000	45 000	72 000	90 000	230 000	270 000	500 000	700 000
Republic of Moldova République de Moldova	...	...	...	...	36	150	200	1 200	11 000	15 000
Romania Roumanie	...	...	...	850	6 000	17 000	50 000	100 000	500 000	600 000
Russian Federation Fédération de Russie	...	...	1 000	20 000	80 000	220 000	400 000	700 000	1 200 000	2 700 000
Slovakia Slovaquie	...	...	...	6 800	17 000	28 000	100 000	190 000	500 000	600 000
Slovenia Slovénie	...	...	...	8 000	21 000	57 000	100 000	150 000	200 000	250 000
Spain Espagne	...	10 000	30 000	50 000	110 000	150 000	525 000	1 100 000	2 747 000	4 652 000
Sweden Suède	...	100 000	130 000	150 000	300 000	450 000	800 000	2 100 000	2 961 000	3 666 000
Switzerland Suisse	...	80 000	120 000	150 000	190 000	250 000	322 000	548 000	853 000	1 427 000
TFYR Macedonia L'ex-R.y. Macédoine	...	...	...	...	...	800	1 500	10 000	20 000	30 000
Ukraine Ukraine	...	...	...	400	7 000	22 000	50 000	100 000	150 000	200 000
United Kingdom [1] Royaume-Uni [1]	...	100 000	150 000	300 000	600 000	1 100 000	2 400 000	4 310 000	8 000 000	12 500 000
Yugoslavia Yougoslavie	...	...	...	...	...	...	20 000	50 000	65 000	80 000
Oceania · Océanie										
Australia [2] Australie [2]	...	190 000	310 000	350 000	400 000	500 000	600 000	1 600 000	3 000 000	6 000 000
Micronesia (Fed. States of) Micron (Etats fédérés de)	...	...	...	...	...	...	300	616	976	2 000
Fiji Fidji	...	...	...	50	60	70	500	1 750	5 000	7 500
French Polynesia Polynésie française	...	...	...	...	...	...	200	480	3 000	5 000
Guam Guam	...	...	...	...	...	500	2 000	3 000	4 000	5 000
Kiribati Kiribati	...	...	...	...	...	...	...	...	500	1 000
Marshall Islands Iles Marshall	...	...	0	0	0	0	19	...	...	500
New Caledonia Nouvelle-Calédonie	...	...	...	...	...	10	500	2 000	4 000	5 000
New Zealand [1] Nouvelle-Zélande [1]	...	...	10 000	22 500	115 000	180 000	300 000	550 000	600 000	700 000
Papua New Guinea Papouasie-Nvl-Guinée	...	...	...	...	...	...	50	...	...	2 000
Samoa Samoa	...	...	...	...	...	...	...	300	400	500

17
Internet users
Estimated number [*cont.*]
        Usagers d'Internet
        Nombre estimatif [*suite*]

Country or area Pays ou zone	1990	1991	1992	1993	1994	1995	1996	1997	1998	1999
Solomon Islands[1] Iles Salomon[1]	...	...	...	...	...	90	1 000	1 500	2 000	2 000
Tonga Tonga	...	...	...	...	...	120	160	500	750	1 000
Vanuatu Vanuatu	...	...	...	...	...	...	100	1 000	2 000	3 000

Source:
International Telecommunication Union (ITU), Geneva,
"Yearbook of Statistics, 1989-1998" and the ITU database.

† For information on recent changes in country or
area nomenclature pertaining to former Czechoslovakia,
Germany, Hong Kong Special Administrative Region (SAR) of
China, Macao Special Administrative Region (SAR) of China,
SFR of Yugoslavia and the former USSR, see Annex I - Country
or area nomenclature, regional and other groupings.

†† For statistical purposes, the data for
China do not include those for Hong Kong Special
Administrative Region (Hong Kong SAR), Macao Special
Administrative Region (Macao SAR) and Taiwan province of
China.

1 Data refer to fiscal years beginning 1 April of the year
   indicated.
2 Data refer to fiscal years ending 30 June of the year
   indicated.
3 Number of subscribers.
4 Data refer to fiscal years ending 30 September of the year
   indicated.
5 Data refer to fiscal years beginning 22 March of the year
   indicated.
6 Data refer to fiscal years ending 15 July of the year
   indicated.

Source:
Union internationale des télécommunications (UIT), Genève,
"Annuaire statistique, 1989-1998" et la base de données de
l'UIT.

† Pour les modifications récentes de nomenclature
de pays ou de zone concernant l'Allemagne, Hong Kong, région
administrative spéciale (RAS) de Chine, Macao, région
administrative spéciale (RAS) de Chine,
l'ex-Tchécoslovaquie, l'ex-URSS et l'ex-Rfs de Yougoslavie,
voir annexe I - Nomenclature des pays ou des zones,
groupements régionaux et autres groupements.

†† Les données statistiques relatives à
la Chine ne comprennent pas celles qui concernent la région
administrative spéciale de Hong Kong (la RAS de Hong Kong),
la région administrative spéciale de Macao (la RAS de Macao)
et la province chinoise de Taiwan.

1 Les données se réfèrent à l'année fiscale commençant le 1er
   avril de l'année indiquée.
2 Les données se réfèrent à l'année fiscale finissant le 30e
   juin de l'année indiquée.
3 Nombre d'abonnés.
4 Les données se réfèrent à l'année fiscale finissant le 30e
   septembre de l'année indiquée.
5 Les données se réfèrent à l'année fiscale commençant le 22e
   mars de l'année indiquée.
6 Les données se réfèrent à l'année fiscale finissant le 15e
   juillet de l'année indiquée.

Technical notes, tables 14-17

Table 14: The data on cinemas presented in this table have been compiled from the UNESCO *Statistical Yearbook* [29] and the UNESCO statistics database. The statistics refer to fixed cinemas and mobile units regularly used for commercial exhibition of long films of 1,600 metres and over.

The term fixed cinema used in this table refers to establishments possessing their own equipment and includes indoor cinemas (those with a permanent fixed roof over most of the seating accommodation), outdoor cinemas and drive-ins (establishments designed to enable the audience to watch a film while seated in their automobile). Mobile units are defined as projection units equipped and used to serve more than one site.

The capacity of fixed cinemas refers to the number of seats in indoor and outdoor cinemas plus the number of places for automobiles, multiplied by a factor of 4 in the case of drive-ins.

Cinema attendance is calculated from the number of tickets sold during a given year.

As a rule, figures refer only to commercial establishments but in the case of mobile units, it is possible that the figures for some countries may also include non-commercial units. Gross receipts are given in the national currency of each country.

The statistics included in *Tables 15-17* were obtained from the statistics database and the *Yearbook of Statistics, Telecommunication Services* [17] of the International Telecommunication Union.

Table 15: The data on the number of facsimile machines are estimates which are generally based on Telefax directories or sales data.

The number of mobile cellular subscribers refers to users of portable telephones subscribing to an automatic public mobile telephone service using cellular technology which provides access to the Public Switched Telephone Network (PSTN).

Table 16: This table shows the number of main lines in operation and the main lines in operation per 100 inhabitants for the years indicated. Main telephone lines refer to the telephone lines connecting a customer's equipment to the Public Switched Telephone Network (PSTN) and which have a dedicated port on a telephone exchange. Note that in most countries, main lines also include public telephones. Main telephone lines per 100 inhabitants is calculated by dividing the number of main lines by the population and multiplying by 100.

Table 17: Internet user data is based on reported estimates, derivations based on reported Internet Access Provider subscriber counts, or calculated by multiplying

Notes techniques, tableaux 14 à 17

Tableau 14: Les données sur les cinémas présentées dans ce tableau proviennent de l'*Annuaire statistique* [29] et de la base de données de l'UNESCO. Les statistiques concernent les établissements fixes et les cinémas itinérants d'exploitation commerciale de films d'une longueur de 1600 mètres et plus.

Dans ce tableau, le terme établissement fixe désigne tout établissement doté de son propre équipement; il englobe les salles fermées (c'est-à-dire celles où un toit fixe recouvre la plupart des places assises), les cinémas de plein air et les cinémas pour automobilistes ou drive-ins (conçus pour permettre aux spectateurs d'assister à la projection sans quitter leur voiture). Les cinémas itinérants sont définis comme groupes mobiles de projection équipés de manière à pouvoir être utilisés dans des lieux différents.

La capacité des cinémas fixes se réfère au nombre de sièges dans les salles fermées et les cinémas de plein air, plus le nombre de places d'automobiles multiplié par le facteur 4 dans le cas des drive-ins.

La fréquentation des cinémas est calculée sur la base du nombre de billets vendus au cours d'une année donnée.

En général, les statistiques présentées ne concernent que les établissements commerciaux: toutefois, dans le cas des cinémas itinérants, il se peut que les données relatives à certains pays tiennent compte aussi des établissements non-commerciaux. Les recettes brutes sont indiquées en monnaie nationale de chaque pays.

Les données présentées dans les *Tableaux 15 à 17* proviennent de la base de données et *l'Annuaire statistique, Services de télécommunications* [17] de l'Union internationale des télécommunications.

Tableau 15: Les données sur le nombre de télécopieurs sont estimations, basées généralement sur les annuaires de télécopie ou sur les données des ventes.

Les abonnés mobiles désignent les utilisateurs de téléphones portatifs abonnés à un service automatique public de téléphones mobiles ayant accès au Réseau de téléphone public connecté (RTPC).

Tableau 16: Ce tableau indique le nombre de lignes principales en service et les lignes principales en service pour 100 habitants pour les années indiquées. Les lignes principales sont des lignes téléphoniques qui relient l'équipement terminal de l'abonné au Réseau de téléphone public connecté (RTPC) et qui possèdent un accès individualisé aux équipements d'un central téléphonique. Pour la plupart des pays, le nombre de lignes principales en service indiqué comprend également les lignes publiques. Le nombre de lignes principales pour 100 habitants se calcule en divisant le nombre de lignes

the number of hosts by an estimated multiplier. However, comparisons of user data are misleading because there is no standard definition of frequency (e.g., daily, weekly, monthly) or services used (e.g., e-mail, World Wide Web).

principales par la population et en multipliant par 100.

Tableau 17: Les chiffres relatifs aux usagers d'Internet sont basés sur les estimations communiquées, calculés à partir des chiffres issus de dénombrements d'abonnés aux services de fournisseurs d'accès, ou obtenus en multipliant le nombre d'hôtes par un facteur estimatif. Mais les comparaisons de chiffres relatifs aux usagers prêtent à confusion, car il n'existe pas de définition normalisée de la fréquence (quotidienne, hebdomadaire, mensuelle) ni des services utilisés (courrier électronique, Web).

Part Three
Economic Activity

VI
National accounts and industrial production (tables 18-22)
VII
Financial statistics (tables 23 and 24)
VIII
Labour force (tables 25 and 26)
IX
Wages and prices (tables 27-29)
X
Agriculture, hunting, forestry and fishing (tables 30-36)
XI
Manufacturing (tables 37-56)
XII
Transport (tables 57-61)
XIII
Energy (tables 62 and 63)
XIV
Environment (tables 64-67)
XV
Intellectual property (table 68)

Part Three of the *Yearbook* presents statistical series on production and consumption for a wide range of economic activities, and other basic series on major economic topics, for all countries or areas of the world for which data are available. Included are basic tables on national accounts, finance, labour force, wages and prices, a wide range of agricultural, mined and manufactured commodities, transport, energy, environment and intellectual property. In most cases, tables present statistics on production; in a few cases, data are presented on stocks and consumption.

International economic topics such as external trade are covered in Part Four.

Troisième partie
Activité économique

VI
Comptabilités nationales et production industrielle (tableaux 18 à 22)
VII
Statistiques financières (tableaux 23 et 24)
VIII
Main-d'oeuvre (tableaux 25 et 26)
IX
Salaires et prix (tableaux 27 à 29)
X
Agriculture, chasse, forêts et pêche (tableaux 30 à 36)
XI
Industries manufacturières (tableaux 37 à 56)
XII
Transports (tableaux 57 à 61)
XIII
Energie (tableaux 62 et 63)
XIV
Environnement (tableaux 64 à 67)
XV
Propriété intellectuelle (tableau 68)

La troisième partie de l'*Annuaire* présente, pour une large gamme d'activités économiques, des séries statistiques sur la production et la consommation, et, pour tous les pays ou zones du monde pour lesquels des données sont disponibles, d'autres séries fondamentales ayant trait à des questions économiques importantes. Y figurent des tableaux de base consacrés à la comptabilité nationale, aux finances, à la main-d'oeuvre, aux salaires et aux prix, à un large éventail de produits agricoles, miniers et manufacturés, aux transports, à l'énergie, à l'environnement et à la propriété intellectuelle. On y trouve, dans la plupart des cas, des statistiques sur la production et parfois des données relatives aux stocks et à la consommation.

Les questions économiques internationales comme le commerce extérieur sont traitées dans la quatrième partie.

18
Gross domestic product: total and per capita
Produit intérieur brut : total et par habitant

In US dollars (millions) [1] at current and constant 1990 prices; per capita US dollars;
real rates of growth

En dollars E.–U. (millions) [1] aux prix courants et constants de 1990; par habitant en dollars E.–U.;
taux de l'accroissement réels

Country or area Pays ou zone	1990	1991	1992	1993	1994	1995	1996	1997	1998
World Monde									
At current prices	22 667 128	23 351 962	23 883 143	24 494 354	26 315 038	29 127 966	29 847 347	29 706 258	29 547 914
Per capita	4 309	4 369	4 401	4 449	4 712	5 144	5 199	5 105	5 010
At constant prices	22 667 128	22 883 958	23 153 720	23 393 890	24 002 707	24 655 538	25 468 081	26 343 657	26 889 874
Growth rates	2.0	1.0	1.2	1.0	2.6	2.7	3.3	3.4	2.1
Afghanistan Afghanistan									
At current prices	21 769	21 943	22 163	21 476	31 041	22 781	9 832	9 240	11 166
Per capita	1 475	1 416	1 344	1 218	1 657	1 159	483	442	523
At constant prices	21 769	21 943	22 163	21 476	20 831	26 289	27 866	29 538	31 311
Growth rates	−3.1	0.8	1.0	−3.1	−3.0	26.2	6.0	6.0	6.0
Albania Albanie									
At current prices	2 171	1 010	676	1 228	1 949	2 479	2 689	2 294	3 032
Per capita	660	306	206	378	607	780	853	733	972
At constant prices	2 171	1 563	1 450	1 589	1 721	1 950	2 128	1 979	2 137
Growth rates	−10.0	−28.0	−7.2	9.6	8.3	13.3	9.1	−7.0	8.0
Algeria Algérie									
At current prices	61 891	46 670	49 216	50 962	42 426	42 017	46 845	48 046	50 816
Per capita	2 482	1 827	1 881	1 903	1 548	1 497	1 631	1 635	1 689
At constant prices	61 891	61 210	62 067	61 322	61 690	64 158	66 724	69 393	72 030
Growth rates	3.2	−1.1	1.4	−1.2	0.6	4.0	4.0	4.0	3.8
Andorra Andorre									
At current prices	675	753	857	743	784	946	1 027	980	1 062
Per capita	13 069	14 009	15 275	12 658	12 772	14 766	15 377	14 101	14 690
At constant prices	675	690	695	687	702	721	738	766	797
Growth rates	3.7	2.3	0.7	−1.2	2.2	2.7	2.3	3.8	4.0
Angola Angola									
At current prices	10 269	8 314	4 967	3 302	3 473	5 273	6 605	7 768	6 382
Per capita	1 112	871	503	323	328	481	582	663	528
At constant prices	10 269	10 106	10 224	8 077	8 190	9 116	10 182	10 854	10 963
Growth rates	−0.4	−1.6	1.2	−21.0	1.4	11.3	11.7	6.6	1.0
Anguilla Anguilla									
At current prices	54	56	61	66	74	75	79	89	95
Per capita	7 459	7 546	8 108	8 728	9 633	9 617	10 028	11 094	11 678
At constant prices	54	53	57	62	67	65	67	74	77
Growth rates	25.5	−2.0	7.5	7.4	8.2	−2.1	2.5	10.8	4.1
Antigua and Barbuda Antigua−et−Barbuda									
At current prices	392	409	424	457	500	494	543	584	626
Per capita	6 135	6 376	6 563	7 028	7 653	7 509	8 213	8 791	9 370
At constant prices	392	402	406	426	453	430	453	479	499
Growth rates	3.5	2.7	0.8	5.1	6.2	−5.0	5.4	5.7	4.2
Argentina Argentine									
At current prices	141 353	189 710	228 990	236 754	257 695	258 096	272 242	293 005	298 280
Per capita	4 346	5 753	6 852	6 990	7 509	7 423	7 730	8 214	8 257
At constant prices	141 353	156 312	171 332	181 135	191 706	186 252	196 545	212 487	220 723
Growth rates	−1.8	10.6	9.6	5.7	5.8	−2.8	5.5	8.1	3.9
Armenia Arménie									
At current prices	15 119	9 117	321	463	648	1 287	1 597	1 639	1 885
Per capita	4 265	2 558	90	129	181	360	448	461	533
At constant prices	15 119	13 789	8 025	7 319	7 714	8 247	8 733	9 021	9 671
Growth rates	0.8	−8.8	−41.8	−8.8	5.4	6.9	5.9	3.3	7.2
Australia Australie									
At current prices	310 040	316 591	313 887	305 860	346 954	376 651	417 598	420 080	372 723
Per capita	18 359	18 495	18 107	17 433	19 550	20 988	23 019	22 914	20 125
At constant prices	310 040	311 221	322 696	335 965	351 162	367 063	380 959	398 937	417 031
Growth rates	−0.2	0.4	3.7	4.1	4.5	4.5	3.8	4.7	4.5
Austria Autriche									
At current prices	161 514	168 757	189 571	185 019	198 559	235 597	231 731	206 668	210 913
Per capita	20 961	21 753	24 250	23 478	24 998	29 447	28 777	25 518	25 911
At constant prices	161 514	167 045	169 286	170 154	174 479	178 069	181 596	183 755	189 039
Growth rates	4.6	3.4	1.3	0.5	2.5	2.1	2.0	1.2	2.9

18

Gross domestic product: total and per capita
In US dollars (millions) [1] at current and constant 1990 prices; per capita US dollars;
real rates of growth [cont.]
Produit intérieur brut : total et par habitant
En dollars E.−U. (millions) [1] aux prix courants et constants de 1990; par habitant en dollars E.−U.;
taux de l'accroissement réels [suite]

Country or area Pays ou zone	1990	1991	1992	1993	1994	1995	1996	1997	1998
Azerbaijan Azerbaïdjan									
At current prices	22 012	15 269	445	1 571	1 193	2 417	3 177	3 962	4 117
Per capita	3 075	2 106	61	212	159	320	417	518	537
At constant prices	22 012	21 858	16 931	13 020	10 461	9 224	9 340	9 882	10 969
Growth rates	−9.9	−0.7	−22.5	−23.1	−19.7	−11.8	1.3	5.8	11.0
Bahamas Bahamas									
At current prices	2 944	3 047	2 888	2 857	2 854	3 053	3 069	3 243	3 374
Per capita	11 540	11 718	10 898	10 579	10 369	10 889	10 747	11 150	11 395
At constant prices	2 944	2 798	2 755	2 596	2 542	2 592	2 620	2 730	2 790
Growth rates	5.6	−5.0	−1.5	−5.8	−2.1	2.0	1.1	4.2	2.2
Bahrain Bahreïn									
At current prices	4 006	4 241	4 433	4 648	4 861	5 054	5 361	5 579	5 757
Per capita	8 177	8 409	8 554	8 742	8 924	9 064	9 402	9 577	9 684
At constant prices	4 006	4 189	4 515	4 888	5 004	5 112	5 270	5 248	5 179
Growth rates	4.6	4.6	7.8	8.3	2.4	2.2	3.1	−0.4	−1.3
Bangladesh Bangladesh									
At current prices	24 137	24 770	24 340	26 041	29 103	32 315	33 570	35 107	37 288
Per capita	221	223	215	227	249	272	278	286	299
At constant prices	24 137	25 157	26 285	27 393	28 611	30 143	31 915	33 694	35 446
Growth rates	3.4	4.2	4.5	4.2	4.4	5.4	5.9	5.6	5.2
Barbados Barbados									
At current prices	1 720	1 697	1 589	1 651	1 737	1 883	1 994	2 183	2 337
Per capita	6 689	6 565	6 113	6 315	6 608	7 123	7 506	8 178	8 717
At constant prices	1 720	1 653	1 559	1 571	1 634	1 682	1 769	1 845	1 935
Growth rates	−3.3	−3.9	−5.7	0.8	4.0	2.9	5.2	4.3	4.9
Belarus Bélarus									
At current prices	64 414	49 486	4 746	6 723	5 922	10 409	14 240	13 714	14 024
Per capita	6 278	4 804	459	648	570	1 002	1 372	1 325	1 360
At constant prices	64 414	63 665	57 529	53 133	46 444	41 628	42 797	47 676	51 633
Growth rates	−1.4	−1.2	−9.6	−7.6	−12.6	−10.4	2.8	11.4	8.3
Belgium Belgique									
At current prices	197 285	202 332	226 230	214 792	232 925	275 744	268 208	243 540	250 392
Per capita	19 827	20 279	22 608	21 403	23 146	27 334	26 531	24 049	24 692
At constant prices	197 285	201 165	204 335	201 259	207 228	212 407	214 494	222 066	228 047
Growth rates	2.7	2.0	1.6	−1.5	3.0	2.5	1.0	3.5	2.7
Belize Belize									
At current prices	405	433	485	530	552	587	604	615	630
Per capita	2 163	2 250	2 455	2 617	2 655	2 750	2 759	2 744	2 741
At constant prices	405	415	450	469	481	500	507	524	531
Growth rates	11.5	2.4	8.2	4.2	2.6	3.9	1.4	3.3	1.5
Benin Bénin									
At current prices	1 845	1 878	2 152	2 106	1 497	2 009	2 208	2 141	2 306
Per capita	396	392	437	416	288	377	403	380	399
At constant prices	1 845	1 932	2 011	2 082	2 172	2 270	2 398	2 534	2 647
Growth rates	3.2	4.7	4.1	3.6	4.3	4.5	5.6	5.7	4.5
Bermuda Bermudes									
At current prices	1 635	1 705	1 720	1 864	1 914	2 083	2 194	2 330	2 457
Per capita	27 559	28 492	28 489	30 599	31 141	33 597	35 088	36 954	38 652
At constant prices	1 635	1 661	1 592	1 665	1 677	1 794	1 846	1 914	1 944
Growth rates	−3.5	1.6	−4.1	4.6	0.7	6.9	2.9	3.7	1.5
Bhutan Bhoutan									
At current prices	285	242	245	236	271	307	331	399	398
Per capita	168	140	140	132	150	166	175	205	199
At constant prices	285	295	308	327	347	373	396	425	450
Growth rates	6.6	3.5	4.5	6.1	6.4	7.4	6.1	7.3	5.8
Bolivia Bolivie									
At current prices	4 868	5 343	5 644	5 735	5 981	6 715	7 397	7 967	8 571
Per capita	741	794	819	812	826	906	974	1 025	1 077
At constant prices	4 868	5 124	5 208	5 431	5 684	5 950	6 210	6 486	6 794
Growth rates	4.6	5.3	1.6	4.3	4.7	4.7	4.4	4.4	4.7
Bosnia & Herzegovina Bosnie−Herzégovine									
At current prices	13 012	14 377	1 377	1 222	1 088	2 029	2 778	3 300	3 900
Per capita	3 020	3 451	349	329	309	594	812	938	1 061

18

Gross domestic product: total and per capita
In US dollars (millions) [1] at current and constant 1990 prices; per capita US dollars;
real rates of growth [*cont.*]
Produit intérieur brut : total et par habitant
En dollars E.−U. (millions) [1] aux prix courants et constants de 1990; par habitant en dollars E.−U.;
taux de l'accroissement réels [*suite*]

Country or area Pays ou zone	1990	1991	1992	1993	1994	1995	1996	1997	1998
At constant prices	13 012	11 438	8 452	6 170	6 571	8 740	11 187	12 865	15 438
Growth rates	−8.9	−12.1	−26.1	−27.0	6.5	33.0	28.0	15.0	20.0
Botswana Botswana									
At current prices	3 489	3 708	3 934	3 733	4 087	4 420	4 272	4 790	4 819
Per capita	2 734	2 816	2 896	2 669	2 843	2 998	2 832	3 109	3 069
At constant prices	3 489	3 791	4 029	4 026	4 194	4 307	4 590	4 915	5 308
Growth rates	5.5	8.7	6.3	−0.1	4.2	2.7	6.6	7.1	8.0
Brazil Brésil									
At current prices	465 051	407 751	390 594	438 433	546 222	704 175	775 025	801 577	775 022
Per capita	3 144	2 713	2 559	2 830	3 476	4 419	4 798	4 897	4 673
At constant prices	465 051	470 020	467 284	490 491	519 054	540 975	555 151	575 410	574 773
Growth rates	0.5	1.1	−0.6	5.0	5.8	4.2	2.6	3.6	−0.1
British Virgin Islands Iles Vierges britanniques									
At current prices	299	315	345	364	414	457	504	566	604
Per capita	18 517	18 942	20 098	20 640	22 788	24 463	26 270	28 712	29 795
At constant prices	299	305	313	324	342	360	368	390	395
Growth rates	8.5	2.0	2.5	3.5	5.7	5.0	2.3	5.9	1.3
Brunei Darussalam Brunéi Darussalam									
At current prices	3 591	3 832	4 030	4 075	4 377	5 217	5 450	5 422	4 323
Per capita	13 972	14 496	14 823	14 582	15 252	17 723	18 078	17 582	13 719
At constant prices	3 591	3 736	3 695	3 713	3 781	3 895	4 034	4 199	4 241
Growth rates	2.7	4.0	−1.1	0.5	1.8	3.0	3.6	4.1	1.0
Bulgaria Bulgarie									
At current prices	20 726	7 628	8 605	10 835	9 709	13 106	9 830	10 141	12 257
Per capita	2 377	880	997	1 262	1 136	1 542	1 164	1 208	1 470
At constant prices	20 726	19 294	17 894	17 630	17 950	18 323	16 472	15 313	15 854
Growth rates	−17.5	−6.9	−7.3	−1.5	1.8	2.1	−10.1	−7.0	3.5
Burkina Faso Burkina Faso									
At current prices	2 859	2 877	3 070	2 940	1 940	2 378	2 470	2 302	2 495
Per capita	316	309	320	298	192	228	231	209	221
At constant prices	2 859	3 131	3 143	3 302	3 341	3 482	3 666	3 868	4 061
Growth rates	−1.0	9.5	0.4	5.1	1.2	4.2	5.3	5.5	5.0
Burundi Burundi									
At current prices	1 104	1 158	1 046	933	937	1 014	889	789	667
Per capita	202	207	182	158	155	165	142	124	103
At constant prices	1 104	1 163	1 184	1 101	1 067	992	907	910	951
Growth rates	3.5	5.3	1.8	−7.0	−3.1	−7.0	−8.6	0.4	4.5
Cambodia Cambodge									
At current prices	1 431	1 900	1 980	2 263	2 436	3 078	3 172	3 063	2 736
Per capita	165	213	215	239	251	308	310	292	255
At constant prices	1 431	1 540	1 648	1 659	1 724	1 839	1 940	1 991	2 016
Growth rates	1.2	7.6	7.0	0.7	3.9	6.7	5.5	2.6	1.3
Cameroon Cameroun									
At current prices	13 187	11 102	11 568	11 936	7 339	9 072	9 296	9 039	10 047
Per capita	1 149	941	954	957	572	688	686	649	702
At constant prices	13 187	12 791	12 382	12 060	12 446	13 093	13 551	14 243	14 983
Growth rates	2.1	−3.0	−3.2	−2.6	3.2	5.2	3.5	5.1	5.2
Canada Canada									
At current prices	572 676	586 979	568 680	552 968	553 374	579 249	602 212	621 307	594 106
Per capita	20 674	20 940	20 040	19 265	19 058	19 733	20 296	20 719	19 642
At constant prices	572 676	561 739	566 859	579 905	607 325	623 965	634 524	659 705	680 124
Growth rates	0.2	−1.9	0.9	2.3	4.7	2.7	1.7	4.0	3.1
Cape Verde Cap−Vert									
At current prices	308	321	358	362	409	491	480	446	443
Per capita	903	921	1 007	994	1 100	1 289	1 232	1 120	1 085
At constant prices	308	312	322	345	369	397	412	425	438
Growth rates	0.7	1.4	3.0	7.3	6.9	7.5	3.8	3.2	3.0
Cayman Islands Iles Caïmanes									
At current prices	495	514	573	621	712	768	845	891	972
Per capita	18 796	18 750	20 091	20 937	23 104	23 995	25 425	25 854	27 187
At constant prices	495	494	498	503	549	460	600	723	800
Growth rates	13.2	−0.2	0.9	0.9	9.1	−16.2	30.3	20.5	10.8
Central African Rep. Rép. centrafricaine									
At current prices	1 297	1 284	1 339	1 213	797	1 065	1 016	951	1 032

18

Gross domestic product: total and per capita

In US dollars (millions) [1] at current and constant 1990 prices; per capita US dollars;

real rates of growth [*cont.*]

Produit intérieur brut : total et par habitant

En dollars E.−U. (millions) [1] aux prix courants et constants de 1990; par habitant en dollars E.−U.;

taux de l'accroissement réels [*suite*]

Country or area Pays ou zone	1990	1991	1992	1993	1994	1995	1996	1997	1998
Per capita	441	426	435	385	247	324	303	278	296
At constant prices	1 297	1 295	1 261	1 294	1 344	1 408	1 378	1 439	1 518
Growth rates	2.1	−0.1	−2.6	2.6	3.9	4.7	−2.1	4.4	5.5
Chad Tchad									
At current prices	1 224	1 321	1 325	1 030	830	1 006	1 060	994	1 091
Per capita	213	223	217	163	128	150	154	140	150
At constant prices	1 224	1 356	1 460	1 225	1 375	1 411	1 440	1 484	1 573
Growth rates	−4.7	10.8	7.7	−16.1	12.3	2.6	2.0	3.1	6.0
Chile Chili									
At current prices	30 323	34 650	41 881	44 474	50 919	65 216	68 568	75 779	72 949
Per capita	2 315	2 601	3 092	3 229	3 639	4 589	4 755	5 182	4 921
At constant prices	30 323	32 740	36 760	39 328	41 573	45 991	49 393	53 142	54 955
Growth rates	3.7	8.0	12.3	7.0	5.7	10.6	7.4	7.6	3.4
China †† Chine ††									
At current prices	387 772	406 090	483 047	601 078	542 534	700 219	816 490	898 244	959 001
Per capita	342	353	415	511	457	584	674	735	777
At constant prices	387 772	423 447	483 576	548 859	618 015	682 907	748 466	814 331	877 849
Growth rates	3.8	9.2	14.2	13.5	12.6	10.5	9.6	8.8	7.8
China, Hong Kong SAR † Chine, Hong Kong RAS †									
At current prices	74 784	86 024	100 681	116 017	130 801	139 242	154 197	171 142	163 712
Per capita	13 110	14 877	17 140	19 404	21 455	22 372	24 235	26 287	24 581
At constant prices	74 784	78 566	83 487	88 606	93 392	97 028	101 466	106 421	100 901
Growth rates	3.4	5.1	6.3	6.1	5.4	3.9	4.6	4.9	−5.2
Colombia Colombie									
At current prices	46 908	48 033	51 411	59 241	79 936	92 503	97 147	106 671	102 932
Per capita	1 341	1 347	1 414	1 598	2 114	2 400	2 473	2 664	2 523
At constant prices	46 908	47 847	49 782	52 463	55 514	58 402	59 602	61 450	61 573
Growth rates	4.3	2.0	4.0	5.4	5.8	5.2	2.1	3.1	0.2
Comoros Comores									
At current prices	250	247	264	261	186	214	213	193	201
Per capita	475	455	474	456	315	354	342	302	305
At constant prices	250	237	255	264	250	241	240	240	242
Growth rates	3.4	−5.4	7.7	3.8	−5.3	−3.9	−0.4	0.0	1.1
Congo Congo									
At current prices	2 871	2 722	2 932	2 685	1 769	2 116	2 541	2 322	1 925
Per capita	1 293	1 191	1 247	1 110	711	826	965	857	691
At constant prices	2 871	2 939	2 989	2 960	2 798	2 860	3 031	3 060	3 020
Growth rates	2.2	2.4	1.7	−1.0	−5.5	2.2	6.0	1.0	−1.3
Cook Islands Iles Cook									
At current prices	64	70	72	81	96	102	103	102	87
Per capita	3 485	3 756	3 855	4 293	5 080	5 384	5 393	5 352	4 521
At constant prices	64	68	73	75	78	75	75	77	78
Growth rates	7.9	7.1	6.0	3.9	3.9	−4.4	−0.2	2.5	2.0
Costa Rica Costa Rica									
At current prices	5 709	5 637	6 738	7 521	8 317	9 233	9 391	9 952	10 731
Per capita	1 873	1 793	2 076	2 246	2 409	2 598	2 571	2 655	2 793
At constant prices	5 709	5 838	6 290	6 688	6 991	7 169	7 129	7 394	7 851
Growth rates	3.6	2.3	7.7	6.3	4.5	2.5	−0.6	3.7	6.2
Côte d'Ivoire Côte d'Ivoire									
At current prices	11 893	11 531	12 033	11 153	8 314	11 105	12 075	11 596	12 702
Per capita	1 022	959	969	870	630	821	874	824	889
At constant prices	11 893	11 900	11 826	11 779	12 031	12 880	13 748	14 311	15 098
Growth rates	−1.2	0.1	−0.6	−0.4	2.1	7.1	6.7	4.1	5.5
Croatia Croatie									
At current prices	24 782	22 464	10 241	10 904	14 583	18 811	19 871	20 145	21 321
Per capita	5 486	4 974	2 269	2 420	3 241	4 187	4 428	4 493	4 758
At constant prices	24 782	19 556	17 265	15 880	16 812	17 961	19 038	20 276	20 823
Growth rates	−7.1	−21.1	−11.7	−8.0	5.9	6.8	6.0	6.5	2.7
Cuba Cuba									
At current prices	19 645	16 248	14 905	15 095	19 198	21 737	22 815	22 952	23 901
Per capita	1 848	1 517	1 382	1 391	1 760	1 983	2 071	2 074	2 150
At constant prices	19 645	17 544	15 513	13 205	13 299	13 626	14 694	15 060	15 248
Growth rates	−2.9	−10.7	−11.6	−14.9	0.7	2.5	7.8	2.5	1.2

18

Gross domestic product: total and per capita
In US dollars (millions) [1] at current and constant 1990 prices; per capita US dollars;
real rates of growth [*cont.*]

Produit intérieur brut : total et par habitant
En dollars E.−U. (millions) [1] aux prix courants et constants de 1990; par habitant en dollars E.−U.;
taux de l'accroissement réels [*suite*]

Country or area Pays ou zone	1990	1991	1992	1993	1994	1995	1996	1997	1998
Cyprus Chypre									
At current prices	5 557	5 734	6 902	6 583	7 417	8 823	8 867	8 447	8 970
Per capita	8 165	8 289	9 796	9 163	10 134	11 859	11 754	11 065	11 631
At constant prices	5 557	5 589	6 134	6 176	6 538	6 937	7 069	7 246	7 608
Growth rates	7.4	0.6	9.8	0.7	5.9	6.1	1.9	2.5	5.0
Czech Republic République tchèque									
At current prices	34 886	25 570	29 816	35 000	41 092	52 035	57 921	53 000	56 402
Per capita	3 385	2 480	2 890	3 390	3 979	5 040	5 615	5 145	5 486
At constant prices	34 886	30 835	30 676	30 695	31 377	33 242	34 513	34 623	33 817
Growth rates	−1.2	−11.6	−0.5	0.1	2.2	5.9	3.8	0.3	−2.3
Dem. Rep. of the Congo Rép. dém. du Congo									
At current prices	11 195	9 078	8 205	8 975	5 170	5 680	5 896	5 612	4 836
Per capita	300	234	202	212	118	125	126	117	98
At constant prices	11 195	9 818	8 797	7 689	7 389	7 440	7 507	7 079	6 676
Growth rates	3.0	−12.3	−10.4	−12.6	−3.9	0.7	0.9	−5.7	−5.7
Denmark Danemark									
At current prices	133 360	134 081	147 093	138 829	151 828	180 249	183 087	168 736	174 348
Per capita	25 946	26 017	28 450	26 757	29 157	34 499	34 933	32 103	33 085
At constant prices	133 360	135 217	136 944	138 096	146 042	151 425	155 734	160 615	164 930
Growth rates	1.2	1.4	1.3	0.8	5.8	3.7	2.8	3.1	2.7
Djibouti Djibouti									
At current prices	457	466	482	482	511	510	496	491	498
Per capita	884	866	864	840	868	848	814	796	800
At constant prices	457	443	445	453	446	441	416	421	430
Growth rates	4.0	−3.1	0.5	2.0	−1.8	−0.9	−5.7	1.2	2.1
Dominica Dominica									
At current prices	171	184	192	200	215	224	236	244	257
Per capita	2 396	2 590	2 696	2 821	3 035	3 159	3 337	3 452	3 630
At constant prices	171	172	176	179	181	184	189	192	197
Growth rates	9.3	0.6	2.0	1.7	1.4	1.7	2.8	1.4	2.6
Dominican Republic Rép. dominicaine									
At current prices	7 074	7 590	8 822	9 610	10 453	11 935	13 324	15 076	15 845
Per capita	995	1 046	1 192	1 274	1 360	1 526	1 674	1 862	1 925
At constant prices	7 074	7 142	7 715	7 948	8 292	8 691	9 323	10 083	10 814
Growth rates	−5.5	1.0	8.0	3.0	4.3	4.8	7.3	8.2	7.3
Ecuador Equateur									
At current prices	10 686	11 752	12 656	14 304	16 606	17 939	19 040	19 768	19 723
Per capita	1 041	1 119	1 178	1 303	1 480	1 565	1 627	1 656	1 620
At constant prices	10 686	11 222	11 622	11 858	12 371	12 661	12 911	13 348	13 403
Growth rates	3.0	5.0	3.6	2.0	4.3	2.3	2.0	3.4	0.4
Egypt Egypte									
At current prices	48 050	33 371	41 664	46 652	51 607	60 472	67 385	75 635	79 867
Per capita	853	580	709	779	845	971	1 061	1 168	1 211
At constant prices	48 050	48 569	50 722	52 184	54 244	56 717	59 634	63 142	66 615
Growth rates	8.6	1.1	4.4	2.9	3.9	4.6	5.1	5.9	5.5
El Salvador El Salvador									
At current prices	4 544	5 272	5 435	6 981	8 070	9 477	10 290	11 183	11 707
Per capita	889	1 012	1 023	1 286	1 455	1 672	1 777	1 892	1 941
At constant prices	4 544	4 706	5 061	5 435	5 760	6 128	6 233	6 496	6 704
Growth rates	3.4	3.6	7.5	7.4	6.0	6.4	1.7	4.2	3.2
Equatorial Guinea Guinée équatoriale									
At current prices	163	165	185	181	133	155	158	147	162
Per capita	463	457	501	478	342	389	386	349	377
At constant prices	163	169	174	179	174	176	180	183	186
Growth rates	4.7	3.5	3.2	2.7	−2.8	1.2	2.5	1.6	1.4
Eritrea Erythrée									
At current prices	...	...	715	504	619	629	670	702	751
Per capita	...	...	240	167	200	197	203	205	210
At constant prices	...	...	780	756	830	855	913	985	1014
Growth rates	...	...	...	−3.0	9.8	2.9	6.8	7.9	3.0
Estonia Estonie									
At current prices	11 977	10 466	1 100	1 634	2 278	3 550	4 358	4 634	5 210
Per capita	7 624	6 693	710	1 069	1 512	2 390	2 973	3 202	3 645

18

Gross domestic product: total and per capita
In US dollars (millions) [1] at current and constant 1990 prices; per capita US dollars;
real rates of growth [cont.]

Produit intérieur brut : total et par habitant
En dollars E.−U. (millions) [1] aux prix courants et constants de 1990; par habitant en dollars E.−U.;
taux de l'accroissement réels [suite]

Country or area Pays ou zone	1990	1991	1992	1993	1994	1995	1996	1997	1998
At constant prices	11 977	10 357	8 881	8 127	7 964	8 306	8 631	9 547	9 997
Growth rates	−6.6	−13.5	−14.2	−8.5	−2.0	4.3	3.9	10.6	4.7
Ethiopia including Eritrea Ethiopie y compris Erythrée									
At current prices	8 634	9 573	...	...	...	...	...	...	...
Per capita	173	186	...	...	...	...	...	...	...
At constant prices	8 634	8 113	...	...	...	...	...	...	...
Growth rates	−0.4	−6.0	...	...	...	...	...	...	...
Ethiopia Ethiopie									
At current prices	...	...	7 419	5 304	5 189	5 531	6 001	6 209	6 383
Per capita	...	...	145	101	96	100	106	107	107
At constant prices	...	...	7 621	8 553	8 698	9 165	10 141	10 699	10 753
Growth rates	...	...	...	12.2	1.7	5.4	10.6	5.5	0.5
Fiji Fidji									
At current prices	1 337	1 384	1 532	1 636	1 826	1 990	2 121	2 101	1 578
Per capita	1 841	1 888	2 067	2 183	2 408	2 592	2 730	2 672	1 982
At constant prices	1 337	1 301	1 352	1 375	1 445	1 482	1 532	1 505	1 446
Growth rates	8.4	−2.7	3.9	1.7	5.1	2.5	3.4	−1.8	−3.9
Finland Finlande									
At current prices	136 795	123 481	108 703	86 237	99 992	129 289	127 539	122 420	128 505
Per capita	27 433	24 652	21 592	17 040	19 661	25 312	24 880	23 812	24 934
At constant prices	136 795	128 236	123 976	122 553	127 399	132 253	137 555	146 210	153 577
Growth rates	0.0	−6.3	−3.3	−1.1	4.0	3.8	4.0	6.3	5.0
France France									
At current prices	1 215 887	1 220 137	1 346 108	1 276 051	1 350 811	1 553 125	1 554 367	1 409 170	1 451 763
Per capita	21 437	21 405	23 503	22 179	23 378	26 769	26 684	24 100	24 739
At constant prices	1 215 887	1 227 599	1 245 734	1 233 348	1 257 421	1 278 270	1 292 370	1 318 305	1 362 279
Growth rates	2.6	1.0	1.5	−1.0	2.0	1.7	1.1	2.0	3.3
French Guiana Guyane française									
At current prices	1 199	1 312	1 507	1 411	1 482	1 675	1 672	1 500	1 518
Per capita	10 243	10 698	11 730	10 499	10 554	11 415	10 911	9 373	9 094
At constant prices	1 199	1 341	1 448	1 406	1 492	1 516	1 540	1 565	1 590
Growth rates	12.2	11.9	8.0	−2.9	6.1	1.6	1.6	1.6	1.6
French Polynesia Polynesie française									
At current prices	2 930	2 975	3 265	3 479	3 741	4 112	4 123	3 742	3 610
Per capita	14 971	14 897	16 033	16 766	17 702	19 104	18 815	16 770	15 900
At constant prices	2 930	3 045	3 160	3 263	3 682	3 597	3 656	3 698	3 737
Growth rates	4.0	3.9	3.8	3.3	12.8	−2.3	1.6	1.1	1.1
Gabon Gabon									
At current prices	5 426	5 403	5 593	5 406	4 191	5 122	5 564	5 309	5 586
Per capita	5 806	5 614	5 646	5 305	3 999	4 755	5 027	4 670	4 787
At constant prices	5 426	5 759	5 572	5 792	6 006	6 234	6 483	6 775	6 917
Growth rates	10.2	6.1	−3.2	4.0	3.7	3.8	4.0	4.5	2.1
Gambia Gambie									
At current prices	287	298	329	337	339	375	382	432	436
Per capita	312	311	330	326	316	338	332	363	355
At constant prices	287	292	305	308	312	301	317	334	348
Growth rates	5.2	1.7	4.5	0.9	1.3	−3.4	5.3	5.4	4.0
Georgia Géorgie									
At current prices	22 470	10 941	716	1 335	1 246	2 842	4 238	4 948	4 927
Per capita	4 115	2 009	132	249	235	541	817	966	974
At constant prices	22 470	17 729	9 769	6 906	6 188	6 349	7 060	7 858	8 086
Growth rates	−15.1	−21.1	−44.9	−29.3	−10.4	2.6	11.2	11.3	2.9
Germany † Allemagne †									
At current prices	...	1 770 413	2 020 362	1 956 935	2 091 693	2 458 307	2 383 041	2 114 411	2 150 480
Per capita	...	22 171	25 140	24 200	25 726	30 104	29 094	25 768	26 183
At constant prices	...	1 807 239	1 847 748	1 827 656	1 870 541	1 902 841	1 917 208	1 945 024	1 986 883
Growth rates	...	...	2.2	−1.1	2.3	1.7	0.8	1.5	2.2
F. R. Germany R.F. Allemagne									
At current prices	1 501 516	...	...	...	...	...	...	...	...
Per capita	24 485	...	...	...	...	...	...	...	...
At constant prices	1 501 516	...	...	...	...	...	...	...	...
Growth rates	5.7	...	...	...	...	...	...	...	...
former German D. R. l'ex−R.d. allemande									
At current prices	169 475	...	...	...	...	...	...	...	...

18
Gross domestic product: total and per capita
In US dollars (millions) [1] at current and constant 1990 prices; per capita US dollars;
real rates of growth [cont.]
Produit intérieur brut : total et par habitant
En dollars E.−U. (millions) [1] aux prix courants et constants de 1990; par habitant en dollars E.−U.;
taux de l'accroissement réels [suite]

Country or area Pays ou zone	1990	1991	1992	1993	1994	1995	1996	1997	1998
Per capita	10 430	...	...	...	...	...	...	...	...
At constant prices	169 475	...	...	...	...	...	...	...	...
Growth rates	−15.1	...	...	...	...	...	...	...	...
Ghana Ghana									
At current prices	6 226	6 600	6 413	5 662	5 174	6 179	6 495	6 884	6 639
Per capita	412	423	398	341	302	350	358	369	346
At constant prices	6 226	6 556	6 812	7 148	7 420	7 754	8 155	8 570	8 896
Growth rates	3.3	5.3	3.9	4.9	3.8	4.5	5.2	5.1	3.8
Greece Grèce									
At current prices	83 999	90 213	99 734	93 401	100 153	117 565	124 362	120 933	121 513
Per capita	8 219	8 778	9 651	8 990	9 592	11 208	11 808	11 442	11 463
At constant prices	83 999	86 590	87 208	85 781	87 535	89 362	91 469	94 598	98 059
Growth rates	0.0	3.1	0.7	−1.6	2.0	2.1	2.4	3.4	3.7
Grenada Grenade									
At current prices	200	210	214	213	224	236	251	263	279
Per capita	2 209	2 309	2 346	2 331	2 439	2 558	2 713	2 832	2 997
At constant prices	200	206	209	206	213	220	226	237	245
Growth rates	6.7	3.0	1.1	−1.2	3.3	3.1	3.1	4.6	3.6
Guadeloupe Guadeloupe									
At current prices	2 791	2 909	3 395	3 461	3 946	4 439	4 575	4 453	4 697
Per capita	7 145	7 315	8 393	8 418	9 446	10 463	10 620	10 187	10 591
At constant prices	2 791	2 293	2 460	2 639	2 835	2 711	2 828	3 089	3 217
Growth rates	3.1	−17.9	7.3	7.3	7.4	−4.3	4.3	9.2	4.1
Guatemala Guatemala									
At current prices	7 650	9 406	10 441	11 400	12 983	14 656	15 783	17 797	19 008
Per capita	874	1 048	1 133	1 205	1 336	1 469	1 541	1 692	1 760
At constant prices	7 650	7 930	8 314	8 640	8 989	9 434	9 712	10 129	10 612
Growth rates	3.1	3.7	4.8	3.9	4.0	5.0	2.9	4.3	4.8
Guinea Guinée									
At current prices	2 764	3 016	2 974	3 177	3 395	3 682	3 932	3 916	3 779
Per capita	480	501	469	477	489	515	540	535	515
At constant prices	2 764	2 895	2 982	3 122	3 247	3 390	3 542	3 654	3 837
Growth rates	5.1	4.8	3.0	4.7	4.0	4.4	4.5	3.2	5.0
Guinea−Bissau Guinée−Bissau									
At current prices	233	234	221	170	255	179	138	109	116
Per capita	240	235	217	164	240	165	124	96	100
At constant prices	233	240	249	253	270	284	296	311	319
Growth rates	3.3	3.0	3.6	1.6	6.9	4.9	4.4	5.1	2.4
Guyana Guyana									
At current prices	396	348	374	467	545	622	705	743	719
Per capita	498	436	464	573	663	749	843	881	846
At constant prices	396	428	475	516	565	592	611	649	640
Growth rates	−5.0	7.9	11.2	8.6	9.4	4.9	3.1	6.3	−1.3
Haiti Haïti									
At current prices	2 614	2 352	1 532	1 551	2 057	2 334	2 722	3 097	3 522
Per capita	378	333	213	212	277	309	354	396	443
At constant prices	2 614	2 621	2 276	2 221	2 037	2 126	2 184	2 214	2 282
Growth rates	−0.1	0.3	−13.2	−2.4	−8.3	4.4	2.7	1.4	3.1
Holy See [2] Saint−Siège [2]									
At current prices	16	15	15	11	10	10	10	10	10
Per capita	19 333	20 341	21 543	17 358	17 898	19 136	21 421	20 207	20 659
At constant prices	16	16	16	16	16	17	17	17	18
Growth rates	2.0	1.4	0.8	−0.9	2.2	2.9	0.9	1.5	1.3
Honduras Honduras									
At current prices	3 049	3 068	3 419	3 506	3 432	3 960	4 081	4 698	5 348
Per capita	625	610	660	657	625	700	702	785	870
At constant prices	3 049	3 148	3 325	3 532	3 486	3 628	3 762	3 929	4 052
Growth rates	0.1	3.3	5.6	6.2	−1.3	4.1	3.7	4.5	3.1
Hungary Hongrie									
At current prices	36 111	33 743	37 604	38 958	41 896	44 669	45 163	45 724	46 977
Per capita	3 484	3 266	3 649	3 789	4 085	4 368	4 431	4 502	4 644
At constant prices	36 111	31 816	30 842	30 664	31 568	32 035	32 464	33 949	35 625
Growth rates	−3.5	−11.9	−3.1	−0.6	2.9	1.5	1.3	4.6	4.9

18
Gross domestic product: total and per capita
In US dollars (millions) [1] at current and constant 1990 prices; per capita US dollars;
real rates of growth [cont.]
Produit intérieur brut : total et par habitant
En dollars E. – U. (millions) [1] aux prix courants et constants de 1990; par habitant en dollars E. – U.;
taux de l'accroissement réels [suite]

Country or area Pays ou zone	1990	1991	1992	1993	1994	1995	1996	1997	1998
Iceland Islande									
At current prices	6 245	6 729	6 910	6 086	6 220	6 980	7 315	7 474	8 266
Per capita	24 512	26 130	26 548	23 138	23 405	26 006	26 993	27 323	29 946
At constant prices	6 245	6 321	6 109	6 167	6 390	6 429	6 796	7 159	7 523
Growth rates	1.1	1.2	−3.3	0.9	3.6	0.6	5.7	5.3	5.1
India Inde									
At current prices	305 949	271 211	272 365	265 878	307 099	345 071	360 391	405 870	414 010
Per capita	360	313	308	295	335	370	379	420	422
At constant prices	305 949	307 245	323 899	339 948	367 587	394 688	423 729	449 178	476 129
Growth rates	5.7	0.4	5.4	5.0	8.1	7.4	7.4	6.0	6.0
Indonesia Indonésie									
At current prices	114 426	128 168	139 116	158 007	176 888	202 131	227 397	214 593	98 638
Per capita	626	690	737	825	909	1 024	1 135	1 055	478
At constant prices	114 426	124 642	133 643	143 337	154 144	166 814	180 126	188 500	162 717
Growth rates	9.0	8.9	7.2	7.3	7.5	8.2	8.0	4.6	−13.7
Iran (Islamic Rep. of) Iran (Rép. islamique d')									
At current prices	92 960	97 923	101 455	73 838	73 414	102 335	134 361	158 496	187 423
Per capita	1 651	1 697	1 721	1 228	1 199	1 642	2 117	2 452	2 850
At constant prices	92 960	102 845	109 120	111 415	112 397	115 644	122 017	126 155	128 752
Growth rates	11.2	10.6	6.1	2.1	0.9	2.9	5.5	3.4	2.1
Iraq Iraq									
At current prices	54 942	18 771	35 999	51 959	52 417	50 320	51 377	64 216	73 848
Per capita	3 039	1 014	1 905	2 698	2 668	2 504	2 493	3 032	3 388
At constant prices	54 942	18 614	21 365	14 892	15 023	14 422	14 725	18 404	21 165
Growth rates	0.0	−66.1	14.8	−30.3	0.9	−4.0	2.1	25.0	15.0
Ireland Irlande									
At current prices	47 180	47 615	53 437	50 073	54 558	65 801	72 359	78 667	85 024
Per capita	13 468	13 562	15 142	14 086	15 229	18 232	19 913	21 508	23 098
At constant prices	47 180	48 058	49 645	50 954	53 890	59 010	63 574	70 378	76 664
Growth rates	7.1	1.9	3.3	2.6	5.8	9.5	7.7	10.7	8.9
Israel Israël									
At current prices	55 140	62 762	69 893	70 066	79 020	91 627	100 442	103 111	101 972
Per capita	11 833	13 033	13 984	13 486	14 663	16 461	17 553	17 595	17 041
At constant prices	55 140	59 174	63 588	65 976	70 794	75 666	79 393	80 980	82 777
Growth rates	7.0	7.3	7.5	3.8	7.3	6.9	4.9	2.0	2.2
Italy Italie									
At current prices	1 102 439	1 161 241	1 231 407	993 392	1 025 404	1 097 230	1 228 869	1 159 426	1 185 192
Per capita	19 333	20 341	21 543	17 358	17 898	19 136	21 421	20 207	20 659
At constant prices	1 102 439	1 117 764	1 126 266	1 116 312	1 140 955	1 174 315	1 184 478	1 202 032	1 218 110
Growth rates	2.0	1.4	0.8	−0.9	2.2	2.9	0.9	1.5	1.3
Jamaica Jamaïque									
At current prices	4 246	3 732	3 354	4 306	4 309	5 239	5 864	6 722	6 871
Per capita	1 792	1 564	1 394	1 773	1 758	2 119	2 351	2 671	2 707
At constant prices	4 246	4 277	4 342	4 405	4 454	4 475	4 396	4 292	4 262
Growth rates	5.5	0.7	1.5	1.5	1.1	0.5	−1.7	−2.4	−0.7
Japan Japon									
At current prices	2 970 093	3 402 116	3 719 074	4 275 010	4 688 975	5 137 361	4 599 280	4 197 469	3 782 834
Per capita	24 042	27 441	29 898	34 260	37 469	40 944	36 569	33 303	29 956
At constant prices	2 970 093	3 082 889	3 114 396	3 124 101	3 144 242	3 190 495	3 351 615	3 399 434	3 303 324
Growth rates	5.1	3.8	1.0	0.3	0.6	1.5	5.1	1.4	−2.8
Jordan Jordanie									
At current prices	4 020	4 193	5 138	5 487	6 036	6 596	7 259	7 621	8 069
Per capita	870	874	1 024	1 043	1 096	1 150	1 223	1 244	1 280
At constant prices	4 020	4 093	4 752	5 017	5 444	5 767	5 825	5 900	6 030
Growth rates	−6.2	1.8	16.1	5.6	8.5	5.9	1.0	1.3	2.2
Kazakhstan Kazakhstan									
At current prices	69 595	46 286	6 237	11 722	11 915	16 640	21 036	22 165	22 324
Per capita	4 157	2 759	372	703	718	1 008	1 280	1 354	1 368
At constant prices	69 595	62 816	55 673	46 988	41 067	37 700	37 888	38 532	37 569
Growth rates	−4.6	−9.7	−11.4	−15.6	−12.6	−8.2	0.5	1.7	−2.5
Kenya Kenya									
At current prices	8 533	8 043	7 951	5 520	7 024	8 960	9 148	10 133	10 809
Per capita	362	331	317	214	265	329	328	356	373

18

Gross domestic product: total and per capita
In US dollars (millions) [1] at current and constant 1990 prices; per capita US dollars;
real rates of growth [cont.]
Produit intérieur brut : total et par habitant
En dollars E.–U. (millions) [1] aux prix courants et constants de 1990; par habitant en dollars E.–U.;
taux de l'accroissement réels [suite]

Country or area Pays ou zone	1990	1991	1992	1993	1994	1995	1996	1997	1998
At constant prices	8 533	8 655	8 587	8 617	8 844	9 237	9 664	9 886	10 153
Growth rates	4.2	1.4	−0.8	0.4	2.6	4.4	4.6	2.3	2.7
Kiribati Kiribati									
At current prices	28	33	34	33	40	46	54	54	48
Per capita	383	456	454	439	520	594	680	680	594
At constant prices	28	31	30	31	33	34	36	37	38
Growth rates	−2.1	10.1	−1.5	2.1	7.7	3.4	6.3	2.5	2.0
Korea, Dem. P. R. Corée, R.p. dém.									
At current prices	16 752	15 598	13 881	11 711	9 360	5 229	10 588	10 323	10 273
Per capita	819	750	656	545	428	235	468	449	440
At constant prices	16 752	15 881	14 674	14 043	13 790	13 156	12 669	11 808	11 678
Growth rates	−3.7	−5.2	−7.6	−4.3	−1.8	−4.6	−3.7	−6.8	−1.1
Korea, Republic of Corée, République de									
At current prices	252 623	295 235	314 737	345 717	402 523	489 258	520 205	476 486	320 748
Per capita	5 893	6 821	7 202	7 835	9 037	10 885	11 472	10 419	6 956
At constant prices	252 623	275 934	290 938	306 915	332 235	361 869	386 296	405 653	381 972
Growth rates	9.0	9.2	5.4	5.5	8.3	8.9	6.8	5.0	−5.8
Kuwait Kowëit									
At current prices	18 471	11 015	19 869	23 957	24 859	26 555	31 086	30 368	25 306
Per capita	8 619	5 259	9 980	12 863	14 190	15 717	18 434	17 533	13 976
At constant prices	18 471	11 289	21 141	28 327	30 717	31 049	34 139	33 108	28 804
Growth rates	−32.8	−38.9	87.3	34.0	8.4	1.1	10.0	−3.0	−13.0
Kyrgyzstan Kirghizistan									
At current prices	12 823	10 571	767	993	1 109	1 492	1 754	1 767	1 701
Per capita	2 918	2 378	171	220	244	326	382	383	366
At constant prices	12 823	11 832	10 300	8 663	6 921	6 548	7 013	7 708	7 985
Growth rates	4.2	−7.7	−12.9	−15.9	−20.1	−5.4	7.1	9.9	3.6
Lao People's Dem. Rep. Rép. dém. pop. lao									
At current prices	866	1 028	1 180	1 328	1 544	1 764	1 873	1 747	1 292
Per capita	209	241	268	294	332	369	382	347	250
At constant prices	866	900	964	1 020	1 103	1 181	1 262	1 349	1 403
Growth rates	6.7	4.0	7.0	5.8	8.1	7.0	6.9	6.9	4.0
Latvia Lettonie									
At current prices	18 751	16 380	1 364	2 172	3 647	4 449	5 134	5 637	6 397
Per capita	6 986	6 130	515	831	1 416	1 754	2 055	2 290	2 638
At constant prices	18 751	16 799	10 943	9 316	9 375	9 300	9 613	10 440	10 815
Growth rates	−1.5	−10.4	−34.9	−14.9	0.6	−0.8	3.4	8.6	3.6
Lebanon Liban									
At current prices	2 635	3 644	3 808	4 075	4 401	4 687	4 874	5 069	5 323
Per capita	1 031	1 396	1 411	1 452	1 510	1 558	1 581	1 613	1 668
At constant prices	2 635	3 644	3 808	4 075	4 401	4 687	4 874	5 069	5 323
Growth rates	−7.9	38.3	4.5	7.0	8.0	6.5	4.0	4.0	5.0
Lesotho Lesotho									
At current prices	622	690	827	818	837	933	940	1 023	877
Per capita	361	392	459	444	444	484	477	508	425
At constant prices	622	646	677	703	727	760	835	902	853
Growth rates	6.2	3.8	4.8	3.8	3.4	4.5	10.0	8.0	−5.5
Liberia Libéria									
At current prices	1 259	1 133	968	968	638	638	651	739	759
Per capita	488	453	410	439	304	305	296	308	285
At constant prices	1 259	1 133	968	968	638	638	651	739	759
Growth rates	−16.3	−10.0	−14.6	0.0	−34.1	0.0	2.0	13.5	2.7
Libyan Arab Jamah. Jamah. arabe libyenne									
At current prices	30 846	33 292	33 923	32 709	32 151	30 793	29 893	29 920	31 661
Per capita	6 985	7 352	7 317	6 895	6 625	6 200	5 877	5 742	5 930
At constant prices	30 846	32 390	28 147	24 882	24 287	24 774	25 146	25 254	25 398
Growth rates	6.9	5.0	−13.1	−11.6	−2.4	2.0	1.5	0.4	0.6
Liechtenstein Liechtenstein									
At current prices	959	981	1 032	1 009	1 120	1 324	1 283	1 117	1 150
Per capita	33 422	33 734	34 976	33 705	36 892	43 015	41 118	35 314	35 910
At constant prices	959	951	950	945	950	955	958	974	994
Growth rates	3.7	−0.8	−0.1	−0.5	0.5	0.5	0.3	1.7	2.1

18

Gross domestic product: total and per capita
In US dollars (millions) [1] at current and constant 1990 prices; per capita US dollars;
real rates of growth [cont.]
Produit intérieur brut : total et par habitant
En dollars E.−U. (millions) [1] aux prix courants et constants de 1990; par habitant en dollars E.−U.;
taux de l'accroissement réels [suite]

Country or area Pays ou zone	1990	1991	1992	1993	1994	1995	1996	1997	1998
Lithuania Lituanie									
At current prices	20 135	23 697	1 921	2 670	4 249	6 026	7 892	9 585	10 692
Per capita	5 388	6 320	512	713	1 137	1 617	2 124	2 587	2 895
At constant prices	20 135	18 993	14 956	12 529	11 305	11 677	12 231	12 978	13 549
Growth rates	−3.6	−5.7	−21.3	−16.2	−9.8	3.3	4.7	6.1	4.4
Luxembourg Luxembourg									
At current prices	10 929	11 520	13 329	13 565	15 397	18 265	18 200	17 459	18 340
Per capita	28 698	29 893	34 135	34 260	38 350	44 888	44 164	41 858	43 475
At constant prices	10 929	11 600	12 118	13 174	13 727	14 247	14 659	15 723	16 512
Growth rates	2.2	6.1	4.5	8.7	4.2	3.8	2.9	7.3	5.0
Madagascar Madagascar									
At current prices	3 080	2 673	2 996	3 366	2 972	3 208	3 679	3 133	3 136
Per capita	265	223	241	262	223	233	259	214	208
At constant prices	3 080	2 886	2 920	2 982	2 982	3 041	3 148	3 274	3 388
Growth rates	3.1	−6.3	1.2	2.1	0.0	2.0	3.5	4.0	3.5
Malawi Malawi									
At current prices	1 752	2 024	1 818	1 999	1 181	1 369	2 216	2 463	1 615
Per capita	188	213	190	209	123	142	225	245	156
At constant prices	1 752	1 878	1 711	1 876	2 171	2 271	2 215	2 358	2 432
Growth rates	4.6	7.2	−8.9	9.6	15.7	4.6	−2.5	6.5	3.1
Malaysia Malaisie									
At current prices	42 775	48 137	58 310	64 180	72 506	87 315	99 170	97 884	71 023
Per capita	2 397	2 631	3 109	3 341	3 688	4 342	4 826	4 665	3 317
At constant prices	42 775	46 452	50 074	54 254	59 300	64 852	70 432	75 858	70 776
Growth rates	9.7	8.6	7.8	8.3	9.3	9.4	8.6	7.7	−6.7
Maldives Maldives									
At current prices	145	163	191	216	239	269	301	340	366
Per capita	672	735	833	916	987	1 080	1 176	1 290	1 350
At constant prices	145	156	166	176	188	201	217	237	258
Growth rates	16.3	7.7	6.3	6.2	6.6	7.2	7.9	9.1	9.1
Mali Mali									
At current prices	2 510	2 451	2 786	2 590	1 813	2 310	2 669	2 535	2 716
Per capita	284	271	301	273	187	232	262	243	254
At constant prices	2 510	2 505	2 747	2 633	2 738	2 904	3 196	3 403	3 597
Growth rates	2.4	−0.2	9.7	−4.2	4.0	6.1	10.1	6.5	5.7
Malta Malte									
At current prices	2 312	2 496	2 743	2 459	2 722	3 246	3 333	3 340	3 495
Per capita	6 528	6 979	7 579	6 709	7 335	8 654	8 809	8 761	9 110
At constant prices	2 312	2 457	2 572	2 687	2 839	3 019	3 135	3 273	3 522
Growth rates	6.3	6.3	4.7	4.5	5.7	6.3	3.8	4.4	7.6
Marshall Islands Iles Marshall									
At current prices	69	72	79	84	89	99	92	92	91
Per capita	1 486	1 505	1 606	1 636	1 690	1 817	1 633	1 569	1 509
At constant prices	69	69	69	72	70	76	64	58	57
Growth rates	7.0	1.1	0.0	4.1	−3.8	9.8	−15.9	−9.4	−2.8
Martinique Martinique									
At current prices	3 548	3 684	4 173	4 055	4 273	4 838	4 863	4 377	4 617
Per capita	9 848	10 116	11 341	10 909	11 387	12 771	12 719	11 348	11 866
At constant prices	3 548	3 408	3 463	3 520	3 577	3 635	3 695	3 755	3 910
Growth rates	2.9	−4.0	1.6	1.6	1.6	1.6	1.6	1.6	4.1
Mauritania Mauritanie									
At current prices	1 050	1 136	1 146	894	903	971	985	959	830
Per capita	518	545	535	406	398	417	411	390	328
At constant prices	1 050	1 085	1 127	1 162	1 193	1 248	1 295	1 342	1 382
Growth rates	3.6	3.4	3.8	3.1	2.7	4.6	3.7	3.6	3.0
Mauritius Maurice									
At current prices	2 559	2 738	3 189	3 205	3 510	3 973	4 307	4 203	4 253
Per capita	2 422	2 565	2 956	2 938	3 182	3 567	3 833	3 711	3 727
At constant prices	2 559	2 665	2 830	2 988	3 106	3 251	3 440	3 640	3 832
Growth rates	7.2	4.1	6.2	5.6	3.9	4.7	5.8	5.8	5.3
Mexico Mexique									
At current prices	262 710	314 454	363 609	403 196	420 776	286 167	332 339	400 858	414 350
Per capita	3 157	3 708	4 209	4 583	4 698	3 140	3 584	4 252	4 324

18
Gross domestic product: total and per capita
In US dollars (millions) [1] at current and constant 1990 prices; per capita US dollars;
real rates of growth [*cont.*]

Produit intérieur brut : total et par habitant
En dollars E.−U. (millions) [1] aux prix courants et constants de 1990; par habitant en dollars E.−U.;
taux de l'accroissement réels [*suite*]

Country or area Pays ou zone	1990	1991	1992	1993	1994	1995	1996	1997	1998
At constant prices	262 710	273 802	283 737	289 272	302 044	283 417	298 022	318 164	333 494
Growth rates	5.1	4.2	3.6	2.0	4.4	−6.2	5.2	6.8	4.8
Micronesia (Fed. States of) Micron (Etats fédérés de)									
At current prices	148	166	176	189	193	203	213	210	210
Per capita	1 535	1 691	1 762	1 851	1 843	1 889	1 940	1 876	1 841
At constant prices	148	159	161	164	161	162	163	157	152
Growth rates	4.7	7.4	1.3	1.4	−1.9	0.8	0.8	−4.0	−2.8
Monaco Monaco									
At current prices	642	649	722	689	735	852	859	784	814
Per capita	21 437	21 405	23 503	22 179	23 378	26 769	26 684	24 100	24 739
At constant prices	642	648	658	652	664	675	683	696	720
Growth rates	2.6	1.0	1.5	−1.0	2.0	1.7	1.1	2.0	3.3
Mongolia Mongolie									
At current prices	3 135	2 565	1 435	793	886	1 235	1 203	1 071	992
Per capita	1 415	1 130	619	336	368	504	482	422	384
At constant prices	3 135	2 846	2 575	2 498	2 555	2 717	2 783	2 893	2 994
Growth rates	−2.5	−9.2	−9.5	−3.0	2.3	6.3	2.4	4.0	3.5
Montserrat Montserrat									
At current prices	72	60	63	66	68	64	52	40	38
Per capita	6 547	5 466	5 779	6 112	6 295	5 971	4 842	3 755	3 570
At constant prices	72	57	58	60	60	56	44	32	31
Growth rates	14.3	−20.9	2.7	2.5	0.9	−7.6	−21.4	−26.5	−3.2
Morocco Maroc									
At current prices	25 824	27 835	28 450	26 798	30 351	32 985	36 672	33 514	35 651
Per capita	1 079	1 143	1 150	1 066	1 188	1 270	1 388	1 246	1 302
At constant prices	25 824	27 619	26 505	26 237	28 954	27 050	30 328	29 710	31 579
Growth rates	3.9	6.9	−4.0	−1.0	10.4	−6.6	12.1	−2.0	6.3
Mozambique Mozambique									
At current prices	1 481	1 371	1 098	1 248	1 232	1 337	1 710	1 734	1 737
Per capita	104	93	72	78	74	77	95	94	92
At constant prices	1 481	1 510	1 481	1 736	1 834	1 871	1 991	2 148	2 275
Growth rates	0.9	1.9	−1.9	17.2	5.7	2.0	6.4	7.9	5.9
Myanmar Myanmar									
At current prices	8 235	8 159	9 026	9 630	10 099	10 639	11 324	11 964	12 557
Per capita	203	199	218	230	238	248	261	272	282
At constant prices	8 235	8 181	8 972	9 514	10 225	10 936	11 640	12 298	12 907
Growth rates	2.8	−0.7	9.7	6.0	7.5	6.9	6.4	5.7	5.0
Namibia Namibie									
At current prices	2 340	2 483	2 823	2 628	2 978	3 224	3 122	3 234	3 044
Per capita	1 734	1 790	1 980	1 794	1 980	2 089	1 972	1 994	1 834
At constant prices	2 340	2 532	2 712	2 666	2 835	2 940	3 003	3 082	3 156
Growth rates	2.0	8.2	7.1	−1.7	6.4	3.7	2.1	2.6	2.4
Nauru Nauru									
At current prices	51	51	46	41	42	41	41	37	32
Per capita	5 352	5 208	4 611	4 013	4 057	3 867	3 837	3 420	2 900
At constant prices	51	49	46	42	39	36	34	31	31
Growth rates	−2.1	−3.7	−7.3	−7.3	−7.3	−7.3	−7.3	−7.3	−1.9
Nepal Népal									
At current prices	3 521	3 231	3 499	3 528	4 034	4 224	4 391	4 836	4 495
Per capita	188	168	177	174	194	199	201	217	197
At constant prices	3 521	3 745	3 899	4 049	4 382	4 534	4 776	5 017	5 134
Growth rates	4.6	6.4	4.1	3.8	8.2	3.5	5.3	5.0	2.3
Netherlands Pays−Bas									
At current prices	295 369	302 162	335 204	325 977	351 426	414 794	411 826	376 597	391 269
Per capita	19 755	20 070	22 109	21 352	22 869	26 832	26 499	24 119	24 956
At constant prices	295 369	302 077	308 195	310 544	320 552	327 785	337 743	350 537	363 378
Growth rates	4.1	2.3	2.0	0.8	3.2	2.3	3.0	3.8	3.7
Netherlands Antilles Antilles néerlandaises									
At current prices	1 817	1 906	1 982	2 104	2 356	2 516	2 697	2 914	2 941
Per capita	9 681	10 001	10 214	10 628	11 678	12 260	12 964	13 841	13 827
At constant prices	1 817	1 745	1 836	1 803	1 834	1 858	1 813	1 808	1 753
Growth rates	7.6	−4.0	5.2	−1.8	1.7	1.3	−2.4	−0.3	−3.0

18

Gross domestic product: total and per capita
In US dollars (millions) [1] at current and constant 1990 prices; per capita US dollars;
real rates of growth [*cont.*]

Produit intérieur brut : total et par habitant
En dollars E.–U. (millions) [1] aux prix courants et constants de 1990; par habitant en dollars E.–U.;
taux de l'accroissement réels [*suite*]

Country or area Pays ou zone	1990	1991	1992	1993	1994	1995	1996	1997	1998
New Caledonia Nouvelle–Calédonie									
At current prices	2 529	2 654	2 924	3 070	3 039	3 628	3 607	3 275	3 022
Per capita	15 100	15 443	16 528	16 835	16 177	18 799	18 238	16 198	14 647
At constant prices	2 529	2 629	2 655	2 673	2 743	2 905	3 050	3 203	3 315
Growth rates	−4.3	3.9	1.0	0.7	2.6	5.9	5.0	5.0	3.5
New Zealand Nouvelle–Zélande									
At current prices	43 102	41 694	40 057	43 677	51 322	60 035	65 281	64 991	53 087
Per capita	12 826	12 220	11 526	12 321	14 208	16 352	17 547	17 279	13 985
At constant prices	43 102	42 574	43 082	45 805	48 271	50 103	51 388	52 404	51 999
Growth rates	−0.6	−1.2	1.2	6.3	5.4	3.8	2.6	2.0	−0.8
Nicaragua Nicaragua									
At current prices	2 214	1 738	1 843	1 967	1 831	1 888	1 973	2 023	2 125
Per capita	579	442	455	471	426	427	433	432	442
At constant prices	2 214	2 210	2 219	2 210	2 284	2 382	2 494	2 622	2 728
Growth rates	0.0	−0.2	0.4	−0.4	3.3	4.3	4.7	5.1	4.0
Niger Niger									
At current prices	2 506	2 252	2 269	2 257	1 495	1 598	1 629	1 530	1 602
Per capita	324	282	274	264	169	175	172	157	159
At constant prices	2 506	2 569	2 402	2 407	2 440	2 178	2 148	2 238	2 314
Growth rates	2.8	2.5	−6.5	0.2	1.4	−10.7	−1.4	4.2	3.4
Nigeria Nigéria									
At current prices	32 424	32 695	31 784	31 791	41 568	66 759	72 967	75 251	77 023
Per capita	373	366	347	338	431	675	720	724	724
At constant prices	32 424	33 966	34 951	35 871	36 230	37 169	38 407	39 609	40 542
Growth rates	8.2	4.8	2.9	2.6	1.0	2.6	3.3	3.1	2.4
Norway Norvège									
At current prices	115 453	117 757	126 307	116 111	122 926	146 601	157 616	153 962	146 729
Per capita	27 220	27 631	29 492	26 976	28 413	33 708	36 049	35 026	33 203
At constant prices	115 453	119 051	122 941	126 302	133 239	138 365	145 140	151 347	154 550
Growth rates	2.0	3.1	3.3	2.7	5.5	3.8	4.9	4.3	2.1
Oman Oman									
At current prices	11 685	11 341	12 452	12 493	12 919	13 803	15 278	15 837	14 162
Per capita	6 548	6 103	6 444	6 227	6 209	6 405	6 851	6 870	5 946
At constant prices	11 685	12 391	13 443	14 269	14 818	15 534	15 983	16 971	17 470
Growth rates	8.4	6.0	8.5	6.1	3.8	4.8	2.9	6.2	2.9
Pakistan Pakistan									
At current prices	47 016	50 897	54 720	57 258	62 992	69 248	69 681	68 108	67 917
Per capita	395	415	435	443	475	508	498	473	458
At constant prices	47 016	50 700	51 671	53 684	56 432	59 259	59 986	61 966	64 388
Growth rates	5.5	7.8	1.9	3.9	5.1	5.0	1.2	3.3	3.9
Palau Palaos									
At current prices	85	94	100	100	109	116	144	143	119
Per capita	5 562	6 049	6 272	6 086	6 508	6 748	8 145	7 925	6 448
At constant prices	85	88	89	91	89	90	91	92	88
Growth rates	7.0	3.9	1.5	2.0	−1.9	0.8	0.8	0.8	−4.0
Panama Panama									
At current prices	5 313	5 842	6 641	7 253	7 734	7 906	8 110	8 613	9 097
Per capita	2 216	2 390	2 666	2 858	2 992	3 005	3 030	3 164	3 287
At constant prices	5 313	5 814	6 290	6 634	6 823	6 942	7 110	7 425	7 732
Growth rates	8.1	9.4	8.2	5.5	2.9	1.8	2.4	4.4	4.1
Papua New Guinea Papouasie–Nvl–Guinée									
At current prices	3 221	3 788	4 378	5 128	5 469	5 033	5 272	4 639	3 480
Per capita	839	965	1 090	1 248	1 301	1 170	1 198	1 031	756
At constant prices	3 221	3 528	4 017	4 598	4 839	4 697	4 882	4 566	4 871
Growth rates	−3.0	9.5	13.9	14.5	5.2	−2.9	3.9	−6.5	6.7
Paraguay Paraguay									
At current prices	5 265	6 249	6 446	6 875	7 826	8 982	9 601	9 555	8 505
Per capita	1 248	1 440	1 445	1 501	1 664	1 860	1 937	1 878	1 629
At constant prices	5 265	5 395	5 492	5 719	5 896	6 173	6 252	6 413	6 387
Growth rates	3.1	2.5	1.8	4.1	3.1	4.7	1.3	2.6	−0.4
Peru Pérou									
At current prices	36 117	42 608	41 870	40 246	49 670	58 919	60 448	64 711	62 518
Per capita	1 674	1 940	1 873	1 770	2 147	2 504	2 525	2 656	2 521

18

Gross domestic product: total and per capita

In US dollars (millions) [1] at current and constant 1990 prices; per capita US dollars;

real rates of growth [*cont.*]

Produit intérieur brut : total et par habitant

En dollars E.-U. (millions) [1] aux prix courants et constants de 1990; par habitant en dollars E.-U.;

taux de l'accroissement réels [*suite*]

Country or area Pays ou zone	1990	1991	1992	1993	1994	1995	1996	1997	1998
At constant prices	36 117	37 129	36 601	38 940	44 025	47 214	48 444	51 814	51 749
Growth rates	−5.4	2.8	−1.4	6.4	13.1	7.2	2.6	7.0	−0.1
Philippines Philippines									
At current prices	44 312	45 418	52 976	54 368	64 084	74 120	82 847	82 159	65 221
Per capita	730	731	833	834	960	1 084	1 185	1 150	894
At constant prices	44 312	44 055	44 204	45 140	47 120	49 325	52 208	54 900	54 605
Growth rates	3.0	−0.6	0.3	2.1	4.4	4.7	5.8	5.2	−0.5
Poland Pologne									
At current prices	58 976	76 478	84 357	85 995	98 533	126 317	142 965	143 132	158 574
Per capita	1 547	2 000	2 199	2 236	2 556	3 272	3 698	3 699	4 096
At constant prices	58 976	54 838	56 264	58 389	61 401	65 675	69 647	74 383	78 128
Growth rates	−11.5	−7.0	2.6	3.8	5.2	7.0	6.0	6.8	5.0
Portugal Portugal									
At current prices	70 324	79 744	96 189	85 205	89 730	106 561	110 857	104 252	109 344
Per capita	7 126	8 086	9 758	8 646	9 105	10 812	11 244	10 569	11 080
At constant prices	70 324	72 488	74 104	73 099	74 957	77 162	79 621	82 381	85 258
Growth rates	5.3	3.1	2.2	−1.4	2.5	2.9	3.2	3.5	3.5
Puerto Rico Porto Rico									
At current prices	32 287	34 630	36 923	39 691	42 647	45 511	48 102	50 932	55 194
Per capita	9 152	9 719	10 253	10 903	11 592	12 250	12 832	13 475	14 488
At constant prices	32 287	33 761	35 330	36 808	38 482	39 546	41 386	42 669	43 992
Growth rates	2.3	4.6	4.6	4.2	4.5	2.8	4.7	3.1	3.1
Qatar Qatar									
At current prices	7 360	6 884	7 646	7 157	7 374	8 138	9 059	11 298	10 460
Per capita	15 165	13 695	14 806	13 562	13 710	14 851	16 226	19 867	18 065
At constant prices	7 360	7 302	8 011	7 964	8 151	8 391	8 795	10 909	11 345
Growth rates	2.7	−0.8	9.7	−0.6	2.3	2.9	4.8	24.0	4.0
Republic of Moldova République de Moldova									
At current prices	19 039	14 800	463	500	1 109	1 441	1 694	1 929	1 639
Per capita	4 363	3 383	106	114	253	329	387	441	374
At constant prices	19 039	15 708	11 153	11 019	7 592	7 486	6 902	6 992	6 390
Growth rates	−1.4	−17.5	−29.0	−1.2	−31.1	−1.4	−7.8	1.3	−8.6
Réunion Réunion									
At current prices	5 211	5 554	6 382	5 953	6 352	7 420	7 564	6 929	7 172
Per capita	8 627	9 043	10 219	9 375	9 847	11 330	11 386	10 290	10 513
At constant prices	5 211	5 292	5 475	5 711	5 839	5 998	6 169	6 360	6 553
Growth rates	4.0	1.6	3.5	4.3	2.3	2.7	2.9	3.1	3.0
Romania Roumanie									
At current prices	38 248	28 851	19 579	26 361	30 073	35 477	35 315	34 945	38 157
Per capita	1 648	1 245	848	1 148	1 316	1 561	1 560	1 550	1 698
At constant prices	38 248	37 838	34 521	35 048	36 426	39 026	40 567	37 704	34 960
Growth rates	−6.5	−1.1	−8.8	1.5	3.9	7.1	3.9	−7.1	−7.3
Russian Federation Fédération de Russie									
At current prices	967 267	799 143	85 572	172 945	278 777	347 654	429 664	449 846	285 464
Per capita	6 523	5 377	575	1 164	1 879	2 347	2 906	3 047	1 936
At constant prices	967 267	918 905	785 662	717 309	626 930	601 083	580 046	584 854	557 951
Growth rates	−3.6	−5.0	−14.5	−8.7	−12.6	−4.1	−3.5	0.8	−4.6
Rwanda Rwanda									
At current prices	2 335	1 701	1 630	1 576	954	1 060	945	1 169	1 484
Per capita	334	253	261	275	178	202	173	196	225
At constant prices	2 335	2 353	2 365	1 990	1 017	1 267	1 416	1 600	1 768
Growth rates	2.0	0.8	0.5	−15.9	−48.9	24.6	11.8	13.0	10.5
Saint Kitts and Nevis Saint-Kitts-et-Nevis									
At current prices	160	165	182	198	222	231	246	271	290
Per capita	3 811	3 970	4 429	4 874	5 497	5 766	6 195	6 899	7 440
At constant prices	160	170	177	184	194	200	212	227	235
Growth rates	1.3	6.8	3.6	4.0	5.5	3.5	5.9	7.0	3.6
Saint Lucia Sainte-Lucie									
At current prices	416	448	497	498	519	554	571	585	613
Per capita	3 103	3 291	3 604	3 554	3 650	3 845	3 910	3 945	4 081
At constant prices	416	418	450	452	458	463	477	486	500
Growth rates	1.9	0.4	7.7	0.4	1.3	1.1	3.1	1.8	2.8

18

Gross domestic product: total and per capita

In US dollars (millions) [1] at current and constant 1990 prices; per capita US dollars;

real rates of growth [*cont.*]

Produit intérieur brut : total et par habitant

En dollars E.−U. (millions) [1] aux prix courants et constants de 1990; par habitant en dollars E.−U.;

taux de l'accroissement réels [*suite*]

Country or area Pays ou zone	1990	1991	1992	1993	1994	1995	1996	1997	1998
St. Vincent−Grenadines St. Vincent−Grenadines									
At current prices	198	212	233	239	243	264	278	294	316
Per capita	1 874	1 993	2 170	2 205	2 229	2 400	2 514	2 633	2 815
At constant prices	198	201	213	218	214	230	233	242	254
Growth rates	6.7	1.5	5.9	2.3	−2.0	7.6	1.5	3.7	5.2
Samoa Samoa									
At current prices	112	112	118	119	186	193	215	237	219
Per capita	700	695	726	723	1 123	1 151	1 266	1 378	1 255
At constant prices	112	109	107	109	105	112	119	121	122
Growth rates	−7.5	−2.4	−2.3	2.4	−3.7	6.8	6.0	1.3	1.1
San Marino Saint−Marin									
At current prices	448	477	512	419	439	476	540	516	535
Per capita	19 333	20 341	21 543	17 358	17 898	19 136	21 421	20 207	20 659
At constant prices	448	454	458	454	464	477	481	488	495
Growth rates	2.0	1.4	0.8	−0.9	2.2	2.9	0.9	1.5	1.3
Sao Tome and Principe Sao Tomé−et−Principe									
At current prices	50	57	46	48	50	45	45	44	30
Per capita	421	468	370	375	382	342	331	316	210
At constant prices	50	51	52	52	53	54	55	56	58
Growth rates	3.8	1.6	1.5	1.5	1.4	2.6	1.9	1.7	2.6
Saudi Arabia Arabie saoudite									
At current prices	82 996	104 671	118 034	123 204	118 516	120 167	127 811	141 322	146 494
Per capita	5 173	6 327	6 958	7 101	6 671	6 584	6 788	7 255	7 259
At constant prices	82 996	81 119	85 987	88 386	87 823	88 274	88 688	89 923	92 327
Growth rates	1.2	−2.3	6.0	2.8	−0.6	0.5	0.5	1.4	2.7
Senegal Sénégal									
At current prices	5 699	5 500	6 027	5 431	3 642	4 476	4 653	4 377	4 666
Per capita	778	731	781	686	449	537	544	499	518
At constant prices	5 699	5 676	5 802	5 673	5 836	6 136	6 454	6 780	7 163
Growth rates	3.9	−0.4	2.2	−2.2	2.9	5.2	5.2	5.0	5.6
Seychelles Seychelles									
At current prices	369	374	434	469	483	508	499	548	559
Per capita	5 303	5 322	6 096	6 527	6 643	6 920	6 728	7 304	7 378
At constant prices	369	379	406	431	428	425	433	532	571
Growth rates	7.5	2.7	7.2	6.2	−0.8	−0.6	1.9	22.8	7.4
Sierra Leone Sierra Leone									
At current prices	635	652	655	823	927	941	930	978	703
Per capita	159	161	161	202	225	225	217	221	154
At constant prices	635	617	533	500	501	487	494	478	483
Growth rates	1.0	−2.8	−13.6	−6.2	0.2	−2.8	1.6	−3.4	1.1
Singapore Singapour									
At current prices	37 450	43 719	49 685	58 372	70 849	85 161	92 748	96 319	85 425
Per capita	12 415	14 199	15 816	18 222	21 711	25 645	27 479	28 107	24 577
At constant prices	37 450	40 167	42 668	47 109	52 064	56 568	60 453	65 145	66 114
Growth rates	9.0	7.3	6.2	10.4	10.5	8.7	6.9	7.8	1.5
Slovakia Slovaquie									
At current prices	15 489	10 844	11 757	11 996	13 747	17 392	18 781	19 452	20 362
Per capita	2 947	2 055	2 218	2 254	2 574	3 248	3 500	3 621	3 787
At constant prices	15 489	13 236	12 364	11 881	12 464	13 324	14 202	15 130	15 796
Growth rates	−2.5	−14.5	−6.6	−3.9	4.9	6.9	6.6	6.5	4.4
Slovenia Slovénie									
At current prices	17 382	12 673	12 523	12 673	14 386	18 743	18 878	18 206	19 524
Per capita	9 063	6 561	6 428	6 449	7 266	9 419	9 463	9 124	9 798
At constant prices	17 382	15 835	14 970	15 395	16 215	16 881	17 478	18 274	18 995
Growth rates	−4.5	−8.9	−5.5	2.8	5.3	4.1	3.5	4.6	3.9
Solomon Islands Iles Salomon									
At current prices	168	186	209	245	282	322	355	376	297
Per capita	525	561	608	690	768	848	908	931	712
At constant prices	168	172	190	195	205	219	226	224	219
Growth rates	6.7	2.2	10.7	2.4	5.1	6.7	3.5	−1.0	−2.2
Somalia Somalie									
At current prices	1 071	619	556	1 015	1 136	1 132	1 271	1 495	1 631
Per capita	138	79	70	127	141	138	150	169	177

18
Gross domestic product: total and per capita
In US dollars (millions) [1] at current and constant 1990 prices; per capita US dollars;
real rates of growth [*cont.*]
Produit intérieur brut : total et par habitant
En dollars E.–U. (millions) [1] aux prix courants et constants de 1990; par habitant en dollars E.–U.;
taux de l'accroissement réels [*suite*]

Country or area Pays ou zone	1990	1991	1992	1993	1994	1995	1996	1997	1998
At constant prices	1 071	1 061	933	933	737	737	766	745	764
Growth rates	−1.6	−1.0	−12.0	0.0	−21.0	0.0	3.9	−2.7	2.5
South Africa Afrique du Sud									
At current prices	112 014	120 226	130 514	130 406	135 778	151 113	143 840	148 366	133 962
Per capita	3 293	3 464	3 686	3 612	3 690	4 033	3 773	3 828	3 404
At constant prices	112 014	110 873	108 504	109 842	113 395	116 928	121 782	124 856	125 639
Growth rates	−0.3	−1.0	−2.1	1.2	3.2	3.1	4.2	2.5	0.6
Spain Espagne									
At current prices	513 664	551 939	602 811	500 114	505 013	584 281	608 812	558 567	582 138
Per capita	13 069	14 009	15 275	12 658	12 772	14 766	15 377	14 101	14 690
At constant prices	513 664	525 315	528 925	522 770	534 383	548 964	561 811	583 359	606 435
Growth rates	3.7	2.3	0.7	−1.2	2.2	2.7	2.3	3.8	4.0
Sri Lanka Sri Lanka									
At current prices	7 935	8 937	9 623	10 341	11 720	12 924	13 957	15 095	15 711
Per capita	466	519	553	588	660	721	771	826	851
At constant prices	7 935	8 318	8 682	9 282	9 807	10 349	10 738	11 414	11 955
Growth rates	6.2	4.8	4.4	6.9	5.6	5.5	3.8	6.3	4.7
Sudan Soudan									
At current prices	24 469	27 697	4 329	5 953	6 496	7 645	5 309	7 895	8 642
Per capita	1 017	1 127	173	233	249	287	195	285	305
At constant prices	24 469	24 763	33 219	34 473	35 086	38 208	39 929	42 404	44 947
Growth rates	−1.4	1.2	34.1	3.8	1.8	8.9	4.5	6.2	6.0
Suriname Suriname									
At current prices	1 000	1 034	1 006	836	479	519	758	848	1 015
Per capita	2 489	2 560	2 483	2 057	1 174	1 269	1 846	2 059	2 454
At constant prices	1 000	1 034	1 006	836	857	911	1 115	1 224	1 217
Growth rates	−3.9	3.4	−2.6	−16.9	2.4	6.3	22.4	9.8	−0.6
Swaziland Swaziland									
At current prices	859	869	931	947	1 019	1 216	1 172	1 261	1 218
Per capita	1 141	1 121	1 165	1 152	1 203	1 394	1 305	1 363	1 279
At constant prices	859	880	891	920	952	981	1 016	1 054	1 086
Growth rates	8.9	2.5	1.3	3.3	3.5	3.0	3.6	3.7	3.0
Sweden Suède									
At current prices	237 927	247 838	256 361	192 415	206 889	240 186	261 908	237 479	237 764
Per capita	27 799	28 785	29 594	22 082	23 617	27 294	29 655	26 816	26 790
At constant prices	237 927	235 271	231 926	226 775	236 111	244 826	247 465	252 367	259 816
Growth rates	1.4	−1.1	−1.4	−2.2	4.1	3.7	1.1	2.0	3.0
Switzerland Suisse									
At current prices	228 408	232 679	243 468	236 734	261 361	307 255	295 981	256 039	262 113
Per capita	33 422	33 734	34 976	33 705	36 892	43 015	41 118	35 314	35 910
At constant prices	228 408	226 579	226 293	225 203	226 402	227 544	228 269	232 097	236 874
Growth rates	3.7	−0.8	−0.1	−0.5	0.5	0.5	0.3	1.7	2.1
Syrian Arab Republic Rép. arabe syrienne									
At current prices	23 904	27 756	33 107	36 860	45 087	50 866	36 173	36 641	38 473
Per capita	1 930	2 175	2 522	2 734	3 258	3 582	2 483	2 451	2 509
At constant prices	23 904	25 793	29 268	30 783	33 139	35 045	36 620	37 094	38 948
Growth rates	4.6	7.9	13.5	5.2	7.7	5.8	4.5	1.3	5.0
Tajikistan Tadjikistan									
At current prices	11 032	7 661	2 581	680	730	568	1 044	922	1 320
Per capita	2 080	1 415	469	122	129	99	179	156	219
At constant prices	11 032	10 072	7 050	5 901	4 644	4 068	3 389	3 447	3 629
Growth rates	−2.4	−8.7	−30.0	−16.3	−21.3	−12.4	−16.7	1.7	5.3
Thailand Thaïlande									
At current prices	85 344	98 235	111 453	125 210	144 534	168 011	181 865	150 619	113 990
Per capita	1 535	1 745	1 958	2 177	2 489	2 867	3 074	2 521	1 890
At constant prices	85 344	92 648	100 137	108 532	118 232	128 759	136 392	134 023	123 242
Growth rates	11.2	8.6	8.1	8.4	8.9	8.9	5.9	−1.7	−8.0
TFYR Macedonia L'ex−R.y. Macédoine									
At current prices	4 471	4 685	2 317	2 544	3 384	4 475	4 526	3 699	3 504
Per capita	2 342	2 437	1 198	1 309	1 733	2 279	2 292	1 862	1 753
At constant prices	4 471	4 326	3 972	3 924	3 855	3 812	3 857	3 913	4 028
Growth rates	−6.5	−3.2	−8.2	−1.2	−1.8	−1.1	1.2	1.4	2.9

18

Gross domestic product: total and per capita
In US dollars (millions) [1] at current and constant 1990 prices; per capita US dollars;
real rates of growth [*cont.*]
     Produit intérieur brut : total et par habitant
     En dollars E.−U. (millions) [1] aux prix courants et constants de 1990; par habitant en dollars E.−U.;
     taux de l'accroissement réels [*suite*]

Country or area Pays ou zone	1990	1991	1992	1993	1994	1995	1996	1997	19
Togo Togo									
At current prices	1 571	1 469	1 676	1 244	982	1 307	1 450	1 400	1 5
Per capita	447	406	450	324	249	322	348	327	3
At constant prices	1 571	1 585	1 526	1 317	1 532	1 666	1 733	1 816	1 9
Growth rates	0.1	0.9	−3.7	−13.7	16.3	8.8	4.0	4.8	6
Tonga Tonga									
At current prices	124	149	147	145	159	171	187	180	1
Per capita	1 292	1 552	1 528	1 503	1 643	1 758	1 920	1 838	1 6
At constant prices	124	130	135	139	144	151	149	139	1
Growth rates	−2.7	5.4	3.5	2.8	3.8	5.2	−1.5	−6.6	−
Trinidad and Tobago Trinité−et−Tobago									
At current prices	5 068	5 308	5 439	4 577	4 947	5 324	5 770	5 914	5 9
Per capita	4 171	4 338	4 410	3 680	3 946	4 217	4 543	4 632	4 6
At constant prices	5 068	5 204	5 118	5 044	5 224	5 423	5 631	5 812	6 0
Growth rates	1.5	2.7	−1.6	−1.5	3.6	3.8	3.8	3.2	
Tunisia Tunisie									
At current prices	12 314	13 010	15 497	14 609	15 632	18 029	19 587	18 899	19 9
Per capita	1 510	1 564	1 827	1 690	1 777	2 016	2 157	2 052	2 1
At constant prices	12 314	12 795	13 794	14 096	14 544	15 252	16 335	17 217	18 0
Growth rates	7.1	3.9	7.8	2.2	3.2	4.9	7.1	5.4	
Turkey Turquie									
At current prices	150 679	151 042	159 096	180 422	130 652	169 319	181 464	189 878	198 0
Per capita	2 686	2 642	2 733	3 047	2 169	2 763	2 911	2 995	3 0
At constant prices	150 679	152 075	161 175	174 137	164 637	176 476	188 839	203 056	208 7
Growth rates	9.3	0.9	6.0	8.0	−5.5	7.2	7.0	7.5	
Turkmenistan Turkménistan									
At current prices	11 023	8 492	4 145	5 725	2 460	1 612	1 949	1 899	2 5
Per capita	3 005	2 262	1 080	1 461	615	395	469	449	5
At constant prices	11 023	10 505	14 245	14 458	12 044	11 117	11 128	9 859	10 3
Growth rates	1.8	−4.7	35.6	1.5	−16.7	−7.7	0.1	−11.4	
Tuvalu Tuvalu									
At current prices	10	10	11	10	11	12	15	15	
Per capita	1 073	1 110	1 139	990	1 148	1 149	1 427	1 407	1 2
At constant prices	10	10	10	11	12	11	13	14	
Growth rates	15.4	3.6	2.8	4.1	10.3	−5.0	20.4	2.5	
Uganda Ouganda									
At current prices	3 736	3 028	3 252	3 367	5 280	6 170	6 344	6 865	7 1
Per capita	227	179	187	188	287	326	326	343	3
At constant prices	3 736	3 941	4 124	4 415	4 882	5 352	5 665	6 119	6 2
Growth rates	6.2	5.5	4.6	7.1	10.6	9.6	5.9	8.0	
Ukraine Ukraine									
At current prices	250 901	171 086	20 970	32 731	36 756	37 008	44 558	50 150	41 8
Per capita	4 835	3 296	404	633	712	720	869	982	8
At constant prices	250 901	224 305	186 173	159 737	123 157	108 132	97 275	94 367	93 3
Growth rates	−3.4	−10.6	−17.0	−14.2	−22.9	−12.2	−10.0	−3.0	−
United Arab Emirates Emirats arabes unis									
At current prices	33 780	33 914	34 977	35 305	37 797	42 280	47 403	48 745	45 8
Per capita	17 589	17 100	17 114	16 798	17 522	19 134	20 978	21 127	19 5
At constant prices	33 780	33 834	34 789	34 497	35 256	37 760	41 688	42 500	39 5
Growth rates	17.8	0.2	2.8	−0.8	2.2	7.1	10.4	1.9	−
United Kingdom Royaume−Uni									
At current prices	984 580	1 028 105	1 064 609	956 606	1 034 612	1 124 757	1 178 460	1 316 529	1 403 6
Per capita	17 105	17 807	18 388	16 481	17 783	19 290	20 168	22 488	23 9
At constant prices	984 580	969 866	970 368	992 861	1 036 460	1 065 424	1 092 666	1 131 038	1 155 4
Growth rates	0.6	−1.5	0.1	2.3	4.4	2.8	2.6	3.5	
United Rep.Tanzania Rép.−Unic de Tanzanie									
At current prices	3 878	4 401	3 925	3 555	3 665	4 264	5 276	6 265	6 8
Per capita	152	167	144	126	126	142	172	199	2
At constant prices	3 878	4 099	4 244	4 421	4 555	4 787	5 007	5 158	5 3
Growth rates	4.5	5.7	3.5	4.2	3.0	5.1	4.6	3.0	
United States Etats−Unis									
At current prices	5 793 517	5 957 181	6 287 428	6 614 963	7 012 700	7 341 800	7 751 100	8 239 000	8 699 2
Per capita	22 802	23 210	24 249	25 256	26 512	27 495	28 768	30 316	31 7

18
Gross domestic product: total and per capita
In US dollars (millions) [1] at current and constant 1990 prices; per capita US dollars;
real rates of growth [cont.]
Produit intérieur brut : total et par habitant
En dollars E.–U. (millions) [1] aux prix courants et constants de 1990; par habitant en dollars E.–U.;
taux de l'accroissement réels [suite]

Country or area Pays ou zone	1990	1991	1992	1993	1994	1995	1996	1997	1998
At constant prices	5 793 517	5 735 504	5 896 826	6 039 756	6 263 299	6 445 263	6 675 270	6 958 476	7 258 449
Growth rates	1.2	−1.0	2.8	2.4	3.7	2.9	3.6	4.2	4.3
Uruguay Uruguay									
At current prices	8 355	10 047	11 858	13 832	16 279	18 046	19 124	19 967	20 831
Per capita	2 690	3 213	3 766	4 361	5 096	5 607	5 899	6 115	6 333
At constant prices	8 355	8 624	9 303	9 582	10 190	10 011	10 539	11 072	11 570
Growth rates	0.9	3.2	7.9	3.0	6.3	−1.8	5.3	5.1	4.5
Uzbekistan Ouzbékistan									
At current prices	48 694	35 171	2 298	5 479	6 516	10 050	7 680	15 373	11 073
Per capita	2 374	1 680	108	252	295	447	336	662	470
At constant prices	48 694	48 448	43 049	42 067	39 858	39 515	40 202	42 263	44 123
Growth rates	−0.8	−0.5	−11.1	−2.3	−5.3	−0.9	1.7	5.1	4.4
Vanuatu Vanuatu									
At current prices	153	182	190	196	214	243	253	254	232
Per capita	1 023	1 189	1 210	1 216	1 301	1 440	1 461	1 436	1 276
At constant prices	153	171	170	178	182	191	196	200	205
Growth rates	4.8	12.1	−0.7	4.5	2.5	4.7	2.6	2.4	2.1
Venezuela Venezuela									
At current prices	48 598	53 462	60 423	60 048	58 418	77 389	70 538	88 704	95 450
Per capita	2 492	2 676	2 955	2 871	2 733	3 543	3 162	3 894	4 107
At constant prices	48 598	53 326	56 558	56 714	55 381	57 570	57 456	61 116	61 050
Growth rates	6.5	9.7	6.1	0.3	−2.3	4.0	−0.2	6.4	−0.1
Viet Nam Viet Nam									
At current prices	6 472	7 443	9 867	13 181	16 286	20 743	24 657	27 609	26 030
Per capita	97	109	142	185	225	281	328	361	336
At constant prices	6 472	6 848	7 443	8 045	8 755	9 591	10 486	11 341	11 999
Growth rates	5.1	5.8	8.7	8.1	8.8	9.5	9.3	8.2	5.8
Yemen Yémen									
At current prices	12 628	12 177	15 227	18 392	22 556	11 001	6 946	5 719	5 985
Per capita	1 090	999	1 184	1 353	1 575	732	443	351	354
At constant prices	12 628	12 668	13 288	13 677	13 615	14 737	15 387	16 187	16 511
Growth rates	−3.0	0.3	4.9	2.9	−0.5	8.2	4.4	5.2	2.0
Yugoslavia Yougoslavie									
At current prices	28 390	25 754	18 696	13 169	13 862	14 681	15 548	17 000	11 956
Per capita	2 795	2 515	1 810	1 263	1 320	1 389	1 466	1 600	1 124
At constant prices	28 390	25 091	18 090	12 525	12 843	13 628	14 428	15 496	15 899
Growth rates	−7.9	−11.6	−27.9	−30.8	2.5	6.1	5.9	7.4	2.6
Zambia Zambie									
At current prices	3 742	3 377	3 308	3 274	3 348	3 470	3 286	3 922	3 627
Per capita	517	455	435	419	419	423	392	457	413
At constant prices	3 742	3 741	3 676	3 926	3 787	3 701	3 942	4 081	3 999
Growth rates	−0.5	0.0	−1.7	6.8	−3.5	−2.3	6.5	3.5	−2.0
Zimbabwe Zimbabwe									
At current prices	8 780	8 641	6 751	6 563	6 891	7 134	7 537	8 388	6 232
Per capita	890	855	654	624	644	656	682	748	548
At constant prices	8 780	9 266	8 429	8 541	9 125	9 066	9 728	10 042	10 202
Growth rates	7.0	5.5	−9.0	1.3	6.8	−0.6	7.3	3.2	1.6

Source:
United Nations Secretariat, national accounts database
of the Statistics Division.

† For information on recent changes in country or area
nomenclature pertaining to former Czechoslovakia, Germany,
Hong Kong Special Administrative Region (SAR) of China,
Macao Special Administrative Region (SAR) of China,
SFR of Yugoslavia and the former USSR, see Annex I –
Country or area nomenclature, regional and other groupings.

Source:
Secrétariat de l'Organisation des Nations Unies, la base de données
sur les comptes nationaux de la Division de statistique.

† Pour les modifications récentes de nomenclature de pays
ou de zone concernant l'Allemagne, Hong Kong, région
administrative spéciale (RAS) de Chine, Macao, région
administrative spéciale (RAS) de Chine, l'ex–Tchécoslovaquie,
l'ex–URSS et l'ex–Rfs de Yougoslavie, voir annexe I –
Nomenclature des pays ou des zones, groupements
régionaux et autres groupements.

18
Gross domestic product: total and per capita
In US dollars (millions) [1] at current and constant 1990 prices; per capita US dollars;
real rates of growth [*cont.*]

Produit intérieur brut : total et par habitant
En dollars E.–U. (millions) [1] aux prix courants et constants de 1990; par habitant en dollars E.–U.;
taux de l'accroissement réels [*suite*]

†† For statistical purposes, the data for China do not include those for the Hong Kong Special Administrative Region (Hong Kong SAR), Macao Special Administrative Region (Macao SAR) and Taiwan province of China.

1   The conversion rates used to translate national currency data into United States dollars are the period averages of market exchange rates (MERs) for members of the International Monetary Fund (IMF). These rates, which are published in the *International Financial Statistics*, are communicated to the IMF by national central banks and consist of three types of rates:

   a) Market rates, determined largely by market forces;
   b) Official rates, determined by government authorities;
   c) Principal rates, for countries maintaining multiple exchange rate arrangements.

Market rates always take priority and official rates are used only when a free market rate is not available.

For non–members of the IMF, averages of the United Nations operational rates, used for accounting purposes in UN transactions with member countries, are applied. These are based on official, commercial and/or tourist rates of exchange.

For Afghanistan, Iraq, Lebanon, Liberia, Myanmar, Nigeria, Suriname and Syrian Arab Republic price–adjusted rates of exchange (PARE) were used due to large distortions in the levels of per capita GDP with the use of IMF market exchange rates.

It should be noted that there are practical constraints in the use of MERs for conversion purposes, particularly in the case of countries with multiple exchange rates, those coping with inordinate levels of inflation or experiencing misalignments caused by market fluctuations, the use of which may result in excessive fluctuations or distortions in the dollar income levels of a number of countries. Caution is therefore urged when making inter–country comparisons of incomes as expressed in US dollars.

2   Data refer to the Vatican City State.

†† Les données statistiques relatives à la Chine ne comprennent pas celles qui concernent la région administrative spéciale de Hong Kong (la RAS de Hong Kong), la région administrative spéciale de Macao (la RAS de Macao) et la province chinoise de Taiwan.

1   Les taux de conversion utilisés pour exprimer les données nationales en dollars des États–Unis sont, pour les membres du Fonds monétaire international (FMI), les moyennes pour la période considérée des taux de change du marché. Ces derniers, qui sont publiés dans "Statistiques financières internationales," sont communiqués au FMI par les banques centrales nationales et reposent sur trois types de taux :

   a) Taux du marché, déterminés surtout par les facteurs du marché;
   b) Taux officiels, déterminés par les pouvoirs publics;
   c) Taux principaux, pour les pays pratiquant différents arrangements en matière de taux de change.

On donne toujours la priorité aux taux du marché, n'utilisant les taux officiels que lorsqu'il n'y a pas de taux du marché libre.

Pour les pays qui ne sont pas membres du FMI, on utilise des moyennes des taux de change opérationnels de l'ONU (qui servent à des fins comptables, pour les opérations de l'ONU avec les les pays qui en sont membres). Ces taux reposent sur les taux de change officiels, les taux du commerce et/ou les taux touristiques.

Pour l'Afghanistan, l'Iraq, le Liban, le Libéria, le Myanmar, le Nigéria, le Suriname et le République arabe syrienne on a utilisé des taux de change corrigés des prix, car les taux de change du marché publiés par le FMI induisent des distorsions importantes dans les montants du produit intérieur brut par habitant.

Il est à noter qu'on se heurte à des difficultés pratiques en utilisant les taux de change du marché pour convertir les données en monnaie nationale, surtout dans le cas des pays qui pratiquent plusieurs taux de change et de ceux qui connaissent des taux d'inflation exceptionnels ou des décalages provenant des fluctuations du marché; on risque en les utilisant d'aboutir à des fluctuations excessives ou à des distorsions du revenu en dollars de certains pays. Les comparaisons de revenu entre pays sont donc sujettes à caution lorsqu'on se fonde sur le revenu en dollars des États–Unis.

2   Les données se rapportent à l'Etat de la Cité du Vatican.

19
Expenditure on gross domestic product at current prices
Dépenses imputées au produit intérieur brut aux prix courants

Percentage distribution
Répartition en pourcentage

Country or area Pays ou zone	Year Année	GDP at current prices (Million nat. cur.) PIB aux prix courants (Mil. monnaie nat.)	% of GDP − en % du PIB					
			Govt. final consumption expenditure Consom. finale des admin. publiques	Household final consumption expenditure Consom. finale des ménages	Changes in inventories Variation des stocks	Gross fixed capital formation Formation brute de capital fixe	Exports of goods and services Exportations de biens et services	Imports of goods and services Importations de biens et services
Albania Albanie	1988	17 001	9.5	63.3	−2.6	31.9	−2.0[1]	...
	1989	18 674	8.8	61.0	0.4	31.3	−1.5[1]	...
	1990	16 812	10.2	72.7	−10.1	34.6	−7.4[1]	...
Algeria Algérie	1994	1 487 404	17.7	56.3	4.1	27.4	23.0	28.5
	1995	2 002 638	17.0	55.5	4.6	27.1	26.6	30.8
	1996	2 564 739	15.8	52.0	0.2	24.9	30.9	23.9
Angola Angola	1988	239 640	32.9	45.5	−0.0	14.6	32.8	25.8
	1989	278 866	28.9	48.2	0.9	11.2	33.8	23.1
	1990	308 062	28.5	44.7	0.6	11.1	38.9	23.8
Anguilla Anguilla	1995	202[2]	17.1	77.9	...	28.9[3]	75.8	99.7
	1996	214[2]	18.0	82.4	...	29.1[3]	72.1	101.6
	1997	238[2]	18.8	69.5	...	25.3[3]	72.8	86.3
Antigua and Barbuda Antigua−et−Barbuda	1984	468	18.5	69.8	...	23.6[3]	73.7	85.6
	1985	541	18.3	71.5	...	28.0[3]	75.7	93.5
	1986	642	18.9	69.7	...	36.1[3]	75.2	99.9
Argentina Argentine	1996	272 150	12.5	70.0	...	18.1[3]	10.5	11.1
	1997	292 859	12.1	70.7	...	19.4[3]	10.6	12.7
	1998	298 131	11.9	70.7	...	19.9[3]	10.4	12.9
Aruba Aruba	1994	2 381	16.8	48.6	0.5	29.3	80.4	75.6
Australia [4] [5] Australie [4] [5]	1996	533 632	18.3	58.8	−0.0	22.7	19.7	19.4
	1997	565 881	18.2	58.9	0.2	23.5	20.1	21.0
	1998	593 311[2]	18.2	59.4	0.8	23.8	18.8	21.3
Austria [5] Autriche [5]	1996	2 453 240[2]	20.2	57.3	0.2	23.2	39.5	40.6
	1997	2 522 222[2]	19.8	56.8	0.5	23.1	42.6	44.0
	1998	2 610 914[2]	19.8	56.1	0.4	24.2	44.9	45.4
Azerbaijan [5] Azerbaïdjan [5]	1996	13 663 200[2]	12.0	87.7	−0.1	29.1	24.9	55.9
	1997	15 791 400[2]	12.6	74.5	−2.8	37.0	29.0	53.0
	1998	15 929 700[2]	12.8	80.9	−0.0	40.6	25.3	58.3
Bahamas Bahamas	1993	2 854[2]	14.3	69.6	1.1	18.4	53.2	51.8
	1994	3 053[2]	16.7	67.3	1.1	20.1	51.4	53.5
	1995	3 069[2]	15.8	67.7	0.4	22.8	54.7	59.3
Bahrain Bahreïn	1994	1 828	24.4	29.4	1.8	32.3	98.4	86.3
	1995	1 900	24.0	26.4	−7.5	28.3	112.1	83.2
	1996	2 016	21.2	24.5	−2.8	22.2	120.9	86.1
Bangladesh [4] Bangladesh [4]	1995	1 301 600[2]	13.6	78.8	...	17.0[3]	14.2	23.9
	1996	1 403 045[2]	14.1	78.4	...	17.3[3]	15.4	23.2
	1997	1 540 923[2]	14.8	77.3	...	16.3[3]	16.8	23.4
Barbados Barbade	1993	3 301	22.2	59.9	0.4	13.3	51.8	46.6
	1994	3 474	20.4	61.7	0.7	12.7	52.2	47.5
	1995	3 765	20.2	67.5	0.3	13.5	50.3	51.8
Belarus [5] Bélarus [5]	1994	17 814 500	20.1	60.2	−0.3	33.2	71.0	84.1
	1995	119 813 100	19.3	60.4	0.1	25.0	50.0	54.8
	1996	184 174 000	19.9	59.5	2.5	22.0	48.3	52.2
Belgium [5] Belgique [5]	1996	8 304 112	21.8	54.2	−0.3	20.3	71.3	67.2
	1997	8 712 360	21.2	53.6	−0.2	20.9	75.8	71.3
	1998	9 088 844	21.1	53.8	0.3	20.8	75.6	71.5
Belize Belize	1990	793	19.6	43.4	2.3	26.2	89.5	81.0
	1991	861	19.4	66.3	1.7	28.5	70.7	86.6
	1992	936	18.7	64.4	1.2	29.7	68.7	82.8
Benin Bénin	1989	479 200	13.0	81.4	−0.6	12.5	18.3	24.5
	1990	502 300	13.2	80.4	0.8	13.4	20.4	28.2
	1991	535 500	12.0	82.6	0.9	13.6	22.0	31.1
Bermuda [6] Bermudes [6]	1996	2 194	12.2	64.8	...	13.5[3]	59.9	50.3
	1997	2 330	11.7	63.7	...	13.7[3]	60.0	49.2
	1998	2 457	12.9	64.4	...	15.1[3]	58.4	50.8
Bhutan Bhoutan	1996	11 714	21.4	40.3	1.1	46.9	34.0	43.7
	1997	14 477	25.5	35.8	2.1	46.0	33.0	42.3
	1998	16 420	25.8	36.3	2.5	44.8	33.2	42.6

19
Expenditure on gross domestic product at current prices
Percentage distribution [cont.]
Dépenses imputées au produit intérieur brut aux prix courants
Répartition en pourcentage [suite]

Country or area Pays ou zone	Year Année	GDP at current prices (Million nat. cur.) PIB aux prix courants (Mil. monnaie nat.)	% of GDP – en % du PIB					Import goods serv Importati de bi et serv
			Govt. final consumption expenditure Consom. finale des admin. publiques	Household final consumption expenditure Consom. finale des ménages	Changes in inventories Variation des stocks	Gross fixed capital formation Formation brute de capital fixe	Exports of goods and services Exportations de biens et services	
Bolivia	1994	27 603	13.6	77.7	−0.5	14.9	21.7	2
Bolivie	1995	31 485	13.7	76.7	−0.4	15.7	19.8	2
	1996	36 194	13.6	78.1	−0.1	15.6	19.7	2
Botswana [7]	1996	14 202[2]	29.4	32.1	−2.0	25.0	53.2	3
Botswana [7]	1997	17 486[2]	28.1	30.9	−0.9	23.9	57.1	3
	1998	20 363[2]	28.5	32.4	3.4	24.8	55.8	4
Brazil	1996	778 887	18.5	62.5	1.7	19.3	7.0	
Brésil	1997	864 111	17.8	63.1	1.8	19.9	7.6	
	1998	899 814	17.8	63.6	1.4	19.9	7.4	
British Virgin Islands	1987	117	17.3	73.7	2.3	36.9	95.5	12
Iles Vierges brit.	1988	131	20.1	68.9	2.7	34.3	107.6	13
	1989	156	20.7	64.9	2.6	31.6	104.8	12
Brunei Darussalam	1982	9 126	10.0	5.5	−0.0	12.4	89.3	
Brunéi Darussalam	1983	8 124	11.4	9.5	−0.0	9.9	88.3	
	1984	8 069	31.1	−5.6	0.0	6.5	84.5	
Bulgaria [5]	1996	1 748 701	11.9	76.6[8]	−5.2	13.6	62.9	
Bulgarie [5]	1997	17 055 205	12.8	70.3[8]	0.6	10.8	61.9	
	1998	21 577 020[2]	15.1	72.9[8]	3.2	11.6	45.2	4
Burkina Faso	1991	811 676	14.7	76.2	1.4	21.8	11.4	
Burkina Faso	1992	812 590	14.4	76.2	−0.2	21.3	9.7	
	1993	832 349	14.4	77.2	0.8	20.4	9.7	
Burundi	1990	196 656	19.5	83.0	−0.6	16.4	8.0	2
Burundi	1991	211 898	17.0	83.9	−0.5	18.1	10.0	2
	1992	226 384	15.6	82.9	0.4	21.1	9.0	2
Cambodia	1996	8 324 792[2]	6.4	88.3	1.7	13.5	25.7	4
Cambodge	1997	9 025 268[2]	6.1	89.1	1.4	13.3	43.7	4
	1998	10 243 942[2]	5.7	90.8	0.6	12.8	45.6	
Cameroon [4 5]	1996	4 793 080	79.8[9]	...	−0.2	13.1	24.7	
Cameroun [4 5]	1997	5 370 580	82.0[9]	0.1	12.8	24.0	1	
	1998	5 744 000	82.9[9]	...	−0.1	13.5	24.0	
Canada [5]	1996	821 116	20.9	57.3	0.4	17.5	38.9	
Canada [5]	1997	860 261	20.1	58.0	1.0	19.2	39.9	
	1998	881 356	20.0	58.7	0.5	19.4	41.8	
Cape Verde	1993	29 078	23.3	83.5	−1.0	40.0	18.0	
Cap–Vert	1994	33 497	21.6	83.0	0.7	43.7	18.4	
	1995	37 705	22.8	86.3	2.0	38.8	16.6	
Cayman Islands	1989	474[2]	14.1	65.0	...	23.2[3]	60.1	
Iles Caïmanes	1990	590[2]	14.2	62.5	...	21.4[3]	64.1	
	1991	616[2]	15.1	62.5	...	21.8[3]	58.9	
Central African Rep.	1986	388 647	15.6	82.1	−0.1	12.9	18.2	2
Rép. centrafricaine	1987	360 942	17.5	80.6	−0.2	12.9	17.8	2
	1988	376 748	16.1	80.7	0.7	9.8	17.7	2
Chad	1992	350 632	17.6	75.6	...	8.7[3]	17.6	
Tchad	1993	291 691	24.1	83.1	...	7.7[3]	19.9	
	1994	460 851	12.8	56.0	...	9.8[3]	22.7	
Chile	1994	21 395 185	9.9	64.6	0.8	23.3	29.3	2
Chili	1995	25 875 727	9.8	62.6	1.9	23.9	30.5	
	1996	28 536 186	10.2	65.3	1.8	24.8	28.2	
China †† [5]	1996	6 833 040	11.5	47.1	5.2	34.2	2.1[1]	
Chine †† [5]	1997	7 489 430	11.6	46.5	4.4	33.6	3.8[1]	
	1998	7 985 330	11.9	46.2	2.8	35.3	3.8[1]	
China, Hong Kong SAR †	1996	1 192 000	8.8	60.6	0.9	31.2	142.1	1
Chine, Hong Kong RAS †	1997	1 325 000	8.6	60.5	0.9	33.7	132.4	13
	1998	1 268 000	9.3	58.4	−1.0	30.7	127.4	12
Colombia [5]	1994	67 532 862	14.5	65.9	2.2	23.3	15.0	2
Colombie [5]	1995	84 439 109	14.9	65.7	3.3	22.4	14.5	2
	1996	100 711 389	18.0	65.5	0.5	21.6	15.2	2
Comoros	1989	63 397	27.6	77.8	4.6	14.4	14.9	3
Comores	1990	66 370	25.7	79.7	8.0	12.2	11.7	3
	1991	69 248	25.3	80.9	4.0	12.3	15.5	3

19
Expenditure on gross domestic product at current prices
Percentage distribution [cont.]
Dépenses imputées au produit intérieur brut aux prix courants
Répartition en pourcentage [suite]

Country or area Pays ou zone	Year Année	GDP at current prices (Million nat. cur.) PIB aux prix courants (Mil. monnaie nat.)	% of GDP − en % du PIB					
			Govt. final consumption expenditure Consom. finale des admin. publiques	Household final consumption expenditure Consom. finale des ménages	Changes in inventories Variation des stocks	Gross fixed capital formation Formation brute de capital fixe	Exports of goods and services Exportations de biens et services	Imports of goods and services Importations de biens et services
Congo Congo	1987	690 523	20.6	56.6	−1.1	20.9	41.7	38.6
	1988	658 964	21.1	60.1	−1.0	19.6	40.6	40.4
	1989	773 524	18.7	52.8	−0.5	16.4	47.6	35.0
Costa Rica Costa Rica	1993	1 069 259	16.7	60.6	6.6	23.2	38.6	45.8
	1994	1 306 302	17.3	59.7	7.1	19.7	39.4	43.2
	1995	1 659 385	16.8	59.0	7.1	18.3	40.9	42.1
Côte d'Ivoire Côte d'Ivoire	1994	4 616 000	18.1	60.4	2.2	10.2	39.6	30.5
	1995	5 543 000	16.9	64.1	1.9	12.2	37.0	32.1
	1996	6 177 000	16.0	65.1	−4.1	13.7	41.0	31.7
Croatia [5] Croatie [5]	1995	98 382	29.4	62.7	1.9	15.7	38.6	49.5
	1996	107 981	27.0	59.0	1.4	20.5	40.2	49.7
	1997	122 905	26.2	59.1	3.9	24.4	42.1	57.3
Cuba Cuba	1996	22 815[2]	24.2	70.6	−2.8	9.9	15.6	18.3
	1997	22 952[2]	24.0	71.7	−2.2	9.9	16.5	19.4
	1998	23 901[2]	23.6	71.0	−2.3	10.2	16.2	19.3
Cyprus Chypre	1997	4 366[2]	18.8	66.1	0.7	19.0	47.0	52.1
	1998	4 680[2]	19.3	68.5	1.1	18.5	43.6	51.3
	1999	4 943[2]	18.0	66.9	1.3	17.8	48.6	49.3
Czech Republic [5] République tchèque [5]	1996	1 572 257	19.9	51.6	3.0	31.8	52.9	59.3
	1997	1 680 000	19.7	53.1	2.9	30.2	56.5	62.5
	1998	1 820 700	19.3	52.2	2.3	27.5	60.0	61.4
Dem. Rep. of the Congo Rép. dém. du Congo	1985	147 263	11.6	47.8	7.7	21.7	72.2	61.1
	1986	203 416	19.0	48.1	8.3	23.0	61.4	59.6
	1987	326 946	22.4	77.1	5.3	20.3	63.2	88.2
Denmark [5] Danemark [5]	1996	1 061 720	25.8	50.1	0.2	18.9	35.7	30.8
	1997	1 114 332	25.4	50.5	0.3	20.2	36.5	33.1
	1998	1 168 306	25.6	50.7	0.9	20.9	35.0	33.2
Djibouti Djibouti	1996	88 233	33.6	63.7	−0.9	19.3	40.3	56.8
	1997	87 289	34.7	59.5	0.2	21.4	42.2	57.8
	1998	88 461	29.0	67.4	0.2	23.2	43.4	63.0
Dominica Dominique	1989	423	20.5	71.5	1.5	38.8	41.0	73.4
	1990	452	20.3	64.1	1.1	39.7	50.1	75.3
	1991	479	20.0	71.4	1.1	40.2	46.4	79.1
Dominican Republic Rép. dominicaine	1991	100 070	4.1	82.5	0.1	16.9	24.6	28.1
	1992	112 369	5.1	81.2	0.1	21.0	23.6	31.0
	1993	120 572	5.7	76.9	0.2	22.2	23.4	28.4
Ecuador Equateur	1991	12 296 000	7.6	68.6	2.5	19.6	31.4	29.7
	1992	19 414 000	7.2	67.7	1.7	19.5	31.5	27.7
	1993	27 451 000	7.7	70.6	1.2	19.9	26.2	25.5
Egypt [4] Egypte [4]	1989	87 741	11.0	71.7	5.5	25.6	22.0	35.8
	1990	110 143	10.0	76.3	−0.6	22.4	28.1	36.2
	1991	136 190	8.9	80.8	0.1	17.9	29.5	37.2
El Salvador El Salvador	1992	49 841	9.4	88.4	1.4	17.2	16.1	32.4
	1993	60 522	8.7	87.2	0.7	17.9	19.5	34.0
	1994	70 613	8.2	87.4	1.1	18.7	20.0	35.3
Equatorial Guinea Guinée équatoriale	1989	42 256	22.2	54.3	−0.0	19.6	40.4	36.6
	1990	44 349	15.3	53.2	−3.1	34.6	59.7	59.7
	1991	46 429	14.4	75.9	−2.3	18.4	28.4	34.7
Estonia [5] Estonie [5]	1996	52 446[2]	24.1	60.7	1.1	26.7	67.1	78.6
	1997	64 324[2]	22.1	59.1	2.9	27.9	78.1	89.6
	1998	73 325[2]	21.8	59.5	−0.3	29.7	79.9	90.4
Ethiopia [10] Ethiopie [10]	1997	41 465	11.1	80.6	...	19.1[3]	15.5	26.3
	1998	45 035	14.2	77.1	...	18.9[3]	16.1	26.3
	1999	49 994	13.3	79.2	...	20.4[3]	13.6	26.5
Fiji Fidji	1994	2 674[2]	16.5	71.1	1.5	12.3	56.4	59.4
	1995	2 799[2]	16.1	71.0	1.1	12.0	54.7	58.2
	1996	2 976[2]	16.2	69.2	1.4	9.6	59.4	59.0
Finland [5] Finlande [5]	1996	585 865[2]	23.2	52.7	−0.3	17.0	37.5	30.0
	1997	635 532[2]	22.4	50.9	0.4	18.0	39.1	30.9
	1998	686 742[2]	21.7	50.3	1.1	18.6	39.0	30.1

19
Expenditure on gross domestic product at current prices
Percentage distribution *[cont.]*
Dépenses imputées au produit intérieur brut aux prix courants
Répartition en pourcentage *[suite]*

Country or area Pays ou zone	Year Année	GDP at current prices (Million nat. cur.) PIB aux prix courants (Mil. monnaie nat.)	% of GDP – en % du PIB					
			Govt. final consumption expenditure Consom. finale des admin. publiques	Household final consumption expenditure Consom. finale des ménages	Changes in inventories Variation des stocks	Gross fixed capital formation Formation brute de capital fixe	Exports of goods and services Exportations de biens et services	Imports of goods and services Importations de biens et services
France [5]	1996	7 951 366	24.2	55.8	-0.2	18.5	23.1	21.
France [5]	1997	8 224 901	24.0	54.9	-0.0	18.1	25.5	22.
	1998	8 564 678	23.6	55.0	0.3	18.4	26.0	23.
French Guyana	1990	6 526	35.0	64.4	-0.2	47.8	67.3	114.
Guyane française	1991	7 404	34.4	60.1	1.5	40.5	81.1	117.
	1992	7 976	34.2	58.9	1.5	30.8	65.4	90.
French Polynesia	1991	305 211	39.3	63.9	-0.2	18.4	9.3	30.
Polynésie française	1992	314 265[2]	47.8	63.9	0.0	16.7	8.3	27.
	1993	329 266	38.3	61.5	-0.2	16.2	10.5	26.
Gabon	1986	1 201 100	25.3	46.8	...	45.2[3]	39.6	57.
Gabon	1987	1 020 600	23.7	48.6	...	26.7[3]	41.3	40.
	1988	1 013 600	21.8	48.1	...	36.2[3]	37.3	43.
Gambia [4]	1991	2 920	13.0	83.7	...	18.2[3]	45.3	60.
Gambie [4]	1992	3 078	13.2	81.2	...	22.4[3]	45.2	61.
	1993	3 243	15.1	78.1	...	27.1[3]	36.6	56.
Georgia [5]	1994	1 806 633 000[2] [15]	6.6	98.9	6.0	10.8	23.3	45.
Georgie [5]	1995	3694[2] [15]	8.0	83.2	4.7	19.3	14.0	28.
	1996	5300[2] [15]	6.2	87.0	4.3	13.6	11.2	18.
Germany [5]	1997	3 666 600	19.5	57.5	0.2	21.4	27.8	26.
Allemagne [5]	1998	3 784 200	19.0	57.5	0.8	21.1	28.9	27.
	1999	3 871 600	19.0	57.8	0.9	20.9	29.1	27.
Ghana	1994	5 205 200	13.7	73.7	1.4	22.6	22.5	33.
Ghana	1995	7 752 600	12.1	76.2	-1.1	21.1	24.5	32.
	1996	11 339 200	12.0	76.1	0.9	20.6	24.9	34.
Greece [5]	1996	29 935 080	14.5	73.7	0.3	19.5	17.5	25.
Grèce [5]	1997	33 021 832	14.7	72.4	-0.0	21.0	17.8	25
	1998	35 910 654	14.8	71.1	-0.1	22.1	17.6	25
Grenada	1990	541	20.5	64.9	3.1	38.9	44.4	71
Grenade	1991	567	18.8	69.2	3.7	40.0	45.4	77
	1992	578	19.9	66.5	2.1	32.4	38.6	59
Guadeloupe	1990	15 201	30.8	92.8	1.1	33.9	4.9	63
Guadeloupe	1991	16 415	31.0	87.3	1.0	33.0	6.1	58
	1992	17 972	29.3	84.1	1.3	27.8	4.5	47
Guatemala	1996	95 479	5.1	87.0	-0.6	13.3	17.8	22
Guatemala	1997	107 943	4.9	86.9	-1.0	14.8	17.9	23
	1998	121 548	6.2	86.6	-0.2	15.7	17.9	26
Guinea–Bissau	1990	510 094	11.4	100.9	0.9	13.8	12.0	39
Guinée–Bissau	1991	854 985	12.6	100.6	0.9	10.4	13.4	38
	1992	1 530 010	10.7	111.1	...	26.5[3]	8.2	56
Guyana	1997	106 678	20.4	44.2	...	44.2[3]	...	
Guyana	1998	109 055	21.5	49.6	...	40.5[3]	...	
	1999	115 150	20.2	50.5	...	40.0[3]	...	
Haiti [11]	1997	51 578	103.1[9]	...	...	12.5[3]	11.5	27
Haïti [11]	1998	59 055	102.5[9]	...	...	12.9[3]	13.2	28
	1999	66 425	101.8[9]	...	...	13.1[3]	13.3	28
Honduras	1995	37 507	9.3	63.5	7.6	24.0	43.7	48
Honduras	1996	47 774	9.5	65.1	7.1	23.3	47.0	52
	1997	61 084	8.8	64.9	6.4	23.6	46.5	50
Hungary [5]	1996	6 893 934	22.0	52.2	5.4	21.4	38.9	39
Hongrie [5]	1997	8 540 669[2]	21.9	50.6	5.4	22.2	45.5	46
	1998	10 071 939	...	49.9	6.6	23.1	50.7	53
Iceland	1996	486 454	20.6	61.0	-0.2	18.0	36.4	35
Islande	1997	529 949	20.3	60.4	-0.0	18.6	36.0	35
	1998	586 572	21.1	61.6	0.2	21.4	34.9	39
India [6]	1995	12 179 630[2]	10.4	61.7	1.8	23.8	10.7	11
Inde [6]	1996	14 098 490[2]	10.2	62.4	-0.1	23.2	10.3	11
	1997	15 635 520[2]	11.1	61.1	0.5	22.9	10.3	11
Indonesia	1996	532 567 000	7.6	62.4	1.1	29.6	25.8	26
Indonésie	1997	627 695 000	6.8	61.7	3.4	28.3	27.9	28
	1998	1 002 334 000	5.4	66.2	-3.0	22.1	50.5	41

19
Expenditure on gross domestic product at current prices
Percentage distribution *[cont.]*
Dépenses imputées au produit intérieur brut aux prix courants
Répartition en pourcentage *[suite]*

Country or area Pays ou zone	Year Année	GDP at current prices (Million nat. cur.) PIB aux prix courants (Mil. monnaie nat.)	% of GDP – en % du PIB					
			Govt. final consumption expenditure Consom. finale des admin. publiques	Household final consumption expenditure Consom. finale des ménages	Changes in inventories Variation des stocks	Gross fixed capital formation Formation brute de capital fixe	Exports of goods and services Exportations de biens et services	Imports of goods and services Importations de biens et services
Iran (Islamic Republic of) [12]	1996	235 233 000	13.6	59.7	−4.8[2]	25.7	18.5	12.8
Iran (Rép. islamique d') [12]	1997	277 831 000	13.8	62.0	−3.5[2]	24.9	13.1	10.3
	1998	328 337 000	13.3	64.8	−0.1[2]	22.1	8.3	8.3
Iraq	1989	21 026	28.5	53.4	−11.0	30.0	21.3	22.2
Iraq	1990	23 297	26.4	50.5	−4.2	26.7	18.5	17.8
	1991	19 940	35.3	48.2	2.6	16.5	2.7	5.3
Ireland [5]	1996	45 210[2]	15.8	54.1	0.8	19.1	76.0	65.0
Irlande [5]	1997	51 823[2]	15.1	51.9	1.1	20.7	78.4	66.2
	1998	59 637[2]	14.6	50.2	1.3	22.5	84.4	72.7
Israel [5]	1996	324 929	28.4	56.6	1.2	21.9	28.8	37.0
Israël [5]	1997	362 209	28.1	57.1	0.2	20.4	29.6	35.4
	1998	394 022	28.0	57.2	−0.6	19.1	30.9	34.7
Italy [5]	1996	1 896 022 000	18.2	58.3	0.2	18.2	25.9	20.9
Italie [5]	1997	1 974 618 000	18.2	58.9	0.7	18.0	26.7	22.5
	1998	2 057 731 000	18.1	58.9	1.2	18.1	26.1	22.6
Jamaica	1994	139 655	11.8	64.0	0.2	31.1	60.0	67.2
Jamaïque	1995	179 686	13.0	67.1	0.3	32.2	56.1	68.8
	1996	219 103	14.5	65.2	0.3	32.0	50.9	62.8
Japan	1996	500 309 700	9.7	59.8	0.5	29.5	9.9	9.4
Japon	1997	507 851 800	9.7	60.3	0.4	28.4	11.1	9.9
	1998	495 210 800	10.1	61.5	0.3	26.2	11.2	9.2
Jordan	1996	4711	25.6	69.0	1.1	30.7	55.1	81.5
Jordanie	1997	4 946	26.6	69.8	−0.1	26.8	51.2	74.3
	1998	5 180	26.4	71.2	0.7	22.8	48.6	69.7
Kazakhstan [5]	1994	423 469[2]	10.7	77.7	2.6	26.1	37.1	47.1
Kazakhstan [5]	1995	1 014 190[2]	13.6	68.8	2.6	23.1	39.0	43.5
	1996	1 415 750[2]	12.6	67.1	1.1	17.2	35.3	36.0
Kenya	1993	16 007	15.1	61.6	0.7	17.6	42.1	37.2
Kenya	1994	19 684	15.4	61.7	0.4	19.2	37.6	34.5
	1995	23 040	15.0	69.4	0.4	21.6	33.1	39.5
Kiribati								
Kiribati	1980	21	36.4	92.8	...	44.0[3]	22.5	95.7
Korea, Republic of [5]	1996	418 478 988[2]	10.2	55.8	1.1	36.8	29.5	33.6
Corée, Rép. de [5]	1997	453 276 389[2]	10.1	56.3	−0.9	35.1	34.7	35.7
	1998	449 508 816[2]	10.9	55.7	−8.6	29.4	48.7	35.8
Kuwait	1995	7 925	33.0	41.3	1.2	13.9	53.6	43.0
Koweït	1996	9 307	27.6	45.9	...	13.3[3]	52.9	39.7
	1997	9 212	27.6	47.2	...	13.5[3]	52.6	40.8
Kyrgyzstan [5]	1995	16 145	19.5	75.0	−2.3	20.7	29.5	42.4
Kirghizistan [5]	1996	23 399	18.5	79.9	2.6	22.6	30.7	56.6
	1997	30 438[2]	15.2	80.0	2.0	13.7	38.7	50.0
Latvia [5]	1995	2 349	22.2	62.6	2.5	15.1	46.9	49.3
Lettonie [5]	1996	2 829	21.6	67.6	0.7	18.1	50.9	59.0
	1997	3 211	23.3	67.2	0.4	19.3	50.5	60.6
Lebanon	1994	14 992 000	121.4[9]	...	...	36.4[3]	8.4	66.3
Liban	1995	17 779 000	117.7[9]	...	...	36.3[3]	11.0	64.9
Lesotho	1996	4 040	16.3	119.7	0.2	58.1	24.6	118.9
Lesotho	1997	4 715	17.0	113.9	−1.0	54.7	27.6	112.2
	1998	4 849	20.0	115.6	−3.3	49.4	27.2	109.0
Liberia	1987	1 090[2]	13.2	65.5	0.6	11.1	40.2	32.7
Libéria	1988	1 158[2]	11.8	63.3	0.3	10.0	39.0	27.8
	1989	1 194[2]	11.9	55.0	0.3	8.1	43.7	23.1
Libyan Arab Jamah.	1983	8 805	32.7	39.2	−1.1	25.1	42.1	38.0
Jamah. arabe libyenne	1984	8 013	33.6	38.6	0.5	25.3	41.4	39.4
	1985	8 277	31.7	37.6	0.4	19.7	37.4	26.7
Lithuania [5]	1995	24 103	19.7	67.4	1.7	23.0	53.0	64.8
Lithuanie [5]	1996	31 569	18.9	66.4	1.5	23.0	53.4	63.2
	1997	38 201	19.6	67.1	1.5	22.0	54.6	64.8
Luxembourg [5]	1996	563 513	18.2	48.6	0.0	20.3	106.1	93.0
Luxembourg [5]	1997	624 581	17.3	46.3	0.2	20.1	109.8	93.8
	1998	665 735	16.8	45.2	0.3	19.2	113.7	95.1

19
Expenditure on gross domestic product at current prices
Percentage distribution *[cont.]*
Dépenses imputées au produit intérieur brut aux prix courants
Répartition en pourcentage *[suite]*

Country or area Pays ou zone	Year Année	GDP at current prices (Million nat. cur.) PIB aux prix courants (Mil. monnaie nat.)	% of GDP – en % du PIB Govt. final consumption expenditure Consom. finale des admin. publiques	Household final consumption expenditure Consom. finale des ménages	Changes in inventories Variation des stocks	Gross fixed capital formation Formation brute de capital fixe	Exports of goods and services Exportations de biens et services	Imports of goods and services Importations de biens et services
Madagascar Madagascar	1990	4 601 600	8.0	86.0	...	17.0[3]	15.9	26
	1991	4 906 400	8.6	92.2	...	8.2[3]	17.3	26
	1992	5 584 500	8.2	90.0	...	11.6[3]	15.6	25
Malawi Malawi	1992	6 551[2]	18.9	88.3[13]	...	16.4	23.9	40
	1993	8 802[2]	16.2	88.0[13]	...	12.3	16.9	29
	1994	10 319[2]	28.3	74.4[13]	...	12.0	31.8	40
Malaysia Malaisie	1997	281 795	10.8	45.3	-0.2	43.1	93.2	92
	1998	284 475	10.0	41.5	-0.1	26.8	114.4	92
	1999	299 193	11.2	41.7	0.1	22.3	121.7	97
Maldives Maldives	1982	454	14.3	80.8	0.4	22.7	-18.3[1]	
	1983	466	16.3	82.6	2.6	35.6	-37.1[1]	
	1984	537	17.7	77.5	1.5	39.5	-36.1[1]	
Mali Mali	1990	683 300	15.2	79.0	2.2	20.0	17.3	33
	1991	691 400	15.3	85.1	-2.4	20.0	17.5	35
	1992	737 400	14.2	82.2	2.7	17.6	17.8	34
Malta Malte	1997	1 288	20.5	62.4	0.2[2]	25.3	85.1	93
	1998	1 362	19.7	62.1	-0.8[2]	24.5	87.7	93
	1999	1 447	18.7	62.8	0.7[2]	22.7	91.9	96
Martinique Martinique	1990	19 320	29.7	83.6	1.9	26.7	8.4	50
	1991	20 787	28.8	84.0	1.4	25.6	7.4	47
	1992	22 093	28.7	84.3	-0.9	23.6	6.8	42
Mauritania Mauritanie	1986	59 715	14.3	85.4	1.5	22.7	55.4	79
	1987	67 216	13.6	82.6	1.7	20.8	48.3	67
	1988	72 635	14.2	79.6	1.4	17.0	49.1	61
Mauritius Maurice	1996	77 310	12.2	63.8	-1.2	26.0	65.0	65
	1997	86 428	12.1	63.5	2.2	27.1	62.9	67
	1998	96 985	11.7	63.0	0.8	23.8	67.2	66
Mexico [5] Méxique [5]	1995	1 837 019	10.5	67.1	3.7	16.2	30.4	27
	1996	2 525 575	9.6	65.1	5.2	17.9	32.2	30
	1997	3 174 193	9.9	64.2	6.4	19.5	30.4	30
Mongolia Mongolie	1996	659 698	71.2[9]	...	...	22.4[3]	...	
	1997	846 344	70.0[9]	...	...	25.3[3]	...	
	1998	833 727	81.0[9]	...	...	27.3[3]	...	
Montserrat Montserrat	1984	94	20.6	96.4	2.7	23.7	13.6	56
	1985	100	20.3	96.3	1.5	24.7	11.7	54
	1986	114	18.7	89.5	2.8	33.0	10.1	53
Morocco Maroc	1995	281 700	17.4	68.4	-0.7	21.4	27.6	34
	1996	319 630	16.7	67.3	0.3	19.4	25.9	29
	1997	319 290	17.9	65.3	-0.1	20.7	27.9	31
Mozambique Mozambique	1992	2 764 000	21.6	93.5	...	43.5[3]	26.7	85
	1997[5]	40 126 200	8.4	89.2	...	18.9[3]	12.8	29
	1998[5]	43 557 100	9.4	88.2	...	23.3[3]	11.6	32
Myanmar [6] Myanmar [6]	1996	791 980	88.5[9]	...	-2.7	14.9	0.7	1
	1997	1 109 554	88.1[9]	...	-0.9	13.5	0.6	1
	1998	1 559 996	89.4[9]	...	-0.7	11.8	0.5	1
Namibia [5] Namibie [5]	1996	13 421	33.0	55.8	-1.0	23.9	55.8	67
	1997	14 901	32.8	62.3	-0.5	18.3	53.3	66
	1998	16 826	31.5	58.5	1.8	18.1	52.7	62
Nepal [14] Népal [14]	1996	248 913	9.2	76.9	4.8	22.5	22.3	35
	1997	280 513	8.9	77.1	3.7	21.7	26.3	37
	1998	296 547	9.3	81.2	-0.5	21.2	23.1	34
Netherlands [5] Pays–Bas [5]	1996	694 298	23.1	49.9	0.2	21.1	57.9	52
	1997	734 853	22.9	49.4	0.1	21.4	61.2	55
	1998	776 161	23.0	49.5	0.2	21.7	60.9	55
Netherlands Antilles Antilles néerlandaises	1992	3 548	25.3	58.3	2.3	22.1	81.5	89
	1993	3 766	27.7	57.6	0.4	20.9	76.1	82
	1994	4 218	26.2	64.2	0.7	18.5	72.8	82
New Caledonia Nouvelle–Calédonie	1990	250 427[2]	32.6	57.3	-1.1	24.4	22.0	35
	1991	272 235[2]	32.8	53.8	1.3	23.9	20.1	32
	1992	281 427[2]	33.7	56.7	0.1	23.7	16.8	31

19
Expenditure on gross domestic product at current prices
Percentage distribution *[cont.]*
Dépenses imputées au produit intérieur brut aux prix courants
Répartition en pourcentage *[suite]*

Country or area Pays ou zone	Year Année	GDP at current prices (Million nat. cur.) PIB aux prix courants (Mil. monnaie nat.)	Govt. final consumption expenditure Consom. finale des admin. publiques	Household final consumption expenditure Consom. finale des ménages	Changes in inventories Variation des stocks	Gross fixed capital formation Formation brute de capital fixe	Exports of goods and services Exportations de biens et services	Imports of goods and services Importations de biens et services
New Zealand [6]	1996	94 940[2]	14.5	63.0	0.7	21.3	29.0	28.2
Nouvelle-Zélande [6]	1997	98 025[2]	15.1	63.6	0.9	20.2	29.0	28.4
	1998	98 913[2]	15.3	65.0	-0.1	19.2	30.7	30.0
Nicaragua	1985	115 404	35.7	48.2	2.4	20.7	14.8	21.8
Nicaragua	1986	435 742	35.4	55.8	3.1	13.8	12.8	20.8
	1987	2 389 500	24.7	58.1	3.0	7.9	22.1	15.7
Niger	1988	678 200	15.5	65.9	7.9	11.9	20.7	21.9
Niger	1989	692 600	18.0	73.0	-0.1	12.3	18.6	21.8
	1990	682 300	17.2	74.1	1.1	11.7	16.8	20.9
Nigeria	1992	549 809	3.7	73.5	0.1	10.7	35.8	23.8
Nigéria	1993	701 473	3.9	76.6	0.1	11.5	32.6	24.8
	1994	914 334	3.5	82.1	0.0	9.3	23.8	18.6
Norway [5]	1996	1 016 589	20.3	48.2	1.6	21.3	40.8	32.2
Norvège [5]	1997	1 089 032[2]	20.0	47.8	1.7	23.3	41.2	34.1
	1998	1 107 082	21.5	49.8	2.7	25.9	37.4	37.2
Oman [5]	1996	5 874	24.6	47.6	0.2	13.5	48.2	34.1
Oman [5]	1997	6 090	23.2	47.5	0.1	17.6	48.3	36.7
	1998	5 445	25.7	57.2	-0.0	24.1	39.0	46.0
Pakistan [4]	1996	2 457 381	11.8	75.1	1.6	16.2	15.9	20.5
Pakistan [4]	1997	2 736 919	11.0	72.9	2.6	14.5	16.1	17.1
	1998	3 025 683	11.1	73.8	1.5	13.2	15.1	14.7
Panama	1996	8 151	15.6	52.7	5.3	25.3	93.0	91.8
Panama	1997	8 658	16.2	54.3	4.6	26.5	98.1	99.7
	1998	9 144	16.5	57.7	4.1	28.7	89.8	96.8
Papua New Guinea	1990	3 076	24.8	59.0	-0.7	25.1	40.6	48.9
Papouasie-Nouvelle-	1991	3 606	22.4	60.1	-0.6	28.0	42.3	52.2
Guinée	1992	4 140	22.5	57.9	...	23.8[3]	45.2	49.3
Paraguay	1993	11 991 719	6.7	81.3	0.9	22.0	36.9	47.9
Paraguay	1994	14 960 131	6.8	88.4	0.9	22.5	34.2	52.8
	1995	17 699 000	7.2	85.3	0.9	23.1	35.0	51.2
Peru	1996	148 278	9.5	71.2	2.1	21.9	12.2	16.8
Pérou	1997	172 389	9.3	69.4	1.6	23.4	13.0	16.7
	1998	183 179	9.5	71.4	1.3	22.9	11.7	16.8
Philippines	1995	1 905 951	11.4	74.1	0.2	22.2	36.4	44.2
Philippines	1996	2 171 922	11.9	73.5	0.6	23.4	40.5	49.3
	1997	2 423 640	13.0	72.7	0.4	24.5	49.0	59.4
Poland [5]	1995	306 318	16.6	61.2	1.1	18.7	25.5	23.2
Pologne [5]	1996	385 448	16.5	63.1	1.1	20.9	24.4	26.0
	1997	469 372	16.1	63.5	1.1	23.6	25.7	30.0
Portugal [5]	1996	17 098 600[2]	19.1	63.1	-0.2	24.5	29.7	36.7
Portugal [5]	1997	18 276 364[2]	19.3	62.3	0.6	25.9	30.4	38.7
	1998	19 692 907[2]	19.7	62.2	0.6	26.5	30.9	40.3
Puerto Rico [4]	1996	48 187	14.3	62.3	0.9	17.7	63.6	58.8
Porto Rico [4]	1997	53 875	13.2	59.3	0.1	17.2	68.6	58.3
	1998	59 946	12.4	57.7	0.8	19.4	69.7	60.1
Qatar	1996	32 976	33.0	27.3	0.8	35.0	43.7	39.8
Qatar	1997	41 124	29.8	22.7	0.8	34.6	48.3	36.2
	1998	38 074	34.0	24.9	1.0	35.7	43.5	39.1
Republic of Moldova [5]	1995	6 480	27.1	57.0	8.9	16.0	60.1	67.9
Rép. de Moldova [5]	1996	7 658	27.2	69.9	4.6	19.8	53.9	74.1
	1997	8 917	27.4	70.1	3.8	19.2	-19.6[1]	...
Réunion	1992	33 787	28.4	76.1	2.1	28.6	3.4	38.6
Réunion	1993	33 711	28.6	76.4	-0.4	25.7	3.1	36.2
	1994	35 266	28.9	78.0	0.1	28.1	2.9	38.0
Romania [5]	1995	72 135 500	13.7	67.6	2.9	21.4	27.6	33.2
Roumanie [5]	1996	108 919 600	13.1	69.5	2.9	23.0	28.1	36.6
	1997	250 480 200	9.7	75.6	-0.2	22.0	29.6	36.6
Russian Federation [5]	1996	2 145 700 000[2]	20.4	51.6	3.5	21.2	4.2[1]	...
Féderation de Russie [5]	1997	2 522 000 000[2]	21.6	53.3	3.7	19.4	2.9[1]	...
	1998	2 684 500 000[2]	18.1	58.2	-1.3	17.6	7.9[1]	...

19

Expenditure on gross domestic product at current prices
Percentage distribution *[cont.]*

Dépenses imputées au produit intérieur brut aux prix courants
Répartition en pourcentage *[suite]*

Country or area Pays ou zone	Year Année	GDP at current prices (Million nat. cur.) PIB aux prix courants (Mil. monnaie nat.)	% of GDP − en % du PIB					
			Govt. final consumption expenditure Consom. finale des admin. publiques	Household final consumption expenditure Consom. finale des ménages	Changes in inventories Variation des stocks	Gross fixed capital formation Formation brute de capital fixe	Exports of goods and services Exportations de biens et services	Imports goods a servic Importatio de bie et servic
Rwanda	1990	192 900	17.2	82.9	−0.9	12.4	7.7	1
Rwanda	1991	212 900	21.6	82.2	−1.5	11.9	9.8	2
	1992	217 300	25.1	76.8	−0.0	14.9	7.4	2
Saint Kitts−Nevis	1994	599	18.6	67.4	...	38.1[3]	54.2	7
Saint−Kitts−et−Nevis	1995	624	20.3	63.0	...	46.2[3]	50.8	8
	1996	667	19.9	63.0	...	46.6[3]	45.8	7
Saint Lucia	1982	364	24.2	75.5	6.7	33.3	55.0	9
Sainte−Lucie	1983	380	25.7	64.1	5.0	24.9	63.5	8
	1984	408	25.2	65.3	5.1	25.7	64.0	8
Saint Vincent−Grenadines	1995	710[2]	20.3	68.2	2.8	30.4	51.4	6
St.−Vincent−et−	1996	744[2]	20.4	67.6	2.8	28.6	54.2	6
Grenadines	1997	766[2]	21.0	81.9	2.7	30.7	50.3	7
Sao Tome and Principe	1986	2 478	30.3	76.1	0.9	13.6	...	5
Sao Tomé−et−Principe	1987	3 003	24.8	63.1	1.1	15.4	...	4
	1988	4 221	21.2	71.8	...	15.7[3]	...	6
Saudi Arabia	1993	443 842	28.8	43.7	2.1	22.2	40.4	3
Arabie saoudite	1994	450 025	26.6	41.3	1.4	18.7	40.4	2
	1995	470 702	26.1	40.6	1.4	18.5	44.5	3
Senegal	1996	2 380 000[2]	12.0	78.9	2.2	16.3	30.6	4
Sénégal	1997	2 555 000	11.3	76.4	...	18.0[3]	34.0	3
	1998	2 753 000	11.2	74.5	...	20.2[3]	32.8	3
Seychelles	1996	2 482	29.7	48.0	−0.8	33.1	−10.0[1]	
Seychelles	1997	2 910	25.2	50.4	3.7	29.7	−9.0[1]	
	1998	3 127	27.1	51.3	...	37.0[3]	−15.4[1]	
Sierra Leone [4]	1988	43 947	7.5	86.7	0.8	12.7	14.5	2
Sierra Leone [4]	1989	82 837	6.6	84.7	0.5	13.5	19.7	2
	1990	150 175	10.4	77.9	1.8	10.1	25.4	2
Singapore	1995	120 704[2]	8.2	41.4	0.6	33.1	16.9[1]	
Singapour	1996	130 775[2]	9.4	41.2	−1.5	36.8	15.2[1]	
	1997	143 014[2]	9.4	40.6	0.4	37.0	13.9[1]	
Slovakia [5]	1995	516 760	20.3	49.6	1.0	27.4	63.0	6
Slovaquie [5]	1996	575 700	22.5	50.1	2.4	36.9	58.0	7
	1997	653 900	21.7	50.0	−3.2	38.6	56.4	6
Slovenia [5]	1995	2 221 500	20.2	58.1	2.0	21.4	55.2	5
Slovénie [5]	1996	2 552 700	20.3	57.3	0.9	22.5	55.6	5
	1997	2 906 700	20.4	57.1	0.2	23.5	57.1	5
Solomon Islands	1986	253	33.3	63.1	1.0	25.2	52.6	7
Iles Salomon	1987	293	36.3	63.1	2.7	20.4	55.9	7
	1988	367	31.4	68.6	2.7	30.0	52.4	8
Somalia	1985	87 290	10.6	90.5	2.9	8.9	4.2	1
Somalie	1986	118 781	9.7	89.1	1.0	16.8	5.8	2
	1987	169 608	11.1	88.8	4.8	16.8	5.9	2
South Africa [5]	1996	618 417[2]	19.4	62.3	1.0	16.1	24.5	2
Afrique du Sud [5]	1997	683 666[2]	19.8	63.1	−0.2	16.3	24.6	2
	1998	740 581[2]	19.8	62.8	−0.6	16.5	25.7	2
Spain [5]	1996	77 113 358	18.0	59.6	0.3	21.6	23.9	2
Espagne [5]	1997	81 782 027	17.6	59.3	0.2	21.9	26.8	2
	1998	86 968 544	17.4	59.2	0.3	22.8	27.1	2
Sri Lanka	1996	771 414[2]	14.5	68.7	0.3	25.7	35.0	4
Sri Lanka	1997	891 067	14.2	67.0	0.1	25.7	36.6	4
	1998	1 011 326	14.1	66.7	0.1	25.6	36.1	4
Sudan [4]	1991	421 819	10.4	75.6	7.4	10.0	3.8	
Soudan [4]	1992	948 448	5.9	82.3	6.4	13.4	4.5	1
	1993	1 881 289	5.5	82.8	6.6	16.1	4.8	1
Suriname	1996	303 970	14.7	58.9	6.2	29.1	65.5	7
Suriname	1997	340 220	17.7	60.2	5.9	24.0	57.4	6
	1998	407 130	18.7	71.5	...	23.2[3]	42.3	5
Swaziland [7]	1992	2 761	17.7	63.6	0.9	25.3	78.6	8
Swaziland [7]	1993	3 206	24.4	49.1	0.9	25.9	85.3	8
	1994	3 712	23.5	51.3	0.9	24.3	82.7	8

19
Expenditure on gross domestic product at current prices
Percentage distribution *[cont.]*
Dépenses imputées au produit intérieur brut aux prix courants
Répartition en pourcentage *[suite]*

Country or area Pays ou zone	Year Année	GDP at current prices (Million nat. cur.) PIB aux prix courants (Mil. monnaie nat.)	% of GDP − en % du PIB					
			Govt. final consumption expenditure Consom. finale des admin. publiques	Household final consumption expenditure Consom. finale des ménages	Changes in inventories Variation des stocks	Gross fixed capital formation Formation brute de capital fixe	Exports of goods and services Exportations de biens et services	Imports of goods and services Importations de biens et services
Sweden [5]	1996	1 756 358	27.1	50.3	0.2	15.7	39.1	32.4
Suède [5]	1997	1 813 128	26.7	50.7	0.6	14.9	42.7	35.6
	1998	1 890 202	26.7	50.3	0.9	15.8	43.8	37.5
Switzerland	1996	365 833[2]	14.6	61.0	0.1	20.2	35.9	31.8
Suisse	1997	371 590[2]	14.2	61.2	0.6	19.6	39.7	35.4
	1998	380 011[2]	13.7	61.3	1.3	19.9	40.2	36.4
Syrian Arab Rep.	1995	570 975	13.4	66.3	...	27.1[3]	31.0	37.9
Rép. arabe syrienne	1996	676 441	12.0	70.5	...	23.9[3]	32.5	38.9
	1997	728 794	11.7	67.3	...	22.5[3]	33.2	34.6
Thailand	1995	4 186 000[2]	9.9	53.2	0.4	41.0	41.8	48.5
Thaïlande	1996	4 609 000[2]	10.2	54.5	0.6	41.1	39.2	45.5
	1997	4 724 000[2]	10.0	56.0	-0.6	33.8	48.0	46.6
TFYR Macedonia [5]	1991	935	21.3	64.2	-1.7	19.1	22.5	25.5
L'ex−République yougo−	1992	12 005	19.2	64.6	-3.8	19.0	53.4	52.4
slave de Macédonie [5]	1993	58 145	21.4	67.4	-0.7	17.0	47.5	52.7
Togo	1984	304 800	14.0	66.0	-1.5	21.2	51.9	51.6
Togo	1985	332 500	14.2	66.0	5.2	22.9	48.3	56.7
	1986	363 600	14.4	69.0	5.3	23.8	35.6	48.2
Trinidad and Tobago	1992	23 118	17.8	57.5	0.2	13.6	39.4	28.5
Trinité−et−Tobago	1993	24 491	16.4	61.9	0.4	12.9	40.5	30.6
	1994	29 312	14.8	55.4	0.4	12.3	42.6	27.8
Tunisia	1995	17 052	16.3	62.9	0.5	24.2	44.9	48.8
Tunisie	1996	19 066	15.6	60.9	1.9	23.2	42.1	43.7
	1997	20 901	15.7	60.1	2.1	24.6	43.9	46.4
Turkey	1996	14 772 111 000[2]	11.6	67.3	-0.5	25.1	21.5	27.8
Turquie	1997	28 835 883 000[2]	12.3	68.0	-1.3	26.4	24.6	30.4
	1998	51 625 143 000[2]	...	81.0	-0.2	24.8	24.8	28.2
Uganda	1993	4 024 186[2]	10.6	87.5	0.1	16.1	7.7	20.0
Ouganda	1994	5 129 772[2]	9.3	84.9	-0.5	14.3	10.8	18.6
	1995	5 813 893[2]	9.5	84.0	-0.2	16.8	11.1	20.8
Ukraine [5]	1996	81 519	21.8	58.1	1.8	20.7	45.7	48.2
Ukraine [5]	1997	93 365	23.9	57.7	1.4	19.8	40.6	43.7
	1998	102 593	21.6	59.9	1.1	19.6	41.9	44.2
United Arab Emirates	1990	124 008	16.3	38.6	1.0	19.4	65.4	40.8
Emirats arabes unis	1991	124 500	16.9	41.4	1.1	20.7	67.6	47.7
	1992	128 400	17.8	45.5	1.2	23.2	69.1	56.8
United Kingdom [5]	1996	754 601	19.4	64.3	0.2	16.7	29.2	29.7
Royaume−Uni [5]	1997	803 889	18.4	64.3	0.5	16.7	28.5	28.5
	1998	847 421[2]	18.2	64.6	0.4	17.6	26.6	27.5
United Rep. of Tanzania	1992	1 130 596	7.1	90.7	2.8	29.9	15.1	45.7
Rép.−Unie de Tanzanie	1993	1 404 369	9.1	86.8	3.2	29.0	20.5	48.6
	1994	1 822 570	7.7	89.6	3.2	27.5	26.4	54.3
United States	1995	7 038 400	15.9	68.2	0.4	16.8	11.4	12.8
Etats−Unis	1996	7 418 700[2]	15.6	68.1	0.4	17.3	11.6	13.0
	1997	7 844 000	15.2	67.7	0.9	17.7	12.1	13.5
Uruguay	1996	152 449	13.7	73.8	0.9	11.8	21.1	21.3
Uruguay	1997	188 529	13.7	73.8	0.8	12.0	22.6	22.8
	1998	218 145	13.7	71.0	3.1	12.7	21.9	22.5
Uzbekistan [5]	1991	61 549	20.8	56.3	1.8	25.1	35.3	39.1
Ouzbékistan [5]	1992	443 887	20.1	45.3	17.4	26.5	33.9	43.2
	1993	5 095 202	24.6	57.5	-10.5	25.2	33.8	30.6
Vanuatu	1993	23 779	28.4	49.2	2.3	25.5	45.3	53.8
Vanuatu	1994	24 961	27.7	49.2	2.3	26.5	47.3	57.2
	1995	27 255	25.4	46.9	2.1	29.8	44.2	53.6
Venezuela	1997	43 343 669	6.5	65.8	2.3	18.7	28.4	21.7
Venezuela	1998	52 264 273	7.7	72.1	2.1	19.1	20.0	20.9
	1999	61 917 874	7.6	70.2	1.3	14.3	22.0	15.4
Viet Nam [5]	1996	272 036 000[2]	8.4	74.4	1.8	26.3	-11.0[1]	...
Viet Nam [5]	1997	313 623 000[2]	8.1	71.8	1.6	26.7	-8.1[1]	...
	1998	361 017 000[2]	7.6	70.9	2.0	27.0	-7.3[1]	...

19
Expenditure on gross domestic product at current prices
Percentage distribution *[cont.]*
Dépenses imputées au produit intérieur brut aux prix courants
Répartition en pourcentage *[suite]*

Country or area Pays ou zone	Year Année	GDP at current prices (Million nat. cur.) PIB aux prix courants (Mil. monnaie nat.)	% of GDP – en % du PIB					
			Govt. final consumption expenditure Consom. finale des admin. publiques	Household final consumption expenditure Consom. finale des ménages	Changes in inventories Variation des stocks	Gross fixed capital formation Formation brute de capital fixe	Exports of goods and services Exportations de biens et services	Imports of goods and service Importation de bien et service
Yemen	1994	270 900	21.3	78.1	1.1	21.4	16.1	37.
Yémen	1995	449 271	16.5	81.3	4.5	20.9	24.9	48.
	1996	654 036	14.5	70.0	4.5	20.9	40.4	50.
Yugoslavia [5] Yougoslavie [5]	1994	24 578	27.1	59.3	3.6	12.4	−2.4	.
Yugoslavia, SFR † Yougoslavie, SFR †	1988	15 833[2]	14.2	50.1	19.9	17.2	29.5	30.
	1989	235 395[2]	14.4	47.4	28.0	14.5	25.3	29.
	1990	1 147 787	17.6	66.1	7.3	14.7	23.7	29.
Zambia	1989	58 706	73.3	13.5	...	19.9[3]	25.2	31.
Zambie	1990	123 487	54.7	14.1	...	30.7[3]	34.3	33.
	1991	234 504	60.4	14.3	...	24.6[3]	26.4	25.
Zimbabwe	1994	56 441	16.6	61.2	2.3	21.7	34.4	36.
Zimbabwe	1995	66 551	16.7	62.6	−0.7	24.0	35.4	37.
	1996	85 585	14.7	59.4	3.7	22.0	36.1	35.

Source:
United Nations Secretariat, national accounts database of the Statistics Division.

Source:
Secrétariat de l'ONU, la base de données sur les comptes nationaux de la Division de statistique.

† For information on recent changes in country or area nomenclature pertaining to former Czechoslovakia, Germany, Hong Kong Special Administrative Region (SAR) of China, Macao Special Administrative Region (SAR) of China, SFR of Yugoslavia and the former USSR, see Annex I – Country or area nomenclature, regional and other groupings.

†† For statistical purposes, the data for China do not include those for the Hong Kong Special Administrative Region (Hong Kong SAR), Macao Special Administrative Region (Hong Kong SAR) and Taiwan province of China.

1   Net exports.
2   Including statistical discrepancy.
3   Gross capital formation.
4   Data refer to fiscal year beginning 1 July.
5   Data classified according to SNA 93.
6   Data refer to fiscal year beginning 1 April.
7   Data refer to fiscal year ending 30 June.
8   Including government consumption expenditure on individual goods.
9   Including household final consumption expenditure.
10 Data refer to fiscal year ending 7 July.
11 Data refer to fiscal year ending 30 September.
12 Data refer to fiscal year beginning 21 March.
13 Including changes in inventories.
14 Data refer to fiscal year ending 15 July.
15 1990–1992: roubles; 1993–1994: coupous; 1995–1996: laris.

† Pour les modifications récentes de nomenclature de pays ou de zone concernant l'Allemagne, Hong Kong région administrative spéciale (RAS) de Chine, Macao région administrative spéciale (RAS) de Chine, l'ex–Tchécoslovaquie, l'ex–URSS et l'ex–Rfs de Yougoslavie, voir annex I – Nomenclature des pays ou des zones, groupements régionaux et autres groupments.

†† Les données statistiques relatives à la Chine ne comprennent pas celles qui concernent la région administrative spéciale de Hong Kong (la RAS de Hong Kong), la région administrative spéciale de Macao (la RAS de Macao) et la province chinoise de Taiwan.

1   Exportations nettes.
2   Y compris divergence statistique.
3   Formation brute de capital.
4   Les données se réfèrent à l'année fiscale commençant le 1er juillet.
5   Les données sont classifiées selon le SCN 1993.
6   Les données se réfèrent à l'année fiscale commençant le 1er avril.
7   Les données se réfèrent à l'année fiscale finissant le 30e juin.
8   Y compris consommation des administrations publiques biens pris séparément.
9   Y compris la consommation finale des ménages.
10 Les données se réfèrent à l'année fiscale commençant le 7e juillet.
11 Les données se réfèrent à l'année fiscale finissant le 30e septembre.
12 Les données se réfèrent à l'année fiscale commençant le 21e mars.
13 Y compris les variations des stocks.
14 Les données se réfèrent à l'année fiscale finissant le 15e juillet.
15 1990 à 1992 : roubles; 1993 à 1994 : coupous; 1995 à 1996 : laris.

20
Value added by kind of economic activity at current prices
Valeur ajoutée par genre d'activité économique aux prix courants

Percentage distribution
Répartition en pourcentage

Country or area Pays ou zone	Year Année	Value added (Mil. nat.cur.) Valeur ajoutée (Mil. mon.nat.)	Agriculture, hunting, forestry & fishing Agriculture, chasse, sylviculture et pêche	Mining & quarrying Industries extractives	Manufac- turing Industries manufac- turières	Electricity, gas and water Electricité, gaz et eau	Con- struc- tion Con- struc- tion	Wholesale/ retail trade, restaurants and hotels Commerce, restaurants, hôtels	Transport, storage & commu- nication Transports, entrepôts, communi- cations	Other activities Autres activités
Albania [1]	1994	184 393	54.6	12.5[2]	...	...	9.6	19.8[3]	3.4	...
Albanie [1]	1995	229 793	54.6	11.7[2]	...	...	10.3	19.9[3]	3.5	...
	1996	280 998	52.8	12.5[2]	...	...	11.4	20.0[3]	3.3	...
Algeria	1994	1 155 644	12.6	30.1	12.5	1.2	13.1	21.0	6.5	2.9
Algérie	1995	1 566 580	12.5	33.8	10.9	1.2	12.2	19.8	6.4	3.2
	1996	2 039 189	13.6	37.6	9.4	1.2	10.7	17.3	7.3	2.9
Angola	1988	236 682	16.0	27.1	8.3	0.2	4.1	11.7[4]	3.5	29.1
Angola	1989	276 076	19.3	29.7	6.2	0.2	3.3	11.4[4]	3.0	27.1
	1990	305 831	18.0	32.9	5.0	0.1	2.9	10.7[4]	3.2	27.0
Anguilla	1993	162[5]	3.7	0.7	0.7	3.4	13.2	37.5	13.2	27.5
Anguilla	1994	182[5]	3.9	0.6	0.7	3.2	11.8	39.4	13.3	27.0
	1995	183[5]	3.5	0.7	0.7	3.5	12.7	38.9	12.7	27.2
Antigua and Barbuda	1986	567[5]	4.3	1.7	3.8	3.5	8.9	23.6	15.6	38.5
Antigua–et–Barbuda	1987	649[5]	4.5	2.2	3.5	3.5	11.3	24.1	15.6	35.3
	1988	776[5]	4.1	2.2	3.1	4.0	12.7	23.7	14.3	35.9
Argentina	1990	69 709	8.0	2.8	26.5	1.9	4.4	15.4	5.2	35.7
Argentine	1991	182 050	6.8	2.1	24.2	1.6	4.6	15.8	5.2	39.9
	1992	226 921	6.0	1.8	21.8	1.7	5.3	15.4	5.2	42.8
Aruba										
Aruba	1994	2 225	0.6[6]	...	5.8	3.5	7.0	28.6	9.2	45.4
Australia [7]	1994	469 419	2.8	3.6	14.2	3.0	6.1	19.5	7.9	42.9
Australie [7]	1995	503 460	3.3	3.6	14.0	2.8	5.9	19.7	7.7	43.1
	1996	527 667	3.1	3.5	13.7	2.6	5.8	19.7	7.7	43.9
Austria [1]	1995	2 253 793	2.5	0.4	19.7	2.8	7.9	16.7	7.4	42.7
Autriche [1]	1996	2 323 022	2.5	0.4	19.4	2.8	8.1	16.5	7.3	43.0
	1997	2 375 526	2.4	0.4	19.9	2.6	8.0	16.5	7.5	42.7
Azerbaijan [1]	1995	9 843 000	27.3	29.5[2]	...	...	4.0	5.2	18.8	17.3
Azerbaïdjan [1]	1996	12 288 000	27.6	28.7[2]	...	...	10.4	5.8	11.4	17.3
	1997	14 624 000	21.1	26.0[2]	...	...	14.5	5.7	12.5	16.5
Bahrain	1994	2 009	0.9	14.3	16.0	1.5	5.5	10.4	10.8	40.7
Bahreïn	1995	2 071	1.0	15.4	20.2	1.7	5.1	9.8	7.9	38.9
	1996	2 188	1.0	18.1	18.0	1.6	4.5	9.5	8.4	38.9
Bangladesh [7]	1995	1 301 600	30.0	0.0	9.6	2.2	5.9	9.0	11.4	32.0
Bangladesh [7]	1996	1 403 045	29.3	0.0	9.3	2.2	5.9	8.9	11.5	32.9
	1997	1 540 923	28.9	0.0	9.4	2.1	5.9	8.9	11.2	33.5
Barbados	1993	2 791[5]	5.8	0.5	7.4	3.8	4.3	31.1	9.1	37.9
Barbade	1994	2 921[5]	5.1	0.6	7.1	3.5	4.6	31.6	9.2	38.2
	1995	3 173[5]	6.4	0.6	6.8	3.4	4.7	31.8	9.2	37.1
Belarus [1]	1993	10 076 800	16.8	0.1	28.4[8]	...	7.7	10.3	12.8	24.0
Bélarus [1]	1994	17 336 600	13.9	0.1	28.7[8]	...	5.7	14.7	12.7	24.2
	1995	112 164 900	17.0	0.1	30.2[8]	...	5.9	11.1	13.6	22.0
Belgium	1995	7 695 197[9][10]	1.3	...	19.8	4.3	5.3	18.2	8.5	43.2
Belgique	1996	7 955 097[9][10]	1.2	...	18.9	4.5	5.1	18.5	8.4	43.8
	1997	8 267 700[9][10]	1.2	...	19.3	4.5	5.2	18.3	8.6	43.5
Belize	1991	759[5]	19.2	0.8	14.8	2.5	7.8	17.4	11.1	26.5
Belize	1992	829[5]	19.3	0.7	13.2	2.9	7.6	16.9	11.4	28.0
	1993	865[5]	17.6	0.8	12.8	3.4	8.1	17.0	12.3	27.9
Benin	1987	430 800[5]	36.3	1.2	7.8	0.9	3.5	17.0	8.5	24.7
Bénin	1988	451 080[5]	37.2	0.9	8.9	1.0	3.3	18.7	8.1	21.9
	1989	465 735[5]	38.0	0.9	9.2	0.9	3.3	17.6	7.8	22.2
Bhutan	1996	11 558[5]	39.3	2.3	12.1	9.5	9.0	7.8	7.4	12.6
Bhoutan	1997	14 498[5]	36.4	2.1	11.0	11.9	10.1	7.0	7.1	14.4
	1998	16 288[5]	36.7	2.4	11.1	11.0	10.6	7.0	7.5	13.7
Bolivia	1994	25 397	16.6	5.4	18.0	3.7	3.4	12.4	11.8	28.7
Bolivie	1995	28 944	15.4	5.8	19.0	4.0	3.3	12.6	11.0	29.0
	1996	33 065	14.7	5.4	20.2	4.1	3.4	13.1	9.5	29.7

20
Value added by kind of economic activity at current prices
Percentage distribution [cont.]
Valeur ajoutée par genre d'activité économique aux prix courants
Répartition en pourcentage [suite]

% of Value added – % de la valeur ajoutée

Country or area Pays ou zone	Year Année	Value added (Mil. nat.cur.) Valeur ajoutée (Mil. mon.nat.)	Agriculture, hunting, forestry & fishing Agriculture, chasse, sylviculture et pêche	Mining & quarrying Industries extractives	Manufacturing Industries manufacturières	Electricity, gas and water Electricité, gaz et eau	Construction Construction	Wholesale/retail trade, restaurants and hotels Commerce, restaurants, hôtels	Transport, storage & communication Transports, entrepôts, communications	Other activities Autres activités
Botswana [11]	1996	13 742	4.0	35.3	5.1	2.0	6.4	12.0	4.1	3
Botswana [11]	1997	16 974	3.6	38.1	5.1	1.9	6.0	12.1	4.0	2
	1998	19 693	3.2	39.0	5.0	1.9	5.9	11.7	4.0	2
Brazil	1992	617[5]	10.7	1.6	22.7	2.8	6.8	6.6	5.0	4
Brésil	1993	14 361[5]	10.7	1.5	21.6	2.6	6.9	6.5	5.3	4
	1994	348 092[5]	12.6	1.0	21.0	2.6	7.4	6.4	5.0	4
British Virgin Islands	1987	108[5]	4.0	0.2	3.2	3.8	6.0	29.8	11.4	4
Iles Vierges brit.	1988	121[5]	3.6	0.2	3.1	4.0	6.1	28.3	11.9	4
	1989	141[5]	3.4	0.2	3.0	3.7	6.7	27.9	15.0	4
Brunei Darussalam	1992	6 722	2.5	42.2[12]	...	1.0	4.7	11.8	4.6	3
Brunéi Darussalam	1993	6 749	2.6	38.9[12]	...	1.0	4.9	11.9	4.7	3
	1994	6 862	2.6	35.8[12]	...	1.0	5.3	11.6	4.9	3
Bulgaria [1]	1996	1 650 372	15.4	1.8	21.0	3.2	4.3	12.1	7.5	3
Bulgarie[1]	1997	15 294 482	26.6	2.3	18.7	4.5	2.8	10.0	7.6	2
	1998	19 203 204	21.1	1.5	19.1	4.3	3.7	9.7	8.2	3
Burkina Faso	1983	369 658	41.1	0.0	13.0	1.1	2.1	12.5	6.5	2
Burkina Faso	1984	381 868	43.0	0.1	12.4	1.1	1.3	11.0	7.6	2
	1985	441 490	48.5	0.1	11.5	0.7	1.2	10.3	7.0	2
Burundi	1988	149 067	48.9	1.0[8]	16.5	...	2.9	12.9	2.6	1
Burundi	1989	175 627	47.0	1.2[8]	18.5	...	3.3	10.8	3.3	1
	1990	192 050	52.4	0.8[8]	16.8	...	3.4	4.9	3.1	1
Cambodia	1996	7 904 514	43.9	0.2	9.5	0.5	5.1	18.1	6.5	1
Cambodge	1997	8 584 514	42.0	0.2	12.8	0.5	4.8	17.9	6.3	1
	1998	9 760 033	40.7	0.2	14.2	0.5	4.5	17.3	6.8	1
Cameroon [1][7]	1996	4 467 110	22.0	5.5	21.3	0.9	3.2	21.0	5.2	2
Cameroun [1][7]	1997	5 013 530	23.6	5.6	21.3	0.8	2.1	19.9	5.8	2
	1998	5 362 130	23.6	5.6	21.3	0.8	2.1	19.9	5.8	2
Canada [1]	1994	664 376	2.6	4.1	17.9	3.6	5.6	13.4	7.5	4
Canada [1]	1995	699 685	2.8	4.0	19.2	3.6	5.1	13.4	7.5	4
	1996	723 146	2.9	4.7	19.0	3.6	5.1	13.3	7.4	4
Cape Verde	1993	27 264	14.7	1.0	7.5	1.4	11.6	17.8	18.9	2
Cap–Vert	1994	31 175	13.8	0.9	7.5	1.4	11.1	18.9	20.2	2
	1995	35 256	14.6	1.1	7.3	1.9	10.1	18.6	18.0	2
Cayman Islands	1989	473	0.4	0.6	1.9	3.2	11.0	24.5	11.0	4
Iles Caïmanes	1990	580	0.3	0.3	1.6	3.1	9.7	24.5	10.9	4
	1991	605	0.3	0.3	1.5	3.1	9.1	22.8	10.7	5
Central African Rep.	1983	243 350	40.8	2.5	7.8	0.5	2.1	21.2	4.2	2
Rép. centrafricaine	1984	268 725	40.7	2.8	8.1	0.9	2.7	21.7	4.3	1
	1985	308 549	42.4	2.5	7.5	0.8	2.6	22.0	4.2	1
Chad	1992	297 361	34.7	0.3	18.1	0.7	1.2	34.3[14]	...	1
Tchad	1993	250 850	32.1	0.2	18.7	0.9	1.1	33.8[14]	...	1
	1994	347 578	29.4	0.3	17.9	0.7	1.6	40.1[14]	...	1
Chile	1994	19 976 720	8.0	7.9	20.6	3.4	7.4	14.0	7.4	3
Chili	1995	24 163 509	7.5	9.5	20.7	3.3	7.3	13.9	7.0	3
	1996	26 603 983	7.1	7.6	20.6	3.2	7.9	13.8	7.3	3
China ††	1995	5 847 810	20.5	42.3[2]	...	...	6.5	8.4	5.2	1
Chine ††	1996	6 788 460	20.4	42.8[2]	...	...	6.7	8.2	5.1	1
	1997	7 477 240	18.7	42.5[2]	...	...	6.7	8.4	6.1	1
China, Hong Kong SAR †	1995	1 096 472[5]	0.1	0.0	7.7	2.2	5.0	24.7	9.3	5
Chine, Hong Kong RAS †	1996	1 219 986[5]	0.1	0.0	6.8	2.2	5.3	24.7	9.1	5
	1997	1 324 000[5]	0.1	0.0	6.0	2.2	5.4	23.6	8.5	5
Colombia [1]	1994	65 353 067	15.3	3.6	15.5	3.3	7.7	12.8	7.5	3
Colombie [1]	1995	82 058 289	14.4	4.0	15.2	3.2	7.7	12.4	7.4	3
	1996	99 204 630	13.0	4.2	14.6	3.4	6.7	12.0	7.0	3
Comoros	1989	64 731	40.0	...	3.9	0.8	3.4	25.1	3.9	2
Comores	1990	67 992	40.4	...	4.1	0.9	3.1	25.1	4.1	2
	1991	71 113	40.8	...	4.2	0.9	2.7	25.1	4.2	2

20

Value added by kind of economic activity at current prices
Percentage distribution *[cont.]*
Valeur ajoutée par genre d'activité économique aux prix courants
Répartition en pourcentage *[suite]*

% of Value added — % de la valeur ajoutée

Country or area Pays ou zone	Year Année	Value added (Mil. nat.cur.) Valeur ajoutée (Mil. mon.nat.)	Agriculture, hunting, forestry & fishing Agriculture, chasse, sylviculture et pêche	Mining & quarrying Industries extractives	Manufac- turing Industries manufac- turières	Electricity, gas and water Electricité, gaz et eau	Con- struc- tion Con- struc- tion	Wholesale/ retail trade, restaurants and hotels Commerce, restaurants, hôtels	Transport, storage & commu- nication Transports, entrepôts, communi- cations	Other activities Autres activités
Congo	1987	678 106	12.2	22.9	8.8	1.6	3.2	15.1	10.5	25.8
Congo	1988	643 830	14.2	17.1	8.8	2.0	2.7	16.7	11.3	27.2
	1989	757 088	13.3	28.6	7.2	1.9	1.8	14.7	9.3	23.3
Cook Islands	1984	44	14.9	0.2	4.8	1.0	2.1	25.4	10.3	41.3
Iles Cook	1985	53	14.1	0.1	4.5	0.1	2.6	25.6	10.6	42.3
	1986	64	12.5	0.1	5.0	1.1	3.7	22.6	12.0	43.1
Costa Rica	1993	1 069 259	16.0	19.3[12]	...	3.7	2.7	20.8	5.4	31.9
Costa Rica	1994	1 306 302	16.6	18.6[12]	...	3.6	2.7	20.2	5.3	33.0
	1995	1 659 385	17.4	18.6[12]	...	3.4	2.3	20.2	5.3	32.8
Côte d'Ivoire	1986	3 075 000	29.3	1.3	16.0	2.3	2.5	22.4	7.4	18.8
Côte d'Ivoire	1987	2 935 700	30.1	1.0	17.2	2.1	2.8	17.3	8.4	21.1[9]
	1988	2 964 000	33.0	0.7	17.8	2.2	2.6	14.7	8.1	20.9[9]
Croatia [1]	1995	81 108	10.4	0.3	23.6	3.7	5.7	14.2	9.6	32.4
Croatie [1]	1996	90 860	10.0	0.3	21.6	3.8	6.6	15.2	8.8	33.7
	1997	104 682	9.3	0.6	21.8	3.5	7.1	15.6	8.7	33.5
Cuba	1989	19 230	11.2	0.8	24.7	2.6	6.6	23.3	7.1	23.7
Cuba	1990	19 645	11.4	0.6	23.6	2.5	7.3	24.7	6.2	23.6
	1991	16 248	11.2	0.7	25.9	2.9	6.2	18.6	6.4	28.1
Cyprus	1997	4 157	4.3	0.3	11.8	2.1	8.4	22.0	8.6	42.5
Chypre	1998	4 482	4.4	0.3	11.4	2.1	8.1	22.0	8.9	42.9
	1999	4 774	4.2	0.3	10.9	2.2	7.7	21.8	8.8	44.0
Czech Republic	1994	1 083 421	4.4	1.6	25.2	5.4	7.6	16.2	7.2	32.5
République tchèque	1995[1]	1 290 592	4.7	2.2	26.0	5.1	8.7	15.0	8.1	30.2
	1996[1]	1 450 979	4.7	2.5	25.7	4.3	8.4	16.3	8.0	30.2
Denmark	1993	775 414[5]	3.6	0.9	18.6	2.0	5.3	13.6	9.2	46.8
Danemark	1994	818 061[5]	3.7	0.9	19.0	2.0	5.1	13.5	9.0	46.8
	1995	852 423[5]	4.1	0.8	19.5	1.9	5.3	13.0	8.9	46.4
Djibouti	1981	50 486[5]	4.2	...	9.4	2.2	7.9	21.0	11.2	44.2
Djibouti	1982	52 124[5]	4.9	...	9.2	3.0	8.5	18.5	11.1	44.8
	1983	53 014[5]	4.9	...	9.3	3.6	8.6	17.8	11.1	44.8
Dominica	1989	367[5]	24.4	0.8	6.7	2.7	6.8	11.9	14.7	32.1
Dominique	1990	402[5]	24.1	0.8	6.6	2.8	7.0	12.1	14.9	31.8
	1991	427[5]	23.8	0.9	6.4	3.0	6.8	12.3	15.2	31.6
Dominican Republic	1991	100 070	17.8	4.0	13.5[15 16]	0.4	7.1	13.7[4]	6.7	36.8
Rép. dominicaine	1992	112 369	17.5	3.0	14.1[15 16]	0.5	8.2	14.1[4]	6.9	35.8
	1993	120 572	17.5	3.0	14.1[15 16]	0.5	8.2	14.1[4]	6.9	35.8
Ecuador	1991	11 938 000	14.8	11.5	21.4	−0.1	4.7	22.8	8.9	16.1
Equateur	1992	18 953 000	13.0	12.9	22.6	0.1	4.7	22.0	7.9	16.8
	1993	26 844 000	12.4	11.0	22.2	0.3	5.0	20.7	9.1	19.3
Egypt [7]	1989	81 341[5]	19.5	4.8	18.0	1.3[17]	5.5	21.9	9.2	19.8
Egypte [7]	1990	103 344[5]	17.2	10.6	16.9	1.4[17]	5.1	21.0	10.5	17.3
	1991	125 485[5]	16.5	10.6	17.1	1.6[17]	4.8	21.2	11.3	16.8
El Salvador	1992	49 751	14.3	0.4	23.9	0.9	4.4	19.0[4]	7.7	29.5
El Salvador	1993	58 104	14.5	0.4	23.3	1.0	4.5	19.5[4]	7.8	28.9
	1994	67 677	14.5	0.5	23.3	1.1	4.8	20.3[4]	7.8	28.2[9]
Equatorial Guinea	1989	40 948	56.1	...	1.3	3.1	3.7	8.8	2.0	25.0
Guinée équatoriale	1990	42 765	53.6	...	1.3	3.4	3.8	7.6	2.2	28.0
	1991	43 932	53.1	...	1.4	3.1	3.0	7.6	1.9	30.0
Estonia [1]	1996	46 959	7.5	1.6	16.6	4.0	5.8	18.4	10.8	35.3
Estonie [1]	1997	56 858	6.9	1.5	16.5	3.5	5.8	18.3	12.2	35.4
	1998	65 918	6.3	1.2	16.4	3.7	6.4	17.7	13.8	34.5
Ethiopia incl. Eritrea [18]	1990	11 436[5]	41.1	0.2	11.1	1.5	3.6	9.6[4]	7.2	25.7
Ethiopie y comp. Eryth. [18]	1991	12 295[5]	41.0	0.3	10.3	1.5	3.2	9.4[4]	7.1	27.3
	1992	12 544[5]	50.3	0.3	9.1	1.3	2.8	10.2[4]	5.4	20.6
Fiji	1987	1 399[5]	21.9	2.2	11.2	3.1	3.6	14.9	9.5	33.5
Fidji	1988	1 518[5]	18.4	4.1	9.0	3.4	4.0	18.6	10.7	31.8
	1989	1 759[5]	18.5	3.2	9.9	3.1	3.8	21.5	9.6	30.3

20

Value added by kind of economic activity at current prices
Percentage distribution *[cont.]*
Valeur ajoutée par genre d'activité économique aux prix courants
Répartition en pourcentage *[suite]*

% of Value added — % de la valeur ajoutée

Country or area Pays ou zone	Year Année	Value added (Mil. nat.cur.) Valeur ajoutée (Mil. mon.nat.)	Agriculture, hunting, forestry & fishing Agriculture, chasse, sylviculture et pêche	Mining & quarrying Industries extractives	Manufac- turing Industries manufac- turières	Electricity, gas and water Electricité, gaz et eau	Con- struc- tion Cons- truc- tion	Wholesale/ retail trade, restaurants and hotels Commerce, restaurants, hôtels	Transport, storage & commu- nication Transports, entrepôts, communi- cations	Other activities Autres activités
Finland	1995	496 109	4.4	0.4	26.0	2.6	5.7	10.7	8.4	41.8
Finlande	1996	511 958	3.9	0.4	24.7	2.7	5.7	10.8	8.6	43.2
	1997	553 010	3.9	0.4	25.7	2.5	6.2	10.8	8.7	41.9
France	1995	7 349 082	2.5	0.4	20.1	2.4	4.7	15.8	5.9	48.1
France	1996	7 505 238	2.4	0.4	20.0	2.5	4.5	15.6	5.9	48.6
	1997	7 747 705	2.4	0.4	20.3	2.4	4.5	15.4	5.9	48.8
French Guiana	1990	6 454	10.1	7.6	...	0.7	12.8	13.5	7.7	47.5
Guyane française	1991	7 385	7.4	7.6	...	0.5	12.1	13.1	12.3	47.0
	1992	8 052	7.2	9.0	...	0.6	10.8	11.9	11.4	49.1
French Polynesia	1982	141 574	4.2	...	7.2[19]	0.8[19]	10.0	23.9	6.2	47.7
Polynésie française	1983	170 489	3.9	...	7.6[19]	0.8[19]	9.8	24.6	6.2	47.1
	1984	201 807	4.0	...	8.3[19]	0.8[19]	10.0	25.3	5.9	45.7
Gabon	1987	986 000	10.9	28.4	7.1[16]	2.7	7.2	9.2	8.1	26.5
Gabon	1988	965 700	11.2	22.6	7.3[16]	3.0	5.2	14.4	9.1	27.3
	1989	1 128 400	10.4	32.3	5.7[16]	2.5	5.5	12.4	8.2	23.1
Gambia [7]	1991	2 962	22.3	0.0	5.5	0.9	4.4	39.1	10.9	17.0
Gambie [7]	1992	3 100	18.4	0.0	5.7	1.0	4.7	41.7	11.2	17.4
	1993	3 296	20.2	0.0	5.1	1.0	4.5	38.3	12.5	18.4
Georgia [1]	1995	3 488[20]	44.3	1.2	6.3	2.6	2.4	27.6	9.0	6.7
Géorgie [1]	1996	5 116[20]	32.1	1.3	6.6	2.8	4.8	23.0	6.5	22.8
	1997	6 093[20]	29.8	1.2	6.3	2.6	5.0	23.2	10.5	21.4
Germany † Allemagne †										
F. R. Germany	1991	2 555 340	1.3	0.5[21]	30.9[21]	2.4	5.4	10.8	5.6	43.0
R. F. Allemagne	1992	2 719 240	1.2	0.5[21]	29.4[21]	2.3	5.6	10.6	5.7	44.8
	1993	2 747 940	1.1	0.5[21]	27.2[21]	2.3	5.6	10.3	5.7	47.5
Ghana	1994	4 686 000[5]	42.0	6.3	10.1	3.0	8.3	6.4	4.8	18.2
Ghana	1995	7 040 200[5]	42.7	5.3	10.3	2.9	8.3	6.5	4.3	18.8
	1996	10 067 000[5]	43.9	5.3	9.7	3.0	8.5	6.5	4.2	17.9
Greece [1]	1996	27 489 066	9.1	0.7	13.1	2.1	6.5	21.4[4]	6.2	41.0
Grèce [1]	1997	30 248 596	8.4	0.6	12.2	2.0	7.4	21.5[4]	6.2	41.7
	1998	32 717 675	8.1	0.6	11.6	1.9	8.3	21.5[4]	6.4	41.6
Grenada	1989	393[5]	18.7	0.4	5.3	2.9	10.3	18.8	13.9	34.4
Grenade	1990	440[5]	16.2	0.4	5.1	3.0	10.1	18.7	13.7	32.8
	1991	463[5]	14.9	0.4	5.3	3.1	10.4	19.5	14.3	32.1
Guadeloupe	1990	15 036	6.7	5.4[12]	...	1.0	7.4	18.3	5.9	55.2
Guadeloupe	1991	16 278	7.3	6.1[12]	...	1.4	7.0	16.5	6.0	55.5
	1992	17 968	6.7	6.9[12]	...	1.7	6.5	16.2	7.9	54.1
Guinea–Bissau	1989	358 875	44.6	7.9[2]	...	...	9.7	25.7	3.6	8.5
Guinée–Bissau	1990	510 094	44.6	8.2[2]	...	...	10.0	25.7	3.7	7.8
	1991	854 985	44.7	8.5[2]	...	...	8.4	25.8	3.9	8.7
Guyana	1997	89 744[5]	35.4[22]	17.3	11.4[8]	...	5.0	4.3	5.8	20.7
Guyana	1998	92 610[5]	35.6[22]	16.0	9.8[8]	...	5.3	4.5	6.7	22.1
	1999	98 315[5]	35.4[22]	15.6	10.0[8]	...	5.4	4.6	6.7	22.2
Honduras	1995	32 626[5]	21.5	1.9	17.8	5.4	5.5	12.0	4.7	31.0
Honduras	1996	41 171[5]	22.3	1.9	18.1	6.2	4.6	11.9	4.4	30.6
	1997	52 872[5]	22.6	1.7	18.0	6.2	4.3	11.8	4.8	30.4
Hungary [1]	1995	4 932 855	6.7	0.5	22.5	3.3	4.6	13.3	9.0	40.1
Hongrie [1]	1996	6 061 312	6.6	0.4	22.5	3.4	4.3	13.3	9.2	40.4
	1997	7 555 986	5.9	0.4	23.9	3.8	4.6	13.5	9.7	38.2
Iceland	1993	337 080[5]	11.7	...	15.6	4.0	7.1	12.6	7.0	42.0
Islande	1994	356 040[5]	11.1	...	16.6	3.8	6.5	12.8	7.7	41.5
	1995	366 880[5]	11.6	...	16.1	4.0	6.4	12.7	7.6	41.6
India [23]	1995	11 032 380[5]	28.4	2.2	17.4	2.5	5.0	14.9	7.1	22.5
Inde [23]	1996	12 852 590[5]	29.3	2.1	16.8	2.3	4.9	15.3	7.2	22.1
	1997	14 266 700[5]	27.5	2.1	16.8	2.5	4.7	15.5	7.6	23.3
Indonesia	1996	532 567 000	16.7	8.7	25.6	1.3	7.9	16.4	6.6	17.0
Indonésie	1997	627 695 000	16.1	8.9	26.8	1.2	7.5	15.9	6.1	17.6
	1998	1 002 334 000	18.1	13.7	24.5	1.1	5.6	16.7	5.2	15.2

20
Value added by kind of economic activity at current prices
Percentage distribution *[cont.]*
Valeur ajoutée par genre d'activité économique aux prix courants
Répartition en pourcentage *[suite]*

			% of Value added − % de la valeur ajoutée							
Country or area Pays ou zone	Year Année	Value added (Mil. nat.cur.) Valeur ajoutée (Mil. mon.nat.)	Agriculture, hunting, forestry & fishing Agriculture, chasse, sylviculture et pêche	Mining & quarrying Industries extractives	Manufac- turing Industries manufac- turières	Electricity, gas and water Electricité, gaz et eau	Con- struc- tion Con- struc- tion	Wholesale/ retail trade, restaurants and hotels Commerce, restaurants, hôtels	Transport, storage & commu- nication Transports, entrepôts, communi- cations	Other activities Autres activités
Iran (Islamic Rep. of) [24]	1996	236 957 000	20.2	15.7[25]	14.4	1.7	4.3	15.8	7.2	20.8
Iran (Rép. islamique d') [24]	1997	278 206 000	20.1	11.4[25]	15.9	1.7	4.0	16.9	8.0	22.0
	1998	328 003 000	22.1	7.2[25]	17.4	1.8	3.4	17.7	8.4	22.0
Iraq	1993	146 912[5]	30.9	0.1	5.5	0.3	5.3	24.4	13.0	20.5
Iraq	1994	721 603[5]	42.1	0.0	3.2	0.1	1.3	27.2	14.8	11.3
	1995	2 320 671[5]	54.1	−0.1	3.8	0.0	1.2	8.8	22.2	10.0
Ireland	1984	15 177	11.1	30.4	...	...	6.6	11.0	4.7	36.1
Irlande	1985	16 559	9.4	32.4	...	...	5.8	11.7	5.2	35.5
	1986	17 448	8.8	32.1	...	...	5.5	11.0	5.6	36.9
Israel	1995	204 335	2.3	17.8[12]	...	1.1	8.0	11.4	7.2	52.0[9]
Israël	1996	236 833	2.0	17.5[12]	...	1.0	8.1	11.2[16]	6.4	53.6[9]
	1997	242 650	2.0	19.5[12]	...	1.1	0.8	11.9[16]	6.5	58.1[9]
Italy [1]	1996	1 786 327 000	3.2	0.5	21.6	2.2	5.1	16.8	7.2	43.3
Italie [1]	1997	1 850 267 000	3.1	0.5	21.6	2.1	5.0	16.7	7.1	43.8
	1998	1 911 943 000	3.0	0.4	21.5	2.3	4.9	16.6	7.3	44.0
Jamaica	1991	46 568	6.6	10.3	18.1	1.7	11.9	19.9	7.6	23.7
Jamaïque	1992	77 519	7.5	8.8	18.4	2.4	12.1	22.1	7.2	21.6
	1993	101 720	7.9	6.8	17.4	2.2	12.1	22.3	7.5	23.8
Japan	1994	499 162 700	2.1	0.2	23.5	2.7	10.4	12.2[4]	6.1	42.9
Japon	1995	504 804 500	1.9	0.2	23.6	2.7	10.0	12.1[4]	6.2	43.3
	1996	520 867 400	1.8	0.2	23.3	2.7	10.1	11.7[4]	6.4	43.8
Jordan	1989	2 271[5]	6.2	7.4	14.2	2.3	4.5	7.9	16.3	41.3
Jordanie	1990	2 521[5]	7.5	7.4	17.0	2.2	4.2	9.0	14.7	38.0
	1991	2 714[5]	7.9	5.8	16.0	2.3	4.7	9.4	14.4	39.5
Kazakhstan [1]	1994	415 086	15.2	29.7[2]	...	...	9.8	12.4	11.4	21.5
Kazakhstan [1]	1995	970 854	12.9	24.6[2]	...	...	6.7	18.0	11.1	26.6
	1996	1 352 549	12.7	22.2[2]	...	...	4.6	18.1	11.8	30.6
Kenya	1993	14 239[5]	27.3	0.2	10.0	1.3	5.4	13.5	7.0	35.4
Kenya	1994	17 713[5]	26.3	0.2	10.2	1.3	4.8	14.7	7.1	35.4
	1995	21 139[5]	27.4	0.2	10.2	1.3	4.3	14.3	7.2	35.1
Korea, Republic of [1]	1996	421 139 006	5.8	0.4	28.7	2.1	11.5	11.9	6.5	33.0
Corée, Rép. de [1]	1997	455 590 846	5.3	0.4	28.7	2.1	11.6	11.4	6.5	33.9
	1998	454 421 587	4.9	0.4	30.3	2.3	10.0	10.5	6.9	34.8
Kuwait	1995	8 022	0.4	39.1	11.1	−0.4	3.0	7.7	4.5	34.5
Koweït	1996	9 421	0.4	43.8	11.7	−0.1	2.6	6.7	4.2	30.7
	1997	9 402	0.4	39.2	13.1	0.1	2.6	6.9	4.5	33.2
Kyrgyzstan [1]	1994	11 556	39.9	4.3	10.8	7.2	3.5	11.7	4.7	17.9
Kirghizistan [1]	1995	15 247	43.1	2.4	8.2	2.6	6.5	12.5	4.8	19.9
	1996	21 922	49.4	2.8	4.8	4.9	6.8	11.3	4.5	15.5
Latvia [1]	1994	1 809	9.5	0.2	19.9	5.2	5.9	11.4	20.5	27.4
Lettonie [1]	1995	2 034	10.8	0.2	22.4	5.5	5.1	12.4	16.0	27.7
	1996	2 469	9.0	0.2	20.9	5.3	4.7	16.4	17.0	26.4
Lebanon	1980	14 000	9.2	...	12.2	5.1	3.2	28.6	3.8	38.0
Liban	1981	16 800	8.5	...	13.0	5.4	3.4	28.3	3.7	37.5
	1982	12 600	8.5	...	13.0	5.4	3.4	28.3	3.7	37.5
Lesotho	1989	1 146[5]	23.0	0.4	14.6[15]	1.1	15.1	9.1	7.1	32.2
Lesotho	1990	1 329[5]	23.4	0.5	13.7[15]	1.6	17.8	9.0	7.2	29.4
	1991	1 582[5]	17.0	0.2	14.1[15]	1.8	22.5	9.7	7.3	30.2
Liberia	1987	1 009[5]	37.8	10.4	7.2	1.9	3.2	6.0	7.5	26.0
Libéria	1988	1 080[5]	38.2	10.7	7.4	1.7	2.7	5.9	7.3	26.1
	1989	1 119[5]	36.7	10.9	7.3	1.7	2.4	5.7	7.1	28.3
Libyan Arab Jamah.	1983	8 482[5]	3.0	48.8[26]	3.2	0.9	10.4	6.1	4.6	23.0
Jamah. arabe libyenne	1984	7 681[5]	3.4	40.9[26]	3.9	1.2	11.1	7.9	5.3	26.4
	1985	8 050[5]	3.5	41.6[26]	4.5	1.3	11.4	7.0	5.0	25.8
Lithuania [1]	1995	22 081	11.7	0.4	22.2	3.5	7.1	19.3	9.4	26.3
Lithuanie [1]	1996	29 051	12.2	0.5	21.8	3.5	7.1	18.4	9.5	27.0
	1997	34 138	12.7	0.5	20.3	3.3	7.3	18.5	9.2	28.3

20
Value added by kind of economic activity at current prices
Percentage distribution *[cont.]*
Valeur ajoutée par genre d'activité économique aux prix courants
Répartition en pourcentage *[suite]*

% of Value added — % de la valeur ajoutée

Country or area Pays ou zone	Year Année	Value added (Mil. nat.cur.) Valeur ajoutée (Mil. mon.nat.)	Agriculture, hunting, forestry & fishing Agriculture, chasse, sylviculture et pêche	Mining & quarrying Industries extractives	Manufac- turing Industries manufac- turières	Electricity, gas and water Electricité, gaz et eau	Con- struc- tion Con- struc- tion	Wholesale/ retail trade, restaurants and hotels Commerce, restaurants, hôtels	Transport, storage & commu- nication Transports, entrepôts, communi- cations	Other activities Autres activités
Luxembourg Luxembourg	1993 1994 1995	442 790[10] 499 315[10] 518 765[10]	1.1 1.0 1.0	... ...	16.8 15.7 15.2	1.6 1.5 1.6	7.1 6.8 6.9	13.3 12.4 12.6	6.5 6.8 7.4	53.5 55.7 55.3
Madagascar Madagascar	1983 1984 1985	1 187 400 1 323 100 1 500 600	44.2 43.9 43.5	15.6[2 27] 16.2[2 27] 16.9[2 27]	... ...	... ...	... ...	30.4 30.3 30.1	... ...	9.7 9.7 9.4
Malawi Malawi	1984 1985 1986	1 322 1 540 1 694	37.4[28] 34.7[28] 34.5[28]	... ...	18.6 17.5 20.3	1.8 1.5 1.2	2.0 2.2 2.0	6.8 12.8 11.5	4.9 4.8 3.5	28.6 26.4 27.1
Malaysia Malaisie	1997 1998 1999	292 838 301 554 313 517	10.7 12.5 10.2	6.6 6.4 6.5	27.3 27.0 30.2	2.6 2.8 2.8	6.3 4.9 4.5	14.2 14.4 13.9	6.4 6.6 6.7	25.8 25.5 25.2
Mali Mali	1990 1991 1992	655 600 662 500 707 000	47.8 46.1 47.2	1.6 1.7 1.5	8.1[15] 6.9[15] 7.0[15]	3.8[27] 4.3[27] 4.4[27]	... ...	18.8 20.2 19.3	4.9 5.0 5.0	15.1 15.9 15.6
Malta Malte	1995 1996 1997	989[5] 1 058[5] 1 111[5]	2.8 2.9 3.0	3.5[27] 3.4[27] 3.4[27]	24.4 23.4 22.7	6.2 5.6 6.7	... ...	13.3[4] 12.6[4] 12.2[4]	6.7 6.4 6.2	43.1 45.2 46.1
Marshall Islands Iles Marshall	1995 1996 1997	105 95 90	14.9 14.3 14.3	0.3 0.3 0.4	2.6 1.6 1.7	2.0 2.7 3.1	10.2 7.0 7.0	17.0 18.7 17.9	6.2 7.3 7.9	46.8 48.2 47.7
Martinique Martinique	1990 1991 1992	18 835 20 377 21 869	5.7 5.7 5.1	7.9[12] 7.8[12] 8.1[12]	... ...	2.5 2.4 2.2	4.9 5.3 5.2	18.9 18.9 18.4	6.2 6.3 6.5	53.9 53.6 54.5
Mauritania Mauritanie	1986 1987 1988	53 464[5] 60 302[5] 65 069[5]	26.6 32.3 32.4	11.2 8.3 7.7	13.1[8] 12.1[8] 13.0[8]	... ...	6.8 6.3 6.3	13.2 13.0 13.2	5.6 5.1 5.1	23.4 22.8 22.3
Mauritius Maurice	1996 1997 1998	70 440[5] 78 023[5] 87 152[5]	9.4 8.5 8.4	0.2 0.2 0.1	23.4 23.4 24.0	2.2 2.0 1.6	6.3 5.8 5.8	16.7 16.9 16.8	10.5 11.4 11.4	31.4 31.8 31.9
Mexico [1] Mexique [1]	1995 1996 1997	1 769 049 2 353 489 2 915 519	5.2 5.9 5.5	1.6[29] 1.5[29] 1.5[29]	19.8 21.0 21.1	1.2 1.1 1.2	3.9 4.1 4.4	19.9 21.0 21.1	9.5 9.9 10.4	38.9 35.4 34.9
Mongolia Mongolie	1996 1997 1998	625 005 792 989 775 578	45.2 37.6 39.5	10.8 15.0 8.8	5.2 5.7 5.0	2.4 3.2 4.3	2.8 2.3 2.6	11.8 16.4 15.3	7.7 8.1 10.4	14.1 12.1 14.2
Montserrat Montserrat	1985 1986 1987	90[5] 103[5] 118[5]	4.8 4.3 4.1	1.3 1.4 1.3	5.7 5.6 5.7	3.7 3.7 3.2	7.9 11.3 11.5	18.0 18.7 22.1	11.5 11.6 11.1	47.2 43.4 41.0
Morocco Maroc	1995 1996 1997	271 520 310 240 309 810	15.2 19.9 15.8	1.9 1.8 2.3	19.0 17.6 18.1	8.7[30 31] 8.3[30 31] 9.0[30 31]	4.6 4.3 4.8	13.9 13.8 13.9	6.4 5.8 6.0	30.2 28.5 30.1
Myanmar [23] Myanmar [23]	1996 1997 1998	791 980 1 109 554 1 559 996	60.1 59.4 59.1	0.6 0.6 0.5	7.1 7.1 7.2	0.3 0.1 0.1	2.4 2.4 2.4	22.6 23.2 23.9	3.5 3.9 4.0	3.4 3.1 2.7
Namibia [1] Namibie [1]	1989 1990 1991	5 179[5] 5 479[5] 6 223[5]	9.8 9.4 9.5	26.7 19.8 17.7	12.0 13.8 13.0	1.6 1.9 1.7	2.6 2.5 2.3	8.9 7.7 7.6	4.7 5.1 4.9	32.0 36.0 38.9
Nepal [32] Népal [32]	1996 1997 1998	239 388[5] 269 570[5] 285 702[5]	40.5 40.4 39.4	0.6 0.6 0.5	9.4[33] 9.2[33] 9.3[33]	1.5 1.7 1.6	10.9 10.9 10.2	11.8 11.3 11.8	6.6 7.2 7.8	18.7 18.9 19.5
Netherlands Pays–Bas	1993 1994 1995	553 740 582 050 604 180	3.3 3.5 3.3	2.8 2.7 2.7	18.6 18.6 18.7	1.7 1.8 1.8	5.3 5.2 5.2	15.2 15.1 14.9	6.9 6.9 7.0	46.0 46.2 46.4
Netherlands Antilles Antilles néerlandaises	1992 1993 1994	3 755 3 994 4 476	0.7 0.8 0.8	... ...	6.9 6.1 6.3	4.2 3.4 2.8	6.1 6.0 5.7	25.3 24.4 24.1	11.6 12.3 13.8	45.3 46.9 46.4

20
Value added by kind of economic activity at current prices
Percentage distribution *[cont.]*
Valeur ajoutée par genre d'activité économique aux prix courants
Répartition en pourcentage *[suite]*

% of Value added − % de la valeur ajoutée

Country or area Pays ou zone	Year Année	Value added (Mil. nat.cur.) Valeur ajoutée (Mil. mon.nat.)	Agriculture, hunting, forestry & fishing Agriculture, chasse, sylviculture et pêche	Mining & quarrying Industries extractives	Manufac-turing Industries manufac-turières	Electricity, gas and water Electricité, gaz et eau	Con-struc-tion Con-struc-tion	Wholesale/ retail trade, restaurants and hotels Commerce, restaurants, hôtels	Transport, storage & commu-nication Transports, entrepôts, communi-cations	Other activities Autres activités
New Caledonia	1994	306 748	1.9	7.4	6.6	1.5	6.0	23.0	6.3	47.4
Nouvelle−Calédonie	1995	329 296	1.8	8.7	6.0	1.5	5.7	22.2	6.3	47.7
	1996	335 482	1.7	8.5	5.7	1.6	5.0	22.8	6.7	47.8
New Zealand [23]	1992	71 699	7.9	1.5	18.7	3.0	3.2	15.5	8.7	41.5
Nouvelle−Zélande [23]	1993	77 567	8.7	1.5	18.7	2.9	3.4	16.2	8.4	40.3
	1994	83 119	7.8	1.3	19.3	2.8	3.7	16.7	8.6	40.0
Niger	1985	627 027	37.9	8.3	7.4	2.3	3.6	16.3	4.4	19.9
Niger	1986	622 426	37.3	7.6	7.9	2.6	4.6	14.6	4.2	21.1
	1987	632 248	34.6	7.8	9.0	2.8	5.3	14.1	4.3	22.2
Nigeria	1992	549 809[5]	26.5	46.6	5.7	0.3	1.1	11.5	1.7	6.7
Nigéria	1993	701 473[5]	33.1	35.9	6.2	0.2	1.1	14.6	2.2	6.8
	1994	914 334[5]	38.2	25.0	7.1	0.2	1.1	17.5	3.5	7.3
Norway [1]	1995	831 067	2.8	13.4	13.4	2.8	3.8	11.9	10.5	41.4
Norvège [1]	1996	911 370	2.4	17.2	12.5	2.3	3.9	11.3	10.2	40.2
	1997	970 655	2.2	16.8	12.4	2.4	4.2	11.5	10.3	40.1
Oman	1993	4 853	2.4	36.9	4.2	0.9	3.3	13.6	5.9	32.9
Oman	1994	5 035	2.5	36.3	4.3	1.0	3.0	13.2	6.2	33.6
	1995	5 375	2.8	37.9	4.5	0.9	2.6	13.3	6.2	31.8
Pakistan [7]	1996	2 255 649	26.4	0.5	17.0	3.4	3.6	15.8[4]	9.7	23.6
Pakistan [7]	1997	2 540 147	26.4	0.5	16.9	3.7	3.5	15.8[4]	10.1	23.0
	1998	2 784 986	25.8	0.5	16.7	4.7	3.4	15.1[4]	10.1	23.8
Panama	1991	5 748[5]	9.1	0.1	9.8	4.1	2.6	16.9	15.4	41.9
Panama	1992	6 585[5]	8.2	0.2	9.4	3.5	3.3	19.0	14.3	42.1
	1993	7 163[5]	7.8	0.2	9.0	3.9	4.3	20.7	13.5	40.6
Papua New Guinea	1989	2 964	28.9	11.9	11.4	1.7	5.4	11.1	5.5	24.2
Papouasie−Nouv.− Guinée	1990	2 996	29.7	15.1	9.2	1.7	5.2	9.9	6.4	22.8
	1991	3 515	26.6	17.4	9.8	1.7	6.4	10.2	6.9	20.9
Paraguay	1993	11 991 719	24.5	0.4	16.5	3.4	5.9	30.4	3.9	15.0
Paraguay	1994	14 960 131	23.7	0.4	15.7	3.9	6.0	30.5	3.9	15.9
	1995	17 699 000	24.8	0.3	15.7	4.3	6.0	29.5	3.7	15.8
Peru	1996	149 092	7.0	1.9	22.1	1.6	10.8	16.9	5.0	34.7
Pérou	1997	174 201	6.5	1.9	21.8	1.7	11.5	16.8	5.2	34.6
	1998	185 055	6.6	1.7	21.4	1.8	11.3	16.7	5.3	35.3
Philippines	1995	1 905 951	21.6	0.9	23.0	2.6	5.6	15.5	4.7	26.2
Philippines	1996	2 171 922	20.6	0.8	22.8	2.6	5.9	15.4	4.7	27.2
	1997	2 423 640	18.7	0.7	22.3	2.7	6.4	14.9	4.9	29.3
Poland [1]	1995	266 504	7.0	4.2	23.8	4.0	7.3	20.9	6.6	26.3
Pologne [1]	1996	334 475	6.5	3.8	22.7	3.8	7.5	22.0	6.5	27.3
	1997	409 892	5.6	3.6	22.5	3.4	8.0	22.1	6.5	28.3
Portugal	1994	14 190 807	4.1	...	26.4	4.0	6.0	16.6	5.9	36.8
Portugal	1995	15 294 193	4.1	...	26.2	3.9	6.4	16.5	6.1	36.9
Puerto Rico [7]	1996	48 951	1.0	0.1	39.4	2.6	2.5[34]	14.8	5.1	34.6
Porto Rico [7]	1997	54 407	0.8	0.1	42.2	2.5	2.4[34]	14.5	4.8	32.6
	1998	60 250	0.5	0.1	43.9	2.2	2.4[34]	14.1	5.0	31.8
Qatar	1996	33 770	0.9	37.8	7.4	1.3	6.7	7.5	3.6	34.8
Qatar	1997	41 958	0.7	41.4	8.1	1.1	6.8	6.6	3.5	31.7
	1998	38 899	0.8	36.1	8.8	1.3	7.4	7.2	3.9	34.5
Republic of Moldova [1]	1995	5 888	32.2	0.2	25.1	2.3	3.9	9.7	5.7	21.1
Rép. de Moldova [1]	1996	6 968	30.0	0.2	25.6	2.1	4.2	9.0	6.2	22.8
	1997	7 645	29.4	28.4[2]	...	...	5.5	9.3	5.8	22.5
Réunion	1990	27 417	4.0	9.1[12]	...	4.7	5.9	20.5	4.0	51.7
Réunion	1991	30 371	3.7	9.1[12]	...	4.1	7.1	19.9	4.6	51.5
	1992	32 832[9]	3.5	9.0[12]	...	4.1	6.8	20.0	4.5	50.1
Romania [1]	1995	68 773 500	20.7	3.4	27.1	4.0	6.9	11.0	8.1	18.7
Roumanie [1]	1996	104 076 900	20.1	2.7	29.5	2.5	6.8	12.2	9.4	16.7
	1997	230 699 200	19.7	38.6	...	...	5.7	10.8	11.0	14.3

20
Value added by kind of economic activity at current prices
Percentage distribution *[cont.]*
Valeur ajoutée par genre d'activité économique aux prix courants
Répartition en pourcentage *[suite]*

Country or area Pays ou zone	Year Année	Value added (Mil. nat.cur.) Valeur ajoutée (Mil. mon.nat.)	% of Value added – % de la valeur ajoutée							
			Agriculture, hunting, forestry & fishing Agriculture, chasse, sylviculture et pêche	Mining & quarrying Industries extractives	Manufac- turing Industries manufac- turières	Electricity, gas and water Electricité, gaz et eau	Con- struc- tion Con- struc- tion	Wholesale/ retail trade, restaurants and hotels Commerce, restaurants, hôtels	Transport, storage & commu- nication Transports, entrepôts, communi- cations	Other activities Autres activités
Russian Federation [1]	1991	1 378 100	14.0	...	39.3	...	9.4	12.3	7.5	17.5
Fédération de Russie [1]	1993	162 000 000	8.9	...	40.9	...	7.7	15.4	8.6	22.9
	1994	587 000 000	7.6	...	30.7	...	10.0	17.5	9.6	27.4
Rwanda	1987	166 760	39.2	0.2	15.0	0.6	7.2	14.2	7.1	16.5
Rwanda	1988	171 700	39.3	0.2	14.5	0.7	7.1	13.2	7.4	17.6
	1989	184 380	41.1	0.4	13.5	0.5	7.0	13.2	7.0	17.3
Saint Kitts–Nevis	1994	538[5]	5.4	0.3	9.6	1.6	10.4	23.5	7.2	42.1
Saint–Kitts–et–Nevis	1995	566[5]	5.0	0.3	10.0	1.5	11.3	21.4	7.2	43.4
	1996	602[5]	5.2	0.3	9.9	1.5	11.1	21.8	7.0	43.0
Saint Lucia	1981	317[5]	9.1	1.3	8.0	2.3	11.9	23.0	10.9	33.5
Sainte–Lucie	1982	333[5]	10.8	1.0	8.0	2.6	9.9	21.9	10.6	35.2
	1983	344[5]	12.3	0.6	8.8	3.3	5.7	22.0	10.9	36.4
Saint Vincent–Grenadines	1995	640[5]	13.3	0.3	8.0	4.7	10.6	16.6	19.4	27.2
St.–Vincent–et–Gren.	1996	672[5]	11.9	0.3	7.9	4.9	9.8	16.7	20.4	28.1
	1997	691[5]	9.7	0.3	7.5	5.1	11.4	16.5	20.3	29.2
Sao Tome and Principe	1986	2 259	29.2	...	2.3	0.3	3.4	19.4	5.3	40.1
Sao Tomé–et–Principe	1987	2 797	31.5	...	1.3	1.4	3.8	17.1	5.6	39.2
	1988	3 800	32.1	...	1.7	1.0	4.2	18.8	4.1	38.1
Saudi Arabia [7]	1993	440 065	6.9	34.0	8.6	0.2	9.4	7.3	6.7	26.9
Arabie saoudite [7]	1994	447 676	7.0	33.3	8.8	0.2	9.5	7.4	6.8	27.0
	1995	467 680	6.8	33.8	9.1	0.2	9.3	7.1	6.6	27.2
Senegal	1996	2 380 000	20.6	0.8	12.8	2.2	3.6	26.3	10.0	23.6
Sénégal	1997	2 555 000	20.0	1.1	12.5	2.2	3.8	26.7	10.9	22.7
	1998	2 753 000	18.2	1.0	12.8	2.2	4.0	27.7	11.1	23.0
Seychelles	1996	2 321	4.2	...	13.9	3.1	8.5	10.7	29.4	30.2
Seychelles	1997	2 725	3.4	...	14.9	3.2	7.8	9.9	32.4	28.4
	1998	2 918	3.1	...	15.1	3.1	9.5	9.3	32.6	27.3
Sierra Leone [7]	1988	42 364	39.3	6.3	7.7	0.3	2.6	20.9	10.5	12.3
Sierra Leone [7]	1989	81 921	37.3	7.0	7.1	0.2	1.9	25.0	10.8	10.6
	1990	148 652	35.3	9.5	8.7	0.1	1.3	20.3	8.9	15.9
Singapore	1995	128 395	0.1	0.0	24.6	1.5	6.9	18.5	11.1	37.2
Singapour	1996	139 324	0.1	0.0	23.8	1.6	7.9	17.9	10.5	38.0
	1997	152 801	0.1	0.0	22.7	1.7	8.4	17.6	10.3	39.1
Slovakia [1]	1995	480 815	6.0	1.1	29.0	4.5	4.9	19.3	9.0	26.2
Slovaquie [1]	1996	540 168	5.5	1.1	26.7	4.2	5.0	23.7	8.9	24.8
	1997	622 169	5.1	1.0	24.8	3.8	5.5	22.9	8.5	28.4
Slovenia [1]	1994	1 617 900[5]	4.5	1.5	30.0	3.2	4.7	14.8	7.5	33.8
Slovénie [1]	1995	1 928 200[5]	4.5	1.3	28.3	2.9	5.0	15.0	7.7	35.1
	1996	2 224 800[5]	4.4	1.4	27.7	2.9	5.6	14.6	7.6	35.7
Solomon Islands	1984	199	53.5	−0.2	3.6	0.9	3.8	10.6	5.2	22.6
Iles Salomon	1985	213	50.4	−0.7	3.8	1.0	4.2	10.4	5.1	25.8
	1986	224	48.3	−1.2	4.5	1.2	5.1	8.4	5.8	27.9
Somalia	1985	84 050[5]	66.1	0.3	4.9	0.1	2.2	10.1	6.7	9.5
Somalie	1986	112 584[5]	62.5	0.4	5.5	0.2	2.7	10.3	7.3	11.1
	1987	163 175[5]	64.9	0.3	5.1	−0.5	2.9	10.7	6.8	9.8
South Africa [1]	1996	565 978	4.2	6.8	20.2	3.2	3.1	14.0	9.2	39.3
Afrique du Sud [1]	1997	625 340	4.0	6.5	19.9	3.3	3.1	13.7	9.2	40.2
	1998	675 878	3.8	6.5	19.0	3.3	3.1	13.2	9.6	41.4
Spain	1992	59 380 400	3.5	0.5	21.0	2.7	8.5	21.6	5.4	36.8
Espagne	1993	61 625 600	3.5	0.5	20.2	2.7	8.0	22.2	5.5	37.3
	1994	64 878 000	3.3	0.5	20.5	2.7	7.9	22.5	5.7	36.8
Sri Lanka	1996	744 865	19.0	1.2	18.3	2.2	7.3	23.0	10.4	18.6
Sri Lanka	1997	863 283	18.4	1.1	19.1	1.9	7.0	23.3	10.7	18.5
	1998	985 586	17.8	0.9	18.8	1.9	6.9	23.7	10.9	19.0
Sudan [7]	1994	4 440 648	40.5	6.5[12]	...	0.7	3.8	46.6[14]	...	1.9
Soudan [7]	1996	9 015 824	37.1	9.6[12]	...	0.9	5.0	44.4[14]	...	3.0
	1997	15 865 432	40.5	9.1[12]	...	0.8	6.9	39.8[14]	...	2.8

20
Value added by kind of economic activity at current prices
Percentage distribution *[cont.]*
Valeur ajoutée par genre d'activité économique aux prix courants
Répartition en pourcentage *[suite]*

% of Value added — % de la valeur ajoutée

Country or area Pays ou zone	Year Année	Value added (Mil. nat.cur.) Valeur ajoutée (Mil. mon.nat.)	Agriculture, hunting, forestry & fishing Agriculture, chasse, sylviculture et pêche	Mining & quarrying Industries extractives	Manufac- turing Industries manufac- turières	Electricity, gas and water Electricité, gaz et eau	Con- struc- tion Con- struc- tion	Wholesale/ retail trade, restaurants and hotels Commerce- restaurants, hôtels	Transport, storage & commu- nication Transports, entrepôts, communi- cations	Other activities Autres activités
Suriname	1994	60 620[5]	16.6	12.8	15.3	8.6	2.5	15.2	13.0	17.8
Suriname	1995	205 370[5]	15.9	9.4	15.4	7.4	2.5	24.3	10.2	17.4
	1996	272 100[5]	14.3	8.9	10.9	7.5	2.5	24.8	11.2	24.0
Swaziland [35]	1992	2 340[5]	12.1	1.9	33.6	2.0	3.3	8.6	5.9	32.6
Swaziland [35]	1993	2 737[5]	13.6	1.7	32.3	1.8	3.7	8.6	5.7	32.5
	1994	3 089[5]	13.1	1.7	32.8	1.6	4.2	8.9	7.1	29.7
Sweden	1992	1 308 666[5]	2.3	0.3	18.9	3.3	7.0	10.6	6.9	50.8
Suède	1993	1 328 816[5]	2.1	0.3	19.6	3.2	6.0	10.5	6.4	52.0
	1994	1 396 953[5]	2.2	0.3	21.4	3.0	5.3	10.8	6.4	50.7
Switzerland	1985	234 650	3.5	...	25.1	2.1	7.4	17.8	6.2	37.9
Suisse	1990	324 289	3.0	...	23.7	1.9	8.1	18.7	5.7	39.0
	1991	343 983	2.9	...	22.6	1.9	7.8	16.6	5.8	42.4
Syrian Arab Rep.	1995	570 975	28.2	6.7	6.2	0.9	4.3	26.0	11.6	16.0
Rép. arabe syrienne	1996	676 441	28.3	13.3	5.8	1.0	4.1	22.0	10.7	14.7
	1997	728 794	25.9	17.1	4.9	1.0	4.1	19.9	12.4	14.6
Thailand	1995	3 687 000	12.7	1.1	26.7	2.5	7.9	19.0	8.2	21.8
Thaïlande	1996	4 049 000	12.6	1.3	26.6	2.5	8.0	18.9	8.4	21.6
	1997	4 183 000	12.7	1.8	26.2	2.6	6.0	20.4	8.7	21.6
TFYR of Macedonia [1]	1991	774	13.4	29.4	...	0.4	5.5	7.2	5.6	34.6
L'ex-R.y. Macédoine [1]	1992	10 296	18.1	32.0	...	0.6	4.0	7.8	6.0	27.0
	1993	50 856	11.4	29.5	...	0.6	5.9	9.6	6.8	32.1
Trinidad and Tobago	1995	31 141	1.8	14.6	16.4	1.5	9.2	17.7	9.3	29.4
Trinité-et-Tobago	1996	34 062	1.8	13.9	18.0	1.3	8.9	18.6	9.1	28.4
	1997	36 380	1.6	12.7	18.9	1.7	10.2	19.3	8.9	26.8
Tunisia	1994	14 253	13.9	4.3	20.5	2.0	5.5	15.9	8.4	29.3
Tunisie	1995	15 410	12.6	4.0	21.0	2.2	5.2	17.0	8.3	29.8
	1996	17 280	15.1	4.2	20.2	2.1	4.8	16.3	8.2	28.9
Turkey	1995	7 748 670 000	15.7	1.3	22.6	2.5	5.5	20.5	12.7	19.3
Turquie	1996	15 022 757 000	16.6	1.2	20.8	2.7	5.7	20.1	12.9	19.9
	1997	29 634 717 000	14.8	1.1	21.0	2.5	5.9	20.5	13.7	20.6
Uganda	1993	3 732 424[5]	48.9	0.4	6.4	0.9	6.4	12.5	4.2	20.4
Ouganda	1994	4 752 827[5]	52.5	0.3	6.1	1.2	5.7	12.2	3.7	18.4
	1995	5 304 443[5]	48.3	0.3	6.7	1.1	6.7	12.7	4.2	20.0
Ukraine [1]	1993	1 595[9]	20.0	27.6[2]	...	...	6.4	7.1	10.9	5.7
Ukraine [1]	1994	11 483[9]	15.3	36.7[2]	...	...	7.8	5.4	8.5	6.6
	1995	49 986[9]	15.0	33.8[2]	...	...	7.5	5.8	13.1	10.1
United Arab Emirates	1988	90 137[5]	1.8	33.2	9.1	2.3	9.8	11.3	5.6	26.8
Emirats arabes unis	1989	104 730[5]	1.8	37.3	8.3	2.1	9.1	10.2	5.4	25.7
	1990	127 737[5]	1.6	45.4	7.2	1.8	7.8	8.8	4.6	22.7
United Kingdom	1993	571 363[5]	1.8	2.1	20.3	2.6	5.1	13.8	8.1	46.2
Royaume-Uni	1994	607 800[5]	1.7	2.2	20.4	2.4	5.1	13.7	8.1	46.6
	1995	634 789[5]	1.8	2.4	20.7	2.2	5.1	13.8	8.0	45.9
United Rep. of Tanzania	1992	1 060 631[5]	54.4	1.8	7.8[15]	1.9	4.5	15.4	5.1	9.1
Rép.-Unie de Tanzanie	1993	1 343 237[5]	54.4	1.4	7.8[15]	2.1	4.9	14.6	6.3	8.5
	1994	1 740 521[5]	54.5	1.5	7.3[15]	2.2	5.0	14.6	6.2	8.8
United States	1994	6 919 100	1.8	1.4	17.7	2.8	3.9	16.3	5.9	48.7
Etats-Unis	1995	7 293 800	1.6	1.4	17.8	2.8	4.0	16.1	5.8	49.1
	1996	7 696 300	1.7	1.5	17.5	2.7	4.0	16.1	5.7	49.3
Uruguay	1996	157 521	8.6	0.2	17.8	3.9	4.2	12.0	7.2	46.2
Uruguay	1997	194 700	8.2	0.2	17.7	4.1	4.2	12.0	7.1	46.5
	1998	226 426	8.2	0.3	17.1	4.4	4.7	11.4	7.0	47.0
Uzbekistan [1]	1991	61 887	37.1	26.1[2]	...	...	10.4	3.9	4.3	18.3
Ouzbékistan [1]	1992	452 130	34.8	26.1[2]	...	...	9.3	5.4	5.1	19.2
	1993	4 749 005	29.9	24.0[2]	...	...	9.6	6.7	5.9	23.9
Vanuatu	1996	28 227	24.9	...	5.0	1.7	5.6	32.0	7.3	23.5
Vanuatu	1997	29 477	25.2	...	4.9	1.7	5.5	32.4	7.3	23.1
	1998	29 545	23.1	...	4.9	1.8	4.6	34.3	7.4	23.9

20
Value added by kind of economic activity at current prices
Percentage distribution [cont.]
Valeur ajoutée par genre d'activité économique aux prix courants
Répartition en pourcentage [suite]

% of Value added − % de la valeur ajoutée

Country or area Pays ou zone	Year Année	Value added (Mil. nat.cur.) Valeur ajoutée (Mil. mon.nat.)	Agriculture, hunting, forestry & fishing Agriculture, chasse, sylviculture et pêche	Mining & quarrying Industries extractives	Manufacturing Industries manufacturières	Electricity, gas and water Electricité, gaz et eau	Construction Construction	Wholesale/retail trade, restaurants and hotels Commerce, restaurants, hôtels	Transport, storage & communication Transports, entrepôts, communications	Oth activiti Autr activit
Venezuela Venezuela	1997	41 288 574	4.3	17.8[36]	16.7[31]	1.6[30]	5.9	16.2	9.0	28
	1998	50 352 678	4.9	10.6[36]	14.9[31]	1.7[30]	6.8	17.1	9.8	34
	1999	59 780 921	4.9	14.1[36]	14.0[31]	1.8[30]	5.5	15.6	9.6	34
Viet Nam[1] Viet Nam[1]	1996	272 036 000	27.8	5.6	15.2	2.4	6.5	19.4	3.8	19
	1997	313 623 000	25.8	6.3	16.5	2.7	6.5	19.2	4.0	19
	1998	361 017 000	25.8	6.7	17.1	2.9	5.8	18.9	3.9	18
Yemen Yémen	1994	274 824	25.4	7.3	9.0	2.2	3.6	15.8	8.5	28
	1995	449 111	21.5	16.5	10.2	2.0	3.8	14.6	7.4	23
	1996	651 430	16.6	30.5	10.8	1.3	3.6	11.2	6.4	19
Yugoslavia[1] Yougoslavie[1]	1994	24 578	18.1	1.8	27.5	1.6	6.3	13.0	6.5	25
Yugoslavia, SFR † Yougoslavie, SFR †	1988	14 645	11.2	2.7	40.3	2.2	6.2	7.6	11.1	18
	1989	224 684	11.3	2.4	41.4	1.7	6.4	6.6	10.5	19
	1990	966 420	12.9	2.5	31.2	1.7	7.9	8.5	12.3	23
Zambia Zambie	1989	55 850[5]	11.4	18.0	23.3	0.6	5.4	16.0	5.6	19
	1990	114 675[5]	12.4	22.0	22.2	0.6	5.5	11.5	6.0	19
	1991	220 351[5]	12.8	15.3	28.0	0.9	5.0	10.9	7.2	20
Zimbabwe Zimbabwe	1982	4 803[5]	13.9	4.5	23.3	1.5	4.0	15.4	7.6	29
	1983	5 605[5]	9.7	7.0	25.7	3.5	4.6	14.0	7.2	28
	1984	5 817[5]	12.9	5.5	25.4	2.4	3.5	12.8	7.5	30

Source:
United Nations Secretariat, national accounts database of the
Statistics Division.

† For information on recent changes in country or area
nomenclature pertaining to former Czechoslovakia, Germany,
Hong Kong Special Administrative Region (SAR) of China,
Macao Special Administrative Region (SAR) of China,
SFR of Yugoslavia and the former USSR, see Annex I −
Country or area nomenclature, regional and other groupings.

†† For statistical purposes, the data for China do not
include those for the Hong Kong Special Administrative
Region (Hong Kong SAR), Macao Special Administrative
Region (Macao SAR) and Taiwan province of China.

1 Data classified according to 1993 SNA.
2 Including manufacturing and electricity, gas and water.
3 Including "other activities".
4 Restaurants and hotels are included in "other activities".
5 Value added at basic values
6 Including mining and quarrying.
7 Data refer to fiscal year beginning 1 July of the year indicated.
8 Including electricity, gas and water.
9 Including statistical discrepancy.
10 The breakdown by kind of economic activity used in this table is
according to the classification NACE/CLIO.

Source:
Secrétariat de l'ONU, la base de données sur les comptes nationaux
de la division statistique.

† Pour les modifications récentes de nomenclature de pays
ou de zone concernant l'Allemagne, Hong Kong, région
administrative spéciale (RAS) de Chine, Macao, région
administrative spéciale (RAS) de Chine, l'ex−Tchécoslovaquie,
l'ex−URSS et l'ex−Rfs de Yougoslavie, voir annexe I −
Nomenclature des pays ou des zones, groupements
régionaux et autres groupements.

††Les données statistiques relatives à la Chine ne comprennent
pas celles qui concernent la région administrative spéciale de
Hong Kong (la RAS de Hong Kong), la région administrative
spéciale de Macao (la RAS de Macao) et la province chinoise
de Taiwan.

1 Les données sont classifiées selon le SCN 1993.
2 Y compris les industries manufacturières, l'électricité, le gaz et l'eau.
3 Y compris "autres activités".
4 Restaurants et hôtels sont incluses dans "autres activités".
5 Valeur ajoutée au coût de base.
6 Y compris industries extractives.
7 Les données se réfèrent à l'année fiscale commençant le 1er juillet
de l'année indiquée.
8 Y compris l'électricité, le gaz et l'eau.
9 Y compris divergence statistique.
10 La ventilation par branche utilisée est conforme à la nomenclature
NACE/CLIO.

20
Value added by kind of economic activity at current prices
Percentage distribution *[cont.]*
Valeur ajoutée par genre d'activité économique aux prix courants
Répartition en pourcentage *[suite]*

11 Data refer to fiscal year ending 30 June of the year indicated.

12 Including manufacturing.
13 Excluding banks and insurance companies registered in Cayman Islands but with no physical presence in the Islands.
14 Including "Transport, storage and communication" and financial and financial and community services.
15 Including handiworks.
16 Including repair services.
17 Electricity only. Gas and water are included in "other activities".

18 Data refer to fiscal year ending 7 July of the year indicated.

19 Manufacturing of energy–producing product is included in electricity, gas and water
20 1990 – 1992: roubles; 1993 – 1994: coupons; 1995 – 1997: laris
21 Quarrying is included in manufacturing.
22 Excluding hunting.
23 Data refer to fiscal year beginning 1 April of the year indicated.

24 Data refer to fiscal year beginning 21 March of the year indicated.

25 Including oil production.
26 Including gas and oil production.
27 Including construction.
28 Including non–monetary output.
29 Including basic petroleum manufacturing.
30 Excluding gas.
31 Including petroleum refining.
32 Data refer to fiscal year ending 15 July of the year indicated.

33 Including cottage industries.
34 Contract construction only.
35 Data refer to fiscal year ending 30 June of the year indicated.

36 Including crude petroleum and natural gas production.

11 Les données se réfèrent à l'année fiscale finissant le 30e juin de l'année indiquée.
12 Y compris les industries manufacturières.
13 Non compris les banques et les compagnies d'assurances enregistrées aux îles Caïmanes, mais sans présence matérielle dans ce territoire.
14 Y compris transports, entrepôts et communications et les services financiers et communautaires.
15 Y compris l'artisanat.
16 Y compris les services de réparation.
17 Seulement électricité. Le gaz et l'eau sont incluses dans "autres activités".
18 Les données se réfèrent à l'année fiscale finissant le 7e juillet de l'année indiquée.
19 La fabrication de produits énergétiques est incluse à la rubrique Électricité, gaz et eau.
20 1990 à 1992: roubles; 1993 à 1994: coupons; 1995 à 1997: laris.
21 Les carrières sont incluses dans "industries manufacturières".
22 Non compris le chasse.
23 Les données se réfèrent à l'année fiscale commençant le 1er avril de l'année indiquée.
24 Les données se réfèrent à l'année fiscale commençant le 21e mars de l'année indiquée.
25 Y compris la production de pétrole.
26 Y compris la production de gaz et de pétrole.
27 Y compris construction.
28 Y compris la production non commercialisée.
29 Y compris la production de pétrole.
30 Non compris le gaz.
31 Y compris le raffinage du pétrole.
32 Les données se réfèrent à l'année fiscale finissant le 15e juillet de l'année indiquée.
33 Y compris artisanat.
34 Construction sous contrat seulement.
35 Les données se réfèrent à l'année fiscale finissant le 30e juin de l'année indiquée.
36 Y compris la production de pétrole brut et de gas naturel.

21
Relationships between the principal national accounting aggregates
Relations entre les principaux agrégats de comptabilité nationale

As a percentage of GDP
En pourcentage du PIB

As a percentage of GDP − En pourcentage du PIB

Country or area Pays ou zone	Year Année	GDP at current prices (Mil. nat.cur.) PIB aux prix courants (Mil. mon.nat.)	Plus: Net factor income from the rest of world Plus : Rev. net des facteurs reçu du reste du monde	Equals: Gross national income Égal : Revenue national brut	Plus: Net curr. transfers from the rest of the world Plus : Transferts courants nets reçus du reste du monde	Equals: Gross national disposable income Égal : Revenu national brut disponible	Less: Final consump− tion Moins : Consom− mation finale	Equals: Gross savings Égal : Épargne brute	Consump− tion of fixed capital Consom− mation de capital fixe
Algeria	1994	1487404	−3.9	96.1	6.7	102.8	74.0	28.8	8.2
Algiers	1995	2002638	−5.1	94.9	5.8	100.7	72.5	28.2	7.1
	1996	2564739	−4.6	95.4	3.5	98.9	67.8	31.1	10.7
Angola	1988	239640	−11.1	88.9	−1.9	87.0	78.4	8.6	...
Angola	1989	278866	−10.5	89.5	−1.6	87.9	77.1	10.8	...
	1990	308062	−12.4	87.6	−4.2	83.4	73.2	10.2	...
Argentina	1996	272150	−1.9	98.1	0.2	...	...	...	...
Argentine	1997	292859	−2.1	97.9	0.2	...	...	...	...
	1998	298131	−2.6	97.4	0.2	...	...	...	...
Australia [1] [2]	1996	533632	−3.6	96.4	0.0	96.4	77.0	19.3	15.3
Australie [1] [2]	1997	565881	−3.2	96.8	0.0	96.8	77.1	19.7	15.5
	1998	593311	...	97.7	0.0	97.7	77.6	20.1	15.7
Austria [1]	1996	2453240	−0.5	99.5	−0.5	99.1	77.6	21.5	13.2
Autriche [1]	1997	2522222	−0.6	99.4	−0.4	99.0	76.6	22.4	13.3
	1998	2610914	−0.9	99.1	−0.6	98.5	75.9	22.6	13.3
Azerbaijan [1]	1995	10669000	−0.2	99.8	4.6	104.4	97.1	20.9	14.1
Azerbaïdjan [1]	1996	13663200	0.1	100.1	2.1	102.2	99.7	19.8	11.1
	1997	15791400	0.1	100.1	1.2	101.3	87.1	...	14.1
Bahamas	1993	2854	...	97.4	...	...	83.9	...	...
Bahamas	1994	3053	...	97.1	...	...	84.0	...	...
	1995	3069	...	96.8	...	...	83.4	...	...
Bahrain	1994	1828	...	82.4	...	...	53.8	...	...
Bahreïn	1995	1900	...	85.3	...	...	50.3	...	...
	1996	2016	...	83.9	...	...	45.7	...	...
Bangladesh [2]	1995	1301600	...	104.6	...	106.7	92.5	14.3	7.2
Bangladesh [2]	1996	1403045	...	105.1	...	107.3	92.5	14.8	7.2
	1997	1540923	...	104.9	...	106.9	92.1	14.8	7.1
Belgium [1]	1996	8304112	1.3	101.3	−0.8	100.5	76.0	24.5	14.3
Belgique [1]	1997	8712360	0.9	100.9	−0.8	100.2	74.9	25.3	14.4
	1998	9088844	0.9	100.9	−0.9	100.0	74.9	25.2	14.5
Belize	1990	793	...	98.3	...	...	...	...	6.3
Belize	1991	861	...	97.5	...	...	...	...	6.4
	1992	936	...	97.6	...	...	...	...	6.3
Benin	1987	469554	...	98.2	8.7	106.9	96.5	10.4	...
Bénin	1988	482434	...	97.9	9.3	107.2	95.3	11.9	...
	1989	479200	...	99.2	11.1	110.2	97.6	12.6	...
Bermuda [3]	1994	1914	...	202.3	...	...	...	...	...
Bermudes [3]	1995	2083	...	206.1	...	...	...	...	...
	1996	2194	...	206.0	...	...	...	...	...
Bhutan	1996	11714	−10.6	89.4	3.2	92.6	61.7	30.9	8.1
Bhoutan	1997	14477	−7.9	92.1	4.9	97.0	61.2	35.8	8.2
	1998	16420	...	93.6	4.9	98.5	62.1	36.5	8.2
Bolivia	1990	15443	−4.6	95.4	2.9	98.3	88.6	9.7	...
Bolivie	1991	19132	−4.0	96.0	2.6	98.6	89.9	8.7	...
	1992	22014	−3.5	96.5	2.8	99.3	92.3	7.0	...
Botswana [2]	1996	14202	−3.3	96.7	−2.1	94.7	61.5	33.2	13.9
Botswana [2]	1997	17486	−3.9	96.1	−0.4	95.7	59.0	36.7	13.0
	1998	20363	−2.1	97.9	−0.4	97.4	60.9	36.5	12.2
Brazil	1993	14116	−2.8	96.7	...	...	...	...	...
Brésil	1994	360919	−1.9	96.6	...	...	...	...	...
	1995	658141	−1.7	...	...	...	...	...	...

21
Relationships between the principal national accounting aggregates
As a percentage of GDP [cont.]
Relations entre les printicpaux agrégats de comptabilité nationale
En pourcentage du PIB [suite]

As a percentage of GDP – En pourcentage du PIB

Country or area Pays ou zone	Year Année	GDP at current prices (Mil. nat.cur.) PIB aux prix courants (Mil. mon.nat.)	Plus: Net factor income from the rest of world Plus : Rev. net des facteurs reçu du reste du monde	Equals: Gross national income Égal : Revenue national brut	Plus: Net curr. transfers from the rest of the world Plus : Transferts courants nets reçus du reste du monde	Equals: Gross national disposable income Égal : Revenu national brut disponible	Less: Final consump- tion Moins : Consom- mation finale	Equals: Gross savings Égal : Épargne brute	Consump- tion of fixed capital Consom- mation de capital fixe
British Virgin Islands	1987	117	9.3	109.3	1.7	110.9	91.0	19.9	11.6
Iles Vierges britanniques	1988	131	8.8	108.8	1.6	110.4	88.9	21.5	10.8
	1989	156	8.5	108.5	1.5	109.9	85.6	24.3	14.9
Bulgaria [1]	1995	880322	-3.3	96.7	0.1	96.8	85.9	...	8.7
Bulgarie [1]	1996	1748701	-4.0	96.0	1.0	97.0	88.5	...	8.2
	1997	17055205	-3.5	96.5	2.3	98.9	83.1	...	6.8
Burkina Faso	1991	811676	0.3	100.3	1.5	...	90.9	...	...
Burkina Faso	1992	812590	0.2	100.2	1.9	...	90.6	...	...
	1993	832349	-0.1	99.9	1.9	...	91.6	...	...
Burundi	1990	196656	...	98.0	...	...	...	...	4.2
Burundi	1991	211898	...	99.0	...	...	...	...	
	1992	226384	...	98.7	...	...	...	...	
Cambodia	1994	6201001	...	92.1	...	...	104.7	...	
Cambodge	1995	7542711	...	95.1	...	...	95.6	...	
	1996	8324792	...	93.6	...	...	95.5	...	
Cameroon [1,2]	1994	3754530	...	94.6	0.0	94.7	84.4	10.2	
Cameroun [1,2]	1995	4465080	...	95.2	0.5	95.8	80.3	15.5	...
	1996	4793080	...	95.7	0.3	95.9	79.8	16.1	...
Canada [1]	1996	821116	-3.4	96.6	0.1	96.6	78.2	18.5	12.9
Canada [1]	1997	860261	-3.3	96.7	0.1	96.8	78.0	18.8	12.8
	1998	881356	-3.4	96.6	0.1	96.7	78.7	18.0	13.0
Cape Verde	1993	29078	...	166.4	...	...	106.8	...	...
Cap–Vert	1994	33497	...	161.3	...	...	104.5	...	...
	1995	37705	...	163.5	...	...	109.1	...	...
Cayman Islands	1989	474	-10.8	89.2	...	92.0	79.3	12.7	8.0
Iles Caïmanes	1990	590	-10.3	89.7	...	92.2	76.8	15.4	7.1
	1991	616	-9.4	90.6	...	93.0	77.6	15.4	7.6
Chile	1994	21395185	...	95.0	...	...	73.5	...	...
Chili	1995	25875727	...	95.7	...	...	73.0	...	...
	1996	28536186	...	95.6	...	...	...	...	...
China †† [1]	1996	6788460	...	98.5	...	...	...	...	...
Chine †† [1]	1997	7446260	...	98.2	...	...	...	...	...
	1998	7939570	...	98.3	...	...	...	...	...
China, Hong Kong SAR †	1995	1077145	1.9	101.9	...	...	...	...	...
Chine, Hong Kong RAS †	1996	1192000	...	100.0	...	...	...	...	...
	1997	1325000	...	100.8	...	...	...	...	...
Colombia [1]	1994	67532862	-1.8	98.2	5.1	103.3	80.4	23.0	...
Colombie [1]	1995	84439109	-1.7	98.3	5.4	103.7	80.6	23.0	...
	1996	100711389	-2.1	97.9	4.5	102.4	83.5	18.9	...
Comoros	1989	63397	...	100.7	...	...	...	...	...
Comores	1990	66370	...	99.8	12.3	112.1	105.5	6.7	...
	1991	69248	...	99.6	...	...	...	...	...
Congo	1986	640407	-6.5	93.5	-1.3	92.2	84.4	40.9	24.4
Congo	1987	690523	-11.1	88.9	-1.6	87.3	77.2	37.4	23.8
	1988	658964	-13.7	86.3	-1.8	84.5	81.2	40.6	22.0
Costa Rica	1993	1069259	-2.3	97.0	...	98.8	77.3	21.4	2.4
Costa Rica	1994	1306302	-1.8	98.4	...	100.3	77.0	23.3	2.3
	1995	1659385	...	98.0	...	99.5	75.8	23.8	2.3
Côte d'Ivoire	1994	4616000	-8.0	91.9	2.4	...	78.5	...	...
Côte d'Ivoire	1995	5543000	-7.8	92.4	-1.2	...	81.0	...	...
	1996	6177000	-8.6	91.4	-2.7	...	81.1	...	...
Cuba	1996	22815	...	97.8	1.7	101.1	94.8	6.3	...
Cuba	1997	22952	...	97.9	1.9	101.3	95.7	5.6	...
	1998	23901	...	97.5	1.3	100.9	94.6	6.4	...

21
Relationships between the principal national accounting aggregates
As a percentage of GDP [cont.]
Relations entre les printicpaux agrégats de comptabilité nationale
En pourcentage du PIB [suite]

As a percentage of GDP – En pourcentage du PIB

Country or area Pays ou zone	Year Année	GDP at current prices (Mil. nat.cur.) PIB aux prix courants (Mil. mon.nat.)	Plus: Net factor income from the rest of world Plus : Rev. net des facteurs reçu du reste du monde	Equals: Gross national income Égal : Revenue national brut	Plus: Net curr. transfers from the rest of the world Plus : Transferts courants nets reçus du reste du monde	Equals: Gross national disposable income Égal : Revenu national brut disponible	Less: Final consump- tion Moins : Consom- mation finale	Equals: Gross savings Égal : Épargne brute	Consump- tion of fixed capital Consom- mation de capital fixe
Cyprus	1997	4366	...	100.9	...	...	84.9	...	10.6
Chypre	1998	4680	...	100.6	...	...	87.8	...	10.6
	1999	4943	...	100.3	...	...	84.9	...	10.5
Czech Republic [1]	1994	1182800	-0.1	99.9	0.3	97.3	72.9	27.4	22.1
République tchèque [1]	1995	1381049	-0.5	99.5	1.1	100.6	70.7	29.9	17.8
	1996	1572257	-1.1	98.9	0.7	99.6	71.4	28.1	17.0
Dem. Rep. of the Congo	1983	59134	...	95.7	...	...	...	...	2.9
Rép. dém. du Congo	1984	99723	...	88.5	...	...	...	...	2.5
	1985	147263	...	97.2	...	...	...	...	2.9
Denmark [1]	1996	1061720	-1.3	98.7	-2.1	96.5	75.9	20.7	15.5
Danemark [1]	1997	1114332	-1.4	98.6	-1.7	96.9	75.9	21.0	15.7
	1998	1168306	-1.6	98.4	-1.7	96.7	76.3	20.4	15.0
Djibouti	1996	88233	...	100.0	9.4	109.4	97.3	12.2	...
Djibouti	1997	87289	...	99.9	8.3	108.2	94.2	14.0	...
	1998	88461	...	99.9	8.3	108.3	96.4	11.8	...
Dominica	1989	423	...	101.0	...	...	...	...	...
Dominique	1990	452	...	101.1	...	...	...	...	...
	1991	479	...	101.0	...	...	...	...	...
Dominican Republic	1991	100070	...	97.3	...	102.2	86.6	15.6	5.9
Rép. dominicaine	1992	112369	...	97.3	...	102.1	86.3	16.3	6.0
	1993	120572	...	95.9	...	100.5	82.6	18.5	5.9
Ecuador	1991	12296000	-6.0	94.0	1.0	95.0	76.2	18.8	16.5
Equateur	1992	19414000	-4.8	95.2	1.0	96.2	75.0	21.2	15.5
	1993	27451000	-4.0	96.0	0.9	96.9	78.3	18.6	15.9
Egypt [2]	1980	17149	4.3	104.3	1.5	105.8	81.6	24.2	...
Egypte [2]	1981	20222	1.3	101.3	1.3	102.6	81.7	21.0	...
El Salvador	1992	49841	...	96.8	...	...	97.8	...	...
El Salvador	1993	60522	...	98.8	...	...	95.9	...	...
	1994	70613	...	99.4	...	...	95.5	...	...
Estonia [1]	1996	52446	0.0	100.0	2.3	102.4	84.8	17.6	10.8
Estonie [1]	1997	64324	-3.1	96.9	2.5	99.4	81.2	18.2	11.5
	1998	73325	-1.6	98.4	2.8	101.3	81.3	19.9	13.7
Ethiopia [4]	1997	41465	-0.3	99.7	...	...	...	...	...
Ethiopie [4]	1998	45035	-0.4	99.6	...	...	...	...	...
	1999	49994	-0.4	99.6	...	...	...	...	...
Fiji	1991	2042	-1.4	105.1	-1.6	103.6	92.1	11.5	8.2
Fidji	1992	2302	-1.7	101.5	-0.9	100.7	88.1	12.5	7.9
	1993	2522	-0.6	100.2	-0.5	99.7	87.4	12.3	7.3
Finland [1]	1996	585865	-2.9	97.1	-0.6	96.5	75.8	20.7	17.6
Finlande [1]	1997	635532	-2.0	98.0	-0.6	97.4	73.4	24.1	16.7
	1998	686742	-2.2	97.8	-0.8	97.0	72.1	24.9	16.2
France [1]	1996	7951366	-0.1	99.9	-0.7	99.3	80.0	19.2	12.8
France [1]	1997	8224901	0.1	100.1	-0.8	99.4	78.9	20.5	12.7
	1998	8564678	0.3	100.3	-0.8	99.5	78.6	20.9	12.7
French Guiana	1990	6526	-1.9	98.1	36.3	134.4	99.4	35.0	...
Guyane française	1991	7404	-5.8	94.2	35.9	130.1	94.5	35.6	...
	1992	7976	-6.9	93.1	36.4	129.6	93.1	36.4	...
Gabon	1987	1020600	-6.2	93.8	-4.2	89.7	72.4	21.0	19.2
Gabon	1988	1013600	-7.4	92.6	-7.6	85.0	69.9	15.1	12.0
	1989	1168066	-8.6	91.4	-6.1	85.3	66.8	18.5	14.5
Gambia [2]	1991	2920	...	98.3	...	115.7	96.7	19.0	11.7
Gambie [2]	1992	3078	...	98.7	...	114.1	94.4	19.7	12.3
	1993	3243	...	98.5	...	114.4	93.3	21.1	12.9

21
Relationships between the principal national accounting aggregates
As a percentage of GDP [cont.]
Relations entre les printicpaux agrégats de comptabilité nationale
En pourcentage du PIB [suite]

As a percentage of GDP − En pourcentage du PIB

Country or area Pays ou zone	Year Année	GDP at current prices (Mil. nat.cur.) PIB aux prix courants (Mil. mon.nat.)	Plus: Net factor income from the rest of world Plus : Rev. net des facteurs reçu du reste du monde	Equals: Gross national income Égal : Revenue national brut	Plus: Net curr. transfers from the rest of the world Plus : Transferts courants nets reçus du reste du monde	Equals: Gross national disposable income Égal : Revenu national brut disponible	Less: Final consump− tion Moins : Consom− mation finale	Equals: Gross savings Égal : Épargne brute	Consump− tion of fixed capital Consom− mation de capital fixe
Georgia [1]	1995	3694	...	97.9	4.0	101.9	91.2	11.7	11.2
Georgie [1]	1996	5300	...	101.7	2.0	103.7	93.2	12.8	11.6
	1997	6431	...	102.6	3.9	106.5	100.0	16.8	11.7
Germany [1]	1997	3666600	−0.5	99.5	−1.0	98.5	76.9	21.6	14.9
Allemagne [1]	1998	3784200	−0.8	99.2	−1.0	98.2	76.5	21.7	14.8
	1999	3871600	−1.0	99.0	−1.0	98.0	76.8	21.3	14.8
Ghana	1994	5205200	...	98.0	...	...	...	...	7.9
Ghana	1995	7752600	...	98.0	...	...	...	...	6.6
	1996	11339200	...	98.1	...	...	...	...	7.1
Greece [1]	1996	29935080	2.8	102.8	2.8	105.6	88.2	17.4	9.1
Grèce [1]	1997	33021832	3.1	103.1	2.7	105.8	87.1	18.7	9.9
	1998	35910654	3.1	103.1	2.9	106.0	85.9	20.1	10.4
Grenada	1984	275	...	98.9	...	...	...	...	...
Grenade	1985	311	...	98.9	...	...	...	...	...
	1986	350	...	99.2	...	...	...	...	...
Guadeloupe	1990	15201	−2.5	97.5	37.3	...	123.6	...	...
Guadeloupe	1991	16415	−3.4	96.6	35.4	...	118.3	...	...
	1992	17972	−3.0	97.0	36.6	...	113.4	...	...
Guatemala	1996	95479	−1.5	98.5	3.4	101.9	91.7	10.2	...
Guatemala	1997	107943	−1.3	98.7	3.4	...	84.5	...	...
	1998	121548	−0.8	99.2	3.8	103.0	92.4	10.6	...
Guinea−Bissau	1986	46973	−1.7	98.3	2.9	101.3	102.8	−1.5	...
Guinée−Bissau	1987	92375	−0.5	99.5	4.1	103.6	100.8	2.8	...
Guyana	1997	106678	...	90.2	...	...	64.6	...	...
Guyana	1998	109055	...	92.2	...	...	71.1	...	...
	1999	115150	...	91.8	...	...	70.8	...	...
Haiti [5]	1995	35207	...	98.7	...	121.5	108.1	13.4	2.2
Haïti [5]	1996	43234	...	99.6	...	116.7	104.9	11.8	2.3
	1997	51789	...	99.6	...	113.7	103.7	10.0	2.0
Honduras	1995	37507	...	93.2	6.7	99.9	72.8	27.0	6.0
Honduras	1996	47774	...	93.6	6.8	100.3	74.6	25.7	5.9
	1997	61084	...	94.9	6.6	101.5	73.7	27.4	5.5
Hungary [1]	1995	5614042	...	93.1	...	...	77.3	...	...
Hongrie [1]	1996	6893934	...	92.7	...	...	74.3	...	...
	1997	8540669	...	91.6	...	...	72.6	...	...
Iceland	1994	435028	−3.1	96.9	−0.1	96.8	79.6	17.1	13.0
Islande	1995	451548	−2.8	97.2	−0.1	97.2	81.2	15.9	12.8
	1996	485168	−2.2	97.8	−0.1	97.7	81.9	15.8	12.3
India [3]	1995	12179630	−1.1	98.9	...	100.7	72.1	24.1	9.4
Inde [3]	1996	14098490	−0.9	99.1	...	102.2	72.6	24.4	9.3
	1997	15635520	−0.9	99.1	...	101.9	72.2	23.1	9.5
Indonesia	1996	532567000	...	97.3	...	...	69.9	...	5.0
Indonésie	1997	627695000	...	97.1	...	...	68.5	...	5.0
	1998	1002334000	...	94.6	...	...	71.6	...	4.9
Iran (Islamic Rep. of) [6]	1996	235233000	−0.9	99.1	...	97.7	74.4	25.8	16.2
Iran (Rép. islamique d') [6]	1997	277831000	−0.6	99.4	...	...	...	23.5	16.7
	1998	328337000	−0.3	99.7	...	...	...	21.5	17.0
Iraq	1989	21026	...	96.7	...	95.9	81.9	14.0	8.7
Iraq	1990	23297	...	96.7	...	96.5	76.8	19.6	8.8
	1991	19940	...	96.7	...	97.4	83.5	13.9	9.6
Ireland [1]	1996	45210	−8.7	91.3	0.5	91.8	69.8	22.0	10.0
Irlande [1]	1997	51823	−10.3	89.7	0.6	90.3	67.0	23.3	9.9
	1998	59637	−11.1	88.9	0.4	89.2	64.8	24.4	10.2

21
Relationships between the principal national accounting aggregates
As a percentage of GDP *[cont.]*
Relations entre les printicpaux agrégats de comptabilité nationale
En pourcentage du PIB *[suite]*

Country or area Pays ou zone	Year Année	GDP at current prices (Mil. nat.cur.) PIB aux prix courants (Mil. mon.nat.)	Plus: Net factor income from the rest of world Plus : Rev. net des facteurs reçu du reste du monde	Equals: Gross national income Égal : Revenue national brut	Plus: Net curr. transfers from the rest of the world Plus : Transferts courants nets reçus du reste du monde	Equals: Gross national disposable income Égal : Revenu national brut disponible	Less: Final consump-tion Moins : Consom-mation finale	Equals: Gross savings Égal : Épargne brute	Consump-tion of fixed capital Consom-mation de capital fixe
Israel [1] Israël [1]	1996	324929	−3.2	96.8	6.2	103.0	85.0	18.0	13.1
	1997	362209	−3.3	96.7	5.9	102.6	85.2	17.4	13.4
	1998	394022	−2.7	97.3	6.0	103.3	85.2	18.1	13.9
Italy [1] Italie [1]	1996	1896022000	−1.4	98.6	−0.4	98.2	76.5	21.7	14.1
	1997	1974618000	−0.9	99.1	−0.3	98.7	77.1	21.6	14.2
	1998	2057731000	−1.1	98.9	−0.6	98.3	77.0	21.3	14.2
Jamaica Jamaïque	1987	16640	−11.4	84.8	3.7	88.4	73.5	14.9	7.9
	1988	19458	−10.1	86.2	12.2	98.4	74.4	24.0	7.0
	1989	23400	−10.5	84.5	7.5	92.0	72.6	19.3	7.5
Japan Japon	1995	483220200	0.8	100.8	−0.1	100.8	69.9	30.8	16.0
	1996	500309700	1.1	101.1	−0.2	101.1	69.5	31.6	16.0
	1997	507851800	1.3	101.3	−0.2	101.1	70.1	31.0	16.1
Jordan Jordanie	1996	4711	...	97.6	25.4	...	94.6	...	11.0
	1997	4946	...	99.0	24.5	...	96.4	...	11.4
	1998	5180	...	99.9	21.5	...	97.6	...	11.5
Kazakhstan [1] Kazakhstan [1]	1994	423469	0.5	99.5	1.7	101.2	88.3	26.9	19.9
	1995	1014190	0.9	99.1	0.8	99.9	82.4	18.7	18.1
	1996	1415750	0.0	99.1	0.7	99.8	79.8	20.1	14.3
Kenya Kenya	1993	16007	...	92.5	4.4	...	76.7	...	...
	1994	19684	...	94.4	3.9	...	77.2	...	...
	1995	23040	...	96.4	5.6	...	84.4	...	...
Korea, Republic of [1] Corée, Rép. de [1]	1996	418478988	−0.3	99.7	0.0	99.6	66.0	33.7	11.2
	1997	453276389	−0.5	99.5	0.2	99.6	66.3	33.3	11.3
	1998	449508816	−1.4	98.6	1.0	99.6	66.6	33.0	11.9
Kuwait Koweït	1995	7925	...	118.4	−5.5	112.9	74.3	38.6	9.0
	1996	9307	...	116.7	−4.8	111.9	73.5	38.4	7.4
	1997	9212	...	120.7	−4.7	116.0	74.8	41.2	7.6
Krygyzstan [1] Kirghizistan [1]	1994	12019	−1.6	98.4	5.5	104.0	97.3	13.6	10.2
	1995	16145	−1.2	98.8	5.1	103.8	94.5	11.1	10.2
	1996	23399	−2.1	97.9	6.1	104.1	100.6	21.9	12.7
Latvia [1] Lettonie [1]	1994	2043	−0.2	99.8	3.6	103.4	78.8	24.6	12.5
	1995	2349	0.5	100.5	1.5	102.0	84.8	17.2	12.2
	1996	2829	0.8	100.8	1.8	102.6	89.3	13.4	10.7
Lesotho Lesotho	1996	4040	41.7	141.7	24.6	153.9	93.2	60.7	...
	1997	4715	38.4	138.4	24.1	...	...	...	...
	1998	4849	32.8	132.8	19.8	...	...	...	...
Liberia Libéria	1987	1090	...	83.2	...	...	...	...	8.6
	1988	1158	...	84.2	...	...	...	...	8.3
	1989	1194	...	84.9	...	...	...	...	8.5
Libyan Arab Jamah. Jamah. arabe libyenne	1983	8805	...	91.0	−0.2	90.9	72.0	18.9	5.0
	1984	8013	...	92.7	−0.3	92.4	72.2	20.2	5.7
	1985	8277	...	96.7	−0.2	96.5	69.2	27.3	5.8
Lithuania [1] Lituanie [1]	1995	24103	−0.2	99.8	1.8	101.6	87.1	14.5	8.7
	1996	31569	−1.2	98.8	1.8	100.7	85.3	15.3	9.7
	1997	38201	−2.1	97.9	2.4	100.3	86.7	13.6	10.0
Luxembourg [1] Luxembourg [1]	1996	563513	5.3	105.3	...	...	66.8	...	14.8
	1997	624581	2.2	102.2	...	...	63.6	...	13.4
	1998	665735	−3.6	96.4	...	...	61.9	...	13.1
Madagascar Madagascar	1980	689800	...	99.9	...	...	...	...	...
Malawi Malawi	1994	10319	...	104.7	...	...	...	...	...
	1995	20923	...	93.7	...	...	...	...	...
	1996	33918	...	69.5	...	...	...	...	...

21
Relationships between the principal national accounting aggregates
As a percentage of GDP *[cont.]*
Relations entre les princtpaux agrégats de comptabilité nationale
En pourcentage du PIB *[suite]*

As a percentage of GDP – En pourcentage du PIB

Country or area Pays ou zone	Year Année	GDP at current prices (Mil. nat.cur.) PIB aux prix courants (Mil. mon.nat.)	Plus: Net factor income from the rest of world Plus : Rev. net des facteurs reçu du reste du monde	Equals: Gross national income Égal : Revenue national brut	Plus: Net curr. transfers from the rest of the world Plus : Transferts courants nets reçus du reste du monde	Equals: Gross national disposable income Égal : Revenu national brut disponible	Less: Final consump- tion Moins : Consom- mation finale	Equals: Gross savings Égal : Épargne brute	Consump- tion of fixed capital Consom- mation de capital fixe
Malaysia	1997	281795	−5.4	94.6	−1.2	93.5	56.1	37.3	...
Malaisie	1998	284472	−5.4	94.6	−3.5	91.1	51.5	39.6	...
	1999	299193	−6.5	93.5	−2.7	90.9	52.9	38.0	...
Mali	1990	683300	−1.2	98.8	11.5	110.3	94.3	16.1	3.9
Mali	1991	691400	−1.3	98.7	13.0	111.9	100.4	11.5	4.0
	1992	737400	−1.2	98.8	11.4	110.2	96.4	13.8	3.5
Malta	1997	1288	0.3	100.3	...	...	...	...	...
Malte	1998	1362	−2.0	98.0	...	...	...	...	...
	1999	1447	−0.2	99.8	...	...	...	...	...
Martinique	1990	19320	−4.2	95.8	33.7	...	113.3	...	...
Martinique	1991	20787	−4.4	95.6	30.7	...	112.8	...	...
	1992	22093	−3.9	96.1	33.4	...	113.1	...	...
Mauritania	1987	67216	−5.1	94.9	8.1	103.0	96.2	6.7	...
Mauritanie	1988	72635	−5.6	94.4	7.9	102.3	93.7	8.5	...
	1989	83520	−3.6	96.4	9.0	105.4	...	...	...
Mauritius	1996	77310	−1.0	99.0	2.6	101.5	76.0	25.5	...
Maurice	1997	86428	−0.4	99.6	2.8	102.3	75.5	26.8	...
	1998	96985	−0.7	99.3	2.5	101.8	74.8	27.0	...
Mexico [1]	1995	1837019	−4.6	95.4	1.4	96.8	77.5	19.3	11.5
Mexique [1]	1996	2525575	−4.1	95.9	1.4	97.2	74.8	22.5	10.8
	1997	3174193	−3.1	96.9	1.3	98.2	74.1	24.1	10.2
Mongolia	1996	659698	...	98.8	...	...	...	...	6.0
Mongolie	1997	846344	...	95.0	...	...	...	...	8.4
	1998	833727	...	99.3	...	...	...	...	10.5
Morocco	1995	281700	−4.0	96.1	7.0	103.1	85.8	17.3	...
Maroc	1996	319630	...	...	7.0	...	83.9	...	...
	1997	319290	...	...	6.6	...	83.2	...	...
Mozambique	1984	109000	...	100.0	...	...	...	...	3.7
Mozambique	1985	147000	...	100.0	...	...	...	...	2.7
	1986	167000	...	100.6	...	...	...	...	...
Myanmar [3]	1996	791980	0.0	100.0	...	100.0	88.5	11.4	2.3
Myanmar [3]	1997	1109554	0.0	100.0	...	100.0	88.1	11.9	1.9
	1998	1559996	0.0	100.0	...	100.0	89.4	10.6	1.7
Namibia [1]	1996	13421	2.2	102.3	13.3	...	88.8	...	15.6
Namibie [1]	1997	14901	2.2	102.2	13.7	...	95.1	...	15.0
	1998	16826	2.0	102.0	13.3	...	89.9	...	14.2
Nepal [7]	1996	248913	1.4	101.4	0.4	101.8	86.2	15.6	1.8
Népal [7]	1997	280513	1.7	101.7	0.4	102.0	86.0	16.0	2.0
	1998	296547	2.0	102.0	0.4	102.4	90.5	11.9	2.4
Netherlands [1]	1996	694298	0.5	100.5	−0.8	99.7	73.0	26.7	15.1
Pays−Bas [1]	1997	734853	1.8	101.8	−0.9	100.9	72.3	28.6	14.9
	1998	776161	1.1	101.1	−0.8	100.3	72.5	27.9	14.8
Netherlands Antilles	1992	3548	3.4	103.4	...	107.9	83.6	24.3	11.4
Antilles néerlandaises	1993	3766	1.6	101.6	...	105.8	85.4	20.4	12.6
	1994	4218	3.8	103.8	...	106.6	90.4	16.2	13.1
New Zealand [3]	1994	86577	−6.0	94.0	0.2	94.2	75.6	18.6	9.5
Nouvelle−Zélande [3]	1995	91740	−6.5	93.5	0.2	93.6	76.1	17.5	9.5
	1996	95816	−8.0	92.0	0.8	92.7	76.8	16.0	9.7
Nicaragua	1981	24483	...	95.9	...	...	...	...	4.2
Nicaragua	1982	28350	...	95.1	...	...	...	...	4.2
	1983	32920	...	98.0	...	...	...	...	4.5
Niger	1982	663022	−3.1	96.9	1.5	98.4	85.1	13.3	8.7
Niger	1983	687142	−3.1	96.9	1.1	98.0	88.8	9.5	9.3
	1984	638406	...	96.2	1.6	97.8	88.2	11.3	10.4

21
Relationships between the principal national accounting aggregates
As a percentage of GDP [cont.]
Relations entre les printicpaux agrégats de comptabilité nationale
En pourcentage du PIB [suite]

As a percentage of GDP – En pourcentage du PIB

Country or area Pays ou zone	Year Année	GDP at current prices (Mil. nat.cur.) PIB aux prix courants (Mil. mon.nat.)	Plus: Net factor income from the rest of world Plus : Rev. net des facteurs reçu du reste du monde	Equals: Gross national income Égal : Revenue national brut	Plus: Net curr. transfers from the rest of the world Plus : Transferts courants nets reçus du reste du monde	Equals: Gross national disposable income Égal : Revenu national brut disponible	Less: Final consump- tion Moins : Consom- mation finale	Equals: Gross savings Égal : Épargne brute	Consump- tion of fixed capital Consom- mation de capital fixe
Nigeria	1992	549809	−11.7	88.3	2.3	90.6	77.2	13.4	3.0
Nigéria	1993	701473	−10.5	89.5	2.5	92.0	80.6	11.5	2.5
	1994	914334	−7.2	92.8	1.2	94.0	85.5	8.5	2.0
Norway [1]	1996	1016589	−1.2	98.8	−1.0	97.9	68.6	29.3	15.5
Norvège [1]	1997	1089032	−1.0	99.0	−0.9	98.1	67.9	30.2	15.3
	1998	1107081	−0.6	99.4	−1.1	98.3	71.2	27.1	16.3
Oman [1]	1996	5874	...	96.9	...	...	72.2	...	10.0
Oman [1]	1997	6090	...	97.3	...	...	70.8	...	10.3
	1998	5445	...	96.3	...	...	83.0	...	11.9
Pakistan [2]	1996	2457381	...	99.2	...	...	86.9	...	6.5
Pakistan [2]	1997	2736919	...	99.1	...	...	83.9	...	6.7
	1998	3025683	...	99.1	...	...	84.9	...	6.7
Panama	1996	8151	...	95.6	1.7	97.2	68.3	28.9	7.1
Panama	1997	8658	...	94.8	1.7	96.5	70.5	26.0	6.9
	1998	9144	...	93.8	1.7	95.6	74.2	21.3	7.0
Papua New Guinea	1990	3076	−3.8	96.2	3.2	99.4	83.9	15.5	11.0
Papouasie−Nouv.−Guinée	1991	3606	−3.3	96.7	3.4	100.2	82.5	17.7	11.6
	1992	4140	...	97.3	...	...	...	...	...
Paraguay	1993	11991719	...	100.4	...	100.4	88.0	12.4	7.8
Paraguay	1994	14960131	...	100.5	...	100.5	95.2	10.2	7.8
	1995	17699000	...	100.9	...	100.9	92.5	8.4	7.8
Peru	1996	148278	...	97.3	...	...	80.6	...	...
Pérou	1997	172389	...	97.5	...	...	78.7	...	...
	1998	183179	...	97.7	...	...	80.9	...	...
Philippines	1995	1905951	2.8	102.8	1.6	104.4	85.5	18.9	9.0
Philippines	1996	2171922	4.1	104.1	0.6	104.7	85.4	19.3	8.8
	1997	2423640	4.3	104.3	2.6	106.8	85.7	21.1	8.6
Poland [1]	1995	306318	...	98.4	−0.3	...	77.8	...	...
Pologne [1]	1996	385448	...	99.2	0.1	...	79.6	...	...
	1997	469372	...	99.2	...	...	79.6	...	...
Portugal [1]	1996	17098600	−1.0	99.0	3.7	102.7	82.2	20.4	...
Portugal [1]	1997	18276363	−0.5	99.5	3.1	102.6	81.6	21.0	...
	1998	19692907	−0.6	99.4	3.2	102.6	81.9	20.6	...
Puerto Rico [2]	1996	48187	−33.4	66.6	14.3	80.9	76.6	8.6	6.4
Porto Rico [2]	1997	53875	−35.5	64.5	13.3	77.8	72.4	7.2	6.3
	1998	59946	−36.8	63.2	14.8	78.0	70.1	7.9	6.1
Republic of Moldova [1]	1994	4737	−0.5	99.5	2.7	102.2	75.4	26.7	...
Rép. de Moldova [1]	1995	6480	...	100.0	1.5	101.5	82.9	18.6	...
	1996	7658	3.6	103.6	0.7	104.2	95.8	8.4	...
Réunion	1990	28374	−2.5	97.5	44.3	141.7	108.1	33.6	...
Réunion	1991	31339	0.7	100.7	42.7	143.4	103.5	39.9	...
	1992	33787	−1.5	98.4	43.6	142.1	104.5	37.6	...
Romania [1]	1993	20035700	...	...	2.9	...	76.0	...	...
Roumanie [1]	1994	49773200	...	...	2.2	...	77.3	...	...
	1995	72135500	...	...	1.2	...	81.3	...	...
Russian Federation [1]	1992	19005500	...	98.0	3.1	101.1	48.3	52.7	12.8
Fédération de Russie [1]	1993	171509500	...	98.5	0.7	99.2	60.2	39.0	16.9
	1994	610745200	...	99.4	0.0	99.4	68.6	30.8	20.2
Rwanda	1987	171430	−1.6	98.4	2.5	100.9	93.5	7.4	6.5
Rwanda	1988	177920	−2.0	98.0	2.9	100.9	93.6	7.3	6.9
	1989	190220	−1.2	98.8	2.4	101.3	95.4	9.4	7.6
Saint Kitts−Nevis	1982	158	...	94.2	...	...	...	...	...
Saint−Kitts−et−Nevis	1983	154	...	98.6	...	...	...	...	...
	1984	167	...	99.5	...	...	...	...	...

21
Relationships between the principal national accounting aggregates
As a percentage of GDP *[cont.]*
Relations entre les princtipaux agrégats de comptabilité nationale
En pourcentage du PIB *[suite]*

Country or area Pays ou zone	Year Année	GDP at current prices (Mil. nat.cur.) PIB aux prix courants (Mil. mon.nat.)	Plus: Net factor income from the rest of world Plus : Rev. net des facteurs reçu du reste du monde	Equals: Gross national income Égal : Revenue national brut	Plus: Net curr. transfers from the rest of the world Plus : Transferts courants nets reçus du reste du monde	Equals: Gross national disposable income Égal : Revenu national brut disponible	Less: Final consumption Moins : Consommation finale	Equals: Gross savings Égal : Épargne brute	Consumption of fixed capital Consommation de capital fixe
Saint Vincent−Grenadines	1995	710	−4.4	95.6	...	...	...	...	...
St.−Vincent−et−Gren.	1996	744	−3.0	96.1	...	...	...	...	...
	1997	766	−6.0	94.0	...	...	...	...	...
Saudi Arabia [2]	1992	461398	−1.9	98.1	−18.3	79.8	72.2	12.3	10.0
Arabie saoudite [2]	1993	443842	−1.6	98.4	−16.2	82.2	72.5	10.3	10.0
	1994	450025	−3.1	96.9	−13.9	83.0	69.9	13.1	10.0
Senegal	1996	2380000	...	108.1	...	...	...	...	...
Sénégal	1997	2555000	...	104.1	...	...	...	...	...
	1998	2753000	...	104.2	...	...	...	...	...
Seychelles	1995	2420	−3.6	96.4	1.5	...	76.4	...	8.7
Seychelles	1996	2482	−3.0	97.0	3.1	...	77.6	...	9.7
	1997	2910	...	98.3	...	...	75.6	...	...
Sierra Leone [2]	1988	43947	0.9	100.9	0.6	101.5	94.3	7.3	5.8
Sierra Leone [2]	1989	82837	0.8	100.8	0.5	101.3	91.3	10.0	5.9
	1990	150175	−5.0	95.0	0.7	95.7	88.4	7.3	5.6
Singapore	1995	120704	...	101.0	...	99.9	49.6	50.5	12.6
Singapour	1996	130775	...	101.8	...	100.5	50.7	51.0	12.7
	1997	143014	...	102.7	...	101.3	50.0	52.5	12.7
Slovakia [1]	1993	369117	−0.3	99.7	0.9	100.6	78.2	22.4	16.9
Slovaquie [1]	1994	440514	−0.9	99.1	0.5	99.6	71.7	27.9	14.6
	1995	516760	−0.1	99.9	0.4	100.3	69.8	30.5	13.5
Slovenia [1] Slovénie [1]	1993	1435095	−0.4	...	...	...	...	...	...
Solomon Islands	1984	222	...	94.2	...	100.8	78.2	22.6	5.9
Iles Salomon	1985	237	...	95.0	...	101.0	91.6	9.4	6.7
	1986	253	...	92.6	...	115.7	94.8	20.9	7.6
Somalia	1985	87290	...	97.8	...	...	101.1	...	...
Somalie	1986	118781	...	96.3	...	...	98.8	...	...
	1987	169608	...	96.8	...	...	99.9	...	...
South Africa [1]	1996	618417	−2.2	97.8	−0.5	97.5	81.7	15.8	12.8
Afrique du Sud [1]	1997	683666	−2.2	97.8	−0.5	97.4	82.9	14.5	12.7
	1998	740581	−2.3	97.7	−0.6	96.9	82.6	14.3	12.8
Spain [1]	1996	77113358	−0.6	99.4	0.3	99.6	77.6	22.0	11.5
Espagne [1]	1997	81782027	−0.8	99.2	0.3	99.5	76.9	22.5	11.5
	1998	86968544	−0.9	99.1	0.2	99.3	76.6	22.7	11.5
Sri Lanka	1996	771414	−1.4	98.6	5.1	103.7	83.2	20.9	5.2
Sri Lanka	1997	891067	−1.1	98.9	5.2	104.1	81.2	22.9	5.2
	1998	1011326	−1.1	98.9	5.4	104.3	80.8	23.5	5.1
Sudan [2]	1991	421819	...	85.5	...	104.0	86.0	18.0	7.0
Soudan [2]	1992	948448	...	99.7	...	102.2	88.2	14.0	6.4
	1993	1881289	...	99.8	...	100.6	88.3	12.3	7.1
Suriname	1996	303970	0.3	100.3	0.2	100.5	73.6	26.9	9.6
Suriname	1997	340220	−0.3	99.7	−0.3	99.8	77.9	21.9	9.3
	1998	407130	...	100.1	−0.2	...	...	...	9.5
Swaziland [8]	1992	2761	...	104.3	...	110.9	81.4	29.5	...
Swaziland [8]	1993	3206	...	98.4	...	100.9	73.5	27.4	...
	1994	3712	...	98.0	...	98.7	74.8	23.9	...
Sweden [1]	1996	1756358	−3.2	96.8	−0.4	96.3	77.4	18.9	13.6
Suède [1]	1997	1813128	−2.8	97.2	−0.6	96.5	77.4	19.1	13.6
	1998	1890202	−2.0	98.0	−0.9	97.1	77.0	20.1	13.8
Switzerland	1994	357463	3.5	103.5	−1.2	102.3	74.4	27.9	17.6
Suisse	1995	363490	4.3	104.3	−1.2	103.1	74.5	28.5	16.6
	1996	364763	4.3	104.3	−1.2	103.1	75.5	27.6	16.4

21
Relationships between the principal national accounting aggregates
As a percentage of GDP [cont.]
    Relations entre les printicpaux agrégats de comptabilité nationale
    En pourcentage du PIB [suite]

As a percentage of GDP – En pourcentage du PIB

Country or area Pays ou zone	Year Année	GDP at current prices (Mil. nat.cur.) PIB aux prix courants (Mil. mon.nat.)	Plus: Net factor income from the rest of world Plus : Rev. net des facteurs reçu du reste du monde	Equals: Gross national income Égal : Revenue national brut	Plus: Net curr. transfers from the rest of the world Plus : Transferts courants nets reçus du reste du monde	Equals: Gross national disposable income Égal : Revenu national brut disponible	Less: Final consump- tion Moins : Consom- mation finale	Equals: Gross savings Égal : Épargne brute	Consump- tion of fixed capital Consom- mation de capital fixe
Thailand	1995	4186000	−1.6	98.4	0.3	98.6	63.1	35.5	11.2
Thaïlande	1996	4609000	−2.2	97.8	0.4	98.2	64.6	33.5	12.0
	1997	4724000	−2.6	97.4	0.3	97.7	66.0	31.7	13.4
TYFR of Macedonia [1]	1991	935	...	99.4	−0.4	99.0	85.5	13.5	12.0
L'ex−R.y. Macédoine [1]	1992	12005	...	96.9	−0.4	96.6	83.8	41.3	27.1
	1993	58145	...	97.7	0.7	98.4	88.9	34.9	22.2
Togo									
Togo	1980	238872	−1.8	98.2	6.3	104.4	80.3	24.1	7.5
Tonga [8]	1981	54	6.3	106.3	23.7	130.0	136.9	15.1	4.6
Tonga [8]	1982	64	6.9	106.9	35.8	142.7	137.9	29.0	4.5
	1983	73	4.4	104.4	27.1	130.5	140.0	10.2	4.0
Trinidad and Tobago	1995	31665	−9.2	90.8	...	...	...	...	...
Trinité−et−Tobago	1996	34648	−9.1	90.9	...	...	...	...	...
	1997	36970	−6.2	93.8	...	...	...	...	...
Tunisia	1995	17052	...	95.3	4.0	99.4	79.2	20.2	10.6
Tunisie	1996	19066	...	94.7	4.2	98.8	76.5	22.3	10.2
	1997	20901	...	95.2	4.1	99.3	75.8	23.5	...
Turkey	1995	7762456000	...	101.2	...	101.2	81.4	19.7	6.5
Turquie	1996	14772110000	...	101.4	...	...	0.0	...	6.3
	1997	29137554000	...	101.9	...	...	0.0	...	...
Ukraine [1]	1996	81519	−1.3	98.7	1.1	99.9	79.9	20.0	18.0
Ukraine [1]	1997	93365	−1.3	98.7	1.7	100.4	81.6	18.8	18.6
	1998	102593	−2.0	98.0	2.6	100.6	81.5	19.1	18.8
United Arab Emirates	1988	87106	0.3	100.3	−1.2	99.1	65.8	33.3	16.5
Emirats arabes unis	1989	100976	0.4	100.4	−0.7	99.7	61.7	38.0	15.0
	1990	124008	−1.0	99.0	−8.9	90.1	54.9	35.1	13.0
United Kingdom [1]	1996	754601	0.6	100.6	−0.1	100.5	83.7	16.8	11.1
Royaume−Uni [1]	1997	803889	1.1	101.1	−0.3	100.8	82.7	18.1	10.7
	1998	847421	1.3	101.3	−0.4	100.9	82.8	18.4	10.7
United Rep. of Tanzania	1992	1130596	...	93.8	25.0	118.8	97.8	20.9	3.2
Rép.−Unie de Tanzanie	1993	1404369	...	95.7	20.8	116.5	95.9	20.6	2.6
	1994	1822570	...	96.2	20.9	117.1	97.3	19.8	2.7
United States	1994	6722900	0.3	100.3	−0.6	99.8	84.2	15.4	10.7
Etats−Unis	1995	7038400	0.3	100.5	−0.5	100.0	84.1	16.2	10.6
	1996	7418700	0.2	100.4	−0.6	99.8	83.7	16.6	10.5
Uruguay	1996	152449	...	99.0	0.4	99.4	87.6	11.9	...
Uruguay	1997	188529	...	99.0	0.4	99.4	87.5	11.9	...
	1998	218145	...	99.1	0.3	99.4	84.7	14.6	...
Vanuatu	1996	28227	...	91.1	...	...	...	...	...
Vanuatu	1997	29477	...	91.7	...	...	...	...	...
	1998	29545	...	93.5	...	...	...	...	...
Venezuela	1997	43344000	−2.7	97.3	−0.2	97.1	72.3	24.8	6.8
Venezuela	1998	52264000	−1.6	98.4	−0.2	98.2	79.8	18.4	7.8
	1999	61918000	−1.2	98.8	0.0	98.8	77.8	21.1	7.6
Yemen	1994	270900	−1.9	98.1	30.5	128.6	99.4	29.3	7.6
Yémen	1995	449271	−3.6	96.4	28.5	124.9	97.8	27.1	8.4
	1996	654036	−12.1	87.9	19.8	107.7	84.5	23.3	10.5
Yugoslavia, SFR †	1988	15833	...	105.0	...	...	64.3	...	12.2
Yougoslavie, SFR †	1989	235395	...	106.9	...	...	61.9	...	12.1
	1990	1147787	...	108.7	...	...	83.7	...	11.2
Zimbabwe	1995	61763	−4.5	95.5	...	...	83.3	16.5	...
Zimbabwe	1996	84767	−3.5	96.5	...	...	76.5	22.8	...
	1997	99737	−5.0	95.0	...	...	87.3	...	...

21
Relationships between the principal national accounting aggregates
As a percentage of GDP *[cont.]*
Relations entre les printicpaux agrégats de comptabilité nationale
En pourcentage du PIB *[suite]*

Source:
United Nations Secretariat, national accounts database
of the Statistics Division.

† For information on recent changes in country or area
nomenclature pertaining to former Czechoslovakia, Germany,
Hong Kong Special Administrative Region (SAR) of China,
Macao Special Administrative Region (SAR) of China,
SFR of Yugoslavia and the former USSR, see Annex I – Country
or area nomenclature, regional and other groupings.

†† For statistical purposes, the data for China do not
include those for the Hong Kong Special Administrative
Region (Hong Kong SAR), Macao Special Administrative
Region (Hong Kong SAR) and Taiwan province of China.

1   Data classified according to 1993 SNA.
2   Data refer to fiscal years beginning 1 July of the year indicated.

3   Data refer to fiscal years beginning 1 April of the year indicated.

4   Data refer to fiscal years ending 7 July of the year indicated.

5   Data refer to fiscal years ending 30 September of the year indicated.

6   Data refer to fiscal years beginning 21 March of the year indicated.

7   Data refer to fiscal years ending 15 July of the year indicated.

8   Data refer to fiscal years ending 30 June of the year indicated.

Source:
Secrétariat de l'Organisation des Nations Unies, la base de données
sur les comptes nationaux de la Division de statistique.

† Pour les modifications récentes de nomenclature de pays
ou de zone concernant l'Allemagne, Hong Kong région
administrative spéciale (RAS) de Chine, Macao région administrati·
spéciale (RAS) de Chine, l'ex–Tchécoslovaquie, l'ex–URSS et l'ex
Rfs de Yougoslavie, voir annex I – Nomenclature des pays ou des
zones, groupements régionaux et autres groupments.

†† Les données statistiques relatives à la Chine ne comprennent
pas celles qui concernent la région administrative spéciale de
Hong Kong (la RAS de Hong Kong), la région administrative
spéciale de Macao (la RAS de Macao) et la province chinoise
de Taiwan.

1   Les données sont classifiées selon le SCN 1993.
2   Les données se réfèrent aux années fiscales commençant le
1er juillet de l'année indiquée.
3   Les données se réfèrent aux années fiscales commençant le
1er avril de l'année indiquée.
4   Les données se réfèrent aux années fiscales finissant le
7e juillet de l'année indiquée.
5   Les données se réfèrent aux années fiscales finissant le
30e septembre de l'année indiquée.
6   Les données se réfèrent aux années fiscales commençant le
21e mars de l'année indiquée.
7   Les données se réfèrent aux années fiscales finissant le
15e juillet de l'année indiquée.
8   Les données se réfèrent aux années fiscales finissant le
30e juin de l'année indiquée.

22
Index numbers of industrial production
Indices de la production industrielle
1990=100

Country or area and industry [ISIC Rev.3] Pays ou zone et industrie [CITI Rév.3]	1992	1993	1994	1995	1996	1997	1998	1999
Africa · Afrique								
Algeria　Algérie								
Total industry [CDE]								
Total, industrie [CDE]	93.3	92.9	86.8	86.0	79.6	77.0	82.2	...
Total mining [C]								
Total, industries extractives [C]	93.1	83.0	80.9	79.7	76.2	69.8	69.0	...
Total manufacturing [D]								
Total, industries manufacturières [D]	88.9	87.5	79.7	78.3	67.8	62.9	68.4	...
Food, beverages, tobacco								
Aliments, boissons, tabac	93.7	99.0	95.0	87.7	83.7	81.9	93.5	...
Textiles,wearing apparel, leather, footwear								
Textiles, habillement, cuir et chaussures	85.9	79.2	72.3	64.6	46.1	41.8	45.5	
Chemicals, petroleum, rubber and plastic prod.								
Prod. chimiques, pétroliers, caoutch. et plast.	96.1	94.7	92.6	94.1	88.6	94.8	93.7	...
Basic metals								
Métaux de base	85.1	93.1	85.5	96.9	64.4	53.4	58.6	...
Metal products								
Produits métalliques	89.0	80.0	64.3	75.0	56.7	45.0	48.1	...
Electricity [E]								
Electricité [E]	114.2	122.7	125.8	125.1	130.7	135.8	147.6	...
Cameroon [1]　Cameroun [1]								
Total industry [DE]								
Total, industrie [DE]	97.5	98.5	99.4	106.7	126.9	124.9	129.2	...
Total manufacturing [D]								
Total, industries manufacturières [D]	95.8	94.8	96.7	106.1	127.5	124.7	128.5	...
Electricity, gas and water [E]								
Electricité, gaz et eau [E]	103.7	110.0	108.8	109.2	118.5	124.2	132.1	
Central African Republic　République centrafricaine								
Total industry [CDE]								
Total, industrie [CDE]	85.7	85.4	93.3	83.9	84.7	...	...	...
Total mining [C]								
Total, industries extractives [C]	97.3	114.5	120.6	110.3	103.4	...	...	...
Total manufacturing [D]								
Total, industries manufacturières [D]	72.4	69.4	65.7	93.2	76.2	...	...	...
Electricity, gas and water [E]								
Electricité, gaz et eau [E]	97.6	100.3	90.2	106.8	103.1	...	...	...
Côte d'Ivoire　Côte d'Ivoire								
Total industry [CDE]								
Total, industrie [CDE]	96.9	97.9	101.0	111.5	125.0	139.6	155.2	159.4
Total mining [C]								
Total, industries extractives [C]	63.6	27.3	27.3	290.9	709.1	654.5	490.9	500.0
Total manufacturing [D]								
Total, industries manufacturières [D]	97.3	97.3	99.1	101.8	108.2	120.9	141.8	142.7
Food, beverages, tobacco								
Aliments, boissons, tabac	127.7	107.2	99.3	97.1	105.1	113.3	123.4	135.6
Textiles and wearing apparel								
Textiles et habillement	91.8	95.9	97.9	128.9	129.9	151.5	211.3	203.1
Chemicals, petroleum, rubber and plastic prod.								
Prod. chimiques, pétroliers, caoutch. et plast.	95.6	90.0	101.6	98.1	104.9	117.7	129.0	123.5
Metal products								
Produits métalliques	85.5	80.6	84.2	98.9	102.8	101.1	111.2	98.7
Electricity and water [E]								
Electricité et eau [E]	96.4	109.9	116.2	139.6	154.1	185.6	188.3	218.9
Egypt [2]　Egypte [2]								
Total industry [CDE]								
Total, industrie [CDE]	100.4	103.3	104.8	105.8	117.5	131.7	...	...
Total mining [C]								
Total, industries extractives [C]	105.0	107.7	108.0	106.1	104.2	120.7	...	...
Total manufacturing [D]								
Total, industries manufacturières [D]	96.5	99.5	101.3	101.2	121.8	135.7	...	...
Food, beverages, tobacco								
Aliments, boissons, tabac	98.6	113.1	118.7	124.4	140.3	146.8	...	...

22
Index numbers of industrial production [*cont.*]
Indices de la production industrielle [*suite*]
1990=100

Country or area and industry [ISIC Rev.3] Pays ou zone et industrie [CITI Rév.3]	1992	1993	1994	1995	1996	1997	1998	1999
Textiles and wearing apparel								
Textiles et habillement	93.6	88.7	89.2	93.4	81.1	105.5	...	...
Chemicals, petroleum, rubber and plastic prod.								
Prod. chimiques, pétroliers, caoutch. et plast.	106.1	105.3	104.3	96.8	121.0	119.3	...	...
Basic metals								
Métaux de base	90.5	89.5	97.0	102.8	124.2	113.1	...	...
Metal products								
Produits métalliques	90.5	92.0	95.3	96.3	131.7	175.6	...	...
Electricity, gas and water [E]								
Electricité, gaz et eau [E]	**119.5**	**125.4**	**126.8**	**129.4**	**136.6**	**143.2**	**...**	**...**
Ethiopia [2] Ethiopie [2]								
Total industry [CDE]								
Total, industrie [CDE]	74.6	96.1	102.1	110.6	115.9	123.1	131.9	143.1
Total mining [C]								
Total, industries extractives [C]	203.1	297.4	234.4	255.2	288.5	326.0	366.7	410.9
Total manufacturing [D]								
Total, industries manufacturières [D]	64.3	87.5	95.2	103.7	111.6	118.1	127.1	134.4
Electricity and water [E]								
Electricité et eau [E]	**102.2**	**113.0**	**119.1**	**125.6**	**116.4**	**123.2**	**127.8**	**152.6**
Gabon Gabon								
Total industry [CDE]								
Total, industrie [CDE]	74.3	71.0	71.0	86.0	87.2	84.4	...	...
Total mining [C]								
Total, industries extractives [C]	66.9	60.0	64.0	81.6	81.3	77.3	...	...
Total manufacturing [D]								
Total, industries manufacturières [D]	104.7	109.7	97.3	102.9	108.2	107.8	...	...
Food, beverages, tobacco								
Aliments, boissons, tabac	105.1	107.2	96.0	99.4	103.4	103.8	...	...
Textiles								
Textiles	84.9	78.7	55.8	61.4	48.7	44.5	...	...
Chemicals and chemical products								
Produits chimiques	110.6	100.7	96.1	101.1	101.1	89.5	...	...
Electricity and water [E]								
Electricité et eau [E]	**104.3**	**104.3**	**104.3**	**105.8**	**120.9**	**127.9**	**...**	**...**
Ghana Ghana								
Total industry [CDE] [3]								
Total, industrie [CDE] [3]	128.3	143.1	161.4	176.6	183.6	170.9	...	...
Total mining [C]								
Total, industries extractives [C]	177.5	200.2	216.8	250.9	251.7	274.2	...	...
Total manufacturing [D]								
Total, industries manufacturières [D]	121.1	137.5	159.4	173.1	181.1	159.1	...	...
Food, beverages, tobacco								
Aliments, boissons, tabac	103.9	116.3	118.6	121.7	126.7	133.0	...	...
Textiles,wearing apparel, leather, footwear								
Textiles, habillement, cuir et chaussures	62.9	159.7	127.3	145.4	148.8	147.2	...	...
Chemicals, petroleum, rubber and plastic prod.								
Prod. chimiques, pétroliers, caoutch. et plast.	95.0	81.2	175.4	188.9	197.0	209.1	...	...
Basic metals								
Métaux de base	293.4	307.0	364.2	414.3	421.2	447.1	...	...
Metal products								
Produits métalliques	156.9	185.9	203.6	182.1	210.7	221.6	...	...
Electricity [E]								
Electricité [E]	**113.8**	**107.9**	**104.8**	**105.7**	**114.3**	**118.7**	**...**	**...**
Kenya Kenya								
Total industry [CD] [3]								
Total, industrie [CD] [3]	103.8	106.0	107.8	111.7	117.2	124.9	135.9	...
Total mining [C]								
Total, industries extractives [C]	87.8	103.5	95.7	100.4	121.0	142.7	144.6	...
Total manufacturing [D]								
Total, industries manufacturières [D]	104.2	106.1	108.1	112.0	117.1	124.5	135.8	...
Food, beverages, tobacco								
Aliments, boissons, tabac	103.3	103.1	100.8	113.4	110.1	109.9	111.9	...
Textiles,wearing apparel, leather, footwear								
Textiles, habillement, cuir et chaussures	102.8	109.9	86.6	63.1	60.3	56.5	55.7	...

22
Index numbers of industrial production [*cont.*]
Indices de la production industrielle [*suite*]
1990=100

Country or area and industry [ISIC Rev.3] Pays ou zone et industrie [CITI Rév.3]	1992	1993	1994	1995	1996	1997	1998	1999
Chemicals, petroleum, rubber and plastic prod.								
Prod. chimiques, pétroliers, caoutch. et plast.	143.9	144.9	140.8	147.5	153.7	170.4	177.9	...
Metal products								
Produits métalliques	113.9	105.8	113.6	117.0	138.2	138.8	121.1	...
Malawi Malawi								
Total industry [DE]								
Total, industrie [DE]	**103.9**	**98.0**	**93.2**	**94.5**	**97.8**	**97.0**	**93.9**	**85.4**
Total manufacturing [D]								
Total, industries manufacturières [D]	**102.2**	**95.1**	**88.2**	**89.7**	**92.8**	**89.8**	**84.6**	**72.8**
Food, beverages, tobacco								
Aliments, boissons, tabac	97.7	99.7	101.2	96.2	97.9	99.1	99.1	48.1
Textiles,wearing apparel, leather, footwear								
Textiles, habillement, cuir et chaussures	129.4	103.1	93.4	73.7	67.2	107.6	107.6	163.7
Electricity and water [E]								
Electricité et eau [E]	**113.3**	**114.4**	**121.2**	**121.0**	**125.2**	**136.4**	**145.6**	**143.6**
Mali Mali								
Total industry [DE]								
Total, industrie [DE]	**105.2**	**93.3**	**102.8**	**124.7**	**132.4**	**151.5**	**174.7**	**166.3**
Food, beverages, tobacco								
Aliments, boissons, tabac	104.3	90.9	93.5	93.2	97.2	102.6	97.2	92.0
Wearing apparel								
Habillement	87.3	128.9	108.6	121.4	131.5	168.0	171.6	147.8
Chemicals and chemical products								
Produits chimiques	82.9	78.4	80.2	87.6	98.6	93.3	88.6	79.9
Morocco Maroc								
Total industry [CD] [3]								
Total, industrie [CD] [3]	**103.0**	**102.6**	**108.2**	**112.3**	**116.0**	**121.6**	**124.1**	**125.5**
Total mining [C] [4]								
Total, industries extractives [C] [4]	**91.7**	**90.1**	**98.1**	**96.9**	**99.3**	**108.1**	**106.4**	**104.1**
Total manufacturing [D] [5]								
Total, industries manufacturières [D] [5]	**104.2**	**103.6**	**108.0**	**111.6**	**115.1**	**119.9**	**122.9**	**125.7**
Food, beverages, tobacco								
Aliments, boissons, tabac	97.8	98.3	107.1	108.9	113.4	113.1	117.6	116.5
Textiles,wearing apparel, leather, footwear								
Textiles, habillement, cuir et chaussures	105.8	105.3	107.4	111.6	115.2	121.7	124.4	122.6
Chemicals, petroleum, rubber and plastic prod.								
Prod. chimiques, pétroliers, caoutch. et plast.	103.7	105.2	110.3	108.2	107.8	115.5	115.1	126.9
Basic metals								
Métaux de base	103.6	99.6	101.3	114.6	112.5	126.7	125.3	139.8
Metal products								
Produits métalliques	105.6	102.8	104.2	106.3	108.9	114.1	112.7	119.2
Electricity [E]								
Electricité [E]	**105.3**	**107.5**	**118.6**	**130.3**	**136.0**	**144.8**	**146.7**	**142.9**
Namibia Namibie								
Total industry [CDE]								
Total, industrie [CDE]	**125.6**	**104.4**	**115.4**	**...**	**...**	**...**	**...**	**...**
Total mining [C]								
Total, industries extractives [C]	**133.0**	**104.0**	**115.0**	**...**	**...**	**...**	**...**	**...**
Total manufacturing [D]								
Total, industries manufacturières [D]	**103.9**	**118.3**	**128.8**	**...**	**...**	**...**	**...**	**...**
Electricity and water [E]								
Electricité et eau [E]	**126.5**	**59.3**	**72.8**	**...**	**...**	**...**	**...**	**...**
Nigeria Nigéria								
Total industry [CDE]								
Total, industrie [CDE]	**104.3**	**100.8**	**98.9**	**98.5**	**101.3**	**107.6**	**102.5**	**...**
Total mining [C]								
Total, industries extractives [C]	**104.2**	**108.3**	**105.2**	**108.1**	**112.1**	**122.9**	**116.5**	**...**
Total manufacturing [D]								
Total, industries manufacturières [D]	**104.1**	**89.3**	**88.5**	**83.7**	**84.7**	**85.0**	**81.7**	**...**
Electricity [E]								
Electricité [E]	**111.5**	**113.9**	**122.4**	**120.4**	**117.5**	**115.1**	**111.0**	**...**
Senegal Sénégal								
Total industry [CDE]								
Total, industrie [CDE]	**93.8**	**87.9**	**89.0**	**103.4**	**99.7**	**101.5**	**105.5**	**107.6**

22
Index numbers of industrial production [*cont.*]
Indices de la production industrielle [*suite*]
1990=100

Country or area and industry [ISIC Rev.3] Pays ou zone et industrie [CITI Rév.3]	1992	1993	1994	1995	1996	1997	1998	1999
Total mining [C]								
Total, industries extractives [C]	**102.3**	**78.8**	**74.4**	**75.4**	**74.9**	**84.0**	**80.7**	**93.4**
Total manufacturing [D] [3]								
Total, industries manufacturières [D] [3]	**93.8**	**87.9**	**89.0**	**103.4**	**99.7**	**101.5**	**105.5**	**107.6**
Food, beverages, tobacco								
Aliments, boissons, tabac	84.7	88.3	90.9	98.9	88.3	82.1	90.5	92.5
Textiles								
Textiles	88.7	73.6	75.2	66.0	71.4	70.9	69.0	55.5
Chemicals, petroleum, rubber and plastic prod.								
Prod. chimiques, pétroliers, caoutch. et plast.	108.1	106.4	98.2	128.2	119.4	137.2	136.6	124.8
Metal products								
Produits métalliques	85.1	90.6	92.1	125.7	118.6	118.3	121.5	123.7
Electricity and water [E]								
Electricité et eau [E]	**108.9**	**104.2**	**110.3**	**116.2**	**120.0**	**130.9**	**136.9**	**140.8**
South Africa Afrique du Sud								
Total industry [CDE] [3]								
Total, industrie [CDE] [3]	**95.4**	**97.1**	**98.8**	**102.9**	**103.8**	**107.2**	**104.7**	**104.2**
Total mining [C]								
Total, industries extractives [C]	**99.5**	**102.4**	**100.9**	**100.1**	**98.4**	**100.4**	**99.4**	**97.5**
Total manufacturing [D]								
Total, industries manufacturières [D]	**92.8**	**93.9**	**96.3**	**102.5**	**104.0**	**106.9**	**103.6**	**103.8**
Food and beverages								
Aliments et boissons	101.8	98.9	99.5	103.5	105.1	105.6	104.3	103.1
Textiles, wearing apparel, leather, footwear								
Textiles, habillement, cuir et chaussures	93.4	96.6	102.5	110.6	104.4	108.3	100.0	99.1
Chemicals, petroleum, rubber and plastic prod.								
Prod. chimiques, pétroliers, caoutch. et plast.	98.8	102.9	105.8	111.6	112.1	115.0	114.2	117.3
Basic metals								
Métaux de base	87.5	87.8	95.0	109.8	119.2	124.2	120.8	123.4
Metal products								
Produits métalliques	90.2	89.5	94.0	105.3	108.3	112.0	107.6	106.2
Electricity [E]								
Electricité [E]	**101.6**	**105.6**	**109.9**	**112.9**	**121.0**	**127.2**	**124.2**	**122.8**
Swaziland Swaziland								
Total industry [CDE] [3]								
Total, industrie [CDE] [3]	**101.3**	**102.5**	**108.5**	**113.2**	**114.4**	...	...	...
Total mining [C]								
Total, industries extractives [C]	**95.7**	**99.3**	**106.4**	**102.8**	**103.5**	...	...	...
Total manufacturing [D]								
Total, industries manufacturières [D]	**100.5**	**101.4**	**107.5**	**112.7**	**112.7**	...	...	...
Electricity, gas and water [E]								
Electricité, gaz et eau [E]	**114.7**	**119.3**	**122.0**	**123.9**	**140.4**	...	...	...
Tunisia Tunisie								
Total industry [CDE]								
Total, industrie [CDE]	**111.8**	**112.1**	**117.7**	**121.4**	**124.7**	**130.1**	**138.9**	**145.9**
Total mining [C]								
Total, industries extractives [C]	**111.9**	**100.4**	**96.5**	**97.6**	**102.9**	**100.1**	**107.2**	**110.2**
Total manufacturing [D]								
Total, industries manufacturières [D]	**112.1**	**116.4**	**125.7**	**130.0**	**132.5**	**140.7**	**150.4**	**158.4**
Food, beverages, tobacco								
Aliments, boissons, tabac	116.8	112.5	118.4	116.7	121.7	136.2	136.3	147.7
Textiles, wearing apparel, leather, footwear								
Textiles, habillement, cuir et chaussures	117.1	130.7	145.4	157.4	158.3	166.2	179.7	184.8
Chemicals, petroleum, rubber and plastic prod.								
Prod. chimiques, pétroliers, caoutch. et plast.	108.1	109.3	121.2	128.6	134.5	138.6	149.3	151.7
Basic metals								
Métaux de base	97.6	99.3	96.5	96.3	97.1	101.1	96.6	115.2
Metal products								
Produits métalliques	112.6	111.9	121.6	120.6	127.8	135.4	156.4	172.6
Electricity and water [E]								
Electricité et eau [E]	**108.4**	**113.0**	**119.6**	**126.0**	**128.7**	**136.5**	**144.3**	**157.1**
Uganda Ouganda								
Total manufacturing [D]								
Total, industries manufacturières [D]	**123.0**	**138.6**	**167.4**	**212.8**	**247.2**	**293.3**	**323.4**	**354.3**

22
Index numbers of industrial production [*cont.*]
Indices de la production industrielle [*suite*]
1990=100

Country or area and industry [ISIC Rev.3] Pays ou zone et industrie [CITI Rév.3]	1992	1993	1994	1995	1996	1997	1998	1999
Food, beverages, tobacco								
Aliments, boissons, tabac	122.0	126.7	163.2	203.2	248.5	255.9	286.2	300.0
Textiles,wearing apparel, leather, footwear								
Textiles, habillement, cuir et chaussures	95.9	80.8	69.2	86.2	92.1	125.8	130.4	130.0
Chemicals, rubber and plastic prod.								
Prod. chimiques, caoutchouc et plastiques	150.1	212.0	259.3	376.2	388.9	526.3	586.4	665.6
Basic metals								
Métaux de base	177.1	240.5	362.0	455.4	446.3	416.2	481.1	577.6
Metal products								
Produits métalliques	112.2	307.6	361.9	381.2	486.3	402.7	278.9	264.5
United Rep. Tanzania Rép.−Unie de Tanzanie								
Total manufacturing [D]								
Total, industries manufacturières [D]	**96.5**	**96.5**	**87.8**	**91.2**	**92.1**	**97.4**	**105.3**	...
Food, beverages, tobacco								
Aliments, boissons, tabac	108.3	99.8	90.5	93.8	107.1	121.2	125.1	...
Textiles, leather and footwear								
Textiles, cuir et chaussures	85.5	81.2	68.2	65.6	63.2	58.9	69.1	...
Chemicals, rubber and plastic prod.								
Prod. chimiques, caoutchouc et plastiques	86.2	83.8	92.1	82.0	70.7	68.9	73.4	...
Basic metals								
Métaux de base	112.4	128.6	105.7	45.7	14.3	13.3	37.1	...
Metal products								
Produits métalliques	73.6	42.8	45.5	33.9	38.8	35.7	33.4	...
Zambia Zambie								
Total industry [CDE] [3]								
Total, industrie [CDE] [3]	**101.0**	**92.3**	**80.6**	**75.5**	**77.3**	**79.4**	**80.5**	**69.0**
Total mining [C]								
Total, industries extractives [C]	**102.0**	**93.2**	**77.2**	**69.1**	**79.0**	**79.1**	**89.5**	**66.9**
Total manufacturing [D]								
Total, industries manufacturières [D]	**100.3**	**89.2**	**80.6**	**78.5**	**71.9**	**74.5**	**64.4**	**65.6**
Food, beverages, tobacco								
Aliments, boissons, tabac	129.4	124.8	121.5	127.1	94.6	66.1	63.0	69.0
Textiles and wearing apparel								
Textiles et habillement	80.9	57.1	54.1	48.0	61.5	104.6	79.1	86.0
Chemicals, petroleum, rubber and plastic prod.								
Prod. chimiques, pétroliers, caoutch. et plast.	82.4	86.5	66.7	60.0	83.4	69.3	67.7	57.8
Basic metals								
Métaux de base	119.5	116.2	108.9	103.7	81.8	68.9	77.1	79.3
Metal products								
Produits métalliques	98.8	74.8	63.8	67.0	45.5	43.8	46.9	39.0
Electricity and water [E]								
Electricité et eau [E]	**97.9**	**101.2**	**104.7**	**106.4**	**91.9**	**106.5**	**97.9**	**101.9**
Zimbabwe Zimbabwe								
Total industry [CDE] [3]								
Total, industrie [CDE] [3]	**94.7**	**87.8**	**97.2**	**89.4**	**90.2**	**91.8**	**90.7**	...
Total mining [C]								
Total, industries extractives [C]	**100.1**	**96.2**	**109.3**	**116.0**	**111.4**	**110.8**	**119.7**	**113.9**
Total manufacturing [D]								
Total, industries manufacturières [D]	**93.4**	**85.8**	**94.0**	**81.2**	**84.0**	**86.7**	**82.6**	**78.4**
Food, beverages, tobacco								
Aliments, boissons, tabac	103.7	92.7	94.7	94.2	96.0	99.3	100.7	96.3
Textiles,wearing apparel, leather, footwear								
Textiles, habillement, cuir et chaussures	83.3	88.5	91.6	50.3	50.5	50.5	51.6	52.7
Chemicals, petroleum, rubber and plastic prod.								
Prod. chimiques, pétroliers, caoutch. et plast.	87.0	81.5	93.6	84.1	86.2	118.0	88.2	84.6
Basic metals and metal products								
Métaux de base et produtis métalliques	91.2	71.2	83.8	81.4	88.4	92.6	78.9	66.6
Electricity [E]								
Electricité [E]	**89.0**	**78.5**	**86.8**	**83.3**	**80.1**	**78.3**	**73.1**	...
America, North · Amérique du Nord								
Barbados Barbade								
Total industry [CDE]								
Total, industrie [CDE]	**91.0**	**88.5**	**93.4**	**100.3**	**101.1**	**105.2**	**112.5**	**113.2**

22
Index numbers of industrial production [*cont.*]
Indices de la production industrielle [*suite*]
1990=100

Country or area and industry [ISIC Rev.3] Pays ou zone et industrie [CITI Rév.3]	1992	1993	1994	1995	1996	1997	1998	1999
Total mining [C]								
Total, industries extractives [C]	**87.6**	**87.6**	**90.3**	**90.8**	**90.9**	**94.3**	**128.4**	**149.6**
Total manufacturing [D]								
Total, industries manufacturières [D]	**89.1**	**85.9**	**91.0**	**98.4**	**98.5**	**102.6**	**107.3**	**105.4**
Food, beverages, tobacco								
Aliments, boissons, tabac	101.3	104.5	109.2	114.3	116.4	123.4	132.2	128.7
Wearing apparel								
Habillement	52.3	44.1	26.9	24.6	22.4	23.2	17.0	16.0
Chemicals, petroleum products								
Produits chimiques et pétroliers	78.6	81.4	80.5	94.9	96.4	110.5	54.4	48.1
Metal products								
Produits métalliques	128.6	102.3	94.1	102.2	108.8	105.6	89.4	82.6
Electricity and gas [E]								
Electricité et gaz [E]	**103.8**	**104.3**	**108.4**	**115.8**	**120.2**	**124.8**	**135.8**	**143.1**
Belize Belize								
Total industry [DE]								
Total, industrie [DE]	**106.4**	**111.5**	**118.4**	**122.7**	**123.1**	**129.9**	**124.5**	...
Total manufacturing [D]								
Total, industries manufacturières [D]	**105.0**	**109.3**	**115.9**	**120.2**	**120.4**	**126.4**	**118.2**	...
Food, beverages, tobacco								
Aliments, boissons, tabac	104.6	108.5	115.9	123.5	124.2	131.5	122.2	...
Wearing apparel								
Habillement	113.3	118.9	91.8	54.9	55.3	55.4	59.6	...
Chemicals and chemical products								
Produits chimiques	128.0	162.5	249.3	241.8	224.8	195.6	193.8	...
Metal products								
Produits métalliques	57.0	43.0	33.3	27.4	22.1	18.4	15.5	...
Electricity and water [E]								
Electricité et eau [E]	**120.0**	**132.4**	**141.7**	**146.4**	**148.9**	**163.5**	**185.1**	...
Canada Canada								
Total industry [CDE]								
Total, industrie [CDE]	**97.0**	**101.3**	**107.9**	**112.8**	**114.3**	**119.3**	**122.2**	**127.6**
Total mining [C]								
Total, industries extractives [C]	**107.3**	**111.5**	**116.7**	**120.7**	**122.2**	**126.0**	**123.8**	**119.6**
Total manufacturing [D]								
Total, industries manufacturières [D]	**93.8**	**98.6**	**106.1**	**111.4**	**112.8**	**119.3**	**124.2**	**132.0**
Food, beverages, tobacco								
Aliments, boissons, tabac	102.6	102.7	106.1	107.2	106.5	105.8	109.5	111.2
Textiles,wearing apparel, leather, footwear								
Textiles, habillement, cuir et chaussures	93.5	96.0	102.4	108.5	106.0	113.7	113.3	112.6
Chemicals, petroleum, rubber and plastic prod.								
Prod. chimiques, pétroliers, caoutch. et plast.	94.4	101.2	108.6	112.2	115.9	120.7	126.6	132.6
Basic metals								
Métaux de base	106.7	113.0	114.1	116.9	119.2	125.8	126.9	129.1
Metal products								
Produits métalliques	89.2	98.8	112.8	125.3	125.4	137.8	146.5	163.5
Electricity, gas and water [E]								
Electricité, gaz et eau [E]	**101.6**	**104.4**	**107.4**	**111.6**	**114.0**	**113.0**	**111.4**	**114.8**
Costa Rica Costa Rica								
Total industry [DE] [3]								
Total, industrie [DE] [3]	**110.9**	**118.8**	**123.6**	**128.2**	**124.4**	...	...	...
Total manufacturing [D]								
Total, industries manufacturières [D]	**111.0**	**119.0**	**122.9**	**127.6**	**122.5**	**129.4**	...	...
Food, beverages, tobacco								
Aliments, boissons, tabac	111.2	120.6	120.2	129.2	126.4	129.6	139.1	...
Textiles,wearing apparel, leather, footwear								
Textiles, habillement, cuir et chaussures	104.6	106.7	99.0	96.7	85.0	88.8	93.4	...
Chemicals, petroleum, rubber and plastic prod.								
Prod. chimiques, pétroliers, caoutch. et plast.	121.1	128.3	149.2	157.9	149.7	152.4	158.2	...
Metal products								
Produits métalliques	118.8	134.4	146.3	143.2	137.0	151.8	157.7	...
Electricity and water [E]								
Electricité et eau [E]	**110.5**	**117.7**	**127.4**	**131.4**	**135.0**	...	...	...

22
Index numbers of industrial production [*cont.*]
Indices de la production industrielle [*suite*]
1990=100

Country or area and industry [ISIC Rev.3] Pays ou zone et industrie [CITI Rév.3]	1992	1993	1994	1995	1996	1997	1998	1999
Dominican Republic Rép. dominicaine								
Total industry [CDE]								
Total, industrie [CDE]	**114.8**	**110.8**	**120.7**	**123.8**	**128.4**	**137.4**	**143.4**	**152.2**
Total mining [C]								
Total, industries extractives [C]	**77.6**	**49.7**	**93.5**	**102.3**	**104.7**	**108.0**	**90.8**	**89.4**
Total manufacturing [D]								
Total, industries manufacturières [D]	**120.0**	**118.2**	**122.3**	**125.1**	**129.1**	**138.6**	**147.1**	**157.0**
Electricity [E]								
Electricité [E]	**134.8**	**155.8**	**161.6**	**155.1**	**171.0**	**188.3**	**214.2**	**231.3**
El Salvador El Salvador								
Total industry [CDE]								
Total, industrie [CDE]	**113.2**	**111.8**	**120.1**	**128.3**	**131.0**	**141.4**	**150.8**	**156.3**
Total mining [C]								
Total, industries extractives [C]	**115.3**	**127.5**	**141.4**	**150.9**	**152.5**	**162.3**	**170.9**	**176.1**
Total manufacturing [D]								
Total, industries manufacturières [D]	**116.4**	**114.6**	**123.0**	**131.5**	**133.8**	**144.5**	**154.0**	**159.7**
Food, beverages, tobacco								
Aliments, boissons, tabac	110.3	110.7	116.4	121.1	123.0	128.3	134.6	104.0
Textiles,wearing apparel, leather, footwear								
Textiles, habillement, cuir et chaussures	112.6	101.3	102.7	112.1	110.3	117.0	121.3	124.3
Chemicals, petroleum, rubber and plastic prod.								
Prod. chimiques, pétroliers, caoutch. et plast.	129.6	115.3	127.8	132.4	130.7	137.1	151.0	156.2
Basic metals and metal products								
Métaux de base et produtis métalliques	109.3	104.5	113.7	126.9	137.4	144.7	158.7	167.5
Electricity [E]								
Electricité [E]	**28.4**	**31.6**	**34.2**	**36.3**	**50.5**	**51.5**	**57.5**	**58.1**
Guatemala Guatemala								
Total industry [CDE]								
Total, industrie [CDE]	**107.9**	**112.4**	**116.2**	**121.2**	**125.0**	...	...	...
Total mining [C]								
Total, industries extractives [C]	**140.6**	**156.2**	**162.9**	**185.6**	**229.9**	...	...	...
Total manufacturing [D]								
Total, industries manufacturières [D]	**105.7**	**108.8**	**112.0**	**115.6**	**117.8**	...	...	...
Food, beverages, tobacco								
Aliments, boissons, tabac	106.1	109.3	112.7	116.8	119.4	...	...	...
Textiles,wearing apparel, leather, footwear								
Textiles, habillement, cuir et chaussures	105.6	108.6	111.9	114.5	116.1	...	...	...
Chemicals, rubber and plastic products								
Prod. chimiques, caoutchouc et plastiques	105.6	108.8	112.4	116.4	118.6	...	...	...
Basic metals and metal products								
Métaux de base et produtis métalliques	105.3	108.3	111.6	115.1	117.2	...	...	...
Electricity and water [E]								
Electricité et eau [E]	**118.1**	**129.5**	**136.8**	**148.6**	**157.5**	...	...	...
Haiti [6] Haïti [6]								
Total manufacturing [D]								
Total, industries manufacturières [D]	**55.3**	**45.6**	**32.7**	**39.2**	**42.7**	**46.8**	**45.0**	...
Food, beverages, tobacco								
Aliments, boissons, tabac	55.9	44.6	43.7	42.3	52.4	56.6	...	...
Chemicals and chemical products								
Produits chimiques	113.0	109.7	100.1	126.6	224.6	240.0	...	...
Honduras Honduras								
Total industry [CDE]								
Total, industrie [CDE]	**107.7**	**114.4**	**111.9**	**119.7**	**127.3**	**135.2**	**140.4**	**144.5**
Total mining [C]								
Total, industries extractives [C]	**115.3**	**119.4**	**122.2**	**133.3**	**143.1**	**150.0**	**158.3**	**170.8**
Total manufacturing [D]								
Total, industries manufacturières [D]	**107.9**	**114.4**	**112.6**	**118.8**	**124.3**	**131.9**	**136.4**	**139.9**
Food, beverages, tobacco								
Aliments, boissons, tabac	146.1	160.9	207.1	261.0	316.1	388.0	427.5	481.5
Textiles,wearing apparel, leather, footwear								
Textiles, habillement, cuir et chaussures	169.0	182.4	218.8	301.5	401.3	483.4	539.4	607.1
Chemicals, petroleum, rubber and plastic prod.								
Prod. chimiques, pétroliers, caoutch. et plast.	140.8	157.6	190.3	287.8	298.0	358.4	415.2	467.3

22
Index numbers of industrial production [*cont.*]
Indices de la production industrielle [*suite*]
1990=100

Country or area and industry [ISIC Rev.3] Pays ou zone et industrie [CITI Rév.3]	1992	1993	1994	1995	1996	1997	1998	1999
Basic metals								
Métaux de base	113.3	122.2	147.8	200.6	231.6	277.5	288.2	324.3
Metal products								
Produits métalliques	114.3	126.2	159.8	193.2	226.0	256.9	291.9	328.5
Electricity, gas and water [E]								
Electricité, gaz et eau [E]	**101.6**	**109.4**	**101.6**	**116.4**	**134.4**	**144.5**	**151.6**	**153.9**
Mexico Mexique								
Total industry [CDE] [7]								
Total, industrie [CDE] [7]	**107.9**	**108.2**	**113.4**	**104.5**	**115.2**	**125.8**	**133.7**	**138.7**
Total mining [C]								
Total, industries extractives [C]	**102.3**	**104.2**	**107.3**	**104.0**	**112.4**	**117.4**	**120.6**	**116.7**
Total manufacturing [D]								
Total, industries manufacturières [D]	**107.8**	**107.1**	**111.5**	**105.9**	**117.3**	**129.0**	**138.5**	**144.2**
Food, beverages, tobacco								
Aliments, boissons, tabac	107.4	110.9	114.5	114.5	118.4	122.2	130.3	136.9
Textiles and wearing apparel								
Textiles et habillement	102.5	99.7	100.8	94.4	109.2	120.6	125.0	128.3
Chemicals, petroleum, rubber and plastic prod.								
Prod. chimiques, pétroliers, caoutch. et plast.	102.8	101.0	104.4	103.5	110.3	117.8	124.9	128.4
Basic metals								
Métaux de base	96.8	99.8	106.0	110.3	130.9	145.5	151.3	150.9
Metal products								
Produits métalliques	114.9	110.1	117.5	105.4	129.0	153.5	171.0	180.8
Electricity, gas and water [E]								
Electricité, gaz et eau [E]	**103.5**	**106.2**	**111.3**	**113.6**	**118.8**	**125.1**	**127.3**	**132.9**
Panama Panama								
Total industry [CDE] [3]								
Total, industrie [CDE] [3]	**115.6**	**124.1**	**129.4**	**131.4**	**134.4**	**144.2**	**150.1**	**147.2**
Total mining [C]								
Total, industries extractives [C]	**258.9**	**318.0**	**351.9**	**341.9**	**277.0**	**534.0**	**674.3**	**691.9**
Total manufacturing [D]								
Total, industries manufacturières [D]	**117.6**	**125.7**	**129.9**	**130.1**	**130.5**	**137.9**	**143.6**	**137.6**
Food, beverages, tobacco								
Aliments, boissons, tabac	109.6	116.1	122.4	121.5	125.3	133.7	143.5	135.2
Textiles,wearing apparel, leather, footwear								
Textiles, habillement, cuir et chaussures	117.6	119.7	113.2	112.0	101.4	96.2	90.9	78.4
Chemicals, petroleum, rubber and plastic prod.								
Prod. chimiques, pétroliers, caoutch. et plast.	134.7	131.1	119.9	128.3	153.8	158.6	165.6	165.7
Basic metals								
Métaux de base	169.4	196.0	170.0	202.4	226.9	301.3	251.5	358.4
Metal products								
Produits métalliques	107.3	120.4	129.3	140.5	146.9	157.7	168.1	157.5
Electricity and water [E]								
Electricité et eau [E]	**108.5**	**117.0**	**124.5**	**129.6**	**141.0**	**152.5**	**156.6**	**160.5**
Trinidad and Tobago Trinité−et−Tobago								
Total industry [DE]								
Total, industrie [DE]	**122.3**	**114.5**	**130.7**	**140.6**	**148.6**	**157.9**	**176.2**	**207.6**
Total manufacturing [D] [3]								
Total, industries manufacturières [D] [3]	**122.6**	**114.6**	**131.2**	**141.2**	**149.3**	**158.8**	**177.1**	**209.2**
Food, beverages, tobacco								
Aliments, boissons, tabac	100.3	93.6	103.6	104.0	104.8	107.4	159.5	191.5
Textiles, leather and footwear								
Textiles, cuir et chaussures	85.5	56.9	48.6	46.8	47.5	67.8	96.5	231.7
Chemicals and petroleum products								
Produits chimiques et pétroliers	100.3	91.0	90.9	82.9	90.8	119.4	171.3	200.4
Metal products								
Produits métalliques	142.0	124.3	133.4	145.5	174.0	158.0	214.7	220.0
Electricity [E]								
Electricité [E]	**111.3**	**110.3**	**116.6**	**122.3**	**125.5**	**130.0**	**147.0**	**155.4**
United States Etats−Unis								
Total industry [CDE]								
Total, industrie [CDE]	**101.1**	**104.6**	**110.3**	**115.7**	**120.7**	**128.5**	**133.9**	**138.6**
Total mining [C]								
Total, industries extractives [C]	**95.4**	**95.3**	**97.7**	**97.3**	**99.0**	**101.0**	**99.2**	**93.5**

22

Index numbers of industrial production [*cont.*]

Indices de la production industrielle [*suite*]

1990=100

Country or area and industry [ISIC Rev.3] Pays ou zone et industrie [CITI Rév.3]	1992	1993	1994	1995	1996	1997	1998	1999
Total manufacturing [D]								
Total, industries manufacturières [D]	**101.5**	**105.3**	**111.7**	**117.6**	**123.1**	**132.1**	**138.5**	**144.5**
Food, beverages, tobacco								
Aliments, boissons, tabac	102.0	101.9	105.8	108.7	108.5	110.5	111.1	110.4
Textiles,wearing apparel, leather, footwear								
Textiles, habillement, cuir et chaussures	103.8	107.4	111.2	110.9	108.7	108.7	104.9	101.2
Chemicals, petroleum, rubber and plastic prod.								
Prod. chimiques, pétroliers, caoutch. et plast.	103.6	106.7	111.2	113.8	116.6	121.5	123.3	126.1
Basic metals								
Métaux de base	96.2	101.1	109.5	111.7	115.0	121.8	120.8	121.8
Metal products								
Produits métalliques	101.3	107.0	116.4	127.6	139.8	157.2	176.2	196.5
Electricity and gas [E]								
Electricité et gaz [E]	**101.7**	**105.7**	**107.1**	**110.9**	**114.5**	**114.6**	**116.4**	**117.6**
America, South · Amérique du Sud								
Argentina Argentine								
Total manufacturing [D]								
Total, industries manufacturières [D]	**124.5**	**128.7**	**134.6**	**125.2**	**133.2**	**145.7**	**148.6**	**136.3**
Food, beverages, tobacco								
Aliments, boissons, tabac	123.6	124.1	133.0	135.1	135.6	142.5	149.9	151.3
Textiles,wearing apparel, leather, footwear								
Textiles, habillement, cuir et chaussures	116.9	102.7	107.4	99.1	109.0	106.3	96.1	81.4
Chemicals, petroleum, rubber and plastic prod.								
Prod. chimiques, pétroliers, caoutch. et plast.	124.3	132.4	140.5	128.9	141.4	154.2	157.0	148.2
Basic metals								
Métaux de base	85.6	90.2	98.9	104.5	116.7	129.8	132.1	114.0
Metal products								
Produits métalliques	147.1	161.5	167.5	138.0	152.1	179.0	185.4	142.7
Bolivia Bolivie								
Total industry [CDE] [3]								
Total, industrie [CDE] [3]	**109.4**	**120.2**	**121.9**	**136.1**	**135.5**	**139.5**	**142.4**	**136.8**
Total mining [C]								
Total, industries extractives [C]	**109.7**	**123.7**	**120.2**	**142.0**	**135.3**	**137.2**	**136.6**	**127.2**
Total manufacturing [D]								
Total, industries manufacturières [D]	**108.7**	**115.9**	**122.4**	**127.9**	**133.2**	**138.8**	**144.9**	**142.8**
Food, beverages, tobacco								
Aliments, boissons, tabac	110.2	116.5	120.6	127.6	134.7	135.4	141.9	146.4
Textiles,wearing apparel, leather, footwear								
Textiles, habillement, cuir et chaussures	117.3	142.2	155.8	172.6	176.1	194.7	198.6	180.2
Chemicals, petroleum, rubber and plastic prod.								
Prod. chimiques, pétroliers, caoutch. et plast.	101.8	101.0	110.7	116.5	132.3	147.6	149.8	156.5
Basic metals								
Métaux de base	119.3	130.4	134.0	102.5	95.7	111.1	86.8	89.1
Metal products								
Produits métalliques	111.1	116.3	135.9	131.9	121.3	122.6	125.2	118.5
Electricity, gas and water [E]								
Electricité, gaz et eau [E]	**113.4**	**123.7**	**142.0**	**155.5**	**170.0**	**184.2**	**196.2**	**204.6**
Brazil Brésil								
Total industry [CD]								
Total, industrie [CD]	**93.8**	**100.8**	**108.5**	**110.4**	**112.4**	**116.7**	**114.3**	**113.6**
Total mining [C]								
Total, industries extractives [C]	**101.7**	**102.3**	**107.2**	**110.7**	**121.5**	**130.3**	**146.4**	**159.8**
Total manufacturing [D]								
Total, industries manufacturières [D]	**93.7**	**101.3**	**109.2**	**111.0**	**112.3**	**116.3**	**112.6**	**110.7**
Food, beverages, tobacco								
Aliments, boissons, tabac	104.4	106.2	108.2	117.0	122.3	124.8	123.7	126.3
Textiles,wearing apparel, leather, footwear								
Textiles, habillement, cuir et chaussures	89.3	93.3	94.3	88.3	84.5	78.9	74.4	74.1
Chemicals, petroleum, rubber and plastic prod.								
Prod. chimiques, pétroliers, caoutch. et plast.	91.9	96.7	102.6	103.5	109.1	114.3	116.8	116.9
Basic metals and metal products								
Métaux de base et produtis métalliques	88.0	100.5	116.2	121.9	122.4	127.3	116.3	108.5

22
Index numbers of industrial production [*cont.*]
Indices de la production industrielle [*suite*]
1990=100

Country or area and industry [ISIC Rev.3] Pays ou zone et industrie [CITI Rév.3]	1992	1993	1994	1995	1996	1997	1998	1999
Chile Chili								
Total industry [CDE] [3]								
Total, industrie [CDE] [3]	**119.1**	**122.4**	**127.0**	**136.5**	**148.3**	**158.5**	**163.1**	**171.9**
Total mining [C]								
Total, industries extractives [C]	**118.5**	**123.2**	**131.4**	**146.2**	**178.8**	**197.1**	**209.3**	**240.6**
Total manufacturing [D]								
Total, industries manufacturières [D]	**119.0**	**121.5**	**124.1**	**131.8**	**135.4**	**142.3**	**143.6**	**143.2**
Food, beverages, tobacco								
Aliments, boissons, tabac	116.5	121.2	131.1	137.9	138.9	138.8	133.9	135.7
Textiles,wearing apparel, leather, footwear								
Textiles, habillement, cuir et chaussures	109.6	103.7	94.4	93.0	91.7	85.7	74.7	65.8
Chemicals, petroleum, rubber and plastic prod.								
Prod. chimiques, pétroliers, caoutch. et plast.	120.4	123.4	132.2	144.3	155.0	170.9	179.7	186.3
Basic metals								
Métaux de base	106.4	103.6	99.6	106.8	109.7	118.8	126.8	130.6
Metal products								
Produits métalliques	128.0	142.7	145.5	153.7	155.5	174.4	164.5	151.9
Electricity [E]								
Electricité [E]	**121.7**	**127.0**	**137.5**	**146.2**	**164.7**	**177.2**	**189.9**	**204.1**
Colombia Colombie								
Total industry [CDE] [3]								
Total, industrie [CDE] [3]	**103.7**	**106.2**	**108.9**	**118.0**	**125.6**	**130.2**	**135.2**	...
Total mining [C]								
Total, industries extractives [C]	**100.8**	**99.6**	**98.5**	**120.6**	**149.2**	**157.6**	**176.0**	...
Total manufacturing [D]								
Total, industries manufacturières [D]	**106.7**	**109.5**	**113.5**	**115.9**	**112.8**	**115.5**	**113.8**	**98.5**
Food, beverages, tobacco								
Aliments, boissons, tabac	106.0	103.6	104.4	108.9	109.1	109.7	110.3	100.0
Textiles,wearing apparel, leather, footwear								
Textiles, habillement, cuir et chaussures	106.5	102.0	93.9	92.4	91.0	95.5	112.8	98.1
Chemicals, petroleum, rubber and plastic prod.								
Prod. chimiques, pétroliers, caoutch. et plast.	103.7	107.2	112.3	114.7	112.0	112.8	109.0	98.2
Basic metals								
Métaux de base	110.5	112.0	126.8	129.4	122.7	139.0	127.0	121.5
Metal products								
Produits métalliques	101.6	118.1	128.2	134.5	128.4	137.2	127.3	95.0
Electricity [E]								
Electricité [E]	**94.5**	**108.5**	**116.4**	**122.9**	**125.4**	**128.3**	**129.6**	**124.6**
Ecuador Equateur								
Total manufacturing [D]								
Total, industries manufacturières [D]	**118.2**	**120.6**	**135.1**	**141.8**	**145.2**	**148.1**	**149.3**	**141.8**
Food, beverages, tobacco								
Aliments, boissons, tabac	109.6	108.1	110.6	113.4	115.6	117.2	120.4	118.2
Textiles, leather and footwear								
Textiles, cuir et chaussures	88.8	77.8	81.6	82.9	84.6	86.3	84.1	79.3
Chemicals, petroleum, rubber and plastic prod.								
Prod. chimiques, pétroliers, caoutch. et plast.	130.1	140.2	157.1	161.4	165.1	168.9	172.3	156.1
Basic metals								
Métaux de base	126.4	139.0	154.3	152.8	154.9	156.5	156.9	145.9
Metal products								
Produits métalliques	134.5	144.8	184.2	194.7	192.9	195.0	196.5	129.7
Paraguay Paraguay								
Total manufacturing [D]								
Total, industries manufacturières [D]	**101.5**	**103.5**	**105.1**	**108.2**	**105.8**	**105.6**	**106.2**	...
Food, beverages, tobacco								
Aliments, boissons, tabac	108.3	108.6	117.0	121.6	122.7	127.3	128.6	...
Textiles,wearing apparel, leather and footwear								
Textiles, habillement, cuir et chaussures	98.1	100.8	89.7	98.3	96.4	80.8	85.7	...
Chemicals, petroleum, rubber and plastic prod.								
Prod. chimiques, pétroliers, caoutch. et plast.	89.6	92.3	89.9	76.3	67.8	62.8	59.8	...
Basic metals								
Métaux de base	101.2	106.0	85.2	88.6	85.2	80.5	76.7	...
Metal products								
Produits métalliques	106.4	86.2	54.6	54.8	54.6	54.3	54.3	...

22

Index numbers of industrial production [*cont.*]

Indices de la production industrielle [*suite*]

1990=100

Country or area and industry [ISIC Rev.3] Pays ou zone et industrie [CITI Rév.3]	1992	1993	1994	1995	1996	1997	1998	1999
Peru Pérou								
Total industry [CDE]								
Total, industrie [CDE]	100.3	106.9	120.7	129.2	132.7	141.3	144.8	148.7
Total mining [C]								
Total, industries extractives [C]	94.4	103.9	113.3	115.9	119.4	126.5	121.3	132.3
Total manufacturing [D]								
Total, industries manufacturières [D]	104.3	109.4	134.1	145.5	149.1	157.3	152.1	152.0
Food, beverages, tobacco								
Aliments, boissons, tabac	100.4	100.5	120.3	120.1	120.8	124.0	118.7	134.2
Textiles,wearing apparel, leather, footwear								
Textiles, habillement, cuir et chaussures	99.8	99.7	134.8	147.6	149.4	156.2	147.0	143.2
Chemicals, petroleum, rubber and plastic prod.								
Prod. chimiques, pétroliers, caoutch. et plast.	115.2	130.0	156.5	164.5	175.6	198.1	186.7	189.1
Basic metals								
Métaux de base	112.6	125.5	170.6	179.6	193.3	202.6	212.4	212.9
Metal products								
Produits métalliques	86.6	77.9	106.2	128.7	104.6	109.1	110.1	84.3
Electricity [E]								
Electricité [E]	95.8	107.4	120.9	124.3	126.5	139.0	145.9	162.0
Suriname Suriname								
Total industry [CDE]								
Total, industrie [CDE]	111.0	100.0	96.0	104.0	108.0	109.0	...	...
Total mining [C]								
Total, industries extractives [C]	102.0	98.0	101.0	103.0	107.0	174.0	200.0	...
Total manufacturing [D]								
Total, industries manufacturières [D]	143.0	107.0	84.0	107.0	110.0	95.0	...	...
Food, beverages, tobacco								
Aliments, boissons, tabac	122.6	87.6	92.9	83.3	103.7	106.1	...	...
Leather, leather products and footwear								
Cuir, produits en cuir et chaussures	97.0	76.0	85.0	...	...	...	...	...
Rubber and plastics products								
Prod. caoutchouc et plastiques	101.0	124.0	151.0	...	...	...	...	...
Electricity, gas and water [E]								
Electricité, gaz et eau [E]	109.0	96.0	67.0	94.0	114.0	132.0	150.0	...
Uruguay Uruguay								
Total manufacturing [D]								
Total, industries manufacturières [D]	91.9	81.1	83.4	86.1	89.6	94.7	99.9	91.3
Food, beverages, tobacco								
Aliments, boissons, tabac	105.4	101.5	108.0	109.4	117.1	127.3	129.9	129.5
Textiles,wearing apparel, leather, footwear								
Textiles, habillement, cuir et chaussures	100.7	97.2	101.0	84.4	89.7	92.9	78.3	61.0
Chemicals, petroleum, rubber and plastic prod.								
Prod. chimiques, pétroliers, caoutch. et plast.	95.4	87.4	89.9	97.7	96.8	96.9	99.9	93.2
Basic metals								
Métaux de base	98.4	85.5	78.4	74.3	72.9	79.5	82.8	78.2
Metal products								
Produits métalliques	92.9	87.0	107.3	67.1	51.4	64.0	87.8	69.9
Asia · Asie								
Armenia [8] Arménie [8]								
Total industry [CDE]								
Total, industrie [CDE]	...	...	...	100.0	101.4	102.4	100.2	105.5
Total mining [C]								
Total, industries extractives [C]	...	...	...	100.0	116.1	110.2	143.1	166.3
Total manufacturing [D]								
Total, industries manufacturières [D]	...	...	...	100.0	99.0	101.9	97.1	107.3
Electricity [E]								
Electricité [E]	...	...	...	100.0	108.3	105.2	105.7	100.0
Azerbaijan Azerbaïdjan								
Total industry [CDE]								
Total, industrie [CDE]	63.4	50.9	38.3	30.1	28.1	28.2	28.8	29.9
Total mining [C]								
Total, industries extractives [C]	89.6	81.8	76.0	72.9	71.4	71.0	88.4	106.0
Total manufacturing [D]								
Total, industries manufacturières [D]	74.6	69.4	50.3	39.1	35.2	35.5	31.3	28.5

22
Index numbers of industrial production [*cont.*]
Indices de la production industrielle [*suite*]
1990=100

Country or area and industry [ISIC Rev.3] Pays ou zone et industrie [CITI Rév.3]	1992	1993	1994	1995	1996	1997	1998	1999
Electricity [E] **Electricité [E]**	**81.0**	**76.5**	**67.7**	**63.5**	**67.2**	**61.8**	**65.0**	**66.1**
Bangladesh Bangladesh								
Total industry [CDE] **Total, industrie [CDE]**	113.6	129.9	140.5	150.0	159.3	165.4	168.8	182.1
Total mining [C] **Total, industries extractives [C]**	112.1	125.2	132.9	146.9	157.6	156.4	166.8	168.5
Total manufacturing [D] **Total, industries manufacturières [D]**	113.4	131.1	142.2	150.9	160.4	165.7	181.1	186.8
Food, beverages, tobacco Aliments, boissons, tabac	118.0	133.6	147.5	160.8	156.0	154.9	164.3	165.0
Textiles,wearing apparel, leather, footwear Textiles, habillement, cuir et chaussures	121.8	133.7	135.0	148.3	167.7	181.8	212.3	228.7
Chemicals, petroleum, rubber and plastic prod. Prod. chimiques, pétroliers, caoutch. et plast.	113.9	139.5	154.5	157.2	168.9	162.5	169.0	161.2
Basic metals Métaux de base	61.6	66.4	117.6	195.8	170.4	184.7	205.8	174.8
Metal products Produits métalliques	84.3	85.5	79.4	85.5	79.5	89.9	129.8	99.0
Electricity [E] **Electricité [E]**	**115.1**	**119.2**	**126.6**	**140.4**	**148.5**	**153.5**	**166.9**	**178.8**
China, Hong Kong SAR † Chine, Hong Kong RAS †								
Total industry [DE] [3] **Total, industrie [DE] [3]**	104.8	104.7	101.3	102.8	99.7	99.3	92.6	87.1
Total manufacturing [D] **Total, industries manufacturières [D]**	102.6	102.0	101.8	102.8	98.9	98.2	89.7	84.0
Food, beverages, tobacco Aliments, boissons, tabac	109.4	111.8	113.5	113.0	112.0	111.5	101.3	99.7
Textiles and wearing apparel Textiles and habillement	102.6	100.6	100.3	99.4	94.3	93.2	85.8	83.8
Chemicals and other non−metallic mineral prod. Prod. chimiques et minéraux non−métalliques	86.6	75.4	64.8	57.9	56.9	55.6	46.6	38.9
Basic metals and metal products Métaux de base et produtis métalliques	102.6	102.8	105.4	113.0	106.5	103.4	95.4	91.3
Electricity and gas [E] **Electricité et gaz [E]**	**121.1**	**124.5**	**98.1**	**102.7**	**105.1**	**107.4**	**114.9**	**109.7**
Cyprus Chypre								
Total industry [CDE] **Total, industrie [CDE]**	105.0	98.0	101.4	102.9	99.6	99.5	102.3	104.0
Total mining [C] **Total, industries extractives [C]**	105.0	122.0	132.1	121.7	118.8	123.4	147.4	157.4
Total manufacturing [D] **Total, industries manufacturières [D]**	103.0	93.0	96.3	96.8	91.9	91.3	92.3	92.6
Food, beverages, tobacco Aliments, boissons, tabac	104.2	98.8	108.2	108.4	102.7	100.2	100.0	103.4
Textiles,wearing apparel, leather, footwear Textiles, habillement, cuir et chaussures	89.1	75.1	74.6	71.7	60.2	57.6	58.7	54.5
Chemicals, petroleum, rubber and plastic prod. Prod. chimiques, pétroliers, caoutch. et plast.	109.6	94.3	100.4	103.6	101.8	106.5	105.3	105.3
Metal products Produits métalliques	108.7	115.4	117.0	122.2	121.0	122.0	124.2	128.0
Electricity, gas and water [E] **Electricité, gaz et eau [E]**	**115.0**	**125.0**	**133.4**	**143.5**	**151.5**	**154.7**	**166.4**	**177.2**
India [9] Inde [9]								
Total industry [CDE] **Total, industrie [CDE]**	103.0	109.1	118.8	134.3	142.5	151.8	157.6	170.3
Total mining [C] **Total, industries extractives [C]**	103.2	105.6	113.6	124.5	122.0	129.2	126.9	127.9
Total manufacturing [D] **Total, industries manufacturières [D]**	101.4	107.6	117.2	133.9	143.7	153.3	159.6	174.2
Food, beverages, tobacco Aliments, boissons, tabac	99.8	97.9	113.3	121.3	127.9	133.9	137.3	144.1
Textiles,wearing apparel, leather, footwear Textiles, habillement, cuir et chaussures	111.0	122.5	124.1	145.3	160.0	171.8	165.2	176.1

22
Index numbers of industrial production [*cont.*]
Indices de la production industrielle [*suite*]
1990=100

Country or area and industry [ISIC Rev.3] Pays ou zone et industrie [CITI Rév.3]	1992	1993	1994	1995	1996	1997	1998	1999
Chemicals, petroleum, rubber and plastic prod.								
Prod. chimiques, pétroliers, caoutch. et plast.	101.7	106.0	112.3	123.9	129.0	143.9	154.8	180.5
Basic metals								
Métaux de base	107.0	131.1	148.4	171.8	183.3	186.2	183.5	192.6
Metal products								
Produits métalliques	97.2	98.4	111.6	130.7	141.8	146.8	158.7	172.7
Electricity [E]								
Électricité [E]	**113.9**	**122.5**	**132.9**	**143.7**	**149.4**	**159.2**	**169.5**	**179.8**
Indonesia Indonésie								
Total industry [CDE] [3]								
Total, industrie [CDE] [3]	**104.9**	**120.6**	**132.1**	**141.2**	**148.1**	**160.6**	**149.3**	**168.1**
Total mining [C]								
Total, industries extractives [C]	**89.1**	**106.4**	**107.2**	**108.7**	**110.6**	**112.3**	**112.9**	**107.2**
Total manufacturing [D]								
Total, industries manufacturières [D]	**123.4**	**137.3**	**161.5**	**179.2**	**191.0**	**216.1**	**187.3**	**235.4**
Food, beverages, tobacco								
Aliments, boissons, tabac	109.4	136.1	180.3	206.7	245.3	329.7	500.6	1080.0
Textiles,wearing apparel, leather, footwear								
Textiles, habillement, cuir et chaussures	143.5	151.1	164.0	185.2	189.1	188.4	172.4	187.0
Chemicals, petroleum, rubber and plastic prod.								
Prod. chimiques, pétroliers, caoutch. et plast.	128.7	145.4	155.8	159.0	158.3	161.8	155.6	208.3
Basic metals								
Métaux de base	164.8	213.3	229.5	290.5	283.0	280.9	221.4	221.0
Metal products								
Produits métalliques	98.1	92.1	103.5	107.5	102.0	121.7	70.1	65.5
Electricity [E]								
Électricité [E]	**124.1**	**137.6**	**155.8**	**180.3**	**206.2**	**234.5**	**266.1**	**302.0**
Iran (Islamic Rep. of) Iran (Rép. islamique d')								
Total manufacturing [D]								
Total, industries manufacturières [D]	**124.7**	**121.3**	**129.4**	**138.1**	**146.1**	**150.0**	**180.0**	...
Food and beverages								
Aliments et boissons	122.7	129.5	134.4	150.1	163.8	178.3	185.6	...
Textiles, wearing apparel, leather, footwear								
Textiles, habillement, cuir et chaussures	117.7	120.8	129.1	127.8	138.5	140.9	137.1	...
Chemical, rubber and plastic products								
Prod. chimiques, caoutchouc et plastiques	108.3	109.3	116.9	128.6	146.0	154.6	148.2	...
Metal products								
Produits métalliques	194.6	191.1	157.0	181.7	194.8	264.9	284.7	...
Israel Israël								
Total industry [CD]								
Total, industrie [CD]	**115.6**	**124.1**	**132.5**	**143.7**	**151.4**	**154.0**	**158.4**	**160.6**
Total mining [C]								
Total, industries extractives [C]	**113.8**	**124.3**	**134.8**	**148.7**	**160.3**	**156.0**	**162.4**	**160.9**
Total manufacturing [D]								
Total, industries manufacturières [D]	**115.6**	**124.1**	**132.5**	**143.4**	**151.1**	**153.9**	**158.3**	**160.7**
Food, beverages, tobacco								
Aliments, boissons, tabac	104.5	112.6	119.7	130.3	130.5	134.4	135.4	137.3
Textiles								
Textiles	110.6	110.5	119.8	128.4	121.4	121.4	125.4	131.4
Chemicals, petroleum, rubber and plastic prod.								
Prod. chimiques, pétroliers, caoutch. et plast.	118.4	131.3	145.7	157.7	170.4	171.3	187.0	185.8
Basic metals								
Métaux de base	115.9	121.4	138.7	165.9	175.6	178.1	167.7	166.9
Metal products								
Produits métalliques	115.6	123.3	133.9	146.4	150.8	153.9	157.6	156.7
Japan Japon								
Total industry [CDE]								
Total, industrie [CDE]	**95.5**	**91.2**	**92.4**	**95.4**	**97.7**	**101.1**	**94.4**	**95.3**
Total mining [C]								
Total, industries extractives [C]	**102.5**	**100.0**	**99.8**	**96.2**	**97.6**	**89.3**	**83.2**	**82.9**
Total manufacturing [D]								
Total, industries manufacturières [D]	**95.5**	**91.2**	**92.1**	**95.1**	**97.3**	**100.8**	**93.7**	**94.4**
Food, beverages, tobacco								
Aliments, boissons, tabac	101.0	100.0	101.6	100.9	101.8	101.3	98.6	99.9

22
Index numbers of industrial production [*cont.*]
Indices de la production industrielle [*suite*]
1990=100

Country or area and industry [ISIC Rev.3] Pays ou zone et industrie [CITI Rév.3]	1992	1993	1994	1995	1996	1997	1998	1999
Textiles,wearing apparel, leather, footwear								
Textiles, habillement, cuir et chaussures	94.0	84.2	80.4	74.8	72.2	69.9	62.0	57.8
Chemicals, petroleum, rubber and plastic prod.								
Prod. chimiques, pétroliers, caoutch. et plast.	102.1	100.3	104.0	109.0	110.3	113.7	108.9	112.0
Basic metals								
Métaux de base	93.2	91.2	90.9	94.1	93.3	97.6	86.5	86.1
Metal products								
Produits métalliques	94.7	89.2	90.4	95.1	99.9	104.9	97.6	98.4
Electricity and gas [E]								
Electricité et gaz [E]	**106.2**	**107.0**	**114.0**	**116.6**	**120.3**	**123.1**	**124.5**	**126.1**
Jordan Jordanie								
Total industry [CD]								
Total, industrie [CD]	**106.1**	**114.4**	**120.9**	**131.9**	**126.9**	**133.8**	**136.1**	**136.7**
Total mining [C]								
Total, industries extractives [C]	**86.4**	**86.9**	**93.4**	**108.5**	**110.0**	**112.9**	**107.9**	**115.7**
Total manufacturing [D]								
Total, industries manufacturières [D]	**110.5**	**120.6**	**127.0**	**136.8**	**130.2**	**138.1**	**142.4**	**139.6**
Food, beverages, tobacco								
Aliments, boissons, tabac	118.3	124.1	132.8	150.5	138.7	125.6	162.2	163.3
Textiles,wearing apparel, leather, footwear								
Textiles, habillement, cuir et chaussures	81.2	87.7	84.4	82.2	94.4	89.8	88.6	71.0
Chemicals, petroleum, rubber and plastic prod.								
Prod. chimiques, pétroliers, caoutch. et plast.	95.8	91.8	91.4	120.9	96.1	124.6	117.8	103.8
Basic metals								
Métaux de base	133.4	105.1	89.0	84.6	91.9	66.0	54.5	63.6
Korea, Republic of Corée, Rép. de								
Total industry [CDE]								
Total, industrie [CDE]	**116.1**	**121.2**	**134.5**	**150.6**	**163.3**	**171.1**	**159.9**	**198.6**
Total mining [C]								
Total, industries extractives [C]	**85.8**	**79.9**	**78.7**	**73.6**	**72.1**	**69.1**	**53.6**	**57.8**
Total manufacturing [D]								
Total, industries manufacturières [D]	**116.3**	**121.1**	**134.5**	**150.6**	**163.1**	**170.5**	**159.2**	**199.1**
Food, beverages, tobacco								
Aliments, boissons, tabac	110.3	112.1	119.9	119.9	126.0	124.9	114.9	123.8
Textiles,wearing apparel, leather, footwear								
Textiles, habillement, cuir et chaussures	90.2	77.3	75.2	72.2	67.9	59.2	48.4	51.6
Chemicals, petroleum, rubber and plastic prod.								
Prod. chimiques, pétroliers, caoutch. et plast.	137.7	149.7	159.7	172.6	193.6	218.6	199.6	221.6
Basic metals								
Métaux de base	115.8	128.9	139.9	153.6	163.0	172.4	151.5	173.0
Metal products								
Produits métalliques	119.1	129.2	153.4	185.3	210.0	225.3	218.5	310.8
Electricity and gas [E]								
Electricité et gaz [E]	**124.4**	**139.2**	**160.5**	**182.1**	**204.6**	**224.6**	**216.9**	**243.7**
Malaysia Malaisie								
Total industry [CDE]								
Total, industrie [CDE]	**120.7**	**132.4**	**148.9**	**168.3**	**186.9**	**206.7**	**191.9**	**290.2**
Total mining [C]								
Total, industries extractives [C]	**108.0**	**109.3**	**113.2**	**123.3**	**130.5**	**133.7**	**135.1**	**130.8**
Total manufacturing [D]								
Total, industries manufacturières [D]	**125.8**	**142.0**	**163.2**	**186.3**	**209.2**	**235.2**	**211.0**	**238.0**
Food, beverages, tobacco								
Aliments, boissons, tabac	102.1	106.5	114.6	121.5	132.2	142.7	137.3	155.7
Textiles,wearing apparel, leather, footwear								
Textiles, habillement, cuir et chaussures	113.8	133.2	147.4	155.8	156.4	164.6	154.5	160.8
Chemicals, petroleum, rubber and plastic prod.								
Prod. chimiques, pétroliers, caoutch. et plast.	121.3	137.1	155.1	173.8	201.8	239.3	237.5	270.2
Basic metals								
Métaux de base	130.9	148.1	170.0	191.6	224.5	253.8	179.6	257.9
Metal products								
Produits métalliques	155.4	174.7	213.8	256.0	283.7	319.8	277.0	317.5
Electricity [E]								
Electricité [E]	**129.0**	**144.9**	**164.8**	**188.2**	**212.2**	**242.3**	**250.6**	**260.2**

22

Index numbers of industrial production [*cont.*]

Indices de la production industrielle [*suite*]

1990=100

Country or area and industry [ISIC Rev.3] Pays ou zone et industrie [CITI Rév.3]	1992	1993	1994	1995	1996	1997	1998	1999
Mongolia Mongolie								
Total industry [CDE]								
Total, industrie [CDE]	**67.9**	**59.1**	**61.3**	**68.6**	**66.9**	**69.9**	**127.7**	**73.2**
Total mining [C]								
Total, industries extractives [C]	**108.2**	**121.2**	**154.8**	**187.4**	**201.1**	**235.1**	**218.4**	**226.7**
Total manufacturing [D]								
Total, industries manufacturières [D]	**55.2**	**42.4**	**36.5**	**40.8**	**36.5**	**33.5**	**29.9**	**29.0**
Food and beverages								
Aliments et boissons	47.8	40.8	35.6	42.5	32.1	30.1	29.6	25.8
Textiles,wearing apparel, leather, footwear								
Textiles, habillement, cuir et chaussures	50.5	31.4	25.8	30.6	23.7	22.3	20.9	23.7
Chemicals and chemical products								
Produits chimiques	82.7	74.3	68.1	69.9	68.1	67.2	72.0	75.5
Basic metals								
Métaux de base	101.4	34.4	49.6	102.1	94.8	170.8	146.1	148.1
Electricity and gas [E]								
Electricité et gaz [E]	**108.9**	**101.7**	**123.6**	**130.2**	**125.3**	**122.0**	**127.7**	**131.6**
Myanmar [1] Myanmar [1]								
Total industry [CDE] [3]								
Total, industrie [CDE] [3]	**107.8**	**118.3**	**128.5**	**139.0**	**145.3**	...	...	...
Total mining [C]								
Total, industries extractives [C]	**109.7**	**130.4**	**152.3**	**173.5**	**186.1**	...	...	...
Total manufacturing [D]								
Total, industries manufacturières [D]	**107.5**	**116.9**	**126.1**	**135.5**	**141.2**	...	...	...
Food and beverages								
Aliments et boissons	105.5	118.0	122.8	128.5	132.5	...	...	...
Textiles,wearing apparel, leather, footwear								
Textiles, habillement, cuir et chaussures	128.7	116.0	160.9	175.7	174.7	...	...	...
Chemicals and petroleum products								
Prod. chimiques, pétroliers, caoutch. et plast.	98.1	96.6	127.7	182.0	173.0	...	...	...
Basic metals and other non−metallic mineral prod.								
Métaux de base et minéraux non−métalliques	103.4	113.9	103.6	107.2	112.8	...	...	...
Metal products								
Produits métalliques	102.6	116.6	132.8	175.3	236.3	...	...	...
Electricity [E]								
Electricité [E]	**113.8**	**128.1**	**137.4**	**153.5**	**161.0**	...	...	...
Pakistan [1] Pakistan [1]								
Total industry [CDE] [3]								
Total, industrie [CDE] [3]	**112.2**	**116.7**	**114.2**	**123.6**	**122.4**	**130.6**	**134.3**	**134.1**
Total mining [C]								
Total, industries extractives [C]	**101.2**	**100.0**	**98.4**	**107.8**	**111.0**	**109.9**	**108.5**	**109.7**
Total manufacturing [D]								
Total, industries manufacturières [D]	**112.3**	**117.1**	**118.9**	**122.7**	**120.0**	**129.2**	**133.9**	**132.9**
Electricity and gas [E]								
Electricité et gaz [E]	**116.7**	**122.8**	**130.1**	**137.8**	**142.9**	**150.1**	**150.3**	**154.6**
Singapore Singapour								
Total manufacturing [D]								
Total, industries manufacturières [D]	**107.8**	**118.8**	**134.2**	**148.0**	**152.9**	**160.0**	**159.4**	**181.4**
Food, beverages, tobacco								
Aliments, boissons, tabac	111.8	114.4	120.8	121.4	122.3	115.6	102.5	97.0
Textiles,wearing apparel, leather, footwear								
Textiles, habillement, cuir et chaussures	91.5	75.3	66.8	54.3	44.0	43.0	46.0	47.9
Chemicals, petroleum, rubber and plastic prod.								
Prod. chimiques, pétroliers, caoutch. et plast.	106.1	115.1	124.8	126.1	131.4	149.1	166.9	192.1
Basic metals								
Métaux de base	103.4	109.3	111.2	101.4	101.6	106.7	88.6	94.1
Metal products								
Produits métalliques	108.7	111.0	123.7	131.6	130.1	134.7	131.7	148.7
Sri Lanka Sri Lanka								
Total manufacturing [D]								
Total, industries manufacturières [D]	**98.5**	**171.3**	**184.3**	**198.5**	**187.1**	**151.9**	...	...
Food, beverages, tobacco								
Aliments, boissons, tabac	97.5	117.3	124.8	146.4	146.7	91.7	...	...

22
Index numbers of industrial production [*cont.*]
Indices de la production industrielle [*suite*]
1990=100

Country or area and industry [ISIC Rev.3] Pays ou zone et industrie [CITI Rév.3]	1992	1993	1994	1995	1996	1997	1998	1999
Textiles,wearing apparel, leather, footwear Textiles, habillement, cuir et chaussures	115.8	303.4	330.6	241.2	228.4	251.7	...	...
Chemicals, petroleum, rubber and plastic prod. Prod. chimiques, pétroliers, caoutch. et plast.	98.1	137.4	135.4	163.1	174.7	154.8	...	...
Basic metals Métaux de base	63.6	71.7	93.8	52.9	64.5	49.2	...	...
Metal products Produits métalliques	100.6	123.7	154.1	212.5	263.9	102.1		
Syrian Arab Republic Rép. arabe syrienne **Total industry [CDE]** **Total, industrie [CDE]**	**114.0**	**116.6**	**125.7**	**129.5**	**130.8**	**138.6**	**141.2**	...
Total mining [C] **Total, industries extractives [C]**	**125.0**	**136.9**	**142.9**	**148.8**	**148.8**	**150.3**	**151.8**	...
Total manufacturing [D] **Total, industries manufacturières [D]**	**107.0**	**107.0**	**114.1**	**117.6**	**118.8**	**128.2**	**129.3**	...
Food, beverages, tobacco Aliments, boissons, tabac	110.2	103.8	108.2	120.4	120.6	133.7	123.5	...
Textiles,wearing apparel, leather, footwear Textiles, habillement, cuir et chaussures	101.3	95.4	97.1	96.5	95.7	104.5	105.6	...
Chemicals, petroleum, rubber and plastic prod. Prod. chimiques, pétroliers, caoutch. et plast.	101.5	114.9	130.4	121.1	128.0	142.8	154.1	
Basic metals Métaux de base	109.0	108.3	74.6	73.2	106.8	119.2	116.3	...
Metal products Produits métalliques	163.4	180.5	246.1	292.9	276.4	254.8	230.7	...
Electricity and water [E] **Electricité et eau [E]**	**100.0**	**101.3**	**118.2**	**129.9**	**140.3**	**149.4**	**167.5**	...
Tajikistan Tadjikistan **Total industry [CDE]** **Total, industrie [CDE]**	**73.0**	**67.0**	**50.0**	**43.0**	**33.0**	**32.0**	**35.0**	**37.0**
Total mining [C] **Total, industries extractives [C]**	**74.0**	**75.0**	**65.0**	**64.0**	**62.0**	**76.0**	**84.0**	**84.0**
Total manufacturing [D] **Total, industries manufacturières [D]**	**73.0**	**66.0**	**49.0**	**41.0**	**30.0**	**27.0**	**28.0**	**32.0**
Electricity, gas and water [E] **Electricité, gaz et eau [E]**	**93.0**	**99.0**	**96.0**	**95.0**	**93.0**	**104.0**	**107.0**	**120.0**
Thailand Thaïlande **Total manufacturing [D]** **Total, industries manufacturières [D]**	**121.0**	**130.2**	**138.8**	**150.8**	**163.3**	**162.6**	**145.6**	**164.3**
Turkey Turquie **Total industry [CDE]** **Total, industrie [CDE]**	**108.6**	**115.0**	**107.8**	**117.0**	**123.9**	**137.2**	**138.4**	**131.1**
Total mining [C] **Total, industries extractives [C]**	**105.4**	**95.2**	**104.1**	**104.7**	**108.1**	**114.5**	**125.9**	**115.0**
Total manufacturing [D] **Total, industries manufacturières [D]**	**105.1**	**112.3**	**101.8**	**110.5**	**117.7**	**131.2**	**130.8**	**123.4**
Food, beverages, tobacco Aliments, boissons, tabac	108.1	114.1	118.7	125.0	136.5	147.2	152.6	149.6
Textiles,wearing apparel, leather, footwear Textiles, habillement, cuir et chaussures	92.5	92.5	89.3	102.5	111.6	119.7	114.5	107.3
Chemicals, petroleum, rubber and plastic prod. Prod. chimiques, pétroliers, caoutch. et plast.	103.2	110.6	106.2	122.6	125.4	138.2	140.7	137.2
Basic metals Métaux de base	96.3	110.1	104.1	110.7	119.2	130.7	131.4	129.0
Metal products Produits métalliques	115.0	134.8	96.9	120.7	138.5	172.3	172.6	157.6
Electricity, gas and water [E] **Electricité, gaz et eau [E]**	**116.8**	**128.1**	**136.0**	**149.8**	**165.6**	**179.2**	**192.8**	**202.3**
Europe · Europe								
Austria Autriche **Total industry [CDE]** **Total, industrie [CDE]**	**93.8**	**92.5**	**93.6**	**112.3**	**113.4**	**120.6**	**130.5**	**138.4**
Total mining [C] **Total, industries extractives [C]**	**84.7**	**78.6**	**75.4**	**89.7**	**89.9**	**86.7**	**93.2**	**96.3**

22
Index numbers of industrial production [cont.]
Indices de la production industrielle [suite]
1990=100

Country or area and industry [ISIC Rev.3] Pays ou zone et industrie [CITI Rév.3]	1992	1993	1994	1995	1996	1997	1998	1999
Total manufacturing [D]								
Total, industries manufacturières [D]	**92.0**	**90.5**	**91.9**	**112.8**	**113.6**	**121.8**	**132.9**	**140.9**
Food, beverages, tobacco								
Aliments, boissons, tabac	96.8	99.7	94.5	97.9	98.0	106.2	110.9	114.8
Textiles,wearing apparel, leather, footwear								
Textiles, habillement, cuir et chaussures	98.3	87.2	79.5	75.9	72.1	73.9	75.8	70.9
Chemicals, petroleum, rubber and plastic prod.								
Prod. chimiques, pétroliers, caoutch. et plast.	102.0	102.8	98.8	109.7	111.4	114.1	122.6	126.7
Basic metals								
Métaux de base	89.0	83.4	89.8	105.0	101.1	116.8	120.3	119.6
Metal products								
Produits métalliques	85.4	82.2	90.1	121.4	124.8	135.2	159.5	185.1
Electricity, gas and water [E]								
Electricité, gaz et eau [E]	**118.4**	**121.4**	**119.2**	**114.1**	**117.4**	**119.6**	**121.6**	**128.8**
Belgium Belgique								
Total industry [CDE]								
Total, industrie [CDE]	**97.9**	**93.0**	**94.7**	**100.6**	**101.4**	**106.0**	**109.6**	**110.8**
Total mining [C]								
Total, industries extractives [C]	**113.9**	**101.4**	**103.3**	**145.1**	**154.8**	**164.5**	**169.2**	**181.7**
Total manufacturing [D]								
Total, industries manufacturières [D]	**98.8**	**98.3**	**100.1**	**106.5**	**107.0**	**112.2**	**115.4**	**116.8**
Food, beverages, tobacco								
Aliments, boissons, tabac	102.8	101.8	99.8	107.5	108.4	113.4	115.9	111.2
Textiles,wearing apparel, leather, footwear								
Textiles, habillement, cuir et chaussures	98.7	93.5	93.1	86.9	79.0	81.1	78.4	73.3
Chemicals, petroleum, rubber and plastic prod.								
Prod. chimiques, pétroliers, caoutch. et plast.	109.8	105.2	104.9	112.9	117.2	129.6	130.4	139.2
Basic metals								
Métaux de base	89.3	95.0	103.3	106.8	104.5	104.9	108.1	108.4
Metal products								
Produits métalliques	94.9	87.6	89.8	99.3	100.5	105.4	110.8	115.2
Electricity, gas and water [E]								
Electricité, gaz et eau [E]	**102.5**	**101.1**	**102.7**	**106.0**	**109.9**	**112.0**	**119.5**	**119.9**
Bulgaria [8] Bulgarie [8]								
Total industry [CDE]								
Total, industrie [CDE]	...	...	...	100.0	105.1	94.6	82.6	...
Total mining [C]								
Total, industries extractives [C]	...	...	...	100.0	115.5	105.2	100.9	...
Total manufacturing [D]								
Total, industries manufacturières [D]	...	...	...	100.0	104.8	92.2	77.1	...
Electricity, gas and water [E]								
Electricité, gaz et eau [E]	...	...	...	100.0	101.6	108.3	119.2	...
Croatia Croatie								
Total industry [CDE]								
Total, industrie [CDE]	**61.1**	**57.4**	**55.9**	**56.1**	**57.8**	**61.7**	**64.0**	**63.2**
Total mining [C]								
Total, industries extractives [C]	**74.9**	**77.6**	**73.9**	**75.7**	**73.4**	**73.1**	**71.4**	**72.7**
Total manufacturing [D]								
Total, industries manufacturières [D]	**58.9**	**54.7**	**53.4**	**53.2**	**53.9**	**56.0**	**57.8**	**56.1**
Food, beverages, tobacco								
Aliments, boissons, tabac	71.9	63.8	66.5	68.2	70.1	65.3	67.5	64.0
Textiles,wearing apparel, leather, footwear								
Textiles, habillement, cuir et chaussures	58.3	58.9	55.3	49.6	43.0	44.6	44.6	40.0
Chemicals, petroleum, rubber and plastic prod.								
Prod. chimiques, pétroliers, caoutch. et plast.	62.5	58.7	60.3	62.3	60.3	60.0	58.0	58.7
Basic metals								
Métaux de base	41.3	42.2	42.1	34.7	31.5	39.6	46.3	40.1
Metal products								
Produits métalliques	49.7	43.9	40.1	41.0	42.6	47.7	50.6	51.0
Electricity, gas and water [E]								
Electricité, gaz et eau [E]	**101.4**	**108.1**	**99.8**	**104.7**	**131.3**	**163.0**	**177.2**	**189.5**
Czech Republic Rép. tchèque								
Total industry [CDE]								
Total, industrie [CDE]	**72.1**	**68.3**	**69.8**	**75.9**	**77.4**	**80.8**	**83.3**	**80.9**

22
Index numbers of industrial production [*cont.*]
Indices de la production industrielle [*suite*]
1990=100

Country or area and industry [ISIC Rev.3] Pays ou zone et industrie [CITI Rév.3]	1992	1993	1994	1995	1996	1997	1998	1999
Total mining [C]								
Total, industries extractives [C]	**69.7**	**69.7**	**70.1**	**69.1**	**70.1**	**68.1**	**64.1**	**56.3**
Total manufacturing [D]								
Total, industries manufacturières [D]	**56.7**	**56.7**	**56.7**	**61.4**	**62.4**	**66.4**	**69.1**	**67.5**
Electricity, gas and water [E]								
Electricité, gaz et eau [E]	**94.5**	**94.5**	**94.5**	**98.5**	**102.1**	**99.4**	**98.9**	**96.0**
Denmark Danemark								
Total industry [CD]								
Total, industrie [CD]	**104.0**	**101.0**	**111.0**	**116.0**	**118.0**	**124.1**	**126.8**	**129.2**
Total mining [C]								
Total, industries extractives [C]	**100.0**	**91.0**	**97.0**	**97.0**	**100.3**	**85.7**	**91.5**	**91.2**
Total manufacturing [D]								
Total, industries manufacturières [D]	**104.0**	**101.0**	**111.0**	**116.0**	**118.0**	**124.4**	**126.9**	**129.3**
Food, beverages, tobacco								
Aliments, boissons, tabac	105.3	106.6	113.4	109.6	107.5	113.5	112.3	112.0
Textiles,wearing apparel, leather, footwear								
Textiles, habillement, cuir et chaussures	98.4	93.5	98.5	97.1	100.2	98.4	102.9	97.6
Chemicals, petroleum, rubber and plastic prod.								
Prod. chimiques, pétroliers, caoutch. et plast.	107.9	106.5	118.3	126.3	131.0	141.0	147.1	165.8
Basic metals								
Métaux de base	117.8	121.8	129.9	132.7	125.2	138.4	135.9	133.8
Metal products								
Produits métalliques	102.0	95.5	108.8	117.6	121.9	127.1	130.9	130.6
Estonia Estonie								
Total industry [CDE]								
Total, industrie [CDE]	**60.1**	**48.9**	**47.4**	**48.3**	**49.7**	**57.0**	**59.3**	**54.8**
Total mining [C]								
Total, industries extractives [C]	**74.4**	**54.1**	**53.5**	**51.1**	**54.1**	**53.8**	**51.6**	**48.2**
Total manufacturing [D]								
Total, industries manufacturières [D]	**57.3**	**46.6**	**45.2**	**46.5**	**47.5**	**56.3**	**59.4**	**54.7**
Electricity [E]								
Electricité [E]	**69.2**	**57.9**	**56.5**	**55.4**	**58.8**	**57.0**	**55.0**	**51.3**
Finland Finlande								
Total industry [CDE]								
Total, industrie [CDE]	**92.2**	**97.1**	**107.9**	**114.5**	**118.6**	**129.7**	**140.2**	**147.8**
Total mining [C]								
Total, industries extractives [C]	**95.8**	**94.4**	**106.8**	**105.4**	**106.1**	**130.5**	**99.7**	**131.7**
Total manufacturing [D]								
Total, industries manufacturières [D]	**91.1**	**96.2**	**107.4**	**114.9**	**118.4**	**130.3**	**142.5**	**150.6**
Food, beverages, tobacco								
Aliments, boissons, tabac	99.3	103.9	103.3	106.6	110.5	114.4	114.9	118.5
Textiles,wearing apparel, leather, footwear								
Textiles, habillement, cuir et chaussures	74.6	73.3	80.1	73.8	75.3	75.8	76.1	74.1
Chemicals, petroleum, rubber and plastic prod.								
Prod. chimiques, pétroliers, caoutch. et plast.	98.8	103.5	116.2	118.1	121.9	127.1	135.7	139.4
Basic metals								
Métaux de base	110.2	117.0	126.2	133.9	141.5	150.5	158.1	164.4
Metal products								
Produits métalliques	89.0	97.9	118.9	143.9	155.7	178.5	221.7	254.5
Electricity, gas and water [E]								
Electricité, gaz et eau [E]	**102.9**	**107.5**	**113.8**	**112.0**	**122.2**	**121.9**	**123.5**	**123.1**
France France								
Total industry [CDE]								
Total, industrie [CDE]	**98.8**	**95.0**	**99.1**	**101.5**	**102.4**	**106.2**	**111.7**	**114.0**
Total mining [C]								
Total, industries extractives [C]	**91.4**	**84.0**	**82.6**	**82.2**	**75.4**	**73.6**	**73.0**	**75.0**
Total manufacturing [D]								
Total, industries manufacturières [D]	**97.5**	**93.1**	**97.6**	**99.8**	**100.4**	**105.1**	**111.2**	**113.5**
Food, beverages, tobacco								
Aliments, boissons, tabac	100.8	101.2	103.2	104.8	107.0	110.1	111.2	113.4
Textiles,wearing apparel, leather, footwear								
Textiles, habillement, cuir et chaussures	90.1	82.8	84.3	80.1	70.9	69.3	66.9	60.5
Chemicals, petroleum, rubber and plastic prod.								
Prod. chimiques, pétroliers, caoutch. et plast.	105.1	104.8	110.5	113.2	115.7	120.6	126.7	129.3

22
Index numbers of industrial production [*cont.*]
Indices de la production industrielle [*suite*]
1990=100

Country or area and industry [ISIC Rev.3] Pays ou zone et industrie [CITI Rév.3]	1992	1993	1994	1995	1996	1997	1998	1999
Basic metals								
Métaux de base	95.4	87.4	96.6	97.1	94.6	102.0	105.0	102.7
Metal products								
Produits métalliques	95.1	88.6	93.0	96.2	98.6	104.3	113.4	117.0
Electricity and gas [E]								
Electricité et gaz [E]	**110.9**	**113.1**	**113.4**	**118.2**	**122.5**	**120.3**	**121.5**	**124.0**
Germany [10] **Allemagne** [10]								
Total industry [CDE]								
Total, industrie [CDE]	**97.6**	**90.5**	**93.9**	**95.9**	**96.5**	**99.8**	**104.1**	**105.7**
Total mining [C]								
Total, industries extractives [C]	**92.6**	**85.7**	**82.8**	**79.6**	**75.1**	**72.5**	**67.5**	**66.6**
Total manufacturing [D]								
Total, industries manufacturières [D]	**97.7**	**90.1**	**93.9**	**96.0**	**96.4**	**100.2**	**105.1**	**106.8**
Food, beverages, tobacco								
Aliments, boissons, tabac	99.3	99.9	102.0	102.4	103.7	104.9	104.3	107.2
Textiles,wearing apparel, leather, footwear								
Textiles, habillement, cuir et chaussures	89.3	79.6	72.7	69.6	64.8	63.2	62.2	57.5
Chemicals, petroleum, rubber and plastic prod.								
Prod. chimiques, pétroliers, caoutch. et plast.	98.5	93.2	99.2	102.1	105.2	110.7	112.7	116.3
Basic metals								
Métaux de base	95.5	85.5	92.3	93.6	88.6	97.2	98.0	94.7
Metal products								
Produits métalliques	97.1	86.7	90.9	92.3	93.3	98.1	106.2	108.8
Electricity and gas [E]								
Electricité et gaz [E]	**99.8**	**98.2**	**99.1**	**101.1**	**106.7**	**105.9**	**106.1**	**106.7**
Greece Grèce								
Total industry [CDE]								
Total, industrie [CDE]	**98.0**	**95.1**	**95.6**	**97.9**	**99.1**	**100.8**	**106.7**	**110.0**
Total mining [C]								
Total, industries extractives [C]	**92.4**	**86.6**	**89.5**	**91.7**	**95.3**	**94.4**	**92.9**	**87.4**
Total manufacturing [D]								
Total, industries manufacturières [D]	**97.8**	**94.6**	**93.8**	**95.7**	**95.9**	**97.5**	**101.9**	**102.6**
Food, beverages, tobacco								
Aliments, boissons, tabac	112.2	112.0	115.1	119.2	117.3	114.1	117.3	119.1
Textiles,wearing apparel, leather, footwear								
Textiles, habillement, cuir et chaussures	89.0	86.2	81.7	75.6	69.7	69.4	65.8	62.1
Chemicals, petroleum, rubber and plastic prod.								
Prod. chimiques, pétroliers, caoutch. et plast.	91.8	93.0	98.0	102.2	108.8	110.0	119.7	122.4
Basic metals								
Métaux de base	98.5	92.4	94.6	101.7	98.1	109.6	114.6	109.5
Metal products								
Produits métalliques	106.2	98.6	94.5	98.8	100.2	106.9	116.9	124.5
Electricity and gas [E]								
Electricité et gaz [E]	**105.4**	**108.1**	**114.1**	**118.3**	**123.5**	**124.9**	**142.1**	**158.4**
Hungary Hongrie								
Total industry [CDE]								
Total, industrie [CDE]	**73.7**	**76.7**	**84.0**	**87.9**	**90.9**	**100.9**	**113.4**	**125.2**
Total mining [C]								
Total, industries extractives [C]	**73.5**	**72.6**	**60.1**	**52.1**	**53.4**	**48.9**	**38.9**	**39.2**
Total manufacturing [D]								
Total, industries manufacturières [D]	**72.4**	**74.7**	**81.7**	**85.9**	**88.8**	**101.8**	**118.2**	**132.9**
Food, beverages, tobacco								
Aliments, boissons, tabac	85.2	81.4	85.8	87.4	87.0	80.7	81.3	83.5
Textiles,wearing apparel, leather, footwear								
Textiles, habillement, cuir et chaussures	61.3	63.1	66.2	63.2	61.8	62.4	72.0	78.6
Chemicals, petroleum, rubber and plastic prod.								
Prod. chimiques, pétroliers, caoutch. et plast.	73.7	74.0	78.1	78.1	76.5	78.3	84.8	76.8
Basic metals								
Métaux de base	53.4	55.9	65.2	74.0	80.9	90.6	87.9	83.9
Metal products								
Produits métalliques	60.7	71.1	83.0	91.7	139.6	305.6	518.7	941.5
Electricity and gas [E]								
Electricité et gaz [E]	**83.5**	**81.7**	**83.1**	**84.7**	**89.0**	**89.8**	**89.7**	**88.5**

22
Index numbers of industrial production [cont.]
Indices de la production industrielle [suite]
1990=100

Country or area and industry [ISIC Rev.3] Pays ou zone et industrie [CITI Rév.3]	1992	1993	1994	1995	1996	1997	1998	1999
Ireland Irlande								
Total industry [CDE]								
Total, industrie [CDE]	**112.9**	**119.3**	**133.4**	**160.8**	**173.0**	**198.6**	**228.9**	**252.7**
Total mining [C]								
Total, industries extractives [C]	**90.1**	**101.7**	**104.5**	**154.1**	**151.6**	**129.7**	**119.6**	**142.2**
Total manufacturing [D]								
Total, industries manufacturières [D]	**113.7**	**119.8**	**135.0**	**163.7**	**176.8**	**205.6**	**239.3**	**264.3**
Food, beverages, tobacco								
Aliments, boissons, tabac	111.7	116.4	125.0	138.7	140.9	144.0	151.6	158.8
Textiles,wearing apparel, leather, footwear								
Textiles, habillement, cuir et chaussures	93.6	92.2	91.7	76.2	76.4	76.6	78.0	68.6
Chemicals, rubber and plastic prod.								
Prod. chimiques, caoutch. et plast.	137.9	150.4	178.0	226.0	258.8	326.1	410.1	466.4
Basic metals								
Métaux de base	92.1	94.6	99.3	119.5	117.7	113.5	107.9	109.8
Metal products								
Produits métalliques	105.3	110.4	124.8	165.4	179.5	208.1	238.5	267.4
Electricity, gas and water [E]								
Electricité, gaz et eau [E]	**111.3**	**117.5**	**123.3**	**125.3**	**132.5**	**138.1**	**142.0**	**154.0**
Italy Italie								
Total industry [CDE]								
Total, industrie [CDE]	**98.9**	**96.5**	**101.5**	**107.0**	**106.0**	**109.6**	**111.6**	**111.7**
Total mining [C]								
Total, industries extractives [C]	**95.2**	**99.2**	**106.1**	**114.1**	**116.8**	**123.8**	**123.1**	**123.0**
Total manufacturing [D]								
Total, industries manufacturières [D]	**98.6**	**95.9**	**100.9**	**106.5**	**105.3**	**108.8**	**110.7**	**110.3**
Food, beverages, tobacco								
Aliments, boissons, tabac	102.9	104.1	104.3	105.1	104.8	107.5	109.9	113.8
Textiles,wearing apparel, leather, footwear								
Textiles, habillement, cuir et chaussures	99.9	97.9	104.5	107.6	106.0	110.0	107.3	102.5
Chemicals, petroleum, rubber and plastic prod.								
Prod. chimiques, pétroliers, caoutch. et plast.	100.9	98.4	102.6	105.3	104.9	110.8	112.1	112.1
Basic metals								
Métaux de base	101.8	100.9	111.4	115.7	115.6	118.0	117.8	108.9
Metal products								
Produits métalliques	93.4	89.0	94.5	105.5	105.5	108.1	109.8	107.8
Electricity and gas [E]								
Electricité et gaz [E]	**103.8**	**103.2**	**107.2**	**111.5**	**112.2**	**115.3**	**119.6**	**124.2**
Latvia Lettonie								
Total industry [CDE]								
Total, industrie [CDE]	**65.1**	**44.2**	**39.8**	**38.4**	**40.5**	**46.1**	**47.5**	**39.0**
Total mining [C]								
Total, industries extractives [C]	**56.6**	**38.0**	**46.6**	**38.7**	**39.7**	**42.8**	**45.4**	**48.0**
Total manufacturing [D]								
Total, industries manufacturières [D]	**64.3**	**41.8**	**36.8**	**35.2**	**37.7**	**44.2**	**45.8**	**36.4**
Food, beverages, tobacco								
Aliments, boissons, tabac	66.0	44.9	39.0	38.8	47.1	56.2	59.3	52.5
Textiles,wearing apparel, leather, footwear								
Textiles, habillement, cuir et chaussures	59.8	36.8	29.0	24.5	32.8	35.0	34.5	25.9
Chemicals, rubber and plastic prod.								
Prod. chimiques, caoutch. et plast.	81.2	54.9	35.8	36.9	36.4	43.1	40.8	21.9
Basic metals								
Métaux de base	49.0	61.0	68.0	56.0	55.8	78.2	133.1	82.5
Metal products								
Produits métalliques	57.8	32.9	29.7	26.5	27.8	34.4	31.7	22.3
Electricity, gas and water [E]								
Electricité, gaz et eau [E]	**74.5**	**59.7**	**58.6**	**58.4**	**57.3**	**56.9**	**57.6**	**54.1**
Lithuania [8] Lituanie [8]								
Total industry [CDE]								
Total, industrie [CDE]	...	...	...	100.0	104.1	108.8	117.8	106.1
Total mining [C]								
Total, industries extractives [C]	...	...	...	100.0	122.0	136.3	185.7	173.2
Total manufacturing [D]								
Total, industries manufacturières [D]	...	...	...	100.0	100.9	106.6	115.4	104.7

22
Index numbers of industrial production [*cont.*]
Indices de la production industrielle [*suite*]
1990=100

Country or area and industry [ISIC Rev.3] Pays ou zone et industrie [CITI Rév.3]	1992	1993	1994	1995	1996	1997	1998	1999
Electricity, gas and water [E]								
Electricité, gaz et eau [E]	...	...	...	100.0	106.7	96.8	99.9	80.0
Luxembourg Luxembourg								
Total industry [CDE]								
Total, industrie [CDE]	99.5	95.2	100.9	102.0	102.1	107.4	116.8	118.6
Total mining [C]								
Total, industries extractives [C]	128.8	114.8	105.6	96.7	86.9	86.4	96.9	104.2
Total manufacturing [D]								
Total, industries manufacturières [D]	98.9	94.3	100.1	101.0	101.3	107.2	116.9	118.9
Food and beverages								
Aliments et boissons	103.9	101.8	105.2	103.7	103.2	103.3	104.9	109.5
Textiles,wearing apparel, leather, footwear								
Textiles, habillement, cuir et chaussures	112.9	108.9	119.4	116.0	94.4	108.1	114.6	106.3
Chemicals, rubber and plastic products								
Prod. chimiques, caoutchouc et plastiques	104.4	94.7	107.5	111.2	116.8	123.2	148.1	135.7
Basic metals								
Métaux de base	93.3	92.2	91.0	83.7	78.4	86.1	75.4	95.6
Metal products								
Produits métalliques	94.3	90.8	96.4	105.7	112.7	113.1	128.6	128.9
Electricity and gas [E]								
Electricité et gaz [E]	103.5	106.0	111.0	117.5	116.6	115.4	119.8	117.3
Malta Malte								
Total industry [CDE]								
Total, industrie [CDE]	128.4	132.8	149.6	166.0	158.2	...	...	...
Total mining [C]								
Total, industries extractives [C]	152.2	159.0	195.4	247.3	274.7	...	...	...
Total manufacturing [D]								
Total, industries manufacturières [D]	128.1	134.2	152.6	165.0	154.8	...	...	...
Food, beverages, tobacco								
Aliments, boissons, tabac	111.1	116.1	122.3	126.7	132.5	...	...	...
Textiles,wearing apparel, leather, footwear								
Textiles, habillement, cuir et chaussures	86.5	102.4	116.7	102.5	110.6	...	...	...
Chemicals, petroleum, rubber and plastic prod.								
Prod. chimiques, pétroliers, caoutch. et plast.	127.0	141.6	154.8	170.3	176.9	...	...	...
Metal products								
Produits métalliques	129.1	132.0	151.4	175.8	161.6	...	...	...
Electricity and water [E]								
Electricité et eau [E]	118.5	124.6	131.7	137.5	142.7	...	...	...
Netherlands Pays−Bas								
Total industry [CDE]								
Total, industrie [CDE]	101.6	100.4	105.3	108.5	111.1	111.3	114.0	116.5
Total mining [C]								
Total, industries extractives [C]	110.5	112.5	111.3	112.2	127.2	116.8	114.0	106.7
Total manufacturing [D]								
Total, industries manufacturières [D]	99.8	98.0	104.0	107.6	108.1	110.9	114.6	118.1
Food, beverages, tobacco								
Aliments, boissons, tabac	106.8	107.6	114.2	118.1	120.2	120.6	120.0	124.0
Textiles,wearing apparel, leather, footwear								
Textiles, habillement, cuir et chaussures	87.7	85.9	84.1	79.7	78.9	79.1	81.3	80.0
Chemicals, petroleum, rubber and plastic prod.								
Prod. chimiques, pétroliers, caoutch. et plast.	98.7	98.3	108.4	114.2	111.8	111.3	112.1	119.9
Basic metals								
Métaux de base	97.6	97.3	108.9	110.1	107.3	116.2	118.6	119.5
Metal products								
Produits métalliques	100.2	95.7	100.4	104.5	106.5	110.0	117.5	120.1
Electricity, gas and water [E]								
Electricité, gaz et eau [E]	104.4	104.9	106.8	109.3	114.5	106.5	107.7	113.1
Norway Norvège								
Total industry [CDE]								
Total, industrie [CDE]	108.4	112.2	120.1	127.2	134.1	138.7	137.8	137.5
Total mining [C] [11]								
Total, industries extractives [C] [11]	96.6	97.0	103.2	106.3	105.7	109.8	105.6	104.5
Total manufacturing [D]								
Total, industries manufacturières [D]	99.7	102.1	108.1	111.5	114.6	118.4	122.0	119.3

22
Index numbers of industrial production [cont.]
Indices de la production industrielle [suite]
1990=100

Country or area and industry [ISIC Rev.3] Pays ou zone et industrie [CITI Rév.3]	1992	1993	1994	1995	1996	1997	1998	1999
Food, beverages, tobacco								
Aliments, boissons, tabac	103.4	104.0	108.6	110.4	112.5	113.6	112.7	109.1
Textiles,wearing apparel, leather, footwear								
Textiles, habillement, cuir et chaussures	95.9	93.7	102.8	99.2	100.5	99.1	94.3	82.4
Chemicals, petroleum, rubber and plastic prod.								
Prod. chimiques, pétroliers, caoutch. et plast.	94.0	98.5	102.7	103.6	105.4	107.6	109.7	109.7
Basic metals								
Métaux de base	99.6	101.6	109.9	108.6	111.6	115.7	121.6	125.4
Metal products								
Produits métalliques	109.3	116.2	120.1	123.9	128.7	133.8	145.4	142.7
Electricity and gas [E]								
Electricité et gaz [E]	**96.5**	**98.6**	**93.4**	**101.5**	**86.4**	**92.2**	**96.5**	**101.3**
Poland Pologne								
Total industry [CDE]								
Total, industrie [CDE]	**94.6**	**100.7**	**112.9**	**123.8**	**135.5**	**150.7**	**157.7**	**165.3**
Total mining [C]								
Total, industries extractives [C]	**92.2**	**88.4**	**92.4**	**91.9**	**93.1**	**91.6**	**79.6**	**76.5**
Total manufacturing [D]								
Total, industries manufacturières [D]	**94.3**	**104.2**	**118.4**	**132.1**	**147.3**	**167.3**	**178.2**	**188.2**
Food, beverages, tobacco								
Aliments, boissons, tabac	108.0	118.1	132.8	143.8	155.7	167.9	180.3	182.4
Textiles,wearing apparel, leather, footwear								
Textiles, habillement, cuir et chaussures	83.0	89.3	100.9	102.4	107.5	125.4	125.4	120.7
Chemicals, petroleum, rubber and plastic prod.								
Prod. chimiques, pétroliers, caoutch. et plast.	104.6	116.3	131.6	146.4	156.7	173.3	173.6	183.2
Basic metals								
Métaux de base	73.5	74.9	87.4	100.7	100.7	113.8	108.0	97.9
Metal products								
Produits métalliques	75.7	86.2	100.5	116.2	135.4	167.7	191.7	208.9
Electricity, gas and water [E]								
Electricité, gaz et eau [E]	**98.8**	**87.7**	**91.9**	**92.7**	**93.1**	**95.3**	**97.1**	**99.3**
Portugal Portugal								
Total industry [CDE]								
Total, industrie [CDE]	**99.6**	**95.2**	**94.9**	**99.4**	**100.8**	**103.3**	**107.4**	**110.8**
Total mining [C]								
Total, industries extractives [C]	**100.8**	**94.4**	**89.3**	**87.5**	**86.4**	**86.4**	**88.0**	**85.6**
Total manufacturing [D]								
Total, industries manufacturières [D]	**97.8**	**92.2**	**92.5**	**95.9**	**97.4**	**101.7**	**104.3**	**105.8**
Food, beverages, tobacco								
Aliments, boissons, tabac	97.3	98.0	94.8	97.1	99.3	102.1	106.6	110.9
Textiles,wearing apparel, leather, footwear								
Textiles, habillement, cuir et chaussures	98.1	88.5	86.5	88.6	85.3	83.9	80.8	76.3
Chemicals, petroleum, rubber and plastic prod.								
Prod. chimiques, pétroliers, caoutch. et plast.	86.6	78.9	82.9	84.3	87.0	92.0	94.2	97.2
Basic metals								
Métaux de base	100.2	96.2	97.9	103.8	100.3	114.0	116.7	131.1
Metal products								
Produits métalliques	98.9	91.1	92.3	100.7	109.4	117.1	127.0	141.6
Electricity and gas [E]								
Electricité et gaz [E]	**107.0**	**108.0**	**106.7**	**117.1**	**118.2**	**113.4**	**124.6**	**144.6**
Romania Roumanie								
Total industry [CDE]								
Total, industrie [CDE]	**57.6**	**58.0**	**59.9**	**65.5**	**69.2**	**64.6**	**53.6**	**48.9**
Total mining [C]								
Total, industries extractives [C]	**82.1**	**82.1**	**83.4**	**83.0**	**83.5**	**78.8**	**67.7**	**61.1**
Total manufacturing [D]								
Total, industries manufacturières [D]	**54.2**	**53.9**	**55.9**	**62.6**	**67.1**	**63.1**	**51.7**	**47.1**
Food, beverages, tobacco								
Aliments, boissons, tabac	70.9	61.2	68.4	70.7	71.8	62.1	61.9	60.1
Textiles,wearing apparel, leather, footwear								
Textiles, habillement, cuir et chaussures	62.3	60.2	67.5	73.5	78.5	78.1	52.3	48.0
Chemicals, petroleum, rubber and plastic prod.								
Prod. chimiques, pétroliers, caoutch. et plast.	55.9	57.6	54.5	58.1	53.2	44.6	38.8	30.9

22
Index numbers of industrial production [*cont.*]
Indices de la production industrielle [*suite*]
1990=100

Country or area and industry [ISIC Rev.3] Pays ou zone et industrie [CITI Rév.3]	1992	1993	1994	1995	1996	1997	1998	1999
Basic metals								
Métaux de base	52.0	55.2	57.1	67.4	61.8	62.7	62.2	39.5
Metal products								
Produits métalliques	57.7	60.3	60.4	73.8	87.3	88.3	68.2	62.2
Electricity, gas and water [E]								
Electricité, gaz et eau [E]	72.6	76.8	76.7	79.2	79.7	70.3	61.6	57.8
Russian Federation Fédération de Russie								
Total industry [CDE]								
Total, industrie [CDE]	74.7	64.9	51.3	49.4	47.4	48.1	45.5	...
Total mining [C]								
Total, industries extractives [C]	84.6	76.9	71.5	70.8	60.0	61.5	...	...
Total manufacturing [D]								
Total, industries manufacturières [D]	73.6	62.9	45.3	43.4	37.1	34.0	...	...
Food, beverages, tobacco								
Aliments, boissons, tabac	86.1	82.0	67.4	58.6	52.1	50.0	50.3	...
Textiles,wearing apparel, leather, footwear								
Textiles, habillement, cuir et chaussures	65.2	51.1	25.9	18.4	14.0	12.7	9.8	...
Chemicals, petroleum, rubber and plastic prod.								
Prod. chimiques, pétroliers, caoutch. et plast.	72.5	57.5	43.2	45.3	41.1	40.3	39.7	...
Basic metals								
Métaux de base	76.6	64.9	55.8	59.7	59.1	59.7	57.1	...
Metal products								
Produits métalliques	74.8	62.9	37.1	29.6	16.4	12.6	10.7	...
Electricity and gas [E]								
Electricité et gaz [E]	95.5	90.9	80.9	80.9	78.2	77.3	76.4	...
Slovakia Slovaquie								
Total industry [CDE]								
Total, industrie [CDE]	73.0	70.2	73.7	79.8	81.8	82.8	86.7	83.8
Total mining [C]								
Total, industries extractives [C]	61.0	44.5	43.0	42.8	45.2	50.5	44.9	47.8
Total manufacturing [D]								
Total, industries manufacturières [D]	71.9	67.8	70.9	78.2	80.0	81.3	86.3	81.8
Electricity, gas and water [E]								
Electricité, gaz et eau [E]	83.3	102.0	118.8	116.8	122.3	118.6	111.7	115.9
Slovenia Slovénie								
Total industry [CDE]								
Total, industrie [CDE]	76.0	73.9	78.7	80.2	81.0	81.8	84.8	84.4
Total mining [C]								
Total, industries extractives [C]	88.0	79.0	75.0	75.6	75.9	77.3	77.1	73.9
Total manufacturing [D]								
Total, industries manufacturières [D]	74.3	72.4	77.2	79.3	80.2	80.4	83.6	83.6
Food, beverages, tobacco								
Aliments, boissons, tabac	80.2	77.5	79.4	79.7	83.4	80.0	79.1	79.0
Textiles,wearing apparel, leather, footwear								
Textiles, habillement, cuir et chaussures	75.1	74.6	72.1	73.5	71.4	70.4	71.0	70.3
Chemicals, petroleum, rubber and plastic prod.								
Prod. chimiques, pétroliers, caoutch. et plast.	72.3	71.7	80.2	82.5	85.2	70.9	72.9	72.6
Basic metals								
Métaux de base	73.5	69.4	75.7	79.3	72.1	62.8	63.9	59.5
Metal products								
Produits métalliques	69.6	66.5	74.9	79.5	81.7	70.3	76.2	75.4
Electricity [E]								
Electricité [E]	97.0	93.5	100.8	100.5	101.3	109.6	113.3	107.2
Spain Espagne								
Total industry [CDE]								
Total, industrie [CDE]	96.1	91.6	98.3	102.9	102.2	109.2	115.1	118.1
Total mining [C]								
Total, industries extractives [C]	92.3	87.0	93.3	98.0	92.5	90.2	90.3	88.4
Total manufacturing [D]								
Total, industries manufacturières [D]	95.4	90.5	98.2	103.3	102.6	110.1	116.9	119.6
Food, beverages, tobacco								
Aliments, boissons, tabac	98.6	100.2	104.1	102.3	99.3	106.7	111.5	111.5
Textiles,wearing apparel, leather, footwear								
Textiles, habillement, cuir et chaussures	88.0	78.5	86.5	84.7	80.8	84.4	86.0	83.5

22
Index numbers of industrial production [*cont.*]
Indices de la production industrielle [*suite*]
1990=100

Country or area and industry [ISIC Rev.3] Pays ou zone et industrie [CITI Rév.3]	1992	1993	1994	1995	1996	1997	1998	1999
Chemicals, petroleum, rubber and plastic prod. Prod. chimiques, pétroliers, caoutch. et plast.	98.3	95.1	105.7	109.2	109.4	116.8	122.7	129.3
Basic metals Métaux de base	96.0	93.8	103.3	109.7	106.6	113.9	119.1	120.2
Metal products Produits métalliques	93.2	84.5	94.3	107.0	109.4	119.1	129.1	130.3
Electricity and gas [E] **Electricité et gaz [E]**	**102.5**	**99.6**	**100.1**	**101.5**	**102.1**	**108.6**	**110.0**	**116.8**
Sweden Suède								
Total industry [CD] **Total, industrie [CD]**	**92.8**	**91.9**	**101.9**	**112.1**	**114.7**	**122.8**	**127.9**	**129.1**
Total mining [C] **Total, industries extractives [C]**	**100.1**	**94.6**	**98.7**	**105.3**	**104.3**	**100.8**	**99.9**	**94.9**
Total manufacturing [D] **Total, industries manufacturières [D]**	**92.7**	**91.9**	**101.9**	**112.2**	**114.8**	**123.1**	**128.4**	**129.7**
Food, beverages, tobacco Aliments, boissons, tabac	96.7	99.0	103.0	106.5	111.3	109.9	107.9	108.5
Textiles,wearing apparel, leather, footwear Textiles, habillement, cuir et chaussures	78.2	70.5	76.8	78.8	76.7	77.1	73.3	66.8
Chemicals, petroleum, rubber and plastic prod. Prod. chimiques, pétroliers, caoutch. et plast.	109.7	116.2	114.2	113.0	117.3	123.1	125.3	127.0
Basic metals Métaux de base	94.3	103.5	122.7	130.2	132.2	137.5	137.4	134.5
Metal products Produits métalliques	89.7	87.3	108.0	136.3	143.1	160.3	175.7	181.4
Switzerland Suisse								
Total industry [CDE] **Total, industrie [CDE]**	**99.0**	**96.9**	**101.0**	**103.1**	**103.0**	**107.8**	**111.8**	**115.5**
Total manufacturing [D] **Total, industries manufacturières [D]**	**99.0**	**96.9**	**100.0**	**103.1**	**103.4**	**108.1**	**112.5**	**116.1**
Food, beverages, tobacco Aliments, boissons, tabac	99.0	101.0	100.0	102.0	102.6	95.8	95.3	96.7
Textiles and wearing apparel Textiles et habillement	93.6	89.6	90.4	93.5	89.9	88.8	85.8	81.0
Chemicals and chemical products Produits chimiques	105.7	112.9	130.0	142.9	157.4	179.6	194.0	217.1
Basic metals and metal products Métaux de base et produtis métalliques	101.7	97.1	98.9	101.0	99.4	106.1	110.0	110.6
Electricity, gas and water [E] **Electricité, gaz et eau [E]**	**106.8**	**110.2**	**118.2**	**113.6**	**110.8**	**115.5**	**116.4**	**122.7**
TFYR Macedonia L'ex−R.y. Macédonie								
Total industry [CDE] **Total, industrie [CDE]**	**70.0**	**60.0**	**54.0**	**48.2**	**49.8**	**50.5**	**52.5**	**51.2**
Ukraine Ukraine								
Total industry [CDE] **Total, industrie [CDE]**	**89.1**	**82.0**	**59.6**	**52.4**	...	...	...	...
Total mining [C] **Total, industries extractives [C]**	**81.0**	**67.8**	**52.0**	**45.7**	...	...	...	...
Total manufacturing [D] **Total, industries manufacturières [D]**	**97.2**	**94.7**	**62.8**	**52.1**	...	...	...	...
Food, beverages, tobacco Aliments, boissons, tabac	77.6	71.4	60.7	54.4	...	...	...	...
Textiles,wearing apparel, leather, footwear Textiles, habillement, cuir et chaussures	109.8	96.6	59.3	38.0	...	...	...	...
Chemicals, petroleum, rubber and plastic prod. Prod. chimiques, pétroliers, caoutch. et plast.	81.7	64.0	46.7	41.6	...	...	...	...
Basic metals Métaux de base	82.7	64.5	41.8	38.9	...	...	...	...
Metal products Produits métalliques	102.7	108.9	70.2	57.1	...	...	...	...
Electricity, gas and water [E] **Electricité, gaz et eau [E]**	**92.0**	**88.7**	**81.1**	**78.1**	...	...	...	...

22
Index numbers of industrial production [cont.]
Indices de la production industrielle [suite]
1990=100

Country or area and industry [ISIC Rev.3] Pays ou zone et industrie [CITI Rév.3]	1992	1993	1994	1995	1996	1997	1998	1999
United Kingdom Royaume – Uni								
Total industry [CDE]								
Total, industrie [CDE]	**97.1**	**99.3**	**104.5**	**106.3**	**107.4**	**108.5**	**109.4**	**109.9**
Total mining [C]								
Total, industries extractives [C]	**107.6**	**114.9**	**132.1**	**136.4**	**140.9**	**139.3**	**142.4**	**147.3**
Total manufacturing [D]								
Total, industries manufacturières [D]	**95.1**	**96.4**	**100.8**	**102.4**	**102.8**	**104.1**	**104.6**	**104.6**
Food, beverages, tobacco								
Aliments, boissons, tabac	101.6	101.8	105.0	103.0	104.8	107.0	105.2	104.8
Textiles,wearing apparel, leather, footwear								
Textiles, habillement, cuir et chaussures	90.2	90.2	92.0	89.2	87.4	86.6	79.5	73.9
Chemicals, petroleum, rubber and plastic prod.								
Prod. chimiques, pétroliers, caoutch. et plast.	104.5	107.1	113.4	119.2	118.2	119.5	120.6	121.7
Basic metals								
Métaux de base	87.9	88.2	89.9	93.0	94.0	95.3	92.2	87.6
Metal products								
Produits métalliques	91.0	91.5	97.3	100.6	102.6	105.5	109.9	112.4
Electricity, gas and water [E]								
Electricité, gaz et eau [E]	**107.4**	**111.9**	**113.1**	**115.6**	**121.7**	**122.2**	**124.4**	**126.4**
Yugoslavia Yougoslavie								
Total industry [CDE]								
Total, industrie [CDE]	**63.8**	**40.1**	**40.5**	**42.4**	**45.5**	**49.6**	**51.3**	**38.9**
Total mining [C]								
Total, industries extractives [C]	**87.6**	**73.6**	**73.4**	**77.1**	**76.5**	**81.8**	**81.3**	**66.3**
Total manufacturing [D]								
Total, industries manufacturières [D]	**62.0**	**34.2**	**34.5**	**35.5**	**39.4**	**45.3**	**47.3**	**33.6**
Food, beverages, tobacco								
Aliments, boissons, tabac	80.1	58.0	59.1	62.8	64.2	61.9	71.2	68.7
Textiles,wearing apparel, leather, footwear								
Textiles, habillement, cuir et chaussures	61.5	33.9	33.5	28.3	30.0	31.8	36.0	25.6
Chemicals, petroleum, rubber and plastic prod.								
Prod. chimiques, pétroliers, caoutch. et plast.	64.5	26.7	30.6	33.6	45.8	65.3	75.3	41.3
Basic metals								
Métaux de base	55.4	22.3	23.2	27.7	39.7	49.1	53.3	29.1
Metal products								
Produits métalliques	51.6	26.9	25.0	24.9	28.1	31.2	37.0	25.1
Electricity, gas and water [E]								
Electricité, gaz et eau [E]	**89.2**	**83.5**	**86.4**	**90.8**	**93.1**	**98.5**	**99.2**	**93.6**
Oceania · Océanie								
Australia [2] Australie [2]								
Total industry [CDE]								
Total, industrie [CDE]	**100.0**	**101.6**	**105.3**	**108.7**	**111.8**	**113.7**	**117.7**	**120.5**
Total mining [C] [12]								
Total, industries extractives [C] [12]	**112.7**	**113.0**	**114.9**	**122.5**	**131.8**	**133.4**	**139.4**	**136.4**
Total manufacturing [D]								
Total, industries manufacturières [D]	**94.8**	**96.9**	**101.2**	**103.3**	**105.5**	**107.7**	**111.1**	**115.5**
Food, beverages, tobacco								
Aliments, boissons, tabac	102.9	103.9	107.6	108.8	111.8	113.6	119.3	125.2
Textiles,wearing apparel, leather, footwear								
Textiles, habillement, cuir et chaussures	92.1	88.4	89.6	87.6	82.7	82.2	83.3	84.5
Chemicals, petroleum, rubber and plastic prod.								
Prod. chimiques, pétroliers, caoutch. et plast.	99.1	100.6	105.6	108.8	115.0	117.2	119.2	124.1
Basic metals and metal products								
Métaux de base et produtis métalliques	93.6	94.9	100.9	103.3	107.0	110.2	114.0	117.9
Electricity, gas and water [E]								
Electricité, gaz et eau [E]	**103.3**	**105.2**	**108.9**	**111.8**	**111.8**	**111.6**	**116.2**	**118.3**
Fiji Fidji								
Total industry [CDE]								
Total, industrie [CDE]	**104.6**	**110.7**	**116.2**	**119.4**	**103.7**	**108.6**	**110.5**	**117.4**
Total mining [C]								
Total, industries extractives [C]	**89.9**	**92.0**	**94.0**	**92.9**	**118.3**	**124.1**	**99.0**	**117.7**
Total manufacturing [D]								
Total, industries manufacturières [D]	**103.1**	**110.7**	**116.2**	**118.8**	**87.7**	**93.2**	**96.3**	**100.1**

22
Index numbers of industrial production [*cont.*]
Indices de la production industrielle [*suite*]
1990=100

Country or area and industry [ISIC Rev.3] Pays ou zone et industrie [CITI Rév.3]	1992	1993	1994	1995	1996	1997	1998	1999
Food, beverages, tobacco Aliments, boissons, tabac	106.6	106.0	116.0	111.7	110.6	96.1	99.5	108.0
Textiles and wearing apparel Textiles et habillement	88.7	124.8	106.3	144.2	190.2	244.0	318.4	346.9
Chemicals and chemical products Produits chimiques	109.3	114.4	113.7	107.3	100.0	121.8	133.8	117.2
Electricity and water [E] **Electricité et eau [E]**	**111.9**	**115.3**	**123.9**	**129.3**	**139.0**	**142.4**	**147.3**	**161.4**
New Zealand [13] Nouvelle–Zélande [13]								
Total industry [CDE] **Total, industrie [CDE]**	**96.4**	**99.3**	**105.7**	**111.3**	**113.4**	**113.6**	**116.6**	**112.7**
Total mining [C] [14] **Total, industries extractives [C] [14]**	**110.8**	**113.1**	**117.0**	**113.5**	**116.2**	**121.0**	**121.8**	**119.6**
Total manufacturing [D] **Total, industries manufacturières [D]**	**93.5**	**97.5**	**104.2**	**111.4**	**113.2**	**114.3**	**116.7**	**112.3**
Food, beverages, tobacco Aliments, boissons, tabac	102.5	105.7	109.7	114.4	119.8	119.2	126.7	121.3
Textiles,wearing apparel, leather, footwear Textiles, habillement, cuir et chaussures	88.6	87.9	92.5	95.1	90.1	87.3	78.6	77.6
Chemicals, petroleum, rubber and plastic prod. Prod. chimiques, pétroliers, caoutch. et plast.	94.0	98.9	108.8	120.0	122.1	117.5	115.2	120.0
Basic metals and metal products Métaux de base et produtis métalliques	86.1	96.9	107.8	113.8	115.1	120.2	122.7	115.5
Electricity, gas and water [E] **Electricité, gaz et eau [E]**	**102.7**	**98.9**	**104.7**	**108.4**	**112.4**	**111.6**	**110.9**	**108.7**

Source:
United Nations Secretariat, industrial statistics database
of the Statistics Division.

† For information on recent changes in country or area
  nomenclature pertaining to former Czechoslovakia, Germany,
  Hong Kong Special Administrative Region (SAR) of China,
  Macao Special Administrative Region (SAR) of China,
  SFR of Yugolasvia and the former USSR, see Annex I –
  Country or area nomenclature, regional and other groupings.

1 Figures relate to 12 months beginning 1 July of the year stated.
2 Figures relate to 12 months ending 30 June of the year stated.
3 Calculated by the Statistics Division of the United Nations
  from component national indices.
4 Excluding coal mining and crude petroleum.
5 Excluding petroleum refineries.
6 Figures relate to 12 months ending 30 September of
  the year stated.
7 Including construction.
8 Base: 1995 = 100.
9 Figures relate to 12 months beginning 1 April of the year stated.
10 Base: 1991 = 100.
11 Excluding gas and oil extraction.
12 Excluding services to mining.
13 Figures relate to 12 months ending 31 March of the year stated.
14 Including forestry and fishing.

Source:
Secrétariat de l'Organisation des Nations Unies, la base de
données de statistiques industrielles de la Division de statistique.

† Pour les modifications récentes de nomenclature de pays ou
  de zone concernant l'Allemagne, Hong Kong (Région
  administrative spéciale de Chine), Macao (Région
  administrative spéciale de Chine), l'ex–Tchécoslovaquie,
  l'ex–URSS, Rfs de Yougoslavie, voir annexe I –
  Nomenclature des pays ou des zones, groupements
  régionaux et autres groupments.

1 Les chiffres se rapportent à 12 mois commençant le 1 juillet
  de l'année indiquée.
2 Les chiffres se rapportent à 12 mois finissant le 30 juin
  de l'année indiquée.
3 Calculé par la Division de Statistiques de l'Organisation
  des Nations Unies à partir d'indices nationaux plus détaillés.
4 Non compris l'extraction du charbon et de pétrole brut.
5 Non compris les raffineries de pétrole.
6 Les chiffres se rapportent à 12 mois finissant le 30 septembre
  de l'année indiquée.
7 Y compris la construction.
8 Base de référence: 1995=100.
9 Les chiffres se rapportent à 12 mois commençant le 1 avril
  de l'année indiquée.
10 Base de référence: 1991=100.
11 Non compris l'extraction de gaz et de pétrole brut.
12 Non compris les services relatifs aux mines.
13 Les chiffres se rapportent à 12 mois finissant le 31 mars
  de l'année indiquée.
14 Y compris l'exploitation forestière et la pêche.

Technical notes, tables 18-22

Detailed internationally comparable data on national accounts are compiled and published annually by the Statistics Division, Department of Economic and Social Affairs of the United Nations Secretariat. Data for national accounts aggregates for countries or areas are based on the concepts and definitions contained in *A System of National Accounts* (1968 SNA) [55] and in *System of National Accounts 1993* (1993 SNA) [56]. A summary of the conceptual framework, classifications and definitions of transactions is found in the annual United Nations publication, *National Accounts Statistics: Main Aggregates and Detailed Tables* [26].

The national accounts data shown in this publication offer, in the form of analytical tables, a summary of selected principal national accounts aggregates based on official detailed national accounts data of some 180 countries and areas. Every effort has been made to present the estimates of the various countries or areas in a form designed to facilitate international comparability. The data for the majority of countries or areas has been compiled according to the 1968 SNA. Data for those countries or areas which have started to follow the concepts and definitions of the 1993 SNA is indicated with a footnote. To the extent possible, any other differences in concept, scope, coverage and classification are footnoted as well. Detailed footnotes identifying these differences are also available in the annual national accounts publication mentioned above. Such differences should be taken into account in order to avoid misleading comparisons among countries or areas.

Table 18 shows gross domestic product (GDP) and GDP per capita in US dollars at current prices, and GDP at constant 1990 prices and the corresponding rates of growth. The table is designed to facilitate international comparisons of levels of income generated in production. In order to present comparable coverage for as many countries as possible, the official GDP national currency data are supplemented by estimates prepared by the Statistics Division, based on a variety of data derived from national and international sources. The conversion rates used to translate national currency data into US dollars are the period averages of market exchange rates (MERs) for members of the International Monetary Fund (IMF). These rates, which are published in the *International Financial Statistics* [14], are communicated to the IMF by national central banks and consist of three types: (a) market rates, determined largely by market forces; (b) official rates, determined by government authorities; and (c) principal rates for countries maintaining multiple exchange rate arrangements. Market rates always take priority and official rates are used only when a free market rate is not available.

Notes techniques, tableaux 18 à 22

La Division de statistique du Département des affaires économiques et sociales du Secrétariat de l'Organisation des Nations Unies établit et publie chaque année des données détaillées, comparables au plan international, sur les comptes nationaux. Les données relatives aux agrégats des différents pays et territoires sont établies en fonction des concepts et des définitions du *Système de comptabilité nationale* (SCN de 1968) [55] et du *Système de comptabilité nationale* (SCN de 1993) [56]. On trouvera un résumé de l'appareil conceptuel, des classifications et des définitions des opérations dans *National Accounts Statistics: Main Aggregates and Detailed Tables* [26], publication annuelle des Nations Unies.

Les chiffres de comptabilité nationale présentés ici récapitulent sous forme de tableaux analytiques un choix d'agrégats essentiels de comptabilité nationale, issus des comptes nationaux détaillés de quelque 180 pays et territoires. On n'a rien négligé pour présenter les chiffres des différents pays et territoires sous une forme facilitant les comparaisons internationales. Pour la plupart des pays, les chiffres ont été établis selon le SCN de 1968. Les données des pays et territoires qui ont commencé à appliquer les concepts et les définitions du SCN de 1993 sont signalées par une note. Dans toute la mesure possible, on signale également au moyen de notes les cas où les concepts, la portée, la couverture et la classification ne seraient pas les mêmes. Il y a en outre des notes détaillées explicitant ces différences dans la publication annuelle mentionnée plus haut. Il y a lieu de tenir compte de ces différences pour éviter de tenter des comparaisons qui donneraient matière à confusion.

Le *tableau 18* fait apparaître le produit intérieur brut (PIB) total et par habitant, exprimé en dollars des États-Unis aux prix courants et à prix constants (base 1990), ainsi que les taux de croissance correspondants. Le tableau est conçu pour faciliter les comparaisons internationales du revenu issu de la production. Afin que la couverture soit comparable pour le plus grand nombre possible de pays, la Division de statistique s'appuie non seulement sur les chiffres officiels du PIB exprimé dans la monnaie nationale, mais aussi sur diverses données provenant de sources nationales et internationales. Les taux de conversion utilisés pour exprimer les données nationales en dollars des États-Unis sont, pour les membres du Fonds monétaire international (FMI), les moyennes pour la période considérée des taux de change du marché. Ces derniers, publiés dans *Statistiques financières internationales* [14], sont communiqués au FMI par les banques centrales des pays et reposent sur trois types de taux : a) taux du marché, déterminés dans une large mesure par les facteurs du marché; b) taux officiels, déterminés par les pouvoirs publics; c) taux principaux, pour les pays

For non-members of the IMF, averages of the United Nations operational rates, used for accounting purposes in United Nations transactions with member countries, are applied. These are based on official, commercial and/or tourist rates of exchange.

It should be noted that there are practical constraints in the use of MERs for conversion purposes. Their use may result in excessive fluctuations or distortions in the dollar income levels of a number of countries particularly in those with multiple exchange rates, those coping with inordinate levels of inflation or countries experiencing misalignments caused by market fluctuations. Caution is therefore urged when making inter-country comparisons of incomes as expressed in US dollars.

The GDP constant price series, based primarily on data officially provided by countries or areas and partly on estimates made by the Statistics Division, are transformed into index numbers and rebased to 1990=100. The resulting data are then converted into US dollars at the rate prevailing in the base year 1990. The growth rates are based on the estimates of GDP at constant 1990 prices. The growth rate of the year in question is obtained by dividing the GDP of that year by the GDP of the preceding year.

Table 19 features the percentage distribution of GDP at current prices by expenditure breakdown. It shows the portions of GDP spent on consumption by the government and the household (including the non-profit institutions serving households) sector, the portions spent on gross fixed capital formation, on changes in inventories, and on exports of goods and services, deducting imports of goods and services. The percentages are derived from official data reported to the United Nations by the countries and published in the annual national accounts publication.

Table 20 shows the percentage distribution of value added originating from the various industry components of the *International Standard Industrial Classification of All Economic Activities, Revision 3* (ISIC Rev. 3) [47]. This table reflects the economic structure of production in the different countries or areas. The percentages are based on official value added estimates at current prices broken down by the kind of economic activity: agriculture, hunting, forestry and fishing (categories A+B); mining and quarrying (C); manufacturing (D); electricity, gas and water supply (E); construction (F); wholesale and retail trade, repair of motor vehicles, motorcycles and personal and household goods, restaurants and hotels (G+H); transport, storage and communications (I) and other activities comprised of financial intermediation (J), real estate, renting and business activities (K), public administration and defence, compulsory social security (L), education (M), health and social

pratiquant différents arrangements en matière de taux de change. On donne toujours la priorité aux taux du marché, n'utilisant les taux officiels que lorsqu'on n'a pas de taux du marché libre.

Pour les pays qui ne sont pas membres du FMI, on utilise les moyennes des taux de change opérationnels de l'ONU (qui servent à des fins comptables pour les opérations de l'ONU avec les pays qui en sont membres). Ces taux reposent sur les taux de change officiels, les taux du commerce et/ou les taux touristiques.

Il est à noter que l'utilisation des taux de change du marché pour la conversion des données se heurte à des obstacles pratiques. On risque, ce faisant, d'aboutir à des fluctuations excessives ou à des distorsions du revenu en dollars de certains pays, surtout dans le cas des pays qui pratiquent plusieurs taux de change et de ceux qui connaissent des taux d'inflation exceptionnels ou des décalages provenant des fluctuations du marché. Les comparaisons de revenu entre pays sont donc sujettes à caution lorsqu'on se fonde sur le revenu exprimé en dollars des États-Unis.

La série de statistiques du PIB à prix constants est fondée principalement sur des données officiellement communiquées par les pays, et en partie sur des estimations de la Division de statistique; les données permettent de calculer des indices, la base 100 correspondant à 1990. Les chiffres ainsi obtenus sont alors convertis en dollars des États-Unis au taux de change de l'année de base (1990). Les taux de croissance sont calculés à partir des estimations du PIB aux prix constants de 1990. Le taux de croissance de l'année considérée est obtenu en divisant le PIB de l'année par celui de l'année précédente.

Le *tableau 19* montre la répartition (en pourcentage) du PIB aux prix courants par catégorie de dépense. Il indique la part du PIB consacrée aux dépenses de consommation des administrations publiques et du secteur des ménages (y compris les institutions sans but lucratif au service des ménages), celle qui est consacrée à la formation brute de capital fixe, celle qui correspond aux variations de stocks et celle qui correspond aux exportations de biens et services, déduction faite des importations de biens et services. Ces pourcentages sont calculés à partir des chiffres officiels communiqués à l'ONU par les pays, publiés dans l'ouvrage annuel.

Le *tableau 20* montre la répartition (en pourcentage) de la valeur ajoutée par branche d'activité, selon le classement retenu dans la *Classification internationale type, par industrie, de toutes les branches d'activité économique, Révision 3* (CITI Rev. 3) [47]. Il rend donc compte de la structure économique de la production dans chaque pays. Les pourcentages sont établis à partir des chiffres officiels de valeur ajoutée, aux prix courants, ventilés selon les différentes catégories d'activité économique : agriculture, chasse, sylviculture et pêche (catégories

work (N), other community, social and personal service activities (O) and private households with employed persons (P).

Table 21 presents the relationships between the principal national accounting aggregates, namely: gross domestic product (GDP), gross national income (GNI), gross national disposable income (GNDI) and gross saving. GNI is the term used in the 1993 SNA instead of the term Gross National Product (GNP) which was used in the 1968 SNA. The ratio of each aggregate to GDP is derived cumulatively by adding net primary income (or net factor income) from the rest of the world, (GNI); adding net current transfers from the rest of the world, (GNDI) and deducting final consumption to arrive at gross saving. Net national income, net national disposable income and net saving can be derived by deducting consumption of fixed capital from the corresponding gross values mentioned above.

Table 22:The national indices in this table are shown for the categories "Mining", "Manufacturing" and "Electricity, gas and water". These categories are classified according to Tabulation Categories C, D and E of the ISIC Revision 3 [47]. Major deviations from ISIC in the scope of the indices for the above categories are indicated by footnotes to the table.

The category "Total industry" covers Mining, Manufacturing and Electricity, gas and water. The indices for "Total industry", however, are the combination of the components shown and share all deviations from ISIC as footnoted for the component series.

For the purpose of presentation, the national indices have been rebased to 1990=100, where necessary.

A + B); activités extractives (C); activités de fabrication (D); production et distribution d'électricité, de gaz et d'eau (E); construction (F); commerce de gros et de détail, réparation de véhicules automobiles, de motocycles et de biens personnels et domestiques, hôtels et restaurants (G + H); transports, entreposage et communications (I) et intermédiation financière (J); immobilier, locations et activités de services aux entreprises (K); administration publique et défense, sécurité sociale obligatoire (L); éducation (M); santé et action sociale (N); autres activités de services collectifs, sociaux et personnels (O); et ménages privés employant du personnel domestique (P).

Le *tableau 21* montre les rapports entre les principaux agrégats de la comptabilité nationale, à savoir le produit intérieur brut (PIB), le revenu national brut (RNB), le revenu national brut disponible et l'épargne brute. Le revenu national brut est l'agrégat qui remplace dans le SCN de 1993 le produit national brut, utilisé dans le SCN de 1968. Chacun d'entre eux est obtenu par rapport au PIB, en ajoutant les revenus primaires nets (ou revenus nets de facteurs) engendrés dans le reste du monde, pour obtenir le revenu national brut; en ajoutant les transferts courants nets reçus de non-résidents, pour obtenir le revenu national disponible; en soustrayant la consommation finale pour obtenir l'épargne brute. Le revenu national net, le revenu national disponible net et l'épargne nette s'obtiennent en déduisant de la valeur brute correspondante la consommation de capital fixe.

Tableau 22: Les définitions des catégories "Mines", "Industries manufacturières" et "Electricité, gaz et eau", pour lesquelles des indices nationaux sont donnés dans ce tableau correspondent aux catégories C, D et E des tableaux de la CITI Révision 3 [47]. Toutes différences importantes par rapport à la CITI dans la portée des indices de ces catégories sont indiquées dans les notes du tableau.

La catégorie "Total, industrie" couvre Mines, Industries manufacturières et Electricité, gaz et eau. Toutefois, les indices de cette catégorie "Total, industrie" ne portent que sur la combinaison des indices partiels indiqués, et partagent toutes les différences par rapport à la CITI notées dans le cas des indices partiels.

Pour les besoins de la présentation, les indices nationaux ont été dans certains cas recalculés en prenant 1990=100 comme base de référence.

23
Rates of discount of central banks
Taux d'escompte des banques centrales
Per cent per annum, end of period
Pour cent par année, fin de la période

Country or area Pays ou zone	1990	1991	1992	1993	1994	1995	1996	1997	1998	1999
Albania Albanie	...	...	40.00	34.00	25.00	20.50	24.00	32.00	23.44	18.00
Algeria Algérie	10.50	11.50	11.50	11.50	21.00	...	13.00	11.00	9.50	8.50
Angola Angola	...	...	...	...	...	160.00	2.00	48.00	58.00	120.00
Armenia Arménie	...	...	30.00	210.00	210.00	77.80	26.00	65.10	...	...
Aruba Aruba	9.50	9.50	9.50	9.50	9.50	9.50	9.50	9.50	9.50	6.50
Australia Australie	15.24	10.99	6.96	5.83	5.75	5.75	...	...	...	...
Austria Autriche	6.50	8.00	8.00	5.25	4.50	3.00	2.50	2.50	2.50	...
Azerbaijan Azerbaïdjan	...	...	12.00	100.00	200.00	80.00	20.00	12.00	14.00	10.00
Bahamas Bahamas	9.00	9.00	7.50	7.00	6.50	6.50	6.50	6.50	6.50	5.75
Bangladesh Bangladesh	9.75	9.25	8.50	6.00	5.50	6.00	7.00	8.00	8.00	7.00
Barbados Barbade	13.50	18.00	12.00	8.00	9.50	12.50	12.50	9.00	9.00	10.00
Belarus Bélarus	...	...	30.00	210.00	480.00	66.00	8.30	8.90	9.60	23.40
Belgium Belgique	10.50	8.50	7.75	5.25	4.50	3.00	2.50	2.75	2.75	...
Belize Belize	12.00	12.00	12.00	12.00	12.00	12.00	12.00	12.00	12.00	12.00
Benin Bénin	11.00	11.00	12.50	10.50	10.00	7.50	6.50	6.00	6.25	5.75
Bolivia Bolivie	...	...	...	...	...	...	16.50	13.25	14.10	12.50
Botswana Botswana	8.50	12.00	14.25	14.25	13.50	13.00	13.00	12.50	12.50	13.25
Brazil Brésil	...	...	...	...	...	...	25.34	45.09	39.41	21.37
Bulgaria Bulgarie	...	54.00	41.00	52.00	78.50	37.31	192.00	...	...	...
Burkina Faso Burkina Faso	11.00	11.00	12.50	10.50	10.00	7.50	6.50	6.00	6.25	5.75
Burundi Burundi	8.00	10.70	9.80	9.80	9.40	9.90	...	...	12.40	12.09
Cameroon Cameroun	11.00	10.75	12.00	11.50	# 7.75	8.60	7.75	7.50	7.00	7.30
Canada Canada	11.78	7.67	7.36	4.11	7.43	5.79	3.25	4.50	5.25	5.00
Central African Rep. Rép. centrafricaine	11.00	10.75	12.00	11.50	# 7.75	8.60	7.75	7.50	7.00	7.60

23
Rates of discount of central banks
Per cent per annum, end of period [cont.]
Taux d'escompte des banques centrales
Pour cent par année, fin de la période [suite]

Country or area Pays ou zone	1990	1991	1992	1993	1994	1995	1996	1997	1998	1999
Chad Tchad	11.00	10.75	12.00	11.50	# 7.75	8.60	7.75	7.50	7.00	7.60
China †† Chine ††	7.92	7.20	7.20	10.08	10.08	10.44	9.00	8.55	4.59	3.24
China, Hong Kong SAR† Chine, Hong Kong RAS†	...	...	4.00	4.00	5.75	6.25	6.00	7.00	6.25	7.00
Colombia Colombie	46.45	44.98	34.42	33.49	44.90	40.42	35.05	31.32	42.28	23.05
Congo Congo	11.00	10.75	12.00	11.50	# 7.75	8.60	7.75	7.50	7.00	7.60
Costa Rica Costa Rica	37.80	42.50	29.00	35.00	37.75	38.50	35.00	31.00	37.00	34.00
Côte d'Ivoire Côte d'Ivoire	11.00	11.00	12.50	10.50	10.00	7.50	6.50	6.00	6.25	5.75
Croatia Croatie	...	...	1 889.39	34.49	8.50	8.50	6.50	5.90	5.90	7.90
Cyprus Chypre	6.50	6.50	6.50	6.50	6.50	6.50	# 7.50	7.00	7.00	7.00
Czech Republic République tchèque	...	...	...	8.00	8.50	9.50	10.50	13.00	7.50	5.00
Dem. Rep. of the Congo Rép. dém. du Congo	45.00	55.00	55.00	95.00	145.00	125.00	238.00	13.00	22.00	120.00
Denmark Danemark	8.50	9.50	9.50	6.25	5.00	4.25	3.25	3.50	3.50	3.00
Ecuador Equateur	35.00	49.00	49.00	33.57	44.88	59.41	46.38	37.46	61.84	64.40
Egypt Egypte	14.00	20.00	18.40	16.50	14.00	13.50	13.00	12.25	12.00	12.00
Equatorial Guinea Guinée équatoriale	11.00	10.75	12.00	11.50	# 7.75	8.60	7.75	7.50	7.00	7.60
Ethiopia Ethiopie	3.00	3.00	5.25	12.00	12.00	12.00	...	...	...	...
Fiji Fidji	8.00	8.00	6.00	6.00	6.00	6.00	6.00	1.88	2.50	2.50
Finland Finlande	8.50	8.50	9.50	5.50	5.25	4.88	4.00	4.00	3.50	...
Gabon Gabon	11.00	10.75	12.00	11.50	# 7.75	8.60	7.75	7.50	7.00	7.60
Gambia Gambie	16.50	15.50	17.50	13.50	13.50	14.00	14.00	14.00	12.00	10.50
Germany Allemagne	6.00	8.00	8.25	5.75	4.50	3.00	2.50	2.50	2.50	...
Ghana Ghana	33.00	20.00	30.00	35.00	33.00	45.00	45.00	45.00	37.00	27.00
Greece Grèce	19.00	19.00	19.00	21.50	20.50	18.00	16.50	14.50	...	11.81
Guinea Guinée	15.00	19.00	19.00	17.00	17.00	18.00	18.00	15.00	...	...
Guinea-Bissau Guinée-Bissau	42.00	42.00	45.50	41.00	26.00	39.00	54.00	6.00	6.25	5.75

23
Rates of discount of central banks
Per cent per annum, end of period [cont.]
Taux d'escompte des banques centrales
Pour cent par année, fin de la période [suite]

Country or area Pays ou zone	1990	1991	1992	1993	1994	1995	1996	1997	1998	1999
Guyana Guyana	30.00	32.50	24.30	17.00	20.25	17.25	12.00	11.00	11.25	13.25
Hungary Hongrie	22.00	22.00	21.00	22.00	25.00	28.00	23.00	20.50	17.00	14.50
Iceland Islande	21.00	21.00	# 16.63	...	4.70	5.93	5.70	6.55	...	...
India Inde	10.00	12.00	12.00	12.00	12.00	12.00	12.00	9.00	9.00	8.00
Indonesia Indonésie	18.83	18.47	13.50	8.82	12.44	13.99	12.80	20.00	38.44	12.51
Ireland Irlande	11.25	10.75	...	7.00	6.25	6.50	6.25	6.75	4.06	...
Israel Israël	13.00	14.23	10.39	9.78	17.01	14.19	...	...	...	...
Italy Italie	12.50	12.00	12.00	8.00	7.50	9.00	7.50	5.50	3.00	...
Japan Japon	6.00	4.50	3.25	1.75	1.75	0.50	0.50	0.50	0.50	0.50
Jordan Jordanie	8.50	8.50	8.50	8.50	8.50	8.50	8.50	7.75	9.00	8.00
Kazakhstan Kazakhstan	...	...	...	170.00	230.00	# 52.50	35.00	18.50	25.00	18.00
Kenya Kenya	19.43	20.27	20.46	45.50	21.50	24.50	26.88	32.27	17.07	26.46
Korea, Republic of Corée, République de	7.00	7.00	7.00	5.00	5.00	5.00	5.00	5.00	3.00	3.00
Kuwait Koweït	...	7.50	7.50	5.75	7.00	7.25	7.25	7.50	7.00	6.75
Lao People's Dem. Rep. Rép. dém. pop. lao	...	...	23.67	25.00	30.00	32.08	35.00	...	35.00	34.89
Latvia Lettonie	...	...	...	27.00	25.00	24.00	9.50	4.00	4.00	4.00
Lebanon Liban	21.84	18.04	16.00	20.22	16.49	19.01	25.00	30.00	30.00	25.00
Lesotho Lesotho	15.75	18.00	15.00	13.50	13.50	15.50	17.00	15.60	19.50	19.00
Libyan Arab Jamah. Jamah. arabe libyenne	5.00	5.00	5.00	5.00	...	...	...	...	3.00	5.00
Malawi Malawi	14.00	13.00	20.00	25.00	40.00	50.00	27.00	23.00	43.00	47.00
Malaysia Malaisie	7.23	7.70	7.10	5.24	4.51	6.47	7.28	...	...	...
Mali Mali	11.00	11.00	12.50	10.50	10.00	7.50	6.50	6.00	6.25	5.75
Malta Malte	5.50	5.50	5.50	5.50	5.50	5.50	5.50	5.50	5.50	4.75
Mauritania Mauritanie	7.00	7.00	7.00	...	...	...	...	...	...	...
Mauritius Maurice	12.00	11.30	8.30	8.30	13.80	11.40	11.82	10.46	17.19	...

23
Rates of discount of central banks
Per cent per annum, end of period [cont.]
Taux d'escompte des banques centrales
Pour cent par année, fin de la période [suite]

Country or area Pays ou zone	1990	1991	1992	1993	1994	1995	1996	1997	1998	1999
Mongolia Mongolie	...	...	...	628.80	180.00	150.00	109.00	45.50	23.30	11.40
Morocco Maroc	...	...	...	...	7.17	...	...	...	6.04	5.42
Myanmar Myanmar	...	11.00	11.00	11.00	11.00	12.50	15.00	15.00	15.00	12.00
Namibia Namibie	...	20.50	16.50	14.50	15.50	17.50	17.75	16.00	18.75	11.50
Nepal Népal	11.00	13.00	13.00	11.00	11.00	11.00	11.00	9.00	9.00	9.00
Netherlands Pays-Bas	7.25	8.50	7.75	5.00	...	...	...	...	...	...
Netherlands Antilles Antilles néerlandaises	6.00	6.00	6.00	5.00	5.00	6.00	6.00	6.00	6.00	6.00
New Zealand Nouvelle-Zélande	13.25	8.30	9.15	5.70	9.75	9.80	8.80	9.70	5.60	5.00
Nicaragua Nicaragua	10.00	15.00	15.00	11.75	10.50	...	...	...	...	...
Niger Niger	11.00	11.00	12.50	10.50	10.00	7.50	6.50	6.00	6.25	5.75
Nigeria Nigéria	18.50	15.50	17.50	26.00	13.50	13.50	13.50	13.50	13.50	18.00
Norway Norvège	10.50	10.00	11.00	7.00	6.75	6.75	6.00	5.50	10.00	7.50
Pakistan Pakistan	10.00	10.00	10.00	10.00	# 15.00	17.00	20.00	18.00	16.50	13.00
Papua New Guinea Papouasie-Nvl-Guinée	9.30	9.30	7.12	# 6.39	...	...	...	...	...	...
Paraguay Paraguay	33.00	19.75	24.00	27.17	19.15	20.50	15.00	20.00	20.00	20.00
Peru Pérou	289.60	67.65	48.50	28.63	16.08	18.44	18.16	15.94	18.72	17.80
Philippines Philippines	14.00	14.00	14.30	9.40	8.30	10.83	11.70	14.64	12.40	7.89
Poland Pologne	48.00	36.00	32.00	29.00	28.00	25.00	22.00	24.50	18.25	19.00
Portugal Portugal	14.50	# 20.00	21.96	11.00	8.88	8.50	6.70	5.31	3.00	...
Russian Federation Fédération de Russie	...	...	...	...	...	160.00	48.00	28.00	60.00	55.00
Rwanda Rwanda	14.00	14.00	11.00	11.00	11.00	16.00	16.00	10.75	11.38	11.19
Sao Tome and Principe Sao Tomé-et-Principe	25.00	45.00	45.00	30.00	32.00	50.00	35.00	55.00	29.50	17.00
Senegal Sénégal	11.00	11.00	12.50	10.50	10.00	7.50	6.50	6.00	6.25	5.75
Seychelles Seychelles	1.00	1.00	1.00	1.00	1.00	1.00	1.00	1.00	1.00	1.00
Slovakia Slovaquie	...	...	...	12.00	12.00	9.75	8.80	8.80	8.80	8.80

23
Rates of discount of central banks
Per cent per annum, end of period [cont.]
Taux d'escompte des banques centrales
Pour cent par année, fin de la période [suite]

Country or area Pays ou zone	1990	1991	1992	1993	1994	1995	1996	1997	1998	1999
Slovenia Slovénie	...	...	...	...	...	14.62	11.42	13.78	8.55	8.35
South Africa Afrique du Sud	18.00	17.00	14.00	12.00	13.00	15.00	17.00	16.00	# 19.32	12.00
Spain Espagne	14.71	12.50	13.25	9.00	7.38	9.00	6.25	4.75	3.00	...
Sri Lanka Sri Lanka	15.00	17.00	17.00	17.00	17.00	17.00	17.00	17.00	17.00	16.00
Swaziland Swaziland	12.00	13.00	12.00	11.00	12.00	15.00	16.75	15.75	18.00	12.00
Sweden Suède	11.50	8.00	# 10.00	5.00	7.00	7.00	3.50	2.50	2.00	1.50
Switzerland Suisse	6.00	7.00	6.00	4.00	3.50	1.50	1.00	1.00	1.00	0.50
Syrian Arab Republic Rép. arabe syrienne	5.00	5.00	5.00	5.00	5.00	...	...	...	...	...
Thailand Thaïlande	12.00	11.00	11.00	9.00	9.50	10.50	10.50	12.50	12.50	4.00
TFYR Macedonia L'ex-R.y. Macédoine	...	...	...	295.00	33.00	15.00	9.20	8.90	8.90	8.90
Togo Togo	11.00	11.00	12.50	10.50	10.00	7.50	6.50	6.00	6.25	5.75
Trinidad and Tobago Trinité-et-Tobago	9.50	11.50	13.00	13.00	13.00	13.00	13.00	13.00	13.00	13.00
Tunisia Tunisie	11.88	11.88	11.38	8.88	8.88	8.88	7.88	...	...	...
Turkey Turquie	45.00	48.00	48.00	48.00	55.00	50.00	...	...	...
Uganda Ouganda	50.00	46.00	41.00	24.00	15.00	13.30	15.85	14.08	9.10	15.75
Ukraine Ukraine	...	...	80.00	240.00	252.00	110.00	40.00	35.00	60.00	45.00
United Rep.Tanzania Rép.-Unie de Tanzanie	...	...	14.50	14.50	67.50	47.90	19.00	16.20	17.60	20.20
United States Etats-Unis	6.50	3.50	3.00	3.00	4.75	5.25	5.00	5.00	4.50	5.00
Uruguay Uruguay	251.60	219.00	162.40	164.30	182.30	178.70	160.30	95.50	73.70	66.39
Venezuela Venezuela	43.00	43.00	52.20	71.25	48.00	49.00	45.00	45.00	60.00	38.00
Zambia Zambie	...	...	47.00	72.50	20.50	40.20	47.00	17.70	...	...
Zimbabwe Zimbabwe	10.25	20.00	29.50	28.50	29.50	29.50	27.00	31.50	39.50	74.41

Source:
International Monetary Fund (IMF), Washington, D.C.,
"International Financial Statistics," November 2000 and the
IMF database.

Source:
Fonds monétaire international (FMI), Washington,
D.C.,"Statistiques Financières Internationales," novembre
2000 et la base de données du FMI.

23
Rates of discount of central banks
Per cent per annum, end of period [*cont.*]

Taux d'escompte des banques centrales
Pour cent par année, fin de la période [*suite*]

† For information on recent changes in country or
area nomenclature pertaining to former Czechoslovakia,
Germany, Hong Kong Special Administrative Region (SAR) of
China, Macao Special Administrative Region (SAR) of China,
SFR of Yugoslavia and the former USSR, see Annex I - Country
or area nomenclature, regional and other groupings.

†† For statistical purposes, the data for
China do not include those for Hong Kong Special
Administrative Region (Hong Kong SAR), Macao Special
Administrative Region (Macao SAR) and Taiwan province of
China.

† Pour les modifications récentes de nomenclature
de pays ou de zone concernant l'Allemagne, Hong Kong, région
administrative spéciale (RAS) de Chine, Macao, région
administrative spéciale (RAS) de Chine,
l'ex-Tchécoslovaquie, l'ex-URSS et l'ex-Rfs de Yougoslavie,
voir annexe I - Nomenclature des pays ou des zones,
groupements régionaux et autres groupements.

†† Les données statistiques relatives à
la Chine ne comprennent pas celles qui concernent la région
administrative spéciale de Hong Kong (la RAS de Hong Kong),
la région administrative spéciale de Macao (la RAS de Macao)
et la province chinoise de Taiwan.

24
Short-term interest rates
Taux d'intérêt à court terme
Treasury bill and money market rates: per cent per annum
Taux des bons du Trésor et du marché monétaire : pour cent par année

Country or area Pays ou zone	1990	1991	1992	1993	1994	1995	1996	1997	1998	1999
Albania Albanie										
Treasury bill										
Bons du Trésor	...	...	...	...	...	13.84	17.81	32.59	27.49	17.54
Algeria Algérie										
Treasury bill										
Bons du Trésor	3.25	9.50	9.50	9.50	16.50	...	...	...	9.96	10.05
Money market										
Marché monétaire	...	...	...	...	19.80	...	18.50	11.80	10.40	10.40
Antigua and Barbuda Antigua-et-Barbuda										
Treasury bill										
Bons du Trésor	7.00	7.00	7.00	7.00	7.00	7.00	7.00	7.00	7.00	7.00
Argentina Argentine										
Money market										
Marché monétaire	...	71.33	15.11	6.31	7.66	9.46	6.23	6.63	6.81	6.99
Armenia Arménie										
Treasury bill										
Bons du Trésor	...	...	...	...	...	37.81	41.40	55.84	45.84	53.28
Money market										
Marché monétaire	...	...	...	...	...		48.56	36.41	27.84	23.65
Australia Australie										
Treasury bill										
Bons du Trésor	14.15	9.96	6.27	5.00	5.69	# 7.64	7.02	5.29	4.84	4.76
Money market										
Marché monétaire	14.81	10.47	6.44	5.11	5.18	# 7.50	7.20	5.50	4.99	4.78
Austria Autriche										
Money market										
Marché monétaire	8.53	9.10	9.35	7.22	5.03	4.36	3.19	3.27	3.36	...
Bahamas Bahamas										
Treasury bill										
Bons du Trésor	5.85	6.49	5.32	3.96	1.88	3.01	4.45	4.35	3.84	1.97
Bahrain Bahreïn										
Treasury bill										
Bons du Trésor	...	5.90	3.78	3.33	4.81	6.07	5.49	5.68	5.53	5.46
Money market										
Marché monétaire	8.54	6.31	3.99	3.53	5.18	6.24	5.69	...	5.69	5.58
Barbados Barbade										
Treasury bill										
Bons du Trésor	7.07	9.34	10.88	5.44	7.26	8.01	6.85	3.61	5.61	5.83
Belgium Belgique										
Treasury bill										
Bons du Trésor	9.62	9.24	9.36	8.52	5.57	4.67	3.19	3.38	3.51	2.72
Money market										
Marché monétaire	8.29	9.38	9.38	8.21	5.72	4.80	3.24	3.46	3.58	...
Belize Belize										
Treasury bill										
Bons du Trésor	7.37	6.71	5.38	4.59	4.27	4.10	3.78	3.51	3.83	5.91
Benin Bénin										
Money market										
Marché monétaire	10.98	10.94	11.44	...	...	...	...	...	4.81	4.95
Bolivia Bolivie										
Treasury bill										
Bons du Trésor	...	...	...	...	17.89	24.51	19.93	13.65	12.33	14.07
Money market										
Marché monétaire	...	...	...	...	...	22.42	20.27	13.97	12.57	13.49

24
Short-term interest rates
Treasury bill and money market rates: per cent per annum [cont.]
Taux d'intérêt à court terme
Taux des bons du Trésor et du marché monétaire : pour cent par année [suite]

Country or area Pays ou zone	1990	1991	1992	1993	1994	1995	1996	1997	1998	1999
Brazil Brésil										
Treasury bill										
Bons du Trésor	...	...	...	...	...	49.93	25.73	24.79	28.57	26.39
Money market										
Marché monétaire	15 778.60	847.54	1 574.28	3 284.44	4 820.64	53.37	27.45	25.00	29.50	26.26
Bulgaria Bulgarie										
Treasury bill										
Bons du Trésor	...	...	48.11	45.45	57.72	48.27	114.31	78.35	6.02	5.43
Money market										
Marché monétaire	...	48.67	52.39	48.07	66.43	53.09	119.88	66.43	2.48	2.93
Burkina Faso Burkina Faso										
Money market										
Marché monétaire	10.98	10.94	11.44	...	...	...	...	...	4.81	4.95
Canada Canada										
Treasury bill										
Bons du Trésor	12.81	8.73	6.59	4.84	5.54	6.89	4.21	3.26	4.73	4.72
Money market										
Marché monétaire	11.62	7.40	6.79	3.79	5.54	5.71	3.01	4.34	5.11	4.76
China, Hong Kong SAR† Chine, Hong Kong RAS†										
Treasury bill										
Bons du Trésor	...	...	3.83	3.17	5.66	5.55	4.45	7.50	5.04	4.94
Money market										
Marché monétaire	11.50	4.63	3.81	4.00	5.44	6.00	5.13	4.50	5.50	5.75
Colombia Colombie										
Money market										
Marché monétaire	...	...	...	...	...	22.40	28.37	23.83	35.00	18.81
Côte d'Ivoire Côte d'Ivoire										
Money market										
Marché monétaire	10.98	10.94	11.44	...	...	...	...	...	4.81	4.95
Croatia Croatie										
Money market										
Marché monétaire	...	...	951.20	1 370.50	26.93	21.13	19.26	10.18	14.48	13.72
Denmark Danemark										
Money market										
Marché monétaire	10.97	9.78	11.35	# 11.49	6.30	6.19	3.98	3.71	4.27	3.37
Dominica Dominique										
Treasury bill										
Bons du Trésor	6.50	6.50	6.48	6.40	6.40	6.40	6.40	6.40	6.40	6.40
Dominican Republic Rép. dominicaine										
Money market										
Marché monétaire	...	...	...	...	...	...	14.70	13.01	16.68	15.30
Egypt Egypte										
Treasury bill										
Bons du Trésor	...	...	...	...	...	...	...	8.80	8.80	9.00
El Salvador El Salvador										
Money market										
Marché monétaire	...	...	...	...	...	...	...	10.43	9.43	10.68
Estonia Estonie										
Money market										
Marché monétaire	...	...	...	...	5.67	4.94	3.53	6.45	11.66	4.92
Ethiopia Ethiopie										
Treasury bill										
Bons du Trésor	3.00	3.00	5.25	12.00	12.00	12.00	7.22	3.97	3.48	3.65

24
Short-term interest rates
Treasury bill and money market rates: per cent per annum [*cont.*]
Taux d'intérêt à court terme
Taux des bons du Trésor et du marché monétaire : pour cent par année [*suite*]

Country or area Pays ou zone	1990	1991	1992	1993	1994	1995	1996	1997	1998	1999
Fiji　Fidji										
Treasury bill 　Bons du Trésor	4.40	5.61	3.65	2.91	2.69	3.15	2.98	2.60	2.00	2.00
Money market 　Marché monétaire	2.92	4.28	3.06	2.91	4.10	3.95	2.43	1.91	1.27	1.27
Finland　Finlande										
Money market 　Marché monétaire	14.00	13.08	13.25	7.77	5.35	5.75	3.63	3.23	3.57	2.97
France　France										
Treasury bill 　Bons du Trésor	10.18	9.69	10.49	8.41	5.79	6.58	3.84	3.35	3.45	2.72
Money market 　Marché monétaire	9.85	9.49	10.35	8.75	5.69	6.35	3.73	3.24	3.39	...
Georgia　Géorgie										
Money market 　Marché monétaire	...	...	...	...	...	...	43.39	26.58	43.26	34.61
Germany　Allemagne										
Treasury bill 　Bons du Trésor	8.13	8.27	8.32	6.22	5.05	4.40	3.30	3.32	3.42	2.88
Money market 　Marché monétaire	7.92	8.84	9.42	7.49	5.35	4.50	3.27	3.18	3.41	2.73
Ghana　Ghana										
Treasury bill 　Bons du Trésor	21.78	29.23	19.38	30.95	27.72	35.38	41.64	42.77	34.33	26.37
Greece　Grèce										
Treasury bill 　Bons du Trésor	18.50	18.79	17.69	18.23	18.23	14.29	11.92	9.51	11.98	9.54
Grenada　Grenade										
Treasury bill 　Bons du Trésor	6.50	6.50	6.50	6.50	6.50	6.50	6.50	6.50	6.50	6.50
Guatemala　Guatemala										
Money market 　Marché monétaire	...	...	...	...	...	...	...	7.77	6.62	9.23
Guinea-Bissau　Guinée-Bissau										
Money market 　Marché monétaire	10.98	10.94	11.45	...	...	...	...	...	4.81	4.95
Guyana　Guyana										
Treasury bill 　Bons du Trésor	30.00	30.94	25.75	16.83	17.66	17.51	11.35	8.91	8.33	11.31
Haiti　Haïti										
Treasury bill 　Bons du Trésor	...	...	...	...	...	...	...	14.13	16.21	7.71
Hungary　Hongrie										
Treasury bill 　Bons du Trésor	30.13	34.48	22.65	17.22	26.93	32.04	23.96	20.13	17.83	14.68
Iceland　Islande										
Treasury bill 　Bons du Trésor	12.92	14.25	# 11.30	8.35	4.95	7.22	6.97	7.04	7.40	8.61
Money market 　Marché monétaire	12.73	14.85	12.38	8.61	4.96	6.58	6.96	7.38	8.12	9.24
India　Inde										
Money market 　Marché monétaire	15.57	19.35	15.23	8.64	7.14	15.57	11.04	5.29	...	...

24
Short-term interest rates
Treasury bill and money market rates: per cent per annum [cont.]
Taux d'intérêt à court terme
Taux des bons du Trésor et du marché monétaire : pour cent par année [suite]

Country or area Pays ou zone	1990	1991	1992	1993	1994	1995	1996	1997	1998	1999
Indonesia Indonésie Money market Marché monétaire	13.97	14.91	11.99	8.66	9.74	13.64	13.96	27.82	62.79	23.58
Ireland Irlande Treasury bill Bons du Trésor	10.90	10.12	...	# 9.06	5.87	6.19	5.36	6.03	5.37	...
Money market Marché monétaire	11.10	10.45	15.12	10.49	# 5.75	5.45	5.74	6.43	3.23	3.14
Israel Israël Treasury bill Bons du Trésor	15.08	14.50	11.79	10.54	11.77	14.37	15.54	13.88	12.17	...
Italy Italie Treasury bill Bons du Trésor	12.38	12.54	14.32	10.58	9.17	10.85	8.46	6.33	4.59	3.01
Money market Marché monétaire	12.38	# 12.21	14.02	10.20	8.51	10.46	8.82	6.88	4.99	2.95
Jamaica Jamaïque Treasury bill Bons du Trésor	26.21	25.56	34.36	28.85	42.98	27.65	37.95	21.14	25.65	20.75
Japan Japon Money market Marché monétaire	7.24	7.46	4.58	# 3.06	2.20	1.21	0.47	0.48	0.37	0.06
Kazakhstan Kazakhstan Treasury bill Bons du Trésor	...	...	...	...	214.34	48.98	28.91	15.15	23.59	15.63
Kenya Kenya Treasury bill Bons du Trésor	14.78	16.59	16.53	49.80	23.32	18.29	22.25	22.87	22.83	13.87
Korea, Republic of Corée, République de Money market Marché monétaire	14.03	17.03	14.32	12.12	12.45	12.57	12.44	13.24	14.98	5.01
Kuwait Koweït Treasury bill Bons du Trésor	...	...	...	...	6.32	7.35	6.93	6.98	...	...
Money market Marché monétaire	...	...	...	7.43	6.31	7.43	6.98	7.05	7.24	6.32
Kyrgyzstan Kirghizistan Treasury bill Bons du Trésor	...	...	...	...	143.13	34.90	40.10	35.83	43.67	47.19
Money market Marché monétaire	...	...	...	...	...	...	...	...	43.98	43.71
Lao People's Dem. Rep. Rép. dém. pop. lao Treasury bill Bons du Trésor	...	...	...	...	...	20.46	...	...	23.66	30.00
Latvia Lettonie Treasury bill Bons du Trésor	...	...	...	...	...	28.24	16.27	4.73	5.27	6.23
Money market Marché monétaire	...	...	...	37.18	22.39	13.08	3.76	4.42	4.72
Lebanon Liban Treasury bill Bons du Trésor	18.84	17.47	22.40	18.27	15.09	19.40	15.19	13.42	12.70	11.57

24
Short-term interest rates
Treasury bill and money market rates: per cent per annum [*cont.*]
Taux d'intérêt à court terme
Taux des bons du Trésor et du marché monétaire : pour cent par année [*suite*]

Country or area Pays ou zone	1990	1991	1992	1993	1994	1995	1996	1997	1998	1999
Lesotho Lesotho										
Treasury bill Bons du Trésor	16.33	15.75	14.20	13.10	# 9.44	12.40	13.89	14.83	15.47	12.45
Libyan Arab Jamah. Jamah. arabe libyenne										
Money market Marché monétaire	4.00	4.00	4.00	4.00	...	...	...	...	4.00	4.00
Lithuania Lituanie										
Treasury bill Bons du Trésor	...	...	...	...	...	26.82	20.95	8.64	10.69	11.14
Money market Marché monétaire	...	...	...	...	69.48	26.73	20.26	9.55	6.12	6.26
Luxembourg Luxembourg										
Money market Marché monétaire	9.67	9.10	8.93	8.09	5.16	4.26	3.29	3.36	3.48	...
Madagascar Madagascar										
Money market Marché monétaire	15.00	15.00	15.00	...	0.00	29.00	10.00	...	11.24	...
Malawi Malawi										
Treasury bill Bons du Trésor	12.92	11.50	15.62	23.54	27.68	46.30	30.83	18.31	32.98	42.85
Malaysia Malaisie										
Treasury bill Bons du Trésor	6.12	7.27	7.66	6.48	3.68	5.50	6.41	6.41	6.86	3.53
Money market Marché monétaire	6.81	7.83	8.01	6.53	4.65	5.78	6.98	7.61	8.46	3.38
Maldives Maldives										
Money market Marché monétaire	7.00	7.00	7.00	5.00	5.00	6.80	6.80	6.80	6.80	6.80
Mali Mali										
Money market Marché monétaire	10.98	10.94	11.44	...	...	...	...	...	4.81	4.95
Malta Malte										
Treasury bill Bons du Trésor	4.25	4.46	4.58	4.60	4.29	4.65	4.99	5.08	5.41	5.15
Mauritius Maurice										
Money market Marché monétaire	13.26	12.24	9.05	7.73	10.23	10.35	9.96	9.43	8.99	10.01
Mexico Mexique										
Treasury bill Bons du Trésor	34.76	19.28	15.62	14.99	14.10	48.44	31.39	19.80	24.76	21.41
Money market Marché monétaire	37.36	23.58	18.87	17.39	16.47	# 60.92	33.61	21.91	26.89	24.10
Morocco Maroc										
Money market Marché monétaire	...	...	...	...	12.29	10.06	8.42	7.89	6.30	5.64
Namibia Namibie										
Treasury bill Bons du Trésor	...	...	13.88	12.16	11.35	13.91	15.25	15.69	17.24	13.28
Nepal Népal										
Treasury bill Bons du Trésor	7.93	8.80	9.00	4.50	6.50	9.90	11.51	2.52	3.70	4.30
Netherlands Pays-Bas										
Money market Marché monétaire	8.29	9.01	9.27	7.10	5.14	4.22	2.89	3.07	3.21	...

24
Short-term interest rates
Treasury bill and money market rates: per cent per annum [cont.]
Taux d'intérêt à court terme
Taux des bons du Trésor et du marché monétaire : pour cent par année [suite]

Country or area Pays ou zone	1990	1991	1992	1993	1994	1995	1996	1997	1998	1999
Netherlands Antilles Antilles néerlandaises										
Treasury bill										
Bons du Trésor	6.10	...	...	4.83	4.48	5.46	5.66	5.77	5.82	6.15
New Zealand Nouvelle-Zélande										
Treasury bill										
Bons du Trésor	13.78	9.74	6.72	6.21	6.69	8.82	9.09	7.53	7.10	4.58
Money market										
Marché monétaire	12.61	7.59	7.59	4.96	9.44	8.77	7.89	8.84	4.91	5.63
Niger Niger										
Money market										
Marché monétaire	10.98	10.94	11.44	...	...	...	...	...	4.81	4.95
Nigeria Nigéria										
Treasury bill										
Bons du Trésor	...	...	17.89	24.50	12.87	12.50	12.25	12.00	12.26	17.82
Norway Norvège										
Money market										
Marché monétaire	11.45	10.58	13.71	7.64	5.70	5.54	4.97	3.77	6.03	6.87
Pakistan Pakistan										
Treasury bill										
Bons du Trésor	...	...	12.47	13.03	11.26	12.49	13.61	# 15.74	...	...
Money market										
Marché monétaire	7.29	7.64	7.51	11.00	8.36	11.52	11.40	12.10	10.76	9.04
Papua New Guinea Papouasie-Nvl-Guinée										
Treasury bill										
Bons du Trésor	11.40	10.33	8.88	6.25	6.85	17.40	14.44	9.94	21.18	22.70
Paraguay Paraguay										
Money market										
Marché monétaire	...	12.39	21.59	22.55	18.64	20.18	16.35	12.48	20.74	17.26
Philippines Philippines										
Treasury bill										
Bons du Trésor	23.67	21.48	16.02	12.45	12.71	11.76	12.34	12.89	15.00	10.00
Poland Pologne										
Treasury bill										
Bons du Trésor	...	...	44.03	33.16	28.81	25.62	20.32	21.58	19.09	13.14
Money market										
Marché monétaire	...	49.93	# 29.49	24.51	23.32	25.82	20.63	22.43	20.59	13.58
Portugal Portugal										
Treasury bill										
Bons du Trésor	13.51	14.20	12.88	...	...	7.75	5.75	4.43	...	...
Money market										
Marché monétaire	13.12	15.50	# 17.48	13.25	10.62	8.91	7.38	5.78	4.34	2.71
Republic of Moldova République de Moldova										
Treasury bill										
Bons du Trésor	...	...	...	...	...	52.90	39.01	23.63	30.54	28.49
Money market										
Marché monétaire	...	...	...	...	...	...	...	28.10	30.91	32.60
Romania Roumanie										
Treasury bill										
Bons du Trésor	...	...	...	...	...	...	51.09	85.72	63.99	74.21
Russian Federation Fédération de Russie										
Treasury bill										
Bons du Trésor	...	...	...	...	...	168.04	86.07	23.43	...	...
Money market										
Marché monétaire	...	...	...	...	...	190.43	47.65	20.97	50.56	14.79

24
Short-term interest rates
Treasury bill and money market rates: per cent per annum [*cont.*]
Taux d'intérêt à court terme
Taux des bons du Trésor et du marché monétaire : pour cent par année [*suite*]

Country or area Pays ou zone	1990	1991	1992	1993	1994	1995	1996	1997	1998	1999
Saint Kitts and Nevis Saint-Kitts-et-Nevis										
Treasury bill										
Bons du Trésor	6.50	6.50	6.50	6.50	6.50	6.50	6.50	6.50	6.50	6.50
Saint Lucia Sainte-Lucie										
Treasury bill										
Bons du Trésor	7.00	7.00	7.00	7.00	7.00	7.00	7.00	7.00	7.00	7.00
St. Vincent-Grenadines St. Vincent-Grenadines										
Treasury bill										
Bons du Trésor	6.50	6.50	6.50	6.50	6.50	6.50	6.50	6.50	6.50	6.50
Senegal Sénégal										
Money market										
Marché monétaire	10.98	10.94	11.44	...	...	...	...	...	4.81	4.95
Seychelles Seychelles										
Treasury bill										
Bons du Trésor	13.00	13.00	13.00	12.91	12.36	12.15	11.47	10.50	7.96	4.50
Sierra Leone Sierra Leone										
Treasury bill										
Bons du Trésor	47.50	50.67	78.63	28.64	12.19	14.73	29.25	12.71	22.10	32.42
Singapore Singapour										
Money market										
Marché monétaire	6.61	4.76	2.74	2.50	3.68	2.56	2.93	4.35	5.00	2.04
Slovenia Slovénie										
Money market										
Marché monétaire	...	...	67.58	39.15	29.08	12.18	13.98	9.71	7.45	6.87
Solomon Islands Iles Salomon										
Treasury bill										
Bons du Trésor	11.00	13.71	13.50	12.15	11.25	12.50	12.75	12.88	6.00	6.00
South Africa Afrique du Sud										
Treasury bill										
Bons du Trésor	17.80	16.68	13.77	11.31	10.93	13.53	15.04	15.26	16.53	12.85
Money market										
Marché monétaire	19.46	17.02	14.11	10.83	10.24	13.07	15.54	15.59	17.11	13.06
Spain Espagne										
Treasury bill										
Bons du Trésor	14.17	12.45	12.44	10.53	8.11	9.79	7.23	5.02	3.79	3.01
Money market										
Marché monétaire	14.76	13.20	13.01	12.33	7.81	8.98	7.65	5.49	4.34	2.72
Sri Lanka Sri Lanka										
Treasury bill										
Bons du Trésor	14.08	13.75	16.19	16.52	12.68	16.81	# 17.40	...	12.59	12.51
Money market										
Marché monétaire	21.56	25.42	21.63	25.65	18.54	41.87	24.33	18.42	15.74	16.69
Swaziland Swaziland										
Treasury bill										
Bons du Trésor	11.14	12.67	12.34	8.25	8.35	10.87	13.68	14.37	13.09	11.19
Money market										
Marché monétaire	10.50	10.61	10.25	9.73	7.01	8.52	9.77	10.35	10.63	8.86
Sweden Suède										
Treasury bill										
Bons du Trésor	13.66	11.59	12.85	8.35	7.40	8.75	5.79	4.11	4.19	3.12
Money market										
Marché monétaire	13.45	11.81	18.42	9.08	7.36	8.54	6.28	4.21	4.24	3.14

24
Short-term interest rates
Treasury bill and money market rates: per cent per annum [*cont.*]
Taux d'intérêt à court terme
Taux des bons du Trésor et du marché monétaire : pour cent par année [*suite*]

Country or area Pays ou zone	1990	1991	1992	1993	1994	1995	1996	1997	1998	1999
Switzerland Suisse										
Treasury bill										
Bons du Trésor	8.32	7.74	7.76	4.75	3.97	2.78	1.72	1.45	1.32	1.17
Money market										
Marché monétaire	8.33	7.73	7.47	4.94	3.85	2.89	1.78	1.35	1.22	0.93
Thailand Thaïlande										
Money market										
Marché monétaire	12.87	11.15	6.93	6.54	7.25	10.96	9.23	14.59	13.02	1.77
Togo Togo										
Money market										
Marché monétaire	10.98	10.94	11.44	...	...	...	...	...	4.81	4.95
Trinidad and Tobago Trinité-et-Tobago										
Treasury bill										
Bons du Trésor	7.50	7.67	9.26	9.45	10.00	8.41	10.44	9.83	11.93	10.40
Tunisia Tunisie										
Money market										
Marché monétaire	11.53	11.79	11.73	10.48	8.81	8.81	8.64	6.88	6.89	5.99
Turkey Turquie										
Treasury bill										
Bons du Trésor	43.46	67.01	72.17	...	...	...	...	...	...	...
Money market										
Marché monétaire	51.91	72.75	65.35	62.83	136.47	72.30	76.24	70.32	74.60	73.53
Uganda Ouganda										
Treasury bill										
Bons du Trésor	41.00	34.17	...	# 21.30	12.52	8.75	11.71	10.59	7.77	7.43
Ukraine Ukraine										
Money market										
Marché monétaire	...	...	...	...	...	...	...	22.05	40.41	44.98
United Kingdom Royaume-Uni										
Treasury bill										
Bons du Trésor	14.09	10.85	8.94	5.25	5.15	6.33	5.77	6.48	6.82	5.04
Money market										
Marché monétaire	14.64	11.77	9.39	5.46	4.76	5.98	5.89	6.56	7.09	5.11
United Rep.Tanzania Rép.-Unie de Tanzanie										
Treasury bill										
Bons du Trésor	...	...	...	34.00	35.09	40.33	15.30	9.59	11.83	10.05
United States Etats-Unis										
Treasury bill										
Bons du Trésor[2]	7.51	5.41	3.46	3.02	4.27	5.51	5.02	5.07	4.82	4.66
Money market[2]										
Marché monétaire[2]	8.10	5.69	3.52	3.02	4.20	5.84	5.30	5.46	5.35	4.97
Uruguay Uruguay										
Treasury bill										
Bons du Trésor	...	...	...	...	44.60	39.40	29.20	23.18	...	...
Money market										
Marché monétaire	...	...	...	...	39.82	36.81	28.47	23.43	20.48	13.96
Vanuatu Vanuatu										
Money market										
Marché monétaire	7.00	7.00	5.92	6.00	6.00	6.00	6.00	6.00	8.65	6.99
Venezuela Venezuela										
Money market										
Marché monétaire	...	...	...	...	...	...	16.70	12.47	18.58	7.48
Zambia Zambie										
Treasury bill										
Bons du Trésor	25.92	...	...	124.03	74.21	39.81	52.78	29.48	24.94	36.19

24
Short-term interest rates
Treasury bill and money market rates: per cent per annum [*cont.*]
Taux d'intérêt à court terme
Taux des bons du Trésor et du marché monétaire : pour cent par année [*suite*]

Country or area Pays ou zone	1990	1991	1992	1993	1994	1995	1996	1997	1998	1999
Zimbabwe Zimbabwe										
Treasury bill Bons du Trésor	8.39	14.44	26.16	33.04	29.22	27.98	24.53	22.07	32.78	50.48
Money market Marché monétaire	8.68	17.49	34.77	34.18	30.90	29.64	26.18	25.15	37.22	53.13

Source:
International Monetary Fund (IMF), Washington, D.C.,
"International Financial Statistics," November 2000 and the
IMF database.

† For information on recent changes in country or
area nomenclature pertaining to former Czechoslovakia,
Germany, Hong Kong Special Administrative Region (SAR) of
China, Macao Special Administrative Region (SAR) of China,
SFR of Yugoslavia and the former USSR, see Annex I - Country
or area nomenclature, regional and other groupings.

1 Rate = 9,695,422.00.
2 Federal funds rate.

Source:
Fonds monétaire international (FMI), Washington,
D.C.,"Statistiques Financières Internationales," novembre
2000 et la base de données du FMI.

† Pour les modifications récentes de nomenclature
de pays ou de zone concernant l'Allemagne, Hong Kong, région
administrative spéciale (RAS) de Chine, Macao, région
administrative spéciale (RAS) de Chine,
l'ex-Tchécoslovaquie, l'ex-URSS et l'ex-Rfs de Yougoslavie,
voir annexe I - Nomenclature des pays ou des zones,
groupements régionaux et autres groupements.

1 Taux = 9 695 422.00.
2 Taux des fonds du système fédérale.

Technical notes, tables 23 and 24

Detailed information and current figures relating to tables 23 and 24 are contained in *International Financial Statistics*, published by the International Monetary Fund [14] and in the United Nations *Monthly Bulletin of Statistics* [25].

Table 23: The discount rates shown represent the rates at which the central bank lends or discounts eligible paper for deposit money banks, typically shown on an end-of-period basis.

Table 24: The rates shown represent short-term treasury bill rates and money market rates. The treasury bill rate is the rate at which short-term securities are issued or traded in the market. The money market rate is the rate on short-term lending between financial institutions.

Notes techniques, tableaux 23 et 24

Les informations détaillées et les chiffres courants concernant les tableaux 23 et 24 figurent dans les *Statistiques financières internationales* publiées par le Fonds monétaire international [14] et dans le *Bulletin mensuel de statistique* des Nations Unies [25].

Tableau 23: Les taux d'escomptes indiqués représentent les taux que la banque centrale applique à ses prêts ou auquel elle réescompte les effets escomptables des banques créatrices de monnaie (généralement, taux de fin de période).

Tableau 24: Les taux indiqués représentent le taux des bons du Trésor et le taux du marché monétaire à court terme. Le taux des bons du Trésor est le taux auquel les effets à court terme sont émis ou négociés sur le marché. Le taux du marché monétaire est le taux prêteur à court terme entre institutions financières.

Table 25 follows overleaf

Le tableau 25 est présenté au verso

25
Employment by industry
Emploi par industrie

A. ISIC Rev. 2 [+] · CITI Rév. 2 [+]

Persons employed, by branch of economic activity (000s)
Personnes employées, par branches d'activité économique (000s)

Country or area / Pays ou zone	Year / Année	Total employment (000s) Emploi total (000s) M	F	Agriculture, hunting, forestry and fishing Agriculture, chasse, sylviculture, pêche M	F	Mining and quarrying Industries extractives M	F	Manufacturing Industries manufacturières M	F	Electricity, gas, wa... Electricité, gaz, ea... M	F
Australia [1 2 3 4 5]	1993	4420.5	3259.1	286.3	122.5	80.7	8.2	777.1	290.8	82.5	1...
Australie [1 2 3 4 5]	1994	4545.4	3375.2	281.0	122.6	76.6	9.7	811.5	294.5	77.3	1...
Austria [2 6]	1993	2078.8	1496.6	129.3	117.2	9.3	0.9	658.0	244.8	31.8	4
Autriche [2 6]	1994	2146.8	1595.2	141.8	127.5	8.0	1.2	585.6	232.0	30.7	4
Azerbaijan [7]	1993	3714.6	...	1203.5	...	...	...	391.8[8]	...	107.7	
Azerbaïdjan [7]	1998	3701.5	...	1085.4				240.2[8]	...	126.6	
Bangladesh [9]	1990	30443.0	19716.0	16560.0	16743.0	15.0	...	4240.0	1685.0	39.0	1
Bangladesh [9]	1996[10]	33765.0	20832.0	18382.0	16148.0	22.0	1.0	2586.0	1499.0	90.0	13
Barbados [12]	1993	51.2	44.2	3.2	2.0	...	...	4.9	5.1	1.1	0
Barbade [12]	1995	57.7	52.1	3.2	1.9			5.4	6.3	0.8	0
Belarus [7]	1993	4827.7	...	1048.8	...	29.6	...	1311.8	...	38.1	
Belarus [7]	1994	4700.9	...	995.7	...	27.2	...	1245.6	...	38.7	
Belgium [13 14 15]	1991	2295.4	1435.1	68.0	27.3	7.2	0.7	655.2	189.1	41.5	6
Belgique [13 14 15]	1992	2287.6	1484.9	70.6	29.4	7.9	0.4	657.8	207.7	35.5	6
Belize [16]	1993	43.4	18.7	14.7	0.9	0.3	0.0	5.0	2.2	1.0	0
Belize [16]	1994	43.0	19.0	13.3	0.8	0.3	0.0	5.0	1.7	1.0	0
Bolivia [1 17]	1991	525.8	361.9	12.3	3.7	18.6	1.8	109.6	49.3	6.3	1
Bolivie [1 17]	1992	616.3	432.1	16.7	5.4	18.8	0.9	136.5	67.0	8.2	1
Brazil [9 13 18]	1993	40585.0	25985.0	12004.0	6250.0	795.0[19]	152.0[19]	6113.0	2426.0	...	
Brésil [9 13 18]	1997	41978.0	27354.0	11254.0	5516.0	658.0[19]	116.0[19]	6101.0	2406.0	...	
Bulgaria [7 24]	1993	3221.8	...	712.6[25]	...	...	...	978.7[26]	...	...	
Bulgarie [7 24]	1996	3279.5	...	809.8[25]	...	...	...	893.5[26]	...	...	
Canada [2 28]	1993	6753.0	5630.0	395.0	155.0	129.0	20.0	1297.0[29]	503.0[29]	108.0[30]	34
Canada [2 28]	1997	7648.8	6291.7	384.5	153.0	151.3	25.9	1556.1	610.7	106.0	33
Chile [1 2 32]	1996[33]	3609.0	1689.7	727.3	89.1	87.2	3.4	631.1	228.6	36.6	5
Chili [1 2 32]	1998	3624.8	1807.6	702.1	82.3	76.6	5.3	591.3	227.3	34.0	3
China †† [7 13 34 35]	1993	663730.0	...	339660.0	...	9320.0	...	92950.0	...	2400.0	
Chine †† [7 13 34 35]	1997	696000.0	...	330049.0	...	8676.0	...	96108.0	...	2834.0	
China, Hong Kong SAR † [1 2 37]	1993	1758.9	1041.2	14.0	3.9	0.3	...	369.3	224.7	17.1	2
Chine, Hong Kong RAS † [1 2 37]	1998	1935.1	1265.8	6.7	2.8	0.2	...	251.9	139.9	16.2	2
China, Macao SAR † [1 15 38]	1993	99.6	71.8	0.3	0.1	0.0	...	17.6	25.2	0.6	0
Chine, Macao RAS † [1 15 38]	1997	110.9	89.7	0.2	0.1	...	...	14.0	27.4	1.3	0
Colombia [13 39 40 41]	1993	3107.2	2225.6	45.2	15.6	14.2	5.7	709.6	533.8	26.1	7
Colombie [13 39 40 41]	1998	3194.6	2460.3	43.3	14.8	11.0	3.4	624.7	474.4	23.4	9
Costa Rica [1 13 39]	1993	772.5	324.0	228.2	19.7	1.3	0.3	127.2	69.6	13.7	2
Costa Rica [1 13 39]	1996	808.1	336.9	228.7	19.2	2.0	0.1	128.6	60.3	10.1	1
Cyprus [1]	1993	165.7	103.0	18.7	12.8	0.7	...	25.5	19.3	1.4	0
Chypre [1]	1995	173.0	112.1	18.8	11.7	0.8	...	25.9	18.1	1.3	0
Denmark [32 42]	1992	1427.3	1224.9	103.4	32.5	2.0	0.6	362.4	168.4	16.4	2
Danemark [32 42]	1993[43]	1383.1	1200.9	100.5	31.3	1.8	0.7	346.6	155.1	13.9	2
Dominican Republic	1993	1701.0	715.6	387.6	19.7	7.6	0.4	295.8	152.6	15.3	1
Rep. dominicaine	1996	1734.9	736.2	341.6	16.0	7.9	0.8	301.7	131.3	11.8	1
Ecuador [9 13 17]	1993	1636.4	1014.4	169.4	24.6	16.6	1.9	302.7	159.8	16.0	3
Equateur [9 13 17]	1998	1920.8	1230.4	202.4	28.2	10.4	0.2	303.7	159.3	12.9	2
Egypt [1 38 44]	1993	11762.8	2940.6	3821.5	1366.9	43.1	2.4	1837.3	207.9	135.2	12
Egypte [1 38 44]	1995	12395.8	2948.4	3962.7	1252.9	38.2	2.5	1944.5	239.0	152.9	13
El Salvador [9]	1994	1200.2	750.8	483.7	62.3	1.3	0.3	190.6	192.1	7.1	1
El Salvador [9]	1997	1292.1	783.9	492.4	54.7	1.6	0.1	175.8	158.3	14.1	1
Finland [42 45]	1993	1071.0	993.0	117.0	56.0	4.0	...	265.0	131.0	18.0	5
Finlande [42 45]	1995	1104.0	988.0	104.0	54.0	4.0	...	296.0	130.0	21.0	4
France [14]	1992	12647.8	9659.8	777.9	372.3	...	...	4771.9[46]	1551.3[46]	...	
France [14]	1993	12446.3	9629.9	748.7	352.1	...	...	4551.8[46]	1479.8[46]	...	
Germany [2 13]	1993	21296.0	15085.0	742.0	514.0	268.0	39.0	7308.0	2923.0	312.0	81
Allemagne [2 13]	1994	20987.0	15088.0	714.0	477.0	234.0	32.0	6877.0	2765.0	295.0	79
Greece [14 15 32]	1991	2406.8	1225.7	479.2	327.3	17.7	1.6	491.8[48]	207.2[48]	31.8	4
Grèce [14 15 32]	1992	2403.2	1281.3	468.7	338.0	17.6	0.7	487.3[48]	211.4[48]	30.9	5
Honduras [1 9 13]	1995	1266.6	539.9	638.4	34.4	2.2	0.6	173.5	152.2	6.0	1
Honduras [1 9 13]	1998	1400.8	734.2	680.9	57.6	4.4	0.1	177.1	191.3	5.8	1

Construction Construction		Trade, restaurants and hotels Commerce, restaurants, hôtels		Transport, storage, communications Transports, entrepôts, communications		Financing, insurance, real est.,bus. services Services financières, immob., et apparentées		Community, social and personal services Services fournis à la collectivité, services soc. et pe	
M	F	M	F	M	F	M	F	M	F
473.6	76.9	1033.1	917.7	370.4	114.2	510.7	441.9	782.2	1263.2
490.0	79.6	1066.1	948.5	384.2	126.5	537.5	488.7	800.1	1278.1
280.7	25.1	273.2	401.1	188.1	44.4	133.7	131.6	366.4	516.0
316.7	36.0	341.3	431.1	191.8	54.2	163.5	180.6	367.4	528.1
212.3	...	445.8	...	196.2	...	12.6	...	607.8	...
150.2		772.3	...	166.8	...	10.2	...	618.3	...
485.0	41.0	4262.0	123.0	1600.0	11.0	284.0	12.0	1647.0	262.0
936.0	80.0	5573.0	488.0	2263.0	45.0	197.0	16.0	3343.0	1748.0
6.6[11]	0.3[11]	7.0[12]	7.6[12]	3.4	1.2	2.3	3.2	18.4	19.7
8.5[11]	0.3[11]	8.1[12]	8.5[12]	3.7	1.3	2.3	5.3	20.3	21.8
369.1	...	405.3	...	328.9	...	33.6	...	1075.6	...
328.9	...	422.3	...	318.0	...	40.9	...	1099.7	...
217.7	14.1	349.4	292.8	229.9	48.2	174.0	129.0	543.8	706.3
230.0	15.5	344.7	312.6	221.2	47.7	192.9	132.8	520.8	710.5
3.8	0.1	1.1	2.0	2.9	0.5	0.3	0.6	1.6	1.1
3.5	0.1	1.3	1.9	3.2	0.5	0.5	0.7	1.4	1.4
74.1	2.0	103.4	156.7	60.6	4.1	22.8	9.3	118.0	134.4
95.9	1.3	121.8	183.4	70.7	4.8	26.5	13.9	120.4	154.3
4134.0	155.0	5290.0[20]	3185.0[20]	2105.0[21]	179.0[21]	894.0[22]	496.0[22]	9250.0[23]	13142.0
4486.0	98.0	5614.0[20]	3609.0[20]	2507.0[21]	252.0[21]	818.0[22]	460.0[22]	10538.0[23]	14898.0
200.0	...	352.3	...	241.0[21]	...	66.8	...	670.4[27]	...
171.9	...	397.4	...	246.2[21]	...	68.7	...	692.0[27]	...
585.0	75.0	1514.0	1398.0	559.0	208.0	699.0	767.0	1468.0[31]	2469.0
664.9	82.4	1707.3	1576.6	662.3	234.8	880.4	919.4	1536.2	2655.0
402.6	14.4	522.5	409.4	349.9	44.0	231.3	138.1	620.4	757.5
434.6	13.9	545.1	460.4	373.6	59.1	252.4	153.3	615.2	802.5
30500.0	...	34590.0	...	16880.0	...	3360.0[36]	...	15730.0	...
34479.0	...	47943.0	...	20599.0	...	3952.0[36]	...	18031.0	...
211.2	9.9	457.1	338.7	263.6	51.3	173.7	115.5	252.5	295.2
300.8	18.7	531.8	442.0	296.5	66.8	251.3	167.7	279.7	425.6
15.3	1.8	25.0	19.5	8.7	1.8	4.4	4.8	27.4	18.1
12.8	1.6	27.9	25.3	9.7	3.7	8.3	5.4	36.5	25.9
356.4	18.7	744.1	603.8	314.4	39.7	243.3	152.7	648.2	842.8
326.2	26.2	763.7	668.1	355.4	56.3	312.3	206.8	730.5	997.6
66.5	0.8	119.3	75.2	46.5	5.5	34.2	12.4	126.4	133.9
63.3	0.8	141.2	83.6	53.1	5.5	37.2	13.3	135.4	150.3
23.5	1.5	37.3	30.2	12.2	4.6	10.3	9.1	33.5	24.7
24.1	1.6	40.3	34.3	13.4	5.1	11.8	10.8	34.2	29.6
143.7	19.6	194.2	183.1	136.3	49.5	131.8	107.8	330.5	655.5
131.9	15.9	216.5	185.6	132.5	51.5	134.6	122.9	300.2	632.0
102.8	1.6	369.7	197.9	132.1	8.6	44.1	23.2	344.6	308.0
123.3	3.8	362.3	210.6	173.6	12.3	57.2	37.4	353.5	318.4
156.6	3.8	395.7	390.6	140.4	15.6	81.7	37.7	356.6	377.4
181.0	4.9	489.9	462.6	181.3	17.7	113.0	50.8	425.3	502.6
934.4	15.1	1257.0	180.0	769.2	37.3	229.3	47.1	2733.9	1071.5
951.5	16.1	1378.6	209.1	863.2	44.4	238.5	44.2	2864.9	1125.9
109.2	3.0	161.6	222.3	71.9	5.5	13.9	12.5	160.9	251.8
134.7	4.0	187.4	257.7	90.1	6.6	16.9	13.3	179.1	288.0
113.0	12.0	132.0	169.0	116.0	42.0	84.0	95.0	219.0	480.0
110.0	10.0	138.0	160.0	117.0	41.0	88.0	87.0	221.0	500.0
...	...	7098.0[47]	7736.2[47]	...	...	...	...	...	...
...	...	7145.8[47]	7798.0[47]	...	...	...	...	...	...
2619.0	327.0	2234.0	3074.0	1596.0	624.0	1575.0	1494.0	4734.0	6010.0
2753.0	355.0	2273.0	3111.0	1555.0	614.0	1636.0	1523.0	4651.0	6133.0
242.9	2.9	411.8	248.6	225.3	27.1	116.3	76.4	390.0	329.8
242.5	3.7	423.9	263.4	220.7	29.5	120.1	80.5	391.5	348.1
101.4	1.0	127.9	166.2	53.5	4.3	24.5	10.8	139.0	169.1
108.8	1.8	183.5	256.4	48.9	5.7	36.5	15.9	154.8	204.3

25
Employment by industry [cont.]
Emploi par industrie [suite]

A. ISIC Rev. 2 + – CITI Rév. 2 +

Persons employed, by branch of economic activity (000s)
Personnes employées, par branches d'activité économique (000s)

Country or area Pays ou zone	Year Année	Total employment (000s) Emploi total (000s) M	F	Agriculture, hunting, forestry and fishing Agriculture, chasse, sylviculture, pêche M	F	Mining and quarrying Industries extractives M	F	Manufacturing Industries manufacturières M	F	Electricity, gas, wa Electricité, gaz, ea M
Hungary [35] Hongrie [35]	1991	2411.3	2300.8	468.7	291.4	...	...	786.6[49]	606.2[49]	...
	1992	2185.2	2131.3	364.8	204.7	...	...	718.2[49]	599.6[49]	...
Indonesia [13] Indonésie [13]	1993[9]	48735.0	30465.0	24485.0	15586.0	534.0	119.0	4619.0	4165.0	157.0	1
	1997[2]	53971.0	33079.0	21960.0	13889.0	710.0	186.0	6189.0	5026.0	214.0	1
Ireland [2][13] Irlande [2][13]	1990	754.5	371.5	153.7	13.7	7.7	0.4	154.6	65.0	11.3
	1991	748.1	377.0	141.9	12.3	6.1	0.5	157.8	63.4	12.5
Israel [1][2][51] Israël [1][2][51]	1993	1033.1	718.1	48.5	13.5	...	...	271.1[8]	100.2[8]	14.9
	1994	1090.3	781.1	48.3	14.0	...	...	285.4[8]	110.7[8]	17.1
Italy [14][15][52] Italie [14][15][52]	1992	14021.0	7588.0	1105.0	644.0	212.0[53]	26.0[53]	3179.0	1500.0	...
	1994	12972.0	7030.0	998.0	574.0	267.0[53]	27.0[53]	3120.0	1421.0	...
Jamaica [1][15] Jamaïque [1][15]	1993	509.2	397.1	173.2	47.6	6.9	0.9	55.9	41.9	3.6
	1998	553.7	400.6	160.5	39.6	4.5	0.7	55.7	29.1	4.0
Japan [2][54] Japon [2][54]	1993	38400.0	26100.0	2070.0	1760.0	50.0	10.0	9450.0	5850.0	300.0	50
	1998	38580.0	26560.0	1860.0	1580.0	50.0	10.0	8920.0	4900.0	330.0	40
Korea, Republic of [1][2] Corée, République de [1][2]	1993	11515.0	7738.0	1495.0	1373.0	49.0	3.0	2866.0	1785.0	56.0	9
	1994	11832.0	8005.0	1427.0	1272.0	37.0	3.0	2930.0	1765.0	59.0	12
Luxembourg [45] Luxembourg [45]	1989	120.3	61.6	4.3	1.9	0.2	...	33.1	4.1	1.2
	1990	125.0	64.6	4.3	1.9	0.2	...	33.1	4.1	1.2
Malaysia [1][58] Malaisie [1][58]	1993	4853.8	2529.6	1077.0	481.6	34.0	3.6	960.7	766.3	54.6
	1998	5718.9	2880.7	1185.0	431.5	25.3	3.1	1146.9	761.0	44.2
Mexico [32][39] Mexique [32][39]	1993	22748.0	10084.6	7721.2	1121.5	165.0	6.0	3371.9	1705.8	86.8	12
	1995	23026.8	10854.3	7172.0	1206.3	128.6	18.4	3621.2	1547.1	67.4	12
Morocco [2][17] Maroc [2][17]	1991	2590.9	809.1	109.2	23.2	39.1	1.9	634.8	378.0	28.6	2
	1992	2733.5	760.8	104.0	21.1	43.9	1.5	548.4	340.9	30.5	2
Myanmar [1][7] Myanmar [1][7]	1993	16469.0	...	11347.0	...	83.0	...	1195.0	...	17.0
	1997	17964.0	...	11381.0	...	132.0	...	1573.0	...	21.0
Netherlands [45][58] Pays–Bas [45][58]	1993	3980.0	2668.0	189.0	66.0	8.0	...	889.0	238.0	36.0	6
	1994	3979.0	2713.0	193.0	71.0	9.0	...	855.0	220.0	40.0	7
Netherlands Antilles [2][7][13][59] Antilles néerlandaises [2][7][13][59]	1993	52.4	...	0.4	...	0.1	...	6.0	...	0.9
	1997	56.2	...	0.4	...	0.1	...	5.7	...	0.9
New Zealand [1][2] Nouvelle–Zélande [1][2]	1993	838.4	657.4	108.3	49.4	3.7	...	175.4	79.5	8.8	2
	1998	947.5	777.5	102.3	44.7	3.6	0.6	202.1	87.6	8.1	2
Norway [45][60] Norvège [45][60]	1993	1086.0	918.0	82.0	29.0	20.0	5.0	216.0	76.0	18.0	4
	1995	1126.0	953.0	77.0	28.0	18.0	6.0	229.0	79.0	17.0	4
Pakistan [1][9][61] Pakistan [1][9][61]	1993	26258.0	4276.0	11545.0	2872.0	30.0	...	2864.0	465.0	254.0	4
	1997	29581.0	4599.0	12040.0	3051.0	35.0	...	3336.0	457.0	332.0	2
Panama [2][13] Panama [2][13]	1991	495.2	224.9	185.7	6.2	0.7	...	47.8	21.6	7.0	1
	1992	560.5	234.6	202.0	7.2	1.7	0.4	53.7	21.8	7.8	2
Paraguay [19] Paraguay [19]	1993[62]	326.5	243.2	8.0	1.2	0.2	...	68.2	32.5	3.5	0
	1996[17]	684.8	505.6	48.1	14.1	0.1	...	121.3	49.2	6.3	2
Philippines [2][13][63] Philippines [2][13][63]	1993	15468.0	8975.0	8263.0	2931.0	119.0	11.0	1321.0	1134.0	90.0	16
	1998	17654.0	10608.0	8375.0	2898.0	98.0	6.0	1480.0	1207.0	119.0	21
Poland [17] Pologne [17]	1991	16285.3	...	4140.2	...	480.8	...	4026.9	...	147.2
	1992	15462.3	...	3860.8	...	477.9	...	3589.7	...	149.6
Portugal [14][39][65] Portugal [14][39][65]	1992	2548.7	1994.4	265.3	257.0	21.4	1.1	610.6	462.4	25.8	7
	1993	2486.0	1971.6	262.7	252.9	19.0	0.7	598.2	444.4	25.8	6
Puerto Rico [1][66] Porto Rico [1][66]	1993	593.0	411.0	32.0	2.0	1.0	...	94.0	74.0	13.0	3
	1998	666.0	470.0	27.0	1.0	1.0	...	98.0	62.0	12.0	2
Republic of Moldova [1][7] Rép. de Moldova [1][7]	1993	1688.0	...	728.0	...	0.4	...	233.0	...	8.0
	1994	1681.0	...	765.0	...	0.3	...	218.0	...	8.0
Romania [1][67] Roumanie [1][67]	1992	5570.2	4887.8	1605.0	1843.8	227.6	44.4	1568.3	1296.9	127.4	36
	1993	5415.3	4646.7	1742.3	1878.8	216.8	42.4	1430.8	1175.5	128.8	36
San Marino [15][67] Saint–Marin [15][67]	1992	8.2	5.4	0.2	0.1	...	...	3.1	1.5	...
	1993	8.6	5.6	0.2	0.1	...	...	3.2	1.5	...
Seychelles [7][69] Seychelles [7][69]	1989	22.3	...	2.2	...	...	...	2.5	...	...
	1990	23.5	...	...	...	...	...	2.6	...	...
Singapore [2][13] Singapour [2][13]	1992	944.3	631.8	4.4	0.6	0.4	0.1	243.6	190.5	7.0	1
	1993	952.3	639.7	3.6	0.3	0.3	...	247.8	181.7	5.9	1

Construction Construction		Trade, restaurants and hotels Commerce, restaurants, hôtels		Transport, storage, communications Transports, entrepôts, communications		Financing, insurance, real est.,bus. services Services financières, immob., et apparentées		Community, social and personal services Services fournis à la collectivité, services soc. et pers.	
M	F	M	F	M	F	M	F	M	F
238.0	69.0	198.1	406.0	274.0	135.0	...	...	445.9[50]	793.2[50]
211.2	60.1	205.4	412.3	250.4	123.6	...	...	435.2[50]	791.0[50]
2727.0	84.0	6110.0	6398.0	2832.0	99.0	412.0	153.0	6801.0	3765.0
4050.0	150.0	8404.0	8817.0	4023.0	115.0	447.0	209.0	7972.0	4666.0
75.8	2.6	114.3	79.4	54.7	13.1	49.7	41.0	130.0	153.3
76.3	3.5	113.9	85.7	52.3	12.9	51.0	43.5	133.7	151.3
111.7	6.6	147.4	103.3	81.2	24.9	96.6	87.3	255.1	376.9
111.5	6.5	162.2	118.6	83.8	25.2	111.2	95.2	262.3	405.0
1824.0	110.0	2893.0	1723.0	971.0	180.0	638.0	441.0	3200.0	2962.0
1554.0	88.0	2663.0	1557.0	914.0	168.0	959.0	557.0	2496.0	2638.0
60.3	1.8	69.2	121.9	31.9	8.2	18.8	24.6	85.3	143.6
75.8	2.6	77.2	127.2	46.6	11.3	27.5	30.4	101.0	157.6
5370.0	1030.0	7300.0[55]	7180.0[55]	3300.0	640.0	3020.0	2450.0	7360.0	7020.0[56]
5550.0	1070.0	7290.0[55]	7540.0[55]	3290.0	760.0	3310.0	2630.0	7770.0	7890.0[56]
1522.0	162.0	2386.0	2451.0	903.0	102.0	796.0	563.0	1439.0	1329.0
1616.0	161.0	2554.0	2645.0	901.0	106.0	850.0	645.0	1458.0	1398.0
16.6	1.1	20.2	18.6	10.2	2.3	8.3	7.1	26.2[57]	26.3[57]
17.7	1.1	20.9	19.3	10.6	2.3	9.1	7.7	27.9[57]	28.0[57]
508.1	30.7	770.5	495.7	309.5	34.4	208.1	121.9	931.2	589.7
700.4	45.5	982.6	633.3	364.7	57.0	247.4	178.4	1022.6	764.9
1815.8	63.4	3646.4	3246.3	1243.3	119.1	656.9	423.2	3837.0	3368.2
1768.8	50.2	3908.0	3891.2	1336.4	125.0	695.9	408.1	4189.8	3575.4
261.1	3.0	649.2	63.3	171.8	9.1	52.7	22.9	639.3[48]	304.0[48]
278.1	3.8	698.6	62.8	189.8	10.3	52.8	23.3	779.8[48]	293.0[48]
288.0	...	1407.0	...	412.0	...	1238.0	...	482.0	...
378.0	...	1746.0	...	470.0	...	1686.0	...	577.0	...
367.0	28.0	627.0	549.0	317.0	92.0	428.0	271.0	1033.0	1311.0
364.0	29.0	654.0	573.0	323.0	96.0	425.0	279.0	1032.0	1339.0
4.5	...	13.1	...	3.7	...	6.6	...	17.2	...
4.9	...	14.6	...	3.9	...	7.3	...	18.4	...
72.4	8.5	161.6	154.5	65.8	24.8	76.9	72.2	164.2	265.2
97.7	13.3	181.8	188.3	72.2	31.0	111.4	103.1	165.7	304.8
107.0	9.0	163.0	186.0	111.0	47.0	88.0	65.0	278.0	497.0
117.0	8.0	171.0	186.0	119.0	51.0	92.0	68.0	282.0	521.0
2076.0	41.0	3943.0	125.0	1668.0	17.0	244.0	5.0	3582.0	642.0
2284.0	23.0	4868.0	128.0	1934.0	16.0	333.0	3.0	4407.0	917.0
25.5	0.4	91.1	51.9	42.9	6.8	17.5	12.5	76.7	123.5
42.1	0.9	104.4	52.9	40.8	6.5	21.7	13.9	85.4	128.9
41.8	...	79.4	73.4	24.0	3.6	29.1	15.3	72.2	116.5
82.5	...	198.8	199.7	56.5	5.2	41.0	15.9	130.0	219.5
1080.0	22.0	1168.0[20]	2247.0[20]	1299.0	60.0	298.0	198.0	1821.0[64]	2352.0[64]
1480.0	31.0	1511.0[20]	2817.0[20]	1780.0	105.0	408.0	287.0	2398.0[64]	3234.0[64]
1203.8	...	1750.5	...	999.7	...	341.7	...	3099.3	...
1131.8	...	1827.3	...	1023.5	...	405.0	...	2895.8	...
354.2	16.4	524.0	373.8	167.8	51.8	175.3	111.2	404.4	713.0
349.5	15.8	498.1	369.1	160.9	47.0	182.1	117.9	389.7	717.6
54.0	2.0	128.0[55]	74.0[55]	30.0	7.0	16.0	17.0	225.0	232.0
70.0	3.0	134.0[55]	96.0[55]	33.0	13.0	18.0	23.0	272.0	271.0
101.0	...	92.0	...	75.0	...	10.0	...	401.0	...
86.0	...	97.0	...	73.0	...	11.0	...	385.0	...
502.9	76.3	408.6	520.6	503.6	145.0	242.5	255.7	384.3	668.8
500.7	73.3	332.5	383.2	451.5	140.4	235.3	246.9	376.6	669.9
1.1	0.0	1.2	1.3	0.2	0.0	0.2	0.1	2.3	2.3
1.2	0.0	1.2	1.3	0.2	0.1	0.2	0.2	2.4	2.4
1.7	...	4.4	...	3.1	...	0.7	...	4.6	...
1.7	...	...	...	3.3	...	...	...	...	...
92.3	11.0	214.0	142.0	122.0	36.4	87.9	83.5	172.6	166.6
91.1	11.0	216.2	147.4	131.0	35.8	88.1	85.3	167.6	176.5

25
Employment by industry [cont.]
Emploi par industrie [suite]

A. ISIC Rev. 2 + – CITI Rév. 2 +

Persons employed, by branch of economic activity (000s)
Personnes employées, par branches d'activité économique (000s)

Country or area Pays ou zone	Year Année	Total employment (000s) Emploi total (000s)		Agriculture, hunting, forestry and fishing Agriculture, chasse, sylviculture, pêche		Mining and quarrying Industries extractives		Manufacturing Industries manufacturières		Electricity, gas, wat Electricité, gaz, eau	
		M	F	M	F	M	F	M	F	M	
Spain [66 70]	1992	8277.8	4088.4	906.9	345.8	64.5	2.6	2056.2	603.9	71.3	5
Espagne [66 70]	1993[43]	7850.3	3987.3	869.7	328.1	55.6	2.6	1859.4	542.3	73.5	6.
Sri Lanka [9 32 71]	1994	3542.2	1606.2	1445.2	746.4	30.3	0.5	371.0	411.1	19.7	
Sri Lanka [9 32 71]	1998	3855.3	2090.8	1451.6	1020.7	68.3	9.8	479.5	435.1	30.2	5.
Suriname [15]	1993	53.7	29.8	3.1	0.7	2.4	0.2	6.2	1.6	0.9	0.
Suriname [15]	1996	57.8	29.4	4.6	0.5	4.1	0.1	6.0	1.3	1.2	0.
Sweden [14 72]	1992	2159.0	2034.0	102.0	39.0	10.0	1.0	578.0	216.0	29.0	7.
Suède [14 72]	1994	2016.0	1911.0	101.0	35.0	8.0	1.0	527.0	193.0	26.0	6.
Syrian Arab Republic [19 13]	1989	2441.4	441.2	554.0	208.9	10.5	0.2	361.4	49.1	26.6	2.
Rép. arabe syrienne [19 13]	1991	2710.3	539.6	625.0	292.0	6.7	...	421.5	34.6	7.9	0
Thailand [1 38 73]	1993	17450.6	15000.2	9794.6	8749.9	45.0	12.1	2031.5[29]	1929.5[29]	121.4[30]	23
Thaïlande [1 38 73]	1998	17666.8	14471.1	9231.2	7240.5	33.1	8.1	2135.4[29]	2054.0[29]	149.8[30]	27
Trinidad and Tobago [2]	1993	261.8	142.8	37.7	8.0	13.1	1.9	28.1	12.2	6.2	0.
Trinité-et-Tobago [2]	1998	305.5	173.8	33.1	5.9	16.0	2.5	37.2	14.3	5.1	1.
Turkey [1 13 39 76]	1993	13781.0	6124.0	4213.0	4430.0	161.0	3.0	2311.0	690.0	108.0	6.
Turquie [1 13 39 76]	1998	15587.0	6371.0	5074.0	4460.0	167.0	4.0	2667.0	632.0	96.0	10.
Ukraine [7]	1993	23427.0	...	4948.0	...	970.0	...	4560.0	...	...	
Ukraine [7]	1998	19427.0	...	5074.0	...	687.0	...	3540.0	...	...	
United States [1 66 77 78]	1993	65349.0	54910.0	2623.0	677.0	563.0	108.0	13358.0	6354.0	1253.0[30]	346.
Etats-Unis [1 66 77 78]	1998	70693.0	60771.0	2657.0	852.0	535.0	85.0	14138.0	6595.0	1162.0[30]	334
Uruguay [14 15 17]	1993	679.2	476.8	40.7	4.5	1.9	0.1	149.2	89.9	13.1	2.
Uruguay [14 15 17]	1998	640.0	474.4	36.7	6.9	1.4	0.2	117.0	62.6	8.5	2.
Uzbekistan	1993	...	...	...	...	...	...	560.2	519.2	...	
Ouzbékistan	1995	...	...	...	...	...	...	498.3	469.3	...	
Venezuela [1 2]	1993	4879.6	2223.1	763.3	36.7	62.1	8.8	798.1	296.3	48.1	16.
Venezuela [1 2]	1997	5451.8	2835.0	852.8	41.3	80.1	10.4	789.9	332.6	55.3	10.
Viet Nam [7]	1993	...	...	...	...	...	...	3521.8	...	...	
Viet Nam [7]	1997	...	...	...	...	...	...	3292.5	...	...	

Labour force   Main–d'œuvre

Construction		Trade, restaurants and hotels Commerce, restaurants, hôtels		Transport, storage, communications Transports, entrepôts, communications		Financing, insurance, real est.,bus. services Services financières, immob., et apparentées		Community, social and personal services Services fournis à la collectivité, services soc. et pers.	
M	F	M	F	M	F	M	F	M	F
1153.2	43.1	1438.9	1098.2	637.1	90.9	505.1	236.3	1444.5	1662.0
1046.1	42.3	1596.5	1095.5	606.5	88.4	554.5	372.2	1188.6	1509.3
171.6	...	560.4	105.9	197.4	8.0	59.1	38.5	546.4	279.0
295.2	14.0	469.5	124.2	251.5	16.5	85.5	31.6	607.7	398.9
4.1	0.2	8.1	5.0	4.7	0.3	1.8	1.7	20.4	19.2
7.6	0.2	8.9	6.0	5.6	1.2	2.2	1.7	13.9	18.1
247.0	24.0	304.0	297.0	206.0	94.0	212.0	171.0	468.0	1185.0
202.0	18.0	292.0	276.0	187.0	84.0	213.0	166.0	457.0	1131.0
333.3	4.1	328.3	9.7	172.9	4.0	32.5	4.2	621.8	159.0
334.3	6.4	369.0	9.3	158.4	8.6	20.2	4.5	767.4	183.7
1214.4	260.3	1735.8[74]	1968.3	770.0	109.3	...	...	1731.0[75]	1936.7[75]
1082.4	197.1	2076.5[74]	2387.0	798.7	124.0	...	...	2156.8[75]	2427.4[75]
39.7	4.6	35.5	35.6	25.2	4.8	15.4	12.5	60.5	62.2
53.9	4.9	38.4	44.9	29.3	6.2	19.0	20.0	73.2	73.9
1153.0	19.0	2349.0	196.0	892.0	67.0	372.0	119.0	2222.0	593.0
1306.0	30.0	2601.0	300.0	917.0	36.0	358.0	157.0	2400.0	742.0
1771.0	...	1648.0	...	1714.0	...	178.0	...	...	...
1092.0	...	1514.0	...	1400.0	...	213.0	...	...	...
6660.0	616.0	13445.0[55]	11698.0[55]	4843.0	2084.0	6169.0	6887.0	16435.0[79]	26141.0[79]
7721.0	798.0	14367.0[55]	12836.0[55]	5436.0	2375.0	7431.0	8021.0	17246.0[79]	28875.0[79]
80.4	1.7	126.5	90.7	55.2	9.1	38.7	25.5	173.5	252.3
81.6	1.7	128.7	97.1	57.4	10.1	39.9	31.2	168.8	262.1
...	...	...	...	...	...	...	...	...	...
...	...	...	...	...	...	...	...	...	...
617.9	24.5	993.6	581.0	418.7	45.4	268.3	176.8	906.0	1042.3
668.0	26.4	1130.7	854.9	487.8	46.6	281.0	185.3	1092.3	1319.4
848.3	...	...	...	549.2	...	...	...	...	...
976.5	...	...	...	856.0	...	...	...	...	...

25
Employment by industry [*cont.*]
Emploi par industrie [*suite*]

B. ISIC Rev. 3 [+] · CITI Rév. 3 [+]

Persons employed, by branch of economic activity (000s)
Personnes employées, par branches d'activité économique (000s)

Country or area Pays ou zone	Sex	Year Année	Total employment (000s) Emploi total (000s)	Agriculture, hunting and forestry Agriculture, chasse et sylviculture	Fishing Pêche	Mining and quarrying Activités extractives	Manufacturing Activités de fabrication	Electricity, gas and water supply Production et distribution d'électricité, de gaz et d'eau	Construc...
Argentina [9][13] Argentine [9][13]	M	1995	6479.9	...	...	...	1227.5	88.5	8
	F	1995	3868.1	...	...	...	412.7	10.6	
	M	1996	6576.4	...	...	...	1217.4	87.7	8.
	F	1996	3965.6	...	...	...	419.8	18.4	
Australia [1][2][3][4][5] Australie [1][2][3][4][5]	M	1993	4396.6	274.3	11.6	74.3	783.4	82.5	4
	F	1993	3248.2	119.0	3.4	6.5	295.6	13.0	
	M	1998	4836.6	279.8	10.6	69.4	812.5	54.0	5
	F	1998	3714.6	127.6	2.7	7.3	285.8	11.1	
Austria [2] Autriche [2]	M	1994	2146.8	141.6	0.2	8.0	585.6	30.7	3
	F	1994	1595.2	127.4	0.1	1.1	232.0	4.5	
	M	1998	2125.7	124.5	0.2	9.8	560.3	31.8	29
	F	1998	1597.5	117.2	0.1	1.8	196.7	4.1	
Bahamas [13][24] Bahamas [13][24]	M	1993	62.7	3.6	2.1	0.1	2.8	1.4	
	F	1993	56.3	0.7	0.1	0.0	2.2	0.3	
	M	1997	71.3	4.3	...	1.4	2.7	...	
	F	1997	63.9	0.9	0.5		2.7	...	
Belgium [13][14][15] Belgique [13][14][15]	M	1996	2269.3	...	...	...	...	...	
	F	1996	1522.6	...	...	...	...	...	
	M	1997	2277.0	...	...	...	...	...	
	F	1997	1562.1	...	...	...	...	...	
Bolivia [1][9][17] Bolivie [1][9][17]	M	1993	617.5	17.0	...	13.7	130.3	4.1	8
	F	1993	473.4	3.4	...	1.1	69.3	0.3	
	M	1996[13]	736.0	15.7	0.3	17.6	156.9	8.7	10
	F	1996[13]	618.6	12.5	...	2.1	92.1	1.5	
Botswana [1][39][80] Botswana [1][39][80]	M	1995	189.3	...	...	12.8	14.2	2.6	2
	F	1995	156.1	...	...	2.4	15.4	0.2	1
Bulgaria [7][24] Bulgarie [7][24]	T	1996	3285.9	...	...	65.0	782.3	57.2	16
	T	1998	3106.2	...	...	56.2	706.5	58.2	13
Canada [2][28] Canada [2][28]	M	1993	7126.1	364.3	35.9	139.2	1318.7	96.3	61
	F	1993	5888.6	139.6	4.7	23.5	488.5	33.1	7
	M	1998	7802.6	359.0	29.2	151.6	1556.7	90.8	67
	F	1998	6523.8	141.1	4.8	30.0	589.9	26.6	8
China, Macao SAR † [1][15][38] Chine, Macao RAS † [1][15][38]	M	1998	109.8	...	...	...	13.4	1.1	1
	F	1998	91.2	...	...	...	28.0	0.3	
Costa Rica [1][13][39] Costa Rica [1][13][39]	M	1996	808.1	223.4	5.3	2.0	128.6	10.1	6
	F	1996	336.9	19.0	0.2	0.1	60.3	1.8	
	M	1998	887.5	233.1	5.6	1.6	132.4	11.1	8
	F	1998	412.5	22.7	0.1	...	71.1	2.0	
Croatia [2] Croatie [2]	M	1996[13]	838.4	154.8	2.4	7.0	184.9	22.5	8
	F	1996[13]	701.9	148.6	...	...	135.6	3.8	
	M	1998	832.2	264.0	2.4	7.3	184.3	22.8	8
	F	1998	711.6	123.1	...		139.1	5.8	1
Czech Republic [2] Rép. tchèque [2]	M	1994	2711.0[81]	...	...	83.0	828.0	72.0	40
	F	1994	2334.0[81]	...	...	15.0	648.0	28.0	4
	M	1997	2791.0	148.0	43.0	75.0	826.0	69.0	43
	F	1997	2151.0	82.0	12.0	14.0	548.0	23.0	4

Wholesale and retail trade; repair of motor vehicles motorcycles and personal and household goods Commerce de gros et détail; répa-n de véhicules automobiles, de torcycles et de ens personnels et domestiques	Hotels and restaurants Hôtels et restaurants	Transport, storage and communications Transports, entreposage et communications	Financial inter-mediation Inter médiation financière	Real estate, renting and business activities Immobilier, locations et activités de services aux entreprises	Public admin. and defence; compulsory social sec. Admin. publique et défense; séc. sociale obligatoire	Education Education	Health and social work Santé et action sociale	Other community, social and personal service act. Autres act. de services collectifs, sociaux et personnels	Private households with employed persons Ménages privés employant du personnel domestique	Extra-territorial org. and bodies Org. et organismes extra-territoriaux
1130.2	198.9	667.9	139.3	376.9	602.5	180.2	202.0	637.8	67.4	...
667.1	113.5	73.0	92.6	218.4	297.1	608.4	371.9	196.4	761.1	
1191.7	172.1	679.2	129.7	392.8	628.9	150.9	207.4	636.6	69.8	...
665.7	112.1	73.8	89.9	258.4	327.6	565.5	392.7	247.5	741.6	
881.5	150.6	370.8	144.7	357.4	279.9	193.0	165.7	151.7	2.2	0.6
725.3	190.0	114.2	168.4	270.6	181.6	360.7	524.9	185.1	13.1	0.5
975.2	183.4	401.2	140.1	541.1	254.0	194.1	184.8	198.6	1.7	0.6
799.5	224.4	143.6	182.6	411.4	174.3	399.0	625.5	224.8	9.0	0.7
265.3	76.0	191.8	76.6	86.9	167.8	70.1	59.6	66.3	1.1	2.5
304.3	126.8	54.2	67.3	113.3	89.4	134.7	201.7	84.0	15.6	2.7
265.7	82.5	190.9	71.8	113.2	161.7	69.8	72.4	73.2	0.4	4.0
315.9	133.5	51.0	67.1	119.7	90.8	148.0	226.3	85.2	13.6	1.8
11.5	8.2	6.0	1.7	3.3	6.0	1.7	1.1	3.0	2.5	...
10.2	10.3	3.1	3.9	2.3	4.3	4.7	3.8	4.1	5.8	...
8.0	9.2	7.9	5.0	...	...	...	...	...	20.7	...
9.6	12.2	4.0	7.4	...	...	...	...	...	25.9	...
...	...	...	...	...	...	...	...	...	...	...
...	...	...	...	...	...	...	...	...	...	...
...	...	...	...	...	...	...	...	...	...	...
113.7	15.8	86.8	8.3	24.7	43.5		...	...	...	0.7
167.0	40.4	4.9	5.3	9.8	14.1		...	...	...	0.8
149.7	18.9	93.7	8.2	27.3	51.9	30.9	17.3	22.6	6.2	0.7
209.4	61.9	5.4	6.3	13.8	22.8	46.7	26.7	22.4	92.5	0.3
19.5	2.5	5.8	1.8	5.8	37.9	12.4	2.1	4.3	2.0	0.2
24.6	7.5	1.9	2.3	1.9	22.0	20.9	7.3	3.0	17.0	0.0
321.4	76.5	252.1	42.9	102.0	73.2	255.8	187.2	104.0	...	...
326.0	75.8	223.9	40.8	96.7	80.1	233.0	170.0	105.0	...	...
1259.3	358.3	648.1	196.4	697.3	499.2	344.5	280.1	258.5	14.5	...
1007.0	461.4	295.7	385.7	539.9	377.6	559.5	1090.5	320.2	83.6	1.5
1359.7	383.6	737.6	207.7	903.4	435.5	349.3	281.2	267.5	14.7	...
1092.8	532.9	343.5	387.9	730.1	352.7	593.4	1184.0	353.3	77.0	1.5
19.2	12.0	10.3	2.2	6.2	11.0	2.1	1.3	11.0	0.4	...
14.3	11.1	3.4	3.4	2.1	5.4	4.6	2.8	9.0	4.5	...
113.3	28.0	53.1	16.3	2.8	...	19.5	21.5	100.0	11.3	1.1
58.0	25.7	5.5	6.5	0.9	...	41.6	31.2	30.6	52.3	0.6
129.4	26.3	65.4	19.0	3.5	...	21.5	27.4	114.8	6.9	1.9
63.9	32.2	7.9	10.5	1.1	...	50.3	32.0	42.9	71.1	1.0
96.1	34.4	77.1	8.8	25.5	73.0	19.7	19.9	24.8	...	...
108.4	39.7	21.7	26.2	23.7	38.2	54.7	65.2	24.2	2.7	...
89.0	38.7	86.9	7.9	34.0	67.4	21.1	20.0	28.9	...	...
117.1	43.7	23.6	24.9	26.4	41.0	54.2	72.6	23.0	3.8	...
257.0	64.0	246.0	24.0	135.0	160.0	85.0	59.0	77.0	...	1.0
371.0	89.0	136.0	61.0	112.0	122.0	239.0	236.0	91.0	1.0	...
295.0	74.0	256.0	31.0	135.0	198.0	73.0	53.0	76.0	...	1.0
365.0	91.0	127.0	66.0	118.0	123.0	234.0	219.0	84.0	1.0	1.0

25
Employment by industry [cont.]
Emploi par industrie [suite]

B. ISIC Rev. 3 [+] — CITI Rév. 3 [+]

Persons employed, by branch of economic activity (000s)
Personnes employées, par branches d'activité économique (000s)

Country or area Pays ou zone	Sex	Year Année	Total employment (000s) Emploi total (000s)	Agriculture, Agriculture, hunting and forestry Agriculture, chasse et sylviculture	Fishing Pêche	Mining and quarrying Activités extractives	Manufacturing Activités de fabrication	Electricity, gas Electricity, gas and water supply Production et distribution d'électricité, de gaz et d'eau	Construc Construc
Denmark [82] Danemark [82]	M	1995[32]	1448.6	77.8	7.0	2.2	361.7	14.4	1!
	F	1995[32]	1161.1	29.3	...	1.9	158.5	1.7	!
	M	1998	1460.1	72.0	4.7	2.4	356.1	16.9	1!
	F	1998	1232.3	19.9	0.0	0.8	160.0	3.6	!
Dominican Republic Rép. dominicaine	M	1997	1891.4	502.5	...	7.5	332.7	13.7	1!
	F	1997	760.6	16.5	...	0.9	150.7	6.6	
Estonia Estonie	M	1993[16]	373.9	64.7	12.8	8.7	77.9	12.8	4
	F	1993[16]	334.2	36.8	3.2	2.6	73.6	5.4	
	M	1998[32 42]	333.0	34.4	6.0	6.3	77.3	12.8	4
	F	1998[32 42]	310.0	19.7	...	...	63.4	4.4	
Finland [42] Finlande [42]	M	1993	1091.0	121.0	2.0	4.0	267.0	19.0	1!
	F	1993	1008.0	60.0	1.0	...	132.0	5.0	!
	M	1998	1199.0	95.0	2.0	5.0	314.0	18.0	12
	F	1998	1048.0	47.0	...	1.0	133.0	4.0	!
Germany [2 13] Allemagne [2 13]	M	1996	20706.0	655.0	7.0	216.0	6126.0	268.0	304
	F	1996	15276.0	412.0	...	27.0	2410.0	67.0	42
	M	1998	20509.0	639.0	6.0	167.0	6068.0	241.0	276
	F	1998	15351.0	377.0	...	15.0	2393.0	64.0	4!
Greece [14 15 32] Grèce [14 15 32]	M	1994	2452.2	443.6	13.8	14.8	398.6	34.8	2!
	F	1994	1337.4	331.1	1.2	0.8	179.2	5.9	
	M	1997	2439.0	424.5	13.2	16.6	380.5	33.4	24
	F	1997	1415.1	326.1	1.2	0.7	178.2	7.4	
Hungary [42] Hongrie [42]	M	1995	2049.6	...	...	28.8	498.1	71.8	19
	F	1995	1629.2	...	...	5.2	352.1	24.8	2
	M	1998	2041.7	...	...	21.4	535.5	72.6	21
	F	1998	1656.0	...	...	4.3	376.6	23.9	1
Iceland [1 38 60] Islande [1 38 60]	M	1993	73.3	4.1	6.4	...	14.0	1.0	
	F	1993	63.3	1.9	0.2	...	8.9	0.4	
	M	1998	79.1	3.9	5.6	0.1	15.3	1.2	1
	F	1998	68.9	2.7	0.6	...	9.4	0.3	
Ireland [2 38] Irlande [2 38]	M	1993	749.4	131.5	2.4	4.9	157.0	10.0	7
	F	1993	433.7	15.4	0.4	0.3	66.5	1.6	
	M	1998	899.9	116.1	3.4	4.7	193.8	9.9	12
	F	1998	594.6	16.1	0.4	0.4	90.4	2.0	
Israel [1 2 51] Israël [1 2 51]	M	1996	1146.9	...	...	...	...	15.6	14
	F	1996	865.8	...	...	...	...	2.9	
	M	1998	1163.0	...	...	...	...	16.7	12
	F	1998	913.6	...	...	...	...	3.5	
Italy [15 52 70] Italie [15 52 70]	M	1995	12886.0	915.0	40.0	79.0	3101.0	185.0	152
	F	1995	7055.0	530.0	4.0	9.0	1433.0	19.0	8
Korea, Republic of [1 2] Corée, République de [1 2]	M	1993	11515.0	1406.0	89.0	49.0	2866.0	56.0	152
	F	1993	7738.0	1307.0	26.0	3.0	1785.0	9.0	16
	M	1998	11897.0	1212.0	58.0	20.0	2545.0	52.0	143
	F	1998	8030.0	1130.0	23.0	...	1339.0	9.0	14
Kyrgyzstan Kirghizistan	M	1996	897.1	416.7	...	6.1	54.1	12.0	4
	F	1996	754.4	356.8	...	1.9	52.8	3.5	1
	M	1998	918.7	447.9	...	4.8	44.5	12.5	4
	F	1998	786.2	383.0	...	1.4	36.7	4.1	!
Latvia [2 13 70] Lettonie [2 13 70]	M	1996	505.0	103.3	4.9	1.9	99.4	16.9	4'
	F	1996	460.5	63.4	1.5	0.3	76.9	5.1	
	M	1998	533.5	108.5	3.7	1.1	105.3	17.8	4!
	F	1998	473.7	75.6	1.2	0.2	77.1	6.6	

Wholesale and retail trade; repair of motor vehicles motorcycles and personal and household goods Commerce de gros et de détail; réparation de véhicules automobiles, de motorcycles et de biens personnels et domestiques	Hotels and restaurants Hôtels et restaurants	Transport, storage and communications Transports, entreposage et communications	Financial intermediation Intermédiation financière	Real estate, renting and business activities Immobilier, locations et activités de services aux entreprises	Public admin. and defence; compulsory social sec. Admin. publique et défense; séc. sociale obligatoire	Education Education	Health and social work Santé et action sociale	Other community, social and personal service act. Autres act. de services collectifs, sociaux et personnels	Private households with employed persons Ménages privés employant du personnel domestique	Extra-territorial org. and bodies Org. et organismes extra-territoriaux
221.6	20.7	140.0	38.4	111.3	88.7	85.2	71.3	53.6	0.9	0.4
147.9	43.0	48.7	38.5	73.2	77.2	99.7	361.7	61.6	4.8	0.7
211.6	28.1	131.9	37.9	138.1	89.5	80.1	70.5	56.7	0.8	0.4
156.1	43.2	50.0	41.3	89.5	78.8	113.7	388.3	61.8	4.6	0.5
356.1	59.5	190.0	17.3	...	99.5	...	...	152.2	...	...
176.1	55.8	12.9	16.8	...	25.9	...	...	295.3	...	...
36.0	5.3	41.9	...	14.5	19.2	11.7	6.9	11.3	...	...
45.0	11.7	17.0	4.6	13.3	15.6	38.0	40.4	16.0	...	...
40.9	2.4	42.0	1.9	20.6	19.1	12.3	4.9	9.7	...	...
48.9	13.2	17.5	5.2	16.4	17.8	45.1	30.2	20.2	...	...
119.0	15.0	116.0	18.0	92.0	88.0	46.0	31.0	38.0	...	...
126.0	45.0	42.0	53.0	71.0	55.0	88.0	249.0	69.0	...	...
141.0	22.0	122.0	15.0	117.0	81.0	50.0	37.0	47.0	...	...
128.0	49.0	47.0	31.0	87.0	56.0	104.0	277.0	68.0	3.0	...
2393.0	466.0	1394.0	623.0	1171.0	1959.0	676.0	853.0	829.0	10.0	20.0
2734.0	650.0	547.0	653.0	1114.0	1368.0	1217.0	2514.0	990.0	127.0	18.0
2435.0	482.0	1382.0	638.0	1348.0	1872.0	697.0	914.0	820.0	9.0	22.0
2719.0	648.0	538.0	635.0	1233.0	1302.0	1230.0	2620.0	1006.0	141.0	14.0
383.1	124.5	219.7	53.5	87.9	197.6	85.9	62.4	70.5	3.2	0.7
219.1	87.5	32.5	36.1	53.5	86.6	128.0	98.9	44.9	27.9	0.7
407.4	131.6	214.5	53.2	96.7	188.3	87.3	64.9	76.9	3.9	0.5
235.2	98.3	32.2	43.6	63.5	91.0	142.6	105.2	48.6	37.8	0.3
208.1	52.3	238.1	23.6	68.6	201.4	85.5	56.2	98.4	0.2	3.1
251.8	64.3	81.5	58.6	62.0	116.7	249.9	175.2	88.3	0.8	0.5
220.2	57.2	216.0	26.6	91.4	160.7	73.5	57.0	84.4	0.7	1.8
252.0	64.4	85.9	55.2	71.6	133.6	232.0	180.8	87.4	0.8	1.2
11.2	1.5	6.0	1.4	4.2	4.0	2.9	3.2	3.7	...	0.2
9.4	2.4	3.0	3.7	3.1	3.3	5.8	16.1	4.3	...	0.1
11.2	2.0	6.6	1.8	5.7	4.1	3.1	3.0	4.4	...	0.7
9.4	2.5	4.1	2.8	3.8	2.9	6.5	17.7	5.4	...	0.1
103.7	29.7	42.9	21.5	38.6	43.9	31.1	21.2	27.6	1.3	0.3
68.8	34.9	10.4	22.3	29.6	21.3	50.7	70.9	30.3	4.4	0.3
115.3	39.4	59.9	22.8	58.8	45.0	33.9	25.8	33.9	0.6	0.1
92.3	53.7	20.2	32.5	51.5	27.4	66.2	86.9	34.4	8.3	0.1
158.9	41.6	93.7	27.2	111.3	61.9	61.1	44.4	49.1	3.3	0.3
96.4	34.3	30.6	40.4	82.3	46.2	181.9	135.0	46.2	30.5	0.7
164.7	45.7	94.3	32.1	121.2	67.0	64.8	52.2	51.1	2.2	1.2
106.3	35.5	29.9	41.3	95.4	46.1	197.5	150.8	45.4	29.7	1.1
2194.0	469.0	884.0	439.0	568.0	1018.0	458.0	516.0	449.0	34.0	9.0
1173.0	384.0	174.0	217.0	374.0	484.0	1024.0	622.0	354.0	169.0	5.0
1956.0	430.0	903.0	299.0	497.0	497.0	433.0	96.0	402.0	11.0	18.0
1521.0	910.0	102.0	342.0	221.0	122.0	505.0	178.0	360.0	163.0	4.0
2161.0	565.0	1044.0	357.0	785.0	567.0	489.0	115.0	470.0	5.0	19.0
1654.0	1184.0	125.0	403.0	324.0	173.0	655.0	246.0	420.0	198.0	1.0
...	...	67.3	3.7	3.8	44.6	44.7	25.3	15.2	...	...
...	...	13.9	5.4	4.1	17.6	94.2	68.6	9.6	...	...
...	...	61.9	4.4	3.8	45.7	47.7	27.4	16.3	...	...
...	...	13.4	3.7	3.0	15.3	91.6	66.8	8.5	...	...
58.8	5.1	56.3	4.9	17.2	36.0	19.0	9.5	23.5	0.7	...
61.9	10.0	29.3	9.1	14.0	26.7	76.8	45.7	29.7	0.7	...
65.2	3.8	57.4	4.6	20.0	41.3	20.5	11.8	21.4	1.0	0.1
86.6	13.0	24.6	8.0	16.7	29.5	62.1	41.6	24.1	0.9	...

25
Employment by industry [*cont.*]
Emploi par industrie [*suite*]

B. ISIC Rev. 3 + — CITI Rév. 3 +

Persons employed, by branch of economic activity (000s)
Personnes employées, par branches d'activité économique (000s)

Country or area Pays ou zone	Sex	Year Année	Total employment (000s) Emploi total (000s)	Agriculture, hunting and forestry Agriculture, chasse et sylviculture	Fishing Pêche	Mining and quarrying Activités extractives	Manufacturing Activités de fabrication	Electricity, gas and water supply Production et distribution d'électricité, de gaz et d'eau	Constructi Constructi
Lithuania [1] [15]	M	1997	823.0	...	...	...	...	30.7	9.
Lituanie [1] [15]	F	1997	740.9	...	...	...	...	10.9	1
	M	1998	818.4	...	...	...	...	30.0	9
	F	1998	769.6	...	...	...	...	11.2	1
Mauritius [1] [39]	M	1995	299.3	...	...	1.9	68.1	4.1	4
Maurice [1] [39]	F	1995	137.0	...	...	0.1	57.4	0.3	
Mexico [32] [39]	M	1995	23026.8	6825.8	346.3	128.6	3621.2	67.4	176
Mexique [32] [39]	F	1995	10854.3	1160.0	46.3	18.4	1547.1	12.2	5
	M	1998	25663.1	6508.6	171.4	140.8	4473.5	155.1	205
	F	1998	12954.4	1133.3	4.0	11.9	2510.5	27.6	6
Netherlands [58]	M	1996	4109.0	188.0	...	9.0	849.0	34.0	39
Pays–Bas [58]	F	1996	2862.0	71.0	...	...	229.0	7.0	3
	M	1998	4289.0	167.0	...	10.0	856.0	40.0	41
	F	1998	3109.0	70.0	...	...	247.0	7.0	38
Netherlands Antilles [2] [13] [59]	M	1993	29.6	...	...	0.1	5.1	0.8	
Antilles néerlandaises [2] [13] [59]	F	1993	22.9	...	...	0.0	1.0	0.2	0
	M	1998	29.5	...	...	0.0	3.9	0.8	4
	F	1998	24.7	...	...	0.1	0.9	0.1	
Norway [60]	M	1996	1157.0	64.0	17.0	22.0	232.0	17.0	11
Norvège [60]	F	1996	980.0	26.0	2.0	6.0	82.0	4.0	
	M	1998	1207.0	60.0	17.0	28.0	239.0	16.0	13
	F	1998	1036.0	26.0	2.0	6.0	82.0	3.0	1
Panama [2] [13]	M	1993	560.4	174.3	6.4	1.0	59.2	6.9	48
Panama [2] [13]	F	1993	255.1	7.2	0.5	0.1	25.2	1.7	
	M	1998	604.3	154.0	13.1	1.8	70.1	6.0	57
	F	1998	298.8	6.7	0.4	0.1	27.8	1.8	
Peru [15] [17] [32]	M	1996	3622.5	246.1	29.6	82.8	617.8	23.7	291
Pérou [15] [17] [32]	F	1996	2508.0	89.6	1.3	3.1	289.4	4.8	6
	M	1998	3885.4	246.0	26.2	59.3	602.8	21.5	377
	F	1998	2948.5	92.7	0.4	3.3	310.6	3.0	5
Poland [2] [83]	M	1995	8095.0	1829.0	12.0	396.0	1912.0	212.0	803
Pologne [2] [83]	F	1995	6696.0	1502.0	3.0	50.0	1207.0	54.0	94
	M	1998	8470.0	1631.0	11.0	339.0	1970.0	210.0	977
	F	1998	6884.0	1304.0	1.0	41.0	1235.0	55.0	94
Portugal	M	1993[15]	2521.5	247.3	15.4	19.0	598.2	25.8	349
Portugal	F	1993[15]	1971.6	248.8	4.2	0.7	444.4	6.3	15
	M	1998[2]	2641.4	299.9	20.5	14.0	635.5	27.9	497
	F	1998[2]	2110.5	317.4	1.6	1.9	494.6	4.0	19
Republic of Moldova [17]	T	1996	1660.0	710.0	1.0	4.0	169.0	22.0	55
République de Moldova [17]	T	1998	1642.0	749.0	1.0	4.0	155.0	23.0	58
Romania	M	1995[13] [15]	6026.6	2118.1	10.7	241.6	1404.6	163.0	398
Roumanie	F	1995[13] [15]	5125.7	2367.2	1.5	40.0	1093.5	41.4	70
	M	1998[2]	5885.1	2166.3	6.6	171.1	1284.9	183.2	379
	F	1998[2]	4959.8	2168.3	...	30.8	1028.8	51.8	54
Russian Federation [7]	T	1993	70851.5	10992.5	...	1233.4	18057.4	1066.3	6581
Fédération de Russie [7]	T	1997	64638.5	...	...	1149.8	12074.8	1379.9	5341
San Marino [15] [67]	M	1996	10.3	0.2	...	...	3.7	...	1
Saint–Marin [15] [67]	F	1996	6.4	0.1	...	...	1.6	...	0.
	M	1998	11.0	0.1	...	...	4.1	...	1.
	F	1998	6.9	0.1	...	...	1.7	...	0.

Wholesale and retail trade; repair of motor vehicles motorcycles and personal and household goods Commerce de gros et de détail; répa- ration de véhicules automobiles, de motorcycles et de biens personnels et domestiques	Hotels and restaurants Hôtels et restaurants	Transport, storage and communi- cations Transports, entreposage et communi- cations	Financial inter- mediation Inter médiation financière	Real estate, renting and business activities Immobilier, locations et activités de services aux entreprises	Public admin. and defence; compulsory social sec. Admin. publique et défense; séc. sociale obligatoire	Education Education	Health and social work Santé et action sociale	Other community, social and personal service act. Autres act. de services collectifs, sociaux et personnels	Private households with employed persons Ménages privés employant du personnel domestique	Extra- territorial org. and bodies Org. et organismes extra- territoriaux
110.0	8.3	69.2	5.2	26.9	41.2	31.8	21.7	33.0	...	...
125.4	18.5	31.6	7.7	25.1	30.7	100.5	78.9	35.9	...	...
115.3	6.6	71.0	6.7	23.7	48.7	35.5	19.0	28.0	...	...
118.7	19.3	35.3	12.3	23.1	28.5	113.8	88.1	39.0	...	...
41.9	11.2	24.9	...	...	21.2	...	...	...	...	...
15.4	3.3	2.7	...	...	5.4	...	...	...	...	...
3182.2	725.9	1336.4	190.2	505.6	905.3	641.4	280.8	2261.8	100.4	110.3
3096.8	821.4	125.0	115.5	292.5	377.2	1022.5	506.1	634.3	1035.3	15.3
3643.5	815.2	1539.5	175.8	766.1	1134.1	785.2	341.6	2628.1	187.6	120.0
3160.7	1009.6	153.6	140.0	390.1	472.9	1108.0	668.8	482.1	1583.8	24.4
648.0	113.0	321.0	132.0	423.0	343.0	214.0	210.0	136.0	...	...
512.0	131.0	102.0	104.0	297.0	157.0	228.0	736.0	145.0	25.0	...
686.0	120.0	333.0	148.0	498.0	348.0	219.0	221.0	147.0	...	...
534.0	147.0	109.0	116.0	334.0	117.0	246.0	807.0	171.0	20.0	...
4.9	1.3	2.5	1.3	1.9	4.2	0.8	0.9	1.2	0.0	0.0
5.3	1.7	1.2	2.1	1.2	1.9	1.6	3.0	2.0	1.5	0.0
5.1	1.6	2.8	1.4	2.5	3.6	0.9	0.9	1.2	0.1	0.0
5.3	2.1	1.3	2.3	1.4	2.1	1.8	3.3	1.8	1.9	0.1
173.0	23.0	115.0	27.0	91.0	87.0	65.0	65.0	38.0	...	...
150.0	45.0	49.0	27.0	61.0	57.0	100.0	307.0	47.0	6.0	...
181.0	25.0	119.0	25.0	109.0	89.0	64.0	65.0	37.0	...	...
160.0	45.0	51.0	26.0	70.0	63.0	109.0	324.0	51.0	6.0	...
89.0	12.4	51.3	8.3	15.3	35.9	16.3	9.2	18.4	4.8	3.2
46.0	12.6	8.0	9.6	8.7	24.6	29.6	17.0	16.1	46.2	0.9
104.3	18.2	51.1	9.2	21.0	41.0	17.7	9.1	22.7	4.8	2.9
58.8	18.6	9.9	13.0	9.7	27.4	30.7	21.9	28.2	40.5	1.6
909.7	123.2	465.3	33.2	229.7	202.0	182.2	58.1	114.1	13.4	...
944.7	265.6	37.8	20.5	82.7	61.5	255.2	111.6	119.7	213.6	...
917.4	137.9	517.3	39.2	260.6	231.4	230.0	72.2	126.9	19.0	...
1093.2	365.9	56.8	35.1	95.2	72.6	283.1	98.0	152.6	280.2	...
840.0	58.0	619.0	92.0	196.0	389.0	259.0	176.0	293.0	1.0	...
972.0	136.0	237.0	204.0	141.0	296.0	740.0	798.0	248.0	10.0	...
1003.0	72.0	710.0	110.0	275.0	440.0	239.0	188.0	294.0	...	1.0
1114.0	147.0	247.0	244.0	189.0	340.0	732.0	868.0	263.0	8.0	...
400.3	97.8	160.9	88.1	94.0	236.3	72.0	52.5	61.7	0.8	1.9
256.7	112.4	47.0	41.7	76.1	120.9	234.3	146.5	110.5	104.8	0.6
388.4	103.3	140.2	55.8	91.0	196.1	67.1	38.8	62.2	1.7	1.6
266.2	141.7	37.4	31.4	84.7	104.4	208.3	161.7	91.5	143.2	1.0
256.0	15.0	66.0	11.0	36.0	30.0	155.0	94.0	36.0	...	...
190.0	18.0	77.0	10.0	37.0	52.0	148.0	88.0	32.0	...	...
340.2	46.1	415.8	33.1	73.5	456.3	135.1	84.1	106.3	...	...
376.7	92.1	140.9	54.0	79.9	106.5	301.3	261.2	99.6	...	...
421.4	49.8	399.6	26.8	85.6	392.5	125.8	80.4	112.0	...	...
504.5	92.3	129.7	54.9	68.4	112.1	302.3	255.0	105.6	...	...
...	...	5407.5	...	...	1508.0	6164.0	4121.5	2371.3	...	...
...	...	5120.4	...	...	2612.8	6019.1	4327.0	2648.0	...	...
1.1	0.3	0.3	0.3	0.5	1.4	0.2	0.3	0.3	...	...
1.1	0.3	0.1	0.2	0.3	0.7	0.7	0.6	0.4	0.1	0.0
1.1	0.3	0.3	0.3	0.5	1.5	0.2	0.3	0.3	0.0	...
1.1	0.3	0.1	0.2	0.4	0.8	0.8	0.7	0.4	0.1	0.0

25
Employment by industry [cont.]
Emploi par industrie [suite]

B. ISIC Rev. 3 ⁺ − CITI Rév. 3 ⁺

Persons employed, by branch of economic activity (000s)
Personnes employées, par branches d'activité économique (000s)

Country or area Pays ou zone	Sex	Year Année	Total employment (000s) Emploi total (000s)	Agriculture, Agriculture, hunting and forestry Agriculture, chasse et sylviculture	Fishing Pêche	Mining and quarrying Activités extractives	Manufacturing Activités de fabrication	Electricity, gas Electricity, gas and water supply Production et distribution d'électricité, de gaz et d'eau	Construc Construc
Singapore [2][13]	M	1993	952.3	...	...	0.3	247.8	5.9	
Singapour [2][13]	F	1993	639.7	...	...	...	181.7	1.6	
	M	1998	1089.6	...	...	1.3	245.2	6.7	1
	F	1998	780.1	...	...	0.2	159.2	1.6	
Slovakia [1][2][84]	M	1995	1193.3	...	...	25.7	331.8	37.6	1
Slovaquie [1][2][84]	F	1995	953.5	...	...	3.7	242.9	8.9	
	M	1998	1188.7	...	...	26.7	339.2	42.7	1
	F	1998	978.1	...	...	4.4	235.2	7.7	
Slovenia [2]	M	1994[13]	454.0	54.0	...	8.0	169.0	7.0	
Slovénie [2]	F	1994[13]	397.0	44.0	...	...	124.0	3.0	
	M	1998[32]	487.0	57.0	...	8.0	171.0	7.0	
	F	1998[32]	420.0	51.0	...	...	118.0	1.0	
Spain [66][70]	M	1994	7740.4	767.4	73.7	62.4	1805.9	77.9	10
Espagne [66][70]	F	1994	3989.7	304.9	5.0	3.0	525.7	8.9	
	M	1998	8517.4	741.7	49.6	54.4	1984.3	77.0	12
	F	1998	4687.4	263.7	5.6	5.3	578.9	8.0	
Sweden [72]	M	1993[68]	2026.0	97.0	3.0	10.0	527.0	29.0	2
Suède [72]	F	1993[68]	1938.0	36.0	...	1.0	199.0	7.0	
	M	1998	2079.0	74.0	2.0	8.0	560.0	25.0	2
	F	1998	1901.0	26.0	...	1.0	202.0	7.0	
Switzerland [1]	M	1993	2276.0	...	...	5.0	541.0	22.0	2
Suisse [1]	F	1993	1527.0	...	...	1.0	203.0	3.0	
	M	1998	2239.0	...	...	5.0	493.0	20.0	2
	F	1998	1611.0	...	...	1.0	192.0	3.0	
Tajikistan [7]	T	1993	1854.0	949.0	...	...	219.0	37.0	1
Tadjikistan [7]	T	1997	1143.4	527.6	0.2	...	136.5	18.0	
United Kingdom [38][66]	M	1993	14034.6	379.4	16.4	134.6	3827.9	223.7	14
Rouyame−Uni [38][66]	F	1993	11476.5	121.7	1.0	16.8	1538.2	71.6	18
	M	1998	14905.8	336.8	17.3	85.9	3655.6	137.1	17
	F	1998	12041.6	108.4	2.5	13.9	1331.2	41.5	1

Wholesale and retail trade; repair of motor vehicles motorcycles and personal and household goods Commerce de gros de détail; répa- tion de véhicules automobiles, de motorcycles et de biens personnels et domestiques	Hotels and restaurants Hôtels et restaurants	Transport, storage and communi- cations Transports, entreposage et communi- cations	Financial inter- mediation Inter médiation financière	Real estate, renting and business activities Immobilier, locations et activités de services aux entreprises	Public admin. and defence; compulsory social sec. Admin. publique et défense; séc. sociale obligatoire	Education Education	Health and social work Santé et action sociale	Other community, social and personal service act. Autres act. de services collectifs, sociaux et personnels	Private households with employed persons Ménages privés employant du personnel domestique	Extra- territorial org. and bodies Org. et organismes extra- territoriaux
160.5	55.7	131.0	27.9	60.2	89.0	...	...	...	...	...
100.7	46.7	35.8	39.7	45.6	17.2	...	...	...	...	...
166.1	61.0	157.2	45.4	104.3	93.4	...	...	...	...	...
115.1	57.9	49.2	63.1	80.0	25.1	...	...	...	...	...
93.5	22.9	113.2	8.4	56.5	80.1	39.1	28.6	50.4	0.3	0.6
128.7	36.6	54.0	21.4	39.1	57.2	131.1	113.0	38.5	0.3	0.2
113.2	21.7	118.3	10.0	47.5	77.9	32.7	29.3	37.2	0.2	...
153.2	41.4	49.8	26.8	34.6	71.3	131.4	114.4	34.8	2.5	0.3
46.0	13.0	38.0	6.0	16.0	19.0	13.0	10.0	14.0	...	...
54.0	18.0	13.0	12.0	14.0	19.0	32.0	42.0	14.0	...	...
55.0	15.0	39.0	5.0	26.0	19.0	14.0	9.0	15.0	...	...
56.0	23.0	12.0	13.0	21.0	22.0	46.0	33.0	15.0	1.0	...
1193.2	422.0	583.8	214.6	326.8	493.2	250.7	181.3	229.9	48.6	0.2
829.5	286.8	97.1	98.1	274.4	257.4	387.0	404.8	186.6	279.8	1.0
1252.5	437.1	640.2	228.6	454.7	532.7	293.3	205.8	256.5	48.8	0.5
927.0	360.6	131.4	104.6	403.8	293.4	493.5	508.4	240.0	313.4	2.4
278.0	38.0	185.0	37.0	193.0	...	94.0	109.0	...	...	...
227.0	54.0	86.0	51.0	120.0	...	204.0	709.0	...	...	...
288.0	44.0	192.0	36.0	250.0	...	94.0	103.0	...	...	...
215.0	67.0	79.0	48.0	161.0	...	199.0	667.0	...	...	...
353.0	101.0	182.0	118.0	200.0	98.0	100.0	86.0	68.0	1.0	...
316.0	132.0	67.0	85.0	117.0	48.0	109.0	254.0	76.0	30.0	...
342.0	98.0	177.0	121.0	227.0	97.0	103.0	93.0	69.0	3.0	...
318.0	142.0	67.0	87.0	137.0	56.0	125.0	291.0	79.0	28.0	...
87.0	...	72.0	...	...	...	188.0	103.0	...	...	...
40.2	...	50.9	...	...	...	160.0	82.0	...	...	...
1968.8	405.5	1243.7	541.5	1150.1	918.6	546.4	500.7	542.5	11.3	21.7
1979.0	692.5	401.2	651.3	893.8	725.1	1273.0	2126.1	609.7	128.9	7.6
2115.9	489.8	1321.6	584.4	1597.4	870.7	593.2	578.4	699.0	32.1	16.5
2001.4	748.9	433.9	599.9	1170.6	693.0	1447.7	2385.7	753.4	111.1	4.2

25
Employment by industry [*cont.*]
Emploi par industrie [*suite*]

Source:

International Labour Office (ILO), Geneva, "Yearbook of Labour Statistics 1999" and the ILO labour statistics database.

+ Countries using the latest version of the International Standard Industrial Classification of all Economic Activities, Revision 3 (ISIC Revision 3), are presented in Part B. Countries using the former classification, ISIC Revision 2, are presented in Part A. Countries that report both classifications, ISIC 2 and ISIC 3, are presented in both part A and part B.

† For information on the recent changes in country or area nomenclature pertaining to former Czechoslovakia, Germany, Hong Kong Special Administrative Region (SAR) of China, Macao Special Administrative Region (SAR) of China, SFR of Yugoslavia and the former USSR, see Annex I − Country or area nomenclature, regional and other groupings.

†† For statistical purposes the data for China do not include those for Hong Kong Special Administrative Region (Hong Kong SAR), Macao Special Administrative Region (Macao SAR) and Taiwan province of China.

1 Civilian labour force employed.
2 Persons aged 15 years and over.
3 Estimates based on 1986 census benchmarks.
4 Data classified according to ANZSIC; previously classified by ASIC.

5 Estimates based on the 1991 Census of Population and Housing.

6 Including armed forces, except conscripts not employed before their military service.
7 Both sexes.
8 Including mining and quarrying.
9 Persons aged 10 years and over.
10 Year ending in June of the year indicated.
11 Including quarrying.
12 Wholesale and retail trade.
13 One month of each year.
14 Including professional army; excluding compulsory military service.

15 Persons aged 14 years and over.
16 Persons aged 15 to 69 years.
17 Urban areas.
18 Excluding rural population of Rondônia, Acre, Amazonas, Roraima, Pará and Amapá.
19 Including electricity, gas, water and sanitary services.
20 Excluding restaurants and hotels.
21 Excluding storage.
22 Including international and other extra−territorial bodies and activities not adequately defined.
23 Including restaurants, hotels and storage; excluding sanitary services and international bodies.
24 Excluding armed forces.
25 Including veterinary services.
26 Including major divisions 2 and 4.
27 Excluding veterinary services, radio and TV broadcasting, repair and installation services.
28 Excluding full−time members of the armed forces.
29 Including repair and installation services.
30 Including sanitary services.
31 Excluding repair and installation services and sanitary services.

32 One quarter of each year.
33 Beginning 1996, sample design revised.
34 Excluding armed forces and reemployed retired persons.
35 Whole national economy.
36 Excluding business services.

Source:

Bureau international du travail (BIT), Genève, "Annuaire des statistiques du travail 1999" et la base de données du BIT.

+ On trouvera ans la partie B les chiffres relatifs aux pays qui appliquent le version la plus récente de la Classification internationale type, par industrie, de toutes les branches d'activité économique, Révision 3 (CITI Rév. 3). Les pays, qui utilisent encore la classification dans sa version précédente (Révision 2) figurent à la partie A. Les pays qui utilisent les deux classifications, CITI 2 et CITI 3, figurent à la fois dans les parties A et B.

† Pour les modifications récentes de nomenclature de pays ou de zone concernant l'Allemagne, Hong Kong, région administrative spéciale (RAS) de Chine, Macao, région administrative spéciale (RAS) de Chine, l'ex−Tchécoslovaquie, l'ex−URSS et l'ex−Rfs de Yougoslavie, voir annex I − Nomenclature des pays ou des zones, groupements régionaux et autres groupements.

†† Les données statistiques relatives à la Chine ne comprennent pas celles qui concernent la région administrative spéciale de Hong Kong (la RAS de Hong Kong), la région administrative spéciale de Macao (la RAS de Macao) et la province chinoise de Taiwan.

1 Main−d'oeuvre civile occupée.
2 Personnes âgées de 15 ans et plus.
3 Estimations basées sur les données de calage du recensement de 1986.
4 Données classifiées selon l'ANZSIC; précédemment classifiées par l'ASIC.

5 Estimations basées sur le recensement de la population et de l'habitat de 1991.

6 Y compris les forces armées, sauf les conscrits n'ayant pas travaillé avant leur service militaire.
7 Les deux sexes.
8 Y compris les industries extractives.
9 Personnes âgées de 10 ans et plus.
10 Année se terminant en juin de l'année indiquée.
11 Y compris les carrières.
12 Commerce de gros et de détail.
13 Un mois de chaque année.
14 Y compris les militaires de carrière; non compris les militaires du contingent.

15 Personnes âgées de 14 ans et plus.
16 Personnes âgées de 15 à 69 ans.
17 Régions urbaines.
18 Non compris la population rurale de Rondônia, Acre, Amazonas, Romaima, Pará et Amapá.
19 Y compris l'électricité, le gaz, l'eau et les services sanitaires.
20 Non compris les restaurants et hôtels.
21 Non compris les entrepôts.
22 Y compris les organisations internationales et autres organismes extra−territoriaux et les activiités mal désignées.
23 Y compris les restaurants, hôtels et entrepôts; non compris les services sanitaires et les organismes internationaux.
24 Non compris les forces armées.
25 Y compris les services vétérinaires.
26 Y compris les branches 2 et 4.
27 Non compris les services vétérinaires, de réparation et d'installation, et la radiodiffusion et télévision.
28 Non compris les membres à temps complet des forces armées.
29 Y compris les services de réparation et d'installation.
30 Y compris les services sanitaires.
31 Non compris les services de réparation et d'installation, et les services sanitaires.

32 Un trimestre de chaque année.
33 A partir de 1996, plan d'échantillonnage révisé.
34 Non compris les forces armées et les retraités réemployés.
35 Ensemble de l'économie nationale.
36 Non compris les services aux entreprises.

25
Employment by industry [*cont.*]
Emploi par industrie [*suite*]

37 Including unpaid family workers who worked for one hour or more.	37 Y compris les travailleurs familiaux non rémunérés ayant travaillé une heure ou plus.
38 Average of less than 12 months.	38 Moyenne de moins de douze mois.
39 Persons aged 12 years and over.	39 Personnes âgées de 12 ans et plus.
40 7 main cities of the country.	40 7 villes principales du pays.
41 Estimates based on the 1993 Census results.	41 Estimations basées sur les résultats du Recensement de 1993.
42 Persons aged 15 to 74 years.	42 Personnes âgées de 15 à 74 ans.
43 Data classified according to ISIC Rev. 3.	43 Données classifiées selon la CITI Rév. 3.
44 Persons aged 12 to 64 years.	44 Personnes âgées de 12 à 64 ans.
45 Including armed forces.	45 Y compris les forces armées.
46 Including major divisions 2, 4 and 5.	46 Y compris les branches 2, 4 et 5.
47 Including major divisions 7, 8 and 9.	47 Y compris les branches 7, 8 et 9.
48 Including repairs.	48 Y compris les réparations.
49 Including mining and quarrying, electricity, gas and water.	49 Y compris les industries extractives, l'électricité, le gaz et l'eau.
50 Non–material activities; including major division 8.	50 Activités non matérielles; y compris la branche 8.
51 Including the residents of East Jerusalem.	51 Y compris les résidents de Jérusalem–Est.
52 Including permanent members of institutional households.	52 Y compris les membres permanents des ménages collectifs.
53 Including electricity, gas and water.	53 Y compris l'électricité, le gaz et l'eau.
54 Including self–defence forces.	54 Y compris les forces d'autodéfense.
55 Excluding hotels.	55 Non compris les hôtels.
56 Paper products.	56 Articles en papier.
57 Including activities not adequately defined.	57 Y compris les activités mal désignées.
58 Persons aged 15 to 64 years.	58 Personnes âgées de 15 à 64 ans.
59 Curaçao.	59 Curaçao.
60 Persons aged 16 to 74 years.	60 Personnes âgées de 16 à 74 ans.
61 July of preceding year to June of current year.	61 Juillet de l'année précédente à juin de l'année en cours.
62 Asunción metropolitan area.	62 Région métropolitaine d'Asunción.
63 Including members of the armed forces living in private households.	63 Y compris les membres des forces armées vivant en ménages privés.
64 Including restaurants and hotels.	64 Y compris les restaurants et hôtels.
65 Including the Azores and Madeira.	65 Y compris les Açores et Madère.
66 Persons aged 16 years and over.	66 Personnes âgées de 16 ans et plus.
67 31st Dec. of each year.	67 31 déc. de chaque année.
68 Beginning 1993, methodology revised; data not strictly comparable.	68 A partir de 1993, méthodologie révisée; les données ne sont pas strictement comparables.
69 Excluding domestic workers (private households), self–employed and family workers.	69 Non compris le personnel domestique (ménages privés), les travailleurs indépendants et les travailleurs familiaux.
70 Excluding compulsory military service.	70 Non compris les militaires du contingent.
71 Excluding Northern and Eastern provinces.	71 Non compris les provinces du Nord et de l'Est.
72 Persons aged 16 to 64 years.	72 Personnes âgées de 16 à 64 ans.
73 Persons aged 13 years and over.	73 Personnes âgées de 13 ans et plus.
74 Including financing, insurance and real estate; excluding restaurants and hotels.	74 Y compris les banques, les assurances et affaires immobilières; non compris les restaurants et hôtels.
75 Including restaurants and hotels; excluding repair and installation services and sanitary services.	75 Y compris les restaurants et hôtels; non compris les services de réparation et d'installation, et les services sanitaires.
76 Figures revised on the basis of the 1990 census results.	76 Données révisées sur la base des résultats du Recensement de 1990.
77 1990 Census industrial classification.	77 Classification par industrie du recensement de 1990.
78 Estimates based on 1990 census benchmarks.	78 Estimations basées sur les données de calage du recensement de 1990.
79 Including hotels; excluding sanitary services.	79 Y compris les hôtels; non compris les services sanitaires.
80 Year beginning in August of year indicated.	80 Année commençant en août de l'année indiquée.
81 Including persons on child–care leave.	81 Y compris les personnes en congé parental.
82 Persons aged 15 to 66 years.	82 Personnes âgées de 15 à 66 ans.
83 Excluding regular military living in barracks and conscripts.	83 Non compris les militaires de carrière vivant dans des casernes et les conscrits.
84 Excluding persons on child–care leave.	84 Non compris les personnes en congé parental.

26
Unemployment
Chômage
Number (thousands) and percentage of unemployed
Nombre (milliers) et pourcentage des chômeurs

Country or area § Pays ou zone §	1989	1990	1991	1992	1993	1994	1995	1996	1997	1998
Albania Albanie										
MF [IV]	113.4	150.7	139.8	...	...	...	...	...	...	...
% MF [IV]	7.3	9.5	9.1	...	...	...	...	...	...	...
Algeria Algérie										
MF [IV] [1]	946.0	1 156.0	1 261.0	1 482.0	1 519.0	1 660.0	2 104.7	...	2 311.0	...
M [IV] [1]	876.0	1 069.0	1 155.0	1 348.0	...	...	1 626.0	...	2 031.0	...
F [IV] [1]	70.0	87.0	106.0	134.0	...	...	478.0	...	280.0	...
% MF [IV] [1]	16.9	19.8	20.6	23.0	23.2	24.4	27.9	...	28.7	...
% M [IV] [1]	17.2	...	21.7	24.2	...	...	26.0	...	26.9	...
% F [IV] [1]	15.9	...	17.0	20.3	...	...	38.4	...	24.0	...
Angola Angola										
MF [III] [2]	...	...	...	...	...	...	...	19.0	...	...
M [III] [2]	...	...	...	...	...	...	...	15.5	...	...
F [III] [2]	...	...	...	...	...	...	...	3.5	...	...
Argentina Argentine										
MF [I] [3]	...	...	696.0	827.0	1 062.0	1 400.0	1 959.0	2 047.0	...	...
M [I] [3]	...	...	...	...	...	761.3	1 123.1	1 199.4	...	...
F [I] [3]	...	...	...	...	...	638.7	835.9	847.6	...	...
% MF [I] [3]	...	...	6.3	7.2	9.1	11.7	15.9	16.3	...	...
% M [I] [3]	...	...	...	...	...	10.3	14.8	15.4	...	...
% F [I] [3]	...	...	...	...	...	14.1	17.8	17.6	...	...
Armenia Arménie										
MF [I] [4]	...	...	...	...	...	...	...	...	166.1	139.1
M [I] [4]	...	...	...	...	...	...	...	...	47.2	41.0
F [I] [4]	...	...	...	...	...	...	...	...	118.9	98.1
% MF [I] [4]	...	...	...	...	...	...	...	...	10.8	9.3
% M [I] [4]	...	...	...	...	...	...	...	...	5.5	4.9
% F [I] [4]	...	...	...	...	...	...	...	...	17.4	15.0
Australia Australie										
MF [I] [156]	508.1	584.8	814.5	925.1	939.2	855.5	764.5	779.4	786.5	746.5
M [I] [156]	276.5	332.3	489.5	566.2	574.0	505.6	453.4	456.0	457.9	434.5
F [I] [156]	231.6	252.5	325.0	358.9	365.1	349.9	311.1	323.4	328.7	312.0
% MF [I] [156]	6.2	6.9	9.6	10.8	10.9	9.7	8.5	8.5	8.6	8.0
% M [I] [156]	5.7	6.7	9.9	11.4	11.5	10.0	8.8	8.8	8.7	8.2
% F [I] [156]	6.8	7.2	9.2	10.0	10.1	9.4	8.1	8.3	8.3	7.7
Austria Autriche										
MF [I] [1]	108.6	114.8	125.4	132.4	158.8	138.4	143.7	160.4	164.8	165.0
M [I] [1]	58.2	63.0	70.9	74.4	88.1	72.6	71.4	86.5	87.3	88.4
F [I] [1]	50.4	51.8	54.5	58.0	70.7	65.7	72.2	73.9	77.5	76.6
MF [III] [1]	149.2	165.8	185.0	193.1	222.3	214.9	215.7	230.5	233.3	237.8
M [III] [1]	81.0	89.0	99.0	107.2	126.7	120.6	120.0	128.0	128.6	129.4
F [III] [1]	68.2	76.8	86.0	85.9	95.6	94.4	95.7	102.5	104.8	108.4
% MF [I] [1]	3.1	3.2	3.5	3.7	4.3	3.6	3.7	4.1	4.2	4.2
% M [I] [1]	2.8	3.0	3.3	3.5	4.1	3.3	3.2	3.9	3.9	4.0
% F [I] [1]	3.6	3.6	3.7	3.8	4.5	4.0	4.3	4.5	4.6	4.6
% MF [III] [1]	5.0	5.4	5.8	5.9	6.8	6.5	6.6	7.0	7.1	7.2
% M [III] [1]	4.6	4.9	5.3	5.7	6.7	6.4	6.4	6.9	6.9	6.9
% F [III] [1]	5.5	6.0	6.5	6.2	6.9	6.7	6.8	7.3	7.4	7.5
Azerbaijan Azerbaïdjan										
MF [III] [7]	...	...	4.0	6.4	19.5	23.6	28.3	31.9	38.3	42.3
M [III] [7]	...	...	1.5	2.8	7.7	9.2	11.4	13.1	16.2	18.2
F [III] [7]	...	...	2.5	3.6	11.8	14.4	16.9	18.8	22.1	24.1
% MF [III] [7]	...	...	0.1	0.2	0.5	0.7	0.8	0.9	1.0	1.1
% M [III] [7]	...	...	0.1	0.1	0.4	0.5	0.6	0.7	0.8	0.9
% F [III] [7]	...	...	0.2	0.2	0.7	0.9	1.0	1.1	1.2	1.4
Bahamas Bahamas										
MF [I] [18]	14.9	...	16.0	20.0	18.0	18.4	15.6	16.9	14.7	...
M [I] [18]	7.4	...	8.4	9.8	9.2	9.2	7.5	6.6	6.5	...
F [I] [18]	7.5	...	7.7	10.2	8.7	9.3	8.1	10.3	8.2	...
% MF [I] [18]	11.7	...	12.3	14.8	13.1	13.3	10.9	11.5	9.8	...
% M [I] [18]	11.0	...	12.2	13.8	12.8	12.6	10.1	8.6	8.3	...
% F [I] [18]	12.5	...	12.4	16.0	13.4	14.0	11.8	14.7	11.3	...

26
Unemployment
Number (thousands) and percentage of unemployed [cont.]
Chômage
Nombre (milliers) et pourcentage des chômeurs [suite]

Country or area [§] Pays ou zone [§]	1989	1990	1991	1992	1993	1994	1995	1996	1997	1998
Bahrain Bahreïn										
MF [III] [9]	3.4	3.0	3.3	3.0	3.6	4.2	5.1	...	6.1	4.1
M [III] [9]	2.5	2.1	2.4	2.2	2.9	2.7	3.4	...	4.1	2.7
F [III] [9]	0.9	0.8	0.9	0.9	0.7	1.4	1.7	...	2.0	1.4
Bangladesh Bangladesh										
MF [I] [3]	595.0	997.0	...	...	...	...	...	1 417.0[10]	...	...
M [I] [3]	372.0	616.0	...	...	...	...	...	933.0[10]	...	...
F [I] [3]	223.0	379.0	...	...	...	...	...	484.0[10]	...	...
% MF [I] [3]	1.2	1.9	...	...	...	...	...	2.5[10]	...	...
% M [I] [3]	1.3	2.0	...	...	...	...	...	2.7[10]	...	...
% F [I] [3]	1.1	1.9	...	...	...	...	...	2.3[10]	...	...
Barbados Barbade										
MF [I] [1]	17.1[11]	18.6[12]	20.9	28.7	30.9	28.2	26.9	...	...	...
M [I] [1]	5.9[11]	6.6[12]	8.6	13.2	14.0	12.1	11.4	...	...	...
F [I] [1]	11.2[11]	12.0[12]	12.3	15.5	16.9	16.1	15.5	...	...	...
% MF [I] [1]	13.7[11]	15.0[12]	17.1	23.0	24.5	21.9	19.7	...	...	...
% M [I] [1]	9.1[11]	10.3[12]	13.3	20.4	21.5	18.3	16.5	...	...	...
% F [I] [1]	18.7[11]	20.2[12]	21.4	25.7	27.7	25.6	22.9	...	...	...
Belarus Bélarus										
MF [III] [8]	...	...	2.3	24.0	66.3	101.2	131.0	182.5	126.2	105.9
M [III] [8]	...	...	0.5	4.4	22.3	36.7	46.7	66.1	42.1	35.3
F [III] [8]	...	...	1.8	19.6	44.0	64.5	84.3	116.4	84.1	70.6
% MF [III] [8]	...	...	0.1	0.5	1.4	2.1	2.7	3.9	2.8	2.3
% M [III] [8]	...	...	...	0.2	0.9	1.6	2.2			
% F [III] [8]	...	...	0.1	0.7	1.6	2.4	3.3	...	...	...
Belgium Belgique										
MF [I] [28]	326.0	285.1	282.4	316.1	335.2	405.4	390.1	404.0	375.1	384.0
M [I] [28]	127.9	109.1	110.9	137.1	149.1	188.5	178.9	181.7	173.2	179.3
F [I] [28]	198.1	176.1	171.5	179.0	186.1	216.9	211.2	222.3	201.9	204.7
MF [III]	419.3[13]	402.8[13]	429.5[13]	472.9[13]	549.7[13]	588.7[13]	596.9[13]	588.2[13]	570.0[13]	541.0
M [III]	167.5[13]	161.3[13]	178.0[13]	199.1[13]	237.5[13]	257.0[13]	259.6[13]	255.6[13]	249.6[13]	237.4
F [III]	251.8[13]	241.5[13]	251.5[13]	273.8[13]	312.2[13]	331.6[13]	337.3[13]	332.7[13]	320.5[13]	303.6
% MF [I] [28]	8.3	7.2	7.0	7.7	8.2	9.8	9.3	9.6	8.9	9.1
% M [I] [28]	5.3	4.5	4.6	5.7	6.2	7.7	7.3	7.4	7.1	7.3
% F [I] [28]	13.0	11.4	10.7	10.7	11.1	12.7	12.2	12.8	11.4	11.4
% MF [III]	10.1[13]	9.6[13]	10.2[13]	11.2[13]	12.9[13]	13.8[13]	13.9[13]	13.7[13]	13.1[13]	12.4
% M [III]	6.9[13]	6.6[13]	7.3[13]	8.1[13]	9.7[13]	10.6[13]	10.7[13]	10.5[13]	10.2[13]	9.7
% F [III]	14.7[13]	13.9[13]	14.3[13]	15.3[13]	17.1[13]	18.0[13]	18.1[13]	17.7[13]	16.8[13]	15.9
Belize Belize										
MF [I] [14]	...	...	...	...	6.7	7.7	...	...	...	...
M [I] [14]	...	...	...	...	3.5	4.3	...	...	...	...
F [I] [14]	...	...	...	...	3.2	3.5	...	...	...	...
% MF [I] [14]	...	...	...	...	9.8	11.1	...	...	...	...
% M [I] [14]	...	...	...	...	7.5	9.0	...	...	...	...
% F [I] [14]	...	...	...	...	14.5	15.1	...	...	...	...
Bermuda Bermudes										
MF [III]	0.0	0.1	0.2	...	...	...	...	...	...	...
Bolivia Bolivie										
MF [I] [3 15]	95.3	71.8	62.1	59.3	69.6	38.8	47.5	58.7[8]	...	...
M [I] [3 15]	54.1	39.7	34.6	34.5	43.2	23.5	24.3	29.5[8]	...	...
F [I] [3 15]	41.3	32.1	27.4	24.8	26.3	15.3	23.1	29.2[8]	...	...
% MF [I] [3 15]	10.0	7.3	5.9	5.5	6.0	3.1	3.6	4.2[8]	...	...
% M [I] [3 15]	9.9	6.9	5.7	5.5	6.5	3.4	3.3	3.7[8]	...	...
% F [I] [3 15]	10.1	7.8	6.2	5.6	5.3	2.9	4.0	4.5[8]	...	...
Botswana Botswana										
MF [I] [16 17]	...	...	...	...	...	...	94.5	...	...	...
M [I] [16 17]	...	...	...	...	...	...	45.5	...	...	...
F [I] [16 17]	...	...	...	...	...	...	49.1	...	...	...
% MF [I] [16 17]	...	...	...	...	...	...	21.5	...	...	...
% M [I] [16 17]	...	...	...	...	...	...	19.4	...	...	...
% F [I] [16 17]	...	...	...	...	...	...	23.9	...	...	...

26
Unemployment
Number (thousands) and percentage of unemployed [*cont.*]
Chômage
Nombre (milliers) et pourcentage des chômeurs [*suite*]

Country or area [§] Pays ou zone [§]	1989	1990	1991	1992	1993	1994	1995	1996	1997	1998
Brazil Brésil										
MF [I] [3 8 18]	1 891.0	2 367.5	...	4 573.3[19]	4 395.6	...	4 509.8	5 076.2	5 881.8	...
M [I] [3 8 18]	1 244.0	1 582.4	...	2 355.1[19]	2 305.9	...	2 327.9	2 498.3	2 854.9	...
F [I] [3 8 18]	647.0	785.1	...	2 218.2[19]	2 089.7	...	2 181.9	2 577.9	3 026.9	...
% MF [I] [3 8 18]	3.0	3.7	...	6.5[19]	6.2	...	6.1	7.0	7.8	...
% M [I] [3 8 18]	3.1	3.8	...	5.6[19]	5.4	...	5.3	5.7	6.4	...
% F [I] [3 8 18]	2.9	3.4	...	8.0[19]	7.4	...	7.3	8.8	10.0	...
Bulgaria Bulgarie										
MF [I] [1]	...	...	...	...	814.7	731.1	589.7	505.2	512.8	497.4
M [I] [1]	...	...	...	...	421.3	392.0	305.9	268.6	271.9	269.2
F [I] [1]	...	...	...	...	393.4	339.1	283.8	236.6	240.9	228.2
MF [III] [8]	...	65.1	419.1	576.9	626.1	488.4	423.8	478.8	523.5	465.2
M [III] [8 20]	...	22.7	190.7	274.5	298.4	223.0	188.0	215.4	236.5	211.1
F [III] [8 21]	...	42.4	228.4	302.4	327.7	265.4	235.8	263.4	287.1	254.1
% MF [I] [1]	...	...	...	...	21.4	20.2	16.5	14.2	14.4	...
% M [I] [1]	...	...	...	...	20.9	20.2	16.2	14.2	14.3	...
% F [I] [1]	...	...	...	...	22.0	20.3	16.8	14.1	14.4	...
% MF [III] [8]	...	1.7	11.1	15.3	16.4	12.4	11.1	12.5	13.7	...
Burkina Faso Burkina Faso										
MF [III] [22]	38.1	42.0	34.8	29.8	29.6	26.6	...	...	...	...
M [III] [22]	32.4	37.4	30.4	25.9	24.9	24.0	...	...	...	...
F [III] [22]	5.7	4.6	4.4	3.9	4.6	2.7	...	...	...	...
Burundi Burundi										
MF [III] [23]	11.1	14.5	13.8	7.3	...	...	...	...	...	...
M [III] [23]	9.8	...	9.6	...	...	...	...	...	...	...
F [III] [23]	1.3	...	4.2	...	...	...	...	...	...	...
Canada Canada										
MF [I] [1 24 25]	1 065.3	1 163.9	1 491.7	1 640.2	1 648.8	1 540.7	1 422.1	1 469.2	1 413.5	1 305.1
M [I] [1 24 25]	577.9	649.2	866.1	966.2	952.0	884.5	801.1	822.5	779.1	727.4
F [I] [1 24 25]	487.3	514.7	625.6	674.0	696.8	656.2	621.0	646.7	634.3	577.7
% MF [I] [1 24 25]	7.5	8.1	10.4	11.3	11.2	10.4	9.5	9.7	9.2	8.3
% M [I] [1 24 25]	7.3	8.1	10.9	12.1	11.8	10.8	9.8	9.9	9.2	8.5
% F [I] [1 24 25]	7.8	8.1	9.7	10.4	10.6	9.9	9.2	9.4	9.2	8.1
Cape Verde Cap–Vert										
MF [III]	0.3	0.3	0.3	0.2	0.6	0.6	0.6	...	...	...
Central African Republic République centrafricaine										
MF [III] [26]	7.8	7.8	7.7	5.8	5.6	9.9	7.6	...	...	...
M [III] [26]	7.2	7.1	7.2	5.2	5.2	9.2	6.7	...	...	...
F [III] [26]	0.6	0.7	0.5	0.5	0.4	0.6	0.9	...	...	...
Chile Chili										
MF [I] [1 11]	249.8	268.9	253.6	217.1	233.6	311.3	248.1	302.0[27]	303.6	419.2
M [I] [1 11]	162.4	184.8	168.6	132.1	147.6	193.9	158.4	180.9[27]	180.8	271.1
F [I] [1 11]	87.4	84.0	85.0	85.1	86.0	117.4	89.8	121.1[27]	122.8	148.1
% MF [I] [1 11]	5.3	5.7	5.3	4.4	4.5	5.9	4.7	5.4[27]	5.3	7.2
% M [I] [1 11]	5.0	5.7	5.1	4.1	4.2	5.4	4.4	4.8[27]	4.7	7.0
% F [I] [1 11]	6.1	5.7	5.8	5.6	5.1	6.8	5.3	6.7[27]	6.6	7.6
China †† Chine ††										
MF [IV] [8 28]	3 779.0	3 832.0	3 522.0	3 603.0	4 201.0	4 764.0	5 196.0	5 528.0	5 768.0	5 710.0
M [IV] [8 28 29]	1 942.0	1 313.0	1 207.0	1 298.0	1 394.0	1 258.0	...	2 637.0	2 737.0	...
F [IV] [8 28 29]	1 837.0	1 814.0	1 677.0	1 700.0	1 925.0	1 752.0	...	2 891.0	3 031.0	...
% MF [IV] [8 28]	2.6	2.5	2.3	2.3	2.6	2.8	2.9	3.0	3.0	3.1
% M [IV] [8 28 29]	1.3	0.9	0.8	...	0.9	0.8	...	...	...	...
% F [IV] [8 28 29]	1.3	1.2	1.1	...	1.2	1.1	...	...	...	...
China, Hong Kong SAR † Chine, Hong Kong RAS †										
MF [I] [1 30]	29.7	36.6	50.4	54.7	56.3	56.2	95.6	86.1	71.3	157.6
M [I] [1 30]	19.1	23.3	33.8	35.3	35.8	37.7	62.3	58.0	45.7	105.0
F [I] [1 30]	10.6	13.3	16.6	19.4	20.6	18.6	33.3	28.1	25.6	52.7
% MF [I] [1 30]	1.1	1.3	1.8	2.0	2.0	1.9	3.2	2.8	2.2	4.7
% M [I] [1 30]	1.1	1.3	1.9	2.0	2.0	2.1	3.4	3.1	2.3	5.1
% F [I] [1 30]	1.1	1.3	1.6	1.9	1.9	1.7	2.9	2.3	2.0	4.0

26
Unemployment
Number (thousands) and percentage of unemployed [*cont.*]
Chômage
Nombre (milliers) et pourcentage des chômeurs [*suite*]

Country or area [§] Pays ou zone [§]	1989	1990	1991	1992	1993	1994	1995	1996	1997	1998
China, Macao SAR † Chine, Macao RAS †										
MF [I] [2]	6.2[8]	5.3[8]	5.3[8]	3.8[12]	3.7[12]	4.4[12]	6.7[12]	8.7[12]	6.5[12]	9.6[12]
M [I] [2]	2.6[8]	2.5[8]	2.6[8]	2.1[12]	2.2[12]	2.4[12]	4.3[12]	5.4[12]	4.2[12]	6.6[12]
F [I] [2]	3.6[8]	2.8[8]	2.7[8]	1.8[12]	1.5[12]	2.0[12]	2.4[12]	3.3[12]	2.3[12]	3.1[12]
% MF [I] [2]	3.7[8]	3.2[8]	3.0[8]	2.2[12]	2.1[12]	2.5[12]	3.6[12]	4.3[12]	3.2[12]	4.6[12]
% M [I] [2]	2.7[8]	2.5[8]	2.5[8]	2.1[12]	2.2[12]	2.4[12]	4.1[12]	4.7[12]	2.7[12]	5.7[12]
% F [I] [2]	5.1[8]	4.1[8]	3.7[8]	2.4[12]	2.0[12]	2.6[12]	3.0[12]	3.7[12]	2.5[12]	3.3[12]
Colombia Colombie										
MF [I] [8 17 31]	356.5	491.6	527.5[32]	509.2[32]	450.2[32]	443.6[32]	524.6[32]	739.6[32]	786.3[32]	998.3[32]
M [I] [8 17 31]	159.4	232.8	228.1[32]	205.6[32]	175.1[32]	163.7[32]	231.4[32]	338.2[32]	355.3[32]	457.2[32]
F [I] [8 17 31]	197.1	258.8	299.4[32]	303.5[32]	275.1[32]	279.8[32]	293.2[32]	401.3[32]	431.0[32]	541.1[32]
% MF [I] [8 17 31]	8.9	10.2	9.8[32]	9.2[32]	7.8[32]	7.6[32]	8.7[32]	11.9[32]	12.1[32]	15.0[32]
% M [I] [8 17 31]	6.8	8.1	7.4[32]	6.5[32]	5.3[32]	4.9[32]	6.8[32]	9.6[32]	9.8[32]	12.5[32]
% F [I] [8 17 31]	11.8	13.2	13.1[32]	12.6[32]	11.0[32]	11.2[32]	11.3[32]	15.1[32]	15.1[32]	18.0[32]
Costa Rica Costa Rica										
MF [I] [8 17]	38.7	49.5	59.1	44.0	46.9	49.4	63.5	75.9	74.3	76.5
M [I] [8 17]	23.4	31.7	35.5	26.4	28.9	28.7	39.1	45.3	43.5	40.6
F [I] [8 17]	15.3	17.8	23.5	17.6	18.0	20.7	24.4	30.6	30.8	36.0
% MF [I] [8 17]	3.8	4.6	5.5	4.1	4.1	4.2	5.2	6.2	5.7	5.6
% M [I] [8 17]	3.2	4.2	4.8	3.5	3.6	3.5	4.6	5.3	4.9	4.4
% F [I] [8 17]	5.3	5.9	7.4	5.4	5.3	5.8	6.5	8.3	7.5	8.0
Côte d'Ivoire Côte d'Ivoire										
MF [III] [7 33]	128.5	140.2	136.9	114.9	...	...	...	...	...	...
M [III] [7 33]	89.4	99.0	...	88.2	...	...	...	...	...	...
F [III] [7 33]	39.1	41.3	...	26.7	...	...	...	...	...	...
Croatia Croatie										
MF [I] [1]	...	...	...	...	...	...	...	170.2[8]	175.2[8]	198.5
M [I] [1]	...	...	...	...	...	...	...	88.3[8]	90.7[8]	100.9
F [I] [1]	...	...	...	...	...	...	...	82.0[8]	84.5[8]	97.5
MF [III]	140.0	161.0	254.0	267.0	251.0	243.0	241.0	261.0	278.0	288.0
M [III]	57.0	70.0	121.0	126.0	113.0	113.0	117.0	131.0	141.0	139.0
F [III]	83.0	91.0	133.0	141.0	138.0	130.0	124.0	130.0	137.0	149.0
% MF [I] [1]	...	...	...	...	...	...	...	10.0[8]	9.9[8]	11.4
% M [I] [1]	...	...	...	...	...	...	...	9.5[8]	9.5[8]	11.9
% F [I] [1]	...	...	...	...	...	...	...	10.5[8]	10.4[8]	12.1
% MF [III]	7.2	8.2	14.9	17.2	16.8	...	...	...	...	...
% M [III]	5.0	6.2	12.8	14.8	14.0	...	...	...	...	...
% F [III]	10.0	10.9	17.6	20.1	20.1	...	...	...	...	...
Cyprus Chypre										
MF [III] [2 34]	6.2	5.1	8.3	5.2	7.6	8.0	7.9	9.4	10.4	10.4
M [III] [2 34]	2.9	2.5	3.8	2.4	3.2	3.7	3.6	4.3	5.0	5.4
F [III] [2 34]	3.3	2.6	4.5	2.8	4.4	4.3	4.3	5.1	5.4	5.0
% MF [III] [2 34]	2.3	1.8	3.0	1.8	2.7	2.7	2.6	3.1	3.4	3.3
% M [III] [2 34]	1.7	1.4	2.2	1.8	1.8	2.0	1.9	2.3	2.7	2.8
% F [III] [2 34]	3.3	2.5	4.4	2.6	4.1	3.9	3.7	4.3	4.5	4.2
Czech Republic République tchèque										
MF [I] [1]	...	...	...	...	199.6	201.5	181.4	199.4	241.8	...
M [I] [1]	...	...	...	...	87.1	95.2	84.5	94.3	110.4	...
F [I] [1]	...	...	...	...	112.5	106.3	96.9	105.0	131.4	...
MF [III] [8]	...	39.0	222.0	135.0	185.0	166.0	153.0	186.0	269.0	387.0
M [III] [8]	...	19.0	95.0	57.0	81.0	70.0	65.0	81.0	117.0	182.0
F [III] [8]	...	20.0	127.0	78.0	104.0	96.0	88.0	105.0	152.0	205.0
% MF [I] [1]	...	...	...	...	4.0	4.1	4.1	3.9	4.7	...
% M [I] [1]	...	...	...	...	3.3	3.7	3.5	3.3	3.8	...
% F [I] [1]	...	...	...	...	4.8	4.7	4.8	4.6	5.8	...
% MF [III] [8]	...	0.7	4.1	2.6	3.5	3.2	2.9	3.5	5.2	7.5
% M [III] [8]	...	0.7	3.5	2.2	3.0	2.5	2.3	2.8	4.1	6.3
% F [III] [8]	...	0.8	4.8	3.0	4.1	4.0	3.6	4.3	6.7	9.0

26
Unemployment
Number (thousands) and percentage of unemployed [*cont.*]
Chômage
Nombre (milliers) et pourcentage des chômeurs [*suite*]

Country or area [§] Pays ou zone [§]	1989	1990	1991	1992	1993	1994	1995	1996	1997	1998
Denmark Danemark										
MF [I] [11]	253.9[35]	242.4[35]	264.8[35]	261.8[35]	308.8[35]	222.0[36]	195.5[36]	194.5[36]	174.2[36]	155.3[36]
M [I] [11]	124.3[35]	122.8[35]	129.3[35]	127.9[35]	159.2[35]	107.0[36]	85.6[36]	87.6[36]	74.8[36]	68.5[36]
F [I] [11]	129.6[35]	119.6[35]	135.5[35]	134.0[35]	149.6[35]	115.0[36]	109.9[36]	107.0[36]	99.5[36]	86.9[36]
MF [III] [37]	264.9	271.7	296.1	318.3	348.8	343.4	288.4	245.6	220.2	182.7
M [III] [37]	120.0	124.0	137.2	148.8	168.6	163.9	134.1	115.8	99.4	81.0
F [III] [37]	145.0	147.7	158.9	169.5	180.2	179.6	154.3	129.8	120.8	101.8
% MF [I] [11 36]	...	...	...	...	...	8.0	7.0	6.9	6.1	5.5
% M [I] [11 36]	...	...	...	...	...	7.1	5.6	5.7	4.9	4.5
% F [I] [11 36]	...	...	...	...	...	9.0	8.6	8.3	7.6	6.6
% MF [III] [37]	9.5	9.7	10.6	11.3	12.4	12.2	10.3	8.8	7.9	6.6
% M [III] [37]	8.1	8.4	9.2	10.0	11.3	11.0	9.0	7.8	6.7	5.5
% F [III] [37]	11.1	11.3	12.1	12.9	13.7	13.6	12.0	10.1	9.4	7.8
Dominican Republic République dominicaine										
MF [IV]	...	...	547.5[2]	611.8[2]	599.3[2]	456.6[2]	452.1[2]	505.7[3]	503.7[3]	...
M [IV]	...	...	229.7[2]	223.5[2]	217.9[2]	185.1[2]	187.3[2]	218.6[3]	199.0[3]	...
F [IV]	...	...	317.8[2]	388.3[2]	381.4[2]	271.6[2]	264.8[2]	287.2[3]	304.7[3]	...
% MF [IV]	...	...	19.7[2]	20.3[2]	19.9[2]	16.0[2]	15.8[2]	16.6[3]	15.9[3]	...
% M [IV]	...	...	12.5[2]	11.7[2]	11.4[2]	10.0[2]	10.2[2]	10.6[3]	9.5[3]	...
% F [IV]	...	...	33.1[2]	34.9[2]	34.8[2]	26.0[2]	26.2[2]	28.4[3]	28.6[3]	...
Ecuador Equateur										
MF [I] [8 15]	187.0[17]	150.2[3]	158.0[3]	263.2[3]	240.8[3]	207.2[3]	212.7[3]	334.6[3]	311.6[3]	409.3[3]
M [I] [8 15]	88.1[17]	67.0[3]	69.0[3]	105.3[3]	108.6[3]	101.8[3]	104.2[3]	156.1[3]	143.4[3]	174.5[3]
F [I] [8 15]	98.9[17]	83.2[3]	89.1[3]	157.9[3]	132.3[3]	105.4[3]	108.4[3]	178.5[3]	168.3[3]	233.8[3]
% MF [I] [8 15]	7.9[17]	6.1[3]	5.8[3]	8.9[3]	8.3[3]	7.1[3]	6.9[3]	10.4[3]	9.2[3]	11.5[3]
% M [I] [8 15]	5.9[17]	4.3[3]	4.1[3]	6.0[3]	6.2[3]	5.8[3]	5.5[3]	8.0[3]	7.0[3]	8.4[3]
% F [I] [8 15]	11.1[17]	9.1[3]	8.5[3]	13.2[3]	11.5[3]	9.3[3]	8.8[3]	14.0[3]	12.7[3]	16.0[3]
Egypt Egypte										
MF [I] [38]	1 107.9[8]	1 346.4[8]	1 463.4[8]	1 415.7[12]	1 800.6[12]	1 877.4[12]	1 916.9[12]	...	...	...
M [I] [38]	615.8[8]	602.3[8]	692.1[8]	768.1[12]	955.8[12]	963.3[12]	997.2[12]	...	...	...
F [I] [38]	492.1[8]	744.1[8]	771.3[8]	647.6[12]	844.8[12]	914.1[12]	919.7[12]	...	...	...
% MF [I] [38]	6.9[8]	8.6[8]	9.6[8]	9.0[12]	10.9[12]	11.0[12]	11.3[12]	...	...	...
% M [I] [38]	5.4[8]	5.2[8]	5.9[8]	6.4[12]	7.5[12]	7.4[12]	7.6[12]	...	...	...
% F [I] [38]	10.7[8]	17.9[8]	21.3[8]	17.0[12]	22.3[12]	22.8[12]	24.1[12]	...	...	...
El Salvador El Salvador										
MF [I] [3]	72.0[15]	97.9[15]	72.5[15]	81.0[15]	109.0	162.3	163.4	171.0	180.0	...
M [I] [3]	46.2[15]	54.8[15]	43.9[15]	47.5[15]	148.0	110.7	116.8	117.5	136.0	...
F [I] [3]	25.8[15]	43.1[15]	28.6[15]	33.5[15]	51.0	51.6	46.6	53.4	44.0	...
% MF [I] [3]	8.4[15]	10.0[15]	7.5[15]	7.9[15]	9.9	7.7	7.7	7.7	8.0	...
% M [I] [3]	9.9[15]	10.1[15]	8.3[15]	8.4[15]	11.8	8.4	8.7	8.4	9.5	...
% F [I] [3]	6.8[15]	9.8[15]	6.6[15]	7.2[15]	6.8	6.4	5.9	6.5	5.3	...
Estonia Estonie										
MF [I]	4.7[14]	5.3[14]	12.0[14]	29.1[14]	49.6[14]	56.7[14]	70.9[14]	71.9[14]	69.4[35]	68.0[11]
M [I]	...	2.5[14]	6.1[14]	16.3[14]	26.0[14]	28.9[14]	40.6[14]	40.4[14]	37.9[35]	38.8[11]
F [I]	...	2.8[14]	6.0[14]	12.8[14]	23.7[14]	27.8[14]	30.3[14]	31.6[14]	31.5[35]	29.2[11]
MF [III] [4]	...	...	0.9	14.9	16.3	15.3	15.6	17.3	...	...
M [III] [4]	...	...	0.3	7.5	7.5	6.4	5.1	5.2	...	...
F [III] [4]	...	...	0.6	7.4	8.8	8.9	10.5	12.1	...	...
% MF [I]	0.6[14]	0.6[14]	1.5[14]	3.7[14]	6.5[14]	7.6[14]	9.7[14]	10.0[14]	9.7[35]	9.6[11]
% M [I]	...	0.6[14]	1.4[14]	3.9[14]	6.5[14]	7.3[14]	10.6[14]	10.7[14]	10.1[35]	10.4[11]
% F [I]	...	0.7[14]	1.5[14]	3.4[14]	6.6[14]	7.9[14]	8.8[14]	9.2[14]	9.2[35]	8.6[11]
% MF [III] [4]	...	...	0.1	1.7	1.9	2.2	...	...	...	...
% M [III] [4]	...	...	0.1	1.6	1.7	...	...	...	...	...
% F [III] [4]	...	...	0.2	1.8	2.1	...	...	...	...	...
Ethiopia Ethiopie										
MF [III] [10]	...	...	44.3	70.9	62.9	64.7	37.5	44.9	34.6	...
M [III] [10]	...	...	24.9	52.0	40.4	37.5	14.0	16.6	19.1	...
F [III] [10]	...	...	19.4	18.8	22.6	27.2	23.5	28.3	15.4	...
Ethiopia incl. Eritrea Ethiopie y compris Erythrée										
MF [III] [10]	51.3	44.2	...	...	...	...	...	...	...	...
M [III] [10]	28.6	25.8	...	...	...	...	...	...	...	...
F [III] [10]	22.7	18.4	...	...	...	...	...	...	...	...
Fiji Fidji										
MF [IV] [1]	15.0	16.0	15.0	14.2	15.8	16.1	15.4	...	...	...
% MF [IV] [1]	6.1	6.4	5.9	5.4	5.9	5.7	5.4	...	...	...

26
Unemployment
Number (thousands) and percentage of unemployed [*cont.*]
Chômage
Nombre (milliers) et pourcentage des chômeurs [*suite*]

Country or area [§] Pays ou zone [§]	1989	1990	1991	1992	1993	1994	1995	1996	1997	1998
Finland Finlande										
MF [I] [35]	80.0	82.0	169.0	292.0	405.0	408.0	382.0	363.0	314.0	285.0
M [I] [35]	43.0	49.0	106.0	178.0	235.0	235.0	204.0	186.0	160.0	143.0
F [I] [35]	38.0	33.0	62.0	114.0	170.0	174.0	178.0	176.0	154.0	142.0
MF [III] [1 39 40]	97.0	94.0	181.0	319.0	436.0	467.0	451.0	434.0	398.0	362.0
M [III] [1 39 40]	50.0	52.0	108.0	186.0	245.0	257.0	244.0	231.0	207.0	183.0
F [III] [1 39 40]	47.0	42.0	73.0	133.0	191.0	210.0	207.0	203.0	191.0	179.0
% MF [I] [35]	3.1	3.1	6.6	11.6	16.2	16.4	15.2	14.4	12.5	11.3
% M [I] [35]	3.1	3.5	7.8	13.3	17.7	17.8	15.3	14.0	12.1	10.7
% F [I] [35]	3.0	2.7	5.1	9.6	14.4	14.9	15.1	14.8	13.0	11.9
France France										
MF [I] [18]	...	...	...	...	2 781.0	3 115.0	2 935.0	3 098.7	3 152.0	3 050.2
M [I] [18]	...	...	...	...	1 302.0	1 503.0	1 360.0	1 460.9	1 523.0	1 436.7
F [I] [18]					1 479.0	1 612.0	1 575.0	1 637.8	1 629.0	1 613.4
MF [III] [4]	2 531.9	2 504.7	2 709.1	2 911.2	3 172.0	3 329.2	2 976.2[41]	3 063.0	3 102.4	...
M [III] [4]	1 177.4	1 148.7	1 266.4	1 404.6	1 603.9	1 664.5	1 457.7[41]	1 519.8	1 545.7	...
F [III] [4]	1 354.5	1 355.9	1 442.7	1 506.6	1 568.1	1 664.7	1 518.5[41]	1 543.2	1 556.7	...
MF [IV] [1]	2 323.0	2 204.9	2 348.9	2 590.7	2 929.0	3 104.0	2 931.0	3 137.0	3 192.0	...
M [IV] [1]	998.9	947.8	1 031.8	1 168.3	1 401.0	1 488.0	1 371.0	1 502.0	1 554.0	...
F [IV] [1]	1 324.1	1 257.0	1 317.1	1 422.5	1 528.0	1 616.0	1 559.0	1 635.0	1 638.0	...
% MF [I] [18]	...	...	...	10.1	11.1	12.4	11.6	12.1	12.3	11.8
% M [I] [18]	...	...	...	7.9	9.4	10.8	9.8	10.4	10.8	10.2
% F [I] [18]	...	...	...	12.8	13.3	14.3	13.9	14.2	14.2	13.8
% MF [IV] [1]	9.4	8.9	9.4	10.3	11.6	12.3	11.6	12.3	12.4	...
% M [IV] [1]	7.1	6.7	7.3	8.3	10.0	10.6	9.8	10.6	11.0	...
% F [IV] [1]	12.4	11.7	12.0	12.9	13.7	14.3	13.8	14.3	14.3	...
French Guiana Guyane française										
MF [III] [4 42]	3.8	4.4	4.7	6.9	8.1	...	...	...	...	...
M [III] [4 42]	1.9	2.3	2.5	4.0	4.7	...	...	...	...	...
F [III] [4 42]	2.0	2.1	2.2	3.0	3.4	...	...	...	...	...
% MF [III] [4 42]	12.2	13.9	9.7	...	...	...	...	...	...	...
% M [III] [4 42]	9.4	11.7	8.2	...	...	...	...	...	...	...
% F [III] [4 42]	16.8	17.6	11.6	...	...	...	...	...	...	...
French Polynesia Polynésie française										
MF [III] [2]	0.6	0.6	0.6	...	...	...	...	...	...	3.8
Germany Allemagne										
MF [I] [18]	...	...	2 642.0	3 186.0	3 799.0	4 160.0	4 035.0	3 473.0	3 890.0	3 849.0
M [I] [18]	...	...	1 251.0	1 422.0	1 792.0	2 051.0	1 991.0	1 858.0	2 083.0	2 074.0
F [I] [18]	...	...	1 392.0	1 764.0	2 007.0	2 110.0	2 044.0	1 614.0	1 806.0	1 775.0
MF [III] [8 43]	...	...	...	2 894.2	3 447.1	3 493.3	3 521.0	3 848.4	4 308.1	3 965.4
M [III] [8 43]	...	...	...	1 344.6	1 672.3	1 721.2	1 764.9	1 996.1	2 220.5	2 046.8
F [III] [8 43]	...	...	...	1 549.6	1 774.8	1 772.1	1 756.1	1 852.3	2 087.6	1 918.6
% MF [I] [18]	...	...	6.6	7.9	9.5	10.3	10.1	8.8	9.8	9.7
% M [I] [18]	...	...	5.4	6.2	7.8	8.9	8.7	8.2	9.2	9.2
% F [I] [18]	...	...	8.2	10.3	11.7	12.3	11.9	9.6	10.6	10.4
% MF [III] [8 43]	...	...	...	8.2	9.9	10.0	10.2	11.2	12.5	11.4
% M [III] [8 43]	...	...	...	...	...	...	9.2	10.4	11.6	10.7
% F [III] [8 43]	...	...	...	...	...	...	11.4	12.1	13.5	12.2
Ghana Ghana										
MF [III] [44]	27.4	30.2	30.7	30.6	39.4	37.0	...	...	...	...
M [III] [44]	24.7	26.6	27.5	27.5	36.2	34.5	...	...	...	...
F [III] [44]	2.7	3.2	3.3	3.1	3.2	2.4	...	...	...	...
Gibraltar Gibraltar										
MF [III] [45]	0.6	0.4	0.9	1.8	2.1	2.4	2.1	1.9	...	...
M [III] [45]	0.5	0.3	0.7	1.3	1.4	1.5	1.3	1.2	...	...
F [III] [45]	0.1	0.1	0.2	0.5	0.8	0.9	0.8	0.7	...	...

26
Unemployment
Number (thousands) and percentage of unemployed [cont.]
Chômage
Nombre (milliers) et pourcentage des chômeurs [suite]

Country or area [§] Pays ou zone [§]	1989	1990	1991	1992	1993	1994	1995	1996	1997	1998
Greece Grèce										
MF [I] [2 11]	296.0	280.8	301.1	349.8	398.2	403.8	424.7	446.4	440.4	...
M [I] [2 11]	114.6	107.1	120.8	137.9	164.5	170.4	176.1	167.1	173.0	...
F [I] [2 11]	181.4	173.7	180.3	211.9	233.7	233.4	248.6	279.3	267.3	...
MF [III] [1]	133.9	140.2	173.2	184.7	175.9	179.8	...	...	...	...
M [III] [1]	64.6	68.1	83.9	89.7	87.9	87.3	...	...	...	...
F [III] [1]	69.3	72.1	89.3	95.0	87.9	92.4	...	...	...	...
% MF [I] [2 11]	7.5	7.0	7.7	8.7	9.7	9.6	10.0	10.3	10.3	...
% M [I] [2 11]	4.6	4.3	4.8	5.4	6.4	6.5	6.7	6.3	6.6	...
% F [I] [2 11]	12.4	11.7	12.9	14.2	15.2	14.9	15.4	16.6	15.9	...
% MF [III] [1]	6.5	6.4	7.3	7.6	7.1	7.2	...	...	...	...
Greenland Groënland										
MF [III]	1.0	1.3	1.7	1.9	1.8	1.8	2.0	2.0	1.9	...
Guadeloupe Guadeloupe										
MF [III] [4]	30.8	29.4[8]	34.3[8]	...	38.8	42.9	...	...	...	...
M [III] [4]	13.5	11.7[8]	13.9[8]	...	...	...	...	...	...	...
F [III] [4]	21.3	17.6[8]	20.4[8]	...	...	...	...	...	...	...
% MF [III] [4]	24.0	17.0	19.9	...	...	...	...	...	...	...
% M [III] [4]	16.0	...	...	...	...	...	...	...	...	...
% F [III] [4]	34.0	...	...	...	...	...	...	...	...	...
Guam Guam										
MF [I] [4]	1.1	1.3	1.7	1.8	2.6	...	...	...	...	...
% MF [I] [4]	2.8	2.8	3.5	3.9	5.5	...	...	...	...	...
Guatemala Guatemala										
MF [III] [3 46]	1.7	1.8	1.7	1.6	1.0	1.3	1.4	...	...	...
M [III] [3 46]	1.2	1.3	1.0	1.1	0.7	0.9	0.9	...	...	...
F [III] [3 46]	0.5	0.5	0.7	0.5	0.3	0.4	0.5	...	...	...
Honduras Honduras										
MF [I] [3]	...	61.7	72.1	53.9	...	...	59.1[8]	89.4[8]	69.4[8]	87.7[8]
M [I] [3]	...	41.4	46.0	37.8	...	...	40.3[8]	58.9[8]	45.4[8]	55.5[8]
F [I] [3]	...	20.3	26.1	16.1	...	...	18.8[8]	30.4[8]	23.9[8]	32.2[8]
% MF [I] [3]	...	4.8	4.6	3.1	...	...	3.2[8]	4.3[8]	3.2[8]	3.9[8]
% M [I] [3]	...	4.4	4.2	3.2	...	...	3.1[8]	4.2[8]	3.2[8]	3.8[8]
% F [I] [3]	...	6.2	5.6	3.0	...	...	3.4[8]	4.4[8]	3.2[8]	4.2[8]
Hungary Hongrie										
MF [I] [35]	...	...	...	444.2	518.9	451.2	416.5	400.1	348.8	313.0
M [I] [35]	...	...	...	265.9	316.0	274.8	261.5	243.7	214.1	189.2
F [I] [35]	...	...	...	178.3	202.9	176.4	155.0	156.4	134.7	123.8
MF [III] [8]	...	79.5[47]	406.1[47]	663.0[47]	632.1[47]	519.6[47]	495.9	477.5	464.0	404.1
M [III] [8]	...	49.1[47]	239.0[47]	390.0[47]	376.1[47]	302.6[47]	285.3	275.4	...	...
F [III] [8]	...	30.4[47]	167.1[47]	273.0[47]	256.0[47]	217.0[47]	210.6	202.1	...	...
% MF [I] [35]	...	...	...	9.8	11.9	10.7	10.2	9.9	8.7	7.8
% M [I] [35]	...	...	...	10.7	13.2	11.8	10.7	10.7	9.5	8.5
% F [I] [35]	...	...	...	8.7	10.4	9.4	8.7	8.8	7.8	7.0
% MF [III] [8]	...	1.7[47]	8.5[47]	12.3[47]	12.1[47]	10.4[47]	12.0	10.7	10.4	9.6
% M [III] [8]	...	1.8	9.2	14.0	14.2	11.7	...	...	...	...
% F [III] [8]	...	1.4	7.6	10.5	10.1	8.9	...	...	...	...
Iceland Islande										
MF [I] [12 48]	...	...	3.6	6.2	7.6	7.7	7.2	5.5	5.7	4.2
M [I] [12 48]	...	...	1.7	2.9	3.8	4.0	3.8	2.7	2.6	1.8
F [I] [12 48]	...	...	1.9	3.2	3.8	3.8	3.4	2.8	3.1	2.3
MF [III] [4]	2.1	2.3	1.9	3.9	5.6	6.2	6.5	5.8	5.2	3.8
M [III] [4]	0.9	1.1	1.0	1.9	2.7	2.9	3.1	2.5	2.0	1.4
F [III] [4]	1.2	1.2	0.9	1.9	2.9	3.4	3.5	3.3	3.2	2.4
% MF [I] [12 48]	...	...	2.5	4.3	5.3	5.3	4.9	3.7	3.9	2.7
% M [I] [12 48]	...	...	2.3	3.8	5.0	5.1	4.8	3.4	3.3	2.3
% F [I] [12 48]	...	...	2.9	4.9	5.6	5.5	4.9	4.1	4.5	3.3
% MF [III] [4]	1.7	1.8	1.5	3.0	4.3	4.8	5.0	4.3	3.9	2.8
% M [III] [4]	1.2	1.4	1.3	2.6	3.6	3.9	4.1	3.2	2.6	1.8
% F [III] [4]	2.2	2.2	1.7	3.6	5.4	6.1	6.2	5.8	5.6	5.5
India Inde										
MF [III] [28]	32 776.2	34 631.8	36 300.0	36 758.4	36 275.5	36 691.5	36 742.3	37 430.0	39 140.0	40 090.0
M [III] [28]	26 667.6	27 932.0	28 992.0	29 105.0	28 410.0	28 647.0	28 722.0	29 050.0	30 107.0	30 563.0
F [III] [28]	6 108.6	6 700.0	7 308.0	7 653.0	7 865.0	8 045.0	8 020.0	8 380.0	9 033.0	9 526.0

26
Unemployment
Number (thousands) and percentage of unemployed [*cont.*]
Chômage
Nombre (milliers) et pourcentage des chômeurs [*suite*]

Country or area [§] Pays ou zone [§]	1989	1990	1991	1992	1993	1994	1995	1996	1997	1998
Indonesia Indonésie										
MF [I] [8]	2 083.2[3]	1 951.6[3]	2 032.4[3]	2 198.8[3]	...	...	...	3 624.8[3]	4 197.3[1]	5 062.5[1]
M [I] [3 8]	1 251.1	1 155.2	1 147.3	1 292.1	...	...	...	1 851.8	...	...
F [I] [3 8]	832.1	796.4	885.1	906.7	...	...	...	1 773.0	...	...
MF [III] [1]	1 214.1	862.0	782.9	814.9	754.1	1 198.3	953.2	1 041.8	1 542.2	1 191.7
% MF [I] [8]	...	...	...	...	...	...	...	4.0	4.7[1]	5.5[1]
Ireland Irlande										
MF [I] [1 12]	196.8	172.4	198.5	206.6	220.1	211.0	177.4	179.0	159.0	126.6
M [I] [1 12]	128.4	108.4	124.9	132.3	138.6	131.9	110.4	109.8	97.1	78.8
F [I] [1 12]	68.4	63.9	73.6	74.4	81.4	79.1	67.1	69.1	62.0	47.8
MF [III] [4]	231.6	224.7	254.0	283.1	294.3	282.4	276.9	279.2	254.4	227.1
M [III] [4]	160.0	152.1	170.5	187.2	193.8	184.4	178.5	175.6	155.8	135.7
F [III] [4]	71.6	72.6	83.5	96.0	100.5	98.0	99.3	103.6	98.5	91.4
% MF [I] [1 12]	15.0	12.9	14.7	15.1	15.7	14.7	12.2	11.9	10.3	7.8
% M [I] [1 12]	14.9	12.5	14.2	15.0	15.6	14.7	12.1	11.9	10.4	8.1
% F [I] [1 12]	15.4	13.8	15.5	15.2	15.8	14.8	12.2	11.9	10.3	7.4
Isle of Man Ile de Man										
MF [III]	0.6	0.6	1.0	1.4	1.7	1.6	1.5	1.2	0.7	0.4
M [III]	0.4	0.4	0.7	1.0	1.2	1.2	1.1	0.9	0.5	0.3
F [III]	0.2	0.1	0.3	0.4	0.4	0.4	0.4	0.3	0.2	0.1
% MF [III]	2.0	2.1	3.0[49]	4.3[49]	4.9[49]	4.7[49]	4.4[49]	3.4[49]	...	...
% M [III]	2.3	2.6	3.9[49]	5.4[49]	...	...	...	4.4[49]	...	...
% F [III]	1.6	1.3	1.9[49]	2.7[49]	...	...	...	2.1[49]	...	...
Israel Israël										
MF [I] [1 51]	142.5[50]	158.0[50]	187.4[50]	207.5[50]	194.9[50]	158.3[50]	145.0	144.1	169.8	195.0
M [I] [1 51]	75.7[50]	82.2[50]	89.9[50]	99.7[50]	96.2[50]	71.7[50]	66.6	70.8	84.6	102.7
F [I] [1 51]	66.8[50]	75.8[50]	97.5[50]	107.8[50]	98.7[50]	86.6[50]	78.4	73.3	85.2	92.3
% MF [I] [1 51]	8.9[50]	9.6[50]	10.6[50]	11.2[50]	10.0[50]	7.8[50]	6.9	6.7	7.7	8.6
% M [I] [1 51]	7.9[50]	8.4[50]	8.6[50]	9.2[50]	8.5[50]	6.2[50]	5.6	5.8	6.8	8.1
% F [I] [1 51]	10.3[50]	11.3[50]	13.4[50]	13.9[50]	12.1[50]	10.0[50]	8.6	7.8	8.8	9.2
Italy Italie										
MF [I]	2 865.0[2]	2 621.0[2]	2 653.0[2]	2 799.0[2]	2 335.0[1 52]	2 541.0[1]	2 725.0[1]	2 763.0[1]	2 805.0[1]	...
M [I]	1 220.0[2]	1 102.0[2]	1 142.0[2]	1 226.0[2]	1 098.0[1 52]	1 251.0[1]	1 311.0[1]	1 335.0[1]	1 348.0[1]	...
F [I]	1 646.0[2]	1 519.0[2]	1 511.0[2]	1 572.0[2]	1 237.0[1 52]	1 290.0[1]	1 414.0[1]	1 428.0[1]	1 457.0[1]	...
% MF [I]	12.0[2]	11.0[2]	10.9[2]	11.4[2]	10.2[1 52]	11.3[1]	12.0[1]	12.1[1]	12.3[1]	...
% M [I]	8.1[2]	7.3[2]	7.5[2]	7.9[2]	7.6[1 52]	8.7[1]	9.2[1]	9.4[1]	9.5[1]	...
% F [I]	18.7[2]	17.1[2]	16.8[2]	17.2[2]	14.8[1 52]	15.6[1]	16.7[1]	16.6[1]	16.8[1]	...
Jamaica Jamaïque										
MF [I] [2]	177.4	166.6	168.7	169.2	176.7	167.4	186.7	183.0	186.9	175.0
M [I] [2]	54.1	52.8	54.2	54.1	62.1	54.9	66.9	61.3	64.8	61.4
F [I] [2]	123.3	113.8	114.5	115.2	114.6	112.5	119.8	121.7	122.1	113.5
% MF [I] [2]	16.8	15.7	15.7	15.4	16.3	15.4	16.2	16.0	...	...
% M [I] [2]	9.5	9.3	9.4	9.4	10.9	9.6	10.8	9.9	...	...
% F [I] [2]	25.2	23.1	22.8	22.2	22.4	21.8	22.5	23.0	...	...
Japan Japon										
MF [I] [1]	1 420.0	1 340.0	1 360.0	1 420.0	1 660.0	1 920.0	2 100.0	2 250.0	2 300.0	2 769.0
M [I] [1]	830.0	770.0	780.0	820.0	950.0	1 120.0	1 230.0	1 340.0	1 350.0	1 680.0
F [I] [1]	590.0	570.0	590.0	600.0	710.0	800.0	870.0	910.0	950.0	1 110.0
% MF [I] [1]	2.3	2.1	2.1	2.2	2.5	2.9	3.2	3.4	3.4	4.1
% M [I] [1]	2.2	2.0	2.0	2.1	2.4	2.8	3.1	3.4	3.4	4.2
% F [I] [1]	2.3	2.2	2.2	2.2	2.6	3.0	3.2	3.3	3.4	4.0
Kazakhstan Kazakhstan										
MF [III] [7]	...	...	6.0	34.0	40.5	70.1	139.6	282.4	257.5	251.9
M [III] [7]	...	...	2.0	9.0	12.1	24.7	55.7	104.0	86.0	95.5
F [III] [7]	...	...	4.0	25.0	28.4	45.4	83.9	178.4	171.5	156.4
MF [IV]	...	...	6.0	70.5	78.1	170.0	203.2	391.7	382.8	382.0
M [IV]	...	...	1.0	21.0	...	103.8	88.5	156.6	139.5	161.9
F [IV]	...	...	5.0	19.0	...	66.2	114.7	235.1	243.3	220.1
% MF [III] [7]	...	...	0.1	0.4	0.6	1.1	2.1	4.2	3.8	3.7
% M [III] [7]	...	...	...	...	...	0.7	1.6	2.9	2.4	2.6
% F [III] [7]	...	...	...	...	...	1.4	2.7	5.6	5.5	5.0
% MF [IV]	...	...	...	...	...	7.5	11.0	13.0	13.0	13.7

26
Unemployment
Number (thousands) and percentage of unemployed [*cont.*]
Chômage
Nombre (milliers) et pourcentage des chômeurs [*suite*]

Country or area § Pays ou zone §	1989	1990	1991	1992	1993	1994	1995	1996	1997	1998
Korea, Republic of Corée, République de										
MF [I] [1]	463.0	454.0	436.0	465.0	550.0	489.0	419.0	425.0	556.0	1 463.0
M [I] [1]	329.0	321.0	288.0	305.0	375.0	334.0	280.0	290.0	352.0	986.0
F [I] [1]	134.0	133.0	149.0	160.0	175.0	155.0	139.0	134.0	204.0	477.0
% MF [I] [1]	2.6	2.4	2.3	2.4	2.8	2.4	2.0	2.0	2.6	6.8
% M [I] [1]	3.1	2.9	2.5	2.6	3.2	2.7	2.3	2.3	2.8	7.7
% F [I] [1]	1.8	1.8	1.9	2.1	2.2	1.9	1.7	1.6	2.3	5.6
Kuwait Koweït										
MF [III] [7]	...	...	...	...	...	...	...	...	8.6	8.9
M [III] [7]	...	...	...	...	...	...	...	...	7.2	7.3
F [III] [7]	...	...	...	...	...	...	...	...	1.4	1.6
Kyrgyzstan Kirghizistan										
MF [III]	...	...	...	1.8	2.9	12.6	50.4	77.2	54.6	55.9
M [III]	...	...	...	0.5	0.9	4.9	20.5	32.5	22.7	22.6
F [III]	...	...	...	1.3	2.0	7.7	29.9	44.7	31.9	33.3
Latvia Lettonie										
MF [I] [8]	...	...	...	...	...	...	227.0[14]	216.7[1]	171.2[1]	160.6[1]
M [I] [8]	...	...	...	...	...	...	126.5[14]	117.9[1]	88.0[1]	82.9[1]
F [I] [8]	...	...	...	...	...	...	100.5[14]	98.8[1]	83.2[1]	77.7[1]
MF [III] [7]	...	...	...	31.3	76.7	83.9	83.2	90.8	84.9	111.4
M [III] [7]	...	...	...	12.9	35.9	40.4	39.7	41.1	34.5	46.2
F [III] [7]	...	...	...	18.4	40.8	43.6	43.5	49.7	50.4	65.2
% MF [I] [8]	...	...	...	...	...	...	18.9[14]	18.3[1]	14.4[1]	13.8[1]
% M [I] [8]	...	...	...	...	...	...	19.7[14]	18.9[1]	14.3[1]	13.5[1]
% F [I] [8]	...	...	...	...	...	...	18.0[14]	17.7[1]	14.6[1]	14.1[1]
% MF [III] [7]	...	...	...	2.3	5.8	6.5	6.6	7.2	7.0	9.2
% M [III] [7]	...	...	...	1.8	5.2	6.1	6.1	6.4	5.6	7.5
% F [III] [7]	...	...	...	2.8	6.4	6.9	7.0	8.1	8.5	11.0
Lebanon Liban										
MF [IV]	...	...	...	...	...	...	...	...	116.1	...
Lithuania Lituanie										
MF [I] [2]	...	...	...	...	...	347.2	347.1	317.4	255.9	247.3
M [I] [2]	...	...	...	...	...	...	...	155.4	135.3	138.5
F [I] [2]	...	...	...	...	...	...	...	162.0	120.6	108.8
MF [III] [7]	...	...	4.8	66.5	65.5	78.0	127.7	109.4	120.2	122.8
M [III] [7]	...	...	...	38.1	33.5	36.7	57.4	49.8	58.3	61.7
F [III] [7]	...	...	...	28.4	32.0	41.3	70.3	59.6	61.9	61.1
% MF [I] [2]	...	...	...	...	...	17.4	17.1	16.4	14.1	13.5
% M [I] [2]	...	...	...	...	...	...	...	...	14.1	14.5
% F [I] [2]	...	...	...	...	...	...	...	...	14.0	12.4
% MF [III] [7]	...	...	0.3	3.5	3.5	4.5	7.3	6.2	6.7	6.5
% M [III] [7]	...	...	...	4.3	3.7	4.4	6.6	5.7	6.6	6.5
% F [III] [7]	...	...	...	2.8	3.3	4.5	8.1	6.7	6.9	7.0
Luxembourg Luxembourg										
MF [III] [53]	2.3	2.1	2.3	2.7	3.5	4.6	5.1	5.6	5.9[54]	5.5
M [III] [53]	1.4	1.2	1.4	1.6	2.0	2.7	2.9	3.2	3.3[54]	2.9
F [III] [53]	0.9	0.8	0.9	1.2	1.5	1.9	2.2	2.5	2.6[54]	2.6
% MF [III] [53]	1.4	1.3	1.4	1.6	2.1	2.7	3.0	3.3	3.3[54]	3.1
Madagascar Madagascar										
MF [III] [8 55]	15.7	16.8	9.3	6.2	5.3	3.6	3.3	...	...	...
Malaysia Malaisie										
MF [I] [43]	388.5	315.2	...	271.2	316.8	...	248.1	216.8	214.9	284.0
MF [III] [1]	75.6	61.2	48.6	45.2	35.6	26.8	24.0	23.3	23.1	...
% MF [I] [43]	6.3	5.1	...	3.7	3.0	...	2.8	2.5	2.5	...
Malta Malte										
MF [III] [8 56]	4.8	5.1	4.9	5.5	6.2	5.6	5.2	6.2	7.1	7.4
M [III] [8 56]	4.1	4.3	4.0	4.5	5.3	4.8	4.4	5.2	6.0	...
F [III] [8 56]	0.8	0.8	0.9	1.1	0.9	0.8	0.8	1.1	1.1	...
% MF [III] [8 56]	3.7	3.9	3.6	4.0	4.5	4.0	3.6	4.3	5.0	...
% M [III] [8 56]	4.1	4.4	4.0	4.4	5.2	4.7	4.2	4.9	5.8	...
% F [III] [8 56]	2.3	2.3	2.6	3.0	2.5	2.0	2.1	2.6	2.8	...
Mauritius Maurice										
MF [III] [1 57]	18.1	12.8	10.6	7.9	6.7	6.6	8.5	10.4	10.7	10.7
M [III] [1 57]	11.8	7.3	5.2	3.4	2.6	2.5	3.4	4.5	4.6	4.6
F [III] [1 57]	6.3	5.5	5.4	4.6	4.1	4.2	5.0	5.9	6.0	6.1

26
Unemployment
Number (thousands) and percentage of unemployed [cont.]
Chômage
Nombre (milliers) et pourcentage des chômeurs [suite]

Country or area § / Pays ou zone §	1989	1990	1991	1992	1993	1994	1995	1996	1997	1998
Mexico Mexique										
MF [I] [17]	...	...	694.9	...	819.1	...	1 677.4[11]	1 354.7[11]	984.9[11]	889.6
M [I] [17]	...	...	373.1	...	495.4	...	1 100.2[11]	860.7[11]	544.7[11]	513.0
F [I] [17]	...	...	321.8	...	323.7	...	577.2[11]	494.0[11]	440.2[11]	376.6
% MF [I] [17]	...	...	2.2	...	2.4	...	4.7[11]	3.7[11]	2.6[11]	2.3
% M [I] [17]	...	...	1.7	...	2.1	...	4.6[11]	3.5[11]	2.1[11]	2.0
% F [I] [17]	...	...	3.4	...	3.1	...	5.0[11]	4.1[11]	3.4[11]	2.8
Mongolia Mongolie										
MF [III] [7]	...	...	...	...	...	...	...	...	...	48.3
M [III] [7]	...	...	...	...	...	...	...	...	...	22.7
F [III] [7]	...	...	...	...	...	...	...	...	...	25.6
% MF [III] [7]	...	...	...	...	...	...	...	...	...	5.7
% M [III] [7]	...	...	...	...	...	...	...	...	...	5.2
% F [III] [7]	...	...	...	...	...	...	...	...	...	6.3
Morocco Maroc										
MF [I] [1 15]	...	601.2	695.5	649.9	680.8	...	1 111.7	871.2	...	...
M [I] [1 15]	...	401.4	459.3	400.7	469.1	...	631.5	568.1	...	...
F [I] [1 15]	...	199.8	236.2	249.2	211.7	...	480.2	303.1	...	...
% MF [I] [1 15]	16.3	15.4	17.3	16.0	15.7	...	22.3	17.8	...	...
% M [I] [1 15]	15.0	13.9	15.1	13.0	14.0	...	18.4	15.8	...	...
% F [I] [1 15]	19.8	19.6	22.6	25.3	21.2	...	31.0	23.0	...	...
Myanmar Myanmar										
MF [III] [58]	485.8	555.3	559.0	502.6	518.2	541.5	...	...	535.3	...
Netherlands Pays-Bas										
MF [I] [43]	558.0	516.0	490.0	386.0	437.0[59]	492.0[59]	523.0[59]	489.0[59]	422.0[59]	337.0[59]
M [I] [43]	261.0	227.0	226.0	181.0	217.0[59]	254.0[59]	255.0[59]	228.0[59]	196.0[59]	155.0[59]
F [I] [43]	297.0	288.0	264.0	205.0	220.0[59]	239.0[59]	268.0[59]	262.0[59]	227.0[59]	181.0[59]
MF [III] [43 60]	390.0	346.0	319.0	336.0	415.0	486.0	464.0	440.0	375.0	286.0
M [III] [43 60]	241.0	209.0	187.0	195.0	241.0	283.0	260.0	240.0	199.0	156.0
F [III] [43 60]	149.0	137.0	132.0	141.0	174.0	203.0	204.0	201.0	176.0	132.0
% MF [I] [43]	8.0	7.5	7.0	5.5	6.2[59]	6.8[59]	7.1[59]	6.6[59]	5.5[59]	4.4[59]
% M [I] [43]	6.0	5.4	5.3	4.3	5.2[59]	6.0[59]	5.9[59]	5.3[59]	4.5[59]	3.5[59]
% F [I] [43]	12.0	10.7	9.5	7.3	7.6[59]	8.1[59]	8.8[59]	8.4[59]	7.0[59]	5.5[59]
% MF [III] [43]	6.9	5.9	5.4	5.3	6.5	7.5	7.0	6.6	5.5	4.1
% M [III] [43]	6.4	5.4	4.9	4.9	6.0	7.0	6.4	5.9	4.8	...
% F [III] [43]	7.8	6.8	6.3	6.1	7.3	8.3	8.1	7.8	6.5	...
Netherlands Antilles Antilles néerlandaises										
MF [I] [1 61]	11.4	9.8	8.6	8.2	8.2	8.0	8.2	9.3	10.1	10.8
M [I] [1 61]	...	...	3.8	3.5	3.8	3.7	3.3	3.7	4.3	4.8
F [I] [1 61]	...	...	4.7	4.8	4.4	4.3	4.9	5.6	5.8	6.0
% MF [I] [1 61]	20.1	17.0	14.6	13.9	13.6	12.8	13.1	14.0	15.3	16.7
% M [I] [1 61]	...	...	11.7	10.5	11.4	11.0	9.9	10.5	12.4	14.1
% F [I] [1 61]	...	...	18.1	17.9	16.2	15.0	17.0	10.1	10.4	19.4
New Caledonia Nouvelle-Calédonie										
MF [III] [4]	5.2	5.7	6.3	6.6	6.8	7.4	7.4	7.7	7.9	8.3
New Zealand Nouvelle-Zélande										
MF [I] [1]	112.6	124.5	167.6	169.8	158.8	140.4	111.5	112.3	123.3	139.1
M [I] [1]	66.0	74.0	99.8	101.1	94.0	81.7	61.8	61.9	67.9	77.4
F [I] [1]	46.5	50.5	67.7	68.7	64.8	58.6	49.7	50.4	55.5	61.8
MF [III] [62]	153.6[44]	163.8[44]	196.0[44]	216.9[44]	212.7[44]	186.5[44]	157.7[44]	154.0[44]	168.9[44]	189.3[8]
M [III] [62]	106.6[44]	112.1[44]	135.9[44]	149.8[44]	143.2[44]	124.1[44]	103.1[44]	100.0[44]	107.3[44]	117.8[8]
F [III] [62]	47.0[44]	51.7[44]	60.1[44]	67.1[44]	69.4[44]	62.4[44]	54.6[44]	54.0[44]	61.6[44]	72.5[8]
% MF [I] [1]	7.1	7.8	10.3	10.3	9.5	8.1	6.3	6.1	6.6	7.5
% M [I] [1]	7.3	8.2	10.9	10.9	10.0	8.5	6.2	6.1	6.6	7.6
% F [I] [1]	6.9	7.2	9.5	9.6	8.9	7.7	6.3	6.1	6.7	7.4
Nicaragua Nicaragua										
MF [IV] [3]	107.2	145.6	194.2	...	...	...	244.7	225.1	208.4	215.5
M [IV] [3]	57.8	78.5	104.8	...	...	...	162.3	149.2	138.2	142.9
F [IV] [3]	49.4	67.1	89.4	...	...	...	82.4	75.9	70.2	72.6
% MF [IV] [3]	8.4	11.1	14.0	...	...	...	16.9	14.9	13.3	13.3
% M [IV] [3]	6.9	9.0	11.3	...	...	...	15.9	14.0	12.6	8.8
% F [IV] [3]	12.0	15.4	19.4	...	...	...	19.3	17.1	14.8	14.5
Niger Niger										
MF [III]	24.6	20.9	20.9	...	...	...	...	...	...	...
M [III]	23.4	19.9	19.9	...	...	...	...	...	...	...
F [III]	1.3	1.1	1.0	...	...	...	...	...	...	...

26
Unemployment
Number (thousands) and percentage of unemployed [*cont.*]
Chômage
Nombre (milliers) et pourcentage des chômeurs [*suite*]

Country or area [§] Pays ou zone [§]	1989	1990	1991	1992	1993	1994	1995	1996	1997	1998
Nigeria Nigéria										
MF [III] [1]	57.6	57.1	60.2	64.0	68.6	...	...	...	...	...
Norway Norvège										
MF [I] [48]	106.0	112.0	116.0	126.0	127.0	116.0	107.0	108.0	93.0	75.0
M [I] [48]	61.0	66.0	68.0	76.0	77.0	70.0	61.0	58.0	49.0	40.0
F [I] [48]	45.0	46.0	48.0	50.0	50.0	46.0	46.0	50.0	44.0	35.0
MF [III] [4]	82.9	92.7[63]	100.7	114.4	118.1	110.3	102.2	90.9	73.5	56.0
M [III] [4]	51.6	57.1[63]	62.8	71.0	73.3	65.7	57.7	50.4	39.9	29.8
F [III] [4]	31.3	35.6[63]	37.9	43.3	44.8	44.5	44.5	40.6	33.6	26.2
% MF [I] [48]	4.9	5.2	5.5	5.9	6.0	5.4	4.9	4.9	4.1	...
% M [I] [48]	5.1	5.6	5.9	6.5	6.6	6.0	5.2	4.8	4.0	...
% F [I] [48]	4.7	4.8	5.0	5.1	5.2	4.7	4.6	4.9	4.2	...
% MF [III] [4]	3.8	4.3[63]	4.7	5.4	5.5	5.2	4.7	4.2	3.3	2.4
% M [III] [4]	4.3	4.8[63]	5.3	6.1	6.3	5.6	4.9	4.1	...	...
% F [III] [4]	3.2	3.7[63]	3.9	4.5	4.7	4.5	4.5	3.9	...	...
Pakistan Pakistan										
MF [I] [3 65]	939.0[64]	963.0[64]	1 922.0	1 845.0	1 516.0	1 591.0	1 783.0	1 827.0	2 227.0	...
M [I] [3 65]	909.0[64]	932.0[64]	1 190.0	1 134.0	1 024.0	1 083.0	1 179.0	1 208.0	1 302.0	...
F [I] [3 65]	30.0[64]	31.0[64]	732.0	711.0	492.0	508.0	604.0	619.0	925.0	...
MF [III] [66]	251.8	238.8	221.7	204.3	...	...	...	...	...	...
% MF [I] [3 65]	3.1[64]	3.1[64]	6.3	5.9	4.7	4.8	5.4	5.4	6.1	...
% M [I] [3 65]	3.4[64]	3.4[64]	4.5	4.3	3.8	3.9	4.1	4.1	4.2	...
% F [I] [3 65]	0.9[64]	0.9[64]	16.8	14.2	10.3	10.0	13.7	13.7	16.8	...
Panama Panama										
MF [I] [18]	133.7	...	138.4	134.4	124.7	135.5	141.2	144.9	140.3	145.9
M [I] [18]	75.0	...	72.8	65.6	60.2	67.7	70.7	74.8	72.5	72.5
F [I] [18]	58.7	...	65.6	68.7	64.5	67.7	70.5	70.1	67.8	73.4
% MF [I] [18]	16.3	...	16.2	14.7	13.3	14.0	14.0	14.3	13.4	13.9
% M [I] [18]	13.7	...	12.6	10.8	9.7	10.7	10.8	11.3	10.7	10.7
% F [I] [18]	21.6	...	22.6	22.3	20.2	20.4	20.1	20.0	18.1	19.7
Paraguay Paraguay										
MF [I]	32.0[17 67]	34.1[17 67]	26.6[17 67]	29.1[17 67]	30.5[3 67]	48.1[3 15]	...	105.7	...	...
M [I]	19.3[17 67]	20.3[17 67]	16.6[17 67]	20.1[17 67]	19.1[3 67]	31.7[3 15]	...	58.1	...	...
F [I]	12.7[17 67]	13.8[17 67]	10.0[17 67]	8.9[17 67]	11.4[3 67]	16.5[3 15]	...	47.5	...	...
% MF [I]	6.1[17 67]	6.6[17 67]	5.1[17 67]	5.3[17 67]	5.1[3 67]	4.4[3 15]	...	8.2	...	...
% M [I]	6.6[17 67]	6.6[17 67]	5.4[17 67]	6.4[17 67]	5.5[3 67]	4.9[3 15]	...	7.8	...	...
% F [I]	5.6[17 67]	6.5[17 67]	4.7[17 67]	3.8[17 67]	4.5[3 67]	3.7[3 15]	...	8.6	...	...
Peru Pérou										
MF [I] [2 11 15]	...	...	...	...	...	...	...	461.6	565.0	573.4
M [I] [2 11 15]	...	...	...	...	...	...	...	247.4	279.9	272.0
F [I] [2 11 15]	...	...	...	...	...	...	...	214.2	285.1	301.4
% MF [I] [2 11 15]	...	...	...	...	...	...	...	7.0	7.7	7.7
% M [I] [2 11 15]	...	...	...	...	...	...	...	6.4	6.8	6.5
% F [I] [2 11 15]	...	...	...	...	...	...	...	7.9	8.9	9.3
Philippines Philippines										
MF [I] [18]	2 009.0	1 993.0	2 267.0	2 263.0	2 379.0	2 317.0	2 342.0	2 195.0	2 377.0	3 016.0
M [I] [18]	1 101.0	1 099.0	1 290.0	1 303.0	1 384.0	1 362.0	1 354.0	1 293.0	1 411.0	1 857.0
F [I] [18]	908.0	893.0	977.0	959.0	995.0	955.0	988.0	902.0	966.0	1 159.0
% MF [I] [18]	8.4	8.1	9.0	8.6	8.9	8.4	8.4	7.4	7.9	9.6
% M [I] [18]	7.3	7.1	8.1	7.9	8.2	7.9	7.7	7.0	7.5	9.5
% F [I] [18]	10.3	9.8	10.5	9.8	10.0	9.4	9.4	8.2	8.5	9.8
Poland Pologne										
MF [I] [1]	...	...	...	...	2 427.0	2 474.0	2 277.0	2 108.0	1 923.0	1 808.0
M [I] [1]	...	...	...	...	1 183.0	1 207.0	1 119.0	1 015.0	889.0	843.0
F [I] [1]	...	...	...	...	1 244.0	1 266.0	1 157.0	1 093.0	1 035.0	965.0
MF [III] [1 7]	...	1 126.1	2 155.6	2 509.3	2 889.6	2 838.0	2 628.8	2 359.5	1 826.4	1 831.4
M [III] [1 7]	...	552.4	1 021.5	1 170.5	1 382.3	1 343.0	1 180.2	983.9	723.2	760.1
F [III] [1 7]	...	573.7	1 134.1	1 338.8	1 507.3	1 495.0	1 448.6	1 375.6	1 103.2	1 071.3
% MF [I] [1]	...	...	...	...	14.0	14.4	13.3	12.3	11.2	10.5
% M [I] [1]	...	...	...	...	12.6	13.1	12.1	11.0	9.6	9.1
% F [I] [1]	...	...	...	...	15.6	16.0	14.7	13.9	13.2	12.3
% MF [III] [1 7]	...	6.5	11.8	13.6	16.4	16.0	15.2	13.2	10.5	10.4
% M [III] [1 7]	...	5.8	10.6	11.9	15.0	14.7	...	...	...	...
% F [III] [1 7]	...	7.1	13.5	15.5	17.9	17.3	...	...	...	...

26
Unemployment
Number (thousands) and percentage of unemployed [*cont.*]
Chômage
Nombre (milliers) et pourcentage des chômeurs [*suite*]

Country or area [§] Pays ou zone [§]	1989	1990	1991	1992	1993	1994	1995	1996	1997	1998
Portugal Portugal										
MF [I]	243.3[68]	231.1[68]	207.5[68]	194.1[2]	257.5[2]	323.8[2]	338.4[2]	343.9[2]	324.1[2]	247.9[1]
M [I]	95.1[68]	90.0[68]	77.6[68]	90.7[2]	120.0[2]	155.8[2]	165.8[2]	167.0[2]	158.5[2]	107.6[1]
F [I]	148.3[68]	141.1[68]	129.9[68]	103.4[2]	137.5[2]	168.1[2]	172.1[2]	177.0[2]	165.6[2]	140.4[1]
% MF [I]	5.0[68]	4.7[68]	4.1[68]	4.1[2]	5.4[2]	6.7[2]	7.1[2]	7.2[2]	6.7[2]	5.0[1]
% M [I]	3.4[68]	3.2[68]	2.8[68]	3.4[2]	4.5[2]	5.9[2]	6.3[2]	6.4[2]	6.0[2]	3.9[1]
% F [I]	7.2[68]	6.6[68]	5.8[68]	4.9[2]	6.5[2]	7.8[2]	8.1[2]	8.2[2]	7.5[2]	6.2[1]
Puerto Rico Porto Rico										
MF [I] [4 39]	163.0	160.0	186.0	197.0	206.0	175.0	170.0	172.0	176.0	175.0
M [I] [4 39]	118.0	115.0	131.0	139.0	144.0	121.0	117.0	114.0	112.0	112.0
F [I] [4 39]	45.0	45.0	55.0	58.0	62.0	54.0	53.0	58.0	64.0	63.0
% MF [I] [4 39]	14.6	14.1	16.0	16.6	17.0	14.6	13.7	13.4	13.5	13.3
% M [I] [4 39]	16.9	16.2	17.9	19.0	19.5	16.5	15.6	14.9	14.4	14.4
% F [I] [4 39]	10.8	10.7	12.6	12.8	13.2	11.5	10.8	11.2	12.1	11.8
Republic of Moldova Réublique de Moldova										
MF [III] [8]	...	...	0.1	15.0	14.1	20.6	24.5	23.4	28.0	32.0
M [III] [8]	...	...	...	5.9	5.5	7.7	8.4	7.5	10.3	13.0
F [III] [8]	...	...	0.1	9.1	8.9	12.9	16.1	15.9	17.7	19.0
% MF [III] [8]	...	...	...	0.7	0.7	1.1	1.0	...	...	...
Réunion Réunion										
MF [III] [4]	59.5	53.8	59.3	80.1	80.2	...	...	...	...	...
M [III] [4 8]	30.2	28.4	30.4	41.9	43.1	...	...	...	...	...
F [III] [4 8]	27.3	25.4	28.8	38.2	37.1	...	...	...	...	...
% MF [III] [4]	...	23.0	25.4	34.3	34.4	...	...	...	...	...
Romania Roumanie										
MF [I] [1]	...	...	...	...	...	971.0[2 8]	967.9[2 8]	790.9	706.5	732.4
M [I] [1]	...	...	...	...	...	488.2[2 8]	487.6[2 8]	399.1	364.2	410.3
F [I] [1]	...	...	...	...	...	482.8[2 8]	480.3[2 8]	391.7	342.2	322.1
MF [III] [8]	...	...	337.4	929.0	1 164.7	1 223.9	998.4	657.6	881.4	1 025.1
M [III] [8]	...	...	129.0	366.0	479.2	530.6	446.9	302.2	452.8	539.9
F [III] [8]	...	...	208.4	563.0	685.5	693.3	551.5	355.4	428.6	485.2
% MF [I] [1]	...	...	...	...	...	8.2[2 8]	8.0[2 8]	6.7	6.0	6.3
% M [I] [1]	...	...	...	...	...	7.7[2 8]	7.5[2 8]	6.3	5.7	6.5
% F [I] [1]	...	...	...	...	...	8.7[2 8]	8.6[2 8]	7.3	6.4	6.1
% MF [III] [8]	...	...	3.0	8.2	10.4	10.9	9.5	6.6	8.8	10.3
% M [III] [8]	...	...	2.2	6.2	8.1	9.0	7.9	5.7	8.5	10.2
% F [III] [8]	...	...	4.0	10.3	12.9	12.9	11.4	7.5	9.1	10.5
Russian Federation Fédération de Russie										
MF [I] [8 69]	...	...	...	3 877.0	4 305.0	5 702.0	6 712.0	6 732.0	8 058.0	8 876.0
M [I] [8 69]	...	...	...	2 026.0	2 280.0	3 074.0	3 616.0	3 662.0	4 371.0	4 787.0
F [I] [8 69]	...	...	...	1 851.0	2 025.0	2 628.0	3 096.0	3 070.0	3 687.0	4 090.0
MF [III] [8]	...	...	61.9	577.7	836.0	1 637.0	2 327.0	2 506.0	1 990.0	1 929.0
M [III] [8]	...	...	18.8	160.7	...	...	...	...	...	682.0
F [III] [8]	...	...	43.1	417.0	...	...	...	...	...	1 247.0
% MF [I] [8 69]	...	...	...	5.2	5.9	8.1	9.5	9.7	11.8	13.3
% M [I] [8 69]	...	...	...	5.2	5.9	8.3	9.7	10.0	12.2	13.6
% F [I] [8 69]	...	...	...	5.2	5.8	7.9	9.2	9.3	11.5	13.0
% MF [III] [8]	...	...	0.1	0.8	5.7	7.5	8.9	9.9	11.3	13.3
Saint Helena Sainte–Hélène										
MF [III]	0.2	0.2	0.2	0.2	0.2	0.3	0.3	0.4	0.4	...
M [III]	0.0	0.1	0.1	0.1	0.1	0.2	0.2	0.2	0.3	...
F [III]	0.1	0.1	0.1	0.1	0.1	0.1	0.1	0.1	0.1	...
Saint Pierre and Miquelon Sainte–Pierre–et–Miquelon										
MF [III] [20]	0.3	...	...	...	0.4	...	...	...	...	...
San Marino Saint–Marin										
MF [IV] [7]	0.6[2]	0.6[2]	0.5[2]	0.5[2]	0.6[2]	0.6[2]	0.5[2]	0.6[1]	0.5[1]	0.6[1]
M [IV] [7]	0.1[2]	0.2[2]	0.1[2]	0.1[2]	0.2[2]	0.1[2]	0.1[2]	0.1[1]	0.1[1]	0.1[1]
F [IV] [7]	0.5[2]	0.5[2]	0.3[2]	0.4[2]	0.4[2]	0.4[2]	0.4[2]	0.5[1]	0.4[1]	0.4[1]
% MF [IV] [7]	5.3[2]	5.5[2]	4.3[2]	4.2[2]	5.1[2]	3.9[2]	3.9[2]	5.1[1]	4.4[1]	4.1[1]
% M [IV] [7]	2.1[2]	2.4[2]	2.3[2]	2.0[2]	2.6[2]	1.6[2]	1.5[2]	2.0[1]	1.9[1]	1.8[1]
% F [IV] [7]	9.5[2]	9.7[2]	6.9[2]	7.1[2]	8.1[2]	7.4[2]	7.0[2]	8.8[1]	7.3[1]	6.9[1]
Senegal Sénégal										
MF [III] [33 70]	8.3	10.4	14.4	12.0	10.2	...	...	...	...	...
M [III] [33 70]	7.1	8.3	13.1	10.0	9.0	...	...	...	...	...
F [III] [33 70]	1.2	2.1	1.3	2.0	1.2	...	...	...	...	...

26
Unemployment
Number (thousands) and percentage of unemployed [cont.]
Chômage
Nombre (milliers) et pourcentage des chômeurs [suite]

Country or area [§] Pays ou zone [§]	1989	1990	1991	1992	1993	1994	1995	1996	1997	1998
Singapore Singapour										
MF [I] [18]	30.7	25.8[71]	30.0	43.4	43.7	43.8	47.2	53.8	45.5	62.1
M [I] [18]	20.2	17.6[71]	18.7	26.4	25.2	24.9	28.4	31.0	26.8	35.5
F [I] [18]	10.4	8.2[71]	11.3	17.0	18.5	18.9	18.8	22.8	18.7	26.6
MF [III] [2]	2.7	1.7	1.2	1.0	1.0	1.0	1.1	1.5	2.6	4.4
M [III] [2]	1.9	1.2	0.8	0.7	0.7	0.7	0.7	0.8	1.2	2.3
F [III] [2]	0.8	0.5	0.4	0.3	0.3	0.4	0.4	0.7	1.4	2.1
% MF [I] [18]	2.2	1.7[71]	1.9	2.7	2.7	2.6	2.7	3.0	2.4	3.2
% M [I] [18]	2.3	1.9[71]	2.0	2.7	2.6	2.5	2.7	2.9	2.4	3.2
% F [I] [18]	1.9	1.3[71]	1.8	2.6	2.8	2.8	2.8	3.1	2.4	3.3
Slovakia Slovaquie										
MF [I] [1][72]	...	...	...	...	...	333.6	324.5	277.6	287.1	297.0
M [I] [1][72]	...	...	...	...	...	180.0	171.8	136.6	146.6	156.1
F [I] [1][72]	...	...	...	...	...	153.7	152.8	141.0	140.6	140.9
MF [III]	...	...	169.0	285.5	323.2	366.2	349.8	324.3	336.7	379.5
M [III]	...	...	83.4	141.1	167.2	189.5	174.8	155.1	162.9	193.0
F [III]	...	...	85.6	144.4	156.0	176.6	175.0	169.2	173.8	186.5
% MF [I] [1][72]	...	...	...	...	...	13.7	13.1	11.1	11.6	11.9
% M [I] [1][72]	...	...	...	...	...	13.3	12.6	10.0	10.8	11.4
% F [I] [1][72]	...	...	...	...	...	14.2	13.8	12.5	12.5	12.6
% MF [III]	...	...	6.6	11.4	12.9	14.4	13.8	12.6	12.9	14.6
% M [III]	...	...	6.4	11.1	12.7	13.9	12.8	11.3	11.7	13.9
% F [III]	...	...	6.9	11.7	13.0	15.0	14.8	14.1	14.3	15.3
Slovenia Slovénie										
MF [I] [1]	...	...	...	...	85.0[8]	85.0[8]	70.0[8]	69.0[8]	69.0[11]	75.0[1]
M [I] [1]	...	...	...	...	49.0[8]	48.0[8]	39.0[8]	38.0[8]	36.0[11]	40.0[1]
F [I] [1]	...	...	...	...	36.0[8]	37.0[8]	31.0[8]	31.0[8]	32.0[11]	35.0[1]
MF [III] [1]	28.2	44.6	75.1	102.6	129.1	127.1	...	...	125.2	126.1
M [III] [1]	14.4	23.2	41.5	57.5	72.5	70.0	...	...	64.1	63.2
F [III] [1]	13.8	21.4	33.6	45.1	56.6	57.0	...	...	61.1	62.9
% MF [I] [1]	...	...	...	...	9.1[8]	9.0[8]	7.4[8]	7.3[8]	7.1[11]	7.7[1]
% M [I] [1]	...	...	...	...	9.9[8]	9.5[8]	7.7[8]	7.5[8]	7.0[11]	7.6[1]
% F [I] [1]	...	...	...	...	8.3[8]	8.4[8]	7.0[8]	7.0[8]	7.3[11]	7.7[1]
% MF [III] [1]	2.9	4.7	8.2	11.5	14.4	14.4	...	...	...	...
% M [III] [1]	2.8	4.5	8.5	12.1	15.3	15.1	...	...	...	...
% F [III] [1]	3.1	4.8	7.9	10.8	13.5	13.7	...	...	...	...
Spain Espagne										
MF [I] [4]	2 560.8	2 441.2	2 463.7	2 788.5	3 481.3	3 738.1	3 583.5	3 540.0	3 356.5	3 060.3
M [I] [4]	1 263.0	1 166.1	1 191.9	1 384.5	1 836.7	1 911.9	1 753.9	1 724.0	1 581.6	1 364.3
F [I] [4]	1 297.8	1 275.1	1 271.8	1 404.1	1 644.6	1 826.2	1 829.7	1 816.1	1 774.9	1 696.1
MF [III] [53]	2 550.3	2 350.0	2 289.0	2 259.9	2 537.9	2 647.0	2 449.0	2 275.4	2 118.7	1 889.5
M [III] [53]	1 087.5	942.5	910.7	954.2	1 193.0	1 283.5	1 156.0	1 064.9	968.4	818.2
F [III] [53]	1 462.8	1 407.5	1 378.3	1 305.7	1 344.9	1 363.5	1 292.9	1 210.4	1 150.3	1 071.3
% MF [I] [4]	17.3	16.3	16.4	18.4	22.7	24.2	22.9	22.2	20.8	18.8
% M [I] [4]	13.0	12.0	12.3	14.3	19.0	18.8	18.2	17.6	16.1	13.8
% F [I] [4]	25.4	24.2	23.8	25.6	29.2	31.4	30.6	29.6	28.3	26.6
% MF [III] [53]	17.2	15.7	15.2	14.9	16.6	17.1	20.3	...	...	...
% M [III] [53]	11.2	9.7	9.4	9.9	12.3	13.3	12.0	...	...	...
% F [III] [53]	28.6	26.7	25.8	23.8	23.9	23.4	21.6	...	...	...
Sri Lanka Sri Lanka										
MF [I] [3][11][74]	...	1 005.1[73]	843.3	817.6	874.1	813.3	759.1	710.3	...	701.0
M [I] [3][11][74]	...	395.8[73]	380.0	408.7	349.3	390.5	352.9	328.2	...	296.2
F [I] [3][11][74]	...	609.2[73]	463.3	409.0	524.8	422.8	406.2	382.0	...	404.8
% MF [I] [3][11][74]	...	14.4[73]	14.1	14.1	14.7	13.6	12.5	11.3	...	10.6
% M [I] [3][11][74]	...	9.1[73]	10.0	10.6	9.1	9.9	8.8	8.0	...	7.1
% F [I] [3][11][74]	...	23.5[73]	21.2	21.0	25.2	20.8	19.7	17.6	...	16.2
Sudan Soudan										
MF [III]	25.4	70.1	19.9[75]	5.3[75]	...	...	...	...	...	...
M [III]	15.5	44.4	10.2[75]	3.7[75]	...	...	...	...	...	...
F [III]	9.9	25.7	9.7[75]	1.6[75]	...	...	...	...	...	...

26
Unemployment
Number (thousands) and percentage of unemployed [*cont.*]
Chômage
Nombre (milliers) et pourcentage des chômeurs [*suite*]

Country or area § Pays ou zone §	1989	1990	1991	1992	1993	1994	1995	1996	1997	1998
Suriname Suriname										
MF [I] [2]	15.4	15.4[11]	...	18.5	14.4	11.3	7.6	10.7	...	...
M [I] [2]	7.6	7.2[11]	...	9.1	7.3	6.6	4.1	4.9	...	...
F [I] [2]	7.9	8.2[11]	...	9.4	7.1	4.7	3.4	5.8	...	...
MF [III]	2.4	3.9	3.7	1.4	1.0	0.6	0.9	0.9	...	...
M [III]	1.2	1.2	1.1	0.5	0.4	0.1	0.3	0.3	...	...
F [III]	1.2	2.8	2.6	0.9	0.6	0.4	0.6	0.6	...	...
% MF [I] [2]	...	15.8[11]	...	17.2	14.7	12.7	8.4	11.0	...	...
% M [I] [2]	...	12.5[11]	...	13.7	12.0	11.4	7.0	7.9	...	...
% F [I] [2]	...	20.6[11]	...	23.1	19.2	15.0	10.9	16.4	...	...
Sweden Suède										
MF [I] [53]	66.0	75.0	134.0	233.0	356.0[52]	340.0	333.0	347.0	342.0	276.0
M [I] [53]	34.0	40.0	78.0	144.0	218.0[52]	202.0	190.0	192.0	188.0	154.0
F [I] [53]	33.0	36.0	56.0	89.0	137.0[52]	138.0	142.0	155.0	154.0	122.0
MF [III] [53]	56.3	66.4	114.6	309.8	447.4	438.4	436.2	407.6	367.0	285.6
M [III] [53]	29.2	35.6	66.4	186.1	262.6	250.7	238.2	220.2	199.5	156.3
F [III] [53]	27.1	30.9	48.1	123.7	184.8	187.7	198.0	187.3	167.4	129.3
% MF [I] [53]	1.5	1.6	3.0	5.2	8.2[52]	8.0	7.7	8.0	8.0	6.5
% M [I] [53]	1.4	1.7	3.3	6.3	9.7[52]	9.1	8.5	8.5	8.4	6.9
% F [I] [53]	1.5	1.6	2.6	4.2	6.6[52]	6.7	6.9	7.5	7.5	6.0
Switzerland Suisse										
MF [I] [111]	...	...	68.0	109.0	145.0	150.0	129.0	145.0	162.0	142.0
M [I] [111]	...	...	27.0	50.0	68.0	76.0	64.0	75.0	95.0	70.0
F [I] [111]	...	...	41.0	59.0	77.0	74.0	65.0	70.0	67.0	72.0
MF [III] [1]	17.5	18.1	39.2	92.3	163.1	171.0	153.3	168.6	188.3	139.7
M [III] [1]	9.1	9.8	22.7	54.7	96.6	98.0	85.5	96.8	108.7	77.1
F [III] [1]	8.4	8.3	16.5	37.6	66.6	73.1	67.8	71.8	79.6	62.6
% MF [I] [111]	...	...	1.8	2.8	3.7	3.9	3.3	3.7	4.1	3.6
% M [I] [111]	...	...	1.2	2.3	3.1	3.5	2.9	3.4	4.3	3.2
% F [I] [111]	...	...	2.5	3.5	4.6	4.4	3.9	4.1	3.9	4.1
% MF [III] [1]	0.6	0.5	1.1	2.5	4.5	4.7	4.2	4.7	5.2	3.9
% M [III] [1]	0.5	0.4	1.1	2.5	4.4	4.4	3.9	4.4	4.9	3.5
% F [III] [1]	0.8	0.6	1.2	2.7	4.7	5.2	4.8	5.1	5.7	4.4
Syrian Arab Republic Rép. arabe syrienne										
MF [I] [3 8]	177.3	...	235.4	...	...	...	...	...	...	...
M [I] [3 8]	130.8	...	147.3	...	...	...	...	...	...	...
F [I] [3 8]	46.5	...	88.2	...	...	...	...	...	...	...
% MF [I] [3 8]	5.8	...	6.8	...	...	...	...	...	...	...
% M [I] [3 8]	5.1	...	5.2	...	...	...	...	...	...	...
% F [I] [3 8]	9.5	...	14.0	...	...	...	...	...	...	...
Tajikistan Tadjikistan										
MF [III]	...	...	...	6.8	21.6	32.1	37.5	45.7	51.1	...
M [III]	...	...	...	4.2	12.4	17.1	20.2	22.8	24.1	...
F [III]	...	...	...	2.6	9.2	15.0	17.3	22.9	27.0	...
% MF [III]	...	...	...	0.4	1.2	1.7	2.0	2.6	2.7	...
% M [III]	...	...	...	0.4	1.2	1.6	1.9	2.4	2.4	...
% F [III]	...	...	...	0.4	1.1	1.8	2.1	2.8	2.9	...
Thailand Thaïlande										
MF [I] [12 76]	433.1	710.0	869.3	456.3	494.4	422.8	375.0	353.9	292.5	1 137.9
M [I] [12 76]	204.5	347.4	350.1	224.1	217.3	196.2	167.1	186.5	154.4	625.2
F [I] [12 76]	228.6	362.5	519.1	232.2	277.0	226.5	207.9	167.4	138.1	512.7
% MF [I] [12 76]	1.4	2.2	2.7	1.4	1.5	1.3	1.1	1.1	0.9	3.4
% M [I] [12 76]	1.2	2.1	2.0	1.3	1.2	1.1	0.9	1.0	0.8	3.4
% F [I] [12 76]	1.6	2.4	3.5	1.5	1.8	1.5	1.4	1.1	0.9	3.4
TFYR Macedonia L'ex–R.y. Macédoine										
MF [III]	150.4	156.3	164.8	172.1	174.8	185.9	216.2	238.0	253.0	...
M [III]	72.0	76.0	82.0	87.0	89.0	96.0	101.0	110.0	138.0	...
F [III]	78.0	80.0	83.0	85.0	86.0	90.0	115.0	128.0	115.0	...
% MF [III]	22.6[77]	23.6[77]	24.5	26.3	27.7	30.0	35.6	38.8	...	...
% M [III]	18.3[77]	19.4[77]	20.1	22.1	23.6	25.8	31.9	35.0	...	...
% F [III]	28.8[77]	29.7[77]	31.3	32.5	33.7	36.4	41.7	44.5	...	...

26
Unemployment
Number (thousands) and percentage of unemployed [*cont.*]
Chômage
Nombre (milliers) et pourcentage des chômeurs [*suite*]

Country or area [§] Pays ou zone [§]	1989	1990	1991	1992	1993	1994	1995	1996	1997	1998
Trinidad and Tobago Trinité−et−Tobago										
MF [I] [1 78 79]	103.4	93.6	91.2	99.2	99.9	93.9	89.4	86.1	81.2	79.4
M [I] [1 78 79]	64.8	55.1	49.6	54.3	56.3	51.5	49.5	43.1	41.3	39.0
F [I] [1 78 79]	38.6	38.5	41.5	44.9	43.7	42.4	39.9	43.0	39.9	40.4
% MF [I] [1 78 79]	22.0	20.0	18.5	19.6	19.8	18.4	17.2	16.2	15.0	14.2
% M [I] [1 78 79]	20.8	17.8	15.7	17.0	17.6	16.1	15.1	13.2	12.3	11.3
% F [I] [1 78 79]	24.5	24.2	23.4	23.9	23.4	22.3	20.6	21.0	19.4	18.9
Tunisia Tunisie										
MF [III] [58]	105.9	152.2	133.1	136.9	142.2	160.2	189.7	180.9	...	...
M [III] [58]	80.5	103.6	89.4	89.0	94.8	132.7	160.4	115.9	...	...
F [III] [58]	25.5	48.6	43.7	47.9	47.4	27.5	29.3	64.9	...	...
Turkey Turquie										
MF [I] [8 17]	1 821.0	1 615.0	1 787.0	1 745.0	1 722.0	1 740.0	1 522.0	1 332.0	1 545.0	1 547.0
M [I] [8 17]	1 198.0	1 103.0	1 300.0	1 237.0	1 225.0	1 218.0	1 052.0	956.0	994.0	1 041.0
F [I] [8 17]	623.0	512.0	486.0	508.0	497.0	522.0	470.0	376.0	550.0	416.0
MF [III] [2 8]	1 076.2[80]	979.5[80]	859.0[80]	840.1[80]	682.6[80]	469.3	401.3	416.8	463.0	...
M [III] [2 8]	887.6[80]	808.8[80]	706.8[80]	695.5[80]	571.7[80]	382.2	324.7	341.8	382.1	...
F [III] [2 8]	188.6[80]	170.7[80]	152.2[80]	144.6[80]	111.0[80]	87.1	76.6	75.0	81.2	...
% MF [I] [8 17]	8.8	7.5	8.4	8.0	8.0	7.9	6.6	5.8	6.9	6.2
% M [I] [8 17]	8.5	7.5	8.9	8.2	8.2	7.7	6.6	5.9	6.1	6.3
% F [I] [8 17]	9.4	7.5	7.3	7.6	7.5	8.2	6.8	5.5	9.2	6.1
Ukraine Ukraine										
MF [I] [8 81]	...	...	...	...	...	...	1 437.0	1 997.5	2 330.1	2 937.1
M [I] [8 81]	...	...	...	...	...	...	805.7	1 057.2	1 216.9	1 515.1
F [I] [8 81]	...	...	...	...	...	...	631.3	940.3	1 113.2	1 422.0
MF [III] [7]	...	...	...	...	83.9	82.2	126.9	351.1	637.1	1 003.2
M [III] [7]	...	...	...	...	21.2	22.5	34.7	115.3	220.6	620.4
F [III] [7]	...	...	...	...	62.7	59.7	92.2	235.8	416.5	382.8
% MF [I] [8 81]	...	...	...	...	...	...	5.6	7.6	8.9	11.3
% M [I] [8 81]	...	...	...	...	...	...	6.3	8.0	9.5	11.9
% F [I] [8 81]	...	...	...	...	...	...	4.9	7.3	8.4	10.8
United Kingdom Royaume−Uni										
MF [I] [4 12]	2 074.9	1 973.8	2 413.6	2 769.2	2 935.5	2 735.8	2 453.6	2 335.5	2 034.2	1 765.6
M [I] [4 12]	1 215.1	1 164.6	1 513.9	1 865.2	1 986.4	1 825.4	1 607.3	1 545.8	1 303.7	1 091.4
F [I] [4 12]	859.9	809.1	899.7	903.9	949.2	910.4	846.3	787.7	730.6	674.2
MF [II] [39 82 83 84 85]	1 798.7	1 664.5	2 291.9	2 778.6	2 919.2	2 636.5	2 325.7	2 122.2	1 602.4	1 362.4
M [II] [39 82 83 84 85]	1 290.8	1 232.3	1 737.1	2 126.0	2 236.0	2 014.4	1 770.0	1 610.3	...	...
F [II] [39 85]	507.9	432.2[83]	554.9[83]	652.6[83]	683.1[83]	622.6[83]	555.6[83]	511.9[83]	...	...
% MF [I] [4 12]	7.2	6.8	8.4	9.7	10.3	9.6	8.6	8.2	7.1	6.1
% M [I] [4 12]	7.4	7.1	9.2	11.5	12.4	11.4	10.1	9.7	8.1	6.8
% F [I] [4 12]	7.0	6.5	7.2	7.3	7.6	7.3	6.8	6.3	5.8	5.3
% MF [II] [39 82 83 84 85]	6.3	5.9	8.1	9.9	10.4	9.4	8.3	7.6	5.7	4.7
% M [II] [39 82 83 84 85]	7.9	7.6	10.7	13.3	14.0	12.6	11.3	10.3	...	...
% F [II] [39 85]	4.2	3.5[83]	4.6[83]	5.4[83]	5.6[83]	5.1[83]	4.5[83]	4.2[83]	...	...
United States Etats−Unis										
MF [I] [4 86 87]	6 528.0	7 047.0	8 628.0	9 613.0	8 940.0	7 996.0[88]	7 404.0	7 236.0	6 739.0[89]	6 210.0
M [I] [4 86 87]	3 525.0	3 906.0	4 946.0	5 523.0	5 055.0	4 367.0[88]	3 983.0	3 880.0	3 577.0[89]	3 266.0
F [I] [4 86 87]	3 003.0	3 140.0	3 683.0	4 090.0	3 885.0	3 629.0[88]	3 421.0	3 356.0	3 162.0[89]	2 944.0
% MF [I] [4 86 87]	5.3	5.6	6.8	7.5	6.9	6.1[88]	5.6	5.4	4.9[89]	4.5
% M [I] [4 86 87]	5.2	5.7	7.2	7.9	7.2	6.2[88]	5.6	5.4	4.9[89]	4.4
% F [I] [4 86 87]	5.4	5.5	6.4	7.0	6.6	6.0[88]	5.6	5.4	5.0[89]	4.6
United States Virgin Is. Iles Vierges américaines										
MF [III] [90]	1.7	1.3	1.4	1.7	1.9	2.8	2.7	2.4	2.7	...
% MF [III] [90]	3.7	2.8	2.8	3.5	3.5	5.6	5.7	5.2	5.9	...
Uruguay Uruguay										
MF [I] [2 15]	98.4	105.7	111.0	112.8	105.0	120.1	137.5	...	...	125.0
M [I] [2 15]	44.9	50.6	52.6	49.6	46.9	53.2	61.5	...	...	53.9
F [I] [2 15]	53.5	55.1	58.4	63.2	58.1	66.9	76.0	...	...	71.1
% MF [I] [2 15]	8.0	8.5	9.0	9.0	8.3	9.2	10.2	...	...	10.1
% M [I] [2 15]	6.1	6.9	7.2	6.9	6.5	7.1	8.0	...	...	7.8
% F [I] [2 15]	10.8	10.9	11.6	11.9	10.9	12.1	13.2	...	...	13.0

26
Unemployment
Number (thousands) and percentage of unemployed [*cont.*]
Chômage
Nombre (milliers) et pourcentage des chômeurs [*suite*]

Country or area [§] Pays ou zone [§]	1989	1990	1991	1992	1993	1994	1995	1996	1997	1998
Uzbekistan Ouzbékistan										
MF [III]	...	...	...	20.2	29.0	29.4	31.0	...	...	...
M [III]	...	...	...	7.9	11.3	12.1	12.1	...	...	...
F [III]	...	...	...	12.3	17.7	17.3	18.9	...	...	...
% MF [III]	...	...	...	0.2	0.4	0.4	0.4	...	...	...
% M [III]	...	...	...	0.2	0.2	0.3	0.3	...	...	...
% F [III]	...	...	...	0.3	0.5	0.5	0.5	...	...	...
Venezuela Venezuela										
MF [I] [1]	672.3	743.4	701.7	582.4	503.5	687.4	874.7	1 042.9	1 060.7	...
M [I] [1]	487.1	514.1	481.7	418.7	371.2	442.4	1 016.8	1 210.0	592.4	...
F [I] [1]	185.2	229.2	220.0	163.7	132.3	245.0	366.3	437.9	468.3	...
% MF [I] [1]	9.9	10.4	9.5	7.7	6.7	8.7	10.3	11.8	11.4	...
% M [I] [1]	10.3	10.4	9.6	8.1	7.1	8.2	9.1	10.4	9.8	...
% F [I] [1]	9.2	10.3	9.4	6.8	5.6	9.7	12.9	14.5	14.2	...

Source:
International Labour Office (ILO), Geneva, "Yearbook of Labour Statistics 1999" and the ILO labour statistics database.

§   I   = Labour force sample surveys.
     II   = Social insurance statistics.
     III   = Employment office statistics.
     IV   = Official estimates.

†   For information on recent changes in country or area nomenclature pertaining to former Czechoslovakia, Germany, Hong Kong Special Administrative Region of China, Macao Special Administrative Region of China, SFR Yugoslavia and former USSR, see Annex I – Country or area nomenclature, regional and other groupings.

††   For statistical purposes, the data for China do not include those for the Hong Kong Special Administrative Region, Macao Special Administrative Region of China and Taiwan province of China.

1   Persons aged 15 years and over.
2   Persons aged 14 years and over.
3   Persons aged 10 years and over.
4   Persons aged 16 years and over.
5   Estimates based on 1986 census benchmarks.
6   Estimates based on the 1991 Census of Population and Housing.
7   31st Dec. of each year.
8   One month of each year.
9   Private sector.
10   Year ending in June of the year indicated.
11   One quarter of each year.
12   Average of less than 12 months.
13   Excluding some elderly unemployed no longer applicants for work.
14   Persons aged 15 to 69 years.
15   Urban areas.
16   Year beginning in August of year indicated.
17   Persons aged 12 years and over.
18   Excluding rural population of Rondônia, Acre, Amazonas, Roraima, Pará and Amapá.
19   Beginning 1992, methodology revised; data not strictly comparable.

Source:
Bureau international du Travail (BIT), Genève, "Annuaire des statistiques du travail 1999" et la base de données du BIT.

§   I   = Enquêtes par sondage sur la main-d'oeuvre.
     II   = Statistiques d'assurances sociales.
     III   = Statistiques des bureaux de placement.
     IV   = Evaluations officielles.

†   Pour les modifications récentes de nomenclature de pays ou de zone concernant l'Allemagne, Hong-Kong (Région administrative spéciale de Chine), Macao (Région administrative spéciale de Chine), l'ex-Tchécoslovaquie, l'ex-URSS et l'ex-Rfs de Yougoslavie, voir annexe I – Nomenclature de pays ou des zones, groupements régionaux et autres groupements.

††   Les données statistiques relatives à la Chine ne comprennent pas celles qui concernent la région administrative spéciale de Hong-Kong, la région administrative spéciale de Macao et la province chinoise de Taiwan.

1   Personnes âgées de 15 ans et plus.
2   Personnes âgées de 14 ans et plus.
3   Personnes âgées de 10 ans et plus.
4   Personnes âgées de 16 ans et plus.
5   Estimations basées sur les données de calage du recensement de 1986.
6   Estimations basées sur le recensement de la population et de l'habitat de 1991.
7   31 déc. de chaque année.
8   Un mois de chaque année.
9   Secteur privé.
10   Année se terminant en juin de l'année indiquée.
11   Un trimestre de chaque année.
12   Moyenne de moins de douze mois.
13   Non compris certains chômeurs âgés devenus non demandeurs d'emploi.
14   Personnes âgées de 15 à 69 ans.
15   Régions urbaines.
16   Année commençant en août de l'année indiquée.
17   Personnes âgées de 12 ans et plus.
18   Non compris la population rurale de Rondônia, Acre, Amazonas, Roraima, Pará et Amapá.
19   A partir de 1992, méthodologie révisée; les données ne sont pas strictement comparables.

26
Unemployment
Number (thousands) and percentage of unemployed [*cont.*]
Chômage
Nombre (milliers) et pourcentage des chômeurs [*suite*]

20 Persons aged 16 to 60 years.	20 Personnes âgées de 16 à 60 ans.
21 Persons aged 16 to 55 years.	21 Personnes âgées de 16 à 55 ans.
22 Four employment offices.	22 Quatre bureaux de placement.
23 Bujumbura.	23 Bujumbura.
24 Excluding full-time members of the armed forces.	24 Non compris les membres à temps complet des forces armées.
25 Excluding residents of the Territories and indigenous persons living on reserves.	25 Non compris les habitants des Territoires et les populations indigènes vivant dans les réserves.
26 Bangui.	26 Bangui.
27 Beginning 1996, sample design revised.	27 A partir de 1996, plan d'échantillonnage révisé.
28 Unemployed in urban areas.	28 Chômeurs dans les régions urbaines.
29 Young people aged 16 to 25 years.	29 Jeunes gens de 16 à 25 ans.
30 Excluding unpaid family workers who worked for one hour or more.	30 Non compris les travailleurs familiaux non rémunérés ayant travaillé une heure ou plus.
31 7 main cities of the country.	31 7 villes principales du pays.
32 Estimates based on the 1993 Census results.	32 Estimations basées sur les résultats du Recensement de 1993.
33 Persons aged 14 to 55 years.	33 Personnes âgées de 14 à 55 ans.
34 The data relate to the government-controlled areas.	34 Les données se réfèrent aux régions sous contrôle gouvernemental.
35 Persons aged 15 to 74 years.	35 Personnes âgées de 15 à 74 ans.
36 Persons aged 15 to 66 years.	36 Personnes âgées de 15 à 66 ans.
37 Persons aged 16 to 66 years.	37 Personnes âgées de 16 à 66 ans.
38 Persons aged 12 to 64 years.	38 Personnes âgées de 12 à 64 ans.
39 Excluding persons temporarily laid off.	39 Non compris les personnes temporairement mises à pied.
40 Excluding elderly unemployment pensioners no longer seeking work.	40 Non compris les chômeurs indemnisés âgés ne recherchant plus de travail.
41 Excluding registered applicants for work who worked more than 78 hours during the month.	41 Non compris les demandeurs d'emploi inscrits ayant travaillé plus de 78 heures dans le mois.
42 Cayenne and Kourou.	42 Cayenne et Kourou.
43 Persons aged 15 to 64 years.	43 Personnes âgées de 15 à 64 ans.
44 Persons aged 15 to 60 years.	44 Personnes âgées de 15 à 60 ans.
45 Persons aged 15 to 65 years.	45 Personnes âgées de 15 à 65 ans.
46 Guatemala City.	46 Ville de Guatemala.
47 Including unemployed temporarily unable to undertake work (child-care allowance, military service, etc.).	47 Y compris chômeurs qui temporairement ne peuvent travailler (allocation congé parental, service militaire, etc.).
48 Persons aged 16 to 74 years.	48 Personnes âgées de 16 à 74 ans.
49 Rates calculated on basis of 1991 Census.	49 Taux calculés sur la base du Recensement de 1991.
50 Including workers from the Judea, Samaria and Gaza areas.	50 Y compris les travailleurs des régions de Judée, Samarie et Gaza.
51 Including the residents of East Jerusalem.	51 Y compris les résidents de Jérusalem-Est.
52 Beginning 1993, methodology revised.	52 A partir de 1993, méthodologie révisée.
53 Persons aged 16 to 64 years.	53 Personnes âgées de 16 à 64 ans.
54 Beginning 1997, revised series.	54 A partir de 1997, série révisée.
55 6 provincial capitals.	55 6 chefs-lieux de province.
56 Persons aged 16 to 61 years.	56 Personnes âgées de 16 à 61 ans.
57 Excluding Rodrigues.	57 Non compris Rodrigues.
58 Persons aged 18 years and over.	58 Personnes âgées de 18 ans et plus.
59 Persons working or seeking work for less than 12 hours per week are no longer included.	59 Ne sont plus comprises les personnes qui travaillent, ou qui cherchent moins de 12 heures de travail par semaine.
60 Persons seeking work for 20 hours or more a week.	60 Personnes à la recherche d'un travail de 20 heures ou plus par semaine.
61 Curaçao.	61 Curaçao.
62 Including students seeking vacation work.	62 Y compris les étudiants qui cherchent un emploi pendant les vacances.
63 Annual average calculated using December data as at 12 Dec.	63 Moyenne annuelle calculée en utilisant pour le mois de décembre les données du 12 déc.
64 Computed from 1987-88 survey results.	64 Calculé sur la base des résultats de l'enquête de 1987-88.
65 July of preceding year to June of current year.	65 Juillet de l'année précédente à juin de l'année en cours.
66 Persons aged 18 to 60 years.	66 Personnes âgées de 18 à 60 ans.
67 Asunción metropolitan area.	67 Région métropolitaine d'Asunción.
68 Persons of 10 years and over.	68 Personnes de 10 ans et plus.
69 Persons aged 15 to 72 years.	69 Personnes âgées de 15 à 72 ans.
70 Dakar.	70 Dakar.
71 Population census.	71 Recensement de population.
72 Excluding persons on child-care leave.	72 Non compris les personnes en congé parental.
73 Whole country.	73 Ensemble du pays.
74 Excluding Northern and Eastern provinces.	74 Non compris les provinces du Nord et de l'Est.
75 Khartoum province.	75 Province de Khartoum.
76 Persons aged 13 years and over.	76 Personnes âgées de 13 ans et plus.

26
Unemployment
Number (thousands) and percentage of unemployed [*cont.*]
Chômage
Nombre (milliers) et pourcentage des chômeurs [*suite*]

77   Labour force denominator excluded self–employed.

78   Beginning 1987, excluding unemployed not previously employed.
79   New series according to 1980 population census; 1980: second semester.
80   Annual averages.
81   Persons aged 15–70 years.
82   Excluding some categories of men aged 60 and over.

83   Beginning September 1988, excluding most under 18–year–olds.

84   Beginning September 1989, excluding some men formerly employed in the coalmining industry.
85   Claimants at unemployment benefits offices.
86   Beginning 1990, estimates based on 1990 census benchmarks.

87   Beginning 1992, 1990 Census industrial classification.
88   Beginning 1994, methodology revised; data not strictly comparable.
89   Beginning 1997, methodology revised; data not strictly comparable.
90   Persons aged 16 to 65 years.

77   La main–d'œuvre du dénominateur excluait les travailleurs indépendants.
78   A partir de 1987, non compris les chômeurs n'ayant jamais travaillé.
79   Nouvelle série selon le recensement de population de 1980; 1980: second semestre.
80   Moyennes annuelles.
81   Personnes âgées de 15 à 70 ans.
82   Non compris certaines catégories d'hommes âgés de 60 ans et plus.
83   A partir de septembre 1988, non compris la plupart des moins de 18 ans.
84   A partir de septembre 1989, non compris certains hommes ayant précédemment travaillé dans l'industrie charbonnière.
85   Demandeurs auprès des bureaux de prestations de chômage.
86   A partir de 1990, estimations basées sur les données de calage du recensement de 1990.
87   A partir de 1992, classification par industrie du recensement de 1990.
88   A partir de 1994, méthodologie révisée; les données ne sont pas strictement comparables.
89   A partir de 1997, méthodologie révisée; les données ne sont pas strictement comparables.
90   Personnes âgées de 16 à 65 ans.

Technical notes, tables 25 and 26

Detailed data on labour force and related topics are published in the ILO *Yearbook of Labour Statistics* [12]. The series shown in the *Statistical Yearbook* give an overall picture of the availability and disposition of labour resources and, in conjunction with other macro-economic indicators, can be useful for an overall assessment of economic performance. The ILO *Yearbook of Labour Statistics* provides a comprehensive description of the methodology underlying the labour series. Brief definitions of the major categories of labour statistics are given below.

"Employment" is defined to include persons above a specified age who, during a specified period of time, were in one of the following categories:

(a) "Paid employment", comprising persons who perform some work for pay or profit during the reference period or persons with a job but not at work due to temporary absence, such as vacation, strike, education leave;

(b) "Self-employment", comprising employers, own-account workers, members of producers' cooperatives, persons engaged in production of goods and services for own consumption and unpaid family workers;

(c) Members of the armed forces, students, homemakers and others mainly engaged in non-economic activities during the reference period who, at the same time, were in paid employment or self-employment are considered as employed on the same basis as other categories.

"Unemployment" is defined to include persons above a certain age and who, during a specified period of time were:

(a) "Without work", i.e. were not in paid employment or self-employment;

(b) "Currently available for work", i.e. were available for paid employment or self-employment during the reference period; and

(c) "Seeking work", i.e. had taken specific steps in a specified period to find paid employment or self-employment.

Persons not considered to be unemployed include:

(a) Persons intending to establish their own business or farm, but who had not yet arranged to do so and who were not seeking work for pay or profit;

(b) Former unpaid family workers not at work and not seeking work for pay or profit.

For various reasons, national definitions of employment and unemployment often differ from the recommended international standard definitions and thereby limit international comparability. Intercountry comparisons are also complicated by a variety of types

Notes techniques, tableaux 25 et 26

Des données détaillées sur la main-d'oeuvre et des sujets connexes sont publiées dans l'*Annuaire des Statistiques du Travail* du BIT [12]. Les séries indiquées dans l'*Annuaire des Statistiques* donnent un tableau d'ensemble des disponibilités de main-d'œuvre et de l'emploi de ces ressources et, combinées à d'autres indicateurs économiques, elles peuvent être utiles pour une évaluation générale de la performance économique. L'*Annuaire des statistiques du Travail* du BIT donne une description complète de la méthodologie employée pour établir les séries sur la main-d'œuvre. On trouvera ci-dessous quelques brèves définitions des grandes catégories de statistiques du travail.

Le terme "Emploi" désigne les personnes dépassant un âge déterminé qui, au cours d'une période donnée, se trouvaient dans l'une des catégories suivantes:

(a) La catégorie "emploi rémunéré", composée des personnes faisant un certain travail en échange d'une rémunération ou d'un profit pendant la période de référence, ou les personnes ayant un emploi, mais qui ne travaillaient pas en raison d'une absence temporaire (vacances, grève, congé d'études);

(b) La catégorie "emploi indépendant" regroupe les employeurs, les travailleurs indépendants, les membres de coopératives de producteurs et les personnes s'adonnant à la production de biens et de services pour leur propre consommation et la main-d'œuvre familiale non rémunérée;

(c) Les membres des forces armées, les étudiants, les aides familiales et autres personnes qui s'adonnaient essentiellement à des activités non économiques pendant la période de référence et qui, en même temps, avaient un emploi rémunéré ou indépendant, sont considérés comme employés au même titre que les personnes des autres catégories.

Par "chômeurs", on entend les personnes dépassant un âge déterminé et qui, pendant une période donnée, étaient:

(a) "sans emploi", c'est-à-dire sans emploi rémunéré ou indépendant;

(b) "disponibles", c'est-à-dire qui pouvaient être engagées pour un emploi rémunéré ou pouvaient s'adonner à un emploi indépendant au cours de la période de référence; et

(c) "à la recherche d'un emploi", c'est-à-dire qui avaient pris des mesures précises à un certain moment pour trouver un emploi rémunéré ou un emploi indépendant.

Ne sont pas considérés comme chômeurs:

(a) Les personnes qui, pendant la période de référence, avaient l'intention de créer leur propre entre-

of data collection systems used to obtain information on employed and unemployed persons.

Table 25 presents absolute figures on the distribution of employed persons by economic activity. In part A the figures are according to Revision 2 (ISIC 2) of the *International Standard Industrial Classification*, and in part B according to ISIC 3. In part A, the column for total employment includes economic activities not adequately defined and that are not accounted for in the other categories. Data are arranged as far as possible according to the major divisions of economic activity of the *International Standard Industrial Classification of All Economic Activities* [47].

Table 26: Figures are presented in absolute numbers and in percentages. Data are normally annual averages of monthly, quarterly or semi-annual data.

The series generally represent the total number of persons wholly unemployed or temporarily laid off. Percentage figures, where given, are calculated by comparing the number of unemployed to the total members of that group of the labour force on which the unemployment data are based.

prise ou exploitation agricole, mais n'avaient pas encore pris les dispositions nécessaires à cet effet et qui n'étaient pas à la recherche d'un emploi en vue d'une rémunération ou d'un profit;

(b)   Les anciens travailleurs familiaux non rémunérés qui n'avaient pas d'emploi et n'étaient pas à la recherche d'un emploi en vue d'une rémunération ou d'un profit.

Pour diverses raisons, les définitions nationales de l'emploi et du chômage diffèrent souvent des définitions internationales types recommandées, limitant ainsi les possibilités de comparaison entre pays. Ces comparaisons se trouvent en outre compliquées par la diversité des systèmes de collecte de données utilisés pour recueillir des informations sur les personnes employées et les chômeurs.

Le *tableau 25* présente les effectifs de personnes employées par activité économique. Dans la partie A, les chiffres sont classés en fonction de la Révision 2 de la *Classification internationale type, par Industrie, de toutes les branches d'activité économique* et dans la partie B en fonction de la Révision 3. Dans la partie A, l'emploi total inclut les personnes employées à des activités économiques mal définies et qui ne sont pas classées ailleurs. Les données sont ventilées autant que possible selon les branches d'activité économique de la *Classification internationale type, par industrie, de toutes les activités économiques* [47].

Tableau 26: Les chiffres sont présentés en valeur absolue et en pourcentage. Les données sont normalement des moyennes annuelles des données mensuelles, trimestrielles ou semestrielles.

Les séries représentent généralement le nombre total des chômeurs complets ou des personnes temporairement mises à pied. Les données en pourcentage, lorsqu'elles figurent au tableau, sont calculées par comparaison du nombre de chômeurs au nombre total des personnes du groupe de main-d'œuvre sur lequel sont basées les données relatives au chômage.

27
Wages in manufacturing
Salaires dans les industries manufacturières
By hour, day, week or month
Par heure, jour, semaine ou mois

Country or area and unit Pays ou zone et unité	1989	1990	1991	1992	1993	1994	1995	1996	1997	1998
Albania: lek Albanie : lek										
MF - month mois[1][2]	542.0	554.0	665.0	...	...	...	...	...	...	...
Algeria: Algerian dinar Algérie : dinar algérien										
MF - month mois[3]	...	...	...	6 430.0	8 012.0	8 937.0	10 462.0	12 323.0	...	...
Antigua and Barbuda: EC dollar Antigua-et-Barbuda : dollar des Caraïbes orientales										
MF - week semaine[4][5]	416.0	...	505.0	505.0	...	...	...	...	...	...
Argentina: Argentine peso Argentine : peso argentin										
MF - hour heure[3][5][7]	...	10 030.8[6]	24 941.2[6]	3.2	3.6	3.8	3.9	4.1	4.1	4.1
Australia: Australian dollar Australie : dollar australien										
MF - hour heure[8][9]	...	12.9	13.3	13.7	14.0	14.7[10]	15.6	16.4[3]	...	17.4[3]
M - hour heure[8][9]	...	13.5	13.8	14.2	14.6	15.2[10]	16.1	16.9[3]	...	18.0[3]
F - hour heure[8][9]	...	11.1	11.7	12.0	12.4	13.0[10]	13.7	14.3[3]	...	15.2[3]
Austria: Austrian schilling Autriche : schilling autrichien										
MF - month mois[15]	19 130.0	20 496.0	21 547.0	22 784.0	23 758.0	24 743.0	25 898.0	...	...	...
MF - month mois[3]	...	...	...	...	...	...	26 020.0	27 239.0	27 776.0	...
M - month mois[3]	...	...	...	...	...	...	28 815.0	30 084.0	30 667.0	...
F - month mois[3]	...	...	...	...	...	...	19 903.0	20 667.0	21 051.0	...
Azerbaijan: manat Azerbaïdjan : manat										
MF - month mois	209.4[11]	218.7[11]	400.2[11]	3 282.6[11]	3 109.2	21 009.0	95 556.7	146 174.7	8 887.0[3]	91 210.0[3]
Bahrain: Bahrain dinar Bahreïn : dinar de Bahreïn										
MF - month mois[12][13]	240.5	224.5	220.2	203.9	190.0	188.0	...	...	200.0	...
Bangladesh: taka Bangladesh : taka										
MF - day jour[14][15]	...	...	56.1	59.9	...	...	...	...	...	...
M - day jour[14][15]	...	...	60.9	62.1	...	...	...	...	...	...
F - day jour[14][15]	...	...	30.1	31.3	...	...	...	...	...	...
MF - day jour[14][16]	...	...	21.8	23.0	...	...	...	...	...	...
M - day jour[14][16]	...	...	22.8	24.0	...	...	...	...	...	...
F - day jour[14][16]	...	...	15.9	17.2	...	...	...	...	...	...
Belarus: Belarussian rouble Bélarus : rouble bélarussien										
MF - month mois	249.0[17]	283.0[17]	596.0	5 852.0	68 866.0	115 536.0	...	...	...	...
Belgium: Belgian franc Belgique : franc belge										
MF - hour heure[5][8]	327.1	342.4	363.1	379.6	395.9	411.8	388.2[3]	398.2[3]	406.8[3]	...
M - hour heure[5][8]	348.2	364.0	385.7	403.8	420.7	438.0	405.5[3]	416.2[3]	425.2[3]	...
F - hour heure[5][8]	257.6	271.2	287.7	300.2	313.4	325.3	320.9[3]	331.0[3]	335.8[3]	...
MF - month mois[8][18]	81 756.0	86 673.0	91 950.0	95 615.0	98 702.0	101 426.0	104 773.0[3]	106 983.0[3]	109 980.0[3]	...
M - month mois[8][18]	89 869.0	95 285.0	101 007.0	104 757.0	107 877.0	110 656.0	113 618.0[3]	116 279.0[3]	119 233.0[3]	...
F - month mois[8][18]	56 822.0	60 211.0	64 116.0	67 524.0	70 506.0	73 061.0	80 118.0[3]	82 096.0[3]	85 194.0[3]	...
Bolivia: boliviano Bolivie : boliviano										
MF - month mois[8][19]	436.7	493.1	620.9	689.6	761.3	891.5	959.0	1 094.0	...	...
Botswana: pula Botswana : pula										
MF - month mois[8][20]	345.0	383.0	403.0	511.0	606.0	537.0	582.0	617.0	633.0	632.0[3]

27
Wages in manufacturing
By hour, day, week or month [*cont.*]
Salaires dans les industries manufacturières
Par heure, jour, semaine ou mois [*suite*]

Country or area and unit Pays ou zone et unité	1989	1990	1991	1992	1993	1994	1995	1996	1997	1998
M - month mois[3 8 20]	...	...	...	...	...	...	...	...	...	821.0
F - month mois[3 8 20]	...	...	...	...	...	...	...	...	...	447.0
Brazil: real Brésil : real										
MF - month mois	1 110.7[21]	26 076.0[21]	136 699.0[21]	1 562.0[22]	33 978.0[22]	793 056.6[22]	504.9	597.2	637.1	...
M - month mois	1 275.8[21]	29 850.0[21]	156 457.0[21]	2 779.0[22]	38 861.0[22]	905 566.4[22]	569.7	669.6	711.0	...
F - month mois	664.3[21]	15 990.0[21]	84 818.0[21]	963.0[22]	20 895.0[22]	491 201.2[22]	333.0	403.9	438.8	...
British Virgin Islands: US dollar Iles Vierges britanniques : dollar des Etats-Unis										
MF - hour heure[3]	...	7.3	6.1	6.0	6.3	6.1	...	...	...	...
M - hour heure[3]	...	...	...	...	...	7.2	...	...	...	...
F - hour heure[3]	...	...	...	...	...	4.4	...	...	...	...
Bulgaria: lev Bulgarie : lev										
MF - month mois[23]	281.8	335.8	916.9	2 244.2[24]	3 481.2[24]	5 356.0[24]	8 448.0[24]	15 276.0[3]	148 460.0[3]	198 116.0[3]
M - month mois[3 25]	...	...	...	...	...	...	...	17 794.0	172 043.0	...
F - month mois[3 25]	...	...	...	...	...	...	...	12 658.0	123 423.0	...
Canada: Canadian dollar Canada : dollar canadien										
MF - week semaine[3]	570.6	599.4	624.7	652.9	669.4	685.8	694.6	716.6	736.7	755.9
Chile: Chilean peso Chili : peso chilien										
MF - month mois[8 26]	103 250.0	130 650.0	173 012.0	211 780.0	116 457.0[27]	141 844.0	159 085.0	176 480.0	189 753.0	200 773.0
China ††: yuan Chine †† : yuan										
MF - month mois[3 28]	158.3	172.3	190.8	219.6	279.0	356.9	430.8	470.2	494.4	588.7
China, Hong Kong SAR†: Hong Kong dollar Chine, Hong Kong RAS† : dollar de Hong Kong										
MF - month mois[18 19]	4 954.9	5 685.8	6 382.8	7 163.5	7 897.5	8 780.4	9 508.3	10 323.8	11 331.2	11 711.6
M - month mois[18 19]	5 481.1	6 262.3	7 020.7	7 878.2	8 677.8	9 499.6	10 421.4	11 260.0	12 165.2	12 555.7
F - month mois[18 19]	4 332.7	5 022.6	5 718.4	6 445.4	7 180.2	8 098.4	8 684.2	9 390.4	10 467.0	10 915.9
MF - day jour[5 14]	157.0	179.5	200.7	218.6	241.7	266.6	278.0	296.9	322.6	335.3
M - day jour[5 14]	191.7	224.5	249.9	274.8	313.8	333.5	357.7	386.3	423.8	430.6
F - day jour[5 14]	140.3	155.8	173.6	189.6	206.8	226.3	233.5	245.3	258.8	262.9
China, Macao SAR †: Macao pataca Chine, Macao RAS † : pataca de Macao										
MF - month mois[29]	1 859.0[8]	2 058.0[8]	2 232.0[8]	2 509.0	2 926.0	3 111.0	3 210.0	3 124.0	3 323.0	3 138.0[3]
M - month mois[29]	...	...	...	3 321.0	3 865.0	4 015.0	4 388.0	4 541.0	5 016.0	4 789.0[3]
F - month mois[29]	...	...	...	2 222.0	2 447.0	2 624.0	2 682.0	2 677.0	2 842.0	2 694.0[3]
Colombia: Colombian peso Colombie : peso colombien										
MF - month mois	76 942.0	98 730.0	140 031.0	167 106.0	217 741.0	271 109.0	326 421.0	368 180.0	456 955.0	...
Cook Islands: Cook Islands dollar Iles Cook : dollar des Iles Cook										
MF - week semaine[8]	134.0	137.0	...	...	187.0	...	...	...	...	...
M - week semaine[8]	134.0	160.0	...	...	194.0	...	...	...	...	...
F - week semaine[8]	87.0	111.0	...	...	177.0	...	...	...	...	...
Costa Rica: Costa Rican colón Costa Rica : colón costa-ricien										
MF - month mois[8]	16 784.0	20 037.0	27 229.0	32 949.0	38 631.0	44 720.0	54 365.0	63 894.0	75 672.0	85 899.0[3]

27
Wages in manufacturing
By hour, day, week or month [cont.]
Salaires dans les industries manufacturières
Par heure, jour, semaine ou mois [suite]

Country or area and unit Pays ou zone et unité	1989	1990	1991	1992	1993	1994	1995	1996	1997	1998
M - month mois[8]	18 534.0	21 887.0	30 152.0	36 427.0	42 225.0	49 059.0	60 273.0	69 627.0	78 917.0	91 493.0[3]
F - month mois[8]	13 505.0	16 262.0	21 733.0	26 282.0	30 556.0	35 335.0	42 739.0	50 028.0	67 531.0	73 122.0[3]
Côte d'Ivoire: CFA franc	**Côte d'Ivoire : franc CFA**									
MF - month mois[24 30]	161.4	179.4	...	...	...	...	...	...	...	...
Croatia: kuna	**Croatie : kuna**									
MF - month mois	764.0[31]	4 218.0[31]	7 447.0[31]	34 024.0[31]	518.0	1 186.0	1 672.0	1 916.0[3]	2 196.0[3]	...
Cyprus: Cyprus pound	**Chypre : livre chypriote**									
MF - month mois[8 18 26 32]	475.0	504.0	542.0	558.0	640.0	672.0	710.0	758.0	762.0	...
M - month mois[8 18 26 32]	553.0	586.0	626.0	678.0	738.0	770.0	822.0	864.0	871.0	...
F - month mois[8 18 26 32]	288.0	314.0	349.0	384.0	419.0	455.0	476.0	504.0	530.0	...
MF - week semaine[5 8 26 32]	68.0	74.2	80.3	89.0	101.0	104.1	113.4	130.1	117.5	...
M - week semaine[5 8 26 32]	89.4	98.8	105.6	116.4	134.2	132.3	143.4	170.8	145.0	...
F - week semaine[5 8 26 32]	52.1	56.8	63.0	69.9	75.8	81.2	86.1	90.1	92.4	...
Czech Republic: Czech koruna	**République tchèque : couronne tchèque**									
MF - month mois[5]	3 015.0[33]	3 057.0[33]	3 620.0[34]	4 276.0[3 35]	5 150.0[3 35]	5 857.0[3 35]	6 838.0[3 34]	7 965.0[3 34]	8 874.0[3 36]	9 757.0[3 36]
M - month mois[3 5]	...	...	...	4 891.0[35]	5 891.0[35]	6 699.0[35]	7 821.0[34]	9 026.0[34]	10 056.0[36]	11 057.0[36]
F - month mois[3 5]	...	...	...	3 320.0[35]	3 998.0[35]	4 547.0[35]	5 309.0[34]	6 169.0[34]	6 873.0[36]	7 557.0[36]
MF - month mois[3]	...	...	...	...	5 652.0[35]	6 631.0[35]	7 854.0[34]	9 259.0[34]	10 418.0[36]	11 493.0[36]
Denmark: Danish krone	**Danemark : couronne danoise**									
MF - hour heure[5 32 37]	96.0	99.9	104.6	108.3	...	...	...	...	...	...
M - hour heure[5 32 37]	99.6	103.8	108.5	112.2	...	...	...	...	...	...
F - hour heure[5 32 37]	84.3	87.8	92.1	95.4	...	...	...	...	...	...
MF - hour heure[3]	...	...	...	...	...	...	...	158.7	...	...
M - hour heure[3]	...	...	...	...	...	...	...	167.5	...	...
F - hour heure[3]	...	...	...	...	...	...	...	139.6	...	...
Dominican Republic: Dominican peso	**Rép. dominicaine : peso dominicain**									
MF - hour heure[38]	...	...	10.4	12.2	11.3	17.4	16.6	18.0	21.6	...
MF - month mois[19]	700.0	1 120.0	1 456.0	1 456.0	1 456.0	1 675.0	2 010.0	...	...	...
Ecuador: sucre	**Equateur : sucre**									
MF - hour heure[5]	337.0	467.9	669.4	1 088.6	1 676.1	2 113.1	2 469.3[3]	3 226.7[3]	4 380.4[3]	...
MF - month mois[3 39]	...	...	...	...	...	...	1 302.7	1 726.4	2 179.7	...
Egypt: Egyptian pound	**Egypte : livre égyptienne**									
MF - week semaine[5 8 13]	46.0	54.0	55.0	62.0	70.0	77.0	84.0	93.0[3]	...	...
M - week semaine[5 8 13]	48.0	56.0	57.0	64.0	72.0	80.0	87.0	97.0[3]	...	...
F - week semaine[5 8 13]	34.0	38.0	41.0	48.0	54.0	57.0	64.0	97.0[3]	...	...
El Salvador: El Salvadoran colón	**El Salvador : cólon salvadorien**									
MF - hour heure[5]	3.3	3.3	4.1	4.6	5.4	6.2	6.9	7.5	...	...
M - hour heure[5]	3.4	3.4	4.5	4.8	5.6	6.4	7.0	7.7	...	...
F - hour heure[5]	3.1	3.2	3.7	4.5	5.2	6.0	6.8	7.3	...	...

27
Wages in manufacturing
By hour, day, week or month [cont.]
Salaires dans les industries manufacturières
Par heure, jour, semaine ou mois [suite]

Country or area and unit Pays ou zone et unité	1989	1990	1991	1992	1993	1994	1995	1996	1997	1998
Eritrea: Birr Erythrée : Birr										
MF - month mois[3][19]	...	...	...	...		...	...	478.5	...	...
M - month mois[3][19]	...	...	...	...		...	...	522.0	...	...
F - month mois[3][19]	...	...	...	...		...	...	346.5	...	...
Estonia: Estonian kroon Estonie : couronne estonienne										
MF - month mois	292.6[40]	359.8[40]	850.7[40]	536.0[3]	1 076.0[3]	1 849.0[3][41]	2 498.0[3][41]	3 078.0[3][41]	3 733.0[3][42]	...
Fiji: Fiji dollar Fidji : dollar des Fidji										
MF - day jour[5][14]	11.4	11.4	12.0	12.9	13.9	14.3	14.5	16.3	...	...
Finland: Finnish markka Finlande : markka finlandais										
MF - hour heure[5][43]	43.5	47.7	50.7	52.3	53.5	55.8	60.1	...	...	...
M - hour heure[5][43]	46.7	51.1	53.9	55.4	56.8	59.2	63.4	...	...	...
F - hour heure[5][43]	35.8	39.5	42.1	43.4	44.4	46.6	50.3	...	...	...
MF - month mois[3][44]	...	...	...	...	...	...	11 004.0	11 434.0	11 677.0	...
M - month mois[3][44]	...	...	...	...	...	...	11 810.0	12 240.0	12 523.0	...
F - month mois[3][44]	...	...	...	...	...	...	9 232.0	9 674.0	9 842.0	...
France: French franc France : franc français										
MF - hour heure[5][1]	43.4	45.5	47.5	49.4	50.6	51.8	52.8	54.2	55.4	...
M - hour heure[5][1]	46.2	48.4	50.5	52.4	53.7	54.9	55.8	57.2	58.5	...
F - hour heure[5][1]	36.3	38.2	39.7	41.2	42.5	43.3	44.3	45.4	46.3	...
Germany Allemagne										
MF - hour heure[3][5]	...	...	...	...	...	...	...	25.7	26.2	26.8
M - hour heure[3][5]	...	...	...	...	...	...	...	27.0	27.4	28.0
F - hour heure[3][5]	...	...	...	...	...	...	...	20.0	20.3	20.8
F. R. Germany: deutsche mark R. f. Allemagne : deutsche mark										
MF - hour heure[5][45]	19.1	20.1	21.3	22.5	23.8	24.6	25.5[3]	26.4[3]	26.8[3]	27.4[3]
M - hour heure[5][45]	20.3	21.3	22.6	23.8	25.0	25.8	26.8[3]	27.7[3]	28.0[3]	28.6[3]
F - hour heure[5][45]	14.7	15.5	16.5	17.5	18.5	19.0	19.7[3]	20.5[3]	20.8[3]	21.3[3]
former German D. R.: deutsche mark l'ex-R. d. allemande : deutsche mark										
MF - hour heure[5]	...	...	9.4	11.9	13.9	15.5	17.0[3]	18.0[3]	18.6[3]	19.2[3]
M - hour heure[5]	...	...	9.7	12.3	14.4	16.2	17.8[3]	18.8[3]	19.5[3]	20.1[3]
F - hour heure[5]	...	...	8.4	10.5	11.9	13.0	14.1[3]	15.0[3]	15.4[3]	15.9[3]
Ghana: cedi Ghana : cedi										
MF - month mois[8]	36 793.0	45 045.0	34 226.0	...	...	...	...	...	...	...
Gibraltar: Gibraltar pound Gibraltar : livre de Gibraltar										
MF - week semaine[5][1]	190.1	238.5	214.1	239.4	252.2	233.3	279.3	...	...	...
M - week semaine[5][1]	194.3	247.7	254.4	254.5	272.7	246.0	295.3	...	...	...
F - week semaine[5][1]	137.7	151.7	148.8	161.7	166.0	171.5	193.8	...	...	...
Greece: drachma Grèce : drachme										
MF - hour heure[5][13]	554.0	661.3	772.1	878.2	970.8	1 097.9	1 243.3	1 349.9	1 470.5	...
M - hour heure[5][13]	614.5	733.8	854.7	967.5	1 063.6	1 200.1	1 353.3	1 459.8	1 585.9	...

27
Wages in manufacturing
By hour, day, week or month [cont.]
Salaires dans les industries manufacturières
Par heure, jour, semaine ou mois [suite]

Country or area and unit Pays ou zone et unité	1989	1990	1991	1992	1993	1994	1995	1996	1997	1998
F - hour heure[5][13]	481.0	575.3	673.2	765.3	851.4	963.4	1 088.6	1 183.4	1 287.8	...
MF - month mois[13][18]	139 492.0	169 842.0	200 303.0	229 596.0	259 853.0	293 627.0	332 568.0	363 857.0	399 599.0	...
M - month mois[13][18]	150 484.0	183 440.0	216 176.0	247 723.0	280 219.0	319 082.0	358 318.0	391 700.0	430 889.0	...
F - month mois[13][18]	102 591.0	125 467.0	148 938.0	171 921.0	195 542.0	218 400.0	244 904.0	278 996.0	303 900.0	...
Guam: US dollar Guam : dollar des Etats-Unis										
MF - hour heure[5][8][12]	7.3	8.1	9.1	9.3	10.1	10.4	10.6	...	...	...
Guatemala: quetzal Guatemala : quetzal										
MF - month mois	435.1	473.6	577.9	686.2	775.2	868.1	1 138.0	1 368.9	1 430.0	1 541.0
Guinea: Guinean franc Guinée : franc guinéen										
MF - month mois[19]	...	80 000.0	85 000.0	110 000.0	110 000.0	130 000.0	130 000.0	153 000.0	...	...
Hungary: forint Hongrie : forint										
MF - month mois[5][47]	9 121.0[46]	11 167.0[46]	13 992.0[46]	17 636.0	21 751.0	...	...	...	...	...
MF - month mois[3][44]	...	...	...	21 107.0[47]	26 317.0[47]	32 500.0[47]	39 554.0[47]	48 195.0[47]	58 915.0[47]	67 169.0[48]
M - month mois[3][44][47]	...	...	...	24 319.0	30 422.0	37 429.0	45 466.0	55 437.0	68 396.0	...
F - month mois[3][44][47]	...	...	...	17 014.0	21 109.0	26 175.0	31 853.0	38 897.0	46 897.0	...
India: Indian rupee Inde : roupie indienne										
MF - month mois[5]	841.2	988.4	1 019.3	932.6	977.4	960.5	1 211.0	1 188.8	...	...
Ireland: Irish pound Irlande : livre irlandaise										
MF - hour heure[5][8][49]	5.1	5.4	5.6	5.9	6.2	6.3	6.5	6.6	6.9	7.3
M - hour heure[5][8][32]	5.7	6.0	6.3	6.6	7.0	7.0	7.1	7.3	7.5	...
F - hour heure[5][8][32]	4.0	4.2	4.4	4.7	5.0	5.1	5.3	5.4	5.6	...
Isle of Man: pound sterling Ile de Man : livre sterling										
MF - week semaine[8]	...	...	...	207.0	225.0	238.1	285.2[3]	272.4[3]	292.7[3]	313.3[3]
M - week semaine[8]	...	...	...	...	276.0	251.8	288.6[3]	294.6[3]	320.5[3]	366.0[3]
F - week semaine[8]	...	...	...	148.0	199.4	266.2[3]	196.1[3]	215.8[3]	209.6[3]	
Israel: new sheqel Israël : nouveau sheqel										
MF - month mois[50]	...	2 668.8	3 080.0	3 514.0	3 917.0	4 427.0[3]	5 061.0[3]	5 757.0[3]	6 676.0[3]	7 418.0[3]
Italy: Italian lira Italie : lire italienne										
MF - hour heure[3][5]	...	100.0[51]	109.5[51]	115.7[51]	120.5[51]	124.3[51]	128.7[51]	101.8[52]	105.7[52]	108.6[52]
MF - hour heure[3][18]	...	100.0[51]	110.2[51]	116.8[51]	121.9[51]	126.1[51]	131.3[51]	102.2[52]	106.4[52]	109.6[52]
Jamaica: Jamaican dollar Jamaïque : dollar jamaïcain										
MF - week semaine	391.8	450.6[53]	701.0	895.0	...	...	...	...	...	...
Japan: yen Japon : yen										
MF - month mois	336 648.0[54]	352 020.0[54]	368 011.0[54]	372 594.0[54]	371 356.0[54]	276 700.0[55]	278 800.0[55]	283 700.0[55]	287 200.0[55]	289 600.0[55]
M - month mois	414 981.0[54]	436 135.0[54]	450 336.0[54]	454 482.0[54]	...	317 000.0[55]	318 200.0[55]	322 500.0[55]	325 600.0[55]	327 900.0[55]
F - month mois	173 097.0[54]	180 253.0[54]	193 112.0[54]	198 058.0[54]	...	175 500.0[55]	177 900.0[55]	181 800.0[55]	184 500.0[55]	187 300.0[55]
Jordan: Jordan dinar Jordanie : dinar jordanien										
MF - day jour[8]	4.4	4.6	4.6	4.8	4.9	5.2	5.3	...	...	...
M - day jour[8]	4.6	4.8	4.9	5.0	5.1	5.4	5.5	...	...	...
F - day jour[8]	2.8	2.7	3.0	2.9	3.1	3.3	3.4	...	...	...

27
Wages in manufacturing
By hour, day, week or month [*cont.*]
Salaires dans les industries manufacturières
Par heure, jour, semaine ou mois [*suite*]

Country or area and unit Pays ou zone et unité	1989	1990	1991	1992	1993	1994	1995	1996	1997	1998
Kazakhstan: tenge Kazakhstan : tenge										
MF - month mois	250.0[56]	277.0[56]	489.0[56]	5 675.0[56]	144.0	2 263.0	6 520.0	9 288.0	11 092.0	11 632.0[3]
Kenya: Kenya shilling Kenya : shilling du Kenya										
MF - month mois[8 57]	2 797.5	3 064.6	3 324.2	3 698.7	5 275.3	4 920.5	6 228.7	4 998.6	5 510.8	...
M - month mois[8 57]	2 890.9	3 159.8	3 430.1	3 692.7	4 239.7	4 878.6	6 867.7	...	5 294.3	...
F - month mois[8 57]	2 001.7	2 317.7	2 515.8	3 313.4	3 830.0	5 168.5	3 314.4	...	6 509.5	...
Korea, Republic of: Korean won Corée, République de : won coréen										
MF - month mois[26 39]	491.6	590.8	690.3	798.5	885.4[3]	1 022.5[3]	1 123.9[3]	1 261.2[3]	1 326.2[3]	1 284.5[3]
M - month mois[26 39]	608.9	724.5	842.8	963.8	1 055.5[3]	1 206.7[3]	1 314.7[3]	1 463.4[3]	1 527.2[3]	1 467.3[3]
F - month mois[26 39]	307.5	364.3	428.1	497.3	551.4[3]	638.9[3]	711.1[3]	795.6[3]	852.0[3]	820.1[3]
Kyrgyzstan: Kyrgyz som Kirghizistan : som kirghize										
MF - month mois[3]	1.2	1.3	2.1	15.1	118.1	280.4	377.1	652.1	844.7	988.8
Latvia: lats Lettonie : lats										
MF - month mois[3]	...	1.6[2]	3.2[2]	22.5	46.2	60.5	86.5	95.2	114.7[37]	128.3[37]
M - month mois[3]	...	...	...	24.0	...	66.2	94.6	101.4	121.5[37]	136.1[37]
F - month mois[3]	...	...	...	20.1	...	54.8	77.8	88.3	107.9[37]	119.2[37]
Lithuania: litas Lituanie : litas										
M - month mois[3 8]	...	...	...	...	...	...	...	...	909.0	1 089.0
F - month mois[3 8]	...	...	...	...	...	...	...	...	733.0	847.0
Luxembourg: Luxembourg franc Luxembourg : franc luxembourgeois										
MF - hour heure[5 8]	374.0	379.0	400.0	425.0	446.0	468.0	478.0	484.0	...	...
M - hour heure[5 8]	393.0	399.0	420.0	446.0	466.0	486.0	495.0	504.0	...	...
F - hour heure[5 8]	234.0	248.0	265.0	278.0	300.0	314.0	316.0	320.0	...	...
MF - month mois[8 18]	112 273.0	118 555.0	124 885.0	133 958.0	136 802.0	138 170.0	139 190.0	140 155.0	...	...
M - month mois[8 18]	122 207.0	129 207.0	135 258.0	144 648.0	146 876.0	148 197.0	147 878.0	148 131.0	...	...
F - month mois[8 18]	66 793.0	72 152.0	77 096.0	83 632.0	88 607.0	89 493.0	93 576.0	95 441.0	...	...
Malawi: Malawi kwacha Malawi : kwacha malawien										
MF - month mois	147.0	176.8	154.8	167.8	173.8	184.7	195.8	...	...	...
Malaysia: ringgit Malaisie : ringgit										
MF - month mois	640.0	660.0	719.0	794.0	848.0	928.0	1 002.0	1 115.0	...	...
M - month mois	864.0	885.0	952.0	1 037.0	1 082.0	1 161.0	1 242.0	1 343.0	...	...
F - month mois	420.0	443.0	495.0	558.0	612.0	677.0	719.0	842.0	...	...
Mauritius: Mauritian rupee Maurice : roupie mauricienne										
MF - month mois[8 18]	2 799.0[58]	3 105.0[58]	3 684.0	4 016.0	4 411.0	5 162.0	5 659.0	5 972.0	6 282.0	6 912.0
MF - day jour[8 59]	52.6[58]	60.5[58]	84.0	93.0	109.0	122.0	132.0	138.0	148.7	161.4
Mexico: Mexican new peso Mexique : nouveau peso mexicain										
MF - hour heure[3 5]	3.3	4.2	5.2	6.4	6.5	7.2	8.3	10.2	12.1	...
MF - month mois[3]	...	...	947.9	...	1 013.9	...	1 178.1	1 327.3	1 575.3	1 927.4
M - month mois[3]	...	...	1 124.4	...	1 120.9	...	1 288.0	1 435.5	1 726.5	2 154.3
F - month mois[3]	...	...	558.9	...	750.1	...	897.3	1 061.4	1 236.0	1 499.5

27
Wages in manufacturing
By hour, day, week or month [*cont.*]
Salaires dans les industries manufacturières
Par heure, jour, semaine ou mois [*suite*]

Country or area and unit Pays ou zone et unité	1989	1990	1991	1992	1993	1994	1995	1996	1997	1998
Myanmar: kyat Myanmar : kyat										
M - month mois[53 60]	729.5	...	631.9	880.5	985.3	...	...	...	1 043.3	
F - month mois[53 60]	705.6	...	670.9	866.8	940.2	...	...	...	998.9	
Netherlands: Netherlands guilder Pays-Bas : florin néerlandais										
MF - hour heure[8 49]	20.8	21.5	22.3	22.7	23.4	27.9[3]	28.9[3]	...	...	...
M - hour heure[8 32]	21.9	22.8	23.5	23.9	24.5	29.1[3]	30.1[3]	...	...	...
F - hour heure[8 32]	16.5	17.1	17.8	18.3	19.0	22.2[3]	22.6[3]	...	...	...
MF - hour heure[32]	126.0[61]	100.0[3 51]	103.9[3 51]	108.3[3 51]	111.8[3 51]	113.7[3 51]	115.0[3 51]	117.2[3 51]	120.7[3 51]	124.6[3 51]
Netherlands Antilles: Netherlands Antillean guilder Antilles néerlandaises : florin des Antilles néerlandaises										
MF - month mois[3 62]	...	...	2 319.0	2 416.0	2 441.0	2 445.0	2 364.0	2 475.0	2 546.0	2 507.0
New Zealand: New Zealand dollar Nouvelle-Zélande : dollar néo-zélandais										
MF - hour heure[8 63]	12.6	13.3	13.8	14.2	14.3	14.4[3]	14.8[3]	15.4[3]	15.9[3]	16.3[3]
M - hour heure[8 63]	13.5	14.3	14.8	15.1	15.2	15.3[3]	15.7[3]	16.3[3]	16.8[3]	17.2[3]
F - hour heure[8 63]	10.1	10.6	11.0	11.5	11.6	11.9[3]	12.2[3]	12.7[3]	13.2[3]	13.7[3]
Nicaragua: córdoba Nicaragua : córdoba										
MF - month mois	1 407.6[39 64]	143 589.0[39 64]	1 140.6	1 951.2	2 150.0	2 282.4	2 443.6	2 672.0	2 724.0	2 846.0
Norway: Norwegian krone Norvège : couronne norvégienne										
MF - hour heure[5 32 57]	87.3	92.5	97.3	100.4	103.2	106.1	109.8	114.4	118.9	125.5
M - hour heure[5 32 57]	89.5	94.6	99.5	102.7	105.4	108.5	112.3	117.0	121.6	128.3
F - hour heure[5 32 57]	76.5	81.8	86.7	89.2	91.8	94.6	97.8	102.2	106.1	112.4
Pakistan: Pakistan rupee Pakistan : roupie pakistanaise										
MF - month mois	1 289.7	1 735.0	...	...	1 502.0	1 956.0	2 970.0	2 878.0	...	...
Panama: balboa Panama : balboa										
MF - month mois	459.0	515.0	537.0	524.0	590.0	587.0	...	597.0[3]	...	...
Paraguay: guaraní Paraguay : guaraní										
MF - month mois	177 464.0	220 548.0	273 537.0	298 682.0	380 096.0	480 081.0	...	...	...	...
M - month mois	170 222.0	234 234.0	292 787.0	342 552.0	407 117.0	507 072.0	...	...	...	...
F - month mois	212 743.0	155 744.0	196 738.0	177 754.0	298 952.0	389 558.0	...	...	...	...
Peru: new sol Pérou : nouveau sol										
MF - month mois[18 19]	1 344.6[8 65 66]	14.9[8 66]	322.7[8 66]	565.0[8 66]	860.6[8 66]	1 451.1[8 66]	...	1 624.6[3 67]	1 875.2[3 67]	2 067.0[3 67]
MF - day jour[5 14]	18 636.6[8 66 68]	0.3[8 66]	6.0[8 66]	10.1[8 66]	14.8[8 66]	21.9[8 66]	24.0[3 8 66]	22.6[3 67]	24.5[3 67]	24.9[3 67]
Philippines: Philippine peso Philippines : peso philippin										
MF - month mois[13 69]	3 441.0	4 263.0	4 831.0	5 386.0	5 584.0	6 272.0	6 654.0	...	...	...
M - month mois[13 69]	...	...	...	...	6 223.0	7 063.0	7 529.0	...	...	...
F - month mois[13 69]	...	...	...	...	4 741.0	5 277.0	5 592.0	...	...	...
Poland: zloty Pologne : zloty										
MF - month mois[57]	212 170.0[17 70]	995.5[17 71]	1 620.1[39 70]	2 679.4[39 70]	361.9[3]	494.9[3]	656.7[3]	832.8[3]	1 014.9[3]	1 206.7[3]
Portugal: Portuguese escudo Portugal : escudo portugais										
MF - hour heure[5]	281.0	324.0	370.0	419.0	436.4	...	470.0	498.0	539.0	703.0[3]
M - hour heure[5]	320.0	368.0	419.0	480.0	485.7	...	551.0	586.0	626.0	832.0[3]

27
Wages in manufacturing
By hour, day, week or month [cont.]
Salaires dans les industries manufacturières
Par heure, jour, semaine ou mois [suite]

Country or area and unit Pays ou zone et unité	1989	1990	1991	1992	1993	1994	1995	1996	1997	1998
F - hour heure[5]	222.0	254.0	295.0	326.0	390.1	...	378.0	402.0	434.0	545.0[3]
MF - month mois	...	...	...	...	...	...	100 700.0	107 800.0	116 100.0	120 803.0[3]
M - month mois	...	...	...	...	...	...	118 900.0	127 200.0	136 900.0	140 720.0[3]
F - month mois	...	...	...	...	...	...	78 100.0	83 900.0	88 900.0	94 837.0[3]
Puerto Rico: US dollar Porto Rico : dollar des Etats-Unis										
MF - hour heure[5]	5.8	6.0	6.3	6.6	7.0	7.2	7.4	7.7	8.0	8.4
Republic of Moldova: Moldovan leu République de Moldova : leu moldove										
MF - month mois	244.4[72]	287.6[72]	475.2[72]	3 676.2[72]	37.8	143.2	209.5	282.2[3]	352.0[3]	399.0[3]
Romania: Romanian leu Roumanie : leu roumain										
MF - month mois[5]	2 920.0[23]	3 146.0[23]	6 842.0[23]	17 959.0	54 245.0	126 260.0	...	...	...	...
MF - month mois[3]	...	...	...	23 582.0	71 779.0	169 435.0	268 436.0	424 587.0	826 902.0	...
Russian Federation: ruble Fédération de Russie : ruble										
MF - month mois	...	...	...	...	...	...	...	...	833 428.0	1 026.0[3 73]
San Marino: Italian lira Saint-Marin : lire italienne										
MF - day jour	84 782.0	84 835.0	102 579.0	111 611.0	113 772.0	120 131.0	127 347.0	135 278.0	142 712.0	149 357.0
Seychelles: Seychelles rupee Seychelles : roupie seychelloises										
MF - month mois[75]	1 975.0[74]	2 187.0[74]	2 259.0[74]	2 349.0	2 454.0	2 422.0	2 513.0	2 646.0	2 727.0	...
Singapore: Singapore dollar Singapour : dollar singapourien										
MF - month mois	1 242.9	1 395.0	1 551.8	1 686.2	1 817.8	1 995.3	2 157.3	2 319.5	2 486.7	2 553.0[3]
M - month mois	1 623.0	1 797.5	1 970.1	2 127.4	2 266.2	2 473.8	2 644.0	2 815.2	2 999.7	3 066.0[3]
F - month mois	876.2	983.3	1 096.8	1 190.7	1 294.5	1 415.4	1 541.2	1 674.4	1 811.0	1 864.0[3]
Slovakia: Slovak koruna Slovaquie : couronne slovaque										
MF - month mois	3 156.0	3 262.0	3 757.0[3 76]	4 370.0[3 76]	5 234.0[3 76]	6 193.0[3 76]	7 194.0[3 76]	8 230.0[3 76]	9 197.0[3 77]	10 001.0[3 77]
Slovenia: tolar Slovénie : tolar										
MF - month mois[3]	1 895.0	8 698.0	14 737.0	43 305.0	62 491.0	79 347.0	92 877.0	106 144.0	118 960.0	132 080.0
Solomon Islands: Solomon Islands dollar Iles Salomon : dollar des Iles Salomon										
MF - month mois[18]	...	433.0	403.0	...	572.0	579.0	632.0	...	...	...
South Africa: rand Afrique du Sud : rand										
MF - month mois[78]	1 438.0	1 660.0	1 890.0	2 195.0	2 446.0	...	...	...	...	...
Spain: peseta Espagne : peseta										
MF - hour heure	780.0	902.0	994.0	1 080.0	1 159.0	1 221.0	1 263.0	1 311.0[3]	1 372.0[3]	1 429.0[3]
Sri Lanka: Sri Lanka rupee Sri Lanka : roupie sri-lankaise										
MF - hour heure[5 53]	7.5	9.5	11.2	11.8	13.7	15.1	16.5	17.9	18.2	20.3
M - hour heure[5 53]	8.2	9.8	11.7	12.3	14.1	15.6	17.1	17.9	18.4	20.8
F - hour heure[5 53]	5.4	8.9	9.4	10.4	12.7	13.8	16.2	17.6	16.3	16.4
Sudan: Sudanese pound Soudan : livre soudanaise										
MF - month mois[5]	...	375.4	...	1 210.3	...	...	...	...	...	...
Swaziland: lilangeni Swaziland : lilangeni										
M - month mois[5 8 12 79]	1 040.0	1 380.0	1 415.0	1 486.0	1 146.0	1 861.0	2 134.0	2 388.0	...	...
F - month mois[5 8 12 79]	561.0	1 001.0	845.0	835.0	1 869.0	1 252.0	1 507.0	1 530.0	...	...

273 Wages and prices   Salaires et prix

27
Wages in manufacturing
By hour, day, week or month [cont.]
Salaires dans les industries manufacturières
Par heure, jour, semaine ou mois [suite]

Country or area and unit Pays ou zone et unité	1989	1990	1991	1992	1993	1994	1995	1996	1997	1998
M - month mois[5 8 12 80]	257.0	324.0	318.0	372.0	409.0	424.0	558.0	681.0	...	...
F - month mois[5 8 12 80]	207.0	284.0	286.0	305.0	382.0	346.0	483.0	572.0	...	...
Sweden: Swedish krona Suède : couronne suédoise										
MF - hour heure[5 32 37]	79.3[81]	87.3[81]	91.7[81]	98.3[81]	98.5[3 81]	102.4[3 81]	107.0[3 81]	115.0[3 81]	101.2[3 82]	
M - hour heure[5 32 37]	81.1[81]	89.5[81]	93.8[81]	100.7[81]	100.7[3 81]	104.5[3 81]	109.1[3 81]	117.4[3 81]	103.3[3 82]	
F - hour heure[5 32 37]	72.6[81]	79.5[81]	83.7[81]	90.1[81]	90.1[3 81]	94.2[3 81]	98.2[3 81]	105.7[3 81]	93.3[3 82]	
Switzerland: Swiss franc Suisse : franc suisse										
M - hour heure[5 8 32]	22.1	23.4	25.0	26.2	26.8	...	...	...	...	...
F - hour heure[5 8 32]	15.0	15.9	17.0	17.8	18.4	...	...	...	...	...
MF - month mois[3]	...	...	...	...	...	5 462.0	...	5 565.0	...	
M - month mois[3]	...	...	...	...	...	5 881.0	...	5 970.0	...	
F - month mois[3]	...	...	...	...	...	4 151.0	...	4 280.0	...	
Tajikistan: Tajik ruble Tadjikistan : ruble tadjik										
MF - month mois[24]	...	...	405.4[83]	2 522.9[83]	26 905.1[83]	65 162.0[83]	1 559.0	8 080.0	14 977.0	
Thailand: baht Thaïlande : baht										
MF - month mois[8 19 84]	2 996.0	3 357.0	3 688.0	3 986.0	4 138.0	4 229.0[85]	4 994.0[85]	5 502.0[85]	5 935.0[85]	
M - month mois[8 19 84]	...	...	4 728.0	5 159.0	5 145.0	5 205.0[85]	6 234.0[85]	...	...	
F - month mois[8 19 84]	...	...	3 016.0	3 329.0	3 558.0	3 715.0[85]	4 250.0[85]	...	...	
Tonga: pa'anga Tonga : pa'anga										
MF - week semaine[8]	43.0	42.6	51.4	51.3	...	...	...	...	...	
Trinidad and Tobago: Trinidad and Tobago dollar Trinité-et-Tobago : dollar de la Trinité-et-Tobago										
MF - week semaine[3]	703.0	724.5	731.3	732.3	755.0	739.9	790.6	810.1	865.4	908.7
Turkey: Turkish lira Turquie : livre turque										
MF - day jour[8]	17 820.5	30 582.2	61 620.4	88 144.3	135 236.0	191 118.5	...	757 277.0	1 640 856.4	...
M - day jour[8]	18 679.1	31 231.1	62 140.3	91 204.1	138 746.1	191 858.8	...	758 475.1	1 661 886.1	...
F - day jour[8]	13 830.0	25 299.5	56 660.2	84 558.2	122 720.8	189 297.3	...	747 788.8	1 611 526.4	...
Ukraine: hryvnia Ukraine : hryvnia										
MF - month mois	236.0[86]	263.0[86]	532.2[86]	7 494.8[86]	173.3[39 87]	1 499.9[39 87]	7 716.7[39 87]	131.7	148.9	157.4
United Kingdom: pound sterling Royaume-Uni : livre sterling										
MF - hour heure[3 8 88 89 90]	5.5	6.1	6.7	7.1	7.5	7.6	7.9	8.2	8.5	9.1
M - hour heure[3 8 88 89 90]	6.0	6.5	7.2	7.7	8.0	8.1	8.4	8.8	9.1	9.7
F - hour heure[3 8 88 89 90]	4.0	4.5	4.9	5.3	5.6	5.7	6.0	6.2	6.6	7.0
United States: US dollar Etats-Unis : dollar des Etats-Unis										
MF - hour heure[5 12 91]	10.5	10.8	11.2	11.5	11.7	12.1	12.4	12.8	13.2	13.5
United States Virgin Is.: US dollar Iles Vierges américaines : dollar des Etats-Unis										
MF - hour heure[5]	10.9	11.9	12.5	13.7	15.0	15.2	15.8	17.0	18.1	...
Uruguay: Uruguayan peso Uruguay : peso uruguayen										
MF - month mois[92]	1 751.6	3 453.2	7 371.5	12 564.4	20 197.5	28 849.4	38 710.5	...	...	...
Zimbabwe: Zimbabwe dollar Zimbabwe : dollar zimbabwéen										
MF - month mois[93]	665.5	796.1	928.1	1 123.3	1 242.1	1 559.1	1 913.8	2 301.1	2 951.5	...

27
Wages in manufacturing
By hour, day, week or month [cont.]

Salaires dans les industries manufacturières
Par heure, jour, semaine ou mois [suite]

Source:
International Labour Office (ILO), Geneva, "Yearbook of
Labour Statistics, 1999" and ILO database.

† For information on recent changes in country or
area nomenclature pertaining to former Czechoslovakia,
Germany, Hong Kong Special Administrative Region (SAR) of
China, Macao Special Administrative Region (SAR) of China,
SFR of Yugoslavia and the former USSR, see Annex I - Country
or area nomenclature, regional and other groupings.

†† For statistical purposes, the data for
China do not include those for Hong Kong Special
Administrative Region (Hong Kong SAR), Macao Special
Administrative Region (Macao SAR) and Taiwan province of
China.

1 Including mining and quarrying.
2 State sector only.
3 Data classified according to ISIC, Rev.3.
4 Weekly wage rates.
5 Wage earners.
6 Australes, 1 peso is equivalent to 10,000 australes.
7 Hourly wage rates.
8 One month of each year.
9 Full-time adult non-managerial employees.

10 New industrial classification.
11 Roubles; 1 manat is equivalent to 10 roubles.
12 Private sector.
13 Establishments with 10 or more persons employed.
14 Daily wage rates.
15 Skilled - managerial, administrative, technical, and
   production workers.
16 Unskilled - clerical, sales and service workers.

17 Socialised sector.
18 Salaried employees.
19 Monthly wage rates.
20 Citizens only.
21 Cruzeiros; 1 real - approximately 2750 x 1000 cruzeiros.
22 Figures in thousands. Cruzeiros; 1 real - approximately 2750
   x 1000 cruzeiros.
23 State and cooperative sector.
24 Including mining and quarrying and manufacturing.
25 Employees under labour contract.
26 Including family allowances and the value of payments in
   kind.
27 Beginning April 1993, sample design and methodology revised.

28 State-owned units, urban collective-owned units and other
   ownership units.
29 Median.
30 Modern sector.
31 Dinars; 1 kuna - 1,000 dinars.
32 Adults.
33 State-owned enterprises, excluding local and cooperative
   industry.
34 Enterprises with 100 or more employees.
35 Enterprises with 25 or more employees.
36 Enterprises with 20 or more employees.
37 One quarter of each year.

Source:
Bureau international du Travail (BIT), Genève, "Annuaire des
statistiques du travail, 1999" et la base de données du BIT.

† Pour les modifications récentes de nomenclature
de pays ou de zone concernant l'Allemagne, Hong Kong, région
administrative spéciale (RAS) de Chine, Macao, région
administrative spéciale (RAS) de Chine,
l'ex-Tchécoslovaquie, l'ex-URSS et l'ex-Rfs de Yougoslavie,
voir annexe I - Nomenclature des pays ou des zones,
groupements régionaux et autres groupements.

†† Les données statistiques relatives à
la Chine ne comprennent pas celles qui concernent la région
administrative spéciale de Hong Kong (la RAS de Hong Kong),
la région administrative spéciale de Macao (la RAS de Macao)
et la province chinoise de Taiwan.

1 Y compris les industries extractives.
2 Seulement le secteur d'Etat.
3 Données classifiées selon la CITI, Rév.3.
4 Taux de salaire hebdomadaires.
5 Ouvriers.
6 Australes, 1 peso équivant à 10,000 australes.
7 Taux de salaire horaires.
8 Un mois de chaque année.
9 Salariés adultes à plein temps, non compris les cadres
   dirigeants.
10 Nouvelle classification industrielle.
11 Roubles; 1 manat équivaut à 10 roubles.
12 Secteur privé.
13 Etablissements occupant 10 personnes et plus.
14 Taux de salaire journaliers.
15 Qualifiés - directeurs, cadres administratifs supérieurs,
   personnel technique et travailleurs à la production.
16 Non qualifiés - personnel administratif, personnel
   commercial et spécialisé dans les services.
17 Secteur socialisé.
18 Employés.
19 Taux de salaire mensuels.
20 Nationaux seulement.
21 Cruzeiros; 1 real - environ 2750 x 1000 cruzeiros.
22 Données en milliers. Cruzeiros; 1 real - environ 2750 x 1000
   cruzeiros.
23 Secteur d'Etat et coopératif.
24 Y compris les industries extractives et manufacturières.
25 Salariés sous contrat de travail.
26 Y compris les allocations familiales et la valeur des
   paiements en nature.
27 A partir d'avril 1993, plan d'échantillonnage et
   méthodologie révisés.
28 Unités d'Etat, unités collectives urbaines et autres.

29 Médiane.
30 Secteur moderne.
31 Dinars; 1 kuna - 1000 dinars.
32 Adultes.
33 Entreprises d'Etat, non compris industrie local et
   coopératives.
34 Entreprises occupant 100 salariés et plus.
35 Entreprises occupant 25 salariés et plus.
36 Entreprises occupant 20 salariés et plus.
37 Un trimestre de chaque année.

27
Wages in manufacturing
By hour, day, week or month [*cont.*]
Salaires dans les industries manufacturières
Par heure, jour, semaine ou mois [*suite*]

38 Estimations based on National Accounts.	38 Estimations basées sur la Comptabilité nationale.
39 Figures in thousands.	39 Données en milliers.
40 Roubles; 1 kroon is equivalent to 10 roubles.	40 Roubles; 1 couronne équivaut à 10 roubles.
41 Enterprises with 20 or more employees. State-owned and municipal enterprises, institutions and organizations.	41 Entreprises occupant 20 salariés et plus. Entreprises d'Etat et municipales, institutions et organisations.
42 Enterprises with 50 or more employees. State-owned and municipal enterprises, institutions and organizations.	42 Entreprises occupant 50 salariés et plus. Entreprises d'Etat et municipales, institutions et organisations.
43 Including mining, quarrying and electricity.	43 Y compris les industries extractives et l'électricité.
44 Full-time employees.	44 Salariés à plein temps.
45 Including family allowances paid directly by the employers.	45 Y compris les allocations familiales payées directement par l'employeur.
46 All legal economic units.	46 Ensemble des unités économiques dotées d'un statut juridique.
47 Enterprises with more than 20 employees.	47 Entreprises avec plus de 20 salariés.
48 Enterprises with more than 10 employees.	48 Entreprises avec plus de 10 salariés.
49 Including juveniles.	49 Y compris les jeunes gens.
50 Including payments subject to income tax.	50 Y compris les versements soumis à l'impôt sur le revenu.
51 Index of hourly wage rates (1990 = 100).	51 Indice des taux de salaires horaires (1990 = 100).
52 Index of hourly wage rates (Dec. 1995 = 100).	52 Indice des taux de salaires horaires (déc. 1995 = 100).
53 Average of less than 12 months.	53 Moyenne de moins de douze mois.
54 Including family allowances and mid- and end-of-year bonuses.	54 Y compris les allocations familiales et les primes de milieu et de fin d'année.
55 One month of each year. Private sector. Regular scheduled cash earnings. Establishments with 10 or more employees.	55 Un mois de chaque année. Secteur privé. Gains en espèce tarifés réguliers. Etablissements occupant 10 salariés stables ou plus.
56 Roubles; 1 tenge = 500 roubles.	56 Roubles; 1 tenge = 500 roubles.
57 Including the value of payments in kind.	57 Y compris la valeur des paiements en nature.
58 Excluding sugar and tea factories.	58 Non compris les fabriques de sucre et de thé.
59 Wage-earners on daily rates of pay.	59 Ouvriers rémunérés sur la base de taux de salaire journaliers.
60 Regular employees.	60 Salariés stables.
61 Index of hourly wage rates (1980 = 100).	61 Indices des taux de salaires horaires (1980 = 100).
62 Curaçao.	62 Curaçao.
63 Establishments with the equivalent of more than 2 full-time paid employees.	63 Etablissements occupant plus de l'équivalent de 2 salariés à plein temps.
64 Old córdobas; 1 new córdoba = 1,000 old córdobas.	64 Anciens córdobas; 1 nouveau córdoba = 1000 anciens córdobas.
65 Figures in thousands. Intís; 1 new sol = 1 million intís.	65 Données en milliers. Intís; 1 nouveau sol = 1 million d'intís.
66 Lima.	66 Lima.
67 Annual averages. Urban areas.	67 Moyennes annuelles. Régions urbaines.
68 Intís; 1 new sol = 1 million intís.	68 Intís; 1 nouveau sol = 1 million d'intís.
69 Computed on the basis of annual wages.	69 Calculés sur la base de salaires annuels.
70 Zlotyche; 1 new zloty = 10,000 zlotyche.	70 Zlotyche; 1 nouveau zloty = 10,000 zlotyche.
71 Figures in thousands. Zlotyche; 1 new zloty = 10,000 zlotyche.	71 Données en milliers. Zlotyche; 1 nouveau zloty = 10,000 zlotyche.
72 Roubles; 1 leu is equivalent to approximately 417 roubles.	72 Roubles; 1 leu équivaut à environ 417 roubles.
73 Rouble redenominated at 1 new rouble = 1000 old roubles.	73 Nouvelle dénomination du rouble: 1 nouveau rouble = 1000 anciens roubles.
74 Including electricity and water.	74 Y compris l'électricité et l'eau.
75 Earnings are exempted from income tax.	75 Les gains sont exempts de l'impôt sur le revenu.
76 Excluding enterprises with less than 25 employees.	76 Non compris les entreprises occupant moins de 25 salariés.
77 Excluding enterprises with less than 20 employees.	77 Non compris les entreprises occupant moins de 20 salariés.
78 Including employers' non-statutory contributions to certain funds.	78 Y compris les cotisations des employeurs à certains fonds privés.
79 Skilled wage earners.	79 Ouvriers qualifiés.
80 Unskilled wage earners.	80 Ouvriers non qualifiés.
81 Including holidays and sick-leave payments and the value of payments in kind.	81 Y compris les versements pour les vacances et congés de maladie et la valeur des paiements en nature.
82 Excluding holidays, sick-leave and overtime payments.	82 Non compris les versements pour les vacances, congés maladie ainsi que la rémunération des heures supplémentaires.
83 Roubles; 1 Tajik rouble = 100 roubles.	83 Roubles; 1 rouble Tajik = 100 roubles.
84 Average wage rates for normal/usual hours of work.	84 Taux de salaire moyens pour la durée normale/usuelle du travail.
85 Excluding public enterprises.	85 Non compris les entreprises publiques.

27
Wages in manufacturing
By hour, day, week or month [*cont.*]

Salaires dans les industries manufacturières
Par heure, jour, semaine ou mois [*suite*]

86 Roubles; 1 rouble is equivalent to 25 karbovanets.
87 Karbovanets: 1 hrivna is equivalent to 100,000 karbovanets.
88 Excluding overtime payments.
89 Excluding Northern Ireland.
90 Full-time employees on adult rates of pay.

91 Production workers.
92 Index of average monthly earnings (Oct.-Dec. 1984 = 100).
93 Including employers' contributions to pension, provident and other funds.

86 Roubles; 1 rouble équivaut à 25 karbovanets.
87 Karbovanets; 1 hrivna équivaut à 100 000 karbovanets.
88 Non compris la rémunération des heures supplémentaires.
89 Non compris l'Irlande du Nord.
90 Salariés à plein temps rémunérés sur la base de taux de salaire pour adultes.
91 Travailleurs à la production.
92 Indices des gains mensuels moyens (oct.-déc. 1984 = 100).
93 Y compris les cotisations des employeurs aux fonds de pension, de prévoyance et autres fonds.

28
Producers prices and wholesale prices
Prix à la production et des prix de gros
Index numbers: 1990 = 100
Indices : 1990 = 100

Country or area and groups	1993	1994	1995	1996	1997	1998	1999	Pays ou zone et groupes
Argentina								**Argentine**
Domestic supply[1][2]	227	226	241	248	249	241	232	Offre intérieure[1][2]
Domestic production	230	229	243	252	253	245	236	Production intérieure
Agricultural products[2]	243	223	245	283	254	237	189	Produits agricoles[2]
Industrial products[2][3]	228	232	247	248	252	249	241	Produits industriels[2][3]
Import products[3]	189	190	211	204	196	187	177	Produits importés[3]
Australia								**Australie**
Industrial products[2][3][4][5][6]	105	106	110	111	112	113	113	Produits industriels[2][3][4][5][6]
Exported goods[5][6]	97	100	101	97	104	101	97	Produits exportés[5][6]
Raw materials[5][6]	101	103	106	102	103	102	104	Matières premières[5][6]
Austria								**Autriche**
Domestic supply[2][7][8]	100	101	102	102	102	102	101	Offre intérieure[2][7][8]
Agricultural products	89	91	86	76	74	77	75	Produits agricoles
Producers' material[2][7][8]	97	98	97	98	98	97	96	Matériaux de production[2][7][8]
Consumers' goods[2][7]	103	105	107	106	106	107	106	Biens de consommation[2][7]
Capital goods[2][7]	99	100	100	101	101	100	98	Biens d'équipement[2][7]
Bangladesh								**Bangladesh**
Domestic supply[2][5][7][8]	110	115	121	127	128	135	144	Offre intérieure[2][5][7][8]
Agricultural products[2][5][7][9]	106	113	119	126	126	133	146	Produits agricoles[2][5][7][9]
Industrial products[2][3][5][7][9]	119	122	125	131	132	137	128	Produits industriels[2][3][5][7][9]
Raw materials[5][7]	110	107	117	120	123	...	134	Matières premières[5][7]
Finished goods[5][7]	117	118	130	133	132	...	126	Produits finis[5][7]
Belgium								**Belgique**
Domestic supply	98	99	102	102	104	103	...	Offre intérieure
Agricultural products[2]	102	104	106	107	111	109	107	Produits agricoles[2]
Industrial products	97	99	101	102	104	103	102	Produits industriels
Intermediate products	93	94	97	98	99	97	97	Produits intermédiaires
Consumers' goods	103	101	107	108	111	110	109	Biens de consommation
Capital goods	106	107	108	109	109	109	108	Biens d'équipement
Bolivia								**Bolivie**
Agricultural products	147	151	167	185	...	...	...	Produits agricoles
Industrial products	...	...	...	174	179	187	190	Produits industriels
Import products	149	167	179	194	...	...	...	Produits importés
Brazil								**Brésil**
Domestic supply[10][11]	4	100	159	169	181	189	220	Offre intérieure[10][11]
Agricultural products[10][11]	3	100	163	172	200	215	252	Produits agricoles[10][11]
Industrial products[10][11]	5	100	155	165	172	175	203	Produits industriels[10][11]
Raw materials[10][11]	4	100	150	162	179	179	212	Matières premières[10][11]
Producers' material[10][11]	4	100	153	165	176	180	209	Matériaux de production[10][11]
Consumers' goods[10][11]	4	100	169	177	192	212	243	Biens de consommation[10][11]
Capital goods[10]	4	100	155	172	176	178	198	Biens d'équipement[10]
Canada								**Canada**
Raw materials[12]	100	108	118	122	120	103	111	Matières premières[12]
Chile								**Chili**
Domestic supply	147	159	171	181	184	188	198	Offre intérieure
Domestic production	151	163	178	190	195	197	205	Production intérieure

28
Producers prices and wholesale prices
Index numbers: 1990 = 100 [cont.]
Prix à la production et des prix de gros
Indices : 1990 = 100 [suite]

Country or area and groups	1993	1994	1995	1996	1997	1998	1999	Pays ou zone et groupes
Agricultural products	150	163	180	193	197	204	200	Produits agricoles
Industrial products[8]	155	168	179	190	193	198	210	Produits industriels [8]
Import products	128	136	140	147	145	152	165	Produits importés
China, Hong Kong SAR†								**Chine, Hong Kong RAS†**
Industrial products[6][13]	106	108	111	111	111	109	107	Produits industriels[6][13]
Colombia								**Colombie**
Domestic supply[2][7]	164	198	229	262	308	...	...	Offre intérieure [2][7]
Domestic production[7]	170	208	238	276	325	...	...	Production intérieure[7]
Agricultural products[7]	172	236	267	307	378	...	...	Produits agricoles [7]
Industrial products[7]	165	191	223	255	295	...	...	Produits industriels [7]
Import products[7]	136	150	179	190	203	...	...	Produits importés [7]
Exported goods[7]	112	156	163	175	239	...	...	Produits exportés [7]
Raw materials[7]	176	201	225	257	302	...	...	Matières premières [7]
Intermediate products[7]	155	188	218	245	286	...	...	Produits intermédiaires [7]
Finished goods[7]	183	223	258	304	362	...	...	Produits finis[7]
Croatia								**Croatie**
Industrial products[14]	54	97	98	99	100	98	101	Produits industriels[14]
Producers' material[14]	56	97	97	97	100	97	98	Matériaux de production[14]
Consumers' goods[14]	49	92	94	98	100	99	99	Biens de consommation [14]
Capital goods[14]	62	103	100	102	100	101	105	Biens d'équipement[14]
Cyprus								**Chypre**
Industrial products	110	112	117	122	122	124	126	Produits industriels
Czech Republic								**République tchèque**
Agricultural products	113	120	129	140	146	147	131	Produits agricoles
Denmark								**Danemark**
Domestic supply[2][11]	99	100	103	104	106	105	106	Offre intérieure[2][11]
Domestic production[2][11]	100	100	103	105	107	106	107	Production intérieure[2][11]
Import products[11]	99	100	103	103	105	104	104	Produits importés [11]
Producers' material	98	100	103	104	106	105	106	Matériaux de production
Consumers' goods	99	101	103	104	106	106	106	Biens de consommation
Egypt								**Egypte**
Domestic supply[5][7][8]	144	153	163	176	183	186	188	Offre intérieure [5][7][8]
Raw materials[5][7]	124	104	113	133	140	133	132	Matières premières [5][7]
Intermediate products[5][7]	131	138	151	162	165	169	163	Produits intermédiaires [5][7]
Finished goods[5][7]	137	144	154	169	175	178	180	Produits finis [5][7]
Capital goods[5][7]	143	145	153	158	163	165	159	Biens d'équipement[5][7]
El Salvador								**El Salvador**
Domestic supply[15]	116	125	138	145	147	138	136	Offre intérieure[15]
Domestic production	123	131	133	147	148	142	147	Production intérieure
Import products	113	117	125	130	126	119	119	Produits importés
Exported goods	101	122	179	155	170	150	135	Produits exportés
Finland								**Finlande**
Domestic supply	105	106	107	106	108	106	106	Offre intérieure
Domestic production	101	103	104	102	104	105	104	Production intérieure
Import products	119	119	119	120	121	115	115	Produits importés
Raw materials	104	105	108	105	107	100	98	Matières premières

28
Producers prices and wholesale prices
Index numbers: 1990 = 100 [cont.]
Prix à la production et des prix de gros
Indices : 1990 = 100 [suite]

Country or area and groups	1993	1994	1995	1996	1997	1998	1999	Pays ou zone et groupes
Finished goods	108	109	110	110	111	107	106	Produits finis
Consumers' goods	109	110	107	108	109	112	113	Biens de consommation
Capital goods	104	105	105	105	108	109	109	Biens d'équipement
France								**France**
Agricultural products	89	88	89	89	90	90	87	Produits agricoles
Germany								**Allemagne**
Domestic supply[16][17]	102	102	104	104	105	103	102	Offre intérieure[16][17]
Domestic production[16][17]	99	100	103	100	101	100	...	Production intérieure[16][17]
Agricultural products[16][17]	91	92	92	91	93	88	84	Produits agricoles[16][17]
Import products[16][17]	96	97	97	96	97	97	97	Produits importés[16][17]
Exported goods[16][17]	101	102	103	103	105	105	104	Produits exportés[16][17]
Raw materials[16][17]	...	95	97	92	99	88	...	Matières premières[16][17]
Intermediate products[16][17]	...	...	...	100	101	100	...	Produits intermédiaires[16][17]
Finished goods[16][17]	104	105	106	107	108	108	...	Produits finis[16][17]
Producers' material[16][17]	101	101	103	102	103	103	...	Matériaux de production[16][17]
Consumers' goods[16][17]	104	105	106	107	108	108	...	Biens de consommation[16][17]
Capital goods[16][17]	104	105	106	107	108	109	...	Biens d'équipement[16][17]
Greece								**Grèce**
Domestic supply[18][19][20]	141	153	166	176	182	189	193	Offre intérieure[18][19][20]
Domestic production[19][20]	141	154	166	179	186	192	199	Production intérieure[19][20]
Agricultural products[19][21]	131	152	164	171	178	192	198	Produits agricoles[19][21]
Industrial products[19][20]	143	154	166	180	187	193	200	Produits industriels[19][20]
Import products[18][19][20]	144	157	166	170	174	183	184	Produits importés[18][19][20]
Exported goods[19][20][22]	135	147	163	174	179	185	185	Produits exportés[19][20][22]
Guatemala								**Guatemala**
Domestic supply	143	155	166	202	222	228	234	Offre intérieure
India								**Inde**
Domestic supply[23]	137	151	165	174	184	197	203	Offre intérieure[23]
Agricultural products[23]	147	158	173	189	201	225	237	Produits agricoles[23]
Industrial products[3][23]	133	146	162	169	176	184	188	Produits industriels[3][23]
Raw materials[23][24]	138	154	170	181	189	210	219	Matières premières[23][24]
Indonesia								**Indonésie**
Domestic supply[7][20]	115	121	135	145	158	319	355	Offre intérieure[7][20]
Domestic production	126	139	157	168	179	296	326	Production intérieure
Agricultural products[7]	131	156	186	209	233	393	533	Produits agricoles[7]
Industrial products[3][7]	124	131	146	151	156	258	325	Produits industriels[3][7]
Import products[7][20]	110	113	120	127	136	313	325	Produits importés[7][20]
Exported goods[7]	99	99	112	128	150	372	346	Produits exportés[7]
Raw materials[7]	103	108	125	141	161	357	352	Matières premières[7]
Intermediate products[7]	118	123	135	141	148	317	342	Produits intermédiaires[7]
Finished goods[7]	118	125	137	146	157	285	369	Produits finis[7]
Producers' material[7]	111	116	130	141	151	337	343	Matériaux de production[7]
Consumers' goods[7]	118	127	141	151	164	299	395	Biens de consommation[7]
Capital goods[7]	117	121	128	132	139	248	291	Biens d'équipement[7]

28
Producers prices and wholesale prices
Index numbers: 1990 = 100 [cont.]
Prix à la production et des prix de gros
Indices : 1990 = 100 [suite]

Country or area and groups	1993	1994	1995	1996	1997	1998	1999	Pays ou zone et groupes
Iran (Islamic Rep. of)								**Iran (Rép. islamique d')**
Domestic supply[29]	212	301	483	582	644	740	860	Offre intérieure[29]
Domestic production[29]	192	302	423	573	619	749	868	Production intérieure[29]
Agricultural products[29]	171	268	409	505	541	690	822	Produits agricoles[29]
Industrial products[29]	188	291	415	493	486	536	663	Produits industriels[29]
Import products[29]	193	314	477	668	731	798	910	Produits importés[29]
Exported goods[29]	167	248	356	429	466	445	600	Produits exportés[29]
Raw materials[29]	155	287	410	572	598	608	691	Matières premières[29]
Ireland								**Irlande**
Domestic supply[2,18,25]	107	108	110	111	110	112	112	Offre intérieure[2,18,25]
Agricultural products[2,25]	104	106	108	103	96	96	91	Produits agricoles[2,25]
Industrial products[2,3,25]	107	108	111	112	111	112	113	Produits industriels[2,3,25]
Capital goods[9]	107	110	113	115	117	120	123	Biens d'équipement[9]
Israel								**Israël**
Industrial products[20]	139	150	166	180	192	201	214	Produits industriels[20]
Italy								**Italie**
Domestic supply[2,20]	113	117	130	132	134	135	...	Offre intérieure[2,20]
Agricultural products[2,9]	105	109	122	127	124	...	...	Produits agricoles[2,9]
Industrial products[2,20]	114	119	130	133	136	...	...	Produits industriels[2,20]
Producers' material	111	116	122	124	125	123	...	Matériaux de production
Consumers' goods	115	120	129	133	134	136	...	Biens de consommation
Capital goods	112	116	130	133	137	139	...	Biens d'équipement
Japan								**Japon**
Domestic supply[2,7]	96	95	94	93	95	93	91	Offre intérieure[2,7]
Domestic production[7]	99	97	96	95	94	94	92	Production intérieure[7]
Agricultural products[7,9]	98	98	90	90	90	85	88	Produits agricoles[7,9]
Industrial products[7,9]	99	97	96	95	95	94	92	Produits industriels[7,9]
Import products[7,18]	96	98	104	103	102	92	93	Produits importés[7,18]
Exported goods[22]	102	105	108	103	98	94	93	Produits exportés[22]
Raw materials[7]	83	80	80	88	93	83	78	Matières premières[7]
Intermediate products[7]	95	93	93	92	94	92	90	Produits intermédiaires[7]
Finished goods[7]	99	98	96	95	96	95	93	Produits finis[7]
Producers' material[7]	94	92	92	92	94	91	89	Matériaux de production[7]
Consumers' goods[7]	100	99	97	96	97	96	95	Biens de consommation[7]
Capital goods[7]	99	97	95	93	93	93	90	Biens d'équipement[7]
Jordan								**Jordanie**
Domestic supply[2,6,7]	114	119	117	119	121	122	116	Offre intérieure[2,6,7]
Korea, Republic of								**Corée, République de**
Domestic supply	109	112	117	121	125	141	107	Offre intérieure
Agricultural products[9,26]	114	128	134	134	136	142	157	Produits agricoles[9,26]
Industrial products	108	109	115	117	121	139	134	Produits industriels
Raw materials	108	110	118	126	140	169	157	Matières premières
Intermediate products	106	108	116	117	123	153	139	Produits intermédiaires
Finished goods	111	116	118	121	125	143	142	Produits finis
Producers' material	107	108	116	118	125	155	141	Matériaux de production
Consumers' goods	112	118	121	126	131	144	147	Biens de consommation

28
Producers prices and wholesale prices
Index numbers: 1990 = 100 [cont.]
Prix à la production et des prix de gros
Indices : 1990 = 100 [suite]

Country or area and groups	1993	1994	1995	1996	1997	1998	1999	Pays ou zone et groupes
Capital goods	108	110	112	112	114	139	132	Biens d'équipement
Kuwait								**Koweït**
Domestic supply	108	108	110	115	114	112	...	Offre intérieure
Agricultural products	107	105	113	111	112	115	109	Produits agricoles
Raw materials	102	103	103	110	115	114	115	Matières premières
Intermediate products	115	110	111	119	123	121	114	Produits intermédiaires
Finished goods	104	106	109	112	107	106	107	Produits finis
Producers' material	108	111	113	112	111	110	107	Matériaux de production
Consumers' goods	119	115	117	126	128	128	126	Biens de consommation
Capital goods	87	92	95	98	89	84	86	Biens d'équipement
Latvia								**Lettonie**
Domestic supply[27]	217	254	284	323	336	343	329	Offre intérieure[27]
Lithuania								**Lituanie**
Domestic supply	19 650	28 445	36 504	42 796	44 611	41 636	42 912	Offre intérieure
Luxembourg								**Luxembourg**
Industrial products	94	94	98	94	95	97	93	Produits industriels
Import products	106	107	111	106	109	112	110	Produits importés
Exported goods	91	89	90	87	89	91	87	Produits exportés
Intermediate products	88	88	92	86	88	90	84	Produits intermédiaires
Consumers' goods[28]	113	101	103	104	104	104	104	Biens de consommation[28]
Capital goods	105	106	108	111	112	114	113	Biens d'équipement
Malaysia								**Malaisie**
Domestic supply	104	109	113	115	118	131	127	Offre intérieure
Domestic production	105	110	115	118	121	135	130	Production intérieure
Import products	103	103	104	104	107	117	116	Produits importés
Mexico								**Mexique**
Domestic supply[8 29]	142	151	214	287	363	379	439	Offre intérieure[8 29]
Agricultural products	159	167	206	287	333	349	434	Produits agricoles
Exported goods	104	117	213	314	311	317	372	Produits exportés
Raw materials	129	138	211	287	325	358	400	Matières premières
Consumers' goods[9 29]	150	158	222	288	349	404	455	Biens de consommation[9 29]
Capital goods[8 9 29]	143	150	207	266	312	363	418	Biens d'équipement[8 9 29]
Morocco								**Maroc**
Domestic supply	114	117	125	130	128	132	134	Offre intérieure
Agricultural products	118	119	132	140	134	138	139	Produits agricoles
Industrial products	112	116	120	124	126	129	130	Produits industriels
Netherlands								**Pays-Bas**
Industrial products	102	102	100	101	104	102	102	Produits industriels
Import products	91	92	100	104	109	102	106	Produits importés
Exported goods[22]	94	95	98	99	103	100	100	Produits exportés[22]
Raw materials	93	95	100	101	104	99	99	Matières premières
Intermediate products	99	100	100	101	104	100	100	Produits intermédiaires
Producers' material	92	94	100	103	106	100	102	Matériaux de production
Consumers' goods	107	105	100	102	104	103	104	Biens de consommation
Capital goods	102	104	100	101	103	105	106	Biens d'équipement

28

Producers prices and wholesale prices
Index numbers: 1990 = 100 [*cont.*]

Prix à la production et des prix de gros
Indices : 1990 = 100 [*suite*]

Country or area and groups	1993	1994	1995	1996	1997	1998	1999	Pays ou zone et groupes
New Zealand								**Nouvelle-Zélande**
Agricultural products[26 14]	...	...	101	99	100	99	99	Produits agricoles[26 14]
Industrial products[26 14 30]	...	...	102	101	100	101	102	Produits industriels[26 14 30]
Intermediate products[6 14 31]	...	...	99	100	100	101	102	Produits intermédiaires[6 14]
Finished goods[6 14 32]	...	...	99	99	100	101	101	Produits finis[6 14 32]
Norway								**Norvège**
Domestic supply	103	105	107	108	110	110	112	Offre intérieure
Import products[6]	97	98	99	98	97	98	96	Produits importés[6]
Exported goods[6]	88	86	88	95	97	86	96	Produits exportés[6]
Raw materials	92	96	98	97	101	100	101	Matières premières
Intermediate products	102	104	109	110	111	113	113	Produits intermédiaires
Finished goods	99	101	106	107	108	110	121	Produits finis
Consumers' goods	106	108	109	111	113	114	116	Biens de consommation
Pakistan								**Pakistan**
Domestic supply[2 5 7 8]	133	144	168	199	237	227	229	Offre intérieure[2 5 7 8]
Agricultural products[5 7]	140	165	184	206	221	236	237	Produits agricoles[5 7]
Industrial products[5 7]	131	151	165	185	189	195	201	Produits industriels[5 7]
Raw materials[5 7]	121	155	179	216	233	256	245	Matières premières[5 7]
Panama								**Panama**
Domestic supply[6]	105	108	111	113	111	106	109	Offre intérieure[6]
Peru								**Pérou**
Domestic supply	942	1 111	1 228	1 344	1 443	1 548	1 624	Offre intérieure
Domestic production	929	1 103	1 226	1 341	...	1 545	...	Production intérieure
Agricultural products[33]	1 050	1 330	1 468	1 592	1 763	2 061	...	Produits agricoles[33]
Industrial products[39]	888	1 035	1 155	1 264	1 355	1 437	...	Produits industriels[39]
Import products	948	1 035	1 116	1 230	1 295	1 376	1 513	Produits importés
Philippines								**Philippines**
Domestic supply[34]	...	127	131	143	...	151	172	Offre intérieure[34]
Romania								**Roumanie**
Industrial products	2 094	3 999	7 391	11 236	28 390	37 810	53 757	Produits industriels
Singapore								**Singapour**
Domestic supply[8]	89	87	87	85	81	79	80	Offre intérieure[8]
Domestic production[2 3 35]	83	80	81	77	70	67	67	Production intérieure[2 3 35]
Import products[18 35]	92	91	91	87	84	83	85	Produits importés[18 35]
Exported goods	86	83	81	78	73	73	73	Produits exportés
Slovenia								**Slovénie**
Agricultural products	778	858	972	1 077	1 149	1 198	1 206	Produits agricoles
Industrial products	862	1 015	1 145	1 222	1 297	1 374	1 404	Produits industriels
Producers' material	815	951	1 090	1 153	1 207	1 245	1 296	Matériaux de production
Consumers' goods	909	1 082	1 212	1 305	1 408	1 533	1 535	Biens de consommation
Capital goods	840	973	1 028	1 104	1 115	1 136	1 217	Biens d'équipement
South Africa								**Afrique du Sud**
Domestic supply[36]	129	139	152	164	175	181	190	Offre intérieure[36]
Domestic production[36]	131	143	157	168	181	188	197	Production intérieure[36]
Agricultural products	137	155	166	174	188	191	194	Produits agricoles

28
Producers prices and wholesale prices
Index numbers: 1990 = 100 [*cont.*]
Prix à la production et des prix de gros
Indices : 1990 = 100 [*suite*]

Country or area and groups	1993	1994	1995	1996	1997	1998	1999	Pays ou zone et groupes
Industrial products[3]	127	139	153	166	180	188	195	Produits industriels[3]
Import products	118	125	134	141	148	153	164	Produits importés
Spain								**Espagne**
Domestic supply[20]	106	111	118	120	121	120	121	Offre intérieure[20]
Producers' material	103	108	117	116	117	115	115	Matériaux de production
Consumers' goods	110	115	121	126	127	127	129	Biens de consommation
Capital goods	107	109	113	116	117	118	119	Biens d'équipement
Sri Lanka								**Sri Lanka**
Domestic supply	128	134	146	172	188	199	...	Offre intérieure
Domestic production	125	141	151	168	179	188	...	Production intérieure
Import products	116	121	134	151	161	161	...	Produits importés
Exported goods	141	134	148	208	222	247	...	Produits exportés
Producers' material	122	144	166	183	185	186	...	Matériaux de production
Consumers' goods	129	130	138	173	189	203	...	Biens de consommation
Capital goods	134	156	172	182	192	210	...	Biens d'équipement
Sweden								**Suède**
Domestic supply[2,20,37]	106	111	120	118	119	119	120	Offre intérieure[2,20,37]
Domestic production[2,20,37]	103	107	116	116	117	117	117	Production intérieure[2,20,37]
Import products[20,37]	112	117	124	120	122	121	124	Produits importés[20,37]
Exported goods[20,37]	108	113	126	120	121	120	119	Produits exportés[20,37]
Producers' material	106	111	121	119	119	119	118	Matériaux de production
Switzerland								**Suisse**
Domestic supply[2,8]	101	100	100	98	98	97	95	Offre intérieure[2,8]
Domestic production[2,8]	103	102	102	99	99	98	98	Production intérieure[2,8]
Agricultural products[2]	95	97	91	85	84	81	79	Produits agricoles[2]
Industrial products	103	102	103	101	100	99	98	Produits industriels
Import products[8]	96	96	96	92	94	92	90	Produits importés[8]
Raw materials	98	103	93	88	89	84	81	Matières premières
Consumers' goods	104	104	104	103	103	103	104	Biens de consommation
Thailand								**Thaïlande**
Domestic supply[2,11]	106	109	119	125	130	147	138	Offre intérieure[2,11]
Agricultural products	108	113	133	145	148	171	147	Produits agricoles
Industrial products[3]	105	108	117	120	125	139	136	Produits industriels[3]
Exported goods[11]	101	115	131	132	131	158	139	Produits exportés[11]
Raw materials	100	110	134	138	144	173	138	Matières premières
Intermediate products	108	109	118	123	128	150	144	Produits intermédiaires
Finished goods	110	115	121	126	135	165	156	Produits finis
Consumers' goods	111	119	123	130	137	160	148	Biens de consommation
TFYR Macedonia								**L'ex-R.y. Macédoine**
Domestic supply[38]	47	88	93	92	96	100	100	Offre intérieure[38]
Producers' material[38]	50	92	94	91	95	100	100	Matériaux de production[38]
Consumers' goods[38]	50	89	90	92	97	100	101	Biens de consommation[38]
Capital goods[38]	50	89	90	92	96	100	102	Biens d'équipement[38]
Trinidad and Tobago								**Trinité-et-Tobago**
Domestic supply	106	112	116	...	...	...	...	Offre intérieure

28
Producers prices and wholesale prices
Index numbers: 1990 = 100 [cont.]

Prix à la production et des prix de gros
Indices : 1990 = 100 [suite]

Country or area and groups	1993	1994	1995	1996	1997	1998	1999	Pays ou zone et groupes
Tunisia								**Tunisie**
Agricultural products	122	122	135	...	...	...	...	Produits agricoles
Industrial products	105	108	192	199	...	...	...	Produits industriels
Turkey								**Turquie**
Domestic supply[2 20 39]	399	880	1 638	2 881	5 238	9 000	13 776	Offre intérieure[2 20 39]
Agricultural products	398	788	1 638	3 054	5 707	10 659	15 117	Produits agricoles
Industrial products	388	890	1 611	2 746	4 959	8 265	12 991	Produits industriels
United Kingdom								**Royaume-Uni**
Agricultural products[4]	119	125	130	139	136	...	...	Produits agricoles[4]
Industrial products[3 4]	111	116	120	121	123	123	123	Produits industriels[3 4]
Raw materials	93	95	103	102	94	85	87	Matières premières
Finished goods	117	120	125	128	130	130	132	Produits finis
United States								**Etats-Unis**
Domestic supply[2]	102	104	107	110	110	107	108	Offre intérieure[2]
Agricultural products[2]	96	95	96	109	101	93	88	Produits agricoles[2]
Industrial products[2 40]	103	104	109	110	111	108	109	Produits industriels[2 40]
Raw materials	94	93	94	104	102	89	90	Matières premières
Intermediate products	102	103	109	110	110	107	108	Produits intermédiaires
Finished goods	105	105	107	110	111	110	112	Produits finis
Consumers' goods	104	104	106	110	110	109	111	Biens de consommation
Capital goods	107	109	111	113	113	112	112	Biens d'équipement
Uruguay								**Uruguay**
Domestic supply[2 8 41]	384	515	703	887	1 032	1 128	1 118	Offre intérieure[2 8 41]
Domestic production[41]	398	534	735	919	1 069	1 168	1 158	Production intérieure[41]
Agricultural products[41]	381	523	748	918	1 067	1 170	1 062	Produits agricoles[41]
Industrial products[8 41]	410	546	742	934	1 086	1 184	1 208	Produits industriels[8 41]
Venezuela								**Venezuela**
Domestic supply[7 8]	205	363	573	1 164	1 511	...	...	Offre intérieure[7 8]
Domestic production[7 8]	211	372	597	1 191	1 580	...	...	Production intérieure[7 8]
Agricultural products[7 8]	211	316	500	793	1 089	...	...	Produits agricoles[7 8]
Industrial products[7 8]	204	367	579	1 194	1 545	...	...	Produits industriels[7 8]
Import products[7 8]	189	341	514	1 098	1 339	...	...	Produits importés[7 8]
Yugoslavia								**Yougoslavie**
Domestic supply[42]	...	23	44	100	118	157	212	Offre intérieure[42]
Agricultural products[42]	...	24	44	100	118	157	226	Produits agricoles[42]
Industrial products[42]	...	33	53	100	119	150	216	Produits industriels[42]
Producers' material[42]	...	37	52	100	119	151	217	Matériaux de production[42]
Consumers' goods[42]	...	30	53	100	122	152	216	Biens de consommation[42]
Capital goods[42]	...	33	53	100	110	148	236	Biens d'équipement[42]
Zambia								**Zambie**
Domestic supply	...	1 743	2 603	...	...	...	...	Offre intérieure
Domestic production	...	1 475	2 081	...	...	...	...	Production intérieure
Exported goods	...	2 429	4 014	...	...	...	...	Produits exportés
Zimbabwe								**Zimbabwe**
Domestic supply	258	315	380	445	...	...	...	Offre intérieure

28
Producers prices and wholesale prices
Index numbers: 1990 = 100 [*cont.*]

Prix à la production et des prix de gros
Indices : 1990 = 100 [*suite*]

Source:
United Nations Secretariat, price statistics database of the
Statistics Division.

† For information on recent changes in country or
area nomenclature pertaining to former Czechoslovakia,
Germany, Hong Kong Special Administrative Region (SAR) of
China, Macao Special Administrative Region (SAR) of China,
SFR of Yugoslavia and the former USSR, see Annex I - Country
or area nomenclature, regional and other groupings.

1 Domestic agricultural products only.
2 Including exported products.
3 Manufacturing industry only.
4 Prices relate only to products for sale or transfer to other
  sectors or for use as capital equipment.

5 Annual average refers to average of 12 months beginning July
  of stated year.
6 Data are derived from quarterly figures.
7 Prices are collected from wholesalers.
8 Excluding mining and quarrying.
9 Including imported products.
10 Base: 1994=100.
11 Agricultural products and products of manufacturing
   industry.
12 Valued at purchasers' values.
13 Footnote text not found
14 Base: 1997=100.
15 San Salvador.
16 Footnote text not found
17 Base: 1991=100.
18 Imports are valued C.I.F.
19 Finished products only.
20 Excluding electricity, gas and water.
21 Including mining and quarrying.
22 Exports are valued F.O.B.
23 Annual average refers to average of 12 months beginning
   April of stated year.
24 Primary articles include food, non-food articles and
   minerals.
25 Excluding Value Added Tax.
26 Including marine foods.
27 Base: 1992=100.
28 Beginning 1994, durable goods only.
29 Mexico City.
30 Including all outputs of manufacturing.
31 Including all industrial inputs.
32 Including services.
33 Excluding fishing.
34 Manila.
35 Not a sub-division of the domestic supply index.
36 Excluding gold mining.
37 Excluding agriculture.
38 Base: 1998=100.
39 Excluding industrial finished goods.
40 Excluding foods and feeds production.
41 Montevideo.
42 Base: 1996=100.

Source:
Secrétariat de l'Organisation des Nations Unies, la base de
données pour les statistiques des prix de la Division de
statistique.

† Pour les modifications récentes de nomenclature
de pays ou de zone concernant l'Allemagne, Hong Kong, région
administrative spéciale (RAS) de Chine, Macao, région
administrative spéciale (RAS) de Chine,
l'ex-Tchécoslovaquie, l'ex-URSS et l'ex-Rfs de Yougoslavie,
voir annexe I - Nomenclature des pays ou des zones,
groupements régionaux et autres groupements.

1 Produits agricoles interiéurs seulement.
2 Y compris les produits exportés.
3 Industries manufacturières seulement.
4 Uniquement les prix des produits destinés à être vendus ou
  transférés à d'autres secteurs ou à être utilisés comme
  biens d'équipment.
5 La moyenne annuelle est la moyenne de douze mois de compter
  à partir de juillet de ladite année.
6 Données tirées de chiffres trimestriels.
7 Prix recueillis auprès des grossistes.
8 Non compris les industries extractives.
9 Y compris les produits importés.
10 Base: 1994=100.
11 Produits agricoles et produits des industries
   manufacturières.
12 A la valeur d'acquisition.
13 Le texte de la note n'est pas trouvé
14 Base: 1997=100.
15 San Salvador.
16 Le texte de la note n'est pas trouvé
17 Base : 1991=100.
18 Les importations sont évaluées c.a.f.
19 Produits finis uniquement.
20 Non compris l'électricité, le gaz et l'eau.
21 Y compris les industries extractives.
22 Les exportations sont évaluées f.o.b.
23 La moyenne annuelle est la moyenne de 12 mois de compter à
   partir d'avril de ladite année.
24 Les articles primaires comprennent des articles des produits
   alimentaires, non-alimentaires et des minéraux.
25 Non compris taxe sur la valeur ajoutée.
26 Y compris l'alimentation marine.
27 Base : 1992=100.
28 De compter à partir de 1994, biens durables seulement.
29 Mexico.
30 Y compris toute la production du secteur manufacturière.
31 Tous les intrants industriels.
32 Y compris services.
33 Non compris la pêche.
34 Manille.
35 N'est pas un élément de l'indice de l'offre intérieure.
36 Non compris l'extraction de l'or.
37 Non compris l'agriculture.
38 Base : 1998=100.
39 Non compris les produits finis industriels.
40 Non compris les produits alimentaires et d'affouragement.
41 Montevideo.
42 Base : 1996=100.

29
Consumer price index numbers
Indices des prix à la consommation
All items and food; 1990 = 100
Ensemble des prix et alimentation; 1990 = 100

Country or area Pays ou zone	1989	1990	1991	1992	1993	1994	1995	1996	1997	1998
Albania[2]										
Albanie[2]	22[1]	23[1]	31	100	185	227	244	276	...	...
Food[2]										
Aliments[2]	21[1]	21[1]	45[1]	100	187	214	229	263	...	...
Algeria										
Algérie	83	100	126	164	200	263	338	407	431	458
Food										
Aliments	81	100	121	152	189	266	343	417	437	467
American Samoa[3]										
Samoa américaines[3]	93	100	104	109	109	111	113	118	...	...
Food										
Aliments	94	100	104	108	107	108	109	112	...	...
Angola[5]										
Angola[5]	...	...	100[4]	399[4]	5 905[4]	61 982[4]	2 771[6]	117 653[6]	375 531[6]	...
Food[5]										
Aliments[5]	...	...	100[4]	409[4]	6 856[4]	70 425[4]	2 533[6]	100 167[6]	201 844[6]	...
Anguilla										
Anguilla	95	100	105	108	111	116	117	121	122	125
Food										
Aliments	95	100	104	107	111	113	116	119	120	119
Argentina[5 7]										
Argentine[5 7]	4	100	272	339	375	391	404	405	407	411
Food[5 7]										
Aliments[5 7]	5	100	261	340	375	380	391	389	387	393
Aruba										
Aruba	95	100	106	110	115	123	127[8]	131	135	137
Food										
Aliments	92	100	105	109	113	120	125[8]	130	134	136
Australia										
Australie	93	100[8]	103	104	106	108	113	116	116	117
Food										
Aliments	96	100[8]	104	105	107	109	113	116	119	122
Austria										
Autriche	97	100	103	108	111	115	117	120	121[8]	122
Food										
Aliments	97	100	104	108	111	113	113	114	116[8]	118
Azerbaijan[9]										
Azerbaïdjan[9]	...	...	1	8	100	1 764	9 025	10 817	11 218	11 131
Food[9 10]										
Aliments[9 10]	...	...	1	7	100	1 793	9 369	11 016	10 964	10 817
Bahamas										
Bahamas	96	100	107	113	117	118	121[8]	122	...	...
Food										
Aliments	93	100	109	111	112	111	114[8]	116	...	...
Bahrain										
Bahreïn	99	100	101	101	103	104	107	107	109	109
Food										
Aliments	100	100	102	102	102	101	107	108	107	108
Bangladesh[6 11]										
Bangladesh[6 11]	...	...	...	...		100	110	113	119	129
Food[6 11]										
Aliments[6 11]	...	...	...	...	...	100	111	113	118	130
Barbados										
Barbade	97	100	106	113	114	114	117[8]	120	129	127

29
Consumer price index numbers
All items and food; 1990 = 100 [cont.]
Indices des prix à la consommation
Ensemble des prix et alimentation; 1990 = 100 [suite]

Country or area Pays ou zone	1989	1990	1991	1992	1993	1994	1995	1996	1997	1998
Food Aliments	96	100	105	105	105	105	110[8]	115	130	125
Belarus[2] Bélarus[2]	5	5	9	100	1 290	29 950	242 300	370 000	606 300	1 049 000
Food[2] Aliments[2]	4	5	9	100	1 520	37 480	285 500	427 000	725 400	1 275 700
Belgium Belgique	97	100	103[8]	106	109	111	113	115[8]	117	118
Food Aliments	96	100	102[8]	102	101	103	104	105[8]	107	109
Belize Belize	97	100	106	102[4]	104[4]	107[4]	110[4]	117[4]	...	...
Food Aliments	98	100	106[10]	103[4 10]	105[4 10]	106[4 10]	109[4 10]	116[4 10]	...	...
Benin[2 5] Bénin[2 5]	...	...	...	100[12]	101	140	161	166	173	...
Food[5] Aliments[5]	101	100	100	100[2]	100[2 12]	135[2]	161[2]	...	189[2]	...
Bermuda Bermudes	94	100	104	107	110	112	115	118	121	123
Food Aliments	95	100	103	104	105	107	110	113	116	119
Bhutan Bhoutan	91	100	112	130	145	155	170	185	197	217
Food[10] Aliments[10]	92	100	113	134	145	150	165	180	187	208
Bolivia[13] Bolivie[13]	85	100	121	136	148	159	176	197	207	223
Food[13] Aliments[13]	84	100	121	138	147	161	180	205	212	224
Botswana Botswana	90	100	112	130[8]	149	164	181	200[8]	217	231
Food Aliments	90	100	112	133[8]	151	165	183	207[8]	228	242
Brazil Brésil	3	2[2]	10[2]	100[2]	2 027[2]	100[6]	166[6]	192[6]	206[6]	212[6]
Food Aliments	4	2[2]	9[2]	100[2]	2 049[2]	100[6]	159[6]	168[6]	169[6]	174[6]
British Virgin Islands Iles Vierges britanniques	95	100	106	110	113	117	123	129	...	...
Food Aliments	97	100	107	109	109	115	120	124	...	...
Brunei Darussalam Brunéi Darussalam	98[11]	100[11]	102[14]	103	107	110	117	119	121	120
Food Aliments	100[11]	100[11]	103[14]	103	106	107	110	113	118	118
Bulgaria Bulgarie	...	100	439	787	1 228	2 296	3 722	8 300	98 132	120 008
Food Aliments	...	100	475	830	1 296	2 484	3 968	8 664	106 100	128 552
Burkina Faso[5] Burkina Faso[5]	101	100	103	101	101	126	136	144	...	...

29
Consumer price index numbers
All items and food; 1990 = 100 [cont.]
Indices des prix à la consommation
Ensemble des prix et alimentation; 1990 = 100 [suite]

Country or area Pays ou zone	1989	1990	1991	1992	1993	1994	1995	1996	1997	1998
Food[5] Aliments[5]	101	100	110	101	96	113	126	145	...	...
Burundi[5] **Burundi[5]**	**93**	**100**	**109**	**111**[8]	**122**	**140**	**166**	...	...	...
Food[5] Aliments[5]	93	100	107	105[8]	121	143	171	...	...	...
Cambodia[5 15] **Cambodge[5 15]**	...	...	...	...	...	...	**100**	**107**	**116**	**133**
Food[5 15] Aliments[5 15]	...	...	...	...	...	...	100	108	115[10]	131[10]
Cameroon[5 16] **Cameroun[5 16]**	**98**[12]	**100**[12]	**102**[17]	**103**[17]	...	**115**	**127**	...	...	...
Food[5 16] Aliments[5 16]	93[12]	83[12]	83[17]	81[17]	...	87	103	...	...	...
Canada **Canada**	**95**	**100**	**106**	**107**	**109**	**109**	**112**	**114**	**115**	**116**
Food Aliments	96	100	105	104	106	107	109	111	112	114
Cape Verde **Cap-Vert**	**92**	**100**	**106**	**112**	**119**	**123**	**133**	**141**	**153**	...
Food Aliments	89	100	109	119	123	126	140	148	162	...
Cayman Islands **Iles Caïmanes**	**93**	**100**	**108**	**111**	**114**	**118**	**120**	**123**	**126**	...
Food Aliments	92	100	102	103	106	108	111	114	119	...
Central African Rep.[3 5] **Rép. centrafricaine[3 5]**	**100**	**100**	**97**	**96**	**94**	**117**	**139**	**144**	**146**	...
Food[5] Aliments[5]	99	100	96	95	91	113	139	147	148	...
Chad[5] **Tchad[5]**	**100**	**100**	**104**	**101**	**92**	**132**	**143**	**161**	**170**	**193**
Food[5] Aliments[5]	100	100	109	104	90	136	143	164	178	184
Chile[5] **Chili[5]**	**79**	**100**	**122**	**141**	**159**	**177**	**191**	**205**	**218**	**229**
Food[5] Aliments[5]	79	100	126	148	165	181	196	208	222	231
China †† **Chine ††**	**99**	**100**	**105**	**113**	**133**	**166**	**194**	**210**	**215**	**214**
Food Aliments	99	100	103	114	132	174	214	230	230	223
China, Hong Kong SAR† **Chine, Hong Kong RAS†**	**91**	**100**	**111**	**122**	**133**	**144**	**157**	**167**	**177**	**182**
Food Aliments	91	100	112	122	131	140	150	155	161	164
China, Macao SAR †[3] **Chine, Macao RAS †[3]**	**93**	**100**	**110**	**118**	**126**	**134**[8]	**145**	**152**	**158**[8]	**158**
Food Aliments	92	100	109	118	126	135[8]	146	152	158[8]	159
Colombia[18] **Colombie[18]**	**77**[8]	**100**	**130**	**167**	**203**	**250**	**302**	**364**	**432**	**520**
Food[18] Aliments[18]	79[8]	100	130	168	194	234	280	326	379	466

29
Consumer price index numbers
All items and food; 1990 = 100 [cont.]
Indices des prix à la consommation
Ensemble des prix et alimentation; 1990 = 100 [suite]

Country or area Pays ou zone	1989	1990	1991	1992	1993	1994	1995	1996	1997	1998
Congo[5] Congo[5]	97	100	98	94	99	141	154	170	...	...
Food[5] Aliments[5]	99	100	96	88	94	139	149	159	...	...
Cook Islands[5] Iles Cook[5]	95	100	106	110	118	121	122	121	121	121
Food[5 19] Aliments[5 19]	96	100	102	106	113	115	115	114	114	116
Costa Rica[20] Costa Rica[20]	84	100	129	157	172	195	241	283	320	358
Food[20] Aliments[20]	85[21]	100[21]	126[21]	156[21]	173[21]	197[21]	100[15 22]	119[15 22]	136[15 22]	156[15 22]
Côte d'Ivoire[4 5 18] Côte d'Ivoire[4 5 18]	99[12]	98[12]	100	104	107	135[8]	...	...	...	...
Food[4 5 18] Aliments[4 5 18]	99[12]	98[12]	100	103	107	131[8]	...	...	...	...
Croatia Croatie	14	100	224	1 646	26 104	54 088	56 251	58 670	61 076	64 985
Food Aliments	16	100	223	1 832	26 707	53 696	54 112	55 844	58 301	62 220
Cyprus Chypre	96	100	105	112	117	123[8]	126	130	135	138
Food Aliments	96	100	107	115	117	126[8]	128	132	139	145
Czech Republic République tchèque	...	100	157	174	210	231[8]	252	275	298	330
Food Aliments	...	...	144	158	184	201[8]	222	240	252	268
Denmark Danemark	98	100	102	105	106	108	110	113	115	117
Food Aliments	100	100	101	102	102	105	108	110	114	116
Dominica Dominique	97	100	106	111	113	113	115	116	119	...
Food Aliments	102	100	105	114	116	112	114	116	120	...
Dominican Republic[23] Rép. dominicaine[23]	67	100	147	153	161	175	197	207	224	...
Food Aliments	67	100	149	149	154	164	188	197	212	...
Ecuador Equateur	68	100	149	230	333	424	522	649	847	1 153
Food[10] Aliments[10]	68	100	148	229	324	405	489	598	814	1 146
Egypt Egypte	86	100	120	136	153	165	179	192	200	208
Food[10] Aliments[10]	86	100	117	127	136	149	164	177	184	191
El Salvador[13] El Salvador[13]	81	100	114	127	151	167	184	202	211	...
Food[10 13] Aliments[10 13]	79	100	118	133	167	193	206	233	244	...
Estonia Estonie	...	...	100[4]	1 176[4]	2 232[4]	3 296[4]	4 252[4]	5 232[4]	5 817[4]	108[24]

29
Consumer price index numbers
All items and food; 1990 = 100 [*cont.*]
Indices des prix à la consommation
Ensemble des prix et alimentation; 1990 = 100 [*suite*]

Country or area Pays ou zone	1989	1990	1991	1992	1993	1994	1995	1996	1997	1998
Food Aliments	...	...	100[4]	1 037[4]	1 804[4]	2 451[4]	2 838[4]	3 355[4]	3 540[4]	105[24]
Ethiopia[5] **Ethiopie**[5]	**95**[3]	**100**[3]	**136**[3]	**150**[3]	**155**[3]	**167**[3]	**184**[3]	**178**[3 12]	**100**[24 25]	**101**[24]
Food[5] Aliments[5]	95	100	141	158	160	177	199	189[12]	100[19 24]	102[19]
Faeroe Islands **Iles Féroé**	**95**	**100**	**104**	**106**	**111**	**114**	**118**	**121**	...	...
Food Aliments	95	100	105	110	116	123	133	138	...	...
Falkland Is. (Malvinas)[5 25] **Iles Falkland (Malvinas)**[5 25]	...	**100**[8]	**105**	**112**	**113**	**114**	**117**	**123**	**125**	...
Food[5] Aliments[5]	94	100[8]	104	110	116	119	124	128	124	...
Fiji **Fidji**	**93**	**100**	**107**	**112**	**118**	**119**[8]	**121**	**125**	**129**	**136**
Food Aliments	92	100	102	101	108	109[8]	109	112	117	126
Finland **Finlande**	**94**	**100**	**104**	**107**	**110**	**111**	**112**	**113**	**114**	**116**
Food[26] Aliments[26]	96	100	103	103	102	102	95	93	94	96
France **France**	**97**	**100**[8]	**103**	**106**	**108**	**110**	**112**	**114**	**115**	**116**
Food Aliments	96	100[8]	103	104	104	105	106	107	109	111
French Guiana **Guyane française**	**97**[5]	**100**	...	**105**	**107**	**109**	**111**	**112**	**113**	**114**
Food Aliments	96[5]	100	...	102	104	105	107	108	109	111
French Polynesia **Polynésie française**	**99**[8]	**100**	**101**	**102**	**104**	**106**	**107**	**108**	**109**	**111**
Food Aliments	98[8]	100	99	100	102	105	107	108	111	112
Gabon[4 5] **Gabon**[4 5]	**93**	**100**[12]	**100**	**91**	**91**	**124**	**136**[12]	**142**[12]	...	...
Food[4 5] Aliments[4 5]	91	101[12]	100	84	85	111	120[12]	128[12]	...	...
Gambia[5] **Gambie**[5]	**89**	**100**	**119**	**119**	**127**	**129**	**138**	**139**	**143**	...
Food[5] Aliments[5]	88	100	108	118	128	126	137	139	141	...
Georgia[6] **Géorgie**[6]	...	...	...	...	...	**100**	**263**	**366**	**393**	...
Food[6 10] Aliments[6 10]	...	...	...	...	...	100	240	319	335	...
Germany[4] **Allemagne**[4]	...	...	**100**	**105**	**110**	**113**	**115**	**116**	**119**	**120**
Food[4 27] Aliments[4 27]	...	...	100	102	102	101	102	102	104	105
Ghana **Ghana**	**73**	**100**	**118**	**130**	**163**	**203**	**323**	**474**	**606**	...
Food Aliments	71	100	109	120	150	189	307	417	...	...

29
Consumer price index numbers
All items and food; 1990 = 100 [cont.]
Indices des prix à la consommation
Ensemble des prix et alimentation; 1990 = 100 [suite]

Country or area Pays ou zone	1989	1990	1991	1992	1993	1994	1995	1996	1997	1998
Gibraltar **Gibraltar**	**94**	**100**	**108**	**115**	**121**	**121**	**124**	**126**	**128**	**130**
Food Aliments	94	100	107	112	114	113	114	118	120	123
Greece **Grèce**	**83**	**100**	**120**	**139**	**159**	**176**	**191**	**207**	**219**	**229**
Food Aliments	83	100	118	132	145	164	178	190	198	207
Greenland **Groenland**	**95**	**100**	**104**	**106**	**107**	**108**	**109**	**111**	**112**	**113**
Food[10] Aliments[10]	94	100	105	106	107	108	113	118	120	122
Grenada **Grenade**	**97**	**100**	**103**	**107**	**110**	**112**	**115**	**118**	**120**	...
Food[10] Aliments[10]	96	100	102	102	107	112	118	123	123	...
Guadeloupe[13] **Guadeloupe[13]**	**97**	**100**	**103**	**106**	**108**[8 28]	**110**	**112**	**114**	**115**	...
Food[13] Aliments[13]	97	100	102	103	106[8 28]	108	111	113	114	...
Guam **Guam**	**88**	**100**	**110**	**121**	**132**	**154**	**162**	...	...	...
Food Aliments	85	100	118	136	160	208	226	...	...	...
Guatemala[5] **Guatemala[5]**	**71**	**100**	**135**	**149**	**169**	**190**	**206**	**229**	**250**	**266**
Food[5] Aliments[5]	68	100	132	142	162	189	205	229	244	256
Guinea[5] **Guinée[5]**	**84**	**100**	**119**	**140**	**149**	**156**	**164**	**169**	...	...
Food[5] Aliments[5]	78	100	116	135	148	155	167	169	...	...
Guyana[13] **Guyana[13]**	**167**[12 16]	**62**[4 12]	**100**[4]	**126**[4]	**138**[4]	**100**[6]	**112**[6]	**120**[6]	**124**[6]	**130**[6]
Food[13] Aliments[13]	170[12 16]	65[4 12]	100[4]	125[4]	133[4]	100[6]	117[6]	126[6]	127[6]	132[6]
Haiti[7] **Haïti[7]**	**83**	**100**	**115**	**131**	**166**	**243**	**228**	...	...	...
Food[7] Aliments[7]	81	100	115	126	160	227	216	...	...	...
Honduras **Honduras**	**81**	**100**	**134**	**146**	**161**	**196**	**254**	**315**	**378**	**430**
Food Aliments	79	100	144	153	172	219	281	351	420	469
Hungary **Hongrie**	**78**	**100**	**135**	**166**[8]	**203**	**242**	**310**	**383**	**453**	**518**
Food Aliments	74	100	122	146[8]	188	232	304	357	419	480
Iceland[5] **Islande[5]**	**87**	**100**	**107**	**111**	**115**	**117**	**119**	**122**	**124**	**126**
Food[5 19] Aliments[5 19]	89	100	103	104	106	104	107	110	114	117
India[29] **Inde[29]**	**92**[8]	**100**	**114**	**127**	**136**	**150**	**165**	**180**	**193**	**218**
Food[29] Aliments[29]	92[8]	100	116	131	139	155	173	188	199	229

29
Consumer price index numbers
All items and food; 1990 = 100 [cont.]
Indices des prix à la consommation
Ensemble des prix et alimentation; 1990 = 100 [suite]

Country or area Pays ou zone	1989	1990	1991	1992	1993	1994	1995	1996	1997	1998
Indonesia **Indonésie**	93	100[8]	109	118	129	140	153	165	176	150
Food Aliments	93	100[8]	108	116	125	138	156	171	186	191
Iran (Islamic Rep. of) **Iran (Rép. islamique d')**	93	100	118	148	180	236	353	455	534	637
Food[10] Aliments[10]	97	100	119	159	193	255	405	506	557	689
Ireland **Irlande**	97	100[8]	103	106	108	111	113	115	117[8]	120
Food Aliments	98	100[8]	101	103	104	107	110	113	114[8]	119
Isle of Man **Ile de Man**	92	100	107	112	115	118	121	125	127	131
Food Aliments	91	100	108	113	118	121	126	133	135	143
Israel **Israël**	85	100	119	133	148[8]	166	183	203	222	234
Food Aliments	92	100	114	129	135[8]	150	161	177	193	204
Italy **Italie**	94	100	106[8]	112	117	121	128	133[8]	136	138
Food Aliments	94	100	107[8]	112[30]	114[30]	118[30]	126[30]	131[8][30]	131[30]	132[30]
Jamaica **Jamaïque**	82	100	151	268	327	442	530	670	734	798
Food Aliments	82	100	155	275	333	461	554	688	742	794
Japan **Japon**	97	100	103	105	106	107	107	107	109	110
Food Aliments	96	100	105	105	107	107	106	106	108	109
Jordan **Jordanie**	86	100	108	113	116	120	123	131	135	141
Food Aliments	83	100	111	114	117	124	126	135	144	151
Kazakhstan[2] **Kazakhstan**[2]	...	...	3[1]	100	2 265[1]	13 899	38 389	53 476	62 776	67 246
Food[2] Aliments[2]	...	...	5[1]	100	2 297[1]	13 465	35 521	47 882	50 946	53 208
Kenya[5][18] **Kenya**[5][18]	90	100[14]	119	155	225	291	297	319	357	378
Food[5][18] Aliments[5][18]	92	100[14]	124	167	242	317	310	335	388	402
Kiribati[5] **Kiribati**[5]	96	100	106	110	117	123	127	127	127[12]	...
Food[5] Aliments[5]	97	100	104	107	113	117	123	121	120[12]	...
Korea, Republic of **Corée, République de**	92	100	109	116	122	129	135	142	148	159
Food Aliments	91	100	113	119	124	135	140	146	151	164
Kuwait[31] **Koweït**[31]	100	110[12]	120[12]	119	120	123	126	130	131	...

29

Consumer price index numbers
All items and food; 1990 = 100 [*cont.*]

Indices des prix à la consommation
Ensemble des prix et alimentation; 1990 = 100 [*suite*]

Country or area Pays ou zone	1989	1990	1991	1992	1993	1994	1995	1996	1997	1998
Food[31] Aliments[31]	100	112[12]	124[12]	121	115	117	120	127	128	...
Kyrgyzstan[2] **Kirghizistan[2]**	...	...	...	**100**	**1 186**	**3 330**	**4 776**	**6 303**	**7 780**	**8 593**
Food[2] Aliments[2]	...	...	...	100	1 066	2 785	3 898	5 504	6 874	7 593
Latvia[4] **Lettonie[4]**	...	...	**100**	**1 052**	**2 199**[8]	**2 989**	**3 736**	**4 393**	**4 767**	**4 987**
Food[4] Aliments[4]	...	...	100	848	1 104[8]	1 470	1 708	1 920	1 969	1 995
Lebanon[5] **Liban[5]**	**61**	**100**	**148**	**268**	**310**	**331**	**413**	**438**	**447**	...
Food[5] Aliments[5]	64	100	143	258	301	324	350	379	377	...
Lesotho **Lesotho**	**90**	**100**	**118**	**138**	**157**	**168**	**185**	**202**	...	...
Food[10] Aliments[10]	90	100	118	146	161	171	193	214	...	...
Lithuania **Lituanie**	**100**[31]	...	**100**[4]	**1 121**[4]	**5 718**[4]	**9 845**[4]	**13 749**[4]	**17 135**[4]	**18 656**[4]	**19 602**[4]
Food Aliments	100[31]	...	100[4]	1 038[4]	5 204[4]	8 380[4]	11 679[4]	14 812[4]	15 815[4]	16 036[4]
Luxembourg **Luxembourg**	...	**100**	**103**	**106**	**110**	**113**	**115**	**116**	**118**	**119**
Food Aliments	96	100[8]	103	104	104	105	108	109	110[8]	113
Madagascar[3 5 32] **Madagascar[3 5 32]**	**90**	**100**	**109**	**124**	**137**	**190**	**283**	**339**	**355**	**377**
Food[5 32] Aliments[5 32]	88	100	109	127	138	193	291	346	360	382
Malawi **Malawi**	**89**[3 5 18]	**100**	**108**	**133**	**164**	**221**	**404**	**556**	**607**	...
Food Aliments	89[5 18]	100	108	139	176	243	469	681	737	...
Malaysia **Malaisie**	**97**	**100**[14]	**104**	**109**	**113**	**117**	**121**	**126**	**129**	**136**
Food Aliments	96	100[14]	105	112	114	120	126	134	139	151
Maldives[5] **Maldives[5]**	**97**	**100**	**115**	**134**	**161**	**167**	**176**	**187**	**201**	**196**
Food[5 10] Aliments[5 10]	94	100	113	129	152	158	177	193	231	219
Mali **Mali**	**99**	**100**	**101**	**96**	**95**	**117**	...	**142**	...	...
Food Aliments	99	100	103	94	93	116	...	147	...	...
Malta **Malte**	**97**	**100**	**103**	**104**[8]	**109**	**113**	**118**	**120**[8]	**124**	**127**
Food Aliments	96	100	102	102[8]	107	111	115	119[8]	121	123
Marshall Islands[2 5] **Iles Marshall[2 5]**	...	...	...	**100**	**105**	**111**	**119**	...	...	...
Food[2 5] Aliments[2 5]	...	...	...	100	103	...	...	...	...	...

29
Consumer price index numbers
All items and food; 1990 = 100 [*cont.*]
Indices des prix à la consommation
Ensemble des prix et alimentation; 1990 = 100 [*suite*]

Country or area Pays ou zone	1989	1990	1991	1992	1993	1994	1995	1996	1997	1998
Martinique										
Martinique	**96**	**100**	**103**	**107**	**111**[8]	**113**	**116**	**117**	**119**	**120**
Food[10]										
Aliments[10]	96	100	103	107	109[8]	111	113	114	116	119
Mauritius										
Maurice	**88**	**100**	**107**	**112**[8]	**124**	**133**	**141**	**150**	**160**[8]	**171**
Food										
Aliments	90	100	104	100[2]	114[2]	124[2]	132[2]	139[2]	146[2 8]	158[2]
Mexico										
Mexique	**79**	**100**	**123**	**142**	**156**	**166**	**225**	**302**	**364**	**422**
Food[10]										
Aliments[10]	80	100	120	134	142	150	209	296	352	409
Morocco										
Maroc	**94**[14]	**100**	**108**	**114**	**120**	**126**	**134**	**138**	**139**	**143**
Food[10]										
Aliments[10]	93[14]	100	109	116	123	132	143	144	142	146
Myanmar[5]										
Myanmar[5]	**85**	**100**	**132**	**161**	**213**	**264**	**330**	**384**	**498**	...
Food[5]										
Aliments[5]	84	100	138	168	234	281	354	421	548	...
Namibia[5]										
Namibie[5]	**90**	**100**	**113**	**133**	**144**	**159**	**175**	**189**	**206**	**219**
Food[5]										
Aliments[5]	86	100	106	126	135	152	170	181	195	201
Nepal										
Népal	**91**	**100**	**116**	**135**	**146**	**158**	**170**	**186**	**193**	...
Food										
Aliments	93[8]	100	118	140	147	159	171	189	194	...
Netherlands										
Pays-Bas	**98**	**100**[14]	**103**	**106**	**109**	**112**	**114**	**117**[8]	**119**	**122**
Food[10]										
Aliments[10]	98	100[14]	103	106	107	109	109	110[8]	112	114
Netherlands Antilles[5]										
Antilles néerlandaises[5]	**96**	**100**	**104**	**105**	**108**	**110**	**113**	**117**	**120**	**122**
Food[5]										
Aliments[5]	93	100	107	110	114	117	122	129	132	113
New Caledonia[5]										
Nouvelle-Calédonie[5]	**98**	**100**	**104**	**107**	**109**[8]	**113**	**114**	**116**	**118**	**119**
Food[5]										
Aliments[5]	100	100	103	106	110[8]	114	115	118	123	124
New Zealand										
Nouvelle-Zélande	**94**	**100**	**103**	**104**	**105**	**107**	**111**	**113**	**115**	**116**
Food										
Aliments	93	100	101	101	102	102	103	105	107	110
Nicaragua										
Nicaragua	**1**	**100**	**2 842**	**3 767**	**4 534**	**4 886**	**111**[6]	**124**[6]	**135**[6]	**153**[6]
Food										
Aliments	1	100	2 851	3 503	3 904	4 208	112[6]	125[6]	136[6]	156[6]
Nigeria[33]										
Nigéria[33]	**93**	**100**	**113**	**163**	**257**	**403**	**688**	**901**	**975**	**1 076**
Food[33]										
Aliments[33]	96	100	112	164	259	380	654	851	924	985
Niue										
Nioué	**94**	**100**	**105**	**110**	**112**	**114**	**115**	...	...	...

29
Consumer price index numbers
All items and food; 1990 = 100 [cont.]
Indices des prix à la consommation
Ensemble des prix et alimentation; 1990 = 100 [suite]

Country or area Pays ou zone	1989	1990	1991	1992	1993	1994	1995	1996	1997	1998
Food Aliments	94	100	104	107	110	111	113	...	...	...
Northern Mariana Islands[5] **Iles Marianas du Nord**[5]	**116**	**100**	**107**	**117**	**122**	**125**	**128**	**132**	**133**	**133**
Food[5] Aliments[5]	99	100	107	112	116	118	119	121	121	120
Norway **Norvège**	**96**	**100**	**103**	**106**	**108**	**110**	**113**	**114**	**117**	**120**
Food Aliments	97	100	102	103	102	103	105	107	110	116
Oman[5] **Oman**[5]	...	**100**	**105**	**106**	**107**	**106**	**105**	**105**	**105**	**104**
Food[5] Aliments[5]	100	100[8]	103	102	101	100	101	104	105	104
Pakistan **Pakistan**	**92**	**100**	**112**	**122**[8]	**135**	**151**	**170**	**188**	**209**	**222**
Food Aliments	92	100	111	123[8]	135	155	177	193	217	229
Panama[5] **Panama**[5]	**99**	**100**	**101**	**103**	**104**	**105**	**106**	**107**	**109**	**109**
Food[5] Aliments[5]	99	100	102	106	106	108	108	109	110	110
Papua New Guinea **Papouasie-Nvl-Guinée**	**94**	**100**	**107**	**112**	**117**	**120**	**141**	**158**	...	...
Food Aliments	91	100	108	111	114	116	137	156	...	...
Paraguay[5] **Paraguay**[5]	**72**	**100**	**124**	**143**	**169**	**204**	**231**	**254**	**272**	**303**
Food[5] Aliments[5]	68	100	120	138	161	196	224	237	247	275
Peru[5 7] **Pérou**[5 7]	**1**	**100**	**510**	**884**	**1 314**	**1 626**	**1 806**	**2 015**	**2 187**	**2 346**
Food[5 7] Aliments[5 7]	1	100	447	766	1 144	1 352	1 479	1 659	1 776	1 923
Philippines **Philippines**	**88**	**100**	**119**	**129**	**138**	**149**	**161**	**176**	**186**	**204**
Food[10] Aliments[10]	90	100	116	124	131	141	154	170	175	191
Poland **Pologne**	**15**	**100**	**170**	**244**	**330**	**436**	**557**	**668**	**767**	**858**
Food[34] Aliments[34]	16	100	151	207	274	363	462	550	620	671
Portugal[3] **Portugal**[3]	**88**	**100**	**111**	**121**[8]	**129**	**136**	**142**	**146**	**149**[8]	**153**
Food Aliments	88	100	110	118[8]	121	127	132	135	136[8]	140
Puerto Rico **Porto Rico**	**95**	**100**	**103**	**106**	**109**	**113**	**118**	**125**	**131**	**138**
Food Aliments	92	100	105	111	118	127	140	153	169	188
Qatar **Qatar**	**97**	**100**	**104**	**108**	**107**	**108**	**111**	...	...	...
Food Aliments	99	100	106	106	98	93	104	...	...	...

29
Consumer price index numbers
All items and food; 1990 = 100 [cont.]
Indices des prix à la consommation
Ensemble des prix et alimentation; 1990 = 100 [suite]

Country or area Pays ou zone	1989	1990	1991	1992	1993	1994	1995	1996	1997	1998
Republic of Moldova[2] **République de Moldova**[2]	...	...	**8**	**100**	**1 714**	**10 059**	**13 064**	**16 135**	**18 034**	**19 422**
Food[2] Aliments[2]	...	...	7	100	1 418	7 844	10 168	12 148	13 004	13 525
Réunion[13] **Réunion**[13]	96	100[8][28]	**104**	**107**	**111**	**114**	**116**	**118**	**119**	**121**
Food[13] Aliments[13]	98	100[8][28]	105	107	111	112	113	115	117	120
Romania **Roumanie**	95	100	275	310[4]	1 105[4]	2 617[4]	3 461[4]	4 805[4]	12 241[4]	19 474[4]
Food Aliments	96	100	299	337[4]	1 174[4]	2 774[4]	3 657[4]	4 987[4]	12 536[4]	18 607[4]
Russian Federation[4] **Fédération de Russie**[4]	...	...	**100**	**1 629**	**15 869**	**64 688**	**192 521**	**284 429**[8]	**326 484**	**416 814**
Food[4] Aliments[4]	...	...	100	1 690	16 760	67 339	210 974	287 151[8]	323 749	412 044
Rwanda[5] **Rwanda**[5]	96	100	120	131	147	...	...	...	...	...
Food[5] Aliments[5]	95	100	114	122	...	...	...	...	...	...
Saint Helena **Sainte-Hélène**	97	100	104	109[8]	118	123	128	134	137	139
Food Aliments	96	100	102	106[8]	112	116	121	126	126	124
Saint Kitts and Nevis[5] **Saint-Kitts-et-Nevis**[5]	96	100	104	107	109	111	114	116	...	...
Food[5] Aliments[5]	98	100	106	111	113	117	119	123	...	...
Saint Lucia **Sainte-Lucie**	96	100	107	113	113	116	123	124	124	128
Food Aliments	96	100	109	114	114	119	128	128	124	130
St. Vincent-Grenadines[5] **St. Vincent-Grenadines**[5]	93	100	106	110	115	115	118	123	124	126
Food[5] Aliments[5]	93	100	109	113	116	116	120	128	127	124
Samoa[3] **Samoa**[3]	87	100	99	107	109	129	130	139	155	...
Food Aliments	83	100	92	102	102	127	128	144	160	...
San Marino **Saint-Marin**	94	100	107	115	121	126[8]	132	137[8]	140	143
Food Aliments	95	100	105	111	118	123[8]	128	132[8]	136	139
Saudi Arabia[35] **Arabie saoudite**[35]	98	100	105	104	105	106	111	112	112	111
Food[10][35] Aliments[10][35]	98	100	108	112	113	111	112	114	116	117
Senegal[5] **Sénégal**[5]	100	100	98	98	98	129	139	143	...	...
Food[5] Aliments[5]	100	100	97	96	94	131	143	145	...	...
Seychelles[5] **Seychelles**[5]	96	100	102	105	107	109	108	107	108	...

29
Consumer price index numbers
All items and food; 1990 = 100 [cont.]
Indices des prix à la consommation
Ensemble des prix et alimentation; 1990 = 100 [suite]

Country or area Pays ou zone	1989	1990	1991	1992	1993	1994	1995	1996	1997	1998
Food[5] Aliments[5]	95	100	103	104	107	100	99	96	98	...
Singapore **Singapour**	**97**	**100**	**103**	**106**	**108**	**112**	**114**	**115**	**117**	**117**
Food Aliments	99	100	102	103	104	107	110	112	115	115
Slovakia **Slovaquie**	**91**	**100**	**161**[8]	**177**	**218**	**248**	**272**	**288**	**305**[8]	**326**
Food Aliments	90[34]	100[34]	147[8,34]	158[34]	191[34]	222[34]	249[34]	258	276[8]	292
Slovenia[13] **Slovénie**[13]	**15**	**100**	**215**	**662**	**880**	**1 065**	**1 208**	**1 327**	**1 438**	**1 552**
Food[13,19] Aliments[13,19]	16	100	212	649	816	1 005	1 162	1 271	1 378	1 495
Solomon Islands[5] **Iles Salomon**[5]	**91**	**100**	**114**	**126**	**134**[8]	**152**	**167**	**186**	**202**	**227**
Food[5] Aliments[5]	92	100	117	130	136[8]	152	163	185	205	232
South Africa **Afrique du Sud**	**88**	**100**	**115**	**131**	**144**	**157**	**171**	**183**	**199**	**213**
Food Aliments	86	100	120	150	160	182	198	210	230	244
Spain **Espagne**	**94**	**100**	**106**	**112**	**117**	**123**	**129**	**133**	**136**	**138**
Food[10] Aliments[10]	94	100	104	107	109	115	121	125	126	128
Sri Lanka[5] **Sri Lanka**[5]	**82**	**100**	**112**	**125**	**140**	**151**	**163**	**189**	**207**	**227**
Food[5] Aliments[5]	81	100	112	125	139	152	162	193	214	238
Sudan[18] **Soudan**[18]	**59**	**100**	**222**	**473**	**953**	**2 068**	**3 482**	**8 192**	**...**	**...**
Food[10,18] Aliments[10,18]	59	100	236	457	...	...	...	...	...	...
Suriname[5] **Suriname**[5]	**82**	**100**	**126**	**181**	**441**	**2 065**	**6 935**	**6 879**	**7 371**	**8 773**
Food[5] Aliments[5]	77	100	119	184	485	2 365	7 843	7 267	7 209	8 244
Swaziland[18] **Swaziland**[18]	**89**[8]	**100**	**102**	**122**	**137**	**157**	**180**	**204**	**212**[8]	**228**
Food[18] Aliments[18]	85[8]	100	114	128	145	172	206	233	265[8]	281
Sweden **Suède**	**91**	**100**	**109**	**112**	**117**	**120**	**123**	**123**	**124**	**124**
Food Aliments	93	100	105	99	100	102	103	96	96	97
Switzerland **Suisse**	**95**	**100**	**106**	**110**	**114**[8]	**115**	**117**	**118**	**118**	**118**
Food Aliments	95	100	105	106	106[8]	106	107	106	107	108
Syrian Arab Republic **Rép. arabe syrienne**	**90**	**100**	**109**	**121**	**137**	**154**	**170**	**185**	**189**	**188**
Food Aliments	84	100	106	113	126	145	155	169	173	169

29
Consumer price index numbers
All items and food; 1990 = 100 [cont.]
Indices des prix à la consommation
Ensemble des prix et alimentation; 1990 = 100 [suite]

Country or area Pays ou zone	1989	1990	1991	1992	1993	1994	1995	1996	1997	1998
Tajikistan **Tadjikistan**	...	**100**	**184**	**1 951**	**43 620**	**148 100**	**804 300**	**2 977 500**	**5 112 400**	...
Food Aliments	...	100	189	2 477	75 100	189 920	1 066 000	4 065 800	7 172 000	...
Thailand **Thaïlande**	**94**	**100**	**106**	**110**	**114**	**120**	**126**	**134**	**141**	**153**
Food Aliments	93	100	107	112	114	122	132	144	154	168
TFYR Macedonia **L'ex-R.y. Macédoine**	**14**	**100**	**203**	**3 375**	**15 625**	**35 672**	**41 266**	**42 219**	**43 313**	...
Food Aliments	16	100	203	3 500	15 625	34 844	37 844	37 797	39 391	...
Togo[5] **Togo[5]**	**99**	**100**	**101**	**102**	**102**	**143**	...	...	...	...
Food[5] Aliments[5]	98	100	96	99	98	130	...	...	...	...
Tonga[3] **Tonga[3]**	**90**	**100**	**110**	**118**	**119**	**120**	**122**	**126**	**129**	**133**
Food Aliments	93	100	106	119	115	114	117	126	130	138
Trinidad and Tobago **Trinité-et-Tobago**	**90**	**100**	**104**	**111**	**123**	**133[8]**	**140**	**145**	**150**	**159**
Food Aliments	85	100	106	115	137	161[8]	188	208	228	262
Tunisia **Tunisie**	**94**	**100[14]**	**108**	**115**	**119**	**125**	**132**	**137**	**142**	**147**
Food Aliments	94	100[14]	109	114	117	122	132	137	143	147
Turkey **Turquie**	**62**	**100**	**166**	**282**	**469**	**967**	**1 872**	**339[6]**	**630[6]**	**1 163[6]**
Food[10] Aliments[10]	61	100	167	286	468	983	1 938	331[6]	637[6]	1 162[6]
Tuvalu[5] **Tuvalu[5]**	**96**	**100**	**106**	**100**	**102**	**104**	**109**	**110**	**112**	**112**
Food[5] Aliments[5]	98	100	106	97	99	103	109	110	110	110
Uganda[13] **Ouganda[13]**	...	**100**	**128**	**197**	**207**	**228**	**243**	**261**	...	...
Food[13] Aliments[13]	...	100	124	205	197	228	238	254	...	...
Ukraine[2] **Ukraine[2]**	...	...	...	**100**	**4 835**	**47 923**	**228 471**	**411 775**	**477 190**	**527 663**
Food[2 10] Aliments[2 10]	...	...	...	100	5 514	49 582	226 059	357 921	399 575	446 690
United Kingdom **Royaume-Uni**	**91**	**100**	**106**	**110**	**112**	**114**	**118**	**121**	**125**	**129**
Food Aliments	93	100	105	108	109	111	115	118	119	120
United Rep.Tanzania[36] **Rép.-Unie de Tanzanie[36]**	**74[8]**	**100**	**129**	**157**	**197**	**254**	**336**	**406**	**471**	**532**
Food[36] Aliments[36]	74[8]	100	132	160	196	260	347	418	490	562
United States **Etats-Unis**	**95**	**100**	**104**	**107**	**111**	**113**	**117**	**120**	**123**	**125**

29
Consumer price index numbers
All items and food; 1990 = 100 [cont.]
Indices des prix à la consommation
Ensemble des prix et alimentation; 1990 = 100 [suite]

Country or area Pays ou zone	1989	1990	1991	1992	1993	1994	1995	1996	1997	1998
Food Aliments	95	100	104	105	107	110	113	116	119	122
Uruguay[5] Uruguay[5]	47	100	202	340	524	759	1 080	1 385	1 661[8]	1 839
Food[5] Aliments[5]	45	100	185	297	449	632	894	1 105	1 308[8]	1 444
Vanuatu[13] Vanuatu[13]	95	100	106	111	115	117	120	121	125	129
Food[13] Aliments[13]	98	100	103	104	108	109	113	112	113	117
Venezuela Venezuela	...	100	133	175	239	381	609	1 224	2 112	...
Food Aliments	...	100	134	175	231	366	585	1 096	1 848	...
Yugoslavia Yougoslavie	...	100	222	20 021	...	24[24]	43[24]	82[24]	100[24]	130[24]
Food Aliments	...	100	200	19 217	...	27[24]	46[24]	84[24]	100[24]	134[24]
Zambia[18] Zambie[18]	47	100	193	573	1 655	2 521	3 381	4 591[14]	5 662	7 045
Food[18] Aliments[18]	48	100	191	608	1 781	2 665	3 568	5 203[14]	6 279	7 803
Zimbabwe Zimbabwe[19 30]	...	100	123	175	224	273	335	407	484	637
Food[19 30] Aliments[19 30]	...	100	113	193	267	337	429	545	641	893

Source:
International Labour Office (ILO), Geneva, "Yearbook of
Labour Statistics 1999" and the ILO labour statistics
database.

†   For information on recent changes in country or
area nomenclature pertaining to former Czechoslovakia,
Germany, Hong Kong Special Administrative Region (SAR) of
China, Macao Special Administrative Region (SAR) of China,
SFR of Yugoslavia and the former USSR, see Annex I - Country
or area nomenclature, regional and other groupings.

††   For statistical purposes, the data for
China do not include those for Hong Kong Special
Administrative Region (Hong Kong SAR), Macao Special
Administrative Region (Macao SAR) and Taiwan province of
China.

1   One month of each year.
2   Index base: 1992 = 100.
3   Excluding Rent.
4   Index base: 1991 = 100.

Source:
Bureau international du Travail (BIT), Genève, "Annuaire des
statistiques du travail 1999" et la base de données du BIT.

†   Pour les modifications récentes de nomenclature
de pays ou de zone concernant l'Allemagne, Hong Kong, région
administrative spéciale (RAS) de Chine, Macao, région
administrative spéciale (RAS) de Chine,
l'ex-Tchécoslovaquie, l'ex-URSS et l'ex-Rfs de Yougoslavie,
voir annexe I - Nomenclature des pays ou des zones,
groupements régionaux et autres groupements.

††   Les données statistiques relatives à
la Chine ne comprennent pas celles qui concernent la région
administrative spéciale de Hong Kong (la RAS de Hong Kong),
la région administrative spéciale de Macao (la RAS de Macao)
et la province chinoise de Taiwan.

1   Un mois de chaque année.
2   Indices base : 1992 = 100.
3   Non compris le groupe "Loyer".
4   Indices base : 1991 = 100.

29

Consumer price index numbers
All items and food; 1990 = 100 [cont.]

Indices des prix à la consommation
Ensemble des prix et alimentation; 1990 = 100 [suite]

5 Data refer to the index of the capital city.	5 Les données se réfèrent à l'indice de la capitale.
6 Index base: 1994 = 100.	6 Indices base : 1994 = 100.
7 Metropolitan area.	7 Région métropolitaine.
8 Series linked to former series.	8 Série enchaînée à la précédente.
9 Index base: 1993 = 100	9 Indices base : 1993 = 100.
10 Including tobacco.	10 Y compris le tabac.
11 Government officials.	11 Fonctionnaires.
12 Average of less than 12 months.	12 Moyenne de moins de douze mois.
13 Urban areas.	13 Régions urbaines.
14 Series replacing former series.	14 Série remplaçant la précédente.
15 Index base: 1995 = 100.	15 Indices base: 1995 = 100
16 Index base: 1988 = 100.	16 Indices base : 1988 = 100.
17 Official estimates.	17 Estimations officielles.
18 Low income group.	18 Familles à revenu modique.
19 Excluding beverages.	19 Non compris les boissons.
20 Central area.	20 Région centrale.
21 Including non-alcoholic beverages only.	21 Y compris les boissons non alcoolisées seulement.
22 Including beverages, alcoholic beverages and tobacco.	22 Y compris les boissons, les boissons alcoholisées et le tabac.
23 Including direct taxes.	23 Y compris les impôts directs.
24 Index base: 1997=100.	24 Indices base: 1997=100.
25 Including rent.	25 Y compris le groupe loyer.
26 Excluding alcoholic beverages and tobacco.	26 Non compris les boissons alcoolisées et le tabac.
27 Excluding alcoholic beverages.	27 Non compris les boissons alcoolisées.
28 All households.	28 Ensemble des ménages.
29 Industrial workers.	29 Travailleurs de l'industrie.
30 Excluding tobacco.	30 Non compris le tabac.
31 Index base: 1989 = 100.	31 Indices base : 1989 = 100.
32 Madagascans.	32 Malgaches.
33 Rural and urban areas.	33 Régions rurales et urbaines.
34 Including alcoholic beverages.	34 Y compris les boissons alcoolisées.
35 All cities.	35 Ensemble des villes.
36 Tanganyika.	36 Tanganyika.

Technical notes, tables 27-29

Table 27: The series generally relate to the average earnings per worker in manufacturing industries, according to the *International Standard Industrial Classification of All Economic Activities* (ISIC) Revision 2 or Revision 3 [47]. The data cover all employees (i.e. wage earners and salaried employees) of both sexes, irrespective of age. Data which refer exclusively to wage earners (i.e. manual or production workers), or to salaried employees (i.e. non-manual workers) are footnoted. Earnings generally include bonuses, cost of living allowances, taxes, social insurance contributions payable by the employed person and, in some cases, payments in kind, and normally exclude social insurance contributions payable by the employers, family allowances and other social security benefits. The time of year to which the figures refer is not the same for all countries. In some cases, the series may show wage rates instead of earnings; this is indicated in footnotes.

Table 28: Producer prices are prices at which producers sell their output on the domestic market or for export. Wholesale prices, in the strict sense, are prices at which wholesalers sell their goods on the domestic market or for export. In practice, many national wholesale price indexes are a mixture of producer and wholesale prices for domestic goods representing prices for purchases in large quantities from either source. In addition, these indexes may cover the prices of goods imported in quantity for the domestic market either by producers or by retail or wholesale distributors.

Producer or wholesale price indexes normally cover the prices of the characteristic products of agriculture, forestry and fishing, mining and quarrying, manufacturing, and electricity, gas and water supply. Prices are normally measured in terms of transaction prices, including non-deductible indirect taxes less subsidies, in the case of domestically-produced goods and import duties and other non-deductible indirect taxes less subsidies in the case of imported goods.

The Laspeyres index number formula is generally used and, for the purpose of the presentation, the national index numbers have been recalculated, where necessary, on the reference base 1990=100.

The price index numbers for each country are arranged according to the following scheme:

 (a) Components of supply
   Domestic supply
   Domestic production for domestic market
   Agricultural products
   Industrial products
   Imported products
   Exported goods

Notes techniques, tableaux 27 à 29

Tableau 27: Les séries se rapportent généralement aux gains moyens des salariés des industries manufacturières (activités de fabrication), suivant la *Classification internationale type, par industrie, de toutes les branches d'activité économique* (CITI, Rev. 2 ou Rev.3) [47]. Les données portent sur l'ensemble des salariés (qu'ils perçoivent un salaire ou un traitement au mois) des deux sexes, indépendamment de leur âge. Lorsque les données portent exclusivement sur les salariés horaires (ouvriers, travailleurs manuels) ou sur les employés percevant un traitement (travailleurs autres que manuels, cadres), le fait est signalé par une note. Les gains comprennent en général les primes, les indemnités pour coût de la vie, les impôts, les cotisations de sécurité sociale à la charge de l'employé, et dans certains cas des paiements en nature, mais ne comprennent pas en règle générale la part patronale des cotisations d'assurance sociale, les allocations familiales et les autres prestations de sécurité sociale. La période de l'année visée par les données n'est pas la même pour tous les pays. Dans certains cas, les séries visent les taux horaires et non pas les gains, ce qui est alors signalé en note.

Tableau 28: Les prix à la production sont les prix auxquels les producteurs vendent leur production sur le marché intérieur ou à l'exportation. Les prix de gros, au sens strict du terme, sont les prix auxquels les grossistes vendent sur le marché intérieur ou à l'exportation. En pratique, les indices nationaux des prix de gros combinent souvent les prix à la production et les prix de gros de biens nationaux représentant les prix d'achat par grandes quantités au producteur ou au grossiste. En outre, ces indices peuvent s'appliquer aux prix de biens importés en quantités pour être vendus sur le marché intérieur par les producteurs, les détaillants ou les grossistes.

Les indices de prix de gros ou de prix à la production comprennent aussi en général les prix des produits provenant de l'agriculture, de la sylviculture et de la pêche, des industries extractives (mines et carrières), de l'industrie manufacturière ainsi que les prix de l'électricité, de gaz et de l'eau. Les prix sont normalement ceux auxquels s'effectue la transaction, y compris les impôts indirects non déductibles, mais non compris les subventions dans le cas des biens produits dans le pays et y compris les taxes à l'importation et autres impôts indirects non déductibles, mais non compris les subventions dans le cas des biens importés.

On utilise généralement la formule de Laspeyres et, pour la présentation, on a recalculé les indices nationaux, le cas échéant, en prenant comme base de référence 1990=100.

(b)   Stage of processing
     Raw materials
     Intermediate products
     Finished goods
(c)   End-use
     Producers' materials
     Consumers' goods
     Capital goods

A description of the general methods used in compiling the related national indexes is given in the United Nations *1977 Supplement to the Statistical Yearbook and the Monthly Bulletin of Statistics* [54].

Table 29: Unless otherwise stated, the consumer price index covers all the main classes of expenditure on all items and on food. Monthly data for many of these series and descriptions of them may be found in the United Nations *Monthly Bulletin of Statistics* [25] and the United Nations *1977 Supplement to the Statistical Yearbook and the Monthly Bulletin of Statistics* [54].

Les indices des prix pour chaque pays sont présentés suivant la classification ci-après:
(a)   Eléments de l'offre
     Offre intérieure
     Production nationale pour le marché intérieur
     Produits agricoles
     Produits industriels
     Produits importés
     Produits exportés
(b)   Stade de la transformation
     Matières premières
     Produits intermédiaires
     Produits finis
(c)   Utilisation finale
     Biens de production
     Biens de consommation
     Biens d'équipement

Les méthodes générales utilisées pour calculer les indices nationaux correspondants sont exposées dans: *1977 Supplément à l'Annuaire statistique et au Bulletin mensuel de statistique* des Nations Unies [54].

Tableau 29: Sauf indication contraire, les indices des prix à la consommation donnés englobent tous les groupes principaux de dépenses pour l'ensemble des prix et alimentation. Les données mensuelles pour plusieurs de ces séries et définitions figurent dans le *Bulletin mensuel de statistique* [25] et dans le *1977 Supplément à l'Annuaire statistique et au Bulletin mensuel de statistique* des Nations Unies [54].

30
Agricultural production
Production agricole
Index numbers: 1989-91 = 100
Indices : 1989-91 = 100

Country or area Pays ou zone	Agriculture Agriculture					Food Produits alimentaires				
	1995	1996	1997	1998	1999	1995	1996	1997	1998	1999
Africa · Afrique										
Algeria Algérie	119.6	140.6	112.6	128.3	130.4	120.5	142.6	113.5	129.5	131.5
Angola Angola	121.8	126.8	127.4	146.1	138.6	123.2	128.4	128.9	148.2	141.4
Benin Bénin	138.6	154.7	166.6	162.1	186.8	125.9	135.0	151.8	147.8	169.7
Botswana Botswana	105.7	105.5	93.9	95.8	98.3	105.7	105.5	94.0	95.9	98.5
Burkina Faso Burkina Faso	117.2	128.6	133.9	142.9	142.9	120.7	129.1	124.2	136.0	136.0
Burundi Burundi	96.7	96.6	94.1	89.2	90.9	97.9	98.3	96.9	91.4	92.2
Cameroon Cameroun	115.3	120.0	117.2	119.2	122.2	116.6	123.1	120.2	121.2	125.0
Cape Verde Cap-Vert	125.5	124.8	126.1	140.0	138.5	125.9	125.2	126.5	140.4	138.9
Central African Rep. Rép. centrafricaine	112.1	129.3	126.3	127.5	132.3	114.9	129.2	125.2	129.3	134.7
Chad Tchad	116.8	127.2	135.2	158.5	158.5	119.8	125.4	134.7	157.2	157.2
Comoros Comores	112.6	110.0	112.5	121.2	114.3	113.6	111.1	114.0	121.9	115.1
Congo Congo	114.1	114.9	112.2	115.2	118.2	114.5	115.7	113.0	116.1	119.1
Côte d'Ivoire Côte d'Ivoire	115.9	118.6	126.9	129.1	131.4	123.8	128.1	130.1	128.7	129.7
Dem. Rep. of the Congo Rép. dém. du Congo	107.8	94.4	93.7	93.8	94.0	108.6	94.6	94.4	94.9	95.6
Djibouti Djibouti	84.1	85.8	86.5	87.1	87.5	84.1	85.8	86.5	87.1	87.5
Egypt Egypte	122.5	135.0	138.4	135.4	142.4	124.9	136.2	139.9	138.8	145.1
Equatorial Guinea Guinée équatoriale	91.3	98.3	92.2	95.0	94.4	87.2	97.5	91.8	97.2	96.3
Eritrea Erythrée	109.8	101.1	103.6	143.1	123.9	110.1	101.1	103.7	144.0	124.4
Ethiopia Ethiopie	108.4	123.5	124.4	119.8	121.2	108.3	124.6	125.7	120.7	122.1
Gabon Gabon	105.8	109.3	113.0	115.5	117.9	105.3	107.7	110.2	112.4	114.8
Gambia Gambie	87.7	70.4	91.7	90.6	128.1	87.7	70.2	92.4	90.7	128.7
Ghana Ghana	138.1	149.5	144.8	158.7	167.7	137.7	148.7	143.9	157.4	166.5
Guinea Guinée	126.5	129.4	134.9	142.3	141.9	127.7	132.0	137.2	143.5	143.1
Guinea-Bissau Guinée-Bissau	117.4	115.2	117.7	119.7	119.7	117.5	115.3	118.0	119.9	119.9

30
Agricultural production
Index numbers: 1989-91 = 100 [*cont.*]
Production agricole
Indices : 1989-91 = 100 [*suite*]

Country or area Pays ou zone	Agriculture Agriculture					Food Produits alimentaires				
	1995	1996	1997	1998	1999	1995	1996	1997	1998	1999
Kenya Kenya	104.1	106.3	105.8	108.0	103.0	102.3	104.4	106.1	105.8	103.9
Lesotho Lesotho	98.5	116.1	117.2	108.4	108.6	90.2	116.4	116.6	106.9	107.2
Libyan Arab Jamah. Jamah. arabe libyenne	123.4	132.4	144.7	154.5	160.9	124.7	133.7	146.5	156.8	163.4
Madagascar Madagascar	105.5	107.3	108.6	108.7	111.8	107.2	109.0	111.2	110.6	113.8
Malawi Malawi	109.0	117.1	111.4	117.1	128.3	105.0	111.9	100.8	116.0	131.4
Mali Mali	117.7	118.8	122.1	129.8	129.8	116.9	112.5	113.5	118.5	118.5
Mauritania Mauritanie	101.1	106.9	106.3	104.9	106.2	101.1	106.9	106.3	104.9	106.2
Mauritius Maurice	103.1	104.2	110.6	106.8	80.5	105.3	108.2	116.0	112.3	84.0
Morocco Maroc	73.1	113.6	97.4	111.1	96.5	72.4	114.2	97.3	111.4	96.3
Mozambique Mozambique	109.6	123.2	130.9	140.6	142.9	109.1	123.2	130.0	138.9	141.2
Namibia Namibie	110.1	118.3	85.8	96.3	97.8	110.1	118.4	85.2	96.0	97.4
Niger Niger	106.3	120.8	96.7	145.5	138.3	106.3	121.0	96.7	145.8	138.5
Nigeria Nigéria	133.1	141.2	137.8	150.1	156.0	133.4	141.9	138.7	151.7	157.7
Réunion Réunion	110.3	110.4	119.8	114.0	116.3	110.9	111.0	120.5	114.7	117.0
Rwanda Rwanda	65.4	69.6	77.3	83.7	89.0	65.4	70.2	77.6	84.3	89.8
Sao Tome and Principe Sao Tomé-et-Principe	124.4	153.6	172.3	183.2	196.1	124.3	153.6	172.2	183.1	195.9
Senegal Sénégal	116.3	107.4	101.8	102.9	121.9	117.2	108.1	101.7	101.0	120.5
Seychelles Seychelles	141.1	136.1	143.0	128.1	134.4	142.9	137.7	143.7	128.4	134.8
Sierra Leone Sierra Leone	92.0	96.9	102.2	95.7	79.1	91.5	96.9	101.0	93.7	81.1
South Africa Afrique du Sud	85.3	100.6	99.0	94.7	96.1	86.7	103.0	101.8	97.0	98.2
Sudan Soudan	140.3	153.2	154.2	154.7	151.5	141.2	155.0	156.7	158.3	153.9
Swaziland Swaziland	84.4	94.8	90.7	90.2	87.7	88.9	97.9	92.8	92.1	89.4
Togo Togo	114.8	134.4	142.5	139.0	139.0	117.1	135.6	141.1	133.7	133.7
Tunisia Tunisie	82.0	141.2	96.0	118.6	122.5	82.2	143.3	96.7	119.9	124.0

30
Agricultural production
Index numbers: 1989-91 = 100 [*cont.*]
Production agricole
Indices : 1989-91 = 100 [*suite*]

Country or area Pays ou zone	Agriculture Agriculture					Food Produits alimentaires				
	1995	1996	1997	1998	1999	1995	1996	1997	1998	1999
Uganda Ouganda	112.9	109.4	109.7	116.6	121.8	111.4	102.5	105.5	113.6	119.3
United Rep.Tanzania Rép.-Unie de Tanzanie	102.2	105.1	99.7	103.6	102.6	100.4	102.9	97.2	104.1	102.6
Zambia Zambie	93.5	111.8	95.9	91.1	100.8	93.2	113.2	97.8	93.0	103.1
Zimbabwe Zimbabwe	82.8	112.4	116.7	111.9	109.0	74.7	106.1	109.3	96.5	101.7
America, North · Amérique du Nord										
Antigua and Barbuda Antigua-et-Barbuda	99.3	98.6	98.6	98.6	98.6	99.6	98.9	98.9	98.9	98.9
Bahamas Bahamas	117.4	128.6	137.9	148.5	139.8	117.4	128.6	137.9	148.5	139.8
Barbados Barbade	90.4	105.6	96.7	97.2	98.6	90.4	105.6	96.7	97.2	98.6
Belize Belize	135.6	147.4	161.7	153.5	153.5	135.6	147.4	161.7	153.5	153.5
Bermuda Bermudes	84.7	78.1	78.4	78.4	78.4	84.7	78.1	78.4	78.4	78.4
British Virgin Islands Iles Vierges britanniques	104.0	104.0	104.0	104.0	104.0	104.0	104.0	104.0	104.0	104.0
Canada Canada	111.1	117.4	117.2	121.7	130.7	110.6	117.4	117.0	121.4	130.5
Cayman Islands Iles Caïmanes	84.9	84.9	84.9	84.9	84.9	84.9	84.9	84.9	84.9	84.9
Costa Rica Costa Rica	122.3	127.4	126.5	124.3	126.0	126.1	130.1	132.4	130.4	131.4
Cuba Cuba	54.9	64.3	62.8	61.5	61.5	54.3	63.7	62.0	60.3	60.3
Dominica Dominique	76.9	91.3	92.1	85.2	85.5	76.1	90.5	91.3	84.4	84.7
Dominican Republic Rép. dominicaine	98.1	104.4	104.8	105.9	99.6	100.2	106.0	105.4	104.3	103.1
El Salvador El Salvador	102.8	102.2	105.9	108.6	116.8	105.1	102.9	112.4	117.4	122.9
Greenland Groenland	105.6	105.7	105.9	105.8	105.8	106.0	106.1	106.3	106.1	106.1
Grenada Grenade	95.3	94.1	96.9	89.7	88.4	95.2	94.0	96.8	89.7	88.4
Guadeloupe Guadeloupe	83.5	90.6	113.8	108.2	108.2	83.5	90.6	113.8	108.2	108.2
Guatemala Guatemala	111.3	114.2	120.9	122.6	117.2	117.5	120.1	125.8	128.6	125.1
Haiti Haïti	87.9	91.2	94.1	93.3	94.2	88.7	92.6	95.7	94.9	95.7
Honduras Honduras	104.0	115.2	115.5	117.5	115.3	100.8	112.3	110.6	111.6	107.7
Jamaica Jamaïque	117.6	124.4	117.7	118.2	118.8	117.6	124.6	117.7	118.3	118.9

30
Agricultural production
Index numbers: 1989-91 = 100 [*cont.*]
Production agricole
Indices : 1989-91 = 100 [*suite*]

Country or area Pays ou zone	Agriculture Agriculture 1995	1996	1997	1998	1999	Food Produits alimentaires 1995	1996	1997	1998	1999
Martinique Martinique	90.7	112.8	120.2	120.0	120.0	90.7	112.8	120.2	120.0	120.0
Mexico Mexique	118.9	115.9	120.2	123.5	125.7	121.4	117.1	122.3	125.8	128.8
Montserrat Montserrat	110.2	110.2	110.2	110.2	110.2	110.2	110.2	110.2	110.2	110.2
Netherlands Antilles Antilles néerlandaises	188.1	130.0	163.4	151.5	157.6	188.1	130.0	163.4	151.5	157.6
Nicaragua Nicaragua	111.5	114.2	117.2	115.2	121.3	116.5	121.4	122.8	119.1	127.3
Panama Panama	103.4	106.5	100.2	101.1	101.3	103.5	106.8	100.4	101.2	101.5
Puerto Rico Porto Rico	87.1	83.0	81.8	81.8	81.8	86.8	82.7	81.7	81.7	81.7
Saint Kitts and Nevis Saint-Kitts-et-Nevis	94.3	101.9	133.8	113.1	98.7	94.5	102.1	134.1	113.4	98.9
Saint Lucia Sainte-Lucie	97.2	91.6	81.0	67.2	67.2	97.2	91.6	81.0	67.2	67.2
St. Vincent-Grenadines St. Vincent-Grenadines	88.5	82.7	72.1	77.2	77.2	88.2	82.2	71.5	76.7	76.7
Trinidad and Tobago Trinité-et-Tobago	110.0	112.8	102.4	86.9	92.9	111.0	114.3	102.9	88.0	94.1
United States Etats-Unis	110.2	114.6	118.7	119.4	119.7	110.2	114.4	118.6	120.7	120.3
United States Virgin Is. Iles Vierges américaines	103.4	103.4	103.4	103.4	103.4	103.4	103.4	103.4	103.4	103.4
America, South · Amérique du Sud										
Argentina Argentine	115.6	119.4	121.8	132.4	132.3	117.4	121.1	124.5	135.7	136.2
Bolivia Bolivie	123.1	130.0	138.6	138.6	131.8	122.9	128.9	138.1	138.5	131.4
Brazil Brésil	120.2	125.2	128.9	129.6	135.1	123.6	128.4	132.6	132.0	137.5
Chile Chili	126.1	128.0	128.8	131.0	129.2	126.7	128.7	129.8	132.1	130.1
Colombia Colombie	109.5	107.1	108.4	111.0	111.6	113.0	112.1	115.1	116.1	118.5
Ecuador Equateur	129.9	141.5	147.7	119.8	124.4	132.2	142.2	154.4	126.2	130.8
Falkland Is. (Malvinas) Iles Falkland (Malvinas)	98.1	84.4	91.9	90.3	90.3	107.8	71.6	87.0	86.4	86.4
French Guiana Guyane française	122.6	136.7	129.5	127.6	127.6	122.6	136.7	129.5	127.6	127.6
Guyana Guyana	176.2	187.6	191.0	175.2	193.3	176.6	188.1	191.5	175.7	193.9
Paraguay Paraguay	106.8	106.1	108.2	111.1	119.2	114.5	117.2	124.4	124.6	134.4
Peru Pérou	124.2	133.3	140.9	142.4	153.7	126.7	134.9	145.3	147.5	158.6

30
Agricultural production
Index numbers: 1989-91 = 100 [cont.]
Production agricole
Indices : 1989-91 = 100 [suite]

Country or area Pays ou zone	Agriculture Agriculture					Food Produits alimentaires				
	1995	1996	1997	1998	1999	1995	1996	1997	1998	1999
Suriname Suriname	100.8	89.1	90.0	84.7	75.8	100.8	89.1	90.1	84.7	75.8
Uruguay Uruguay	111.0	120.6	129.1	129.8	130.6	114.6	127.0	135.8	138.0	141.9
Venezuela Venezuela	105.7	111.1	117.9	114.9	114.2	107.0	112.3	119.5	116.6	115.5
Asia · Asie										
Armenia Arménie	77.2	83.3	71.1	74.8	74.2	77.6	84.1	71.8	75.6	74.9
Azerbaijan Azerbaïdjan	55.2	57.8	53.7	52.1	55.5	57.1	61.1	56.3	56.5	61.7
Bahrain Bahreïn	111.5	116.1	105.4	96.3	97.4	111.5	116.1	105.4	96.3	97.4
Bangladesh Bangladesh	103.3	109.5	111.6	111.8	115.1	103.7	109.8	111.3	111.6	115.9
Bhutan Bhoutan	107.2	107.2	107.2	107.2	107.2	107.2	107.2	107.2	107.2	107.2
Brunei Darussalam Brunéi Darussalam	145.4	126.7	166.0	152.4	152.4	146.1	127.2	166.8	153.0	153.0
Cambodia Cambodge	125.1	128.5	130.7	131.6	137.6	125.0	128.4	130.7	131.6	137.9
China †† Chine ††	135.8	143.8	152.5	157.6	158.6	138.8	147.4	155.6	162.9	164.2
China, Hong Kong SAR† Chine, Hong Kong RAS†	55.9	25.4	20.3	11.3	28.3	55.9	25.4	20.3	11.3	28.3
China, Macao SAR † Chine, Macao RAS †	102.6	103.7	104.1	154.6	154.6	102.6	103.7	104.1	154.6	154.6
Cyprus Chypre	115.6	112.6	103.6	111.1	116.7	114.9	112.1	103.3	111.1	116.8
Georgia Géorgie	73.8	72.9	72.9	68.4	76.4	83.2	82.8	83.3	75.4	83.2
India Inde	115.7	118.2	122.2	121.6	125.1	115.7	117.9	121.8	120.8	124.6
Indonesia Indonésie	119.7	122.2	119.3	117.1	117.2	120.2	122.5	119.6	117.2	117.3
Iran (Islamic Rep. of) Iran (Rép. islamique d')	132.7	140.5	136.9	160.6	151.9	132.9	140.6	137.1	161.6	152.1
Iraq Iraq	99.7	100.6	90.6	95.0	86.4	101.0	102.4	91.7	96.2	87.5
Israel Israël	106.8	109.9	106.4	104.7	104.5	106.9	109.3	105.3	103.5	103.2
Japan Japon	97.7	95.7	96.2	92.9	92.4	98.2	96.2	96.7	93.3	92.9
Jordan Jordanie	155.5	119.5	139.6	145.1	126.9	155.8	118.8	140.4	146.6	127.8
Kazakhstan Kazakhstan	63.5	61.2	59.1	48.2	64.2	63.9	62.0	60.5	49.4	66.2
Korea, Republic of Corée, République de	112.1	118.7	124.4	122.9	100.3	112.3	119.8	125.7	124.2	100.7

30
Agricultural production
Index numbers: 1989-91 = 100 [cont.]
Production agricole
Indices : 1989-91 = 100 [suite]

Country or area Pays ou zone	Agriculture Agriculture					Food Produits alimentaires				
	1995	1996	1997	1998	1999	1995	1996	1997	1998	1999
Kuwait Koweït	125.3	158.2	146.4	163.4	191.5	126.8	160.1	147.7	165.2	193.3
Kyrgyzstan Kirghizistan	82.1	89.0	95.7	97.9	99.4	89.0	98.8	105.6	107.1	107.9
Lao People's Dem. Rep. Rép. dém. pop. lao	110.2	110.7	123.8	132.3	150.9	114.2	115.6	129.5	134.6	155.9
Lebanon Liban	130.7	137.8	139.4	146.1	147.0	129.1	135.7	137.0	143.6	144.5
Malaysia Malaisie	115.1	118.3	119.0	118.0	120.3	121.9	125.8	128.5	127.3	130.1
Maldives Maldives	113.3	112.4	115.3	115.3	115.3	113.3	112.4	115.3	115.3	115.3
Mongolia Mongolie	84.1	91.4	84.9	91.8	91.5	79.7	91.1	84.6	91.7	91.3
Myanmar Myanmar	131.3	138.9	138.5	139.4	145.9	132.1	138.8	138.3	137.3	144.7
Nepal Népal	111.0	114.7	117.0	119.2	121.6	111.3	115.0	117.3	119.6	122.0
Occupied Palestinian Terr.[1] Terr. palestinien occupé[1]	100.6	101.3	102.0	102.0	102.0	100.6	101.3	102.0	102.0	102.0
Oman Oman	98.4	109.2	114.7	111.8	111.8	97.4	108.4	113.9	110.9	110.9
Pakistan Pakistan	123.2	125.3	127.8	135.1	134.0	127.2	131.8	135.0	144.4	143.0
Philippines Philippines	116.9	122.8	128.6	123.2	128.8	118.3	124.6	130.5	124.8	130.7
Qatar Qatar	157.6	163.8	184.5	185.4	185.8	157.6	163.8	184.5	185.4	185.8
Saudi Arabia Arabie saoudite	78.6	71.9	77.6	77.5	77.5	78.0	70.8	76.6	76.5	76.5
Singapore Singapour	43.3	35.9	30.3	34.8	34.9	43.3	35.9	30.3	34.8	34.9
Sri Lanka Sri Lanka	116.3	106.8	110.7	114.4	114.4	119.1	104.8	108.2	113.3	113.3
Syrian Arab Republic Rép. arabe syrienne	132.3	147.7	137.7	165.2	136.7	135.1	150.4	132.4	166.1	134.6
Tajikistan Tadjikistan	62.4	57.0	54.7	59.0	54.3	67.3	61.7	55.8	60.2	61.5
Thailand Thaïlande	112.4	116.2	117.2	113.3	116.1	110.6	114.4	115.3	111.1	114.1
Turkey Turquie	104.7	109.7	109.0	115.9	113.7	104.3	110.1	108.3	116.4	114.1
Turkmenistan Turkménistan	106.6	64.4	74.6	88.8	112.3	120.7	90.0	98.4	124.3	128.4
United Arab Emirates Emirats arabes unis	174.1	199.5	237.9	241.4	248.3	175.0	200.6	239.3	243.0	249.8
Uzbekistan Ouzbékistan	100.8	92.0	95.5	95.4	102.1	111.9	105.2	111.1	116.3	120.6

30
Agricultural production
Index numbers: 1989-91 = 100 [cont.]
Production agricole
Indices : 1989-91 = 100 [suite]

Country or area Pays ou zone	Agriculture Agriculture					Food Produits alimentaires				
	1995	1996	1997	1998	1999	1995	1996	1997	1998	1999
Viet Nam Viet Nam	130.3	137.8	144.6	151.8	163.1	128.7	135.1	140.0	147.3	157.8
Yemen Yémen	114.2	115.0	121.9	134.2	132.2	113.6	113.7	120.3	132.4	130.1
Europe · Europe										
Austria Autriche	102.6	102.0	104.6	106.7	105.8	102.6	102.0	104.6	106.7	105.8
Belarus Bélarus	64.0	66.6	63.0	65.8	59.9	63.7	66.5	62.8	65.7	59.7
Belgium-Luxembourg Belgique-Luxembourg	113.3	115.5	113.9	111.2	104.9	113.3	115.5	113.9	111.1	104.8
Bulgaria Bulgarie	77.9	64.2	68.6	67.6	70.7	80.8	65.4	69.4	69.2	72.4
Croatia Croatie	58.8	62.4	57.6	69.7	65.2	58.6	61.9	57.0	69.2	64.8
Czech Republic République tchèque	80.3	79.1	77.8	79.2	85.5	80.0	79.2	78.1	79.4	85.8
Denmark Danemark	101.8	102.2	104.0	106.4	105.9	101.8	102.2	104.0	106.4	105.9
Estonia Estonie	53.2	48.9	45.2	46.4	44.4	53.2	48.9	45.2	46.5	44.4
Faeroe Islands Iles Féroé	101.4	106.0	106.0	106.0	106.0	101.4	106.0	106.0	106.0	106.0
Finland Finlande	91.1	92.2	95.3	85.1	89.8	91.1	92.2	95.3	85.1	89.8
France France	100.7	105.8	106.3	106.1	105.6	100.7	105.9	106.4	106.2	105.6
Germany Allemagne	89.3	91.8	92.6	93.9	94.8	89.3	91.8	92.6	93.8	94.7
Greece Grèce	111.5	102.6	101.6	101.4	99.7	107.0	100.4	98.1	97.6	95.9
Hungary Hongrie	70.8	76.0	78.3	78.2	75.6	70.9	76.2	78.6	78.4	75.7
Iceland Islande	96.0	92.7	92.2	91.7	91.7	97.5	93.8	93.3	92.8	92.8
Ireland Irlande	102.3	106.2	103.1	108.6	109.0	102.7	106.7	103.6	109.1	109.6
Italy Italie	99.4	100.9	99.6	101.1	105.3	100.0	101.5	100.1	101.6	105.9
Latvia Lettonie	56.6	46.8	51.6	46.0	41.4	56.8	47.0	51.8	46.1	41.5
Liechtenstein Liechtenstein	91.1	91.1	91.1	91.1	91.1	91.1	91.1	91.1	91.1	91.1
Lithuania Lituanie	66.1	67.8	72.3	66.3	63.5	66.0	67.9	72.6	66.5	63.7
Malta Malte	119.9	137.2	126.8	127.6	126.2	119.9	137.4	126.9	127.7	126.3
Netherlands Pays-Bas	103.0	103.8	96.3	96.6	95.3	103.1	104.0	96.4	96.6	95.4

30
Agricultural production
Index numbers: 1989-91 = 100 [*cont.*]
Production agricole
Indices : 1989-91 = 100 [*suite*]

Country or area Pays ou zone	Agriculture Agriculture					Food Produits alimentaires				
	1995	1996	1997	1998	1999	1995	1996	1997	1998	1999
Norway Norvège	99.6	101.1	100.5	97.3	97.6	99.5	100.9	100.4	97.1	97.6
Poland Pologne	83.8	87.9	85.0	91.1	89.7	84.1	88.3	85.5	91.6	90.2
Portugal Portugal	98.5	102.7	97.4	91.2	95.0	98.5	102.7	97.4	90.9	94.8
Republic of Moldova République de Moldova	65.6	56.6	59.2	47.3	46.5	66.4	57.5	60.0	47.4	46.9
Romania Roumanie	98.9	92.4	103.9	94.1	96.9	100.0	93.4	105.0	95.2	98.1
Russian Federation Fédération de Russie	64.3	67.2	67.6	59.0	58.5	64.6	67.8	68.4	59.7	59.2
Slovakia Slovaquie	75.6	76.4	81.6	77.4	60.0	75.5	76.9	82.2	77.9	60.3
Slovenia Slovénie	97.6	104.3	102.4	106.5	106.4	97.6	104.3	102.4	106.5	106.4
Spain Espagne	86.7	107.9	113.9	108.2	106.6	86.8	107.9	113.7	108.1	106.3
Sweden Suède	93.4	99.6	103.2	100.3	98.4	93.4	99.5	103.0	100.2	98.3
Switzerland Suisse	96.8	97.8	93.2	101.2	94.9	96.8	97.7	93.3	101.2	94.9
TFYR Macedonia L'ex-R.y. Macédoine	91.6	92.3	95.1	99.5	99.8	93.0	94.1	94.8	97.0	97.3
Ukraine Ukraine	60.6	52.2	54.8	46.2	45.3	60.8	52.5	55.2	46.5	45.6
United Kingdom Royaume-Uni	101.3	101.2	99.8	99.3	100.4	101.3	101.3	99.8	99.1	100.0
Yugoslavia Yougoslavie	95.7	103.6	100.0	103.8	92.6	95.8	103.8	100.1	104.0	92.7
Oceania · Océanie										
American Samoa Samoa américaines	96.2	96.2	96.2	96.2	96.2	96.2	96.2	96.2	96.2	96.2
Australia Australie	107.7	117.5	119.0	122.5	123.1	118.2	130.6	130.0	135.8	134.6
Cocos (Keeling) Islands Iles des Cocos (Keeling)	101.7	101.7	101.7	101.7	101.7	101.7	101.7	101.7	101.7	101.7
Cook Islands Iles Cook	77.2	80.5	89.4	103.4	97.2	76.8	80.0	89.0	103.1	97.1
Fiji Fidji	102.6	107.7	110.4	106.9	106.9	102.9	108.0	110.6	107.1	107.1
French Polynesia Polynésie française	95.8	95.2	95.6	95.6	95.6	95.8	95.2	95.6	95.6	95.6
Guam Guam	110.8	110.8	110.8	110.8	110.8	110.8	110.8	110.8	110.8	110.8
Kiribati Kiribati	109.0	113.8	113.8	113.8	113.8	109.0	113.8	113.8	113.8	113.8
Nauru Nauru	105.5	105.4	105.6	105.6	105.6	105.5	105.4	105.6	105.6	105.6

30
Agricultural production
Index numbers: 1989-91 = 100 [cont.]
Production agricole
Indices : 1989-91 = 100 [suite]

Country or area Pays ou zone	Agriculture Agriculture					Food Produits alimentaires				
	1995	1996	1997	1998	1999	1995	1996	1997	1998	1999
New Caledonia Nouvelle-Calédonie	119.6	125.0	131.3	133.1	133.1	121.1	126.7	133.1	134.9	134.9
New Zealand Nouvelle-Zélande	112.5	113.4	119.8	118.6	113.5	117.0	119.6	127.3	126.5	122.4
Niue Nioué	100.7	100.7	100.7	100.7	100.7	100.7	100.7	100.7	100.7	100.7
Papua New Guinea Papouasie-Nvl-Guinée	106.8	111.2	110.4	112.4	113.0	107.9	111.8	111.2	112.4	113.1
Samoa Samoa	94.2	94.2	94.2	94.2	94.2	93.8	93.8	93.8	93.8	93.8
Solomon Islands Iles Salomon	109.8	112.5	117.8	119.7	122.3	109.8	112.5	117.8	119.7	122.3
Tokelau Tokélaou	108.5	108.5	108.5	108.5	108.5	108.5	108.5	108.5	108.5	108.5
Tonga Tonga	76.5	76.6	76.5	76.1	76.1	76.5	76.6	76.6	76.2	76.2
Tuvalu Tuvalu	99.2	99.2	99.2	99.2	99.2	99.2	99.2	99.2	99.2	99.2
Vanuatu Vanuatu	104.3	104.0	131.5	118.4	118.4	104.3	104.0	131.5	118.4	118.4
Wallis and Futuna Islands Iles Wallis et Futuna	101.5	101.5	101.5	101.5	101.5	101.5	101.5	101.5	101.5	101.5

Source:
Food and Agriculture Organization of the United
Nations (FAO), Rome, "FAO Production Yearbook 1999" and the
FAOSTAT database.

† For information on recent changes in country or
area nomenclature pertaining to former Czechoslovakia,
Germany, Hong Kong Special Administrative Region (SAR) of
China, Macao Special Administrative Region (SAR) of China,
SFR of Yugoslavia and the former USSR, see Annex I - Country
or area nomenclature, regional and other groupings.

†† For statistical purposes, the data for
China do not include those for Hong Kong Special
Administrative Region (Hong Kong SAR) and Macao Special
Administrative Region (Macao SAR).

1 Data refer to the Gaza Strip.

Source:
Organisation des Nations Unies pour l'alimentation et
l'agriculture (FAO), Rome, "Annuaire FAO de la production
1999" et la base de données FAOSTAT.

† Pour les modifications récentes de nomenclature
de pays ou de zone concernant l'Allemagne, Hong Kong, région
administrative spéciale (RAS) de Chine, Macao, région
administrative spéciale (RAS) de Chine,
l'ex-Tchécoslovaquie, l'ex-URSS et l'ex-Rfs de Yougoslavie,
voir annexe I - Nomenclature des pays ou des zones,
groupements régionaux et autres groupements.

†† Les données statistiques relatives à
la Chine ne comprennent pas celles qui concernent la région
administrative spéciale de Hong Kong (la RAS de Hong Kong)
et la région administrative spéciale de Macao (la RAS de
Macao).

1 Les données se rapportent à la Zone de Gaza.

31
Cereals
Céréales
Production: thousand metric tons
Production : milliers de tonnes

Region, country or area Région, pays ou zone	1990	1991	1992	1993	1994	1995	1996	1997	1998	1999
World *Monde*	1 953 438	1 888 769	1 973 866	1 902 079	1 957 882	1 903 107	2 070 061	2 097 471	2 075 256	2 062 427
Africa Afrique	93 150	103 922	89 493	99 391	110 568	96 911	124 746	110 314	114 101	110 815
Algeria Algérie	1 627	3 810	3 330	1 454	965	2 140	4 902	870	3 026	2 029
Angola Angola	249	372	402	322	285	296	525	457	621	550
Benin Bénin	546	587	609	627	646	725	714	906	867	1 047
Botswana Botswana	53	50	20	44	52	42	106	31	12	20
Burkina Faso Burkina Faso	1 518	2 455	2 477	2 552	2 492	2 308	2 470	2 274	2 662	2 662[1]
Burundi Burundi	293	300	306	300	* 225	* 269	* 273	* 305	261	269
Cameroon Cameroun	816	1 048	917	959	910	1 238	1 314	1 136	1 186	1 236[1]
Cape Verde Cap-Vert	11	8	10	12	8[1]	8	10	10[1]	10[1]	10[1]
Central African Rep. Rép. centrafricaine	95	92	94	94	101	113	126	138	148	157
Chad Tchad	601	812	976	683	1 059	907	975	1 077	1 369	1 369[1]
Comoros Comores	19	20	20	21	21	21	21	21	21[1]	21[1]
Congo Congo	6	6	6	7	7	6	* 5	* 4	2	2[1]
Côte d'Ivoire Côte d'Ivoire	1 239	1 286	1 319	1 511	1 599	1 690	1 494	1 963	1 870	1 832
Dem. Rep. of the Congo Rép. dém. du Congo	1 491	1 507	1 553	1 655	1 708	1 766	1 566	1 633	1 692	1 700[1]
Egypt Egypte	13 022	13 864	14 611	14 961	15 012	16 097	16 542	17 492	17 047	18 822
Eritrea Erythrée	...	...	...	87	259	153	84[1]	99[1]	* 458	270[1]
Ethiopia incl. Eritrea Ethiopie comp. Erythrée	6 138	5 811	5 035	...	...	...	...	...	...	...
Ethiopia Ethiopie	...	...	...	5 295	5 245	6 740	9 379	9 473	7 197	7 197[1]
Gabon Gabon	24	25	26	27	29	30[1]	31[1]	32[1]	32[1]	32[1]
Gambia Gambie	90	111	96	97	95	98	103	104	114	144
Ghana Ghana	844	1 436	1 254	1 645	1 594	1 797	1 770	1 669	1 788	1 686
Guinea Guinée	627	686	683	711	718	825	879	927	985	971
Guinea-Bissau Guinée-Bissau	167	179	169	181	190	201	174	183	191[1]	191[1]

31
Cereals
Production: thousand metric tons [*cont.*]
Céréales
Production : milliers de tonnes [*suite*]

Region, country or area Région, pays ou zone	1990	1991	1992	1993	1994	1995	1996	1997	1998	1999
Kenya Kenya	2 728	2 773	2 849	2 530	3 663	3 275	2 773	2 767	3 082	2 514
Lesotho Lesotho	242	67	94	153	223	81	256	206	172	175
Liberia Libéria	185[1]	130[1]	110[1]	* 65	* 50	* 56	* 94	* 168	* 210	210[1]
Libyan Arab Jamah. Jamah. arabe libyenne	273	258[1]	218[1]	180[1]	165[1]	146	160	206	238[1]	251[1]
Madagascar Madagascar	2 581	2 497	2 591	2 724	2 517	2 642	2 685	2 742	2 610	2 829
Malawi Malawi	1 413	1 680	644	2 137	1 110	1 778	1 943	1 349	1 860	2 655
Mali Mali	2 157	1 772	2 414	1 809	2 228	2 457	2 173	2 163	2 149	2 149[1]
Mauritania Mauritanie	103	105	107	169	215	223	231	154	169	196
Mauritius Maurice	2	2	2	2	1	0	0	0	0	0[1]
Morocco Maroc	6 276	8 665	2 950	2 818	9 639	1 783	10 104	4 098	6 641	3 860
Mozambique Mozambique	734	546	242	765	791	1 127	1 379	1 531	1 688	1 770[1]
Namibia Namibie	98	115	31	75	116	62	89	173	55	75
Niger Niger	2 134	2 384	2 253	2 022	2 430	2 095	2 260	1 702	2 957	2 806
Nigeria Nigéria	17 678	18 615	19 597	20 091	20 373	21 206	21 655	21 949	21 621	23 234
Réunion Réunion	11	13	16	14	17	17	16	17[1]	17[1]	17[1]
Rwanda Rwanda	265	341	251	221	126	157	183	222	192	176
Sao Tome and Principe Sao Tomé-et-Principe	3	4	4	4	4	* 3	2[1]	1	2[1]	1
Senegal Sénégal	977	946	856	1 086	943	1 059	976	783	719	963
Sierra Leone Sierra Leone	563	560	534	542	466	408	444	467	373	280
Somalia Somalie	581[1]	256	209	165	405	285	290	284[1]	197[1]	207[1]
South Africa Afrique du Sud	11 553	11 290	5 045	12 793	15 967	7 492	13 651	13 236	10 026	8 887
Sudan Soudan	1 702	4 637	5 438	3 102	5 146	3 305	5 202	4 503	6 102	3 779
Swaziland Swaziland	99	142	58	75	101	79	152	110	126	114
Togo Togo	484	465	495	634	559	550	687	744	620	620[1]
Tunisia Tunisie	1 638	2 556	2 199	1 917	660	623	2 869	1 056	1 667	1 825

31

Cereals
Production: thousand metric tons [*cont.*]
Céréales
Production : milliers de tonnes [*suite*]

Region, country or area Région, pays ou zone	1990	1991	1992	1993	1994	1995	1996	1997	1998	1999
Uganda Ouganda	1 580	1 576	1 743	1 880	1 936	2 030	1 588	1 625	1 931	1 977
United Rep.Tanzania Rép.-Unie de Tanzanie	3 842	3 777	3 533	3 917	3 547	4 626	4 717	3 389	4 492	3 977
Zambia Zambie	1 210	1 225	612	1 758	1 170	882	1 573	1 137	798	1 062
Zimbabwe Zimbabwe	2 560	2 060	481	2 498	2 780	987	3 127	2 723	1 829	1 987
America, North **Amérique du Nord**	**400 181**	**362 743**	**435 367**	**341 267**	**434 334**	**366 751**	**429 034**	**419 615**	**435 026**	**424 252**
Bahamas Bahamas	1[1]	1[1]	1[1]	0[1]	0	0	0	0	0	0[1]
Barbados[1] Barbade[1]	2	2	2	2	2	2	2	2	2	2
Belize Belize	23	37	32	37	30	38	50	54	46	46[1]
Canada Canada	56 803	53 855	49 698	51 676	46 724	49 315	58 465	49 526	50 851	53 776
Costa Rica Costa Rica	281	260	272	204	207	206	211	250	316	292
Cuba Cuba	540	484	418	227	301	305	474	546	551[1]	551[1]
Dominica[1] Dominique[1]	0	0	0	0	0	0	0	0	0	0
Dominican Republic Rép. dominicaine	488	526	629	498	417	548	535	564	530	601
El Salvador El Salvador	825	729	992	909	727	889	857	764	841	925
Guatemala Guatemala	1 435	1 382	1 514	1 446	1 296	1 164	1 140	1 223	1 093	1 209
Haiti Haïti	361	400	452	420[1]	425[1]	410[1]	412	490[1]	403	413[1]
Honduras Honduras	683	692	687	691	674	770	784	757	576	532
Jamaica Jamaïque	2	3	4	4	4	4	4	3	2	2[1]
Mexico Mexique	25 562	23 673	26 889	25 200	26 810	26 883	29 311	28 062	29 265	28 998
Nicaragua Nicaragua	488	388	498	588	521	622	674	619	565	522
Panama Panama	345	337	337	329	348	310	364	239	339	339[1]
St. Vincent-Grenadines St. Vincent-Grenadines	3	2[1]	2	2	2	2	1	1	2	2
Trinidad and Tobago Trinité-et-Tobago	17	19	26	21	23	15	23	12	12	12[1]
United States Etats-Unis	312 322	279 954	352 914	259 010	355 823	285 269	335 726	336 502	349 631	336 028
America, South **Amérique du Sud**	**68 056**	**74 066**	**85 027**	**84 354**	**88 039**	**91 338**	**94 732**	**101 990**	**94 879**	**99 413**

31
Cereals
Production: thousand metric tons [cont.]
Céréales
Production : milliers de tonnes [suite]

Region, country or area Région, pays ou zone	1990	1991	1992	1993	1994	1995	1996	1997	1998	1999
Argentina Argentine	20 079	21 591	25 444	25 097	25 270	24 209	30 495	35 819	36 733	33 435
Bolivia Bolivie	788	1 011	819	1 078	1 008	1 096	1 254	1 252	1 073	1 164
Brazil Brésil	32 469	36 803	44 068	42 981	45 777	49 612	46 371	47 321	40 625	47 635
Chile Chili	2 981	2 864	2 901	2 643	2 619	2 766	2 578	3 077	3 098	2 168
Colombia Colombie	4 314	3 948	3 674	3 522	3 631	3 435	3 177	3 207	2 893	3 286
Ecuador Equateur	1 383	1 444	1 631	1 902	2 061	1 900	1 947	1 815	1 485	1 655
French Guiana Guyane française	22	29	24	27	25	25	31	31	31[1]	31[1]
Guyana Guyana	159	254	288	349	396	506	547	571	535	603
Paraguay Paraguay	893	761	888	1 000	982	1 187	1 353	1 621	1 205	1 597
Peru Pérou	1 778	1 729	1 522	2 013	2 408	2 135	2 338	2 586	2 830	3 248
Suriname Suriname	196	229	261	217	218	242	220	229	213	181
Uruguay Uruguay	1 121	1 098	1 541	1 424	1 464	1 795	2 194	2 068	2 025	2 394
Venezuela Venezuela	1 874	2 305	1 966	2 100	2 181	2 428	2 225	2 391	2 132	2 017
Asia Asie	874 257	868 963	931 089	936 459	924 681	943 830	995 107	993 788	1 012 769	1 020 956
Afghanistan Afghanistan	2 705	2 724	2 770[1]	2 970	3 202[1]	3 322[1]	3 522[1]	3 683	3 876	3 876[1]
Armenia Arménie	...	...	307	344	226	260	368	278	325	296
Azerbaijan Azerbaïdjan	...	...	1 325	1 137	1 024	910	1 010	1 119	940	932
Bangladesh Bangladesh	27 747	28 462	28 654	28 297	26 513	27 702	29 622	29 673	30 162	31 832
Bhutan Bhoutan	106	106	106	105[1]	107[1]	112[1]	112[1]	112[1]	112[1]	112[1]
Brunei Darussalam Brunéi Darussalam	1	1	1	1	1	0	0	0	0[1]	0[1]
Cambodia Cambodge	2 588	2 460	2 281	2 429	2 268	3 373	3 455	3 457	3 558	3 850
China †† Chine ††	404 413	398 464	404 269	407 931	396 460	418 665	453 665	445 931	458 395	456 588
Cyprus Chypre	109	65	182	205	162	145	141	48	66	133
Georgia Géorgie	...	...	496	402	471	498	669	892	589	766
India Inde	193 919	193 101	201 619	208 121	213 167	209 778	216 918	223 615	224 027	229 173

31
Cereals
Production: thousand metric tons [cont.]
Céréales
Production : milliers de tonnes [suite]

Region, country or area Région, pays ou zone	1990	1991	1992	1993	1994	1995	1996	1997	1998	1999
Indonesia Indonésie	51 913	50 944	56 235	54 641	53 510	57 990	60 409	58 148	59 406	58 668
Iran (Islamic Rep. of) Iran (Rép. islamique d')	13 684	14 447	15 811	16 287	16 691	17 031	16 077	15 812	18 971	13 851
Iraq Iraq	3 455	2 673	2 959	3 239	2 829	2 538	2 999	2 211	2 511	1 644[1]
Israel Israël	303	190	267	230	121	248	195	126	163	90
Japan Japon	14 449	13 070	14 286	10 737	15 787	14 122	13 668	13 326	11 942	11 979
Jordan Jordanie	129	107	157	114	111	125	97	97	92	29
Kazakhstan Kazakhstan	...	...	29 658	21 540	16 375	9 476	11 210	12 359	6 380	15 555
Korea, Dem. P. R. Corée, R. p. dém. de	8 071	8 836	8 681	9 137	7 215	3 787	2 596	2 866	4 412	3 957
Korea, Republic of Corée, République de	8 434	7 853	7 846	7 042	7 305	6 876	7 616	7 675	7 131	7 698
Kuwait Koweït	2[1]	0[1]	2[1]	2[1]	2	2	3	4	4	4[1]
Kyrgyzstan Kirghizistan	...	...	1 603	1 597	1 065	1 045	1 407	1 730	1 619	1 621
Lao People's Dem. Rep. Rép. dém. pop. lao	1 558	1 292	1 561	1 298	1 633	1 468	1 492	1 738	1 784	2 199
Lebanon Liban	77	83	88	81	79	100	94	94[1]	94	93[1]
Malaysia Malaisie	1 995	2 175	2 106	2 142	2 179	2 170	2 273	2 178	* 1 990	1 990[1]
Mongolia Mongolie	720	597	496	474	328	261	219	240	194	172
Myanmar Myanmar	14 424	13 652	15 342	17 263	18 727	18 483	18 391	18 208	17 231	17 632
Nepal Népal	5 847	5 520	4 902	5 816	5 381	6 113	6 367	6 280	6 361	6 465
Occupied Palestinian Terr.[2] Terr. palestinien occupé[2]	1	1	1	1	1	1	1	1	1	1
Oman Oman	5	5[1]	5[1]	5[1]	6[1]	6[1]	6[1]	6[1]	6[1]	6[1]
Pakistan Pakistan	20 957	21 138	22 123	23 870	22 338	24 816	25 163	24 994	27 621	26 661
Philippines Philippines	14 739	14 329	14 132	14 232	14 669	14 702	15 629	15 601	14 059	16 031
Qatar Qatar	3	4	4	5	4	4	5	6	6[1]	6[1]
Saudi Arabia Arabie saoudite	4 137	4 574	4 703	5 043	4 875	2 669	1 938	2 435	2 440	2 440
Sri Lanka Sri Lanka	2 579	2 430	2 374	2 549	2 722	2 850	2 099	2 269	2 731	2 731[1]
Syrian Arab Republic Rép. arabe syrienne	3 103	3 294	4 368	5 393	5 397	6 098	5 995	4 325	5 295	3 247

31
Cereals
Production: thousand metric tons [cont.]
Céréales
Production : milliers de tonnes [suite]

Region, country or area Région, pays ou zone	1990	1991	1992	1993	1994	1995	1996	1997	1998	1999
Tajikistan Tadjikistan	...	...	260	258	248	242	477	527	521	521
Thailand Thaïlande	21 170	24 462	23 864	22 013	25 339	26 399	27 124	27 605	27 982	28 105
Turkey Turquie	30 201	31 148	29 157	31 749	27 014	28 134	29 344	29 747	33 182	30 282
Turkmenistan Turkménistan	...	...	732	1 009	1 120	1 102	545	759	1 278	1 567
United Arab Emirates Emirats arabes unis	3	2	3	1	1	1	1	1[1]	1[1]	1[1]
Uzbekistan Ouzbékistan	...	...	2 178	2 165	2 502	3 223	3 558	3 771	3 691	4 337
Viet Nam Viet Nam	19 898	20 296	22 341	23 721	24 675	26 144	27 936	29 167	30 759	33 149
Yemen Yémen	767	448	811	834	802	810	659	646	830	635
Europe **Europe**	**284 737**	**303 522**	**407 027**	**413 066**	**383 951**	**376 163**	**390 639**	**439 859**	**385 952**	**374 929**
Albania Albanie	897	446	430	686	666	662	519	616	620	579
Austria Autriche	5 290	5 045	4 323	4 206	4 436	4 455	4 493	5 009	4 771	4 756
Belarus Bélarus	...	...	7 061	7 240	5 872	5 314	5 478	5 919	4 493	* 3 353
Belgium-Luxembourg Belgique-Luxembourg	2 119	2 215	2 165	2 311	2 174	2 144	2 571	2 393	2 625	2 378
Bosnia and Herzegovina Bosnie-Herzégovine	...	...	1 269[1]	1 174[1]	1 085	717	842	297	514	438
Bulgaria Bulgarie	8 115	8 974	6 560	5 666	6 409	6 514	3 380	6 152	5 345	4 888
Croatia Croatie	...	...	2 356	2 733	2 596	2 780	2 762	3 179	3 202	2 883
former Czechoslovakia† l'ex-Tchécoslovaquie†	12 626	11 939	10 198	...	...	...	...	...	...	...
Czech Republic République tchèque	...	...	...	6 486	6 788	6 609	6 651	6 990	6 677	6 964
Denmark Danemark	9 607	9 231	6 954	8 203	7 800	9 043	9 218	9 529	9 334	9 183[1]
Estonia Estonie	...	...	592	811	510	513	629	650	576	485
Finland Finlande	4 296	3 429	2 603	3 340	3 400	3 333	3 697	3 807	2 773	3 418
France France	55 111	60 335	60 639	55 626	53 407	53 545	62 599	63 432	68 446	64 364
Germany Allemagne	37 580	39 268	34 758	35 549	36 336	39 863	42 136	45 486	44 575	44 352
Greece Grèce	4 464	6 183	5 035	4 856	5 272	4 903	4 591	4 705	4 569	4 554
Hungary Hongrie	12 561	15 797	9 981	8 520	11 720	11 277	11 324	14 141	13 103	11 346

31
Cereals
Production: thousand metric tons [*cont.*]
Céréales
Production : milliers de tonnes [*suite*]

Region, country or area Région, pays ou zone	1990	1991	1992	1993	1994	1995	1996	1997	1998	1999
Ireland Irlande	1 966	1 964	2 017	1 627	1 610	1 796	2 142	1 944	1 865	2 022
Italy Italie	17 411	19 219	19 891	19 772	19 187	19 692	20 911	19 912	20 731	21 005
Latvia Lettonie	...	...	1 135	1 187	893	692	961	1 036	957	754
Lithuania Lituanie	...	...	2 198	2 673	2 098	1 907	2 615	2 945	2 717	* 2 114
Malta Malte	8 [1]	7	7	7	7	7	7	6	6	6
Netherlands Pays-Bas	1 361	1 252	1 350	1 466	1 355	1 505	1 659	1 373	1 434	1 345
Norway Norvège	1 568	1 482	1 010	1 402	1 271	1 227	1 345	1 288	1 412	1 299
Poland Pologne	28 014	27 812	19 962	23 417	21 763	25 905	25 298	25 400	27 159	26 883
Portugal Portugal	1 427	1 789	1 338	1 449	1 645	1 446	1 673	1 563	1 380	1 855
Republic of Moldova République de Moldova	...	...	1 976	3 219	1 628	2 683	1 977	3 487	2 511	2 116
Romania Roumanie	17 174	19 307	12 288	15 493	18 184	19 883	14 199	22 097	15 450	15 723
Russian Federation Fédération de Russie	...	...	103 794	96 225	78 650	61 902	67 589	86 802	46 969	53 783
Slovakia Slovaquie	...	...	...	3 157	3 700	3 489	3 322	3 740	3 485	2 829
Slovenia Slovénie	...	...	429	457	571	453	487	544	557	534
Spain Espagne	18 762	19 457	14 479	17 479	15 231	11 574	22 328	19 318	22 478	17 218
Sweden Suède	6 380	5 160	3 760	5 242	4 472	4 860	5 995	5 986	5 618	5 112
Switzerland Suisse	1 268	1 313	1 213	1 292	1 249	1 281	1 348	1 223	1 264	1 040
TFYR Macedonia L'ex-R.y. Macédoine	...	...	624	479	648	725	546	610	742	760
Ukraine Ukraine	...	...	35 550	42 725	32 960	32 360	23 486	34 396	25 720	23 841
United Kingdom Royaume-Uni	22 569	22 635	22 063	19 482	19 948	21 859	24 567	23 527	22 783	22 045
Yugoslavia Yougoslavie	...	...	7 019	7 411	8 409	9 245	7 294	10 355	9 093	8 704
Yugoslavia, SFR† Yougoslavie, Rfs†	14 165	19 263	...	...	...	...	...	...	...	...
Oceania Océanie	**23 948**	**19 592**	**25 863**	**27 542**	**16 308**	**28 113**	**35 804**	**31 905**	**32 529**	**32 062**
Australia Australie	23 045	18 748	25 097	26 709	15 437	27 331	34 870	30 829	31 667	31 117
Fiji Fidji	28	30	23	23	20	20	19	19	18	18 [1]

31

Cereals
Production: thousand metric tons [cont.]
Céréales
Production : milliers de tonnes [suite]

Region, country or area Région, pays ou zone	1990	1991	1992	1993	1994	1995	1996	1997	1998	1999
New Caledonia Nouvelle-Calédonie	1	1	1	1	1	1	2	2[1]	2[1]	2[1]
New Zealand Nouvelle-Zélande	868	808	736	803	843	752	904	1 046	830	910
Papua New Guinea Papouasie-Nvl-Guinée	4[1]	5[1]	5[1]	6[1]	7[1]	8[1]	9[1]	10	10[1]	10[1]
Solomon Islands Iles Salomon	0[1]	0[1]	0[1]	0[1]	0[1]	0[1]	0[1]	0[1]	* 1	* 5
Vanuatu Vanuatu	1[1]	1[1]	1[1]	1[1]	1[1]	1[1]	1[1]	1	1	1[1]
former USSR† l'ex-URSS†	209 109	155 960	...	...	...	...	...	...	...	...

Source:
Food and Agriculture Organization of the United
Nations (FAO), Rome, "FAO Production Yearbook 1999" and the
FAOSTAT database.

† For information on recent changes in country or
area nomenclature pertaining to former Czechoslovakia,
Germany, Hong Kong Special Administrative Region (SAR) of
China, Macao Special Administrative Region (SAR) of China,
SFR of Yugoslavia and the former USSR, see Annex I - Country
or area nomenclature, regional and other groupings.

†† For statistical purposes, the data for
China do not include those for Hong Kong Special
Administrative Region (Hong Kong SAR) and Macao Special
Administrative Region (Macao SAR).

1 FAO estimate.
2 Data refer to the Gaza Strip.

Source:
Organisation des Nations Unies pour l'alimentation et
l'agriculture (FAO), Rome, "Annuaire FAO de la production
1999" et la base de données FAOSTAT.

† Pour les modifications récentes de nomenclature
de pays ou de zone concernant l'Allemagne, Hong Kong, région
administrative spéciale (RAS) de Chine, Macao, région
administrative spéciale (RAS) de Chine,
l'ex-Tchécoslovaquie, l'ex-URSS et l'ex-Rfs de Yougoslavie,
voir annexe I - Nomenclature des pays ou des zones,
groupements régionaux et autres groupements.

†† Les données statistiques relatives à
la Chine ne comprennent pas celles qui concernent la région
administrative spéciale de Hong Kong (la RAS de Hong Kong)
et la région administrative spéciale de Macao (la RAS de
Macao).

1 Estimation de la FAO.
2 Les données se rapportent à la Zone de Gaza.

32
Oil crops, in oil equivalent
Cultures d'huile, en équivalent d'huile
Production: thousand metric tons
Production : milliers de tonnes

Region, country or area Région, pays ou zone	1990	1991	1992	1993	1994	1995	1996	1997	1998	1999
World *Monde*	**74 296**	**76 435**	**77 392**	**79 683**	**87 959**	**91 437**	**92 816**	**97 243**	**100 654**	**103 472**
Africa Afrique	**5 866**	**6 210**	**5 972**	**6 446**	**6 600**	**6 939**	**8 007**	**7 488**	**7 670**	**8 197**
Algeria Algérie	70	52	94	81	73	64	105	106	64	105
Angola Angola	56	59	62	63	66	65	67	66	68	60
Benin Bénin	78	78	74	89	90	109	113	114	109	125
Botswana Botswana	1	1	1[1]	1[1]	1[1]	1[1]	1[1]	1[1]	1[1]	1[1]
Burkina Faso Burkina Faso	90	75	90	102	103	109	117	108	129	129[1]
Burundi Burundi	8	8	8	8	6	7	6	7	6	6
Cameroon Cameroun	274	253	253	260	265	284	303	275	274	300
Cape Verde Cap-Vert	1	1	1	1	1	1	1	1	1	1
Central African Rep. Rép. centrafricaine	65	57	61	61	66	70	73	77	78	81
Chad Tchad	63	105	98	86	93	122	134	156	193	193[1]
Comoros Comores	6	7	7	7	7	* 9	* 9	* 10	10[1]	9[1]
Congo Congo	27	27	26	27	28	27	27[1]	25	26[1]	27[1]
Côte d'Ivoire Côte d'Ivoire	334	342	357	371	367	358	367	342	368	328
Dem. Rep. of the Congo Rép. dém. du Congo	396	399	405	422	425	426	357	337	331	342[1]
Egypt Egypte	159	171	187	233	195	219	244	225	192	214[1]
Equatorial Guinea[1] Guinée équatoriale[1]	9	9	9	9	9	9	9	9	9	9
Eritrea Erythrée	...	...	...	7	9	9[1]	8[1]	7[1]	8	8[1]
Ethiopia incl. Eritrea Ethiopie comp. Erythrée	138	144	145	...	...	...	...	...	...	...
Ethiopia Ethiopie	...	...	...	145	143	144	147	147	149	149[1]
Gabon Gabon	10	12	12	13	13	13	12	13	12[1]	12[1]
Gambia Gambie	31	34	25	32	33	31	22	32	31	47
Ghana Ghana	249	236	250	266	281	272	264	262	311	311[1]

32
Oil crops, in oil equivalent
Production: thousand metric tons [cont.]
Cultures d'huile, en équivalent d'huile
Production : milliers de tonnes [suite]

Region, country or area Région, pays ou zone	1990	1991	1992	1993	1994	1995	1996	1997	1998	1999
Guinea Guinée	160	175	177	200	203	207	217	222	228	228 [1]
Guinea-Bissau Guinée-Bissau	25	30	26	25	27	28	27	28	28	28
Kenya Kenya	30	33	28	30	34	32	33	36	36	33 [1]
Liberia [1] Libéria [1]	26	23	23	24	26	28	31	33	33	33
Libyan Arab Jamah. Jamah. arabe libyenne	20	22	26	31	35	42	46	46	47	47
Madagascar Madagascar	30	29	27	31	28	29	31	31	32	31
Malawi Malawi	16	25	13	25	17	22	29	29	42	42 [1]
Mali Mali	102	114	116	102	101	128	121	119	130	130
Mauritania Mauritanie	2	2	1	1	1	2	2	2	2 [1]	2 [1]
Mauritius Maurice	1	1	1	1	1	1	0	1	0	0 [1]
Morocco Maroc	163	169	156	123	146	107	252	158	184	119
Mozambique Mozambique	115	115	106	108	104	114	121	127	135	135
Namibia Namibie	1	0	0	1	0	0	0	0	0	0 [1]
Niger Niger	6	15	19	9	22	36	63	29	36	35
Nigeria Nigéria	1 708	1 855	1 874	2 040	2 193	2 277	2 621	2 674	2 758	2 831
Réunion Réunion	0	0	0 [1]	0	1	0	0	0 [1]	0 [1]	0 [1]
Rwanda Rwanda	6	5	8	4	4	4	4	3	3	3
Sao Tome and Principe [1] Sao Tomé-et-Principe [1]	4	7	7	7	6	6	7	7	7	8
Senegal Sénégal	242	247	199	215	233	272	225	195	203	282
Seychelles [1] Seychelles [1]	1	1	0	0	0	0	0	0	0	0
Sierra Leone Sierra Leone	58	58	55	55	61	58	59	60	60	43
Somalia Somalie	24	19	9	13	13	15	14	14	12 [1]	13 [1]
South Africa Afrique du Sud	344	333	138	210	228	276	415	271	322	560
Sudan Soudan	130	152	298	267	374	448	515	523	382	471 [1]

32
Oil crops, in oil equivalent
Production: thousand metric tons [*cont.*]
Cultures d'huile, en équivalent d'huile
Production : milliers de tonnes [*suite*]

Region, country or area Région, pays ou zone	1990	1991	1992	1993	1994	1995	1996	1997	1998	1999
Swaziland Swaziland	4	4	2	2	2	2	3	3	3	3[1]
Togo Togo	48	45	50	49	52	55	64	60	58	58[1]
Tunisia Tunisie	186	296	153	236	82	72	347	116	215	215[1]
Uganda Ouganda	97	97	101	109	105	106	103	107	112	135
United Rep.Tanzania Rép.-Unie de Tanzanie	122	140	141	133	126	143	145	138	126	126[1]
Zambia Zambie	24	24	11	33	23	29	33	26	25	29[1]
Zimbabwe Zimbabwe	105	104	39	80	79	51	92	111	81	97
America, North **Amérique du Nord**	**13 996**	**15 164**	**15 456**	**14 573**	**19 371**	**17 080**	**17 534**	**19 718**	**20 717**	**20 624**
Canada Canada	1 783	2 045	1 792	2 584	3 396	3 135	2 535	3 125	3 645	4 064
Costa Rica Costa Rica	70	76	75	77	99	102	90	90	92	92
Cuba Cuba	8	8	7	8	8	8	8	8	8	8
Dominica Dominique	1[1]	2[1]	2	2	2[1]	2[1]	2[1]	2[1]	1[1]	1[1]
Dominican Republic Rép. dominicaine	41	44	42	45	50	50	50	48	49	52
El Salvador El Salvador	19	18	18	18	14	15	15	15	15	15
Grenada[1] Grenade[1]	1	1	1	1	1	1	1	1	1	1
Guatemala Guatemala	45	46	55	49	56	62	76	94	95	97
Haiti Haïti	19[1]	17[1]	14	14[1]	14[1]	14[1]	14	14[1]	13	13[1]
Honduras Honduras	73	73	85	78	89	98	107	116	109	109[1]
Jamaica Jamaïque	11	13	16	16	16	16	16	16	16	16[1]
Mexico Mexique	427	422	330	321	346	350	377	385	398	389
Nicaragua Nicaragua	23	25	22	23	38	31	35	33	31	30
Panama Panama	3	3	3	3[1]	2	2	2	2[1]	2[1]	2[1]
Puerto Rico Porto Rico	1	1	1	1	1	1	1	1	1[1]	1[1]

32
Oil crops, in oil equivalent
Production: thousand metric tons [*cont.*]
Cultures d'huile, en équivalent d'huile
Production : milliers de tonnes [*suite*]

Region, country or area Région, pays ou zone	1990	1991	1992	1993	1994	1995	1996	1997	1998	1999
Saint Lucia[1] Sainte-Lucie[1]	4	3	3	3	2	2	2	3	2	2
St. Vincent-Grenadines St. Vincent-Grenadines	3	3	3	3	3	3	3	3	3	3
Trinidad and Tobago[1] Trinité-et-Tobago[1]	5	5	7	7	4	3	3	3	3	3
United States Etats-Unis	11 460	12 358	12 981	11 321	15 229	13 184	14 197	15 757	16 233	15 725
America, South **Amérique du Sud**	**9 244**	**8 524**	**8 955**	**9 164**	**10 309**	**11 495**	**11 218**	**11 439**	**14 052**	**14 220**
Argentina Argentine	3 855	4 008	3 744	3 425	3 987	4 824	4 906	4 459	6 067	6 170
Bolivia Bolivie	52	85	80	104	146	183	181	231	248	186
Brazil Brésil	4 053	3 192	3 931	4 400	4 877	5 019	4 604	5 122	6 031	5 988
Chile Chili	32	36	34	16	13	14	15	15	22	29
Colombia Colombie	379	427	407	408	414	511	520	544	555	580
Ecuador Equateur	213	220	218	228	263	233	234	285	309	311
Guyana Guyana	6	6	6	7	8	10	10	10	8	8
Paraguay Paraguay	466	389	401	438	444	513	540	560	618	707
Peru Pérou	54	50	36	44	54	59	64	57	52	55
Suriname Suriname	3	3	4	3	3	3	2	1	1	1
Uruguay Uruguay	20	29	30	26	30	52	49	50	36	79
Venezuela Venezuela	112	78	64	65	69	72	94	105	105	106
Asia **Asie**	**33 060**	**33 620**	**36 040**	**39 148**	**41 241**	**43 514**	**44 648**	**45 913**	**45 197**	**45 875**
Afghanistan Afghanistan	26	30	30	30	30	30	30	30	30[1]	30[1]
Armenia Arménie	...	...	...	...	...	...	...	...	4	4
Azerbaijan Azerbaïdjan	...	...	37	31	31	30	30	14	13	11[1]
Bangladesh Bangladesh	145	146	155	159	153	156	154	157	158	159
Bhutan[1] Bhoutan[1]	1	1	1	1	1	1	1	1	1	1
Cambodia Cambodge	15	19	20	19	17	16	19	24	19	19

32
Oil crops, in oil equivalent
Production: thousand metric tons [*cont.*]
        Cultures d'huile, en équivalent d'huile
        Production : milliers de tonnes [*suite*]

Region, country or area Région, pays ou zone	1990	1991	1992	1993	1994	1995	1996	1997	1998	1999
China †† Chine ††	9 633	9 995	9 741	10 811	11 810	12 366	12 031	12 321	12 714	12 869
Cyprus Chypre	3	2	5	3	3	3	3	2	3	4
Georgia Géorgie	...	...	3	1	4	3	3	13	9	17
India Inde	7 211	7 405	8 464	8 255	8 715	8 866	9 470	9 679	8 962	9 234
Indonesia Indonésie	4 500	4 814	5 140	5 973	6 501	7 028	7 483	7 905	8 216	8 210
Iran (Islamic Rep. of) Iran (Rép. islamique d')	101	92	85	85	102	115	128	112	115	115 [1]
Iraq Iraq	37	18	36	44	37	39	41	40	41	38 [1]
Israel Israël	35	29	40	32	28	38	40	36	40	40 [1]
Japan Japon	58	52	50	31	36	38	45	45	45	49
Jordan Jordanie	14	9	18	7	21	14	20	13	30	12
Kazakhstan Kazakhstan	...	...	109	82	88	84	60	58	66	85
Korea, Dem. P. R. Corée, R. p. dém. de	85 [1]	82	75	72	76	74	76	68	65	65 [1]
Korea, Republic of Corée, République de	76	64	64	53	55	58	54	55	51	50
Kyrgyzstan Kirghizistan	...	...	6	5	6	8	9	8	9	11
Lao People's Dem. Rep. Rép. dém. pop. lao	5	6	7	7	7	9	9	9	10	10
Lebanon Liban	16	13	26	14 [1]	21	15 [1]	24	17 [1]	25	25 [1]
Malaysia Malaisie	6 373	6 456	6 802	8 110	7 923	8 608	8 901	9 409	8 669 [1]	8 669 [1]
Maldives Maldives	* 2	* 2	2	* 2	* 2	* 2	2 [1]	2 [1]	2 [1]	2 [1]
Myanmar Myanmar	317	329	277	328	315	397	455	436	411	424
Nepal Népal	36	34	33	35	36	38	38	39	38	40
Occupied Palestinian Terr.[2] Terr. palestinien occupé[2]	1	1	1	1	1	1	1	1	1	1
Pakistan Pakistan	683	866	669	603	640	777	729	735	704	708
Philippines Philippines	1 484	1 178	1 277	1 530	1 513	1 639	1 531	1 626	1 466	1 478 [1]
Saudi Arabia Arabie saoudite	2	2	2	2	2	2	2	2 [1]	2 [1]	2 [1]

32
Oil crops, in oil equivalent
Production: thousand metric tons [cont.]
Cultures d'huile, en équivalent d'huile
Production : milliers de tonnes [suite]

Region, country or area Région, pays ou zone	1990	1991	1992	1993	1994	1995	1996	1997	1998	1999
Sri Lanka Sri Lanka	255	220	230	222	264	277	255	265	245	245 [1]
Syrian Arab Republic Rép. arabe syrienne	174	134	219	175	198	183	252	225	297	202
Tajikistan Tadjikistan	...	...	57	58	58	45	35	39	42	35
Thailand Thaïlande	679	678	689	799	813	854	942	925	889	1 101
Turkey Turquie	845	697	772	668	842	781	988	755	999	999 [1]
Turkmenistan Turkménistan	...	...	142	148	141	142	48	70	78	143
Uzbekistan Ouzbékistan	...	...	462	473	442	442	378	417	366	416
Viet Nam Viet Nam	211	242	250	271	273	298	324	322	323	309
Yemen Yémen	5	5	6	7	7	8	9	10	11	11
Europe **Europe**	**7 588**	**8 800**	**10 231**	**9 582**	**9 714**	**11 590**	**10 542**	**11 633**	**11 696**	**13 030**
Albania Albanie	12	10	6	6	7	9	7	8	11	9
Austria Autriche	62	84	94	108	135	126	67	72	85	92 [1]
Belarus Bélarus	...	...	18	15	15	20	19	21	32	35 [1]
Belgium-Luxembourg Belgique-Luxembourg	11	14	9	9	12	13	12	* 11	* 12	12 [1]
Bosnia and Herzegovina Bosnie-Herzégovine	...	...	3 [1]	2 [1]	1 [1]	1	2	2 [1]	1	1
Bulgaria Bulgarie	168	188	248	179	246	316	217	182	216	206
Croatia Croatie	...	...	37	38	32	37	26	28	51	64
former Czechoslovakia† l'ex-Tchécoslovaquie†	178	230	202	...	...	...	...	...	...	...
Czech Republic République tchèque	...	...	...	149	180	259	205	215	262	409
Denmark Danemark	278	254	142	146	130	110	89	103	117	117 [1]
Estonia Estonie	...	...	1 [1]	1 [1]	1	2	4	3	6	11
Finland Finlande	41	33	46	45	38	45	31	33	24	24 [1]
France France	1 741	1 908	1 523	1 253	1 516	1 842	1 879	2 096	2 066	2 413
Germany Allemagne	766	1 099	1 009	1 096	1 151	1 150	760	1 081	1 276	1 560

32
Oil crops, in oil equivalent
Production: thousand metric tons [*cont.*]
Cultures d'huile, en équivalent d'huile
Production : milliers de tonnes [*suite*]

Region, country or area / Région, pays ou zone	1990	1991	1992	1993	1994	1995	1996	1997	1998	1999
Greece / Grèce	318	531	517	494	589	646	554	555	605	567
Hungary / Hongrie	331	386	337	292	295	357	408	279	336	459
Ireland / Irlande	7	8	6	3	6	5	4	4	6	6[1]
Italy / Italie	722	1 285	857	908	969	1 131	880	1 233	1 008	1 081
Latvia / Lettonie	...	...	4	4	2	1	1	1	1	1[1]
Lithuania / Lituanie	...	...	4	2	6	9	9	14	21	21[1]
Netherlands / Pays-Bas	12	11	6	6	6	5	3	4	4	4
Norway / Norvège	3	2	3	5	5	* 5	* 5	* 5	5	3
Poland / Pologne	434	371	269	212	272	491	164	214	391	442
Portugal / Portugal	71	115	61	85	73	87	84	89	86	78
Republic of Moldova / République de Moldova	...	...	80	79	60	93	127	70	80	114
Romania / Roumanie	265	290	341	307	329	401	466	376	483	560
Russian Federation / Fédération de Russie	...	...	1 432	1 273	1 174	1 813	1 236	1 244	1 321	1 528
Slovakia / Slovaquie	...	...	...	49	58	88	94	98	86	137
Slovenia / Slovénie	...	...	2	2	2	1	1	0	0	0[1]
Spain / Espagne	1 314	1 104	1 271	1 159	1 044	657	1 536	1 870	1 347	915
Sweden / Suède	148	101	99	126	75	71	50	47	45	46
Switzerland / Suisse	16	18	16	18	13	17	17	20	19	17
TFYR Macedonia / L'ex-R.y. Macédoine	...	...	16	8	8	9	10	7	6	6[1]
Ukraine / Ukraine	...	...	928	869	647	1 171	863	944	938	1 159
United Kingdom / Royaume-Uni	465	514	482	462	482	461	524	572	600	687
Yugoslavia / Yougoslavie	...	...	161	170	135	143	191	135	149	244
Yugoslavia, SFR† / Yougoslavie, Rfs†	227	245	...	...	...	...	...	...	...	...
Oceania / Océanie	**587**	**687**	**739**	**770**	**724**	**818**	**866**	**1 052**	**1 321**	**1 526**

32
Oil crops, in oil equivalent
Production: thousand metric tons [*cont.*]
Cultures d'huile, en équivalent d'huile
Production : milliers de tonnes [*suite*]

Region, country or area Région, pays ou zone	1990	1991	1992	1993	1994	1995	1996	1997	1998	1999
American Samoa[1] Samoa américaines[1]	1	1	1	1	1	1	1	1	1	1
Australia Australie	177	278	268	277	252	357	394	555	844	1 046
Cocos (Keeling) Islands[1] Iles des Cocos (Keeling)[1]	1	1	1	1	1	1	1	1	1	1
Cook Islands Iles Cook	1[1]	1[1]	0	1	0	1[1]	1[1]	1	1	1[1]
Fiji Fidji	33	26	32	26	25	25[1]	28[1]	28	27	27[1]
French Polynesia[1] Polynésie française[1]	13	11	11	11	11	11	11	11	11	11
Guam[1] Guam[1]	5	5	5	5	5	5	5	5	5	5
Kiribati Kiribati	* 8	* 10	* 11	* 11	* 11	* 11	* 11	* 11	11[1]	11
New Caledonia[1] Nouvelle-Calédonie[1]	2	2	2	2	2	2	2	2	2	2
New Zealand Nouvelle-Zélande	1	1	1	1	2	2	2	2	2	2
Papua New Guinea Papouasie-Nvl-Guinée	216	235	282	309	286	288	299	302	294	294[1]
Samoa[1] Samoa[1]	18	12	13	17	17	17	17	17	17	17
Solomon Islands Iles Salomon	43	46	54	51	54	55	53	58	56	59[1]
Tonga Tonga	4	4	4[1]	4[1]	4[1]	3	3[1]	3[1]	3[1]	3[1]
Vanuatu Vanuatu	47	35	34	34	34	37	37	53	45	45[1]
former USSR† l'ex-URSS†	3 955	3 430	...	...	...	...	...	...	...	...

Source:
Food and Agriculture Organization of the United
Nations (FAO), Rome, "FAO Production Yearbook 1999" and the
FAOSTAT database.

† For information on recent changes in country or
area nomenclature pertaining to former Czechoslovakia,
Germany, Hong Kong Special Administrative Region (SAR) of
China, Macao Special Administrative Region (SAR) of China,
SFR of Yugoslavia and the former USSR, see Annex I - Country
or area nomenclature, regional and other groupings.

†† For statistical purposes, the data for
China do not include those for Hong Kong Special
Administrative Region (Hong Kong SAR) and Macao Special
Administrative Region (Macao SAR).

1 FAO estimate.
2 Data refer to the Gaza Strip.

Source:
Organisation des Nations Unies pour l'alimentation et
l'agriculture (FAO), Rome, "Annuaire FAO de la production
1999" et la base de données FAOSTAT.

† Pour les modifications récentes de nomenclature
de pays ou de zone concernant l'Allemagne, Hong Kong, région
administrative spéciale (RAS) de Chine, Macao, région
administrative spéciale (RAS) de Chine,
l'ex-Tchécoslovaquie, l'ex-URSS et l'ex-Rfs de Yougoslavie,
voir annexe I - Nomenclature des pays ou des zones,
groupements régionaux et autres groupements.

†† Les données statistiques relatives à
la Chine ne comprennent pas celles qui concernent la région
administrative spéciale de Hong Kong (la RAS de Hong Kong)
et la région administrative spéciale de Macao (la RAS de
Macao).

1 Estimation de la FAO.
2 Les données se rapportent à la Zone de Gaza.

33
Livestock
Cheptel
Thousand head
Milliers de têtes

Region, country or area	1992	1993	1994	1995	1996	1997	1998	1999	Région, pays ou zone
World									**Monde**
Cattle and buffaloes	1455459	1459333	1474887	1479633	1491938	1484859	1495820	1500608	Bovine et buffles
Sheep and goats	1751840	1743160	1756833	1750636	1777884	1747678	1771473	1781543	Ovine et caprins
Pigs	871 429	879 991	885 958	894 988	915 915	840 964	880 795	915 266	Porcine
Horses	61 315	61 282	61 426	61 993	62 277	60 852	60 885	60 991	Chevaline
Asses	44 307	44 078	44 266	44 513	44 307	43 186	43 403	43 447	Asine
Mules	15 028	14 968	14 843	14 891	14 779	14 150	14 170	14 101	Mulassière
Africa									**Afrique**
Cattle and buffaloes	196 590	197 350	200 201	205 188	215 121	220 387	225 785	227 589	Bovine et buffles
Sheep and goats	382 377	392 606	410 372	414 033	421 943	434 924	446 693	448 375	Ovine et caprins
Pigs	18 974	20 584	21 235	21 623	21 759	26 198	26 764	27 238	Porcine
Horses	4 681	4 765	4 800	4 825	4 843	4 862	4 878	4 886	Chevaline
Asses	14 487	14 615	14 813	14 919	14 789	14 903	14 946	14 967	Asine
Mules	1 376	1 372	1 367	1 379	1 357	1 344	1 348	1 348	Mulassière
Algeria									**Algérie**
Cattle and buffaloes	1 342	1 314	1 269	1 267	1 228	1 255	1 317	1 350[1]	Bovine et buffles
Sheep and goats	20 498	21 348	20 386	20 081	20 460	19 876	20 900	21 200[1]	Ovine et caprins
Pigs [1]	6	6	6	6	6	6	6	6	Porcine [1]
Horses	77	73	67	62	60	52	55[1]	55[1]	Chevaline
Asses	278	259	226	224	210	199	200[1]	200[1]	Asine
Mules	92	88	81	80	76	69	70[1]	70[1]	Mulassière
Angola									**Angola**
Cattle and buffaloes	3 200	3 100[1]	3 000[1]	3 000	3 309	* 3 556	* 3 898	* 3 900	Bovine et buffles
Sheep and goats	1 800	1 745[1]	1 690[1]	* 1 700	1 850[1]	* 2 000	* 2 166	* 2 336	Ovine et caprins
Pigs	810	800[1]	790[1]	800	810[1]	820[1]	810[1]	800[1]	Porcine
Horses [1]	1	1	1	1	1	1	1	1	Chevaline [1]
Asses [1]	5	5	5	5	5	5	5	5	Asine [1]
Benin									**Bénin**
Cattle and buffaloes	* 1 141	* 1 140	1 223	1 294	1 350	1 399	1 345	1 345[1]	Bovine et buffles
Sheep and goats	* 2 040[1]	2 120[1]	2 150[1]	1 575[1]	1 614	1 688[1]	1 721	1 721[1]	Ovine et caprins
Pigs	* 513	* 536	555	566	584	580[1]	470	470[1]	Porcine
Horses [1]	6	6	6	6	6	6	6	6	Chevaline [1]
Asses [1]	1	1	1	1	1	1	1	1	Asine [1]
Botswana									**Botswana**
Cattle and buffaloes	2 220	1 821	2 200[1]	* 2 668	2 400[1]	2 420[1]	2 370[1]	2 380[1]	Bovine et buffles
Sheep and goats	2 400[1]	2 088	2 088	2 150[1]	2 090[1]	2 120[1]	2 060[1]	2 085[1]	Ovine et caprins
Pigs	10[1]	4	5[1]	4[1]	3[1]	5[1]	6[1]	7[1]	Porcine
Horses	32[1]	31[1]	31	32[1]	32[1]	33[1]	32[1]	33[1]	Chevaline
Asses	200[1]	220[1]	231	235[1]	232[1]	233[1]	234[1]	235[1]	Asine
Mules [1]	3	3	3	3	3	3	3	3	Mulassière [1]
Burkina Faso									**Burkina Faso**
Cattle and buffaloes	4 096	4 178	4 261	4 346	4 433	4 522	4 550[1]	4 550[1]	Bovine et buffles
Sheep and goats	12 214	12 580	* 12 928	13 200[1]	13 500[1]	14 121	14 300[1]	14 300[1]	Ovine et caprins
Pigs	530	540	551	563	575	587	590[1]	590[1]	Porcine
Horses	22	23	* 23	24[1]	24[1]	25[1]	25[1]	25[1]	Chevaline
Asses	427	436[1]	* 445	455[1]	465[1]	475[1]	475[1]	475[1]	Asine
Burundi									**Burundi**
Cattle and buffaloes	* 459	465[1]	460[1]	453[1]	* 449	* 311	346	345[1]	Bovine et buffles
Sheep and goats	1 325[1]	1 340[1]	1 270[1]	1 150[1]	1 000[1]	850[1]	822	845[1]	Ovine et caprins
Pigs	85[1]	90[1]	85[1]	80[1]	75[1]	70[1]	73	71[1]	Porcine
Cameroon									**Cameroun**
Cattle and buffaloes	4 970[1]	5 110[1]	5 250[1]	5 400[1]	5 550[1]	5 700[1]	5 900[1]	5 900[1]	Bovine et buffles
Sheep and goats	7 120[1]	7 530[1]	7 550[1]	7 600[1]	7 640[1]	7 670[1]	7 700[1]	7 730[1]	Ovine et caprins
Pigs	1 380[1]	1 390[1]	1 400[1]	1 410[1]	1 415[1]	1 420[1]	1 425[1]	1 430[1]	Porcine
Horses [1]	15	15	15	16	16	16	16	17	Chevaline [1]
Asses [1]	36	36	36	36	36	36	36	36	Asine [1]
Cape Verde									**Cap−Vert**
Cattle and buffaloes	18	18	18	19	21	21[1]	22[1]	22	Bovine et buffles
Sheep and goats	140	152	143[1]	122	118	119[1]	135[1]	121	Ovine et caprins
Pigs	207	326	512	450	455[1]	560[1]	636[1]	636[1]	Porcine
Asses	13[1]	13[1]	13[1]	13	14[1]	14[1]	14[1]	14[1]	Asine
Mules	2[1]	2[1]	2[1]	2[1]	2[1]	2[1]	2[1]	2[1]	Mulassière

33
Livestock
Thousand head [*cont.*]
Cheptel
Milliers de têtes [*suite*]

Region, country or area	1992	1993	1994	1995	1996	1997	1998	1999	Région, pays ou zone
Central African Rep.									**Rép. centrafricaine**
Cattle and buffaloes	2 680	2 674	2 735	2 797	2 861	2 926	* 2 992	2 992[1]	Bovine et buffles
Sheep and goats	1 821	1 927	2 037	2 152	2 274	2 404	* 2 540	2 551[1]	Ovine et caprins
Pigs	467	502	524	547	571	596	* 622	622[1]	Porcine
Chad									**Tchad**
Cattle and buffaloes	4 506	4 517	4 528	4 539	4 860	5 451	5 582	5 582[1]	Bovine et buffles
Sheep and goats	5 024	5 175	5 330	5 490	6 235	7 184	7 400	7 400[1]	Ovine et caprins
Pigs	15	16	17	18	* 18	* 19	23[1]	23[1]	Porcine
Horses	206	210	214	218[1]	* 224	* 228	230[1]	230[1]	Chevaline
Asses	243	248	253	258[1]	* 275	* 280	285[1]	285[1]	Asine
Comoros									**Comores**
Cattle and buffaloes [1]	49	50	51	51	51	51	51	50	Bovine et buffles [1]
Sheep and goats	141[1]	144[1]	145[1]	146[1]	147[1]	* 149	149[1]	149[1]	Ovine et caprins
Asses [1]	5	5	5	5	5	5	5	5	Asine [1]
Congo									**Congo**
Cattle and buffaloes	65[1]	68[1]	69[1]	70[1]	72[1]	75	72	75[1]	Bovine et buffles
Sheep and goats	405[1]	407[1]	409[1]	409[1]	409[1]	401	394[1]	400[1]	Ovine et caprins
Pigs	45[1]	46[1]	47[1]	46[1]	46[1]	45	44[1]	45[1]	Porcine
Côte d'Ivoire									**Côte d'Ivoire**
Cattle and buffaloes	1 180	1 205	1 231	1 258	1 286	1 312	1 330[1]	1 330[1]	Bovine et buffles
Sheep and goats	2 121	2 173	2 229	2 284	2 341	2 399	2 440[1]	2 440[1]	Ovine et caprins
Pigs	382	392	403	414	290	271	275[1]	275[1]	Porcine
Dem. Rep. of the Congo									**Rép. dém. du Congo**
Cattle and buffaloes	1 381	1 225	1 127	1 150[1]	1 060	982	909	950[1]	Bovine et buffles
Sheep and goats	5 031	5 135	5 372	* 5 395	5 286	5 403	5 525	5 550[1]	Ovine et caprins
Pigs	1 124	1 142	1 152	1 170	1 117	1 144	1 170	1 180[1]	Porcine
Djibouti									**Djibouti**
Cattle and buffaloes	190[1]	200[1]	* 213	* 247	* 266	267[1]	268[1]	269[1]	Bovine et buffles
Sheep and goats	976[1]	967[1]	* 971	* 965	* 972	973[1]	974[1]	974[1]	Ovine et caprins
Asses	8[1]	8[1]	8[1]	* 8	* 8	8[1]	9[1]	9[1]	Asine
Egypt									**Egypte**
Cattle and buffaloes	6 135[1]	6 227[1]	* 5 909	6 014	* 6 014	6 213	6 270[1]	6 330[1]	Bovine et buffles
Sheep and goats	6 140	6 724	* 7 003	7 352	* 7 352	7 447	7 500[1]	7 700[1]	Ovine et caprins
Pigs	27[1]	27[1]	27	27[1]	27[1]	28[1]	29[1]	29[1]	Porcine
Horses	30[1]	35[1]	* 39	* 42	* 41	43[1]	45[1]	46[1]	Chevaline
Asses [1]	2 750	2 950	3 100	3 112	2 980	2 990	2 995	3 000	Asine [1]
Mules [1]	1	1	1	1	1	1	1	1	Mulassière [1]
Equatorial Guinea									**Guinée équatoriale**
Cattle and buffaloes [1]	5	5	5	5	5	5	5	5	Bovine et buffles [1]
Sheep and goats [1]	44	44	44	44	44	44	44	44	Ovine et caprins [1]
Pigs [1]	5	5	5	5	5	5	5	5	Porcine [1]
Eritrea									**Erythrée**
Cattle and buffaloes	...	* 1 269	* 1 290	* 1 312	1 400[1]	1 450[1]	* 1 500	1 550[1]	Bovine et buffles
Sheep and goats [1]	...	2 910	2 970	3 030	3 090	3 150	3 210	3 270	Ovine et caprins [1]
Ethiopia									**Ethiopie**
Cattle and buffaloes	...	29 450[1]	29 450[1]	29 825	31 755	33 083	35 372	36 000[1]	Bovine et buffles
Sheep and goats [1]	...	38 400	38 400	38 500	38 600	38 700	38 800	38 950	Ovine et caprins [1]
Pigs [1]	...	20	20	21	22	23	24	25	Porcine [1]
Horses [1]	...	2 750	2 750	2 750	2 750	2 750	2 750	2 750	Chevaline [1]
Asses [1]	...	5 200	5 200	5 200	5 200	5 200	5 200	5 200	Asine [1]
Mules [1]	...	630	630	630	630	630	630	630	Mulassière [1]
Ethiopia incl.Eritrea									**Ethiopie comp. Erythrée**
Cattle and buffaloes [1]	31 000	...	...	...	...	...	...	...	Bovine et buffles [1]
Sheep and goats [1]	41 300	...	...	...	...	...	...	...	Ovine et caprins [1]
Pigs [1]	20	...	...	...	...	...	...	...	Porcine [1]
Horses [1]	2 750	...	...	...	...	...	...	...	Chevaline [1]
Asses [1]	5 200	...	...	...	...	...	...	...	Asine [1]
Mules [1]	630	...	...	...	...	...	...	...	Mulassière [1]
Gabon									**Gabon**
Cattle and buffaloes	37	37	38[1]	* 38	36	33	34[1]	35[1]	Bovine et buffles
Sheep and goats	251	256	260[1]	265[1]	270[1]	275[1]	280[1]	285[1]	Ovine et caprins
Pigs	195	207	207[1]	208[1]	209[1]	210[1]	211[1]	212[1]	Porcine
Gambia									**Gambie**
Cattle and buffaloes	296	305	279	290	322	346	360[1]	360[1]	Bovine et buffles
Sheep and goats	369	329	370	376[1]	398	432	455[1]	455[1]	Ovine et caprins

33

Livestock
Thousand head [*cont.*]
Cheptel
Milliers de têtes [*suite*]

Region, country or area	1992	1993	1994	1995	1996	1997	1998	1999	Région, pays ou zone
Pigs	14	14	14	14	14	14	14[1]	14[1]	Porcine
Horses	17[1]	17	18	18[1]	13	16	17[1]	17[1]	Chevaline
Asses	32[1]	36	33	34[1]	25	33	34[1]	34[1]	Asine
Ghana									**Ghana**
Cattle and buffaloes	1 159	1 169	1 187	1 217	1 248	1 260	1 273	1 273[1]	Bovine et buffles
Sheep and goats	4 283	4 350	4 473	4 420	4 759	5 101	5 256	5 256[1]	Ovine et caprins
Pigs	413	408	419	351	318	353	352	352[1]	Porcine
Horses	2	2	2	2[1]	2[1]	2[1]	2[1]	2[1]	Chevaline
Asses	13	12	12	12[1]	13[1]	13[1]	13[1]	13[1]	Asine
Guinea									**Guinée**
Cattle and buffaloes	1 663	1 768	1 874	2 202	2 246	2 291	2 337	2 368	Bovine et buffles
Sheep and goats	1 006	1 038	1 074	1 341	1 389	1 438	1 489	1 551	Ovine et caprins
Pigs	30	35	41	46	48	51	53	54	Porcine
Horses [1]	2	2	2	3	3	3	3	3	Chevaline [1]
Asses	2[1]	2[1]	2[1]	* 2	2[1]	2[1]	2[1]	2[1]	Asine
Guinea–Bissau									**Guinée–Bissau**
Cattle and buffaloes	450	475[1]	480[1]	490[1]	500[1]	510[1]	520[1]	520[1]	Bovine et buffles
Sheep and goats	500	525[1]	540[1]	550[1]	565[1]	580[1]	595[1]	595[1]	Ovine et caprins
Pigs	300	310[1]	320[1]	325[1]	330[1]	335[1]	340[1]	340[1]	Porcine
Horses	2	2[1]	2[1]	2[1]	2[1]	2[1]	2[1]	2[1]	Chevaline
Asses	5	5[1]	5[1]	5[1]	5[1]	5[1]	5[1]	5[1]	Asine
Kenya									**Kenya**
Cattle and buffaloes	13 200[1]	13 000[1]	13 250[1]	* 13 567	* 13 838	13 414	* 13 002	* 13 392	Bovine et buffles
Sheep and goats	13 500[1]	12 800[1]	12 800[1]	13 000[1]	13 200[1]	13 000[1]	13 200[1]	13 400[1]	Ovine et caprins
Pigs	105[1]	100[1]	102[1]	104[1]	106[1]	105[1]	108[1]	110[1]	Porcine
Horses [1]	2	2	2	2	2	2	2	2	Chevaline [1]
Lesotho									**Lesotho**
Cattle and buffaloes	623	658	578	580	585[1]	590[1]	580[1]	575[1]	Bovine et buffles
Sheep and goats	1 916	1 988	2 152	1 880	1 900[1]	1 960[1]	1 830[1]	1 830[1]	Ovine et caprins
Pigs	36	60	46	66	70[1]	75[1]	65[1]	65[1]	Porcine
Horses	89	107	113	113[1]	114[1]	115[1]	114[1]	114[1]	Chevaline
Asses	145[1]	139	140	145[1]	150[1]	155[1]	150[1]	150[1]	Asine
Mules [1]	1	1	1	1	1	1	1	1	Mulassière [1]
Liberia									**Libéria**
Cattle and buffaloes [1]	36	36	36	36	36	36	36	36	Bovine et buffles [1]
Sheep and goats [1]	435	430	430	430	430	430	430	430	Ovine et caprins [1]
Pigs [1]	120	120	120	120	120	120	120	120	Porcine [1]
Libyan Arab Jamah.									**Jamah. arabe libyenne**
Cattle and buffaloes	180[1]	155[1]	* 140	* 145	* 145	142[1]	140[1]	140[1]	Bovine et buffles
Sheep and goats	6 300[1]	6 220[1]	* 6 010[1]	* 6 400[1]	* 7 200[1]	7 820[1]	8 550[1]	8 600[1]	Ovine et caprins
Horses	28[1]	29[1]	* 30	* 35	* 40	43[1]	44[1]	45[1]	Chevaline
Asses	40[1]	30[1]	* 20	* 21	* 25	27[1]	28[1]	29[1]	Asine
Madagascar									**Madagascar**
Cattle and buffaloes	10 276	10 287	10 298	10 309	10 320	10 331	10 342	10 353	Bovine et buffles
Sheep and goats	* 2 081	* 2 127	* 2 173	* 2 220	2 085	2 120[1]	2 160[1]	2 200[1]	Ovine et caprins
Pigs	1 493	1 526	1 558	1 592	1 629	1 662	1 680[1]	1 700[1]	Porcine
Malawi									**Malawi**
Cattle and buffaloes	* 967	800[1]	680[1]	690[1]	700	750[1]	800[1]	830[1]	Bovine et buffles
Sheep and goats	* 1 082	1 000[1]	1 100[1]	1 200[1]	1 358	1 370[1]	1 390[1]	1 405[1]	Ovine et caprins
Pigs	* 238	240[1]	245[1]	247	220	230[1]	240[1]	250[1]	Porcine
Asses	2[1]	2[1]	2[1]	2	2[1]	2[1]	2[1]	2[1]	Asine
Mali									**Mali**
Cattle and buffaloes	5 092	5 227	5 380	5 541	5 708	5 882	6 058	6 058[1]	Bovine et buffles
Sheep and goats	13 315	11 955	12 553	13 179	13 838	14 500[1]	14 500	14 500[1]	Ovine et caprins
Pigs	61	61	62	63	64	65	65	65[1]	Porcine
Horses	85	92	101	112	123	136	136[1]	136[1]	Chevaline
Asses	600	600	612	625	638	652	652[1]	652[1]	Asine
Mauritania									**Mauritanie**
Cattle and buffaloes	1 200	1 200	1 100	1 125	1 312	1 312[1]	1 312[1]	1 312[1]	Bovine et buffles
Sheep and goats	* 8 500	* 8 800	* 8 800	* 8 814	10 332	10 332	10 333[1]	10 333[1]	Ovine et caprins
Horses	18[1]	18[1]	* 19	* 19	* 19	20[1]	20[1]	20[1]	Chevaline
Asses [1]	154	155	155	155	155	155	155	155	Asine [1]
Mauritius									**Maurice**
Cattle and buffaloes [1]	33	29	29	25	26	* 22	* 25	* 27	Bovine et buffles [1]
Sheep and goats [1]	102	102	97	98	97	98	99	100	Ovine et caprins [1]
Pigs	14	15	17[1]	18[1]	19[1]	* 20	* 20	* 20	Porcine

33

Livestock
Thousand head [*cont.*]
Cheptel
Milliers de têtes [*suite*]

Region, country or area	1992	1993	1994	1995	1996	1997	1998	1999	Région, pays ou zone
Morocco									**Maroc**
Cattle and buffaloes	3 005	2 348	2 343	2 371	2 408	2 547	2 600	2 560	Bovine et buffles
Sheep and goats	17 827	15 735	17 282	17 403	19 131	20 077	22 559	21 691	Ovine et caprins
Pigs	9[1]	10[1]	10[1]	10[1]	10[1]	10	8	8[1]	Porcine
Horses	186	162	165	162	156	145	150[1]	150[1]	Chevaline
Asses	982	905	916	954	919	949	950[1]	950[1]	Asine
Mules	528	526	527	540	523	516	520[1]	520[1]	Mulassière
Mozambique									**Mozambique**
Cattle and buffaloes [1]	1 250	1 260	1 240	1 250	1 270	1 290	1 300	1 310	Bovine et buffles [1]
Sheep and goats [1]	498	501	497	501	504	508	511	514	Ovine et caprins [1]
Pigs [1]	170	170	168	170	172	174	176	178	Porcine [1]
Asses [1]	17	19	18	19	20	21	22	23	Asine [1]
Namibia									**Namibie**
Cattle and buffaloes	2 206	2 074	2 036	2 031	1 990	2 055	2 192	2 000[1]	Bovine et buffles
Sheep and goats	4 614	4 232	4 259	4 026	3 985	4 250	3 797	3 800[1]	Ovine et caprins
Pigs	15	20	18	20	19	17	15	14[1]	Porcine
Horses	55	57	59	58	57	57	53	52[1]	Chevaline
Asses	* 70	71[1]	72[1]	71[1]	70[1]	71[1]	69[1]	68[1]	Asine
Mules	* 7	7[1]	7[1]	7[1]	7[1]	7[1]	7[1]	6[1]	Mulassière
Niger									**Niger**
Cattle and buffaloes	* 1 909	1 872	1 968	2 008	2 048	2 089	2 131	2 174	Bovine et buffles
Sheep and goats	* 9 100	8 885	9 244	9 504	9 718	* 10 044	* 10 447	* 10 781	Ovine et caprins
Pigs [1]	38	39	39	39	39	39	39	39	Porcine [1]
Horses	86[1]	88[1]	* 90	* 91	* 92	* 93	* 93	94[1]	Chevaline
Asses	450[1]	450[1]	* 486	* 496	* 506	* 516	* 526	530[1]	Asine
Nigeria									**Nigéria**
Cattle and buffaloes	14 087	14 807	14 881	15 405	18 680	19 610	19 700[1]	19 850[1]	Bovine et buffles
Sheep and goats	37 500	38 500[1]	38 500[1]	38 500[1]	38 500[1]	42 660[1]	43 700[1]	44 800[1]	Ovine et caprins
Pigs	5 328	6 660	6 926	7 150[1]	7 400[1]	11 550[1]	12 000[1]	12 400[1]	Porcine
Horses	205[1]	204[1]	204[1]	204[1]	204[1]	204[1]	204[1]	204[1]	Chevaline
Asses	1 000[1]	1 000[1]	1 000[1]	1 000[1]	1 000[1]	1 000[1]	1 000[1]	1 000[1]	Asine
Réunion									**Réunion**
Cattle and buffaloes	23	25	26	26	26	* 27	27[1]	27[1]	Bovine et buffles
Sheep and goats	34	33	33	32	32	* 40	40[1]	40[1]	Ovine et caprins
Pigs	92	86	82	86	86	* 89	89[1]	89[1]	Porcine
Rwanda									**Rwanda**
Cattle and buffaloes	550[1]	500[1]	454	465	500[1]	570[1]	650[1]	726	Bovine et buffles
Sheep and goats	* 1 575	* 1 615	* 1 655	* 770	* 869	* 921	* 977	* 924	Ovine et caprins
Pigs	* 142	* 146	* 150	* 120	* 134	* 142	* 149	160	Porcine
Sao Tome and Principe									**Sao Tomé−et−Principe**
Cattle and buffaloes [1]	4	4	4	4	4	4	4	4	Bovine et buffles [1]
Sheep and goats [1]	6	7	7	7	7	7	7	7	Ovine et caprins [1]
Pigs [1]	3	2	2	2	2	2	2	2	Porcine [1]
Senegal									**Sénégal**
Cattle and buffaloes	* 2 692	* 2 754	* 2 760	* 2 829	2 835[1]	2 913	2 955[1]	2 955[1]	Bovine et buffles
Sheep and goats	* 7 293	* 7 518	* 7 800	7 900[1]	7 750[1]	7 811	7 895[1]	7 895[1]	Ovine et caprins
Pigs	310[1]	320[1]	322[1]	324[1]	326[1]	328[1]	330[1]	330[1]	Porcine
Horses	431	498	500[1]	502[1]	504[1]	506[1]	508[1]	508[1]	Chevaline
Asses	362	364	364[1]	368[1]	372[1]	376[1]	380[1]	380[1]	Asine
Seychelles									**Seychelles**
Cattle and buffaloes [1]	2	2	2	2	1	1	1	1	Bovine et buffles [1]
Sheep and goats [1]	5	5	5	5	5	5	5	5	Ovine et caprins [1]
Pigs [1]	18	18	18	18	18	18	18	18	Porcine [1]
Sierra Leone									**Sierra Leone**
Cattle and buffaloes	349	360	370[1]	380[1]	390[1]	400[1]	400[1]	400[1]	Bovine et buffles
Sheep and goats	446	468	488[1]	510[1]	525[1]	540[1]	540[1]	540[1]	Ovine et caprins
Pigs	50[1]	50[1]	50[1]	50[1]	50[1]	50[1]	50[1]	52	Porcine
Somalia									**Somalie**
Cattle and buffaloes	3 300[1]	4 200[1]	5 000	5 200[1]	5 400[1]	5 600[1]	5 300[1]	5 000[1]	Bovine et buffles
Sheep and goats	20 000[1]	22 500[1]	25 000	26 000[1]	26 600[1]	27 000[1]	26 000[1]	25 000[1]	Ovine et caprins
Pigs [1]	3	4	4	4	4	5	4	4	Porcine [1]
Horses [1]	1	1	1	1	1	1	1	1	Chevaline [1]
Asses [1]	15	18	19	20	20	21	19	19	Asine [1]
Mules [1]	17	18	19	19	20	20	18	18	Mulassière [1]

33

Livestock
Thousand head [*cont.*]
Cheptel
Milliers de têtes [*suite*]

Region, country or area	1992	1993	1994	1995	1996	1997	1998	1999	Région, pays ou zone
South Africa									**Afrique du Sud**
Cattle and buffaloes	13 074	12 503	12 584	13 015	13 389	13 667	13 800	13 900[1]	Bovine et buffles
Sheep and goats	37 373	35 017	35 536	35 241	35 608	35 830	* 36 980	37 100[1]	Ovine et caprins
Pigs	1 529	1 493	1 511	1 628	1 603	1 617	1 641	1 640[1]	Porcine
Horses [1]	230	235	240	245	250	255	260	265	Chevaline [1]
Asses [1]	210	210	210	210	210	210	210	210	Asine [1]
Mules [1]	14	14	14	14	14	14	14	14	Mulassière [1]
Sudan									**Soudan**
Cattle and buffaloes	* 25 092	* 27 571	29 000[1]	30 077	31 669	33 103	34 584	35 000[1]	Bovine et buffles
Sheep and goats	* 49 211	* 58 545	70 464	72 395[1]	72 418	75 872	79 709	80 000[1]	Ovine et caprins
Horses [1]	23	23	23	24	24	25	25	26	Chevaline [1]
Asses [1]	681	670	675	678	680	700	720	730	Asine [1]
Mules [1]	1	1	1	1	1	1	1	1	Mulassière [1]
Swaziland									**Swaziland**
Cattle and buffaloes	753	608	626	642	656	658	650[1]	652[1]	Bovine et buffles
Sheep and goats	438	449	455	459	465	467[1]	460[1]	464[1]	Ovine et caprins
Pigs	31	30	30[1]	30	31	32[1]	30[1]	31[1]	Porcine
Horses	1	1	1	1[1]	1[1]	1[1]	1[1]	1[1]	Chevaline
Asses	12	15	15	15[1]	15[1]	15[1]	15[1]	15[1]	Asine
Togo									**Togo**
Cattle and buffaloes	251	248	248[1]	239	217	206	223	223[1]	Bovine et buffles
Sheep and goats	3 100	3 100	2 850[1]	2 740[1]	1 932	1 598	1 850	1 850[1]	Ovine et caprins
Pigs	800[1]	850[1]	850[1]	850[1]	850[1]	850[1]	850[1]	850[1]	Porcine
Horses [1]	2	2	2	2	2	2	2	2	Chevaline [1]
Asses	3[1]	3[1]	3[1]	3[1]	3[1]	3[1]	3[1]	3[1]	Asine
Tunisia									**Tunisie**
Cattle and buffaloes	* 636	659	662	654	680[1]	701	770[1]	780[1]	Bovine et buffles
Sheep and goats	7 750[1]	8 527	7 488	7 426	7 650[1]	7 554	7 900[1]	7 900[1]	Ovine et caprins
Pigs [1]	6[1]	6[1]	6[1]	6[1]	6[1]	6[1]	6[1]	6[1]	Porcine [1]
Horses [1]	56	56	56	56	56	56	56	56	Chevaline [1]
Asses [1]	229	230	230	230	230	230	230	230	Asine [1]
Mules [1]	80	81	81	81	81	81	81	81	Mulassière [1]
Uganda									**Ouganda**
Cattle and buffaloes	5 209	5 370	5 106	5 233	5 301	5 363	5 651	5 700[1]	Bovine et buffles
Sheep and goats	* 4 910	* 5 160	5 300[1]	5 400[1]	5 470[1]	* 5 544	5 560[1]	5 620[1]	Ovine et caprins
Pigs	880[1]	900[1]	910[1]	920[1]	930[1]	940	950[1]	960[1]	Porcine
Asses [1]	17	17	17	17	18	18	18	18	Asine [1]
United Rep.Tanzania									**Rép.–Unie de Tanzanie**
Cattle and buffaloes	13 230	* 13 618	* 13 752	* 13 888	* 14 025	* 14 163	* 14 302	14 350[1]	Bovine et buffles
Sheep and goats	12 665	* 13 201	* 13 637	13 670[1]	13 750[1]	13 850[1]	13 950[1]	14 050[1]	Ovine et caprins
Pigs	* 330	* 335	* 335	340[1]	330[1]	335[1]	340[1]	345[1]	Porcine
Asses [1]	176	177	178	178	176	177	178	178	Asine [1]
Zambia									**Zambie**
Cattle and buffaloes	* 3 095	* 3 204	3 200[1]	3 000[1]	2 800[1]	* 2 100	* 2 176	* 2 273	Bovine et buffles
Sheep and goats	* 623	* 667	700[1]	724[1]	747[1]	* 780	* 989	* 1 189	Ovine et caprins
Pigs	290[1]	300[1]	310[1]	300[1]	320[1]	* 316	* 320	* 324	Porcine
Asses [1]	2	2	2	2	2	2	2	2	Asine [1]
Zimbabwe									**Zimbabwe**
Cattle and buffaloes	6 024	* 4 180	4 300[1]	4 500	5 436	5 400[1]	5 450	5 500[1]	Bovine et buffles
Sheep and goats	3 034	2 920[1]	3 030[1]	3 102	3 236	3 210[1]	3 270	3 295[1]	Ovine et caprins
Pigs	285	* 210	* 246	277	266	260[1]	270	272[1]	Porcine
Horses [1]	24	23	24	25	25	25	25	26	Chevaline [1]
Asses [1]	104	103	104	105	105	104	105	106	Asine [1]
Mules [1]	1	1	1	1	1	1	1	1	Mulassière [1]
America, North									**Amérique du Nord**
Cattle and buffaloes	160 141	161 992	163 997	165 367	166 169	165 503	163 237	160 970	**Bovine et buffles**
Sheep and goats	34 607	33 920	32 811	31 825	30 975	29 966	29 829	28 181	**Ovine et caprins**
Pigs	91 264	92 554	91 373	93 783	92 208	90 529	95 606	95 545	**Porcine**
Horses	14 696	14 792	14 887	14 925	15 016	15 207	15 213	15 334	**Chevaline**
Asses	3 685	3 689	3 699	3 730	3 750	3 750	3 751	3 751	**Asine**
Mules	3 685	3 696	3 706	3 736	3 755	3 753	3 753	3 753	**Mulassière**
Antigua and Barbuda									**Antigua–et–Barbuda**
Cattle and buffaloes [1]	16	16	16	16	16	16	16	16	Bovine et buffles [1]
Sheep and goats [1]	25	25	25	24	24	24	24	24	Ovine et caprins [1]

33
Livestock
Thousand head [*cont.*]
Cheptel
Milliers de têtes [*suite*]

Region, country or area	1992	1993	1994	1995	1996	1997	1998	1999	Région, pays ou zone
Pigs [1]	2	2	2	2	2	2	2	2	Porcine [1]
Horses [1]	1	1	1	0	0	0	0	0	Chevaline [1]
Asses [1]	2	2	2	1	1	1	1	1	Asine [1]
Bahamas									**Bahamas**
Cattle and buffaloes	1[1]	1[1]	1	1	1	1[1]	1[1]	1[1]	Bovine et buffles
Sheep and goats	20[1]	20[1]	20	21	22	22[1]	22[1]	22[1]	Ovine et caprins
Pigs	5[1]	5[1]	5	* 5	5	5[1]	5[1]	5[1]	Porcine
Barbados									**Barbade**
Cattle and buffaloes [1]	30	28	28	28	28	24	23	23	Bovine et buffles [1]
Sheep and goats [1]	46	46	46	46	46	46	46	46	Ovine et caprins [1]
Pigs [1]	30	30	30	30	30	31	33	33	Porcine [1]
Horses [1]	1	1	1	1	1	1	1	1	Chevaline [1]
Asses [1]	2	2	2	2	2	2	2	2	Asine [1]
Mules [1]	2	2	2	2	2	2	2	2	Mulassière [1]
Belize									**Belize**
Cattle and buffaloes	* 54	* 58	59[1]	60	62[1]	60[1]	58[1]	58[1]	Bovine et buffles
Sheep and goats [1]	5	5	4	4	4	4	4	4	Ovine et caprins [1]
Pigs	25[1]	25[1]	24[1]	22	23[1]	23[1]	23[1]	23[1]	Porcine
Horses [1]	5	5	5	5	5	5	5	5	Chevaline [1]
Mules [1]	4	4	4	4	4	4	4	4	Mulassière [1]
Bermuda									**Bermudes**
Cattle and buffaloes [1]	1	1	1	1	1	1	1	1	Bovine et buffles [1]
Sheep and goats	1[1]	1[1]	1	0[1]	0	0[1]	0[1]	0[1]	Ovine et caprins
Pigs	1[1]	1[1]	1[1]	1[1]	1	1[1]	1[1]	1[1]	Porcine
Horses	1[1]	1[1]	1	1[1]	1[1]	1[1]	1[1]	1[1]	Chevaline
British Virgin Islands									**Iles Vierges britanniques**
Cattle and buffaloes [1]	2	2	2	2	2	2	2	2	Bovine et buffles [1]
Sheep and goats [1]	16	16	16	16	16	16	16	16	Ovine et caprins [1]
Pigs [1]	2	2	2	2	2	2	2	2	Porcine [1]
Canada									**Canada**
Cattle and buffaloes	11 869	11 860	12 012	12 709	13 402	13 453	13 272	12 981	Bovine et buffles
Sheep and goats [1]	675	660	667	645	672	656	642	685	Ovine et caprins [1]
Pigs	10 596	10 744	10 534	11 291	11 588	11 480	11 985	12 403	Porcine
Horses [1]	350	370	350	380	376	508	508	508	Chevaline [1]
Mules [1]	4	4	4	4	4	4	4	4	Mulassière [1]
Cayman Islands									**Iles Caïmanes**
Cattle and buffaloes	1	1[1]	1[1]	1[1]	1[1]	1[1]	1[1]	1[1]	Bovine et buffles
Costa Rica									**Costa Rica**
Cattle and buffaloes *	2 132	2 122	1 894	1 645	1 585	1 529	1 527	1 617	Bovine et buffles *
Sheep and goats [1]	4	4	4	4	4	4	4	4	Ovine et caprins [1]
Pigs	310[1]	340	350	300	300	300[1]	280[1]	290[1]	Porcine
Horses [1]	114	114	114	115	115	115	115	115	Chevaline [1]
Asses [1]	7	7	7	8	8	8	8	8	Asine [1]
Mules [1]	5	5	5	5	5	5	5	5	Mulassière [1]
Cuba									**Cuba**
Cattle and buffaloes	4 609	4 583	4 617	4 632	4 601	4 606	4 650[1]	4 650[1]	Bovine et buffles
Sheep and goats [1]	450	410	410	415	429	449	448	450	Ovine et caprins [1]
Pigs [1]	2 200	2 300	2 300	2 300	2 400	2 400	2 400	2 400	Porcine [1]
Horses	607	608	597	583	568	525	530[1]	620[1]	Chevaline
Asses	6	6	6	6	6	6	6[1]	6[1]	Asine
Mules	33	33	33	32	30	28	28[1]	28[1]	Mulassière
Dominica									**Dominique**
Cattle and buffaloes [1]	14	13	13	13	13	13	13	13	Bovine et buffles [1]
Sheep and goats [1]	17	17	17	17	17	17	17	17	Ovine et caprins [1]
Pigs [1]	5	5	5	5	5	5	5	5	Porcine [1]
Dominican Republic									**Rép. dominicaine**
Cattle and buffaloes	* 2 356	* 2 371	* 2 366	2 302	2 435	2 481	2 528	1 904	Bovine et buffles
Sheep and goats	682[1]	691[1]	700[1]	705[1]	705[1]	705	705[1]	269	Ovine et caprins
Pigs	750[1]	850[1]	900[1]	950[1]	950[1]	960	960	540	Porcine
Horses [1]	320	329	329	329	329	329	329	329	Chevaline [1]
Asses [1]	143	145	145	145	145	145	145	145	Asine [1]
Mules [1]	133	135	135	135	135	135	135	135	Mulassière [1]
El Salvador									**El Salvador**
Cattle and buffaloes	1 257	1 197	1 262	1 125	1 287	1 162	1 038	1 141	Bovine et buffles
Sheep and goats [1]	20	20	20	21	21	21	21	21	Ovine et caprins [1]
Pigs	316	336	223	295	306	294	312	335	Porcine

33
Livestock
Thousand head [*cont.*]
Cheptel
Milliers de têtes [*suite*]

Region, country or area	1992	1993	1994	1995	1996	1997	1998	1999	Région, pays ou zone
Horses [1]	95	96	96	96	96	96	96	96	Chevaline [1]
Asses [1]	3	3	3	3	3	3	3	3	Asine [1]
Mules [1]	23	24	24	24	24	24	24	24	Mulassière [1]
Greenland									**Groenland**
Sheep and goats [1]	22	22	22	22	22	22	22	22	Ovine et caprins [1]
Grenada									**Grenade**
Cattle and buffaloes	4[1]	4[1]	4[1]	4	4[1]	4[1]	4[1]	4[1]	Bovine et buffles
Sheep and goats	21[1]	21[1]	21[1]	20	20[1]	20[1]	20[1]	20[1]	Ovine et caprins
Pigs	4[1]	5[1]	5[1]	5	5[1]	5[1]	5[1]	5[1]	Porcine
Asses [1]	1	1	1	1	1	1	1	1	Asine [1]
Guadeloupe									**Guadeloupe**
Cattle and buffaloes	64	56	60	63[1]	65[1]	80	80[1]	80[1]	Bovine et buffles
Sheep and goats [1]	63	66	66	66	64	67	67	67	Ovine et caprins [1]
Pigs	16[1]	14[1]	14[1]	17[1]	15[1]	15[1]	15[1]	15[1]	Porcine
Horses [1]	1	1	1	1	1	1	1	1	Chevaline [1]
Guatemala									**Guatemala**
Cattle and buffaloes	2 250	2 400	2 300	2 293	2 291	* 2 337	* 2 330	2 300[1]	Bovine et buffles
Sheep and goats	534	545	604	628	660	660[1]	660[1]	661[1]	Ovine et caprins
Pigs	650	715	796	753	773	802	826	825[1]	Porcine
Horses [1]	114	115	116	117	118	118	118	118	Chevaline [1]
Asses [1]	9	9	9	9	10	10	10	10	Asine [1]
Mules [1]	38	38	38	38	38	38	38	38	Mulassière [1]
Haiti									**Haïti**
Cattle and buffaloes	* 1 339	* 1 251	* 1 234	1 250	1 246	1 270	1 300	1 300[1]	Bovine et buffles
Sheep and goats	1 237[1]	1 243[1]	1 245[1]	* 1 242	* 1 380	* 1 605	* 1 756	1 756[1]	Ovine et caprins
Pigs	* 380	* 350	* 360	390	485	600	800	800[1]	Porcine
Horses [1]	450	460	470	480	490	490	490	490	Chevaline [1]
Asses [1]	210	210	210	210	210	210	210	210	Asine [1]
Mules [1]	81	80	80	80	80	80	80	80	Mulassière [1]
Honduras									**Honduras**
Cattle and buffaloes	* 2 351	2 077	* 2 286	2 111	2 127	2 061	2 200	2 070[1]	Bovine et buffles
Sheep and goats	40[1]	40	41[1]	41[1]	41[1]	43[1]	43[1]	43[1]	Ovine et caprins
Pigs	591	596	600[1]	600[1]	640[1]	670[1]	700[1]	700[1]	Porcine
Horses [1]	172	172	173	174	175	176	177	178	Chevaline [1]
Asses [1]	22	22	23	23	23	23	23	23	Asine [1]
Mules [1]	69	69	69	69	69	69	69	70	Mulassière [1]
Jamaica									**Jamaïque**
Cattle and buffaloes [1]	460	460	440	450	420	400	400	400	Bovine et buffles [1]
Sheep and goats [1]	442	441	441	441	441	442	442	442	Ovine et caprins [1]
Pigs [1]	170	200	200	200	180	180	180	180	Porcine [1]
Horses [1]	4	4	4	4	4	4	4	4	Chevaline [1]
Asses [1]	23	23	23	23	23	23	23	23	Asine [1]
Mules [1]	10	10	10	10	10	10	10	10	Mulassière [1]
Martinique									**Martinique**
Cattle and buffaloes	35	30	30	30[1]	30[1]	30[1]	30[1]	30[1]	Bovine et buffles
Sheep and goats [1]	75	72	70	64	64	64	64	64	Ovine et caprins [1]
Pigs [1]	39	36	36	33	33	33	33	33	Porcine [1]
Horses [1]	2	2	2	2	2	2	2	2	Chevaline [1]
Mexico									**Mexique**
Cattle and buffaloes	* 30 157	* 30 649	* 30 702	* 30 191	29 301	30 772	30 500	30 293	Bovine et buffles
Sheep and goats	17 192	17 176[1]	* 16 355[1]	16 328	15 750	* 15 195	* 15 371[1]	14 700[1]	Ovine et caprins
Pigs	16 502	16 832	16 200	15 923	15 405	15 735	14 994	13 855	Porcine
Horses [1]	6 180	6 185	6 190	6 200	6 250	6 250	6 250	6 250	Chevaline [1]
Asses [1]	3 189	3 190	3 200	3 230	3 250	3 250	3 250	3 250	Asine [1]
Mules [1]	3 200	3 210	3 220	3 250	3 270	3 270	3 270	3 270	Mulassière [1]
Montserrat									**Montserrat**
Cattle and buffaloes [1]	10	10	10	10	10	10	10	10	Bovine et buffles [1]
Sheep and goats [1]	11	12	12	12	12	12	12	12	Ovine et caprins [1]
Pigs [1]	1	1	1	1	1	1	1	1	Porcine [1]
Netherlands Antilles									**Antilles néerlandaises**
Cattle and buffaloes [1]	1	1	1	1	1	1	1	1	Bovine et buffles [1]
Sheep and goats [1]	20	19	20	19	20	19	20	20	Ovine et caprins [1]
Pigs [1]	2	2	2	2	2	2	2	2	Porcine [1]
Asses [1]	3	3	3	3	3	3	3	3	Asine [1]

33
Livestock
Thousand head [*cont.*]
Cheptel
Milliers de têtes [*suite*]

Region, country or area	1992	1993	1994	1995	1996	1997	1998	1999	Région, pays ou zone
Nicaragua									**Nicaragua**
Cattle and buffaloes	1 641	1 688	1 730	1 750	1 807	* 1 712	* 1 668	* 1 693	Bovine et buffles
Sheep and goats [1]	10	10	10	10	11	10	10	10	Ovine et caprins [1]
Pigs [1]	447	430	330	392	366	385	400	400	Porcine [1]
Horses [1]	250	248	247	246	245	245	245	245	Chevaline [1]
Asses [1]	8	8	8	8	8	9	9	9	Asine [1]
Mules [1]	45	45	46	46	46	46	46	46	Mulassière [1]
Panama									**Panama**
Cattle and buffaloes	1 427	1 437	1 454	1 456	1 442	1 362	1 382	1 400[1]	Bovine et buffles
Sheep and goats	5[1]	5[1]	* 5	5[1]	5[1]	5[1]	5[1]	5[1]	Ovine et caprins
Pigs	292	266	257	261	244	240	252	252[1]	Porcine
Horses	155[1]	156[1]	* 164	165[1]	165[1]	165[1]	165[1]	165[1]	Chevaline
Mules	4[1]	4[1]	* 4	4[1]	4[1]	4[1]	4[1]	4[1]	Mulassière
Puerto Rico									**Porto Rico**
Cattle and buffaloes	429	429	429	368	371	388	388[1]	388[1]	Bovine et buffles
Sheep and goats [1]	31	29	28	26	16	21	21	21	Ovine et caprins [1]
Pigs	197	194	196	205	182	175	175[1]	175[1]	Porcine
Horses [1]	23	23	24	24	24	24	24	24	Chevaline [1]
Asses [1]	2	2	2	2	2	2	2	2	Asine [1]
Mules [1]	3	3	3	3	3	3	3	3	Mulassière [1]
Saint Kitts and Nevis									**Saint-Kitts-et-Nevis**
Cattle and buffaloes	4[1]	4	4[1]	4[1]	4[1]	4	4[1]	4[1]	Bovine et buffles
Sheep and goats	24[1]	24	24[1]	24	26	24[1]	23[1]	23[1]	Ovine et caprins
Pigs	2[1]	2[1]	2	2	3	3[1]	3[1]	3[1]	Porcine
Saint Lucia									**Sainte-Lucie**
Cattle and buffaloes [1]	12	12	12	12	12	12	12	12	Bovine et buffles [1]
Sheep and goats	26[1]	25[1]	24[1]	23[1]	22	22[1]	22[1]	22[1]	Ovine et caprins
Pigs	13[1]	14[1]	14[1]	14[1]	15	15[1]	15[1]	15[1]	Porcine
Horses [1]	1	1	1	1	1	1	1	1	Chevaline [1]
Asses [1]	1	1	1	1	1	1	1	1	Asine [1]
Mules [1]	1	1	1	1	1	1	1	1	Mulassière [1]
St. Vincent-Grenadines									**St. Vincent-Grenadines**
Cattle and buffaloes	6[1]	6[1]	6[1]	6[1]	6[1]	6[1]	6[1]	6[1]	Bovine et buffles
Sheep and goats	18[1]	18[1]	18[1]	19[1]	19[1]	19[1]	19[1]	19[1]	Ovine et caprins
Pigs	9[1]	9[1]	9[1]	9[1]	9[1]	9[1]	9[1]	9[1]	Porcine
Asses [1]	1	1	1	1	1	1	1	1	Asine [1]
Trinidad and Tobago									**Trinité-et-Tobago**
Cattle and buffaloes	46[1]	41	41	41	41[1]	40[1]	39[1]	39[1]	Bovine et buffles
Sheep and goats [1]	72	71	71	71	71	71	71	71	Ovine et caprins [1]
Pigs	54[1]	45[1]	31	32	34	30[1]	28[1]	28[1]	Porcine
Horses [1]	1	1	1	1	1	1	1	1	Chevaline [1]
Asses [1]	2	2	2	2	2	2	2	2	Asine [1]
Mules [1]	2	2	2	2	2	2	2	2	Mulassière [1]
United States									**Etats-Unis**
Cattle and buffaloes	97 556	99 176	100 974	102 785	103 548	101 656	99 744	98 522	Bovine et buffles
Sheep and goats	12 797	12 161	11 796	10 839	10 365	9 674	9 225	8 638[1]	Ovine et caprins
Pigs	57 649	58 202	57 940	59 738	58 201	56 124	61 158	62 206	Porcine
Horses [1]	5 850	5 900	6 000	6 000	6 050	6 150	6 150	6 180	Chevaline [1]
Asses [1]	51	52	52	52	52	52	52	52	Asine [1]
Mules [1]	28	28	28	28	28	28	28	28	Mulassière [1]
United States Virgin Is.									**Iles Vierges américaines**
Cattle and buffaloes [1]	8	8	8	8	8	8	8	8	Bovine et buffles [1]
Sheep and goats [1]	7	7	7	7	7	7	7	7	Ovine et caprins [1]
Pigs [1]	3	3	3	3	3	3	3	3	Porcine [1]
America, South									**Amérique du Sud**
Cattle and buffaloes	282 868	285 101	290 980	285 394	290 444	296 552	301 053	306 022	**Bovine et buffles**
Sheep and goats	123 606	118 353	116 544	114 945	111 606	111 102	108 283	106 612	**Ovine et caprins**
Pigs	54 065	54 288	56 337	49 505	49 474	50 141	50 598	51 268	**Porcine**
Horses	15 060	15 129	15 308	15 587	15 699	15 651	15 651	15 652	**Chevaline**
Asses	4 091	4 018	4 030	4 062	4 069	4 070	4 071	4 072	**Asine**
Mules	3 395	3 346	3 342	3 311	3 325	3 326	3 327	3 327	**Mulassière**
Argentina									**Argentine**
Cattle and buffaloes	53 011	52 665	53 157	53 500	54 000	54 500	54 600	55 000[1]	Bovine et buffles
Sheep and goats *	29 206[1]	28 210	27 478	25 173	21 330	20 723	18 660[1]	17 428[1]	Ovine et caprins *
Pigs	2 600[1]	2 850[1]	3 300	3 100	3 100	3 200	3 200[1]	3 200[1]	Porcine

33
Livestock
Thousand head [*cont.*]
Cheptel
Milliers de têtes [*suite*]

Region, country or area	1992	1993	1994	1995	1996	1997	1998	1999	Région, pays ou zone
Horses	* 3 300	* 3 300	3 300[1]	3 300[1]	3 300[1]	3 300[1]	3 300[1]	3 300[1]	Chevaline
Asses [1]	90	90	90	90	90	90	90	90	Asine [1]
Mules [1]	173	174	175	175	175	175	175	175	Mulassière [1]
Bolivia									**Bolivie**
Cattle and buffaloes	5 779	5 794	5 912	6 000	6 118	6 238	6 387	6 556	Bovine et buffles
Sheep and goats	8 913	8 982	9 165	9 380	9 539[1]	9 728	9 905	10 075[1]	Ovine et caprins
Pigs	2 226	2 273	2 331	2 405	2 482	2 569	2 637	2 715	Porcine
Horses [1]	322	322	322	322	322	322	322	322	Chevaline [1]
Asses [1]	631	631	631	631	631	631	631	631	Asine [1]
Mules [1]	81	81	81	81	81	81	81	81	Mulassière [1]
Brazil									**Brésil**
Cattle and buffaloes	155 652	156 633	159 815	151 679	154 758[1]	157 989[1]	161 452[1]	165 170[1]	Bovine et buffles
Sheep and goats	32 115	28 627	29 315	29 608	30 200[1]	30 900[1]	30 900[1]	30 900[1]	Ovine et caprins
Pigs	34 532	34 184	35 142	27 964	27 811	27 670	27 542	27 425	Porcine
Horses	6 329	6 314	6 356	6 394	6 400[1]	6 400[1]	6 400[1]	6 400[1]	Chevaline
Asses	1 381	1 302	1 313	1 344	1 350[1]	1 350[1]	1 350[1]	1 350[1]	Asine
Mules	2 046	1 993	1 987	1 990	2 000[1]	2 000[1]	2 000[1]	2 000[1]	Mulassière
Chile									**Chili**
Cattle and buffaloes	3 461	3 557	3 692	3 814	3 858	4 142	4 160	4 134	Bovine et buffles
Sheep and goats	5 289[1]	5 229[1]	5 249[1]	5 225[1]	5 116[1]	4 573	4 494[1]	4 856[1]	Ovine et caprins
Pigs	1 226	1 288	1 407	1 490	1 486	1 655	1 962	2 221	Porcine
Horses [1]	530	500	500	550	580	590	590	590	Chevaline [1]
Asses [1]	28	28	28	28	28	28	28	28	Asine [1]
Mules [1]	10	10	10	10	10	10	10	10	Mulassière [1]
Colombia									**Colombie**
Cattle and buffaloes	24 773	25 324	* 25 634	25 551	* 26 088	* 27 945	* 28 261	* 28 479	Bovine et buffles
Sheep and goats	3 521	3 500	3 500[1]	* 3 505	* 3 503	* 3 331	3 335[1]	3 335[1]	Ovine et caprins
Pigs	2 644	2 635	2 600[1]	2 500	2 431	2 480	2 500[1]	2 500[1]	Porcine
Horses	2 100[1]	2 200[1]	2 300[1]	2 450	2 450[1]	2 450[1]	2 450[1]	2 450[1]	Chevaline
Asses [1]	705	710	710	710	710	710	710	710	Asine [1]
Mules	620[1]	622[1]	622[1]	586	590[1]	590[1]	590[1]	590[1]	Mulassière
Ecuador									**Equateur**
Cattle and buffaloes	4 682	4 803	4 937	4 995	5 105	5 150	5 329	5 534	Bovine et buffles
Sheep and goats	1 895	1 979	2 059	1 987	2 018	2 243[1]	2 366[1]	2 492[1]	Ovine et caprins
Pigs	2 425	2 461	2 546	2 618	2 621	2 708	2 795	2 892	Porcine
Horses	512	510[1]	515[1]	520[1]	520[1]	520[1]	520[1]	521[1]	Chevaline
Asses	262	263[1]	264[1]	265[1]	266[1]	267[1]	268[1]	269[1]	Asine
Mules	151	152[1]	153[1]	154[1]	155[1]	156[1]	157[1]	157[1]	Mulassière
Falkland Is. (Malvinas)									**Iles Falkland (Malvinas)**
Cattle and buffaloes	5	5	5	5	4	5	4	4[1]	Bovine et buffles
Sheep and goats	713	721	727	717	686	707	708	708[1]	Ovine et caprins
Horses	2	1	1	1	1	1	1	1[1]	Chevaline
French Guiana									**Guyane française**
Cattle and buffaloes	12	8	8	8	9	9[1]	9[1]	9[1]	Bovine et buffles
Sheep and goats	* 6	4	4	4	4[1]	4[1]	4[1]	4[1]	Ovine et caprins
Pigs	11	9	9	9	10	11[1]	11[1]	11[1]	Porcine
Guyana									**Guyana**
Cattle and buffaloes [1]	220	240	260	250	240	230	220	220	Bovine et buffles [1]
Sheep and goats [1]	209	209	209	209	209	209	209	209	Ovine et caprins [1]
Pigs [1]	35	35	25	20	20	20	20	20	Porcine [1]
Horses [1]	2	2	2	2	2	2	2	2	Chevaline [1]
Asses [1]	1	1	1	1	1	1	1	1	Asine [1]
Paraguay									**Paraguay**
Cattle and buffaloes	7 886	8 600[1]	9 100[1]	9 788	9 765	9 794	* 9 833	* 9 863	Bovine et buffles
Sheep and goats	485[1]	500[1]	508	509[1]	511[1]	510	* 522	* 527	Ovine et caprins
Pigs	2 510[1]	2 485[1]	2 500[1]	2 525[1]	2 268[1]	2 300[1]	2 300[1]	2 500[1]	Porcine
Horses	327	339	370	411[1]	478[1]	400[1]	400[1]	400[1]	Chevaline
Asses [1]	31	32	32	32	32	32	32	32	Asine [1]
Mules [1]	14	14	14	14	14	14	14	14	Mulassière [1]
Peru									**Pérou**
Cattle and buffaloes	3 972	3 955	4 062	4 513	4 646	4 560	4 657	4 750[1]	Bovine et buffles
Sheep and goats	13 688	13 660	13 950	14 614	14 736	15 156	15 581	15 723[1]	Ovine et caprins
Pigs	2 396	2 317	2 442	2 401	2 533	2 481	2 531	2 600[1]	Porcine
Horses [1]	665	665	665	665	665	665	665	665	Chevaline [1]
Asses [1]	520	520	520	520	520	520	520	520	Asine [1]
Mules [1]	224	224	224	224	224	224	224	224	Mulassière [1]

33
Livestock
Thousand head [*cont.*]
Cheptel
Milliers de têtes [*suite*]

Region, country or area	1992	1993	1994	1995	1996	1997	1998	1999	Région, pays ou zone
Suriname									**Suriname**
Cattle and buffaloes	97[1]	98[1]	100[1]	103	99	98	101	103[1]	Bovine et buffles
Sheep and goats	18	17[1]	16[1]	13	16	17	18	21	Ovine et caprins
Pigs	38	36[1]	37	20	20	21	20	25	Porcine
Uruguay									**Uruguay**
Cattle and buffaloes	9 670	10 093	10 504	10 451	10 651	10 557	* 10 392	* 10 700	Bovine et buffles
Sheep and goats [1]	25 049	24 029	21 245	20 220	19 762	18 202	* 16 761	* 15 515	Ovine et caprins [1]
Pigs	240[1]	260[1]	280	270[1]	270	270[1]	330[1]	360[1]	Porcine
Horses [1]	475	480	480	470	480	500	500	500	Chevaline [1]
Asses [1]	1	1	1	1	1	1	1	1	Asine [1]
Mules [1]	4	4	4	4	4	4	4	4	Mulassière [1]
Venezuela									**Venezuela**
Cattle and buffaloes	* 13 648	13 325	13 796	14 737	15 103	15 337	15 648	15 500[1]	Bovine et buffles
Sheep and goats	2 500[1]	2 687[1]	3 119[1]	3 781	3 978	4 800[1]	4 820[1]	4 820[1]	Ovine et caprins
Pigs	3 183	3 456	3 716	4 182	4 422	4 756	4 750[1]	4 800[1]	Porcine
Horses [1]	495	495	495	500	500	500	500	500	Chevaline [1]
Asses [1]	440	440	440	440	440	440	440	440	Asine [1]
Mules [1]	72	72	72	72	72	72	72	72	Mulassière [1]
Asia									**Asie**
Cattle and buffaloes	578 616	586 918	596 627	609 675	611 408	601 219	613 459	618 878	**Bovine et buffles**
Sheep and goats	776 666	785 681	801 097	820 218	857 817	821 591	842 045	859 233	**Ovine et caprins**
Pigs	464 712	479 662	489 863	511 446	539 793	464 969	503 725	527 232	**Porcine**
Horses	18 381	18 211	18 211	18 343	18 478	16 994	17 263	17 244	**Chevaline**
Asses	21 042	20 791	20 788	20 901	20 813	19 580	19 827	19 847	**Asine**
Mules	6 307	6 295	6 171	6 221	6 112	5 499	5 531	5 462	**Mulassière**
Afghanistan									**Afghanistan**
Cattle and buffaloes [1]	1 500	1 500	1 500	1 500	1 500	1 500	1 500	1 500	Bovine et buffles [1]
Sheep and goats [1]	16 350	16 350	16 350	16 500	16 500	16 500	16 500	16 500	Ovine et caprins [1]
Horses	340[1]	320[1]	300[1]	300[1]	300[1]	300[1]	300[1]	300[1]	Chevaline
Asses [1]	1 200	1 180	1 160	1 160	1 160	1 160	1 160	1 160	Asine [1]
Mules [1]	25	24	23	23	23	23	23	23	Mulassière [1]
Armenia									**Arménie**
Cattle and buffaloes	566	499[1]	502[1]	504[1]	497[1]	510[1]	505[1]	505[1]	Bovine et buffles
Sheep and goats	* 1 023	873	* 736	* 636	604	* 579	562[1]	562[1]	Ovine et caprins
Pigs	224	84	81	82	79	55	52[1]	52[1]	Porcine
Horses	9	9	9[1]	10[1]	11[1]	11[1]	12[1]	12[1]	Chevaline
Asses	3	4[1]	3[1]	3[1]	3[1]	3[1]	3[1]	3[1]	Asine
Azerbaijan									**Azerbaïdjan**
Cattle and buffaloes	2 111[1]	2 017[1]	1 911[1]	1 928[1]	1 980	2 083	2 137	2 203[1]	Bovine et buffles
Sheep and goats	5 292	* 4 901	* 4 539	* 4 558	4 644	4 922	5 267	5 503[1]	Ovine et caprins
Pigs	137	67	48	33	30	23	21	26	Porcine
Horses	35	35	35	38	43	49	53	56	Chevaline
Asses	27	24	20	22	25	28	31	33	Asine
Bahrain									**Bahreïn**
Cattle and buffaloes	13[1]	13[1]	12[1]	11	12	12	13	13[1]	Bovine et buffles
Sheep and goats	37[1]	36[1]	35[1]	33	34	35	33	33[1]	Ovine et caprins
Bangladesh									**Bangladesh**
Cattle and buffaloes	24 312	24 435	* 24 643	* 24 859	24 401	* 24 816	24 220	24 220[1]	Bovine et buffles
Sheep and goats	24 919	26 956	* 29 080[1]	* 31 400[1]	34 436	35 636	34 610	34 610[1]	Ovine et caprins
Bhutan									**Bhoutan**
Cattle and buffaloes [1]	426	433	439	439	439	439	439	439	Bovine et buffles [1]
Sheep and goats [1]	92	95	101	101	101	101	101	101	Ovine et caprins [1]
Pigs [1]	74	74	75	75	75	75	75	75	Porcine [1]
Horses [1]	28	29	30	30	30	30	30	30	Chevaline [1]
Asses [1]	18	18	18	18	18	18	18	18	Asine [1]
Mules [1]	10	10	10	10	10	10	10	10	Mulassière [1]
Brunei Darussalam									**Brunéi Darussalam**
Cattle and buffaloes	7	5	6	6	6	8	8[1]	8[1]	Bovine et buffles
Sheep and goats	4	5	4	4	3	3	3[1]	3[1]	Ovine et caprins
Pigs	4	5[1]	5[1]	4[1]	5[1]	5[1]	5[1]	5[1]	Porcine
Cambodia									**Cambodge**
Cattle and buffaloes	3 272	3 366	3 431	3 543	3 544	3 514	3 514[1]	3 514[1]	Bovine et buffles
Pigs	2 043	2 123	2 024	2 039	2 151	2 438	2 438[1]	2 438[1]	Porcine
Horses [1]	19	20	21	21	22	22	22	22	Chevaline [1]

33
Livestock
Thousand head [*cont.*]
      Cheptel
      Milliers de têtes [*suite*]

Region, country or area	1992	1993	1994	1995	1996	1997	1998	1999	Région, pays ou zone
China †††									**Chine †††**
Cattle and buffaloes	104 745	107 998	113 471	123 483	123 053	* 110 481	* 121 923	* 124 519	Bovine et buffles
Sheep and goats	206 386	207 532	217 669	240 839	277 542	237 593	256 036	269 120	Ovine et caprins
Pigs	379 735	393 965	402 846	424 681	452 201	373 534	408 315	429 102	Porcine
Horses	10 095	10 018	9 960	10 038	10 073	8 716	8 913	8 982	Chevaline
Asses	11 158	10 983	10 891	10 923	10 745	9 444	9 528	9 558	Asine
Mules	5 606	5 610	5 498	5 552	5 389	4 780	4 806	4 739[1]	Mulassière
China, Hong Kong SAR †									**Chine, Hong Kong RAS †**
Cattle and buffaloes	2	2	2	2	2	3[1]	40[1]	32[1]	Bovine et buffles
Pigs	175	104	97	107	109	110[1]	110[1]	110[1]	Porcine
Horses	1	1	1	2[1]	2[1]	2[1]	2[1]	2[1]	Chevaline
Cyprus									**Chypre**
Cattle and buffaloes	55	56	61	64	68	70	62	63[1]	Bovine et buffles
Sheep and goats	500	485	473	465	470	492	540	550[1]	Ovine et caprins
Pigs	296	342	369	356	374	400	415	436	Porcine
Horses [1]	1	1	1	1	1	1	1	1	Chevaline [1]
Asses [1]	5	5	5	5	5	5	5	5	Asine [1]
Mules [1]	2	2	2	2	2	2	2	2	Mulassière [1]
Georgia									**Géorgie**
Cattle and buffaloes	1 228[1]	1 022[1]	* 964	* 994	* 994	1 027[1]	1 043[1]	1 067[1]	Bovine et buffles
Sheep and goats	1 500	1 211	958	793	725	* 652	* 584	* 587	Ovine et caprins
Pigs	732	476	367	367	353	333	330	366	Porcine
Horses	18	17	20	22[1]	24	26	22[1]	22[1]	Chevaline
Asses [1]	2	2	2	3	3	3	3	3	Asine [1]
India									**Inde**
Cattle and buffaloes	288 772	* 290 570	293 220	295 868	298 552	301 273	* 303 030	* 306 967	Bovine et buffles
Sheep and goats	166 078	* 168 186	170 358	172 550	174 773	177 032	* 178 462	* 180 130	Ovine et caprins
Pigs	12 795	* 13 500	13 783	14 306	14 848	15 411	* 16 005	16 005[1]	Porcine
Horses [1]	970	980	990	990	990	990	990	990	Chevaline [1]
Asses	970	1 000[1]	1 000[1]	1 000[1]	1 000[1]	1 000[1]	1 000[1]	1 000[1]	Asine
Mules	200	200[1]	200[1]	200[1]	200[1]	200[1]	200[1]	200[1]	Mulassière
Indonesia									**Indonésie**
Cattle and buffaloes	14 440[1]	13 886	14 472	14 663	14 987	15 145	15 384	15 384[1]	Bovine et buffles
Sheep and goats	18 280	17 742	19 511	20 478	21 565	22 008	23 349	23 349[1]	Ovine et caprins
Pigs	8 140	8 704	8 858	7 825	7 597	8 589	10 069	10 069[1]	Porcine
Horses	630[1]	582	611	609	579	582	* 740	740[1]	Chevaline
Iran (Islamic Rep. of)									**Iran (Rép. islamique d')**
Cattle and buffaloes	* 7 340[1]	8 426	8 640	8 794	8 948	9 103	9 259	8 521	Bovine et buffles
Sheep and goats	70 986[1]	75 443	76 042	76 646	77 256	78 117	79 002	79 657	Ovine et caprins
Horses	250[1]	250[1]	250[1]	250[1]	250[1]	250[1]	250[1]	250[1]	Chevaline
Asses	1 600[1]	* 1 400	* 1 400	* 1 400	* 1 400	1 400[1]	1 400[1]	1 400[1]	Asine
Mules	136[1]	* 137	* 137	* 137	* 137	137[1]	137[1]	137[1]	Mulassière
Iraq									**Iraq**
Cattle and buffaloes	1 365[1]	1 588[1]	* 1 441[1]	* 1 260[1]	1 100[1]	* 1 363	1 384[1]	1 160[1]	Bovine et buffles
Sheep and goats	8 775[1]	11 050[1]	9 825[1]	8 850[1]	6 405[1]	* 8 050	8 200[1]	7 300[1]	Ovine et caprins
Horses	52[1]	51[1]	51[1]	* 47	46[1]	47[1]	48[1]	46[1]	Chevaline
Asses	355[1]	360[1]	380[1]	* 396	368[1]	380[1]	385[1]	375[1]	Asine
Mules [1]	12	12	12	12	12	12	13	11	Mulassière [1]
Israel									**Israël**
Cattle and buffaloes	349	366	387	391	391	375	390[1]	390[1]	Bovine et buffles
Sheep and goats	471	430	435	421	420	420	420[1]	420[1]	Ovine et caprins
Pigs [1]	126	118	120	143	145	165	168	168	Porcine [1]
Horses [1]	4	4	4	4	4	4	4	4	Chevaline [1]
Asses [1]	5	5	5	5	5	5	5	5	Asine [1]
Mules [1]	2	2	2	2	2	2	2	2	Mulassière [1]
Japan									**Japon**
Cattle and buffaloes	4 980	5 024	4 989	4 916	4 828	4 749	4 708	4 656	Bovine et buffles
Sheep and goats	64	61	56	50	47	45	45[1]	45[1]	Ovine et caprins
Pigs	10 966	10 783	10 621	10 250	9 900	9 809	9 904	9 873	Porcine
Horses	26	27	28	27[1]	27[1]	27[1]	27[1]	27[1]	Chevaline
Jordan									**Jordanie**
Cattle and buffaloes	64[1]	64[1]	61	58	62	62	65[1]	65[1]	Bovine et buffles
Sheep and goats	3 586	4 029	3 025	3 034	3 182	2 795	2 795[1]	2 795[1]	Ovine et caprins
Horses [1]	4	4	4	4	4	4	4	4	Chevaline [1]
Asses [1]	19	19	19	18	18	18	18	18	Asine [1]
Mules [1]	3	3	3	3	3	3	3	3	Mulassière [1]

33

Livestock
Thousand head [*cont.*]
Cheptel
Milliers de têtes [*suite*]

Region, country or area	1992	1993	1994	1995	1996	1997	1998	1999	Région, pays ou zone
Kazakhstan									**Kazakhstan**
Cattle and buffaloes	9 096	9 587	9 358	8 083	6 870	5 435	4 316	3 967	Bovine et buffles
Sheep and goats	34 600	34 420	34 209	25 132	19 585	13 679	10 384	* 9 556	Ovine et caprins
Pigs	2 794	2 591	2 445	1 983	1 623	1 036	879	892	Porcine
Horses	1 666	1 704	1 777	1 636	1 557	1 310	1 083	986	Chevaline
Asses [1]	45	45	40	40	40	35	29	29	Asine [1]
Korea, Dem. P. R.									**Corée, R. p. dém. de**
Cattle and buffaloes	880[1]	900[1]	911	886	629	545	565	565[1]	Bovine et buffles
Sheep and goats	1 200[1]	1 250[1]	1 401	972[1]	961	1 237	1 673	2 085	Ovine et caprins
Pigs	5 000[1]	4 000[1]	3 572	2 674	2 290	1 859	2 475	2 970	Porcine
Horses [1]	46	46	47	45	40	40	40	40	Mulassière [1]
Korea, Republic of									**Corée, République de**
Cattle and buffaloes	2 527	2 814	2 945	3 147	3 395	3 280	2 922	2 486	Bovine et buffles
Sheep and goats	505	560	605	682	676	605	540	540[1]	Ovine et caprins
Pigs	5 463	5 928	5 955	6 461	6 517	7 096	7 544	7 864	Porcine
Horses	5	5	6	6	7	8	8[1]	8[1]	Chevaline
Kuwait									**Koweït**
Cattle and buffaloes	6	11	15	20	19	21	18	20[1]	Bovine et buffles
Sheep and goats	81	192	258	376	491	564	551	595[1]	Ovine et caprins
Horses [1]	0	1	1	1	1	1	1	1	Chevaline [1]
Kyrgyzstan									**Kirghizistan**
Cattle and buffaloes	1 190	1 122	1 062	920	869	848	830[1]	830[1]	Bovine et buffles
Sheep and goats	9 525	* 8 742	7 322	5 076	4 275	3 716	3 518[1]	3 570[1]	Ovine et caprins
Pigs	358	247	169	118	114	88	85[1]	85[1]	Porcine
Horses	321	313	322	299	308	314	320[1]	320[1]	Chevaline
Asses [1]	10	10	10	10	10	9	8	8	Asine [1]
Lao People's Dem. Rep.									**Rép. dém. pop. lao**
Cattle and buffaloes	2 124	2 154	2 249	2 337	2 398	2 451	2 220	2 783	Bovine et buffles
Sheep and goats	104	126	142	153	159	165	186	200	Ovine et caprins
Pigs	1 561	1 625	1 673	1 724	1 772	1 813	1 464	1 937	Porcine
Horses	29	29[1]	29[1]	29[1]	26[1]	26[1]	27[1]	28[1]	Chevaline
Lebanon									**Liban**
Cattle and buffaloes	73[1]	75[1]	77	* 60	70	70[1]	80	82[1]	Bovine et buffles
Sheep and goats	705[1]	686[1]	662	* 688[1]	795	820[1]	800	815[1]	Ovine et caprins
Pigs	45[1]	48[1]	53	54[1]	58	59[1]	60	62[1]	Porcine
Horses	9[1]	8[1]	* 7	* 5	5	5[1]	6[1]	6[1]	Chevaline
Asses	22[1]	23[1]	23[1]	24[1]	24[1]	25[1]	25[1]	25[1]	Asine
Mules	8[1]	7[1]	7[1]	6[1]	5	6[1]	6[1]	6[1]	Mulassière
Malaysia									**Malaisie**
Cattle and buffaloes	912	901	893	881	851	843	843[1]	843[1]	Bovine et buffles
Sheep and goats	625	581	554	504	441	414	414[1]	414[1]	Ovine et caprins
Pigs	2 843	2 718	3 203	3 150	2 978	3 148	3 148[1]	3 148[1]	Porcine
Horses [1]	5	5	5	4	4	4	4	4	Chevaline [1]
Mongolia									**Mongolie**
Cattle and buffaloes	2 822	2 819	2 731	3 005	3 317	3 476	3 613	3 816	Bovine et buffles
Sheep and goats	19 971	20 260	19 886	21 028	22 239	22 695	24 431	26 185	Ovine et caprins
Pigs	83	49	29	23	24	19	21	21[1]	Porcine
Horses	2 259	2 200	2 190	2 409	2 648	2 771	2 900[1]	2 900[1]	Chevaline
Myanmar									**Myanmar**
Cattle and buffaloes	11 609	11 722	11 821	12 060	12 386	12 600	12 829	13 131	Bovine et buffles
Sheep and goats	1 360	1 397	1 417	1 492	1 558	1 632	1 688	1 732	Ovine et caprins
Pigs	2 630	2 655	2 728	2 944	3 229	3 358	3 501	3 715	Porcine
Horses	116	120	121[1]	122[1]	122[1]	122[1]	122[1]	122[1]	Chevaline
Mules [1]	8	8	8	8	8	8	8	8	Mulassière [1]
Nepal									**Népal**
Cattle and buffaloes	9 304	9 310	9 722	10 116	10 311	10 387	10 468	10 501	Bovine et buffles
Sheep and goats	6 318	6 363	6 439	6 568	6 642	6 792	6 949	7 060	Ovine et caprins
Pigs	599	605	612	636	670	724	766	825	Porcine
Occupied Palestinian Terr. [2]									**Terr. palestinien occupé [2]**
Cattle and buffaloes [1]	3	3	3	3	3	3	3	3	Bovine et buffles [1]
Sheep and goats [1]	40	40	40	40	40	40	40	40	Ovine et caprins [1]
Oman									**Oman**
Cattle and buffaloes	140[1]	142[1]	144[1]	144[1]	145[1]	146[1]	146[1]	146[1]	Bovine et buffles
Sheep and goats [1]	875	883	884	884	870	880	880	880	Ovine et caprins [1]
Asses [1]	26	26	26	26	27	27	27	27	Asine [1]

33
Livestock
Thousand head [*cont.*]
Cheptel
Milliers de têtes [*suite*]

Region, country or area	1992	1993	1994	1995	1996	1997	1998	1999	Région, pays ou zone
Pakistan									**Pakistan**
Cattle and buffaloes	36 018	36 519	37 033	37 559	38 097	38 648	39 300	39 300[1]	Bovine et buffles
Sheep and goats	65 559	67 893	70 315	72 829	75 438	78 147	81 000	81 000[1]	Ovine et caprins
Horses	358	354	350	346	334	331	327	327[1]	Chevaline
Asses	3 653	3 775	3 901	4 000	4 200	4 300	4 500	4 500[1]	Asine
Mules	75	76	77	78	132	142	151	151[1]	Mulassière
Philippines									**Philippines**
Cattle and buffaloes	4 306	4 490	4 496	4 728	4 970	5 234	5 408	5 401[1]	Bovine et buffles
Sheep and goats [1]	5 245	5 760	6 025	6 213	6 260	6 530	6 810	6 810	Ovine et caprins [1]
Pigs	8 022	7 954	8 227	8 941	9 026	9 752	* 10 210	* 10 390	Porcine
Horses [1]	210	210	220	220	220	230	230	230	Chevaline [1]
Qatar									**Qatar**
Cattle and buffaloes	11	12	13	14	14	14	14[1]	14[1]	Bovine et buffles
Sheep and goats	265	308	340	360	372	376	380[1]	380[1]	Ovine et caprins
Horses	1	1	1	1[1]	2[1]	2[1]	2[1]	2[1]	Chevaline
Saudi Arabia									**Arabie saoudite**
Cattle and buffaloes	224	229	242	253	259	243[1]	253[1]	253[1]	Bovine et buffles
Sheep and goats	10 789	11 270	11 840	11 961	12 193	* 12 442[1]	12 442[1]	12 442[1]	Ovine et caprins
Horses [1]	3[1]	3[1]	3	3	3	3[1]	3[1]	3[1]	Chevaline [1]
Asses [1]	102[1]	100[1]	107	102	101	101[1]	101[1]	101[1]	Asine [1]
Singapore									**Singapour**
Sheep and goats [1]	1	1	1	0	0	0	0	0	Ovine et caprins [1]
Pigs [1]	200	150	180	190	190	190	190	190	Porcine [1]
Sri Lanka									**Sri Lanka**
Cattle and buffaloes	2 463	2 498	2 494	2 468	2 405	2 305	2 320	2 320[1]	Bovine et buffles
Sheep and goats	520	602	608	610	547	531	531	531[1]	Ovine et caprins
Pigs	91	90	94	87	85	80	76	76[1]	Porcine
Horses [1]	2	2	2	2	2	2	2	2	Chevaline [1]
Syrian Arab Republic									**Rép. arabe syrienne**
Cattle and buffaloes	766	708	722	776	812	858	902[1]	907[1]	Bovine et buffles
Sheep and goats	15 616	11 133	12 292	13 138	14 201	14 930	15 550[1]	16 200[1]	Ovine et caprins
Pigs	1[1]	1[1]	1	1[1]	1[1]	1[1]	1[1]	1[1]	Porcine
Horses	37	27	27	27	28	27	28[1]	28[1]	Chevaline
Asses	158	185	201	200	191	190	195[1]	195[1]	Asine
Mules	27	21	18	17	18	18	19[1]	19[1]	Mulassière
Tajikistan									**Tadjikistan**
Cattle and buffaloes	1 222	1 244	1 250	1 199	1 147	1 082	1 040[1]	1 050[1]	Bovine et buffles
Sheep and goats	3 324	2 997	* 2 906	* 2 700	* 2 494	* 2 293	2 228[1]	2 245[1]	Ovine et caprins
Pigs	128	46	46	32	6	2	2[1]	2[1]	Porcine
Horses	48	53[1]	50[1]	48[1]	47[1]	45[1]	45[1]	46[1]	Chevaline
Asses [1]	36	36	35	34	33	32	33	32	Asine [1]
Thailand									**Thaïlande**
Cattle and buffaloes	11 849	12 277	11 862	11 004	10 611	9 762	* 9 828[1]	* 9 177[1]	Bovine et buffles
Sheep and goats	336	262	232	208	140	167	167[1]	167[1]	Ovine et caprins
Pigs	4 655	4 985	5 435	5 369	6 129	6 894	7 000[1]	7 200[1]	Porcine
Horses	19	18	14	17	12	16[1]	16[1]	16[1]	Chevaline
Turkey									**Turquie**
Cattle and buffaloes	12 339	12 303	12 226	12 206	12 044	12 121	11 379	11 379[1]	Bovine et buffles
Sheep and goats	51 197	49 870	47 674	45 210	42 902	42 023	38 614	38 614[1]	Ovine et caprins
Pigs	10	12	9	8	5	5	5[1]	5[1]	Porcine
Horses	496	483	450	437	415	391	391[1]	391[1]	Chevaline
Asses	944	895	841	809	731	689	650[1]	650[1]	Asine
Mules	192	181	172	169	169	154	150[1]	150[1]	Mulassière
Turkmenistan									**Turkménistan**
Cattle and buffaloes	777	1 004	1 104	1 181	1 199	* 959	950[1]	880[1]	Bovine et buffles
Sheep and goats	5 600	* 6 265	* 6 314	* 6 503	* 6 574	* 5 775	5 870[1]	6 025[1]	Ovine et caprins
Pigs	237	212	159	128	82	65[1]	55[1]	48[1]	Porcine
Horses [1]	20	22	20	18	17	17	16	16	Chevaline [1]
Asses [1]	26	26	25	25	26	26	25	25	Asine [1]
United Arab Emirates									**Emirats arabes unis**
Cattle and buffaloes	56	60	65	69	74	75[1]	76[1]	76[1]	Bovine et buffles
Sheep and goats	1 043	1 116	1 194	1 277	1 367	1 375[1]	1 385[1]	1 440[1]	Ovine et caprins
Uzbekistan									**Ouzbékistan**
Cattle and buffaloes	5 113	5 275	5 431	5 484	5 204	* 5 217	5 300[1]	5 400[1]	Bovine et buffles
Sheep and goats	9 192	9 368	* 10 400	10 049	* 9 322	* 9 544	8 800[1]	8 650[1]	Ovine et caprins

33
Livestock
Thousand head [*cont.*]
Cheptel
Milliers de têtes [*suite*]

Region, country or area	1992	1993	1994	1995	1996	1997	1998	1999	Région, pays ou zone
Pigs	654	529	391	350	208	* 200	205[1]	192[1]	Porcine
Horses	113	123	120[1]	145	146	* 146	150[1]	155[1]	Chevaline
Asses	143	158	162[1]	165[1]	168[1]	169[1]	165[1]	165[1]	Asine
Viet Nam									**Viet Nam**
Cattle and buffaloes	6 088	6 294	6 444	6 602	6 754	6 849	6 936	7 019	Bovine et buffles
Sheep and goats	312	353	428	551	513	515	514	471	Ovine et caprins
Pigs	13 892	14 874	15 588	16 306	16 921	17 636	18 132	18 886	Porcine
Horses	133	133	131	127	126	120	123	123[1]	Chevaline
Yemen									**Yémen**
Cattle and buffaloes	1 139	1 163	1 151	1 174	1 181	1 201	1 263	1 289	Bovine et buffles
Sheep and goats	6 870	7 012	6 941	7 080	7 480	8 148	8 616	8 745	Ovine et caprins
Horses [1]	3	3	3	3	3	3	3	3	Chevaline [1]
Asses	500	500	* 500	500[1]	500[1]	500[1]	500[1]	500[1]	Asine
Europe									**Europe**
Cattle and buffaloes	**204 506**	**194 857**	**187 680**	**178 247**	**172 642**	**164 650**	**156 086**	**150 809**	**Bovine et buffles**
Sheep and goats	**232 658**	**223 313**	**213 159**	**199 070**	**186 281**	**182 098**	**178 107**	**172 715**	**Ovine et caprins**
Pigs	**237 440**	**227 965**	**221 946**	**213 477**	**207 603**	**204 003**	**198 843**	**208 722**	**Porcine**
Horses	**8 042**	**7 955**	**7 808**	**7 910**	**7 848**	**7 746**	**7 498**	**7 493**	**Chevaline**
Asses	**993**	**956**	**927**	**892**	**876**	**873**	**800**	**800**	**Asine**
Mules	**266**	**259**	**257**	**246**	**230**	**228**	**212**	**211**	**Mulassière**
Albania									**Albanie**
Cattle and buffaloes	618	656	820	840	806	771	705	780[1]	Bovine et buffles
Sheep and goats	3 030	3 205	4 177	4 130	3 232	3 006	2 923	2 000[1]	Ovine et caprins
Pigs	90	93	98	100	98	97	83	90[1]	Porcine
Horses	44	58	62	71	74	70	65	65[1]	Chevaline
Asses	104	114	113[1]	113[1]	113[1]	113[1]	113[1]	113[1]	Asine
Mules	20	26	25[1]	25[1]	25[1]	25[1]	25[1]	25[1]	Mulassière
Austria									**Autriche**
Cattle and buffaloes	2 501	2 532	2 334	2 329	2 326	2 272	2 198	* 2 172	Bovine et buffles
Sheep and goats	351	364	381	392	419	435	442	442[1]	Ovine et caprins
Pigs	3 720	3 629	3 820	3 729	3 706	3 664	3 680	* 3 810	Porcine
Horses	61	57	65	67	72	73	74	74[1]	Chevaline
Belarus									**Bélarus**
Cattle and buffaloes	6 577	6 221	5 851	5 403	5 054	4 855	4 801	* 4 515	Bovine et buffles
Sheep and goats	434	381	301	284	262	213	187[1]	182[1]	Ovine et caprins
Pigs	4 703	4 308	4 181	4 005	3 895	3 715	3 682	* 3 608	Porcine
Horses	212	215	215	220	229	232	233	233[1]	Chevaline
Asses [1]	8	8	8	8	8	8	8	8	Asine [1]
Belgium−Luxembourg									**Belgique−Luxembourg**
Cattle and buffaloes	3 311	3 303	3 289	3 369	3 363	3 280	3 184	3 185	Bovine et buffles
Sheep and goats	181	180	176	170	173	174	* 167	167[1]	Ovine et caprins
Pigs	6 597	6 963	6 948	7 053	7 225	7 194	7 436	7 671	Porcine
Horses	64	65	66	66	66	67	67[1]	67[1]	Chevaline
Bosnia & Herzegovina									**Bosnie−Herzégovine**
Cattle and buffaloes [1]	501	426	391	274	315	261	261	261	Bovine et buffles
Sheep and goats	854[1]	400[1]	300[1]	260[1]	276	276[1]	276[1]	276[1]	Ovine et caprins
Pigs	590[1]	500[1]	* 223	147	165	70[1]	70[1]	70[1]	Porcine
Horses [1]	70	56	50	50	50	50	50	50	Chevaline [1]
Bulgaria									**Bulgarie**
Cattle and buffaloes	1 336	996	768	652	645	593	622	681	Bovine et buffles
Sheep and goats	7 256	5 426	4 440	4 193	4 216	3 868	3 814	3 822	Ovine et caprins
Pigs	3 141	2 680	2 071	1 986	2 140	1 500	1 480	1 721	Porcine
Horses	114	114	113	133	151	170	126	126[1]	Chevaline
Asses	329	303	297	276	281	287	225	225[1]	Asine
Mules	17	21	23	16	17	17	17	17[1]	Mulassière
Croatia									**Croatie**
Cattle and buffaloes	590	590	519	493	462	451	443	439	Bovine et buffles
Sheep and goats	653	629	552	560	532	552	511	566	Ovine et caprins
Pigs	1 183	1 262	1 347	1 175	1 196	1 175	1 166	1 362	Porcine
Horses	27	22	22	21	21	19	16	16[1]	Chevaline
Asses	13	12	7	4[1]	4[1]	4[1]	4[1]	4[1]	Mulassière
former Czechoslovakia †									**l'ex−Tchécoslovaquie †**
Cattle and buffaloes	4 347	...	...	...	...	...	...	...	Bovine et buffles
Sheep and goats	* 940	...	...	...	...	...	...	...	Ovine et caprins
Pigs	7 139	...	...	...	...	...	...	...	Porcine
Horses	34	...	...	...	...	...	...	...	Chevaline

33
Livestock
Thousand head [*cont.*]
Cheptel
Milliers de têtes [*suite*]

Region, country or area	1992	1993	1994	1995	1996	1997	1998	1999	Région, pays ou zone
Czech Republic									**République tchèque**
Cattle and buffaloes	...	2 512	2 161	2 030	1 989	1 866	1 690	* 1 657	Bovine et buffles
Sheep and goats	...	299	241	210	176	159	128	128[1]	Ovine et caprins
Pigs	...	4 599	4 071	3 867	4 016	4 080	3 995	* 4 001	Porcine
Horses	...	19	18	19	19	19	20	20[1]	Chevaline
Denmark									**Danemark**
Cattle and buffaloes	2 190	2 195	2 105	2 091	2 093	2 030	1 974	* 1 968	Bovine et buffles
Sheep and goats	182	157	145	145	170	142	156	156[1]	Ovine et caprins
Pigs	10 345	10 870	10 923	11 084	10 842	11 383	12 004	* 11 991	Porcine
Horses	28	20	18	18	20	39	38	38[1]	Chevaline
Estonia									**Estonie**
Cattle and buffaloes	708	615	463	420	370	343	326	308	Bovine et buffles
Sheep and goats	142	124	83	62	50	39	36	31	Ovine et caprins
Pigs	799	541	424	460	449	298	306	326	Porcine
Horses	8	7	5	5	5	4	4	4[1]	Chevaline
Faeroe Islands									**Iles Féroé**
Cattle and buffaloes [1]	2	2	2	2	2	2	2	2	Bovine et buffles [1]
Sheep and goats [1]	68	68	68	68	68	68	68	68	Ovine et caprins [1]
Finland									**Finlande**
Cattle and buffaloes	1 263	1 232	1 230	1 185	1 179	1 150	1 101	1 101[1]	Bovine et buffles
Sheep and goats	66	67	84	85	120	157	135	135[1]	Ovine et caprins
Pigs	1 357	1 309	1 300	1 295	1 395	1 467	1 541	1 541[1]	Porcine
Horses	49	49	49	50	52	53	55	55[1]	Chevaline
France									**France**
Cattle and buffaloes	20 970	20 328	20 099	20 524	20 661	20 664	20 371	20 214	Bovine et buffles
Sheep and goats	11 761	11 451	12 560	11 389	11 744	11 665	11 516	11 439	Ovine et caprins
Pigs	12 539	13 015	14 291	14 593	14 530	14 976	14 501	16 190	Porcine
Horses	328	329	332	338	338	340	347	348	Chevaline
Asses [1]	25	25	25	25	25	25	25	25	Asine [1]
Mules	12	12	13	13	14	14	14	14	Mulassière
Germany									**Allemagne**
Cattle and buffaloes	17 134	16 207	15 897	15 962	15 890	15 760	15 227	14 942	Bovine et buffles
Sheep and goats	2 571	2 474	2 458	2 429	2 489	2 427	2 412	* 2 408[1]	Ovine et caprins
Pigs	26 063	26 514	26 075	24 698	23 737	24 283	24 795	26 294	Porcine
Horses	492	531	599	652	652	670	670[1]	670[1]	Chevaline
Greece									**Grèce**
Cattle and buffaloes	603	588	580	579	551	598[1]	580[1]	* 586[1]	Bovine et buffles
Sheep and goats	14 028	14 031	14 084	14 246	14 716	14 564	14 830	* 14 456	Ovine et caprins
Pigs	986	1 001	1 014	1 009	917	928	905	875	Porcine
Horses	42	40	38	36	35	33	33[1]	33[1]	Chevaline
Asses	118	111	103	95	89	83	83[1]	83[1]	Asine
Mules	54	50	47	44	41	38	38[1]	38[1]	Mulassière
Hungary									**Hongrie**
Cattle and buffaloes	1 420	1 159	999	910	928	909	871	873	Bovine et buffles
Sheep and goats	1 832	* 1 781	1 288	999	1 065	980	963	1 018	Ovine et caprins
Pigs	5 993	5 364	5 002	4 356	5 032	5 289	4 931	5 479	Porcine
Horses	75	73	72	78	71	70	72	74[1]	Chevaline
Asses	4[1]	4[1]	4[1]	4[1]	4[1]	4[1]	4[1]	4[1]	Asine
Iceland									**Islande**
Cattle and buffaloes	76	74	72	73	75	75	75[1]	75[1]	Bovine et buffles
Sheep and goats	488	489	499	459	464	478[1]	477[1]	477[1]	Ovine et caprins
Pigs [1]	40	40	41	42	43	43	43	43	Porcine [1]
Horses	75	77	79	78	81	80	80[1]	80[1]	Chevaline
Ireland									**Irlande**
Cattle and buffaloes	6 158	6 265	6 308	6 410	6 757	6 757	6 992	7 093	Bovine et buffles
Sheep and goats	5 988	6 125	5 991	5 775	5 583	5 391	5 634	5 624	Ovine et caprins
Pigs	1 346	1 423	1 487	1 498	1 542	1 665	1 717	1 801	Porcine
Horses	51[1]	52[1]	48[1]	40[1]	45[1]	52[1]	50[1]	50[1]	Chevaline
Asses [1]	11	11	10	10	10	10	10	10	Asine [1]
Mules [1]	1	1	1	1	1	1	1	1	Mulassière [1]
Italy									**Italie**
Cattle and buffaloes	8 087	7 704	7 560	7 272	7 414	7 334	7 328	7 320	Bovine et buffles
Sheep and goats	11 749	11 667	11 839	12 129	12 041	12 366	12 237	12 135	Ovine et caprins
Pigs	8 549	8 244	8 348	8 023	8 061	8 171	8 281	8 225	Porcine

33
Livestock
Thousand head [*cont.*]
Cheptel
Milliers de têtes [*suite*]

Region, country or area	1992	1993	1994	1995	1996	1997	1998	1999	Région, pays ou zone
Horses	316	316	323	324	315	310[1]	310[1]	310[1]	Chevaline
Asses	40	39	33	* 30	26	26[1]	26[1]	26[1]	Asine
Mules	19	18	17	16	12	12[1]	12[1]	12[1]	Mulassière
Latvia									**Lettonie**
Cattle and buffaloes	1 383	1 144	678	551	509	477	434	434[1]	Bovine et buffles
Sheep and goats	189	171	120	93	64	49	40	40[1]	Ovine et caprins
Pigs	1 246	867	482	501	460	430	421	421[1]	Porcine
Horses	30	28	27	27	27	26	23	23[1]	Chevaline
Liechtenstein									**Liechtenstein**
Cattle and buffaloes	6	6[1]	6[1]	6[1]	6[1]	6[1]	6[1]	6[1]	Bovine et buffles
Sheep and goats	3	3[1]	3[1]	3[1]	3[1]	3[1]	3[1]	3[1]	Ovine et caprins
Pigs	3	3[1]	3[1]	3[1]	3[1]	3[1]	3[1]	3[1]	Porcine
Lithuania									**Lituanie**
Cattle and buffaloes	2 197	1 701	1 384	1 152	1 065	1 054	1 016	928	Bovine et buffles
Sheep and goats	64	61	55	52	47	45	45	45[1]	Ovine et caprins
Pigs	2 180	1 360	1 196	1 260	1 270	1 128	1 200	1 168	Porcine
Horses	80	80	81	78	78	81	78	75	Chevaline
Malta									**Malte**
Cattle and buffaloes	22[1]	22	20	19	21	21[1]	21[1]	21[1]	Bovine et buffles
Sheep and goats	24[1]	25[1]	26[1]	27	25	25[1]	25[1]	25[1]	Ovine et caprins
Pigs	107[1]	109[1]	111[1]	103	69	69[1]	69[1]	69[1]	Porcine
Horses [1]	1	1	1	1	1	1	1	1	Chevaline [1]
Asses [1]	1	1	1	1	1	1	1	1	Asine [1]
Netherlands									**Pays—Bas**
Cattle and buffaloes	4 920	4 797	4 716	4 654	4 557	* 4 366	* 4 292	* 4 184	Bovine et buffles
Sheep and goats	* 2 017	1 973	1 830	1 750	1 729	1 584	1 584[1]	1 584[1]	Ovine et caprins
Pigs	14 161	14 964	14 565	14 397	* 13 958	* 14 253	* 11 438	* 13 418	Porcine
Horses	86	92	97	100	107	112	112[1]	112[1]	Chevaline
Norway									**Norvège**
Cattle and buffaloes	984	975	980	998	1 006	1 018	1 036	1 042	Bovine et buffles
Sheep and goats	2 452	2 375	2 524	2 586	2 620	2 511	2 481	2 481[1]	Ovine et caprins
Pigs	766	748	748	768	768[1]	692	689	690	Porcine
Horses	21	21	22	22	23	24	24[1]	24[1]	Chevaline
Poland									**Pologne**
Cattle and buffaloes	8 221	7 643	7 696	7 306	7 136	7 307	6 955	* 6 600	Bovine et buffles
Sheep and goats	1 870	1 268	870	713	552	491	453	437[1]	Ovine et caprins
Pigs	22 086	18 860	19 467	20 418	17 964	18 135	19 168	22 000[1]	Porcine
Horses	900	841	622	636	569	558	561	567[1]	Chevaline
Portugal									**Portugal**
Cattle and buffaloes *	1 416	1 345	1 323	1 329	1 324	1 311	1 285	1 270	Bovine et buffles *
Sheep and goats	* 6 502	6 983	6 827	6 719[1]	6 599[1]	7 081[1]	6 585[1]	* 6 643[1]	Ovine et caprins
Pigs	2 535	2 547	2 666	2 416	2 402	2 344	2 365	2 341	Porcine
Horses [1]	25	25	25	23	25	22	23	25	Chevaline [1]
Asses [1]	170	160	160	160	150	150	140	140	Asine [1]
Mules [1]	80	70	70	70	60	60	50	50	Mulassière [1]
Republic of Moldova									**République de Moldova**
Cattle and buffaloes	1 000	971	916	832	726	646	551	* 525	Bovine et buffles
Sheep and goats	1 289	1 357	1 445	1 507	1 423	1 372	1 128	* 1 035	Ovine et caprins
Pigs	1 753	1 487	1 165	1 061	1 015	950	798	807	Porcine
Horses	48	51	55	59	61	63	66	68[1]	Chevaline
Asses	2	2	2	2[1]	2[1]	2[1]	2[1]	2[1]	Asine
Romania									**Roumanie**
Cattle and buffaloes	4 355	3 683	3 957	3 481	3 496	3 435	3 235	3 100	Bovine et buffles
Sheep and goats	14 833	12 884	12 275	11 642	11 086	10 317	9 547	8 500	Ovine et caprins
Pigs	10 954	9 852	9 262	7 758	7 960	8 235	7 097	7 000	Porcine
Horses	749	721	751	784	806	816	820[1]	825[1]	Chevaline
Asses [1]	35	34	33	32	31	30	30	30	Asine [1]
Russian Federation									**Fédération de Russie**
Cattle and buffaloes	54 700	52 248	48 932	43 320	39 720	35 124	31 536	28 651[1]	Bovine et buffles
Sheep and goats	55 255	51 369	43 713	34 540	28.027	22 772	18 774	* 17 372[1]	Ovine et caprins
Pigs	35 384	31 520	28 557	24 859	22 631	19 115	17 348	16 400[1]	Porcine
Horses	2 590	2 556	2 500	2 431	2 363	2 197	2 013	2 000[1]	Chevaline
Asses	22	22	26	26[1]	27[1]	26[1]	25[1]	25[1]	Asine
Slovakia									**Slovaquie**
Cattle and buffaloes	...	1 203	993	916	929	892	803	705	Bovine et buffles
Sheep and goats	...	592	436	422	453	445	444	377	Ovine et caprins

33
Livestock
Thousand head [*cont.*]
Cheptel
Milliers de têtes [*suite*]

Region, country or area	1992	1993	1994	1995	1996	1997	1998	1999	Région, pays ou zone
Pigs	...	2 269	2 179	2 037	2 076	1 985	1 810	1 593	Porcine
Horses	...	11	11	10	10	10	10[1]	10[1]	Chevaline
Slovenia									**Slovénie**
Cattle and buffaloes	484	504	478	477	496	486	446	453	Bovine et buffles
Sheep and goats	36[1]	30	39	50	52	61[1]	81[1]	81[1]	Ovine et caprins
Pigs	529	602	592	571	592	552	578	592	Porcine
Horses	11	9	9	8	8	8	10	10[1]	Chevaline
Spain									**Espagne**
Cattle and buffaloes	5 063	4 976	5 018	5 248	5 512	5 925	5 884	6 065	Bovine et buffles
Sheep and goats	27 597	27 452	26 819	26 215	23 928	26 917	27 752	* 26 651	Ovine et caprins
Pigs	17 110	18 260	18 234	18 345	18 163	18 652	19 479	21 715	Porcine
Horses	240	263	262[1]	260[1]	260[1]	260[1]	250[1]	260[1]	Chevaline
Asses [1]	90	90	90	90	90	90	90	90	Asine [1]
Mules [1]	60	60	60	60	60	60	54	53	Mulassière [1]
Sweden									**Suède**
Cattle and buffaloes	1 773	1 809	1 827	1 777	1 790	1 781	1 706	* 1 757	Bovine et buffles
Sheep and goats	447	471	484	462	469	442	421	420	Ovine et caprins
Pigs	2 279	2 277	2 328	2 313	2 349	2 351	2 309	2 321	Porcine
Horses	78[1]	79[1]	86	83	85[1]	87	87[1]	87[1]	Chevaline
Switzerland									**Suisse**
Cattle and buffaloes	1 783	1 745	1 755	1 756	1 772	1 673	1 641	1 615	Bovine et buffles
Sheep and goats	473	481	496	489	495	478	480	555	Ovine et caprins
Pigs	1 706	1 692	1 660	1 611	1 580	1 395	1 487	1 420	Porcine
Horses	52	54	55[1]	55[1]	43	46	46[1]	46[1]	Chevaline
Asses [1]	2	2	2	2	2	2	2	2	Asine [1]
TFYR Macedonia									**L'ex–R.y. Macédoine**
Cattle and buffaloes	284	286	281	282	284	296	299[1]	291[1]	Bovine et buffles
Sheep and goats	2 251	2 351	2 459	2 466	2 320	1 814	1 805	1 550	Ovine et caprins
Pigs	171	173	185	172	175	192	193	185	Porcine
Horses	65	62	62	62	66	67[1]	67[1]	67[1]	Chevaline
Ukraine									**Ukraine**
Cattle and buffaloes	23 728	22 457	21 607	19 624	17 557	15 313	12 759	11 722	Bovine et buffles
Sheep and goats	7 829	7 237	6 863	5 574	4 098	3 047	2 362	2 026	Ovine et caprins
Pigs	17 839	16 175	15 298	13 946	13 144	11 236	9 479	10 083	Porcine
Horses	717	707	716	737	756	754	737	721	Chevaline
Asses [1]	19	19	15	15	14	13	13	13	Asine [1]
United Kingdom									**Royaume–Uni**
Cattle and buffaloes	11 804	11 729	11 834	11 733	11 913	11 633	11 519	11 423	Bovine et buffles
Sheep and goats	43 998	43 901	43 295	42 771	41 530	42 823	44 471	44 656	Ovine et caprins
Pigs	7 609	7 754	7 892	7 627	7 590	8 072	8 146	7 284	Porcine
Horses [1]	172	173	173	173	173	173	173	173	Chevaline [1]
Yugoslavia									**Yougoslavie**
Cattle and buffaloes	1 994	2 010	1 832	1 968	1 944	1 915	1 910	1 847[1]	Bovine et buffles
Sheep and goats	2 955[1]	3 014	2 914	3 004	2 966	2 859	2 714	2 704[1]	Ovine et caprins
Pigs	3 844	4 092	3 693	4 192	4 446	4 216	4 150	4 115	Porcine
Horses	89	82	82	96	93	90	86	86[1]	Chevaline
Oceania									**Océanie**
Cattle and buffaloes	**32 738**	**33 115**	**35 402**	**35 762**	**36 155**	**36 548**	**36 200**	**36 340**	**Bovine et buffles**
Sheep and goats	**201 926**	**189 287**	**182 851**	**170 546**	**169 262**	**167 996**	**166 516**	**166 428**	**Ovine et caprins**
Pigs	**4 974**	**4 938**	**5 205**	**5 154**	**5 078**	**5 125**	**5 259**	**5 261**	**Porcine**
Horses	**454**	**429**	**412**	**402**	**392**	**392**	**382**	**382**	**Chevaline**
Asses	**10**	**9**	**9**	**9**	**9**	**9**	**9**	**9**	**Asine**
American Samoa									**Samoa américaines**
Pigs [1]	11	11	11	11	11	11	11	11	Porcine [1]
Australia									**Australie**
Cattle and buffaloes	23 880	24 062	25 758	25 731	26 377	26 780	26 710	26 710[1]	Bovine et buffles
Sheep and goats	148 551	138 343	132 801	121 092[1]	121 346[1]	120 458[1]	119 820	119 780[1]	Ovine et caprins
Pigs	2 792	2 646	2 775	2 653	2 526	2 555	2 680	2 680[1]	Porcine
Horses	289	272	250[1]	240[1]	230[1]	230[1]	220[1]	220[1]	Chevaline
Asses	3	2	2[1]	2[1]	2[1]	2[1]	2[1]	2[1]	Asine
Cook Islands									**Iles Cook**
Sheep and goats	7	7	8	7	3	3[1]	3[1]	3[1]	Ovine et caprins
Pigs	18	25	28	32	40	40[1]	40[1]	40[1]	Porcine

33
Livestock
Thousand head [*cont.*]
Cheptel
Milliers de têtes [*suite*]

Region, country or area	1992	1993	1994	1995	1996	1997	1998	1999	Région, pays ou zone
Fiji									**Fidji**
Cattle and buffaloes	288[1]	315	334	354	350[1]	350[1]	345	345[1]	Bovine et buffles
Sheep and goats	187	204	211	218	214	227[1]	237	237[1]	Ovine et caprins
Pigs	97[1]	110	115	121	120[1]	115[1]	112	112[1]	Porcine
Horses [1]	43	43	44	44	44	44	44	44	Chevaline [1]
French Polynesia									**Polynésie française**
Cattle and buffaloes	7[1]	8[1]	7	8[1]	6[1]	7[1]	7[1]	7[1]	Bovine et buffles
Sheep and goats	15[1]	15[1]	16	16[1]	16[1]	16[1]	16[1]	16[1]	Ovine et caprins
Pigs	36[1]	38	40	39[1]	37[1]	33[1]	33[1]	33[1]	Porcine
Horses [1]	2[1]	2[1]	2[1]	2[1]	2[1]	2[1]	2[1]	2[1]	Chevaline [1]
Guam									**Guam**
Sheep and goats	1[1]	1[1]	1[1]	1[1]	1[1]	1[1]	1[1]	1[1]	Ovine et caprins
Pigs [1]	4	4	4	4	4	4	4	4	Porcine [1]
Kiribati									**Kiribati**
Pigs	9[1]	9[1]	9[1]	9[1]	10[1]	10[1]	10[1]	10	Porcine
Micronesia (Federated States of)									**Micron (Etats fédérés de)**
Cattle and buffaloes	...	...	...	14[1]	14[1]	14[1]	14[1]	14[1]	Bovine et buffles
Sheep and goats	...	...	...	4[1]	4[1]	4[1]	4[1]	4[1]	Ovine et caprins
Pigs	...	...	...	32[1]	32[1]	32[1]	32[1]	32[1]	Porcine
Nauru									**Nauru**
Pigs [1]	3	3	3	3	3	3	3	3	Porcine [1]
New Caledonia									**Nouvelle-Calédonie**
Cattle and buffaloes	125[1]	120[1]	113	110[1]	120[1]	120[1]	120[1]	120[1]	Bovine et buffles
Sheep and goats	20[1]	20[1]	20[1]	20[1]	21[1]	21[1]	21[1]	21[1]	Ovine et caprins
Pigs	39[1]	39[1]	38[1]	37[1]	38[1]	38[1]	38[1]	38[1]	Porcine
Horses	12[1]	12[1]	12[1]	12[1]	12[1]	12[1]	12[1]	12[1]	Chevaline
New Zealand									**Nouvelle-Zélande**
Cattle and buffaloes	8 144	8 308	8 887	9 272	9 017	9 008	8 736	8 876	Bovine et buffles
Sheep and goats	53 101	50 651	49 750	49 153	47 622	47 230	46 378	46 330[1]	Ovine et caprins
Pigs	411	395	423	431	424	400	413	413	Porcine
Horses	88	80	85[1]	85[1]	85[1]	85[1]	85[1]	85[1]	Chevaline
Niue									**Nioué**
Pigs	2[1]	2[1]	2[1]	2[1]	2[1]	2[1]	2[1]	2[1]	Porcine
Papua New Guinea									**Papouasie-Nvl-Guinée**
Cattle and buffaloes	96[1]	94[1]	92[1]	90[1]	88[1]	87	86[1]	86[1]	Bovine et buffles
Sheep and goats	6[1]	6[1]	7[1]	7[1]	6[1]	* 8	8[1]	8[1]	Ovine et caprins
Pigs	1 100[1]	1 200[1]	1 300[1]	1 400[1]	1 450[1]	1 500	1 500[1]	1 500[1]	Porcine
Horses [1]	2	2	2	2	2	2	2	2	Chevaline [1]
Samoa									**Samoa**
Cattle and buffaloes [1]	24	25	26	26	26	26	26	26	Bovine et buffles [1]
Pigs [1]	175	178	179	179	179	179	179	179	Porcine [1]
Horses [1]	3	3	3	3	3	3	3	3	Chevaline [1]
Asses [1]	7	7	7	7	7	7	7	7	Asine [1]
Solomon Islands									**Iles Salomon**
Cattle and buffaloes [1]	10	10	10	10	10	10	10	10	Bovine et buffles [1]
Pigs	54[1]	55[1]	55[1]	55[1]	56[1]	57[1]	57[1]	58[1]	Porcine
Tokelau									**Tokélaou**
Pigs [1]	1	1	1	1	1	1	1	1	Porcine [1]
Tonga									**Tonga**
Cattle and buffaloes	10[1]	10[1]	10[1]	9	9[1]	9[1]	9[1]	9[1]	Bovine et buffles
Sheep and goats	16[1]	16[1]	16[1]	14	14[1]	14[1]	14[1]	14[1]	Ovine et caprins
Pigs	94[1]	94[1]	94[1]	81	81[1]	81[1]	81[1]	81[1]	Porcine
Horses	12[1]	11[1]	11[1]	11[1]	11[1]	11[1]	11[1]	11[1]	Chevaline
Tuvalu									**Tuvalu**
Pigs	13[1]	13[1]	13[1]	13[1]	13[1]	13[1]	13[1]	13[1]	Porcine
Vanuatu									**Vanuatu**
Cattle and buffaloes	140[1]	150	* 151	* 151	151[1]	151[1]	151[1]	151[1]	Bovine et buffles
Sheep and goats	12	12	12	12	12[1]	12[1]	12[1]	12[1]	Ovine et caprins
Pigs	60	60	60	60	60[1]	60[1]	60[1]	60[1]	Porcine
Horses [1]	3	3	3	3	3	3	3	3	Chevaline [1]
Wallis and Futuna Islands									**Iles Wallis et Futuna**
Sheep and goats [1]	7	7	7	7	7	7	7	7	Ovine et caprins [1]
Pigs [1]	25	25	25	25	25	25	25	25	Porcine [1]

33
Livestock [*cont.*]
Cheptel [*suite*]

Source:
Food and Agriculture Organization of the United Nations (FAO),
Rome, FAOSTAT Database.

† For information on recent changes in country or area
nomenclature pertaining to former Czechoslovakia, Germany,
Hong Kong Special Administrative Region (SAR) of China,
Macao Special Administrative Region (SAR) of China,
SFR Yugoslavia and former USSR, see Annex I − Country or
area nomenclature, regional and other groupings.

†† For statistical purposes, the data for China do not
include those for the Hong Kong Special Administrative
Region and Macao Special Administrative Region.

1   FAO estimate.
2   Data refer to the Gaza Strip.

Source:
Organisation des Nations Unies pour l'alimentation et
l'agriculture (FAO), Rome, la base de données FAOSTAT.

† Pour les modifications récentes de nomenclature de pays
ou de zone concernant l'Allemagne, Hong−Kong (Région
administrative spéciale de Chine), l'ex−Tchécoslovaquie, Macao
(Région administrative spéciale de chine), l'ex−URSS,
Rfs de Yougoslavie, voir annexe I − Nomenclature des pays ou des
zones, groupements régionaux et autres groupments.

†† Les données statistiques relatives à la Chine ne comprennent
pas celles qui concernent la région administrative spéciale de
Hong−Kong et la région administrative spéciale de Macao.

1   Estimation de la FAO.
2   Les données se rapportent à la Zone de Gaza.

34
Roundwood
Bois rond

Production (solid volume of roundwood without bark): million cubic metres
Production (volume solide de bois rond sans écorce) : millions de mètres cubes

Region, country or area Région, pays ou zone	1990	1991	1992	1993	1994	1995	1996	1997	1998	1999
World *Monde*	**3 326.3**	**3 207.9**	**3 146.2**	**3 141.4**	**3 161.9**	**3 214.1**	**3 218.9**	**3 297.5**	**3 549.9**	**3 590.5**
Africa Afrique	**439.7**	**438.1**	**460.2**	**474.7**	**491.0**	**502.0**	**512.4**	**523.8**	**531.4**	**531.7**
Algeria Algérie	2.2	2.3	2.3	2.5	2.5	2.5	2.6	2.7	2.7	2.7
Angola Angola	5.0	5.1	5.3	5.5	5.7	5.9	6.1	6.3	6.5	6.5
Benin Bénin	4.9	5.0[1]	5.1[1]	5.3[1]	5.4[1]	5.5[1]	5.7[1]	5.8[1]	6.0[1]	6.0[1]
Botswana[1] Botswana[1]	1.4	1.4	1.4	1.5	1.5	1.6	1.6	1.6	1.7	1.7
Burkina Faso[1] Burkina Faso[1]	8.7	8.9	9.1	9.4	9.7	9.9	10.2	10.5	10.8	10.8
Burundi Burundi	1.3	1.4	1.4	1.5	1.5	1.6	1.6	1.6[1]	1.8	1.8[1]
Cameroon Cameroun	12.9	13.1	13.3	13.6	14.2	14.8	15.3	15.1	15.2	15.2[1]
Central African Rep. Rép. centrafricaine	3.5	3.4	3.7	3.7	3.6	3.6	3.2	3.4	3.5	3.5
Chad Tchad	1.5	1.6	1.6	1.7	1.7[1]	1.8[1]	1.8[1]	1.9[1]	1.9[1]	1.9[1]
Congo Congo	3.6	3.2	3.5	3.5	3.6	3.8	3.6	4.1	3.9	3.9
Côte d'Ivoire Côte d'Ivoire	11.8	11.5	11.6	11.9	12.6	12.7	12.8	12.9	13.3	13.2
Dem. Rep. of the Congo Rép. dém. du Congo	38.0	39.4	41.0	42.7	44.3	45.8	47.2	48.4	49.5	49.5[1]
Djibouti Djibouti	0.0	0.0	0.0	0.0	0.0[1]	0.0[1]	0.0[1]	0.0[1]	0.0[1]	0.0[1]
Egypt[1] Egypte[1]	2.4	2.5	2.5	2.6	2.6	2.7	2.7	2.8	2.8	2.8
Equatorial Guinea Guinée équatoriale	0.6	0.6	0.6	0.6	0.7	0.8	0.8[1]	0.8[1]	0.8[1]	0.8[1]
Eritrea[1] Erythrée[1]	...	...	...	1.9	1.9	2.0	2.0	2.1	2.2	2.2
Ethiopia incl. Eritrea Ethiopie comp. Erythrée	42.1	43.3	44.5	...	...	...	...	...	...	...
Ethiopia Ethiopie	...	...	...	44.1	45.3	46.5	47.8	49.0	50.1	50.1
Gabon Gabon	3.7	3.4	3.7	4.1	4.4	4.7	4.8	5.3	5.3[1]	5.3[1]
Gambia Gambie	0.5[1]	0.5[1]	0.5[1]	0.6	0.6	0.6	0.6	0.6	0.6	0.6
Ghana Ghana	14.3	12.4	16.3	19.9	22.5	22.0	21.9	22.0	21.9	21.9
Guinea Guinée	4.0	4.2	8.2	8.3	8.6	8.6[1]	8.6[1]	8.7	8.7	8.7[1]
Guinea-Bissau[1] Guinée-Bissau[1]	0.6	0.6	0.6	0.6	0.6	0.6	0.6	0.6	0.6	0.6

34
Roundwood
Production (solid volume of roundwood without bark): million cubic metres [cont.]
Bois rond
Production (volume solide de bois rond sans écorce) : millions de mètres cubes [suite]

Region, country or area Région, pays ou zone	1990	1991	1992	1993	1994	1995	1996	1997	1998	1999
Kenya Kenya	23.9	24.8	25.5	26.2	26.9	27.6	28.2	28.8	29.4	29.4
Lesotho Lesotho	1.3	1.3	1.4	1.4	1.4	1.5	1.5	1.6	1.6	1.6
Liberia Libéria	3.8	3.4	3.7	3.6	3.3[1]	2.9[1]	2.9	2.9	3.0	3.0[1]
Libyan Arab Jamah.[1] Jamah. arabe libyenne[1]	0.6	0.6	0.6	0.6	0.6	0.6	0.6	0.7	0.7	0.7
Madagascar Madagascar	8.2	8.5	8.9	9.1	9.4	9.8	10.1	10.2	10.3	10.6
Malawi Malawi	8.7	8.9	9.0	9.0	9.0[1]	9.1[1]	9.2[1]	9.4[1]	9.7[1]	9.7[1]
Mali Mali	5.6[1]	5.5[1]	5.6[1]	5.7[1]	5.9[1]	6.0	6.1	6.3[1]	6.4[1]	6.4[1]
Mauritania[1] Mauritanie[1]	0.0	0.0	0.0	0.0	0.0	0.0	0.0	0.0	0.0	0.0
Mauritius Maurice	0.0	0.0	0.0	0.0	0.0	0.0	0.0	0.0[1]	0.0[1]	0.0[1]
Morocco Maroc	1.4	2.0	1.8	1.4	1.6	1.5	1.5	0.8	1.7	1.7
Mozambique Mozambique	15.7	16.0	16.4	16.8[1]	17.3	17.9	17.9[1]	18.0[1]	18.0[1]	18.0[1]
Niger[1] Niger[1]	5.0	5.1	5.3	5.5	5.7	5.9	6.1	6.3	6.5	6.5
Nigeria Nigéria	88.8	83.1	85.1	87.1	89.1	91.1	93.4	96.1	98.5	98.5[1]
Réunion Réunion	0.0	0.0	0.0[1]	0.0[1]	0.0[1]	0.0[1]	0.0[1]	0.0[1]	0.0[1]	0.0[1]
Rwanda Rwanda	3.0	3.0	3.1	3.1	2.6	2.2	3.2	3.3	3.3	3.3
Sao Tome and Principe[1] Sao Tomé-et-Principe[1]	0.0	0.0	0.0	0.0	0.0	0.0	0.0	0.0	0.0	0.0
Senegal Sénégal	4.0	4.1	4.2	4.3[1]	4.4[1]	4.5[1]	4.7[1]	4.8[1]	4.9[1]	4.9[1]
Sierra Leone Sierra Leone	2.9	2.9	3.0	3.0	3.0[1]	3.0[1]	3.1[1]	3.2[1]	3.3[1]	3.3[1]
Somalia[1] Somalie[1]	7.4	6.8	6.8	6.9	6.9	7.1	7.3	7.6	8.0	8.0
South Africa Afrique du Sud	24.8	24.8	27.9	28.2	30.5	32.0	32.4	33.2	30.6	30.6
Sudan Soudan	8.1	8.1	8.3	8.5	8.7	8.9[1]	9.1[1]	9.3[1]	9.5[1]	9.5[1]
Swaziland Swaziland	1.5	1.5	1.5	1.5	1.5	1.5	1.5	1.5	0.9	0.9
Togo Togo	0.9	0.9	0.9	1.0	1.0	1.1	1.1	1.2	1.2	1.2
Tunisia Tunisie	2.4	2.5	2.5	2.6	2.7	2.7	2.7	2.8	2.8	2.8
Uganda Ouganda	12.6	12.8	13.3	13.6	14.0[1]	14.4[1]	14.8[1]	15.2[1]	15.6[1]	15.6[1]

34

Roundwood
Production (solid volume of roundwood without bark): million cubic metres [cont.]
Bois rond
Production (volume solide de bois rond sans écorce) : millions de mètres cubes [suite]

Region, country or area Région, pays ou zone	1990	1991	1992	1993	1994	1995	1996	1997	1998	1999
United Rep.Tanzania Rép.-Unie de Tanzanie	31.1	32.1	33.5	34.4	35.4	36.4	37.4	38.2	39.0	39.0
Zambia Zambie	7.1	7.3	7.6	7.9	8.3	8.2[1]	8.1[1]	8.0[1]	8.0[1]	8.0[1]
Zimbabwe Zimbabwe	7.9	8.0	8.0	8.0	8.0	8.1	7.8	8.4	8.4	8.4
America, North **Amérique du Nord**	**734.5**	**700.3**	**724.5**	**727.4**	**745.9**	**752.8**	**745.9**	**745.0**	**948.9**	**956.0**
Bahamas Bahamas	0.1	0.1	0.1	0.1	0.1	0.1	0.1	0.1	0.0	0.0
Barbados Barbade	0.0	0.0	0.0[1]	0.0[1]	0.0[1]	0.0[1]	0.0[1]	0.0[1]	0.0[1]	0.0[1]
Belize[1] Belize[1]	0.2	0.2	0.2	0.2	0.2	0.2	0.2	0.2	0.2	0.2
Canada Canada	162.1	160.2	169.9	176.2	183.2	188.4	189.8	191.2	216.7	216.6
Costa Rica Costa Rica	3.9	3.9	4.1	4.3	4.9	5.0	5.1	5.2	5.3	5.3
Cuba Cuba	2.6	2.3	1.9	1.8	1.8[1]	1.8[1]	1.8[1]	1.8[1]	1.8[1]	1.6
Dominican Republic Rép. dominicaine	0.6	0.6	0.6	0.6	0.6[1]	0.6[1]	0.6[1]	0.6[1]	0.6[1]	0.6[1]
El Salvador El Salvador	5.8[1]	4.7	4.7[1]	4.7[1]	4.7[1]	4.7	4.3	5.2	5.1	5.1[1]
Guadeloupe Guadeloupe	0.0[1]	0.0	0.0	0.0	0.0[1]	0.0[1]	0.0[1]	0.0[1]	0.0[1]	0.0[1]
Guatemala Guatemala	11.3	11.3	11.3	13.0	13.4	13.6	13.1	13.0	13.0[1]	13.0[1]
Haiti[1] Haïti[1]	5.3	5.7	5.8	5.9	6.0	6.1	6.2	6.3	6.4	6.4
Honduras Honduras	5.8	5.9	5.9	6.1	6.4	6.4	6.7	6.9	7.2	7.2[1]
Jamaica Jamaïque	1.1	0.9	0.6	0.5	0.5	0.3	0.3[1]	0.3[1]	0.3[1]	0.3[1]
Martinique Martinique	0.0[1]	0.0[1]	0.0	0.0	0.0	0.0[1]	0.0[1]	0.0[1]	0.0[1]	0.0[1]
Mexico Mexique	21.4	21.3	21.4	20.6	20.9	21.2	22.0	23.0	23.9	23.9
Nicaragua Nicaragua	3.2	3.5	3.5	3.6	3.7	3.8	4.0	4.1	4.2[1]	4.2[1]
Panama Panama	1.0[1]	1.0	1.0	1.0[1]	1.1[1]	1.1[1]	1.1	1.1	1.1[1]	1.1[1]
Trinidad and Tobago Trinité-et-Tobago	0.1	0.1	0.1	0.1	0.1	0.1	0.1	0.1	0.1	0.1[1]
United States Etats-Unis	510.1	478.6	493.4	488.8	498.4	499.3	490.6	485.9	663.1	670.4
America, South **Amérique du Sud**	**283.1**	**286.3**	**289.5**	**288.4**	**294.9**	**296.7**	**294.1**	**297.1**	**268.0**	**268.0**
Argentina Argentine	9.8	9.9	10.4	9.8	10.1	10.6	11.4	11.4	11.4	11.4

34
Roundwood
Production (solid volume of roundwood without bark): million cubic metres [*cont.*]
Bois rond
Production (volume solide de bois rond sans écorce) : millions de mètres cubes [*suite*]

Region, country or area Région, pays ou zone	1990	1991	1992	1993	1994	1995	1996	1997	1998	1999
Bolivia Bolivie	1.5	1.6	1.8	2.0	2.1	2.1	2.2	2.2	1.6	1.6
Brazil Brésil	205.6	205.6	203.2	202.6	201.0	198.6	198.7	198.7	167.1	167.1
Chile Chili	22.1	24.0	28.4	29.9	31.1	34.9	29.8	30.0	31.7	31.7
Colombia Colombie	17.0	18.2	17.7	17.8	18.0	18.2	18.5	18.8	18.6	18.6
Ecuador Equateur	6.6	6.3	6.4	4.7	9.4	10.0	10.6	11.3	11.3	11.3
French Guiana Guyane française	0.2[1]	0.2[1]	0.2[1]	0.1	0.1	0.1[1]	0.1[1]	0.1[1]	0.1[1]	0.1[1]
Guyana Guyana	0.2	0.2	0.2	0.3	0.4	0.5	0.5	0.6	0.4	0.4
Paraguay Paraguay	* 7.5	* 7.6	* 7.7	* 7.4	* 8.1	8.1[1]	8.1[1]	8.1[1]	8.1[1]	8.1[1]
Peru Pérou	7.6	7.7	7.8	8.2	9.0	8.0	7.9	8.4	9.2	9.2
Suriname Suriname	0.1	0.1	0.1	0.1	0.1	0.1	0.2	0.2	0.2[1]	0.2[1]
Uruguay Uruguay	3.2	3.3	3.5	3.5	3.5	3.5	4.0	5.0	6.2	6.2
Venezuela Venezuela	1.7	1.6	2.0	2.1	2.0	1.9	2.1	2.3	2.0	2.0
Asia **Asie**	**1 053.3**	**1 067.6**	**1 089.8**	**1 103.9**	**1 113.5**	**1 128.0**	**1 151.3**	**1 159.1**	**1 127.0**	**1 126.4**
Afghanistan[1] Afghanistan[1]	5.9	6.1	6.4	6.8	7.2	7.5	7.8	7.9	8.1	8.1
Armenia Arménie	...	...	0.0	0.0	0.0	0.0	0.0	0.1	0.0	0.0
Bangladesh Bangladesh	29.2	29.6	30.1	30.6	31.0	31.4	32.0	32.5	33.1	33.1
Bhutan Bhoutan	1.4	1.5	1.5	1.5	1.6[1]	1.6[1]	1.6[1]	1.7[1]	1.7[1]	1.7[1]
Brunei Darussalam Brunéi Darussalam	0.3	0.3	0.3	0.3	0.3[1]	0.3[1]	0.3[1]	0.3[1]	0.3[1]	0.3[1]
Cambodia Cambodge	6.2[1]	6.5[1]	6.7	6.8	7.3	7.5	7.7[1]	7.9[1]	8.0[1]	8.0[1]
China †† Chine ††	280.0	282.3	288.9	298.7	303.4	305.6	312.7	312.7	291.9	291.9
China, Hong Kong SAR†[1] Chine, Hong Kong RAS†[1]	0.0	0.0	0.0	0.0	0.0	0.0	0.0	0.0	0.0	0.0
Cyprus Chypre	0.1	0.1	0.0	0.1	0.0	0.0	0.0	0.0	0.0	0.0
East Timor Timor oriental	0.0	0.0	0.0	0.0	0.0[1]	0.0[1]	0.0[1]	0.0[1]	0.0[1]	0.0[1]
India Inde	262.0	266.8	271.5	276.3	281.0	285.7	290.3	294.9	298.3	298.3
Indonesia Indonésie	177.5	183.4	186.7	189.9	190.7	193.5	199.8	202.1	193.2	193.2

34
Roundwood
Production (solid volume of roundwood without bark): million cubic metres [cont.]
Bois rond
Production (volume solide de bois rond sans écorce) : millions de mètres cubes [suite]

Region, country or area Région, pays ou zone	1990	1991	1992	1993	1994	1995	1996	1997	1998	1999
Iran (Islamic Rep. of) Iran (Rép. islamique d')	6.7	6.9	6.8	6.9	7.0	6.9	6.9	6.9	6.8	6.8
Iraq Iraq	0.1[1]	0.1[1]	0.1[1]	0.1[1]	0.1[1]	0.1[1]	0.1[1]	0.2	0.2	0.2[1]
Israel Israël	0.1	0.1	0.1	0.1	0.1	0.1	0.1	0.1	0.1	0.1
Japan Japon	29.4	28.1	27.3	25.7	24.8	23.4	23.2	22.3	19.6	19.0
Jordan[1] Jordanie[1]	0.0	0.0	0.0	0.0	0.0	0.0	0.0	0.0	0.0	0.0
Kazakhstan Kazakhstan	...	...	0.5	0.3	0.3	0.3	0.3	0.3[1]	0.3[1]	0.3[1]
Korea, Dem. P. R. Corée, R. p. dém. de	4.5	4.6	4.6	4.6	4.7	4.7	5.5[1]	6.2[1]	7.0[1]	7.0[1]
Korea, Republic of Corée, République de	3.2	2.6	2.1	1.9	1.7	1.8	1.6	1.5	1.8	1.8
Kyrgyzstan Kirghizistan	...	...	0.0	0.0	0.0	0.0	0.0	0.0	0.0	0.0[1]
Lao People's Dem. Rep. Rép. dém. pop. lao	3.6	3.9	3.7	4.0	4.2	4.6	4.5	4.5	4.6[1]	4.6[1]
Lebanon Liban	0.3	0.3	0.3	0.4	0.4[1]	0.4[1]	0.4[1]	0.4[1]	0.4[1]	0.4[1]
Malaysia Malaisie	47.6	47.8	51.7	44.8	43.4	42.9	43.0	38.9	29.3	29.3
Mongolia[1] Mongolie[1]	1.4	0.9	0.9	0.9	0.8	0.6	0.6	0.6	0.6	0.6
Myanmar Myanmar	21.3	21.5	21.7	21.2	20.7	21.1	21.5	22.1	22.4	22.4[1]
Nepal Népal	17.7	18.2	18.7[1]	19.1[1]	19.6[1]	20.0[1]	20.5[1]	21.0[1]	21.5[1]	21.5[1]
Pakistan Pakistan	25.9	26.4	27.2	27.5	27.9	28.2	29.4	32.1	33.0	33.0
Philippines Philippines	37.5	37.6	37.9	38.4	39.4	40.1	40.9	41.6	42.5	42.5
Sri Lanka Sri Lanka	9.7	9.9	9.7	9.9	10.2	10.4	10.4	10.4	10.3	10.3
Syrian Arab Republic Rép. arabe syrienne	0.0	0.1	0.1	0.1	0.1[1]	0.1[1]	0.1[1]	0.1[1]	0.1[1]	0.1[1]
Thailand Thaïlande	33.9	34.1	34.3	34.6	35.0	35.3	35.6	36.0	36.3	36.3
Turkey Turquie	15.8	15.3	17.0	18.9	16.8	19.3	19.4	18.1	19.3	19.2
Viet Nam Viet Nam	31.9	32.7	32.9	33.4	34.0[1]	34.6[1]	35.2[1]	35.7[1]	36.2[1]	36.2[1]
Europe **Europe**	**388.2**	**316.4**	**538.8**	**500.6**	**468.0**	**485.1**	**466.2**	**522.2**	**625.2**	**659.9**
Albania Albanie	2.1	2.6[1]	2.6[1]	0.6	0.4	0.4[1]	0.4[1]	0.4[1]	0.4[1]	0.4[1]
Austria Autriche	16.8	15.6	12.8	12.9	15.0	14.4	15.6	15.3	16.7	17.0

34
Roundwood
Production (solid volume of roundwood without bark): million cubic metres [*cont.*]
Bois rond
Production (volume solide de bois rond sans écorce) : millions de mètres cubes [*suite*]

Region, country or area Région, pays ou zone	1990	1991	1992	1993	1994	1995	1996	1997	1998	1999
Belarus Bélarus	...	...	11.4	10.0	10.0	10.0	15.7	17.6	17.7	17.7
Belgium-Luxembourg Belgique-Luxembourg	5.6	4.8	4.2	4.2	4.3	4.1	4.0	4.0	5.0	6.4
Bosnia and Herzegovina[1] Bosnie-Herzégovine[1]	...	...	0.0	0.0	0.0	0.0	0.0	0.0	0.0	0.0
Bulgaria Bulgarie	4.1	3.7	3.5	3.5	2.7	2.8	3.2	3.0	3.0	3.0
Croatia Croatie	...	...	2.0	2.5	2.8	2.6	2.5	3.1	3.7	3.8
former Czechoslovakia† l'ex-Tchécoslovaquie†	18.2	15.3	...	...	...	...	...	...	...	...
Czech Republic République tchèque	...	...	...	10.4	12.0	12.4	12.6	13.5	19.3	19.5
Denmark Danemark	2.3	2.3	2.2	2.3	2.3	2.3	2.3	2.1	1.5	1.5
Estonia Estonie	...	...	2.1	2.4	3.6	3.7	3.9	5.4	9.1	10.1
Finland Finlande	43.2	34.9	38.5	42.2	48.7	50.2	46.6	51.3	77.6	78.4
France France	44.7	43.6	42.4	39.4	42.2	43.4	40.4	41.1	45.8	46.9
Germany Allemagne	84.7	33.6	33.0	33.2	39.8	39.3	37.0	38.2	49.5	47.9
Greece Grèce	2.5	2.5	2.3	2.2	2.1	2.0	2.0	1.7	1.8	2.3
Hungary Hongrie	6.0	5.5	5.0	4.5	4.5	4.3	3.7	4.2	4.5	4.6
Ireland Irlande	1.6	1.7	2.0	1.8	2.0	2.2	2.3	2.2	3.1	3.6
Italy Italie	8.0	8.3	8.4	8.8	9.5	9.7	9.1	9.1	10.3	12.1
Latvia Lettonie	...	...	2.5	4.9	5.7	6.9	8.1	8.7	12.6	16.2
Lithuania Lituanie	...	...	3.2	4.5	4.0	6.0	5.5	5.1	6.1	6.2
Netherlands Pays-Bas	1.4	1.1	1.3	1.1	1.0	1.1	1.0	1.1	1.3	1.3
Norway Norvège	11.8	11.3	10.1	9.7	8.7	9.0	8.4	8.3	11.7	11.9
Poland Pologne	17.6	17.0	18.8	18.6	18.8	19.1	20.3	21.7	32.4	34.4
Portugal Portugal	11.2	10.8	10.3	10.2	9.8	9.4	9.0	9.0	12.9	13.9
Republic of Moldova République de Moldova	...	...	0.0	0.0	0.0	0.0	0.4	0.4	0.4	0.0
Romania Roumanie	12.6	13.0	12.4	8.8	11.9	12.2	12.3	13.5	11.6	11.6
Russian Federation Fédération de Russie	...	...	227.9	174.6	111.8	116.2	96.8	134.7	125.4	149.7

34
Roundwood
Production (solid volume of roundwood without bark): million cubic metres [cont.]
Bois rond
Production (volume solide de bois rond sans écorce) : millions de mètres cubes [suite]

Region, country or area Région, pays ou zone	1990	1991	1992	1993	1994	1995	1996	1997	1998	1999
Slovakia Slovaquie	...	...	...	5.2	5.3	5.3	5.5	4.9	8.4	8.7
Slovenia Slovénie	...	...	1.7	1.1	1.9	1.9	2.0	2.2	2.1	2.1
Spain Espagne	15.6	15.2	13.9	13.8	15.3	16.1	15.6	15.6	21.6	20.6
Sweden Suède	52.9	51.4	53.5	54.0	56.3	63.6	56.3	60.2	82.8	80.2
Switzerland Suisse	6.3	4.6	4.6	4.4	4.7	4.7	4.1	4.5	4.8	5.5
TFYR Macedonia L'ex-R.y. Macédoine	...	...	...	0.9	0.8	0.8	0.8	0.8	0.7	0.8
Ukraine Ukraine	...	...	...	...	...	...	10.4	10.1	10.1[1]	10.1[1]
United Kingdom Royaume-Uni	6.4	6.4	6.3	7.8	8.6	7.6	7.1	7.5	9.9	10.1
Yugoslavia Yougoslavie	...	...	0.0	0.0	1.3	1.3	1.3	1.3	1.1	1.1
Yugoslavia, SFR† Yougoslavie, Rfs†	12.7	11.4	...	...	...	...	...	...	...	...
Oceania **Océanie**	**41.1**	**42.8**	**43.4**	**46.4**	**48.5**	**49.6**	**48.9**	**50.4**	**49.5**	**48.5**
Australia Australie	19.9	19.3	19.4	20.4	21.5	22.3	22.0	22.6	23.9	22.9
Cook Islands Iles Cook	0.0	0.0	0.0	0.0[1]	0.0[1]	0.0[1]	0.0[1]	0.0[1]	0.0[1]	0.0[1]
Fiji Fidji	0.3	0.3	0.3	0.5	0.6	0.6	0.6	0.8	0.6	0.6
New Caledonia Nouvelle-Calédonie	0.0[1]	0.0	0.0	0.0	0.0	0.0[1]	0.0[1]	0.0[1]	0.0[1]	0.0[1]
New Zealand Nouvelle-Zélande	12.0	14.3	15.1	16.0	16.3	16.9	16.4	17.1	15.3	15.3
Papua New Guinea Papouasie-Nvl-Guinée	8.2	8.2	8.0	8.8	9.3	8.8	8.8	8.8	8.6	8.6
Samoa[1] Samoa[1]	0.1	0.1	0.1	0.1	0.1	0.1	0.1	0.1	0.1	0.1
Solomon Islands Iles Salomon	0.5	0.5	0.5	0.5	0.8	0.9	0.9[1]	0.9[1]	0.9[1]	0.9[1]
Tonga[1] Tonga[1]	0.0	0.0	0.0	0.0	0.0	0.0	0.0	0.0	0.0	0.0
Vanuatu[1] Vanuatu[1]	0.1	0.1	0.1	0.1	0.1	0.1	0.1	0.1	0.1	0.1
former USSR† **l'ex-URSS†**	**386.4**	**356.4**	...	...	...	...	...	...	...	...

34

Roundwood
Production (solid volume of roundwood without bark): million cubic metres [*cont.*]

Bois rond
Production (volume solide de bois rond sans écorce) : millions de mètres cubes [*suite*]

Source:
Food and Agriculture Organization of the United
Nations (FAO), Rome, "FAO Yearbook of Forest Products 1999"
and the FAOSTAT database.

† For information on recent changes in country or
area nomenclature pertaining to former Czechoslovakia,
Germany, Hong Kong Special Administrative Region (SAR) of
China, Macao Special Administrative Region (SAR) of China,
SFR of Yugoslavia and the former USSR, see Annex I - Country
or area nomenclature, regional and other groupings.

†† For statistical purposes, the data for
China do not include those for Hong Kong Special
Administrative Region (Hong Kong SAR) and Macao Special
Administrative Region (Macao SAR).

1 FAO estimate.

Source:
Organisation des Nations Unies pour l'alimentation et
l'agriculture (FAO), Rome, "Annuaire FAO des produits
forestiers 1999" et la base de données FAOSTAT.

† Pour les modifications récentes de nomenclature
de pays ou de zone concernant l'Allemagne, Hong Kong, région
administrative spéciale (RAS) de Chine, Macao, région
administrative spéciale (RAS) de Chine,
l'ex-Tchécoslovaquie, l'ex-URSS et l'ex-Rfs de Yougoslavie,
voir annexe I - Nomenclature des pays ou des zones,
groupements régionaux et autres groupements.

†† Les données statistiques relatives à
la Chine ne comprennent pas celles qui concernent la région
administrative spéciale de Hong Kong (la RAS de Hong Kong)
et la région administrative spéciale de Macao (la RAS de
Macao).

1 Estimation de la FAO.

35
Fish catches
Quantités pêchées

All fishing areas, catch and culture production: thousand metric tons
Toutes les zones de pêche, captures et production de l'aquaculture : milliers de tonnes

Country or area Pays ou zone	1989	1990	1991	1992	1993	1994	1995	1996	1997	1998
World *Monde*	**101 618.3**	**98 594.8**	**98 220.6**	**100 776.9**	**104 404.0**	**112 256.4**	**116 128.9**	**120 294.2**	**122 443.3**	**117 162.4**
Afghanistan[1] Afghanistan[1]	1.0	1.1	1.1	1.2	1.2	1.3	1.3	1.3	1.3	1.2
Albania Albanie	12.0	15.0	3.9	3.1	3.0[1]	2.6[1]	1.7	2.4	1.1	2.7
Algeria Algérie	99.6	91.0	79.8	95.4	102.2	135.8	106.2	116.7	91.9	92.6
American Samoa Samoa américaines	0.1	0.0	0.0	0.1	0.0	0.1	0.2	0.2	0.6	0.9
Angola Angola	137.5	133.1	117.1	114.5	126.2	132.4	122.8	137.8	136.1	145.8
Anguilla Anguilla	0.4	0.4	0.4	0.4	0.3	0.3	0.4	0.3	0.4	0.4
Antigua and Barbuda Antigua-et-Barbuda	1.0[1]	0.9	1.5	1.7	0.6	0.6	0.5	0.5[1]	0.5[1]	0.5[1]
Argentina Argentine	486.6	555.6	640.5	703.8	931.8	949.5	1 148.8	1 250.1	1 352.4	1 130.2
Armenia Arménie	7.3	7.8	4.5	4.5	4.1	2.6	1.9	1.2	1.3	1.1
Aruba Aruba	0.5[1]	0.4[1]	0.4[1]	0.3	0.3	0.3	0.1	0.2	0.2	0.2
Australia Australie	183.4	220.5	237.6	248.9	246.8	220.2	226.5	228.6	225.0	229.0
Austria Autriche	5.0	3.7	3.6	3.6	3.6	3.5	3.3	3.4	3.5	3.4
Azerbaijan Azerbaïdjan	54.4	41.7	39.7	32.0	22.8	19.7	11.0	7.0	5.5	4.9
Bahamas Bahamas	8.2	7.5	9.2	9.9	10.1	9.7	9.6	9.9	10.4	10.1
Bahrain Bahreïn	9.2	8.1	7.6	8.0	9.0	7.6	9.4	12.9	10.1	9.8
Bangladesh Bangladesh	843.6	847.8	892.7	966.7	1 047.2	1 090.6	1 172.9	1 264.4	1 342.2	1 423.0
Barbados Barbade	2.5	3.0	2.1	3.3	2.9	2.6	3.3	3.4	2.8	3.6
Belarus Bélarus	21.5	19.6	15.5	9.9	10.0	7.7	6.2	6.9	4.8	5.2
Belgium Belgique	40.4	42.1	40.7	38.0	36.9	35.1	36.4	31.8	31.3	31.7
Belize Belize	1.8	1.5	1.6	2.2	2.1	2.0	2.2	2.0	2.6	4.0
Benin Bénin	41.9	38.2	35.1	32.5	39.2	39.9	44.4	42.2	43.8	43.2
Bermuda Bermudes	0.8	0.5	0.4	0.4	0.4	0.4	0.4	0.5	0.5	0.5
Bhutan[1] Bhoutan[1]	0.3	0.3	0.3	0.4	0.4	0.3	0.3	0.3	0.3	0.3
Bolivia Bolivie	6.0	7.4	5.4	5.2	6.2	6.0	6.3	6.4	6.4	6.4

35
Fish catches
All fishing areas, catch and culture production: thousand metric tons [*cont.*]
Quantités pêchées
Toutes les zones de pêche, captures et production de l'aquaculture : milliers de tonnes [*suite*]

Country or area Pays ou zone	1989	1990	1991	1992	1993	1994	1995	1996	1997	1998
Bosnia and Herzegovina[1] Bosnie-Herzégovine[1]	...	...	...	3.0	2.5	2.4	2.5	2.6	2.6	2.5
Botswana Botswana	1.9	1.9[1]	1.9[1]	1.9[1]	2.0[1]	2.0[1]	2.0[1]	2.1[1]	2.0[1]	2.0[1]
Brazil Brésil	850.0	801.6[1]	789.7[1]	771.1[1]	747.5[1]	771.0[1]	752.9	793.2	832.3	855.0
British Virgin Islands Iles Vierges britanniques	1.4	1.4	1.4	1.0[1]	0.8	1.0	1.2	1.1	0.8	0.9
Brunei Darussalam Brunéi Darussalam	2.3	2.4	1.7	1.7	1.8	4.5	4.8	7.5	4.7	5.2
Bulgaria Bulgarie	103.0	57.1	57.9	32.1	21.6	12.5[1]	12.8	13.6	16.7	15.0
Burkina Faso Burkina Faso	8.0	7.0	7.0	7.5	7.0	8.0	8.0	8.0	8.0	8.4
Burundi Burundi	10.8	17.4	21.0	23.1	22.1	20.7[1]	21.2	3.1	20.3	32.0
Cambodia Cambodge	82.1	111.4	117.8	111.2	108.9	103.2	112.5	104.3	114.6	122.0
Cameroon Cameroun	69.8	70.8[1]	69.4[1]	72.0	65.3	75.0[1]	91.8[1]	92.5[1]	94.1[1]	97.1[1]
Canada Canada	1 637.3	1 673.0	1 502.0	1 336.6	1 190.4	1 081.9	918.7	981.8	1 046.0	1 085.6
Cape Verde Cap-Vert	8.6	6.6	7.4	6.6	7.0	8.3	8.5	8.9	11.1	10.0
Cayman Islands Iles Caïmanes	0.6[1]	0.8[1]	0.6	0.6	0.4	0.4	0.3	0.3	0.3[1]	0.3
Central African Rep. Rép. centrafricaine	13.1	13.1	13.6	13.3	13.5[1]	12.9[1]	13.1[1]	12.8[1]	12.6[1]	13.1[1]
Chad Tchad	64.4	70.0	60.0	80.0	87.3	80.0	90.0	100.0	85.0	84.0
Channel Islands Iles Anglo-Normandes	2.9	3.1[1]	2.9[1]	2.9	2.9[1]	2.9	3.1[1]	4.5	4.4	4.3
Chile Chili	6 454.2	5 195.2	6 006.5	6 500.8	6 036.0	7 838.5	7 591.0	6 908.9	6 083.9	3 558.4
China †† Chine ††	12 210.2	13 136.8	14 253.6	16 579.0	19 708.2	23 833.6	28 418.4	31 896.7	35 038.0	38 025.3
China, Hong Kong SAR† Chine, Hong Kong RAS†	242.5	234.5	230.9	229.5	226.8	220.0	203.6	192.3	194.3	186.4
China, Macao SAR † Chine, Macao RAS †	3.5	2.6	2.3	2.7	1.9	1.9	1.6	1.4	1.5[1]	1.5[1]
Colombia Colombie	98.4	127.9	113.4	164.7	147.8	123.7	157.6	161.1	193.1	213.4
Comoros Comores	11.7	12.2	12.6	11.8	11.6	13.0	13.2[1]	13.0[1]	12.5[1]	12.5[1]
Congo Congo	45.8	48.2	45.6	40.2	47.0	42.8	45.9	45.6	38.2	40.1[1]
Cook Islands Iles Cook	1.1[1]	1.2[1]	1.1	1.0	1.0[1]	0.9[1]	1.1	1.0[1]	1.0[1]	1.0[1]
Costa Rica Costa Rica	17.4[1]	17.6[1]	18.0	18.1	18.9	20.9	27.9	31.2	31.2	29.3

35
Fish catches
All fishing areas, catch and culture production: thousand metric tons [cont.]
Quantités pêchées
Toutes les zones de pêche, captures et production de l'aquaculture : milliers de tonnes [suite]

Country or area Pays ou zone	1989	1990	1991	1992	1993	1994	1995	1996	1997	1998
Côte d'Ivoire Côte d'Ivoire	99.2	104.4	85.0	87.3	70.2	74.1	70.6	69.1	67.7	67.5[1]
Croatia Croatie	...	...	...	32.8	30.3	21.3	19.2	20.2	20.0	28.3
Cuba Cuba	192.1	188.2	171.1	109.0	93.7	87.7	94.2	109.7	123.6	100.2
Cyprus Chypre	2.6	2.7	2.7	2.8	3.0	3.1	3.0	3.4	3.4	3.7
former Czechoslovakia† l'ex-Tchécoslovaquie†	25.2	26.6	26.3[1]	28.5[1]	...	...	...	...	...	...
Czech Republic République tchèque	...	...	...	...	23.4	22.6	22.6	21.7	20.9	21.2
Dem. Rep. of the Congo Rép. dém. du Congo	166.0[1]	162.0[1]	166.6	188.6	197.5	156.6	159.4	163.8	163.0	178.8
Denmark Danemark	1 929.3	1 517.7	1 793.3	1 997.1	1 657.5	1 916.2	2 043.8	1 722.9	1 865.8	1 599.7
Djibouti Djibouti	0.4	0.4	0.3	0.3[1]	0.3[1]	0.3[1]	0.4[1]	0.4[1]	0.3[1]	0.4[1]
Dominica Dominique	0.5[1]	0.4	0.6	0.7	0.8	0.9	0.8	0.9	1.0	1.2
Dominican Republic Rép. dominicaine	21.8	20.1[1]	17.3	13.6	14.4	26.9	20.2	14.6	15.2	11.0
Ecuador Equateur	682.8	366.6	437.7	343.5	375.2	345.0	611.8	811.7	684.3	456.6
Egypt Egypte	293.6	313.0	299.9	322.6	326.8	340.5	372.6	396.1	418.7	505.0
El Salvador El Salvador	11.6	9.2	11.3	12.6	13.0	14.4	15.1	13.2	11.0	15.4
Equatorial Guinea Guinée équatoriale	4.0[1]	3.7[1]	3.5[1]	3.6[1]	3.5[1]	5.1[1]	2.3[1]	5.0	6.1[1]	6.0
Eritrea Erythrée	...	...	...	...	0.5	2.7	3.7	3.2	1.0	1.6
Estonia Estonie	404.8	367.7	359.1	132.0	147.5	124.1	132.3	108.7	123.9	119.0
Ethiopia Ethiopie	4.3	5.0	4.3	4.6	4.2	5.3	6.4	8.8	10.4	14.0
Faeroe Islands Iles Féroé	308.6	286.1	246.6	267.5	265.2	253.1	297.5	324.4	352.3	396.8
Falkland Is. (Malvinas) Iles Falkland (Malvinas)	4.6	6.0	1.5	1.9	2.0	8.8	29.1	32.2	17.9	44.7
Fiji Fidji	28.9	32.4	28.6	24.8	28.2	29.3[1]	29.1	25.2	28.1	28.5
Finland Finlande	169.1	160.4	147.4	169.7	173.8	181.0	184.8	196.7	196.5	197.3
France France	858.9	875.7	824.7	835.7	895.7	904.2	892.4	845.8	854.9	810.1
French Guiana Guyane française	6.5	6.5	7.1	7.6	6.9	7.8	8.1	8.0	7.7	7.7
French Polynesia Polynésie française	3.2	4.1	3.8	3.2	8.2	9.0	8.6	9.0	10.9	11.5

35
Fish catches
All fishing areas, catch and culture production: thousand metric tons [*cont.*]
Quantités pêchées
Toutes les zones de pêche, captures et production de l'aquaculture : milliers de tonnes [*suite*]

Country or area Pays ou zone	1989	1990	1991	1992	1993	1994	1995	1996	1997	1998
Gabon Gabon	20.5[1]	20.0[1]	22.0[1]	24.0[1]	31.8[1]	31.0[1]	40.5[1]	45.4	44.8	53.7
Gambia Gambie	19.8	17.9	22.8	16.6	20.0	22.3	23.3	31.6	32.3	29.0
Georgia Géorgie	148.3	105.2	60.8	39.1[1]	18.8[1]	7.6[1]	3.7[1]	2.6	2.6	3.1
Germany Allemagne	412.3	391.1	300.8	307.2	316.0	272.5	297.9	311.6	318.8	333.6
Ghana Ghana	362.1	396.3	363.1	424.0	373.2	336.1	353.5	477.6	447.2	443.1
Greece Grèce	140.1	146.4	156.8	179.6	199.5	224.1	198.0	202.3	219.3	188.2
Greenland Groenland	168.8	143.3	114.2	113.3	116.7	117.4	128.9	116.0	120.6	128.6
Grenada Grenade	1.7	1.8	2.0	2.1	2.1	1.6	1.5	1.3	1.4	1.7
Guadeloupe Guadeloupe	8.5	8.6	8.5	8.5	8.6	8.8	9.5	9.6	10.5	9.1
Guam Guam	0.6	0.7	0.8	0.5	0.6	0.7	0.4	0.3	0.4	0.5
Guatemala Guatemala	4.3	7.8	7.3	7.8	10.9	11.6	11.9	11.1	11.3	14.0
Guinea Guinée	41.0[1]	44.0[1]	49.5[1]	55.0[1]	60.6[1]	63.8[1]	67.9	63.4	62.4	69.8
Guinea-Bissau Guinée-Bissau	5.4[1]	5.4[1]	5.0[1]	5.2[1]	5.4[1]	6.0[1]	6.3	7.0[1]	7.3[1]	7.0[1]
Guyana Guyana	35.3	36.9	40.8	41.3	44.3	46.6	48.1[1]	48.8	54.2	57.2
Haiti[1] Haïti[1]	5.5	5.2	5.2	5.0	5.2	5.5	5.5	5.2	5.3	5.2
Honduras Honduras	17.4	15.6	24.7	22.7	31.7	27.7	27.0	25.0[1]	26.6[1]	23.0[1]
Hungary Hongrie	35.5	33.9	22.9	22.9	17.4	18.2	16.7	15.7	16.7	17.5
Iceland Islande	1 502.4	1 508.1	1 050.3	1 577.2	1 718.5	1 560.2	1 616.0	2 063.9	2 209.6	1 685.8
India Inde	3 640.7	3 794.7	4 045.5	4 232.7	4 545.7	4 737.8	4 905.9	5 257.5	5 379.3	5 244.4
Indonesia Indonésie	2 948.4	3 044.2	3 352.5	3 439.4	3 685.4	3 913.2	4 139.1	4 290.7	4 453.6	4 395.7
Iran (Islamic Rep. of) Iran (Rép. islamique d')	260.2	269.5	275.7	334.2	317.4	332.2	368.0	381.7	380.2	400.1
Iraq Iraq	24.6	24.2	15.2	22.8	23.9	29.2	30.8	33.2	34.7	23.2
Ireland Irlande	208.1	242.4	261.0	276.3	308.7	322.6	412.8	368.0	329.5	365.1
Isle of Man Ile de Man	5.7	4.1	4.6	4.5	4.9	3.6	3.7	3.5	4.3	2.2
Israel Israël	26.5	23.6	20.6	17.7	18.7	19.5	19.8	22.4	23.5	24.9

35
Fish catches
All fishing areas, catch and culture production: thousand metric tons [cont.]
            Quantités pêchées
            Toutes les zones de pêche, captures et production de l'aquaculture : milliers de tonnes [suite]

Country or area Pays ou zone	1989	1990	1991	1992	1993	1994	1995	1996	1997	1998
Italy Italie	551.8	530.6	576.4	561.8	567.2	599.0	626.6	575.3	552.7	562.2
Jamaica Jamaïque	11.4	11.4[1]	11.6[1]	12.2[1]	13.0[1]	13.5[1]	13.6[1]	15.9	11.5	10.1
Japan Japon	11 173.5	10 354.3	9 301.2	8 502.2	8 080.8	7 398.3	6 787.4	6 765.5	6 722.7	6 025.9
Jordan Jordanie	0.4	0.4	0.4	0.4	0.5	0.5	0.6	0.6	0.7	0.8
Kazakhstan Kazakhstan	89.5	87.0	82.7	68.5	59.6	47.6	50.4	46.0	33.7	24.2
Kenya Kenya	146.6	202.1	198.9	163.3	183.2	204.0	194.0	181.6	161.3	172.7
Kiribati Kiribati	29.2	25.1	27.4	28.3	27.1	27.8	30.4	32.0	31.5[1]	34.0[1]
Korea, Dem. P. R. Corée, R. p. dém. de	1 723.1[1]	1 355.0[1]	1 105.0[1]	960.0[1]	930.0[1]	449.7	401.0	334.0	306.6	288.5[1]
Korea, Republic of Corée, République de	2 840.4	2 843.3	2 514.3	2 696.6	2 649.4	2 700.7	2 688.1	2 771.8	2 596.4	2 354.4
Kuwait Koweït	7.7	4.5	2.0	7.9	8.5	7.8	8.7	8.3	8.0	7.9
Kyrgyzstan Kirghizistan	1.4	1.3	1.2	0.8	0.4	0.3	0.4	0.3[1]	0.3[1]	0.3[1]
Lao People's Dem. Rep. Rép. dém. pop. lao	28.0[1]	28.0[1]	29.0[1]	30.0[1]	30.5	35.0	40.3	40.3	40.0	40.9
Latvia Lettonie	551.6	467.3	416.6	157.4	142.3	138.7	149.7	143.0	106.0	102.8
Lebanon Liban	1.8	1.5	1.8	1.9[1]	2.2	2.4	4.4	4.5	4.0	3.9
Liberia Libéria	14.8	6.5	9.6	8.9	7.8	7.7	9.2	7.2	8.6	10.8
Libyan Arab Jamah.[1] Jamah. arabe libyenne[1]	22.1	24.8	26.1	28.9	31.2	34.1	34.5	34.8	33.8	33.7
Lithuania Lituanie	421.4	350.2	475.0	192.4	120.1	51.0	49.5	56.7	19.8	22.3
Madagascar Madagascar	97.7	103.7	99.1	106.0	116.6	119.7	120.4	119.6	121.5	121.3
Malawi Malawi	70.8	74.1	63.7	69.5	68.2	58.8	53.9	63.8	56.6	41.3
Malaysia Malaisie	936.7	1 004.9	978.2	1 105.0	1 154.6	1 181.8	1 245.1	1 239.4	1 276.3	1 282.7
Maldives Maldives	71.2	78.7	80.7	82.2	90.0	104.1	104.6	105.6	107.7	118.2
Mali Mali	71.8	70.5	68.8	68.5	64.4	63.0	133.0	112.0	99.6	98.1
Malta Malte	0.9	6.4	5.2	5.3	1.4	1.8	1.8	2.4	2.7	2.9
Marshall Islands Iles Marshall	0.3[1]	0.3[1]	0.3	0.3[1]	0.5[1]	0.4[1]	0.4[1]	0.4	0.4[1]	0.4[1]
Martinique Martinique	3.3	3.6	6.4	4.6	6.0	5.9	5.4	3.3	5.1	5.6

35
Fish catches
All fishing areas, catch and culture production: thousand metric tons [cont.]
Quantités pêchées
Toutes les zones de pêche, captures et production de l'aquaculture : milliers de tonnes [suite]

Country or area Pays ou zone	1989	1990	1991	1992	1993	1994	1995	1996	1997	1998
Mauritania[1] Mauritanie[1]	92.6	80.5	88.7	93.9	100.4	85.0	90.0	95.0	84.0	85.0
Mauritius Maurice	17.2	14.7	18.9	19.2	21.2	19.0	17.0	12.5	13.9	12.1
Mayotte Mayotte	1.7	1.4	1.3	1.1	0.4	0.5	0.6	1.2	1.5	1.6
Mexico Mexique	1 465.1	1 383.5	1 398.1	1 184.1	1 131.0	1 223.2	1 355.0	1 495.4	1 528.5	1 222.4
Micronesia (Fed. States of) Micron (Etats fédérés de)	2.1[1]	2.1[1]	12.3	16.5[1]	17.2[1]	23.4[1]	9.0[1]	9.7[1]	10.4[1]	15.4
Mongolia Mongolie	0.3	0.1	0.1	0.1[1]	0.2	0.2	0.2	0.2	0.2	0.2
Montserrat Montserrat	0.0	0.2	0.1	0.1	0.2	0.2	0.2[1]	0.1[1]	0.0	0.1
Morocco Maroc	520.5	565.9	593.4	548.3	623.0	752.1	846.4	640.0	785.9	710.4
Mozambique Mozambique	31.1	36.4	29.4	31.6	30.2	27.6	26.9	34.9	42.1	36.8
Myanmar Myanmar	733.8	743.8	769.2	800.0[1]	836.9	824.5	832.5	873.0	917.7	958.2
Namibia Namibie	21.2	262.5	206.2	294.6	330.2	301.0	292.4	267.0	279.5	352.2
Nauru Nauru	0.2[1]	0.2[1]	0.2	0.4	0.5	0.5	0.5[1]	0.4[1]	0.4[1]	0.5[1]
Nepal Népal	12.5	14.5	15.6	16.5	17.0	17.0	21.1	21.9	23.2	24.9
Netherlands Pays-Bas	530.2	507.2	458.8	487.1	532.9	529.4	522.0	510.7	550.0	656.7
Netherlands Antilles[1] Antilles néerlandaises[1]	1.2	1.2	1.1	1.2	1.2	1.1	1.0	1.0	1.1	1.0
New Caledonia Nouvelle-Calédonie	3.4	5.4	4.9	4.0	3.4	4.0	3.6	4.0	3.6	4.5
New Zealand Nouvelle-Zélande	333.6	372.5	417.2	503.5	471.3	492.9	614.6	495.9	672.9	729.5
Nicaragua Nicaragua	4.7	3.2	5.8	6.8	8.8	12.3	13.5	18.0	19.9	24.7
Niger Niger	4.7	3.4	3.1	2.5	2.2	2.5	3.7	4.2	6.3	7.0
Nigeria Nigéria	299.8[1]	316.3	267.2	318.4	255.5	282.1	366.1	355.9	383.4	354.8
Niue Nioué	0.1	0.1	0.1	0.1	0.1	0.1	0.1	0.1	0.1	0.1
Northern Mariana Islands Iles Marianas du Nord	0.2	0.2	0.1	0.1	0.1	0.2	0.2	0.2	0.3	0.2
Norway Norvège	1 908.9	1 753.0	2 172.8	2 568.4	2 588.6	2 584.6	2 801.7	2 960.1	3 223.3	3 259.3
Occupied Palestinian Terr.[2] Terr. palestinien occupé[2]	...	...	...	...	...	...	1.2	2.5	3.8	3.6
Oman Oman	117.7	123.1	117.8	112.3	116.5	118.6	139.9	119.8	117.5	100.1

35
Fish catches
All fishing areas, catch and culture production: thousand metric tons [cont.]
Quantités pêchées
Toutes les zones de pêche, captures et production de l'aquaculture : milliers de tonnes [suite]

Country or area Pays ou zone	1989	1990	1991	1992	1993	1994	1995	1996	1997	1998
Pakistan Pakistan	446.3	479.1	515.6	553.2	621.8	552.0	541.9	555.5	611.8	621.0
Palau Palaos	1.4[1]	1.4[1]	1.4	1.4[1]	1.4[1]	1.4[1]	1.4[1]	1.4[1]	1.4[1]	1.4[1]
Panama Panama	185.2	137.7	152.7	160.4	165.7	168.9	180.5	145.4	173.8	219.0
Papua New Guinea[1] Papouasie-Nvl-Guinée[1]	26.0	26.2	25.0	25.4	25.8	29.0	39.3	37.3	43.8	67.7
Paraguay Paraguay	11.1	12.6	13.1	18.1	16.1[1]	17.0[1]	18.0[1]	22.0	28.0	26.1[1]
Peru Pérou	6 853.9	6 874.1	6 905.0	7 507.7	9 009.6	12 005.1	8 943.1	9 522.0	7 877.3	4 346.2
Philippines Philippines	2 098.8	2 208.8	2 311.8	2 271.9	2 226.4	2 232.9	2 222.0	2 133.0	2 136.2	2 139.9
Poland Pologne	564.8	473.0	457.4	505.9	423.0	460.2	451.3	369.0	390.5	276.8
Portugal Portugal	333.2	323.1	325.9	299.6	293.8	269.7	265.6	265.8	229.1	231.5
Puerto Rico Porto Rico	2.1	2.2	2.6	2.2	1.9	2.2	2.6	2.4	2.7	2.2
Qatar Qatar	4.4	5.7	8.1	7.8	7.0	5.1	4.3	4.7	5.0	5.3
Republic of Moldova République de Moldova	8.6	9.5	5.2	3.3	2.9	1.9	2.1	1.7	1.8	1.6
Réunion Réunion	1.7	1.7	2.3	2.5	2.8	4.5	4.8	5.2	6.0	6.5
Romania Roumanie	224.8	127.7	125.0	95.4	34.9	42.7	69.1	32.2	19.3	18.6
Russian Federation Fédération de Russie	8 385.0	7 807.9	7 006.4	5 613.7	4 461.4	3 780.5	4 373.8	4 729.6	4 715.0	4 518.0
Rwanda Rwanda	1.5	2.5	3.6	3.7	3.6[1]	3.5[1]	3.4[1]	3.1	4.5	6.8
Saint Helena Sainte-Hélène	1.0	0.8	0.6	0.7	0.7	0.6	0.8	0.7	0.9	1.0
Saint Kitts and Nevis Saint-Kitts-et-Nevis	0.7[1]	0.6[1]	0.5[1]	0.3[1]	0.3[1]	0.2	0.1	0.3	0.2	0.3
Saint Lucia Sainte-Lucie	0.8	0.9	1.0	1.0	1.2	1.2	1.2	1.3	1.3	1.3
Saint Pierre and Miquelon Saint-Pierre-et-Miquelon	18.5	23.2	23.8	16.4	0.3	0.3	0.3	0.7	3.6	6.1
St. Vincent-Grenadines St. Vincent-Grenadines	5.8	9.0	8.4	2.1	1.9	1.5	1.3	1.3[1]	1.4	1.3
Samoa Samoa	1.9	0.6	0.6	1.3	0.7	1.3	1.9	4.0	7.1	7.2
Sao Tome and Principe Sao Tomé-et-Principe	3.1	3.6	2.2	2.1	2.3	3.4	3.6	4.0	3.3	3.3
Saudi Arabia Arabie saoudite	48.4	42.6	42.4	48.3	50.5	56.8	48.4	51.5	54.1	59.3
Senegal Sénégal	287.1	314.5	324.4	370.3	382.2	350.5	358.7	436.3	507.0	425.8

35
Fish catches
All fishing areas, catch and culture production: thousand metric tons [cont.]
Quantités pêchées
Toutes les zones de pêche, captures et production de l'aquaculture : milliers de tonnes [suite]

Country or area Pays ou zone	1989	1990	1991	1992	1993	1994	1995	1996	1997	1998
Seychelles Seychelles	4.4	5.5	8.2	6.7	5.3	4.6	4.2	4.9	5.9	18.4
Sierra Leone Sierra Leone	52.2[l]	50.1[l]	60.2	60.7	61.0	62.0	62.4	61.6[l]	68.8	62.7
Singapore Singapour	12.6	13.3	13.1	11.6	11.7	13.7	13.7	13.5	13.3	11.9
Slovakia Slovaquie	...	...	...	...	2.8	3.5	3.6	2.4	2.6	2.0
Slovenia Slovénie	...	...	...	4.8	3.0	3.1	2.9	3.2	3.3	3.1
Solomon Islands Iles Salomon	51.3	43.8	63.4	47.8[l]	45.1[l]	48.6[l]	65.8[l]	56.9[l]	62.1[l]	58.6[l]
Somalia[l] Somalie[l]	19.8	21.3	23.5	21.3	19.3	17.3	16.3	16.0	15.7	16.0
South Africa Afrique du Sud	878.5	538.0	501.1	696.6	565.6	527.9	579.1	443.3	518.6	563.9
Spain Espagne	1 520.8	1 302.5[l]	1 282.3[l]	1 238.9[l]	1 196.5[l]	1 262.5[l]	1 365.2[l]	1 358.3	1 382.3	1 420.1[l]
Sri Lanka Sri Lanka	206.0	166.4	199.6	208.2	223.4	227.1	235.8	232.1	247.0	273.0
Sudan Soudan	30.3	31.7	33.3	35.2	40.2	44.2	45.0	46.0	48.0	50.5
Suriname Suriname	6.2	6.5[l]	7.4	10.9	9.5	14.5	13.0[l]	13.2[l]	13.0[l]	13.0[l]
Swaziland[l] Swaziland[l]	0.1	0.1	0.1	0.1	0.1	0.1	0.1	0.2	0.1	0.2
Sweden Suède	257.7	260.1	245.0	314.7	347.8	394.2	412.1	379.1	364.1	416.4
Switzerland Suisse	4.5	4.2	4.8	3.9	3.0	2.7	2.7	3.0	3.0	2.9
Syrian Arab Republic Rép. arabe syrienne	5.1	5.8	7.7	9.7	9.2	10.0	11.6	12.1	11.7	14.3
Tajikistan Tadjikistan	3.5	3.9	3.9	2.0	2.7	1.1	0.4	0.1	0.1	0.1
Thailand Thaïlande	2 704.1	2 790.0	2 972.1	3 246.4	3 385.0	3 522.1	3 572.8	3 562.1	3 430.0	3 469.9
TFYR Macedonia L'ex-R.y. Macédoine	...	...	...	1.2	1.2	1.2	1.5	1.0	1.6	1.4[l]
Togo Togo	16.5	15.8	12.5	10.9	17.1	13.2	12.2	15.1	14.3	16.7
Tokelau Tokélaou	0.2[l]	0.2[l]	0.2	0.2	0.2[l]	0.2[l]	0.2[l]	0.2[l]	0.2[l]	0.2[l]
Tonga Tonga	2.7	1.6	1.9	2.2	2.4	2.5	2.6	2.9	2.7	3.9
Trinidad and Tobago Trinité-et-Tobago	8.2[l]	8.5	12.4	15.6	11.0	14.3	13.3[l]	14.4	15.0	14.5[l]
Tunisia Tunisie	95.5	88.9	86.4	87.3	84.0	87.0	84.4	85.2	89.0	91.2
Turkey Turquie	454.8	384.9	364.8	456.6	561.2	605.8	655.6	561.0	504.6	543.9

35
Fish catches
All fishing areas, catch and culture production: thousand metric tons [cont.]
Quantités pêchées
Toutes les zones de pêche, captures et production de l'aquaculture : milliers de tonnes [suite]

Country or area Pays ou zone	1989	1990	1991	1992	1993	1994	1995	1996	1997	1998
Turkmenistan Turkménistan	53.0	44.9	43.0	33.7	18.2	17.3	11.4	9.3	8.8	7.6
Turks and Caicos Islands Iles Turques et Caïques	1.2	0.9	1.1	1.2	1.5	1.4[1]	1.4[1]	1.3[1]	1.3[1]	1.3
Tuvalu Tuvalu	0.5	0.5	0.5	0.5	1.5	0.6	0.4	0.4	0.4[1]	0.4[1]
Uganda Ouganda	212.2	245.3	214.6	265.0	219.9	213.3	209.0	195.3	218.4	221.0
Ukraine Ukraine	1 134.0	1 048.4	865.2	525.8	371.5	310.9	413.9	449.8	403.0	490.6
United Arab Emirates Emirats arabes unis	91.2	95.1	92.3	95.0	99.6	108.6	105.9	107.0	114.4	114.7
United Kingdom Royaume-Uni	906.4	810.5	851.4	869.9	929.0	963.7	1 003.8	975.0	1 016.0	1 057.3
United Rep.Tanzania Rép.-Unie de Tanzanie	377.1	414.0	326.8	331.6	331.5	288.5	360.0	356.8	357.2	348.3
United States Etats-Unis	5 777.7	5 870.9	5 490.3	5 604.2	5 940.6	5 926.1	5 638.0	5 394.8	5 421.8	5 154.1
United States Virgin Is. Iles Vierges américaines	0.8	0.7	0.9	0.9[1]	0.9[1]	0.9[1]	0.9[1]	0.9[1]	0.9[1]	0.9[1]
Uruguay Uruguay	121.7	90.8	143.7	125.8	118.8	120.7	126.5	123.4	137.0	140.6
Uzbekistan Ouzbékistan	25.5	26.8	27.4	28.1	23.4	17.7	13.8	6.5	10.6	9.8
Vanuatu Vanuatu	3.2[1]	5.5[1]	3.1	2.4	2.8[1]	3.3[1]	10.2[1]	13.9[1]	30.7[1]	40.9[1]
Venezuela Venezuela	329.5	339.3	344.4	333.6	397.3	441.3	505.5	491.9	471.8	516.8
Viet Nam Viet Nam	921.0[1]	912.5[1]	965.5[1]	955.0	1 061.6[1]	1 177.6[1]	1 451.8[1]	1 461.0[1]	1 572.7	1 652.5
Wallis and Futuna Islands Iles Wallis et Futuna	0.1	0.1	0.1	0.1	0.2	0.2	0.2	0.2	0.2	0.2
Yemen Yémen	71.9	77.4	82.5	79.5	85.9	82.6	103.0	101.2	112.8	110.0[1]
Yugoslavia Yougoslavie	...	...	...	7.6	6.5	6.8	6.5	6.9	7.4	7.9
Yugoslavia, SFR† Yougoslavie, Rfs†	72.0	65.8	35.8[1]	...	...	...	...	...	...	...
Zambia Zambie	66.8	64.8	65.4	67.3	65.3	70.1	70.5	66.3	70.6	72.3
Zimbabwe Zimbabwe	24.1	25.8	22.2	21.7	21.4	20.3	16.6	16.5	18.2	16.6

Source:
Food and Agriculture Organization of the United
Nations (FAO), Rome, FAOSTAT Fisheries database.

Source:
Organisation des Nations Unies pour l'alimentation et
l'agriculture (FAO), Rome, les données des pêches de
FAOSTAT.

35

Fish catches

All fishing areas, catch and culture production: thousand metric tons [*cont.*]

Quantités pêchées

Toutes les zones de pêche, captures et production de l'aquaculture : milliers de tonnes [*suite*]

† For information on recent changes in country or area nomenclature pertaining to former Czechoslovakia, Germany, Hong Kong Special Administrative Region (SAR) of China, Macao Special Administrative Region (SAR) of China, SFR of Yugoslavia and the former USSR, see Annex I - Country or area nomenclature, regional and other groupings.

†† For statistical purposes, the data for China do not include those for Hong Kong Special Administrative Region (Hong Kong SAR) and Macao Special Administrative Region (Macao SAR).

1 FAO estimate.
2 Data refer to the Gaza Strip.

† Pour les modifications récentes de nomenclature de pays ou de zone concernant l'Allemagne, Hong Kong, région administrative spéciale (RAS) de Chine, Macao, région administrative spéciale (RAS) de Chine, l'ex-Tchécoslovaquie, l'ex-URSS et l'ex-Rfs de Yougoslavie, voir annexe I - Nomenclature des pays ou des zones, groupements régionaux et autres groupements.

†† Les données statistiques relatives à la Chine ne comprennent pas celles qui concernent la région administrative spéciale de Hong Kong (la RAS de Hong Kong) et la région administrative spéciale de Macao (la RAS de Macao).

1 Estimation de la FAO.
2 Les données se rapportent à la Zone de Gaza.

36
Fertilizers
Engrais
Nitrogenous, phosphate and potash: thousand metric tons
Azotés, phosphatés et potassiques : milliers de tonnes

Region, country or area Région, pays ou zone	Production Production					Consumption Consommation				
	1994/95	1995/96	1996/97	1997/98	1998/99	1994/95	1995/96	1996/97	1997/98	1998/99
World Monde										
Nitrogenous fertilizers										
Engrais azotés	80 553.1	86 049.8	90 636.9	87 443.5	88 450.6	72 599.3	77 905.2	82 492.6	81 162.6	82 421.4
Phosphate fertilizers										
Engrais phosphatés	32 163.9	33 463.2	33 729.0	32 772.9	33 040.3	29 566.6	30 653.0	31 089.3	33 393.7	32 911.5
Potash fertilizers										
Engrais potassiques	23 038.3	22 703.6	22 962.8	26 140.4	25 761.8	20 123.9	20 676.2	20 588.7	22 457.9	22 022.2
Africa Afrique										
Nitrogenous fertilizers										
Engrais azotés	2 428.3	2 521.1	2 610.8	2 433.2	2 566.4	2 007.3	2 100.8	2 313.5	2 210.8	2 342.1
Phosphate fertilizers										
Engrais phosphatés	2 212.0	2 306.6	2 458.5	2 259.2	2 380.5	946.6	926.7	971.7	951.2	944.1
Potash fertilizers										
Engrais potassiques	...	...	...	...	...	444.6	418.4	468.1	473.3	508.5
Algeria Algérie										
Nitrogenous fertilizers *										
Engrais azotés *	82.9	12.0	8.3	28.4	58.7	58.2	18.4	14.0	36.0	40.0
Phosphate fertilizers										
Engrais phosphatés	* 29.6	* 12.3	...	...	5.4	* 36.7	* 15.2	* 11.0	* 35.0	* 25.8
Potash fertilizers *										
Engrais potassiques *	...	...	...	...	...	24.4	12.8	13.0	26.0	30.0
Angola Angola										
Nitrogenous fertilizers *										
Engrais azotés *	...	...	...	...	...	2.0	2.0	2.0	2.0	3.0
Phosphate fertilizers *										
Engrais phosphatés *	...	...	...	...	...	5.0	3.0	2.0	...	...
Potash fertilizers *										
Engrais potassiques *	...	...	...	...	...	3.0	3.0	2.0	...	2.2
Benin Bénin										
Nitrogenous fertilizers										
Engrais azotés	...	...	...	...	...	7.7	* 14.0	14.5	18.8	* 15.3
Phosphate fertilizers										
Engrais phosphatés	...	...	...	...	...	6.0	* 15.0	10.3	12.6	* 14.6
Potash fertilizers										
Engrais potassiques	...	...	...	...	...	3.3	* 7.0	* 5.9	* 7.6	* 7.8
Botswana Botswana										
Nitrogenous fertilizers										
Engrais azotés	...	...	...	...	...	* 0.5	2.1	3.2	* 3.5	3.7
Phosphate fertilizers										
Engrais phosphatés	...	...	...	...	...	* 0.4	0.1	0.1	* 0.2	* 0.3
Potash fertilizers										
Engrais potassiques	...	...	...	...	...	* 0.1	0.0	0.0	* 0.1	* 0.2
Burkina Faso Burkina Faso										
Nitrogenous fertilizers										
Engrais azotés	...	...	...	...	...	11.5	11.4	11.5	24.4	* 16.4
Phosphate fertilizers										
Engrais phosphatés	* 0.3	* 0.3	* 0.3	* 0.3	* 0.3	5.9	6.7	6.3	9.9	* 17.8
Potash fertilizers										
Engrais potassiques	...	...	...	...	...	5.2	6.3	6.3	8.3	* 16.0
Burundi Burundi										
Nitrogenous fertilizers *										
Engrais azotés *	...	...	...	...	...	1.0	1.0	1.0	1.0	1.3
Phosphate fertilizers										
Engrais phosphatés	...	...	...	...	...	* 2.0	* 2.0	* 1.8	...	0.8
Potash fertilizers *										
Engrais potassiques *	...	...	...	...	...	0.1	...	...	...	...

36
Fertilizers
Nitrogenous, phosphate and potash: thousand metric tons [*cont.*]
Engrais
Azotés, phosphatés et potassiques : milliers de tonnes [*suite*]

Region, country or area	Production Production					Consumption Consommation				
Région, pays ou zone	1994/95	1995/96	1996/97	1997/98	1998/99	1994/95	1995/96	1996/97	1997/98	1998/99
Cameroon Cameroun										
Nitrogenous fertilizers										
Engrais azotés	...	...	...	...	...	* 15.0	* 15.0	* 18.0	* 18.9	16.5
Phosphate fertilizers										
Engrais phosphatés	...	...	...	...	...	* 5.0	* 5.0	* 5.0	* 7.0	7.6
Potash fertilizers										
Engrais potassiques	...	...	...	...	...	* 10.0	* 10.0	* 11.0	* 13.3	15.4
Central African Rep. Rép. centrafricaine										
Nitrogenous fertilizers *										
Engrais azotés *	...	...	...	...	...	0.1	0.1	0.1	0.1	0.2
Phosphate fertilizers *										
Engrais phosphatés *	...	...	...	...	...	0.1	0.1	0.1	0.1	0.2
Potash fertilizers *										
Engrais potassiques *	...	...	...	...	...	0.1	0.1	0.1	0.1	0.2
Chad Tchad										
Nitrogenous fertilizers										
Engrais azotés	...	...	...	...	...	* 2.0	3.6	* 7.5	* 3.5	* 10.7
Phosphate fertilizers										
Engrais phosphatés	...	...	...	...	...	* 2.0	* 2.0	* 2.4	* 2.4	1.7
Potash fertilizers										
Engrais potassiques	...	...	...	...	...	* 3.0	* 3.0	* 2.0	* 2.0	4.4
Comoros Comores										
Nitrogenous fertilizers *										
Engrais azotés *	...	...	...	...	...	0.1	0.1	0.1	0.1	0.1
Phosphate fertilizers *										
Engrais phosphatés *	...	...	...	...	...	0.1	0.1	0.1	0.1	0.1
Potash fertilizers *										
Engrais potassiques *	...	...	...	...	...	0.1	0.1	0.1	0.1	0.1
Congo Congo										
Nitrogenous fertilizers *										
Engrais azotés *	...	...	...	...	...	0.9	1.0	2.0	2.0	2.0
Phosphate fertilizers *										
Engrais phosphatés *	...	...	...	...	...	...	...	1.0	1.0	1.0
Potash fertilizers *										
Engrais potassiques *	...	...	...	...	...	1.0	1.0	1.0	1.0	2.0
Côte d'Ivoire Côte d'Ivoire										
Nitrogenous fertilizers *										
Engrais azotés *	...	...	...	...	...	34.0	36.0	41.5	60.0	60.9
Phosphate fertilizers *										
Engrais phosphatés *	...	...	...	...	...	16.0	16.0	15.0	25.0	27.5
Potash fertilizers *										
Engrais potassiques *	...	...	...	...	...	15.0	14.0	14.0	25.0	25.0
Dem. Rep. of the Congo Rép. dém. du Congo										
Nitrogenous fertilizers										
Engrais azotés	...	...	...	...	...	3.5	* 3.0	* 2.0	...	...
Phosphate fertilizers										
Engrais phosphatés	...	...	...	...	...	3.5	* 3.0	* 2.0	...	...
Potash fertilizers										
Engrais potassiques	...	...	...	...	...	3.5	* 3.0	* 2.0	...	...
Egypt Egypte										
Nitrogenous fertilizers										
Engrais azotés	900.3	931.0	1 019.4	* 943.8	942.1	729.0	956.8	* 1 002.6	* 841.6	974.0
Phosphate fertilizers										
Engrais phosphatés	157.1	162.9	* 201.6	197.2	148.1	* 104.3	* 135.0	* 121.9	* 134.5	116.1
Potash fertilizers										
Engrais potassiques	...	...	...	...	...	* 18.2	* 21.4	* 33.0	28.2	22.5

36
Fertilizers
Nitrogenous, phosphate and potash: thousand metric tons [*cont.*]
Engrais
Azotés, phosphatés et potassiques : milliers de tonnes [*suite*]

Region, country or area	Production Production					Consumption Consommation				
Région, pays ou zone	1994/95	1995/96	1996/97	1997/98	1998/99	1994/95	1995/96	1996/97	1997/98	1998/99
Eritrea Erythrée										
Nitrogenous fertilizers										
Engrais azotés	...	...	...	...	...	* 1.1	1.4	3.8	* 5.0	* 5.0
Phosphate fertilizers *										
Engrais phosphatés *	...	...	...	...	...	0.2	0.2	1.2	1.0	1.5
Ethiopia Ethiopie										
Nitrogenous fertilizers										
Engrais azotés	...	...	...	...	...	45.3	42.6	81.0	54.2	* 75.3
Phosphate fertilizers										
Engrais phosphatés	...	...	...	...	...	* 75.9	* 88.8	* 96.5	77.6	89.0
Potash fertilizers *										
Engrais potassiques *	...	...	...	...	...	0.4	...	...	...	...
Gabon Gabon										
Nitrogenous fertilizers *										
Engrais azotés *	...	...	...	...	...	0.1	0.1	0.1	0.1	0.2
Phosphate fertilizers *										
Engrais phosphatés *	...	...	...	...	...	0.1	0.1	0.1	0.1	0.2
Potash fertilizers										
Engrais potassiques	...	...	...	...	...	* 0.2	* 0.2	0.0	0.0	* 0.0
Gambia Gambie										
Nitrogenous fertilizers										
Engrais azotés	...	...	...	...	...	* 0.2	0.3	0.2	* 0.3	* 0.5
Phosphate fertilizers *										
Engrais phosphatés *	...	...	...	...	...	0.4	0.4	0.4	0.5	0.6
Potash fertilizers *										
Engrais potassiques *	...	...	...	...	...	0.2	0.2	0.2	0.3	0.4
Ghana Ghana										
Nitrogenous fertilizers										
Engrais azotés	...	...	...	...	...	2.7[1]	3.2[1]	* 7.2	8.7	7.2
Phosphate fertilizers										
Engrais phosphatés	...	...	...	...	...	2.0[1]	2.5[1]	* 3.5	6.0	3.7
Potash fertilizers										
Engrais potassiques	...	...	...	...	...	* 3.0	4.0[1]	* 6.7	6.7	4.3
Guinea Guinée										
Nitrogenous fertilizers										
Engrais azotés	...	...	...	...	...	2.3[1]	2.8	2.4	0.7	1.1
Phosphate fertilizers										
Engrais phosphatés	...	...	...	...	...	1.0[1]	1.4	1.0	0.6	1.4
Potash fertilizers										
Engrais potassiques	...	...	...	...	...	0.7[1]	0.9	0.8	0.5	0.7
Guinea-Bissau Guinée-Bissau										
Nitrogenous fertilizers *										
Engrais azotés *	...	...	...	...	...	0.1	0.1	0.1	0.1	0.2
Phosphate fertilizers										
Engrais phosphatés	...	...	...	...	...	0.1[1]	0.1[1]	* 0.1	* 0.1	* 0.2
Potash fertilizers										
Engrais potassiques	...	...	...	...	...	* 0.1	0.1[1]	* 0.1	* 0.1	* 0.2
Kenya Kenya										
Nitrogenous fertilizers										
Engrais azotés	...	...	...	...	...	50.8	32.3	* 63.0	* 58.0	* 61.5
Phosphate fertilizers *										
Engrais phosphatés *	...	...	...	...	...	71.0	40.0	75.8	67.8	57.1
Potash fertilizers *										
Engrais potassiques *	...	...	...	...	...	8.0	5.4	22.0	14.0	9.0
Lesotho Lesotho										
Nitrogenous fertilizers										
Engrais azotés	...	...	...	...	...	1.3[1]	1.9	2.1	1.6	* 1.8

36

Fertilizers
Nitrogenous, phosphate and potash: thousand metric tons [*cont.*]
Engrais
Azotés, phosphatés et potassiques : milliers de tonnes [*suite*]

Region, country or area	Production Production					Consumption Consommation				
Région, pays ou zone	1994/95	1995/96	1996/97	1997/98	1998/99	1994/95	1995/96	1996/97	1997/98	1998/99
Phosphate fertilizers										
Engrais phosphatés	...	...	...	...	...	2.0[1]	2.0[1]	* 2.0	* 2.0	* 2.1
Potash fertilizers										
Engrais potassiques	...	...	...	...	...	2.0[1]	2.0[1]	* 2.0	* 2.0	* 2.1
Libyan Arab Jamah. Jamah. arabe libyenne										
Nitrogenous fertilizers *										
Engrais azotés *	346.6	409.5	398.8	383.4	408.2	24.4	30.0	16.6	17.5	20.0
Phosphate fertilizers *										
Engrais phosphatés *	...	...	...	...	...	44.5	55.0	40.4	40.9	26.8
Potash fertilizers *										
Engrais potassiques *	...	...	...	...	...	5.6	4.0	5.4	3.3	3.5
Madagascar Madagascar										
Nitrogenous fertilizers										
Engrais azotés	...	...	...	...	...	6.0	7.7	8.9	3.6	3.6
Phosphate fertilizers										
Engrais phosphatés	...	...	...	...	...	2.7	2.7	4.6	3.0	2.7
Potash fertilizers										
Engrais potassiques	...	...	...	...	...	2.6	2.1	3.1	2.9	2.4
Malawi Malawi										
Nitrogenous fertilizers *										
Engrais azotés *	...	...	...	...	...	9.1	28.2	37.9	41.2	34.8
Phosphate fertilizers										
Engrais phosphatés	...	...	...	...	...	7.2	10.3	* 14.3	* 12.6	* 11.9
Potash fertilizers *										
Engrais potassiques *	...	...	...	...	...	5.0	5.0	6.0	3.0	3.5
Mali Mali										
Nitrogenous fertilizers *										
Engrais azotés *	...	...	...	...	...	12.0	12.0	12.0	25.6	18.0
Phosphate fertilizers *										
Engrais phosphatés *	...	...	...	...	...	6.0	8.0	8.7	12.0	19.0
Potash fertilizers *										
Engrais potassiques *	...	...	...	...	...	7.0	7.0	6.6	10.2	15.6
Mauritania Mauritanie										
Nitrogenous fertilizers										
Engrais azotés	...	...	...	...	...	* 4.0	* 4.0	* 5.0	1.5	1.8
Phosphate fertilizers *										
Engrais phosphatés *	...	...	...	...	...	...	...	...	0.2	0.3
Mauritius Maurice										
Nitrogenous fertilizers										
Engrais azotés	15.4	14.6	16.2	14.3	* 15.9	11.8	12.3	13.1	11.8	* 12.4
Phosphate fertilizers *										
Engrais phosphatés *	...	...	...	...	...	3.2	5.1	8.0	7.0	6.0
Potash fertilizers										
Engrais potassiques	...	...	...	...	...	* 14.2	* 14.3	* 16.7	14.7	* 14.7
Morocco Maroc										
Nitrogenous fertilizers										
Engrais azotés	* 265.5	* 269.2	* 257.7	* 261.9	* 271.0	* 134.8	* 144.9	* 124.5	174.1	* 180.0
Phosphate fertilizers										
Engrais phosphatés	* 894.0	* 935.8	* 990.0	923.9	* 958.6	* 104.8	* 79.5	* 109.0	* 98.0	* 110.4
Potash fertilizers *										
Engrais potassiques *	...	...	...	...	...	55.5	57.8	56.5	55.2	60.0
Mozambique Mozambique										
Nitrogenous fertilizers *										
Engrais azotés *	...	...	...	...	...	5.0	5.0	7.0	1.5	2.5
Phosphate fertilizers *										
Engrais phosphatés *	...	...	...	...	...	0.3	0.3	0.3	2.6	0.5

36
Fertilizers
Nitrogenous, phosphate and potash: thousand metric tons [*cont.*]
Engrais
Azotés, phosphatés et potassiques : milliers de tonnes [*suite*]

Region, country or area	Production Production					Consumption Consommation				
Région, pays ou zone	1994/95	1995/96	1996/97	1997/98	1998/99	1994/95	1995/96	1996/97	1997/98	1998/99
Potash fertilizers *										
Engrais potassiques *	...	...	...	...	...	1.0	2.5	0.8	2.4	2.0
Niger Niger										
Nitrogenous fertilizers										
Engrais azotés	...	...	...	...	...	2.6	5.2	* 5.5	* 0.5	* 0.5
Phosphate fertilizers										
Engrais phosphatés	...	...	...	...	...	1.8	2.6	* 2.0	...	* 0.2
Potash fertilizers										
Engrais potassiques	...	...	...	...	...	1.7	2.2	* 1.5	* 0.2	* 0.2
Nigeria Nigéria										
Nitrogenous fertilizers										
Engrais azotés	* 151.4	* 138.0	* 114.3	* 41.2	* 71.0	* 186.0	* 100.0	105.0	* 77.3	* 100.0
Phosphate fertilizers *										
Engrais phosphatés *	6.3	0.9	9.5	5.0	10.5	50.0	50.0	32.5	21.4	45.3
Potash fertilizers *										
Engrais potassiques *	...	...	...	...	...	60.0	33.0	36.0	39.0	43.0
Réunion Réunion										
Nitrogenous fertilizers *										
Engrais azotés *	...	...	...	...	...	3.0	3.5	3.5	2.0	2.1
Phosphate fertilizers *										
Engrais phosphatés *	...	...	...	...	...	2.0	2.0	1.6	2.0	1.5
Potash fertilizers *										
Engrais potassiques *	...	...	...	...	...	2.4	0.9	4.0	3.0	2.0
Rwanda Rwanda										
Nitrogenous fertilizers *										
Engrais azotés *	...	...	...	...	...	...	...	0.1	0.1	0.1
Phosphate fertilizers *										
Engrais phosphatés *	...	...	...	...	...	...	...	0.1	0.2	0.1
Potash fertilizers *										
Engrais potassiques *	...	...	...	...	...	...	...	0.1	0.1	0.1
Senegal Sénégal										
Nitrogenous fertilizers *										
Engrais azotés *	25.9	28.7	24.8	24.4	29.8	12.9	5.2	8.0	7.1	8.8
Phosphate fertilizers *										
Engrais phosphatés *	35.2	39.5	35.4	55.0	61.7	10.0	8.0	9.6	10.8	11.0
Potash fertilizers *										
Engrais potassiques *	...	...	...	...	...	3.0	3.0	4.0	6.0	7.0
Sierra Leone Sierra Leone										
Nitrogenous fertilizers *										
Engrais azotés *	...	...	...	...	...	1.0	1.0	1.0	1.0	1.0
Phosphate fertilizers *										
Engrais phosphatés *	...	...	...	...	...	1.0	1.0	1.0	1.0	1.0
Potash fertilizers *										
Engrais potassiques *	...	...	...	...	...	1.0	1.0	1.0	1.0	1.0
Somalia Somalie										
Nitrogenous fertilizers *										
Engrais azotés *	...	...	...	...	...	...	...	0.5	0.5	0.5
South Africa Afrique du Sud										
Nitrogenous fertilizers										
Engrais azotés	* 365.0	* 420.0	452.0	453.0	* 462.7	375.1	* 386.0	405.0	424.8	* 430.0
Phosphate fertilizers										
Engrais phosphatés	* 328.2	* 373.2	* 397.7	371.5	* 378.5	* 247.0	* 240.0	255.9	232.6	* 212.6
Potash fertilizers										
Engrais potassiques	...	...	...	...	...	* 130.0	* 141.0	143.0	131.0	* 140.0
Sudan Soudan										
Nitrogenous fertilizers *										
Engrais azotés *	...	...	...	...	...	39.4	31.7	76.8	69.0	26.0

36

Fertilizers
Nitrogenous, phosphate and potash: thousand metric tons [*cont.*]
Engrais
Azotés, phosphatés et potassiques : milliers de tonnes [*suite*]

Region, country or area Région, pays ou zone	Production Production					Consumption Consommation				
	1994/95	1995/96	1996/97	1997/98	1998/99	1994/95	1995/96	1996/97	1997/98	1998/99
Phosphate fertilizers * Engrais phosphatés *	...	...	...	...	...	19.0	20.0	18.6	8.4	11.5
Swaziland Swaziland										
Nitrogenous fertilizers Engrais azotés	...	...	...	...	...	* 1.6	1.6	1.5	* 1.6	* 1.7
Phosphate fertilizers Engrais phosphatés	...	...	...	...	...	* 2.3	2.5	1.7	* 1.8	* 1.9
Potash fertilizers * Engrais potassiques *	...	...	...	...	...	1.0	1.0	1.0	1.8	1.9
Togo Togo										
Nitrogenous fertilizers Engrais azotés	...	...	...	...	...	5.2	5.9	8.1	* 6.0	* 6.6
Phosphate fertilizers Engrais phosphatés	...	...	...	...	...	3.6	7.8	4.7	* 5.4	* 5.3
Potash fertilizers Engrais potassiques	...	...	...	...	...	2.4	2.8	4.8	* 5.4	* 5.3
Tunisia Tunisie										
Nitrogenous fertilizers Engrais azotés	175.3	214.2	229.2	* 190.4	* 230.7	* 47.0	* 40.0	* 52.0	54.6	63.3
Phosphate fertilizers Engrais phosphatés	* 719.3	* 741.7	* 788.0	* 673.3	* 781.9	* 39.0	* 35.0	* 41.0	* 40.0	44.5
Potash fertilizers * Engrais potassiques *	...	...	...	...	...	3.0	2.0	4.0	5.0	13.0
Uganda Ouganda										
Nitrogenous fertilizers * Engrais azotés *	...	...	...	...	...	1.0	0.8	0.2	0.2	1.3
Phosphate fertilizers * Engrais phosphatés *	...	...	...	...	...	0.4	0.2	0.2	0.2	0.3
Potash fertilizers * Engrais potassiques *	...	...	...	...	...	0.5	0.3	0.2	0.2	0.3
United Rep.Tanzania Rép.-Unie de Tanzanie										
Nitrogenous fertilizers Engrais azotés	...	...	...	...	...	* 25.4	* 15.0	20.2	21.9	19.3
Phosphate fertilizers Engrais phosphatés	...	...	...	...	...	* 6.9	* 7.0	7.0	9.5	6.0
Potash fertilizers Engrais potassiques	...	...	...	...	...	* 3.6	* 5.0	4.0	6.7	2.6
Zambia Zambie										
Nitrogenous fertilizers * Engrais azotés *	6.0	4.0	4.1	4.0	2.3	38.0	34.0	27.5	32.9	16.0
Phosphate fertilizers * Engrais phosphatés *	...	...	...	...	...	13.0	13.0	13.9	14.1	14.3
Potash fertilizers * Engrais potassiques *	...	...	...	...	...	8.0	8.0	10.0	10.0	10.0
Zimbabwe Zimbabwe										
Nitrogenous fertilizers Engrais azotés	* 94.0	79.9	* 86.0	* 88.4	* 74.1	92.7	77.6	93.6	* 94.0	* 94.8
Phosphate fertilizers * Engrais phosphatés *	42.0	40.0	36.0	33.0	35.5	42.3	38.0	37.0	44.0	41.6
Potash fertilizers * Engrais potassiques *	...	...	...	...	...	35.5	31.0	37.0	37.0	38.0
America, North Amérique du Nord										
Nitrogenous fertilizers Engrais azotés	19 370.6	19 939.0	20 966.5	19 124.8	19 321.9	13 687.8	14 312.2	14 636.5	14 677.4	14 814.1
Phosphate fertilizers Engrais phosphatés	11 783.0	11 304.0	11 717.0	9 846.5	9 868.1	5 177.0	5 125.4	5 391.7	5 413.8	5 091.5

36

Fertilizers
Nitrogenous, phosphate and potash: thousand metric tons [*cont.*]
Engrais
Azotés, phosphatés et potassiques : milliers de tonnes [*suite*]

Region, country or area	Production Production					Consumption Consommation				
Région, pays ou zone	1994/95	1995/96	1996/97	1997/98	1998/99	1994/95	1995/96	1996/97	1997/98	1998/99
Potash fertilizers										
Engrais potassiques	**9 877.3**	**8 809.2**	**8 985.4**	**10 970.4**	**9 970.7**	**5 216.0**	**5 399.7**	**5 622.1**	**5 632.0**	**5 315.3**
Bahamas Bahamas										
Nitrogenous fertilizers *										
Engrais azotés *	...	...	...	...	...	0.1	0.1	0.2	0.1	0.1
Phosphate fertilizers *										
Engrais phosphatés *	...	...	...	...	...	...	...	0.1	0.1	0.1
Potash fertilizers										
Engrais potassiques	...	...	...	...	...	* 0.1	* 0.1	* 0.1	0.1	* 0.1
Barbados Barbade										
Nitrogenous fertilizers *										
Engrais azotés *	...	...	...	...	...	1.5	2.0	2.0	2.0	1.8
Phosphate fertilizers *										
Engrais phosphatés *	...	...	...	...	...	0.2	0.2	0.2	0.2	0.2
Potash fertilizers *										
Engrais potassiques *	...	...	...	...	...	1.0	1.0	1.0	1.0	1.0
Belize Belize										
Nitrogenous fertilizers *										
Engrais azotés *	...	...	...	...	...	1.2	1.3	1.0	1.3	1.0
Phosphate fertilizers										
Engrais phosphatés	...	...	...	...	...	* 1.4	* 2.7	* 1.3	2.5	* 2.7
Potash fertilizers *										
Engrais potassiques *	...	...	...	...	...	2.0	1.0	1.0	1.0	1.0
Bermuda Bermudes										
Nitrogenous fertilizers *										
Engrais azotés *	...	...	...	...	...	0.1	0.1	0.1	0.1	0.1
Canada Canada										
Nitrogenous fertilizers										
Engrais azotés	3 801.3	4 018.9	* 3 864.2	* 3 670.2	* 3 734.0	1 456.1	1 576.2	1 670.6	* 1 652.7	* 1 626.0
Phosphate fertilizers *										
Engrais phosphatés *	355.0	381.0	383.0	372.6	357.8	628.5	658.4	703.5	717.3	667.0
Potash fertilizers										
Engrais potassiques	9 050.3	* 7 966.2	* 8 151.4	* 9 535.1	* 8 605.9	* 310.0	* 333.2	* 322.2	* 356.2	* 357.0
Costa Rica Costa Rica										
Nitrogenous fertilizers *										
Engrais azotés *	40.6	44.0	56.0	41.0	32.0	70.0	70.0	89.0	100.0	104.0
Phosphate fertilizers *										
Engrais phosphatés *	...	...	...	...	...	27.0	20.0	28.2	31.0	33.0
Potash fertilizers *										
Engrais potassiques *	...	...	...	...	...	32.0	32.0	32.0	60.0	60.9
Cuba Cuba										
Nitrogenous fertilizers *										
Engrais azotés *	15.0	55.0	60.0	62.0	50.0	72.0	100.0	100.0	124.0	107.0
Phosphate fertilizers *										
Engrais phosphatés *	...	...	...	...	...	13.0	40.0	32.0	35.0	15.2
Potash fertilizers *										
Engrais potassiques *	...	...	...	...	...	39.0	104.0	103.0	71.0	47.5
Dominica Dominique										
Nitrogenous fertilizers										
Engrais azotés	...	...	...	...	...	1.8	1.1	0.9	* 1.0	* 1.0
Phosphate fertilizers										
Engrais phosphatés	...	...	...	...	...	1.3	1.1	0.9	* 1.0	* 1.0
Potash fertilizers										
Engrais potassiques	...	...	...	...	...	1.3	1.1	0.9	* 1.0	* 1.0
Dominican Republic Rép. dominicaine										
Nitrogenous fertilizers										
Engrais azotés	...	...	...	...	...	* 45.7	* 50.0	* 50.0	55.4	* 51.8

36
Fertilizers
Nitrogenous, phosphate and potash: thousand metric tons [*cont.*]
Engrais
Azotés, phosphatés et potassiques : milliers de tonnes [*suite*]

Region, country or area Région, pays ou zone	Production Production					Consumption Consommation				
	1994/95	1995/96	1996/97	1997/98	1998/99	1994/95	1995/96	1996/97	1997/98	1998/99
Phosphate fertilizers * Engrais phosphatés *	...	...	...	...	...	22.0	21.0	17.9	16.8	15.5
Potash fertilizers * Engrais potassiques *	...	...	...	...	...	23.0	23.0	24.0	31.6	28.2
El Salvador El Salvador Nitrogenous fertilizers Engrais azotés	...	...	...	...	...	46.4	41.9	* 60.0	* 72.1	* 56.8
Phosphate fertilizers * Engrais phosphatés *	...	...	...	...	...	15.0	21.0	22.0	18.0	16.0
Potash fertilizers * Engrais potassiques *	...	...	...	...	...	5.0	7.0	9.8	9.2	9.8
Guadeloupe Guadeloupe Nitrogenous fertilizers * Engrais azotés *	...	...	...	...	...	1.0	1.0	1.5	1.5	4.8
Phosphate fertilizers * Engrais phosphatés *	...	...	...	...	...	1.0	1.0	1.0	1.0	...
Potash fertilizers * Engrais potassiques *	...	...	...	...	...	5.0	1.0	1.0	1.0	1.9
Guatemala Guatemala Nitrogenous fertilizers Engrais azotés	...	...	...	...	...	* 112.0	* 115.0	* 110.0	118.6	* 114.8
Phosphate fertilizers * Engrais phosphatés *	...	...	...	...	...	37.0	39.0	37.0	88.6	80.6
Potash fertilizers * Engrais potassiques *	...	...	...	...	...	20.0	32.0	36.0	42.0	27.0
Haiti Haïti Nitrogenous fertilizers Engrais azotés	...	...	...	...	...	* 4.0	* 5.4	* 4.0	8.5	5.4
Phosphate fertilizers Engrais phosphatés	...	...	...	...	...	* 0.5	* 1.0	* 2.0	2.0	1.2
Potash fertilizers Engrais potassiques	...	...	...	...	...	* 0.6	* 1.0	* 1.0	2.0	1.5
Honduras Honduras Nitrogenous fertilizers * Engrais azotés *	...	...	...	...	...	12.0	72.3	49.8	82.9	93.9
Phosphate fertilizers Engrais phosphatés	...	...	...	...	...	* 13.0	8.3[1]	* 19.2	* 24.2	* 23.0
Potash fertilizers Engrais potassiques	...	...	...	...	...	4.5[1]	* 8.3	* 13.6	* 36.6	* 23.0
Jamaica Jamaïque Nitrogenous fertilizers Engrais azotés	...	...	...	...	...	* 8.2	8.1	* 8.1	9.0	8.9
Phosphate fertilizers Engrais phosphatés	...	...	...	...	...	* 5.4	* 5.0	* 5.3	6.0	5.2
Potash fertilizers Engrais potassiques	...	...	...	...	...	* 9.6	13.4	* 10.4	8.4	9.3
Martinique Martinique Nitrogenous fertilizers * Engrais azotés *	...	...	...	...	...	3.0	3.0	5.3	3.9	4.3
Phosphate fertilizers * Engrais phosphatés *	...	...	...	...	...	1.0	1.0	0.6	1.0	3.7
Potash fertilizers * Engrais potassiques *	...	...	...	...	...	9.0	5.8	9.8	4.7	8.9
Mexico Mexique Nitrogenous fertilizers Engrais azotés	* 1 268.1	* 1 314.0	* 1 487.4	* 1 287.9	1 137.4	* 1 182.4	* 1 049.0	1 207.4	* 1 193.6	* 1 284.0

36
Fertilizers
Nitrogenous, phosphate and potash: thousand metric tons [cont.]
Engrais
Azotés, phosphatés et potassiques : milliers de tonnes [suite]

Region, country or area Région, pays ou zone	Production Production					Consumption Consommation				
	1994/95	1995/96	1996/97	1997/98	1998/99	1994/95	1995/96	1996/97	1997/98	1998/99
Phosphate fertilizers * Engrais phosphatés *	373.0	423.0	434.0	468.8	479.4	375.5	182.0	309.0	259.0	260.0
Potash fertilizers * Engrais potassiques *	...	...	...	...	...	90.0	55.0	120.0	178.1	161.7
Nicaragua Nicaragua										
Nitrogenous fertilizers Engrais azotés	...	...	...	...	...	* 10.8	* 25.0	25.9	37.1	* 34.4
Phosphate fertilizers * Engrais phosphatés *	...	...	...	...	...	7.4	3.0	10.6	8.9	10.5
Potash fertilizers Engrais potassiques	...	...	...	...	...	* 3.6	* 3.0	4.2	6.8	* 7.7
Panama Panama										
Nitrogenous fertilizers Engrais azotés	...	...	...	...	...	18.0	* 16.7	* 27.4	21.4	14.0
Phosphate fertilizers Engrais phosphatés	...	...	...	...	...	* 9.0	* 9.0	* 12.5	9.5	8.8
Potash fertilizers Engrais potassiques	...	...	...	...	...	* 3.0	* 2.0	* 4.4	5.5	9.4
Saint Kitts and Nevis Saint-Kitts-et-Nevis										
Nitrogenous fertilizers Engrais azotés	...	...	...	...	...	0.7	0.6	0.6	* 0.8	* 0.8
Phosphate fertilizers Engrais phosphatés	...	...	...	...	...	0.4	0.4	0.4	* 0.5	* 0.5
Potash fertilizers Engrais potassiques	...	...	...	...	...	0.5	0.3	0.3	* 0.4	* 0.4
Saint Lucia Sainte-Lucie										
Nitrogenous fertilizers Engrais azotés	...	...	...	...	...	5.0[1]	7.0[1]	9.0	9.6	* 9.9
Phosphate fertilizers * Engrais phosphatés *	...	...	...	...	...	2.0	2.0	2.0	2.0	2.5
Potash fertilizers * Engrais potassiques *	...	...	...	...	...	2.0	2.0	2.0	2.0	2.5
St. Vincent-Grenadines St. Vincent-Grenadines										
Nitrogenous fertilizers * Engrais azotés *	...	...	...	...	...	1.0	1.0	1.0	1.0	1.3
Phosphate fertilizers * Engrais phosphatés *	...	...	...	...	...	1.0	1.0	1.0	1.0	1.3
Potash fertilizers * Engrais potassiques *	...	...	...	...	...	1.0	1.0	1.0	1.0	1.3
Trinidad and Tobago Trinité-et-Tobago										
Nitrogenous fertilizers * Engrais azotés *	228.6	263.1	272.9	277.5	240.7	3.0	3.0	6.0	6.0	5.6
Phosphate fertilizers * Engrais phosphatés *	...	...	...	...	...	1.0	1.0	1.0	1.0	1.0
Potash fertilizers Engrais potassiques	...	...	...	...	...	* 1.4	* 3.0	3.4	* 3.6	* 4.0
United States Etats-Unis										
Nitrogenous fertilizers Engrais azotés	14 017.0	14 244.0	15 226.0	13 786.1	* 14 127.8	10 630.8	11 161.4	11 205.6	11 173.6	* 11 281.5
Phosphate fertilizers Engrais phosphatés	11 055.0	10 500.0	10 900.0	9 005.2	* 9 030.9	4 014.1	4 107.1	4 183.7	4 187.0	* 3 942.1
Potash fertilizers Engrais potassiques	827.0	843.0	834.0	1 435.3	* 1 364.8	4 652.4	4 769.5	4 921.0	4 808.8	* 4 550.2
United States Virgin Is. Iles Vierges américaines										
Nitrogenous fertilizers * Engrais azotés *	...	...	...	...	...	1.0	1.0	1.0	1.0	1.0

36
Fertilizers
Nitrogenous, phosphate and potash: thousand metric tons [cont.]
Engrais
Azotés, phosphatés et potassiques : milliers de tonnes [suite]

Region, country or area Région, pays ou zone	Production Production					Consumption Consommation				
	1994/95	1995/96	1996/97	1997/98	1998/99	1994/95	1995/96	1996/97	1997/98	1998/99
Phosphate fertilizers * Engrais phosphatés *	...	...	...	...	...	0.3	0.3	0.3	0.3	0.3
America, South Amérique du Sud										
Nitrogenous fertilizers Engrais azotés	1 396.7	1 529.5	1 565.8	1 592.1	1 389.1	2 294.1	2 314.3	2 663.0	2 715.2	2 869.9
Phosphate fertilizers Engrais phosphatés	1 554.4	1 358.0	1 400.3	1 436.9	1 476.1	2 468.9	1 867.7	2 495.3	2 904.3	2 907.5
Potash fertilizers Engrais potassiques	281.4	276.1	419.5	516.4	641.5	2 191.5	2 118.4	2 428.4	2 656.5	2 673.8
Argentina Argentine										
Nitrogenous fertilizers Engrais azotés	43.5	58.3	* 80.7	* 88.3	70.0	* 281.8	* 318.8	* 510.3	* 476.4	* 460.0
Phosphate fertilizers * Engrais phosphatés *	7.0	...	...	...	...	153.8	182.5	306.9	302.6	320.0
Potash fertilizers * Engrais potassiques *	...	...	...	...	...	26.4	23.4	38.0	34.0	29.5
Bolivia Bolivie										
Nitrogenous fertilizers Engrais azotés	...	...	...	...	...	4.3	2.8	4.0	4.9	3.7
Phosphate fertilizers Engrais phosphatés	...	...	...	...	...	5.1	3.6	4.3	7.1	2.9
Potash fertilizers Engrais potassiques	...	...	...	...	...	1.4	0.3	0.8	0.6	0.8
Brazil Brésil										
Nitrogenous fertilizers Engrais azotés	768.3	795.6	779.0	808.4	728.0	1 220.8[1]	1 140.1[1]	1 250.9[1]	* 1 302.0	* 1 455.0
Phosphate fertilizers Engrais phosphatés	1 428.6	1 264.7	1 305.1	* 1 354.0	1 369.0	* 1 931.0	* 1 275.2	* 1 704.8	* 2 015.1	* 2 020.3
Potash fertilizers Engrais potassiques	229.4	224.1	240.7	281.4	326.5	* 1 866.0	* 1 790.6	* 2 064.3	* 2 241.7	* 2 261.2
Chile Chili										
Nitrogenous fertilizers * Engrais azotés *	97.0	111.0	111.0	115.0	117.0	195.0	215.0	225.0	203.8	214.4
Phosphate fertilizers * Engrais phosphatés *	5.0	5.0	4.0	...	...	136.0	140.0	145.0	195.0	175.0
Potash fertilizers * Engrais potassiques *	52.0	52.0	178.8	235.0	315.0	50.0	50.0	53.0	55.0	57.0
Colombia Colombie										
Nitrogenous fertilizers * Engrais azotés *	95.0	92.7	109.0	117.3	68.8	252.8	241.4	236.0	265.2	297.0
Phosphate fertilizers * Engrais phosphatés *	10.5	9.3	10.0	27.5	28.0	95.6	108.0	113.0	148.8	158.0
Potash fertilizers * Engrais potassiques *	...	...	...	...	...	149.4	136.8	136.0	168.4	172.0
Ecuador Equateur										
Nitrogenous fertilizers * Engrais azotés *	...	...	...	...	...	48.0	56.0	65.0	90.6	96.0
Phosphate fertilizers Engrais phosphatés	...	...	...	...	...	* 25.0	* 21.0	23.0	25.0	32.0
Potash fertilizers * Engrais potassiques *	...	...	...	...	...	20.0	24.0	30.0	45.0	44.5
French Guiana Guyane française										
Nitrogenous fertilizers * Engrais azotés *	...	...	...	...	...	1.0	1.0	1.0	1.0	1.2
Phosphate fertilizers * Engrais phosphatés *	...	...	...	...	...	0.3	0.3	0.3	0.3	0.4

36

Fertilizers
Nitrogenous, phosphate and potash: thousand metric tons [cont.]
Engrais
Azotés, phosphatés et potassiques : milliers de tonnes [suite]

Region, country or area	Production					Consumption				
Région, pays ou zone	1994/95	1995/96	1996/97	1997/98	1998/99	1994/95	1995/96	1996/97	1997/98	1998/99
Potash fertilizers *										
Engrais potassiques *	...	...	...	...	...	0.1	0.1	0.1	0.1	0.2
Guyana Guyana										
Nitrogenous fertilizers										
Engrais azotés	...	...	...	...	...	* 8.1	* 12.0	* 10.9	14.0	* 14.5
Phosphate fertilizers *										
Engrais phosphatés *	...	...	...	...	...	1.0	1.0	1.4	0.7	0.7
Potash fertilizers *										
Engrais potassiques *	...	...	...	...	...	2.0	2.0	1.0	1.0	1.0
Paraguay Paraguay										
Nitrogenous fertilizers *										
Engrais azotés *	...	...	...	...	...	9.9	10.0	14.0	15.0	15.5
Phosphate fertilizers *										
Engrais phosphatés *	...	...	...	...	...	5.0	5.0	5.0	22.0	23.0
Potash fertilizers *										
Engrais potassiques *	...	...	...	...	...	8.0	8.0	14.0	22.0	23.0
Peru Pérou										
Nitrogenous fertilizers										
Engrais azotés	* 14.0	* 15.9	* 12.6	* 11.5	* 3.0	* 109.4	* 124.2	120.9	* 120.0	* 115.0
Phosphate fertilizers										
Engrais phosphatés	1.7	* 1.0	* 2.4	* 2.5	* 3.0	* 24.0	* 24.0	* 25.0	* 45.9	* 50.0
Potash fertilizers *										
Engrais potassiques *	...	...	...	...	...	10.0	15.0	17.0	25.2	25.7
Suriname Suriname										
Nitrogenous fertilizers *										
Engrais azotés *	...	...	...	...	...	4.0	4.0	7.0	6.8	5.0
Phosphate fertilizers *										
Engrais phosphatés *	...	...	...	...	...	0.1	0.1	0.1	0.1	0.2
Potash fertilizers *										
Engrais potassiques *	...	...	...	...	...	0.2	0.2	0.2	0.2	0.3
Uruguay Uruguay										
Nitrogenous fertilizers *										
Engrais azotés *	...	...	...	...	...	25.0	21.0	47.0	47.3	52.6
Phosphate fertilizers *										
Engrais phosphatés *	10.0	5.0	9.3	9.3	9.3	35.0	40.0	102.5	80.4	74.6
Potash fertilizers *										
Engrais potassiques *	...	...	...	...	...	3.0	5.0	4.0	1.9	6.1
Venezuela Venezuela										
Nitrogenous fertilizers										
Engrais azotés	* 379.0	* 456.0	* 473.5	* 451.6	402.2	* 134.0	* 168.0	* 171.0	* 168.3	* 140.0
Phosphate fertilizers										
Engrais phosphatés	* 91.6	* 73.0	* 69.5	* 43.6	66.8	* 57.0	* 67.0	* 64.0	* 61.3	* 50.4
Potash fertilizers *										
Engrais potassiques *	...	...	...	...	...	55.0	63.0	70.0	61.4	52.4
Asia Asie										
Nitrogenous fertilizers										
Engrais azotés	36 640.5	40 136.9	42 825.6	43 436.3	45 075.6	39 934.3	44 661.7	47 587.2	46 535.8	47 336.4
Phosphate fertilizers										
Engrais phosphatés	10 880.9	11 995.2	11 865.3	12 563.9	12 930.5	14 827.9	16 480.6	15 761.5	17 827.8	17 954.1
Potash fertilizers										
Engrais potassiques	2 373.5	2 648.2	2 801.6	2 654.2	3 095.0	6 124.3	6 561.8	5 929.5	7 441.5	7 631.4
Afghanistan Afghanistan										
Nitrogenous fertilizers										
Engrais azotés	* 14.0	* 10.0	...	5.0	5.0	...	...	* 5.0	5.0	5.0
Armenia Arménie										
Nitrogenous fertilizers *										
Engrais azotés *	...	...	...	...	...	7.0	7.0	8.0	0.0	0.0

36

Fertilizers
Nitrogenous, phosphate and potash: thousand metric tons [*cont.*]
Engrais
Azotés, phosphatés et potassiques : milliers de tonnes [*suite*]

Region, country or area	Production Production					Consumption Consommation				
Région, pays ou zone	1994/95	1995/96	1996/97	1997/98	1998/99	1994/95	1995/96	1996/97	1997/98	1998/99
Azerbaijan Azerbaïdjan										
Nitrogenous fertilizers *										
Engrais azotés *	...	...	...	...	...	34.0	34.0	16.6	20.0	20.0
Phosphate fertilizers *										
Engrais phosphatés *	...	...	...	...	...	...	...	...	2.7	2.7
Potash fertilizers										
Engrais potassiques	* 30.0	* 8.0	* 3.0	* 5.0	* 0.0	* 5.0	* 5.0	...	1.0	1.0
Bahrain Bahreïn										
Nitrogenous fertilizers										
Engrais azotés	...	...	...	...	214.3	* 0.2	* 0.2	* 0.2	* 0.2	* 0.2
Phosphate fertilizers *										
Engrais phosphatés *	...	...	...	...	...	0.2	0.2	0.2	0.2	0.2
Potash fertilizers *										
Engrais potassiques *	...	...	...	...	...	0.2	0.2	0.2	0.2	0.2
Bangladesh Bangladesh										
Nitrogenous fertilizers										
Engrais azotés	911.6	981.6	* 965.7	868.2	1 010.1	803.5	942.1	* 996.1	875.3	* 883.0
Phosphate fertilizers										
Engrais phosphatés	* 50.2	* 60.0	* 49.4	38.9	* 41.1	* 153.4	* 158.0	* 117.5	116.8	* 161.4
Potash fertilizers										
Engrais potassiques	...	...	...	...	...	92.4	* 94.0	74.9	115.8	* 126.6
Bhutan Bhoutan										
Nitrogenous fertilizers *										
Engrais azotés *	...	...	...	...	...	0.1	0.1	0.1	0.1	0.1
Cambodia Cambodge										
Nitrogenous fertilizers *										
Engrais azotés *	...	...	...	...	...	6.0	6.0	4.3	5.0	8.0
Phosphate fertilizers *										
Engrais phosphatés *	...	...	...	...	...	4.6	3.0	2.7	3.0	4.7
Potash fertilizers *										
Engrais potassiques *	...	...	...	...	...	...	0.8	0.8	...	...
China †† Chine ††										
Nitrogenous fertilizers *										
Engrais azotés *	16 696.0	18 635.1	21 042.8	20 278.6	21 082.1	19 216.0	23 382.5	25 275.8	23 010.0	22 445.6
Phosphate fertilizers *										
Engrais phosphatés *	4 946.0	6 091.3	5 822.0	6 419.0	6 441.0	7 329.0	8 911.7	8 118.0	9 277.0	9 185.0
Potash fertilizers *										
Engrais potassiques *	116.5	223.0	218.0	170.0	340.0	2 444.0	2 887.0	2 336.9	3 420.0	3 447.0
Cyprus Chypre										
Nitrogenous fertilizers										
Engrais azotés	...	...	...	...	...	14.4	13.9	13.8	10.8	10.8
Phosphate fertilizers										
Engrais phosphatés	...	...	...	...	...	9.9	10.2	9.5	7.8	7.7
Potash fertilizers										
Engrais potassiques	...	...	...	...	...	* 2.0	* 2.4	* 2.2	1.8	2.0
Georgia Géorgie										
Nitrogenous fertilizers *										
Engrais azotés *	34.0	42.5	53.7	73.6	55.3	26.0	26.0	27.2	31.5	30.0
Phosphate fertilizers *										
Engrais phosphatés *	...	...	...	...	...	5.0	5.0	5.0	5.0	5.0
India Inde										
Nitrogenous fertilizers										
Engrais azotés	7 944.3	8 768.8	8 593.1	10 083.0	* 10 477.3	9 507.1	9 822.8	10 301.8	10 901.8	* 11 353.8
Phosphate fertilizers										
Engrais phosphatés	2 586.7	2 625.6	2 614.8	3 079.5	* 3 186.2	2 931.7	2 897.5	2 976.8	* 3 913.6	* 4 112.2

36
Fertilizers
Nitrogenous, phosphate and potash: thousand metric tons [cont.]
Engrais
Azotés, phosphatés et potassiques : milliers de tonnes [suite]

Region, country or area	Production Production					Consumption Consommation				
Région, pays ou zone	1994/95	1995/96	1996/97	1997/98	1998/99	1994/95	1995/96	1996/97	1997/98	1998/99
Potash fertilizers										
Engrais potassiques	...	...	...	...	...	* 1 124.8	1 155.8	1 043.1	1 372.6	* 1 331.5
Indonesia Indonésie										
Nitrogenous fertilizers *										
Engrais azotés *	2 542.2	2 822.0	2 986.4	3 059.4	2 895.4	1 649.0	1 844.0	2 084.0	1 706.6	2 129.9
Phosphate fertilizers *										
Engrais phosphatés *	541.0	325.2	355.0	282.9	235.2	518.0	385.2	331.9	280.0	360.0
Potash fertilizers *										
Engrais potassiques *	...	...	...	...	...	300.0	300.0	300.0	242.0	283.0
Iran (Islamic Rep. of) Iran (Rép. islamique d')										
Nitrogenous fertilizers										
Engrais azotés	460.5	* 500.1	* 688.8	* 727.8	863.6	603.7	624.8	685.1	777.3	* 878.0
Phosphate fertilizers										
Engrais phosphatés	* 110.0	* 82.5	* 136.1	* 93.3	113.6	* 368.0	* 379.0	* 374.1	338.0	* 314.5
Potash fertilizers *										
Engrais potassiques *	...	...	...	...	...	27.0	5.2	20.0	37.1	60.0
Iraq Iraq										
Nitrogenous fertilizers *										
Engrais azotés *	218.0	218.0	235.0	235.0	235.0	238.0	225.0	240.5	242.7	251.3
Phosphate fertilizers *										
Engrais phosphatés *	90.0	90.0	90.0	90.0	90.0	141.0	108.4	103.9	111.6	132.1
Potash fertilizers										
Engrais potassiques	...	...	...	...	...	* 5.0	* 0.5	* 10.0	* 2.5	0.0
Israel Israël										
Nitrogenous fertilizers *										
Engrais azotés *	65.0	75.0	76.0	88.0	87.0	50.0	50.0	65.0	61.3	61.1
Phosphate fertilizers *										
Engrais phosphatés *	190.0	216.0	222.0	235.0	270.0	22.0	22.0	19.0	23.0	23.0
Potash fertilizers *										
Engrais potassiques *	1 260.0	1 326.0	1 500.0	1 488.0	1 668.0	32.0	32.0	35.0	36.0	37.0
Japan Japon										
Nitrogenous fertilizers										
Engrais azotés	891.0	869.0	884.0	830.0	782.0	581.0	528.0	512.0	494.0	476.0
Phosphate fertilizers										
Engrais phosphatés	336.0	307.0	278.0	263.0	249.0	703.0	631.0	611.0	594.0	562.0
Potash fertilizers										
Engrais potassiques	* 36.8	* 23.2	* 21.4	...	...	* 479.5	* 482.2	* 441.2	422.0	382.0
Jordan Jordanie										
Nitrogenous fertilizers										
Engrais azotés	* 134.9	* 131.2	120.8	127.9	149.6	* 4.0	* 6.0	5.1	10.9	14.8
Phosphate fertilizers										
Engrais phosphatés	* 344.8	* 335.5	308.7	279.4	397.5	* 8.0	* 8.0	11.2	9.1	4.6
Potash fertilizers										
Engrais potassiques	* 930.2	* 1 068.0	* 1 059.2	* 986.7	1 079.0	* 2.0	* 2.0	* 4.0	* 4.0	* 4.0
Kazakhstan Kazakhstan										
Nitrogenous fertilizers *										
Engrais azotés *	61.0	74.0	78.7	40.0	0.0	65.0	64.0	67.1	26.4	15.3
Phosphate fertilizers *										
Engrais phosphatés *	70.0	129.0	125.0	74.0	36.0	50.0	25.0	57.9	55.0	25.0
Potash fertilizers *										
Engrais potassiques *	...	...	...	...	...	6.0	6.0	6.0	6.0	6.0
Korea, Dem. P. R. Corée, R. p. dém. de										
Nitrogenous fertilizers *										
Engrais azotés *	314.0	75.0	72.0	72.0	72.0	300.0	84.0	72.4	149.3	129.1
Phosphate fertilizers *										
Engrais phosphatés *	20.0	20.0	20.0	20.0	47.0	20.0	20.0	20.0	21.0	25.2

36
Fertilizers
Nitrogenous, phosphate and potash: thousand metric tons [*cont.*]
Engrais
Azotés, phosphatés et potassiques : milliers de tonnes [*suite*]

Region, country or area Région, pays ou zone	Production Production					Consumption Consommation				
	1994/95	1995/96	1996/97	1997/98	1998/99	1994/95	1995/96	1996/97	1997/98	1998/99
Potash fertilizers * Engrais potassiques *	...	...	...	...	...	3.0	0.2	0.6	0.8	2.9
Korea, Republic of Corée, République de										
Nitrogenous fertilizers Engrais azotés	* 669.0	615.7	660.0	* 666.7	* 570.0	475.0	471.6	455.9	* 506.0	* 451.0
Phosphate fertilizers * Engrais phosphatés *	447.0	421.0	409.0	420.0	420.0	222.0	227.0	209.0	222.0	188.0
Potash fertilizers * Engrais potassiques *	...	...	...	...	...	263.0	274.0	244.0	262.0	235.0
Kuwait Koweït										
Nitrogenous fertilizers * Engrais azotés *	324.1	390.8	356.3	348.5	361.3	1.0	1.0	2.0	1.2	2.0
Potash fertilizers * Engrais potassiques *	...	...	...	...	...	...	...	...	...	0.1
Kyrgyzstan Kirghizistan										
Nitrogenous fertilizers * Engrais azotés *	...	...	...	...	...	22.0	22.0	25.0	25.0	50.6
Phosphate fertilizers * Engrais phosphatés *	...	...	...	...	...	1.0	1.0	1.0	1.0	1.0
Potash fertilizers * Engrais potassiques *	...	...	...	...	...	5.0	5.0	5.0	5.0	5.0
Lao People's Dem. Rep. Rép. dém. pop. lao										
Nitrogenous fertilizers Engrais azotés	...	...	...	...	...	0.7	2.1	* 2.0	* 5.0	* 7.0
Phosphate fertilizers Engrais phosphatés	...	...	...	...	...	* 1.0	3.9	* 1.3	* 2.6	* 3.0
Potash fertilizers Engrais potassiques	...	...	...	...	...	* 0.1	0.1	* 0.5	* 0.2	* 0.2
Lebanon Liban										
Nitrogenous fertilizers Engrais azotés	...	...	...	...	...	* 10.0	25.5	* 22.0	21.9	* 23.5
Phosphate fertilizers * Engrais phosphatés *	89.0	81.0	95.0	115.0	134.0	14.0	15.0	30.0	32.0	32.0
Potash fertilizers Engrais potassiques	...	...	...	...	...	4.0	4.0	* 4.0	* 5.0	* 5.0
Malaysia Malaisie										
Nitrogenous fertilizers Engrais azotés	* 284.3	* 290.0	* 290.0	* 231.7	* 316.6	* 287.0	* 286.0	* 255.0	344.0	* 417.0
Phosphate fertilizers * Engrais phosphatés *	...	...	...	...	...	170.3	201.0	230.0	238.3	233.1
Potash fertilizers * Engrais potassiques *	...	...	...	...	...	700.0	600.0	646.0	670.0	756.0
Mongolia Mongolie										
Nitrogenous fertilizers Engrais azotés	...	...	...	...	...	* 0.5	* 2.0	* 2.0	5.0	5.0
Phosphate fertilizers Engrais phosphatés	...	...	...	...	...	...	...	...	1.0	...
Myanmar Myanmar										
Nitrogenous fertilizers Engrais azotés	67.8	65.7	73.6	54.1	51.6	* 110.6	114.9	130.9	135.5	* 135.0
Phosphate fertilizers Engrais phosphatés	...	...	...	...	...	* 31.9	* 57.2	* 33.0	35.2	34.5
Potash fertilizers Engrais potassiques	...	...	...	...	...	* 2.2	* 7.6	* 10.0	5.5	2.3
Nepal Népal										
Nitrogenous fertilizers Engrais azotés	...	...	...	...	...	64.4	* 70.0	* 75.0	* 77.4	* 87.2

36

Fertilizers
Nitrogenous, phosphate and potash: thousand metric tons [*cont.*]
Engrais
Azotés, phosphatés et potassiques : milliers de tonnes [*suite*]

Region, country or area / Région, pays ou zone	Production					Consumption / Consommation				
	1994/95	1995/96	1996/97	1997/98	1998/99	1994/95	1995/96	1996/97	1997/98	1998/99
Phosphate fertilizers / Engrais phosphatés	...	...	...	...	...	24.9	* 21.3	* 25.0	* 28.5	* 32.3
Potash fertilizers / Engrais potassiques	...	...	...	...	...	1.7	2.4	* 3.0	* 3.0	* 1.8
Oman Oman										
Nitrogenous fertilizers / Engrais azotés	...	...	...	...	...	* 6.0	* 6.0	4.9	3.5	4.0
Phosphate fertilizers / Engrais phosphatés	...	...	...	...	...	* 0.8	* 0.9	* 0.9	1.0	* 1.0
Potash fertilizers / Engrais potassiques	...	...	...	...	...	* 0.8	* 0.9	* 0.9	1.0	* 1.0
Pakistan Pakistan										
Nitrogenous fertilizers / Engrais azotés	1 547.0	1 693.4	1 681.5	1 660.5	1 745.5	1 738.1	1 983.6	1 985.1	2 087.6	2 043.0
Phosphate fertilizers / Engrais phosphatés	* 105.8	* 95.6	* 80.6	67.5	69.5	* 428.9	* 494.4	* 419.4	551.3	402.3
Potash fertilizers / Engrais potassiques	...	...	...	...	...	16.6	29.7	8.4	20.4	16.0
Philippines Philippines										
Nitrogenous fertilizers / Engrais azotés	168.7	215.3	253.2	213.0	184.3	402.6	397.2	427.1	546.5	409.0
Phosphate fertilizers / Engrais phosphatés	* 205.1	* 264.4	* 273.4	217.1	192.7	* 105.6	* 129.7	* 145.8	149.2	121.1
Potash fertilizers / Engrais potassiques	...	...	...	4.5	8.0	92.6	* 71.4	* 108.5	112.4	97.8
Qatar Qatar										
Nitrogenous fertilizers / Engrais azotés	* 394.6	411.1	403.8	* 672.3	* 767.3	* 6.0	* 6.0	1.2	1.2	* 1.0
Saudi Arabia Arabie saoudite										
Nitrogenous fertilizers / Engrais azotés	* 1 050.5	* 1 027.0	* 1 063.7	* 981.1	* 1 079.8	* 196.0	* 153.0	* 171.0	* 181.0	200.0
Phosphate fertilizers * / Engrais phosphatés *	147.9	122.8	129.7	119.8	138.0	155.0	121.0	138.0	131.0	122.0
Potash fertilizers * / Engrais potassiques *	...	...	...	...	...	9.0	10.0	8.0	9.0	0.0
Singapore Singapour										
Nitrogenous fertilizers / Engrais azotés	...	...	...	...	...	3.0	3.4	2.8	1.9	* 2.1
Phosphate fertilizers / Engrais phosphatés	...	...	...	...	...	0.2	0.1	0.2	0.1	* 0.2
Potash fertilizers * / Engrais potassiques *	...	...	...	...	...	1.5	1.0	0.2	0.1	0.1
Sri Lanka Sri Lanka										
Nitrogenous fertilizers / Engrais azotés	...	...	...	...	...	119.3	115.9	117.6	122.9	142.2
Phosphate fertilizers / Engrais phosphatés	7.5	9.0	9.5	8.3	10.4	34.9	28.2	35.0	31.2	29.0
Potash fertilizers / Engrais potassiques	...	...	...	...	...	58.8	55.7	58.8	56.7	61.9
Syrian Arab Republic Rép. arabe syrienne										
Nitrogenous fertilizers / Engrais azotés	* 83.4	* 48.7	* 71.3	* 68.7	* 112.2	217.1	236.3	227.4	236.8	218.4
Phosphate fertilizers / Engrais phosphatés	...	* 28.0	* 92.0	* 84.2	* 96.5	* 127.9	* 99.0	124.0	117.6	103.3
Potash fertilizers / Engrais potassiques	...	...	...	...	...	6.3	6.5	5.8	7.0	7.4

36

Fertilizers
Nitrogenous, phosphate and potash: thousand metric tons [*cont.*]
Engrais
Azotés, phosphatés et potassiques : milliers de tonnes [*suite*]

Region, country or area Région, pays ou zone	Production Production					Consumption Consommation				
	1994/95	1995/96	1996/97	1997/98	1998/99	1994/95	1995/96	1996/97	1997/98	1998/99
Tajikistan Tadjikistan										
Nitrogenous fertilizers *										
Engrais azotés *	10.0	14.0	4.1	4.0	4.0	40.0	40.0	32.1	41.2	28.2
Phosphate fertilizers *										
Engrais phosphatés *	...	...	...	...	...	25.0	25.0	25.0	25.0	25.0
Potash fertilizers *										
Engrais potassiques *	...	...	...	...	...	5.0	5.0	5.0	5.0	5.0
Thailand Thaïlande										
Nitrogenous fertilizers										
Engrais azotés	...	...	...	* 56.0	* 79.4	* 740.0	728.0	* 811.0	* 783.6	* 902.5
Phosphate fertilizers										
Engrais phosphatés	...	...	...	43.0	85.0	* 374.0	* 453.0	* 436.0	* 423.0	* 455.2
Potash fertilizers										
Engrais potassiques	...	...	...	...	...	* 246.0	326.0	* 273.0	* 274.0	* 303.1
Turkey Turquie										
Nitrogenous fertilizers										
Engrais azotés	701.5	938.8	923.5	* 728.2	* 729.1	1 006.6	1 053.7	1 147.7	* 1 167.0	* 1 392.0
Phosphate fertilizers										
Engrais phosphatés	344.7	* 392.1	* 424.9	* 355.8	* 392.0	* 444.3	* 579.6	* 578.0	* 592.4	* 700.2
Potash fertilizers										
Engrais potassiques	...	...	...	...	...	* 56.4	67.1	* 73.5	* 66.3	* 88.5
Turkmenistan Turkménistan										
Nitrogenous fertilizers *										
Engrais azotés *	102.6	105.0	110.0	100.0	57.0	102.0	105.0	110.0	153.0	117.0
Phosphate fertilizers *										
Engrais phosphatés *	1.4	2.0	...	...	...	13.0	16.0	20.0	20.0	20.0
Potash fertilizers *										
Engrais potassiques *	...	...	...	...	...	10.0	10.0	12.0	14.0	14.0
United Arab Emirates Emirats arabes unis										
Nitrogenous fertilizers *										
Engrais azotés *	230.0	293.6	258.4	299.6	258.9	23.0	25.0	24.5	24.2	23.6
Phosphate fertilizers *										
Engrais phosphatés *	...	...	...	...	...	3.4	4.0	3.3	3.7	5.0
Potash fertilizers *										
Engrais potassiques *	...	...	...	...	...	3.0	3.0	3.0	3.0	3.0
Uzbekistan Ouzbékistan										
Nitrogenous fertilizers *										
Engrais azotés *	673.0	775.5	825.3	809.3	800.0	300.0	300.0	220.0	678.0	643.0
Phosphate fertilizers *										
Engrais phosphatés *	129.0	168.2	194.3	122.1	141.4	123.0	124.0	150.0	122.1	141.4
Potash fertilizers *										
Engrais potassiques *	...	...	...	...	...	50.0	50.0	75.0	75.0	75.0
Viet Nam Viet Nam										
Nitrogenous fertilizers *										
Engrais azotés *	47.5	50.0	54.0	54.0	29.9	949.2	843.0	947.0	1 039.0	1 300.0
Phosphate fertilizers *										
Engrais phosphatés *	118.7	129.0	136.0	136.0	144.4	261.6	313.0	398.0	342.0	377.4
Potash fertilizers *										
Engrais potassiques *	...	...	...	...	...	68.4	58.0	110.0	185.0	270.0
Yemen Yémen										
Nitrogenous fertilizers *										
Engrais azotés *	...	...	...	...	...	9.2	10.1	8.1	19.3	19.9
Phosphate fertilizers										
Engrais phosphatés	...	...	...	...	...	* 1.5	* 2.0	...	...	1.8
Potash fertilizers *										
Engrais potassiques *	...	...	...	...	...	1.0	1.0	...	...	...

36
Fertilizers
Nitrogenous, phosphate and potash: thousand metric tons [*cont.*]
Engrais
Azotés, phosphatés et potassiques : milliers de tonnes [*suite*]

Region, country or area	Production					Consumption				
Région, pays ou zone	1994/95	1995/96	1996/97	1997/98	1998/99	1994/95	1995/96	1996/97	1997/98	1998/99
Europe Europe										
Nitrogenous fertilizers										
Engrais azotés	20 403.1	21 565.3	22 319.5	20 517.8	19 677.1	13 949.2	13 670.7	14 306.8	14 026.0	13 994.8
Phosphate fertilizers										
Engrais phosphatés	5 065.3	5 845.2	5 714.5	6 013.0	5 796.6	4 829.7	4 892.2	5 090.5	4 818.9	4 618.7
Potash fertilizers										
Engrais potassiques	10 506.2	10 970.1	10 756.3	11 999.5	12 054.6	5 784.4	5 800.2	5 792.1	5 862.7	5 541.9
Albania Albanie										
Nitrogenous fertilizers										
Engrais azotés	3.7	...	...	...	...	12.7	* 10.0	* 5.5	* 4.2	* 18.0
Phosphate fertilizers *										
Engrais phosphatés *	1.1	1.0	3.0	3.0	2.0	2.1	1.0	1.0	1.0	6.9
Potash fertilizers										
Engrais potassiques	...	...	...	...	...	...	...	...	...	0.1
Austria Autriche										
Nitrogenous fertilizers *										
Engrais azotés *	223.0	222.0	240.0	227.0	245.0	121.0	125.0	133.0	127.0	128.0
Phosphate fertilizers										
Engrais phosphatés	* 58.0	* 44.0	* 72.0	* 64.0	* 66.0	* 56.0	52.0	* 60.0	* 57.0	* 57.0
Potash fertilizers *										
Engrais potassiques *	...	...	...	...	...	73.0	60.0	72.0	69.0	67.0
Belarus Bélarus										
Nitrogenous fertilizers *										
Engrais azotés *	404.8	429.0	449.6	378.9	443.2	200.0	230.0	260.0	282.3	280.0
Phosphate fertilizers *										
Engrais phosphatés *	27.7	46.1	91.5	128.2	122.0	40.0	43.0	95.0	100.0	100.0
Potash fertilizers *										
Engrais potassiques *	2 510.0	2 789.0	2 716.0	3 247.0	3 451.0	300.0	250.0	422.0	475.0	535.0
Belgium-Luxembourg Belgique-Luxembourg										
Nitrogenous fertilizers *										
Engrais azotés *	897.1	907.3	660.0	838.0	840.0	168.0	165.0	172.0	171.0	172.0
Phosphate fertilizers *										
Engrais phosphatés *	84.0	140.0	108.0	132.0	134.1	51.0	51.0	46.0	44.0	42.0
Potash fertilizers *										
Engrais potassiques *	...	...	...	...	...	100.0	91.0	96.0	92.0	90.0
Bosnia and Herzegovina Bosnie-Herzégovine										
Nitrogenous fertilizers *										
Engrais azotés *	...	...	...	...	...	...	5.0	3.0	3.0	19.0
Phosphate fertilizers										
Engrais phosphatés	...	...	...	...	...	...	5.0	* 3.0	* 3.0	* 5.9
Potash fertilizers *										
Engrais potassiques *	...	...	...	...	...	...	5.0	3.0	3.0	6.0
Bulgaria Bulgarie										
Nitrogenous fertilizers										
Engrais azotés	675.9	833.0	835.2	* 694.9	* 362.0	* 207.7	* 112.0	* 152.0	* 157.8	* 135.0
Phosphate fertilizers										
Engrais phosphatés	50.6	53.1	* 80.0	109.8	* 91.1	14.8	11.1	13.0	11.0	* 9.0
Potash fertilizers										
Engrais potassiques	...	...	...	...	...	2.6	...	* 0.5	* 31.0	* 25.2
Croatia Croatie										
Nitrogenous fertilizers										
Engrais azotés	283.8	290.7	* 305.9	323.4	248.3	* 95.0	93.4	* 101.6	124.2	97.2
Phosphate fertilizers										
Engrais phosphatés	87.2	89.6	86.8	88.7	75.5	48.4	44.2	48.2	55.2	38.3
Potash fertilizers										
Engrais potassiques	...	...	...	...	...	* 48.0	* 47.0	52.5	67.9	67.2

36

Fertilizers
Nitrogenous, phosphate and potash: thousand metric tons [cont.]
Engrais
Azotés, phosphatés et potassiques : milliers de tonnes [suite]

Region, country or area	Production					Consumption				
Région, pays ou zone	1994/95	1995/96	1996/97	1997/98	1998/99	1994/95	1995/96	1996/97	1997/98	1998/99
Czech Republic République tchèque										
Nitrogenous fertilizers										
Engrais azotés	* 246.6	* 259.8	* 305.0	269.1	284.4	* 239.4	* 232.7	* 262.3	237.9	219.3
Phosphate fertilizers										
Engrais phosphatés	* 25.0	* 30.0	* 24.8	24.6	25.7	* 41.7	* 61.3	* 50.4	46.9	51.8
Potash fertilizers										
Engrais potassiques	...	...	...	...	...	* 55.6	* 54.0	* 34.0	* 41.4	29.9
Denmark Danemark										
Nitrogenous fertilizers										
Engrais azotés	* 163.0	* 130.0	* 150.0	* 149.0	* 138.0	315.9	* 291.0	* 288.0	* 283.0	* 262.0
Phosphate fertilizers *										
Engrais phosphatés *	72.0	58.0	46.0	46.0	46.0	51.0	49.0	53.0	50.0	44.0
Potash fertilizers *										
Engrais potassiques *	...	...	...	...	...	99.0	98.0	108.0	103.0	97.0
Estonia Estonie										
Nitrogenous fertilizers										
Engrais azotés	50.9	55.8	* 52.3	41.4	31.0	* 26.3	* 19.0	* 16.6	20.5	24.9
Phosphate fertilizers										
Engrais phosphatés	3.5	* 1.3	...	...	...	5.0	3.8	2.6	5.1	4.4
Potash fertilizers										
Engrais potassiques	...	...	...	...	...	10.3	* 5.0	2.9	* 3.0	3.1
Finland Finlande										
Nitrogenous fertilizers										
Engrais azotés	* 241.0	* 246.5	* 231.0	235.0	252.0	198.5	183.0	174.0	177.0	176.0
Phosphate fertilizers										
Engrais phosphatés	* 130.0	* 122.0	105.0	101.0	97.0	* 82.0	* 72.0	* 57.0	56.0	* 53.0
Potash fertilizers										
Engrais potassiques	...	...	...	...	...	* 90.0	* 85.0	* 82.0	78.0	* 76.0
France France										
Nitrogenous fertilizers										
Engrais azotés	* 1 493.0	* 1 490.0	* 1 616.0	* 1 484.0	* 1 463.6	2 308.5	2 392.0	2 525.1	* 2 513.1	* 2 488.0
Phosphate fertilizers *										
Engrais phosphatés *	323.0	513.0	558.0	527.6	528.3	1 030.0	1 031.4	1 051.9	1 038.8	1 011.0
Potash fertilizers										
Engrais potassiques	* 870.0	* 802.0	* 751.0	* 665.3	* 417.1	1 373.4	1 491.1	1 488.2	* 1 436.9	* 1 332.0
Germany Allemagne										
Nitrogenous fertilizers										
Engrais azotés	* 1 167.0	* 1 174.0	* 1 269.0	1 075.0	* 1 175.0	1 787.4	1 769.2	1 758.0	1 788.4	1 903.0
Phosphate fertilizers										
Engrais phosphatés	* 19.0	* 110.0	* 203.0	194.0	* 184.0	450.7	401.7	415.1	409.6	406.8
Potash fertilizers										
Engrais potassiques	* 3 286.0	* 3 278.0	* 3 334.0	* 3 423.0	* 3 582.0	668.0	649.0	645.8	658.9	628.7
Greece Grèce										
Nitrogenous fertilizers *										
Engrais azotés *	317.0	275.0	316.0	240.0	290.8	346.0	315.0	340.0	307.0	298.0
Phosphate fertilizers *										
Engrais phosphatés *	114.0	146.0	162.0	125.0	127.0	126.0	136.0	145.0	132.0	128.0
Potash fertilizers *										
Engrais potassiques *	...	...	...	...	...	55.0	54.0	75.0	65.0	60.0
Hungary Hongrie										
Nitrogenous fertilizers										
Engrais azotés	238.5	219.7	260.9	251.4	* 218.7	* 243.1	246.8	321.1	287.0	* 320.8
Phosphate fertilizers										
Engrais phosphatés	* 13.2	* 26.0	* 28.5	* 26.5	* 27.0	* 28.6	* 56.0	* 74.7	74.8	* 73.0
Potash fertilizers										
Engrais potassiques	...	...	...	...	...	* 42.0	* 65.4	* 61.7	67.8	* 62.0

36

Fertilizers
Nitrogenous, phosphate and potash: thousand metric tons [cont.]
Engrais
Azotés, phosphatés et potassiques : milliers de tonnes [suite]

Region, country or area	Production Production					Consumption Consommation				
Région, pays ou zone	1994/95	1995/96	1996/97	1997/98	1998/99	1994/95	1995/96	1996/97	1997/98	1998/99
Iceland Islande										
Nitrogenous fertilizers										
Engrais azotés	11.5	8.7	12.3	* 12.0	* 12.5	11.2	10.0	11.6	* 11.8	* 12.4
Phosphate fertilizers *										
Engrais phosphatés *	...	...	...	...	...	5.0	5.1	3.5	4.1	4.2
Potash fertilizers										
Engrais potassiques	...	...	...	...	...	* 3.9	* 3.5	* 3.8	* 3.4	2.0
Ireland Irlande										
Nitrogenous fertilizers *										
Engrais azotés *	320.0	307.4	288.1	326.0	310.5	433.0	425.0	394.0	433.0	433.0
Phosphate fertilizers *										
Engrais phosphatés *	...	...	...	...	...	141.0	141.0	128.0	113.0	124.0
Potash fertilizers										
Engrais potassiques	...	...	...	...	...	* 178.0	* 182.0	* 160.0	149.0	149.0
Italy Italie										
Nitrogenous fertilizers										
Engrais azotés	* 621.0	* 660.0	* 535.0	* 537.0	* 469.7	879.2	918.9	894.0	* 855.0	* 843.0
Phosphate fertilizers *										
Engrais phosphatés *	282.0	216.0	198.0	170.0	172.0	582.0	542.0	575.0	501.0	490.0
Potash fertilizers *										
Engrais potassiques *	...	...	...	...	...	431.0	405.0	414.0	413.0	409.0
Latvia Lettonie										
Nitrogenous fertilizers *										
Engrais azotés *	...	...	...	...	...	40.0	12.0	14.0	19.0	31.5
Phosphate fertilizers *										
Engrais phosphatés *	...	...	...	...	...	2.3	4.0	6.0	6.0	6.0
Potash fertilizers *										
Engrais potassiques *	...	...	...	...	...	53.0	6.0	5.0	8.0	7.0
Lithuania Lituanie										
Nitrogenous fertilizers *										
Engrais azotés *	189.0	294.4	300.2	322.9	447.2	43.0	40.0	79.0	81.1	83.4
Phosphate fertilizers *										
Engrais phosphatés *	69.0	120.0	146.1	192.8	230.5	14.0	30.0	10.0	18.2	18.4
Potash fertilizers										
Engrais potassiques	...	...	...	...	...	* 22.0	* 48.0	* 30.0	38.0	38.0
Malta Malte										
Nitrogenous fertilizers *										
Engrais azotés *	...	...	...	...	...	1.0	1.0	1.0	1.0	1.0
Netherlands Pays-Bas										
Nitrogenous fertilizers										
Engrais azotés	1 785.5	* 1 595.0	1 772.2	* 1 586.0	* 1 566.0	405.8	* 390.0	400.6	367.8	* 350.0
Phosphate fertilizers										
Engrais phosphatés	* 382.0	* 338.0	* 271.0	* 402.0	* 405.0	* 62.0	* 70.0	* 65.0	60.0	* 55.0
Potash fertilizers										
Engrais potassiques	...	...	...	...	...	* 77.0	* 75.0	* 72.0	66.7	* 60.0
Norway Norvège										
Nitrogenous fertilizers										
Engrais azotés	558.0	* 595.0	* 595.0	* 570.0	* 571.0	110.7	* 112.0	* 112.0	* 111.0	* 112.0
Phosphate fertilizers *										
Engrais phosphatés *	207.0	236.0	265.0	236.0	236.0	31.0	32.0	32.0	30.0	30.0
Potash fertilizers *										
Engrais potassiques *	...	...	...	...	...	66.0	66.0	65.0	63.0	63.0
Poland Pologne										
Nitrogenous fertilizers										
Engrais azotés	1 354.3	1 575.1	1 548.0	* 1 557.4	* 1 673.5	836.1	851.9	* 910.0	* 899.6	* 915.0

36

Fertilizers
Nitrogenous, phosphate and potash: thousand metric tons [*cont.*]
Engrais
Azotés, phosphatés et potassiques : milliers de tonnes [*suite*]

Region, country or area Région, pays ou zone	Production Production					Consumption Consommation				
	1994/95	1995/96	1996/97	1997/98	1998/99	1994/95	1995/96	1996/97	1997/98	1998/99
Phosphate fertilizers										
Engrais phosphatés	* 326.0	* 496.0	* 442.0	* 473.6	* 503.0	* 276.0	* 302.0	308.8	* 289.6	325.7
Potash fertilizers										
Engrais potassiques	...	...	...	...	...	* 316.0	* 358.0	376.1	* 400.9	386.7
Portugal Portugal										
Nitrogenous fertilizers *										
Engrais azotés *	99.0	124.0	135.0	121.0	135.0	128.0	125.0	132.0	121.0	127.0
Phosphate fertilizers *										
Engrais phosphatés *	56.0	56.0	57.0	55.0	57.0	73.0	71.0	76.0	67.0	73.0
Potash fertilizers *										
Engrais potassiques *	...	...	...	...	...	47.0	48.0	50.0	48.0	48.0
Republic of Moldova République de Moldova										
Nitrogenous fertilizers *										
Engrais azotés *	...	...	...	...	...	60.0	60.0	60.0	62.0	62.0
Phosphate fertilizers *										
Engrais phosphatés *	...	...	...	...	...	40.0	40.0	40.0	42.0	42.0
Potash fertilizers *										
Engrais potassiques *	...	...	...	5.0	5.0	15.0	15.0	16.0	17.0	17.0
Romania Roumanie										
Nitrogenous fertilizers										
Engrais azotés	926.4	* 1 227.0	* 1 250.0	668.7	* 313.2	* 227.6	* 233.0	* 266.0	* 220.0	* 268.0
Phosphate fertilizers										
Engrais phosphatés	* 207.0	* 197.0	201.8	* 135.5	* 96.2	* 111.8	* 127.0	* 141.0	* 85.0	* 79.7
Potash fertilizers *										
Engrais potassiques *	...	...	...	...	...	34.7	3.4	15.0	10.0	12.0
Russian Federation Fédération de Russie										
Nitrogenous fertilizers *										
Engrais azotés *	4 129.0	4 856.0	4 900.0	4 187.0	4 135.0	900.0	1 000.0	984.0	950.0	738.0
Phosphate fertilizers *										
Engrais phosphatés *	1 716.0	1 933.0	1 575.0	1 777.0	1 602.0	260.0	350.0	376.0	320.0	211.0
Potash fertilizers *										
Engrais potassiques *	2 498.2	2 814.0	2 618.0	3 403.0	3 461.0	350.0	400.0	220.0	280.0	138.0
Slovakia Slovaquie										
Nitrogenous fertilizers										
Engrais azotés	* 231.2	* 185.9	* 210.8	* 283.8	* 266.9	78.7	72.0	77.6	* 72.5	* 71.8
Phosphate fertilizers										
Engrais phosphatés	* 12.0	* 36.6	* 36.7	* 16.0	* 10.0	* 16.6	16.8	20.9	* 17.8	* 18.0
Potash fertilizers *										
Engrais potassiques *	...	...	...	...	...	13.8	18.7	20.2	17.1	16.5
Slovenia Slovénie										
Nitrogenous fertilizers										
Engrais azotés	...	...	...	...	...	44.7	* 35.0	24.2	34.1	34.8
Phosphate fertilizers										
Engrais phosphatés	...	...	...	...	...	* 18.0	* 17.0	* 17.5	17.5	18.8
Potash fertilizers										
Engrais potassiques	...	...	...	...	...	* 22.0	* 22.0	* 21.6	22.3	23.0
Spain Espagne										
Nitrogenous fertilizers										
Engrais azotés	788.3	844.7	881.7	918.5	* 861.8	982.5	912.8	1 153.1	1 041.9	* 1 047.5
Phosphate fertilizers										
Engrais phosphatés	421.9	413.3	477.8	488.0	* 496.0	520.9	509.9	559.9	540.2	* 548.3
Potash fertilizers										
Engrais potassiques	* 684.0	* 650.0	* 680.0	639.0	* 496.5	* 424.0	* 446.0	* 458.0	479.4	* 511.0
Sweden Suède										
Nitrogenous fertilizers										
Engrais azotés	117.5	* 123.0	* 107.0	* 103.0	* 104.0	210.2	192.3	204.6	205.6	* 179.2

36
Fertilizers
Nitrogenous, phosphate and potash: thousand metric tons [*cont.*]
Engrais
Azotés, phosphatés et potassiques : milliers de tonnes [*suite*]

Region, country or area / Région, pays ou zone	Production Production					Consumption Consommation				
	1994/95	1995/96	1996/97	1997/98	1998/99	1994/95	1995/96	1996/97	1997/98	1998/99
Phosphate fertilizers / Engrais phosphatés	* 20.0	* 18.0	* 16.0	* 15.0	* 16.0	* 54.0	* 49.0	* 50.0	49.7	* 48.0
Potash fertilizers / Engrais potassiques	...	...	...	...	...	* 53.0	* 52.0	* 53.0	53.7	* 53.0
Switzerland Suisse										
Nitrogenous fertilizers * / Engrais azotés *	14.0	22.0	13.0	13.0	10.8	63.0	65.0	62.0	60.0	277.0
Phosphate fertilizers * / Engrais phosphatés *	...	3.0	...	2.0	2.0	27.0	27.0	26.0	17.0	17.0
Potash fertilizers * / Engrais potassiques *	...	...	...	...	...	55.0	43.0	37.0	36.0	35.0
TFYR Macedonia L'ex-R.y. Macédoine										
Nitrogenous fertilizers / Engrais azotés	11.2	7.9	* 6.0	* 6.5	* 6.0	36.0	25.2	* 30.4	* 28.1	* 30.0
Phosphate fertilizers / Engrais phosphatés	8.1	6.3	* 8.0	* 7.0	* 7.5	8.8	6.0	* 7.0	* 9.2	* 9.5
Potash fertilizers * / Engrais potassiques *	...	...	...	...	...	14.0	6.0	6.0	9.4	4.5
Ukraine Ukraine										
Nitrogenous fertilizers / Engrais azotés	* 1 966.0	* 1 830.0	2 083.3	2 021.8	* 1 725.0	* 774.0	* 625.0	* 373.0	* 413.0	* 406.0
Phosphate fertilizers * / Engrais phosphatés *	270.0	294.0	326.5	266.7	213.7	140.0	130.0	97.0	104.0	76.0
Potash fertilizers / Engrais potassiques	* 78.0	* 55.1	* 39.3	* 52.2	* 33.6	* 217.1	175.1	81.8	* 45.0	* 40.0
United Kingdom Royaume-Uni										
Nitrogenous fertilizers * / Engrais azotés *	800.0	729.0	896.0	952.0	965.0	1 339.0	1 328.0	1 451.0	1 370.0	1 290.0
Phosphate fertilizers * / Engrais phosphatés *	66.0	88.0	111.0	190.0	200.0	405.0	390.0	416.0	408.0	369.0
Potash fertilizers * / Engrais potassiques *	580.0	582.0	618.0	565.0	608.4	475.0	473.0	509.0	487.0	425.0
Yugoslavia Yougoslavie										
Nitrogenous fertilizers * / Engrais azotés *	76.0	47.5	95.0	124.0	112.0	76.0	47.5	160.5	185.1	141.0
Phosphate fertilizers * / Engrais phosphatés *	14.0	14.0	14.0	16.0	24.0	14.0	14.0	19.0	35.2	24.0
Potash fertilizers * / Engrais potassiques *	...	...	...	...	...	...	...	35.0	24.0	25.0
Oceania Océanie										
Nitrogenous fertilizers / Engrais azotés	313.9	357.9	348.7	339.4	420.5	726.5	845.5	985.6	997.3	1 064.1
Phosphate fertilizers / Engrais phosphatés	668.4	654.2	573.4	653.4	588.5	1 316.5	1 360.4	1 378.7	1 477.6	1 395.7
Potash fertilizers / Engrais potassiques	...	...	...	...	...	363.1	377.7	348.5	391.8	351.3
Australia Australie										
Nitrogenous fertilizers * / Engrais azotés *	228.9	281.0	278.7	258.4	328.0	583.2	671.3	825.0	839.4	890.0
Phosphate fertilizers / Engrais phosphatés	* 425.4	* 407.3	* 333.4	383.4	328.5	* 922.7	* 965.3	* 985.3	* 1 090.1	* 1 010.0
Potash fertilizers * / Engrais potassiques *	...	...	...	...	...	219.6	230.8	206.0	254.6	210.0
Fiji Fidji										
Nitrogenous fertilizers * / Engrais azotés *	...	...	...	...	...	9.0	10.0	10.0	10.2	10.9

36
Fertilizers
Nitrogenous, phosphate and potash: thousand metric tons [*cont.*]
Engrais
Azotés, phosphatés et potassiques : milliers de tonnes [*suite*]

Region, country or area Région, pays ou zone	Production Production 1994/95	1995/96	1996/97	1997/98	1998/99	Consumption Consommation 1994/95	1995/96	1996/97	1997/98	1998/99
Phosphate fertilizers * Engrais phosphatés *	...	...	...	...	...	3.0	3.0	4.0	4.0	4.8
Potash fertilizers * Engrais potassiques *	...	...	...	...	...	6.0	5.0	5.0	5.0	6.3
French Polynesia Polynésie française										
Nitrogenous fertilizers * Engrais azotés *	...	...	...	...	...	0.4	0.4	0.4	0.4	0.4
Phosphate fertilizers * Engrais phosphatés *	...	...	...	...	...	0.4	0.4	0.4	0.4	0.4
Potash fertilizers * Engrais potassiques *	...	...	...	...	...	0.2	0.2	0.2	0.2	0.2
New Caledonia Nouvelle-Calédonie										
Nitrogenous fertilizers * Engrais azotés *	...	...	...	...	...	0.3	0.3	0.3	0.3	0.3
Phosphate fertilizers * Engrais phosphatés *	...	...	...	...	...	1.0	1.0	1.0	1.0	1.0
Potash fertilizers Engrais potassiques	...	...	...	...	...	* 0.3	* 0.3	* 0.3	* 0.3	0.3
New Zealand Nouvelle-Zélande										
Nitrogenous fertilizers * Engrais azotés *	85.0	76.9	70.0	81.0	92.5	125.6	155.5	140.0	138.9	153.5
Phosphate fertilizers * Engrais phosphatés *	243.0	246.9	240.0	270.0	260.0	386.4	387.7	385.0	379.1	376.0
Potash fertilizers * Engrais potassiques *	...	...	...	...	...	135.0	139.4	135.0	129.7	132.0
Palau Palaos										
Nitrogenous fertilizers Engrais azotés	...	...	...	...	...	...	...	* 1.9	0.0	0.0
Papua New Guinea Papouasie-Nvl-Guinée										
Nitrogenous fertilizers * Engrais azotés *	...	...	...	...	...	8.0	8.0	8.0	8.1	9.0
Phosphate fertilizers * Engrais phosphatés *	...	...	...	...	...	3.0	3.0	3.0	3.0	3.5
Potash fertilizers * Engrais potassiques *	...	...	...	...	...	2.0	2.0	2.0	2.0	2.5

Source:
Food and Agriculture Organization of the United Nations (FAO), Rome, FAOSTAT Agriculture Database.

† For information on recent changes in country or area nomenclature pertaining to former Czechoslovakia, Germany, Hong Kong Special Administrative Region (SAR) of China, Macao Special Administrative Region (SAR) of China, SFR of Yugoslavia and the former USSR, see Annex I - Country or area nomenclature, regional and other groupings.

†† For statistical purposes, the data for China do not include those for Hong Kong Special Administrative Region (Hong Kong SAR) and Macao Special Administrative Region (Macao SAR).

1 FAO estimate.

Source:
Organisation des Nations Unies pour l'alimentation et l'agriculture (FAO), Rome, les données de l'agriculture de FAOSTAT.

† Pour les modifications récentes de nomenclature de pays ou de zone concernant l'Allemagne, Hong Kong, région administrative spéciale (RAS) de Chine, Macao, région administrative spéciale (RAS) de Chine, l'ex-Tchécoslovaquie, l'ex-URSS et l'ex-Rfs de Yougoslavie, voir annexe I - Nomenclature des pays ou des zones, groupements régionaux et autres groupements.

†† Les données statistiques relatives à la Chine ne comprennent pas celles qui concernent la région administrative spéciale de Hong Kong (la RAS de Hong Kong) et la région administrative spéciale de Macao (la RAS de Macao).

1 Estimation de la FAO.

Technical notes, tables 30-36

The series shown on agriculture and fishing have been furnished by the Food and Agriculture Organization of the United Nations (FAO). They refer mainly to:

(a)   Long-term trends in the growth of agricultural output and the food supply;

(b)   Output of principal agricultural commodities.

Agricultural production is defined to include all crops and livestock products except those used for seed and fodder and other intermediate uses in agriculture; for example deductions are made for eggs used for hatching. Intermediate input of seeds and fodder and similar items refer to both domestically produced and imported commodities. For further details, reference may be made to FAO Yearbooks [4, 6, 7, 8, 9]. FAO data are also available through the Internet (http://www.fao.org).

Table 30: "Agriculture" relates to the production of all crops and livestock products. The "Food Index" includes those commodities which are considered edible and contain nutrients.

The index numbers of agricultural output and food production are calculated by the Laspeyres formula with the base year period 1989-1991. The latter is provided in order to diminish the impact of annual fluctuations in agricultural output during base years on the indices for the period. Production quantities of each commodity are weighted by 1989-1991 average national producer prices and summed for each year. The index numbers are based on production data for a calendar year. These may differ in some instances from those actually produced and published by the individual countries themselves due to variations in concepts, coverage, weights and methods of calculation. Efforts have been made to estimate these methodological differences to achieve a better international comparability of data. The series include a large amount of estimates made by FAO in cases where no official or semi-official figures are available from the countries.

Detailed data on agricultural production and trade are published by FAO in its *Production Yearbook* [6] and *Trade Yearbook* [7].

Table 31: The data on the production of cereals relate to crops harvested for dry grain only. Cereals harvested for hay, green feed or used for grazing are excluded.

Table 32: Oil crops, or oil-bearing crops, are those crops yielding seeds, nuts or fruits which are used mainly for the extraction of culinary or industrial oils, excluding essential oils. In this table, data for oil crops represent the total production of oil seeds, oil nuts and oil fruits harvested in the year indicated and expressed

Notes techniques, tableaux 30 à 36

Les séries présentées sur l'agriculture et la pêche ont été fournies par l'Organisation des Nations Unies pour l'alimentation et l'agriculture (FAO) et portent principalement sur:

(a)   Les tendances à long terme de la croissance de la production agricole et des approvisionnements alimentaires;

(b)   La production des principales denrées agricoles.

La production agricole se définit comme comprenant l'ensemble des produits agricoles et des produits de l'élevage à l'exception de ceux utilisés comme semences et comme aliments pour les animaux, et pour les autres utilisations intermédiaires en agriculture; par exemple, on déduit les œufs utilisés pour la reproduction. L'apport intermédiaire de semences et d'aliments pour les animaux et d'autres éléments similaires se rapportent à la fois à des produits locaux et importés. Pour tous détails complémentaires, on se reportera aux annuaires de la FAO [4, 6, 7, 8, 9]. Des statistiques peuvent également être consultées sur le site Web de la FAO (http://www.fao.org).

Tableau 30: L'"Agriculture" se rapporte à la production de tous les produits de l'agriculture et de l'élevage. L'"Indice des produits alimentaires" comprend les produits considérés comme comestibles et qui contiennent des éléments nutritifs.

Les indices de la production agricole et de la production alimentaire sont calculés selon la formule de Laspeyres avec les années 1989-1991 pour période de base. Le choix d'une période de plusieurs années permet de diminuer l'incidence des fluctuations annuelles de la production agricole pendant les années de base sur les indices pour cette période. Les quantités produites de chaque denrée sont pondérées par les prix nationaux moyens à la production de 1989-1991, et additionnées pour chaque année. Les indices sont fondés sur les données de production d'une année civile. Ils peuvent différer dans certains cas des indices effectivement établis et publiés par les pays eux-mêmes par suite de différences dans les concepts, la couverture, les pondérations et les méthodes de calcul. On s'est efforcé d'estimer ces différences méthodologiques afin de rendre les données plus facilement comparables à l'échelle internationale. Les séries comprennent une grande quantité d'estimations faites par la FAO dans les cas où les pays n'avaient pas fourni de chiffres officiels ou semi-officiels.

Des chiffres détaillés de production et d'échange sont publiés dans l'*Annuaire FAO de la production* [6] et l'*Annuaire FAO du commerce* [7].

Tableau 31: Les données sur la production de cé-

in terms of oil equivalent and cake/meal equivalent. That is to say, these figures do not relate to the actual production of vegetable oils and cake/meal, but to the potential production if the total amounts produced from all oil crops were processed into oil and cake/meal in producing countries in the same year in which they were harvested. Naturally, the total production of oil crops is never processed into oil in its entirety, since depending on the crop, important quantities are also used for seed, feed and food. However, although oil and cake/meal extraction rates vary from country to country, in this table the same extraction rate for each crop has been applied for all countries. Moreover. it should be borne in mind that the crops harvested during the latter months of the year are generally processed into oil during the following year.

In spite of these deficiencies in coverage, extraction rates and time reference, the data reported here are useful as they provide a valid indication of year-to-year changes in the size of total oil-crop production. The actual production of vegetable oils in the world is about 80 percent of the production reported here. In addition, about two million tonnes of vegetable oils are produced every year from crops which are not included among those defined above. The most important of these oils are maize-germ oil and rice-bran oil. The actual world production of cake/meal derived from oil crops is also about 80 percent of the production reported in the table.

Table 33: The data refer to livestock numbers grouped into twelve-month periods ending 30 September of the year stated and cover all domestic animals irrespective of their age and place or purpose of their breeding.

Table 34: The data on roundwood refer to wood in the rough, wood in its natural state as felled or otherwise harvested, with or without bark, round, split, roughly squared or in other form (i.e. roots, stumps, burls, etc.). It may also be impregnated (e.g. telegraph poles) or roughly shaped or pointed. It comprises all wood obtained from removals, i.e. the quantities removed from forests and from trees outside the forest, including wood recovered from natural, felling and logging losses during the period — calendar year or forest year.

Table 35: The data cover as far as possible both sea and inland fisheries and aquaculture and are expressed in terms of live weight. They generally include crustaceans and molluscs but exclude seaweed and aquatic mammals such as whales and dolphins. Data include landings by domestic craft in foreign ports and exclude the landings by foreign craft in domestic ports. The flag of the vessel is considered as the paramount indication of the nationality of the catch.

Table 36: The data generally refer to the fertilizer

réales se rapportent uniquement aux céréales récoltées pour le grain sec; celles cultivées pour le foin, le fourrage vert ou le pâturage en sont exclues.

Tableau 32: On désigne sous le nom de cultures oléagineuses l'ensemble des cultures produisant des graines, des noix ou des fruits, essentiellement destinées à l'extraction d'huiles alimentaires ou industrielles, à l'exclusion des huiles essentielles. Dans ce tableau, les chiffres se rapportent à la production totale de graines, noix et fruits oléagineux récoltés au cours de l'année de référence et sont exprimés en équivalent d'huile et en équivalent de tourteau/farine. En d'autres termes, ces chiffres ne se rapportent pas à la production effective mais à la production potentielle d'huiles végétales et de tourteau/farine dans l'hypothèse où les volumes totaux de produits provenant de toutes les cultures d'oléagineux seraient transformés en huile et en tourteau/farine dans les pays producteurs l'année même où ils ont été récoltés. Bien entendu, la production totale d'oléagineux n'est jamais transformée intégralement en huile, car des quantités importantes qui varient suivant les cultures sont également utilisées pour les semailles, l'alimentation animale et l'alimentation humaine. Toutefois, bien que les taux d'extraction d'huile et de tourteau/farine varient selon les pays, on a appliqué dans ce tableau le même taux à tous les pays pour chaque oléagineux. En outre, il ne faut pas oublier que les produits récoltés au cours des derniers mois de l'année sont généralement transformés en huile dans le courant de l'année suivante.

En dépit de ces imperfections qui concernent le champ d'application, les taux d'extraction et les périodes de référence, les chiffres présentés ici sont utiles, car ils donnent une indication valable des variations de volume que la production totale d'oléagineux enregistre d'une année à l'autre. La production mondiale effective d'huiles végétales atteint 80 pour cent environ de la production indiquée ici. En outre, environ 2 millions de tonnes d'huiles végétales sont produites chaque année à partir de cultures non comprises dans les catégories définies ci-dessus. Les principales sont l'huile de germes de maïs et l'huile de son de riz. La production mondiale effective tourteau/farine d'oléagineux représente environ 80 pour cent de production indiquée dans le tableau.

Tableau 33: Les statistiques sur les effectifs du cheptel sont groupées en périodes de 12 mois se terminant le 30 septembre de l'année indiquée et s'entendent de tous les animaux domestiques, quel que soit leur âge, leur emplacement ou le but de leur élevage.

Tableau 34: Les données sur le bois rond se réfèrent au bois brut, bois à l'état naturel, tel qu'il a été abattu ou récolté autrement, avec ou sans écorce, fendu, grossièrement équarri ou sous une autre forme (par

year 1 July-30 June.

Nitrogenous fertilizers: data refer to the nitrogen content of commercial inorganic fertilizers.

Phosphate fertilizers: data refer to commercial phosphoric acid (P_2O_5) and cover the P_2O_5 of superphosphates, ammonium phosphate and basic slag.

Potash fertilizers: data refer to K_2O content of commercial potash, muriate, nitrate and sulphate of potash, manure salts, kainit and nitrate of soda potash.

Data on fertilizer production, consumption and trade are available in FAO's *Fertilizer Yearbook* [4].

exemple, racines, souches, loupes, etc.). Il peut être également imprégné (par exemple, dans le cas des poteaux télégraphiques) et dégrossi ou taillé en pointe. Cette catégorie comprend tous les bois provenant des quantités enlevées en forêt ou provenant des arbres poussant hors forêt, y compris le volume récupéré sur les déchets naturels et les déchets d'abattage et de transport pendant la période envisagée (année civile ou forestière).

Tableau 35: Les données englobent autant que possible la pêche maritime et intérieure et l'aquaculture, et sont exprimées en poids vif. Elles comprennent, en général, crustacés et mollusques, mais excluent les plantes marines et les mammifères aquatiques (baleines, dauphins, etc.). Les données comprennent les quantités débarquées par des bateaux nationaux dans des ports étrangers et excluent les quantités débarquées par des bateaux étrangers dans des ports nationaux. Le pavillon du navire est considéré comme la principale indication de la nationalité de la prise.

Tableau 36: Les données sur les engrais se rapportent en général à une période d'un an comptée du 1er juillet au 30 juin.

Engrais azotés: les données se rapportent à la teneur en azote des engrais commerciaux inorganiques.

Engrais phosphatés: les données se rapportent à l'acide phosphorique (P_2O_5) et englobent la teneur en (P_2O_5) des superphosphates, du phosphate d'ammonium et des scories de déphosphoration.

Engrais potassiques: les données se rapportent à la teneur en K_2O des produits potassiques commerciaux, muriate, nitrate et sulfate de potasse, sels d'engrais, kainite et nitrate de soude potassique.

On trouvera des chiffres relatifs à la production, à la consommation et aux échanges d'engrais dans l'*Annuaire FAO des engrais* [4].

37
Sugar
Sucre

Production and consumption: thousand metric tons; consumption per capita: kilograms

Production et consommation : milliers de tonnes ; consommation par habitant : kilogrammes

Country or area Pays ou zone	1990	1991	1992	1993	1994	1995	1996	1997	1998	1999
World Monde										
Production	110 650	112 254	117 443	111 942	110 414	117 831	124 952	125 203	126 694	136 325
Consumption	107 870	108 860	112 237	111 347	112 954	116 590	120 032	122 931	124 417	126 221
Consumption per cap.(kg)	21	19	21	20	20	20	21	21	20	20
Africa · Afrique										
Algeria Algérie										
Consumption *	810	850	880	825	800	775	750	650	800	900
Consumption per cap.(kg)	32	33	34	31	29	28	26	22	25	27
Angola Angola										
Production *	25	30	25	20	20	30	25	28	32	32
Consumption *	95	100	110	110	95	100	110	110	85	120
Consumption per cap.(kg)	10	11	10	11	9	9	10	9	7	9
Benin Bénin										
Production *	5	5	4	5	4	5	5	4	0	0
Consumption *	15	20	25	30	35	45	45	40	45	45
Consumption per cap.(kg)	3	4	5	6	7	8	8	7	7	7
Botswana Botswana										
Consumption	50	55	50	45	45	40	40	30	45	45
Consumption per cap.(kg)	38	41	37	31	32	27	27	19	28	28
Burkina Faso Burkina Faso										
Production	* 28	* 29	31	* 32	* 33	* 32	* 33	* 34	* 30	30
Consumption	* 35	* 30	32	* 35	* 35	* 35	* 35	* 42	* 50	* 50
Consumption per cap.(kg)	4	3	3	4	3	3	3	4	5	5
Burundi Burundi										
Production	8	14	10	10	12	10	8	8	24	23
Consumption	17	11	15	17	20	25	20	12	22	23
Consumption per cap.(kg)	3	2	3	3	3	4	3	2	3	3
Cameroon Cameroun										
Production	* 77	* 76	* 72	* 67	* 57	* 59	* 52	* 44	* 46	52
Consumption *	75	80	80	80	83	85	85	80	95	100
Consumption per cap.(kg)	7	7	7	6	6	6	6	6	7	7
Cape Verde Cap–Vert										
Consumption *	11	12	13	15	15	15	17	18	12	12
Consumption per cap.(kg)	32	37	39	41	39	39	43	44	28	27
Central African Rep. Rép. centrafricaine										
Consumption *	3	3	3	4	4	3	5	5	5	4
Consumption per cap.(kg)	1	1	1	1	1	1	2	1	2	1
Chad Tchad										
Production	* 25	* 30	* 30	32	* 32	* 30	* 30	* 34	* 31	32
Consumption *	50	40	40	40	43	47	50	46	55	55
Consumption per cap.(kg)	9	7	7	6	7	8	9	9	11	11
Comoros Comores										
Consumption	3	4	4	4	3	3	3	2	5	5
Consumption per cap.(kg)	6	7	7	7	5	5	4	3	7	7
Congo Congo										
Production	* 35	21	30	26	* 29	38	42	* 45	* 45	* 60
Consumption	* 20	* 17	18	16	* 17	* 28	* 28	* 50	* 60	* 60
Consumption per cap.(kg)	9	7	8	7	7	11	11	18	21	21
Côte d'Ivoire Côte d'Ivoire										
Production	* 160	* 155	* 160	* 155	141	* 160	* 134	* 132	126	152
Consumption	* 160	* 160	* 165	* 165	126	* 160	* 170	* 170	137	* 170
Consumption per cap.(kg)	13	13	13	12	9	11	12	11	9	10
Dem. Rep. of the Congo Rép. dém. du Congo										
Production *	85	88	90	85	85	80	50	86	51	65
Consumption *	95	95	100	105	105	110	110	90	80	75
Consumption per cap.(kg)	3	3	3	3	3	3	2	2	2	2
Djibouti Djibouti										
Consumption	10	9	12	10	11	12	11	10	10	12
Consumption per cap.(kg)	19	17	22	18	19	21	19	17	16	19
Egypt Egypte										
Production	* 955	* 1 060	* 1 060	* 1 090	* 1 190	* 1 125	* 1 222	* 1 228	* 1 152	1 269
Consumption	* 1 725	* 1 745	1 750	* 1 675	* 1 700	* 1 775	* 1 850	* 2 000	* 2 200	* 2 300
Consumption per cap.(kg)	33	32	32	30	29	30	31	33	36	37

37
Sugar
Production and consumption: thousand metric tons; consumption per capita: kilograms [*cont.*]
Sucre
Production et consommation : milliers de tonnes ; consommation par habitant : kilogrammes [*suite*]

Country or area Pays ou zone	1990	1991	1992	1993	1994	1995	1996	1997	1998	1999
Eritrea Erythrée										
Consumption	...	...	...	...	...	...	...	10	10	8
Ethiopia Ethiopie										
Production	* 184	* 161	165	* 185	95	128	* 180	* 126	* 219	235
Consumption	* 160	* 160	* 160	* 160	* 145	113	* 175	* 200	* 200	* 211
Consumption per cap.(kg)	3	3	3	3	3	2	3	3	3	3
Gabon Gabon										
Production *	20	22	15	18	17	16	15	16	17	16
Consumption *	18	16	10	15	17	17	16	16	17	20
Consumption per cap.(kg)	15	15	10	15	16	16	14	14	5	5
Gambia Gambie										
Consumption *	33	35	35	40	40	45	30	40	35	35
Consumption per cap.(kg)	35	37	40	39	37	40	25	32	27	26
Ghana Ghana										
Consumption *	90	95	105	120	123	120	120	130	200	200
Consumption per cap.(kg)	6	6	7	7	7	7	7	7	11	10
Guinea Guinée										
Production *	20	18	18	20	19	20	21	22	22	25
Consumption *	50	55	65	70	75	75	75	80	80	100
Consumption per cap.(kg)	9	9	11	11	11	11	11	11	11	13
Guinea−Bissau Guinée−Bissau										
Consumption	3	3	3	2	3	4	4	7	4	5
Consumption per cap.(kg)	3	3	3	2	3	3	4	6	4	4
Kenya Kenya										
Production	496	471	404	414	329	418	423	436	488	512
Consumption	585	537	600	609	620	* 510	* 500	* 525	798	662
Consumption per cap.(kg)	22	21	22	22	21	17	16	18	27	18
Liberia Libéria										
Production	1	1	1	1	1	0	...	...	...	...
Consumption	11	6	6	6	8	8	7	6	10	8
Consumption per cap.(kg)	5	2	2	2	3	3	3	2	3	3
Libyan Arab Jamah. Jamah. arabe libyenne										
Consumption *	155	160	160	160	160	150	180	225	225	230
Consumption per cap.(kg)	37	37	36	34	33	29	34	41	39	38
Madagascar Madagascar										
Production	118	96	97	104	83	94	* 95	* 96	95	* 85
Consumption	87	87	88	85	90	78	* 90	* 110	* 120	* 120
Consumption per cap.(kg)	8	8	7	6	6	5	6	7	7	7
Malawi Malawi										
Production	204	210	209	137	213	241	234	210	210	187
Consumption	124	130	152	162	149	164	173	178	158	137
Consumption per cap.(kg)	15	15	17	18	16	17	17	16	14	12
Mali Mali										
Production	* 25	* 30	25	* 25	* 25	* 25	* 26	* 26	* 33	* 31
Consumption	* 75	* 80	80	* 85	* 90	* 90	* 65	* 60	* 80	* 75
Consumption per cap.(kg)	9	8	8	8	9	8	7	5	7	6
Mauritania Mauritanie										
Consumption *	55	60	60	55	70	80	85	90	130	150
Consumption per cap.(kg)	27	29	28	26	32	35	36	38	54	61
Mauritius Maurice										
Production	661	648	681	604	530	572	624	658	667	396
Consumption	41	42	41	39	39	39	40	42	43	42
Consumption per cap.(kg)	38	40	38	36	36	36	36	37	37	36
Morocco Maroc										
Production	* 520	498	453	507	482	455	400	406	* 533	* 500
Consumption	* 775	778	811	829	830	894	950	975	* 1 050	* 1 050
Consumption per cap.(kg)	32	31	32	32	31	33	34	36	38	38
Mozambique Mozambique										
Production	* 32	* 25	* 30	* 20	* 20	* 30	* 30	* 42	* 39	46
Consumption *	45	45	50	70	73	60	55	50	121	90
Consumption per cap.(kg)	3	3	3	5	4	3	3	3	8	4
Namibia Namibie										
Consumption	...	...	...	...	...	...	...	...	25	20

37
Sugar
Production and consumption: thousand metric tons; consumption per capita: kilograms [cont.]
Sucre
Production et consommation : milliers de tonnes ; consommation par habitant : kilogrammes [suite]

Country or area Pays ou zone	1990	1991	1992	1993	1994	1995	1996	1997	1998	1999
Niger Niger										
Consumption *	25	25	23	25	25	30	30	24	35	35
Consumption per cap.(kg)	3	3	3	3	3	3	3	2	3	3
Nigeria Nigéria										
Production *	60	56	46	46	48	37	27	15	15	17
Consumption *	415	480	600	625	600	500	600	650	900	752
Consumption per cap.(kg)	4	5	6	6	6	5	5	6	7	6
Réunion [1] Réunion [1]										
Production	193	215	227	184	177	195	205	207	* 195	* 234
Rwanda Rwanda										
Production	3	4	4	4	3	1	...	...	...	...
Consumption	10	11	12	12	7	4	4	4	3	3
Consumption per cap.(kg)	1	2	2	2	1	1	1	1	0	0
Senegal Sénégal										
Production	* 80	* 85	* 90	* 90	* 95	* 81	* 85	* 91	90	* 95
Consumption	* 98	* 115	128	* 135	* 145	* 165	* 175	* 180	* 180	* 170
Consumption per cap.(kg)	13	15	16	17	18	21	20	23	23	22
Sierra Leone Sierra Leone										
Production *	5	5	3	4	4	4	5	6	6	7
Consumption *	18	18	19	17	17	18	19	14	20	15
Consumption per cap.(kg)	5	4	5	4	4	4	4	3	4	3
Somalia Somalie										
Production *	35	30	28	20	18	20	20	19	19	20
Consumption *	40	37	43	47	80	110	110	135	185	200
Consumption per cap.(kg)	5	4	5	5	9	12	12	14	19	21
South Africa Afrique du Sud										
Production	2 226	2 462	1 715	1 282	1 777	1 732	2 471	2 419	2 985	2 547
Consumption	1 433	1 382	1 327	1 303	1 480	1 381	1 330	1 656	1 367	1 223
Consumption per cap.(kg)	39	36	34	33	37	34	32	38	32	27
Sudan Soudan										
Production	* 445	* 490	* 515	* 485	* 510	486	543	538	610	635
Consumption *	455	475	480	500	515	460	480	480	391	396
Consumption per cap.(kg)	18	19	18	18	18	15	18	19	13	12
Swaziland Swaziland										
Production	527	517	495	458	474	419	458	457	537	571
Consumption	47	52	73	103	141	174	188	187	250	275
Consumption per cap.(kg)	61	65	100	122	160	191	196	200	260	287
Togo Togo										
Production *	5	5	5	5	5	5	5	3	3	3
Consumption *	35	30	30	19	28	32	35	45	50	50
Consumption per cap.(kg)	10	8	8	5	7	8	9	11	12	12
Tunisia Tunisie										
Production	25	22	28	25	25	29	29	28	15	9
Consumption	212	215	246	250	258	257	272	283	287	292
Consumption per cap.(kg)	27	27	30	30	29	28	30	30	30	33
Uganda Ouganda										
Production *	25	45	58	54	48	76	109	145	111	137
Consumption *	35	45	46	55	65	100	100	150	150	150
Consumption per cap.(kg)	2	2	2	3	3	5	5	7	6	6
United Rep. Tanzania Rép.–Unie de Tanzanie										
Production	* 115	* 115	* 105	* 120	* 130	* 110	* 100	84	110	114
Consumption *	100	115	120	120	115	120	160	175	200	200
Consumption per cap.(kg)	4	4	4	4	4	4	5	6	6	6
Zambia Zambie										
Production	135	134	155	147	* 150	151	166	174	173	210
Consumption	116	105	111	86	* 105	152	154	74	75	* 100
Consumption per cap.(kg)	14	13	13	10	11	16	16	8	8	10
Zimbabwe Zimbabwe										
Production	493	346[2]	9	51	524	512	337	574	572	583
Consumption	297	294	234	229	253	292	287	335	305	376
Consumption per cap.(kg)	32	29	22	21	23	25	25	27	25	29
America, North · Amerique du Nord										
Bahamas Bahamas										
Consumption	11	10	10	10	9	11	12	10	10	10
Consumption per cap.(kg)	42	39	39	36	35	41	43	37	37	37

37

Sugar

Production and consumption: thousand metric tons; consumption per capita: kilograms [*cont.*]

Sucre

Production et consommation : milliers de tonnes ; consommation par habitant : kilogrammes [*suite*]

Country or area Pays ou zone	1990	1991	1992	1993	1994	1995	1996	1997	1998	1999
Barbados Barbade										
Production	70	67	* 55	* 48	* 51	* 55	59	62	46	53
Consumption	12	11	* 12	* 11	* 13	* 14	16	16	15	* 15
Consumption per cap.(kg)	49	42	46	42	48	52	58	60	56	56
Belize Belize										
Production	108	103	108	108	108	115	113	131	123	124
Consumption	9	9	9	11	13	13	15	16	15	15
Consumption per cap.(kg)	46	47	47	54	63	63	69	68	65	70
Bermuda Bermudes										
Consumption	2	2	2	2	2	2	2	1	2	1
Consumption per cap.(kg)	33	33	27	33	24	21	21	13	18	11
Canada Canada										
Production	* 140	* 150	* 125	* 124	* 169	* 167	* 158	* 115	* 104	118
Consumption *	1 050	1 100	1 120	1 150	1 175	1 200	1 225	1 225	1 200	1 200
Consumption per cap.(kg)	41	41	41	40	40	41	41	40	39	39
Costa Rica Costa Rica										
Production	246	279	301	* 305	* 325	* 355	* 332	* 319	* 381	* 378
Consumption	178	183	186	* 190	* 193	* 195	* 225	* 230	* 230	* 240
Consumption per cap.(kg)	64	64	63	63	63	62	66	67	68	70
Cuba Cuba										
Production	8 445	7 233	7 219	4 246	4 017	3 259	4 529	4 318	3 291	3 875
Consumption [3]	937	956	942	796	664	581	* 670	733	713	711
Consumption per cap.(kg)	88	89	87	73	61	53	61	66	64	63
Dominican Republic Rép. dominicaine										
Production	590	628	593	621	579	508	* 670	687	409	421
Consumption	201	251	277	290	295	300	* 350	274	337	* 350
Consumption per cap.(kg)	28	34	37	38	38	38	44	33	40	41
El Salvador El Salvador										
Production	* 220	186	233	* 250	* 275	* 300	* 352	414	487	585
Consumption	* 165	* 150	116	* 165	* 175	* 190	* 210	232	237	234
Consumption per cap.(kg)	32	28	21	30	32	33	36	41	39	37
Guadeloupe [1] Guadeloupe [1]										
Production	26	53	38	63	58	33	49	57	38	38[4]
Guatemala Guatemala										
Production	939	1 038	1 165	1 226	1 131	1 362	1 318	1 390	1 682	1 687
Consumption	360	348	368	391	416	417	372	392	408	460
Consumption per cap.(kg)	39	37	38	39	40	39	34	35	39	47
Haiti Haïti										
Production *	35	25	20	20	15	5	8	9	10	10
Consumption *	85	90	95	85	85	120	115	120	130	170
Consumption per cap.(kg)	15	14	14	12	12	17	16	16	17	22
Honduras Honduras										
Production	* 205	175	* 185	* 190	* 185	* 215	* 240	* 251	* 277	190
Consumption	* 175	161	* 170	* 180	* 200	* 225	* 235	* 235	* 230	* 235
Consumption per cap.(kg)	34	31	31	32	35	38	38	37	35	35
Jamaica Jamaïque										
Production	209	234	228	219	223	214	236	233	183	212
Consumption	114	116	117	123	120	92	115	113	120	98
Consumption per cap.(kg)	48	48	48	50	48	37	45	45	48	37
Martinique [1] Martinique [1]										
Production	7	7	6	7	7	8	8	7	7[4]	7[4]
Mexico Mexique										
Production	3 486	3 882	3 885	4 353	3 849	4 588	4 784	5 048	5 287	5 030
Consumption	3 879	4 545	4 301	4 449	4 370	4 423	4 229	4 231	4 293	* 4 500
Consumption per cap.(kg)	55	56	48	49	47	49	44	44	44	44
Netherlands Antilles Antilles néerlandaises										
Consumption *	10	10	10	6	8	9	8	12	15	20
Consumption per cap.(kg)	40	39	39	23	30	33	30	44	56	74
Nicaragua Nicaragua										
Production	212	* 225	* 190	* 185	* 210	* 220	* 314	* 354	330	351
Consumption	* 150	* 140	* 135	* 150	* 155	* 160	* 180	* 180	217	179
Consumption per cap.(kg)	39	35	33	35	35	35	39	37	44	35

37

Sugar
Production and consumption: thousand metric tons; consumption per capita: kilograms [*cont.*]
Sucre
Production et consommation : milliers de tonnes ; consommation par habitant : kilogrammes [*suite*]

Country or area Pays ou zone	1990	1991	1992	1993	1994	1995	1996	1997	1998	1999
Panama Panama										
Production	* 90	* 127	* 157	* 150	* 148	* 127	* 142	* 166	* 181	177
Consumption	* 85	* 64	63	* 63	* 63	* 66	* 69	* 73	* 75	* 85
Consumption per cap.(kg)	37	36	25	25	25	25	26	27	27	30
Saint Kitts and Nevis Saint–Kitts–et–Nevis										
Production	* 25	20	* 20	* 25	* 30	* 25	20	30	24	* 20
Consumption	* 2	2	* 2	* 2	* 2	* 2	* 2	* 2	* 2	* 2
Consumption per cap.(kg)	40	41	41	41	43	50	50	50	50	50
Trinidad and Tobago Trinité–et–Tobago										
Production	122	104	114	108	127	117	117	120	79	92
Consumption	63	61	55	59	63	84	73	87	72	70
Consumption per cap.(kg)	49	49	43	47	48	66	57	67	56	55
United States Etats–Unis										
Production	5 740	6 477	6 805	7 045	6 921	7 238	6 593	6 731	7 159	8 243
Consumption	7 848	7 887	8 098	8 192	8 454	8 580	8 701	8 800	9 049	9 200
Consumption per cap.(kg)	31	31	32	32	32	33	33	33	34	34
America, South · Amerique du Sud										
Argentina Argentine										
Production	1 351	* 1 560	1 379	1 093	1 202	1 612	1 393	1 649	1 749	1 882
Consumption	1 070	* 1 140	1 174	* 1 200	1 296	1 350	1 347	* 1 350	* 1 350	1 450
Consumption per cap.(kg)	33	35	36	36	38	39	38	38	38	40
Bolivia Bolivie										
Production	* 225	* 230	* 220	* 220	* 235	* 230	* 270	* 277	282	293
Consumption	* 185	* 185	* 190	* 200	* 210	* 215	* 225	* 235	287	* 290
Consumption per cap.(kg)	28	28	28	28	29	29	30	30	36	36
Brazil Brésil										
Production	* 8 007	9 453	9 925	10 097	12 270	13 835	14 718	16 371	19 168	20 646
Consumption	* 6 615	7 276	* 7 349	* 7 575	* 7 874	* 8 230	* 8 490	* 8 900	* 9 150	* 9 500
Consumption per cap.(kg)	46	50	49	50	51	53	54	56	56	58
Chile Chili										
Production	371	363	529	492	503	596	459	390	511	487
Consumption	508	518	588	598	615	650	* 700	* 720	728	729
Consumption per cap.(kg)	39	39	43	43	44	46	49	49	49	48
Colombia Colombie										
Production	1 593	1 633	1 813	1 833	1 964	2 069	2 149	2 136	2 126	2 241
Consumption [5]	1 195	1 318	1 262	1 158	1 140	1 128	1 206	1 192	1 240	1 281
Consumption per cap.(kg)	37	40	38	34	32	32	31	30	30	38
Ecuador Equateur										
Production	334	* 335	387	366	312	358	419	190	186	556
Consumption	360	* 375	439	361	* 400	355	* 375	396	360	* 400
Consumption per cap.(kg)	35	36	41	33	36	31	32	33	30	32
Guyana Guyana										
Production	134	168	255	255	265	258	287	283	263	336
Consumption	29	26	24	22	23	24	24	25	25	25
Consumption per cap.(kg)	35	32	30	27	28	29	30	35	35	30
Paraguay Paraguay										
Production	89	* 105	* 95	* 105	* 100	* 90	* 116	* 108	114	* 112
Consumption	79	90	* 91	* 100	* 103	* 105	* 110	* 120	125	* 125
Consumption per cap.(kg)	19	21	20	22	22	22	22	24	24	23
Peru Pérou										
Production	592	579	474	434	543	633	612	693	570	* 655
Consumption	782	673	665	669	715	730	745	826	* 850	* 900
Consumption per cap.(kg)	29	31	30	30	31	31	31	34	34	36
Suriname Suriname										
Production	* 10	* 5	* 5	* 5	* 7	* 10	* 7	* 7	...	...
Consumption *	18	18	18	16	17	20	18	15	15	15
Consumption per cap.(kg)	45	45	43	39	41	47	41	32	38	32
Uruguay Uruguay										
Production	84	79	73	* 35	* 22	* 20	* 15	* 19	* 14	* 9
Consumption	* 75	88	92	* 95	100	* 105	* 125	* 145	* 115	101
Consumption per cap.(kg)	24	28	30	30	32	33	39	45	35	31
Venezuela Venezuela										
Production	542	567	483	* 569	* 530	* 523	* 559	* 594	* 590	* 535
Consumption	732	731	642	* 725	* 780	* 850	* 900	* 925	* 975	* 975
Consumption per cap.(kg)	37	37	34	35	37	39	41	42	44	43

37

Sugar
Production and consumption: thousand metric tons; consumption per capita: kilograms [cont.]

Sucre
Production et consommation : milliers de tonnes ; consommation par habitant : kilogrammes [suite]

Country or area Pays ou zone	1990	1991	1992	1993	1994	1995	1996	1997	1998	1999
Asia · Asie										
Afghanistan Afghanistan										
Consumption *	39	40	50	50	46	50	45	50	50	70
Consumption per cap.(kg)	2	2	3	3	2	3	2	2	2	3
Armenia Arménie										
Consumption *	...	...	70	60	50	50	60	55	60	65
Consumption per cap.(kg)	...	...	19	17	14	13	16	13	13	14
Azerbaijan Azerbaïdjan										
Consumption	...	...	* 220	* 205	* 180	* 170	* 170	123	157	* 135
Consumption per cap.(kg)	...	...	30	28	24	23	23	16	21	17
Bangladesh Bangladesh										
Production	* 206	* 231	* 231	* 205	* 249	* 278	* 194	* 138	* 159	162
Consumption *	250	275	285	300	315	285	290	300	270	300
Consumption per cap.(kg)	2	3	3	3	3	2	2	3	2	2
Brunei Darussalam Brunéi Darussalam										
Consumption	10	9	8	8	8	8	6	4	7	5
Consumption per cap.(kg)	39	35	28	27	27	27	21	13	23	18
Cambodia Cambodge										
Consumption *	5	5	10	15	20	22	40	55	65	100
Consumption per cap.(kg)	1	1	1	2	2	2	4	5	6	9
China †† Chine ††										
Production	* 6 250	6 944	8 864	8 093	6 325	6 148	* 7 091	7 415	8 904	9 274
Consumption	* 7 125	* 7 350	7 615	* 7 720	* 7 900	* 8 200	* 8 250	* 7 800	* 8 300	* 8 700
Consumption per cap.(kg)	6	6	6	7	7	7	7	6	7	7
China, Hong Kong SAR † Chine, Hong Kong RAS †										
Consumption *	150	153	155	158	160	160	180	200	200	200
Consumption per cap.(kg)	26	27	27	27	26	26	29	31	30	30
China, Macao SAR † Chine, Macao RAS †										
Consumption	3	3	3	3	4	5	6	7	7	7
Consumption per cap.(kg)	9	9	8	8	10	12	13	16	16	16
Cyprus Chypre										
Consumption *	25	27	28	30	32	35	30	30	50	40
Consumption per cap.(kg)	36	38	39	42	44	49	42	42	69	56
Georgia Géorgie										
Production	...	...	2	1	0	0	0	0	0	0
Consumption *	...	...	153	100	60	70	90	120	180	200
Consumption per cap.(kg)	...	...	28	18	11	13	17	22	33	36
India Inde										
Production	12 068	13 113	13 873	* 11 750	11 745	15 337	16 892	14 440	14 281	17 406
Consumption	11 075	11 721	12 387	* 12 989	* 13 700	* 13 900	15 254	14 971	15 272	* 15 750
Consumption per cap.(kg)	13	14	14	15	15	15	16	16	15	14
Indonesia Indonésie										
Production	2 126	2 259	2 313	2 490	2 461	2 103	2 100	2 189	1 493	1 490
Consumption	2 389	2 526	2 441	2 724	2 941	3 341	3 074	3 350	2 736	* 2 750
Consumption per cap.(kg)	15	14	13	15	15	17	16	17	13	13
Iran (Islamic Rep. of) Iran (Rép. islamique d')										
Production *	631	813	933	930	902	905	692	848	863	940
Consumption *	1 200	1 400	1 500	1 550	1 600	1 675	1 750	1 800	1 800	1 900
Consumption per cap.(kg)	22	25	26	27	27	27	29	30	28	29
Iraq Iraq										
Consumption *	450	300	325	350	375	285	250	350	350	400
Consumption per cap.(kg)	25	16	17	18	19	14	12	16	16	18
Israel Israël										
Production	...	0	0	0	0	0	0	0	0	0
Consumption *	265	280	295	305	315	320	325	330	330	335
Consumption per cap.(kg)	57	57	58	58	58	58	57	56	55	54
Japan Japon										
Production	982	1 005	1 023	861	826	870	882	783	870	913
Consumption	2 833	2 846	2 773	2 678	2 657	2 600	2 579	2 471	2 427	2 541
Consumption per cap.(kg)	23	23	22	22	21	21	21	20	19	20
Jordan Jordanie										
Consumption	* 170	* 175	* 185	171	183	174	170	* 170	* 150	* 180
Consumption per cap.(kg)	40	39	40	35	35	32	30	28	24	27

37

Sugar
Production and consumption: thousand metric tons; consumption per capita: kilograms [*cont.*]

Sucre
Production et consommation : milliers de tonnes ; consommation par habitant : kilogrammes [*suite*]

Country or area Pays ou zone	1990	1991	1992	1993	1994	1995	1996	1997	1998	1999
Kazakhstan Kazakhstan										
Production	...	...	* 105	* 100	* 87	45	* 84	* 87	* 85	* 91
Consumption *	...	...	495	465	400	400	380	380	380	340
Consumption per cap.(kg)	...	...	29	28	24	24	23	24	25	22
Korea, Dem. P. R. Corée, R.p. dém. de										
Consumption	120	120	125	* 125	* 81	* 55	* 55	* 48	* 30	* 50
Consumption per cap.(kg)	6	5	6	5	3	2	2	2	1	2
Korea, Republic of Corée, République de										
Consumption [6]	817	857	860	852	945	1 041	1 107	1 113	986	814
Consumption per cap.(kg)	19	20	20	19	19	23	25	24	21	18
Kuwait Koweït										
Consumption *	60	40	48	50	55	60	65	65	70	70
Consumption per cap.(kg)	28	19	34	34	34	36	37	35	37	35
Kyrgyzstan Kirghizistan										
Production	...	...	* 15	* 10	* 23	* 35	* 35	26	36	45
Consumption *	...	...	135	145	130	125	125	110	110	100
Consumption per cap.(kg)	...	...	30	32	28	27	27	24	23	20
Lao People's Dem. Rep. Rép. dém. pop. lao										
Consumption *	7	8	9	12	14	15	15	15	16	20
Consumption per cap.(kg)	2	2	2	3	3	3	3	3	3	4
Lebanon Liban										
Production	...	...	5	19	23	29	30	32	37	40
Consumption	* 110	* 115	* 115	* 113	* 110	* 113	109	96	126	150
Consumption per cap.(kg)	43	44	43	40	38	37	35	28	38	43
Malaysia Malaisie										
Production *	110	105	105	105	110	110	107	108	100	107
Consumption *	670	700	720	800	875	950	1 025	1 100	1 000	1 050
Consumption per cap.(kg)	38	39	39	42	45	47	49	51	45	46
Maldives Maldives										
Consumption	7	8	9	9	9	8	8	7	8	5
Consumption per cap.(kg)	41	36	39	38	36	31	30	25	27	16
Mongolia Mongolie										
Consumption	50	55	50	45	43	45	40	40	19	10
Consumption per cap.(kg)	23	25	22	19	18	19	16	16	8	4
Myanmar Myanmar										
Production	38	35	50	47	48	42	46	55	51	43
Consumption *	34	36	42	47	50	50	55	50	31	69
Consumption per cap.(kg)	1	1	1	1	1	1	1	1	1	1
Nepal Népal										
Production	15	25	20	25	25	20	25	20	15	15
Consumption	40	40	40	41	37	35	28	20	50	40
Consumption per cap.(kg)	2	2	2	2	2	2	1	1	2	1
Pakistan Pakistan										
Production	1 930	2 227	2 543	2 750	3 196	3 116	2 662	2 914	* 3 909	3 712
Consumption	2 290	2 555	2 670	2 747	2 945	2 971	3 033	3 105	3 139	* 3 250
Consumption per cap.(kg)	20	21	22	22	23	23	23	23	24	26
Philippines Philippines										
Production	1 686	1 911	1 919	2 091	2 098	1 562	1 895	1 954	1 549	1 913
Consumption	1 582	1 565	1 643	1 739	1 922	1 765	1 956	1 959	1 958	1 854
Consumption per cap.(kg)	26	25	26	27	29	26	27	28	27	25
Saudi Arabia Arabie saoudite										
Consumption *	475	475	500	520	535	550	550	550	550	520
Consumption per cap.(kg)	32	29	30	30	31	31	30	30	29	27
Singapore Singapour										
Consumption *	195	200	210	210	250	250	280	290	250	285
Consumption per cap.(kg)	72	73	75	73	85	84	92	93	79	88
Sri Lanka Sri Lanka										
Production	* 57	67	60	69	* 70	* 70	* 73	63	20	19
Consumption *	350	360	360	405	450	500	525	550	550	550
Consumption per cap.(kg)	21	21	21	23	25	28	29	30	29	29
Syrian Arab Republic Rép. arabe syrienne										
Production	* 50	195	193	199	198	172	197	191	107	* 102
Consumption	395	* 430	* 450	* 550	* 600	* 650	* 700	* 750	* 750	* 750
Consumption per cap.(kg)	33	34	39	41	43	45	48	50	48	46

37

Sugar
Production and consumption: thousand metric tons; consumption per capita: kilograms [cont.]
Sucre
Production et consommation : milliers de tonnes ; consommation par habitant : kilogrammes [suite]

Country or area Pays ou zone	1990	1991	1992	1993	1994	1995	1996	1997	1998	1999
Tajikistan Tadjikistan										
Consumption *	...	...	110	115	100	95	80	70	65	60
Consumption per cap.(kg)	...	...	20	20	17	16	14	12	11	10
Thailand Thaïlande										
Production	3 542	4 248	5 078	3 825	4 168	5 447	6 154	6 243	4 143	5 456
Consumption	1 105	1 189	1 264	1 368	1 480	1 645	1 706	1 829	1 834	1 776
Consumption per cap.(kg)	20	21	22	23	25	27	28	30	30	28
Turkey Turquie										
Production	1 565	1 983	1 961	1 894	1 877	1 405	2 002	2 187	2 784	2 491
Consumption	1 715	1 737	* 1 752	* 1 810	* 1 795	* 1 800	* 1 900	2 107	2 074	1 836
Consumption per cap.(kg)	31	30	30	30	29	29	30	34	33	29
Turkmenistan Turkménistan										
Consumption *	...	...	100	105	95	80	75	70	70	70
Consumption per cap.(kg)	...	...	26	27	24	20	16	16	16	16
Uzbekistan Ouzbékistan										
Production	...	...	...	...	...	...	...	...	11	* 20
Consumption *	...	...	475	450	375	360	350	350	350	300
Consumption per cap.(kg)	...	...	22	21	17	16	15	15	15	12
Viet Nam Viet Nam										
Production	* 465	* 475	* 495	* 510	* 475	* 525	* 550	* 559	657	* 878
Consumption *	520	510	520	570	590	625	625	625	675	700
Consumption per cap.(kg)	8	8	8	8	8	8	8	8	9	9
Yemen Yémen										
Consumption *	...	250	285	300	285	285	350	375	375	375
Consumption per cap.(kg)		22	24	24	23	22	22	27	26	26
Europe · Europe										
Albania Albanie										
Production	17	* 15	* 17	* 10	* 10	* 10	9	* 3	* 3	* 3
Consumption	70	* 68	* 65	* 85	* 80	* 80	* 80	* 65	* 65	* 65
Consumption per cap.(kg)	22	21	19	25	24	24	24	20	20	20
Austria Autriche										
Production	432	507	436	497	501	* 481[1]	* 535[1]	* 529[1]	* 533[1]	* 545[1]
Consumption [7]	396	425	426	412	406	...	...	...	...	...
Consumption per cap.(kg)	51	54	54	52	50	...	...	...	...	...
Belarus Bélarus										
Production	...	...	106	129	134	139	144	179	180	151
Consumption	...	...	345	337	376	355	358	380	4058	357
Consumption per cap.(kg)	...	...	34	33	27	34	35	37	40	35
Belgium−Luxembourg [1] Belgique−Luxembourg [1]										
Production	1 146	1 049	1 039	1 118	1 005	999	1 036	1 106	* 912	* 1 187
Bosnia−Herzegovina Bosnie−Herzégovine										
Production *	...	...	...	25	15	10	15	15	10	10
Consumption *	...	...	...	30	30	30	30	45	85	100
Consumption per cap.(kg)	...	...	...	7	7	7	7	10	19	22
Bulgaria Bulgarie										
Production *	35	65	35	15	10	15	7	6	5	2
Consumption	289	160	* 250	* 250	* 250	* 260	* 260	* 260	* 260	* 225
Consumption per cap.(kg)	18	18	29	30	30	31	31	31	32	27
Croatia Croatie										
Production	...	...	...	86	125	191	212	154	151	114
Consumption *	...	...	...	150	155	200	220	220	220	180
Consumption per cap.(kg)	...	...	...	31	32	42	46	48	46	38
former Czechoslovakia † l'ex−Tchécoslovaquie †										
Production	717	* 790	743	...	...	...	...	...	...	...
Consumption	741	* 800	* 795	...	...	...	...	...	...	...
Consumption per cap.(kg)	48	51	51	...	...	...	...	...	...	...
Czech Republic République tchèque										
Production	...	...	...	563	465	550	654	648	535	420
Consumption	...	...	...	* 485	435	* 435	412	* 425	438	* 450
Consumption per cap.(kg)	...	...	...	47	42	42	40	41	43	44
Denmark [1] Danemark [1]										
Production	572	527	446	542	510	448	536	603	585	* 601
Estonia Estonie										
Consumption	...	...	* 40	* 40	* 40	* 40	37	* 50	* 55	* 80
Consumption per cap.(kg)	...	...	26	26	26	27	25	35	38	55

37

Sugar
Production and consumption: thousand metric tons; consumption per capita: kilograms [cont.]
Sucre
Production et consommation : milliers de tonnes ; consommation par habitant : kilogrammes [suite]

Country or area Pays ou zone	1990	1991	1992	1993	1994	1995	1996	1997	1998	1999
Finland Finlande										
Production [9]	169	163	153	154	113	164[1]	135[1]	175[1]	125[1]	* 175[1]
Consumption [10]	189	213	227	242	219	...	...	...	...	...
Consumption per cap.(kg)	38	42	45	48	43	...	...	...	...	...
France [1] France [1]										
Production	4 736	4 413	4 723	4 724	4 364	4 564	4 543	5 134	4 637	4 914
Germany [1] Allemagne [1]										
Production	4 675	4 251	4 401	4 359	3 672	3 826	4 203	4 045	4 037	4 300
Gibraltar Gibraltar										
Consumption	3	3	3	3	4	4	4	4	3	...
Consumption per cap.(kg)	75	79	76	74	81	100	100	93	70	63
Greece [1] Grèce [1]										
Production	304	262	320	* 333	* 271	* 312	* 288	* 396	* 217	* 252
Hungary Hongrie										
Production	580	* 700	391	248	434	515	554	460	461	446
Consumption	657	575	608	382	398	430	462	448	386	399
Consumption per cap.(kg)	61	56	59	37	39	42	45	44	39	40
Iceland Islande										
Consumption	* 14	* 14	* 15	* 15	16	* 16	* 15	* 13	* 13	* 12
Consumption per cap.(kg)	54	54	58	58	58	57	50	48	47	48
Ireland [1] Irlande [1]										
Production *	245	232	242	191	230	242	247	223	228	235
Italy [1] Italie [1]										
Production	1 585	1 641	2 032	1 542	1 621	1 621	1 561	1 891	* 1 735	* 1 851
Latvia Lettonie										
Production	...	...	* 30	* 35	* 25	* 35	* 40	* 49	71	* 70
Consumption *	...	...	151	145	140	135	130	150	150	140
Consumption per cap.(kg)	...	...	57	56	55	54	52	62	62	57
Lithuania Lituanie										
Production	...	...	85	* 70	59	105	* 75	117	137	121
Consumption	...	...	116	* 110	* 105	104	* 125	98	119	* 125
Consumption per cap.(kg)	...	...	31	30	28	28	34	27	32	34
Malta Malte										
Consumption	18	13	17	17	* 18	* 19	* 20	* 20	* 20	* 22
Consumption per cap.(kg)	51	37	46	47	49	51	54	53	53	60
Netherlands [1] Pays–Bas [1]										
Production *	1 304	1 137	1 295	1 232	1 051	1 074	1 125	1 120	896	1 215
Norway Norvège										
Consumption	171	177	178	177	184	177	* 180	* 185	* 190	* 190
Consumption per cap.(kg)	40	42	41	41	43	41	41	42	42	42
Poland Pologne										
Production	2 142	1 778	1 595	2 155	1 503	1 734	2 380	2 112	2 242	1 968
Consumption	1 624	1 660	1 618	1 691	* 1 700	* 1 700	* 1 700	* 1 750	1 708	* 1 773
Consumption per cap.(kg)	43	43	42	44	44	44	44	45	44	46
Portugal [1] Portugal [1]										
Production *	2	1	2	4	6	6	3	71	66	76
Republic of Moldova République de Moldova										
Production	...	...	* 180	* 220	167	215	231	203	186	108
Consumption *	...	...	175	175	175	175	175	175	175	100
Consumption per cap.(kg)	...	...	40	40	40	40	40	41	41	23
Romania Roumanie										
Production	408	344	280	141	206	202	226	204	189	86
Consumption *	555	565	615	475	480	480	480	480	480	480
Consumption per cap.(kg)	24	24	24	21	21	21	21	21	21	21
Russian Federation Fédération de Russie										
Production	...	...	2 437	* 2 717	* 1 650	2 241	1 851	1 337	1 370	1 651
Consumption *	...	...	6 145	5 034	4 957	5 108	5 235	5 308	5 450	5 565
Consumption per cap.(kg)	...	...	41	34	34	35	35	36	37	38

37
Sugar
Production and consumption: thousand metric tons; consumption per capita: kilograms [*cont.*]
Sucre
Production et consommation : milliers de tonnes ; consommation par habitant : kilogrammes [*suite*]

Country or area Pays ou zone	1990	1991	1992	1993	1994	1995	1996	1997	1998	1999
Slovakia Slovaquie										
Production	...	...	...	* 150	* 130	* 145	* 140	237	170	213
Consumption *	...	...	...	150	150	175	200	220	220	220
Consumption per cap.(kg)	...	...	...	28	28	33	37	42	41	41
Slovenia Slovénie										
Production *	...	...	...	41	45	65	71	67	51	60
Consumption *	...	...	...	100	100	120	120	120	120	120
Consumption per cap.(kg)	...	...	...	50	52	61	60	58	61	56
Spain [1] Espagne [1]										
Production	994	949	1 032	1 237	1 116	1 111	1 228	1 142	1 210	1 074
Sweden Suède										
Production [11]	445	266	333	413	370	357[1]	398[1]	396[1]	400[1]	* 467[1]
Consumption	379	380	382	388	457	...	...	...	...	...
Consumption per cap.(kg)	44	44	44	44	52	...	...	...	...	...
Switzerland Suisse										
Production	160	136	137	* 150	* 130	* 140	* 194	* 200	191	177
Consumption	305	307	311	* 310	* 310	* 315	* 310	* 315	206	328
Consumption per cap.(kg)	46	46	46	45	44	45	44	44	29	45
TFYR Macedonia L'ex–R.y. Macédoine										
Production	...	...	...	7	6	7	18	* 15	40	43
Consumption *	...	...	...	35	40	45	50	50	60	90
Consumption per cap.(kg)	...	...	...	17	19	21	25	23	27	40
Ukraine Ukraine										
Production	...	...	3 824	* 4 160	3 632	3 801	* 2 935	* 2 170	2 041	1 640
Consumption	...	...	2 881	* 2 575	2 492	* 2 200	* 2 100	* 1 800	1 739	* 1 700
Consumption per cap.(kg)	...	...	55	49	48	43	41	35	35	35
United Kingdom [1] Royaume–Uni [1]										
Production	1 349	1 326	1 476	1 436	1 373	* 1 326	1 605	1 592	1 439	1 500
Yugoslavia Yougoslavie										
Production	...	* 900	* 500	* 127	* 210	* 156	* 285	239	213	248
Consumption	...	* 810	* 725	* 350	* 350	* 300	* 300	239	* 300	* 300
Consumption per cap.(kg)	...	...	69	33	33	29	28	28	28	28
Yugoslavia, SFR † Yougoslavie, Rfs †										
Production	* 945	900	...	...	...	...	...	...	...	...
Consumption *	950	810	...	...	...	...	...	...	...	...
Consumption per cap.(kg)	40	34	...	...	...	...	...	...	...	...
			Oceania · Océanie							
Australia Australie										
Production	3 612	3 195	4 363	4 488	5 222	5 119	5 618	5 883	5 085	5 514
Consumption	864	835	829	909	911	926	976	1 003	1 003	1 005
Consumption per cap.(kg)	51	48	47	52	51	51	53	54	53	53
Fiji Fidji										
Production	378	456	451	451	543	458	474	369	278	377
Consumption [12]	40	44	45	46	43	48	48	51	44	38
Consumption per cap.(kg)	54	59	60	60	56	63	62	66	56	50
New Zealand Nouvelle–Zélande										
Consumption	* 175	* 175	* 178	* 180	* 183	* 185	* 200	* 220	158	198
Consumption per cap.(kg)	52	52	52	52	52	52	56	60	42	53
Papua New Guinea Papouasie–Nvl–Guinée										
Production	28	* 35	* 30	* 30	* 35	* 35	* 35	39	41	47
Consumption	27	* 27	* 27	* 28	* 27	* 27	* 30	37	36	38
Consumption per cap.(kg)	7	7	7	7	7	7	7	9	8	9
Samoa Samoa										
Production	2	2	2	2	2	2	2	2	2	...
Consumption	3	3	3	3	4	4	3	3	3	2
Consumption per cap.(kg)	13	13	12	12	14	14	10	10	10	8
			former USSR · ancienne URSS							
former USSR † l'ex–URSS †										
Production	9 159	6 898	...	...	...	...	...	...	...	...
Consumption *	13 400	11 908	...	...	...	...	...	...	...	...
Consumption per cap.(kg)	46	41	...	...	...	...	...	...	...	...

37
Sugar
Production and consumption: thousand metric tons; consumption per capita: kilograms [*cont.*]
Sucre
Production et consommation : milliers de tonnes ; consommation par habitant : kilogrammes [*suite*]

Source:
International Sugar Organization (ISO), London, "Sugar Yearbook 1999" and the ISO database.

† For information on recent changes in country or area nomenclature pertaining to former Czechoslovakia, Germany, Hong Kong Special Administrative Region (SAR) of China, Macao Special Administrative Region (SAR) of China, SFR of Yugoslavia and the former USSR, see Annex I – Country or area nomenclature, regional and other groupings.

†† For statistical purposes, the data for China do not include those for Hong Kong Special Administrative Region (Hong Kong SAR), Macao Special Administrative Region (Macao SAR) and Taiwan province of China.

1 Source: Food and Agriculture Organization of the United Nations.
2 3,268 t lost in fire.
3 Including non–human consumption: 1984– 31,191t; 1985– 77,946t; 1986– 8,831t; 1987– 64,646t; 1988– 46,834t; 1989– 167,173t; 1990– 129,608t; 1991– 92,446t; 1993– 94,156t; 1994– 92,313t.
4 FAO estimate.
5 Including non–human consumption: 1983 – 6,710t; 1984 – 19,797t; 1985–79,908t; 1986– 98,608t; 1987– 147,262t; 1988– 122,058t; 1989– 52,230t; 1991– 13,541t; 1994– 12,178t; 1995– 10,211t; 1996– 14,648t.
6 Including consumption of mono–sodium glutamate, lysine and other products: 1987– 44,600t; 1988– 92,200t; 1989– 94,500t; 1990– 89,400t; 1991– 77,300t; 1992– 75,800t; 1993– 89,800t; 1994– 170,384t; 1995– 200,863t; 1996– 257,763t; 1997– 257,310t; 1998– 258,247t.
7 Including non–human consumption: 1981 – 7,255t; 1982 – 11,501t; 1983–4,988t; 1984– 9,002t; 1986– 7,862t; 1987– 9,989t; 1988– 12,384t; 1989– 8,288t; 1990– 5,387t; 1991– 11,799t; 1993– 9,348t.
8 Including non–human consumption: 1998 – 15,652t.
9 Of which 1,041 t of sugar produced from imported Estonian beet in 1993 and 1,145 t in 1994.
10 Including non–human consumption: 1980–22,850t; 1981–18,840t; 1982–17,270t; 1983–15,075t; 1984–16,775t; 1985–12,812t; 1986–26,552t; 1987–31,312t; 1988–20,912t.
11 Including sales from government stocks: 1983–4,238t; 1984–3,602t; 1985–3,181t; 1988–4,324t; 1989–2,771t.
12 Including 11,572 t sold to other Pacific Island nations in 1994; 12,520t in 1995; 14,154t in 1996; 13,109t in 1997; 5,305t in 1998.

Source:
Organisation internationale du sucre (OIS), Londres, "Annuaire du sucre 1999" et la base de données de l'OIS.

† Pour les modifications récentes de nomenclature de pays ou de zone concernant l'Allemagne, Hong Kong, région administrative spéciale (RAS) de Chine, Macao, région administrative spéciale (RAS) de Chine, l'ex–Tchécoslovaquie, l'ex–URSS et l'ex–Rfs de Yougoslavie, voir annexe I – Nomenclature des pays ou des zones, groupements régionaux et autres groupements.

†† Les données statistiques relatives à la Chine ne comprennent pas celles qui concernent la région administrative spéciale de Hong Kong (la RAS de Hong Kong), la région administrative spéciale de Macao (la RAS de Macao) et la province chinoise de Taiwan.

1 Source: Organisation des Nations Unies pour l'alimentation et l'agriculture.
2 Dont 3 268 tonnes détruites par le feu.
3 Dont la consommation non humaine : 1984– 31 119t; 1985– 77 946t; 1986– 8 831t; 1987– 64 646t; 1988– 46 834t; 1989– 167 173t; 1990– 129 608t; 1991– 92 446t; 1993– 94 156t; 1994– 82 313t.
4 Estimation de FAO.
5 Dont la consommation non humaine : 1983 – 6 701t; 1984– 19 797t; 1985– 79 908t; 1986– 98 608t; 1987– 147 262t; 1988– 122 058t; 1989– 52 230t; 1991– 13 541t; 1994– 12 178t; 1995– 10 211t; 1996– 14 648t.
6 Y compris la consommation des produits du glutamate monosodium, lysine et autres: 1987– 44 600t ; 1988– 92 200t; 1989– 94 500t ; 1990– 89 400t ; 1991– 77 300t ; 1992– 75 800t ; 1993– 89 800t ; 1994– 170 384t ; 1995– 200 863t; 1996– 257 763t; 1997– 257 310t; 1998– 258 247t.
7 Y compris la consommation non humaine : 1981–7 255t; 1982– 11 501t; 1983–4 988t; 1986– 7 862t; 1987– 9 989t; 1988– 12 384t; 1989– 8 288t; 1990– 5 387t; 1991– 11 799t; 1993– 9 348t.
8 Dont la consommation non humaine: 1998 – 15 652t.
9 Dont 1 041 tonnes de sucre à l'aide de betteraves importées d'Estonie en 1993 et 1 145 t en 1994.
10 Dont la consommation non humaine : 1980–22 850t; 1981– 18 640t; 1982–17 270t; 1983– 15 075t; 1984–16 775t; 1985– 12 812t; 1986–26 552t; 1987–31 312t; 1988–20 912t.
11 Dont les ventes par prélèvement dans les réserves publiques : 1983–4 238t; 1984–3 602t; 1985–3 181t; 1988–4 324t; 1989– 2 771t.
12 Y compris 11 572 tonnes vendues à autres îles pacifiques en 1994; 12 520t en 1995; 14 154t en 1996; 13 109t en 1997; et 5 305t en 1998.

38

Meat
Viande

Production: thousand metric tons
Production : milliers de tonnes

Region, country or area Région, pays ou zone	1990	1991	1992	1993	1994	1995	1996	1997	1998	1999
World *Monde*	135 249	137 139	138 525	140 685	144 206	146 332	146 874	151 916	157 631	158 674
Beef,veal & buffalo Boeuf,veau et buffle	55 644	56 292	55 494	55 040	55 848	56 819	57 385	58 137	58 317	58 951
Pork Porc	69 908	70 953	73 088	75 480	77 963	78 883	78 830	82 731	88 000	88 430
Mutton,lamb & goat Mouton,agneau et caprin	9 697	9 894	9 943	10 165	10 395	10 631	10 658	11 048	11 314	11 294
Africa Afrique	5 633	5 820	6 000	6 043	6 004	6 136	6 297	6 641	6 703	6 850
Beef,veal & buffalo Boeuf,veau et buffle	3 480	3 604	3 682	3 625	3 521	3 561	3 660	3 779	3 783	3 891
Pork Porc	604	624	693	743	759	790	794	956	977	990
Mutton,lamb & goat Mouton,agneau et caprin	1 549	1 591	1 625	1 675	1 725	1 785	1 843	1 906	1 943	1 970
Algeria Algérie	232	247	260	276	279	279	289	281	282	293
Beef,veal & buffalo Boeuf,veau et buffle	90	94	97	98	101	101	99	102	103	117
Mutton,lamb & goat Mouton,agneau et caprin	142	152	164	178	178	178	190	179	179	175
Angola Angola	86	88	95	96	96	97	107	115	123	124
Beef,veal & buffalo Boeuf,veau et buffle	59	60	66	66	65	65	71	77	85	85
Pork Porc	22	23	24	25	25	26	28	29	29	29
Mutton,lamb & goat Mouton,agneau et caprin	5	5	5	6	6	6	8	9	9	10
Benin Bénin	26	27	28	29	30	32	33	34	33	36
Beef,veal & buffalo Boeuf,veau et buffle	15	16	16	16	17	18	19	20	20	23
Pork Porc	5	6	6	6	6	7	8	8	6	6
Mutton,lamb & goat Mouton,agneau et caprin	6	6	6	6	6	7	6	6	7	6
Botswana Botswana	50	54	56	55	41	53	51	45	47	48
Beef,veal & buffalo Boeuf,veau et buffle	42	44	47	49	35	46	44	39	40	41
Pork Porc	1	1	0	0	0	0	1	0	0	0
Mutton,lamb & goat Mouton,agneau et caprin	7	9	8	7	6	6	6	7	6	6
Burkina Faso Burkina Faso	73	75	75	77	77	78	88	91	88	88
Beef,veal & buffalo Boeuf,veau et buffle	37	38	39	40	40	40	47	50	45	45
Pork Porc	6	6	6	6	6	6	7	8	8	8
Mutton,lamb & goat Mouton,agneau et caprin	29	30	31	31	31	32	33	34	35	35
Burundi Burundi	23	22	24	25	23	22	22	18	19	18
Beef,veal & buffalo Boeuf,veau et buffle	12	12	14	14	12	12	13	10	11	9

38
Meat
Production: thousand metric tons [cont.]
Viande
Production : milliers de tonnes [suite]

Region, country or area Région, pays ou zone	1990	1991	1992	1993	1994	1995	1996	1997	1998	1999
Pork Porc	6	5	5	5	5	5	5	4	4	4
Mutton,lamb & goat Mouton,agneau et caprin	5	5	5	6	6	5	5	4	3	4
Cameroon **Cameroun**	**116**	**119**	**122**	**126**	**129**	**132**	**134**	**137**	**139**	**139**
Beef,veal & buffalo Boeuf,veau et buffle	72	74	77	79	81	83	85	88	90	90
Pork Porc	16	17	17	17	17	18	18	18	18	18
Mutton,lamb & goat Mouton,agneau et caprin	27	28	28	30	30	31	31	31	31	31
Cape Verde **Cap-Vert**	**5**	**5**	**5**	**8**	**6**	**9**	**4**	**6**	**8**	**7**
Beef,veal & buffalo Boeuf,veau et buffle	0	0	0	0	0	0	1	1	1	0
Pork Porc	4	4	4	7	5	8	3	5	6	6
Mutton,lamb & goat Mouton,agneau et caprin	0	0	0	1	1	0	0	0	1	1
Central African Rep. **Rép. centrafricaine**	**54**	**56**	**58**	**60**	**61**	**65**	**81**	**70**	**72**	**72**
Beef,veal & buffalo Boeuf,veau et buffle	41	42	44	45	45	48	61	50	51	51
Pork Porc	8	8	8	9	9	10	11	12	12	12
Mutton,lamb & goat Mouton,agneau et caprin	5	6	6	6	7	8	8	8	9	9
Chad **Tchad**	**55**	**58**	**60**	**57**	**58**	**58**	**63**	**64**	**66**	**66**
Beef,veal & buffalo Boeuf,veau et buffle	38	39	40	36	36	36	38	39	40	40
Pork Porc	0	0	0	0	0	0	0	0	1	1
Mutton,lamb & goat Mouton,agneau et caprin	17	19	20	21	21	22	24	25	26	26
Comoros **Comores**	**1**	**1**	**1**	**1**	**1**	**1**	**1**	**1**	**1**	**1**
Beef,veal & buffalo Boeuf,veau et buffle	1	1	1	1	1	1	1	1	1	1
Congo **Congo**	**5**	**5**	**5**	**5**	**5**	**5**	**5**	**5**	**5**	**5**
Beef,veal & buffalo Boeuf,veau et buffle	2	2	2	2	2	2	2	2	2	2
Pork Porc	2	2	2	2	2	2	2	2	2	2
Mutton,lamb & goat Mouton,agneau et caprin	1	1	1	1	1	1	1	1	1	1
Côte d'Ivoire **Côte d'Ivoire**	**54**	**56**	**58**	**59**	**60**	**64**	**60**	**61**	**69**	**69**
Beef,veal & buffalo Boeuf,veau et buffle	31	33	34	34	34	36	37	38	46	46
Pork Porc	14	15	15	16	16	19	14	13	13	13
Mutton,lamb & goat Mouton,agneau et caprin	9	8	9	9	9	9	10	10	10	10
Dem. Rep. of the Congo **Rép. dém. du Congo**	**80**	**79**	**82**	**84**	**85**	**84**	**82**	**82**	**82**	**80**

38
Meat
Production: thousand metric tons [cont.]
Viande
Production : milliers de tonnes [suite]

Region, country or area Région, pays ou zone	1990	1991	1992	1993	1994	1995	1996	1997	1998	1999
Beef,veal & buffalo										
Boeuf,veau et buffle	22	19	20	20	19	17	17	16	14	15
Pork										
Porc	39	39	41	42	43	44	42	43	43	41
Mutton,lamb & goat										
Mouton,agneau et caprin	20	20	21	22	23	23	23	24	24	24
Djibouti										
Djibouti	**6**	**7**	**7**	**8**	**8**	**8**	**8**	**8**	**8**	**8**
Beef,veal & buffalo										
Boeuf,veau et buffle	2	3	3	3	3	3	3	4	4	4
Mutton,lamb & goat										
Mouton,agneau et caprin	4	4	4	4	4	4	4	4	4	4
Egypt										
Egypte	**396**	**426**	**436**	**464**	**492**	**511**	**572**	**658**	**607**	**653**
Beef,veal & buffalo										
Boeuf,veau et buffle	304	335	343	361	382	394	453	536	483	527
Pork										
Porc	2	3	3	3	3	3	3	3	3	3
Mutton,lamb & goat										
Mouton,agneau et caprin	90	88	90	100	107	114	117	120	121	123
Eritrea										
Erythrée	...	...	...	**19**	**20**	**20**	**21**	**22**	**22**	**24**
Beef,veal & buffalo										
Boeuf,veau et buffle	...	...	...	9	10	10	11	11	12	13
Mutton,lamb & goat										
Mouton,agneau et caprin	...	...	...	9	10	10	10	10	11	11
Ethiopia incl. Eritrea										
Ethiopie comp. Erythrée	**394**	**395**	**394**	...	...	...	...	...	...	...
Beef,veal & buffalo										
Boeuf,veau et buffle	245	245	244	...	...	...	...	...	...	...
Pork										
Porc	1	1	1	...	...	...	...	...	...	...
Mutton,lamb & goat										
Mouton,agneau et caprin	148	149	149	...	...	...	...	...	...	...
Ethiopia										
Ethiopie	...	...	...	**370**	**374**	**379**	**412**	**415**	**420**	**436**
Beef,veal & buffalo										
Boeuf,veau et buffle	...	...	...	230	230	235	267	270	274	290
Pork										
Porc	...	...	...	1	1	1	1	1	1	1
Mutton,lamb & goat										
Mouton,agneau et caprin	...	...	...	139	143	143	144	144	144	145
Gabon										
Gabon	**4**	**4**	**5**	**5**	**5**	**5**	**5**	**5**	**5**	**5**
Beef,veal & buffalo										
Boeuf,veau et buffle	1	1	1	1	1	1	1	1	1	1
Pork										
Porc	2	3	3	3	3	3	3	3	3	3
Mutton,lamb & goat										
Mouton,agneau et caprin	1	1	1	1	1	1	1	1	1	1
Gambia										
Gambie	**4**	**4**	**4**	**4**	**4**	**5**	**5**	**5**	**5**	**5**
Beef,veal & buffalo										
Boeuf,veau et buffle	3	3	3	3	3	3	3	3	3	3
Mutton,lamb & goat										
Mouton,agneau et caprin	1	1	1	1	1	1	1	2	2	2
Ghana										
Ghana	**41**	**42**	**40**	**40**	**41**	**40**	**40**	**33**	**35**	**35**

38
Meat
Production: thousand metric tons [*cont.*]
Viande
Production : milliers de tonnes [*suite*]

Region, country or area Région, pays ou zone	1990	1991	1992	1993	1994	1995	1996	1997	1998	1999
Beef,veal & buffalo Boeuf,veau et buffle	20	21	20	20	20	21	21	12	14	14
Pork Porc	11	10	9	9	9	8	7	8	8	8
Mutton,lamb & goat Mouton,agneau et caprin	11	11	11	11	11	11	12	13	13	13
Guinea **Guinée**	**13**	**14**	**15**	**16**	**17**	**20**	**20**	**21**	**22**	**22**
Beef,veal & buffalo Boeuf,veau et buffle	10	10	11	12	12	15	15	15	15	15
Pork Porc	1	1	1	1	1	1	1	1	2	2
Mutton,lamb & goat Mouton,agneau et caprin	3	3	3	3	3	4	4	4	5	5
Guinea-Bissau **Guinée-Bissau**	**13**	**14**	**14**	**15**	**15**	**15**	**16**	**16**	**16**	**16**
Beef,veal & buffalo Boeuf,veau et buffle	3	3	4	4	4	4	4	4	4	4
Pork Porc	9	9	9	10	10	10	10	10	10	10
Mutton,lamb & goat Mouton,agneau et caprin	1	1	1	1	1	1	1	2	2	2
Kenya **Kenya**	**312**	**312**	**297**	**281**	**286**	**297**	**318**	**328**	**302**	**312**
Beef,veal & buffalo Boeuf,veau et buffle	250	250	238	225	230	240	260	270	243	252
Pork Porc	5	5	5	5	5	5	6	6	6	6
Mutton,lamb & goat Mouton,agneau et caprin	56	56	53	51	51	51	52	52	54	54
Lesotho **Lesotho**	**23**	**22**	**23**	**25**	**22**	**23**	**21**	**24**	**20**	**20**
Beef,veal & buffalo Boeuf,veau et buffle	13	13	14	15	13	14	12	15	12	12
Pork Porc	3	2	2	3	2	3	3	3	3	3
Mutton,lamb & goat Mouton,agneau et caprin	7	7	7	7	7	6	6	6	5	5
Liberia **Libéria**	**6**	**6**	**6**	**6**	**6**	**6**	**6**	**6**	**6**	**6**
Beef,veal & buffalo Boeuf,veau et buffle	1	1	1	1	1	1	1	1	1	1
Pork Porc	4	4	4	4	4	4	4	4	4	4
Mutton,lamb & goat Mouton,agneau et caprin	1	1	1	1	1	1	1	1	1	1
Libyan Arab Jamah. **Jamah. arabe libyenne**	**53**	**60**	**56**	**61**	**55**	**68**	**74**	**88**	**101**	**102**
Beef,veal & buffalo Boeuf,veau et buffle	24	31	27	26	22	22	15	14	14	14
Mutton,lamb & goat Mouton,agneau et caprin	29	30	29	35	33	46	60	74	87	88
Madagascar **Madagascar**	**197**	**200**	**202**	**205**	**207**	**209**	**210**	**213**	**214**	**216**
Beef,veal & buffalo Boeuf,veau et buffle	143	143	144	145	145	146	147	147	148	149
Pork Porc	45	47	48	50	51	52	54	56	56	57

38

Meat
Production: thousand metric tons [*cont.*]
Viande
Production : milliers de tonnes [*suite*]

Region, country or area Région, pays ou zone	1990	1991	1992	1993	1994	1995	1996	1997	1998	1999
Mutton,lamb & goat Mouton,agneau et caprin	9	9	9	10	10	11	10	10	10	10
Malawi **Malawi**	**31**	**31**	**32**	**32**	**30**	**31**	**32**	**35**	**33**	**34**
Beef,veal & buffalo Boeuf,veau et buffle	17	17	17	18	14	14	16	18	17	18
Pork Porc	10	11	11	11	12	12	11	12	11	12
Mutton,lamb & goat Mouton,agneau et caprin	4	4	4	4	4	4	5	5	5	5
Mali **Mali**	**117**	**122**	**128**	**126**	**130**	**135**	**138**	**141**	**152**	**152**
Beef,veal & buffalo Boeuf,veau et buffle	72	74	78	81	83	85	86	86	91	91
Pork Porc	2	2	2	2	2	2	2	2	3	3
Mutton,lamb & goat Mouton,agneau et caprin	44	46	48	43	45	48	50	52	58	58
Mauritania **Mauritanie**	**38**	**41**	**38**	**29**	**30**	**31**	**35**	**35**	**34**	**33**
Beef,veal & buffalo Boeuf,veau et buffle	17	20	18	9	9	10	10	10	10	10
Mutton,lamb & goat Mouton,agneau et caprin	21	21	20	20	21	21	25	25	24	23
Mauritius **Maurice**	**3**	**3**	**4**	**4**	**4**	**4**	**4**	**4**	**4**	**4**
Beef,veal & buffalo Boeuf,veau et buffle	2	2	2	3	3	2	2	2	3	3
Pork Porc	1	1	1	1	1	1	1	1	1	1
Morocco **Maroc**	**267**	**270**	**274**	**273**	**250**	**255**	**216**	**268**	**256**	**267**
Beef,veal & buffalo Boeuf,veau et buffle	145	149	145	150	125	122	103	125	120	125
Pork Porc	1	1	1	1	1	1	1	1	1	1
Mutton,lamb & goat Mouton,agneau et caprin	122	120	128	122	125	132	112	142	135	141
Mozambique **Mozambique**	**56**	**53**	**51**	**53**	**51**	**52**	**52**	**53**	**53**	**54**
Beef,veal & buffalo Boeuf,veau et buffle	41	39	36	38	36	37	37	38	38	38
Pork Porc	12	12	12	12	12	12	12	13	13	13
Mutton,lamb & goat Mouton,agneau et caprin	3	3	3	3	3	3	3	3	3	3
Namibia **Namibie**	**57**	**66**	**67**	**69**	**70**	**63**	**61**	**47**	**53**	**52**
Beef,veal & buffalo Boeuf,veau et buffle	39	46	49	49	49	48	46	30	38	38
Pork Porc	3	2	2	2	3	3	2	2	2	2
Mutton,lamb & goat Mouton,agneau et caprin	16	18	16	18	17	13	13	15	12	12
Niger **Niger**	**61**	**57**	**66**	**67**	**68**	**70**	**72**	**74**	**75**	**77**
Beef,veal & buffalo Boeuf,veau et buffle	28	25	32	33	33	34	35	36	36	37

38

Meat
Production: thousand metric tons [cont.]
    Viande
    Production : milliers de tonnes [suite]

Region, country or area Région, pays ou zone	1990	1991	1992	1993	1994	1995	1996	1997	1998	1999
Pork										
Porc	1	1	1	1	1	1	1	1	1	1
Mutton,lamb & goat										
Mouton,agneau et caprin	31	32	33	33	34	35	36	37	38	39
Nigeria										
** Nigéria**	**499**	**538**	**588**	**677**	**710**	**722**	**782**	**972**	**994**	**1 020**
Beef,veal & buffalo										
Boeuf,veau et buffle	204	205	210	244	264	267	280	294	297	299
Pork										
Porc	131	163	204	255	265	275	284	444	457	475
Mutton,lamb & goat										
Mouton,agneau et caprin	165	170	174	178	180	180	218	234	240	246
Réunion										
** Réunion**	**9**	**10**	**11**	**11**	**12**	**12**	**12**	**14**	**14**	**14**
Beef,veal & buffalo										
Boeuf,veau et buffle	1	1	1	1	1	1	1	1	1	1
Pork										
Porc	8	9	10	10	10	10	10	12	13	13
Rwanda										
** Rwanda**	**22**	**22**	**21**	**20**	**18**	**16**	**17**	**19**	**22**	**24**
Beef,veal & buffalo										
Boeuf,veau et buffle	14	14	13	12	10	10	11	14	16	18
Pork										
Porc	3	3	3	3	3	2	2	2	2	2
Mutton,lamb & goat										
Mouton,agneau et caprin	5	5	5	5	5	3	4	4	4	4
Senegal										
** Sénégal**	**71**	**75**	**78**	**80**	**82**	**83**	**82**	**84**	**85**	**85**
Beef,veal & buffalo										
Boeuf,veau et buffle	43	44	44	45	46	46	46	48	48	48
Pork										
Porc	7	7	7	7	7	7	7	7	7	7
Mutton,lamb & goat										
Mouton,agneau et caprin	22	25	27	28	29	29	29	29	29	29
Seychelles										
** Seychelles**	**1**	**1**	**1**	**1**	**1**	**1**	**1**	**1**	**1**	**1**
Pork										
Porc	1	1	1	1	1	1	1	1	1	1
Sierra Leone										
** Sierra Leone**	**9**	**9**	**9**	**9**	**9**	**10**	**10**	**10**	**10**	**10**
Beef,veal & buffalo										
Boeuf,veau et buffle	5	5	5	6	6	6	6	6	6	6
Pork										
Porc	2	2	2	2	2	2	2	2	2	2
Mutton,lamb & goat										
Mouton,agneau et caprin	1	1	1	1	1	1	1	1	2	2
Somalia										
** Somalie**	**135**	**114**	**88**	**95**	**99**	**107**	**114**	**121**	**116**	**112**
Beef,veal & buffalo										
Boeuf,veau et buffle	46	41	36	42	44	50	54	59	56	53
Mutton,lamb & goat										
Mouton,agneau et caprin	88	73	52	53	55	57	60	61	60	59
South Africa										
** Afrique du Sud**	**959**	**981**	**1 042**	**930**	**828**	**794**	**744**	**732**	**773**	**783**
Beef,veal & buffalo										
Boeuf,veau et buffle	661	700	745	651	554	521	481	484	521	527
Pork										
Porc	131	113	130	120	119	127	128	120	124	117

38
Meat
Production: thousand metric tons [cont.]
Viande
Production : milliers de tonnes [suite]

Region, country or area Région, pays ou zone	1990	1991	1992	1993	1994	1995	1996	1997	1998	1999
Mutton,lamb & goat Mouton,agneau et caprin	168	168	167	159	155	146	135	128	128	139
Sudan **Soudan**	**323**	**361**	**379**	**394**	**417**	**462**	**469**	**478**	**492**	**499**
Beef,veal & buffalo Boeuf,veau et buffle	218	231	226	215	212	225	226	230	235	240
Mutton,lamb & goat Mouton,agneau et caprin	105	129	153	179	205	237	242	248	257	259
Swaziland **Swaziland**	**15**	**17**	**18**	**19**	**18**	**18**	**17**	**18**	**17**	**17**
Beef,veal & buffalo Boeuf,veau et buffle	11	13	14	15	14	14	13	14	13	13
Pork Porc	1	1	1	1	1	1	1	1	1	1
Mutton,lamb & goat Mouton,agneau et caprin	3	3	3	3	3	3	3	3	3	3
Togo **Togo**	**22**	**22**	**24**	**24**	**24**	**25**	**26**	**27**	**28**	**28**
Beef,veal & buffalo Boeuf,veau et buffle	5	5	5	5	5	7	7	7	7	7
Pork Porc	10	10	11	12	12	12	12	12	12	12
Mutton,lamb & goat Mouton,agneau et caprin	7	7	7	7	7	7	7	7	8	8
Tunisia **Tunisie**	**85**	**88**	**91**	**99**	**101**	**105**	**108**	**106**	**112**	**108**
Beef,veal & buffalo Boeuf,veau et buffle	39	41	44	48	49	50	52	50	53	50
Mutton,lamb & goat Mouton,agneau et caprin	46	46	47	51	52	54	56	55	58	58
Uganda **Ouganda**	**146**	**151**	**155**	**163**	**158**	**161**	**163**	**165**	**171**	**172**
Beef,veal & buffalo Boeuf,veau et buffle	81	84	86	92	84	86	88	89	93	94
Pork Porc	45	46	48	49	50	51	51	52	53	54
Mutton,lamb & goat Mouton,agneau et caprin	20	21	22	23	24	24	24	25	25	25
United Rep.Tanzania **Rép.-Unie de Tanzanie**	**235**	**238**	**241**	**247**	**250**	**251**	**254**	**257**	**259**	**260**
Beef,veal & buffalo Boeuf,veau et buffle	195	197	199	203	205	206	209	211	213	214
Pork Porc	9	9	9	9	9	10	9	9	10	10
Mutton,lamb & goat Mouton,agneau et caprin	31	32	33	34	35	36	36	36	36	37
Zambia **Zambie**	**48**	**49**	**50**	**54**	**56**	**50**	**53**	**41**	**42**	**44**
Beef,veal & buffalo Boeuf,veau et buffle	36	37	38	42	43	38	40	28	27	29
Pork Porc	9	10	9	10	10	10	10	10	10	11
Mutton,lamb & goat Mouton,agneau et caprin	2	2	2	2	3	3	3	3	4	4
Zimbabwe **Zimbabwe**	**101**	**103**	**113**	**90**	**85**	**94**	**87**	**89**	**92**	**93**

38

Meat
Production: thousand metric tons [*cont.*]
Viande
Production : milliers de tonnes [*suite*]

Region, country or area Région, pays ou zone	1990	1991	1992	1993	1994	1995	1996	1997	1998	1999
Beef,veal & buffalo										
Boeuf,veau et buffle	78	80	90	71	64	69	62	65	66	68
Pork										
Porc	11	11	11	8	10	13	13	12	13	13
Mutton,lamb & goat										
Mouton,agneau et caprin	11	11	11	11	11	11	12	12	12	13
America, North										
Amérique du Nord	**22 474**	**22 847**	**23 616**	**23 512**	**24 626**	**25 249**	**25 030**	**25 185**	**26 278**	**26 936**
Beef,veal & buffalo										
Boeuf,veau et buffle	**13 119**	**13 156**	**13 290**	**13 239**	**13 999**	**14 453**	**14 632**	**14 661**	**14 861**	**15 182**
Pork										
Porc	**9 104**	**9 434**	**10 071**	**10 024**	**10 392**	**10 571**	**10 183**	**10 313**	**11 206**	**11 550**
Mutton,lamb & goat										
Mouton,agneau et caprin	**251**	**257**	**255**	**250**	**235**	**224**	**214**	**211**	**210**	**203**
Antigua and Barbuda										
Antigua-et-Barbuda	**1**	**1**	**1**	**1**	**1**	**1**	**1**	**1**	**1**	**1**
Beef,veal & buffalo										
Boeuf,veau et buffle	1	1	1	1	1	1	1	1	1	1
Barbados										
Barbade	**5**	**5**	**5**	**5**	**5**	**5**	**5**	**5**	**5**	**5**
Beef,veal & buffalo										
Boeuf,veau et buffle	1	1	1	1	1	1	1	1	1	1
Pork										
Porc	4	4	4	4	4	4	4	4	4	4
Belize										
Belize	**3**	**3**	**3**	**3**	**3**	**3**	**3**	**3**	**2**	**2**
Beef,veal & buffalo										
Boeuf,veau et buffle	1	1	2	1	1	1	1	2	1	1
Pork										
Porc	1	1	1	1	1	1	1	1	1	1
Canada										
Canada	**2 033**	**1 973**	**2 118**	**2 065**	**2 139**	**2 222**	**2 255**	**2 343**	**2 499**	**2 746**
Beef,veal & buffalo										
Boeuf,veau et buffle	900	866	899	860	899	936	1 016	1 076	1 151	1 210
Pork										
Porc	1 124	1 096	1 208	1 194	1 229	1 276	1 228	1 257	1 338	1 525
Mutton,lamb & goat										
Mouton,agneau et caprin	9	10	11	11	11	10	11	10	10	11
Costa Rica										
Costa Rica	**102**	**111**	**100**	**102**	**115**	**116**	**117**	**106**	**97**	**99**
Beef,veal & buffalo										
Boeuf,veau et buffle	87	94	81	82	91	92	96	86	78	80
Pork										
Porc	14	17	19	20	23	24	20	20	19	19
Cuba										
Cuba	**239**	**184**	**126**	**130**	**130**	**137**	**144**	**143**	**150**	**150**
Beef,veal & buffalo										
Boeuf,veau et buffle	136	90	77	66	60	64	68	68	75	75
Pork										
Porc	101	91	47	63	69	72	74	73	73	73
Mutton,lamb & goat										
Mouton,agneau et caprin	2	2	2	1	1	1	2	2	2	2
Dominica										
Dominique	**1**	**1**	**1**	**1**	**1**	**1**	**1**	**1**	**1**	**1**
Beef,veal & buffalo										
Boeuf,veau et buffle	0	0	0	0	0	0	1	1	1	1
Dominican Republic										
Rép. dominicaine	**106**	**125**	**129**	**141**	**140**	**144**	**146**	**146**	**143**	**106**

38

Meat
Production: thousand metric tons [*cont.*]
Viande
Production : milliers de tonnes [*suite*]

Region, country or area Région, pays ou zone	1990	1991	1992	1993	1994	1995	1996	1997	1998	1999
Beef,veal & buffalo										
Boeuf,veau et buffle	82	84	83	86	81	80	80	79	77	74
Pork										
Porc	21	38	43	53	57	62	63	64	64	30
Mutton,lamb & goat										
Mouton,agneau et caprin	2	2	3	3	3	3	3	3	3	3
El Salvador										
El Salvador	**38**	**34**	**33**	**36**	**35**	**38**	**38**	**45**	**45**	**46**
Beef,veal & buffalo										
Boeuf,veau et buffle	27	24	22	25	27	27	27	35	34	34
Pork										
Porc	11	11	11	11	8	11	11	11	11	11
Guadeloupe										
Guadeloupe	**5**	**4**	**4**	**4**	**5**	**5**	**4**	**5**	**5**	**5**
Beef,veal & buffalo										
Boeuf,veau et buffle	3	3	3	3	3	3	3	3	3	3
Pork										
Porc	2	1	1	1	1	1	1	1	1	1
Guatemala										
Guatemala	**83**	**68**	**57**	**67**	**70**	**73**	**74**	**74**	**75**	**68**
Beef,veal & buffalo										
Boeuf,veau et buffle	67	52	41	48	52	54	54	54	54	47
Pork										
Porc	14	13	14	17	15	16	16	17	18	18
Mutton,lamb & goat										
Mouton,agneau et caprin	2	2	2	2	3	3	3	3	3	3
Haiti										
Haïti	**41**	**44**	**49**	**52**	**53**	**51**	**57**	**59**	**64**	**64**
Beef,veal & buffalo										
Boeuf,veau et buffle	24	25	27	29	28	24	28	28	31	31
Pork										
Porc	13	15	18	19	21	23	24	25	27	27
Mutton,lamb & goat										
Mouton,agneau et caprin	4	4	4	4	4	4	5	5	6	6
Honduras										
Honduras	**59**	**58**	**58**	**58**	**59**	**37**	**40**	**41**	**45**	**39**
Beef,veal & buffalo										
Boeuf,veau et buffle	46	45	44	45	45	23	25	26	28	22
Pork										
Porc	13	13	13	13	14	14	15	15	16	17
Jamaica										
Jamaïque	**24**	**23**	**26**	**24**	**25**	**25**	**24**	**23**	**23**	**23**
Beef,veal & buffalo										
Boeuf,veau et buffle	15	16	18	16	16	17	16	15	14	14
Pork										
Porc	7	5	6	7	7	7	7	7	7	7
Mutton,lamb & goat										
Mouton,agneau et caprin	2	2	2	2	2	2	2	2	2	2
Martinique										
Martinique	**5**	**5**	**5**	**5**	**4**	**4**	**4**	**4**	**4**	**4**
Beef,veal & buffalo										
Boeuf,veau et buffle	3	3	3	2	2	2	3	3	3	3
Pork										
Porc	2	2	2	2	2	2	2	2	2	2
Mexico										
Mexique	**1 932**	**2 066**	**2 138**	**2 148**	**2 307**	**2 401**	**2 306**	**2 345**	**2 409**	**2 450**
Beef,veal & buffalo										
Boeuf,veau et buffle	1 114	1 189	1 247	1 256	1 365	1 412	1 330	1 340	1 380	1 390

38
Meat
Production: thousand metric tons [cont.]
Viande
Production : milliers de tonnes [suite]

Region, country or area Région, pays ou zone	1990	1991	1992	1993	1994	1995	1996	1997	1998	1999
Pork Porc	757	812	820	822	873	922	910	939	961	990
Mutton,lamb & goat Mouton,agneau et caprin	61	66	71	70	69	68	65	65	69	70
Montserrat **Montserrat**	**1**	**1**	**1**	**1**	**1**	**1**	**1**	**1**	**1**	**1**
Beef,veal & buffalo Boeuf,veau et buffle	1	1	1	1	1	1	1	1	1	1
Nicaragua **Nicaragua**	**68**	**55**	**56**	**61**	**56**	**54**	**55**	**58**	**51**	**69**
Beef,veal & buffalo Boeuf,veau et buffle	57	45	48	52	51	49	50	52	45	63
Pork Porc	10	9	9	8	5	5	5	6	6	6
Panama **Panama**	**76**	**74**	**73**	**76**	**76**	**78**	**84**	**79**	**82**	**82**
Beef,veal & buffalo Boeuf,veau et buffle	64	61	59	60	60	61	66	60	64	64
Pork Porc	12	12	15	16	16	17	19	19	19	19
Puerto Rico **Porto Rico**	**50**	**50**	**39**	**36**	**34**	**32**	**29**	**29**	**29**	**29**
Beef,veal & buffalo Boeuf,veau et buffle	21	19	21	19	18	16	14	16	16	16
Pork Porc	28	30	18	17	15	15	15	13	13	13
Saint Lucia **Sainte-Lucie**	**1**	**1**	**1**	**1**	**1**	**1**	**1**	**1**	**1**	**1**
Beef,veal & buffalo Boeuf,veau et buffle	1	1	1	1	1	1	1	1	1	1
Pork Porc	1	1	1	1	1	1	1	1	1	1
St. Vincent-Grenadines **St. Vincent-Grenadines**	**1**	**1**	**1**	**1**	**1**	**1**	**1**	**1**	**1**	**1**
Pork Porc	1	1	1	1	1	1	1	1	1	1
Trinidad and Tobago **Trinité-et-Tobago**	**4**	**4**	**4**	**3**	**3**	**3**	**3**	**3**	**3**	**3**
Beef,veal & buffalo Boeuf,veau et buffle	1	1	1	1	1	1	1	1	1	1
Pork Porc	2	2	2	2	2	2	2	1	1	1
United States **Etats-Unis**	**17 594**	**17 956**	**18 587**	**18 488**	**19 361**	**19 812**	**19 635**	**19 667**	**20 539**	**20 940**
Beef,veal & buffalo Boeuf,veau et buffle	10 465	10 534	10 612	10 584	11 194	11 585	11 749	11 714	11 803	12 050
Pork Porc	6 964	7 258	7 817	7 751	8 027	8 097	7 764	7 835	8 623	8 785
Mutton,lamb & goat Mouton,agneau et caprin	165	165	158	153	140	130	122	118	113	105
United States Virgin Is. **Iles Vierges américaines**	**1**	**1**	**1**	**1**	**1**	**1**	**1**	**1**	**1**	**1**
Beef,veal & buffalo Boeuf,veau et buffle	0	1	1	1	1	1	1	1	1	1
America, South **Amérique du Sud**	**11 634**	**11 951**	**12 048**	**12 304**	**12 760**	**13 409**	**14 195**	**14 045**	**14 044**	**14 522**

38
Meat
Production: thousand metric tons [cont.]
Viande
Production : milliers de tonnes [suite]

Region, country or area Région, pays ou zone	1990	1991	1992	1993	1994	1995	1996	1997	1998	1999
Beef,veal & buffalo										
Boeuf,veau et buffle	**9 369**	**9 598**	**9 578**	**9 739**	**10 114**	**10 639**	**11 265**	**11 174**	**11 005**	**11 365**
Pork										
Porc	**1 900**	**1 992**	**2 124**	**2 214**	**2 274**	**2 412**	**2 572**	**2 514**	**2 693**	**2 808**
Mutton,lamb & goat										
Mouton,agneau et caprin	**365**	**362**	**346**	**351**	**372**	**358**	**358**	**358**	**346**	**349**
Argentina										
Argentine	**3 239**	**3 151**	**3 014**	**3 062**	**3 057**	**2 955**	**2 914**	**2 907**	**2 867**	**2 858**
Beef,veal & buffalo										
Boeuf,veau et buffle	3 007	2 918	2 784	2 808	2 783	2 688	2 694	2 705	2 656	2 650
Pork										
Porc	141	142	157	182	182	178	148	137	156	156
Mutton,lamb & goat										
Mouton,agneau et caprin	92	92	73	72	92	88	71	65	55	52
Bolivia										
Bolivie	**215**	**215**	**210**	**205**	**214**	**221**	**229**	**236**	**244**	**250**
Beef,veal & buffalo										
Boeuf,veau et buffle	130	132	126	130	136	140	143	147	151	155
Pork										
Porc	65	65	67	58	60	62	66	69	72	74
Mutton,lamb & goat										
Mouton,agneau et caprin	19	17	17	17	19	20	20	20	21	21
Brazil										
Brésil	**5 277**	**5 745**	**6 019**	**6 176**	**6 556**	**7 265**	**7 915**	**7 571**	**7 578**	**8 065**
Beef,veal & buffalo										
Boeuf,veau et buffle	4 115	4 511	4 716	4 807	5 136	5 710	6 187	5 922	5 794	6 182
Pork										
Porc	1 050	1 120	1 188	1 250	1 300	1 430	1 600	1 518	1 652	1 752
Mutton,lamb & goat										
Mouton,agneau et caprin	112	114	115	119	120	125	128	131	131	131
Chile										
Chili	**385**	**376**	**355**	**389**	**417**	**445**	**458**	**486**	**508**	**488**
Beef,veal & buffalo										
Boeuf,veau et buffle	242	230	200	224	240	258	259	262	256	226
Pork										
Porc	123	129	138	147	161	172	185	209	235	244
Mutton,lamb & goat										
Mouton,agneau et caprin	19	18	17	18	17	15	13	15	17	18
Colombia										
Colombie	**892**	**846**	**742**	**750**	**793**	**849**	**881**	**915**	**918**	**873**
Beef,veal & buffalo										
Boeuf,veau et buffle	746	701	595	603	646	702	730	763	766	720
Pork										
Porc	133	133	135	134	133	133	135	135	135	135
Mutton,lamb & goat										
Mouton,agneau et caprin	13	12	13	13	13	14	16	17	17	17
Ecuador										
Equateur	**176**	**194**	**200**	**213**	**216**	**245**	**264**	**270**	**266**	**282**
Beef,veal & buffalo										
Boeuf,veau et buffle	100	113	113	126	127	149	153	156	158	164
Pork										
Porc	71	76	82	81	82	89	103	107	100	110
Mutton,lamb & goat										
Mouton,agneau et caprin	5	5	5	6	6	7	7	8	8	8
Falkland Is. (Malvinas)										
Iles Falkland (Malvinas)	**1**	**1**	**1**	**1**	**1**	**1**	**1**	**1**	**1**	**1**
Mutton,lamb & goat										
Mouton,agneau et caprin	1	1	1	1	1	1	1	1	1	1

38
Meat
Production: thousand metric tons [cont.]
Viande
Production : milliers de tonnes [suite]

Region, country or area Région, pays ou zone	1990	1991	1992	1993	1994	1995	1996	1997	1998	1999
French Guiana **Guyane française**	**1**	**1**	**1**	**1**	**1**	**2**	**2**	**2**	**2**	**2**
Beef,veal & buffalo Boeuf,veau et buffle	1	1	0	0	0	0	0	0	0	0
Pork Porc	1	1	1	1	1	1	1	1	1	1
Guyana **Guyana**	**4**	**5**	**6**	**6**	**6**	**5**	**5**	**4**	**4**	**4**
Beef,veal & buffalo Boeuf,veau et buffle	2	3	4	4	5	4	4	3	3	3
Pork Porc	1	1	1	1	1	1	1	1	1	1
Mutton,lamb & goat Mouton,agneau et caprin	1	1	1	1	1	1	1	1	1	1
Paraguay **Paraguay**	**311**	**343**	**363**	**355**	**356**	**359**	**345**	**347**	**353**	**369**
Beef,veal & buffalo Boeuf,veau et buffle	189	219	233	225	225	226	226	226	231	246
Pork Porc	118	121	126	127	128	130	116	117	119	120
Mutton,lamb & goat Mouton,agneau et caprin	3	3	3	3	3	3	3	3	3	3
Peru **Pérou**	**216**	**206**	**212**	**209**	**205**	**213**	**220**	**233**	**243**	**263**
Beef,veal & buffalo Boeuf,veau et buffle	117	109	111	107	102	107	110	118	124	133
Pork Porc	67	69	73	76	78	80	83	87	91	93
Mutton,lamb & goat Mouton,agneau et caprin	33	28	28	26	26	26	27	28	29	37
Suriname **Suriname**	**4**	**5**	**4**	**4**	**3**	**3**	**2**	**3**	**3**	**3**
Beef,veal & buffalo Boeuf,veau et buffle	2	3	3	2	2	2	2	2	2	2
Pork Porc	2	2	1	1	2	1	1	1	1	1
Uruguay **Uruguay**	**418**	**405**	**415**	**396**	**450**	**412**	**491**	**536**	**531**	**536**
Beef,veal & buffalo Boeuf,veau et buffle	335	320	329	310	361	338	407	454	450	458
Pork Porc	22	22	22	23	23	22	21	22	26	27
Mutton,lamb & goat Mouton,agneau et caprin	61	63	64	64	66	52	64	60	55	51
Venezuela **Venezuela**	**496**	**458**	**507**	**536**	**483**	**435**	**469**	**535**	**527**	**528**
Beef,veal & buffalo Boeuf,veau et buffle	382	337	365	394	351	316	350	415	413	424
Pork Porc	107	111	133	133	125	112	113	111	105	95
Mutton,lamb & goat Mouton,agneau et caprin	7	9	8	10	8	7	7	9	9	9
Asia **Asie**	**40 822**	**43 206**	**48 025**	**51 694**	**55 388**	**57 103**	**57 042**	**62 899**	**66 452**	**66 546**
Beef,veal & buffalo Boeuf,veau et buffle	**7 431**	**7 817**	**9 504**	**10 396**	**10 975**	**11 741**	**11 776**	**12 850**	**13 296**	**13 394**
Pork Porc	**29 599**	**31 422**	**33 940**	**36 451**	**39 350**	**40 006**	**39 807**	**44 165**	**47 066**	**47 046**

38
Meat
Production: thousand metric tons [cont.]
Viande
Production : milliers de tonnes [suite]

Region, country or area Région, pays ou zone	1990	1991	1992	1993	1994	1995	1996	1997	1998	1999
Mutton,lamb & goat Mouton,agneau et caprin	3 793	3 968	4 580	4 847	5 063	5 356	5 459	5 885	6 090	6 105
Afghanistan Afghanistan	203	203	203	203	203	206	206	206	206	206
Beef,veal & buffalo Boeuf,veau et buffle	65	65	65	65	65	65	65	65	65	65
Mutton,lamb & goat Mouton,agneau et caprin	138	138	138	138	138	141	141	141	141	141
Armenia Arménie	...	...	57	43	43	41	45	44	46	45
Beef,veal & buffalo Boeuf,veau et buffle	...	...	33	30	29	30	33	32	34	35
Pork Porc	...	...	16	5	6	4	6	6	6	6
Mutton,lamb & goat Mouton,agneau et caprin	...	...	9	8	8	7	6	6	7	5
Azerbaijan Azerbaïdjan	...	...	82	73	68	66	71	76	84	86
Beef,veal & buffalo Boeuf,veau et buffle	...	...	50	44	44	41	44	48	50	52
Pork Porc	...	...	5	3	2	2	2	2	1	1
Mutton,lamb & goat Mouton,agneau et caprin	...	...	27	26	22	23	26	26	32	33
Bahrain Bahreïn	8	8	8	8	10	9	9	9	8	8
Beef,veal & buffalo Boeuf,veau et buffle	1	1	1	1	1	1	1	1	1	1
Mutton,lamb & goat Mouton,agneau et caprin	7	7	7	7	9	9	9	9	7	7
Bangladesh Bangladesh	218	223	230	240	250	258	273	294	293	293
Beef,veal & buffalo Boeuf,veau et buffle	143	143	145	147	150	151	156	169	165	165
Mutton,lamb & goat Mouton,agneau et caprin	75	80	86	93	100	107	118	126	129	129
Bhutan Bhoutan	7	7	7	7	7	7	7	7	7	7
Beef,veal & buffalo Boeuf,veau et buffle	5	6	6	6	6	6	6	6	6	6
Pork Porc	1	1	1	1	1	1	1	1	1	1
Brunei Darussalam Brunéi Darussalam	2	2	2	2	2	1	2	2	2	2
Beef,veal & buffalo Boeuf,veau et buffle	2	2	2	1	2	1	2	2	2	2
Cambodia Cambodge	99	103	127	132	129	134	139	142	142	142
Beef,veal & buffalo Boeuf,veau et buffle	39	41	45	47	48	52	53	54	54	54
Pork Porc	61	62	82	85	81	82	86	88	88	88
China †† Chine ††	26 149	28 369	30 538	33 395	36 696	38 553	38 227	43 569	46 833	47 180
Beef,veal & buffalo Boeuf,veau et buffle	1 261	1 540	1 808	2 341	2 775	3 571	3 563	4 415	4 804	5 004
Pork Porc	23 820	25 649	27 479	29 679	32 439	33 233	32 849	36 993	39 729	39 858

38

Meat
Production: thousand metric tons [*cont.*]
Viande
Production : milliers de tonnes [*suite*]

Region, country or area Région, pays ou zone	1990	1991	1992	1993	1994	1995	1996	1997	1998	1999
Mutton,lamb & goat Mouton,agneau et caprin	1 068	1 180	1 251	1 375	1 482	1 749	1 814	2 162	2 300	2 318
China, Hong Kong SAR† **Chine, Hong Kong RAS†**	**227**	**206**	**195**	**181**	**195**	**185**	**176**	**168**	**180**	**175**
Beef,veal & buffalo Boeuf,veau et buffle	39	38	35	32	29	25	20	15	19	18
Pork Porc	188	168	160	149	166	159	156	153	161	157
China, Macao SAR † **Chine, Macao RAS †**	**9**	**9**	**9**	**9**	**10**	**10**	**10**	**9**	**9**	**9**
Beef,veal & buffalo Boeuf,veau et buffle	2	2	2	2	2	2	2	1	1	1
Pork Porc	8	7	8	8	8	8	8	8	8	8
Cyprus **Chypre**	**44**	**43**	**45**	**51**	**54**	**56**	**58**	**60**	**62**	**62**
Beef,veal & buffalo Boeuf,veau et buffle	4	5	5	5	4	5	5	5	5	4
Pork Porc	31	32	34	39	43	43	46	46	47	48
Mutton,lamb & goat Mouton,agneau et caprin	8	7	7	7	7	8	8	8	10	10
Georgia **Géorgie**	...	...	**103**	**92**	**94**	**114**	**124**	**111**	**99**	**92**
Beef,veal & buffalo Boeuf,veau et buffle	...	...	40	40	40	55	59	52	49	46
Pork Porc	...	...	57	45	48	51	56	50	42	39
Mutton,lamb & goat Mouton,agneau et caprin	...	...	6	7	6	8	9	8	8	7
India **Inde**	**3 431**	**3 505**	**3 606**	**3 737**	**3 814**	**3 875**	**3 937**	**3 995**	**3 937**	**3 994**
Beef,veal & buffalo Boeuf,veau et buffle	2 403	2 452	2 535	2 632	2 682	2 716	2 751	2 782	2 781	2 832
Pork Porc	417	434	445	469	477	495	514	533	469	469
Mutton,lamb & goat Mouton,agneau et caprin	611	619	626	635	655	663	672	680	688	694
Indonesia **Indonésie**	**944**	**978**	**1 035**	**1 117**	**1 144**	**1 042**	**1 094**	**1 175**	**1 241**	**1 242**
Beef,veal & buffalo Boeuf,veau et buffle	309	312	347	398	385	359	396	402	400	399
Pork Porc	545	572	589	622	660	589	600	666	759	759
Mutton,lamb & goat Mouton,agneau et caprin	90	94	99	98	100	94	99	107	82	84
Iran (Islamic Rep. of) **Iran (Rép. islamique d')**	**557**	**572**	**595**	**612**	**628**	**642**	**668**	**715**	**744**	**703**
Beef,veal & buffalo Boeuf,veau et buffle	220	228	237	246	256	265	287	309	326	306
Mutton,lamb & goat Mouton,agneau et caprin	338	344	358	366	372	377	380	406	418	397
Iraq **Iraq**	**87**	**54**	**74**	**92**	**84**	**73**	**59**	**73**	**75**	**67**
Beef,veal & buffalo Boeuf,veau et buffle	51	33	45	55	51	43	37	46	47	41
Mutton,lamb & goat Mouton,agneau et caprin	36	22	29	38	33	31	22	27	28	26

38

Meat
Production: thousand metric tons [*cont.*]
Viande
Production : milliers de tonnes [*suite*]

Region, country or area Région, pays ou zone	1990	1991	1992	1993	1994	1995	1996	1997	1998	1999
Israel **Israël**	**51**	**53**	**52**	**51**	**57**	**58**	**61**	**65**	**64**	**64**
Beef,veal & buffalo Boeuf,veau et buffle	36	38	37	36	41	41	44	46	46	46
Pork Porc	9	9	9	9	9	11	11	12	12	12
Mutton,lamb & goat Mouton,agneau et caprin	6	6	6	7	7	7	7	6	6	6
Japan **Japon**	**2 105**	**2 058**	**2 026**	**2 034**	**1 993**	**1 923**	**1 821**	**1 814**	**1 816**	**1 798**
Beef,veal & buffalo Boeuf,veau et buffle	549	575	592	594	602	601	555	530	529	515
Pork Porc	1 555	1 483	1 434	1 440	1 390	1 322	1 266	1 283	1 286	1 283
Jordan **Jordanie**	**13**	**18**	**17**	**19**	**16**	**14**	**16**	**15**	**22**	**21**
Beef,veal & buffalo Boeuf,veau et buffle	3	3	2	3	4	2	3	4	3	3
Mutton,lamb & goat Mouton,agneau et caprin	11	15	14	16	12	12	13	12	19	18
Kazakhstan **Kazakhstan**	...	...	**1 056**	**1 131**	**1 052**	**867**	**740**	**623**	**546**	**527**
Beef,veal & buffalo Boeuf,veau et buffle	...	...	596	662	642	548	463	398	351	331
Pork Porc	...	...	217	194	158	113	110	82	79	77
Mutton,lamb & goat Mouton,agneau et caprin	...	...	243	275	252	206	167	143	117	119
Korea, Dem. P. R. **Corée, R. p. dém. de**	**265**	**271**	**211**	**187**	**173**	**146**	**131**	**108**	**139**	**163**
Beef,veal & buffalo Boeuf,veau et buffle	35	30	30	31	32	27	22	19	20	20
Pork Porc	225	235	175	150	135	115	105	84	112	134
Mutton,lamb & goat Mouton,agneau et caprin	6	6	6	6	6	4	4	6	8	10
Korea, Republic of **Corée, République de**	**679**	**664**	**928**	**977**	**1 003**	**1 023**	**1 138**	**1 237**	**1 318**	**984**
Beef,veal & buffalo Boeuf,veau et buffle	128	132	174	204	214	221	248	338	376	240
Pork Porc	550	530	752	770	786	799	887	896	939	741
Mutton,lamb & goat Mouton,agneau et caprin	1	2	2	3	3	3	3	4	3	3
Kuwait **Koweït**	**19**	**9**	**18**	**26**	**50**	**40**	**41**	**41**	**33**	**34**
Beef,veal & buffalo Boeuf,veau et buffle	1	0	1	1	1	2	2	2	1	2
Mutton,lamb & goat Mouton,agneau et caprin	17	9	17	25	49	38	39	39	32	32
Kyrgyzstan **Kirghizistan**	...	...	**193**	**194**	**177**	**167**	**169**	**164**	**169**	**174**
Beef,veal & buffalo Boeuf,veau et buffle	...	...	88	88	82	85	86	95	94	97
Pork Porc	...	...	36	25	18	28	29	26	31	32
Mutton,lamb & goat Mouton,agneau et caprin	...	...	70	82	76	54	54	44	44	45

38

Meat
Production: thousand metric tons [*cont.*]
Viande
Production : milliers de tonnes [*suite*]

Region, country or area Région, pays ou zone	1990	1991	1992	1993	1994	1995	1996	1997	1998	1999
Lao People's Dem. Rep. **Rép. dém. pop. lao**	**37**	**40**	**42**	**45**	**48**	**58**	**58**	**61**	**63**	**70**
Beef,veal & buffalo Boeuf,veau et buffle	16	18	19	21	22	28	28	30	31	38
Pork Porc	21	22	23	25	26	29	30	31	31	32
Lebanon **Liban**	**29**	**31**	**34**	**38**	**38**	**33**	**32**	**39**	**40**	**41**
Beef,veal & buffalo Boeuf,veau et buffle	14	15	16	16	15	12	10	15	16	16
Pork Porc	4	4	4	5	6	7	8	8	8	9
Mutton,lamb & goat Mouton,agneau et caprin	11	13	14	16	17	14	14	15	16	16
Malaysia **Malaisie**	**235**	**243**	**240**	**239**	**252**	**253**	**245**	**256**	**243**	**243**
Beef,veal & buffalo Boeuf,veau et buffle	15	18	18	19	19	20	21	22	21	21
Pork Porc	219	225	222	220	232	232	223	233	221	221
Mutton,lamb & goat Mouton,agneau et caprin	1	1	1	1	1	1	1	1	1	1
Mongolia **Mongolie**	**206**	**224**	**194**	**178**	**177**	**182**	**212**	**191**	**199**	**204**
Beef,veal & buffalo Boeuf,veau et buffle	66	84	76	65	64	69	90	87	86	87
Pork Porc	8	4	2	1	1	1	0	0	1	1
Mutton,lamb & goat Mouton,agneau et caprin	132	136	116	113	112	112	121	104	112	117
Myanmar **Myanmar**	**189**	**197**	**203**	**205**	**208**	**218**	**231**	**240**	**245**	**251**
Beef,veal & buffalo Boeuf,veau et buffle	107	108	109	110	111	113	116	119	121	121
Pork Porc	75	83	87	88	90	97	107	113	116	121
Mutton,lamb & goat Mouton,agneau et caprin	7	7	7	7	7	8	8	8	9	9
Nepal **Népal**	**177**	**179**	**181**	**182**	**188**	**195**	**199**	**211**	**217**	**220**
Beef,veal & buffalo Boeuf,veau et buffle	136	137	137	138	144	150	152	161	165	167
Pork Porc	10	10	10	10	11	11	12	12	13	14
Mutton,lamb & goat Mouton,agneau et caprin	32	32	33	33	34	34	35	37	39	39
Occupied Palestinian Terr. **Terr. palestinien occupé**	**3**	**2**	**2**	**2**	**3**	**3**	**3**	**3**	**3**	**3**
Beef,veal & buffalo Boeuf,veau et buffle	1	1	1	1	1	1	1	1	1	1
Mutton,lamb & goat Mouton,agneau et caprin	2	1	1	1	1	1	1	1	1	1
Oman **Oman**	**18**	**19**	**18**	**19**	**19**	**18**	**18**	**18**	**18**	**19**
Beef,veal & buffalo Boeuf,veau et buffle	3	3	3	3	3	3	3	3	3	3
Mutton,lamb & goat Mouton,agneau et caprin	15	16	16	16	16	15	15	15	16	16

38
Meat
Production: thousand metric tons [*cont.*]
Viande
Production : milliers de tonnes [*suite*]

Region, country or area Région, pays ou zone	1990	1991	1992	1993	1994	1995	1996	1997	1998	1999
Pakistan **Pakistan**	**1 151**	**1 215**	**1 287**	**1 363**	**1 444**	**1 530**	**1 622**	**1 719**	**1 822**	**1 822**
Beef,veal & buffalo Boeuf,veau et buffle	667	696	731	768	807	847	891	937	984	984
Mutton,lamb & goat Mouton,agneau et caprin	484	519	556	595	637	683	731	782	838	838
Philippines **Philippines**	**860**	**849**	**880**	**1 146**	**1 191**	**1 192**	**1 272**	**1 340**	**1 377**	**1 428**
Beef,veal & buffalo Boeuf,veau et buffle	125	127	130	137	136	147	161	177	196	223
Pork Porc	709	691	710	953	997	970	1 036	1 085	1 100	1 123
Mutton,lamb & goat Mouton,agneau et caprin	27	31	40	55	58	74	75	78	82	82
Qatar **Qatar**	**12**	**14**	**12**	**12**	**13**	**12**	**8**	**8**	**8**	**8**
Mutton,lamb & goat Mouton,agneau et caprin	12	14	12	12	13	12	8	8	8	8
Saudi Arabia **Arabie saoudite**	**111**	**106**	**112**	**117**	**123**	**126**	**119**	**114**	**122**	**122**
Beef,veal & buffalo Boeuf,veau et buffle	28	27	28	29	30	26	18	16	17	17
Mutton,lamb & goat Mouton,agneau et caprin	83	79	84	88	93	100	101	98	105	105
Singapore **Singapour**	**77**	**82**	**85**	**86**	**88**	**87**	**84**	**84**	**84**	**50**
Pork Porc	76	81	84	85	87	86	84	84	84	50
Mutton,lamb & goat Mouton,agneau et caprin	1	1	1	1	1	0	0	0	0	0
Sri Lanka **Sri Lanka**	**29**	**32**	**35**	**33**	**36**	**37**	**33**	**34**	**33**	**33**
Beef,veal & buffalo Boeuf,veau et buffle	26	28	31	29	31	32	29	30	29	29
Pork Porc	2	2	2	2	2	2	2	2	2	2
Mutton,lamb & goat Mouton,agneau et caprin	2	2	2	2	3	3	2	2	2	2
Syrian Arab Republic **Rép. arabe syrienne**	**152**	**162**	**146**	**127**	**156**	**171**	**190**	**196**	**204**	**207**
Beef,veal & buffalo Boeuf,veau et buffle	32	33	29	29	31	34	40	42	44	45
Mutton,lamb & goat Mouton,agneau et caprin	120	129	118	98	126	137	150	154	160	162
Tajikistan **Tadjikistan**	**...**	**...**	**65**	**55**	**58**	**51**	**45**	**29**	**29**	**29**
Beef,veal & buffalo Boeuf,veau et buffle	...	...	41	34	36	31	34	20	19	21
Pork Porc	...	...	4	1	1	1	0	0	0	0
Mutton,lamb & goat Mouton,agneau et caprin	...	...	20	20	21	19	11	9	10	8
Thailand **Thaïlande**	**655**	**723**	**753**	**798**	**839**	**827**	**842**	**849**	**750**	**694**
Beef,veal & buffalo Boeuf,veau et buffle	317	320	318	338	348	337	330	300	275	267
Pork Porc	338	402	433	459	489	489	511	549	475	426

38

Meat
Production: thousand metric tons [*cont.*]
Viande
Production : milliers de tonnes [*suite*]

Region, country or area Région, pays ou zone	1990	1991	1992	1993	1994	1995	1996	1997	1998	1999
Mutton,lamb & goat Mouton,agneau et caprin	1	1	2	1	1	1	1	1	1	1
Turkey **Turquie**	**742**	**715**	**674**	**666**	**697**	**671**	**672**	**764**	**739**	**739**
Beef,veal & buffalo Boeuf,veau et buffle	372	348	309	303	325	299	305	385	364	364
Pork Porc	0	0	0	0	0	0	1	1	1	1
Mutton,lamb & goat Mouton,agneau et caprin	370	367	365	363	372	372	366	378	374	374
Turkmenistan **Turkménistan**	...	...	**88**	**100**	**100**	**104**	**107**	**107**	**123**	**127**
Beef,veal & buffalo Boeuf,veau et buffle	...	...	46	50	51	51	52	55	61	63
Pork Porc	...	...	7	5	4	3	1	1	1	1
Mutton,lamb & goat Mouton,agneau et caprin	...	...	35	45	45	50	53	51	61	63
United Arab Emirates **Emirats arabes unis**	**31**	**37**	**36**	**41**	**44**	**46**	**48**	**50**	**43**	**43**
Beef,veal & buffalo Boeuf,veau et buffle	5	6	6	6	7	9	10	13	13	13
Mutton,lamb & goat Mouton,agneau et caprin	26	31	30	35	36	38	39	37	30	30
Uzbekistan **Ouzbékistan**	...	...	**427**	**479**	**483**	**491**	**447**	**474**	**497**	**503**
Beef,veal & buffalo Boeuf,veau et buffle	...	...	323	378	390	392	362	382	400	403
Pork Porc	...	...	36	27	20	16	9	12	15	16
Mutton,lamb & goat Mouton,agneau et caprin	...	...	68	74	73	83	76	80	82	84
Viet Nam **Viet Nam**	**896**	**883**	**995**	**1 051**	**1 137**	**1 191**	**1 232**	**1 284**	**1 408**	**1 501**
Beef,veal & buffalo Boeuf,veau et buffle	164	165	173	171	176	180	175	175	176	178
Pork Porc	729	716	820	878	958	1 007	1 052	1 104	1 228	1 318
Mutton,lamb & goat Mouton,agneau et caprin	3	2	2	3	3	4	5	5	5	5
Yemen **Yémen**	**76**	**77**	**79**	**79**	**78**	**79**	**81**	**86**	**90**	**92**
Beef,veal & buffalo Boeuf,veau et buffle	38	37	38	39	40	41	42	43	45	46
Mutton,lamb & goat Mouton,agneau et caprin	38	40	41	40	38	38	39	43	45	45
Europe **Europe**	**34 455**	**34 177**	**44 816**	**43 140**	**41 413**	**40 358**	**40 376**	**39 086**	**39 911**	**39 660**
Beef,veal & buffalo **Boeuf,veau et buffle**	**11 256**	**11 535**	**17 092**	**15 622**	**14 856**	**13 973**	**13 654**	**13 190**	**12 762**	**12 542**
Pork **Porc**	**21 641**	**21 083**	**25 830**	**25 620**	**24 741**	**24 645**	**25 033**	**24 336**	**25 591**	**25 564**
Mutton,lamb & goat **Mouton,agneau et caprin**	**1 558**	**1 558**	**1 894**	**1 898**	**1 816**	**1 740**	**1 688**	**1 561**	**1 558**	**1 555**
Albania **Albanie**	**47**	**43**	**49**	**52**	**60**	**63**	**56**	**55**	**55**	**58**
Beef,veal & buffalo Boeuf,veau et buffle	22	21	23	24	28	31	33	33	32	34

38
Meat
Production: thousand metric tons [*cont.*]
Viande
Production : milliers de tonnes [*suite*]

Region, country or area Région, pays ou zone	1990	1991	1992	1993	1994	1995	1996	1997	1998	1999
Pork Porc	13	9	11	13	14	14	6	7	7	6
Mutton,lamb & goat Mouton,agneau et caprin	12	13	15	15	19	18	17	16	17	18
Austria **Autriche**	**747**	**759**	**780**	**767**	**757**	**723**	**766**	**769**	**796**	**709**
Beef,veal & buffalo Boeuf,veau et buffle	224	236	247	223	212	196	221	206	197	203
Pork Porc	517	517	527	538	539	521	538	556	592	499
Mutton,lamb & goat Mouton,agneau et caprin	6	6	6	6	6	7	7	7	7	7
Belarus **Bélarus**	...	...	824	701	641	582	554	557	593	574
Beef,veal & buffalo Boeuf,veau et buffle	...	...	495	411	384	316	277	256	271	261
Pork Porc	...	...	323	284	252	263	273	298	320	310
Mutton,lamb & goat Mouton,agneau et caprin	...	...	6	6	5	4	4	3	3	3
Belgium-Luxembourg **Belgique-Luxembourg**	**1 114**	**1 305**	**1 316**	**1 378**	**1 380**	**1 405**	**1 436**	**1 377**	**1 393**	**1 395**
Beef,veal & buffalo Boeuf,veau et buffle	323	381	359	373	355	357	362	340	303	320
Pork Porc	784	915	951	1 001	1 019	1 043	1 070	1 033	1 085	1 070
Mutton,lamb & goat Mouton,agneau et caprin	7	8	6	4	5	5	5	4	4	5
Bosnia and Herzegovina **Bosnie-Herzégovine**	...	...	102	85	52	34	37	20	16	16
Beef,veal & buffalo Boeuf,veau et buffle	...	...	43	37	30	16	18	13	9	9
Pork Porc	...	...	50	44	20	16	16	5	5	5
Mutton,lamb & goat Mouton,agneau et caprin	...	...	8	4	2	3	3	3	3	3
Bulgaria **Bulgarie**	**590**	**543**	**506**	**449**	**343**	**366**	**388**	**334**	**356**	**376**
Beef,veal & buffalo Boeuf,veau et buffle	121	108	135	117	89	65	80	57	56	65
Pork Porc	406	362	311	277	207	256	252	227	247	258
Mutton,lamb & goat Mouton,agneau et caprin	63	73	60	56	47	45	56	50	53	53
Croatia **Croatie**	...	...	123	103	90	78	74	72	63	58
Beef,veal & buffalo Boeuf,veau et buffle	...	...	40	36	31	28	26	26	21	19
Pork Porc	...	...	81	65	57	48	46	44	40	37
Mutton,lamb & goat Mouton,agneau et caprin	...	...	3	2	2	2	2	2	2	2
former Czechoslovakia† **l'ex-Tchécoslovaquie†**	**1 326**	**1 190**	**1 162**	...	...	...	...	...	...	...
Beef,veal & buffalo Boeuf,veau et buffle	403	354	319	...	...	...	...	...	...	...
Pork Porc	913	827	834	...	...	...	...	...	...	...

38
Meat
Production: thousand metric tons [cont.]
Viande
Production : milliers de tonnes [suite]

Region, country or area Région, pays ou zone	1990	1991	1992	1993	1994	1995	1996	1997	1998	1999
Mutton,lamb & goat Mouton,agneau et caprin	10	9	8	...	...	...	...	...	...	...
Czech Republic République tchèque	...	...	...	**834**	**643**	**674**	**667**	**621**	**611**	**591**
Beef,veal & buffalo Boeuf,veau et buffle	...	...	...	216	170	170	164	156	134	136
Pork Porc	...	...	...	615	471	502	502	464	476	452
Mutton,lamb & goat Mouton,agneau et caprin	...	...	...	3	2	2	2	2	1	3
Denmark Danemark	**1 412**	**1 486**	**1 589**	**1 709**	**1 712**	**1 677**	**1 673**	**1 697**	**1 793**	**1 800**
Beef,veal & buffalo Boeuf,veau et buffle	202	213	217	203	189	182	178	175	162	157
Pork Porc	1 208	1 272	1 370	1 504	1 521	1 494	1 494	1 521	1 629	1 642
Mutton,lamb & goat Mouton,agneau et caprin	1	2	2	2	2	2	2	2	2	1
Estonia Estonie	...	...	**97**	**79**	**63**	**62**	**54**	**49**	**52**	**54**
Beef,veal & buffalo Boeuf,veau et buffle	...	...	45	43	31	26	22	19	19	20
Pork Porc	...	...	50	35	30	35	32	30	32	34
Mutton,lamb & goat Mouton,agneau et caprin	...	...	2	1	1	1	1	0	0	0
Faeroe Islands Iles Féroé	**1**	**1**	**1**	**1**	**1**	**1**	**1**	**1**	**1**	**1**
Mutton,lamb & goat Mouton,agneau et caprin	1	1	1	1	1	1	1	1	1	1
Finland Finlande	**306**	**300**	**295**	**277**	**280**	**265**	**270**	**281**	**279**	**280**
Beef,veal & buffalo Boeuf,veau et buffle	118	122	117	106	108	96	97	100	94	93
Pork Porc	187	177	176	169	171	168	172	180	185	186
Mutton,lamb & goat Mouton,agneau et caprin	1	1	1	1	1	2	1	1	1	1
France France	**3 833**	**3 968**	**3 936**	**3 893**	**3 890**	**3 975**	**4 072**	**4 088**	**4 087**	**4 092**
Beef,veal & buffalo Boeuf,veau et buffle	1 912	2 026	1 877	1 704	1 627	1 683	1 735	1 718	1 630	1 567
Pork Porc	1 727	1 773	1 903	2 034	2 116	2 144	2 183	2 220	2 313	2 386
Mutton,lamb & goat Mouton,agneau et caprin	194	170	156	155	147	148	153	149	144	139
Germany Allemagne	**6 619**	**6 043**	**5 419**	**5 257**	**5 064**	**5 052**	**5 160**	**5 056**	**5 248**	**5 404**
Beef,veal & buffalo Boeuf,veau et buffle	2 112	2 181	1 790	1 570	1 420	1 408	1 482	1 448	1 459	1 420
Pork Porc	4 457	3 813	3 585	3 646	3 604	3 602	3 635	3 564	3 745	3 940
Mutton,lamb & goat Mouton,agneau et caprin	50	50	44	41	40	42	43	44	44	44
Greece Grèce	**360**	**359**	**360**	**350**	**353**	**343**	**344**	**346**	**341**	**332**
Beef,veal & buffalo Boeuf,veau et buffle	79	79	76	73	74	72	71	70	69	70

38
Meat
Production: thousand metric tons [cont.]
Viande
Production : milliers de tonnes [suite]

Region, country or area Région, pays ou zone	1990	1991	1992	1993	1994	1995	1996	1997	1998	1999
Pork										
Porc	140	140	145	136	137	142	142	145	142	138
Mutton,lamb & goat										
Mouton,agneau et caprin	140	140	139	141	142	128	131	131	130	125
Hungary										
Hongrie	**1 137**	**1 059**	**894**	**771**	**682**	**652**	**736**	**636**	**638**	**655**
Beef,veal & buffalo										
Boeuf,veau et buffle	114	123	123	97	72	69	63	63	65	57
Pork										
Porc	1 018	931	764	672	608	578	671	570	569	595
Mutton,lamb & goat										
Mouton,agneau et caprin	5	6	6	2	1	5	3	3	3	3
Iceland										
Islande	**15**	**15**	**15**	**15**	**16**	**15**	**15**	**15**	**15**	**15**
Beef,veal & buffalo										
Boeuf,veau et buffle	3	3	3	3	4	3	3	3	3	3
Pork										
Porc	3	3	3	3	3	3	4	4	4	4
Mutton,lamb & goat										
Mouton,agneau et caprin	9	9	9	9	9	9	8	8	8	8
Ireland										
Irlande	**758**	**825**	**861**	**837**	**753**	**779**	**836**	**868**	**914**	**893**
Beef,veal & buffalo										
Boeuf,veau et buffle	515	554	565	526	445	477	535	569	590	566
Pork										
Porc	157	179	202	212	215	212	211	221	241	239
Mutton,lamb & goat										
Mouton,agneau et caprin	86	92	95	99	93	89	90	79	84	88
Italy										
Italie	**2 583**	**2 599**	**2 645**	**2 640**	**2 619**	**2 603**	**2 670**	**2 633**	**2 598**	**2 597**
Beef,veal & buffalo										
Boeuf,veau et buffle	1 165	1 182	1 218	1 188	1 171	1 181	1 182	1 161	1 113	1 101
Pork										
Porc	1 333	1 333	1 342	1 371	1 369	1 346	1 410	1 396	1 412	1 425
Mutton,lamb & goat										
Mouton,agneau et caprin	85	85	86	81	79	76	78	76	73	71
Latvia										
Lettonie	...	...	**224**	**179**	**124**	**112**	**67**	**63**	**63**	**56**
Beef,veal & buffalo										
Boeuf,veau et buffle	...	...	120	107	68	48	27	26	26	19
Pork										
Porc	...	...	101	68	54	63	40	37	37	37
Mutton,lamb & goat										
Mouton,agneau et caprin	...	...	4	4	2	2	1	0	0	0
Lithuania										
Lituanie	...	...	**383**	**254**	**199**	**182**	**173**	**178**	**195**	**201**
Beef,veal & buffalo										
Boeuf,veau et buffle	...	...	226	162	116	87	83	90	99	102
Pork										
Porc	...	...	155	90	82	93	89	87	96	98
Mutton,lamb & goat										
Mouton,agneau et caprin	...	...	2	2	2	2	1	1	1	1
Malta										
Malte	**10**	**10**	**10**	**10**	**11**	**10**	**10**	**10**	**11**	**11**
Beef,veal & buffalo										
Boeuf,veau et buffle	2	2	2	2	2	2	2	2	2	2
Pork										
Porc	8	8	8	9	9	9	9	9	9	9

38

Meat
Production: thousand metric tons [*cont.*]
Viande
Production : milliers de tonnes [*suite*]

Region, country or area Région, pays ou zone	1990	1991	1992	1993	1994	1995	1996	1997	1998	1999
Netherlands **Pays-Bas**	**2 197**	**2 232**	**2 238**	**2 376**	**2 294**	**2 218**	**2 222**	**1 956**	**2 266**	**2 226**
Beef,veal & buffalo Boeuf,veau et buffle	521	623	635	611	603	580	580	565	535	510
Pork Porc	1 661	1 591	1 585	1 747	1 673	1 622	1 624	1 376	1 715	1 700
Mutton,lamb & goat Mouton,agneau et caprin	15	18	18	18	17	16	18	15	16	16
Norway **Norvège**	**191**	**190**	**201**	**200**	**206**	**208**	**217**	**221**	**221**	**224**
Beef,veal & buffalo Boeuf,veau et buffle	83	80	85	84	88	85	86	89	91	91
Pork Porc	83	85	91	90	91	96	103	105	106	108
Mutton,lamb & goat Mouton,agneau et caprin	25	24	25	26	27	27	27	26	24	25
Poland **Pologne**	**2 609**	**2 643**	**2 602**	**2 401**	**2 111**	**2 354**	**2 483**	**2 323**	**2 459**	**2 426**
Beef,veal & buffalo Boeuf,veau et buffle	725	663	544	480	421	386	415	429	430	397
Pork Porc	1 855	1 947	2 036	1 903	1 681	1 962	2 064	1 891	2 026	2 026
Mutton,lamb & goat Mouton,agneau et caprin	29	33	23	18	8	6	5	3	3	3
Portugal **Portugal**	**424**	**420**	**416**	**451**	**438**	**435**	**450**	**466**	**451**	**493**
Beef,veal & buffalo Boeuf,veau et buffle	116	127	124	117	95	104	99	109	96	107
Pork Porc	279	263	265	307	316	305	325	330	330	360
Mutton,lamb & goat Mouton,agneau et caprin	28	30	27	27	27	27	26	27	26	26
Republic of Moldova **République de Moldova**	...	...	**193**	**151**	**127**	**110**	**106**	**104**	**88**	**87**
Beef,veal & buffalo Boeuf,veau et buffle	...	...	75	68	62	47	39	35	27	25
Pork Porc	...	...	114	79	61	60	64	66	58	59
Mutton,lamb & goat Mouton,agneau et caprin	...	...	4	3	4	3	3	3	4	4
Romania **Roumanie**	**1 213**	**1 245**	**1 138**	**1 105**	**1 114**	**950**	**880**	**916**	**862**	**834**
Beef,veal & buffalo Boeuf,veau et buffle	317	317	250	252	258	202	177	185	183	170
Pork Porc	788	834	789	761	775	673	631	667	620	610
Mutton,lamb & goat Mouton,agneau et caprin	109	94	100	92	81	75	71	64	60	54
Russian Federation **Fédération de Russie**	...	...	**6 746**	**6 150**	**5 659**	**4 859**	**4 565**	**4 140**	**3 931**	**3 607**
Beef,veal & buffalo Boeuf,veau et buffle	...	...	3 632	3 359	3 240	2 733	2 630	2 394	2 247	2 229
Pork Porc	...	...	2 784	2 432	2 103	1 865	1 705	1 546	1 505	1 205
Mutton,lamb & goat Mouton,agneau et caprin	...	...	330	359	316	261	230	200	178	174
Slovakia **Slovaquie**	...	...	...	**337**	**314**	**304**	**314**	**322**	**288**	**311**

38

Meat
Production: thousand metric tons [*cont.*]
Viande
Production : milliers de tonnes [*suite*]

Region, country or area Région, pays ou zone	1990	1991	1992	1993	1994	1995	1996	1997	1998	1999
Beef,veal & buffalo										
Boeuf,veau et buffle	...	...	...	93	67	59	61	66	59	50
Pork										
Porc	...	...	...	241	244	243	251	255	227	259
Mutton,lamb & goat										
Mouton,agneau et caprin	...	...	...	3	2	2	2	2	2	2
Slovenia										
Slovénie	...	...	**79**	**117**	**123**	**112**	**117**	**114**	**108**	**108**
Beef,veal & buffalo										
Boeuf,veau et buffle	...	...	38	52	52	51	54	54	45	45
Pork										
Porc	...	...	41	65	71	61	63	59	63	63
Spain										
Espagne	**2 537**	**2 630**	**2 690**	**2 817**	**2 849**	**2 925**	**3 159**	**3 238**	**3 644**	**3 824**
Beef,veal & buffalo										
Boeuf,veau et buffle	514	509	539	488	484	508	565	592	651	675
Pork										
Porc	1 789	1 877	1 918	2 089	2 124	2 175	2 356	2 401	2 744	2 900
Mutton,lamb & goat										
Mouton,agneau et caprin	234	244	233	241	241	242	238	245	249	249
Sweden										
Suède	**441**	**409**	**412**	**437**	**454**	**456**	**460**	**482**	**477**	**477**
Beef,veal & buffalo										
Boeuf,veau et buffle	145	137	130	142	142	143	138	149	143	143
Pork										
Porc	291	268	278	291	308	309	319	329	330	330
Mutton,lamb & goat										
Mouton,agneau et caprin	5	4	4	4	4	3	4	4	3	4
Switzerland										
Suisse	**440**	**445**	**436**	**422**	**394**	**404**	**385**	**373**	**386**	**382**
Beef,veal & buffalo										
Boeuf,veau et buffle	165	174	165	156	142	147	159	152	147	148
Pork										
Porc	270	265	264	260	246	251	220	214	232	227
Mutton,lamb & goat										
Mouton,agneau et caprin	5	6	6	6	6	6	6	6	6	7
TFYR Macedonia										
L'ex-R.y. Macédoine	...	...	**30**	**31**	**30**	**26**	**26**	**23**	**22**	**22**
Beef,veal & buffalo										
Boeuf,veau et buffle	...	...	8	8	8	7	7	8	7	7
Pork										
Porc	...	...	10	10	10	9	9	9	9	9
Mutton,lamb & goat										
Mouton,agneau et caprin	...	...	12	13	13	10	10	7	6	6
Ukraine										
Ukraine	...	...	**2 870**	**2 422**	**2 387**	**2 035**	**1 855**	**1 689**	**1 488**	**1 473**
Beef,veal & buffalo										
Boeuf,veau et buffle	...	...	1 656	1 379	1 427	1 186	1 037	930	793	786
Pork										
Porc	...	...	1 180	1 013	916	807	789	735	675	668
Mutton,lamb & goat										
Mouton,agneau et caprin	...	...	35	30	44	42	29	24	20	19
United Kingdom										
Royaume-Uni	**2 318**	**2 384**	**2 361**	**2 292**	**2 387**	**2 409**	**2 094**	**2 111**	**2 190**	**2 087**
Beef,veal & buffalo										
Boeuf,veau et buffle	1 002	1 020	971	881	943	996	708	696	697	678
Pork										
Porc	946	979	992	1 012	1 053	1 012	1 004	1 094	1 142	1 048

38

Meat
Production: thousand metric tons [*cont.*]

Viande
Production : milliers de tonnes [*suite*]

Region, country or area Région, pays ou zone	1990	1991	1992	1993	1994	1995	1996	1997	1998	1999
Mutton,lamb & goat Mouton,agneau et caprin	370	385	398	399	391	401	382	321	351	361
Yugoslavia **Yougoslavie**	...	...	**816**	**790**	**794**	**899**	**986**	**883**	**913**	**913**
Beef,veal & buffalo Boeuf,veau et buffle	...	...	201	231	197	227	242	209	258	258
Pork Porc	...	...	592	534	571	644	713	644	625	625
Mutton,lamb & goat Mouton,agneau et caprin	...	...	23	25	26	29	31	31	30	30
Yugoslavia, SFR† **Yougoslavie, Rfs†**	**1 230**	**1 075**	...	...	...	...	...	...	...	...
Beef,veal & buffalo Boeuf,veau et buffle	352	301	...	...	...	...	...	...	...	...
Pork Porc	810	716	...	...	...	...	...	...	...	...
Mutton,lamb & goat Mouton,agneau et caprin	67	57	...	...	...	...	...	...	...	...
Oceania **Océanie**	**3 755**	**3 965**	**4 020**	**3 991**	**4 015**	**4 078**	**3 935**	**4 059**	**4 243**	**4 161**
Beef,veal & buffalo Boeuf,veau et buffle	2 176	2 321	2 347	2 418	2 383	2 452	2 398	2 483	2 610	2 577
Pork Porc	**405**	**401**	**430**	**429**	**448**	**459**	**441**	**449**	**466**	**472**
Mutton,lamb & goat Mouton,agneau et caprin	**1 174**	**1 243**	**1 242**	**1 144**	**1 184**	**1 167**	**1 096**	**1 128**	**1 167**	**1 113**
Australia **Australie**	**2 635**	**2 755**	**2 807**	**2 809**	**2 827**	**2 786**	**2 662**	**2 737**	**2 931**	**2 982**
Beef,veal & buffalo Boeuf,veau et buffle	1 677	1 760	1 791	1 826	1 825	1 803	1 745	1 816	1 955	2 009
Pork Porc	317	312	336	328	344	351	334	339	356	362
Mutton,lamb & goat Mouton,agneau et caprin	641	683	681	655	658	631	583	582	619	611
Cook Islands **Iles Cook**	**0**	**0**	**0**	**0**	**0**	**0**	**1**	**1**	**1**	**1**
Pork Porc	0	0	0	0	0	0	1	1	1	1
Fiji **Fidji**	**14**	**14**	**14**	**13**	**13**	**13**	**13**	**14**	**14**	**14**
Beef,veal & buffalo Boeuf,veau et buffle	11	10	10	9	9	9	9	9	9	9
Pork Porc	3	3	3	3	4	3	3	4	3	3
Mutton,lamb & goat Mouton,agneau et caprin	1	1	1	1	1	1	1	1	1	1
French Polynesia **Polynésie française**	**2**	**1**	**1**	**1**	**2**	**2**	**1**	**1**	**1**	**1**
Pork Porc	1	1	1	1	1	1	1	1	1	1
Kiribati **Kiribati**	**1**	**1**	**1**	**1**	**1**	**1**	**1**	**1**	**1**	**1**
Pork Porc	1	1	1	1	1	1	1	1	1	1
Micronesia (Fed. States of) **Micron (Etats fédérés de)**	**0**	**0**	**0**	**0**	**0**	**1**	**1**	**1**	**1**	**1**

38

Meat
Production: thousand metric tons [*cont.*]
Viande
Production : milliers de tonnes [*suite*]

Region, country or area Région, pays ou zone	1990	1991	1992	1993	1994	1995	1996	1997	1998	1999
Pork Porc	0	0	0	0	0	1	1	1	1	1
New Caledonia **Nouvelle-Calédonie**	**4**	**4**	**5**	**5**	**6**	**5**	**6**	**6**	**6**	**6**
Beef,veal & buffalo Boeuf,veau et buffle	3	3	3	4	4	4	4	4	4	4
Pork Porc	1	1	1	1	1	1	1	1	1	1
New Zealand **Nouvelle-Zélande**	**1 054**	**1 143**	**1 143**	**1 109**	**1 111**	**1 215**	**1 194**	**1 240**	**1 231**	**1 097**
Beef,veal & buffalo Boeuf,veau et buffle	479	540	536	572	537	629	633	646	634	547
Pork Porc	43	44	47	49	49	51	50	49	50	50
Mutton,lamb & goat Mouton,agneau et caprin	532	559	560	488	525	535	511	544	547	500
Papua New Guinea **Papouasie-Nvl-Guinée**	**29**	**29**	**32**	**35**	**38**	**41**	**42**	**44**	**44**	**44**
Beef,veal & buffalo Boeuf,veau et buffle	2	2	2	2	2	2	2	2	2	2
Pork Porc	27	27	30	33	36	39	40	42	42	42
Samoa **Samoa**	**5**	**5**	**4**	**5**	**5**	**5**	**5**	**5**	**5**	**5**
Beef,veal & buffalo Boeuf,veau et buffle	1	1	1	1	1	1	1	1	1	1
Pork Porc	4	4	4	4	4	4	4	4	4	4
Solomon Islands **Iles Salomon**	**2**	**2**	**2**	**2**	**2**	**2**	**2**	**2**	**2**	**2**
Beef,veal & buffalo Boeuf,veau et buffle	1	1	0	0	0	0	0	0	0	0
Pork Porc	2	2	2	2	2	2	2	2	2	2
Tonga **Tonga**	**2**	**2**	**2**	**2**	**2**	**2**	**2**	**2**	**2**	**2**
Pork Porc	2	2	2	1	1	1	1	1	1	1
Vanuatu **Vanuatu**	**5**	**6**	**6**	**6**	**7**	**6**	**6**	**7**	**6**	**6**
Beef,veal & buffalo Boeuf,veau et buffle	3	3	3	4	4	4	4	4	4	4
Pork Porc	2	2	3	3	3	3	3	3	3	3
former USSR† **l'ex-URSS†**	**16 476**	**15 174**	...	...	...	...	...	...	...	...
Beef,veal & buffalo Boeuf,veau et buffle	8 814	8 261	...	...	...	...	...	...	...	...
Pork Porc	6 654	5 997	...	...	...	...	...	...	...	...
Mutton,lamb & goat Mouton,agneau et caprin	1 008	916	...	...	...	...	...	...	...	...

38
Meat
Production: thousand metric tons [*cont.*]
Viande
Production : milliers de tonnes [*suite*]

Source:
Food and Agriculture Organization of the United
Nations (FAO), Rome, "FAO Production Yearbook 1999" and the
FAOSTAT database.

† For information on recent changes in country or
area nomenclature pertaining to former Czechoslovakia,
Germany, Hong Kong Special Administrative Region (SAR) of
China, Macao Special Administrative Region (SAR) of China,
SFR of Yugoslavia and the former USSR, see Annex I - Country
or area nomenclature, regional and other groupings.

†† For statistical purposes, the data for
China do not include those for Hong Kong Special
Administrative Region (Hong Kong SAR) and Macao Special
Administrative Region (Macao SAR).

1 Data refer to the Gaza Strip.

Source:
Organisation des Nations Unies pour l'alimentation et
l'agriculture (FAO), Rome, "Annuaire FAO de la production
1999" et la base de données FAOSTAT.

† Pour les modifications récentes de nomenclature
de pays ou de zone concernant l'Allemagne, Hong Kong, région
administrative spéciale (RAS) de Chine, Macao, région
administrative spéciale (RAS) de Chine,
l'ex-Tchécoslovaquie, l'ex-URSS et l'ex-Rfs de Yougoslavie,
voir annexe I - Nomenclature des pays ou des zones,
groupements régionaux et autres groupements.

†† Les données statistiques relatives à
la Chine ne comprennent pas celles qui concernent la région
administrative spéciale de Hong Kong (la RAS de Hong Kong)
et la région administrative spéciale de Macao (la RAS de
Macao).

1 Les données se rapportent à la Zone de Gaza.

39

Beer
Bière

Production: thousand hectolitres
Production : milliers d'hectolitres

Country or area Pays ou zone	1989	1990	1991	1992	1993	1994	1995	1996	1997	1998
Albania Albanie	228	187	76	18	5	72	89	9	151	92
Algeria Algérie	365	325	301	337	421	398	402	377	379	382
Angola Angola	479	410	484	345	...	...	...	...	...	...
Argentina Argentine	6 102	6 170	7 979	9 518	10 305	11 272	10 913	11 615	12 687	...
Armenia Arménie	567	513	419	149	70	70	53	29	50	132
Australia Australie	19 508 [1] [2]	19 540	18 970	18 040	17 760	17 840	17 700	17 118	17 615	17 452
Austria Autriche	9 174	9 799	9 971	10 176	11 465	10 070	9 474	9 445	9 303	8 837
Azerbaijan Azerbaïdjan	4 928	5 876	5 159	1 855	148	114	22	13	16	11
Barbados Barbade	80	77	66	58	67	73	74	76	75	87
Belarus Bélarus	3 222	3 283	3 389	2 736	2 146	1 489	1 518	2 013	2 413	2 604
Belgium Belgique	13 164	14 141	13 799	14 259	...	15 055	15 110	14 408	14 758	14 763
Belize Belize	27	34	36	38	68	56	49	41	37	42
Bolivia Bolivie	965	1 031	1 278	1 333	1 121	1 262	* 1 429	...	...	...
Botswana Botswana	1 076	1 214	1 211	1 289	1 374	1 305	1 366	1 351	1 005	1 019
Brazil Brésil	42 343	43 849	54 545	43 509	45 336	52 556	67 284	63 559	66 582	66 243
Bulgaria Bulgarie	6 720	6 507	4 880	4 695	4 247	4 792	4 331	4 402	3 031	3 796
Burkina Faso Burkina Faso	398	350	394	71	258	...	...	...	...	...
Burundi Burundi	919	1 107	981	1 007	1 044	...	...	...	...	...
Cameroon Cameroun	...	...	4 324	3 834	4 373	2 073	2 933	...	...	...
Central African Rep. Rép. centrafricaine	...	...	270	285	124	450	269	...	...	...
Chad Tchad	115	116	144	129	117	110	95	...	...	...
Chile Chili	2 765	2 658	2 791	3 349	3 623	3 303	3 551	3 459	3 640	3 666
China ††[3] Chine ††[3]	52 662	56 657	68 590	83 536	97 565	115 752	128 406	137 664	154 610	162 693
Colombia Colombie	14 027	15 098	...	14 574	...	15 739	20 525	...	18 290	16 461

39

Beer
Production: thousand hectolitres [*cont.*]
Bière
Production : milliers d'hectolitres [*suite*]

Country or area Pays ou zone	1989	1990	1991	1992	1993	1994	1995	1996	1997	1998
Congo Congo	618	566	686	708	759	...	...	...	...	...
Croatia Croatie	2 279	2 800	2 248	2 720	2 481	3 122	3 166	3 292	3 607	3 759
Cuba Cuba	3 333	...	...	...	...	...	...	...	...	...
Cyprus Chypre	318	342	331	370	341	359	352	331	333	365
Czech Republic République tchèque	18 854	18 936	17 902	18 982	17 366	17 876	17 687	18 057	18 558	18 289
Denmark[4] Danemark[4]	9 217	9 362		9 775	9 435	9 410	9 903	9 591	9 181	8 044
Dominica Dominique	...	...	...	...	...	...	3	14	11	...
Dominican Republic Rép. dominicaine	...	1 376	1 459	2 057	1 837	2 190	2 082	447	2 593	2 993
Ecuador Equateur	...	...	...	1 826	1 525	1 131	3 201	2 163	...	...
Egypt Egypte	490	500	440	420	350	360	360	380	...	...
Estonia Estonie	89	77	675	426	419	477	492	459	543	744
Ethiopia[5] Ethiopie[5]	777	500	435	428	522	634	724	876	843	831
Fiji Fidji	175	194	183	173	167	160	150	170	170	170
Finland Finlande	3 947	4 151	4 418	4 685	4 579	4 524	4 702	4 980	4 840	4 341
France France	...	19 109	18 654	18 512	18 291	17 688	18 311	17 140	...	...
French Polynesia Polynésie française	121	121	124	129	...	...	...	...	...	...
Gabon Gabon	786	819	814	785	905	801	816	...	...	...
Georgia Géorgie	...	...	...	235	120	63	65	48	79	74
Germany Allemagne	...	...	112 071	114 089	111 075	113 428	111 875	108 938	108 729	106 993
F. R. Germany R. f. Allemagne	87 761	99 150	...	...	...	...	...	...	...	...
former German D. R. l'ex-R. d. allemande	24 843	15 885	...	...	...	...	...	...	...	...
Greece Grèce	3 869	3 961	3 772	4 025	4 088	4 376	4 024	3 766	3 950	...
Grenada Grenade	21	25	25	26	18	24	...	...	...	...
Guatemala Guatemala	...	...	974	1 172	1 327	805	1 471	1 655	1 303	1 363

39
Beer
Production: thousand hectolitres [cont.]
Bière
Production : milliers d'hectolitres [suite]

Country or area Pays ou zone	1989	1990	1991	1992	1993	1994	1995	1996	1997	1998
Guyana Guyana	106	109	124	143	145	97	...	...	...	...
Hungary Hongrie	9 722	9 918	9 570	9 162	7 877	8 082	7 697	7 270	6 973	7 163
Iceland Islande	44	35	30	32	41	54	52	63	64	71
India[6] Inde[6]	1 972	1 915	2 136	2 233	3 053	2 778	3 700	4 255	4 331	4 332
Indonesia Indonésie	952	1 042	1 043	1 145	871	779	1 136	...	531	...
Ireland Irlande	5 094[7]	5 236[7]	...	...	...	...	8 132	10 765	12 095	12 580
Israel Israël	511	567	532	511	587	508	...	...	...	...
Italy Italie	10 615	11 248	11 049	10 489	9 873	10 258	10 616	9 559	10 379	11 073
Jamaica Jamaïque	852	887	715	828	786	760	662	690	674	670
Japan[8] Japon[8]	62 869	65 636	69 157	70 106	69 642	71 007	67 971	69 082	66 370	61 759
Jordan Jordanie	46	...	...	...	...	...	...	...	...	...
Kazakhstan Kazakhstan	2 936	2 980	31 330	23 011	1 692	129	812	636	693	850
Kenya Kenya	3 154	3 311	3 140	3 686	3 589	3 250	3 474	2 759	...	...
Korea, Republic of Corée, République de	12 108	13 045	15 928	15 673	15 252	17 176	17 554	17 210	16 907	14 080
Kyrgyzstan Kirghizistan	42	40	44	31	19	12	12	14	14	13
Lao People's Dem. Rep. Rép. dém. pop. lao	...	...	...	...	...	102	151	...	...	...
Latvia Lettonie	856	874	1 295	859	546	638	653	645	715	721
Lithuania Lituanie	1 603	1 502	1 412	1 426	1 164	1 353	1 093	1 139	1 413	1 559
Luxembourg Luxembourg	618	600	572	569	558	531	518	484	481	469
Madagascar Madagascar	232	298	236	226	228	...	...	...	...	...
Malawi Malawi	757	752	763	774	763	811	289	277	292	206
Malaysia Malaisie	1 263	1 401	1 413	...	...	...	...	...	...	...
Mali Mali	34	34	38	41	40	43	52	60	...	...
Mauritius Maurice	254	281	291	295	292	283	309	312	339	376
Mexico Mexique	37 355	38 734	41 092	42 262	43 630	45 060	44 205	48 111	51 315	54 569

39
Beer
Production: thousand hectolitres [*cont.*]
Bière
Production : milliers d'hectolitres [*suite*]

Country or area Pays ou zone	1989	1990	1991	1992	1993	1994	1995	1996	1997	1998
Mongolia Mongolie	67	...	...	...	...	...	...	...	...	...
Mozambique Mozambique	413	353	227	211	204	118	244	374	631	...
Myanmar[9] Myanmar[9]	21	24	30	19	24	13	...	...	...	...
Nepal[10] Népal[10]	73	...	...	123	144	149	168	183	215	205
Netherlands[4][11] Pays-Bas[4][11]	18 908	20 055	19 863	20 419	19 720	21 200	22 380	22 670	23 780	23 040
New Zealand[4] Nouvelle-Zélande[4]	3 916	3 890	3 627	3 637	3 519	3 568	3 488	3 435	3 214	3 206
Nigeria Nigéria	8 179	7 877	8 108	11 438	16 860	1 561	1 461	...	...	...
Norway Norvège	2 229	2 281	...	2 273	...	...	2 255	...	2 396	1 833
Panama Panama	1 042	1 066	1 219	1 163	1 204	1 291	1 274	1 206	...	...
Paraguay Paraguay	1 060	1 070	1 150	1 140	1 710	...	...	...	...	...
Peru Pérou	5 548	5 685	6 774	6 764	7 060	6 957	7 815	7 493	7 428	6 556
Poland Pologne	12 082	11 294	13 633	14 139	12 585	14 099	15 205	16 667	19 281	21 017
Portugal Portugal	6 874	6 919	6 309	6 923	6 662	6 902	7 220	6 958	6 766	7 072
Puerto Rico Porto Rico	630	751	773	654	477	438	397	360	317	258
Republic of Moldova République de Moldova	711	762	660	410	297[12]	233[12]	276[12]	226[12]	238[12]	278[12]
Romania Roumanie	11 513	10 527	9 803	10 014	9 929	9 047	8 768	8 118	7 651	9 989
Russian Federation Fédération de Russie	31 600	33 600	33 300	27 900	24 700	21 800	21 400	20 800	26 100	33 500
Saint Kitts and Nevis Saint-Kitts-et-Nevis	17	17	17	16	17	17	20	...	...	...
Seychelles Seychelles	52	53	59	70	65	58	58	63	71	72
Slovakia Slovaquie	4 538	4 607	4 082	3 686	3 967	4 974	4 369	4 666	5 577	4 478
Slovenia Slovénie	2 023	2 456	2 203	1 783	1 978	2 075	2 087	2 223	2 138	2 000
South Africa Afrique du Sud	18 610	17 750	17 710	18 290	...	...	...	...	...	...
Spain Espagne	27 546	27 940	26 482	24 279	21 353	25 587	25 396	24 520	24 786	22 428
Sri Lanka Sri Lanka	60	...	...	...	...	...	...	...	...	...

39
Beer
Production: thousand hectolitres [cont.]
Bière
Production : milliers d'hectolitres [suite]

Country or area Pays ou zone	1989	1990	1991	1992	1993	1994	1995	1996	1997	1998
Suriname Suriname	117	122	122	71	107	69	65	72	...	...
Sweden Suède	4 722	4 711	4 663	4 969	5 087	5 379	5 471	5 318	5 078	4 765
Switzerland[4] Suisse[4]	4 121	4 143	4 137	4 020	3 804	3 828	3 672	...	...	...
Syrian Arab Republic Rép. arabe syrienne	95	99	99	102	104	102	102	102	97	97
Tajikistan Tadjikistan	267	317	364	135	82	67	47	6	6	9
Thailand Thaïlande	1 801	2 635	2 840	3 252	4 153	5 230	6 473	7 591	8 742	9 770
TFYR Macedonia L'ex-R.y. Macédoine	691	958	928	861	952	725	620	622	600	578
Trinidad and Tobago Trinité-et-Tobago	527	412	487	395	424	482	428	419	407	517
Tunisia Tunisie	394	426	407	494	601	689	659	662	780	813
Turkey Turquie	2 994	3 544	4 188	4 843	5 524	6 019	6 946	7 381	7 658	7 130
Turkmenistan Turkménistan	322	442	465	372	287	218	113	17	44	29
Uganda Ouganda	195	194	195	187	239	308	512	642	896	...
Ukraine Ukraine	13 749	13 778	13 093	10 997	9 086	9 087	7 102	6 025	6 125	6 842
former USSR† l'ex-URSS†	60 182	62 507	...	...	...	...	...	...	...	...
United Kingdom Royaume-Uni	54 950	70 800	...	...	...	66 161	59 337	61 262	64 736	60 806
United Rep.Tanzania Rép.-Unie de Tanzanie	537	450	498	493	570	568	893	125	148	...
United States[7] Etats-Unis[7]	232 510	236 670	...	237 029	237 345	237 987	...	233 485	...	...
Uruguay Uruguay	...	...	...	...	817	...	998	815	921	860
Uzbekistan Ouzbékistan	1 620	1 746	1 759	1 434	1 363	1 291	724	677	619	...
Viet Nam Viet Nam	892	1 000	1 312	1 685	...	...	...	...	...	...
Yemen Yémen	60	50	100	40	...	...	...	...	...	...
Yugoslavia Yougoslavie	4 991	6 105	5 460	4 413	3 019	5 043	5 611	5 987	6 106	6 630
Yugoslavia, SFR† Yougoslavie, Rfs†	11 286	...	...	...	...	...	...	...	...	...

39
Beer
Production: thousand hectolitres [*cont.*]

Bière
Production : milliers d'hectolitres [*suite*]

Source:
United Nations Secretariat, "Industrial Commodity Statistics
Yearbook 1998" and the industrial statistics database of
the Statistics Division.

† For information on recent changes in country or
area nomenclature pertaining to former Czechoslovakia,
Germany, Hong Kong Special Administrative Region (SAR) of
China, Macao Special Administrative Region (SAR) of China,
SFR of Yugoslavia and the former USSR, see Annex I - Country
or area nomenclature, regional and other groupings.

†† For statistical purposes, the data for
China do not include those for Hong Kong Special
Administrative Region (Hong Kong SAR), Macao Special
Administrative Region (Macao SAR) and Taiwan province of
China.

1 Twelve months ending 30 June of year stated.

2 Excluding light beer containing less than 1.15% by volume of
alcohol.
3 Original data in metric tons.
4 Sales.
5 Twelve months ending 7 July of the year stated.

6 Production by large and medium scale establishments only.
7 Twelve months ending 30 September of year stated.

8 Twelve months beginning 1 April of year stated.

9 Government production only.
10 Twelve months beginning 16 July of year stated.

11 Production by establishments employing 20 or more persons.
12 Excluding Transnistria region.

Source:
Secrétariat de l'Organisation des Nations Unies, "Annuaire
de statistiques industrielles par produit 1998" et la base
de données pour les statistiques industrielles de la
Division de statistique.

† Pour les modifications récentes de nomenclature
de pays ou de zone concernant l'Allemagne, Hong Kong, région
administrative spéciale (RAS) de Chine, Macao, région
administrative spéciale (RAS) de Chine,
l'ex-Tchécoslovaquie, l'ex-URSS et l'ex-Rfs de Yougoslavie,
voir annexe I - Nomenclature des pays ou des zones,
groupements régionaux et autres groupements.

†† Les données statistiques relatives à
la Chine ne comprennent pas celles qui concernent la région
administrative spéciale de Hong Kong (la RAS de Hong Kong),
la région administrative spéciale de Macao (la RAS de Macao)
et la province chinoise de Taiwan.

1 Période de douze mois finissant le 30e juin de l'année
indiquée.
2 Non compris la bière légère contenant moins de 1.15 p. 100
en volume d'alcool.
3 Données d'origine exprimées en tonnes.
4 Ventes.
5 Période de douze mois finissant le 7e juillet de l'année
indiquée.
6 Production des grandes et moyennes entreprises seulement.
7 Période de douze mois finissant le 30e septembre de l'année
indiquée.
8 Période de douze mois commençant le 1er avril de l'année
indiquée.
9 Production de l'Etat seulement.
10 Période de douze mois commençant le 16e juillet de l'année
indiquée.
11 Production des établissements occupant 20 personnes ou plus.
12 Non compris la région de Transnistria.

40
Cigarettes
Cigarettes
Production: millions
Production : millions

Country or area Pays ou zone	1989	1990	1991	1992	1993	1994	1995	1996	1997	1998
Albania [1] Albanie [1]	6 184	4 947	1 703	1 393	1 395	929	685	4 830	414	764
Algeria [1] Algérie [1]	15 850	18 775	17 848	16 426	16 260	16 345	...	...	...	...
Angola [2] Angola [2]	2 400	2 400	2 400	2 400	...	...	...	...	...	...
Argentina Argentine	1 677	1 657	1 727	1 845	1 929	1 975	1 963	1 971	1 940	...
Armenia Arménie	9 006	8 102	6 614	3 927	1 878	2 014	1 043	152	815	2 490
Australia [3] Australie [3]	34 736	36 263	34 977	* 34 000	...	...	...	...	...	...
Austria Autriche	14 402	14 961	16 406	15 836	16 247	16 429	16 298	...	...	...
Azerbaijan Azerbaïdjan	7 049	6 453	7 256	4 855	5 277	3 179	1 926	766	827	232
Bangladesh [4] Bangladesh [4]	14 088	12 289	13 604	12 535	11 516	12 655	17 379	16 222	18 601	...
Barbados Barbade	143 [1]	135 [1]	124 [1]	115 [1]	133 [1]	150 [1]	65	...	...	...
Belarus Bélarus	15 953	16 399	15 009	8 847	8 670	7 378	6 228	6 267	6 787	7 296
Belgium Belgique	27 489 [5]	27 758 [5]	27 303 [5]	29 576 [5]	27 173 [5]	21 366	18 826	17 471	18 061	17 519
Belize Belize	95	101	104	104	105	101	95	79	88	94
Bolivia Bolivie	101	97	102	116	119	1 490	* 170	...	...	...
Brazil [2] Brésil [2]	162 700	173 987	175 396	169 000	...	...	...	...	...	...
Bulgaria Bulgarie	82 600	73 000	79 749	48 558	32 098	53 664	74 603	57 238	43 315	33 181
Burkina Faso Burkina Faso	609	822	983	979	943	...	...	...	...	...
Burundi Burundi	286	384	450	453	517	...	...	...	...	...
Cambodia [2] Cambodge [2]	4 200	4 200	4 200	4 200	...	...	...	...	...	...
Cameroon [2] Cameroun [2]	4 800	4 900	5 000	5 000	...	...	...	...	...	...
Canada Canada	48 792 [2]	46 111 [2]	46 815 [2]	45 500 [2]	...	...	50 775	49 362	47 263	...
Central African Rep. Rép. centrafricaine	19	25	26	21	12	21	30	...	...	...
Chad Tchad	187	248	476	415	499	508	569	...	...	...
Chile Chili	9 686	10 198	10 259	11 167	10 793	10 801	10 891	11 569	12 522	12 904

40
Cigarettes
Production: millions [*cont.*]
Cigarettes
Production : millions [*suite*]

Country or area Pays ou zone	1989	1990	1991	1992	1993	1994	1995	1996	1997	1998
China †† Chine ††	1 597 530	1 648 765	1 613 245	1 642 340	1 655 630	...	...	...	...	...
China, Hong Kong SAR†[5] Chine, Hong Kong RAS†[5]	20 901	21 700	32 721	36 513	25 759	24 747	22 767	21 386	20 929	13 470
China, Macao SAR †[167] Chine, Macao RAS †[167]	500	500	500	500	500	450	450	450	...	...
Colombia Colombie	16 570[2]	14 490[2]	13 585[2]	14 877	...	11 566	10 491	...	11 662	12 472
Congo Congo	709[1]	* 645	581[1]	431[1]	...	...	...	...	...	...
Costa Rica Costa Rica	2 050[2]	2 030[2]	2 000[2]	2 000[2]	16[16]	16[16]	16[16]	16[16]	...	...
Côte d'Ivoire[2] Côte d'Ivoire[2]	4 500	4 500	4 500	4 500	...	...	...	...	...	...
Croatia Croatie	13 301	12 437	11 655	12 833	11 585	12 672	12 110	11 548	11 416	11 987
Cuba Cuba	16 520	...	...	...	...	...	...	...	...	...
Cyprus Chypre	3 935	4 601	5 497	6 177	3 530	2 493	2 528	2 728	3 484	4 362
Czech Republic République tchèque	16 965	18 119	...	...	...	...	...	...	...	...
Dem. Rep. of the Congo[2] Rép. dém. du Congo[2]	5 200	5 200	5 200	5 200	...	...	...	...	...	...
Denmark[8] Danemark[8]	11 209	11 387	11 407	11 439	10 980	11 448	11 902	11 804	12 262	12 392
Dominican Republic Rép. dominicaine	4 473[2]	4 535	4 170	4 432	4 356	4 513	4 092	4 192	3 972	4 098
Ecuador Equateur	* 4 600	* 4 600	* 4 600	3 000	3 079	2 515	1 734	1 745	...	...
Egypt Egypte	43 208	39 837	40 154	42 516	38 844	39 145	42 469	46 000	50 000	52 000
El Salvador El Salvador	1 970[2]	1 655[2]	1 620[2]	1 620[2]	...	...	1 701	1 756	...	...
Estonia Estonie	4 726	4 165	3 577	1 780	2 630	2 287	1 864	954		
Ethiopia[9] Ethiopie[9]	2 711	2 258	2 416	1 879	1 932	1 468	1 583	1 862	2 024	2 029
Fiji Fidji	505	531	514	484	506	483	437	439	450	410
Finland Finlande	8 931	8 974	8 180	8 106	7 237	7 232	6 542	5 910	...	...
France France	* 54 225	55 495	50 311	* 53 312	47 912	48 188	46 361	46 931	...	...
Gabon Gabon	362	328	358	399	334	288	297	...	...	...
Georgia Géorgie	...	...	...	4 953	3 593	3 256	1 840	1 183	917	595

40
Cigarettes
Production: millions [cont.]
Cigarettes
Production : millions [suite]

Country or area Pays ou zone	1989	1990	1991	1992	1993	1994	1995	1996	1997	1998
Germany Allemagne	...	...	...	...	204 730	222 791	...	...	...	...
F. R. Germany R. f. Allemagne	159 477	177 905	...	...	...	...	...	...	...	...
former German D. R. l'ex-R. d. allemande	28 625	22 469	...	...	...	...	...	...	...	...
Ghana Ghana	1 616	1 805	* 2 100	* 2 100	...	...	...	...	...	...
Greece Grèce	26 123	26 175	27 700	* 29 250	30 427	32 843	39 291	38 268	36 909	...
Grenada Grenade	24	22	20	20	19	15	...	...	...	...
Guatemala Guatemala	1 997 [2]	1 955 [2]	870	2 001 [2]	2 010	1 390	2 616	1 725	2 198	4 184
Guyana Guyana	266	247	307	318	302	314	...	...	...	...
Haiti Haïti	870 [2]	1 027	985	970	1 110	722	...	...	...	...
Honduras [2] Honduras [2]	2 582	2 862	2 300	2 200	...	...	...	...	...	...
Hungary Hongrie	26 540	28 212	26 124	26 835	28 728	29 518	25 709	27 594	26 057	26 849
India [10] Inde [10]	58 066	61 162	65 130	61 413	71 842	71 038	69 589	73 841	83 162	...
Indonesia Indonésie	...	...	...	34 382	34 757	36 421	38 768			
Iran (Islamic Rep. of) Iran (Rép. islamique d')	9 923 [11]	12 319 [11]	* 11 565 [11]	10 171 [11]	7 835 [11]	7 939 [11]	9 787 [12]	11 860 [12]	10 304 [12]	...
Iraq [2] Iraq [2]	27 000	26 000	13 000	5 794	...	...	...	...	...	...
Ireland Irlande	6 161	6 218	6 377	* 7 850	7 300 [16]	7 000 [16]	7 500 [16]	7 500 [16]	461	645
Israel Israël	5 245	5 440	5 590 [1]	5 742 [1]	5 525 [1]	5 638 [1]	4 933 [1]	4 793 [1]	...	...
Italy Italie	67 942 [1]	61 736 [1]	57 634 [1]	53 799 [1]	54 943 [1]	55 175 [1]	50 247 [1]	51 489 [1]	51 894 [1]	50 785
Jamaica Jamaïque	1 383	1 380	1 219	1 299	1 224	1 273	1 216	...	...	...
Japan [13] Japon [13]	268 400	268 100	275 000	279 000	...	...	...	...	...	...
Jordan Jordanie	2 926	3 185	3 719	3 091	3 465	4 191	3 675	4 738	...	...
Kazakhstan Kazakhstan	...	...	9 536	8 997	10 664	9 393	12 080	19 121	24 109	21 747
Kenya Kenya	6 661	6 647	6 473	7 193	7 267	7 319	7 932	8 436	...	...
Korea, Republic of Corée, République de	86 759	91 923	94 336	96 648	96 887	90 774	87 959	94 709	96 725	101 011
Kyrgyzstan Kirghizistan	4 010	3 974	4 015	3 120	3 428	1 943	1 332	975	716	862

40
Cigarettes
Production: millions [*cont.*]
Cigarettes
Production : millions [*suite*]

Country or area Pays ou zone	1989	1990	1991	1992	1993	1994	1995	1996	1997	1998
Lao People's Dem. Rep. Rép. dém. pop. lao	1 200 [2]	1 200 [2]	1 200 [2]	1 200 [2]	...	936	1 062	...	...	...
Latvia Lettonie	5 522	5 209	4 765	3 435	2 589	2 093	2 101	1 876	1 775	2 018
Lebanon Liban	4 000 [2]	4 000 [2]	4 000 [2]	4 000 [2]	...	...	535 [1]	539 [1]	...	...
Liberia [2] Libéria [2]	22	22	22	22	...	...	...	...	...	
Libyan Arab Jamah. [2] Jamah. arabe libyenne [2]	3 500	3 500	3 500	3 500						
Lithuania Lituanie	7 828	6 654	6 438	5 269	3 435	3 860	4 876	...	...	
Madagascar [1] Madagascar [1]	2 341	1 476	1 950	2 223	2 304	...	...	...		
Malawi Malawi	* 1 080	1 061	951	1 000	1 020	1 127	1 160	975	731	501
Malaysia [1] Malaisie [1]	16 169	17 331	17 498	16 574	15 568	15 762	15 918	16 896	20 236	18 410
Mali Mali	...	17	23	24	23	20	22	21	...	...
Malta [2] Malte [2]	1 450	1 475	1 475	1 475	...	...	...	...	...	
Mauritius Maurice	1 050	1 000	1 034	1 060	1 269	1 300	1 215	1 193	1 144	1 038
Mexico Mexique	53 920	55 380	54 680	55 988	53 435	53 402	56 821	59 907	57 618	60 407
Morocco Maroc	615	640	602	515	...	...	...	...	...	
Mozambique Mozambique	1 044	1 030	217	124	377	343	106	250	250	...
Myanmar [14] Myanmar [14]	505	979	682	396	426	440	752	1 727	1 991	2 040
Nepal [15] Népal [15]	6 706	...	...	6 963	7 846	6 894	7 430	8 067	7 944	7 699
Netherlands [8][16] Pays-Bas [8][16]	63 148	71 992	74 767	78 479	71 254	88 069	97 727	...	...	...
New Zealand Nouvelle-Zélande	4 270	4 489	4 014	3 466	3 381	3 396 [8]	3 338 [8]	3 660 [8]	3 449 [8]	3 263 [8]
Nicaragua [2] Nicaragua [2]	2 400	2 400	2 400	2 400	...	...	...	...	...	
Nigeria Nigéria	9 284	10 380	9 405	8 608	9 384	338	256	...	...	
Norway [2] Norvège [2]	1 750	1 480	1 730	1 825	...	...	...	...	...	
Pakistan [4] Pakistan [4]	31 567	32 279	29 887	29 673	29 947	35 895	32 747	45 506	46 101	48 215
Panama Panama	637	810	771	806	903	1 204	1 136	663	...	...
Paraguay Paraguay	2 730	992	827	777	...	...	...	...	...	...

40
Cigarettes
Production: millions [cont.]
Cigarettes
Production : millions [suite]

Country or area Pays ou zone	1989	1990	1991	1992	1993	1994	1995	1996	1997	1998
Peru Pérou	2 439	2 585	2 696	2 501	2 511	2 752	2 970	3 279	2 960	3 061
Philippines[16] Philippines[16]	6 970	7 175	7 071	6 771	7 135	7 300	7 440	7 440	...	...
Poland Pologne	81 342	91 497	90 407	86 571	90 713	98 394	100 627	95 293	95 798	96 741
Portugal Portugal	15 424 [1]	17 547	17 361	15 619	15 335	13 610	13 215	12 780	13 234	15 781
Republic of Moldova République de Moldova	9 452	9 088	9 164	8 582	8 790 [17]	8 001 [17]	7 108 [17]	9 657 [17]	9 539 [17]	7 512
Romania[3] Roumanie[3]	22 121	18 090	17 722	17 781	15 222	14 532	14 747	16 536	25 943	...
Russian Federation Fédération de Russie	121 756	115 321	112 326	107 763	100 162	91 601	99 545	112 319	140 077	195 806
Senegal[2] Sénégal[2]	3 350	3 350	3 350	3 350	...	...	...	...	...	...
Seychelles Seychelles	58	67	69	62	65	49	56	62	70	61
Sierra Leone[2] Sierra Leone[2]	1 200	1 200	1 200	1 200	...	...	...	...	...	...
Singapore[2] Singapour[2]	5 982	9 620	10 500	11 760	...	...	...	...	...	...
Slovakia Slovaquie	8 463	8 589	8 721	...	...	...	...	...	...	...
Slovenia Slovénie	6 409	5 179	4 798	5 278	4 851	4 722	4 543	4 909	5 767	7 555
South Africa Afrique du Sud	36 665	40 792	40 163	35 563	34 499	...	...	...	...	...
Spain Espagne	75 817	75 995	81 843	76 696	80 103	81 886	78 676	77 675	77 315	81 940
Sri Lanka Sri Lanka	5 136	5 621	5 789	5 359	5 649	5 656	5 822	6 160	* 5 712	5 653
Sudan[2] Soudan[2]	750	750	750	750	...	...	...	...	...	...
Suriname Suriname	526	487	337	419	454	443	472	483		
Sweden Suède	10 107	9 648	9 594	9 841	7 420	8 032	7 193	7 251	6 237	5 692
Switzerland Suisse	28 059	31 771	32 943	33 740	34 713	39 906	41 976	42 955	37 638	34 453
Syrian Arab Republic[1] Rép. arabe syrienne [1]	6 345	6 855	7 974	8 093	7 185	7 773	9 699	8 528	10 137	10 398
Tajikistan Tadjikistan	5 248	5 022	4 467	2 607	1 901	1 644	964	604	153	191
Thailand Thaïlande	37 365	38 180	39 697	40 691	42 043	45 359	43 020	48 173	43 387	34 585
Trinidad and Tobago Trinité-et-Tobago	726 [1]	701 [1]	881 [1]	656 [1]	638	593	920	1 102	1 386	1 680

40
Cigarettes
Production: millions [*cont.*]
Cigarettes
Production : millions [*suite*]

Country or area Pays ou zone	1989	1990	1991	1992	1993	1994	1995	1996	1997	1998
Tunisia Tunisie	6 571	6 852	7 790	7 797	6 965	7 128	7 421	7 159	7 735	7 606
Turkey Turquie	46 570	63 055	71 106	67 549	74 845	85 093	80 700	73 787	74 984	81 616
Uganda Ouganda	1 586	1 290	1 688	1 575	1 412	1 459	1 576	1 702	1 810	...
Ukraine Ukraine	78 446	69 397	66 645	60 990	40 571	47 083	48 033	44 900	54 488	59 268
former USSR† l'ex-URSS†	343 288	313 082	...	...	...	...	...	...	...	...
United Kingdom Royaume-Uni	104 155[1 18]	112 000[1 18]	127 000[1 18]	* 126 538[1 18]	146 138	165 479	155 103	166 496	167 670	152 998
United Rep.Tanzania Rép.-Unie de Tanzanie	2 845	3 742	3 870	3 789	3 893	3 383	3 699	3 733	4 710	...
United States Etats-Unis	677 200	709 700	694 500	718 500	661 000	725 500	746 500	754 500	719 600	679 700
Uruguay Uruguay	3 900[2]	3 900[2]	3 900[2]	3 900[2]	3 736	...	3 561	6 044	6 870	9 209
Uzbekistan Ouzbékistan	6 103	4 370	4 897	4 150	4 151	3 379	2 742	5 172	8 521	...
Venezuela[2] Venezuela[2]	20 599	23 560	24 236	24 400	...	...	...	...	...	...
Viet Nam Viet Nam	23 288	24 990	25 960	* 24 600	...	...	...	...	...	...
Yemen Yémen	6 029[16]	5 968[16]	6 790[16]	6 294[16]	8 844[16]	5 423[16]	6 540	6 740	6 800	...
Yugoslavia Yougoslavie	...		17 605	15 654	16 053	12 972	12 686	13 176	10 988	14 597
Yugoslavia, SFR† Yougoslavie, Rfs†	51 287	58 200	...	...	...	...	...	...	...	...
Zambia[2] Zambie[2]	1 500	1 500	1 500	1 500	...	...	...	...	...	...
Zimbabwe[2] Zimbabwe[2]	2 518	2 600	3 240	3 025	...	...	...	...	...	...

Source:
United Nations Secretariat, "Industrial Commodity Statistics
Yearbook 1998" and the industrial statistics database of
the Statistics Division.

† For information on recent changes in country or
area nomenclature pertaining to former Czechoslovakia,
Germany, Hong Kong Special Administrative Region (SAR) of
China, Macao Special Administrative Region (SAR) of China,
SFR of Yugoslavia and the former USSR, see Annex I - Country
or area nomenclature, regional and other groupings.

†† For statistical purposes, the data for
China do not include those for Hong Kong Special
Administrative Region (Hong Kong SAR), Macao Special

Source:
Secrétariat de l'Organisation des Nations Unies, "Annuaire
de statistiques industrielles par produit 1998" et la base
de données pour les statistiques industrielles de la
Division de statistique.

† Pour les modifications récentes de nomenclature
de pays ou de zone concernant l'Allemagne, Hong Kong, région
administrative spéciale (RAS) de Chine, Macao, région
administrative spéciale (RAS) de Chine,
l'ex-Tchécoslovaquie, l'ex-URSS et l'ex-Rfs de Yougoslavie,
voir annexe I - Nomenclature des pays ou des zones,
groupements régionaux et autres groupements.

†† Les données statistiques relatives à

40

Cigarettes
Production: millions [*cont.*]

Cigarettes
Production : millions [*suite*]

Administrative Region (Macao SAR) and Taiwan province of China.

1   Original data in units of weight. Computed on the basis of one million cigarettes par tonne.
2   Source: U. S. Department of Agriculture, (Washington, D. C.).
3   Including cigars.
4   Twelve months ending 30 June of year stated.

5   Including cigarillos.
6   Source: Food and Agriculture Organization of the United Nations (FAO), (Rome).
7   1997 data are confidential.
8   Sales.
9   Twelve months ending 7 July of the year stated.

10 Production by large and medium scale establishments only.
11 Production by establishments employing 50 or more persons.
12 Production by establishments employing 10 or more persons.
13 Twelve months beginning 1 April of year stated.

14 Government production only.
15 Twelve months beginning 16 July of year stated.

16 Beginning 1986, production by establishments employing 20 or more persons.
17 Excluding Transnistria region.
18 Sales by manufacturers employing 25 or more persons.

la Chine ne comprennent pas celles qui concernent la région administrative spéciale de Hong Kong (la RAS de Hong Kong), la région administrative spéciale de Macao (la RAS de Macao) et la province chinoise de Taiwan.

1   Données d'origine exprimées en poids. Calcul sur la base d'un million cigarettes par tonne.
2   Source: "U.S. Department of Agriculture," (Washington, D.C.).
3   Y compris les cigares.
4   Période de douze mois finissant le 30e juin de l'année indiquée.
5   Y compris les cigarillos.
6   Source: Organisation des Nations Unies pour l'alimentation et l'agriculture (FAO), (Rome).
7   Pour 1997, les données sont confidentielles.
8   Ventes.
9   Période de douze mois finissant le 7e juillet de l'année indiquée.
10 Production des grandes et moyennes entreprises seulement.
11 Production des établissements occupant 50 personnes ou plus.
12 Production des établissements occupant 10 personnes ou plus.
13 Période de douze mois commençant le 1er avril de l'année indiquée.
14 Production de l'Etat seulement.
15 Période de douze mois commençant le 16e juillet de l'année indiquée.
16 A partir de 1986, production des établissements occupant 20 personnes ou plus.
17 Non compris la région de Transnistria.
18 Ventes des fabricants employant 25 personnes ou plus.

41
Fabrics
Tissus
Woven cotton and wool, cellulosic and non−cellulosic fibres: million square metres
Tissus de coton, laines, fibres cellulosiques et non cellulosiques : millions de mètres carrés

Country or area Pays ou zone	1989	1990	1991	1992	1993	1994	1995	1996	1997	1998
A. Cotton · Coton										
Armenia Arménie	29	34	10	5	2	0	...	...	...	...
Australia [1] Australie [1]	36[2]	38	36[2]	40	41	50	52	64	61	62
Austria Autriche	88	108	100	86	83	83	89	14	15	16
Azerbaijan Azerbaïdjan	121	102	95	77	98	78	58	24	17	7
Bangladesh [1] Bangladesh [1]	63	63	63	63	63	63	63	63	63	...
Belarus Bélarus	138	144	144	119	92	25	34	45	48	72
Belgium Belgique	386	399	379	337	331	...	...	...	...	...
Bolivia [3] Bolivie [3]	2	2	1	1	0	0	* 0	...	...	...
Brazil [3][4][5] Brésil [3][4][5]	2 178	1 901	1 679	1 616	1 568	1 566	1 354	1 298		
Bulgaria [6] Bulgarie [6]	367	254	138	102	83	86	93	85	98	
Cameroon [3] Cameroun [3]	...	...	18	21	18	35	24	...	...	
Chad Tchad	57	58	60	81	...	...	...	...	...	
Chile [3] Chili [3]	38	31	24	23	32	28	29	34		
China †† [3] Chine †† [3]	22 609	22 557	21 719	22 783	24 263	25 243	31 091	...	...	...
China, Hong Kong SAR † Chine, Hong Kong RAS †	734	* 818	753	807	755	692	658	540	506	...
China, Macao SAR † Chine, Macao RAS †	...	...	...	...	15	10	8	9	9	10
Congo [3] Congo [3]	14	11	7	6	2	...	...	...	...	...
Croatia Croatie	55	39	30	29	29	23	22	19	34	39
Cuba [5] Cuba [5]	184	...	...	...	...	...	...	...	...	...
Czech Republic République tchèque	523	529	381	293	337	340	358	330	346	337
Egypt Egypte	601	603	609	613	329	494	414	321	290	...
Estonia Estonie	187	169	168	111	55	74	90	120	130	127
Ethiopia [7] Ethiopie [7]	68	65	32	30	36	61	50	48	35	38
Finland [6] Finlande [6]	46	41	24	20	20	19	8	9	...	...
France [8] France [8]	883	836	760	753	761	691	...	...	...	...
Georgia Géorgie	...	...	...	13	7	2	1	1	0	0
Germany † Allemagne †	...	...	929	763	687	635	444	466	489	506
F. R. Germany † [6] R. f. Allemagne † [6]	943	896	...	...	...	...	...	...	...	...
former German D. R. † l'ex−R. d. allemande †	304	213	...	...	...	...	...	...	...	...

41

Fabrics
Woven cotton and wool, cellulosic and non−cellulosic fibres: million square metres [*cont.*]
Tissus
Tissus de coton, laines, fibres cellulosiques et non cellulosiques : millions de mètres carrés [*suite*]

Country or area Pays ou zone	1989	1990	1991	1992	1993	1994	1995	1996	1997	1998
Greece Grèce	* 394	...	...	...	119[4]	94[4]	72[4]	...	...	...
Hungary [6] Hongrie [6]	247	206	133	86	78	76	66	...	79	44
India Inde	13 750	15 177	16 478	17 582	19 648	...	...	...	...	...
Italy [8] Italie [8]	1 777	1 780	1 682	1 487	1 422	1 521	1 585	...	...	...
Japan Japon	1 915	1 765	1 603	1 465	1 205	1 180	1 029	916	917	842
Kazakhstan Kazakhstan	...	...	134	135	136	85	21	21	14	10
Kenya Kenya	38	45	27	31	28	27	22	28	...	...
Korea, Republic of [6] Corée, République de [6]	648	620	608	483	480	447	379	...	...	...
Kyrgyzstan Kirghizistan	122	105	119	119	65	49	21	25	20	13
Latvia Lettonie	60	54	45	22	0	0	2	6	9	12
Lithuania Lituanie	98	98	106	89	48	42	35	35	62	64
Madagascar Madagascar	72	...	...	50	42	...	...	...	...
Mexico [8] Mexique [8]	463	408	368	313	454	321	305	256	...	...
Myanmar [9] Myanmar [9]	21	47[3]	27[3]	22[3]	16[3]	13[3]	16[3]	...	...	...
Netherlands [8] Pays−Bas [8]	99	83	81	70	...	...	...	...	...
Nigeria Nigéria	279	316	395	420	393	124	113	...	...	...
Norway [8] Norvège [8]	13	* 13	11	10	7	8	6	6	...	...
Pakistan [11] Pakistan [11]	270[10]	295[10]	293[10]	308[10]	325[10]	315	322	327	333	340
Paraguay [3] Paraguay [3]	16	18	23	23	24	...	...	...	...	...
Poland [6 12] Pologne [6 12]	811	474	332	290	284	321	263	295	303	275
Portugal Portugal	...	...	...	367	388	421	418	401	410	445
Republic of Moldova République de Moldova	156	170	165	150	1[13]	0[13]	0[13]	0[13]	0[13]	0[13]
Romania [6] Roumanie [6]	709	536	437	289	271	294	275	212	173	170
Russian Federation Fédération de Russie	6 417	6 201	5 949	3 799	2 822	1 631	1 401	1 120	1 374	1 241
Slovakia Slovaquie	...	...	...	...	78	76	90	57	...	...
Slovenia Slovénie	101[12]	136[12]	102[12]	78[12]	81	81	71	53	...	...
South Africa Afrique du Sud	188	175	170	138	166	195	228	246	269	...
Spain Espagne	775[8 14]	766[8 14]	773[8 14]	748[8 14]	523	622	689	...	...	...
Sweden * Suède *	65	...	...	...	...	...	...	...	...	...
Switzerland [3] Suisse [3]	101	103	81	77	74	82	70	...	...	...
Syrian Arab Republic [8] Rép. arabe syrienne [8]	237[15]	214[15]	221	205	222	213	...	...	...	...

41

Fabrics
Woven cotton and wool, cellulosic and non−cellulosic fibres: million square metres [*cont.*]
Tissus
Tissus de coton, laines, fibres cellulosiques et non cellulosiques : millions de mètres carrés [*suite*]

Country or area Pays ou zone	1989	1990	1991	1992	1993	1994	1995	1996	1997	1998
Tajikistan Tadjikistan	129	122	102	58	57	34	28	17	8	13
TFYR Macedonia L'ex−R.y. Macédoine	49	39	25	21	19	23	15	16	8	12
Turkey [3] Turquie [3]	661[16]	715[16]	626	648	532	432	414	395	...	...
Turkmenistan Turkménistan	28	29	28	29	29	20	17	18	14	15
Uganda [6] Ouganda [6]	12[17]	8[17]	9[17]	10[17]	7[17]	4	...	...	...	...
Ukraine Ukraine	620	614	561	509	262	145	87	54	28	57
former USSR † [6] l'ex−URSS † [6]	8 906	8 647	...	...	...	...	...	...	...	...
United Kingdom * Royaume−Uni *	246	198	185	...	...	...	...	...	...	...
United Rep. Tanzania Rép.−Unie de Tanzanie	46	46	38	49	40	24	10	13	27	...
United States Etats−Unis	3 837	3 732	3 682	3 846	3 682	3 740	3 753	4 010	4 246	3 974
Uzbekistan Ouzbékistan	468	469	392	474	482	433	456	445	425	...
Viet Nam Viet Nam	403	380	...	...	...	...	...	...	...	...
Yugoslavia [5][17] Yougoslavie [5][17]	82	65	45	39	27	24	19	22	19	23
Yugoslavia, SFR † [17] Yougoslavie. Rfs † [17]	339	...	...	...	...	...	...	...	...	...
Zambia Zambie	11	...	...	...	...	...	...	...	...	...

B. Wool · Laines

Country or area Pays ou zone	1989	1990	1991	1992	1993	1994	1995	1996	1997	1998
Algeria [3] Algérie [3]	10	13	16	13	...	...	...	...	...	...
Armenia Arménie	7	8	4	3	1	0	0	0	0	0
Australia [1] Australie [1]	10	8	8	8	8	8	8	7	6	7
Austria Autriche	9	9	8	8	5	3	2	3	3	4
Azerbaijan Azerbaïdjan	14	11	9	7	5	2	1	0	0	0
Belarus Bélarus	53	51	49	39	40	20	8	8	9	10
Belgium [18] Belgique [18]	5	5	6	4	4	...	...	...	...	...
Bolivia [3] Bolivie [3]	0	0	0	0	0	0	* 0	...	...	...
Bulgaria [6] Bulgarie [6]	51	47	26	22	23	21	20	18	17	...
China †† [3] Chine †† [3]	461	487	514	558	388	413	1 079	...	...	...
China, Hong Kong SAR † Chine, Hong Kong RAS †	0	0	0	...	...	...	...	...	...	...
Croatia Croatie	12	9	5	6	7	7	7	5	3	2
Cuba [19] Cuba [19]	0	...	...	...	...	...	...	...	...	...
Czech Republic République tchèque	68	58	49	46	43	34	32	30	28	29
Denmark [20] Danemark [20]	1[10]	1[10]	1[10]	1[10]	1	1	1	1	1	...

41

Fabrics

Woven cotton and wool, cellulosic and non–cellulosic fibres: million square metres [*cont.*]

Tissus

Tissus de coton, laines, fibres cellulosiques et non cellulosiques : millions de mètres carrés [*suite*]

Country or area Pays ou zone	1989	1990	1991	1992	1993	1994	1995	1996	1997	1998
Egypt Egypt	* 28	23	23	23	9	14	14	8	8	...
Estonia Estonie	8	7	7	4	1	0	0	0	0	0
Finland [6] Finlande [6]	1	* 0	* 0	* 0	* 0	...	...	...	...	...
France France	21	16	14	13	9	37	...	...	...	...
Georgia Géorgie	...	...	...	0	2	1	0	0	0	0
Germany † Allemagne †	...	...	121	119	97	...	87	87	87	79
F. R. Germany † [6] R. f. Allemagne † [6]	109	108	...	...	...	...	...	...	...	...
former German D. R. † l'ex–R. d. allemande †	50	38	...	...	...	...	...	...	...	...
Greece Grèce	...	...	...	...	3	2	2	2	3	...
Hungary [6] Hongrie [6]	21	11	7	4	3	1	1	...	0	...
Iceland Islande	0	0	0	0	0	0	...	...	...	...
Ireland [6] Irlande [6]	2	2	...	...	...	...	...	...	...	...
Italy [8] Italie [8]	457	418	428	445	426	443	433	431	...	...
Japan [10] Japon [10]	351	335	345	326	287	286	249	247	247	213
Kazakhstan Kazakhstan	...	...	31	23	20	10	3	2	2	1
Kenya Kenya	1	0	...	...	0	9	1	1	...	...
Korea, Republic of Corée, République de	21[6]	20[6]	20[6]	20[6]	19[6]	20	18	17	14	7
Kyrgyzstan Kirghizistan	15	15	13	11	9	4	2	3	3	2
Latvia Lettonie	18	17	11	8	2	0[6]	0[6]	0[6]	0[6]	0[6]
Lithuania Lituanie	23	22	22	17	12	9	10	13	12	14
Mexico [8] Mexique [8]	8	9	8	11	12	9	12	16	...	...
Mongolia [3] Mongolie [3]	3	...	1	1	0	0	0	...	...	...
Netherlands [6] Pays–Bas [6]	5	4	4	4	...	...	...	...	...	...
Norway Norvège	1[6 21]	...	1[8]	2[8]	1[8]	2[8]	2[8]	2[8]	2[8]	2[8]
Poland [6 22] Pologne [6 22]	146	98	67	50	48	51	50	50	49	45
Portugal Portugal	32[8]	34[8]	29[8]	12	10	9	8	6	6	8
Republic of Moldova République de Moldova	0	0	0	0	0[13]	0[13]	0[13]	0[13]	0[13]	0[13]
Romania [6] Roumanie [6]	141	107	100	69	68	65	68	50	34	22
Russian Federation Fédération de Russie	597	583	492	351	270	114	107	67	63	52
Slovakia [6] Slovaquie [6]	19	19	12	11	10	10	...	...	...	...
Slovenia Slovénie	19	10	15	15	13	10	7	3	...	...

41

Fabrics
Woven cotton and wool, cellulosic and non−cellulosic fibres: million square metres [*cont.*]

Tissus
Tissus de coton, laines, fibres cellulosiques et non cellulosiques : millions de mètres carrés [*suite*]

Country or area Pays ou zone	1989	1990	1991	1992	1993	1994	1995	1996	1997	1998
South Africa [21] Afrique du Sud [21]	19	19	15	11	10	11	10	9	...	...
Spain [8] Espagne [8]	40[14]	31[14]	31[14]	28[14]	17	14	15	...	...	...
Sweden Suède	1	1	...	...	0[9]	...	...	...	...	...
Switzerland [21] Suisse [21]	9	9	10	8	7	7	5	...	...	...
Syrian Arab Republic [8] Rép. arabe syrienne [8]	1	1	0	1	2	1	1	...	...	...
Tajikistan Tadjikistan	2	2	2	3	3	1	0	0	0	0
TFYR Macedonia L'ex−R.y. Macédoine	14	11	10	9	7	5	6	4	4	4
Turkey [3] Turquie [3]	29	42	36	35	38	38	50	...	...	...
Turkmenistan Turkménistan	3	3	3	3	3	3	3	3	3	3
Ukraine Ukraine	90	86	79	76	60	26	19	12	14	8
former USSR † l'ex−URSS †	890	865	...	...	...	...	...	...	...	...
United Kingdom Royaume−Uni	25[23]	20[23]	* 39	* 37	* 33	* 38	...	...	...	...
United States Etats−Unis	147	118	142	147	154	149	136	127	138	111
Uzbekistan Ouzbékistan	1	1	1	1	1	1	1	1	0	...
Yugoslavia [17] [19] Yougoslavie [17] [19]	44	39	24	21	13	13	11	11	10	9
Yugoslavia, SFR † [17] Yougoslavie. Rfs † [17]	100	...	...	...	...	...	...	...	...	...

C. Cellulosic and non−cellulosic fibres · Fibres cellulosiques et non cellulosique

Country or area	1989	1990	1991	1992	1993	1994	1995	1996	1997	1998
Australia [1] Australie [1]	191	179	184	185	185	...	...	...	...	...
Austria Autriche	97	101	66	72	47	42	60	...	...	...
Belarus Bélarus	215[15]	210[15]	175	147	135	80	35	39	67	77
Belgium [24] [25] Belgique [24] [25]	3 638	3 955	3 883	4 259	4 776	...	...	...	...	...
China, Hong Kong SAR † Chine, Hong Kong RAS †	1	0	2	2	3	3	1	...	21	...
Colombia Colombie	...	...	...	...	...	...	...	...	15	16
Croatia Croatie	25	18	12	12	14	11	9	8	11	12
Czech Republic République tchèque	86	85	32	35	29					
Ethiopia [7] Ethiopie [7]	5	5	3	2	4	4	5	5	4	5
Finland [6] Finlande [6]	* 33	27	* 17	* 14	* 14	* 12	* 8	* 8	...	...
France France	2 446	2 668	2 763	3 517	2 891	2 884	...	...	...	...
Germany † Allemagne †	...	...	1 476	1 359	1 154	1 116	1 329	1 176	1 225	1 269
F. R. Germany † [6] R. f. Allemagne † [6]	1 473	1 471	...	...	...	...	...	...	...	...
former German D. R. † l'ex−R. d. allemande †	250	...	...	...	...	...	...	...	...	...

41

Fabrics

Woven cotton and wool, cellulosic and non−cellulosic fibres: million square metres [*cont.*]

Tissus

Tissus de coton, laines, fibres cellulosiques et non cellulosiques : millions de mètres carrés [*suite*]

Country or area Pays ou zone	1989	1990	1991	1992	1993	1994	1995	1996	1997	1998
Greece [26] [27] Grèce [26] [27]	...	...	...	...	19	29	15	...	...	...
Hungary [6] Hongrie [6]	67	45	35	22	20	18	18	...	...	# 97
Japan [10] Japon [10]	3 365	3 376	3 263	3 175	2 758	2 578	2 459	2 438	2 497	2 133
Korea, Republic of Corée, République de	2 908	3 428	3 479	3 094	2 459	2 540	2 594	...	...	...
Lithuania Lituanie	52	40	35	26	18	...	8	6	47	53
Poland [6] Pologne [6]	147	113	88	97	86	106	104	95	95	87
Portugal Portugal	...	...	...	142	134	129	127	131	138	144
Republic of Moldova [15] République de Moldova [15]	45	51	44	22	...	...	...	...	...	...
Slovakia Slovaquie	29	29	27	...	...	13	...	...	...	...
Slovenia Slovénie	10	8	7	6	5	10	24	42	...	...
Sweden [8] Suède [8]	9	10	6	...	...	...	...	...	...	...
TFYR Macedonia L'ex−R.y. Macédoine	6	6	5	3	2	1	1	1	1	1
Ukraine [15] Ukraine [15]	300	...	...	...	...	...	...	...	...	...
former USSR † l'ex−URSS †	2 049	...	...	...	...	...	...	...	...	...
Yugoslavia Yougoslavie	...	...	4	4	4	2	2	1	1	1
Yugoslavia, SFR † Yougoslavie. Rfs †	37	...	...	...	...	...	...	...	...	...

Source:
United Nations Secretariat, "Industrial Commodity Statistics
Yearbook 1998" and the industrial statistics database of
the Statistics Division.

Source:
Secrétariat de l'Organisation des Nations Unies, "Annuaire
de statistiques industrielles par produit 1998" et la base
de données pour les statistiques industrielles de la
Division de statistique.

†   For information on recent changes in country or
    area nomenclature pertaining to former Czechoslovakia,
    Germany, Hong Kong Special Administrative Region (SAR) of
    China, Macao Special Administrative Region (SAR) of China,
    SFR of Yugoslavia and the former USSR, see Annex I − Country
    or area nomenclature, regional and other groupings.

†   Pour les modifications récentes de nomenclature
    de pays ou de zone concernant l'Allemagne, Hong Kong, régi
    administrative spéciale (RAS) de Chine, Macao, région
    administrative spéciale (RAS) de Chine,
    l'ex−Tchécoslovaquie, l'ex−URSS et l'ex−Rfs de Yougoslav
    voir annexe I − Nomenclature des pays ou des zones,
    groupements régionaux et autres groupements.

†† For statistical purposes, the data for
    China do not include those for Hong Kong Special
    Administrative Region (Hong Kong SAR), Macao Special
    Administrative Region (Macao SAR) and Taiwan province of
    China.

†† Les données statistiques relatives à la Chine ne comprennent
    pas celles qui concernent la région administrative spéciale
    de Hong Kong (la RAS de Hong Kong), la région
    administrative spéciale de Macao (la RAS de Macao)
    et la province chinoise de Taiwan.

1   Twelve months ending 30 June of year stated.

1   Période de douze mois finissant le 30e juin de l'année
    indiquée.

2   Including pile and chenille fabrics of non−cellulosic fibres.

2   Y compris les tissus bouclés et tissus chenille de fibres
    non−cellulosiques.

3   Original data in metres.

3   Données d'origine exprimées en mètres.

4   Including cotton fabrics after undergoing finishing
    processes.

4   Y compris les tissus de cotton, après opérations de
    finition.

41

Fabrics
Woven cotton and wool, cellulosic and non−cellulosic fibres: million square metres [*cont.*]
Tissus
Tissus de coton, laines, fibres cellulosiques et non cellulosiques : millions de mètres carrés [*suite*]

5 Including mixed cotton fabrics.	5 Y compris les tissus de cotton mélangé.
6 After undergoing finishing processes.	6 Après opérations de finition.
7 Twelve months ending 7 July of the year stated.	7 Période de douze mois finissant le 7e juillet de l'année indiquée.
8 Original data in metric tons.	8 Données d'origine exprimées en tonnes.
9 Production by government−owned enterprises only.	9 Production des établissements d'Etat seulement.
10 Including finished fabrics and blanketing made of synthetic fibers.	10 Y compris les tissus finis et les couvertures en fibres synthétiques.
11 Factory production only.	11 Production des fabriques seulement.
12 Including fabrics of cotton substitutes.	12 Y compris les tissus de succédanés de coton.
13 Excluding Transnistria region.	13 Non compris la région de Transnistria.
14 Including household production.	14 Y compris la production ménagère.
15 Including silk fabrics.	15 Y compris les tissus de soie.
16 Government production only.	16 Production de l'Etat seulement.
17 Including cellulosic fabrics.	17 Y compris les tissus en fibres cellulosiques.
18 Including woollen blankets and carpets.	18 Y compris les couvertures et tapis en laine.
19 Including mixed wool fabrics.	19 Y compris les tissus de laine mélangée.
20 Sales.	20 Ventes.
21 Pure woollen fabrics only.	21 Tissus de laine pure seulement.
22 Including fabrics of wool substitutes.	22 Y compris les tissus de succédanés de laine.
23 Deliveries of woollen and worsted fabrics, except blankets, containing, by weight, more than 15 per cent wool or animal fibres. Including finished fabrics.	23 Quantités livrées de tissus de laine cardée et peignée, à l'exception des couvertures, contenant, en poids, de 15 p. 100 de laine ou de fibres animales. Y compris les tissus finis.
24 Including blankets and carpets of cellulosic fibres.	24 Y compris les couvertures et les tapis en fibres cellulosiques.
25 Including blankets and carpets of non−cellulosic fibres.	25 Y compris les couvertures et les tapis en fibres non cellulosiques.
26 Including fabrics after undergoing finishing processes.	26 Y compris les tissus, après opérations de finition.
27 Including mixed fabrics.	27 Y compris les tissus mélangés.

42
Leather footwear
Chaussures de cuir

Production: thousand pairs
Production : milliers de paires

Country or area Pays or zone	1989	1990	1991	1992	1993	1994	1995	1996	1997	1998
Albania Albanie	6 103	5 990	1 881	1 214	1 818	266	267	...	...	...
Algeria Algérie	14 943	16 376	11 824	9 040	7 171	6 467	3 986	2 320	2 542	2 207
Angola Angola	155	143	95	48	...	...	...	...	...	...
Armenia Arménie	17 952	18 740	11 340	5 661	3 517	1 612	656	305	85	63
Australia Australie	29 032 [1]	1 875	1 935	383	283	315	278	...	...	...
Austria Autriche	16 769	16 553	16 760	14 842	13 229	12 767	12 743	10 120	10 615	10 919
Azerbaijan Azerbaïdjan	17 156	15 207	10 262	5 221	4 068	3 043	799	495	313	315
Belarus Bélarus	45 282	46 764	45 343	37 207	33 412	26 358	13 004	11 381	15 587	16 159
Belgium Belgique	3 810	3 562	3 454	3 190	2 267	...	...	...	...	...
Bolivia Bolivie	938	833	862	1 152	1 308	1 381	* 1 222	...	...	...
Brazil Brésil	157 749	141 000	152 925	156 540	190 026	146 540	124 272	163 042	159 861	142 734
Bulgaria Bulgarie	33 206	27 214	17 048	13 421	10 785	10 244	11 980	8 915	6 838	6 401
Burkina Faso Burkina Faso	500	500	1 271	1 200 [2]	...	...	...	...	...	...
Cameroon Cameroun	1 800 [3]	1 800 [3]	1 800 [2]	1 900 [2]	...	...	...	...	...	...
Canada [2] Canada [2]	15 100	15 100	16 000	16 000	...	...	...	...	...	...
Central African Rep. Rép. centrafricaine	200	200	200 [2]	200 [2]	...	...	...	...	...	...
Chile Chili	7 601	7 577	9 231	9 311	9 270	8 317	7 410	7 134	7 008	6 777
China †† Chine ††	1 103 933	1 202 565	1 328 950	1 613 647	...	...	...	...	...	...
China, Hong Kong SAR† Chine, Hong Kong RAS†	48 710	73 496	140 000 [2]	8 433	...	...	...	1 499	752 [4]	178 [4]
Colombia Colombie	26 700 [2]	28 100 [2]	30 000 [2]	20 651	19 471	20 933	18 277	...	18 736 [5]	16 635 [5]
Congo Congo	147 [5]	* 300 [5]	300 [2]	300 [2]	...	...	...	...	...	...
Côte d'Ivoire Côte d'Ivoire	1 800	1 800	1 800 [2]	1 800 [2]	...	...	...	...	...	...
Croatia Croatie	29 332	26 107	11 717	11 240	13 449	12 459	9 521	9 271	9 598	8 742
Cuba Cuba	11 004	13 400	13 000 [2]	13 400 [2]	...	...	...	...	...	...

42
Leather footwear
Production: thousand pairs [cont.]
Chaussures de cuir
Production : milliers de paires [suite]

Country or area Pays or zone	1989	1990	1991	1992	1993	1994	1995	1996	1997	1998
Cyprus Chypre	11 643	10 447	10 591	6 199	3 835	3 820[6]	3 367[6]	2 507[6]	2 686[6]	2 190[6]
Czech Republic République tchèque	73 102	71 047	41 400	36 948	32 293	23 323	22 115	21 572	13 455	9 246
Dem. Rep. of the Congo[2] Rép. dém. du Congo[2]	900	900	900	900	...	...	...	...	...	...
Denmark[2] Danemark[2]	4 400	4 400	4 400	4 600	...	...	...	...	...	...
Dominican Republic[2] Rép. dominicaine[2]	2 100	2 100	2 000	2 200	...	...	...	...	...	...
Ecuador Equateur	1 500	1 500	1 600[2]	1 936	1 691	1 672	1 744	1 507		
Egypt Egypte	50 375	48 325	48 311	48 390	48 385	48 394	48 444	48 300	48 131	...
El Salvador El Salvador	3 600	3 600	3 700[2]	3 800[2]	...	...	...	...	...	...
Estonia Estonie	7 060	7 209	6 301	3 208	1 035	827	682	711	793	705
Ethiopia[7] Ethiopie[7]	12 957[8]	5 367	3 374	2 419	3 083	2 871	3 751	3 773	6 925	6 252
Finland Finlande	5 243	4 752	3 683	3 606	3 291	3 421	3 186	3 220	2 928	3 499
France[3] France[3]	169 788	194 700	168 084	160 320	151 124	131 051	...	...	...	...
Georgia Géorgie	...	...	...	2 614	1 046	224	50	48	101	45
Germany Allemagne	...	...	84 435	63 672	55 485	47 193	45 491	40 675	36 948	38 441
F. R. Germany R. f. Allemagne	68 697	64 358	...	...	...	...	...	...	...	...
former German D. R. l'ex-R. d. allemande	91 518	61 822	...	...	...	...	...	...	...	...
Greece Grèce	12 359	12 260	10 712	9 264	8 166	6 922	7 032	6 769	6 202	...
Haiti[2] Haïti[2]	500	500	500	600	...	...	...	...	...	...
Hungary Hongrie	33 107	27 426	20 757	14 752	12 783	12 499	12 178	...	...	...
Iceland Islande	29	39	46	18	...	...	...	9	8	...
India[9] Inde[9]	198 761	198 404	188 309	187 493	188 746	158 263	181 462	157 095	137 837	180 490
Indonesia[10] Indonésie[10]	38 722	61 657	87 565	...	#250 053	272 529	245 227	...	238 335	...
Iran (Islamic Rep. of) Iran (Rép. islamique d')	21 849[11]	23 374[11]	18 849[11]	25 129[11]	21 756[11]	17 598[11]	29 807[12]	28 310[12]	27 267[12]	...
Iraq Iraq	4 600	4 400	5 000[2]	4 087	...	...	...	...	...	...
Ireland Irlande	1 913	1 403	3 000[2]	3 200[2]						

42
Leather footwear
Production: thousand pairs [cont.]
Chaussures de cuir
Production : milliers de paires [suite]

Country or area Pays or zone	1989	1990	1991	1992	1993	1994	1995	1996	1997	1998
Italy[2] Italie[2]	311 900	320 200	310 200	295 000	...	...	...	...	...	...
Jamaica[2] Jamaïque[2]	700	700	700	800	...	...	...	...	...	...
Japan[12 13] Japon[12 13]	53 819	54 054	53 351	52 455	47 703	51 503	49 525	48 819	47 573	...
Kenya Kenya	1 696	1 605	1 190	1 480	1 571	1 774	2 018	2 089	...	...
Korea, Republic of Corée, République de	24 023	24 440	26 384	25 409	19 085	16 806	15 309	...	...	...
Kyrgyzstan Kirghizistan	11 899	11 569	9 507	5 751	3 528	1 512	755	605	436	196
Lao People's Dem. Rep. Rép. dém. pop. lao	...	...	...	...	...	240	150	...	...	...
Latvia Lettonie	10 175	10 648	7 778	5 738	2 687	1 633	1 032	939	753	753
Lithuania Lituanie	11 864	11 884	11 154	7 702	3 657	1 565	1 961	2 004	1 663	1 631
Madagascar[10] Madagascar[10]	1 356	807	837	702	306	...	...	...	...	...
Mali Mali	...	...	127	104	86	106	99	98	...	...
Mexico Mexique	15 986	16 249	14 685	14 570	27 645	25 275	21 215	23 004	25 117	24 397
Mongolia Mongolie	4 140	3 000	4 438	2 654	1 283	497	325	146	...	...
Mozambique Mozambique	346	347	242	148	153	87	29	...	12	...
Nepal Népal	124[14]	600[2]	700[2]	800[14]	823[14]	700[14]	685[14]	649[14]	550[14]	550[14]
Netherlands[3 15 16] Pays-Bas[3 15 16]	6 197	5 598	5 255	5 289	6 315	5 455	5 492	...	...	...
New Zealand[1] Nouvelle-Zélande[1]	5 073	4 977	4 022	3 764	3 525	3 590	3 110	2 656	2 222[17]	1 484[17]
Nicaragua Nicaragua	* 1 100	* 1 100	1 200[2]	1 300[2]	...	...	...	...	...	...
Nigeria Nigéria	3 423	3 779	7 093	4 538	4 554	1 182	1 255	...	...	...
Norway Norvège	800[5]	900[5]	900[2]	1 000[2]	...	...	...	...	...	...
Panama Panama	999	1 508	1 600[2]	1 377	1 483	1 294	1 287	1 004	...	...
Paraguay Paraguay	5 094	5 300	5 500[2]	5 600[2]	...	...	...	...	...	...
Peru[2] Pérou[2]	18 400	18 800	19 000	20 000	...	...	...	...	...	...
Philippines[2] Philippines[2]	10 100	10 000	12 000	15 000	...	...	...	...	...	...
Poland Pologne	150 833	98 200	66 857	55 181	47 905	53 236	59 783	66 620	68 513	54 491

42
Leather footwear
Production: thousand pairs [cont.]
Chaussures de cuir
Production : milliers de paires [suite]

Country or area Pays or zone	1989	1990	1991	1992	1993	1994	1995	1996	1997	1998
Portugal Portugal	43 667	75 378	39 658	60 463	75 422	71 648	68 070	69 439	71 425	66 881
Republic of Moldova République de Moldova	23 716	23 196	20 751	14 504	4 897[18]	2 267[18]	1 506[18]	1 429[18]	1 032[18]	739[18]
Romania Roumanie	110 733	80 670	63 196	41 237	41 893	45 666	48 239	44 838	34 365	30 341
Russian Federation Fédération de Russie	377 669	385 262	336 411	220 415	145 889	76 531	51 618	36 764	33 030	23 816
Senegal Sénégal	186	302	153	644	508	...	...	...	...	...
Singapore Singapour	2 800[5]	2 800[5]	3 000[2]	3 100[2]	...	...	...	...	...	...
Slovakia Slovaquie	47 385	44 330	26 744	22 875	17 257	12 636	46 438	13 188	10 300	9 772
Slovenia Slovénie	11 795	11 042	9 124	9 492	8 923	6 005	5 052	5 739	5 976	5 641
South Africa[3] Afrique du Sud[3]	50 658	51 633	49 318	42 251	44 492	41 078	39 071[19]	38 858[19]	35 486[19]	29 581[19]
Spain Espagne	114 089	117 199	115 190	106 959	74 883	104 788	140 141	155 218	165 417	179 534
Sri Lanka Sri Lanka	270	339	276	272	274	...	...	...	...	...
Sudan[2] Soudan[2]	4 000	4 000	3 000	3 000	...	...	...	...	...	...
Sweden Suède	2 088	1 904	2 500[2]	3 000[2]	1 013	676	372	1 104	1 202	1 283
Switzerland Suisse	4 285	4 039	3 353	3 035	3 261	3 203	2 480	...	...	...
Tajikistan Tadjikistan	10 759	10 903	8 567	5 476	4 044	929	612	394	107	123
TFYR Macedonia L'ex-R.y. Macédoine	6 283	6 340	4 238	3 786	2 031	1 760	1 121	1 200	1 507	1 722
Togo Togo	100	100	100[2]	100[2]	...	...	...	...	...	...
Tunisia Tunisie	9 800	10 380	11 590	13 220	12 870	14 100	16 580	18 380	20 300	...
Turkmenistan Turkménistan	4 831	5 142	4 246	3 231	3 358	1 938	1 910	1 546	1 108	561
Ukraine Ukraine	193 673	196 466	177 336	143 970	104 479	39 873	20 591	13 116	10 408	9 555
former USSR† l'ex-URSS†	826 988	843 245	...	...	...	...	...	...	...	...
United Kingdom Royaume-Uni	101 318[20]	92 673[20]	41 000[2]	43 000[2]	70 837	69 637	61 141	62 157	54 423	45 155
United Rep.Tanzania Rép.-Unie de Tanzanie	445	459	328	168	55	89	339	121	152	...
United States Etats-Unis	218 025	184 568	168 992	164 904	171 733	156 712	146 979	127 315	127 876	117 627
Uzbekistan Ouzbékistan	44 200	46 685	45 443	40 491	40 466	28 202	5 654	5 591	5 547	...

42
Leather footwear
Production: thousand pairs [cont.]
Chaussures de cuir
Production : milliers de paires [suite]

Country or area Pays or zone	1989	1990	1991	1992	1993	1994	1995	1996	1997	1998
Viet Nam Viet Nam	...	5 827	6 188	5 672	...	...	...	...	...	...
Yugoslavia Yougoslavie	30 005	26 191	18 149	16 169	10 590	8 824	5 982	6 461	6 848	6 976
Yugoslavia, SFR† Yougoslavie, Rfs†	91 616	...	...	...	...	...	...	...	...	...

Source:
United Nations Secretariat, "Industrial Commodity Statistics Yearbook 1998" and the industrial statistics database of the Statistics Division.

† For information on recent changes in country or area nomenclature pertaining to former Czechoslovakia, Germany, Hong Kong Special Administrative Region (SAR) of China, Macao Special Administrative Region (SAR) of China, SFR of Yugoslavia and the former USSR, see Annex I - Country or area nomenclature, regional and other groupings.

†† For statistical purposes, the data for China do not include those for Hong Kong Special Administrative Region (Hong Kong SAR), Macao Special Administrative Region (Macao SAR) and Taiwan province of China.

1 Twelve months ending 30 June of year stated.

2 Source: Food and Agriculture Organization of the United Nations (FAO), (Rome).
3 Including rubber footwear.
4 Excluding other footwear for confidentiality purposes.

5 Including rubber and plastic footwear.

6 Including other footwear, house footwear, sandals and other light footwear. Also including rubber footwear.

7 Twelve months ending 7 July of the year stated.

8 Including canvas, plastic and rubber footwear.

9 Production by large and medium scale establishments only.
10 Including plastic footwear.
11 Production by establishments employing 50 or more persons.
12 Production by establishments employing 10 or more persons.
13 Shipments.
14 Twelve months beginning 16 July of year stated.

15 Sales.
16 Beginning 1986, production by establishments employing 20 or more persons.
17 Including non-leather footwear.
18 Excluding Transnistria region.
19 Excluding children's footwear.
20 Manufacturers' sales.

Source:
Secrétariat de l'Organisation des Nations Unies, "Annuaire de statistiques industrielles par produit 1998" et la base de données pour les statistiques industrielles de la Division de statistique.

† Pour les modifications récentes de nomenclature de pays ou de zone concernant l'Allemagne, Hong Kong, région administrative spéciale (RAS) de Chine, Macao, région administrative spéciale (RAS) de Chine, l'ex-Tchécoslovaquie, l'ex-URSS et l'ex-Rfs de Yougoslavie, voir annexe I - Nomenclature des pays ou des zones, groupements régionaux et autres groupements.

†† Les données statistiques relatives à la Chine ne comprennent pas celles qui concernent la région administrative spéciale de Hong Kong (la RAS de Hong Kong), la région administrative spéciale de Macao (la RAS de Macao) et la province chinoise de Taiwan.

1 Période de douze mois finissant le 30e juin de l'année indiquée.
2 Source: Organisation des Nations Unies pour l'alimentation et l'agriculture (FAO), (Rome).
3 Y compris les chaussures en caoutchouc.
4 A l'exclusion d'autres chaussures, pour raisons de confidentialité.
5 Y compris les chaussures en caoutchouc et en matière plastique.
6 Y compris les autres chaussures, chaussures de maison, sandales et autres chaussures légères. Y compris également les chaussures en caoutchouc.
7 Période de douze mois finissant le 7e juillet de l'année indiquée.
8 Y compris les chaussures en toile, en matière plastique et en caoutchouc.
9 Production des grandes et moyennes entreprises seulement.
10 Y compris les chaussures en matière plastique.
11 Production des établissements occupant 50 personnes ou plus.
12 Production des établissements occupant 10 personnes ou plus.
13 Expéditions.
14 Période de douze mois commençant le 16e juillet de l'année indiquée.
15 Ventes.
16 A partir de 1986, production des établissements occupant 20 personnes ou plus.
17 Y compris les chaussures en matières autres que le cuir.
18 Non compris la région de Transnistria.
19 Non compris les chaussures pour enfants.
20 Ventes des fabricants.

43
Sawnwood
Sciages
Production (sawn): thousand cubic metres
Production (sciés) : milliers de mètres cubes

Region, country or area Région, pays ou zone	1990	1991	1992	1993	1994	1995	1996	1997	1998	1999
World *Monde*	505 276	457 134	437 287	431 087	433 242	425 526	430 902	431 099	421 108	434 080
Africa **Afrique**	**8 257**	**7 947**	**8 088**	**7 833**	**8 275**	**8 013**	**7 538**	**7 275**	**7 310**	**7 215**
Algeria[1] Algérie[1]	13	13	13	13	13	13	13	13	13	13
Angola Angola	5	5[1]	5[1]	5[1]	5[1]	5[1]	5[1]	5[1]	5[1]	5[1]
Benin Bénin	14[1]	27	24	24[1]	24[1]	24[1]	24[1]	24[1]	24[1]	24[1]
Burkina Faso Burkina Faso	2	2	2[1]	2[1]	2[1]	2[1]	2[1]	2[1]	2[1]	2[1]
Burundi Burundi	2	3	3	20	21	43	33	33[1]	33[1]	33[1]
Cameroon Cameroun	591[1]	563[1]	577[1]	579[1]	647[1]	676[1]	685[1]	560	588	588[1]
Central African Rep. Rép. centrafricaine	63	60	68	60[1]	73	70	61	72	91	79
Chad Tchad	1	2	2	2	2[1]	2	2	2[1]	2[1]	2[1]
Congo Congo	50	54	52	52[1]	57	62	59	64	78	78[1]
Côte d'Ivoire Côte d'Ivoire	753	608	623	587	708	706	596	613	623	611
Dem. Rep. of the Congo Rép. dém. du Congo	117	105	105[1]	105[1]	* 80	* 100	* 85	* 90	* 80	80[1]
Equatorial Guinea Guinée équatoriale	12	13	8	7	4	4	4[1]	4[1]	4[1]	4[1]
Ethiopia incl. Eritrea Ethiopie comp. Erythrée	22	12	12[1]	...	...	...	...	...	...	...
Ethiopia[1] Ethiopie[1]	...	...	...	40	33	33	33	33	33	33
Gabon Gabon	* 37	* 85	* 155	* 153	* 173	100[1]	50[1]	30[1]	60	98
Gambia[1] Gambie[1]	1	1	1	1	1	1	1	1	1	1
Ghana Ghana	472	400	420	504	801	612	604	575	590	475
Guinea Guinée	70	70	63	65	72	85	85[1]	25	26	26[1]
Guinea-Bissau[1] Guinée-Bissau[1]	16	16	16	16	16	16	16	16	16	16
Kenya[1] Kenya[1]	185	185	185	185	185	185	185	185	185	185
Liberia Libéria	* 85	* 75	* 125	* 90	90[1]	90[1]	90[1]	90[1]	90[1]	90[1]
Libyan Arab Jamah.[1] Jamah. arabe libyenne[1]	31	31	31	31	31	31	31	31	31	31
Madagascar Madagascar	234	233	238[1]	144	74	84[1]	84[1]	84[1]	84[1]	84[1]

43
Sawnwood
Production (sawn): thousand cubic metres [cont.]
Sciages
Production (sciés) : milliers de mètres cubes [suite]

Region, country or area Région, pays ou zone	1990	1991	1992	1993	1994	1995	1996	1997	1998	1999
Malawi Malawi	* 43	* 43	43[1]	45	45[1]	45[1]	45[1]	45[1]	45[1]	45[1]
Mali[1] Mali[1]	13	13	13	13	13	13	13	13	13	13
Mauritius Maurice	4	5	4	5	4	2	3	3[1]	3[1]	3[1]
Morocco[1] Maroc[1]	83	83	83	83	83	83	83	83	83	83
Mozambique Mozambique	26	18	16[1]	30[1]	30	42	42[1]	33	28	28[1]
Niger Niger	0	0	1[1]	4[1]	4[1]	4[1]	4[1]	4[1]	4[1]	4[1]
Nigeria Nigéria	2 729	2 719	2 715	2 711	2 533	2 356	2 178	2 000	2 000[1]	2 000[1]
Réunion Réunion	3	2	2[1]	2[1]	2[1]	2[1]	2[1]	2[1]	2[1]	2[1]
Rwanda Rwanda	36	36	36	36	26	54	59	74	76	79
Sao Tome and Principe[1] Sao Tomé-et-Principe[1]	5	5	5	5	5	5	5	5	5	5
Senegal Sénégal	22	23	23[1]	23[1]	23[1]	23[1]	23[1]	23[1]	23[1]	23[1]
Sierra Leone Sierra Leone	11	9	9[1]	5	5[1]	5[1]	5[1]	5[1]	5[1]	5[1]
Somalia[1] Somalie[1]	14	14	14	14	14	14	14	14	14	14
South Africa Afrique du Sud	* 1 936	* 1 792	1 818	1 383	1 499	1 574	1 574[1]	1 574[1]	1 498	1 498[1]
Sudan Soudan	4	2	3	3	45	45	45[1]	45[1]	51[1]	51[1]
Swaziland Swaziland	77	75	75	75	80[1]	90[1]	100[1]	102	102[1]	102[1]
Togo Togo	6	2	3	3[1]	8	14	15	17	18	21
Tunisia Tunisie	16	17	6	19	20	20[1]	20[1]	20[1]	20[1]	20[1]
Uganda Ouganda	28[1]	28[1]	82	83	83[1]	83[1]	83[1]	83[1]	83[1]	83[1]
United Rep.Tanzania[1] Rép.-Unie de Tanzanie[1]	156	156	48	39	24	24	24	24	24	24
Zambia Zambie	81	94	112	318	367	320[1]	245[1]	157[1]	157[1]	157
Zimbabwe Zimbabwe	190[1]	250	250[1]	250[1]	250[1]	250[1]	207	396[1]	396[1]	396[1]
America, North **Amérique du Nord**	**168 302**	**158 270**	**168 640**	**169 803**	**175 794**	**169 897**	**176 955**	**181 132**	**184 028**	**194 214**
Bahamas[1] Bahamas[1]	1	1	1	1	1	1	1	1	1	1
Belize[1] Belize[1]	14	14	14	14	20	35	35	35	35	35

43

Sawnwood
Production (sawn): thousand cubic metres [*cont.*]
Sciages
Production (sciés) : milliers de mètres cubes [*suite*]

Region, country or area Région, pays ou zone	1990	1991	1992	1993	1994	1995	1996	1997	1998	1999
Canada Canada	54 906	52 040	56 318	59 774	61 650	60 436	62 828	64 764	65 109	69 286
Costa Rica Costa Rica	412	412	772	798	746[1]	780[1]	780[1]	780[1]	780[1]	780
Cuba[1] Cuba[1]	130	130	130	130	130	130	130	130	130	146
El Salvador[1] El Salvador[1]	70	70	70	70	70	70	70	70	70	70
Guadeloupe[1] Guadeloupe[1]	1	1	1	1	1	1	1	1	1	1
Guatemala Guatemala	37[1]	55[1]	90[1]	398	417	355	355[1]	355[1]	355[1]	355[1]
Haiti[1] Haïti[1]	14	14	14	14	14	14	14	14	14	14
Honduras Honduras	328	303	411	364	361	231	322	379	369	369[1]
Jamaica Jamaïque	40	32	27	24	20	12	12[1]	12[1]	12[1]	12[1]
Martinique Martinique	1[1]	1[1]	1	1[1]	1[1]	1[1]	1[1]	1[1]	1[1]	1[1]
Mexico Mexique	2 366	* 2 696	2 696[1]	2 560	2 693	2 329	2 543	2 961	3 260	3 260[1]
Nicaragua Nicaragua	80	80[1]	61	65	27	74	160	148	148[1]	148[1]
Panama Panama	48[1]	16	37	37[1]	37[1]	37[1]	19	17	17[1]	17[1]
Trinidad and Tobago Trinité-et-Tobago	53	42	59	35	58	64	29	38	27	27[1]
United States Etats-Unis	109 800	102 363	107 937	105 516	109 547	105 326	109 654	111 425	113 698	119 692
America, South **Amérique du Sud**	**25 282**	**25 930**	**26 705**	**25 474**	**27 190**	**28 390**	**29 990**	**30 471**	**29 970**	**29 970**
Argentina Argentine	950[1]	950[1]	1 472	998	1 080	1 329	1 711	1 711[1]	1 711[1]	1 711[1]
Bolivia Bolivie	102	125[1]	230	268	185	162	181	180	218	218[1]
Brazil Brésil	17 179[1]	18 628[1]	18 628[1]	18 628[1]	18 691	19 091	19 091[1]	19 091[1]	18 591	18 591[1]
Chile Chili	3 327	3 218	3 020	3 113	3 364	3 802	4 140	4 661	4 551	4 551[1]
Colombia Colombie	813[1]	813[1]	758	694	644	644	1 134	1 085	1 019	1 019[1]
Ecuador Equateur	1 641	865	908	196	1 600	1 696	1 886	2 079	2 079[1]	2 079[1]
French Guiana Guyane française	19[1]	19[1]	19[1]	18	15	15[1]	15[1]	15[1]	15[1]	15[1]
Guyana Guyana	50[1]	50[1]	50[1]	50[1]	77	101	97	57	57[1]	57[1]
Paraguay Paraguay	228	313	357	357[1]	357[1]	400[1]	500[1]	550[1]	550[1]	550[1]

43

Sawnwood
Production (sawn): thousand cubic metres [*cont.*]
Sciages
Production (sciés) : milliers de mètres cubes [*suite*]

Region, country or area Région, pays ou zone	1990	1991	1992	1993	1994	1995	1996	1997	1998	1999
Peru Pérou	499	477	500	592	649	630	693	482	590	590[1]
Suriname Suriname	44	40	43	33	29	29[1]	40	41	41[1]	41[1]
Uruguay Uruguay	229	205	269	269[1]	269[1]	269[1]	269[1]	269[1]	269[1]	269[1]
Venezuela Venezuela	201	227	451	258	230	222	233	250	279	279[1]
Asia **Asie**	**104 713**	**100 069**	**97 200**	**101 601**	**98 045**	**95 767**	**98 248**	**88 723**	**73 833**	**73 519**
Afghanistan[1] Afghanistan[1]	400	400	400	400	400	400	400	400	400	400
Bangladesh[1] Bangladesh[1]	79	79	79	79	79	70	70	70	70	70
Bhutan Bhoutan	35	35	21	18	18[1]	18[1]	18[1]	18[1]	18[1]	18[1]
Brunei Darussalam Brunéi Darussalam	90	90	90	90	90[1]	90[1]	90[1]	90[1]	90[1]	90[1]
Cambodia Cambodge	71	122	132[1]	155[1]	195	140	100	71	40	40[1]
China †† Chine ††	23 160[1]	20 521[1]	19 317[1]	25 268[1]	25 162[1]	25 162[1]	26 969[1]	20 541	18 292[1]	18 292[1]
China, Hong Kong SAR† Chine, Hong Kong RAS†	421	421[1]	439	441	441[1]	441[1]	441[1]	441[1]	441[1]	441[1]
Cyprus Chypre	22	16	14	17	15	15	16	14	11	12
India Inde	17 460[1]	17 460	17 460[1]	17 460[1]	17 460[1]	17 460[1]	17 460[1]	17 460[1]	17 460[1]	17 460[1]
Indonesia Indonésie	9 145	8 638	8 438	8 338	6 838	6 638	7 338	7 238	2 545	2 545[1]
Iran (Islamic Rep. of) Iran (Rép. islamique d')	169	173	187	170	178	159	144	141	129	129[1]
Iraq Iraq	8[1]	8[1]	8[1]	8[1]	8[1]	8[1]	8[1]	8[1]	12	12[1]
Japan Japon	29 781[1]	28 264[1]	27 277[1]	26 260[1]	25 906[1]	24 493[1]	23 844[1]	21 709	18 625	17 952
Korea, Dem. P. R.[1] Corée, R. p. dém. de[1]	280	280	280	280	280	280	280	280	280	280
Korea, Republic of Corée, République de	3 897	4 041	3 513	3 249	3 862	3 440	4 291	4 759	2 240	2 240[1]
Kyrgyzstan Kirghizistan	...	...	0	0	0	0	0	2	3	3[1]
Lao People's Dem. Rep. Rép. dém. pop. lao	100	300	170[1]	262	331	465	320	560	560[1]	560[1]
Lebanon Liban	13	11	9	9	9[1]	9[1]	9[1]	9[1]	9[1]	9[1]
Malaysia Malaisie	8 849	8 993	9 369	9 395	8 858	8 382[1]	8 382[1]	7 326	5 241	5 241[1]
Mongolia Mongolie	509	270	124	84	50	61	170[1]	200[1]	300[1]	300[1]

43

Sawnwood
Production (sawn): thousand cubic metres [*cont.*]
Sciages
Production (sciés) : milliers de mètres cubes [*suite*]

Region, country or area Région, pays ou zone	1990	1991	1992	1993	1994	1995	1996	1997	1998	1999
Myanmar Myanmar	296	282	302	339	347[1]	347[1]	351	372	326	326[1]
Nepal Népal	570	620	620[1]	620[1]	620[1]	620[1]	620[1]	620[1]	620[1]	620[1]
Pakistan Pakistan	1 450	1 520	1 450	1 503	1 127	1 266	1 280	1 024	1 051	1 051[1]
Philippines Philippines	846	729	647	440	407	286	313	351	216	216[1]
Singapore[1] Singapour[1]	55	30	25	25	25	25	25	25	25	25
Sri Lanka Sri Lanka	10	5	5	5[1]	5[1]	6	5	5[1]	5[1]	5[1]
Syrian Arab Republic[1] Rép. arabe syrienne[1]	9	9	9	9	9	9	9	9	9	9
Thailand Thaïlande	1 170	939	1 076	715	568	426	307	426	103	195
Turkey Turquie	4 923[1]	4 928	4 891	5 241	4 037	4 331	4 268	3 833	3 990	4 257
Viet Nam Viet Nam	896	885	849	721	721[1]	721[1]	721[1]	721[1]	721[1]	721[1]
Europe **Europe**	**88 112**	**80 191**	**130 748**	**120 108**	**117 271**	**116 454**	**111 245**	**116 487**	**118 713**	**121 948**
Albania Albanie	382	382[1]	382[1]	4	5	5[1]	5[1]	5	5[1]	5[1]
Austria Autriche	7 509	7 239	7 020	6 786	7 572	7 804	8 200	8 450	8 737	9 786
Belarus Bélarus	...	...	1 693	1 545	1 545[1]	1 545[1]	1 545[1]	1 545[1]	1 545[1]	1 545[1]
Belgium-Luxembourg Belgique-Luxembourg	1 194	1 244	1 184	1 184[1]	1 209	1 150	1 100	1 150	1 267	1 190
Bosnia and Herzegovina[1] Bosnie-Herzégovine[1]	...	...	20	20	20	20	20	20	20	20
Bulgaria Bulgarie	1 108	1 114	324	253	253[1]	253[1]	253[1]	253[1]	253[1]	253[1]
Croatia Croatie	...	...	651	699	601	578	598	644	676	685
former Czechoslovakia† l'ex-Tchécoslovaquie†	4 764	3 621	...	...	...	...	...	...	...	...
Czech Republic République tchèque	...	...	...	3 025	3 155	3 490	3 405	3 393	3 427	3 584
Denmark Danemark	861[1]	861	620	583	583[1]	583[1]	583[1]	583[1]	238	350
Estonia Estonie	...	...	300	300[1]	341	350	400	729[1]	850	945
Finland Finlande	7 503	5 983	6 983	8 375	9 748	9 480	9 370	11 430	12 300	12 770
France France	10 960	10 974	10 488	9 132	9 649	9 848	9 600	9 607	10 220	10 500
Germany Allemagne	14 724[1]	13 322	13 496	11 522	13 567	14 105	14 267	14 730	14 972	16 329

43
Sawnwood
Production (sawn): thousand cubic metres [cont.]
Sciages
Production (sciés) : milliers de mètres cubes [suite]

Region, country or area Région, pays ou zone	1990	1991	1992	1993	1994	1995	1996	1997	1998	1999
Greece Grèce	355	387	337	337[1]	337[1]	337[1]	337[1]	130	137	140
Hungary Hongrie	1 098	936	667	480	417	230	285	317	298	308
Ireland Irlande	386	386[1]	575	637	709	678	687	642	675	811
Italy Italie	1 950	1 850	1 823	1 700	1 808	1 850	1 650	1 751	1 600	1 630
Latvia Lettonie	...	...	740	446	950	1 300	1 614	2 700	3 200	3 640
Lithuania Lituanie	...	...	105[1]	699	760	940	1 450	1 250	1 150	1 150
Netherlands Pays-Bas	455	425	405	389	383	426	359	401	349	362
Norway Norvège	2 413	2 262	2 362	2 315	2 415	2 210	2 420	2 520	2 525	2 551
Poland Pologne	4 129	3 205	4 082	4 260	5 300	5 650	5 060	5 910	6 521	6 395
Portugal Portugal	2 090	1 970	1 550	1 494	1 670	1 731	1 731[1]	1 731[1]	1 490	1 430
Republic of Moldova République de Moldova	...	...	...	...	31	25	29	30	30	31
Romania Roumanie	2 911	2 233	2 460	2 460[1]	1 727	1 777	1 693	1 861	2 200	2 200[1]
Russian Federation Fédération de Russie	...	...	53 370	40 890	30 720	26 500	21 913	20 600	19 580	18 980
Slovakia Slovaquie	...	...	...	550	700	646	629	767	1 265	1 308
Slovenia Slovénie	...	...	403	513	513	511	496	510	664	664[1]
Spain Espagne	3 267	3 162	2 468	2 717	2 755	3 262	3 080	3 080	3 178	3 087[1]
Sweden Suède	12 018	11 463	12 128	12 738	13 816	14 944	14 370	15 669	15 124	14 858
Switzerland Suisse	1 985	1 727	1 525	1 410	1 320	1 479	1 355	1 280	1 400[1]	1 500
TFYR Macedonia L'ex-R.y. Macédoine	...	...	...	63	57	42	40	34	27	30
United Kingdom Royaume-Uni	2 271	2 241	2 097	2 112	2 225	2 295	2 291	2 356	2 382	2 502
Yugoslavia Yougoslavie	...	...	490[1]	470[1]	410[1]	410	410[1]	410[1]	410[1]	410[1]
Yugoslavia, SFR† Yougoslavie, Rfs†	3 779	3 204	...	...	...	...	...	...	...	...
Oceania **Océanie**	**5 610**	**5 427**	**5 907**	**6 268**	**6 667**	**7 006**	**6 927**	**7 013**	**7 255**	**7 214**
Australia Australie	3 151	2 858	3 041	3 187	3 431	3 691	3 530	3 481	3 711	3 670
Fiji Fidji	94[1]	141[1]	91[1]	111	112	102	102[1]	133	131	131[1]

43
Sawnwood
Production (sawn): thousand cubic metres [*cont.*]
Sciages
Production (sciés) : milliers de mètres cubes [*suite*]

Region, country or area Région, pays ou zone	1990	1991	1992	1993	1994	1995	1996	1997	1998	1999
New Caledonia Nouvelle-Calédonie	5	3	2	2	3	3[1]	3[1]	3[1]	3[1]	3[1]
New Zealand Nouvelle-Zélande	2 198	2 263	2 544	2 805	2 861	2 950	3 032	3 136	3 150	3 150[1]
Papua New Guinea Papouasie-Nvl-Guinée	117[1]	117[1]	183	118	218	218	218[1]	218[1]	218[1]	218[1]
Samoa Samoa	21	21	21	21	21[1]	21[1]	21[1]	21[1]	21[1]	21[1]
Solomon Islands Iles Salomon	16[1]	16[1]	16[1]	16[1]	12	12[1]	12[1]	12[1]	12[1]	12[1]
Tonga[1] Tonga[1]	1	1	1	1	1	1	1	1	1	1
Vanuatu Vanuatu	7	7	7	7	7[1]	7[1]	7[1]	7[1]	7[1]	7[1]
former USSR† **l'ex-URSS†**	**105 000**	**79 300**	...	...	...	...	...	...	...	...

Source:
Food and Agriculture Organization of the United
Nations (FAO), Rome, "FAO Yearbook of Forest Products 1999"
and the FAOSTAT database.

† For information on recent changes in country or
area nomenclature pertaining to former Czechoslovakia, Hong
Kong Special Administrative Region (SAR) of China, Macao
Special Administrative Region (SAR) of China, SFR of
Yugoslavia and the former USSR, see Annex I - Country or
area nomenclature, regional and other groupings.

†† For statistical purposes, the data for
China do not include those for Hong Kong Special
Administrative Region (Hong Kong SAR) and Macao Special
Administrative Region (Macao SAR).

1 FAO estimate.

Source:
Organisation des Nations Unies pour l'alimentation et
l'agriculture (FAO), Rome, "Annuaire FAO des produits
forestiers 1999" et la base de données FAOSTAT.

† Pour les modifications récentes de nomenclature
de pays ou de zone concernant l'Allemagne, Hong Kong, région
administrative spéciale (RAS) de Chine, Macao, région
administrative spéciale (RAS) de Chine,
l'ex-Tchécoslovaquie, l'ex-URSS et l'ex-Rfs de Yougoslavie,
voir annexe I - Nomenclature des pays ou des zones,
groupements régionaux et autres groupements.

†† Les données statistiques relatives à
la Chine ne comprennent pas celles qui concernent la région
administrative spéciale de Hong Kong (la RAS de Hong Kong)
et la région administrative spéciale de Macao (la RAS de
Macao).

1 Estimation de la FAO.

44
Paper and paperboard
Papiers et cartons
Production: thousand metric tons
Production : milliers de tonnes

Region, country or area Région, pays ou zone	1990	1991	1992	1993	1994	1995	1996	1997	1998	1999
World *Monde*	240 099	243 336	245 002	252 029	268 278	282 045	281 976	289 247	300 739	309 487
Africa **Afrique**	2 698	2 658	2 605	2 520	2 437	2 628	2 637	2 871	2 947	2 883
Algeria Algérie	* 91	* 91	91[1]	93	87	* 78	* 56	* 65	65[1]	65[1]
Angola Angola	0	0	0	0	0[1]	0[1]	0[1]	0[1]	0[1]	0[1]
Cameroon Cameroun	5[1]	5[1]	5[1]	5[1]	5[1]	5[1]	5[1]	0	0	0[1]
Dem. Rep. of the Congo Rép. dém. du Congo	1[1]	1[1]	3	3[1]	3[1]	3[1]	3[1]	3[1]	3[1]	3[1]
Egypt Egypte	* 223	208	201	* 220	* 219	* 221	221[1]	* 282	* 287	287[1]
Ethiopia incl. Eritrea Ethiopie comp. Erythrée	* 8	6	3	...	...	...	...	...	...	...
Ethiopia Ethiopie	...	...	...	8	8	7	8	8	10	10[1]
Kenya Kenya	* 93	* 92	176	176[1]	* 108	* 113	129	129[1]	129[1]	129[1]
Libyan Arab Jamah.[1] Jamah. arabe libyenne[1]	6	6	6	6	6	6	6	6	6	6
Madagascar Madagascar	6	5	5	6	5	4	3	4	4[1]	4[1]
Morocco Maroc	* 119	* 117	102	99	103	106	106[1]	107	110	110[1]
Mozambique Mozambique	* 1	2[1]	2[1]	1[1]	1[1]	1[1]	1[1]	0	0	0[1]
Nigeria Nigéria	43	29	21	5	3	6	21	19	19	19
South Africa Afrique du Sud	* 1 904	* 1 905	* 1 800	* 1 710	* 1 684	1 871	1 871[1]	2 047	2 105	2 041
Sudan Soudan	* 4	* 3	3[1]	3[1]	3[1]	3[1]	3[1]	3[1]	3[1]	3[1]
Tunisia Tunisie	78	72	71	* 80	* 92	* 90	90[1]	97	105	105[1]
Uganda Ouganda	* 3	* 3	3[1]	3[1]	3[1]	3[1]	3[1]	3[1]	3[1]	3[1]
United Rep. Tanzania Rép.-Unie de Tanzanie	25	25[1]	25[1]	25[1]	25[1]	25[1]	25[1]	25[1]	25[1]	25[1]
Zambia Zambie	2	2	2	4	2	2[1]	2[1]	4[1]	4[1]	4[1]
Zimbabwe Zimbabwe	86	86[1]	86[1]	* 73	* 81	84[1]	84[1]	69[1]	69[1]	69[1]
America, North **Amérique du Nord**	91 519	92 389	94 724	97 399	101 968	107 536	103 748	99 214	108 534	112 281
Canada Canada	16 466	16 559	16 585	17 557	18 348	18 713	18 414	18 969	18 725	20 147
Costa Rica Costa Rica	19	19[1]	19[1]	19[1]	* 20	20[1]	20[1]	20[1]	20[1]	20[1]

44
Paper and paperboard
Production: thousand metric tons [cont.]
Papiers et cartons
Production : milliers de tonnes [suite]

Region, country or area Région, pays ou zone	1990	1991	1992	1993	1994	1995	1996	1997	1998	1999
Cuba Cuba	* 123	* 118	* 60	* 57	57[1]	57[1]	57[1]	57[1]	57[1]	57[1]
Dominican Republic Rép. dominicaine	10	10	10	7	7	7	21	21[1]	130	130[1]
El Salvador El Salvador	17	17	17	17	17	17	56	56[1]	56[1]	56[1]
Guatemala Guatemala	14	14	14	14	25	31	31[1]	31[1]	31[1]	31[1]
Honduras Honduras	0	0	0	0	0	90	103	89	95	95[1]
Jamaica Jamaïque	4	4	5	3	3[1]	...	...	...	...	...
Mexico Mexique	2 873	2 896[1]	* 2 825	2 447	2 518	* 3 047	3 047[1]	3 491	3 673	3 673[1]
Panama Panama	28	28	28	28	28[1]	28[1]	28[1]	28[1]	28[1]	28[1]
United States Etats-Unis	71 965	72 724	75 161	77 250	80 945	85 526	81 971	76 452	85 719	88 044
America, South Amérique du Sud	7 686	7 986	8 082	8 208	8 812	9 204	9 247	9 981	9 930	9 930
Argentina Argentine	891	* 963	976	850	* 961	1 025	991	* 1 144	* 1 159	1 159[1]
Bolivia Bolivie	5	0	0	0	0[1]	2	2	2[1]	2[1]	2[1]
Brazil Brésil	4 844	4 888	4 913	5 352	5 730	5 856	5 885	6 475	6 524	6 524[1]
Chile Chili	462	486	508	526	553	573	680	614	642	642[1]
Colombia Colombie	494	521	629	595	672	690	693	704	711	711[1]
Ecuador Equateur	44	129	160	103	78	83	86	91	91[1]	91[1]
Paraguay Paraguay	12	13	13	13	13[1]	13[1]	13[1]	13[1]	13[1]	13[1]
Peru Pérou	263	279	141	79	94	140	140[1]	140[1]	63	63[1]
Uruguay Uruguay	61	75	83	83[1]	83[1]	86	86[1]	* 90	* 88	88[1]
Venezuela Venezuela	610	632	659	607	628	736	671	708	637	637[1]
Asia Asie	57 057	60 339	63 168	65 822	71 791	77 457	81 636	85 286	85 264	87 182
Bangladesh Bangladesh	104	104	97[1]	* 150	* 160	120[1]	90[1]	70	46	46[1]
China †† Chine ††	17 328	18 525	19 929	21 884	25 377	28 237	30 633	31 483	* 32 053	32 053[1]
China, Hong Kong SAR† Chine, Hong Kong RAS†	* 80	* 115	* 120	* 193	* 250	* 280	280[1]	280[1]	280[1]	280[1]
India Inde	2 185	2 362	2 528	2 626	* 2 859	* 3 025	3 025[1]	* 3 000	* 3 285	3 285[1]

44
Paper and paperboard
Production: thousand metric tons [cont.]
Papiers et cartons
Production : milliers de tonnes [suite]

Region, country or area Région, pays ou zone	1990	1991	1992	1993	1994	1995	1996	1997	1998	1999
Indonesia Indonésie	* 1 438	* 1 755	* 2 263	2 600[1]	* 3 054	* 3 425	* 4 121	* 4 822	* 5 487	5 487[1]
Iran (Islamic Rep. of) Iran (Rép. islamique d')	* 211	* 235	190	* 260	205	205[1]	205[1]	205[1]	130	130[1]
Iraq Iraq	55	13	13[1]	13[1]	* 18	18[1]	18[1]	18[1]	20	20[1]
Israel Israël	194	200	215	213	229	275	275[1]	275[1]	275[1]	275[1]
Japan Japon	28 088	29 053	28 324	27 764	28 527	29 664	30 014	31 014	29 886	30 359
Jordan Jordanie	* 15	* 15	15[1]	29	31	31[1]	31[1]	32	32[1]	32[1]
Korea, Dem. P. R.[1] Corée, R. p. dém. de[1]	80	80	80	80	80	80	80	80	80	80
Korea, Republic of Corée, République de	4 524	4 922	5 504	5 804	6 435	* 6 878	7 681	8 334	7 749	* 8 875
Lebanon Liban	37[1]	42	42[1]	42[1]	42[1]	42[1]	42[1]	42[1]	42[1]	42[1]
Malaysia Malaisie	275	293	636	663	574	665	674	711	761	761[1]
Myanmar Myanmar	11	11[1]	11[1]	15	15[1]	15[1]	15[1]	39	37	37[1]
Nepal Népal	13	13	13[1]	13[1]	13[1]	13[1]	13[1]	13[1]	13[1]	13[1]
Pakistan Pakistan	229	206	229	362	403	420	447	500	513	513[1]
Philippines Philippines	245	473	570	* 518	* 518	* 613	613[1]	613[1]	613[1]	613[1]
Singapore Singapour	* 80	* 85	85[1]	* 96	* 97	* 87	87[1]	87[1]	87[1]	87[1]
Sri Lanka Sri Lanka	16	23	26	29	31	28	25	25[1]	25[1]	25[1]
Syrian Arab Republic Rép. arabe syrienne	19[1]	1	1[1]	1[1]	1[1]	1[1]	1[1]	1[1]	1[1]	1[1]
Thailand Thaïlande	877	958	1 150	1 306	1 664	1 970	2 036	2 271	2 367	2 692
Turkey Turquie	891	747	1 013	1 032	1 102	1 240	1 105	1 246	1 357	1 351
Viet Nam Viet Nam	62	108	115	129	* 106	* 125	125[1]	125[1]	125[1]	125[1]
Europe Europe	**67 654**	**67 541**	**73 695**	**75 205**	**80 208**	**82 065**	**81 524**	**88 588**	**90 688**	**93 812**
Albania Albanie	44	44[1]	44[1]	44[1]	44[1]	44[1]	44[1]	44[1]	44[1]	44[1]
Austria Autriche	2 932	3 090	3 252	3 301	3 603	3 599	3 653	3 816	4 009	4 142
Belarus Bélarus	...	...	267[1]	175[1]	131	131[1]	131[1]	131[1]	131[1]	131[1]
Belgium-Luxembourg Belgique-Luxembourg	1 196	1 233	1 147	1 147[1]	1 088	1 088[1]	1 432	1 432[1]	1 831	1 971

44
Paper and paperboard
Production: thousand metric tons [*cont.*]
Papiers et cartons
Production : milliers de tonnes [*suite*]

Region, country or area Région, pays ou zone	1990	1991	1992	1993	1994	1995	1996	1997	1998	1999
Bulgaria Bulgarie	322	258	153	* 139	* 148	150	150	150	150[1]	150[1]
Croatia Croatie	...	...	100	114	248	325	304	393	403	417
former Czechoslovakia† l'ex-Tchécoslovaquie†	1 300	1 087	...	...	...	...	...	...	...	...
Czech Republic République tchèque	...	...	...	643	700	738	714	772	768	770
Denmark Danemark	335	356	317	339	345	345[1]	345[1]	391	393	397
Estonia Estonie	...	...	42	42	42	42	53	35	43	48
Finland Finlande	8 968	8 777	9 153	9 990	10 909	10 942	10 442	12 149	12 703	12 947
France France	7 049	7 442	7 691	7 975	8 701	8 619	8 556	9 143	9 161	9 500
Germany Allemagne	13 224[1]	12 904	13 214	13 034	14 457	14 827	14 733	15 930	16 311	16 692
Greece Grèce	361	387	387[1]	750[1]	750[1]	750[1]	750[1]	478	517	538
Hungary Hongrie	443	364	348	292	328	321	363	820	718	456
Ireland Irlande	35	36	0	0	0	0	0[1]	0[1]	42	42
Italy Italie	5 587	5 795	6 040	6 019	6 705	6 810	6 954	8 032	8 254	8 568
Latvia Lettonie	...	...	45	10	4	6	8	16	18	16
Lithuania Lituanie	...	...	50	31	23	29	31	25	37	37
Netherlands Pays-Bas	2 770	2 862	2 835	2 855	3 011	2 967	2 987	3 159	3 180	3 256
Norway Norvège	1 819	1 784	1 683	1 958	2 148	2 261	2 096	2 129	2 260	2 242
Poland Pologne	1 064	1 066	1 147	1 183	1 326	1 477	1 528	1 660	1 718	1 830
Portugal Portugal	780	877	959	878	949	977	1 026	1 080	1 136	1 163
Romania Roumanie	547	359	359[1]	359[1]	288	364	332	324	294	294[1]
Russian Federation Fédération de Russie	...	...	5 765	4 459	3 412	4 073	3 224	3 339	3 595	4 468
Slovakia Slovaquie	...	...	...	303	299	327	467	526	597	602
Slovenia Slovénie	...	...	413	401	460	449	456	430	491	491[1]
Spain Espagne	3 446	3 576	3 449	3 348	3 503	3 684	3 768	3 968	3 545	3 807

44
Paper and paperboard
Production: thousand metric tons [cont.]
Papiers et cartons
Production : milliers de tonnes [suite]

Region, country or area Région, pays ou zone	1990	1991	1992	1993	1994	1995	1996	1997	1998	1999
Sweden Suède	8 419	8 349	8 378	8 781	9 284	9 159	9 018	9 756	9 879	10 071
Switzerland Suisse	1 295	1 259[1]	1 305	1 332	1 450	1 435	1 461	1 583	1 592	1 755
TFYR Macedonia L'ex-R.y. Macédoine	...	...	...	22	24	34	21	21	15	14
Ukraine Ukraine	...	...	...	...	...	...	288	261	261[1]	261[1]
United Kingdom Royaume-Uni	4 824	4 951	5 152	5 282	5 829	6 093	6 189	6 479	6 477	6 576
Yugoslavia Yougoslavie	...	...	...	...	...	...	...	117	117[1]	117[1]
Yugoslavia, SFR† Yougoslavie, Rfs†	894	685	...	...	...	...	...	...	...	...
Oceania **Océanie**	**2 768**	**2 833**	**2 728**	**2 875**	**3 061**	**3 155**	**3 185**	**3 308**	**3 376**	**3 399**
Australia Australie	2 011	2 018	1 990	2 039	2 197	2 252	2 320	2 418	2 541	2 564
New Zealand Nouvelle-Zélande	757	815	738	836	864	903	865	890	835	835[1]
former USSR† **l'ex-URSS†**	**10 718**	**9 590**	...	...	...	...	...	...	...	...

Source:
Food and Agriculture Organization of the United
Nations (FAO), Rome, "FAO Yearbook of Forest Products 1999"
and the FAOSTAT database.

† For information on recent changes in country or
area nomenclature pertaining to former Czechoslovakia, Hong
Kong Special Administrative Region (SAR) of China, Macao
Special Administrative Region (SAR) of China, SFR of
Yugoslavia and the former USSR, see Annex I - Country or
area nomenclature, regional and other groupings.

†† For statistical purposes, the data for
China do not include those for Hong Kong Special
Administrative Region (Hong Kong SAR) and Macao Special
Administrative Region (Macao SAR).

1 FAO estimate.

Source:
Organisation des Nations Unies pour l'alimentation et
l'agriculture (FAO), Rome, "Annuaire FAO des produits
forestiers 1999" et la base de données FAOSTAT.

† Pour les modifications récentes de nomenclature
de pays ou de zone concernant l'Allemagne, Hong Kong, région
administrative spéciale (RAS) de Chine, Macao, région
administrative spéciale (RAS) de Chine,
l'ex-Tchécoslovaquie, l'ex-URSS et l'ex-Rfs de Yougoslavie,
voir annexe I - Nomenclature des pays ou des zones,
groupements régionaux et autres groupements.

†† Les données statistiques relatives à
la Chine ne comprennent pas celles qui concernent la région
administrative spéciale de Hong Kong (la RAS de Hong Kong)
et la région administrative spéciale de Macao (la RAS de
Macao).

1 Estimation de la FAO.

45

Tires
Pneumatiques

Production: thousands
Production : milliers

Country or area Pays ou zone	1989	1990	1991	1992	1993	1994	1995	1996	1997	1998
Angola[1] Angola[1]	60	46	20	...	...	...	...	...	...	...
Argentina Argentine	4 594	4 677	4 568	5 365	6 038	7 083	6 940	7 297	8 138	...
Armenia Arménie	861	560	485	97	65	104	90	54	1	17
Australia[2,3] Australie[2,3]	7 450	7 600	...	...	...	...	...	...	...	...
Azerbaijan Azerbaïdjan	366	287	271	222	134	65	21	6	5	0
Belarus Bélarus	4 360	4 018	3 367	2 862	1 916	1 027	1 163	1 733	2 178	2 098
Brazil Brésil	29 215[4]	29 162[4]	28 926[4]	30 306[4]	31 795[4]	33 395[4]	35 076[5]	34 539[5]	...	...
Bulgaria Bulgarie	1 762	1 795	1 125	1 034	783	553	642	532	391	124
Canada[6] Canada[6]	20 664	21 692	...	...	...	...	...	...	...	...
Chile Chili	1 562	1 632	1 825	2 002	2 198	2 285	2 330	2 269	2 509	2 350
China ††[1] Chine ††[1]	32 262	32 091	38 723	51 834	6 391	9 302	7 945	...	...	...
Colombia Colombie	1 875	1 408	1 437	1 159	927	1 234	769	...	605	...
Croatia Croatie	337	255	34	...	...	...	...	...	...	...
Cuba Cuba	230	373[5]	88[5]	126[5]	63[5]	112[5]	194[5]	212[5]	...	...
Cyprus Chypre	89	* 99	* 72	38	* 38	* 42	56	60	46	47
Czech Republic République tchèque	2 706	2 660	2 501	3 123	3 572	...	...	...	...	...
Denmark Danemark	...	...	...	0	0[7]	0[7]	0[7]	...	...	...
Ecuador Equateur	128[5]	102[5]	115[5]	894[5]	837	924	920	1 244	...	...
Egypt Egypte	1 126	1 171	1 243	1 186	1 162	1 869	1 932	1 763	1 277	1 498
Ethiopia Ethiopie	83	118	65	66	100	171	168	80	151	152
France France	61 678	54 536	57 876	59 928	53 390	66 744	...	...	...	...
Germany Allemagne	...	...	...	50 993	45 595	46 415	48 534	48 703	53 605	57 745
F. R. Germany R. f. Allemagne	49 467	48 247	...	...	...	...	...	...	...	...
former German D. R. l'ex-R. d. allemande	6 259	4 052	...	...	...	...	...	...	...	...
Hungary Hongrie	736	605	425	355	146	...	...	391	429	464

45
Tires
Production: thousands [cont.]
Pneumatiques
Production : milliers [suite]

Country or area Pays ou zone	1989	1990	1991	1992	1993	1994	1995	1996	1997	1998
India Inde	8 066	8 460	8 312	8 756	9 702	10 456	12 333	12 434	...	...
Indonesia Indonésie	6 396	7 848	6 396	8 460	14 376	20 842	12 033	...	23 388	...
Iran (Islamic Rep. of) Iran (Rép. islamique d')	4 814[8]	6 012[8]	6 255[8]	6 170[8]	5 284[8]	5 942[8]	5 956[9]	5 624[9]	6 319[9]	...
Israel Israël	751	778	786	892	854	966	918	900	...	...
Italy Italie	33 625	30 767	32 447	29 978	29 138	31 520	33 551	33 600	32 761	36 072
Jamaica Jamaïque	286	347	326	308	359	352	146	782	0	...
Japan Japon	155 038	153 226	153 677	154 900	142 595	139 172	152 040	157 819	163 006	158 999
Kenya[10] Kenya[10]	797	813	462	474	456	478	469	530	...	...
Korea, Republic of Corée, République de	24 535	28 129	33 710	38 120	42 285	47 105	53 558	57 835	59 380	60 192
Malaysia[1] Malaisie[1]	6 156	6 764	7 970	8 540	9 486	10 156	11 368	12 221	13 716	13 567
Mexico Mexique	11 038	11 855	12 148	12 568	10 490	10 787	9 292	10 772	13 450	16 646
Morocco Maroc	...	...	1 015	886	863	976	1 073	1 206	1 254	...
Mozambique Mozambique	29	23	5	...	...	...	...	...	...	...
New Zealand[11] Nouvelle-Zélande[11]	1 460	1 550	...	...	...	...	...	...	...	...
Pakistan[3] Pakistan[3]	907	915	952	784	712	783	912	1 003	525	767
Panama Panama	23[5]	16	30[5]	31	33	43	32	34	37[5]	...
Peru Pérou	710	637	686	575	717	783	813	797	868	1 033
Philippines Philippines	* 2 016	2 208	...	...	...	...	...	...	...	...
Poland Pologne	6 025	4 704	4 516	5 607	6 479	7 612	9 502	10 930	11 939	14 410
Portugal Portugal	3 292	2 976	2 184	...	1 824	...	...	...	...	...
Romania[11] Roumanie[11]	4 804	3 702	2 822	2 877	3 294	2 781	3 038	3 304	2 761	2 646
Russian Federation Fédération de Russie	35 339	35 592	33 522	33 682	31 208	17 449	17 462	19 732	22 954	22 008
Slovakia Slovaquie	2 557	2 655	2 276	...	...	3 797	4 387	4 528	...	3 984
Slovenia Slovénie	3 377	4 397	3 289	4 133	4 371	4 627	5 184	5 679	6 472	6 320
South Africa Afrique du Sud	6 817	7 478	7 236	7 136	7 421	7 811	8 635	8 429	8 958	9 602

45

Tires
Production: thousands [*cont.*]
Pneumatiques
Production : milliers [*suite*]

Country or area Pays ou zone	1989	1990	1991	1992	1993	1994	1995	1996	1997	1998
Spain Espagne	24 696	23 361	23 812	25 670	24 116	...	...	28 161	...	30 441
Sri Lanka Sri Lanka	339	382	392	276	184	...	...	...	...	...
Sweden Suède	* 2 915	* 2 162	2 158	2 517	2 336	2 406	2 543	2 943	3 507	3 942
Thailand Thaïlande	4 320	4 183	4 518	...	...	...	...	8 818	10 945	11 602
TFYR Macedonia L'ex-R.y. Macédoine	12	12	1	...	...	...	...	...	...	...
Tunisia Tunisie	505	480	510	439	568	463	505	502	563	567
Turkey Turquie	6 633	4 754	7 541	8 463	9 137	8 729	11 377	12 018	13 658	13 602
Ukraine Ukraine	8 730	8 539	7 859	7 886	7 699	5 726	5 356	5 832	6 940	7 941
former USSR†[12] l'ex-URSS†[12]	69 705	...	...	...	...	...	...	...	...	...
United Kingdom Royaume-Uni	31 080	29 376	28 500	30 408	...	...	...	...	...	...
United Rep.Tanzania Rép.-Unie de Tanzanie	213	208	185	158	190	177	151	159	167	...
United States Etats-Unis	212 868	210 660	202 391	230 256	237 444	243 600	...	...	...	...
Venezuela Venezuela	4 177	3 951	4 787	4 713	5 119[5]	5 385[5]	5 361[5]	5 162[5]	5 717[5]	5 383[5]
Yugoslavia Yougoslavie	...	...	4 680	2 782	544	965	1 186	2 254	3 103	3 666
Yugoslavia, SFR†[2] Yougoslavie, Rfs†[2]	13 201	12 744	...	...	...	...	...	...	...	...

Source:
United Nations Secretariat, "Industrial Commodity Statistics
Yearbook 1998" and the industrial statistics database of
the Statistics Division.

† For information on recent changes in country or
area nomenclature pertaining to former Czechoslovakia,
Germany, Hong Kong Special Administrative Region (SAR) of
China, Macao Special Administrative Region (SAR) of China,
SFR of Yugoslavia and the former USSR, see Annex I - Country
or area nomenclature, regional and other groupings.

†† For statistical purposes, the data for
China do not include those for Hong Kong Special
Administrative Region (Hong Kong SAR), Macao Special
Administrative Region (Macao SAR) and Taiwan province of
China.

Source:
Secrétariat de l'Organisation des Nations Unies, "Annuaire
de statistiques industrielles par produit 1998" et la base
de données pour les statistiques industrielles de la
Division de statistique.

† Pour les modifications récentes de nomenclature
de pays ou de zone concernant l'Allemagne, Hong Kong, région
administrative spéciale (RAS) de Chine, Macao, région
administrative spéciale (RAS) de Chine,
l'ex-Tchécoslovaquie, l'ex-URSS et l'ex-Rfs de Yougoslavie,
voir annexe I - Nomenclature des pays ou des zones,
groupements régionaux et autres groupements.

†† Les données statistiques relatives à
la Chine ne comprennent pas celles qui concernent la région
administrative spéciale de Hong Kong (la RAS de Hong Kong),
la région administrative spéciale de Macao (la RAS de Macao)

45

Tires
Production: thousands [*cont.*]

Pneumatiques
Production : milliers [*suite*]

et la province chinoise de Taiwan.

1   Tires of all types.
2   Including motorcycle tires.
3   Twelve months ending 30 June of year stated.

4   Including tires for motorcycles and bicycles.

5   Source: United Nations Economic Commission for Latin America and the Caribbean (ECLAC), (Santiago).
6   Source: International Rubber Study Group, (London).
7   Sales.
8   Production by establishments employing 50 or more persons.
9   Production by establishments employing 10 or more persons.
10 Including retreaded tires.
11 Including tires for vehicles operating off-the-road.
12 Including tires for agricultural vehicles, motorcycles and scooters.

1   Pneumatiques de tous genres.
2   Y compris les pneumatiques pour motocyclettes.
3   Période de douze mois finissant le 30e juin de l'année indiquée.
4   Y compris les pneumatiques pour motocyclettes et bicyclettes.
5   Source: Commission économique des Nations Unies pour l'Amérique Latine et les Caraïbes (CEPALC), (Santiago).
6   Source: ″International Rubber Study Group″, (Londres).
7   Ventes.
8   Production des établissements occupant 50 personnes ou plus.
9   Production des établissements occupant 10 personnes ou plus.
10 Y compris les pneumatiques rechapés.
11 Y compris les pneumatiques pour véhicules tous terrains.
12 Y compris les pneumatiques pour véhicules agricoles, motocyclettes et scooters.

46
Cement
Ciment
Production: thousand metric tons
Production : milliers de tonnes

Country or area Pays ou zone	1989	1990	1991	1992	1993	1994	1995	1996	1997	1998
Afghanistan Afghanistan	* 100	100[1]	109[1]	115[2]	115[2]	115[2]	115[2]	116[2]	116[2]	...
Albania Albanie	753	644	311	197	198	240	240	204	100	84
Algeria Algérie	6 778	6 337	6 323	7 093	6 951	6 093	6 783	7 470	7 146	7 836
Angola Angola	298	305	314	370	* 250[2]	* 250[2]	* 250[2]	* 270[2]	* 301[2]	...
Argentina Argentine	4 449	3 612	4 399	5 051	5 647	6 306	5 477	5 117	6 769	7 195[3]
Armenia Arménie	1 639	1 466	1 507	368	198	122	228	281	293	314
Australia Australie	6 901	6 535	5 725	5 897	6 628	7 017	6 606	6 524	6 952	...
Austria Autriche	4 749	4 903	5 017	5 029	4 941	4 828	3 806	3 900	3 944	...
Azerbaijan Azerbaïdjan	1 058	990	923	827	643	467	196	223	303	201
Bangladesh[4] Bangladesh[4]	344	337	275	272	207	324	316	426	610	...
Barbados Barbade	225	213	144	71	64	76	76	108	176	257
Belarus Bélarus	2 283	2 258	2 402	2 263	1 908	1 488	1 235	1 467	1 876	2 035
Belgium Belgique	6 720	6 924	7 184	8 073	7 569	7 542	7 501	6 996	7 001	6 929
Benin[2] Bénin[2]	250	300	320	370	380	380	380	...	...	...
Bhutan[2] Bhoutan[2]	...	...	...	...	108	* 120	* 140	* 160	* 160	...
Bolivia Bolivie	501	524	621	630	629	789	869	859[3]	970[3]	1 094[3]
Brazil Brésil	25 921	25 850	27 491	23 902	24 845	25 229	28 256	34 597	34 115	35 359
Bulgaria Bulgarie	5 036	4 710	2 374	2 132	2 007	1 910	2 070	2 137	1 654	1 742
Cameroon Cameroun	614[2]	624[2]	622[2]	620[2]	* 620[2]	* 620[2]	522	* 600[2]	* 600[2]	...
Canada Canada	12 591	11 745	9 372	8 592	9 394	10 584	10 440	11 587	* 11 736	12 064
Chile Chili	2 010	2 115	2 251	2 660	3 024	3 001	3 304	3 627	3 718	3 890
China †† Chine ††	210 295	209 711	244 656	308 217	267 878	421 180	475 606	491 189	511 738	536 000
China, Hong Kong SAR† Chine, Hong Kong RAS†	2 141	1 808	1 677	1 644	1 712	1 927	1 913	2 027	1 925	1 539
Colombia Colombie	6 648	6 360	6 389	9 163	18 205	9 273	9 908	...	10 878	8 673
Congo Congo	121	90	102	124	95	* 114[2]	* 100[2]	43	20	0

46
Cement
Production: thousand metric tons [*cont.*]
Ciment
Production : milliers de tonnes [*suite*]

Country or area Pays ou zone	1989	1990	1991	1992	1993	1994	1995	1996	1997	1998
Costa Rica Costa Rica	315[3]	...	* 700[2]	* 700[2]	* 860[2]	* 940[2]	* 865[2]	* 830[2]	* 850[2]	...
Côte d'Ivoire *[2] Côte d'Ivoire *[2]	700	500	500	510	500	500	500	...	...	...
Croatia Croatie	2 900	2 655	1 742	1 771	1 683	2 055	1 708	1 842	2 184	3 873
Cuba Cuba	3 759	3 696	1 851[3]	1 134[3]	1 049[3]	1 085[3]	1 456[3]	1 438[3]	1 701[3]	...
Cyprus Chypre	1 042	1 133	1 134	1 132	1 089	1 053	1 024	1 021	909	1 204
Czech Republic République tchèque	6 788	6 434	5 610	6 145	5 393	5 252	4 831	5 016	4 874	4 604
Dem. Rep. of the Congo[2] Rép. dém. du Congo[2]	460	461	* 250	174	149	* 150	* 200	241	125	...
Denmark[5] Danemark[5]	2 000	1 656	2 019	2 072	2 270	2 427	2 580	2 629	2 683	2 667
Dominican Republic Rép. dominicaine	1 269	1 109	1 235	1 365	1 271[3]	1 303	1 450	1 642	1 822	1 872
Ecuador Equateur	* 1 548	1 792	1 774	2 072	2 155	2 452	2 549	2 601	...	...
Egypt Egypte	12 480	14 111	16 427	15 454	12 576	13 544	14 237	15 569	15 569	15 480
El Salvador[3] El Salvador[3]	353	641	694	760	659	915	914	938	1 029	988
Estonia Estonie	1 129	938	905	483	354	403	418	388	422	321
Ethiopia[6] Ethiopie[6]	412	324	270	237	377	464	609	672	775	497
Fiji Fidji	58	78	79	85	80	94	91	84	96	89
Finland Finlande	1 693	1 649	1 343	1 133	835	864	907	975	* 960[2]	...
France France	25 994	26 497	25 089	21 584	19 320	20 184	19 896	18 340[2]	* 18 600[2]	...
Gabon Gabon	117	112	126	116[2]	141[2]	148[2]	154[2]	180[2]	* 200[2]	...
Georgia Géorgie	...	...	...	426	278	89	59	85	94	199
Germany Allemagne	...	...	...	37 331	36 649	40 217	38 858	37 006	37 210	38 464
F. R. Germany R. f. Allemagne	28 499	30 456	...	...	...	...	...	...	...	
former German D. R. l'ex-R. d. allemande	12 229	7 316	...	...	...	...	...	...	...	
Ghana[2] Ghana[2]	565	675	750	1 020	1 200	1 350	* 1 300	* 1 300	* 1 400	...
Greece Grèce	12 319	13 142	13 151	12 761	12 492	12 633	10 914	13 391	13 660	...
Guadeloupe Guadeloupe	215	291	339	292	276	283	* 230	...	...	...

46
Cement
Production: thousand metric tons [*cont.*]
Ciment
Production : milliers de tonnes [*suite*]

Country or area Pays ou zone	1989	1990	1991	1992	1993	1994	1995	1996	1997	1998
Guatemala Guatemala	935[3]	897[3]	450	658[3]	1 018[3]	1 163[3]	1 257	1 173	1 480	1 496
Haiti Haïti	223	180	211	216[3]	228[3]	228[3]	...	...	...	...
Honduras Honduras	321	326	402	390[3]	368[3]	368[3]	366[3]	334[3]	...	...
Hungary Hongrie	3 857	3 933	2 529	2 236	2 533	2 793	2 875	2 747	2 811	2 999
Iceland Islande	* 116	114	106	100	86	81	82	90	110	118
India Inde	44 197	46 170	52 013	53 936	57 326	63 461	67 722	73 261	82 873	87 646
Indonesia Indonésie	14 788	14 786	13 480	14 048	19 610	24 564	23 136	...	20 702	...
Iran (Islamic Rep. of)[7] Iran (Rép. islamique d')[7]	12 587	14 429	13 996	15 094	16 321	16 250	16 904	17 703	18 349	...
Iraq Iraq	12 500	13 000	* 5 000	2 453	* 2 000[2]	* 2 000[2]	* 2 108[2]	* 2 100[2]	* 2 500[2]	...
Ireland * [2] Irlande * [2]	1 624	1 630	1 600	1 600	1 600	1 550	2 100	2 100	2 000	...
Israel Israël	2 289	2 868	3 340	3 960	4 536	4 800	6 204	6 723	...	...
Italy Italie	39 692	40 544	40 301	41 034	33 771	32 698	33 716	33 327	33 718	35 512
Jamaica Jamaïque	361	421	390	480	441	445	518	559	588	558
Japan Japon	79 717	84 445	89 564	88 252	88 046	91 624	90 474	94 492	91 938	81 328
Jordan Jordanie	1 930	1 733	1 675	2 651	3 437	3 392	3 415	3 512	3 250	2 650
Kazakhstan Kazakhstan	8 650	8 301	7 575	6 436	3 963	2 033	1 772	1 115	657	622
Kenya Kenya	1 316	1 515	1 423	1 507	1 417	1 470	1 670	1 575	...	...
Korea, Dem. P. R. * [2] Corée, R. p. dém. de * [2]	16 300	16 000	16 000	17 000	17 000	17 000	17 000	17 000	17 000	...
Korea, Republic of Corée, République de	30 821	33 914	39 167	44 444	47 313	52 088	56 101	58 434	60 317	46 791
Kuwait Koweït	1 108	800	300[2]	534	956	1 232	* 1 363	...	...	2 310
Kyrgyzstan Kirghizistan	1 408	1 387	1 320	1 096	692	426	310	546	658	709
Lao People's Dem. Rep. Rép. dém. pop. lao	...	...	...	...	...	7	59	...	...	...
Latvia Lettonie	776	744	720	340	114	244	204	325	246	366
Lebanon Liban	* 900[2]	* 900[2]	* 900[2]	2 163	2 591	2 948	3 470	3 430	...	...
Liberia Libéria	* 85	50	* 2[2]	* 8[2]	* 8[2]	...	...	...	...	...

46
Cement
Production: thousand metric tons [*cont.*]
Ciment
Production : milliers de tonnes [*suite*]

Country or area Pays ou zone	1989	1990	1991	1992	1993	1994	1995	1996	1997	1998
Libyan Arab Jamah. Jamah. arabe libyenne	4	4	4	4	4	4	3	3	...	...
Lithuania Lituanie	3 410	3 359	3 126	1 485	727	736	649	656	714	788
Luxembourg Luxembourg	590	636	688	695	719	711	714	667	683	699
Madagascar Madagascar	24	29	32	30	36	* 60[2]	* 60[2]	* 60[2]	* 60[2]	...
Malawi Malawi	79	101	112	108	117	122	124	88	70	83
Malaysia Malaisie	4 794	5 881	7 451	8 366	8 797	9 928	10 713	12 349	12 668	10 397
Mali Mali	0	4	11	16	14	14	13	21	...	...
Martinique Martinique	244	277	291	262	234	231	* 225	...	...	...
Mauritania[2] Mauritanie[2]	...	...	105	122	111	374	120	120	* 125	
Mexico Mexique	24 210	24 683	25 208	27 114	28 725	31 594	25 295	26 174	29 685	30 915
Mongolia Mongolie	513	510	227	133	82	86	109	106	* 112[2]	...
Morocco Maroc	4 641	5 381	5 777	6 223	6 175	6 284	6 399	6 585	7 236	7 155
Mozambique Mozambique	79	80	63	73	60	62	146	179	217	...
Myanmar[8] Myanmar[8]	441	420	443	472	400	477	525	513	524	371
Nepal[9] Népal[9]	114	107	136[2]	237	248	315	327	309	227	276
Netherlands Pays-Bas	3 546[5 10]	3 682[5 10]	3 571[5 10]	3 296[5 10]	3 142[5 10]	* 3 400[2]	* 3 400[2]	* 3 300[2]	* 3 300[2]	...
New Caledonia Nouvelle-Calédonie	67	64	* 68	90	100	97	98	89	84	...
New Zealand Nouvelle-Zélande	729	681	581	599	684	* 900[2]	* 950[2]	* 974[2]	* 976[2]	...
Nicaragua Nicaragua	225[3]	* 140[3]	* 239[2]	* 277[2]	* 255[2]	* 309[2]	* 350[2]	...	...	...
Niger Niger	16	19	20	29	31	26	31	* 30[2]	* 30[2]	...
Nigeria Nigéria	4 229	2 974	3 418	3 367	3 247	1 275	1 573	...	...	...
Norway Norvège	1 380	1 260	1 293	1 242	1 368	1 464	1 613	1 690	...	...
Oman[2] Oman[2]	...	...	...	...	1 000	1 200	1 177	1 260	* 1 300	...
Pakistan[4] Pakistan[4]	7 125	7 488	7 762	8 321	8 558	8 100	7 913	9 567	9 536	9 364
Panama Panama	185[3]	325	300[2]	473	620[3]	678[3]	658[3]	651	756[3]	...

46
Cement
Production: thousand metric tons [cont.]
Ciment
Production : milliers de tonnes [suite]

Country or area Pays ou zone	1989	1990	1991	1992	1993	1994	1995	1996	1997	1998
Paraguay Paraguay	256	344	343	476	480	529	* 625	700[3]	...	...
Peru Pérou	2 105	2 185	2 137	2 080	2 327	3 177	3 792	3 848	4 300	4 339
Philippines Philippines	3 624	6 360	6 804	6 540	7 932	9 576	10 566	* 12 000[2]	* 15 000[2]	...
Poland Pologne	17 125	12 518	12 012	11 908	12 200	13 834	13 914	13 959	15 003	14 970
Portugal Portugal	6 673	7 188	7 342	7 728	7 662	7 756	8 030	8 444	9 395	9 784
Puerto Rico Porto Rico	1 257	1 305	1 296	1 266	1 303	1 356	1 398	1 508	1 586	1 632
Qatar Qatar	295	267	367	354	400	470	475	486	584	...
Republic of Moldova République de Moldova	2 259	2 288	1 809	705	110[11]	39[11]	49[11]	40[11]	122[11]	74[11]
Réunion Réunion	322	336	350	344	325	321	313	290	268	275
Romania Roumanie	12 225	9 468	6 692	6 271	6 158	5 998	6 842	6 956	6 553	7 300
Russian Federation Fédération de Russie	84 518	83 034	77 463	61 699	49 903	37 220	36 466	27 791	26 688	25 974
Rwanda *[2] Rwanda *[2]	68	60	60	60	60	10	10	10	10	...
Saudi Arabia[2] Arabie saoudite[2]	* 9 500	12 000	11 400	15 300	15 300	16 000	15 773	16 437	* 15 400	...
Senegal Sénégal	391	471	503	602	591	697	694	810	854	847
Sierra Leone Sierra Leone	9	...	...	...	...	...	...	...	...	...
Singapore Singapour	1 704	1 848	2 199	* 1 900[2]	* 1 900[2]	* 1 900[2]	* 1 900[2]	...	...	...
Slovakia Slovaquie	4 100	3 781	2 680	3 374	2 656	2 879	2 981	4 234	5 856	3 066
Slovenia Slovénie	1 175	1 142	1 801	1 568	1 291	1 667	1 807	1 064	1 113	1 149
South Africa Afrique du Sud	7 261	6 563	6 147	5 850	6 135	7 068	7 437	7 664	7 891	7 676
Spain Espagne	27 375	28 092	27 576	24 612	21 658	25 884	27 220	26 339	27 860	...
Sri Lanka Sri Lanka	596	579	620	553	466	* 925[2]	956	670	* 966	...
Sudan *[2] Soudan *[2]	150	167	170	250	250	250	250	...	...	...
Suriname Suriname	52	55	24	11	17	18	* 50[2]	* 50[2]	* 50[2]	...
Sweden Suède	4 541	5 000	4 493	2 289	2 152	2 138	2 550	2 503	2 272	2 372
Switzerland Suisse	5 461	5 206	4 716	4 260	* 4 000[2]	* 4 000[2]	* 4 000[2]	...	...	...

46
Cement
Production: thousand metric tons [*cont.*]
Ciment
Production : milliers de tonnes [*suite*]

Country or area Pays ou zone	1989	1990	1991	1992	1993	1994	1995	1996	1997	1998
Syrian Arab Republic Rép. arabe syrienne	3 976	3 049	3 078	3 515	3 906	4 344	4 804	4 817	4 838	5 016
Tajikistan Tadjikistan	1 111	1 067	1 013	447	262	178	78	49	36	18
Thailand Thaïlande	15 024	18 054	19 164	21 711	26 300	29 929	34 051	38 749	37 136	22 722
TFYR Macedonia L'ex-R.y. Macédoine	769	639	606	516	499	486	523	490	610	461
Togo Togo	389[2]	399[2]	388[2]	350[2]	* 350[2]	* 350[2]	* 350[2]	* 350[12]	* 350[2]	...
Trinidad and Tobago Trinité-et-Tobago	384	438	486	482	527	583	559	617	677	700
Tunisia Tunisie	3 984	4 311	4 195	4 184	4 508	4 605	4 998	4 566	4 378	4 588
Turkey Turquie	23 704	24 299	26 029	28 455	31 134	29 356	33 084	35 090	36 054	37 447
Turkmenistan Turkménistan	1 057	1 085	904	1 050	1 118	690	437	438	601	750
Uganda Ouganda	17	27	27	38	52	45	84	195	290	...
Ukraine Ukraine	23 416	22 729	21 745	20 121	15 012	11 435	7 627	5 021	5 101	5 591
former USSR† l'ex-URSS†	140 436	137 321	...	...	...	...	...	...	...	...
United Arab Emirates[2] Emirats arabes unis[2]	3 112	3 110	3 473	* 3 800	* 4 000	* 5 000	* 6 000	* 6 000	...	...
United Kingdom Royaume-Uni	16 849	14 736	12 002	11 004	...	12 330	12 822	15 518	14 361	14 995
United Rep.Tanzania Rép.-Unie de Tanzanie	595	664	1 022	677	749	686	739	726	621	...
United States Etats-Unis	71 308	70 944	67 193	69 585	73 807	77 948	76 906	79 266	82 582	83 931
Uruguay Uruguay	* 465	469	458	552	610	701	593	656	753[3]	907[3]
Uzbekistan Ouzbékistan	6 194	6 385	6 191	5 934	5 277	4 780	3 419	3 277	3 286	...
Venezuela Venezuela	5 259	5 996	6 336	6 585	6 876	4 562	* 6 900	7 568[3]	7 867[3]	7 869[3]
Viet Nam Viet Nam	2 088	2 534	3 127	3 926	* 4 200[2]	* 4 700[2]	* 5 200[2]	* 5 700[2]	* 6 000[2]	...
Yemen Yémen	718	828	718	820	1 000	898	1 100	1 028	1 038	...
Yugoslavia Yougoslavie	...	2 723	2 411	2 036	1 088	1 612	1 696	2 212	2 011	...
Yugoslavia, SFR† Yougoslavie, Rfs†	8 560	7 956	...	...	...	...	...	...	...	...

46
Cement
Production: thousand metric tons [*cont.*]
Ciment
Production : milliers de tonnes [*suite*]

Country or area Pays ou zone	1989	1990	1991	1992	1993	1994	1995	1996	1997	1998
Zambia Zambie	385	432	376	* 347[2]	* 310[2]	* 280[2]	* 250[2]	* 350[2]	...	...
Zimbabwe Zimbabwe	827	924	949	829	816	624	948	996	954	...

Source:
United Nations Secretariat, "Industrial Commodity Statistics Yearbook 1998" and the industrial statistics database of the Statistics Division.

† For information on recent changes in country or area nomenclature pertaining to former Czechoslovakia, Germany, Hong Kong Special Administrative Region (SAR) of China, Macao Special Administrative Region (SAR) of China, SFR of Yugoslavia and the former USSR, see Annex I - Country or area nomenclature, regional and other groupings.

†† For statistical purposes, the data for China do not include those for Hong Kong Special Administrative Region (Hong Kong SAR), Macao Special Administrative Region (Macao SAR) and Taiwan province of China.

1 Twelve months beginning 21 March of year stated.

2 Source: U. S. Bureau of Mines, (Washington, D. C.).
3 Source: United Nations Economic Commission for Latin America and the Caribbean (ECLAC), (Santiago).
4 Twelve months ending 30 June of year stated.

5 Sales.
6 Twelve months ending 7 July of the year stated.

7 Production by establishments employing 50 or more persons.
8 Government production only.
9 Twelve months beginning 16 July of year stated.

10 Production by establishments employing 20 or more persons.
11 Excluding Transnistria region.
12 Including calf hides.

Source:
Secrétariat de l'Organisation des Nations Unies, "Annuaire de statistiques industrielles par produit 1998" et la base de données pour les statistiques industrielles de la Division de statistique.

† Pour les modifications récentes de nomenclature de pays ou de zone concernant l'Allemagne, Hong Kong, région administrative spéciale (RAS) de Chine, Macao, région administrative spéciale (RAS) de Chine, l'ex-Tchécoslovaquie, l'ex-URSS et l'ex-Rfs de Yougoslavie, voir annexe I - Nomenclature des pays ou des zones, groupements régionaux et autres groupements.

†† Les données statistiques relatives à la Chine ne comprennent pas celles qui concernent la région administrative spéciale de Hong Kong (la RAS de Hong Kong), la région administrative spéciale de Macao (la RAS de Macao) et la province chinoise de Taiwan.

1 Période de douze mois commençant le 21e mars de l'année indiquée.
2 Source: "U.S. Bureau of Mines," (Washington, D.C.).
3 Source: Commission économique des Nations Unies pour l'Amérique Latine et les Caraïbes (CEPALC), (Santiago).
4 Période de douze mois finissant le 30e juin de l'année indiquée.
5 Ventes.
6 Période de douze mois finissant le 7e juillet de l'année indiquée.
7 Production des établissements occupant 50 personnes ou plus.
8 Production de l'Etat seulement.
9 Période de douze mois commençant le 16e juillet de l'année indiquée.
10 Production des établissements occupant 20 personnes ou plus.
11 Non compris la région de Transnistria.
12 Y compris les peaux de veaux.

47
Sulphuric acid
Acide sulfurique
Production: thousand metric tons
Production : milliers de tonnes

Country or area Pays ou zone	1989	1990	1991	1992	1993	1994	1995	1996	1997	1998
Albania Albanie	82	68	21	11	6	4	...	0	0	0
Algeria Algérie	49	39	46	52	55	40	45	42	55	45
Argentina Argentine	214	209	243	219	206	204	226	220	...	...
Armenia Arménie	38	...	...	...	...	...	...	...	...	...
Australia[1] Australie[1]	1 904	1 464	986	816	868	833	...	...	...	...
Azerbaijan Azerbaïdjan	768	603	552	269	141	56	24	31	53	24
Bangladesh[1] Bangladesh[1]	6	3	10	8	7	6	5	9	4	...
Belarus Bélarus	1 179	1 177	998	616	399	291	437	549	698	640
Belgium Belgique	1 956[2]	1 906[2]	1 936[2]	1 906[2]	1 593[2]	717[3]	673[3]	678[3]	649[3]	587[3]
Bolivia Bolivie	1	1	1	0	1	3	* 1	...	...	...
Brazil Brésil	3 809	3 451	3 634	3 257	3 724	4 112	4 043	4 308	4 638	4 624
Bulgaria Bulgarie	846	522	356	404	409	428	454	525	556	499
Canada Canada	3 719	3 830	3 676	3 776	3 713	4 059	3 844	4 278	* 4 100	4 333
Chile Chili	...	347	804	887	920	1 174	1 427	1 518	1 864	1 983
China †† Chine ††	11 533	11 969	13 329	14 087	13 365	15 365	18 110	18 836	20 369	21 710
Colombia Colombie	95	76	...	91	77	103	86	...	95	93
Croatia Croatie	271	242	187	278	178	206	233	223	202	164
Cuba Cuba	377	...	...	...	...	...	...	...	...	...
Cyprus Chypre	1	0	0	...	...	...	...	...	...	...
Czech Republic République tchèque	987	910	588	522	383	337	340	345	333	327
Denmark[5] Danemark[5]	122[4]	90[4]	37[4]	38[4]	...	5	25	19	2	...
Egypt Egypte	60	92	101	111	122	112	133	299	84	...
Estonia Estonie	552	547	460	46	...	0	...	...	...	...
Finland Finlande	1 129	1 010	1 015	1 087	1 179	1 084	1 159	1 288	2 182	2 496
France France	4 187	3 771	3 627	2 871	2 357	2 227	2 382[6]	2 263[6]	2 243[6]	2 231[6]

47
Sulphuric acid
Production: thousand metric tons [cont.]
Acide sulfurique
Production : milliers de tonnes [suite]

Country or area Pays ou zone	1989	1990	1991	1992	1993	1994	1995	1996	1997	1998
Germany Allemagne	...	...	3 064	...	...	2 781[6]	1 387	1 225	1 370	1 601
F. R. Germany R. f. Allemagne	4 028	3 221	...	...	...	...	...	...	...	...
former German D. R. l'ex-R. d. allemande	835	431	...	...	...	...	...	...	...	...
Greece Grèce	1 023	950	841	617	550	623	753	1 544	1 655	...
Hungary[7] Hongrie[7]	502	263	141	99	77	80	114	94	89	62
India Inde	3 293	3 272	3 904	4 183	3 730	3 745	4 402	4 988	4 830	5 366
Indonesia Indonésie	...	40	52	52	42	35	35	...	224	...
Israel Israël	161	154	...	...	...	...	...	...	...	...
Italy Italie	2 212	2 038	1 853	1 733	1 430	1 975	2 161	2 214	2 214	2 097
Japan Japon	6 885	6 887	7 057	7 100	6 937	6 594	6 888	6 851	6 828	6 739
Kazakhstan Kazakhstan	3 455	3 151	2 815	2 349	1 179	681	695	653	635	605
Lithuania Lituanie	512	412	368	141	129	212	344	425	504	619
Mexico Mexique	414	455	362	195	178	375	...	...	...	...
Netherlands[6] Pays-Bas[6]	...	...	...	...	...	...	500	418	356	429
Norway Norvège	...	...	...	615	...	...	...	...	...	...
Pakistan[1] Pakistan[1]	79	90	93	98	100	102	80	69	31	28
Peru Pérou	193	172	207	143	229	215	211	230	410	541
Poland Pologne	3 115	1 721	1 088	1 244	1 145	1 452	1 861	1 761	1 741	1 707
Portugal Portugal	289	260	51	...	...	2[6]	3[6]	10[6]	11[6]	15[6]
Romania Roumanie	1 687	1 111	745	572	527	491	477	422	329	229
Russian Federation Fédération de Russie	12 422	12 767	11 597	9 704	8 243	6 334	6 946	5 764	6 247	5 840
Slovakia Slovaquie	155	178	94	...	...	...	...	62[6]	73	68
Slovenia Slovénie	189	125	86	121	114	123	116	103	109	128
Spain Espagne	3 325	2 848	1 628	1 724	1 199	1 375	2 847	2 265	2 817	3 134[6]
Sweden Suède	902	855	928	...	...	487	507	572[6]	566	548

47
Sulphuric acid
Production: thousand metric tons [cont.]
Acide sulfurique
Production : milliers de tonnes [suite]

Country or area Pays ou zone	1989	1990	1991	1992	1993	1994	1995	1996	1997	1998
Syrian Arab Republic Rép. arabe syrienne	7	8	8	10	10	...	...	...	...	...
Thailand[a] Thaïlande[a]	64	72	82	...	...	...	...	...	...	...
TFYR Macedonia L'ex-R.y. Macédoine	92	97	102	95	89	72	82	99	105	101
Tunisia Tunisie	...	3 425	3 421	3 644	3 547	4 161	4 239	4 423	3 948	...
Turkey Turquie	617	716	532	642	757	730	630	798[6]	947	913
Turkmenistan Turkménistan	799	843	788	353	206	70	76	120	31	47
Ukraine Ukraine	5 144	5 011	4 186	3 000	1 843	1 646	1 593	1 577	1 438	1 354
former USSR† l'ex-URSS†	28 276	27 267	...	...	...	...	...	...	...	...
United Kingdom Royaume-Uni	2 156	1 997	1 852	1 568	1 268	1 266	1 293	643[6]	613[6]	716
United States Etats-Unis	39 282[9]	40 222[9]	12 842[10]	12 340[10]	11 900[10]	11 300[10]	11 500[10]	10 900[10]	10 700[10]	10 500[10]
Uzbekistan Ouzbékistan	3 054	2 859	2 393	1 476	1 361	805	1 016	984	870	...
Venezuela Venezuela	163	210	277	253	...	...	...	...	...	...
Viet Nam Viet Nam	10	8	9	7	...	...	...	...	...	...
Yugoslavia Yougoslavie	...	886	582	302	80	24	87	231	177	211
Yugoslavia, SFR† Yougoslavie, Rfs†	1 617	...	...	...	...	...	...	...	...	...

Source:
United Nations Secretariat, "Industrial Commodity Statistics
Yearbook 1998" and the industrial statistics database of
the Statistics Division.

† For information on recent changes in country or
area nomenclature pertaining to former Czechoslovakia,
Germany, Hong Kong Special Administrative Region (SAR) of
China, Macao Special Administrative Region (SAR) of China,
SFR of Yugoslavia and the former USSR, see Annex I - Country
or area nomenclature, regional and other groupings.

†† For statistical purposes, the data for
China do not include those for Hong Kong Special
Administrative Region (Hong Kong SAR), Macao Special
Administrative Region (Macao SAR) and Taiwan province of
China.

Source:
Secrétariat de l'Organisation des Nations Unies, "Annuaire
de statistiques industrielles par produit 1998" et la base
de données pour les statistiques industrielles de la
Division de statistique.

† Pour les modifications récentes de nomenclature
de pays ou de zone concernant l'Allemagne, Hong Kong, région
administrative spéciale (RAS) de Chine, Macao, région
administrative spéciale (RAS) de Chine,
l'ex-Tchécoslovaquie, l'ex-URSS et l'ex-Rfs de Yougoslavie,
voir annexe I - Nomenclature des pays ou des zones,
groupements régionaux et autres groupements.

†† Les données statistiques relatives à
la Chine ne comprennent pas celles qui concernent la région
administrative spéciale de Hong Kong (la RAS de Hong Kong),
la région administrative spéciale de Macao (la RAS de Macao)

47
Sulphuric acid
Production: thousand metric tons [*cont.*]

Acide sulfurique
Production : milliers de tonnes [*suite*]

	et la province chinoise de Taiwan.
1 Twelve months ending 30 June of year stated.	1 Période de douze mois finissant le 30e juin de l'année indiquée.
2 Production by establishments employing 5 or more persons.	2 Production des établissements occupant 5 personnes ou plus.
3 Incomplete coverage.	3 Couverture incomplète.
4 Excluding quantities consumed by superphosphate industry.	4 Non compris les quantités utilisées par l'industrie des superphosphates.
5 Sales.	5 Ventes.
6 Source: United Nations Economic Commission for Europe (ECE), (Geneva).	6 Source: Commission économique des Nations Unies pour l'Europe (CEE), (Genève).
7 Including regenerated sulphuric acid.	7 Y compris l'acide sulfurique régénéré.
8 Strength of acid not known.	8 Titre de l'acide inconnu.
9 Including data for government-owned, but privately-operated plants.	9 Y compris les données relatives à des usines appartenant à l'Etat mais exploitées par des entreprises privées.
10 Sold or used by producers.	10 Vendu ou utilisé par les producteurs.

48
Soap, washing powders and detergents
Savons, poudres pour lessives et détersifs
Production: thousand metric tons
Production : milliers de tonnes

Country or area Pays ou zone	1989	1990	1991	1992	1993	1994	1995	1996	1997	1998
Albania[1] Albanie[1]	24	21	5	2	4	3	2	2	2	2
Algeria Algérie	231	261	247	185	206	223	198	156	168	186
Angola[1] Angola[1]	8	8	5	4	...	...	...	...	...	...
Argentina[2] Argentine[2]	85	153	162	178	189	214	211	232	225	...
Armenia Arménie	32	17	12	1[3]	0[3]	0[3]	0[3]	0[3]	0[3]	0[3]
Austria Autriche	146	153	162	188	156	122	121	1[1]	1[1]	0[1]
Azerbaijan Azerbaïdjan	99	97	82	54	40	10	3	2	0	1
Belarus[4] Bélarus[4]	86	83	71	58	45	24	23	34	40	32
Belgium Belgique	405	417	440	423	420	477	526	582	604	561
Bolivia Bolivie	5	8	4	4	4	7	* 7	...	...	...
Bosnia and Herzegovina[3 5] Bosnie-Herzégovine[3 5]	...	...	...	...	...	0	1	...	1	...
Bulgaria Bulgarie	28[1]	24[1]	17[1]	20	7	6	8	9	6	15
Burkina Faso[1] Burkina Faso[1]	10	14	26	14	14	...	...	...	...	...
Burundi[1] Burundi[1]	3	3	3	3	5	...	...	...	...	...
Cameroon[1] Cameroun[1]	...	...	...	14	29	* 29	33	...	...	...
Cape Verde[1] Cap-Vert[1]	...	...	...	...	1	1	2	...	...	...
Central African Rep.[1] Rép. centrafricaine[1]	...	...	0	0	0	0	0	...	...	...
Chad[1] Tchad[1]	4	4	3	3	3	3	5	...	...	...
Chile Chili	68	69	73	73	77	77	80	78	77	86
China †† Chine ††	2 577	2 581	2 366	2 500	2 728	2 974	3 824	3 355	3 442	3 317
China, Hong Kong SAR†[3] Chine, Hong Kong RAS†[3]	62	84	56	46	42	278	66	46	116	49[6]
Colombia Colombie	148[1]	179[1]	...	318	311	334	375	...	533	421
Congo[1] Congo[1]	1	3	5	3	1	...	...	...	...	...
Croatia Croatie	145	113	67	52	44	31	31	31	40	40
Cuba[7] Cuba[7]	68	...	...	...	...	...	...	...	...	...

48
Soap, washing powders and detergents
Production: thousand metric tons [cont.]
Savons, poudres pour lessives et détersifs
Production : milliers de tonnes [suite]

Country or area Pays ou zone	1989	1990	1991	1992	1993	1994	1995	1996	1997	1998
Cyprus Chypre	11	* 13	* 15	14	* 13	* 14	13	12	10	10
Czech Republic République tchèque	95	97	82	24[1]	28[1]	195	230	289	361	453
Denmark[35] Danemark[35]	...	...	...	...	...	...	...	194	192	196
Dominica[1] Dominique[1]	...	...	...	...	11	11	11	14	12	15
Ecuador Equateur	...	95	...	57	59	54	50	65	...	...
Egypt Egypte	399	417	370	358	382	307	243	210	214	290
Estonia Estonie	42	40[3]	28[3]	4[3]	3[3]	4[3]	2[3]	1[3]	1[3]	1[3]
Ethiopia[18] Ethiopie[18]	12	9	0	5	17	15	15	18	14	11
Fiji[1] Fidji[1]	6	7	7	7	7	7	7	6	8	9
Finland Finlande	98	93	82	72	75	73	74	76	77	90
France France	808	811	781	822	778	830	...	...	...	...
Gabon Gabon	132	137	153	169	3[1]	3[1]	3[1]	...	...	...
Georgia Géorgie	...	...	...	1	2	1[5]	0[5]	0[5]	0	0
Germany: deutsche mark Allemagne : deutsche mark	...	...	122[1]	113[1]	140	2 498[5]	2 130[3]	2 166[3]	2 393	2 237[3]
F. R. Germany[1] R. f. Allemagne[1]	113	126	...	...	...	...	...	...	...	...
former German D. R. l'ex-R. d. allemande	527	291	...	...	...	...	...	...	...	...
Greece Grèce	163	158	150	154	240	257	274	545	518	...
Guyana Guyana	1[1]	0[1]	1	1	0	0	...	...	...	...
Haiti[7] Haïti[7]	49	45	50	35	36	30	...	...	...	...
Hungary Hongrie	129	144	104	92	92	91	91	119	96	92
Iceland[3] Islande[3]	3	3	1	2	2	2	2[5]	3	3	4
India[9] Inde[9]	1 739	1 794	1 795	1 752	1 773	1 952	2 314	1 993	2 104	2 506
Indonesia Indonésie	...	502	455	568	553	430	405	...	769	...
Iran (Islamic Rep. of)[3] Iran (Rép. islamique d')[3]	169[10]	212[10]	192[10]	170[10]	181[10]	191[10]	225[11]	227[11]	246[11]	...
Israel[1] Israël[1]	4	4	...	...	...	...	...	...	...	...

48
Soap, washing powders and detergents
Production: thousand metric tons [cont.]

Savons, poudres pour lessives et détersifs
Production : milliers de tonnes [suite]

Country or area Pays ou zone	1989	1990	1991	1992	1993	1994	1995	1996	1997	1998
Italy[35] Italie [35]	...	...	...	...	...	1 749	1 712	1 808	2 041	...
Jamaica Jamaïque	16	16	14	11	0	0	0	0	0	0
Japan[12] Japon[12]	1 245	1 310	1 370	1 394	1 310	1 347	1 302	1 251	1 281	1 189
Jordan[1] Jordanie[1]	26	...	...	...	...	...	...	...	...	...
Kazakhstan Kazakhstan	119[1]	124[1]	38[1]	24[1]	19[1]	43[5]	27[5]	16[5]	10[5]	5[5]
Kenya Kenya	79	73	63	60	62	64	76	89	...	...
Korea, Republic of Corée, République de	474	524	508	503	461	485	471	369[3]	375[3]	327[3]
Kuwait[3] Koweït[3]	3	...	...	1	1	1	1	...	...	...
Kyrgyzstan[1] Kirghizistan[1]	0	0	0	0	0	0	0	0	0	0
Lao People's Dem. Rep.[3] Rép. dém. pop. lao[3]	...	...	...	...	...	1	1	...	...	...
Latvia[4] Lettonie[4]	23	24	18	8	2	4	3	2	1	1
Lithuania Lituanie	32[13]	31[13]	28[13]	13[13]	5[13]	3[13]	6[13]	6	5	6
Madagascar[1] Madagascar[1]	15	14	16	16	19	...	...	...	...	...
Malaysia[14] Malaisie [14]	67	80	88	102	105	136	124	126	138	119
Mali[1] Mali[1]	9	10	11	10	9	11	13	16	...	...
Malta[35] Malte[35]	...	...	...	...	...	...	...	10	...	...
Mauritania[1] Mauritanie[1]	...	3	5	5	4	...	...	...	...	...
Mexico Mexique	1 099	1 166	1 231	1 257	1 137	1 190	1 135	1 140	1 180	1 267
Mongolia[1] Mongolie[1]	3	...	1	1	0	1	1	1	...	...
Mozambique[1] Mozambique[1]	12	9	9	7	11	11	13	14	9	...
Myanmar[1][15] Myanmar[1][15]	12	15	23	18	12	25	36	30	27	35
Nepal[1][16] Népal[1][16]	...	...	...	21	23	21	23	25	29	30
Netherlands[35] Pays-Bas[35]	...	...	...	...	...	331	384	436	461	424
Nigeria[1] Nigéria[1]	249	241	243	262	303	124	111	...	...	...
Norway Norvège	55	7[1]	...	6[1]	...	...	...	...	103[35]	...

48
Soap, washing powders and detergents
Production: thousand metric tons [cont.]
Savons, poudres pour lessives et détersifs
Production : milliers de tonnes [suite]

Country or area Pays ou zone	1989	1990	1991	1992	1993	1994	1995	1996	1997	1998
Pakistan[14] Pakistan[14]	103	59	75	86	89	82	84	98	104	113
Panama Panama	18	15	...	31	28	24	24	27	...	...
Paraguay[1] Paraguay[1]	8	8	7	6	...	...	...	...	...	...
Peru Pérou	74	79	79	85	97	107	108	112	75[3]	68[3]
Poland[13] Pologne[13]	332	215	199	174	194	222	211	262	301	317
Portugal Portugal	209	213	177	205	203	181	185	216	213	326
Republic of Moldova République de Moldova	35	34	23	12	7[17]	2[17]	2[17]	2[17]	1[17]	0[17]
Romania[18] Roumanie[18]	46	49	37	20	27	19	25	16	14	13
Russian Federation Fédération de Russie	1 329	1 393	1 106	876	699	517	502	453	436	354
Saint Lucia[1] Sainte-Lucie[1]	0	0	0	0	0	0	0	0	0	...
Senegal[1] Sénégal[1]	26	37	37	42	36	23	44	38	40	39
Sierra Leone[1] Sierra Leone[1]	...	...	1	2	3	...	...	...	...	...
Singapore[1] Singapour[1]	28	...	...	...	...	...	...	...	...	...
Slovakia Slovaquie	40	42	23	...	28[3]	23[3]	25[3 5]	32[3]	42[3]	44[5]
Slovenia Slovénie	65	63	64	47	46	49	45	45	37	39
South Africa Afrique du Sud	241	262	280	286	286	312	330	345	349	344
Spain Espagne	1 283	1 376	1 414	1 489	1 900	2 012	2 094	1 817	1 836	2 066
Sweden Suède	185[3]	158[3]	127[3]	121[3]	...	18[1]	13[1]	173	137	138
Switzerland[19 20] Suisse[19 20]	163[1]	168[1]	165[1]	156[1]	152[1]	297[5]	308[5]	...	...	...
Syrian Arab Republic Rép. arabe syrienne	31	40	38	44	57	57	59	57	59	...
Tajikistan[1] Tadjikistan[1]	23	21	16	11	3	2	2	1	1	1
Thailand Thaïlande	197	190	196	...	...	...	...	258	281	273
TFYR Macedonia L'ex-R.y. Macédoine	29	21	20	16	21	21	23	21	24	23
Trinidad and Tobago[1] Trinité-et-Tobago[1]	3	2	2	2	2	2	2	2	2	2
Turkey Turquie	448	442	380	378	434	505	548	737	963	888

48
Soap, washing powders and detergents
Production: thousand metric tons [*cont.*]
Savons, poudres pour lessives et détersifs
Production : milliers de tonnes [*suite*]

Country or area Pays ou zone	1989	1990	1991	1992	1993	1994	1995	1996	1997	1998
Turkmenistan Turkménistan	41	39	25	21	9	8	7	3	1	2
Uganda[1] Ouganda[1]	27	31	33	39	48	49	55	44	67	...
Ukraine[4] Ukraine[4]	575	600	530	482	321	267	170	117	80	69
former USSR†[4] l'ex-URSS†[4]	3 128	3 208	...	...	...	...	...	...	...	...
United Kingdom Royaume-Uni	1 415 [3] [21]	...	...	...	1 815 [3]	1 882	2 112	2 195	1 335	1 639
United Rep. Tanzania[1] Rép.-Unie de Tanzanie[1]	20	23	24	20	22	20	25	25	30	...
Uzbekistan Ouzbékistan	152	158	134	102	89	79	78	64	54	...
Viet Nam[1] Viet Nam[1]	40	55	68	72	...	...	...	...	...	...
Yemen[1] Yémen[1]	0	0	41	39	36	30	32	24	23	...
Yugoslavia Yougoslavie	...	83	98	92	56	53	64	72	90	82
Yugoslavia, SFR† Yougoslavie, Rfs†	412	...	...	...	...	...	...	...	...	...

Source:
United Nations Secretariat, "Industrial Commodity Statistics
Yearbook 1998" and the industrial statistics database of
the Statistics Division.

† For information on recent changes in country or
area nomenclature pertaining to former Czechoslovakia,
Germany, Hong Kong Special Administrative Region (SAR) of
China, Macao Special Administrative Region (SAR) of China,
SFR of Yugoslavia and the former USSR, see Annex I - Country
or area nomenclature, regional and other groupings.

†† For statistical purposes, the data for
China do not include those for Hong Kong Special
Administrative Region (Hong Kong SAR), Macao Special
Administrative Region (Macao SAR) and Taiwan province of
China.

1 Soap only.
2 Excluding liquid toilet soap.
3 Washing powder and detergent only.
4 Soap: in terms of 40 per cent fat content.
5 Source: United Nations Economic Commission for Europe (ECE),
(Geneva).
6 Excluding washing and cleaning powder, for confidentiality
purposes.
7 Excluding washing powder.
8 Twelve months ending 7 July of the year stated.

9 Production by large and medium scale establishments only.
10 Production by establishments employing 50 or more persons.

Source:
Secrétariat de l'Organisation des Nations Unies, "Annuaire
de statistiques industrielles par produit 1998" et la base
de données pour les statistiques industrielles de la
Division de statistique.

† Pour les modifications récentes de nomenclature
de pays ou de zone concernant l'Allemagne, Hong Kong, région
administrative spéciale (RAS) de Chine, Macao, région
administrative spéciale (RAS) de Chine,
l'ex-Tchécoslovaquie, l'ex-URSS et l'ex-Rfs de Yougoslavie,
voir annexe I - Nomenclature des pays ou des zones,
groupements régionaux et autres groupements.

†† Les données statistiques relatives à
la Chine ne comprennent pas celles qui concernent la région
administrative spéciale de Hong Kong (la RAS de Hong Kong),
la région administrative spéciale de Macao (la RAS de Macao)
et la province chinoise de Taiwan.

1 Les savons seulement.
2 Non compris le savon liquide de toilette.
3 Les poudres pour lessives et détersifs seulement.
4 Savons : sur la base de 40 p. 100 de matières grasses.
5 Source: Commission économique des Nations Unies pour
l'Europe (CEE), (Genève).
6 A l'exclusion des poudres à laver et à récurer, pour raisons
de confidentialité.
7 Non compris les poudres.
8 Période de douze mois finissant le 7e juillet de l'année
indiquée.
9 Production des grandes et moyennes entreprises seulement.
10 Production des établissements occupant 50 personnes ou plus.

48

Soap, washing powders and detergents
Production: thousand metric tons [*cont.*]

Savons, poudres pour lessives et détersifs
Production : milliers de tonnes [*suite*]

11 Production by establishments employing 10 or more persons.	11 Production des établissements occupant 10 personnes ou plus.
12 Surface-active agents and soap.	12 Produits tensio-actifs et les savons.
13 Excluding detergents.	13 Non compris les détersifs.
14 Soap: toilet soap only.	14 Savons de toilette Savons : seulement.
15 Government production only.	15 Production de l'Etat seulement.
16 Twelve months beginning 16 July of year stated.	16 Période de douze mois commençant le 16e juillet de l'année indiquée.
17 Excluding Transnistria region.	17 Non compris la région de Transnistria.
18 Washing powder and detergents: on the basis of 100 per cent active substances.	18 Les poudres pour lessives et détersifs : sur la base de 100 p. 100 de substances actives.
19 Soap: sales.	19 Savons : ventes.
20 Including other cleaning products.	20 Y compris les autres produits de nettoyage.
21 Estimates of manufacturers' sales of finished detergents for washing purposes, in terms of actual weight sold.	21 Estimations des ventes de détersifs pour lessives par les fabricants, sur la base du poids de produits effectivement ecoulé.

49
Pig iron and crude steel
Fonte et acier brut
Production: thousand metric tons
Production : milliers de tonnes

Country or area Pays ou zone	1989	1990	1991	1992	1993	1994	1995	1996	1997	1998
A. Pig-iron • Fonte										
Algeria Algérie	1 315	1 054	893	944	925	919	962	850	526	757
Argentina Argentine	2 100	1 908	1 366	971	980	1 392	1 524	1 966[1]	2 066[1]	* 2 000[1]
Australia[2] Australie[2]	5 875	6 188	5 600	6 394	7 209	7 449	7 554	7 560	7 692	7 716
Austria Autriche	3 823	3 452	3 439	3 074[3]	3 070[3]	3 320[3]	3 878[3]	3 416[3]	3 966[3]	4 021[3]
Belgium[4] Belgique[4]	8 863	9 416	9 353	8 524	8 179	8 976	9 204	8 604	8 064	8 616
Brazil Brésil	24 363	21 141	22 695	23 057	23 900	25 092	25 021	23 978	24 962	25 111
Bulgaria Bulgarie	1 487	1 143	961	849	1 014	1 470	1 607	1 504	1 643	1 500[1]
Canada Canada	10 200	7 344	8 268	8 621	8 628	8 112	8 460	8 638	8 670	8 937
Chile[4] Chili[4]	679	722	700	873[1]	917[1]	886[1]	855[1]	* 850[1]	* 860[1]	* 870[1]
China †† Chine ††	58 200	62 380	67 000	75 890	87 389	97 410	105 293	107 225	115 114	118 629
Colombia Colombie	297	347	300	308[1]	238[1]	245[1]	282[1]	274[1]	322[1]	* 195[1]
Croatia[4] Croatie[4]	240	209	69	* 40[1]	* 40[1]	* 40[1]	* 0[1]	* 0[1]	* 0[1]	...
Czech Republic République tchèque	6 396	6 107	5 090	5 010[3]	4 656[3]	5 274[3]	5 263[3]	4 898	5 276	4 980
Egypt Egypte	112	108	113	60	92	109	69	15	15	...
Finland[4] Finlande[4]	2 284	2 283	2 332	2 452	2 595	2 597	2 242	2 457	2 784	2 916
France France	14 724	14 100	13 416	13 057[3]	12 396	13 008	13 758[3]	12 987[3]	14 399[3]	13 896[3]
Georgia Géorgie	...	...	501[3]	242	12	1	4	4	4	1
Germany[3] Allemagne †[3]	...	...	30 608	28 202	26 705	29 632	29 599	27 340	30 462	29 705
F. R. Germany R. f. Allemagne	32 112	29 585	...	...	...	...	...	...	...	...
former German D. R. l'ex-R. d. allemande	2 722	2 128	...	...	...	...	...	...	...	...
Greece[1] Grèce[1]	160	160	160	...	...	...	...	...	...	...
Hungary Hongrie	1 954	1 697	1 314	1 179	1 407[3]	1 595[3]	1 515[3]	1 496[3]	1 140[3]	1 259[3]
India Inde	12 080[1]	12 600[1]	14 176[1]	15 126[1]	* 15 679	* 17 805	* 18 623	* 19 864	* 19 997	* 20 996
Iran (Islamic Rep. of) Iran (Rép. islamique d')	* 1 000[4]	* 1 000[4]	1 952[1 4]	2 053[1 4]	1 961[1 4]	1 883[1 4]	1 532[1 4]	1 867[1 4]	2 153[1]	* 2 100[1]

49
Pig iron and crude steel
Production: thousand metric tons [cont.]
Fonte et acier brut
Production : milliers de tonnes [suite]

Country or area Pays ou zone	1989	1990	1991	1992	1993	1994	1995	1996	1997	1998
Italy Italie	11 762	11 852	10 561	10 432	11 188	11 161	11 677	10 321	11 477	10 791
Japan Japon	80 196	80 229	79 985	73 144	73 738	73 776	74 905	74 597	78 520	74 981
Kazakhstan[5] Kazakhstan[5]	5 279	5 226	4 953	4 666	3 552	2 435	2 530	2 536	3 089	2 594
Korea, Dem. P. R. *[1] Corée, R. p. dém. de *[1]	6 500	6 500	6 500	6 600	6 600	6 600	6 600	6 600	6 600	6 600
Korea, Republic of Corée, République de	14 937	15 477	18 883	19 581	22 193	21 169	22 344	23 010	22 712	23 093
Luxembourg[4] Luxembourg[4]	2 684	2 645	2 463	2 255	2 412	1 927	1 028	829	438	0
Mexico Mexique	* 2 076	* 2 378	2 313	2 220	2 515	3 359	3 660	4 404	4 464	4 532
Morocco[14] Maroc[14]	15	15	15	15	15	* 15	* 15	* 15	* 15	* 15
Netherlands[4] Pays-Bas[4]	5 163	4 960	4 697	4 849	5 405	5 443[67]	5 530[67]	5 544[67]	5 805[67]	5 562[67]
Norway[4] Norvège[4]	240	54[1]	61[1]	70[1]	73[1]	* 70[1]	* 70[1]	* 70[1]	* 70[1]	* 70[1]
Peru[1] Pérou[1]	199	93	207	147	147	* 150	* 150	* 150	* 150	* 150
Poland Pologne	9 075	8 352	6 297	6 315	6 105	6 866	7 373	6 540	7 295	6 129
Portugal[4] Portugal[4]	377	336	252	408	396	420	408	420	431[1]	365[1]
Romania Roumanie	9 052	6 355	4 525	3 110	3 190	3 496	4 203	4 025	4 557	4 541
Russian Federation Fédération de Russie	61 199	59 078	48 628	45 990	40 744	36 480	39 676	37 079	37 277	34 582
Slovakia[4] Slovaquie[4]	3 515	3 561	3 163	2 952[3]	3 205	3 330	3 207	2 928	3 072[3]	2 756[3]
South Africa[1] Afrique du Sud[1]	6 543	6 257	6 968	7 352	6 940	6 982	7 137	6 876	6 192	* 6 000
Spain Espagne	5 479	5 440[3]	5 397[3]	4 764[3]	5 394[3]	5 447[3]	5 106[3]	4 127[3]	3 927[3]	4 236[3]
Sweden Suède	2 648	2 696	2 851	2 883	2 844	3 036	3 020	3 130	3 072	3 156
Switzerland Suisse	141	129	105	102	82	88	97	100[1]	* 100[3]	* 100[3]
TFYR Macedonia[4] L'ex-R.y. Macédoine[4]	279	84	...	13	20	20	* 20[1]	* 20[1]	* 20[1]	* 20[1]
Tunisia[5] Tunisie[5]	155	148	162	147	154	145	152	145	152	123
Turkey Turquie	300	354	332	286	296	326	246[5]	363[5]	337[5]	171[5]
Ukraine Ukraine	46 128	44 612	36 435	36 948	28 160	20 837	18 314	18 110	21 060	21 239
former USSR†[8] l'ex-URSS†[8]	113 928	110 166	...	...	...	...	...	...	...	...

49
Pig iron and crude steel
Production: thousand metric tons [*cont.*]
Fonte et acier brut
Production : milliers de tonnes [*suite*]

Country or area Pays ou zone	1989	1990	1991	1992	1993	1994	1995	1996	1997	1998
United Kingdom Royaume-Uni	12 551	12 320[3]	11 884[3]	11 542[3]	11 534[3]	11 943[3]	12 236[3]	12 830[3]	13 056[3]	12 746[3]
United States Etats-Unis	50 687	49 668	44 123	47 377	48 200	49 400	50 900	49 400	49 600	48 200
Venezuela Venezuela	455	314	0[9]	0[9]	0[9]	0[9]	0[9]	...	...	...
Yugoslavia[4] Yougoslavie[4]	...	...	526	512	62	17	109	565	907[3]	792
Yugoslavia, SFR† Yougoslavie, Rfs†	2 899	2 313	...	...	...	...	...	...	...	...
Zimbabwe[4] Zimbabwe[4]	520	521	* 535[1]	* 507[1]	* 211[1]	* 100[1]	* 209[1]	* 210[1]	* 210[1]	* 210[1]

B. Crude steel · Acier brut

Country or area Pays ou zone	1989	1990	1991	1992	1993	1994	1995	1996	1997	1998
Albania Albanie	112	79	16	0	15	19	22	22	22	22
Algeria Algérie	945	769	797	768	798	772	780	590	361	581
Angola *[1 10] Angola *[1 10]	10	10	10	10	9	9	9	9	9	9
Argentina Argentine	* 3 874	3 636	2 972	2 680	2 870	3 274	3 575	4 069	4 157	4 150[1]
Australia[2] Australie[2]	6 651	7 576	7 141	5 205	7 628	7 807	7 951	7 944	8 088	8 088
Austria[3] Autriche[3]	4 901	4 395	4 186	3 953	4 149	4 398	4 991	5 390	6 359	6 525
Azerbaijan Azerbaïdjan	1 586	1 361	1 127	809	461	77	39	3	25	8
Bangladesh[2 10] Bangladesh[2 10]	86	90	58[1]	36[1]	32[1]	34[1]	36[1]	27	23	35[1]
Belarus Bélarus	1 104	1 112	1 123	1 105[3]	946[3]	880	744	886	1 220	1 411
Belgium Belgique	11 053	11 546	11 419	10 386	10 237	11 331[3]	11 606[3]	10 817[3]	10 739[3]	11 425[3]
Bosnia and Herzegovina[3 10] Bosnie-Herzégovine[3 10]	...	...	...	...	...	...	...	52	72	...
Brazil Brésil	25 084	20 631	22 617	23 934	25 207	25 747	25 076	25 237	26 153	25 760
Bulgaria Bulgarie	2 899	2 184	1 615	1 551	1 941	2 491	2 724	2 457	2 628	2 237[3]
Canada Canada	15 005	12 281	13 079	14 027	14 369[1]	13 897[1]	14 415[1]	14 735[1]	15 554[1]	15 800[1]
Chile[10] Chili[10]	816	768	804	1 008	1 020	996	948	1 178[1]	1 167[1]	1 170[1]
China †† Chine ††	64 209	68 858	73 881	84 252	89 556	92 617	95 360	100 056	108 942	115 590
Colombia Colombie	711	733	700	657	715	702	714[1]	677[1]	710[1]	* 700[1]
Croatia Croatie	486	424	214	102	74[3]	63	45	46	70	6

49
Pig iron and crude steel
Production: thousand metric tons [cont.]
Fonte et acier brut
Production : milliers de tonnes [suite]

Country or area Pays ou zone	1989	1990	1991	1992	1993	1994	1995	1996	1997	1998
Cuba[10] Cuba[10]	314	270	270	134[1]	91[1]	131[1]	207[1]	231[1]	342[1]	284[1]
Czech Republic République tchèque	10 724	9 997	7 972	7 349	6 732	7 075	7 003	6 519	6 593	6 061
Denmark Danemark	624	612	636	600	612	720	660	732	792	792
Ecuador[10] Equateur[10]	23	20	20	20[1]	27[1]	32[1]	35[1]	35[18]	44[1]	40[1]
Egypt[1] Egypte[1]	* 2 117	2 326	2 541	2 524	2 772	2 622	2 642	2 618	2 717	* 2 700
Finland Finlande	2 921	2 860	2 890	3 077	3 257	3 420	3 176	3 301	3 734	3 929[3]
France France	19 535	19 304	18 708	18 190	17 313	18 242	18 101[3]	17 633[3]	19 767[3]	20 126[3]
Georgia Géorgie	...	...	...	532	224	122	89	83	104	56
Germany Allemagne †	...	...	41 997	39 962	37 705	40 963	42 051[3]	39 792[3]	10 591	10 218
F. R. Germany R. f. Allemagne	41 078	38 433	...	...	...	...	...	...	...	...
former German D. R.[10] l'ex-R. d. allemande[10]	7 829	5 339	...	...	...	...	...	...	...	...
Greece Grèce	960	999	980	924	980	852	936	852	1 020	1 104
Hungary Hongrie	3 263	2 808[3]	1 860[3]	1 560[3]	1 752[3]	1 932[3]	1 860[3]	1 878[3]	1 690[3]	1 940
India Inde	15 522	16 479	17 577	18 723	13 351	13 356	13 378	13 439	13 416	18 547[1]
Indonesia Indonésie	* 2 000	2 890[1]	3 250[1]	3 171[1]	1 948[1]	3 220[1]	3 500[1]	3 400[1]	3 450[1]	* 3 330[1]
Iran (Islamic Rep. of) Iran (Rép. islamique d')	* 1 000	1 430[1]	2 200[1]	2 940[1]	3 672[1]	4 498[1]	4 696[1]	5 420[1]	6 322[1]	* 6 300[1]
Iraq *[1 10] Iraq *[1 10]	...	150	20	100	300	300	300	300	300	300
Ireland Irlande	324	325	293	257	326	288	312	336	336[3]	355[3]
Israel *[1] Israël *[1]	118	144	90	109	120	180	200	203	203	203
Italy Italie	25 507	25 647	25 270	24 924	25 967	26 212	27 907	24 391	25 870	25 782
Japan Japon	107 907	110 339	109 648	98 132	99 632	98 295	101 640	98 801	104 545	93 548
Kazakhstan Kazakhstan	6 831	6 753	6 377	6 063	4 557	2 968	3 026	3 216	3 880	...
Korea, Dem. P. R. *[1] Corée, R. p. dém. de *[1]	7 300	8 000	8 000	8 100	8 100	8 100	8 100	8 100	8 100	8 000
Korea, Republic of Corée, République de	21 992	23 247	26 126	28 177	33 141	33 887	37 639	39 643	43 405	40 299
Latvia Lettonie	555	550	374	246	300	332	280	293	465	471

49
Pig iron and crude steel
Production: thousand metric tons [cont.]
Fonte et acier brut
Production : milliers de tonnes [suite]

Country or area Pays ou zone	1989	1990	1991	1992	1993	1994	1995	1996	1997	1998
Lithuania[11] Lituanie[11]	7	7	4	3	2	1	1	0	1	1
Luxembourg[10] Luxembourg[10]	3 721	3 560	3 379	3 068	3 293	3 073	2 613	2 501	2 580	2 477
Mexico Mexique	7 329	8 221	7 462	7 848	8 188	8 690	9 948	9 852	10 560	10 812
Morocco[1] Maroc[1]	* 7	* 7	* 7	* 7	* 7	* 7	* 7	* 5	5	* 5
Netherlands Pays-Bas	5 681	5 412	5 171	5 439	6 000	6 172	6 409	6 326	6 641	6 377
New Zealand[1 10] Nouvelle-Zélande[1 10]	608	719	806	759	853	766	842	680	680	* 700
Nigeria[10] Nigéria[10]	213	220	200	* 200[1]	* 150[1]	* 58[1]	* 36[1]	* 20[1]	* 0[1]	* 0[1]
Norway Norvège	677	376	438[3]	446[3]	505[3]	456[3]	503[3]	511[3]	564[3]	639[3]
Peru Pérou	364	284	404	343	417	506[1]	* 515[1]	* 510[1]	* 510[1]	* 510[1]
Philippines[1] Philippines[1]	300	# 600	605	497	623	473	* 923	* 920	* 950	* 950
Poland Pologne	12 466	11 501	10 440	9 864	9 936	11 112	11 892	10 668[3]	11 592	9 916[3]
Portugal Portugal	1 061	744	576	768	780	744	828	871[1]	905[1]	* 854[1]
Republic of Moldova[11] République de Moldova[11]	685	712	623	653	# 1[12]	1[12]	0[12]	0[12]	0[12]	0[12]
Romania Roumanie	15 165	10 624	7 509	5 614	5 629	5 943	6 697	6 216	6 790	6 405
Russian Federation Fédération de Russie	92 526	89 623	77 100	67 028	58 346	48 812	51 590	49 253	48 502	43 673
Saudi Arabia[1 10] Arabie saoudite[1 10]	1 810	1 833	1 785	1 825	2 318	2 411	2 451	2 683	2 539	* 2 550
Slovakia[10] Slovaquie[10]	4 741	4 779	4 107	4 498	3 922	3 974	3 958	3 718	3 866	3 388[3]
Slovenia Slovénie	609	505	289	401	357	424	408	94	99	98
South Africa Afrique du Sud	9 337	8 691	9 358	8 970[1]	8 726[1]	8 525[1]	8 741[1]	7 999[1]	8 311[1]	* 8 500[1]
Spain Espagne	* 12 564	* 12 818	12 846	12 600	12 960	13 440	13 932	12 166[3]	13 677[3]	14 819[3]
Sweden Suède	4 692	4 455	4 248	4 356	4 596	4 956	4 920	4 908	5 148	5 172
Switzerland[10] Suisse[10]	1 064[3]	1 105[3]	955[3]	1 238[3]	1 254[3]	1 100[3]	850[3]	750[3]	1 000[1]	* 1 000[1]
Thailand[10] Thaïlande[10]	689[1]	685[1]	711[1]	779[1]	972[1]	1 391[1]	2 134[1]	2 143[1]	2 101	1 619
TFYR Macedonia[10] L'ex-R.y. Macédoine[10]	295	227	209	162	133	67	31	21	27	45
Tunisia[11] Tunisie[11]	188	176	193	182	182	183	201	186	195	171

49
Pig iron and crude steel
Production: thousand metric tons [cont.]
Fonte et acier brut
Production : milliers de tonnes [suite]

Country or area Pays ou zone	1989	1990	1991	1992	1993	1994	1995	1996	1997	1998
Turkey Turquie	10 809	12 225	12 323	15 387	15 198	15 861	14 438	17 189	17 795	17 002
Uganda Ouganda	0	0	* 20[1]	* 20[1]	* 20[1]	* 10[1]	* 12[1]	* 12[1]	* 15[1]	* 15[1]
Ukraine Ukraine	56 821	54 555	46 767	43 285	33 709	24 635	22 761	22 718	25 972	24 789
former USSR† l'ex-URSS†	168 421	162 326	...	...	...	...	...	...	...	...
United Kingdom Royaume-Uni	18 740	17 841	16 511	16 212[3]	16 625[3]	17 286[3]	17 604[3]	17 992[3]	18 510	11 681
United States Etats-Unis	88 852	89 726	79 738	84 322	88 800	91 200	95 200	95 500	98 500	98 600
Uruguay[10] Uruguay[10]	37	34	41[1]	55[1]	36[1]	36[1]	40[1]	34[1]	39[1]	* 52[1]
Venezuela Venezuela	3 404	3 140	2 933	2 446	2 568	3 524[1]	3 568[1]	3 941[1]	4 019[1]	3 700[1]
Viet Nam[10] Viet Nam[10]	85	101	149	196	* 270[1]	* 301[1]	* 271[1]	* 311[1]	* 330	* 320[1]
Yugoslavia Yougoslavie	...	...	164	96	51	44	28	45	46	45
Yugoslavia, SFR† Yougoslavie, Rfs†	4 542	3 608	...	...	...	...	...	...	...	...
Zimbabwe[1][10] Zimbabwe[1][10]	650	580	581	547	221	187	210	212	240	* 250

Source:
United Nations Secretariat, "Industrial Commodity Statistics
Yearbook 1998" and the industrial statistics database of
the Statistics Division.

† For information on recent changes in country or
area nomenclature pertaining to former Czechoslovakia,
Germany, Hong Kong Special Administrative Region (SAR) of
China, Macao Special Administrative Region (SAR) of China,
SFR of Yugoslavia and the former USSR, see Annex I - Country
or area nomenclature, regional and other groupings.

†† For statistical purposes, the data for
China do not include those for Hong Kong Special
Administrative Region (Hong Kong SAR), Macao Special
Administrative Region (Macao SAR) and Taiwan province of
China.

1 Source: U. S. Bureau of Mines, (Washington, D. C.).
2 Twelve months ending 30 June of year stated.

3 Source: Annual Bulletin of Steel Statistics for Europe,
America and Asia, United Nations Economic Commission of
Europe (Geneva).

Source:
Secrétariat de l'Organisation des Nations Unies, "Annuaire
de statistiques industrielles par produit 1998" et la base
de données pour les statistiques industrielles de la
Division de statistique.

† Pour les modifications récentes de nomenclature
de pays ou de zone concernant l'Allemagne, Hong Kong, région
administrative spéciale (RAS) de Chine, Macao, région
administrative spéciale (RAS) de Chine,
l'ex-Tchécoslovaquie, l'ex-URSS et l'ex-Rfs de Yougoslavie,
voir annexe I - Nomenclature des pays ou des zones,
groupements régionaux et autres groupements.

†† Les données statistiques relatives à
la Chine ne comprennent pas celles qui concernent la région
administrative spéciale de Hong Kong (la RAS de Hong Kong),
la région administrative spéciale de Macao (la RAS de Macao)
et la province chinoise de Taiwan.

1 Source: "U.S. Bureau of Mines," (Washington, D.C.).
2 Période de douze mois finissant le 30 juin de l'année
indiquée.

3 Source: Bulletin annuel de statistiques de l'acier pour
l'Europe, l'Amérique et l'Asie, Commission économique des
Nations Unies pour l'Europe (Genève).

49
Pig iron and crude steel
Production: thousand metric tons [*cont.*]

Fonte et acier brut
Production : milliers de tonnes [*suite*]

4 Pig iron for steel making only.
5 Foundry pig iron only.
6 Production by establishments employing 20 or more persons.
7 Sales.
8 Including other ferro-alloys.
9 Source: United Nations Economic Commission for Latin America and the Caribbean (ECLAC), (Santiago).
10 Ingots only.
11 Crude steel for casting only.
12 Excluding Transnistria region.

4 La fonte d'affinage seulement.
5 La fonte de moulage seulement.
6 Production des établissements occupant 20 personnes ou plus.
7 Ventes.
8 Y compris les autres ferro-alliages.
9 Source: Commission économique des Nations Unies pour l'Amérique Latine et des Caraïbes (CEPAL), (Santiago).
10 Les lingots seulement.
11 L'acier brut pour moulages seulement.
12 Non compris la région de Transnistria.

50
Aluminium
Aluminium

Production: thousand metric tons
Production : milliers de tonnes

Country or area Pays ou zone	1989	1990	1991	1992	1993	1994	1995	1996	1997	1998
Argentina **Argentine**	**167**	**169**	**184**	**172**	**185**	**188**	**193**	**200**	***203**	**203**[1]
Primary 1re fusion	162	163	166	153	171	173	183	185	187	187[1]
Secondary[1] 2ème fusion[1]	5	6	18	19	14	14	10	16	16	16
Australia[2] **Australie**[2]	***1 289**	***1 268**	**1 265**	**1 234**	**1 341**	**1 439**	**1 370**	**1 426**	***1 590**	***1 722**
Primary[2] 1re fusion[2]	1 241	1 235	1 235	1 194	1 306	1 384	1 285	1 330	1 489	1 618
Secondary[2] 2ème fusion[2]	48[1]	33	30	40[1]	35[1]	55[1]	85[1]	96[1]	101[1]	104[1]
Austria **Autriche**	**334**	**246**	**206**	***78**	**43**[1]	**52**[1]	**94**[1]	**98**[1]	**119**[1]	**126**[1]
Primary 1re fusion	169	159	89	33	0[1]	0[1]	0[1]	0[1]	0[1]	0[1]
Secondary 2ème fusion	165[3]	87[3]	117[3]	45[1]	43[1]	52[1]	94[1]	98[1]	119[1]	126[1]
Bahrain[4] **Bahreïn**[4]	**187**	**212**	**214**	**292**	**448**	**451**	**449**	**456**	**480**[5]	**499**[5]
Belgium[16] **Belgique**[16]	**3**	**3**	**3**	**0**	**0**	**0**	**0**	**0**	**0**	**0**
Brazil[1] **Brésil**[1]	**954**	**996**	**1 206**	**1 260**	**1 249**	**1 276**	**1 305**	**1 343**	**1 369**	**1 371**
Primary[1] 1re fusion[1]	888	931	1 139	1 193	1 172	1 185	1 188	1 197	1 189	1 208
Secondary[1] 2ème fusion[1]	67	65	66	67	77	91	117	146	180	163
Cameroon[4] **Cameroun**[4]	**87**[1]	**88**[1]	**86**[1]	**82**[1]	**86**[1]	**81**[1]	**71**	**82**[1]	**91**[1]	**82**[1]
Canada[1] **Canada**[1]	**1 615**	**1 635**	**1 889**	**2 058**	**2 399**	**2 350**	**2 269**	**2 384**	**2 433**	**2 485**
Primary 1re fusion	1 555[1]	1 567[1]	1 822	1 972[1]	2 309[1]	2 255[1]	2 172[1]	2 283[1]	2 327[1]	2 374[1]
Secondary[1] 2ème fusion[1]	60	68	68	86	90	97	97	101	106	111
China ††[4] **Chine ††**[4]	**758**	**854**	**900**	**1 096**	**1 255**	**1 498**	**1 870**	**1 896**	**2 180**	**2 362**
Colombia **Colombie**	...	...	...	0	1	...	0	...	...	...
Croatia[4] **Croatie**[4]	**73**	**75**	**54**	**29**	**26**	**26**	**31**	**33**	**35**[5]	**16**
former Czechoslovakia† **l'ex-Tchécoslovaquie†**	**69**	**70**	**66**	...	...	...	...	...	...	...
Primary 1re fusion	33	30	49	...	...	...	...	...	...	...
Secondary 2ème fusion	37	40	17	...	...	...	...	...	...	...
Denmark[6] **Danemark**[6]	**16**[1]	**11**[1]	**12**[1]	**16**[7]	**21**[7]	**22**[7]	**28**[7]	**27**[7]	**35**[7]	***35**[7]
Egypt[41] **Egypte**[41]	**146**	**141**	**141**	**139**	**139**	**149**	**136**	**150**	**119**	**187**[1]
Finland * [6] **Finlande *** [6]	**4**	**5**	**4**	**5**	**4**	**4**	**5**	**5**	...	...

50
Aluminium
Production: thousand metric tons [*cont.*]
Aluminium
Production : milliers de tonnes [*suite*]

Country or area Pays ou zone	1989	1990	1991	1992	1993	1994	1995	1996	1997	1998
France[9] **France[9]**	**555**	**533**	**472**	**637**	**627**	**709**	**618**[1]	**617**[1]	**641**[1]	**669**[1]
Primary 1re fusion	329	325	255	414	425	481	365[1]	380[1]	399[1]	424[1]
Secondary[9] 2ème fusion[9]	226	208	217	222	203	227	254[1]	237[1]	242[1]	245[1]
Germany **Allemagne**	...	...	**740**	**654**	**610**	**559**	**430**	**358**	**349**	**375**
Primary 1re fusion	...	...	690	603	552	503	...	...	...	...
Secondary 2ème fusion	...	...	50	52	58	56	...	...	...	...
F. R. Germany **R. f. Allemagne**	**785**	**760**	...	...	...	...	...	...	...	...
Primary 1re fusion	742	720[10]	...	...	...	...	...	...	...	...
former German D. R.[9] **l'ex-R. d. allemande[9]**	**108**	**83**	...	...	...	...	...	...	...	...
Primary[9] 1re fusion[9]	54	41	...	...	...	...	...	...	...	...
Secondary[9] 2ème fusion[9]	54	42	...	...	...	...	...	...	...	...
Ghana[4] **Ghana[4]**	**169**	**174**	**175**	**180**[1]	**175**[1]	**141**[1]	**135**[1]	**137**[1]	**152**[1]	**56**[1]
Greece[4] **Grèce[4]**	**209**	**226**	**175**	**174**	**148**	**142**	**132**	**141**	**132**	**146**
Hungary **Hongrie**	**85**	**81**	**63**	**27**	**29**	**31**	**35**	**94**	**98**	**92**
Primary 1re fusion	75	75	63	27	29	31	35	94	98	92
Secondary 2ème fusion	10	6	...	...	...	...	...	...	...	...
Iceland[4] **Islande[4]**	**89**	**87**	**89**	**89**	**94**	**99**	**100**	**102**	**123**	**160**
India[4] **Inde[4]**	**425**	**428**	**504**	**499**	**478**	**479**	**518**	**516**	**539**	**542**[5]
Indonesia[4] **Indonésie[4]**	**197**	**192**	**173**	**214**	**202**	**222**[1]	**228**[1]	**223**[1]	**219**[1]	**133**[1]
Iran (Islamic Rep. of) **Iran (Rép. islamique d')**[1]	**28**	**73**	**110**	**119**	**107**[1]	**142**[1]	**145**[1]	**96**[1]	**125**[1]	**135**[1]
Primary[1] 1re fusion[1]	20	59	70	79	92	116	119	70	99	109
Secondary[1] 2ème fusion[1]	9	14	39	39	15	26	26	26	26	26
Italy **Italie**	**610**	**581**	**566**	**514**	**502**	**551**	**590**	**561**	**631**	**690**
Primary 1re fusion	220	232	218	161	156	175	178	184	188	187
Secondary 2ème fusion	390	350	348	353	346	376	412	377	443	503
Japan[9] **Japon[9]**	**1 082**	**1 141**	**1 148**	**1 112**	**1 044**	**1 215**	**1 227**	**1 238**	**1 330**	**1 207**
Primary 1re fusion	51	51	52	38	39	41	46	46	53	51

50
Aluminium
Production: thousand metric tons [*cont.*]
Aluminium
Production : milliers de tonnes [*suite*]

Country or area Pays ou zone	1989	1990	1991	1992	1993	1994	1995	1996	1997	1998
Secondary[9] 2ème fusion[9]	1 031	1 090	1 096	1 074	1 006	1 175	1 181	1 191	1 277	1 155
Korea, Republic of[4] **Corée, République de**[4]	**16**	**13**	**14**	...	...	...	...	...	...	...
Mexico * **Mexique ***	**81**	**117**	**97**	**77**	**95**	**174**	**162**	**154**	**194**	**286**
Primary 1re fusion	68	57	43	17	25	29	33	69	71	68
Secondary[1] 2ème fusion[1]	13	60	54	60	70	145	129	85	123	218
Netherlands **Pays-Bas**	**409**	**392**	**368**	**378**	**367**	**405**	**408**	**298**[1]	**312**[1]	**366**[1]
Primary 1re fusion	279	258	254	227	228	230	216	227[1]	232[1]	264[1]
Secondary 2ème fusion	130	134	114	150	139	175	192	71[1]	80[1]	102[1]
New Zealand[1] **Nouvelle-Zélande**[1]	**262**	**264**	**263**	**250**	**285**	**277**	**281**	**293**	**318**	**326**
Primary[1] 1re fusion[1]	257	260	258	243	277	269	273	285	310	318
Secondary[1] 2ème fusion[1]	4	5	5	7	7	8	8	8	8	8
Norway **Norvège**	**874**	***887**	***889**	**878**	***943**	***906**	***919**	***923**	**977**[1]	**1 058**[1]
Primary 1re fusion	867	867	858	838	887	857	847	863	919[1]	996[1]
Secondary 2ème fusion	7	20[1]	31[1]	40[1]	56[1]	49[1]	72[1]	60[1]	59[1]	62[1]
Poland[4] **Pologne**[4]	**48**	**46**	**46**	**44**	**47**	**50**	**56**	**52**	**54**	**54**
Portugal[6] **Portugal**[6]	**4**	**9**	**8**	**12**	**12**	**12**	**3**[1]	**3**[1]	**3**[1]	**3**[1]
Romania[9 11] **Roumanie**[9 11]	**280**	**178**	**167**	**120**	**116**	**122**	**144**	**145**	**164**	**175**
Primary[9 11] 1re fusion[9 11]	269	168	158	112	112	120	140	141	162	174
Secondary[9] 2ème fusion[9]	11	10	9	8	4	3	3	4	2	1[11]
Russian Federation[4 5] **Fédération de Russie**[4 5]	...	...	...	**2 700**	**2 820**	**2 670**	**2 724**	**2 874**	**2 906**	**3 005**
Slovakia **Slovaquie**	**69**	**70**	**66**	...	**19**	**4**	**25**	**311**	**110**[1]	**121**
Primary 1re fusion	32	30	49	...	18	4	25	311	110[1]	115
Secondary 2ème fusion	37	40	17	...	1	...	...	...	...	6
Slovenia[4] **Slovénie**[4]	**98**	**100**	**90**	**85**	**83**	**77**	**58**	**27**	**9**	**10**
South Africa[4 5] **Afrique du Sud**[4 5]	**166**	**170**	**169**	**173**	**175**	**172**	**195**	**570**	**673**	**650**
Spain[1] **Espagne**[1]	**430**	**442**	**451**	**456**	**456**	**442**	**469**	**515**	**533**	**570**
Primary[1] 1re fusion[1]	352	355	355	359	356	338	362	362	360	360

50
Aluminium
Production: thousand metric tons [cont.]
Aluminium
Production : milliers de tonnes [suite]

Country or area Pays ou zone	1989	1990	1991	1992	1993	1994	1995	1996	1997	1998
Secondary[1] 2ème fusion[1]	78	87	96	96	100	104	107	154	173	210
Suriname[4] Suriname[4]	28	31	31	32	30	27	28	29	32[5]	29[5]
Sweden Suède	130[1]	126[1]	116	94[1]	101[1]	105[1]	117[1]	123[1]	123[1]	123[1]
Primary[1] 1re fusion[1]	97	96	97	77	82	84	94	98	98	96
Secondary 2ème fusion	33[1]	30[1]	16	19	19[1]	22[1]	23[1]	24[1]	25[1]	27
Switzerland Suisse	* 103	* 106	* 102	* 63	* 41	* 30	26[1]	33[1]	35[1]	47
Primary 1re fusion	71	72	66	52	36	24	21	27[1]	27[1]	32[1]
Secondary[1] 2ème fusion[1]	31	34	36	11	4	6	5	6	8	15
Tajikistan[4] Tadjikistan[4]	...	...	...	* 400[5]	252	236	237	198	189	196
TFYR Macedonia L'ex-R.y. Macédoine	5	5	6	6	6	7	5	5	5	7
Turkey[4] Turquie[4]	57	61	56	61	58	60	62	62	62	62
Ukraine *[4,5] Ukraine *[4,5]	...	...	...	100	100	100	98	90	101	107
former USSR†*[5] l'ex-URSS†*[5]	3 000	2 800	...	...	...	...	...	...	...	...
Primary *[5] 1re fusion *[5]	2 400	2 200	...	...	...	...	...	...	...	...
Secondary *[5] 2ème fusion *[5]	600	600	...	...	...	...	...	...	...	...
United Kingdom Royaume-Uni	367[11]	363[11]	350[11]	496[1]	475[1]	456[1]	468[1]	497[1]	492[1]	533[1]
Primary 1re fusion	297[11]	290[11]	294[11]	244[1]	239[1]	231[1]	238[1]	240[1]	248[1]	258[1]
Secondary 2ème fusion	70	73	56	252[1]	236[1]	224[1]	230[1]	257[1]	244[1]	275[1]
United States[9] Etats-Unis[9]	6 084	6 441	6 411	6 802	6 635	6 389	6 565	6 887	7 153	7 153
Primary 1re fusion	4 030	4 048	4 121	4 042	3 695	3 299	3 375	3 577	3 603	3 713
Secondary[9] 2ème fusion[9]	2 054	2 393	2 290	2 760	2 940	3 090	3 190	3 310	3 550	3 440
Venezuela Venezuela	576	609	620	542	602	617[1]	654[1]	656[1]	662[1]	606[1]
Primary 1re fusion	566	599	610	508	568	585[1]	627[1]	635[1]	641[1]	584[1]
Secondary[1] 2ème fusion[1]	10	10	10	35	35	32	28	21	21	21
Yugoslavia Yougoslavie	...	...	76	67	26	4	17	37	67	61
Primary 1re fusion	...	...	76	67	26	4	17	37	66	61
Secondary 2ème fusion	...	...	0	0	0	0	0	0	1	0

50
Aluminium
Production: thousand metric tons [cont.]
Aluminium
Production : milliers de tonnes [suite]

Country or area Pays ou zone	1989	1990	1991	1992	1993	1994	1995	1996	1997	1998
Yugoslavia, SFR† **Yougoslavie, Rfs†**	332	291	...	...	...	...	...	...	...	...
Primary 1re fusion	331	* 290	...	...	...	...	...	...	...	...
Secondary 2ème fusion	1	* 1	...	...	...	...	...	...	...	...

Source:
United Nations Secretariat, "Industrial Commodity Statistics Yearbook 1998" and the industrial statistics database of the Statistics Division.

† For information on recent changes in country or area nomenclature pertaining to former Czechoslovakia, Germany, Hong Kong Special Administrative Region (SAR) of China, Macao Special Administrative Region (SAR) of China, SFR of Yugoslavia and the former USSR, see Annex I - Country or area nomenclature, regional and other groupings.

†† For statistical purposes, the data for China do not include those for Hong Kong Special Administrative Region (Hong Kong SAR), Macao Special Administrative Region (Macao SAR) and Taiwan province of China.

1 Source: World Metal Statistics, (London).
2 Twelve months ending 30 June of year stated.

3 Secondary aluminium produced from old scrap only.

4 Primary metal production only.
5 Source: U. S. Bureau of Mines, (Washington, D. C.).
6 Secondary metal production only.
7 Sales.
8 Including aluminium plates, shapes and bars.
9 Including alloys.
10 Source: Metallgesellschaft Aktiengesellschaft, (Frankfurt).

11 Including pure content of virgin alloys.

Source:
Secrétariat de l'Organisation des Nations Unies, "Annuaire de statistiques industrielles par produit 1998" et la base de données pour les statistiques industrielles de la Division de statistique.

† Pour les modifications récentes de nomenclature de pays ou de zone concernant l'Allemagne, Hong Kong, région administrative spéciale (RAS) de Chine, Macao, région administrative spéciale (RAS) de Chine, l'ex-Tchécoslovaquie, l'ex-URSS et l'ex-Rfs de Yougoslavie, voir annexe I - Nomenclature des pays ou des zones, groupements régionaux et autres groupements.

†† Les données statistiques relatives à la Chine ne comprennent pas celles qui concernent la région administrative spéciale de Hong Kong (la RAS de Hong Kong), la région administrative spéciale de Macao (la RAS de Macao) et la province chinoise de Taiwan.

1 Source: "World Metal Statistics," (Londres).
2 Période de douze mois finissant le 30e juin de l'année indiquée.
3 Aluminium de deuxième fusion obtenu à partir de vieux déchets seulement.
4 Production du métal de première fusion seulement.
5 Source: "U.S. Bureau of Mines," (Washington, D.C.).
6 Production du métal de deuxième fusion seulement.
7 Ventes.
8 Y compris les tôles, les profilés et les barres d'aluminium.
9 Y compris les alliages.
10 Source: "Metallgesellschaft Aktiengesellschaft", (Francfort).
11 Y compris la teneur pure des alliages de première fusion.

51
Radio and television receivers
Récepteurs radio et télévision
Production: thousands
Production : milliers

Country or area Pays ou zone	Radio receivers Récepteurs radio					Television receivers Récepteurs télévision				
	1994	1995	1996	1997	1998	1994	1995	1996	1997	1998
Albania Albanie	0	0	0	0	0	0	0	0	0	0
Algeria Algérie	107	...	...	...	...	165	194	250	172	251
Argentina Argentine	...	...	...	...	...	1 523	949	1 089	1 601	...
Azerbaijan Azerbaïdjan	3	0	0	0	0	2	4	1	1	1
Bangladesh Bangladesh	3	4	11	20	...	77	79	64	94	...
Belarus Bélarus	545	277	138	170	114	473	250	314	454	468
Brazil Brésil	4 665	4 729	2 941	4 211	2 753	5 522	6 424	8 644	7 976	5 711
Bulgaria Bulgarie	2	2	0	...	...	19	10	11	6	3
China †† Chine ††	41 320	...	...	...	...	32 833	34 962	35 418	36 372	42 809
China, Hong Kong SAR†[1] Chine, Hong Kong RAS†[1]	3 390	1 698	...	...	...	...	...	...	...	...
Colombia Colombie	...	...	...	...	...	141	129	...	58	50
Croatia Croatie	0	0	0	...	...	0	0	0	...	...
Czech Republic République tchèque	...	...	...	...	...	128	66	74	180	567
Ecuador Equateur	...	...	...	...	...	54	5	0	...	...
Egypt Egypte	52	...	...	...	...	281	288	336	114	...
Finland Finlande	70	82	...	...	...	339	308	191	...	...
France France	2 804	...	...	...	...	2 796	...	...	...	...
Georgia Géorgie	...	...	...	...	...	0	0	2	2	1
Germany Allemagne	5 404	3 182	3 342	3 632	3 884	3 234	3 218	1 965	...	1 269
Hungary Hongrie	126	103	310	528	2 328	272	274	...	...	...
India Inde	210	117	47	33	2	1 562	2 190	1 956	2 370	2 461
Indonesia [2] Indonésie [2]	3 372	...	...	4 177	...	...	...	...	...	...
Iran (Islamic Rep. of) Iran (Rép. islamique d')	138 [3]	45 [4]	56 [4]	76 [4]	...	360 [3]	253 [4]	453 [4]	751 [4]	...
Italy Italie	...	...	...	...	...	2 780	2 780	2 677	1 920	1 659

51
Radio and television receivers
Production: thousands [*cont.*]
Récepteurs radio et télévision
Production : milliers [*suite*]

Country or area Pays ou zone	Radio receivers Récepteurs radio					Television receivers Récepteurs télévision				
	1994	1995	1996	1997	1998	1994	1995	1996	1997	1998
Japan Japon	7 569	7 181	2 638	2 434	2 623	11 192	9 022	7 568	7 559	6 567
Kazakhstan Kazakhstan	4	12	3	3	3	43	47	74	61	103
Korea, Republic of Corée, République de	28	0	...	...	...	17 102	18 722	21 469	16 428	12 763
Kyrgyzstan Kirghizistan	...	...	...	...	...	43	7	0	0	4
Latvia Lettonie	33	9	10	10	2	...	...	...	...	...
Lithuania Lituanie	...	...	...	...	...	181	55	57	52	84
Malaysia Malaisie	36 310	38 767	29 431	33 491	30 265	7 702	9 461	8 901	7 774	8 035
Mexico Mexique	...	...	...	...	...	423	181	205	...	...
Pakistan Pakistan	...	...	...	...	...	185	101	278	186	107
Poland Pologne	309	225	206	143	154	888	1 138	1 615	3 020	4 436
Portugal Portugal	...	...	4 372	4 552	5 076	...	...	...	...	...
Republic of Moldova[5] République de Moldova[5]	3	16	67	94	51	108	47	31	19	9
Romania Roumanie	28[2]	29[2]	76[2]	28[2]	10[2]	452	369	275	89	134
Russian Federation Fédération de Russie	1 087	988	477	342	235	2 240	1 005	313	327	329
Slovenia Slovénie	...	...	0	0	0	124	130	179	0	231
Spain Espagne	...	54	82	313	508	4 103	5 392	...	...	...
Syrian Arab Republic Rép. arabe syrienne	...	...	...	...	...	77	71	124	128	151
Trinidad and Tobago Trinité-et-Tobago	...	0	0	...	...	11	3	1	...	...
Tunisia Tunisie	...	...	...	...	...	103	93	90	108	90
Turkey Turquie	32	...	...	...	...	1 528	1 859	2 510	4 657	5 795
Ukraine Ukraine	302	125	47	25	10	821	315	118	50	93
United Kingdom Royaume-Uni	1 176	1 480	1 531	2 095	2 164	...	...	...	...	...
United Rep.Tanzania Rép.-Unie de Tanzanie	54	76	54	56		...	...	...	...	...
United States[6] Etats-Unis[6]	...	...	...	...	...	13 881	12 132	11 440	11 476	10 240

51
Radio and television receivers
Production: thousands [*cont.*]
Récepteurs radio et télévision
Production : milliers [*suite*]

Country or area Pays ou zone	Radio receivers Récepteurs radio					Television receivers Récepteurs télévision				
	1994	1995	1996	1997	1998	1994	1995	1996	1997	1998
Uzbekistan Ouzbékistan	...	...	...	...	...	52	65	140	269	...
Yugoslavia Yougoslavie	0	0	1	0	0	40	31	24	25	30

Source:
United Nations Secretariat, "Industrial Commodity Statistics
Yearbook 1998" and the industrial statistics database of
the Statistics Division.

† For information on recent changes in country or
area nomenclature pertaining to former Czechoslovakia,
Germany, Hong Kong Special Administrative Region (SAR) of
China, Macao Special Administrative Region (SAR) of China,
SFR of Yugoslavia and the former USSR, see Annex I - Country
or area nomenclature, regional and other groupings.

†† For statistical purposes, the data for
China do not include those for Hong Kong Special
Administrative Region (Hong Kong SAR), Macao Special
Administrative Region (Macao SAR) and Taiwan province of
China.

1 Beginning 1996, data are confidential.
2 Including radio with tape recording unit.

3 Production by establishments employing 50 or more persons.
4 Production by establishments employing 10 or more persons.
5 Excluding Transnistria region.
6 Shipments.

Source:
Secrétariat de l'Organisation des Nations Unies, "Annuaire
de statistiques industrielles par produit 1998" et la base
de données pour les statistiques industrielles de la
Division de statistique.

† Pour les modifications récentes de nomenclature
de pays ou de zone concernant l'Allemagne, Hong Kong, région
administrative spéciale (RAS) de Chine, Macao, région
administrative spéciale (RAS) de Chine,
l'ex-Tchécoslovaquie, l'ex-URSS et l'ex-Rfs de Yougoslavie,
voir annexe I - Nomenclature des pays ou des zones,
groupements régionaux et autres groupements.

†† Les données statistiques relatives à
la Chine ne comprennent pas celles qui concernent la région
administrative spéciale de Hong Kong (la RAS de Hong Kong),
la région administrative spéciale de Macao (la RAS de Macao)
et la province chinoise de Taiwan.

1 A partir de 1996, les données sont confidentielles.
2 Y compris les récepteurs de radio avec appareil enregistreur
à bande magnétique incorporés.
3 Production des établissements occupant 50 personnes ou plus.
4 Production des établissements occupant 10 personnes ou plus.
5 Non compris la région de Transnistria.
6 Expéditions.

52
Passenger cars
Voitures de tourisme
Production: thousands
Production : milliers

Country or area Pays ou zone	1989	1990	1991	1992	1993	1994	1995	1996	1997	1998
Argentina[1] Argentine[1]	108	81	114	221	287	338	227	269	366	...
Australia Australie	333[1 2]	361	278	270	285	310	294	305	...	...
Austria Autriche	7	15	14	...	...	...	...	...	...	...
Brazil[3] Brésil[3]	313	267	293	338	392	367	271	245	253	242
Canada Canada	984	940	890	901	838	...	...	...	...	...
China ††* Chine ††*	...	...	40	...	...	...	...	...	...	...
Czech Republic République tchèque	184	188	...	...	...	...	...	...	...	...
Egypt Egypte	13	10	9	7	4	7	8	14	13	13
Finland[1] Finlande[1]	37	30	39	13	7	...	...	0	...	...
France France	3 415	3 293	3 190	3 326	2 837	3 176	...	...	...	...
Germany Allemagne	...	...	4 647	4 895	3 875	4 222	...	4 713[1]	...	...
F. R. Germany R. f. Allemagne	4 536	4 634	...	...	...	...	...	...	...	...
former German D. R. l'ex-R. d. allemande	217	145	...	...	...	...	...	...	...	...
Hungary Hongrie	...	...	...	...	...	...	...	...	...	90
India[4] Inde[4]	178	177	164	162	210	262	331	399	384	...
Indonesia Indonésie	17	16	26	28	20	85	19	...	11	...
Italy[4] Italie[4]	1 971	1 873	1 632	1 475	1 116	1 340	1 422	1 244	1 563	1 379
Japan Japon	9 052	9 948	9 753	9 379	8 494	7 801	7 611	7 864	8 491	8 056
Korea, Republic of[1] Corée, République de[1]	846	935	1 119	1 259	1 528	1 755	1 999	2 256	2 313	1 577
Mexico Mexique	448[1]	611[1]	730[1]	799[1]	861	887	705	802	858	947
Netherlands[1 5 6] Pays-Bas[1 5 6]	133	122	84	95	80	92	98	...	...	...
Poland Pologne	285	266	167	219	334	338	366	441	520	592
Romania Roumanie	144	100	84	74	93	56	70	97	109	104
Russian Federation Fédération de Russie	1 062	1 103	1 030	963	956	798	835	868	986	840

52
Passenger cars
Production: thousands [cont.]
Voitures de tourisme
Production : milliers [suite]

Country or area Pays ou zone	1989	1990	1991	1992	1993	1994	1995	1996	1997	1998
Slovakia Slovaquie	5	3	4	...	5	8	22	32	42	125
Slovenia Slovénie	47	68	79	84	58	74	88	89	...	...
Spain Espagne	1 651	1 696	1 787	1 817	1 774[1 5]	2 146[1 5]	2 254[1 5]	2 334[1 5]	2 278[1 5]	2 469[1 5]
Sweden Suède	240	216	178	205	173	193	...	207	219	214
Ukraine Ukraine	155	156	156	135	140	94	59	7	2	26
former USSR† l'ex-URSS†	1 217	1 259	...	...	...	...	...	...	...	...
United Kingdom Royaume-Uni	1 308	1 302	1 340	1 291	1 504	1 654	1 735	1 707	1 818	1 709
United States[7] Etats-Unis[7]	6 808	6 081	5 441	5 684	5 956	* 6 614	...	...	...	...
Yugoslavia Yougoslavie	...	179	76	22	8	8	8	9	10	12
Yugoslavia, SFR† Yougoslavie, Rfs†	227	289	...	...	...	...	...	...	...	...

Source:
United Nations Secretariat, "Industrial Commodity Statistics
Yearbook 1998" and the industrial statistics database of
the Statistics Division.

† For information on recent changes in country or
area nomenclature pertaining to former Czechoslovakia,
Germany, Hong Kong Special Administrative Region (SAR) of
China, Macao Special Administrative Region (SAR) of China,
SFR of Yugoslavia and the former USSR, see Annex I - Country
or area nomenclature, regional and other groupings.

†† For statistical purposes, the data for
China do not include those for Hong Kong Special
Administrative Region (Hong Kong SAR), Macao Special
Administrative Region (Macao SAR) and Taiwan province of
China.

1 Including assembly.
2 Twelve months ending 30 June of year stated.

3 Excluding station wagons.
4 Excluding production for armed forces.
5 Sales.
6 Production by establishments employing 20 or more persons.
7 Factory sales.

Source:
Secrétariat de l'Organisation des Nations Unies, "Annuaire
de statistiques industrielles par produit 1998" et la base
de données pour les statistiques industrielles de la
Division de statistique.

† Pour les modifications récentes de nomenclature
de pays ou de zone concernant l'Allemagne, Hong Kong, région
administrative spéciale (RAS) de Chine, Macao, région
administrative spéciale (RAS) de Chine,
l'ex-Tchécoslovaquie, l'ex-URSS et l'ex-Rfs de Yougoslavie,
voir annexe I - Nomenclature des pays ou des zones,
groupements régionaux et autres groupements.

†† Les données statistiques relatives à
la Chine ne comprennent pas celles qui concernent la région
administrative spéciale de Hong Kong (la RAS de Hong Kong),
la région administrative spéciale de Macao (la RAS de Macao)
et la province chinoise de Taiwan.

1 Y compris le montage.
2 Période de douze mois finissant le 30e juin de l'année
indiquée.
3 Non compris les stations-wagons.
4 Non compris la production destinée aux forces armées.
5 Ventes.
6 Production des établissements occupant 20 personnes ou plus.
7 Ventes des fabriques.

53
Refrigerators for household use
Réfrigérateurs à usage domestique
Production: thousands
Production : milliers

Country or area Pays ou zone	1989	1990	1991	1992	1993	1994	1995	1996	1997	1998
Algeria Algérie	369	387	388	317	183	119	131	137	175	215
Angola Angola	3	1	2	2	...	...	...	...	...	...
Antigua and Barbuda[1] Antigua-et-Barbuda[1]	...	...	...	...	3	3	...	...	...	...
Argentina Argentine	...	265	439	554	688	494	389	379	410	...
Australia Australie	380[2]	329	389	363	421	444	423	403	...	...
Azerbaijan Azerbaïdjan	354	330	313	223	228	97	25	7	0	3
Belarus Bélarus	718	728	743	740	738	742	746	754	795	802
Brazil Brésil	2 381	2 441	2 445	1 704	2 098	2 721	3 242	3 776	3 592	3 034
Bulgaria Bulgarie	101	82	65	106	81	69	49	36	21	55
Chile Chili	79	89	86	136	192	221	272	213	268	229
China †† Chine ††	6 708	4 631	4 699	4 858	5 967	7 681	9 185	9 797	10 444	10 600
Colombia Colombie	...	...	...	306	396	465	465	...	...	...
Cuba Cuba	9	...	...	...	...	...	...	...	...	...
former Czechoslovakia† l'ex-Tchécoslovaquie†	502	449	515	...	...	...	...	...	...	...
Denmark[3] Danemark[3]	257	278	269	294	261	285	265	223	247	271
Ecuador Equateur	...	...	...	66	72	111	156	17	...	...
Egypt Egypte	477	246	260	232	204	236	236	250	...	...
Finland Finlande	198	166	150	144	128	134	104	68	102	107
France France	614	596	556	566	487	554	...	...	...	...
Germany Allemagne	...	...	4 226	4 298	3 838	3 794	...	2 747	...	...
F. R. Germany R. f. Allemagne	3 614	4 037	...	...	...	...	...	...	...	...
former German D. R. l'ex-R. d. allemande	1 140	1 005	...	...	...	...	...	...	...	...
Greece Grèce	130	119	85	80	...	...	...	...	...	...
Guyana Guyana	7	6	8	6	5	5	...	...	...	...

53
Refrigerators for household use
Production: thousands [cont.]

Réfrigérateurs à usage domestique
Production : milliers [suite]

Country or area Pays ou zone	1989	1990	1991	1992	1993	1994	1995	1996	1997	1998
Hungary Hongrie	390	438	443	483	520	603	714	736	835	708
India Inde	991	1 220	1 133	997	1 382	1 668	1 913	1 705	1 600	1 902
Indonesia Indonésie	115	196	194	...	172	469	...	...	573	...
Iran (Islamic Rep. of) Iran (Rép. islamique d')	351[4]	649[4]	829[4]	896[4]	789[4]	629[4]	575[5]	756[5]	702[5]	
Iraq Iraq	...	...	...	35	...	...	...	...	...	...
Italy Italie	4 082	4 199	4 484	4 285	4 753	5 033	5 908	5 402	5 562	6 280
Japan Japon	5 018	5 048	5 212	4 425	4 351	4 952	5 013	5 163	5 369	4 851
Kazakhstan Kazakhstan	...	...	...	...	13	...	...	...	...	...
Kenya Kenya	21	21	...	...	...	...	...	...	...	...
Korea, Republic of Corée, République de	2 803	2 827	3 228	3 296	3 585	3 943	3 975	4 292	4 257	3 790
Kyrgyzstan Kirghizistan	...	...	0	1	0	3	1	0	0	...
Lithuania Lituanie	350	263	254	137	207	183	187	138	172	153
Malaysia Malaisie	185	212	266	288	250	266	295	257	249	206
Mexico Mexique	372	396	487	541	1 065	1 356	1 256	1 447	1 942	1 986
Mozambique Mozambique	3	1	...	...	...	...	...	...	...	...
Myanmar[6] Myanmar[6]	0	0	0	...	...	...	...	...	...	...
Nigeria Nigéria	...	...	77	52	53	20	19	...	...	...
Peru Pérou	32	46	70	54	57	86	111	56	87	115
Poland Pologne	516	604	553	500	588	605	585	584	705	714
Portugal Portugal	376	464	529	251	224	244	...	173	211	257
Republic of Moldova République de Moldova	204	133	118	55	58[7]	53[7]	24[7]	1[7]	2[7]	0[7]
Romania[8] Roumanie[8]	470	393	389	402	435	383	435	446	429	366
Russian Federation Fédération de Russie	3 447	3 615	3 566	2 972	3 049	2 283	1 531	966	1 108	956
Slovakia Slovaquie	502	449	515	552	482	371	330	393	258	228
Slovenia Slovénie	797	844	720	661	665	797	863	592	692	756

53
Refrigerators for household use
Production: thousands [*cont.*]
Réfrigérateurs à usage domestique
Production : milliers [*suite*]

Country or area Pays ou zone	1989	1990	1991	1992	1993	1994	1995	1996	1997	1998
South Africa[9] Afrique du Sud[9]	338	352	356	318	318	321	365	411	388	...
Spain Espagne	1 268	1 285	1 410	1 322	1 240	1 461	1 269	1 260	1 960	2 415
Sweden Suède	631	584	562	562	549	582	610	478	523	545
Syrian Arab Republic Rép. arabe syrienne	89	40	85	129	150	148	156	155	138	...
Tajikistan Tadjikistan	...	167	145	61	18	3	0	1	2	1
Thailand Thaïlande	730	855	789	...	...	...	...	2 246	2 384	1 631
TFYR Macedonia L'ex-R.y. Macédoine	214	156	136	139	98	95	51	20	12	7
Trinidad and Tobago Trinité-et-Tobago	12	14	13	10	3	3	1	0	...	...
Tunisia Tunisie	...	64	82	123	141	129	...	...	...	...
Turkey Turquie	815	986	1 019	1 040	1 254	1 258	1 663	1 656	1 946	1 993
Ukraine Ukraine	882	903	883	838	757	653	562	431	382	390
former USSR†[8] l'ex-URSS†[8]	6 465	6 499	...	...	...	...	...	...	...	...
United Kingdom Royaume-Uni	1 244	1 312	...	...	1 033	1 094	1 256	1 225	1 249	1 096
United States[10][11] Etats-Unis[10][11]	8 013	7 015	7 599	9 676	10 306	11 276	11 005	11 132	12 092	12 618
Uzbekistan Ouzbékistan	192	201	212	85	82	20	19	13	13	...
Yugoslavia Yougoslavie	...	215	109	85	39	41	50	51	81	48
Yugoslavia, SFR†[12] Yougoslavie, Rfs†[12]	971	...	...	...	...	...	...	...	...	...

Source:
United Nations Secretariat, "Industrial Commodity Statistics
Yearbook 1998" and the industrial statistics database of
the Statistics Division.

† For information on recent changes in country or
area nomenclature pertaining to former Czechoslovakia,
Germany, Hong Kong Special Administrative Region (SAR) of
China, Macao Special Administrative Region (SAR) of China,
SFR of Yugoslavia and the former USSR, see Annex I - Country
or area nomenclature, regional and other groupings.

†† For statistical purposes, the data for
China do not include those for Hong Kong Special
Administrative Region (Hong Kong SAR), Macao Special

Source:
Secrétariat de l'Organisation des Nations Unies, "Annuaire
de statistiques industrielles par produit 1998" et la base
de données pour les statistiques industrielles de la
Division de statistique.

† Pour les modifications récentes de nomenclature
de pays ou de zone concernant l'Allemagne, Hong Kong, région
administrative spéciale (RAS) de Chine, Macao, région
administrative spéciale (RAS) de Chine,
l'ex-Tchécoslovaquie, l'ex-URSS et l'ex-Rfs de Yougoslavie,
voir annexe I - Nomenclature des pays ou des zones,
groupements régionaux et autres groupements.

†† Les données statistiques relatives à

53

Refrigerators for household use
Production: thousands [*cont.*]

Réfrigérateurs à usage domestique
Production : milliers [*suite*]

Administrative Region (Macao SAR) and Taiwan province of China.

la Chine ne comprennent pas celles qui concernent la région administrative spéciale de Hong Kong (la RAS de Hong Kong), la région administrative spéciale de Macao (la RAS de Macao) et la province chinoise de Taiwan.

1 Twelve months beginning 21 March of year stated.

2 Twelve months ending 30 June of year stated.

3 Sales.
4 Production by establishments employing 50 or more persons.
5 Production by establishments employing 10 or more persons.
6 Government production only.
7 Excluding Transnistria region.
8 Including freezers.
9 Including deep freezers and deep freeze-refrigerator combinations.
10 Electric domestic refrigerators only.
11 Shipments.
12 Including refrigerators other than domestic.

1 Période de douze mois commençant le 21e mars de l'année indiquée.

2 Période de douze mois finissant le 30e juin de l'année indiquée.

3 Ventes.
4 Production des établissements occupant 50 personnes ou plus.
5 Production des établissements occupant 10 personnes ou plus.
6 Production de l'Etat seulement.
7 Non compris la région de Transnistria.
8 Y compris les congélateurs.
9 Y compris congélateurs-conservateurs et congélateurs combinés avec un réfrigérateur.
10 Réfrigérateurs électriques de ménage seulement.
11 Expéditions.
12 Y compris les réfrigérateurs autres que ménagers.

54
Washing machines for household use
Machines à laver à usage domestique
Production: thousands
Production : en milliers

Country or area Pays or zone	1989	1990	1991	1992	1993	1994	1995	1996	1997	1998
Argentina Argentine	...	...	436	756	801	702	458	524	603	...
Armenia Arménie	118	110	74	9	0	0	1	0	...	...
Australia Australie	397 [1]	343	295	295	328	314	310	266	...	...
Austria Autriche	72	77	...	...	...	...	...	...	...	...
Belarus Bélarus	22	33	57	62	71	77	37	61	88	91
Belgium [2 3] Belgique [2 3]	81	60	99	138	49	...	...	...	...	...
Brazil Brésil	578	552	948	849	1 167	1 461	1 681	2 160	2 095	1 851
Bulgaria Bulgarie	177	90	74	69	42	41	26	24	5	...
Chile Chili	108	177	203	301	386	447	434	310	...	...
China †† Chine ††	8 254	6 627	6 872	7 079	8 959	10 941	9 484	10 747	12 545	12 073
Colombia Colombie	...	...	...	41	41	50	45	...	...	...
Croatia Croatie	13	3	1	1	0	0	0	0	0	...
Czech Republic République tchèque	255	249	...	...	...	...	...	...	...	...
Denmark [4] Danemark [4]	...	...	...	...	...	0	0	...	...	...
Ecuador Equateur	...	...	...	...	...	...	11	12	...	...
Egypt Egypte	212	179	202	198	200	209	198	200	201	...
France [3] France [3]	1 670	1 636	1 645	1 713	1 943	2 245	...	...	...	...
Germany Allemagne	...	...	...	...	...	...	2 703	2 816	3 035	3 370
F. R. Germany [5] R. f. Allemagne [5]	2 430	...	...	...	...	...	...	...	...	...
former German D. R. l'ex-R. d. allemande	521	556	...	...	...	...	...	...	...	...
Greece Grèce	48	...	...	...	31	20	15	10	...	...
Hungary Hongrie	383	315	220	219	...	...	...	...	...	...
Indonesia Indonésie	10	17	19	27	32	44	...	...	86	...
Iran (Islamic Rep. of) Iran (Rép. islamique d')	41 [6]	19 [6]	43 [6]	63 [6]	59 [6]	79 [6]	98 [7]	159 [7]	194 [7]	...
Israel [8] Israël [8]	8	13	...	...	...	...	...	...	...	...

54
Washing machines for household use
Production: thousands [*cont.*]

Machines à laver à usage domestique
Production : en milliers [*suite*]

Country or area Pays or zone	1989	1990	1991	1992	1993	1994	1995	1996	1997	1998
Italy Italie	4 338	4 372	5 044	5 140	5 693	6 251	6 996	7 135	7 967	8 119
Japan Japon	5 141	5 576	5 587	5 225	5 163	5 042	4 876	5 006	4 818	4 468
Kazakhstan Kazakhstan	...	...	391	370	255	88	46	23	11	3
Korea, Republic of Corée, République de	1 864	2 163	2 157	1 896	2 199	2 443	2 827	2 878	2 967	2 643
Kyrgyzstan Kirghizistan	250	234	209	94	77	17	4	3	2	0
Latvia Lettonie	612	570	427	18	18	10	8	3	3	2
Mexico Mexique	442	558	611	646	1 085	1 185	882	1 091	1 448	1 512
Peru Pérou	10	9	6	5	3	5	5	2	...	...
Poland Pologne	811	482	336	363	402	449	419	445	412	416
Portugal Portugal	16	34	7	...	...	...	...	...	...	...
Republic of Moldova République de Moldova	280	298	194	102	123[9]	81[9]	49[9]	54[9]	46[9]	43[9]
Romania Roumanie	204	205	188	159	161	109	125	138	82	36
Russian Federation Fédération de Russie	4 501	5 419	5 541	4 289	3 901	2 122	1 294	762	800	862
Slovakia Slovaquie	199	202	144	122	100	...	...	...	...	...
Slovenia Slovénie	322	315	318	188	189	200	220	291	405	474
South Africa Afrique du Sud	68	109	87	44	52	55	57	55	44	...
Spain Espagne	1 378	1 425	1 522	1 540	1 334	1 632	1 655	1 945	2 270	2 281
Sweden Suède	104	107	103	91	94	113	106	103	120	119
Syrian Arab Republic Rép. arabe syrienne	34	44	29	41	47	50	78	80	72	...
Thailand Thaïlande	...	...	...	...	...	...	...	541	794	800
Turkey Turquie	621	743	837	802	980	780	866	1 051	1 485	1 408
Ukraine Ukraine	651	788	830	805	643	422	213	149	147	138
former USSR† l'ex-URSS†	6 698	7 818	...	...	...	...	...	...	...	...
United States[3] Etats-Unis[3]	6 375	6 428	6 404	6 566	6 739	7 081	6 605	6 873	6 942	7 504
Uzbekistan Ouzbékistan	...	...	13	9	10	9	14	4	4	...

54
Washing machines for household use
Production: thousands [*cont.*]
Machines à laver à usage domestique
Production : en milliers [*suite*]

Country or area Pays or zone	1989	1990	1991	1992	1993	1994	1995	1996	1997	1998
Yugoslavia Yougoslavie	...	...	94	68	39	63	36	33	33	30
Yugoslavia, SFR†[10] Yougoslavie, Rfs†[10]	529	...	...	...	...	...	...	...	...	...

Source:
United Nations Secretariat, "Industrial Commodity Statistics Yearbook 1998" and the industrial statistics database of the Statistics Division.

†   For information on recent changes in country or area nomenclature pertaining to former Czechoslovakia, Germany, Hong Kong Special Administrative Region (SAR) of China, Macao Special Administrative Region (SAR) of China, SFR of Yugoslavia and the former USSR, see Annex I - Country or area nomenclature, regional and other groupings.

††   For statistical purposes, the data for China do not include those for Hong Kong Special Administrative Region (Hong Kong SAR), Macao Special Administrative Region (Macao SAR) and Taiwan province of China.

1 Twelve months ending 30 June of year stated.
2 Production by establishments employing 5 or more persons.
3 Shipments.
4 Sales.
5 Automatic washing machines only.
6 Production by establishments employing 50 or more persons.
7 Production by establishments employing 10 or more persons.
8 Marketed local production.
9 Excluding Transnistria region.
10 Including drying machines.

Source:
Secrétariat de l'Organisation des Nations Unies, "Annuaire de statistiques industrielles par produit 1998" et la base de données pour les statistiques industrielles de la Division de statistique.

†   Pour les modifications récentes de nomenclature de pays ou de zone concernant l'Allemagne, Hong Kong, région administrative spéciale (RAS) de Chine, Macao, région administrative spéciale (RAS) de Chine, l'ex-Tchécoslovaquie, l'ex-URSS et l'ex-Rfs de Yougoslavie, voir annexe I - Nomenclature des pays ou des zones, groupements régionaux et autres groupements.

††   Les données statistiques relatives à la Chine ne comprennent pas celles qui concernent la région administrative spéciale de Hong Kong (la RAS de Hong Kong), la région administrative spéciale de Macao (la RAS de Macao) et la province chinoise de Taiwan.

1 Période de douze mois finissant le 30e juin de
2 Production des établissements occupant 5 personnes ou plus.
3 Expéditions.
4 Ventes.
5 Machines à laver automatiques seulement.
6 Production des établissements occupant 50 personnes ou plus.
7 Production des établissements occupant 10 personnes ou plus.
8 Production locale commercialisée.
9 Non compris la région de Transnistria.
10 Y compris les machines à sécher.

55
Machine tools
Machines-outils
Production: number
Production : nombre

Country or area Pays ou zone	1989	1990	1991	1992	1993	1994	1995	1996	1997	1998
A. Drilling and boring machines • Perceuses										
Algeria Algérie	32	412	210	122	30	...	...	...	...	...
Austria Autriche	1 443	...	...	...	...	...	...	...	...	...
Azerbaijan Azerbaïdjan	754	594	643	428	86	102	112	49	24	29
Bangladesh Bangladesh	125	131	...	...	...	...	...	...	...	...
Bulgaria Bulgarie	6 496	4 729	1 959	996	759	850	864	953	906	955
Croatia Croatie	644	619	458	346	255	...	4 369	3 212	1 134	31
Czech Republic République tchèque	871	897	1 131	...	...	...	...	1 235	1 263	1 162
Denmark[1] Danemark[1]	338	348	394	223	197	...	...	...	...	...
Finland Finlande	74	59	42	54	78	88	106	109	...	67
France[2] France[2]	...	2 500	1 460	1 212	...	...	...	...	...	...
Germany Allemagne	...	...	...	15 085	21 222	15 955	13 049	11 730	...	11 396
F. R. Germany R. f. Allemagne	14 336	14 158	...	...	...	...	...	...		
Hungary Hongrie	2 027	1 929	1 257	75	78	15	4	...	...	...
Indonesia Indonésie	139	89	437	1 000	52	...	12 155	...	...	...
Japan Japon	39 152	40 171	33 929	22 973	14 496	11 936	14 678	16 414	17 097	12 531
Korea, Republic of[3] Corée, République de[3]	8 347	7 662	8 150	7 336	7 416	11 107	10 861	8 025	8 741	1 491
Lithuania Lituanie	...	...	...	...	...	...	749	437	333	192
Mexico Mexique	4 518	2 138	2 187	855	487	...	...	...	...	...
Poland Pologne	5 339	2 238	2 995	1 858	1 348	998	771	840	1 253	917
Portugal Portugal	...	...	...	75	52	...	...	...	...	...
Russian Federation Fédération de Russie	20 136	16 192	16 020	12 835	10 607	5 291	5 021	3 088	2 522	1 877
Slovakia Slovaquie	0	4	10	...	0	...	...	...	...	...
Slovenia Slovénie	542	137	114	60	0	...	...	...	4	0
Spain Espagne	5 043	3 688	2 567	2 060	886	1 738	2 313	2 185	2 689	3 380

55
Machine tools
Production: number [*cont.*]
　　　Machines-outils
　　　Production : nombre [*suite*]

Country or area Pays ou zone	1989	1990	1991	1992	1993	1994	1995	1996	1997	1998
Sweden Suède	...	...	...	...	...	...	...	...	3 158	3 667
Turkey Turquie	22	8	57	239	41	185	12	37	50	0
Ukraine Ukraine	...	4 482	7 970	11 113	12 996	3 745	1 337	563	667	418
United Kingdom Royaume-Uni	...	...	...	...	901	1 061	...	...	...	...
United States[4] Etats-Unis[4]	10 508	8 828	7 603	7 542	7 182	...	10 465	7 927	6 234	5 812
Yugoslavia Yougoslavie	...	...	924	607	276	206	328	100	106	133
Yugoslavia, SFR† Yougoslavie, Rfs†	2 355	...	...	...	...	...	...	...	...	...

B. Lathes • Tours

Country or area Pays ou zone	1989	1990	1991	1992	1993	1994	1995	1996	1997	1998
Algeria Algérie	150	270	273	310	194	118	196	189	110	14
Armenia Arménie	2 535	2 735	2 633	1 079	486	395	190	141	81	51
Austria Autriche	4 556	1 726	1 647	1 421	915	709	848	1 452	801	1 914
Bangladesh[5] Bangladesh[5]	23	4	13	3	1	1	...	...	...	...
Belarus Bélarus	...	...	...	162	332	57	70	93	117	131
Bulgaria Bulgarie	5 438	5 014	4 744	3 587	2 197	1 979	2 496	2 513	2 315	1 761
Colombia Colombie	...	...	...	97	103	155	112	...	...	...
Croatia Croatie	803	605	584	463	358	...	52	68	98	144
Czech Republic République tchèque	2 065	1 736	1 405	1 017	709	685	735	943	932	994
Denmark[1] Danemark[1]	...	545	384	279	374	...	...	...	...	...
Finland Finlande	2	4	1	1	1	2	3	2	...	...
France[4] France[4]	...	1 400	988	942	11	546	...	...	...	...
Georgia Géorgie	...	...	...	1 001	348	109	57	18	28	21
Germany Allemagne	...	...	...	7 689	4 755	5 322	8 232	6 375	5 542	6 070
F. R. Germany R. f. Allemagne	7 155	7 612	...	...	...	...	...	...	...	...
former German D. R.[6] l'ex-R. d. allemande[6]	2 481	...	...	...	...	...	...	...	...	...
Hungary Hongrie	943	663	304	63	135	33	7	...	...	...

55
Machine tools
Production: number [cont.]
Machines-outils
Production : nombre [suite]

Country or area Pays ou zone	1989	1990	1991	1992	1993	1994	1995	1996	1997	1998
Indonesia Indonésie	19	2	45	42	46	96	166	...	23	...
Japan Japon	32 748	32 659	26 216	16 155	12 343	14 961	20 339	21 443	23 357	22 652
Korea, Republic of Corée, République de	9 156	10 597	11 324	6 643	6 931	10 265	12 526	11 094	8 357	4 809
Latvia Lettonie	...	...	...	...	28	87	36	26	20	29
Lithuania Lituanie	9	81	95	110	93	27	64	4	1	6
Poland Pologne	3 824	5 178	2 184	1 105	910	900	1 012	1 037	900	963
Portugal Portugal	124	101	87	...	...	...	...	...	...	...
Romania Roumanie	4 747	3 702	2 883	1 583	489	312	471	587	681	573
Russian Federation Fédération de Russie	13 875	14 747	9 850	7 079	6 506	3 807	3 269	2 095	2 135	1 798
Slovakia Slovaquie	4 328	4 326	4 417	...	1 637	1 566	1 549	3 121	3 084	1 660
Spain Espagne	2 074	1 353	1 265	925	1 237	1 713	2 475	2 887	3 080	3 577
Sweden Suède	...	...	...	...	...	...	...	259	40	22
Turkey Turquie	47	43	23	2	10	59	11	16	0	0
Ukraine Ukraine	3 456	3 283	3 300	2 420	1 619	867	808	338	352	234
United Kingdom Royaume-Uni	5 275	5 742	...	...	2 429	2 941	3 568	3 845	3 077	3 377
United States[4] Etats-Unis[4]	3 789	3 247	2 658	2 409	3 042	3 662	4 643	4 190	5 058	5 089
Yugoslavia Yougoslavie	...	...	514	338	67	135	206	110	256	213
Yugoslavia, SFR† Yougoslavie, Rfs†	2 059	...	...	...	...	...	...	...	...	...

C. Milling machines · Fraiseuses

	1989	1990	1991	1992	1993	1994	1995	1996	1997	1998
Algeria Algérie	44	267	150	103	81	124	119	124	75	80
Armenia Arménie	1 088	951	759	410	0	63	73	47	188	80
Austria Autriche	1 142	458	526	844	223	209	284	362	249	279
Bangladesh Bangladesh	139	144	...	...	...	...	...	...	...	...
Belarus Bélarus	153	143	150	56	13	0	1	3	5	3
Bulgaria Bulgarie	1 450	1 240	961	432	324	200	227	295	412	173

55
Machine tools
Production: number [*cont.*]
Machines-outils
Production : nombre [*suite*]

Country or area Pays ou zone	1989	1990	1991	1992	1993	1994	1995	1996	1997	1998
Croatia Croatie	614	623	212	168	192	...	77	90	165	224
Czech Republic République tchèque	1 596	1 470	1 706	1 358	...	...	...	1 109	1 039	1 117
Denmark[1] Danemark[1]	292	...	201	200	0	0	0	...	...	...
Finland Finlande	100	...	...	...	...	...	...	...	...	...
France[4] France[4]	...	700	496	401	7	394	...	...	...	...
Germany Allemagne	...	...	...	...	6 680	6 327	...	5 213	5 335	5 348
F. R. Germany R. f. Allemagne	...	12 150	...	...	...	...	...	...	...	...
former German D. R. l'ex-R. d. allemande	3 135	3 051	...	...	...	...	...	...	...	...
Greece Grèce	1 890	1 805	1 452	...	...	...	...	...	...	...
Hungary Hongrie	66	136	297	256	50	3	...	...	...	...
Indonesia Indonésie	...	21	...	...	50	...	...	...	...	...
Japan Japon	8 612	8 492	7 584	3 913	2 007	1 791	1 832	2 198	2 368	2 019
Korea, Republic of Corée, République de	3 062	3 775	3 994	2 509	2 824	4 667	5 293	3 952	2 900	825
Latvia Lettonie	...	...	...	...	12	44	44	9	26	78
Lithuania Lituanie	1 873	1 538	1 303	1 035	450	341	255	213	161	130
Poland Pologne	1 448	1 196	834	500	248	260	274	281	354	257
Portugal Portugal	134	...	...	...	...	...	...	...	...	...
Romania Roumanie	2 073	1 196	1 355	764	436	162	341	458	403	321
Russian Federation Fédération de Russie	4 930	4 555	4 233	4 144	3 424	1 560	897	622	591	641
Slovenia Slovénie	...	...	13	12	15	26	27	...	...	...
Spain Espagne	8 057	7 062	4 169	4 553	788	1 458	1 600	1 852	1 605	3 086
Sweden Suède	...	98	...	48	22	27	25	...	...	...
Turkey Turquie	52	169	86	39	85	107	84	169	75	1
Ukraine Ukraine	1 180	1 341	1 208	1 040	752	195	90	48	161	168
United Kingdom Royaume-Uni	...	...	...	...	824	856	493	268	240	245

55
Machine tools
Production: number [*cont.*]
Machines-outils
Production : nombre [*suite*]

Country or area Pays ou zone	1989	1990	1991	1992	1993	1994	1995	1996	1997	1998
United States[4] Etats-Unis[4]	6 872	4 787	2 772	2 581	3 386	4 087	4 747	4 102	4 240	3 416
Yugoslavia Yougoslavie	...	...	15	...	...	...	...	...	...	...
Yugoslavia, SFR† Yougoslavie, Rfs†	921	...	...	...	...	...	...	...	...	...

D. Metal-working presses • Presses pour le travail des métaux

Country or area Pays ou zone	1989	1990	1991	1992	1993	1994	1995	1996	1997	1998
Armenia Arménie	124	292	206	45	100	29	43	34	31	18
Austria Autriche	52	...	...	...	...	...	...	...	...	...
Brazil Brésil	1 415	1 182	1 853	1 194	1 763	1 836	1 858	1 657	1 678	1 533
Colombia Colombie	...	...	...	16 992	13 366	22 661	26 344	...	...	...
Czech Republic République tchèque	132	113	82	106	47	60	114	231	239	...
Finland Finlande	121	126	98	17	6	180	1 764	2 159	2 101	2 285
France[4] France[4]	781	1 300	1 235	1 385	970	605	...	...	...	...
Germany Allemagne	...	...	17 726	55 997	18 939	23 284	16 399	...	21 531	...
F. R. Germany R. f. Allemagne	16 460	16 643	...	...	...	...	...	...	...	...
former German D. R. l'ex-R. d. allemande	2 366	1 781	...	...	...	...	...	...	...	...
Greece Grèce	405	328	320	355	...	...	...	...	...	...
Indonesia Indonésie	...	...	...	...	54	...	...	...	...	...
Japan Japon	21 574	22 571	19 173	12 458	9 516	9 531	10 512	10 068	11 575	8 546
Latvia Lettonie	78	15	3	...	...	...	...	...	...	...
Poland Pologne	63	50	44	13	11	8	2	2	15	...
Portugal Portugal	315	255	102	742	670	649	...	...	...	...
Slovakia Slovaquie	1 354	1 311	829	261	184	301	282	199	73	276
Slovenia Slovénie	603	1 334	119	92	145	153	215	719	...	...
Spain Espagne	2 035	1 600	2 152	1 687	2 436	723	5 452	...	...	...
Ukraine Ukraine	600	575	666	268	277	117	146	35	42	38
United Kingdom Royaume-Uni	...	...	...	...	667	615	...	...	827	...

55
Machine tools
Production: number [*cont.*]
    Machines-outils
    Production : nombre [*suite*]

Country or area Pays ou zone	1989	1990	1991	1992	1993	1994	1995	1996	1997	1998
United States[4] Etats-Unis[4]	8 959	7 285	5 912	5 822	6 236	10 947	5 045	11 023	12 084	12 559
Yugoslavia Yougoslavie	...	...	979	1 046	167	54	114	53	47	66
Yugoslavia, SFR[†] Yougoslavie, Rfs[†]	2 280	...	...	...	...	...	...	...	...	...

Source:
United Nations Secretariat, "Industrial Commodity Statistics Yearbook 1998" and the industrial statistics database of the Statistics Division.

† For information on recent changes in country or area nomenclature pertaining to former Czechoslovakia, Germany, Hong Kong Special Administrative Region (SAR) of China, Macao Special Administrative Region (SAR) of China, SFR of Yugoslavia and the former USSR, see Annex I - Country or area nomenclature, regional and other groupings.

1 Sales.
2 Limited coverage.
3 Drilling machines only.
4 Shipments.
5 Twelve months ending 30 June of year stated.

6 Excluding turning lathes for clock-makers.

Source:
Secrétariat de l'Organisation des Nations Unies, "Annuaire de statistiques industrielles par produit 1998" et la base de données pour les statistiques industrielles de la Division de statistique.

† Pour les modifications récentes de nomenclature de pays ou de zone concernant l'Allemagne, Hong Kong, région administrative spéciale (RAS) de Chine, Macao, région administrative spéciale (RAS) de Chine, l'ex-Tchécoslovaquie, l'ex-URSS et l'ex-Rfs de Yougoslavie, voir annexe I - Nomenclature des pays ou des zones, groupements régionaux et autres groupements.

1 Ventes.
2 Couverture limitée.
3 Perceuses seulement.
4 Expéditions.
5 Période de douze mois finissant le 30e juin de l'année indiquée.
6 Non compris les tours d'horloger.

56
Lorries (trucks)
Camions
Production: number
Production : nombre

Country or area Pays ou zone	1989	1990	1991	1992	1993	1994	1995	1996	1997	1998
A. Assembled • Assemblés										
Algeria Algérie	3 656	3 564	3 164	2 434	2 304	1 230	2 570	2 136	1 293	1 798
Bangladesh Bangladesh	806	504	1 090	715	452	642	1 047	922	1 000	...
Belgium[12] Belgique[12]	75 357	65 667	88 937	70 532	56 244	...	...	...	...	...
Chile[3] Chili[3]	8 377	8 028	9 400	14 352	16 584	15 960	...	...	...	...
Colombia Colombie	13 572[3]	12 660[3]	8 900[3]	10 116[3]	13 992[3]	15 660[3]	...	...	736	903
Cuba Cuba	542	...	...	...	...	...	...	...	...	...
Greece Grèce	2 897	1 715	1 534	1 920	62	...	57	128	...	...
Iran (Islamic Rep. of) Iran (Rép. islamique d')	8 086[4]	22 198[4]	32 672[4]	34 842[4]	21 234[4]	15 785[4]	8 836[5]	19 777[5]	16 761[5]	...
Israel Israël	1 174	1 074	864	852	836	1 260	1 217	1 199	...	...
Kenya Kenya	1 679	1 701	1 296	315	310	428	1 103	1 430	...	...
Malaysia[6] Malaisie[6]	38 607	73 733	78 926	34 711	34 711	42 618	55 961	78 571	94 977	19 693
Morocco[3] Maroc[3]	9 621	10 784	12 775	11 976	9 734	...	...	...	...	...
Myanmar[7] Myanmar[7]	229	166	117	85	172	846	500	550	255	31
Netherlands[8,9] Pays-Bas[8,9]	4 092	...	...	...	...	...	...	...	...	...
New Zealand * [6] Nouvelle-Zélande * [6]	...	13 500	13 500	10 210	...	...	...	...	...	...
Nigeria Nigéria	...	...	4 378	2 683	1 097	696	715	...	...	...
Pakistan[10] Pakistan[10]	13 756	13 324	13 911	13 270	13 700	6 522	5 857	9 864	12 733	11 736
Peru[3] Pérou[3]	3 019	2 921	2 000	600	768	...	...	...	...	...
Portugal Portugal	61 996	...	...	...	...	...	...	...	...	...
Slovakia Slovaquie	...	...	...	...	...	...	...	1 421	709	312
Slovenia Slovénie	434	451	611	...	1	...	...	...	...	...
South Africa Afrique du Sud	119 591	107 922	97 178	93 599	96 772	118 221	147 792	132 383	132 338	...
Thailand[3] Thaïlande[3]	155 094	236 221	206 172	223 680	323 508	324 780	...	...	...	...
Trinidad and Tobago[3] Trinité-et-Tobago[3]	381	1 124	1 711	1 698	1 083	621	0	0	...	...

56
Lorries (trucks)
Production: number [*cont.*]
Camions
Production : nombre [*suite*]

Country or area Pays ou zone	1989	1990	1991	1992	1993	1994	1995	1996	1997	1998
Tunisia Tunisie	478	1 024	1 065	768	922	1 084	616	954	1 003	1 016
Turkey Turquie	19 045	27 014	29 967	37 195	49 827	21 591	35 930	50 471	73 946	67 985
United Rep.Tanzania [11] Rép.-Unie de Tanzanie [11]	470	637	479	171	40	115	0	0	0	...
Venezuela Venezuela	6 000	12 000	24 000	30 000	...	...	...	...	...	...
Yugoslavia Yougoslavie	...	...	0	0	0	...	0	...	...	...
Yugoslavia, SFR† Yougoslavie, Rfs†	434	451	...	...	...	...	...	...	...	...

B. Produced · Fabriqués

Country or area Pays ou zone	1989	1990	1991	1992	1993	1994	1995	1996	1997	1998
Argentina [12] Argentine [12]	18 368	16 869	22 388	36 999	50 805	64 022	...	...	...	...
Armenia Arménie	10 864	9 410	6 823	3 171	1 247	446	232	114	27	51
Australia [10][13] Australie [10][13]	29 557	25 958	17 666	14 550	15 459	...	...	...	...	...
Austria Autriche	557	736	5 168	4 089	3 565	3 098	2 903	...	...	...
Azerbaijan Azerbaïdjan	3 028	3 104	3 246	402	93	8	2	1	0	0
Belarus Bélarus	43 036	42 034	38 178	32 951	30 771	21 264	12 902	10 671	13 002	12 792
Brazil [14] Brésil [14]	62 699	51 597	49 295	32 025	47 876	64 137	70 495	48 712	63 744	63 773
Bulgaria Bulgarie	7 888 [12]	7 285 [12]	2 778 [12]	945 [12]	406 [12]	321	259	66	43	...
Canada [15] Canada [15]	949 200	789 932	789 600	901 000	838 000	...	...	...	...	...
China †† Chine ††	363 400	289 700	382 500	476 700	597 897	662 600	595 997	625 100	573 600	...
Croatia Croatie	...	...	...	4	7	...	5	8	10	96
Czech Republic République tchèque	33 293	36 322	20 419	14 030	33 873	30 103	22 052	27 036	39 537	38 985
Egypt Egypte	1 475	1 371	1 127	1 529	1 208	1 379	1 241	738	328	...
Finland [12] Finlande [12]	852	910	545	578	435	546	540	492	493	687
France France	577 495	539 796	461 640	494 124	373 200	453 344	...	...	...	...
Georgia Géorgie	...	...	...	650	384	137	209	95	82	39
Germany Allemagne	...	...	356 059	325 901	240 014	259 575	...	240 604 [12]	272 916 [12]	292 581 [12]
F. R. Germany R. f. Allemagne	274 496	315 010	...	...	...	...	...	...	...	...

56
Lorries (trucks)
Production: number [cont.]
Camions
Production : nombre [suite]

Country or area Pays ou zone	1989	1990	1991	1992	1993	1994	1995	1996	1997	1998
former German D. R. l'ex-R. d. allemande	38 786	31 360	...	...	...	...	...	...	...	...
Hungary[3] Hongrie[3]	1 320	840	480	360	...	...	...	...	...	...
India[3 15] Inde[3 15]	115 200	145 200	146 400	141 600	148 800	163 200	...	...	...	...
Indonesia Indonésie	1 145	1 280	26	174	...	2 890	...	...	575	...
Italy Italie	240 807	234 393	229 860	194 616	155 476	191 288	234 354	188 852	256 062	278 322
Japan Japon	3 918 400	3 486 618	3 433 790	3 053 477	2 674 941	2 689 340	2 519 319	2 417 370	2 410 124	1 930 965
Korea, Republic of[12] Corée, République de[12]	169 703	237 384	245 232	293 260	310 639	332 263	331 328	340 179	297 565	182 218
Kyrgyzstan Kirghizistan	23 757	24 270	23 621	14 818	5 026	206	8	1	12	...
Mexico Mexique	184 725[12]	199 123[12]	238 804[12]	269 591[12]	222 807	217 359	210 072	396 377	468 931	445 125
Netherlands[8 16] Pays-Bas[8 16]	9 994	11 305	10 316	10 034	9 538	13 938	15 818	...	...	...
Poland[17] Pologne[17]	43 853	38 956	20 100	17 657	18 811	21 356	30 662	44 159	57 254	56 080
Romania Roumanie	13 515	8 457	7 592	4 456	4 433	3 044	3 098	3 142	1 956	1 263
Russian Federation Fédération de Russie	...	665 201	615 868	582 963	466 925	185 018	142 483	134 130	145 850	141 484
Slovakia Slovaquie	...	...	...	...	744	369	663	1 421	709	312
Slovenia Slovénie	2 875	1 721	1 513	377	424	397	277	195		
Spain Espagne	343 899[15]	302 400[15]	244 164	256 070	17 923[8 12]	32 217[8 12]	50 255[8 12]	73 319[8 12]	280 708[8 12]	342 632[8 12]
Sweden Suède	81 670[15]	74 400[15]	75 000[15]	...	...	...	...	...	51 378	61 348
Ukraine Ukraine	28 111	27 680	25 096	33 386	23 052	11 741	6 492	4 164	3 386	4 857
former USSR†*[15] l'ex-URSS†*[15]	900 000	...	...	...	...	...	...	...	...	...
United Kingdom Royaume-Uni	311 732	258 026	207 304	239 936	320 456	372 633	247 022	188 215	189 464	185 152
United States Etats-Unis	4 061 950[18]	3 720 000	3 372 000	4 118 578	...	...	...	...	...	...
Yugoslavia Yougoslavie	...	8 421	8 601	4 169	287	685	708	824	1 278	1 139
Yugoslavia, SFR† Yougoslavie, Rfs†	11 194	9 989	...	...	...	...	...	...	...	...

56
Lorries (trucks)
Production: number [*cont.*]

Camions
Production : nombre [*suite*]

Source:
United Nations Secretariat, "Industrial Commodity Statistics Yearbook 1998" and the industrial statistics database of the Statistics Division.

† For information on recent changes in country or area nomenclature pertaining to former Czechoslovakia, Germany, Hong Kong Special Administrative Region (SAR) of China, Macao Special Administrative Region (SAR) of China, SFR of Yugoslavia and the former USSR, see Annex I - Country or area nomenclature, regional and other groupings.

†† For statistical purposes, the data for China do not include those for Hong Kong Special Administrative Region (Hong Kong SAR), Macao Special Administrative Region (Macao SAR) and Taiwan province of China.

1 Production by establishments employing 5 or more persons.
2 Shipments.
3 Including motor coaches and buses.
4 Production by establishments employing 50 or more persons.
5 Production by establishments employing 10 or more persons.
6 Including vans and buses.
7 Government production only.
8 Sales.
9 Production by establishments employing 20 or more persons.
10 Twelve months ending 30 June of year stated.

11 Including buses.
12 Including assembly.
13 Finished and partly finished.
14 Trucks only.
15 Excluding production for armed forces.
16 Beginning 1986, production by establishments employing 20 or more persons.
17 Including special-purpose vehicles.
18 Factory sales.

Source:
Secrétariat de l'Organisation des Nations Unies, "Annuaire de statistiques industrielles par produit 1998" et la base de données pour les statistiques industrielles de la Division de statistique.

† Pour les modifications récentes de nomenclature de pays ou de zone concernant l'Allemagne, Hong Kong, région administrative spéciale (RAS) de Chine, Macao, région administrative spéciale (RAS) de Chine, l'ex-Tchécoslovaquie, l'ex-URSS et l'ex-Rfs de Yougoslavie, voir annexe I - Nomenclature des pays ou des zones, groupements régionaux et autres groupements.

†† Les données statistiques relatives à la Chine ne comprennent pas celles qui concernent la région administrative spéciale de Hong Kong (la RAS de Hong Kong), la région administrative spéciale de Macao (la RAS de Macao) et la province chinoise de Taiwan.

1 Production des établissements occupant 5 personnes ou plus.
2 Expéditions.
3 Y compris les autocars et autobus.
4 Production des établissements occupant 50 personnes ou plus.
5 Production des établissements occupant 10 personnes ou plus.
6 Y compris les autobus et les camionnettes.
7 Production de l'Etat seulement.
8 Ventes.
9 Production des établissements occupant 20 personnes ou plus.
10 Période de douze mois finissant le 30e juin de l'année indiquée.

11 Y compris les autobus.
12 Y compris le montage.
13 Finis et semi-finis.
14 Les camions seulement.
15 Non compris la production destinée aux forces armées.
16 A partir de 1986, production des établissements occupant 20 personnes ou plus.
17 Y compris véhicules à usages spéciaux.
18 Ventes des fabriques.

Technical notes, tables 37-56

Industrial activity includes mining and quarrying, manufacturing and the production of electricity, gas and water. These activities correspond to the major divisions 2, 3 and 4 respectively of the *International Standard Industrial Classification of All Economic Activities* [47].

Many of the tables are based primarily on data compiled for the United Nations *Industrial Commodity Statistics Yearbook* [23]. Data taken from alternate sources are footnoted.

The methods used by countries for the computation of industrial output are, as a rule, consistent with those described in the United Nations *International Recommendations for Industrial Statistics* [46] and provide a satisfactory basis for comparative analysis. In some cases, however, the definitions and procedures underlying computations of output differ from approved guidelines. The differences, where known, are indicated in the footnotes to each table.

A. Food, beverages and tobacco

Table 37: The statistics on sugar were obtained from the database and the *Sugar Yearbook* [15] of the International Sugar Organization. The data shown cover the production and consumption of centrifugal sugar from both beet and cane, and refer to calendar years.

The consumption data relate to the apparent consumption of centrifugal sugar in the country concerned, including sugar used for the manufacture of sugar-containing products whether exported or not and sugar used for purposes other than human consumption as food. Unless otherwise specified, the statistics are expressed in terms of raw value (i.e. sugar polarizing at 96 degrees). However, where exact information is lacking, data are expressed in terms of sugar "tel quel" and are footnoted accordingly. The world and regional totals also include data for countries not shown separately whose sugar consumption was less than 10 thousand metric tons.

Table 38: The data refer to meat from animals slaughtered within the national boundaries irrespective of the origin of the animals. Production figures of beef, veal, buffalo meat, pork (including bacon and ham), mutton, lamb and goat meat are in terms of carcass weight, excluding edible offals, tallow and lard. All data refer to total meat production, i.e from both commercial and farm slaughter.

Table 39: The data refer to beer made from malt, including ale, stout, porter.

Table 40 presents data on cigarettes only.

Notes techniques, tableaux 37 à 56

L'activité industrielle comprend les industries extractives (mines et carrières), les industries manufacturières et la production d'électricité, de gaz et d'eau. Ces activités correspondent aux grandes divisions 2, 3 et 4, respectivement, de la *Classification internationale type par industrie de toutes les branches d'activité économique* [47].

Un grand nombre de ces tableaux sont établis principalement sur la base de données compilées pour l'*Annuaire de statistiques industrielles par produit* des Nations Unies [23]. Les données tirées des autres sources sont signalées par une note.

En règle générale, les méthodes employées par les pays pour le calcul de leur production industrielle sont conformes à celles dans *Recommandations internationales concernant les statistiques industrielles* des Nations Unies [46] et offrent une base satisfaisante pour une analyse comparative. Toutefois, dans certains cas, les définitions des méthodes sur lesquelles reposent les calculs de la production diffèrent des directives approuvées. Lorsqu'elles sont connues, les différences sont indiquées par une note.

A. Alimentation, boissons et tabac

Tableau 37: Les données sur le sucre proviennent de la base de données et de l'*Annuaire du sucre* [15] de l'Organisation internationale du sucre. Les données présentées portent sur la production et la consommation de sucre centrifugé à partir de la betterave et de la canne à sucre, et se rapportent à des années civiles.

Les données de la consommation se rapportent à la consommation apparente de sucre centrifugé dans le pays en question, y compris le sucre utilisé pour la fabrication de produits à base de sucre, exportés ou non, et le sucre utilisé à d'autres fins que pour la consommation alimentaire humaine. Sauf indication contraire, les statistiques sont exprimés en valeur brute (sucre polarisant à 96°). Toutefois, en l'absence d'informations exactes, les données sont exprimées en sucre tel quel, accompagnées d'une note. Les totaux mondiaux et régionaux comprennent également les données relatives aux pays où la consommation de sucre est inférieure à 10.000 tonnes.

Le *tableau 38* indique la production de viande provenant des animaux abattus à l'intérieur des frontières nationales, quelle que soit leur origine. Les chiffres de production de viande de bœuf, de veau, de la viande de buffle, de porc (y compris le bacon et le jambon), de mouton et d'agneau (y compris la viande de chèvre) se rapportent à la production en poids de carcasses et ne comprennent pas le saindoux, le suif et les abats comestibles. Toutes les données se rapportent à la production totale de viande, c'est-à-dire à la fois aux animaux abattus

B.   *Textiles, wearing apparel, leather and leather products*

Table 41: The data on cotton fabrics refer to woven fabrics of cotton at the loom stage before undergoing finishing processes such as bleaching, dyeing, printing, mercerizing, lazing, etc.; those on wool refer to woollen and worsted fabrics before undergoing finishing processes. Fabrics of fine hair are excluded.

The data on woven fabrics of cellulosic and non-cellulosic fibres include fabrics of continuous and discontinuous rayon and acetate fibres, and non-cellulosic fibres other than textile glass fibres. Pile and chenille fabrics at the loom stage are also included.

Table 42: The data refer to the total production of leather footwear for children, men and women and all other footwear such as footwear with outer soles of wood or cork, sports footwear and orthopedic leather footwear. House slippers and sandals of various types are included, but rubber footwear is excluded.

C.   *Wood and wood products; paper and paper products*

Table 43: The data refer to the aggregate of sawnwood and sleepers, coniferous or non-coniferous. The data cover wood planed, unplaned, grooved, tongued and the like, sawn lengthwise or produced by a profile-chipping process, and planed wood which may also be finger-jointed, tongued or grooved, chamfered, rabbeted, V-jointed, beaded and so on. Wood flooring is excluded. Sleepers may be sawn or hewn.

Table 44 presents statistics on the production of all paper and paper board. The data cover newsprint, printing and writing paper, construction paper and paperboard, household and sanitary paper, special thin paper, wrapping and packaging paper and paperboard.

D.   *Chemicals and related products*

Table 45: The data refer to the production of rubber tires for passenger cars and commercial vehicles. Unless otherwise stated, the data do not cover tires for vehicles operating off the road, motorcycles, bicycles and animal-drawn road vehicles, or the production of inner tubes.

Table 46: Statistics on all hydraulic cements used for construction (portland, metallurgic, aluminous, natural, and so on) are shown.

Table 47: The data refer to H_2SO_4 in terms of pure monohydrate sulphuric acid, including the sulphuric acid equivalent of oleum or fuming sulphuric acid.

Table 48: The data on soaps refer to normal soaps of commerce, including both hard and soft soaps. Included are, in particular, household soaps, toilet soaps, transparent soaps, shaving soaps, medicated soaps, disinfectant soaps, abrasive soaps, resin and naphthenate

à des fins commerciales et des animaux sacrifiés à la ferme.

Tableau 39: Les données se rapportent à la bière produite à partir du malte, y compris ale, stout et porter (bière anglaise, blonde et brune).

Le *Tableau 40* se rapporte seulement aux cigarettes.

B.   *Textiles, articles d' habillement, cuir et articles en cuir*

Tableau 41: Les données sur les tissus de coton et de laine se rapportent aux tissus de coton, avant les opérations de finition, c'est-à-dire avant d'être blanchis teints, imprimés, mercerisés, glacés, etc., et aux tissus de laine cardée ou peignée, avant les opérations de finition. A l'exclusion des tissus de poils fins.

Les données sur les tissus de fibres cellulosiques et non-cellulosiques comprennent les tissus sortant du métier à tisser de fibres de rayonne et d'acétate et tissus composés de fibres non cellulosiques, autres que les fibres de verre, continues ou discontinues. Cette rubrique comprend les velours, peluches, tissus boucles et tissus chenille.

Tableau 42: Les données se rapportent à la production totale de chaussures de cuir pour enfants, hommes et dames et toutes les autres chaussures telles que chaussures à semelles en bois ou en liège, chaussures pour sports et orthopédiques en cuir. Chaussures en caoutchouc ne sont pas compris.

C.   *Bois et produits dérivés; papier et produits dérivés*

Tableau 43: Les données sont un agrégat des sciages de bois de conifères et de non-conifères et des traverses de chemins de fer. Elles comprennent les bois rabotés, non rabotés, rainés, languetés, etc. sciés en long ou obtenus à l'aide d'un procédé de profilage par enlèvement de copeaux et les bois rabotés qui peuvent être également à joints digitiformes languetés ou rainés, chanfreinés, à feuillures, à joints en V, à rebords, etc. Cette rubrique ne comprend pas les éléments de parquet en bois. Les traverses de chemin de fer comprennent les traverses sciées ou équaries à la hache.

Le *tableau 44* présente les statistiques sur la production de tout papier et carton. Les données comprennent le papier journal, les papiers d'impression et d'écriture, les papiers et cartons de construction, les papiers de ménage et les papiers hygiéniques, les papiers minces spéciaux, les papiers d'empaquetage et d'emballage et carton.

D.   *Produits chimiques et apparentés*

Tableau 45: Les données se rapportent à la production de pneus en caoutchouc pour voitures particulières et véhicules utilitaires. Sauf indication contraire, elles ne couvrent pas les pneus pour véhicules non routiers, motocyclettes, bicyclettes et véhicules routiers à traction ani-

soaps, and industrial soaps.

Washing powders and detergents refer to organic surface-active agents, surface-active preparations and washing preparations whether or not containing soap.

E.   *Basic metal industries*

Table 49 includes foundry and steel making pig-iron. Figures on crude steel include both ingots and steel for castings. In selected cases, data are obtained from the United States Bureau of Mines (Washington, D.C.), the Latin American Iron and Steel Institute (Santiago) and the United Nations Economic Commission for Europe. Detailed references to sources of data are given in the United Nations *Industrial Commodity Statistics Yearbook* [23].

Table 50: The data refer to aluminium obtained by electrolytic reduction of alumina (primary) and re-melting metal waste or scrap (secondary).

F.   *Fabricated metal products, machinery and equipment*

Table 51 presents data on the total production of all kinds of radio and television receivers.

Table 52: Passenger cars include three-and four-wheeled road motor vehicles other than motorcycle combinations, intended for the transport of passengers and seating not more than nine persons (including the driver), which are manufactured wholly or mainly from domestically-produced parts and passenger cars shipped in "knocked-down" form for assembly abroad.

Table 53: The data refer to refrigerators of the compression type or of the absorption type, of the sizes commonly used in private households. Insulated cabinets to contain an active refrigerating element (block ice) but no machine are excluded.

Table 54: These washing machines usually include electrically-driven paddles or rotating cylinders (for keeping the cleaning solution circulating through the fabrics) or alternative devices. Washing machines with attached wringers or centrifugal spin driers, and centrifugal spin driers designed as independent units, are included.

Table 55: The data on machine tools presented in this table include drilling and boring machines, lathes, milling machines, and metal-working presses. Drilling and boring machines refer to metal-working machines fitted with a baseplate, stand or other device for mounting on the floor, or on a bench, wall or another machine. Lathes refer to metal-working lathes of all kinds, whether or not automatic, including slide lathes, vertical lathes, capstan and turret lathes, production (or copying) lathes. Milling machines refer to metal-working machines designed to work a plane or profile surface by means of rotating tools, known as milling cutters. Metal-

male, ni la production de chambres à air.

Tableau 46: Les données sur tous les ciments hydrauliques utilisés dans la construction (portland métallurgique, alumineux, naturel, etc.) sont présentées.

Tableau 47: Les données se rapportent au H_2SO_4 sur la base de l'acide sulfurique monohydraté, y compris l'équivalent en acide sulfurique de l'oléum ou acide sulfurique fumant.

Tableau 48: Les données sur les savons se rapportent aux produits commercialement désignés sous le nom de savon, y compris les savons durs et les savons mous. Cette rubrique comprend notamment: les savons de ménage, les savons de toilette, les savons translucides, les savons à barbe, les savons médicinaux, les savons désinfectants, les savons abrasifs, les savons de résines ou de naphténates et les savons industriels.

Les poudres pour lessives et les détersifs se rapportent aux produits organiques tensio-actifs, préparations tensio-actives et préparations pour lessives contenant ou non du savon.

E.   *Industries métallurgiques de base*

Tableau 49: Les données se rapportent à la production de fonte et d'acier. Les données sur l'acier brut comprennent les lingots et l'acier pour moulage. Dans certains cas, les données proviennent du United States Bureau of Mines (Washington, D.C.), de l'Institut latino-américain du fer et de l'acier (Santiago) et de la Commission économique pour l'Europe. Pour plus de détails sur les sources de données, se reporter à *l'Annuaire des statistiques industrielles par produit* des Nations Unies [23].

Tableau 50: Les données se rapportent à la production d'aluminium obtenue par réduction électrolytique de l'alumine (production primaire) et par refusion de déchets métalliques (production secondaire).

F.   *Fabrications métallurgiques, machines et équipements*

Tableau 51: Les données sur la production totale de postes récepteurs de radiodiffusion et de télévision de toutes sortes sont présentées.

Tableau 52: Les voitures de tourisme comprennent les véhicules automobiles routiers à trois ou quatre roues, autres que les motocycles, destinés au transport de passagers, dont le nombre de places assises (y compris celle du conducteur) n'est pas supérieur à neuf et qui sont construits entièrement ou principalement avec des pièces fabriqués dans le pays, et les voitures destinées au transport de passagers exportées en pièces détachées pour être montées à l'étranger.

Tableau 53: Les données se rapportent aux appareils frigorifiques du type à compression ou à absorption de la taille des appareils communément utilisés dans les ménages. Cette rubrique ne comprend pas les glacières conçues

working presses are mechanical, hydraulic and pneumatic presses used for forging, stamping, cutting out, etc. Forge hammers are excluded. Detailed product definitions are given in the United Nations *Industrial Commodity Statistics Yearbook* [23].

Table 56 presents data on lorries, distinguishing between lorries assembled from imported parts and those manufactured wholly or mainly from domestically-produced parts. Both include road motor vehicles designed for the conveyance of goods, including vehicles specially equipped for the transport of certain goods, and articulated vehicles (that is, units made up of a road motor vehicle and a semi-trailer). Ambulances, prison vans and special purpose lorries and vans, such as fire-engines are excluded.

pour contenir un élément frigorifique actif (glace en bloc) mais non un équipement frigorifique.

Tableau 54: Ces machines à laver comprennent généralement des pales ou des cylindres rotatifs (destinés à assurer le brassage continu du liquide et du linge) ou des dispositifs à mouvements alternés, mus électriquement. Cette rubrique comprend les machines à laver avec essoreuses à rouleau ou essoreuses centrifuges et les essoreuses centrifuges conçues comme des appareils indépendants.

Tableau 55: Les données sur les machines-outils présentés dans ce tableau comprennent les perceuses, tours, fraiseuses, et presses pour le travail des métaux. Perceuses se rapportent aux machines-outils pour le travail des métaux, munies d'un socle, d'un pied ou d'un autre dispositif permettant de les fixer au sol, à un établi, à une paroi ou à une autre machine. Tours se rapportent aux tours à métaux, de tous types, automatiques ou non, y compris les tours parallèles, les tours verticaux, les tours à revolver, les tours à reproduire. Fraiseuses se rapportent aux machines-outils pour le travail des métaux conçues pour usiner une surface plane ou un profil au moyen d'outils tournants appelés fraises. Presses pour le travail des métaux se rapportent aux presses à commande mécanique, hydraulique et pneumatique servant à forger, à estamper, à matricer etc. Cette rubrique ne comprend pas les outils agissant par chocs. Pour plus de détails sur les description des produits se reporter à l'*Annuaire des statistiques industrielles par produit* [23] des Nations Unies.

Tableau 56 présente les données sur les camions et fait la distinction entre les camions assemblés à partir de pièces importées et les camions qui sont montés entièrement ou principalement avec des pièces importées. Les deux comprennent les véhicules automobiles routiers conçus pour le transport des marchandises, y compris les véhicules spécialement équipés pour le transport de certaines marchandises, et les véhicules articulés (c'est-à-dire les ensembles composés d'un véhicule automobile routier et d'une semi-remorque). Cette rubrique ne comprend pas les ambulances, les voitures cellulaires et les camions à usages spéciaux, tels que les voitures-pompes à incendie.

57
Railways: traffic
Chemins de fer : trafic
Passenger and net ton-kilometres: millions
Voyageurs et tonnes-kilomètres nettes : millions

Country or area Pays ou zone	1990	1991	1992	1993	1994	1995	1996	1997	1998	1999
Albania Albanie										
Passenger-kilometres Voyageurs-kilomètres	779	317	191	223	215	197	168	95	116	121
Net ton-kilometres Tonnes-kilomètres	584	278	60	54	53	53	42	23	25	26
Algeria Algérie										
Passenger-kilometres Voyageurs-kilomètres	2 991	3 192	2 904	3 009	2 234	1 574	1 826	1 360	1 163	· 1 069
Net ton-kilometres Tonnes-kilomètres	2 690	2 710	2 523	2 296	2 261	1 946	2 194	2 882	2 174	2 099
Argentina Argentine										
Passenger-kilometres[1] Voyageurs-kilomètres[1]	10 512	8 882	6 749	4 171	4 905	7 017	8 524	9 324	9 652	9 102
Net ton-kilometres Tonnes-kilomètres	7 578	5 460	4 388	4 477	6 613	7 613	8 505	9 835	9 852	9 094
Armenia Arménie										
Passenger-kilometres Voyageurs-kilomètres	316	320	446	435	353	166	84	84	52	...
Net ton-kilometres Tonnes-kilomètres	4 884	4 177	1 260	451	378	403	351	381	420	...
Australia Australie										
Net ton-kilometres[2] Tonnes-kilomètres[2]	85 840	88 260	89 276	92 123	97 779	99 727	104 311	114 500	125 200	127 200
Austria Autriche										
Passenger-kilometres Voyageurs-kilomètres	9 017	9 428	9 799	9 599	9 384	9 755	9 824	8 477	8 313	...
Net ton-kilometres Tonnes-kilomètres	12 796	12 981	12 321	11 922	13 164	13 857	14 066	14 993	15 552	...
Azerbaijan Azerbaïdjan										
Passenger-kilometres Voyageurs-kilomètres	1 827	1 975	1 629	1 330	1 081	791	558	491	533	422
Net ton-kilometres Tonnes-kilomètres	37 288	30 477	13 781	7 300	3 312	2 384	2 778	3 515	4 702	5 052
Bangladesh Bangladesh										
Passenger-kilometres[3] Voyageurs-kilomètres[3]	5 070	4 587	5 348	5 112	4 570	4 037	3 333	3 754	3 855	...
Net ton-kilometres[3] Tonnes-kilomètres[3]	643	651	718	641	641	760	689	782	804	...
Belarus Bélarus										
Passenger-kilometres[4] Voyageurs-kilomètres[4]	16 852	15 795	18 017	19 500	16 063	12 505	11 657	12 909	13 268	16 874
Net ton-kilometres Tonnes-kilomètres	75 430	65 551	56 441	42 919	27 963	25 510	26 018	30 636	30 370	30 529
Belgium Belgique										
Passenger-kilometres Voyageurs-kilomètres	6 539	6 771	6 798	6 694	6 638	6 757	6 788	6 984	7 097	...
Net ton-kilometres Tonnes-kilomètres	8 354	8 187	8 346	7 581	8 081	7 287	7 244	7 465	7 600	...
Benin Bénin										
Passenger-kilometres Voyageurs-kilomètres	97	63	62	75	107	...	...	...	...	...
Net ton-kilometres Tonnes-kilomètres	245	277	238	225	253	...	...	...	...	...
Bolivia Bolivie										
Passenger-kilometres Voyageurs-kilomètres	388	350	334	279	277	240	197	225	270	271

57
Railways: traffic
Passenger and net ton-kilometres: millions [*cont.*]
Chemins de fer : trafic
Voyageurs et tonnes-kilomètres nettes : millions [*suite*]

Country or area Pays ou zone	1990	1991	1992	1993	1994	1995	1996	1997	1998	1999
Net ton-kilometres Tonnes-kilomètres	541	682	714	695	782	758	780	839	908	832
Botswana Botswana										
Passenger-kilometres Voyageurs-kilomètres	82	103	75	95	119	110	81	82	71	...
Net ton-kilometres Tonnes-kilomètres	904	...	...	585	569	687	668	1 049	1 278	...
Brazil Brésil										
Passenger-kilometres[5] Voyageurs-kilomètres[5]	18 202	18 859	15 668	14 040	15 758	14 506	13 999	12 650	...	...
Net ton-kilometres[6] Tonnes-kilomètres[6]	120 439	121 414	116 599	124 677	133 734	136 060	128 088	138 867		
Bulgaria Bulgarie										
Passenger-kilometres Voyageurs-kilomètres	7 793	4 866	5 393	5 837	5 059	4 693	5 065	5 886	4 740	3 819
Net ton-kilometres[7] Tonnes-kilomètres[7]	14 132	8 585	7 758	7 702	7 774	8 595	7 549	7 444	6 152	5 297
Cambodia Cambodge										
Passenger-kilometres Voyageurs-kilomètres	33	42	69	97	39	38	22	51	44	50
Net ton-kilometres Tonnes-kilomètres	24	12	22	28	16	6	4	37	76	76
Cameroon Cameroun										
Passenger-kilometres Voyageurs-kilomètres	442	530	445	352	...	...	...	...	...	...
Net ton-kilometres Tonnes-kilomètres	684	679	613	653	...	...	...	...	...	...
Canada Canada										
Passenger-kilometres Voyageurs-kilomètres	2 004	1 426	1 439	1 413	1 440	1 473	1 519	1 515	...	...
Net ton-kilometres[7] Tonnes-kilomètres[7]	250 117	262 425	252 454	257 805	288 864	282 444	283 887	308 460	...	...
Chile Chili										
Passenger-kilometres Voyageurs-kilomètres	1 077	1 125	1 010	938	816	691	644	552	737	546
Net ton-kilometres Tonnes-kilomètres	2 787	2 717	2 738	2 496	2 371	2 262	2 366	2 330	2 650	2 647
China †† Chine ††										
Passenger-kilometres[8] Voyageurs-kilomètres[8]	261 263	282 810	315 224	348 330	363 605	354 570	332 537	354 825	369 598	...
Net ton-kilometres[8] Tonnes-kilomètres[8]	1 062 238	1 097 200	1 157 555	1 195 464	1 245 750	1 287 025	1 297 046	1 309 708	1 231 224	...
China, Hong Kong SAR† Chine, Hong Kong RAS†										
Passenger-kilometres[9] Voyageurs-kilomètres[9]	2 533	2 912	3 121	3 269	3 497	3 662	3 914	4 172	4 252	4 321
Net ton-kilometres[9] Tonnes-kilomètres[9]	70	65	61	51	47	41	30	24	15	15
Colombia Colombie										
Passenger-kilometres Voyageurs-kilomètres	141	79	16	...	...	...	...	...	...	...
Net ton-kilometres[7] Tonnes-kilomètres[7]	391	298	243	459	666	753	747	736	658	373
Congo Congo										
Passenger-kilometres Voyageurs-kilomètres	410	435	421	312	227	301	360	235	...	9
Net ton-kilometres Tonnes-kilomètres	421	397	350	257	122	267	289	139	...	21

57
Railways: traffic
Passenger and net ton-kilometres: millions [*cont.*]
Chemins de fer : trafic
Voyageurs et tonnes-kilomètres nettes : millions [*suite*]

Country or area Pays ou zone	1990	1991	1992	1993	1994	1995	1996	1997	1998	1999
Croatia Croatie										
Passenger-kilometres										
Voyageurs-kilomètres	3 429	1 503	981	951	962	943	1 029	981	921	943
Net ton-kilometres										
Tonnes-kilomètres	6 535	3 617	1 770	1 592	1 563	1 974	1 717	1 876	2 001	1 849
Cuba Cuba										
Passenger-kilometres										
Voyageurs-kilomètres	2 867	3 026	2 594	2 512	2 353	2 188	2 156	1 962	1 750	1 499
Net ton-kilometres										
Tonnes-kilomètres	1 995	1 368	1 059	764	653	745	871	859	822	806
Czech Republic République tchèque										
Passenger-kilometres										
Voyageurs-kilomètres	13 313	13 557	11 753	8 548	8 481	8 023	8 111	7 710	7 001	6 929
Net ton-kilometres[10]										
Tonnes-kilomètres[10]	41 150	32 679	31 116	25 579	24 393	25 395	24 174	22 173	19 529	17 625
Dem. Rep. of the Congo Rép. dém. du Congo										
Passenger-kilometres										
Voyageurs-kilomètres	469	...	...	...	...	...	...	...	...	...
Net ton-kilometres										
Tonnes-kilomètres	1 655	...	...	...	...	...	...	...	...	...
Denmark Danemark										
Passenger-kilometres										
Voyageurs-kilomètres	4 729	4 659	4 798	4 737	4 847	4 783	4 718	4 990	5 369	...
Net ton-kilometres[11]										
Tonnes-kilomètres[11]	1 787	1 858	1 870	1 751	2 008	1 985	1 757	1 983	2 058	...
Ecuador Equateur										
Passenger-kilometres										
Voyageurs-kilomètres	82	53	53	39	27	47	51	47	44	...
Net ton-kilometres										
Tonnes-kilomètres	5	2	3	3	9	3	1	...	...	...
Egypt Egypte										
Passenger-kilometres[2]										
Voyageurs-kilomètres[2]	28 684	20 950	36 644	49 025	51 098	52 839	55 638	60 617	64 077	...
Net ton-kilometres[2]										
Tonnes-kilomètres[2]	3 045	3 162	3 213	3 141	3 621	4 073	4 117	3 969	4 012	...
El Salvador El Salvador										
Passenger-kilometres										
Voyageurs-kilomètres	6	8	6	6	6	5	7	7	6	8
Net ton-kilometres										
Tonnes-kilomètres	38	35	38	35	30	13	17	17	24	19
Estonia Estonie										
Passenger-kilometres										
Voyageurs-kilomètres	1 510	1 273	950	722	537	421	309	261	236	238
Net ton-kilometres										
Tonnes-kilomètres	6 977	6 545	3 646	4 152	3 612	3 846	4 198	5 141	6 079	7 295
Ethiopia Ethiopie										
Passenger-kilometres[12 13]										
Voyageurs-kilomètres[12 13]	277	291	204	230	280	293	218	206	151	...
Net ton-kilometres[12 13]										
Tonnes-kilomètres[12 13]	126	122	84	112	102	93	104	106	90	...
Finland Finlande										
Passenger-kilometres										
Voyageurs-kilomètres	3 331	3 230	3 057	3 007	3 037	3 184	3 254	3 376	3 377	3 415
Net ton-kilometres[14]										
Tonnes-kilomètres[14]	8 357	7 634	7 848	9 259	9 949	9 293	8 806	9 856	9 885	9 753

57
Railways: traffic
Passenger and net ton-kilometres: millions [cont.]
Chemins de fer : trafic
Voyageurs et tonnes-kilomètres nettes : millions [suite]

Country or area Pays ou zone	1990	1991	1992	1993	1994	1995	1996	1997	1998	1999
France France										
Passenger-kilometres										
Voyageurs-kilomètres	63 740	62 300	62 230	58 610	58 930	55 560	59 770	61 830	64 450	...
Net ton-kilometres[15]										
Tonnes-kilomètres[15]	51 530	51 480	50 380	45 830	49 720	49 170	50 500	54 820	55 090	...
Georgia Géorgie										
Passenger-kilometres										
Voyageurs-kilomètres	2 457	2 135	1 210	917	1 165	371	380	294	397	349
Net ton-kilometres										
Tonnes-kilomètres	15 477	12 117	3 512	1 554	955	1 246	1 141	2 006	2 574	3 139
Germany Allemagne										
Passenger-kilometres										
Voyageurs-kilomètres	61 985	57 034	57 240	58 003	61 962	74 970	75 975	73 917	72 389	73 586
Net ton-kilometres										
Tonnes-kilomètres	103 093	82 219	72 848	66 660	71 814	70 863	69 713	73 763	74 051	71 455
Greece Grèce										
Passenger-kilometres										
Voyageurs-kilomètres	1 978	1 995	2 004	1 726	1 399	1 569	1 752	1 783	1 552	...
Net ton-kilometres[16]										
Tonnes-kilomètres[16]	647	605	563	523	325	306	350	330	322	...
Guatemala Guatemala										
Passenger-kilometres										
Voyageurs-kilomètres	15 960	12 531	9 151	3 427	991	...	...	...		
Net ton-kilometres										
Tonnes-kilomètres	44 134	47 233	66 472	29 186	25 295	14 242	836	...	...	...
Hungary Hongrie										
Passenger-kilometres										
Voyageurs-kilomètres	11 403	9 861	9 184	8 432	8 508	8 441	8 582	8 669	8 884	9 479
Net ton-kilometres										
Tonnes-kilomètres	16 781	11 938	10 015	7 708	7 707	8 422	7 634	8 149	8 150	7 715
India Inde										
Passenger-kilometres[17]										
Voyageurs-kilomètres[17]	295 644	314 564	300 103	296 245	319 365	341 999	357 013	379 897	403 884	...
Net ton-kilometres[17]										
Tonnes-kilomètres[17]	235 785	250 238	252 388	252 411	249 564	270 489	277 567	284 249	281 513	...
Indonesia Indonésie										
Passenger-kilometres										
Voyageurs-kilomètres	9 290	9 767	10 458	12 337	13 728	15 500	15 223	15 518	16 970	18 512
Net ton-kilometres										
Tonnes-kilomètres	3 190	3 470	3 779	3 955	3 854	4 172	4 700	5 030	4 963	5 035
Iran (Islamic Rep. of) Iran (Rép. islamique d')										
Passenger-kilometres										
Voyageurs-kilomètres	4 573	4 585	5 298	6 422	6 479	7 294	7 044	6 103	5 426	...
Net ton-kilometres										
Tonnes-kilomètres	7 629	7 701	8 002	9 124	10 700	11 865	13 638	14 400	12 638	...
Iraq Iraq										
Passenger-kilometres										
Voyageurs-kilomètres	1 316	436	926	1 566	2 334	2 198	...	...	...	...
Net ton-kilometres[18]										
Tonnes-kilomètres[18]	3 060	326	1 100	1 587	1 901	1 120	...	...	...	...
Ireland Irlande										
Passenger-kilometres										
Voyageurs-kilomètres	1 226	1 290	1 226	1 274	1 260	1 291	1 295	1 388	...	...
Net ton-kilometres										
Tonnes-kilomètres	582	600	633	575	569	602	570	522	469	...
Israel Israël										
Passenger-kilometres										
Voyageurs-kilomètres	166	186	198	214	238	269	294	346	383	529

57
Railways: traffic
Passenger and net ton-kilometres: millions [*cont.*]
Chemins de fer : trafic
Voyageurs et tonnes-kilomètres nettes : millions [*suite*]

Country or area Pays ou zone	1990	1991	1992	1993	1994	1995	1996	1997	1998	1999
Net ton-kilometres Tonnes-kilomètres	1 041	1 091	1 098	1 072	1 079	1 176	1 152	992	1 049	1 128
Italy Italie										
Passenger-kilometres Voyageurs-kilomètres	45 513	46 427	48 361	47 101	48 900	49 700	50 300	...	...	...
Net ton-kilometres [18] Tonnes-kilomètres [18]	21 217	21 680	21 830	20 226	22 564	24 050	23 314	...	...	...
Japan Japon										
Passenger-kilometres Voyageurs-kilomètres	383 735	396 472	403 245	401 864	402 513	393 907	400 712	301 510	391 073	...
Net ton-kilometres Tonnes-kilomètres	26 656	27 292	26 899	25 619	25 946	23 695	24 991	18 661	23 136	
Jordan Jordanie										
Passenger-kilometres Voyageurs-kilomètres	2	2	2	2	2	1	1	2	2	2
Net ton-kilometres Tonnes-kilomètres	711	791	797	711	676	698	735	625	596	585
Kazakhstan Kazakhstan										
Passenger-kilometres Voyageurs-kilomètres	19 734	19 365	19 671	20 507	17 362	13 159	14 188	12 802	10 681	...
Net ton-kilometres Tonnes-kilomètres	406 963	374 230	286 109	192 258	146 778	124 502	112 688	106 425	99 371	...
Kenya Kenya										
Passenger-kilometres Voyageurs-kilomètres	707	715	563	395	401	363	371	393	432	...
Net ton-kilometres Tonnes-kilomètres	1 992	1 943	1 784	1 479	1 172	1 456	1 309	1 068	1 111	...
Korea, Republic of Corée, République de										
Passenger-kilometres Voyageurs-kilomètres	29 932	33 470	34 787	33 693	31 912	29 292	29 580	30 073	32 976	...
Net ton-kilometres Tonnes-kilomètres	13 663	14 494	14 256	14 658	14 070	13 838	12 947	12 710	10 372	...
Kyrgyzstan Kirghizistan										
Passenger-kilometres Voyageurs-kilomètres	205	200	235	296	172	87	92	93	59	39
Net ton-kilometres Tonnes-kilomètres	2 620	2 415	1 589	923	629	403	481	472	466	354
Latvia Lettonie										
Passenger-kilometres Voyageurs-kilomètres	5 366	3 930	3 656	2 359	1 794	1 256	1 149	1 154	1 059	984
Net ton-kilometres [11] Tonnes-kilomètres [11]	18 538	16 739	10 115	9 852	9 520	9 757	12 412	13 970	12 966	12 210
Lithuania Lituanie [19]										
Passenger-kilometres [19] Voyageurs-kilomètres [19]	3 640	3 225	2 740	2 700	1 574	1 130	954	842	800	745
Net ton-kilometres [19] Tonnes-kilomètres [19]	19 258	17 748	11 337	11 030	7 996	7 220	8 103	8 622	8 265	7 849
Luxembourg Luxembourg										
Passenger-kilometres Voyageurs-kilomètres	261	272	255	262	289	286	284	295	300	310
Net ton-kilometres Tonnes-kilomètres	709	713	672	647	686	566	574	613	624	660
Madagascar Madagascar										
Passenger-kilometres Voyageurs-kilomètres [7]	198	...	...	...	...	...	...	...	...	...
Net ton-kilometres [7] Tonnes-kilomètres [7]	209	...	...	...	...	...	...	...	...	...

57
Railways: traffic
Passenger and net ton-kilometres: millions [cont.]
Chemins de fer : trafic
Voyageurs et tonnes-kilomètres nettes : millions [suite]

Country or area Pays ou zone	1990	1991	1992	1993	1994	1995	1996	1997	1998	1999
Malawi Malawi										
Passenger-kilometres [17]										
Voyageurs-kilomètres [17]	107	92	72	46	20	22	26	17	21	19
Net ton-kilometres [17]										
Tonnes-kilomètres [17]	76	56	52	43	58	74	57	46	55	62
Malaysia Malaisie										
Passenger-kilometres [20]										
Voyageurs-kilomètres [20]	1 830	1 763	1 618	1 543	1 348	1 270	1 370	1 492	1 397	1 313
Net ton-kilometres [20]										
Tonnes-kilomètres [20]	1 405	1 262	1 081	1 157	1 463	1 416	1 397	1 336	992	908
Mali Mali										
Passenger-kilometres										
Voyageurs-kilomètres	184	...	...	...	...	...	...	...	...	...
Net ton-kilometres										
Tonnes-kilomètres	273	...	208	191	220	254	405	...	...	...
Mexico Mexique										
Passenger-kilometres										
Voyageurs-kilomètres	5 336	4 686	4 794	3 219	1 855	1 899	1 799	1 508	460	218
Net ton-kilometres										
Tonnes-kilomètres	36 417	32 698	34 197	35 672	37 314	35 662	41 723	42 442	46 873	49 955
Mongolia Mongolie										
Passenger-kilometres										
Voyageurs-kilomètres	570	596	630	583	790	680	733	951	981	...
Net ton-kilometres										
Tonnes-kilomètres	5 088	3 013	2 756	2 531	2 132	2 280	2 529	2 254	2 815	...
Morocco Maroc										
Passenger-kilometres										
Voyageurs-kilomètres	2 237	2 345	2 233	1 904	1 881	1 564	1 776	1 856	1 875	...
Net ton-kilometres										
Tonnes-kilomètres	5 107	4 523	5 001	4 415	4 679	4 621	4 757	4 835	4 827	...
Myanmar Myanmar										
Passenger-kilometres										
Voyageurs-kilomètres	4 370	4 481	4 606	4 706	4 390	4 178	4 294	3 784	3 948	4 112
Net ton-kilometres [7]										
Tonnes-kilomètres [7]	525	581	601	663	726	659	748	674	988	1 043
Netherlands Pays-Bas										
Passenger-kilometres										
Voyageurs-kilomètres	11 060	15 195	14 980	14 788	14 439	13 977	14 131	14 485	14 879	...
Net ton-kilometres										
Tonnes-kilomètres	3 070	3 038	2 764	2 681	2 830	3 097	3 123	3 406	3 778	...
New Zealand Nouvelle-Zélande										
Net ton-kilometres [2]										
Tonnes-kilomètres [2]	2 744	2 364	2 475	2 468	2 835	3 202	3 260	3 505	3 547	3 636
Nigeria Nigéria										
Passenger-kilometres										
Voyageurs-kilomètres	555	475	451	55	220	161	170	179	...	...
Net ton-kilometres										
Tonnes-kilomètres	374	282	203	162	141	108	114	120	...	...
Norway Norvège										
Passenger-kilometres										
Voyageurs-kilomètres	2 136	2 153	2 201	2 341	2 398	2 381	2 120	2 426	2 496	2 691
Net ton-kilometres										
Tonnes-kilomètres	2 354	2 675	2 294	2 873	2 678	2 715	2 641	2 401	2 144	2 454
Pakistan Pakistan										
Passenger-kilometres [3]										
Voyageurs-kilomètres [3]	19 963	18 159	16 759	16 274	18 044	18 905	19 114	18 771	18 979	...
Net ton-kilometres [3]										
Tonnes-kilomètres [3]	5 704	5 964	5 860	5 940	5 660	5 078	4 538	4 444	3 939	...

57
Railways: traffic
Passenger and net ton-kilometres: millions [*cont.*]
Chemins de fer : trafic
Voyageurs et tonnes-kilomètres nettes : millions [*suite*]

Country or area Pays ou zone	1990	1991	1992	1993	1994	1995	1996	1997	1998	1999
Panama Panama										
Passenger-kilometres										
Voyageurs-kilomètres	44 260[21]	62 951[21]	54 234[21]	46 440[21]	59 590[22]	39 240[22]	11 740[22]	5 684[22]	...	...
Net ton-kilometres[23]										
Tonnes-kilomètres[23]	30 020	37 856	48 380	42 482	38 173	34 119	27 971	24 115	...	...
Paraguay Paraguay										
Passenger-kilometres										
Voyageurs-kilomètres	2	1	1	1	...	...	...	...	...	...
Net ton-kilometres										
Tonnes-kilomètres	4	3	3	3	...	...	...	...	...	...
Peru Pérou										
Passenger-kilometres[7]										
Voyageurs-kilomètres[7]	469	320	226	165	240	231	222	210	180	144
Net ton-kilometres[7]										
Tonnes-kilomètres[7]	809	860	837	850	864	843	878	833	892	891
Philippines Philippines										
Passenger-kilometres										
Voyageurs-kilomètres	271	182	121	102	106	163	69	172	181	171
Net ton-kilometres										
Tonnes-kilomètres	7	2	1	5	3	4	0[24]	0	0	...
Poland Pologne										
Passenger-kilometres										
Voyageurs-kilomètres	50 373	40 115	32 571	30 865	27 610	26 635	26 569	25 806	25 664	26 198
Net ton-kilometres										
Tonnes-kilomètres	83 530	65 146	57 763	64 359	65 788	69 116	68 332	68 651	61 760	55 471
Portugal Portugal										
Passenger-kilometres										
Voyageurs-kilomètres	5 664	5 692	5 494	5 397	5 149	4 840	4 503[25]	4 563[25]	4 602[25]	...
Net ton-kilometres										
Tonnes-kilomètres	1 588	1 784	1 767	1 786	1 826	2 342	2 178	2 632	2 340	...
Republic of Moldova République de Moldova										
Passenger-kilometres										
Voyageurs-kilomètres	1 464	1 280	1 718[4]	1 661[4]	1 204[4]	1 019[4]	882[4]	789[4]	656[4]	343[4]
Net ton-kilometres										
Tonnes-kilomètres	15 007	11 883	7 861	4 965	3 533	3 134	2 897	2 937	2 575	1 191
Romania Roumanie[26]										
Passenger-kilometres[26]										
Voyageurs-kilomètres[26]	30 582	25 429	24 269	19 402	18 313	18 879	18 356	15 795	13 422	12 304
Net ton-kilometres										
Tonnes-kilomètres	57 253	37 853	28 170	25 170	24 704	27 179	26 877	24 789	19 708	15 927
Russian Federation Fédération de Russie										
Passenger-kilometres										
Voyageurs-kilomètres	274 400	255 000	253 200	272 200	227 100	192 200	181 200	170 300	152 900	141 000
Net ton-kilometres										
Tonnes-kilomètres	2 523 000	2 326 000	1 967 000	1 608 000	1 195 000	1 214 000	1 131 000	1 100 000	1 020 000	1 205 000
Saudi Arabia Arabie saoudite										
Passenger-kilometres										
Voyageurs-kilomètres	159	144	135	136	153	159	170	192	222	224
Net ton-kilometres										
Tonnes-kilomètres	645	726	915	868	927	728	691	726	856	938
Senegal Sénégal										
Passenger-kilometres										
Voyageurs-kilomètres	183	173								
Net ton-kilometres										
Tonnes-kilomètres	612	485								
Slovakia Slovaquie										
Passenger-kilometres										
Voyageurs-kilomètres	6 381	6 002	5 453	4 569	4 548	4 202	3 769	3 057	3 092	2 967

57
Railways: traffic
Passenger and net ton-kilometres: millions [*cont.*]
Chemins de fer : trafic
Voyageurs et tonnes-kilomètres nettes : millions [*suite*]

Country or area Pays ou zone	1990	1991	1992	1993	1994	1995	1996	1997	1998	1999
Net ton-kilometres Tonnes-kilomètres	23 181	17 255	16 697	14 201	12 236	13 674	12 017	12 373	11 754	9 859
Slovenia Slovénie										
Passenger-kilometres Voyageurs-kilomètres	1 429	814	547	566	590	595	613	616	645	625
Net ton-kilometres Tonnes-kilomètres	4 209	3 246	2 573	2 262	2 448	3 076	2 550	2 852	2 859	2 784
South Africa Afrique du Sud										
Passenger-kilometres[27][28] Voyageurs-kilomètres[27][28]	1 628	1 205	1 038	895	686	1 007	1 198	1 393	1 775	1 794
Net ton-kilometres[27][28] Tonnes-kilomètres[27][28]	100 696	93 255	88 817	91 472	92 538	98 798	99 818	99 773	103 866	102 777
Spain Espagne										
Passenger-kilometres Voyageurs-kilomètres[7]	16 733	16 333	17 553	16 465	16 114	16 582	16 804	17 883	18 833	...
Net ton-kilometres[7] Tonnes-kilomètres[7]	11 613	10 755	9 513	8 059	8 966	10 419	10 449	11 488	11 739	...
Sri Lanka Sri Lanka										
Passenger-kilometres[29] Voyageurs-kilomètres[29]	2 781	2 698	2 613	2 822	2 230	3 433	3 220	3 290	3 267	...
Net ton-kilometres[29] Tonnes-kilomètres[29]	164	170	173	159	154	137	114	105	134	...
Sudan Soudan										
Passenger-kilometres Voyageurs-kilomètres	985	1 020	1 130	1 183	...	...	...	...	...	...
Net ton-kilometres Tonnes-kilomètres	1 970	2 030	2 120	2 240	...	...	...	...	...	...
Swaziland Swaziland										
Net ton-kilometres[2] Tonnes-kilomètres[2]	...	...	...	675	743	684	670	653	677	...
Sweden Suède										
Passenger-kilometres Voyageurs-kilomètres	6 353	5 745	5 587	6 001	6 063	6 364	6 216[10]	6 770[10]	6 997[10]	7 434[10]
Net ton-kilometres Tonnes-kilomètres	19 105	18 818	19 204	18 581	19 062	19 390	18 835[10]	19 114[10]	19 019[10]	18 905[10]
Switzerland Suisse										
Passenger-kilometres Voyageurs-kilomètres	12 678	13 834	13 209	13 384	13 836	13 408	13 326	...	...	...
Net ton-kilometres Tonnes-kilomètres	8 794	8 659	8 212	7 821	8 586	8 626	7 907	...	...	...
Syrian Arab Republic Rép. arabe syrienne										
Passenger-kilometres Voyageurs-kilomètres	1 140	1 314	1 254	855	769	498	454	294	182	...
Net ton-kilometres Tonnes-kilomètres	1 265	1 238	1 699	1 097	1 190	1 285	1 864	1 472	1 430	...
Tajikistan Tadjikistan										
Passenger-kilometres[30] Voyageurs-kilomètres[30]	842	888	103	117	366	134	95	129	121	61
Net ton-kilometres[30] Tonnes-kilomètres[30]	10 657	9 881	641	329	2 169	2 115	1 719	1 384	1 458	1 282
Thailand Thaïlande										
Passenger-kilometres[29] Voyageurs-kilomètres[29]	11 612	12 820	13 669	13 702	13 814	12 975	12 205	11 804	10 947	9 894
Net ton-kilometres[29] Tonnes-kilomètres[29]	3 291	3 365	3 075	3 059	3 072	3 242	3 286	3 410	2 874	2 929

57
Railways: traffic
Passenger and net ton-kilometres: millions [*cont.*]
Chemins de fer : trafic
Voyageurs et tonnes-kilomètres nettes : millions [*suite*]

Country or area Pays ou zone	1990	1991	1992	1993	1994	1995	1996	1997	1998	1999
TFYR Macedonia L'ex-R.y. Macédoine										
Passenger-kilometres										
Voyageurs-kilomètres	355	200	109	66	67	65	120	141	150	150
Net ton-kilometres										
Tonnes-kilomètres	769	712	577	493	151	169	271	279	408	380
Tunisia Tunisie										
Passenger-kilometres [16]										
Voyageurs-kilomètres [16]	1 019	1 020	1 078	1 057	1 038	996	988	1 094	1 130	1 200
Net ton-kilometres [7 31]										
Tonnes-kilomètres [7 31]	1 834	1 813	2 015	2 012	2 225	2 317	2 329	2 338	2 351	2 365
Turkey Turquie										
Passenger-kilometres										
Voyageurs-kilomètres	6 410	6 048	6 259	7 147	6 335	5 797	5 229	5 840	6 160	6 147
Net ton-kilometres										
Tonnes-kilomètres	8 031	8 093	8 383	8 517	8 339	8 632	9 018	9 717	8 377	8 265
Uganda Ouganda										
Passenger-kilometres										
Voyageurs-kilomètres	108	60	63	60	35	30	...	...	...	...
Net ton-kilometres										
Tonnes-kilomètres	103	139	119	130	208	245	...	...	...	...
Ukraine Ukraine										
Passenger-kilometres										
Voyageurs-kilomètres	76 038	70 968	76 196	75 896	70 882	63 759	59 080	54 540	49 938	47 600
Net ton-kilometres										
Tonnes-kilomètres	473 953	402 290	307 761	246 356	200 422	195 762	160 384	160 433	158 693	156 336
United Kingdom Royaume-Uni										
Passenger-kilometres [17 32]										
Voyageurs-kilomètres [17 32]	33 191	32 466	31 718	30 363	28 650	30 039	32 135	34 660	36 270	38 349
Net ton-kilometres [17 32]										
Tonnes-kilomètres [17 32]	16 000	15 300	15 550	13 765	12 979	13 136	15 144	16 949	17 369	18 409
United Rep.Tanzania Rép.-Unie de Tanzanie										
Passenger-kilometres										
Voyageurs-kilomètres	809	990	...	...	...	...	...	...	...	...
Net ton-kilometres										
Tonnes-kilomètres	956	983	...	...	...	...	...	...	...	...
United States Etats-Unis										
Passenger-kilometres [33]										
Voyageurs-kilomètres [33]	9 748	10 095	9 803	9 976	9 529	8 924	8 127	8 314	8 568	8 509
Net ton-kilometres [34]										
Tonnes-kilomètres [34]	1 509 592	1 516 754	1 557 492	1 619 588	1 753 020	1 906 300	1 979 719	1 969 428	2 009 696	2 237 707
Uruguay Uruguay										
Passenger-kilometres [35]										
Voyageurs-kilomètres [35]	-	-	-	221	467	...	...	17	14	...
Net ton-kilometres										
Tonnes-kilomètres	204	203	215	178	188	184	182	204	244	...
Uzbekistan Ouzbékistan										
Passenger-kilometres										
Voyageurs-kilomètres	4	5	6	5	5	3	2	2	2	2
Net ton-kilometres										
Tonnes-kilomètres	57	71	41	36	19	17	20	17	16	14
Venezuela Venezuela										
Passenger-kilometres										
Voyageurs-kilomètres	64	55	47	44	31	12	...	...	...	...
Net ton-kilometres										
Tonnes-kilomètres	35	40	36	26	47	53	...	...	...	...

57
Railways: traffic
Passenger and net ton-kilometres: millions [*cont.*]
Chemins de fer : trafic
Voyageurs et tonnes-kilomètres nettes : millions [*suite*]

Country or area Pays ou zone	1990	1991	1992	1993	1994	1995	1996	1997	1998	1999
Viet Nam Viet Nam										
Passenger-kilometres Voyageurs-kilomètres	1 913	1 767	1 752	1 921	1 796	2 133	2 261	2 476	2 542	2 723
Net ton-kilometres Tonnes-kilomètres	847	1 103	1 077	978	1 370	1 751	1 684	1 533	1 369	1 387
Yemen Yémen										
Passenger-kilometres Voyageurs-kilomètres	...	...	...	...	1 714	2 051	2 260	2 492	...	...
Yugoslavia Yougoslavie										
Passenger-kilometres Voyageurs-kilomètres	..	...	2 800	3 379	2 525	2 580	1 830	1 744	1 622	...
Net ton-kilometres [7] Tonnes-kilomètres [7]	..	...	4 409	1 699	1 387	1 460	2 062	2 432	2 743	
Yugoslavia, SFR† Yougoslavie, Rfs†										
Passenger-kilometres Voyageurs-kilomètres	4 794	2 935		..	..	..	..	...	...	...
Net ton-kilometres [7] Tonnes-kilomètres [7]	7 744	5 760		..	..	..	..	...	...	...
Zambia Zambie										
Passenger-kilometres Voyageurs-kilomètres	476	584	547	690	702	778	749	755	586	...
Net ton-kilometres Tonnes-kilomètres	...	141	...	123	151	90	666	758	702	...
Zimbabwe Zimbabwe										
Net ton-kilometres [2][36] Tonnes-kilomètres [2][36]	5 590	5 413	5 887	4 581	4 489	7 180	4 990	5 115	9 122	4 375

Source:
United Nations Secretariat, transport statistics database of
the Statistics Division.

† For information on recent changes in country or
area nomenclature pertaining to former Czechoslovakia,
Germany, Hong Kong Special Administrative Region (SAR) of
China, Macao Special Administrative Region (SAR) of China,
SFR of Yugoslavia and the former USSR, see Annex I - Country
or area nomenclature, regional and other groupings.

†† For statistical purposes, the data for
China do not include those for Hong Kong Special
Administrative Region (Hong Kong SAR), Macao Special
Administrative Region (Macao SAR) and Taiwan province of
China.

1 Including urban transport only.
2 Data refer to fiscal years ending 30 June of the year
indicated.
3 Data refer to fiscal years beginning 1 July of the year
indicated.
4 Including passengers carried without revenues.
5 Including urban railways traffic.

Source:
Secrétariat de l'Organisation des Nations Unies, la base de
données pour les statistiques des transports de la Division
de statistique.

† Pour les modifications récentes de nomenclature
de pays ou de zone concernant l'Allemagne, Hong Kong, région
administrative spéciale (RAS) de Chine, Macao, région
administrative spéciale (RAS) de Chine,
l'ex-Tchécoslovaquie, l'ex-URSS et l'ex-Rfs de Yougoslavie,
voir annexe I - Nomenclature des pays ou des zones,
groupements régionaux et autres groupements.

†† Les données statistiques relatives à
la Chine ne comprennent pas celles qui concernent la région
administrative spéciale de Hong Kong (la RAS de Hong Kong),
la région administrative spéciale de Macao (la RAS de Macao)
et la province chinoise de Taiwan.

1 Les chemins de fer urbains seulement.
2 Les données se réfèrent aux années fiscales finissant le 30e
juin de l'année indiquée.
3 Les données se réfèrent aux années fiscales commençant le
1er juillet de l'année indiquée.
4 Y compris passagers transportés gratuitement.
5 Y compris le trafic de chemins de fer urbains.

57

Railways: traffic
Passenger and net ton-kilometres: millions [*cont.*]

Chemins de fer : trafic
Voyageurs et tonnes-kilomètres nettes : millions [*suite*]

6 Including service traffic, animals, baggage and parcels.

7 Including service traffic.
8 May include service traffic.
9 Kowloon - Canton Railway only.
10 Including only state-owned railways.
11 Including passengers' baggage and parcel post (Latvia: also mail).
12 Including traffic of Djibouti portion of Djibouti-Addis Ababa line.
13 Data refer to fiscal years beginning 7 July of the year indicated.
14 Beginning 1995, wagon loads traffic only.
15 Including passengers' baggage.
16 Including military traffic (Greece: also government traffic).
17 Data refer to fiscal years beginning 1 April of the year indicated.
18 Excluding livestock.
19 Prior to 1994, data refer to operated ton-kilometres which is the weight in tons of freight carried multiplied by the distance in kilometres actually run; beginning 1994, data refer to net ton-kilometres which is the weight in tons of freight carried multiplied by distance in kilometres for which payments were made.
20 Peninsular Malaysia only.
21 National Railway of Chiriqui only.
22 Panama Railway and National Railway of Chiriqui.

23 Panama Railway only.
24 Freight train operations suspended from November 1995 to August 1996 due to typhoon damages.

25 Excluding river traffic of the railway company.

26 Including military, government and railway personnel (Latvia: railway personnel only; Romania: military and government only).

27 Data refer to fiscal years ending 31 March of the year indicated.
28 Beginning 1998, excluding Namibia.
29 Data refer to fiscal years ending 30 September of the year indicated.
30 Beginning 1992, decline due to border changes affecting the Dushanbe branch of the Csredniya Niyatskaya (Central Asia) Railway Co.
31 Ordinary goods only.
32 Excluding Northern Ireland.
33 Beginning 1986, excluding commuter railroads.

34 Class I railways only.
35 Passenger transport suspended from 1988 to 1992.

36 Including traffic in Botswana.

6 Y compris le trafic de service, les animaux, les bagages et les colis.
7 Y compris le trafic de service.
8 Le trafic de service peut être compris.
9 Chemin de fer de Kowloon - Canton seulement.
10 Y compris chemins de fer de l'état seulement.
11 Y compris les bagages des voyageurs et les colis postaux (Lettonie : courrier aussi).
12 Y compris le trafic de la ligne Djibouti-Addis Abéba en Djibouti.
13 Les données se réfèrent aux années fiscales commençant le 7e juillet de l'année indiquée.
14 A compter de 1995, trafic de charge de wagon seulement.
15 Y compris les bagages des voyageurs.
16 Y compris le trafic militaire (Grèce: et de l'Etat aussi).
17 Les données se réfèrent aux années fiscales commençant le 1er avril de l'année indiquée.
18 Non compris le bétail.
19 Avant de 1994, les données se réfèrent aux tonnes-kilomètres transportées, c'est-à-dire le produit du poids et de la distance effectivement parcourue. A partir de l'année 1994, l'unité utilisée est la tonne-kilomètre nette, c'est-à-dire le produit du poids et de la distance pour lequel un paiement à été effectué.
20 Malaisie péninsulaire seulement.
21 Chemin de fer national de Chiriqui seulement.
22 Chemin de fer de Panama et chemin de fer national de Chiriqui.
23 Chemin de fer de Panama seulement.
24 Les opérations de train de marchandises interrompues pendant la période de novembre 1995 à août 1996 à cause des dommages de typhon.
25 Non compris le trafic fluvial de la compagnie des chemins de fer.
26 Y compris le militaires, les fonctionnaires et le personnel de chemin de fer (Lettonie : le personnel de chemins de fer seulement ; Roumanie : les militaires et les fonctionnaires seulement).
27 Les données se réfèrent aux années fiscales finissant le 31e mars de l'année indiquée.
28 A partir de 1988, non compris la Namibie.
29 Les données se réfèrent aux années fiscales finissant le 30e septembre de l'année indiquée.
30 A compter de 1992, réduction imputable à des changements de frontière affectant la ligne de Douchanbé de la Compagnie Csredniya Niyatskaya (Asie centrale).
31 Petite vitesse seulement.
32 Non compris l'Irlande du Nord.
33 A partir de 1986, non compris les chemins de fer de banlieue.
34 Réseaux de catégorie 1 seulement.
35 Transport passager interrompu pendant la période 1988 à 1992.
36 Y compris le trafic en Botswana.

58
Motor vehicles in use
Véhicules automobiles en circulation

Passenger cars and commercial vehicles: thousand units
Voitures de tourisme et véhicules utilitaires : milliers de véhicules

Country or area Pays or zone	1990	1991	1992	1993	1994	1995	1996	1997	1998	1999
World Monde [1]										
Passenger cars [1]										
Voitures de tourisme [1]	441 957.6	451 927.6	445 741.8	449 989.7	469 302.6	457 762.8	470 586.6	481 755.2	...	...
Commercial vehicles [1]										
Véhicules utilitaires [1]	137 869.4	141 929.8	139 575.4	141 022.8	149 548.2	165 367.5	186 867.0	196 055.6	...	...
Afghanistan Afghanistan										
Passenger cars										
Voitures de tourisme	31.0	31.0	31.0	1.6	1.6	1.6	4.1	4.6	4.9	...
Commercial vehicles										
Véhicules utilitaires	25.0	25.0	25.0	0.6	0.6	0.6	...	...	...	...
Albania Albanie										
Passenger cars										
Voitures de tourisme	...	...	...	56.7	67.9	58.6	67.2	76.8	90.7	99.0
Commercial vehicles										
Véhicules utilitaires	...	...	...	39.3	51.1	29.1	30.6	33.2	37.1	40.9
Algeria Algérie										
Passenger cars										
Voitures de tourisme	1 465.8	1 502.6	1 528.3	1 547.8	1 555.8	1 562.1	1 588.0	1 615.1	1 634.4	...
Commercial vehicles										
Véhicules utilitaires	885.8	903.9	917.2	926.0	930.8	933.1	958.1	952.7	963.9	...
American Samoa Samoa américaines										
Passenger cars										
Voitures de tourisme	4.3	4.2	5.0	4.6	4.6	4.7	5.4	5.3	5.7	6.2
Commercial vehicles										
Véhicules utilitaires	0.4	0.3	0.3	0.5	0.4	0.4	0.5	0.5	0.7	0.7
Angola Angola										
Passenger cars [1]										
Voitures de tourisme [1]	122.0	122.0	122.0	19.3	20.4	22.1	24.1	26.2	...	...
Commercial vehicles [1]										
Véhicules utilitaires [1]	41.0	41.0	42.2	16.6	17.5	19.1	21.7	26.2	...	...
Antigua and Barbuda Antigua-et-Barbuda										
Passenger cars										
Voitures de tourisme	18.1	19.2	13.5	14.8	15.0	15.1	21.6 [2]	23.7 [2]	24.0 [2]	...
Commercial vehicles										
Véhicules utilitaires	4.3	3.8	3.5	4.6	4.8	4.8	...	...	...	...
Argentina Argentine										
Passenger cars										
Voitures de tourisme	4 283.7	4 405.0	4 809.0	4 856.0	4 427.0	4 665.0	4 783.9	4 904.3	6 047.8	...
Commercial vehicles										
Véhicules utilitaires	1 500.8	1 554.0	1 648.0	1 664.0	1 239.0	1 238.0	1 286.9	1 372.5	1 496.5	...
Australia Australie [3]										
Passenger cars [3]										
Voitures de tourisme [3]	7 672.2	7 734.1	7 913.2	8 050.0	8 209.0	8 660.6	9 021.5	9 239.5	9 560.6	...
Commercial vehicles [3]										
Véhicules utilitaires [3]	2 104.3	1 915.4	2 041.3	2 043.0	2 151.0	1 990.3	2 075.6	2 111.7	2 177.4	...
Austria Autriche										
Passenger cars [4]										
Voitures de tourisme [4]	2 991.3	3 100.0	3 244.9	3 367.6	3 479.6	3 599.6	3 691.7	3 782.5	3 887.2	4 009.6
Commercial vehicles [4,5]										
Véhicules utilitaires [4,5]	648.3	657.6	674.6	685.7	698.2	710.1	721.1	736.2	752.1	758.0
Azerbaijan Azerbaïdjan										
Passenger cars										
Voitures de tourisme	260.2	260.0	258.3	263.3	276.4	278.3	273.7	271.3	281.3	311.6
Commercial vehicles										
Véhicules utilitaires	154.4	148.5	141.3	132.3	127.5	125.5	122.9	115.6	117.6	122.8
Bahamas Bahamas										
Passenger cars										
Voitures de tourisme	69.0 [1]	69.0 [1]	44.7 [1]	46.1 [1]	54.4	67.1	48.6 [1]	66.1 [1]	...	...

58
Motor vehicles in use
Passenger cars and commercial vehicles: thousand units [cont.]
Véhicules automobiles en circulation
Voitures de tourisme et véhicules utilitaires : milliers de véhicules [suite]

Country or area / Pays or zone	1990	1991	1992	1993	1994	1995	1996	1997	1998	1999
Commercial vehicles / Véhicules utilitaires	14.0[1]	14.0[1]	11.5[1]	11.9[1]	9.3	13.7	12.7[1]	16.2[1]	...	...
Bahrain Bahreïn										
Passenger cars / Voitures de tourisme	103.2	105.7	113.8	122.9	130.7	135.4	140.0	147.9	...	...
Commercial vehicles / Véhicules utilitaires	24.2	25.0	26.5	28.2	29.4	30.5	31.5	39.7	...	...
Bangladesh Bangladesh										
Passenger cars / Voitures de tourisme	42.1	44.2	45.6	46.6	48.1	51.1	55.8	61.2	65.0	...
Commercial vehicles / Véhicules utilitaires	76.6	82.2	87.5	92.4	99.4	111.7	126.8	138.1	145.9	...
Barbados Barbade										
Passenger cars[4] / Voitures de tourisme[4]	41.9	42.5	41.0	45.5	42.6	...	...	...	...	...
Commercial vehicles[4,6] / Véhicules utilitaires[4,6]	6.8	8.6	6.6	6.6	6.8	...	...	...	...	...
Belarus Bélarus										
Passenger cars / Voitures de tourisme	604.5	657.2	722.8	773.6	875.6	939.6	1 035.8	1 132.8	1 279.2	1 351.1
Belgium Belgique										
Passenger cars / Voitures de tourisme	3 814.6	3 934.0	3 991.6	4 079.5	4 208.1	4 270.3	4 336.1	4 412.1	4 488.5	4 580.0
Commercial vehicles / Véhicules utilitaires	396.0	414.3	420.0	427.7	444.4	457.1	471.8	491.3	510.1	539.0
Belize Belize										
Passenger cars[8] / Voitures de tourisme[8]	2.6[7]	2.8[7]	1.7[9]	1.9[9]	1.9[9]	1.7[9]	1.8[9]	1.9[9]	1.9[9]	...
Commercial vehicles[8] / Véhicules utilitaires[8]	1.0[7]	1.2[7]	0.3[10]	0.4[10]	0.4[10]	0.4[10]	0.4[10]	0.4[10]	0.5[10]	...
Benin Bénin										
Passenger cars[1] / Voitures de tourisme[1]	22.0	22.0	22.0	7.1	7.3	7.3	7.3	7.3	...	...
Commercial vehicles[1] / Véhicules utilitaires[1]	12.0	12.0	12.2	5.3	5.5	5.7	5.8	6.0	...	...
Bermuda Bermudes										
Passenger cars / Voitures de tourisme	19.7	20.1	19.7	20.1	20.7	21.1	21.2	21.6	22.0	...
Commercial vehicles / Véhicules utilitaires	3.8	3.6	3.9	4.0	4.2	4.4	4.1	4.2	5.0	...
Bolivia Bolivie										
Passenger cars / Voitures de tourisme	119.1	131.2	146.6	164.7	183.7	201.9	220.3	234.1	254.1	264.7
Commercial vehicles / Véhicules utilitaires	73.1	80.2	87.7	95.3	103.4	112.2	119.8	124.8	132.0	137.0
Botswana Botswana										
Passenger cars / Voitures de tourisme	22.0	20.8	23.4	26.3	27.1	30.5	26.7	28.2	37.0	43.6
Commercial vehicles / Véhicules utilitaires	41.3	45.3	49.2	55.0	60.9	63.7	48.1	52.3	58.7	67.9
Brazil Brésil										
Passenger cars[1] / Voitures de tourisme[1]	...	12 128.0	7 855.5	8 098.4	9 524.0	10 320.5	12 666.0	12 723.5	...	...
Commercial vehicles[1] / Véhicules utilitaires[1]	...	1 075.0	1 170.8	1 839.0	2 378.7	2 520.4	2 896.0	2 907.6	...	...
British Virgin Islands Iles Vierges britanniques										
Passenger cars[2] / Voitures de tourisme[2]	6.2	6.5	6.9	6.7	7.0	...	...	...	...	...

58
Motor vehicles in use
Passenger cars and commercial vehicles: thousand units [cont.]
Véhicules automobiles en circulation
Voitures de tourisme et véhicules utilitaires : milliers de véhicules [suite]

Country or area Pays or zone	1990	1991	1992	1993	1994	1995	1996	1997	1998	1999
Brunei Darussalam Brunéi Darussalam										
Passenger cars										
Voitures de tourisme	106.6	114.1	122.0	130.0	135.9	141.7	150.1	163.1	170.2	176.0
Commercial vehicles										
Véhicules utilitaires	11.4	11.9	13.7	14.5	15.4	16.3	17.3	18.3	19.1	19.4
Bulgaria Bulgarie										
Passenger cars										
Voitures de tourisme	1 317.4	1 359.0	1 411.3	1 505.5	1 587.9	1 647.6	1 707.0	1 730.5	1 809.4	1 908.4
Commercial vehicles										
Véhicules utilitaires	195.4	209.8	224.5	243.2	255.4	264.2	270.7	273.2	283.8	293.5
Burkina Faso Burkina Faso										
Passenger cars										
Voitures de tourisme	22.4	25.0	27.4	29.9	32.0	...	...	...	...	...
Commercial vehicles										
Véhicules utilitaires	19.3	21.0	22.2	23.4	24.0	...	...	...	...	...
Burundi Burundi										
Passenger cars										
Voitures de tourisme	15.0	16.4	17.5	18.5	17.5	...	...	...	...	...
Commercial vehicles										
Véhicules utilitaires	10.4	11.3	11.8	12.3	10.2	...	...	...	...	...
Cambodia Cambodge										
Passenger cars										
Voitures de tourisme	5.3	5.6	10.8	6.8	7.4	8.0	6.3	8.4	8.0	8.5
Commercial vehicles										
Véhicules utilitaires	0.9	2.9	0.9	0.7	1.7	2.1	1.4	1.8	1.6	1.5
Cameroon Cameroun										
Passenger cars										
Voitures de tourisme	63.4	57.2	90.0[1]	90.0[1]	60.3[1]	60.3[1]	50.4[1]	50.4[1]	...	...
Commercial vehicles										
Véhicules utilitaires	34.3	30.9	79.0[1]	79.0[1]	47.6[1]	48.3[1]	47.1[1]	47.4[1]	...	...
Canada Canada										
Passenger cars[4]										
Voitures de tourisme[4]	12 622.0	13 061.1	13 322.5	13 477.9	13 639.4	13 182.9	13 217.3	13 486.9	...	...
Commercial vehicles[4]										
Véhicules utilitaires[4]	3 931.3	3 679.8	3 688.0	3 712.4	3 764.9	3 485.2	3 644.5	3 526.9	...	...
Cape Verde Cap-Vert										
Passenger cars										
Voitures de tourisme	4.0	4.4	5.5	6.5	7.7	8.0	9.3	10.3	11.4	13.2
Commercial vehicles										
Véhicules utilitaires	1.0	1.2	1.2	1.3	2.0	2.0	2.2	2.5	2.8	3.3
Cayman Islands Iles Caïmanes										
Passenger cars										
Voitures de tourisme	10.7	10.8	11.3	11.6	12.3	13.5	14.9	16.0	...	...
Commercial vehicles										
Véhicules utilitaires	2.4	2.6	2.6	2.7	2.8	9.1	3.4	3.7	...	...
Central African Rep. Rép. centrafricaine										
Passenger cars										
Voitures de tourisme	12.2	9.2	8.0	10.4	11.9	8.9	...	...	...	...
Commercial vehicles										
Véhicules utilitaires	3.0	2.3	1.7	2.4	2.8	3.5	...	...	...	...
Chad Tchad										
Passenger cars[11]										
Voitures de tourisme[11]	8.5	8.5	9.0	9.5	9.5	8.7	...	...	...	...
Commercial vehicles[11]										
Véhicules utilitaires[11]	6.5	6.5	7.0	7.2	7.2	12.4	...	...	...	...
Chile Chili										
Passenger cars										
Voitures de tourisme	710.4	765.5	826.8	896.5	914.3	1 026.0	1 121.2	1 175.8	1 236.9	1 323.8

58
Motor vehicles in use
Passenger cars and commercial vehicles: thousand units [cont.]
Véhicules automobiles en circulation
Voitures de tourisme et véhicules utilitaires : milliers de véhicules [suite]

Country or area Pays or zone	1990	1991	1992	1993	1994	1995	1996	1997	1998	1999
Commercial vehicles[13] Véhicules utilitaires[13]	178.2[12]	192.0[12]	198.8[12]	211.0[12]	492.7[14]	540.0[14]	585.7[14]	620.5[14]	656.0[14]	691.1[14]
China †† Chine ††										
Passenger cars Voitures de tourisme	1 621.9	1 852.4	2 261.6	2 859.8	3 497.4	4 179.0	4 880.2	5 805.6	6 548.3	...
Commercial vehicles Véhicules utilitaires	3 684.8	3 986.2	4 414.5	5 010.0	5 603.3	5 854.3	5 750.3	6 012.3	6 278.9	...
China, Hong Kong SAR† Chine, Hong Kong RAS†										
Passenger cars Voitures de tourisme	214.9	229.3	254.6	277.5	297.3	303.3	311.2	332.8	336.2	339.6
Commercial vehicles Véhicules utilitaires	131.8	132.4	134.4	135.6	137.0	134.2	133.7	135.9	133.4	132.3
China, Macao SAR † Chine, Macao RAS †										
Passenger cars[13] Voitures de tourisme[13]	24.7	26.2	29.9	32.6	34.0	34.5	38.9	42.9	46.3	47.8
Commercial vehicles[13] Véhicules utilitaires[13]	6.4	6.5	6.5	6.6	6.3	6.2	6.3	6.6	6.6	7.4
Colombia Colombie										
Passenger cars[1] Voitures de tourisme[1]	715.0	715.0	715.0	761.7	688.1	718.9	800.0	823.0	...	...
Commercial vehicles[1] Véhicules utilitaires[1]	665.0	665.0	665.0	672.6	385.1	405.6	530.0	380.4	...	...
Congo Congo										
Passenger cars[1] Voitures de tourisme[1]	26.0	26.0	26.0	29.0	29.0	29.0	29.0	29.0	...	...
Commercial vehicles[1] Véhicules utilitaires[1]	20.0	20.0	20.1	16.6	16.6	16.6	16.6	16.6	...	...
Costa Rica Costa Rica										
Passenger cars Voitures de tourisme	168.8[4]	180.8[4]	204.2[4]	220.1[4]	238.5[4]	254.8[4]	272.9[4]	294.1	316.8	...
Commercial vehicles Véhicules utilitaires	95.1[4]	96.3[4]	110.3[4]	114.9[4]	127.1[4]	141.4[4]	151.1[4]	153.1	164.8	
Côte d'Ivoire Côte d'Ivoire										
Passenger cars[1] Voitures de tourisme[1]	155.0	155.0	155.3	109.9	109.9	111.9	74.2	76.2	...	...
Commercial vehicles[1] Véhicules utilitaires[1]	90.0	90.0	90.3	46.1	47.1	50.3	35.3	35.3	...	...
Croatia Croatie										
Passenger cars Voitures de tourisme	795.4	735.7	669.8	646.2	698.4	710.9	835.7	932.3	1 000.0	1 063.5
Commercial vehicles Véhicules utilitaires	68.0	58.4	53.6	55.0	68.5	77.4	99.5	114.5	120.6	123.4
Cyprus[15] Chypre										
Passenger cars[15] Voitures de tourisme[15]	177.8[4]	189.7[4]	197.8[4]	203.2[4]	210.0[4]	219.4[4]	226.5[4]	234.6	248.8	256.6
Commercial vehicles Véhicules utilitaires	76.6[4]	84.3[4]	89.2[4]	92.6[4]	97.1[4]	103.9[4]	106.8[4]	108.5	112.0	114.0
Czech Republic République tchèque										
Passenger cars Voitures de tourisme	2 366.7	2 435.6	2 522.4	2 693.9	2 967.3[16]	3 113.5[16]	3 349.0[16]	3 547.7[16]	3 687.5[16]	3 695.8[16]
Commercial vehicles[17] Véhicules utilitaires[17]	500.2	511.8	523.3	515.2	469.5[18]	490.0[18]	537.1[18]	562.3[18]	604.0[18]	583.3[18]
Dem. Rep. of the Congo Rép. dém. du Congo										
Passenger cars Voitures de tourisme	145.1	...	...	...	...	...	...	...	...	...
Commercial vehicles Véhicules utilitaires	92.8	...	...	...	...	...	...	...	...	...

58
Motor vehicles in use
Passenger cars and commercial vehicles: thousand units [*cont.*]
Véhicules automobiles en circulation
Voitures de tourisme et véhicules utilitaires : milliers de véhicules [*suite*]

Country or area Pays or zone	1990	1991	1992	1993	1994	1995	1996	1997	1998	1999
Denmark Danemark										
Passenger cars[4][19]										
Voitures de tourisme[4][19]	1 590.3	1 593.9	1 604.6	1 618.3	1 611.2	1 679.0	1 738.9	1 783.1	1 817.1	...
Commercial vehicles[4][19]										
Véhicules utilitaires[4][19]	302.4	309.4	376.6	326.4	335.6	347.6	353.6	359.8	371.5	...
Djibouti Djibouti										
Passenger cars[11]										
Voitures de tourisme[11]	13.0	13.0	13.0	13.5	13.5	...	...	...	...	...
Commercial vehicles[11]										
Véhicules utilitaires[11]	2.0	2.5	3.0	3.0	3.0	...	...	...	...	...
Dominica Dominique										
Passenger cars										
Voitures de tourisme	4.1	4.5	4.8	5.8	7.0	7.4	7.9	8.3	8.7	...
Commercial vehicles[20]										
Véhicules utilitaires[20]	3.1	3.4	2.8	2.7	2.8	2.9	3.3	3.3	3.4	...
Dominican Republic Rép. dominicaine										
Passenger cars										
Voitures de tourisme	148.0	144.7	138.1	174.4	...	183.8	271.0	331.0	394.6	...
Commercial vehicles										
Véhicules utilitaires	94.1[21]	98.6[21]	97.5[21]	118.5[21]	...	106.2	145.1	174.9	...	...
Ecuador Equateur										
Passenger cars										
Voitures de tourisme	165.6	181.2	194.5	202.4	219.8	253.5	268.2	276.5	301.4	...
Commercial vehicles										
Véhicules utilitaires	207.3	206.0	232.7	231.4	243.4	244.0	248.4	256.3	257.6	...
Egypt Egypte										
Passenger cars										
Voitures de tourisme	1 054.0	1 081.0	1 117.0	1 143.0	1 225.0	1 313.0	1 372.0	1 435.0	1 525.0	...
Commercial vehicles										
Véhicules utilitaires	380.0	389.0	408.0	423.0	445.0	466.0	484.0	508.0	539.0	...
El Salvador El Salvador										
Passenger cars										
Voitures de tourisme	52.0[1]	53.0[1]	80.5	88.4	86.9	113.8	...	...	...	508.6[22]
Commercial vehicles										
Véhicules utilitaires	65.0[1]	65.0[1]	140.2	165.9	195.5	209.9	...	...	...	...
Estonia Estonie										
Passenger cars										
Voitures de tourisme	242.0	261.1	283.5	317.4	337.8	383.4	406.6	427.7	451.0	458.7
Commercial vehicles										
Véhicules utilitaires	75.6	85.7	83.0	82.8	60.0	72.6	78.0	83.1	86.9	87.2
Ethiopia Ethiopie										
Passenger cars[23]										
Voitures de tourisme[23]	38.5	40.2	40.0	29.9	42.1	45.6	...	...	...	...
Commercial vehicles[23]										
Véhicules utilitaires[23]	20.3	20.2	18.8	16.6	18.1	20.9	...	...	...	...
Fiji Fidji										
Passenger cars[24]										
Voitures de tourisme[24]	40.2	42.0	44.0	45.3	47.7	49.7	51.7	50.4	51.7	...
Commercial vehicles[25]										
Véhicules utilitaires[25]	39.9	41.9	43.8	44.8	46.4	47.5	48.5	48.0	48.6	...
Finland Finlande										
Passenger cars[26]										
Voitures de tourisme[26]	1 938.9	1 922.5	1 936.3	1 872.9	1 872.6	1 900.9	1 942.8	1 948.1	2 021.1	2 082.6
Commercial vehicles[26][27]										
Véhicules utilitaires[26][27]	273.5	273.4	271.2	261.4	257.5	260.1	266.9	275.4	289.7	303.2

58
Motor vehicles in use
Passenger cars and commercial vehicles: thousand units [*cont.*]
Véhicules automobiles en circulation
Voitures de tourisme et véhicules utilitaires : milliers de véhicules [*suite*]

Country or area Pays or zone	1990	1991	1992	1993	1994	1995	1996	1997	1998	1999
France France										
Passenger cars										
Voitures de tourisme	23 550.0	23 810.0	24 020.0	24 385.0	24 900.0	25 100.0	25 500.0	26 090.0	26 810.0	...
Commercial vehicles[28]										
Véhicules utilitaires[28]	5 075.0	5 190.0	5 209.0	5 238.0	5 314.0	5 374.0	5 437.0	5 561.0	5 680.0	...
French Guiana Guyane française										
Passenger cars[1]										
Voitures de tourisme[1]	25.0	27.0	27.7	29.1	24.4	26.5	28.2	28.2	...	...
Commercial vehicles[1]										
Véhicules utilitaires[1]	9.0	10.0	10.4	10.6	7.6	8.1	8.9	9.4	...	...
Gabon Gabon										
Passenger cars[11]										
Voitures de tourisme[11]	22.0	23.0	23.0	24.0	24.0	23.0	...			
Commercial vehicles[11]										
Véhicules utilitaires[11]	16.0	17.0	17.0	17.5	18.0	10.0	...	...		
Gambia Gambie										
Passenger cars										
Voitures de tourisme	5.0	6.7	7.4	6.1	6.2	6.4	...	...	...	...
Commercial vehicles										
Véhicules utilitaires	2.2	2.5	2.8	3.4	3.5	3.5	...	...	...	...
Georgia Géorgie										
Passenger cars										
Voitures de tourisme	481.9	479.3	479.0	485.9	452.3	360.6	323.6	265.6	260.4	247.9
Commercial vehicles										
Véhicules utilitaires	98.4	96.5	138.6	147.7	101.2	104.3	90.7	79.6	71.0	51.3
Germany Allemagne										
Passenger cars										
Voitures de tourisme	30 684.8	32 087.6	36 042.4	38 772.5	39 765.4	40 404.3	40 987.5	41 372.0	41 673.8	42 323.7
Commercial vehicles										
Véhicules utilitaires	...	...	...	...	2 619.3	2 754.9	2 851.4	2 931.3	3 068.1	...
Ghana Ghana										
Passenger cars[1]										
Voitures de tourisme[1]	82.2	90.0	90.0	30.4	30.7	30.8	31.2	31.9	...	...
Commercial vehicles[1]										
Véhicules utilitaires[1]	42.1	43.0	44.2	31.5	33.1	35.7	38.4	38.4	...	...
Gibraltar Gibraltar										
Passenger cars										
Voitures de tourisme	19.8	18.1	24.0	18.0	18.5	18.4	...	...	...	...
Commercial vehicles										
Véhicules utilitaires	2.5	2.6	2.9	1.1	1.2	1.0	...	...	...	...
Greece Grèce										
Passenger cars										
Voitures de tourisme	1 735.5	1 777.5	1 829.1	1 958.5	2 074.1	2 204.8	2 339.4	2 500.1	2 676.0	2 929.0
Commercial vehicles										
Véhicules utilitaires	787.9	814.9	820.5	848.9	872.6	908.4	939.9	977.5	1 014.0	1 051.0
Greenland Groenland										
Passenger cars[4]										
Voitures de tourisme[4]	2.0	1.9	2.0	2.1	1.9	1.9	2.6	1.8	2.0	2.4
Commercial vehicles[4]										
Véhicules utilitaires[4]	1.2	1.5	1.5	1.4	1.6	1.4	1.2	1.5	1.4	1.5
Guadeloupe Guadeloupe										
Passenger cars[1]										
Voitures de tourisme[1]	86.0	89.0	94.7	101.6	90.5	97.0	106.5	107.6	...	...
Commercial vehicles[1]										
Véhicules utilitaires[1]	34.0	35.0	36.0	37.5	26.6	28.9	32.5	34.1	...	...
Guam Guam										
Passenger cars										
Voitures de tourisme	...	72.8	76.7	74.7	...	79.8	79.1	...	...	...

58
Motor vehicles in use
Passenger cars and commercial vehicles: thousand units [*cont.*]
Véhicules automobiles en circulation
Voitures de tourisme et véhicules utilitaires : milliers de véhicules [*suite*]

Country or area Pays or zone	1990	1991	1992	1993	1994	1995	1996	1997	1998	1999
Commercial vehicles Véhicules utilitaires	...	29.7	30.2	30.6	...	34.7	33.8	...	...	...
Guatemala Guatemala										
Passenger cars Voitures de tourisme	...	...	...	...	...	...	...	...	646.5	...
Commercial vehicles Véhicules utilitaires	...	...	...	...	...	...	...	...	21.2	...
Guinea Guinée										
Passenger cars Voitures de tourisme	60.9	65.6	23.1[11]	24.0[11]	24.0[11]	23.2[11]	...	...	...	...
Commercial vehicles Véhicules utilitaires	27.8	29.0	13.0[11]	13.5[11]	14.0[11]	13.0[11]	...	...	...	...
Guinea-Bissau Guinée-Bissau										
Passenger cars[11] Voitures de tourisme[11]	3.3	3.3	3.5	...	...	...	...	...	...	...
Commercial vehicles[11] Véhicules utilitaires[11]	2.4	2.4	2.5	...	...	...	...	...	...	...
Guyana Guyana										
Passenger cars[1] Voitures de tourisme[1]	24.0	24.0	24.0	9.5	9.5	9.5	9.5	9.5	...	...
Commercial vehicles[1] Véhicules utilitaires[1]	9.0	9.0	9.0	2.6	2.7	2.9	3.0	3.1	...	...
Haiti Haïti										
Passenger cars Voitures de tourisme	25.8	32.0	32.0	32.0	30.0	49.0	59.0	...	...	93.0
Commercial vehicles Véhicules utilitaires	9.6	21.0	21.0	21.0	30.0	29.0	35.0	...	...	61.6
Honduras Honduras										
Passenger cars Voitures de tourisme	38.6	43.7	68.5	...	15.1[1]	16.1[1]	16.3[1]	16.5[1]	...	...
Commercial vehicles Véhicules utilitaires	80.4	92.9	102.0	...	45.3[1]	48.0[1]	48.6[1]	49.1[1]	...	...
Hungary Hongrie										
Passenger cars Voitures de tourisme	1 944.6	2 015.5	2 058.3	2 091.6	2 176.9	2 245.4	2 264.2	2 297.1	2 218.0	2 255.5
Commercial vehicles Véhicules utilitaires	288.5	289.6	288.9	296.2	318.5	345.0	351.3	360.9	355.4	363.0
Iceland Islande										
Passenger cars Voitures de tourisme	119.7	120.9	120.1	116.2	116.2	119.2	124.9	132.5	140.4	151.4
Commercial vehicles[29] Véhicules utilitaires[29]	14.5	16.0	16.0	15.6	15.6	16.0	16.6	17.5	18.1	19.3
India Inde										
Passenger cars Voitures de tourisme	2 694.0	2 954.0	3 205.0	3 361.0	3 569.0	3 841.0	4 204.0	4 662.0	...	...
Commercial vehicles[30] Véhicules utilitaires[30]	2 847.0	4 220.0	4 641.0	4 961.0	5 192.0	5 623.0	6 327.0	6 876.0	...	...
Indonesia Indonésie										
Passenger cars Voitures de tourisme	1 313.2	1 494.6	1 590.8	1 700.5	1 890.3	2 107.3	...	...	...	...
Commercial vehicles Véhicules utilitaires	1 492.8	1 592.7	1 666.0	1 729.0	1 903.6	2 024.7	...	...	...	...
Iran (Islamic Rep. of) Iran (Rép. islamique d')										
Passenger cars[1 31] Voitures de tourisme[1 31]	1 557.0	1 557.0	1 557.0	779.8	819.6	819.6	454.2	572.9	...	...
Commercial vehicles[1 31] Véhicules utilitaires[1 31]	533.0	561.0	584.1	589.2	589.2	589.2	346.4	346.4	...	...

58
Motor vehicles in use
Passenger cars and commercial vehicles: thousand units [cont.]
Véhicules automobiles en circulation
Voitures de tourisme et véhicules utilitaires : milliers de véhicules [suite]

Country or area Pays or zone	1990	1991	1992	1993	1994	1995	1996	1997	1998	1999
Iraq Iraq										
Passenger cars										
Voitures de tourisme	732.7	660.1	670.2	672.4	678.5	680.1	...	...	...	...
Commercial vehicles										
Véhicules utilitaires	288.2	295.0	299.5	309.3	317.2	319.9	...	...	...	...
Ireland Irlande										
Passenger cars[32 33 34]										
Voitures de tourisme[32 33 34]	802.7	843.2	865.4	898.3	947.2	999.7	1 067.8	1 145.9	1 209.2	
Commercial vehicles[20 32]										
Véhicules utilitaires[20 32]	149.5	155.2	152.0	142.9	143.9	150.5	155.9	168.2	181.0	
Israel Israël										
Passenger cars										
Voitures de tourisme	812.0	857.0	932.0	993.0	1 065.0	1 131.0	1 195.0	1 252.0	1 298.0	1 341.3
Commercial vehicles										
Véhicules utilitaires	166.0	178.0	200.0	217.0	250.0	263.0	279.0	292.0	298.0	308.9
Italy Italie										
Passenger cars										
Voitures de tourisme	27 415.8	28 434.9	29 429.6	29 652.0	29 665.3	30 149.6	...	...	...	...
Commercial vehicles										
Véhicules utilitaires	2 416.7	2 529.6	2 763.0	2 663.0	2 745.5	...	...	...	...	...
Jamaica Jamaïque										
Passenger cars										
Voitures de tourisme	68.5	77.8	73.0	81.1	86.8	104.0	120.7	156.8	...	...
Commercial vehicles										
Véhicules utilitaires	28.2	29.8	30.5	36.2	41.3	49.1	52.8	56.1	...	...
Japan Japon										
Passenger cars[35 36]										
Voitures de tourisme[35 36]	34 924.0	37 076.0	38 964.0	40 772.0	42 679.0	44 680.0	46 869.0	48 611.0	49 896.0	51 165.0
Commercial vehicles[35]										
Véhicules utilitaires[35]	21 571.0	21 575.0	21 383.0	21 132.0	20 916.0	20 676.0	20 334.0	19 859.0	19 821.0	18 869.0
Jordan Jordanie										
Passenger cars[4]										
Voitures de tourisme[4]	172.0	166.8	181.5	175.3	164.0	188.0	212.2	202.1	200.0	213.0
Commercial vehicles[4]										
Véhicules utilitaires[4]	68.3	61.4	51.5	63.8	75.3	76.7	80.6	85.1	106.9	109.0
Kazakhstan Kazakhstan										
Passenger cars										
Voitures de tourisme	809.7	848.9	916.1	955.9	991.7	1 034.1	997.5	973.3	971.2	987.7
Commercial vehicles										
Véhicules utilitaires	459.6	453.5	456.9	456.4	...	390.9	360.4	315.3	277.1	257.4
Kenya Kenya										
Passenger cars										
Voitures de tourisme	157.7	163.5	165.4	171.5	171.6	187.1	202.7	215.9	236.1	...
Commercial vehicles										
Véhicules utilitaires	114.7	130.8	158.1	162.2	162.3	174.9	187.7	199.1	204.3	
Korea, Republic of Corée, République de										
Passenger cars[37]										
Voitures de tourisme[37]	2 074.9	2 727.9	3 461.1	4 271.3	5 148.7	6 006.3	6 893.6	7 586.5	7 580.9	
Commercial vehicles[37]										
Véhicules utilitaires[37]	1 308.4	1 505.1	1 745.1	1 976.6	2 226.7	2 429.2	2 625.6	2 791.2	2 854.0	...
Kuwait Koweït										
Passenger cars										
Voitures de tourisme	...	554.7	579.8	600.0	629.7	662.9	701.2	540.0	585.0	624.0
Commercial vehicles										
Véhicules utilitaires	...	149.8	151.1	147.0	148.7	153.5	160.0	115.0	124.0	130.0
Kyrgyzstan Kirghizistan										
Passenger cars										
Voitures de tourisme	194.6	212.6	215.0	188.3	140.0	197.5	172.4	176.1	187.7	188.0

58

Motor vehicles in use
Passenger cars and commercial vehicles: thousand units [cont.]
Véhicules automobiles en circulation
Voitures de tourisme et véhicules utilitaires : milliers de véhicules [suite]

Country or area Pays or zone	1990	1991	1992	1993	1994	1995	1996	1997	1998	1999
Latvia Lettonie										
Passenger cars										
Voitures de tourisme	282.7	328.5	350.0	367.5	251.6	331.8	379.9	431.8	482.7	525.6
Commercial vehicles										
Véhicules utilitaires	79.0	83.3	83.3	72.1	73.5	85.1	90.2	95.4	96.5	101.8
Lebanon Liban										
Passenger cars										
Voitures de tourisme	...	...	...	943.1[38]	1 141.7[38]	1 197.5[38]	1 250.5	...	...	...
Commercial vehicles										
Véhicules utilitaires	...	...	...	77.3[38]	82.9[38]	84.7[38]	87.4		...	...	...
Liberia Libéria										
Passenger cars[1]										
Voitures de tourisme[1]	...	...	...	17.4	17.4	17.4	17.4	17.4	...	...
Commercial vehicles[1]										
Véhicules utilitaires[1]	...	...	...	10.7	10.7	10.7	10.7	10.7	...	...
Libyan Arab Jamah. Jamah. arabe libyenne										
Passenger cars										
Voitures de tourisme	448.0[11]	450.0[11]	448.0[11]	448.0[11]	448.0[11]	448.0[11]	829.0	859.0	...	...
Commercial vehicles										
Véhicules utilitaires	322.0[11]	330.0[11]	322.0[11]	322.0[11]	322.0[11]	322.0[11]	357.5	362.4	...	...
Lithuania Lituanie										
Passenger cars										
Voitures de tourisme	493.0	530.8	565.3	597.7	652.8	718.5	785.1	882.1	980.9	...
Commercial vehicles										
Véhicules utilitaires	105.9	107.7	112.5	115.1	118.2	125.9	104.8	108.6	114.6	...
Luxembourg Luxembourg										
Passenger cars										
Voitures de tourisme	183.4	191.6	200.7	208.8	217.8	229.0	231.7	236.8	244.1	253.4
Commercial vehicles[5]										
Véhicules utilitaires[5]	35.9	38.0	40.2	42.2	45.6	48.1	47.8	49.2	51.1	53.6
Madagascar Madagascar										
Passenger cars[1]										
Voitures de tourisme[1]	46.6	47.0	10.9	11.1	11.1	11.1	11.1	11.3	...	...
Commercial vehicles[1]										
Véhicules utilitaires[1]	33.1	33.0	12.6	13.3	13.3	13.3	13.9	15.5	...	...
Malawi Malawi										
Passenger cars[4]										
Voitures de tourisme[4]	35.3	# 6.6	5.3	1.8	2.3	1.5	1.6	...	...	...
Commercial vehicles[4]										
Véhicules utilitaires[4]	3.3	2.7	2.7	1.4	1.8	2.2	1.9	...	...	...
Malaysia Malaisie										
Passenger cars										
Voitures de tourisme	156.4	170.1	131.0	132.8	186.6	256.4	325.7	379.5	163.8	300.4
Commercial vehicles[27]										
Véhicules utilitaires[27]	47.7	49.3	43.7	33.5	49.9	74.9	102.7	96.5	19.0	28.6
Maldives Maldives										
Passenger cars										
Voitures de tourisme	0.1	0.1	0.1	0.1	0.2	0.1	0.2	0.2	0.2	0.2
Commercial vehicles										
Véhicules utilitaires	0.1	0.1	0.1	0.2	0.2	0.1	0.1	0.2	0.2	0.2
Mali Mali										
Passenger cars										
Voitures de tourisme	21.0	21.0	21.0	6.3	6.3	6.3	4.0	3.3	...	...
Commercial vehicles										
Véhicules utilitaires	8.0	8.0	8.4	6.6	6.8	7.2	5.6	3.4	...	...

58
Motor vehicles in use
Passenger cars and commercial vehicles: thousand units [cont.]
Véhicules automobiles en circulation
Voitures de tourisme et véhicules utilitaires : milliers de véhicules [suite]

Country or area Pays or zone	1990	1991	1992	1993	1994	1995	1996	1997	1998	1999
Malta Malte										
Passenger cars										
Voitures de tourisme	109.2	121.6	125.0	152.6	170.6	199.3	166.2	183.8	191.8	201.8
Commercial vehicles										
Véhicules utilitaires	20.5	21.7	35.4	50.9	55.7	40.8	39.4	47.4	49.5	51.2
Martinique Martinique										
Passenger cars[1]										
Voitures de tourisme[1]	92.0	96.0	102.6	80.8	86.7	95.0	...	...	...	...
Commercial vehicles[1]										
Véhicules utilitaires[1]	30.0	31.0	31.9	19.3	20.0	21.5	...	...	...	...
Mauritania Mauritanie										
Passenger cars[1]										
Voitures de tourisme[1]	8.0	8.0	8.0	5.0	5.1	5.1	5.2	5.3	...	...
Commercial vehicles[1]										
Véhicules utilitaires[1]	5.0	5.0	5.5	5.0	5.3	5.6	6.0	6.3	...	...
Mauritius Maurice										
Passenger cars										
Voitures de tourisme	45.5	48.6	52.4	55.8	59.6	63.6	68.1	73.4	78.5	83.0
Commercial vehicles										
Véhicules utilitaires	16.9	18.7	20.6	22.1	23.3	24.4	25.3	26.6	29.1	31.7
Mexico Mexique										
Passenger cars										
Voitures de tourisme	6 839.0	7 220.0	7 750.0	8 112.0	7 772.0	8 074.0	8 437.0	9 023.0	9 181.0	9 600.0
Commercial vehicles										
Véhicules utilitaires	3 077.0	3 404.0	3 601.0	3 695.0	3 759.0	3 751.0	3 773.0	4 034.0	4 404.0	4 629.0
Morocco Maroc										
Passenger cars[13]										
Voitures de tourisme[13]	669.6	707.1	778.9	849.3	944.0	992.0	1 018.1	1 060.3	1 108.7	...
Commercial vehicles[13]										
Véhicules utilitaires[13]	282.9	295.5	307.4	316.7	332.1	343.2	351.6	365.7	382.0	...
Mozambique Mozambique										
Passenger cars[1]										
Voitures de tourisme[1]	84.0	84.0	84.0	84.0	27.2	27.2	27.2	27.2	...	...
Commercial vehicles[1]										
Véhicules utilitaires[1]	25.0	26.0	26.2	26.8	14.3	14.4	14.5	14.5	...	...
Myanmar Myanmar										
Passenger cars[4]										
Voitures de tourisme[4]	78.1	88.6	100.2	115.9	125.4	145.4	171.3	177.9	177.6	171.3
Commercial vehicles[4]										
Véhicules utilitaires[4]	54.9	56.6	59.7	66.6	58.2	63.1	68.3	74.8	75.9	83.4
Nepal Népal										
Passenger cars										
Voitures de tourisme	21.2	24.1	26.2	28.4	31.5	34.5	39.8	42.8	46.9	49.4
Commercial vehicles										
Véhicules utilitaires	...	...	9.3	103.7	99.5	113.8	131.8	147.9	164.2	185.8
Netherlands Pays-Bas										
Passenger cars[4 39]										
Voitures de tourisme[4 39]	5 118.0	5 205.0	5 247.0	5 341.0	5 456.0	5 581.0	5 664.0	5 810.0	5 931.0	6 120.0
Commercial vehicles[4 39]										
Véhicules utilitaires[4 39]	539.0	565.0	590.0	631.0	652.0	654.0	666.0	695.0	738.0	806.0
New Caledonia Nouvelle-Calédonie										
Passenger cars										
Voitures de tourisme	54.0[1]	55.0[1]	56.7[1]	58.5[1]	50.4[1]	52.8[1]	55.1[1]	57.9[1]	76.4[2]	80.3[2]
Commercial vehicles[1]										
Véhicules utilitaires[1]	19.0	20.0	21.2	22.6	17.2	18.4	20.8	23.0	...	...

58
Motor vehicles in use
Passenger cars and commercial vehicles: thousand units [cont.]
Véhicules automobiles en circulation
Voitures de tourisme et véhicules utilitaires : milliers de véhicules [suite]

Country or area Pays or zone	1990	1991	1992	1993	1994	1995	1996	1997	1998	1999
New Zealand Nouvelle-Zélande										
Passenger cars										
Voitures de tourisme	1 500.5	1 551.3	1 554.9	1 575.6	1 615.9	1 665.0	1 655.8	1 697.2	1 768.2	1 905.6
Commercial vehicles										
Véhicules utilitaires	317.0	323.6	330.9	344.9	396.2	411.9	403.0	407.8	422.6	438.1
Nicaragua Nicaragua										
Passenger cars										
Voitures de tourisme	39.8	61.4	67.2	68.4	72.4	72.7	65.1	58.1	63.1	...
Commercial vehicles										
Véhicules utilitaires	33.9	54.8	69.5	66.3	69.5	81.8	82.9	70.6	78.9	...
Niger Niger										
Passenger cars										
Voitures de tourisme	17.0[11]	18.0[11]	16.0[1]	16.0[11]	16.0[11]	16.0[11]	...	...	...	...
Commercial vehicles										
Véhicules utilitaires	18.0[11]	18.0[11]	18.0[1]	18.0[11]	18.0[11]	18.0[11]	...	...	...	...
Nigeria Nigéria										
Passenger cars[40]										
Voitures de tourisme[40]	6.0	27.3	37.4	63.6	45.4	46.1	40.7	52.3	...	...
Commercial vehicles[40]										
Véhicules utilitaires[40]	0.8	1.1	4.6	1.4	6.8	8.6	10.5	13.5	...	...
Norway Norvège										
Passenger cars[4 41]										
Voitures de tourisme[4 41]	1 612.0	1 614.6	1 619.4	1 633.0	1 653.7	1 684.7	1 661.2	1 758.0	1 786.0	1 813.6
Commercial vehicles[4 41]										
Véhicules utilitaires[4 41]	330.6	334.3	341.6	352.5	366.3	382.0	392.1	412.2	427.0	437.4
Oman Oman										
Passenger cars[42]										
Voitures de tourisme[42]	143.5	169.2	171.3	184.3	194.5	204.0	220.4	245.1	279.1	281.1
Commercial vehicles[43]										
Véhicules utilitaires[43]	77.3	88.1	84.4	86.6	88.2	89.3	92.0	101.2	110.7	117.6
Pakistan Pakistan										
Passenger cars[4]										
Voitures de tourisme[4]	558.7	594.9	659.0	670.0	690.9	772.6	816.1	863.0	919.8	966.5
Commercial vehicles[4]										
Véhicules utilitaires[4]	224.8	235.8	262.9	269.6	285.8	305.8	333.6	351.7	378.9	396.8
Panama Panama										
Passenger cars										
Voitures de tourisme	132.9	144.2	149.9	161.2	169.8	178.3	188.3	198.7	212.6	...
Commercial vehicles										
Véhicules utilitaires	42.2	47.3	50.4	55.0	56.5	60.4	60.5	64.2	68.4	...
Papua New Guinea Papouasie-Nvl-Guinée										
Passenger cars[11]										
Voitures de tourisme[11]	...	...	11.5	13.0	11.5	20.0	...	...	...	...
Commercial vehicles[11]										
Véhicules utilitaires[11]	...	...	29.8	32.0	30.8	35.0	...	...	...	...
Paraguay Paraguay										
Passenger cars										
Voitures de tourisme	165.2	190.9	221.1	250.7	...	...	...	...	...	...
Commercial vehicles										
Véhicules utilitaires	25.7	30.7	34.9	37.7	...	...	...	...	...	...
Peru Pérou										
Passenger cars										
Voitures de tourisme	368.2	379.1	402.4	418.6	444.2	505.8	557.0	579.5	...	...
Commercial vehicles										
Véhicules utilitaires	237.4	244.9	270.6	288.8	316.6	356.8	379.5	410.8	...	...

58
Motor vehicles in use
Passenger cars and commercial vehicles: thousand units [cont.]
Véhicules automobiles en circulation
Voitures de tourisme et véhicules utilitaires : milliers de véhicules [suite]

Country or area Pays or zone	1990	1991	1992	1993	1994	1995	1996	1997	1998	1999
Philippines Philippines										
Passenger cars										
Voitures de tourisme	1 057.8	1 118.6	1 223.9	1 364.0	1 483.9	1 623.5	1 802.5	1 930.1	1 989.0	...
Commercial vehicles										
Véhicules utilitaires	147.4	156.1	172.2	189.7	207.3	220.9	249.6	274.7	263.0	...
Poland Pologne										
Passenger cars										
Voitures de tourisme	5 260.6	6 112.2	6 504.7	6 770.6	7 153.1	7 517.3	8 054.4	8 533.5	8 890.9	...
Commercial vehicles[44]										
Véhicules utilitaires[44]	1 138.1	1 240.2	1 299.5	1 321.9	1 395.1	1 442.3	1 522.2	1 579.0	1 657.1	...
Portugal Portugal										
Passenger cars[45][46]										
Voitures de tourisme[45][46]	2 552.3	2 774.7	3 049.8	3 295.1	3 532.0	3 751.0	4 002.6[47]	4 272.5[47]	4 587.3[47]	...
Commercial vehicles[46]										
Véhicules utilitaires[46]	812.8	881.2[13]	964.0	1 050.1	1 158.6	1 218.8	1 292.2[47]	1 383.9[47]	1 492.4[47]	...
Puerto Rico Porto Rico										
Passenger cars[3]										
Voitures de tourisme[3]	1 305.1	1 321.9	1 347.0	1 393.3	1 484.7	1 597.0	1 726.4	1 835.8	1 962.3	2 048.4
Commercial vehicles[3]										
Véhicules utilitaires[3]	188.4	192.1	201.5	239.6	257.7	270.6	290.2	288.8	298.8	339.0
Qatar Qatar										
Passenger cars										
Voitures de tourisme	105.8	114.5	123.6	132.1	137.6	143.4	151.9	164.7	178.0	188.0
Commercial vehicles										
Véhicules utilitaires	46.8	53.9	57.5	61.5	65.8	69.5	73.8	79.1	85.0	88.9
Republic of Moldova République de Moldova										
Passenger cars										
Voitures de tourisme	209.0	218.1	166.3[48]	166.4[48]	169.4[48]	165.9[48]	177.3[48]	206.0[48]	222.8[48]	...
Commercial vehicles[49]										
Véhicules utilitaires[49]	15.0	14.3	10.1[48]	8.9[48]	7.8[48]	12.9[48]	11.5[48]	10.4[48]	9.2[48]	8.1[48]
Réunion Réunion										
Passenger cars										
Voitures de tourisme	106.3	112.0	119.3	127.8	133.1	142.1	150.6	159.3	167.9	180.6
Commercial vehicles										
Véhicules utilitaires	32.7	34.4	36.6	39.2	40.9	43.6	46.2	49.0	51.6	54.0
Romania Roumanie										
Passenger cars										
Voitures de tourisme	1 292.0	1 432.0	1 593.0	1 793.0	2 020.0	2 197.0	2 392.0	2 605.0	2 822.0	...
Commercial vehicles										
Véhicules utilitaires	287.0	291.0	311.0	336.0	362.0	385.0	409.0	428.0	456.0	...
Russian Federation Fédération de Russie										
Passenger cars										
Voitures de tourisme	8 963.8	9 712.7	10 531.3	11 518.3	12 863.5	14 195.3	15 815.0	17 613.6	18 819.6	19 717.8
Commercial vehicles										
Véhicules utilitaires	2 743.6	2 779.3	2 847.9	2 924.0	3 006.0	3 078.1	3 041.1	3 103.1	3 108.2	...
Rwanda Rwanda										
Passenger cars										
Voitures de tourisme	7.2	15.0[11]	7.9[11]	...	...	...	...	...	...	...
Commercial vehicles										
Véhicules utilitaires	7.0	10.0[11]	2.0[11]	...	...	...	...	...	...	...
Saint Kitts and Nevis Saint-Kitts-et-Nevis										
Passenger cars										
Voitures de tourisme	4.0	3.9	4.1	4.5	4.8	5.2	5.5	6.3	6.3	7.7
Commercial vehicles										
Véhicules utilitaires	2.0	2.7	2.3	2.4	2.4	2.3	2.5	2.4	2.9	3.9

58
Motor vehicles in use
Passenger cars and commercial vehicles: thousand units [*cont.*]
Véhicules automobiles en circulation
Voitures de tourisme et véhicules utilitaires : milliers de véhicules [*suite*]

Country or area Pays or zone	1990	1991	1992	1993	1994	1995	1996	1997	1998	1999
Saint Lucia Sainte-Lucie										
Passenger cars										
Voitures de tourisme	8.1	9.1	9.3	10.1	11.4	12.5	13.5	...	...	...
Commercial vehicles										
Véhicules utilitaires	7.3	8.4	9.3	10.5	9.5	...	10.8	...	...	...
St. Vincent-Grenadines St. Vincent-Grenadines										
Passenger cars										
Voitures de tourisme	5.3	5.3	5.0	5.4	5.7	5.3	6.1	7.4	8.0	8.7
Commercial vehicles										
Véhicules utilitaires	.2.8	2.8	2.0	3.1	3.2	3.7	3.2	3.8	4.1	3.9
Saudi Arabia Arabie saoudite										
Passenger cars[2][50]										
Voitures de tourisme[2][50]	4 950.5	5 117.4	5 328.5	5 588.0	5 861.6	6 111.1	6 333.9	6 580.0	7 046.0	...
Senegal Sénégal										
Passenger cars										
Voitures de tourisme	92.0[11]	97.0[11]	100.0[11]	# 65.4	105.0[11]	106.0[11]	...	...	...	...
Commercial vehicles										
Véhicules utilitaires	43.0[11]	40.0[11]	45.0[11]	# 24.0	45.0[11]	48.0[11]	...	...	...	...
Seychelles Seychelles										
Passenger cars										
Voitures de tourisme	4.3	4.7	4.9	6.1	5.6	5.5	6.2	6.7	6.5	6.4
Commercial vehicles										
Véhicules utilitaires	1.2	1.3	1.5	1.8	1.8	1.9	2.0	2.1	2.2	2.2
Sierra Leone Sierra Leone										
Passenger cars[1]										
Voitures de tourisme[1]	35.9	36.0	36.0	32.4	32.4	32.4	32.4	32.4	...	...
Commercial vehicles[1]										
Véhicules utilitaires[1]	11.8	12.0	12.0	11.9	11.9	11.9	11.9	11.9	...	...
Singapore Singapour										
Passenger cars										
Voitures de tourisme	286.8	300.1	302.8	321.9	340.6	363.9	384.5	396.4	395.2	403.2
Commercial vehicles										
Véhicules utilitaires	126.9	130.1	131.5	135.2	136.8	140.0	142.7	144.8	142.6	141.3
Slovakia Slovaquie										
Passenger cars										
Voitures de tourisme	875.6	906.1	953.2	994.9	994.0	1 015.8	1 058.4	1 135.9	1 196.1	1 236.4
Commercial vehicles										
Véhicules utilitaires	122.6	127.5	134.7	130.6	131.2	131.5	127.2	135.0	144.4	149.4
Slovenia Slovénie										
Passenger cars										
Voitures de tourisme	587.1	602.9	615.7	641.7	667.2	709.6	740.9	778.3	813.8	848.6
Commercial vehicles										
Véhicules utilitaires	33.8	33.6	34.0	34.7	36.6	40.2	42.6	44.9	42.5	44.4
Somalia Somalie										
Passenger cars[11]										
Voitures de tourisme[11]	20.0	10.5	10.5	10.7	11.8	12.0	...	...	...	...
Commercial vehicles[11]										
Véhicules utilitaires[11]	12.0	12.0	11.5	12.0	12.2	12.0	...	...	...	...
South Africa Afrique du Sud										
Passenger cars										
Voitures de tourisme	3 599.8[34]	3 698.2[34]	3 739.2[34]	3 488.6[1]	3 814.9[1]	3 830.8[1]	3 846.8[1]	3 900.0[1]	...	3 966.3[51]
Commercial vehicles										
Véhicules utilitaires	1 486.9[52]	1 519.9[52]	1 551.4[52]	1 784.9[1]	1 596.8[1]	1 625.5[1]	1 653.5[1]	2 000.0[1]	...	2 248.1[53]
Spain Espagne										
Passenger cars										
Voitures de tourisme	11 995.6	12 537.1	13 102.3	13 440.7	13 733.8	14 212.3	14 753.8	15 297.4	16 050.1	...

58
Motor vehicles in use
Passenger cars and commercial vehicles: thousand units [*cont.*]
Véhicules automobiles en circulation
Voitures de tourisme et véhicules utilitaires : milliers de véhicules [*suite*]

Country or area Pays or zone	1990	1991	1992	1993	1994	1995	1996	1997	1998	1999
Commercial vehicles Véhicules utilitaires	2 446.9	2 615.0	2 773.4	2 859.6	2 952.8	3 071.6	3 200.3	3 360.1	3 561.5	...
Sri Lanka Sri Lanka										
Passenger cars[4] Voitures de tourisme[4]	173.5	180.1	189.5	197.3	210.1	228.9	246.5	261.6	284.3	...
Commercial vehicles[4] Véhicules utilitaires[4]	146.0	152.7	159.9	166.3	175.3	184.3	191.5	199.2	211.2	
Sudan Soudan										
Passenger cars[11] Voitures de tourisme[11]	116.0	116.0	116.0	30.8	30.8	30.8	...	...	...	...
Commercial vehicles[11] Véhicules utilitaires[11]	56.9	57.0	57.0	35.9	35.9	35.9	...	...	...	...
Suriname Suriname										
Passenger cars Voitures de tourisme	36.2	38.7	42.6	46.6	42.2	49.3	46.4	50.2	55.4	59.9
Commercial vehicles Véhicules utilitaires	14.4	15.5	16.0	18.2	17.9	17.3	19.5	20.5	21.1	22.5
Swaziland Swaziland										
Passenger cars Voitures de tourisme	26.9	...	...	25.4[7]	26.6[7]	28.1[7]	29.8[7]	31.9[7]	...	...
Commercial vehicles Véhicules utilitaires	26.3	...	...	32.9[7]	32.1[7]	35.4[7]	37.2[7]	39.7[7]	...	...
Sweden Suède										
Passenger cars Voitures de tourisme	3 600.5	3 619.4	3 588.4	3 566.0	3 594.2	3 630.8	3 654.9	3 702.8	3 790.7	3 890.2
Commercial vehicles Véhicules utilitaires	324.1	324.1	319.2	316.0	317.8	322.3	326.5	336.6	352.9	369.2
Switzerland Suisse										
Passenger cars[4 32] Voitures de tourisme[4 32]	2 985.4	3 057.8	3 091.2	3 109.5	3 165.0	3 229.2	3 268.1	3 323.4	3 383.3	3 467.3
Commercial vehicles[4 32] Véhicules utilitaires[4 32]	283.4	291.3	291.3	288.8	292.4	299.3	300.7	302.7	306.4	313.6
Syrian Arab Republic Rép. arabe syrienne										
Passenger cars Voitures de tourisme	126.0	126.9	128.0	149.8	159.1	166.5	173.6	175.9	178.7	...
Commercial vehicles Véhicules utilitaires	118.5	121.9	136.7	162.3	188.4	224.0	251.4	269.1	282.6	...
Tajikistan Tadjikistan										
Passenger cars Voitures de tourisme	...	...	...	...	175.0	166.4	151.5	154.1	146.6	141.7
Commercial vehicles Véhicules utilitaires	...	...	...	...	10.9	9.8	9.6	10.2	13.3	16.4
Thailand Thaïlande										
Passenger cars[54] Voitures de tourisme[54]	1 222.4	1 279.2	1 396.6	1 598.2	1 798.8	1 913.2	2 098.6	2 350.4	2 529.2	...
Commercial vehicles[55] Véhicules utilitaires[55]	1 457.4	1 541.2	1 763.5	2 091.1	2 384.1	2 735.6	3 149.3	3 534.9	3 746.7	...
TFYR Macedonia L'ex-R.y. Macédoine										
Passenger cars Voitures de tourisme	231.0	250.0	280.0	290.0	263.0	286.0	284.0	289.0	289.0	290.0
Commercial vehicles Véhicules utilitaires	17.8	18.9	22.1	23.0	19.9	22.1	21.8	22.2	22.6	22.5
Togo Togo										
Passenger cars[1] Voitures de tourisme[1]	25.0	25.0	25.0	18.2	74.6	74.7	74.7	74.7	...	...
Commercial vehicles[1] Véhicules utilitaires[1]	15.0	16.0	16.1	11.6	34.6	34.6	34.6	34.6	...	...

58
Motor vehicles in use
Passenger cars and commercial vehicles: thousand units [cont.]
Véhicules automobiles en circulation
Voitures de tourisme et véhicules utilitaires : milliers de véhicules [suite]

Country or area Pays or zone	1990	1991	1992	1993	1994	1995	1996	1997	1998	1999
Tonga Tonga										
Passenger cars										
Voitures de tourisme	2.0	2.8	3.3	4.7	5.3	7.7	8.6	8.4	9.6	...
Commercial vehicles										
Véhicules utilitaires	2.6	3.1	3.7	5.0	5.9	8.1	9.7	8.7	9.3	...
Trinidad and Tobago Trinité-et-Tobago										
Passenger cars										
Voitures de tourisme	199.7	162.5	166.7	159.0	162.1	166.8	180.2	194.3	213.4	229.4
Commercial vehicles										
Véhicules utilitaires	47.6	39.4	40.8	39.2	40.2	42.2	44.9	47.7	51.1	53.9
Tunisia Tunisie										
Passenger cars										
Voitures de tourisme	251.2	262.7	277.6	299.1	327.0	356.3	379.2	415.2	445.6	482.7
Commercial vehicles[56]										
Véhicules utilitaires[56]	131.0	140.3	151.6	165.3	177.7	189.3	201.5	217.1	233.0	250.3
Turkey Turquie[57]										
Passenger cars[57]										
Voitures de tourisme[57]	1 649.9	1 864.3	2 181.4	2 619.9	2 861.6	3 058.5	3 274.1	3 570.1	3 838.3	4 072.3
Commercial vehicles[29]										
Véhicules utilitaires[29]	452.9	469.0	490.9	518.4	530.4	617.1	642.3	683.5	715.1	730.7
Uganda Ouganda										
Passenger cars										
Voitures de tourisme	13.0	17.8	19.0	20.5	24.2	25.9	...	...	...	...
Commercial vehicles										
Véhicules utilitaires	15.0	25.2	26.9	29.4	35.0	42.3	...	...	...	...
Ukraine Ukraine										
Passenger cars										
Voitures de tourisme	3 362.0	3 657.0	3 884.8	4 206.5	4 384.1	4 603.1	4 872.3	5 024.0	5 127.3	5 210.8
United Arab Emirates Emirats arabes unis										
Passenger cars										
Voitures de tourisme	224.9	241.3	257.8	297.1	332.5	321.6	346.3	...	...	...
Commercial vehicles										
Véhicules utilitaires	57.3	47.1	65.8	78.8	87.2	84.2	89.3	...	...	...
United Kingdom Royaume-Uni										
Passenger cars[58]										
Voitures de tourisme[58]	21 485.0	21 515.0	20 973.0	21 291.0	21 740.0	21 949.9	...	...	...	...
Commercial vehicles[58]										
Véhicules utilitaires[58]	2 520.0	2 438.0	3 008.0	2 990.0	2 994.0	2 987.3	...	...	...	...
United Rep.Tanzania Rép.-Unie de Tanzanie										
Passenger cars										
Voitures de tourisme	44.0	44.0[1]	44.0[1]	13.6[1]	13.6[1]	13.8[1]	13.8[1]	13.8[1]	...	...
Commercial vehicles										
Véhicules utilitaires	54.0	55.0[1]	57.2[1]	33.7[1]	35.4[1]	37.5[1]	42.5[1]	42.5[1]	...	...
United States Etats-Unis										
Passenger cars [59]										
Voitures de tourisme[59]	198 022.0	202 333.0	203 798.0	207 535.0	191 071.6	198 022.0	202 333.0	203 798.0	207 535.0	...
Commercial vehicles										
Véhicules utilitaires	7 404.9	7 703.0	7 780.8	7 959.6	7 258.3	7 404.9	7 703.0	7 780.8	7 959.6	...
Uruguay Uruguay										
Passenger cars										
Voitures de tourisme	379.6	389.6	418.0	425.6	444.8	464.5	485.1	516.9	578.3	...
Commercial vehicles										
Véhicules utilitaires	49.9	48.6	45.0	44.3	46.2	45.8	48.4	50.3	53.9	...
Vanuatu Vanuatu										
Passenger cars[1]										
Voitures de tourisme[1]	4.0	4.5	4.0	2.7	7.1	7.4	2.7	2.7	...	...

58
Motor vehicles in use
Passenger cars and commercial vehicles: thousand units [*cont.*]
Véhicules automobiles en circulation
Voitures de tourisme et véhicules utilitaires : milliers de véhicules [*suite*]

Country or area Pays or zone	1990	1991	1992	1993	1994	1995	1996	1997	1998	1999
Commercial vehicles[1] Véhicules utilitaires[1]	2.0	2.1	2.2	2.7	1.7	1.8	3.2	3.5	...	...
Venezuela Venezuela										
Passenger cars Voitures de tourisme	1 582.0	1 688.0	1 753.0	1 805.0	1 813.0	1 823.0	...	...	...	...
Commercial vehicles Véhicules utilitaires	464.0	538.0	559.0	576.0	578.0	581.0	...	...	...	...
Viet Nam Viet Nam										
Commercial vehicles Véhicules utilitaires	27.4	28.2	38.7	41.5	33.8	39.1	41.5	41.5	49.4	...
Yemen Yémen										
Passenger cars Voitures de tourisme	94.9	118.3	140.6	176.1	196.5	224.1	259.4	327.1	380.6	...
Commercial vehicles Véhicules utilitaires	190.3	204.6	223.0	251.8	266.4	291.7	345.3	413.1	422.1	...
Zambia Zambie										
Passenger cars Voitures de tourisme	...	...	3.0	3.0	3.9	5.7	3.7	...	...	...
Commercial vehicles Véhicules utilitaires	...	...	4.0	2.7	4.2	7.3	3.9	...	...	...
Zimbabwe Zimbabwe										
Passenger cars Voitures de tourisme	290.0	300.0	310.0	328.3	349.1	384.0	422.4	464.7	521.0	534.6
Commercial vehicles Véhicules utilitaires	27.4	28.4	30.4	32.5	34.5	37.9	42.2	46.4	54.3	58.5

Source:
United Nations Secretariat, transport statistics database of
the Statistics Division.

† For information on recent changes in country or
area nomenclature pertaining to former Czechoslovakia,
Germany, Hong Kong Special Administrative Region (SAR) of
China, Macao Special Administrative Region (SAR) of China,
SFR of Yugoslavia and the former USSR, see Annex I - Country
or area nomenclature, regional and other groupings.

†† For statistical purposes, the data for
China do not include those for Hong Kong Special
Administrative Region (Hong Kong SAR), Macao Special
Administrative Region (Macao SAR) and Taiwan province of
China.

1 Source: World Automotive Market Report, Auto and Truck
   International (Illinois).
2 Including commercial vehicles.
3 Data refer to fiscal years beginning 1 July of the year
   indicated.
4 Including vehicles operated by police or other governmental
   security organizations.
5 Including farm tractors.
6 Including jeeps.
7 Excluding government vehicles.
8 Number of licensed vehicles.
9 Including taxis only.
10 Including buses only.
11 Source: AAMA Motor Vehicle Facts and Figures, American
   Automobile Manufacturers Association (Michigan).
12 Excluding pick-ups.

Source:
Secrétariat de l'Organisation des Nations Unies, la base de
données pour les statistiques des transports de la Division
de statistique.

† Pour les modifications récentes de nomenclature
de pays ou de zone concernant l'Allemagne, Hong Kong, région
administrative spéciale (RAS) de Chine, Macao, région
administrative spéciale (RAS) de Chine,
l'ex-Tchécoslovaquie, l'ex-URSS et l'ex-Rfs de Yougoslavie,
voir annexe I - Nomenclature des pays ou des zones,
groupements régionaux et autres groupements.

†† Les données statistiques relatives à
la Chine ne comprennent pas celles qui concernent la région
administrative spéciale de Hong Kong (la RAS de Hong Kong),
la région administrative spéciale de Macao (la RAS de Macao)
et la province chinoise de Taiwan.

1 Source : "World Automotive Market Report, Auto and Truck
   International" (Illinois).
2 Y compris véhicules utilitaires.
3 Les données se réfèrent aux années fiscales commençant le
   1er juillet de l'année indiquée.
4 Y compris véhicules de la police ou d'autres services
   gouvernementales d'ordre public.
5 Y compris tracteurs agricoles.
6 Y compris jeeps.
7 Non compris les véhicules des administrations publiques.
8 Nombre de véhicules automobiles licensés.
9 Y compris taxis seulement.
10 Y compris autobus seulement.
11 Source: AAMA Motor Vehicle Facts and Figures, American
   Automobile Manufacturers Association (Michigan).
12 Non compris fourgonnettes.

58
Motor vehicles in use
Passenger cars and commercial vehicles: thousand units [*cont.*]
Véhicules automobiles en circulation
Voitures de tourisme et véhicules utilitaires : milliers de véhicules [*suite*]

13 Including special-purpose vehicles.	13 Y compris véhicules à usages spéciaux.
14 Including minibuses.	14 Y compris minibuses.
15 Excluding learners' vehicles.	15 Non compris les voitures écoles.
16 Including vans.	16 Y compris fourgons.
17 Including special-purpose commercial vehicles and farm tractors.	17 Y compris véhicules utilitaires à usages spéciaux et tracteurs agricoles.
18 Excluding vans.	18 Non compris fourgons.
19 Excluding Faeroe Islands.	19 Non compris Iles Féroés.
20 Including large public service excavators and trench diggers.	20 Y compris les grosses excavatrices et machines d'excavation de tranchées de travaux publics.
21 Including dump trucks and motor scooters.	21 Y compris camions-bennes et scooters.
22 Including commercial vehicles, motorcycles and trailers.	22 Y compris véhicules utilitaires, motocyclettes y remorques.
23 Data refer to fiscal years ending 7 July of the year indicated.	23 Les données se réfèrent aux années fiscales finissant le 7e juillet de l'année indiquée.
24 Including private and government cars, rental and hired cars.	24 Y compris les voitures particulières et celles des administrations publiques, les voitures de location et de louage.
25 Including pick-ups, ambulances, light and heavy fire engines and all other vehicles such as trailers, cranes, loaders, forklifts, etc.	25 Y compris les fourgonnettes, les ambulances, les voitures depompiers légères et lourdes, et tous autres véhicules telsque remoques, grues, chargeuses, chariots élévateurs à fourches, etc.
26 Data refer to 31 December of the year indicated.	26 Les données se réfèrent au 31e décembre de l'année indiquée.
27 Excluding tractors.	27 Non compris tracteurs.
28 Including only trailers and semi-trailer combinations less than 10 years old.	28 Y compris les remorques et semi-remorques de moins de 10 ans seulement.
29 Excluding tractors and semi-trailer combinations.	29 Non compris ensembles tracteur-remorque et semi-remorque.
30 Including goods vehicles, tractors, trailers, three-wheeled passengers and goods vehicles and other miscellaneous vehicles which are not separately classified.	30 Y compris véhicules de transport de marchandises, camions-remorques, remorques, véhicules à trois roues (passagers et marchandises) et autres véhicules divers qui ne font pas l'objet d'une catégorie separée.
31 Data refer to fiscal years ending 20 March of the year indicated.	31 Les données se réfèrent aux années fiscales finissant le 20e mars de l'années indiquée.
32 Data refer to fiscal years ending 30 September of the year indicated.	32 Les données se réfèrent aux années fiscales finissant le 30e septembre de l'année indiquée.
33 Including school buses.	33 Y compris l'autobus de l'école.
34 Including mini-buses equipped for transport of nine to fifteen passengers.	34 Y compris mini-buses ayant une capacité de neuf à quinze passagers.
35 Excluding small vehicles.	35 Non compris véhicules petites.
36 Including cars with a seating capacity of up to 10 persons.	36 Y compris véhicules comptant jusqu'à 10 places.
37 Number of registered motor vehicles.	37 Nombre de véhicules automobiles enregistrés.
38 Source: United Nations Economic and Social Commission for Western Asia (ESCWA).	38 Source : Commission économique et sociale pour l'Asie occidentale (CESAO).
39 Excluding diplomatic corps vehicles.	39 Non compris véhicules des diplomates.
40 Newly registered.	40 Enregistrés récemment.
41 Including hearses (Norway: registered before 1981).	41 Y compris corbillards (Norvège : enregistrés avant de 1981).
42 Excluding taxis.	42 Non compris taxis.
43 Trucks only.	43 Camions seulement.
44 Excluding buses and tractors, but including special lorries.	44 Non compris autobus et tracteurs, mais y compris camions spéciaux.
45 Including light miscellaneous vehicles.	45 Y compris les véhicules légers divers.
46 Excluding Madeira and Azores.	46 Non compris Madère et Azores.
47 Including vehicles no longer in circulation.	47 Y compris véhicules retirés de la circulation.
48 Excluding Transnistria region.	48 Non compris région de Transnistria.
49 For the period 1980 - 1994, including motor vehicles for general use owned by Ministry of Transport. For the period 1995 – 1999, including motorvehicles owned by enterprises with main activity as road transport enterprises.	49 Pour la période 1980 - 1994, y compris les véhicules à moteur d'usage général appartenant au Ministère des transports. Pour la période 1995 – 1999, y compris les véhicules pour les enterprises de transport.
50 Including motorcycles.	50 Y compris motocyclettes.
51 Including all minibuses and passenger vehicles which transport fewer than 12 persons.	51 Y compris tous les minibus et véhicules qui transportant moins de 12 passagers.
52 Including hearses, ambulances, fire-engines and jeeps specifically registered as commercial vehicles.	52 Y compris corbillards, ambulances, voitures de pompiers et jeeps spécifiquement immatriculés comme véhicules utilitaires.
53 Including vehicles which transport 12 persons or more and	53 Y compris véhicules transportant 12 personnes ou plus et

58
Motor vehicles in use
Passenger cars and commercial vehicles: thousand units [*cont.*]
Véhicules automobiles en circulation
Voitures de tourisme et véhicules utilitaires : milliers de véhicules [*suite*]

all light and heavy load vehicles, whether self-propelled or semi-trailer.
54 Including micro-buses and passenger pick-ups.

55 Including pick-ups, taxis, cars for hire, small rural buses.

56 Beginning 1987, including trailers.
57 Including vehicles seating not more than eight persons, including the driver.
58 Figures prior to 1992 were derived from vehicle taxation class; beginning 1992, figures derived from vehicle body type.
59 Including motorcycles, mini-vans, sport-utility vehicles and pick-up trucks.

tous véhicules poids légèrs ou poids lourds, auto-propulsés ou semi-remorque.
54 Y compris les microbus et les camionnettes de transport de passagers.
55 Y compris les camionnettes, les taxis, les voitures de louage, les petits autobus ruraux.
56 A compter de l'année 1987, y compris remorques.
57 Y compris véhicules dont le nombre de places assises (y compris celle du conducteur) n'est pas supérieur à huit.
58 Les chiffres antérieurs à 1992 ont été calculés selon les catégories fiscales de véhicules; à partir de 1992, ils ont été calculés selon les types de carrosserie.
59 Y compris motocyclettes , fourgonettes, véhicules de la classe quatre-x-quatre et camionette légères.

59
Merchant shipping: fleets
Transports maritimes : flotte marchande
Total, Oil tankers and Ore and bulk carrier fleets: thousand gross registered tons
Total, Pétroliers et Minéraliers et transporteurs de vracs : milliers de tonneaux de jauge brute

Flag Pavillon	1990	1991	1992	1993	1994	1995	1996	1997	1998	1999
A. Total · Totale										
World *Monde*	**423 627**	**436 027**	**445 169**	**457 915**	**475 859**	**490 662**	**507 873**	**522 197**	**531 893**	**543 610**
Africa · Afrique										
Algeria Algérie	906	921	921	921	936	980	983	983	1 005	1 005
Angola Angola	93	93	94	88	90	90	82	68	74	66
Benin Bénin	5	2	2	1	1	1	1	1	1	1
Cameroon Cameroun	33	34	35	36	36	37	37	11	13	14
Cape Verde Cap-Vert	21	22	22	23	22	16	15	21	20	21
Comoros Comores	2	3	2	2	2	2	2	2	1	1
Congo Congo	9	9	9	10	9	12	6	7	4	4
Côte d'Ivoire Côte d'Ivoire	82	82	75	103	62	40	13	11	10	10
Dem. Rep. of the Congo Rép. dém. du Congo	56	56	29	15	15	15	15	15	13	13
Djibouti Djibouti	3	3	3	4	4	4	4	4	4	4
Egypt Egypte	1 257	1 257	1 122	1 149	1 262	1 269	1 230	1 288	1 368	1 368
Equatorial Guinea Guinée équatoriale	6	6	7	2	3	3	21	35	59	44
Eritrea Erythrée	...	...	...	0	0	12	1	7	7	16
Ethiopia incl. Eritrea Ethiopie comp. Erythrée	75	84	70	...	...	...	...	...	...	...
Ethiopia Ethiopie	...	...	...	69	83	80	86	86	83	96
Gabon Gabon	24	25	25	36	28	32	33	35	27	16
Gambia Gambie	2	3	2	2	3	1	1	2	2	2
Ghana Ghana	126	135	135	118	106	114	135	130	115	118
Guinea Guinée	9	9	5	6	8	7	7	9	11	11
Guinea-Bissau Guinée-Bissau	4	4	4	4	5	5	6	6	6	6
Kenya Kenya	7	13	14	16	16	18	20	21	21	21
Liberia Libéria	54 700	52 427	55 918	53 919	57 648	59 801	59 989	60 058	60 492	54 107
Libyan Arab Jamah. Jamah. arabe libyenne	835	840	720	721	739	733	681	686	567	439

59
Merchant shipping: fleets
Total, Oil tankers and Ore and bulk carrier fleets: thousand gross registered tons [*cont.*]
Transports maritimes : flotte marchande
Total, Pétroliers et Minéraliers et transporteurs de vracs : milliers de tonneaux de jauge brute [*suite*]

Flag Pavillon	1990	1991	1992	1993	1994	1995	1996	1997	1998	1999
Madagascar Madagascar	74	73	45	34	36	38	39	40	42	43
Mauritania Mauritanie	41	42	43	44	42	39	43	43	48	49
Mauritius Maurice	99	82	122	194	206	238	244	275	206	150
Morocco Maroc	488	483	479	393	362	383	403	417	444	448
Mozambique Mozambique	40	37	39	36	36	38	45	39	35	36
Namibia Namibie	...	0	17	36	44	52	59	55	55	55
Nigeria Nigéria	496	493	516	515	473	479	447	452	452	432
Réunion Réunion	21	21	21	...	...	...	...	...	...	...
Saint Helena Sainte-Hélène	3	...	...	...	...	...	0	1	1	1
Sao Tome and Principe Sao Tomé-et-Principe	1	1	3	3	3	3	3	3	10	42
Senegal Sénégal	52	55	58	66	50	48	50	51	51	48
Seychelles Seychelles	3	4	4	4	4	5	4	5	18	24
Sierra Leone Sierra Leone	21	21	26	26	24	23	19	19	19	17
Somalia Somalie	17	17	17	18	17	16	14	11	11	6
South Africa Afrique du Sud	352	340	336	346	331	340	371	383	384	379
Sudan Soudan	58	45	45	64	57	48	42	42	43	43
Togo Togo	52	22	12	12	1	1	1	2	2	43
Tunisia Tunisie	278	276	280	269	141	160	158	180	193	200
United Rep.Tanzania Rép.-Unie de Tanzanie	32	39	41	43	43	46	45	46	36	36
America, North · Amérique du Nord										
Anguilla Anguilla	3	5	5	4	3	2	2	2	1	1
Antigua and Barbuda Antigua-et-Barbuda	359	811	802	1 063	1 507	1 842	2 176	2 214	2 788	3 622
Bahamas Bahamas	13 626	17 541	20 616	21 224	22 915	23 603	24 409	25 523	27 716	29 483
Barbados Barbade	8	8	51	49	76	292	497	888	688	725
Belize Belize	1	...	37	148	280	517	1 016	1 761	2 382	2 368
Bermuda Bermudes	4 258	3 037	3 338	3 140	2 904	3 048	3 462	4 610	4 811	6 187

59
Merchant shipping: fleets
Total, Oil tankers and Ore and bulk carrier fleets: thousand gross registered tons [cont.]
Transports maritimes : flotte marchande
Total, Pétroliers et Minéraliers et transporteurs de vracs : milliers de tonneaux de jauge brute [suite]

Flag Pavillon	1990	1991	1992	1993	1994	1995	1996	1997	1998	1999
British Virgin Islands Iles Vierges britanniques	7	7	7	6	5	5	5	5	4	4
Canada Canada	2 744	2 685	2 610	2 541	2 490	2 401	2 406	2 527	2 501	2 496
Cayman Islands Iles Caïmanes	415	395	363	383	383	368	827	844	1 282	1 165
Costa Rica Costa Rica	14	14	8	8	8	7	6	6	6	6
Cuba Cuba	836	770	671	626	444	410	291	203	158	130
Dominica Dominique	2	2	2	4	2	2	2	3	3	2
Dominican Republic Rép. dominicaine	36	12	12	13	12	12	12	11	9	10
El Salvador El Salvador	2	2	2	2	1	1	1	1	1	2
Greenland Groenland	57	57	55	...	...	...	...	...	...	...
Grenada Grenade	1	1	1	1	1	5	1	1	1	1
Guadeloupe Guadeloupe	4	5	6	...	...	...	...	...	...	...
Guatemala Guatemala	5	1	2	1	1	1	1	1	1	5
Haiti Haïti	1	1	1	1	1	0	1	2	1	1
Honduras Honduras	712	816	1 045	1 116	1 206	1 206	1 198	1 053	1 083	1 220
Jamaica Jamaïque	14	14	11	11	7	9	9	10	4	4
Martinique Martinique	8	1	1	...	...	...	...	...	...	...
Mexico Mexique	1 320	1 196	1 114	1 125	1 179	1 129	1 128	1 145	1 085	918
Montserrat Montserrat	1	1	1	...	...	...	...	...	...	...
Netherlands Antilles Antilles néerlandaises	455 [1]	568 [1]	841 [1]	1 039	1 047	1 197	1 168	1 067	971	1 110
Nicaragua Nicaragua	5	5	4	4	4	4	4	4	4	4
Panama Panama	39 298	44 949	52 486	57 619	64 710	71 922	82 131	91 128	98 222	105 248
Puerto Rico Porto Rico	21	16	9	...	...	...	...	...	...	...
Saint Kitts and Nevis Saint-Kitts-et-Nevis	0	0	0	0	0	0	0	0	0	0
Saint Lucia Sainte-Lucie	2	2	2	2	2	1	1	...	...	...
Saint Pierre and Miquelon Saint-Pierre-et-Miquelon	4	3	6	...	...	...	...	...	...	...

59
Merchant shipping: fleets
Total, Oil tankers and Ore and bulk carrier fleets: thousand gross registered tons [cont.]
Transports maritimes : flotte marchande
Total, Pétroliers et Minéraliers et transporteurs de vracs : milliers de tonneaux de jauge brute [suite]

Flag Pavillon	1990	1991	1992	1993	1994	1995	1996	1997	1998	1999
St. Vincent-Grenadines St. Vincent-Grenadines	1 937	4 221	4 698	5 287	5 420	6 165	7 134	8 374	7 875	7 105
Trinidad and Tobago Trinité-et-Tobago	22	22	24	23	27	28	19	19	19	22
Turks and Caicos Islands Iles Turques et Caïques	3	5	4	4	3	2	2	2	1	1
United States Etats-Unis	19 744	18 565	14 435	14 087	13 655	12 761	12 025	11 789	11 852	12 026
America, South · Amérique du Sud										
Argentina Argentine	1 890	1 709	873	773	716	595	586	579	499	477
Bolivia Bolivie	...	...	...	...	...	...	...	2	16	179
Brazil Brésil	6 016	5 883	5 348	5 216	5 283	5 077	4 530	4 372	4 171	3 933
Chile Chili	616	619	580	624	721	761	691	722	753	820
Colombia Colombie	372	313	250	238	142	144	122	118	112	97
Ecuador Equateur	385	384	348	286	270	168	178	145	171	309
Falkland Is. (Malvinas) Iles Falkland (Malvinas)	10	10	14	15	16	20	30	38	39	45
French Guiana Guyane française	1	1	1	...	...	...	...	...	...	...
Guyana Guyana	15	16	17	17	15	15	16	17	16	14
Paraguay Paraguay	37	35	33	31	33	39	44	44	45	43
Peru Pérou	617	605	433	411	321	341	346	337	270	285
Suriname Suriname	13	13	13	13	8	8	8	8	6	6
Uruguay Uruguay	104	105	127	149	125	124	100	121	107	62
Venezuela Venezuela	935	970	871	971	920	787	697	705	665	657
Asia · Asie										
Azerbaijan Azerbaïdjan	...	...	637	667	621	655	636	633	651	654
Bahrain Bahreïn	47	262	138	103	167	166	164	194	284	292
Bangladesh Bangladesh	464	456	392	388	380	379	436	419	414	378
Brunei Darussalam Brunéi Darussalam	358	348	364	365	366	366	369	369	362	362
Cambodia Cambodge	...	...	4	6	6	60	206	439	616	999
China †† Chine ††	13 899	14 299	13 899	14 945	15 827	16 943	16 993	16 339	16 503	16 315

59
Merchant shipping: fleets
Total, Oil tankers and Ore and bulk carrier fleets: thousand gross registered tons [*cont.*]
Transports maritimes : flotte marchande
Total, Pétroliers et Minéraliers et transporteurs de vracs : milliers de tonneaux de jauge brute [*suite*]

Flag Pavillon	1990	1991	1992	1993	1994	1995	1996	1997	1998	1999
China, Hong Kong SAR† Chine, Hong Kong RAS†	6 565	5 876	7 267	7 664	7 703	8 795	7 863	5 771	6 171	7 973
China, Macao SAR † Chine, Macao RAS †	3	3	3	2	2	2	2	2	2	4
Cyprus Chypre	18 336	20 298	20 487	22 842	23 293	24 653	23 799	23 653	23 302	23 641
Georgia Géorgie	...	...	...	0	439	282	206	128	118	132
India Inde	6 476	6 517	6 546	6 575	6 485	7 127	7 127	6 934	6 777	6 915
Indonesia Indonésie	2 179	2 337	2 367	2 440	2 678	2 771	2 973	3 195	3 252	3 241
Iran (Islamic Rep. of) Iran (Rép. islamique d')	4 738	4 583	4 571	4 444	3 803	2 902	3 567	3 553	3 347	3 546
Iraq Iraq	1 044	931	902	902	885	858	857	572	511	511
Israel Israël	530	604	664	652	646	599	679	794	752	728
Japan Japon	27 078	26 407	25 102	24 248	22 102	19 913	19 201	18 516	17 780	17 063
Jordan Jordanie	42	135	61	71	61	21	41	43	42	42
Kazakhstan Kazakhstan	...	...	...	...	9	12	9	10	9	9
Korea, Dem. P. R. Corée, R. p. dém. de	442	511	602	671	696	715	693	667	631	658
Korea, Republic of Corée, République de	7 783	7 821	7 407	7 047	7 004	6 972	7 558	7 430	5 694	5 735
Kuwait Koweït	1 855	1 373	2 258	2 218	2 017	2 057	2 028	1 984	2 459	2 456
Lao People's Dem. Rep. Rép. dém. pop. lao	0	0	0	3	3	3	3	3	2	2
Lebanon Liban	307	274	293	249	258	285	275	297	263	322
Malaysia Malaisie	1 717	1 755	2 048	2 166	2 728	3 283	4 175	4 842	5 209	5 245
Maldives Maldives	78	42	52	55	68	85	96	98	101	90
Myanmar Myanmar	827	1 046	947	711	683	523	687	568	492	540
Oman Oman	23	23	15	16	15	16	16	15	15	17
Pakistan Pakistan	354	358	380	360	375	398	444	435	401	308
Philippines Philippines	8 515	8 626	8 470	8 466	9 413	8 744	9 034	8 849	8 508	7 650
Qatar Qatar	359	485	392	431	557	482	562	648	744	749
Saudi Arabia Arabie saoudite	1 683	1 321	1 016	998	1 064	1 187	1 208	1 164	1 278	1 208
Singapore Singapour	7 928	8 488	9 905	11 035	11 895	13 611	16 448	18 875	20 370	21 780

59
Merchant shipping: fleets
Total, Oil tankers and Ore and bulk carrier fleets: thousand gross registered tons [cont.]
Transports maritimes : flotte marchande
Total, Pétroliers et Minéraliers et transporteurs de vracs : milliers de tonneaux de jauge brute [suite]

Flag Pavillon	1990	1991	1992	1993	1994	1995	1996	1997	1998	1999
Sri Lanka Sri Lanka	350	333	285	294	294	227	242	217	189	195
Syrian Arab Republic Rép. arabe syrienne	80	109	144	209	279	352	420	415	428	440
Thailand Thaïlande	615	725	917	1 116	1 374	1 743	2 042	2 158	1 999	1 956
Turkey Turquie	3 719	4 107	4 136	5 044	5 453	6 268	6 426	6 567	6 251	6 325
Turkmenistan Turkménistan	...	...	...	...	23	32	40	39	38	44
United Arab Emirates Emirats arabes unis	750	889	884	804	1 016	961	890	924	933	786
Viet Nam Viet Nam	470	574	616	728	773	700	808	766	784	865
Yemen Yémen	17	17	16	24	25	27	25	26	25	25
Europe · Europe										
Albania Albanie	56	59	59	59	59	63	43	30	29	21
Austria Autriche	139	139	140	160	134	92	95	83	68	71
Belgium Belgique	1 954	314	241	218	233	240	278	169	127	132
Bulgaria Bulgarie	1 360	1 367	1 348	1 314	1 295	1 166	1 150	1 128	1 091	1 036
Channel Islands Iles Anglo-Normandes	8	4	3	3	3	2	3	3	2	2
Croatia Croatie	...	...	210	193	247	333	580	871	896	869
former Czechoslovakia† l'ex-Tchécoslovaquie†	326	361	238	...	...	...	...	...	...	...
Czech Republic République tchèque	...	...	...	228	173	140	78	16		
Denmark Danemark	5 008	5 698	5 269	5 293	5 698	5 747	5 885	5 754	5 687	5 809
Estonia Estonie	...	...	680	686	695	598	545	602	522	453
Faeroe Islands Iles Féroé	124	115	111	100	100	104	109	105	103	104
Finland Finlande	1 069	1 053	1 197	1 354	1 404	1 519	1 511	1 559	1 629	1 658
France[2] France[2]	3 721	3 879	3 869	4 252	4 242	4 086	4 291	4 570	4 738	4 766
Germany † Allemagne †	...	5 971	5 360	4 979	5 696	5 626	5 842	6 950	8 084	6 514
F. R. Germany R. f. Allemagne	4 301	...	...	...	...	...	...	...	...	...
former German D. R. l'ex-R. d. allemande	1 437	...	...	...	...	...	...	...	...	...
Gibraltar Gibraltar	2 008	1 410	492	384	331	307	306	297	314	451

59
Merchant shipping: fleets
Total, Oil tankers and Ore and bulk carrier fleets: thousand gross registered tons [cont.]
Transports maritimes : flotte marchande
Total, Pétroliers et Minéraliers et transporteurs de vracs : milliers de tonneaux de jauge brute [suite]

Flag Pavillon	1990	1991	1992	1993	1994	1995	1996	1997	1998	1999
Greece Grèce	20 522	22 753	25 739	29 134	30 162	29 435	27 507	25 288	25 225	24 833
Hungary Hongrie	98	104	92	45	45	45	50	27	15	12
Iceland Islande	177	168	177	174	175	209	218	215	198	192
Ireland Irlande	181	195	199	184	190	213	219	235	184	219
Isle of Man Ile de Man	1 824	1 937	1 628	1 563	2 093	2 300	3 140	4 759	4 203	4 729
Italy Italie	7 991	8 122	7 513	7 030	6 818	6 699	6 594	6 194	6 819	8 048
Latvia Lettonie	...	...	1 207	1 155	1 034	798	723	319	118	118
Lithuania Lituanie	...	...	668	639	661	610	572	510	481	424
Luxembourg Luxembourg	3	1 703	1 656	1 327	1 143	881	878	820	932	1 343
Malta Malte	4 519	6 916	11 005	14 163	15 455	17 678	19 479	22 984	24 075	28 205
Netherlands Pays-Bas	3 330	3 305	3 346	3 086	3 349	3 409	3 995	3 880	4 263	4 814
Norway Norvège	23 429	23 586	22 231	21 536	22 388	21 551	21 806	22 839	23 136	23 446
Poland Pologne	3 369	3 348	3 109	2 646	2 610	2 358	2 293	1 878	1 424	1 319
Portugal Portugal	851	887	972	1 002	882	897	676	952	1 130	1 165
Romania Roumanie	4 005	3 828	2 981	2 867	2 689	2 536	2 568	2 345	2 088	1 221
Russian Federation Fédération de Russie	...	...	16 302	16 814	16 504	15 202	13 755	12 282	11 090	10 649
Slovakia Slovaquie	...	...	...	...	6	19	19	15	15	15
Slovenia Slovénie	...	...	2	2	9	2	2	2	2	2
Spain Espagne	3 807 [3]	3 617 [3]	2 643 [3]	1 752	1 560	1 619	1 675	1 688	1 838	1 903
Sweden Suède	2 775	3 174	2 884	2 439	2 797	2 955	3 002	2 754	2 552	2 947
Switzerland Suisse	287	286	346	300	336	381	400	434	383	439
Ukraine Ukraine	...	...	5 222	5 265	5 279	4 613	3 825	2 690	2 033	1 775
United Kingdom Royaume-Uni	4 887	4 670	4 081	4 117	4 430	4 413	3 872	3 486	4 085	4 331
Yugoslavia Yougoslavie	...	...	2	2	2	2	2	2	5	4
Yugoslavia, SFR† Yougoslavie, Rfs†	3 816	3 293	...	...	...	...	...	...	...	...

59
Merchant shipping: fleets
Total, Oil tankers and Ore and bulk carrier fleets: thousand gross registered tons [*cont.*]
Transports maritimes : flotte marchande
Total, Pétroliers et Minéraliers et transporteurs de vracs : milliers de tonneaux de jauge brute [*suite*]

Flag Pavillon	1990	1991	1992	1993	1994	1995	1996	1997	1998	1999
Oceania · Océanie										
Australia Australie	2 512	1 709	2 689	2 862	3 012	2 853	2 718	2 607	2 188	2 084
Cook Islands Iles Cook	6	7	5	5	5	4	5	6	7	7
Fiji Fidji	55	50	64	39	31	32	36	36	29	29
French Polynesia Polynésie française	20	20	23	...	...	...	...	...	...	...
Guam Guam	4	1	1	...	...	...	...	...	...	...
Kiribati Kiribati	4	4	5	5	5	6	6	6	4	4
Marshall Islands Iles Marshall	1 551	1 698	1 676	2 198	2 149	3 099	4 897	6 314	6 442	6 762
Micronesia (Fed. States of) Micron (Etats fédérés de)	6	8	9	9	9	8	9	9	10	10
Nauru Nauru	32	15	5	1	...	...	...	...	...	...
New Caledonia Nouvelle-Calédonie	14	14	14	...	...	...	...	...	...	...
New Zealand Nouvelle-Zélande	254	269	238	218	246	307	386	367	336	265
Papua New Guinea Papouasie-Nvl-Guinée	37	36	46	47	47	49	57	60	61	65
Samoa Samoa	27	6	6	6	6	6	...	1	3	3
Solomon Islands Iles Salomon	8	8	8	7	8	8	10	10	10	10
Tonga Tonga	52	40	11	12	10	12	11	12	22	25
Tuvalu Tuvalu	1	1	12	70	51	64	57	55	49	43
Vanuatu Vanuatu	2 164	2 173	2 064	1 946	1 998	1 874	1 711	1 578	1 602	1 444
Wallis and Futuna Islands Iles Wallis et Futuna	39	42	80	80	105	108	92	111	111	159
former USSR† · l'ex-URSS†										
former USSR† l'ex-URSS†	26 737	26 405	...	...	...	...	...	...	...	...

B. Oil tankers · Pétroliers

World *Monde*	134 836	138 897	138 149	143 077	144 595	143 521	146 366	147 108	151 036	154 092
Africa · Afrique										
Algeria Algérie	39	39	32	32	35	35	34	34	33	33
Angola Angola	2	2	2	2	2	2	2	3	3	3

59
Merchant shipping: fleets
Total, Oil tankers and Ore and bulk carrier fleets: thousand gross registered tons [cont.]
Transports maritimes : flotte marchande
Total, Pétroliers et Minéraliers et transporteurs de vracs : milliers de tonneaux de jauge brute [suite]

Flag Pavillon	1990	1991	1992	1993	1994	1995	1996	1997	1998	1999
Cape Verde Cap-Vert	1	1	0	0	0	0	0	1	1	1
Côte d'Ivoire Côte d'Ivoire	0	0	0	0	1	1	1	1	1	1
Egypt Egypte	263	262	170	195	245	222	222	223	210	209
Equatorial Guinea Guinée équatoriale	...	...	...	...	...	...	...	...	5	...
Eritrea Erythrée	...	...	...	...	...	...	...	...	2	2
Ethiopia incl. Eritrea Ethiopie comp. Erythrée	4	4	4	...	...	...	...	...	...	...
Ethiopia Ethiopie	...	...	...	4	4	4	4	...	2	2
Gabon Gabon	0	1	1	1	1	1	1	1	1	1
Ghana Ghana	1	1	1	1	1	1	1	2	6	6
Kenya Kenya	...	4	4	4	4	4	5	5	5	5
Liberia Libéria	28 763	26 700	27 440	26 273	28 275	29 002	28 044	26 699	26 361	21 298
Libyan Arab Jamah. Jamah. arabe libyenne	707	581	581	581	579	572	505	511	395	267
Madagascar Madagascar	5	5	9	9	9	11	11	11	11	11
Mauritius Maurice	...	...	...	...	...	53	53	53	...	...
Morocco Maroc	10	10	14	14	14	14	12	12	12	12
Mozambique Mozambique	1	1	1	1	0	0	0	...	...	...
Nigeria Nigéria	225	225	235	236	245	251	252	250	252	265
Sao Tome and Principe Sao Tomé-et-Principe	...	...	...	...	...	...	...	...	...	1
Sierra Leone Sierra Leone	0	1	1	1	1	1	1	1	1	3
South Africa Afrique du Sud	1	1	1	1	1	1	4	3	3	3
Sudan Soudan	1	1	1	1	1	1	1	1	1	1
Tunisia Tunisie	27	27	27	6	6	9	7	7	22	20
United Rep.Tanzania Rép.-Unie de Tanzanie	3	3	4	5	4	5	5	5	4	4
America, North · Amérique du Nord										
Antigua and Barbuda Antigua-et-Barbuda	11	14	5	7	2	4	4	4	7	5
Bahamas Bahamas	6 780	8 738	9 812	9 680	10 393	10 326	10 863	10 810	11 982	13 158

59
Merchant shipping: fleets
Total, Oil tankers and Ore and bulk carrier fleets: thousand gross registered tons [cont.]
Transports maritimes : flotte marchande
Total, Pétroliers et Minéraliers et transporteurs de vracs : milliers de tonneaux de jauge brute [suite]

Flag Pavillon	1990	1991	1992	1993	1994	1995	1996	1997	1998	1999
Barbados Barbade	...	...	44	44	44	44	22	350	350	350
Belize Belize	...	...	4	9	59	22	67	338	360	321
Bermuda Bermudes	3 285	1 987	2 058	1 838	1 569	1 586	1 586	2 069	2 144	2 652
Canada Canada	242	233	162	153	153	118	110	254	255	250
Cayman Islands Iles Caïmanes	79	72	31	31	6	6	87	114	318	123
Cuba Cuba	80	78	71	67	71	64	27	8	8	3
Dominican Republic Rép. dominicaine	1	1	1	1	1	1	1	1	...	...
Honduras Honduras	112	149	144	119	85	97	103	107	108	131
Jamaica Jamaïque	2	2	2	2	2	2	2	2	2	2
Mexico Mexique	507	507	479	478	425	425	425	435	409	464
Netherlands Antilles Antilles néerlandaises	...	...	32[1]	32	32	139	215	158	135	135
Panama Panama	10 080	13 976	16 454	18 273	18 649	19 513	20 910	21 272	22 680	23 856
St. Vincent-Grenadines St. Vincent-Grenadines	295	378	834	1 112	941	1 101	1 228	1 061	913	569
Trinidad and Tobago Trinité-et-Tobago	...	...	...	...	...	...	...	...	...	1
Turks and Caicos Islands Iles Turques et Caïques	0	1	1	1	1	...	...	...	...	...
United States Etats-Unis	8 532	8 069	5 493	5 013	4 500	3 987	3 630	3 372	3 436	3 491
America, South · Amérique du Sud										
Argentina Argentine	568	542	221	107	124	107	114	105	102	100
Bolivia Bolivie	...	...	...	...	...	...	...	...	...	18
Brazil Brésil	1 897	1 947	1 930	2 068	2 112	2 090	1 803	1 854	1 825	1 770
Chile Chili	26	26	4	4	41	71	93	93	100	100
Colombia Colombie	14	11	6	6	6	6	6	6	6	6
Ecuador Equateur	120	116	112	75	77	77	81	80	93	223
Paraguay Paraguay	1	1	2	2	2	2	4	4	4	4
Peru Pérou	190	177	131	131	68	80	76	76	31	31
Suriname Suriname	2	2	2	2	2	2	2	2	2	2

59
Merchant shipping: fleets
Total, Oil tankers and Ore and bulk carrier fleets: thousand gross registered tons [cont.]
Transports maritimes : flotte marchande
Total, Pétroliers et Minéraliers et transporteurs de vracs : milliers de tonneaux de jauge brute [suite]

Flag Pavillon	1990	1991	1992	1993	1994	1995	1996	1997	1998	1999
Uruguay Uruguay	47	47	46	46	46	46	48	48	48	6
Venezuela Venezuela	463	478	455	437	420	361	275	275	222	222
Asia · Asie										
Azerbaijan Azerbaïdjan	...	...	197	222	180	188	181	180	176	176
Bahrain Bahreïn	2	2	2	2	55	54	54	55	54	54
Bangladesh Bangladesh	50	51	51	51	51	51	59	59	59	61
Cambodia Cambodge	...	...	...	...	...	...	...	...	...	7
China †† Chine ††	1 810	1 840	1 721	2 117	2 278	2 295	2 190	2 014	2 029	2 084
China, Hong Kong SAR† Chine, Hong Kong RAS†	1 000	756	880	818	697	669	396	22	340	515
Cyprus Chypre	5 390	5 996	4 677	4 960	4 634	4 341	3 733	3 779	3 848	3 987
Georgia Géorgie	...	...	...	...	220	136	115	73	73	76
India Inde	1 734	1 805	2 009	2 112	2 337	2 553	2 622	2 515	2 530	2 698
Indonesia Indonésie	582	595	594	608	646	738	849	844	841	830
Iran (Islamic Rep. of) Iran (Rép. islamique d')	3 101	2 945	2 944	2 765	2 135	1 234	1 860	1 844	1 592	1 754
Iraq Iraq	829	725	720	719	719	698	698	422	361	361
Israel Israël	0	0	1	1	1	1	1	1	1	1
Japan Japon	7 584	7 204	7 167	7 249	6 421	6 033	5 819	5 510	5 434	5 006
Jordan Jordanie	...	50	50	50	50	...	...	...	...	...
Korea, Dem. P. R. Corée, R. p. dém. de	13	13	112	115	115	116	4	5	6	6
Korea, Republic of Corée, République de	593	543	612	620	524	399	380	385	328	404
Kuwait Koweït	1 101	1 044	1 706	1 548	1 343	1 343	1 343	1 313	1 662	1 644
Lebanon Liban	14	2	2	2	2	1	2	2	1	1
Malaysia Malaisie	179	249	256	257	382	412	589	689	854	918
Maldives Maldives	5	5	6	6	6	6	6	6	6	4
Myanmar Myanmar	6	9	3	3	3	3	45	3	3	3
Oman Oman	0	0	...	1	0	0	0	0	0	0

59
Merchant shipping: fleets
Total, Oil tankers and Ore and bulk carrier fleets: thousand gross registered tons [*cont.*]
Transports maritimes : flotte marchande
Total, Pétroliers et Minéraliers et transporteurs de vracs : milliers de tonneaux de jauge brute [*suite*]

Flag Pavillon	1990	1991	1992	1993	1994	1995	1996	1997	1998	1999
Pakistan Pakistan	43	43	50	50	50	49	49	50	50	50
Philippines Philippines	372	376	388	414	419	147	158	163	162	159
Qatar Qatar	160	160	125	125	177	105	183	263	263	263
Saudi Arabia Arabie saoudite	928	561	265	277	210	238	258	203	220	218
Singapore Singapour	3 165	3 543	4 182	4 684	4 959	5 102	6 614	7 787	8 781	9 619
Sri Lanka Sri Lanka	78	78	74	74	74	3	5	5	5	5
Thailand Thaïlande	85	100	172	184	190	196	385	411	364	361
Turkey Turquie	777	772	828	903	954	821	709	514	503	584
Turkmenistan Turkménistan	...	...	...	...	1	3	3	3	2	2
United Arab Emirates Emirats arabes unis	332	334	458	326	502	519	410	426	369	248
Viet Nam Viet Nam	18	91	15	91	94	19	20	22	63	105
Yemen Yémen	2	2	2	2	2	2	2	2	2	2
Europe · Europe										
Belgium Belgique	272	12	2	2	3	2	2	2	4	4
Bulgaria Bulgarie	288	293	283	284	256	216	194	163	145	145
Croatia Croatie	...	...	7	7	19	6	8	13	11	11
Denmark Danemark	2 024	2 061	834	787	788	1 053	1 024	741	379	494
Estonia Estonie	...	...	6	6	10	10	6	6	7	8
Faeroe Islands Iles Féroé	...	...	1	1	1	1	3	2	2	2
Finland Finlande	245	209	256	307	303	303	303	303	303	303
France France	1 717	1 674	1 696[2]	1 869[2]	1 957[2]	1 943[2]	1 797[2]	2 049[2]	2 248[2]	2 198[2]
Germany † Allemagne †	...	249	89	89	83	14	11	17	9	8
F. R. Germany R. f. Allemagne	228	...	...	...	...	...	...	...	...	...
former German D. R. l'ex-R. d. allemande	6	...	...	...	...	...	...	...	...	...
Gibraltar Gibraltar	1 552	1 123	319	276	271	272	272	263	233	288
Greece Grèce	7 856	9 095	10 876	13 273	13 386	12 836	13 066	11 894	12 587	13 158

59
Merchant shipping: fleets
Total, Oil tankers and Ore and bulk carrier fleets: thousand gross registered tons [*cont.*]
Transports maritimes : flotte marchande
Total, Pétroliers et Minéraliers et transporteurs de vracs : milliers de tonneaux de jauge brute [*suite*]

Flag Pavillon	1990	1991	1992	1993	1994	1995	1996	1997	1998	1999
Iceland Islande	1	1	0	2	2	2	2	2	2	2
Ireland Irlande	19	19	8	8	9	9	3	3	0	0
Isle of Man Ile de Man	...	...	801	744	1 059	872	1 023	2 401	1 893	2 409
Italy Italie	2 560	2 685	2 115	1 949	2 181	1 956	1 781	1 608	1 547	1 660
Latvia Lettonie	...	...	533	536	483	323	279	137	9	9
Lithuania Lituanie	...	...	17	12	13	8	5	5	4	4
Luxembourg Luxembourg	2	264	107	55	3	3	165	165	244	543
Malta Malte	1 646	2 412	3 086	5 176	5 699	6 793	7 370	9 043	9 848	12 151
Netherlands Pays-Bas	590	618	364	407	403	405	412	18	16	25
Norway Norvège	10 794	10 904	9 220	9 265	8 962	8 779	8 895	9 244	8 993	9 195
Poland Pologne	154	136	89	89	88	7	6	5	5	5
Portugal Portugal	393	460	657	723	552	490	217	349	416	416
Romania Roumanie	645	679	520	446	438	429	429	249	204	68
Russian Federation Fédération de Russie	...	...	2 436	2 507	2 378	2 294	1 917	1 646	1 608	1 429
Spain Espagne	1 472	1 488	917[3]	452	430	437	515	510	585	583
Sweden Suède	534	862	692	368	370	385	392	307	105	102
Ukraine Ukraine	...	...	80	80	84	81	79	89	62	56
United Kingdom Royaume-Uni	2 367	2 316	1 179	1 176	1 185	1 115	876	476	625	544
Yugoslavia, SFR† Yougoslavie, Rfs†	306	264	...	...	...	...	...	...	...	...
Oceania · Océanie										
Australia Australie	677	708	780	780	779	579	467	380	226	226
Fiji Fidji	4	4	4	3	3	3	3	3	3	3
Kiribati Kiribati	...	...	...	...	...	2	2	2	...	...
Marshall Islands Iles Marshall	...	...	1 146	1 601	1 560	1 502	2 721	3 388	3 561	4 313
New Caledonia Nouvelle-Calédonie	...	...	1	...	...	...	...	...	...	...

59
Merchant shipping: fleets
Total, Oil tankers and Ore and bulk carrier fleets: thousand gross registered tons [*cont.*]
Transports maritimes : flotte marchande
Total, Pétroliers et Minéraliers et transporteurs de vracs : milliers de tonneaux de jauge brute [*suite*]

Flag Pavillon	1990	1991	1992	1993	1994	1995	1996	1997	1998	1999
New Zealand Nouvelle-Zélande	80	80	73	54	54	76	61	61	73	73
Papua New Guinea Papouasie-Nvl-Guinée	2	2	3	3	3	3	7	4	3	3
Vanuatu Vanuatu	233	233	184	24	15	38	40	14	11	11
Wallis and Futuna Islands Iles Wallis et Futuna	...	...	50	50	75	75	75	75	75	75
	former USSR† · l'ex-URSS†									
former USSR† l'ex-URSS†	4 167	4 068	...	...	...	...	...	...	...	...

C. Ore and bulk carrier fleets · Minéraliers et transporteurs de vracs

World Monde	133 190	135 884	139 042	140 915	144 914	151 694	157 382	162 169	158 565	158 957
	Africa · Afrique									
Algeria Algérie	153	172	172	172	172	172	172	172	172	172
Egypt Egypte	343	343	343	343	420	510	487	575	613	601
Gabon Gabon	...	...	...	11	11	24	24	24	12	...
Liberia Libéria	16 099	15 629	17 035	15 640	15 970	16 373	16 744	17 711	16 739	14 426
Mauritius Maurice	47	47	80	116	120	2	2	4	4	4
Morocco Maroc	92	92	92	...	...	...	...	...	...	...
Nigeria Nigéria	...	...	1	1	1	...	...	...	...	...
Tunisia Tunisie	37	37	37	37	37	38	38	38	27	17
	America, North · Amérique du Nord									
Antigua and Barbuda Antigua-et-Barbuda	3	3	43	90	93	102	174	174	294	196
Bahamas Bahamas	3 698	4 872	4 312	4 515	4 269	4 501	4 425	4 728	4 990	4 943
Barbados Barbade	...	...	...	...	...	74	226	268	174	174
Belize Belize	...	...	...	5	5	20	160	195	190	210
Bermuda Bermudes	161	199	213	147	165	248	301	1 018	1 089	1 910
Canada Canada	1 462	1 414	1 425	1 377	1 371	1 335	1 347	1 352	1 352	1 338
Cayman Islands Iles Caïmanes	89	54	69	100	136	104	282	282	455	526
Cuba Cuba	62	62	31	30	1	1	1	2	2	2

59
Merchant shipping: fleets
Total, Oil tankers and Ore and bulk carrier fleets: thousand gross registered tons [cont.]
Transports maritimes : flotte marchande
Total, Pétroliers et Minéraliers et transporteurs de vracs : milliers de tonneaux de jauge brute [suite]

Flag Pavillon	1990	1991	1992	1993	1994	1995	1996	1997	1998	1999
Dominican Republic Rép. dominicaine	11	...	...	...	...	...	...	...	...	...
Honduras Honduras	56	57	92	90	118	138	115	114	77	133
Mexico Mexique	178	48	...	...	...	...	...	...	...	...
Netherlands Antilles Antilles néerlandaises	...	...	113[1]	131	146	71	108	108	...	...
Panama Panama	13 293	13 669	17 327	19 280	22 169	26 726	33 019	38 617	40 319	42 726
St. Vincent-Grenadines St. Vincent-Grenadines	651	1 004	1 816	1 798	1 939	2 328	2 627	3 202	2 858	2 656
United States Etats-Unis	2 140	2 168	1 550	1 539	1 546	1 513	1 301	1 275	1 268	1 268
America, South · Amérique du Sud										
Argentina Argentine	502	365	62	62	62	62	34	34	34	34
Bolivia Bolivie	...	...	...	...	...	...	...	...	7	49
Brazil Brésil	2 971	2 855	2 378	2 199	2 214	2 077	1 890	1 706	1 501	1 453
Chile Chili	296	296	279	297	306	294	191	213	188	203
Colombia Colombie	81	81	63	63	...	...	...	...	...	...
Ecuador Equateur	27	27	22	22	22	...	...	...	...	...
Peru Pérou	129	129	64	49	31	31	15	...	...	15
Venezuela Venezuela	147	147	96	147	147	111	111	111	126	116
Asia · Asie										
Bahrain Bahreïn	...	...	8	8	8	8	8	33	33	33
Bangladesh Bangladesh	...	...	...	...	7	7	7	6	6	
Cambodia Cambodge	...	...	...	...	...	95	146	169	305	
China †† Chine ††	4 907	5 206	5 405	5 714	5 960	6 677	6 781	6 464	6 832	6 648
China, Hong Kong SAR† Chine, Hong Kong RAS†	4 396	3 925	4 864	5 466	5 570	6 405	5 749	4 211	4 208	5 233
Cyprus Chypre	9 226	10 234	10 816	12 277	12 317	13 084	12 653	11 819	11 090	11 511
Georgia Géorgie	...	...	...	...	170	104	48	0	0	0
India Inde	3 182	3 134	2 912	2 939	2 740	3 183	3 081	3 013	2 832	2 748
Indonesia Indonésie	138	149	170	170	170	205	222	335	358	380

59
Merchant shipping: fleets
Total, Oil tankers and Ore and bulk carrier fleets: thousand gross registered tons [cont.]
Transports maritimes : flotte marchande
Total, Pétroliers et Minéraliers et transporteurs de vracs : milliers de tonneaux de jauge brute [suite]

Flag Pavillon	1990	1991	1992	1993	1994	1995	1996	1997	1998	1999
Iran (Islamic Rep. of) Iran (Rép. islamique d')	1 059	1 059	1 047	1 049	1 048	1 015	1 015	1 015	990	957
Israel Israël	32	22	22	22	23	12	12	12	...	...
Japan Japon	8 788	8 652	8 509	7 336	6 615	5 445	4 956	4 558	3 869	3 556
Jordan Jordanie	25	13	...	10	10	21	40	40	21	21
Korea, Dem. P. R. Corée, R. p. dém. de	79	79	84	130	128	107	107	96	50	53
Korea, Republic of Corée, République de	4 708	4 463	3 931	3 575	3 659	3 706	3 650	3 542	2 809	2 708
Kuwait Koweït	...	...	...	...	...	...	...	...	17	17
Lebanon Liban	44	44	55	46	46	81	73	124	108	152
Malaysia Malaisie	347	319	449	556	798	982	1 272	1 305	1 448	1 513
Maldives Maldives	32	21	19	11	11	11	11	...	...	...
Myanmar Myanmar	518	569	553	415	358	215	310	298	283	301
Pakistan Pakistan	...	...	17	17	88	115	159	158	125	30
Philippines Philippines	6 344	6 262	6 040	5 999	6 496	6 138	6 334	5 951	5 597	4 822
Qatar Qatar	...	...	...	70	141	142	142	142	142	142
Saudi Arabia Arabie saoudite	26	...	12	12	12	12	12	12	12	...
Singapore Singapour	2 190	2 132	2 626	2 889	3 209	3 766	4 344	4 358	4 585	4 695
Sri Lanka Sri Lanka	103	93	93	93	93	93	93	95	77	77
Syrian Arab Republic Rép. arabe syrienne	...	14	24	32	48	48	45	14	22	30
Thailand Thaïlande	10	32	69	158	224	387	480	567	491	476
Turkey Turquie	1 932	2 331	2 263	3 036	3 253	4 007	4 168	4 444	4 023	3 939
Turkmenistan Turkménistan	...	...	...	...	...	...	...	...	...	5
United Arab Emirates Emirats arabes unis	34	32	60	27	47	35	37	20	20	20
Viet Nam Viet Nam	14	21	21	21	21	21	63	94	94	94
Europe · Europe										
Austria Autriche	71	71	63	85	49	...	...	...	...	...
Belgium Belgique	979	...	...	...	...	...	56	...	...	...

59
Merchant shipping: fleets
Total, Oil tankers and Ore and bulk carrier fleets: thousand gross registered tons [cont.]
Transports maritimes : flotte marchande
Total, Pétroliers et Minéraliers et transporteurs de vracs : milliers de tonneaux de jauge brute [suite]

Flag Pavillon	1990	1991	1992	1993	1994	1995	1996	1997	1998	1999
Bulgaria Bulgarie	611	601	613	589	578	502	532	542	532	518
Croatia Croatie	...	...	32	3	19	19	186	469	517	504
former Czechoslovakia† l'ex-Tchécoslovaquie†	241	276	153	...	...	...	...	...	...	...
Czech Republic République tchèque	...	...	...	153	112	98	78	16	...	...
Denmark Danemark	353	525	563	498	569	493	521	522	522	464
Estonia Estonie	...	...	160	160	160	160	160	160	96	65
Finland Finlande	120	89	72	71	71	80	80	80	90	90
France France	357	406	343[2]	463[2]	462[2]	291[2]	448[2]	355[2]	354[2]	539[2]
Germany † Allemagne †	...	695	377	308	285	238	48	2	2	2
F. R. Germany R. f. Allemagne	397	...	...	...	...	...	...	...	...	...
former German D. R. l'ex-R. d. allemande	324	...	...	...	...	...	...	...	...	...
Gibraltar Gibraltar	344	192	73	58	28	...	...	...	...	16
Greece Grèce	9 783	10 802	11 638	12 482	12 988	12 795	10 705	9 472	8 771	7 709
Iceland Islande	4	...	0	0	0	0	0	0	0	0
Ireland Irlande	9	9	3	3	3	...	...	...	...	8
Isle of Man Ile de Man	...	...	304	171	223	414	756	831	783	732
Italy Italie	2 346	2 228	2 200	1 829	1 549	1 535	1 553	1 303	1 525	1 851
Lithuania Lituanie	...	...	112	116	111	111	110	110	110	110
Luxembourg Luxembourg	...	993	879	669	555	365	86	86	86	93
Malta Malte	1 774	2 772	5 103	5 854	6 196	6 857	7 478	8 623	8 616	9 984
Netherlands Pays-Bas	328	359	244	98	99	99	68	68	77	77
Norway Norvège	7 283	7 091	5 912	4 924	4 865	4 010	3 858	3 908	4 041	3 913
Poland Pologne	1 603	1 636	1 667	1 524	1 511	1 455	1 455	1 360	1 082	993
Portugal Portugal	223	197	75	27	85	127	128	128	188	160
Romania Roumanie	1 891	1 698	1 082	1 089	980	850	865	865	788	320
Russian Federation Fédération de Russie	...	...	1 903	1 821	1 757	1 768	1 767	1 568	1 031	889

59
Merchant shipping: fleets
Total, Oil tankers and Ore and bulk carrier fleets: thousand gross registered tons [*cont.*]
Transports maritimes : flotte marchande
Total, Pétroliers et Minéraliers et transporteurs de vracs : milliers de tonneaux de jauge brute [*suite*]

Flag Pavillon	1990	1991	1992	1993	1994	1995	1996	1997	1998	1999
Spain Espagne	850	732	504	223	59	68	23	39	42	42
Sweden Suède	383	415	209	119	45	52	44	38	32	32
Switzerland Suisse	252	252	312	268	307	351	370	389	349	393
Ukraine Ukraine	...	...	1 199	1 195	1 196	729	452	254	207	161
United Kingdom Royaume-Uni	749	743	122	104	74	74	67	64	48	33
Yugoslavia, SFR† Yougoslavie, Rfs†	2 018	1 707	...	...	...	...	...	...	...	...
Oceania · Océanie										
Australia Australie	1 112	1 004	987	1 030	1 049	1 011	1 039	1 036	893	801
Marshall Islands Iles Marshall	...	...	440	506	539	701	1 095	1 666	1 602	1 255
Nauru Nauru	17	...	...	...	...	...	...	...	...	...
New Zealand Nouvelle-Zélande	26	13	22	25	25	25	25	12	12	12
Vanuatu Vanuatu	1 133	1 132	1 052	1 117	1 008	841	706	620	708	518
former USSR† · l'ex-URSS†										
former USSR† l'ex-URSS†	4 183	3 902	...	...	...	...	...	...	...	...

Source:
Lloyd's Register of Shipping, London, "World Fleet
Statistics 1999" and previous issues.

† For information on recent changes in country or
area nomenclature pertaining to former Czechoslovakia,
Germany, Hong Kong Special Administrative Region (SAR) of
China, Macao Special Administrative Region (SAR) of China,
SFR of Yugoslavia and the former USSR, see Annex I - Country
or area nomenclature, regional and other groupings.

†† For statistical purposes, the data for
China do not include those for Hong Kong Special
Administrative Region (Hong Kong SAR), Macao Special
Administrative Region (Macao SAR) and Taiwan province of
China.

1 Including Aruba.
2 Including French Antarctic Territory.
3 Including Canary Islands.

Source:
"Lloyd's Register of Shipping", Londres, "World Fleet
Statistics 1999" et éditions précédentes.

† Pour les modifications récentes de nomenclature
de pays ou de zone concernant l'Allemagne, Hong Kong, région
administrative spéciale (RAS) de Chine, Macao, région
administrative spéciale (RAS) de Chine,
l'ex-Tchécoslovaquie, l'ex-URSS et l'ex-Rfs de Yougoslavie,
voir annexe I - Nomenclature des pays ou des zones,
groupements régionaux et autres groupements.

†† Les données statistiques relatives à
la Chine ne comprennent pas celles qui concernent la région
administrative spéciale de Hong Kong (la RAS de Hong Kong),
la région administrative spéciale de Macao (la RAS de Macao)
et la province chinoise de Taiwan.

1 Y compris Aruba.
2 Y compris le territoire antarctique français.
3 Y compris les Iles Canaries.

60
International maritime transport
Transports maritimes internationaux
Vessels entered and cleared: thousand net registered tons
Navires entrés et sortis : milliers de tonneaux de jauge nette

Country or area Pays ou zone	1990	1991	1992	1993	1994	1995	1996	1997	1998	1999
Albania Albanie										
Vessels entered Navires entrés	...	...	...	288	576	1 002	1 218	1 053	1 419	1 115
Vessels cleared Navires sortis	...	...	...	121	198	309	213	123	61	29
Algeria Algérie										
Vessels entered Navires entrés	86 861	86 254	85 577	84 744	86 500	88 502	93 913	103 201	106 256	111 525
Vessels cleared Navires sortis	86 693	86 213	85 730	84 659	86 767	88 865	93 676	103 187	108 036	...
American Samoa Samoa américaines										
Vessels entered[1] Navires entrés[1]	...	848	618	440	581	526	452	725	589	884
Antigua and Barbuda Antigua-et-Barbuda										
Vessels entered Navires entrés	...	...	...	...	...	...	57 386	94 907	...	...
Vessels cleared Navires sortis	...	...	...	...	...	...	544 328	667 126	...	...
Argentina Argentine										
Vessels entered[2] Navires entrés[2]	38 283	36 664[3]	11 379[4]	20 092[5]	12 345[4]	...	...	...	...	...
Vessels cleared[2] Navires sortis[2]	44 611					...	...	...	...	...
Australia Australie										
Vessels entered[1 6] Navires entrés[1 6]	...	...	...	...	...	2 299	2 268	2 238	2 248	2 294
Azerbaijan Azerbaïdjan										
Vessels entered Navires entrés	...	...	115	142	127	925	1 022	2 007	3 967	4 015
Vessels cleared Navires sortis	...	...	1 849	1 568	2 289	1 751	1 702	1 737	1 483	624
Bahrain Bahreïn										
Vessels entered Navires entrés	1	1	1	1	1	1	2	2	...	...
Bangladesh Bangladesh										
Vessels entered[7] Navires entrés[7]	5 512	4 997	5 375	4 835	4 832	6 013	5 928	5 488	5 794	6 509
Vessels cleared[7] Navires sortis[7]	3 208	2 816	2 943	3 103	2 556	3 094	3 136	2 866	2 556	2 949
Belgium Belgique										
Vessels entered Navires entrés	204 857	211 767	236 323	229 915	239 678	253 427	297 664	337 862	367 684	...
Vessels cleared Navires sortis	162 236	165 185	189 286	190 795	201 448	210 144	297 610	333 694	360 987	...
Benin Bénin										
Vessels entered Navires entrés	933	993	937	1 134	1 163	...	...	...	...	...
Brazil Brésil										
Vessels entered Navires entrés	61 852	65 461	65 794	74 314	78 757	79 732	82 593	86 720	92 822	...
Vessels cleared Navires sortis	170 917	166 047	164 152	173 624	185 291	197 955	192 889	209 330	216 273	...
Cambodia Cambodge										
Vessels entered[8] Navires entrés[8]	257	135	468	463	608	647	726	715	781	1 056
Vessels cleared Navires sortis	163	158	124	193	182	214	145	293	319	191

60
International maritime transport
Vessels entered and cleared: thousand net registered tons [cont.]
Transports maritimes internationaux
Navires entrés et sortis : milliers de tonneaux de jauge nette [suite]

Country or area Pays ou zone	1990	1991	1992	1993	1994	1995	1996	1997	1998	1999
Cameroon Cameroun										
Vessels entered[29]										
Navires entrés[29]	5 521	5 426	5 344	5 279	...	...	...	...	...	...
Canada Canada										
Vessels entered[10]										
Navires entrés[10]	64 163	58 690	58 724	56 769	60 417	62 415	66 166	74 422	...	...
Vessels cleared[10]										
Navires sortis[10]	114 272	116 974	109 263	108 587	116 279	114 040	117 452	124 999	...	...
Cape Verde Cap-Vert										
Vessels entered										
Navires entrés	...	...	...	...	3 409	3 628	3 601	3 590	4 296	...
China, Hong Kong SAR† Chine, Hong Kong RAS†										
Vessels entered										
Navires entrés	129 864	138 102	160 193	184 166	201 919	216 437	229 444	250 303	261 694	267 255
Vessels cleared										
Navires sortis	130 001	138 023	160 436	184 023	201 607	217 539	229 474	250 399	261 552	267 419
Colombia Colombie										
Vessels entered[2]										
Navires entrés[2]	22 713	23 732	21 967	24 874	28 138	32 191	35 787	40 863	50 712	68 649
Vessels cleared										
Navires sortis	22 448	23 809	22 056	24 967	27 919	31 813	34 585	39 562	48 530	65 790
Congo Congo										
Vessels entered										
Navires entrés	7 148	6 480	...	...	...	...	...	...	...	...
Costa Rica Costa Rica										
Vessels entered										
Navires entrés	2 565	2 942	3 326	3 684	4 004	4 202	4 135	3 555	4 024	...
Vessels cleared										
Navires sortis	2 007	2 045	2 510	2 760	2 983	3 070	2 992	2 941	3 405	...
Croatia Croatie										
Vessels entered										
Navires entrés	43 736	30 801	27 591	29 753	31 438	34 306	86 065[6]	93 270[6]	101 914[6]	118 029[6]
Vessels cleared										
Navires sortis	35 624	25 133	24 542	27 701	33 505	32 214	81 757[6]	91 599[6]	96 306[6]	114 168[6]
Cyprus Chypre										
Vessels entered										
Navires entrés	14 964	12 860	14 791	14 918	15 350	15 700	19 033	16 478	15 955	18 017
Dominica Dominique										
Vessels entered										
Navires entrés	...	...	...	...	2 214	2 252	2 289	2 145	2 218	...
Dominican Republic Rép. dominicaine										
Vessels entered										
Navires entrés	6 536	6 698	7 489	7 563	8 421	8 751	9 238	10 113	10 719	13 603
Vessels cleared										
Navires sortis	794	736	796	788	770	1 162	1 341	1 822	1 673	1 609
Ecuador Equateur										
Vessels entered										
Navires entrés	1 958	2 389	2 563	2 719	3 006	3 665	3 283	3 263	3 158	...
Vessels cleared										
Navires sortis	11 783	13 916	15 208	15 459	16 958	18 010	17 450	18 277	16 937	...
Egypt Egypte										
Vessels entered										
Navires entrés	29 765	38 555	39 606	41 253	44 726	48 008	47 824	48 866	40 834	...
Vessels cleared										
Navires sortis	23 193	28 047	33 059	34 307	37 377	41 257	43 386	40 924	33 711	...
El Salvador El Salvador										
Vessels entered										
Navires entrés	2 208	2 270	3 008	3 012	3 393	3 185	3 345	5 633	7 969	3 374

60
International maritime transport
Vessels entered and cleared: thousand net registered tons [*cont.*]
Transports maritimes internationaux
Navires entrés et sortis : milliers de tonneaux de jauge nette [*suite*]

Country or area Pays ou zone	1990	1991	1992	1993	1994	1995	1996	1997	1998	1999
Vessels cleared Navires sortis	551	589	834	938	861	625	822	550	490	566
Estonia Estonie										
Vessels entered Navires entrés	..	...	...	3 419	2 376[6]	...	...	...	...	...
Vessels cleared Navires sortis	..	...	...	3 087	3 813[6]	...	...	...	...	...
Fiji Fidji										
Vessels entered Navires entrés	3 262	3 136	3 381	2 876	2 843	4 065	4 070	...	...	...
Finland Finlande										
Vessels entered[2] Navires entrés[2]	102 500	112 418	119 238	117 003	111 934	127 711	131 338	144 923	148 690	153 149
Vessels cleared[2] Navires sortis[2]	102 995	111 948	119 040	121 946	117 143	132 879	135 650	148 366	150 969	154 700
France France										
Vessels entered[11][12] Navires entrés[11][12]	1 681 491	1 751 943	1 825 276	1 861 742	1 941 433	1 893 000	1 975 705	1 989 767	2 133 346	
Gambia Gambie										
Vessels entered[1] Navires entrés[1]	1 044	1 075	1 117	1 153	...	...	...	...	...	...
Germany † Allemagne †										
Vessels entered Navires entrés	..	...	225 984	221 741	223 363	221 226	251 500	260 553	263 470	271 978
Vessels cleared Navires sortis	..	...	199 441	196 456	201 316	197 339	229 959	235 110	237 071	249 225
F. R. Germany R. f. Allemagne										
Vessels entered Navires entrés	171 906	181 086	..	..	..	...	...	...	...	...
Vessels cleared Navires sortis	150 514	156 178	..	..	..	...	...	...	...	...
former German D. R. l'ex-R. d. allemande										
Vessels entered Navires entrés	8 713	..	..	..	..	...	...	...	...	...
Vessels cleared Navires sortis	8 327	..	..	..	..	...	...	...	...	...
Gibraltar Gibraltar										
Vessels entered Navires entrés	209	291	321	307	276	256	...	...	...	...
Greece Grèce										
Vessels entered Navires entrés	35 153	36 679	37 789	32 429	33 048	38 573	38 549	38 704	...	...
Vessels cleared Navires sortis	22 262	20 118	20 401	18 467	21 087	21 940	21 356	19 359	...	...
Guadeloupe Guadeloupe										
Vessels entered[2] Navires entrés[2]	2 557	2 579	...	...	...	...	...	...	...	...
Guatemala Guatemala										
Vessels entered Navires entrés	2 111	2 349	2 747	3 367	4 008	3 976	3 680	4 505	...	...
Vessels cleared Navires sortis	1 772	1 740	2 025	2 266	2 280	2 854	3 275	3 815	...	...
Haiti Haïti										
Vessels entered[13] Navires entrés[13]	995	987	583	897	529	1 285	1 680	1 304	...	...
India Inde										
Vessels entered[14][15] Navires entrés[14][15]	34 260	18 982	30 125	27 825	39 619	47 857	48 358	47 055	48 512	...

60

International maritime transport
Vessels entered and cleared: thousand net registered tons [cont.]
Transports maritimes internationaux
Navires entrés et sortis : milliers de tonneaux de jauge nette [suite]

Country or area Pays ou zone	1990	1991	1992	1993	1994	1995	1996	1997	1998	1999
Vessels cleared[14][15] Navires sortis[14][15]	35 666	23 423	34 660	36 325	42 885	48 497	44 494	45 819	39 031	...
Indonesia Indonésie										
Vessels entered Navires entrés	109 490	113 380	128 571	140 861	155 869	163 597	259 096	286 314	249 159	248 616
Vessels cleared Navires sortis	26 105	34 903	38 178	41 993	48 857	48 753	75 055	97 885	82 711	73 938
Iran (Islamic Rep. of) Iran (Rép. islamique d')										
Vessels entered Navires entrés	9 795	12 218	12 772	11 218	13 795	14 686	17 155	27 756	46 985	61 048
Ireland Irlande										
Vessels entered[2] Navires entrés[2]	31 769	32 892	33 857	36 408	37 896	45 968	54 602	165 925[6]	176 228[6]	...
Vessels cleared Navires sortis	12 523	12 495	12 109	13 199	15 113	15 890	16 787	16 463	16 669	...
Italy Italie										
Vessels entered Navires entrés	173 360	184 693	175 940	168 545	180 175	181 733	190 910	226 977	250 830	...
Vessels cleared Navires sortis	74 000	80 303	79 600	84 044	91 288	96 505	160 757	132 532	152 655	...
Jamaica Jamaïque										
Vessels entered Navires entrés	...	...	...	...	9 892	10 531	12 339	12 815	...	...
Vessels cleared Navires sortis	...	...	4 859	5 576	5 599	5 730	6 043	6 457	6 553	...
Japan Japon										
Vessels entered[2] Navires entrés[2]	385 110	402 190	398 240	397 582	410 164	412 163	422 256	438 111	425 193	446 482
Jordan Jordanie										
Vessels entered Navires entrés	1 678	1 690	2 041	2 143	1 910	2 382	2 735	2 997	2 608	2 551
Vessels cleared Navires sortis	544	385	392	347	576	...	...	...	...	...
Kenya Kenya										
Vessels entered[2][9] Navires entrés[2][9]	6 134	5 897	7 112	7 917	8 269	7 973	8 694	8 442	8 413	
Korea, Republic of Corée, République de										
Vessels entered Navires entrés	279 004	317 046	348 767	383 311	430 872	487 851	537 163	578 373	586 629	...
Vessels cleared Navires sortis	278 423	316 670	350 906	381 545	429 538	485 357	542 600	584 164	595 072	...
Kuwait Koweït										
Vessels entered Navires entrés	1 482	...	6 230	6 248	9 775	10 723	9 676	9 171	9 357	...
Vessels cleared Navires sortis	1 131	...	619	944	1 184	1 222	1 223	1 285	1 178	...
Libyan Arab Jamah. Jamah. arabe libyenne										
Vessels entered Navires entrés	6 081	6 592	5 850	6 492	5 277	5 142	5 638	5 980	6 245	5 304
Vessels cleared Navires sortis	334	327	456	556	572	751	624	647	739	815
Lithuania Lituanie										
Vessels entered[2][6] Navires entrés[2][6]	...	...	...	...	...	25 642	32 187	34 259	35 680	32 438
Vessels cleared[2][6] Navires sortis[2][6]	...	...	...	...	...	25 477	31 383	34 161	35 658	32 419

60
International maritime transport
Vessels entered and cleared: thousand net registered tons [*cont.*]
Transports maritimes internationaux
Navires entrés et sortis : milliers de tonneaux de jauge nette [*suite*]

Country or area Pays ou zone	1990	1991	1992	1993	1994	1995	1996	1997	1998	1999
Madagascar Madagascar										
Vessels entered[2]										
Navires entrés [2]	2 161	...	...	...	...	...	...	...	...	...
Vessels cleared[2]										
Navires sortis[2]	2 160	...	...	...	...	...	...	...	...	...
Malaysia Malaisie										
Vessels entered[16]										
Navires entrés[16]	95 724	101 170	108 170	109 300	110 330	...	...	...	...	...
Vessels cleared[16]										
Navires sortis[16]	94 713	101 230	109 070	109 000	110 650	...	...	...	...	...
Malta Malte										
Vessels entered										
Navires entrés	4 068	5 087	7 049	6 802	7 657	9 404	9 830	11 597	13 738	16 725
Vessels cleared										
Navires sortis	1 670	2 377	3 160	3 534	2 471	2 887	3 779	4 976	2 493	5 084
Mauritius Maurice										
Vessels entered[2]										
Navires entrés[2]	4 364	6 157	5 277	5 271	5 500	5 356	4 999	5 485	5 925	6 725
Vessels cleared										
Navires sortis	4 357	6 188	5 447	5 219	5 550	5 313	5 140	5 263	5 924	6 129
Mexico Mexique										
Vessels entered										
Navires entrés	19 020	19 069	21 520	20 241	21 918	19 696	27 533	33 317	43 185	43 505
Vessels cleared										
Navires sortis	88 897	94 440	97 464	101 688	100 757	103 355	117 598	125 571	125 682	126 044
Morocco Maroc										
Vessels entered[17]										
Navires entrés[17]	20 855	19 769	21 578	22 436	22 633	24 034	26 271	27 088	27 478	...
Myanmar Myanmar										
Vessels entered										
Navires entrés	610	698	879	1 278	1 587	2 388	2 286	2 230	2 955	2 729
Vessels cleared										
Navires sortis	577	667	1 205	1 408	1 612	1 624	1 108	794	1 235	1 656
Netherlands Pays-Bas										
Vessels entered[6]										
Navires entrés[6]	365 350	374 428	383 164	375 906	403 355	431 997	441 281	456 522	472 977	...
Vessels cleared[6]										
Navires sortis[6]	224 415	232 349	239 572	237 817	258 152	280 667	291 089	290 813	301 559	...
New Zealand Nouvelle-Zélande										
Vessels entered[6]										
Navires entrés[6]	32 592	38 069	27 983	37 603	39 700	48 827	...	...	...	...
Vessels cleared[6]										
Navires sortis[6]	31 967	36 158	27 508	35 128	37 421	42 985	...	...	...	...
Nicaragua Nicaragua										
Vessels entered										
Navires entrés	2	1	1	1	1	2	2	2	2	2
Nigeria Nigéria										
Vessels entered										
Navires entrés	2 160	2 350	2 352	2 776	1 908	1 846[18]	2 043	2 464	...	...
Vessels cleared										
Navires sortis	2 132	3 092	2 275	2 830	1 879	1 852[18]	2 104	2 510	...	...
Oman Oman										
Vessels entered										
Navires entrés	1	1	1	2	1	1	1	2	1	...
Vessels cleared										
Navires sortis	4 816	5 156	2 745	1 146	1 192	1 309	5 529	6 781	7 147	...
Pakistan Pakistan										
Vessels entered[7]										
Navires entrés[7]	15 057	16 289	19 401	18 785	20 195	21 268	22 632	26 915	26 502	...

60
International maritime transport
Vessels entered and cleared: thousand net registered tons [*cont.*]
Transports maritimes internationaux
Navires entrés et sortis : milliers de tonneaux de jauge nette [*suite*]

Country or area Pays ou zone	1990	1991	1992	1993	1994	1995	1996	1997	1998	1999
Vessels cleared[7] Navires sortis[7]	6 743	7 692	7 382	7 284	8 287	7 411	7 728	5 748	6 983	...
Panama Panama										
Vessels entered Navires entrés	1 337	1 660	1 959	2 178	2 404	2 766	3 263	4 431	7 814	...
Vessels cleared Navires sortis	1 377	1 492	1 513	1 560	1 643	1 972	2 367	2 927	5 454	...
Peru Pérou										
Vessels entered Navires entrés	4 363	6 115	7 012	6 066	7 145	7 454	7 516	6 693	...	...
Vessels cleared Navires sortis	9 076	9 815	8 852	9 186	4 930	4 640	4 731	5 961	...	...
Philippines Philippines										
Vessels entered Navires entrés	30 441	28 969	29 876	32 388	38 222	40 876	...	...	...	...
Vessels cleared Navires sortis	22 810	22 442	19 411	22 431	25 582	27 829	...	...	...	...
Poland Pologne										
Vessels entered Navires entrés	12 959	13 116	15 573	15 544	14 816	18 316	20 997	24 280	25 549	24 161
Vessels cleared Navires sortis	21 131	18 277	20 031	23 222	25 552	25 269	25 566	28 877	30 065	30 062
Portugal Portugal										
Vessels entered Navires entrés	35 757	34 909	36 415	32 654	34 544	36 095	...	...	...	...
Réunion Réunion										
Vessels entered[17] Navires entrés[17]	2 051	2 103	2 375	2 421	2 349	2 715	2 595	2 755	3 065	...
Romania Roumanie										
Vessels entered Navires entrés	...	...	...	...	...	...	23 985	21 748	18 966	11 093
Vessels cleared Navires sortis	...	...	...	...	...	...	14 016	12 643	11 673	12 276
Russian Federation Fédération de Russie										
Vessels entered[2] Navires entrés[2]	...	...	...	...	...	...	...	...	67 110	82 544
Vessels cleared[2] Navires sortis[2]	...	...	...	...	...	...	...	...	68 830	82 939
Saint Helena Sainte-Hélène										
Vessels entered Navires entrés	78	216	244	319	254	55	...	...	...	...
Saint Lucia Sainte-Lucie										
Vessels entered Navires entrés	2 063	1 761	1 331	...	...	4 755	5 317	6 803	...	...
St. Vincent-Grenadines St. Vincent-Grenadines										
Vessels entered Navires entrés	1 185	1 143	1 233	1 336	1 037	932	1 204	1 253	1 274	1 478
Vessels cleared Navires sortis	1 120	1 083	1 233	1 336	1 037	932	1 204	1 253	1 274	1 478
Samoa Samoa										
Vessels entered Navires entrés	501	527	425	530	563	579	544	662	685	827
Senegal Sénégal										
Vessels entered Navires entrés	...	8 985	9 447	9 625	...	...	...	...	...	...

60
International maritime transport
Vessels entered and cleared: thousand net registered tons [*cont.*]
Transports maritimes internationaux
Navires entrés et sortis : milliers de tonneaux de jauge nette [*suite*]

Country or area Pays ou zone	1990	1991	1992	1993	1994	1995	1996	1997	1998	1999
Vessels cleared Navires sortis	...	8 987	9 477	9 769	...	...	...	...	...	...
Seychelles Seychelles										
Vessels entered Navires entrés	953	769	778	871	764	879	872	1 059	1 099	1 139
Singapore Singapour										
Vessels entered[19] Navires entrés[19]	60 347	70 345	81 334	92 655	101 107	104 014	117 723	130 333	140 922	...
Vessels cleared[19] Navires sortis[19]	...	70 119	81 245	92 477	101 017	104 123	117 662	130 237	140 838	
Slovakia Slovaquie										
Vessels entered Navires entrés	...	...	...	387	379	374	401	367	381	336
Slovenia Slovénie										
Vessels entered Navires entrés	6 111	4 721	4 594	4 997	4 903	5 530	6 099	7 734	9 111	9 318
Vessels cleared Navires sortis	9 709	4 904	4 713	5 008	4 872	5 473	6 086	7 862	8 421	9 273
South Africa Afrique du Sud										
Vessels entered[6] Navires entrés[6]	15 138	13 396	13 309	13 437	13 037	...	...	...	...	...
Vessels cleared[6] Navires sortis[6]	389 880	402 011	439 645	441 053	472 025	...	...	...	...	...
Spain Espagne										
Vessels entered Navires entrés	125 881	132 398	134 847	130 171	137 951	154 134	149 874	152 951	170 817	...
Vessels cleared Navires sortis	43 208	43 226	43 255	46 942	47 813	48 176	51 657	54 243	56 449	...
Sri Lanka Sri Lanka										
Vessels entered Navires entrés	20 148	20 545	22 087	24 955	25 120	25 368	29 882	33 188	36 011	...
Suriname Suriname										
Vessels entered Navires entrés	1 308	1 294	1 335	1 265	1 301	1 167	1 270	1 307	1 411	1 344
Vessels cleared Navires sortis	1 729	1 617	1 723	1 595	1 714	1 926	2 018	2 137	2 206	2 391
Sweden Suède										
Vessels entered[6] Navires entrés[6]	68 025	63 922	64 654	62 159	74 334	82 386	88 828	95 655	101 977	...
Vessels cleared[6] Navires sortis[6]	59 213	56 475	58 075	55 058	63 026	73 139	79 888	82 877	84 722	...
Syrian Arab Republic Rép. arabe syrienne										
Vessels entered[29] Navires entrés[29]	2 087	2 446	2 836	3 525	3 433	2 884	2 901	2 640	2 622	...
Vessels cleared[2] Navires sortis[2]	2 143	2 351	2 992	3 459	3 537	2 701	2 792	2 573	2 562	...
Thailand Thaïlande										
Vessels entered Navires entrés	38 587	40 878	47 639	39 647	46 527	58 759	53 033	54 489	35 764	...
Vessels cleared Navires sortis	23 233	22 741	23 584	22 205	24 692	28 689	22 231	23 757	24 920	...
Tonga Tonga										
Vessels entered Navires entrés	1 816	1 950	...	...	...	...	...	...	...	...
Tunisia Tunisie										
Vessels entered[6] Navires entrés[6]	23 354	23 725	26 842	28 746	32 498	36 205	38 513	42 749	43 546	...

60
International maritime transport
Vessels entered and cleared: thousand net registered tons [cont.]
Transports maritimes internationaux
Navires entrés et sortis : milliers de tonneaux de jauge nette [suite]

Country or area Pays ou zone	1990	1991	1992	1993	1994	1995	1996	1997	1998	1999
Vessels cleared[6] Navires sortis[6]	23 338	23 695	26 883	28 753	32 462	36 232	38 541	42 561	43 513	...
Turkey Turquie										
Vessels entered Navires entrés	62 689	47 818	46 990	56 687	52 925	57 170	59 861	78 174	142 303[6]	136 456[6]
Vessels cleared Navires sortis	60 651	45 719	45 961	55 329	51 303	56 221	58 766	77 952	89 712[6]	88 661[6]
Ukraine Ukraine										
Vessels entered Navires entrés	..	19 236	16 640	5 072	3 381	4 270	3 287	3 108	4 843	5 085
Vessels cleared Navires sortis	..	40 142	45 374	29 120	25 189	21 916	21 550	28 765	36 027	44 030
United States Etats-Unis										
Vessels entered[10 20] Navires entrés[10 20]	379 612	320 439	321 169	340 507	363 896	352 411	371 107	410 157	431 565	440 341
Vessels cleared[10 20] Navires sortis[10 20]	323 183	298 837	293 452	277 520	281 709	303 707	305 250	318 435	327 092	302 344
Uruguay Uruguay										
Vessels entered Navires entrés	3 603	3 764	3 862	4 036	5 297	5 414	5 505	5 844	5 262	...
Vessels cleared Navires sortis	12 696	12 553	13 141	16 059	20 266	24 608	24 975	26 844	24 499	...
Venezuela Venezuela										
Vessels entered Navires entrés	15 774	19 882	19 758	22 087	21 657	21 009	...	...	...	...
Vessels cleared Navires sortis	18 294	11 500	15 194	17 211	12 045	8 461	...	...	...	...
Yemen Yémen										
Vessels entered Navires entrés	...	10 075	11 439	12 459	9 323	10 353	10 477	10 268	11 210	...
Vessels cleared Navires sortis	...	3 238	11 207	12 243	10 386	10 524	4 562	5 958	9 851	...
Yugoslavia Yougoslavie										
Vessels entered Navires entrés	3 190	1 180	626	...	...	805	1 960	1 828	1 589	1 810
Vessels cleared Navires sortis	3 244	1 128	511	...	...	769	1 155	1 360	1 398	1 082

Source:
United Nations Secretariat, transport statistics database of
the Statistics Division.

† For information on recent changes in country or
area nomenclature pertaining to former Czechoslovakia,
Germany, Hong Kong Special Administrative Region (SAR) of
China, Macao Special Administrative Region (SAR) of China,
SFR of Yugoslavia and the former USSR, see Annex I - Country
or area nomenclature, regional and other groupings.

1 Data refer to fiscal years ending 30 June of the year
indicated.
2 Including vessels in ballast.
3 Comprises Buenos Aires, Bahía Blanca, La Plata, Quequén, Mar
del Plata, Paraná Inferior, Paraná Medio and Rosario only.
4 Buenos Aires only.
5 Comprising Buenos Aires, Rosario, Lib, Gral. San Martin,

Source:
Secrétariat de l'Organisation des Nations Unies, la base de
données pour les statistiques des transports de la Division
de statistique.

† Pour les modifications récentes de nomenclature
de pays ou de zone concernant l'Allemagne, Hong Kong, région
administrative spéciale (RAS) de Chine, Macao, région
administrative spéciale (RAS) de Chine,
l'ex-Tchécoslovaquie, l'ex-URSS et l'ex-Rfs de Yougoslavie,
voir annexe I - Nomenclature des pays ou des zones,
groupements régionaux et autres groupements.

1 Les données se réfèrent aux années fiscales finissant le 30e
juin de l'année indiquée.
2 Y compris navires sur lest.
3 Buenos Aires, Bahía Blanca, La Plata, Quequén, Mar del
Plata, Paraná Inferior, Paraná Medio et Rosario.
4 Buenos Aires seulement.
5 Buenos Aires, Rosario, Lib. Gral, San Martín, Quequén et La

60

International maritime transport
Vessels entered and cleared: thousand net registered tons [*cont.*]

Transports maritimes internationaux
Navires entrés et sortis : milliers de tonneaux de jauge nette [*suite*]

Quequén and La Plata.	Plata.
6 Gross registered tons.	6 Tonneaux de jauge brute.
7 Data refer to fiscal years beginning 1 July of the year indicated.	7 Les données se réfèrent aux années fiscales finissant le 1er juillet de l'année indiquée.
8 Sihanoukville Port and Phnom Penh Port.	8 Port de Sihanoukville et Port de Phnom Penh.
9 All entrances counted.	9 Toutes entrées comprises.
10 Including Great Lakes international traffic (Canada: also St. Lawrence).	10 Y compris trafic international des Grands Lacs (Canada: et du St. Laurent).
11 Taxable volume in thousands of cubic metres.	11 Volume taxable en milliers de mètres cubes.
12 Including national maritime transport.	12 Y compris transports martimes nationaux.
13 Port-au-Prince.	13 Port-au-Prince.
14 Data refer to fiscal years beginning 1 April of the year indicated.	14 Les données se réfèrent aux années fiscales finissant le 1er avril de l'année indiquée.
15 Excluding minor and intermediate ports.	15 Non compris les ports petits et moyens.
16 Data for Sarawak include vessels in ballast and all entrances counted.	16 Les données pour Sarawak comprennent navires sur lest et toutes entrées comprises.
17 Including vessels cleared.	17 Y compris navires sortis.
18 Data cover only the first three quarters of the year.	18 Les données se réfèrent aux premieres trois trimestres de l'année.
19 Vessels exceeding 75 gross registered tons.	19 Navires dépassant 75 tonneaux de jauge brute.
20 Excluding traffic with United States Virgin Islands.	20 Non compris le trafic avec les Iles Vierges américaines.

61
Civil Aviation
Aviation civile

Passengers on scheduled services (000); Kilometres (millions)
Passagers sur les services réguliers (000); Kilomètres (millions)

Country or area and traffic	Total Totale 1995	1996	1997	1998	International Internationaux 1995	1996	1997	1998	Pays ou zone et trafic
World									**Monde**
Kilometres flown	**19470**	**20601**	**21635**	**22430**	**8529**	**9322**	**9963**	**10589**	**Kilomètres parcourus**
Passengers carried	**1303645**	**1391085**	**1456147**	**1470730**	**375160**	**412084**	**437688**	**457151**	**Passagers transportés**
Passenger−km	**2248215**	**2431695**	**2571962**	**2627056**	**1249156**	**1380670**	**1467863**	**1511533**	**Passagers−km**
Total ton−km	**293934**	**317154**	**344013**	**348480**	**189421**	**206871**	**227282**	**231389**	**Total tonnes−km**
Africa [1]									**Afrique** [1]
Kilometres flown	**451**	**488**	**522**	**532**	**329**	**355**	**388**	**408**	**Kilomètres parcourus**
Passengers carried	**27131**	**28399**	**29696**	**29076**	**13789**	**14320**	**15517**	**16062**	**Passagers transportés**
Passenger−km	**49922**	**53070**	**56258**	**55736**	**40989**	**43580**	**46988**	**47448**	**Passagers−km**
Total ton−km	**5876**	**6279**	**6657**	**6830**	**4983**	**5353**	**5778**	**6031**	**Total tonnes−km**
Algeria									**Algérie**
Kilometres flown	31	31	34	31	14	14	17	16	Kilomètres parcourus
Passengers carried	3478	3494	3518	3382	1352	1406	1525	1436	Passagers transportés
Passenger−km	2855	2863	3130	3012	1561	1616	1874	1785	Passagers−km
Total ton−km	278	274	299	292	157	158	183	177	Total tonnes−km
Angola									**Angola**
Kilometres flown	8	8	8	8	5	5	5	5	Kilomètres parcourus
Passengers carried	553	585	555	553	155	165	125	125	Passagers transportés
Passenger−km	833	880	620	622	625	660	368	369	Passagers−km
Total ton−km	133	141	97	95	113	120	73	71	Total tonnes−km
Benin [2]									**Bénin** [2]
Kilometres flown	3	3	3	3	3	3	3	3	Kilomètres parcourus
Passengers carried	74	75	86	91	74	75	86	91	Passagers transportés
Passenger−km	223	225	242	258	223	225	242	258	Passagers−km
Total ton−km	36	37	38	38	36	37	38	38	Total tonnes−km
Botswana									**Botswana**
Kilometres flown	2	2	2	3	1	1	2	2	Kilomètres parcourus
Passengers carried	100	104	116	124	70	75	88	92	Passagers transportés
Passenger−km	53	51	55	57	38	37	41	42	Passagers−km
Total ton−km	5	5	5	5	4	3	4	4	Total tonnes−km
Burkina Faso [2]									**Burkina Faso** [2]
Kilometres flown	3	4	3	3	3	3	3	3	Kilomètres parcourus
Passengers carried	137	138	97	102	111	112	94	99	Passagers transportés
Passenger−km	256	258	248	264	248	250	247	263	Passagers−km
Total ton−km	40	40	39	39	39	39	39	39	Total tonnes−km
Burundi									**Burundi**
Kilometres flown	...	...	1	1	...	...	1	1	Kilomètres parcourus
Passengers carried	9	9	12	12	8	8	12	12	Passagers transportés
Passenger−km	2	2	8	8	2	2	8	8	Passagers−km
Total ton−km	...	...	1	1	...	...	1	1	Total tonnes−km
Cameroon									**Cameroun**
Kilometres flown	7	7	6	6	6	6	5	5	Kilomètres parcourus
Passengers carried	345	362	279	290	192	202	175	189	Passagers transportés
Passenger−km	615	649	547	568	530	560	490	492	Passagers−km
Total ton−km	94	100	84	108	86	91	78	100	Total tonnes−km
Cape Verde									**Cap−Vert**
Kilometres flown	3	3	5	5	1	1	3	3	Kilomètres parcourus
Passengers carried	124	129	237	236	30	31	87	87	Passagers transportés
Passenger−km	181	188	268	269	152	157	218	219	Passagers−km
Total ton−km	17	18	25	26	14	14	20	21	Total tonnes−km
Central African Rep. [2]									**Rép. centrafricaine** [2]
Kilometres flown	3	3	3	3	3	3	3	3	Kilomètres parcourus
Passengers carried	74	75	86	91	74	75	86	91	Passagers transportés
Passenger−km	223	225	242	258	223	225	242	258	Passagers−km
Total ton−km	36	37	38	38	36	37	38	38	Total tonnes−km
Chad [2]									**Tchad** [2]
Kilometres flown	3	3	3	3	3	3	3	3	Kilomètres parcourus
Passengers carried	92	93	93	98	77	78	86	91	Passagers transportés
Passenger−km	231	233	247	263	224	226	242	258	Passagers−km
Total ton−km	37	37	39	38	37	37	38	38	Total tonnes−km

61
Civil Aviation
Passengers on scheduled services (000); Kilometres (millions) [*cont.*]
Aviation civile
Passagers sur les services réguliers (000); Kilomètres (millions) [*suite*]

Country or area and traffic	Total Totale				International Internationaux				Pays ou zone et trafic
	1995	1996	1997	1998	1995	1996	1997	1998	
Comoros									**Comores**
Kilometres flown	...	...	...	...	...	...	...	...	Kilomètres parcourus
Passengers carried	27	27	...	...	5	5	...	...	Passagers transportés
Passenger–km	3	3	...	...	1	1	...	...	Passagers–km
Total ton–km	...	...	...	...	...	...	...	...	Total tonnes–km
Congo [2]									**Congo** [2]
Kilometres flown	4	4	5	5	3	3	3	3	Kilomètres parcourus
Passengers carried	267	253	237	241	80	80	88	93	Passagers transportés
Passenger–km	283	279	305	321	226	227	245	261	Passagers–km
Total ton–km	43	42	44	44	37	37	39	38	Total tonnes–km
Côte d'Ivoire [2]									**Côte d'Ivoire** [2]
Kilometres flown	4	5	4	4	4	4	4	4	Kilomètres parcourus
Passengers carried	175	179	158	162	151	154	148	153	Passagers transportés
Passenger–km	302	307	302	318	288	292	297	313	Passagers–km
Total ton–km	44	44	44	44	42	43	43	43	Total tonnes–km
Egypt									**Egypte**
Kilometres flown	55	62	65	63	50	57	59	58	Kilomètres parcourus
Passengers carried	3897	4282	4416	4022	2594	2802	2931	2793	Passagers transportés
Passenger–km	7678	8742	9018	8036	7067	8040	8310	7470	Passagers–km
Total ton–km	864	993	1029	989	808	929	965	938	Total tonnes–km
Equatorial Guinea									**Guinée équatoriale**
Kilometres flown	...	...	0	0	...	...	0	0	Kilomètres parcourus
Passengers carried	15	15	21	21	15	15	8	7	Passagers transportés
Passenger–km	7	7	4	4	7	7	1	1	Passagers–km
Total ton–km	1	1	0	0	1	1	0	0	Total tonnes–km
Ethiopia									**Ethiopie**
Kilometres flown	25	26	28	27	21	23	24	22	Kilomètres parcourus
Passengers carried	750	743	772	790	480	477	496	460	Passagers transportés
Passenger–km	1796	1889	1966	1881	1681	1781	1834	1743	Passagers–km
Total ton–km	290	302	317	318	279	292	305	304	Total tonnes–km
Gabon									**Gabon**
Kilometres flown	7	7	8	8	4	5	6	6	Kilomètres parcourus
Passengers carried	508	431	469	467	165	167	195	194	Passagers transportés
Passenger–km	623	728	826	829	520	650	745	748	Passagers–km
Total ton–km	89	100	112	111	78	93	105	103	Total tonnes–km
Ghana									**Ghana**
Kilometres flown	5	6	6	6	5	6	6	6	Kilomètres parcourus
Passengers carried	186	197	211	210	186	197	211	210	Passagers transportés
Passenger–km	611	655	702	705	611	655	702	705	Passagers–km
Total ton–km	86	91	99	97	86	91	99	97	Total tonnes–km
Guinea									**Guinée**
Kilometres flown	1	1	1	1	1	1	1	1	Kilomètres parcourus
Passengers carried	35	36	36	36	30	31	31	31	Passagers transportés
Passenger–km	52	55	55	55	48	50	50	50	Passagers–km
Total ton–km	5	6	6	6	5	5	5	5	Total tonnes–km
Guinea–Bissau									**Guinée–Bissau**
Kilometres flown	...	...	0	0	...	...	0	0	Kilomètres parcourus
Passengers carried	21	21	21	20	8	8	8	8	Passagers transportés
Passenger–km	10	10	10	10	6	6	6	6	Passagers–km
Total ton–km	1	1	1	1	1	1	1	1	Total tonnes–km
Kenya									**Kenya**
Kilometres flown	16	17	19	21	13	14	15	17	Kilomètres parcourus
Passengers carried	740	779	836	1138	427	463	470	658	Passagers transportés
Passenger–km	1757	1838	1824	2091	1616	1709	1689	1883	Passagers–km
Total ton–km	211	214	216	243	198	203	203	223	Total tonnes–km
Lesotho									**Lesotho**
Kilometres flown	1	1	0	1	1	1	0	1	Kilomètres parcourus
Passengers carried	25	17	10	28	20	17	7	23	Passagers transportés
Passenger–km	8	6	3	9	7	6	3	8	Passagers–km
Total ton–km	1	1	0	1	1	1	0	1	Total tonnes–km
Libyan Arab Jamahiriya									**Jamah. arabe libyenne**
Kilometres flown	3	4	4	4	...	...	...	...	Kilomètres parcourus
Passengers carried	623	639	571	571	...	...	...	...	Passagers transportés
Passenger–km	398	412	377	377	...	...	...	...	Passagers–km
Total ton–km	32	33	30	27	...	...	...	...	Total tonnes–km

61
Civil Aviation
Passengers on scheduled services (000); Kilometres (millions) [*cont.*]
Aviation civile
Passagers sur les services réguliers (000); Kilomètres (millions) [*suite*]

Country or area and traffic	Total Totale				International Internationaux				Pays ou zone et trafic
	1995	1996	1997	1998	1995	1996	1997	1998	
Madagascar									**Madagascar**
Kilometres flown	8	8	9	9	4	4	4	7	Kilomètres parcourus
Passengers carried	497	542	575	318	109	119	131	145	Passagers transportés
Passenger–km	631	659	758	718	471	484	570	646	Passagers–km
Total ton–km	89	85	98	94	73	68	79	86	Total tonnes–km
Malawi									**Malawi**
Kilometres flown	3	3	3	3	2	2	2	2	Kilomètres parcourus
Passengers carried	149	153	158	158	72	76	79	79	Passagers transportés
Passenger–km	110	115	336	337	75	80	299	300	Passagers–km
Total ton–km	14	14	33	33	10	10	31	31	Total tonnes–km
Mali [2]									**Mali** [2]
Kilometres flown	3	3	3	3	3	3	3	3	Kilomètres parcourus
Passengers carried	74	75	86	91	74	75	86	91	Passagers transportés
Passenger–km	223	225	242	258	223	225	242	258	Passagers–km
Total ton–km	36	37	38	38	36	37	38	38	Total tonnes–km
Mauritania [2]									**Mauritanie** [2]
Kilometres flown	4	4	4	4	3	3	3	3	Kilomètres parcourus
Passengers carried	228	235	245	250	98	99	110	115	Passagers transportés
Passenger–km	301	306	324	340	247	250	267	283	Passagers–km
Total ton–km	44	44	46	46	39	39	41	40	Total tonnes–km
Mauritius									**Maurice**
Kilometres flown	20	22	26	24	19	21	25	23	Kilomètres parcourus
Passengers carried	676	717	804	810	639	674	743	743	Passagers transportés
Passenger–km	3225	3515	3917	3826	3203	3488	3881	3788	Passagers–km
Total ton–km	425	458	538	526	423	456	535	523	Total tonnes–km
Morocco									**Maroc**
Kilometres flown	44	45	49	56	41	42	45	51	Kilomètres parcourus
Passengers carried	2147	2301	2638	3012	1735	1790	2023	2265	Passagers transportés
Passenger–km	4602	4665	5321	5868	4456	4489	5124	5625	Passagers–km
Total ton–km	379	396	417	573	366	380	401	549	Total tonnes–km
Mozambique									**Mozambique**
Kilometres flown	3	3	4	4	1	1	1	2	Kilomètres parcourus
Passengers carried	168	163	188	201	60	54	65	73	Passagers transportés
Passenger–km	290	260	291	295	172	151	170	163	Passagers–km
Total ton–km	32	27	32	33	19	15	19	19	Total tonnes–km
Namibia									**Namibie**
Kilometres flown	8	8	8	9	6	6	7	7	Kilomètres parcourus
Passengers carried	225	237	214	229	203	213	183	200	Passagers transportés
Passenger–km	844	890	906	630	826	870	882	614	Passagers–km
Total ton–km	103	109	118	59	101	107	116	57	Total tonnes–km
Niger [2]									**Niger** [2]
Kilometres flown	3	3	3	3	3	3	3	3	Kilomètres parcourus
Passengers carried	74	75	86	91	74	75	86	91	Passagers transportés
Passenger–km	223	225	242	258	223	225	242	258	Passagers–km
Total ton–km	36	37	38	38	36	37	38	38	Total tonnes–km
Nigeria									**Nigéria**
Kilometres flown	6	4	5	5	3	2	2	2	Kilomètres parcourus
Passengers carried	548	221	318	313	192	66	44	49	Passagers transportés
Passenger–km	819	273	221	245	533	164	100	122	Passagers–km
Total ton–km	81	30	27	32	54	21	14	18	Total tonnes–km
Sao Tome and Principe									**Sao Tomé–et–Principe**
Kilometres flown	...	...	0	0	...	...	0	0	Kilomètres parcourus
Passengers carried	22	23	25	24	13	14	15	15	Passagers transportés
Passenger–km	8	9	9	9	4	4	5	5	Passagers–km
Total ton–km	1	1	1	1	...	...	0	0	Total tonnes–km
Senegal [2]									**Sénégal** [2]
Kilometres flown	3	4	4	3	3	3	3	3	Kilomètres parcourus
Passengers carried	150	155	166	121	120	124	135	91	Passagers transportés
Passenger–km	244	247	265	267	235	238	256	258	Passagers–km
Total ton–km	38	39	40	39	38	38	40	38	Total tonnes–km
Seychelles									**Seychelles**
Kilometres flown	7	8	8	9	6	7	7	8	Kilomètres parcourus
Passengers carried	314	373	384	369	117	132	133	113	Passagers transportés
Passenger–km	708	784	847	755	699	773	836	743	Passagers–km
Total ton–km	82	94	106	84	81	93	105	83	Total tonnes–km

61
Civil Aviation
Passengers on scheduled services (000); Kilometres (millions) [*cont.*]
Aviation civile
Passagers sur les services réguliers (000); Kilomètres (millions) [*suite*]

Country or area and traffic	Total Totale				International Internationaux				Pays ou zone et trafic
	1995	1996	1997	1998	1995	1996	1997	1998	
Sierra Leone									**Sierra Leone**
Kilometres flown	...	...	...	...	...	...	...	...	Kilomètres parcourus
Passengers carried	14	15	...	...	14	15	...	...	Passagers transportés
Passenger−km	23	24	...	...	23	24	...	...	Passagers−km
Total ton−km	2	2	...	...	2	2	...	...	Total tonnes−km
South Africa									**Afrique du Sud**
Kilometres flown	98	121	131	128	47	60	69	75	Kilomètres parcourus
Passengers carried	6396	7183	7274	6480	1456	1625	1808	1913	Passagers transportés
Passenger−km	14496	15957	16825	16997	9952	10723	11928	12869	Passagers−km
Total ton−km	1551	1747	1918	2046	1096	1239	1449	1636	Total tonnes−km
Sudan									**Soudan**
Kilometres flown	13	13	7	6	7	6	5	4	Kilomètres parcourus
Passengers carried	497	491	333	499	344	315	211	311	Passagers transportés
Passenger−km	681	650	471	148	516	522	384	126	Passagers−km
Total ton−km	121	107	66	19	79	73	50	16	Total tonnes−km
Swaziland									**Swaziland**
Kilometres flown	1	1	1	1	1	1	1	1	Kilomètres parcourus
Passengers carried	49	54	41	41	49	54	41	41	Passagers transportés
Passenger−km	49	57	43	43	49	57	43	43	Passagers−km
Total ton−km	5	5	4	4	5	5	4	4	Total tonnes−km
Togo [2]									**Togo** [2]
Kilometres flown	3	3	3	3	3	3	3	3	Kilomètres parcourus
Passengers carried	74	75	86	91	74	75	86	91	Passagers transportés
Passenger−km	223	225	242	258	223	225	242	258	Passagers−km
Total ton−km	36	37	38	38	36	37	38	38	Total tonnes−km
Tunisia									**Tunisie**
Kilometres flown	19	18	24	27	19	18	24	27	Kilomètres parcourus
Passengers carried	1419	1371	1779	1888	1418	1371	1779	1888	Passagers transportés
Passenger−km	1955	2118	2479	2683	1954	2118	2479	2683	Passagers−km
Total ton−km	197	212	249	266	197	212	249	266	Total tonnes−km
Uganda									**Ouganda**
Kilometres flown	2	2	2	2	2	2	2	2	Kilomètres parcourus
Passengers carried	95	100	100	100	95	100	100	100	Passagers transportés
Passenger−km	103	110	110	110	103	110	110	110	Passagers−km
Total ton−km	10	11	11	11	10	11	11	11	Total tonnes−km
United Rep.Tanzania									**Rép.−Unie de Tanzanie**
Kilometres flown	4	4	4	5	2	2	3	3	Kilomètres parcourus
Passengers carried	236	224	218	220	85	85	93	89	Passagers transportés
Passenger−km	189	190	231	236	107	119	165	171	Passagers−km
Total ton−km	20	20	26	25	11	12	18	18	Total tonnes−km
Zambia									**Zambie**
Kilometres flown	...	...	1	1	...	...	1	1	Kilomètres parcourus
Passengers carried	...	...	50	49	...	...	42	42	Passagers transportés
Passenger−km	...	...	45	44	...	...	43	42	Passagers−km
Total ton−km	...	...	5	4	...	...	4	4	Total tonnes−km
Zimbabwe									**Zimbabwe**
Kilometres flown	13	13	16	19	11	11	13	16	Kilomètres parcourus
Passengers carried	626	654	771	706	279	290	302	310	Passagers transportés
Passenger−km	840	881	914	955	705	740	724	791	Passagers−km
Total ton−km	216	234	224	234	204	220	208	221	Total tonnes−km
America, North [1]									**Amérique du Nord** [1]
Kilometres flown	**9107**	**9547**	**9912**	**10224**	**1941**	**2102**	**2240**	**2473**	**Kilomètres parcourus**
Passengers carried	**577675**	**617339**	**639612**	**640789**	**73865**	**80372**	**82704**	**85779**	**Passagers transportés**
Passenger−km	**937107**	**1005200**	**1058636**	**1086197**	**290053**	**312073**	**328718**	**339436**	**Passagers−km**
Total ton−km	**109970**	**118516**	**127555**	**130124**	**39554**	**43073**	**47720**	**49173**	**Total tonnes−km**
Antigua and Barbuda									**Antigua−et−Barbuda**
Kilometres flown	12	12	12	12	12	12	12	12	Kilomètres parcourus
Passengers carried	1050	1098	1250	1245	1050	1098	1250	1245	Passagers transportés
Passenger−km	252	267	250	251	252	267	250	251	Passagers−km
Total ton−km	23	24	23	23	23	24	23	23	Total tonnes−km
Bahamas									**Bahamas**
Kilometres flown	4	5	2	2	2	2	1	1	Kilomètres parcourus
Passengers carried	937	978	704	701	449	472	296	294	Passagers transportés
Passenger−km	220	234	140	140	159	170	76	76	Passagers−km
Total ton−km	20	21	13	13	15	16	7	7	Total tonnes−km

61
Civil Aviation
Passengers on scheduled services (000); Kilometres (millions) [*cont.*]
Aviation civile
Passagers sur les services réguliers (000); Kilomètres (millions) [*suite*]

Country or area and traffic	Total Totale				International Internationaux				Pays ou zone et trafic
	1995	1996	1997	1998	1995	1996	1997	1998	
Canada									**Canada**
Kilometres flown	449	497	519	547	223	273	293	317	Kilomètres parcourus
Passengers carried	20291	22856	23981	24653	8230	10045	10945	11382	Passagers transportés
Passenger−km	49288	56018	61862	63801	31421	36764	40928	42071	Passagers−km
Total ton−km	6214	6961	7667	7751	4231	4838	5382	5402	Total tonnes−km
Costa Rica									**Costa Rica**
Kilometres flown	22	23	24	28	21	22	23	25	Kilomètres parcourus
Passengers carried	870	918	992	1070	793	865	899	933	Passagers transportés
Passenger−km	1838	1965	1915	2004	1827	1958	1903	1983	Passagers−km
Total ton−km	234	245	248	289	233	242	247	287	Total tonnes−km
Cuba									**Cuba**
Kilometres flown	16	20	26	34	10	15	20	28	Kilomètres parcourus
Passengers carried	824	929	1117	1138	311	416	592	647	Passagers transportés
Passenger−km	2006	2649	3543	4791	1702	2340	3228	4470	Passagers−km
Total ton−km	219	292	388	524	194	267	362	497	Total tonnes−km
Dominican Republic									**Rép. dominicaine**
Kilometres flown	1	1	1	1	1	1	1	1	Kilomètres parcourus
Passengers carried	67	30	34	34	67	30	34	34	Passagers transportés
Passenger−km	28	14	16	16	28	14	16	16	Passagers−km
Total ton−km	3	1	1	1	3	1	1	1	Total tonnes−km
El Salvador									**El Salvador**
Kilometres flown	21	22	17	22	21	22	17	22	Kilomètres parcourus
Passengers carried	1698	1800	1006	1585	1698	1800	1006	1525	Passagers transportés
Passenger−km	2077	2181	1898	2292	2077	2181	1898	2284	Passagers−km
Total ton−km	227	212	190	253	227	212	190	252	Total tonnes−km
Guatemala									**Guatemala**
Kilometres flown	6	6	5	7	6	6	4	7	Kilomètres parcourus
Passengers carried	300	300	508	794	300	300	432	760	Passagers transportés
Passenger−km	500	530	368	480	500	530	337	469	Passagers−km
Total ton−km	70	71	77	50	70	71	75	49	Total tonnes−km
Jamaica									**Jamaïque**
Kilometres flown	13	18	22	23	12	17	22	23	Kilomètres parcourus
Passengers carried	1126	1388	1400	1454	1060	1322	1400	1454	Passagers transportés
Passenger−km	1592	2117	2677	2961	1583	2107	2677	2961	Passagers−km
Total ton−km	166	217	264	293	166	216	264	293	Total tonnes−km
Mexico									**Mexique**
Kilometres flown	231	245	308	360	83	101	141	176	Kilomètres parcourus
Passengers carried	14969	14678	17752	18685	3410	3844	4773	4728	Passagers transportés
Passenger−km	19403	19636	24065	25976	7884	8971	11228	11703	Passagers−km
Total ton−km	1799	1861	2333	2566	780	883	1142	1241	Total tonnes−km
Nicaragua									**Nicaragua**
Kilometres flown	1	1	1	1	1	1	1	1	Kilomètres parcourus
Passengers carried	48	51	51	52	48	51	51	52	Passagers transportés
Passenger−km	79	85	85	93	79	85	85	93	Passagers−km
Total ton−km	16	17	17	10	16	17	17	10	Total tonnes−km
Panama									**Panama**
Kilometres flown	14	14	18	21	14	14	18	21	Kilomètres parcourus
Passengers carried	661	689	772	856	661	689	772	856	Passagers transportés
Passenger−km	862	872	1094	1373	862	872	1094	1373	Passagers−km
Total ton−km	111	114	152	174	111	114	152	174	Total tonnes−km
Trinidad and Tobago									**Trinité−et−Tobago**
Kilometres flown	33	20	18	21	33	20	18	21	Kilomètres parcourus
Passengers carried	1727	897	807	880	1280	897	807	880	Passagers transportés
Passenger−km	4330	2658	2392	2567	4300	2658	2392	2567	Passagers−km
Total ton−km	428	265	239	315	425	265	239	315	Total tonnes−km
United States									**Etats−Unis**
Kilometres flown	8285	8665	8928	9134	1502	1598	1659	1809	Kilomètres parcourus
Passengers carried	533512	571072	587992	586402	54803	58813	58580	60126	Passagers transportés
Passenger−km	858629	919816	957379	978498	240219	255916	261741	268253	Passagers−km
Total ton−km	100914	108684	115856	117773	33376	36228	39541	40540	Total tonnes−km
America, South									**Amérique du Sud**
Kilometres flown	**839**	**927**	**1023**	**1099**	**398**	**444**	**466**	**445**	**Kilomètres parcourus**
Passengers carried	**48611**	**53497**	**58522**	**63745**	**11736**	**12711**	**13332**	**13731**	**Passagers transportés**
Passenger−km	**72379**	**77786**	**86036**	**91204**	**45819**	**48653**	**53012**	**53043**	**Passagers−km**
Total ton−km	**10239**	**10400**	**12035**	**12559**	**7289**	**7280**	**8277**	**8568**	**Total tonnes−km**

61
Civil Aviation
Passengers on scheduled services (000); Kilometres (millions) [*cont.*]
Aviation civile
Passagers sur les services réguliers (000); Kilomètres (millions) [*suite*]

Country or area and traffic	Total Totale				International Internationaux				Pays ou zone et trafic
	1995	1996	1997	1998	1995	1996	1997	1998	
Argentina									**Argentine**
Kilometres flown	108	133	155	157	47	64	74	54	Kilomètres parcourus
Passengers carried	6642	7913	8603	8623	1972	2193	2120	2108	Passagers transportés
Passenger−km	11892	13360	14348	14379	7885	8267	8602	8447	Passagers−km
Total ton−km	1338	1447	1566	1597	956	994	1055	1055	Total tonnes−km
Bolivia									**Bolivie**
Kilometres flown	16	24	28	28	12	15	17	19	Kilomètres parcourus
Passengers carried	1224	1783	2251	2115	452	542	705	773	Passagers transportés
Passenger−km	1234	1634	2143	2179	956	1166	1548	1629	Passagers−km
Total ton−km	187	223	274	273	157	177	215	218	Total tonnes−km
Brazil									**Brésil**
Kilometres flown	391	428	468	535	146	166	172	173	Kilomètres parcourus
Passengers carried	20196	22011	24196	29137	3699	4174	4582	4648	Passagers transportés
Passenger−km	34781	37671	42242	46978	20116	22296	25492	25479	Passagers−km
Total ton−km	4866	5166	5716	5980	3077	3348	3697	3627	Total tonnes−km
Chile									**Chili**
Kilometres flown	92	97	109	117	60	55	59	63	Kilomètres parcourus
Passengers carried	3197	3622	4693	5095	1201	1224	1613	1768	Passagers transportés
Passenger−km	6333	6787	8769	9679	4448	4481	5691	6300	Passagers−km
Total ton−km	1348	1419	1865	2124	1150	1175	1543	1768	Total tonnes−km
Colombia									**Colombie**
Kilometres flown	98	97	117	125	45	43	50	57	Kilomètres parcourus
Passengers carried	7863	8342	9099	9051	1062	1115	1136	1320	Passagers transportés
Passenger−km	5772	5991	6934	7350	2932	2980	3400	3835	Passagers−km
Total ton−km	1108	836	1392	1436	832	551	855	1061	Total tonnes−km
Ecuador									**Equateur**
Kilometres flown	15	15	23	23	9	9	18	18	Kilomètres parcourus
Passengers carried	1671	1925	1791	2048	355	385	503	674	Passagers transportés
Passenger−km	1591	1663	2035	2282	1095	1123	1455	1788	Passagers−km
Total ton−km	174	181	235	286	126	130	180	239	Total tonnes−km
Guyana									**Guyana**
Kilometres flown	2	3	3	3	2	2	2	2	Kilomètres parcourus
Passengers carried	121	126	126	126	56	59	59	59	Passagers transportés
Passenger−km	235	248	248	249	218	230	230	231	Passagers−km
Total ton−km	25	26	26	26	22	23	23	24	Total tonnes−km
Paraguay									**Paraguay**
Kilometres flown	4	7	4	5	4	6	4	5	Kilomètres parcourus
Passengers carried	105	260	196	222	105	213	196	222	Passagers transportés
Passenger−km	283	474	215	247	283	454	215	247	Passagers−km
Total ton−km	32	42	19	22	32	40	19	22	Total tonnes−km
Peru									**Pérou**
Kilometres flown	34	33	40	41	17	17	17	18	Kilomètres parcourus
Passengers carried	2508	2328	2725	2774	600	555	510	508	Passagers transportés
Passenger−km	2884	2634	2964	3014	1759	1613	1521	1526	Passagers−km
Total ton−km	294	251	276	286	186	153	140	144	Total tonnes−km
Suriname									**Suriname**
Kilometres flown	5	5	7	7	4	5	7	7	Kilomètres parcourus
Passengers carried	162	195	279	278	154	190	275	274	Passagers transportés
Passenger−km	618	883	1068	1072	617	883	1067	1071	Passagers−km
Total ton−km	81	106	127	127	81	106	127	127	Total tonnes−km
Uruguay									**Uruguay**
Kilometres flown	5	5	6	7	5	5	6	7	Kilomètres parcourus
Passengers carried	477	504	544	557	477	504	544	557	Passagers transportés
Passenger−km	636	640	627	642	636	640	627	642	Passagers−km
Total ton−km	62	62	57	70	62	62	57	70	Total tonnes−km
Venezuela									**Venezuela**
Kilometres flown	68	80	63	52	45	57	40	22	Kilomètres parcourus
Passengers carried	4445	4487	4020	3720	1604	1557	1090	820	Passagers transportés
Passenger−km	6120	5800	4444	3133	4874	4520	3164	1848	Passagers−km
Total ton−km	724	639	483	332	609	520	364	213	Total tonnes−km
Asia [1]									**Asie** [1]
Kilometres flown	3596	3864	4102	4189	2152	2353	2540	2593	**Kilomètres parcourus**
Passengers carried	319381	337237	345483	336963	105582	113764	117496	116720	**Passagers transportés**
Passenger−km	556656	605604	636050	621807	382399	423548	445638	439870	**Passagers−km**
Total ton−km	79956	86943	93944	91631	63901	69987	76098	74427	**Total tonnes−km**

61
Civil Aviation
Passengers on scheduled services (000); Kilometres (millions) [*cont.*]
Aviation civile
Passagers sur les services réguliers (000); Kilomètres (millions) [*suite*]

Country or area and traffic	Total Totale				International Internationaux				Pays ou zone et trafic
	1995	1996	1997	1998	1995	1996	1997	1998	
Afghanistan									**Afghanistan**
Kilometres flown	6	6	6	3	3	3	6	2	Kilomètres parcourus
Passengers carried	250	256	90	53	107	112	51	27	Passagers transportés
Passenger–km	276	286	158	88	202	212	136	72	Passagers–km
Total ton–km	38	40	50	24	31	32	48	22	Total tonnes–km
Armenia									**Arménie**
Kilometres flown	...	9	8	9	...	9	8	9	Kilomètres parcourus
Passengers carried	...	358	368	365	...	358	368	365	Passagers transportés
Passenger–km	...	747	767	765	...	747	767	765	Passagers–km
Total ton–km	...	79	80	80	...	79	80	80	Total tonnes–km
Azerbaijan									**Azerbaïdjan**
Kilometres flown	21	21	17	9	4	5	13	7	Kilomètres parcourus
Passengers carried	1156	1233	982	669	119	175	517	311	Passagers transportés
Passenger–km	1650	1743	1283	843	250	291	1021	632	Passagers–km
Total ton–km	183	183	159	169	39	36	119	145	Total tonnes–km
Bahrain [3]									**Bahreïn** [3]
Kilometres flown	21	22	19	19	21	22	19	19	Kilomètres parcourus
Passengers carried	1073	1200	1165	1207	1073	1200	1165	1207	Passagers transportés
Passenger–km	2766	2759	2501	2653	2766	2759	2501	2653	Passagers–km
Total ton–km	395	367	333	357	395	367	333	357	Total tonnes–km
Bangladesh									**Bangladesh**
Kilometres flown	19	19	20	20	18	17	19	19	Kilomètres parcourus
Passengers carried	1261	1252	1315	1162	815	765	846	855	Passagers transportés
Passenger–km	3058	2995	3233	3422	2969	2897	3141	3358	Passagers–km
Total ton–km	398	406	494	524	390	396	486	519	Total tonnes–km
Bhutan									**Bhoutan**
Kilometres flown	1	1	1	1	1	1	1	1	Kilomètres parcourus
Passengers carried	30	35	36	36	30	35	36	36	Passagers transportés
Passenger–km	40	46	49	49	40	46	49	49	Passagers–km
Total ton–km	4	4	4	4	4	4	4	4	Total tonnes–km
Brunei Darussalam									**Brunéi Darussalam**
Kilometres flown	22	24	28	35	22	24	28	35	Kilomètres parcourus
Passengers carried	916	857	1088	877	916	857	1088	877	Passagers transportés
Passenger–km	2403	2712	2906	2972	2403	2712	2906	2972	Passagers–km
Total ton–km	327	353	378	386	327	353	378	386	Total tonnes–km
China ††									**Chine ††**
Kilometres flown	519	590	639	730	97	111	107	127	Kilomètres parcourus
Passengers carried	47565	51770	52277	53481	6004	6778	4790	5086	Passagers transportés
Passenger–km	64204	70605	72964	75823	13900	16128	15781	17181	Passagers–km
Total ton–km	6779	7649	8259	8893	2238	2498	2709	3047	Total tonnes–km
China, Hong Kong SAR † [8]									**Chine, Hong Kong RAS † [8]**
Kilometres flown	...	...	112	228	...	...	112	228	Kilomètres parcourus
Passengers carried	...	...	5957	12203	...	...	5957	12203	Passagers transportés
Passenger–km	...	...	20283	42964	...	...	20283	42964	Passagers–km
Total ton–km	...	...	4278	8274	...	...	4278	8274	Total tonnes–km
Cyprus									**Chypre**
Kilometres flown	20	19	20	20	20	19	20	20	Kilomètres parcourus
Passengers carried	1219	1214	1278	1346	1219	1214	1278	1346	Passagers transportés
Passenger–km	2667	2561	2657	2711	2667	2561	2657	2711	Passagers–km
Total ton–km	279	272	278	284	279	272	278	284	Total tonnes–km
Georgia									**Géorgie**
Kilometres flown	4	5	3	7	4	4	3	5	Kilomètres parcourus
Passengers carried	177	152	110	205	167	149	110	175	Passagers transportés
Passenger–km	308	288	206	409	305	287	206	340	Passagers–km
Total ton–km	30	28	20	45	29	28	20	34	Total tonnes–km
India									**Inde**
Kilometres flown	168	171	194	200	65	68	66	68	Kilomètres parcourus
Passengers carried	14261	13395	16536	16547	3025	3229	3447	3478	Passagers transportés
Passenger–km	21880	22317	24620	24722	11916	12198	12700	12947	Passagers–km
Total ton–km	2622	2566	2737	2776	1648	1579	1573	1607	Total tonnes–km
Indonesia									**Indonésie**
Kilometres flown	248	256	199	155	90	92	88	56	Kilomètres parcourus
Passengers carried	15977	17139	12937	9603	3535	3633	3120	2017	Passagers transportés
Passenger–km	24754	25081	23718	15974	15411	14929	15670	9770	Passagers–km
Total ton–km	2965	2986	2797	1826	2032	2015	2007	1173	Total tonnes–km

61
Civil Aviation
Passengers on scheduled services (000); Kilometres (millions) [cont.]
Aviation civile
Passagers sur les services réguliers (000); Kilomètres (millions) [suite]

Country or area and traffic	Total Totale				International Internationaux				Pays ou zone et trafic
	1995	1996	1997	1998	1995	1996	1997	1998	
Iran (Islamic Rep. of)									**Iran (Rép. islamique d')**
Kilometres flown	40	50	70	68	14	15	21	22	Kilomètres parcourus
Passengers carried	6291	7610	9804	9303	774	938	1309	1404	Passagers transportés
Passenger−km	5634	6634	8963	8539	1832	1933	2642	2632	Passagers−km
Total ton−km	621	708	901	856	264	270	324	322	Total tonnes−km
Israel									**Israël**
Kilometres flown	70	74	75	79	66	67	69	72	Kilomètres parcourus
Passengers carried	3453	3695	3754	3699	2787	2715	2714	2741	Passagers transportés
Passenger−km	11412	11793	11776	12418	11287	11512	11493	12152	Passagers−km
Total ton−km	2103	2179	2195	2241	2091	2154	2175	2217	Total tonnes−km
Japan									**Japon**
Kilometres flown	692	727	777	828	348	370	399	426	Kilomètres parcourus
Passengers carried	91797	95914	94998	101701	13943	15641	16235	16388	Passagers transportés
Passenger−km	129981	141812	151048	154402	70157	79049	84098	85608	Passagers−km
Total ton−km	17922	19142	20627	20896	12622	13607	14755	14905	Total tonnes−km
Jordan									**Jordanie**
Kilometres flown	38	42	40	35	38	42	40	35	Kilomètres parcourus
Passengers carried	1270	1299	1353	1187	1219	1293	1353	1187	Passagers transportés
Passenger−km	4395	4750	4900	4065	4382	4748	4900	4065	Passagers−km
Total ton−km	664	731	721	596	663	731	721	596	Total tonnes−km
Kazakhstan									**Kazakhstan**
Kilometres flown	35	20	20	35	9	7	7	25	Kilomètres parcourus
Passengers carried	1117	568	568	726	209	158	158	318	Passagers transportés
Passenger−km	2429	1330	1330	1533	760	640	640	1149	Passagers−km
Total ton−km	237	137	137	162	81	72	72	123	Total tonnes−km
Korea, Dem. P. R.									**Corée, R. p. dém. de**
Kilometres flown	3	3	5	3	1	1	3	3	Kilomètres parcourus
Passengers carried	254	254	280	64	38	38	64	64	Passagers transportés
Passenger−km	207	207	286	192	113	113	192	192	Passagers−km
Total ton−km	22	22	30	19	11	11	19	19	Total tonnes−km
Korea, Republic of									**Corée, République de**
Kilometres flown	285	323	365	319	237	271	306	266	Kilomètres parcourus
Passengers carried	29345	33003	35506	27109	8932	9938	10262	8973	Passagers transportés
Passenger−km	48441	55751	59372	47711	41296	47664	50485	40982	Passagers−km
Total ton−km	10018	11549	13210	11605	9325	10770	12346	10929	Total tonnes−km
Kuwait									**Koweït**
Kilometres flown	38	43	43	45	38	43	43	45	Kilomètres parcourus
Passengers carried	1951	2133	2114	2190	1951	2133	2114	2190	Passagers transportés
Passenger−km	5124	6073	5997	6207	5124	6073	5997	6207	Passagers−km
Total ton−km	797	929	912	932	797	929	912	932	Total tonnes−km
Kyrgyzstan									**Kirghizistan**
Kilometres flown	9	10	8	9	1	2	2	6	Kilomètres parcourus
Passengers carried	439	488	423	427	17	30	52	143	Passagers transportés
Passenger−km	573	625	531	519	71	136	189	407	Passagers−km
Total ton−km	54	59	52	60	7	13	19	50	Total tonnes−km
Lao People's Dem. Rep.									**Rép. dém. pop. lao**
Kilometres flown	1	1	1	1	1	1	1	1	Kilomètres parcourus
Passengers carried	125	125	125	124	31	31	31	31	Passagers transportés
Passenger−km	48	48	48	48	20	20	20	20	Passagers−km
Total ton−km	5	5	5	5	2	2	2	2	Total tonnes−km
Lebanon									**Liban**
Kilometres flown	20	19	21	20	20	19	21	20	Kilomètres parcourus
Passengers carried	770	775	857	716	770	775	857	716	Passagers transportés
Passenger−km	1720	1857	2116	1504	1720	1857	2116	1504	Passagers−km
Total ton−km	287	252	319	247	287	252	319	247	Total tonnes−km
Malaysia									**Malaisie**
Kilometres flown	148	173	183	189	104	121	128	140	Kilomètres parcourus
Passengers carried	15418	15118	15592	13654	7085	6086	6274	6105	Passagers transportés
Passenger−km	23431	26862	28698	29372	19807	22377	24004	25392	Passagers−km
Total ton−km	3146	3620	3777	3777	2811	3199	3332	3407	Total tonnes−km
Maldives									**Maldives**
Kilometres flown	1	2	3	4	1	1	2	3	Kilomètres parcourus
Passengers carried	159	207	189	247	120	167	170	192	Passagers transportés
Passenger−km	71	252	292	355	67	247	283	331	Passagers−km
Total ton−km	8	26	33	42	8	26	32	40	Total tonnes−km

61
Civil Aviation
Passengers on scheduled services (000); Kilometres (millions) [*cont.*]
Aviation civile
Passagers sur les services réguliers (000); Kilomètres (millions) [*suite*]

Country or area and traffic	Total Totale				International Internationaux				Pays ou zone et trafic
	1995	1996	1997	1998	1995	1996	1997	1998	
Mongolia									**Mongolie**
Kilometres flown	13	13	4	8	2	2	2	4	Kilomètres parcourus
Passengers carried	662	662	240	255	45	45	121	95	Passagers transportés
Passenger–km	516	525	195	469	121	130	147	331	Passagers–km
Total ton–km	47	48	18	50	12	13	14	35	Total tonnes–km
Myanmar									**Myanmar**
Kilometres flown	8	8	9	8	4	5	6	5	Kilomètres parcourus
Passengers carried	662	676	575	522	162	205	192	148	Passagers transportés
Passenger–km	379	392	385	345	164	197	206	156	Passagers–km
Total ton–km	42	44	46	40	26	33	33	25	Total tonnes–km
Nepal									**Népal**
Kilometres flown	10	11	11	11	7	7	7	7	Kilomètres parcourus
Passengers carried	717	755	755	754	364	385	385	385	Passagers transportés
Passenger–km	856	908	908	908	805	855	855	855	Passagers–km
Total ton–km	93	99	99	99	89	94	94	94	Total tonnes–km
Oman [3]									**Oman** [3]
Kilometres flown	26	27	26	27	25	26	24	26	Kilomètres parcourus
Passengers carried	1453	1620	1678	1768	1293	1461	1507	1590	Passagers transportés
Passenger–km	3226	3277	3197	3405	3094	3146	3055	3257	Passagers–km
Total ton–km	436	413	384	415	424	402	374	404	Total tonnes–km
Pakistan									**Pakistan**
Kilometres flown	73	74	78	75	51	52	56	53	Kilomètres parcourus
Passengers carried	5343	5375	5883	5414	2415	2473	2632	2568	Passagers transportés
Passenger–km	10384	10580	11658	10972	8341	8574	9413	8922	Passagers–km
Total ton–km	1400	1398	1479	1408	1177	1180	1243	1186	Total tonnes–km
Philippines									**Philippines**
Kilometres flown	74	81	96	40	51	58	73	28	Kilomètres parcourus
Passengers carried	7180	7263	7475	3944	2470	2816	2902	1306	Passagers transportés
Passenger–km	14374	15132	16392	7503	11977	12848	13966	5918	Passagers–km
Total ton–km	1798	1893	2086	925	1561	1663	1847	785	Total tonnes–km
Qatar [3]									**Qatar** [3]
Kilometres flown	21	22	19	19	21	22	19	19	Kilomètres parcourus
Passengers carried	1073	1200	1165	1207	1073	1200	1165	1207	Passagers transportés
Passenger–km	2766	2759	2501	2653	2766	2759	2501	2653	Passagers–km
Total ton–km	395	367	333	357	395	367	333	357	Total tonnes–km
Saudi Arabia									**Arabie saoudite**
Kilometres flown	115	118	117	120	67	68	68	71	Kilomètres parcourus
Passengers carried	11524	11706	11738	11816	3597	3873	3895	3895	Passagers transportés
Passenger–km	18501	18980	18949	18820	12781	13126	13061	12875	Passagers–km
Total ton–km	2583	2592	2650	2645	1998	1991	2038	2030	Total tonnes–km
Singapore									**Singapour**
Kilometres flown	222	245	270	293	222	245	270	293	Kilomètres parcourus
Passengers carried	10779	11841	12981	13316	10779	11841	12981	13316	Passagers transportés
Passenger–km	48400	53647	55459	58174	48400	53647	55459	58174	Passagers–km
Total ton–km	8389	9296	10128	10381	8389	9296	10128	10381	Total tonnes–km
Sri Lanka									**Sri Lanka**
Kilometres flown	22	21	22	23	22	21	22	23	Kilomètres parcourus
Passengers carried	1156	1171	1232	1213	1156	1171	1232	1213	Passagers transportés
Passenger–km	3966	3816	4249	4136	3966	3816	4249	4136	Passagers–km
Total ton–km	519	507	569	553	519	507	569	553	Total tonnes–km
Syrian Arab Republic									**Rép. arabe syrienne**
Kilometres flown	10	11	12	13	10	11	11	13	Kilomètres parcourus
Passengers carried	563	599	694	665	515	578	615	643	Passagers transportés
Passenger–km	948	1068	1235	1410	940	1058	1205	1398	Passagers–km
Total ton–km	103	113	127	140	102	113	124	139	Total tonnes–km
Tajikistan									**Tadjikistan**
Kilometres flown	10	7	7	5	2	2	2	3	Kilomètres parcourus
Passengers carried	822	594	594	217	40	44	44	105	Passagers transportés
Passenger–km	2427	1825	1825	322	200	222	222	275	Passagers–km
Total ton–km	223	166	166	32	19	19	19	28	Total tonnes–km
Thailand									**Thaïlande**
Kilometres flown	134	140	153	158	114	118	131	136	Kilomètres parcourus
Passengers carried	12771	14078	14236	15015	7497	8175	8445	9147	Passagers transportés
Passenger–km	27053	29801	30827	34340	24087	26498	27633	31049	Passagers–km
Total ton–km	3788	4075	4460	4682	3487	3744	4139	4355	Total tonnes–km

61
Civil Aviation
Passengers on scheduled services (000); Kilometres (millions) [*cont.*]
Aviation civile
Passagers sur les services réguliers (000); Kilomètres (millions) [*suite*]

Country or area and traffic	Total Totale				International Internationaux				Pays ou zone et trafic
	1995	1996	1997	1998	1995	1996	1997	1998	
Turkey									**Turquie**
Kilometres flown	94	101	113	123	69	74	84	90	Kilomètres parcourus
Passengers carried	7749	8464	9380	10132	2839	3376	3812	3988	Passagers transportés
Passenger−km	9475	10947	12379	13037	6810	8199	9372	9792	Passagers−km
Total ton−km	1065	1192	1363	1371	834	953	1107	1092	Total tonnes−km
Turkmenistan									**Turkménistan**
Kilometres flown	21	15	15	11	...	...	...	6	Kilomètres parcourus
Passengers carried	748	523	523	890	...	...	...	250	Passagers transportés
Passenger−km	1562	1093	1093	832	...	...	...	511	Passagers−km
Total ton−km	143	101	101	79	...	...	...	49	Total tonnes−km
United Arab Emirates [3]									**Emirats arabes unis** [3]
Kilometres flown	73	82	85	94	73	82	85	94	Kilomètres parcourus
Passengers carried	3551	4063	4720	5264	3551	4063	4720	5264	Passagers transportés
Passenger−km	9958	11352	13519	15633	9958	11352	13519	15633	Passagers−km
Total ton−km	1517	1743	2107	2403	1517	1743	2107	2403	Total tonnes−km
Uzbekistan									**Ouzbékistan**
Kilometres flown	32	23	23	33	2	2	2	23	Kilomètres parcourus
Passengers carried	2217	1566	1566	1401	32	36	36	673	Passagers transportés
Passenger−km	4855	3460	3460	2609	127	145	145	2258	Passagers−km
Total ton−km	447	321	321	284	18	20	20	252	Total tonnes−km
Viet Nam									**Viet Nam**
Kilometres flown	25	29	35	33	9	17	22	20	Kilomètres parcourus
Passengers carried	2290	2108	2527	2373	1031	713	925	899	Passagers transportés
Passenger−km	2303	2954	3785	3644	1185	1884	2511	2371	Passagers−km
Total ton−km	209	352	448	426	108	234	306	285	Total tonnes−km
Yemen									**Yémen**
Kilometres flown	6	11	13	12	5	9	12	11	Kilomètres parcourus
Passengers carried	375	588	707	765	176	366	408	462	Passagers transportés
Passenger−km	486	849	1076	1104	381	790	987	1017	Passagers−km
Total ton−km	49	86	115	120	39	80	106	111	Total tonnes−km
Europe [1]									**Europe** [1]
Kilometres flown	**4793**	**5050**	**5299**	**5629**	**3376**	**3714**	**3969**	**4310**	**Kilomètres parcourus**
Passengers carried	**289363**	**309630**	**337120**	**356166**	**157958**	**177827**	**195590**	**212517**	**Passagers transportés**
Passenger−km	**539424**	**584821**	**627072**	**669007**	**427432**	**479774**	**518162**	**560344**	**Passagers−km**
Total ton−km	**76362**	**82232**	**90617**	**94522**	**65265**	**71718**	**79625**	**83633**	**Total tonnes−km**
Albania									**Albanie**
Kilometres flown	...	...	1	0	...	...	1	0	Kilomètres parcourus
Passengers carried	...	13	55	21	...	13	55	21	Passagers transportés
Passenger−km	...	4	35	7	...	4	35	7	Passagers−km
Total ton−km	...	...	3	1	...	...	3	1	Total tonnes−km
Austria									**Autriche**
Kilometres flown	97	111	118	126	93	106	113	121	Kilomètres parcourus
Passengers carried	4265	4719	5154	5880	3937	4402	4829	5510	Passagers transportés
Passenger−km	6727	8791	10066	11923	6643	8693	9959	11814	Passagers−km
Total ton−km	814	1035	1201	1411	807	1026	1191	1400	Total tonnes−km
Belarus									**Bélarus**
Kilometres flown	36	36	9	9	1	11	9	9	Kilomètres parcourus
Passengers carried	805	843	231	226	42	293	231	226	Passagers transportés
Passenger−km	2604	2342	399	397	98	537	399	397	Passagers−km
Total ton−km	237	216	39	40	9	52	39	40	Total tonnes−km
Belgium									**Belgique**
Kilometres flown	141	153	159	197	141	153	159	197	Kilomètres parcourus
Passengers carried	5001	5174	6872	8748	5001	5174	6872	8748	Passagers transportés
Passenger−km	8620	9011	11277	15338	8620	9011	11277	15338	Passagers−km
Total ton−km	1390	1419	1706	1853	1390	1419	1706	1853	Total tonnes−km
Bosnia and Herzegovina									**Bosnie−Herzégovine**
Kilometres flown	...	...	...	1	...	...	...	1	Kilomètres parcourus
Passengers carried	...	...	...	50	...	...	...	50	Passagers transportés
Passenger−km	...	...	...	40	...	...	...	40	Passagers−km
Total ton−km	...	...	...	5	...	...	...	5	Total tonnes−km
Bulgaria									**Bulgarie**
Kilometres flown	24	21	20	22	23	20	19	21	Kilomètres parcourus
Passengers carried	863	718	722	828	771	637	655	750	Passagers transportés
Passenger−km	2260	1812	1796	2026	2221	1776	1766	1992	Passagers−km
Total ton−km	235	188	194	214	231	185	192	211	Total tonnes−km

61
Civil Aviation
Passengers on scheduled services (000); Kilometres (millions) [*cont.*]
Aviation civile
Passagers sur les services réguliers (000); Kilomètres (millions) [*suite*]

Country or area and traffic	Total Totale 1995	1996	1997	1998	International Internationaux 1995	1996	1997	1998	Pays ou zone et trafic
Croatia									**Croatie**
Kilometres flown	8	9	9	10	6	7	8	8	Kilomètres parcourus
Passengers carried	644	727	767	828	317	402	417	465	Passagers transportés
Passenger–km	414	486	469	544	289	369	367	436	Passagers–km
Total ton–km	41	48	45	52	29	37	35	42	Total tonnes–km
Czech Republic									**République tchèque**
Kilometres flown	27	28	30	32	27	28	29	32	Kilomètres parcourus
Passengers carried	1285	1394	1448	1606	1272	1380	1437	1606	Passagers transportés
Passenger–km	2317	2368	2442	2637	2313	2364	2439	2637	Passagers–km
Total ton–km	235	237	244	264	235	236	244	264	Total tonnes–km
Denmark [4]									**Danemark** [4]
Kilometres flown	68	75	80	81	54	61	66	69	Kilomètres parcourus
Passengers carried	5689	5892	6236	5947	3246	3498	3832	3976	Passagers transportés
Passenger–km	5301	5466	5669	5658	4432	4661	4891	4990	Passagers–km
Total ton–km	621	679	729	725	538	599	651	657	Total tonnes–km
Estonia									**Estonie**
Kilometres flown	4	4	5	6	4	4	5	6	Kilomètres parcourus
Passengers carried	169	149	231	297	167	149	231	294	Passagers transportés
Passenger–km	107	114	147	177	106	114	147	177	Passagers–km
Total ton–km	10	11	14	17	10	11	14	17	Total tonnes–km
Finland									**Finlande**
Kilometres flown	78	82	92	95	60	63	72	73	Kilomètres parcourus
Passengers carried	5212	5597	6002	6771	3190	3301	3577	3986	Passagers transportés
Passenger–km	8562	8731	9575	10714	7659	7748	8475	9467	Passagers–km
Total ton–km	990	1031	1170	1250	910	945	1073	1140	Total tonnes–km
France [5]									**France** [5]
Kilometres flown	528	609	669	726	363	418	432	486	Kilomètres parcourus
Passengers carried	36020	41253	42344	43826	14598	17795	17329	18494	Passagers transportés
Passenger–km	68192	81594	84037	90225	45003	55978	54823	59584	Passagers–km
Total ton–km	11570	13151	13750	14033	9114	10475	10622	10784	Total tonnes–km
Germany									**Allemagne**
Kilometres flown	622	653	704	736	533	566	593	625	Kilomètres parcourus
Passengers carried	34680	40118	45805	49417	20273	26068	29202	31281	Passagers transportés
Passenger–km	64233	77765	86189	90393	58430	72011	79338	82922	Passagers–km
Total ton–km	12415	13850	14822	15301	11781	13215	14093	14522	Total tonnes–km
Greece									**Grèce**
Kilometres flown	62	66	68	68	46	50	52	53	Kilomètres parcourus
Passengers carried	6006	6396	7061	6403	2486	2599	2872	2621	Passagers transportés
Passenger–km	7945	8533	9261	8561	6895	7427	8026	7455	Passagers–km
Total ton–km	843	933	1013	936	738	822	891	829	Total tonnes–km
Hungary									**Hongrie**
Kilometres flown	27	30	32	35	27	30	32	35	Kilomètres parcourus
Passengers carried	1311	1563	1635	1749	1311	1563	1635	1749	Passagers transportés
Passenger–km	1694	2077	2346	2510	1694	2077	2346	2510	Passagers–km
Total ton–km	185	219	249	267	185	219	249	267	Total tonnes–km
Iceland									**Islande**
Kilometres flown	22	26	28	33	20	24	25	31	Kilomètres parcourus
Passengers carried	1097	1239	1334	1593	830	958	1056	1298	Passagers transportés
Passenger–km	2498	2872	3216	3774	2429	2800	3147	3712	Passagers–km
Total ton–km	276	317	351	426	270	310	344	420	Total tonnes–km
Ireland									**Irlande**
Kilometres flown	50	59	70	78	49	58	68	77	Kilomètres parcourus
Passengers carried	6587	7677	8964	10401	6206	7253	8522	9917	Passagers transportés
Passenger–km	5854	6732	7260	8510	5782	6664	7201	8442	Passagers–km
Total ton–km	626	700	767	889	619	694	762	883	Total tonnes–km
Italy									**Italie**
Kilometres flown	265	300	338	344	190	218	242	239	Kilomètres parcourus
Passengers carried	23666	25838	28184	28037	10146	11195	11507	11113	Passagers transportés
Passenger–km	33390	36157	38240	38122	26246	28432	29289	28889	Passagers–km
Total ton–km	4505	5060	5247	5261	3831	4274	4327	4338	Total tonnes–km
Latvia									**Lettonie**
Kilometres flown	6	9	6	6	6	9	6	6	Kilomètres parcourus
Passengers carried	173	276	229	222	173	276	229	222	Passagers transportés
Passenger–km	195	260	217	174	195	260	217	174	Passagers–km
Total ton–km	18	23	20	16	18	23	20	16	Total tonnes–km

61
Civil Aviation
Passengers on scheduled services (000); Kilometres (millions) [*cont.*]
Aviation civile
Passagers sur les services réguliers (000); Kilomètres (millions) [*suite*]

Country or area and traffic	Total Totale 1995	1996	1997	1998	International Internationaux 1995	1996	1997	1998	Pays ou zone et trafic
Lithuania									**Lituanie**
Kilometres flown	8	8	9	10	8	8	9	10	Kilomètres parcourus
Passengers carried	210	214	237	259	210	214	236	259	Passagers transportés
Passenger–km	308	304	301	307	308	304	301	307	Passagers–km
Total ton–km	29	29	30	31	29	29	30	31	Total tonnes–km
Luxembourg									**Luxembourg**
Kilometres flown	5	6	36	43	5	6	36	43	Kilomètres parcourus
Passengers carried	570	639	560	701	570	639	560	701	Passagers transportés
Passenger–km	380	421	281	454	380	421	281	454	Passagers–km
Total ton–km	35	39	2286	2287	35	39	2286	2287	Total tonnes–km
Malta									**Malte**
Kilometres flown	20	20	20	20	20	20	20	20	Kilomètres parcourus
Passengers carried	1066	1038	1054	1143	1066	1038	1054	1143	Passagers transportés
Passenger–km	1723	1663	1681	1888	1723	1663	1681	1888	Passagers–km
Total ton–km	165	155	157	177	165	155	157	177	Total tonnes–km
Monaco									**Monaco**
Kilometres flown	...	...	0	0	...	...	0	0	Kilomètres parcourus
Passengers carried	44	44	44	44	44	44	44	44	Passagers transportés
Passenger–km	1	1	1	1	1	1	1	1	Passagers–km
Total ton–km	...	...	0	0	...	...	0	0	Total tonnes–km
Netherlands [6]									**Pays–Bas** [6]
Kilometres flown	365	386	364	390	356	377	363	390	Kilomètres parcourus
Passengers carried	16378	17114	17161	17950	16021	16724	17084	17879	Passagers transportés
Passenger–km	57580	62397	66132	68597	57356	62160	66124	68590	Passagers–km
Total ton–km	9345	9959	10590	10864	9323	9937	10589	10864	Total tonnes–km
Norway [4]									**Norvège** [4]
Kilometres flown	112	121	130	134	51	56	60	62	Kilomètres parcourus
Passengers carried	11695	12727	13759	14279	3199	3461	3871	4068	Passagers transportés
Passenger–km	8034	8688	9158	9480	4461	4751	5041	5171	Passagers–km
Total ton–km	869	969	1061	1082	543	606	663	673	Total tonnes–km
Poland									**Pologne**
Kilometres flown	41	40	45	46	38	37	42	42	Kilomètres parcourus
Passengers carried	1657	1806	1998	2061	1413	1521	1690	1724	Passagers transportés
Passenger–km	4242	3917	4204	4255	4146	3830	4111	4155	Passagers–km
Total ton–km	457	430	478	483	448	422	470	475	Total tonnes–km
Portugal									**Portugal**
Kilometres flown	82	96	95	98	66	78	76	78	Kilomètres parcourus
Passengers carried	4590	4806	5296	5832	2633	2813	3170	3462	Passagers transportés
Passenger–km	8057	8423	9342	10107	6702	7041	7889	8475	Passagers–km
Total ton–km	933	985	1094	1157	788	836	936	981	Total tonnes–km
Republic of Moldova									**République de Moldova**
Kilometres flown	4	5	2	4	4	5	2	4	Kilomètres parcourus
Passengers carried	170	190	46	118	170	190	46	118	Passagers transportés
Passenger–km	211	240	61	146	211	240	61	146	Passagers–km
Total ton–km	20	23	6	14	20	23	6	14	Total tonnes–km
Romania									**Roumanie**
Kilometres flown	30	24	26	22	27	21	23	20	Kilomètres parcourus
Passengers carried	1245	913	995	921	979	739	775	758	Passagers transportés
Passenger–km	2526	1823	1702	1712	2426	1753	1617	1647	Passagers–km
Total ton–km	246	180	167	167	237	173	159	161	Total tonnes–km
Russian Federation									**Fédération de Russie**
Kilometres flown	821	724	609	581	186	214	198	212	Kilomètres parcourus
Passengers carried	26525	22117	20419	18685	4338	6001	5915	5960	Passagers transportés
Passenger–km	61035	52710	49278	46158	15972	18715	18135	18811	Passagers–km
Total ton–km	6433	5643	5269	4931	1980	2222	2145	2179	Total tonnes–km
Slovakia									**Slovaquie**
Kilometres flown	1	2	2	3	1	2	2	3	Kilomètres parcourus
Passengers carried	41	63	81	107	26	41	59	82	Passagers transportés
Passenger–km	43	80	103	128	38	72	95	119	Passagers–km
Total ton–km	4	7	10	11	4	7	9	10	Total tonnes–km
Slovenia									**Slovénie**
Kilometres flown	6	7	7	8	6	7	7	8	Kilomètres parcourus
Passengers carried	371	393	404	460	370	393	404	460	Passagers transportés
Passenger–km	357	380	375	411	357	380	375	411	Passagers–km
Total ton–km	36	38	37	41	36	38	37	41	Total tonnes–km

61
Civil Aviation
Passengers on scheduled services (000); Kilometres (millions) [*cont.*]
Aviation civile
Passagers sur les services réguliers (000); Kilomètres (millions) [*suite*]

Country or area and traffic	Total Totale				International Internationaux				Pays ou zone et trafic
	1995	1996	1997	1998	1995	1996	1997	1998	
Spain									**Espagne**
Kilometres flown	265	285	305	331	146	156	159	179	Kilomètres parcourus
Passengers carried	25766	27759	30316	31594	7171	7674	8227	8971	Passagers transportés
Passenger–km	31070	34102	37240	40042	19775	21715	23595	26027	Passagers–km
Total ton–km	3485	3807	4093	4378	2399	2618	2780	3038	Total tonnes–km
Sweden [4]									**Suède** [4]
Kilometres flown	110	120	132	143	71	78	83	89	Kilomètres parcourus
Passengers carried	9498	9879	11327	11878	4417	4782	5264	5571	Passagers transportés
Passenger–km	8538	8925	9749	10249	6256	6611	6972	7198	Passagers–km
Total ton–km	980	1073	1191	1234	773	863	939	959	Total tonnes–km
Switzerland									**Suisse**
Kilometres flown	192	211	230	263	184	206	225	258	Kilomètres parcourus
Passengers carried	9859	10468	12482	14299	8754	9299	11204	12868	Passagers transportés
Passenger–km	20359	22264	26314	29415	20016	22035	26072	29147	Passagers–km
Total ton–km	3557	3743	4462	4897	3517	3717	4438	4870	Total tonnes–km
TFYR Macedonia									**L'ex–R.y. Macédoine**
Kilometres flown	5	7	5	5	5	7	5	5	Kilomètres parcourus
Passengers carried	215	287	250	295	215	287	250	295	Passagers transportés
Passenger–km	340	410	285	328	340	410	285	328	Passagers–km
Total ton–km	31	38	27	31	31	38	27	31	Total tonnes–km
Ukraine									**Ukraine**
Kilometres flown	32	36	36	37	19	22	29	30	Kilomètres parcourus
Passengers carried	1005	1151	1190	1064	485	630	887	807	Passagers transportés
Passenger–km	1726	1792	1853	1720	1235	1330	1658	1556	Passagers–km
Total ton–km	180	176	186	188	135	133	168	173	Total tonnes–km
United Kingdom [79]									**Royaume–Uni** [79]
Kilometres flown	863	940	809	885	762	834	698	768	Kilomètres parcourus
Passengers carried	59689	64209	56227	61625	45672	49181	40360	45017	Passagers transportés
Passenger–km	152698	167577	136371	151880	146938	161366	129725	144933	Passagers–km
Total ton–km	21757	24104	17912	19589	21258	23562	17331	18984	Total tonnes–km
Oceania [1]									**Océanie** [1]
Kilometres flown	**684**	**726**	**777**	**757**	**335**	**354**	**360**	**360**	**Kilomètres parcourus**
Passengers carried	**41484**	**44982**	**45714**	**43990**	**12230**	**13091**	**13048**	**12343**	**Passagers transportés**
Passenger–km	**92726**	**105214**	**107911**	**103104**	**62464**	**73043**	**75345**	**71392**	**Passagers–km**
Total ton–km	**11530**	**12783**	**13205**	**12813**	**8429**	**9461**	**9783**	**9558**	**Total tonnes–km**
Australia									**Australie**
Kilometres flown	456	466	500	479	185	189	196	193	Kilomètres parcourus
Passengers carried	28831	30075	30954	30180	6187	6777	6783	6894	Passagers transportés
Passenger–km	64495	72594	75873	73647	38428	45238	47771	46525	Passagers–km
Total ton–km	8127	8707	9137	8929	5487	5898	6243	6116	Total tonnes–km
Fiji									**Fidji**
Kilometres flown	13	17	20	20	9	13	13	13	Kilomètres parcourus
Passengers carried	495	480	517	516	320	305	334	334	Passagers transportés
Passenger–km	1282	1217	2000	2000	1260	1195	1956	1956	Passagers–km
Total ton–km	198	195	200	200	196	193	196	196	Total tonnes–km
Kiribati									**Kiribati**
Kilometres flown	1	1	1	1	...	...	0	0	Kilomètres parcourus
Passengers carried	27	28	28	28	3	3	3	3	Passagers transportés
Passenger–km	10	11	11	11	6	7	7	7	Passagers–km
Total ton–km	2	2	2	2	1	1	1	1	Total tonnes–km
Marshall Islands									**Iles Marshall**
Kilometres flown	2	2	2	1	1	1	1	1	Kilomètres parcourus
Passengers carried	46	41	33	32	23	13	11	9	Passagers transportés
Passenger–km	57	45	26	20	49	28	17	12	Passagers–km
Total ton–km	16	7	2	2	15	5	2	1	Total tonnes–km
Nauru									**Nauru**
Kilometres flown	3	2	2	2	3	2	2	2	Kilomètres parcourus
Passengers carried	123	137	137	137	123	137	137	137	Passagers transportés
Passenger–km	216	243	243	243	216	243	243	243	Passagers–km
Total ton–km	21	24	24	24	21	24	24	24	Total tonnes–km
New Zealand									**Nouvelle–Zélande**
Kilometres flown	131	156	173	174	85	92	93	98	Kilomètres parcourus
Passengers carried	7677	9597	9435	8655	3188	3122	3324	2773	Passagers transportés
Passenger–km	18008	22052	20983	19014	15797	19148	18273	16352	Passagers–km
Total ton–km	2208	2841	2816	2700	1987	2555	2492	2479	Total tonnes–km

61

Civil Aviation
Passengers on scheduled services (000); Kilometres (millions) [*cont.*]
Aviation civile
Passagers sur les services réguliers (000); Kilomètres (millions) [*suite*]

Country or area and traffic	Total Totale				International Internationaux				Pays ou zone et trafic
	1995	1996	1997	1998	1995	1996	1997	1998	
Papua New Guinea									**Papouasie – Nvl – Guinée**
Kilometres flown	14	14	15	15	5	5	5	5	Kilomètres parcourus
Passengers carried	970	970	1114	1110	206	206	159	159	Passagers transportés
Passenger – km	830	830	735	736	470	470	361	361	Passagers – km
Total ton – km	94	94	86	87	58	58	49	49	Total tonnes – km
Samoa									**Samoa**
Kilometres flown	...	4	3	4	...	4	3	3	Kilomètres parcourus
Passengers carried	...	270	75	149	...	270	75	77	Passagers transportés
Passenger – km	...	265	247	250	...	265	247	242	Passagers – km
Total ton – km	...	26	30	24	...	26	30	23	Total tonnes – km
Solomon Islands									**Iles Salomon**
Kilometres flown	3	3	3	3	1	1	1	1	Kilomètres parcourus
Passengers carried	89	94	94	94	27	28	28	28	Passagers transportés
Passenger – km	70	74	74	74	55	58	58	58	Passagers – km
Total ton – km	8	9	9	9	7	7	7	7	Total tonnes – km
Tonga									**Tonga**
Kilometres flown	1	1	1	1	...	...	...	...	Kilomètres parcourus
Passengers carried	53	56	49	49	...	...	...	...	Passagers transportés
Passenger – km	11	11	10	10	...	...	...	...	Passagers – km
Total ton – km	1	1	1	1	...	...	...	...	Total tonnes – km
Vanuatu									**Vanuatu**
Kilometres flown	2	2	2	3	2	2	2	3	Kilomètres parcourus
Passengers carried	66	73	75	89	66	73	75	89	Passagers transportés
Passenger – km	146	150	156	179	146	150	156	179	Passagers – km
Total ton – km	15	15	15	19	15	15	15	19	Total tonnes – km

Source:
International Civil Aviation Organization (ICAO), Montreal, "Digest of Statistics – Traffic, 1994 – 1998" and the ICAO database.

† For information on recent changes in country or area nomenclature pertaining to former Czechoslovakia, Germany, Hong Kong Special Administrative Region (SAR) of China, Macao Special Administrative Region (SAR) of China, SFR of Yugoslavia and the former USSR, see Annex I – Country or area nomenclature, regional and other groupings.

†† For statistical purposes, the data for China do not include those for the Hong Kong Special Administrative Region, (Hong Kong SAR), Macao Special Administrative Region (Macao SAR) and Taiwan Province of China.

1 The statistics of France, Netherlands, Portugal, United Kingdom and United States have been distributed between two or more regions – France (Europe, Africa, North America and Oceania), Netherlands (Europe and North America), Portugal (1997 only; Europe and Asia), United Kingdom (Europe, Asia and North America) and United States (North America and Oceania).

2 Includes apportionment (1/10) of the traffic of Air Afrique, a multinational airline with headquarters in Côte d'Ivoire and operated by 10 African States until 1991. From 1992 includes apportionment (1/11) of the traffic of Air Afrique operated by 11 African States.

3 Includes apportionment (1/4) of the traffic of Gulf Air, a multinational airline with headquarters in Bahrain and operated by four Gulf States.

4 Includes an apportionment of international operations performed by Scandinavian Airlines System (SAS); Denmark (2/7), Norway (2/7), Sweden (3/7).

Source:
Organisation de l'aviation civile international (OACI), Montréal, "Recueil de statistiques – trafic, 1994 – 1998" et la base de données de l'OACI.

† Pour les modifications récentes de nomenclature de pays ou de zone concernant l'Allemagne, Hong Kong (Région administrative spéciale de Chine), Macao (Région administrative spéciale de Chine), l'ex – Tchécoslovaquie, l'ex – URSS et l'ex – Rfs de Yougoslavie, voir annexe I – Nomenclature des pays ou des zones, groupements régionaux et autres groupements.

†† Les données statistiques relatives à la Chine ne comprennent pas celles qui concernent la région administrative spéciale de Hong Kong (la RAS de Hong Kong (la RAS de Hong Kong), la région administrative spéciale de Macao (la RAS de Macao), et la province chinoise de Taiwan.

1 Les statistiques de la France, des Pays – Bas, du Portugal, du Royaume – Uni et des Etats – Unis concernent deux régions ou plus; France (Europe, Afrique, Amérique du Nord et Océanie), Pays – Bas (Europe et Amérique du Nord), Portugal (1997 seulement; Europe et Asie), Royaume – Uni (Europe, Asie et Amérqiue du Nord) et Etats – Unis (Amérique du Nord et Océanie).

2 Ces chiffres comprennent une partie du trafic (1/10) assurée par Air Afrique, compagnie aérienne multinationale dont le siège est situé   en Côte d'Ivoire et est exploitée conjointement par 10 Etats Africains jusqu'à 1991. A partir de 1992 ces chiffres comprennent une partie du trafic (1/11) assurée par Air Afrique et exploitée conjointement par 11 Etats Africains.

3 Ces chiffres comprennent une partie du trafic (1/4) assurée par Gulf Air, compagnie aérienne multinationale dont le siège est situé en Bahreïn et est exploitée conjointement par 4 Etats Gulf.

4 Y compris une partie des vols internationaux effectués par le SAS; Danemark (2/7), Norvège (2/7) et Suède (3/7).

61
Civil Aviation
Passengers on scheduled services (000); Kilometres (millions) [*cont.*]
Aviation civile
Passagers sur les services réguliers (000); Kilomètres (millions) [*suite*]

5   Including data for airlines based in the territories and dependencies of France.

6   Including data for airlines based in the territories and dependencies of Netherlands.

7   Including data for airlines based in the territories and dependencies of United Kingdom.

8   For 1997, data refer to the last six months of 1997.

9   Beginning the second half of 1997, data exlude those for Hong Kong Special Administrative Region (SAR) of China.

5   Y compris les données relatives aux compagnies aériennes ayant des bases d'opérations dans les territoires et dépendances de France.

6   Y compris les données relatives aux compagnies aériennes ayant des bases d'opérations dans les territoires et dépendances des Pays-Bas.

7   Y compris les données relatives aux compagnies aériennes ayant des bases d'opération dans les territoires et dépendances du Royaume-Uni.

8   Pour 1997, les données se rapportent au second semestre de 1997.

9   A partir du second semestre de 1997, les données ne comprennent pas celles relatives à la RAS de Hong Kong de la Chine.

Technical notes, tables 57-61

Table 57: Data refer to domestic and international traffic on all railway lines within each country shown, except railways entirely within an urban unit, and plantation, industrial mining, funicular and cable railways. The figures relating to passenger-kilometres include all passengers except military, government and railway personnel when carried without revenue. Those relating to ton-kilometres are freight net ton-kilometres and include both fast and ordinary goods services but exclude service traffic, mail, baggage and non-revenue governmental stores.

Table 58: For years in which a census or registration took place, the census or registration figure is shown; for other years, unless otherwise indicated, the officially estimated number of vehicles in use is shown. The time of year to which the figures refer is variable. Special purpose vehicles such as two- or three-wheeled cycles and motorcycles, trams, trolley-buses, ambulances, hearses, military vehicles operated by police or other governmental security organizations are excluded. Passenger cars includes vehicles seating not more than nine persons (including the driver), such as taxis, jeeps and station wagons. Commercial vehicles include: vans, lorries (trucks), buses, tractor and semi-trailer combinations but excludes trailers and farm tractors.

Table 59: Data refer to merchant fleets registered in each country as at 31 December, except for data prior to 1992 which refer to 30 June of the year stated. They are given in gross registered tons (100 cubic feet or 2.83 cubic metres) and represent the total volume of all the permanently enclosed spaces of the vessels to which the figures refer. Vessels without mechanical means of propulsion are excluded, but sailing vessels with auxiliary power are included.

Part A of the table refers to the total of merchant fleets registered. Part B shows data for oil tanker fleets and part C data for ore/oil and bulk carrier fleets. The data are published by Lloyd's Register of Shipping in *World Fleet Statistics* [18].

Table 60: The figures for vessels entered and cleared, unless otherwise stated, represent the sum of the net registered tonnage of sea-going foreign and domestic merchant vessels (power and sailing) entered with cargo from or cleared with cargo to a foreign port and refer to only one entrance or clearance for each foreign voyage. Where possible, the data exclude vessels "in ballast", i.e. entering without unloading or clearing without loading goods.

Table 61: Data for total services cover both domestic and international scheduled services operated by airlines registered in each country. Scheduled services

Notes techniques, tableaux 57 à 61

Tableau 57: Les données se rapportent au trafic intérieur et international de toutes les lignes de chemins de fer du pays indiqué, à l'exception des lignes situées entièrement à l'intérieur d'une agglomération urbaine ou desservant une plantation ou un complexe industriel minier, des funiculaires et des téléfériques. Les chiffres relatifs aux voyageurs-kilomètres se rapportent à tous les voyageurs sauf les militaires, les fonctionnaires et le personnel des chemins de fer, qui sont transportés gratuitement. Les chiffres relatifs aux tonnes-kilomètres se rapportent aux tonnes-kilomètres nettes de fret et comprennent les services rapides et ordinaires de transport de marchandises, à l'exception des transports pour les besoins du service, du courrier, des bagages et des marchandises transportées gratuitement pour les besoins de l'Etat.

Tableau 58: Pour les années où a eu lieu un recensement ou un enregistrement des véhicules, le chiffre indiqué est le résultat de cette opération; pour les autres années, sauf indication contraire, le chiffre indiqué correspond à l'estimation officielle du nombre de véhicules en circulation. L'époque de l'année à laquelle se rapportent les chiffres varie. Les véhicules à usage spécial, tels que les cycles à deux ou trois roues et motocyclettes, les tramways, les trolley-bus, les ambulances, les corbillards, les véhicules militaires utilisés par la police ou par d'autres services publics de sécurité ne sont pas compris dans ces chiffres. Les voitures de tourisme comprennent les véhicules automobiles dont le nombre de places assises (y compris celle du conducteur) n'est pas supérieur à neuf, tels que les taxis, jeeps et breaks. Les véhicules utilitaires comprennent les fourgons, camions, autobus et autocars, les ensembles tracteurs-remorques et semi-remorques, mais ne comprennent pas les remorques et les tracteurs agricoles.

Tableau 59: Les données se rapportent à la flotte marchande enregistrée dans chaque pays au 31 décembre de l'année indiquée à l'exception des données qui se rapportent aux années avant 1992, qui se réfèrent à la flotte marchande au 30 juin. Elles sont exprimées en tonneaux de jauge brute (100 pieds cubes ou 2,83 mètres cubes) et représentent le volume total de tous les espaces clos en permanence dans les navires auxquels elle s'appliquent. Elles excluent les navires sans moteur, mais pas les voiliers avec moteurs auxiliaires.

Les données de la Partie A du tableau se rapportent au total de la flotte marchande enregistrée. Celles de la Partie B se rapportent à la flotte des pétroliers, et celles de la Partie C à la flotte des minéraliers et des transporteurs de vrac et d'huile. Les données sont publiées par Lloyd's Register of Shipping dans *World*

include supplementary services occasioned by overflow traffic on regularly scheduled trips and preparatory flights for newly scheduled services. Freight means all goods, except mail and excess baggage, carried for remuneration. The data are published by the International Civil Aviation Organization in *Civil Aviation Statistics of the World* [10] and in the *Digest of Statistics—Traffic* [11].

Fleet Statistics [18].

Tableau 60: Sauf indication contraire, les données relatives aux navires entrés et sortis représentent la jauge nette totale des navires marchands de haute mer (à moteur ou à voile) nationaux ou étrangers, qui entrent ou sortent chargés, en provenance ou à destination d'un port étranger. On ne compte qu'une seule entrée et une seule sortie pour chaque voyage international. Dans la mesure du possible, le tableau exclut les navires sur lest (c'est-à-dire les navires entrant sans décharger ou sortant sans avoir chargé).

Tableau 61: Les données relatives au total des services se rapportent aux services réguliers, intérieurs ou internationaux des compagnies de transport aérien enregistrées dans chaque pays. Les services réguliers comprennent aussi les vols supplémentaires nécessités par un surcroît d'activité des services réguliers et les vols préparatoires en vue de nouveaux services réguliers. Par fret, on entend toutes les marchandises transportées contre paiement, mais non le courrier et les excédents de bagage. Les données sont publiées par l'Organisation de l'aviation civile internationale dans les *Statistiques de l'Aviation civile dans le monde* [10] et dans le *Recueil de statistiques—trafic* [11].

62
Production, trade and consumption of commercial energy
Production, commerce et consommation d'énergie commerciale
Thousand metric tons of oil equivalent and kilograms per capita
Milliers de tonnes d'équivalent pétrole et kilogrammes par habitant

| Region, country or area | Year | Primary energy production – Production d'énergie primaire | | | | | Changes in stocks | Imports | Exports |
		Total Totale	Solids Solides	Liquids Liquides	Gas Gaz	Electricity Electricité	Variations des stocks	Imports Importations	Exports Exportatio
World	**1994**	**8 262 109**	**2 224 045**	**3 295 097**	**1 929 519**	**813 448**	**44 374**	**2 999 937**	**2 908**
	1995	**8 517 778**	**2 291 139**	**3 326 687**	**2 052 164**	**847 788**	**14 802**	**3 075 475**	**3 025**
	1996	**8 743 802**	**2 330 496**	**3 371 941**	**2 152 705**	**888 659**	**3 876**	**3 251 140**	**3 170**
	1997	**8 840 353**	**2 349 117**	**3 449 857**	**2 155 122**	**886 257**	**51 314**	**3 364 732**	**3 272**
Africa	**1994**	**526 339**	**109 312**	**338 828**	**70 483**	**7 715**	**−2 371**	**53 832**	**342**
	1995	**554 667**	**115 036**	**347 587**	**83 921**	**8 122**	**−1 177**	**56 044**	**370**
	1996	**567 066**	**114 880**	**353 302**	**90 353**	**8 532**	**−3 732**	**55 385**	**382**
	1997	**589 166**	**120 896**	**359 660**	**99 862**	**8 748**	**−2 044**	**56 248**	**395**
Algeria	1994	107 111	14	59 405	47 677	14	− 302	888	74
	1995	119 352	15	61 257	58 063	17	− 108	859	83
	1996	125 429	15	62 853	62 549	11	− 416	850	88
	1997	135 408	16	64 806	70 579	6	227	846	96
Angola	1994	27 462	...	27 188	155	119	...	15	2
	1995	32 402	...	32 127	156	119	...	15	30
	1996	35 058	...	34 771	167	120	...	16	33
	1997	35 189	...	34 894	174	121	...	16	33
Benin	1994	121	...	121	...	...	...	197	
	1995	89	...	89	...	...	...	200	
	1996	75	...	75	...	...	...	203	
	1997	62	...	62	...	...	...	205	
Burkina Faso	1994	6	...	...	...	6	...	322	
	1995	8	...	...	...	8	...	323	
	1996	10	...	...	...	10	...	326	
	1997	10	...	...	...	10	...	328	
Burundi	1994	14	4	...	...	10	2	74	
	1995	14	4	...	...	10	1	75	
	1996	14	4	...	...	10	1	77	
	1997	15	4	...	...	10	...	79	
Cameroon	1994	6 037	1	5 808	...	229	882	77	3
	1995	5 609	1	5 379	...	229	450	83	3
	1996	5 444	1	5 214	...	229	− 325	98	4
	1997	5 819	1	5 589	...	229	− 95	98	5
Cape Verde	1994	...	...	...	...	...	...	39	
	1995	...	...	...	...	...	...	38	
	1996	...	...	...	...	...	...	40	
	1997	...	...	...	...	...	...	40	
Central African Rep.	1994	7	...	...	...	7	2	94	
	1995	7	...	...	...	7	1	94	
	1996	7	...	...	...	7	1	95	
	1997	7	...	...	...	7	1	98	
Chad	1994	...	...	...	...	...	3	55	
	1995	...	...	...	...	...	3	55	
	1996	...	...	...	...	...	3	56	
	1997	...	...	...	...	...	...	57	
Comoros	1994	...	...	...	...	...	...	22	
	1995	...	...	...	...	...	...	23	
	1996	...	...	...	...	...	...	23	
	1997	...	...	...	...	...	...	23	
Congo	1994	9 600	...	9 560	3	37	301	15	8
	1995	9 307	...	9 266	3	37	− 109	15	8
	1996	10 409	...	10 368	3	37	− 209	16	10
	1997	11 625	...	11 584	3	38	...	16	11
Côte d'Ivoire	1994	457	...	348	...	109	...	3 390	
	1995	400	...	314	...	86	...	3 399	
	1996	1 382	...	1 263	...	120	...	3 382	
	1997	1 417	...	1 272	...	145	...	3 393	
Dem. Rep. of the Congo	1994	1 643	64	1 124	...	455	...	726	1
	1995	1 672	65	1 146	...	461	...	746	1
	1996	1 678	66	1 148	...	464	...	754	1
	1997	1 682	66	1 151	...	465	...	768	1
Djibouti	1994	...	...	...	...	...	...	539	
	1995	...	...	...	...	...	...	545	
	1996	...	...	...	...	...	...	545	
	1997	...	...	...	...	...	...	550	

Air Avion	Sea Maritime	Unallocated Nondistribué	Per capita Par habitant	Total Totale	Solids Solides	Liquids Liquides	Gas Gaz	Electricity Electricité	Année	Région, pays ou zone
296	125 385	311 972	1 395	7 820 371	2 244 729	2 842 044	1 920 180	813 417	1994	Monde
441	132 236	305 396	1 418	8 062 332	2 299 602	2 858 149	2 056 720	847 861	1995	
017	136 507	315 365	1 442	8 312 817	2 366 930	2 920 459	2 137 740	887 689	1996	
176	139 811	344 937	1 427	8 337 926	2 346 286	2 953 472	2 151 710	886 458	1997	
441	6 342	23 361	305	207 537	73 814	85 049	41 028	7 646	1994	Afrique
386	6 341	20 812	303	211 663	69 290	85 253	49 055	8 065	1995	
620	6 913	15 973	305	218 067	69 354	87 809	52 595	8 309	1996	
551	7 095	14 629	312	228 032	75 410	90 167	53 924	8 531	1997	
206	201	3 021	1 091	29 911	896	10 945	18 152	− 82	1994	Algérie
258	202	3 974	1 151	32 298	855	8 521	22 928	− 7	1995	
258	248	4 831	1 157	33 233	841	7 841	24 552	− 1	1996	
258	331	4 615	1 168	34 320	835	8 502	24 977	6	1997	
165	675	387	59	623	...	349	155	119	1994	Angola
163	660	840	57	628	...	352	156	119	1995	
165	670	363	57	645	...	358	167	120	1996	
165	680	376	56	653	...	358	174	121	1997	
19	...	...	33	171	...	148	...	22	1994	Bénin
20	...	...	32	173	...	150	...	23	1995	
20	...	− 20	32	176	...	153	...	23	1996	
20	...	2	32	178	...	156	...	23	1997	
...	...	...	32	328	...	322	...	6	1994	Burkina Faso
...	...	...	32	331	...	323	...	8	1995	
...	...	...	31	336	...	326	...	10	1996	
...	...	...	31	338	...	328	...	10	1997	
5	...	...	13	81	4	65	...	12	1994	Burundi
6	...	...	13	83	4	66	...	13	1995	
6	...	...	14	85	4	68	...	13	1996	
6	...	...	14	87	4	70	...	13	1997	
17	...	62	102	1 312	1	1 083	...	229	1994	Cameroun
19	...	144	102	1 344	1	1 115	...	229	1995	
21	...	− 514	101	1 368	1	1 138	...	229	1996	
21	...	− 390	99	1 373	1	1 143	...	229	1997	
...	...	...	105	39	...	39	...	...	1994	Cap−Vert
...	...	...	100	38	...	38	...	...	1995	
...	...	...	103	40	...	40	...	...	1996	
...	...	...	100	40	...	40	...	...	1997	
13	...	...	26	85	...	78	...	7	1994	Rép. centrafricaine
13	...	...	26	86	...	79	...	7	1995	
14	...	...	26	86	...	79	...	7	1996	
14	...	...	26	89	...	82	...	7	1997	
20	...	...	5	32	...	32	...	...	1994	Tchad
20	...	...	5	32	...	32	...	...	1995	
20	...	...	5	33	...	33	...	...	1996	
20	...	...	5	37	...	37	...	...	1997	
...	...	...	37	22	...	22	...	...	1994	Comores
...	...	...	38	23	...	23	...	...	1995	
...	...	...	37	23	...	23	...	...	1996	
...	...	...	36	23	...	23	...	...	1997	
...	8	93	231	575	...	526	3	46	1994	Congo
...	10	20	216	554	...	504	3	47	1995	
...	10	17	214	564	...	514	3	47	1996	
...	10	− 482	211	571	...	520	3	48	1997	
89	7	1 316	164	2 164	...	2 055	...	109	1994	Côte d'Ivoire
92	8	1 414	148	2 008	...	1 922	...	86	1995	
94	8	2 064	168	2 317	...	2 198	...	120	1996	
95	8	2 062	168	2 363	...	2 217	...	145	1997	
111	2	− 14	24	1 042	221	454	...	367	1994	Rép. Dém. du Congo
114	2	15	23	1 060	224	464	...	372	1995	
114	2	20	23	1 079	226	475	...	379	1996	
116	2	21	23	1 089	228	482	...	380	1997	
66	351	...	207	122	...	122	...	...	1994	Djibouti
68	354	...	205	123	...	123	...	...	1995	
68	356	...	198	121	...	121	...	...	1996	
69	360	...	196	121	...	121	...	...	1997	

62
Production, trade and consumption of commercial energy
Thousand metric tons of oil equivalent and kilograms per capita [*cont.*]
Production, commerce et consommation d'énergie commerciale
Milliers de tonnes d'équivalent pétrole et kilogrammes par habitant [*suite*]

Region, country or area	Year	Primary energy production – Production d'énergie primaire					Changes in stocks Variations des stocks	Imports Importations	Exports Exportation
		Total Totale	Solids Solides	Liquids Liquides	Gas Gaz	Electricity Electricité			
Egypt	1994	57 674	...	46 923	9 827	923	500	1 194	25
	1995	60 440	...	46 840	12 650	950	600	970	25
	1996	59 824	...	45 412	13 453	959	− 660	2 002	22
	1997	59 357	...	44 468	13 884	1 006	− 190	2 216	20
Equatorial Guinea	1994	242	...	242	...	...	...	42	
	1995	339	...	339	...	...	...	42	
	1996	857	...	857	...	...	...	43	
	1997	2 997	...	2 996	...	...	...	46	2
Ethiopia	1994	116	...	...	...	116	43	1 250	
	1995	122	...	...	...	122	4	1 038	
	1996	130	...	...	...	130	2	608	
	1997	135	...	...	...	135	2	686	
Gabon	1994	17 988	...	17 211	712	64	152	176	16
	1995	19 080	...	18 243	769	68	198	156	17
	1996	18 946	...	18 274	606	66	130	173	17
	1997	19 288	...	18 594	624	70	162	249	17
Gambia	1994	...	...	...	...	...	...	72	
	1995		...	...	...	...	...	74	
	1996	...	...	...	...	...	...	74	
	1997	...	...	...	...	...	...	74	
Ghana	1994	523	...	...	...	523	...	1 264	
	1995	526	...	...	...	526	...	1 277	
	1996	570	...	...	...	570	...	1 282	
	1997	571	...	...	...	571	...	1 282	
Guinea	1994	16	...	...	...	16	...	364	
	1995	16	...	...	...	16	...	370	
	1996	16	...	...	...	16	...	374	
	1997	16	...	...	...	16	...	374	
Guinea−Bissau	1994	...	...	...	...	...	...	81	
	1995		...	...	...	...	...	82	
	1996	...	...	...	...	...	...	82	
	1997	...	...	...	...	...	...	82	
Kenya	1994	488	...	...	...	488	...	2 595	
	1995	517	...	...	...	517	...	2 494	
	1996	517	...	...	...	517	...	2 657	
	1997	627	...	...	...	627	...	2 813	
Liberia	1994	15	...	...	...	15	...	120	
	1995	15	...	...	...	15	...	123	
	1996	15	...	...	...	15	...	125	
	1997	15	...	...	...	15	...	126	
Libyan Arab Jamah.	1994	74 601	...	68 645	5 956	...	−2 262	7	61
	1995	74 768	...	68 885	5 883	...	− 761	7	60
	1996	74 639	...	68 682	5 957	...	−2 175	7	61
	1997	75 475	...	69 378	6 097	...	−2 561	7	62
Madagascar	1994	30	...	...	...	30	3	421	
	1995	32	...	...	...	32	− 7	430	
	1996	37	...	...	...	37	1	431	
	1997	37	...	...	...	37		433	
Malawi	1994	70	...	...	...	70	...	228	
	1995	72	...	...	...	72	...	229	
	1996	74	...	...	...	74	...	233	
	1997	74	...	...	...	74	...	233	
Mali	1994	19	...	...	...	19	...	168	
	1995	19	...	...	...	19	...	173	
	1996	18	...	...	...	18	...	176	
	1997	20	...	...	...	20	...	176	
Mauritania	1994	2	...	...	...	2	...	1 057	
	1995	2	...	...	...	2	...	1 059	
	1996	2	...	...	...	2	...	1 062	
	1997	2	...	...	...	2	...	1 062	
Mauritius	1994	7	...	...	...	7	− 32	709	
	1995	12	...	...	...	12	13	785	
	1996	9	...	...	...	9	− 28	799	
	1997	9	...	...	...	9	− 7	809	

| Bunkers – Soutes | | | Consumption – Consommation | | | | | | | |
Air Avion	Sea Maritime	Unallocated Nondistribué	Per capita Par habitant	Total Totale	Solids Solides	Liquids Liquides	Gas Gaz	Electricity Electricité	Année	Région, pays ou zone
361	1 369	1 957	475	29 039	974	17 354	9 787	923	1994	Egypte
258	1 372	1 355	517	32 196	646	17 970	12 630	950	1995	
361	1 883	2 127	559	35 519	902	20 206	13 453	959	1996	
272	1 965	2 079	576	37 269	900	21 479	13 884	1 006	1997	
...	...	1	108	42	...	42	...	...	1994	Guinée équatoriale
...	...	20	105	42	...	42	...	...	1995	
...	...	5	105	43	...	43	...	...	1996	
...	...	154	110	46	...	46	...	...	1997	
52	14	109	18	988	...	872	...	116	1994	Ethiopie
53	14	8	15	891	...	770	...	122	1995	
55	14	1	10	630	...	501	...	130	1996	
55	14	22	10	629	...	495	...	135	1997	
51	307	- 19	1 142	1 197	...	421	712	64	1994	Gabon
26	310	194	1 124	1 211	...	374	769	68	1995	
39	319	99	942	1 043	...	371	606	66	1996	
34	290	136	1 080	1 228	...	534	624	70	1997	
...	...	...	65	70	...	70	...	...	1994	Gambie
...	...	...	65	72	...	72	...	...	1995	
...	...	...	63	72	...	72	...	...	1996	
...	...	...	61	72	...	72	...	...	1997	
28	24	- 39	98	1 687	2	1 181	...	504	1994	Ghana
29	24	65	90	1 597	2	1 088	...	507	1995	
29	25	54	91	1 654	2	1 102	...	550	1996	
29	25	53	89	1 657	2	1 103	...	552	1997	
14	...	...	53	366	...	350	...	16	1994	Guinée
14	...	...	52	372	...	356	...	16	1995	
14	...	...	52	377	...	361	...	16	1996	
14	...	...	51	377	...	361	...	16	1997	
6	...	...	71	75	...	75	...	...	1994	Guinée–Bissau
6	...	...	70	76	...	76	...	...	1995	
6	...	...	68	76	...	76	...	...	1996	
6	...	...	67	76	...	76	...	...	1997	
...	136	189	87	2 305	77	1 717	...	511	1994	Kenya
...	55	- 67	97	2 650	66	2 051	...	532	1995	
...	55	85	95	2 659	65	2 062	...	532	1996	
...	57	229	87	2 485	80	1 764	...	640	1997	
4	12	...	56	118	...	103	...	15	1994	Libéria
4	12	...	58	121	...	106	...	15	1995	
4	12	...	56	124	...	108	...	15	1996	
4	12	...	52	125	...	109	...	15	1997	
155	79	3 209	2 528	12 270	3	7 690	4 577	...	1994	Jamah. arabe libyenne
155	89	2 493	2 464	12 239	3	7 741	4 494	...	1995	
155	99	2 576	2 501	12 719	3	7 877	4 839	...	1996	
155	99	2 733	2 483	12 935	3	7 860	5 072	...	1997	
1	13	14	23	399	12	357	...	30	1994	Madagascar
2	15	24	30	408	12	364	...	32	1995	
2	15	15	29	414	12	366	...	37	1996	
2	15	14	29	417	12	369	...	37	1997	
15	...	...	30	283	12	201	...	70	1994	Malawi
17	...	...	29	285	12	201	...	72	1995	
17	...	...	29	290	12	205	...	73	1996	
17	...	...	29	291	12	205	...	74	1997	
15	...	...	18	171	...	152	...	19	1994	Mali
17	...	...	18	176	...	157	...	19	1995	
18	...	...	17	177	...	159	...	18	1996	
18	...	...	17	178	...	159	...	20	1997	
12	10	97	415	939	4	933	...	2	1994	Mauritanie
12	10	95	405	944	4	937	...	2	1995	
12	10	89	398	953	4	946	...	2	1996	
12	10	84	389	958	4	951	...	2	1997	
127	138	...	437	482	27	449	...	7	1994	Maurice
124	157	...	451	502	46	444	...	12	1995	
128	131	...	513	577	47	521	...	9	1996	
129	133	...	498	564	48	507	...	9	1997	

62
Production, trade and consumption of commercial energy
Thousand metric tons of oil equivalent and kilograms per capita [*cont.*]
Production, commerce et consommation d'énergie commerciale
Milliers de tonnes d'équivalent pétrole et kilogrammes par habitant [*suite*]

| Region, country or area | Year | Primary energy production – Production d'énergie primaire | | | | | Changes in stocks Variations des stocks | Imports Importations | Exports Exportatio |
		Total Totale	Solids Solides	Liquids Liquides	Gas Gaz	Electricity Electricité			
Morocco	1994	558	455	8	23	72	105	8 733	
	1995	535	455	5	23	52	211	9 036	
	1996	544	354	5	19	167	− 236	8 577	
	1997	480	263	12	28	177	178	9 279	
Mozambique	1994	32	28	...	...	4	...	357	
	1995	31	27	...	...	4	...	412	
	1996	32	28	...	...	4	...	416	
	1997	32	28	...	...	4	...	422	
Niger	1994	120	120	...	...	...	...	242	
	1995	121	121	...	...	...	...	247	
	1996	121	121	...	...	...	...	248	
	1997	122	122	...	...	...	...	248	
Nigeria	1994	95 821	35	91 030	4 241	516	...	2 307	80
	1995	97 207	35	92 142	4 515	516	...	2 237	83
	1996	98 429	35	92 789	5 089	516	...	2 238	86
	1997	99 301	35	93 624	5 126	516	...	2 223	88
Réunion	1994	43	...	...	...	43	...	527	
	1995	43	...	...	...	43	...	535	
	1996	43	...	...	...	43	...	536	
	1997	43	...	...	...	43	...	538	
Rwanda	1994	14	...	...	...	14	...	168	
	1995	14	...	...	...	14	...	172	
	1996	14	...	...	...	14	...	172	
	1997	14	...	...	...	14	...	174	
Saint Helena	1994	...	...	...	...	...	...	2	
	1995	...	...	...	...	...	...	2	
	1996	...	...	...	...	...	...	2	
	1997	...	...	...	...	...	...	2	
Sao Tome and Principe	1994	1	...	...	...	1	...	25	
	1995	1	...	...	...	1	...	26	
	1996	1	...	...	...	1	...	26	
	1997	1	...	...	...	1	...	26	
Senegal	1994	...	...	...	...	...	...	1 203	
	1995	...	...	...	...	...	...	1 212	
	1996	...	...	...	...	...	...	1 215	
	1997	...	...	...	...	...	...	1 224	
Seychelles	1994	...	...	...	...	...	...	171	
	1995	...	...	...	...	...	...	174	
	1996	...	...	...	...	...	...	175	
	1997	...	...	...	...	...	...	181	
Sierra Leone	1994	...	...	...	...	...	...	282	
	1995	...	...	...	...	...	...	286	
	1996	...	...	...	...	...	...	288	
	1997	...	...	...	...	...	...	292	
South Africa Customs Union	1994	115 698	104 535	6 816	1 714	2 633	−1 814	14 294	39
	1995	122 218	110 227	7 272	1 715	3 004	−1 426	16 331	49
	1996	122 670	110 372	7 388	1 715	3 195	...	14 628	50
	1997	128 893	116 575	7 399	1 717	3 202	...	14 695	50
Sudan	1994	81	...	...	...	81	...	1 331	
	1995	81	...	...	...	81	...	1 337	
	1996	81	...	...	...	81	...	1 344	
	1997	82	...	...	...	82	...	1 345	
Togo	1994	...	...	...	...	...	...	214	
	1995	1	...	...	...	1	...	224	
	1996	1	...	...	...	1	...	226	
	1997	1	...	...	...	1	...	234	
Tunisia	1994	4 576	...	4 398	175	3	62	4 697	4
	1995	4 431	...	4 284	144	3	− 225	4 585	4
	1996	5 003	...	4 203	794	6	115	5 205	4
	1997	5 463	...	3 830	1 629	4	238	4 681	4
Uganda	1994	90	...	...	...	90	...	248	
	1995	94	...	...	...	94	...	310	
	1996	100	...	...	...	100	...	315	
	1997	108	...	...	...	108	...	336	

Air Avion	Sea Maritime	Unallocated Nondistribué	Per capita Par habitant	Total Totale	Solids Solides	Liquids Liquides	Gas Gaz	Electricity Electricité	Année	Région, pays ou zone
83	...	860	323	8 244	1 555	6 514	23	151	1994	Maroc
82	...	904	323	8 375	1 854	6 360	23	138	1995	
77	...	796	321	8 483	2 213	5 994	19	257	1996	
77	...	800	324	8 704	2 119	6 285	28	272	1997	
34	25	...	20	330	42	256	...	32	1994	Mozambique
35	36	...	21	372	39	277	...	56	1995	
36	36	...	21	376	42	278	...	56	1996	
38	36	...	21	381	42	282	...	56	1997	
20	...	...	39	343	120	206	...	17	1994	Niger
22	...	...	38	347	121	209	...	17	1995	
22	...	...	37	348	121	210	...	17	1996	
22	...	...	36	348	122	210	...	17	1997	
366	369	6 184	114	10 984	39	6 188	4 241	516	1994	Nigéria
366	379	3 247	116	11 458	39	6 388	4 515	516	1995	
377	379	1 277	118	12 011	39	6 367	5 089	516	1996	
372	369	− 39	116	12 069	39	6 388	5 126	516	1997	
12	1	...	864	557	...	514	...	43	1994	Réunion
12	1	...	863	565	...	521	...	43	1995	
12	1	...	852	566	...	522	...	43	1996	
12	1	...	844	568	...	524	...	43	1997	
8	...	...	32	173	...	158	...	14	1994	Rwanda
9	...	...	33	176	...	161	...	15	1995	
9	...	...	32	176	...	161	...	15	1996	
9	...	...	30	178	...	163	...	15	1997	
...	...	...	333	2	...	2	...	...	1994	Saint−Hélène
...	...	...	333	2	...	2	...	...	1995	
...	...	...	333	2	...	2	...	...	1996	
...	...	...	333	2	...	2	...	...	1997	
...	...	...	192	25	...	25	...	1	1994	Sao Tomé−et−Principe
...	...	...	195	26	...	26	...	1	1995	
...	...	...	193	26	...	26	...	1	1996	
...	...	...	188	26	...	26	...	1	1997	
108	140	4	112	913	...	913	...	...	1994	Sénégal
109	144	3	110	917	...	917	...	...	1995	
109	144	...	108	923	...	923	...	...	1996	
110	148	− 3	106	928	...	928	...	...	1997	
33	80	...	795	58	...	58	...	...	1994	Seychelles
34	78	...	849	62	...	62	...	...	1995	
34	78	...	851	63	...	63	...	...	1996	
35	80	...	867	65	...	65	...	...	1997	
19	80	53	31	128	...	128	...	...	1994	Sierra Leone
19	83	52	31	130	...	130	...	...	1995	
19	83	53	31	131	...	131	...	...	1996	
19	85	52	30	134	...	134	...	...	1997	
...	2 268	5 702	1 994	84 672	65 716	14 741	1 714	2 502	1994	Union douanière
...	2 295	5 845	1 898	82 136	61 205	16 457	1 715	2 759	1995	d'Afrique australe
...	2 305	1 913	1 878	82 795	60 955	17 407	1 715	2 718	1996	
...	2 335	1 968	1 984	88 993	67 155	17 396	1 717	2 725	1997	
34	7	163	45	1 169	...	1 088	...	81	1994	Soudan
37	8	156	44	1 178	...	1 097	...	81	1995	
38	8	150	44	1 188	...	1 107	...	81	1996	
38	8	145	43	1 192	...	1 111	...	82	1997	
...	...	...	53	209	...	181	...	27	1994	Togo
...	...	...	54	218	...	190	...	28	1995	
...	...	...	53	220	...	192	...	28	1996	
...	...	...	53	229	...	201	...	28	1997	
105	2	− 27	572	5 031	70	3 265	1 664	32	1994	Tunisie
104	1	− 29	554	4 954	62	3 063	1 822	6	1995	
196	...	− 69	592	5 377	63	3 155	2 152	7	1996	
217	...	− 46	618	5 695	68	3 304	2 318	4	1997	
...	...	...	17	315	...	246	...	69	1994	Ouganda
...	...	...	20	385	...	308	...	77	1995	
...	...	...	21	400	...	313	...	87	1996	
...	...	...	21	427	...	334	...	93	1997	

62

Production, trade and consumption of commercial energy
Thousand metric tons of oil equivalent and kilograms per capita [cont.]
Production, commerce et consommation d'énergie commerciale
Milliers de tonnes d'équivalent pétrole et kilogrammes par habitant [suite]

Region, country or area	Year	Primary energy production – Production d'énergie primaire					Changes in stocks Variations des stocks	Imports Importations	Exports Exportations
		Total Totale	Solids Solides	Liquids Liquides	Gas Gaz	Electricity Electricité			
United Rep. of Tanzania	1994	131	3	...	...	128	...	733	2
	1995	132	3	...	...	129	...	745	2
	1996	133	3	...	...	129	...	751	2
	1997	133	3	...	...	129	...	760	3
Western Sahara	1994	...	...	...	...	...	...	71	4
	1995	...	...	...	...	...	...	73	
	1996	...	...	...	...	...	...	73	
	1997	...	...	...	...	...	...	73	
Zambia	1994	890	224	...	...	666	...	565	17
	1995	879	212	...	...	666	...	575	17
	1996	873	206	...	...	667	...	585	17
	1997	879	212	...	...	667	...	590	17
Zimbabwe	1994	4 033	3 828	...	...	204	− 17	1 463	13
	1995	4 057	3 870	...	...	187	− 23	1 746	9
	1996	3 859	3 673	...	...	186	63	1 756	8
	1997	3 757	3 570	...	...	187		1 740	8
America, North	**1994**	**2 189 660**	**575 967**	**676 551**	**668 594**	**268 548**	**21 589**	**665 461**	**332 10**
	1995	**2 206 264**	**573 332**	**672 864**	**680 679**	**279 389**	**−10 902**	**655 502**	**354 49**
	1996	**2 254 645**	**590 424**	**665 213**	**701 207**	**297 800**	**−7 514**	**690 841**	**368 32**
	1997	**2 272 937**	**606 037**	**677 442**	**707 404**	**282 054**	**8 337**	**737 602**	**383 74**
Antigua and Barbuda	1994	...	...	...	...	...	...	154	
	1995	...	...	...	...	...	...	158	
	1996	...	...	...	...	...	...	158	
	1997	...	...	...	...	...	...	164	
Aruba	1994	...	...	...	...	...	...	584	
	1995	...	...	...	...	...	...	591	
	1996	...	...	...	...	...	...	602	.
	1997	...	...	...	...	...	...	615	.
Bahamas	1994	...	...	...	...	...	− 43	2 848	2 10
	1995	...	...	...	...	...	− 18	2 879	2 10
	1996	...	...	...	...	...	− 18	2 877	2 09
	1997	...	...	...	...	...	− 5	2 889	2 09
Barbados	1994	83	...	62	21	...	− 26	271	2
	1995	87	...	63	24	...	− 1	327	2
	1996	77	...	50	27	...	7	364	2
	1997	67	...	45	22	...	5	416	2
Belize	1994	...	...	...	...	...	...	141	
	1995	3	...	...	...	3	...	138	..
	1996	5	...	...	...	5	...	117	..
	1997	6	...	...	...	6	...	148	..
Bermuda	1994	...	...	...	...	...	...	168	..
	1995	...	...	...	...	...	...	168	..
	1996	...	...	...	...	...	...	171	..
	1997	...	...	...	...	...	...	171	..
British Virgin Islands	1994	...	...	...	...	...	...	17	..
	1995	...	...	...	...	...	...	17	..
	1996	...	...	...	...	...	...	20	..
	1997	...	...	...	...	...	...	20	..
Canada	1994	337 363	37 509	107 592	137 741	54 521	500	42 971	147 723
	1995	349 478	38 899	111 464	146 588	52 526	−2 856	41 759	160 772
	1996	357 834	39 721	112 873	152 161	53 078	40	47 504	167 506
	1997	365 083	41 103	118 317	153 997	51 667	2 070	54 607	174 774
Cayman Islands	1994	...	...	...	...	...	...	108	...
	1995	...	...	...	...	...	...	110	...
	1996	...	...	...	...	...	...	111	...
	1997	...	...	...	...	...	...	111	...
Costa Rica	1994	599	...	...	...	599	44	1 744	96
	1995	713	...	...	...	713	8	1 693	182
	1996	778	...	...	...	778	− 50	1 600	165
	1997	885	...	...	...	885	− 88	1 645	175
Cuba	1994	1 282	...	1 258	19	5	12	9 335	88
	1995	1 473	...	1 449	16	8	10	10 190	72
	1996	1 482	...	1 454	18	10	− 8	10 085	74
	1997	1 541	...	1 511	20	10	− 2	6 844	69

Air Avion	Sea Maritime	Unallocated Nondistribué	Per capita Par habitant	Total Totale	Solids Solides	Liquids Liquides	Gas Gaz	Electricity Electricité	Année	Région, pays ou zone
28	22	− 4	27	793	3	662	...	128	1994	République–Unie de
28	23	− 2	27	800	3	668	...	129	1995	Tanzanie
31	23	− 2	26	803	3	670	...	129	1996	
31	23	− 3	26	809	3	676	...	129	1997	
4	...	...	280	67	...	67	...	...	1994	Sahara occidental
4	...	...	278	69		69	...	...	1995	
4	...	...	268	69		69	...	...	1996	
4	...	...	259	69	...	69	...	...	1997	
35	...	43	151	1 204	221	444	...	539	1994	Zambie
36	...	42	147	1 201	209	453	...	539	1995	
36	...	43	144	1 206	204	463	...	540	1996	
36	...	46	141	1 214	209	465	...	540	1997	
...	...	...	503	5 382	3 814	1 185	...	382	1994	Zimbabwe
...	...	...	527	5 731	3 879	1 435	...	417	1995	
...	...	...	495	5 467	3 594	1 414	...	459	1996	
...	...	...	483	5 412	3 522	1 436	...	454	1997	
323	31 380	59 075	5 348	2 409 647	508 171	965 934	666 995	268 547	1994	**Amérique du Nord**
379	33 063	49 983	5 335	2 433 750	510 637	950 547	693 105	279 461	1995	
563	31 367	53 382	5 410	2 498 367	534 621	964 398	701 542	297 806	1996	
406	27 691	65 598	5 402	2 523 767	551 399	982 680	707 209	282 479	1997	
43	...		1 600	104	...	104		...	1994	Antigua–et–Barbuda
43	...		1 636	108	...	108	...	...	1995	
43	...		1 636	108	...	108	...	...	1996	
44	...		1 712	113	...	113	...	...	1997	
...	...	310	3 558	274	...	274	...	...	1994	Aruba
...	...	312	3 402	279	...	279	...	...	1995	
...	...	315	3 337	287	...	287	...	...	1996	
...	...	321	3 267	294	...	294	...	...	1997	
36	184	...	2 069	569	1	568	...	...	1994	Bahamas
38	184	...	2 046	573	1	571	...	...	1995	
41	184	...	2 003	573	1	571	...	...	1996	
36	184	...	1 983	577	1	575	...	...	1997	
115	...	− 48	1 110	292	...	271	21	...	1994	Barbade
123	...	− 43	1 189	314	...	290	24	...	1995	
136	...	− 44	1 195	318	...	291	27	...	1996	
179	...	− 55	1 247	333	...	311	22	...	1997	
13	...	...	615	128	...	126	...	2	1994	Belize
9	...	...	620	132	...	127	...	6	1995	
7	4	...	507	111	...	103	...	7	1996	
5	9	...	621	139	...	131	...	8	1997	
15	...	...	2 508	153	...	153	...	...	1994	Bermudes
17	...	...	2 452	152	...	152	...	...	1995	
17	...	...	2 460	155	...	155	...	...	1996	
17	...	...	2 460	155	...	155	...	...	1997	
...	...	...	944	17	...	17	...	...	1994	Iles Vierges britanniques
...	...	...	895	17	...	17	...	...	1995	
...	...	...	1 053	20	...	20	...	...	1996	
...	...	...	1 000	20	...	20	...	...	1997	
787	640	6 050	7 674	224 634	22 966	79 109	71 814	50 745	1994	Canada
834	628	4 808	7 666	227 051	23 453	78 301	75 868	49 429	1995	
983	636	3 333	7 775	232 840	23 975	78 777	80 248	49 840	1996	
784	546	4 523	7 832	236 995	25 495	82 996	79 910	48 594	1997	
12	...	...	3 065	95	...	95	...	...	1994	Iles Caïmanes
14	...	...	3 000	96	...	96	...	...	1995	
17	...	...	2 848	94	...	94	...	...	1996	
17	...	...	2 765	94	...	94	...	...	1997	
...	...	15	634	2 187	...	1 592	...	595	1994	Costa Rica
...	...	58	607	2 159	...	1 444	...	715	1995	
...	...	50	606	2 213	...	1 422	...	791	1996	
...	...	46	640	2 397	...	1 501	...	896	1997	
58	...	3 556	633	6 903	49	6 830	19	5	1994	Cuba
58	...	3 957	690	7 566	44	7 498	16	8	1995	
63	...	3 929	681	7 507	8	7 471	18	10	1996	
58	...	833	671	7 427	29	7 367	20	10	1997	

62

Production, trade and consumption of commercial energy
Thousand metric tons of oil equivalent and kilograms per capita [cont.]
Production, commerce et consommation d'énergie commerciale
Milliers de tonnes d'équivalent pétrole et kilogrammes par habitant [suite]

Region, country or area	Year	Primary energy production – Production d'énergie primaire					Changes in stocks Variations des stocks	Imports Importations	Exports Exportation
		Total Totale	Solids Solides	Liquids Liquides	Gas Gaz	Electricity Electricité			
Dominica	1994	1	...	...	...	1	...	24	
	1995	2	...	...	...	2	...	27	
	1996	2	...	...	...	2	...	27	
	1997	2	...	...	...	2	...	27	
Dominican Republic	1994	161	...	...	...	161	− 9	3 910	
	1995	171	...	...	...	171	− 9	3 986	
	1996	181	...	...	...	181	− 10	3 973	
	1997	192	...	...	...	192	− 130	3 968	
El Salvador	1994	474	...	...	...	474	− 49	1 360	
	1995	507	...	...	...	507	34	1 618	
	1996	532	...	...	...	532	25	1 551	1
	1997	549	...	...	...	549	49	1 907	1
Greenland	1994	...	...	...	...	...	...	174	
	1995	...	...	...	...	...	...	174	
	1996	...	...	...	...	...	...	178	
	1997	...	...	...	...	...	...	180	
Grenada	1994	...	...	...	...	...	− 1	57	
	1995	...	...	...	...	...	− 1	58	
	1996	...	...	...	...	...	...	59	
	1997	...	...	...	...	...	...	64	
Guadeloupe	1994	...	...	...	...	...	...	534	
	1995	...	...	...	...	...	...	541	
	1996	...	...	...	...	...	...	544	
	1997	...	...	...	...	...	...	551	
Guatemala	1994	550	...	365	9	176	− 2	1 935	2
	1995	641	...	467	10	164	1	2 141	4
	1996	937	...	729	10	198	4	1 922	6
	1997	1 166	...	975	10	181	26	2 276	9
Haiti	1994	17	...	...	...	17	...	108	
	1995	19	...	...	...	19	...	311	
	1996	22	...	...	...	22	...	357	
	1997	22	...	...	...	22	...	477	
Honduras	1994	210	...	...	...	210	16	1 036	
	1995	180	...	...	...	180	38	1 229	
	1996	186	...	...	...	186	28	1 219	
	1997	118	...	...	...	118	1	1 248	
Jamaica	1994	10	...	...	...	10	− 48	2 789	
	1995	10	...	...	...	10	− 81	3 049	
	1996	11	...	...	...	11	− 112	3 199	
	1997	12	...	...	...	12	− 122	3 389	
Martinique	1994	...	...	...	...	...	...	851	18
	1995	...	...	...	...	...	...	855	19
	1996	...	...	...	...	...	...	857	19
	1997	...	...	...	...	...	...	861	20
Mexico	1994	202 998	2 859	164 332	27 300	8 507	382	11 466	76 68
	1995	200 334	2 873	160 394	26 791	10 277	− 395	9 092	76 49
	1996	208 968	3 153	165 680	30 443	9 692	468	9 271	84 00
	1997	219 987	3 202	175 074	31 404	10 308	376	15 162	94 39
Montserrat	1994	...	...	...	...	...	...	13	
	1995	...	...	...	...	...	...	15	
	1996	...	...	...	...	...	...	15	
	1997	...	...	...	...	...	...	16	
Netherland Antilles	1994	...	...	...	...	...	...	15 606	9 31
	1995	...	...	...	...	...	...	15 619	9 35
	1996	...	...	...	...	...	...	15 633	9 37
	1997	...	...	...	...	...	...	15 657	9 39
Nicaragua	1994	469	...	...	...	469	− 46	768	1
	1995	502	...	...	...	502	10	898	
	1996	546	...	...	...	546	45	958	
	1997	546	...	...	...	546	2	978	
Panama	1994	206	...	...	...	206	20	2 450	92
	1995	208	...	...	...	208	− 40	1 752	78
	1996	258	...	...	...	258	4	2 862	1 36
	1997	250	...	...	...	250	86	2 907	37

Air Avion	Sea Maritime	Unallocated Nondistribué	Per capita Par habitant	Total Totale	Solids Solides	Liquids Liquides	Gas Gaz	Electricity Electricité	Année	Région, pays ou zone
...	...	...	352	25	...	24	...	1	1994	Dominique
...	...	...	408	29	...	27	...	2	1995	
...	...	...	408	29	...	27	...	2	1996	
...	...	...	408	29	...	27	...	2	1997	
...	...	349	486	3 731	73	3 497	...	161	1994	Rép. dominicaine
...	...	297	495	3 870	78	3 621	...	171	1995	
...	...	149	504	4 015	90	3 744	...	181	1996	
...	...	13	528	4 277	97	3 988	...	192	1997	
...	...	39	332	1 841	...	1 368	...	473	1994	El Salvador
...	...	46	359	2 033	...	1 529	...	504	1995	
...	...	42	327	1 895	...	1 361	...	534	1996	
...	...	47	369	2 181	...	1 624	...	556	1997	
...	...	...	2 982	167	...	167	...	...	1994	Groenland
...	...	...	2 982	167	...	167	...	...	1995	
...	...	...	3 054	171	...	171	...	...	1996	
...	...	...	3 089	173	...	173	...	...	1997	
2	...	...	609	56	...	56	...	...	1994	Grenade
2	...	...	620	57	...	57	...	...	1995	
2	...	...	620	57	...	57	...	...	1996	
2	...	...	667	62	...	62	...	...	1997	
78	...	...	1 089	455	...	455	...	...	1994	Guadeloupe
78	...	...	1 090	462	...	462	...	...	1995	
78	...	...	1 079	465	...	465	...	...	1996	
80	...	...	1 080	472	...	472	...	...	1997	
...	...	168	215	2 084	...	1 899	9	177	1994	Guatemala
...	...	49	233	2 322	...	2 145	10	167	1995	
...	...	− 14	217	2 224	...	2 018	10	196	1996	
...	...	102	229	2 413	...	2 229	10	173	1997	
6	...	...	16	119	...	102	...	17	1994	Haïti
7	...	...	43	323	...	304	...	19	1995	
8	...	...	48	371	...	349	...	22	1996	
15	...	...	62	483	...	461	...	22	1997	
...	...	...	223	1 224	...	1 009	...	215	1994	Honduras
...	...	...	239	1 353	...	1 174	...	178	1995	
...	...	...	230	1 338	...	1 158	...	180	1996	
...	...	...	225	1 344	...	1 212	...	132	1997	
31	...	− 172	1 198	2 937	37	2 890	...	10	1994	Jamaïque
31	...	− 39	1 250	3 092	38	3 044	...	10	1995	
36	...	1	1 294	3 229	45	3 173	...	11	1996	
36	...	49	1 343	3 380	47	3 321	...	12	1997	
...	37	55	1 523	571	...	571	...	...	1994	Martinique
...	37	48	1 522	577	...	577	...	...	1995	
...	39	43	1 510	577	...	577	...	...	1996	
...	39	44	1 492	576	...	576	...	...	1997	
10	620	10 037	1 415	126 730	3 552	86 209	28 533	8 436	1994	Mexique
10	613	8 855	1 359	123 850	4 081	81 381	28 179	10 210	1995	
10	575	9 226	1 337	123 959	4 647	78 738	30 873	9 701	1996	
10	796	10 484	1 369	129 091	4 776	81 838	32 045	10 433	1997	
...	1	...	1 091	12	...	12	...	...	1994	Montserrat
...	1	...	1 273	14	...	14	...	...	1995	
...	1	...	1 273	14	...	14	...	...	1996	
...	1	...	1 364	15	...	15	...	...	1997	
60	1 704	3 661	4 267	862	...	862	...	...	1994	Antilles néerlandaises
61	1 710	3 626	4 220	865	...	865	...	...	1995	
63	1 714	3 612	4 168	867	...	867	...	...	1996	
65	1 720	3 601	4 142	874	...	874	...	...	1997	
...	...	15	292	1 255	...	788	...	467	1994	Nicaragua
...	...	16	309	1 366	...	865	...	501	1995	
...	...	19	316	1 438	...	892	...	546	1996	
...	...	4	324	1 518	...	958	...	560	1997	
...	...	54	641	1 657	38	1 351	56	213	1994	Panama
...	...	− 44	480	1 263	25	966	56	215	1995	
...	...	25	646	1 729	70	1 344	57	258	1996	
...	...	861	676	1 840	40	1 472	57	271	1997	

62
Production, trade and consumption of commercial energy
Thousand metric tons of oil equivalent and kilograms per capita [*cont.*]
Production, commerce et consommation d'énergie commerciale
Milliers de tonnes d'équivalent pétrole et kilogrammes par habitant [*suite*]

Region, country or area	Year	Primary energy production – Production d'énergie primaire					Changes in stocks Variations des stocks	Imports Importations	Exports Exportatior
		Total Totale	Solids Solides	Liquids Liquides	Gas Gaz	Electricity Electricité			
Puerto Rico	1994	28	...	...	...	28	− 271	8 004	
	1995	28	...	...	...	28	− 34	7 961	
	1996	29	...	...	...	29	− 74	7 982	
	1997	29	...	...	...	29	− 79	7 996	
Saint Kitts and Nevis	1994	...	...	...	...	...	...	30	
	1995	...	...	...	...	...	...	32	
	1996	...	...	...	...	...	...	34	
	1997	...	...	...	...	...	...	34	
Saint Lucia	1994	...	...	...	...	...	...	63	
	1995	...	...	...	...	...	...	64	
	1996	...	...	...	...	...	...	64	
	1997	...	...	...	...	...	...	67	
Saint Pierre and Miquelon	1994	...	...	...	...	...	...	42	
	1995	...	...	...	...	...	...	28	
	1996	...	...	...	...	...	...	28	
	1997	...	...	...	...	...	...	19	
Saint Vincent and the Grenadines	1994	2	...	...	...	2	...	40	
	1995	2	...	...	...	2	...	43	
	1996	2	...	...	...	2	...	44	
	1997	2	...	...	...	2	...	44	
Trinidad and Tobago	1994	12 933	...	6 807	6 126	...	− 421	1 737	7 (
	1995	13 072	...	6 783	6 289	...	− 341	1 859	6 9
	1996	13 817	...	6 710	7 107	...	87	2 300	7)
	1997	13 777	...	6 210	7 567	...	33	2 063	6 (
United States	1994	1 632 275	535 599	396 136	497 378	203 162	21 247	536 994	74 (
	1995	1 638 833	531 560	392 244	500 960	214 069	−7 426	528 704	82 5
	1996	1 668 979	547 550	377 718	511 441	232 271	−8 065	556 589	80 8
	1997	1 668 703	561 732	375 310	514 384	217 277	5 940	592 357	79 8
U.S. Virgin Islands	1994	...	...	...	...	...	285	17 130	12 8
	1995	...	...	...	...	...	200	17 416	13 9
	1996	...	...	...	...	...	115	17 568	13 9
	1997	...	...	...	...	...	174	17 724	13 9
America, South	**1994**	**407 044**	**21 433**	**269 966**	**75 965**	**39 679**	**−2 304**	**71 315**	**184 3**
	1995	**427 641**	**23 395**	**283 637**	**78 715**	**41 894**	**−6 902**	**74 257**	**203 5**
	1996	**446 445**	**24 836**	**295 619**	**82 398**	**43 593**	**−4 899**	**79 771**	**213 4**
	1997	**480 139**	**28 489**	**314 746**	**91 424**	**45 480**	**−3 046**	**84 865**	**231 3**
Argentina	1994	63 803	205	35 277	23 800	4 520	− 448	5 165	13 7
	1995	66 950	180	37 241	25 371	4 158	− 14	6 162	17 3
	1996	70 456	183	41 712	24 645	3 916	− 67	4 888	19 4
	1997	77 965	147	44 309	29 015	4 493	241	4 527	20 7
Bolivia	1994	4 589	...	1 426	3 048	115	− 47	77	2 (
	1995	5 271	...	1 640	3 513	118	− 5	151	2 2
	1996	5 532	...	1 823	3 585	125	− 45	159	2 (
	1997	5 135	...	1 803	3 203	129	− 270	165	2 (
Brazil	1994	62 283	2 281	34 829	4 289	20 883	− 58	47 333	4 5
	1995	65 266	2 310	35 867	4 601	22 487	−2 503	45 935	2 6
	1996	71 148	2 135	40 372	5 157	23 484	962	51 862	1 7
	1997	76 128	2 509	43 094	5 706	24 819	67	52 307	1 9
Chile	1994	5 116	844	1 076	1 739	1 456	439	9 877	1
	1995	4 862	743	864	1 672	1 583	34	10 837	1
	1996	5 171	799	925	1 830	1 618	...	11 778	1
	1997	4 923	746	754	1 795	1 629	− 109	15 034	1
Colombia	1994	45 377	14 732	23 764	4 119	2 761	−1 022	1 940	24 5
	1995	54 294	16 815	30 388	4 322	2 769	746	1 595	30 8
	1996	59 643	19 237	32 591	4 761	3 055	213	1 119	36 2
	1997	62 538	21 185	33 930	4 695	2 728	151	1 406	39 1
Ecuador	1994	18 452	...	17 553	351	548	...	472	13 9
	1995	21 185	...	20 240	364	580	...	848	14 2
	1996	20 704	...	19 408	618	679	...	731	12 8
	1997	21 493	...	20 289	580	624	...	906	15 4
Falkland Is. (Malvinas)	1994	3	3	...	...	...	...	8	
	1995	3	3	...	...	...	...	9	
	1996	3	3	...	...	...	...	10	
	1997	3	3	...	...	...	...	11	

Energy   Energie

Air vion	Sea Maritime	Unallocated Nondistribué	Per capita Par habitant	Total Totale	Solids Solides	Liquids Liquides	Gas Gaz	Electricity Electricité	Année	Région, pays ou zone
...	150	– 114	2 072	7 624	113	7 482	...	28	1994	Porto Rico
...	170	239	1 870	6 947	115	6 803	...	28	1995	
...	172	215	1 874	7 026	119	6 879	...	29	1996	
...	175	192	1 864	7 046	121	6 896	...	29	1997	
...	...	...	750	30	...	30	...	...	1994	Saint–Kitts–et–Nevis
...	...	...	800	32	...	32	...	...	1995	
...	...	...	850	34	...	34	...	...	1996	
...	...	...	872	34	...	34	...	...	1997	
...	...	...	444	63	...	63	...	...	1994	Saint–Lucie
...	...	...	444	64	...	64	...	...	1995	
...	...	...	438	64	...	64	...	...	1996	
...	...	...	453	67	...	67	...	...	1997	
...	18	...	3 833	23	...	23	...	...	1994	Saint–Pierre–et–
...	4	...	3 833	23	...	23	...	...	1995	Miquelon
...	4	...	3 833	23	...	23	...	...	1996	
...	4	...	2 143	15	...	15	...	...	1997	
...	...	...	385	42	...	40	...	2	1994	Saint–Vincent–et–les–
...	...	...	409	45	...	43	...	2	1995	Grenadines
...	...	...	414	46	...	44	...	2	1996	
...	...	...	411	46	...	44	...	2	1997	
55	224	139	6 046	7 582	...	1 456	6 126	...	1994	Trinité–et–Tobago
53	171	633	5 947	7 505	...	1 216	6 289	...	1995	
58	221	125	6 681	8 485	...	1 378	7 107	...	1996	
58	221	59	6 944	8 868	...	1 301	7 567	...	1997	
...	27 631	34 319	7 606	2 011 992	481 169	763 405	560 417	207 001	1994	Etats–Unis
...	29 354	26 520	7 627	2 036 570	482 626	753 986	582 663	217 295	1995	
...	27 625	31 556	7 770	2 093 567	505 491	769 377	583 202	235 497	1996	
...	23 801	43 624	7 756	2 107 891	520 616	779 110	587 578	220 587	1997	
...	171	643	32 724	3 207	171	3 035	...	...	1994	Iles Vierges américaines
...	191	645	25 515	2 475	175	2 300	...	...	1995	
...	193	798	26 240	2 519	175	2 344	...	...	1996	
...	195	850	26 632	2 530	176	2 354	...	...	1997	
177	**2 183**	**21 710**	**860**	**271 279**	**18 752**	**136 935**	**76 012**	**39 581**	**1994**	**Amérique du Sud**
278	**2 424**	**17 388**	**886**	**284 160**	**19 868**	**143 708**	**78 702**	**41 882**	**1995**	
412	**2 712**	**19 716**	**902**	**293 780**	**20 048**	**147 905**	**82 264**	**43 564**	**1996**	
428	**3 043**	**17 530**	**952**	**314 698**	**21 864**	**156 018**	**91 344**	**45 472**	**1997**	
...	391	3 918	1 496	51 355	939	19 822	25 973	4 621	1994	Argentine
...	479	1 856	1 538	53 456	977	20 788	27 352	4 340	1995	
...	579	4 453	1 446	50 926	818	19 440	26 463	4 205	1996	
...	704	5 628	1 546	55 142	733	18 995	30 475	4 940	1997	
...	...	173	340	2 460	...	1 313	1 031	116	1994	Bolivie
...	...	21	426	3 156	...	1 439	1 599	119	1995	
...	...	268	446	3 387	...	1 545	1 717	126	1996	
...	...	422	396	3 076	...	1 581	1 366	129	1997	
590	1 224	6 795	614	96 468	11 088	57 476	4 289	23 615	1994	Brésil
680	1 172	7 388	639	101 799	11 730	59 940	4 601	25 527	1995	
779	1 347	9 023	676	109 178	12 376	65 018	5 157	26 627	1996	
779	1 703	8 339	706	115 577	12 271	69 300	5 706	28 299	1997	
...	...	383	1 005	14 069	2 488	8 527	1 597	1 456	1994	Chili
...	...	302	1 073	15 247	2 741	9 361	1 561	1 583	1995	
...	...	– 15	1 168	16 845	2 878	10 604	1 746	1 618	1996	
6	...	547	1 322	19 328	4 928	10 678	2 093	1 629	1997	
...	...	1 686	586	22 140	3 591	11 644	4 119	2 785	1994	Colombie
...	...	1 870	581	22 401	3 730	11 548	4 322	2 801	1995	
...	...	1 947	570	22 400	3 301	11 269	4 761	3 069	1996	
...	...	2 425	554	22 188	3 242	11 505	4 695	2 745	1997	
42	206	– 1 171	524	5 877	...	4 979	351	548	1994	Equateur
43	211	1 129	563	6 448	...	5 504	364	580	1995	
46	223	1 108	614	7 189	...	5 893	618	679	1996	
41	151	– 193	586	7 000	...	5 796	580	624	1997	
...	...	...	6 000	12	3	8	...	...	1994	Iles Falkland (Malvinas)
...	...	...	6 500	13	3	9	...	...	1995	
...	...	...	7 000	14	3	10	...	...	1996	
...	...	...	7 500	15	3	11	...	...	1997	

62
Production, trade and consumption of commercial energy
Thousand metric tons of oil equivalent and kilograms per capita [*cont.*]
Production, commerce et consommation d'énergie commerciale
Milliers de tonnes d'équivalent pétrole et kilogrammes par habitant [*suite*]

Region, country or area	Year	Primary energy production – Production d'énergie primaire					Changes in stocks Variations des stocks	Imports Importations	Exports Exportations
		Total Totale	Solids Solides	Liquids Liquides	Gas Gaz	Electricity Electricité			
French Guiana	1994	...	...	...	...	...	...	302	
	1995	...	...	...	...	...	...	304	
	1996	...	...	...	...	...	...	304	
	1997	...	...	...	...	...	...	304	
Guyana	1994	...	...	...	...	...	...	360	
	1995	...	...	...	...	...	...	322	
	1996	...	...	...	...	...	...	337	
	1997	...	...	...	...	...	...	354	
Paraguay	1994	3 129	...	...	...	3 129	29	1 110	2 8:
	1995	3 619	...	...	...	3 619	− 88	1 124	3 2'
	1996	4 130	...	...	...	4 130	− 128	961	3 4!
	1997	4 352	...	...	...	4 352	− 61	1 128	3 9:
Peru	1994	7 833	51	6 571	115	1 097	− 142	2 390	2 0'
	1995	7 645	98	6 338	24	1 185	544	4 383	2 5!
	1996	7 478	40	6 245	28	1 165	412	4 681	3 6(
	1997	7 469	15	6 201	117	1 136	− 528	5 802	3 2(
Suriname	1994	381	...	272	...	110	1	473	:
	1995	385	...	275	...	110	1	477	:
	1996	355	...	245	...	110	...	483	∠
	1997	357	...	246	...	111	1	488	∠
Uruguay	1994	642	...	...	...	642	123	1 606	1∠
	1995	503	...	...	...	503	86	2 031	:
	1996	496	...	...	...	496	− 48	2 191	:
	1997	558	...	...	...	558	− 16	2 150	∠
Venezuela	1994	195 435	3 317	149 196	38 505	4 418	−1 178	200	120 18
	1995	197 657	3 246	150 784	38 846	4 781	−5 704	79	130 1:
	1996	201 326	2 439	152 297	41 775	4 815	−6 199	266	133 8(
	1997	219 216	3 884	164 120	46 311	4 901	−2 524	283	144 4!
Asia	1994	2 813 836	938 566	1 356 720	364 765	153 784	19 979	954 636	1 103 95
	1995	2 930 182	1 003 485	1 367 320	392 601	166 777	24 272	1 006 693	1 126 85
	1996	3 028 425	1 036 360	1 390 604	427 644	173 818	23 865	1 082 887	1 163 20
	1997	3 073 395	1 032 859	1 427 901	432 270	180 365	30 014	1 140 871	1 210 46
Afghanistan	1994	208	4	...	163	41	12	317	
	1995	196	3	...	156	36	10	303	
	1996	183	2	...	149	31	10	286	:
	1997	167	1	...	137	28	10	268	:
Armenia	1994	302	...	...	...	302	...	1 171	:
	1995	244	...	...	...	244	...	1 529	:
	1996	740	...	...	...	740	...	1 135	:
	1997	536	...	...	...	536	171	1 378	:
Azerbaijan	1994	15 483	...	9 582	5 744	157	...	3 389	1 76
	1995	15 294	...	9 178	5 983	134	...	675	2 17
	1996	14 925	...	9 115	5 677	132	...	188	2 03
	1997	14 601	...	9 087	5 367	147	...	211	1 71
Bahrain	1994	8 451	...	2 502	5 949	...	150	10 216	10 16
	1995	8 755	...	2 447	6 308	...	− 6	10 439	10 32
	1996	8 699	...	2 168	6 532	...	33	9 621	10 54
	1997	9 121	...	2 237	6 883	...	208	9 998	9 90
Bangladesh	1994	5 755	...	113	5 570	73	− 63	2 197	
	1995	6 501	...	10	6 459	32	− 23	2 797	
	1996	7 063	...	66	6 933	64	− 274	2 723	
	1997	6 919	...	44	6 813	62	− 25	3 275	
Bhutan	1994	190	45	...	...	145	...	31	15
	1995	188	48	...	...	140	...	35	14
	1996	214	45	...	...	170	...	44	15
	1997	196	38	...	...	158	...	75	14
Brunei Darussalam	1994	18 557	...	9 409	9 148	...	12	...	16 55
	1995	18 882	...	8 961	9 922	...	− 33	7	16 96
	1996	18 624	...	8 669	9 955	...	89	59	16 61
	1997	18 503	...	8 549	9 954	...	25	80	16 45
Cambodia	1994	6	...	...	...	6	...	162	:
	1995	6	...	...	...	6	...	166	:
	1996	7	...	...	...	7	...	166	:
	1997	7	...	...	...	7	...	170	:

Air Avion	Sea Maritime	Unallocated Nondistribué	Per capita Par habitant	Total Totale	Solids Solides	Liquids Liquides	Gas Gaz	Electricity Electricité	Année	Région, pays ou zone
17	...	...	2 043	286	...	286	...	...	1994	Guyane française
17	...	...	1 959	288	...	288	...	...	1995	
17	...	...	1 882	288	...	288	...	...	1996	
17	...	...	1 800	288	...	288	...	...	1997	
10	3	...	423	348	...	346	...	1	1994	Guyana
9	2	...	375	311	...	310	...	2	1995	
12	2	...	386	323	...	322	...	2	1996	
11	2	...	405	341	...	339	...	2	1997	
2	...	− 15	297	1 395	...	1 068	...	326	1994	Paraguay
2	...	− 17	326	1 572	...	1 206	...	367	1995	
2	...	− 3	351	1 740	...	1 072	...	668	1996	
2	...	7	312	1 585	...	1 161	...	425	1997	
...	...	300	345	7 973	328	6 434	115	1 097	1994	Pérou
...	...	659	350	8 239	367	6 662	24	1 185	1995	
...	...	177	330	7 907	383	6 330	28	1 165	1996	
...	...	915	395	9 616	334	8 029	117	1 136	1997	
...	...	210	1 451	592	...	482	...	110	1994	Suriname
...	...	212	1 457	596	...	486	...	110	1995	
...	...	189	1 468	602	...	492	...	110	1996	
...	...	189	1 476	608	...	497	...	111	1997	
41	218	...	539	1 722	...	1 223	...	499	1994	Uruguay
32	408	11	600	1 930	...	1 430	...	500	1995	
39	409	36	676	2 193	1	1 700	...	493	1996	
45	331	54	687	2 244	1	1 698	...	545	1997	
475	142	9 431	3 115	66 584	314	23 327	38 536	4 407	1994	Venezuela
495	152	3 958	3 145	68 704	319	24 738	38 877	4 770	1995	
516	152	2 534	3 173	70 787	288	23 922	41 775	4 802	1996	
526	152	− 802	3 411	77 692	352	26 142	46 311	4 888	1997	
14 931	**47 506**	**159 153**	**712**	**2 422 947**	**1 051 734**	**851 546**	**364 871**	**154 796**	**1994**	**Asie**
16 099	**50 995**	**164 378**	**739**	**2 554 273**	**1 113 985**	**882 548**	**390 305**	**167 435**	**1995**	
17 099	**53 278**	**171 794**	**765**	**2 682 071**	**1 157 887**	**926 109**	**423 728**	**174 346**	**1996**	
17 585	**55 642**	**190 777**	**762**	**2 709 786**	**1 146 075**	**942 704**	**440 069**	**180 938**	**1997**	
5	...	...	27	507	4	288	163	52	1994	Afghanistan
5	...	...	25	483	3	277	156	46	1995	
5	...	...	22	454	2	261	149	41	1996	
5	...	...	20	419	1	244	137	37	1997	
...	...	...	411	1 473	25	359	785	304	1994	Arménie
...	...	...	496	1 773	2	255	1 271	245	1995	
...	...	...	526	1 874	3	141	990	740	1996	
...	...	...	491	1 742	3	141	1 063	536	1997	
432	...	1 516	2 021	15 159	1	6 884	8 095	180	1994	Azerbaïdjan
520	...	381	1 705	12 894	1	6 265	6 461	168	1995	
544	...	1 435	1 459	11 102	1	5 232	5 699	170	1996	
597	...	1 393	1 453	11 107	1	5 520	5 367	219	1997	
...	...	1 805	12 009	6 545	...	596	5 949	...	1994	Bahreïn
...	...	1 969	12 384	6 910	...	602	6 308	...	1995	
...	...	366	12 937	7 374	...	843	6 532	...	1996	
...	...	1 053	13 642	7 953	...	1 070	6 883	...	1997	
...	...	714	63	7 302	27	1 633	5 570	73	1994	Bangladesh
...	12	663	73	8 645	321	1 833	6 459	32	1995	
...	14	773	77	9 272	179	2 097	6 933	64	1996	
...	9	619	78	9 590	323	2 393	6 813	62	1997	
...	...	...	38	68	17	31	...	20	1994	Bhoutan
...	...	...	45	83	20	35	...	28	1995	
...	...	...	55	104	24	43	...	36	1996	
...	...	...	65	127	50	41	...	36	1997	
...	...	− 238	7 749	2 224	...	949	1 275	...	1994	Brunéi Darussalam
...	...	− 349	7 840	2 305	...	977	1 328	...	1995	
...	...	− 338	7 708	2 320	...	949	1 371	...	1996	
...	...	− 294	7 802	2 403	...	979	1 423	...	1997	
...	...	...	17	168	...	162	...	6	1994	Cambodge
...	...	...	17	173	...	166	...	6	1995	
...	...	...	17	173	...	166	...	7	1996	
...	...	...	17	177	...	170	...	7	1997	

62
Production, trade and consumption of commercial energy
Thousand metric tons of oil equivalent and kilograms per capita [*cont.*]
Production, commerce et consommation d'énergie commerciale
Milliers de tonnes d'équivalent pétrole et kilogrammes par habitant [*suite*]

Region, country or area	Year	Primary energy production – Production d'énergie primaire					Changes in stocks Variations des stocks	Imports Importations	Exports Exportations
		Total Totale	Solids Solides	Liquids Liquides	Gas Gaz	Electricity Electricité			
China ††	1994	799 843	619 331	146 058	16 347	18 107	−4 665	28 848	37 361
	1995	866 126	679 685	150 019	16 699	19 724	7 101	35 123	43 930
	1996	895 624	697 801	157 308	20 811	19 704	−4 161	43 552	46 621
	1997	889 741	685 724	160 714	23 489	19 814	9 153	63 411	51 453
China, Hong Kong SAR †	1994	...	...	...	...	...	332	18 939	5 425
	1995	...	...	...	...	...	− 382	21 716	8 145
	1996	...	...	...	...	...	− 5	21 493	8 822
	1997	...	...	...	...	...	177	22 758	10 320
China, Macao SAR †	1994	...	...	...	...	...	10	439	1
	1995	...	...	...	...	...	...	419	...
	1996	...	...	...	...	...	2	480	...
	1997	...	...	...	...	...	− 11	489	...
Cyprus	1994	...	...	...	...	...	165	2 044	...
	1995	...	...	...	...	...	174	2 055	...
	1996	...	...	...	...	...	56	1 992	...
	1997	...	...	...	...	...	− 8	1 998	2
Georgia	1994	514	26	74	9	405	...	2 640	17
	1995	538	25	47	9	457	...	984	15
	1996	664	13	128	3	520	38	1 630	130
	1997	659	3	134	3	520	65	1 850	174
India	1994	210 112	152 137	33 512	15 866	8 598	− 790	47 680	64
	1995	219 889	159 140	35 232	17 156	8 361	−1 068	51 712	65
	1996	240 119	170 750	36 616	24 389	8 365	−1 026	60 904	591
	1997	241 318	177 148	37 596	17 477	9 097	471	64 429	889
Indonesia	1994	181 561	21 867	102 680	54 679	2 336	556	12 775	97 021
	1995	190 889	29 062	100 627	58 364	2 836	3 462	16 459	95 114
	1996	209 552	33 137	102 304	71 245	2 866	8 805	18 965	101 730
	1997	213 971	36 452	103 338	71 248	2 933	7 127	19 075	108 746
Iran (Islamic Rep. of)	1994	223 458	905	184 261	37 652	640	207	4 904	136 124
	1995	222 116	797	184 720	35 974	626	1 000	5 056	134 526
	1996	225 048	848	185 914	37 652	634	595	6 474	135 391
	1997	233 454	847	189 701	42 312	594	3 674	7 623	133 524
Iraq	1994	40 418	...	37 415	2 955	48	5 827	...	3 905
	1995	40 771	...	37 767	2 955	49	4 979	...	4 161
	1996	41 040	...	37 970	3 020	50	3 846	...	6 747
	1997	61 666	...	58 241	3 374	51	−3 999	...	33 806
Israel	1994	108	84	4	18	2	− 841	16 719	2 949
	1995	131	103	7	18	2	− 98	18 117	1 675
	1996	110	93	4	12	2	− 801	16 959	1 511
	1997	123	104	5	12	2	256	19 751	2 445
Japan	1994	85 242	4 027	723	2 227	78 265	3 687	391 187	8 326
	1995	92 830	3 637	718	2 164	86 310	256	391 976	9 571
	1996	96 078	3 764	696	2 185	89 433	3 354	401 532	8 510
	1997	100 249	2 486	700	2 233	94 831	3 468	402 520	9 376
Jordan	1994	3	...	2	...	1	− 101	3 896	...
	1995	4	...	2	...	2	− 40	4 067	...
	1996	4	...	2	...	2	72	4 446	2
	1997	2	...	...	...	2	...	4 550	...
Kazakhstan	1994	71 226	45 981	20 414	4 041	789	...	12 191	22 296
	1995	63 332	36 642	20 647	5 327	716	...	13 258	18 823
	1996	63 390	33 761	23 124	5 875	630	...	10 335	26 692
	1997	65 481	32 009	25 607	7 306	559	...	4 784	29 574
Korea, Dem. People's Republic of	1994	63 201	61 180	...	...	2 021	...	5 633	306
	1995	62 598	60 620	...	...	1 978	...	5 526	289
	1996	61 925	59 990	...	...	1 935	...	5 439	278
	1997	61 392	59 500	...	...	1 892	...	5 315	267
Korea, Republic of	1994	18 951	3 346		...	15 605	4 502	127 238	11 865
	1995	20 475	2 573		...	17 902	3 117	141 048	14 167
	1996	21 899	2 227		...	19 671	2 074	158 415	17 702
	1997	22 541	2 030		...	20 511	543	179 205	26 516
Kuwait [1]	1994	109 627	...	104 063	5 564	...	2 811	1	88 961
	1995	113 824	...	105 368	8 457	...	1 452	1	91 108
	1996	114 028	...	105 549	8 479	...	331	1	91 639
	1997	114 180	...	105 734	8 447	...	1 679	1	90 702

Air Avion	Sea Maritime	Unallocated Nondistribué	Per capita Par habitant	Total Totale	Solids Solides	Liquids Liquides	Gas Gaz	Electricity Electricité	Année	Région, pays ou zone
...	852	30 365	644	764 779	612 587	117 913	16 347	17 931	1994	Chine ††
...	1 012	29 536	683	819 670	656 713	126 724	16 699	19 535	1995	
...	983	37 684	709	858 049	683 572	135 914	19 167	19 396	1996	
...	990	45 399	692	846 156	659 419	146 613	20 923	19 202	1997	
2 492	1 712	...	1 473	8 979	4 521	3 899	...	558	1994	Chine, Hong Kong RAS †
2 783	2 319	...	1 422	8 851	4 874	3 456	...	521	1995	
2 858	2 389	...	1 168	7 429	3 623	3 183	...	623	1996	
2 990	2 159	...	1 092	7 112	3 055	3 427	...	629	1997	
...	...	...	1 024	429	...	417	...	11	1994	Chine, Macao RAS †
...	...	...	974	419	...	403	...	15	1995	
...	...	...	1 086	478	...	463	...	15	1996	
...	...	...	1 111	500	...	485	...	15	1997	
245	62	18	2 124	1 555	19	1 536	...	...	1994	Chypre
268	69	25	2 042	1 519	14	1 505	...	...	1995	
257	90	20	2 082	1 570	12	1 558	...	...	1996	
253	98	24	2 134	1 628	13	1 615	...	...	1997	
...	...	79	576	3 058	89	274	2 221	474	1994	Géorgie
...	...	8	286	1 499	42	124	819	514	1995	
...	...	4	409	2 122	42	849	704	527	1996	
...	...	8	442	2 263	3	871	853	536	1997	
660	...	16 181	263	241 676	159 121	57 970	15 866	8 720	1994	Inde
666	...	19 964	270	251 975	165 947	60 380	17 156	8 492	1995	
671	...	20 161	295	280 626	178 512	69 233	24 389	8 493	1996	
676	...	19 175	294	284 536	186 954	70 879	17 477	9 225	1997	
464	230	27 962	350	68 101	7 931	38 045	19 790	2 336	1994	Indonésie
516	250	27 079	410	80 926	13 523	40 035	24 533	2 836	1995	
619	271	25 188	459	91 905	11 088	41 710	36 241	2 866	1996	
645	296	25 408	447	90 824	7 299	43 483	37 110	2 933	1997	
5	517	4 299	1 425	87 210	921	47 998	37 652	640	1994	Iran (Rép. islamique d')
5	537	4 086	1 396	87 018	1 081	49 337	35 974	626	1995	
5	552	3 221	1 446	91 757	1 071	52 491	37 561	634	1996	
5	552	5 467	1 514	97 854	1 072	53 967	42 221	594	1997	
...	...	5 913	1 261	24 773	...	21 770	2 955	48	1994	Iraq
...	...	5 944	1 278	25 686	...	22 682	2 955	49	1995	
...	...	5 885	1 192	24 563	...	21 493	3 020	50	1996	
...	...	6 480	1 198	25 379	...	21 955	3 374	51	1997	
5	202	1 414	2 431	13 098	4 303	8 838	18	− 61	1994	Israël
4	207	998	2 778	15 462	5 010	10 511	18	− 76	1995	
4	93	874	2 689	15 388	5 559	9 899	12	− 82	1996	
4	180	1 240	2 688	15 749	6 152	9 673	12	− 89	1997	
4 921	6 877	17 641	3 476	434 977	83 369	216 475	56 868	78 265	1994	Japon
5 566	6 233	16 270	3 562	446 911	87 558	215 228	57 815	86 310	1995	
5 908	4 336	16 958	3 646	458 544	90 012	216 797	62 303	89 433	1996	
6 286	5 187	20 634	3 632	457 817	92 706	209 210	61 071	94 831	1997	
213	...	98	670	3 689	...	3 688	...	1	1994	Jordanie
250	2	79	659	3 780	...	3 778	...	2	1995	
303	1	85	671	3 987	...	3 985	...	2	1996	
329	...	117	670	4 106	...	4 104	...	2	1997	
498	...	3 146	3 465	57 475	34 993	11 546	9 027	1 910	1994	Kazakhstan
428	...	2 826	3 302	54 514	31 925	10 027	11 210	1 352	1995	
386	...	3 780	2 608	42 868	25 083	7 852	8 714	1 220	1996	
310	...	2 940	2 287	37 441	21 908	7 506	6 892	1 135	1997	
...	...	− 651	3 163	69 178	62 701	4 457	...	2 021	1994	Corée, Rép. populaire démocratique de
...	...	− 675	3 081	68 510	62 123	4 409	...	1 978	1995	
...	...	− 699	2 998	67 784	61 483	4 367	...	1 935	1996	
...	...	− 698	2 921	67 138	60 951	4 295	...	1 892	1997	
632	4 232	8 067	2 624	116 890	27 325	66 493	7 468	15 605	1994	Corée, République de
686	4 727	10 292	2 860	128 534	29 411	72 010	9 212	17 902	1995	
756	5 387	13 668	3 103	140 726	32 818	76 294	11 942	19 671	1996	
759	5 984	20 655	3 221	147 289	34 685	77 535	14 558	20 511	1997	
330	169	6 101	6 424	11 255	...	5 692	5 564	...	1994	Koweït ¹
371	189	5 449	9 027	15 255	...	6 798	8 457	...	1995	
390	189	6 107	9 117	15 372	...	6 893	8 479	...	1996	
427	189	4 882	9 412	16 301	...	7 855	8 447	...	1997	

62
Production, trade and consumption of commercial energy
Thousand metric tons of oil equivalent and kilograms per capita [*cont.*]
Production, commerce et consommation d'énergie commerciale
Milliers de tonnes d'équivalent pétrole et kilogrammes par habitant [*suite*]

Region, country or area	Year	Primary energy production – Production d'énergie primaire					Changes in stocks Variations des stocks	Imports Importations	Exports Exportations
		Total Totale	Solids Solides	Liquids Liquides	Gas Gaz	Electricity Electricité			
Kyrgystan	1994	1 612	479	88	36	1 008	...	2 180	853
	1995	1 359	281	89	34	956	− 175	2 147	820
	1996	1 416	238	100	24	1 054	61	2 527	854
	1997	1 384	297	85	37	965	...	2 252	832
Lao People's Dem. Rep.	1994	100	1	...	...	99	...	103	71
	1995	87	1	...	...	86	...	107	61
	1996	104	1	...	...	104	...	115	67
	1997	102	1	...	...	101	...	120	66
Lebanon	1994	83	...	...	...	83	...	3 788	...
	1995	63	...	...	...	63	...	4 091	...
	1996	73	...	...	...	73	...	4 501	...
	1997	78	...	...	...	78	...	4 737	...
Malaysia	1994	55 534	94	33 340	21 540	561	435	10 257	33 582
	1995	67 909	78	34 631	32 669	530	41	10 203	35 101
	1996	68 526	58	35 156	32 870	442	524	11 619	36 450
	1997	72 292	70	34 569	37 189	464	673	13 223	38 476
Maldives	1994	...	...	...	...	...	...	116	42
	1995							144	50
	1996	...	...	...	...	...	...	114	15
	1997	...	...	...	...	...	...	117	17
Mongolia	1994	1 793	1 793	...	...	...	...	421	67
	1995	1 730	1 730	...	...	...	...	486	72
	1996	1 828	1 828	...	...	...	...	437	75
	1997	1 687	1 687	...	...	...	...	481	69
Myanmar	1994	2 076	32	695	1 209	139	− 91	402	...
	1995	2 012	36	483	1 355	140	− 159	665	...
	1996	2 049	33	407	1 469	140	− 244	687	...
	1997	2 163	29	401	1 587	145	− 311	940	...
Nepal	1994	75	...	...	...	75	− 19	441	35
	1995	78	...	...	...	78	7	500	29
	1996	99	...	...	...	99	...	600	34
	1997	100	...	...	...	100	2	646	35
Oman	1994	44 357	...	40 169	4 188	...	− 176	41	38 169
	1995	46 369	...	42 335	4 033	...	− 372	137	39 763
	1996	48 258	...	44 040	4 219	...	41	65	41 443
	1997	49 945	...	44 942	5 003	...	169	275	42 975
Pakistan	1994	20 143	1 671	2 816	13 856	1 800	...	12 894	291
	1995	20 298	1 439	2 762	13 999	2 098	...	13 371	307
	1996	21 673	1 720	2 956	14 875	2 121	...	15 115	289
	1997	21 891	1 680	2 977	15 351	1 883	...	14 794	472
Philippines	1994	6 482	686	223	...	5 574	323	15 129	339
	1995	6 434	624	142	...	5 668	628	18 992	275
	1996	6 623	496	47	...	6 080	331	20 559	821
	1997	6 966	517	43	...	6 406	− 70	22 728	781
Qatar	1994	33 419	...	20 837	12 582	...	− 138	...	20 077
	1995	33 936	...	21 354	12 582	...	− 197	...	20 658
	1996	34 332	...	21 564	12 768	...	−1 484	...	22 154
	1997	45 588	...	28 905	16 682	...	1 196	...	26 545
Saudi Arabia [1]	1994	461 190	...	426 053	35 137	...	9 609	...	348 802
	1995	460 343	...	424 890	35 453	...	5 373	164	350 988
	1996	467 512	...	428 984	38 528	...	11 997	178	345 173
	1997	464 972	...	424 524	40 448	...	8 032	194	346 906
Singapore	1994	...	...	...	...	...	−4 654	74 760	41 886
	1995	...	...	...	...	...	−6 367	73 575	41 087
	1996	...	...	...	...	...	−3 532	83 741	42 995
	1997	...	...	...	...	...	−3 113	85 523	41 272
Sri Lanka	1994	352	...	...	...	352	− 38	2 307	90
	1995	388	...	...	...	388	− 13	2 486	95
	1996	280	...	...	...	280	− 14	2 900	78
	1997	296	...	...	...	296	28	3 033	79
Syrian Arab Republic	1994	32 373	...	30 251	1 911	211	1 910	454	17 041
	1995	33 317	...	30 951	2 150	216	− 492	445	19 827
	1996	33 109	...	30 454	2 436	219	243	584	18 926
	1997	32 110	...	28 543	3 344	224	−1 556	713	18 695

| \|| | \|| | Bunkers – Soutes | Consumption – Consommation | | | | | | | |
Air Avion	Sea Maritime	Unallocated Nondistribué	Per capita Par habitant	Total Totale	Solids Solides	Liquids Liquides	Gas Gaz	Electricity Electricité	Année	Région, pays ou zone
...	...	19	642	2 920	1 005	288	834	793	1994	Kirghizistan
...	...	71	610	2 790	597	532	823	838	1995	
...	...	91	639	2 937	502	579	981	875	1996	
...	...	110	583	2 694	932	375	569	819	1997	
...	...	...	28	132	1	98	...	33	1994	Rép. démocratique
...	...	...	28	133	1	104	...	29	1995	populaire lao
...	...	...	31	152	1	111	...	41	1996	
...	...	...	31	156	1	116	...	39	1997	
140	...	...	1 280	3 730	78	3 565	...	87	1994	Liban
169	...	...	1 324	3 985	133	3 785	...	67	1995	
175	...	...	1 427	4 398	143	4 156	...	98	1996	
181	...	...	1 474	4 634	143	4 391	...	101	1997	
...	242	1 966	1 504	29 566	1 644	16 487	10 871	565	1994	Malaisie
...	248	2 714	1 990	40 009	1 670	17 414	20 396	528	1995	
...	162	3 863	1 905	39 146	2 041	19 063	17 601	441	1996	
...	156	3 977	2 013	42 232	1 928	20 168	19 675	461	1997	
...	...	...	302	73	...	73	...	...	1994	Maldives
...	...	...	382	95	...	95	...	...	1995	
...	...	...	387	99	...	99	...	...	1996	
...	...	...	384	101	...	101	...	...	1997	
...	...	...	891	2 146	1 761	367	...	18	1994	Mongolie
...	...	...	875	2 145	1 769	343	...	33	1995	
...	...	...	877	2 189	1 770	387	...	33	1996	
...	...	...	827	2 098	1 687	378	...	32	1997	
2	5	236	55	2 325	36	941	1 209	139	1994	Myanmar
6	2	89	64	2 739	38	1 207	1 355	140	1995	
12	5	66	67	2 897	37	1 251	1 469	140	1996	
17	4	131	74	3 263	50	1 481	1 587	145	1997	
...	...	...	24	499	38	383	...	78 [19]	1994	Népal
...	...	...	25	542	35	423	...	83 [19]	1995	
...	...	...	31	666	83	485	...	98 [19]	1996	
...	...	...	32	709	83	523	...	103 [19]	1997	
167	308	− 207	2 949	6 137	...	1 949	4 188	.. [19]	1994	Oman
160	417	270	2 908	6 267	...	2 234	4 033	.. [19]	1995	
131	454	− 143	2 869	6 397	...	2 179	4 219	.. [19]	1996	
36	396	− 308	3 016	6 951	...	1 948	5 003	.. [19]	1997	
133	17	845	239	31 752	2 429	13 666	13 856	1 800	1994	Pakistan
138	15	846	238	32 362	2 198	14 067	13 999	2 098	1995	
129	12	899	253	35 459	2 469	15 994	14 875	2 121	1996	
135	18	708	245	35 351	2 262	15 855	15 351	1 883	1997	
506	100	485	297	19 859	1 551	12 734	...	5 574	1994	Philippines
516	120	2 647	311	21 240	1 578	13 994	...	5 668	1995	
531	73	314	359	25 110	2 671	16 359	...	6 080	1996	
593	94	866	384	27 429	3 534	17 489	...	6 406	1997	
103	...	79	24 717	13 298	...	716	12 582	...	1994	Qatar
93	...	56	24 316	13 325	...	744	12 582	...	1995	
124	...	− 34	24 324	13 573	...	805	12 768	...	1996	
124	...	137	30 909	17 587	...	904	16 682	...	1997	
1 238	8 884	13 484	4 457	79 173	...	44 036	35 137	...	1994	Arabie saoudite [1]
1 290	10 620	14 596	4 254	77 640	...	42 187	35 453	...	1995	
1 393	11 542	12 296	4 530	85 290	...	46 763	38 528	...	1996	
1 264	11 168	11 110	4 450	86 687	...	46 239	40 448	...	1997	
887	9 834	7 517	5 912	19 290	25	19 272	...	− 8	1994	Singapour
903	10 381	7 257	6 117	20 315	29	20 286	...	...	1995	
1 187	13 167	7 155	6 747	22 770	30	22 740	...	...	1996	
1 027	14 202	7 368	7 227	24 767	6	24 762	...	...	1997	
70	341	163	115	2 033	2	1 679	...	352	1994	Sri Lanka
79	336	163	124	2 214	1	1 825	...	388	1995	
101	379	125	139	2 511	1	2 230	...	280	1996	
104	273	101	150	2 744	2	2 446	...	296	1997	
233	...	1 457	881	12 186	1	10 063	1 911	211	1994	Rép. arabe syrienne
102	...	1 641	893	12 684	4	10 315	2 150	216	1995	
98	...	1 013	920	13 412	3	10 754	2 436	219	1996	
108	...	1 389	949	14 187	3	10 617	3 344	224	1997	

62
Production, trade and consumption of commercial energy
Thousand metric tons of oil equivalent and kilograms per capita [*cont.*]
Production, commerce et consommation d'énergie commerciale
Milliers de tonnes d'équivalent pétrole et kilogrammes par habitant [*suite*]

Region, country or area	Year	Primary energy production – Production d'énergie primaire					Changes in stocks Variations des stocks	Imports Importations	Exports Exportations
		Total Totale	Solids Solides	Liquids Liquides	Gas Gaz	Electricity Electricité			
Tajikistan	1994	1 525	28	32	30	1 435	...	2 338	53
	1995	1 322	7	24	35	1 255	...	2 362	36
	1996	1 241	5	20	44	1 171	...	2 552	42
	1997	1 245	3	25	38	1 179	...	2 493	36
Thailand	1994	20 766	7 523	3 741	9 112	389	− 412	28 209	1 12
	1995	21 828	8 105	3 682	9 463	578	− 639	33 630	1 12
	1996	24 966	9 449	4 152	10 733	632	1 199	41 596	4 28
	1997	29 231	10 291	4 931	13 389	620	229	41 265	5 67
Turkey	1994	18 682	12 107	3 695	182	2 698	1 048	33 375	1 95
	1995	18 834	12 022	3 515	166	3 130	1 098	38 576	1 54
	1996	19 596	12 356	3 499	188	3 552	544	42 883	1 25
	1997	20 282	13 107	3 448	232	3 495	− 444	44 524	1 00
Turkmenistan	1994	35 855	...	3 359	32 495	...	...	693	22 10
	1995	35 811	...	3 499	32 311	...	...	629	21 57
	1996	35 704	...	4 024	31 680	...	...	330	23 15
	1997	20 058	...	4 480	15 578	...	...	839	7 99
United Arab Emirates	1994	133 817	...	109 753	24 064	...	258	12 647	105 95
	1995	140 055	...	110 865	29 190	...	765	13 167	110 25
	1996	143 388	...	111 887	31 501	...	150	12 754	111 77
	1997	145 958	...	112 537	33 421	...	−1 328	12 754	114 56
Uzbekistan	1994	50 861	1 059	7 496	41 691	615	...	4 811	5 83
	1995	51 396	836	7 652	42 377	532	2 231	2 761	6 66
	1996	51 625	777	7 695	42 591	561	135	5 057	9 77
	1997	53 441	804	7 992	44 148	497	− 481	3 607	10 56
Viet Nam	1994	12 357	3 983	6 999	2	1 373	− 226	4 592	8 38
	1995	15 026	5 845	7 619	5	1 558	465	4 769	9 62
	1996	17 416	6 876	8 802	7	1 731	486	5 637	11 25
	1997	19 985	7 972	10 088	11	1 914	1 073	5 769	12 05
Yemen	1994	16 294	...	16 294	...	...	10	373	12 94
	1995	17 015	...	17 015	...	...	15	2 099	14 22
	1996	17 125	...	17 125	...	...	−1 430	1 200	14 43
	1997	17 671	...	17 671	...	...	1 847	2 003	12 43
Europe	1994	2 134 684	457 429	618 990	720 193	338 071	9 805	1 226 449	840 499
	1995	2 193 858	442 371	621 292	784 173	346 022	7 293	1 254 299	855 789
	1996	2 238 412	428 198	633 125	817 693	359 395	−3 062	1 310 391	927 003
	1997	2 206 313	415 733	635 807	790 549	364 225	16 042	1 312 357	929 708
Albania	1994	948	42	535	47	324	40	89	36
	1995	949	41	521	26	361	...	94	6
	1996	1 024	26	488	21	489	...	126	...
	1997	859	19	360	17	464	...	133	...
Austria	1994	5 923	362	1 151	1 238	3 172	− 613	18 775	1 639
	1995	6 086	338	1 082	1 358	3 308	− 77	19 894	1 644
	1996	5 705	288	991	1 367	3 059	129	21 429	1 692
	1997	5 805	294	998	1 307	3 207	− 439	21 486	2 080
Belarus	1994	3 064	791	2 000	271	2	− 672	26 690	2 991
	1995	2 892	713	1 932	245	2	338	25 933	3 376
	1996	2 738	647	1 860	230	1	−1 414	25 677	4 043
	1997	2 679	629	1 822	227	2	455	27 114	3 518
Belgium	1994	10 871	203	...	1	10 667	70	63 720	18 786
	1995	11 032	172	...	...	10 861	908	63 216	17 417
	1996	11 526	151	...	2	11 373	253	69 090	20 490
	1997	11 953	115	...	...	11 837	93	69 365	20 606
Bosnia & Herzegovina	1994	544	436	...	...	107	− 141	810	35
	1995	633	511	...	...	122	32	794	16
	1996	742	511	...	...	231	11	565	49
	1997	715	511	...	...	204	− 48	764	47
Bulgaria	1994	8 987	4 792	36	45	4 114	− 238	13 861	2 036
	1995	9 912	5 142	43	40	4 688	190	15 457	2 019
	1996	9 711	4 689	32	37	4 953	451	15 175	1 817
	1997	9 399	4 472	28	31	4 869	5	13 178	1 931
Croatia	1994	4 056	69	2 108	1 455	424	65	5 403	2 033
	1995	4 355	54	2 063	1 785	453	− 56	5 283	1 911
	1996	4 206	45	1 919	1 621	621	146	5 682	1 739
	1997	3 987	34	1 938	1 559	456	92	5 579	1 408

Air Avion	Sea Maritime	Unallocated Nondistribué	Per capita Par habitant	Total Totale	Solids Solides	Liquids Liquides	Gas Gaz	Electricity Electricité	Année	Région, pays ou zone
...	...	22	584	3 309	28	1 167	722	1 392	1994	Tadjikistan
...	...	24	574	3 299	7	1 167	812	1 312	1995	
...	...	20	574	3 352	50	1 167	1 043	1 092	1996	
...	...	25	565	3 348	47	1 167	946	1 188	1997	
...	...	1 377	808	46 887	8 477	28 837	9 112	460	1994	Thaïlande
...	...	2 662	892	52 307	9 667	32 546	9 463	631	1995	
...	...	3 098	980	57 983	11 725	34 831	10 733	694	1996	
...	...	3 904	1 016	60 692	12 018	34 609	13 389	675	1997	
258	112	2 082	774	46 606	15 991	22 940	5 023	2 651	1994	Turquie
264	187	2 753	842	51 567	16 483	25 584	6 430	3 070	1995	
328	126	3 197	915	57 034	19 002	26 723	7 763	3 546	1996	
448	160	3 698	945	59 941	21 094	25 893	9 268	3 686	1997	
...	...	432	3 503	14 010	...	2 418	11 820	- 228	1994	Turkménistan
...	...	439	3 539	14 431	...	2 151	12 452	- 173	1995	
...	...	652	2 943	12 231	70	2 332	10 069	- 240	1996	
...	...	1 047	2 802	11 861	...	2 364	9 725	- 227	1997	
248	10 664	1 146	13 069	28 189	...	7 993	20 196	...	1994	Emirats arabes unis
258	10 674	302	14 014	30 970	...	7 866	23 104	...	1995	
120	10 674	450	14 588	32 970	...	7 751	25 219	...	1996	
199	10 674	361	14 842	34 240	...	7 362	26 878	...	1997	
...	...	3 912	2 077	45 921	1 320	6 074	37 946	581	1994	Ouzbékistan
...	...	1 828	1 932	43 437	830	5 804	36 381	421	1995	
...	...	1 728	1 971	45 042	930	5 745	37 712	655	1996	
...	...	1 831	1 944	45 133	766	5 959	37 832	577	1997	
...	...	1	121	8 785	2 811	4 599	2	1 373	1994	Viet Nam
...	...	1	131	9 703	3 357	4 783	5	1 558	1995	
...	...	1	150	11 309	3 898	5 673	7	1 731	1996	
...	...	1	165	12 625	4 903	5 797	11	1 914	1997	
42	100	353	225	3 219	...	3 219	...	...	1994	Yémen
53	100	1 255	231	3 468	...	3 468	...	...	1995	
63	100	1 745	218	3 415	...	3 415	...	...	1996	
63	150	110	311	5 071	...	5 071	...	...	1997	
8 725	36 452	49 811	3 294	2 395 840	548 874	760 352	749 417	3 378	1994	Europe
9 390	37 865	54 955	3 383	2 462 865	541 124	753 659	822 650	345 434	1995	
0 239	40 693	54 678	3 431	2 499 252	536 673	750 403	854 033	358 142	1996	
2 024	44 845	54 692	3 350	2 441 359	501 307	741 245	835 154	363 653	1997	
...	...	41	287	920	43	522	47	308	1994	Albanie
...	...	217	258	820	41	399	26	355	1995	
...	...	189	305	961	26	408	21	506	1996	
...	...	82	291	910	19	394	17	481	1997	
208	...	364	2 908	23 100	2 994	10 557	6 448	3 102	1994	Autriche
231	...	490	2 961	23 692	3 291	10 315	6 990	3 096	1995	
256	...	318	3 072	24 740	3 400	10 705	7 495	3 141	1996	
265	...	410	3 084	24 975	3 624	10 988	7 222	3 141	1997	
...	...	1 943	2 454	25 491	1 511	10 125	13 525	330	1994	Bélarus
...	...	1 250	2 296	23 861	1 380	9 097	12 767	617	1995	
...	...	1 598	2 331	24 189	1 296	8 688	13 469	736	1996	
...	...	1 180	2 380	24 640	1 072	7 601	15 310	657	1997	
817	4 187	2 315	4 811	48 415	9 292	17 366	10 747	11 009	1994	Belgique
884	3 985	2 367	4 826	48 688	8 916	16 771	11 790	11 211	1995	
998	4 592	2 688	5 104	51 594	8 594	18 139	13 129	11 733	1996	
1 280	5 198	3 187	5 031	50 953	8 449	17 869	12 516	12 119	1997	
...	...	...	415	1 460	436	526	376	121	1994	Bosnie-Herzégovine
...	...	...	404	1 380	511	494	235	140	1995	
...	...	...	364	1 247	511	345	205	186	1996	
...	...	...	420	1 480	511	701	108	161	1997	
...	264	836	2 334	19 950	7 117	4 982	3 744	4 108	1994	Bulgarie
...	274	1 298	2 540	21 589	7 235	5 098	4 582	4 674	1995	
...	238	1 090	2 520	21 289	6 823	4 354	5 197	4 915	1996	
...	339	891	2 313	19 411	7 060	3 676	4 111	4 563	1997	
52	45	1 061	1 379	6 206	239	3 155	2 081	731	1994	Croatie
59	33	1 092	1 469	6 599	185	3 426	2 149	839	1995	
65	37	1 077	1 520	6 824	150	3 443	2 408	822	1996	
59	24	835	1 594	7 149	265	3 592	2 496	795	1997	

62
Production, trade and consumption of commercial energy
Thousand metric tons of oil equivalent and kilograms per capita [cont.]
Production, commerce et consommation d'énergie commerciale
Milliers de tonnes d'équivalent pétrole et kilogrammes par habitant [suite]

Region, country or area	Year	Total Totale	Solids Solides	Liquids Liquides	Gas Gaz	Electricity Electricité	Changes in stocks Variations des stocks	Imports Importations	Exports Exportations
Czech Republic	1994	33 796	29 928	128	212	3 527	− 399	16 918	8 700
	1995	31 123	27 381	146	220	3 376	− 247	18 125	8 799
	1996	31 432	27 529	152	202	3 548	636	20 092	8 570
	1997	30 360	26 587	163	181	3 428	641	19 543	7 988
Denmark	1994	13 808	6	9 116	4 569	117	− 762	18 020	12 126
	1995	14 313	13	9 167	5 010	122	1 240	17 664	10 965
	1996	15 979	38	10 119	5 694	128	− 865	17 668	13 290
	1997	18 533	14	11 358	6 970	191	1 449	17 371	15 263
Estonia	1994	3 422	3 422	...	...	...	33	2 681	347
	1995	3 133	3 133	...	...	...	− 106	2 454	616
	1996	3 481	3 481	...	...	...	− 79	2 287	488
	1997	3 372	3 372	...	...	...	− 99	2 679	902
Faeroe Islands	1994	7	...	...	...	7	...	170	...
	1995	7	...	...	...	7	...	205	...
	1996	7	...	...	...	7	...	210	...
	1997	7	...	...	...	7	...	211	...
Finland	1994	8 196	2 130	...	...	6 066	2 372	22 545	3 556
	1995	8 142	2 032	...	...	6 109	− 600	19 157	3 951
	1996	8 301	2 216	...	...	6 085	− 831	21 672	4 846
	1997	9 114	2 627	...	...	6 488	875	21 629	3 882
France [2]	1994	112 945	5 840	3 265	3 210	100 630	490	132 142	22 451
	1995	116 823	6 047	2 945	3 103	104 728	76	136 537	19 654
	1996	120 048	5 360	2 545	2 674	109 469	−1 841	147 173	22 688
	1997	117 723	4 501	2 160	1 834	109 229	672	146 985	23 675
Germany	1994	148 010	88 643	2 938	15 165	41 264	6 898	213 133	21 505
	1995	139 427	78 346	2 926	15 969	42 186	−2 056	214 209	20 171
	1996	138 028	73 504	2 874	17 462	44 188	−3 242	229 396	21 510
	1997	136 405	70 140	2 804	17 357	46 105	1 948	228 474	21 565
Gibraltar	1994	...	...	...	...	...	...	966	...
	1995	...	...	...	...	...	...	1 184	...
	1996	...	...	...	...	...	...	1 739	...
	1997	...	...	...	...	...	...	2 202	...
Greece	1994	8 795	7 416	533	51	794	−1 608	19 953	3 416
	1995	8 854	7 508	459	48	840	165	22 115	3 400
	1996	9 274	7 783	516	50	923	− 93	23 289	3 793
	1997	9 155	7 709	467	49	930	384	22 635	2 764
Hungary	1994	13 104	2 873	2 395	4 169	3 667	87	14 166	2 258
	1995	13 872	2 970	3 036	4 204	3 662	238	14 849	2 185
	1996	13 687	3 123	2 862	3 997	3 705	758	16 586	2 052
	1997	13 306	3 214	2 711	3 729	3 651	561	16 166	2 073
Iceland	1994	611	...	...	...	611	− 2	733	...
	1995	652	...	...	...	652	50	733	...
	1996	711	...	...	...	711	− 24	798	...
	1997	770	...	...	...	770	− 12	794	...
Ireland	1994	3 742	1 192	...	2 437	112	− 324	8 081	1 004
	1995	4 384	1 785	...	2 497	102	775	8 640	913
	1996	3 773	1 261	...	2 409	103	166	9 359	953
	1997	2 961	740	...	2 118	103	− 70	10 892	1 259
Italy [3]	1994	30 374	62	4 896	18 378	7 038	617	147 915	19 798
	1995	30 043	88	5 237	18 163	6 554	357	152 729	16 129
	1996	30 984	69	5 453	18 182	7 280	1 960	153 591	17 595
	1997	30 871	24	5 949	17 533	7 366	−1 033	156 146	19 707
Latvia	1994	429	145	...	...	284	− 78	3 748	157
	1995	331	79	...	...	253	− 4	3 459	88
	1996	248	88	...	...	160	252	3 758	129
	1997	343	89	...	...	254	− 169	2 911	63
Lithuania	1994	2 179	21	93	...	2 066	− 181	8 554	2 790
	1995	3 281	14	128	...	3 139	337	8 065	2 424
	1996	3 873	18	155	...	3 701	82	8 285	3 278
	1997	3 425	20	212	...	3 193	27	8 978	4 097
Luxembourg	1994	59	...	...	...	59	...	3 814	55
	1995	71	...	...	...	71	− 19	3 363	66
	1996	75	...	...	...	75	16	3 500	75
	1997	81	...	...	...	81	− 8	3 426	78

Bunkers – Soutes			Consumption – Consommation							
Air Avion	Sea Maritime	Unallocated Nondistribué	Per capita Par habitant	Total Totale	Solids Solides	Liquids Liquides	Gas Gaz	Electricity Electricité	Année	Région, pays ou zone
172	...	1 636	3 931	40 599	24 833	5 844	6 433	3 489	1994	République tchèque
186	...	1 577	3 771	38 934	22 260	5 982	7 280	3 412	1995	
133	...	1 664	3 928	40 521	22 366	6 229	8 379	3 548	1996	
125	...	1 281	3 870	39 867	21 932	6 089	8 521	3 326	1997	
629	1 505	– 277	3 574	18 608	7 874	8 245	2 788	– 300	1994	Danemark
645	1 627	– 115	3 371	17 615	6 453	7 797	3 312	54	1995	
709	1 518	– 134	3 650	19 129	8 879	7 943	3 502	–1 196 19	1996	
696	1 508	– 132	3 257	17 121	6 583	7 440	3 530	– 433	1997	
...	133	– 298	3 908	5 889	3 787	1 693	511	– 102	1994	Estonie
...	90	– 310	3 565	5 297	3 606	1 173	582	– 65	1995	
...	93	– 340	3 824	5 606	3 750	1 287	642	– 74	1996	
...	102	– 364	3 808	5 510	3 719	1 250	624	– 83	1997	
...	...	...	3 911	176	...	170	...	7	1994	Iles Féroé
...	...	...	4 711	212	...	205	...	7	1995	
...	...	...	4 909	216	...	210	...	7	1996	
...	...	...	4 932	217	...	211	...	7	1997	
271	424	–2 105	5 156	26 223	6 535	9 900	3 159	6 629	1994	Finlande
293	336	–2 497	5 054	25 816	6 102	9 737	3 268	6 709	1995	
314	380	–2 402	5 397	27 666	7 438	10 531	3 297	6 400	1996	
326	413	–1 341	5 172	26 588	6 823	9 390	3 230	7 146	1997	
3 677	2 167	4 107	3 670	212 194	14 924	71 157	30 915	958	1994	France [2]
3 880	2 530	8 624	3 766	218 597	16 279	70 634	32 961	98 723	1995	
4 138	2 750	8 372	3 965	231 114	16 752	74 491	36 319	103 553	1996	
4 246	2 994	7 708	3 853	225 414	14 791	72 727	34 291	103 606	1997	
5 401	2 038	6 313	3 923	318 987	93 826	116 394	67 301	41 465	1994	Allemagne
5 602	2 056	5 568	3 947	322 294	91 107	115 275	73 311	42 601	1995	
5 870	2 040	5 214	4 102	336 031	90 606	118 712	82 978	43 735	1996	
6 063	2 166	6 233	3 984	326 905	86 316	116 051	78 636	45 903	1997	
4	845	...	4 500	117	...	117	...	...	1994	Gibraltar
4	1 100	...	3 077	80	...	80	...	...	1995	
4	1 654	...	3 115	81	...	81	...	...	1996	
2	2 125	...	2 885	75	...	75	...	...	1997	
853	3 348	–1 318	2 304	24 057	8 545	14 633	51	827	1994	Grèce
854	3 598	–1 628	2 343	24 579	8 374	15 249	48	908	1995	
818	3 166	– 898	2 447	25 777	9 032	15 652	54	1 040	1996	
791	3 174	–1 042	2 433	25 718	8 447	15 955	189	1 127	1997	
190	...	1 372	2 278	23 363	4 216	6 810	8 495	3 842	1994	Hongrie
183	...	2 061	2 352	24 055	4 137	6 475	9 575	3 868	1995	
194	...	1 669	2 512	25 600	4 210	6 133	11 363	3 894	1996	
185	...	1 700	2 457	24 952	3 991	6 349	10 777	3 836	1997	
69	29	...	4 688	1 247	67	568	...	611	1994	Islande
67	46	...	4 560	1 222	55	516	...	652	1995	
85	38	...	5 203	1 410	64	635	...	711	1996	
93	47	...	5 245	1 437	56	611	...	770	1997	
382	39	61	2 975	10 660	3 147	4 964	2 437	112	1994	Irlande
354	114	25	3 005	10 844	3 137	5 014	2 592	101	1995	
345	160	15	3 163	11 493	3 103	5 352	2 946	92	1996	
414	152	60	3 291	12 038	3 133	5 724	3 080	102	1997	
2 598	2 355	–6 074	2 774	158 995	11 399	92 289	45 035	10 271	1994	Italie [3]
2 764	2 430	–3 691	2 873	164 782	12 294	93 102	49 614	9 772	1995	
2 890	2 297	–1 384	2 809	161 216	11 279	88 256	51 185	10 495	1996	
2 723	2 392	–3 436	2 903	166 665	11 265	91 933	52 762	10 705	1997	
...	...	...	1 592	4 099	291	2 540	827	440	1994	Latvie
...	...	...	1 461	3 707	225	2 025	1 010	447	1995	
...	...	...	1 451	3 626	213	2 101	874	437	1996	
...	...	...	1 365	3 360	173	1 712	1 065	411	1997	
...	...	– 148	2 214	8 272	355	4 010	1 743	2 164	1994	Lettonie
...	...	49	2 291	8 538	283	3 318	2 028	2 909	1995	
...	...	– 316	2 453	9 114	255	3 433	2 169	3 257	1996	
...	55	– 259	2 290	8 484	198	3 394	2 002	2 890	1997	
167	...	...	9 107	3 652	905	1 762	542	442	1994	Luxembourg
190	...	...	7 855	3 197	507	1 570	619	501	1995	
206	...	...	7 956	3 278	478	1 624	679	497	1996	
252	...	...	7 638	3 185	305	1 658	696	526	1997	

62

Production, trade and consumption of commercial energy
Thousand metric tons of oil equivalent and kilograms per capita [*cont.*]
Production, commerce et consommation d'énergie commerciale
Milliers de tonnes d'équivalent pétrole et kilogrammes par habitant [*suite*]

| Region, country or area | Year | Primary energy production – Production d'énergie primaire | | | | | Changes in stocks | Imports | Exports |
		Total Totale	Solids Solides	Liquids Liquides	Gas Gaz	Electricity Electricité	Variations des stocks	Importations	Exportations
Malta	1994	...	...	...	...	...	...	603	
	1995	...	...	...	...	...	...	606	
	1996	...	...	...	...	...	...	615	
	1997	...	...	...	...	...	...	616	
Netherlands	1994	71 835	...	4 393	66 379	1 063	2 299	93 293	78 0!
	1995	71 625	...	3 539	67 006	1 080	−1 532	95 291	80 0
	1996	79 979	...	3 108	75 745	1 126	282	100 201	87 2
	1997	70 883	...	2 998	67 209	675	947	105 838	83 8!
Norway [4]	1994	168 837	202	128 769	30 166	9 701	385	4 806	147 1!
	1995	166 962	196	138 786	17 452	10 528	309	5 183	159 6‹
	1996	207 716	154	157 100	41 517	8 944	1 631	4 979	184 5!
	1997	212 288	259	156 795	45 696	9 538	− 42	6 091	190 1!
Poland	1994	93 474	89 456	284	3 409	326	620	21 489	19 7.
	1995	94 584	90 475	292	3 486	331	−1 170	23 358	21 9!
	1996	95 562	91 306	317	3 604	336	439	27 596	19 7‹
	1997	95 287	91 110	289	3 560	328	4 085	30 501	21 0!
Portugal	1994	1 010	60	...	...	950	− 246	19 416	4 1‹
	1995	764	...	...	...	764	182	20 437	3 5:
	1996	1 321	...	...	...	1 321	− 284	18 266	2 31
	1997	1 180	...	...	...	1 180	393	19 493	2 1!
Republic of Moldova	1994	24	...	...	...	24	− 53	4 938	4:
	1995	28	...	...	...	28	59	4 694	1
	1996	31	...	...	...	31	− 145	4 710	
	1997	33	...	...	...	33	92	4 768	
Romania	1994	30 050	7 315	6 790	14 824	1 122	− 315	16 233	5 02
	1995	30 214	7 364	6 968	14 446	1 435	16	19 275	4 69
	1996	29 879	7 531	6 869	13 764	1 715	− 106	18 731	3 80
	1997	27 815	6 229	6 768	11 908	2 910	1 151	17 570	2 86
Russian Federation	1994	944 542	113 188	315 711	474 964	40 678	15 974	23 162	329 65
	1995	998 691	110 329	305 056	542 156	41 150	13 401	25 794	341 15
	1996	977 116	107 144	299 448	528 792	41 732	1 895	22 768	372 84
	1997	955 588	101 955	303 949	507 729	41 955	2 040	19 612	366 84
Slovakia	1994	4 529	692	60	225	3 552	193	13 334	1 67
	1995	4 853	1 101	62	267	3 424	− 244	13 412	1 82‹
	1996	4 755	1 121	71	244	3 318	368	15 087	2 03
	1997	4 617	1 146	64	225	3 182	6	14 778	2 22
Slovenia	1994	2 559	1 055	2	11	1 491	50	2 391	21.
	1995	2 601	1 062	2	16	1 521	− 22	3 344	21.
	1996	2 551	1 037	1	11	1 502	56	3 734	22
	1997	2 659	1 077	1	10	1 571	58	3 849	22.
Spain	1994	27 933	9 880	959	200	16 894	211	76 027	8 83'
	1995	27 344	9 536	793	416	16 598	1 414	80 778	6 26(
	1996	28 706	9 353	658	467	18 228	− 738	79 501	5 51‹
	1997	27 518	9 293	517	178	17 531	−1 528	84 934	5 43:
Sweden	1994	24 431	283	5	...	24 142	529	29 081	9 14‹
	1995	24 267	304	4	...	23 959	−1 539	27 807	11 09‹
	1996	23 993	351	4	...	23 638	− 472	30 690	9 95!
	1997	24 406	252	...	...	24 154	513	30 005	10 86‹
Switzerland [5]	1994	9 777	...	...	1	9 776	− 438	16 499	3 01‹
	1995	9 566	...	...	...	9 566	− 328	16 238	2 75(
	1996	9 089	...	...	...	9 089	− 14	17 495	2 74‹
	1997	9 631	...	...	...	9 631	76	17 517	2 88'
TFYR Macedonia	1994	1 909	1 849	...	...	60	− 45	862	16
	1995	2 022	1 954	...	...	69	107	1 040	46
	1996	1 999	1 926	...	...	73	− 6	1 292	37
	1997	1 883	1 806	...	...	77	...	1 078	5
Ukraine	1994	88 278	48 636	4 199	16 478	18 964	−3 411	85 142	5 234
	1995	83 482	43 209	4 057	16 926	19 290	...	92 027	3 836
	1996	81 718	39 011	4 097	17 156	21 454	...	91 283	5 003
	1997	82 155	39 611	4 127	16 898	21 519	...	78 870	4 725
United Kingdom	1994	240 669	28 266	127 547	61 539	23 317	−11 604	75 886	102 317
	1995	255 189	31 955	130 981	68 535	23 718	−4 898	70 268	102 901
	1996	267 627	30 244	130 458	81 842	25 084	−2 441	72 683	101 925
	1997	267 236	29 218	128 350	83 605	26 063	2 927	73 646	103 517

Air Avion	Sea Maritime	Unallocated Nondistribué	Per capita Par habitant	Total Totale	Solids Solides	Liquids Liquides	Gas Gaz	Electricity Electricité	Année	Région, pays ou zone
52	30	...	1 404	521	179	342	...	...	1994	Malte
52	30	...	1 397	524	179	345	...	...	1995	
52	31	...	1 407	532	185	347	...	...	1996	
52	31	...	1 399	533	185	348	...	...	1997	
2 193	11 306	−6 541	5 061	77 779	8 640	30 246	36 920	1 972	1994	Pays−Bas
2 531	11 442	−6 661	5 244	81 060	9 011	32 284	37 706	2 059	1995	
2 704	11 648	−9 247	5 635	87 578	9 214	34 910	41 417	2 037	1996	
2 929	12 356	−6 358	5 318	83 041	9 003	33 132	39 145	1 761	1997	
91	576	2 889	5 199	22 511	988	7 934	3 899	9 690	1994	Norvège [4]
92	681	2 653	2 013	8 764	1 058	7 852	−10 093	9 947	1995	
57	775	3 317	5 119	22 404	1 005	8 558	3 985	8 856	1996	
511	965	2 507	5 517	24 282	1 029	8 910	4 477	9 866	1997	
531	90	288	2 430	93 662	70 760	13 768	9 039	95	1994	Pologne
517	194	− 144	2 501	96 547	71 717	14 845	9 894	90	1995	
479	224	− 31	2 646	102 283	74 110	17 496	10 609	68	1996	
451	153	471	2 573	99 576	70 925	18 046	10 464	140	1997	
295	496	1 034	1 490	14 682	3 269	10 386	...	1 026	1994	Portugal
506	491	645	1 608	15 846	3 631	11 372	...	843	1995	
468	507	815	1 599	15 767	3 425	10 926	...	1 417	1996	
482	504	757	1 657	16 340	3 453	11 362	96	1 429	1997	
...	...	...	1 048	4 585	969	1 122	2 440	54	1994	Rép. de Moldova
...	...	...	1 063	4 651	592	1 026	2 844	189	1995	
...	...	...	1 117	4 886	511	952	3 253	170	1996	
...	...	...	1 076	4 707	151	880	3 475	201	1997	
165	...	1 740	1 737	39 673	9 711	10 219	18 559	1 184	1994	Roumanie
185	...	2 836	1 837	41 760	10 077	10 982	19 240	1 461	1995	
10	...	2 762	1 862	42 135	9 938	10 995	19 418	1 785	1996	
124	...	2 246	1 729	38 997	9 087	11 043	15 939	2 929	1997	
...	...	27 069	4 011	595 003	114 548	130 025	311 514	38 916	1994	Fédération de Russie
...	...	24 611	4 357	645 324	109 914	121 427	374 518	39 465	1995	
...	...	22 083	4 078	603 064	111 154	109 132	342 722	40 056	1996	
...	...	23 793	3 945	582 518	98 023	104 781	339 453	40 261	1997	
...	...	813	2 844	15 186	4 622	2 334	4 749	3 480	1994	Slovaquie
...	...	905	2 946	15 775	5 221	2 172	4 841	3 542	1995	
...	...	1 256	3 017	16 184	5 041	2 168	5 353	3 621	1996	
...	...	1 287	2 956	15 882	4 680	2 035	5 636	3 531	1997	
...	...	50	2 340	4 633	1 179	1 500	630	1 325	1994	Slovénie
...	...	22	2 880	5 731	1 248	2 357	746	1 379	1995	
...	...	60	2 980	5 945	1 205	2 675	706	1 359	1996	
...	...	65	3 089	6 162	1 283	2 662	791	1 425	1997	
1 925	3 150	6 348	2 111	83 489	18 192	40 750	7 494	17 054	1994	Espagne
2 038	3 238	7 443	2 217	87 729	19 013	43 156	8 575	16 984	1995	
2 149	4 727	7 761	2 243	88 790	18 471	42 403	9 597	18 319	1996	
2 322	5 831	7 252	2 351	93 144	18 124	45 192	12 562	17 267	1997	
430	1 086	682	4 754	41 644	2 761	14 007	711	24 165	1994	Suède
435	1 085	281	4 627	40 716	2 902	13 246	756	23 812	1995	
431	1 131	1 316	4 792	42 322	3 117	14 230	809	24 166	1996	
446	1 341	1 039	4 540	40 208	2 496	12 992	799	23 921	1997	
1 174	18	− 53	3 171	22 560	180	11 409	2 213	8 757	1994	Suisse [5]
1 229	16	− 25	3 089	22 163	192	10 590	2 440	8 941	1995	
1 287	14	40	3 114	22 514	144	10 721	2 640	9 008	1996	
1 342	13	− 88	3 147	22 917	110	11 207	2 549	9 050	1997	
...	...	− 40	1 454	2 840	2 005	762	...	74	1994	L'ex−Rép. yougoslave
...	...	7	1 478	2 902	2 065	769	...	69	1995	de Macédoine
...	...	− 24	1 662	3 283	2 007	1 203	...	73	1996	
...	...	12	1 482	2 944	1 876	991	...	77	1997	
1 076	...	936	3 287	169 584	50 839	20 401	79 469	18 874	1994	Ukraine
918	...	2 036	3 280	168 719	51 491	22 098	76 093	19 036	1995	
771	...	1 088	3 241	166 139	44 899	17 189	82 770	21 280	1996	
658	...	1 019	3 028	154 622	43 622	15 791	73 704	21 506	1997	
5 261	2 322	4 335	3 663	213 924	49 485	75 847	63 823	24 769	1994	Royaume−Uni
4 649	2 470	3 653	3 702	216 682	47 867	74 321	69 373	25 121	1995	
4 750	2 670	4 045	3 910	229 362	44 783	76 113	81 947	26 518	1996	
5 090	2 963	2 452	3 810	223 933	39 824	74 215	82 406	27 488	1997	

62
Production, trade and consumption of commercial energy
Thousand metric tons of oil equivalent and kilograms per capita [*cont.*]
Production, commerce et consommation d'énergie commerciale
Milliers de tonnes d'équivalent pétrole et kilogrammes par habitant [*suite*]

Region, country or area	Year	Primary energy production – Production d'énergie primaire					Changes in stocks Variations des stocks	Imports Importations	Exports Exportations
		Total Totale	Solids Solides	Liquids Liquides	Gas Gaz	Electricity Electricité			
Yugoslavia	1994	10 957	8 174	1 078	748	957	...	398	
	1995	11 352	8 523	1 066	799	965	...	586	..
	1996	10 816	8 193	1 030	604	989	...	3 612	1.
	1997	11 312	8 668	979	619	1 046	...	4 528	..
Oceania	**1994**	**190 548**	**121 338**	**34 042**	**29 518**	**5 650**	**−2 324**	**28 173**	**104 91**
	1995	**205 166**	**133 519**	**33 987**	**32 075**	**5 584**	**2 219**	**28 607**	**113 67**
	1996	**208 809**	**135 798**	**34 078**	**33 411**	**5 522**	**− 783**	**31 790**	**115 72**
	1997	**218 403**	**145 102**	**34 301**	**33 615**	**5 385**	**2 011**	**32 717**	**122 51**
American Samoa	1994	...	...	...	...	...	...	186	..
	1995							183	..
	1996	...	...	...	...	...	...	186	..
	1997	...		...				186	
Australia	1994	172 679	119 647	26 614	24 986	1 432	−2 278	19 289	97 505
	1995	188 110	131 568	27 369	27 776	1 396	2 409	19 688	106 821
	1996	191 647	133 798	27 957	28 507	1 385	− 559	22 462	109 347
	1997	200 652	143 212	27 559	28 397	1 483	2 115	23 241	115 892
Cook Islands	1994	...	...	...	...	...	...	15	...
	1995	...	...	...	...	...	...	15	...
	1996	...	...	...	...	...	...	15	...
	1997	...	...	...	...	...	...	15	..
Fiji	1994	35	...	...	...	35	...	396	119
	1995	37	...	...	...	37	...	408	119
	1996	37	...	...	...	37	...	416	120
	1997	37	...	...	...	37	...	408	119
French Polynesia	1994	8	...	...	...	8	...	223	...
	1995	11	...	...	...	11	...	230	..
	1996	12	...	...	...	12	...	230	..
	1997	12	...	...	...	12	...	230	...
Guam	1994	...	...	...	...	...	...	1 633	...
	1995	...	...	...	...	...	...	1 481	...
	1996	...	...	...	...	...	...	1 465	...
	1997	...	...	...	...	...	...	1 465	...
Kiribati	1994	...	...	...	...	...	...	7	...
	1995	...	...	...	...	...	...	7	...
	1996	...	...	...	...	...	...	7	...
	1997	...	...	...	...	...	...	7	...
Nauru	1994		...	...	...	...	...	49	...
	1995						...	50	...
	1996	...					...	50	...
	1997	...	...	...		...	...	50	...
New Caledonia	1994	33	...	...	...	33	...	555	12
	1995	36	...	...	...	36	...	555	12
	1996	41	...	...	...	41	...	567	12
	1997	41	...	...	...	41	...	567	12
New Zealand	1994	12 176	1 691	1 929	4 458	4 097	− 46	4 425	1 842
	1995	11 849	1 951	1 619	4 222	4 056	− 190	4 590	1 757
	1996	12 948	2 000	2 121	4 826	4 000	− 224	4 986	2 285
	1997	13 577	1 889	2 783	5 140	3 764	− 104	5 130	2 572
Niue	1994	...	...	...	...	...	...	1	...
	1995	...		...	...	...	...	1	
	1996	...		...	...	...	...	1	
	1997	...	...	...	...	...	...	1	...
Palau	1994	3	...	...	...	3	...	92	...
	1995	3	...	...	...	3	...	95	...
	1996	3	...	...	...	3	...	98	...
	1997	3	...	...	...	3	...	96	...
Papua New Guinea	1994	5 613	...	5 499	74	40	...	733	5 434
	1995	5 118	...	4 999	76	43	...	724	4 959
	1996	4 120	...	3 999	78	43	...	724	3 960
	1997	4 080	...	3 959	78	43	...	736	3 915
Samoa	1994	2	...	...	...	2	...	41	...
	1995	2	...	...	...	2	...	44	...
	1996	2	...	...	...	2	...	44	...
	1997	2	...	...	...	2	...	44	...

Air Avion	Sea Maritime	Unallocated Nondistribué	Per capita Par habitant	Total Totale	Solids Solides	Liquids Liquides	Gas Gaz	Electricity Electricité	Année	Région, pays ou zone
39	...	429	1 036	10 887	8 211	971	748	957	1994	Yougoslavie
43	...	319	1 095	11 576	8 567	1 065	979	965	1995	
57	...	1 017	1 258	13 341	8 237	1 634	2 495	975	1996	
98	...	1 242	1 364	14 500	8 706	2 270	2 478	1 046	1997	
2 698	1 457	−1 138	4 025	113 115	43 384	42 224	21 858	5 650	1994	Oceanie
2 909	1 481	−2 120	4 055	115 614	44 699	42 429	22 902	5 584	1995	
3 084	1 477	− 177	4 195	121 274	48 347	43 828	23 578	5 522	1996	
3 183	1 426	1 710	4 107	120 279	50 231	40 653	24 011	5 385	1997	
...	91	...	1 727	95	...	95	...	...	1994	Samoa américaines
...	91	...	1 614	92	...	92	...	...	1995	
...	91	...	1 610	95	...	95	...	...	1996	
...	91	...	1 557	95	...	95	...	...	1997	
1 719	761	− 737	5 353	94 997	42 018	34 222	17 326	1 432	1994	Australie
1 882	856	−1 887	5 445	97 716	43 304	34 413	18 604	1 396	1995	
2 029	871	− 44	5 648	102 465	46 846	35 559	18 675	1 385	1996	
2 102	805	1 940	5 511	101 039	48 643	32 121	18 792	1 483	1997	
8	...	...	368	7	...	7	...	...	1994	Iles Cook
8	...	...	368	7	...	7	...	...	1995	
8	...	...	368	7	...	7	...	...	1996	
8	...	...	368	7	...	7	...	...	1997	
26	28	...	340	258	14	208	...	35	1994	Fidji
26	29	...	352	270	14	220	...	37	1995	
26	29	...	356	277	15	225	...	37	1996	
26	29	...	345	271	15	219	...	37	1997	
5	35	...	900	190	...	182	...	8	1994	Polynésie française
5	38	...	921	198	...	187	...	11	1995	
5	38	...	909	199	...	187	...	12	1996	
5	38	...	892	199	...	187	...	12	1997	
8	101	...	10 297	1 524	...	1 524	...	...	1994	Guam
8	90	...	9 152	1 382	...	1 382	...	...	1995	
11	90	...	8 794	1 363	...	1 363	...	...	1996	
11	90	...	8 627	1 363	...	1 363	...	...	1997	
...	...	...	91	7	...	7	...	...	1994	Kiribati
...	...	...	90	7	...	7	...	...	1995	
...	...	...	89	7	...	7	...	...	1996	
...	...	...	88	7	...	7	...	...	1997	
5	...	...	4 400	44	...	44	...	...	1994	Nauru
5	...	...	4 091	45	...	45	...	...	1995	
5	...	...	4 091	45	...	45	...	...	1996	
5	...	...	4 091	45	...	45	...	...	1997	
15	9		2 926	550	115	402	...	33	1994	Nouvelle−Calédonie
15	9		2 870	554	115	402	...	36	1995	
17	9	...	2 879	570	118	411	...	41	1996	
17	9	...	2 822	570	118	411	...	41	1997	
473	416	− 430	3 972	14 346	1 236	4 555	4 458	4 097	1994	Nouvelle−Zélande
518	353	− 237	3 879	14 238	1 265	4 695	4 222	4 056	1995	
540	333	− 137	4 069	15 138	1 367	4 946	4 825	4 000	1996	
563	347	− 237	4 139	15 565	1 455	5 205	5 141	3 764	1997	
...	...	...	500	1	...	1	...	...	1994	Nioué
...	...	...	500	1	...	1	...	...	1995	
...	...	...	500	1	...	1	...	...	1996	
...	...	...	500	1	...	1	...	...	1997	
15	...	...	4 706	80	...	77	...	3	1994	Palaos
15	...	...	4 882	83	...	80	...	3	1995	
15	...	...	4 722	85	...	82	...	3	1996	
15	...	...	4 611	83	...	80	...	3	1997	
21	3	29	204	859	1	744	74	40	1994	Papouasie−Nouvelle−
21	3	4	199	856	1	736	76	43	1995	Guinée
21	3	4	195	857	1	736	78	43	1996	
23	3	7	193	869	1	747	78	43	1997	
...	...	...	259	43	...	41	...	2	1994	Samoa
...	...	...	274	46	...	44	...	2	1995	
...	...	...	271	46	...	44	...	2	1996	
...	...	...	267	46	...	44	...	2	1997	

62

Production, trade and consumption of commercial energy
Thousand metric tons of oil equivalent and kilograms per capita [*cont.*]
Production, commerce et consommation d'énergie commerciale
Milliers de tonnes d'équivalent pétrole et kilogrammes par habitant [*suite*]

Region, country or area	Year	Primary energy production – Production d'énergie primaire					Changes in stocks Variations des stocks	Imports Importations	Exports Exportations
		Total Totale	Solids Solides	Liquids Liquides	Gas Gaz	Electricity Electricité			
Solomon Islands	1994	...	...	...	...	...	...	53	...
	1995	...	...	...	...	...	...	55	...
	1996	...	...	...	...	...	...	55	...
	1997	...	...	...	...	...	...	55	...
Tonga	1994	...	...	...	...	...	...	39	...
	1995	...	...	...	...	...	...	41	...
	1996	...	...	...	...	...	...	42	...
	1997	...	...	...	...	...	...	43	...
Vanuatu	1994	...	...	...	...	...	...	20	...
	1995	...	...	...	...	...	...	20	...
	1996	...	...	...	...	...	...	20	...
	1997	...	...	...	...	...	...	20	...
Wake Island	1994	...	...	...	...	...	...	415	...
	1995	...	...	...	...	...	...	418	...
	1996	...	...	...	...	...	...	421	...
	1997	...	...	...	...	...	...	421	...

Source:
United Nations Secretariat, "Energy Statistics Yearbook 1997" and the energy statistics database of the Statistics Division.

† For information on recent changes in country or area nomenclature pertaining to former Czechoslovakia, Germany, Hong Kong Special Administrative Region (SAR) of China, Macao Special Administrative Region (SAR) of China, SFR of Yugoslavia and former USSR, see Annex I – Country or area nomenclature, regional and other groupings.

†† For statistical purposes, the data for China do not include those for Hong Kong Special Administrative Region (Hong Kong SAR), Macao Special Administrative Region (Macao SAR) and Taiwan province of China.

1 Including part of the Neutral Zone.
2 Including Monaco.
3 Including San Marino.
4 Including Svalbard and Jan Mayen Islands.
5 Including Liechtenstein

Source:
Secrétariat de l'Organisation des Nations Unies, "Annuaire des statistique de l'énergie 1997" et la base de données pour les statistiques énergétiques de la Division de statistique.

† Pour les modifications récentes de nomenclature de pays ou de zone concernant l'Allemagne, Hong Kong (Région administrative spéciale de Chine), Macao, (Région administrative spéciale de Chine), l'ex Tchécoslovaquie, l'ex–URSS, Rfs de Yougoslavie, voir annexe I – Nomenclature des pays ou des zones, groupements régiounax et autres groupements.

†† Les données statistiques relatives à la Chine ne comprennent pas celles qui concernent la région administrative spéciale de Hong Kong (la RAS de Hong Kong), la région administrative spéciale de Macao (la RAS de Macao) et la province chinoise de Taiwan.

1 Y compris une partie de la Zone Neutral.
2 Y compris Monaco.
3 Y compris Saint–Marin.
4 Y compris îles Svalbard et Jan Mayen.
5 Y compris Liechtenstein.

Bunkers – Soutes			Consumption – Consommation							
Air Avion	Sea Maritime	Unallocated Nondistribué	Per capita Par habitant	Total Totale	Solids Solides	Liquids Liquides	Gas Gaz	Electricity Electricité	Année	Région, pays ou zone
2	...	...	139	51	...	51	...	...	1994	Iles Salomon
2	...	...	140	53	...	53	...	...	1995	
2	...	...	135	53	...	53	...	...	1996	
2	...	...	131	53	...	53	...	...	1997	
3	...	...	371	36	...	36	...	...	1994	Tonga
3	...	...	392	38	...	38	...	...	1995	
3	...	...	402	39	...	39	...	...	1996	
3	...	...	408	40	...	40	...	...	1997	
...	...	...	121	20	...	20	...	...	1994	Vanuatu
...	...	...	118	20	...	20	...	...	1995	
...	...	...	116	20	...	20	...	...	1996	
...	...	...	113	20	...	20	...	...	1997	
397	12	...	6 000	6	...	6	...	...	1994	Ile de Wake
400	12	...	6 000	6	...	6	...	...	1995	
402	13	...	6 000	6	...	6	...	...	1996	
402	13	...	6 000	6	...	6	...	...	1997	

63
Production of selected energy commodities
Production des principaux biens de l'énergie

Thousand metric tons of oil equivalent
Milliers de tonnes d'équivalent pétrole

Region, country or area / Région, pays ou zone	Year / Anneé	Hard coal, lignite & peat / Houille, lignite et tourbe	Briquettes & cokes / Agglomérés et cokes	Crude petroleum & NGL / Pétrole brut et GNL	Light petroleum products / Produits pétroliers légers	Heavy petroleum products / Produits pétroliers lourds	Other petroleum products / Autres produits pétroliers	LPG & refinery gas / GLP et gaz de raffinerie	Natural gas / Gaz naturel	Electrici...
World Monde	1994	2 224 045	229 162	3 295 097	1 220 371	1 551 251	242 996	173 908	1 929 519	1 505 25
	1995	2 291 139	253 841	3 326 687	1 257 888	1 547 610	242 507	177 840	2 052 164	1 558 73
	1996	2 330 496	249 638	3 371 941	1 297 402	1 595 416	240 740	178 808	2 152 705	1 628 60
	1997	2 349 117	248 661	3 449 857	1 333 365	1 638 709	251 775	184 464	2 155 122	1 648 04
Africa Afrique	1994	109 312	3 578	338 828	39 124	63 360	3 287	2 282	70 483	33 08
	1995	115 036	3 754	347 587	39 105	65 007	3 518	2 284	83 921	33 82
	1996	114 880	3 747	353 302	39 966	64 975	3 446	2 317	90 353	34 35
	1997	120 896	3 761	359 660	40 146	66 417	3 504	2 337	99 862	35 10
Algeria Algérie	1994	14	0	59 405	8 930	12 758	391	566	47 677	1 71
	1995	15	0	61 257	8 409	12 783	411	555	58 063	1 69
	1996	15	0	62 853	8 231	12 211	421	566	62 549	1 77
	1997	16	0	64 806	7 913	12 862	431	587	70 579	1 84
Angola Angola	1994	...	...	27 188	334	959	15	20	155	16
	1995	...	...	32 127	334	944	16	20	156	16
	1996	...	...	34 771	346	954	18	22	167	16
	1997	...	...	34 894	346	964	18	22	174	16
Benin Bénin	1994	...	...	121	...	...	...	...	...	
	1995	...	...	89	...	...	...	...	...	
	1996	...	...	75	...	...	...	...	...	
	1997	...	...	62	...	...	...	...	...	
Burkina Faso Burkina Faso	1994	...	...	...	...	...	...	...	...	1
	1995	...	...	...	...	...	...	...	...	2
	1996	...	...	...	...	...	...	...	...	2
	1997	...	...	...	...	...	...	...	...	2
Burundi Burundi	1994	4	0	...	...	...	...	...	...	1
	1995	4	0	...	...	...	...	...	...	1
	1996	4	0	...	...	...	...	...	...	1
	1997	4	0	...	...	...	...	...	...	1
Cameroon Cameroun	1994	1	...	5 808	596	425	50	22	...	23
	1995	1	...	5 379	599	444	60	23	...	23
	1996	1	...	5 214	606	448	63	24	...	23
	1997	1	...	5 589	610	449	67	24	...	23
Cape Verde Cap-Vert	1994	...	...	...	...	...	...	...	...	3
	1995	...	...	...	...	...	...	...	...	3
	1996	...	...	...	...	...	...	...	...	4
	1997	...	...	...	...	...	...	...	...	4
Central African Republic Rép. centrafricaine	1994	...	...	...	...	...	...	...	...	9
	1995	...	...	...	...	...	...	...	...	9
	1996	...	...	...	...	...	...	...	...	9
	1997	...	...	...	...	...	...	...	...	9
Chad Tchad	1994	...	...	...	...	...	...	...	...	7
	1995	...	...	...	...	...	...	...	...	8
	1996	...	...	...	...	...	...	...	...	8
	1997	...	...	...	...	...	...	...	...	8
Comoros Comores	1994	...	...	...	...	...	...	...	...	1
	1995	...	...	...	...	...	...	...	...	1
	1996	...	...	...	...	...	...	...	...	1
	1997	...	...	...	...	...	...	...	...	1
Congo Congo	1994	0	...	9 560	184	359	13	4	3	37
	1995	0	...	9 266	179	347	11	4	3	37
	1996	0	...	10 368	186	351	11	4	3	38
	1997	0	...	11 584	187	356	12	4	3	38
Côte d'Ivoire Côte d'Ivoire	1994	...	...	348	1 013	1 045	92	18	...	176
	1995	...	...	314	1 019	909	94	20	...	151
	1996	...	...	1 263	1 024	1 181	95	20	...	204
	1997	...	...	1 272	1 029	1 194	96	21	...	237

63
Production of selected energy commodities
Thousand metric tons of oil equivalent [*cont.*]
Production des principaux biens de l'énergie
Milliers de tonnes d'équivalent pétrole [*suite*]

Region, country or area Région, pays ou zone	Year Anneé	Hard coal, lignite & peat Houille, lignite et tourbe	Briquettes & cokes Agglo- mérés et cokes	Crude petroleum & NGL Pétrole brut et GNL	Light petroleum products Produits pétroliers légers	Heavy petroleum products Produits pétroliers lourds	Other petroleum products Autres produits pétroliers	LPG & refinery gas GLP et gaz de raffinerie	Natural gas Gaz naturel	Electricity Electricité
Dem. Rep. of the Congo	1994	64	...	1 124	20	30	14	0	...	457
Rép. dém. du Congo	1995	65	...	1 146	23	26	13	0	...	462
	1996	66	...	1 148	23	26	12	0	...	466
	1997	66	...	1 151	23	27	13	0	...	466
Djibouti	1994	...	...	...	...	...	...	...	...	16
Djibouti	1995	...	...	...	...	...	...	...	...	16
	1996	...	...	...	...	...	...	...	...	16
	1997	...	...	...	...	...	...	...	...	16
Egypt	1994	...	1 165	46 923	6 834	17 289	1 171	445	9 827	4 256
Egypte	1995	...	1 171	46 840	6 845	17 817	1 322	499	12 650	4 321
	1996	...	1 175	45 412	7 276	18 370	1 240	482	13 453	4 356
	1997	...	1 189	44 468	7 471	18 772	1 287	499	13 884	4 723
Equatorial Guinea	1994	...	...	242	...	...	...	...	...	2
Guinée équatoriale	1995	...	...	339	...	...	...	...	...	2
	1996	...	...	857	...	...	...	...	...	2
	1997	...	...	2 996	...	...	...	...	...	2
Ethiopia	1994	...	...	...	133	465	9	7	...	124
Ethiopie	1995	...	...	...	63	438	7	6	...	129
	1996	...	...	...	24	57	2	3	...	137
	1997	...	...	...	19	118	2	4	...	143
Gabon	1994	...	...	17 211	216	488	20	10	712	91
Gabon	1995	...	...	18 243	163	484	29	12	769	98
	1996	...	...	18 274	184	473	33	12	606	104
	1997	...	...	18 594	186	516	28	11	624	108
Gambia	1994	...	...	...	...	...	...	...	...	6
Gambie	1995	...	...	...	...	...	...	...	...	6
	1996	...	...	...	...	...	...	...	...	7
	1997	...	...	...	...	...	...	...	...	7
Ghana	1994	...	...	0	409	601	54	18	...	524
Ghana	1995	...	...	0	361	549	59	20	...	528
	1996	...	...	0	367	558	59	20	...	570
	1997	...	...	0	368	558	59	20	...	572
Guinea	1994	...	...	...	...	...	...	...	...	46
Guinee	1995	...	...	...	...	...	...	...	...	46
	1996	...	...	...	...	...	...	...	...	47
	1997	...	...	...	...	...	...	...	...	47
Guinea−Bissau	1994	...	...	...	...	...	...	...	...	4
Guinée−Bissau	1995	...	...	...	...	...	...	...	...	4
	1996	...	...	...	...	...	...	...	...	4
	1997	...	...	...	...	...	...	...	...	5
Kenya	1994	...	...	...	780	1 172	110	33	...	506
Kenya	1995	...	...	...	706	1 006	119	35	...	546
	1996	...	...	...	707	1 013	117	35	...	546
	1997	...	...	...	632	912	106	26	...	667
Liberia	1994	...	...	...	0	...	0	...	...	41
Libéria	1995	...	...	...	0	...	0	...	...	42
	1996	...	...	...	0	...	0	...	...	42
	1997	...	...	...	0	...	0	...	...	42
Libyan Arab Jamahiriya	1994	...	...	68 645	4 970	9 018	100	250	5 956	1 531
Jamah. arabe libyenne	1995	...	...	68 885	4 980	9 318	100	261	5 883	1 548
	1996	...	...	68 682	5 138	9 442	105	272	5 957	1 574
	1997	...	...	69 378	5 171	9 530	108	286	6 097	1 574
Madagascar	1994	...	0	...	69	120	10	1	...	52
Madagascar	1995	...	0	...	70	121	10	1	...	54
	1996	...	0	...	71	122	10	1	...	59
	1997	...	0	...	71	124	10	1	...	59
Malawi	1994	...	...	...	...	...	...	...	...	72
Malawi	1995	...	...	...	...	...	...	...	...	74
	1996	...	...	...	...	...	...	...	...	75
	1997	...	...	...	...	...	...	...	...	75

63
Production of selected energy commodities
Thousand metric tons of oil equivalent [cont.]
Production des principaux biens de l'énergie
Milliers de tonnes d'équivalent pétrole [suite]

Region, country or area Région, pays ou zone	Year Anneé	Hard coal, lignite & peat Houille, lignite et tourbe	Briquettes & cokes Agglo-mérés et cokes	Crude petroleum & NGL Pétrole brut et GNL	Light petroleum products Produits pétroliers légers	Heavy petroleum products Produits pétroliers lourds	Other petroleum products Autres produits pétroliers	LPG & refinery gas GLP et gaz de raffinerie	Natural gas Gaz naturel	Electricity Electricité
Mali Mali	1994	...	...	...	...	...	...	...	...	2
	1995	...	...	...	...	...	...	...	...	2
	1996	...	...	...	...	...	...	...	...	2
	1997	...	...	...	...	...	...	...	...	3
Mauritania Mauritanie	1994	...	...	...	304	499	97	39	...	1
	1995	...	...	...	305	501	98	40	...	1
	1996	...	...	...	310	505	98	41	...	1
	1997	...	...	...	313	507	99	41	...	1
Mauritius Maurice	1994	...	...	...	...	...	...	...	...	8
	1995									9
	1996	...	...	...	...	...	...	...	...	10
	1997	...	...	...	...	...	...	...	...	11
Morocco Maroc	1994	455	0	8	1 097	4 717	282	286	23	94
	1995	455	0	5	1 120	4 360	269	256	23	1 02
	1996	354	0	5	981	3 893	254	264	19	1 06
	1997	263	0	12	1 061	4 126	260	260	28	1 12
Mozambique Mozambique	1994	28	...	...	...	...	...	...	...	4
	1995	27	...						...	4
	1996	28	...	...	...	...	...	...	...	4
	1997	28	...	...	...	...	...	...	...	4
Niger Niger	1994	120	...	...	...	...	...	...	...	1
	1995	121	...						...	1
	1996	121	...						...	1
	1997	122	...	...	...	...	...	...	...	1
Nigeria Nigéria	1994	35	...	91 030	2 614	2 680	...	65	4 241	1 27
	1995	35	...	92 142	2 504	3 094	...	60	4 515	1 27
	1996	35	...	92 789	2 487	3 095	...	65	5 089	1 27
	1997	35	...	93 624	2 508	3 105	...	65	5 126	1 27
Réunion Réunion	1994	...	...	...	...	...	...	...	...	9
	1995	...	...	...	...	...	...	...	...	9
	1996	...	...	...	...	...	...	...	...	9
	1997	...	...	...	...	...	...	...	...	9
Rwanda Rwanda	1994	...	...	...	...	...	...	...	0	1
	1995	...						...	0	1
	1996	...						...	0	1
	1997	...						...	0	1
Saint Helena Sainte−Hélène	1994	...	...	...	...	...	...	...	...	
	1995	...	...	...	...	...	...	...	...	
	1996	...	...	...	...	...	...	...	...	
	1997	...	...	...	...	...	...	...	...	
Sao Tome and Principe Sao Tomé−et−Principe	1994	...	...	...	...	...	...	...	...	
	1995	...	...	...	...	...	...	...	...	
	1996	...	...	...	...	...	...	...	...	
	1997	...	...	...	...	...	...	...	...	
Senegal Sénégal	1994	...	...	...	339	523	11	3	...	8
	1995	...	...	...	342	523	12	3	...	9
	1996	...	...	...	344	525	12	3	...	10
	1997	...	...	...	348	527	12	3	...	10
Seychelles Seychelles	1994	...	...	...	...	...	...	...	...	1
	1995	...	...	...	...	...	...	...	...	1
	1996	...	...	...	...	...	...	...	...	1
	1997	...	...	...	...	...	...	...	...	1
Sierra Leone Sierra Leone	1994	...	...	...	61	120	27	...	...	2
	1995	...	...	...	63	122	27			2
	1996	...	...	...	64	122	27			2
	1997	...	...	...	64	125	27			2
Somalia Somalie	1994	...	...	...	...	...	...	...	...	2
	1995	...	...	...	...	...	...	...	...	2
	1996	...	...	...	...	...	...	...	...	2
	1997	...	...	...	...	...	...	...	...	2

63
Production of selected energy commodities
Thousand metric tons of oil equivalent [*cont.*]
Production des principaux biens de l'énergie
Milliers de tonnes d'équivalent pétrole [*suite*]

Region, country or area Région, pays ou zone	Year Anneé	Hard coal, lignite & peat Houille, lignite et tourbe	Briquettes & cokes Agglo-mérés et cokes	Crude petroleum & NGL Pétrole brut et GNL	Light petroleum products Produits pétroliers légers	Heavy petroleum products Produits pétroliers lourds	Other petroleum products Autres produits pétroliers	LPG & refinery gas GLP et gaz de raffinerie	Natural gas Gaz naturel	Electricity Electricité
South Africa Customs Union	1994	104 535	2 253	6 816	9 110	7 622	692	326	1 714	18 016
Union douanière d'Afrique	1995	110 227	2 269	7 272	9 856	8 643	730	303	1 715	18 492
australe	1996	110 372	2 269	7 388	10 405	9 052	739	305	1 715	18 657
	1997	116 575	2 269	7 399	10 418	9 058	739	305	1 717	18 674
Sudan	1994	...	...	...	246	645	106	7	...	114
Soudan	1995	...	...	...	251	647	107	8	...	114
	1996	...	...	...	257	650	107	8	...	115
	1997	...	...	...	259	652	107	8	...	115
Togo	1994	...	...	...	...	...	...	...	...	8
Togo	1995	...	...	...	...	...	...	...	...	8
	1996	...	...	...	...	...	...	...	...	8
	1997	...	...	...	...	...	...	...	...	8
Tunisia	1994	...	...	4 398	492	1 123	...	144	175	577
Tunisie	1995	...	...	4 284	528	1 224	...	141	144	628
	1996	...	...	4 203	546	1 217	...	154	794	674
	1997	...	...	3 830	756	1 220	...	133	1 629	721
Uganda	1994	...	...	...	...	...	...	...	...	91
Ouganda	1995	...	...	...	...	...	...	...	...	94
	1996	...	...	...	...	...	...	...	...	101
	1997	...	...	...	...	...	...	...	...	108
United Rep. of Tanzania	1994	3	...	...	186	392	2	7	...	147
Rép.–Unie de Tanzanie	1995	3	...	...	190	394	2	7	...	148
	1996	3	...	...	191	395	2	7	...	149
	1997	3	...	...	194	397	2	7	...	150
Western Sahara	1994	...	...	...	...	...	...	...	...	7
Sahara occidental	1995	...	...	...	...	...	...	...	...	7
	1996	...	...	...	...	...	...	...	...	7
	1997	...	...	...	...	...	...	...	...	7
Zambia	1994	224	21	...	189	307	20	11	...	669
Zambie	1995	212	20	...	195	312	20	11	...	670
	1996	206	19	...	199	316	20	11	...	670
	1997	212	19	...	200	317	20	11	...	670
Zimbabwe	1994	3 828	139	...	...	...	...	...	...	711
Zimbabwe	1995	3 870	294	...	...	...	...	...	...	689
	1996	3 673	283	...	...	...	...	...	...	672
	1997	3 570	283	...	...	...	...	...	...	673
America, North	1994	575 967	17 237	676 551	492 903	311 335	98 825	66 480	668 594	492 313
Amérique du Nord	1995	573 332	17 716	672 864	505 029	302 441	99 557	66 559	680 679	506 149
	1996	590 424	17 387	665 213	516 900	311 368	99 987	63 753	701 207	535 079
	1997	606 037	16 794	677 442	525 022	316 988	105 125	65 144	707 404	526 971
Antigua and Barbuda	1994	...	...	...	...	...	...	...	...	8
Antigua–et–Barbuda	1995	...	...	...	...	...	...	...	...	8
	1996	...	...	...	...	...	...	...	...	8
	1997	...	...	...	...	...	...	...	...	9
Aruba	1994	...	...	...	...	...	...	...	...	36
Aruba	1995	...	...	...	...	...	...	...	...	40
	1996	...	...	...	...	...	...	...	...	40
	1997	...	...	...	...	...	...	...	...	40
Bahamas	1994	...	...	...	...	...	...	...	...	110
Bahamas	1995	...	...	...	...	...	...	...	...	112
	1996	...	...	...	...	...	...	...	...	115
	1997	...	...	...	...	...	...	...	...	122
Barbados	1994	...	...	62	64	181	6	2	21	50
Barbade	1995	...	...	63	68	197	5	2	24	53
	1996	...	...	50	61	195	5	1	27	56
	1997	...	...	45	74	204	5	1	22	58
Belize	1994	...	...	...	...	...	...	...	...	12
Belize	1995	...	...	...	...	...	...	...	...	13
	1996	...	...	...	...	...	...	...	...	13
	1997	...	...	...	...	...	...	...	...	14

63
Production of selected energy commodities
Thousand metric tons of oil equivalent [*cont.*]
Production des principaux biens de l'énergie
Milliers de tonnes d'équivalent pétrole [*suite*]

Region, country or area / Région, pays ou zone	Year / Anneé	Hard coal, lignite & peat Houille, lignite et tourbe	Briquettes & cokes Agglo- mérés et cokes	Crude petroleum & NGL Pétrole brut et GNL	Light petroleum products Produits pétroliers légers	Heavy petroleum products Produits pétroliers lourds	Other petroleum products Autres produits pétroliers	LPG & refinery gas GLP et gaz de raffinerie	Natural gas Gaz naturel	Electrici Electrici
Bermuda	1994	...	...	...	...	...	...	...	...	
Bermudes	1995	...	...	...	...	...	...	...	...	
	1996	...	...	...	...	...	...	...	...	
	1997	...	...	...	...	...	...	...	...	
British Virgin Islands	1994	...	...	...	...	...	...	...	...	
Iles Vierges britaniques	1995	...	...	...	...	...	...	...	...	
	1996	...	...	...	...	...	...	...	...	
	1997	...	...	...	...	...	...	...	...	
Canada	1994	37 509	2 410	107 592	38 224	30 089	10 747	5 928	137 741	64 0
Canada	1995	38 899	2 148	111 464	39 405	29 343	10 477	5 305	146 588	62 7
	1996	39 721	2 196	112 873	40 704	31 945	10 217	5 282	152 161	63 0
	1997	41 103	2 205	118 317	40 408	34 686	11 741	6 101	153 997	63 1
Cayman Islands	1994	...	...	...	...	...	...	...	...	
Iles Caïmanes	1995	...	...	...	...	...	...	...	...	
	1996	...	...	...	...	...	...	...	...	
	1997	...	...	...	...	...	...	...	...	
Costa Rica	1994	...	...	...	164	383	16	4	...	6
Costa Rica	1995	...	...	...	152	523	25	2	...	7
	1996	...	...	...	128	485	23	2	...	8
	1997	...	...	...	135	501	26	2	...	9
Cuba	1994	...	...	1 258	1 764	903	323	106	19	1 0
Cuba	1995	...	...	1 449	1 768	826	294	147	16	1 0
	1996	...	...	1 454	1 752	1 076	264	146	18	1 1
	1997	...	...	1 511	1 146	1 182	196	142	20	1 2
Dominica	1994	...	...	...	...	...	...	...	...	
Dominique	1995	...	...	...	...	...	...	...	...	
	1996	...	...	...	...	...	...	...	...	
	1997	...	...	...	...	...	...	...	...	
Dominican Republic	1994	...	...	...	600	1 400	...	38	...	5
Rép. dominicaine	1995	...	...	...	621	1 444	...	40	...	5
	1996	...	...	...	642	1 490	...	42	...	5
	1997	...	...	...	664	1 567	...	39	...	6
El Salvador	1994	...	...	...	246	528	18	18	...	5
El Salvador	1995	...	...	...	237	436	21	17	...	6
	1996	...	...	...	280	415	29	15	...	6
	1997	...	...	...	212	503	25	16	...	6
Greenland	1994	0	...	...	...	...	...	...	...	
Groenland	1995	0	...	...	...	...	...	...	...	
	1996	0	...	...	...	...	...	...	...	
	1997	0	...	...	...	...	...	...	...	
Grenada	1994	...	...	...	...	...	...	...	...	
Grenade	1995	...	...	...	...	...	...	...	...	
	1996	...	...	...	...	...	...	...	...	
	1997	...	...	...	...	...	...	...	...	
Guadeloupe	1994	...	...	...	...	...	...	...	...	8
Guadeloupe	1995	...	...	...	...	...	...	...	...	9
	1996	...	...	...	...	...	...	...	...	9
	1997	...	...	...	...	...	...	...	...	10
Guatemala	1994	...	...	365	172	566	...	11	9	2
Guatemala	1995	...	...	467	157	573	...	8	10	2
	1996	...	...	729	147	527	...	8	10	3
	1997	...	...	975	154	564	...	5	10	3
Haiti	1994	...	...	...	...	...	...	...	...	2
Haïti	1995	...	...	...	...	...	...	...	...	
	1996	...	...	...	...	...	...	...	...	
	1997	...	...	...	...	...	...	...	...	
Honduras	1994	...	...	...	...	...	...	...	...	2
Honduras	1995	...	...	...	...	...	...	...	...	2
	1996	...	...	...	...	...	...	...	...	2
	1997	...	...	...	...	...	...	...	...	2

63
Production of selected energy commodities
Thousand metric tons of oil equivalent [*cont.*]
Production des principaux biens de l'énergie
Milliers de tonnes d'équivalent pétrole [*suite*]

Region, country or area Région, pays ou zone	Year Anneé	Hard coal, lignite & peat Houille, lignite et tourbe	Briquettes & cokes Agglo- mérés et cokes	Crude petroleum & NGL Pétrole brut et GNL	Light petroleum products Produits pétroliers légers	Heavy petroleum products Produits pétroliers lourds	Other petroleum products Autres produits pétroliers	LPG & refinery gas GLP et gaz de raffinerie	Natural gas Gaz naturel	Electricity Electricité
Jamaica	1994	...	...	...	244	731	18	27	...	411
Jamaïque	1995	...	...	...	246	749	16	23	...	501
	1996	...	...	...	273	770	17	24	...	519
	1997	...	...	...	301	791	14	25	...	538
Martinique	1994	...	...	...	287	428	...	22	...	78
Martinique	1995	...	...	...	293	431	...	22	...	84
	1996	...	...	...	296	433	...	23	...	88
	1997	...	...	...	296	435	...	23	...	93
Mexico	1994	2 859	1 324	164 332	24 948	40 627	3 812	3 868	27 300	17 894
Mexique	1995	2 873	1 432	160 394	24 181	38 880	3 381	3 552	26 791	19 776
	1996	3 153	1 456	165 680	22 162	37 776	1 863	3 216	30 443	19 771
	1997	3 202	1 426	175 074	20 434	38 251	3 404	2 766	31 404	20 813
Montserrat	1994	...	...	...	...	...	...	...	...	1
Montserrat	1995	...	...	...	...	...	...	...	...	1
	1996	...	...	...	...	...	...	...	...	1
	1997	...	...	...	...	...	...	...	...	2
Netherlands Antilles	1994	...	...	...	2 765	7 200	2 380	65	...	122
Antilles néerlandaises	1995	...	...	...	2 771	7 214	2 388	66	...	126
	1996	...	...	...	2 775	7 220	2 394	69	...	127
	1997	...	...	...	2 785	7 224	2 400	70	...	128
Nicaragua	1994	...	...	...	134	487	25	34	...	543
Nicaragua	1995	...	...	...	139	403	23	30	...	579
	1996	...	...	...	144	424	24	32	...	628
	1997	...	...	...	137	575	24	30	...	627
Panama	1994	...	...	...	148	937	10	45	...	299
Panama	1995	...	...	...	125	748	10	43	...	303
	1996	...	...	...	277	1 701	10	61	...	340
	1997	...	...	...	314	1 125	10	57	...	360
Puerto Rico	1994	...	...	...	3 542	3 000	1 569	98	...	1 537
Porto Rico	1995	...	...	...	3 263	3 108	1 620	120	...	1 635
	1996	...	...	...	3 290	3 129	1 627	122	...	1 636
	1997	...	...	...	3 323	3 141	1 635	125	...	1 638
Saint Kitts and Nevis	1994	...	...	...	...	...	...	...	...	6
Saint−Kitts−et−Nevis	1995	...	...	...	...	...	...	...	...	7
	1996	...	...	...	...	...	...	...	...	7
	1997	...	...	...	...	...	...	...	...	8
Saint Lucia	1994	...	...	...	...	...	...	...	...	10
Sainte−Lucie	1995	...	...	...	...	...	...	...	...	10
	1996	...	...	...	...	...	...	...	...	10
	1997	...	...	...	...	...	...	...	...	10
St. Pierre and Miquelon	1994	...	...	...	...	...	...	...	...	4
St.−Pierre−et−Miquelon	1995	...	...	...	...	...	...	...	...	4
	1996	...	...	...	...	...	...	...	...	4
	1997	...	...	...	...	...	...	...	...	4
St. Vincent and Grenadines	1994	...	...	...	...	...	...	...	...	6
St.−Vincent−et−Grenad.	1995	...	...	...	...	...	...	...	...	6
	1996	...	...	...	...	...	...	...	...	7
	1997	...	...	...	...	...	...	...	...	7
Trinidad and Tobago	1994	...	...	6 807	1 546	3 321	162	427	6 126	350
Trinité−et−Tobago	1995	...	...	6 783	1 485	3 262	37	473	6 289	370
	1996	...	...	6 710	1 434	3 613	43	491	7 107	390
	1997	...	...	6 210	1 284	3 583	42	466	7 567	417
United States	1994	535 599	13 503	396 136	414 095	213 824	75 329	55 638	497 378	403 118
Etats−Unis	1995	531 560	14 136	392 244	426 010	207 602	76 747	56 556	500 960	415 892
	1996	547 550	13 735	377 718	438 409	213 464	78 958	54 066	511 441	444 206
	1997	561 732	13 163	375 310	449 214	215 942	81 069	55 118	514 384	434 613

63

Production of selected energy commodities
Thousand metric tons of oil equivalent [cont.]
Production des principaux biens de l'énergie
Milliers de tonnes d'équivalent pétrole [suite]

Region, country or area Région, pays ou zone	Year Anneé	Hard coal, lignite & peat Houille, lignite et tourbe	Briquettes & cokes Agglomérés et cokes	Crude petroleum & NGL Pétrole brut et GNL	Light petroleum products Produits pétroliers légers	Heavy petroleum products Produits pétroliers lourds	Other petroleum products Autres produits pétroliers	LPG & refinery gas GLP et gaz de raffinerie	Natural gas Gaz naturel	Electricit Electricit
U.S. Virgin Islands	1994	...	...	...	3 961	6 729	4 408	147	...	9
Iles Vierges américaines	1995	...	...	...	4 107	6 700	4 513	152	...	9
	1996	...	...	...	4 125	6 707	4 513	154	...	9
	1997	...	...	...	4 141	6 715	4 534	158	...	9
America, South	**1994**	**21 433**	**6 283**	**269 966**	**62 318**	**91 206**	**8 078**	**11 893**	**75 965**	**47 88**
Amérique du Sud	**1995**	**23 395**	**6 246**	**283 637**	**64 941**	**92 776**	**8 053**	**11 092**	**78 715**	**50 89**
	1996	**24 836**	**7 208**	**295 619**	**66 134**	**98 087**	**8 641**	**11 348**	**82 398**	**53 05**
	1997	**28 489**	**7 068**	**314 746**	**69 998**	**103 480**	**9 328**	**11 991**	**91 424**	**55 85**
Argentina	1994	205	447	35 277	8 441	11 649	1 906	1 560	23 800	7 08
Argentine	1995	180	379	37 241	9 005	11 018	1 869	1 544	25 371	6 99
	1996	183	467	41 712	7 765	11 536	1 850	1 507	24 645	7 30
	1997	147	478	44 309	7 489	13 082	2 071	1 465	29 015	7 66
Bolivia	1994	...	...	1 426	519	372	19	52	3 048	24
Bolivie	1995	...	...	1 640	568	354	21	61	3 513	25
	1996	...	...	1 823	620	340	22	59	3 585	27
	1997	...	...	1 803	704	344	19	60	3 203	29
Brazil	1994	2 281	5 207	34 829	19 737	34 910	3 489	6 773	4 289	22 36
Brésil	1995	2 310	5 249	35 867	19 472	34 434	3 307	6 501	4 601	24 13
	1996	2 135	6 096	40 372	20 595	36 932	3 919	6 526	5 157	25 46
	1997	2 509	5 993	43 094	22 578	39 461	4 164	7 138	5 706	27 03
Chile	1994	844	326	1 076	2 600	4 074	121	456	1 739	2 17
Chili	1995	743	301	864	2 706	4 460	130	539	1 672	2 57
	1996	799	318	925	2 980	5 119	121	602	1 830	2 68
	1997	746	304	754	3 165	4 629	133	616	1 795	2 86
Colombia	1994	14 732	303	23 764	5 024	5 821	277	1 254	4 119	3 70
Colombie	1995	16 815	317	30 388	5 279	5 893	281	1 268	4 322	3 89
	1996	19 237	328	32 591	6 079	6 255	281	1 354	4 761	3 85
	1997	21 185	293	33 930	5 729	6 356	295	1 362	4 695	3 98
Ecuador	1994	...	...	17 553	1 632	4 269	141	275	351	70
Equateur	1995	...	...	20 240	1 609	4 536	141	234	364	71
	1996	...	...	19 408	1 906	4 928	89	275	618	79
	1997	...	...	20 289	1 705	5 636	95	224	580	82
Falkland Is. (Malvinas)	1994	3	...	...	...	...	...	...	...	
Iles Falkland (Malvinas)	1995	3	...	...	...	...	...	...	...	
	1996	3	...	...	...	...	...	...	...	
	1997	3	...	...	...	...	...	...	...	
French Guiana	1994	...	...	...	...	...	...	...	...	3
Guyane française	1995	...	...	...	...	...	...	...	...	3
	1996	...	...	...	...	...	...	...	...	3
	1997	...	...	...	...	...	...	...	...	3
Guyana	1994	...	...	...	...	...	...	...	...	2
Guyana	1995	...	...	...	...	...	...	...	...	2
	1996	...	...	...	...	...	...	...	...	3
	1997	...	...	...	...	...	...	...	...	3
Paraguay	1994	...	...	...	77	195	...	2	...	3 13
Paraguay	1995	...	...	...	66	155	...	1	...	3 63
	1996	...	...	...	33	125	...	1	...	4 14
	1997	...	...	...	35	115	...	1	...	4 35
Peru	1994	51	...	6 571	2 364	4 808	65	199	115	1 34
Pérou	1995	98	...	6 338	2 193	4 307	92	228	24	1 50
	1996	40	...	6 245	2 439	4 428	128	228	28	1 48
	1997	15	...	6 201	2 353	4 435	265	279	117	1 54
Suriname	1994	...	...	272	...	...	...	...	...	13
Suriname	1995	...	...	275	...	...	...	...	...	13
	1996	...	...	245	...	...	...	...	...	13
	1997	...	...	246	...	...	...	...	...	14
Uruguay	1994	...	1	...	0	0	0	0	...	65
Uruguay	1995	...	0	...	347	911	43	59	...	54
	1996	...	0	...	348	1 199	61	70	...	57
	1997	...	0	...	360	920	80	81	...	61

63
Production of selected energy commodities
Thousand metric tons of oil equivalent [*cont.*]
Production des principaux biens de l'énergie
Milliers de tonnes d'équivalent pétrole [*suite*]

Region, country or area Région, pays ou zone	Year Anneé	Hard coal, lignite & peat Houille, lignite et tourbe	Briquettes & cokes Agglo– mérés et cokes	Crude petroleum & NGL Pétrole brut et GNL	Light petroleum products Produits pétroliers légers	Heavy petroleum products Produits pétroliers lourds	Other petroleum products Autres produits pétroliers	LPG & refinery gas GLP et gaz de raffinerie	Natural gas Gaz naturel	Electricity Electricité
Venezuela	1994	3 317	0	149 196	21 921	25 108	2 059	1 322	38 505	6 287
Venezuela	1995	3 246	0	150 784	23 695	26 707	2 169	657	38 846	6 439
	1996	2 439	0	152 297	23 368	27 225	2 170	725	41 775	6 249
	1997	3 884	0	164 120	25 880	28 500	2 207	764	46 311	6 475
Asia	**1994**	**938 566**	**116 271**	**1 356 720**	**302 625**	**553 809**	**46 524**	**39 689**	**364 765**	**381 615**
Asie	**1995**	**1 003 485**	**141 640**	**1 367 320**	**320 993**	**568 160**	**48 465**	**42 790**	**392 601**	**407 129**
	1996	**1 036 360**	**141 231**	**1 390 604**	**342 515**	**590 727**	**50 655**	**45 163**	**427 644**	**429 302**
	1997	**1 032 859**	**142 759**	**1 427 901**	**360 857**	**617 036**	**52 473**	**47 735**	**432 270**	**449 348**
Afghanistan	1994	4	...	...	...	...	...	...	163	59
Afghanistan	1995	3	...	...	...	...	...	...	156	54
	1996	2	...	...	...	...	...	...	149	49
	1997	1	...	...	...	...	...	...	137	44
Armenia	1994	...	...	...	...	...	...	...	...	487
Arménie	1995	...	...	...	...	...	...	...	...	531
	1996	...	...	...	...	...	...	...	...	939
	1997	...	...	...	...	...	...	...	...	796
Azerbaijan	1994	...	...	9 582	2 346	6 331	332	242	5 744	1 512
Azerbaïdjan	1995	...	...	9 178	2 318	6 429	208	111	5 983	1 466
	1996	...	...	9 115	1 473	6 103	360	104	5 677	1 469
	1997	...	...	9 087	1 567	6 023	206	103	5 367	1 459
Bahrain	1994	...	...	2 502	4 617	7 254	384	26	5 949	391
Bahreïn	1995	...	...	2 447	5 370	7 046	218	53	6 308	396
	1996	...	...	2 168	4 995	7 714	291	36	6 532	431
	1997	...	...	2 237	5 051	7 375	374	34	6 883	433
Bangladesh	1994	...	...	113	432	260	34	14	5 570	911
Bangladesh	1995	...	...	10	448	304	0	16	6 459	1 005
	1996	...	...	66	418	251	0	14	6 933	1 067
	1997	...	...	44	467	279	0	17	6 813	1 102
Bhutan	1994	45	...	...	...	...	...	...	...	145
Bhoutan	1995	48	...	...	...	...	...	...	...	140
	1996	45	...	...	...	...	...	...	...	170
	1997	38	...	...	...	...	...	...	...	158
Brunei Darussalam	1994	...	...	9 409	355	199	...	12	9 148	133
Brunéi Darussalam	1995	...	...	8 961	373	213	...	11	9 922	140
	1996	...	...	8 669	369	192	...	10	9 955	144
	1997	...	...	8 549	381	204	...	9	9 954	147
Cambodia	1994	...	...	...	0	0	...	...	...	16
Cambodge	1995	...	...	...	0	0	...	...	...	17
	1996	...	...	...	0	0	...	...	...	17
	1997	...	...	...	0	0	...	...	...	18
China ††	1994	619 331	66 411	146 058	34 269	65 539	6 842	9 026	16 347	82 245
Chine ††	1995	679 685	91 677	150 019	36 743	69 668	8 781	10 362	16 699	88 883
	1996	697 801	92 637	157 308	39 937	69 677	8 939	11 092	20 811	95 347
	1997	685 724	93 023	160 714	43 276	72 892	9 180	12 607	23 489	99 932
China, Hong Kong SAR †	1994	...	...	...	...	...	...	...	...	2 299
Chine, Hong Kong RAS †	1995	...	...	...	...	...	...	...	...	2 400
	1996	...	...	...	...	...	...	...	...	2 445
	1997	...	...	...	...	...	...	...	...	2 489
China, Macao SAR	1994	...	...	...	...	...	...	...	...	108
Chine, Macao RAS	1995	...	...	...	...	...	...	...	...	109
	1996	...	...	...	...	...	...	...	...	118
	1997	...	...	...	...	...	...	...	...	121
Cyprus	1994	...	...	...	179	642	35	58	...	231
Chypre	1995	...	...	...	138	619	37	46	...	213
	1996	...	...	...	120	575	30	45	...	223
	1997	...	...	...	174	789	37	56	...	233
Georgia	1994	26	...	74	52	143	...	...	9	585
Géorgie	1995	25	...	47	10	29	...	...	9	593
	1996	13	...	128	0	11	...	...	3	621
	1997	3	...	134	5	17	...	...	3	617

63
Production of selected energy commodities
Thousand metric tons of oil equivalent [*cont.*]
Production des principaux biens de l'énergie
Milliers de tonnes d'équivalent pétrole [*suite*]

Region, country or area Région, pays ou zone	Year Anneé	Hard coal, lignite & peat Houille, lignite et tourbe	Briquettes & cokes Agglo–mérés et cokes	Crude petroleum & NGL Pétrole brut et GNL	Light petroleum products Produits pétroliers légers	Heavy petroleum products Produits pétroliers lourds	Other petroleum products Autres produits pétroliers	LPG & refinery gas GLP et gaz de raffinerie	Natural gas Gaz naturel	Electricity Electricité
India	1994	152 137	6 920	33 512	17 490	29 744	5 187	1 516	15 866	34 13?
Inde	1995	159 140	6 997	35 232	18 113	30 045	5 385	1 674	17 156	37 33?
	1996	170 750	7 579	36 616	19 709	31 967	5 693	2 139	24 389	39 14?
	1997	177 148	7 949	37 596	20 242	34 334	5 492	1 807	17 477	41 67?
Indonesia	1994	21 867	...	102 680	14 396	24 301	1 547	3 683	54 679	6 77?
Indonésie	1995	29 062	...	100 627	13 673	24 997	1 539	3 498	58 364	7 58?
	1996	33 137	...	102 304	17 639	24 726	1 607	3 769	71 245	8 42?
	1997	36 452	...	103 338	16 755	26 307	1 493	3 528	71 248	9 11?
Iran (Islamic Republic of)	1994	905	279	184 261	13 122	28 592	2 810	1 632	37 652	7 05?
Iran (Rép. islamique d')	1995	797	108	184 720	13 487	28 693	2 810	2 093	35 974	7 30?
	1996	848	80	185 914	14 147	30 125	2 901	2 121	37 652	7 81?
	1997	847	80	189 701	14 021	30 536	2 926	2 110	42 312	8 40?
Iraq	1994	...	...	37 415	5 946	15 904	724	653	2 955	2 408
Iraq	1995	...	...	37 767	5 988	15 924	724	653	2 955	2 49?
	1996	...	...	37 970	6 014	16 044	734	653	3 020	2 55?
	1997	...	...	58 241	6 061	16 224	734	664	3 374	2 57?
Israel	1994	84	...	4	4 270	6 657	316	468	18	2 43?
Israël	1995	103	...	7	4 197	6 395	392	500	18	2 61?
	1996	93	...	4	3 974	5 805	363	481	12	2 79?
	1997	104	...	5	4 271	5 769	356	536	12	3 01?
Japan	1994	4 027	26 572	723	80 791	108 694	11 288	13 363	2 227	131 35?
Japon	1995	3 637	26 937	718	82 488	107 511	11 240	13 931	2 164	138 26?
	1996	3 764	26 083	696	83 110	104 966	11 597	14 155	2 185	142 22?
	1997	2 486	26 021	700	87 020	106 468	11 687	14 821	2 233	147 87?
Jordan	1994	...	...	2	949	1 765	160	197	...	43?
Jordanie	1995	...	...	2	1 012	1 871	154	211	...	48?
	1996	...	...	2	1 074	1 877	168	209	...	52?
	1997	...	...	0	1 147	2 001	177	222	...	53?
Kazakhstan	1994	45 981	...	20 414	3 338	7 716	731	87	4 041	5 70?
Kazakhstan	1995	36 642	...	20 647	3 084	6 596	569	67	5 327	5 73?
	1996	33 761	...	23 124	3 175	6 463	547	65	5 875	5 04?
	1997	32 009	...	25 607	2 458	5 854	678	65	7 306	4 47?
Korea, Dem. People's Rep.	1994	61 180	2 236	...	1 235	1 665	...	...	...	3 18?
Corée, Rép. pop. dém. de	1995	60 620	2 205	...	1 220	1 655	...	...	...	3 09?
	1996	59 990	2 173	...	1 204	1 645	...	...	...	3 00?
	1997	59 500	2 142	...	1 173	1 625	...	...	...	2 92?
Korea, Republic of	1994	3 346	9 095	...	22 323	53 135	2 505	1 374	...	26 11?
Corée, Rép. de	1995	2 573	9 287	...	28 429	56 728	2 629	1 498	...	29 30?
	1996	2 227	8 286	...	33 256	62 563	2 950	1 498	...	32 43?
	1997	2 030	8 496	...	43 559	71 601	3 403	1 947	...	34 79?
Kuwait [1]	1994	...	...	104 063	10 390	22 900	370	358	5 564	1 99?
Koweït [1]	1995	...	...	105 368	13 926	22 507	577	361	8 457	2 07?
	1996	...	...	105 549	13 914	21 029	611	363	8 479	2 22?
	1997	...	...	105 734	14 528	24 833	643	373	8 447	2 34?
Kyrgyzstan	1994	479	...	88	...	...	...	...	36	1 11?
Kirghizistan	1995	281	...	89	...	...	...	...	34	1 06?
	1996	238	...	100	...	...	...	...	24	1 18?
	1997	297	...	85	...	...	...	...	37	1 08?
Lao People's Dem. Rep.	1994	1	...	...	...	...	...	...	...	10?
Rép. dém. populaire lao	1995	1	...	...	...	...	...	...	...	9?
	1996	1	...	...	...	...	...	...	...	10?
	1997	1	...	...	...	...	...	...	...	10?
Lebanon	1994	...	0	...	...	...	...	...	...	45?
Liban	1995	...	0	...	...	...	...	...	...	47?
	1996	...	0	...	...	...	...	...	...	52?
	1997	...	0	...	...	...	...	...	...	60?
Malaysia	1994	94	...	33 340	4 257	7 945	318	481	21 540	3 44?
Malaisie	1995	78	...	34 631	4 336	8 192	335	517	32 669	4 01?
	1996	58	...	35 156	4 441	9 047	350	548	32 870	4 55?
	1997	70	...	34 569	4 567	9 842	365	521	37 189	5 04?

63
Production of selected energy commodities
Thousand metric tons of oil equivalent [*cont.*]
Production des principaux biens de l'énergie
Milliers de tonnes d'équivalent pétrole [*suite*]

Region, country or area Région, pays ou zone	Year Anneé	Hard coal, lignite & peat Houille, lignite et tourbe	Briquettes & cokes Agglo– mérés et cokes	Crude petroleum & NGL Pétrole brut et GNL	Light petroleum products Produits pétroliers légers	Heavy petroleum products Produits pétroliers lourds	Other petroleum products Autres produits pétroliers	LPG & refinery gas GLP et gaz de raffinerie	Natural gas Gaz naturel	Electricity Electricité
Maldives	1994	...	...	...	...	...	...	...	...	4
Maldives	1995	...	...	...	...	...	...	...	...	5
	1996	...	...	...	...	...	...	...	...	5
	1997	...	...	...	...	...	...	...	...	6
Mongolia	1994	1 793	...	...	...	...	...	...	...	233
Mongolie	1995	1 730	...	...	...	...	...	...	...	226
	1996	1 828	...	...	...	...	...	...	...	225
	1997	1 687	...	...	...	...	...	...	...	234
Myanmar	1994	32	...	695	251	506	53	2	1 209	309
Myanmar	1995	36	...	483	287	556	52	4	1 355	349
	1996	33	...	407	236	447	50	4	1 469	366
	1997	29	...	401	324	574	53	7	1 587	362
Nepal	1994	...	...	...	...	...	...	...	...	80
Népal	1995	...	...	...	...	...	...	...	...	87
	1996	...	...	...	...	...	...	...	...	105
	1997	...	...	...	...	...	...	...	...	106
Oman	1994	...	...	40 169	762	2 841	25	37	4 188	675
Oman	1995	...	...	42 335	754	2 832	0	66	4 033	722
	1996	...	...	44 040	906	2 835	0	38	4 219	772
	1997	...	...	44 942	856	2 648	0	39	5 003	831
Pakistan	1994	1 671	481	2 816	2 250	3 649	439	44	13 856	4 441
Pakistan	1995	1 439	...	2 762	2 147	3 346	454	40	13 999	4 694
	1996	1 720	...	2 956	2 320	3 619	470	39	14 875	4 981
	1997	1 680	...	2 977	2 149	3 398	436	45	15 351	5 144
Philippines	1994	686	...	223	3 621	8 135	119	299	...	7 138
Philippines	1995	624	...	142	3 987	9 325	123	348	...	7 470
	1996	496	...	47	4 441	12 107	128	424	...	8 096
	1997	517	...	43	4 581	12 255	141	496	...	8 638
Qatar	1994	...	...	20 837	1 014	1 692	...	95	12 582	503
Qatar	1995	...	...	21 354	998	1 778	...	94	12 582	504
	1996	...	...	21 564	1 059	1 888	...	97	12 768	565
	1997	...	...	28 905	999	1 805	...	75	16 682	591
Saudi Arabia [1]	1994	...	...	426 053	25 219	47 296	2 073	979	35 137	8 330
Arabie saoudite [1]	1995	...	...	424 890	24 110	47 227	2 153	990	35 453	8 584
	1996	...	...	428 984	25 929	53 986	2 213	1 001	38 528	8 953
	1997	...	...	424 524	25 076	51 709	2 234	1 001	40 448	9 199
Singapore	1994	...	...	...	20 661	33 341	1 710	609	...	1 778
Singapour	1995	...	...	...	21 528	34 644	1 760	734	...	1 897
	1996	...	...	...	24 286	35 545	1 803	952	...	2 017
	1997	...	...	...	22 299	36 643	1 941	1 050	...	2 252
Sri Lanka	1994	...	...	...	571	1 318	70	63	...	377
Sri Lanka	1995	...	...	...	549	1 204	70	59	...	413
	1996	...	...	...	593	1 382	68	68	...	389
	1997	...	...	...	508	1 235	67	55	...	442
Syrian Arab Republic	1994	...	...	30 251	2 145	9 066	410	185	1 911	1 305
Rép. arabe syrienne	1995	...	...	30 951	2 130	9 105	446	151	2 150	1 316
	1996	...	...	30 454	2 111	9 319	531	149	2 436	1 486
	1997	...	...	28 543	2 194	9 319	550	152	3 344	1 570
Tajikistan	1994	28	1	32	34	...	...	...	30	1 460
Tadjikistan	1995	7	0	24	26	...	...	...	35	1 270
	1996	5	0	20	22	...	...	...	44	1 196
	1997	3	0	25	27	...	...	...	38	1 204
Thailand	1994	7 523	...	3 741	5 687	12 772	291	521	9 112	6 402
Thaïlande	1995	8 105	...	3 682	6 664	14 326	281	770	9 463	7 194
	1996	9 449	...	4 152	8 806	19 860	341	1 017	10 733	7 866
	1997	10 291	...	4 931	9 899	23 036	591	1 147	13 389	8 389
Turkey	1994	12 107	2 089	3 695	6 365	16 076	1 405	1 395	182	6 796
Turquie	1995	12 022	2 193	3 515	6 984	17 523	1 584	1 477	166	7 577
	1996	12 356	2 249	3 499	6 820	16 680	1 723	1 448	188	8 338
	1997	13 107	2 253	3 448	7 388	16 091	1 968	1 491	232	9 109

63
Production of selected energy commodities
Thousand metric tons of oil equivalent [*cont.*]
Production des principaux biens de l'énergie
Milliers de tonnes d'équivalent pétrole [*suite*]

Region, country or area Région, pays ou zone	Year Anneé	Hard coal, lignite & peat Houille, lignite et tourbe	Briquettes & cokes Agglo-mérés et cokes	Crude petroleum & NGL Pétrole brut et GNL	Light petroleum products Produits pétroliers légers	Heavy petroleum products Produits pétroliers lourds	Other petroleum products Autres produits pétroliers	LPG & refinery gas GLP et gaz de raffinerie	Natural gas Gaz naturel	Electricity Electricité
Turkmenistan Turkmenistan	1994	...	...	3 359	734	2 612	...	...	32 495	902
	1995	...	...	3 499	673	2 388	...	...	32 311	843
	1996	...	...	4 024	711	2 561	...	...	31 680	868
	1997	...	...	4 480	804	3 129	...	...	15 578	808
United Arab Emirates Emirats arabes unis	1994	...	...	109 753	3 560	5 454	60	435	24 064	1 623
	1995	...	...	110 865	5 133	4 851	60	431	29 190	1 640
	1996	...	...	111 887	5 275	5 226	60	439	31 501	1 697
	1997	...	...	112 537	5 957	5 829	65	503	33 421	1 769
Uzbekistan Ouzbékistan	1994	1 059	...	7 496	1 698	3 386	1 288	3	41 691	4 110
	1995	836	...	7 652	1 573	4 200	695	47	42 377	4 080
	1996	777	...	7 695	1 648	4 051	723	49	42 591	3 905
	1997	804	...	7 992	1 773	4 027	829	57	44 148	3 960
Viet Nam Viet Nam	1994	3 983	...	6 999	11	27	1	...	2	1 540
	1995	5 845	...	7 619	11	27	1	...	5	1 728
	1996	6 876	...	8 802	11	27	1	...	7	1 937
	1997	7 972	...	10 088	11	27	1	...	11	2 142
Yemen Yémen	1994	...	...	16 294	1 106	1 872	35	65	...	186
	1995	...	...	17 015	1 622	1 611	29	109	...	204
	1996	...	...	17 125	1 647	1 527	40	109	...	201
	1997	...	...	17 671	2 147	3 235	59	109	...	213
Europe Europe	**1994**	**457 429**	**82 717**	**618 990**	**302 949**	**517 247**	**83 163**	**51 270**	**720 193**	**530 614**
	1995	**442 371**	**81 370**	**621 292**	**307 153**	**504 595**	**79 772**	**52 844**	**784 173**	**540 614**
	1996	**428 198**	**77 025**	**633 125**	**310 539**	**515 362**	**74 671**	**53 817**	**817 693**	**556 500**
	1997	**415 733**	**75 376**	**635 807**	**315 716**	**519 363**	**78 102**	**54 781**	**790 549**	**559 907**
Albania Albanie	1994	42	1	535	108	264	35	...	47	336
	1995	41	0	521	154	150	40	...	26	380
	1996	26	0	488	149	155	36	...	21	510
	1997	19	0	360	137	147	14	...	17	488
Austria Autriche	1994	362	975	1 151	3 065	5 162	1 123	381	1 238	4 584
	1995	338	986	1 082	2 824	4 923	1 339	369	1 358	4 866
	1996	288	1 061	991	2 911	5 067	1 519	381	1 367	4 715
	1997	294	1 066	998	3 055	5 501	1 577	400	1 307	4 888
Belarus Bélarus	1994	791	...	2 000	2 655	8 017	595	242	271	2 700
	1995	713	...	1 932	2 679	9 060	639	271	245	2 143
	1996	647	...	1 860	2 600	7 987	681	268	230	2 040
	1997	629	...	1 822	2 760	7 646	756	200	227	2 240
Belgium Belgique	1994	203	2 628	...	9 085	16 941	5 159	1 212	1	13 287
	1995	172	2 602	...	7 999	16 038	4 451	1 039	0	13 601
	1996	151	2 500	...	9 504	19 591	5 517	1 197	2	14 117
	1997	115	2 389	...	9 872	20 086	6 110	1 224	0	14 637
Bosnia and Herzegovina Bosnie-Herzégovine	1994	436	...	...	...	...	...	...	...	165
	1995	511	...	...	...	...	...	...	...	189
	1996	511	...	...	...	...	...	...	...	351
	1997	511	...	...	...	...	...	...	...	429
Bulgaria Bulgarie	1994	4 792	1 209	36	2 017	4 358	131	261	45	5 948
	1995	5 142	1 253	43	2 414	4 640	68	275	40	6 598
	1996	4 689	1 248	32	2 203	4 106	0	238	37	6 820
	1997	4 472	1 241	28	1 978	3 535	0	214	31	6 770
Croatia Croatie	1994	69	175	2 108	1 487	2 759	421	342	1 455	712
	1995	54	0	2 063	1 659	2 909	335	432	1 785	762
	1996	45	0	1 919	1 428	2 869	449	399	1 621	907
	1997	34	0	1 938	1 442	2 985	346	374	1 559	833
Czech Republic République tchèque	1994	29 928	3 511	128	1 813	3 189	1 749	439	212	7 307
	1995	27 381	3 378	146	1 838	3 866	1 495	198	220	7 361
	1996	27 529	3 414	152	1 970	4 239	1 524	245	202	7 762
	1997	26 587	2 955	163	1 856	4 001	1 386	306	181	7 729
Denmark Danemark	1994	6	0	9 116	2 078	6 436	0	464	4 569	3 565
	1995	13	0	9 167	2 676	6 708	0	533	5 010	3 285
	1996	38	0	10 119	3 319	6 934	0	587	5 694	4 728
	1997	14	0	11 358	2 973	5 409	0	527	6 970	4 160

63
Production of selected energy commodities
Thousand metric tons of oil equivalent [*cont.*]
Production des principaux biens de l'énergie
Milliers de tonnes d'équivalent pétrole [*suite*]

Region, country or area Région, pays ou zone	Year Anneé	Hard coal, lignite & peat Houille, lignite et tourbe	Briquettes & cokes Agglo— mérés et cokes	Crude petroleum & NGL Pétrole brut et GNL	Light petroleum products Produits pétroliers légers	Heavy petroleum products Produits pétroliers lourds	Other petroleum products Autres produits pétroliers	LPG & refinery gas GLP et gaz de raffinerie	Natural gas Gaz naturel	Electricity Electricité
Estonia	1994	3 422	23	...	...	298	...	...	...	787
Estonie	1995	3 133	24	...	...	310	...	...	...	747
	1996	3 481	26	...	...	340	...	...	...	783
	1997	3 372	25	...	...	364	...	...	...	793
Faeroe Islands	1994	0	0	...	...	...	...	...	...	15
Iles Féroé	1995	0	0	...	...	...	...	...	...	15
	1996	0	0	...	...	...	...	...	...	15
	1997	0	0	...	...	...	...	...	...	16
Finland	1994	2 130	581	...	5 308	5 461	321	905	...	9 026
Finlande	1995	2 032	580	...	5 652	5 111	264	832	...	8 839
	1996	2 216	573	...	5 669	5 942	274	968	...	9 914
	1997	2 627	554	...	5 049	5 535	335	864	...	9 585
France [2]	1994	5 840	4 274	3 265	27 844	41 453	9 779	5 063	3 210	103 607
France [2]	1995	6 047	4 023	2 945	29 214	40 605	9 736	5 097	3 103	108 121
	1996	5 360	4 022	2 545	30 183	44 261	9 709	5 438	2 674	113 277
	1997	4 501	3 897	2 160	32 797	46 593	10 394	5 489	1 834	113 162
Germany	1994	88 643	13 324	2 938	40 887	63 418	10 178	7 766	15 165	71 629
Allemagne	1995	78 346	12 193	2 926	40 694	59 488	9 513	7 323	15 969	72 816
	1996	73 504	11 653	2 874	40 783	61 407	8 820	7 102	17 462	74 929
	1997	70 140	10 943	2 804	39 658	58 312	8 833	6 759	17 357	76 631
Gibraltar	1994	...	...	...	...	...	...	...	...	9
Gibraltar	1995	...	...	...	...	...	...	...	...	9
	1996	...	...	...	...	...	...	...	...	9
	1997	...	...	...	...	...	...	...	...	10
Greece	1994	7 416	39	533	5 960	9 040	615	935	51	4 039
Grèce	1995	7 508	34	459	6 301	10 054	641	952	48	4 084
	1996	7 783	32	516	6 617	12 190	693	1 082	50	4 583
	1997	7 709	36	467	6 845	12 307	697	1 114	49	4 316
Hungary	1994	2 873	721	2 395	2 691	4 160	781	271	4 169	5 327
Hongrie	1995	2 970	699	3 036	2 665	4 109	933	289	4 204	5 366
	1996	3 123	643	2 862	2 647	3 806	671	280	3 997	5 486
	1997	3 214	615	2 711	2 820	3 971	775	283	3 729	5 475
Iceland	1994	...	...	...	...	...	...	...	...	612
Islande	1995	...	...	...	...	...	...	...	...	652
	1996	...	...	...	...	...	...	...	...	712
	1997	...	...	...	...	...	...	...	...	770
Ireland	1994	1 192	184	...	539	1 664	10	79	2 437	1 478
Irlande	1995	1 785	166	...	594	1 604	64	81	2 497	1 553
	1996	1 261	146	...	619	1 562	26	86	2 409	1 665
	1997	740	134	...	805	2 028	19	101	2 118	1 794
Italy [3]	1994	62	3 705	4 896	29 914	53 904	5 719	5 616	18 378	22 577
Italie [3]	1995	88	3 629	5 237	30 785	51 156	5 297	5 468	18 163	23 526
	1996	69	3 473	5 453	30 327	50 330	5 035	5 345	18 182	23 893
	1997	24	3 653	5 949	32 443	54 328	5 655	5 595	17 533	24 579
Latvia	1994	145	...	...	...	...	...	...	...	382
Lettonie	1995	79	...	...	...	...	...	...	...	342
	1996	88	...	...	...	...	...	...	...	269
	1997	89	...	...	...	...	...	...	...	387
Lithuania	1994	21	...	93	1 322	2 406	289	166	...	2 203
Lituanie	1995	14	...	128	1 119	1 839	411	181	...	3 253
	1996	18	...	155	1 628	2 195	139	255	...	3 870
	1997	20	...	212	1 979	3 018	70	278	...	3 437
Luxembourg	1994	...	0	...	...	...	...	...	...	102
Luxembourg	1995	...	0	...	...	...	...	...	...	106
	1996	...	0	...	...	...	...	...	...	112
	1997	...	0	...	...	...	...	...	...	110
Malta	1994	...	0	...	...	...	...	...	...	130
Malte	1995	...	0	...	...	...	...	...	...	130
	1996	...	0	...	...	...	...	...	...	130
	1997	...	0	...	...	...	...	...	...	130

63
Production of selected energy commodities
Thousand metric tons of oil equivalent [*cont.*]
Production des principaux biens de l'énergie
Milliers de tonnes d'équivalent pétrole [*suite*]

Region, country or area Région, pays ou zone	Year Anneé	Hard coal, lignite & peat Houille, lignite et tourbe	Briquettes & cokes Agglo- mérés et cokes	Crude petroleum & NGL Pétrole brut et GNL	Light petroleum products Produits pétroliers légers	Heavy petroleum products Produits pétroliers lourds	Other petroleum products Autres produits pétroliers	LPG & refinery gas GLP et gaz de raffinerie	Natural gas Gaz naturel	Electricity Electricité
Netherlands	1994	0	1 965	4 393	33 079	31 979	6 126	7 190	66 379	7 542
Pays−Bas	1995	0	1 971	3 539	34 129	33 565	7 302	7 248	67 006	7 650
	1996	0	1 988	3 108	33 926	36 038	5 161	7 885	75 745	8 040
	1997	0	1 977	2 998	33 594	34 647	5 532	7 764	67 209	7 869
Norway [4]	1994	202	0	128 769	5 242	8 530	185	998	30 166	9 750
Norvège [4]	1995	196	0	138 786	4 782	7 557	145	913	17 452	10 588
	1996	154	0	157 100	5 211	8 397	131	1 056	41 517	9 007
	1997	259	0	156 795	5 344	8 928	166	1 106	45 696	9 592
Poland	1994	89 456	7 707	284	4 839	8 337	1 115	451	3 409	11 638
Pologne	1995	90 475	7 743	292	4 742	8 682	1 087	477	3 486	11 951
	1996	91 306	6 927	317	5 301	9 249	1 433	505	3 604	12 309
	1997	91 110	7 153	289	4 947	9 421	1 604	610	3 560	12 275
Portugal	1994	60	194	...	4 574	8 070	576	817	...	2 723
Portugal	1995	0	222	...	4 945	7 754	473	459	...	2 892
	1996	0	222	...	4 596	6 828	777	413	...	3 006
	1997	0	228	...	5 039	7 026	791	494	...	2 979
Republic of Moldova	1994	...	...	...	...	...	...	...	...	707
République de Moldova	1995	...	...	...	...	...	...	...	...	522
	1996	...	...	...	...	...	...	...	...	526
	1997	...	...	...	...	...	...	...	...	453
Romania	1994	7 315	1 821	6 790	4 342	8 123	1 258	1 247	14 824	4 741
Roumanie	1995	7 364	2 132	6 968	4 375	7 726	1 358	1 314	14 446	5 096
	1996	7 531	1 986	6 869	4 048	6 645	1 661	1 087	13 764	5 516
	1997	6 229	2 089	6 768	3 998	6 073	1 267	1 147	11 908	5 854
Russian Federation	1994	113 188	16 961	315 711	41 851	119 080	21 594	7 111	474 964	92 364
Fédération de Russie	1995	110 329	19 449	305 056	43 092	115 285	17 795	9 441	542 156	91 297
	1996	107 144	17 745	299 448	41 104	112 399	16 162	9 421	528 792	91 846
	1997	101 955	16 753	303 949	40 803	112 138	16 921	10 111	507 729	90 715
Slovakia	1994	692	1 210	60	835	2 806	605	104	225	4 240
Slovaquie	1995	1 101	1 201	62	894	2 758	1 616	104	267	4 253
	1996	1 121	1 102	71	982	2 884	899	129	244	4 134
	1997	1 146	1 116	64	964	2 945	1 379	129	225	4 014
Slovenia	1994	1 055	...	2	163	214	3	...	11	1 888
Slovénie	1995	1 062	...	2	232	369	4	...	16	1 919
	1996	1 037	...	1	219	312	3	...	11	1 892
	1997	1 077	...	1	174	375	3	...	10	2 006
Spain	1994	9 880	2 165	959	16 473	30 683	5 621	3 347	200	23 516
Espagne	1995	9 536	1 763	793	16 544	30 579	5 720	3 470	416	24 024
	1996	9 353	1 745	658	16 205	29 975	5 067	3 147	467	24 811
	1997	9 293	1 914	517	16 652	32 313	5 090	3 363	178	25 980
Sweden	1994	283	764	5	5 538	12 523	1 045	297	...	25 033
Suède	1995	304	770	4	5 930	12 177	1 113	251	...	24 816
	1996	351	770	4	6 358	13 006	1 104	283	...	24 880
	1997	252	777	0	6 485	13 907	1 113	295	...	25 058
Switzerland [5]	1994	...	...	...	1 477	2 927	146	396	1	9 959
Suisse [5]	1995	...	...	...	1 418	2 806	154	360	0	9 757
	1996	...	...	...	1 590	3 214	134	420	0	9 283
	1997	...	...	...	1 682	2 873	126	424	0	9 823
TFYR Macedonia	1994	1 849	...	...	83	97	0	2	...	474
L'ex−R.y. Macédonie	1995	1 954	...	...	23	88	0	1	...	526
	1996	1 926	...	...	61	611	0	8	...	558
	1997	1 806	...	...	37	348	0	3	...	578
Ukraine	1994	48 636	13 975	4 199	4 299	13 035	1 729	539	16 478	29 432
Ukraine	1995	43 209	12 393	4 057	3 676	11 188	1 431	460	16 926	29 036
	1996	39 011	11 232	4 097	2 942	8 946	1 068	357	17 156	29 500
	1997	39 611	11 326	4 127	3 594	8 124	996	341	16 898	29 132
United Kingdom	1994	28 266	4 607	127 547	43 053	41 248	6 040	4 619	61 539	43 112
Royaume−Uni	1995	31 955	4 161	130 981	42 725	40 747	6 124	4 995	68 535	44 345
	1996	30 244	4 515	130 458	44 758	43 019	5 658	5 206	81 842	46 320
	1997	29 218	4 536	128 350	44 880	43 148	5 854	5 213	83 605	46 745

63
Production of selected energy commodities
Thousand metric tons of oil equivalent [*cont.*]
Production des principaux biens de l'énergie
Milliers de tonnes d'équivalent pétrole [*suite*]

Region, country or area Région, pays ou zone	Year Anneé	Hard coal, lignite & peat Houille, lignite et tourbe	Briquettes & cokes Agglo- mérés et cokes	Crude petroleum & NGL Pétrole brut et GNL	Light petroleum products Produits pétroliers légers	Heavy petroleum products Produits pétroliers lourds	Other petroleum products Autres produits pétroliers	LPG & refinery gas GLP et gaz de raffinerie	Natural gas Gaz naturel	Electricity Electricité
Yugoslavia	1994	8 174	...	1 078	329	663	214	11	748	2 969
Yougoslavie	1995	8 523	...	1 066	376	740	225	12	799	3 197
	1996	8 193	...	1 030	684	859	321	29	604	3 275
	1997	8 668	...	979	1 053	1 330	293	51	619	3 466
Oceania	**1994**	**121 338**	**3 076**	**34 042**	**20 452**	**14 295**	**3 118**	**2 293**	**29 518**	**19 739**
Océanie	**1995**	**133 519**	**3 115**	**33 987**	**20 666**	**14 631**	**3 142**	**2 271**	**32 075**	**20 128**
	1996	**135 798**	**3 040**	**34 078**	**21 348**	**14 896**	**3 339**	**2 410**	**33 411**	**20 315**
	1997	**145 102**	**2 903**	**34 301**	**21 625**	**15 426**	**3 243**	**2 475**	**33 615**	**20 850**
American Samoa	1994	...	...	...	...	...	...	...	...	11
Samoa américaines	1995	...	...	...	...	...	...	...	...	11
	1996	...	...	...	...	...	...	...	...	11
	1997	...	...	...	...	...	...	...	...	11
Australia	1994	119 647	3 076	26 614	17 799	12 167	2 891	2 063	24 986	14 404
Australie	1995	131 568	3 115	27 369	18 209	12 632	2 900	2 106	27 776	14 908
	1996	133 798	3 040	27 957	18 989	12 947	3 105	2 219	28 507	15 277
	1997	143 212	2 903	27 559	19 122	13 272	3 044	2 225	28 397	15 741
Cook Islands	1994	...	...	...	...	...	...	...	...	1
Iles Cook	1995	...	...	...	...	...	...	...	...	1
	1996	...	...	...	...	...	...	...	...	1
	1997	...	...	...	...	...	...	...	...	1
Fiji	1994	...	...	...	...	...	...	...	...	45
Fidji	1995	...	...	...	...	...	...	...	...	47
	1996	...	...	...	...	...	...	...	...	47
	1997	...	...	...	...	...	...	...	...	47
French Polynesia	1994	...	...	...	...	...	...	...	...	29
Polynésie française	1995	...	...	...	...	...	...	...	...	30
	1996	...	...	...	...	...	...	...	...	31
	1997	...	...	...	...	...	...	...	...	31
Guam	1994	...	...	...	...	...	...	...	...	69
Guam	1995	...	...	...	...	...	...	...	...	71
	1996	...	...	...	...	...	...	...	...	71
	1997	...	...	...	...	...	...	...	...	71
Kiribati	1994	...	...	...	...	...	...	...	...	1
Kiribati	1995	...	...	...	...	...	...	...	...	1
	1996	...	...	...	...	...	...	...	...	1
	1997	...	...	...	...	...	...	...	...	1
Nauru	1994	...	...	...	...	...	...	...	...	3
Nauru	1995	...	...	...	...	...	...	...	...	3
	1996	...	...	...	...	...	...	...	...	3
	1997	...	...	...	...	...	...	...	...	3
New Caledonia	1994	...	...	...	...	...	...	...	...	110
Nouvelle – Caledonie	1995	...	...	...	...	...	...	...	...	142
	1996	...	...	...	...	...	...	...	...	135
	1997	...	...	...	...	...	...	...	...	135
New Zealand	1994	1 691	0	1 929	2 632	2 097	227	230	4 458	4 883
Nouvelle – Zélande	1995	1 951	0	1 619	2 437	1 969	242	166	4 222	4 728
	1996	2 000	0	2 121	2 338	1 919	234	191	4 826	4 553
	1997	1 889	0	2 783	2 482	2 122	198	250	5 140	4 623
Niue	1994	...	...	...	...	...	...	...	...	0
Niue	1995	...	...	...	...	...	...	...	...	0
	1996	...	...	...	...	...	...	...	...	0
	1997	...	...	...	...	...	...	...	...	0
Palau	1994	...	...	...	...	...	...	...	...	17
Palaos	1995	...	...	...	...	...	...	...	...	18
	1996	...	...	...	...	...	...	...	...	18
	1997	...	...	...	...	...	...	...	...	18
Papua New Guinea	1994	...	...	5 499	21	30	...	...	74	154
Papouasie – Nouv. – Guinée	1995	...	...	4 999	21	30	...	...	76	154
	1996	...	...	3 999	21	30	...	...	78	154
	1997	...	...	3 959	21	32	...	...	78	154

63
Production of selected energy commodities
Thousand metric tons of oil equivalent [*cont.*]
Production des principaux biens de l'énergie
Milliers de tonnes d'équivalent pétrole [*suite*]

Region, country or area Région, pays ou zone	Year Anneé	Hard coal, lignite & peat Houille, lignite et tourbe	Briquettes & cokes Agglo-mérés et cokes	Crude petroleum & NGL Pétrole brut et GNL	Light petroleum products Produits pétroliers légers	Heavy petroleum products Produits pétroliers lourds	Other petroleum products Autres produits pétroliers	LPG & refinery gas GLP et gaz de raffinerie	Natural gas Gaz naturel	Electricity Electricité
Samoa	1994	...	...	...	...	...	...	...	...	6
Samoa	1995	...	...	...	...	...	...	...	...	6
	1996	...	...	...	...	...	...	...	...	6
	1997	...	...	...	...	...	...	...	...	6
Solomon Islands	1994	...	...	...	...	...	...	...	...	3
Iles Salomon	1995	...	...	...	...	...	...	...	...	3
	1996	...	...	...	...	...	...	...	...	3
	1997	...	...	...	...	...	...	...	...	3
Tonga	1994	...	...	...	...	...	...	...	...	2
Tonga	1995	...	...	...	...	...	...	...	...	3
	1996	...	...	...	...	...	...	...	...	3
	1997	...	...	...	...	...	...	...	...	3
Vanuatu	1994	...	...	...	...	...	...	...	...	2
Vanuatu	1995	...	...	...	...	...	...	...	...	3
	1996	...	...	...	...	...	...	...	...	3
	1997	...	...	...	...	...	...	...	...	3

Source:
United Nations Secretariat, "Energy Statistics Yearbook 1997" and the energy statistics database of the Statistics Division.

† For information on recent changes in country or area nomenclature pertaining to former Czechoslovakia, Germany, Hong Kong Special Administrative Region (SAR) of China, Macao Special Administrative Region of China (SAR), SFR of Yugoslavia and former USSR, see Annex I – Country or area nomenclature, regional and other groupings.

†† For statistical purposes, the data for China do not include those for the Hong Kong Special Administrative Region (Hong Kong SAR), Macao Special Administrative Region (Macao SAR) and Taiwan province of China.

1 Including part of the Neutral Zone.
2 Including Monaco.
3 Including San Marino.
4 Including Svalbard and Jan Mayen Islands.
5 Including Liechtenstein.

Source:
Secrétariat de l'Organisation des Nations Unies, "Annuaire des statistique de l'énergie 1997" et la base de données pour les statistiques énergétiques de la Division de statistique.

† Pour les modifications récentes de nomenclature de pays ou de zone ou de zone concernant l'Allemagne, Hong Kong (Région administrative spéciale de Chine), Macao (Région administrative spéciale de Chine), l'ex Tchécoslovaquie, Rfs de Yougoslavie et l'ex–URSS, voir annexe I – Nomenclature des pays ou des zones, groupements régionaux et autres groupements.

†† Les données statistiques relatives à la Chine ne comprennent pas celles qu concernent la région administrative spéciale de Hong Kong (la RAS de Hong Kong), la région administrative spéciale de Macao (la RAS de Macao) et la province chinoise de Taiwan.

1 Y compris une partie de la Zone Neutral.
2 Y compris Monaco.
3 Y compris Saint–Marin.
4 Y compris îles Svalbard et Jan Mayen.
5 Y compris Liechtenstein.

Technical notes, tables 62 and 63

Tables 62 and 63: Data are presented in metric tons of oil equivalent (TOE), to which the individual energy commodities are converted in the interests of international uniformity and comparability.

To convert from original units to TOE, the data in original units (metric tons, terajoules, kilowatt hours, cubic metres) are multiplied by conversion factors. For a list of the relevant conversion factors and a detailed description of methods, see the United Nations *Energy Statistics Yearbook* and related methodological publications [22, 42, 43].

Table 62: Included in the production of commercial primary energy for *solids* are hard coal, lignite, peat and oil shale; *liquids* are comprised of crude petroleum and natural gas liquids; *gas* comprises natural gas; and *electricity* is comprised of primary electricity generation from hydro, nuclear, geothermal, wind, tide, wave and solar sources.

In general, data on stocks refer to changes in stocks of producers, importers and/or industrial consumers at the beginning and end of each year.

International trade of energy commodities is based on the "general trade" system, that is, all goods entering and leaving the national boundary of a country are recorded as imports and exports.

Sea/air bunkers refer to the amounts of fuels delivered to ocean-going ships or aircraft of all flags engaged in international traffic. Consumption by ships engaged in transport in inland and coastal waters, or by aircraft engaged in domestic flights, is not included.

Data on consumption refer to "apparent consumption" and are derived from the formula "production + imports - exports - bunkers +/- stock changes". Accordingly, the series on apparent consumption may in some cases represent only an indication of the magnitude of actual gross inland availability.

Included in the consumption of commercial energy for *solids* are consumption of primary forms of solid fuels, net imports and changes in stocks of secondary fuels; *liquids* are comprised of consumption of energy petroleum products including feedstocks, natural gasolene, condensate, refinery gas and input of crude petroleum to thermal power plants; *gases* include the consumption of natural gas, net imports and changes in stocks of gasworks and coke-oven gas; and *electricity* is comprised of production of primary electricity and net imports of electricity.

Table 63: The definitions of the energy commodities are as follows:

— Hard coal: Coal that has a high degree of coalification with a gross calorific value above 23,865 KJ/kg (5,700 kcal/kg) on an ash-free but moist basis, and a mean random reflectance of vitrinite of at least 0.6. Slurries, middlings and

Notes techniques, tableaux 62 et 63

Tableaux 62 et 63: Les données relatives aux divers produits énergétiques ont été converties en tonnes d'équivalent pétrole (TEP), dans un souci d'uniformité et pour permettre les comparaisons entre la production de différents pays.

Pour passer des unités de mesure d'origine à l'unité commune, les données en unités d'origine (tonnes, terajoules, kilowatt-heures, mètres cubes) sont multipliées pour les facteurs de conversion. Pour une liste des facteurs de conversion appropriée et pour des descriptions détaillées des méthodes appliquées, se reporter à *l'Annuaire des statistiques de l'énergie* des Nations Unies et aux publications méthodologiques connexes [22, 42, 43].

Tableau 62: Sont compris dans la production d'énergie primaire commerciale: pour *les solides*, la houille, la lignite, la tourbe et le schiste bitumineux; pour *les liquides*, le pétrole brut et les liquides de gaz naturel; pour *les gaz*, le gaz naturel; pour *l'électricité*, l'électricité primaire de source hydraulique, nucléaire, géothermique, éolienne, marémotrice, des vagues et solaire.

En général, les variations des stocks se rapportent aux différences entre les stocks des producteurs, des importateurs ou des consommateurs industriels au début et à la fin de chaque année.

Le commerce international des produits énergétiques est fondé sur le système du "commerce général", c'est-à-dire que tous les biens entrant sur le territoire national d'un pays ou en sortant sont respectivement enregistrés comme importations et exportations.

Les soutages maritimes/aériens se rapportent aux quantités de combustibles livrées aux navires de mer et aéronefs assurant des liaisons commerciales internationales, quel que soit leur pavillon. La consommation des navires effectuant des opérations de transport sur les voies navigables intérieures ou dans les eaux côtières n'est pas incluse, non plus que celle des aéronefs effectuant des vols intérieurs.

Les données sur la consommation se rapportent à la "consommation apparente" et sont obtenues par la formule "production + importations - exportations - soutage +/- variations des stocks". En conséquence, les séries relatives à la consommation apparente peuvent occasionnellement ne donner qu'une indication de l'ordre de grandeur des disponibilités intérieures brutes réelles.

Sont compris dans la consommation d'énergie commerciale: pour *les solides*, la consommation de combustibles solides primaires, les importations nettes et les variations de stocks de combustibles solides secondaires; pour *les liquides*, la consommation de produits pétroliers énergétiques y compris les charges d'alimentation des usines de traitement, l'essence naturelle, le condensat et le gaz de raffinerie ainsi que le pétrole brut consommé dans les centrales thermiques pour la production d'électricité; pour *les gaz*, la consommation de gaz naturel, les importations nettes et

other low-grade coal products, which cannot be classified according to the type of coal from which they are obtained, are included under hard coal.

— Lignite: Non-agglomerating coal with a low degree of coalification which retained the anatomical structure of the vegetable matter from which it was formed. Its gross calorific value is less than 17,435 KJ/kg (4,165 kcal/kg), and it contains greater than 31 per cent volatile matter on a dry mineral matter free basis.

— Peat: A solid fuel formed from the partial decomposition of dead vegetation under conditions of high humidity and limited air access (initial stage of coalification). Only peat used as fuel is included.

— Patent fuel (hard coal briquettes): A composition fuel manufactured from coal fines by shaping with the addition of a binding agent (pitch).

— Lignite briquettes: A composition fuel manufactured from lignite. The lignite is crushed, dried and molded under high pressure into an even-shaped briquette without the addition of binders.

— Peat briquettes: A composition fuel manufactured from peat. Raw peat, after crushing and drying, is molded under high pressure into an even-shaped briquette without the addition of binders.

— Coke: The solid residue obtained from coal or lignite by heating it to a high temperature in the absence or near absence of air. It is high in carbon and low in moisture and volatile matter. Several categories are distinguished: coke-oven coke; gas coke; and brown coal coke.

— Crude oil: A mineral oil consisting of a mixture of hydrocarbons of natural origin, yellow to black in color, of variable density and viscosity. Data in this category also includes lease or field condensate (separator liquids) which is recovered from gaseous hydrocarbons in lease separation facilities, as well as synthetic crude oil, mineral oils extracted from bituminous minerals such as shales and bituminous sand, and oils from coal liquefaction.

— Natural gas liquids (NGL): Liquid or liquefied hydrocarbons produced in the manufacture, purification and stabilization of natural gas. NGLs include, but are not limited to, ethane, propane, butane, pentane, natural gasolene, and plant condensate.

— Light petroleum products: Light products are defined in the table as liquid products obtained by distillation of crude petroleum at temperatures between 30°C and 350°C, and/or which have a specific gravity between 0.625 and 0.830. They comprise: aviation gasolene; motor gasolene; natural gasolene; jet fuel; kerosene; naphtha; and white spirit/industrial spirit.

— Heavy petroleum products: are defined in the table as products obtained by the distillation of crude petroleum at temperatures above 350°C, and which have a specific gravity higher than 0.83. Products which are

les variations de stocks de gaz d'usines à gaz et de gaz de cokerie; pour *l'électricité*, la production d'électricité primaire et les importations nettes d'électricité.

Tableau 63: Les définitions des produits énergétiques sont données ci-après :

— Houille: Charbon à haut degré de houillification et de pouvoir calorifique brut supérieur à 23 865 kJ/kg (5 700 kcal/kg), valeur mesurée pour un combustible exempt de cendres, mais humide et ayant un indice moyen de réflectance de la vitrinite au moins égal à 0,6. Les schlamms, les mixtes et autres produits du charbon de faible qualité qui ne peuvent être classés en fonction du type de charbon dont ils sont dérivés, sont inclus dans cette rubrique.

— Lignite: Le charbon non agglutinant d'un faible degré de houillification qui a gardé la structure anatomique des végétaux dont il est issu. Son pouvoir calorifique supérieur est inférieur à 17 435 kJ/kg (4 165 kcal/kg) et il contient plus de 31% de matières volatiles sur produit sec exempt de matières minérales.

— Tourbe: Combustible solide issu de la décomposition partielle de végétaux morts dans des conditions de forte humidité et de faible circulation d'air (phase initiale de la houillification). N'est prise en considération ici que la tourbe utilisée comme combustible.

— Agglomérés (briquettes de houille): Combustibles composites fabriqués par moulage au moyen de fines de charbon avec l'addition d'un liant (brai).

— Briquettes de lignite: Combustibles composites fabriqués au moyen de lignite. Le lignite est broyé, séché et moulé sous pression élevée pour donner une briquette de forme régulière sans l'addition d'un élément liant.

— Briquettes de tourbe: Combustibles composites fabriqués au moyen de tourbe. La tourbe brute, après broyage et séchage, est moulée sous pression élevée pour donner une briquette de forme régulière sans l'addition d'un élément liant.

— Coke: Résidu solide obtenu lors de la distillation de houille ou de lignite en l'absence totale ou presque total d'air. Il a un haut contenu de carbone, et a peu d'humidité et matières volatiles. On distingue plusieurs catégories de coke: coke de four; coke de gaz; et coke de lignite.

— Pétrole brut: Huile minérale constituée d'un mélange d'hydrocarbures d'origine naturelle, de couleur variant du jaune au noir, d'une densité et d'une viscosité variable. Figurent également dans cette rubrique les condensats directement récupérés sur les sites d'exploitation des hydrocarbures gazeux (dans les installations prévues pour la séparation des phases liquide et gazeuse), le pétrole brut synthétique, les huiles minérales brutes extraites des roches bitumineuses telles que schistes, sables asphaltiques et les huiles issues de la liquéfaction du charbon.

— Liquides de gaz naturel (LGN): Hydrocarbures liquides ou liquéfiés produits lors de la fabrication, de la purification et de la stabilisation du gaz naturel. Les liquides de gaz naturel comprennent l'éthane, le propane,

not used for energy purposes, such as insulating oils, lubricants, paraffin wax, bitumen and petroleum coke, are excluded. Heavy products comprise residual fuel oil and gas-diesel oil (distillate fuel oil).

— Liquefied petroleum gas (LPG): Hydrocarbons which are gaseous under conditions of normal temperature and pressure but are liquefied by compression or cooling to facilitate storage, handling and transportation. It comprises propane, butane, or a combination of the two. Also included is ethane from petroleum refineries or natural gas producers' separation and stabilization plants.

— Refinery gas: Non-condensable gas obtained during distillation of crude oil or treatment of oil products (e.g. cracking) in refineries. It consists mainly of hydrogen, methane, ethane and olefins.

— Natural gas: Gases consisting mainly of methane occurring naturally in underground deposits. It includes both non-associated gas (originating from fields producing only hydrocarbons in gaseous form) and associated gas (originating from fields producing both liquid and gaseous hydrocarbons), as well as methane recovered from coal mines and sewage gas. Production of natural gas refers to dry marketable production, measured after purification and extraction of natural gas liquids and sulphur. Extraction losses and the amounts that have been reinjected, flared, and vented are excluded from the data on production.

— Electricity production refers to gross production, which includes the consumption by station auxiliaries and any losses in the transformers that are considered integral parts of the station. Included also is total electric energy produced by pumping installations without deduction of electric energy absorbed by pumping.

le butane, le pentane, l'essence naturelle et les condensats d'usine, sans que la liste soit limitative.

— Produits pétroliers légers: Les produits légers sont définis ici comme des produits liquides obtenus par distillation du pétrole brut à des températures comprises entre 30°C et 350°C et/ou ayant une densité comprise entre 0,625 et 0,830. Ces produits sont les suivants: l'essence aviation; l'essence auto; l'essence naturelle; les carburéacteurs du type essence et du type kérosène; le pétrole lampant; les naphtas; et le white spirit/essences spéciales.

— Produits pétroliers lourds sont définis ici comme des produits obtenus par distillation du pétrole brut à des températures supérieures à 350°C et ayant une densité supérieure à 0,83. En sont exclus les produits qui ne sont pas utilisés à des fins énergétiques, tels que les huiles isolantes, les lubrifiants, les paraffines, le bitume et le coke de pétrole. Les produits lourds comprennent le mazout résiduel et le gazole/carburant diesel (mazout distillé).

— Gaz de pétrole liquéfiés (GPL): Hydrocarbures qui sont à l'état gazeux dans des conditions de température et de pression normales mais sont liquéfiés par compression ou refroidissement pour en faciliter l'entreposage, la manipulation et le transport. Dans cette rubrique figurent le propane et le butane ou un mélange de ces deux hydrocarbures. Est également inclus l'éthane produit dans les raffineries ou dans les installations de séparation et de stabilisation des producteurs de gaz naturel.

— Gaz de raffinerie: Comprend les gaz non condensables obtenus dans les raffineries lors de la distillation du pétrole brut ou du traitement des produits pétroliers (par craquage par exemple). Il s'agit principalement d'hydrogène, de méthane, d'éthane et d'oléfines.

— Gaz naturel: Est constitué de gaz, méthane essentiellement, extraits de gisements naturels souterrains. Il peut s'agir aussi bien de gaz non associé (provenant de gisements qui produisent uniquement des hydrocarbures gazeux) que de gaz associé (provenant de gisements qui produisent à la fois des hydrocarbures liquides et gazeux) ou de méthane récupéré dans les mines de charbon et le gaz de gadoues. La production de gaz naturel se rapporte à la production de gaz commercialisable sec, mesurée après purification et extraction des condensats de gaz naturel et du soufre. Les quantités réinjectées, brûlées à la torchère ou éventées et les pertes d'extraction sont exclus des données sur la production.

— Production d'électricité se rapporte à la production brute, qui comprend la consommation des équipements auxiliaires des centrales et les pertes au niveau des transformateurs considérés comme faisant partie intégrante de ces centrales, ainsi que la quantité totale d'énergie électrique produits par les installations de pompage sans déductions de l'énergie électrique absorbée par ces dernières.

64
Land use
Utilisation des terres

Country or area Pays ou zone	Land use, 10³ hectares (1998) Utilisation des terres, 10³ hectares (1998)				Net change, 10³ ha (1990 − 1998) Variation nette, 10³ ha (1990−1998)	
	Total area Superficie totale	Total land Superficie totale des terres	Arable land Terres arables	Permanent crops Cultures permanentes	Arable land Terres arables	Permanent crops Cultures permanentes
Africa · Afrique						
Algeria Algérie	238174	238174	7661	512	580	−42
Angola Angola	124670	124670	3000[1]	500[1]	100	0
Benin Bénin	11262	11062	1700[1]	150[1]	85	45
Botswana Botswana	58173	56673	343[1]	3[1]	−75	0
British Indian Ocean Terr. Terr. brit. de l'océan indien	8	8	...	...	...	...
Burkina Faso Burkina Faso	27400	27360	3400[1]	50[1]	−120	−5
Burundi Burundi	2783	2568	770[1]	330[1]	−40	−10
Cameroon Cameroun	47544	46540	5960[1]	1200[1]	20	−30
Cape Verde Cap−Vert	403	403	39[1]	2[1]	−2	0
Central African Rep. Rép. centrafricaine	62298	62298	1930[1]	90[1]	10	4
Chad Tchad	128400	125920	3520[1]	30[1]	247	3
Comoros Comores	223	223	78[1]	40[1]	0	5
Congo Congo	34200	34150	173[1]	45[1]	19	3
Côte d'Ivoire Côte d'Ivoire	32246	31800	2950[1]	4400[1]	520	900
Dem. Rep. of the Congo Rép. dém. du Congo	234486	226705	6700[1]	1180[1]	30	−10
Djibouti Djibouti	2320	2318	...	...	...	...
Egypt Egypte	100145	99545	2834[1]	466[1]	550	102
Equatorial Guinea Guinée équatoriale	2805	2805	130[1]	100[1]	0	0
Eritrea Erythrée	11760	10100	498	2	...	...
Ethiopia Ethiopie	110430	100000	9950[1]	650[1]	...	...
Gabon Gabon	26767	25767	325[1]	170[1]	30	8
Gambia Gambie	1130	1000	195[1]	5[1]	13	0
Ghana Ghana	23854	22754	3600	1700	900	200
Guinea Guinée	24586	24572	885[1]	600[1]	157	100
Guinea−Bissau Guinée−Bissau	3612	2812	300[1]	50[1]	0	10
Kenya Kenya	58037	56914	4000[1]	520[1]	0	20
Lesotho Lesotho	3035	3035	325[1]	...	8	...
Liberia Libéria	11137	9632	190[1]	200[1]	20	−30
Libyan Arab Jamahiriya Jamah. arabe libyenne	175954	175954	1815[1]	300[1]	10	0

64
Land use [*cont.*]
Utilisation des terres [*suite*]

Country or area Pays ou zone	Land use, 10³ hectares (1998) Utilisation des terres, 10³ hectares (1998)				Net change, 10³ ha (1990 − 1998) Variation nette, 10³ ha (1990−1998)	
	Total area Superficie totale	Total land Superficie totale des terres	Arable land Terres arables	Permanent crops Cultures permanentes	Arable land Terres arables	Permanent crops Cultures permanentes
Madagascar Madagascar	58704	58154	2565[1]	543[1]	63	−57
Malawi Malawi	11848	9408	1875[1]	125[1]	60	10
Mali Mali	124019	122019	4606[1]	44[1]	2553	4
Mauritania Mauritanie	102552	102522	488[1]	12[1]	88	6
Mauritius Maurice	204[6]	203	100[1]	6[1]	0	0
Morocco Maroc	44655	44630	9033	943	326	207
Mozambique Mozambique	80159	78409	3120[1]	230[1]	50	0
Namibia Namibie	82429	82329	816[1]	4[1]	156	2
Niger Niger	126700	126670	4994[1]	6[1]	1394	1
Nigeria Nigéria	92377	91077	28200[1]	2538[1]	−1339	3
Reunion Réunion	251	250	33	5	−14	0
Rwanda Rwanda	2634	2467	820[1]	250[1]	−60	−55
Saint Helena Sainte−Hélène	31	31	4[1]	...	2	...
Sao Tome and Principe Sao Tomé−et−Principe	96	96	2[1]	39[1]	0	−1
Senegal Sénégal	19672	19253	2230[1]	36[1]	−95	11
Seychelles Seychelles	45	45	1[1]	6[1]	0	1
Sierra Leone Sierra Leone	7174	7162	484[1]	56[1]	−2	2
Somalia Somalie	63766	62734	1040[1]	22[1]	18	2
South Africa Afrique du Sud	122104	122104	14791[1]	959	1351	99
Sudan Soudan	250581	237600	16700[1]	200[1]	3700	−35
Swaziland Swaziland	1736	1720	168[1]	12[1]	−12	0
Togo Togo	5679	5439	2200[1]	100[1]	100	10
Tunisia Tunisie	16361	15536	2900[1]	2000[1]	−9	58
Uganda Ouganda	24104	19965	5060[1]	1750[1]	60	40
United Rep. Tanzania Rép.−Unie de Tanzanie	94509	88359	3750[1]	900[1]	250	0
Zambia Zambie	75261	74339	5260[1]	19[1]	11	0
Zimbabwe Zimbabwe	39076	38685	3220[1]	130[1]	330	10
America, North · Amérique du Nord						
Antigua and Barbuda Antigua−et−Barbuda	44	44	8[1]	...	0	...
Aruba Aruba	19	19	2[1]	...	0	...
Bahamas Bahamas	1388	1001	6[1]	4[1]	−2	2

64
Land use [*cont.*]
Utilisation des terres [*suite*]

Country or area Pays ou zone	Land use, 10^3 hectares (1998) Utilisation des terres, 10^3 hectares (1998)				Net change, 10^3 ha (1990 − 1998) Variation nette, 10^3 ha (1990−1998)	
	Total area Superficie totale	Total land Superficie totale des terres	Arable land Terres arables	Permanent crops Cultures permanentes	Arable land Terres arables	Permanent crops Cultures permanentes
Barbados Barbade	43	43	16[1]	1[1]	0	0
Belize Belize	2296	2280	64[1]	25[1]	14	7
Bermuda Bermudes	5	5	...	...	...	...
British Virgin Islands Iles Vierges britanniques	15	15	3[1]	1[1]	0	0
Canada Canada	997061	922097	45560[1]	140[1]	−260	10
Cayman Islands Iles Caïmanes	26	26	...	...	...	...
Costa Rica Costa Rica	5110	5106	225[1]	280[1]	−35	30
Cuba Cuba	11086	10982	3630[1]	835[1]	380	25
Dominica Dominique	75	75	3	12	−2	1
Dominican Republic Rép. dominicaine	4873	4838	1070[1]	480[1]	20	30
El Salvador El Salvador	2104	2072	560[1]	250[1]	10	−10
Greenland Groenland	34170[2]	34170	...	...	...	...
Grenada Grenade	34	34	2[1]	9[1]	0	−1
Guadeloupe Guadeloupe	171	169	18[1]	7[1]	−3	−1
Guatemala Guatemala	10889	10843	1360[1]	545[1]	60	60
Haiti Haïti	2775	2756	560[1]	350[1]	5	0
Honduras Honduras	11209	11189	1695[1]	350[1]	85	140
Jamaica Jamaïque	1099	1083	174[1]	100[1]	55	0
Martinique Martinique	110	106	10[1]	12[1]	0	2
Mexico Mexique	195820	190869	25200[1]	2100[1]	1200	200
Montserrat Montserrat	10	10	2[1]	...	0	...
Netherland Antilles Antilles néerlandaises	80	80	8[1]	...	0	...
Nicaragua Nicaragua	13000	12140	2457[1]	289[1]	494	38
Panama Panama	7552	7443	500[1]	155[1]	1	0
Puerto Rico Porto Rico	895	887	33[1]	45[1]	−32	−5
Saint Kitts and Nevis Saint−Kitts−et−Nevis	36	36	6[1]	1[1]	−2	−1
Saint Lucia Sainte−Lucie	62	61	3[1]	14[1]	−2	1
Saint Pierre and Miquelon Saint−Pierre−et−Miquelon	24	23	3[1]	...	0	...
Saint Vincent and the Grenadines Saint−Vincent−Grenadines	39	39	4[1]	7[1]	0	0
Trinidad and Tobago Trinité−et−Tobago	513	513	75[1]	47[1]	1	1
Turks and Caicos Islands Iles Turques et Caïques	43	43	1[1]	...	0	...

64
Land use [*cont.*]
Utilisation des terres [*suite*]

Country or area Pays ou zone	Land use, 10³ hectares (1998) Utilisation des terres, 10³ hectares (1998)				Net change, 10³ ha (1990 – 1998) Variation nette, 10³ ha (1990–1998)	
	Total area Superficie totale	Total land Superficie totale des terres	Arable land Terres arables	Permanent crops Cultures permanentes	Arable land Terres arables	Permanent crops Cultures permanentes
United States Etats–Unis	936352	915912	176950[1]	2050[1]	−8792	16
United States Virgin Islands Iles Vierges américaines	34	34	5[1]	2[1]	0	0
America, South · Amérique du Sud						
Argentina Argentine	278040	273669	25000[1]	2200[1]	0	0
Bolivia Bolivie	109858	108438	1974	229	74	8
Brazil Brésil	854740	845651	53200[1]	12000[1]	7600	1000
Chile Chili	75663	74880	1979[1]	315	−823	68
Colombia Colombie	113891	103870	2079[1]	2036	−921	36
Ecuador Equateur	28356	27684	1574[1]	1427[1]	−30	106
Falkland Islands (Malvinas) Iles Falkland (Malvinas)	1217	1217	...	...	...	...
French Guiana Guyane française	9000	8815	10[1]	3[1]	0	1
Guyana Guyana	21497	19685	480[1]	16[1]	0	1
Paraguay Paraguay	40675	39730	2200[1]	85[1]	90	−4
Peru Pérou	128522	128000	3670[1]	500[1]	170	80
Suriname Suriname	16327	15600	57[1]	10[1]	0	−1
Uruguay Uruguay	17741	17481	1260[1]	47[1]	0	2
Venezuela Venezuela	91205	88205	2640[1]	850[1]	−340	−65
Asia · Asie						
Afghanistan Afghanistan	65209	65209	7910[1]	144[1]	0	0
Armenia Arménie	2980	2820	495	65[1]	...	...
Azerbaijan Azerbaïdjan	8660	8660	1672[1]	263[1]	...	...
Bahrain Bahreïn	69	69	3[1]	3[1]	1	1
Bangladesh Bangladesh	14400	13017	7992[1]	340[1]	−1145	40
Bhutan Bhoutan	4700	4700	140[1]	20[1]	27	1
Brunei Darussalam Brunéi Darussalam	577	527	3[1]	4[1]	0	0
Cambodia Cambodge	18104	17652	3700[1]	107[1]	5	7
China †† [3] Chine †† [3]	959696	932641	124139[1]	11420[1]	467	3702
China, Hong Kong SAR † Chine, Hong Kong RAS †	107	99	5[1]	1[1]	−1	0
China, Macao SAR † Chine, Macao RAS†	2	2	...[1]	...	...	...
Cyprus Chypre	925	924	100	43	−6	−8
East Timor Timor oriental	1487	1487	70[1]	10[1]	0	0
Georgia Géorgie	6970	6970	785[1]	285[1]	...	...

64
Land use [*cont.*]
Utilisation des terres [*suite*]

Country or area Pays ou zone	Land use, 10³ hectares (1998) Utilisation des terres, 10³ hectares (1998)				Net change, 10³ ha (1990 – 1998) Variation nette, 10³ ha (1990 – 1998)	
	Total area Superficie totale	Total land Superficie totale des terres	Arable land Terres arables	Permanent crops Cultures permanentes	Arable land Terres arables	Permanent crops Cultures permanentes
India Inde	328759	297319	161500[1]	8000[1]	−1638	1700
Indonesia Indonésie	190457	181157	17941[1]	13046[1]	−2312	1326
Iran (Islamic Rep. of) Iran (Rép. islamique d')	163319	162200	16837	1966	1647	656
Iraq Iraq	43832	43737	5200[1]	340[1]	−100	50
Israel Israël	2106	2062	351[1]	86[1]	3	−2
Japan Japon	37780	37652	4535	370	−233	−105
Jordan Jordanie	8921	8893	255[1]	135[1]	−35	45
Kazakhstan Kazakhstan	271730	267073	30000[1]	135[1]	...	...
Korea, Dem.People's Rep. Corée, R. p. dém. de	12054	12041	1700[1]	300[1]	0	0
Korea, Republic of Corée, République de	9926	9873	1708	202	−245	46
Kuwait Koweït	1782	1782	6[1]	1[1]	2	0
Kyrgyzstan Kirghizistan	19850	19180	1350[1]	75[1]	...	...
Lao People's Dem. Rep. Rép. dém. pop. lao	23680	23080	800[1]	52[1]	−7	9
Lebanon Liban	1040	1023	180[1]	128[1]	−3	6
Malaysia Malaisie	32975	32855	1820[1]	5785[1]	120	585
Maldives Maldives	30	30	1[1]	2[1]	0	0
Mongolia Mongolie	156650	156650	1321[1]	1[1]	−49	0
Myanmar Myanmar	67658	65755	9548	595[1]	−19	93
Nepal Népal	14718	14300	2898[1]	70[1]	612	6
Occupied Palestinian Territory [4] Terr. palestinien occupé [4]	38	38	10[1]	15[1]	1	0
Oman Oman	21246	21246	16[1]	47[1]	0	2
Pakistan Pakistan	79610	77088	21425[1]	615[1]	941	159
Philippines Philippines	30000	29817	5500[1]	4500[1]	20	100
Qatar Qatar	1100	1100	14[1]	3[1]	4	2
Saudi Arabia Arabie saoudite	214969	214969	3700[1]	130[1]	310	39
Singapore Singapour	62	61	1	0	0	0
Sri Lanka Sri Lanka	6561	6463	869[1]	1020[1]	−6	−5
Syrian Arab Republic Rep. arabe syrienne	18518	18378	4709	775	−176	34
Tajikistan Tadjikistan	14310	14060	760[1]	130[1]	...	...
Thailand Thaïlande	51312	51089	16800[1]	3575[1]	−694	466
Turkey Turquie	77482	76963	24438	2530	−209	−500

64
Land use [*cont.*]
    Utilisation des terres [*suite*]

Country or area Pays ou zone	Land use, 10³ hectares (1998) Utilisation des terres, 10³ hectares (1998)				Net change, 10³ ha (1990 – 1998) Variation nette, 10³ ha (1990 – 1998)	
	Total area Superficie totale	Total land Superficie totale des terres	Arable land Terres arables	Permanent crops Cultures permanentes	Arable land Terres arables	Permanent crops Cultures permanentes
Turkmenistan Turkménistan	48810	46993	1630[1]	65[1]	...	...
United Arab Emirates Emirats arabes unis	8360	8360	40[1]	41[1]	5	21
Uzbekistan Ouzbékistan	44740	41424	4475[1]	375[1]	...	...
Viet Nam Viet Nam	33169	32549	5700[1]	1550[1]	361	505
Yemen Yémen	52797	52797	1500[1]	113[1]	122	10
Europe · Europe						
Albania Albanie	2875	2740	577[1]	122	−2	−3
Andorra Andorre	45	45	1[1]	...	0	...
Austria Autriche	8386	8273	1397[1]	82[1]	−29	3
Belarus Bélarus	20760	20748	6187	124	...	...
Belgium–Luxembourg Belgique–Luxembourg	3310	3282	812	20	46	5
Bosnia and Herzegovina Bosnie–Herzégovine	5113	5100	500[1]	150[1]	...	...
Bulgaria Bulgarie	11091	11055	4291	220	435	−80
Croatia Croatie	5654	5592	1458	129	...	...
Czech Republic République tchèque	7886	7728	3101	232	...	...
Denmark Danemark	4309	4243	2365[1]	9[1]	−196	−1
Estonia Estonie	4510	4227	1120	15	...	...
Faeroe Islands Iles Féroé	140	140	3[1]	...	0	...
Finland Finlande	33815	30459	2167	3	−104	0
France France	55150	55010	18362	1155	363	−36
Germany Allemagne	35698	34927	11879	228	−92	−215
Gibraltar Gibraltar	1	1	...	...	...	...
Greece Grèce	13196	12890	2843	1098	9	27
Hungary Hongrie	9303	9234	4819	226	−235	−8
Iceland Islande	10300	10025	6[1]	...	−1	...
Ireland Irlande	7028	6889	1355	3	108	0
Italy Italie	30127	29406	8280[1]	2750[1]	−732	−210
Latvia Lettonie	6460	6205	1841	30	...	...
Liechtenstein Liechtenstein	16	16	4[1]	...	0	...
Lithuania Lituanie	6520	6480	2945	59	...	...
Malta Malte	32	32	10	1	−2	0

64
Land use [*cont.*]
Utilisation des terres [*suite*]

Country or area Pays ou zone	Land use, 10³ hectares (1998) Utilisation des terres, 10³ hectares (1998)				Net change, 10³ ha (1990 – 1998) Variation nette, 10³ ha (1990 – 1998)	
	Total area Superficie totale	Total land Superficie totale des terres	Arable land Terres arables	Permanent crops Cultures permanentes	Arable land Terres arables	Permanent crops Cultures permanentes
Netherlands Pays – Bas	4084	3392	906[1]	35[1]	27	5
Norway Norvège	32388	30683	908[1]	...	44	...
Poland Pologne	32325	30442	13999[1]	380[1]	−389	35
Portugal Portugal	9198	9150	1880[1]	700[1]	−493	−100
Republic of Moldova Rép. de Moldova	3370	3297	1796[1]	386	...	...
Romania Roumanie	23839	23034	9325	518	−125	−73
Russian Federation Fédération de Russie	1707540	1688850	126000[1]	1827	...	...
San Marino Saint – Marin	6	6	1[1]	...	0	
Slovakia Slovaquie	4901	4808	1471	133	...	...
Slovenia Slovénie	2025	2012	231[1]	54[1]		
Spain Espagne	50599	49944	14280[1]	4800[1]	−1055	−37
Sweden Suède	44996	41162	2784	...	−61	...
Switzerland Suisse	4129	3955	415	24	24	3
TFYR Macedonia L'ex – R.y. Macédoine	2571	2543	587	48	...	...
Ukraine Ukraine	60370	57935	32858	963	...	...
United Kingdom Royaume – Uni	24488	24160	6267	41	−340	−9
Yugoslavia Yougoslavie	10217	10200	3696	351	...	...
Oceania · Océanie						
American Samoa Samoa américaines	20	20	1[1]	2[1]	−1	0
Australia Australie	774122	768230	53775[1, 5]	225[1]	5875	44
Cocos Island Iles Cocos	1	1	...	...	...	...
Cook Islands Iles Cook	23	23	4[1]	3[1]	2	−1
Fiji Fidji	1827	1827	200[1]	85[1]	40	5
French Polynesia Polynésie française	400	366	6[1]	22[1]	1	0
Guam Guam	55	55	6[1]	6[1]	0	0
Kiribati Kiribati	73	73	...	37[1]	...	0
Nauru Nauru	2	2	...	...	...	...
New Caledonia Nouvelle – Calédonie	1858	1828	7[1]	6[1]	0	0
New Zealand Nouvelle – Zélande	27053	26799	1555[1]	1725[1]	−1006	421
Niue Nioué	26	26	5[1]	2[1]	0	0
Norfolk Island Ile Norfolk	4	4	...	...	...	...

64
Land use [*cont.*]
Utilisation des terres [*suite*]

Country or area Pays ou zone	Land use, 10³ hectares (1998) Utilisation des terres, 10³ hectares (1998)				Net change, 10³ ha (1990 − 1998) Variation nette, 10³ ha (1990−1998)	
	Total area Superficie totale	Total land Superficie totale des terres	Arable land Terres arables	Permanent crops Cultures permanentes	Arable land Terres arables	Permanent crops Cultures permanentes
Palau Palaos	46	46	10[1]	...	10	...
Papua New Guinea Papouasie−Nvl−Guinée	46284	45286	60[1]	610[1]	25	30
Samoa Samoa	284	283	55[1]	67[1]	0	0
Solomon Islands Iles Salomon	2890	2799	42[1]	18[1]	2	1
Tokelau Tokélaou	1	1	...	...	...	...
Tonga Tonga	75	72	17[1]	31[1]	0	0
Tuvalu Tuvalu	3	3	...	...	...	...
Vanuatu Vanuatu	1219	1219	30[1]	90[1]	0	0
Wallis and Futuna Islands Iles Wallis et Futuna	20	20	1[1]	4[1]	0	0

Sources:
Food and Agriculture Organization of the United Nations (FAO),
Rome, "FAO Production Yearbook 1999" and the FAOSTAT database.

† For information on recent changes in country or area
nomenclature pertaining to former Czechoslovakia, Germany,
Hong Kong Special Administrative Region (SAR) of China,
Macao Special Administrative Region (SAR) of China,
SFR of Yugoslavia and the former USSR, see Annex I −
Country or area nomenclature, regional and other groupings.

†† For statistical purposes, the data for China do not
include those for the Hong Kong Special Administrative
Region (Hong Kong SAR) and Macao Special
Administrative Region (Macao SAR).

1   FAO estimate.
2   Total area refers to area free from ice.
3   Data generally include those for Taiwan Province of China.
4   Data refer to the Gaza Strip.
5   Includes about 27 million hectares of cultivated grassland.
6   Data on total area exclude dependencies.

Sources:
Organisation des Nations Unies pour l'alimentation et l'agric
(FAO), Rome, "Annuaire FAO de la production 1999" et la b
données FAOSTAT.

† Pour les modifications récentes de nomenclature de pays ou
zone concernant l'Allemagne, Hong Kong, région administ
spéciale (RAS) de Chine, Macao, région administrative spé
(RAS) de Chine, l'ex−Tchécoslovaquie, l'ex−URSS, et l'ex
de Yougoslavie, voir annexe I − Nomenclature des pays ou
zones, groupements de régionaux et autres groupements.

††Les données statistiques relatives à la Chine ne comprenne
celles qui concernent la région administrative spéciale de
Hong Kong (la RAS de Hong Kong) et la région administra
spéciale de Macao (la RAS de Macao).

1 Estimation de la FAO.
2 La superficie totale est la superficie non couverte de glace.
3 Les données comprennent en général les chiffres pour la pr
de Taiwan.
4 Les données se rapportent à la Zone de Gaza.
5 Y compris 27 millions d'hectares d'herbages cultivés.
6 La superficie totale ne comprend pas les dépendances.

65
CO₂ emission estimates
Estimations des émissions de CO₂

From fossil fuel combustion, cement production and gas flared (thousand metric tons of carbon dioxide)
Dues à la combustion de combustibles fossiles, à la production de ciment et au gaz brûlés à la torche
(milliers de tonnes de dioxyde de carbone)

Country or area Pays ou zone	1990	1991	1992	1993	1994	1995	1996	1997	1998	Change: 1990– latest year (%) Variation: 1990 à l'année la plus récente (%)
Africa · Afrique										
Algeria Algérie	80441	79701	79931	83812	83343	91656	94243	95167	...	18
Angola Angola	4650	4419	4620	4935	5111	6515	5093	5163	...	11
Benin Bénin	564	572	601	674	674	736	685	744	...	32
Botswana Botswana	2169	2132	3268	3466	3466	3499	3085	3356	...	55
Burkina Faso Burkina Faso	993	912	923	920	953	956	967	971	...	−2
Burundi Burundi	194	213	191	205	209	213	220	224	...	15
Cameroon Cameroun	1488	887	3547	3620	3642	3957	1990	2371	...	59
Cape Verde Cap–Vert	84	84	106	106	117	114	121	121	...	43
Central African Rep. Rép. centrafricaine	198	205	216	220	234	234	234	242	...	22
Chad Tchad	143	62	77	92	95	95	99	110	...	−23
Comoros Comores	66	66	66	66	66	66	66	66	...	0
Congo Congo	2037	1953	1326	1891	2089	1795	1817	264	...	−87
Côte d'Ivoire Côte d'Ivoire	9908	10003	10204	10344	10300	10182	13022	13073	...	32
Dem. Rep. of the Congo Rép. dém. du Congo	4096	3774	3386	3459	2136	2253	2305	2334	...	−43
Djibouti Djibouti	352	348	366	377	366	370	366	366	...	4
Egypt Egypte	75436	77583	80906	88623	87934	92473	104737	109295	...	45
Equatorial Guinea Guinée équatoriale	117	121	125	161	128	187	143	612	...	422
Ethiopia Ethiopie	2964	2931	2898	2957	3206	2660	1850	1894	...	−36
Gabon Gabon	6676	4074	2818	3430	2682	3290	2660	3331	...	−50
Gambia Gambie	191	198	198	209	209	216	216	216	...	13
Ghana Ghana	3528	3565	3741	3910	4001	3997	4052	4052	...	15
Guinea Guinée	1011	1030	1030	1063	1063	1081	1092	1092	...	8
Guinea–Bissau Guinée–Bissau	209	213	216	227	227	231	231	231	...	11
Kenya Kenya	5822	4807	5459	6236	6386	6496	6987	6643	...	14
Lesotho [1] Lesotho [1]	...	...	...	...	636	...	...	...	...	...
Liberia Libéria	465	278	278	315	315	322	330	333	...	−28
Libyan Arab Jamahiriya Jamah. arabe libyenne	37773	39572	35728	36838	40081	39367	40807	41719	...	10
Madagascar Madagascar	945	1026	1004	1030	1165	1220	1198	1202	...	27
Malawi Malawi	601	649	645	682	703	711	725	725	...	21

65

CO$_2$ emission estimates
From fossil fuel combustion, cement production and gas flared (thousand metric tons of carbon dioxide) [cont.]

Estimations des émissions de CO$_2$
Dues à la combustion de combustibles fossiles, à la production de ciment et au gaz brûlés à la torche
(milliers de tonnes de dioxyde de carbone) [suite]

Country or area Pays ou zone	1990	1991	1992	1993	1994	1995	1996	1997	1998	Change: 1990– latest year (%) Variation: 1990 à l'année la plus récente (%)
Mali Mali	421	432	443	454	462	473	480	480	...	14
Mauritania Mauritanie	2634	2715	2884	2906	3063	2942	2950	2950	...	12
Mauritius Maurice	1154	1216	1400	1528	1455	1513	1744	1704	...	48
Morocco Maroc	23487	24806	26022	28195	29613	30254	31427	31885	...	36
Mozambique Mozambique	997	1026	997	982	960	1011	1048	1110	...	11
Niger Niger	1048	1059	1077	1096	1088	1099	1103	1107	...	6
Nigeria Nigéria	88667	91975	110959	112421	99629	92151	87871	82203	...	−7
Réunion Réunion	1227	1488	1462	1521	1535	1557	1561	1568	...	28
Rwanda Rwanda	528	476	487	502	484	491	491	495	...	−6
Saint Helena Sainte−Hélène	7	7	7	7	7	7	7	7	...	0
Sao Tome and Principe Sao Tomé−et−Principe	66	70	73	73	73	77	77	77	...	17
Senegal Sénégal	2898	3005	3059	3059	3059	3092	3129	3133	...	8
Seychelles Seychelles	114	143	154	161	176	187	191	198	...	74
Sierra Leone Sierra Leone	333	407	407	436	451	454	462	465	...	40
Somalia Somalie	18	4	11	11	11	11	15	15	...	−20
South Africa Afrique du Sud	291113	298111	305011	287174	319649	307539	293601	317058	...	9
Sudan Soudan	3459	3404	3507	3382	3547	3620	3624	3620	...	5
Swaziland Swaziland	425	326	264	132	484	454	341	399	...	−6
Togo Togo	689	736	696	711	718	744	751	802	...	16
Tunisia Tunisie	13260	15547	14997	16474	15928	15711	16371	16638	...	25
Uganda Ouganda	813	850	861	821	751	956	1004	1070	...	32
United Rep. Tanzania Rép.−Unie de Tanzanie	2272	2334	2261	2275	2257	2440	2448	2466	...	9
Western Sahara Sahara occidental	198	198	198	202	202	209	209	209	...	6
Zambia Zambie	2444	2415	2455	2495	2418	2378	2444	2455	...	0
Zimbabwe Zimbabwe	16646	16913	18053	17324	18533	19533	18412	18203	...	9
America, North · Amérique du Nord										
Antigua and Barbuda Antigua−et−Barbuda	300	289	289	304	311	322	322	337	...	12
Aruba Aruba	1839	1927	1718	1766	1781	1799	1832	1872	...	2
Bahamas Bahamas	1949	1781	1792	1715	1718	1729	1729	1740	...	−11
Barbados Barbade	1077	1205	978	1114	747	828	850	898	...	−17

65

CO$_2$ emission estimates
From fossil fuel combustion, cement production and gas flared (thousand metric tons of carbon dioxide) [*cont.*]

Estimations des émissions de CO$_2$
Dues à la combustion de combustibles fossiles, à la production de ciment et au gaz brûlés à la torche
(milliers de tonnes de dioxyde de carbone) [*suite*]

Country or area Pays ou zone	1990	1991	1992	1993	1994	1995	1996	1997	1998	Change: 1990– latest year (%) Variation: 1990 à l'année la plus récente (%)
Belize Belize	311	359	355	377	374	377	308	388	...	25
Bermuda Bermudes	590	491	399	462	458	454	462	462	...	−22
British Virgin Islands Iles Vierges britanniques	48	48	51	51	51	51	59	59	...	23
Canada [1] Canada [1]	465755	456369	469539	468039	482059	493841	506555	518376	529431	14
Cayman Islands Iles Caïmanes	249	271	275	286	286	286	282	282	...	13
Costa Rica Costa Rica	2917	3309	3741	3943	5232	4859	4730	4965	...	70
Cuba Cuba	31690	27960	29056	27814	31049	34658	34471	25113	...	−21
Dominica Dominique	59	59	59	62	70	81	81	81	...	38
Dominican Republic Rép. dominicaine	9435	10131	11197	11787	12593	12722	12879	13224	...	40
El Salvador El Salvador	2616	3232	3415	4155	4642	5152	4631	5456	...	109
Greenland Groenland	553	546	480	498	502	502	517	520	...	−6
Grenada Grenade	121	121	128	143	165	169	169	183	...	52
Guadeloupe Guadeloupe	1282	1348	1411	1440	1484	1506	1513	1532	...	19
Guatemala Guatemala	5086	5045	6013	5654	6863	7207	6603	7684	...	51
Haiti Haïti	993	997	909	663	337	909	1048	1389	...	40
Honduras Honduras	2590	2697	3074	2847	3576	3895	3965	4137	...	60
Jamaica Jamaïque	7958	8167	8090	8413	8625	9541	10094	10728	...	35
Martinique Martinique	2059	1839	2045	2015	2037	2037	2023	2023	...	−2
Mexico Mexique	294979	310489	345598	346448	364237	345283	351376	366274	...	24
Montserrat Montserrat	33	33	37	37	37	44	44	48	...	44
Netherlands Antilles Antilles néerlandaises	895	3964	5454	7223	6977	6856	6801	6771	...	656
Nicaragua Nicaragua	2601	2034	2437	2297	2536	2788	2891	3045	...	17
Panama Panama	3129	3400	4008	4118	4778	3272	4833	7654	...	145
Puerto Rico Porto Rico	11762	10915	13275	14565	17434	16001	16206	16221	...	38
Saint Lucia Sainte−Lucie	161	161	169	172	187	191	191	198	...	23
St. Kitts and Nevis Saint−Kitts−et−Nevis	66	73	73	84	88	95	103	103	...	56
St. Pierre and Miquelon Saint−Pierre−et−Miquelon	92	103	95	73	70	70	70	48	...	−48
St. Vincent and the Grenadines St. Vincent−Grenadines	81	77	84	103	121	128	132	132	...	64
Trinidad and Tobago Trinité−et−Tobago	16924	20574	20698	16759	19255	20816	22234	21966	...	30
United States [1] Etats−Unis [1]	4914351	4862349	4951561	5072271	5150787	5193841	5193841	5449974	5478051	11

65

CO$_2$ emission estimates
From fossil fuel combustion, cement production and gas flared (thousand metric tons of carbon dioxide) [*cont.*]

Estimations des émissions de CO$_2$
Dues à la combustion de combustibles fossiles, à la production de ciment et au gaz brûlés à la torche
(milliers de tonnes de dioxyde de carbone) [*suite*]

Country or area Pays ou zone	1990	1991	1992	1993	1994	1995	1996	1997	1998	Change: 1990– latest year (%) Variation: 1990 à l'année la plus récente (%)
US Virgin Islands Iles Vierges américaines	8446	9702	8581	12150	12938	10761	11362	11564	...	37
America, South · Amérique du Sud										
Argentina Argentine	109731	115517	118895	123713	131433	130448	130701	137875	...	26
Bolivia Bolivie	5500	5731	6577	7962	8805	9999	10498	10816	...	97
Brazil Brésil	202615	213897	215088	224871	234683	249618	276464	288237	...	42
Chile Chili	35333	33585	35102	35754	41008	44269	48208	58200	...	65
Colombia Colombie	55851	55859	60772	63439	66642	67902	66114	67972	...	22
Ecuador Equateur	16569	16177	22801	25139	14455	23395	24487	20332	...	23
Falkland Islands (Malvinas) Iles Falkland (Malvinas)	37	37	37	37	37	40	44	48	...	30
French Guiana Guyane française	804	829	873	866	866	873	873	873	...	9
Guyana Guyana	1132	1114	1044	1048	1052	934	971	1022	...	−10
Paraguay Paraguay	2261	2231	2620	2946	3452	3884	3514	3814	...	69
Peru Pérou	22175	21350	22384	23615	23303	24842	22629	29258	...	32
Suriname Suriname	1810	2100	2110	2125	2132	2147	2096	2110	...	17
Uruguay Uruguay	3910	4485	5075	4404	4012	4492	5386	5383	...	38
Venezuela Venezuela	113571	123325	131353	153927	190718	179176	177809	187395	...	65
Asia · Asie										
Afghanistan Afghanistan	2612	2437	1392	1341	1290	1238	1176	1096	...	−58
Armenia Arménie	...	...	3679	2781	2851	3510	2620	2777		...
Azerbaijan Azerbaïdjan	...	...	47138	44581	41737	33270	31262	31852		...
Bahrain Bahreïn	11710	11157	10270	16027	14381	14781	11469	14847	...	27
Bangladesh Bangladesh	15360	15766	16184	17111	18386	22149	23714	24487	...	59
Bhutan Bhoutan	128	187	216	187	216	253	300	392	...	206
Brunei Darussalam Brunéi Darussalam	5819	5177	5078	5280	5097	5207	5071	5404	...	−7
Cambodia Cambodge	451	462	476	476	487	498	498	513	...	14
China †† Chine ††	2401779	2522484	2646124	2761370	2998837	3212565	3379298	3348099	...	39
China, Hong Kong SAR † Chine, Hong Kong RAS †	26183	27550	31661	34867	29833	29818	24300	22842	...	−13
China, Macao SAR † Chine, Macao RAS †	1026	1088	1081	1180	1271	1231	1407	1473	...	44
Cyprus Chypre	4646	4481	4979	5104	5258	5130	5273	5456	...	17
Georgia Géorgie	...	...	15210	9856	6038	2290	4184	4415	...	...
India Inde	675271	723574	774135	808485	860222	908514	1002252	1025566	...	52

65

CO$_2$ emission estimates
From fossil fuel combustion, cement production and gas flared (thousand metric tons of carbon dioxide) [*cont.*]

Estimations des émissions de CO$_2$
Dues à la combustion de combustibles fossiles, à la production de ciment et au gaz brûlés à la torche
(milliers de tonnes de dioxyde de carbone) [*suite*]

Country or area Pays ou zone	1990	1991	1992	1993	1994	1995	1996	1997	1998	Change: 1990– latest year (%) Variation: 1990 à l'année la plus récente (%)
Indonesia Indonésie	165212	159203	174039	191751	196529	234950	245071	238541	...	44
Iran, Islamic Rep. of Iran, Rép. islamique d'	212358	224226	233269	211838	260555	261064	271411	287940	...	36
Iraq Iraq	49263	43749	61769	77627	88212	90949	87271	91294	...	85
Israel Israël	34629	35234	41451	45471	47765	54360	54983	57090	...	65
Japan [1] Japon [1]	1147845	1162310	1143843	1213940	1219418	1235593	1230831	...	...	7
Jordan Jordanie	10182	9794	12014	11806	13143	13121	13689	14037	...	38
Kazakhstan Kazakhstan	...	...	252699	207448	190461	178388	142514	122640	...	...
Korea, Dem.People's Rep. Corée, R. p. dém. de	244638	250944	255209	261929	259434	256990	254330	252065	...	3
Korea, Republic of Corée, République de	241183	265091	290193	317348	342835	373606	408033	427599	...	77
Kuwait [2 3] Koweït [2 3]	42206	494010	20918	31947	42335	49505	51564	50025	...	19
Kyrgyzstan Kirghizistan	...	...	11040	8350	6669	5925	6192	6507	...	...
Lao People's Dem. Rep. Rép. dém. pop. lao	231	253	275	275	300	315	337	352	...	52
Lebanon Liban	9094	9494	11348	11648	12733	13612	14858	15755	...	73
Malaysia Malaisie	55280	67679	74329	90411	92646	117957	123138	130844	...	137
Maldives Maldives	154	172	253	216	220	286	297	304	...	98
Mongolia Mongolie	9981	12146	11010	9277	7936	7914	8035	7706	...	−23
Myanmar Myanmar	4148	4038	4892	5404	6313	6998	7284	8493	...	105
Nepal Népal	630	964	1301	1341	1451	1561	1916	2026	...	222
Oman Oman	11538	11252	12029	13301	15341	17239	16246	17771	...	54
Pakistan Pakistan	67873	67884	72673	77740	84479	85193	94335	93756	...	38
Philippines Philippines	44306	45640	50535	48300	49710	60157	64209	74194	...	67
Qatar Qatar	13652	17734	24868	28594	28613	28635	29041	37916	...	178
Saudi Arabia [2] Arabie saoudite [2]	177099	223141	245049	239937	251226	254802	267835	266069	...	50
Singapore Singapour	41920	44804	51322	56412	62622	64777	71812	80276	...	91
Sri Lanka Sri Lanka	3855	4162	5181	5031	5514	5914	7079	7680	...	99
Syrian Arab Republic Rép. arabe syrienne	35845	41195	42983	45658	44145	45526	45621	47673	...	33
Tajikistan Tadjikistan	...	...	20614	13605	5089	5174	5782	5566	...	...
Thailand Thaïlande	95742	116044	126725	142704	158144	181404	200391	208822	...	118
Turkey Turquie	143822	142895	146504	159768	156397	174446	188171	198013	...	38

65

CO$_2$ emission estimates
From fossil fuel combustion, cement production and gas flared (thousand metric tons of carbon dioxide) [*cont.*]

Estimations des émissions de CO$_2$
Dues à la combustion de combustibles fossiles, à la production de ciment et au gaz brûlés à la torche
(milliers de tonnes de dioxyde de carbone) [*suite*]

Country or area Pays ou zone	1990	1991	1992	1993	1994	1995	1996	1997	1998	Change: 1990– latest year (%) Variation: 1990 à l'année la plus récente (%)
Turkmenistan Turkménistan	...	...	28041	27642	33449	33838	30397	30767	...	...
United Arab Emirates Emirats arabes unis	60856	65370	63172	65828	70529	74043	77726	79499	...	31
Uzbekistan [1] Ouzbékistan [1]	114559	...	...	...	102157	...	...	...	...	−11
Viet Nam Viet Nam	22464	20138	21710	27620	29536	32661	37901	42485	...	89
Yemen Yémen	...	9369	13759	13799	11150	14858	16140	16162	...	...
Europe · Europe										
Albania Albanie	7269	3943	2374	2352	1971	2063	1953	1583	...	−78
Austria [1] Autriche [1]	62130	66022	60152	59899	61754	63694	65911	66788	66604	7
Belarus Bélarus	...	...	69903	62157	63135	61399	97658	103609	...	...
Belgium [1] Belgique [1]	113997	121420	121591	119519	124312	125576	129654	121340	121975	7
Bosnia and Herzegovina Bosnie–Herzégovine	...	...	4723	3741	4155	4067	3550	4437	...	...
Bulgaria [1] Bulgarie [1]	84136	66043	59183	61859	59178	62332	...	59148	55150	−34
Croatia Croatie	...	...	16807	17100	16976	17749	18148	19016	...	...
Czech Republic [1] République tchèque [1]	165490	153142	140220	134851	127745	128817	132538	137125	128268	−22
Denmark [1] Danemark [1]	52894	63516	58191	59928	63414	60348	73657	64347	60125	14
Estonia [1] Estonie [1]	37797	36956	27766	21979	22852	20859	21423	20716	19232	−49
Faeroe Islands Iles Féroé	616	575	638	575	513	619	630	634	...	3
Finland [1] Finlande [1]	60771	60400	57879	58638	64813	62227	68387	66177	63945	5
France [1] France [1]	387590	411325	401632	381065	377852	383817	396515	391113	412860	7
Germany [1] Allemagne [1]	1014500	975950	928308	918268	904112	902916	924128	892426	886181	−13
Gibraltar Gibraltar	62	70	48	293	355	238	242	224	...	259
Greece [1] Grèce [1]	85164	84937	86869	87290	88570	90121	91466	96176	100449	18
Hungary [1] Hongrie [1]	71673	66638	59804	60073	58443	59005	59722	58139	57601	−20
Iceland [1] Islande [1]	2147	2068	2197	2302	2265	2282	...	...	...	6
Ireland [1] Irlande [1]	31575	32256	32893	32421	33987	34501	35700	38071	40019	27
Italy [1] Italie [1]	432565	430912	429331	422324	418104	443184	439479	441232	459461	6
Latvia [1] Lettonie [1]	24771	19420	16423	14482	11910	12027	11065	12842	8287	−67
Liechtenstein [1] Liechtenstein [1]	208	...	...	...	...	...	...	...	...	...
Lituania [1] Lituanie [1]	39535	...	...	...	15200	16200	16200	16694		−58
Luxembourg [1] Luxembourg [1]	12750	...	...	...	11998	9545	...	...	...	−25

65
CO$_2$ emission estimates
From fossil fuel combustion, cement production and gas flared (thousand metric tons of carbon dioxide) [*cont.*]

Estimations des émissions de CO$_2$
Dues à la combustion de combustibles fossiles, à la production de ciment et au gaz brûlés à la torche
(milliers de tonnes de dioxyde de carbone) [*suite*]

Country or area Pays ou zone	1990	1991	1992	1993	1994	1995	1996	1997	1998	Change: 1990– latest year (%) Variation: 1990 à l'année la plus récente (%)
Malta Malte	1660	1652	1660	1707	1715	1726	1755	1759	...	6
Monaco [1] Monaco [1]	108	125	133	135	138	135	141	143	138	28
Netherlands [1] Pays–Bas [1]	161360	166910	165210	167450	168340	177130	184790	183230	181370	12
Norway [1] Norvège [1]	35146	33605	34267	35918	37940	38157	41119	41426	41700	19
Poland [1] Pologne [1]	380697	366958	371591	363160	371588	348172	372530	361626	337450	–11
Portugal [1] Portugal [1]	43132	44976	48928	47774	48587	51531	49822	51505	53891	25
Republic of Moldova Moldova, Rép. de	...	...	20889	15649	12135	11227	11575	10388	...	...
Romania [1] Roumanie [1]	172510	135660	130160	127086	125597	...	...	...	...	–27
Russian Federation [1] Fédération de Russie [1]	2372300	...	...	...	1660000	1590420	1495920	...	...	–37
Slovakia [1] Slovaquie [1]	62237	54500	50312	47982	45176	46624	46993	46404	43772	–30
Slovenia [1] Slovénie [1]	13935	...	...	...	...	...	...	...	...	...
Spain [1] Espagne [1]	226057	233257	242275	229515	242279	252958	240847	264118	273017	21
Sweden [1] Suède [1]	55443	55218	56207	56182	58438	58108	63352	56684	56953	3
Switzerland [1] Suisse [1]	44409	46285	45990	43566	42928	43805	44212	43549	44809	1
TFYR Macedonia L'ex–R.y. Macédoine	...	...	10633	10201	10336	10747	11747	10688	...	...
Ukraine [1] Ukraine [1]	703792	586478	577916	504222	406838	380928	346768	322907	314445	–55
United Kingdom [1] Royaume–Uni [1]	584220	588047	573656	559620	559333	551325	570278	544252	546390	–6
Yugoslavia Yougoslavie	130455	88139	...	...	...	...	...	...	...	...
Oceania · Océanie										
American Samoa Samoa américaines	286	286	300	297	282	275	282	282	...	–1
Australia [1] Australie [1]	278669	280206	282769	286296	290367	302277	312286	319532	337973	21
Cook Islands Iles Cook	22	22	22	22	22	22	22	22	...	0
Fiji Fidji	813	674	707	711	722	755	773	755	...	–7
French Polynesia Polynésie française	613	617	624	628	547	562	562	562	...	–8
Guam Guam	2268	2422	2451	3554	4558	4137	4078	4078	...	80
Kiribati Kiribati	22	22	22	22	22	22	22	22	...	0
Micronesia (Federated States of) [1] Micronésie (États fédérés de) [1]	...	...	...	...	236	...	141	...	...	...
Nauru Nauru	132	132	136	136	136	139	139	139	...	6
New Caledonia Nouvelle–Calédonie	1612	1777	1759	1759	1711	1715	1751	1751	...	9
New Zealand [1] Nouvelle–Zélande [1]	25398	25881	27762	27136	27197	27206	28276	30372	28941	14

65

CO_2 emission estimates
From fossil fuel combustion, cement production and gas flared (thousand metric tons of carbon dioxide) [*cont.*]

Estimations des émissions de CO_2
Dues à la combustion de combustibles fossiles, à la production de ciment et au gaz brûlés à la torche
(milliers de tonnes de dioxyde de carbone) [*suite*]

Country or area Pays ou zone	1990	1991	1992	1993	1994	1995	1996	1997	1998	Change: 1990– latest year (%) Variation: 1990 à l'année la plus récente (%)
Niue Nioué	4	4	4	4	4	4	4	4	...	0
Palau Palaos	234	234	...	...	...	...	...	...	...	...
Papua New Guinea Papouasie–Nvl–Guinée	2429	2587	2528	2528	2503	2407	2407	2451	...	1
Samoa Samoa	125	125	128	128	121	132	132	132	...	6
Solomon Islands Iles Salomon	161	161	161	158	154	161	161	161	...	0
Tonga Tonga	77	92	88	103	106	114	117	121	...	57
Tuvalu [1] Tuvalu [1]	...	...	...	...	5	...	...	...	...	...
Vanuatu Vanuatu	66	66	62	62	62	62	62	62	...	−6
Wake Island Ile de Wake	48	40	44	33	18	18	18	18	...	−62
former USSR · l'ex–URSS										
former USSR † l'ex–URSS †	3706096	3577322	...							...

Sources:
Carbon Dioxide Information Analysis Center (CDIAC) of the
Oak Ridge National Laboratory, Oak Ridge, Tennessee, U.S.A.,
database on national CO_2 emissions estimates from fossil fuel
burning, cement production and gas flaring: 1751–1997 and the
Secretariat of the United Nations Framework Convention on
Climate Change (UNFCCC), Bonn, Secretariat of the UNFCCC
database.

The majority of the data have been taken from the CDIAC database;
all other data have been taken from the UNFCCC database and are
footnoted accordingly.

†   For information on recent changes in country or area
    nomenclature pertaining to former Czechoslovakia, Germany,
    Hong Kong Special Administrative Region (SAR) of China,
    Macao Special Administrative Region (SAR) of China,
    SFR of Yugoslavia and the former USSR, see Annex I – Country
    or area nomenclature, regional and other groupings.

†† For statistical purposes, the data for China do not
    include those for the Hong Kong Special Administrative
    Region (Hong Kong SAR), Macao Special Administrative
    Region (Hong Kong SAR) and Taiwan province of China.

1   Source: Secretariat of the UNFCCC.
2   Including part of the Neutral Zone.
3   In 1991, includes Kuwaiti oil fires : 477932.

Sources:
"Carbon Dioxide Information Analysis Center (CDIAC) of the
Oak Ridge National Laboratory, Oak Ridge, Tennessee, U.S.A.,
database on national CO_2 emissions estimates from fossil fuel
burning, cement production and gas flaring: 1751–1997" et la
Secrétariat de la convention–cadre concernant les changements
climatiques (CCCC) des Nations Unies, Bonn, la base de données du
Secrétariat de la CCCC.

La majorité des données proviennent de la base de données du
CDIAC; les autres, qui proviennent de la base de données
du Secrétariat de la CCCC, sont signalées par une note.

†   Pour les modifications récentes de nomenclature de pays
    ou de zone concernant l'Allemagne, Hong Kong région
    administrative spéciale (RAS) de Chine, Macao région administrative
    spéciale (RAS) de Chine, l'ex–Tchécoslovaquie, l'ex–URSS et l'ex–
    Rfs de Yougoslavie, voir annex I – Nomenclature des pays ou des
    zones, groupements régionaux et autres groupments.

†† Les données statistiques relatives à la Chine ne comprennent
    pas celles qui concernent la région administrative spéciale de
    Hong Kong (la RAS de Hong Kong), la région administrative
    spéciale de Macao (la RAS de Macao) et la province chinoise
    de Taiwan.

1   Source: Secrétariat de la CCCC des Nations Unies.
2   Y compris une partie de la Zone Neutral.
3   En 1991, y compris les feux d'hydrocarbures au Koweït : 477 932.

66
Water supply and sanitation coverage
Accès à l'eau et à l'assainissement

Percent of population covered by: − Pourcentage de la population ayant accès à :

Region, country or area Région, pays ou zone	Year Année	Water supply Un système de distribution d'eau			Sanitation facilities Un système d'assainissement		
		Urban (%) Urbaine (%)	Rural (%) Rurale (%)	Total (%) Totale (%)	Urban (%) Urbaine (%)	Rural (%) Rurale (%)	Total (%) Totale (%)
World [1]	1990	**95**	**66**	**79**	82	35	55
Monde [1]	2000	**94**	**71**	**82**	86	38	60
Africa [2]	1990	**84**	**44**	**57**	85	49	61
Afrique [2]	2000	**85**	**47**	**62**	84	45	60
Algeria	1990	...	...	...	...	...	...
Algérie	2000	98	88	94	90	47	73
Angola	1990	...	...	...	...	...	...
Angola	2000	34	40	38	70	30	44
Benin	1990	...	...	...	46	6	20
Bénin	2000	74	55	63	46	6	23
Botswana	1990	100	91	95	84	44	61
Botswana	2000	100	...	...	...	...	...
Burkina Faso	1990	74	50	53	88	14	24
Burkina Faso	2000	84	...	...	88	16	29
Burundi	1990	94	63	65	67	90	89
Burundi	2000	96	...	...	79	...	...
Cameroon	1990	76	36	52	99	79	87
Cameroun	2000	82	42	62	99	85	92
Cape Verde	1990	...	...	...	...	...	...
Cap−Vert	2000	64	89	74	95	32	71
Central African Rep.	1990	80	46	59	43	23	30
Rép. centrafricaine	2000	80	46	60	43	23	31
Chad	1990	...	...	...	70	4	18
Tchad	2000	31	26	27	81	13	29
Comoros	1990	97	84	88	98	98	98
Comores	2000	98	95	96	98	98	98
Congo	1990	...	...	...	...	...	...
Congo	2000	71	17	51	14	...	...
Côte d'Ivoire	1990	89	49	65	78	30	49
Côte d'Ivoire	2000	90	65	77	...	...	...
Dem. Rep. of the Congo	1990	...	...	...	...	...	...
Rép. dém. du Congo	2000	89	26	45	53	6	20
Djibouti	1990	...	...	...	...	...	...
Djibouti	2000	100	100	100	99	50	91
Egypt	1990	97	91	94	96	80	87
Egypte	2000	96	94	95	98	91	94
Equatorial Guinea	1990	...	...	...	...	...	...
Guinée équatoriale	2000	45	42	43	60	46	53
Eritrea	1990	...	...	...	...	...	...
Erythrée	2000	63	42	46	66	1	13
Ethiopia	1990	77	13	22	58	6	13
Ethiopie	2000	77	13	24	58	6	15
Gabon	1990	...	...	...	...	...	...
Gabon	2000	73	55	70	25	4	21
Gambia	1990	...	...	...	...	...	...
Gambie	2000	80	53	62	41	35	37
Ghana	1990	83	43	56	59	61	60
Ghana	2000	87	49	64	62	64	63
Guinea	1990	72	36	45	94	41	55
Guinée	2000	72	36	48	94	41	58
Guinea−Bissau	1990	...	...	...	...	...	...
Guinée−Bissau	2000	29	55	49	88	34	47
Kenya	1990	89	25	40	94	81	84
Kenya	2000	87	31	49	96	81	86
Lesotho	1990	...	...	...	...	...	...
Lesotho	2000	98	88	91	93	92	92
Libyan Arab Jamahiriya	1990	72	68	71	97	96	97
Jamah. arabe libyenne	2000	72	68	72	97	96	97
Madagascar	1990	85	31	44	70	25	36
Madagascar	2000	85	31	47	70	30	42
Malawi	1990	90	43	49	96	70	73
Malawi	2000	95	44	57	96	70	77

66
Water supply and sanitation coverage [cont.]
Accès à l'eau et à l'assainissement [suite]

| | | Percent of population covered by: — Pourcentage de la population ayant accès à : | | | | | |
| | | Water supply Un système de distribution d'eau | | | Sanitation facilities Un système d'assainissement | | |
Region, country or area Région, pays ou zone	Year Année	Urban (%) Urbaine (%)	Rural (%) Rurale (%)	Total (%) Totale (%)	Urban (%) Urbaine (%)	Rural (%) Rurale (%)	Total (%) Totale (%)
Mali	1990	65	52	55	95	62	70
Mali	2000	74	61	65	93	58	69
Mauritania	1990	34	40	37	44	19	30
Mauritanie	2000	34	40	37	44	19	33
Mauritius	1990	100	100	100	100	100	100
Maurice	2000	100	100	100	100	99	99
Morocco	1990	94	58	75	95	31	62
Maroc	2000	100	58	82	100	42	75
Mozambique	1990	...	...	...	...	...	...
Mozambique	2000	86	43	60	69	26	43
Namibia	1990	98	63	72	84	14	33
Namibie	2000	100	67	77	96	17	41
Niger	1990	65	51	53	71	4	15
Niger	2000	70	56	59	79	5	20
Nigeria	1990	78	33	49	77	51	60
Nigéria	2000	81	39	57	85	45	63
Rwanda	1990	...	...	...	...	...	...
Rwanda	2000	60	40	41	12	8	8
Senegal	1990	90	60	72	86	38	57
Sénégal	2000	92	65	78	94	48	70
Sierra Leone	1990	...	...	...	...	...	...
Sierra Leone	2000	23	31	28	23	31	28
South Africa	1990	...	...	...	...	...	...
Afrique du Sud	2000	92	80	86	99	73	86
Sudan	1990	86	60	67	87	48	58
Soudan	2000	86	69	75	87	48	62
Togo	1990	82	38	51	71	24	37
Togo	2000	85	38	54	69	17	34
Tunisia	1990	94	61	80	97	48	76
Tunisie	2000	...	...	...	...	...	...
Uganda	1990	80	40	44	96	82	84
Ouganda	2000	72	46	50	96	72	75
United Rep. Tanzania	1990	80	42	50	97	86	88
Rép. Unie de Tanzanie	2000	80	42	54	98	86	90
Western Sahara	1990	89	...	...	...	...	...
Sahara occidental	2000	...	...	...	...	...	...
Zambia	1990	88	28	52	86	48	63
Zambie	2000	88	48	64	99	64	78
Zimbabwe	1990	99	68	77	98	51	64
Zimbabwe	2000	100	77	85	99	51	68
Asia [3]	1990	**94**	**67**	**76**	**67**	**23**	**37**
Asie [3]	2000	**93**	**75**	**81**	**78**	**31**	**48**
Afghanistan	1990	...	...	...	...	...	...
Afghanistan	2000	19	11	13	25	8	12
Bangladesh	1990	98	89	91	78	27	37
Bangladesh	2000	99	97	97	82	44	53
Bhutan	1990	...	...	...	...	...	...
Bhoutan	2000	86	60	62	65	70	69
Cambodia	1990	...	...	...	...	...	...
Cambodge	2000	53	25	30	58	10	18
China ††	1990	99	60	71	57	18	29
Chine ††	2000	94	66	75	68	24	38
Cyprus	1990	100	100	100	100	100	100
Chypre	2000	100	100	100	100	100	100
India	1990	92	73	78	58	8	21
Inde	2000	92	86	88	73	14	31
Indonesia	1990	90	60	69	76	44	54
Indonésie	2000	91	65	76	87	52	66
Iran, Islamic Rep. of	1990	95	75	86	86	74	81
Iran, Rép. islamique d'	2000	99	89	95	86	74	81
Iraq	1990	...	...	...	...	...	...
Iraq	2000	96	48	85	93	31	79
Jordan	1990	99	92	97	100	95	98
Jordanie	2000	100	84	96	100	98	99

66
Water supply and sanitation coverage [*cont.*]
Accès à l'eau et à l'assainissement [*suite*]

Region, country or area Région, pays ou zone	Year Année	Water supply Un système de distribution d'eau			Sanitation facilities Un système d'assainissement		
		Urban (%) Urbaine (%)	Rural (%) Rurale (%)	Total (%) Totale (%)	Urban (%) Urbaine (%)	Rural (%) Rurale (%)	Total (%) Totale (%)
Kazakhstan Kazakhstan	1990 2000	... 98	... 82	... 91	... 100	... 98	... 99
Korea, Dem.People's Rep. Corée, R. p. dém. de	1990 2000	... 100	... 100	... 100	... 99	... 100	... 99
Korea, Republic of Corée, République de	1990 2000	... 97	... 71	... 92	... 76	... 4	... 63
Kyrgyzstan Kirghizistan	1990 2000	... 98	... 66	... 77	... 100	... 100	... 100
Lao People's Dem. Rep. Rép. dém. pop. lao	1990 2000	... 59	... 100	... 90	... 84	... 34	... 46
Lebanon Liban	1990 2000	... 100	... 100	... 100	... 100	... 87	... 99
Malaysia Malaisie	1990 2000	... ...	... 94	... ...	... ...	... 98	... ...
Maldives Maldives	1990 2000	... 100	... 100	... 100	... 100	... 41	... 56
Mongolia Mongolie	1990 2000	... 77	... 30	... 60	... 46	... 2	... 30
Myanmar Myanmar	1990 2000	88 88	56 60	64 68	65 65	38 39	45 46
Nepal Népal	1990 2000	96 85	63 80	66 81	68 75	16 20	21 27
Oman Oman	1990 2000	41 41	30 30	37 39	98 98	61 61	84 92
Pakistan Pakistan	1990 2000	96 96	79 84	84 88	78 94	13 42	34 61
Philippines Philippines	1990 2000	94 92	81 80	87 87	85 92	64 71	74 83
Saudi Arabia Arabie saoudite	1990 2000	... 100	... 64	... 95	... 100	... 100	... 100
Singapore Singapour	1990 2000	100 100	... ...	100 100	100 100	... ...	100 100
Sri Lanka Sri Lanka	1990 2000	90 91	59 80	66 83	93 91	79 80	82 83
Syrian Arab Republic Rép. arabe syrienne	1990 2000	... 94	... 64	... 80	... 98	... 81	... 90
Thailand Thaïlande	1990 2000	83 89	68 77	71 80	97 97	83 96	86 96
Turkey Turquie	1990 2000	82 82	76 84	80 83	98 98	70 70	87 91
Uzbekistan Ouzbékistan	1990 2000	... 96	... 78	... 85	... 100	... 100	... 100
Viet Nam Viet Nam	1990 2000	81 81	40 50	48 56	86 86	70 70	73 73
Yemen Yémen	1990 2000	85 85	60 64	66 69	80 87	27 31	39 45
Europe [4] **Europe** [4]	1990 2000	**100** **100**	**100** **87**	**100** **96**	**100** **99**	**100** **74**	**100** **92**
Andorra Andorre	1990 2000	... 100	... 100	... 100	... 100	... 100	... 100
Austria Autriche	1990 2000	100 100	100 100	100 100	100 100	100 100	100 100
Belarus Bélarus	1990 2000	... 100	... 100	... 100	... ...	... ...	... ...
Bulgaria Bulgarie	1990 2000	... 100	... 100	... 100	... 100	... 100	... 100
Denmark Danemark	1990 2000	... 100	... 100	... 100	... ...	... ...	... ...
Estonia Estonie	1990 2000	... ...	... ...	... ...	... 93	... ...	... ...
Finland Finlande	1990 2000	100 100	100 100	100 100	100 100	100 100	100 100
Hungary Hongrie	1990 2000	100 100	98 98	99 99	100 100	98 98	99 99

Percent of population covered by: – Pourcentage de la population ayant accès à :

66
Water supply and sanitation coverage [*cont.*]
Accès à l'eau et à l'assainissement [*suite*]

Region, country or area Région, pays ou zone	Year Année	Percent of population covered by: — Pourcentage de la population ayant accès à :					
		Water supply Un système de distribution d'eau			Sanitation facilities Un système d'assainissement		
		Urban (%) Urbaine (%)	Rural (%) Rurale (%)	Total (%) Totale (%)	Urban (%) Urbaine (%)	Rural (%) Rurale (%)	Total (%) Totale (%)
Malta	1990	100	100	100	100	100	100
Malte	2000	100	100	100	100	100	100
Monaco	1990	...	...	...	...	...	...
Monaco	2000	100	100	100	100	100	100
Netherlands	1990	100	100	100	100	100	100
Pays−Bas	2000	100	100	100	100	100	100
Norway	1990	100	100	100	100	...	...
Norvège	2000	100	100	100	...	...	...
Republic of Moldova	1990	...	...	...	...	...	...
Moldova, Rép. de	2000	100	100	100	100	...	...
Romania	1990	...	...	...	...	...	...
Roumanie	2000	91	16	58	86	10	53
Russian Federation	1990	...	...	...	...	...	...
Fédération de Russie	2000	100	96	99	...	...	...
Slovakia	1990	...	...	...	...	...	...
Slovaquie	2000	100	100	100	100	100	100
Slovenia	1990	100	100	100	100	...	...
Slovénie	2000	100	100	100	...	...	...
Sweden	1990	100	100	100	100	100	100
Suède	2000	100	100	100	100	100	100
Switzerland	1990	100	100	100	100	100	100
Suisse	2000	100	100	100	100	100	100
United Kingdom	1990	100	100	100	100	100	100
Royaume−Uni	2000	100	100	100	100	100	100
Latin America and the Caribbean [5]	1990	**92**	**56**	**82**	**85**	**39**	**72**
Amérique latine et Caraïbes [5]	2000	**93**	**62**	**85**	**87**	**49**	**78**
Anguilla	1990	...	...	...	...	...	...
Anguilla	2000	60	60	60	99	99	99
Antigua and Barbuda	1990	...	...	...	...	...	...
Antigua−et−Barbuda	2000	95	88	91	98	94	96
Argentina	1990	...	...	...	...	...	...
Argentine	2000	85	30	79	89	48	85
Aruba	1990	...	...	...	...	...	...
Aruba	2000	...	...	100	...	...	...
Bahamas	1990	...	...	...	...	...	...
Bahamas	2000	98	86	96	93	94	93
Barbados	1990	100	100	100	100	100	100
Barbade	2000	100	100	100	100	100	100
Belize	1990	...	...	...	...	...	...
Belize	2000	83	69	76	59	21	42
Bolivia	1990	92	52	74	77	28	55
Bolivie	2000	93	55	79	82	38	66
Brazil	1990	93	50	82	84	37	72
Brésil	2000	95	54	87	85	40	77
British Virgin Islands	1990	...	...	...	...	...	...
Iles Vierges britanniques	2000	98	98	98	100	100	100
Chile	1990	98	48	90	98	93	97
Chili	2000	99	66	94	98	93	97
Colombia	1990	95	68	87	95	53	82
Colombie	2000	98	73	91	97	51	85
Costa Rica	1990	...	...	...	...	...	...
Costa Rica	2000	98	98	98	98	95	96
Cuba	1990	...	...	...	...	...	...
Cuba	2000	99	82	95	96	91	95
Dominica	1990	...	...	...	...	...	...
Dominique	2000	100	90	97	...	...	...
Dominican Republic	1990	83	70	78	66	52	60
Rép. dominicaine	2000	83	70	79	75	64	71
Ecuador	1990	...	...	...	...	...	...
Equateur	2000	81	51	71	70	37	59
El Salvador	1990	...	47	...	...	...	...
El Salvador	2000	88	61	74	88	78	83
French Guiana	1990	...	...	...	...	...	...
Guyane française	2000	88	71	84	85	57	79

66
Water supply and sanitation coverage [*cont.*]
Accès à l'eau et à l'assainissement [*suite*]

Region, country or area Région, pays ou zone	Year Année	Percent of population covered by: − Pourcentage de la population ayant accès à :					
		Water supply Un système de distribution d'eau			Sanitation facilities Un système d'assainissement		
		Urban (%) Urbaine (%)	Rural (%) Rurale (%)	Total (%) Totale (%)	Urban (%) Urbaine (%)	Rural (%) Rurale (%)	Total (%) Totale (%)
Grenada	1990	...	...	...	...	...	...
Grenade	2000	97	93	94	96	97	97
Guadeloupe	1990	...	...	...	...	...	...
Guadeloupe	2000	94	94	94	61	61	61
Guatemala	1990	88	72	78	94	66	77
Guatemala	2000	97	88	92	98	76	85
Guyana	1990	...	...	...	...	...	...
Guyana	2000	98	91	94	97	81	87
Haiti	1990	55	42	46	48	15	25
Haïti	2000	49	45	46	50	16	28
Honduras	1990	90	79	84	85	...	...
Honduras	2000	97	82	90	94	57	77
Jamaica	1990	...	...	...	...	...	...
Jamaïque	2000	81	59	71	98	66	84
Mexico	1990	92	61	83	85	28	69
Mexique	2000	94	63	86	87	32	73
Montserrat	1990	100	100	100	100	100	100
Montserrat	2000	100	100	100	100	100	100
Nicaragua	1990	93	44	70	97	53	76
Nicaragua	2000	95	59	79	96	68	84
Panama	1990	...	...	...	...	...	...
Panama	2000	88	86	87	99	87	94
Paraguay	1990	80	47	63	92	87	89
Paraguay	2000	95	58	79	95	95	95
Peru	1990	84	47	72	81	26	64
Pérou	2000	87	51	77	90	40	76
St. Kitts and Nevis	1990	...	...	...	...	...	...
Saint−Kitts−et−Nevis	2000	...	...	98	...	...	96
Saint Lucia	1990	...	...	...	...	...	...
Sainte−Lucie	2000	...	...	98	...	...	...
St. Vincent and the Grenadines	1990	...	...	...	...	...	...
St. Vincent−Grenadines	2000	...	...	93	...	...	96
Suriname	1990	...	...	...	...	...	...
Suriname	2000	94	96	95	100	34	83
Trinidad and Tobago	1990	...	...	...	...	...	...
Trinité−et−Tobago	2000	...	...	86	...	...	88
Turks and Caicos Islands	1990	...	...	...	...	...	...
Iles Turques et Caiques	2000	100	100	100	98	94	96
Uruguay	1990	...	...	...	...	...	...
Uruguay	2000	98	93	98	96	89	95
Venezuela	1990	...	...	...	...	...	...
Venezuela	2000	88	58	84	75	69	74
Northern America [6]	1990	**100**	**100**	**100**	**100**	**100**	**100**
Amérique du Nord [6]	2000	**100**	**100**	**100**	**100**	**100**	**100**
Canada	1990	100	99	100	100	99	100
Canada	2000	100	99	100	100	99	100
United States	2000	100	100	100	100	100	100
Etats−Unis	1990	100	100	100	100	100	100
Oceania [7]	1990	**100**	**62**	**88**	**99**	**89**	**96**
Océanie [7]	2000	**98**	**63**	**88**	**99**	**81**	**93**
American Samoa	1990	100	100	100	...	...	...
Samoa américaines	2000	100	100	100	...	...	...
Australia	1990	100	100	100	100	100	100
Australie	2000	100	100	100	100	100	100
Cook Islands	1990	100	100	100	100	100	100
Iles Cook	2000	100	100	100	100	100	100
Fiji	1990	...	...	...	...	...	...
Fidji	2000	43	51	47	75	12	43
French Polynesia	1990	...	...	...	100	...	...
Polynésie française	2000	100	100	100	99	97	98
Kiribati	1990	...	...	...	...	...	...
Kiribati	2000	82	25	47	54	44	48
New Zealand	1990	100	...	...	...	...	...
Nouvelle−Zélande	2000	100	...	...	...	...	...

66
Water supply and sanitation coverage [*cont.*]
Accès à l'eau et à l'assainissement [*suite*]

Region, country or area Région, pays ou zone	Year Année	Water supply Un système de distribution d'eau			Sanitation facilities Un système d'assainissement		
		Urban (%) Urbaine (%)	Rural (%) Rurale (%)	Total (%) Totale (%)	Urban (%) Urbaine (%)	Rural (%) Rurale (%)	Total (%) Totale (%)
Niue	1990	100	100	100	100	100	100
Nioué	2000	100	100	100	100	100	100
Northern Mariana Islands	1990	...	...	...	...	...	...
Iles Mariannes septentrionales	2000	...	...	...	...	92	...
Palau	1990	...	...	...	...	...	...
Palaos	2000	100	20	79	100	100	100
Papua New Guinea	1990	88	32	42	92	80	82
Papouasie – Nvl – Guinée	2000	88	32	42	92	80	82
Samoa	1990	...	...	...	...	...	...
Samoa	2000	95	100	99	95	100	99
Solomon Islands	1990	...	...	...	...	...	...
Iles Salomon	2000	94	65	71	98	18	34
Tokelau	1990	...	...	...	...	...	...
Tokélaou	2000	97	48	48	...	...	...
Tonga	1990	...	...	...	...	...	...
Tonga	2000	100	100	100	...	...	...
Tuvalu	1990	...	...	...	...	...	...
Tuvalu	2000	100	100	100	100	100	100
Vanuatu	1990	...	...	...	...	...	...
Vanuatu	2000	63	94	88	100	100	100
Wallis and Futuna Islands	1990	...	...	...	...	...	...
Iles Wallis et Futuna	2000	...	...	100	...	...	80

Source:
World Health Organization and United Nations Children's Fund, WHO/UNICEF Joint Monitoring Programme for Water Supply and Sanitation, Geneva, "Global water supply and sanitation assessment 2000 report".

Source:
Organisation mondiale de la santé et Fonds des Nations Unies pour l'enfance, OMS/FISE Programme de surveillance conjointe de l'approvisionnement en eau et l'assainissement, Genève, "Global water supply and sanitation assessement 2000 report".

†† For statistical purposes, the data for China do not include those for the Hong Kong Special Administrative Region (Hong Kong SAR), Macao Special Administrative Region (Hong Kong SAR) and Taiwan province of China.

†† Les données statistiques relatives à la Chine ne comprennent pas celles qui concernent la région administrative spéciale de Hong Kong (la RAS de Hong Kong), la région administrative spéciale de Macao (la RAS de Macao) et la province chinoise de Taiwan.

1 Only 76% of global population represented in 1990 and 89% in 2000.
2 Only 72% of regional population represented in 1990 and 96% in 2000.
3 Only 88% of regional population represented in 1990 and 94% in 2000.
4 Only 15% of regional population represented in 1990 and 44% in 2000.
5 Only 77% of regional population represented in 1990 and 99% in 2000.
6 Only 99.9% of regional population represented in 1990 and 99.9% in 2000.
7 Only 64% of regional population represented in 1990 and 85% in 2000.

1 Seulement 76% de la population mondiale est représentée en 1990 et 89% en 2000.
2 Seulement 72% de la population régionale est représentée en 1990 et 96% en 2000.
3 Seulement 88% de la population régionale est représentée en 1990 et 94% en 2000.
4 Seulement 15% de la population régionale est représentée en 1990 et 44% en 2000.
5 Seulement 77% de la population régionale est représentée en 1990 et 99% en 2000.
6 Seulement 99.9% de la population régionale est représentée en 1990 et 99.9% en 2000.
7 Seulement 64% de la population régionale est représentée en 1990 et 85% en 2000.

67
Threatened species
Espèces menacées

Number by taxonomic group (as assessed between 1996 and 2000)
Nombre par groupe taxonomique (évaluations réalisées entre 1996 et 2000)

Country or area Pays ou zone	Mammals Mammifères	Birds Oiseaux	Reptiles Reptiles	Amphibians Amphibiens	Fishes Poissons	Invertebrates Inverterrés	Plants and trees Plantes et arbres	Total
Africa · Afrique								
Algeria Algérie	13	6	2	0	0	11	2	34
Angola Angola	18	15	4	0	0	6	19	62
Benin Bénin	7	2	1	0	0	0	11	21
Botswana Botswana	5	7	0	0	0	0	0	12
Burkina Faso Burkina Faso	7	2	1	0	0	0	2	12
Burundi Burundi	5	7	0	0	0	3	2	17
Cameroon Cameroun	37	15	1	1	27	4	155	240
Cape Verde Cap–Vert	3	2	0	0	1	0	2	8
Central African Republic Rép. centrafricaine	12	3	1	0	0	0	10	26
Chad Tchad	17	5	1	0	0	1	2	26
Comoros Comores	2	9	2	0	1	4	5	23
Congo Congo	12	4	1	0	1	1	33	52
Côte d'Ivoire Côte d'Ivoire	17	12	2	1	0	1	101	134
Dem. Rep. of the Congo Rép. dém. du Congo	40	28	2	0	1	45	55	171
Djibouti Djibouti	4	5	0	0	0	0	2	11
Egypt Egypte	12	7	6	0	0	1	2	28
Equatorial Guinea Guinée équatoriale	15	5	2	1	0	2	23	48
Eritrea Erythrée	12	7	6	0	0	0	3	28
Ethiopia Ethiopie	34	16	1	0	0	4	22	77
Gabon Gabon	15	6	1	0	1	1	71	95
Gambia Gambie	3	2	1	0	1	0	3	10
Ghana Ghana	13	8	2	0	0	0	115	138
Guinea Guinée	11	10	1	1	0	3	21	47
Guinea–Bissau Guinée–Bissau	2	0	1	0	1	1	4	9
Kenya Kenya	51	24	5	0	18	15	98	211
Lesotho Lesotho	3	7	0	0	1	1	0	12
Liberia Libéria	16	11	2	0	0	2	46	77
Libyan Arab Jamahiriya Jamah. arabe libyenne	9	1	3	0	0	0	1	14
Madagascar Madagascar	50	27	18	2	13	30	162	302
Malawi Malawi	8	11	0	0	0	8	14	41
Mali Mali	13	4	1	0	1	0	6	25

67
Threatened species
Number by taxonomic group (as assessed between 1996 and 2000) [cont]
Espèces menacées
Nombre par groupe taxonomique (évaluations réalisées entre 1996 et 2000) [suite]

Country or area Pays ou zone	Mammals Mammifères	Birds Oiseaux	Reptiles Reptiles	Amphibians Amphibiens	Fishes Poissons	Invertebrates Inverterrés	Plants and trees Plantes et arbres	Total
Mauritania Mauritanie	10	2	2	0	0	0	0	14
Mauritius Maurice	4	9	4	0	0	32	87	136
Mayotte Mayotte	0	3	2	0	0	1	0	6
Morocco Maroc	16	9	2	0	0	7	2	36
Mozambique Mozambique	15	16	5	0	3	7	36	82
Namibia Namibie	14	11	3	1	3	1	5	38
Niger Niger	11	3	0	0	0	1	2	17
Nigeria Nigéria	25	9	2	0	2	1	119	158
Reunion Réunion	3	5	2	0	1	16	14	41
Rwanda Rwanda	8	9	0	0	0	2	3	22
Saint Helena Sainte–Hélène	1	13	1	0	8	2	9	34
Sao Tome and Principe Sao Tomé–et–Principe	3	9	1	0	0	2	27	42
Senegal Sénégal	11	4	6	0	1	0	7	29
Seychelles Seychelles	4	10	4	4	0	4	43	69
Sierra Leone Sierra Leone	11	10	3	0	0	4	43	71
Somalia Somalie	19	10	2	0	3	1	17	52
South Africa Afrique du Sud	41	28	19	9	30	111	45	283
Sudan Soudan	24	6	2	0	0	1	17	50
Swaziland Swaziland	4	5	0	0	0	0	3	12
Togo Togo	9	0	2	0	0	0	9	20
Tunisia Tunisie	11	5	3	0	0	5	0	24
Uganda Ouganda	19	13	0	0	27	10	33	102
United Rep. of Tanzania Rép.–Unie de Tanzanie	43	33	5	0	15	47	236	379
Western Sahara Sahara occidental	3	0	0	0	0	0	0	3
Zambia Zambie	12	11	0	0	0	6	8	37
Zimbabwe Zimbabwe	12	10	0	0	0	2	14	38
America, North · Amérique du Nord								
Anguilla Anguilla	0	0	4	0	0	0	3	7
Antigua and Barbuda Antigua–et–Barbuda	0	1	5	0	0	0	4	10
Aruba Aruba	1	0	2	0	0	1	0	4
Bahamas Bahamas	5	4	5	0	1	1	4	20
Barbados Barbade	0	1	2	0	0	0	2	5

67
Threatened species
Number by taxonomic group (as assessed between 1996 and 2000) [*cont*]
Espèces menacées
Nombre par groupe taxonomique (évaluations réalisées entre 1996 et 2000) [*suite*]

Country or area Pays ou zone	Mammals Mammifères	Birds Oiseaux	Reptiles Reptiles	Amphibians Amphibiens	Fishes Poissons	Invertebrates Inverterrés	Plants and trees Plantes et arbres	Total
Belize Belize	4	2	4	0	4	1	28	43
Bermuda Bermudes	2	2	2	0	1	25	4	36
British Virgin Islands Iles Vierges britanniques	0	2	6	1	0	0	4	13
Canada Canada	14	8	2	1	16	10	1	52
Cayman Islands Iles Caïmanes	0	1	2	0	0	1	2	6
Costa Rica Costa Rica	14	13	7	1	0	9	109	153
Cuba Cuba	11	18	7	0	7	3	160	206
Dominica Dominique	1	3	4	0	0	0	11	19
Dominican Republic Rép. dominicaine	5	15	10	1	0	2	29	62
El Salvador El Salvador	2	0	4	0	1	1	23	31
Greenland Groenland	7	0	0	0	0	0	1	8
Grenada Grenade	0	1	4	0	1	0	3	9
Guadeloupe Guadeloupe	5	1	5	0	0	1	7	19
Guatemala Guatemala	6	6	8	0	1	8	77	106
Haiti Haïti	4	14	7	1	0	2	27	55
Honduras Honduras	9	5	6	0	1	2	108	131
Jamaica Jamaïque	5	12	8	4	0	5	206	240
Martinique Martinique	0	2	5	0	0	1	8	16
Mexico Mexique	69	39	18	4	88	40	161	419
Montserrat Montserrat	1	2	4	0	0	0	3	10
Netherland Antilles Antilles néerlandaises	3	1	6	0	0	0	2	12
Nicaragua Nicaragua	6	5	7	0	1	2	39	60
Panama Panama	20	16	7	0	3	2	193	241
Puerto Rico Porto Rico	2	8	8	3	0	1	48	70
Saint Kitts and Nevis Saint−Kitts−et−Nevis	0	1	3	0	0	0	2	6
Saint Lucia Sainte−Lucie	1	5	6	0	0	0	6	18
Saint Pierre and Miquelon Saint−Pierre−et−Miquelon	0	1	0	0	0	0	0	1
Saint Vincent and the Grenadines St. Vincent−et−Grenadines	2	2	4	0	0	0	4	12
Trinidad and Tobago Trinité−et−Tobago	1	1	5	0	0	0	1	8
Turks and Caicos Islands Iles Turques et Caïques	0	3	4	0	0	0	2	9
United States Etats−Unis	37	55	27	25	131	555	168	998

67
Threatened species
Number by taxonomic group (as assessed between 1996 and 2000) [*cont*]
Espèces menacées
Nombre par groupe taxonomique (évaluations réalisées entre 1996 et 2000) [*suite*]

Country or area Pays ou zone	Mammals Mammifères	Birds Oiseaux	Reptiles Reptiles	Amphibians Amphibiens	Fishes Poissons	Invertebrates Invertérrés	Plants and trees Plantes et arbres	Total
United States Virgin Islands Iles Vierges américaines	1	2	5	0	0	0	7	15
America, South · Amérique du Sud								
Argentina Argentine	32	39	6	5	2	11	41	136
Bolivia Bolivie	23	27	2	1	0	1	70	124
Brazil Brésil	79	113	22	6	17	34	338	609
Chile Chili	21	21	0	3	4	0	40	89
Colombia Colombie	36	77	13	0	6	0	213	345
Ecuador Equateur	31	62	10	0	3	23	197	326
Falkland Island (Malvinas) Iles Falkland (Malvinas)	4	5	0	0	0	0	0	9
French Guyana Guyane française	9	0	7	0	0	0	16	32
Guyana Guyana	9	2	6	0	0	1	23	41
Paraguay Paraguay	9	26	2	0	0	0	10	47
Peru Pérou	47	73	6	1	0	2	269	398
Suriname Suriname	11	1	6	0	0	0	27	45
Uruguay Uruguay	6	11	3	0	3	1	1	25
Venezuela Venezuela	25	24	12	0	5	1	67	134
Asia · Asie								
Afghanistan Afghanistan	13	11	1	1	0	1	1	28
Armenia Arménie	7	4	5	0	1	7	0	24
Azerbaijan Azerbaïdjan	13	8	5	0	5	6	0	37
Bahrain Bahreïn	1	6	0	0	1	0	0	8
Bangladesh Bangladesh	21	23	21	0	0	0	12	77
Bhutan Bhoutan	20	12	0	0	0	1	7	40
British Indian Ocean Territory Terr. brit. de l'océan indien	0	0	2	0	0	0	1	3
Brunei Darussalam Brunéi Darussalam	9	15	3	0	2	0	99	128
Cambodia Cambodge	21	19	10	0	7	0	29	86
China †† Chine ††	76	73	31	1	33	4	167	385
China, Hong Kong SAR † Chine, Hong Kong RAS †	1	11	1	0	0	1	4	18
China, Macao SAR † Chine, Macao RAS †	0	1	0	0	0	0	0	1
Cyprus Chypre	3	3	3	0	0	0	1	10
East Timor Timor oriental	0	6	0	0	0	0	0	6
Georgia Géorgie	14	3	7	1	6	10	0	41

67
Threatened species
Number by taxonomic group (as assessed between 1996 and 2000) [*cont*]
Espèces menacées
Nombre par groupe taxonomique (évaluations réalisées entre 1996 et 2000) [*suite*]

Country or area Pays ou zone	Mammals Mammifères	Birds Oiseaux	Reptiles Reptiles	Amphibians Amphibiens	Fishes Poissons	Invertebrates Inverterrés	Plants and trees Plantes et arbres	Total
India Inde	86	70	25	3	8	23	244	459
Indonesia Indonésie	140	113	28	0	67	31	384	763
Iran (Islamic Republic of) Iran (République islamique d')	23	13	8	2	7	3	1	57
Iraq Iraq	10	11	2	0	2	2	0	27
Israel Israël	14	12	4	0	0	10	0	40
Japan Japon	37	34	11	10	13	45	11	161
Jordan Jordanie	8	8	1	0	0	3	0	20
Kazakhstan Kazakhstan	18	15	2	1	7	4	0	47
Korea, Dem.People's Rep. Corée, R. p. dém. de	13	19	0	0	0	1	3	36
Korea, Republic of Corée, République de	13	25	0	0	0	1	0	39
Kuwait Koweït	1	7	1	0	0	0	0	9
Kyrgyzstan Kirghizistan	7	4	2	0	0	3	0	16
Lao People's Dem. Rep. Rép. dém. pop. lao	27	19	12	0	7	0	18	83
Lebanon Liban	6	7	1	0	0	1	0	15
Malaysia Malaisie	47	37	21	0	16	3	681	805
Maldives Maldives	0	1	2	0	0	0	0	3
Mongolia Mongolie	12	16	0	0	0	3	0	31
Myanmar Myanmar	36	35	20	0	1	2	37	131
Nepal Népal	27	26	5	0	0	1	6	65
Occupied Palestinian Terr. Territoire palestinien occupé	1	1	0	0	0	0	0	2
Oman Oman	9	10	4	0	4	1	6	34
Pakistan Pakistan	18	17	9	0	1	0	2	47
Philippines Philippines	50	67	8	22	28	19	193	387
Qatar Qatar	0	6	1	0	0	0	0	7
Saudi Arabia Arabie saoudite	7	15	2	0	0	1	3	28
Singapore Singapour	3	7	3	0	2	1	54	70
Sri Lanka Sri Lanka	20	14	8	0	9	2	280	333
Syrian Arab Republic Rép. arabe syrienne	4	8	3	0	0	3	0	18
Tajikistan Tadjikistan	9	7	1	0	3	2	1	23
Thailand Thaïlande	34	37	18	0	19	1	78	187
Turkey Turquie	17	11	12	3	22	13	3	81
Turkmenistan Turkménistan	13	6	2	0	7	4	0	32
United Arab Emirates Emirats arabes unis	3	8	1	0	1	0	0	13

67
Threatened species
Number by taxonomic group (as assessed between 1996 and 2000) [*cont*]
Espèces menacées
Nombre par groupe taxonomique (évaluations réalisées entre 1996 et 2000) [*suite*]

Country or area Pays ou zone	Mammals Mammifères	Birds Oiseaux	Reptiles Reptiles	Amphibians Amphibiens	Fishes Poissons	Invertebrates Inverterrés	Plants and trees Plantes et arbres	Total
Uzbekistan Ouzbékistan	11	9	1	0	4	1	0	26
Viet Nam Viet Nam	37	35	24	1	6	0	126	229
Yemen Yémen	4	12	2	0	0	2	52	72
Europe · Europe								
Albania Albanie	3	3	4	0	7	4	0	21
Andorra Andorre	1	0	0	0	0	4	0	5
Austria Autriche	9	3	0	0	7	44	3	66
Belarus Bélarus	5	3	0	0	0	6	6	20
Belgium Belgique	11	2	0	0	0	12	0	25
Bosnia and Herzegovina Bosnie–Herzégovine	10	3	1	1	6	8	1	30
Bulgaria Bulgarie	15	10	2	0	10	9	0	46
Croatia Croatie	9	4	1	1	21	8	0	44
Czech Republic République tchèque	8	2	0	0	7	20	3	40
Denmark Danemark	5	1	0	0	0	11	3	20
Estonia Estonie	5	3	0	0	0	3	0	11
Faeroe Island Iles Féroé	3	0	0	0	0	0	0	3
Finland Finlande	6	3	0	0	0	9	1	19
France France	18	5	3	1	5	64	2	98
Germany Allemagne	12	5	0	0	6	32	12	67
Gibraltar Gibraltar	0	1	0	0	0	2	0	3
Greece Grèce	14	7	6	1	19	10	2	59
Hungary Hongrie	9	8	1	0	8	26	1	53
Iceland Islande	6	0	0	0	0	0	0	6
Ireland Irlande	5	1	0	0	0	2	1	9
Italy Italie	14	5	4	4	8	57	3	95
Latvia Lettonie	5	3	0	0	1	8	0	17
Liechtenstein Liechtenstein	3	1	0	0	0	5	0	9
Lithuania Lituanie	5	4	0	0	1	5	0	15
Luxembourg Luxembourg	6	1	0	0	0	4	0	11
Malta Malte	3	1	0	0	0	3	0	7
Netherlands Pays–Bas	11	4	0	0	0	8	0	23

67
Threatened species
Number by taxonomic group (as assessed between 1996 and 2000) [*cont*]
Espèces menacées
Nombre par groupe taxonomique (évaluations réalisées entre 1996 et 2000) [*suite*]

Country or area Pays ou zone	Mammals Mammifères	Birds Oiseaux	Reptiles Reptiles	Amphibians Amphibiens	Fishes Poissons	Invertebrates Inverterrés	Plants and trees Plantes et arbres	Total
Norway								
Norvège	10	2	0	0	0	9	2	23
Poland								
Pologne	15	4	0	0	1	15	4	39
Portugal								
Portugal	17	7	0	1	9	82	15	131
Republic of Moldova								
Rép. de Moldova	3	5	1	0	9	5	0	23
Romania								
Roumanie	17	8	2	0	10	21	1	59
Russian Federation								
Fédération de Russie	42	38	6	0	14	29	0	129
San Marino								
Saint−Marin	1	0	0	0	0	0	0	1
Slovakia								
Slovaquie	9	4	1	0	8	21	1	44
Slovenia								
Slovénie	9	1	0	1	8	66	0	85
Spain								
Espagne	24	7	6	3	11	35	14	100
Svalbard and Jan Mayen Islands								
Iles Svalbard et Jan Mayen	5	0	0	0	0	0	0	5
Sweden								
Suède	8	2	0	0	0	13	3	26
Switzerland								
Suisse	6	2	0	0	4	29	2	43
TFYR Macedonia								
L'ex−R.y. Macédoine	11	3	2	0	4	3	0	23
Ukraine								
Ukraine	17	8	2	0	12	15	1	55
United Kingdom								
Royaume−Uni	12	2	0	0	1	11	13	39
Yugoslavia								
Yougoslavie	11	5	1	0	10	21	1	49
Oceania · Océanie								
American Samoa								
Samoa américaines	3	2	2	0	0	5	1	13
Australia								
Australie	63	35	39	25	44	280	38	524
Christmas Island								
Ile Christmas	0	5	2	0	0	0	1	8
Cook Islands								
Iles Cook	1	7	2	0	0	0	1	11
Fiji								
Fidji	5	12	6	1	0	2	65	91
French Polynesia								
Polynésie française	3	23	1	0	3	29	47	106
Guam								
Guam	2	2	2	0	1	5	3	15
Kiribati								
Kiribati	0	4	1	0	0	1	0	6
Marshall Islands								
Iles Marshall	1	1	2	0	0	1	0	5
Micronesia (Fed. States of)								
Micronésie (Etats fédérés de)	6	5	2	0	0	4	4	21
Nauru								
Nauru	0	2	0	0	0	0	0	2
New Caledonia								
Nouvelle−Calédonie	6	10	2	0	0	11	214	243
New Zealand								
Nouvelle−Zélande	8	62	11	1	8	13	21	124
Niue								
Nioué	0	1	1	0	0	0	0	2

67
Threatened species
Number by taxonomic group (as assessed between 1996 and 2000) [cont]
Espèces menacées
Nombre par groupe taxonomique (évaluations réalisées entre 1996 et 2000) [suite]

Country or area Pays ou zone	Mammals Mammifères	Birds Oiseaux	Reptiles Reptiles	Amphibians Amphibiens	Fishes Poissons	Invertebrates Inverterrés	Plants and trees Plantes et arbres	Total
Norfolk Island Ile Norfolk	0	7	2	0	0	12	1	22
Northern Mariana Islands Iles Mariannes septentrionales	2	8	2	0	0	2	4	18
Palau Palaos	3	2	2	0	0	5	3	15
Papua New Guinea Papouasie – Nvl – Guinée	58	32	9	0	12	12	142	265
Pitcairn Pitcairn	0	8	0	0	0	5	7	20
Samoa Samoa	3	7	1	0	0	1	2	14
Solomon Islands Iles Salomon	21	23	4	0	0	6	16	70
Tokelau Tokélau	0	1	2	0	0	0	0	3
Tonga Tonga	1	3	2	0	0	2	2	10
Tuvalu Tuvalu	0	1	1	0	0	1	0	3
Vanuatu Vanuatu	4	7	2	0	0	0	9	22
Wallis and Futuna Islands Iles Wallis – et – Futuna	0	1	0	0	0	0	1	2

Source:
World Conservation Union (IUCN) / Species Survival Commission (SSC), Gland, Switzerland and Cambridge, United Kingdom, "2000 IUCN Red List of Threatened Species".

† For information on the recent changes in country or area nomenclature pertaining to former Czechoslovakia, Germany, Hong Kong Special Administrative Region (SAR) of China, Macao Special Administrative Region (SAR) of China, SFR of Yugoslavia and the former USSR, see Annex I – Country or area nomenclature, regional and other groupings.

†† For statistical purposes the data for China do not include those for Hong Kong Special Administrative Region (Hong Kong SAR), Macao Special Administrative Region (Macao SAR) and Taiwan province of China.

Source:
Union mondiale pour la nature (UICN) / Commission de la sauvegarde des espèces, Gland, Suisse, et Cambridge, Royaume – Uni, "La liste rouge des espèces menacées 2000 de l'UICN".

† Pour les modifications récentes de nomenclature de pays ou de zone concernant l'Allemagne, Hong Kong, région administrative spéciale (RAS) de Chine, Macao, région administrative spéciale (RAS) de Chine, l'ex – Tchécoslovaquie, l'ex – URSS et l'ex – Rfs de Yougoslavie, voir annex I – Nomenclature des pays ou des zones, groupements régionaux et autres groupements.

†† Les données statistiques relatives à la Chine ne comprennent pas celles qui concernent la région administrative spéciale de Hong Kong (la RAS de Hong Kong), la région administrative spéciale de Macao (la RAS de Macao), et la province chinoise de Taiwan.

Technical notes, tables 64-67

Table 64: The data on land use is compiled by the Food and Agriculture Organization of the United Nations (FAO). FAO's definitions of land use (land cover) categories are as follows:

Total area: The total area of the country, including area under inland water bodies. The definition of inland water bodies generally includes major rivers and lakes.

Land area: Total area excluding area under inland water bodies.

Data in the two categories above are obtained mainly from the United Nations Statistics Division (UNSD).

Arable land: Land under temporary crops (double-cropped areas are counted only once); temporary meadows for mowing or pasture; land under market and kitchen gardens; and land temporarily fallow (less than five years). Abandoned land resulting from shifting cultivation is not included in this category. Data for "arable land" are not meant to indicate the amount of land that is potentially cultivable.

Permanent crops: Land cultivated with crops that occupy the land for long periods and need not be replanted after each harvest, such as cocoa, coffee and rubber. This category includes land under flowering shrubs, fruit trees, nut trees and vines, but excludes land under trees grown for wood or timber.

Table 65: The sources of the data presented on the emissions of carbon dioxide (CO_2) are the Secretariat of the United Nations Framework Convention on Climate Change (UNFCCC) and the Carbon Dioxide Information Analysis Center (CDIAC) of the Oak Ridge National Laboratory in the USA. The UNFCCC data in the table are indicated by a footnote, and cover (a) the countries that joined the convention (except for Belarus which joined in May 2000) and (b) countries which voluntarily reported time-series data on their emissions to the UNFCCC. The CO_2 data from national reports to the Secretariat of the UNFCCC are based on the methodology of the Intergovernmental Panel for Climate Change (IPCC) 1996 Guidebook. The CDIAC estimates of CO_2 emissions are derived primarily from United Nations energy statistics on the consumption of liquid and solid fuels and gas consumption and flaring, and from cement production estimates from the Bureau of Mines of the U.S. Department of Interior. The emissions presented in the table are in units of 1,000 metric tons of carbon dioxide (CO_2); to convert CO_2 into carbon, multiply the data by 0.272756. Full details of the procedures for calculating emissions are given in the CDIAC Web site. Relative to other industrial sources for which CO_2 emissions are estimated, statistics on gas flaring activities are

Notes techniques, tableaux 64 à 67

Tableau 64: Les données relatives à l'utilisation des terres sont compilées par la FAO. Les définitions de la FAO en ce qui concerne l'utilisation des terres et la couverture végétale des terres sont les suivantes:

Superficie totale: Superficie totale du pays, y compris les eaux intérieures;

Superficie totale des terres: Superficie totale, à l'exception des eaux intérieures. Les eaux intérieures désignent généralement les principaux fleuves et lacs.

Les données de ces deux catégories proviennent en grande partie de la Division de statistique de l'Organisation des Nations Unies.

Terres arables: Terres affectées aux cultures temporaires (les terres sur lesquelles est pratiquée la double culture ne sont comptabilisées qu'une fois), prairies temporaires à faucher ou à pâturer, jardins maraîchers ou potagers et terres en jachère temporaire (moins de cinq ans). Cette définition ne comprend pas les terres abandonnées du fait de la culture itinérante. Les données relatives aux terres arables ne peuvent être utilisées pour calculer la superficie des terres aptes à l'agriculture.

Cultures permanentes: Superficie des terres avec des cultures qui occupent la terre pour de longues périodes et qui ne nécessitent pas d'être replantées après chaque récolte, comme le cacao, le café et le caoutchouc. Cette catégorie comprend les terres plantées d'arbustes à fleurs, d'arbres fruitiers, d'arbres à noix et de vignes, mais ne comprend pas les terres plantées d'arbres destinés à la coupe.

Tableau 65: Les données sur les émissions de dioxyde de carbone (CO_2) proviennent du secrétariat de la Convention-cadre des Nations Unies sur les changements climatiques et du Carbon Dioxide Information Analysis Center du Oak Ridge National Laboratory (États-Unis). Les données provenant du secrétariat de la Convention-cadre, qui sont signalées par une note, couvrent (a) les pays qui ont adhéré à la Convention (sauf pour le Bélarus, qui y a adhéré en mai 2000), et (b) les pays qui ont bénévolement communiqué des séries chronologiques sur leurs émissions au secrétariat. Les données sur le CO_2 tirées des rapports de pays au secrétariat de la Convention-cadre ont été obtenues par les méthodes recommandées dans le Manuel de 1996 du Groupe intergouvernemental d'experts pour l'étude du changement climatique. Les estimations du Carbon Dioxide Information Analysis Center sont obtenues essentiellement à partir des statistiques de l'énergie des Nations Unies relatives à la consommation de combustibles liquides et solides, à la production et à la consommation de gaz de torche, et des chiffres de production de ciment du Bureau of Mines du Department of Interior des États-

sparse and sporadic. In countries where gas flaring activities account for a considerable proportion of the total CO_2 emissions, the sporadic nature of gas flaring statistics may produce spurious or misleading trends in national CO_2 emissions over the period covered by the table.

Table 66: Data were extracted from the *Global water supply and sanitation assessment 2000 report* [33], published by the WHO/UNICEF Joint Monitoring Programme for Water Supply and Sanitation. A review of water and sanitation coverage data from the 1980s and the first part of the 1990s showed that the definition of safe, or improved, water supply and sanitation facilities sometimes differed not only from one country to another, but also for a given country over time. Coverage data were based on estimates by service *providers*, rather than on the responses of *consumers* to household surveys, and these estimates can differ substantially. The Assessment 2000 marks a shift from gathering provider-based information only to include also consumer-based information.

Data were collected from two main sources: assessment questionnaires and household surveys. Assessment questionnaires were sent to all WHO country representatives, to be completed in liaison with local UNICEF staff and relevant national agencies involved in the sector. Household survey results and data obtained from Demographic Health Surveys (DHS) and Multiple Indicator Cluster Surveys (MICS) were collected and reviewed. The DHS and MICS are national cluster sample surveys, covering several thousand households in each country. They collect information on the main source of drinking water used, as well as the sanitation facility.

While the type of water source and the type of excreta disposal facility can be associated with the quality of water and the adequacy of disposal, respectively, they cannot adequately measure population coverage of *safe* water or of *sanitary* excreta disposal. Access to water and sanitation does not imply that the level of service or quality of water is "adequate" or "safe". The assessment questionnaire did not include any methodology for discounting coverage figures to allow for intermittence or poor quality of the water supplies. Hence, the coverage estimates presented represent the population covered by *improved* water sources and *improved* sanitary facilities.

Access to water supply and sanitation is defined in terms of the types of technology and levels of service afforded. For water, this included house connections, public standpipes, boreholes with handpumps, protected dug wells, protected springs and rainwater collection; allowance was also made for other locally-defined technologies. "Reasonable access" was broadly defined as

Unis. Les émissions sont indiquées en milliers de tonnes de dioxyde de carbone (à multiplier par 0,272756 pour avoir les chiffres de carbone). On peut voir dans le détail les méthodes utilisées pour calculer les émissions sur le site Web du Carbon Dioxide Information Analysis Center. Par rapport à d'autres sources industrielles pour lesquelles on calcule les émissions de CO_2 les statistiques sur la production de gaz de torche sont rares et sporadiques. Dans les pays où cette production représente une proportion considérable de l'ensemble des émissions de dioxyde de carbone, on peut voir apparaître de ce fait des chiffres parasites ou trompeurs pour ce qui est des tendances des émissions nationales de dioxyde de carbone durant la période visée par le tableau.

Tableau 66: Les données proviennent du *Bilan mondial de l'approvisionnement en eau et de l'assainissement à l'horizon 2000* [33], publié par l'OMS et l'UNICEF (Programme commun de surveillance de l'eau et de l'assainissement). Lorsqu'on a examiné ce que couvraient les données sur l'eau et l'assainissement des années 80 et de la première moitié des années 90, on a constaté que la définition de l'approvisionnement en eau potable (ou améliorée) et des installations d'assainissement n'étaient pas la même non seulement d'un pays à un autre, mais dans un même pays, d'une période à une autre. Les données sur la couverture proviennent de chiffres communiqués par les *prestataires* de services, et non pas des réponses d'usagers à des enquêtes sur les ménages, qui peuvent donner des chiffres assez différents des premiers. Le Bilan à l'horizon 2000, pour la première fois, présente non seulement des chiffres provenant des prestataires, mais aussi des usagers.

Les données ont été collectées à deux sources principales : les réponses aux questionnaires envoyés pour le bilan, et les enquêtes sur les ménages. Les questionnaires ont été adressés à tous les représentants de pays de l'OMS, remplis en liaison avec les agents locaux de l'UNICEF et les organismes nationaux compétents et actifs dans ce secteur. On a réuni et utilisé les résultats d'enquêtes sur les ménages et les données tirées d'enquêtes sur la démographie et la santé et d'enquêtes en grappe à indicateurs multiples. Ces deux derniers types d'enquête sont des enquêtes réalisées par les pays sur un échantillon en grappe de plusieurs milliers de ménages dans chaque pays participant. Elles permettent de réunir des renseignements sur la principale provenance de l'eau utilisée pour l'alimentation, ainsi que sur les installations d'assainissement.

Si la provenance de l'eau utilisée de même que le type d'installation d'évacuation des excréments peuvent renseigner sur la qualité de l'eau et celle de l'évacuation, ils ne suffisent pas à mesurer la proportion

the availability of at least 20 litres per person per day from a source within one kilometre of the user's dwelling. Sanitation was defined to include connection to a sewer or septic tank system, pour-flush latrine, simple pit or ventilated improved pit latrine, again with allowance for acceptable local technologies.

The Assessment 2000 did not provide a standard definition of urban or rural areas. The countries' own working definition of urban and rural was used. Similarly, when using household survey data, definitions predetermined by those responsible for the survey were accepted.

Estimates of percentage coverage for a region are based upon available data from the reporting countries in the region. When no data were available for countries in a region, estimates were extrapolated from countries in the region for which data were available. Such extrapolation, however, is used only to compute regional statistics: any country data reported in this assessment are based on reports for the country concerned.

Table 67: Data on the numbers of threatened species in each group of animals and plants are compiled by the World Conservation Union (IUCN)/Species Survival Commission (SSC) and published in the 2000 IUCN *Red List of Threatened Species* [32].

This list provides a catalogue of those species that are considered globally threatened. The categories used in the 2000 Red List are as follows: Extinct (EX), Extinct in the Wild (EW),Critically Endangered (CR),Endangered (EN),Vulnerable (VU), Low Risk, conservation dependent (LR/cd),Low Risk, near threatened (LR/nt) and Data Deficient (DD).

de la population qui dispose d'eau *potable* ou d'un système d'évacuation *hygiénique*. L'accès à l'eau ou à l'assainissement ne signifie pas que le service ou la qualité de l'eau soient "suffisants" ou "salubres". On n'avait pas prévu pour le questionnaire du bilan de moyens permettant d'ajuster les chiffres de couverture si le service était intermittent ou l'eau de mauvaise qualité. Les chiffres de population couverte visent donc la population ayant accès à un approvisionnement en eau et à des installations d'assainissement *de qualité améliorée*.

L'accès à la distribution d'eau et à l'assainissement est défini par les types de technologie et le niveau de service accessibles. Pour l'eau, il s'agissait d'eau courante dans le logement, de bornes-fontaines, de points d'eau équipés de pompe à bras, de puits protégés, de sources protégées et de systèmes de captage des eaux pluviales; on a tenu compte aussi d'autres méthodes de définition locale. Un "accès raisonnable" était défini en gros comme la possibilité de se procurer 20 litres d'eau par personne et par jour à moins d'un kilomètre du logement. L'assainissement était défini comme branchement à un égout ou à une fosse septique, à des latrines à chasse d'eau, à une fosse d'aisance ou à des latrines améliorées à fosse autoventilée, compte tenu là aussi de méthodes locales acceptables.

Le Bilan à l'horizon 2000 ne comportait pas de définition normalisée des zones urbaines ou rurales. On a utilisé la définition opérationnelle en usage dans le pays considéré. De même, on a accepté pour les données issues d'enquêtes sur les ménages les définitions choisies par les responsables de l'enquête.

Les chiffres de couverture (en pourcentage) pour une région donnée sont basés sur les données disponibles communiquées par les pays de la région. Lorsqu'il n'y avait pas de données pour des pays d'une région, on a extrapolé les chiffres disponibles des pays de la même région. Mais l'extrapolation n'a servi qu'à calculer des statistiques régionales: les données de pays figurant dans le bilan sont tirés de chiffres effectivement communiqués pour le pays en cause.

Tableau 67: Les données relatives aux espèces menacées pour chaque groupe d'animaux et de plantes, réunies par la Commission de la sauvegarde des espèces de l'Union mondiale pour la nature (UICN), sont publiées dans la *Liste rouge des espèces menacées 2000* de l'UICN [32].

Cette liste répertorie les espèces animales considérées comme menacées à l'échelle mondiale, réparties entre les catégories ci-après: éteintes, éteintes à l'état sauvage, gravement menacées d'extinction, menacées d'extinction, vulnérables, à faible risque (dépendant de mesures de conservation, ou quasi menacées), catégorie à données insuffisantes.

68
Patents
Brevets
Applications, grants, patents in force: number
Demandes, délivrances, brevets en vigueur : nombre

Country or area Pays ou zone	Applications for patents Demandes de brevets			Grants of patents Brevets délivrés			Patents in force Brevets en vigueur		
	1996	1997	1998	1996	1997	1998	1996	1997	1998
African Intellectual Prop. Org[1] Org. africaine de la prop. intel.[1]	20 938	26 088	34 995	231	242	265	...	...	1 229
Albania Albanie	18 762	26 005	35 159	...	...	...	...	...	...
Algeria Algérie	198	240	306	...	863	...	1 354	1 368	...
Argentina Argentine	...	5 859	6 320	1 792	1 228	1 689	...	...	...
Armenia Arménie	20 430	25 122	33 899	127	143	85	...	187	261
Australia Australie	43 321	48 211	57 706	8 987	9 464	14 784	73 884	76 694	83 429
Austria Autriche	78 491	111 224	147 040	16 085	16 025	14 963	15 556	14 184	13 621
Azerbaijan Azerbaïdjan	16 635	24 308	33 507	81	...	19	...	...	...
Bangladesh Bangladesh	...	...	216	...	...	140	...	...	...
Barbados Barbade	20 945	26 322	35 001	...	...	...	...	...	...
Belarus Bélarus	21 048	26 035	35 269	409	483	687	1 631	...	...
Belgium Belgique	60 455	86 645	112 652	18 136	17 673	16 093	88 885	85 663	88 752
Bosnia and Herzegovina Bosnie-Herzégovine	3 056	23 197	34 441	...	...	...	...	...	...
Botswana Botswana	61	93	92	107	32	21	...	...	...
Brazil Brésil	32 106	31 983	41 621	1 487	...	...	15 429	...	...
Bulgaria Bulgarie	22 553	28 000	36 575	530	448	534	2 168	1 908	1 754
Burundi Burundi	5	...	...	5	...	...	60	...	...
Canada Canada	49 254	54 446	65 682	7 145	7 283	9 572	259 379	246 900	235 916
Chile Chili	1 960	...	...	181	...	...	6 300	...	...
China †† Chine ††	52 714	61 382	82 289	2 976	3 494	4 735	20 491	20 310	...
China, Hong Kong SAR† Chine, Hong Kong RAS†	2 100	2 385	14 667	2 205	1 487	2 453	...	...	...
China, Macao SAR † Chine, Macao RAS †	...	...	...	4	19	4	46	...	...
Colombia Colombie	1 259	...	1 736	370	...	476	...	...	417
Croatia Croatie	615	712	12 906	281	119	244	306	...	...
Cuba Cuba	4 918	23 271	33 997	50	50	...	1 293	1 399	...

68
Patents
Applications, grants, patents in force: number [*cont.*]
Brevets
Demandes, délivrances, brevets en vigueur : nombre [*suite*]

Country or area Pays ou zone	Applications for patents Demandes de brevets			Grants of patents Brevets délivrés			Patents in force Brevets en vigueur		
	1996	1997	1998	1996	1997	1998	1996	1997	1998
Cyprus Chypre	...	4	77 374	...	...	...	...	...	...
Czech Republic République tchèque	25 479	30 577	39 196	1 290	1 477	1 451	6 222	6 203	7 001
Dem. Rep. of the Congo Rép. dém. du Congo	29	...	...	14	...	...	644	...	...
Denmark Danemark	74 603	109 061	146 357	11 494	12 103	11 018	26 353	29 322	...
Ecuador Equateur	361	310	...	159	212	...	159	...	...
Egypt Egypte	1 210	...	1 633	250	...	118	7 676	...	...
Estonia Estonie	21 156	26 644	35 501	22	108	82	22	130	212
Ethiopia Ethiopie	3	4	...	...	...	...	...	...	...
European Patent Office[2] Office européen de brevets[2]	86 614	97 943	113 408	40 069	39 646	36 718	...	...	...
Finland Finlande	64 818	109 437	146 884	2 302	2 315	2 329	19 529	19 878	20 274
France France	98 508	112 631	130 015	49 245	50 448	46 213	314 849	324 341	326 447
Gambia Gambie	54	200	60 272	98	29	18	...	...	...
Georgia Géorgie	21 413	26 826	35 728	327	318	536	608	...	961
Germany: deutsche mark Allemagne : deutsche mark	155 095	175 595	202 771	55 444	55 053	51 685	316 305	337 227	354 879
Ghana Ghana	33	34 103	66 173	96	29	13	...	...	...
Greece Grèce	52 805	82 443	111 339	8 603	8 555	7 857	5 182	...	...
Grenada Grenade	...	...	3 330	...	...	...	...	...	...
Guatemala Guatemala	104	135	207	8	15	17	...	...	...
Guinea-Bissau Guinée-Bissau	...	25	15 568	...	...	...	...	...	...
Haiti Haïti	9	...	...	15	...	...	...	...	...
Honduras Honduras	136	...	151	55	...	58	101	...	...
Hungary Hongrie	24 979	30 105	38 707	1 030	1 189	1 257	11 446	10 951	10 896
Iceland Islande	20 518	26 298	35 182	58	41	35	267	261	275
India Inde	8 292	10 155	282	1 020	...	...	9 448	...	...
Indonesia Indonésie	3 997	4 517	32 910	631	...	...	...	...	...

68
Patents
Applications, grants, patents in force: number [cont.]
Brevets
Demandes, délivrances, brevets en vigueur : nombre [suite]

Country or area	Applications for patents Demandes de brevets			Grants of patents Brevets délivrés			Patents in force Brevets en vigueur		
Pays ou zone	1996	1997	1998	1996	1997	1998	1996	1997	1998
Iran (Islamic Rep. of) Iran (Rép. islamique d')	...	418	496	...	258	241	...	...	...
Iraq Iraq	86	...	...	46	...	...	1 168	...	...
Ireland Irlande	53 332	83 430	112 344	4 602	6 889	7 088	15 115	18 513	...
Israel Israël	13 535	30 344	42 271	2 133	2 152	2 021	12 023	12 018	12 017
Italy Italie	80 852	91 410	123 606	37 935	28 096	38 988	...	...	...
Japan Japon	401 251	417 974	437 375	215 100	147 686	141 448	830 565	870 928	935 858
Jordan Jordanie	...	...	...	...	58		...	...	...
Kazakhstan Kazakhstan	21 088	26 169	35 338	1 161	1 525	1 192	4 116	5 337	5 830
Kenya Kenya	39 049	49 960	67 830	132	79	101	384	136	...
Korea, Dem. P. R. Corée, R. p. dém. de	20 575	25 467	33 918	...	...	...	...	...	...
Korea, Republic of Corée, République de	113 994	129 982	46 517	16 516	24 579	...	74 379	...	...
Kyrgyzstan Kirghizistan	20 305	25 103	33 905	125	133	105	355	488	579
Latvia Lettonie	21 695	27 023	35 963	775	403	297	1 886	...	2 160
Lesotho Lesotho	37 045	49 483	67 491	90	26	36	...	...	...
Liberia Libéria	20 497	26 045	34 862	...	...	...	...	...	...
Libyan Arab Jamah. Jamah. arabe libyenne	35	...	...	...	...	...	...	...	...
Lithuania Lituanie	21 350	26 798	35 838	466	183	165	1 336	1 296	1 219
Luxembourg Luxembourg	70 852	106 484	144 401	9 244	8 981	8 023	...	31 237	30 681
Madagascar Madagascar	20 807	26 174	34 941	30	...	...	49	...	...
Malawi Malawi	39 034	49 934	67 756	117	49	76	545	546	631
Malaysia Malaisie	...	6 451	...	...	786	...	...	...	...
Malta Malte	24	46	34	12	2	28	110	158	110
Mauritius Maurice	22	15	15	4	1	3	136	113	96
Mexico Mexique	30 694	35 932	44 721	3 186	3 944	3 219	32 027	34 799	36 817
Monaco Monaco	49 639	81 270	111 088	2 478	3 791	4 061	329	3 907	241

68
Patents
Applications, grants, patents in force: number [cont.]
Brevets
Demandes, délivrances, brevets en vigueur : nombre [suite]

Country or area Pays ou zone	Applications for patents Demandes de brevets			Grants of patents Brevets délivrés			Patents in force Brevets en vigueur		
	1996	1997	1998	1996	1997	1998	1996	1997	1998
Mongolia Mongolie	20 996	26 383	35 154	112	116	172	443	552	...
Morocco Maroc	327	...	...	327	...	...	6 587	...	6 331
Netherlands Pays-Bas	66 842	90 629	115 076	22 642	23 794	22 411	107 005	112 237	117 453
New Zealand Nouvelle-Zélande	28 368	35 137	39 734	2 771	3 823	4 058	...	...	...
Nicaragua Nicaragua	...	105	154	...	38	18	...	...	...
Norway Norvège	27 178	32 007	44 258	1 860	2 942	2 560	15 254	...	...
Pakistan Pakistan	798	...	...	539	...	...	26 440	...	...
Panama Panama	173	...	...	38	...	...	389	...	...
Peru Pérou	617	804	...	181	180	...	...	...	...
Philippines Philippines	2 797	3 565	3 443	778	916	565	...	...	...
Poland Pologne	27 316	32 538	41 352	2 565	2 330	2 416	14 479	13 704	13 589
Portugal Portugal	71 649	106 687	145 142	4 810	7 229	8 947	9 175	14 235	...
Republic of Moldova République de Moldova	20 535	25 325	34 111	235	225	220	501	653	774
Romania Roumanie	23 970	29 055	37 826	1 860	1 417	1 818	22 691	20 380	20 100
Russian Federation Fédération de Russie	46 287	48 220	58 532	19 678	29 692	23 368	109 467	155 247	173 081
Saint Lucia Sainte-Lucie	3 207	22 899	34 087	4	...	...	25	...	...
Samoa Samoa	3	...	...	1	...	...	41	...	...
Saudi Arabia Arabie saoudite	837	1 058	1 331	2	2	3	5	6	8
Seychelles Seychelles	6	...	...	6	...	...	...	...	...
Sierra Leone Sierra Leone	...	9 506	33 154	...	...	...	...	...	...
Singapore Singapour	38 618	37 655	44 948	3 331	...	2 291	...	...	...
Slovakia Slovaquie	23 066	28 207	36 852	198	562	845	2 019	2 252	2 436
Slovenia Slovénie	21 987	27 447	36 297	515	623	466	1 614	2 518	2 905
South Africa Afrique du Sud	...	...	8	...	...	...	...	...	...
Spain Espagne	83 983	113 767	147 889	19 817	20 613	20 128	153 832	197 806	...

68
Patents
Applications, grants, patents in force: number [cont.]
Brevets
Demandes, délivrances, brevets en vigueur : nombre [suite]

Country or area Pays ou zone	Applications for patents Demandes de brevets			Grants of patents Brevets délivrés			Patents in force Brevets en vigueur		
	1996	1997	1998	1996	1997	1998	1996	1997	1998
Sri Lanka Sri Lanka	21 188	26 403	34 974	205	160	...	1 713	1 873	...
St. Vincent-Grenadines St. Vincent-Grenadines	8	...	...	...	...	...	...	...	...
Sudan Soudan	39 061	49 920	67 719	97	37	64	...	...	...
Swaziland Swaziland	20 322	25 672	34 535	91	34	63	...	...	...
Sweden Suède	83 441	115 000	149 493	18 983	19 412	18 482	95 161	96 809	97 435
Switzerland Suisse	78 275	112 852	147 579	17 304	18 083	16 253	...	94 636	87 527
Syrian Arab Republic Rép. arabe syrienne	...	...	...	49	...	...	...	...	...
Tajikistan Tadjikistan	19 602	24 765	33 779	77	109	57	115	181	177
Thailand Thaïlande	4 558	5 443	5 071	884	729	723	...	...	...
TFYR Macedonia L'ex-R.y. Macédoine	18 987	26 153	35 133	95	79	80	352	431	360
Trinidad and Tobago Trinité-et-Tobago	20 811	26 339	34 969	119	171	...	1 261	...	...
Tunisia Tunisie	174	...	...	146	...	...	2 040	...	...
Turkey Turquie	20 035	28 218	37 386	601	458	796	7 798	11 952	12 786
Turkmenistan Turkménistan	19 014	24 636	33 705	...	206	154	...	...	...
Uganda Ouganda	38 497	49 760	67 610	102	30	66	...	...	...
Ukraine Ukraine	26 502	32 728	41 950	4 270	9 121	4 336	11 988	18 823	19 587
United Arab Emirates Emirats arabes unis	...	...	8	...	...	...	...	...	...
United Kingdom Royaume-Uni	129 353	148 209	176 187	44 335	44 754	43 181	...	...	...
United Rep.Tanzania Rép.-Unie de Tanzanie	...	...	...	...	...	10	...	...	...
United States Etats-Unis	223 419	236 692	262 787	109 646	111 984	147 520	1 127 625	1 113 452	1 173 145
Uruguay Uruguay	207	402	496	22	52	73	1 325	367	386
Uzbekistan Ouzbékistan	22 002	27 307	35 110	421	2	...	421	1 644	...
Venezuela Venezuela	2 004	2 524	...	1 271	9 844	...	...	...	...
Viet Nam Viet Nam	22 243	27 440	35 748	61	111	...	225	363	...
Yugoslavia Yougoslavie	809	17 021	34 541	337	293	342	3 290	2 687	2 059

68

Patents
Applications, grants, patents in force: number [cont.]
Brevets
Demandes, délivrances, brevets en vigueur : nombre [suite]

Country or area Pays ou zone	Applications for patents Demandes de brevets			Grants of patents Brevets délivrés			Patents in force Brevets en vigueur		
	1996	1997	1998	1996	1997	1998	1996	1997	1998
Zambia Zambie	99	96	93	144	33	20	1 297	...	...
Zimbabwe Zimbabwe	211	21 969	66 272	184	33	30	1 656	...	...

Source:
World Intellectual Property Organization (WIPO), Geneva,
"Industrial Property Statistics 1998, Publication A" and
previous issues.

† For information on recent changes in country or
area nomenclature pertaining to former Czechoslovakia,
Germany, Hong Kong Special Administrative Region (SAR) of
China, Macao Special Administrative Region (SAR) of China,
SFR of Yugoslavia and the former USSR, see Annex I - Country
or area nomenclature, regional and other groupings.

†† For statistical purposes, the data for
China do not include those for Hong Kong Special
Administrative Region (Hong Kong SAR), Macao Special
Administrative Region (Macao SAR) and Taiwan province of
China.

1 Members of the African Intellectual Property Organization
(OAPI), which includes Benin, Burkina Faso, Cameroon,
Central African Republic, Chad, Congo, Côte d'Ivoire, Gabon,
Guinea, Mali, Mauritania, Niger, Senegal, Togo.
2 In 1992, the European Patent Office (EPO) was constituted by
the following member countries: Austria, Belgium, Denmark,
France, Germany, Greece, Ireland, Italy, Liechtenstein,
Luxembourg, Monaco, Netherlands, Portugal, Spain, Sweden,
Switzerland, United Kingdom.

Source:
Organisation mondiale de la propriété intellectuelle (OMPI),
Genève, "Statistiques de propriété industrielle 1998,
Publication A" et éditions précédentes.

† Pour les modifications récentes de nomenclature
de pays ou de zone concernant l'Allemagne, Hong Kong, région
administrative spéciale (RAS) de Chine, Macao, région
administrative spéciale (RAS) de Chine,
l'ex-Tchécoslovaquie, l'ex-URSS et l'ex-Rfs de Yougoslavie,
voir annexe I - Nomenclature des pays ou des zones,
groupements régionaux et autres groupements.

†† Les données statistiques relatives à
la Chine ne comprennent pas celles qui concernent la région
administrative spéciale de Hong Kong (la RAS de Hong Kong),
la région administrative spéciale de Macao (la RAS de Macao)
et la province chinoise de Taiwan.

1 Les membres de l'Organisation africaine de la propriété
intellectuelle (OAPI): Bénin, Burkina Faso, Cameroun, Congo,
Côte d'Ivoire, Gabon, Guinée, Mali, Mauritanie, Niger,
République centrafricaine, Sénégal, Tchad, Togo.
2 En 1992, l'Office européen de brevets (OEB) comprenait les
pays membres suivants: Allemagne, Autriche, Belgique,
Danemark, Espagne, France, Grèce, Irlande, Italie,
Liechtenstein, Luxembourg, Monaco, Pays-Bas, Portugal,
Royaume-Uni, Suède, Suisse.

Technical notes, table 68

Table 68: Data on patents include patent applications filed directly with the office concerned and grants made on the basis of such applications; inventors' certificates; patents of importation, including patents of introduction, revalidation patents and "patentes precaucionales"; petty patents; patents applied and granted under the Patent Cooperation Treaty (PCT), the European Patent Convention, the Havana Agreement, the Harare Protocol of the African Regional Industrial Property Organization (ARIPO) and the African Intellectual Property Organization (OAPI). The data are compiled and published by the World Intellectual Property Organization [34].

Notes techniques, tableau 68

Tableau 68: Les données relatives aux brevets comprennent les demandes de brevet déposées directement auprès de l'office intéressé et brevets délivrés sur la base de telles demandes; les brevets d'invention; les brevets d'importation; y compris les brevets d'introduction, les brevets de revalidation et les brevets "precaucionales"; les petits brevets, les brevets demandés et délivrés en vertu du traité de coopération sur les brevets, de la Convention européenne relative aux brevets, de l'Accord de la Havane, du Protocole d'Hararé de l'Organisation régionale africaine de la propriété industrielle (ARIPO) et de l'Organisation africaine de la propriété intellectuelle (OAPI). Les données sont compilées et publiées par l'Organisation mondiale de la propriété intellectuelle [34].

Part Four
International Economic Relations

XVI
International merchandise trade
(tables 69-71)
XVII
International tourism (tables 72-74)
XVIII
Balance of payments (table 75)
XIX
International finance (tables 76 and 77)
XX
Development assistance (tables 78-80)

Part Four of the *Yearbook* presents statistics on international economic relations in areas of international merchandise trade, international tourism, balance of payments and assistance to developing countries. The series cover all countries or areas of the world for which data are available.

Quatrième partie
Relations économiques internationales

XVI
Commerce international des marchandises
(tableaux 69 à 71)
XVII
Tourisme international (tableaux 72 à 74)
XVIII
Balance des paiements (tableau 75)
XIX
Finances internationales (tableaux 76 et 77)
XX
Aide au développement (tableaux 78 à 80)

La quatrième partie de l'*Annuaire* présente des statistiques sur les relations économiques internationales dans les domaines du commerce international des marchandises, du tourisme international, de la balance des paiements et de l'assistance aux pays en développement. Les séries couvrent tous les pays ou les zones du monde pour lesquels des données sont disponibles.

69
Total imports and exports
Importations et exportations totales
Value in million US dollars
Valeur en millions de dollars E.-U.

Region, country or area Région, pays ou zone	1990	1991	1992	1993	1994	1995	1996	1997	1998	1999
A. Imports c.i.f. • Importations c.a.f.										
World *Monde*	3 557 011	3 563 918	3 798 610	3 755 627	4 279 142	5 052 714	5 310 932	5 533 424	5 449 884	5 664 891
Developed economies[1][2] Econ. développées[1][2]	2 573 478	2 586 707	2 695 533	2 549 276	2 891 263	3 365 071	3 503 419	3 614 814	3 702 117	3 880 487
Developing economies[2] Econ. en dévelop.[2]	797 125	884 380	1 005 654	1 097 469	1 239 463	1 492 829	1 586 439	1 676 969	1 507 639	1 573 543
Other[3] Autres[3]	186 408	92 831	97 423	108 881	148 416	194 814	221 074	241 641	240 128	210 862
America • Amérique										
Developed economies **Economies développées**	**615 676**	**605 871**	**653 774**	**709 535**	**804 108**	**890 885**	**944 218**	**1 037 793**	**1 085 099**	**1 212 198**
Canada[4][5] Canada[4][5]	123 247	124 782	129 268	139 039	155 076	168 053	174 962	195 980	201 060	214 791
United States[5][6] Etats-Unis[5][6]	516 987	508 363	553 923	603 438	689 215	770 852	822 025	899 019	944 353	1 059 430
Developing economies **Econ. en dévelop.**	**129 394**	**145 373**	**172 167**	**187 339**	**218 800**	**247 952**	**270 452**	**320 980**	**331 131**	**321 597**
LAIA+[7] ALAI+[7]	**97 611**	**116 099**	**142 699**	**155 749**	**186 540**	**209 532**	**233 063**	**279 063**	**286 233**	**275 257**
Argentina[8] Argentine[8]	4 076	8 275	14 872	16 784	21 527	20 122	23 762	30 450	31 404	25 538
Bolivia[5] Bolivie[5]	687	970	1 090	1 206	1 209	1 424	1 635	1 851	1 983	1 755
Brazil[4][5] Brésil[4][5]	22 524	22 950	23 068	27 740	35 997	53 783	56 947	65 007	57 731	49 214
Chile[8] Chili[8]	7 678	8 094	10 129	11 125	11 825	15 900	17 823	19 662	18 779	15 137
Colombia[5] Colombie[5]	5 590	4 906	6 516	9 832	11 883	13 853	13 684	15 378	14 635	10 659
Ecuador[5] Equateur[5]	1 865	2 399	2 431	2 562	3 622	4 153	3 935	4 955	5 576	3 017
Mexico[4][5][9] Mexique[4][5][9]	41 594	49 966	62 129	65 367	79 346	72 453	89 469	109 808	125 373	142 064
Paraguay[8] Paraguay[8]	1 352	1 460	1 422	1 689	2 370	3 144	3 204	3 403	...	...
Peru[8] Pérou[8]	3 470	4 195	4 861	4 859	6 691	9 224	9 473	10 264	8 200	6 728
Uruguay[5] Uruguay[5]	1 343	1 637	2 045	2 326	2 786	2 867	3 323	3 716	3 808	3 357
Venezuela[5] Venezuela[5]	7 443	11 256	14 145	12 269	9 292	12 619	9 814	14 573	15 743	14 522
CACM+[10] MCAC+[10]	**6 473**	**6 840**	**8 562**	**9 900**	**10 573**	**12 362**	**13 098**	**15 430**	**17 986**	**18 405**
Costa Rica[8] Costa Rica[8]	1 990	1 877	2 441	3 515	3 789	4 036	4 300	4 924	6 230	6 320
El Salvador[8] El Salvador[8]	1 263	1 406	1 699	1 912	2 249	2 853	2 671	2 973	3 112	3 130
Guatemala[8] Guatemala[8]	1 649	1 851	2 532	2 599	2 604	3 293	3 146	3 852	4 651	4 382

Region, country or area Région, pays ou zone	1990	1991	1992	1993	1994	1995	1996	1997	1998	1999
B. Exports f.o.b. • Exportations f.o.b.										
World *Monde*	**3 437 607**	**3 444 347**	**3 685 643**	**3 707 921**	**4 228 468**	**5 007 781**	**5 205 638**	**5 447 619**	**5 371 072**	**5 546 317**
Developed economies[1,2] Econ. développées[1,2]	2 455 145	2 489 621	2 633 352	2 578 954	2 899 247	3 402 805	3 488 137	3 613 527	3 631 081	3 690 506
Developing economies[2] Econ. en dévelop.[2]	819 838	865 061	959 695	1 026 657	1 183 025	1 420 189	1 520 146	1 625 666	1 536 018	1 653 481
Other[3] Autres[3]	162 625	89 665	92 596	102 311	146 195	184 787	197 354	208 425	203 974	202 330
America • Amérique										
Developed economies **Economies développées**	**496 668**	**521 619**	**553 187**	**577 014**	**637 824**	**728 927**	**773 941**	**845 918**	**836 158**	**878 497**
Canada[4,5] Canada[4,5]	127 634	127 163	134 441	145 182	165 380	192 204	201 636	214 428	214 335	238 422
United States[5,6] Etats-Unis[5,6]	393 592	421 730	448 163	464 773	512 627	584 743	625 073	688 696	682 138	702 098
Developing economies **Econ. en dévelop.**	**144 617**	**142 653**	**149 389**	**159 055**	**184 961**	**225 138**	**251 443**	**277 911**	**275 482**	**293 903**
LAIA+[7] **ALAI+[7]**	**126 912**	**127 054**	**135 043**	**143 917**	**169 151**	**205 946**	**231 922**	**256 126**	**252 840**	**270 527**
Argentina[8] Argentine[8]	12 353	11 978	12 235	13 118	15 659	20 967	23 811	26 370	26 441	23 309
Bolivia[5] Bolivie[5]	926	849	710	728	1 032	1 101	1 137	1 167	1 104	1 033
Brazil[4,5] Brésil[4,5]	31 414	31 620	35 793	38 555	43 545	46 506	47 747	52 990	51 120	48 011
Chile[8] Chili[8]	8 373	8 942	10 007	9 199	11 604	16 137	15 353	16 663	14 830	15 616
Colombia[5] Colombie[5]	6 766	7 232	6 917	7 116	8 419	10 056	10 587	11 522	10 852	11 576
Ecuador[5] Equateur[5]	2 714	2 852	3 007	2 904	3 820	4 307	4 900	5 264	4 203	4 451
Mexico[4,5,9] Mexique[4,5,9]	40 711	42 688	46 196	51 886	60 882	79 542	96 000	110 431	117 460	136 703
Paraguay[8] Paraguay[8]	959	737	657	725	817	919	1 044	1 089	...	...
Peru[8] Pérou[8]	3 231	3 329	3 484	3 515	4 555	5 575	5 897	6 841	5 735	6 116
Uruguay[5] Uruguay[5]	1 693	1 605	1 703	1 645	1 913	2 106	2 397	2 726	2 769	2 232
Venezuela[5] Venezuela[5]	17 783	15 233	14 343	14 536	16 912	18 739	23 054	21 067	17 168	20 288
CACM+[10] **MCAC+[10]**	**4 354**	**4 453**	**4 758**	**5 778**	**6 429**	**8 194**	**8 772**	**10 120**	**11 504**	**11 622**
Costa Rica[8] Costa Rica[8]	1 448	1 598	1 841	2 625	2 869	3 453	3 730	4 268	5 511	6 577
El Salvador[8] El Salvador[8]	582	588	598	732	844	998	1 024	1 359	1 263	1 164
Guatemala[8] Guatemala[8]	1 163	1 202	1 295	1 340	1 522	2 156	2 031	2 344	2 582	2 398

69
Total imports and exports
Value in million US dollars [*cont.*]
Importations et exportations totales
Valeur en millions de dollars E.-U. [*suite*]

Region, country or area Region, pays ou zone	1990	1991	1992	1993	1994	1995	1996	1997	1998	1999
Honduras[8] Honduras[8]	935	955	1 037	1 130	1 056	1 219	1 840	2 149	2 500	2 728
Nicaragua[5] Nicaragua[5]	638	751	855	744	875	962	1 142	1 532	1 492	1 846
Other America **Autres pays d'Amérique**	**25 309**	**22 434**	**20 905**	**21 689**	**21 687**	**26 058**	**24 291**	**26 487**	**26 913**	**27 935**
Antigua and Barbuda[5] Antigua-et-Barbuda[5]	222	246	...	...	...	...	...	...	...	...
Aruba[8] Aruba[8]	536	481	...	...	...	...	...	...	...	...
Bahamas[5 11] Bahamas[5 11]	1 112	1 091	1 038	954	1 056	1 243	1 343	1 622	1 872	1 808
Barbados[5] Barbade[5]	700	695	521	574	611	766	834	996	1 009	1 021
Belize[5] Belize[5]	211	256	274	281	260	256	255	286	325	366
Bermuda[5] Bermudes[5]	595	510	562	534	550	550	569	619	629	...
Cayman Islands[5] Iles Caïmanes[5]	288	267	334	319	327	399	378	...	...	...
Cuba[8] Cuba[8]	6 745	3 690	2 185	1 990	2 055	2 825	3 205	...	...	...
Dominica[8] Dominique[8]	118	110	105	94	96	117	130	125	136	141
Dominican Republic[5 12 13] Rép. dominicaine[5 12 13]	2 062	1 988	2 501	2 436	2 626	2 976	3 686	4 192	4 897	5 380
French Guiana[8 14] Guyane française[8 14]	785	769	669	524	676	752	...	...	...	...
Greenland[5] Groenland[5]	447	408	457	347	364	435	469	397	411	...
Grenada[8] Grenade[8]	105	121	107	118	119	124	152	173	200	...
Guadeloupe[8 14] Guadeloupe[8 14]	1 650	1 644	1 509	1 393	1 539	1 890	...	...	...	...
Guyana[8] Guyana[8]	312	328	440	485	506	528	598	629	...	...
Haiti[5] Haïti[5]	332	464	278	359	259	654	666	648	800	1 035
Jamaica[5] Jamaïque[5]	1 924	1 811	1 675	2 133	2 221	2 808	2 932	3 113	2 995	2 575
Martinique[8 14] Martinique[8 14]	1 779	1 695	1 750	1 556	1 642	1 963	...	...	...	...
Montserrat[8] Montserrat[8]	48	35	34	...	...	...	...	...	...	...
Netherlands Antilles[8] Antilles néerlandaises[8]	2 141	2 139	1 868	1 947	1 758	1 841	2 519	2 083	...	...
Panama[8] Panama[8]	1 539	1 695	2 024	2 188	2 404	2 511	2 780	3 002	3 074	3 516
Saint Kitts and Nevis[8] Saint-Kitts-et-Nevis[8]	110	110	95	118	128	133	149	148	148	...

Region, country or area Région, pays ou zone	1990	1991	1992	1993	1994	1995	1996	1997	1998	1999
Honduras[1] Honduras[1]	831	792	802	814	842	1 061	1 316	1 446	1 575	940
Nicaragua[5] Nicaragua[5]	331	272	223	267	352	526	671	704	573	544
Other America **Autres pays d'Amérique**	**13 351**	**11 146**	**9 588**	**9 360**	**9 382**	**10 999**	**10 749**	**11 665**	**11 138**	**11 753**
Antigua and Barbuda[5] Antigua-et-Barbuda[5]	19	40	...	...	...	...	...	...	...	...
Aruba[8] Aruba[8]	28	26	...	...	...	...	...	...	...	...
Bahamas[5,11] Bahamas[5,11]	238	225	192	162	167	176	180	181	300	380
Barbados[5] Barbade[5]	214	206	189	186	181	238	281	283	254	229
Belize[5] Belize[5]	133	122	141	136	151	162	168	176	191	169
Bermuda[5] Bermudes[5]	60	55	85	35	32	53	68	57	45	...
Cayman Islands[5] Iles Caïmanes[5]	4	3	4	2	3	4	3	...	...	...
Cuba[8] Cuba[8]	4 910	3 550	2 050	1 275	1 385	1 600	2 015	...	...	...
Dominica[8] Dominique[8]	55	54	53	49	47	45	51	53	63	54
Dominican Republic[5,12,13] Rép. dominicaine[5,12,13]	735	658	562	511	644	872	945	1 017	880	872
French Guiana[8,14] Guyane française[8,14]	93	70	96	95	136	131	...	...	...	...
Greenland[5] Groenland[5]	454	341	333	313	285	373	369	293	255	...
Grenada[8] Grenade[8]	27	23	20	20	24	22	20	23	27	...
Guadeloupe[8,14] Guadeloupe[8,14]	118	147	130	128	152	159	...	...	...	...
Guyana[8] Guyana[8]	256	247	290	414	456	455	517	643	485	523
Haiti[5] Haïti[5]	160	190	72	80	87	112	90	119	175	199
Jamaica[5] Jamaïque[5]	1 158	1 097	1 048	1 071	1 211	1 420	1 382	1 381	1 312	1 127
Martinique[8,14] Martinique[8,14]	278	216	247	191	218	224	...	...	...	...
Montserrat[8] Montserrat[8]	1	1	2	...	...	...	...	...	...	...
Netherlands Antilles[8] Antilles néerlandaises[8]	1 790	1 599	1 559	1 283	1 376	1 522	1 269	1 488	...	...
Panama[8] Panama[8]	340	358	502	553	583	625	623	723	784	821
Saint Kitts and Nevis[8] Saint-Kitts-et-Nevis[8]	28	27	26	27	22	19	22	36	...	...

69
Total imports and exports
Value in million US dollars [cont.]
Importations et exportations totales
Valeur en millions de dollars E.-U. [suite]

Region, country or area Region, pays ou zone	1990	1991	1992	1993	1994	1995	1996	1997	1998	1999
Saint Lucia[8] Sainte-Lucie[8]	271	295	313	300	303	307	314	332	...	...
St. Pierre and Miquelon[8] St.-Pierre-et-Miquelon[8]	86	81	76	70	71	...	...	...	...	...
St. Vincent-Grenadines[8] St. Vincent-Grenadines[8]	136	140	132	134	130	136	132	182	193	201
Suriname[5] Suriname[5]	472	509	543	986	423	585	501	658	552	...
Trinidad and Tobago[8] Trinité-et-Tobago[8]	1 109	1 410	1 168	1 463	1 130	1 714	2 144	2 990	2 999	...

Europe · Europe

Region, country or area Region, pays ou zone	1990	1991	1992	1993	1994	1995	1996	1997	1998	1999
Developed economies **Economies développées**	**1 642 572**	**1 663 906**	**1 728 667**	**1 509 910**	**1 708 862**	**2 017 065**	**2 081 651**	**2 109 547**	**2 216 790**	**2 233 459**
EU+[15] **UE+[15]**	**1 536 408**	**1 567 521**	**1 636 503**	**1 425 452**	**1 613 245**	**1 901 988**	**1 966 344**	**1 997 812**	**2 101 101**	**2 118 167**
Austria[8] Autriche[8]	49 091	50 804	54 122	48 616	55 340	29 646	67 324	64 785	68 187	68 757
Belgium-Luxembourg[8][16] Belgique-Luxembourg[8][16]	120 325	121 060	125 153	114 415	130 081	159 713	163 680	157 280	162 208	160 770
Denmark[8] Danemark[8]	32 230	32 411	35 185	30 546	34 882	45 090	44 435	44 044	45 427	44 157
Finland[5] Finlande[5]	27 003	21 808	21 184	18 033	23 214	28 114	29 265	29 786	32 301	30 727
France[8][14] France[8][14]	233 207	230 832	238 875	200 750	230 639	276 981	235 122	271 945	290 273	289 925
Germany[8][17] Allemagne[8][17]	345 032	390 423	403 268	346 130	384 746	444 554	458 810	445 682	471 447	472 171
Greece[8] Grèce[8]	19 780	21 582	23 232	22 007	21 489	25 509	27 398	27 718	...	...
Ireland[5] Irlande[5]	20 682	20 756	22 483	21 794	25 910	33 068	35 900	39 233	44 620	46 535
Italy[8] Italie[8]	181 983	182 750	188 456	148 308	169 179	206 025	206 969	210 283	218 255	216 626
Luxembourg[8] Luxembourg[8]	...	...	...	7 690	8 389	9 755	9 668	9 380	7 409	10 931
Netherlands[8] Pays-Bas[8]	126 485	127 251	134 670	124 742	141 317	176 873	180 642	178 132	187 733	187 529
Portugal[8] Portugal[8]	25 265	26 426	30 308	24 288	27 304	33 314	35 178	35 063	38 534	38 461
Spain[8] Espagne[8]	87 555	92 992	99 765	79 755	92 189	113 317	121 794	122 721	133 153	144 438
Sweden[5] Suède[5]	54 266	50 001	50 050	42 687	51 732	64 751	72 898	65 710	68 256	68 431
United Kingdom[5] Royaume-Uni[5]	224 550	209 864	221 638	206 321	226 172	265 321	287 537	306 591	314 033	317 958
EFTA+[18] **AELE+[18]**	**98 589**	**93 839**	**89 363**	**81 956**	**92 859**	**111 734**	**112 114**	**108 782**	**112 570**	**111 989**
Iceland[5] Islande[5]	1 679	1 761	1 684	1 342	1 472	1 755	2 027	1 994	2 489	2 502
Norway[5] Norvège[5]	27 219	25 576	25 916	23 892	27 303	32 973	35 616	35 713	36 196	34 047

Region, country or area Region, pays ou zone	1990	1991	1992	1993	1994	1995	1996	1997	1998	1999
Saint Lucia[8] Sainte-Lucie[8]	127	110	123	120	94	109	80	61	...	...
St. Pierre and Miquelon[8] St.-Pierre-et-Miquelon[8]	26	30	25	1	12	...	...	...	...	...
St. Vincent-Grenadines[8] St. Vincent-Grenadines[8]	83	67	78	58	50	43	46	46	50	49
Suriname[5] Suriname[5]	472	359	392	1 190	449	477	433	701	436	...
Trinidad and Tobago[8] Trinité-et-Tobago[8]	1 960	1 775	1 691	1 662	1 866	2 456	2 500	2 542	2 258	...

Europe • Europe

Region, country or area Region, pays ou zone	1990	1991	1992	1993	1994	1995	1996	1997	1998	1999
Developed economies **Economies développées**	**1 593 455**	**1 574 040**	**1 662 630**	**1 556 970**	**1 773 387**	**2 130 239**	**2 192 356**	**2 231 465**	**2 305 579**	**2 291 848**
EU+[15] **UE+[15]**	**1 479 098**	**1 475 167**	**1 562 552**	**1 463 439**	**1 668 984**	**2 006 146**	**2 063 493**	**2 106 604**	**2 186 307**	**2 166 509**
Austria[8] Autriche[8]	41 138	41 125	44 419	40 199	45 031	25 515	57 824	58 598	62 746	63 408
Belgium-Luxembourg[8][16] Belgique-Luxembourg[8][16]	118 328	118 355	123 564	125 894	143 674	175 881	175 455	171 903	177 662	176 140
Denmark[8] Danemark[8]	35 135	36 011	41 067	37 172	41 422	49 763	50 101	47 720	47 481	48 457
Finland[5] Finlande[5]	26 572	23 079	23 955	23 447	29 658	39 573	38 435	39 318	42 963	40 666
France[8][14] France[8][14]	210 169	213 441	231 913	206 231	236 072	287 334	241 072	290 285	306 096	300 161
Germany[8][17] Allemagne[8][17]	409 958	402 982	422 706	382 631	429 075	508 398	524 228	512 503	543 431	541 090
Greece[8] Grèce[8]	8 106	8 675	9 839	8 777	9 392	10 970	9 480	8 656	...	...
Ireland[5] Irlande[5]	23 747	24 223	28 532	29 022	34 155	44 638	48 670	53 449	64 572	70 544
Italy[8] Italie[8]	170 383	169 536	178 164	167 746	191 431	233 980	250 355	240 424	242 147	230 199
Luxembourg[8] Luxembourg[8]	...	...	...	5 894	6 562	7 755	7 211	7 000	7 912	7 890
Netherlands[8] Pays-Bas[8]	131 787	133 672	140 356	139 127	155 554	196 276	197 420	194 909	201 363	200 290
Portugal[8] Portugal[8]	16 422	16 333	18 378	15 419	18 006	23 211	24 606	23 972	24 813	23 864
Spain[8] Espagne[8]	55 528	58 640	64 849	61 084	72 929	91 043	102 002	104 368	109 231	109 966
Sweden[5] Suède[5]	57 542	55 229	56 154	49 864	61 352	79 816	84 904	82 956	84 739	84 771
United Kingdom[5] Royaume-Uni[5]	185 326	185 306	190 542	181 559	204 009	242 036	262 004	281 082	271 849	268 254
EFTA+[18] **AELE+[18]**	**99 429**	**97 197**	**98 124**	**91 872**	**102 546**	**121 860**	**126 798**	**122 900**	**117 138**	**123 028**
Iceland[5] Islande[5]	1 591	1 549	1 528	1 400	1 623	1 803	1 635	1 847	2 050	2 013
Norway[5] Norvège[5]	34 045	34 116	35 193	31 778	34 685	41 995	48 958	48 547	39 649	44 892

69
Total imports and exports
Value in million US dollars [*cont.*]
Importations et exportations totales
Valeur en millions de dollars E.-U. [*suite*]

Region, country or area Region, pays ou zone	1990	1991	1992	1993	1994	1995	1996	1997	1998	1999
Switzerland[1] Suisse[1]	69 691	66 502	61 763	56 722	64 085	77 006	74 471	71 075	73 885	75 440
Other Europe **Autres pays d'Europe**	**2 445**	**2 547**	**2 801**	**2 501**	**2 758**	**3 342**	**3 193**	**2 953**	**3 119**	**3 303**
Faeroe Islands[5] Iles Féroé[5]	338	303	334	219	242	315	365	...	...	...
Malta[5] Malte[5]	1 961	2 114	2 349	2 174	2 441	2 942	2 796	2 555	2 685	2 856
Developing economies[19] **Econ. en dévelop.**[19]	**18 890**	**11 804**	**15 439**	**16 143**	**17 883**	**22 703**	**22 940**	**25 039**	**25 030**	**23 249**
Croatia[5] Croatie[5]	...	...	4 461	4 666	5 229	7 510	7 788	9 104	8 383	7 799
Slovenia[1] Slovénie[1]	...	...	6 142	6 529	7 304	9 490	9 423	9 357	10 110	9 952
TFYR Macedonia[1] L'ex-R.y. Macédoine[1]	...	...	1 206	1 199	1 484	1 719	1 627	1 779	1 915	1 796
Yugoslavia[1][20] Yougoslavie[1][20]	18 890	11 804	3 630	...	...	...	4 102	4 799	4 622	...
Eastern Europe **Europe de l'est**	**57 293**	**45 496**	**50 231**	**64 179**	**71 738**	**94 841**	**112 245**	**117 660**	**131 598**	**130 562**
Albania[5] Albanie[5]	76	61	175	574	603	713	841	649	828	1 140
Bulgaria[1][21] Bulgarie[1][21]	4 710	2 455	4 460	4 767	4 144	5 662	6 850	5 315	4 974	5 430
former Czechoslovakia†[4][5] l'anc. Tchécoslovaquie†[4][5]	13 106	10 014	12 530	...	...	...	...	...	...	...
Czech Republic[4][1] République tchèque[4][1]	...	...	...	14 602	17 500	25 306	29 002	27 188	28 813	28 667
Hungary[1][22] Hongrie[1][22]	8 671	11 416	11 106	12 521	14 383	15 046	15 856	20 652	25 596	27 920
Poland[1] Pologne[1]	8 413	15 757	15 701	18 834	21 383	29 050	37 137	42 308	46 494	45 903
Romania[1] Roumanie[1]	9 843	5 793	6 260	6 522	7 109	10 278	11 435	11 280	11 821	10 392
Slovakia[4][5][23] Slovaquie[4][5][23]	...	...	...	6 360	6 615	8 787	11 124	10 269	13 071	11 110
former USSR†[4][5][24] **ancienne URSS†**[4][5][24]	**120 651**	**43 458**	...	...	...	...	...	...	...	...
former USSR-Europe[25] anc. URSS-Europe[25]	...	...	43 082	40 114	70 296	91 413	99 057	113 457	98 314	71 588
Belarus[5][26] Bélarus[5][26]	...	...	3 495	2 539	3 066	5 563	6 939	8 689	8 549	6 664
Estonia[5][27] Estonie[5][27]	...	...	412	897	1 663	2 545	3 244	4 429	4 611	4 093
Latvia[1] Lettonie[1]	...	...	...	961	1 244	1 819	2 319	2 721	3 191	2 945
Lithuania[5] Lituanie[5]	...	...	602	2 284	2 353	3 649	4 559	5 644	5 794	4 892
Republic of Moldova[5][26] Rép. de Moldova[5][26]	...	...	640	628	703	841	1 079	1 200	1 018	...

Region, country or area Région, pays ou zone	1990	1991	1992	1993	1994	1995	1996	1997	1998	1999
Switzerland[8] **Suisse**[8]	63 793	61 532	61 403	58 694	66 238	78 061	76 205	72 506	75 439	76 124
Other Europe **Autres pays d'Europe**	**1 549**	**1 677**	**1 954**	**1 659**	**1 857**	**2 233**	**2 065**	**1 960**	**2 133**	**2 310**
Faeroe Islands[5] Iles Féroé[5]	418	435	439	327	326	362	437	...	...	
Malta[5] Malte[5]	1 130	1 252	1 543	1 355	1 572	1 913	1 731	1 640	1 820	1 985
Developing economies[19] **Econ. en dévelop.**[19]	**14 312**	**9 548**	**14 957**	**13 362**	**14 335**	**16 152**	**15 813**	**16 148**	**17 504**	**16 281**
Croatia[5] Croatie[5]	...	...	4 598	3 904	4 260	4 633	4 512	4 171	4 541	4 303
Slovenia[8] Slovénie[8]	...	...	6 681	6 083	6 828	8 315	8 312	8 372	9 048	8 604
TFYR Macedonia[8] L'ex-R.y. Macédoine[8]	...	...	1 199	1 055	1 086	1 204	1 147	1 237	1 311	1 192
Yugoslavia[8,20] Yougoslavie[8,20]	14 312	9 548	2 480	...		1 842	2 368	2 604	...	
Eastern Europe **Europe de l'est**	**58 448**	**43 391**	**44 010**	**51 723**	**60 898**	**79 082**	**80 972**	**89 259**	**100 084**	**101 915**
Albania[5] Albanie[5]	46	25	76	122	139	202	207	139	205	264
Bulgaria[8,21] Bulgarie[8,21]	4 822	3 120	3 914	3 729	3 947	5 359	6 602	5 323	4 296	3 937
former Czechoslovakia†[4,5] l'anc. Tchécoslovaquie†[4,5]	11 882	10 878	11 656	...	...	...	...	...	...	...
Czech Republic[4,8] République tchèque[4,8]	...	...	...	14 466	16 234	21 686	20 160	22 751	26 417	26 834
Hungary[8,22] Hongrie[8,22]	9 597	10 199	10 676	8 888	10 689	12 435	12 647	18 613	22 955	24 947
Poland[8] Pologne[8]	13 627	14 903	13 324	14 143	17 042	22 895	24 440	25 751	27 191	27 397
Romania[8] Roumanie[8]	5 775	4 266	4 363	4 892	6 151	7 910	8 085	8 431	8 300	8 505
Slovakia[4,5,23] Slovaquie[4,5,23]	...	...	...	5 482	6 695	8 596	8 831	8 251	10 720	10 031
former USSR†[4,5,24] **ancienne URSS†**[4,5,24]	**104 177**	**46 274**	...	...	...	...	...	...	...	...
former USSR-Europe[25] anc. URSS-Europe[25]	...	...	48 586	50 588	85 296	105 706	116 382	119 166	103 890	100 415
Belarus[5,26] Bélarus[5,26]	...	...	3 559	1 970	2 510	4 707	5 652	7 301	7 070	5 922
Estonia[5,27] Estonie[5,27]	...	...	445	805	1 302	1 838	2 088	2 924	3 129	2 939
Latvia[8] Lettonie[8]	...	...	883	1 004	991	1 304	1 443	1 672	1 811	1 723
Lithuania[5] Lituanie[5]	...	...	852	2 029	2 029	2 705	3 355	3 860	3 711	3 045
Republic of Moldova[5,26] Rép. de Moldova[5,26]	...	...	470	483	619	739	805	890	644	...

69
Total imports and exports
Value in million US dollars [cont.]
Importations et exportations totales
Valeur en millions de dollars E.-U. [suite]

Region, country or area Region, pays ou zone	1990	1991	1992	1993	1994	1995	1996	1997	1998	1999
Russian Federation[5 26] Fédération de Russie[5 26]	...	...	36 984	32 806	50 518	60 945	62 278	73 660	60 476	40 429
Ukraine[5 26 28] Ukraine[5 26 28]	...	...	...	...	10 748	16 052	18 639	17 114	14 676	11 846

Africa • Afrique

Region, country or area	1990	1991	1992	1993	1994	1995	1996	1997	1998	1999
South Africa[5 29 30] Afrique du Sud[5 29 30]	17 665	17 837	18 714	19 090	22 470	29 608	29 105	31 939	28 277	25 890
Developing economies **Econ. en dévelop.**	**78 951**	**68 432**	**72 383**	**70 248**	**75 117**	**88 038**	**84 752**	**89 655**	**94 823**	**96 726**
Northern Africa **Afrique du Nord**	**44 810**	**33 391**	**35 849**	**35 185**	**39 392**	**46 249**	**45 609**	**46 282**	**51 005**	**48 649**
Algeria[8] Algérie[8]	9 574	7 438	8 648	7 770	9 370	10 250	8 690	...	...	...
Egypt[8 31] Egypte[8 31]	16 783	8 310	8 325	8 214	10 218	11 760	13 038	13 211	16 166	16 022
Libyan Arab Jamah.[5] Jamah. arabe libyenne[5]	5 599	5 356	...	...	...	...	...	5 593	5 692	...
Morocco[8] Maroc[8]	6 925	6 894	7 356	7 162	7 188	10 023	9 704	9 526	10 276	9 925
Sudan[5] Soudan[5]	619	890	821	945	1 227	1 219	1 548	1 580	1 915	...
Tunisia[5] Tunisie[5]	5 513	5 189	6 431	6 214	6 581	7 903	7 700	7 914	8 338	8 340
Other Africa **Autres Pays d'Afrique**	**34 141**	**35 041**	**36 534**	**35 063**	**35 726**	**41 789**	**39 143**	**43 373**	**43 817**	**48 077**
CACEU+[32] **UDEAC+[32]**	**3 440**	**3 018**	**2 759**	**2 752**	**2 413**	**2 998**	**3 192**	**3 391**	**3 372**	**3 310**
Cameroon[8] Cameroun[8]	1 400	1 173	1 163	888	721	1 201	1 226	1 358	...	...
Central African Rep.[8] Rép. centrafricaine[8]	154	93	146	125	139	175	141	145	...	...
Chad[8] Tchad[8]	286	252	243	201	136	37	33	33	36	32
Congo[8] Congo[8]	617	599	451	583	634	671	...	...	...	...
Equatorial Guinea[5] Guinée équatoriale[5]	61	68	56	38	24	31	168	79	32	28
Gabon[8] Gabon[8]	922	834	700	917	758	884	956	1 102	...	...
ECOWAS+[33] **CEDEAO+[33]**	**13 747**	**16 749**	**17 855**	**16 538**	**16 137**	**18 801**	**18 324**	**21 578**	**22 353**	**27 272**
Benin[8] Bénin[8]	266	243	579	571	431	746	654	681	672	668
Burkina Faso[8] Burkina Faso[8]	540	536	545	555	390	532	647	587	782	695
Cape Verde[8] Cap-Vert[8]	136	147	180	154	210	252	...	...	...	...
Côte d'Ivoire[8] Côte d'Ivoire[8]	2 098	2 118	2 316	2 121	1 927	2 943	2 902	2 741	3 295	3 258
Gambia[5] Gambie[5]	188	202	217	260	211	182	228	174	245	192

Region, country or area Région, pays ou zone	1990	1991	1992	1993	1994	1995	1996	1997	1998	1999
Russian Federation[5][26] Fédération de Russie[5][26]	...	...	42 376	44 297	67 542	81 096	88 599	88 288	74 888	74 663
Ukraine[5][26][28] Ukraine[5][26][28]	...	...	...	...	10 305	13 317	14 441	14 232	12 637	11 582

Africa · Afrique

Region, country or area Région, pays ou zone	1990	1991	1992	1993	1994	1995	1996	1997	1998	1999
South Africa[5][29][30] Afrique du Sud[5][29][30]	22 834	22 288	22 416	23 339	24 415	26 918	28 145	29 964	25 396	25 901
Developing economies **Econ. en dévelop.**	**77 654**	**71 226**	**68 740**	**63 239**	**65 995**	**78 305**	**85 696**	**85 964**	**77 767**	**79 109**
Northern Africa **Afrique du Nord**	**39 474**	**35 263**	**32 449**	**30 432**	**32 036**	**37 792**	**38 669**	**39 643**	**37 674**	**38 000**
Algeria[8] Algérie[8]	12 675	12 657	11 137	10 230	8 880	10 240	12 621	...	...	...
Egypt[8][31] Egypte[8][31]	4 957	3 790	3 063	2 252	3 475	3 450	3 539	3 921	3 130	3 559
Libyan Arab Jamah.[5] Jamah. arabe libyenne[5]	13 877	11 213	...	...	...	...	...	9 036	6 131	...
Morocco[8] Maroc[8]	4 265	4 285	3 977	3 428	4 005	6 883	6 881	7 033	7 267	7 367
Sudan[5] Soudan[5]	374	305	319	417	503	556	620	594	596	...
Tunisia[5] Tunisie[5]	3 527	3 699	4 019	3 802	4 657	5 475	5 517	5 559	5 750	5 788
Other Africa **Autres Pays d'Afrique**	**38 180**	**35 962**	**36 292**	**32 807**	**33 959**	**40 513**	**47 028**	**46 321**	**40 093**	**41 109**
CACEU+[32] **UDEAC+[32]**	**5 561**	**5 388**	**5 445**	**5 129**	**5 111**	**5 873**	**6 907**	**7 218**	**6 899**	**7 154**
Cameroon[8] Cameroun[8]	2 002	1 834	1 840	1 443	1 370	1 654	1 769	1 860	...	...
Central African Rep.[8] Rép. centrafricaine[8]	120	47	108	110	151	171	147	154	...	...
Chad[8] Tchad[8]	188	195	182	132	212	24	24	24	26	20
Congo[8] Congo[8]	975	1 032	1 183	1 070	963	1 176	1 552	1 664	...	...
Equatorial Guinea[5] Guinée équatoriale[5]	62	37	50	75	67	128	232	497	423	407
Gabon[8] Gabon[8]	2 213	2 243	2 082	2 300	2 348	2 719	3 184	3 020	...	...
ECOWAS+[33] **CEDEAO+[33]**	**20 326**	**19 294**	**20 213**	**17 577**	**17 549**	**21 864**	**26 772**	**25 688**	**20 517**	**22 421**
Benin[8] Bénin[8]	122	213	336	384	398	420	526	423	414	386
Burkina Faso[8] Burkina Faso[8]	151	105	896	801	349	536	234	229	319	254
Cape Verde[8] Cap-Vert[8]	6	6	5	4	5	9	...	...	...	...
Côte d'Ivoire[8] Côte d'Ivoire[8]	3 072	2 705	2 839	2 525	2 755	3 812	4 446	4 459	4 471	4 544
Gambia[5] Gambie[5]	31	38	57	67	35	16	18	15	27	7

69
Total imports and exports
Value in million US dollars [cont.]
Importations et exportations totales
Valeur en millions de dollars E.-U. [suite]

Region, country or area Region, pays ou zone	1990	1991	1992	1993	1994	1995	1996	1997	1998	1999
Ghana[5] Ghana[5]	...	1 053	2 175	3 912	2 095	1 895	2 098	2 307	2 555	3 524
Guinea-Bissau[5 34] Guinée-Bissau[5 34]	1	1	...	61	16	13	9	...	6	9
Mali[8] Mali[8]	609	463	608	635	591	794	843	759	762	751
Niger[8] Niger[8]	389	355	479	376	328	373	387	379	423	390
Nigeria[5 35] Nigéria[5 35]	5 692	8 986	8 275	5 537	7 438	7 912	6 932	10 330	10 002	14 142
Senegal[8] Sénégal[8]	1 220	1 176	1 036	1 090	1 021	1 242	1 267	1 333	1 406	1 468
Sierra Leone[8] Sierra Leone[8]	148	163	146	147	151	134	211	92	95	80
Togo[8] Togo[8]	581	444	395	179	222	593	664	645	624	584
Rest of Africa **Afrique N.D.A.**	**16 954**	**15 274**	**15 920**	**15 773**	**17 176**	**19 991**	**17 628**	**18 404**	**18 093**	**17 495**
Angola Angola	...	...	...	...	...	...	...	...	...	...
Burundi[8] Burundi[8]	235	255	221	205	224	234	127	121	158	118
Comoros[8] Comores[8]	52	58	69	...	...	...	...	...	...	...
Dem. Rep. of the Congo[8] Rép. dém. du Congo[8]	888	711	420	372	382	397	424	...	...	...
Djibouti[5] Djibouti[5]	215	214	219	...	...	...	...	...	...	...
Ethiopia[5] Ethiopie[5]	1 081	472	859	787	1 033	1 142	...	...	...	1 317
Kenya[5] Kenya[5]	2 124	1 937	1 843	1 774	2 090	3 006	2 949	3 296	3 194	2 833
Madagascar[8] Madagascar[8]	651	436	448	468	447	543	507	465	511	...
Malawi[5] Malawi[5]	575	703	735	545	489	475	623	786	606	698
Mauritius[5] Maurice[5]	1 621	1 559	1 624	1 716	1 930	1 959	2 278	2 231	2 183	...
Mozambique[8] Mozambique[8]	878	899	855	955	535	718	774	754	805	1 161
Réunion[8 14] Réunion[8 14]	2 165	2 130	2 320	2 057	2 365	2 625	...	...	...	...
Rwanda[5] Rwanda[5]	285	308	288	332	101	241	256	297	285	253
Seychelles[5] Seychelles[5]	187	173	191	238	207	233	379	340	405	...
Somalia[8] Somalie[8]	81	...	...	...	...	...	...	...	...	...
Uganda[5] Ouganda[5]	291	196	515	...	879	1 055	1 190	1 315	1 412	1 340
United Rep.Tanzania[5] Rép.-Unie de Tanzanie[5]	1 364	1 546	1 453	1 498	1 504	1 679	1 386	1 335	1 452	1 634

Region, country or area Region, pays ou zone	1990	1991	1992	1993	1994	1995	1996	1997	1998	1999
Ghana[5] Ghana[5]	...	...	1 252	981	1 419	1 753	1 667	1 635	1 788	...
Guinea-Bissau[5 34] Guinée-Bissau[5 34]	...	...	...	28	9	4	3	...	3	5
Mali[8] Mali[8]	361	314	343	478	336	443	433	561	556	569
Niger[8] Niger[8]	283	307	333	288	225	289	325	271	298	282
Nigeria[5 35] Nigéria[5 35]	12 961	12 264	11 886	9 908	9 415	11 725	16 153	15 213	9 729	12 082
Senegal[8] Sénégal[8]	762	703	674	709	790	968	986	903	965	981
Sierra Leone[8] Sierra Leone[8]	137	145	149	118	115	25	47	17	7	6
Togo[8] Togo[8]	268	253	275	136	328	378	440	424	421	384
Rest of Africa **Afrique N.D.A.**	**12 293**	**11 281**	**10 634**	**10 101**	**11 298**	**12 776**	**13 349**	**13 414**	**12 678**	**11 534**
Angola[8] Angola[8]	3 910	3 413	3 714	...	...	...	...	...	...	...
Burundi[8] Burundi[8]	75	91	73	62	121	106	40	87	65	54
Comoros[8] Comores[8]	18	25	22	...	...	...	...	...	...	...
Dem. Rep. of the Congo[8] Rép. dm du Congo[8]	888	711	420	372	382	397	424	...	...	...
Djibouti[5] Djibouti[5]	25	17	16	...	...	...	...	...	...	...
Ethiopia[5] Ethiopie[5]	298	189	169	199	372	422	417	587	560	...
Kenya[5] Kenya[5]	1 031	1 188	1 067	1 297	1 565	1 890	2 067	2 054	2 007	1 759
Madagascar[8] Madagascar[8]	319	305	278	261	375	370	299	221	241	...
Malawi[5] Malawi[5]	417	469	396	319	325	405	481	540	558	442
Mauritius[5] Maurice[5]	1 196	1 195	1 301	1 299	1 347	1 537	1 751	1 630	1 734	...
Mozambique[8] Mozambique[8]	126	162	139	132	160	171	222	226	234	268
Réunion[8 14] Réunion[8 14]	189	150	213	168	171	207	...	...	...	...
Rwanda[5] Rwanda[5]	114	93	67	65	20	52	60	87	60	61
Seychelles[5] Seychelles[5]	57	49	48	51	52	53	100	113	...	...
Somalia[8] Somalie[8]	81	...	...	...	...	...	...	...	...	...
Uganda[5] Ouganda[5]	153	200	143	179	410	461	587	554	500	516
United Rep.Tanzania[5] Rép.-Unie de Tanzanie[5]	331	342	412	450	519	685	758	718	675	540

69
Total imports and exports
Value in million US dollars [*cont.*]
Importations et exportations totales
Valeur en millions de dollars E.-U. [*suite*]

Region, country or area Region, pays ou zone	1990	1991	1992	1993	1994	1995	1996	1997	1998	1999
Zambia[8][36] Zambie[8][36]	1 210	830	809	829	530	708	844	818	...	...
Zimbabwe[5] Zimbabwe[5]	1 850	2 037	2 202	1 817	2 241	2 661	2 817	...	2 701	...

Asia • Asie

Region, country or area Region, pays ou zone	1990	1991	1992	1993	1994	1995	1996	1997	1998	1999
Developed economies **Economies développées**	**247 832**	**251 145**	**243 595**	**257 951**	**293 165**	**356 340**	**371 512**	**358 437**	**298 253**	**329 112**
Israel[8] Israël[8]	16 803	18 658	15 535	22 624	25 237	29 579	31 620	30 782	29 342	33 160
Japan[5] Japon[5]	235 423	237 289	233 265	241 652	275 268	335 991	349 176	338 829	280 618	310 012
Developing economies[37] **Econ. en dévelop.**[37]	**564 779**	**653 314**	**740 254**	**818 503**	**921 993**	**1 128 309**	**1 201 990**	**1 235 074**	**1 050 869**	**1 125 746**
Asia Middle East **Moyen-Orient d'Asie**	**98 800**	**119 332**	**133 724**	**130 740**	**114 367**	**136 893**	**153 249**	**165 632**	**159 395**	**160 916**
Bahrain[5] Bahreïn[5]	3 712	4 115	4 263	3 858	3 748	3 716	4 273	4 026	3 566	3 588
Cyprus[5][38] Chypre[5][38]	2 796	2 849	3 662	2 647	3 019	3 694	3 983	3 655	3 687	3 618
Iran (Islamic Rep. of)[8][39] Iran (Rép. islamique d')[8][39]	...	27 927	25 860	21 427	13 774	13 882	16 274	...	...	...
Iraq[8] Iraq[8]	4 834	...	...	...	...	...	...	...	...	...
Jordan[5] Jordanie[5]	2 603	2 508	3 255	3 539	3 382	3 696	4 293	4 102	3 828	3 717
Kuwait[8] Koweït[8]	3 923	4 761	7 251	7 042	6 680	7 792	8 374	8 246	8 617	7 617
Lebanon[8] Liban[8]	2 524	3 744	4 202	2 215	2 856	5 335	7 568	7 469	7 063	...
Oman[5] Oman[5]	2 681	3 194	3 769	4 114	3 915	4 248	4 578	5 026	5 682	4 674
Qatar[5] Qatar[5]	1 695	1 720	2 015	1 891	1 927	3 398	2 868	3 322	3 409	...
Saudi Arabia[8] Arabie saoudite[8]	24 069	29 079	33 271	28 198	23 338	28 091	27 768	28 743	30 013	28 032
Syrian Arab Republic[8] Rép. arabe syrienne[8]	2 400	2 768	3 490	4 140	5 467	4 709	5 380	4 028	3 895	3 832
Turkey[8] Turquie[8]	22 302	21 047	22 872	29 428	23 270	35 709	43 627	48 559	45 921	40 692
United Arab Emirates[5] Emirats arabes unis[5]	11 199	13 746	17 414	19 520	21 024	20 984	22 638	29 952	24 728	34 745
Yemen[8][40] Yémen[8][40]	1 571	2 024	2 588	2 821	2 087	1 817	2 038	2 014	2 172	2 106
Non-petroleum exports Pétrole non compris	...	...	...	...	...	...	...	...	...	...
Other Asia **Autres pays d'Asie**	**465 979**	**533 983**	**603 503**	**681 029**	**798 390**	**980 842**	**1 034 866**	**1 055 660**	**878 533**	**953 583**
ASEAN+[41] **ANASE+**[41]	**161 256**	**183 771**	**198 625**	**231 110**	**280 524**	**353 897**	**374 882**	**371 238**	**281 396**	**299 080**

Region, country or area Region, pays ou zone	1990	1991	1992	1993	1994	1995	1996	1997	1998	1999
Zambia [36] Zambie [36]	1 311	1 077	788	850	827	1 055	1 052	914	...	...
Zimbabwe [5] Zimbabwe [5]	1 729	1 530	1 442	1 565	1 881	2 114	2 397	...	1 864	...

Asia · Asie

Region, country or area Region, pays ou zone	1990	1991	1992	1993	1994	1995	1996	1997	1998	1999
Developed economies **Economies développées**	**294 826**	**322 281**	**344 724**	**370 787**	**406 592**	**453 082**	**422 254**	**432 381**	**399 402**	**429 357**
Israel [8] Israël [8]	11 573	11 921	10 019	14 826	16 884	19 046	20 610	22 502	22 993	25 794
Japan [5] Japon [5]	287 648	315 163	339 911	362 286	397 048	443 265	410 928	421 051	388 117	417 623
Developing economies [37] **Econ. en dévelop. [37]**	**580 518**	**638 584**	**723 144**	**786 786**	**913 297**	**1 095 845**	**1 162 476**	**1 241 371**	**1 161 510**	**1 260 070**
Asia Middle East **Moyen-Orient d'Asie**	**128 779**	**123 678**	**135 171**	**137 806**	**137 749**	**153 673**	**175 705**	**188 029**	**163 146**	**198 279**
Bahrain [5] Bahreïn [5]	3 761	3 511	3 464	3 723	3 617	4 113	4 700	4 384	3 270	4 088
Cyprus [5 38] Chypre [5 38]	948	954	984	867	969	1 231	1 391	1 250	1 062	997
Iran (Islamic Rep. of) [8 39] Iran (Rép. islamique d') [8 39]	...	18 661	19 868	18 080	19 434	18 360	22 391	...	...	...
Iraq Iraq	...	...	...	...	...	...	...	...	...	...
Jordan [5] Jordanie [5]	1 063	1 130	1 219	1 246	1 424	1 769	1 817	1 836	1 802	1 832
Kuwait [8] Koweït [8]	6 956	1 088	6 567	10 244	11 228	12 785	14 889	14 225	9 553	12 217
Lebanon [8] Liban [8]	494	539	560	452	573	733	1 014	717	716	...
Oman [5] Oman [5]	5 508	4 869	5 425	5 298	5 545	6 068	7 346	7 630	5 508	...
Qatar [5] Qatar [5]	3 529	3 107	3 736	3 181	...	...	3 752	...	...	...
Saudi Arabia [8] Arabie saoudite [8]	44 417	47 797	50 286	42 395	42 614	50 040	60 729	62 381	39 775	...
Syrian Arab Republic [8] Rép. arabe syrienne [8]	4 212	3 430	3 093	3 146	3 047	3 563	3 999	3 916	2 890	3 464
Turkey [8] Turquie [8]	12 959	13 594	14 716	15 345	18 106	21 637	23 224	26 261	26 974	26 588
United Arab Emirates [5] Emirats arabes unis [5]	23 544	24 436	24 756	...	26 922	27 753	28 085	39 613	42 666	43 307
Yemen [8 40] Yémen [8 40]	692	659	619	611	934	1 917	2 675	2 504	1 501	2 571
Non-petroleum exports [43] Petrole non compris [43]	49 427	55 155	56 952	70 769	51 479	56 967	64 463	83 789	51 085	86 149
Other Asia **Autres pays d'Asie**	**451 740**	**514 906**	**583 573**	**642 765**	**765 454**	**929 658**	**971 952**	**1 037 766**	**985 109**	**1 048 426**
ASEAN+ [41] **ANASE+ [41]**	**143 771**	**164 533**	**185 374**	**211 978**	**261 501**	**320 020**	**339 724**	**352 217**	**328 937**	**353 998**

69
Total imports and exports
Value in million US dollars [cont.]
Importations et exportations totales
Valeur en millions de dollars E.-U. [suite]

Region, country or area Region, pays ou zone	1990	1991	1992	1993	1994	1995	1996	1997	1998	1999
Brunei Darussalam[8] Brunéi Darussalam[8]	1 001	1 208	1 482	1 822	1 874	2 078	2 487	2 180	1 741	...
Indonesia[8] Indonésie[8]	21 837	25 869	27 280	28 328	31 983	40 630	42 929	41 694	27 337	24 004
Lao People's Dem. Rep.[8] Rép. dém. pop. lao[8]	194	170	270	432	564	589	690	706	553	525
Malaysia[5] Malaisie[5]	29 259	36 649	39 854	45 657	59 581	77 614	78 418	79 030	58 326	64 962
Myanmar[5] Myanmar[5]	270	646	651	814	878	1 335	1 355	2 037	2 667	2 301
Philippines[5] Philippines[5]	12 103	13 180	13 689	18 772	22 641	28 340	34 126	38 622	31 496	32 568
Singapore[5] Singapour[5]	60 774	66 093	72 132	85 229	102 670	124 502	131 340	132 442	104 728	111 062
Thailand[8] Thaïlande[8]	33 031	37 579	40 680	46 076	54 438	70 579	72 330	62 879	42 971	50 301
Viet Nam[5] Viet Nam[5]	2 752	2 338	2 541	3 924	5 826	8 155	11 144	11 592	11 494	...
Rest of Asia **Autres pays d'Asie**	**304 723**	**350 211**	**404 878**	**449 919**	**517 867**	**626 945**	**659 984**	**684 423**	**597 137**	**654 503**
Afghanistan[5] Afghanistan[5]	936	616	...	...	...	...	...	...	...	...
Bangladesh[5] Bangladesh[5]	3 618	3 412	3 731	3 994	4 602	6 501	6 621	6 896	6 978	7 687
China††[8] Chine††[8]	53 345	63 791	80 585	103 088	115 681	129 113	138 944	142 189	140 305	165 788
China, Hong Kong SAR†[5] Chine, Hong Kong RAS†[5]	82 490	100 240	123 407	138 650	161 841	192 751	198 550	208 614	184 518	179 520
China, Macao SAR†[5] Chine, Macao RAS†[5]	1 534	1 843	1 948	1 999	2 090	2 026	1 993	2 079	1 949	...
India[5] Inde[5]	23 583	20 445	23 594	22 789	26 843	34 710	37 944	41 430	42 998	44 889
Korea, Republic of[5] Corée, République de[5]	69 844	81 525	81 775	83 800	102 348	135 119	150 339	144 616	93 282	119 750
Maldives[5] Maldives[5]	138	161	189	191	222	268	302	349	354	402
Mongolia[5] Mongolie[5]	924	361	418	379	258	415	451	443	472	1 010
Nepal[5] Népal[5]	672	737	776	890	1 155	1 333	1 442	1 720	1 243	1 418
Pakistan[5] Pakistan[5]	7 376	8 439	9 379	9 501	8 889	11 461	12 131	11 581	9 284	10 159
Sri Lanka[5] Sri Lanka[5]	2 689	3 062	3 505	3 993	4 767	5 307	5 412	5 851	5 917	5 884
former USSR-Asia **anc. URSS-Asie**	...	...	**3 026**	**6 734**	**9 236**	**10 574**	**13 875**	**13 781**	**12 941**	**11 247**
Armenia[8 26] Arménie[8 26]	...	...	50	254	394	674	856	892	896	800
Azerbaijan[5 26] Azerbaïdjan[5 26]	...	...	998	241	778	668	961	794	1 077	...

Region, country or area Region, pays ou zone	1990	1991	1992	1993	1994	1995	1996	1997	1998	1999
Brunei Darussalam[8] Brunéi Darussalam[8]	2 213	2 675	2 401	2 167	2 234	2 389	2 474	2 442	2 307	...
Indonesia[8] Indonésie[8]	25 675	29 142	33 967	36 823	40 055	45 417	49 814	53 443	48 847	48 665
Lao People's Dem. Rep.[8] Rép. dém. pop. lao[8]	79	97	133	241	301	311	323	359	370	311
Malaysia[5] Malaisie[5]	29 453	34 350	40 772	47 131	58 755	73 715	78 253	78 741	73 304	84 451
Myanmar[5] Myanmar[5]	325	419	531	586	792	851	744	866	1 066	1 125
Philippines[5] Philippines[5]	7 906	8 411	9 140	11 129	13 304	17 502	20 408	24 882	29 414	36 576
Singapore[5] Singapour[5]	52 730	58 964	63 435	74 008	96 825	118 263	125 016	124 990	109 905	114 691
Thailand[8] Thaïlande[8]	23 071	28 439	32 467	36 963	45 236	56 191	55 528	57 413	54 455	58 392
Viet Nam[5] Viet Nam[5]	2 404	2 087	2 581	2 985	4 054	5 449	7 256	9 185	9 361	...
Rest of Asia **Autres pays d'Asie**	**307 969**	**350 373**	**398 199**	**430 787**	**503 952**	**609 638**	**632 229**	**685 549**	**656 172**	**694 429**
Afghanistan[5] Afghanistan[5]	235	188	...	...	...	...	...	...	...	...
Bangladesh[5] Bangladesh[5]	1 671	1 689	2 098	2 278	2 661	3 173	3 297	3 778	3 831	3 919
China††[8] Chine††[8]	62 091	71 910	84 940	90 970	121 047	148 797	151 197	182 877	183 589	195 150
China, Hong Kong SAR†[5] Chine Hong Kong RAS†[5]	82 160	98 577	119 487	135 244	151 399	173 750	180 750	188 059	174 002	173 885
China, Macao SAR†[5] Chine, Macao RAS†[5]	1 694	1 655	1 749	1 763	1 834	1 983	1 989	2 145	2 135	...
India[5] Inde[5]	17 970	17 727	19 641	21 573	25 022	30 629	33 107	35 005	33 463	36 310
Korea, Republic of[5] Corée, République de[5]	65 016	71 870	76 632	82 236	96 013	125 058	129 715	136 164	132 313	144 745
Maldives[5] Maldives[5]	52	54	40	35	46	50	59	73	74	64
Mongolia[5] Mongolie[5]	661	348	389	383	356	473	424	418	317	763
Nepal[5] Népal[5]	204	257	368	384	362	346	385	402	474	600
Pakistan[5] Pakistan[5]	5 589	6 528	7 317	6 688	7 365	7 992	9 321	8 708	8 475	8 383
Sri Lanka[5] Sri Lanka[5]	1 913	1 988	2 462	2 851	3 209	3 798	4 095	4 633	4 734	4 593
former USSR-Asia **anc. URSS-Asie**	...	...	**4 400**	**6 216**	**10 094**	**12 514**	**14 818**	**15 576**	**13 255**	**13 365**
Armenia[8 26] Arménie[8 26]	...	...	26	156	216	271	290	233	223	232
Azerbaijan[5 26] Azerbaïdjan[5 26]	...	...	754	351	638	637	631	781	606	...

69
Total imports and exports
Value in million US dollars [cont.]
Importations et exportations totales
Valeur en millions de dollars E.-U. [suite]

Region, country or area Region, pays ou zone	1990	1991	1992	1993	1994	1995	1996	1997	1998	1999
Georgia[5][26] Géorgie[5][26]	...	...	...	...	236	417	687	944	878	...
Kazakhstan[5][26] Kazakhstan[5][26]	...	...	469	3 887	3 561	3 807	4 241	4 301	4 257	3 683
Kyrgyzstan[8][26] Kirghizistan[8][26]	...	...	...	430	316	522	838	709	842	600
Tajikistan[5][26] Tadjikistan[5][26]	...	...	132	463	578	810	763	750	771	...
Turkmenistan[5][26] Turkménistan[5][26]	...	...	30	501	894	777	...	...	...	...
Uzbekistan[5][26] Ouzbékistan[5][26]	...	...	929	958	2 479	2 900	4 721	4 523	3 289	...

Oceania · Océanie

Region, country or area Region, pays ou zone	1990	1991	1992	1993	1994	1995	1996	1997	1998	1999
Developed economies **Economies développées**	**49 734**	**47 948**	**50 783**	**52 790**	**62 658**	**71 173**	**76 932**	**77 098**	**73 699**	**79 828**
Australia[5] Australie[5]	42 024	41 651	43 808	45 557	53 426	60 317	65 428	65 892	64 630	69 160
New Zealand[5] Nouvelle-Zélande[5]	9 501	8 408	9 218	9 636	11 913	13 959	14 725	14 519	12 495	14 298
Developing economies **Econ. en dévelop.**	**5 111**	**5 456**	**5 412**	**5 237**	**5 669**	**5 827**	**6 305**	**6 222**	**5 786**	**6 225**
American Samoa[8][42] Samoa américaines[8][42]	360	372	418	...	...	...	...	...	...	...
Cook Islands[5] Iles Cook[5]	...	...	...	...	49	49	43	48	46	48
Fiji[5] Fidji[5]	754	652	631	720	829	867	984	965	...	...
French Polynesia[8] Polynésie française[8]	929	915	894	852	881	1 019	1 026	945	...	...
Kiribati[5] Kiribati[5]	27	26	37	28	26	34	38	41	40	...
New Caledonia[8] Nouvelle-Calédonie[8]	883	863	917	858	876	912	1 005	937	...	...
Papua New Guinea[5] Papouasie-Nvl-Guinée[5]	1 192	1 614	1 485	1 299	1 521	1 452	1 741	1 696	1 232	1 191
Samoa[8] Samoa[8]	81	94	110	105	81	95	100	97	97	115
Solomon Islands[8] Iles Salomon[8]	95	110	111	137	139	154	151	170	...	...
Tonga[5] Tonga[5]	62	59	63	61	69	77	75	73	69	73
Vanuatu[5] Vanuatu[5]	96	83	82	79	87	95	97	94	88	...

Additional groups · Groupes supplémentaires

Region, country or area Region, pays ou zone	1990	1991	1992	1993	1994	1995	1996	1997	1998	1999
ANCOM+ ANCOM+	19 045	23 717	29 035	30 719	32 689	41 263	38 536	47 017	46 133	36 679
APEC+ CEAP+	1 316 708	1 378 546	1 531 523	1 668 344	1 943 361	2 257 537	2 402 268	2 521 304	2 337 782	2 554 552
CARICOM+ CARICOM+	6 539	6 789	6 421	7 712	7 027	8 773	9 580	11 373	11 592	11 241

Region, country or area Région, pays ou zone	1990	1991	1992	1993	1994	1995	1996	1997	1998	1999
Georgia[5][26] Géorgie[5][26]	...	...	...	...	134	159	199	240	192	...
Kazakhstan[5][26] Kazakhstan[5][26]	...	...	1 398	3 277	3 231	5 250	5 911	6 497	5 404	5 592
Kyrgyzstan[8][26] Kirghizistan[8][26]	...	...	...	340	340	409	505	604	514	454
Tajikistan[5][26] Tadjikistan[5][26]	...	...	111	322	483	749	651	746	602	...
Turkmenistan[5][26] Turkménistan[5][26]	...	...	908	1 049	2 010	1 939	...	...	...	...
Uzbekistan[5][26] Ouzbékistan[5][26]	...	...	869	721	3 044	3 100	4 590	4 388	3 528	...

Oceania · Océanie

Region, country or area Région, pays ou zone	1990	1991	1992	1993	1994	1995	1996	1997	1998	1999
Developed economies Economies développées	47 362	49 393	50 396	50 842	57 028	63 640	71 441	73 801	64 546	64 903
Australia[5] Australie[5]	39 760	41 855	42 839	42 704	47 525	53 097	60 300	62 910	55 901	56 078
New Zealand[5] Nouvelle-Zélande[5]	9 394	9 649	9 799	10 542	12 185	13 645	14 362	14 203	12 071	12 455
Developing economies Econ. en dévelop.	2 736	3 050	3 465	4 215	4 438	4 749	4 718	4 273	3 756	4 118
American Samoa[8][42] Samoa américaines[8][42]	311	327	318	...	...	...	...	...	...	...
Cook Islands[5] Iles Cook[5]	...	...	...	...	4	5	3	3	4	4
Fiji[5] Fidji[5]	498	451	443	449	550	619	748	590	...	...
French Polynesia[8] Polynésie française[8]	111	127	107	148	226	196	254	224	...	...
Kiribati[5] Kiribati[5]	3	3	5	3	5	7	6	9	8	...
New Caledonia[8] Nouvelle-Calédonie[8]	449	444	409	359	366	515	492	527	...	...
Papua New Guinea[5] Papouasie-Nvl-Guinée[5]	1 177	1 459	1 927	2 584	2 630	2 654	2 531	2 160	1 775	1 880
Samoa[8] Samoa[8]	9	6	6	6	4	9	10	15	15	20
Solomon Islands[8] Iles Salomon[8]	70	84	103	131	142	168	162	173	126	...
Tonga[5] Tonga[5]	12	14	13	17	14	15	13	10	8	12
Vanuatu[5] Vanuatu[5]	19	18	24	23	25	28	30	35	34	...

Additional groups · Groupes supplémentaires

Region, country or area Région, pays ou zone	1990	1991	1992	1993	1994	1995	1996	1997	1998	1999
ANCOM+ ANCOM+	31 411	29 485	28 453	28 789	34 730	39 769	45 571	45 858	39 059	43 462
APEC+ CEAP+	1 233 394	1 344 114	1 507 994	1 614 843	1 860 581	2 177 997	2 255 650	2 411 983	2 309 115	2 448 190
CARICOM+ CARICOM+	4 460	3 986	4 003	4 900	4 479	5 347	5 422	5 878	5 212	5 315

69
Total imports and exports
Value in million US dollars [*cont.*]
Importations et exportations totales
Valeur en millions de dollars E.-U. [*suite*]

Region, country or area Region, pays ou zone	1990	1991	1992	1993	1994	1995	1996	1997	1998	1999
CIS+ CEI+	...	...	44 145	42 707	74 270	93 975	102 810	114 444	97 659	70 905
COMESA+ COMESA+	30 371	20 393	21 044	20 943	24 813	28 728	31 171	32 245	35 056	33 558
LDC+ PMA+	22 691	21 674	23 830	...	...	...	...	...	...	...
MERCOSUR+ MERCOSUR+	29 295	34 322	41 407	48 538	62 681	79 915	87 236	102 576	95 948	81 377
NAFTA+ NAFTA+	657 270	655 837	715 903	774 902	883 454	963 338	1 033 687	1 147 601	1 210 472	1 354 262
OECD+ OCDE+	2 682 260	2 727 377	2 852 065	2 729 613	3 099 028	3 615 225	3 804 931	3 942 272	4 006 858	4 223 131
OPEC+ OPEP+	108 700	136 383	149 514	137 421	130 229	151 333	151 930	168 393	151 787	157 199

Source:
United Nations Secretariat, trade statistics database of the
Statistics Division.

+   For Member States of this grouping, see
Annex I - Other groupings.

†   For information on recent changes in country or
area nomenclature pertaining to former Czechoslovakia,
Germany, Hong Kong Special Administrative Region (SAR) of
China, Macao Special Administrative Region (SAR) of China,
SFR of Yugoslavia and the former USSR, see Annex I - Country
or area nomenclature, regional and other groupings.

††   For statistical purposes, the data for
China do not include those for Hong Kong Special
Administrative Region (Hong Kong SAR), Macao Special
Administrative Region (Macao SAR) and Taiwan province of
China.

1 United States, Canada, Developed Economies of Europe,
Israel, Japan, Australia, New Zealand and South African
Customs Union.
2 This classification is intended for statistical convenience
and does not necessarily express a judgement about the stage
reached by a particular country in the development process.

3 Beginning January 1992, includes Eastern Europe and the
European countries of the former USSR.
4 Imports are f.o.b. Beginning 1998, imports for Brazil, Peru
and Canada are f.o.b.
5 Country or area using general trade system. See technical
notes for explanation of trade systems.

6 Including the trade of the U.S. Virgin Islands and Puerto
Rico, but excluding shipments of merchandise between the
United States and its other possessions (Guam, American

Source:
Secrétariat de l'Organisation des Nations Unies, la base de
données pour les statistiques du commerce extérieur de la
Division de statistique.

+   Les Etats membres de ce groupement, voir
annexe I - Autres groupements.

†   Pour les modifications récentes de nomenclature
de pays ou de zone concernant l'Allemagne, Hong Kong, région
administrative spéciale (RAS) de Chine, Macao, région
administrative spéciale (RAS) de Chine,
l'ex-Tchécoslovaquie, l'ex-URSS et l'ex-Rfs de Yougoslavie,
voir annexe I - Nomenclature des pays ou des zones,
groupements régionaux et autres groupements.

††   Les données statistiques relatives à
la Chine ne comprennent pas celles qui concernent la région
administrative spéciale de Hong Kong (la RAS de Hong Kong),
la région administrative spéciale de Macao (la RAS de Macao)
et la province chinoise de Taiwan.

1 Etats-Unis, Canada, Pays aux économies développés d'Europe,
Israël, Japon, Australie, Nouvelle-Zélande et l'Union
douanière d'Afrique australe.
2 Cette classification est utilisée pour plus de commodité
dans la présentation des statistiques et n'implique pas
nécessairement un jugement quant au stage de développement
auquel est parvenu un pays donné.
3 A partir de janvier 1992, y compris l'Europe de l'est et les
pays européennes de l'ancienne URSS.
4 Importations f.o.b. A partir 1998, importations pour Brésil,
Pérou et Canada sont f.o.b.
5 Pays ou zone utilisant un système générale du commerce. Pour
l'explication du système de commerce, voir les notes
techniques.
6 Y compris le commerce des isles Vierges américaines et de
Porto Rico mais non compris les échanges de merchandises
entre les Etats-Unis et leurs autres possessions (Guam,

Region, country or area Région, pays ou zone	1990	1991	1992	1993	1994	1995	1996	1997	1998	1999
CIS+ CEI+	...	...	50 805	52 966	91 070	112 373	124 315	126 286	108 494	106 074
COMESA+ COMESA+	17 439	15 254	13 828	12 663	15 156	16 625	17 361	17 760	16 181	15 576
LDC+ PMA+	15 036	14 182	15 389	...	...	...	...	...	...	...
MERCOSUR+ MERCOSUR+	46 418	45 940	50 387	54 043	61 935	70 499	74 998	83 174	81 492	74 747
NAFTA+ NAFTA+	537 378	564 306	599 382	628 900	698 707	808 469	869 940	956 349	953 618	1 015 200
OECD+ OCDE+	2 547 720	2 606 990	2 760 507	2 726 093	3 075 058	3 637 860	3 743 503	3 899 073	3 933 868	4 023 715
OPEC+ OPEP+	182 457	175 899	187 630	189 578	190 029	210 810	241 798	252 779	216 911	252 332

Samoa, etc). Data include imports and exports of non-monetary gold.

7 Latin American Integration Association. Formerly Latin American Free Trade Assoc, iztion.

8 Country or area using special trade system. See technical notes for explanation of trade systems.

9 Trade data exclude goods from custom-bonded warehouses. Total exports include revaluation and exports of silver.

10 Central American Common Market.

11 Beginning 1990, trade statistics exclude certain oil and chemical products.

12 Export and import values exclude trade in the processing zone.

13 Beginning January 1997, imports are f.o.b.

14 Beginning January 1996, trade data for France include the import and export values of French Guiana, Guadeloupe, Martinique and Réunion.

15 European Union. Prior to January 1995, excludes Austria, Finland and Sweden. Total EU re-calculated for all periods shown in the table according to the current composition.

16 Economic Union of Belgium and Luxembourg. Inter-trade between the two countries is excluded. Beginning January 1993, data refer only to Belgium.

17 Data prior to January 1991 pertain to the territorial boundaries of the Federal Republic of Germany prior to 3 October 1990.

18 Europen Free Trade Association. Prior to January 1995, includes Austria, Finland and Sweden. Total EFTA re-calculated for all periods shown in the table according to the current composition.

19 Beginning January 1992, data refer to Bosnia and Herzegovina, Croatia, Slovenia, TFYR Macedonia and the Federal Republic of Yugoslavia.

20 Prior to January 1992, data refer to Socialist Federal Republic of Yugoslavia. Beginning 1992, data refer to the Federal Republic of Yugoslavia.

Samoa américaines, etc). Les données comprennent les importations et exportations d'or non monétaire.

7 Association latino-américaine d'intégration. Antérieurement Association latino-américaine de libre-échange.

8 Pays ou zone utilisant un système spécial du commerce. Pour l'explication du système de commerce, voir les notes techniques.

9 Les statistiques du commerce extérieur ne comprennent pas les marchandises provenant des entrepôts en douane. Les exportations comprennent le réevaluation et les données sur les exportations d'argent.

10 Marché commun de l'Amérique central.

11 A partir de l'année 1990, les statistiques commerciales font exclusion de certains produits pétroliers et chimiques.

12 Les valeurs à l'exportation et à l'importation excluent le commerce de la zone de transformation.

13 A partir de janvier 1997, les valuers des importations sont f.o.b.

14 A partir de janvier 1996 les valeurs de commerce pour la France comprennent les valeurs des importations et des exportations de la Guyane française, la Guadeloupe, la Martinique, et la Réunion.

15 L'Union européenne. Avant janvier 1995, non compris Autriche, Finlande, et Suède. Total UE avait été recalculé pour toutes les périodes données au tableau, suivant la composition présente.

16 L'Union économique belgo-luxembourgeoise. Non compris le commerce entre ces pays. A partir de janvier 1993, les données se rapportent à Belgique seulement.

17 Les données relatives à la période précédant janvier 1991 correspondent aux limiutes territoriales de la République fédérale d'Allemagne antérieur au 3 octobre 1990.

18 Association européenne de libre-échange. Avant janvier 1995, y compris Autriche, Finlande, et Suède. Total AELE avait été recalculé pour toutes les périodes données au tableau, suivant la composition présente.

19 A partir de janvier 1992, les données se rapportent aux Bosnie-Herzégovine, Croatie, Slovénie, l'ex-R.y. Macédoine et la République fédéral de Yougoslavie.

20 Avant 1992, les données se rapportent à la République fédérative socialiste de Yougoslavie. A partir de l'année 1992, les données se rapportent à la République fédérative

69
Total imports and exports
Value in million US dollars [cont.]

Importations et exportations totales
Valeur en millions de dollars E.-U. [suite]

21 Prior to 1992, import values are f.o.b.
22 Data excludes re-exports.
23 Includes trade with the Czech Republic.
24 For 1991, data for the former USSR are converted to US dollars using commercial exchange rate of rouble and are not comparable to those shown for prior periods.

25 Excluding inter-trade among countries of the region, except for Estonia, Latvia and Lithuania.
26 Beginning 1994, data includes inter-trade among the Commonwealth of Independent States (CIS).
27 Beginning January 1994, foreign trade statistics exclude re-exports.
28 Prior to 1994, the source for trade values is the CIS Yearbook.
29 Exports include gold exports.
30 The South African Customs Union comprising Botswana, Lesotho, Namibia, South Africa and Swaziland. Trade between the component countries is excluded.
31 Imports exclude petroleum imported without stated value. Exports cover domestic exports.

de Yougoslavie.
21 Avant 1992 les valeurs des importations sont f.o.b.
22 Les données non compris les réexportations.
23 Y compris le commerce avec la République tchèque.
24 Les données de 1991 de l'ancienne URSS sont converties en dollars des E.U. en utilisant le taux de change commercial de rouble et ne sont pas comparables aux données des périodes antérieures.
25 Non compris le commerce avec les autres pays de la région, excepte pour Estonie, Lettonie et Lituanie.
26 A partir de janvier 1994, les données compris le commerce avec les pays du Communauté des Etats indépendants (CEI).
27 A partir de janvier 1994, les statistiques du commerce extérieur non compris les réexportations.
28 Avant 1994, la source des valeurs de commerce est l'Annuaire statistique du CEI.
29 Y compris les exportations d'or.
30 L'Union douanière d'Afrique australe comprend Botswana, Lesotho, Namibie, Afrique du Sud et Swaziland. Non compris le commerce entre ces pays.
31 Non compris le pétrole brut dont la valeur des importations ne sont pas stipulée. Les exportations sont les exportations d'intérieur.

32 Central African Customs and Economic Union. Inter-trade among the members of the Union is excluded.
33 Economic Community of West African States.
34 Beginning May 1997, Guinea-Bissau adopted as the national currency the CFA franc following its membership in the West African Monetary Union and the Central Bank of West African States (BCEAO).
35 Beginning February 1995, trade data for Nigeria are valued at an average (unitary) exchange rate of 70.36 naira to the U.S. dollar. This exchange rate is the weighted average of the official rate and the market rate.
36 Beginning January 1996, imports are f.o.b.

37 Beginning January 1992, includes Armenia, Azerbaijan, Georgia, Kazakhstan, Kyrgyzstan, Tajikistan, Turkmenistan and Uzbekistan. Total developing Asia re-calculated for all periods shown in the table according to the current composition.
38 Imports exclude military goods.
39 Data include oil and gas. Beginning October 1980, data on the value and volume of oil exports and on the value of total exports are rough estimates based on information published in various petroleum industry journals.

40 Comprises trade of the former Democratic Yemen and former Yemen Arab Republic including any inter-trade between them.

41 Association of Southeast Asian Nations.
42 Year ending 30 September of the year stated.
43 Data refer to total exports less petroleum exports of Asia Middle East countries where petroleum, in this case, is the sum of SITC groups 333, 334 and 335.

32 L'Union douanière et économique de l'Afrique centrale. Non compris le commerce avec les autres pays membres de l'UDEAC.
33 Communauté économique des Etats de l'Afrique de l'Ouest.
34 A partir de mai 1997, la Guinée-Bissau a adopté le franc CFA comme monnaie nationale après être devenue membre de l'Union monétaire ouest-africaine et le Banque centrale des états de l'Afrique de l'ouest (BCEAO).
35 A partir de février 1995 les valeurs de commerce pour la Nigéria sont évaluées au taux de change (unitaire) moyen de 70.36 naira pour 1 dollar E.U. Il s'agit de la moyenne pondérée du taux officiel et du taux du marché.
36 A partir de janvier 1996, les valeurs des importations sont f.o.b.

37 A partir de janvier 1992, données compris Arménie, Azerbaidjan, Géorgie, Kazakhstan, Kirghizistan, Tadjikistan, Turkménistan et Ouzbékistan. Total Asie en voie de développement avait été recalculé pour toutes les périodes données au tableau, suivant la composition présente.
38 Non compris les importations des economats militaires.
39 Les données comprennent le pétrole et le gaz. A partir d'octobre 1980, les données relatives à la valeur et au volume des exportations de pétrole et à la valeur des exportations totales sont des estimations approximatives étabiles sur la base des données de diverses publications consacrées à l'industrie pétrolière.
40 Y compris le commerce de l'ancienne République populaire démocratique de Yémen, le commerce de l'ancienne République arabe de Yémen et le commerce entre eux.
41 Association des nations de l'Asie du Sud-Est.
42 Année finissant le 30 septembre de l'année indiquée.
43 Les données se rapportent aux exportations totales moins les exportations pétroliers de moyen-orient d'Asie. Dans ce cas, le pétrole est la somme des groupes CTCI 333, 334 et 335.

70
Total imports and exports: index numbers
Importations et exportations: indices

1990 = 100

Country or area Pays ou zone	1989	1991	1992	1993	1994	1995	1996	1997	1998	1999
A. Imports: Quantum index · Importations: Indice du quantum										
Argentina Argentine	104	213	387	448	569	503	601	597	667	756
Australia Australie	108	99	107	114	133	148	161	180	201	223
Austria Autriche	90	101	107	106	119	125	129	142	151	...
Belgium−Luxembourg Belgique−Luxembourg	95	104	105	106	115	121	126	131	141	141
Bolivia Bolivie	...	...	...	...	...	...	...	...	...	...
Brazil Brésil	92	111	119	136	142	176	190	161	162	150
Bulgaria Bulgarie	130	83	91	108	106	108	...	...	...	...
Canada Canada	100	102	110	120	133	143	151	179	187	208
China, Hong Kong SAR † Chine, Hong Kong RAS †	90	119	145	164	187	213	222	238	221	221
Denmark Danemark	99	108	113	114	118	126	128	139	143	148
Dominica Dominique	93	89	...	...	...	...	...	...	...	...
Dominican Republic Rép. dominicaine	...	...	...	...	...	...	...	...	...	...
Ecuador Equateur	...	...	...	...	...	...	...	...	...	...
Ethiopia Ethiopie	...	...	...	...	...	...	...	...	...	...
Faeroe Islands Iles Féroé	125	100	...	...	...	...	...	...	...	...
Finland Finlande	104	83	81	79	95	102	110	119	128	...
France France	95	102	104	107	117	123	126	135	146	...
Germany Allemagne	90	113	115	104	113	115	122	133	146	153
Greece Grèce	78	113	130	143	150	163	178	125	219	...
Guatemala Guatemala	92	117	125	133	148	...	...	...	...	...
Honduras Honduras	...	...	...	...	...	...	...	...	...	...
Hungary Hongrie	105	105	98	119	136	131	138	175	218	...
Iceland Islande	100	105	97	84	90	96	111	118	146	...
India Inde	97	91	120	138	168	261	186	198	...	...
Indonesia Indonésie	...	...	...	...	...	...	...	...	...	...
Ireland Irlande	94	101	106	113	128	146	161	185	218	233
Israel Israël	93	116	130	146	166	182	194	197	197	222
Italy Italie	96	104	107	114	108	119	113	126	139	...
Japan Japon	94	104	104	107	121	136	141	144	137	150
Jordan Jordanie	96	99	136	224	219	152	164	160	151	149

Country or area Pays ou zone	1989	1991	1992	1993	1994	1995	1996	1997	1998	1999

A. Exports: Quantum index · Exportations: Indice du quantum

Country or area Pays ou zone	1989	1991	1992	1993	1994	1995	1996	1997	1998	1999
Argentina Argentine	78	98	97	104	122	152	162	181	201	211
Australia Australie	94	115	121	128	139	141	157	179	190	196
Austria Autriche	90	106	111	108	119	140	147	172	182	...
Belgium–Luxembourg Belgique–Luxembourg	97	104	104	111	123	131	134	143	151	156
Bolivia Bolivie	95	102	99	93	95	91	93	98	90	85
Brazil Brésil	109	100	100	109	116	120	119	125	138	137
Bulgaria Bulgarie	130	70	75	68	75	76	...	...	...	...
Canada Canada	96	101	110	123	138	152	161	175	189	209
China, Hong Kong SAR † Chine, Hong Kong RAS †	92	117	140	160	176	197	207	219	210	218
Denmark Danemark	98	111	116	113	122	116	119	127	126	135
Dominica Dominique	88	94	97	94	107	68	...	...	...	...
Dominican Republic Rép. dominicaine	117	95	91	95	92	96	101	104	99	...
Ecuador Equateur	98	107	116	124	137	154	157	157	149	143
Ethiopia Ethiopie	115	57	50	125	...	...	...	...	...	...
Faeroe Islands Iles Féroé	102	104	...	...	...	...	...	...	...	...
Finland Finlande	96	91	99	117	133	143	151	169	178	...
France France	95	105	108	110	120	129	134	147	157	...
Germany Allemagne	99	100	102	98	112	116	125	140	152	159
Greece Grèce	105	114	147	143	149	164	175	136	221	...
Guatemala Guatemala	101	125	145	136	147	...	...	...	...	...
Honduras Honduras	99	88	102	90	79	83	99	86	86	...
Hungary Hongrie	104	95	96	84	97	106	110	143	175	...
Iceland Islande	101	92	91	96	108	105	115	117	114	...
India Inde	91	114	116	140	154	189	236	205	...	...
Indonesia Indonésie	112	128	141	148	163	170	179	230	214	...
Ireland Irlande	92	106	121	133	153	184	202	232	289	333
Israel Israël	99	98	107	121	140	150	162	180	191	207
Italy Italie	97	100	102	112	125	141	138	146	149	...
Japan Japon	95	102	104	101	103	107	107	117	116	118
Jordan Jordanie	104	88	96	143	153	137	134	143	147	148

70

Total imports and exports: index numbers
[*cont.*]

Importations et exportations: indices
1990 = 100 [*suite*]

Country or area Pays ou zone	1989	1991	1992	1993	1994	1995	1996	1997	1998	1999
A. Imports: Quantum index [cont.] · Importations: Indice du quantum [suite]										
Kenya										
Kenya	105	93	90	97	121	141	140	149	150	...
Korea, Republic of										
Corée, République de	89	117	222	236	287	187	210	213	168	212
Malaysia										
Malaisie	...	...	...	...	...	...	...	...	...	...
Morocco										
Maroc	87	112	128	120	96	108	100	109	134	...
Myanmar										
Myanmar	...	...	...	...	...	...	...	...	...	...
Netherlands										
Pays—Bas	95	104	106	110	121	136	143	155	174	...
New Zealand										
Nouvelle—Zélande	93	90	100	104	121	129	134	139	142	161
Norway [1]										
Norvège [1]	90	102	106	107	122	134	147	159	175	172
Pakistan										
Pakistan	105	105	122	124	119	129	127	130	111	106
Peru										
Pérou	...	...	...	...	...	...	...	...	...	...
Philippines										
Philippines	93	102	...	...	...	...	...	...	...	...
Poland										
Pologne	138	139	157	186	211	254	325	397	473	492
Portugal										
Portugal	88	106	119	...	...	...	...	...	...	...
Rwanda										
Rwanda	...	...	...	...	...	...	...	...	...	...
Seychelles										
Seychelles	97	95	107	147	124	135	227	200	...	...
Singapore										
Singapour	87	107	114	137	157	177	188	203	184	194
Solomon Islands										
Iles Salomon	...	...	...	...	...	...	...	...	...	...
South Africa										
Afrique du Sud	109	100	103	108	125	136	155	...	...	...
Spain										
Espagne	91	112	122	118	131	...	...	...	...	...
Sri Lanka										
Sri Lanka	95	114	132	136	153	178	158	178	193	191
Sweden										
Suède	100	93	95	97	108	109	102	110	109	103
Switzerland										
Suisse	98	99	94	93	102	108	119	117	126	137
Syrian Arab Republic										
Rép. arabe syrienne	92	107	143	225	276	248	250	218	...	...
Thailand										
Thaïlande	82	109	117	130	151	170	153	137	100	123
Trinidad and Tobago										
Trinité—et—Tobago	106	...	...	...	...	...	...	...	...	...
Tunisia										
Tunisie	101	107	104	115	120	...	...	...	...	...

Country or area Pays ou zone	1989	1991	1992	1993	1994	1995	1996	1997	1998	1999
A. Exports: Quantum index [cont.] · Exportations: Indice du quantum [suite]										
Kenya										
Kenya	94	105	121	133	153	183	...	...	...	...
Korea, Republic of										
Corée, République de	94	110	216	230	264	181	217	271	317	325
Malaysia										
Malaisie	98	97	96	86	84	84	...	...	...	...
Morocco										
Maroc	92	108	101	105	115	114	111	119	122	...
Myanmar										
Myanmar	71	96	108	149	145	150	104	110	...	...
Netherlands										
Pays−Bas	95	105	108	116	129	140	146	160	177	...
New Zealand										
Nouvelle−Zélande	95	110	113	118	130	134	140	147	146	148
Norway [1]										
Norvège [1]	93	106	115	121	136	144	163	170	172	179
Pakistan										
Pakistan	94	113	124	112	139	110	130	123	95	67
Peru										
Pérou	100	104	111	120	132	133	141	153	132	148
Philippines										
Philippines	93	103	...	...	...	...	...	...	...	...
Poland										
Pologne	92	98	95	94	111	130	142	162	173	183
Portugal										
Portugal	89	101	107	...	...	...	...	...	...	...
Rwanda										
Rwanda	72	90	83	73	30	51	49	121	129	...
Seychelles										
Seychelles	102	136	126	106	172	139	256	421	...	...
Singapore										
Singapour	92	113	123	145	187	216	229	245	247	261
Solomon Islands										
Iles Salomon	94	122	136	...	...	...	...	...	...	...
South Africa										
Afrique du Sud	106	100	88	109	115	119	168	...	...	...
Spain										
Espagne	89	116	117	135	160	...	...	...	...	...
Sri Lanka										
Sri Lanka	86	104	108	108	118	145	131	145	143	152
Sweden										
Suède	101	98	99	107	114	112	106	110	107	105
Switzerland										
Suisse	96	99	103	104	109	114	127	123	129	134
Syrian Arab Republic										
Rép. arabe syrienne	78	109	105	158	171	167	164	183	...	...
Thailand										
Thaïlande	89	119	134	149	177	243	219	235	254	284
Trinidad and Tobago										
Trinité−et−Tobago	94	...	...	...	...	...	...	...	...	...
Tunisia										
Tunisie	110	110	111	121	137	...	...	...	...	...

70

Total imports and exports: index numbers
[*cont.*]

Importations et exportations: indices
1990 = 100 [*suite*]

Country or area Pays ou zone	1989	1991	1992	1993	1994	1995	1996	1997	1998	1999
A. Imports: Quantum index [cont.] · Importations: Indice du quantum [suite]										
Turkey										
Turquie	87	96	98	134	99	128	166	205	193	...
United Kingdom										
Royaume – Uni	100	95	101	101	107	112	123	133	144	157
United States										
Etats – Unis	98	98	106	117	131	140	148	166	185	206
B. Imports: Unit value index · Importations: Indice du valeur unitaire										
Argentina										
Argentine	99	96	94	92	93	98	97	95	90	98
Australia [2]										
Australie [2]	96	101	106	114	111	115	109	109	118	116
Austria										
Autriche	103	100	99	95	94	96	91	86	81	...
Bangladesh										
Bangladesh	90	121	...	...	...	...	...	...	...	...
Belgium – Luxembourg										
Belgique – Luxembourg	102	99	95	91	91	94	97	103	101	102
Bolivia										
Bolivie	...	...	...	...	...	...	...	...	...	...
Brazil [3]										
Brésil [3]	89	92	86	91	112	136	126	180	...	...
Canada										
Canada	98	99	103	108	115	120	119	120	125	126
China, Hong Kong SAR †										
Chine, Hong Kong RAS †	98	102	102	102	104	109	108	106	100	98
Colombia										
Colombie	79	121	130	145	158	182	209	224	259	296
Denmark										
Danemark	103	99	96	93	95	97	98	101	100	100
Dominica										
Dominique	94	104	...	...	...	...	...	...	...	...
Dominican Republic										
Rép. dominicaine	...	...	...	...	...	...	...	...	...	...
Ecuador										
Equateur	...	...	...	...	...	...	...	...	...	...
Ethiopia										
Ethiopie	...	...	...	...	...	...	...	...	...	...
Faeroe Islands										
Iles Féroé	103	100	...	...	...	...	...	...	...	...
Finland										
Finlande	99	102	113	127	123	123	125	129	129	...
France										
France	101	99	95	90	94	96	96	98	98	...
Germany										
Allemagne	103	102	99	93	95	98	96	98	96	94
Greece										
Grèce	91	109	110	111	110	112	119	123	123	...
Guatemala										
Guatemala	117	96	123	119	109	...	...	...	...	...
Honduras										
Honduras	...	...	...	...	...	...	...	...	...	...
Hungary										
Hongrie	91	146	161	176	203	269	324	367	409	...

Country or area Pays ou zone	1989	1991	1992	1993	1994	1995	1996	1997	1998	1999
A. Exports: Quantum index [cont.] · Exportations: Indice du quantum [suite]										
Turkey										
Turquie	95	107	110	117	134	143	157	178	188	...
United Kingdom										
Royaume–Uni	94	101	103	103	116	125	136	146	148	153
United States [4]										
Etats–Unis [4]	93	106	113	116	126	136	145	162	166	173
B. Exports: Unit value index · Exportations: Indice du valeur unitaire										
Argentina										
Argentine	99	98	102	102	105	111	119	114	104	106
Australia [2]										
Australie [2]	98	91	93	94	92	99	94	96	101	94
Austria										
Autriche	100	97	95	91	85	86	83	78	73	...
Bangladesh										
Bangladesh	96	105	...	...	...	...	...	...	...	...
Belgium–Luxembourg										
Belgique–Luxembourg	103	98	97	95	94	97	100	105	105	104
Bolivia [3]										
Bolivie [3]	115	96	76	64	66	73	72	55	51	50
Brazil [3]										
Brésil [3]	101	101	114	113	119	124	125	...	...	...
Canada										
Canada	101	96	99	103	110	119	120	120	120	123
China, Hong Kong SAR †										
Chine, Hong Kong RAS †	98	103	104	103	105	108	108	106	102	99
Colombia										
Colombie	73	117	118	134	174	204	217	263	293	336
Denmark										
Danemark	102	100	98	96	97	97	99	100	99	100
Dominica										
Dominique	93	105	100	89	97	100	...	...	...	...
Dominican Republic										
Rép. dominicaine	104	95	83	75	90	101	102	106	83	...
Ecuador [3]										
Equateur [3]	85	88	89	74	83	84	96	94	70	85
Ethiopia										
Ethiopie	108	97	104	157	...	...	...	...	...	...
Faeroe Islands										
Iles Féroé	99	110	...	...	...	...	...	...	...	...
Finland										
Finlande	101	100	106	113	113	121	121	123	125	...
France										
France	102	100	97	94	100	102	102	103	104	...
Germany										
Allemagne	101	99	99	94	93	95	93	94	93	92
Greece										
Grèce	92	109	106	109	121	122	129	110	114	...
Guatemala										
Guatemala	106	79	77	85	88	98	89	...	...	...
Honduras [3]										
Honduras [3]	105	98	77	78	89	123	114	119	116	...
Hungary										
Hongrie	91	131	143	160	189	254	299	343	388	...

70

Total imports and exports: index numbers
[*cont.*]

Importations et exportations: indices
1990 = 100 [*suite*]

Country or area Pays ou zone	1989	1991	1992	1993	1994	1995	1996	1997	1998	1999
B. Imports: Unit value index [cont.] · Importations: Indice du valeur unitaire [suite]										
Iceland										
Islande	83	103	104	113	118	123	128	127	...	...
India										
Inde	86	122	125	117	122	110	168	212	214	...
Indonesia										
Indonésie	...	...	...	...	...	...	...	...	...	...
Ireland										
Irlande	105	102	100	105	108	113	111	112	114	118
Israel [3]										
Israël [3]	93	95	95	92	94	102	101	96	91	89
Italy										
Italie	101	99	99	110	115	100	100	100	95	...
Japan										
Japon	90	91	84	74	69	68	80	84	79	69
Jordan										
Jordanie	74	100	95	90	88	99	108	106	105	103
Kenya										
Kenya	83	111	129	208	187	216	236	252	259	...
Korea, Republic of										
Corée, République de	93	104	108	107	108	113	116	130	154	130
Malaysia										
Malaisie	...	...	...	...	...	...	...	...	...	...
Mauritius										
Maurice	96	105	107	119	127	135	144	147	148	...
Mexico [3]										
Mexique [3]	...	100	101	102	...	...	...	...	...	...
Morocco										
Maroc	91	96	92	101	114	...	...	...	...	...
Myanmar										
Myanmar	...	...	...	...	...	...	...	...	...	...
Netherlands										
Pays–Bas	103	100	97	92	92	92	93	98	92	...
New Zealand										
Nouvelle–Zélande	99	101	108	107	104	103	100	99	103	105
Norway [1]										
Norvège [1]	99	98	96	97	97	98	98	97	98	96
Pakistan										
Pakistan	92	107	110	118	138	156	172	199	143	102
Papua New Guinea										
Papouasie–Nvl–Guinée	...	...	...	...	...	...	...	...	...	...
Peru										
Pérou	...	...	...	...	...	...	...	...	...	...
Philippines [3]										
Philippines [3]	83	108	...	...	...	...	...	...	...	...
Poland [2]										
Pologne [2]	14	130	152	177	225	254	298	338	356	379
Portugal										
Portugal	97	100	95	...	...	...	...	...	...	...
Rwanda										
Rwanda	...	...	...	...	...	...	...	...	...	...
Seychelles										
Seychelles	96	96	92	85	85	83	84	86	...	...
Singapore [2]										
Singapour [2]	101	97	93	92	91	91	90	88	87	88

Country or area Pays ou zone	1989	1991	1992	1993	1994	1995	1996	1997	1998	1999
B. Exports: Unit value index [cont.] • Exportations: Indice du valeur unitaire [suite]										
Iceland Islande	85	108	104	107	113	120	119	122	...	...
India Inde	93	111	142	155	168	167	157	184	190	...
Indonesia [3] Indonésie [3]	82	88	84	77	97	111	117	111	87	...
Ireland [3] Irlande	110	99	97	104	104	106	105	106	109	109
Israel [3] Israël [3]	92	100	101	102	100	105	105	104	101	102
Italy Italie	98	103	136	151	156	131	136	136	136	...
Japan Japon	97	100	100	96	95	94	101	105	105	97
Jordan Jordanie	84	111	107	96	101	117	124	121	114	110
Kenya Kenya	92	128	144	259	266	289	307	359	364	...
Korea, Republic of Corée, République de	97	104	126	129	132	116	104	104	132	110
Malaysia Malaisie	101	102	...	...	...	...	...	...	...	...
Mauritius Maurice	89	106	114	124	130	138	153	158	179	...
Mexico [3] Mexique [3]	...	92	92	89	...	...	...	...	...	...
Morocco Maroc	96	100	95	95	94	128	...	...	...	...
Myanmar Myanmar	111	101	88	81	87	136	130	132	...	...
Netherlands Pays−Bas	101	98	95	92	92	94	94	97	91	...
New Zealand Nouvelle−Zélande	101	96	104	106	102	100	96	94	98	100
Norway [1] Norvège [1]	96	96	88	88	85	88	95	97	86	95
Pakistan Pakistan	91	104	106	116	136	171	189	217	179	131
Papua New Guinea Papouasie−Nvl−Guinée	96	99	101	113	132	185	182	202	231	259
Peru [3] Pérou [3]	104	93	94	74	86	106	112	109	84	90
Philippines [3] Philippines [3]	92	115	...	...	...	...	...	...	...	...
Poland [2] Pologne [2]	16	118	152	190	245	297	321	362	389	417
Portugal Portugal	97	100	98	...	...	...	...	...	...	...
Rwanda Rwanda	115	132	105	127	124	429	400	602	400	...
Seychelles Seychelles	94	88	101	102	91	112	110	111	...	...
Singapore [2] Singapour [2]	100	95	88	86	83	82	81	79	78	78

70

Total imports and exports: index numbers
[*cont.*]

Importations et exportations: indices
1990 = 100 [*suite*]

Country or area Pays ou zone	1989	1991	1992	1993	1994	1995	1996	1997	1998	1999
B. Imports: Unit value index [cont.] · Importations: Indice du valeur unitaire [suite]										
Solomon Islands Iles Salomon	...	...	...	...	...	...	...	...	...	...
South Africa Afrique du Sud	93	110	117	125	138	157	166	...	...	...
Spain [2] Espagne [2]	103	97	96	101	107	112	112	116	113	113
Sri Lanka Sri Lanka	79	104	109	114	121	140	141	161	...	...
Sweden [2] Suède [2]	99	101	99	112	117	124	119	122	121	125
Switzerland Suisse	101	100	102	100	95	93	100	98	95	92
Syrian Arab Republic Rép. arabe syrienne	99	115	98	93	105	118	125	107	...	...
Thailand Thaïlande	95	104	105	106	109	122	138	163	198	172
Trinidad and Tobago Trinité-et-Tobago	99	...	...	...	...	...	...	...	...	...
Tunisia Tunisie	89	99	94	94	...	...	...	...	...	...
Turkey Turquie	95	97	95	89	95	111	105	96	92	...
United Kingdom [2] Royaume-Uni [2]	98	101	102	112	115	127	127	119	114	114
United States [2] Etats-Unis [2]	97	100	101	100	102	106	107	105	99	101
Uruguay Uruguay	...	...	...	...	...	...	...	...	...	...
Venezuela Venezuela	83	119	140	189	341	514	1098	1338	1547	1724
Yugoslavia, SFR † Yougoslavie, Rfs †	90	...	...	...	...	...	...	...	...	...
C. Terms of trade · Termes de l'échange										
Argentina Argentine	100	102	109	111	113	113	123	120	116	108
Australia Australie	102	90	88	82	83	86	86	88	86	81
Austria Autriche	97	97	96	96	90	90	91	91	90	...
Bangladesh Bangladesh	107	87	...	...	...	...	...	...	...	...
Belgium-Luxembourg Belgique-Luxembourg	101	99	102	104	103	103	103	102	104	102
Brazil Brésil	113	110	133	124	106	91	99	...	...	...
Canada Canada	103	97	96	95	96	99	101	100	96	98
China, Hong Kong SAR † Chine, Hong Kong RAS †	100	101	102	101	101	99	100	100	102	101
Colombia Clombie	92	97	91	92	110	112	104	117	113	114
Denmark Danemark	99	101	102	103	102	100	101	99	99	100

Country or area Pays ou zone	1989	1991	1992	1993	1994	1995	1996	1997	1998	1999

B. Exports: Unit value index [cont.] · Exportations: Indice du valeur unitaire [suite]

Country or area Pays ou zone	1989	1991	1992	1993	1994	1995	1996	1997	1998	1999
Solomon Islands Iles Salomon	92	106	103	...	...	...	...	...	...	...
South Africa Afrique du Sud	95	106	112	122	137	161	177	...	...	...
Spain [2] Espagne [2]	103	99	100	105	110	117	118	122	122	121
Sri Lanka Sri Lanka	83	102	128	115	121	169	155	169	195	192
Sweden [2] Suède [2]	98	101	98	108	110	117	111	112	111	110
Switzerland Suisse	99	103	103	103	102	100	109	105	105	105
Syrian Arab Republic Rép. arabe syrienne	77	81	68	67	72	90	95	75	...	...
Thailand Thaïlande	98	103	104	106	109	118	130	155	178	157
Trinidad and Tobago Trinité–et–Tobago	84	...	...	...	...	...	...	...	...	...
Tunisia Tunisie	95	97	95	96	101	...	...	...	...	...
Turkey Turquie	91	99	100	98	95	107	102	97	93	...
United Kingdom [2] Royaume–Uni [2]	97	101	103	116	118	126	127	120	110	109
United States [24] Etats–Unis [24]	99	101	101	101	104	109	109	108	104	102
Uruguay Uruguay	105	100	99	93	95	105	102	...	...	...
Venezuela Venezuela	60	94	108	127	...	...	...	...	...	...
Yugoslavia, SFR † Yougoslavie, Rfs †	90	...	...	...	...	...	...	...	...	...

D. Purchasing power of exports · Pouvoir d'achat des exportations

Country or area Pays ou zone	1989	1991	1992	1993	1994	1995	1996	1997	1998	1999
Argentina Argentine	78	100	105	115	138	172	199	217	232	228
Australia Australie	96	104	106	106	115	121	135	158	163	159
Austria Autriche	87	103	107	103	108	125	134	156	164	...
Bangladesh Bangladesh	...	...	...	...	...	...	...	...	...	...
Belgium–Luxembourg Belgique–Luxembourg	98	103	106	116	127	135	138	146	157	159
Brazil Brésil	124	110	133	135	123	109	118	...	...	...
Canada Canada	99	98	106	117	132	151	162	175	181	204
China, Hong Kong SAR † Chine, Hong Kong RAS †	92	118	143	162	178	195	207	219	214	220
Colombia Colombie	...	...	...	...	...	...	...	...	...	...
Denmark Danemark	97	112	118	117	125	116	120	126	125	135

70

Total imports and exports: index numbers
[*cont.*]

Importations et exportations: indices
1990 = 100 [*suite*]

Country or area Pays ou zone	1989	1991	1992	1993	1994	1995	1996	1997	1998	1999
C. Terms of trade [cont.] • Termes de l'échange [suite]										
Dominica Dominique	99	101	...	...	...	...	...	...	...	...
Faeroe Islands Iles Féroé	96	110	...	...	...	...	...	...	...	...
Finland Finlande	102	98	94	89	92	98	97	95	97	...
France France	101	101	102	104	106	106	106	105	106	...
Germany Allemagne	98	97	100	101	98	97	97	96	97	98
Greece Grèce	101	100	96	98	110	109	108	89	93	...
Guatemala Guatemala	91	82	63	71	81	...	...	...	...	...
Hungary Hongrie	100	90	89	91	93	94	92	93	95	...
Iceland Islande	102	105	100	95	96	98	93	96	...	...
India Inde	108	91	114	132	138	152	93	87	89	...
Ireland Irlande	105	97	97	99	96	94	95	95	96	92
Israel Israël	99	105	106	111	106	103	104	108	111	115
Italy Italie	97	104	137	137	136	131	136	136	143	...
Japan Japon	108	110	119	130	138	138	126	125	133	141
Jordan Jordanie	114	111	113	107	115	118	115	114	109	107
Kenya Kenya	111	115	112	125	142	134	130	142	141	...
Korea. Republic of Corée, République de	104	100	117	121	122	103	90	80	86	85
Mauritius Maurice	93	101	107	104	102	102	106	107	121	...
Mexico Mexique	...	92	91	87	...	...	...	...	...	...
Morocco Maroc	105	104	103	94	82	...	...	...	...	...
Netherlands Pays–Bas	98	98	98	100	100	102	101	99	99	...
New Zealand Nouvelle–Zélande	102	95	96	99	98	97	96	95	95	95
Norway Norvège	97	98	92	91	88	90	97	100	88	99
Pakistan Pakistan	99	97	96	98	99	110	110	109	125	128
Philippines Philippines	111	106	...	...	...	...	...	...	...	...
Poland Pologne	114	91	100	107	109	117	108	107	109	110
Portugal Portugal	100	100	103	...	...	...	...	...	...	...

Country or area Pays ou zone	1989	1991	1992	1993	1994	1995	1996	1997	1998	1999
D. Purchasing power of exports [cont.] · Pouvoir d'achat des exportations [suite]										
Dominica Dominique	87	95	...	...	...	...	...	...	...	...
Faeroe Islands Iles Féroé	98	114	...	...	...	...	...	...	...	...
Finland Finlande	98	89	93	104	122	141	146	161	172	...
France France	96	106	110	115	128	137	142	155	167	...
Germany Allemagne	97	97	102	99	110	112	121	134	147	156
Greece Grèce	106	114	142	140	164	179	190	122	205	...
Guatemala Guatemala	92	103	91	97	119	...	...	...	...	...
Hungary Hongrie	104	85	85	76	90	100	102	134	166	...
Iceland Islande	103	96	91	91	103	102	107	112	...	...
India Inde	98	104	132	185	212	287	221	178	...	...
Ireland Irlande	96	103	117	132	147	173	191	220	276	308
Israel Israël	98	103	114	134	149	154	168	195	212	237
Italy Italie	94	104	140	154	170	185	188	199	213	...
Japan Japon	102	112	124	131	142	148	135	146	154	166
Jordan Jordanie	118	98	108	153	176	162	154	163	160	158
Kenya Kenya	104	121	135	166	218	245	...	...	...	...
Korea, Republic of Corée, République de	98	110	252	277	323	186	195	217	272	275
Mauritius Maurice	...	...	...	...	...	...	...	...	...	...
Mexico Mexique	...	...	...	...	...	...	...	...	...	...
Morocco Maroc	97	113	104	99	95	...	...	...	...	...
Netherlands Pays-Bas	93	103	106	116	129	143	148	158	175	...
New Zealand Nouvelle-Zélande	97	105	109	117	128	130	134	140	139	141
Norway Norvège	90	104	105	110	119	129	158	170	151	177
Pakistan Pakistan	93	110	119	110	137	121	143	134	119	86
Philippines Philippines	103	110	...	...	...	...	...	...	...	...
Poland Pologne	105	89	95	101	121	152	153	174	189	201
Portugal Portugal	89	101	110	...	...	...	...	...	...	...

70
Total imports and exports: index numbers
[*cont.*]

Importations et exportations: indices
1990 = 100 [*suite*]

Country or area Pays ou zone	1989	1991	1992	1993	1994	1995	1996	1997	1998	1999
C. Terms of trade [cont.] · Termes de l'échange [suite]										
Seychelles Seychelles	98	92	110	120	107	135	131	129	...	...
Singapore Singapour	99	98	95	93	91	90	90	90	90	89
South Africa Afrique du Sud	102	96	96	98	99	103	107	...	...	...
Spain Espagne	100	102	104	104	103	104	105	105	108	107
Sri Lanka Sri Lanka	105	98	117	101	100	121	110	105	...	...
Sweden Suède	99	100	99	96	94	94	93	92	92	88
Switzerland Suisse	98	103	101	103	107	108	109	107	111	114
Syrian Arab Republic Rép. arabe syrienne	78	70	69	72	69	76	76	70	...	...
Thailand Thaïlande	103	99	99	100	100	97	94	95	90	91
Trinidad and Tobago Trinité−et−Tobago	85	...	...	...	...	...	...	...	...	...
Tunisia Tunisie	107	98	101	102	...	...	...	...	...	...
Turkey Turquie	96	102	105	110	100	96	97	101	101	...
United Kingdom Royaume−Uni	99	100	101	104	103	99	100	101	96	96
United States Etats−Unis	102	101	100	101	102	103	102	103	105	101
Venezuela Venezuela	72	79	77	67	...	...	...	...	...	...
Yugoslavia Yougoslavie	100	...	...	...	...	...	...	...	...	...

Source:
United Nations Secretariat, trade statistics database of the Statistics Division.

† For information on the recent changes in country or area nomenclature pertaining to former Czechoslovakia, Germany, Hong Kong Special Administrative Region (SAR) of China, Macao Special Administrative Region (SAR) of China, SFR of Yugoslavia and the former USSR, see Annex I − Country or area nomenclature, regional and other groupings.

1 Excluding ships.
2 Price index numbers. For Australia beginning 1981, for the United States beginning 1989, for the United Kingdom starting 1999.

Source:
Secrétariat de l'Organisation des Nations Unies, la base de données pour les statistiques du commerce extérieur de la Division de statistique.

† Pour les modifications récentes de nomenclature de pays ou de zone concernant l'Allemagne, Hong Kong, région administrative spéciale (RAS) de Chine, Macao, région administrative spéciale (RAS) de Chine, l'ex−Tchécoslovaquie. l'ex−URSS et l'ex Rfs de Yougoslavie, voir annex I − Nomenclature des pays ou des zones, groupements régionaux et autres groupements.

1 Non compris les navires.
2 Indices des prix. Pour l'Australie, à partir de 1981; pour les Etats−Unis à partir de 1989; pour le Royaume−Uni, à partir de 1999.

Country or area Pays ou zone	1989	1991	1992	1993	1994	1995	1996	1997	1998	1999
D. Purchasing power of exports [cont.] · Pouvoir d'achat des exportations [suite]										
Seychelles										
Seychelles	100	125	138	127	184	188	335	543	...	...
Singapore										
Singapour	91	111	116	136	171	195	206	220	221	231
South Africa										
Afrique du Sud	108	96	84	106	114	122	179	...	...	...
Spain										
Espagne	89	118	122	140	164	...	...	...	...	...
Sri Lanka										
Sri Lanka	90	102	127	109	118	175	144	152	...	...
Sweden										
Suède	100	98	98	103	107	106	99	101	98	92
Switzerland										
Suisse	94	102	104	107	117	123	138	132	143	153
Syrian Arab Republic										
Rép. arabe syrienne	61	77	73	114	117	127	125	128	...	...
Thailand										
Thaïlande	92	118	133	149	177	235	206	223	228	259
Trinidad and Tobago										
Trinité−et−Tobago	80	...	...	...	...	...	...	...	...	...
Tunisia										
Tunisie	117	108	112	124	...	...	...	...	...	...
Turkey										
Turquie	91	109	116	129	134	138	153	180	190	...
United Kingdom										
Royaume−Uni	93	101	104	107	119	124	136	147	143	146
United States										
Etats−Unis	95	107	113	117	128	140	148	167	174	175
Venezuela										
Venezuela	...	...	...	...	...	...	...	...	...	...
Yugoslavia										
Yougoslavie	...	...	...	...	...	...	...	...	...	...

3   Calculated in terms of US dollars.
4   Excludes military exports.

3   Calculés en dollars des Etats−Unis.
4   Non compris les exportations militaires.

71
Manufactured goods exports
Exportations des produits manufacturés

1990 = 100

Region, country or area Region, pays ou zone	1989	1991	1992	1993	1994	1995	1996	1997	1998	1999
Unit value indices in US dollars • Indices de valeur unitaire en dollars des E.-U.										
Total[1]	93	100	103	99	101	110	106	98	96	...
Developed economies Econ. développées	91	99	103	97	99	110	106	98	96	93
Northern America Amérique septentrionale	100	102	100	99	99	100	100	100	96	95
Canada Canada	98	99	91	88	84	80	83	77	69	67
United States[2] Etats-Unis[2]	101	102	103	103	104	107	106	108	108	108
Europe Europe	87	98	102	91	93	107	104	93	92	89
EU+ UE+	87	97	102	92	93	107	103	92	92	88
Austria[3] Autriche[3]	86	96	99	91	90	104	94	77	68	...
Belgium-Luxembourg[4] Belgique-Luxembourg[4]	89	97	99	90	93	110	105	96	94	...
Denmark Danemark	84	96	102	92	97	112	108	98	97	94
Finland Finlande	90	95	90	74	83	105	99	89	88	85
France France	86	96	100	94	98	111	107	96	96	...
Germany[5] Allemagne †[5]	86	98	103	93	94	108	101	87	89	...
Greece Grèce	87	95	94	81	82	88	84	72	66	...
Ireland[4] Irlande[4]	91	95	97	96	89	98	97	81	75	...
Italy[4] Italie[4]	86	99	105	89	86	96	98	90	91	...
Netherlands[6] Pays-Bas[6]	86	96	102	92	92	109	102	...	...	...
Portugal[4] Portugal[4]	85	101	106	98	94	111	105	96	96	...
Spain[4] Espagne[4]	83	95	109	85	86	99	99	88	86	...
Sweden Suède	90	100	102	82	85	105	106	94	90	...
United Kingdom Royaume-Uni	88	100	102	98	103	114	113	113	112	106
EFTA+ AELE+	86	97	101	87	96	116	113	97	97	96
Iceland[4] Islande[4]	103	88	86	76	80	114	106	101	89	...
Norway Norvège	99	94	92	80	82	102	96	88	85	80

71
Manufactured goods exports
1990 = 100 [*cont.*]

Exportations des produits manufacturés
1990 = 100 [*suite*]

Region, country or area Région, pays ou zone	1989	1991	1992	1993	1994	1995	1996	1997	1998	1999
Switzerland[4] Suisse[4]	84	98	103	88	99	120	117	100	100	...
Other developed economies **Autres écon. développées**	**100**	**105**	**113**	**120**	**129**	**138**	**128**	**121**	**116**	**113**
Australia Australie	102	58	86	81	88	96	94	89	78	78
Israel Israël	92	101	101	102	101	105	105	102	105	114
Japan Japon	100	108	115	124	134	144	133	126	121	119
New Zealand Nouvelle-Zélande	105	94	89	89	98	112	109	102	...	...
South Africa Afrique du Sud	95	96	101	100	101	123	107	...	...	...
Developing economies **Econ. en dévelop.**	**98**	**101**	**101**	**102**	**104**	**111**	**105**	**99**	**96**	...
China, Hong Kong SAR† Chine, Hong Kong RAS†	99	102	104	104	105	108	108	104	101	99
India Inde	...	80	92	89	88	86	69	84	79	...
Korea, Republic of[6] Corée, République de[6]	101	101	97	96	98	102	86	85	76	61
Pakistan Pakistan	94	98	101	98	107	125	123	129	127	118
Singapore Singapour	96	101	103	99	108	112	109	102	92	...
Turkey[7] Turquie[7]	91	99	100	95	90	106	97	89	84	...

Unit value indices in 'SDR'[6]· Indices de valeur unitaire en 'DTS'[6]

Total	98	99	99	96	95	98	99	97	96	...
Developed economies **Econ. développées**	**97**	**99**	**100**	**95**	**94**	**98**	**99**	**96**	**96**	**92**
Developing economies **Econ. en dévelop.**	**104**	**100**	**97**	**99**	**99**	**99**	**98**	**97**	**96**	...

Unit value indices in national currency · Indices de valeur unitaire en monnaie nationale

Northern America · Amérique septentrionale

Canada Canada	99	97	94	98	99	95	97	92	88	86
United States[2] Etats-Unis[2]	101	102	103	103	104	107	106	108	108	108

Europe · Europe
EU+ · UE+

Austria[3] Autriche[3]	100	98	96	93	91	92	88	83	74	...
Denmark Danemark	100	99	100	97	100	102	102	105	105	106
Finland Finlande	101	100	106	112	112	120	119	121	123	124

71
Manufactured goods exports
1990 = 100 [cont.]

Exportations des produits manufacturés
1990 = 100 [suite]

Region, country or area Région, pays ou zone	1989	1991	1992	1993	1994	1995	1996	1997	1998	1999
France France	101	99	97	98	100	101	101	103	104	...
Germany[5] Allemagne †[5]	100	100	100	95	94	96	94	94	97	...
Greece Grèce	90	110	114	112	127	128	128	123	123	...
Netherlands[6] Pays-Bas[6]	101	99	98	94	92	96	95	...	...	...
Sweden Suède	99	102	100	108	111	126	120	121	120	...
United Kingdom Royaume-Uni	96	101	104	117	120	129	129	123	121	117
EFTA+ · AELE+										
Norway Norvège	110	98	92	92	93	104	99	100	103	100
Other developed economies · Autres écon. développées										
Australia Australie	101	58	91	94	94	102	94	94	97	94
Japan Japon	96	100	101	95	95	93	101	106	109	94
New Zealand Nouvelle-Zélande	104	97	99	98	99	101	94	92	...	...
South Africa Afrique du Sud	97	103	111	127	139	173	178	...	...	...
Developing economies · Econ. en dévelop.										
China, Hong Kong SAR† Chine, Hong Kong RAS†	99	102	103	103	105	107	107	103	100	98
India Inde	...	103	136	154	158	160	141	174	187	...
Pakistan Pakistan	89	107	117	127	151	182	203	245	265	270

Quantum indices · Indices de volume

	1989	1991	1992	1993	1994	1995	1996	1997	1998	1999
Total[1]	94	105	111	115	130	142	152	172	171	...
Developed economies Econ. développées	95	104	106	108	121	129	137	155	160	166
Northern America Amérique septentrionale	88	106	114	121	137	155	165	185	194	206
Canada Canada	97	102	119	135	164	202	206	234	274	...
United States Etats-Unis	86	107	113	117	130	142	153	172	172	176
Europe **Europe**	96	103	104	106	119	126	135	153	160	163
EU+ UE+	96	103	105	105	120	127	137	155	162	165

71
Manufactured goods exports
1990 = 100 [cont.]

Exportations des produits manufacturés
1990 = 100 [suite]

Region, country or area Région, pays ou zone	1989	1991	1992	1993	1994	1995	1996	1997	1998	1999
Austria Autriche	90	104	108	107	119	130	147	181	201	...
Belgium-Luxembourg Belgique-Luxembourg	95	102	104	112	126	127	133	144	160	...
Denmark Danemark	93	106	114	111	118	125	128	145	152	170
Finland Finlande	96	90	97	117	132	144	153	172	188	188
France France	94	107	112	104	116	122	129	143	154	...
Germany Allemagne †	99	102	104	100	112	116	126	145	148	...
Greece Grèce	106	109	127	134	133	153	169	195	216	...
Ireland Irlande	93	108	122	124	166	193	232	320	434	...
Italy Italie	97	101	100	112	132	144	153	159	161	...
Netherlands Pays-Bas	95	105	105	107	121	130	139	...	...	...
Portugal Portugal	90	101	110	100	120	132	143	154	166	...
Spain Espagne	94	114	109	132	157	169	191	220	231	...
Sweden Suède	99	97	97	108	128	131	131	156	157	...
United Kingdom Royaume-Uni	94	100	101	95	108	116	128	139	139	140
EFTA+ **AELE+**	**95**	**99**	**101**	**111**	**108**	**106**	**108**	**124**	**129**	**135**
Iceland Islande	107	91	94	102	131	120	130	149	168	...
Norway Norvège	89	103	106	105	96	100	106	136	147	149
Switzerland Suisse	96	98	100	112	111	107	109	120	125	...
Other developed economies **Autres écon. développées**	**96**	**104**	**104**	**104**	**107**	**112**	**115**	**124**	**118**	**133**
Australia Australie	88	192	138	161	180	196	254	277	267	291
Israel Israël	97	98	111	126	146	155	170	194	197	203
Japan Japon	96	102	103	101	103	107	107	115	110	121
New Zealand Nouvelle-Zélande	92	112	120	132	152	155	162	178	...	...
South Africa Afrique du Sud	96	108	107	113	126	134	159	...	...	...

71
Manufactured goods exports
1990 = 100 [*cont.*]

Exportations des produits manufacturés
1990 = 100 [*suite*]

Region, country or area Région, pays ou zone	1989	1991	1992	1993	1994	1995	1996	1997	1998	1999
Developing economies **Econ. en dévelop.**	**91**	**112**	**133**	**146**	**171**	**196**	**218**	**250**	**221**	...
China, Hong Kong SAR† Chine, Hong Kong RAS†	101	100	100	95	93	95	87	90	84	78
India Inde	...	128	132	147	181	215	278	246	253	...
Korea, Republic of Corée, République de	95	109	121	131	150	185	222	231	252	349
Pakistan Pakistan	80	120	130	136	137	124	146	132	128	145
Singapore Singapour	90	112	125	155	195	236	255	274	267	...
Turkey Turquie	96	102	119	130	164	170	197	250	279	...

Value (thousand million US $) • Valeur (millards de dollars des E.-U.)

	1989	1991	1992	1993	1994	1995	1996	1997	1998	1999
Total[1]	2 088.80	2 517.50	2 747.30	2 729.60	3 141.80	3 744.20	3 872.70	4 068.50	3 932.30	...
Developed economies **Econ. développées**	1 688.20	2 014.90	2 148.10	2 064.30	2 346.20	2 774.60	2 847.20	2 959.80	2 990.30	3 030.70
Northern America **Amérique septentrionale**	**319.63**	**389.25**	**413.80**	**435.09**	**490.11**	**557.03**	**593.68**	**667.70**	**675.62**	**703.74**
Canada Canada	74.46	79.42	84.61	93.80	109.17	128.22	134.01	142.90	148.67	...
United States Etats-Unis	245.17	309.83	329.19	341.29	380.94	428.81	459.67	524.79	526.96	538.14
Europe **Europe**	**1 075.30**	**1 290.50**	**1 372.70**	**1 244.10**	**1 432.40**	**1 741.30**	**1 803.10**	**1 830.80**	**1 894.10**	**1 865.90**
EU+ **UE+**	**1 012.70**	**1 216.70**	**1 294.70**	**1 170.60**	**1 352.80**	**1 646.90**	**1 709.30**	**1 739.00**	**1 798.60**	**1 766.80**
Austria Autriche	29.07	37.53	40.66	36.70	40.88	51.38	52.28	53.05	51.65	50.44
Belgium-Luxembourg Belgique-Luxembourg	80.42	93.84	97.60	95.90	110.73	133.05	133.30	131.23	143.26	142.52
Denmark Danemark	16.59	21.40	24.66	21.65	24.30	29.43	29.22	30.17	31.22	33.76
Finland Finlande	19.77	19.65	20.05	20.05	25.11	34.68	34.77	35.12	38.00	36.70
France France	134.56	169.44	184.58	162.83	187.22	222.89	229.44	225.78	244.30	242.53
Germany Allemagne †	309.59	361.85	387.53	334.59	380.38	455.79	459.69	455.26	477.85	461.09
Greece Grèce	4.12	4.59	5.31	4.83	4.88	5.99	6.29	6.21	6.34	5.58
Ireland Irlande	13.95	16.96	19.56	19.58	24.29	31.21	36.99	42.82	53.58	59.86
Italy Italie	125.92	150.98	158.35	150.13	170.55	208.98	226.89	215.04	219.73	206.69
Netherlands Pays-Bas	65.51	80.89	85.31	79.18	89.86	113.91	114.03	133.46	121.70	122.17
Portugal Portugal	10.09	13.39	15.38	12.88	14.86	19.45	19.85	19.48	21.10	...

71
Manufactured goods exports
1990 = 100 [*cont.*]

Exportations des produits manufacturés
1990 = 100 [*suite*]

Region, country or area Region, pays ou zone	1989	1991	1992	1993	1994	1995	1996	1997	1998	1999
Spain Espagne	33.18	46.08	50.61	47.54	57.74	71.35	80.45	82.32	84.75	88.72
Sweden Suède	43.92	47.50	48.49	43.13	53.35	67.44	67.70	71.39	68.70	71.11
United Kingdom Royaume-Uni	125.96	152.62	156.62	141.64	168.65	201.32	218.42	237.73	236.39	225.63
EFTA+ **AELE+**	**61.87**	**72.60**	**76.60**	**72.26**	**78.21**	**92.70**	**92.26**	**90.34**	**93.84**	**97.39**
Iceland Islande	0.32	0.23	0.23	0.23	0.31	0.40	0.40	0.44	0.44	0.56
Norway Norvège	12.55	13.84	13.84	12.05	11.20	14.46	14.39	17.01	17.67	16.84
Switzerland Suisse	49.01	58.52	62.53	59.98	66.70	77.84	77.47	72.88	75.73	79.99
Other developed economies **Autres écon. développées**	**293.25**	**335.15**	**361.60**	**385.08**	**423.70**	**476.20**	**450.37**	**461.27**	**420.65**	**461.04**
Australia Australie	7.44	9.19	9.83	10.85	13.07	15.63	19.75	20.43	17.29	18.73
Israel Israël	9.42	10.47	11.74	13.48	15.50	17.09	18.79	20.84	21.67	24.22
Japan Japon	266.59	304.34	328.52	348.56	381.06	425.75	393.58	402.10	369.56	397.48
New Zealand Nouvelle-Zélande	2.45	2.67	2.73	2.98	3.78	4.38	4.46	4.60	4.32	4.50
South Africa Afrique du Sud	7.35	8.48	8.78	9.22	10.28	13.36	13.79	13.31	7.81	16.12
Developing economies **Econ. en dévelop.**	**400.60**	**502.63**	**599.24**	**665.29**	**795.55**	**969.59**	**1 025.50**	**1 108.70**	**942.00**	...
China, Hong Kong SAR† Chine, Hong Kong RAS†	27.40	28.16	28.42	27.12	27.11	28.22	25.83	25.69	23.26	21.16
India Inde	12.08	12.95	15.35	16.42	20.15	23.34	24.32	25.97	25.28	...
Korea, Republic of Corée, République de	58.26	66.90	71.38	76.79	89.86	115.54	115.97	119.96	116.33	130.55
Pakistan Pakistan	3.27	5.10	5.72	5.79	6.38	6.74	7.76	7.40	7.08	7.41
Singapore Singapour	32.72	43.36	49.33	58.74	80.54	100.99	105.95	106.55	94.15	99.68
Turkey Turquie	7.87	9.10	10.64	11.17	13.30	16.32	17.32	20.02	21.04	21.19

Source:
United Nations Secretariat, trade statistics database of the
Statistics Division.

+   For Member States of this grouping, see
    Annex I - Other groupings.

Source:
Secrétariat de l'Organisation des Nations Unies, la base de
données pour les statistiques du commerce extérieur de la
Division de statistique.

+   Les Etats membres de ce groupement, voir
    annex I - Autres groupements.

71
Manufactured goods exports
[*cont.*]

Exportations des produits manufacturés
1990 = 100 [*suite*]

† For information on recent changes in country or
area nomenclature pertaining to former Czechoslovakia,
Germany, Hong Kong Special Administrative Region (SAR) of
China, Macao Special Administrative Region (SAR) of China,
SFR of Yugoslavia and the former USSR, see Annex I - Country
or area nomenclature, regional and other groupings.

1 Excludes trade of the countries of Eastern Europe and the
former USSR.
2 Beginning 1989, derived from price indices; national unit
value index discontinued.
3 Series linked to 1988 by a factor calculated by the United
Nations Statistics Division.
4 Indices are calculated by the United Nations Statistics
Division.
5 Data prior to January 1991 pertain to the territorial
boundaries of the Federal Republic of Germany prior to 3
October 1990.
6 Derived from sub-indices using current weights.

7 Industrial product.

† Pour les modifications récentes de nomenclature
de pays ou de zone concernant l'Allemagne, Hong Kong, région
administrative spéciale (RAS) de Chine, Macao, région
administrative spéciale (RAS) de Chine,
l'ex-Tchécoslovaquie, l'ex-URSS et l'ex-Rfs de Yougoslavie,
voir annexe I - Nomenclature des pays ou des zones,
groupements régionaux et autres groupements.

1 Non compris le commerce des pays de l'Europe de l'Est et
l'ex-URSS.
2 A partir de 1989, calculés à partir des indices des prix;
l'indice de la valeur unitaire nationale est discontinué.
3 Les séries sont enchaînés à 1988 par un facteur calculé par
la Division de statistique des Nations Unies.
4 Les indices sont calculés par la Division de statistique des
Nations Unies.
5 Les données relatives à la période précédent janvier 1991
correspondent aux limites térritoriales de la République
Fédérale d'Allemagne antérieur au 3 octobre 1990.
6 Calculé à partir de sous-indices à coéfficients de
pondération correspondant à la période en cours.
7 Produit industriel.

Technical notes, tables 69-71

Tables 69-71: Current data (annual, monthly and/or quarterly) for most of the series are published regularly by the Statistics Division in the United Nations *Monthly Bulletin of Statistics* [25]. More detailed descriptions of the tables and notes on methodology appear in the United Nations *1977 Supplement to the Statistical Yearbook and Monthly Bulletin of Statistics* [54], *International Trade Statistics: Concepts and Definitions* [48] and the *International Trade Statistics Yearbook* [24]. More detailed data including series for individual countries showing the value in national currencies for imports and exports and notes on these series can be found in the *International Trade Statistics Yearbook* [24] and in the *Monthly Bulletin of Statistics* [25].

Data are obtained from national published sources; from data supplied by the governments for publication in United Nations publications such as *Commodity Trade Statistics*, *Monthly Bulletin of Statistics* and *Statistical Yearbook*; and from publications of other United Nations agencies.

Territory

The statistics reported by a country refer to the customs area of the country. In most cases, this coincides with the geographical area of the country.

Systems of trade

Two systems of recording trade are in common use, differing mainly in the way warehoused and re-exported goods are recorded:

(a)   Special trade (S): special imports are the combined total of imports for direct domestic consumption (including transformation and repair) and withdrawals from bonded warehouses or free zones for domestic consumption. Special exports comprise exports of national merchandise, namely, goods wholly or partly produced or manufactured in the country, together with exports of nationalized goods. (Nationalized goods are goods which, having been included in special imports, are then exported without transformation);

(b)   General trade (G): general imports are the combined total of imports for direct domestic consumption and imports into bonded warehouses or free zones. General exports are the combined total of national exports and re-exports. Re-exports, in the general trade system, consist of the outward movement of nationalized goods plus goods which, after importation, move outward from bonded warehouses or free zones without having been transformed.

Notes techniques, tableaux 69 à 71

Tableaux 69-71: La Division de statistique des Nations Unies publie régulièrement dans le *Bulletin mensuel de statistique* [25] des données courantes (annuelles, mensuelles et/ou trimestrielles) pour la plupart des séries de ces tableaux. Des descriptions plus détaillées des tableaux et des notes méthodologiques figurent dans *1977 Supplément à l'Annuaire statistique et au Bulletin mensuel de statistique* des Nations Unies [54], dans la publication *Statistiques du commerce international, Concepts et définitions* [48] et dans l'*Annuaire statistique du Commerce international* [24]. Des données plus détaillées, comprenant des séries indiquant la valeur en monnaie nationale des importations et des exportations des divers pays et les notes accompagnant ces séries figurent dans l'*Annuaire statistique du Commerce international* [24] et dans le *Bulletin mensuel de statistique* [25].

Les données proviennent de publications nationales et des informations fournies par les gouvernements pour les publications des Nations Unies telles que: "*Commodity Trade Statistics*", le *Bulletin mensuel de statistique*, et l'*Annuaire statistique*, ainsi que de publications d'autres institutions des Nations Unies.

Territoire

Les statistiques fournies par pays se rapportent au territoire douanier de ce pays. Le plus souvent, ce territoire coïncide avec l'étendue géographique du pays.

Systèmes de commerce

Deux systèmes d'enregistrement du commerce sont couramment utilisés, qui ne diffèrent que par la façon dont sont enregistrées les marchandises entreposées et les marchandises réexportées:

(a)   Commerce spécial (S): les importations spéciales représentent le total combiné des importations destinées directement à la consommation intérieure (transformations et réparations comprises) et les marchandises retirées des entrepôts douaniers ou des zones franches pour la consommation intérieure. Les exportations spéciales comprennent les exportations de marchandises nationales, c'est-à-dire des biens produits ou fabriqués en totalité ou en partie dans le pays, ainsi que les exportations de biens nationalisés. (Les biens nationalisés sont des biens qui, ayant été inclus dans les importations spéciales, sont ensuite réexportés tels quels.)

(b)   Commerce général (G): les importations générales sont le total combiné des importations destinées directement à la consommation intérieure et des importations placées en entrepôt douanier ou destinées aux zones franches. Les exportations générales sont le total combiné des exportations de biens nationaux et des ré-

Valuation

Goods are, in general, valued according to the transaction value. In the case of imports, the transaction value is the value at which the goods were purchased by the importer plus the cost of transportation and insurance to the frontier of the importing country (c.i.f. valuation). In the case of exports, the transaction value is the value at which the goods were sold by the exporter, including the cost of transportation and insurance to bring the goods onto the transporting vehicle at the frontier of the exporting country (f.o.b. valuation).

Currency conversion

Conversion of values from national currencies into United States dollars is done by means of external trade conversion factors which are generally weighted averages of exchange rates, the weight being the corresponding monthly or quarterly value of imports or exports.

Coverage

The statistics relate to merchandise trade. Merchandise trade is defined to include, as far as possible, all goods which add to or subtract from the material resources of a country as a result of their movement into or out of the country. Thus, ordinary commercial transactions, government trade (including foreign aid, war reparations and trade in military goods), postal trade and all kinds of silver (except silver coins after their issue), are included in the statistics. Since their movement affects monetary rather than material resources, monetary gold, together with currency and titles of ownership after their issue into circulation, are excluded.

Commodity classification

The commodity classification of trade is in accordance with the United Nations *Standard International Trade Classification* (SITC) [53].

World and regional totals

The regional, economic and world totals have been adjusted: (a) to include estimates for countries or areas for which full data are not available; (b) to include insurance and freight for imports valued f.o.b.; (c) to include countries or areas not listed separately; (d) to approximate special trade; (e) to approximate calendar years; and (f) where possible, to eliminate incomparabilities owing to geographical changes, by adjusting the figures for periods before the change to be comparable to those for periods after the change.

Quantum and unit value index numbers

These index numbers show the changes in the volume of imports or exports (quantum index) and the average price of imports or exports (unit value index).

exportations. Ces dernières, dans le système du commerce général, comprennent les exportations de biens nationalisés et de biens qui, après avoir été importés, sortent des entrepôts de douane ou des zones franches sans avoir été transformés.

Evaluation

En général, les marchandises sont évaluées à la valeur de la transaction. Dans le cas des importations, cette valeur est celle à laquelle les marchandises ont été achetées par l'importateur plus le coût de leur transport et de leur assurance jusqu'à la frontière du pays importateur (valeur c.a.f.). Dans le cas des exportations, la valeur de la transaction est celle à laquelle les marchandises ont été vendues par l'exportateur, y compris le coût de transport et d'assurance des marchandises jusqu'à leur chargement sur le véhicule de transport à la frontière du pays exportateur (valeur f.à.b.).

Conversion des monnaies

Le conversion en dollars des Etats-Unis de valeurs exprimées en monnaie nationale se fait par application de coefficients de conversion du commerce extérieur, qui sont généralement les moyennes pondérées des taux de change, le poids étant la valeur mensuelle ou trimestrielle correspondante des importations ou des exportations.

Couverture

Les statistiques se rapportent au commerce des marchandises. Le commerce des marchandises se définit comme comprenant, dans toute la mesure du possible, toutes les marchandises qui ajoutent ou retranchent aux ressources matérielles d'un pays par suite de leur importation ou de leur exportation par ce pays. Ainsi, les transactions commerciales ordinaires, le commerce pour le compte de l'Etat (y compris l'aide extérieure, les réparations pour dommages de guerre et le commerce des fournitures militaires), le commerce par voie postale et les transactions de toutes sortes sur l'argent (à l'exception des transactions sur les pièces d'argent après leur émission) sont inclus dans ces statistiques. La monnaie or ainsi que la monnaie et les titres de propriété après leur mise en circulation sont exclus, car leurs mouvements influent sur les ressources monétaires plutôt que sur les ressources matérielles.

Classification par marchandise

La classification par marchandise du commerce extérieur est celle adoptée dans la *Classification type pour le commerce international* des Nations Unies (CTCI) [53].

Totaux mondiaux et régionaux

Les totaux économiques, régionaux et mondiaux

Description of tables

Table 69: World imports and exports are the sum of imports and exports of Developed economies, Developing economies and other. The regional totals for imports and exports and have been adjusted to exclude the re-exports of countries or areas comprising each region. Estimates for certain countries or areas not shown separately as well as for those shown separately but for which no data are yet available are included in the regional and world totals. Export and import values in terms of U.S. dollars are derived by the United Nations Statistics Division from data published in national publications, from data in the replies to the *Monthly Bulletin of Statistics* questionnaires and from data published by the International Monetary Fund (IMF) in the publication *International Financial Statistics* [14].

Table 70: These index numbers show the changes in the volume (quantum index) and the average price (unit value index) of total imports and exports. The terms of trade figures are calculated by dividing export unit value indices by the corresponding import unit value indices. The product of the net terms of trade and the quantum index of exports is called the index of the purchasing power of exports. The footnotes to countries appearing in table 69 also apply to the index numbers in this table.

Table 71: Manufactured goods are defined here to comprise sections 5 through 8 of the Standard International Trade Classification (SITC). These sections are: chemicals and related products, manufactured goods classified chiefly by material, machinery and transport equipment and miscellaneous manufactured articles. The economic and geographic groupings in this table are in accordance with those of table 69, although table 69 includes more detailed geographical sub-groups which make up the groupings "other developed market economies" and "developing market economies" of this table.

The unit value indices are obtained from national sources, except those of a few countries which the United Nations Statistics Division compiles using their quantity and value figures. For countries that do not compile indices for manufactured goods exports conforming to the above definition, sub-indices are aggregated to approximate an index of SITC sections 5-8. Unit value indices obtained from national indices are rebased, where necessary, so that 1990=100. Indices in national currency are converted into US dollars using conversion factors obtained by dividing the weighted average exchange rate of a given currency in the current period by the weighted average exchange rate in the base period. All aggregate unit value indices are current period weighted.

ont été ajustés de manière: (a) à inclure les estimations pour les pays ou régions pour lesquels on ne disposait pas de données complètes; (b) à inclure l'assurance et le fret dans la valeur f.o.b. des importations; (c) à inclure les pays ou régions non indiqués séparément; (d) à donner une approximation du commerce spécial; (e) à les ramener à des années civiles; et (f) à éliminer, dans la mesure du possible, les données non comparables par suite de changements géographiques, en ajustant les chiffres correspondant aux périodes avant le changement de manière à les rendre comparables à ceux des périodes après le changement.

Indices de quantum et de valeur unitaire

Ces indices indiquent les variations du volume des importations ou des exportations (indice de quantum) et du prix moyen des importations ou des exportations (indice de valeur unitaire).

Description des tableaux

Tableau 69: Les importations et les exportations totales pour le monde se composent des importations et exportations des Economies développées, des Economies en développement et des autres. Les totaux régionaux pour importations et exportations ont été ajustés pour exclure les re-exportations des pays ou zones qui comprennent la région. Les totaux régionaux et mondiaux comprennent des estimations pour certains pays ou zones ne figurant pas séparément mais pour lesquels les données ne sont pas encore disponibles. Les valeurs en dollars des E.U. des exportations et des importations ont été obtenues par la Division de statistique des Nations Unies à partir des réponses aux questionnaires du *Bulletin Mensuel de Statistique*, des données publiées par le Fonds Monétaire International dans la publication *Statistiques financières internationales* [14].

Tableau 70: Ces indices indiquent les variations du volume (indice de quantum) et du prix moyen (indice de valeur unitaire) des importations et des exportations totales. Les chiffres relatifs aux termes de l'échange se calculent en divisant les indices de valeur unitaire des exportations par les indices correspondants de valeur unitaire des importations. Le produit de la valeur nette des termes de l'échange et de l'indice du quantum des exportations est appelé indice du pouvoir d'achat des exportations. Les notes figurant au bas du tableau 69 concernant certains pays s'appliquent également aux indices du présent tableau.

Tableau 71: Les produits manufacturés se définissent comme correspondant aux sections 5 à 8 de la Classification type pour le commerce international (CTCI). Ces sections sont: produits chimiques et produits connexes, biens manufacturés classés principalement par matière première, machines et équipements de transport

The indices in Special Drawing Rights (SDRs) are calculated by multiplying the equivalent aggregate indices in United States dollars by conversion factors obtained by dividing the SDR/US $ exchange rate in the current period by the rate in the base period.

The quantum indices are derived from the value data and the unit value indices. All aggregate quantum indices are base period weighted.

et articles divers manufacturés. Les groupements économiques et géographiques de ce tableau sont conformes à ceux du tableau 69; toutefois, le tableau 69 comprend des subdivisions géographiques plus détaillées qui composent les groupements "autres pays développés à économie de marché" et "pays en développement à économie de marché" du présent tableau.

Les indices de valeur unitaire sont obtenus de sources nationales, à l'exception de ceux de certains pays que la Division de statistique des Nations Unies compile en utilisant les chiffres de ces pays relatifs aux quantités et aux valeurs. Pour les pays qui n'établissent pas d'indices conformes à la définition ci-dessus pour leurs exportations de produits manufacturés, on fait la synthèse de sous-indices de manière à établir un indice proche de celui des sections 5 à 8 de la CTCI. Le cas échéant, les indices de valeur unitaire obtenus à partir des indices nationaux sont ajustés sur la base 1990=100. On convertit les indices en monnaie nationale en indices en dollars des Etats-Unis en utilisant des facteurs de conversion obtenus en divisant la moyenne pondérée des taux de change d'une monnaie donnée pendant la période courante par la moyenne pondérée des taux de change de la période de base. Tous les indices globaux de valeur unitaire sont pondérés pour la période courante.

On calcule les indices en droits de tirages spécial (DTS) en multipliant les indices globaux équivalents en dollars des Etats-Unis par les facteurs de conversion obtenus en divisant le taux de change DTS/dollars E.U. de la période courante par le taux correspondant de la période de base.

On détermine les indices de quantum à partir des données de valeur et des indices de valeur unitaire. Tous les indices globaux de quantum sont pondérés par rapport à la période de base.

72
Tourist arrivals by region of origin
Arrivées de touristes par région de provenance

Country or area of destination and region of origin +	1994	1995	1996	1997	1998	Pays ou zone de destination et région de provenance +
Albania[1]	**28 439**	**40 175**	**56 276**	**19 154**	**27 709**	**Albanie**[1]
Africa	47	42	195	...	...	Afrique
Americas	2 584	4 580	4 752	1 177	1 545	Amériques
Europe	25 262	24 504	29 052	11 849	13 854	Europe
Asia, East and South East/Oceania	404	701	1 582	185	310	Asie, Est et Sud-Est et Océanie
Southern Asia	34	48	234	...	...	Asie du Sud
Western Asia	108	1 756	3 594	105	2 370	Asie occidentale
Region not specified	...	8 544	16 867	5 838	9 630	Région non spécifiée
Algeria[2][3]	**804 713**	**519 576**	**604 968**	**634 761**	**678 436**	**Algérie**[2][3]
Africa	252 121	42 878	35 029	34 027	37 373	Afrique
Americas	2 813	2 005	1 770	1 838	2 297	Amériques
Europe	60 383	37 831	45 570	48 440	56 509	Europe
Asia, East and South East/Oceania	3 123	1 661	1 107	1 342	2 609	Asie, Est et Sud-Est et Océanie
Western Asia	17 786	13 275	10 015	9 194	8 414	Asie occidentale
Region not specified	468 487	421 926	511 477	539 920	571 234	Région non spécifiée
American Samoa[4][5]	**17 967**	**17 522**	**21 366**	**...**	**...**	**Samoa américaines**[4][5]
Africa	10	2	19	...	...	Afrique
Americas	7 459	8 695	9 108	...	...	Amériques
Europe	810	888	3 036	...	...	Europe
Asia, East and South East/Oceania	9 603	7 848	8 618	...	...	Asie, Est et Sud-Est et Océanie
Southern Asia	39	62	531	...	...	Asie du Sud
Western Asia	21	18	29	...	...	Asie occidentale
Region not specified	25	9	25	...	...	Région non spécifiée
Angola[5]	**10 943**	**9 546**	**20 978**	**45 139**	**52 011**	**Angola**[5]
Africa	1 308	2 115	4 524	13 863	7 332	Afrique
Americas	1 209	1 145	2 133	3 154	7 509	Amériques
Europe	8 019	6 143	13 097	27 422	34 444	Europe
Asia, East and South East/Oceania	301	...	264	540	2 125	Asie, Est et Sud-Est et Océanie
Southern Asia	66	...	90	26	359	Asie du Sud
Region not specified	40	143	870	134	...	Région non spécifiée
Anguilla[5][6]	**43 705**	**38 531**	**37 498**	**43 181**	**43 874**	**Anguilla**[5][6]
Americas	39 836	35 272	33 748	36 642	34 658	Amériques
Europe	2 742	2 405	2 926	5 455	7 986	Europe
Region not specified	1 127	854	824	1 084	1 230	Région non spécifiée
Antigua and Barbuda[5][6][7]	**254 708**	**211 663**	**220 475**	**232 141**	**226 121**	**Antigua-et-Barbuda**[5][6][7]
Americas	144 877	123 680	128 266	138 028	133 607	Amériques
Europe	105 851	83 799	87 935	89 884	88 082	Europe
Region not specified	3 980	4 184	4 274	4 229	4 432	Région non spécifiée
Argentina[5][6][7]	**2 089 414**	**2 288 694**	**2 613 909**	**2 764 226**	**2 969 774**	**Argentine**[5][6][7]
Americas	1 825 098	1 988 119	2 252 082	2 378 327	2 552 465	Amériques
Europe	217 971	248 348	298 858	319 787	341 402	Europe
Region not specified	46 345	52 227	62 969	66 112	75 907	Région non spécifiée
Armenia[8]	**...**	**12 043**	**13 388**	**23 430**	**31 837**	**Arménie**[8]
Africa	...	15	44	10	32	Afrique
Americas	...	2 061	1 011	3 282	5 028	Amériques
Europe	...	8 376	11 245	16 109	23 099	Europe
Asia, East and South East/Oceania	...	141	232	602	906	Asie, Est et Sud-Est et Océanie
Southern Asia	...	1 181	638	2 203	1 300	Asie du Sud
Western Asia	...	269	218	1 224	1 472	Asie occidentale
Aruba[5]	**582 136**	**618 916**	**640 836**	**649 893**	**647 437**	**Aruba**[5]

72
Tourist arrivals by region of origin [cont.]
Arrivées de touristes par région de provenance [suite]

Country or area of destination and region of origin +	1994	1995	1996	1997	1998	Pays ou zone de destination et région de provenance +
Americas	528 294	564 985	582 140	587 776	595 186	Amériques
Europe	51 968	51 882	55 333	57 335	49 042	Europe
Asia, East and South East/Oceania	188	274	284	346	320	Asie, Est et Sud-Est et Océanie
Region not specified	1 686	1 775	3 079	4 436	2 889	Région non spécifiée
Australia[369]	**3 362 240**	**3 725 800**	**4 164 800**	**4 317 867**	**4 167 204**	**Australie**[369]
Africa	42 900	42 600	53 400	56 220	70 849	Afrique
Americas	361 700	381 800	401 300	420 040	473 551	Amériques
Europe	730 000	762 300	810 500	885 103	963 571	Europe
Asia, East and South East/Oceania	2 190 600	2 490 700	2 842 900	2 892 508	2 583 820	Asie, Est et Sud-Est et Océanie
Southern Asia	19 640	27 500	33 100	37 765	42 741	Asie du Sud
Western Asia	15 000	17 500	20 100	21 120	28 003	Asie occidentale
Region not specified	2 400	3 400	3 500	5 111	4 669	Région non spécifiée
Austria[1]	**17 893 824**	**17 172 968**	**17 089 973**	**16 647 281**	**17 352 477**	**Autriche**[1]
Africa	21 114	22 245	21 783	23 080	32 818	Afrique
Americas	719 100	672 779	707 509	718 578	827 764	Amériques
Europe	16 454 465	15 722 110	15 569 746	15 063 175	15 680 020	Europe
Asia, East and South East/Oceania	447 291	477 316	514 877	530 304	499 515	Asie, Est et Sud-Est et Océanie
Southern Asia	18 288	23 885	27 742	24 174	21 533	Asie du Sud
Western Asia	26 030	21 787	20 582	25 703	25 583	Asie occidentale
Region not specified	207 536	232 846	227 734	262 267	265 244	Région non spécifiée
Bahamas[5]	**1 516 035**	**1 598 135**	**1 633 105**	**1 617 595**	**1 539 999**	**Bahamas**[5]
Americas	1 364 400	1 432 505	1 445 460	1 413 485	1 343 791	Amériques
Europe	109 730	114 950	127 600	130 365	118 246	Europe
Asia, East and South East/Oceania	16 300	20 450	25 680	...	...	Asie, Est et Sud-Est et Océanie
Region not specified	25 605	30 230	34 365	73 745	77 962	Région non spécifiée
Bahrain[36]	**2 582 895**	**2 310 828**	**1 987 604**	**2 600 320**	**2 897 562**	**Bahreïn**[36]
Africa	9 097	10 069	11 713	18 389	21 910	Afrique
Americas	71 851	79 097	76 746	86 358	96 881	Amériques
Europe	156 446	156 142	147 574	173 258	179 472	Europe
Asia, East and South East/Oceania	85 242	74 774	84 318	82 767	96 886	Asie, Est et Sud-Est et Océanie
Southern Asia	258 705	209 067	193 465	221 615	260 817	Asie du Sud
Western Asia	2 001 107	1 781 522	1 473 748	2 017 933	2 241 596	Asie occidentale
Region not specified	447	157	40	...	...	Région non spécifiée
Bangladesh[56]	**140 122**	**156 231**	**165 887**	**182 420**	**171 961**	**Bangladesh**[56]
Africa	1 521	1 429	1 921	1 469	1 997	Afrique
Americas	12 225	13 107	13 988	15 433	15 653	Amériques
Europe	33 500	48 974	51 012	47 934	36 888	Europe
Asia, East and South East/Oceania	24 050	25 624	29 957	33 692	36 063	Asie, Est et Sud-Est et Océanie
Southern Asia	66 064	64 300	66 307	81 728	77 631	Asie du Sud
Western Asia	2 713	2 732	2 698	2 144	3 690	Asie occidentale
Region not specified	49	65	4	20	39	Région non spécifiée
Barbados[5]	**425 632**	**442 107**	**447 083**	**472 290**	**512 397**	**Barbade**[5]
Americas	228 491	237 998	238 721	245 004	254 982	Amériques
Europe	190 596	195 268	200 960	220 618	251 735	Europe
Asia, East and South East/Oceania	1 511	2 556	1 615	1 490	1 515	Asie, Est et Sud-Est et Océanie
Region not specified	5 034	6 285	5 787	5 178	4 165	Région non spécifiée
Belarus[5]	**184 200**	**161 397**	**234 226**	**254 023**	**355 342**	**Bélarus**[5]
Africa	110	305	171	235	703	Afrique
Americas	4 764	5 428	7 808	9 214	9 607	Amériques
Europe	176 985	153 682	222 177	241 549	339 587	Europe

72
Tourist arrivals by region of origin [*cont.*]
Arrivées de touristes par région de provenance [*suite*]

Country or area of destination and region of origin +	1994	1995	1996	1997	1998	Pays ou zone de destination et région de provenance +
Asia, East and South East/Oceania	1 414	1 179	2 883	2 311	4 388	Asie, Est et Sud-Est et Océanie
Southern Asia	309	373	502	508	676	Asie du Sud
Western Asia	618	430	685	206	381	Asie occidentale
Belgium[1]	**5 308 776**	**5 559 875**	**5 829 257**	**6 037 031**	**6 179 254**	**Belgique**[1]
Africa	53 067	55 984	63 451	63 003	61 026	Afrique
Americas	366 368	372 915	388 850	410 712	420 335	Amériques
Europe	4 603 525	4 826 574	5 046 096	5 197 330	5 363 775	Europe
Asia, East and South East/Oceania	204 557	230 481	266 218	286 455	266 801	Asie, Est et Sud-Est et Océanie
Southern Asia	16 759	22 451	30 305	27 946	17 149	Asie du Sud
Western Asia	13 684	14 861	16 036	18 083	19 275	Asie occidentale
Region not specified	50 816	36 609	18 301	33 502	30 893	Région non spécifiée
Belize[3 10]	**357 385**	**362 003**	**367 602**	**328 143**	**299 725**	**Belize**[3 10]
Americas	311 247	314 387	322 529	275 704	248 188	Amériques
Europe	41 145	40 777	38 808	47 489	45 130	Europe
Asia, East and South East/Oceania	2 981	4 724	4 975	3 780	3 972	Asie, Est et Sud-Est et Océanie
Region not specified	2 012	2 115	1 290	1 170	2 435	Région non spécifiée
Benin[1]	**111 000**	**138 000**	...	...	...	**Bénin**[1]
Africa	68 400	90 300	...	...	...	Afrique
Americas	3 755	4 640	...	...	...	Amériques
Europe	36 200	39 800	...	...	...	Europe
Asia, East and South East/Oceania	2 645	3 260	...	...	...	Asie, Est et Sud-Est et Océanie
Bermuda[5 11]	**415 766**	**387 412**	**390 395**	**380 060**	**368 756**	**Bermudes**[5 11]
Americas	377 144	348 841	351 229	338 727	323 609	Amériques
Europe	30 365	29 592	30 273	31 646	37 096	Europe
Asia, East and South East/Oceania	1 266	1 054	1 260	1 010	978	Asie, Est et Sud-Est et Océanie
Region not specified	6 991	7 925	7 633	8 677	7 073	Région non spécifiée
Bhutan[5]	**3 971**	**4 765**	**5 150**	**5 362**	**6 203**	**Bhoutan**[5]
Africa	14	...	...	5	8	Afrique
Americas	806	1 002	1 072	1 046	1 622	Amériques
Europe	1 918	2 229	2 365	2 576	3 145	Europe
Asia, East and South East/Oceania	1 217	1 521	1 597	1 679	1 403	Asie, Est et Sud-Est et Océanie
Southern Asia	16	6	15	33	24	Asie du Sud
Region not specified	...	7	101	23	1	Région non spécifiée
Bolivia[1 12]	**319 578**	**350 687**	**376 855**	**397 517**	**420 491**	**Bolivie**[1 12]
Africa	669	733	683	641	1 016	Afrique
Americas	193 821	211 866	226 084	257 203	269 344	Amériques
Europe	111 834	124 185	135 084	124 895	135 759	Europe
Asia, East and South East/Oceania	13 254	13 903	15 004	14 778	14 372	Asie, Est et Sud-Est et Océanie
Bonaire[5 13]	**55 820**	**59 410**	**65 080**	**62 776**	**61 737**	**Bonaire**[5 13]
Americas	37 921	38 819	41 650	40 495	39 976	Amériques
Europe	17 730	20 381	23 188	22 090	21 605	Europe
Asia, East and South East/Oceania	64	51	74	38	25	Asie, Est et Sud-Est et Océanie
Region not specified	105	159	168	153	131	Région non spécifiée
Botswana[3 14]	**991 000**	**1 020 000**	**1 052 000**	**1 083 000**	...	**Botswana**[3 14]
Africa	890 876	918 000	944 808	972 650	...	Afrique
Americas	12 216	12 000	14 370	14 793	...	Amériques
Europe	77 188	79 000	80 798	83 178	...	Europe
Asia, East and South East/Oceania	10 720	11 000	12 024	12 379	...	Asie, Est et Sud-Est et Océanie
Brazil[5 15]	**1 853 301**	**1 991 416**	**2 665 508**	**2 849 750**	**4 818 084**	**Brésil**[5 15]
Africa	25 229	18 933	23 187	23 747	40 959	Afrique

72
Tourist arrivals by region of origin [cont.]
Arrivées de touristes par région de provenance [suite]

Country or area of destination and region of origin +	1994	1995	1996	1997	1998	Pays ou zone de destination et région de provenance +
Americas	1 357 252	1 374 111	1 830 419	1 998 967	3 449 456	Amériques
Europe	413 560	516 722	681 340	713 059	1 160 672	Europe
Asia, East and South East/Oceania	48 449	66 845	109 638	95 228	121 692	Asie, Est et Sud-Est et Océanie
Western Asia	2 913	4 599	7 344	7 674	13 662	Asie occidentale
Region not specified	5 898	10 206	13 580	11 075	31 643	Région non spécifiée
British Virgin Islands [5]	**238 680**	**219 481**	**243 683**	**244 318**	**279 097**	**Iles Vierges britanniques** [5]
Americas	213 502	193 757	213 311	214 316	223 729	Amériques
Europe	22 536	21 478	23 043	22 137	21 457	Europe
Region not specified	2 642	4 246	7 329	7 865	33 911	Région non spécifiée
Brunei Darussalam [3]	**622 354**	...	...	...	**964 080**	**Brunéi Darussalam** [3]
Americas	7 388	...	...	...	10 184	Amériques
Europe	18 091	...	...	...	40 593	Europe
Asia, East and South East/Oceania	592 329	...	...	...	892 051	Asie, Est et Sud-Est et Océanie
Southern Asia	2 639	...	...	...	12 442	Asie du Sud
Region not specified	1 907	...	...	...	8 810	Région non spécifiée
Bulgaria [3 16]	**10 068 181**	**8 004 584**	**6 810 688**	**7 543 185**	**5 239 691**	**Bulgarie** [3 16]
Africa	8 532	4 406	3 254	6 838	6 675	Afrique
Americas	29 641	21 353	18 672	21 515	39 788	Amériques
Europe	9 730 612	7 687 351	6 406 574	7 247 812	4 821 516	Europe
Asia, East and South East/Oceania	16 005	13 319	13 812	19 054	20 715	Asie, Est et Sud-Est et Océanie
Southern Asia	12 144	9 715	10 086	15 963	14 778	Asie du Sud
Western Asia	48 060	24 665	18 201	21 438	19 840	Asie occidentale
Region not specified	223 187	243 775	340 089	210 565	316 379	Région non spécifiée
Burkina Faso [1]	**118 045**	**124 270**	**131 113**	**138 364**	**160 284**	**Burkina Faso** [1]
Africa	48 568	51 617	54 460	57 459	62 673	Afrique
Americas	7 008	7 374	7 780	8 209	10 062	Amériques
Europe	49 838	52 075	54 942	57 997	77 785	Europe
Asia, East and South East/Oceania	1 845	1 933	2 039	2 153	3 199	Asie, Est et Sud-Est et Océanie
Western Asia	630	608	642	677	1 016	Asie occidentale
Region not specified	10 156	10 663	11 250	11 869	5 549	Région non spécifiée
Burundi [2 5]	**29 944**	**34 125**	**27 391**	**10 553**	**15 404**	**Burundi** [2 5]
Africa	14 217	16 201	13 004	5 011	7 394	Afrique
Americas	1 814	2 068	1 660	639	1 092	Amériques
Europe	11 494	13 099	10 514	4 051	5 700	Europe
Asia, East and South East/Oceania	2 419	2 757	2 213	852	1 218	Asie, Est et Sud-Est et Océanie
Cambodia [5 11]	**176 617**	**219 680**	**260 489**	**218 843**	**186 333**	**Cambodge** [5 11]
Americas	24 000	21 538	27 812	24 561	21 773	Amériques
Europe	36 603	37 907	53 761	43 331	46 165	Europe
Asia, East and South East/Oceania	114 014	155 820	174 406	147 470	105 422	Asie, Est et Sud-Est et Océanie
Southern Asia	...	1 158	3 609	2 735	1 999	Asie du Sud
Western Asia	2 000	...	...	...	...	Asie occidentale
Region not specified	...	3 257	901	746	10 974	Région non spécifiée
Cameroon [1]	**97 619**	**99 749**	**101 106**	**132 839**	...	**Cameroun** [1]
Africa	25 984	26 551	26 912	47 689	...	Afrique
Americas	7 461	7 624	7 728	14 080	...	Amériques
Europe	60 082	61 393	62 228	66 034	...	Europe
Asia, East and South East/Oceania	1 809	1 849	1 874	2 736	...	Asie, Est et Sud-Est et Océanie
Western Asia	1 282	1 310	1 328	1 308	...	Asie occidentale
Region not specified	1 001	1 022	1 036	992	...	Région non spécifiée
Canada [5]	**15 971 800**	**16 932 100**	**17 285 400**	**17 635 700**	**18 866 674**	**Canada** [5]

72
Tourist arrivals by region of origin [cont.]
Arrivées de touristes par région de provenance [suite]

Country or area of destination and region of origin +	1994	1995	1996	1997	1998	Pays ou zone de destination et région de provenance +
Africa	50 200	48 700	55 500	58 700	59 890	Afrique
Americas	12 820 200	13 294 400	13 240 500	13 741 900	15 255 869	Amériques
Europe	1 991 900	2 187 700	2 371 200	2 329 900	2 298 172	Europe
Asia, East and South East/Oceania	1 023 400	1 300 600	1 509 400	1 392 600	1 160 281	Asie, Est et Sud-Est et Océanie
Southern Asia	55 100	68 700	73 400	77 700	61 370	Asie du Sud
Western Asia	31 000	32 000	35 400	34 900	31 092	Asie occidentale
Cape Verde[5][11]	**30 808**	**27 785**	**37 000**	**45 000**	**52 000**	**Cap-Vert**[5][11]
Africa	1 193	981	...	...	...	Afrique
Americas	1 761	1 819	...	...	...	Amériques
Europe	18 422	18 496	31 108	37 834	...	Europe
Region not specified	9 432	6 489	5 892	7 166	52 000	Région non spécifiée
Cayman Islands[5][11]	**341 491**	**361 444**	**373 245**	**381 188**	**404 205**	**Iles Caïmanes**[5][11]
Africa	...	334	374	374	412	Afrique
Americas	301 860	320 271	335 548	344 391	365 319	Amériques
Europe	30 549	37 319	33 440	32 746	34 690	Europe
Asia, East and South East/Oceania	1 269	2 352	2 462	2 861	2 900	Asie, Est et Sud-Est et Océanie
Region not specified	7 813	1 168	1 421	816	884	Région non spécifiée
Central African Rep.[5]	**...**	**...**	**...**	**...**	**7 478**	**Rép. centrafricaine**[5]
Africa	...	...	...	...	3 439	Afrique
Americas	...	...	...	...	455	Amériques
Europe	...	...	...	...	3 054	Europe
Asia, East and South East/Oceania	...	...	...	...	313	Asie, Est et Sud-Est et Océanie
Western Asia	...	...	...	...	89	Asie occidentale
Region not specified	...	...	...	...	128	Région non spécifiée
Chad[1]	**18 933**	**7 382**	**8 891**	**9 375**	**11 249**	**Tchad**[1]
Africa	6 466	2 137	2 400	3 700	4 440	Afrique
Americas	2 263	643	1 023	615	738	Amériques
Europe	9 918	4 141	5 246	4 764	5 716	Europe
Asia, East and South East/Oceania	187	218	98	180	216	Asie, Est et Sud-Est et Océanie
Western Asia	99	243	124	116	139	Asie occidentale
Chile[5]	**1 633 759**	**1 539 593**	**1 449 528**	**1 643 640**	**1 759 279**	**Chili**[5]
Africa	1 295	2 724	...	1 794	2 092	Afrique
Americas	1 430 874	1 345 445	1 242 865	1 402 868	1 492 699	Amériques
Europe	164 662	163 322	167 986	203 373	226 653	Europe
Asia, East and South East/Oceania	31 087	25 749	27 745	32 023	34 281	Asie, Est et Sud-Est et Océanie
Southern Asia	1 198	962	...	1 818	2 442	Asie du Sud
Western Asia	102	151	...	519	455	Asie occidentale
Region not specified	4 541	1 240	10 932	1 245	657	Région non spécifiée
China ††[5][17]	**5 182 060**	**5 886 716**	**6 744 334**	**7 428 006**	**7 107 747**	**Chine ††**[5][17]
Africa	24 685	33 073	38 663	38 099	39 385	Afrique
Americas	633 111	697 255	809 185	867 166	947 927	Amériques
Europe	1 479 622	1 609 431	1 770 216	2 039 424	1 896 160	Europe
Asia, East and South East/Oceania	2 923 492	3 405 199	3 972 408	4 312 645	4 057 595	Asie, Est et Sud-Est et Océanie
Southern Asia	91 489	108 425	119 692	130 716	132 853	Asie du Sud
Western Asia	12 640	16 460	17 769	21 644	20 993	Asie occidentale
Region not specified	17 021	16 873	16 401	18 312	12 834	Région non spécifiée
China, Hong Kong SAR†[3]	**9 331 156**	**10 199 994**	**11 702 735**	**10 406 261**	**9 574 711**	**Chine, Hong Kong RAS†**[3]
Africa	65 861	68 041	60 491	70 224	61 653	Afrique
Americas	1 026 409	986 342	973 132	1 043 787	1 029 405	Amériques
Europe	1 159 659	1 162 107	1 203 141	1 089 714	960 016	Europe

72
Tourist arrivals by region of origin [cont.]
Arrivées de touristes par région de provenance [suite]

Country or area of destination and region of origin +	1994	1995	1996	1997	1998	Pays ou zone de destination et région de provenance +
Asia, East and South East/Oceania	6 918 129	7 805 221	9 285 090	8 028 031	7 344 790	Asie, Est et Sud-Est et Océanie
Southern Asia	138 667	155 263	166 905	158 745	160 154	Asie du Sud
Western Asia	19 343	19 384	13 976	15 760	18 693	Asie occidentale
Region not specified	3 088	3 636	...	...	...	Région non spécifiée
China, Macao SAR †[3][18]	**7 833 754**	**7 752 495**	**8 151 055**	**7 000 370**	**6 948 535**	**Chine, Macao RAS †[3][18]**
Africa	5 648	5 998	6 595	5 546	4 775	Afrique
Americas	139 004	134 527	149 327	121 271	110 543	Amériques
Europe	237 496	241 352	293 355	239 364	262 781	Europe
Asia, East and South East/Oceania	7 291 344	7 188 065	7 493 180	6 434 438	6 497 576	Asie, Est et Sud-Est et Océanie
Southern Asia	12 459	14 628	18 489	16 221	12 532	Asie du Sud
Western Asia	497	561	562	569	719	Asie occidentale
Region not specified	147 306	167 364	189 547	182 961	59 609	Région non spécifiée
Colombia[5]	**1 207 001**	**1 398 997**	**1 253 999**	**968 999**	**...**	**Colombie[5]**
Americas	1 064 944	1 232 974	1 098 697	846 877	...	Amériques
Europe	142 057	166 023	155 302	122 122	...	Europe
Comoros[5][11]	**27 061**	**22 838**	**23 775**	**26 219**	**...**	**Comores[5][11]**
Africa	7 958	7 949	11 355	14 202	...	Afrique
Americas	285	292	130	337	...	Amériques
Europe	18 405	14 151	10 623	11 143	...	Europe
Asia, East and South East/Oceania	413	446	215	537	...	Asie, Est et Sud-Est et Océanie
Region not specified	...	...	1 452	...	...	Région non spécifiée
Congo[1][19]	**30 296**	**37 432**	**39 114**	**25 811**	**25 082**	**Congo[1][19]**
Africa	14 233	16 872	14 337	9 477	9 194	Afrique
Americas	1 555	2 135	2 792	1 830	1 791	Amériques
Europe	13 673	17 375	20 926	13 806	13 410	Europe
Region not specified	835	1 050	1 059	698	687	Région non spécifiée
Cook Islands[5][20]	**57 321**	**48 500**	**48 819**	**49 964**	**48 629**	**Iles Cook[5][20]**
Americas	11 707	7 912	8 866	9 484	8 988	Amériques
Europe	20 310	18 630	17 914	19 924	19 291	Europe
Asia, East and South East/Oceania	25 005	21 713	21 793	20 400	20 239	Asie, Est et Sud-Est et Océanie
Region not specified	299	245	246	156	111	Région non spécifiée
Costa Rica[5]	**761 448**	**784 610**	**781 127**	**811 490**	**942 853**	**Costa Rica[5]**
Africa	491	489	714	689	748	Afrique
Americas	615 454	633 055	629 879	661 574	791 219	Amériques
Europe	131 737	134 656	132 435	130 713	131 657	Europe
Asia, East and South East/Oceania	10 594	13 165	14 638	14 484	14 447	Asie, Est et Sud-Est et Océanie
Region not specified	3 172	3 245	3 461	4 030	4 782	Région non spécifiée
Côte d'Ivoire[5][21]	**156 632**	**187 911**	**236 913**	**274 094**	**301 039**	**Côte d'Ivoire[5][21]**
Africa	85 659	104 739	113 324	137 886	158 808	Afrique
Americas	12 331	13 441	19 478	20 703	23 328	Amériques
Europe	53 397	63 750	96 620	107 304	109 176	Europe
Asia, East and South East/Oceania	3 236	3 360	5 440	5 649	6 172	Asie, Est et Sud-Est et Océanie
Southern Asia	500	702	720	...	1 000	Asie du Sud
Western Asia	1 509	1 919	1 331	2 552	2 555	Asie occidentale
Croatia[1]	**2 292 758**	**1 324 492**	**2 649 424**	**3 834 186**	**4 111 536**	**Croatie[1]**
Americas	27 178	23 535	65 229	60 072	51 743	Amériques
Europe	2 241 434	1 280 865	2 562 039	3 747 869	4 026 662	Europe
Asia, East and South East/Oceania	4 795	3 965	7 987	10 938	15 845	Asie, Est et Sud-Est et Océanie
Region not specified	19 351	16 127	14 169	15 307	17 286	Région non spécifiée
Cuba[3]	**619 218**	**745 495**	**1 004 336**	**1 170 083**	**1 415 832**	**Cuba[3]**

72
Tourist arrivals by region of origin [*cont.*]
Arrivées de touristes par région de provenance [*suite*]

Country or area of destination and region of origin +	1994	1995	1996	1997	1998	Pays ou zone de destination et région de provenance +
Africa	1 492	1 868	3 036	5 178	5 919	Afrique
Americas	306 253	357 189	418 378	496 913	594 354	Amériques
Europe	302 674	375 052	562 575	648 265	793 246	Europe
Asia, East and South East/Oceania	6 112	8 308	15 287	13 775	16 368	Asie, Est et Sud-Est et Océanie
Southern Asia	1 739	1 682	3 141	4 083	4 278	Asie du Sud
Western Asia	782	707	1 045	1 554	1 319	Asie occidentale
Region not specified	166	689	874	315	348	Région non spécifiée
Curaçao[2 5 11]	**238 310**	**232 276**	**218 969**	**208 828**	**...**	**Curaçao**[2 5 11]
Americas	147 850	141 467	130 846	128 009	...	Amériques
Europe	87 660	89 946	87 231	79 861	...	Europe
Asia, East and South East/Oceania	330	191	239	199	...	Asie, Est et Sud-Est et Océanie
Region not specified	2 470	672	653	759	...	Région non spécifiée
Cyprus[5]	**2 069 000**	**2 100 000**	**1 950 000**	**2 088 000**	**2 222 706**	**Chypre**[5]
Africa	10 000	...	...	...	5 769	Afrique
Americas	41 000	...	...	...	26 030	Amériques
Europe	1 883 000	1 840 000	1 772 500	1 978 509	2 111 879	Europe
Asia, East and South East/Oceania	...	...	...	...	9 921	Asie, Est et Sud-Est et Océanie
Southern Asia	...	...	...	...	11 304	Asie du Sud
Western Asia	111 000	105 000	105 000	52 825	51 133	Asie occidentale
Region not specified	24 000	155 000	72 500	56 666	6 670	Région non spécifiée
Czech Republic[3]	**101 140 302**	**98 060 507**	**109 404 686**	**107 884 035**	**102 843 599**	**République tchèque**[3]
Europe	74 436 376	72 947 468	82 935 009	82 786 494	80 036 674	Europe
Region not specified	26 703 926	25 113 039	26 469 677	25 097 541	22 806 925	Région non spécifiée
Dem. Rep. of the Congo[5 22]	**18 429**	**35 700**	**37 000**	**30 000**	**53 139**	**Rép. dém. du Congo**[5 22]
Africa	17 237	20 000	...	...	22 223	Afrique
Americas	217	500	...	...	1 231	Amériques
Europe	761	15 000	...	...	7 975	Europe
Asia, East and South East/Oceania	214	200	...	...	1 333	Asie, Est et Sud-Est et Océanie
Region not specified	...	...	37 000	30 000	20 377	Région non spécifiée
Denmark[8 23]	**2 093 502**	**2 123 956**	**2 124 572**	**2 157 665**	**2 072 800**	**Danemark**[8 23]
Americas	103 162	97 712	93 551	95 437	100 781	Amériques
Europe	1 808 717	1 785 088	1 823 769	1 850 525	1 792 981	Europe
Asia, East and South East/Oceania	51 126	50 008	55 673	51 230	55 921	Asie, Est et Sud-Est et Océanie
Region not specified	130 497	191 148	151 579	160 473	123 117	Région non spécifiée
Dominica[5]	**56 522**	**60 471**	**63 259**	**65 446**	**65 501**	**Dominique**[5]
Americas	43 043	46 676	50 542	52 295	52 776	Amériques
Europe	12 675	12 940	11 898	12 215	11 710	Europe
Asia, East and South East/Oceania	43	54	277	806	339	Asie, Est et Sud-Est et Océanie
Region not specified	761	801	542	130	676	Région non spécifiée
Dominican Republic[2 5 24]	**1 716 789**	**1 775 873**	**1 948 464**	**2 184 688**	**2 334 493**	**Rép. dominicaine**[2 5 24]
Americas	...	...	701 555	732 535	804 941	Amériques
Europe	...	...	863 492	1 013 863	1 063 766	Europe
Asia, East and South East/Oceania	...	...	2 790	2 553	2 455	Asie, Est et Sud-Est et Océanie
Region not specified	1 716 789	1 775 873	380 627	435 737	463 331	Région non spécifiée
Ecuador[3 6]	**471 961**	**439 523**	**493 727**	**529 492**	**510 627**	**Equateur**[3 6]
Africa	498	712	1 023	1 033	980	Afrique
Americas	364 987	330 857	373 652	406 379	387 560	Amériques
Europe	94 698	94 592	105 452	108 473	107 845	Europe
Asia, East and South East/Oceania	11 740	13 278	13 561	13 595	14 195	Asie, Est et Sud-Est et Océanie
Region not specified	38	84	39	12	47	Région non spécifiée

72
Tourist arrivals by region of origin [*cont.*]
Arrivées de touristes par région de provenance [*suite*]

Country or area of destination and region of origin +	1994	1995	1996	1997	1998	Pays ou zone de destination et région de provenance +
Egypt[3]	**2 581 988**	**3 133 461**	**3 895 942**	**3 961 416**	**3 453 866**	**Egypte[3]**
Africa	152 872	130 485	115 808	120 145	130 671	Afrique
Americas	182 378	228 896	259 057	256 668	217 403	Amériques
Europe	1 243 629	1 811 000	2 342 709	2 394 414	1 956 833	Europe
Asia, East and South East/Oceania	160 220	195 029	259 087	237 178	130 835	Asie, Est et Sud-Est et Océanie
Southern Asia	20 732	24 435	29 241	23 140	30 193	Asie du Sud
Western Asia	819 142	741 581	828 727	893 351	985 947	Asie occidentale
Region not specified	3 015	2 035	61 313	36 520	1 984	Région non spécifiée
El Salvador[5][6]	**181 332**	**235 364**	**282 835**	**387 052**	**541 863**	**El Salvador[5][6]**
Africa	86	115	150	...	...	Afrique
Americas	157 903	205 198	244 818	343 209	498 160	Amériques
Europe	19 923	25 340	32 613	27 401	27 107	Europe
Asia, East and South East/Oceania	3 418	4 682	5 224	3 719	3 965	Asie, Est et Sud-Est et Océanie
Western Asia	2	29	30	...	...	Asie occidentale
Region not specified	...	...	...	12 723	12 631	Région non spécifiée
Eritrea[2][3]	**221 582**	**315 417**	**416 596**	**409 544**	**187 647**	**Erythrée[2][3]**
Africa	100 328	181 955	254 996	279 666	119 357	Afrique
Americas	1 452	2 065	2 564	2 960	2 088	Amériques
Europe	7 239	8 959	11 611	11 948	7 757	Europe
Asia, East and South East/Oceania	1 168	2 367	1 521	1 614	1 406	Asie, Est et Sud-Est et Océanie
Southern Asia	253	193	167	475	408	Asie du Sud
Western Asia	4 950	3 259	1 302	1 403	1 543	Asie occidentale
Region not specified	106 192	116 619	144 435	111 478	55 088	Région non spécifiée
Estonia[3]	...	**2 110 926**	**2 443 871**	**2 618 484**	**2 908 819**	**Estonie[3]**
Americas	...	30 000	55 568	44 519	78 590	Amériques
Europe	...	2 072 426	2 364 836	2 547 620	2 783 501	Europe
Asia, East and South East/Oceania	...	7 000	16 196	24 338	28 156	Asie, Est et Sud-Est et Océanie
Region not specified	...	1 500	7 271	2 007	18 572	Région non spécifiée
Ethiopia[2][5][25]	**98 070**	**103 336**	**108 885**	**114 732**	**116 686**	**Ethiopie[2][5][25]**
Africa	27 949	30 595	27 658	29 255	28 202	Afrique
Americas	11 740	13 743	14 917	15 957	14 089	Amériques
Europe	31 804	35 652	39 198	40 905	36 888	Europe
Asia, East and South East/Oceania	7 649	3 925	4 246	4 705	5 131	Asie, Est et Sud-Est et Océanie
Southern Asia	1 961	2 172	2 069	2 066	2 067	Asie du Sud
Western Asia	6 964	9 300	12 739	13 538	10 636	Asie occidentale
Region not specified	10 003	7 949	8 058	8 306	19 673	Région non spécifiée
Fiji[5][6]	**318 874**	**318 495**	**339 560**	**359 441**	**371 342**	**Fidji[5][6]**
Americas	57 369	50 148	50 138	57 735	61 227	Amériques
Europe	54 919	55 377	60 782	67 825	68 675	Europe
Asia, East and South East/Oceania	205 110	211 618	227 211	232 157	239 600	Asie, Est et Sud-Est et Océanie
Region not specified	1 476	1 352	1 429	1 724	1 840	Région non spécifiée
Finland[8][26]	**1 868 000**	**1 779 000**	**1 724 000**	**1 831 325**	**1 866 842**	**Finlande[8][26]**
Africa	4 113	3 916	3 796	4 032	3 505	Afrique
Americas	117 038	111 462	108 015	114 740	113 961	Amériques
Europe	1 541 547	1 468 101	1 422 712	1 511 280	1 539 842	Europe
Asia, East and South East/Oceania	126 415	120 391	116 669	123 933	110 881	Asie, Est et Sud-Est et Océanie
Southern Asia	4 776	4 548	4 408	4 682	4 756	Asie du Sud
Western Asia	1 702	1 621	1 571	1 669	1 729	Asie occidentale
Region not specified	72 409	68 961	66 829	70 989	92 168	Région non spécifiée
France[5][27]	**61 312 000**	**60 033 000**	**62 406 000**	**67 310 000**	**70 040 300**	**France[5][27]**

72
Tourist arrivals by region of origin [cont.]
Arrivées de touristes par région de provenance [suite]

Country or area of destination and region of origin +	1994	1995	1996	1997	1998	Pays ou zone de destination et région de provenance +
Africa	1 068 000	...	996 000	1 086 000	1 117 800	Afrique
Americas	3 916 000	2 184 000	4 191 000	4 433 000	4 703 700	Amériques
Europe	53 679 000	46 438 000	54 788 000	59 180 000	61 556 000	Europe
Asia, East and South East/Oceania	1 702 000	965 000	1 986 000	2 133 000	2 229 000	Asie, Est et Sud-Est et Océanie
Western Asia	336 000	...	262 000	288 000	246 100	Asie occidentale
Region not specified	611 000	10 446 000	183 000	190 000	187 700	Région non spécifiée
French Polynesia[5 6 28]	**166 086**	**172 129**	**163 774**	**180 440**	**188 933**	**Polynésie française**[5 6 28]
Africa	178	268	171	207	161	Afrique
Americas	55 561	59 862	54 970	53 811	62 225	Amériques
Europe	71 078	74 228	73 827	83 697	87 454	Europe
Asia, East and South East/Oceania	38 587	37 209	34 138	42 020	38 381	Asie, Est et Sud-Est et Océanie
Southern Asia	144	36	14	32	33	Asie du Sud
Western Asia	150	137	199	186	213	Asie occidentale
Region not specified	388	389	455	487	466	Région non spécifiée
Gabon[5]	**118 773**	**124 685**	**144 509**	**167 197**	**...**	**Gabon**[5]
Africa	21 517	21 363	28 338	33 341	...	Afrique
Region not specified	97 256	103 322	116 171	133 856	...	Région non spécifiée
Gambia[5 29]	**78 070**	**45 401**	**76 814**	**84 751**	**91 106**	**Gambie**[5 29]
Africa	1 887	1 205	625	1 388	1 541	Afrique
Americas	698	356	528	575	779	Amériques
Europe	71 792	40 365	73 176	81 501	86 998	Europe
Region not specified	3 693	3 475	2 485	1 287	1 788	Région non spécifiée
Georgia[5]	**...**	**85 492**	**116 980**	**313 290**	**317 063**	**Géorgie**[5]
Africa	...	11	57	139	140	Afrique
Americas	...	2 858	2 918	4 248	5 278	Amériques
Europe	...	78 362	106 564	304 547	303 572	Europe
Asia, East and South East/Oceania	...	54	326	1 091	1 513	Asie, Est et Sud-Est et Océanie
Southern Asia	...	1 327	2 071	2 522	4 832	Asie du Sud
Western Asia	...	2	249	685	774	Asie occidentale
Region not specified	...	2 878	4 795	58	954	Région non spécifiée
Germany[8 30 31]	**14 493 812**	**14 846 830**	**15 204 707**	**15 836 797**	**16 511 486**	**Allemagne †**[8 30 31]
Africa	122 206	124 057	124 108	133 811	136 740	Afrique
Americas	1 867 609	1 888 840	1 942 264	2 127 253	2 351 112	Amériques
Europe	10 646 280	10 820 216	11 112 158	11 490 712	11 979 093	Europe
Asia, East and South East/Oceania	1 405 353	1 546 058	1 573 285	1 589 968	1 514 879	Asie, Est et Sud-Est et Océanie
Western Asia	57 259	62 112	75 854	83 888	96 820	Asie occidentale
Region not specified	395 105	405 547	377 038	411 165	432 842	Région non spécifiée
Ghana[5]	**271 310**	**286 000**	**304 860**	**325 434**	**...**	**Ghana**[5]
Africa	92 311	97 309	103 726	110 725	...	Afrique
Americas	22 786	24 019	25 603	27 331	...	Amériques
Europe	67 255	70 897	75 572	80 672	...	Europe
Asia, East and South East/Oceania	13 049	13 756	14 663	15 653	...	Asie, Est et Sud-Est et Océanie
Western Asia	2 058	2 169	2 312	2 468	...	Asie occidentale
Region not specified	73 851	77 850	82 984	88 585	...	Région non spécifiée
Greece[5 32]	**10 641 942**	**10 130 177**	**9 233 295**	**10 070 325**	**10 916 046**	**Grèce**[5 32]
Africa	24 704	27 237	23 706	23 072	21 134	Afrique
Americas	364 062	323 780	298 144	314 057	291 507	Amériques
Europe	9 980 779	9 467 111	8 541 456	9 404 889	10 333 580	Europe
Asia, East and South East/Oceania	227 802	261 070	314 038	280 749	224 193	Asie, Est et Sud-Est et Océanie
Southern Asia	6 458	5 960	5 319	3 730	3 848	Asie du Sud

72
Tourist arrivals by region of origin [cont.]
Arrivées de touristes par région de provenance [suite]

Country or area of destination and region of origin +	1994	1995	1996	1997	1998	Pays ou zone de destination et région de provenance +
Western Asia	38 137	45 019	50 632	43 828	41 784	Asie occidentale
Grenada[5]	**108 957**	**108 007**	**108 230**	**110 749**	**115 794**	**Grenade**[5]
Africa	...	146	144	238	337	Afrique
Americas	50 575	51 718	49 753	51 727	54 578	Amériques
Europe	37 533	36 488	37 587	37 796	38 081	Europe
Asia, East and South East/Oceania	680	655	1 039	977	1 279	Asie, Est et Sud-Est et Océanie
Western Asia	99	27	49	75	104	Asie occidentale
Region not specified	20 070	18 973	19 658	19 936	21 415	Région non spécifiée
Guadeloupe[1]	**144 568**	**152 896**	**146 878**	**147 010**	**133 030**	**Guadeloupe**[1]
Americas	12 803	11 622	11 040	16 740	7 097	Amériques
Europe	131 192	140 641	134 799	129 436	125 231	Europe
Region not specified	573	633	1 039	834	702	Région non spécifiée
Guam[5 7]	**1 086 720**	**1 361 830**	**1 362 600**	**1 381 513**	**1 137 026**	**Guam**[5 7]
Americas	66 847	56 626	35 836	44 087	42 415	Amériques
Europe	...	...	1 278	1 786	1 890	Europe
Asia, East and South East/Oceania	993 467	1 275 948	1 307 561	1 323 597	1 079 175	Asie, Est et Sud-Est et Océanie
Region not specified	26 406	29 256	17 925	12 043	13 546	Région non spécifiée
Guatemala[5]	**537 374**	**563 478**	**520 085**	**576 361**	**636 278**	**Guatemala**[5]
Americas	410 050	446 012	409 374	457 156	504 757	Amériques
Europe	112 442	103 828	96 830	104 475	115 406	Europe
Asia, East and South East/Oceania	12 297	11 917	12 029	13 746	14 739	Asie, Est et Sud-Est et Océanie
Southern Asia	255	222	267	...	...	Asie du Sud
Western Asia	300	364	318	261	296	Asie occidentale
Region not specified	2 030	1 135	1 267	723	1 080	Région non spécifiée
Guinea[5 33]	...	...	...	**17 000**	**23 000**	**Guinée**[5 33]
Africa	...	...	...	2 886	4 400	Afrique
Americas	...	...	...	2 300	2 434	Amériques
Europe	...	...	...	8 966	11 562	Europe
Asia, East and South East/Oceania	...	...	...	353	489	Asie, Est et Sud-Est et Océanie
Western Asia	...	...	...	2 495	4 115	Asie occidentale
Guyana[5]	**112 824**	**105 536**	**91 972**	**75 737**	...	**Guyana**[5]
Africa	128	...	...	...	...	Afrique
Americas	103 093	97 456	84 529	69 309	...	Amériques
Europe	8 325	6 794	6 063	5 212	...	Europe
Asia, East and South East/Oceania	1 278	...	...	...	...	Asie, Est et Sud-Est et Océanie
Region not specified	...	1 286	1 380	1 216	...	Région non spécifiée
Haiti[5]	**70 200**	**145 369**	**150 147**	**148 735**	**146 837**	**Haïti**[5]
Americas	64 800	129 266	133 475	132 706	131 385	Amériques
Europe	5 300	14 245	14 625	14 112	13 607	Europe
Region not specified	100	1 858	2 047	1 917	1 845	Région non spécifiée
Honduras[3]	**233 516**	**270 549**	**263 317**	**306 646**	**321 149**	**Honduras**[3]
Africa	335	206	237	231	168	Afrique
Americas	199 796	227 485	224 926	265 600	280 437	Amériques
Europe	27 826	33 523	31 666	32 954	32 892	Europe
Asia, East and South East/Oceania	5 533	8 157	6 462	7 823	7 618	Asie, Est et Sud-Est et Océanie
Region not specified	26	1 178	26	38	34	Région non spécifiée
Hungary[5 6 34]	**21 424 755**	**20 689 886**	**20 674 199**	**17 248 257**	...	**Hongrie**[5 6 34]
Africa	21 527	19 698	29 757	26 219	...	Afrique
Americas	309 910	298 358	329 686	372 537	...	Amériques
Europe	20 935 982	20 163 497	20 054 714	16 575 893	...	Europe

72
Tourist arrivals by region of origin [cont.]
Arrivées de touristes par région de provenance [suite]

Country or area of destination and region of origin +	1994	1995	1996	1997	1998	Pays ou zone de destination et région de provenance +
Asia, East and South East/Oceania	157 336	208 333	260 042	273 608	...	Asie, Est et Sud-Est et Océanie
Iceland[5]	**179 241**	**189 796**	**200 835**	**201 666**	**232 219**	**Islande**[5]
Africa	300	374	294	407	487	Afrique
Americas	27 674	30 411	33 759	35 757	44 414	Amériques
Europe	145 467	152 812	160 370	158 767	179 783	Europe
Asia, East and South East/Oceania	5 412	5 811	6 129	6 187	7 001	Asie, Est et Sud-Est et Océanie
Southern Asia	152	210	185	205	421	Asie du Sud
Western Asia	99	128	77	314	82	Asie occidentale
Region not specified	137	50	21	29	31	Région non spécifiée
India[5 6]	**1 886 433**	**2 123 683**	**2 287 860**	**2 374 094**	**2 358 629**	**Inde**[5 6]
Africa	61 315	84 148	85 663	98 910	106 045	Afrique
Americas	244 743	283 860	322 240	339 875	348 621	Amériques
Europe	744 735	824 680	897 010	898 929	924 753	Europe
Asia, East and South East/Oceania	251 244	289 348	335 165	358 472	343 102	Asie, Est et Sud-Est et Océanie
Southern Asia	480 142	540 209	543 967	583 706	558 772	Asie du Sud
Western Asia	103 060	100 615	96 857	93 555	77 153	Asie occidentale
Region not specified	1 194	823	6 958	647	183	Région non spécifiée
Indonesia[5]	**4 006 312**	**4 324 229**	**5 034 472**	**5 185 243**	**4 606 416**	**Indonésie**[5]
Africa	9 957	38 128	29 051	24 253	52 312	Afrique
Americas	211 529	201 149	244 497	208 726	201 488	Amériques
Europe	798 870	793 842	754 412	820 340	641 374	Europe
Asia, East and South East/Oceania	2 919 596	3 212 997	3 936 282	4 061 865	3 608 283	Asie, Est et Sud-Est et Océanie
Southern Asia	35 101	50 901	46 370	39 580	58 707	Asie du Sud
Western Asia	31 259	27 212	23 860	30 479	44 252	Asie occidentale
Iran (Islamic Rep. of)[5]	**362 048**	**452 059**	**567 334**	**739 711**	**1 007 597**	**Iran (Rép. islamique d')**[5]
Africa	2 241	1 578	1 966	2 596	2 914	Afrique
Americas	2 642	2 794	3 350	2 640	2 986	Amériques
Europe	166 225	215 157	260 958	449 115	631 020	Europe
Asia, East and South East/Oceania	14 505	16 051	17 063	10 847	17 800	Asie, Est et Sud-Est et Océanie
Southern Asia	122 215	154 549	208 752	194 409	255 776	Asie du Sud
Western Asia	53 846	61 790	75 200	80 104	97 101	Asie occidentale
Region not specified	374	140	45	...	...	Région non spécifiée
Iraq[3]	**89 384**	**60 540**	**51 330**	**...**	**...**	**Iraq**[3]
Africa	1 284	756	777	...	...	Afrique
Americas	833	1 140	761	...	...	Amériques
Europe	8 380	3 869	3 052	...	...	Europe
Asia, East and South East/Oceania	1 025	2 051	1 541	...	...	Asie, Est et Sud-Est et Océanie
Southern Asia	7 981	11 049	9 087	...	...	Asie du Sud
Western Asia	66 555	39 910	34 812	...	...	Asie occidentale
Region not specified	3 326	1 765	1 300	...	...	Région non spécifiée
Ireland[5]	**4 309 000**	**4 821 000**	**5 282 000**	**5 587 000**	**6 064 000**	**Irlande**[5]
Americas	494 000	641 000	729 000	778 000	858 000	Amériques
Europe	3 656 000	3 977 000	4 368 000	4 600 000	4 985 000	Europe
Asia, East and South East/Oceania	90 000	119 000	121 000	143 000	150 000	Asie, Est et Sud-Est et Océanie
Region not specified	69 000	84 000	64 000	66 000	71 000	Région non spécifiée
Israel[5 6]	**1 838 703**	**2 215 285**	**2 100 051**	**2 010 242**	**1 941 620**	**Israël**[5 6]
Africa	42 637	57 302	42 172	42 837	37 085	Afrique
Americas	490 658	581 783	558 964	548 385	571 409	Amériques
Europe	1 121 341	1 289 425	1 246 091	1 178 934	1 117 249	Europe
Asia, East and South East/Oceania	75 954	101 926	111 002	107 478	66 303	Asie, Est et Sud-Est et Océanie

72
Tourist arrivals by region of origin [cont.]
Arrivées de touristes par région de provenance [suite]

Country or area of destination and region of origin +	1994	1995	1996	1997	1998	Pays ou zone de destination et région de provenance +
Southern Asia	8 781	9 931	12 834	14 480	12 715	Asie du Sud
Western Asia	86 751	151 710	106 039	94 094	100 507	Asie occidentale
Region not specified	12 581	23 208	22 949	24 034	36 352	Région non spécifiée
Italy[3][35]	**51 814 449**	**55 706 000**	**57 249 184**	**57 998 188**	**58 499 261**	**Italie**[3][35]
Africa	81 160	95 774	168 162	241 635	181 150	Afrique
Americas	2 364 707	2 403 313	2 034 016	2 645 989	2 474 646	Amériques
Europe	47 514 439	51 111 688	52 905 181	52 920 478	54 049 369	Europe
Asia, East and South East/Oceania	1 029 795	1 100 246	1 973 565	2 018 245	1 626 810	Asie, Est et Sud-Est et Océanie
Southern Asia	...	...	71 851	72 052	73 450	Asie du Sud
Western Asia	224 740	227 160	96 176	99 789	93 751	Asie occidentale
Region not specified	599 608	767 819	233	...	85	Région non spécifiée
Jamaica[2][5][11]	**1 098 287**	**1 147 001**	**1 162 449**	**1 192 194**	**1 225 287**	**Jamaïque**[2][5][11]
Africa	913	1 132	1 063	1 023	1 026	Afrique
Americas	882 178	920 391	925 859	959 027	995 137	Amériques
Europe	189 325	197 544	209 050	211 551	213 893	Europe
Asia, East and South East/Oceania	23 488	25 194	25 266	19 621	14 144	Asie, Est et Sud-Est et Océanie
Southern Asia	368	384	484	700	595	Asie du Sud
Western Asia	...	...	...	63	423	Asie occidentale
Region not specified	2 015	2 356	727	209	69	Région non spécifiée
Japan[5][6]	**3 468 055**	**3 345 274**	**3 837 113**	**4 218 208**	**4 106 057**	**Japon**[5][6]
Africa	10 459	11 534	10 914	11 928	12 556	Afrique
Americas	681 482	695 385	749 000	780 711	828 240	Amériques
Europe	423 232	442 559	484 394	545 783	577 278	Europe
Asia, East and South East/Oceania	2 307 529	2 148 885	2 540 221	2 817 089	2 622 286	Asie, Est et Sud-Est et Océanie
Southern Asia	40 574	42 392	47 123	55 525	57 662	Asie du Sud
Western Asia	2 729	2 642	2 659	2 841	3 095	Asie occidentale
Region not specified	2 050	1 877	2 802	4 331	4 940	Région non spécifiée
Jordan[5]	**857 610**	**1 073 549**	**1 102 752**	**1 127 028**	**1 256 428**	**Jordanie**[5]
Africa	779	2 300	2 313	2 338	2 750	Afrique
Americas	69 878	103 346	107 960	107 676	108 612	Amériques
Europe	202 943	355 575	373 016	365 036	338 706	Europe
Asia, East and South East/Oceania	30 960	45 767	46 806	47 877	33 933	Asie, Est et Sud-Est et Océanie
Western Asia	553 050	566 561	572 657	604 101	772 427	Asie occidentale
Kenya[3][6][36]	**1 008 300**	**973 600**	**1 003 000**	**1 000 599**	**894 300**	**Kenya**[3][6][36]
Africa	246 700	188 170	207 100	272 674	251 243	Afrique
Americas	72 100	58 770	59 200	85 161	79 864	Amériques
Europe	481 200	386 860	393 400	573 672	504 204	Europe
Asia, East and South East/Oceania	44 900	52 260	37 100	44 313	38 145	Asie, Est et Sud-Est et Océanie
Southern Asia	14 500	...	12 100	24 026	20 844	Asie du Sud
Region not specified	148 900	287 540	294 100	753	...	Région non spécifiée
Kiribati[5][37]	**3 888**	**3 153**	**3 406**	**5 007**	**5 464**	**Kiribati**[5][37]
Americas	835	358	278	1 163	1 467	Amériques
Europe	190	135	248	314	288	Europe
Asia, East and South East/Oceania	2 565	2 406	2 500	3 317	3 187	Asie, Est et Sud-Est et Océanie
Region not specified	298	254	380	213	522	Région non spécifiée
Korea, Republic of[3][38]	**3 580 024**	**3 753 197**	**3 683 779**	**3 908 140**	**4 250 176**	**Corée, République de**[3][38]
Africa	7 626	7 519	8 639	10 681	11 368	Afrique
Americas	382 096	417 087	464 509	493 942	471 317	Amériques
Europe	391 808	426 926	444 691	436 078	401 309	Europe
Asia, East and South East/Oceania	2 413 651	2 495 443	2 381 766	2 582 236	2 977 078	Asie, Est et Sud-Est et Océanie

72
Tourist arrivals by region of origin [cont.]
Arrivées de touristes par région de provenance [suite]

Country or area of destination and region of origin +	1994	1995	1996	1997	1998	Pays ou zone de destination et région de provenance +
Southern Asia	58 605	61 815	74 352	71 251	65 727	Asie du Sud
Western Asia	6 073	8 749	7 456	6 907	9 382	Asie occidentale
Region not specified	320 165	335 658	302 366	307 045	313 995	Région non spécifiée
Kuwait[3]	**1 142 131**	**1 443 069**	**1 555 285**	**1 637 805**	**1 762 641**	**Koweït**[3]
Africa	16 519	10 418	10 797	13 885	18 648	Afrique
Americas	21 051	23 159	26 311	31 807	33 428	Amériques
Europe	42 276	52 342	58 383	66 155	65 998	Europe
Asia, East and South East/Oceania	47 057	50 561	56 670	54 516	65 908	Asie, Est et Sud-Est et Océanie
Southern Asia	355 808	417 940	459 051	471 276	513 475	Asie du Sud
Western Asia	659 175	879 387	930 385	983 464	1 045 852	Asie occidentale
Region not specified	245	9 262	13 688	16 702	19 332	Région non spécifiée
Kyrgyzstan[5]	...	**36 423**	**41 650**	**87 386**	**59 363**	**Kirghizistan**[5]
Americas	...	...	...	...	1 386	Amériques
Europe	...	25 710	28 625	72 202	46 287	Europe
Asia, East and South East/Oceania	...	...	...	...	6 791	Asie, Est et Sud-Est et Océanie
Southern Asia	...	...	...	...	2 656	Asie du Sud
Western Asia	...	...	...	...	90	Asie occidentale
Region not specified	...	10 713	13 025	15 184	2 153	Région non spécifiée
Lao People's Dem. Rep.[3]	**146 155**	**345 460**	**403 000**	**463 200**	**500 200**	**Rép. dém. pop. lao**[3]
Americas	1 837	11 019	14 102	18 213	25 326	Amériques
Europe	8 019	20 635	30 582	39 096	52 749	Europe
Asia, East and South East/Oceania	119 413	300 955	337 437	397 253	410 888	Asie, Est et Sud-Est et Océanie
Southern Asia	16 701	12 515	20 255	6 528	10 308	Asie du Sud
Region not specified	185	336	624	2 110	929	Région non spécifiée
Latvia[1]	...	**184 800**	**183 300**	**219 900**	**238 800**	**Lettonie**[1]
Americas	...	8 200	8 800	8 100	9 400	Amériques
Europe	...	149 200	147 100	168 700	186 100	Europe
Region not specified	...	27 400	27 400	43 100	43 300	Région non spécifiée
Lebanon[5][39]	**380 171**	**449 809**	**424 000**	**557 568**	**630 781**	**Liban**[5][39]
Africa	11 705	13 232	13 527	19 380	23 497	Afrique
Americas	40 561	50 568	46 917	59 404	68 321	Amériques
Europe	117 487	151 982	142 100	173 887	195 950	Europe
Asia, East and South East/Oceania	26 476	28 942	33 604	40 683	40 962	Asie, Est et Sud-Est et Océanie
Southern Asia	19 517	20 832	20 213	26 598	35 273	Asie du Sud
Western Asia	118 652	145 666	138 891	207 866	235 992	Asie occidentale
Region not specified	45 773	38 587	28 748	29 750	30 786	Région non spécifiée
Lesotho[3]	**253 310**	**208 906**	**311 802**	**323 868**	**289 819**	**Lesotho**[3]
Africa	247 279	202 007	304 368	313 323	285 734	Afrique
Americas	1 021	1 120	1 242	2 861	794	Amériques
Europe	4 014	4 706	4 708	5 682	2 311	Europe
Asia, East and South East/Oceania	996	1 073	1 484	2 002	980	Asie, Est et Sud-Est et Océanie
Libyan Arab Jamah.[3]	**1 493 127**	**1 831 884**	**1 276 000**	**913 251**	**850 292**	**Jamah. arabe libyenne**[3]
Africa	1 027 628	967 704	829 000	571 868	461 533	Afrique
Americas	1 953	1 821	3 030	861	456	Amériques
Europe	33 380	36 812	54 733	28 140	22 649	Europe
Asia, East and South East/Oceania	10 412	11 052	18 500	3 177	3 088	Asie, Est et Sud-Est et Océanie
Southern Asia	3 688	4 495	8 000	2 100	1 271	Asie du Sud
Western Asia	416 066	810 000	361 938	307 105	361 295	Asie occidentale
Region not specified	...	...	799	...	...	Région non spécifiée
Liechtenstein[1]	**61 741**	**59 447**	**56 168**	**57 077**	**59 228**	**Liechtenstein**[1]

72
Tourist arrivals by region of origin [cont.]
Arrivées de touristes par région de provenance [suite]

Country or area of destination and region of origin +	1994	1995	1996	1997	1998	Pays ou zone de destination et région de provenance +
Africa	164	161	209	155	173	Afrique
Americas	5 780	4 697	4 504	5 252	4 879	Amériques
Europe	53 998	52 183	49 031	49 237	52 319	Europe
Asia, East and South East/Oceania	1 736	2 074	1 733	2 433	1 857	Asie, Est et Sud-Est et Océanie
Region not specified	63	332	691	...	...	Région non spécifiée
Lithuania[5][40]	**222 214**	**210 781**	**255 301**	**288 028**	**306 228**	**Lituanie**[5][40]
Africa	169	269	170	234	208	Afrique
Americas	13 523	11 283	11 344	12 407	14 918	Amériques
Europe	204 311	195 181	237 682	267 822	284 489	Europe
Asia, East and South East/Oceania	4 211	4 048	6 105	7 565	6 613	Asie, Est et Sud-Est et Océanie
Luxembourg[5]	**761 818**	**767 519**	**723 965**	**771 153**	**789 176**	**Luxembourg**[5]
Americas	36 281	33 249	30 463	35 681	31 000	Amériques
Europe	703 680	713 156	671 456	712 614	721 519	Europe
Region not specified	21 857	21 114	22 046	22 858	36 657	Région non spécifiée
Madagascar[5]	**65 839**	**74 619**	**82 681**	**100 762**	**121 207**	**Madagascar**[5]
Africa	7 312	8 331	9 303	5 844	15 515	Afrique
Americas	4 696	5 235	5 606	2 015	2 424	Amériques
Europe	50 644	57 386	63 462	64 488	82 421	Europe
Asia, East and South East/Oceania	3 187	3 667	4 205	1 008	1 454	Asie, Est et Sud-Est et Océanie
Region not specified	...	...	105	27 407	19 393	Région non spécifiée
Malawi[5][34]	**162 559**	**192 169**	**193 628**	**205 248**	**176 573**	**Malawi**[5][34]
Africa	120 618	139 583	154 609	163 887	141 002	Afrique
Americas	4 820	6 397	5 645	5 984	5 146	Amériques
Europe	28 558	36 120	24 739	26 224	22 553	Europe
Region not specified	8 563	10 069	8 635	9 153	7 872	Région non spécifiée
Malaysia[5][41]	**7 197 229**	**7 468 749**	**7 138 452**	**6 210 921**	**5 550 748**	**Malaisie**[5][41]
Africa	29 755	29 171	30 039	23 502	25 519	Afrique
Americas	132 479	136 405	145 991	137 164	121 569	Amériques
Europe	401 200	404 285	407 537	386 790	367 660	Europe
Asia, East and South East/Oceania	6 421 898	6 660 317	6 335 909	5 449 937	4 696 660	Asie, Est et Sud-Est et Océanie
Southern Asia	52 278	63 673	62 985	53 644	56 117	Asie du Sud
Western Asia	26 880	28 923	31 371	16 460	19 571	Asie occidentale
Region not specified	132 739	145 975	124 620	143 424	263 652	Région non spécifiée
Maldives[5][11]	**279 982**	**314 869**	**338 733**	**365 563**	**395 725**	**Maldives**[5][11]
Africa	10 185	8 064	7 584	7 962	7 168	Afrique
Americas	3 278	3 624	4 125	6 101	6 119	Amériques
Europe	193 011	227 375	252 781	273 066	304 905	Europe
Asia, East and South East/Oceania	42 966	48 764	52 634	60 644	56 983	Asie, Est et Sud-Est et Océanie
Southern Asia	29 750	26 207	19 782	16 443	19 284	Asie du Sud
Western Asia	767	830	1 819	1 347	1 266	Asie occidentale
Region not specified	25	5	8	...	...	Région non spécifiée
Mali[1]	**30 877**	**42 897**	**53 893**	**65 649**	**...**	**Mali**[1]
Africa	8 660	12 026	11 541	14 321	...	Afrique
Americas	3 961	4 689	5 814	6 841	...	Amériques
Europe	13 763	22 155	31 137	38 278	...	Europe
Asia, East and South East/Oceania	135	728	1 467	1 621	...	Asie, Est et Sud-Est et Océanie
Western Asia	33	176	171	321	...	Asie occidentale
Region not specified	4 325	3 123	3 763	4 267	...	Région non spécifiée
Malta[5][34]	**1 176 223**	**1 115 971**	**1 053 788**	**1 111 161**	**1 182 240**	**Malte**[5][34]
Africa	2 611	4 969	4 383	5 730	6 342	Afrique

72
Tourist arrivals by region of origin [*cont.*]
Arrivées de touristes par région de provenance [*suite*]

Country or area of destination and region of origin +	1994	1995	1996	1997	1998	Pays ou zone de destination et région de provenance +
Americas	17 836	16 503	17 662	21 197	25 258	Amériques
Europe	1 089 817	1 033 734	952 940	1 023 222	1 087 709	Europe
Asia, East and South East/Oceania	10 313	10 583	11 952	13 930	15 706	Asie, Est et Sud-Est et Océanie
Southern Asia	1 294	1 307	1 336	1 250	1 987	Asie du Sud
Western Asia	42 617	39 485	53 328	42 117	41 067	Asie occidentale
Region not specified	11 735	9 390	12 187	3 715	4 171	Région non spécifiée
Marshall Islands[5][11]	**4 909**	**5 504**	**6 229**	**6 354**	**6 374**	**Iles Marshall**[5][11]
Americas	1 944	1 770	2 055	2 471	2 185	Amériques
Europe	222	299	367	354	131	Europe
Asia, East and South East/Oceania	2 606	3 262	3 664	3 411	3 341	Asie, Est et Sud-Est et Océanie
Region not specified	137	173	143	118	717	Région non spécifiée
Martinique[5]	**419 007**	**457 226**	**476 880**	**513 229**	**548 767**	**Martinique**[5]
Americas	60 165	73 534	66 226	77 759	77 270	Amériques
Europe	349 953	378 663	406 423	431 096	467 263	Europe
Region not specified	8 889	5 029	4 231	4 374	4 234	Région non spécifiée
Mauritius[5]	**400 528**	**422 463**	**486 867**	**536 125**	**558 195**	**Maurice**[5]
Africa	138 498	143 586	163 435	164 082	163 024	Afrique
Americas	3 369	3 617	4 265	5 509	5 842	Amériques
Europe	229 297	244 070	281 817	326 522	352 688	Europe
Asia, East and South East/Oceania	17 696	19 063	23 887	25 283	22 677	Asie, Est et Sud-Est et Océanie
Southern Asia	10 449	11 225	13 075	13 998	13 395	Asie du Sud
Western Asia	...	...	...	682	509	Asie occidentale
Region not specified	1 219	902	388	49	60	Région non spécifiée
Mexico[2][5]	**17 182 004**	**20 241 000**	**21 404 674**	**19 350 900**	**19 809 512**	**Mexique**[2][5]
Americas	16 724 340	19 862 286	21 019 950	18 940 859	19 391 640	Amériques
Europe	411 930	338 620	340 593	346 530	356 720	Europe
Region not specified	45 734	40 094	44 131	63 511	61 152	Région non spécifiée
Monaco[1]	**216 889**	**232 500**	**226 421**	**258 604**	**278 474**	**Monaco**[1]
Africa	369	398	466	576	555	Afrique
Americas	30 558	32 823	31 309	45 817	42 929	Amériques
Europe	157 389	166 881	159 163	172 201	194 000	Europe
Asia, East and South East/Oceania	10 838	12 622	12 051	14 202	12 061	Asie, Est et Sud-Est et Océanie
Western Asia	3 119	2 796	3 516	3 660	4 816	Asie occidentale
Region not specified	14 616	16 980	19 916	22 148	24 113	Région non spécifiée
Mongolia[5]	**124 216**	**108 434**	**70 853**	**82 084**	**197 424**	**Mongolie**[5]
Africa	2	...	...	81	72	Afrique
Americas	4 110	4 322	3 834	5 129	5 442	Amériques
Europe	68 786	42 187	21 800	25 956	79 818	Europe
Asia, East and South East/Oceania	50 696	61 116	44 733	50 328	111 493	Asie, Est et Sud-Est et Océanie
Southern Asia	605	680	464	526	490	Asie du Sud
Western Asia	17	129	22	64	109	Asie occidentale
Montserrat[5][6][11]	**21 285**	**17 675**	**8 703**	**5 132**	**7 467**	**Montserrat**[5][6][11]
Americas	17 176	14 250	6 771	3 770	5 560	Amériques
Europe	3 374	2 749	1 631	1 085	1 496	Europe
Region not specified	735	676	301	277	411	Région non spécifiée
Morocco[2][5]	**3 465 437**	**2 601 641**	**2 693 338**	**3 071 668**	**3 242 105**	**Maroc**[2][5]
Africa	755 189	66 258	75 658	78 327	80 687	Afrique
Americas	122 699	117 453	119 534	129 530	141 676	Amériques
Europe	1 303 649	1 243 178	1 337 213	1 507 819	1 655 935	Europe
Asia, East and South East/Oceania	24 903	31 250	32 480	36 041	38 992	Asie, Est et Sud-Est et Océanie

72
Tourist arrivals by region of origin [*cont.*]
Arrivées de touristes par région de provenance [*suite*]

Country or area of destination and region of origin +	1994	1995	1996	1997	1998	Pays ou zone de destination et région de provenance +
Southern Asia	...	2 793	3 350	3 490	4 013	Asie du Sud
Western Asia	62 805	60 979	62 910	66 022	76 795	Asie occidentale
Region not specified	1 196 192	1 079 730	1 062 193	1 250 439	1 244 007	Région non spécifiée
Myanmar[5 42]	**80 408**	**109 773**	**164 654**	**185 481**	**195 500**	**Myanmar**[5 42]
Americas	7 236	9 103	13 654	14 747	13 304	Amériques
Europe	25 729	33 880	50 818	54 859	51 659	Europe
Asia, East and South East/Oceania	37 191	65 586	98 377	113 927	119 721	Asie, Est et Sud-Est et Océanie
Southern Asia	10 252	1 204	1 805	1 948	10 816	Asie du Sud
Namibia[5]	...	...	**461 310**	**502 012**	**559 674**	**Namibie**[5]
Africa	...	...	351 398	383 515	429 532	Afrique
Americas	...	...	8 452	9 181	10 074	Amériques
Europe	...	...	93 946	101 162	111 113	Europe
Region not specified	...	...	7 514	8 154	8 955	Région non spécifiée
Nepal[5]	**326 531**	**363 395**	**393 613**	**421 857**	**463 684**	**Népal**[5]
Africa	998	1 147	1 982	1 734	1 803	Afrique
Americas	27 471	31 804	33 269	38 797	47 348	Amériques
Europe	134 510	137 890	139 366	146 889	160 539	Europe
Asia, East and South East/Oceania	52 380	63 245	78 522	84 765	87 514	Asie, Est et Sud-Est et Océanie
Southern Asia	110 750	129 283	140 444	149 662	166 475	Asie du Sud
Region not specified	422	26	30	10	5	Région non spécifiée
Netherlands[1]	**6 177 700**	**6 573 700**	**6 580 300**	**7 834 000**	**9 322 000**	**Pays-Bas**[1]
Africa	49 600	49 800	55 000	70 000	80 000	Afrique
Americas	664 700	720 500	664 200	900 000	1 144 000	Amériques
Europe	5 052 300	5 307 200	5 340 000	6 089 000	7 381 000	Europe
Asia, East and South East/Oceania	411 100	496 200	521 100	775 000	717 000	Asie, Est et Sud-Est et Océanie
New Caledonia[2 5]	**85 103**	**86 256**	**91 121**	**105 137**	**103 835**	**Nouvelle-Calédonie**[2 5]
Africa	426	493	472	480	511	Afrique
Americas	1 205	1 193	1 355	1 311	1 529	Amériques
Europe	23 385	26 618	29 823	32 608	31 421	Europe
Asia, East and South East/Oceania	60 080	57 942	59 080	70 475	70 005	Asie, Est et Sud-Est et Océanie
Region not specified	7	10	391	263	369	Région non spécifiée
New Zealand[2 3]	**1 322 565**	**1 408 795**	**1 528 720**	**1 497 183**	**1 484 512**	**Nouvelle-Zélande**[2 3]
Africa	13 258	11 060	13 686	15 529	17 499	Afrique
Americas	198 105	190 885	187 490	185 257	205 738	Amériques
Europe	250 985	258 136	270 179	280 766	294 904	Europe
Asia, East and South East/Oceania	825 046	905 166	982 665	941 659	887 317	Asie, Est et Sud-Est et Océanie
Southern Asia	3 676	4 815	5 838	6 255	6 751	Asie du Sud
Western Asia	3 837	3 754	3 894	3 535	3 691	Asie occidentale
Region not specified	27 658	34 979	64 968	64 182	68 612	Région non spécifiée
Nicaragua[5]	**237 652**	**281 254**	**302 694**	**358 439**	**405 702**	**Nicaragua**[5]
Africa	96	110	106	121	155	Afrique
Americas	208 207	247 452	266 880	322 241	365 011	Amériques
Europe	25 514	29 263	29 761	30 315	33 639	Europe
Asia, East and South East/Oceania	3 474	3 842	5 474	5 318	6 170	Asie, Est et Sud-Est et Océanie
Southern Asia	268	502	410	359	647	Asie du Sud
Western Asia	93	85	63	85	80	Asie occidentale
Niger[5 43]	**10 835**	**16 945**	**17 396**	**19 030**	**20 000**	**Niger**[5 43]
Africa	4 877	7 151	7 388	7 500	8 000	Afrique
Americas	1 276	1 701	1 923	2 030	3 000	Amériques
Europe	4 194	6 775	7 104	8 000	7 902	Europe

72
Tourist arrivals by region of origin [cont.]
Arrivées de touristes par région de provenance [suite]

Country or area of destination and region of origin +	1994	1995	1996	1997	1998	Pays ou zone de destination et région de provenance +
Asia, East and South East/Oceania	330	472	508	500	1 000	Asie, Est et Sud-Est et Océanie
Western Asia	...	...	...	500	...	Asie occidentale
Region not specified	158	846	473	500	98	Région non spécifiée
Nigeria[3]	**327 189**	**1 030 739**	**1 230 155**	...	...	**Nigéria**[3]
Africa	272 115	737 762	866 709	...	...	Afrique
Americas	3 055	33 198	48 018	...	...	Amériques
Europe	41 685	157 055	189 927	...	...	Europe
Asia, East and South East/Oceania	4 085	66 785	75 855	...	...	Asie, Est et Sud-Est et Océanie
Southern Asia	4 506	21 186	28 016	...	...	Asie du Sud
Western Asia	1 535	13 939	20 635	...	...	Asie occidentale
Region not specified	208	814	995	...	...	Région non spécifiée
Niue[5 11 44]	**2 802**	**2 161**	**1 522**	**1 820**	**1 736**	**Nioué**[5 11 44]
Americas	126	32	55	98	86	Amériques
Europe	105	57	74	81	78	Europe
Asia, East and South East/Oceania	2 536	2 048	1 360	1 623	1 552	Asie, Est et Sud-Est et Océanie
Region not specified	35	24	33	18	20	Région non spécifiée
Northern Mariana Islands[3]	**596 033**	**676 161**	**736 117**	**694 888**	**490 165**	**Iles Marianas du Nord**[3]
Africa	26	37	22	39	34	Afrique
Americas	81 826	99 373	84 856	76 217	61 491	Amériques
Europe	2 201	1 840	2 000	2 860	2 852	Europe
Asia, East and South East/Oceania	511 673	574 376	648 188	614 558	425 178	Asie, Est et Sud-Est et Océanie
Southern Asia	235	427	306	187	141	Asie du Sud
Western Asia	34	28	32	63	100	Asie occidentale
Region not specified	38	80	713	964	369	Région non spécifiée
Norway[1]	*** 2 830 000**	*** 2 880 000**	*** 2 746 000**	*** 2 702 000**	**2 829 196**	**Norvège**[1]
Africa	5 382	5 477	5 222	5 138	5 380	Afrique
Americas	259 747	264 336	252 036	247 998	259 700	Amériques
Europe	2 308 271	2 349 051	2 239 758	2 203 867	2 307 590	Europe
Asia, East and South East/Oceania	167 351	170 308	162 384	159 782	167 302	Asie, Est et Sud-Est et Océanie
Region not specified	89 249	90 828	86 600	85 215	89 224	Région non spécifiée
Oman[1]	**283 000**	**279 000**	**349 000**	...	...	**Oman**[1]
Africa	14 000	15 000	22 000	...	...	Afrique
Americas	19 000	18 000	25 000	...	...	Amériques
Europe	100 000	99 000	110 000	...	...	Europe
Asia, East and South East/Oceania	48 000	45 000	65 000	...	...	Asie, Est et Sud-Est et Océanie
Western Asia	37 000	40 000	58 000	...	...	Asie occidentale
Region not specified	65 000	62 000	69 000	...	...	Région non spécifiée
Pakistan[5]	**454 300**	**378 400**	**368 662**	**374 800**	**428 781**	**Pakistan**[5]
Africa	13 328	10 536	9 776	8 261	8 330	Afrique
Americas	58 824	57 789	54 070	54 169	61 073	Amériques
Europe	239 337	165 729	152 998	153 788	183 855	Europe
Asia, East and South East/Oceania	36 910	40 531	43 987	41 935	48 798	Asie, Est et Sud-Est et Océanie
Southern Asia	83 954	83 660	87 502	97 000	107 302	Asie du Sud
Western Asia	21 924	20 066	20 274	19 587	19 375	Asie occidentale
Region not specified	23	89	55	60	48	Région non spécifiée
Palau[5 45]	**44 073**	**53 229**	**69 330**	**73 719**	**64 194**	**Palaos**[5 45]
Americas	9 700	9 846	9 955	10 481	12 487	Amériques
Europe	2 207	2 508	2 870	1 767	2 044	Europe
Asia, East and South East/Oceania	31 658	40 434	55 897	59 909	45 667	Asie, Est et Sud-Est et Océanie
Region not specified	508	441	608	1 562	3 996	Région non spécifiée

72
Tourist arrivals by region of origin [*cont.*]
Arrivées de touristes par région de provenance [*suite*]

Country or area of destination and region of origin +	1994	1995	1996	1997	1998	Pays ou zone de destination et région de provenance +
Panama[3 46]	**342 790**	**359 575**	**376 672**	**418 846**	**422 228**	**Panama**[3 46]
Africa	273	363	215	276	216	Afrique
Americas	305 746	316 519	331 908	370 752	377 594	Amériques
Europe	25 269	31 822	29 985	32 415	30 934	Europe
Asia, East and South East/Oceania	11 451	10 809	14 504	15 338	13 426	Asie, Est et Sud-Est et Océanie
Western Asia	51	62	60	65	58	Asie occidentale
Papua New Guinea[5]	**38 739**	**42 328**	**61 385**	**66 143**	**67 465**	**Papouasie-Nvl-Guinée**[5]
Americas	4 510	5 469	6 192	6 878	7 013	Amériques
Europe	6 866	6 565	5 770	5 984	6 646	Europe
Asia, East and South East/Oceania	27 239	29 894	44 391	53 019	53 478	Asie, Est et Sud-Est et Océanie
Region not specified	124	400	5 032	262	328	Région non spécifiée
Paraguay[5 6 9]	**406 409**	**437 653**	**425 561**	**395 058**	**349 592**	**Paraguay**[5 6 9]
Africa	...	...	...	1 541	723	Afrique
Americas	327 159	354 019	349 283	316 244	282 668	Amériques
Europe	48 972	47 704	40 226	41 995	33 280	Europe
Asia, East and South East/Oceania	18 369	14 179	7 929	11 219	3 852	Asie, Est et Sud-Est et Océanie
Region not specified	11 909	21 751	28 123	24 059	29 069	Région non spécifiée
Peru[5]	**386 120**	**479 231**	**584 388**	**649 287**	**723 668**	**Pérou**[5]
Africa	729	862	1 088	1 435	1 541	Afrique
Americas	243 155	300 485	372 079	436 479	483 106	Amériques
Europe	112 839	140 479	166 648	172 204	199 495	Europe
Asia, East and South East/Oceania	28 170	35 745	42 643	36 940	36 054	Asie, Est et Sud-Est et Océanie
Southern Asia	891	1 306	1 626	1 888	2 566	Asie du Sud
Western Asia	187	199	248	271	349	Asie occidentale
Region not specified	149	155	56	70	557	Région non spécifiée
Philippines[2 5]	**1 573 821**	**1 760 063**	**2 049 367**	**2 222 523**	**2 149 357**	**Philippines**[2 5]
Africa	1 244	1 567	1 802	1 888	2 054	Afrique
Americas	352 483	391 309	434 828	496 213	540 596	Amériques
Europe	205 958	231 902	272 987	294 679	310 762	Europe
Asia, East and South East/Oceania	800 874	929 047	1 133 893	1 232 487	1 050 917	Asie, Est et Sud-Est et Océanie
Southern Asia	20 377	22 068	25 861	27 384	30 954	Asie du Sud
Western Asia	18 115	17 539	18 406	15 104	16 123	Asie occidentale
Region not specified	174 770	166 631	161 590	154 768	197 951	Région non spécifiée
Poland[3]	**74 252 751**	**82 243 621**	**87 438 583**	**87 817 369**	**88 592 355**	**Pologne**[3]
Africa	8 966	5 465	5 543	5 558	6 504	Afrique
Americas	234 324	235 273	251 164	276 272	305 447	Amériques
Europe	73 882 322	81 875 078	87 022 729	87 369 361	88 142 325	Europe
Asia, East and South East/Oceania	47 278	56 514	67 373	74 777	61 856	Asie, Est et Sud-Est et Océanie
Southern Asia	14 712	11 845	11 546	10 558	8 837	Asie du Sud
Western Asia	8 592	8 356	8 147	8 121	6 648	Asie occidentale
Region not specified	56 557	51 090	72 081	72 722	60 738	Région non spécifiée
Portugal[5 6 47]	**9 169 133**	**9 511 490**	**9 730 200**	**10 172 423**	**11 294 973**	**Portugal**[5 6 47]
Americas	339 525	350 077	337 004	373 915	408 580	Amériques
Europe	8 566 004	8 888 759	9 150 847	9 550 552	10 588 648	Europe
Asia, East and South East/Oceania	32 848	35 439	37 502	37 769	44 209	Asie, Est et Sud-Est et Océanie
Region not specified	230 756	237 215	204 847	210 187	253 536	Région non spécifiée
Puerto Rico[5 11]	**3 042 375**	**3 130 662**	**3 065 056**	**3 241 774**	**3 396 115**	**Porto Rico**[5 11]
Americas	2 146 364	2 278 344	2 237 540	2 474 433	2 569 596	Amériques
Region not specified	896 011	852 318	827 516	767 341	826 519	Région non spécifiée
Republic of Moldova[3 48]	**24 719**	**30 610**	**27 167**	**19 890**	**18 718**	**République de Moldova**[3 48]

72
Tourist arrivals by region of origin [*cont.*]
Arrivées de touristes par région de provenance [*suite*]

Country or area of destination and region of origin +	1994	1995	1996	1997	1998	Pays ou zone de destination et région de provenance +
Africa	13	5	23	13	42	Afrique
Americas	378	678	773	1 050	889	Amériques
Europe	24 125	29 378	25 937	18 431	17 486	Europe
Asia, East and South East/Oceania	106	248	200	265	171	Asie, Est et Sud-Est et Océanie
Southern Asia	32	178	52	48	75	Asie du Sud
Western Asia	65	123	182	83	55	Asie occidentale
Réunion[5]	**262 600**	**304 000**	**346 898**	**370 255**	**...**	**Réunion**[5]
Africa	41 909	40 119	40 073	40 626	...	Afrique
Americas	1 296	1 219	794	1 269	...	Amériques
Europe	216 271	259 568	303 772	325 045	...	Europe
Asia, East and South East/Oceania	1 360	1 287	1 402	1 351	...	Asie, Est et Sud-Est et Océanie
Southern Asia	714	608	77	285	...	Asie du Sud
Region not specified	1 050	1 199	780	1 679	...	Région non spécifiée
Romania[5]	**2 796 426**	**2 757 195**	**3 027 596**	**2 957 161**	**2 965 707**	**Roumanie**[5]
Africa	3 113	4 852	4 466	4 224	3 751	Afrique
Americas	46 380	56 997	66 866	70 933	79 351	Amériques
Europe	2 705 754	2 643 000	2 895 069	2 825 926	2 831 628	Europe
Asia, East and South East/Oceania	13 089	20 828	27 435	27 549	27 642	Asie, Est et Sud-Est et Océanie
Southern Asia	4 318	5 350	6 305	5 516	5 332	Asie du Sud
Western Asia	18 279	21 599	20 501	21 458	16 926	Asie occidentale
Region not specified	5 493	4 569	6 954	1 555	1 077	Région non spécifiée
Russian Federation[3][49]	**4 642 899**	**10 290 147**	**16 208 339**	**17 462 627**	**15 805 242**	**Fédération de Russie**[3][49]
Africa	12 676	22 857	25 378	33 593	31 321	Afrique
Americas	148 627	271 453	245 747	293 230	291 751	Amériques
Europe	3 658 892	9 142 771	15 196 814	16 034 061	14 286 682	Europe
Asia, East and South East/Oceania	774 278	736 233	652 297	757 046	754 049	Asie, Est et Sud-Est et Océanie
Southern Asia	18 564	52 040	34 726	51 155	51 851	Asie du Sud
Western Asia	26 788	51 424	45 004	39 429	64 264	Asie occidentale
Region not specified	3 074	13 369	8 373	254 113	325 324	Région non spécifiée
Saba[5][50]	**13 760**	**9 983**	**9 785**	**10 556**	**10 565**	**Saba**[5][50]
Americas	10 677	7 545	7 540	8 295	8 172	Amériques
Europe	1 363	1 306	990	994	1 110	Europe
Region not specified	1 720	1 132	1 255	1 267	1 283	Région non spécifiée
Saint Eustatius[3][11]	**24 210**	**20 556**	**19 912**	**19 128**	**19 072**	**Sainte Eustace**[3][11]
Americas	19 783	16 261	15 331	14 396	14 076	Amériques
Europe	4 182	3 703	3 816	4 125	4 309	Europe
Region not specified	245	592	765	607	687	Région non spécifiée
Saint Kitts and Nevis[5][7]	**94 185**	**78 868**	**84 176**	**88 297**	**93 190**	**Saint-Kitts-et-Nevis**[5][7]
Americas	81 711	68 613	71 365	74 662	77 056	Amériques
Europe	12 025	9 833	11 944	13 068	15 166	Europe
Asia, East and South East/Oceania	31	21	151	62	91	Asie, Est et Sud-Est et Océanie
Region not specified	418	401	716	505	877	Région non spécifiée
Saint Lucia[5][6]	**218 567**	**231 259**	**235 659**	**248 406**	**252 237**	**Sainte-Lucie**[5][6]
Americas	139 233	142 958	148 353	149 334	161 000	Amériques
Europe	76 993	85 802	84 376	96 398	88 642	Europe
Asia, East and South East/Oceania	...	...	...	207	179	Asie, Est et Sud-Est et Océanie
Region not specified	2 341	2 499	2 930	2 467	2 416	Région non spécifiée
Saint Maarten[5][11][51]	**585 701**	**460 070**	**364 706**	**439 234**	**458 486**	**Sainte Martin**[5][11][51]
Americas	388 061	308 046	224 612	285 827	303 465	Amériques
Europe	155 709	131 845	119 394	130 924	132 881	Europe

72
Tourist arrivals by region of origin [cont.]
Arrivées de touristes par région de provenance [suite]

Country or area of destination and region of origin +	1994	1995	1996	1997	1998	Pays ou zone de destination et région de provenance +
Region not specified	41 931	20 179	20 700	22 483	22 140	Région non spécifiée
St. Vincent-Grenadines[5]	**54 982**	**60 206**	**57 882**	**65 143**	**67 228**	**St. Vincent-Grenadines**[5]
Americas	37 854	41 836	39 186	45 722	46 186	Amériques
Europe	16 593	17 551	18 045	18 625	20 301	Europe
Region not specified	535	819	651	796	741	Région non spécifiée
Samoa[5]	**67 089**	**68 392**	**73 155**	**67 960**	**77 926**	**Samoa**[5]
Americas	8 431	6 456	8 434	6 956	8 037	Amériques
Europe	5 342	6 951	4 799	4 494	4 917	Europe
Asia, East and South East/Oceania	51 078	53 462	58 252	55 370	64 695	Asie, Est et Sud-Est et Océanie
Region not specified	2 238	1 523	1 670	1 140	277	Région non spécifiée
San Marino[3 52]	**3 104 231**	**3 368 159**	**3 345 381**	**3 307 983**	**3 264 385**	**Saint-Marin**[3 52]
Region not specified	3 104 231	3 368 159	3 345 381	3 307 983	3 264 385	Région non spécifiée
Sao Tome and Principe[5]	**6 376**	**6 160**	**6 436**	**4 924**	**...**	**Sao Tomé-et-Principe**[5]
Africa	1 813	1 657	1 742	1 109	...	Afrique
Americas	585	441	320	236	...	Amériques
Europe	3 631	3 832	4 101	3 395	...	Europe
Asia, East and South East/Oceania	250	166	219	146	...	Asie, Est et Sud-Est et Océanie
Southern Asia	14	13	17	17	...	Asie du Sud
Western Asia	83	51	37	21	...	Asie occidentale
Saudi Arabia[3]	**3 212 684**	**3 351 549**	**...**	**...**	**...**	**Arabie saoudite**[3]
Africa	638 453	585 114	...	...	...	Afrique
Americas	28 457	29 221	...	...	...	Amériques
Europe	79 901	79 345	...	...	...	Europe
Asia, East and South East/Oceania	2 465 873	2 657 869	...	...	...	Asie, Est et Sud-Est et Océanie
Senegal[1 53]	**239 629**	**280 000**	**282 169**	**313 642**	**352 389**	**Sénégal**[1 53]
Africa	47 352	56 651	67 267	70 224	84 244	Afrique
Americas	10 226	11 244	12 803	11 597	11 632	Amériques
Europe	175 984	205 521	194 705	224 971	247 533	Europe
Asia, East and South East/Oceania	2 855	2 933	3 542	3 583	2 588	Asie, Est et Sud-Est et Océanie
Western Asia	1 029	1 174	1 572	1 335	1 611	Asie occidentale
Region not specified	2 183	2 477	2 280	1 932	4 781	Région non spécifiée
Seychelles[5]	**109 901**	**120 716**	**130 955**	**130 070**	**128 258**	**Seychelles**[5]
Africa	10 967	14 202	13 330	13 966	12 675	Afrique
Americas	3 367	6 274	6 657	6 726	6 787	Amériques
Europe	90 080	93 827	103 495	102 510	102 736	Europe
Asia, East and South East/Oceania	3 316	4 413	4 408	3 523	2 916	Asie, Est et Sud-Est et Océanie
Southern Asia	600	905	1 828	1 875	1 782	Asie du Sud
Western Asia	1 571	1 095	1 237	1 470	1 362	Asie occidentale
Sierra Leone[5 11]	**23 600**	**13 765**	**21 877**	**25 579**	**...**	**Sierra Leone**[5 11]
Africa	6 900	5 087	7 313	8 410	...	Afrique
Americas	3 200	2 117	3 932	4 718	...	Amériques
Europe	7 500	2 553	4 481	5 377	...	Europe
Region not specified	6 000	4 008	6 151	7 074	...	Région non spécifiée
Singapore[3 54]	**6 898 309**	**7 136 538**	**7 292 366**	**7 197 871**	**6 242 152**	**Singapour**[3 54]
Africa	100 692	82 660	75 036	64 978	72 197	Afrique
Americas	428 001	425 707	459 471	460 435	425 424	Amériques
Europe	1 016 520	973 880	1 011 044	996 814	990 805	Europe
Asia, East and South East/Oceania	5 006 027	5 236 745	5 329 485	5 216 166	4 287 819	Asie, Est et Sud-Est et Océanie
Southern Asia	308 130	364 924	367 155	396 068	394 502	Asie du Sud
Western Asia	38 440	52 282	49 913	48 185	60 091	Asie occidentale

72

Tourist arrivals by region of origin [*cont.*]

Arrivées de touristes par région de provenance [*suite*]

Country or area of destination and region of origin +	1994	1995	1996	1997	1998	Pays ou zone de destination et région de provenance +
Region not specified	499	340	262	15 225	11 314	Région non spécifiée
Slovakia[8]	**901 812**	**902 975**	**951 355**	**814 138**	**896 100**	**Slovaquie**[8]
Africa	2 082	2 353	2 481	2 305	3 039	Afrique
Americas	29 955	25 867	28 189	25 982	30 206	Amériques
Europe	849 767	853 974	897 505	762 025	839 445	Europe
Asia, East and South East/Oceania	20 008	20 781	23 180	21 143	22 901	Asie, Est et Sud-Est et Océanie
Region not specified	...	...	...	2 683	509	Région non spécifiée
Slovenia[8]	**748 273**	**732 103**	**831 895**	**974 350**	**976 514**	**Slovénie**[8]
Americas	16 539	15 361	16 926	17 193	20 510	Amériques
Europe	719 319	704 254	800 426	942 022	940 365	Europe
Asia, East and South East/Oceania	3 107	4 134	4 786	5 820	7 775	Asie, Est et Sud-Est et Océanie
Region not specified	9 308	8 354	9 757	9 315	7 864	Région non spécifiée
Solomon Islands[5]	**11 918**	**11 795**	**11 217**	**15 894**	**13 229**	**Iles Salomon**[5]
Americas	1 057	1 089	988	1 145	789	Amériques
Europe	1 521	1 504	1 517	1 356	1 073	Europe
Asia, East and South East/Oceania	9 301	9 158	8 664	13 318	11 278	Asie, Est et Sud-Est et Océanie
Region not specified	39	44	48	75	89	Région non spécifiée
South Africa[3 6 55]	**3 668 956**	**4 488 272**	**4 944 430**	**5 653 447**	**5 898 256**	**Afrique du Sud**[3 6 55]
Africa	2 933 871	3 299 617	3 615 754	4 033 699	4 301 430	Afrique
Americas	109 378	153 391	169 579	223 748	249 935	Amériques
Europe	454 536	710 342	784 040	967 087	996 482	Europe
Asia, East and South East/Oceania	116 761	174 873	180 738	194 586	185 721	Asie, Est et Sud-Est et Océanie
Southern Asia	10 888	14 478	15 713	22 974	23 090	Asie du Sud
Western Asia	7 178	10 069	13 327	15 892	17 236	Asie occidentale
Region not specified	36 344	125 502	165 279	195 461	124 362	Région non spécifiée
Spain[1 56]	**15 310 220**	**16 286 025**	**17 008 452**	**18 249 738**	**20 217 485**	**Espagne**[1 56]
Africa	...	...	...	87 660	104 404	Afrique
Americas	1 425 217	1 476 772	1 616 669	1 858 157	2 170 508	Amériques
Europe	12 953 393	13 664 246	14 024 432	14 895 811	16 527 774	Europe
Asia, East and South East/Oceania	379 892	477 254	616 556	862 233	896 920	Asie, Est et Sud-Est et Océanie
Region not specified	551 718	667 753	750 795	545 877	517 879	Région non spécifiée
Sri Lanka[5 6]	**407 511**	**403 101**	**302 265**	**366 165**	**381 063**	**Sri Lanka**[5 6]
Africa	744	798	2 376	1 533	1 035	Afrique
Americas	16 152	15 177	12 798	16 455	17 937	Amériques
Europe	258 285	254 730	171 888	218 481	246 198	Europe
Asia, East and South East/Oceania	65 493	61 536	51 402	58 332	54 129	Asie, Est et Sud-Est et Océanie
Southern Asia	62 892	67 041	59 919	66 945	57 732	Asie du Sud
Western Asia	3 945	3 819	3 882	4 419	4 032	Asie occidentale
Sudan[5]	**38 406**	**63 040**	**...**	**...**	**...**	**Soudan**[5]
Africa	5 299	5 715	...	...	...	Afrique
Americas	7 624	8 472	...	...	...	Amériques
Europe	9 774	18 086	...	...	...	Europe
Asia, East and South East/Oceania	5 148	9 803	...	...	...	Asie, Est et Sud-Est et Océanie
Southern Asia	1 982	3 020	...	...	...	Asie du Sud
Western Asia	6 379	12 344	...	...	...	Asie occidentale
Region not specified	2 200	5 600	...	...	...	Région non spécifiée
Suriname[5 57]	**42 262**	**43 411**	**53 228**	**61 361**	**54 585**	**Suriname**[5 57]
Africa	221	155	74	70	62	Afrique
Americas	20 060	20 111	10 419	9 553	5 501	Amériques
Europe	15 770	17 600	39 149	49 929	46 061	Europe

72
Tourist arrivals by region of origin [cont.]
Arrivées de touristes par région de provenance [suite]

Country or area of destination and region of origin +	1994	1995	1996	1997	1998	Pays ou zone de destination et région de provenance +
Asia, East and South East/Oceania	6 048	5 149	3 390	1 744	1 714	Asie, Est et Sud-Est et Océanie
Southern Asia	163	394	159	59	45	Asie du Sud
Region not specified	...	2	37	6	1 202	Région non spécifiée
Swaziland[1]	**335 933**	**299 822**	**314 921**	**...**	**...**	**Swaziland**[1]
Africa	283 931	253 409	264 037	...	...	Afrique
Americas	6 459	5 764	6 464	...	...	Amériques
Europe	37 498	33 468	38 122	...	...	Europe
Asia, East and South East/Oceania	4 270	3 810	4 094	...	...	Asie, Est et Sud-Est et Océanie
Region not specified	3 775	3 371	2 204	...	...	Région non spécifiée
**Sweden * **[8]	**1 959 660**	**2 310 000**	**2 374 000**	**...**	**...**	**Suède * **[8]
Americas	101 412	103 000	107 968			Amériques
Europe	1 690 724	2 018 608	2 056 697			Europe
Asia, East and South East/Oceania	30 442	42 945	51 001			Asie, Est et Sud-Est et Océanie
Region not specified	137 082	145 447	158 334	...	...	Région non spécifiée
Switzerland[1]	**7 357 885**	**6 945 983**	**6 729 797**	**7 039 225**	**7 185 379**	**Suisse**[1]
Africa	85 823	83 102	79 804	81 015	82 431	Afrique
Americas	1 041 480	980 212	946 349	990 354	1 074 217	Amériques
Europe	5 191 625	4 784 799	4 556 622	4 846 684	5 050 341	Europe
Asia, East and South East/Oceania	951 895	1 008 010	1 057 519	1 026 559	879 624	Asie, Est et Sud-Est et Océanie
Southern Asia	35 787	36 555	37 276	42 190	55 102	Asie du Sud
Western Asia	51 275	53 305	52 227	52 423	43 664	Asie occidentale
Syrian Arab Republic[3 6]	**2 012 297**	**2 252 787**	**2 435 381**	**2 331 628**	**2 463 724**	**Rép. arabe syrienne**[3 6]
Africa	33 088	52 501	71 636	76 116	70 906	Afrique
Americas	17 186	19 208	21 375	26 265	27 766	Amériques
Europe	304 312	339 429	332 005	342 767	342 615	Europe
Asia, East and South East/Oceania	10 806	11 866	13 027	18 215	16 319	Asie, Est et Sud-Est et Océanie
Southern Asia	188 017	213 064	199 324	139 693	170 143	Asie du Sud
Western Asia	1 415 754	1 581 703	1 745 916	1 696 803	1 799 683	Asie occidentale
Region not specified	43 134	35 016	52 098	31 769	36 292	Région non spécifiée
Thailand[5 58]	**6 166 496**	**6 951 566**	**7 244 400**	**7 293 957**	**7 842 760**	**Thaïlande**[5 58]
Africa	46 438	47 258	47 449	50 963	72 097	Afrique
Americas	373 610	357 674	384 012	388 190	448 761	Amériques
Europe	1 549 119	1 618 379	1 651 788	1 635 581	1 946 154	Europe
Asia, East and South East/Oceania	3 888 374	4 582 307	4 765 104	4 840 429	4 931 506	Asie, Est et Sud-Est et Océanie
Southern Asia	240 893	274 932	275 966	235 623	258 815	Asie du Sud
Western Asia	68 062	71 016	67 826	70 559	107 597	Asie occidentale
Region not specified	...	...	52 255	72 612	77 830	Région non spécifiée
TFYR Macedonia[1]	**185 414**	**147 007**	**136 137**	**121 337**	**156 670**	**L'ex-R.y. Macédoine**[1]
Americas	4 783	3 706	6 083	5 424	8 788	Amériques
Europe	177 825	141 010	126 679	112 752	143 830	Europe
Asia, East and South East/Oceania	1 011	1 034	1 672	1 644	2 280	Asie, Est et Sud-Est et Océanie
Region not specified	1 795	1 257	1 703	1 517	1 772	Région non spécifiée
Togo[1]	**43 767**	**53 061**	**58 049**	**92 081**	**69 461**	**Togo**[1]
Africa	22 423	28 016	30 650	52 275	39 026	Afrique
Americas	2 791	2 601	2 846	4 263	4 853	Amériques
Europe	15 689	20 733	22 683	30 488	21 857	Europe
Asia, East and South East/Oceania	642	675	731	1 739	1 091	Asie, Est et Sud-Est et Océanie
Western Asia	2 159	959	1 057	3 163	2 588	Asie occidentale
Region not specified	63	77	82	153	46	Région non spécifiée
Tonga[5 11]	**28 408**	**29 520**	**26 642**	**26 162**	**27 132**	**Tonga**[5 11]

72
Tourist arrivals by region of origin [cont.]
Arrivées de touristes par région de provenance [suite]

Country or area of destination and region of origin +	1994	1995	1996	1997	1998	Pays ou zone de destination et région de provenance +
Americas	6 302	6 253	5 681	5 166	6 093	Amériques
Europe	5 643	5 192	4 485	4 225	4 031	Europe
Asia, East and South East/Oceania	16 375	17 945	16 389	16 712	16 921	Asie, Est et Sud-Est et Océanie
Southern Asia	79	71	72	51	72	Asie du Sud
Region not specified	9	59	15	8	15	Région non spécifiée
Trinidad and Tobago[5][11]	**253 143**	**259 784**	**265 900**	**324 293**	**347 705**	**Trinité-et-Tobago** [5][11]
Africa	412	543	483	613	766	Afrique
Americas	199 375	203 802	208 398	249 552	265 427	Amériques
Europe	50 146	51 993	52 790	69 887	76 965	Europe
Asia, East and South East/Oceania	1 782	2 177	2 088	1 758	2 149	Asie, Est et Sud-Est et Océanie
Southern Asia	603	926	1 017	937	894	Asie du Sud
Western Asia	156	94	141	233	99	Asie occidentale
Region not specified	669	249	983	1 313	1 405	Région non spécifiée
Tunisia[5][6]	**3 855 546**	**4 119 847**	**3 884 593**	**4 263 107**	**4 717 705**	**Tunisie**[5][6]
Africa	793 069	1 034 479	719 410	671 432	750 322	Afrique
Americas	24 275	24 817	26 945	26 689	27 831	Amériques
Europe	2 415 690	2 357 242	2 522 893	2 845 952	3 011 383	Europe
Asia, East and South East/Oceania	4 008	3 738	4 706	5 506	8 354	Asie, Est et Sud-Est et Océanie
Western Asia	581 091	660 637	571 010	675 264	879 931	Asie occidentale
Region not specified	37 413	38 934	39 629	38 264	39 884	Région non spécifiée
Turkey[5]	**6 033 433**	**7 083 101**	**7 966 004**	**9 039 671**	**8 959 712**	**Turquie**[5]
Africa	74 386	103 766	90 714	95 596	95 504	Afrique
Americas	192 074	203 834	220 032	267 575	317 451	Amériques
Europe	5 115 648	5 979 640	6 854 575	7 874 694	7 786 373	Europe
Asia, East and South East/Oceania	136 346	155 766	169 973	204 510	194 838	Asie, Est et Sud-Est et Océanie
Southern Asia	251 431	384 300	398 671	348 318	320 779	Asie du Sud
Western Asia	255 461	247 076	218 971	233 183	231 436	Asie occidentale
Region not specified	8 087	8 719	13 068	15 795	13 331	Région non spécifiée
Turkmenistan[3]	**61 412**	**232 832**	**281 988**	**332 425**	**...**	**Turkménistan**[3]
Africa	20	91	248	109	...	Afrique
Americas	363	1 876	3 684	2 647	...	Amériques
Europe	9 309	124 518	162 804	150 705	...	Europe
Asia, East and South East/Oceania	114	2 370	2 668	2 189	...	Asie, Est et Sud-Est et Océanie
Southern Asia	51 545	102 803	108 502	175 542	...	Asie du Sud
Western Asia	61	1 174	4 082	1 233	...	Asie occidentale
Turks and Caicos Islands[5]	**71 646**	**78 957**	**87 794**	**93 011**	**110 855**	**Iles Turques et Caïques**[5]
Americas	60 527	67 767	73 446	78 736	90 321	Amériques
Europe	8 383	8 494	11 431	9 121	11 887	Europe
Region not specified	2 736	2 696	2 917	5 154	8 647	Région non spécifiée
Tuvalu[5]	**1 268**	**922**	**1 039**	**1 029**	**1 077**	**Tuvalu**[5]
Americas	133	70	89	76	118	Amériques
Europe	204	168	88	127	123	Europe
Asia, East and South East/Oceania	926	676	849	822	804	Asie, Est et Sud-Est et Océanie
Region not specified	5	8	13	4	32	Région non spécifiée
Uganda[5]	**129 520**	**159 899**	**...**	**...**	**...**	**Ouganda**[5]
Africa	77 895	102 129	...	...	...	Afrique
Americas	10 228	10 675	...	...	...	Amériques
Europe	28 852	31 977	...	...	...	Europe
Asia, East and South East/Oceania	4 969	5 241	...	...	...	Asie, Est et Sud-Est et Océanie
Southern Asia	4 230	6 474	...	...	...	Asie du Sud

72
Tourist arrivals by region of origin [cont.]
Arrivées de touristes par région de provenance [suite]

Country or area of destination and region of origin +	1994	1995	1996	1997	1998	Pays ou zone de destination et région de provenance +
Western Asia	1 906	2 452	...	...	...	Asie occidentale
Region not specified	1 440	951	...	...	...	Région non spécifiée
Ukraine[5]	**3 610 402**	**3 715 994**	**3 853 944**	**7 658 235**	**6 207 640**	**Ukraine**[5]
Africa	2 977	10 046	729	10 551	3 739	Afrique
Americas	61 028	58 698	26 116	79 638	63 940	Amériques
Europe	3 508 389	3 586 084	3 611 514	7 465 648	6 091 006	Europe
Asia, East and South East/Oceania	10 143	13 193	4 009	28 129	22 473	Asie, Est et Sud-Est et Océanie
Southern Asia	4 043	24 689	2 507	36 381	12 675	Asie du Sud
Western Asia	16 335	16 891	205 273	28 585	8 940	Asie occidentale
Region not specified	7 487	6 393	3 796	9 303	4 867	Région non spécifiée
United Arab Emirates[1 59]	**1 239 377**	**1 600 847**	**1 767 638**	**1 791 994**	**2 184 292**	**Emirats arabes unis**[1 59]
Africa	47 400	56 399	84 147	106 612	128 412	Afrique
Americas	43 720	66 617	51 465	49 016	82 778	Amériques
Europe	398 781	567 887	628 686	534 299	658 955	Europe
Asia, East and South East/Oceania	132 269	163 746	148 510	153 641	186 086	Asie, Est et Sud-Est et Océanie
Southern Asia	185 377	212 764	272 255	322 167	354 843	Asie du Sud
Western Asia	431 830	533 434	582 575	626 259	773 218	Asie occidentale
United Kingdom[3 34]	**20 794 000**	**23 537 000**	**25 163 000**	**25 515 000**	**25 744 000**	**Royaume-Uni**[3 34]
Africa	556 000	549 000	510 000	525 000	570 000	Afrique
Americas	3 815 000	4 101 000	4 017 000	4 509 000	5 053 000	Amériques
Europe	13 766 000	15 790 000	17 856 000	17 644 000	17 581 000	Europe
Asia, East and South East/Oceania	1 825 000	2 173 000	2 166 000	2 155 000	1 872 000	Asie, Est et Sud-Est et Océanie
Southern Asia	225 000	265 000	238 000	269 000	264 000	Asie du Sud
Western Asia	607 000	659 000	376 000	413 000	404 000	Asie occidentale
United Rep.Tanzania[3]	**261 579**	**295 312**	**326 188**	**360 000**	**482 331**	**Rép.-Unie de Tanzanie**[3]
Africa	102 041	115 000	127 027	139 842	186 980	Afrique
Americas	58 133	65 800	72 681	80 014	105 720	Amériques
Europe	94 138	106 012	117 098	128 912	175 031	Europe
Asia, East and South East/Oceania	7 267	8 500	9 382	11 232	14 600	Asie, Est et Sud-Est et Océanie
United States[5]	**44 752 895**	**43 317 966**	**46 488 866**	**47 766 476**	**46 395 587**	**Etats-Unis**[5]
Africa	172 941	185 779	204 322	233 972	258 228	Afrique
Americas	29 950 843	26 680 595	27 948 103	28 155 272	27 512 761	Amériques
Europe	8 347 922	9 062 595	10 028 117	10 734 881	11 040 602	Europe
Asia, East and South East/Oceania	5 972 090	7 046 008	7 928 682	8 201 299	7 081 823	Asie, Est et Sud-Est et Océanie
Southern Asia	146 027	168 560	201 723	235 416	282 112	Asie du Sud
Western Asia	163 072	174 429	177 919	205 636	220 061	Asie occidentale
United States Virgin Is.[1]	**432 432**	**363 201**	**229 237**	**386 740**	**480 064**	**Iles Vierges américaines**[1]
Africa	136	165	254	248	539	Afrique
Americas	397 178	332 835	213 318	360 897	453 047	Amériques
Europe	14 525	12 216	11 868	14 875	14 570	Europe
Asia, East and South East/Oceania	911	735	395	1 063	764	Asie, Est et Sud-Est et Océanie
Region not specified	19 682	17 250	3 402	9 657	11 144	Région non spécifiée
Uruguay[2 3]	**2 175 457**	**2 176 930**	**2 258 616**	**2 462 532**	**2 323 993**	**Uruguay**[2 3]
Americas	1 793 799	1 743 468	1 749 878	1 888 852	1 809 579	Amériques
Europe	59 236	83 347	60 101	83 626	96 190	Europe
Asia, East and South East/Oceania	4 669	7 707	...	...	...	Asie, Est et Sud-Est et Océanie
Western Asia	123	323	...	...	...	Asie occidentale
Region not specified	317 630	342 085	448 637	490 054	418 224	Région non spécifiée
Vanuatu[5]	**42 140**	**43 712**	**46 123**	**49 605**	**52 085**	**Vanuatu**[5]

72
Tourist arrivals by region of origin [*cont.*]
Arrivées de touristes par région de provenance [*suite*]

Country or area of destination and region of origin +	1994	1995	1996	1997	1998	Pays ou zone de destination et région de provenance +
Americas	1 140	1 157	1 223	1 248	1 297	Amériques
Europe	2 295	2 352	2 644	2 788	2 337	Europe
Asia, East and South East/Oceania	38 220	39 993	42 199	44 623	47 547	Asie, Est et Sud-Est et Océanie
Region not specified	485	210	57	946	904	Région non spécifiée
Venezuela[5]	**495 921**	**699 837**	**758 503**	**813 862**	**685 429**	**Venezuela**[5]
Africa	566	799	866	929	3 364	Afrique
Americas	276 902	390 761	423 517	454 427	366 315	Amériques
Europe	210 917	297 865	322 606	346 182	301 795	Europe
Asia, East and South East/Oceania	4 334	5 877	6 597	7 065	9 179	Asie, Est et Sud-Est et Océanie
Southern Asia	576	813	900	966	462	Asie du Sud
Western Asia	1 056	1 507	1 619	1 716	1 051	Asie occidentale
Region not specified	1 570	2 215	2 398	2 577	3 263	Région non spécifiée
Viet Nam[2 3 60]	**1 018 244**	**1 351 296**	**1 607 155**	**1 715 637**	**1 520 128**	**Viet Nam**[2 3 60]
Africa	...	...	...	508	...	Afrique
Americas	261 914	189 090	146 488	212 432	176 578	Amériques
Europe	165 794	190 710	128 487	202 974	123 002	Europe
Asia, East and South East/Oceania	315 105	450 557	705 895	1 033 553	679 577	Asie, Est et Sud-Est et Océanie
Southern Asia	...	...	...	5 755	...	Asie du Sud
Region not specified	275 431	520 939	626 285	260 415	540 971	Région non spécifiée
Yemen[1]	**39 929**	**61 346**	**74 476**	**83 754**	**...**	**Yémen**[1]
Africa	1 377	1 611	1 610	2 138	...	Afrique
Americas	3 594	3 207	3 293	4 462	...	Amériques
Europe	26 809	41 474	48 597	58 868	...	Europe
Asia, East and South East/Oceania	3 097	5 335	5 475	8 082	...	Asie, Est et Sud-Est et Océanie
Western Asia	5 052	9 719	15 501	10 204	...	Asie occidentale
Yugoslavia[8]	**246 206**	**227 538**	**301 428**	**298 415**	**282 639**	**Yougoslavie**[8]
Americas	2 064	3 839	5 864	6 288	9 952	Amériques
Europe	239 694	218 412	285 005	280 363	258 992	Europe
Asia, East and South East/Oceania	826	1 119	2 073	1 942	2 156	Asie, Est et Sud-Est et Océanie
Region not specified	3 622	4 168	8 486	9 822	11 539	Région non spécifiée
Zambia[5]	**140 901**	**159 217**	**270 747**	**340 897**	**362 025**	**Zambie**[5]
Africa	107 130	120 092	192 923	203 777	260 162	Afrique
Americas	4 860	5 152	12 438	27 819	14 893	Amériques
Europe	22 143	22 934	44 023	71 427	67 055	Europe
Asia, East and South East/Oceania	3 552	6 962	16 364	34 419	17 494	Asie, Est et Sud-Est et Océanie
Southern Asia	3 058	3 901	4 560	3 455	2 421	Asie du Sud
Western Asia	158	176	353	...	...	Asie occidentale
Region not specified	...	...	86	...	...	Région non spécifiée
Zimbabwe[5 61]	**1 105 849**	**1 539 352**	**1 745 904**	**1 495 676**	**2 090 407**	**Zimbabwe**[5 61]
Africa	949 283	1 122 698	1 137 610	945 652	1 583 343	Afrique
Americas	30 330	40 309	43 864	62 224	121 104	Amériques
Europe	104 021	151 729	179 348	227 847	305 490	Europe
Asia, East and South East/Oceania	15 232	34 302	41 284	56 286	80 470	Asie, Est et Sud-Est et Océanie
Region not specified	6 983	190 314	343 798	203 667	...	Région non spécifiée

Source:
World Tourism Organization (WTO), Madrid, "Yearbook of Tourism Statistics", 52nd edition, 2000 and the WTO Statistics Database.

Source:
Organisation mondiale du tourisme (OMT), Madrid, "Annuaire des statistiques du tourisme", 52e édition, 2000 et la base de données de l'OMT.

72
Tourist arrivals by region of origin
[cont.]

Arrivées de touristes par région de provenance
[suite]

+   For a listing of the Member States of the
regions of origin, see Annex I, with the following
exceptions:
   Africa includes the countries and territories
listed under Africa in Annex I but excludes Egypt,
Guinea-Bissau, Liberia, Libyan Arab Jamahiriya, Mozambique
and Western Sahara.
   Americas is as shown in Annex I, but excludes
Falkland Islands (Malvinas), French Guyana, Greenland and
Saint Pierre and Miquelon.
   Europe is as shown in Annex I, but excludes
Andorra, Channel Islands, Faeroe Islands, Holy See, Isle of
Man and Svalbard and Jan Mayen Islands. The Europe group
also includes Armenia, Azerbaijan, Cyprus, Israel,
Kyrgyzstan, Turkey and Turkmenistan.
   Asia, East and South East/Oceania includes the
countries and territories listed under Eastern Asia and
South-eastern Asia in Annex I (except for East Timor), and
under Oceania except for Christmas Island, Cocos Island,
Norfolk Island, Nauru, Wake Island, Johnston Island, Midway
Islands, Pitcairn, Tokelau and Wallis and Futuna Islands.
The Asia, East and South East/Oceania group also includes
Taiwan Province of China.
   Southern Asia is as shown in Annex I under
South-central Asia, but excludes Kazakhstan, Kyrgyzstan,
Tajikistan, Turkmenistan and Uzbekistan.
   Western Asia is as shown in Annex I but excludes
Armenia, Azerbaijan, Cyprus, Georgia, Israel, Occupied
Palestinian Territory, and Turkey. The Western Asia group
also includes Egypt and the Libyan Arab Jamahiriya.

†   For information on recent changes in country or
area nomenclature pertaining to former Czechoslovakia,
Germany, Hong Kong Special Administrative Region (SAR) of
China, Macao Special Administrative Region (SAR) of China,
SFR of Yugoslavia and the former USSR, see Annex I - Country
or area nomenclature, regional and other groupings.

††   For statistical purposes, the data for
China do not include those for Hong Kong Special
Administrative Region (Hong Kong SAR), Macao Special
Administrative Region (Macao SAR) and Taiwan province of
China.

1   International tourist arrivals at hotels and similar
   establishments.
2   Including nationals of the country residing abroad.
3   International visitor arrivals at frontiers (including
   tourists and same-day visitors).
4   1987 - 1989: including arrivals from Western Samoa.
   Beginning 1990, excluding arrivals from Western Samoa.

5   International tourist arrivals at frontiers (excluding
   same-day visitors).
6   Excluding nationals of the country residing abroad.
7   Air and sea arrivals.
8   International tourist arrivals at collective tourism
   establishments.

+   On se reportera à l'Annexe I pour les États
Membres classés dans les différentes régions de provenance,
avec les exceptions ci-après :
   Afrique - Comprend les États et territoires
énumérés à l'Annexe I, sauf l'Égypte, la Guinée-Bissau, le
Libéria, la Jamahiriya arabe libyenne, le Mozambique et le
Sahara occidental.
   Amériques - Comprend les États et territoires
énumérés à l'Annexe I, sauf les îles Falkland (Malvinas), le
Groënland, la Guyane française et Saint-Pierre-et-Miquelon.
   Europe - Comprend les États et territoires
énumérés à l'Annexe I, sauf l'Andorre, les îles
Anglo-normandes, les îles Féroé, l'île de Man, le
Saint-Siège et les îles Svalbard et Jan Mayen. Le Groupe
comprend en revanche l'Arménie, l'Azerbaïdjan, Chypre,
Israël, l'Kirghizistan, la Turquie et le Turkménistan.
   L'Asie de l'Est et du Sud-Est/Océanie - Comprend
les États et territoires énumérés à l'Annexe I dans les
Groupes Asie de l'Est et Asie du Sud-Est sauf le Timor
oriental, et les États et territoires énumérés dans le
Groupe Océanie sauf les îles Christmas, les îles Cocos,
l'île Johnston, les îles Midway, Nauru, l'île Norfolk,
Pitcairn, Tokélou, l'île Wake et Wallis-et-Futuna. Le
Groupe Asie de l'Est et du Sud-Est/Océanie comprend en
revanche la Province chinoise de Taiwan.
   Asie du Sud - Comprend les États et territoires
énumérés à l'Annexe I, sauf le Kazakhstan, le Kirghizistan,
l'Ouzbékistan, le Tadjikistan et le Turkménistan.
   Asie occidentale - Comprend les États et
territoires énumérés à l'Annexe I, sauf l'Arménie,
l'Azerbaïdjan, Chypre, la Géorgie, Israël, le territoire
Palestinien Occupé et la Turquie. Le Groupe comprend en
revanche l'Égypte et la Jamahiriya arabe libyenne.

†   Pour les modifications récentes de nomenclature
de pays ou de zone concernant l'Allemagne, Hong Kong, région
administrative spéciale (RAS) de Chine, Macao, région
administrative spéciale (RAS) de Chine,
l'ex-Tchécoslovaquie, l'ex-URSS et l'ex-Rfs de Yougoslavie,
voir annexe I - Nomenclature des pays ou des zones,
groupements régionaux et autres groupements.

††   Les données statistiques relatives à
la Chine ne comprennent pas celles qui concernent la région
administrative spéciale de Hong Kong (la RAS de Hong Kong),
la région administrative spéciale de Macao (la RAS de Macao)
et la province chinoise de Taiwan.

1   Arrivées de touristes internationaux dans les hôtels et
   établissements assimilés.
2   Y compris les nationaux du pays résidant à l'étranger.
3   Arrivées de visiteurs internationaux aux frontières (y
   compris touristes et visiteurs de la journée).
4   1987 - 1989: y compris des arrivées en provenance de Samoa
   occidentale. A partir de 1990, à l'exclusion des arrivées
   en provenance de Samoa occidentale.
5   Arrivées de touristes internationaux aux frontières (à
   l'exclusion de visiteurs de la journée).
6   A l'exclusion des nationaux du pays résidant à l'étranger.
7   Arrivées par voie aérienne et maritime.
8   Arrivées de touristes internationaux dans les établissements
   d'hébergement collectifs.

72

Tourist arrivals by region of origin
[cont.]

Arrivées de touristes par région de provenance
[suite]

9 Excluding crew members.
10 Including transit passengers, border permits and returning residents.
11 Air arrivals.
12 International tourist arrivals in hotels of regional capitals.
13 Excluding arrivals from the Netherlands Antilles.

14 Excluding returning residents.
15 1998: Change in methodology.
16 1998: Excluding children without own passports.
17 Excluding ethnic Chinese arriving from "China, Hong Kong SAR", Macao SAR and Taiwan: 1987: 25,174,446; 1988: 29,852,598; 1989: 28,040,424; 1990: 25,714,506; 1991: 30,639,658; 1992: 34,108,578; 1993: 36,871,088; 1994: 38,502,396; 1995: 40,499,795; 1996: 44,383,182; 1997: 50,159,917; 1998: 56,370,654. Also including stateless persons and employees of the United Nations Organizations.

18 Including arrivals by sea, land and by air (helicopter). 1995, Nov.: Arrivals by air began (Macao SAR International Airport). Including stateless and Chinese people who do not have permanent residency in Hong Kong SAR, China: 1992: 93,965; 1993: 92,679; 1994: 147,304; 1995: 167,361; 1996: 189,364; 1997: 182,344.

19 International tourist arrivals at HS in Brazzaville, Pointe Noire, Loubomo, Owando and Sibiti.
20 Air arrivals at Rarotonga.
21 Prior to 1997, air arrivals at the International FHB Airport at Port Bouet. Arrivals at land frontiers, Bouake Airport and Air Ivoire Airport at Abidjan are not taken into consideration. 1997: Air arrivals at the International FHB Airport at Port Bouet and arrivals at land frontiers.

22 1991: January-June; 1992: Incomplete; 1993: July-December; 1994: January-June; 1995: estimate; 1998: Arrivals through "Ndjiti" and "Beach" posts and including nationals of the country residing abroad.
23 Prior to 1996: estimates.
24 1987-1995: Air arrivals. 1996-1998: Departures by air.

25 International tourist arrivals at Addis Ababa Airport.
26 Prior to 1997: estimates.
27 Since 1989 "survey at frontiers and car study realized by SOFRES". 1992, 1993 and 1995: Estimates based on the frontier survey. 1994 and 1996: Frontier survey.

28 1995-1997: Air arrivals.
29 Charter tourists only.
30 From 1992 including camping sites.

31 The data relate to the territory of the Federal Republic of Germany prior to 3 October 1990. As of 1990, tourists from the former German Democratic Republic will be regarded as domestic tourists.

32 Data based on surveys.
33 Air arrivals at Conakry airport.
34 Departures.

9 A l'exclusion des membres des équipages.
10 Y compris passagers en transit, passages à la frontière et résidents de retour de voyage.
11 Arrivées par voie aérienne.
12 Arrivées de touristes internationaux dans les hôtels des capitales de département.
13 A l'exclusion des arrivées en provenance des Antilles Néerlandaises.

14 A l'exclusion des résidants qui retournent au pays.
15 1998: Changement de méthodologie.
16 1998: A l'exclusion d'enfants sans passeports personnels.
17 A l'exclusion des arrivées de personnes d'ethnie chinoise en provenance de "Chine, Hong Kong RAS", Macao RAS et Taiwan: 1987: 25.174.446; 1988: 29.852.598; 1989: 28.040.424; 1990: 25.714.506; 1991: 30.639.658; 1992: 34.108.578; 1993: 36.871.088; 1994: 38.502.396; 1995: 40.499.795; 1996: 44.383.182; 1997: 50.159.917; 1998: 56.370.654. Y compris également les apatrides et les employés des organisations des Nations Unis.

18 Y compris les arrivées par mer, terre et air (hélicoptère). 1995, Nov.: Début de l'inclusion des arrivées par air (Aéroport international de Macao SAR). Y compris les apatrides et les chinois qui ne résident pas de manière permanente à Hong Kong SAR, Chine: 1992: 93.965; 1993: 92.679; 1994: 147.304; 1995: 167.361; 1996: 189.364; 1997: 182.344.

19 Arrivées de touristes internationaux dans HA de Brazzaville, Pointe Noire, Loubomo et Sibiti.
20 Arrivées par voie aérienne à Rarotonga.
21 Avant 1997, arrivées par voie aérienne à l'aéroport international FHB de Port-Bouet. Les arrivées aux frontières terrestres, à l'aéroport de Bouaké, ainsi qu'à l'aéroport Air Ivoire d'Abidjan ne sont pas prises en compte. 1997: Arrivées par voie aérienne à l'aéroport international FHB de Port-Bouet et arrivées aux frontières terrestres.

22 1991: Janvier-juin; 1992: Incomplet; 1993: Juillet-décembre; 1994: Janvier-juin; 1995: estimation; 1998: Arrivées aux postes de "Ndjih" et "Beach" et y compris les nationaux de pays résident à l'étranger.
23 Avant 1996, estimations.
24 1987-1995: Arrivées par voie aérienne. 1996-1998: Départs par voie aérienne.

25 Arrivées par voie aérienne (Aéroport Addis-Abeba).
26 Avant 1997: estimations.
27 A partir de 1989 "enquête aux frontières et étude autocar réalisée par la SOFRES". 1992, 1993 et 1995: Estimation sur la base des enquêtes aux frontières. 1994 et 1996: Enquêtes aux frontières.

28 1995-1997: Arrivées par voie aérienne.
29 Arrivées en vols à la demande seulement.
30 A partir de 1992 les chiffres incluent les terrains de camping.

31 Les données se réfèrent au territoire de la République fédérale d'Allemagne avant le 3 octobre 1990. A partir de 1990, les touristes en provenance de l'ancienne République Démocratique Allemande seront considérés comme des touristes nationaux.

32 Données obtenues au moyen d'enquêtes.
33 Arrivées par voie aérienne à l'aéroport de Conakry.
34 Départs.

72
Tourist arrivals by region of origin
[*cont.*]

Arrivées de touristes par région de provenance
[*suite*]

35 Prior to 1996: travellers; 1996: New methodology, excluding seasonal and border workers.
36 1996: Departures.
37 Arrivals at Tarawa and Christmas Islands.
38 Including nationals residing abroad and from June 1988, also crew members.
39 Excluding Syrian nationals.
40 1992: Excluding sanatoria and rest houses.
41 Foreign tourist departures; includes Singapore residents crossing the frontier by road through Johore Causeway.

42 Arrivals at Yangon by air.
43 Air arrivals (Niamey Airport).
44 Including Niuans residing usually in New Zealand.

45 Air arrivals (Palau International Airport).

46 Total number of visitors broken down by permanent residence who arrived in Panama at Tocumen International Airport and Paso Canoa border post.
47 Including arrivals from abroad to insular possessions of Madeira and the Azores.
48 Persons who enjoyed the services of the economic agents which carry out the tourist's activity in the republic (except left-bank Dniester river regions and municipality of Bender).
49 Data for 1992 correspond to all CIS countries. 1994: Excluding arrivals by road from Belarus, Kazakhstan and Uzbekistan.
50 Prior to 1994, air arrivals. Beginning 1994, air and sea arrivals.
51 Including visitors to St. Maarten (the French side of the island).
52 Including Italian visitors.
53 Data for 1993 cannot be compared to previous years because one of the most important tourist regions, Zinginchor, did not open during that year, resulting in a drop in arrivals and nights.
54 Including Malaysian citizens arriving by land.
55 Beginning January 1992, contract and border traffic concession workers are excluded.
56 Hotels and "hostales" (accommodation establishments providing limited services).
57 Arrivals at Zanderij Airport.
58 Prior to 1996, excluding nationals of the country residing abroad. Beginning 1996, including nationals of the country residing abroad.
59 Data refer to Dubai only.
60 1992: air arrivals only.
61 Excluding transit passengers.

35 Avant 1996: voyageurs; 1996: Nouvelle méthodologie, à l'exclusion des travailleurs saisoniers et frontaliers.
36 1996: Départs.
37 Arrivées aux Iles Tarawa et Christmas.
38 Y compris les nationaux résidant à l'étranger, à partir de juin 1988, également membres des équipages.
39 A l'exclusion des ressortissants syriens.
40 1992: A l'exclusion des sanatoria et des maisons de repos.
41 Départs de touristes étrangers; y compris les résidents de Singapour traversant la frontière par voie terrestre à travers le Johore Causeway.
42 Arrivées à Yangon par voie aérienne.
43 Arrivées par voie aérienne (Aéroport de Niamey).
44 Y compris les nationaux de Niue résidant habituellement en Nouvelle-Zélande.
45 Arrivées par voie aérienne (Aéroport international de Palau).
46 Nombre total de visiteurs arrivées au Panama par l'aéroport international de Tocúmen et le poste frontière de Paso Canoa, classés selon leur résidence permanente.
47 Y compris les arrivées en provenance de l'étranger aux possessions insulaires de Madère et des Açores.
48 Personnes qui ont bénéficié des services des agents économiques chargés de l'activité touristique dans le pays (à l'exception des régions de la rive gauche du Dniester et la municipalité de Bender).
49 Les données de 1992 couvrent l'ensemble des pays CEI. 1994: Exception faite des arrivées par le route en provenance de Bélarus, Kazakhstan et Ouzbékistan.
50 Avant 1996, arrivées par voie aérienne. A partir de 1994, arrivées par voie aérienne et maritime.
51 Y compris les visiteurs à Saint-Martin (partie française de l'île).
52 Y compris les visiteurs italiens.
53 Les données de 1993 ne sont pas comparables à celles des années antérieures, étant donné que région de Ziguinchor, la plus touristique, n'a ouvert durant toute l'année. D'ou les importantes baisses en arrivées et nuitées.
54 Y compris les arrivées de malaysiens par voie terrestre.
55 A partir de janvier 1992, les données excluent les travailleurs contractuels et ceux de la zone frontière.
56 Hôtels et "hostales" (établissements d'hébergement offrant des services limités).
57 Arrivées à l'aéroport de Zanderij.
58 Avant 1996, à l'exclusion des nationaux du pays résidant à l'étranger. A partir de 1996, y compris les nationaux du pays résidant à l'étranger.
59 Les données se réfèrent au Dubai seulement.
60 1992 : arrivées par voie aérienne seulement.
61 A l'exclusion des passagers en transit.

73
Tourist arrivals and international tourism receipts
Arrivées de touristes et recettes touristiques internationales

Region, country or area Région, pays ou zone	Number of tourist arrivals (000) Nombre d'arrivées de touristes (000)					Tourist receipts (million US dollars) Recettes touristiques (millions de dollars E. - U.)				
	1994	1995	1996	1997	1998	1994	1995	1996	1997	1998
World *Monde*	550 322	565 456	597 417	618 345	636 738	355 083	406 067	436 807	438 479	440 313
Africa **Afrique**	**21 305**	**23 083**	**25 390**	**26 956**	**28 223**	**9 504**	**10 763**	**12 457**	**13 133**	**12 452**
Algeria Algérie	805	520	605	635	678	36	27	24	6	24
Angola Angola	11	9	21	45	52	13	10	9	9	8
Benin Bénin	111	138	143	148	152	23	27	29	31	33
Botswana Botswana	625	644	707	734	740	124	162	93	136	175
Burkina Faso Burkina Faso	118	124	131	138	160	24	25	31	39	42
Burundi Burundi	30	34	27	11	15	2	1	1	1	1
Cameroon Cameroun	98	100	101	133	135	28	36	38	39	40
Cape Verde Cap-Vert	31	28	37	45	52	9	10	11	15	20
Central African Rep. Rép. centrafricaine	24	26	21	17	7	6	5	5	5	6
Chad Tchad	19	7	8	9	11	12	10	10	9	10
Comoros Comores	27	23	24	26	27	16	21	23	26	16
Congo Congo	30	37	40	26	25	4	14	10	10	10
Côte d'Ivoire Côte d'Ivoire	157	188	237	274	301	53	89	93	95	108
Dem. Rep. of the Congo Rép. dém. du Congo	18	35	37	30	53	5	5	5	2	2
Djibouti Djibouti	22	21	20	20	21	3	4	4	4	4
Egypt Egypte	2 356	2 872	3 528	3 657	3 213	2 006	2 684	3 204	3 727	2 564
Eritrea Erythrée	222	315	417	410	188	...	58	69	90	91
Ethiopia Ethiopie	98	103	109	115	91	25	26	28	36	11
Gabon Gabon	119	125	145	167	192	5	7	7	7	8
Gambia Gambie	78	45	77	85	91	30	23	31	32	33
Ghana Ghana	271	286	305	325	335	228	233	249	266	274

73
Tourist arrivals and international tourism receipts
[cont.]

Arrivées de touristes et recettes touristiques internationales
[suite]

Region, country or area Région, pays ou zone	Number of tourist arrivals (000) Nombre d'arrivées de touristes (000)					Tourist receipts (million US dollars) Recettes touristiques (millions de dollars E. - U.)				
	1994	1995	1996	1997	1998	1994	1995	1996	1997	1998
Guinea Guinée	...	...	12	17	23	1	1	6	5	1
Kenya Kenya	928	896	925	907	857	627	447	465	361	233
Lesotho Lesotho	97	87	134	144	150	17	27	32	22	18
Libyan Arab Jamah. Jamah. arabe libyenne	52	56	88	50	32	7	6	6	6	18
Madagascar Madagascar	66	75	83	101	121	46	58	65	74	91
Malawi Malawi	163	192	194	206	178	9	9	5	11	15
Mali Mali	27	42	98	75	83	24	25	29	26	50
Mauritania Mauritanie	...	...	...	...	...	11	11	19	21	21
Mauritius Maurice	401	422	487	536	558	357	430	452	485	503
Morocco Maroc	3 465	2 602	2 693	3 072	3 242	1 236	1 304	1 674	1 449	1 675
Namibia Namibie	326	399	461	502	560	226	278	293	333	288
Niger Niger	11	17	17	19	20	16	15	17	18	18
Nigeria Nigéria	196	656	822	611	739	34	54	85	118	142
Réunion Réunion	263	304	347	370	391	176	216	258	249	265
Rwanda Rwanda	1	1	1	1	2	2	2	4	17	19
Sao Tome and Principe Sao Tomé-et-Principe	6	6	6	5	5	2	2	2	2	2
Senegal Sénégal	240	280	282	314	352	115	161	149	153	178
Seychelles Seychelles	110	121	131	130	128	103	98	107	122	111
Sierra Leone Sierra Leone	72	38	46	48	50	10	6	10	3	3
Somalia Somalie	15	10	10	10	10	...	...	...	...	...
South Africa Afrique du Sud	3 669	4 488	4 944	5 653	5 898	2 064	2 125	2 575	2 769	2 738
Sudan Soudan	38	63	57	30	39	4	8	8	4	8
Swaziland Swaziland	336	300	339	340	319	35	48	38	39	37

73
Tourist arrivals and international tourism receipts
[*cont.*]

Arrivées de touristes et recettes touristiques internationales
[*suite*]

Region, country or area Région, pays ou zone	Number of tourist arrivals (000) Nombre d'arrivées de touristes (000)					Tourist receipts (million US dollars) Recettes touristiques (millions de dollars E. - U.)				
	1994	1995	1996	1997	1998	1994	1995	1996	1997	1998
Togo Togo	44	53	58	92	69	11	13	13	13	15
Tunisia Tunisie	3 856	4 120	3 885	4 263	4 718	1 317	1 402	1 451	1 414	1 557
Uganda Ouganda	153	188	205	227	238	40	78	117	135	142
United Rep.Tanzania Rép.-Unie de Tanzanie	254	285	315	347	450	192	259	322	392	570
Zambia Zambie	141	163	264	341	362	43	47	60	75	75
Zimbabwe Zimbabwe	1 105	1 539	1 746	1 495	2 090	125	154	219	230	177
America, North **Amérique du Nord**	**94 002**	**97 146**	**102 171**	**103 052**	**104 468**	**84 813**	**91 174**	**99 866**	**105 532**	**105 679**
Anguilla Anguilla	44	39	37	43	44	54	49	48	57	58
Antigua and Barbuda Antigua-et-Barbuda	255	212	220	232	226	293	247	258	269	256
Aruba Aruba	582	619	641	650	647	468	521	614	668	715
Bahamas Bahamas	1 516	1 598	1 633	1 618	1 540	1 327	1 346	1 398	1 416	1 408
Barbados Barbade	426	442	447	472	512	598	612	644	657	703
Belize Belize	129	131	133	146	157	71	77	89	87	99
Bermuda Bermudes	416	387	390	380	369	525	488	472	478	487
British Virgin Islands Iles Vierges britanniques	239	219	244	244	279	215	211	227	219	230
Canada Canada	15 972	16 932	17 285	17 636	18 867	6 998	7 882	8 616	8 828	9 396
Cayman Islands Iles Caïmanes	341	361	373	381	404	334	394	368	436	450
Costa Rica Costa Rica	761	785	781	811	943	626	660	689	719	884
Cuba Cuba	617	742	999	1 153	1 390	763	977	1 185	1 354	1 571
Dominica Dominique	57	60	63	65	66	31	34	37	40	38
Dominican Republic Rép. dominicaine	1 717	1 776	1 926	2 211	2 309	1 429	1 576	1 763	2 099	2 142
El Salvador El Salvador	181	235	283	387	542	29	41	44	75	125
Grenada Grenade	109	108	108	111	116	56	54	55	55	59

73
Tourist arrivals and international tourism receipts
[*cont.*]

Arrivées de touristes et recettes touristiques internationales
[*suite*]

Region, country or area Région, pays ou zone	Number of tourist arrivals (000) Nombre d'arrivées de touristes (000)					Tourist receipts (million US dollars) Recettes touristiques (millions de dollars E. - U.)				
	1994	1995	1996	1997	1998	1994	1995	1996	1997	1998
Guadeloupe Guadeloupe	556	640	625	660	693	389	458	496	372	466
Guatemala Guatemala	537	563	520	576	636	258	277	284	325	394
Haiti Haïti	70	145	150	149	147	27	56	58	57	57
Honduras Honduras	228	264	255	303	318	72	80	115	146	164
Jamaica Jamaïque	1 098	1 147	1 162	1 192	1 225	973	1 069	1 092	1 131	1 197
Martinique Martinique	419	457	477	513	549	379	384	382	400	415
Mexico Mexique	17 182	20 241	21 405	19 351	19 810	6 363	6 179	6 934	7 593	7 897
Montserrat Montserrat	24	19	9	5	7	24	20	10	5	8
Netherlands Antilles Antilles néerlandaises	923[1]	786[1]	681[1]	747[1]	751[1]	642[2]	565[2]	554[2]	624[2]	749[2]
Nicaragua Nicaragua	238	281	303	358	406	40	50	54	74	90
Panama Panama	324	345	362	421	431	262	310	343	374	379
Puerto Rico Porto Rico	3 042	3 131	3 065	3 242	3 396	1 728	1 828	1 898	2 046	2 233
Saint Kitts and Nevis Saint-Kitts-et-Nevis	94	79	84	88	93	77	65	67	72	76
Saint Lucia Sainte-Lucie	219	231	236	248	252	224	268	269	284	291
St. Vincent-Grenadines St. Vincent-Grenadines	55	60	58	65	67	44	53	64	71	74
Trinidad and Tobago Trinité-et-Tobago	266	260	266	324	348	87	73	108	193	201
Turks and Caicos Islands Iles Turques et Caïques	72	79	88	93	111	70	53	99	113	196
United States Etats-Unis	44 753	43 318	46 489	47 766	46 395	58 417	63 395	69 751	73 301	71 250
United States Virgin Is. Iles Vierges américaines	540	454	373	411	422	920	822	781	894	921
America, South **Amérique du Sud**	**10 837**	**11 793**	**12 936**	**13 520**	**15 513**	**8 347**	**9 307**	**10 746**	**11 352**	**12 340**
Argentina Argentine	2 089	2 289	2 614	2 764	3 012	1 862	2 144	2 542	2 693	2 936
Bolivia Bolivie	255	284	313	355	434	131	145	159	166	174
Brazil Brésil	1 853	1 991	2 666	2 850	4 818	1 925	2 097	2 469	2 595	3 678

73
Tourist arrivals and international tourism receipts
[*cont.*]

Arrivées de touristes et recettes touristiques internationales
[*suite*]

Region, country or area Région, pays ou zone	Number of tourist arrivals (000) Nombre d'arrivées de touristes (000)					Tourist receipts (million US dollars) Recettes touristiques (millions de dollars E. - U.)				
	1994	1995	1996	1997	1998	1994	1995	1996	1997	1998
Chile Chili	1 634	1 540	1 450	1 644	1 759	846	900	905	1 020	1 062
Colombia Colombie	1 207	1 399	1 254	969	841	660	657	1 120	1 043	939
Ecuador Equateur	472	440	494	529	511	252	255	281	290	291
Guyana Guyana	113	106	92	76	66	85	78	70	60	52
Paraguay Paraguay	406	438	426	395	350	700	1 010	869	753	595
Peru Pérou	386	541	663	747	820	331	428	632	824	913
Suriname Suriname	42	43	53	61	54	13	31	38	63	44
Uruguay Uruguay	1 884	2 022	2 152	2 316	2 163	632	611	717	759	695
Venezuela Venezuela	496	700	759	814	685	910	951	944	1 086	961
Asia Asie	92 233	98 834	107 038	108 910	111 086	69 065	79 750	87 713	84 465	79 289
Afghanistan Afghanistan	5	4	4	4	4	1	1	1	1	1
Armenia Arménie	9	12	13	23	32	...	5	5	7	10
Azerbaijan Azerbaïdjan	77	93	90	123	117	64	70	46	162	125
Bahrain Bahreïn	1 560	1 396	1 201	1 571	1 750	303	247	263	311	366
Bangladesh Bangladesh	140	156	166	182	172	19	23	32	59	51
Bhutan Bhoutan	4	5	5	5	6	4	5	6	6	8
Brunei Darussalam Brunéi Darussalam	622	498	837	850	964	36	37	38	39	37
Cambodia Cambodge	177	220	260	219	286	88	100	118	103	166
China †† Chine ††	19 147	20 034	22 765	23 770	25 073	7 323	8 733	10 200	12 074	12 602
China, Hong Kong SAR† Chine, Hong Kong RAS†	9 331	10 200	11 703	10 406	9 575	8 239	9 604	10 836	9 242	7 083
China, Macao SAR † Chine, Macao RAS †	4 489	4 202	4 690	3 836	4 517	2 701	3 126	3 127	2 956	2 622
Cyprus Chypre	2 069	2 100	1 950	2 088	2 223	1 645	1 788	1 669	1 639	1 671
Georgia Géorgie	...	85	117	313	317	...	...	170	416	423

73
Tourist arrivals and international tourism receipts
[cont.]

Arrivées de touristes et recettes touristiques internationales
[suite]

Region, country or area Région, pays ou zone	Number of tourist arrivals (000) Nombre d'arrivées de touristes (000)					Tourist receipts (million US dollars) Recettes touristiques (millions de dollars E. - U.)				
	1994	1995	1996	1997	1998	1994	1995	1996	1997	1998
India Inde	1 886	2 124	2 288	2 374	2 359	2 320	2 609	2 832	2 913	2 935
Indonesia Indonésie	4 006	4 324	5 034	5 185	4 606	4 785	5 228	6 308	5 321	4 045
Iran (Islamic Rep. of) Iran (Rép. islamique d')	362	452	567	740	1 008	153	190	244	327	477
Iraq Iraq	89	61	51	51	51	12	13	13	13	13
Israel Israël	1 839	2 215	2 100	2 010	1 942	2 440	2 964	2 955	2 836	2 657
Japan Japon	3 468	3 345	3 837	4 218	4 106	3 477	3 226	4 078	4 326	3 742
Jordan Jordanie	858	1 074	1 103	1 127	1 256	581	661	743	774	853
Kazakhstan Kazakhstan	...	...	...	...	...	...	122	199	289	289
Korea, Dem. P. R. Corée, R. p. dém. de	126	128	127	128	130	...	...	...	...	...
Korea, Republic of Corée, République de	3 580	3 753	3 684	3 908	4 250	3 806	5 587	5 430	5 116	5 890
Kuwait Koweït	70	69	73	76	77	101	121	184	188	207
Kyrgyzstan Kirghizistan	...	36	42	87	59	3	5	4	7	7
Lao People's Dem. Rep. Rép. dém. pop. lao	36	60	93	193	200	8	25	44	73	80
Lebanon Liban	380	450	424	558	600	672	710	715	1 000	1 221
Malaysia Malaisie	7 197	7 469	7 138	6 211	5 551	3 440	3 909	4 447	2 702	2 456
Maldives Maldives	280	315	339	366	396	181	210	266	286	303
Mongolia Mongolie	124	108	71	82	197	7	21	10	13	33
Myanmar Myanmar	71	117	172	189	201	24	38	33	34	35
Nepal Népal	327	363	394	422	464	88	117	117	116	153
Oman Oman	283	279	349	375	612	88	92	99	108	112
Pakistan Pakistan	454	378	369	375	429	128	114	146	117	98
Philippines Philippines	1 574	1 760	2 049	2 223	2 149	2 283	2 454	2 701	2 831	2 413
Qatar Qatar	241	294	327	435	451	...	...	...	...	...

73
Tourist arrivals and international tourism receipts
[*cont.*]

Arrivées de touristes et recettes touristiques internationales
[*suite*]

Region, country or area	Number of tourist arrivals (000) Nombre d'arrivées de touristes (000)					Tourist receipts (million US dollars) Recettes touristiques (millions de dollars E. - U.)				
Région, pays ou zone	1994	1995	1996	1997	1998	1994	1995	1996	1997	1998
Saudi Arabia Arabie saoudite	3 229	3 325	3 458	3 594	3 700	1 140	1 210	1 308	1 420	1 462
Singapore Singapour	6 268	6 422	6 608	6 531	5 631	7 811	8 390	8 012	6 066	5 162
Sri Lanka Sri Lanka	408	403	302	366	381	230	225	173	216	231
Syrian Arab Republic Rép. arabe syrienne	718	815	830	891	1 267	1 149	1 338	1 206	1 035	1 190
Tajikistan Tadjikistan	...	...	...	...	511	...	...	...	...	...
Thailand Thaïlande	6 166	6 952	7 244	7 294	7 843	5 762	7 664	8 664	7 048	5 934
Turkey Turquie	6 033	7 083	7 966	9 040	8 960	4 321	4 957	5 962	8 088	7 809
Turkmenistan Turkménistan	61	218	217	257	300	...	...	66	74	192
United Arab Emirates Emirats arabes unis	1 239	1 601	1 768	1 792	2 184	318	389	459	535	562
Uzbekistan Ouzbékistan	45	92	174	253	272	...	...	15	19	21
Viet Nam Viet Nam	1 018	1 351	1 607	1 716	1 520	85	86	87	88	86
Yemen Yémen	40	61	74	81	88	19	50	46	69	84
Europe **Europe**	**324 684**	**326 520**	**341 122**	**356 984**	**369 118**	**172 626**	**202 030**	**211 410**	**209 731**	**218 498**
Albania Albanie	28	40	56	19	28	58	65	77	27	54
Austria Autriche	17 894	17 173	17 090	16 647	17 352	12 250	13 492	12 780	10 991	11 184
Belarus Bélarus	184	161	234	254	355	39	23	55	25	22
Belgium Belgique	5 309	5 560	5 829	6 037	6 179	5 182	5 859	5 963	5 270	5 437
Bosnia and Herzegovina Bosnie-Herzégovine	6	37	99	100	100	...	7	16	15	15
Bulgaria Bulgarie	3 896	3 466	2 795	2 980	2 667	362	473	450	496	966
Croatia Croatie	2 293	1 324	2 649	3 834	4 112	1 801	1 346	2 014	2 530	2 733
Czech Republic République tchèque	17 000	16 500	17 000	16 830	16 325	2 230	2 875	4 075	3 647	3 719
Denmark Danemark	2 094	2 124	2 125	2 158	2 073	3 174	3 672	3 425	3 185	3 211
Estonia Estonie	550	530	665	730	825	92	353	470	465	534

73
Tourist arrivals and international tourism receipts
[*cont.*]

Arrivées de touristes et recettes touristiques internationales
[*suite*]

Region, country or area Région, pays ou zone	Number of tourist arrivals (000) Nombre d'arrivées de touristes (000)					Tourist receipts (million US dollars) Recettes touristiques (millions de dollars E. - U.)				
	1994	1995	1996	1997	1998	1994	1995	1996	1997	1998
Finland Finlande	1 868	1 779	1 724	1 832	2 644	1 358	1 643	1 637	1 644	1 631
France France	61 312	60 033	62 406	67 310	70 040	24 678	27 527	28 357	28 009	29 931
Germany Allemagne †	14 494	14 847	15 205	15 837	16 511	14 816	17 867	17 445	16 488	16 429
Gibraltar Gibraltar	70	72	66	74	74	149	215	282	178	180
Greece Grèce	10 642	10 130	9 233	10 070	10 916	3 905	4 136	3 723	3 772	5 182
Hungary Hongrie	21 425	20 690	20 674	17 248	15 000	1 428	2 640	3 222	3 440	3 514
Iceland Islande	179	190	201	202	232	147	185	176	173	207
Ireland Irlande	4 309	4 821	5 282	5 587	6 064	2 236	2 691	3 022	3 189	3 252
Italy Italie	27 480	31 052	32 943	34 692	34 933	24 739	28 729	30 017	29 714	29 866
Latvia Lettonie	622	523	560	625	567	18	20	215	192	182
Liechtenstein Liechtenstein	62	59	56	57	59	...	...	...	...	...
Lithuania Lituanie	760	650	832	1 012	1 416	69	77	316	360	460
Luxembourg Luxembourg	762	768	724	771	789	291	292	295	297	309
Malta Malte	1 176	1 116	1 054	1 111	1 182	641	660	635	648	661
Monaco Monaco	217	233	226	259	278	...	...	...	...	...
Netherlands Pays-Bas	6 178	6 574	6 580	7 834	9 320	5 418	6 563	6 548	6 304	6 788
Norway Norvège	2 830	2 880	2 746	2 702	4 538	2 229	2 362	2 356	2 216	2 212
Poland Pologne	18 825	19 215	19 410	19 520	18 780	6 150	6 614	8 444	8 679	7 946
Portugal Portugal	9 169	9 511	9 730	10 172	11 295	3 828	4 339	4 265	4 619	5 321
Republic of Moldova République de Moldova	21	32	29	21	19	2	4	4	4	2
Romania Roumanie	2 796	2 757	3 028	2 957	2 966	414	590	529	526	260
Russian Federation Fédération de Russie	5 823	9 262	14 587	15 350	15 805	2 412	4 312	6 868	7 164	6 508
San Marino Saint-Marin	533	535	530	532	532	...	...	...	...	...

73
Tourist arrivals and international tourism receipts
[cont.]

Arrivées de touristes et recettes touristiques internationales
[suite]

Region, country or area Région, pays ou zone	Number of tourist arrivals (000) Nombre d'arrivées de touristes (000)					Tourist receipts (million US dollars) Recettes touristiques (millions de dollars E. - U.)				
	1994	1995	1996	1997	1998	1994	1995	1996	1997	1998
Slovakia Slovaquie	902	903	951	814	896	568	620	673	546	489
Slovenia Slovénie	748	732	832	974	977	911	1 082	1 230	1 188	1 117
Spain Espagne	43 232	38 803	40 541	43 252	47 403	21 474	25 388	26 690	26 651	29 737
Sweden Suède	1 960	2 310	2 376	2 388	2 573	2 815	3 464	3 657	3 730	4 189
Switzerland Suisse	12 200	11 500	10 600	10 600	10 900	8 298	9 365	8 826	7 915	7 815
TFYR Macedonia L'ex-R.y. Macédoine	185	147	136	121	157	29	19	21	14	15
Ukraine Ukraine	3 610	3 716	3 854	7 658	6 208	3 398	3 865	3 416	5 340	5 407
United Kingdom Royaume-Uni	20 794	23 537	25 163	25 515	25 745	14 986	18 554	19 173	20 039	20 978
Yugoslavia Yougoslavie	246	228	301	298	283	31	42	43	41	35
Oceania Océanie	7 261	8 080	8 760	8 923	8 330	10 728	13 043	14 615	14 266	12 055
American Samoa Samoa américaines	18	18	21	22	21	10	10	9	10	10
Australia Australie	3 362	3 726	4 165	4 318	4 167	6 559	7 857	9 113	9 057	7 335
Cook Islands Iles Cook	57	49	49	50	49	33	28	50	35	34
Fiji Fidji	319	318	340	359	371	279	283	299	294	266
French Polynesia Polynésie française	166	172	164	180	189	235	326	322	345	354
Guam Guam	1 087	1 362	1 363	1 382	1 137	1 095	1 275	1 415	1 450	1 378
Kiribati Kiribati	4	3	3	5	5	1	1	1	2	1
Marshall Islands Iles Marshall	5	6	6	6	6	2	3	3	3	3
Micronesia (Fed. States of)[3] Micron (Etats fédérés de)[3]	11	11	11	11	11	...	...	...	...	...
New Caledonia Nouvelle-Calédonie	85	86	91	105	104	96	108	114	117	110
New Zealand Nouvelle-Zélande	1 323	1 409	1 529	1 497	1 485	1 663	2 318	2 432	2 093	1 726
Niue Nioué	3	2	2	2	2	...	2	1	2	1
Northern Mariana Islands Iles Marianas du Nord	588	669	728	685	481	584	655	670	672	647

73
Tourist arrivals and international tourism receipts
[*cont.*]

Arrivées de touristes et recettes touristiques internationales
[*suite*]

Region, country or area Région, pays ou zone	Number of tourist arrivals (000) Nombre d'arrivées de touristes (000)					Tourist receipts (million US dollars) Recettes touristiques (millions de dollars E. - U.)				
	1994	1995	1996	1997	1998	1994	1995	1996	1997	1998
Palau Palaos	44	53	69	74	64	...	...	...	...	...
Papua New Guinea Papouasie-Nvl-Guinée	39	42	61	66	67	55	60	68	71	75
Samoa Samoa	67	68	73	68	78	34	33	41	37	38
Solomon Islands Iles Salomon	12	12	11	16	13	17	16	14	16	13
Tonga Tonga	28	29	27	26	27	10	10	13	16	12
Tuvalu Tuvalu	1	1	1	1	1	...	...	...	...	...
Vanuatu Vanuatu	42	44	46	50	52	55	58	50	46	52

Source:
World Tourism Organization (WTO), Madrid, "Yearbook of Tourism Statistics", 52nd edition, 2000 and the WTO Statistics Database.

† For information on recent changes in country or area nomenclature pertaining to former Czechoslovakia, Germany, Hong Kong Special Administrative Region (SAR) of China, Macao Special Administrative Region (SAR) of China, SFR of Yugoslavia and the former USSR, see Annex I - Country or area nomenclature, regional and other groupings.

†† For statistical purposes, the data for China do not include those for Hong Kong Special Administrative Region (Hong Kong SAR), Macao Special Administrative Region (Macao SAR) and Taiwan province of China.

1 Data refer to Bonaire, Curaçao, Saba, Saint Eustatius and Saint Maarten.
2 Data refer to Bonaire, Curaçao, Saba and Saint Maarten.

3 Data refer to the states of Pohnpei, Truk and Yap.

Source:
Organisation mondiale du tourisme (OMT), Madrid, "Annuaire des statistiques du tourisme", 52e édition, 2000 et la base de données de l'OMT.

† Pour les modifications récentes de nomenclature de pays ou de zone concernant l'Allemagne, Hong Kong, région administrative spéciale (RAS) de Chine, Macao, région administrative spéciale (RAS) de Chine, l'ex-Tchécoslovaquie, l'ex-URSS et l'ex-Rfs de Yougoslavie, voir annexe I - Nomenclature des pays ou des zones, groupements régionaux et autres groupements.

†† Les données statistiques relatives à la Chine ne comprennent pas celles qui concernent la région administrative spéciale de Hong Kong (la RAS de Hong Kong), la région administrative spéciale de Macao (la RAS de Macao) et la province chinoise de Taiwan.

1 Les données se rapportent à Bonaire, Curaçao, Saba, Saint-Eustache et Saint-Martin.
2 Les données se rapportent à Bonaire, Curaçao, Saba et Saint-Martin.
3 Les données se rapportent aux États de Pohnpei, Truk et Yap.

74
International tourism expenditures
Dépenses provenant du tourisme international
Million US dollars
Millions de dollars E.-U.

Region, country or area Région, pays ou zone	1989	1990	1991	1992	1993	1994	1995	1996	1997	1998
World *Monde*	202 499	243 731	249 228	286 094	279 818	312 642	358 679	378 278	375 918	...
Africa **Afrique**	**4 284**	**4 666**	**5 594**	**5 529**	**6 013**	**6 452**	**7 233**	**7 638**	**8 386**	...
Algeria Algérie	212	149	140	163	163	24	42	40	40	...
Angola Angola	37	38	65	75	66	88	75	73	70	...
Benin Bénin	10	12	10	12	12	6	5	6	7	7
Botswana Botswana	49	56	67	75	79	76	145	78	92	126
Burkina Faso Burkina Faso	32	32	22	21	21	23	30	32	32	...
Burundi Burundi	14	17	18	21	20	18	25	12	10	12
Cameroon Cameroun	321	279	414	228	225	58	105	107	107	...
Cape Verde Cap-Vert	3	5	3	8	9	12	16	18	17	24
Central African Rep. Rép. centrafricaine	45	51	43	51	50	43	37	39	39	...
Chad Tchad	53	70	63	80	86	26	23	24	24	...
Comoros Comores	5	6	7	7	6	6	7	8	8	3
Congo Congo	86	113	106	95	70	34	52	77	64	...
Côte d'Ivoire Côte d'Ivoire	168	169	163	168	169	157	190	221	215	237
Dem. Rep. of the Congo Rép. dém. du Congo	17	16	16	16	16	12	10	7	7	...
Djibouti Djibouti	...	...	...	3	5	3	4	5	5	...
Egypt Egypte	87	129	225	918	1 048	1 067	1 278	1 317	1 347	1 153
Equatorial Guinea Guinée équatoriale	8	8	9	9	9	8	7	8	8	...
Ethiopia Ethiopie	10	11	7	10	11	15	25	25	40	46
Gabon Gabon	124	137	112	143	154	143	173	178	178	...
Gambia Gambie	5	8	15	13	14	14	14	15	16	...
Ghana Ghana	13	13	14	17	20	20	21	22	23	24
Guinea Guinée	23	30	27	17	28	24	21	27	23	27

74
International tourism expenditures
Million US dollars [cont.]

Dépenses provenant du tourisme international
Millions de dollars E.-U. [suite]

Region, country or area Région, pays ou zone	1989	1990	1991	1992	1993	1994	1995	1996	1997	1998
Kenya Kenya	27	38	24	29	48	114	145	167	194	147
Lesotho Lesotho	10	12	11	11	6	7	13	12	13	12
Libyan Arab Jamah. Jamah. arabe libyenne	512	424	877	154	206	210	212	215	154	143
Madagascar Madagascar	38	40	32	37	34	47	59	72	80	119
Malawi Malawi	10	16	27	24	11	15	16	17	17	...
Mali Mali	56	62	60	71	58	42	49	46	42	29
Mauritania Mauritanie	31	23	26	31	20	18	23	36	48	43
Mauritius Maurice	79	94	110	142	128	143	159	179	177	194
Morocco Maroc	153	184	190	242	245	303	304	300	316	426
Namibia Namibie	...	63	69	72	71	77	90	89	99	88
Niger Niger	32	44	40	30	29	21	21	23	24	25
Nigeria Nigéria	417	576	839	348	298	858	906	1 304	1 816	1 567
Rwanda Rwanda	17	23	17	17	18	18	10	12	13	17
Sao Tome and Principe Sao Tomé-et-Principe	2	2	2	2	2	1	1	1	1	...
Senegal Sénégal	72	105	105	112	50	48	72	53	53	...
Seychelles Seychelles	29	34	24	28	35	31	39	30	30	...
Sierra Leone Sierra Leone	4	4	4	3	4	4	2	2	2	...
South Africa Afrique du Sud	936	1 117	1 148	1 554	1 868	1 861	1 849	1 754	1 961	1 842
Sudan Soudan	144	51	12	33	15	47	43	28	34	30
Swaziland Swaziland	31	35	41	40	43	38	43	42	38	44
Togo Togo	34	40	29	30	20	18	18	19	19	...
Tunisia Tunisie	134	179	128	167	203	216	251	174	160	168
Uganda Ouganda	10	8	16	18	40	78	80	135	137	...
United Rep.Tanzania Rép.-Unie de Tanzanie	23	23	60	73	180	206	360	412	407	493

74
International tourism expenditures
Million US dollars [cont.]
Dépenses provenant du tourisme international
Millions de dollars E.-U. [suite]

Region, country or area Région, pays ou zone	1989	1990	1991	1992	1993	1994	1995	1996	1997	1998
Zambia Zambie	98	54	87	56	56	58	57	59	59	...
Zimbabwe Zimbabwe	63	66	70	55	44	96	106	118	120	131
America, North **Amérique du Nord**	**47 921**	**55 856**	**55 253**	**58 771**	**59 834**	**61 866**	**61 375**	**65 920**	**70 887**	**...**
Anguilla Anguilla	...	4	3	4	5	6	6	6	6	...
Antigua and Barbuda Antigua-et-Barbuda	16	18	20	23	23	24	23	26	26	...
Aruba Aruba	28	40	47	51	58	65	73	120	156	127
Bahamas Bahamas	184	196	200	187	171	193	213	235	250	256
Barbados Barbade	45	47	44	42	53	59	71	74	79	82
Belize Belize	8	7	8	14	20	19	21	26	18	21
Bermuda Bermudes	121	119	126	134	140	143	145	148	148	...
British Virgin Islands Iles Vierges britanniques	...	...	26	30	33	36	40	42	42	...
Canada Canada	8 301	10 931	12 002	11 796	11 133	10 014	10 267	11 253	11 464	10 765
Costa Rica Costa Rica	114	148	149	223	267	300	321	335	358	408
Dominica Dominique	4	4	5	6	5	6	6	7	7	...
Dominican Republic Rép. dominicaine	136	144	154	164	128	145	173	198	221	254
El Salvador El Salvador	104	61	57	58	61	70	72	73	75	81
Grenada Grenade	4	5	5	4	4	4	5	5	5	5
Guatemala Guatemala	126	100	67	103	117	151	141	135	119	157
Haiti Haïti	33	37	35	11	10	14	35	37	35	37
Honduras Honduras	38	38	37	38	55	57	57	60	62	61
Jamaica Jamaïque	114	114	71	87	82	81	148	157	181	198
Mexico Mexique	4 248	5 519	5 812	6 107	5 562	5 338	3 171	3 387	3 891	4 268
Montserrat Montserrat	2	2	2	1	3	3	2	3	3	...
Netherlands Antilles[1] Antilles néerlandaises[1]	63	82	95	105	125	147	209	236	243	128

74
International tourism expenditures
Million US dollars [cont.]
Dépenses provenant du tourisme international
Millions de dollars E.-U. [suite]

Region, country or area Région, pays ou zone	1989	1990	1991	1992	1993	1994	1995	1996	1997	1998
Nicaragua Nicaragua	1	15	28	30	31	30	40	60	65	70
Panama Panama	86	99	109	120	123	123	128	136	164	176
Puerto Rico Porto Rico	589	630	689	736	776	797	833	821	869	874
Saint Kitts and Nevis Saint-Kitts-et-Nevis	3	4	5	5	5	6	5	6	6	6
Saint Lucia Sainte-Lucie	13	17	18	21	20	23	25	29	29	...
St. Vincent-Grenadines St. Vincent-Grenadines	5	4	4	4	5	6	7	8	7	8
Trinidad and Tobago Trinité-et-Tobago	119	122	113	115	106	90	69	75	72	67
Turks and Caicos Islands Iles Turques et Caïques	...	...	...	...	...	134	153	174	235	...
United States ·Etats-Unis	33 416	37 349	35 322	38 552	40 713	43 782	44 916	48 048	52 051	56 105
America, South **Amérique du Sud**	**4 074**	**5 459**	**5 911**	**6 991**	**8 559**	**9 901**	**10 176**	**13 513**	**14 048**	**13 609**
Argentina Argentine	1 014	1 171	1 739	2 212	2 446	2 575	2 067	2 340	2 680	2 111
Bolivia Bolivie	106	130	129	135	137	140	153	162	165	172
Brazil Brésil	751	1 559	1 224	1 332	1 892	2 931	3 412	5 825	5 446	5 731
Chile Chili	397	426	409	536	560	535	774	806	945	906
Colombia Colombie	494	454	509	641	694	841	878	1 117	1 209	1 124
Ecuador Equateur	169	175	177	178	190	203	235	219	227	241
Guyana Guyana	...	...	...	14	18	23	21	22	22	...
Paraguay Paraguay	75	103	118	135	138	177	235	224	285	142
Peru Pérou	263	295	263	255	269	266	297	351	420	466
Suriname Suriname	10	12	16	21	3	3	3	4	4	...
Uruguay Uruguay	167	111	100	104	129	234	236	192	264	265
Venezuela Venezuela	628	1 023	1 227	1 428	2 083	1 973	1 865	2 251	2 381	2 451
Asia **Asie**	**39 563**	**44 835**	**46 978**	**55 462**	**57 816**	**64 589**	**75 263**	**79 950**	**77 357**	**...**
Afghanistan Afghanistan	1	1	1	1	1	1	1	1	1	...

74
International tourism expenditures
Million US dollars [*cont.*]
Dépenses provenant du tourisme international
Millions de dollars E.-U. [*suite*]

Region, country or area Région, pays ou zone	1989	1990	1991	1992	1993	1994	1995	1996	1997	1998
Armenia Arménie	...	...	...	...	...	1	3	22	41	45
Azerbaijan Azerbaïdjan	...	...	...	...	...	...	146	100	186	170
Bahrain Bahreïn	77	94	98	141	130	146	122	109	122	142
Bangladesh Bangladesh	123	78	83	111	153	210	229	200	170	198
Cambodia Cambodge	...	...	...	...	4	8	8	13	12	13
China †† Chine ††	429	470	511	2 512	2 797	3 036	3 688	4 474	8 130	9 205
China, Macao SAR † Chine, Macao RAS †	32	39	49	59	71	102	116	137	153	167
Cyprus Chypre	78	111	113	132	133	176	241	263	278	276
Georgia Géorgie	...	...	...	...	...	...	...	92	228	262
India Inde	416	393	434	470	474	769	996	913	1 342	1 713
Indonesia Indonésie	722	836	969	1 166	1 539	1 900	2 172	2 399	2 411	2 102
Iran (Islamic Rep. of) Iran (Rép. islamique d')	129	340	734	1 109	862	149	241	258	382	788
Israel Israël	1 261	1 442	1 551	1 674	2 052	2 135	2 120	2 278	2 283	2 376
Japan Japon	22 490	24 928	23 983	26 837	26 860	30 715	36 792	37 040	33 041	28 815
Jordan Jordanie	419	336	281	350	344	394	426	381	398	451
Kazakhstan Kazakhstan	...	...	...	...	...	...	283	319	241	143
Korea, Republic of Corée, République de	2 602	3 166	3 784	3 794	3 259	4 088	5 903	6 963	6 262	2 069
Kuwait Koweït	2 250	1 837	2 012	1 797	1 819	2 146	2 248	2 492	2 377	2 517
Kyrgyzstan Kirghizistan	...	...	...	...	...	2	7	6	4	...
Lao People's Dem. Rep. Rép. dém. pop. lao	2	1	6	10	11	18	30	22	21	23
Malaysia Malaisie	1 365	1 450	1 584	1 770	1 838	1 994	2 314	2 575	2 478	...
Maldives Maldives	10	15	19	22	29	28	31	38	40	42
Mongolia Mongolie	...	1	2	4	3	3	20	19	14	45
Myanmar Myanmar	8	16	24	16	10	12	18	28	33	27

74
International tourism expenditures
Million US dollars [*cont.*]
Dépenses provenant du tourisme international
Millions de dollars E.-U. [*suite*]

Region, country or area Région, pays ou zone	1989	1990	1991	1992	1993	1994	1995	1996	1997	1998
Nepal Népal	48	45	38	52	93	112	136	125	103	78
Oman Oman	47	47	47	47	47	47	47	47	47	...
Pakistan Pakistan	337	440	555	680	633	397	449	900	364	352
Philippines Philippines	77	111	61	102	130	196	422	1 266	1 936	1 950
Singapore Singapour	1 373	1 893	2 080	2 489	3 412	3 368	3 860	3 701	3 224	2 676
Sri Lanka Sri Lanka	69	74	97	111	121	170	186	176	180	202
Syrian Arab Republic Rép. arabe syrienne	246	249	256	260	300	512	498	513	545	580
Thailand Thaïlande	750	854	1 266	1 590	2 092	2 906	3 373	4 171	1 888	1 448
Turkey Turquie	565	520	592	776	934	886	912	1 265	1 716	1 754
Turkmenistan Turkménistan	...	...	...	...	...	...	...	73	125	...
Yemen Yémen	81	64	70	101	80	78	76	78	81	83
Europe Europe	101 520	127 322	130 147	153 954	143 005	164 511	198 607	204 159	197 442	...
Albania Albanie	...	4	3	1	7	6	7	12	5	5
Austria Autriche	6 250	7 748	7 362	7 891	7 776	8 788	10 864	11 020	10 102	9 511
Belarus Bélarus	...	...	...	...	56	74	87	119	114	124
Belgium Belgique	4 320	5 477	5 543	6 714	6 338	7 773	9 003	9 330	8 288	8 842
Bulgaria Bulgarie	113	189	128	313	257	244	195	199	222	519
Croatia Croatie	...	729	231	158	375	396	422	510	530	600
Czech Republic République tchèque	300	455	274	467	527	1 585	1 633	2 953	2 380	1 869
Denmark Danemark	2 932	3 676	3 377	3 779	3 214	3 583	4 280	4 142	4 137	4 462
Estonia Estonie	...	...	...	19	25	48	90	98	118	133
Finland Finlande	2 037	2 791	2 677	2 386	1 617	1 608	2 272	2 287	2 082	2 063
France France	10 031	12 423	12 321	13 914	12 836	13 773	16 328	17 746	16 576	17 791
Germany Allemagne †	26 678	33 771	35 819	41 174	40 878	45 198	52 093	51 017	46 317	46 939

74
International tourism expenditures
Million US dollars [*cont.*]

Dépenses provenant du tourisme international
Millions de dollars E.-U. [*suite*]

Region, country or area Région, pays ou zone	1989	1990	1991	1992	1993	1994	1995	1996	1997	1998
Greece Grèce	816	1 090	1 015	1 186	1 003	1 125	1 323	1 210	1 327	1 756
Hungary Hongrie	947	477	443	640	739	925	1 056	957	924	1 115
Iceland Islande	204	286	299	294	270	247	282	308	324	396
Ireland Irlande	989	1 163	1 128	1 361	1 220	1 615	2 034	2 198	2 210	2 374
Italy Italie	6 809	10 304	12 288	19 583	15 903	13 941	14 827	15 805	16 631	17 653
Latvia Lettonie	...	...	...	13	29	31	24	373	326	305
Lithuania Lituanie	...	...	...	...	12	50	106	266	277	292
Malta Malte	107	137	133	138	154	177	214	219	191	193
Netherlands Pays-Bas	6 461	7 376	8 149	9 634	8 920	9 371	11 661	11 528	10 309	10 975
Norway Norvège	2 986	3 679	3 413	3 870	3 364	3 712	4 247	4 509	4 496	4 608
Poland Pologne	215	423	143	132	181	316	5 500	6 240	5 750	4 430
Portugal Portugal	583	867	1 024	1 165	1 893	1 698	2 141	2 283	2 161	2 416
Romania Roumanie	35	103	143	260	195	449	697	666	783	451
Russian Federation Fédération de Russie	...	...	...	...	...	7 092	11 599	10 270	9 363	8 279
Slovakia Slovaquie	131	181	119	155	262	284	330	483	439	475
Slovenia Slovénie	...	...	...	282	305	369	524	543	544	575
Spain Espagne	3 080	4 254	4 544	5 542	4 735	4 129	4 461	4 919	4 467	5 005
Sweden Suède	5 073	6 286	6 286	7 059	4 483	4 864	5 624	6 448	6 898	7 723
Switzerland Suisse	4 978	5 873	5 735	6 099	5 954	6 370	7 346	7 570	6 960	7 094
TFYR Macedonia L'ex-R.y. Macédoine	...	...	...	...	...	22	27	26	27	30
Ukraine Ukraine	...	...	...	...	...	2 650	3 042	2 596	4 454	4 482
United Kingdom Royaume-Uni	15 314	17 560	17 550	19 725	19 477	21 998	24 268	25 309	27 710	32 267
Yugoslavia, SFR† Yougoslavie, Rfs†	131	...	...	...	...	...	...	...	...	...
Oceania **Océanie**	**5 137**	**5 593**	**5 345**	**5 387**	**4 591**	**5 323**	**6 025**	**7 098**	**7 798**	**...**

74
International tourism expenditures
Million US dollars [*cont.*]
Dépenses provenant du tourisme international
Millions de dollars E.-U. [*suite*]

Region, country or area Région, pays ou zone	1989	1990	1991	1992	1993	1994	1995	1996	1997	1998
Australia Australie	4 103	4 535	4 247	4 301	3 451	3 969	4 587	5 445	6 150	5 388
Fiji Fidji	31	32	36	34	47	62	64	70	69	51
Kiribati Kiribati	2	3	2	3	3	3	3	4	4	5
New Zealand Nouvelle-Zélande	944	958	987	977	1 002	1 194	1 289	1 480	1 475	1 405
Papua New Guinea Papouasie-Nvl-Guinée	42	50	57	57	69	71	58	72	78	52
Samoa Samoa	2	2	2	2	2	4	3	4	5	4
Solomon Islands Iles Salomon	10	11	12	11	12	13	13	15	9	6
Tonga Tonga	2	1	1	1	1	3	3	3	3	...
Vanuatu Vanuatu	1	1	1	1	4	4	5	5	5	8

Source:
World Tourism Organization (WTO), Madrid, "Yearbook of
Tourism Statistics", 52nd edition, 2000 and the WTO
Statistics Database.

† For information on recent changes in country or
area nomenclature pertaining to former Czechoslovakia,
Germany, Hong Kong Special Administrative Region (SAR) of
China, Macao Special Administrative Region (SAR) of China,
SFR of Yugoslavia and the former USSR, see Annex I - Country
or area nomenclature, regional and other groupings.

†† For statistical purposes, the data for
China do not include those for Hong Kong Special
Administrative Region (Hong Kong SAR), Macao Special
Administrative Region (Macao SAR) and Taiwan province of
China.

1 Data refer to Curaçao and Saint Maarten.

Source:
Organisation mondiale du tourisme (OMT), Madrid, "Annuaire
des statistiques du tourisme", 52e édition, 2000 et la base
de données de l'OMT.

† Pour les modifications récentes de nomenclature
de pays ou de zone concernant l'Allemagne, Hong Kong, région
administrative spéciale (RAS) de Chine, Macao, région
administrative spéciale (RAS) de Chine,
l'ex-Tchécoslovaquie, l'ex-URSS et l'ex-Rfs de Yougoslavie,
voir annexe I - Nomenclature des pays ou des zones,
groupements régionaux et autres groupements.

†† Les données statistiques relatives à
la Chine ne comprennent pas celles qui concernent la région
administrative spéciale de Hong Kong (la RAS de Hong Kong),
la région administrative spéciale de Macao (la RAS de Macao)
et la province chinoise de Taiwan.

1 Les données se rapportent à Curaçao et Saint-Martin.

Technical notes, tables 72-74

Tables 72 and 73: For statistical purposes, the term "international visitor" describes "any person who travels to a country other than that in which he/she has his/her usual residence but outside his/her usual environment for a period not exceeding 12 months and whose main purpose of visit is other than the exercise of an activity remunerated from within the country visited".

International visitors include:

(a) *Tourists* (overnight visitors): "visitors who stay at least one night in a collective or private accommodation in the country visited"; and

(b) *Same-day visitors*: "visitors who do not spend the night in a collective or private accommodation in the country visited".

The figures do not include immigrants, residents in a frontier zone, persons domiciled in one country or area and working in an adjoining country or area, members of the armed forces and diplomats and consular representatives when they travel from their country of origin to the country in which they are stationed and vice-versa.

The figures also exclude persons in transit who do not formally enter the country through passport control, such as air transit passengers who remain for a short period in a designated area of the air terminal or ship passengers who are not permitted to disembark. This category would include passengers transferred directly between airports or other terminals. Other passengers in transit through a country are classified as visitors.

These data are based generally on a frontier check. In the absence of frontier check figures, data based on arrivals at accommodation establishments are given but these are not strictly comparable with frontier check data as they exclude certain types of tourists such as campers and tourists staying in private houses, while on the other hand they may contain some duplication when a tourist moves from one establishment to another.

Unless otherwise stated, table 72 shows the number of tourist arrivals at frontiers classified by their region of origin. Totals correspond to the total number of arrivals from the regions indicated in the table. However, these totals may not correspond to the number of tourist arrivals shown in table 73. The latter excludes same-day visitors whereas they may be included in table 72. More detailed information can be found in the *Yearbook of Tourism Statistics* [35], published by the World Tourism Organization.

For detailed information on methods of collection for frontier statistics, accommodation statistics and foreign exchange statistics see the *Methodological Supple-*

Notes techniques, tableaux 72 à 74

Tableaux 72 et 73: A des fins statistiques, l'expression *"visiteur international"* désigne "toute personne qui se rend dans un pays autre que celui où elle a son lieu de résidence habituelle, mais différent de son environnement habituel, pour une période de 12 mois au maximum, dans un but principal autre que celui d'y exercer une profession rémunérée".

Entrent dans cette catégorie:

(a) Les *touristes* (visiteurs passant la nuit), c'est à dire "les visiteurs qui passent une nuit au moins en logement collectif ou privé dans le pays visité";

(b) Les *visiteurs ne restant que la journée*, c'est à dire "les visiteurs qui ne passent pas la nuit en logement collectif ou privé dans le pays visité".

Ces chiffres ne comprennent pas les immigrants, les résidents frontaliers, les personnes domiciliées dans une zone ou un pays donné et travaillant dans une zone ou pays limitrophe, les membres des forces armées et les membres des corps diplomatique et consulaire lorsqu'ils se rendent de leur pays d'origine au pays où ils sont en poste, et vice versa.

Ne sont pas non plus inclus les voyageurs en transit, qui ne pénètrent pas officiellement dans le pays en faisant contrôler leurs passeports, tels que les passagers d'un vol en escale, qui demeurent pendant un court laps de temps dans une aire distincte de l'aérogare, ou les passagers d'un navire qui ne sont pas autorisés à débarquer. Cette catégorie comprend également les passagers transportés directement d'une aérogare à l'autre ou à un autre terminal. Les autres passagers en transit dans un pays sont classés parmi les visiteurs.

Ces données reposent en général sur un contrôle à la frontière. A défaut, les données sont tirées des établissements d'hébergement, mais elles ne sont alors pas strictement comparables à celles du contrôle à la frontière, en ce qu'elles excluent, d'une part, certaines catégories de touristes telles que les campeurs et les touristes séjournant dans des maisons privées, et que, d'autre part, elles peuvent compter deux fois le même touriste si celui-ci change d'établissement d'hébergement.

Sauf indication contraire, le tableau 72 indique le nombre d'arrivées de touristes par région de provenance. Les totaux correspondent au nombre total d'arrivées de touristes des régions indiquées sur le tableau. Les chiffres totaux peuvent néanmoins, ne pas coïncider avec le nombre des arrivées de touristes indiqué dans le tableau 73, qui ne comprend pas les visiteurs ne restant que la journée, lesquels peuvent au contraire être inclus dans les chiffres du tableau 72. Pour plus de renseignements, consulter l'*Annuaire des statistiques du tourisme* [35] publié par l'Organisation mondiale du tourisme.

ment to World Travel and Tourism Statistics [59] published by the World Tourism Organization; see also [51] and [52].

Unless otherwise stated, the data on tourist receipts have been supplied by the World Tourism Organization. Tourist receipts are defined as "expenditure of international inbound visitors including their payments to national carriers for international transport. They should also include any other prepayments made for goods/services received in the destination country. They should in practice also include receipts from same-day visitors, except in cases when these are so important as to justify a separate classification. It is also recommended that, for the sake of consistancy with the Balance of Payments recommendations of the International Monetary Fund, international fare receipts be classified separately".

For detailed definitions of tourist receipts, see the *Balance of Payments Yearbook* published by the International Monetary Fund [13].

Table 74: International tourism expenditure are defined as "expenditure of outbound visitors in other countries including their payments to foreign carriers for international transport. They should in practice also include expenditure of residents travelling abroad as same-day visitors, except in cases when these are so important as to justify a separate classification. It is also recommended that, for the sake of consistency with the Balance of Payments recommendations of the International Monetary Fund, international fare expenditure be classified separately".

For more detailed statistics on the number of tourists and expenditures, see the *Yearbook of Tourism Statistics* published by the World Tourism Organization [35]. For detailed information on methods of collection for frontier statistics, accommodation statistics and foreign exchange statistics see the *Methodological Supplement to World Travel and Tourism Statistics* [59] published by the World Tourism Organization; see also [51] and [52].

Pour plus de renseignements sur les méthodes de collecte de données statistiques sur les contrôles aux frontières, l'hébergement et les mouvements de devises, voir *Supplément méthodologique aux statistiques des voyages et du tourisme mondiaux* [59] publié par l'Organisation mondiale du tourisme; voir aussi [51] et [52].

Sauf indication contraire, les données sur les recettes du tourisme ont été fournies par l'Organisation mondiale du tourisme et sont définies comme "les sommes dépensées par les visiteurs internationaux arrivant dans le pays, y compris les sommes versées aux transporteurs nationaux en paiement de transports internationaux. Il faut également y inclure tout autre versement effectué à l'avance pour des biens ou services à recevoir dans le pays de destination. Dans la pratique, il faut également y inclure les recettes provenant de visiteurs ne restant que la journée, sauf dans les cas où elles sont suffisamment importantes pour justifier une classification distincte. Il est recommandé aussi, dans un souci de cohérence avec les recommandations du Fonds monétaire international visant la balance des paiements, de classer à part les recettes au titre des transports internationaux".

Pour des définitions détaillées des recettes touristiques, voir "*Balance of Payments Yearbook*" publié par le Fonds monétaire international [13].

Tableau 74: Les dépenses du tourisme international sont définies comme étant les dépenses effectuées par les résidents du pays en visite à l'étranger, y compris les sommes versées aux transporteurs étrangers en règlement des transports internationaux. En pratique, ce poste devrait également inclure les dépenses des résidents qui voyagent à l'étranger pour la journée, sauf dans le cas où ces dépenses sont suffisamment importantes pour justifier une classification distincte. Il est recommandé aussi, dans un souci de cohérence avec les recommandations du Fonds monétaire international visant la balance des paiements, de classer à part les dépenses au titre des transports internationaux.

Pour des statistiques plus détaillées sur le nombre de touristes et les dépenses, voir l'*Annuaire des statistiques du tourisme* publié par l'Organisation mondiale du tourisme [35].

Pour plus de renseignements sur les méthodes de collecte de données statistiques sur les contrôles aux frontières, l'hébergement et les mouvements de devises, voir *Supplément méthodologique aux statistiques des voyages et du tourisme mondiaux* [59] publié par l'Organisation mondiale du tourisme; voir aussi [51] et [52].

75
Summary of balance of payments
Résumé des balances des paiements
Millions of US dollars
Millions de dollars des E.-U.

Country or area	1993	1994	1995	1996	1997	1998	1999	Pays ou zone
Africa · Afrique								
Angola								**Angola**
Goods: Exports fob	2 900.5	3 016.6	3 722.7	5 095.0	...	...	...	Biens : exportations,fàb
Goods: Imports fob	−1 462.6	−1 454.1	−1 467.7	−2 040.5	...	...	...	Biens : importations,fàb
Serv. & Income: Credit	117.1	163.2	129.0	311.0	...	...	...	Serv. & revenu : crédit
Serv. & Income: Debit	−2 389.3	−2 310.6	−2 834.6	−3 940.0	...	...	...	Serv. & revenu : débit
Current Trans.,nie: Credit	253.4	333.2	312.2	3 949.4	...	...	...	Transf. cour.,nia : crédit
Current Transfers: Debit	−87.6	−88.1	−156.7	−108.6	...	...	...	Transf. courants : débit
Capital Acct.,nie: Credit	0.0	0.0	0.0	0.0	...	...	...	Compte de cap.,nia : crédit
Capital Account: Debit	0.0	0.0	0.0	0.0	...	...	...	Compte de capital : débit
Financial Account,nie	−274.3	−443.4	−924.8	−654.5	...	...	...	Compte d'op. fin., nia
Net Errors and Omissions	−377.1	−244.5	−19.4	149.2	...	...	...	Erreurs et omissions nettes
Reserves and Related Items	1 319.9	1 027.7	1 239.3	−2 761.0	...	...	...	Rés. et postes appareutés
Benin								**Bénin**
Goods: Exports fob	393.5	397.9	419.9	527.7	424.0	414.3	...	Biens : exportations,fàb
Goods: Imports fob	−561.4	−451.5	−622.5	−559.7	−576.9	−572.6	...	Biens : importations,fàb
Serv. & Income: Credit	184.4	161.0	217.8	162.7	141.4	173.4	...	Serv. & revenu : crédit
Serv. & Income: Debit	−207.9	−203.1	−303.3	−246.3	−217.7	−235.9	...	Serv. & revenu : débit
Current Trans.,nie: Credit	118.5	98.5	105.4	92.4	77.8	102.0	...	Transf. cour.,nia : crédit
Current Transfers: Debit	−28.1	−25.9	−30.5	−34.2	−18.5	−32.7	...	Transf. courants : débit
Capital Acct.,nie: Credit	75.5	75.2	85.6	6.4	84.5	66.6	...	Compte de cap.,nia : crédit
Capital Account: Debit	0.0	0.0	0.0	0.0	0.0	0.0	...	Compte de capital : débit
Financial Account,nie	−123.3	−17.6	−126.3	−104.2	−21.3	−8.9	...	Compte d'op. fin., nia
Net Errors and Omissions	−8.1	−16.3	−1.0	6.3	6.7	7.1	...	Erreurs et omissions nettes
Reserves and Related Items	156.9	−18.1	254.9	149.0	100.0	86.7	...	Rés. et postes appareutés
Botswana								**Botswana**
Goods: Exports fob	1 722.2	1 874.3	2 160.2	2 217.5	2 819.8	2 060.6	2 671.0	Biens : exportations,fàb
Goods: Imports fob	−1 455.4	−1 364.3	−1 605.4	−1 467.7	−1 924.5	−1 983.1	−1 996.5	Biens : importations,fàb
Serv. & Income: Credit	745.9	416.9	743.6	664.7	832.3	878.0	802.4	Serv. & revenu : crédit
Serv. & Income: Debit	−586.5	−777.1	−959.8	−1 098.4	−1 207.5	−1 025.5	−1 211.9	Serv. & revenu : débit
Current Trans.,nie: Credit	275.9	356.8	330.7	355.4	456.8	460.9	474.4	Transf. cour.,nia : crédit
Current Transfers: Debit	−275.1	−295.1	−369.5	−176.6	−255.5	−220.8	−222.6	Transf. courants : débit
Capital Acct.,nie: Credit	86.1	19.6	15.4	18.0	29.4	44.2	33.5	Compte de cap.,nia : crédit
Capital Account: Debit	−1.3	−0.4	−0.9	−11.9	−12.5	−12.4	−12.9	Compte de capital : débit
Financial Account,nie	−40.3	41.1	−33.9	42.4	5.6	−202.4	−175.2	Compte d'op. fin., nia
Net Errors and Omissions	−74.5	−136.7	−73.6	−32.9	−108.9	44.6	8.7	Erreurs et omissions nettes
Reserves and Related Items	−397.0	−135.2	−206.6	−510.7	−635.1	−44.2	−371.0	Rés. et postes appareutés
Burkina Faso								**Burkina Faso**
Goods: Exports fob	226.1	215.6	...	...	...	...	...	Biens : exportations,fàb
Goods: Imports fob	−469.1	−344.3	...	...	...	...	...	Biens : importations,fàb
Serv. & Income: Credit	86.1	65.1	...	...	...	...	...	Serv. & revenu : crédit
Serv. & Income: Debit	−237.6	−176.5	...	...	...	...	...	Serv. & revenu : débit
Current Trans.,nie: Credit	389.6	308.0	...	...	...	...	...	Transf. cour.,nia : crédit
Current Transfers: Debit	−66.3	−53.0	...	...	...	...	...	Transf. courants : débit
Capital Acct.,nie: Credit	0.0	0.0	...	...	...	...	...	Compte de cap.,nia : crédit
Capital Account: Debit	0.0	0.0	...	...	...	...	...	Compte de capital : débit
Financial Account,nie	69.1	−13.9	...	...	...	...	...	Compte d'op. fin., nia
Net Errors and Omissions	4.6	−8.3	...	...	...	...	...	Erreurs et omissions nettes
Reserves and Related Items	−2.5	7.3	...	...	...	...	...	Rés. et postes appareutés
Burundi								**Burundi**
Goods: Exports fob	73.9	80.7	112.9	40.4	87.5	64.0	55.0	Biens : exportations,fàb
Goods: Imports fob	−172.8	−172.6	−175.6	−100.0	−96.1	−123.5	−97.3	Biens : importations,fàb
Serv. & Income: Credit	25.8	23.0	26.8	16.9	13.0	11.2	8.2	Serv. & revenu : crédit
Serv. & Income: Debit	−137.0	−113.4	−106.3	−58.7	−62.2	−61.4	−43.9	Serv. & revenu : débit
Current Trans.,nie: Credit	183.8	167.0	154.7	62.5	61.3	59.3	52.9	Transf. cour.,nia : crédit
Current Transfers: Debit	−1.8	−1.6	−2.1	−1.1	−4.5	−3.3	−1.8	Transf. courants : débit
Capital Acct.,nie: Credit	0.0	0.0	0.0	0.0	0.0	0.0	0.0	Compte de cap.,nia : crédit
Capital Account: Debit	−1.2	−0.2	−0.8	−0.3	−0.1	0.0	0.0	Compte de capital : débit
Financial Account,nie	52.5	31.1	21.1	14.1	13.7	63.9	38.7	Compte d'op. fin., nia
Net Errors and Omissions	−7.2	21.1	5.9	−9.2	−2.4	−29.7	−13.0	Erreurs et omissions nettes
Reserves and Related Items	−16.0	−35.2	−36.7	35.3	−10.2	19.5	1.2	Rés. et postes appareutés

75
Summary of balance of payments
Millions of US dollars
Résumé des balances des paiements
Millions de dollars des E.−U.

Country or area	1993	1994	1995	1996	1997	1998	1999	Pays ou zone
Cameroon								**Cameroun**
Goods: Exports fob	1 507.7	1 454.2	1 735.9	...	...	...	...	Biens : exportations,fàb
Goods: Imports fob	−1 005.3	−1 052.3	−1 109.0	...	...	...	...	Biens : importations,fàb
Serv. & Income: Credit	407.9	350.8	316.7	...	...	...	...	Serv. & revenu : crédit
Serv. & Income: Debit	−1 410.6	−829.5	−923.3	...	...	...	...	Serv. & revenu : débit
Current Trans.,nie: Credit	65.2	83.8	100.7	...	...	...	...	Transf. cour.,nia : crédit
Current Transfers: Debit	−130.2	−63.0	−31.2	...	...	...	...	Transf. courants : débit
Capital Acct.,nie: Credit	6.4	14.1	21.1	...	...	...	...	Compte de cap.,nia : crédit
Capital Account: Debit	−0.1	0.0	−0.7	...	...	...	...	Compte de capital : débit
Financial Account,nie	−310.0	−626.4	43.3	...	...	...	...	Compte d'op. fin., nia
Net Errors and Omissions	−16.2	117.0	−138.1	...	...	...	...	Erreurs et omissions nettes
Reserves and Related Items	885.3	551.3	−15.4	...	...	...	...	Rés. et postes appareutés
Cape Verde								**Cap−Vert**
Goods: Exports fob	9.1	14.2	16.6	23.9	43.2	32.7	...	Biens : exportations,fàb
Goods: Imports fob	−152.0	−195.3	−233.6	−207.5	−215.1	−218.3	...	Biens : importations,fàb
Serv. & Income: Credit	44.9	51.2	70.9	80.5	96.2	89.0	...	Serv. & revenu : crédit
Serv. & Income: Debit	−33.2	−39.1	−67.1	−77.4	−80.4	−98.6	...	Serv. & revenu : débit
Current Trans.,nie: Credit	110.4	125.6	156.0	148.4	129.9	142.5	...	Transf. cour.,nia : crédit
Current Transfers: Debit	−3.1	−2.3	−4.4	−2.9	−3.6	−5.1	...	Transf. courants : débit
Capital Acct.,nie: Credit	19.0	20.1	20.9	12.8	6.3	19.0	...	Compte de cap.,nia : crédit
Capital Account: Debit	0.0	0.0	0.0	0.0	0.0	0.0	...	Compte de capital : débit
Financial Account,nie	17.5	39.6	44.5	46.0	44.1	37.0	...	Compte d'op. fin., nia
Net Errors and Omissions	2.4	8.3	−35.6	−1.3	−20.4	12.8	...	Erreurs et omissions nettes
Reserves and Related Items	−15.0	−22.2	31.9	−22.5	−0.2	−10.8	...	Rés. et postes appareutés
Central African Rep.								**Rép. centrafricaine**
Goods: Exports fob	132.5	145.9	...	...	...	...	...	Biens : exportations,fàb
Goods: Imports fob	−158.1	−130.6	...	...	...	...	...	Biens : importations,fàb
Serv. & Income: Credit	53.7	33.1	...	...	...	...	...	Serv. & revenu : crédit
Serv. & Income: Debit	−155.1	−136.5	...	...	...	...	...	Serv. & revenu : débit
Current Trans.,nie: Credit	152.4	92.6	...	...	...	...	...	Transf. cour.,nia : crédit
Current Transfers: Debit	−38.3	−29.2	...	...	...	...	...	Transf. courants : débit
Capital Acct.,nie: Credit	0.0	0.0	...	...	...	...	...	Compte de cap.,nia : crédit
Capital Account: Debit	0.0	0.0	...	...	...	...	...	Compte de capital : débit
Financial Account,nie	−7.1	52.8	...	...	...	...	...	Compte d'op. fin., nia
Net Errors and Omissions	6.3	−15.0	...	...	...	...	...	Erreurs et omissions nettes
Reserves and Related Items	13.7	−13.1	...	...	...	...	...	Rés. et postes appareutés
Chad								**Tchad**
Goods: Exports fob	151.8	135.3	...	...	...	...	...	Biens : exportations,fàb
Goods: Imports fob	−215.2	−212.1	...	...	...	...	...	Biens : importations,fàb
Serv. & Income: Credit	51.4	59.8	...	...	...	...	...	Serv. & revenu : crédit
Serv. & Income: Debit	−250.8	−211.8	...	...	...	...	...	Serv. & revenu : débit
Current Trans.,nie: Credit	192.4	209.4	...	...	...	...	...	Transf. cour.,nia : crédit
Current Transfers: Debit	−46.2	−18.4	...	...	...	...	...	Transf. courants : débit
Capital Acct.,nie: Credit	0.0	0.0	...	...	...	...	...	Compte de cap.,nia : crédit
Capital Account: Debit	0.0	0.0	...	...	...	...	...	Compte de capital : débit
Financial Account,nie	68.8	76.3	...	...	...	...	...	Compte d'op. fin., nia
Net Errors and Omissions	−0.1	−33.0	...	...	...	...	...	Erreurs et omissions nettes
Reserves and Related Items	47.9	−5.5	...	...	...	...	...	Rés. et postes appareutés
Comoros								**Comores**
Goods: Exports fob	21.6	10.8	11.3	...	...	...	...	Biens : exportations,fàb
Goods: Imports fob	−49.5	−44.9	−53.5	...	...	...	...	Biens : importations,fàb
Serv. & Income: Credit	34.4	31.5	37.9	...	...	...	...	Serv. & revenu : crédit
Serv. & Income: Debit	−51.1	−48.3	−52.2	...	...	...	...	Serv. & revenu : débit
Current Trans.,nie: Credit	59.8	50.0	41.1	...	...	...	...	Transf. cour.,nia : crédit
Current Transfers: Debit	−5.5	−6.2	−3.5	...	...	...	...	Transf. courants : débit
Capital Acct.,nie: Credit	0.0	0.0	0.0	...	...	...	...	Compte de cap.,nia : crédit
Capital Account: Debit	0.0	0.0	0.0	...	...	...	...	Compte de capital : débit
Financial Account,nie	4.0	18.5	10.9	...	...	...	...	Compte d'op. fin., nia
Net Errors and Omissions	−5.8	−6.3	−1.8	...	...	...	...	Erreurs et omissions nettes
Reserves and Related Items	−7.8	−5.0	9.9	...	...	...	...	Rés. et postes appareutés
Congo								**Congo**
Goods: Exports fob	1 119.2	958.9	1 167.0	1 554.5	1 744.1	...	...	Biens : exportations,fàb
Goods: Imports fob	−500.1	−612.7	−650.7	−1 361.0	−802.9	...	...	Biens : importations,fàb
Serv. & Income: Credit	67.5	69.0	79.3	102.8	60.8	...	...	Serv. & revenu : crédit
Serv. & Income: Debit	−1 230.4	−1 286.9	−1 237.9	−1 391.3	−1 234.1	...	...	Serv. & revenu : débit
Current Trans.,nie: Credit	50.5	111.3	30.9	29.9	24.7	...	...	Transf. cour.,nia : crédit

75
Summary of balance of payments
Millions of US dollars
Résumé des balances des paiements
Millions de dollars des E.−U.

Country or area	1993	1994	1995	1996	1997	1998	1999	Pays ou zone
Current Transfers: Debit	−59.3	−33.0	−38.3	−44.0	−44.5	...	...	Transf. courants : débit
Capital Acct.,nie: Credit	0.0	0.0	0.0	0.0	0.0	...	...	Compte de cap.,nia : crédit
Capital Account: Debit	0.0	0.0	0.0	0.0	0.0	...	...	Compte de capital : débit
Financial Account,nie	−111.2	605.4	−80.3	657.2	−173.7	...	...	Compte d'op. fin., nia
Net Errors and Omissions	244.0	33.1	120.7	102.1	−122.1	...	...	Erreurs et omissions nettes
Reserves and Related Items	420.0	154.9	609.3	349.7	547.7	...	...	Rés. et postes appareutés
Côte d'Ivoire								**Côte d'Ivoire**
Goods: Exports fob	2 518.7	2 895.9	3 805.9	4 446.1	4 298.7	4 575.1	...	Biens : exportations,fàb
Goods: Imports fob	−1 770.4	−1 606.8	−2 430.3	−2 622.4	−2 479.5	−2 705.1	...	Biens : importations,fàb
Serv. & Income: Credit	773.8	641.6	720.4	737.0	699.7	719.7	...	Serv. & revenu : crédit
Serv. & Income: Debit	−2 219.6	−1 828.6	−2 351.8	−2 382.9	−2 263.1	−2 353.9	...	Serv. & revenu : débit
Current Trans.,nie: Credit	270.9	246.8	277.7	55.5	50.0	50.9	...	Transf. cour.,nia : crédit
Current Transfers: Debit	−465.1	−362.6	−514.3	−546.6	−547.6	−599.2	...	Transf. courants : débit
Capital Acct.,nie: Credit	0.0	527.6	291.3	49.8	39.7	36.3	...	Compte de cap.,nia : crédit
Capital Account: Debit	0.0	0.0	0.0	0.0	0.0	0.0	...	Compte de capital : débit
Financial Account,nie	−356.0	−523.1	−88.6	−697.3	−455.6	−533.9	...	Compte d'op. fin., nia
Net Errors and Omissions	11.1	−11.1	35.6	−36.2	64.8	171.3	...	Erreurs et omissions nettes
Reserves and Related Items	1 236.6	20.3	254.2	997.0	592.8	638.9	....	Rés. et postes appareutés
Djibouti								**Djibouti**
Goods: Exports fob	71.2	56.4	33.5	...	...	...	...	Biens : exportations,fàb
Goods: Imports fob	−255.1	−237.1	−205.0	...	...	...	...	Biens : importations,fàb
Serv. & Income: Credit	187.1	176.0	177.3	...	...	...	...	Serv. & revenu : crédit
Serv. & Income: Debit	−118.0	−96.7	−95.9	...	...	...	...	Serv. & revenu : débit
Current Trans.,nie: Credit	96.6	73.7	85.4	...	...	...	...	Transf. cour.,nia : crédit
Current Transfers: Debit	−16.1	−18.3	−18.4	...	...	...	...	Transf. courants : débit
Capital Acct.,nie: Credit	0.0	0.0	0.0	...	...	...	...	Compte de cap.,nia : crédit
Capital Account: Debit	0.0	0.0	0.0	...	...	...	...	Compte de capital : débit
Financial Account,nie	16.6	39.1	−2.1	...	...	...	...	Compte d'op. fin., nia
Net Errors and Omissions	6.0	7.9	0.7	...	...	...	...	Erreurs et omissions nettes
Reserves and Related Items	11.7	−0.8	24.5	...	...	...	...	Rés. et postes appareutés
Egypt								**Egypte**
Goods: Exports fob	3 545.0	4 044.0	4 670.0	4 779.0	5 525.3	4 403.0	5 236.5	Biens : exportations,fàb
Goods: Imports fob	−9 923.0	−9 997.0	−12 267.0	−13 169.0	−14 156.8	−14 617.0	−15 164.8	Biens : importations,fàb
Serv. & Income: Credit	9 005.0	9 400.0	10 168.0	11 172.0	11 501.4	10 171.0	11 281.5	Serv. & revenu : crédit
Serv. & Income: Debit	−7 334.0	−7 759.0	−6 856.0	−6 640.0	−7 955.0	−7 567.0	−7 496.4	Serv. & revenu : débit
Current Trans.,nie: Credit	7 006.0	4 622.0	4 284.0	3 888.0	4 737.1	5 166.0	4 563.8	Transf. cour.,nia : crédit
Current Transfers: Debit	0.0	−279.0	−253.0	−222.0	−363.1	−122.0	−55.4	Transf. courants : débit
Capital Acct.,nie: Credit	0.0	0.0	0.0	0.0	0.0	0.0	0.0	Compte de cap.,nia : crédit
Capital Account: Debit	0.0	0.0	0.0	0.0	0.0	0.0	0.0	Compte de capital : débit
Financial Account,nie	−762.0	−1 450.0	−1 845.0	−1 459.0	1 957.8	1 901.0	−1 421.4	Compte d'op. fin., nia
Net Errors and Omissions	−1 519.1	255.4	272.0	−73.6	−1 882.3	−721.9	−1 557.6	Erreurs et omissions nettes
Reserves and Related Items	−17.9	1 163.6	1 827.0	1 724.6	635.1	1 386.9	4 613.8	Rés. et postes appareutés
Equatorial Guinea								**Guinée équatoriale**
Goods: Exports fob	61.1	62.0	89.9	175.3	...	...	...	Biens : exportations,fàb
Goods: Imports fob	−51.0	−36.9	−120.6	−292.0	...	...	...	Biens : importations,fàb
Serv. & Income: Credit	9.0	3.4	4.3	5.0	...	...	...	Serv. & revenu : crédit
Serv. & Income: Debit	−47.8	−32.6	−100.6	−229.8	...	...	...	Serv. & revenu : débit
Current Trans.,nie: Credit	37.8	5.7	6.8	4.0	...	...	...	Transf. cour.,nia : crédit
Current Transfers: Debit	−6.1	−1.9	−3.3	−6.6	...	...	...	Transf. courants : débit
Capital Acct.,nie: Credit	0.0	0.0	0.0	0.0	...	...	...	Compte de cap.,nia : crédit
Capital Account: Debit	0.0	0.0	0.0	0.0	...	...	...	Compte de capital : débit
Financial Account,nie	13.9	−15.0	101.6	313.8	...	...	...	Compte d'op. fin., nia
Net Errors and Omissions	−27.2	−2.9	10.3	24.8	...	...	...	Erreurs et omissions nettes
Reserves and Related Items	10.4	18.4	11.5	5.5	...	...	....	Rés. et postes appareutés
Ethiopia								**Ethiopie**
Goods: Exports fob	198.8	372.0	423.0	417.5	588.3	560.3	447.7	Biens : exportations,fàb
Goods: Imports fob	−706.0	−925.7	−1 136.7	−1 002.2	−1 001.6	−1 309.8	−1 244.9	Biens : importations,fàb
Serv. & Income: Credit	303.2	337.5	412.9	418.4	415.0	449.8	493.1	Serv. & revenu : crédit
Serv. & Income: Debit	−377.4	−385.0	−445.1	−424.9	−459.7	−540.3	−491.7	Serv. & revenu : débit
Current Trans.,nie: Credit	532.6	728.5	737.3	679.0	425.5	589.8	499.7	Transf. cour.,nia : crédit
Current Transfers: Debit	−1.2	−2.0	−1.1	−7.5	−7.6	−15.7	−20.2	Transf. courants : débit
Capital Acct.,nie: Credit	0.0	3.7	0.0	0.0	0.0	0.0	0.0	Compte de cap.,nia : crédit
Capital Account: Debit	0.0	0.0	0.0	−1.7	−0.8	0.0	0.0	Compte de capital : débit
Financial Account,nie	97.7	−199.0	158.3	−499.6	241.2	−23.5	−255.2	Compte d'op. fin., nia
Net Errors and Omissions	−15.2	69.5	−49.0	−44.1	−627.9	−75.6	384.5	Erreurs et omissions nettes
Reserves and Related Items	−32.4	0.4	−99.6	465.0	427.7	364.9	186.9	Rés. et postes appareutés

75
Summary of balance of payments
Millions of US dollars
Résumé des balances des paiements
Millions de dollars des E.−U.

Country or area	1993	1994	1995	1996	1997	1998	1999	Pays ou zone
Gabon								**Gabon**
Goods: Exports fob	2 326.2	2 365.3	2 642.9	...	...	...	...	Biens : exportations,fàb
Goods: Imports fob	−845.1	−776.7	−898.5	...	...	...	...	Biens : importations,fàb
Serv. & Income: Credit	343.3	231.4	286.3	...	...	...	...	Serv. & revenu : crédit
Serv. & Income: Debit	−1 681.0	−1 336.6	−1 733.0	...	...	...	...	Serv. & revenu : débit
Current Trans.,nie: Credit	48.0	18.7	4.4	...	...	...	...	Transf. cour.,nia : crédit
Current Transfers: Debit	−240.5	−184.8	−202.3	...	...	...	...	Transf. courants : débit
Capital Acct.,nie: Credit	0.0	0.0	0.0	...	...	...	...	Compte de cap.,nia : crédit
Capital Account: Debit	0.0	0.0	0.0	...	...	...	...	Compte de capital : débit
Financial Account,nie	−389.2	−745.0	−412.7	...	...	...	...	Compte d'op. fin., nia
Net Errors and Omissions	−13.6	254.6	−108.2	...	...	...	...	Erreurs et omissions nettes
Reserves and Related Items	451.9	173.0	421.2	...	...	...	...	Rés. et postes appareutés
Gambia								**Gambie**
Goods: Exports fob	152.2	123.9	122.1	117.3	116.5	...	...	Biens : exportations,fàb
Goods: Imports fob	−207.8	−180.1	−161.4	−214.5	−201.7	...	...	Biens : importations,fàb
Serv. & Income: Credit	82.8	94.5	57.7	105.9	110.1	...	...	Serv. & revenu : crédit
Serv. & Income: Debit	−77.2	−71.6	−78.3	−85.3	−83.7	...	...	Serv. & revenu : débit
Current Trans.,nie: Credit	48.5	45.5	55.4	34.7	43.9	...	...	Transf. cour.,nia : crédit
Current Transfers: Debit	−3.5	−4.1	−3.7	−5.3	−8.0	...	...	Transf. courants : débit
Capital Acct.,nie: Credit	0.0	0.0	0.0	8.4	5.6	...	...	Compte de cap.,nia : crédit
Capital Account: Debit	0.0	0.0	0.0	0.0	0.0	...	...	Compte de capital : débit
Financial Account,nie	38.2	32.8	24.6	57.9	38.4	...	...	Compte d'op. fin., nia
Net Errors and Omissions	−21.9	−34.8	−15.5	−4.8	−13.7	...	...	Erreurs et omissions nettes
Reserves and Related Items	−11.1	−6.2	−1.0	−14.4	−7.4	...	...	Rés. et postes appareutés
Ghana								**Ghana**
Goods: Exports fob	1 063.6	1 237.7	1 431.2	1 570.1	1 489.9	2 090.8	2 116.6	Biens : exportations,fàb
Goods: Imports fob	−1 728.0	−1 579.9	−1 687.8	−1 937.0	−2 128.2	−2 896.5	−3 228.1	Biens : importations,fàb
Serv. & Income: Credit	156.3	159.3	164.3	180.3	191.6	467.6	482.8	Serv. & revenu : crédit
Serv. & Income: Debit	−569.2	−543.5	−575.6	−619.8	−663.1	−775.8	−757.3	Serv. & revenu : débit
Current Trans.,nie: Credit	532.0	487.3	539.0	497.9	576.5	751.0	637.8	Transf. cour.,nia : crédit
Current Transfers: Debit	−14.5	−15.5	−15.7	−16.2	−16.4	−17.1	−17.8	Transf. courants : débit
Capital Acct.,nie: Credit	0.0	0.0	0.0	0.0	0.0	0.0	0.0	Compte de cap.,nia : crédit
Capital Account: Debit	−1.0	−1.0	−1.0	−1.0	−1.0	−1.0	−1.0	Compte de capital : débit
Financial Account,nie	642.6	481.7	462.1	285.1	493.8	515.8	391.8	Compte d'op. fin., nia
Net Errors and Omissions	−28.5	−54.0	−65.7	20.2	83.7	−27.0	327.3	Erreurs et omissions nettes
Reserves and Related Items	−53.3	−172.1	−250.8	20.4	−26.7	−107.8	47.9	Rés. et postes appareutés
Guinea								**Guinée**
Goods: Exports fob	561.1	515.7	582.8	636.5	630.1	693.0	677.9	Biens : exportations,fàb
Goods: Imports fob	−582.7	−685.4	−621.7	−525.3	−512.5	−572.0	−583.4	Biens : importations,fàb
Serv. & Income: Credit	196.0	159.4	130.4	136.9	118.4	119.7	137.9	Serv. & revenu : crédit
Serv. & Income: Debit	−427.4	−445.8	−486.8	−527.9	−442.9	−516.3	−449.0	Serv. & revenu : débit
Current Trans.,nie: Credit	260.3	280.6	258.3	137.8	131.4	116.2	80.1	Transf. cour.,nia : crédit
Current Transfers: Debit	−64.2	−72.5	−79.3	−35.3	−15.6	−24.3	−15.1	Transf. courants : débit
Capital Acct.,nie: Credit	5.0	0.0	0.0	0.0	0.0	0.0	0.0	Compte de cap.,nia : crédit
Capital Account: Debit	0.0	0.0	0.0	0.0	0.0	0.0	0.0	Compte de capital : débit
Financial Account,nie	62.6	84.2	109.2	47.5	−89.3	8.0	117.2	Compte d'op. fin., nia
Net Errors and Omissions	−107.5	39.8	34.8	69.9	49.8	17.8	−45.0	Erreurs et omissions nettes
Reserves and Related Items	96.7	124.1	72.5	59.9	130.6	157.8	79.5	Rés. et postes appareutés
Guinea−Bissau								**Guinée−Bissau**
Goods: Exports fob	16.0	33.2	23.9	21.6	48.9	...	...	Biens : exportations,fàb
Goods: Imports fob	−53.8	−53.8	−59.3	−56.8	−62.5	...	...	Biens : importations,fàb
Serv. & Income: Credit	9.8	5.6	5.7	7.0	8.0	...	...	Serv. & revenu : crédit
Serv. & Income: Debit	−50.1	−53.4	−51.0	−47.9	−40.5	...	...	Serv. & revenu : débit
Current Trans.,nie: Credit	14.4	21.8	31.4	15.7	15.8	...	...	Transf. cour.,nia : crédit
Current Transfers: Debit	−1.7	−1.1	−1.3	0.0	0.0	...	...	Transf. courants : débit
Capital Acct.,nie: Credit	36.6	44.4	49.2	40.7	32.2	...	...	Compte de cap.,nia : crédit
Capital Account: Debit	0.0	0.0	0.0	0.0	0.0	...	...	Compte de capital : débit
Financial Account,nie	−15.8	−27.0	−28.3	−12.3	2.0	...	...	Compte d'op. fin., nia
Net Errors and Omissions	−16.0	−24.3	−10.9	−11.5	−19.2	...	...	Erreurs et omissions nettes
Reserves and Related Items	60.7	54.5	40.6	43.5	15.2	...	...	Rés. et postes appareutés
Kenya								**Kenya**
Goods: Exports fob	1 262.6	1 537.0	1 923.7	2 083.3	2 062.6	2 013.1	1 740.5	Biens : exportations,fàb
Goods: Imports fob	−1 509.6	−1 775.3	−2 673.9	−2 598.2	−2 948.4	−3 028.7	−2 569.7	Biens : importations,fàb
Serv. & Income: Credit	1 066.8	1 138.3	1 050.2	957.6	937.3	878.8	940.0	Serv. & revenu : crédit
Serv. & Income: Debit	−961.7	−1 072.5	−1 218.6	−1 096.2	−1 078.0	−880.5	−774.0	Serv. & revenu : débit
Current Trans.,nie: Credit	276.0	333.7	563.6	585.4	649.3	654.4	674.2	Transf. cour.,nia : crédit

75
Summary of balance of payments
Millions of US dollars
Résumé des balances des paiements
Millions de dollars des E.−U.

Country or area	1993	1994	1995	1996	1997	1998	1999	Pays ou zone
Current Transfers: Debit	−63.0	−63.2	−45.5	−5.4	0.0	0.0	0.0	Transf. courants : débit
Capital Acct.,nie: Credit	28.5	0.0	0.0	0.0	0.0	0.0	55.4	Compte de cap.,nia : crédit
Capital Account: Debit	−0.4	−0.4	−0.4	−0.4	0.0	0.0	0.0	Compte de capital : débit
Financial Account,nie	55.1	−41.7	247.9	589.1	362.7	562.2	124.9	Compte d'op. fin., nia
Net Errors and Omissions	257.5	5.8	11.4	−128.2	134.8	−125.6	−104.7	Erreurs et omissions nettes
Reserves and Related Items	−411.8	−61.6	141.6	−387.0	−120.2	−73.7	−86.6	Rés. et postes appareutés
Lesotho								**Lesotho**
Goods: Exports fob	134.0	143.5	160.0	186.9	196.1	193.4	172.5	Biens : exportations,fàb
Goods: Imports fob	−868.1	−810.2	−985.2	−998.6	−1 024.4	−866.0	−779.2	Biens : importations,fàb
Serv. & Income: Credit	481.5	407.3	510.6	495.6	534.3	411.2	368.7	Serv. & revenu : crédit
Serv. & Income: Debit	−93.3	−103.6	−218.5	−175.4	−177.6	−175.8	−130.7	Serv. & revenu : débit
Current Trans.,nie: Credit	376.5	472.1	211.3	190.2	202.9	158.0	149.4	Transf. cour.,nia : crédit
Current Transfers: Debit	−1.3	−0.9	−1.2	−1.1	−0.5	−1.2	−1.6	Transf. cour.,nia : débit
Capital Acct.,nie: Credit	0.0	0.0	43.7	45.5	44.5	22.9	18.0	Compte de cap.,nia : crédit
Capital Account: Debit	0.0	0.0	0.0	0.0	0.0	0.0	0.0	Compte de capital : débit
Financial Account,nie	55.2	33.0	349.1	350.6	323.7	316.1	135.8	Compte d'op. fin., nia
Net Errors and Omissions	17.8	−20.3	28.1	23.3	42.1	56.8	26.2	Erreurs et omissions nettes
Reserves and Related Items	−102.3	−120.9	−97.8	−116.9	−141.0	−115.6	40.8	Rés. et postes appareutés
Libyan Arab Jamahiriya								**Jamahiriya arabe libyenne**
Goods: Exports fob	8 522.1	8 365.0	9 037.9	9 577.9	9 876.1	6 328.0	7 276.0	Biens : exportations,fàb
Goods: Imports fob	−8 409.1	−7 339.0	−6 257.1	−7 059.2	−7 159.8	−5 857.1	−4 302.1	Biens : importations,fàb
Serv. & Income: Credit	623.9	526.7	563.0	603.9	673.3	680.0	605.0	Serv. & revenu : crédit
Serv. & Income: Debit	−1 770.9	−1 218.0	−1 080.9	−1 306.8	−1 274.2	−1 274.5	−1 223.8	Serv. & revenu : débit
Current Trans.,nie: Credit	7.9	5.0	4.9	3.0	3.9	5.1	6.9	Transf. cour.,nia : crédit
Current Transfers: Debit	−336.2	−311.0	−270.1	−342.0	−244.0	−271.9	−226.0	Transf. courants : débit
Capital Acct.,nie: Credit	0.0	0.0	0.0	0.0	0.0	0.0	0.0	Compte de cap.,nia : crédit
Capital Account: Debit	0.0	0.0	0.0	0.0	0.0	0.0	0.0	Compte de capital : débit
Financial Account,nie	−201.2	159.9	−250.1	224.2	−884.0	−554.7	−1 045.3	Compte d'op. fin., nia
Net Errors and Omissions	−148.4	106.3	299.1	−234.1	877.7	432.1	−402.8	Erreurs et omissions nettes
Reserves and Related Items	1 711.9	−294.8	−2 046.7	−1 467.0	−1 868.9	513.2	−688.0	Rés. et postes appareutés
Madagascar								**Madagascar**
Goods: Exports fob	334.6	450.1	506.6	509.3	516.1	538.2	...	Biens : exportations,fàb
Goods: Imports fob	−514.4	−545.8	−628.1	−629.0	−694.1	−692.7	...	Biens : importations,fàb
Serv. & Income: Credit	190.2	208.0	249.6	299.5	292.0	315.6	...	Serv. & revenu : crédit
Serv. & Income: Debit	−455.9	−486.2	−532.7	−542.4	−500.9	−538.6	...	Serv. & revenu : débit
Current Trans.,nie: Credit	201.8	113.7	141.1	94.4	156.3	109.5	...	Transf. cour.,nia : crédit
Current Transfers: Debit	−14.4	−16.9	−12.4	−22.6	−35.3	−32.7	...	Transf. courants : débit
Capital Acct.,nie: Credit	78.1	61.9	45.1	5.1	115.4	102.7	...	Compte de cap.,nia : crédit
Capital Account: Debit	0.0	0.0	0.0	0.0	0.0	0.0	...	Compte de capital : débit
Financial Account,nie	−158.1	−122.4	−197.5	133.3	109.7	−76.3	...	Compte d'op. fin., nia
Net Errors and Omissions	3.8	61.3	98.5	58.8	24.6	−25.0	...	Erreurs et omissions nettes
Reserves and Related Items	334.4	276.3	330.0	93.7	16.1	299.2	...	Rés. et postes appareutés
Malawi								**Malawi**
Goods: Exports fob	317.5	362.6	...	...	...	...	...	Biens : exportations,fàb
Goods: Imports fob	−340.2	−639.0	...	...	...	...	...	Biens : importations,fàb
Serv. & Income: Credit	32.1	24.1	...	...	...	...	...	Serv. & revenu : crédit
Serv. & Income: Debit	−330.9	−321.5	...	...	...	...	...	Serv. & revenu : débit
Current Trans.,nie: Credit	167.9	139.7	...	...	...	...	...	Transf. cour.,nia : crédit
Current Transfers: Debit	−11.9	−15.4	...	...	...	...	...	Transf. courants : débit
Capital Acct.,nie: Credit	0.0	0.0	...	...	...	...	...	Compte de cap.,nia : crédit
Capital Account: Debit	0.0	0.0	...	...	...	...	...	Compte de capital : débit
Financial Account,nie	188.9	122.0	...	...	...	...	...	Compte d'op. fin., nia
Net Errors and Omissions	0.7	292.6	...	...	...	...	...	Erreurs et omissions nettes
Reserves and Related Items	−24.0	35.1	...	...	...	...	...	Rés. et postes appareutés
Mali								**Mali**
Goods: Exports fob	371.9	334.9	441.8	433.5	561.6	...	...	Biens : exportations,fàb
Goods: Imports fob	−492.4	−449.2	−556.8	−551.5	−551.9	...	...	Biens : importations,fàb
Serv. & Income: Credit	105.0	78.3	95.8	98.5	92.7	...	...	Serv. & revenu : crédit
Serv. & Income: Debit	−404.0	−366.7	−483.5	−449.8	−407.3	...	...	Serv. & revenu : débit
Current Trans.,nie: Credit	294.6	281.3	266.8	246.1	170.0	...	...	Transf. cour.,nia : crédit
Current Transfers: Debit	−63.7	−41.2	−48.0	−50.0	−43.5	...	...	Transf. courants : débit
Capital Acct.,nie: Credit	112.0	99.1	126.2	136.4	108.6	...	...	Compte de cap.,nia : crédit
Capital Account: Debit	0.0	0.0	0.0	0.0	0.0	...	...	Compte de capital : débit
Financial Account,nie	−14.5	−7.0	118.6	174.6	52.7	...	...	Compte d'op. fin., nia
Net Errors and Omissions	−6.0	5.6	−13.0	−8.8	7.9	...	...	Erreurs et omissions nettes
Reserves and Related Items	97.2	65.0	52.0	−29.0	9.2	...	...	Rés. et postes appareutés

75
Summary of balance of payments
Millions of US dollars
Résumé des balances des paiements
Millions de dollars des E.−U.

Country or area	1993	1994	1995	1996	1997	1998	1999	Pays ou zone
Mauritania								**Mauritanie**
Goods: Exports fob	403.0	399.7	476.4	480.0	423.6	358.6	...	Biens : exportations,fàb
Goods: Imports fob	−400.4	−352.3	−292.6	−346.1	−316.5	−318.7	...	Biens : importations,fàb
Serv. & Income: Credit	22.2	27.1	29.2	32.5	36.3	36.4	...	Serv. & revenu : crédit
Serv. & Income: Debit	−282.6	−228.7	−266.5	−277.2	−240.2	−186.6	...	Serv. & revenu : débit
Current Trans.,nie: Credit	110.3	113.3	94.7	217.5	157.9	198.3	...	Transf. cour.,nia : crédit
Current Transfers: Debit	−26.5	−28.9	−19.2	−15.5	−13.3	−10.8	...	Transf. courants : débit
Capital Acct.,nie: Credit	0.0	0.0	0.0	0.0	0.0	0.0	...	Compte de cap.,nia : crédit
Capital Account: Debit	0.0	0.0	0.0	0.0	0.0	0.0	...	Compte de capital : débit
Financial Account,nie	−134.8	−11.4	−10.2	−86.1	−17.3	−25.9	...	Compte d'op. fin., nia
Net Errors and Omissions	26.7	−23.5	−18.1	−1.0	−3.0	−8.1	...	Erreurs et omissions nettes
Reserves and Related Items	282.1	104.7	6.2	−4.2	−27.6	−43.2	...	Rés. et postes appareutés
Mauritius								**Maurice**
Goods: Exports fob	1 334.4	1 376.9	1 571.7	1 810.6	1 600.1	1 669.3	1 589.3	Biens : exportations,fàb
Goods: Imports fob	−1 576.0	−1 773.9	−1 812.2	−2 136.3	−2 036.1	−1 933.3	−2 136.5	Biens : importations,fàb
Serv. & Income: Credit	636.2	664.5	829.9	991.9	940.6	964.8	1 105.2	Serv. & revenu : crédit
Serv. & Income: Debit	−588.2	−602.8	−712.6	−748.0	−720.9	−792.4	−714.2	Serv. & revenu : débit
Current Trans.,nie: Credit	115.9	129.6	146.8	182.8	206.4	186.8	196.6	Transf. cour.,nia : crédit
Current Transfers: Debit	−14.4	−26.3	−45.4	−67.0	−79.0	−91.8	−92.7	Transf. courants : débit
Capital Acct.,nie: Credit	0.0	0.0	0.0	0.0	0.0	0.0	0.0	Compte de cap.,nia : crédit
Capital Account: Debit	−1.5	−1.3	−1.1	−0.8	−0.5	−0.8	−0.5	Compte de capital : débit
Financial Account,nie	19.3	41.4	25.1	91.9	−18.6	−26.0	60.9	Compte d'op. fin., nia
Net Errors and Omissions	81.2	148.5	106.7	−76.8	73.4	−41.9	181.6	Erreurs et omissions nettes
Reserves and Related Items	−7.0	43.5	−108.8	−48.3	34.6	65.4	−189.7	Rés. et postes appareutés
Morocco								**Maroc**
Goods: Exports fob	4 935.7	5 540.9	6 871.0	6 886.2	7 039.1	7 143.7	...	Biens : exportations,fàb
Goods: Imports fob	−7 001.0	−7 647.6	−9 353.1	−9 079.6	−8 903.0	−9 462.6	...	Biens : importations,fàb
Serv. & Income: Credit	2 273.9	2 238.5	2 424.5	2 932.0	2 643.4	3 020.3	...	Serv. & revenu : crédit
Serv. & Income: Debit	−3 024.6	−3 124.2	−3 458.7	−3 279.9	−3 071.8	−3 190.1	...	Serv. & revenu : débit
Current Trans.,nie: Credit	2 361.0	2 355.2	2 298.0	2 565.4	2 204.2	2 347.3	...	Transf. cour.,nia : crédit
Current Transfers: Debit	−66.4	−85.6	−78.0	−82.5	−80.6	−94.9	...	Transf. courants : débit
Capital Acct.,nie: Credit	0.1	0.3	0.0	78.1	0.5	0.1	...	Compte de cap.,nia : crédit
Capital Account: Debit	−3.2	−3.7	−5.7	−4.8	−5.0	−10.2	...	Compte de capital : débit
Financial Account,nie	965.8	1 247.7	−984.4	−896.6	−989.8	−653.1	...	Compte d'op. fin., nia
Net Errors and Omissions	−5.0	−38.7	391.1	208.7	174.8	180.6	...	Erreurs et omissions nettes
Reserves and Related Items	−436.3	−482.6	1 895.4	673.1	988.2	719.0	...	Rés. et postes appareutés
Mozambique								**Mozambique**
Goods: Exports fob	131.8	149.5	168.9	226.1	230.0	244.6	...	Biens : exportations,fàb
Goods: Imports fob	−859.2	−916.7	−705.2	−704.4	−684.0	−735.6	...	Biens : importations,fàb
Serv. & Income: Credit	239.8	245.9	301.5	314.2	342.3	332.5	...	Serv. & revenu : crédit
Serv. & Income: Debit	−462.0	−510.5	−549.1	−481.1	−496.8	−584.0	...	Serv. & revenu : débit
Current Trans.,nie: Credit	503.3	564.6	339.2	224.7	312.9	313.2	...	Transf. cour.,nia : crédit
Current Transfers: Debit	0.0	0.0	0.0	0.0	0.0	0.0	...	Transf. courants : débit
Capital Acct.,nie: Credit	0.0	0.0	0.0	0.0	0.0	0.0	...	Compte de cap.,nia : crédit
Capital Account: Debit	0.0	0.0	0.0	0.0	0.0	0.0	...	Compte de capital : débit
Financial Account,nie	246.9	344.4	366.7	235.0	182.2	300.4	...	Compte d'op. fin., nia
Net Errors and Omissions	−447.4	−443.2	−308.6	−238.3	−364.8	−263.8	...	Erreurs et omissions nettes
Reserves and Related Items	646.8	566.0	386.6	423.8	478.2	392.7	...	Rés. et postes appareutés
Namibia								**Namibie**
Goods: Exports fob	1 293.1	1 320.4	1 418.4	1 403.7	1 343.3	1 278.3	...	Biens : exportations,fàb
Goods: Imports fob	−1 335.0	−1 406.3	−1 548.2	−1 530.9	−1 615.0	−1 450.9	...	Biens : importations,fàb
Serv. & Income: Credit	440.8	472.9	689.3	656.5	632.1	553.8	...	Serv. & revenu : crédit
Serv. & Income: Debit	−640.0	−628.2	−786.6	−829.9	−714.3	−622.8	...	Serv. & revenu : débit
Current Trans.,nie: Credit	373.2	349.2	426.9	437.3	462.2	418.2	...	Transf. cour.,nia : crédit
Current Transfers: Debit	−21.9	−22.7	−23.9	−21.0	−18.0	−14.7	...	Transf. courants : débit
Capital Acct.,nie: Credit	27.6	43.8	40.7	42.5	33.9	24.2	...	Compte de cap.,nia : crédit
Capital Account: Debit	−0.6	−0.6	−0.6	−0.5	−0.4	−0.4	...	Compte de capital : débit
Financial Account,nie	−62.1	−102.1	−205.3	−174.0	−71.4	−145.6	...	Compte d'op. fin., nia
Net Errors and Omissions	16.2	48.5	13.4	39.1	15.3	15.7	...	Erreurs et omissions nettes
Reserves and Related Items	−91.3	−75.0	−24.2	−22.9	−67.8	−55.8	...	Rés. et postes appareutés
Niger								**Niger**
Goods: Exports fob	300.4	226.8	288.1	...	...	...	...	Biens : exportations,fàb
Goods: Imports fob	−312.1	−271.3	−305.6	...	...	...	...	Biens : importations,fàb
Serv. & Income: Credit	55.8	46.0	39.1	...	...	...	...	Serv. & revenu : crédit
Serv. & Income: Debit	−215.8	−194.3	−204.7	...	...	...	...	Serv. & revenu : débit
Current Trans.,nie: Credit	139.5	115.1	60.6	...	...	...	...	Transf. cour.,nia : crédit

75
Summary of balance of payments
Millions of US dollars
Résumé des balances des paiements
Millions de dollars des E.−U.

Country or area	1993	1994	1995	1996	1997	1998	1999	Pays ou zone
Current Transfers: Debit	−65.0	−48.5	−29.1	...	...	...	...	Transf. courants : débit
Capital Acct.,nie: Credit	109.3	88.2	65.3	...	...	...	...	Compte de cap.,nia : crédit
Capital Account: Debit	0.0	0.0	0.0	...	...	...	...	Compte de capital : débit
Financial Account,nie	−123.3	29.9	−46.1	...	...	...	...	Compte d'op. fin., nia
Net Errors and Omissions	87.2	−67.8	114.4	...	...	...	...	Erreurs et omissions nettes
Reserves and Related Items	23.9	75.8	18.1	...	...	...	...	Rés. et postes appareutés
Nigeria								**Nigéria**
Goods: Exports fob	9 910.0	9 459.1	11 734.4	16 117.0	15 207.3	8 971.2	12 875.7	Biens : exportations,fàb
Goods: Imports fob	−6 661.7	−6 511.5	−8 221.5	−6 438.4	−9 501.4	−9 211.3	−8 587.6	Biens : importations,fàb
Serv. & Income: Credit	1 220.4	419.5	708.3	847.5	1 044.9	1 216.6	1 219.3	Serv. & revenu : crédit
Serv. & Income: Debit	−6 061.4	−5 993.0	−7 598.4	−7 964.1	−8 115.7	−6 789.5	−6 293.3	Serv. & revenu : débit
Current Trans.,nie: Credit	856.5	549.9	803.5	946.6	1 920.3	1 574.2	1 301.1	Transf. cour.,nia : crédit
Current Transfers: Debit	−44.2	−52.0	−4.7	−1.7	−3.8	−4.7	−9.4	Transf. courants : débit
Capital Acct.,nie: Credit	0.0	0.0	0.0	0.0	0.0	0.0	0.0	Compte de cap.,nia : crédit
Capital Account: Debit	0.0	0.0	−66.2	−68.1	−49.4	−54.3	−47.7	Compte de capital : débit
Financial Account,nie	−1 043.1	329.2	−46.2	−4 155.0	−424.9	1 502.5	−4 002.4	Compte d'op. fin., nia
Net Errors and Omissions	−87.6	−139.3	−82.9	−44.8	−62.1	−77.5	6.8	Erreurs et omissions nettes
Reserves and Related Items	1 911.2	1 938.0	2 773.7	761.0	−15.1	2 872.8	3 537.6	Rés. et postes appareutés
Rwanda								**Rwanda**
Goods: Exports fob	67.7	32.2	56.7	61.7	93.2	64.5	62.3	Biens : exportations,fàb
Goods: Imports fob	−267.8	−367.4	−219.1	−218.5	−278.2	−234.0	−202.8	Biens : importations,fàb
Serv. & Income: Credit	37.3	0.0	42.2	27.0	59.2	48.2	44.0	Serv. & revenu : crédit
Serv. & Income: Debit	−154.6	−109.6	−172.2	−168.5	−223.1	−138.6	−113.3	Serv. & revenu : débit
Current Trans.,nie: Credit	208.5	398.6	354.9	293.9	311.6	252.6	220.3	Transf. cour.,nia : crédit
Current Transfers: Debit	−20.1	0.0	−4.9	−4.1	−24.9	−16.9	−12.8	Transf. courants : débit
Capital Acct.,nie: Credit	1.0	0.0	0.0	0.0	0.0	0.0	0.0	Compte de cap.,nia : crédit
Capital Account: Debit	−2.4	0.0	0.0	0.0	0.0	0.0	0.0	Compte de capital : débit
Financial Account,nie	88.5	−12.5	−10.7	24.8	46.8	7.8	−9.1	Compte d'op. fin., nia
Net Errors and Omissions	−8.1	62.4	5.8	4.1	46.0	−33.1	−66.3	Erreurs et omissions nettes
Reserves and Related Items	49.9	−3.7	−52.6	−20.3	−30.5	49.5	77.9	Rés. et postes appareutés
Senegal								**Sénégal**
Goods: Exports fob	736.8	818.8	993.3	988.0	904.6	...	...	Biens : exportations,fàb
Goods: Imports fob	−1 086.7	−1 022.0	−1 242.9	−1 264.0	−1 176.0	...	...	Biens : importations,fàb
Serv. & Income: Credit	496.7	475.7	599.7	459.9	439.6	...	...	Serv. & revenu : crédit
Serv. & Income: Debit	−743.6	−657.2	−789.7	−550.0	−531.6	...	...	Serv. & revenu : débit
Current Trans.,nie: Credit	267.0	267.0	284.7	244.3	258.8	...	...	Transf. cour.,nia : crédit
Current Transfers: Debit	−103.2	−69.7	−89.6	−77.8	−80.3	...	...	Transf. courants : débit
Capital Acct.,nie: Credit	165.9	200.5	201.2	169.3	96.3	...	...	Compte de cap.,nia : crédit
Capital Account: Debit	−12.2	−9.9	−14.2	−0.1	−0.3	...	...	Compte de capital : débit
Financial Account,nie	129.4	48.5	44.2	−4.4	204.3	...	...	Compte d'op. fin., nia
Net Errors and Omissions	8.4	−28.9	−19.6	8.0	−9.2	...	...	Erreurs et omissions nettes
Reserves and Related Items	141.5	−22.8	32.9	26.8	−106.1	...	...	Rés. et postes appareutés
Seychelles								**Seychelles**
Goods: Exports fob	51.3	52.1	53.1	78.0	115.2	123.4	145.2	Biens : exportations,fàb
Goods: Imports fob	−216.3	−188.6	−214.1	−262.7	−302.7	−351.6	−377.6	Biens : importations,fàb
Serv. & Income: Credit	218.4	201.7	223.9	241.9	247.5	284.5	321.7	Serv. & revenu : crédit
Serv. & Income: Debit	−109.0	−99.0	−125.1	−129.1	−137.3	−172.7	−196.5	Serv. & revenu : débit
Current Trans.,nie: Credit	31.8	21.3	19.5	27.6	27.1	3.6	3.9	Transf. cour.,nia : crédit
Current Transfers: Debit	−15.1	−13.4	−11.3	−12.1	−13.1	−11.7	−10.8	Transf. courants : débit
Capital Acct.,nie: Credit	0.0	0.0	0.0	0.0	0.0	21.7	16.5	Compte de cap.,nia : crédit
Capital Account: Debit	0.0	0.0	0.0	0.0	0.0	0.0	0.0	Compte de capital : débit
Financial Account,nie	25.6	7.4	16.7	22.9	49.6	73.3	82.5	Compte d'op. fin., nia
Net Errors and Omissions	3.2	6.8	23.1	20.6	8.4	−4.8	−23.0	Erreurs et omissions nettes
Reserves and Related Items	10.1	11.7	14.0	13.0	5.2	34.4	38.1	Rés. et postes appareutés
Sierra Leone								**Sierra Leone**
Goods: Exports fob	118.3	116.0	41.5	...	...	...	...	Biens : exportations,fàb
Goods: Imports fob	−187.1	−188.7	−168.1	...	...	...	...	Biens : importations,fàb
Serv. & Income: Credit	60.8	101.6	87.6	...	...	...	...	Serv. & revenu : crédit
Serv. & Income: Debit	−67.1	−164.6	−113.2	...	...	...	...	Serv. & revenu : débit
Current Trans.,nie: Credit	19.1	47.5	35.3	...	...	...	...	Transf. cour.,nia : crédit
Current Transfers: Debit	−1.7	−0.9	−9.5	...	...	...	...	Transf. courants : débit
Capital Acct.,nie: Credit	0.1	0.1	0.0	...	...	...	...	Compte de cap.,nia : crédit
Capital Account: Debit	0.0	0.0	0.0	...	...	...	...	Compte de capital : débit
Financial Account,nie	49.1	−25.5	61.6	...	...	...	...	Compte d'op. fin., nia
Net Errors and Omissions	16.1	55.1	19.3	...	...	...	...	Erreurs et omissions nettes
Reserves and Related Items	−7.5	59.5	45.6	...	...	...	...	Rés. et postes appareutés

75
Summary of balance of payments
Millions of US dollars
Résumé des balances des paiements
Millions de dollars des E.-U.

Country or area	1993	1994	1995	1996	1997	1998	1999	Pays ou zone
South Africa								**Afrique du Sud**
Goods: Exports fob	24 717.3	26 333.5	30 071.3	30 263.2	31 171.1	29 234.2	28 361.2	Biens : exportations,fàb
Goods: Imports fob	−18 485.2	−21 852.1	−27 404.4	−27 568.6	−28 847.5	−27 215.8	−24 610.7	Biens : importations,fàb
Serv. & Income: Credit	3 971.6	4 722.1	5 754.3	6 104.9	6 631.9	6 610.5	6 370.3	Serv. & revenu : crédit
Serv. & Income: Debit	−8 059.0	−8 481.0	−9 979.7	−9 926.6	−10 504.3	−9 818.7	−9 658.8	Serv. & revenu : débit
Current Trans.,nie: Credit	126.8	143.5	195.6	54.3	138.4	60.3	66.2	Transf. cour.,nia : crédit
Current Transfers: Debit	−769.5	−752.2	−841.3	−808.0	−862.5	−806.0	−992.6	Transf. courants : débit
Capital Acct.,nie: Credit	0.0	0.0	0.0	0.0	0.0	0.0	25.4	Compte de cap.,nia : crédit
Capital Account: Debit	−57.0	−66.9	−39.9	−46.9	−192.4	−56.2	−67.9	Compte de capital : débit
Financial Account,nie	−344.1	1 087.1	4 002.9	3 018.2	8 131.1	4 895.6	4 098.1	Compte d'op. fin., nia
Net Errors and Omissions	−2 442.2	−450.9	−852.5	−2 362.3	−1 070.2	−1 983.6	363.7	Erreurs et omissions nettes
Reserves and Related Items	1 341.1	−683.2	−906.3	1 271.8	−4 595.6	−920.2	−3 954.9	Rés. et postes appareutés
Sudan								**Soudan**
Goods: Exports fob	306.3	523.9	555.7	620.3	594.2	595.7	780.1	Biens : exportations,fàb
Goods: Imports fob	−532.8	−1 045.4	−1 066.0	−1 339.5	−1 421.9	−1 732.2	−1 256.0	Biens : importations,fàb
Serv. & Income: Credit	70.1	77.8	127.2	57.0	48.4	29.5	100.7	Serv. & revenu : crédit
Serv. & Income: Debit	−130.7	−239.6	−177.2	−201.5	−178.1	−214.6	−398.6	Serv. & revenu : débit
Current Trans.,nie: Credit	84.9	120.1	346.2	236.3	439.1	731.8	702.3	Transf. cour.,nia : crédit
Current Transfers: Debit	0.0	−38.5	−285.8	−199.4	−309.8	−366.7	−393.7	Transf. courants : débit
Capital Acct.,nie: Credit	0.0	0.0	0.0	0.0	0.0	13.0	45.8	Compte de cap.,nia : crédit
Capital Account: Debit	0.0	0.0	0.0	0.0	0.0	−67.2	−68.7	Compte de capital : débit
Financial Account,nie	326.6	276.0	473.7	136.8	195.0	333.4	435.3	Compte d'op. fin., nia
Net Errors and Omissions	−82.6	344.8	89.3	727.5	651.2	750.5	167.6	Erreurs et omissions nettes
Reserves and Related Items	−41.8	−19.1	−63.1	−37.5	−18.1	−73.2	−114.8	Rés. et postes appareutés
Swaziland								**Swaziland**
Goods: Exports fob	684.7	790.9	867.8	849.4	960.1	966.1	941.3	Biens : exportations,fàb
Goods: Imports fob	−788.6	−841.0	−1 064.4	−1 054.4	−1 088.6	−1 082.6	−1 052.1	Biens : importations,fàb
Serv. & Income: Credit	248.0	251.3	314.4	301.6	307.1	266.3	245.4	Serv. & revenu : crédit
Serv. & Income: Debit	−363.6	−356.8	−291.5	−309.4	−288.1	−299.4	−251.9	Serv. & revenu : débit
Current Trans.,nie: Credit	248.1	252.6	257.2	268.7	231.2	243.4	239.6	Transf. cour.,nia : crédit
Current Transfers: Debit	−92.3	−95.1	−113.3	−108.9	−112.7	−110.6	−105.1	Transf. courants : débit
Capital Acct.,nie: Credit	0.3	0.1	0.3	0.1	0.1	0.1	0.0	Compte de capital : crédit
Capital Account: Debit	−0.3	−0.3	−0.4	0.0	0.0	0.0	0.0	Compte de capital : débit
Financial Account,nie	−2.4	−63.1	−74.5	−4.6	−2.9	41.6	−34.9	Compte d'op. fin., nia
Net Errors and Omissions	2.3	48.8	134.1	72.9	19.2	25.6	39.2	Erreurs et omissions nettes
Reserves and Related Items	63.7	12.5	−29.8	−15.4	−25.3	−50.5	−21.5	Rés. et postes appareutés
Togo								**Togo**
Goods: Exports fob	264.0	328.4	377.4	440.6	422.5	420.3	...	Biens : exportations,fàb
Goods: Imports fob	−375.3	−365.5	−506.5	−567.8	−530.6	−553.5	...	Biens : importations,fàb
Serv. & Income: Credit	111.5	80.0	96.1	161.8	123.5	120.4	...	Serv. & revenu : crédit
Serv. & Income: Debit	−145.9	−179.3	−206.6	−273.4	−231.7	−217.0	...	Serv. & revenu : débit
Current Trans.,nie: Credit	82.6	91.3	129.7	106.8	120.2	101.8	...	Transf. cour.,nia : crédit
Current Transfers: Debit	−19.3	−11.2	−12.1	−21.9	−20.8	−12.2	...	Transf. courants : débit
Capital Acct.,nie: Credit	0.0	0.0	0.0	5.6	5.8	6.1	...	Compte de cap.,nia : crédit
Capital Account: Debit	0.0	0.0	0.0	0.0	0.0	0.0	...	Compte de capital : débit
Financial Account,nie	−105.1	−40.5	−52.8	151.3	126.9	114.1	...	Compte d'op. fin., nia
Net Errors and Omissions	−2.1	−0.2	−19.3	−27.9	−2.7	2.7	...	Erreurs et omissions nettes
Reserves and Related Items	189.6	97.1	194.0	24.9	−13.1	17.2	...	Rés. et postes appareutés
Tunisia								**Tunisie**
Goods: Exports fob	3 746.0	4 643.4	5 469.7	5 518.8	5 559.2	5 724.0	5 873.3	Biens : exportations,fàb
Goods: Imports fob	−5 810.3	−6 210.3	−7 458.6	−7 279.6	−7 514.2	−7 875.5	−8 014.5	Biens : importations,fàb
Serv. & Income: Credit	2 113.1	2 338.0	2 628.6	2 697.7	2 690.1	2 847.9	3 008.7	Serv. & revenu : crédit
Serv. & Income: Debit	−1 984.6	−2 106.7	−2 187.7	−2 274.5	−2 121.3	−2 203.3	−2 212.1	Serv. & revenu : débit
Current Trans.,nie: Credit	628.6	815.6	804.7	879.4	821.0	851.8	919.7	Transf. cour.,nia : crédit
Current Transfers: Debit	−15.9	−16.8	−30.7	−19.5	−29.8	−20.2	−17.7	Transf. courants : débit
Capital Acct.,nie: Credit	5.0	4.9	46.5	46.2	94.9	82.5	72.5	Compte de cap.,nia : crédit
Capital Account: Debit	−7.0	−7.9	−14.8	−9.2	−18.1	−22.0	−13.5	Compte de capital : débit
Financial Account,nie	1 272.2	1 143.8	958.0	815.7	699.0	489.1	1 075.7	Compte d'op. fin., nia
Net Errors and Omissions	119.3	−77.5	−118.9	67.0	205.6	−12.0	46.0	Erreurs et omissions nettes
Reserves and Related Items	−66.5	−526.5	−96.8	−442.0	−386.5	137.6	−738.1	Rés. et postes appareutés
Uganda								**Ouganda**
Goods: Exports fob	200.0	463.0	560.3	639.3	592.6	510.2	500.1	Biens : exportations,fàb
Goods: Imports fob	−478.3	−714.2	−926.8	−986.9	−1 042.6	−1 166.3	−1 096.5	Biens : importations,fàb
Serv. & Income: Credit	100.0	77.9	121.7	174.4	205.1	227.0	222.8	Serv. & revenu : crédit
Serv. & Income: Debit	−358.4	−507.3	−676.0	−753.8	−724.6	−788.0	−807.6	Serv. & revenu : débit
Current Trans.,nie: Credit	312.4	473.1	581.9	674.7	602.6	714.6	630.3	Transf. cour.,nia : crédit

75
Summary of balance of payments
Millions of US dollars
Résumé des balances des paiements
Millions de dollars des E.–U.

Country or area	1993	1994	1995	1996	1997	1998	1999	Pays ou zone
Current Transfers: Debit	0.0	0.0	0.0	0.0	0.0	0.0	0.0	Transf. courants : débit
Capital Acct.,nie: Credit	42.4	36.1	48.3	61.4	31.9	49.5	26.3	Compte de cap.,nia : crédit
Capital Account: Debit	0.0	0.0	0.0	0.0	0.0	0.0	0.0	Compte de capital : débit
Financial Account,nie	56.6	76.8	210.7	140.5	298.8	372.8	368.9	Compte d'op. fin., nia
Net Errors and Omissions	−0.1	32.5	28.8	41.3	−4.8	39.7	49.7	Erreurs et omissions nettes
Reserves and Related Items	125.4	62.1	51.2	9.1	40.9	40.6	105.9	Rés. et postes appareutés
United Rep.Tanzania								**Rép.–Unie de Tanzanie**
Goods: Exports fob	446.9	519.4	682.5	764.1	715.3	589.5	...	Biens : exportations,fàb
Goods: Imports fob	−1 304.0	−1 309.3	−1 340.0	−1 213.1	−1 164.5	−1 365.3	...	Biens : importations,fàb
Serv. & Income: Credit	339.8	449.1	614.4	658.4	539.0	590.0	...	Serv. & revenu : crédit
Serv. & Income: Debit	−889.8	−656.7	−941.4	−1 058.7	−965.5	−1 161.8	...	Serv. & revenu : débit
Current Trans.,nie: Credit	389.8	311.5	370.5	370.9	313.6	426.6	...	Transf. cour.,nia : crédit
Current Transfers: Debit	−30.7	−25.0	−32.3	−32.3	−67.7	−35.5	...	Transf. courants : débit
Capital Acct.,nie: Credit	205.2	262.6	190.9	191.0	360.6	422.9	...	Compte de cap.,nia : crédit
Capital Account: Debit	0.0	0.0	0.0	0.0	0.0	0.0	...	Compte de capital : débit
Financial Account,nie	130.5	−91.7	66.7	−92.8	3.6	77.6	...	Compte d'op. fin., nia
Net Errors and Omissions	137.3	121.4	30.0	158.6	−31.9	−53.5	...	Erreurs et omissions nettes
Reserves and Related Items	575.1	418.6	358.7	254.0	297.5	509.4	...	Rés. et postes appareutés
Zimbabwe								**Zimbabwe**
Goods: Exports fob	1 609.1	1 961.1	...	...	...	...	...	Biens : exportations,fàb
Goods: Imports fob	−1 487.0	−1 803.5	...	...	...	...	...	Biens : importations,fàb
Serv. & Income: Credit	407.1	410.8	...	...	...	...	...	Serv. & revenu : crédit
Serv. & Income: Debit	−850.9	−1 032.9	...	...	...	...	...	Serv. & revenu : débit
Current Trans.,nie: Credit	270.6	69.4	...	...	...	...	...	Transf. cour.,nia : crédit
Current Transfers: Debit	−64.7	−29.8	...	...	...	...	...	Transf. courants : débit
Capital Acct.,nie: Credit	0.6	285.4	...	...	...	...	...	Compte de cap.,nia : crédit
Capital Account: Debit	−1.0	−1.0	...	...	...	...	...	Compte de capital : débit
Financial Account,nie	327.2	−25.5	...	...	...	...	...	Compte d'op. fin., nia
Net Errors and Omissions	14.9	80.2	...	...	...	...	...	Erreurs et omissions nettes
Reserves and Related Items	−225.9	85.8	...	...	...	...	...	Rés. et postes appareutés
America, North · Amérique du Nord								
Anguilla								**Anguilla**
Goods: Exports fob	1.1	1.6	...	...	...	...	...	Biens : exportations,fàb
Goods: Imports fob	−34.4	−38.3	...	...	...	...	...	Biens : importations,fàb
Serv. & Income: Credit	54.5	63.0	...	...	...	...	...	Serv. & revenu : crédit
Serv. & Income: Debit	−34.9	−35.2	...	...	...	...	...	Serv. & revenu : débit
Current Trans.,nie: Credit	7.3	5.1	...	...	...	...	...	Transf. cour.,nia : crédit
Current Transfers: Debit	−6.5	−6.7	...	...	...	...	...	Transf. courants : débit
Capital Acct.,nie: Credit	7.0	7.2	...	...	...	...	...	Compte de cap.,nia : crédit
Capital Account: Debit	−1.3	−1.3	...	...	...	...	...	Compte de capital : débit
Financial Account,nie	4.3	8.4	...	...	...	...	...	Compte d'op. fin., nia
Net Errors and Omissions	4.0	−4.2	...	...	...	...	...	Erreurs et omissions nettes
Reserves and Related Items	−1.2	0.2	...	...	...	...	...	Rés. et postes appareutés
Antigua and Barbuda								**Antigua–et–Barbuda**
Goods: Exports fob	62.1	44.4	53.1	54.0	...	...	...	Biens : exportations,fàb
Goods: Imports fob	−282.6	−298.1	−301.8	−316.6	...	...	...	Biens : importations,fàb
Serv. & Income: Credit	380.3	400.6	353.9	373.3	...	...	...	Serv. & revenu : crédit
Serv. & Income: Debit	−157.6	−165.7	−175.0	−178.4	...	...	...	Serv. & revenu : débit
Current Trans.,nie: Credit	9.1	10.4	77.9	31.5	...	...	...	Transf. cour.,nia : crédit
Current Transfers: Debit	−11.7	−9.5	−8.7	−3.6	...	...	...	Transf. courants : débit
Capital Acct.,nie: Credit	6.8	6.5	7.0	3.6	...	...	...	Compte de cap.,nia : crédit
Capital Account: Debit	0.0	−0.6	...	...	...	...	...	Compte de capital : débit
Financial Account,nie	0.1	13.8	12.1	61.7	...	...	...	Compte d'op. fin., nia
Net Errors and Omissions	−18.6	6.3	−5.0	−36.8	...	...	...	Erreurs et omissions nettes
Reserves and Related Items	12.2	−8.1	−13.6	11.3	...	...	...	Rés. et postes appareutés
Aruba								**Aruba**
Goods: Exports fob	1 154.4	1 296.8	1 347.2	1 735.7	1 728.7	1 164.8	1 413.5	Biens : exportations,fàb
Goods: Imports fob	−1 546.5	−1 607.3	−1 772.5	−2 043.4	−2 115.9	−1 518.2	−2 005.2	Biens : importations,fàb
Serv. & Income: Credit	617.4	633.8	661.5	789.1	836.5	932.6	1 027.0	Serv. & revenu : crédit
Serv. & Income: Debit	−193.7	−250.2	−270.1	−546.9	−634.0	−593.2	−781.9	Serv. & revenu : débit
Current Trans.,nie: Credit	43.4	47.5	71.5	18.4	18.4	29.3	59.3	Transf. cour.,nia : crédit
Current Transfers: Debit	−33.3	−38.7	−37.9	−22.0	−29.5	−34.1	−45.9	Transf. courants : débit
Capital Acct.,nie: Credit	0.9	0.3	3.1	28.7	21.6	10.2	0.9	Compte de cap.,nia : crédit
Capital Account: Debit	−2.8	−4.4	−3.6	−0.7	−0.6	−5.0	−0.9	Compte de capital : débit
Financial Account,nie	−8.4	−75.4	41.6	10.7	158.9	64.2	336.4	Compte d'op. fin., nia

75
Summary of balance of payments
Millions of US dollars
Résumé des balances des paiements
Millions de dollars des E. – U.

Country or area	1993	1994	1995	1996	1997	1998	1999	Pays ou zone
Net Errors and Omissions	2.0	−4.7	2.0	4.3	−2.5	0.6	−0.7	Erreurs et omissions nettes
Reserves and Related Items	−33.4	3.2	−42.7	26.1	18.4	−51.3	−2.5	Rés. et postes appareutés
Bahamas								**Bahamas**
Goods: Exports fob	192.2	198.5	225.4	273.3	295.0	362.9	379.9	Biens : exportations,fàb
Goods: Imports fob	−930.2	−1 013.8	−1 156.7	−1 287.4	−1 410.7	−1 737.1	−1 808.1	Biens : importations,fàb
Serv. & Income: Credit	1 571.2	1 571.8	1 617.4	1 662.8	1 698.6	1 680.9	2 040.9	Serv. & revenu : crédit
Serv. & Income: Debit	−808.3	−826.0	−849.9	−949.2	−1 094.3	−1 336.3	−1 321.0	Serv. & revenu : débit
Current Trans.,nie: Credit	33.1	33.1	25.1	45.9	50.0	45.0	49.0	Transf. cour.,nia : crédit
Current Transfers: Debit	−9.3	−5.8	−7.2	−8.7	−10.7	−10.8	−12.5	Transf. courants : débit
Capital Acct.,nie: Credit	0.0	0.0	0.0	0.0	0.0	0.0	0.0	Compte de cap.,nia : crédit
Capital Account: Debit	−9.4	−11.6	−12.5	−24.4	−12.9	−11.7	−14.5	Compte de capital : débit
Financial Account,nie	9.3	66.8	104.6	181.1	412.0	817.7	611.4	Compte d'op. fin., nia
Net Errors and Omissions	−30.0	−3.9	50.9	99.0	129.5	308.6	140.2	Erreurs et omissions nettes
Reserves and Related Items	−18.6	−9.1	2.9	7.6	−56.5	−119.2	−65.2	Rés. et postes appareutés
Barbados								**Barbade**
Goods: Exports fob	187.8	190.0	245.4	286.7	289.0	257.1	...	Biens : exportations,fàb
Goods: Imports fob	−514.3	−544.7	−691.2	−743.0	−887.7	−901.1	...	Biens : importations,fàb
Serv. & Income: Credit	729.5	859.7	961.6	1 014.3	1 019.7	1 087.1	...	Serv. & revenu : crédit
Serv. & Income: Debit	−353.6	−405.7	−459.3	−493.4	−517.6	−551.7	...	Serv. & revenu : débit
Current Trans.,nie: Credit	41.8	54.5	56.2	64.8	71.7	78.3	...	Transf. cour.,nia : crédit
Current Transfers: Debit	−22.5	−20.2	−23.6	−26.6	−25.1	−26.2	...	Transf. courants : débit
Capital Acct.,nie: Credit	0.0	0.0	0.0	0.4	0.0	0.7	...	Compte de cap.,nia : crédit
Capital Account: Debit	0.0	0.0	0.0	0.0	−0.1	0.0	...	Compte de capital : débit
Financial Account,nie	0.6	−6.4	−26.4	−22.2	20.0	55.2	...	Compte d'op. fin., nia
Net Errors and Omissions	−49.7	−89.4	−20.6	5.2	47.5	−5.5	...	Erreurs et omissions nettes
Reserves and Related Items	−19.6	−37.8	−42.1	−86.4	−17.4	6.1	...	Rés. et postes appareutés
Belize								**Belize**
Goods: Exports fob	132.0	156.5	164.6	171.3	193.4	186.2	201.5	Biens : exportations,fàb
Goods: Imports fob	−250.5	−231.9	−230.6	−229.5	−282.9	−290.9	−330.3	Biens : importations,fàb
Serv. & Income: Credit	156.4	124.0	135.6	144.2	145.3	147.7	161.4	Serv. & revenu : crédit
Serv. & Income: Debit	−115.9	−116.2	−120.0	−123.7	−122.5	−138.3	−146.5	Serv. & revenu : débit
Current Trans.,nie: Credit	33.8	34.4	38.3	34.2	38.2	38.4	40.0	Transf. cour.,nia : crédit
Current Transfers: Debit	−4.3	−6.9	−5.2	−3.1	−3.4	−2.8	−3.5	Transf. courants : débit
Capital Acct.,nie: Credit	0.0	0.0	0.0	0.0	0.0	0.0	0.5	Compte de cap.,nia : crédit
Capital Account: Debit	0.0	0.0	0.0	−2.2	−3.4	−1.9	−2.4	Compte de capital : débit
Financial Account,nie	32.8	3.6	−1.0	11.0	27.6	23.5	66.8	Compte d'op. fin., nia
Net Errors and Omissions	1.5	32.8	22.4	18.4	9.1	24.5	4.3	Erreurs et omissions nettes
Reserves and Related Items	14.2	3.6	−4.1	−20.6	−1.4	13.7	8.3	Rés. et postes appareutés
Canada								**Canada**
Goods: Exports fob	147 418.0	166 990.0	193 373.0	205 443.0	217 739.0	217 406.0	242 820.0	Biens : exportations,fàb
Goods: Imports fob	−137 281.0	−152 155.0	−167 517.0	−174 352.0	−200 516.0	−204 631.0	−220 064.0	Biens : importations,fàb
Serv. & Income: Credit	32 564.9	39 401.6	45 015.6	48 446.4	53 908.5	53 678.5	56 136.9	Serv. & revenu : crédit
Serv. & Income: Debit	−63 944.7	−66 912.2	−75 082.1	−76 660.9	−81 746.5	−78 094.3	−81 843.2	Serv. & revenu : débit
Current Trans.,nie: Credit	2 593.2	2 625.1	2 878.2	3 593.5	3 653.3	3 341.5	3 654.4	Transf. cour.,nia : crédit
Current Transfers: Debit	−3 172.4	−2 972.8	−2 995.0	−3 091.8	−3 103.8	−2 833.9	−2 977.6	Transf. courants : débit
Capital Acct.,nie: Credit	8 908.4	7 875.8	5 415.9	6 262.1	5 862.3	3 793.7	3 886.8	Compte de cap.,nia : crédit
Capital Account: Debit	−616.8	−377.6	−466.2	−428.7	−433.0	−458.7	−458.6	Compte de capital : débit
Financial Account,nie	19 504.9	5 159.4	−1 277.4	−9 276.8	3 835.2	9 397.0	−1 868.4	Compte d'op. fin., nia
Net Errors and Omissions	−5 069.6	−26.0	3 366.2	5 562.8	−1 592.2	3 397.2	6 646.6	Erreurs et omissions nettes
Reserves and Related Items	−904.4	392.4	−2 710.8	−5 497.7	2 393.1	−4 996.3	−5 933.2	Rés. et postes appareutés
Costa Rica								**Costa Rica**
Goods: Exports fob	1 866.8	2 122.0	3 481.8	3 774.1	4 349.5	5 546.8	...	Biens : exportations,fàb
Goods: Imports fob	−2 627.6	−2 727.8	−3 804.4	−4 023.3	−4 583.9	−5 791.3	...	Biens : importations,fàb
Serv. & Income: Credit	1 150.5	1 349.6	1 115.5	1 196.0	1 309.5	1 509.6	...	Serv. & revenu : crédit
Serv. & Income: Debit	−1 153.0	−1 143.1	−1 284.9	−1 360.3	−1 404.2	−1 830.4	...	Serv. & revenu : débit
Current Trans.,nie: Credit	149.3	164.5	165.2	190.1	182.2	197.2	...	Transf. cour.,nia : crédit
Current Transfers: Debit	−6.2	−9.2	−31.3	−43.1	−67.8	−92.2	...	Transf. courants : débit
Capital Acct.,nie: Credit	0.0	0.0	0.0	28.2	0.0	0.0	...	Compte de cap.,nia : crédit
Capital Account: Debit	0.0	0.0	0.0	0.0	0.0	0.0	...	Compte de capital : débit
Financial Account,nie	62.8	−108.4	517.3	47.6	199.6	192.4	...	Compte d'op. fin., nia
Net Errors and Omissions	299.0	249.1	57.1	121.4	−117.2	−236.7	...	Erreurs et omissions nettes
Reserves and Related Items	258.4	103.3	−216.2	69.3	132.3	504.6	...	Rés. et postes appareutés
Dominica								**Dominique**
Goods: Exports fob	48.2	47.8	46.1	52.7	53.8	62.3	...	Biens : exportations,fàb
Goods: Imports fob	−92.0	−95.8	−103.2	−100.5	−104.3	−98.8	...	Biens : importations,fàb
Serv. & Income: Credit	51.4	56.0	57.2	64.1	78.1	80.4	...	Serv. & revenu : crédit

75
Summary of balance of payments
Millions of US dollars
Résumé des balances des paiements
Millions de dollars des E.−U.

Country or area	1993	1994	1995	1996	1997	1998	1999	Pays ou zone
Serv. & Income: Debit	−39.7	−53.6	−57.7	−66.5	−71.6	−72.2	...	Serv. & revenu : débit
Current Trans.,nie: Credit	12.4	14.9	16.3	17.8	17.6	17.5	...	Transf. cour.,nia : crédit
Current Transfers: Debit	−3.7	−7.8	−8.4	−7.7	−7.1	−6.7	...	Transf. courants : débit
Capital Acct.,nie: Credit	11.2	9.4	24.6	25.4	22.6	14.0	...	Compte de cap.,nia : crédit
Capital Account: Debit	−1.5	−0.8	−0.1	−0.1	−0.1	−0.1	...	Compte de capital : débit
Financial Account,nie	20.0	29.8	45.0	9.7	15.3	2.2	...	Compte d'op. fin., nia
Net Errors and Omissions	−5.7	−3.2	−11.8	7.1	−2.4	5.3	...	Erreurs et omissions nettes
Reserves and Related Items	−0.6	3.2	−8.0	−2.2	−1.8	−4.0	...	Rés. et postes appareutés
Dominican Republic								**Rép. dominicaine**
Goods: Exports fob	3 211.0	3 452.5	3 779.5	4 052.8	4 613.7	4 980.5	5 136.7	Biens : exportations,fàb
Goods: Imports fob	−4 654.2	−4 903.2	−5 170.4	−5 727.0	−6 608.7	−7 597.3	−8 041.1	Biens : importations,fàb
Serv. & Income: Credit	1 640.7	1 889.3	2 079.4	2 270.3	2 587.0	2 669.7	3 068.6	Serv. & revenu : crédit
Serv. & Income: Debit	−1 624.4	−1 704.4	−1 863.5	−1 976.5	−2 107.1	−2 377.8	−2 441.2	Serv. & revenu : débit
Current Trans.,nie: Credit	908.4	996.8	1 007.7	1 187.6	1 373.1	2 016.9	1 997.1	Transf. cour.,nia : crédit
Current Transfers: Debit	−14.4	−14.0	−15.5	−19.9	−21.0	−30.4	−149.3	Transf. courants : débit
Capital Acct.,nie: Credit	0.0	0.0	0.0	0.0	0.0	0.0	0.0	Compte de cap.,nia : crédit
Capital Account: Debit	0.0	0.0	0.0	0.0	0.0	0.0	0.0	Compte de capital : débit
Financial Account,nie	−226.6	368.0	253.6	64.1	447.6	688.1	1 061.0	Compte d'op. fin., nia
Net Errors and Omissions	215.1	−596.0	75.3	108.8	−193.7	−338.6	−480.4	Erreurs et omissions nettes
Reserves and Related Items	544.4	511.0	−146.1	39.8	−90.9	−11.1	−151.4	Rés. et postes appareutés
El Salvador								**El Salvador**
Goods: Exports fob	1 031.8	1 252.3	1 651.1	1 787.4	2 414.2	2 450.5	...	Biens : exportations,fàb
Goods: Imports fob	−1 994.0	−2 422.3	−3 113.5	−3 029.7	−3 520.9	−3 717.5	...	Biens : importations,fàb
Serv. & Income: Credit	366.3	422.7	442.6	458.5	366.7	401.5	...	Serv. & revenu : crédit
Serv. & Income: Debit	−529.0	−559.1	−630.5	−639.1	−526.6	−726.3	...	Serv. & revenu : débit
Current Trans.,nie: Credit	1 004.7	1 290.9	1 393.2	1 258.6	1 362.7	1 514.7	...	Transf. cour.,nia : crédit
Current Transfers: Debit	−2.5	−2.5	−4.6	−4.8	0.0	−7.3	...	Transf. courants : débit
Capital Acct.,nie: Credit	0.0	0.0	0.0	0.0	0.0	1.3	...	Compte de cap.,nia : crédit
Capital Account: Debit	0.0	0.0	0.0	0.0	0.0	0.0	...	Compte de capital : débit
Financial Account,nie	73.9	115.8	438.3	358.1	379.6	635.6	...	Compte d'op. fin., nia
Net Errors and Omissions	107.6	15.4	−28.4	−24.2	−111.4	−249.4	...	Erreurs et omissions nettes
Reserves and Related Items	−58.6	−113.3	−148.3	−164.8	−364.3	−303.0	...	Rés. et postes appareutés
Grenada								**Grenade**
Goods: Exports fob	22.5	26.5	25.9	24.9	...	...	...	Biens : exportations,fàb
Goods: Imports fob	−118.1	−115.6	−125.4	−147.5	...	...	...	Biens : importations,fàb
Serv. & Income: Credit	90.5	105.1	104.1	111.0	...	...	...	Serv. & revenu : crédit
Serv. & Income: Debit	−52.2	−53.7	−56.9	−65.7	...	...	...	Serv. & revenu : débit
Current Trans.,nie: Credit	16.1	19.7	21.6	23.4	...	...	...	Transf. cour.,nia : crédit
Current Transfers: Debit	−2.4	−3.9	−4.5	−4.1	...	...	...	Transf. courants : débit
Capital Acct.,nie: Credit	18.3	23.0	27.3	30.9	...	...	...	Compte de cap.,nia : crédit
Capital Account: Debit	−1.4	−1.4	−1.4	−1.5	...	...	...	Compte de capital : débit
Financial Account,nie	19.0	4.1	3.1	26.2	...	...	...	Compte d'op. fin., nia
Net Errors and Omissions	8.7	0.7	12.3	2.6	...	...	...	Erreurs et omissions nettes
Reserves and Related Items	−1.0	−4.5	−6.0	−0.3	...	...	...	Rés. et postes appareutés
Guatemala								**Guatemala**
Goods: Exports fob	1 363.2	1 550.1	2 157.5	2 236.9	2 602.9	2 846.9	2 780.6	Biens : exportations,fàb
Goods: Imports fob	−2 384.0	−2 546.6	−3 032.6	−2 880.3	−3 542.7	−4 255.7	−4 225.7	Biens : importations,fàb
Serv. & Income: Credit	721.5	761.1	712.5	599.2	661.2	731.3	775.7	Serv. & revenu : crédit
Serv. & Income: Debit	−765.6	−838.5	−900.6	−929.8	−961.6	−1 066.9	−1 071.4	Serv. & revenu : débit
Current Trans.,nie: Credit	371.4	456.4	508.2	537.1	628.8	742.9	754.4	Transf. cour.,nia : crédit
Current Transfers: Debit	−8.2	−7.8	−17.0	−14.6	−22.1	−37.6	−39.5	Transf. courants : débit
Capital Acct.,nie: Credit	0.0	0.0	61.6	65.0	85.0	71.0	68.4	Compte de cap.,nia : crédit
Capital Account: Debit	0.0	0.0	0.0	0.0	0.0	0.0	0.0	Compte de capital : débit
Financial Account,nie	816.2	655.2	494.8	672.3	737.4	1 136.7	637.5	Compte d'op. fin., nia
Net Errors and Omissions	85.2	−23.6	−136.2	−71.7	40.7	66.8	195.0	Erreurs et omissions nettes
Reserves and Related Items	−199.7	−6.3	151.8	−214.1	−229.6	−235.4	125.0	Rés. et postes appareutés
Haiti								**Haïti**
Goods: Exports fob	80.3	60.3	88.3	82.5	205.4	299.3	...	Biens : exportations,fàb
Goods: Imports fob	−260.5	−171.5	−517.2	−498.6	−559.6	−640.7	...	Biens : importations,fàb
Serv. & Income: Credit	37.8	6.7	104.1	109.1	173.7	180.0	...	Serv. & revenu : crédit
Serv. & Income: Debit	−42.8	−75.1	−315.2	−293.2	−345.1	−392.3	...	Serv. & revenu : débit
Current Trans.,nie: Credit	173.4	156.2	552.9	462.5	477.9	515.6	...	Transf. cour.,nia : crédit
Current Transfers: Debit	0.0	0.0	0.0	0.0	0.0	0.0	...	Transf. courants : débit
Capital Acct.,nie: Credit	0.0	0.0	0.0	0.0	0.0	0.0	...	Compte de cap.,nia : crédit
Capital Account: Debit	0.0	0.0	0.0	0.0	0.0	0.0	...	Compte de capital : débit
Financial Account,nie	−46.5	−15.8	99.2	67.9	61.5	193.1	...	Compte d'op. fin., nia

75
Summary of balance of payments
Millions of US dollars
Résumé des balances des paiements
Millions de dollars des E.−U.

Country or area	1993	1994	1995	1996	1997	1998	1999	Pays ou zone
Net Errors and Omissions	35.3	18.6	97.0	−2.8	36.9	−138.8	...	Erreurs et omissions nettes
Reserves and Related Items	23.0	20.6	−109.2	72.6	−50.7	−16.2	...	Rés. et postes appareutés
Honduras								**Honduras**
Goods: Exports fob	999.6	1 101.5	1 377.2	1 638.4	1 856.5	2 016.5	1 848.9	Biens : exportations,fàb
Goods: Imports fob	−1 203.1	−1 351.1	−1 518.6	−1 925.8	−2 150.4	−2 339.6	−2 558.0	Biens : importations,fàb
Serv. & Income: Credit	240.5	266.4	289.9	344.5	404.9	475.5	534.4	Serv. & revenu : crédit
Serv. & Income: Debit	−510.0	−549.1	−591.9	−619.8	−642.7	−661.2	−726.1	Serv. & revenu : débit
Current Trans.,nie: Credit	165.5	190.2	243.7	271.7	306.8	268.6	365.4	Transf. cour.,nia : crédit
Current Transfers: Debit	−1.2	−1.2	−1.2	−44.4	−47.3	−76.7	−1.4	Transf. courants : débit
Capital Acct.,nie: Credit	0.0	0.0	0.0	29.2	15.3	48.4	75.2	Compte de cap.,nia : crédit
Capital Account: Debit	0.0	0.0	0.0	−0.7	−0.7	−0.8	0.0	Compte de capital : débit
Financial Account,nie	22.8	157.5	114.6	70.2	243.3	260.7	351.4	Compte d'op. fin., nia
Net Errors and Omissions	−47.5	115.5	45.0	157.9	196.5	6.7	52.5	Erreurs et omissions nettes
Reserves and Related Items	333.4	70.3	41.3	78.8	−182.2	1.9	57.7	Rés. et postes appareutés
Jamaica								**Jamaïque**
Goods: Exports fob	1 105.4	1 548.0	1 796.0	1 721.0	1 700.3	1 613.4	1 489.9	Biens : exportations,fàb
Goods: Imports fob	−1 920.5	−2 099.2	−2 625.3	−2 715.2	−2 832.6	−2 743.9	−2 627.6	Biens : importations,fàb
Serv. & Income: Credit	1 377.7	1 601.6	1 759.4	1 766.3	1 861.9	1 942.4	2 031.6	Serv. & revenu : crédit
Serv. & Income: Debit	−1 136.4	−1 417.1	−1 611.2	−1 507.3	−1 665.0	−1 749.3	−1 798.9	Serv. & revenu : débit
Current Trans.,nie: Credit	415.9	504.2	669.6	709.3	705.7	732.1	756.3	Transf. cour.,nia : crédit
Current Transfers: Debit	−26.1	−44.3	−62.6	−85.7	−80.9	−97.1	−107.0	Transf. courants : débit
Capital Acct.,nie: Credit	0.0	33.2	34.5	42.5	21.7	20.3	19.1	Compte de cap.,nia : crédit
Capital Account: Debit	−12.9	−1.5	−3.4	−4.8	−4.8	−4.8	−6.0	Compte de capital : débit
Financial Account,nie	257.1	256.1	108.3	288.6	163.5	337.2	172.6	Compte d'op. fin., nia
Net Errors and Omissions	49.7	−23.3	−38.3	56.7	−40.2	−6.4	−66.4	Erreurs et omissions nettes
Reserves and Related Items	−109.9	−357.7	−27.0	−271.4	170.4	−43.9	136.4	Rés. et postes appareutés
Mexico								**Mexique**
Goods: Exports fob	51 885.0	60 882.2	79 541.6	96 000.0	110 431.0	117 459.0	136 703.0	Biens : exportations,fàb
Goods: Imports fob	−65 366.0	−79 346.0	−72 453.0	−89 469.0	−109 808.0	−125 374.0	−142 063.0	Biens : importations,fàb
Serv. & Income: Credit	12 211.0	13 667.9	13 492.8	14 932.6	15 830.0	16 975.0	16 847.0	Serv. & revenu : crédit
Serv. & Income: Debit	−25 770.0	−28 648.1	−26 117.7	−28 321.6	−29 154.0	−30 799.0	−31 819.0	Serv. & revenu : débit
Current Trans.,nie: Credit	3 656.0	3 821.7	3 995.0	4 560.2	5 272.0	6 042.0	6 341.0	Transf. cour.,nia : crédit
Current Transfers: Debit	−16.0	−39.8	−35.0	−30.0	−25.0	−28.0	−25.0	Transf. courants : débit
Capital Acct.,nie: Credit	0.0	0.0	0.0	0.0	0.0	0.0	0.0	Compte de cap.,nia : crédit
Capital Account: Debit	0.0	0.0	0.0	0.0	0.0	0.0	0.0	Compte de capital : débit
Financial Account,nie	33 760.0	15 786.8	−10 487.3	6 132.0	19 253.4	18 540.0	17 826.0	Compte d'op. fin., nia
Net Errors and Omissions	−3 128.3	−3 323.5	−4 247.8	58.5	2 198.0	377.6	468.4	Erreurs et omissions nettes
Reserves and Related Items	−7 231.7	17 198.8	16 311.5	−3 862.6	−13 997.4	−3 192.6	−4 278.4	Rés. et postes appareutés
Montserrat								**Montserrat**
Goods: Exports fob	2.3	2.9	...	...	...	...	...	Biens : exportations,fàb
Goods: Imports fob	−24.2	−30.0	...	...	...	...	...	Biens : importations,fàb
Serv. & Income: Credit	23.8	27.6	...	...	...	...	...	Serv. & revenu : crédit
Serv. & Income: Debit	−15.2	−19.7	...	...	...	...	...	Serv. & revenu : débit
Current Trans.,nie: Credit	9.7	3.3	...	...	...	...	...	Transf. cour.,nia : crédit
Current Transfers: Debit	−6.4	−3.4	...	...	...	...	...	Transf. courants : débit
Capital Acct.,nie: Credit	5.4	10.1	...	...	...	...	...	Compte de cap.,nia : crédit
Capital Account: Debit	0.0	0.0	...	...	...	...	...	Compte de capital : débit
Financial Account,nie	5.5	−4.3	...	...	...	...	...	Compte d'op. fin., nia
Net Errors and Omissions	−1.2	15.1	...	...	...	...	...	Erreurs et omissions nettes
Reserves and Related Items	0.4	−1.6	...	...	...	...	...	Rés. et postes appareutés
Netherlands Antilles								**Antilles néerlandaises**
Goods: Exports fob	306.0	351.1	354.2	...	...	...	...	Biens : exportations,fàb
Goods: Imports fob	−1 143.8	−1 271.6	−1 318.7	...	...	...	...	Biens : importations,fàb
Serv. & Income: Credit	1 468.7	1 547.9	1 809.4	...	...	...	...	Serv. & revenu : crédit
Serv. & Income: Debit	−736.3	−769.9	−855.8	...	...	...	...	Serv. & revenu : débit
Current Trans.,nie: Credit	250.3	217.9	245.9	...	...	...	...	Transf. cour.,nia : crédit
Current Transfers: Debit	−143.7	−173.3	−148.5	...	...	...	...	Transf. courants : débit
Capital Acct.,nie: Credit	0.8	1.0	1.4	...	...	...	...	Compte de cap.,nia : crédit
Capital Account: Debit	−1.7	−1.7	−2.2	...	...	...	...	Compte de capital : débit
Financial Account,nie	32.2	−2.3	31.1	...	...	...	...	Compte d'op. fin., nia
Net Errors and Omissions	11.5	24.9	22.5	...	...	...	...	Erreurs et omissions nettes
Reserves and Related Items	−44.0	75.9	−139.3	...	...	...	...	Rés. et postes appareutés
Nicaragua								**Nicaragua**
Goods: Exports fob	267.0	339.2	448.4	489.8	630.9	579.4	550.0	Biens : exportations,fàb
Goods: Imports fob	−659.4	−769.7	−850.0	−940.8	−1 329.3	−1 383.1	−1 683.2	Biens : importations,fàb
Serv. & Income: Credit	105.6	131.8	149.0	184.3	231.3	270.6	315.7	Serv. & revenu : crédit

75
Summary of balance of payments
Millions of US dollars
Résumé des balances des paiements
Millions de dollars des E.−U.

Country or area	1993	1994	1995	1996	1997	1998	1999	Pays ou zone
Serv. & Income: Debit	−591.1	−648.5	−596.4	−583.7	−516.5	−483.1	−554.7	Serv. & revenu : débit
Current Trans.,nie: Credit	233.6	248.4	285.5	350.2	427.4	518.0	720.0	Transf. cour.,nia : crédit
Current Transfers: Debit	0.0	0.0	0.0	0.0	0.0	0.0	0.0	Transf. courants : débit
Capital Acct.,nie: Credit	0.0	0.0	0.0	0.0	0.0	0.0	0.0	Compte de cap.,nia : crédit
Capital Account: Debit	0.0	0.0	0.0	0.0	0.0	0.0	0.0	Compte de capital : débit
Financial Account,nie	−502.8	−901.9	−601.8	−378.2	−61.0	83.6	391.9	Compte d'op. fin., nia
Net Errors and Omissions	128.1	72.1	64.2	79.5	322.6	13.8	−192.8	Erreurs et omissions nettes
Reserves and Related Items	1 019.0	1 528.6	1 101.1	798.9	294.6	400.8	453.1	Rés. et postes appareutés
Panama								**Panama**
Goods: Exports fob	5 416.9	6 044.8	6 090.9	5 822.9	6 655.4	6 325.2	5 198.2	Biens : exportations,fàb
Goods: Imports fob	−5 751.1	−6 294.9	−6 679.8	−6 467.0	−7 355.7	−7 696.2	−6 595.9	Biens : importations,fàb
Serv. & Income: Credit	2 352.1	2 606.6	3 163.5	2 980.7	3 084.4	3 422.6	3 254.5	Serv. & revenu : crédit
Serv. & Income: Debit	−2 316.7	−2 489.6	−3 096.3	−2 773.2	−3 138.2	−3 422.2	−3 353.6	Serv. & revenu : débit
Current Trans.,nie: Credit	236.5	185.5	184.1	167.7	185.2	195.2	202.7	Transf. cour.,nia : crédit
Current Transfers: Debit	−33.4	−36.6	−31.5	−33.0	−34.6	−36.2	−38.5	Transf. courants : débit
Capital Acct.,nie: Credit	0.0	0.0	8.5	2.5	72.7	50.9	3.0	Compte de cap.,nia : crédit
Capital Account: Debit	0.0	0.0	0.0	0.0	0.0	0.0	0.0	Compte de capital : débit
Financial Account,nie	−521.4	−297.2	159.3	533.0	788.3	878.6	1 118.4	Compte d'op. fin., nia
Net Errors and Omissions	309.0	−80.4	−130.0	33.2	85.8	−181.1	63.4	Erreurs et omissions nettes
Reserves and Related Items	308.1	361.8	331.3	−266.8	−343.3	463.2	147.8	Rés. et postes appareutés
Saint Kitts and Nevis								**Saint−Kitts−et−Nevis**
Goods: Exports fob	31.9	29.3	...	...	...	...	...	Biens : exportations,fàb
Goods: Imports fob	−94.6	−98.3	...	...	...	...	...	Biens : importations,fàb
Serv. & Income: Credit	85.9	94.5	...	...	...	...	...	Serv. & revenu : crédit
Serv. & Income: Debit	−61.3	−61.5	...	...	...	...	...	Serv. & revenu : débit
Current Trans.,nie: Credit	14.2	15.2	...	...	...	...	...	Transf. cour.,nia : crédit
Current Transfers: Debit	−6.2	−5.7	...	...	...	...	...	Transf. courants : débit
Capital Acct.,nie: Credit	3.5	2.6	...	...	...	...	...	Compte de cap.,nia : crédit
Capital Account: Debit	−0.2	−0.9	...	...	...	...	...	Compte de capital : débit
Financial Account,nie	15.2	26.0	...	...	...	...	...	Compte d'op. fin., nia
Net Errors and Omissions	11.5	−1.3	...	...	...	...	...	Erreurs et omissions nettes
Reserves and Related Items	−3.4	−2.3	...	...	...	...	...	Rés. et postes appareutés
Saint Lucia								**Sainte−Lucie**
Goods: Exports fob	123.5	99.9	114.6	86.3	...	...	...	Biens : exportations,fàb
Goods: Imports fob	−264.0	−265.6	−269.4	−270.7	...	...	...	Biens : importations,fàb
Serv. & Income: Credit	209.0	242.7	271.6	273.0	...	...	...	Serv. & revenu : crédit
Serv. & Income: Debit	−127.1	−143.3	−169.2	−182.9	...	...	...	Serv. & revenu : débit
Current Trans.,nie: Credit	21.9	26.1	28.7	26.5	...	...	...	Transf. cour.,nia : crédit
Current Transfers: Debit	−12.6	−8.3	−9.5	−12.5	...	...	...	Transf. courants : débit
Capital Acct.,nie: Credit	4.2	11.8	13.6	9.5	...	...	...	Compte de cap.,nia : crédit
Capital Account: Debit	−0.3	−1.1	−0.4	−0.7	...	...	...	Compte de capital : débit
Financial Account,nie	56.1	41.7	28.1	61.2	...	...	...	Compte d'op. fin., nia
Net Errors and Omissions	−6.1	−6.3	−2.8	3.5	...	...	...	Erreurs et omissions nettes
Reserves and Related Items	−4.5	2.4	−5.3	6.9	...	...	...	Rés. et postes appareutés
St. Vincent−Grenadines								**St. Vincent−Grenadines**
Goods: Exports fob	57.1	48.9	61.9	52.3	...	...	...	Biens : exportations,fàb
Goods: Imports fob	−118.1	−115.4	−119.4	−127.5	...	...	...	Biens : importations,fàb
Serv. & Income: Credit	65.2	67.4	78.2	98.2	...	...	...	Serv. & revenu : crédit
Serv. & Income: Debit	−55.0	−70.6	−70.8	−69.7	...	...	...	Serv. & revenu : débit
Current Trans.,nie: Credit	15.6	19.4	16.8	18.5	...	...	...	Transf. cour.,nia : crédit
Current Transfers: Debit	−8.6	−7.6	−7.9	−7.2	...	...	...	Transf. courants : débit
Capital Acct.,nie: Credit	7.0	5.4	6.9	5.2	...	...	...	Compte de cap.,nia : crédit
Capital Account: Debit	−0.7	−1.4	−0.7	−1.1	...	...	...	Compte de capital : débit
Financial Account,nie	32.8	50.9	35.8	18.3	...	...	...	Compte d'op. fin., nia
Net Errors and Omissions	3.4	3.5	−1.1	13.2	...	...	...	Erreurs et omissions nettes
Reserves and Related Items	1.3	−0.5	0.3	−0.4	...	...	...	Rés. et postes appareutés
Trinidad and Tobago								**Trinité−et−Tobago**
Goods: Exports fob	1 500.1	1 777.6	2 456.1	2 354.1	2 448.0	2 258.0	...	Biens : exportations,fàb
Goods: Imports fob	−952.9	−1 036.6	−1 868.5	−1 971.6	−2 976.6	−2 998.9	...	Biens : importations,fàb
Serv. & Income: Credit	393.7	383.3	419.2	500.3	610.3	735.8	...	Serv. & revenu : crédit
Serv. & Income: Debit	−832.4	−906.8	−708.6	−770.6	−699.0	−660.7	...	Serv. & revenu : débit
Current Trans.,nie: Credit	23.7	28.3	34.0	34.2	37.0	58.4	...	Transf. cour.,nia : crédit
Current Transfers: Debit	−19.0	−27.9	−38.5	−41.3	−33.2	−36.2	...	Transf. courants : débit
Capital Acct.,nie: Credit	1.3	1.1	1.1	0.0	0.0	0.0	...	Compte de cap.,nia : crédit
Capital Account: Debit	−12.8	−7.5	−13.0	0.0	0.0	0.0	...	Compte de capital : débit
Financial Account,nie	98.8	−32.2	−214.7	43.0	697.2	471.5	...	Compte d'op. fin., nia

75
Summary of balance of payments
Millions of US dollars
Résumé des balances des paiements
Millions de dollars des E.−U.

Country or area	1993	1994	1995	1996	1997	1998	1999	Pays ou zone
Net Errors and Omissions	−41.8	6.3	16.5	90.0	110.1	252.2	...	Erreurs et omissions nettes
Reserves and Related Items	−158.6	−185.5	−83.7	−238.1	−193.6	−80.2	...	Rés. et postes appareutés
United States [1]								**Etats−Unis** [1]
Goods: Exports fob	458.7	504.5	577.7	614.0	681.6	672.3	686.7	Biens : exportations,fàb
Goods: Imports fob	−589.4	−668.6	−749.6	−803.3	−876.4	−917.2	−1 029.9	Biens : importations,fàb
Serv. & Income: Credit	311.8	356.6	420.3	451.6	501.1	511.8	533.4	Serv. & revenu : crédit
Serv. & Income: Debit	−229.4	−277.1	−328.0	−350.9	−412.3	−441.4	−479.6	Serv. & revenu : débit
Current Trans.,nie: Credit	5.9	6.5	7.7	8.9	8.5	9.3	9.4	Transf. cour.,nia : crédit
Current Transfers: Debit	−43.6	−44.7	−41.7	−49.0	−49.3	−53.4	−57.4	Transf. courants : débit
Capital Acct.,nie: Credit	0.5	0.5	0.8	0.7	0.3	0.6	0.5	Compte de cap.,nia : crédit
Capital Account: Debit	−0.5	−0.8	−0.3	0.0	−0.2	0.0	−0.7	Compte de capital : débit
Financial Account,nie	51.1	87.0	98.6	123.8	234.4	39.1	138.2	Compte d'op. fin., nia
Net Errors and Omissions	35.4	36.1	17.9	5.2	−83.9	184.1	193.9	Erreurs et omissions nettes
Reserves and Related Items	−0.6	0.1	−3.3	−0.9	−3.9	−5.2	5.5	Rés. et postes appareutés
**America, South • Amérique du Sud**								
Argentina								**Argentine**
Goods: Exports fob	13 269.0	16 023.0	21 161.0	24 043.0	26 431.0	26 441.0	23 333.0	Biens : exportations,fàb
Goods: Imports fob	−15 633.0	−20 162.0	−18 804.0	−22 283.0	−28 554.0	−29 558.0	−24 115.0	Biens : importations,fàb
Serv. & Income: Credit	5 782.0	6 892.0	8 268.0	8 895.0	10 010.0	10 862.0	10 581.0	Serv. & revenu : crédit
Serv. & Income: Debit	−11 934.0	−14 151.0	−16 123.0	−17 592.0	−20 277.0	−22 648.0	−22 596.0	Serv. & revenu : débit
Current Trans.,nie: Credit	674.0	628.0	623.0	510.0	542.0	634.0	592.0	Transf. cour.,nia : crédit
Current Transfers: Debit	−188.0	−222.0	−110.0	−94.0	−106.0	−107.0	−85.0	Transf. courants : débit
Capital Acct.,nie: Credit	0.0	0.0	0.0	0.0	0.0	0.0	0.0	Compte de cap.,nia : crédit
Capital Account: Debit	0.0	0.0	0.0	0.0	0.0	0.0	0.0	Compte de capital : débit
Financial Account,nie	20 328.0	11 155.0	4 623.0	11 175.0	16 826.0	17 674.0	14 780.0	Compte d'op. fin., nia
Net Errors and Omissions	−1 172.9	−871.8	−1 853.4	−1 316.3	−1 498.5	792.3	−477.5	Erreurs et omissions nettes
Reserves and Related Items	−11 125.1	708.8	2 215.4	−3 337.7	−3 373.6	−4 090.3	−2 012.6	Rés. et postes appareutés
Bolivia								**Bolivie**
Goods: Exports fob	715.5	985.1	1 041.4	1 132.0	1 166.6	1 104.0	1 051.1	Biens : exportations,fàb
Goods: Imports fob	−1 111.7	−1 015.3	−1 223.7	−1 368.0	−1 643.6	−1 759.5	−1 539.1	Biens : importations,fàb
Serv. & Income: Credit	190.6	214.7	220.7	209.5	345.4	380.9	416.4	Serv. & revenu : crédit
Serv. & Income: Debit	−536.8	−538.7	−585.1	−600.2	−713.4	−730.5	−808.0	Serv. & revenu : débit
Current Trans.,nie: Credit	241.0	269.2	248.0	226.2	300.3	341.6	352.2	Transf. cour.,nia : crédit
Current Transfers: Debit	−4.1	−5.2	−3.8	−3.8	−8.8	−11.7	−28.6	Transf. courants : débit
Capital Acct.,nie: Credit	1.0	1.2	2.0	2.8	25.3	9.9	0.0	Compte de cap.,nia : crédit
Capital Account: Debit	0.0	0.0	0.0	0.0	0.0	0.0	0.0	Compte de capital : débit
Financial Account,nie	347.1	315.3	505.2	701.0	889.8	999.1	732.2	Compte d'op. fin., nia
Net Errors and Omissions	123.6	−315.8	−112.3	−31.6	−260.6	−232.1	−218.0	Erreurs et omissions nettes
Reserves and Related Items	33.7	89.5	−92.4	−268.0	−101.0	−101.7	41.8	Rés. et postes appareutés
Brazil								**Brésil**
Goods: Exports fob	39 630.0	44 102.0	46 506.0	47 851.0	53 189.0	51 136.0	48 012.0	Biens : exportations,fàb
Goods: Imports fob	−25 301.0	−33 241.0	−49 663.0	−53 304.0	−59 841.0	−57 739.0	−49 219.0	Biens : importations,fàb
Serv. & Income: Credit	5 273.0	7 110.0	9 592.0	10 005.0	11 333.0	12 545.0	11 663.0	Serv. & revenu : crédit
Serv. & Income: Debit	−21 185.0	−21 547.0	−28 192.0	−30 241.0	−36 986.0	−41 207.0	−37 217.0	Serv. & revenu : débit
Current Trans.,nie: Credit	1 704.0	2 577.0	3 861.0	2 699.0	2 130.0	1 795.0	1 968.0	Transf. cour.,nia : crédit
Current Transfers: Debit	−101.0	−154.0	−240.0	−258.0	−316.0	−359.0	−280.0	Transf. courants : débit
Capital Acct.,nie: Credit	86.0	175.0	363.0	507.0	519.0	488.0	361.0	Compte de cap.,nia : crédit
Capital Account: Debit	−5.0	−2.0	−11.0	−13.0	−37.0	−113.0	−22.0	Compte de capital : débit
Financial Account,nie	7 604.0	8 020.0	29 306.0	33 142.0	24 918.0	20 063.0	7 223.0	Compte d'op. fin., nia
Net Errors and Omissions	−814.8	−441.8	1 446.7	−1 991.6	−3 160.2	−2 910.7	745.6	Erreurs et omissions nettes
Reserves and Related Items	−6 890.2	−6 598.2	−12 968.7	−8 396.4	8 251.2	16 301.7	16 765.4	Rés. et postes appareutés
Chile								**Chili**
Goods: Exports fob	9 198.7	11 604.1	16 025.0	15 405.0	16 663.0	14 831.0	15 616.0	Biens : exportations,fàb
Goods: Imports fob	−10 188.5	−10 872.1	−14 644.0	−16 496.0	−18 221.0	−17 347.0	−13 952.0	Biens : importations,fàb
Serv. & Income: Credit	3 013.9	3 396.3	4 201.4	4 456.0	5 195.3	5 257.0	4 893.0	Serv. & revenu : crédit
Serv. & Income: Debit	−4 898.4	−6 044.5	−7 239.0	−7 382.0	−7 886.0	−7 343.0	−7 089.0	Serv. & revenu : débit
Current Trans.,nie: Credit	535.8	449.2	482.0	664.0	877.0	815.0	793.0	Transf. cour.,nia : crédit
Current Transfers: Debit	−215.9	−117.9	−175.0	−157.0	−356.0	−352.0	−341.0	Transf. courants : débit
Capital Acct.,nie: Credit	0.0	0.0	0.0	0.0	0.0	0.0	0.0	Compte de cap.,nia : crédit
Capital Account: Debit	0.0	0.0	0.0	0.0	0.0	0.0	0.0	Compte de capital : débit
Financial Account,nie	2 994.9	5 293.6	2 356.6	6 664.6	7 355.2	3 181.0	−829.0	Compte d'op. fin., nia
Net Errors and Omissions	−12.9	−557.9	131.5	−650.8	−443.1	−1 177.3	150.8	Erreurs et omissions nettes
Reserves and Related Items	−427.5	−3 150.8	−1 138.5	−2 503.8	−3 184.5	2 135.3	758.2	Rés. et postes appareutés
Colombia								**Colombie**
Goods: Exports fob	7 428.5	9 058.0	10 528.0	10 952.0	12 059.0	11 493.0	12 045.0	Biens : exportations,fàb
Goods: Imports fob	−9 085.7	−11 298.0	−13 167.0	−13 092.0	−14 774.0	−14 007.0	−10 311.0	Biens : importations,fàb

75
Summary of balance of payments
Millions of US dollars
Résumé des balances des paiements
Millions de dollars des E.−U.

Country or area	1993	1994	1995	1996	1997	1998	1999	Pays ou zone
Serv. & Income: Credit	3 081.1	2 349.0	2 430.0	2 894.0	3 025.0	2 974.0	2 700.0	Serv. & revenu : crédit
Serv. & Income: Debit	−4 664.3	−4 795.0	−5 172.0	−6 173.0	−6 871.0	−6 179.0	−6 202.0	Serv. & revenu : débit
Current Trans.,nie: Credit	1 350.0	1 284.0	988.0	811.0	830.0	611.0	970.0	Transf. cour.,nia : crédit
Current Transfers: Debit	−212.0	−194.0	−231.0	−220.0	−219.0	−164.0	−181.0	Transf. courants : débit
Capital Acct.,nie: Credit	0.0	0.0	0.0	0.0	0.0	0.0	0.0	Compte de cap.,nia : crédit
Capital Account: Debit	0.0	0.0	0.0	0.0	0.0	0.0	0.0	Compte de capital : débit
Financial Account,nie	2 701.4	3 421.0	4 687.0	6 707.0	7 095.0	4 542.0	378.0	Compte d'op. fin., nia
Net Errors and Omissions	−134.6	357.0	−67.9	−148.8	−866.5	−659.9	287.9	Erreurs et omissions nettes
Reserves and Related Items	−464.4	−182.0	4.9	−1 730.2	−278.5	1 389.9	313.1	Rés. et postes appareutés
Ecuador								**Equateur**
Goods: Exports fob	3 066.0	3 843.0	4 381.0	4 873.0	5 264.0	4 203.0	4 451.0	Biens : exportations,fàb
Goods: Imports fob	−2 474.0	−3 282.0	−4 057.0	−3 680.0	−4 666.0	−5 198.0	−2 786.0	Biens : importations,fàb
Serv. & Income: Credit	680.0	797.0	936.0	931.0	928.0	890.0	861.0	Serv. & revenu : crédit
Serv. & Income: Debit	−2 080.0	−2 184.0	−2 256.0	−2 330.0	−2 631.0	−2 840.0	−2 672.0	Serv. & revenu : débit
Current Trans.,nie: Credit	145.0	164.0	250.0	359.0	438.0	840.0	1 151.0	Transf. cour.,nia : crédit
Current Transfers: Debit	−15.0	−19.0	−19.0	−69.0	−47.0	−64.0	−50.0	Transf. courants : débit
Capital Acct.,nie: Credit	0.0	0.0	0.0	0.0	0.0	0.0	0.0	Compte de cap.,nia : crédit
Capital Account: Debit	0.0	0.0	0.0	0.0	0.0	0.0	0.0	Compte de capital : débit
Financial Account,nie	1 309.0	998.0	1 883.0	1 514.0	1 454.0	2 114.0	743.0	Compte d'op. fin., nia
Net Errors and Omissions	−91.7	21.7	−1 307.0	−1 343.5	−477.3	−352.4	−2 024.3	Erreurs et omissions nettes
Reserves and Related Items	−539.3	−338.7	189.0	−254.5	−262.7	407.4	326.3	Rés. et postes appareutés
Guyana								**Guyane**
Goods: Exports fob	415.5	463.4	495.7	...	...	...	...	Biens : exportations,fàb
Goods: Imports fob	−483.8	−504.0	−536.5	...	...	...	...	Biens : importations,fàb
Serv. & Income: Credit	120.4	129.4	145.7	...	...	...	...	Serv. & revenu : crédit
Serv. & Income: Debit	−254.9	−275.7	−301.7	...	...	...	...	Serv. & revenu : débit
Current Trans.,nie: Credit	70.0	68.1	67.3	...	...	...	...	Transf. cour.,nia : crédit
Current Transfers: Debit	−7.4	−6.2	−5.3	...	...	...	...	Transf. courants : débit
Capital Acct.,nie: Credit	6.6	11.0	12.5	...	...	...	...	Compte de cap.,nia : crédit
Capital Account: Debit	−2.2	−2.7	−3.0	...	...	...	...	Compte de capital : débit
Financial Account,nie	88.7	126.9	71.1	...	...	...	...	Compte d'op. fin., nia
Net Errors and Omissions	11.0	−16.3	11.2	...	...	...	...	Erreurs et omissions nettes
Reserves and Related Items	36.1	6.0	43.0	...	...	...	...	Rés. et postes appareutés
Paraguay								**Paraguay**
Goods: Exports fob	2 859.0	3 360.1	4 218.6	3 796.9	3 880.0	3 723.2	2 708.3	Biens : exportations,fàb
Goods: Imports fob	−2 779.6	−3 603.5	−4 489.0	−4 383.4	−4 192.4	−3 941.5	−3 039.8	Biens : importations,fàb
Serv. & Income: Credit	636.9	674.1	849.0	869.9	919.3	878.6	760.9	Serv. & revenu : crédit
Serv. & Income: Debit	−735.4	−727.5	−869.9	−828.0	−893.6	−826.3	−710.5	Serv. & revenu : débit
Current Trans.,nie: Credit	78.6	25.6	64.8	46.1	41.0	35.7	47.7	Transf. cour.,nia : crédit
Current Transfers: Debit	−0.4	−2.9	−4.4	−0.8	−1.3	−1.0	−1.2	Transf. courants : débit
Capital Acct.,nie: Credit	22.1	8.8	10.6	14.2	7.5	5.4	10.0	Compte de cap.,nia : crédit
Capital Account: Debit	0.0	0.0	0.0	0.0	0.0	0.0	0.0	Compte de capital : débit
Financial Account,nie	8.5	212.9	238.4	121.2	435.8	184.6	71.5	Compte d'op. fin., nia
Net Errors and Omissions	−46.4	353.0	33.5	317.4	−412.2	−42.0	−149.9	Erreurs et omissions nettes
Reserves and Related Items	−43.3	−300.6	−51.6	46.5	215.9	−16.7	303.0	Rés. et postes appareutés
Peru								**Pérou**
Goods: Exports fob	3 517.0	4 598.2	5 589.0	5 898.0	6 831.0	5 757.0	6 112.0	Biens : exportations,fàb
Goods: Imports fob	−4 122.0	−5 596.9	−7 755.0	−7 885.0	−8 554.0	−8 220.0	−6 729.0	Biens : importations,fàb
Serv. & Income: Credit	1 048.0	1 404.9	1 715.2	2 028.0	2 265.0	2 523.0	2 180.0	Serv. & revenu : crédit
Serv. & Income: Debit	−3 238.0	−3 708.8	−4 478.0	−4 353.0	−4 499.0	−4 611.0	−4 328.0	Serv. & revenu : débit
Current Trans.,nie: Credit	514.0	754.0	817.0	891.0	909.0	923.0	970.0	Transf. cour.,nia : crédit
Current Transfers: Debit	−6.0	−6.7	−5.0	−8.0	−8.0	−11.0	−27.0	Transf. courants : débit
Capital Acct.,nie: Credit	47.0	31.1	66.0	52.0	25.0	21.0	18.0	Compte de cap.,nia : crédit
Capital Account: Debit	−125.0	−123.9	−45.0	−38.0	−100.0	−108.0	−112.0	Compte de capital : débit
Financial Account,nie	1 583.0	3 908.6	3 016.0	3 371.0	5 594.0	1 701.0	721.0	Compte d'op. fin., nia
Net Errors and Omissions	559.2	191.9	494.2	905.6	−290.4	662.9	348.1	Erreurs et omissions nettes
Reserves and Related Items	222.8	−1 452.4	585.6	−861.6	−2 172.6	1 362.1	846.9	Rés. et postes appareutés
Suriname								**Suriname**
Goods: Exports fob	298.3	293.6	415.6	397.2	401.6	349.7	...	Biens : exportations,fàb
Goods: Imports fob	−213.9	−194.3	−292.6	−398.8	−365.5	−376.9	...	Biens : importations,fàb
Serv. & Income: Credit	46.7	73.5	106.8	110.8	99.0	78.5	...	Serv. & revenu : crédit
Serv. & Income: Debit	−108.0	−118.2	−166.7	−173.8	−203.8	−203.9	...	Serv. & revenu : débit
Current Trans.,nie: Credit	26.7	6.2	2.0	3.6	4.0	1.3	...	Transf. cour.,nia : crédit
Current Transfers: Debit	−5.8	−2.2	−2.3	−2.5	−3.0	−3.6	...	Transf. courants : débit
Capital Acct.,nie: Credit	3.5	0.2	22.1	41.6	14.6	6.6	...	Compte de cap.,nia : crédit
Capital Account: Debit	−3.0	−0.4	0.0	0.0	0.0	0.0	...	Compte de capital : débit

75
Summary of balance of payments
Millions of US dollars
Résumé des balances des paiements
Millions de dollars des E.–U.

Country or area	1993	1994	1995	1996	1997	1998	1999	Pays ou zone
Financial Account,nie	−73.1	−84.1	−6.7	27.7	26.9	30.5	...	Compte d'op. fin., nia
Net Errors and Omissions	41.3	60.0	41.6	−7.5	45.3	125.9	...	Erreurs et omissions nettes
Reserves and Related Items	−12.7	−34.3	−119.8	1.7	−19.1	−8.1	...	Rés. et postes appareutés
Uruguay								**Uruguay**
Goods: Exports fob	1 731.6	1 917.6	2 147.6	2 448.5	2 793.1	2 829.3	2 304.5	Biens : exportations,fàb
Goods: Imports fob	−2 118.3	−2 623.6	−2 710.6	−3 135.4	−3 497.5	−3 601.4	−3 172.9	Biens : importations,fàb
Serv. & Income: Credit	1 278.5	1 613.2	1 763.5	1 859.2	1 971.4	1 927.1	1 929.1	Serv. & revenu : crédit
Serv. & Income: Debit	−1 189.0	−1 386.7	−1 489.0	−1 488.2	−1 628.6	−1 689.5	−1 735.7	Serv. & revenu : débit
Current Trans.,nie: Credit	61.2	49.2	84.0	90.7	83.0	75.0	78.4	Transf. cour.,nia : crédit
Current Transfers: Debit	−7.8	−8.0	−8.0	−8.2	−8.8	−16.0	−8.4	Transf. courants : débit
Capital Acct.,nie: Credit	0.0	0.0	0.0	0.0	0.0	0.0	0.0	Compte de cap.,nia : crédit
Capital Account: Debit	0.0	0.0	0.0	0.0	0.0	0.0	0.0	Compte de capital : débit
Financial Account,nie	228.0	537.2	421.7	233.6	608.7	125.7	478.4	Compte d'op. fin., nia
Net Errors and Omissions	208.7	10.2	18.6	152.2	78.8	285.5	96.8	Erreurs et omissions nettes
Reserves and Related Items	−192.9	−109.1	−227.8	−152.4	−400.1	64.3	29.8	Rés. et postes appareutés
Venezuela								**Venezuela**
Goods: Exports fob	14 779.0	16 105.0	19 082.0	23 707.0	23 703.0	17 564.0	20 915.0	Biens : exportations,fàb
Goods: Imports fob	−11 504.0	−8 480.0	−12 069.0	−9 937.0	−13 678.0	−14 816.0	−11 751.0	Biens : importations,fàb
Serv. & Income: Credit	2 939.0	3 202.0	3 538.0	3 152.0	3 628.0	3 885.0	3 263.0	Serv. & revenu : crédit
Serv. & Income: Debit	−7 839.0	−8 202.0	−8 646.0	−8 146.0	−10 042.0	−9 041.0	−7 095.0	Serv. & revenu : débit
Current Trans.,nie: Credit	452.0	606.0	413.0	526.0	221.0	229.0	292.0	Transf. cour.,nia : crédit
Current Transfers: Debit	−820.0	−690.0	−304.0	−388.0	−365.0	−383.0	−257.0	Transf. courants : débit
Capital Acct.,nie: Credit	0.0	0.0	0.0	0.0	0.0	0.0	0.0	Compte de cap.,nia : crédit
Capital Account: Debit	0.0	0.0	0.0	0.0	0.0	0.0	0.0	Compte de capital : débit
Financial Account,nie	2 656.0	−3 204.0	−2 964.0	−1 784.0	1 067.0	844.0	−2 932.0	Compte d'op. fin., nia
Net Errors and Omissions	−538.8	−281.1	−494.2	−891.8	−1 458.6	−1 226.3	−1 409.0	Erreurs et omissions nettes
Reserves and Related Items	−124.2	944.1	1 444.2	−6 238.2	−3 075.4	2 944.3	−1 026.0	Rés. et postes appareutés
Asia · Asie								
Armenia								**Arménie**
Goods: Exports fob	156.2	215.4	270.9	290.4	233.6	228.9	247.3	Biens : exportations,fàb
Goods: Imports fob	−254.2	−393.6	−673.9	−759.6	−793.1	−806.4	−721.3	Biens : importations,fàb
Serv. & Income: Credit	17.3	13.7	83.2	155.8	235.6	234.2	229.4	Serv. & revenu : crédit
Serv. & Income: Debit	−41.4	−44.7	−66.9	−161.8	−199.8	−252.2	−248.0	Serv. & revenu : débit
Current Trans.,nie: Credit	56.3	106.3	170.0	199.0	252.4	203.0	200.6	Transf. cour.,nia : crédit
Current Transfers: Debit	−1.1	−0.8	−1.7	−14.4	−35.2	−25.6	−26.5	Transf. courants : débit
Capital Acct.,nie: Credit	5.1	5.7	8.1	13.4	10.9	9.7	16.9	Compte de cap.,nia : crédit
Capital Account: Debit	0.0	0.0	0.0	0.0	0.0	0.0	−4.3	Compte de capital : débit
Financial Account,nie	57.8	89.9	227.5	216.8	334.8	378.9	279.7	Compte d'op. fin., nia
Net Errors and Omissions	17.2	4.8	12.4	15.1	10.8	30.1	31.1	Erreurs et omissions nettes
Reserves and Related Items	−13.3	3.3	−29.5	45.5	−50.0	−0.6	−4.8	Rés. et postes appareutés
Azerbaijan								**Azerbaïdjan**
Goods: Exports fob	...	...	612.3	643.7	808.3	677.8	1 025.2	Biens : exportations,fàb
Goods: Imports fob	...	...	−985.4	−1 337.6	−1 375.2	−1 723.9	−1 433.4	Biens : importations,fàb
Serv. & Income: Credit	...	...	182.3	164.3	364.6	370.0	267.8	Serv. & revenu : crédit
Serv. & Income: Debit	...	...	−320.6	−468.1	−758.2	−752.3	−541.1	Serv. & revenu : débit
Current Trans.,nie: Credit	...	...	129.3	107.2	95.7	145.0	134.5	Transf. cour.,nia : crédit
Current Transfers: Debit	...	...	−18.5	−40.7	−50.9	−80.9	−52.8	Transf. courants : débit
Capital Acct.,nie: Credit	...	...	0.0	0.0	0.0	0.0	0.0	Compte de cap.,nia : crédit
Capital Account: Debit	...	...	−1.6	0.0	−10.2	−0.7	0.0	Compte de capital : débit
Financial Account,nie	...	...	400.3	822.5	1 092.1	1 326.0	690.2	Compte d'op. fin., nia
Net Errors and Omissions	...	...	59.7	23.6	−27.0	−20.1	42.4	Erreurs et omissions nettes
Reserves and Related Items	...	...	−57.8	85.0	−139.2	59.2	−132.9	Rés. et postes appareutés
Bahrain								**Bahreïn**
Goods: Exports fob	3 723.4	3 617.0	4 114.4	4 702.1	4 383.0	3 270.2	4 088.3	Biens : exportations,fàb
Goods: Imports fob	−3 616.2	−3 497.3	−3 488.3	−4 037.0	−3 778.2	−3 298.7	−3 369.2	Biens : importations,fàb
Serv. & Income: Credit	2 935.6	3 931.4	4 770.2	4 481.4	4 908.0	5 488.6	5 751.9	Serv. & revenu : crédit
Serv. & Income: Debit	−3 059.6	−3 976.9	−4 780.1	−4 452.9	−5 141.8	−5 578.2	−6 072.1	Serv. & revenu : débit
Current Trans.,nie: Credit	73.1	101.1	120.7	126.3	232.7	65.2	36.7	Transf. cour.,nia : crédit
Current Transfers: Debit	−395.7	−430.6	−499.7	−559.3	−634.8	−725.0	−856.1	Transf. courants : débit
Capital Acct.,nie: Credit	202.1	319.1	156.9	50.0	125.0	100.0	100.0	Compte de cap.,nia : crédit
Capital Account: Debit	0.0	0.0	0.0	0.0	0.0	0.0	0.0	Compte de capital : débit
Financial Account,nie	593.9	1 301.1	−1 726.6	−510.4	15.4	22.6	199.5	Compte d'op. fin., nia
Net Errors and Omissions	−569.2	−1 412.2	1 501.4	193.3	−6.5	638.7	146.3	Erreurs et omissions nettes
Reserves and Related Items	112.5	47.5	−168.9	6.4	−102.8	16.6	−25.3	Rés. et postes appareutés

75
Summary of balance of payments
Millions of US dollars
Résumé des balances des paiements
Millions de dollars des E.–U.

Country or area	1993	1994	1995	1996	1997	1998	1999	Pays ou zone
Bangladesh								**Bangladesh**
Goods: Exports fob	2 544.7	2 934.4	3 733.3	4 009.3	4 839.9	5 141.5	5 458.3	Biens : exportations,fàb
Goods: Imports fob	−3 657.3	−4 350.5	−6 057.4	−6 284.6	−6 587.6	−6 715.7	−7 420.4	Biens : importations,fàb
Serv. & Income: Credit	629.6	740.3	968.3	734.2	773.8	815.4	874.6	Serv. & revenu : crédit
Serv. & Income: Debit	−1 108.0	−1 213.8	−1 733.0	−1 359.1	−1 484.0	−1 443.2	−1 694.5	Serv. & revenu : débit
Current Trans.,nie: Credit	1 951.8	2 091.4	2 266.8	1 912.8	2 134.9	2 172.9	2 495.8	Transf. cour.,nia : crédit
Current Transfers: Debit	−1.5	−2.2	−1.8	−4.0	−4.3	−5.9	−5.3	Transf. courants : débit
Capital Acct.,nie: Credit	0.0	0.0	0.0	371.2	368.1	238.7	362.4	Compte de cap.,nia : crédit
Capital Account: Debit	0.0	0.0	0.0	0.0	0.0	0.0	0.0	Compte de capital : débit
Financial Account,nie	268.9	748.8	178.8	92.4	−99.8	−116.0	−526.8	Compte d'op. fin., nia
Net Errors and Omissions	69.4	−257.1	133.3	113.5	−77.3	201.0	264.2	Erreurs et omissions nettes
Reserves and Related Items	−697.6	−691.3	511.7	414.3	136.3	−288.5	191.6	Rés. et postes appareutés
Cambodia								**Cambodge**
Goods: Exports fob	283.7	489.9	855.2	643.6	736.0	705.4	1 002.1	Biens : exportations,fàb
Goods: Imports fob	−471.1	−744.4	−1 186.8	−1 071.8	−1 064.0	−1 096.8	−1 211.6	Biens : importations,fàb
Serv. & Income: Credit	64.4	56.6	123.7	175.4	176.4	127.7	149.4	Serv. & revenu : crédit
Serv. & Income: Debit	−137.1	−188.7	−254.8	−313.1	−246.5	−257.6	−240.4	Serv. & revenu : débit
Current Trans.,nie: Credit	156.4	230.0	277.9	383.4	188.5	298.0	235.9	Transf. cour.,nia : crédit
Current Transfers: Debit	−0.2	0.0	−0.9	−2.4	−0.3	−0.6	−1.4	Transf. courants : débit
Capital Acct.,nie: Credit	123.4	73.2	78.0	75.8	65.2	61.6	44.0	Compte de cap.,nia : crédit
Capital Account: Debit	0.0	0.0	0.0	0.0	0.0	0.0	0.0	Compte de capital : débit
Financial Account,nie	0.2	54.0	122.4	259.1	219.8	122.8	104.0	Compte d'op. fin., nia
Net Errors and Omissions	1.0	65.6	11.5	−78.0	−41.2	55.3	−32.8	Erreurs et omissions nettes
Reserves and Related Items	−20.8	−36.2	−26.2	−72.0	−33.9	−15.8	−49.2	Rés. et postes appareutés
China ††								**Chine ††**
Goods: Exports fob	75 659.0	102 561.0	128 110.0	151 077.0	182 670.0	183 529.0	194 716.0	Biens : exportations,fàb
Goods: Imports fob	−86 313.0	−95 271.0	−110 060.0	−131 542.0	−136 448.0	−136 915.0	−158 509.0	Biens : importations,fàb
Serv. & Income: Credit	15 583.0	22 357.0	24 321.6	27 919.0	30 279.0	29 479.0	34 349.0	Serv. & revenu : crédit
Serv. & Income: Debit	−17 710.0	−23 074.0	−42 187.9	−42 340.0	−44 682.0	−48 900.0	−59 833.0	Serv. & revenu : débit
Current Trans.,nie: Credit	1 290.0	1 269.0	1 826.7	2 368.0	5 477.0	4 661.0	5 368.0	Transf. cour.,nia : crédit
Current Transfers: Debit	−118.0	−934.0	−392.1	−239.0	−333.0	−382.0	−424.0	Transf. courants : débit
Capital Acct.,nie: Credit	0.0	0.0	0.0	0.0	0.0	0.0	0.0	Compte de cap.,nia : crédit
Capital Account: Debit	0.0	0.0	0.0	0.0	−21.0	−47.0	−26.0	Compte de capital : débit
Financial Account,nie	23 474.0	32 645.0	38 673.8	39 966.0	21 037.0	−6 275.0	7 667.0	Compte d'op. fin., nia
Net Errors and Omissions	−10 096.4	−9 100.3	−17 823.2	−15 504.0	−22 121.8	−18 901.8	−14 655.5	Erreurs et omissions nettes
Reserves and Related Items	−1 768.6	−30 452.8	−22 469.0	−31 705.0	−35 857.2	−6 248.2	−8 652.5	Rés. et postes appareutés
China, Hong Kong SAR †								**Chine, Hong Kong RAS †**
Goods: Exports fob	...	...	...	...	...	175 833.0	174 719.0	Biens : exportations,fàb
Goods: Imports fob	...	...	...	...	...	−183 666.0	−177 878.0	Biens : importations,fàb
Serv. & Income: Credit	...	...	...	...	...	82 503.7	84 401.9	Serv. & revenu : crédit
Serv. & Income: Debit	...	...	...	...	...	−69 183.4	−69 232.2	Serv. & revenu : débit
Current Trans.,nie: Credit	...	...	...	...	...	668.7	708.1	Transf. cour.,nia : crédit
Current Transfers: Debit	...	...	...	...	...	−2 265.0	−2 178.5	Transf. courants : débit
Capital Acct.,nie: Credit	...	...	...	...	...	377.4	103.1	Compte de cap.,nia : crédit
Capital Account: Debit	...	...	...	...	...	−2 759.0	−1 880.0	Compte de capital : débit
Financial Account,nie	...	...	...	...	...	−8 475.8	1 497.8	Compte d'op. fin., nia
Net Errors and Omissions	...	...	...	...	...	69.9	−756.6	Erreurs et omissions nettes
Reserves and Related Items	...	...	...	...	...	6 896.2	−9 504.7	Rés. et postes appareutés
Cyprus								**Chypre**
Goods: Exports fob	867.7	967.5	1 228.7	1 392.4	1 245.8	1 064.6	1 000.3	Biens : exportations,fàb
Goods: Imports fob	−2 374.5	−2 703.0	−3 314.2	−3 575.7	−3 317.2	−3 490.4	−3 309.5	Biens : importations,fàb
Serv. & Income: Credit	2 467.0	2 768.2	3 274.0	3 147.0	3 125.1	3 282.6	3 515.1	Serv. & revenu : crédit
Serv. & Income: Debit	−963.4	−1 073.2	−1 418.2	−1 475.6	−1 418.6	−1 488.9	−1 526.5	Serv. & revenu : débit
Current Trans.,nie: Credit	118.4	125.0	134.8	127.8	118.7	132.7	194.7	Transf. cour.,nia : crédit
Current Transfers: Debit	−5.4	−10.2	−65.6	−77.2	−77.8	−101.0	−107.7	Transf. courants : débit
Capital Acct.,nie: Credit	0.0	0.0	0.0	0.0	0.0	0.0	0.0	Compte de cap.,nia : crédit
Capital Account: Debit	0.0	0.0	0.0	0.0	0.0	0.0	0.0	Compte de capital : débit
Financial Account,nie	−3.8	185.7	−150.7	401.9	358.6	595.2	929.7	Compte d'op. fin., nia
Net Errors and Omissions	38.8	−13.2	−51.8	−0.4	−81.6	−77.3	−57.0	Erreurs et omissions nettes
Reserves and Related Items	−144.8	−246.9	363.1	59.8	47.0	82.5	−639.0	Rés. et postes appareutés
Georgia								**Géorgie**
Goods: Exports fob	...	...	...	...	...	300.1	...	Biens : exportations,fàb
Goods: Imports fob	...	...	...	...	...	−1 060.4	...	Biens : importations,fàb
Serv. & Income: Credit	...	...	...	...	...	533.2	...	Serv. & revenu : crédit
Serv. & Income: Debit	...	...	...	...	...	−397.5	...	Serv. & revenu : débit
Current Trans.,nie: Credit	...	...	...	...	...	220.1	...	Transf. cour.,nia : crédit

75
Summary of balance of payments
Millions of US dollars
Résumé des balances des paiements
Millions de dollars des E.–U.

Country or area	1993	1994	1995	1996	1997	1998	1999	Pays ou zone
Current Transfers: Debit	...	...	...	...	...	−11.8	...	Transf. courants : débit
Capital Acct.,nie: Credit	...	...	...	...	...	0.0	...	Compte de cap.,nia : crédit
Capital Account: Debit	...	...	...	...	...	−6.1	...	Compte de capital : débit
Financial Account,nie	...	...	...	...	...	348.8	...	Compte d'op. fin., nia
Net Errors and Omissions	...	...	...	...	...	5.9	...	Erreurs et omissions nettes
Reserves and Related Items	...	...	...	...	...	67.8	...	Rés. et postes appareutés
India								**Inde**
Goods: Exports fob	22 015.9	25 522.5	31 238.5	33 737.3	35 702.1	34 075.7	37 527.6	Biens : exportations,fàb
Goods: Imports fob	−24 108.4	−29 672.6	−37 957.3	−43 789.0	−45 730.1	−44 828.0	−45 556.2	Biens : importations,fàb
Serv. & Income: Credit	5 482.5	6 858.9	8 260.3	8 649.4	10 594.3	13 497.2	16 362.2	Serv. & revenu : crédit
Serv. & Income: Debit	−10 618.0	−12 569.8	−15 487.0	−15 837.6	−17 444.4	−19 982.5	−23 040.6	Serv. & revenu : débit
Current Trans.,nie: Credit	5 375.0	8 207.8	8 409.5	11 349.5	13 975.4	10 401.8	11 957.9	Transf. cour.,nia : crédit
Current Transfers: Debit	−22.8	−23.1	−27.3	−65.8	−62.4	−67.4	−34.9	Transf. courants : débit
Capital Acct.,nie: Credit	0.0	0.0	0.0	0.0	0.0	0.0	0.0	Compte de cap.,nia : crédit
Capital Account: Debit	0.0	0.0	0.0	0.0	0.0	0.0	0.0	Compte de capital : débit
Financial Account,nie	7 074.3	10 575.6	3 860.9	11 847.8	9 634.7	8 583.9	9 154.4	Compte d'op. fin., nia
Net Errors and Omissions	−987.0	1 491.6	969.7	−1 934.1	−1 348.4	1 389.9	293.4	Erreurs et omissions nettes
Reserves and Related Items	−4 211.5	−10 390.9	732.6	−3 957.6	−5 321.1	−3 070.7	−6 663.7	Rés. et postes appareutés
Indonesia								**Indonésie**
Goods: Exports fob	36 607.0	40 223.0	47 454.0	50 188.0	56 298.0	50 371.0	51 242.0	Biens : exportations,fàb
Goods: Imports fob	−28 376.0	−32 322.0	−40 921.0	−44 240.0	−46 223.0	−31 942.0	−30 598.0	Biens : importations,fàb
Serv. & Income: Credit	4 987.0	5 845.0	6 775.0	7 809.0	8 796.0	6 389.0	6 470.0	Serv. & revenu : crédit
Serv. & Income: Debit	−15 861.0	−17 157.0	−20 720.0	−22 357.0	−24 794.0	−22 060.0	−23 243.0	Serv. & revenu : débit
Current Trans.,nie: Credit	537.0	619.0	981.0	937.0	1 034.0	1 338.0	1 914.0	Transf. cour.,nia : crédit
Current Transfers: Debit	0.0	0.0	0.0	0.0	0.0	0.0	0.0	Transf. courants : débit
Capital Acct.,nie: Credit	0.0	0.0	0.0	0.0	0.0	0.0	0.0	Compte de cap.,nia : crédit
Capital Account: Debit	0.0	0.0	0.0	0.0	0.0	0.0	0.0	Compte de capital : débit
Financial Account,nie	5 632.0	3 839.0	10 259.0	10 847.0	−603.0	−9 638.0	−5 941.0	Compte d'op. fin., nia
Net Errors and Omissions	−2 931.6	−263.4	−2 254.6	1 318.7	−2 645.4	1 849.5	2 127.5	Erreurs et omissions nettes
Reserves and Related Items	−594.4	−783.6	−1 573.4	−4 502.7	8 137.4	3 692.5	−1 971.5	Rés. et postes appareutés
Iran (Islamic Rep. of)								**Iran (Rép. islamique d')**
Goods: Exports fob	18 080.0	19 434.0	18 360.0	22 391.0	18 381.0	12 982.0	...	Biens : exportations,fàb
Goods: Imports fob	−19 287.0	−12 617.0	−12 774.0	−14 989.0	−14 123.0	−13 608.0	...	Biens : importations,fàb
Serv. & Income: Credit	1 235.0	580.0	909.0	1 348.0	1 658.0	1 545.0	...	Serv. & revenu : crédit
Serv. & Income: Debit	−5 743.0	−3 639.0	−3 133.0	−3 981.0	−4 096.0	−3 313.0	...	Serv. & revenu : débit
Current Trans.,nie: Credit	1 500.0	1 200.0	0.0	471.0	400.0	500.0	...	Transf. cour.,nia : crédit
Current Transfers: Debit	0.0	−2.0	−4.0	−8.0	−7.0	−3.0	...	Transf. courants : débit
Capital Acct.,nie: Credit	0.0	0.0	0.0	0.0	0.0	0.0	...	Compte de cap.,nia : crédit
Capital Account: Debit	0.0	0.0	0.0	0.0	0.0	0.0	...	Compte de capital : débit
Financial Account,nie	5 563.0	−346.0	−774.0	−5 508.0	−4 822.0	3 099.0	...	Compte d'op. fin., nia
Net Errors and Omissions	−1 120.0	−3 701.9	201.8	2 717.3	−1 088.2	−2 770.7	...	Erreurs et omissions nettes
Reserves and Related Items	−228.0	−908.1	−2 785.8	−2 441.3	3 697.2	1 568.7	...	Rés. et postes appareutés
Israel								**Israël**
Goods: Exports fob	14 922.2	17 225.8	19 393.3	21 332.6	22 698.1	22 974.2	25 564.5	Biens : exportations,fàb
Goods: Imports fob	−20 532.5	−22 752.5	−26 833.9	−28 425.6	−27 823.6	−26 198.9	−29 972.1	Biens : importations,fàb
Serv. & Income: Credit	7 228.5	7 798.1	9 498.0	9 838.8	10 446.3	11 963.6	13 755.1	Serv. & revenu : crédit
Serv. & Income: Debit	−9 636.1	−11 275.9	−12 894.7	−14 320.2	−15 031.3	−15 774.6	−17 552.7	Serv. & revenu : débit
Current Trans.,nie: Credit	5 910.5	5 850.0	5 941.1	6 441.4	6 373.6	6 679.8	7 133.7	Transf. cour.,nia : crédit
Current Transfers: Debit	−303.7	−249.6	−267.9	−304.3	−324.6	−606.9	−809.8	Transf. courants : débit
Capital Acct.,nie: Credit	1 392.1	1 762.8	1 908.9	1 942.2	2 050.2	1 646.6	1 686.4	Compte de cap.,nia : crédit
Capital Account: Debit	0.0	0.0	0.0	0.0	0.0	0.0	0.0	Compte de capital : débit
Financial Account,nie	428.6	−600.4	2 793.6	3 290.8	7 109.1	−792.5	1 812.4	Compte d'op. fin., nia
Net Errors and Omissions	212.7	88.5	899.8	1 381.8	1 585.2	2.7	−1 299.5	Erreurs et omissions nettes
Reserves and Related Items	377.7	2 153.2	−438.2	−1 177.5	−7 083.0	106.0	−318.0	Rés. et postes appareutés
Japan [1]								**Japon** [1]
Goods: Exports fob	352.7	385.7	428.7	400.3	409.2	374.0	403.7	Biens : exportations,fàb
Goods: Imports fob	−213.2	−241.5	−296.9	−316.7	−307.6	−251.7	−280.4	Biens : importations,fàb
Serv. & Income: Credit	201.1	213.5	257.7	292.8	291.5	272.0	249.3	Serv. & revenu : crédit
Serv. & Income: Debit	−203.7	−221.3	−270.8	−301.5	−289.9	−264.8	−253.6	Serv. & revenu : débit
Current Trans.,nie: Credit	1.6	1.8	2.0	6.0	6.0	5.5	6.2	Transf. cour.,nia : crédit
Current Transfers: Debit	−6.7	−7.9	−9.7	−15.0	−14.8	−14.4	−18.4	Transf. courants : débit
Capital Acct.,nie: Credit	0.0	0.0	0.0	1.2	1.5	1.6	0.7	Compte de cap.,nia : crédit
Capital Account: Debit	−1.5	−1.8	−2.2	−4.5	−5.6	−16.0	−17.2	Compte de capital : débit
Financial Account,nie	−102.2	−85.1	−64.0	−28.1	−118.1	−116.8	−31.1	Compte d'op. fin., nia
Net Errors and Omissions	−0.5	−18.0	13.8	0.6	34.3	4.4	17.0	Erreurs et omissions nettes
Reserves and Related Items	−27.5	−25.3	−58.6	−35.1	−6.6	6.2	−76.3	Rés. et postes appareutés

75
Summary of balance of payments
Millions of US dollars
Résumé des balances des paiements
Millions de dollars des E.−U.

Country or area	1993	1994	1995	1996	1997	1998	1999	Pays ou zone
Jordan								**Jordanie**
Goods: Exports fob	1 246.3	1 424.5	1 769.6	1 816.9	1 835.5	1 802.4	1 831.9	Biens : exportations,fàb
Goods: Imports fob	−3 145.2	−3 003.9	−3 287.8	−3 818.1	−3 648.5	−3 404.0	−3 292.0	Biens : importations,fàb
Serv. & Income: Credit	1 672.6	1 634.7	1 824.9	1 958.0	1 985.0	2 132.0	2 002.8	Serv. & revenu : crédit
Serv. & Income: Debit	−1 756.6	−1 780.2	−2 009.5	−2 010.4	−1 994.2	−2 228.8	−2 153.6	Serv. & revenu : débit
Current Trans.,nie: Credit	1 441.2	1 447.4	1 591.8	1 970.2	2 096.1	1 984.3	2 321.3	Transf. cour.,nia : crédit
Current Transfers: Debit	−87.4	−120.5	−147.6	−138.5	−244.6	−271.9	−305.5	Transf. courants : débit
Capital Acct.,nie: Credit	0.0	0.0	197.2	157.7	163.8	81.1	90.3	Compte de cap.,nia : crédit
Capital Account: Debit	0.0	0.0	0.0	0.0	0.0	0.0	0.0	Compte de capital : débit
Financial Account,nie	−530.0	188.9	230.0	233.9	242.3	−177.3	487.9	Compte d'op. fin., nia
Net Errors and Omissions	298.0	−55.8	−339.9	−357.9	−160.8	−454.0	−10.2	Erreurs et omissions nettes
Reserves and Related Items	861.1	264.9	171.3	188.2	−274.6	536.1	−972.9	Rés. et postes appareutés
Kazakhstan								**Kazakhstan**
Goods: Exports fob	...	...	5 440.0	6 291.6	6 899.3	5 870.5	5 988.7	Biens : exportations,fàb
Goods: Imports fob	...	...	−5 325.9	−6 626.7	−7 175.7	−6 671.7	−5 645.0	Biens : importations,fàb
Serv. & Income: Credit	...	...	579.7	731.1	915.7	999.8	1 041.1	Serv. & revenu : crédit
Serv. & Income: Debit	...	...	−965.9	−1 205.4	−1 513.2	−1 545.9	−1 712.5	Serv. & revenu : débit
Current Trans.,nie: Credit	...	...	79.9	83.4	104.7	141.4	174.7	Transf. cour.,nia : crédit
Current Transfers: Debit	...	...	−20.9	−25.0	−30.1	−19.0	−18.0	Transf. courants : débit
Capital Acct.,nie: Credit	...	...	116.1	87.9	58.3	65.9	61.1	Compte de cap.,nia : crédit
Capital Account: Debit	...	...	−496.7	−403.4	−498.1	−435.0	−295.1	Compte de capital : débit
Financial Account,nie	...	...	1 162.5	2 005.1	2 901.6	2 229.1	1 299.2	Compte d'op. fin., nia
Net Errors and Omissions	...	...	−270.1	−780.0	−1 114.1	−1 078.4	−641.6	Erreurs et omissions nettes
Reserves and Related Items	...	...	−298.7	−158.6	−548.4	443.3	−252.6	Rés. et postes appareutés
Korea, Republic of								**Corée, République de**
Goods: Exports fob	82 089.4	94 964.3	124 632.0	129 968.0	138 619.0	132 122.0	145 164.0	Biens : exportations,fàb
Goods: Imports fob	−79 770.9	−97 824.2	−129 076.0	−144 933.0	−141 798.0	−90 494.8	−116 793.0	Biens : importations,fàb
Serv. & Income: Credit	15 459.1	19 640.9	26 313.1	27 078.5	30 179.5	28 239.5	29 773.4	Serv. & revenu : crédit
Serv. & Income: Debit	−17 976.5	−21 928.4	−30 593.5	−35 073.4	−35 834.6	−32 860.5	−35 583.2	Serv. & revenu : débit
Current Trans.,nie: Credit	3 382.1	3 672.3	4 104.0	4 279.0	5 287.9	6 736.6	6 421.3	Transf. cour.,nia : crédit
Current Transfers: Debit	−2 193.7	−2 391.9	−3 885.9	−4 325.1	−4 620.9	−3 384.3	−4 505.5	Transf. courants : débit
Capital Acct.,nie: Credit	1.7	8.0	14.5	18.9	16.6	463.6	95.1	Compte de cap.,nia : crédit
Capital Account: Debit	−476.8	−444.5	−502.1	−616.5	−624.2	−292.5	−484.4	Compte de capital : débit
Financial Account,nie	3 216.5	10 732.9	17 273.2	23 924.4	−9 195.0	−8 381.0	12 708.8	Compte d'op. fin., nia
Net Errors and Omissions	−722.2	−1 815.8	−1 239.9	1 094.6	−5 009.6	−6 218.1	−3 536.2	Erreurs et omissions nettes
Reserves and Related Items	−3 008.7	−4 613.6	−7 039.2	−1 415.7	22 979.4	−25 930.1	−33 260.2	Rés. et postes appareutés
Kuwait								**Koweït**
Goods: Exports fob	10 263.8	11 284.4	12 833.1	14 946.1	14 280.6	9 617.5	12 276.0	Biens : exportations,fàb
Goods: Imports fob	−6 940.8	−6 615.7	−7 254.2	−7 949.0	−7 746.9	−7 714.4	−6 704.7	Biens : importations,fàb
Serv. & Income: Credit	5 731.5	5 588.3	7 525.6	7 929.0	9 503.9	8 925.2	7 893.8	Serv. & revenu : crédit
Serv. & Income: Debit	−5 251.2	−5 534.4	−6 624.3	−6 329.1	−6 596.4	−6 838.3	−6 399.2	Serv. & revenu : débit
Current Trans.,nie: Credit	109.3	94.3	53.6	53.4	79.1	98.4	98.5	Transf. cour.,nia : crédit
Current Transfers: Debit	−1 414.7	−1 589.9	−1 517.9	−1 543.0	−1 585.6	−1 873.6	−2 102.4	Transf. courants : débit
Capital Acct.,nie: Credit	0.0	0.0	0.0	3.3	115.4	288.8	716.1	Compte de cap.,nia : crédit
Capital Account: Debit	−205.4	−205.5	−194.3	−207.1	−211.0	−210.0	−210.2	Compte de capital : débit
Financial Account,nie	420.8	3 304.5	157.5	−7 631.7	−6 210.7	−2 920.4	−6 051.0	Compte d'op. fin., nia
Net Errors and Omissions	−4 192.0	−6 272.6	−5 119.3	704.5	−1 621.4	885.8	1 401.0	Erreurs et omissions nettes
Reserves and Related Items	1 478.7	−53.4	140.2	23.6	−7.0	−259.0	−918.1	Rés. et postes appareutés
Kyrgyzstan								**Kirghizistan**
Goods: Exports fob	339.6	340.0	408.9	531.2	630.8	535.1	...	Biens : exportations,fàb
Goods: Imports fob	−446.7	−426.1	−531.0	−782.9	−646.1	−755.7	...	Biens : importations,fàb
Serv. & Income: Credit	8.7	32.7	42.9	35.9	51.8	73.1	...	Serv. & revenu : crédit
Serv. & Income: Debit	−56.4	−93.1	−234.3	−292.9	−242.6	−272.1	...	Serv. & revenu : débit
Current Trans.,nie: Credit	68.0	63.4	80.4	85.9	69.8	50.8	...	Transf. cour.,nia : crédit
Current Transfers: Debit	−0.8	−0.8	−1.7	−1.9	−2.2	−2.0	...	Transf. courants : débit
Capital Acct.,nie: Credit	0.0	0.3	2.2	9.0	6.2	3.9	...	Compte de cap.,nia : crédit
Capital Account: Debit	−107.1	−62.7	−31.3	−25.0	−14.6	−12.0	...	Compte de capital : débit
Financial Account,nie	181.2	103.4	259.9	362.5	250.7	292.0	...	Compte d'op. fin., nia
Net Errors and Omissions	−16.2	48.0	−76.9	58.4	−57.7	63.1	...	Erreurs et omissions nettes
Reserves and Related Items	29.6	−5.0	80.7	19.8	−46.2	24.0	...	Rés. et postes appareutés
Lao People's Dem. Rep.								**Rép. dém. pop. lao**
Goods: Exports fob	247.9	305.5	310.9	322.8	318.3	342.1	338.2	Biens : exportations,fàb
Goods: Imports fob	−397.4	−519.2	−626.8	−643.7	−601.3	−506.8	−527.7	Biens : importations,fàb
Serv. & Income: Credit	93.8	94.2	104.2	113.6	116.9	151.9	140.5	Serv. & revenu : crédit
Serv. & Income: Debit	−81.5	−161.3	−134.5	−139.5	−139.4	−137.3	−101.7	Serv. & revenu : débit
Current Trans.,nie: Credit	0.0	0.0	0.0	0.0	0.0	0.0	80.2	Transf. cour.,nia : crédit

75
Summary of balance of payments
Millions of US dollars
Résumé des balances des paiements
Millions de dollars des E.−U.

Country or area	1993	1994	1995	1996	1997	1998	1999	Pays ou zone
Current Transfers: Debit	−2.0	−3.2	0.0	0.0	0.0	0.0	−50.6	Transf. courants : débit
Capital Acct.,nie: Credit	9.5	9.5	21.7	44.9	40.3	49.4	0.0	Compte de cap.,nia : crédit
Capital Account: Debit	0.0	0.0	−8.5	−9.9	−6.9	−6.3	0.0	Compte de capital : débit
Financial Account,nie	−21.0	24.3	90.0	135.7	3.5	−43.4	−46.9	Compte d'op. fin., nia
Net Errors and Omissions	13.2	71.8	92.4	17.7	−100.5	−103.8	−165.1	Erreurs et omissions nettes
Reserves and Related Items	137.5	178.4	150.6	158.4	369.1	254.2	333.1	Rés. et postes apparentés
Malaysia								**Malaisie**
Goods: Exports fob	46 238.0	56 897.3	71 767.2	76 985.1	77 538.3	71 882.8	84 051.8	Biens : exportations,fàb
Goods: Imports fob	−43 201.2	−55 320.0	−71 870.6	−73 136.8	−74 028.7	−54 377.8	−61 404.2	Biens : importations,fàb
Serv. & Income: Credit	8 418.5	11 628.4	14 225.0	17 828.3	18 212.0	13 058.9	13 922.1	Serv. & revenu : crédit
Serv. & Income: Debit	−14 733.7	−17 955.2	−21 747.7	−24 956.0	−26 147.6	−18 572.7	−22 235.8	Serv. & revenu : débit
Current Transfers.,nie: Credit	468.9	411.2	700.0	765.9	944.1	727.8	800.8	Transf. cour.,nia : crédit
Current Transfers: Debit	−181.4	−181.8	−1 717.4	−1 948.4	−2 453.4	−3 190.3	−2 529.0	Transf. courants : débit
Capital Acct.,nie: Credit	0.0	0.0	0.0	0.0	0.0	0.0	0.0	Compte de cap.,nia : crédit
Capital Account: Debit	−88.2	−81.5	0.0	0.0	0.0	0.0	0.0	Compte de capital : débit
Financial Account,nie	10 804.6	1 288.0	7 642.5	9 476.8	2 197.5	−2 549.7	−6 619.0	Compte d'op. fin., nia
Net Errors and Omissions	3 624.1	153.6	−761.6	−2 501.6	−136.9	3 038.8	−1 275.0	Erreurs et omissions nettes
Reserves and Related Items	−11 349.6	3 160.1	1 762.7	−2 513.3	3 874.7	−10 017.7	−4 711.9	Rés. et postes apparentés
Maldives								**Maldives**
Goods: Exports fob	52.7	75.4	85.0	79.9	93.0	95.6	91.5	Biens : exportations,fàb
Goods: Imports fob	−177.8	−195.1	−235.8	−265.5	−307.0	−311.5	−354.1	Biens : importations,fàb
Serv. & Income: Credit	163.7	201.2	237.3	294.9	319.6	339.9	362.9	Serv. & revenu : crédit
Serv. & Income: Debit	−79.2	−86.8	−101.1	−115.7	−129.2	−135.5	−148.1	Serv. & revenu : débit
Current Trans.,nie: Credit	13.3	16.3	23.0	26.2	17.2	18.9	18.3	Transf. cour.,nia : crédit
Current Transfers: Debit	−26.5	−22.2	−26.6	−27.3	−27.9	−30.6	−40.5	Transf. courants : débit
Capital Acct.,nie: Credit	0.0	0.0	0.0	0.0	0.0	0.0	0.0	Compte de cap.,nia : crédit
Capital Account: Debit	0.0	0.0	0.0	0.0	0.0	0.0	0.0	Compte de capital : débit
Financial Account,nie	46.3	27.5	67.5	52.2	70.9	60.2	75.6	Compte d'op. fin., nia
Net Errors and Omissions	7.4	−10.8	−32.0	−16.4	−14.5	−16.8	4.0	Erreurs et omissions nettes
Reserves and Related Items	0.1	−5.5	−17.3	−28.3	−22.1	−20.2	−9.6	Rés. et postes apparentés
Mongolia								**Mongolie**
Goods: Exports fob	365.8	367.0	451.0	423.4	568.5	462.4	454.3	Biens : exportations,fàb
Goods: Imports fob	−344.5	−333.3	−425.7	−459.7	−453.1	−524.2	−510.7	Biens : importations,fàb
Serv. & Income: Credit	26.8	48.6	60.3	69.1	58.8	87.9	82.5	Serv. & revenu : crédit
Serv. & Income: Debit	−87.9	−113.7	−123.8	−139.5	−123.2	−156.5	−152.3	Serv. & revenu : débit
Current Trans.,nie: Credit	66.7	77.8	77.1	6.2	4.2	5.5	17.6	Transf. cour.,nia : crédit
Current Transfers: Debit	4.2	0.0	0.0	0.0	0.0	−3.6	−3.6	Transf. courants : débit
Capital Acct.,nie: Credit	0.0	0.0	0.0	0.0	0.0	0.0	0.0	Compte de cap.,nia : crédit
Capital Account: Debit	0.0	0.0	0.0	0.0	0.0	0.0	0.0	Compte de capital : débit
Financial Account,nie	−11.8	−39.0	−15.9	41.3	27.0	126.2	69.6	Compte d'op. fin., nia
Net Errors and Omissions	−4.8	−1.0	9.1	−28.1	−75.6	−50.2	23.6	Erreurs et omissions nettes
Reserves and Related Items	−14.5	−6.4	−32.1	87.3	−6.6	52.5	19.0	Rés. et postes apparentés
Myanmar								**Myanmar**
Goods: Exports fob	630.9	857.4	933.2	937.9	974.5	1 065.2	1 125.2	Biens : exportations,fàb
Goods: Imports fob	−1 260.8	−1 466.8	−1 756.3	−1 869.1	−2 106.6	−2 451.2	−2 115.9	Biens : importations,fàb
Serv. & Income: Credit	251.3	277.8	376.3	436.8	528.2	637.0	532.7	Serv. & revenu : crédit
Serv. & Income: Debit	−193.3	−203.0	−368.0	−355.0	−463.6	−376.1	−294.8	Serv. & revenu : débit
Current Trans.,nie: Credit	344.6	405.2	564.2	598.4	685.1	631.2	531.0	Transf. cour.,nia : crédit
Current Transfers: Debit	−0.5	−0.6	−8.0	−28.8	−29.7	−0.3	−0.3	Transf. courants : débit
Capital Acct.,nie: Credit	0.0	0.0	0.0	0.0	0.0	0.0	0.0	Compte de cap.,nia : crédit
Capital Account: Debit	0.0	0.0	0.0	0.0	0.0	0.0	0.0	Compte de capital : débit
Financial Account,nie	160.8	185.2	242.8	266.8	469.1	535.1	211.9	Compte d'op. fin., nia
Net Errors and Omissions	−10.0	−10.3	−16.2	−11.7	−26.0	18.8	−34.2	Erreurs et omissions nettes
Reserves and Related Items	77.0	−45.0	31.8	24.7	−31.0	−59.7	44.4	Rés. et postes apparentés
Nepal								**Népal**
Goods: Exports fob	397.0	368.7	349.9	388.7	413.8	482.0	708.8	Biens : exportations,fàb
Goods: Imports fob	−858.6	−1 158.9	−1 310.8	−1 494.7	−1 691.9	−1 239.1	−1 589.5	Biens : importations,fàb
Serv. & Income: Credit	362.1	613.8	722.6	790.6	897.6	610.6	555.3	Serv. & revenu : crédit
Serv. & Income: Debit	−275.5	−327.4	−348.1	−274.8	−253.1	−222.7	−240.9	Serv. & revenu : débit
Current Trans.,nie: Credit	155.5	160.7	239.2	281.6	267.4	326.0	603.8	Transf. cour.,nia : crédit
Current Transfers: Debit	−3.0	−8.7	−9.1	−18.0	−21.8	−24.1	−26.9	Transf. courants : débit
Capital Acct.,nie: Credit	0.0	0.0	0.0	0.0	0.0	0.0	111.2	Compte de cap.,nia : crédit
Capital Account: Debit	0.0	0.0	0.0	0.0	0.0	0.0	0.0	Compte de capital : débit
Financial Account,nie	283.5	407.3	368.5	275.2	340.3	212.9	33.8	Compte d'op. fin., nia
Net Errors and Omissions	4.6	7.1	2.8	82.3	216.6	134.0	−25.4	Erreurs et omissions nettes
Reserves and Related Items	−65.6	−62.5	−15.0	−30.9	−168.8	−279.7	−130.2	Rés. et postes apparentés

75
Summary of balance of payments
Millions of US dollars
Résumé des balances des paiements
Millions de dollars des E.-U.

Country or area	1993	1994	1995	1996	1997	1998	1999	Pays ou zone
Oman								**Oman**
Goods: Exports fob	5 365.4	5 542.3	6 065.0	7 339.4	7 630.7	5 508.5	7 218.0	Biens : exportations,fàb
Goods: Imports fob	−4 029.9	−3 693.1	−4 049.9	−4 385.4	−4 649.2	−5 217.4	−4 300.1	Biens : importations,fàb
Serv. & Income: Credit	434.3	270.5	338.1	236.7	364.1	317.3	166.5	Serv. & revenu : crédit
Serv. & Income: Debit	−1 594.5	−1 624.2	−1 684.3	−1 689.7	−1 955.0	−2 146.4	−1 874.8	Serv. & revenu : débit
Current Trans.,nie: Credit	57.2	65.0	67.6	49.4	70.2	39.0	39.0	Transf. cour.,nia : crédit
Current Transfers: Debit	−1 422.6	−1 365.4	−1 537.1	−1 370.6	−1 500.7	−1 472.0	−1 441.0	Transf. courants : débit
Capital Acct.,nie: Credit	0.0	0.0	0.0	0.0	0.0	0.0	0.0	Compte de cap.,nia : crédit
Capital Account: Debit	0.0	0.0	0.0	0.0	0.0	0.0	0.0	Compte de capital : débit
Financial Account,nie	−79.1	229.9	−18.7	275.4	91.8	1 531.6	166.5	Compte d'op. fin., nia
Net Errors and Omissions	210.7	−85.8	387.7	−266.6	484.9	669.7	240.6	Erreurs et omissions nettes
Reserves and Related Items	1 058.5	660.8	431.6	−188.5	−537.0	769.8	−214.6	Rés. et postes appareutés
Pakistan								**Pakistan**
Goods: Exports fob	6 793.4	7 116.8	8 356.4	8 507.3	8 350.7	...	...	Biens : exportations,fàb
Goods: Imports fob	−9 379.9	−9 355.3	−11 247.8	−12 163.7	−10 750.2	...	...	Biens : importations,fàb
Serv. & Income: Credit	1 635.7	1 902.1	2 043.9	2 191.7	1 771.8	...	...	Serv. & revenu : crédit
Serv. & Income: Debit	−4 248.3	−4 359.0	−5 062.9	−5 656.6	−5 024.6	...	...	Serv. & revenu : débit
Current Trans.,nie: Credit	2 336.6	2 918.6	2 610.7	2 739.5	3 980.6	...	...	Transf. cour.,nia : crédit
Current Transfers: Debit	−38.1	−35.2	−49.0	−54.1	−39.9	...	...	Transf. courants : débit
Capital Acct.,nie: Credit	0.0	0.0	0.0	0.0	0.0	...	...	Compte de cap.,nia : crédit
Capital Account: Debit	0.0	0.0	0.0	0.0	0.0	...	...	Compte de capital : débit
Financial Account,nie	3 333.9	2 977.4	2 449.4	3 496.2	2 321.1	...	...	Compte d'op. fin., nia
Net Errors and Omissions	−5.6	177.8	−304.2	159.6	−71.8	...	...	Erreurs et omissions nettes
Reserves and Related Items	−427.8	−1 343.1	1 203.6	780.3	−537.7	...	...	Rés. et postes appareutés
Philippines								**Philippines**
Goods: Exports fob	11 375.0	13 483.0	17 447.0	20 543.0	25 228.0	29 496.0	34 209.6	Biens : exportations,fàb
Goods: Imports fob	−17 597.0	−21 333.0	−26 391.0	−31 885.0	−36 355.0	−29 524.0	−29 252.0	Biens : importations,fàb
Serv. & Income: Credit	7 497.0	10 550.0	15 415.0	19 006.0	22 835.0	13 917.0	12 883.0	Serv. & revenu : crédit
Serv. & Income: Debit	−4 990.0	−6 586.0	−9 331.0	−12 206.0	−17 139.0	−12 778.0	−10 425.0	Serv. & revenu : débit
Current Trans.,nie: Credit	746.0	1 041.0	1 147.0	1 185.0	1 670.0	758.0	610.0	Transf. cour.,nia : crédit
Current Transfers: Debit	−47.0	−105.0	−267.0	−596.0	−590.0	−323.0	−116.0	Transf. courants : débit
Capital Acct.,nie: Credit	0.0	0.0	0.0	0.0	0.0	0.0	44.0	Compte de cap.,nia : crédit
Capital Account: Debit	0.0	0.0	0.0	0.0	0.0	0.0	−53.0	Compte de capital : débit
Financial Account,nie	3 267.0	5 120.0	5 309.0	11 277.0	6 498.0	483.0	−935.0	Compte d'op. fin., nia
Net Errors and Omissions	85.2	156.8	−2 093.6	−2 986.0	−5 241.4	−749.9	−3 306.5	Erreurs et omissions nettes
Reserves and Related Items	−336.2	−2 326.8	−1 235.4	−4 338.0	3 094.4	−1 279.1	−3 659.1	Rés. et postes appareutés
Saudi Arabia								**Arabie saoudite**
Goods: Exports fob	42 395.2	42 614.2	50 040.9	60 728.7	60 731.4	38 821.9	48 482.2	Biens : exportations,fàb
Goods: Imports fob	−25 873.2	−21 325.0	−25 650.5	−25 358.3	−26 369.8	−27 534.6	−25 717.5	Biens : importations,fàb
Serv. & Income: Credit	9 491.3	7 378.9	8 467.6	7 899.1	10 012.3	10 539.1	11 037.4	Serv. & revenu : crédit
Serv. & Income: Debit	−26 764.3	−20 452.9	−21 267.2	−26 975.7	−28 934.0	−19 923.1	−21 428.1	Serv. & revenu : débit
Current Trans.,nie: Credit	0.0	0.0	0.0	0.0	0.0	0.0	0.0	Transf. cour.,nia : crédit
Current Transfers: Debit	−16 517.0	−18 702.0	−16 916.0	−15 613.2	−15 134.4	−15 052.9	−14 075.6	Transf. courants : débit
Capital Acct.,nie: Credit	0.0	0.0	0.0	0.0	0.0	0.0	0.0	Compte de cap.,nia : crédit
Capital Account: Debit	0.0	0.0	0.0	0.0	0.0	0.0	0.0	Compte de capital : débit
Financial Account,nie	18 763.0	10 340.7	6 542.1	5 068.6	343.1	12 430.7	4 516.2	Compte d'op. fin., nia
Net Errors and Omissions	0.0	0.4	0.0	−0.1	−0.5	−0.1	−0.1	Erreurs et omissions nettes
Reserves and Related Items	−1 495.3	145.6	−1 216.9	−5 749.0	−648.1	718.9	−2 814.6	Rés. et postes appareutés
Singapore								**Singapour**
Goods: Exports fob	77 858.0	97 919.0	118 456.0	126 010.0	125 746.0	110 591.0	115 639.0	Biens : exportations,fàb
Goods: Imports fob	−80 582.0	−96 564.6	−117 479.0	−123 786.0	−124 628.0	−95 780.1	−104 337.0	Biens : importations,fàb
Serv. & Income: Credit	26 672.2	32 827.0	42 534.5	44 337.8	45 919.1	33 396.9	39 115.4	Serv. & revenu : crédit
Serv. & Income: Debit	−19 201.2	−22 120.5	−28 189.6	−31 591.3	−28 937.8	−25 999.0	−28 001.3	Serv. & revenu : débit
Current Trans.,nie: Credit	140.2	144.9	155.9	156.7	150.2	136.2	133.9	Transf. cour.,nia : crédit
Current Transfers: Debit	−676.2	−806.0	−1 041.6	−1 229.0	−1 337.6	−1 319.9	−1 296.8	Transf. courants : débit
Capital Acct.,nie: Credit	0.0	0.0	0.0	0.0	0.0	0.0	0.0	Compte de cap.,nia : crédit
Capital Account: Debit	−71.4	−84.1	−71.3	−139.0	−173.1	−225.9	−191.2	Compte de capital : débit
Financial Account,nie	−1 212.0	−8 841.0	−4 733.9	−5 198.4	−13 234.1	−21 312.7	−17 366.8	Compte d'op. fin., nia
Net Errors and Omissions	4 649.9	2 261.5	−1 031.5	−1 165.0	4 435.1	3 479.2	497.7	Erreurs et omissions nettes
Reserves and Related Items	−7 577.7	−4 736.1	−8 599.1	−7 395.9	−7 939.9	−2 965.6	−4 193.7	Rés. et postes appareutés
Sri Lanka								**Sri Lanka**
Goods: Exports fob	2 785.7	3 208.3	3 797.9	4 095.4	4 638.7	4 798.1	4 600.5	Biens : exportations,fàb
Goods: Imports fob	−3 527.8	−4 293.4	−4 782.6	−4 895.0	−5 278.3	−5 300.7	−5 308.5	Biens : importations,fàb
Serv. & Income: Credit	745.7	897.8	1 042.5	940.6	1 108.6	1 128.5	1 132.5	Serv. & revenu : crédit
Serv. & Income: Debit	−1 108.6	−1 364.3	−1 559.7	−1 582.5	−1 695.5	−1 752.2	−1 828.5	Serv. & revenu : débit
Current Trans.,nie: Credit	795.4	882.3	846.7	881.4	966.5	1 051.9	1 080.0	Transf. cour.,nia : crédit

75
Summary of balance of payments
Millions of US dollars
Résumé des balances des paiements
Millions de dollars des E.−U.

Country or area	1993	1994	1995	1996	1997	1998	1999	Pays ou zone
Current Transfers: Debit	−72.6	−88.1	−114.7	−122.4	−134.7	−151.0	−168.8	Transf. courants : débit
Capital Acct.,nie: Credit	0.0	0.0	124.2	99.7	91.3	84.5	80.2	Compte de cap.,nia : crédit
Capital Account: Debit	0.0	0.0	−3.5	−3.8	−4.2	−4.7	−5.2	Compte de capital : débit
Financial Account,nie	1 022.1	958.8	730.1	452.2	466.7	342.7	422.6	Compte d'op. fin., nia
Net Errors and Omissions	128.0	106.3	157.9	143.6	148.0	27.0	−54.0	Erreurs et omissions nettes
Reserves and Related Items	−767.9	−307.7	−238.7	−9.0	−307.2	−224.2	96.6	Rés. et postes appareutés
Syrian Arab Republic								**Rép. arabe syrienne**
Goods: Exports fob	3 253.0	3 329.0	3 858.0	4 178.0	4 057.0	3 135.0	3 806.0	Biens : exportations,fàb
Goods: Imports fob	−3 512.0	−4 604.0	−4 001.0	−4 516.0	−3 603.0	−3 307.0	−3 452.0	Biens : importations,fàb
Serv. & Income: Credit	2 027.0	2 501.0	2 423.0	2 367.0	2 025.0	2 184.0	1 903.0	Serv. & revenu : crédit
Serv. & Income: Debit	−2 506.0	−2 608.0	−2 520.0	−2 572.0	−2 495.0	−2 476.0	−2 451.0	Serv. & revenu : débit
Current Trans.,nie: Credit	543.0	597.0	610.0	630.0	504.0	525.0	466.0	Transf. cour.,nia : crédit
Current Transfers: Debit	−8.0	−6.0	−3.0	−6.0	−5.0	−2.0	−2.0	Transf. courants : débit
Capital Acct.,nie: Credit	28.0	102.0	20.0	26.0	18.0	20.0	8.0	Compte de cap.,nia : crédit
Capital Account: Debit	0.0	0.0	0.0	0.0	0.0	0.0	0.0	Compte de capital : débit
Financial Account,nie	598.1	1 159.0	467.0	674.0	70.0	437.0	87.0	Compte d'op. fin., nia
Net Errors and Omissions	−119.1	96.0	−69.0	98.0	−117.0	−114.9	−106.0	Erreurs et omissions nettes
Reserves and Related Items	−304.0	−566.0	−785.0	−879.0	−454.0	−401.1	−259.0	Rés. et postes appareutés
Thailand								**Thaïlande**
Goods: Exports fob	36 397.6	44 477.8	55 446.6	54 408.4	56 655.9	52 752.9	56 775.1	Biens : exportations,fàb
Goods: Imports fob	−40 694.4	−48 204.1	−63 414.9	−63 896.6	−55 084.3	−36 514.9	−42 761.8	Biens : importations,fàb
Serv. & Income: Credit	13 198.6	14 201.7	18 646.1	20 976.3	19 505.6	16 479.3	17 726.9	Serv. & revenu : crédit
Serv. & Income: Debit	−16 014.9	−19 688.3	−24 718.3	−26 939.3	−24 577.0	−18 889.1	−19 665.6	Serv. & revenu : débit
Current Trans.,nie: Credit	1 222.3	1 901.3	1 190.2	1 651.0	1 392.1	819.8	805.6	Transf. cour.,nia : crédit
Current Transfers: Debit	−472.6	−773.7	−703.7	−891.3	−913.3	−405.4	−452.5	Transf. courants : débit
Capital Acct.,nie: Credit	0.0	0.0	0.0	0.0	0.0	0.0	0.0	Compte de cap.,nia : crédit
Capital Account: Debit	0.0	0.0	0.0	0.0	0.0	0.0	0.0	Compte de capital : débit
Financial Account,nie	10 500.0	12 167.0	21 908.6	19 486.0	−12 055.8	−14 110.3	−11 072.9	Compte d'op. fin., nia
Net Errors and Omissions	−229.6	87.4	−1 196.0	−2 627.3	−3 173.0	−2 828.2	33.4	Erreurs et omissions nettes
Reserves and Related Items	−3 906.8	−4 169.1	−7 158.7	−2 167.3	18 249.8	2 696.0	−1 388.3	Rés. et postes appareutés
Turkey								**Turquie**
Goods: Exports fob	15 611.0	18 390.0	21 975.0	32 446.0	32 631.0	31 220.0	29 326.0	Biens : exportations,fàb
Goods: Imports fob	−29 771.0	−22 606.0	−35 187.0	−43 028.0	−48 029.0	−45 440.0	−39 773.0	Biens : importations,fàb
Serv. & Income: Credit	11 787.0	11 691.0	16 095.0	14 628.0	21 273.0	25 802.0	18 748.0	Serv. & revenu : crédit
Serv. & Income: Debit	−7 828.0	−7 936.0	−9 717.0	−10 930.0	−13 420.0	−15 325.0	−14 840.0	Serv. & revenu : débit
Current Trans.,nie: Credit	3 800.0	3 113.0	4 512.0	4 466.0	4 909.0	5 860.0	5 294.0	Transf. cour.,nia : crédit
Current Transfers: Debit	−32.0	−21.0	−16.0	−19.0	−43.0	−133.0	−119.0	Transf. courants : débit
Capital Acct.,nie: Credit	0.0	0.0	0.0	0.0	0.0	0.0	0.0	Compte de cap.,nia : crédit
Capital Account: Debit	0.0	0.0	0.0	0.0	0.0	0.0	0.0	Compte de capital : débit
Financial Account,nie	8 963.0	−4 194.0	4 643.0	8 763.0	8 616.0	448.0	4 671.0	Compte d'op. fin., nia
Net Errors and Omissions	−2 221.8	1 765.8	2 355.3	−1 782.5	−2 593.8	−1 991.1	1 897.5	Erreurs et omissions nettes
Reserves and Related Items	−308.2	−202.8	−4 660.3	−4 543.5	−3 343.2	−440.9	−5 204.5	Rés. et postes appareutés
Turkmenistan								**Turkménistan**
Goods: Exports fob	...	...	...	1 692.0	774.2	...	...	Biens : exportations,fàb
Goods: Imports fob	...	...	...	−1 388.3	−1 005.1	...	...	Biens : importations,fàb
Serv. & Income: Credit	...	...	...	209.6	428.7	...	...	Serv. & revenu : crédit
Serv. & Income: Debit	...	...	...	−518.4	−746.6	...	...	Serv. & revenu : débit
Current Trans.,nie: Credit	...	...	...	4.8	49.9	...	...	Transf. cour.,nia : crédit
Current Transfers: Debit	...	...	...	0.0	−81.2	...	...	Transf. courants : débit
Capital Acct.,nie: Credit	...	...	...	2.8	14.0	...	...	Compte de cap.,nia : crédit
Capital Account: Debit	...	...	...	−159.7	−22.9	...	...	Compte de capital : débit
Financial Account,nie	...	...	...	113.4	1 060.0	...	...	Compte d'op. fin., nia
Net Errors and Omissions	...	...	...	51.6	−72.9	...	...	Erreurs et omissions nettes
Reserves and Related Items	...	...	...	−7.9	−398.0	...	...	Rés. et postes appareutés
Yemen								**Yémen**
Goods: Exports fob	1 166.9	1 824.0	1 937.2	2 262.8	2 264.0	1 500.7	...	Biens : exportations,fàb
Goods: Imports fob	−2 086.9	−1 521.9	−1 948.2	−2 293.5	−2 406.5	−2 201.2	...	Biens : importations,fàb
Serv. & Income: Credit	199.2	170.0	216.8	232.5	277.2	273.0	...	Serv. & revenu : crédit
Serv. & Income: Debit	−1 594.1	−1 223.2	−1 127.0	−1 283.9	−1 338.4	−1 056.9	...	Serv. & revenu : débit
Current Trans.,nie: Credit	1 092.8	1 133.6	1 120.5	1 207.6	1 268.7	1 273.0	...	Transf. cour.,nia : crédit
Current Transfers: Debit	−25.5	−16.6	−16.6	−19.2	−13.4	−16.7	...	Transf. courants : débit
Capital Acct.,nie: Credit	0.0	0.0	0.0	0.0	0.0	0.0	...	Compte de cap.,nia : crédit
Capital Account: Debit	0.0	0.0	0.0	0.0	0.0	0.0	...	Compte de capital : débit
Financial Account,nie	−87.9	−837.5	−819.0	−252.0	−76.5	−164.4	...	Compte d'op. fin., nia
Net Errors and Omissions	222.4	−181.0	161.8	−222.6	−103.8	−43.7	...	Erreurs et omissions nettes
Reserves and Related Items	1 113.1	652.6	474.5	368.3	128.7	436.2	...	Rés. et postes appareutés

75
Summary of balance of payments
Millions of US dollars
Résumé des balances des paiements
Millions de dollars des E.–U.

Country or area	1993	1994	1995	1996	1997	1998	1999	Pays ou zone
Europe · Europe								
Albania								**Albanie**
Goods: Exports fob	111.6	141.3	204.9	243.7	158.6	208.0	275.0	Biens : exportations,fàb
Goods: Imports fob	−601.5	−601.0	−679.7	−922.0	−693.6	−811.7	−938.0	Biens : importations,fàb
Serv. & Income: Credit	142.5	134.2	170.8	212.9	125.2	172.6	354.9	Serv. & revenu : crédit
Serv. & Income: Debit	−192.9	−173.8	−184.9	−201.3	−127.0	−138.0	−173.3	Serv. & revenu : débit
Current Trans.,nie: Credit	556.9	347.5	521.2	595.9	299.8	560.8	508.9	Transf. cour.,nia : crédit
Current Transfers: Debit	−1.7	−5.5	−43.8	−36.5	−35.2	−56.9	−182.9	Transf. courants : débit
Capital Acct.,nie: Credit	0.0	0.0	389.4	4.8	2.0	31.0	22.6	Compte de cap.,nia : crédit
Capital Account: Debit	0.0	0.0	0.0	0.0	0.0	0.0	0.0	Compte de capital : débit
Financial Account,nie	44.1	40.2	−411.0	61.5	151.4	15.4	33.7	Compte d'op. fin., nia
Net Errors and Omissions	−10.3	123.9	53.7	96.9	158.4	71.1	206.2	Erreurs et omissions nettes
Reserves and Related Items	−48.7	−6.8	−20.6	−55.9	−39.5	−52.4	−107.1	Rés. et postes appareutés
Austria								**Autriche**
Goods: Exports fob	40 271.5	45 175.1	57 695.2	57 937.3	58 662.3	62 826.1	63 694.6	Biens : exportations,fàb
Goods: Imports fob	−46 747.0	−53 089.4	−64 351.6	−65 251.9	−62 936.3	−66 479.8	−67 255.0	Biens : importations,fàb
Serv. & Income: Credit	33 962.8	35 093.0	41 111.6	43 828.9	39 998.0	43 131.0	41 420.7	Serv. & revenu : crédit
Serv. & Income: Debit	−27 495.9	−29 087.6	−38 201.1	−39 621.5	−39 251.5	−42 172.3	−41 575.7	Serv. & revenu : débit
Current Trans.,nie: Credit	1 265.6	1 370.3	2 972.3	3 144.8	2 911.6	2 920.1	2 905.1	Transf. cour.,nia : crédit
Current Transfers: Debit	−2 269.7	−2 453.3	−4 674.3	−4 928.0	−4 605.2	−4 834.0	−4 890.2	Transf. courants : débit
Capital Acct.,nie: Credit	246.4	676.2	540.0	591.3	590.0	476.7	531.0	Compte de cap.,nia : crédit
Capital Account: Debit	−693.9	−744.4	−601.7	−513.0	−563.7	−683.0	−675.7	Compte de capital : débit
Financial Account,nie	3 969.6	4 311.1	7 365.0	5 324.9	1 665.9	8 568.1	4 912.8	Compte d'op. fin., nia
Net Errors and Omissions	−308.1	−417.3	−464.0	562.1	475.5	−250.1	−1 237.9	Erreurs et omissions nettes
Reserves and Related Items	−2 201.3	−833.8	−1 391.3	−1 075.0	3 053.3	−3 502.8	2 170.4	Rés. et postes appareutés
Belarus								**Bélarus**
Goods: Exports fob	1 970.1	2 510.0	4 803.0	5 790.1	7 382.6	7 134.5	5 949.3	Biens : exportations,fàb
Goods: Imports fob	−2 498.0	−2 999.8	−5 468.7	−6 938.6	−8 718.0	−8 568.6	−6 547.8	Biens : importations,fàb
Serv. & Income: Credit	185.0	251.9	468.0	982.1	950.0	902.4	762.8	Serv. & revenu : crédit
Serv. & Income: Debit	−144.3	−228.6	−336.6	−440.8	−480.6	−540.1	−529.4	Serv. & revenu : débit
Current Trans.,nie: Credit	64.6	50.9	107.2	135.5	106.1	165.7	136.2	Transf. cour.,nia : crédit
Current Transfers: Debit	−12.4	−28.2	−31.2	−44.2	−27.7	−25.3	−27.8	Transf. courants : débit
Capital Acct.,nie: Credit	0.0	23.8	7.3	257.2	248.0	261.3	131.1	Compte de cap.,nia : crédit
Capital Account: Debit	0.0	0.0	0.0	−156.1	−114.8	−91.2	−70.7	Compte de capital : débit
Financial Account,nie	294.1	144.6	204.0	346.8	586.4	249.3	249.3	Compte d'op. fin., nia
Net Errors and Omissions	3.4	−41.6	168.6	−146.2	133.1	97.0	34.3	Erreurs et omissions nettes
Reserves and Related Items	137.5	317.0	78.4	214.2	−65.1	415.0	−87.3	Rés. et postes appareutés
Belgium−Luxembourg [2]								**Belgique−Luxembourg** [2]
Goods: Exports fob	106 302.0	122 795.0	155 219.0	154 695.0	149 497.0	153 558.0	154 069.0	Biens : exportations,fàb
Goods: Imports fob	−100 522.0	−115 895.0	−145 664.0	−146 004.0	−141 794.0	−146 577.0	−146 814.0	Biens : importations,fàb
Serv. & Income: Credit	116 377.0	129 843.0	110 264.0	97 586.0	93 740.0	103 332.0	106 869.0	Serv. & revenu : crédit
Serv. & Income: Debit	−108 133.3	−120 666.0	−101 124.0	−87 907.0	−83 546.0	−93 726.0	−97 879.0	Serv. & revenu : débit
Current Trans.,nie: Credit	4 198.2	4 501.0	7 822.0	7 474.0	7 142.0	7 006.0	6 703.0	Transf. cour.,nia : crédit
Current Transfers: Debit	−6 985.6	−8 009.0	−12 285.0	−12 081.0	−11 124.0	−11 426.0	−11 263.0	Transf. courants : débit
Capital Acct.,nie: Credit	0.0	0.0	734.0	673.0	783.0	323.0	459.0	Compte de cap.,nia : crédit
Capital Account: Debit	0.0	0.0	−356.0	−494.0	−379.0	−436.0	−451.0	Compte de capital : débit
Financial Account,nie	−13 562.6	−10 182.0	−12 912.0	−12 257.0	−12 091.0	−16 043.0	−13 291.0	Compte d'op. fin., nia
Net Errors and Omissions	203.5	−2 169.0	−1 456.0	−1 091.0	−1 171.0	1 893.0	−268.0	Erreurs et omissions nettes
Reserves and Related Items	2 122.1	−219.0	−243.0	−593.0	−1 056.0	2 095.0	1 867.0	Rés. et postes appareutés
Bulgaria								**Bulgarie**
Goods: Exports fob	3 726.5	3 935.1	5 345.0	4 890.2	4 939.6	4 193.5	4 006.4	Biens : exportations,fàb
Goods: Imports fob	−4 611.9	−3 951.9	−5 224.0	−4 702.6	−4 559.3	−4 574.2	−5 087.4	Biens : importations,fàb
Serv. & Income: Credit	1 263.9	1 341.5	1 581.0	1 547.0	1 548.2	2 094.5	2 051.8	Serv. & revenu : crédit
Serv. & Income: Debit	−1 514.2	−1 523.2	−1 859.8	−1 823.1	−1 738.4	−2 005.4	−1 955.3	Serv. & revenu : débit
Current Trans.,nie: Credit	285.9	357.1	256.8	231.8	275.5	261.4	328.7	Transf. cour.,nia : crédit
Current Transfers: Debit	−249.0	−190.4	−124.9	−127.6	−38.7	−31.6	−28.9	Transf. courants : débit
Capital Acct.,nie: Credit	0.0	763.3	0.0	65.9	0.0	0.0	0.0	Compte de cap.,nia : crédit
Capital Account: Debit	0.0	0.0	0.0	0.0	0.0	0.0	−2.4	Compte de capital : débit
Financial Account,nie	759.0	−1 018.7	326.6	−715.0	462.0	266.7	777.4	Compte d'op. fin., nia
Net Errors and Omissions	18.1	71.6	143.8	−105.3	256.4	−299.2	6.1	Erreurs et omissions nettes
Reserves and Related Items	321.7	215.6	−444.6	738.7	−1 145.4	94.3	−96.4	Rés. et postes appareutés
Croatia								**Croatie**
Goods: Exports fob	3 903.8	4 260.4	4 632.7	4 545.9	4 210.4	4 604.5	4 372.0	Biens : exportations,fàb
Goods: Imports fob	−4 626.9	−5 402.1	−7 892.0	−8 169.1	−9 406.6	−8 751.9	−7 673.6	Biens : importations,fàb
Serv. & Income: Credit	2 413.8	3 006.1	2 673.3	3 566.3	4 367.8	4 358.9	3 975.4	Serv. & revenu : crédit
Serv. & Income: Debit	−1 395.1	−1 537.1	−1 657.9	−2 056.8	−2 365.8	−2 448.2	−2 710.6	Serv. & revenu : débit

75
Summary of balance of payments
Millions of US dollars
Résumé des balances des paiements
Millions de dollars des E.–U.

Country or area	1993	1994	1995	1996	1997	1998	1999	Pays ou zone
Current Trans.,nie: Credit	509.0	672.0	973.0	1 183.2	966.1	921.1	835.1	Transf. cour.,nia : crédit
Current Transfers: Debit	−180.0	−142.8	−168.9	−150.8	−94.5	−213.3	−334.9	Transf. courants : débit
Capital Acct.,nie: Credit	0.0	0.0	0.0	18.0	23.5	24.1	28.3	Compte de cap.,nia : crédit
Capital Account: Debit	0.0	0.0	0.0	−1.8	−2.2	−5.0	−3.3	Compte de capital : débit
Financial Account,nie	−139.4	43.6	1 146.2	3 047.8	3 026.2	1 594.3	1 827.4	Compte d'op. fin., nia
Net Errors and Omissions	−296.9	−623.6	334.0	−965.4	−334.5	76.0	144.3	Erreurs et omissions nettes
Reserves and Related Items	−188.3	−276.5	−40.4	−1 017.3	−390.4	−160.5	−460.1	Rés. et postes appareutés
Czech Republic								**République tchèque**
Goods: Exports fob	14 231.3	15 964.0	21 476.8	21 693.4	22 736.9	26 394.7	26 258.9	Biens : exportations,fàb
Goods: Imports fob	−14 748.2	−17 371.7	−25 162.2	−27 570.6	−27 324.5	−28 989.3	−28 161.3	Biens : importations,fàb
Serv. & Income: Credit	5 268.6	5 957.9	7 922.5	9 350.6	8 536.6	8 941.5	8 598.0	Serv. & revenu : crédit
Serv. & Income: Debit	−4 373.0	−5 496.9	−6 182.5	−8 156.2	−7 585.4	−8 141.5	−8 236.2	Serv. & revenu : débit
Current Trans.,nie: Credit	241.8	297.8	664.1	616.6	866.0	780.9	1 072.3	Transf. cour.,nia : crédit
Current Transfers: Debit	−154.2	−170.9	−92.1	−232.6	−500.6	−373.1	−563.4	Transf. courants : débit
Capital Acct.,nie: Credit	208.0	0.0	11.7	1.0	16.7	13.8	18.4	Compte de cap.,nia : crédit
Capital Account: Debit	−771.1	0.0	−4.9	−0.5	−5.5	−11.6	−20.5	Compte de capital : débit
Financial Account,nie	3 042.9	4 503.8	8 224.6	4 202.5	1 122.2	2 908.3	2 499.7	Compte d'op. fin., nia
Net Errors and Omissions	95.3	−209.5	595.5	−729.3	379.1	366.8	173.3	Erreurs et omissions nettes
Reserves and Related Items	−3 041.5	−3 474.4	−7 453.4	825.2	1 758.4	−1 890.4	−1 639.3	Rés. et postes appareutés
Denmark								**Danemark**
Goods: Exports fob	36 947.8	41 740.8	50 348.2	50 734.7	48 102.9	47 907.8	49 548.1	Biens : exportations,fàb
Goods: Imports fob	−29 228.8	−34 299.5	−43 820.5	−43 202.5	−42 734.2	−44 021.5	−43 010.9	Biens : importations,fàb
Serv. & Income: Credit	35 654.1	36 404.1	43 739.6	54 128.5	32 817.7	25 612.8	24 424.7	Serv. & revenu : crédit
Serv. & Income: Debit	−37 946.3	−39 451.7	−47 021.5	−57 005.8	−35 929.8	−30 026.4	−26 664.3	Serv. & revenu : débit
Current Trans.,nie: Credit	2 442.2	2 261.5	2 579.6	2 398.3	3 632.9	3 442.8	3 432.7	Transf. cour.,nia : crédit
Current Transfers: Debit	−3 037.3	−3 465.9	−3 970.4	−3 963.4	−4 968.0	−4 923.7	−5 554.5	Transf. courants : débit
Capital Acct.,nie: Credit	0.0	0.0	0.0	0.0	127.8	81.3	166.9	Compte de cap.,nia : crédit
Capital Account: Debit	0.0	0.0	0.0	0.0	0.0	−31.3	−38.3	Compte de capital : débit
Financial Account,nie	−6 545.3	−5 646.9	−431.6	1 882.0	8 496.1	−1 488.1	7 340.6	Compte d'op. fin., nia
Net Errors and Omissions	1 146.3	606.4	1 074.7	−1 408.3	−3 013.0	−793.3	−208.5	Erreurs et omissions nettes
Reserves and Related Items	567.3	1 851.2	−2 497.9	−3 563.3	−6 532.1	4 239.4	−9 437.3	Rés. et postes appareutés
Estonia								**Estonie**
Goods: Exports fob	811.7	1 225.0	1 696.3	1 812.4	2 291.3	2 690.1	2 453.0	Biens : exportations,fàb
Goods: Imports fob	−956.6	−1 581.4	−2 362.3	−2 831.5	−3 415.7	−3 804.9	−3 330.6	Biens : importations,fàb
Serv. & Income: Credit	361.4	552.6	940.4	1 220.5	1 433.1	1 613.2	1 623.5	Serv. & revenu : crédit
Serv. & Income: Debit	−300.2	−477.1	−558.5	−700.2	−987.4	−1 124.7	−1 153.1	Serv. & revenu : débit
Current Trans.,nie: Credit	108.4	120.3	134.5	116.8	135.3	172.9	153.7	Transf. cour.,nia : crédit
Current Transfers: Debit	−3.2	−5.7	−8.2	−16.3	−18.6	−24.5	−41.3	Transf. courants : débit
Capital Acct.,nie: Credit	0.0	0.5	1.4	0.2	0.7	2.1	1.4	Compte de cap.,nia : crédit
Capital Account: Debit	0.0	−1.1	−2.2	−0.8	−0.9	−0.3	−0.2	Compte de capital : débit
Financial Account,nie	188.9	167.2	233.4	540.9	802.8	508.1	418.2	Compte d'op. fin., nia
Net Errors and Omissions	−45.9	17.2	8.7	−35.6	−24.9	5.3	−5.4	Erreurs et omissions nettes
Reserves and Related Items	−164.6	−17.5	−83.5	−106.3	−215.9	−37.3	−119.3	Rés. et postes appareutés
Finland								**Finlande**
Goods: Exports fob	23 587.3	29 880.8	40 558.0	40 725.0	41 148.2	43 393.4	41 983.0	Biens : exportations,fàb
Goods: Imports fob	−17 138.1	−22 157.9	−28 120.7	−29 410.6	−29 604.4	−30 902.9	−30 328.0	Biens : importations,fàb
Serv. & Income: Credit	5 566.1	7 279.3	10 293.5	9 996.7	10 776.1	10 996.0	11 619.4	Serv. & revenu : crédit
Serv. & Income: Debit	−12 722.2	−13 438.5	−16 902.4	−15 319.5	−14 834.7	−15 121.9	−15 326.4	Serv. & revenu : débit
Current Trans.,nie: Credit	475.0	409.9	1 536.4	1 253.0	1 209.8	1 522.7	1 599.8	Transf. cour.,nia : crédit
Current Transfers: Debit	−903.2	−863.2	−2 133.3	−2 242.0	−2 062.2	−2 516.8	−2 611.9	Transf. courants : débit
Capital Acct.,nie: Credit	0.0	0.0	113.7	129.9	247.5	90.7	42.7	Compte de cap.,nia : crédit
Capital Account: Debit	0.0	0.0	−48.0	−74.3	0.0	0.0	−38.4	Compte de capital : débit
Financial Account,nie	373.9	4 092.8	−4 284.3	−7 718.4	−2 975.8	−2 185.6	−4 205.8	Compte d'op. fin., nia
Net Errors and Omissions	1 052.5	−489.4	−1 384.5	−375.5	−1 600.3	−4 980.0	−2 831.8	Erreurs et omissions nettes
Reserves and Related Items	−291.4	−4 713.9	371.7	3 035.7	−2 304.2	−295.6	97.3	Rés. et postes appareutés
France								**France**
Goods: Exports fob	199 044.0	230 811.0	278 627.0	281 846.0	286 071.0	303 025.0	298 148.0	Biens : exportations,fàb
Goods: Imports fob	−191 528.0	−223 561.0	−267 629.0	−266 911.0	−259 172.0	−278 084.0	−278 083.0	Biens : importations,fàb
Serv. & Income: Credit	185 368.5	117 081.6	129 272.1	131 078.2	137 920.3	151 623.6	151 191.4	Serv. & revenu : crédit
Serv. & Income: Debit	−177 693.7	−105 990.3	−120 263.5	−117 529.5	−114 201.3	−125 732.4	−121 062.2	Serv. & revenu : débit
Current Trans.,nie: Credit	16 742.9	18 223.3	22 005.7	22 759.8	19 614.0	19 653.9	18 798.9	Transf. cour.,nia : crédit
Current Transfers: Debit	−22 943.7	−29 148.7	−31 172.6	−30 683.5	−32 430.6	−32 786.3	−31 762.0	Transf. courants : débit
Capital Acct.,nie: Credit	305.0	986.0	1 163.1	1 883.4	2 412.6	2 098.5	2 015.9	Compte de cap.,nia : crédit
Capital Account: Debit	−278.4	−5 164.7	−655.7	−648.9	−933.9	−632.4	−544.1	Compte de capital : débit
Financial Account,nie	−16 674.5	−4 775.6	−7 325.3	−22 344.5	−39 740.5	−31 079.8	−41 816.9	Compte d'op. fin., nia

75
Summary of balance of payments
Millions of US dollars
Résumé des balances des paiements
Millions de dollars des E.−U.

Country or area	1993	1994	1995	1996	1997	1998	1999	Pays ou zone
Net Errors and Omissions	2 652.0	3 986.5	−3 309.7	788.7	4 259.5	9 940.0	1 334.0	Erreurs et omissions nettes
Reserves and Related Items	5 006.2	−2 447.5	−712.4	−239.3	−5 940.0	−19 815.1	1 448.4	Rés. et postes appareutés
Germany [1]								**Allemagne** [1]
Goods: Exports fob	382.7	430.5	523.6	522.6	510.7	542.8	543.0	Biens : exportations,fàb
Goods: Imports fob	−341.5	−379.6	−458.5	−453.2	−439.9	−463.9	−471.0	Biens : importations,fàb
Serv. & Income: Credit	141.8	134.8	166.7	166.9	163.6	167.8	169.0	Serv. & revenu : crédit
Serv. & Income: Debit	−161.6	−167.6	−211.8	−210.2	−206.9	−221.0	−233.0	Serv. & revenu : débit
Current Trans.,nie: Credit	13.4	13.9	16.9	17.9	16.5	16.5	17.0	Transf. cour.,nia : crédit
Current Transfers: Debit	−48.7	−52.9	−55.8	−51.9	−46.8	−46.8	−44.3	Transf. courants : débit
Capital Acct.,nie: Credit	1.4	1.6	1.7	2.8	2.8	3.3	3.0	Compte de cap.,nia : crédit
Capital Account: Debit	−0.9	−1.4	−4.4	−4.9	−2.8	−2.6	−3.1	Compte de capital : débit
Financial Account,nie	16.2	30.4	44.0	16.1	0.5	8.4	−33.9	Compte d'op. fin., nia
Net Errors and Omissions	−17.0	−11.7	−15.1	−7.2	−1.4	−0.5	39.2	Erreurs et omissions nettes
Reserves and Related Items	14.2	2.0	−7.2	1.2	3.8	−4.0	14.1	Rés. et postes appareutés
Greece								**Grèce**
Goods: Exports fob	5 112.0	5 338.0	5 918.0	5 890.0	5 576.0	...	...	Biens : exportations,fàb
Goods: Imports fob	−15 611.0	−16 611.0	−20 343.0	−21 395.0	−20 951.0	...	...	Biens : importations,fàb
Serv. & Income: Credit	9 141.0	10 312.0	10 917.0	10 504.0	10 495.0	...	...	Serv. & revenu : crédit
Serv. & Income: Debit	−5 888.0	−6 121.0	−7 364.0	−7 575.0	−7 490.0	...	...	Serv. & revenu : débit
Current Trans.,nie: Credit	6 516.0	6 964.0	8 039.0	8 053.0	7 538.0	...	...	Transf. cour.,nia : crédit
Current Transfers: Debit	−17.0	−28.0	−31.0	−31.0	−28.0	...	...	Transf. courants : débit
Capital Acct.,nie: Credit	0.0	0.0	0.0	0.0	0.0	...	...	Compte de cap.,nia : crédit
Capital Account: Debit	0.0	0.0	0.0	0.0	0.0	...	...	Compte de capital : débit
Financial Account,nie	4 817.0	6 903.0	3 162.0	8 658.0	119.0	...	...	Compte d'op. fin., nia
Net Errors and Omissions	−631.3	−447.8	−321.3	110.6	225.8	...	...	Erreurs et omissions nettes
Reserves and Related Items	−3 438.7	−6 309.2	23.3	−4 214.6	4 515.2	...	...	Rés. et postes appareutés
Hungary								**Hongrie**
Goods: Exports fob	8 118.7	7 648.2	12 864.1	14 183.8	19 639.9	20 746.6	21 845.7	Biens : exportations,fàb
Goods: Imports fob	−12 139.9	−11 364.1	−15 297.2	−16 835.5	−21 601.7	−23 100.9	−24 036.6	Biens : importations,fàb
Serv. & Income: Credit	3 300.6	3 792.5	5 980.1	7 181.8	7 115.2	7 032.2	6 425.5	Serv. & revenu : crédit
Serv. & Income: Debit	−4 274.6	−5 039.8	−6 217.6	−6 164.2	−6 273.7	−7 130.5	−6 683.0	Serv. & revenu : débit
Current Trans.,nie: Credit	2 693.7	2 871.0	363.6	159.8	334.9	379.4	590.0	Transf. cour.,nia : crédit
Current Transfers: Debit	−1 961.0	−1 961.4	−222.5	−214.5	−196.6	−230.9	−242.7	Transf. courants : débit
Capital Acct.,nie: Credit	0.0	0.0	79.5	266.2	266.5	408.0	509.0	Compte de cap.,nia : crédit
Capital Account: Debit	0.0	0.0	−20.5	−110.3	−149.4	−219.3	−479.5	Compte de capital : débit
Financial Account,nie	6 083.0	3 369.7	7 080.3	−686.7	658.4	3 017.5	4 667.5	Compte d'op. fin., nia
Net Errors and Omissions	724.2	209.0	789.1	975.6	31.7	48.6	−260.7	Erreurs et omissions nettes
Reserves and Related Items	−2 544.8	474.9	−5 399.0	1 244.0	174.9	−950.7	−2 335.0	Rés. et postes appareutés
Iceland								**Islande**
Goods: Exports fob	1 398.0	1 561.0	1 804.0	1 890.0	1 855.0	1 927.0	2 009.0	Biens : exportations,fàb
Goods: Imports fob	−1 217.0	−1 288.0	−1 598.0	−1 871.0	−1 850.0	−2 279.0	−2 316.0	Biens : importations,fàb
Serv. & Income: Credit	693.0	688.0	780.0	881.0	948.0	1 070.0	1 082.0	Serv. & revenu : crédit
Serv. & Income: Debit	−829.0	−844.0	−927.0	−1 011.0	−1 073.0	−1 262.0	−1 357.0	Serv. & revenu : débit
Current Trans.,nie: Credit	18.0	12.0	15.0	10.0	17.0	4.0	5.0	Transf. cour.,nia : crédit
Current Transfers: Debit	−21.0	−20.0	−20.0	−16.0	−22.0	−20.0	−14.0	Transf. courants : débit
Capital Acct.,nie: Credit	12.0	6.0	13.0	10.0	11.0	9.0	18.0	Compte de cap.,nia : crédit
Capital Account: Debit	−11.0	−12.0	−16.0	−11.0	−10.0	−14.0	−18.0	Compte de capital : débit
Financial Account,nie	−55.0	−293.0	−17.0	303.0	197.0	679.0	967.0	Compte d'op. fin., nia
Net Errors and Omissions	−47.0	40.0	−30.1	−32.1	−117.0	−82.0	−301.0	Erreurs et omissions nettes
Reserves and Related Items	59.0	150.0	−3.9	−152.9	44.0	−32.0	−75.0	Rés. et postes appareutés
Ireland								**Irlande**
Goods: Exports fob	28 728.3	33 641.6	44 422.5	49 183.9	55 292.7	78 562.0	66 989.0	Biens : exportations,fàb
Goods: Imports fob	−20 553.0	−24 275.3	−30 865.9	−33 429.7	−36 667.7	−53 172.1	−42 811.3	Biens : importations,fàb
Serv. & Income: Credit	6 549.4	7 831.9	10 126.6	11 325.4	13 538.9	42 165.6	39 674.4	Serv. & revenu : crédit
Serv. & Income: Debit	−14 876.2	−17 371.2	−23 738.1	−27 220.2	−32 254.0	−68 425.3	−64 542.7	Serv. & revenu : débit
Current Trans.,nie: Credit	2 858.2	2 849.5	3 009.0	3 538.2	3 083.4	7 428.5	5 311.3	Transf. cour.,nia : crédit
Current Transfers: Debit	−941.3	−1 099.5	−1 233.1	−1 349.0	−1 127.7	−5 542.6	−4 026.1	Transf. courants : débit
Capital Acct.,nie: Credit	863.4	476.9	913.6	880.8	961.7	1 326.7	674.4	Compte de cap.,nia : crédit
Capital Account: Debit	−88.8	−89.8	−96.2	−96.0	−91.0	−108.3	−81.0	Compte de capital : débit
Financial Account,nie	−900.8	−3 962.7	−33.0	−2 779.7	−7 484.3	4 686.1	−1 675.8	Compte d'op. fin., nia
Net Errors and Omissions	1 020.6	1 823.1	−166.6	−106.0	3 639.4	−3 708.0	−1 485.7	Erreurs et omissions nettes
Reserves and Related Items	−2 659.8	175.5	−2 338.8	52.3	1 108.7	−3 212.4	1 973.5	Rés. et postes appareutés
Italy								**Italie**
Goods: Exports fob	169 153.0	191 421.0	233 998.0	252 039.0	240 404.0	242 572.0	230 831.0	Biens : exportations,fàb
Goods: Imports fob	−140 264.0	−159 854.0	−195 269.0	−197 921.0	−200 527.0	−206 941.0	−210 445.0	Biens : importations,fàb
Serv. & Income: Credit	84 128.7	82 280.2	95 787.2	105 801.3	112 725.1	118 867.5	107 418.3	Serv. & revenu : crédit

75
Summary of balance of payments
Millions of US dollars
Résumé des balances des paiements
Millions de dollars des E.−U.

Country or area	1993	1994	1995	1996	1997	1998	1999	Pays ou zone
Serv. & Income: Debit	−98 000.9	−93 526.7	−104 861.3	−112 706.0	−116 163.1	−127 015.2	−116 103.4	Serv. & revenu : débit
Current Trans.,nie: Credit	12 925.4	12 254.5	14 287.1	14 320.3	15 551.5	14 402.3	16 729.4	Transf. cour.,nia : crédit
Current Transfers: Debit	−20 140.2	−19 366.5	−18 866.1	−21 534.8	−19 587.9	−21 887.4	−22 105.0	Transf. courants : débit
Capital Acct.,nie: Credit	2 807.3	2 212.9	2 796.6	1 414.0	4 582.4	3 359.4	4 572.9	Compte de cap.,nia : crédit
Capital Account: Debit	−1 148.7	−1 187.3	−1 125.5	−1 348.0	−1 147.9	−1 001.5	−1 640.2	Compte de capital : débit
Financial Account,nie	5 259.8	−14 207.0	−2 889.1	−7 982.2	−6 878.3	−18 074.0	−17 931.9	Compte d'op. fin., nia
Net Errors and Omissions	−17 856.0	1 547.5	−21 054.2	−20 176.2	−15 809.8	−25 753.7	623.7	Erreurs et omissions nettes
Reserves and Related Items	3 135.5	−1 575.3	−2 803.6	−11 906.7	−13 149.7	21 471.9	8 051.1	Rés. et postes appareutés
Latvia								**Lettonie**
Goods: Exports fob	1 054.4	1 021.7	1 367.6	1 487.6	1 838.1	2 011.2	1 889.1	Biens : exportations,fàb
Goods: Imports fob	−1 051.3	−1 322.3	−1 947.2	−2 285.9	−2 686.0	−3 141.4	−2 916.1	Biens : importations,fàb
Serv. & Income: Credit	550.6	707.9	791.2	1 266.0	1 210.0	1 315.8	1 182.0	Serv. & revenu : crédit
Serv. & Income: Debit	−214.8	−338.9	−298.5	−841.0	−784.5	−960.0	−890.0	Serv. & revenu : débit
Current Trans.,nie: Credit	80.5	135.7	75.4	98.1	90.9	137.3	113.8	Transf. cour.,nia : crédit
Current Transfers: Debit	−2.6	−3.0	−4.6	−4.6	−13.6	−12.8	−21.0	Transf. courants : débit
Capital Acct.,nie: Credit	0.0	0.0	0.0	0.0	13.7	14.1	12.6	Compte de cap.,nia : crédit
Capital Account: Debit	0.0	0.0	0.0	0.0	0.0	0.0	0.0	Compte de capital : débit
Financial Account,nie	67.0	363.4	635.6	537.1	346.9	601.1	794.1	Compte d'op. fin., nia
Net Errors and Omissions	−186.2	−508.0	−652.6	−46.3	86.5	97.3	0.5	Erreurs et omissions nettes
Reserves and Related Items	−297.6	−56.5	33.2	−211.1	−102.2	−62.6	−165.0	Rés. et postes appareutés
Lithuania								**Lithuanie**
Goods: Exports fob	2 025.8	2 029.2	2 706.1	3 413.2	4 192.4	3 961.6	3 146.7	Biens : exportations,fàb
Goods: Imports fob	−2 180.5	−2 234.1	−3 404.0	−4 309.3	−5 339.9	−5 479.9	−4 551.3	Biens : importations,fàb
Serv. & Income: Credit	210.3	343.3	536.1	849.5	1 112.3	1 233.5	1 206.4	Serv. & revenu : crédit
Serv. & Income: Debit	−257.1	−389.3	−561.8	−819.7	−1 176.1	−1 248.4	−1 158.6	Serv. & revenu : débit
Current Trans.,nie: Credit	115.9	161.6	112.3	149.4	237.0	240.4	167.4	Transf. cour.,nia : crédit
Current Transfers: Debit	0.0	−4.8	−3.0	−5.6	−7.0	−5.4	−4.6	Transf. courants : débit
Capital Acct.,nie: Credit	0.0	12.9	3.3	5.5	4.5	0.9	2.7	Compte de cap.,nia : crédit
Capital Account: Debit	0.0	0.0	−42.3	0.0	−0.4	−2.6	−6.0	Compte de capital : débit
Financial Account,nie	301.5	240.9	534.4	645.6	1 005.6	1 443.9	1 060.7	Compte d'op. fin., nia
Net Errors and Omissions	−7.4	−46.9	287.2	66.7	195.8	282.9	−42.1	Erreurs et omissions nettes
Reserves and Related Items	−208.5	−112.8	−168.3	4.8	−224.2	−426.8	178.7	Rés. et postes appareutés
Luxembourg								**Luxembourg**
Goods: Exports fob	...	...	9 243.7	8 476.8	8 472.7	9 010.0	8 369.8	Biens : exportations,fàb
Goods: Imports fob	...	...	−10 844.8	−10 211.1	−10 465.9	−11 008.6	−10 845.0	Biens : importations,fàb
Serv. & Income: Credit	...	...	57 222.3	48 904.1	47 761.4	53 699.9	54 889.4	Serv. & revenu : crédit
Serv. & Income: Debit	...	...	−52 684.9	−44 350.9	−42 998.8	−49 048.7	−50 846.1	Serv. & revenu : débit
Current Trans.,nie: Credit	...	...	1 741.7	2 225.0	1 935.0	2 124.0	2 181.7	Transf. cour.,nia : crédit
Current Transfers: Debit	...	...	−2 368.7	−2 725.7	−2 446.2	−2 474.6	−2 436.1	Transf. courants : débit
Capital Acct.,nie: Credit	...	...	...	...	...	...	...	Compte de cap.,nia : crédit
Capital Account: Debit	...	...	...	...	...	...	...	Compte de capital : débit
Financial Account,nie	...	...	...	...	...	...	...	Compte d'op. fin., nia
Net Errors and Omissions	...	...	...	...	...	...	...	Erreurs et omissions nettes
Reserves and Related Items	...	...	...	...	...	...	...	Rés. et postes appareutés
Malta								**Malte**
Goods: Exports fob	1 408.1	1 618.5	1 944.9	1 772.8	1 661.4	1 824.3	2 015.7	Biens : exportations,fàb
Goods: Imports fob	−1 976.4	−2 221.0	−2 673.1	−2 536.2	−2 320.7	−2 417.0	−2 589.1	Biens : importations,fàb
Serv. & Income: Credit	1 154.2	1 214.0	1 336.1	1 381.6	1 473.7	1 695.0	2 455.4	Serv. & revenu : crédit
Serv. & Income: Debit	−731.1	−837.1	−991.2	−1 051.6	−1 073.1	−1 381.6	−2 072.7	Serv. & revenu : débit
Current Trans.,nie: Credit	64.9	101.2	65.8	87.1	122.4	114.9	124.3	Transf. cour.,nia : crédit
Current Transfers: Debit	−4.1	−7.1	−13.3	−56.1	−68.0	−56.9	−81.6	Transf. courants : débit
Capital Acct.,nie: Credit	13.1	0.0	0.0	64.2	32.9	33.1	38.0	Compte de cap.,nia : crédit
Capital Account: Debit	0.0	0.0	0.0	−6.1	−24.5	−4.6	−5.5	Compte de capital : débit
Financial Account,nie	188.7	480.9	82.3	204.8	106.7	294.6	404.5	Compte d'op. fin., nia
Net Errors and Omissions	17.4	33.4	−58.5	54.5	96.0	89.1	−50.0	Erreurs et omissions nettes
Reserves and Related Items	−134.8	−382.8	307.1	84.9	−6.8	−190.9	−239.0	Rés. et postes appareutés
Netherlands								**Pays−Bas**
Goods: Exports fob	127 876.0	141 810.0	195 594.0	195 077.0	189 400.0	195 305.0	195 076.0	Biens : exportations,fàb
Goods: Imports fob	−110 972.0	−123 124.0	−171 783.0	−172 310.0	−167 624.0	−174 491.0	−177 122.0	Biens : importations,fàb
Serv. & Income: Credit	66 040.0	70 988.5	82 699.1	84 814.9	89 855.5	89 513.1	93 808.8	Serv. & revenu : crédit
Serv. & Income: Debit	−65 239.7	−67 102.7	−74 270.5	−78 174.6	−78 757.2	−86 817.2	−88 309.9	Serv. & revenu : débit
Current Trans.,nie: Credit	4 359.4	4 197.1	4 725.1	4 318.1	4 345.0	3 788.6	4 555.1	Transf. cour.,nia : crédit
Current Transfers: Debit	−8 860.2	−9 474.3	−11 156.8	−11 085.1	−10 465.3	−10 976.4	−10 732.8	Transf. courants : débit
Capital Acct.,nie: Credit	578.9	563.5	857.1	1 265.0	1 099.7	1 035.4	1 630.1	Compte de cap.,nia : crédit
Capital Account: Debit	−1 293.6	−1 569.5	−1 953.5	−3 290.8	−2 388.4	−1 436.9	−1 730.9	Compte de capital : débit
Financial Account,nie	−11 135.7	−9 969.2	−18 849.5	−5 943.3	−14 330.2	−8 834.6	−15 344.1	Compte d'op. fin., nia

75
Summary of balance of payments
Millions of US dollars
Résumé des balances des paiements
Millions de dollars des E.−U.

Country or area	1993	1994	1995	1996	1997	1998	1999	Pays ou zone
Net Errors and Omissions	5 288.4	−5 819.0	−7 773.3	−20 364.8	−13 841.8	−9 425.5	−6 441.6	Erreurs et omissions nettes
Reserves and Related Items	−6 641.3	−500.1	1 911.6	5 693.7	2 706.9	2 338.8	4 611.0	Rés. et postes appareutés
Norway								**Norvège**
Goods: Exports fob	32 278.0	35 016.4	42 312.2	49 968.3	48 736.7	40 636.5	...	Biens : exportations,fàb
Goods: Imports fob	−25 311.9	−27 520.4	−33 740.9	−37 037.4	−37 584.6	−39 070.3	...	Biens : importations,fàb
Serv. & Income: Credit	14 538.5	15 661.1	17 888.6	19 258.5	20 125.6	20 618.8	...	Serv. & revenu : crédit
Serv. & Income: Debit	−16 638.9	−17 653.3	−19 542.8	−20 438.7	−21 842.7	−22 754.4	...	Serv. & revenu : débit
Current Trans.,nie: Credit	1 533.2	1 291.1	1 276.1	1 324.6	1 234.5	1 261.8	...	Transf. cour.,nia : crédit
Current Transfers: Debit	−2 876.7	−3 034.7	−3 338.9	−2 835.2	−2 652.0	−2 853.0	...	Transf. courants : débit
Capital Acct.,nie: Credit	306.2	93.1	85.8	64.5	29.0	40.7	...	Compte de cap.,nia : crédit
Capital Account: Debit	−337.5	−249.8	−255.4	−191.9	−212.4	−141.4	...	Compte de capital : débit
Financial Account,nie	6 568.3	−1 363.3	−639.9	−1 700.7	−7 413.2	−106.9	...	Compte d'op. fin., nia
Net Errors and Omissions	−1 806.1	−1 987.2	−3 470.0	−1 942.1	−1 619.4	−4 016.4	...	Erreurs et omissions nettes
Reserves and Related Items	−8 253.0	−253.0	−574.8	−6 469.9	1 198.5	6 384.7	...	Rés. et postes appareutés
Poland								**Pologne**
Goods: Exports fob	13 582.0	18 355.0	25 041.0	27 557.0	30 731.0	32 467.0	30 060.0	Biens : exportations,fàb
Goods: Imports fob	−17 087.0	−18 930.0	−26 687.0	−34 844.0	−40 553.0	−45 303.0	−45 132.0	Biens : importations,fàb
Serv. & Income: Credit	4 780.0	7 245.0	11 764.0	11 360.0	10 453.0	13 146.0	10 299.0	Serv. & revenu : crédit
Serv. & Income: Debit	−7 823.0	−6 968.0	−10 222.0	−9 031.0	−8 410.0	−10 108.0	−9 928.0	Serv. & revenu : débit
Current Trans.,nie: Credit	5 840.0	2 174.0	2 459.0	2 825.0	2 700.0	3 520.0	2 898.0	Transf. cour.,nia : crédit
Current Transfers: Debit	−5 080.0	−922.0	−1 501.0	−1 131.0	−665.0	−623.0	−684.0	Transf. courants : débit
Capital Acct.,nie: Credit	0.0	9 215.0	285.0	5 833.0	91.0	117.0	95.0	Compte de cap.,nia : crédit
Capital Account: Debit	0.0	0.0	0.0	−5 739.0	−25.0	−54.0	−40.0	Compte de capital : débit
Financial Account,nie	2 341.0	−9 065.0	9 260.0	6 673.0	7 410.0	13 282.0	10 462.0	Compte d'op. fin., nia
Net Errors and Omissions	218.9	−97.6	−563.6	321.3	1 309.3	−519.6	2 125.6	Erreurs et omissions nettes
Reserves and Related Items	3 228.1	−1 006.5	−9 835.4	−3 824.3	−3 041.3	−5 924.4	−155.6	Rés. et postes appareutés
Portugal								**Portugal**
Goods: Exports fob	15 931.4	18 644.7	24 024.3	25 519.3	24 806.0	26 015.7	25 673.2	Biens : exportations,fàb
Goods: Imports fob	−23 981.3	−26 965.6	−32 934.4	−34 879.7	−34 846.7	−38 292.5	−39 829.9	Biens : importations,fàb
Serv. & Income: Credit	9 301.3	8 987.5	12 331.2	12 353.9	12 086.3	13 164.1	12 627.6	Serv. & revenu : crédit
Serv. & Income: Debit	−7 717.1	−8 282.9	−10 685.1	−11 945.8	−11 247.0	−12 168.5	−11 411.9	Serv. & revenu : débit
Current Trans.,nie: Credit	8 395.1	7 410.0	9 045.9	6 806.0	5 651.9	6 097.9	6 080.4	Transf. cour.,nia : crédit
Current Transfers: Debit	−1 696.5	−1 989.5	−1 913.6	−2 381.5	−1 977.4	−2 066.6	−2 143.6	Transf. courants : débit
Capital Acct.,nie: Credit	0.0	0.0	0.0	2 342.5	2 796.3	2 808.4	2 625.2	Compte de cap.,nia : crédit
Capital Account: Debit	0.0	0.0	0.0	−103.2	−102.0	−220.5	−189.9	Compte de capital : débit
Financial Account,nie	−3 032.3	1 052.2	3 024.7	4 403.6	6 258.3	6 532.4	9 632.1	Compte d'op. fin., nia
Net Errors and Omissions	−48.3	−286.9	−3 192.8	−1 392.4	−2 179.6	−1 362.4	−2 861.2	Erreurs et omissions nettes
Reserves and Related Items	2 847.7	1 430.4	299.8	−722.8	−1 246.1	−507.9	−202.1	Rés. et postes appareutés
Republic of Moldova								**République de Moldova**
Goods: Exports fob	...	618.5	738.9	822.9	889.6	643.3	469.2	Biens : exportations,fàb
Goods: Imports fob	...	−672.4	−809.2	−1 082.5	−1 237.8	−1 031.7	−592.2	Biens : importations,fàb
Serv. & Income: Credit	...	43.6	159.1	212.8	267.7	258.5	231.1	Serv. & revenu : crédit
Serv. & Income: Debit	...	−105.1	−239.7	−224.7	−281.3	−300.2	−240.9	Serv. & revenu : débit
Current Trans.,nie: Credit	...	36.9	66.6	73.1	98.1	101.0	120.0	Transf. cour.,nia : crédit
Current Transfers: Debit	...	−3.6	−14.1	−2.8	−21.8	−18.2	−20.5	Transf. courants : débit
Capital Acct.,nie: Credit	...	0.0	0.0	0.1	0.1	2.1	0.2	Compte de cap.,nia : crédit
Capital Account: Debit	...	−1.0	−0.4	−0.1	−0.4	−2.4	−0.4	Compte de capital : débit
Financial Account,nie	...	211.1	−57.9	45.0	99.9	−6.8	−85.8	Compte d'op. fin., nia
Net Errors and Omissions	...	−115.2	−18.3	11.0	3.8	12.8	−2.5	Erreurs et omissions nettes
Reserves and Related Items	...	−12.9	175.0	145.2	182.1	341.6	122.0	Rés. et postes appareutés
Romania								**Roumanie**
Goods: Exports fob	4 892.0	6 151.0	7 910.0	8 085.0	8 431.0	8 302.0	8 503.0	Biens : exportations,fàb
Goods: Imports fob	−6 020.0	−6 562.0	−9 487.0	−10 555.0	−10 411.0	−10 927.0	−9 595.0	Biens : importations,fàb
Serv. & Income: Credit	862.0	1 160.0	1 575.0	1 641.0	1 728.0	1 530.0	1 517.0	Serv. & revenu : crédit
Serv. & Income: Debit	−1 122.0	−1 460.0	−2 141.0	−2 335.0	−2 464.0	−2 576.0	−2 348.0	Serv. & revenu : débit
Current Trans.,nie: Credit	174.0	317.0	473.0	667.0	731.0	886.0	804.0	Transf. cour.,nia : crédit
Current Transfers: Debit	−17.0	−61.0	−110.0	−82.0	−152.0	−133.0	−178.0	Transf. courants : débit
Capital Acct.,nie: Credit	0.0	0.0	32.0	152.0	43.0	39.0	46.0	Compte de cap.,nia : crédit
Capital Account: Debit	0.0	0.0	0.0	0.0	0.0	0.0	−1.0	Compte de capital : débit
Financial Account,nie	640.0	535.0	812.0	1 486.0	2 458.0	2 042.0	697.0	Compte d'op. fin., nia
Net Errors and Omissions	152.1	90.8	456.4	358.6	1 094.9	194.4	794.5	Erreurs et omissions nettes
Reserves and Related Items	438.9	−170.8	479.6	582.4	−1 458.9	642.6	−239.5	Rés. et postes appareutés
Russian Federation								**Fédération de Russie**
Goods: Exports fob	...	67 826.0	82 913.0	90 564.0	89 008.0	74 883.0	75 306.0	Biens : exportations,fàb
Goods: Imports fob	...	−50 149.0	−62 188.0	−67 630.0	−71 645.0	−57 783.0	−39 460.0	Biens : importations,fàb
Serv. & Income: Credit	...	11 924.0	14 849.0	17 619.0	18 446.0	16 672.0	12 884.0	Serv. & revenu : crédit

75
Summary of balance of payments
Millions of US dollars
Résumé des balances des paiements
Millions de dollars des E.–U.

Country or area	1993	1994	1995	1996	1997	1998	1999	Pays ou zone
Serv. & Income: Debit	...	−20 448.0	−27 621.0	−28 173.0	−32 901.0	−32 324.0	−24 296.0	Serv. & revenu : débit
Current Trans.,nie: Credit	...	238.0	811.0	771.0	411.0	269.0	1 028.0	Transf. cour.,nia : crédit
Current Transfers: Debit	...	−543.0	−738.0	−701.0	−771.0	−679.0	−493.0	Transf. courants : débit
Capital Acct.,nie: Credit	...	5 882.0	3 122.0	3 066.0	2 138.0	1 705.0	887.0	Compte de cap.,nie : crédit
Capital Account: Debit	...	−3 474.0	−3 470.0	−3 529.0	−2 934.0	−2 087.0	−1 214.0	Compte de capital : débit
Financial Account,nie	...	−29 951.8	−7 225.0	−23 501.0	−215.0	−12 788.0	−18 959.0	Compte d'op. fin., nia
Net Errors and Omissions	...	−273.5	−8 750.7	−5 675.9	−8 091.6	−9 136.9	−7 571.6	Erreurs et omissions nettes
Reserves and Related Items	...	18 969.3	8 297.7	17 189.9	6 554.6	21 268.9	1 888.6	Rés. et postes appareutés
Slovakia								**Slovaquie**
Goods: Exports fob	5 452.5	6 706.1	8 590.8	8 823.8	9 640.7	10 720.2	10 201.3	Biens : exportations,fàb
Goods: Imports fob	−6 364.6	−6 645.4	−8 820.0	−11 106.5	−11 725.2	−13 070.9	−11 310.3	Biens : importations,fàb
Serv. & Income: Credit	2 123.8	2 416.8	2 628.1	2 289.1	2 482.5	2 729.4	2 167.7	Serv. & revenu : crédit
Serv. & Income: Debit	−1 889.8	−1 875.1	−2 101.5	−2 297.8	−2 532.7	−2 870.8	−2 411.8	Serv. & revenu : débit
Current Trans.,nie: Credit	216.3	165.8	242.5	482.9	540.4	645.0	466.0	Transf. cour.,nia : crédit
Current Transfers: Debit	−117.8	−97.6	−149.9	−282.0	−367.1	−279.3	−268.1	Transf. courants : débit
Capital Acct.,nie: Credit	771.5	84.0	45.6	30.3	0.0	82.8	171.0	Compte de cap.,nia : crédit
Capital Account: Debit	−207.6	0.0	0.0	0.0	0.0	−12.4	−13.4	Compte de capital : débit
Financial Account,nie	−153.3	70.8	1 211.2	2 267.9	1 780.1	1 911.5	1 788.8	Compte d'op. fin., nia
Net Errors and Omissions	183.2	379.7	144.4	162.2	280.1	−333.1	−14.3	Erreurs et omissions nettes
Reserves and Related Items	−14.1	−1 205.1	−1 791.3	−370.0	−98.9	477.6	−777.0	Rés. et postes appareutés
Slovenia								**Slovénie**
Goods: Exports fob	6 082.9	6 831.7	8 350.2	8 352.6	8 407.4	9 090.9	8 622.7	Biens : exportations,fàb
Goods: Imports fob	−6 237.1	−7 168.1	−9 303.3	−9 177.5	−9 183.8	−9 880.2	−9 867.9	Biens : importations,fàb
Serv. & Income: Credit	1 506.6	2 143.6	2 438.0	2 547.7	2 444.2	2 444.6	2 309.4	Serv. & revenu : crédit
Serv. & Income: Debit	−1 183.4	−1 330.8	−1 680.5	−1 782.1	−1 774.5	−1 924.3	−1 969.7	Serv. & revenu : débit
Current Trans.,nie: Credit	154.9	237.2	247.7	250.9	259.5	299.8	334.4	Transf. cour.,nia : crédit
Current Transfers: Debit	−132.9	−140.6	−151.5	−160.3	−141.5	−178.0	−211.2	Transf. courants : débit
Capital Acct.,nie: Credit	6.7	2.7	3.1	5.5	5.0	3.5	3.3	Compte de cap.,nia : crédit
Capital Account: Debit	−2.6	−5.8	−10.1	−7.4	−3.9	−5.0	−3.9	Compte de capital : débit
Financial Account,nie	−80.9	146.6	541.0	565.8	1 198.7	244.2	674.8	Compte d'op. fin., nia
Net Errors and Omissions	10.7	−70.0	−194.6	−5.2	77.3	62.4	26.9	Erreurs et omissions nettes
Reserves and Related Items	−124.9	−646.5	−240.0	−590.1	−1 288.4	−157.8	81.3	Rés. et postes appareutés
Spain								**Espagne**
Goods: Exports fob	62 021.4	73 924.9	93 439.2	102 735.0	106 926.0	111 986.0	111 005.0	Biens : exportations,fàb
Goods: Imports fob	−77 020.0	−88 817.2	−111 854.0	−119 017.0	−120 333.0	−132 744.0	−140 213.0	Biens : importations,fàb
Serv. & Income: Credit	42 291.4	42 546.2	53 897.8	58 482.4	57 322.2	63 928.4	65 833.1	Serv. & revenu : crédit
Serv. & Income: Debit	−34 358.7	−35 321.8	−39 326.0	−44 185.9	−44 225.9	−49 555.1	−52 418.0	Serv. & revenu : débit
Current Trans.,nie: Credit	8 820.5	9 171.3	12 055.0	11 111.8	11 738.0	12 690.5	13 462.0	Transf. cour.,nia : crédit
Current Transfers: Debit	−7 558.5	−7 892.7	−7 419.6	−8 718.4	−8 915.9	−9 441.2	−10 290.5	Transf. courants : débit
Capital Acct.,nie: Credit	3 997.5	3 571.4	7 374.1	7 713.0	7 274.6	7 159.8	8 062.5	Compte de cap.,nia : crédit
Capital Account: Debit	−1 125.3	−1 266.1	−1 370.0	−1 123.8	−837.2	−829.5	−1 019.3	Compte de capital : débit
Financial Account,nie	−433.6	4 491.0	−7 950.5	20 138.2	8 547.4	−14 155.7	−11 214.4	Compte d'op. fin., nia
Net Errors and Omissions	−1 838.1	−370.6	−5 259.8	−2 856.1	−5 740.9	−3 394.6	−6 001.3	Erreurs et omissions nettes
Reserves and Related Items	5 203.3	−36.3	6 413.9	−24 278.8	−11 755.7	14 355.5	22 793.9	Rés. et postes appareutés
Sweden								**Suède**
Goods: Exports fob	49 348.5	60 199.0	79 903.4	84 689.6	83 193.7	85 179.0	87 568.0	Biens : exportations,fàb
Goods: Imports fob	−41 800.8	−50 641.2	−63 925.6	−66 053.4	−65 194.8	−67 547.3	−71 854.2	Biens : importations,fàb
Serv. & Income: Credit	19 716.0	23 285.5	30 527.6	31 268.4	32 173.3	34 515.3	39 774.8	Serv. & revenu : crédit
Serv. & Income: Debit	−29 615.7	−30 220.3	−38 595.1	−41 396.3	−40 037.1	−44 069.9	−45 907.3	Serv. & revenu : débit
Current Trans.,nie: Credit	455.6	543.9	1 554.6	2 524.0	2 318.6	2 266.0	2 340.6	Transf. cour.,nia : crédit
Current Transfers: Debit	−2 262.9	−2 424.3	−4 524.6	−5 140.0	−5 048.1	−5 703.7	−5 939.6	Transf. courants : débit
Capital Acct.,nie: Credit	37.5	37.5	32.3	31.3	210.9	1 502.2	1 288.6	Compte de cap.,nia : crédit
Capital Account: Debit	−14.9	−14.4	−18.3	−22.4	−438.6	−634.0	−3 431.9	Compte de capital : débit
Financial Account,nie	11 518.3	6 077.9	−5 052.5	−10 046.2	−10 121.2	5 960.7	−1 412.9	Compte d'op. fin., nia
Net Errors and Omissions	−4 852.0	−4 462.2	−1 566.0	−2 240.6	−3 768.9	−8 214.5	−544.6	Erreurs et omissions nettes
Reserves and Related Items	−2 529.6	−2 381.4	1 664.1	6 385.6	6 712.1	−3 253.8	−1 881.4	Rés. et postes appareutés
Switzerland								**Suisse**
Goods: Exports fob	75 424.2	82 624.6	97 139.1	95 543.7	95 039.5	93 781.7	91 732.5	Biens : exportations,fàb
Goods: Imports fob	−73 831.7	−79 278.8	−93 879.8	−93 675.6	−92 302.0	−92 849.2	−91 009.4	Biens : importations,fàb
Serv. & Income: Credit	46 627.8	49 365.6	57 600.6	59 247.1	60 366.7	72 366.5	76 206.3	Serv. & revenu : crédit
Serv. & Income: Debit	−27 555.2	−31 701.6	−34 814.4	−36 073.3	−33 023.9	−43 125.6	−43 660.2	Serv. & revenu : débit
Current Trans.,nie: Credit	2 484.4	2 526.2	2 995.4	2 960.3	2 626.6	2 785.9	2 770.2	Transf. cour.,nia : crédit
Current Transfers: Debit	−5 224.6	−5 949.4	−7 236.6	−6 949.0	−6 027.7	−6 424.3	−6 920.4	Transf. courants : débit
Capital Acct.,nie: Credit	0.0	0.0	0.0	0.0	0.0	0.0	0.0	Compte de cap.,nia : crédit
Capital Account: Debit	−133.3	−146.2	−131.9	−123.0	−78.5	−300.7	−389.1	Compte de capital : débit
Financial Account,nie	−18 984.6	−12 055.3	−8 974.4	−24 344.5	−22 846.9	−21 319.3	−37 609.0	Compte d'op. fin., nia

75
Summary of balance of payments
Millions of US dollars
Résumé des balances des paiements
Millions de dollars des E.−U.

Country or area	1993	1994	1995	1996	1997	1998	1999	Pays ou zone
Net Errors and Omissions	1 679.0	−4 375.9	−12 668.9	5 935.7	−1 599.9	−3 735.9	6 192.1	Erreurs et omissions nettes
Reserves and Related Items	−485.9	−1 009.1	−29.1	−2 521.5	−2 153.9	−1 179.2	2 687.2	Rés. et postes appareutés
TFYR of Macedonia								**L'ex−R.y. Macédoine**
Goods: Exports fob	...	...	...	1 147.4	1 201.4	1 292.9	1 192.1	Biens : exportations,fàb
Goods: Imports fob	...	...	...	−1 464.0	−1 589.1	−1 713.2	−1 602.2	Biens : importations,fàb
Serv. & Income: Credit	...	...	...	199.6	167.3	154.8	270.9	Serv. & revenu : crédit
Serv. & Income: Debit	...	...	...	−384.3	−345.5	−372.7	−390.1	Serv. & revenu : débit
Current Trans.,nie: Credit	...	...	...	475.4	535.0	692.6	750.3	Transf. cour.,nia : crédit
Current Transfers: Debit	...	...	...	−262.3	−244.8	−366.2	−330.2	Transf. courants : débit
Capital Acct.,nie: Credit	...	...	...	0.0	0.0	11.2	4.4	Compte de cap.,nia : crédit
Capital Account: Debit	...	...	...	0.0	0.0	−1.8	0.0	Compte de capital : débit
Financial Account,nie	...	...	...	174.3	186.8	449.2	189.6	Compte d'op. fin., nia
Net Errors and Omissions	...	...	...	18.8	−29.9	−114.8	34.5	Erreurs et omissions nettes
Reserves and Related Items	...	...	...	95.1	118.6	−32.1	−119.2	Rés. et postes appareutés
Ukraine								**Ukraine**
Goods: Exports fob	...	13 894.0	14 244.0	15 547.0	15 418.0	13 699.0	13 189.0	Biens : exportations,fàb
Goods: Imports fob	...	−16 469.0	−16 946.0	−19 843.0	−19 623.0	−16 283.0	−12 945.0	Biens : importations,fàb
Serv. & Income: Credit	...	2 803.0	3 093.0	4 901.0	5 095.0	4 044.0	3 967.0	Serv. & revenu : crédit
Serv. & Income: Debit	...	−1 938.0	−2 015.0	−2 298.0	−3 070.0	−3 538.0	−3 259.0	Serv. & revenu : débit
Current Trans.,nie: Credit	...	583.0	557.0	619.0	942.0	868.0	754.0	Transf. cour.,nia : crédit
Current Transfers: Debit	...	−36.0	−85.0	−110.0	−97.0	−86.0	−48.0	Transf. courants : débit
Capital Acct.,nie: Credit	...	106.0	6.0	5.0	0.0	0.0	0.0	Compte de cap.,nia : crédit
Capital Account: Debit	...	−9.0	0.0	0.0	0.0	−3.0	−10.0	Compte de capital : débit
Financial Account,nie	...	−557.0	−726.0	317.0	1 413.0	−1 340.0	−879.0	Compte d'op. fin., nia
Net Errors and Omissions	...	423.5	248.2	259.3	−780.7	−817.9	−953.1	Erreurs et omissions nettes
Reserves and Related Items	...	1 199.5	1 623.8	602.8	702.7	3 456.9	184.1	Rés. et postes appareutés
United Kingdom [1]								**Royaume−Uni** [1]
Goods: Exports fob	183.0	207.4	242.6	261.6	281.3	271.8	268.1	Biens : exportations,fàb
Goods: Imports fob	−203.1	−224.3	−261.1	−281.8	−300.8	−305.8	−311.4	Biens : importations,fàb
Serv. & Income: Credit	179.2	194.4	231.4	242.9	270.9	282.6	280.0	Serv. & revenu : crédit
Serv. & Income: Debit	−168.3	−172.5	−207.9	−216.3	−232.3	−238.1	−247.9	Serv. & revenu : débit
Current Trans.,nie: Credit	19.9	19.6	21.1	33.4	25.1	25.5	29.6	Transf. cour.,nia : crédit
Current Transfers: Debit	−26.8	−26.7	−32.0	−40.4	−33.3	−36.1	−36.2	Transf. courants : débit
Capital Acct.,nie: Credit	1.7	1.9	1.8	2.2	2.8	2.4	2.5	Compte de cap.,nia : crédit
Capital Account: Debit	−1.2	−1.9	−1.0	−1.0	−1.5	−1.6	−1.3	Compte de capital : débit
Financial Account,nie	19.9	−7.7	1.2	2.4	−25.5	−7.8	8.4	Compte d'op. fin., nia
Net Errors and Omissions	1.1	11.2	3.1	−3.5	9.4	6.9	7.1	Erreurs et omissions nettes
Reserves and Related Items	−5.4	−1.5	0.9	0.7	3.9	0.3	1.0	Rés. et postes appareutés
			Oceania · Océanie					
Australia								**Australie**
Goods: Exports fob	42 636.6	47 370.6	53 219.6	60 396.9	64 892.7	55 848.4	56 047.5	Biens : exportations,fàb
Goods: Imports fob	−42 665.6	−50 648.0	−57 442.8	−61 031.7	−63 043.6	−61 215.2	−65 827.9	Biens : importations,fàb
Serv. & Income: Credit	16 120.6	18 647.6	21 413.4	24 558.0	25 650.3	22 532.7	24 203.8	Serv. & revenu : crédit
Serv. & Income: Debit	−25 674.8	−32 277.9	−36 556.8	−39 865.4	−39 899.4	−35 109.1	−37 248.9	Serv. & revenu : débit
Current Trans.,nie: Credit	2 101.1	2 205.7	2 364.2	2 683.1	2 741.6	2 676.0	3 053.6	Transf. cour.,nia : crédit
Current Transfers: Debit	−2 332.7	−2 588.8	−2 637.5	−2 623.3	−2 972.2	−2 990.6	−3 089.0	Transf. courants : débit
Capital Acct.,nie: Credit	779.5	908.1	1 250.0	1 677.2	1 606.1	1 315.3	1 567.7	Compte de cap.,nia : crédit
Capital Account: Debit	−519.4	−585.5	−691.7	−709.8	−703.3	−645.6	−707.7	Compte de capital : débit
Financial Account,nie	8 733.9	14 618.5	18 821.3	18 669.5	15 607.7	15 785.8	29 413.9	Compte d'op. fin., nia
Net Errors and Omissions	779.2	1 390.1	656.3	−1 283.0	−1 006.6	−237.6	−707.6	Erreurs et omissions nettes
Reserves and Related Items	41.6	959.8	−395.9	−2 471.5	−2 873.3	2 040.0	−6 705.5	Rés. et postes appareutés
Fiji								**Fidji**
Goods: Exports fob	370.9	490.2	519.6	672.2	535.6	428.9	537.7	Biens : exportations,fàb
Goods: Imports fob	−652.8	−719.7	−761.4	−839.9	−818.9	−614.6	−653.3	Biens : importations,fàb
Serv. & Income: Credit	533.3	583.8	619.5	676.2	729.7	557.8	572.4	Serv. & revenu : crédit
Serv. & Income: Debit	−401.5	−471.7	−493.3	−504.5	−504.8	−462.6	−472.6	Serv. & revenu : débit
Current Trans.,nie: Credit	40.2	38.1	36.0	44.1	54.6	45.3	42.7	Transf. cour.,nia : crédit
Current Transfers: Debit	−28.2	−33.5	−33.1	−34.6	−30.3	−14.7	−14.2	Transf. courants : débit
Capital Acct.,nie: Credit	83.7	76.0	120.1	114.5	88.9	100.6	59.3	Compte de cap.,nia : crédit
Capital Account: Debit	−26.7	−32.6	−33.1	−43.8	−40.5	−40.0	−45.3	Compte de capital : débit
Financial Account,nie	45.1	61.0	88.3	3.6	−15.1	28.7	−104.0	Compte d'op. fin., nia
Net Errors and Omissions	22.4	30.9	30.4	−9.7	−24.3	−24.6	32.5	Erreurs et omissions nettes
Reserves and Related Items	13.6	−22.5	−93.0	−78.1	25.1	−4.9	44.9	Rés. et postes appareutés
Kiribati								**Kiribati**
Goods: Exports fob	4.3	6.1	...	...	...	...	...	Biens : exportations,fàb
Goods: Imports fob	−29.3	−27.3	...	...	...	...	...	Biens : importations,fàb

75
Summary of balance of payments
Millions of US dollars
Résumé des balances des paiements
Millions de dollars des E.‑U.

Country or area	1993	1994	1995	1996	1997	1998	1999	Pays ou zone
Serv. & Income: Credit	30.9	34.6	...	...	...	...	...	Serv. & revenu : crédit
Serv. & Income: Debit	−20.9	−19.4	...	...	...	...	...	Serv. & revenu : débit
Current Trans.,nie: Credit	12.9	9.0	...	...	...	...	...	Transf. cour.,nia : crédit
Current Transfers: Debit	−2.0	−1.6	...	...	...	...	...	Transf. courants : débit
Capital Acct.,nie: Credit	5.7	2.5	...	...	...	...	...	Compte de cap.,nia : crédit
Capital Account: Debit	0.0	0.0	...	...	...	...	...	Compte de capital : débit
Financial Account,nie	−7.5	−4.8	...	...	...	...	...	Compte d'op. fin., nia
Net Errors and Omissions	0.8	−5.1	...	...	...	...	...	Erreurs et omissions nettes
Reserves and Related Items	5.1	6.0	...	...	...	...	...	Rés. et postes appareutés
New Zealand								**Nouvelle−Zélande**
Goods: Exports fob	10 467.5	12 176.2	13 478.0	14 342.1	14 241.9	12 271.5	12 618.2	Biens : exportations,fàb
Goods: Imports fob	−8 748.5	−10 768.5	−12 583.5	−13 814.5	−13 380.3	−11 334.1	−13 027.5	Biens : importations,fàb
Serv. & Income: Credit	3 248.4	4 025.0	5 398.5	4 989.9	4 704.4	4 205.6	4 380.1	Serv. & revenu : crédit
Serv. & Income: Debit	−5 844.8	−8 145.8	−9 594.1	−9 995.4	−10 197.0	−8 070.0	−8 553.5	Serv. & revenu : débit
Current Trans.,nie: Credit	309.9	637.8	557.6	900.2	709.8	691.7	616.2	Transf. cour.,nia : crédit
Current Transfers: Debit	−178.0	−309.1	−325.6	−357.7	−386.6	−353.7	−374.7	Transf. courants : débit
Capital Acct.,nie: Credit	833.0	995.4	1 651.6	1 837.5	777.4	516.7	434.7	Compte de cap.,nia : crédit
Capital Account: Debit	−290.8	−378.5	−427.2	−502.4	−541.1	−443.7	−476.8	Compte de capital : débit
Financial Account,nie	2 824.6	2 219.6	4 664.4	3 569.9	4 046.1	824.8	0.0	Compte d'op. fin., nia
Net Errors and Omissions	−2 694.7	280.6	−2 435.8	802.5	−1 417.0	1 207.1	0.0	Erreurs et omissions nettes
Reserves and Related Items	73.6	−732.7	−384.0	−1 772.2	1 442.3	484.2	−167.4	Rés. et postes appareutés
Papua New Guinea								**Papouasie−Nvl−Guinée**
Goods: Exports fob	2 604.4	2 651.0	2 670.4	2 529.8	2 160.1	1 773.3	1 927.4	Biens : exportations,fàb
Goods: Imports fob	−1 134.7	−1 324.9	−1 262.4	−1 513.3	−1 483.3	−1 078.3	−1 071.4	Biens : importations,fàb
Serv. & Income: Credit	338.0	257.9	343.9	464.3	432.1	339.0	266.4	Serv. & revenu : crédit
Serv. & Income: Debit	−1 204.8	−1 031.5	−1 152.8	−1 239.7	−1 268.4	−1 073.6	−1 019.2	Serv. & revenu : débit
Current Trans.,nie: Credit	49.0	58.8	66.7	252.1	69.9	82.4	60.3	Transf. cour.,nia : crédit
Current Transfers: Debit	−178.0	−209.3	−173.9	−304.2	−102.6	−71.6	−68.7	Transf. courants : débit
Capital Acct.,nie: Credit	20.4	19.9	15.7	15.2	13.9	9.7	7.8	Compte de cap.,nia : crédit
Capital Account: Debit	−20.4	−19.9	−15.7	−15.2	−13.9	−9.7	−7.8	Compte de capital : débit
Financial Account,nie	−716.2	−609.2	−444.7	46.6	8.0	−179.7	16.0	Compte d'op. fin., nia
Net Errors and Omissions	−11.3	37.1	−86.6	−33.1	7.3	−12.5	14.3	Erreurs et omissions nettes
Reserves and Related Items	253.4	170.1	39.5	−202.5	177.0	221.0	−125.0	Rés. et postes appareutés
Samoa								**Samoa**
Goods: Exports fob	6.4	3.5	8.8	10.1	14.6	20.4	...	Biens : exportations,fàb
Goods: Imports fob	−87.4	−68.8	−80.3	−90.8	−100.1	−96.9	...	Biens : importations,fàb
Serv. & Income: Credit	40.1	47.0	60.4	70.6	70.8	68.5	...	Serv. & revenu : crédit
Serv. & Income: Debit	−42.7	−32.6	−39.6	−36.8	−44.2	−31.5	...	Serv. & revenu : débit
Current Trans.,nie: Credit	49.9	62.7	66.7	66.9	73.7	64.1	...	Transf. cour.,nia : crédit
Current Transfers: Debit	−5.1	−6.1	−6.6	−7.8	−5.6	−4.6	...	Transf. courants : débit
Capital Acct.,nie: Credit	0.0	0.0	0.0	0.0	0.0	0.0	...	Compte de cap.,nia : crédit
Capital Account: Debit	0.0	0.0	0.0	0.0	0.0	0.0	...	Compte de capital : débit
Financial Account,nie	15.6	−5.5	−5.6	−3.6	−5.9	−5.0	...	Compte d'op. fin., nia
Net Errors and Omissions	13.8	−4.2	−1.7	−1.3	7.9	−9.6	...	Erreurs et omissions nettes
Reserves and Related Items	9.3	3.9	−2.0	−7.4	−11.1	−5.5	...	Rés. et postes appareutés
Solomon Islands								**Iles Salomon**
Goods: Exports fob	129.1	142.2	168.3	161.5	156.4	141.8	164.6	Biens : exportations,fàb
Goods: Imports fob	−136.9	−142.2	−154.5	−150.5	−184.5	−159.9	−110.0	Biens : importations,fàb
Serv. & Income: Credit	43.1	51.5	43.0	55.5	73.0	57.2	61.8	Serv. & revenu : crédit
Serv. & Income: Debit	−85.3	−110.4	−84.9	−94.9	−118.4	−64.5	−109.9	Serv. & revenu : débit
Current Trans.,nie: Credit	47.8	66.6	53.2	57.5	52.6	56.4	41.5	Transf. cour.,nia : crédit
Current Transfers: Debit	−5.5	−11.1	−16.7	−14.5	−17.1	−22.9	−26.5	Transf. courants : débit
Capital Acct.,nie: Credit	0.9	2.9	1.5	0.5	0.3	6.9	9.2	Compte de cap.,nia : crédit
Capital Account: Debit	−0.1	−0.2	−0.9	−2.7	−1.3	−0.3	0.0	Compte de capital : débit
Financial Account,nie	8.2	1.5	−8.3	−1.4	45.7	16.9	−33.8	Compte d'op. fin., nia
Net Errors and Omissions	−3.2	−2.8	−1.4	7.0	2.3	−14.4	−1.6	Erreurs et omissions nettes
Reserves and Related Items	1.7	2.0	0.8	−18.0	−9.1	−17.2	4.7	Rés. et postes appareutés
Tonga								**Tonga**
Goods: Exports fob	16.1	...	...	...	...	...	...	Biens : exportations,fàb
Goods: Imports fob	−56.6	...	...	...	...	...	...	Biens : importations,fàb
Serv. & Income: Credit	21.5	...	...	...	...	...	...	Serv. & revenu : crédit
Serv. & Income: Debit	−23.5	...	...	...	...	...	...	Serv. & revenu : débit
Current Trans.,nie: Credit	49.7	...	...	...	...	...	...	Transf. cour.,nia : crédit
Current Transfers: Debit	−13.1	...	...	...	...	...	...	Transf. courants : débit
Capital Acct.,nie: Credit	1.3	...	...	...	...	...	...	Compte de cap.,nia : crédit
Capital Account: Debit	−0.7	...	...	...	...	...	...	Compte de capital : débit

75
Summary of balance of payments
Millions of US dollars
Résumé des balances des paiements
Millions de dollars des E.-U.

Country or area	1993	1994	1995	1996	1997	1998	1999	Pays ou zone
Financial Account,nie	3.2	...	...	...	...	...	...	Compte d'op. fin., nia
Net Errors and Omissions	−0.3	...	...	...	...	...	...	Erreurs et omissions nettes
Reserves and Related Items	2.4	...	...	...	...	...	...	Rés. et postes appareutés
Vanuatu								**Vanuatu**
Goods: Exports fob	17.4	25.1	28.3	30.2	35.3	33.8	24.9	Biens : exportations,fàb
Goods: Imports fob	−64.7	−74.7	−79.4	−81.1	−79.0	−76.2	−76.4	Biens : importations,fàb
Serv. & Income: Credit	83.8	88.1	94.7	108.6	103.2	134.9	135.8	Serv. & revenu : crédit
Serv. & Income: Debit	−73.4	−80.8	−85.1	−84.0	−81.6	−76.8	−88.6	Serv. & revenu : débit
Current Trans.,nie: Credit	22.5	23.2	23.8	22.4	21.8	30.3	38.4	Transf. cour.,nia : crédit
Current Transfers: Debit	−0.6	−0.7	−0.6	−22.9	−19.0	−31.2	−37.2	Transf. courants : débit
Capital Acct.,nie: Credit	32.0	41.4	38.3	43.4	23.8	25.2	23.9	Compte de cap.,nia : crédit
Capital Account: Debit	−5.7	−4.2	−6.7	−38.5	−29.2	−35.1	−57.2	Compte de capital : débit
Financial Account,nie	14.5	−13.4	25.3	20.9	−16.7	−3.1	43.9	Compte d'op. fin., nia
Net Errors and Omissions	−22.4	−10.2	−33.4	−4.1	39.4	6.3	−11.0	Erreurs et omissions nettes
Reserves and Related Items	−3.4	6.1	−5.3	5.3	2.2	−8.1	3.5	Rés. et postes appareutés

Source:
International Monetary Fund (IMF), Washington, D.C., "International
Financial Statistics," November 2000, and the IMF database.

† For information on recent changes in country or area
nomenclature pertaining to former Czechoslovakia, Germany,
Hong Kong Special Administrative Region (SAR) of China,
Macao Special Administrative Region (SAR) of China,
SFR of Yugoslavia and the former USSR, see Annex I – Country
or area nomenclature, regional and other groupings.

††For statistical purposes, the data for China do not
include those for the Hong Kong Special Administrative
Region (Hong Kong SAR), Macao Special Administrative
Region (Hong Kong SAR) and Taiwan province of China.

1 Billions of US Dollars.
2 BLEU trade data refer to the Belgium–Luxembourg Economic Union
and exclude transactions between the two countries. Beginning in 1997,
trade data are for Belgium only, which includes trade between Belgium
and Luxemboug.

Source:
Fonds Monétaire International (FMI), Washington, D.C., "Statistiques
Financières Internationales," novembre 2000 et la base de données
du FMI.

† Pour les modifications récentes de nomenclature de pays
ou de zone concernant l'Allemagne, Hong Kong région
administrative spéciale (RAS) de Chine, Macao région administrative
spéciale (RAS) de Chine, l'ex–Tchécoslovaquie, l'ex–URSS et l'ex–
Rfs de Yougoslavie, voir annex I – Nomenclature des pays ou des
zones, groupements régionaux et autres groupments.

††Les données statistiques relatives à la Chine ne comprennent
pas celles qui concernent la région administrative spéciale de
Hong Kong (la RAS de Hong Kong), la région administrative
spéciale de Macao (la RAS de Macao) et la province chinoise
de Taiwan.

1 Milliards de dollars des E–U.
2 Les données sur le commerce extérieur se rapportent à l'Union
économique belgo–luxembourgeoise (UEBL) et ne couvrent pas les
transactions entre les deux pays. A compter de 1997, les données
sur le commerce extérieur ne se rapportent qu'à la Belgique, et
recouvrent les échanges entre la Belgique et le Luxembourg.

Technical notes, table 75

A balance of payments can be broadly described as the record of an economy's international economic transactions. It shows (a) transactions in goods, services and income between an economy and the rest of the world, (b) changes of ownership and other changes in that economy's monetary gold, special drawing rights (SDRs) and claims on and liabilities to the rest of the world, and (c) unrequited transfers and counterpart entries needed to balance in the accounting sense any entries for the foregoing transactions and changes which are not mutually offsetting.

The balance of payments are presented on the basis of the methodology and presentation of the fifth edition of the *Balance of Payments Manual* (BPM5)[38], published by the International Monetary Fund in September 1993. The BPM5 incorporates several major changes to take account of developments in international trade and finance over the past decade, and to better harmonize the Fund's balance of payments methodology with the methodology of the 1993 *System of National Accounts* (SNA) [56]. The Fund's balance of payments has been converted for all periods from the BPM4 basis to the BPM5 basis; thus the time series conform to the BPM5 methodology with no methodological breaks.

The detailed definitions concerning the content of the basic categories of the balance of payments are given in the *Balance of Payments Manual (fifth edition)* [38]. Brief explanatory notes are given below to clarify the scope of the major items.

Goods: Exports f.o.b. and *Goods: Imports f.o.b.* are both measured on the "free-on-board" (f.o.b.) basis—that is, by the value of the goods at the border of the exporting country; in the case of imports, this excludes the cost of freight and insurance incurred beyond the border of the exporting country.

Services and income covers transactions in real resources between residents and non-residents other than those classified as merchandise, including (a) shipment and other transportation services, including freight, insurance and other distributive services in connection with the movement of commodities, (b) travel, i.e. goods and services acquired by non-resident travellers in a given country and similar acquisitions by resident travellers abroad, and (c) investment income which covers income of non-residents from their financial assets invested in the compiling economy (debit) and similar income of residents from their financial assets invested abroad (credit).

Current Transfers, n.i.e.: *Credit* comprises all current transfers received by the reporting country, except those made to the country to finance its "overall bal-

Notes techniques, tableau 75

La balance des paiements peut se définir d'une façon générale comme le relevé des transactions économiques internationales d'une économie. Elle indique (a) les transactions sur biens, services et revenus entre une économie et le reste du monde, (b) les transferts de propriété et autres variations intervenues dans les avoirs en or monétaire de cette économie, dans ses avoirs en droits de tirages spéciaux (DTS) ainsi que dans ses créances financières sur le reste du monde ou dans ses engagements financiers envers lui et (c) les "inscriptions de transferts sans contrepartie" et de "contrepartie" destinées à équilibrer, d'un point de vue comptable, les transactions et changements précités qui ne se compensent pas réciproquement.

Les données de balance des paiements sont présentées conformément à la méthodologie et à la classification recommandées dans la cinquième édition du *Manuel de la balance des paiements* [38], publiée en septembre 1993 par le Fonds monétaire international. La cinquième édition fait état de plusieurs changements importants qui ont été opérés de manière à rendre compte de l'évolution des finances et des changes internationaux pendant la décennie écoulée et à harmoniser davantage la méthodologie de la balance des paiements du FMI avec celle du *Système de comptabilité nationale* (SCN) [56] de 1993. Les statistiques incluses dans la balance des paiements du FMI ont été converties et sont désormais établies, pour toutes les périodes, sur la base de la cinquième et non plus de la quatrième édition; en conséquence, les séries chronologiques sont conformes aux principes de la cinquième édition, sans rupture due à des différences d'ordre méthodologique.

Les définitions détaillées relatives au contenu des postes fondamentaux de la balance des paiements figurent dans le *Manuel de la balance des paiements (cinquième édition)* [38]. De brèves notes explicatives sont présentées ci-après pour clarifier la portée de ces principales rubriques.

Les Biens: exportations, f.à.b. et *Biens: importations, f.à.b.* sont évalués sur la base f.à.b. (franco à bord)—c'est-à-dire à la frontière du pays exportateur; dans le cas des importations, cette valeur exclut le coût du fret et de l'assurance au-delà de la frontière du pays exportateur.

Services et revenus: transactions en ressources effectuées entre résidents et non résidents, autres que celles qui sont considérées comme des marchandises, notamment: (a) expéditions et autres services de transport, y compris le fret, l'assurance et les autres services de distribution liés aux mouvements de marchandises; (b) voyages, à savoir les biens et services acquis par des

ance", hence, the label "n.i.e." (not included elsewhere). (Note: some of the capital and financial accounts labeled "n.i.e." denote that *Exceptional Financing items* and *Liabilities Constituting Foreign Authorities' Reserves* (LCFARs) have been excluded.)

Capital Account, n.i.e.: *Credit* refers mainly to capital transfers linked to the acquisition of a fixed asset other than transactions relating to debt forgiveness plus the disposal of nonproduced, nonfinancial assets. *Capital Account*: *Debit* refers mainly to capital transfers linked to the disposal of fixed assets by the donor or to the financing of capital formation by the recipient, plus the acquisition of nonproduced, nonfinancial assets.

Financial Account, n.i.e. is the net sum of the balance of direct investment, portfolio investment, and other investment transactions.

Net Errors and Omissions is a residual category needed to ensure that all debit and credit entries in the balance of payments statement sum to zero and reflects statistical inconsistencies in the recording of the credit and debit entries.

Reserves and Related Items is the sum of transactions in reserve assets, LCFARs, exceptional financing, and use of Fund credit and loans.

For further information see *International Financial Statistics* [14].

voyageurs non résidents dans un pays donné et achats similaires faits par des résidents voyageant à l'étranger; et (c) revenus des investissements, qui correspondent aux revenus que les non résidents tirent de leurs avoirs financiers placés dans l'économie déclarante (débit) et les revenus similaires que les résidents tirent de leurs avoirs financiers placés à l'étranger (crédit).

Les transferts courants, n.i.a: *Crédit* englobent tous les transferts courants reçus par l'économie qui établit sa balance des paiements, à l'exception de ceux qui sont destinés à financer sa "balance globale"—c'est ce qui explique la mention "n.i.a." (non inclus ailleurs). (Note: comptes de capital et d'opérations financières portent la mention "n.i.a.", ce qui signifie que les postes de *Financement exceptionnel* et les *Engagements constituant des réserves pour les autorités étrangères* ont été exclus de ces composantes du compte de capital et d'opérations financières.

Le Compte de capital, n.i.a.: *crédit* retrace principalement les transferts de capital liés à l'acquisition d'un actif fixe autres que les transactions ayant trait à des remises de dettes plus les cessions d'actifs non financiers non produits. Le *Compte de capital*: *débit* retrace principalement les transferts de capital liés à la cession d'actifs fixes par le donateur ou au financement de la formation de capital par le bénéficiaire, plus les acquisitions d'actifs non financiers non produits.

Le solde du *Compte d'op. Fin., n.i.a.* (compte d'opérations financières, n.i.a.) est la somme des soldes des investissements directs, des investissements de portefeuille et des autres investissements.

Le poste des *Erreurs et omissions* nettes est une catégorie résiduelle qui est nécessaire pour assurer que la somme de toutes les inscriptions effectuées au débit et au crédit est égal à zéro et qui laisse apparaître les écarts entre les montants portés au débit et ceux qui sont inscrits au crédit.

Le montant de *Réserves et postes apparentés* est égal à la somme de transactions afférentes aux avoirs de réserve, aux engagements constituant des réserves pour les autorités étrangères, au financement exceptionnel et à l'utilisation des crédits et des prêts du FMI.

Pour plus de renseignements, voir *Statistiques financières internationales* [14].

76
Exchange rates
Cours des changes
National currency per US dollar
Valeur du dollar des Etats-Unis en monnaie nationale

Country (monetary unit) Pays (unité monétaire)	1990	1991	1992	1993	1994	1995	1996	1997	1998	1999
Afghanistan: afghani Afghanistan : afghani										
End of period[1] Fin de période[1]	50.600	50.600	50.600	50.600	500.000	1 000.000	3 000.000	3 000.000	3 000.000	3 000.000
Period average[1] Moyenne sur période[1]	50.600	50.600	50.600	50.600	425.100	833.333	2 333.330	3 000.000	3 000.000	3 000.000
Albania: lek Albanie : lek										
End of period Fin de période	...	...	102.900	98.700	95.590	94.240	103.070	149.140	140.580	135.120
Period average Moyenne sur période	...	...	75.033	102.062	94.623	92.698	104.499	148.933	150.633	137.691
Algeria: Algerian dinar Algérie : dinar algérien										
End of period Fin de période	12.191	21.392	22.781	24.123	42.893	52.175	56.186	58.414	60.353	69.314
Period average Moyenne sur période	8.958	18.473	21.836	23.345	35.059	47.663	54.749	57.707	58.739	66.574
Angola: readjusted kwanza Angola : réajusté kwanza										
End of period Fin de période	0.000	0.000	0.000	0.000	0.001	0.006	0.202	0.262	0.697	5.580
Period average Moyenne sur période	0.000	0.000	0.000	0.000	0.000	0.003	0.128	0.229	0.393	2.791
Antigua and Barbuda: EC dollar Antigua-et-Barbuda : dollar des Caraïbes orientales										
End of period Fin de période	2.700	2.700	2.700	2.700	2.700	2.700	2.700	2.700	2.700	2.700
Argentina: Argentine peso Argentine : peso argentin										
End of period[2] Fin de période[2]	0.559	0.999	0.991	0.999	1.000	1.000	1.000	1.000	1.000	1.000
Period average[2] Moyenne sur période[2]	0.488	0.954	0.991	0.999	0.999	1.000	1.000	1.000	1.000	1.000
Armenia: dram Arménie : dram										
End of period Fin de période	...	...	2.070	75.000	405.510	402.000	435.070	494.980	522.030	523.770
Period average Moyenne sur période	...	...	...	9.105	288.651	405.908	414.041	490.847	504.915	535.062
Aruba: Aruban florin Aruba : florin de Aruba										
End of period Fin de période	1.790	1.790	1.790	1.790	1.790	1.790	1.790	1.790	1.790	1.790
Australia: Australian dollar Australie : dollar australien										
End of period Fin de période	1.293	1.316	1.452	1.477	1.287	1.342	1.255	1.532	1.629	1.530
Period average Moyenne sur période	1.281	1.284	1.362	1.471	1.368	1.349	1.278	1.347	1.592	1.550
Austria: Austrian schilling Autriche : schilling autrichien										
End of period[3] Fin de période[3]	10.677	10.689	11.354	12.143	10.969	10.088	10.954	12.633	11.747	0.995
Period average[3] Moyenne sur période[3]	11.370	11.676	10.989	11.632	11.422	10.082	10.587	12.204	12.379	0.939
Azerbaijan: manat Azerbaïdjan : manat										
End of period Fin de période	...	...	48.600	118.000	4 182.000	4 440.000	4 098.000	3 888.000	3 890.000	4 378.000
Period average Moyenne sur période	...	...	54.200	99.975	1 570.220	4 413.540	4 301.260	3 985.370	3 869.000	4 120.170
Bahamas: Bahamian dollar Bahamas : dollar des Bahamas										
End of period[1] Fin de période[1]	1.000	1.000	1.000	1.000	1.000	1.000	1.000	1.000	1.000	1.000

76
Exchange rates
National currency per US dollar [cont.]
Cours des changes
Valeur du dollar des Etats-Unis en monnaie nationale [suite]

Country (monetary unit) Pays (unité monétaire)	1990	1991	1992	1993	1994	1995	1996	1997	1998	1999
Bahrain: Bahrain dinar Bahreïn : dinar de Bahreïn										
End of period										
Fin de période	0.376	0.376	0.376	0.376	0.376	0.376	0.376	0.376	0.376	0.376
Bangladesh: taka Bangladesh : taka										
End of period[1]										
Fin de période[1]	35.790	38.580	39.000	39.850	40.250	40.750	42.450	45.450	48.500	51.000
Period average[1]										
Moyenne sur période[1]	34.569	36.596	38.951	39.567	40.212	40.278	41.794	43.892	46.906	49.085
Barbados: Barbados dollar Barbade : dollar de la Barbade										
End of period										
Fin de période	2.000	2.000	2.000	2.000	2.000	2.000	2.000	2.000	2.000	2.000
Belarus: Belarussian rouble Bélarus : rouble bélarussien										
Period average										
Moyenne sur période	...	...	...	...	...	...	...	25.964	...	...
Belgium: Belgian franc Belgique : franc belge										
End of period[3]										
Fin de période[3]	30.983	31.270	33.180	36.110	31.838	29.415	32.005	36.920	34.575	0.995
Period average[3]										
Moyenne sur période[3]	33.418	34.148	32.150	34.597	33.457	29.480	30.962	35.774	36.299	0.939
Belize: Belize dollar Belize : dollar du Belize										
End of period										
Fin de période	2.000	2.000	2.000	2.000	2.000	2.000	2.000	2.000	2.000	2.000
Benin: CFA franc Bénin : franc CFA										
End of period[4]										
Fin de période[4]	256.450	259.000	275.325	294.775	534.600	490.000	523.700	598.810	562.210	652.953
Period average[4]										
Moyenne sur période[4]	272.265	282.107	264.692	283.163	555.205	499.148	511.552	583.669	589.952	615.699
Bhutan: ngultrum Bhoutan : ngultrum										
End of period										
Fin de période	18.073	25.834	26.200	31.380	31.380	35.180	35.930	39.280	42.480	43.490
Period average										
Moyenne sur période	17.505	22.742	25.918	30.493	31.374	32.427	35.433	36.313	41.259	43.055
Bolivia: boliviano Bolivie : boliviano										
End of period[5]										
Fin de période[5]	3.400	3.745	4.095	4.475	4.695	4.935	5.185	5.365	5.645	5.990
Period average[5]										
Moyenne sur période[5]	3.173	3.581	3.901	4.265	4.621	4.800	5.075	5.254	5.510	5.812
Botswana: pula Botswana : pula										
End of period										
Fin de période	1.871	2.073	2.257	2.565	2.717	2.822	3.644	3.810	4.458	4.632
Period average										
Moyenne sur période	1.860	2.022	2.110	2.423	2.685	2.772	3.324	3.651	4.226	4.624
Brazil: real Brésil : real										
End of period[1 6]										
Fin de période[1 6]	64.390	388.650	4 504.550	0.119	0.846	0.973	1.039	1.116	1.209	1.789
Period average[1 6]										
Moyenne sur période[1 6]	24.840	147.860	1 641.090	0.032	0.639	0.918	1.005	1.078	1.161	1.815
Brunei Darussalam: Brunei dollar Brunéi Darussalam : dollar du Brunéi										
End of period										
Fin de période	1.745	1.631	1.645	1.608	1.461	1.414	1.400	1.676	1.661	1.666
Period average										
Moyenne sur période	1.813	1.728	1.629	1.616	1.527	1.417	1.410	1.485	1.674	1.695

76
Exchange rates
National currency per US dollar [*cont.*]
Cours des changes
Valeur du dollar des Etats-Unis en monnaie nationale [*suite*]

Country (monetary unit) Pays (unité monétaire)	1990	1991	1992	1993	1994	1995	1996	1997	1998	1999
Bulgaria: lev Bulgarie : lev										
End of period										
Fin de période	0.003	0.022	0.024	0.033	0.066	0.071	0.487	1.777	1.675	1.947
Period average										
Moyenne sur période	0.002	0.018	0.023	0.028	0.054	0.067	0.178	1.682	1.760	1.836
Burkina Faso: CFA franc Burkina Faso : franc CFA										
End of period[4]										
Fin de période[4]	256.450	259.000	275.325	294.775	534.600	490.000	523.700	598.810	562.210	652.953
Period average[4]										
Moyenne sur période[4]	272.265	282.107	264.692	283.163	555.205	499.148	511.552	583.669	589.952	615.699
Burundi: Burundi franc Burundi : franc burundais										
End of period										
Fin de période	165.350	191.100	236.550	264.380	246.940	277.920	322.350	408.380	505.160	628.580
Period average										
Moyenne sur période	171.255	181.513	208.303	242.780	252.662	249.757	302.747	352.351	447.766	563.562
Cambodia: riel Cambodge : riel										
End of period										
Fin de période	600.000	520.000	2 000.000	2 305.000	2 575.000	2 526.000	2 713.000	3 452.000	3 770.000	3 770.000
Period average										
Moyenne sur période	...	...	1 266.580	2 689.000	2 545.250	2 450.830	2 624.080	2 946.250	3 744.420	3 807.830
Cameroon: CFA franc Cameroun : franc CFA										
End of period[4]										
Fin de période[4]	256.450	259.000	275.325	294.775	534.600	490.000	523.700	598.810	562.210	652.953
Period average[4]										
Moyenne sur période[4]	272.265	282.107	264.692	283.163	555.205	499.148	511.552	583.669	589.952	615.699
Canada: Canadian dollar Canada : dollar canadien										
End of period										
Fin de période	1.160	1.156	1.271	1.324	1.403	1.365	1.370	1.429	1.531	1.443
Period average										
Moyenne sur période	1.167	1.146	1.209	1.290	1.366	1.372	1.363	1.385	1.483	1.486
Cape Verde: Cape Verde escudo Cap-Vert : escudo du Cap-Vert										
End of period										
Fin de période	66.085	66.470	73.089	85.992	81.140	77.455	85.165	96.235	94.255	107.575
Period average										
Moyenne sur période	70.031	71.408	68.018	80.427	81.891	76.853	82.592	93.177	98.158	102.700
Central African Rep.: CFA franc Rép. centrafricaine : franc CFA										
End of period[4]										
Fin de période[4]	256.450	259.000	275.325	294.775	534.600	490.000	523.700	598.810	562.210	652.953
Period average[4]										
Moyenne sur période[4]	272.265	282.107	264.692	283.163	555.205	499.148	511.552	583.669	589.952	615.699
Chad: CFA franc Tchad : franc CFA										
End of period[4]										
Fin de période[4]	256.450	259.000	275.325	294.775	534.600	490.000	523.700	598.810	562.210	652.953
Period average[4]										
Moyenne sur période[4]	272.265	282.107	264.692	283.163	555.205	499.148	511.552	583.669	589.952	615.699
Chile: Chilean peso Chili : peso chilien										
End of period[1]										
Fin de période[1]	336.860	374.870	382.330	431.040	404.090	407.130	424.970	439.810	473.770	530.070
Period average[1]										
Moyenne sur période[1]	304.903	349.216	362.576	404.166	420.177	396.773	412.267	419.295	460.287	508.777
China ††: yuan Chine †† : yuan										
End of period[1]										
Fin de période[1]	5.222	5.434	5.752	5.800	8.446	8.317	8.298	8.280	8.279	8.280
Period average[1]										
Moyenne sur période[1]	4.783	5.323	5.515	5.762	8.619	8.351	8.314	8.290	8.279	8.278

76
Exchange rates
National currency per US dollar [cont.]
      Cours des changes
      Valeur du dollar des Etats-Unis en monnaie nationale [suite]

Country (monetary unit) Pays (unité monétaire)	1990	1991	1992	1993	1994	1995	1996	1997	1998	1999
China, Hong Kong SAR†: Hong Kong dollar Chine, Hong Kong RAS† : dollar de Hong Kong										
End of period Fin de période	7.801	7.781	7.743	7.726	7.738	7.732	7.736	7.746	7.746	7.771
Period average Moyenne sur période	7.790	7.771	7.741	7.736	7.728	7.736	7.734	7.742	7.745	7.758
Colombia: Colombian peso Colombie : peso colombien										
End of period Fin de période	568.730	706.860	811.770	917.330	831.270	987.650	1 005.330	1 293.580	1 507.520	1 873.770
Period average Moyenne sur période	502.259	633.045	759.282	863.065	844.836	912.826	1 036.690	1 140.960	1 426.040	1 756.230
Comoros: Comorian franc Comores : franc comorien										
End of period[7] Fin de période[7]	256.448	258.997	275.322	294.772	400.948	367.498	392.773	449.105	421.655	489.715
Period average[7] Moyenne sur période[7]	272.262	282.105	264.690	283.160	416.399	374.357	383.660	437.747	442.459	461.775
Congo: CFA franc Congo : franc CFA										
End of period[4] Fin de période[4]	256.450	259.000	275.325	294.775	534.600	490.000	523.700	598.810	562.210	652.953
Period average[4] Moyenne sur période[4]	272.265	282.107	264.692	283.163	555.205	499.148	511.552	583.669	589.952	615.699
Costa Rica: Costa Rican colón Costa Rica : colón costa-ricien										
End of period Fin de période	103.550	135.425	137.430	151.440	165.070	194.900	220.110	244.290	271.420	298.190
Period average Moyenne sur période	91.579	122.432	134.506	142.172	157.067	179.729	207.689	232.597	257.229	285.685
Côte d'Ivoire: CFA franc Côte d'Ivoire : franc CFA										
End of period[4] Fin de période[4]	256.450	259.000	275.325	294.775	534.600	490.000	523.700	598.810	562.210	652.953
Period average[4] Moyenne sur période[4]	272.265	282.107	264.692	283.163	555.205	499.148	511.552	583.669	589.952	615.699
Croatia: kuna Croatie : kuna										
End of period Fin de période	...	...	0.798	6.562	5.629	5.316	5.540	6.303	6.248	7.648
Period average Moyenne sur période	...	...	...	3.577	5.996	5.230	5.434	6.101	6.362	7.112
Cyprus: Cyprus pound Chypre : livre chypriote										
End of period Fin de période	0.435	0.439	0.483	0.520	0.476	0.457	0.470	0.526	0.498	0.575
Period average Moyenne sur période	0.458	0.464	0.450	0.497	0.492	0.452	0.466	0.514	0.518	0.543
Czech Republic: Czech koruna République tchèque : couronne tchèque										
End of period Fin de période	...	...	...	29.955	28.049	26.602	27.332	34.636	29.855	35.979
Period average[1] Moyenne sur période[1]	...	...	...	29.153	28.785	26.541	27.145	31.698	32.281	34.569
Dem. Rep. of the Congo: new zaïre Rép. dém. du Congo : nouveau zaïre										
End of period[8] Fin de période[8]	666.670	21.220	663.330	35.000	3 250.000	14 831.000	115 600.00	106 000.00	245 000.000	...
Period average[8] Moyenne sur période[8]	239.480	5.190	215.140	2.514	1 194.120	7 024.470	50 184.900	131 345.00	160 666.000	...
Denmark: Danish krone Danemark : couronne danoise										
End of period Fin de période	5.776	5.914	6.256	6.773	6.083	5.546	5.945	6.826	6.387	7.399
Period average Moyenne sur période	6.189	6.396	6.036	6.484	6.361	5.602	5.799	6.604	6.701	6.976

76
Exchange rates
National currency per US dollar [*cont.*]
Cours des changes
Valeur du dollar des Etats-Unis en monnaie nationale [*suite*]

Country (monetary unit) Pays (unité monétaire)	1990	1991	1992	1993	1994	1995	1996	1997	1998	1999
Djibouti: Djibouti franc Djibouti : franc djiboutien										
End of period										
Fin de période	177.721	177.721	177.721	177.721	177.721	177.721	177.721	177.721	177.721	177.721
Dominica: EC dollar Dominique : dollar des Caraïbes orientales										
End of period										
Fin de période	2.700	2.700	2.700	2.700	2.700	2.700	2.700	2.700	2.700	2.700
Dominican Republic: Dominican peso Rép. dominicaine : peso dominicain										
End of period [1]										
Fin de période[1]	11.350	12.660	12.575	12.767	13.064	13.465	14.062	14.366	15.788	16.039
Period average[1]										
Moyenne sur période[1]	8.525	12.692	12.774	12.676	13.160	13.597	13.775	14.266	15.267	16.033
Ecuador: sucre Equateur : sucre										
End of period[1]										
Fin de période[1]	878.200	1 270.580	1 844.250	2 043.780	2 269.000	2 923.500	3 635.000	4 428.000	6 825.000	20 243.000
Period average[1]										
Moyenne sur période[1]	767.751	1 046.250	1 533.960	1 919.100	2 196.730	2 564.490	3 189.470	3 998.270	5 446.570	11 786.800
Egypt: Egyptian pound Egypte : livre égyptienne										
End of period[1]										
Fin de période[1]	2.000	3.332	3.339	3.372	3.391	3.390	3.388	3.388	3.388	3.405
Period average[1]										
Moyenne sur période[1]	1.550	3.138	3.322	3.353	3.385	3.392	3.391	3.389	3.388	3.395
El Salvador: El Salvadoran colón El Salvador : cólon salvadorien										
End of period[1]										
Fin de période[1]	8.030	8.080	9.170	8.670	8.750	8.755	8.755	8.755	8.755	8.755
Period average[1]										
Moyenne sur période[1]	6.848	8.017	8.361	8.703	8.729	8.755	8.755	8.756	8.755	8.755
Equatorial Guinea: CFA franc Guinée équatoriale : franc CFA										
End of period[4]										
Fin de période[4]	256.450	259.000	275.325	294.775	534.600	490.000	523.700	598.810	562.210	652.953
Period average[4]										
Moyenne sur période[4]	272.265	282.107	264.692	283.163	555.205	499.148	511.552	583.669	589.952	615.699
Estonia: Estonian kroon Estonie : couronne estonienne										
End of period										
Fin de période	...	...	12.912	13.878	12.390	11.462	12.440	14.336	13.410	15.562
Period average										
Moyenne sur période	...	...	...	13.223	12.991	11.465	12.034	13.882	14.075	14.678
Ethiopia: Ethiopian birr Ethiopie : birr éthiopien										
End of period										
Fin de période	2.070	2.070	5.000	5.000	5.950	6.320	6.426	6.864	7.503	8.134
Period average										
Moyenne sur période	2.070	2.070	2.803	5.000	5.465	6.158	6.352	6.709	7.116	7.942
Euro Area: euro Zone euro : euro										
End of period[9]										
Fin de période[9]	...	...	...	...	...	...	...	...	...	0.995
Period average[9]										
Moyenne sur période[9]	...	...	...	...	...	...	...	...	...	0.939
Fiji: Fiji dollar Fidji : dollar des Fidji										
End of period										
Fin de période	1.459	1.473	1.564	1.541	1.409	1.429	1.384	1.549	1.986	1.966
Period average										
Moyenne sur période	1.481	1.476	1.503	1.542	1.464	1.406	1.403	1.444	1.987	1.970
Finland: Finnish markka Finlande : markka finlandais										
End of period[3]										
Fin de période[3]	3.634	4.133	5.245	5.785	4.743	4.359	4.644	5.421	5.096	0.995

76
Exchange rates
National currency per US dollar [*cont.*]
Cours des changes
Valeur du dollar des Etats-Unis en monnaie nationale [*suite*]

Country (monetary unit) Pays (unité monétaire)	1990	1991	1992	1993	1994	1995	1996	1997	1998	1999
Period average[3] Moyenne sur période[3]	3.824	4.044	4.479	5.712	5.224	4.367	4.594	5.191	5.344	0.939
France: French franc France : franc français										
End of period[3] Fin de période[3]	5.129	5.180	5.507	5.896	5.346	4.900	5.237	5.988	5.622	0.995
Period average[3] Moyenne sur période[3]	5.445	5.642	5.294	5.663	5.552	4.991	5.116	5.837	5.900	0.939
Gabon: CFA franc Gabon : franc CFA										
End of period[4] Fin de période[4]	256.450	259.000	275.325	294.775	534.600	490.000	523.700	598.810	562.210	652.953
Period average[4] Moyenne sur période[4]	272.265	282.107	264.692	283.163	555.205	499.148	511.552	583.669	589.952	615.699
Gambia: dalasi Gambie : dalasi										
End of period Fin de période	7.495	8.957	9.217	9.535	9.579	9.640	9.892	10.530	10.991	11.547
Period average Moyenne sur période	7.883	8.803	8.887	9.129	9.576	9.546	9.789	10.200	10.643	11.395
Georgia: lari Géorgie : lari										
End of period Fin de période	...	...	...	...	...	1.230	1.276	1.304	1.800	1.930
Period average Moyenne sur période	...	...	...	...	...	...	1.263	1.298	1.390	2.025
Germany: deutsche mark Allemagne : deutsche mark										
End of period[3] Fin de période[3]	1.494	1.516	1.614	1.726	1.549	1.434	1.555	1.792	1.673	0.995
Period average[3] Moyenne sur période[3]	1.616	1.660	1.562	1.653	1.623	1.433	1.505	1.734	1.760	0.939
Ghana: cedi Ghana : cedi										
End of period[1] Fin de période[1]	344.828	390.625	* 520.833	819.672	1 052.630	1 449.280	1 754.390	2 272.730	2 325.580	3 448.280
Period average[1] Moyenne sur période[1]	326.332	367.831	* 437.087	649.061	956.711	1 200.430	1 637.230	2 050.170	2 314.150	2 647.320
Greece: drachma Grèce : drachme										
End of period Fin de période	157.625	175.280	214.580	249.220	240.100	237.040	247.020	282.610	282.570	328.440
Period average Moyenne sur période	158.514	182.266	190.624	229.250	242.603	231.663	240.712	273.058	295.529	305.647
Grenada: EC dollar Grenade : dollar des Caraïbes orientales										
End of period Fin de période	2.700	2.700	2.700	2.700	2.700	2.700	2.700	2.700	2.700	2.700
Guatemala: quetzal Guatemala : quetzal										
End of period Fin de période	5.015	5.043	5.274	5.815	5.649	6.042	5.966	6.177	6.848	7.821
Period average Moyenne sur période	4.486	5.029	5.171	5.635	5.751	5.810	6.050	6.065	6.395	7.386
Guinea: Guinean franc Guinée : franc guinéen										
End of period Fin de période	680.000	802.950	922.410	972.414	981.024	997.984	1 039.130	1 144.950	1 298.030	1 736.000
Period average Moyenne sur période	660.167	753.858	902.001	955.490	976.636	991.411	1 004.020	1 095.330	1 236.830	...
Guinea-Bissau: CFA franc Guinée-Bissau : franc CFA										
End of period[10] Fin de période[10]	38.594	76.295	133.162	176.366	236.451	337.366	537.482	598.810	562.210	652.953
Period average[10] Moyenne sur période[10]	33.622	56.286	106.676	155.106	198.341	278.039	405.745	583.669	589.952	615.699

76
Exchange rates
National currency per US dollar [*cont.*]
Cours des changes
Valeur du dollar des Etats-Unis en monnaie nationale [*suite*]

Country (monetary unit) Pays (unité monétaire)	1990	1991	1992	1993	1994	1995	1996	1997	1998	1999
Guyana: Guyana dollar Guyana : dollar guyanais										
End of period[1] Fin de période[1]	45.000	122.000	126.000	130.750	142.500	140.500	141.250	144.000	162.250	180.500
Period average[1] Moyenne sur période[1]	39.533	111.811	125.002	126.730	138.290	141.989	140.375	142.401	150.519	177.995
Haiti: gourde Haïti : gourde										
End of period Fin de période	4.999[1]	8.240	10.953[1]	12.805[1]	12.947[1]	16.160[1]	15.093[1]	17.311[1]	16.505[1]	17.965[1]
Period average[1] Moyenne sur période[1]	5.000	6.034	9.802	12.823	15.040	15.110	15.701	16.655	16.766	16.938
Honduras: lempira Honduras : lempira										
End of period Fin de période[1]	5.357	5.400	5.830	7.260	9.400	10.343	12.869	13.094	13.808	14.504
Period average[1] Moyenne sur période[1]	4.112	5.317	5.498	6.472	8.409	9.471	11.705	13.004	13.385	14.213
Hungary: forint Hongrie : forint										
End of period Fin de période	61.449	75.620	83.970	100.700	110.690	139.470	164.930	203.500	219.030	252.520
Period average Moyenne sur période	63.206	74.735	78.988	91.933	105.160	125.681	152.647	186.789	214.402	237.146
Iceland: Icelandic króna Islande : couronne islandaise										
End of period Fin de période	55.390	55.620	63.920	72.730	68.300	65.230	66.890	72.180	69.320	72.550
Period average Moyenne sur période	58.284	58.996	57.546	67.603	69.944	64.692	66.500	70.904	70.958	72.335
India: Indian rupee Inde : roupie indienne										
End of period Fin de période	18.073	25.834	26.200	31.380	31.380	35.180	35.930	39.280	42.480	43.490
Period average Moyenne sur période	17.504	22.742	25.918	30.493	31.374	32.427	35.433	36.313	41.259	43.055
Indonesia: Indonesian rupiah Indonésie : roupie indonésien										
End of period Fin de période	1 901.000	1 992.000	2 062.000	2 110.000	2 200.000	2 308.000	2 383.000	4 650.000	8 025.000	7 085.000
Period average Moyenne sur période	1 842.810	1 950.320	2 029.920	2 087.100	2 160.750	2 248.610	2 342.300	2 909.380	10 013.600	7 855.150
Iran (Islamic Rep. of): Iranian rial Iran (Rép. islamique d') : rial iranien										
End of period[1] Fin de période[1]	65.307	64.591	67.039	1 758.560	1 735.970	1 747.500	1 749.140	1 754.260	1 750.930	1 752.290
Period average[1] Moyenne sur période[1]	68.096	67.505	65.552	1 267.770	1 748.750	1 747.930	1 750.760	1 752.920	1 751.860	1 752.930
Iraq: Iraqi dinar Iraq : dinar iraquien										
End of period[1] Fin de période[1]	0.311	0.311	0.311	0.311	0.311	0.311	0.311	0.311	0.311	0.311
Ireland: Irish pound Irlande : livre irlandaise										
End of period[3] Fin de période[3]	0.563	0.571	0.614	0.709	0.646	0.623	0.595	0.699	0.672	0.995
Period average[3] Moyenne sur période[3]	0.605	0.621	0.588	0.677	0.669	0.624	0.625	0.660	0.702	0.939
Israel: new sheqel Israël : nouveau sheqel										
End of period Fin de période	2.048	2.283	2.764	2.986	3.018	3.135	3.251	3.536	4.161	4.153
Period average Moyenne sur période	2.016	2.279	2.459	2.830	3.011	3.011	3.192	3.449	3.800	4.140

76

Exchange rates
National currency per US dollar [*cont.*]
Cours des changes
Valeur du dollar des Etats-Unis en monnaie nationale [*suite*]

Country (monetary unit) Pays (unité monétaire)	1990	1991	1992	1993	1994	1995	1996	1997	1998	1999
Italy: Italian lira Italie : lire italienne										
End of period Fin de période[3]	1 130.150	1 151.060	1 470.860	1 703.970	1 629.740	1 584.720	1 530.570	1 759.190	1 653.100	0.995
Period average Moyenne sur période[3]	1 198.100	1 240.610	1 232.410	1 573.670	1 612.440	1 628.930	1 542.950	1 703.100	1 736.210	0.939
Jamaica: Jamaican dollar Jamaïque : dollar jamaïcain										
End of period Fin de période	8.038	21.493	22.185	32.475	33.202	39.616	34.865	36.341	37.055	41.291
Period average Moyenne sur période	7.184	12.116	22.960	24.949	33.086	35.142	37.120	35.405	36.550	39.044
Japan: yen Japon : yen										
End of period Fin de période	134.400	125.200	124.750	111.850	99.740	102.830	116.000	129.950	115.600	102.200
Period average Moyenne sur période	144.792	134.707	126.651	111.198	102.208	94.060	108.779	120.991	130.905	113.907
Jordan: Jordan dinar Jordanie : dinar jordanien										
End of period Fin de période	0.665	0.675	0.691	0.704	0.701	0.709	0.709	0.709	0.709	0.709
Period average Moyenne sur période	0.664	0.681	0.680	0.693	0.699	0.700	0.709	0.709	0.709	0.709
Kazakhstan: tenge Kazakhstan : tenge										
End of period Fin de période	...	...	...	6.310	54.260	63.950	73.300	75.550	83.800	138.200
Period average Moyenne sur période	...	...	...	...	35.538	60.950	67.303	75.438	78.303	119.523
Kenya: Kenya shilling Kenya : shilling du Kenya										
End of period Fin de période	24.084	28.074	36.216	68.163	44.839	55.939	55.021	62.678	61.906	72.931
Period average Moyenne sur période	22.915	27.508	32.217	58.001	56.051	51.430	57.115	58.732	60.367	70.326
Kiribati: Australian dollar Kiribati : dollar australien										
End of period Fin de période	1.293	1.316	1.452	1.477	1.287	1.342	1.255	1.532	1.629	1.530
Period average Moyenne sur période	1.281	1.284	1.362	1.471	1.368	1.349	1.278	1.347	1.592	1.550
Korea, Republic of: Korean won Corée, République de : won coréen										
End of period Fin de période	716.400	760.800	788.400	808.100	788.700	774.700	844.200	1 695.000	1 204.000	1 138.000
Period average Moyenne sur période	707.764	733.353	780.651	802.671	803.446	771.273	804.453	951.289	1 401.440	1 188.820
Kuwait: Kuwaiti dinar Koweït : dinar koweïtien										
End of period Fin de période	...	0.284	0.303	0.298	0.300	0.299	0.300	0.305	0.302	0.304
Period average Moyenne sur période	0.288	0.284	0.293	0.302	0.297	0.298	0.299	0.303	0.305	0.304
Kyrgyzstan: Kyrgyz som Kirghizistan : som kirghize										
End of period Fin de période	...	...	...	8.030	10.650	11.200	16.700	17.375	29.376	45.429
Period average Moyenne sur période	...	...	...	...	10.842	10.822	12.810	17.363	20.838	39.008
Lao People's Dem. Rep.: kip Rép. dém. pop. lao : kip										
End of period Fin de période	695.500	711.500	717.000	718.000	719.000	# 923.000	935.000	2 634.500	4 274.000	7 600.000
Period average Moyenne sur période	707.750	702.083	716.083	716.250	717.667	# 804.691	921.022	1 259.980	3 298.330	7 102.020

76
Exchange rates
National currency per US dollar [cont.]
Cours des changes
Valeur du dollar des Etats-Unis en monnaie nationale [suite]

Country (monetary unit) Pays (unité monétaire)	1990	1991	1992	1993	1994	1995	1996	1997	1998	1999
Latvia: lats Lettonie : lats										
End of period										
Fin de période	...	...	0.835	0.595	0.548	0.537	0.556	0.590	0.569	0.583
Period average										
Moyenne sur période	...	...	0.736	0.675	0.560	0.528	0.551	0.581	0.590	0.585
Lebanon: Lebanese pound Liban : livre libanaise										
End of period										
Fin de période	842.000	879.000	1 838.000	1 711.000	1 647.000	1 596.000	1 552.000	1 527.000	1 508.000	1 507.500
Period average										
Moyenne sur période	695.089	928.227	1 712.790	1 741.360	1 680.070	1 621.410	1 571.440	1 539.450	1 516.130	1 507.840
Lesotho: loti Lesotho : loti [1]										
End of period [1]										
Fin de période [1]	2.563	2.743	3.053	3.398	3.544	3.648	4.683	4.868	5.860	6.155
Period average [1]										
Moyenne sur période [1]	2.587	2.761	2.852	3.268	3.551	3.627	4.299	4.608	5.528	6.109
Liberia: Liberian dollar Libéria : dollar libérien										
End of period [1]										
Fin de période [1]	1.000	1.000	1.000	1.000	1.000	1.000	1.000	1.000	43.250	39.500
Period average [1]										
Moyenne sur période [1]	1.000	1.000	1.000	1.000	1.000	1.000	1.000	1.000	41.508	41.903
Libyan Arab Jamah.: Libyan dinar Jamah. arabe libyenne : dinar libyen										
End of period										
Fin de période	0.270	0.268	0.301	0.325	0.360	0.353	0.365	0.389	0.378	0.462
Period average										
Moyenne sur période	* 0.283	* 0.281	* 0.285	0.305	0.321	0.346	0.362	0.382	0.394	0.464
Lithuania: litas Lituanie : litas										
End of period										
Fin de période	...	...	3.790	3.900	4.000	4.000	4.000	4.000	4.000	4.000
Period average										
Moyenne sur période	...	...	1.773	4.344	3.978	4.000	4.000	4.000	4.000	4.000
Luxembourg: Luxembourg franc Luxembourg : franc luxembourgeois										
End of period [3]										
Fin de période [3]	30.983	31.270	33.180	36.110	31.838	29.415	32.005	36.920	34.575	0.995
Period average [3]										
Moyenne sur période [3]	33.418	34.148	32.150	34.597	33.457	29.480	30.962	35.774	36.299	0.939
Madagascar: Malagasy franc Madagascar : franc malgache										
End of period										
Fin de période	1 465.830	1 832.660	1 910.170	1 962.670	3 871.080	3 422.970	4 328.470	5 284.670	5 402.210	6 543.200
Period average										
Moyenne sur période	1 494.150	1 835.360	1 863.970	1 913.780	3 067.340	4 265.630	4 061.250	5 090.890	5 441.400	6 283.770
Malawi: Malawi kwacha Malawi : kwacha malawien										
End of period										
Fin de période	2.647	2.664	4.396	4.494	15.299	15.303	15.323	21.228	43.884	46.438
Period average										
Moyenne sur période	2.729	2.803	3.603	4.403	8.736	15.284	15.309	16.444	31.073	44.088
Malaysia: ringgit Malaisie : ringgit										
End of period										
Fin de période	2.702	2.724	2.612	2.702	2.560	2.542	2.529	3.892	3.800	3.800
Period average										
Moyenne sur période	2.705	2.750	2.547	2.574	2.624	2.504	2.516	2.813	3.924	3.800
Maldives: rufiyaa Maldives : rufiyaa										
End of period										
Fin de période	9.620	10.320	10.535	11.105	11.770	11.770	11.770	11.770	11.770	11.770
Period average										
Moyenne sur période	9.552	10.253	10.569	10.957	11.586	11.770	11.770	11.770	11.770	11.770

76
Exchange rates
National currency per US dollar [cont.]
Cours des changes
Valeur du dollar des Etats-Unis en monnaie nationale [suite]

Country (monetary unit) Pays (unité monétaire)	1990	1991	1992	1993	1994	1995	1996	1997	1998	1999
Mali: CFA franc Mali : franc CFA										
End of period[4]										
Fin de période[4]	256.450	259.000	275.325	294.775	534.600	490.000	523.700	598.810	562.210	652.953
Period average[4]										
Moyenne sur période[4]	272.265	282.107	264.692	283.163	555.205	499.148	511.552	583.669	589.952	615.699
Malta: Maltese lira Malte : lire maltaise										
End of period										
Fin de période	0.301	0.306	0.374	0.395	0.368	0.352	0.360	0.391	0.377	0.412
Period average										
Moyenne sur période	0.318	0.323	0.319	0.382	0.378	0.353	0.360	0.386	0.388	0.399
Mauritania: ouguiya Mauritanie : ouguiya										
End of period										
Fin de période	77.840	77.820	115.100	124.160	128.370	137.110	142.450	168.350	205.780	225.000
Period average										
Moyenne sur période	80.609	81.946	87.027	120.806	123.575	129.768	137.222	151.853	188.476	209.514
Mauritius: Mauritian rupee Maurice : roupie mauricienne										
End of period										
Fin de période	14.322	14.794	16.998	18.656	17.863	17.664	17.972	22.265	24.784	25.468
Period average										
Moyenne sur période	14.864	15.652	15.563	17.648	17.960	17.386	17.948	21.057	23.993	25.186
Mexico: Mexican new peso Mexique : nouveau peso mexicain										
End of period[1]										
Fin de période[1]	2.945	3.071	3.115	3.106	5.325	7.643	7.851	8.083	9.865	9.514
Period average[1]										
Moyenne sur période[1]	2.813	3.018	3.095	3.116	3.375	6.419	7.599	7.918	9.136	9.560
Micronesia (Fed. States of): US dollar Micron (Etats fédérés de) : dollar des Etats-Unis										
End of period										
Fin de période	1.000	1.000	1.000	1.000	1.000	1.000	1.000	1.000	1.000	1.000
Mongolia: togrog Mongolie : togrog										
End of period										
Fin de période	14.000	39.400	105.067	# 396.510	414.090	473.620	693.510	813.160	902.000	1 072.370
Period average										
Moyenne sur période	...	9.515	42.559	...	# 412.721	448.613	548.403	789.992	840.828	1 021.870
Morocco: Moroccan dirham Maroc : dirham marocain										
End of period										
Fin de période	8.043	8.150	9.049	9.651	8.960	8.469	8.800	9.714	9.255	10.087
Period average										
Moyenne sur période	8.242	8.707	8.538	9.299	9.203	8.540	8.716	9.527	9.604	9.804
Mozambique: metical Mozambique : metical										
End of period[1]										
Fin de période[1]	1 038.140	1 845.370	# 2 951.400	5 343.160	6 651.000	10 890.000	11 377.000	11 543.000	12 366.000	13 300.000
Period average[1]										
Moyenne sur période[1]	929.088	1 434.470	2 516.550	3 874.240	6 038.590	9 024.330	11 293.700	11 543.600	11 874.600	12 775.100
Myanmar: kyat Myanmar : kyat										
End of period										
Fin de période	6.080	6.014	6.241	6.246	5.903	5.781	5.988	6.363	6.109	6.268
Period average										
Moyenne sur période	6.339	6.284	6.105	6.157	5.975	5.667	5.918	6.242	6.343	6.286
Namibia: Namibia dollar Namibie : Dollar namibia										
End of period										
Fin de période	2.563	2.743	3.053	3.398	3.544	3.648	4.683	4.868	5.860	6.155
Period average										
Moyenne sur période	2.587	2.761	2.852	3.268	3.551	3.627	4.299	4.608	5.528	6.109
Nepal: Nepalese rupee Népal : roupie népalaise										
End of period										
Fin de période	30.400	42.700	43.200	49.240	49.880	56.000	57.030	63.300	67.675	68.725

76
Exchange rates
National currency per US dollar [*cont.*]
  Cours des changes
  Valeur du dollar des Etats-Unis en monnaie nationale [*suite*]

Country (monetary unit) Pays (unité monétaire)	1990	1991	1992	1993	1994	1995	1996	1997	1998	1999
Period average Moyenne sur période	29.369	37.255	42.718	48.607	49.398	51.890	56.692	58.010	65.976	68.239
Netherlands: Netherlands guilder Pays-Bas : florin néerlandais										
End of period[3] Fin de période[3]	1.690	1.710	1.814	1.941	1.735	1.604	1.744	2.017	1.889	0.995
Period average[3] Moyenne sur période[3]	1.821	1.870	1.758	1.857	1.820	1.606	1.686	1.951	1.984	0.939
Netherlands Antilles: Netherlands Antillean guilder Antilles néerlandaises : florin des Antilles néerlandaises										
End of period Fin de période	1.790	1.790	1.790	1.790	1.790	1.790	1.790	1.790	1.790	1.790
New Zealand: New Zealand dollar Nouvelle-Zélande : dollar néo-zélandais										
End of period Fin de période	1.701	1.848	1.944	1.790	1.556	1.531	1.416	1.719	1.898	1.921
Period average Moyenne sur période	1.676	1.734	1.862	1.851	1.687	1.524	1.455	1.512	1.868	1.890
Nicaragua: córdoba Nicaragua : córdoba										
End of period[1,11] Fin de période[1,11]	600.000	5.000	5.000	6.350	7.112	7.965	8.924	9.995	11.194	12.318
Period average[1,11] Moyenne sur période[1,11]	140.920	4.271	5.000	5.620	6.723	7.546	8.435	9.448	10.582	11.809
Niger: CFA franc Niger : franc CFA										
End of period[4] Fin de période[4]	256.450	259.000	275.325	294.775	534.600	490.000	523.700	598.810	562.210	652.953
Period average[4] Moyenne sur période[4]	272.265	282.107	264.692	283.163	555.205	499.148	511.552	583.669	589.952	615.699
Nigeria: naira Nigéria : naira										
End of period[1] Fin de période[1]	9.001	9.862	19.646	21.882	21.997	21.887	21.886	21.886	21.886	97.950
Period average[1] Moyenne sur période[1]	8.038	9.909	17.298	22.065	21.996	21.895	21.884	21.886	21.886	92.338
Norway: Norwegian krone Norvège : couronne norvégienne										
End of period Fin de période	5.908	5.973	6.925	7.518	6.762	6.319	6.443	7.316	7.600	8.040
Period average Moyenne sur période	6.260	6.483	6.215	7.094	7.058	6.335	6.450	7.073	7.545	7.799
Oman: rial Omani Oman : rial omani										
End of period Fin de période	0.385	0.385	0.385	0.385	0.385	0.385	0.385	0.385	0.385	0.385
Pakistan: Pakistan rupee Pakistan : roupie pakistanaise										
End of period Fin de période	21.845	24.658	25.636	30.045	30.723	34.165	40.020	43.940	45.885	# 51.785
Period average Moyenne sur période	21.605	23.689	24.965	27.975	30.423	31.494	35.909	40.918	44.943	49.118
Panama: balboa Panama : balboa										
End of period Fin de période	1.000	1.000	1.000	1.000	1.000	1.000	1.000	1.000	1.000	1.000
Papua New Guinea: kina Papouasie-Nvl-Guinée : kina										
End of period Fin de période	0.953	0.953	0.987	0.981	1.179	1.335	1.347	1.751	2.096	2.695
Period average Moyenne sur période	0.955	0.952	0.965	0.978	1.011	1.280	1.319	1.438	2.074	2.571
Paraguay: guaraní Paraguay : guaraní										
End of period Fin de période	1 258.000	1 380.000	1 630.000	1 880.000	1 924.700	1 979.660	2 109.670	2 360.000	2 840.190	3 328.860

76
Exchange rates
National currency per US dollar [*cont.*]
Cours des changes
Valeur du dollar des Etats-Unis en monnaie nationale [*suite*]

Country (monetary unit) Pays (unité monétaire)	1990	1991	1992	1993	1994	1995	1996	1997	1998	1999
Period average										
Moyenne sur période	1 229.810	1 325.180	1 500.260	1 744.350	1 904.760	1 963.020	2 056.810	2 177.860	2 726.490	3 119.070
Peru: new sol Pérou : nouveau sol										
End of period[12]										
Fin de période[12]	0.517	0.960	1.630	2.160	2.180	2.310	2.600	2.730	3.160	3.510
Period average[12]										
Moyenne sur période[12]	0.188	0.773	1.246	1.988	2.195	2.253	2.453	2.664	2.930	3.383
Philippines: Philippine peso Philippines : peso philippin										
End of period										
Fin de période	28.000	26.650	25.096	27.699	24.418	26.214	26.288	39.975	39.059	40.313
Period average										
Moyenne sur période	24.311	27.479	25.513	27.120	26.417	25.715	26.216	29.471	40.893	39.089
Poland: zloty Pologne : zloty										
End of period[13]										
Fin de période[13]	0.950	1.096	1.577	2.134	2.437	2.468	2.876	3.518	3.504	4.148
Period average[13]										
Moyenne sur période[13]	0.950	1.058	1.363	1.812	2.272	2.425	2.696	3.279	3.475	3.967
Portugal: Portuguese escudo Portugal : escudo portugais										
End of period[3]										
Fin de période[3]	133.600	134.184	146.758	176.812	159.093	149.413	156.385	183.326	171.829	0.995
Period average[3]										
Moyenne sur période[3]	142.555	144.482	134.998	160.800	165.993	151.106	154.244	175.312	180.104	0.939
Qatar: Qatar riyal Qatar : riyal qatarien										
End of period										
Fin de période	3.640	3.640	3.640	3.640	3.640	3.640	3.640	3.640	3.640	3.640
Republic of Moldova: Moldovan leu République de Moldova : leu moldove										
End of period										
Fin de période	...	0.002	0.414	# 3.640	4.270	4.499	4.674	4.661	8.323	11.590
Period average										
Moyenne sur période	...	...	...	...	...	4.496	4.604	4.624	5.371	10.516
Romania: Romanian leu Roumanie : leu roumain										
End of period										
Fin de période	34.710[1]	189.000	460.000[1]	1 276.000[1]	1 767.000[1]	2 578.000[1]	4 035.000[1]	8 023.000[1]	10 951.000[1]	18 255.000[1]
Period average										
Moyenne sur période	22.432[1]	76.387[1]	307.953	760.051[1]	1 655.090[1]	2 033.280[1]	3 084.220[1]	7 167.940[1]	8 875.580[1]	15 332.800[1]
Russian Federation: ruble Fédération de Russie : ruble										
End of period[14]										
Fin de période[14]	...	...	0.415	1.247	3.550	4.640	5.560	5.960	20.650	27.000
Period average[14]										
Moyenne sur période[14]	...	...	...	0.992	2.191	4.559	5.121	5.785	9.705	24.620
Rwanda: Rwanda franc Rwanda : franc rwandais										
End of period										
Fin de période	121.120	119.790	146.270	146.370	138.330	299.811	304.164	304.672	320.338	349.530
Period average										
Moyenne sur période	82.597	125.140	133.350	144.307	220.000	262.197	306.820	301.530	312.314	333.942
Saint Kitts-Nevis: EC dollar Saint-Kitts-et-Nevis : dollar des Caraïbes orientales										
End of period										
Fin de période	2.700	2.700	2.700	2.700	2.700	2.700	2.700	2.700	2.700	2.700
Saint Lucia: EC dollar Sainte-Lucie : dollar des Caraïbes orientales										
End of period										
Fin de période	2.700	2.700	2.700	2.700	2.700	2.700	2.700	2.700	2.700	2.700
St. Vincent-Grenadines: EC dollar St. Vincent-Grenadines : dollar des Caraïbes orientales										
End of period										
Fin de période	2.700	2.700	2.700	2.700	2.700	2.700	2.700	2.700	2.700	2.700

76
Exchange rates
National currency per US dollar [cont.]
Cours des changes
Valeur du dollar des Etats-Unis en monnaie nationale [suite]

Country (monetary unit) Pays (unité monétaire)	1990	1991	1992	1993	1994	1995	1996	1997	1998	1999
Samoa: tala Samoa : tala										
End of period										
Fin de période	2.333	2.449	2.558	2.608	2.452	2.527	2.434	2.766	3.010	3.018
Period average										
Moyenne sur période	2.310	2.400	2.466	2.569	2.535	2.473	2.462	2.559	2.948	3.013
San Marino: Italian lira Saint-Marin : lire italienne										
End of period[3]										
Fin de période[3]	1 130.150	1 151.060	1 470.860	1 703.970	1 629.740	1 584.720	1 530.570	1 759.190	1 653.100	0.995
Period average[3]										
Moyenne sur période[3]	1 198.100	1 240.610	1 232.410	1 573.670	1 612.440	1 628.930	1 542.950	1 703.100	1 736.210	0.939
Sao Tome and Principe: dobra Sao Tomé-et-Principe : dobra										
End of period										
Fin de période	140.982	280.021	375.540	516.700	1 185.310	1 756.870	2 833.210	6 969.730	6 885.000	7 300.000
Period average										
Moyenne sur période	143.331	201.816	321.337	429.854	732.628	1 420.340	2 203.160	4 552.510	6 883.240	7 118.960
Saudi Arabia: Saudi Arabian riyal Arabie saoudite : riyal saoudien										
End of period										
Fin de période	3.745	3.745	3.745	3.745	3.745	3.745	3.745	3.745	3.745	3.745
Senegal: CFA franc Sénégal : franc CFA										
End of period[4]										
Fin de période[4]	256.450	259.000	275.325	294.775	534.600	490.000	523.700	598.810	562.210	652.953
Period average[4]										
Moyenne sur période[4]	272.265	282.107	264.692	283.163	555.205	499.148	511.552	583.669	589.952	615.699
Seychelles: Seychelles rupee Seychelles : roupie seychelloises										
End of period										
Fin de période	5.119	5.063	5.255	5.258	4.970	4.864	4.995	5.125	5.452	5.368
Period average										
Moyenne sur période	5.337	5.289	5.122	5.182	5.056	4.762	4.970	5.026	5.262	5.343
Sierra Leone: leone Sierra Leone : leone										
End of period										
Fin de période	188.679	434.783	526.316	577.634	613.008	943.396	909.091	1 333.330	1 590.760	2 276.050
Period average										
Moyenne sur période	151.446	295.344	499.442	567.459	586.740	755.216	920.732	981.482	1 563.620	1 804.190
Singapore: Singapore dollar Singapour : dollar singapourien										
End of period										
Fin de période	1.745	1.631	1.645	1.608	1.461	1.414	1.400	1.676	1.661	1.666
Period average										
Moyenne sur période	1.813	1.728	1.629	1.616	1.527	1.417	1.410	1.485	1.674	1.695
Slovakia: Slovak koruna Slovaquie : couronne slovaque										
End of period										
Fin de période	...	...	...	33.202	31.277	29.569	31.895	34.782	36.913	42.266
Period average[1]										
Moyenne sur période[1]	...	...	...	30.770	32.045	29.713	30.654	33.616	35.233	41.363
Slovenia: tolar Slovénie : tolar										
End of period										
Fin de période	...	56.693	98.701	131.842	126.458	125.990	141.480	169.180	161.200	196.770
Period average										
Moyenne sur période	...	27.571	81.287	113.242	128.809	118.518	135.364	159.688	166.134	181.769
Solomon Islands: Solomon Islands dollar Iles Salomon : dollar des Iles Salomon										
End of period										
Fin de période	2.614	2.795	3.100	3.248	3.329	3.476	3.622	4.748	4.859	5.076
Period average										
Moyenne sur période	2.529	2.715	2.928	3.188	3.291	3.406	3.566	3.717	4.816	4.838

76

Exchange rates

National currency per US dollar [*cont.*]

Cours des changes

Valeur du dollar des Etats-Unis en monnaie nationale [*suite*]

Country (monetary unit) Pays (unité monétaire)	1990	1991	1992	1993	1994	1995	1996	1997	1998	1999
South Africa: rand Afrique du Sud : rand										
End of period[1]										
Fin de période[1]	2.563	2.743	3.053	3.398	3.544	3.648	4.683	4.868	5.860	6.155
Period average[1]										
Moyenne sur période[1]	2.587	2.761	2.852	3.268	3.551	3.627	4.299	4.608	5.528	6.109
Spain: peseta Espagne : peseta										
End of period[3]										
Fin de période[3]	96.909	96.688	114.623	142.214	131.739	121.409	131.275	151.702	142.607	0.995
Period average[3]										
Moyenne sur période[3]	101.934	103.912	102.379	127.260	133.958	124.689	126.662	146.414	149.395	0.939
Sri Lanka: Sri Lanka rupee Sri Lanka : roupie sri-lankaise										
End of period										
Fin de période	40.240	42.580	46.000	49.562	49.980	54.048	56.705	61.285	67.780	72.115
Period average										
Moyenne sur période	40.063	41.372	43.830	48.322	49.415	51.252	55.271	58.995	64.593	70.402
Sudan: Sudanese pound Soudan : livre soudanaise										
End of period[1]										
Fin de période[1]	0.450	1.499	13.514	21.739	40.000	52.632	144.928	172.200	237.800	257.700
Period average[1]										
Moyenne sur période[1]	0.450	0.696	9.743	15.931	28.961	58.087	125.079	157.574	200.802	252.550
Suriname: Suriname guilder Suriname : florin surinamais										
End of period										
Fin de période	1.785	1.785	1.785	1.785	# 409.500	407.000	401.000	401.000	401.000	987.500
Period average										
Moyenne sur période	1.785	1.785	1.785	1.785	# 134.117	442.228	401.258	401.000	401.000	...
Swaziland: lilangeni Swaziland : lilangeni										
End of period										
Fin de période	2.563	2.743	3.053	3.398	3.544	3.648	4.683	4.868	5.860	6.155
Period average										
Moyenne sur période	2.587	2.761	2.852	3.268	3.551	3.627	4.299	4.608	5.528	6.109
Sweden: Swedish krona Suède : couronne suédoise										
End of period										
Fin de période	5.698	5.530	7.043	8.304	7.462	6.658	6.871	7.877	8.061	8.525
Period average										
Moyenne sur période	5.919	6.047	5.824	7.783	7.716	7.133	6.706	7.635	7.950	8.262
Switzerland: Swiss franc Suisse : franc suisse										
End of period										
Fin de période	1.296	1.356	1.456	1.480	1.312	1.151	1.346	1.455	1.377	1.600
Period average										
Moyenne sur période	1.389	1.434	1.406	1.478	1.368	1.182	1.236	1.451	1.450	1.502
Syrian Arab Republic: Syrian pound Rép. arabe syrienne : livre syrienne										
End of period[1]										
Fin de période[1]	11.225	11.225	11.225	11.225	11.225	11.225	11.225	11.225	11.225	11.225
Tajikistan: Tajik ruble Tadjikistan : ruble tadjik										
End of period										
Fin de période	...	...	4.611	13.856	39.444	293.500	328.000	747.000	9 778.000	...
Period average										
Moyenne sur période	...	...	2.469	10.357	24.494	122.859	295.500	562.333	776.625	...
Thailand: baht Thaïlande : baht										
End of period										
Fin de période	25.290	25.280	25.520	25.540	25.090	25.190	25.610	# 47.247	36.691	37.470
Period average										
Moyenne sur période	25.586	25.517	25.400	25.320	25.150	24.915	25.343	31.364	41.359	37.814
TFYR Macedonia: TFYR Macedonian denar L'ex-R.y. Macédoine : denar de l'ex-R.Y. Macédoine										
End of period										
Fin de période	...	...	...	44.456	40.596	37.980	41.411	55.421	51.836	60.339

76
Exchange rates
National currency per US dollar [*cont.*]
Cours des changes
Valeur du dollar des Etats-Unis en monnaie nationale [*suite*]

Country (monetary unit) Pays (unité monétaire)	1990	1991	1992	1993	1994	1995	1996	1997	1998	1999
Period average Moyenne sur période	...	...	...	...	43.263	37.882	39.981	50.004	54.462	56.900
Togo: CFA franc Togo : franc CFA										
End of period[4] Fin de période[4]	256.450	259.000	275.325	294.775	534.600	490.000	523.700	598.810	562.210	652.953
Period average[4] Moyenne sur période[4]	272.265	282.107	264.692	283.163	555.205	499.148	511.552	583.669	589.952	615.699
Tonga: pa'anga Tonga : pa'anga										
End of period Fin de période	1.296	1.332	1.390	1.379	1.258	1.270	1.213	1.362	1.616	1.611
Period average Moyenne sur période	1.280	1.296	1.347	1.384	1.320	1.271	1.232	1.264	1.492	1.599
Trinidad and Tobago: Trinidad and Tobago dollar Trinité-et-Tobago : dollar de la Trinité-et-Tobago										
End of period Fin de période	4.250	4.250	4.250	5.814	5.933	5.997	6.195	6.300	6.597	6.300
Period average Moyenne sur période	4.250	4.250	4.250	5.351	5.925	5.948	6.005	6.252	6.298	6.299
Tunisia: Tunisian dinar Tunisie : dinar tunisien										
End of period Fin de période	0.837	0.865	0.951	1.047	0.991	0.951	0.999	1.148	1.101	1.253
Period average Moyenne sur période	0.878	0.925	0.884	1.004	1.012	0.946	0.973	1.106	1.139	1.186
Turkey: Turkish lira Turquie : livre turque										
End of period Fin de période	2 930.07	5 079.92	8 564.43	14 472.50	38 726.00	59 650.00	107 775.00	205 605.00	314 464.00	541 400.00
Period average Moyenne sur période	2 608.64	4 171.82	6 872.42	10 984.60	29 608.70	45 845.10	81 404.90	151 865.00	260 724.00	418 783.00
Turkmenistan: Turkmen manat Turkménistan : manat turkmene										
End of period Fin de période	...	...	...	1.990	75.000	200.000	4 070.000	4 165.000	5 200.000	5 200.000
Period average Moyenne sur période	...	...	...	...	19.198	110.917	3 257.670	4 143.420	4 890.170	5 200.000
Uganda: Uganda shilling Ouganda : shilling ougandais										
End of period[1] Fin de période[1]	540.000	915.000	1 217.150	1 130.150	926.770	1 009.450	1 029.590	1 140.110	1 362.690	1 506.040
Period average[1] Moyenne sur période[1]	428.855	734.010	1 133.830	1 195.020	979.445	968.917	1 046.080	1 083.010	1 240.310	1 454.830
Ukraine: hryvnia Ukraine : hryvnia										
End of period Fin de période	...	...	0.006	0.126	1.042	1.794	# 1.889	1.899	3.427	5.216
Period average Moyenne sur période	...	...	...	0.045	0.328	1.473	1.829	1.862	2.450	4.130
United Arab Emirates: UAE dirham Emirats arabes unis : dirham des EAU										
End of period Fin de période	3.671	3.671	3.671	3.671	3.671	3.671	3.671	3.673	3.673	3.673
United Kingdom: pound sterling Royaume-Uni : livre sterling										
End of period Fin de période	0.519	0.535	0.661	0.675	0.640	0.645	0.589	0.605	0.601	0.619
Period average Moyenne sur période	0.563	0.567	0.570	0.667	0.653	0.634	0.641	0.611	0.604	0.618
United Rep.Tanzania: Tanzania shilling Rép.-Unie de Tanzanie : shilling tanzanien										
End of period Fin de période	196.600	233.900	335.000	479.871	523.453	550.360	595.640	624.570	681.000	797.330

76

Exchange rates
National currency per US dollar [*cont.*]
Cours des changes
Valeur du dollar des Etats-Unis en monnaie nationale [*suite*]

Country (monetary unit) Pays (unité monétaire)	1990	1991	1992	1993	1994	1995	1996	1997	1998	1999
Period average Moyenne sur période	195.056	219.157	297.708	405.274	509.631	574.762	579.977	612.122	664.671	744.759
United States: US dollar Etats-Unis : dollar des Etats-Unis										
End of period Fin de période	1.000	1.000	1.000	1.000	1.000	1.000	1.000	1.000	1.000	1.000
Uruguay: Uruguayan peso Uruguay : peso uruguayen										
End of period Fin de période	1.593	2.488	3.480	# 4.416	5.601	7.111	8.713	10.040	10.817	11.615
Period average Moyenne sur période	1.169	2.018	3.025	# 3.941	5.044	6.349	7.972	9.442	10.472	11.339
Vanuatu: vatu Vanuatu : vatu										
End of period Fin de période	109.250	110.790	119.000	120.800	112.080	113.740	110.770	124.310	129.780	128.890
Period average Moyenne sur période	117.061	111.675	113.392	121.581	116.405	112.112	111.719	115.873	127.517	129.075
Venezuela: bolívar Venezuela : bolívar										
End of period Fin de période	50.380	61.554	79.450	105.640	# 170.000	290.000	476.500	504.250	564.500	648.250
Period average Moyenne sur période	46.901	56.816	68.376	90.826	148.503	# 176.842	417.332	488.635	547.556	605.717
Viet Nam: dong Viet Nam : dong										
End of period Fin de période	8 125.000	11 500.000	10 565.000	10 842.500	11 050.000	11 014.000	11 050.000	12 292.000	13 893.000	...
Period average Moyenne sur période	6 482.800	10 037.000	11 202.200	10 641.000	10 962.100	11 034.900	11 032.600	11 359.400	...	...
Yemen: Yemeni rial Yémen : rial yéménite										
End of period Fin de période	12.010	12.010	12.010	12.010	12.010	# 50.040	# 126.910	130.460	141.650	...
Period average Moyenne sur période	...	12.010	12.010	12.010	12.010	# 40.839	# 94.160	129.281	135.882	...
Zambia: Zambia kwacha Zambie : kwacha zambie										
End of period Fin de période	42.753	88.968	359.712	500.000	680.272	956.130	1 282.690	1 414.840	2 298.920	2 632.190
Period average Moyenne sur période	30.289	64.640	172.214	452.763	669.371	864.119	1 207.900	1 314.500	1 862.070	2 388.020
Zimbabwe: Zimbabwe dollar Zimbabwe : dollar zimbabwéen										
End of period Fin de période	2.636	5.051	5.482	6.935	8.387	9.311	10.839	18.608	37.369	38.139
Period average Moyenne sur période	2.452	3.621	5.098	6.483	8.152	8.665	10.002	12.111	23.679	38.301

Source:
International Monetary Fund (IMF), Washington, D.C.,
"International Financial Statistics," November 2000 and the
IMF database.

† For information on recent changes in country or
area nomenclature pertaining to former Czechoslovakia,
Germany, Hong Kong Special Administrative Region (SAR) of
China, Macao Special Administrative Region (SAR) of China,
SFR of Yugoslavia and the former USSR, see Annex I - Country
or area nomenclature, regional and other groupings.

Source:
Fonds monétaire international (FMI), Washington,
D.C.,"Statistiques Financières Internationales," novembre
2000 et la base de données de FMI.

† Pour les modifications récentes de nomenclature
de pays ou de zone concernant l'Allemagne, Hong Kong, région
administrative spéciale (RAS) de Chine, Macao, région
administrative spéciale (RAS) de Chine,
l'ex-Tchécoslovaquie, l'ex-URSS et l'ex-Rfs de Yougoslavie,
voir annexe I - Nomenclature des pays ou des zones,
groupements régionaux et autres groupements.

76

Exchange rates
National currency per US dollar [*cont.*]

Cours des changes
Valeur du dollar des Etats-Unis en monnaie nationale [*suite*]

†† For statistical purposes, the data for
China do not include those for Hong Kong Special
Administrative Region (Hong Kong SAR), Macao Special
Administrative Region (Macao SAR) and Taiwan province of
China.

1 Principal rate.
2 Peso per million US dollars through 1983, per thousand US
  dollars through 1988 and per US dollar thereafter.

3 Beginning 1999, Euros per US dollar.
4 Prior to January 1999, the official rate was pegged to the
  French franc. On January 12, 1994, the CFA franc was
  devalued to CFAF 100 per French franc from CFAF 50 at which
  it had been fixed since 1948. From January 1, 1999, the
  CFAF is pegged to the euro at a rate of CFA franc 655.957
  per euro.

5 Bolivianos per million US dollars through 1983, per thousand
  US dollars for 1984, and per US dollar thereafter.

6 Reals per trillion US dollars through 1983, per billion US
  dollars 1984-1988, per million US dollars 1989-1992, and per
  US dollar thereafter.

7 The official rate is pegged to the French franc. Beginning
  January 12, 1994, the CFA franc was devalued to CFAF 75 per
  French franc from CFAF 50 at which it had been fixed since
  1948.
8 New Zaires per million US dollars through 1990, per thousand
  US dollars for 1991-1992, and per US dollar thereafter.

9 "Euro Area" is an official descriptor for the European
  Economic and Monetary Union (EMU). The participating member
  states of the EMU are Austria, Belgium, Finland, France,
  Germany, Ireland, Italy, Luxembourg, Netherlands, Portugal,
  and Spain.
10 Prior to January 1999, the official rate was pegged to the
   French franc at CFAF 100 per French franc. The CFA franc
   was adopted as national currency as of May 2, 1997. The
   Guinean peso and the CFA franc were set at PG65 per CFA
   franc. From January 1, 1999, the CFAF is pegged to the euro
   at a rate of CFA franc 655.957 per euro.

11 Gold córdoba per billion US dollars through 1987, per
   million US dollars for 1988, per thousand US dollars for
   1989-1990 and per US dollar thereafter.

12 New soles per billion US dollars through 1987, per million
   US dollars for 1988-1989, and per US dollar thereafter.

13 Zlotys per thousand US dollars through 1989, and per US
   dollar thereafter.
14 The post-January 1, 1998 ruble is equal to 1,000 of the
   pre-January 1,1998 rubles.

†† Les données statistiques relatives à
la Chine ne comprennent pas celles qui concernent la région
administrative spéciale de Hong Kong (la RAS de Hong Kong),
la région administrative spéciale de Macao (la RAS de Macao)
et la province chinoise de Taiwan.

1 Taux principal.
2 Peso par million de dollars des États-Unis jusqu'en 1983,
  par millier de dollars des États-Unis jusqu'en 1988 et par
  dollar des États-Unis après cette date.

3 A partir de 1999, euros pour un dollar des États-Unis.
4 Avant janvier 1999, le taux officiel était établi par
  référence au franc français. Le 12 janvier 1994, le franc
  CFA a été dévalué; son taux par rapport au franc français,
  auquel il est rattaché depuis 1948, est passé de 50 à 100
  francs CFA pour 1 franc français. A compter du 1er janvier
  1999, le taux officiel est établi par référence à l'euro à
  un taux de 655 957 francs CFA pour un euro.

5 Bolivianos par million de dollars des États-Unis jusqu'en
  1983, par millier de dollars des États-Unis en 1984, et par
  dollar des États-Unis après cette date.

6 Reals par trillion de dollars des États-Unis jusqu'en 1983,
  par millard de dollars des États-Unis 1984-1988, par million
  de dollars des États-Unis 1989-1992, et par dollar des
  États-Unis après cette date.

7 Le taux de change officiel est raccroché au taux de change
  du franc français. Le 12 janvier 1994, le franc CFA a été
  dévalué de 50 par franc français, valuer qu'il avait
  conservée depuis 1948, à 75 par franc français.

8 Nouveaux zaïres par million de dollars des États-Unis
  jusqu'en 1990, par millier de dollars des États-Unis en 1991
  et 1992, et par dollar des États-Unis après cette date.

9 L'expression "zone euro" est un intitulé officiel pour
  l'Union économique et monétaire (UEM) européenne. L'UEM est
  composée des pays membres suivants : Allemagne, Autriche,
  Belgique, Espagne, Finlande, France, Irlande, Italie,
  Luxembourg, Pays-Bas et Portugal.
10 Avant janvier 1999, le taux de change officiel était
   raccroché au taux de change du franc français à CFA 100 pour
   franc français. Le franc CFA été adopté comme monnaie
   nationale au 2 mai 1997. Le peso guinéen et le franc CFA a
   été établi à 65 pesos guinéen pour 1 franc CFA. A compter
   du 1er janvier 1999, le taux officiel est établi par
   référence à l'euro à un taux de 655 957 francs CFA pour un
   euro.

11 Cordobas or par milliard de dollars des États-Unis jusqu'en
   1987, par million de dollars en 1988, par millier de dollars
   des États-Unis en 1989-1990 et par dollar des États-Unis
   après cette date.

12 Nouveaux soles par milliard de dollars des États-Unis
   jusqu'en 1987, par million de dollars des États-Unis en
   1988-1989 et par dollar des États-Unis après cette date.

13 Zlotys par millier de dollars des États-Unis jusqu'en 1989,
   et par dollar des États-Unis après cette date.
14 Le rouble ayant cours après le 1er janvier 1998 vaut 1 000
   roubles de la période antérieure à cette date.

77

Total external and public/publicly guaranteed long-term debt of developing countries
Total de la dette extérieure et dette publique extérieure à long terme garantie par l'Etat des pays en développement

Million US dollars
Millions de dollars E.-U.

A. Total external debt [1] • Total de la dette extérieure [1]

	1991	1992	1993	1994	1995	1996	1997	1998	
Total long-term debt (LDOD)	**1243408**	**1285920**	**1411179**	**1564438**	**1653951**	**1708479**	**1786391**	**2030343**	**Total de la dette à long terme (LDOD)**
Public/publicly guaranteed	1163817	1185434	1283185	1375599	1432451	1424201	1411963	1529249	Dette publique ou garantie par l'Etat
Official creditors	653604	676857	761027	832031	864278	832236	794444	852901	Créanciers publics
Multilateral	225441	231841	249091	275060	290759	286550	289598	326307	Multilatéraux
IBRD	100103	97945	102691	110108	113869	107160	106036	115927	BIRD
IDA	49755	53606	58310	66505	71630	75219	77474	84159	IDA
Bilateral	428162	445017	511937	556971	573519	545688	504845	526593	Bilatéraux
Private creditors	510213	508576	522158	543569	568174	591963	617519	676348	Créanciers privés
Bonds	116315	128100	161518	234722	257369	293379	308698	345423	Obligations
Commercial banks	252241	240488	221162	168868	173937	174024	207868	236757	Banques commerciales
Other private	141657	139988	139477	139979	136868	124561	100953	94169	Autres institutions privées
Private non-guaranteed	**79591**	**100487**	**127995**	**188838**	**221500**	**284279**	**374428**	**501094**	**Dette privé non garantie**
Undisbursed debt	**233843**	**241444**	**253245**	**256887**	**258895**	**245187**	**231506**	**237009**	**Dette (montants non versés)**
Official creditors	178531	184439	190129	200371	204132	189985	180588	186431	Créanciers publics
Private creditors	55312	57005	63117	56516	54762	55202	50918	50578	Créanciers privés
Commitments	**133850**	**136780**	**143189**	**119600**	**153069**	**171836**	**182474**	**174224**	**Engagements**
Official creditors	74370	67953	62918	61628	79787	60874	69262	69247	Créanciers publics
Private creditors	59479	68828	80270	57971	73282	110962	113212	104977	Créanciers privés
Disbursements	**129639**	**154383**	**175234**	**176408**	**211760**	**268847**	**308387**	**290842**	**Versements**
Public/publicly guaranteed	110194	117648	126263	115726	143262	164473	178944	174531	Dette publique ou garantie par l'Etat
Official creditors	54265	51785	54023	49816	66135	56534	65352	67149	Créanciers publics
Multilateral	28114	27646	31319	29289	32269	33536	40642	44773	Multilatéraux
IBRD	12034	10429	13143	11580	13237	13358	17660	17560	BIRD
IDA	4604	5143	4862	6065	5474	6313	5933	5558	IDA
Bilateral	26151	24139	22704	20528	33866	22998	24710	22375	Bilatéraux
Private creditors	55929	65862	72241	65910	77127	107939	113593	107382	Créanciers privés
Bonds	10277	11062	26023	24143	29902	58610	62526	58631	Obligations
Commercial banks	17514	21938	17968	17773	26614	29653	32053	34766	Banques commerciales
Other private	28138	32864	28250	23995	20611	19676	19013	13986	Autres institutions privées
Private non-guaranteed	**19445**	**36736**	**48971**	**60682**	**68497**	**104373**	**129443**	**116312**	**Dette privé non garantie**
Principal repayments									**Remboursements du principal**
Public/publicly guaranteed	83616	92714	101423	112775	128326	163714	191078	186134	Dette publique ou garantie par l'Etat
	73233	77838	75175	83449	97243	120068	128863	112579	
Official creditors	26998	28254	29010	36625	44924	53529	51487	43631	Créanciers publics
Multilateral	14085	15630	16448	19211	21350	21059	19834	18787	Multilatéraux
IBRD	9428	10314	10383	11887	12134	11998	10934	10729	BIRD
IDA	308	345	398	458	546	593	649	743	IDA
Bilateral	12913	12625	12563	17413	23576	32470	31653	24844	Bilatéraux
Private creditors	46235	49584	46165	46824	52319	66540	77376	68947	Créanciers privés
Bonds	2198	8571	8943	7167	12879	21801	36783	26588	Obligations
Commercial banks	18706	18878	17654	19167	19807	27297	24533	25266	Banques commerciales
Other private	25332	22135	19568	20491	19632	17442	16060	17094	Autres institutions privées
Private non-guaranteed	**10383**	**14876**	**26248**	**29326**	**31084**	**43646**	**62215**	**73556**	**Dette privé non garantie**

77
Total external and public/publicly guaranteed long-term debt of developing countries
Million US dollars [*cont.*]
Total de la dette extérieure et dette publique extérieure à long terme garantie par l'Etat des pays en développement
Millions de dollars E.-U. [*suite*]

A. Total external debt [1] · Total de la dette extérieure [1]

	1991	1992	1993	1994	1995	1996	1997	1998	
Net flows	**46023**	**61669**	**73810**	**63634**	**83433**	**105132**	**117310**	**104708**	**Apports nets**
Public/publicly									**Dette publique ou**
guaranteed	**36961**	**39809**	**51088**	**32278**	**46019**	**44406**	**50081**	**61951**	**garantie par l'Etat**
Official creditors	27268	23531	25013	13192	21211	3007	13865	23517	Créanciers publics
Multilateral	14030	12017	14871	10078	10919	12478	20807	25986	Multilatéraux
IBRD	2605	115	2759	−306	1104	1360	6727	6831	BIRD
IDA	4297	4798	4465	5607	4928	5721	5284	4816	IDA
Bilateral	13238	11514	10142	3114	10291	−9471	−6943	−2468	Bilatéraux
Private creditors	9694	16279	26076	19086	24809	41399	36216	38435	Créanciers privés
Bonds	8079	2491	17080	16976	17023	36808	25743	32043	Obligations
Commercial banks	−1192	3060	314	−1394	6807	2357	7521	9500	Banques commerciales
Other private	2807	10728	8681	3504	979	2235	2953	−3108	Autres institutions privées
Private non−guaranteed	**9062**	**21860**	**22722**	**31356**	**37413**	**60727**	**67228**	**42756**	**Dette privé non garantie**
Interest payments (LINT)	**54782**	**53940**	**52298**	**60765**	**77135**	**80957**	**87074**	**94868**	**Paiements d'intérets (LINT)**
Public/publicly									**Dette publique ou**
guaranteed	**49164**	**47934**	**45356**	**51285**	**63895**	**65022**	**66054**	**68758**	**garantie par l'Etat**
Official creditors	21480	22373	23778	25627	30519	30992	28733	28020	Créanciers publics
Multilateral	12338	12421	13000	13634	14031	13790	12870	13244	Multilatéraux
IBRD	7939	7781	8004	8002	8139	7807	6893	7029	BIRD
IDA	348	372	395	433	504	512	531	554	IDA
Bilateral	9142	9953	10777	11993	16488	17202	15863	14777	Bilatéraux
Private creditors	27684	25561	21578	25659	33376	34029	37321	40738	Créanciers privés
Bonds	7751	7584	8524	11168	16899	16782	19732	22393	Obligations
Commercial banks	12517	11811	7657	7704	9382	10662	11699	13020	Banques commerciales
Other private	7415	6166	5397	6786	7093	6585	5890	5325	Autres institutions privées
Private non−guaranteed	**5618**	**6006**	**6943**	**9480**	**13239**	**15935**	**21020**	**26110**	**Dette privé non garantie**
Net transfers	**−8758**	**7729**	**21511**	**2868**	**6298**	**24176**	**30235**	**9840**	**Transferts nets**
Public/publicly									**Dette publique ou**
guaranteed	**−12202**	**−8124**	**5732**	**−19008**	**−17876**	**−20616**	**−15974**	**−6807**	**garantie par l'Etat**
Official creditors	5787	1157	1235	−12435	−9308	−27986	−14869	−4503	Créanciers publics
Multilateral	1691	−404	1871	−3556	−3112	−1312	7938	12742	Multilatéraux
IBRD	−5333	−7667	−5246	−8309	−7036	−6448	−166	−198	BIRD
IDA	3948	4426	4069	5175	4425	5209	4753	4262	IDA
Bilateral	4096	1562	−636	−8879	−6197	−26674	−22806	−17245	Bilatéraux
Private creditors	−17989	−9282	4498	−6574	−8567	7369	−1105	−2303	Créanciers privés
Bonds	329	−5093	8556	5807	124	20026	6011	9650	Obligations
Commercial banks	−13709	−8751	−7343	−9099	−2576	−8305	−4179	−3521	Banques commerciales
Other private	−4609	4562	3284	−3282	−6115	−4351	−2937	−8432	Autres institutions privées
Private non−guaranteed	**3444**	**15853**	**15779**	**21877**	**24175**	**44793**	**46209**	**16646**	**Dette privé non garantie**
Total debt service									**Total du service de la**
(LTDS)	**138398**	**146654**	**153723**	**173541**	**205461**	**244672**	**278153**	**281003**	**dette (LTDS)**
Public/publicly									**Dette publique ou**
guaranteed	**122397**	**125772**	**120531**	**134735**	**161138**	**185091**	**194918**	**181337**	**garantie par l'Etat**
Official creditors	48479	50628	52788	62251	75444	84522	80220	71651	Créanciers publics
Multilateral	26424	28050	29448	32845	35379	34849	32704	32031	Multilatéraux
IBRD	17368	18095	18389	19889	20273	19806	17826	17757	BIRD
IDA	656	718	792	891	1050	1105	1180	1296	IDA
Bilateral	22055	22578	23340	29406	40063	49673	47516	39621	Bilatéraux
Private creditors	73917	75145	67743	72484	85695	100570	114697	109685	Créanciers privés
Bonds	9948	16155	17467	18336	29779	38584	56515	48980	Obligations
Commercial banks	31223	30689	25311	26871	29190	37959	36232	38286	Banques commerciales
Other private	32746	28301	24965	27276	26726	24027	21951	22418	Autres institutions privées
Private non−guaranteed	**16001**	**20882**	**33191**	**38806**	**44323**	**59581**	**83234**	**99665**	**Dette privé non garantie**

77
Total external and public/publicly guaranteed long–term debt of developing countries
Million US dollars [*cont.*]
Total de la dette extérieure et dette publique extérieure à long terme garantie par l'Etat des pays en développement
Millions de dollars E.–U. [*suite*]

B. Public and publicly guaranteed long–term debt • Dette publique extérieure à long terme garantie par l'Etat

Country or area Pays ou zone	1989	1990	1991	1992	1993	1994	1995	1996	1997	1998
Albania Albanie	...	35.7	86.2	126.9	166.0	215.6	516.7	586.3	603.3	701.3
Algeria Algérie	24612.9	26416.4	25969.0	25489.0	24847.1	28177.8	31042.4	31061.7	28709.8	28468.6
Angola Angola	6677.9	7605.1	7704.4	8132.1	8693.7	9125.9	9552.8	10055.0	10570.6	10616.4
Argentina Argentine	52193.3	47402.5	48199.7	48202.5	46783.2	51254.8	55811.4	63075.7	67561.5	76798.8
Armenia Arménie	...	...	...	...	133.9	188.6	298.3	432.0	511.4	564.0
Azerbaijan Azerbaïdjan	...	...	...	...	35.5	103.2	206.1	247.9	235.9	307.7
Bangladesh Bangladesh	10332.0	11987.0	12536.6	12962.5	13815.0	15391.6	15501.0	15327.2	14577.8	15804.1
Barbados Barbade	480.0	504.1	482.8	400.6	348.8	374.0	372.1	383.7	367.6	387.8
Belarus Bélarus	...	...	...	...	865.1	1099.7	1254.8	690.3	651.8	747.8
Belize Belize	128.9	136.6	151.1	170.2	175.9	182.7	220.3	251.5	269.4	282.2
Benin Bénin	1161.0	1218.5	1239.9	1324.1	1371.4	1487.3	1483.0	1448.4	1393.3	1468.8
Bhutan Bhoutan	71.8	80.3	84.8	88.3	94.9	103.8	105.2	113.6	118.3	119.6
Bolivia Bolivie	3425.6	3687.1	3529.5	3669.4	3694.8	4122.4	4468.2	4265.1	4143.9	4306.7
Botswana Botswana	551.2	557.2	613.2	605.5	651.8	677.5	693.2	607.5	522.0	508.2
Brazil Brésil	88088.2	87668.9	85535.9	90672.4	91987.5	94919.3	97569.0	96321.2	87962.5	98959.1
Bulgaria Bulgarie	9283.1	9834.1	9779.6	9669.6	9717.3	8420.7	8726.2	8160.3	7720.9	7781.2
Burkina Faso Burkina Faso	648.2	749.9	882.6	978.9	1066.0	1039.9	1135.9	1159.5	1138.8	1228.5
Burundi Burundi	832.3	851.4	901.2	947.0	998.0	1061.9	1095.1	1081.0	1022.1	1078.9
Cambodia Cambodge	1548.6	1688.0	1688.6	1679.8	1685.4	1745.2	1946.3	2012.5	2031.0	2101.7
Cameroon Cameroun	4341.3	5368.4	5597.4	6269.0	6236.2	7303.8	8061.7	8001.1	7661.9	8095.7
Cape Verde Cap–Vert	125.3	130.6	130.3	136.1	140.8	166.4	185.0	196.0	200.1	237.3
Central African Rep. Rép. centrafricaine	621.4	624.1	716.9	729.6	773.2	802.4	853.9	850.4	801.5	829.8
Chad Tchad	347.2	463.9	559.6	671.1	713.4	758.5	833.4	914.2	938.5	1004.5
Chile Chili	10865.6	10426.2	10070.5	9577.5	8867.3	8995.0	7178.3	4883.3	4367.3	4986.3
China †† Chine ††	37117.9	45515.2	49479.2	58462.6	70076.2	82391.3	94674.5	102260.2	112821.4	99424.1
Colombia Colombie	13989.0	14670.8	14468.7	13476.1	13242.9	14357.6	13949.6	14854.1	15294.7	16929.8
Comoros Comores	161.0	172.6	166.0	175.2	169.6	179.0	190.3	192.9	183.9	188.1
Congo Congo	3502.4	4206.1	4041.3	3875.6	4114.2	4774.0	4955.4	4665.7	4283.8	4250.4
Costa Rica Costa Rica	3545.2	3062.9	3291.9	3175.7	3130.8	3218.4	3133.4	2923.2	2840.1	3046.6

77
Total external and public/publicly guaranteed long-term debt of developing countries
Million US dollars [cont.]
Total de la dette extérieure et dette publique extérieure à long terme garantie par l'Etat des pays en développement
Millions de dollars E.-U. [suite]

B. Public and publicly guaranteed long-term debt · Dette publique extérieure à long terme garantie par l'Etat

Country or area Pays ou zone	1989	1990	1991	1992	1993	1994	1995	1996	1997	1998
Côte d'Ivoire Côte d'Ivoire	9067.9	10665.5	11264.6	11243.9	11110.6	11241.0	11902.1	11366.7	10427.1	10799.7
Croatia Croatie	...	...	...	...	601.2	643.4	1759.6	3334.1	4221.2	4909.6
Czech Republic République tchèque	3371.8	3983.3	4972.9	4689.2	6008.0	7171.8	9776.7	12149.0	12451.3	12900.6
Dem. Rep. of the Congo Rép. dém. du Congo	7965.8	9006.0	9271.3	8947.8	8769.1	9280.5	9621.3	9261.9	8616.8	8948.9
Djibouti Djibouti	131.2	155.2	204.7	219.3	230.9	254.9	268.9	279.3	253.0	263.8
Dominica Dominique	69.1	80.2	87.8	88.6	92.4	88.7	94.1	97.8	90.6	90.9
Dominican Republic Rép. dominicaine	3319.7	3419.5	3756.7	3736.5	3791.6	3619.4	3652.7	3523.5	3466.9	3530.2
Ecuador Equateur	9427.1	9866.8	9951.0	9831.3	9974.5	10552.3	12067.7	12443.8	12376.2	12588.9
Egypt Egypte	36484.5	27372.4	28466.5	27747.8	27803.1	29814.8	30479.2	28810.3	26804.3	27669.5
El Salvador El Salvador	1828.8	1912.6	2058.3	2148.0	1916.1	2014.2	2079.8	2316.6	2397.1	2443.3
Equatorial Guinea Guinée équatoriale	205.4	209.2	215.5	214.4	214.8	219.3	229.6	222.2	208.6	216.5
Eritrea Erythrée	...	...	...	...	...	29.1	36.7	44.3	75.5	144.1
Estonia Estonie	...	...	...	33.8	84.9	108.6	159.3	216.5	197.5	231.3
Ethiopia Ethiopie	7700.0	8482.5	8843.0	9003.2	9286.6	9570.8	9776.0	9484.5	9426.8	9618.4
Fiji Fidji	301.6	306.0	270.6	226.9	199.4	180.7	167.9	146.7	129.5	140.0
Gabon Gabon	2610.6	3151.1	3224.5	3048.8	2933.3	3694.3	3976.4	3971.6	3664.8	3832.9
Gambia Gambie	289.0	308.4	322.5	346.3	350.3	369.8	388.3	419.7	411.1	451.3
Georgia Géorgie	...	...	...	79.3	558.8	877.6	993.0	1106.3	1189.0	1311.1
Ghana Ghana	2427.4	2783.3	3118.6	3320.0	3639.6	4159.7	4642.3	4974.9	5059.8	5569.7
Grenada Grenade	71.1	89.9	99.7	94.1	92.5	100.2	98.9	105.8	113.8	113.0
Guatemala Guatemala	2130.5	2477.8	2483.7	2376.4	2493.7	2739.2	2823.6	2755.4	2871.9	2989.5
Guinea Guinée	1967.8	2253.0	2399.2	2450.2	2659.2	2886.4	2987.1	2980.6	3008.8	3126.4
Guinea-Bissau Guinée-Bissau	549.9	630.4	676.4	692.3	712.5	761.4	796.6	856.2	838.4	873.1
Guyana Guyana	1261.0	1757.3	1760.2	1673.1	1731.5	1787.0	1781.8	1370.2	1345.0	1369.4
Haiti Haïti	688.0	750.6	620.7	638.0	648.0	634.9	751.1	836.0	897.3	979.8
Honduras Honduras	2867.2	3425.7	3095.8	3231.8	3651.1	3901.8	3972.6	3845.6	3922.2	3946.3
Hungary Hongrie	16634.0	18006.4	18937.9	17896.2	19909.5	22349.1	23914.1	18673.0	15064.2	15941.1
India Inde	64788.6	71061.9	73355.3	77920.8	83906.0	87480.2	80345.8	78049.2	79401.5	85206.6
Indonesia Indonésie	44262.1	47981.8	51891.4	53664.1	57155.9	63926.0	65308.8	60015.8	55869.0	66943.6
Iran (Islamic Rep. of) Iran (Rép. islamique d')	1861.6	1796.8	2064.5	1780.1	5898.8	15529.6	15115.6	11712.0	8262.7	7678.7
Jamaica Jamaïque	3743.4	3933.8	3708.8	3560.2	3449.5	3436.1	3399.4	3124.1	2921.2	3079.1

77
Total external and public/publicly guaranteed long-term debt of developing countries
Million US dollars [*cont.*]
Total de la dette extérieure et dette publique extérieure à long terme garantie par l'Etat des pays en développement
Millions de dollars E.-U. [*suite*]

B. Public and publicly guaranteed long-term debt · Dette publique extérieure à long terme garantie par l'Etat

Country or area Pays ou zone	1989	1990	1991	1992	1993	1994	1995	1996	1997	1998
Jordan Jordanie	6255.6	7042.7	7457.5	6922.2	6770.0	6883.4	7022.9	7091.4	6960.2	7388.0
Kazakhstan Kazakhstan	...	...	...	25.7	1621.1	2227.0	2833.8	1946.5	2621.6	3039.6
Kenya Kenya	4194.7	4761.2	5265.0	5149.0	5245.6	5588.5	5960.0	5684.6	5224.5	5629.4
Korea, Republic of Corée, République de	17037.8	18785.9	22480.5	24049.9	24565.6	19252.7	22123.4	25423.1	33852.4	57956.0
Kyrgyzstan Kirghizistan	...	...	...	3.7	229.8	355.4	471.0	616.1	730.3	909.2
Lao People's Dem. Rep. Rép. dém. pop. lao	1463.2	1757.5	1849.6	1886.7	1948.2	2022.0	2091.2	2185.8	2246.8	2373.1
Latvia Lettonie	...	...	...	30.0	123.6	207.5	271.1	300.4	322.3	413.3
Lebanon Liban	354.3	357.8	336.2	300.5	368.0	778.2	1550.5	1933.4	2352.7	3979.6
Lesotho Lesotho	316.0	377.7	425.7	464.7	500.6	571.8	630.7	627.9	624.2	660.6
Liberia Libéria	1064.0	1115.9	1106.3	1081.2	1101.9	1137.0	1161.4	1109.9	1061.2	1092.2
Lithuania Lituanie	...	...	...	27.4	200.2	268.3	420.0	728.1	1041.9	1215.8
Madagascar Madagascar	3142.5	3334.9	3518.8	3469.0	3316.2	3536.6	3705.7	3552.0	3875.0	4106.5
Malawi Malawi	1258.1	1382.4	1517.6	1568.0	1729.6	1900.4	2083.0	2095.7	2099.2	2309.9
Malaysia Malaisie	12627.8	11592.0	12538.7	12370.5	13460.3	14692.9	16022.7	15702.0	16807.5	18158.4
Maldives Maldives	54.4	64.0	78.0	90.5	109.3	122.5	151.9	163.0	153.6	169.7
Mali Mali	2025.7	2335.8	2461.4	2777.0	2784.9	2544.7	2738.6	2762.2	2691.8	2827.4
Mauritania Mauritanie	1723.8	1788.6	1819.0	1825.3	1903.4	1989.5	2080.8	2125.0	2039.9	2213.5
Mauritius Maurice	645.7	763.6	816.8	747.9	733.0	852.2	1147.9	1152.5	1186.6	1151.6
Mexico Mexique	76102.3	75962.4	77816.4	71149.5	75150.5	79530.6	95167.3	94068.6	84386.5	87995.6
Mongolia Mongolie	...	...	...	272.2	338.5	400.5	463.8	481.1	533.4	633.6
Morocco Maroc	20545.3	23101.3	20791.7	21030.1	20680.2	21529.5	22084.6	21134.0	18978.0	19324.8
Mozambique Mozambique	3860.7	4214.5	4337.4	4701.1	4841.1	5219.0	5208.7	5358.2	5218.3	5651.3
Myanmar Myanmar	4064.6	4466.1	4579.7	5003.0	5394.4	6153.8	5377.7	4803.5	4628.7	5071.1
Nepal Népal	1294.8	1571.8	1712.5	1757.6	1939.6	2209.9	2346.5	2345.7	2332.3	2590.6
Nicaragua Nicaragua	7590.0	8281.1	9153.4	9312.0	9440.7	9761.5	8541.2	5124.7	4838.7	5212.1
Niger Niger	1045.4	1226.2	1137.6	1166.0	1209.9	1268.2	1330.0	1329.6	1328.2	1448.6
Nigeria Nigéria	29251.2	31545.6	32325.0	26477.8	26420.6	27954.5	28140.0	25430.5	22631.2	23455.0
Oman Oman	2620.4	2400.2	2473.5	2340.3	2314.7	2607.5	2637.3	2645.8	2567.1	2228.1
Pakistan Pakistan	14506.8	16505.6	17736.6	18562.7	20402.0	22685.7	23688.7	23518.8	23877.6	26061.4
Panama Panama	3935.2	3987.9	3918.2	3771.2	3799.3	3930.3	3913.5	5135.6	5073.8	5413.4
Papua New Guinea Papouasie–Nvl–Guinée	1324.7	1523.1	1631.1	1592.1	1616.1	1732.1	1668.1	1544.0	1338.0	1410.0

77

Total external and public/publicly guaranteed long-term debt of developing countries
Million US dollars [*cont.*]
Total de la dette extérieure et dette publique extérieure à long terme garantie par l'Etat des pays en développement
Millions de dollars E.-U. [*suite*]

B. Public and publicly guaranteed long-term debt · Dette publique extérieure à long terme garantie par l'Etat

Country or area Pays ou zone	1989	1990	1991	1992	1993	1994	1995	1996	1997	1998
Paraguay Paraguay	2093.6	1712.0	1683.3	1363.2	1281.3	1357.5	1439.3	1397.8	1487.6	1592.6
Peru Pérou	12615.4	13632.8	15442.2	15579.9	16384.8	17680.6	18927.4	20566.6	20204.1	20803.4
Philippines Philippines	22333.4	24040.4	25058.3	25618.1	27481.9	29687.0	28291.9	26867.8	26198.8	28188.8
Poland Pologne	34519.3	39262.7	44866.7	42740.8	41296.5	39503.4	41073.4	39208.4	34177.5	35136.1
Republic of Moldova République de Moldova	...	...	...	38.5	190.2	326.4	449.5	554.5	782.6	808.2
Romania Roumanie	198.8	222.9	218.0	1286.6	2069.9	2925.3	3908.9	6683.3	7157.0	6962.4
Russian Federation Fédération de Russie	35722.1	47997.0	55154.7	64255.3	100971.6	107397.0	100360.3	100259.3	104825.5	119313.8
Rwanda Rwanda	577.4	664.5	747.1	789.9	837.7	905.3	970.1	984.5	993.6	1119.8
Saint Kitts and Nevis Saint-Kitts-et-Nevis	36.5	44.2	48.6	47.4	49.7	55.1	53.8	62.2	108.5	111.3
Saint Lucia Sainte-Lucie	61.6	72.6	73.3	87.6	94.6	101.9	109.8	119.9	118.7	127.1
St. Vincent-Grenadines St. Vincent-Grenadines	49.3	57.0	62.7	70.3	73.4	86.8	86.8	86.2	85.6	101.4
Samoa Samoa	71.9	91.0	113.4	117.8	140.4	156.7	168.1	162.8	148.3	154.3
Sao Tome and Principe Sao Tomé-et-Principe	113.3	132.9	149.8	168.5	181.3	200.4	231.3	223.0	223.3	233.4
Senegal Sénégal	2660.6	2940.1	2879.6	2992.3	3046.5	3048.5	3190.5	3115.7	3092.9	3273.7
Seychelles Seychelles	109.4	117.2	125.5	130.5	132.1	147.8	145.8	138.1	131.3	145.1
Sierra Leone Sierra Leone	553.6	603.9	616.3	677.1	763.8	848.9	905.8	903.0	888.5	944.2
Slovakia Slovaquie	1232.9	1505.2	1764.0	1709.7	2120.3	2862.9	3528.1	3995.4	4617.7	4452.2
Solomon Islands Iles Salomon	98.5	103.2	98.4	92.5	94.3	98.4	99.0	98.0	92.0	108.3
Somalia Somalie	1813.4	1925.9	1945.2	1897.8	1897.0	1934.8	1960.8	1918.2	1852.5	1886.4
South Africa Afrique du Sud	...	...	...	...	...	7789.0	9836.7	10347.5	11465.5	10626.6
Sri Lanka Sri Lanka	4282.7	4946.8	5670.7	5642.8	5981.5	6649.8	7011.1	6818.0	6700.2	7648.7
Sudan Soudan	8468.9	9155.2	9220.1	8983.6	8993.8	9399.9	9779.4	9369.2	8998.2	9225.9
Swaziland Swaziland	248.0	249.2	240.5	215.7	200.0	210.2	223.0	219.6	210.1	222.5
Syrian Arab Republic Rép. arabe syrienne	15693.4	14917.0	16353.2	15913.1	16235.0	16540.2	16756.8	16697.7	16253.8	16328.3
Tajikistan Tadjikistan	...	...	...	9.7	384.9	562.0	590.4	656.8	669.0	706.9
Thailand Thaïlande	12512.5	12530.9	13309.4	13363.0	14775.9	16265.8	16880.5	16929.0	22323.9	28113.2
TFYR Macedonia L'ex-R.y. Macédoine	...	...	...	...	703.9	708.9	1076.5	1178.9	1573.3	1944.2
Togo Togo	937.2	1074.8	1130.0	1121.9	1112.1	1217.7	1274.2	1294.4	1195.4	1301.8
Tonga Tonga	38.1	44.5	44.2	42.6	43.7	63.4	68.7	68.3	60.2	64.1
Trinidad and Tobago Trinité-et-Tobago	1806.0	1781.6	1749.8	1787.7	1807.4	1961.5	1941.2	1869.8	1528.5	1475.8
Tunisia Tunisie	6102.9	6662.2	7109.3	7200.5	7415.3	8002.4	9117.8	9462.8	9426.2	9727.4

77
Total external and public/publicly guaranteed long-term debt of developing countries
Million US dollars [*cont.*]
Total de la dette extérieure et dette publique extérieure à long terme garantie par l'Etat des pays en développement
Millions de dollars E.-U. [*suite*]

B. Public and publicly guaranteed long-term debt · Dette publique extérieure à long terme garantie par l'Etat

Country or area Pays ou zone	1989	1990	1991	1992	1993	1994	1995	1996	1997	1998
Turkey Turquie	34989.9	38870.3	39828.8	40462.7	44066.7	48442.8	50326.0	48215.8	47589.5	49931.6
Turkmenistan Turkménistan	...	...	...	...	276.4	346.3	384.9	464.2	1242.4	1731.2
Uganda Ouganda	1846.6	2160.9	2283.3	2433.2	2599.2	2869.1	3062.4	3151.0	3359.4	3401.9
Ukraine Ukraine	...	...	...	453.6	3682.1	4770.3	6541.2	6608.2	6977.7	8606.0
United Rep.Tanzania Rép.–Unie de Tanzanie	5266.8	5769.4	5790.5	5849.8	5807.7	6128.1	6203.6	6081.7	6015.3	6403.7
Uruguay Uruguay	3007.9	3045.1	2899.8	3142.7	3371.5	3752.4	3835.7	4099.4	4588.2	5141.9
Uzbekistan Ouzbékistan	...	...	...	59.7	939.5	952.8	1417.6	1977.0	2032.1	2485.0
Vanuatu Vanuatu	20.8	30.6	38.1	39.6	39.4	41.5	43.2	42.1	38.9	54.2
Venezuela Venezuela	25166.2	24508.6	24938.6	25829.5	26855.3	28041.9	28500.7	28468.6	26696.8	26691.8
Viet Nam Viet Nam	19185.4	21378.1	21360.5	21648.5	21599.0	21854.5	21777.3	21964.3	18838.8	19774.8
Yemen Yémen	4643.3	5153.9	5255.5	5253.4	5341.1	5459.5	5527.8	5621.8	3418.2	3589.9
Yugoslavia Yougoslavie	14109.5	12986.4	11640.5	11116.9	8231.4	8510.9	8724.8	8479.8	8164.9	8320.9
Zambia Zambie	4114.4	4552.0	4705.8	4513.5	4397.4	5174.2	5284.9	5362.8	5244.8	5319.8
Zimbabwe Zimbabwe	2275.5	2464.3	2612.6	2852.6	3111.0	3420.8	3525.4	3327.8	3108.6	3341.1

Source:
World Bank, Washington, D.C., "Global Development Finance (formerly "World Debt Tables") 1999", volumes 1 and 2.

Source:
Banque mondiale, Washington, D.C., "Global Development Finance (anciennement "World Debt Tables") 1999", volumes 1 et 2.

†† For statistical purposes, the data for China do not include those for the Hong Kong Special Administrative Region (Hong Kong SAR) and Taiwan province of China.

†† Les données statistiques relatives à la Chine ne comprennent pas celles qui concernent la région administrative spéciale de Hong Kong (la RAS de Hong Kong) et la province chinoise de Taiwan.

1 The following abbreviations have been used in the table:
   LDOD: Long-term debt outstanding and disbursed
   IBRD: International Bank for Reconstruction and Development
   IDA: International Development Association
   LINT: Loan Interest
   LTDS: Long-term debt service

1 Les abbréviations ci-après ont été utilisées dans le tableau:
   LDOD: Dette à long terme
   BIRD: Banque internationale pour la réconstruction et le développement
   IDA: Association internationale de développement
   LINT: Paiement de intérêts
   LTDS: Service de la dette à long terme

Technical notes, tables 76 and 77

Table 76: Foreign exchange rates are shown in units of national currency per US dollar. The exchange rates are classified into three broad categories, reflecting both the role of the authorities in the determination of the exchange and/or the multiplicity of exchange rates in a country. The *market rate* is used to describe exchange rates determined largely by market forces; the *official rate* is an exchange rate determined by the authorities, sometimes in a flexible manner. For countries maintaining multiple exchange arrangements, the rates are labeled *principal rate*, *secondary rate*, and *tertiary rate*. Unless otherwise stated, the table refers to end of period and period averages of market exchange rates or official exchange rates. For further information see *International Financial Statistics* [14].

Table 77: Data were extracted from *Global Development Finance 1999* [31], published by the World Bank.

Long term external debt is defined as debt that has an original or extended maturity of more than one year and is owed to non-residents and repayable in foreign currency, goods, or services. A distinction is made between:

— Public debt which is an external obligation of a public debtor, which could be a national government, a political sub-division, an agency of either of the above or, in fact, any autonomous public body;

— Publicly guaranteed debt, which is an external obligation of a private debtor that is guaranteed for repayment by a public entity;

— Private non-guaranteed external debt, which is an external obligation of a private debtor that is not guaranteed for repayment by a public entity.

The data referring to public and publicly guaranteed debt do not include data for (a) transactions with the International Monetary Fund, (b) debt repayable in local currency, (c) direct investment and (d) short-term debt (that is, debt with an original maturity of less than a year).

The data referring to private non-guaranteed debt also exclude the above items but include contractual obligations on loans to direct-investment enterprises by foreign parent companies or their affiliates.

Data are aggregated by type of creditor. The breakdown is as follows:

Official creditors:

(a) Loans from international organizations (multilateral loans), excluding loans from funds administered by an international organization on behalf of a single donor government. The latter are classified as loans from governments;

(b) Loans from governments (bilateral loans) and

Notes techniques, tableaux 76 et 77

Tableau 76: Les taux des changes sont exprimés par nombre d'unités de monnaie nationale pour un dollar des Etats-Unis. Les taux de change sont classés en trois catégories, qui dénotent le rôle des autorités dans l'établissement des taux de change et/ou la multiplicité des taux de change dans un pays. Par *taux du marché*, on entend les taux de change déterminés essentiellement par les forces du marché; le *taux officiel* est un taux de change établi par les autorités, parfois selon des dispositions souples. Pour les pays qui continuent de mettre en œuvre des régimes de taux de change multiples, les taux sont désignés par les appellations suivantes: "taux principal", "taux secondaire" et "taux tertiaire". Sauf indication contraire, le tableau indique des taux de fin de période et les moyennes sur la période, des taux de change du marché ou des taux de change officiels. Pour plus de renseignements, voir *Statistiques financières internationales* [14].

Tableau 77: Les données sont extraites de *Global Development Finance 1999* [31] publié par la Banque mondiale.

La dette extérieure à long terme désigne la dette dont l'échéance initiale ou reportée est de plus d'un an, due à des non résidents et remboursable en devises, biens ou services. On établit les distinctions suivantes:

— La dette publique, qui est une obligation extérieure d'un débiteur public, pouvant être un gouvernement, un organe politique, une institution de l'un ou l'autre ou, en fait, tout organisme public autonome.

— La dette garantie par l'Etat, qui est une obligation extérieure d'un débiteur privé, dont le remboursement est garanti par un organisme public.

— La dette extérieure privée non garantie, qui est une obligation extérieure d'un débiteur privé, dont le remboursement n'est pas garanti par un organisme public.

Les statistiques relatives à la dette publique ou à la dette garantie par l'Etat ne comprennent pas les données concernant: (a) les transactions avec le Fonds monétaire international; (b) la dette remboursable en monnaie nationale; (c) les investissements directs; et (d) la dette à court terme (c'est-à-dire la dette dont l'échéance initiale est inférieure à un an).

Les statistiques relatives à la dette privée non garantie ne comprennent pas non plus les éléments précités, mais comprennent les obligations contractuelles au titre des prêts consentis par des sociétés mères étrangères ou leurs filiales à des entreprises créées dans le cadre d'investissements directs.

Les données sont groupées par type de créancier, comme suit:

Créanciers publics:

(a) Les prêts obtenus auprès d'organisations internationales (prêts multilatéraux), à l'exclusion des prêts au

from autonomous public bodies;

Private creditors:

(a) Suppliers: Credits from manufacturers, exporters, or other suppliers of goods;

(b) Financial markets: Loans from private banks and other private financial institutions as well as publicly issued and privately placed bonds;

(c) Other: External liabilities on account of nationalized properties and unclassified debts to private creditors.

A distinction is made between the following categories of external public debt:

— Debt outstanding (including undisbursed) is the sum of disbursed and undisbursed debt and represents the total outstanding external obligations of the borrower at year-end;

— Debt outstanding (disbursed only) is total outstanding debt drawn by the borrower at year end;

— Commitments are the total of loans for which contracts are signed in the year specified;

— Disbursements are drawings on outstanding loan commitments during the year specified;

— Service payments are actual repayments of principal amortization and interest payments made in foreign currencies, goods or services in the year specified;

— Net flows (or net lending) are disbursements minus principal repayments;

— Net transfers are net flows minus interest payments or disbursements minus total debt-service payments.

The countries included in the table are those for which data are sufficiently reliable to provide a meaningful presentation of debt outstanding and future service payments.

titre de fonds administrés par une organisation internationale pour le compte d'un gouvernement donateur précis, qui sont classés comme prêts consentis par des gouvernements;

(b) Les prêts consentis par des gouvernements (prêts bilatéraux) et par des organisations publiques autonomes.

Créanciers privés:

(a) Fournisseurs: Crédits consentis par des fabricants exportateurs et autre fournisseurs de biens;

(b) Marchés financiers: prêts consentis par des banques privées et autres institutions financières privées, et émissions publiques d'obligations placées auprès d'investisseurs privés;

(c) Autres créanciers: engagements vis-à-vis de l'extérieur au titre des biens nationalisés et dettes diverses à l'égard de créanciers privés.

On fait une distinction entre les catégories suivantes de dette publique extérieure:

— L'encours de la dette (y compris les fonds non décaissés) est la somme des fonds décaissés et non décaissés et représente le total des obligations extérieures en cours de l'emprunteur à la fin de l'année;

— L'encours de la dette (fonds décaissés seulement) est le montant total des tirages effectués par l'emprunteur sur sa dette en cours à la fin de l'année;

— Les engagements représentent le total des prêts dont les contrats ont été signés au cours de l'année considérée;

— Les décaissements sont les sommes tirées sur l'encours des prêts pendant l'année considérée;

— Les paiements au titre du service de la dette sont les remboursements effectifs du principal et les paiements d'intérêts effectués en devises, biens ou services pendant l'année considérée;

— Les flux nets (ou prêts nets) sont les décaissements moins les remboursements de principal;

— Les transferts nets désignent les flux nets moins les paiements d'intérêts, ou les décaissements moins le total des paiements au titre du service de la dette.

Les pays figurant sur ce tableau sont ceux pour lesquels les données sont suffisamment fiables pour permettre une présentation significative de l'encours de la dette et des paiements futurs au titre du service de la dette.

78
Disbursements of bilateral and multilateral official development assistance and official aid to individual recipients
Versements d'aide publique au développement et d'aide publique bilatérales et multilatérales aux bénéficiares

Region, country or area Région, pays ou zone	Year Année	Net disbursements (US $) – Versements nets ($ E.−U.)			
		Bilateral Bilatérale (millions)	Multilateral[1] Multilatérale[1] (millions)	Total (millions)	Per capita[2] Par habitant[2]
Total Total	**1996** 1997 **1998**	**43128.1** 36429.8 **39632.1**	**18254.2** 16870.8 **17085.9**	**61382.3** 53300.5 **56718.0**	... ...
Africa Afrique	**1996** 1997 1998	**12828.1** 11381.2 11213.4	**7048.1** 6366.0 5846.4	**19876.2** 17747.2 17059.8	... ...
Algeria Algérie	1996 1997 1998	263.0 192.5 121.7	34.9 44.1 252.7	297.9 236.6 374.4	10.4 8.0 12.4
Angola Angola	1996 1997 1998	294.4 227.0 214.5	178.7 127.7 120.7	473.1 354.6 335.2	41.7 30.3 27.7
Benin Bénin	1996 1997 1998	164.9 148.0 144.0	117.6 72.8 68.0	282.6 220.7 212.0	51.6 39.2 36.7
Botswana Botswana	1996 1997 1998	67.9 55.8 73.1	8.4 69.2 35.9	76.3 125.0 109.0	50.6 81.1 69.4
Burkina Faso Burkina Faso	1996 1997 1998	269.2 217.9 226.6	144.0 146.8 167.4	413.1 364.8 394.0	38.6 33.2 34.9
Burundi Burundi	1996 1997 1998	67.8 38.2 44.3	44.5 18.3 32.8	112.3 56.5 77.1	17.9 8.9 11.9
Cameroon Cameroun	1996 1997 1998	279.6 330.2 302.9	133.9 170.6 123.2	413.5 500.8 426.1	30.5 36.0 29.8
Cape Verde Cap−Vert	1996 1997 1998	77.5 68.0 85.2	36.4 43.3 44.7	113.9 111.2 129.9	292.8 278.8 318.3
Central African Republic Rép. centrafricaine	1996 1997 1998	121.0 61.3 56.5	44.5 29.7 63.4	165.5 91.0 119.9	49.3 26.6 34.4
Chad Tchad	1996 1997 1998	121.8 96.4 74.5	171.1 126.3 88.2	292.8 222.7 162.7	42.4 31.4 22.4
Comoros Comores	1996 1997 1998	22.0 15.3 18.6	17.4 12.0 16.6	39.4 27.2 35.2	63.2 42.5 53.5
Congo Congo	1996 1997 1998	394.6 260.0 59.4	34.9 8.7 5.2	429.4 268.7 64.6	163.0 99.2 23.2
Côte d'Ivoire Côte d'Ivoire	1996 1997 1998	449.2 232.7 489.3	515.1 212.8 309.0	964.3 445.6 798.3	69.8 31.7 55.9
Dem. Rep. of the Congo Rép. dém. du Congo	1996 1997 1998	106.3 104.5 79.7	57.0 44.4 43.5	163.4 149.0 123.2	3.5 3.1 2.5
Djibouti Djibouti	1996 1997 1998	70.8 62.2 62.3	21.2 18.7 16.9	92.0 80.8 79.2	150.8 131.0 127.2
Egypt Egypte	1996 1997 1998	1933.3 1496.3 1470.8	211.9 388.1 267.3	2145.2 1884.3 1738.1	33.8 29.1 26.3
Equatorial Guinea Guinée équatoriale	1996 1997 1998	23.3 17.8 18.3	7.5 6.5 6.5	30.8 24.3 24.8	75.1 57.8 57.5
Eritrea Erythrée	1996 1997 1998	124.8 80.9 97.7	28.7 25.7 38.1	153.5 106.6 135.8	46.5 31.0 38.0

78
Disbursements of bilateral and multilateral official development assistance
and official aid to individual recipients [*cont.*]
Versements d'aide publique au développement et d'aide publique
bilatérales et multilatérales aux bénéficiares [*suite*]

Region, country or area Région, pays ou zone	Year Année	Net disbursements (US $) — Versements nets ($ E.—U.)			
		Bilateral Bilatérale (millions)	Multilateral[1] Multilatérale[1] (millions)	Total (millions)	Per capita[2] Par habitant[2]
Ethiopia	1996	445.4	369.1	814.5	13.6
Ethiopie	1997	373.6	197.6	571.2	9.3
	1998	364.8	282.2	647.0	10.2
Gabon	1996	113.4	15.0	128.4	116.0
Gabon	1997	30.2	11.2	41.4	36.4
	1998	37.4	8.6	45.9	39.4
Gambia	1996	17.2	21.8	39.0	33.9
Gambie	1997	17.4	23.0	40.4	33.9
	1998	13.5	24.7	38.1	31.0
Ghana	1996	348.9	302.7	651.6	35.9
Ghana	1997	291.9	188.6	480.5	25.8
	1998	374.5	324.1	698.6	36.5
Guinea	1996	134.7	143.4	278.1	38.2
Guinée	1997	125.5	221.6	347.1	47.4
	1998	148.5	187.1	335.6	45.7
Guinea—Bissau	1996	124.8	51.7	176.5	158.8
Guinée—Bissau	1997	58.5	65.5	124.1	109.2
	1998	64.7	31.0	95.7	82.5
Kenya	1996	345.7	247.5	593.2	21.3
Kenya	1997	301.0	144.8	445.8	15.7
	1998	275.3	200.8	476.1	16.4
Lesotho	1996	49.3	51.2	100.5	51.0
Lesotho	1997	44.6	39.9	84.5	41.9
	1998	32.5	34.9	67.4	32.7
Liberia	1996	112.4	58.3	170.7	77.7
Libéria	1997	31.0	43.8	74.7	31.1
	1998	31.3	41.3	72.6	27.2
Libyan Arab Jamahiriya	1996	2.1	6.0	8.1	1.6
Jamah. arabe libyenne	1997	1.8	5.2	7.0	1.3
	1998	3.6	3.4	7.1	1.3
Madagascar	1996	229.8	126.9	356.7	25.1
Madagascar	1997	549.0	284.4	833.4	57.0
	1998	333.1	161.0	494.2	32.8
Malawi	1996	263.9	228.0	491.8	50.0
Malawi	1997	174.1	170.7	344.8	34.2
	1998	203.5	230.1	433.5	41.9
Mali	1996	297.5	201.4	499.0	49.0
Mali	1997	256.6	177.5	434.1	41.6
	1998	236.2	115.9	352.1	32.9
Mauritania	1996	98.8	184.9	283.7	118.5
Mauritanie	1997	96.5	154.2	250.7	101.9
	1998	63.5	115.1	178.6	70.6
Mauritius	1996	−1.1	22.3	21.2	19.0
Maurice	1997	2.7	28.8	31.5	28.1
	1998	19.6	21.1	40.8	36.0
Mayotte	1996	123.9	5.8	129.7	...
Mayotte	1997	102.3	1.9	104.3	...
	1998	104.4	...	104.4	...
Morocco	1996	391.4	232.7	624.1	23.6
Maroc	1997	215.2	217.0	432.2	16.1
	1998	250.4	249.1	499.4	18.2
Mozambique	1996	551.9	333.4	885.3	49.3
Mozambique	1997	621.6	326.7	948.3	51.4
	1998	712.6	329.2	1041.8	55.2
Namibia	1996	136.4	51.4	187.9	118.7
Namibie	1997	122.9	41.6	164.5	101.4
	1998	128.7	51.5	180.1	108.5
Niger	1996	163.2	90.8	254.0	26.9
Niger	1997	181.2	141.2	322.4	33.0
	1998	144.6	145.9	290.4	28.8
Nigeria	1996	47.3	143.5	190.8	1.9
Nigéria	1997	52.2	148.6	200.7	1.9
	1998	34.2	169.8	204.0	1.9

78
Disbursements of bilateral and multilateral official development assistance
and official aid to individual recipients [*cont.*]
Versements d'aide publique au développement et d'aide publique
bilatérales et multilatérales aux bénéficiares [*suite*]

Region, country or area Région, pays ou zone	Year Année	Net disbursements (US $) — Versements nets ($ E.—U.)			
		Bilateral Bilatérale (millions)	Multilateral[1] Multilatérale[1] (millions)	Total (millions)	Per capita[2] Par habitant[2]
Rwanda Rwanda	1996	252.0	213.3	465.3	85.0
	1997	178.7	50.4	229.1	38.4
	1998	209.0	140.9	349.9	53.0
Saint Helena Sainte—Hélène	1996	15.4	0.5	15.9	2646.7
	1997	14.8	0.3	15.1	2511.7
	1998	14.4	1.4	15.8	2625.0
Sao Tome & Principe Sao Tomé—et—Principe	1996	28.9	18.6	47.4	351.4
	1997	21.2	12.2	33.4	241.7
	1998	18.1	10.1	28.3	200.6
Senegal Sénégal	1996	392.0	176.8	568.8	66.5
	1997	292.0	121.6	413.7	47.2
	1998	289.0	211.0	500.0	55.5
Seychelles Seychelles	1996	7.8	8.2	16.0	215.7
	1997	6.3	5.8	12.1	160.9
	1998	17.2	5.8	23.0	302.2
Sierra Leone Sierra Leone	1996	67.0	112.8	179.8	41.9
	1997	41.4	76.2	117.6	26.6
	1998	53.2	50.6	103.7	22.7
Somalia Somalie	1996	39.6	48.5	88.1	10.4
	1997	46.0	33.9	79.9	9.1
	1998	41.7	38.3	80.0	8.7
South Africa Afrique du Sud	1996	311.9	46.2	358.1	9.4
	1997	415.0	80.0	495.0	12.8
	1998	420.7	91.6	512.2	13.0
Sudan Soudan	1996	118.1	100.8	218.9	8.1
	1997	85.7	52.4	138.1	5.0
	1998	150.2	58.5	208.7	7.4
Swaziland Swaziland	1996	20.6	9.8	30.4	33.9
	1997	16.3	10.3	26.6	28.8
	1998	16.8	13.6	30.4	31.9
Togo Togo	1996	97.2	61.8	159.0	38.1
	1997	75.7	50.6	126.3	29.5
	1998	66.1	61.2	127.3	29.0
Tunisia Tunisie	1996	41.5	120.6	162.1	17.8
	1997	69.3	144.1	213.4	23.2
	1998	102.0	76.4	178.4	19.1
Uganda Ouganda	1996	369.9	297.5	667.3	34.3
	1997	438.8	371.2	810.0	40.5
	1998	383.9	87.3	471.2	22.9
United Republic of Tanzania Rép.—Unie de Tanzanie	1996	605.4	274.1	879.5	28.6
	1997	569.1	372.9	942.0	30.0
	1998	769.0	228.3	997.3	31.1
Zambia Zambie	1996	354.1	255.4	609.5	72.7
	1997	367.1	242.9	609.9	71.0
	1998	256.5	93.2	349.7	39.8
Zimbabwe Zimbabwe	1996	280.8	93.3	374.1	33.9
	1997	222.5	115.6	338.1	30.1
	1998	216.3	64.5	280.8	24.7
Other and unallocated Autres et non—ventilés	1996	977.9	514.5	1492.4	...
	1997	1166.6	426.3	1592.8	...
	1998	973.1	187.4	1160.5	...
Americas **Amériques**	**1996**	**5758.8**	**1734.1**	**7492.9**	...
	1997	**3916.9**	**1505.7**	**5422.6**	...
	1998	**3999.0**	**1587.3**	**5586.3**	...
Anguilla Anguilla	1996	2.3	0.2	2.6	320.0
	1997	1.8	0.8	2.6	321.3
	1998	3.2	−0.2	3.1	381.3
Antigua and Barbuda Antigua—et—Barbuda	1996	1.1	8.9	10.0	151.2
	1997	1.0	−0.4	0.6	9.2
	1998	5.0	2.1	7.1	106.1
Argentina Argentine	1996	85.0	39.6	124.6	3.5
	1997	56.9	25.8	82.7	2.3
	1998	28.9	46.4	75.3	2.1

78
Disbursements of bilateral and multilateral official development assistance
and official aid to individual recipients [*cont.*]
Versements d'aide publique au développement et d'aide publique
bilatérales et multilatérales aux bénéficiares [*suite*]

Region, country or area Région, pays ou zone	Year Année	Bilateral Bilatérale (millions)	Multilateral[1] Multilatérale[1] (millions)	Total (millions)	Per capita[2] Par habitant[2]
Aruba Aruba	1996	20.3	−0.8	19.5	227.1
	1997	23.7	1.3	25.1	278.6
	1998	10.7	0.6	11.3	119.8
Bahamas Bahamas	1996	1.3	−1.3	0.0	0.0
	1997	1.1	2.3	3.4	11.7
	1998	0.2	22.4	22.6	76.4
Barbados Barbade	1996	−0.2	4.7	4.5	16.9
	1997	0.1	4.2	4.3	16.1
	1998	0.5	15.2	15.6	58.4
Belize Belize	1996	12.0	3.6	15.7	71.5
	1997	2.4	7.2	9.6	43.0
	1998	2.6	8.8	11.4	49.7
Bermuda Bermudes	1996	−4.1	...	−4.1	−64.6
	1997	−8.2	...	−8.2	−130.2
	1998	0.6	...	0.6	9.4
Bolivia Bolivie	1996	590.9	240.4	831.3	109.5
	1997	453.5	244.9	698.4	89.8
	1998	416.2	211.8	628.1	78.9
Brazil Brésil	1996	190.8	98.9	289.8	1.8
	1997	192.9	81.6	274.6	1.7
	1998	218.9	110.2	329.1	2.0
British Virgin Islands Iles Vierges britanniques	1996	1.1	0.2	1.2	63.7
	1997	1.5	0.3	1.9	93.5
	1998	1.5	−0.3	1.2	58.5
Cayman Islands Iles Caïmanes	1996	−2.1	0.0	−2.0	−61.2
	1997	−2.9	−0.9	−3.8	−111.8
	1998	−1.5	1.7	0.2	5.6
Chile Chili	1996	182.7	13.6	196.3	13.6
	1997	113.1	14.2	127.3	8.7
	1998	95.0	9.5	104.5	7.0
Colombia Colombie	1996	159.8	28.6	188.4	4.8
	1997	171.2	23.3	194.5	4.9
	1998	158.9	6.7	165.6	4.1
Costa Rica Costa Rica	1996	−12.5	0.9	−11.7	−3.2
	1997	−2.1	−4.4	−6.5	−1.7
	1998	20.4	6.9	27.3	7.1
Cuba Cuba	1996	26.9	30.3	57.2	5.2
	1997	31.9	33.0	65.0	5.9
	1998	56.7	23.0	79.6	7.2
Dominica Dominique	1996	25.2	17.3	42.4	597.7
	1997	13.3	0.5	13.8	194.2
	1998	5.7	13.7	19.5	274.1
Dominican Republic Rép. dominicaine	1996	57.3	41.1	98.4	12.37
	1997	31.5	39.5	71.0	8.8
	1998	60.4	60.0	120.4	14.6
Ecuador Equateur	1996	207.1	38.3	245.4	21.0
	1997	139.8	9.5	149.3	12.5
	1998	155.1	21.0	176.1	14.5
El Salvador El Salvador	1996	229.3	67.1	296.4	51.2
	1997	234.0	38.5	272.5	46.1
	1998	154.4	25.4	179.8	29.8
Falkland Islands Iles Falkland	1996	−0.0	2.5	2.5	1235.0
	1997	0.0	−0.2	−0.2	−100.0
	1998	0.0	−0.2	−0.2	−100.0
Grenada Grenade	1996	5.8	1.2	7.0	76.0
	1997	3.8	2.5	6.2	67.0
	1998	3.4	2.6	6.0	64.1
Guatemala Guatemala	1996	141.2	50.9	192.0	18.7
	1997	212.7	50.4	263.0	25.0
	1998	181.6	50.9	232.6	21.5
Guyana Guyana	1996	41.1	100.7	141.8	169.4
	1997	206.0	58.4	264.4	313.7
	1998	51.8	41.2	93.0	109.4

78
Disbursements of bilateral and multilateral official development assistance
and official aid to individual recipients [*cont.*]
Versements d'aide publique au développement et d'aide publique
bilatérales et multilatérales aux bénéficiares [*suite*]

Region, country or area Région, pays ou zone	Year Année	Net disbursements (US $) — Versements nets ($ E.—U.)			
		Bilateral Bilatérale (millions)	Multilateral [1] Multilatérale [1] (millions)	Total (millions)	Per capita [2] Par habitant [2]
Haiti Haïti	1996	150.1	218.8	368.8	48.0
	1997	175.8	148.8	324.6	41.5
	1998	250.9	156.2	407.0	51.2
Honduras Honduras	1996	155.2	191.0	346.2	59.5
	1997	155.0	131.4	286.4	47.9
	1998	190.6	125.0	315.6	51.3
Jamaica Jamaïque	1996	4.0	54.3	58.3	23.4
	1997	−5.0	76.4	71.4	28.4
	1998	3.5	15.1	18.6	7.3
Mexico Mexique	1996	274.3	12.4	286.7	3.1
	1997	88.7	10.3	99.1	1.1
	1998	3.8	10.9	14.8	0.2
Montserrat Montserrat	1996	14.4	0.1	14.4	1310.9
	1997	42.8	0.0	42.8	3886.4
	1998	65.1	0.5	65.6	5968.2
Netherlands Antilles Antilles néerlandaises	1996	116.7	4.1	120.7	580.4
	1997	108.9	1.7	110.6	524.2
	1998	125.7	3.4	129.1	606.0
Nicaragua Nicaragua	1996	764.0	167.3	931.3	204.6
	1997	261.6	148.5	410.1	87.6
	1998	313.3	248.9	562.2	116.9
Panama Panama	1996	47.9	0.1	48.0	17.9
	1997	43.0	−1.4	41.6	15.3
	1998	22.4	−0.6	21.7	7.9
Paraguay Paraguay	1996	62.6	21.7	84.3	17.0
	1997	70.1	32.5	102.6	20.2
	1998	55.7	20.3	76.0	14.6
Peru Pérou	1996	277.7	51.0	328.7	13.7
	1997	364.2	29.2	393.5	16.1
	1998	381.5	119.9	501.5	20.2
Saint Kitts and Nevis Saint−Kitts−et−Nevis	1996	2.6	0.3	2.9	73.0
	1997	0.7	5.2	5.9	151.5
	1998	1.3	2.6	3.9	100.8
Saint Lucia Sainte−Lucie	1996	10.9	24.6	35.4	242.7
	1997	9.9	13.7	23.6	159.5
	1998	0.4	4.8	5.2	34.7
St. Vincent & Grenadines St. Vincent−et−Grenadines	1996	4.7	17.7	22.3	201.2
	1997	5.4	−0.4	5.0	44.4
	1998	3.3	16.4	19.8	176.3
Suriname Suriname	1996	102.3	6.8	109.1	266.1
	1997	69.7	6.6	76.3	185.1
	1998	52.2	6.6	58.8	142.1
Trinidad and Tobago Trinité−et−Tobago	1996	−1.2	17.9	16.7	13.2
	1997	−0.5	33.5	33.0	25.8
	1998	−2.3	16.0	13.7	10.7
Turks & Caicos Islands Iles Turques et Caiques	1996	3.9	0.3	4.2	278.7
	1997	4.1	0.1	4.2	280.0
	1998	4.9	1.2	6.0	376.3
Uruguay Uruguay	1996	29.4	5.5	34.8	10.7
	1997	29.5	4.1	33.6	10.3
	1998	19.4	4.7	24.1	7.3
Venezuela Venezuela	1996	26.0	12.1	38.1	1.7
	1997	−1.8	10.4	8.6	0.4
	1998	21.4	15.2	36.6	1.6
Other and unallocated Autres et non−ventilés	1996	1751.1	141.4	1892.5	...
	1997	615.7	222.9	838.6	...
	1998	855.8	140.7	996.5	...
Asia **Asie**	**1996**	**12001.9**	**6303.3**	**18305.2**	...
	1997	**9358.6**	**5721.4**	**15080.0**	...
	1998	**11499.7**	**5307.6**	**16807.3**	...
Afghanistan Afghanistan	1996	84.3	98.7	183.0	9.0
	1997	123.3	106.5	229.8	11.0
	1998	88.2	65.7	153.9	7.2

78
Disbursements of bilateral and multilateral official development assistance
and official aid to individual recipients [cont.]
Versements d'aide publique au développement et d'aide publique
bilatérales et multilatérales aux bénéficiaires [suite]

Region, country or area Région, pays ou zone	Year Année	Net disbursements (US $) – Versements nets ($ E.–U.)			
		Bilateral Bilatérale (millions)	Multilateral [1] Multilatérale [1] (millions)	Total (millions)	Per capita [2] Par habitant [2]
Armenia	1996	115.3	175.0	290.2	81.4
Arménie	1997	46.4	118.5	164.9	46.4
	1998	62.9	75.6	138.5	39.3
Azerbaijan	1996	25.3	70.9	96.3	12.7
Azerbaïdjan	1997	15.4	160.9	176.3	23.1
	1998	35.6	52.8	88.4	11.5
Bahrain	1996	1.7	0.9	2.6	4.5
Bahreïn	1997	1.6	0.4	2.0	3.4
	1998	1.1	0.7	1.8	2.9
Bangladesh	1996	644.5	591.9	1236.4	10.3
Bangladesh	1997	560.0	452.3	1012.3	8.3
	1998	623.8	630.1	1253.9	10.0
Bhutan	1996	42.1	15.8	57.9	30.6
Bhoutan	1997	45.0	21.2	66.2	34.1
	1998	41.0	16.0	57.0	28.4
Brunei Darussalam	1996	3.0	0.1	3.1	10.3
Brunéi Darussalam	1997	0.3	0.0	0.3	1.0
	1998	0.3	0.0	0.3	1.0
Cambodia	1996	252.5	169.0	421.5	41.2
Cambodge	1997	228.4	105.1	333.4	31.8
	1998	230.6	106.5	337.1	31.5
China ††	1996	1670.9	916.0	2586.8	2.1
Chine ††	1997	1238.2	803.7	2041.9	1.7
	1998	1731.5	639.5	2371.0	1.9
China, Hong Kong SAR †	1996	10.1	3.1	13.2	2.1
Chine, Hong Kong RAS †	1997	3.8	4.7	8.5	1.3
	1998	6.7	0.1	6.8	1.0
China, Macao SAR†	1996	0.2	0.2	0.4	0.9
Chine, Macao RAS †	1997	0.2	0.2	0.4	0.9
	1998	0.1	0.4	0.5	1.2
East Timor	1996	0.1	...	0.1	0.1
Timor oriental	1997	0.4	...	0.4	0.5
	1998	1.7	...	1.7	1.9
Georgia	1996	112.2	197.5	309.7	59.7
Géorgie	1997	69.7	167.6	237.2	46.3
	1998	74.6	87.8	162.4	32.1
India	1996	1025.0	883.6	1908.6	2.0
Inde	1997	928.4	730.6	1659.0	1.7
	1998	915.0	700.2	1615.2	1.6
Indonesia	1996	1061.9	68.8	1130.7	5.6
Indonésie	1997	790.5	45.2	835.7	4.1
	1998	1243.3	13.3	1256.6	6.1
Iran (Islamic Rep. of)	1996	141.3	27.9	169.3	2.7
Iran (Rép. islamique d')	1997	165.2	33.0	198.2	3.1
	1998	142.1	21.8	163.9	2.5
Iraq	1996	284.2	63.6	347.7	16.9
Iraq	1997	180.0	39.9	219.9	10.4
	1998	74.6	40.9	115.4	5.3
Israel	1996	2216.6	0.1	2216.7	387.4
Israël	1997	1185.9	10.3	1196.2	204.1
	1998	1055.3	10.6	1065.9	178.1
Jordan	1996	324.3	180.6	504.9	85.0
Jordanie	1997	288.1	172.3	460.5	75.2
	1998	276.7	131.5	408.2	64.8
Kazakhstan	1996	93.5	30.1	123.5	7.5
Kazakhstan	1997	93.7	35.6	129.4	7.9
	1998	176.5	30.7	207.1	12.7
Korea, Dem. P. R.	1996	9.1	16.8	25.9	1.1
Corée, R. p. dém. de	1997	35.1	53.1	88.3	3.8
	1998	23.5	83.4	106.8	4.6
Korea, Republic of	1996	−149.2	2.3	−146.9	−3.2
Corée, République de	1997	−158.3	−1.1	−159.4	−3.5
	1998	−49.1	−1.3	−50.4	−1.1

78
Disbursements of bilateral and multilateral official development assistance
and official aid to individual recipients [cont.]
Versements d'aide publique au développement et d'aide publique
bilatérales et multilatérales aux bénéficiares [suite]

Region, country or area Région, pays ou zone	Year Année	Net disbursements (US $) – Versements nets ($ E.–U.)			
		Bilateral Bilatérale (millions)	Multilateral[1] Multilatérale[1] (millions)	Total (millions)	Per capita[2] Par habitant[2]
Kuwait Koweït	1996	1.4	1.2	2.6	1.5
	1997	0.5	−0.1	0.4	0.2
	1998	4.9	1.0	5.9	3.3
Kyrgyzstan Kirghizistan	1996	99.4	130.9	230.3	50.1
	1997	50.4	187.6	238.0	51.5
	1998	79.8	135.9	215.7	46.5
Lao People's Dem. Rep. Rép. dém. pop. lao	1996	147.5	184.6	332.1	67.7
	1997	164.8	163.1	327.9	65.2
	1998	165.7	115.7	281.4	54.5
Lebanon Liban	1996	87.1	61.4	148.5	48.2
	1997	69.2	77.5	146.8	46.7
	1998	73.2	125.3	198.5	62.2
Malaysia Malaisie	1996	−455.2	4.8	−450.5	−21.9
	1997	−243.7	4.5	−239.2	−11.4
	1998	198.1	4.0	202.1	9.4
Maldives Maldives	1996	16.5	13.7	30.1	117.6
	1997	16.9	11.1	28.0	106.3
	1998	16.6	9.1	25.7	95.0
Mongolia Mongolie	1996	136.2	63.6	199.8	80.1
	1997	118.1	127.0	245.1	96.6
	1998	141.4	60.2	201.6	78.2
Myanmar Myanmar	1996	45.3	−3.3	42.1	1.0
	1997	23.6	10.0	33.5	0.8
	1998	27.4	31.3	58.7	1.3
Nepal Népal	1996	236.2	155.4	391.6	18.0
	1997	233.4	167.0	400.5	17.9
	1998	212.7	189.3	402.0	17.6
Occupied Palestinian Terr. Territoire palestinien occupé	1996	262.3	257.8	520.1	...
	1997	320.6	248.1	568.7	...
	1998	332.0	243.8	575.8	...
Oman Oman	1996	15.7	1.5	17.2	7.7
	1997	20.3	2.5	22.8	9.9
	1998	19.8	2.7	22.5	9.5
Pakistan Pakistan	1996	338.6	609.4	948.0	6.8
	1997	78.6	527.7	606.2	4.2
	1998	534.7	521.8	1056.5	7.1
Philippines Philippines	1996	748.2	131.7	880.0	12.6
	1997	567.3	115.0	682.2	9.6
	1998	528.0	79.6	607.5	8.3
Qatar Qatar	1996	1.6	0.6	2.2	3.9
	1997	0.6	0.3	0.9	1.6
	1998	1.1	0.2	1.3	2.2
Saudi Arabia Arabie saoudite	1996	12.6	9.9	22.5	1.2
	1997	−2.4	13.0	10.7	0.5
	1998	14.7	10.7	25.4	1.3
Singapore Singapour	1996	14.2	0.7	14.9	4.4
	1997	1.6	1.2	2.8	0.8
	1998	1.3	0.3	1.6	0.5
Sri Lanka Sri Lanka	1996	279.3	209.0	488.2	27.0
	1997	228.3	103.4	331.6	18.1
	1998	282.3	209.9	492.2	26.7
Syrian Arab Republic Rép. arabe syrienne	1996	70.2	50.3	120.5	8.3
	1997	93.0	40.9	134.0	9.0
	1998	82.9	43.8	126.8	8.3
Tajikistan Tadjikistan	1996	44.5	58.8	103.3	17.7
	1997	35.9	49.3	85.2	14.4
	1998	40.0	65.1	105.1	17.5
Thailand Thaïlande	1996	802.6	31.1	833.7	14.1
	1997	600.8	23.5	624.3	10.5
	1998	675.7	14.8	690.5	11.5
Turkmenistan Turkménistan	1996	13.6	10.0	23.7	5.7
	1997	2.2	8.3	10.4	2.5
	1998	8.2	8.4	16.6	3.8

78
Disbursements of bilateral and multilateral official development assistance
and official aid to individual recipients [*cont.*]
Versements d'aide publique au développement et d'aide publique
bilatérales et multilatérales aux bénéficiaires [*suite*]

Region, country or area Région, pays ou zone	Year Année	Net disbursements (US $) – Versements nets ($ E.–U.)			
		Bilateral Bilatérale (millions)	Multilateral[1] Multilatérale[1] (millions)	Total (millions)	Per capita[2] Par habitant[2]
United Arab Emirates	1996	6.6	0.1	6.7	3.0
Emirats arabes unis	1997	1.1	0.7	1.8	0.8
	1998	3.5	0.5	4.0	1.7
Uzbekistan	1996	64.2	22.1	86.2	3.8
Ouzbékistan	1997	110.9	17.0	127.9	5.5
	1998	123.3	19.6	143.0	6.1
Viet Nam	1996	469.5	450.3	919.8	12.2
Viet Nam	1997	585.5	401.3	986.8	12.9
	1998	712.6	451.9	1164.5	15.0
Yemen	1996	133.3	113.2	246.5	15.7
Yémen	1997	174.5	181.5	356.0	21.9
	1998	166.8	143.3	310.2	18.4
Other and unallocated	1996	415.0	221.9	636.9	...
Autres et non–ventilés	1997	259.7	180.1	439.8	...
	1998	220.5	113.2	333.7	...
Europe	**1996**	**5102.4**	**2346.1**	**7448.5**	**...**
Europe	**1997**	**3763.0**	**2258.7**	**6021.7**	**...**
	1998	**4445.0**	**3253.6**	**7698.6**	**...**
Albania	1996	114.2	105.1	219.4	69.6
Albanie	1997	100.0	49.2	149.1	47.6
	1998	77.7	162.8	240.5	76.8
Belarus	1996	61.5	15.0	76.5	7.4
Bélarus	1997	31.9	10.8	42.7	4.1
	1998	20.8	7.5	28.3	2.7
Bosnia–Herzegovina	1996	593.7	206.3	800.1	233.8
Bosnie–Herzégovine	1997	510.1	291.8	801.9	227.8
	1998	576.9	284.5	861.4	234.4
Bulgaria	1996	69.2	112.2	181.4	21.5
Bulgarie	1997	70.8	142.8	213.6	25.4
	1998	134.4	98.0	232.4	27.9
Croatia	1996	126.3	7.0	133.3	29.7
Croatie	1997	22.9	17.4	40.3	9.0
	1998	26.2	12.8	39.0	8.7
Cyprus	1996	13.4	9.4	22.9	30.3
Chypre	1997	−1.1	43.0	41.9	54.9
	1998	12.1	18.7	30.8	39.9
Czech Republic	1996	71.8	57.1	128.9	12.5
République tchèque	1997	56.6	58.3	114.9	11.2
	1998	48.8	398.3	447.1	43.5
Estonia	1996	35.6	23.7	59.3	40.5
Estonie	1997	35.1	29.7	64.8	44.8
	1998	35.9	54.1	90.0	63.0
Gibraltar	1996	−0.2	...	−0.2	−9.2
Gibraltar	1997	0.4	...	0.4	14.2
	1998	0.2	...	0.2	8.8
Hungary	1996	107.0	96.8	203.8	20.0
Hongrie	1997	85.3	78.2	163.5	16.1
	1998	79.8	129.0	208.8	20.6
Latvia	1996	42.3	30.0	72.3	28.9
Lettonie	1997	46.8	33.1	79.9	32.5
	1998	47.0	49.9	96.9	40.0
Lithuania	1996	58.7	32.1	90.8	24.4
Lituanie	1997	53.0	44.3	97.3	26.3
	1998	66.7	54.3	121.0	32.8
Malta	1996	66.1	12.2	78.2	206.9
Malte	1997	22.1	5.1	27.2	71.3
	1998	23.8	1.6	25.4	66.1
Poland	1996	879.4	286.3	1165.7	30.2
Pologne	1997	622.1	237.3	859.4	22.2
	1998	470.9	430.6	901.5	23.3
Republic of Moldova	1996	24.8	11.6	36.4	8.3
République de Moldova	1997	14.3	45.7	59.9	13.7
	1998	20.8	12.6	33.3	7.6

78
Disbursements of bilateral and multilateral official development assistance
and official aid to individual recipients [*cont.*]
Versements d'aide publique au développement et d'aide publique
bilatérales et multilatérales aux bénéficiares [*suite*]

Region, country or area Région, pays ou zone	Year Année	Net disbursements (US $) – Versements nets ($ E.−U.)			
		Bilateral Bilatérale (millions)	Multilateral[1] Multilatérale[1] (millions)	Total (millions)	Per capita[2] Par habitant[2]
Romania Roumanie	1996	100.4	122.7	223.1	9.9
	1997	76.6	134.2	210.8	9.3
	1998	175.0	181.0	356.0	15.8
Russian Federation Fédération de Russie	1996	1094.9	186.8	1281.7	8.7
	1997	549.9	183.5	733.4	5.0
	1998	870.6	146.7	1017.3	6.9
Slovakia Slovaquie	1996	40.8	57.2	98.0	18.3
	1997	30.5	39.8	70.3	13.1
	1998	38.8	115.7	154.5	28.7
Slovenia Slovenie	1996	32.1	50.1	82.2	41.2
	1997	−9.7	106.3	96.6	48.4
	1998	5.6	34.0	39.6	19.9
TFYR Macedonia L'ex−R.y. Macédoine	1996	26.2	79.6	105.8	53.6
	1997	30.2	67.9	98.1	49.4
	1998	31.8	60.2	92.0	46.0
Turkey Turquie	1996	50.6	12.9	63.5	1.0
	1997	−59.3	64.7	5.4	0.1
	1998	−80.7	86.1	5.4	0.1
Ukraine Ukraine	1996	372.6	24.9	397.5	7.8
	1997	164.2	13.8	178.0	3.5
	1998	270.9	108.1	379.0	7.5
Yugoslavia Yugoslavie	1996	69.4	0.1	69.5	6.6
	1997	77.0	19.8	96.8	9.1
	1998	93.4	12.6	105.9	10.0
Yugoslavia, SFR †[3] Yougoslavie, Rfs †[3]	1996	4.0	271.8	275.8	...
	1997	71.2	−2.5	68.7	...
	1998	53.3	52.9	106.2	...
Other and unallocated Autres et non−ventilés	1996	1047.7	535.1	1582.8	...
	1997	1162.5	544.8	1707.3	...
	1998	1344.4	741.6	2086.0	...
Oceania **Océanie**	**1996**	**1698.3**	**77.5**	**1775.8**	...
	1997	**1433.0**	**121.5**	**1554.5**	...
	1998	**1525.7**	**124.4**	**1650.1**	...
Cook Islands Iles Cook	1996	7.1	4.1	11.3	593.2
	1997	7.1	2.9	10.0	528.4
	1998	5.9	2.1	8.1	424.7
Fiji Fidji	1996	40.7	4.5	45.2	58.2
	1997	39.1	4.4	43.5	55.3
	1998	35.8	0.6	36.5	45.8
French Polynesia Polynésie française	1996	402.3	1.8	404.1	1845.1
	1997	364.9	2.5	367.4	1647.5
	1998	368.7	1.7	370.4	1691.2
Kiribati Kiribati	1996	11.4	1.4	12.8	162.0
	1997	14.2	1.5	15.7	195.6
	1998	16.2	1.1	17.3	213.2
Marshall Islands Iles Marshall	1996	69.1	3.7	72.9	1278.2
	1997	52.3	10.6	62.9	1084.5
	1998	42.1	8.2	50.3	838.3
Micronesia (Fed. States of) Micronésie (Etats fédérés de)	1996	111.9	1.0	112.8	1025.6
	1997	83.8	12.2	96.0	857.1
	1998	73.8	6.3	80.1	702.4
Nauru Nauru	1996	2.9	...	2.9	266.4
	1997	2.6	0.0	2.6	236.4
	1998	2.0	0.1	2.1	190.9
New Caledonia Nouvelle−Calédonie	1996	392.1	4.1	396.1	2000.7
	1997	336.6	2.2	338.8	1677.3
	1998	336.3	2.1	338.4	1642.7
Niue Nioué	1996	6.5	0.3	6.7	3360.0
	1997	5.2	0.2	5.3	2660.0
	1998	3.9	0.2	4.1	2040.0
Northern Mariana Islands Iles Mariannes du Nord	1996	−1.6	0.1	−1.6	−25.3
	1997	0.0	0.7	0.7	10.5
	1998	0.0	0.2	0.2	2.9

78
Disbursements of bilateral and multilateral official development assistance
and official aid to individual recipients [cont.]
Versements d'aide publique au développement et d'aide publique
bilatérales et multilatérales aux bénéficiaires [suite]

Region, country or area Région, pays ou zone	Year Année	Net disbursements (US $) – Versements nets ($ E. – U.)			
		Bilateral Bilatérale (millions)	Multilateral [1] Multilatérale [1] (millions)	Total (millions)	Per capita [2] Par habitant [2]
Palau	1996	62.3	0.1	62.4	3463.9
Palaos	1997	38.1	0.1	38.3	2126.1
	1998	89.0	0.1	89.1	4687.4
Papua New Guinea	1996	350.3	29.3	379.6	86.3
Papouasie – Nvl – Guinée	1997	291.9	54.1	346.0	76.9
	1998	311.9	49.6	361.5	78.6
Samoa	1996	30.9	1.8	32.6	192.1
Samoa	1997	26.7	0.9	27.6	160.4
	1998	29.7	6.5	36.1	207.6
Solomon Islands	1996	33.5	8.9	42.4	108.1
Iles Salomon	1997	36.2	5.6	41.7	103.3
	1998	23.6	19.2	42.8	102.8
Tokelau	1996	4.5	0.4	4.9	4880.0
Tokélaou	1997	4.2	0.2	4.4	4410.0
	1998	2.5	0.1	2.7	2660.0
Tonga	1996	26.7	5.3	32.0	329.7
Tonga	1997	22.4	5.1	27.5	280.9
	1998	17.2	8.4	25.6	261.4
Tuvalu	1996	9.2	1.2	10.3	938.2
Tuvalu	1997	9.4	0.7	10.1	915.5
	1998	4.9	0.3	5.2	470.9
Vanuatu	1996	26.6	4.4	31.0	179.4
Vanuatu	1997	23.4	3.7	27.1	153.3
	1998	26.1	14.6	40.6	223.2
Wallis and Futuna Islands	1996	0.1	1.5	1.6	111.4
Iles Wallis et Futuna	1997	0.1	0.5	0.6	39.3
	1998	46.5	0.8	47.3	3377.1
Other and unallocated	1996	111.8	3.9	115.7	...
Autres et non – ventilés	1997	74.9	13.4	88.4	...
	1998	89.7	2.2	91.9	...
Unspecified	**1996**	**5738.6**	**745.2**	**6483.8**	...
Non – specifiés	**1997**	**6577.1**	**897.4**	**7474.6**	...
	1998	**6949.2**	**966.6**	**7915.9**	...

Source:
Organisation for Economic Co – operation and Development (OECD),
Paris, "Geographical Distribution of Financial Flows to Aid Recipients,
1994 – 1998" and the OECD Development Assistance Database. Per
capita calculated by the UN Statistics Division.

Source:
Organisation de coopération et de développement économiques
(OCDE), Paris, "Répartition géographique des ressources financières
allouées aux pays bénéficiaires de l'aide, 1994 – 1998" et la base de
données de l'OCDE sur l'aide au développement. Les données par
habitant ont été calculées par la Division de statistique de l'ONU.

† For information on the recent changes in country or area
nomenclature pertaining to former Czechoslovakia,
Germany, Hong Kong Special Administrative Region (SAR)
of China, Macao Special Administrative Region (SAR) of
China, SFR of Yugoslavia and the former USSR, see Annex I
– Country or area nomenclature, regional and other groupings.

† Pour les modifications récentes de nomenclature de pays ou de
zone concernant l'Allemagne, Hong Kong, région administrative
spéciale (RAS) de Chine, Macao, région administrative spéciale
(RAS) de Chine, l'ex – Tchécoslovaquie, l'ex – URSS et l'ex – Rfs
de Yougoslavie, voir annex I – Nomenclature des pays ou des
zones, groupements régionaux et autres groupements.

†† For statistical purposes, the data for China do not include
those for Hong Kong Special Administrative Region
(Hong Kong SAR), Macao Special Administrative
Region (Macao SAR) and Taiwan province of China.

†† Les données statistiques relatives à la Chine ne comprennent
pas celles qui concernent la région administrative spéciale de
Hong Kong (la RAS de Hong Kong), la région administrative
spéciale de Macao (la RAS de Macao), et la province chinoise
de Taiwan.

1 As reported by OECD/DAC, covers agencies of the United
Nations family, the European Union, IDA and the concessional
lending facilities of regional development banks.
Excludes non – concessional flows (i.e., less than 25%
grant element).

1 Communiqué par le Comité d'aide au développement de
l'OCDE. Comprend les institutions et organismes du système
des Nations Unies, l'Union européene, l'Association
internationale de développement, et les mécanismes de prêt à des
conditions privilégiées des banques régionales de développement.
Les apports aux conditions du marché (élément de libéralité
inférieur à 25%) en sont exclus

2 Population based on estimates of mid – year population.

2 Population d'après des estimations de la population au milieu
de l'année.

3 Data refer to Yugoslavia, SFR unspecified.

3 Les données concernent Yougoslavie, Rfs non spécifié.

79
Net official development assistance from DAC countries to developing countries and multilateral organizations
Aide publique au développement nette de pays du CAD aux pays en développement et aux organisations multilatérales
Net disbursements: million US dollars and as % of GNP
Versements nets: millions de dollars E.-U. et en % de PNB

Country or area Pays ou zone	1993 Million US $ Millions $ E.-U.	As % of GNP En % de PNB	1994 Million US $ Millions $ E.-U.	As % of GNP En % de PNB	1995 Million US $ Millions $ E.-U.	As % of GNP En % de PNB	1996 Million US $ Millions $ E.-U.	As % of GNP En % de PNB	1997 Million US $ Millions $ E.-U.	As % of GNP En % de PNB	1998 Million US $ Millions $ E.-U.	As % of GNP En % de PNB
Total	56486	0.30	59152	0.29	58926	0.27	55438	0.25	48324	0.22	51888	0.23
Australia Australie	953	0.35	1091	0.34	1194	0.36	1074	0.28	1061	0.28	960	0.27
Austria Autriche	544	0.30	655	0.33	767	0.33	557	0.24	527	0.26	456	0.22
Belgium Belgique	810	0.39	727	0.32	1034	0.38	913	0.34	764	0.31	883	0.35
Canada Canada	2400	0.45	2250	0.43	2067	0.38	1795	0.32	2045	0.34	1691	0.29
Denmark Danemark	1340	1.03	1446	1.03	1623	0.96	1772	1.04	1637	0.97	1704	0.99
Finland Finlande	355	0.45	290	0.31	388	0.32	408	0.34	379	0.33	396	0.32
France France	7915	0.63	8466	0.64	8443	0.55	7451	0.48	6307	0.45	5742	0.40
Germany Allemagne	6954	0.36	6818	0.33	7524	0.31	7601	0.32	5857	0.28	5581	0.26
Ireland Irlande	81	0.20	109	0.25	153	0.29	179	0.31	187	0.31	199	0.30
Italy Italie	3043	0.31	2705	0.27	1623	0.15	2416	0.20	1266	0.11	2278	0.20
Japan Japon	11259	0.27	13239	0.29	14489	0.28	9439	0.20	9358	0.22	10640	0.28
Luxembourg Luxembourg	50	0.35	59	0.40	65	0.36	82	0.44	95	0.55	112	0.65
Netherlands Pays-Bas	2525	0.82	2517	0.76	3226	0.81	3246	0.81	2947	0.81	3042	0.80
New Zealand Nouvelle-Zélande	98	0.25	110	0.24	123	0.23	122	0.21	154	0.26	130	0.27
Norway Norvège	1014	1.01	1137	1.05	1244	0.87	1311	0.85	1306	0.86	1321	0.91
Portugal Portugal	235	0.28	303	0.34	258	0.25	218	0.21	250	0.25	259	0.24
Spain Espagne	1304	0.28	1305	0.28	1348	0.24	1251	0.22	1234	0.24	1376	0.24
Sweden Suède	1769	0.99	1819	0.96	1704	0.77	1999	0.84	1731	0.79	1573	0.72
Switzerland Suisse	793	0.33	982	0.36	1084	0.34	1026	0.34	911	0.34	898	0.32
United Kingdom Royaume-Uni	2920	0.31	3197	0.31	3202	0.29	3199	0.27	3433	0.26	3864	0.27
United States Etats-Unis	10123	0.15	9927	0.14	7367	0.10	9377	0.12	6878	0.09	8786	0.10

Source:
Organisation for Economic Co-operation and Development (OECD), Paris. "Development Co-operation, 1999 Report" and previous issues.

Source:
Organisation de Coopération et de Développement Economiques (OCDE), Paris, "Coopération pour le développement, Rapport 1999" et éditions précédentes.

80

Socio-economic development assistance through the United Nations system
Assistance en matière de développement socioéconomique fournie par le système des Nations Unies

Thousand US dollars
Milliers de dollars E.−U.

Development grant expenditures [1] • Aide au développement [1]

Country or area Pays ou zone	Year Année	UNDP PNUD Central resources Ressources centrales	Special funds Fonds gérés	UNFPA FNUAP	UNICEF	WFP PAM	Other UN system Autres organis. −ONU Regular budget Budget ordinaire	Extra−budgetary Extra−budgétaire	Total	Gov't self−supporting Auto−assistance gouverne−mentale
Total	**1997**	**1528700**	**271883**	**214403**	**672635**	**1081148**	**402638**	**603819**	**4775226**	**70450**
Total	**1998**	**1763598**	**367217**	**216603**	**645001**	**1237546**	**297358**	**738335**	**5265658**	**135329**
Regional programmes	**1997**	**41355**	**55451**	**39407**	**14516**	**0**	**132555**	**305282**	**588566**	**5850**
Totaux régionaux	**1998**	**111374**	**74223**	**41907**	**26379**	**0**	**112100**	**302307**	**668290**	**15051**
Africa	1997	0	12502	4742	1983	0	29221	33595	82043	−44
Afrique	1998	62970	14302	5405	2788	0	19788	37069	142322	747
Asia and the Pacific	1997	0	9934	3579	6005	0	23727	36415	79660	−4
Asie et le Pacifique	1998	0	8508	4205	5228	0	14893	34831	67666	89
Europe	1997	0	2493	1184	0	0	20449	32719	56845	117
Europe	1998	0	3561	0	0	0	15675	23852	43088	133
Latin America	1997	0	7008	2307	0	0	22355	18118	49788	958
Amérique latine	1998	0	5687	2320	1449	0	18567	20445	48467	850
Western Asia	1997	0	483	1514	190	0	12787	4265	19239	214
Asie occidentale	1998	0	747	3161	398	0	8520	5274	18101	50
Interregional	1997	16640	14899	26081	0	0	9736	61754	129110	725
Interrégional	1998	13168	23390	26816	16516	0	10103	87572	177564	687
Global	1997	24715	8132	0	6338	0	14280	118416	171881	3788
Global	1998	35236	18028	0	0	0	24555	93263	171082	12495
Country programmes	**1997**	**1412997**	**188296**	**170987**	**632572**	**1064192**	**248975**	**291046**	**4009065**	**64598**
Programmes, pays	**1998**	**1644189**	**259432**	**170786**	**615265**	**1222838**	**182396**	**405757**	**4500663**	**120268**
Afghanistan	1997	18495	523	10	10125	50556	4114	2008	85831	349
Afghanistan	1998	15715	1066	338	8056	18101	2348	4138	49762	−4
Albania	1997	807	5	242	2442	3534	529	2116	9675	0
Albanie	1998	2744	0	559	2039	396	391	2143	8271	0
Algeria	1997	1212	18	666	2049	976	1737	2883	9541	679
Algérie	1998	2072	47	531	610	4982	1319	1105	10666	141
Andorra	1997	0	0	0	0	0	0	0	0	0
Andorre	1998	0	0	0	0	0	60	0	60	0
Angola	1997	8182	7290	2060	14927	59695	1296	2286	95736	172
Angola	1998	7551	12424	2244	14316	38532	941	2137	78146	2
Anguilla	1997	47	2	0	0	0	0	0	49	0
Anguilla	1998	29	5	0	0	0	0	5	39	0
Antigua and Barbuda	1997	192	26	0	0	0	122	28	368	0
Antigua−et−Barbuda	1998	95	3	12	0	0	76	2	188	0
Argentina	1997	122707	2077	61	3891	0	2363	2788	133887	2261
Argentine	1998	166388	1875	51	2840	0	1711	5977	178843	5264
Aruba	1997	480	0	0	0	0	0	0	480	0
Aruba	1998	243	0	0	0	0	58	0	301	0
Azerbaijan	1997	4453	0	709	2804	3472	148	891	12477	9
Azerbaïdjan	1998	1528	3151	678	1610	3442	78	552	11038	0
Bahamas	1997	15	0	0	0	0	618	29	662	23
Bahamas	1998	201	128	0	0	0	407	0	736	0
Bahrain	1997	316	8	27	0	0	276	16	643	0
Bahreïn	1998	328	233	15	0	0	131	0	707	0
Bangladesh	1997	10247	1480	6752	23338	60450	5708	10259	118234	85
Bangladesh	1998	22763	891	6910	25950	68749	4003	5302	134568	32
Barbados	1997	242	157	38	0	0	314	226	977	0
Barbade	1998	69	50	1	0	0	316	67	502	0
Belize	1997	173	454	66	777	0	434	13	1917	3
Belize	1998	215	445	39	706	0	420	16	1 841	1
Benin	1997	5558	1119	2944	2969	4374	1685	471	19120	82
Bénin	1998	4458	746	2607	2665	4810	1065	640	16990	63
Bhutan	1997	3105	3668	1076	1914	1933	1774	707	14177	350
Bhoutan	1998	3517	1935	920	1894	1550	1282	246	11344	31
Bolivia	1997	6418	1368	2185	9696	10943	1976	5124	37710	909
Bolivie	1998	10174	836	1417	7291	4587	1667	6924	32895	768
Botswana	1997	3216	265	911	951	−1	975	323	6640	140
Botswana	1998	3551	427	513	1269	2	679	176	6617	128

80
Socio—economic development assistance through the United Nations system
Thousand US dollars [*cont.*]
Assistance en matière de développement socioéconomique fournie par le système des Nations Unies
Milliers de dollars E.—U. [*suite*]

Development grant expenditures [1] • Aide au développement [1]

Country or area Pays ou zone	Year Année	UNDP PNUD Central resources Ressources centrales	Special funds Fonds gérés	UNFPA FNUAP	UNICEF	WFP PAM	Other UN system Autres organis. —ONU Regular budget Budget ordinaire	Extra— budgetary Extra— budgétaire	Total	Gov't self— supporting Auto— assistance gouverne— mentale
Brazil	1997	196075	4517	2162	20106	−11	3470	19390	245709	17457
Brésil	1998	256111	7670	2380	11923	9	2091	59224	339408	52103
British Virgin Islands	1997	113	5	0	0	0	15	5	138	0
Iles Vierges britanniques	1998	81	8	0	0	0	78	8	175	0
Brunei Darussalam	1997	0	0	0	0	0	22	0	22	0
Brunéi Darussalam	1998	10	0	0	0	0	12	0	22	0
Bulgaria	1997	1237	165	314	75	−15	514	291	2581	0
Bulgarie	1998	5902	350	5	203	0	874	153	7487	0
Burkina Faso	1997	5474	1573	2098	4524	5603	1913	713	21898	13
Burkina Faso	1998	4887	2325	1169	4324	8133	1579	1192	23609	15
Burundi	1997	7166	161	1419	8534	323	1993	1782	21378	0
Burundi	1998	5311	670	1264	6717	71	1449	1998	17480	21
Cambodia	1997	24383	13530	3918	11511	14212	2951	5188	75693	0
Cambodge	1998	11889	29648	6735	12038	12072	1278	3794	77454	0
Cameroon	1997	722	134	1875	2105	805	1340	928	7909	231
Cameroun	1998	1562	143	960	1468	2766	1421	1124	9445	158
Cape Verde	1997	870	393	886	958	2947	1368	1812	9234	421
Cap—Vert	1998	614	1131	972	876	1975	776	1612	7956	377
Cayman Islands	1997	184	0	0	0	0	0	5	189	5
Iles Caïmanes	1998	306	0	0	0	0	0	13	319	13
Central African Rep.	1997	3523	1232	919	1526	1114	1491	159	9964	11
Rép. centrafricaine	1998	6242	588	460	1816	805	879	112	10902	1
Chad	1997	3981	610	1352	3742	6221	1376	482	17764	0
Tchad	1998	5710	1027	1218	3335	4561	1147	308	17306	0
Chile	1997	10268	403	136	743	0	1818	413	13781	−3
Chili	1998	13933	599	185	938	0	1556	820	18031	276
China ††	1997	33599	9547	53	20467	38152	6334	15484	123636	824
Chine ††	1998	23391	11835	1327	21649	24528	3890	16750	103371	688
China, Hong Kong SAR †	1997	19	0	0	0	0	44	0	63	0
Chine, Hong Kong RAS †	1998	0	0	0	0	0	4	0	4	0
China, Macao SAR †	1997	0	0	0	0	0	46	52	98	52
Chine, Macao RAS †	1998	0	0	0	0	0	0	26	26	26
Colombia	1997	77529	3290	764	2569	69	2238	2018	88477	1025
Colombie	1998	99084	694	401	3664	1594	1424	2445	109305	1163
Comoros	1997	1403	718	580	642	−130	1254	64	4531	0
Comores	1998	1040	47	740	538	0	707	23	3094	0
Congo	1997	164	31	258	1376	−71	1165	312	3235	167
Congo	1998	670	187	660	2275	0	1224	165	5181	1
Cook Islands	1997	23	−1	77	0	0	443	1	543	0
Iles Cook	1998	46	11	−21	0	0	222	57	316	0
Costa Rica	1997	2627	3870	260	955	5	1565	2375	11657	133
Costa Rica	1998	2881	2523	178	1018	0	1127	15161	22888	12564
Côte d'Ivoire	1997	2036	586	1845	2634	3097	1600	519	12317	15
Côte d'Ivoire	1998	2215	435	1244	3275	1841	1311	525	10846	32
Cuba	1997	1530	470	911	1763	7338	2465	273	14750	14
Cuba	1998	1061	337	639	2123	3679	2017	170	10026	12
Cyprus	1997	83	7	0	0	0	606	8	704	1
Chypre	1998	1432	0	19	0	0	210	13	1674	13
Czech Republic	1997	388	0	0	0	0	243	485	1116	74
République tchèque	1998	383	0	0	0	0	639	606	1628	428
Dem. Rep. of the Congo	1997	15262	2	140	14571	−3816	2167	43	28369	0
Rép. dém. du Congo	1998	13844	54	158	14858	598	1551	630	31693	0
Djibouti	1997	863	607	362	988	2272	1254	25	6371	0
Djibouti	1998	826	810	391	963	1384	673	−5	5041	0
Dominica	1997	47	57	1	0	0	148	62	315	5
Dominique	1998	106	16	−5	0	0	290	11	418	11
Dominican Republic	1997	4080	1078	1481	1358	1837	1486	66	11386	47
Rép. dominicaine	1998	6933	1395	1295	1673	5612	1561	2802	21271	2720
Ecuador	1997	17247	121	1603	3858	1811	1584	3514	29738	335
Equateur	1998	26332	229	1266	4757	5169	1679	4471	43903	1420

80
Socio—economic development assistance through the United Nations system
Thousand US dollars [cont.]
Assistance en matière de développement socioéconomique fournie par le système des Nations Unies
Milliers de dollars E.—U. [suite]

Country or area Pays ou zone	Year Année	UNDP PNUD — Central resources Ressources centrales	Special funds Fonds gérés	UNFPA FNUAP	UNICEF	WFP PAM	Other UN system Autres organis. —ONU — Regular budget Budget ordinaire	Extra—budgetary Extra—budgétaire	Total	Gov't self—supporting Auto—assistance gouverne—mentale
Egypt	1997	14446	476	3143	5601	6196	3271	5359	38492	681
Egypte	1998	17261	1464	1470	6629	5352	1969	4823	38967	931
El Salvador	1997	21235	2670	970	1419	1459	858	1492	30103	0
El Salvador	1998	33260	4688	587	2309	5348	769	1244	48205	162
Equatorial Guinea	1997	909	129	1006	1065	−273	796	454	4086	0
Guinée équatoriale	1998	1086	88	731	874	0	794	37	3610	0
Eritrea	1997	6665	1009	1122	6246	−2360	1382	1598	15662	0
Erythrée	1998	9676	2737	1497	5461	324	679	1662	22036	0
Ethiopia	1997	25558	1863	5794	14770	83490	2400	1356	135231	203
Ethiopia	1998	17176	2396	1815	17627	71949	1778	2745	115486	224
Fiji	1997	343	80	253	0	0	1517	192	2385	36
Fidji	1998	418	34	−110	0	0	1202	90	1635	1
French Guiana	1997	0	0	0	0	0	36	0	36	0
Guyane française	1998	0	0	0	0	0	12	0	12	0
French Polynesia	1997	0	0	0	0	0	25	0	25	0
Polynésie française	1998	0	0	0	0	0	1	0	1	0
Gabon	1997	768	341	426	556	0	1151	267	3509	40
Gabon	1998	500	167	353	674	0	1075	155	2924	0
Gambia	1997	3357	852	647	1670	2068	1632	1423	11649	31
Gambie	1998	2194	1178	294	1614	2617	1195	611	9703	10
Ghana	1997	6467	265	1922	6188	1054	1895	1297	19088	−10
Ghana	1998	6036	276	4707	7660	1617	1725	751	22772	0
Greece	1997	0	0	0	0	0	138	83	221	81
Grèce	1998	0	0	0	0	0	381	−6	375	−15
Grenada	1997	42	0	60	0	0	99	0	201	0
Grenade	1998	138	166	15	0	0	222	44	586	0
Guam	1997	0	0	0	0	0	29	0	29	0
Guam	1998	0	0	0	0	0	5	0	5	0
Guatemala	1997	30383	2844	568	3240	6756	745	1765	46301	0
Guatemala	1998	43115	2868	544	3727	4608	655	1197	56715	0
Guinea	1997	4062	791	966	3175	−164	1631	491	10952	24
Guinée	1998	6539	708	800	3216	1992	1423	225	14903	0
Guinea—Bissau	1997	2656	245	596	2515	1697	1170	636	9515	−4
Guinée—Bissau	1998	1673	546	271	1864	3543	773	295	8965	0
Guyana	1997	1192	691	22	903	1043	708	116	4675	0
Guyana	1998	1410	355	169	832	815	465	214	4260	10
Haiti	1997	20085	3227	1736	3969	4676	1294	3532	38519	11
Haïti	1998	11697	3644	2708	2186	5227	659	1210	27331	92
Honduras	1997	10811	589	1492	2592	3969	611	2318	22382	157
Honduras	1998	12731	1211	1143	2319	5402	463	5420	28688	3210
Hungary	1997	246	0	0	0	0	482	350	1078	0
Hongrie	1998	443	0	0	0	0	959	269	1671	8
India	1997	17475	6334	8765	52917	23818	7766	5214	122289	2865
Inde	1998	10239	5432	8305	47960	23893	2018	6360	104208	4193
Indonesia	1997	10880	505	2291	14562	−2	6586	3482	38304	1932
Indonésie	1998	6446	841	5385	11075	81554	3958	2092	111351	849
Iran (Islamic Rep. of)	1997	1783	64	1791	1698	3735	3032	3669	15772	365
Iran (Rép. islamique d')	1998	1326	110	2030	1598	3299	1882	1952	12197	30
Iraq	1997	12777	2	140	17940	37605	2460	37844	108768	0
Iraq	1998	29627	0	807	10463	26844	1474	103371	172585	0
Jamaica	1997	1215	650	290	1026	1462	1257	666	6566	0
Jamaïque	1998	2403	200	−36	1594	0	1079	348	5587	0
Jordan	1997	1015	1712	1138	1271	4769	1706	2320	13931	2
Jordanie	1998	1575	1361	155	765	1991	1367	1573	8787	6
Kazakhstan	1997	1929	247	263	1551	0	1096	528	5614	0
Kazakhstan	1998	2482	306	1080	1352	0	787	367	6374	0
Kenya	1997	6528	220	2039	5770	30962	2392	1239	49150	1
Kenya	1998	8464	616	1622	6989	37873	1792	1039	58395	9
Kiribati	1997	323	104	65	0	0	482	89	1063	0
Kiribati	1998	376	132	21	0	0	190	48	767	0

Development grant expenditures [1] • Aide au développement [1]

80

Socio — economic development assistance through the United Nations system
Thousand US dollars [*cont.*]

Assistance en matière de développement socioéconomique fournie par le système des Nations Unies
Milliers de dollars E. — U. [*suite*]

Development grant expenditures [1] • Aide au développement [1]

Country or area / Pays ou zone	Year / Année	UNDP PNUD — Central resources / Ressources centrales	UNDP PNUD — Special funds / Fonds gérés	UNFPA FNUAP	UNICEF	WFP PAM	Other UN system Autres organis. — ONU — Regular budget / Budget ordinaire	Other UN system — Extra-budgetary / Extra-budgétaire	Total	Gov't self-supporting / Auto-assistance gouvernementale
Korea, Dem. P. R.	1997	5604	292	2324	6865	104662	3235	2672	125654	5
Corée, Rep. dém. de	1998	4970	1404	627	11108	126419	1548	3681	149757	0
Korea, Republic of	1997	1800	9	0	0	0	1642	185	3636	123
Corée, République de	1998	1394	0	147	0	0	909	137	2586	97
Kuwait	1997	995	0	0	0	0	234	326	1555	230
Koweït	1998	941	0	0	0	0	146	130	1217	19
Kyrgyzstan	1997	3668	399	1069	1252	1	195	187	6771	0
Kirghizistan	1998	3669	222	851	854	0	216	212	6024	0
Lao People's Dem. Rep.	1997	9864	1739	429	3322	11988	1291	1857	30490	0
Rép. dém. pop. lao	1998	7011	8573	748	2401	2084	944	1732	23492	0
Lebanon	1997	5306	342	298	2262	0	1672	1154	11034	660
Liban	1998	7858	1097	361	1413	0	1294	1814	13837	951
Lesotho	1997	4914	675	690	1167	3423	1229	596	12694	68
Lesotho	1998	3562	652	46	903	2893	791	529	9376	136
Liberia	1997	9783	82	62	8535	19731	2083	663	40939	0
Libéria	1998	9481	108	683	8234	43694	985	754	63939	21
Libyan Arab Jamahiriya	1997	2428	12	11	0	0	706	3256	6413	3116
Jamah. arabe libyenne	1998	1431	2	0	0	0	412	1815	3660	1641
Madagascar	1997	5784	334	1669	4702	2809	2733	3162	21193	511
Madagascar	1998	4319	648	2393	5847	2930	1581	2264	19982	377
Malawi	1997	11030	1460	2826	6670	953	1921	124	24984	0
Malawi	1998	10362	4340	3237	6155	3798	1344	343	29579	0
Malaysia	1997	1533	3652	175	628	0	1555	87	7630	56
Malaisie	1998	1059	2770	138	572	0	931	287	5758	0
Maldives	1997	1856	199	764	694	0	1272	282	5067	6
Maldives	1998	1795	165	435	638	0	939	76	4048	3
Mali	1997	11861	7167	2339	6732	7392	2265	1950	39706	0
Mali	1998	10630	5055	1780	4478	5020	1591	1490	30045	0
Malta	1997	200	0	0	0	0	97	34	331	0
Malte	1998	280	0	0	0	0	186	51	517	10
Marshall Islands	1997	135	76	250	0	0	137	41	639	0
Iles Marshall	1998	15	35	60	0	0	167	76	353	0
Mauritania	1997	3883	3960	992	1975	10119	1828	625	23382	242
Mauritanie	1998	1553	2161	843	2939	2793	1111	557	11957	266
Mauritius	1997	807	143	290	606	13	928	315	3102	63
Maurice	1998	370	34	247	648	2	749	174	2225	78
Mexico	1997	3877	4951	1792	4338	−1	1559	1687	18203	10
Mexique	1998	2846	3881	1950	2562	0	1572	1775	14586	305
Micronesia (Fed. States of)	1997	143	14	183	0	0	256	351	947	278
Micronésie (Etats féd. de)	1998	352	20	20	0	0	90	244	726	204
Mongolia	1997	4592	642	855	1014	0	2245	967	10315	0
Mongolie	1998	3511	1929	1445	1052	0	1811	813	10561	0
Montserrat	1997	202	1	0	0	0	0	1	204	0
Montserrat	1998	−68	0	0	0	0	0	0	−68	0
Morocco	1997	5160	729	1672	1902	4314	2803	2632	19212	965
Maroc	1998	3526	2189	4637	1829	407	1994	2431	17013	1217
Mozambique	1997	12810	13044	3030	10330	5051	1716	3821	49802	0
Mozambique	1998	23796	7787	3940	11680	11373	1485	5282	65343	0
Myanmar	1997	14005	7	955	8386	1564	4217	897	30031	664
Myanmar	1998	16652	8	1000	6973	1317	2637	53	28639	−2
Namibia	1997	739	252	1409	2694	−4	2013	2230	9333	538
Namibie	1998	809	42	1765	2604	0	1164	1707	8091	453
Nauru	1997	0	0	0	0	0	22	0	22	0
Nauru	1998	0	0	0	0	0	76	17	93	17
Nepal	1997	7880	4020	2029	8367	10292	4404	2349	39341	55
Népal	1998	10448	5064	6588	7598	11353	2071	2284	45406	802
Netherlands Antilles	1997	650	0	0	0	0	115	0	765	0
Antilles néerlandaises	1998	367	0	0	0	0	80	0	447	0
New Caledonia	1997	0	0	0	0	0	2	0	2	0
Nouvelle−Calédonie	1998	0	0	0	0	0	0	0	0	0

80

Socio—economic development assistance through the United Nations system

Thousand US dollars [cont.]

Assistance en matière de développement socioéconomique fournie par le système des Nations Unies

Milliers de dollars E.—U. [suite]

Development grant expenditures [1] • Aide au développement [1]

Country or area Pays ou zone	Year Année	UNDP PNUD Central resources Ressources centrales	Special funds Fonds gérés	UNFPA FNUAP	UNICEF	WFP PAM	Other UN system Autres organis. —ONU Regular budget Budget ordinaire	Extra-budgetary Extra-budgétaire	Total	Gov't self-supporting Auto-assistance gouverne-mental
Nicaragua	1997	7095	1191	2715	3403	6931	910	2872	25117	3﹖
Nicaragua	1998	7093	1683	2240	6633	15444	1002	2353	36448	﹖
Niger	1997	4306	1676	2160	4541	8224	1948	4102	26957	6﹖
Niger	1998	4612	2021	3569	6213	6363	1609	2924	27311	2﹖
Nigeria	1997	32583	442	2887	13187	−2	2892	2378	54367	54﹖
Nigéria	1998	13569	1293	3542	17621	0	2720	772	39516	50﹖
Niue	1997	61	54	18	0	0	75	54	262	﹖
Nioué	1998	55	4	4	0	0	119	2	184	﹖
Oman	1997	0	5	66	788	0	778	469	2106	46﹖
Oman	1998	0	128	−4	743	0	543	932	2342	88﹖
Pakistan	1997	9659	1061	4568	12460	16379	3718	2796	50641	46﹖
Pakistan	1998	8785	1013	4263	12577	10553	2236	3423	42850	50﹖
Palau	1997	0	0	0	0	0	95	0	95	﹖
Palaos	1998	0	0	0	0	0	33	23	56	2﹖
Panama	1997	80636	791	345	772	792	1505	365	85206	36﹖
Panama	1998	115196	1093	342	1162	292	984	651	119719	48﹖
Papua New Guinea	1997	2705	855	1868	661	0	2210	406	8705	4﹖
Papouasie—Nvl—Guinée	1998	1966	690	705	611	82	1183	218	5455	4﹖
Paraguay	1997	13773	348	966	1169	505	695	701	18157	34﹖
Paraguay	1998	15290	300	616	1337	0	719	57	18319	5﹖
Peru	1997	95519	491	3092	6782	3160	1862	2692	113598	135﹖
Pérou	1998	90472	869	2025	5593	6079	2143	6369	113549	520﹖
Philippines	1997	7150	667	6115	8810	2	1885	5404	30033	172﹖
Philippines	1998	7232	1566	3473	6821	0	1006	5225	25324	111﹖
Poland	1997	1616	2	226	0	0	1179	1055	4078	2﹖
Pologne	1998	2654	62	140	0	0	1979	91	4926	﹖
Portugal	1997	0	0	0	0	0	154	20	174	2﹖
Portugal	1998	0	0	0	0	0	258	53	310	4﹖
Qatar	1997	108	0	0	0	0	184	569	861	299﹖
Qatar	1998	134	0	0	0	0	126	428	688	9﹖
Réunion	1997	0	0	0	0	0	46	0	46	﹖
Réunion	1998	0	0	0	0	0	22	0	22	﹖
Romania	1997	1587	216	502	1609	0	800	1639	6353	0
Roumanie	1998	1332	53	432	2030	0	1191	1871	6909	5﹖
Rwanda	1997	12364	16732	1487	18321	144992	2757	2265	198918	0
Rwanda	1998	11096	29707	861	11105	111847	1124	1844	167584	0
Saint Helena	1997	247	0	0	0	0	28	0	275	0
Sainte Hélène	1998	281	0	0	0	0	0	0	281	0
Saint Kitts and Nevis	1997	25	7	0	0	0	332	7	371	0
Saint—Kitts—et—Nevis	1998	13	8	0	0	0	143	0	164	0
Saint Lucia	1997	73	0	5	0	0	145	21	244	15﹖
Sainte—Lucie	1998	27	−1	8	0	0	340	57	431	0
Saint Vincent—Grenadines	1997	194	8	21	0	0	127	8	358	0
Saint Vincent—Grenadines	1998	158	15	4	0	0	113	61	351	0
Samoa	1997	61	123	52	0	0	1313	250	1799	0
Samoa	1998	110	8	−8	0	0	887	298	1295	27﹖
Sao Tome and Principe	1997	1074	733	477	669	226	1209	99	4487	42﹖
Sao Tomé—et—Principe	1998	758	605	247	548	528	734	36	3456	6﹖
Saudi Arabia	1997	5332	−1	0	0	0	1220	9620	16171	9384
Arabie saoudite	1998	4017	2	0	0	0	761	9200	13980	8915
Senegal	1997	2826	1437	3061	3865	2404	1798	6175	21566	16﹖
Sénégal	1998	1933	1082	974	2641	3399	1667	4946	16643	13﹖
Seychelles	1997	249	97	101	50	0	893	2	1392	0
Seychelles	1998	16	72	106	21	0	536	14	765	14﹖
Sierra Leone	1997	3154	736	268	3269	11086	1428	1497	21438	655
Sierra Leone	1998	4097	−43	633	5591	23831	1314	707	36130	0
Singapore	1997	0	0	0	0	0	286	0	286	0
Singapour	1998	0	0	0	0	0	146	0	146	0
Solomon Islands	1997	614	37	112	0	0	556	190	1509	16﹖
Iles Salomon	1998	1030	30	67	0	0	480	195	1802	30﹖

80
Socio — economic development assistance through the United Nations system
Thousand US dollars [*cont.*]
Assistance en matière de développement socioéconomique fournie par le système des Nations Unies
Milliers de dollars E. — U. [*suite*]

Development grant expenditures [1] • Aide au développement [1]

Country or area Pays ou zone	Year Année	UNDP PNUD		UNFPA FNUAP	UNICEF	WFP PAM	Other UN system Autres organis. — ONU		Total	Gov't self— supporting Auto— assistance gouverne— mentale
		Central resources Ressources centrales	Special funds Fonds gérés				Regular budget Budget ordinaire	Extra— budgetary Extra— budgétaire		
Somalia	1997	15105	270	596	12955	8986	3231	1096	42239	0
Somalie	1998	15309	751	928	12108	23938	2263	415	55712	0
South Africa	1997	3431	1836	1259	2272	0	1942	1556	12296	10
Afrique du Sud	1998	3719	2609	723	2109	0	1409	2762	13331	5
Sri Lanka	1997	6705	1414	910	5117	3887	3761	769	22563	48
Sri Lanka	1998	5993	570	1711	3543	3501	2340	564	18221	399
Sudan	1997	8607	2474	1792	13867	32357	3511	1280	63888	81
Soudan	1998	5963	1424	2488	14591	166265	2004	1281	194016	27
Suriname	1997	212	154	26	493	0	417	199	1501	126
Suriname	1998	522	209	21	506	0	498	579	2335	2
Swaziland	1997	837	205	678	875	109	1131	95	3930	4
Swaziland	1998	726	370	301	830	0	739	5	2970	0
Syrian Arab Republic	1997	3101	348	2215	913	10520	2315	3091	22503	57
Rép. arabe syrienne	1998	2442	153	2737	844	5756	1718	2389	16040	0
Tajikistan	1997	3591	192	771	2372	12903	304	571	20704	0
Tajikistan	1998	4592	71	392	990	8211	256	1351	15863	0
Thailand	1997	4196	2532	1472	4368	908	3679	1091	18246	302
Thaïlande	1998	2095	1552	102	4767	3812	2340	1533	16202	46
TFYR Macedonia	1997	150	0	0	5142	47120	493	1626	54531	0
L'ex—R.y. Macédoine	1998	285	0	0	3107	0	510	711	4613	0
Togo	1997	3375	732	720	1692	−17	1444	1204	9150	10
Togo	1998	2495	674	997	1557	0	1136	454	7313	22
Tokelau	1997	163	0	21	0	0	37	0	221	0
Tokélaou	1998	78	0	11	0	0	26	0	115	0
Tonga	1997	40	0	53	0	0	851	94	1038	94
Tonga	1998	11	0	−89	0	0	703	58	683	58
Trinidad and Tobago	1997	262	60	0	0	0	610	302	1234	19
Trinité—et—Tobago	1998	221	201	20	0	0	616	299	1357	2
Tunisia	1997	1510	88	673	1024	2798	1741	836	8670	26
Tunisie	1998	1327	96	1274	1085	0	884	1420	6086	59
Turkey	1997	2106	58	723	2273	2	1244	1147	7553	602
Turquie	1998	2730	195	1269	3745	0	1277	1461	10677	255
Turkmenistan	1997	1327	47	773	1046	0	146	85	3424	0
Turkménistan	1998	500	4	667	725	0	131	43	2070	0
Turks and Caicos Islands	1997	2	0	0	0	0	13	0	15	0
Iles Turques et Caïques	1998	20	3	0	0	0	0	3	26	0
Tuvalu	1997	219	17	22	0	0	94	17	369	0
Tuvalu	1998	277	10	27	0	0	14	10	338	0
Uganda	1997	17062	1894	3018	18716	31345	2809	3171	78015	412
Ouganda	1998	15129	2895	6042	15006	30369	2153	1983	73577	219
United Arab Emirates	1997	2952	6	0	0	0	298	29	3285	16
Emirats arabes unis	1998	3446	0	7	0	0	120	525	4098	525
United Rep. Tanzania	1997	13973	898	4176	12445	11965	2883	6389	52729	966
Rép.— Unie de Tanzanie	1998	15635	1915	3652	11100	13852	1928	5025	53106	623
Uruguay	1997	23714	790	275	825	0	698	463	26765	122
Uruguay	1998	30820	1245	256	992	0	561	1726	35600	1354
Uzbekistan	1997	3046	325	394	2487	0	271	323	6846	3
Ouzbékistan	1998	2573	208	1508	2739	0	247	439	7714	0
Vanuatu	1997	212	129	90	0	0	674	74	1179	0
Vanuatu	1998	140	78	28	0	0	377	54	677	0
Venezuela	1997	17849	1125	464	1627	0	1608	197	22870	25
Venezuela	1998	70633	1427	375	1392	0	1292	575	75694	85
Viet Nam	1997	13933	1860	4821	9714	13941	3664	2971	50904	2
Viet Nam	1998	16868	960	5493	12502	11412	1996	3589	52819	29
Yemen	1997	8599	2060	2226	3420	10279	2836	5646	35066	3848
Yémen	1998	7669	3988	756	3518	5854	1389	3788	26963	1717
Yugoslavia	1997	63	16	0	0	0	8	147	234	0
Yougoslavie	1998	68	3	0	0	35460	41	225	35797	0
Zambia	1997	9498	1984	2631	7181	1956	2475	2460	28185	455
Zambie	1998	5992	1257	1577	6307	8499	1842	2521	27995	862

80
Socio—economic development assistance through the United Nations system
Thousand US dollars [*cont.*]

Assistance en matière de développement socioéconomique fournie par le système des Nations Unies
Milliers de dollars E.—U. [*suite*]

| | | Development grant expenditures [1] • Aide au développement [1] | | | | | | Other UN system Autres organis. — ONU | | | Gov't self—supporting |
| | | UNDP PNUD | | | | | | | | | Auto—assistance |
Country or area Pays ou zone	Year Année	Central resources Ressources centrales	Special funds Fonds gérés	UNFPA FNUAP	UNICEF	WFP PAM	Regular budget Budget ordinaire	Extra—budgetary Extra—budgétaire	Total	gouverne—mentale
Zimbabwe	1997	5717	2300	1792	4929	0	2106	1373	18217	29
Zimbabwe	1998	3532	1002	967	4575	155	1305	1261	12796	144
Other countries	1997	27009	5097	2505	22490	8472	8649	10220	84442	1561
Autre pays	1998	34780	26598	1534	36428	9059	14969	13457	136825	1058
Not elsewhere classified	**1997**	**74348**	**28136**	**4009**	**25547**	**16956**	**21108**	**7491**	**177595**	**2**
Non—classé ailleurs	**1998**	**8035**	**33562**	**3909**	**3357**	**14708**	**2862**	**30271**	**96705**	**10**

Source: United Nations, "Operational activities of the United Nations
for international development cooperation, Report of the Secretary—
General, Addendum, Comprehensive statistical data on operational
activities for development for the year 1997" (E/1999/55/Add.2) and
"Operational activities of the United Nations for international
development cooperation, Report of the Secretary—General, Addendum,
Comprehensive statistical data on operational activities for development
for the year 1998" (E/2000/46/Add.2).

Source: Nations Unies, "Activités opérationnelles du système des
Nations Unies au service de la coopération internationale pour
le développement, Rapport du Secrétaire général, Additif,
Données statistiques globales sur les activités opérationnelles
au service du développement pour 1997" (E/1999/55/Add.2) et
"Activités opérationnelles du système des Nations Unies au service
de la coopération internationale pour le développement, Rapport du
Secrétaire général, Additif, Données statistiques globales sur les
activités opérationnelles au service du développement pour 1998"
(E/2000/46/Add.2).

† For information on the recent changes in country or area
nomenclature pertaining to former Czechoslovakia,
Germany, Hong Kong Special Administrative Region (SAR)
of China, Macao Special Administrative Region (SAR) of
China, SFR of Yugoslavia and the former USSR, see
Annex I — Country or area nomenclature, regional and
other groupings.

† Pour les modifications récentes de nomenclature de pays ou de
zone concernant l'Allemagne, Hong Kong, région administrative
spéciale (RAS) de Chine, Macao, région administrative spéciale
(RAS) de Chine, l'ex—Tchécoslovaquie, l'ex—URSS et l'ex—Rfs de
Yougoslavie, voir annex I — Nomenclature des pays ou des zones,
groupements régionaux et autres groupements.

†† For statistical purposes, the data for China do not include
those for Hong Kong Special Administrative Region
(Hong Kong SAR), Macao Special Administrative
Region (Macao SAR) and Taiwan province of China.

†† Les données statistiques relatives à la Chine ne comprennent
pas celles qui concernent la région administrative spéciale de
Hong Kong (la RAS de Hong Kong), la région administrative
spéciale de Macao (la RAS de Macao), et la province chinoise
de Taiwan.

1 The following abbreviations have been used in the table:
UNDP: United Nations Development Programme
UNFPA: United Nations Population Fund
UNICEF: United Nations Children's Fund
WFP: World Food Programme

1 Les abbréviations ci—après ont été utilisées dans le tableau:
PNUD : Programme des Nations Unies pour le développement
FNUAP : Fonds des Nations Unies pour la population
UNICEF : Fonds des Nations Unies pour l'enfance
PAM : Programme alimentaire mondial.

Technical notes, tables 78-80

Table 78 presents estimates of flows of financial resources to individual recipients either directly (bilaterally) or through multilateral institutions (multilaterally).

The multilateral institutions include the World Bank Group, regional banks, financial institutions of the European Union and a number of United Nations institutions, programmes and trust funds.

The main source of data is the Development Assistance Committee of OECD to which member countries reported data on their flow of resources to developing countries and territories and countries and territories in transition, and multilateral institutions.

Additional information on definitions, methods and sources can be found in OECD's *Geographical Distribution of Financial Flows to Aid Recipients* [20].

Table 79 presents the development assistance expenditures of donor countries. This table includes donors' contributions to multilateral agencies, so the overall totals differ from those in table 78, which include disbursements by multilateral agencies.

Table 80 includes data on expenditures on operational activities for development undertaken by the organizations of the United Nations system. Operational activities encompass, in general, those activities of a development cooperation character that seek to mobilize or increase the potential and capacity of countries to promote economic and social development and welfare, including the transfer of resources to developing countries or regions in a tangible or intangible form. The table also covers, as a memo item, expenditures on activities of an emergency character, the purpose of which is immediate relief in crisis situations, such as assistance to refugees, humanitarian work and activities in respect of disasters.

Expenditures on operational activities for development are financed from contributions from governments and other official and non-official sources to a variety of funding channels in the United Nations system. These include United Nations funds and programmes such as contributions to the United Nations Development Programme, contributions to funds administered by the United Nations Development Programme, and regular (assessed) and other extrabudgetary contributions to specialized agencies.

Data are taken from the 1997 and 1998 reports of the Secretary-General to the General Assembly on operational activities for development [27].

Notes techniques, tableaux 78 à 80

Le *Tableau 78* présente les estimations des flux de ressources financières mises à la disposition des pays soit directement (aide bilatérale) soit par l'intermédiaire d'institutions multilatérales (aide multilatérale).

Les institutions multilatérales comprennent le Groupe de la Banque mondiale, les banques régionales, les institutions financières de l'Union européenne et un certain nombre d'institutions, de programmes et de fonds d'affectation spéciale des Nations Unies.

La principale source de données est le Comité d'aide au développement de l'OCDE, auquel les pays membres ont communiqué des données sur les flux de ressources qu'ils mettent à la disposition des pays et territoires en développement et en transition et des institutions multilatérales.

Pour plus de renseignements sur les définitions, méthodes et sources, se reporter à la publication de l'OCDE, la *Répartition géographique des ressources financières de aux pays bénéficiaires de l'Aide* [20].

Le *Tableau 79* présente les dépenses que les pays donateurs consacrent à l'aide publique au développement (APD). Ces chiffres incluent les contributions des donateurs à des agences multilatérales, de sorte que les totaux diffèrent de ceux du tableau 78, qui incluent les dépenses des agences multilatérales.

Le *Tableau 80* présente des données sur les dépenses consacrées à des activités opérationnelles pour le développement par les organisations du système des Nations Unies. Par "activités opérationnelles", on entend en général les activités ayant trait à la coopération au développement, qui visent à mobiliser ou à accroître les potentialités et aptitudes que présentent les pays pour promouvoir le développement et le bien-être économiques et sociaux, y compris les transferts de ressources vers les pays ou régions en développement sous forme tangible ou non. Ce tableau indique également, pour mémoire, les dépenses liées à des activités revêtant un caractère d'urgence, qui ont pour but d'apporter un secours immédiat dans les situations de crise, telles que l'aide aux réfugiés, l'assistance humanitaire et les secours en cas de catastrophe.

Les dépenses consacrées aux activités opérationnelles pour le développement sont financées au moyen de contributions que les gouvernements et d'autres sources officielles et non officielles apportent à divers organes de financement, tels que fonds et programmes du système des Nations Unies. On peut citer notamment les contributions au Programme des Nations Unies pour le développement, les contributions aux fonds gérés par le Programme des Nations Unies pour le développement, les contributions régulières (budgétaires) et les contributions extrabudgétaires aux institutions spécialisées.

Les données sont extraites des rapports annuels de 1997 et de 1998 du Secrétaire général à la session de l'Assemblée générale sur les activités opérationnelles pour le développement [27].

Annex I

Country and area nomenclature, regional and other groupings

A.   Changes in country or area names

In the periods covered by the statistics in the present issue of the *Statistical Yearbook* (in general, 1989-1998 or 1990-1999), and as indicated at the end of each table, the following major changes in designation have taken place:

Czech Republic, Slovakia: Since 1 January 1993, data for the Czech Republic and Slovakia, where available, are shown separately under the appropriate country name. For periods prior to 1 January 1993, where no separate data are available for the Czech Republic and Slovakia, unless otherwise indicated, data for the former Czechoslovakia are shown under the country name "former Czechoslovakia";

Germany: Through the accession of the German Democratic Republic to the Federal Republic of Germany with effect from 3 October 1990, the two German States have united to form one sovereign State. As from the date of unification, the Federal Republic of Germany acts in the United Nations under the designation "Germany". All data shown which pertain to Germany prior to 3 October 1990 are indicated separately for the Federal Republic of Germany and the former German Democratic Republic based on their respective territories at the time indicated;

Hong Kong Special Administrative Region of China: Pursuant to a Joint Declaration signed on 19 December 1984, the United Kingdom restored Hong Kong to the People's Republic of China with effect from 1 July 1997; the People's Republic of China resumed the exercise of sovereignty over the territory with effect from that date;

Macao Special Administrative Region of China: Pursuant to the joint declaration signed on 13 April 1987, Portugal restored Macao to the People's Republic of China with effect from 20 December 1999; the People's Republic of China resumed the exercise of sovereignty over the territory with effect from that date;

Former *USSR*: In 1991, the Union of Soviet Socialist Republics formally dissolved into fifteen independent countries (Armenia, Azerbaijan, Belarus, Estonia, Georgia, Kazakhstan, Kyrgyzstan, Latvia, Lithuania, Republic of Moldova, Russian Federation, Tajikistan, Turkmenistan, Ukraine and Uzbekistan). Whenever possible, data are shown for the individual countries. Otherwise, data are shown for the former USSR;

Yemen: On 22 May 1990 Democratic Yemen and Yemen merged to form a single State. Since that date they have been represented as one Member with the name 'Yemen';

Yugoslavia: Unless otherwise indicated, data provided for Yugoslavia prior to 1 January 1992 refer to the Socialist Federal Republic of Yugoslavia which was composed of six republics. Data provided for Yugoslavia after that date refer to the Federal Republic of Yugoslavia which is composed of two republics (Serbia and

Annexe I

Nomenclature des pays ou zones, groupements régionaux et autres groupements

A.   Changements dans le nom des pays ou zones

Au cours des périodes sur lesquelles portent les statistiques, dans cette édition de l'*Annuaire Statistique* (1989-1998 ou 1990-1999, en générale), et comme indiqués à la fin de chaque tableau les changements principaux de désignation suivants ont eu lieu:

République tchèque, Slovaquie: Depuis le 1er janvier 1993, les données relatives à la République tchèque, et à la Slovaquie, lorsqu'elles sont disponibles, sont présentées séparément sous le nom de chacun des pays. En ce qui concerne la période précédant le 1er janvier 1993, pour laquelle on ne possède pas de données séparées pour les deux Républiques, les données relatives à l'ex-Tchécoslovaquie sont, sauf indication contraire, présentées sous le titre "l'ex-Tchécoslovaquie";

Allemagne: En vertu de l'adhésion de la République démocratique allemande à la République fédérale d'Allemagne, prenant effet le 3 octobre 1990, les deux Etats allemands se sont unis pour former un seul Etat souverain. A compter de la date de l'unification, la République fédérale d'Allemagne est désigné à l'ONU sous le nom d'"Allemagne". Toutes les données se rapportant à l'Allemagne avant le 3 octobre figurent dans deux rubriques séparées basées sur les territoires respectifs de la République fédérale d'Allemagne et l'ex-République démocratique allemande selon la période indiquée;

Hong Kong, région administrative spéciale de Chine: Conformément à une Déclaration commune signée le 19 décembre 1984, le Royaume-Uni a rétrocédé Hong Kong à la République populaire de Chine, avec effet au 1er juillet 1997; la souveraineté de la République populaire de Chine s'exerce à nouveau sur le territoire à compter de cette date;

Macao, région administrative spéciale de Chine: Conformément à une Déclaration commune signée le 13 avril 1987, le Portugal a rétrocédé Macao à la République populaire de Chine, avec effet au 20 décembre 1999; la souveraineté de la République populaire de Chine s'exerce à nouveau sur le territoire à compter de cette date;

L'ex-*URSS*: En 1991, l'Union des républiques socialistes soviétiques s'est séparé en 15 pays distincts (Arménie, Azerbaïdjan, Bélarus, Estonie, Géorgie, Kazakhstan, Kirghizistan, Lettonie, Lituanie, République de Moldova, Fédération de Russie, Tadjikistan, Turkménistan, Ukraine, Ouzbékistan). Les données sont présentées pour ces pays pris séparément quand cela est possible. Autrement, les données sont présentées pour l'ex-URSS;

Yémen: Le Yémen et le Yémen démocratique ont fusionné le 22 mai 1990 pour ne plus former qu'un seul Etat, qui est depuis lors représenté comme tel à l'Organisation, sous le nom 'Yémen';

Yougoslavie: Sauf indication contraire, les données fournies pour la Yougoslavie avant le 1er janvier 1992 se rapportent à la République fédérative socialiste de Yougoslavie, qui était composée de six républiques. Les données fournies pour la Yougoslavie après cette date se rapportent à la République fédérative de Yougoslavie, qui est composée de deux républiques (Serbie et Monténégro);

Les autres changements de désignation couvrant les

Montenegro);

Other changes in designation during the periods are listed below:

Brunei Darussalam was formerly listed as Brunei;

Burkina Faso was formerly listed as Upper Volta;

Cambodia was formerly listed as Democratic Kampuchea;

Cameroon was formerly listed as United Republic of Cameroon;

Côte d'Ivoire was formerly listed as Ivory Coast;

Democratic Republic of the Congo was formerly listed as Zaire;

Myanmar was formerly listed as Burma;

Palau was formerly listed as Pacific Islands and includes data for Federated States of Micronesia, Marshall Islands and Northern Mariana Islands;

Saint Kitts and Nevis was formerly listed as Saint Christopher and Nevis.

Data relating to the People's Republic of China generally include those for Taiwan Province in the field of statistics relating to population, area, natural resources and natural conditions such as climate. In other fields of statistics, they do not include Taiwan Province unless otherwise stated.

B.   *Regional groupings*

The scheme of regional groupings given below presents seven regions based mainly on continents. Five of the seven continental regions are further subdivided into 21 regions that are so drawn as to obtain greater homogeneity in sizes of population, demographic circumstances and accuracy of demographic statistics [21, 57]. This nomenclature is widely used in international statistics and is followed to the greatest extent possible in the present *Yearbook* in order to promote consistency and facilitate comparability and analysis. However, it is by no means universal in international statistical compilation, even at the level of continental regions, and variations in international statistical sources and methods dictate many unavoidable differences in particular fields in the present *Yearbook*. General differences are indicated in the footnotes to the classification presented below. More detailed differences are given in the footnotes and technical notes to individual tables.

Neither is there international standardization in the use of the terms "developed" and "developing" countries, areas or regions. These terms are used in the present publication to refer to regional groupings generally considered as "developed": these are Europe and the former USSR, the United States of America and Canada in Northern America, and Australia, Japan and New Zealand in Asia and Oceania. These designations are intended for statistical convenience and do not necessarily express a judgement about the stage reached by a particular country or area in the development process. Differences from this usage are indicated in the notes to individual tables.

périodes mentionnées sont énumérés ci-dessous:

Le *Brunéi Darussalam* apparaissait antérieurement sous le nom de Brunéi;

Le *Burkino Faso* apparaissait antérieurement sous le nom de la Haute-Volta;

Le *Cambodge* apparaissait antérieurement sous le nom de la Kampuchea démocratique;

Le *Cameroun* apparaissait antérieurement sous le nom de République-Unie du Cameroun;

La *République démocratique du Congo* apparaissait antérieurement sous le nom de Zaïre;

Le *Myanmar* apparaissait antérieurement sous le nom de Birmanie;

Les *Palaos* apparaissait antérieurement sous le nom de Iles du Pacifique y compris les données pour les Etats fédérés de Micronésie, les îles Marshall et îles Mariannes du Nord;

Saint-Kitts-et-Nevis apparaissait antérieurement sous le nom de Saint-Christophe-et-Nevis.

Les données relatives à la République populaire de Chine comprennent en général les données relatives à la province de Taïwan lorsqu'il s'agit de statistiques concernant la population, la superficie, les ressources naturelles, et les conditions naturelles telles que le climat, etc. Dans les statistiques relatives à d'autres domaines, la province de Taïwan n'est pas comprise, sauf indication contraire.

B.   *Groupements régionaux*

Le système de groupements régionaux présenté ci-dessous comporte sept régions basés principalement sur les continents. Cinq des sept régions continentales sont elles-mêmes subdivisées, formant ainsi 21 régions délimitées de manière à obtenir une homogénéité accrue dans les effectifs de population, les situations démographiques et la précision des statistiques démographiques [21, 57]. Cette nomenclature est couramment utilisée aux fins des statistiques internationales et a été appliquée autant qu'il a été possible dans le présent *Annuaire* en vue de renforcer la cohérence et de faciliter la comparaison et l'analyse. Son utilisation pour l'établissement des statistiques internationales n'est cependant rien moins qu'universelle, même au niveau des régions continentales, et les variations que présentent les sources et méthodes statistiques internationales entraînent inévitablement de nombreuses différences dans certains domaines de cet *Annuaire*. Les différences d'ordre général sont indiquées dans les notes figurant au bas de la classification présentée ci-dessous. Les différences plus spécifiques sont mentionnées dans les notes techniques et notes infrapaginales accompagnant les divers tableaux.

L'application des expressions "développés" et "en développement" aux pays, zones ou régions n'est pas non plus normalisée à l'échelle internationale. Ces expressions sont utilisées dans la présente publication en référence aux groupements régionaux généralement considérés comme "développés", à savoir l'Europe et l'ex-URSS, les Etats-Unis d'Amérique et le Canada en Amérique septentrionale, et l'Australie, le Japon et la Nouvelle-Zélande dans la région de l'Asie et du Pacifique. Ces appellations sont employées pour des raisons de commodité statistique et n'expriment pas nécessairement un jugement sur le stade de développement atteint par tel ou tel pays ou zone. Les cas différant de cet usage sont signalés dans les notes accompagnant les tableaux concernés.

Africa

Eastern Africa

Burundi
Comoros
Djibouti
Eritrea
Ethiopia
Kenya
Madagascar
Malawi
Mauritius
Mozambique
Réunion
Rwanda
Seychelles
Somalia
Uganda
United Republic of Tanzania
Zambia
Zimbabwe

Middle Africa

Angola
Cameroon
Central African Republic
Chad
Congo
Democratic Republic of the Congo
Equatorial Guinea
Gabon
Sao Tome and Principe

Northern Africa

Algeria
Egypt
Libyan Arab Jamahiriya
Morocco
Sudan
Tunisia
Western Sahara

Southern Africa

Botswana
Lesotho
Namibia
South Africa
Swaziland

Western Africa

Benin
Burkina Faso
Cape Verde
Côte d'Ivoire
Gambia
Ghana
Guinea

Afrique

Afrique orientale

Burundi
Comores
Djibouti
Erythrée
Ethiopie
Kenya
Madagascar
Malawi
Maurice
Mozambique
Réunion
Rwanda
Seychelles
Somalie
Ouganda
République-Unie de Tanzanie
Zambie
Zimbabwe

Afrique centrale

Angola
Cameroun
République centrafricaine
Tchad
Congo
République démocratique du Congo
Guinée équatoriale
Gabon
Sao Tomé-et-Principe

Afrique septentrionale

Algérie
Egypte
Jamahiriya arabe libyenne
Maroc
Soudan
Tunisie
Sahara occidental

Afrique australe

Botswana
Lesotho
Namibie
Afrique du Sud
Swaziland

Afrique occidentale

Bénin
Burkina Faso
Cap-Vert
Côte d'Ivoire
Gambie
Ghana
Guinée

Guinea-Bissau	Guinée-Bissau
Liberia	Libéria
Mali	Mali
Mauritania	Mauritanie
Niger	Niger
Nigeria	Nigéria
Saint Helena	Sainte-Hélène
Senegal	Sénégal
Sierra Leone	Sierra Leone
Togo	Togo

Americas
Latin America and the Caribbean
Caribbean

Amériques
Amérique latine et Caraïbes
Caraïbes

Anguilla	Anguilla
Antigua and Barbuda	Antigua-et-Barbuda
Aruba	Aruba
Bahamas	Bahamas
Barbados	Barbade
British Virgin Islands	Iles Vierges britanniques
Cayman Islands	Iles Caïmanes
Cuba	Cuba
Dominica	Dominique
Dominican Republic	République dominicaine
Grenada	Grenade
Guadeloupe	Guadeloupe
Haiti	Haïti
Jamaica	Jamaïque
Martinique	Martinique
Montserrat	Montserrat
Netherlands Antilles	Antilles néerlandaises
Puerto Rico	Porto Rico
Saint Kitts and Nevis	Saint-Kitts-et-Nevis
Saint Lucia	Sainte-Lucie
Saint Vincent and the Grenadines	Saint-Vincent-et-les Grenadines
Trinidad and Tobago	Trinité-et-Tobago
Turks and Caicos Islands	Iles Turques et Caïques
United States Virgin Islands	Iles Vierges américaines

Central America

Amérique centrale

Belize	Belize
Costa Rica	Costa Rica
El Salvador	El Salvador
Guatemala	Guatemala
Honduras	Honduras
Mexico	Mexique
Nicaragua	Nicaragua
Panama	Panama

South America

Amérique du Sud

Argentina	Argentine
Bolivia	Bolivie
Brazil	Brésil
Chile	Chili
Colombia	Colombie
Ecuador	Equateur

Falkland Islands (Malvinas)	Iles Falkland (Malvinas)
French Guiana	Guyane française
Guyana	Guyana
Paraguay	Paraguay
Peru	Pérou
Suriname	Suriname
Uruguay	Uruguay
Venezuela	Venezuela

Northern America [a]

Bermuda
Canada
Greenland
Saint Pierre and Miquelon
United States of America

Amérique septentrionale [a]

Bermudes
Canada
Groenland
Saint-Pierre-et-Miquelon
Etats-Unis d'Amérique

Asia

Eastern Asia
China
Hong Kong Special Administrative Region of China
Democratic People's Republic of Korea
Japan
Macao Special Administrative Region of China
Mongolia
Republic of Korea

Asie

Asie orientale
Chine
Hong Kong, région administrative spéciale de Chine
République populaire démocratique de Corée
Japon
Macao, région administrative spéciale de Chine
Mongolie
République de Corée

South-central Asia
Afghanistan
Bangladesh
Bhutan
India
Iran (Islamic Republic of)
Kazakhstan
Kyrgyzstan
Maldives
Nepal
Pakistan
Sri Lanka
Tajikistan
Turkmenistan
Uzbekistan

Asie centrale et du Sud
Afghanistan
Bangladesh
Bhoutan
Inde
Iran (République islamique d')
Kazakhstan
Kirghizistan
Maldives
Népal
Pakistan
Sri Lanka
Tadjikistan
Turkménistan
Ouzbékistan

South-eastern Asia
Brunei Darussalam
Cambodia
East Timor
Indonesia
Lao People's Democratic Republic
Malaysia
Myanmar
Philippines
Singapore
Thailand
Viet Nam

Asie du Sud-Est
Brunéi Darussalam
Cambodge
Timor oriental
Indonésie
République démocratique populaire lao
Malaisie
Myanmar
Philippines
Singapour
Thaïlande
Viet Nam

Western Asia	*Asie occidentale*
Armenia	Arménie
Azerbaijan	Azerbaïdjan
Bahrain	Bahreïn
Cyprus	Chypre
Georgia	Géorgie
Iraq	Iraq
Israel	Israël
Jordan	Jordanie
Kuwait	Koweït
Lebanon	Liban
Occupied Palestinian Territory	Territoire palestinien occupé
Oman	Oman
Qatar	Qatar
Saudi Arabia	Arabie saoudite
Syrian Arab Republic	République arabe syrienne
Turkey	Turquie
United Arab Emirates	Emirats arabes unis
Yemen	Yémen
Europe	**Europe**
Eastern Europe	*Europe orientale*
Belarus	Bélarus
Bulgaria	Bulgarie
Czech Republic	République tchèque
Hungary	Hongrie
Poland	Pologne
Republic of Moldova	République de Moldova
Romania	Roumanie
Russian Federation	Fédération de Russie
Slovakia	Slovaquie
Ukraine	Ukraine
Northern Europe	*Europe septentrionale*
Channel Islands	Iles Anglo-Normandes
Denmark	Danemark
Estonia	Estonie
Faeroe Islands	Iles Féroé
Finland	Finlande
Iceland	Islande
Ireland	Irlande
Isle of Man	Ile de Man
Latvia	Lettonie
Lithuania	Lituanie
Norway	Norvège
Svalbard and Jan Mayen Islands	Iles Svalbard et Jan Mayen
Sweden	Suède
United Kingdom	Royaume-Uni
Southern Europe	*Europe méridionale*
Albania	Albanie
Andorra	Andorre
Bosnia and Herzegovina	Bosnie-Herzégovine
Croatia	Croatie
Gibraltar	Gibraltar
Greece	Grèce

Holy See	Saint-Siège
Italy	Italie
Malta	Malte
Portugal	Portugal
San Marino	Saint-Marin
Slovenia	Slovénie
Spain	Espagne
The former Yugoslav Republic of Macedonia	Ex-République yougoslave de Macédoine
Yugoslavia	Yougoslavie

Western Europe	*Europe occidentale*
Austria	Autriche
Belgium	Belgique
France	France
Germany	Allemagne
Liechtenstein	Liechtenstein
Luxembourg	Luxembourg
Monaco	Monaco
Netherlands	Pays-Bas
Switzerland	Suisse

Oceania	**Océanie**
Australia and New Zealand	*Australie et Nouvelle-Zélande*
Australia	Australie
New Zealand	Nouvelle-Zélande
Norfolk Island	Ile Norfolk

Melanesia	*Mélanésie*
Fiji	Fidji
New Caledonia	Nouvelle-Calédonie
Papua New Guinea	Papouasie-Nouvelle-Guinée
Solomon Islands	Iles Salomon
Vanuatu	Vanuatu

Micronesia-Polynesia	*Micronésie-Polynésie*
Micronesia	*Micronésie*
Guam	Guam
Kiribati	Kiribati
Marshall Islands	Iles Marshall
Micronesia (Federated States of)	Micronésie (Etats fédérés de)
Nauru	Nauru
Northern Mariana Islands	Iles Mariannes septentrionales
Palau	Palaos

Polynesia	*Polynésie*
American Samoa	Samoa américaines
Cook Islands	Iles Cook
French Polynesia	Polynésie française
Niue	Nioué
Pitcairn	Pitcairn
Samoa	Samoa
Tokelau	Tokélaou
Tonga	Tonga
Tuvalu	Tuvalu
Wallis and Futuna Islands	Iles Wallis-et-Futuna

C. Other groupings

Following is a list of other groupings and their compositions presented in the *Yearbook*. These groupings are organized mainly around economic and trade interests in regional associations.

Andean Common Market (ANCOM)
Bolivia
Colombia
Ecuador
Peru
Venezuela

Asia-Pacific Economic Cooperation (APEC)
Australia
Brunei Darussalam
Canada
Chile
China
Hong Kong Special Administrative Region
    of China
Indonesia
Japan
Malaysia
Mexico
New Zealand
Papua New Guinea
Peru
Philippines
Republic of Korea
Russian Federation
Singapore
Taiwan Province of China
Thailand
United States of America
Viet Nam

Association of Southeast Asian Nations (ASEAN)
Brunei Darussalam
Cambodia
Indonesia
Lao People's Democratic Republic
Malaysia
Myanmar
Philippines
Singapore
Thailand
Viet Nam

Caribbean Community and Common Market (CARICOM)
Antigua and Barbuda
Bahamas (member of the Community only)
Barbados
Belize
Dominica
Grenada
Guyana
Jamaica

C. Autres groupements

On trouvera ci-après une liste des autres groupements et de leur composition, présentée dans l'*Annuaire*. Ces groupements correspondent essentiellement à des intérêts économiques et commerciaux d'après les associations régionales.

Marché commun andin (ANCOM)
Bolivie
Colombie
Equateur
Pérou
Vénézuela

Coopération économique Asie-Pacifique (CEAP)
Australie
Brunéi Darussalam
Canada
Chili
Chine
Hong Kong, région administrative spéciale
    de Chine
Indonésie
Japon
Malaisie
Mexique
Nouvelle-Zélande
Papouasie-Nouvelle-Guinée
Pérou
Philippines
République de Corée
Fédération de Russie
Singapour
Province chinoise de Taiwan
Thaïlande
Etats-Unis d'Amérique
Viet Nam

Association des nations de l'Asie du Sud-Est (ANASE)
Brunéi Darussalam
Cambodge
Indonésie
République démocratique populaire lao
Malaisie
Myanmar
Philippines
Singapour
Thaïlande
Viet Nam

Communauté des Caraïbes et Marché commun des Caraïbes (CARICOM)
Antigua-et-Barbuda
Bahamas (membre de la communauté seulement)
Barbade
Belize
Dominique
Grenade
Guyana
Jamaïque

<table>
<tr><td>

Montserrat
Saint Kitts and Nevis
Saint Lucia
Saint Vincent and the Grenadines
Suriname
Trinidad and Tobago

Central African Customs and Economic Union (CACEU)
  Cameroon
  Central African Republic
  Chad
  Congo
  Equatorial Guinea
  Gabon

Central American Common Market (CACM)
  Costa Rica
  El Salvador
  Guatemala
  Honduras
  Nicaragua

Common Market for Eastern and Southern Africa (COMESA)
  Angola
  Burundi
  Comoros
  Democratic Republic of the Congo
  Djibouti
  Egypt
  Eritrea
  Ethiopia
  Kenya
  Madagascar
  Malawi
  Mauritius
  Namibia
  Rwanda
  Seychelles
  Sudan
  Swaziland
  Uganda
  United Republic of Tanzania
  Zambia
  Zimbabwe

Commonwealth of Independent States (CIS)
  Armenia
  Azerbaijan
  Belarus
  Georgia
  Kazakhstan
  Kyrgyzstan
  Republic of Moldova
  Russian Federation
  Tajikistan
  Turkmenistan
  Ukraine
  Uzbekistan

</td><td>

Montserrat
Saint-Kitts-et-Nevis
Sainte-Lucie
Saint-Vincent-et-les Grenadines
Suriname
Trinité-et-Tobago

Union douanière et économique de l'Afrique centrale (UDEAC)
  Cameroun
  République centrafricaine
  Tchad
  Congo
  Guinée équatoriale
  Gabon

Marché commun centraméricain (MCC)
  Costa Rica
  El Salvador
  Guatemala
  Honduras
  Nicaragua

Marché commun de l'Afrique de l'Est et de l'Afrique australe (COMESA)
  Angola
  Burundi
  Comores
  République démocratique du Congo
  Djibouti
  Egypte
  Erythrée
  Ethiopie
  Kenya
  Madagascar
  Malawi
  Maurice
  Namibie
  Rwanda
  Seychelles
  Soudan
  Swaziland
  Ouganda
  République-Unie de Tanzanie
  Zambie
  Zimbabwe

Communauté d'Etats indépendants (CEI)
  Arménie
  Azerbaïdjan
  Bélarus
  Géorgie
  Kazakhstan
  Kirghizistan
  République de Moldova
  Fédération de Russie
  Tadjikistan
  Turkménistan
  Ukraine
  Ouzbékistan

</td></tr>
</table>

Economic Community of West African States
(ECOWAS)
 Benin
 Burkina Faso
 Cape Verde
 Côte d'Ivoire
 Gambia
 Ghana
 Guinea
 Guinea-Bissau
 Liberia
 Mali
 Mauritania
 Niger
 Nigeria
 Senegal
 Sierra Leone
 Togo

European Free Trade Association (EFTA)
 Iceland
 Liechtenstein
 Norway
 Switzerland

European Union (EU)
 Austria
 Belgium
 Denmark
 Finland
 France
 Germany
 Greece
 Ireland
 Italy
 Luxembourg
 Netherlands
 Portugal
 Spain
 Sweden
 United Kingdom

Latin American Integration Association (LAIA)
 Argentina
 Bolivia
 Brazil
 Chile
 Colombia
 Ecuador
 Mexico
 Paraguay
 Peru
 Uruguay
 Venezuela

Least developed countries (LDCs) [b]
 Afghanistan
 Angola
 Bangladesh
 Benin

Communauté économique des Etats de l'Afrique de
l'Ouest (CEDEAO)
 Bénin
 Burkina Faso
 Cap-Vert
 Côte d'Ivoire
 Gambie
 Ghana
 Guinée
 Guinée-Bissau
 Libéria
 Mali
 Mauritanie
 Niger
 Nigéria
 Sénégal
 Sierra Leone
 Togo

Association européenne de libre-échange (AELE)
 Islande
 Liechtenstein
 Norvège
 Suisse

Union européenne (UE)
 Autriche
 Belgique
 Danemark
 Finlande
 France
 Allemagne
 Grèce
 Irlande
 Italie
 Luxembourg
 Pays-Bas
 Portugal
 Espagne
 Suède
 Royaume-Uni

Association latino-américaine pour l'intégration (ALAI)
 Argentine
 Bolivie
 Brésil
 Chili
 Colombie
 Equateur
 Mexique
 Paraguay
 Pérou
 Uruguay
 Venezuela

Pays les moins avancés (PMA) [b]
 Afghanistan
 Angola
 Bangladesh
 Bénin

Bhutan	Bhoutan
Burkina Faso	Burkina Faso
Burundi	Burundi
Cambodia	Cambodge
Cape Verde	Cap-Vert
Central African Republic	République centrafricaine
Chad	Tchad
Comoros	Comores
Democratic Republic of the Congo	République démocratique du Congo
Djibouti	Djibouti
Equatorial Guinea	Guinée équatoriale
Eritrea	Erythrée
Ethiopia	Ethiopie
Gambia	Gambie
Guinea	Guinée
Guinea-Bissau	Guinée-Bissau
Haiti	Haïti
Kiribati	Kiribati
Lao People's Democratic Republic	République démocratique populaire lao
Lesotho	Lesotho
Liberia	Libéria
Madagascar	Madagascar
Malawi	Malawi
Maldives	Maldives
Mali	Mali
Mauritania	Mauritanie
Mozambique	Mozambique
Myanmar	Myanmar
Nepal	Népal
Niger	Niger
Rwanda	Rwanda
Samoa	Samoa
Sao Tome and Principe	Sao Tomé-et-Principe
Sierra Leone	Sierra Leone
Solomon Islands	Iles Salomon
Somalia	Somalie
Sudan	Soudan
Togo	Togo
Tuvalu	Tuvalu
Uganda	Ouganda
United Republic of Tanzania	République-Unie de Tanzanie
Vanuatu	Vanuatu
Yemen	Yémen
Zambia	Zambie

Mercado Común Sudamericano (MERCOSUR) — *Marché commun sud-américain* (Mercosur)

Argentina	Argentine
Brazil	Brésil
Paraguay	Paraguay
Uruguay	Uruguay

North American Free Trade Agreement (NAFTA) — *Accord de libre-échange nord-américain* (ALENA)

Canada	Canada
Mexico	Mexique
United States of America	Etats-Unis d'Amérique

Organisation for Economic Cooperation and Development (OECD) — *Organisation de coopération et de développement économiques* (OCDE)

Australia	Australie
Austria	Autriche

Belgium	Belgique
Canada	Canada
Czech Republic	République tchèque
Denmark	Danemark
Finland	Finlande
France	France
Germany	Allemagne
Greece	Grèce
Hungary	Hongrie
Iceland	Islande
Ireland	Irlande
Italy	Italie
Japan	Japon
Luxembourg	Luxembourg
Mexico	Mexique
Netherlands	Pays-Bas
New Zealand	Nouvelle-Zélande
Norway	Norvège
Poland	Pologne
Portugal	Portugal
Republic of Korea	République de Corée
Spain	Espagne
Sweden	Suède
Switzerland	Suisse
Turkey	Turquie
United Kingdom	Royaume-Uni
United States of America	Etats-Unis d'Amérique

Organization of Petroleum Exporting Countries (OPEC) | *Organisation des pays exportateurs de pétrole* (OPEP)

Algeria	Algérie
Indonesia	Indonésie
Iran (Islamic Republic of)	Iran (République islamique d')
Iraq	Iraq
Kuwait	Koweït
Libyan Arab Jamahiriya	Jamahiriya arabe libyenne
Nigeria	Nigéria
Qatar	Qatar
Saudi Arabia	Arabie saoudite
United Arab Emirates	Emirats arabes unis
Venezuela	Venezuela

Southern African Customs Union (SACU) | *Union douanière d'Afrique australe*

Botswana	Botswana
Lesotho	Lesotho
Namibia	Namibie
South Africa	Afrique du Sud
Swaziland	Swaziland

---

a   The continent of North America comprises Northern America, Caribbean and Central America.
b   As determined by the General Assembly in its resolution 49/133.

---

a   Le continent de l'Amérique du Nord comprend l'Amérique septentrionale, les Caraïbes et l'Amérique centrale.
b   Comme déterminé par l'Assemblée générale dans sa résolution 49/133.

Annex II

Conversion coefficients and factors

The metric system of weights and measures is employed in the *Statistical Yearbook*. In this system, the relationship between units of volume and capacity is: 1 litre = 1 cubic decimetre (dm³) exactly (as decided by the 12th International Conference of Weights and Measures, New Delhi, November 1964).

Section A shows the equivalents of the basic metric, British imperial and United States units of measurements. According to an agreement between the national standards institutions of English-speaking nations, the British and United States units of length, area and volume are now identical, and based on the yard = 0.9144 metre exactly. The weight measures in both systems are based on the pound = 0.45359237 kilogram exactly (Weights and Measures Act 1963 (London), and *Federal Register* announcement of 1 July 1959: *Refinement of Values for the Yard and Pound* (Washington D.C.)).

Section B shows various derived or conventional conversion coefficients and equivalents.

Section C shows other conversion coefficients or factors which have been utilized in the compilation of certain tables in the *Statistical Yearbook*. Some of these are only of an approximate character and have been employed solely to obtain a reasonable measure of international comparability in the tables.

For a comprehensive survey of international and national systems of weights and measures and of units weights for a large number of commodities in different countries, see *World Weights and Measures* (United Nations publication, Sales No. E.66.XVII.3).

Annexe II

Coefficients et facteurs de conversion

L'*Annuaire statistique* utilise le système métrique pour les poids et mesures. La relation entre unités métriques de volume et de capacité est: 1 litre = 1 décimètre cube (dm³) exactement (comme fut décidé à la Conférence internationale des poids et mesures, New Delhi, novembre 1964).

La section A fournit les équivalents principaux des systèmes de mesure métrique, britannique et américain. Suivant un accord entre les institutions de normalisation nationales des pays de langue anglaise, les mesures britanniques et américaines de longueur, superficie et volume sont désormais identiques, et sont basées sur le yard = 0:9144 mètre exactement. Les mesures de poids se rapportent, dans les deux systèmes, à la livre (pound) = 0.45359237 kilogramme exactement ("Weights and Measures Act 1963" (Londres), et "Federal Register Announcement of 1 July 1959: Refinement of Values for the Yard and Pound" (Washington, D.C.)).

La section B fournit divers coeficients et facteurs de conversion conventionnels ou dérivés.

La section C fournit d'autres coefficients ou facteurs de conversion utilisés dans l'élaboration de certains tableaux de l'*Annuaire statistique*. D'aucuns ne sont que des approximations et n'ont été utilisés que pour obtenir un degré raisonnable de comparabilité sur le plan international.

Pour une étude d'ensemble des systèmes internationaux et nationaux de poids et mesures, et d'unités de poids pour un grand nombre de produits dans différents pays, voir "*World Weights and Measures*" (publication des Nations Unies, No de vente E.66.XVII.3).

A. Equivalents of metric, British imperial and United States units of measure

A. Equivalents des unités métriques, britanniques et des Etats-Unis

Metric units / Unités métriques	British imperial and US equivalents / Equivalents en mesures britanniques et des Etats-Unis	British imperial and US units / Unités britanniques et des Etats-Unis	Metric equivalents / Equivalents en mesures métriques	
Length–Longeur				
1 centimetre – centimètre (cm)	0.3937008 inch	1 inch	2.540	cm
1 metre – mètre (m)	3.280840 feet	1 foot	30.480	cm
	1.093613 yard	1 yard	0.9144	m
1 kilometre – kilomètre (km)	0.6213712 mile	1 mile	1609.344	m
	0.5399568 int. naut. mile	1 international nautical mile	1852.000	m
Area – Superficie				
1 square centimetre – (cm²)	0.1550003 square inch	1 square inch	6.45160	cm²
1 square metre – (m²)	10.763910 square feet	1 square foot	9.290304	dm²
	1.195990 square yards	1 square yard	0.83612736	m²
1 hectare – (ha)	2.471054 acres	1 acre	0.4046856	ha
1 square kilometre – (km²)	0.3861022 square mile	1 square mile	2.589988	km²
Volume				
1 cubic centimetre – (cm³)	0.06102374 cubic inch	1 cubic inch	16.38706	cm³
1 cubic metre – (m³)	35.31467 cubic feet	1 cubic foot	28.316847	dm³
	1.307951 cubic yards	1 cubic yard	0.76455486	m³
Capacity – Capacité				
1 litre (l)	0.8798766 imp. quart	1 British imperial quart	1.136523	l
	1.056688 U.S. liq. quart	1 U.S. liquid quart	0.9463529	l
	0.908083 U.S. dry quart	1 U.S. dry quart	1.1012208	l
1 hectolitre (hl)	21.99692 imp. gallons	1 imperial gallon	4.546092	l
	26.417200 U.S. gallons	1 U.S. gallon	3.785412	l
	2.749614 imp. bushels	1 imperial bushel	36.368735	l
	2.837760 U.S. bushels	1 U.S. bushel	35.239067	l
Weight or mass – Poids				
1 kilogram (kg)	35.27396 av. ounces	1 av. ounce	28.349523	g
	32.15075 troy ounces	1 troy ounce	31.10348	g
	2.204623 av. pounds	1 av. pound	453.59237	g
		1 cental (100 lb.)	45.359237	kg
		1 hundredweight (112 lb.)	50.802345	kg
1 ton – tonne (t)	1.1023113 short tons	1 short ton (2 000 lb.)	0.9071847	t
	0.9842065 long tons	1 long ton (2 240 lb.)	1.0160469	t

B.   Various conventional or derived coefficients

Railway and air transport

1 passenger-mile = 1.609344 voyageur (passager) - kilomètre

1 short ton-mile = 1.459972 tonne-kilomètre

1 long ton-mile = 1.635169 tonne kilomètre

Ship tonnage

1 register ton (100 cubic feet) – tonne de jauge = 2.83m³

1 British shipping ton (42 cubic feet) = 1.19m³

1 U.S. shipping ton (40 cubic feet) = 1.13m³

1 deadweight ton (dwt ton = long ton) = 1.016047 metric ton – tonne métrique

Electric energy

1 Kilowatt (kW) =   1.34102 British horsepower (hp)
1.35962 cheval vapeur (cv)

C.   Other coefficients or conversion factors employed in *Statistical Yearbook* tables

Roundwood

Equivalent in solid volume without bark.

Sugar

1 metric ton raw sugar = 0.9 metric ton refined sugar.

For the United States and its possessions:
1 metric ton refined sugar = 1.07 metric tons raw sugar.

B.   Divers coefficients conventionnels ou dérivés

Transport ferroviaire et aérien

1 voyageur (passager) - kilomètre = 0.621371) passenger-mile

1 tonne-kilomètre =   0.684945 short ton-mile
0.611558 long ton-mile

Tonnage de navire

1 cubic metre – m³ = 0.353 register ton – tonne de jauge
0.841 British shipping ton
0.885 US shipping ton

1 metric ton – tonne métrique – 0.984 dwt ton

Energie électrique

1 British horsepower (hp) = 0.7457 kW

1 cheval vapeur (cv) = 0.735499 kW

C.   Autres coefficients ou facteurs de conversion utilisés dans les tableaux de l'*Annuaire statistique*

Bois rond

Equivalences en volume solide sans écorce.

Sucre

1 tonne métrique de sucre brut = 0.9 tonne métrique de sucre raffiné.

Pour les Etats-Unis et leurs possessions:
1 tonne métrique de sucre raffiné = 1.07 t.m. de sucre brut.

Annex III

Tables added and omitted

A. Tables added

The present issue of the *Statistical Yearbook* (1998) includes the following tables which were not presented in the previous issue:

Table 6: Production, trade and consumption of commercial energy (World and region summary);

Table 17: Internet users

Table 62: Production, trade and consumption of commercial energy (by country);

Table 63: Production of selected energy commodities;

Table 66: Water supply and sanitation coverage.

B.

The following tables which were presented in the previous (44th) issue are not presented in the present issue. They will be updated in future issues of the *Yearbook* when new data become available:

Table 8: Population in urban and rural areas, rates of growth and largest urban agglomeration population;

Table 12: Selected indicators of life expectancy, child-bearing and mortality;

Table 15: Book production: number of titles by UDC classes;

Table 16: Daily newspapers;

Table 17: Non-daily newspapers and periodicals;

Table 18: Television and radio receivers;

Table 26: Government final consumption expenditure by function at current prices;

Table 27: Private final consumption expenditure by type and purpose at current prices;

Table 71: Number of researchers, technicians and other supporting staff engaged in research and development;

Table 72: Gross domestic expenditure on R&D by source of funds.

Annexe III

Tableaux ajoutés et supprimés

A. Tableaux ajoutés

Dans ce numéro de l'*Annuaire statistique* (1998), les tableaux suivants qui n'ont pas été présentés dans le numéro antérieur, ont été ajoutés:

Tableau 6: Production, commerce et consommation d'énergie commerciale (Aperçu mondial et régional);

Tableau 17: Usagers d'Internet;

Tableau 62: Production, commerce et consommation d'énergie commerciale (par pays);

Tableau 63: Production des principaux biens de l'énergie;

Table 66: Accès à l'eau et à l'assainissement.

B.

Les tableaux suivants qui ont été repris dans l'édition antérieure (la 44ème édition) n'ont pas été repris dans la présente édition. Ils seront actualisés dans les futures livraisons de l'*Annuaire* à mesure que des données nouvelles deviendront disponibles:

Tableau 8: Population urbaine, population rurale, taux d'accroissement et population de l'agglomération urbaine la plus peuplée;

Tableau 12: Choix d'indicateurs de l'espérance de vie, de maternité et de la mortalité;

Tableau 15: Production de livres: nombre de titres classés d'après la CDU;

Tableau 16: Journaux quotidiens;

Tableau 17: Journaux non quotidiens et périodiques;

Tableau 18: Récepteurs de télévision et de radiodiffusion sonore;

Tableau 26: Consommation finale des administrations publiques par fonction aux prix courants;

Tableau 27: Consommation finale privée par catégorie de dépenses et par fonction aux prix courants;

Tableau 71: Nombre de chercheurs, de techniciens et d'autre personnel de soutien employé à des travaux de recherche et de développement;

Tableau 72: Dépenses intérieures brutes de recherche et développement par source de fonds.

Statistical sources and references

A.   Statistical sources

1.   American Automobile Manufacturers Association, *Motor Vehicle Facts and Figures 1997* (Detroit, USA).

2.   Auto and Truck International, *1999-2000 World Automotive Market Report* (Illinois, USA).

3.   Carbon Dioxide Information Analysis Center, *Global, Regional, and National CO_2 Emissions Estimates from Fossil-Fuel Burning, Hydraulic Cement Production, and Gas Flaring* (Oak Ridge, Tennessee, USA).

4.   Food and Agriculture Organization of the United Nations, *FAO Fertilizer Yearbook 1999* (Rome).

5.   _____, *FAO Food balance sheets, 1996-1998 average,* (Rome).

6.   _____, *FAO Production Yearbook 1999* (Rome).

7.   _____, *FAO Trade Yearbook 1999* (Rome).

8.   _____, *FAO Yearbook of Fishery Statistics, Capture production 1998* (Rome).

9.   _____, *FAO Yearbook of Forest Products 1999* (Rome).

10.   International Civil Aviation Organization, *Civil Aviation Statistics of the World 1998* (Montreal).

11.   _____, *Digest of statistics — Traffic 1994-1998* (Montreal).

12.   International Labour Office, *Yearbook of Labour Statistics 1999* (Geneva).

13.   International Monetary Fund, *Balance of Payments Yearbook 1999* (Washington, D.C.).

14.   _____, *International Financial Statistics,* November 2000 (Washington, D.C.).

15.   International Sugar Organization, *Sugar Yearbook 1999* (London).

16.   International Telecommunication Union, *World Telecommunication Development Report 1998* (Geneva).

17.   _____, *Yearbook of Statistics, Telecommunication Services, Chronological Time Series 1989-1998* (Geneva).

18.   Lloyd's Register of Shipping, *World Fleet Statistics 1999* (London).

19.   Organisation for Economic Cooperation and Development, *Development Cooperation, 1999 Report* (Paris).

20.   _____, *Geographical Distribution of Financial Flows to Aid Recipients, 1994-1998* (Paris).

21.   United Nations, *Demographic Yearbook 1998* (United Nations publication, Sales No. E/F.00.XIII.1).

22.   _____, *Energy Statistics Yearbook 1997* (United Nations publication, Sales No. E/F.00.XVII.8).

Sources statistiques et références

A.   Sources statistiques

1.   "American Automobile Manufacturers Association, *Motor Vehicle Facts and Figures 1997*" (Detroit, USA).

2.   "Auto and Truck International, *1999-2000 World Automotive Market Report*" (Illinois, USA).

3.   "Carbon Dioxide Information Analysis Center, *Global, Regional, and National CO_2 Emissions Estimates from Fossil-Fuel Burning, Hydraulic Cement Production, and Gas Flaring*" (Oak Ridge, Tennessee, USA).

4.   Organisation des Nations Unies pour l'alimentation et l'agriculture, *Annuaire FAO des engrais 1999* (Rome).

5.   _____, *Bilans alimentaires de la FAO, moyenne 1996-1998* (Rome).

6.   _____, *Annuaire FAO de la production 1999* (Rome).

7.   _____, *Annuaire FAO du commerce 1999* (Rome).

8.   _____, *Annuaire statistique des pêches, captures 1998* (Rome).

9.   _____, *Annuaire FAO des produits forestiers 1999* (Rome).

10.   Organisation de l'aviation civile internationale, *Statistiques de l'aviation civile dans le monde 1998* (Montréal).

11.   _____, *Recueil de statistiques — trafic 1994-1998* (Montréal).

12.   Bureau international du Travail, *Annuaire des statistiques du Travail 1999* (Genève).

13.   Fonds monétaire international, "*Balance of Payments Yearbook 1999*", (Washington, D.C.).

14.   _____, *Statistiques financières internationales,* novembre 2000 (Washington, D.C.).

15.   Organisation internationale du sucre, *Annuaire du sucre 1999* (Londres).

16.   Union international de télécommunication, "*World Telecommunication Development Report 1998*" (Genève).

17.   _____, "*Yearbook of Statistics, Telecommunication Services, Chronological Time Series 1989-1998*" (Genève).

18.   "Lloyd's Register of Shipping, *World Fleet Statistics 1999*" (Londres).

19.   Organisation de Coopération et de Développement Economiques, *Coopération pour le développement, Rapport 1999* (Paris).

20.   _____, *Répartition géographique des ressources financières allouées aux pays bénéficiaires de l'aide, 1994-1998* (Paris).

23. _____, *Industrial Commodity Statistics Yearbook 1998* (United Nations publications, Sales No. E/F.01.XVII.3).

24. _____, *International Trade Statistics Yearbook 1998*, vols. I and II (United Nations publication, Sales No. E/F.00.XVII.3).

25. _____, *Monthly Bulletin of Statistics*, various issues up to November 2000 (United Nations publication, Series Q).

26. _____, *National Accounts Statistics: Main Aggregates and Detailed Tables, 1996-1997,* Parts I and II (United Nations publication, Sales No. E.00.XVII.11).

27. _____, *Operational activities of the United Nations for international development cooperation , Report of the Secretary-General, Addendum, Comprehensive statistical data on operational activities for development for the year 1997* (E/1999/55/Add.2) and *Operational activities ... for the year 1998* (E/2000/46/Add.2).

28. _____, *World Population Prospects: The 1998 Revision* (United Nations publication, Sales No. E.99.XIII.8).

29. United Nations Educational, Scientific and Cultural Organization Institute for Statistics, *Statistical Yearbook 1999* (Paris).

30. United Nations Programme on HIV/AIDS and the World Health Organization, *Aids epidemic update: December 2000* (Geneva).

31. World Bank, *Global Development Finance*, Vol. I and II, 2000 (Washington, D.C.).

32. World Conservation Union/Species Survival Commission, *2000 IUCN Red List of Threatened Species* (Gland, Switzerland and Cambridge, United Kingdom).

33. World Health Organization and United Nations Children's Fund, WHO/UNICEF Joint Monitoring Programme for Water Supply and Sanitation, *Global water supply and sanitation assessment 2000 report* (Geneva).

34. World Intellectual Property Organization, *Industrial Property Statistics 1998, Publication A* (Geneva).

35. World Tourism Organization, *Yearbook of Tourism Statistics 52nd edition, 2000* (Madrid).

B.   References

36. Food and Agriculture Organization of the United Nations, *The Fifth World Food Survey 1985* (Rome 1985).

37. International Labour Office, *International Standard Classification of Occupations, Revised Edition 1968* (Geneva, 1969); revised edition, 1988, *ISCO-88* (Geneva, 1990).

21. Nations Unies, *Annuaire démographique 1998* (publication des Nations Unies, No de vente E/F.00.XIII.1).

22. _____, *Annuaire des statistiques de l'énergie 1997* (publication des Nations Unies, No de vente E/F.00.XVII.8).

23. _____, *Annuaire des statistiques industrielles par produit 1998* (publications des Nations Unies, No de vente E/F.01.XVII.3).

24. _____, *Annuaire statistique du commerce international 1998*, Vols. I et II (publication des Nations Unies, No de vente E/F.00.XVII.3).

25. _____, *Bulletin mensuel de statistique*, différentes éditions, jusqu'à novembre 2000 (publication des Nations Unies, Série Q).

26. _____, "*National Accounts Statistics: Main Aggregates and Detailed Tables 1996-1997*, Parties I et II" (publication des Nations Unies, No de vente E.00.XVII.11).

27. _____, *Activités opérationnelles du système des Nations Unies au service de la coopération internationale pour le développement, Rapport du Secrétaire général, Additif, Données statistiques globales sur les activités opérationnelles au service du développement pour 1997* (E/1999/55/Add.2) et *Activités ... pour 1998* (E/2000/46/Add.2).

28. _____, "*World Population Prospects: The 1998 Revision*", (publication des Nations Unies, No de vente E.99.XIII.8).

29. Institut de statististique de l'Organisation des Nations Unies pour l'éducation, la science et la culture, *Annuaire statistique 1999* (Paris).

30. Programme des Nations Unies sur le VIH/SIDA et l'Organisation mondiale de la santé, *Le point sur l'épidémie de SIDA: décembre 2000* (Genève)

31. Banque mondiale, "*Global Development Finance*, Vol. I et II, 2000" (Washington, D.C.).

32. Union mondiale pour la nature/Commission de la sauvegarde des espèces, *Liste rouge des espèces menacées 2000* (Gland, Suisse et Cambridge, Royaume-Uni).

33. Organisation mondiale de la santé et Fonds des Nations Unies pour l'enfance, OMS/FISE Programme de surveillance conjointe de l'approvisionnement en eau et l'assainissement, *Bilan mondial de l'approvisionnement en eau et de l'assainissement à l'horizon 2000* (Genève).

34. Organisation mondiale de la propriété intellectuelle, *Statistiques de propriété industrielle 1998, Publication A* (Genève).

35. Organisation mondiale du tourisme, *Annuaire des statistiques du tourisme 52ème édition, 2000* (Madrid).

38.   International Monetary Fund, *Balance of Payments Manual, Fifth Edition* (Washington, D.C., 1993).

39.   Stanton, C. et al, *Modelling maternal mortality in the developing world*, mimeo, November 1995 (Geneva and New York, WHO, UNICEF).

40.   United Nations, *Basic Methodological Principles Governing the Compilation of the System of Statistical Balances of the National Economy*, Studies in Methods, Series F, No. 17, Rev. 1, vols. 1 and 2 (United Nations publications, Sales No. E.89.XVII.5 and E.89.XVII.3).

41.   _____, *Classifications of Expenditure According to Purpose: Classification of the Functions of Government (COFOG), Classification of Individual Consumption According to Purpose (COICOP), Classification of the Purposes of Non-Profit Institutions Serving Households (COPNI), Classification of the Outlays of Producers According to Purpose (COPP)*, Series M, No. 84 (United Nations publication, Sales No. E.00.XVII.6).

42.   _____, *Energy Statistics: Definitions, Units of Measure and Conversion Factors*, Series F, No. 44 (United Nations publication, Sales No. E.86.XVII.21).

43.   _____, *Energy Statistics: Manual for Developing Countries*, Series F, No. 56 (United Nations publication, Sales No. E.91.XVII.10).

44.   _____, *Handbook of Vital Statistics Systems and Methods*, vol. I, *Legal, Organization and Technical Aspects*, Series F, No. 35, vol. I (United Nations publication, Sales No. E.91.XVII.5).

45.   _____, *Handbook on Social Indicators*, Studies in Methods, Series F, No. 49 (United Nations publication, Sales No. E.89.XVII.6).

46.   _____, *International Recommendations for Industrial Statistics*, Series M, No. 48, Rev. 1 (United Nations publication, Sales No. E.83.XVII.8).

47.   _____, *International Standard Industrial Classification of All Economic Activities*, Statistical Papers, Series M, No. 4, Rev. 2 (United Nations publication, Sales No. E.68.XVII.8); Rev. 3 (United Nations publication, Sales No. E.90.XVII.11).

48   _____, *International Trade Statistics: Concepts and Definitions*, Series M, No. 52, Rev. 1 (United Nations publication, Sales No. E.82.XVII.14).

49.   _____, *Methods Used in Compiling the United Nations Price Indexes for External Trade*, volume 1, Statistical Papers, Series M, No. 82 (United Nations Publication, Sales No. E.87.XVII.4).

50.   _____, *Principles and Recommendations for Population and Housing Censuses*, Statistical Papers, Series M, No. 67 (United Nations publication, Sales No. E.80.XVII.8).

51.   _____, *Provisional Guidelines on Statistics of International Tourism*, Statistical Papers, Series M, No.

B.   *Références*

36.   Organisation des Nations Unies pour l'alimentation et l'agriculture, *Cinquième enquête mondiale sur l'alimentation 1985* (Rome, 1985).

37.   Organisation internationale du Travail, *Classification internationale type des professions, édition révisée* 1968 (Genève, 1969); édition révisée 1988, *CITP-88* (Genève, 1990).

38.   Fonds monétaire international, *Manuel de la balance des paiements, cinquième édition* (Washington, D.C., 1993).

39.   Stanton, C, et al, "*Modelling maternal mortality in the developing world*", novembre 1995 (Genève et New York, WHO, UNICEF).

40.   Organisation des Nations Unies, *Principes méthodologiques de base régissant l'établissement des balances statistiques de l'économie nationale*, Série F, No 17, Rev.1 Vol. 1 et Vol. 2 (publication des Nations Unies, No de vente F.89.XVII.5 et F.89.XVII.3).

41.   _____, "*Classifications of Expenditure According to Purpose: Classification of the Functions of Government (COFOG), Classification of Individual Consumption According to Purpose (COICOP), Classification of the Purposes of Non-Profit Institutions Serving Households (COPNI), Classification of the Outlays of Producers According to Purpose (COPP)*", Série M, No 84 (publication des Nations Unies, No de vente E. 00.XVII.6).

42.   _____, *Statistiques de l'énergie: définitions, unités de mesures et facteurs de conversion*, Série F, No 44 (publication des Nations Unies, No de vente F.86.XVII.21).

43.   _____, *Statistiques de l'énergie: Manuel pour les pays en développement*, Série F, No 56 (publication des Nations Unies, No de vente F.91.XVII.10).

44.   _____, "*Handbook of Vital Statistics System and Methods*, Vol. 1, *Legal, Organization and Technical Aspects*", Série F, No 35, Vol. 1 (publication des Nations Unies, No de vente E.91.XVII.5).

45.   _____, *Manuel des indicateurs sociaux*, Série F, No 49 (publication des Nations Unies, No de vente F.89.XVII.6).

46.   _____, *Recommandations internationales concernant les statistiques industrielles*, Série M, No 48, Rev. 1 (publication des Nations Unies, No de vente F.83.XVII.8).

47.   _____, *Classification internationale type, par industrie, de toutes les branches d'activité économique*, Série M, No 4, Rev. 2 (publication des Nations Unies, No de vente F.68.XVII.8); Rev. 3 (publication des Nations Unies, No de vente F.90.XVII.11).

48.   _____, *Statistiques du commerce international: Concepts et définitions*, Série M, No 52, Rev. 1

62 (United Nations publication, Sales No. E.78.XVII.6).

52. _____ and World Tourism Organization, *Recommendations on Tourism Statistics*, Statistical Papers, Series M, No. 83 (United Nations publication, Sales No. E.94.XVII.6).

53. _____, *Standard International Trade Classification, Revision 3*, Statistical Papers, Series M, No. 34, Rev. 3 (United Nations publication, Sales No. E.86.XVII.12), *Revision 2*, Series M, No. 34, Rev. 2 (United Nations publication), *Revision*, Series M, No. 34, Revision (United Nations publication, Sales No. E.61.XVII.6).

54. _____, *Supplement to the Statistical Yearbook and the Monthly Bulletin of Statistics, 1977,* Series S and Series Q, Supplement 2 (United Nations publication, Sales No. E.78.XVII.10).

55. _____, *System of National Accounts, Studies in Methods*, Series F, No. 2, Rev. 3 (United Nations publication, Sales No. E.69.XVII.3).

56. _____, *System of National Accounts 1993,* Studies in Methods, Series F, No. 2, Rev. 4 (United Nations publication, Sales No. E.94.XVII.4).

57. _____, *Towards a System of Social and Demographic Statistics, Studies in Methods*, Series F, No. 18 (United Nations publication, Sales No. E.74.XVII.8).

58. World Health Organization, *Manual of the International Statistical Classification of Diseases, Injuries and Causes of Death*, vol. 1 (Geneva, 1977).

59. World Tourism Organization, *Methodological Supplement to World Travel and Tourism Statistics* (Madrid, 1985).

(publication des Nations Unies, No de vente F.82.XVII.14).

49. _____, *Méthodes utilisées par les Nations Unies pour établir les indices des prix des produits de base entrant dans le commerce international*, Série M, No 82, Vol. 1 (publication des Nations Unies, No de vente F.87.XVII.4).

50. _____, *Principes et recommandations concernant les recensements de la population et de l'habitation*, Série M, No 67 (publication des Nations Unies, No de vente F.80.XVII.8).

51. _____, *Directives provisoires pour l'établissement des statistiques du tourisme international*, Série M, No 62 (publication des Nations Unies, No de vente 78.XVII.6).

52. _____ et l'Organisation mondiale du tourisme, "*Recommendations on Tourism Statistics*, Statistical Papers", Série M, No. 83 (publication des Nations Unies, No. de vente E.94.XVII.6).

53. _____, *Classification type pour le commerce international (troisième version révisée)*, Série M, No 34, Rev. 3 (publication des Nations Unies, No de vente F.86.XVII.12), *Révision 2*, Série M, No 34, Rev. 2 (publication des Nations Unies), *Révision*, Série M, No. 34, Révision (publication des Nations Unies, No de vente F.61.XVII.6).

54. _____, *Supplément à l'Annuaire statistique et au bulletin mensuel de statistique, 1977,* Série S et Série Q, supplément 2 (publication des Nations Unies, No de vente F.78.XVII.10).

55. _____, *Système de comptabilité nationale,* Série F, No 2, Rev. 3 (publication des Nations Unies, No de vente F.69.XVII.3).

56. _____, *Système de comptabilité nationale 1993*, Série F, No 2, Rev. 4 (publication des Nations Unies, No de vente F.94.XVII.4).

57. _____, *Vers un système de statistiques démographiques et sociales, Etudes méthodologiques,* Série F, No 18 (publication des Nations Unies, No. de vente F.74.XVII.8).

58. Organisation mondiale de la santé, *Manuel de la classification statistique internationale des maladies, traumatismes et causes de décès*, Vol. 1 (Genève, 1977).

59. Organisation mondiale du tourisme, *Supplément méthodologique aux statistiques des voyages et du tourisme mondiaux* (Madrid, 1985).

Index

Note: References to tables are indicated by **boldface** type. For citations of organizations, see the Index of organizations.

Index of Organizations

Litho in United Nations, New York
24796—April 2001—6,000
ISBN 92-1-061189-6
ISSN 0082-8459

United Nations publication
Sales No. E/F.00.XVII.1
ST/ESA/STAT/SER.S/21